Footprint India

13th edition

Robert and Roma Bradnock

'All the convergent influences of the world run through this society: hindu, Moslem, Christian, secular; Stalinist, liberal, Maoist, democratic socialist, Gandhian. There is not a thought that is being though in the West or East that is not active in some Indian mind.'

Rabindranath Tagore: Poet and Dramatist, Edward Thompson

India Highlights

See colour maps at back of book

1 Delhi
The capital city:
Jama Masjid, Red
Fort and the
Qutb Minar

**2 Corbett
National Park**
Tiger country see
from an howdah

3 Amritsar
A golden temple
sparkling in the
dawn light

4 Manali to Leh
Terrifying but
spectacular

5 Agra
The uncomparable
Taj Mahal is white
and almost
transluscent

6 Jaipur
The pink city and
one of the gems of
the 'Golden Triangle'

7 Orchha
Palace and Chhattris
are quiet but very
atmospheric

8 Khajuraho
Erotic temple
architecture

9 Udaipur
Undeniably
romantic with white
palaces, blue lakes
and green hills

10 Jaisalmer
Medieval city
floating in a
desert haze

11 Dwarka
Little visited but
one of India's most
holiest places

12 Sanchi
Crowned on a hill,
a key Buddhist site

13 Mandu
Huge fort with fine
Islamic buildings

The Government of India state that
"the external boundaries of India
are neither correct or authenticated"

14 Auranagab
Visit Ajanta and Ellora caves: both are spectacular

15 Mumbai
Bollywood, tea at the Taj and Queen Victoria's necklace

16 Golconda
Magnificent, medieval fortress

17 Hampi
Hugely impressive ruins: home of the Vijayanagar kings

18 Goa
Beaches, parties and flea markets

19 Bangalore
A 'garden city' at the heart of India's silicon valley

20 Mysore
Be there for the spectacular Dasara celebrations

21 Madurai
Temple elephants, flower sellers and musicians

22 Pondicherry
The old French enclave still retains a gallic flavour

23 Puri
A riot of colour and noise at the car festival

24 Kolkata
The intellectual capital of India

25 Bodh Gaya
Monlam festival is very atmospheric

26 Varanasi
This is India in the raw

27 Darjeeling
Wonderfully scenic tea gardens

TIBET (CHINA)

NEPAL

SIKKIM   BHUTAN

Darjeeling 27

ASSAM

26 Varanasi

BIHAR

25 Bodh Gaya

JHARKHAND   WEST BENGAL

BANGLADESH

MYANMAR (BURMA)

24 Kolkata

ORISSA

Puri
23

Bay of Bengal

Andaman Islands

Nicobar Islands

4

Contents

Brahma and Shakti
The late 10th-century temple complex at Khajuraho is famous for its remarkable erotic sculptures, expressions of the Tantric worship of the Mother Goddess, Shakti.

A foot in the door

The heart of India beats in the densely populated plains of the River Ganges, settled and cultivated for millennia, and the home of great civilizations that shape the lives of nearly one billion people today. To the south lies the Peninsula, politically always more fragmented than the Plains and agriculturally less fertile, but with mineral resources that have supplied empires for over 4000 years. Beyond lies one of India's great natural frontiers, the palm-fringed Indian Ocean, stretching from the Arabian Sea in the west to the Bay of Bengal in the east, with nothing but scattered island chains between Kanniyakumari and Antarctica. To the north of the plains, meanwhile, is the vast wall of the Himalaya, described by a 19th-century Surveyor General of India as "the finest natural combination of boundary and barrier that exists in the world. It stands alone... amidst the eternal silence of vast snowfield and icebound peaks".

India's scenery is among the most varied and exciting anywhere. In the eastern foothills of the Himalaya are some of the wettest regions in the world, still covered in dense rainforest, while in their western ranges are the high-altitude deserts of Ladakh. The Gangetic plains stretch from the fertile and wet delta of Bengal to the deserts of North Rajasthan. Even the Peninsula ranges from the tropical humid climate of the western coast across the beautiful hills of the Western Ghats to the dry plateaus inland.

The range of its landscapes is only one element of the country's enduring appeal: India's openness, friendliness and freedom from personal threat are increasingly rare among major travel destinations and its history and culture are not just packaged and brought out on show for the tourist but lived and experienced daily. All of this is readily accessible to travellers on virtually any budget and travelling over almost any time scale.

10   A vivid history, a varied people

On India's diverse landscape is etched the evidence of a succession of political powers, religions and cultures stretching back over 500,000 years. Cave paintings, such as those at Bhimbetka, show the remains of advanced Stone Age cultures. The cities of the Indus Valley left reminders of one of the world's earliest urban civilizations scattered over northwestern India. Buddhism and Jainism were born in the foothills of the Himalaya, while Hinduism spread to embrace the majority of India's people. Yet Christianity has also found a home here for nearly 2000 years and Islam and Sikhism have made their own distinctive contribution to cities across India.

India's aboriginal peoples are a tiny remnant of the first migrants to scatter out of Africa on their way to Australia. Yet, living in the remote hills of central India, they were precursors of a flow of peoples that continues to contribute colour and variety to the extraordinarily rich texture of India's population. The remaining tribals of Orissa, Rajasthan or Andhra Pradesh illustrate the melting pot that India has become. The dark skinned Dravidians and their lighter skinned cousins in the north both originated in Central Asia, the former coming via the Mediterranean thousands of years before their so-called Aryan successors. All are brought together today in the packed and busy streets of India's rapidly growing cities.

Rush-hour
Rickshaws jostle for customers during rush-hour on the streets of Old Delhi.

Three hundred and thirty million gods

With its colour, noise, public ritual and private devotion, religious faith is expressed with a fervour across the length and breadth of India almost unique in the modern secular world. Hinduism, numerically dominant and historically the most ancient of India's religions, is very much a way of life. You will notice the ubiquitous black stone lingams under shady trees and the brightly painted wayside shrines to Hanuman, the Monkey god. There are startling images of divinities selected from the vast Hindu pantheon – from the amorous Krishna to the blood-thirsty Kali – displayed on taxi dashboards, while the elephant-headed Ganesh is honoured with burning incense sticks, bringing luck to a shopkeeper. You will see the signs at every step – the sacred *tulsi* (basil) bush in humble courtyards of Hindu homes, early morning bathers taking a dip in a holy river at sunrise and bustling temples with their flower sellers, where foreheads of worshippers are marked with vermilion by temple priests. You may pass ash-covered, bearded *sadhus* (holy men) who have renounced all material possessions wandering among pilgrims, young and old, on a journey of a lifetime, and be overtaken by crowds of devotees accompanied by raucous musicians at any of the innumerable festivals. You can't escape the faces of the "three hundred amd thirty million gods" who together represent Hindu divinity.

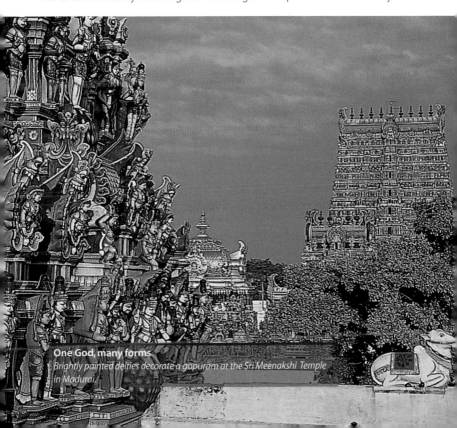

One God, many forms
Brightly painted deities decorate a gopuram at the Sri Meenakshi Temple in Madurai.

1 *Tribals still make up a significant proportion of the population of Rajasthan. The different groups are distinguished by their colourful costumes and jewellery.* ▸▸ *See page 327.*

2 *Coconut husks are poled along the quiet backwaters of Kerala. Travel through the network of rivers, lagoons and canals for a unique glimpse of Keralan village life.* ▸▸ *See page 908.*

3 *The Zanskar River winds through Ladakh's high-altitude desert mountains.* ▸▸ *See page 542.*

4 *The feet of the Gods are moulded from clay in Calcutta. This city has a rich cultural tradition as well as some of the poorest slums in the world.* ▸▸ *See page 579.*

5 *Over 200,000 people, plus droves of cattle and camels, crowd into town for the Pushkar Fair in November.* ▸▸ *See page 353.*

6 *A whitebreasted kingfisher at Keoladeo Ghana National Park. The former hunting reserve is now a UNESCO World Heritage Site due to its protected birdlife.* ▸▸ *See page 347.*

7 *Elephants are often gaily painted when involved in ceremonial duties and festivals.*

8 *The beautiful inlay work of the Mussaman Burj in the Red Fort at Agra.* ▸▸ *See page 160.*

9 *The beaches of Goa range from package resorts to backpacker party destinations, with a few peaceful, undisturbed strands in between.* ▸▸ *See page 1173.*

10 *Pilgrims cross the causeway to Amritsar's holy Har Mandir, the Sikhs' Golden Temple.* ▸▸ *See page 450.*

11 *Elephants stop for a drink in the Kabini River in the Nagarhole National Park.* ▸▸ *See page 986.*

12 *A Hindu deity is decorated with yellow dye and flowers for the spring festival of Vasant Panchami.* ▸▸ *See page 58.*

Land of sacred rivers

India's most holy river, the Ganges, runs across the vital heartland of the country and through the mythology of Hinduism. Joined by other holy rivers along its route, its waters are a vital source of irrigation. Its path is dotted with towns and settlements of great sanctity and it is a vital economic asset. To the south, the great rivers of the peninsula – the Narmada, Krishna, Tungabhadra and Kaveri to name only the largest – also have a spiritual significance to match their roles as providers of water and power.

The heady heights

With a vast stretch of the Himalaya to choose from, the opportunities for trekking in India are virtually limitless. The Garhwal Himalaya, Himachal Pradesh or Ladakh in the northwest all have spectacular routes, while, in the east, the hills around Darjeeling offer wonderful views of Kangchendzonga and its associated ranges. Prepare for the altitude and hard walking, for even though most tracks are in good condition, they can be very demanding. If you fancy something more gentle, try the southern hills of Coorg or the Nilgiris, where you can hike through high-altitude grassland and shola forests.

Golden sands and coral seas

Goa's palm-fringed beaches on the sun-drenched west coast have long provided a magical getaway for travellers. But there are also lesser known strands from Gujarat to Orissa, many ranking as among the most beautiful and sparsely populated in the world. Among them, lushly vegetated and densely populated Kerala in the far southwest adds idyllic backwaters to its coastal fringe. Diving is catching on, too, especially among the coral atolls of the Lakshadweep Islands or in the limpid waters around the scattered Andaman Islands in the Bay of Bengal.

Animal magic

From the foothills of the Himalaya to the forested slopes of the Western Ghats – with a little time and patience – you can see deer, rhino, antelope, wild boar, elephants, panthers and a whole host of other animals. Look out for the flash of a kingfisher, flocks of rose-ringed parakeets or kites and vultures searching for prey or carrion. The forests of Ranthambhore in Rajasthan or Bandhavgarh or Kanha in Madhya Pradesh are among the best places in the world to see tigers in the wild, while the forests, marshes and grasslands of central India, are home to rare species like the gaur, nilgai or sambar. At high altitudes in the Himalaya, the wild yak, snow leopard and bharal are found. The Asiatic lion prowls the open forests of Gir, the blackbuck antelope roams across the arid landscapes of India's northwest and it is now possible to take a camel safari through the distinctive desert landscape of Rajasthan and Gujarat.

Monks signal the start of a religious cermony at the imposing Thikse monastery in Ladakh.

Miracles in stone

The delicately fashioned stone carving of Buddhist-inspired gateways at Sanchi or the almost lace-like fineness of Muslim *jali* windows in Fatehpur Sikri; the towering, richly carved *vimanas* of Hindu temples and the minarets of mosques are all evidence of an extraordinary legacy of architectural skill and craftsmanship. Sites from every region illustrate the flowering of India's diverse cultural traditions. Whether it is a lake-surrounded palace shimmering in the heat, a mountain-top fort towering over a rugged precipice, or an ornately carved temple of latticed stone, every part of India has architectural treasures that are little known to the outside world.

Music and dance

The haunting tones of the sitar and the brilliant rhythms of the tabla capture the unique mystique of India. From its origins in the chants of the ancient scriptures, Indian music has developed into a complex 22-note scale. The Hindustani music of the north is interwoven with Muslim influences, while Carnatic music, which developed in 18th-century South India, uses the distinctive *vina* in place of the sitar Away from the classical tradition, in the villages, local folk dance is used to retell stories of the Hindu epics.

Festivals for all seasons

Every month India is brightened by the colour, sound and feasting that mark religious or seasonal festivals. These moveable feasts are usually linked to the full or the new moon and offer a chance to sample traditional customs, music, dance and theatre. Perhaps the most striking is Diwali, on the dark night of the new moon in October or November. Rows of little clay oil lamps and strings of electric bulbs are lined up on window ledges and balconies, to represent the lights that greeted Rama's return after 14 years in exile, and the night sky bursts with spectacular fireworks and deafening fire crackers.

A monument to love

Of all the world's great monuments the Taj Mahal is one of the most written about, photographed, televised and talked about. To India's Nobel Laureate poet, Tagore, the Taj was a "tear drop on the face of humanity", a building to echo the cry "I have not forgotten, I have not forgotten, O beloved" and its mesmerising power is such that still no one comes away disappointed.

Shah Jahan, fifth of the Great Mughals, was so devoted to his favourite wife, Mumtaz Mahal (Jewel of the Palace) that he could not bear to be parted from her and insisted that she always travel with him, in all states of health. While accompanying him on a military campaign, she died at the age of 39 giving birth to their 14th child. On her deathbed it is said that she asked the emperor to show the world how much they loved one another.

The grief-stricken emperor went into mourning for two years. He turned away from the business of running the empire and devoted himself to architecture, resolving to build his wife the most magnificent memorial on earth. On the right bank of the river Yamuna in full view of his fortress palace, it was to be known as the *Taj-i-Mahal* (The Crown of the Palace).

According to the French traveller Tavernier, work on the Taj commenced in 1632 and took 22 years to complete, employing a workforce of 20,000. The red sandstone was available locally but the white marble was quarried at Makrana in Rajasthan and transported 300 km by a fleet of 1000 elephants. Semi-precious stones for the inlay came from far and wide: red carnelian from Baghdad; red, yellow and brown jasper from the Punjab; green jade and crystal from China; blue lapis lazuli from Ceylon and Afghanistan; turquoise from Tibet; chrysolite from Egypt; amethyst from Persia; agates from the Yemen; dark green malachite from Russia; diamonds from Central India and mother-of-pearl from the Indian Ocean. A three-kilometre ramp was used to lift material up to the dome and, because of the sheer weight of the building, boreholes were filled with metal coins and fragments to provide suitable foundations. The resemblance of the exquisite double dome to a huge pearl is not coincidental: a saying of the Prophet describes the throne of God as a dome of white pearl supported by four pillars.

Myths and controversy surround the Taj Mahal. On its completion it is said that the Emperor ordered the chief mason's right hand to be cut off to prevent him from repeating his masterpiece. Another legend suggests that Shah Jahan intended to build a replica for himself in black marble on the other side of the river, connected to the Taj Mahal by a bridge built with alternate blocks of black and white marble. Some have asserted that architects responsible for designing this superb mausoleum must have come from Turkey, Persia or even Europe (because of the pietra dura work on the tomb). In fact, no one knows who drew the plans. What is certain is that in the Taj Mahal, the traditions of Indian Hindu and Persian Muslim architecture were fused into a completely distinct and perfect art form.

Essentials

⁑ Footprint features

Planning your trip

Where to go

First time visitors are often at a loss when faced with the vast possibilities for travel in India. We have made a few suggestions here for two to three week trips on the basis that some journeys will be flown and that air or rail tickets have been booked in advance. Two or three of these suggested itineraries could be pieced together for those on a longer trip. However, since travelling times are often quite long compared to western standards, it is advisable to stick to a particular region rather than trying to cover too much ground in a short time. Reliable travel agencies are listed through the book, who can make the necessary arrangements for a relatively small fee saving you time and bother. Air tickets can be difficult to get at short notice for some trips, eg Leh-Delhi, Varanasi-Delhi. Indian railways are divided into regions, and despite computerized booking and the growing number of booking offices where all-India reservations can be made there are still places where it is impossible to book train tickets in regions other than the one you are in. Allow a more time if you are planning to travel entirely by road and rail. However, if you use overnight trains for longer journeys you can cover almost as much ground in the same time as flying. Figures in brackets are number of nights we suggest you spend.

The Himalayan Foothills
Two weeks Delhi (2) with both the British built New Delhi and Shah Jahan's 17th-century capital, gives access to some of the most beautiful sights in the Himalayan foothills and awe-inspiring mountain peaks. You can fly to **Shimla** (2), the British summer capital, then continue by road to **Dharamshala** (3) associated with the Dalai Lama and the Tibetan settlement. Spend a night in **Mandi** (1) en route to **Manali** (3) and **Naggar** (2). Fly back to **Delhi** (2) from Kullu to visit **Agra** (1) for the Taj and the splendid fort on the fast Shatabdi Express.

Three weeks Between late June and September the tour could be altered to take in the Tibetan-Buddhist area of **Ladakh** (3) (instead of Dharamshala) by travelling to **Leh** (5) by the spectacular road from **Manali** (2).

Central India - Pre-history to palaces
Two weeks This tour of **Central India** starts in the centre of Muslim influence in **Delhi** (3) and **Agra** (2), and passes through some of the great Rajput palaces and forts in **Gwalior** (3) visiting **Datia** and idyllic **Orchha** (2) via **Jhansi** en route to **Bhopal** (3). Around Bhopal are impressive prehistoric rock art at **Bhimbetka**, and early Hindu and Buddhist remains at **Bhojpur** and **Sanchi**. On the way to **Mumbai** (2) a brief diversion from **Indore** takes you to the quaint fortified site at **Mandu** (2) with its picturesque past.

The Himalayan foothills ———
Central India ············
South India − − −

South India - Historic cultures

One month The **South India** circuit starts at **Mumbai** (2) where you can first visit the rock-cut caves rich in frescoes and carvings at **Ajanta** and **Ellora** and the rugged **Daulatabad** fort near **Aurangabad** (3). Then on to **Hyderabad** (3), with the former capital of the Muslim Nizam with Golconda fort and the tombs nearby. You then visit centres of ancient Tamil culture at **Chidambaram, Gangaikondacholapuram** and **Thanjavur** (2) after **Chennai** (2) fitting in a visit to **Mahabalipuram's** shore temple (2). The tour returns through southern Karnataka via **Mysore** (3), visiting the exquisite carvings in the Hindu and Jain temples at **Belur** and **Halebid** from **Hassan** or **Chikmagalur** (2), and finally to **Bangalore** (2).

The North West - Mughal and Rajput India

One month This route starts in **Delhi** (3) and moves to **Agra** (2) and **Jaipur** (3) before you fly across the desert to **Jaisalmer** (3) and then head for **Jodhpur** (2). On the way to lakeside **Udaipur** (3) you can visit the exquisite Jain temples at **Ranakpur** and the impressive fort at **Kumbhalgarh** from restful **Deogarh** (2). As a bonus, you can sample the charming hospitality at heritage hotels in former palaces and forts in both Rajasthan and Gujarat. Stop at **Poshina** Fort (2) or **Balaram** Palace en route to **Ahmadabad** (3) with its architectural heritage and Calico Museum, before flying back.

The Far South

One month From **Chennai** (2) drive to **Swamimalai** (2) known for traditional bronze casting and continue south to the ancient Tamil temples at **Thanjavur** (2) and **Madurai** (2). A morning start allows a stop at **Padmanabhapuram Palace** on the way across to Kerala on the west coast to relax by the beach at **Kovalam** (3) near Thiruvananthapuram. Take a boat along the backwaters as you move to **Kochi** (3), a fascinating meeting point of Eastern and European cultures. Then drive across to the tea estates of **Munnar** (2), high in the Western Ghats before dropping to the Tamil plains to visit the ancient fort and temples at **Trichy** (2) and **Srirangam**. Before returning home from Chennai, stop by the sea for the rock-cut cave temples at **Mahabalipuram** (3).

Central North India - architectural tradition

One month Across the heart of central North India it is possible to see some of the best examples of Buddhist, Hindu and Muslim art and architecture. Travelling

Essentials Planning your trip

The Northwest ——————
The Far South ·············
Central North India – – –

East India Mountains & Temples ——————
Wildlife Tour North & South ·············

partly by road or rail, you also see a range of India's varied scenery and agriculture, going first across the Deccan plateau, with its rich black lava soils, then over Rajasthan and then Khajuraho on the northern edge of the Peninsula. **Mumbai** (2) - **Aurangabad** (3) for **Ajanta, Ellora** and **Daulatabad** fort - **Udaipur** (3) - **Deogarh** (2) visiting **Ranakpur** Jain temples and **Kumbhalgarh** Fort - **Jaipur** (2) - **Agra** (2) - **Khajuraho** (2) - **Varanasi** (2) - **Delhi** (3).

East India – Mountains and Temples
Two to three weeks The tour starts in **Kolkata** (3), a vibrant city which was once the capital of the Raj, and then takes you to the foothills of the Himalaya starting with **Darjeeling** (3), famous for its tea estates and magnificent views of Kanchengdzonga. Distant **Sikkim** (3) with its distinctive Buddhist influence is a fascinating side trip. Magnificent Orissan temples can be seen at **Bhubaneswar** (3) and **Konark** (with a possible beach diversion near the pilgrimage centre of **Puri** (3), and on to the holy city of **Varanasi** (2) to see India laid bare for the first time visitor. The tour winds up with a visit to see the fabulous carvings at **Khajuraho** (2) and concludes in **Delhi** (3) with a stop en route at **Agra** (2) to see the finest of the Mughal buildings, the Taj Mahal.

Wildlife tours
Each region with its distinctive habitats and outstanding reserves offer many opportunities for seeing wildlife in some of India's 54 national parks and over 370 sanctuaries. The suggested tours take you to the most popular of these and also allow excursions to cultural sites. Most national parks charge foreigners Rs 100-350 per head for entry. Camera/video fees, vehicle charges and guides, usually compulsory, can add a lot to the cost.

One month Northern tour This starts in **Delhi** (2) and goes via **Bhopal** (2) and **Jabalpur** (1) to **Kanha** (3), one of the most outstanding reserves in Central India, with very rich habitat and still little visited. It continues to **Khajuraho** (2), where there is a chance to see magnificent 10th-century temples, en route to **Agra**'s (1) magnificent Taj Mahal and the abandoned city of **Fatehpur Sikri** before arriving at the peaceful bird sanctuary at **Bharatpur** (1), excellent for waterside birds. Not far away, **Ranthambhore** (2), with the semi-arid environment of Rajasthan, is the habitat for a range of wildlife including tigers. Return to **Delhi** (1) via the pink city of **Jaipur** (1) and continue to **Corbett** (3) in the Himalayan foothills. Fly back from Delhi (2).

One month Southern tour This starts in **Chennai** (2) to visit the bird sanctuary of **Vedanthangal** and **Mahabalipuram** (2), by the sea, with its ancient temples. Then travel down to **Trichy** (2) to climb up the rock fort and see the great temple of Srirangam on the banks of the Kaveri. From there the route continues to the hill station of **Coonoor** (1) going up to **Udhagamandalam** (**Ooty**) (1) on the Blue Mountain railway (if it is running), then on to the rich wildlife sanctuary of **Mudumalai-Bandipur** (3). Travelling north into Karnataka, you can visit the beautiful national park of **Nagarhole** (3). A stop in **Mysore** (3) gives a chance to visit and stay in palaces, and to see Tipu Sultan's **Srirangapatnam** before ending the tour at **Bangalore** (3).

Buddhist sites
India has some of the world's most important Buddhist sites. The sacred places of pilgrimage include **Bodh Gaya, Rajgir** and **Sarnath**. The presence of the Dalai Lama draws visitors to **Dharamshala**. The pilgrimage or *Dhammayatra* of old, undertaken by Emperor Asoka in the third century BC, has been extended today to include great centres of Buddhist art and sculpture. **Sanchi, Amaravati, Nagarjunakonda, Ajanta** and **Ellora, Karla** and **Bhaja**.

Forts

A wealth of history awaits you in the forts and citadels of the subcontinent. There are those that still hold rich architectural treasures such as the red forts at **Delhi, Agra** and Meherangarh in **Jodhpur;** those with evocative remains of a bygone lifestyle as in **Gwalior, Orchha** and **Mandu** (Madhya Pradesh), **Kota, Bundi, Jaisalmer** in the desert (Rajasthan) and at **Gingee** (Tamil Nadu) and **Warangal** (Andhra Pradesh). There are desolate ruins at **Cabo de Rama** (Goa) and atmospheric **Hampi-Vijaynagar** (Karnataka) whilst there are marvellous examples of strategic defence at **Kumbhalgarh** (Rajasthan), **Daulatabad** (Maharashtra) and **Golconda** near Hyderabad (Andhra Pradesh). On a smaller scale, the tiny coastal outpost of **Tiracol** in Goa has been restored to accommodate guests. Add to these the numerous fortified 'palaces' now joining the Heritage hotels group in **Rajasthan** and **Gujarat** (Deogarh, Kuchaman, Poshina). Enthusiasts may want to explore the Sivaji forts in **Maharashtra** or the Chandela forts in **Madhya Pradesh.**

When to go → *To check weather conditions try www.wunderground.com.*

In most of India, by far the best time to visit is from the end of the monsoon in October to the end of March. However, there are important exceptions. The hill stations in the Himalaya and the Western Ghats are beautiful in the hot weather months of April to early June. Parts of the western Himalaya can be excellent through to September though it can be very cold and sometimes very wet in the spring. The chart below gives an idea of which states can be visited comfortably during any particular month, indicated by a tick. Because local variations are important, the handbook gives temperatures and rainfall details for all regions and many cities, indicating the most comfortable times to visit.

Some of the country's great festivals such as *Dasara* and *Diwali* across India and *Pongal* in Tamil Nadu are celebrated in the autumn and winter. In Rajasthan, local camel and cattle fairs and the *Desert Festival* among the dunes are added attractions during these seasons.

Tour operators

You may choose to try an inclusive package holiday or let a specialist operator quote for a tailor-made tour. Out of season these can be worth exploring. The lowest prices quoted from the UK vary from about US$550 for a week (flights, hotel and breakfast) in the low season, to over US$3,000 for three weeks during the peak season. Most will chalk out individual itineraries and cover the major sights with small groups. Tour companies are listed here who arrange anything from general tours to wildlife safaris to ashram retreats. See page 67 for a list of trekking operators.

Ace, T01223-835055, ace@studytours.org. Cultural study tours, expert led.
Adventures Abroad, T0114-2473400 (USA & Canada, T800-6653998, Australia T800-890790), info@adventures-abroad.org. Outward bound.
Andrew Brock (*Coromandel*), T01572-821330, abrock@aol.com. Special interest.
Asian Journeys, T01604-234401, F234866, www.asianjourneys.com. Fairs, culture.
Banyan Tours, T01672-564090, www.india-traveldirect.com. Tailored tours, local contact.
Cox & Kings (Taj Group), T020-78735001, F6306038, www.coxandkings.co.uk.

Discovery Initiatives, T020-79786341, www.discoveryinitiatives.com. Wildlife safaris.
Dragoman, T01728-861133, www.dragoman. co.uk. Overland, adventure, camping.
Exodus, T020-8772 3822, www.exodus.co.uk. Adventure holidays.
Gateway to India, T0870-4423204, F4423205, tours@gateway-to-india.com. Tailor-made, off-the-beaten-track, local reps.
Greaves Tours, T020-74879111, F74860722, www.greavesindia.com.
Guerba Expeditions, T01373-826611, info@ guerba.co.uk. Adventure, treks.

	North						East					South				West			
Month	Rajasthan	Uttar Pradesh	Punjab	Madhya Pradesh	Himachal	Ladakh	W Bengal	Orissa	Assam	Sikkim	Bihar	Tamil Nadu	Kerala	Karnataka	Andhra Pradesh	South coast	Maharashtra hills	Goa	Gujarat
January	✓	✓	✓	✓	✓		✓	✓	✓		✓	✓	✓	✓	✓	✓	✓	✓	✓
	Warm days (18-25°), dry, cool nights; very cold and clear in the mountains						Warm days (15-30°C) dry, cool nights					Hot days (30-40°C) dry, cool nights				Hot days (25-35°C) dry, cool nights			
February	✓	✓	✓	✓	✓		✓	✓	✓		✓	✓	✓	✓	✓	✓	✓	✓	✓
	Warm days (18-25°), dry, cool nights; very cold and clear in the mountains						Warm days (20-30°C) dry, cool nights					Hot days (30-40°C) dry; cool and dry in hills				Hot days (25-35°C) dry, cool nights			
March	✓	✓	✓	✓	✓		✓	✓	✓	✓	✓	✓	✓	✓	✓	✓	✓	✓	✓
	Warm days (21-30°), dry, cool nights; cold and clear in the mountains						Cool warm days in hills (20-25°C); cool nights					Hot days (30-40°C) dry; warm and dry in hills by day, cold at night				Hot days (25-35°C) dry, cool nights			
April	✓	✓	✓	✓	✓		✓	✓	✓	✓	✓	✓	✓	✓	✓	✓	✓	✓	✓
	Hot days (30-40°), dry, warm nights; coo and clear in the mountains						Hot on plains (35-42°C); clear warm days in hills (20-25°C), cool nights					Hot (35-42°C) humid on coastal plains; cool and dry in hills				Hot days (25-35°C) dry, cool nights			
May		✓			✓		✓		✓	✓		✓	✓	✓			✓		
	Very hot days (40-50°), dry, hot nights in plains; clear and warm in hills						Very hot (35-45°C) and dry in plains; Warm days in hills (20-30°C), dry, cool nights					Very hot in plains (35-45°C); Warm (20-30°C), dry in hills				Hot days (25-35°C) dry, cool nights			
June				✓											✓			✓	
	Warm days (20-30°C) in hills, rains begins end June, hot (35-45°C) on plains						Warm days in hills (20-30°C), dry, cool nights until rains; hot and wet on plains					Cool, wet & misty in hills, hot (30-35°C) & humid on plains, rains sweep west coast				Hot & wet days (25-35°C), humid nights, coastal Goa & Maharastra have heavy monsoon			
July					✓	✓								✓			✓		
	Warm days (18-25°C), wet except in North & East						Very hot & wet					Hot (30-40°C), showery; wet in hills				Very warm (20-30°C) humid, often wet			
August					✓	✓								✓					
	Warm days (18-25°C), cool nights at atitude						Very hot & wet					Hot (30-40°C), showery; wet in hills				Hot & humid, wet			
September					✓	✓	✓	✓				✓	✓	✓				✓	✓
	Warm days (18-25°C), dry, cool nights; very cold, clear & dry in mountains						In hills warm days (20-25°C), sometimes wet; hotter on plains (35-40°C)					Hot (30-40°C), dry; cooler but still often wet in hills				Hot & humid			

	North						East					South				West			
	Rajasthan	Uttar Pradesh	Punjab	Madhya Pradesh	Himachal	Ladakh	W Bengal	Orissa	Assam	Sikkim	Bihar	Tamil Nadu	Kerala	Karnataka	Andhra Pradesh	South coast	Maharashtra hills	Goa	Gujarat
October	✓	✓	✓	✓	✓		✓	✓	✓	✓	✓	✓	✓			✓	✓	✓	✓
	Hot days (30-40°C), warm nights; mountains getting much cooler						Warm days (20-30°C), dry, cool nights					Hot (30-40°C), cool & dry in hills, monsoon in Tamil Nadu				Hot days (25-35°C), dry, cool nights			
November	✓	✓	✓	✓			✓	✓	✓		✓	✓	✓			✓	✓	✓	✓
	Warm days (18-25°C), dry, cool nights; cold, clear and dry in mountains						Warm days (20-30°C), dry, cool nights					Cyclones in Andhra & Tamil Nadu; hot (30-40°C), hills cooling				Hot days (25-35°C), dry, cool nights			
December	✓	✓	✓	✓	✓		✓	✓	✓		✓	✓	✓			✓	✓	✓	✓
	Warm days (18-25°C), dry, cool nights; very cold, clear & dry in mountains						Warm days (20-30°C), dry, cool nights; cyclones in Orissa					Hot (30- 40°C), dry, cool & dry in hills; cyclones early December in Andhra & Tamil Nadu				Hot days (25-35°C), dry, cool nights			

Indian Magic, T020-84274848, sales@ indiamagic.co.uk. Homestays, small-scale.
Master Travel, T020-86717521, F86742712, www.mastertravel.co.uk. History, ayurveda.
Myths and Mountains, USA T800-6706984, www.mythsandmountains.com. Culture, crafts, religion.
on the go, 68 North End Rd, West Kensington, London W14 9EP, T020- 73711113, F74716414, www.onthegotours.com. Legendary incredible tours and tailormades at amazing prices.
Palanquin Travels, T020-77246022, www.palanquintravels.com. Culture, wildlife.
Pettitts, T01892-515966, F521500, www.pettitts.co.uk. Unusual locations.

Spirit of India, USA T888-3676147, inquire@ spirit-of-india.com. Focused, local experts.
Steppes East, 51 Castle Street, Cirencester, GL7 1QD, UK, T01285-651010, F885888, www.steppeseast.co.uk. Tailor made tours. ATOL protected. Recommended.
Trans Indus, T020-85662729, F8405327, www.transindus.co.uk. Activities, wildlife.
Travelbag Adventures, 15 Turk Street, Alton, Hampshire, GU34 1AG, T01420-593001, www.travelbag- adventures.com. Adventure tours, small groups.
Western & Oriental, T020-73136611, F73136601, enquiries@westernoriental.com. Upmarket, unique heritage hotels.

India Tourist Offices overseas

Australia Level 1, 2 Picadilly, 210 Pitt St, Sydney, NSW 2000, T612-292644855, F92644860.

Canada 60 Bloor St, West Suite No 1003, Toronto, Ontario, T416-9623787, F9626279.

France 11-13 Bis Boulevard Hausmann, F75009, Paris T45233045, F45233345.

Germany Baserler St 48, 60329, Frankfurt AM-Main 1, T069-2429490, F24294977.

Italy Via Albricci 9, Milan 20122, T8053506, F72021681.

Japan Pearl Building, 9-18 Chome Ginza, Chuo Ku, Tokyo 104, T33-5715196, F5715235.

The Netherlands Rokin 9-15, 1012 Amsterdam, T020-6208991, F6383059.

Singapore 20 Kramat Lane, 01-01A United House, Singapore 0922. T2353800, F2358677.

Sweden Sveavagen 9-11 1st Flr, S-III 57 Stockholm 11157, T468-101187, F210186.

Switzerland 1-3 rue de Chantepoulet, 1201 Geneva, T41-227321813, F7315660.

Thailand 3rd Flr, KFC Bldg, 62/5 Thaniya Rd, Bangkok 10500, T662-2352585, F2368411.

UK 7 Cork St, London W1X 2AB, T020-74373677, F74941048.

USA 3550 Wilshire Blvd, Room 204, Los Angeles, California 90010. T213-3808855, F3806111; Suite 1808, 1270 Avenue of Americas, New York, NY 10020, T212-5864901, F5823274.

Finding out more

Tourist offices

There are Government of India Tourist offices in Delhi and the state capitals, as well as State Tourist Offices (usually known as Tourism Development Corporations) in the major cities and a few important sites. In addition, some regions eg Kumaon (KMVN) and Garhwal (GMVN) in Uttaranchal, Darjeeling (DGHC) in West Bengal have their own offices. They produce their own tourist literature, either free or sold at a nominal price, and some also have lists of city hotels and paying guest options. The quality of material is improving though maps handed out are often inadequate. Many offer tours of the city, neighbouring sights and overnight and regional packages. Some run modest hotels and mid-way motels with restaurants, and may also arrange car hire and guides. The staff in the regional and local offices are usually helpful, although the standard of information can be widely variable from town to town. Don't take advice from unofficial 'Tourist Offices' at airports or railway stations.

Websites

www.123india.com Wide ranging current affairs and general India site.

www.fco.gov Advice to travellers from the Foreign Office, London.

www.indev.org British Council site devoted to development issues in India.

www.india.org Contains excellent information on the structure of Indian government. Also **www.indiagov.org.**

www.indiacurrentaffairs.com Regularly updated cuttings from Indian national dailies.

www.indianrail.gov.in Has wide-ranging information on the railways.

www.responsibletravel.com Green tourism.

www.tourindia.com The official government promotional site with useful information but has no objective evaluation of problems and difficulties. 'India Travel Online' is informative and issued fortnightly.

www.travel.indiamart.com Commercial site Details of online bookings for selected hotels.

www.tourismindia.com Yellow pages.

www.travel-health.co.uk/index.html and **www. tripprep.com** Health advice prior to travel.

Language

Hindi, spoken as a mother tongue by over 400 million people, is India's official language. The use of English is also enshrined in the Constitution for a wide range of official purposes, notably communication between Hindi and non-Hindi speaking states. The most widely spoken Indo-Aryan languages are: Bengali (8.3%), Marathi (8%), Urdu (5.7%), Gujarati (5.4%), Oriya (3.7%) and Punjabi (3.2%). Among the Dravidian languages Telugu (8.2%), Tamil (7%), Kannada (4.2%) and Malayalam (3.5%) are the most widely used. Most of these languages have their own scripts. In all, there are 15 major and several hundred minor languages and dialects. In this book many town names are written in the relevant regional language, as many place names on sign boards, buses and stations are only given in a regional script.

English now plays an important role across India. It is widely spoken in towns and cities and even in quite remote villages it is usually not difficult to find someone who speaks at least a little English. Other European languages are almost completely unknown. The accent in which English is spoken is often affected strongly by the mother tongue of the speaker and there have been changes in common grammar which sometimes make it sound unusual. Many of these changes have become standard Indian English usage, as valid as any other varieties of English used around the world. It is possible to study a number of Indian languages at language centres.

Disabled travellers

India is not geared up specially for making provisions for the physically handicapped or wheelchair bound traveller. Access to buildings, toilets (sometimes 'squat' type), pavements, kerbs and public transport can prove frustrating, but it is easy to find people to give a hand with lifting and carrying. Provided there is an able-bodied companion to scout around and arrange help, and so long as you are prepared to pay for at least mid-price hotels or guesthouses, private car-hire and taxis, India should be perfectly rewarding, even if in a somewhat limited way.

Some travel companies are beginning to specialize in exciting holidays, tailor-made for individuals depending on their level of disability. For those with access to the internet, a Global Access - Disabled Travel Network Site is www.geocities.com/Paris/1502. It is dedicated to providing travel information for 'disabled adventurers' and includes a number of reviews and tips from members of the public. You might also want to read *Nothing Ventured*, edited by Alison Walsh (Harper Collins), which gives personal accounts of worldwide journeys by disabled travellers, plus advice and listings.

Gay and lesbian travellers

Indian law forbids homosexual acts for men (but not women) and carries a maximum sentence of life imprisonment. Although it is common to see young males holding hands in public, it doesn't necessarily indicate a gay relationship and is usually an expression of friendship. Overt displays of affection between homosexuals and hetrosexuals give offence and should be avoided.

Student travellers

Full time students qualify for an ISIC (International Student Identity Card) which is issued by student travel and specialist agencies (eg *STA*) at home. It allows certain travel concessions and acts as proof of student status within India which may allow ticket concessions into a few sites. Those intending to study in India may get a one year student visa, see page 27.

Travelling with children → *For further information see www.babygoes2.com.*

Children of all ages are widely welcomed, being greeted with a warmth in their own right which is often then extended to those accompanying them. However, care should be taken when travelling to remote areas where health services are primitive since children can become more rapidly ill than adults. It is best to visit India in the cooler months since you need to protect children from the sun, heat, dehydration and mosquito bites. Cool showers or baths help, and avoid being out during the hottest part of the day. Diarrhoea and vomiting are the most common problems, so take the usual precautions, but more intensively. Breastfeeding is best and most convenient for babies. In the big cities you can get safe baby foods and formula milk. It doesn't harm a baby to eat an unvaried and limited diet of familiar food carried in packets for a few weeks if the local dishes are not acceptable, but it may be an idea to give vitamin and mineral supplements. Wet wipes, always useful, are sometimes difficult to find in India as are disposable nappies. The biggest hotels provide babysitting.

Women travellers

Although it is relatively safe for women to travel around India, most people find it an advantage to travel with a companion. Even then, privacy is rarely respected and there can be a lot of hassle, pressure and intrusion on your personal space, as well as some outright harassment. Backpackers setting out alone often meet like-minded travelling companions at budget hotels. If you are blonde, you are quite naturally likely to attract more attention. Some seasoned travellers find that dyeing their hair dark, helps. See also below and page 41. One way of dealing with people who hassle you on the street is to simply say "thank you", smile and walk away. If you show annoyance, it may result in more pestering or abusive language. Cases of rape in Goa have been reported at late or after late night parties. It is best to walk in a group at night.

Working in the country

Volunteering It is best to arrange voluntary work well in advance with organizations in India (addresses are given in some towns, eg Delhi, Darjeeling, Dharamshala, Kolkata, Leh); alternatively, contact an organisation abroad.

Co-ordinating Committee for International Voluntary Service, 1 rue Miollis, 75732 Paris, France, T01-45684936, www.unesco.org/ccivs.
Council for International Programs, 1101 Wilson Blvd Ste 1708, Arlington, VA 22209.
International Voluntary Service, 7 Upper Bow, Edinburgh EH1 2JN, UK, T0131-2266722, F2266723, www.sci-ivs.org.

VSO, 317 Putney Bridge Rd, London SW15 2PN, UK, T020-87807200, F87807300, www.vso.org.uk.
Volunteer Work Information Service, PO Box 2759, Lewes, BN7 1WU, UK, T01273-470015, www.workingabroad.com. Students in UK may spend part of their 'year off' helping in a school through 'GAP', teach English, or help with a conservation project through 'i to i' International Projects, 1 Cottage Rd, Headingly, Leeds, LS6 4DD, T0870-332332, www.i-to-i.com.

Before you travel

Visas and immigration

Documents Virtually all foreign nationals require a visa to enter India. Nationals of Bhutan and Nepal only require a suitable means of identification. The rules regarding visas change frequently and arrangements for application and collection also vary from town to town so it is essential to check details and costs with the relevant office. These remain closed on Indian national holidays. In London, applications are processed in an hour or two (0800-1200). Visitors from countries which do not have an Indian representation may apply to the resident British representative, or enquire at the *Air India* office. An application on the prescribed form should be accompanied by three passport photographs and your passport which should be valid for at least three months beyond the period of the visit.

Visas Visa fees vary according to nationality. The following visas are available: **Transit** For passengers en route to another country (valid up to 5 days). **Tourist** Six month visa, from the date of issue with multiple entry. Most visitors require this type. **Business** Up to one year from the date of issue. A letter from company giving the nature of business is required. **Five year** For those of Indian origin only, who have held Indian passports, and their spouses. **Student** Valid up to one year from the date of issue. Attach a letter of acceptance from Indian institution, and an AIDS test certificate. Allow up to three months for approval. **Visa extensions** Applications should be made to the Foreigners' Regional Registration Offices at New Delhi, Mumbai, Kolkata or Chennai, or an office of the Superintendent of Police in the District Headquarters. After six months, those with a tourist visa must leave India and apply for a new visa - the Nepal office is known to be difficult.

No foreigner needs to **register** within the 180 day period of their tourist visa. All foreign visitors who stay in India for more than 180 days are required to register at the nearest Foreigners' Registration Office and get an **income tax clearance** exemption certificate from the Foreign Section of the Income Tax Department in Delhi, Mumbai, Kolkata or Chennai.

Embassies

Australia, 3-5 Moonah Place, Yarralumla, Canberra T2733999; Level 27, 25 Bligh St, Sydney T2239500; Melbourne T3840141.
Austria, Kärntner Ring 2, A-1015 Vienna, T01-5058666, F5059219.
Bangladesh, 2 Dhanmondi RA, House 129, Dhaka-2, T503606, Chittagong T654021.
Belgium, 217-Chaussée de Vleurgat, 1050 Brussels, T02-6409802, F02-6489638. Consulates: Ghent T09-263423, Antwerp T03-2341122.
Bhutan, India House Estate, Thimpu, T09752-22162.
Canada, 10 Springfield Rd, Ottawa, Ontario K1M 1C9, T613-7443751. Consulates: Toronto T416-9600751, Vancouver T604-6628811.

Denmark, Vangehusvej 15, 2100 Copenhagen, T31982888, F39270218.
Finland, Satamakatu 2 A8, 00160 Helsinki-16, T608927.
France, 15 Rue Alfred Dehodencq, Paris, 101-40507070. Visas from consulate in next street (deposit passport 0930-1030, collect same day 1600-1700) is in the next street at 20 Rue Albéric Magnard, 75016 Paris, T01 40507171.
Germany, Tiergartenstrasse, visa at Pohlstr 20, 10785 Berlin, T030-4853002, F4853003. Consulates: Willy-Brandt Allee 16, 53113 Bonn T0228-540132, Friedrich Ebert Anlage 26, 60325 Frankfurt T069-271040, Raboisen 6, 20095 Hamburg T040-338036, Munich T089- 92562067, Stuttgart T0711-1530050.
Ireland, 6 Lesson Park, Dublin 6, T01-4970843, F4978074.

Israel, 4 Kaufmann St, Sharbat, Tel Aviv 68012, T03-5101431, F5100894.
Italy, Via XX Settembre 5, 00187 Rome, T06-4884642. Consulates: Milan T02-8690314, Genoa T010-54891.
Japan, 2-11, Kudan Minami 2-Chome, Chiyoda-ku, Tokyo 102, T03-32622391, F03-32344866. Consulate: Kobe T078-2418116.
Korea, 37-3, Hannam-dong, Yongsan-Ku, Seoul, T7984257, F7969534.
Malaysia, 19 Malacca St, Kuala Lumpur, T221766.
Maldives, Mafabbu Aage 37, Orchid Magu, Male 20-02, T323015.
Nepal, Lainchour, PO Box No 292, Kathmandu, T0891-410900.
Netherlands, Buitenrustweg 2, The Hague (2517KD), T070-3469771.
New Zealand, 10th Flr, Princess Tower, 180 Molesworth St (PO Box 4045), Wellington, T4736390.
Norway, 30 Niels Jules Gate, 0272 Oslo-2, T22443194, F22440720.
Pakistan, G5 Diplomatic Enclave, Islamabad, T050-814731, Karachi T021-522275.
Singapore, 31 Grange Rd, Singapore 0923, T7376777.

Spain, Avda Pio XII 30-32, 28016 Madrid, T091-4570209. Consulate: Barcelona T093-2120422.
Sri Lanka, 36-38 Galle Rd, Colombo 3, T01-421605 Kandy, T08-446430.
Sweden, Adolf Fredriks Kyrkogata 12, Box 1340, 11183 Stockholm, T08-107008, F08-248505.
Switzerland, Kirchenfeldstr 28, CH-3005 Bern, T031-3511100.
Thailand, 46, Soi 23 (Prasarn Mitr) Sukhumvit 23, Bangkok 10110, T2580300.
UK, India House, Aldwych, London WC2B 4NA, T020-78368484 (0930-1300, 1400-1730), www.hcilondon.org. Consulates: The Spencers, 20 Augusta St, Hockley, Birmingham, B18 6DS, T0121-2122782; Rutland Sq, Edinburgh EH1 2BB, T0131-2292144; 6th floor, 134 Renfrew St, Glasgow 3 7ST, T0141-3310777, F3310666. (Send SAE for postal applications.)
USA, 2107 Massachusetts Ave, Washington DC 20008, T0202-9397000. Consulates: Houston, Texas, T7136262148, New Orleans T0504-5828105, New York T0212-7740600, San Francisco T0415-6680683, Chicago T0312-5950405.

Restricted and protected areas

Some areas are politically sensitive. The border regions, tribal areas and Himalayan zones are subject to restrictions and special permits may be needed to visit them though the government is relaxing its regulations.

Currently the following require special permits: **Arunachal Pradesh, Manipur** (for five days), **Mizoram** and **Nagaland**. Apply to the Under Secretary, Ministry of Home Affairs, Foreigners Division, Lok Nayak Bhavan, Khan Market, New Delhi 110003 at least four weeks in advance. Special permission is no longer needed to visit Assam, Meghalaya and Tripura. **Andaman Islands** Permits are issued for 30 days to visit some of the islands on arrival at Port Blair, see page 755. **Lakshadweep Islands** Foreigners may visit Bangaram and Suheli Islands only; permits from the Lakshadweep Administration, Willingdon Island, Harbour Rd, Kochi 3. **Sikkim** Permits for 15 days are issued by a large number of government offices.

Work permits

Foreigners should apply to the Indian representative in their country of origin for the latest information about work permits.

Liquor permits

Periodically some Indian states have tried to enforce prohibition. Some degree of prohibition is in force in Gujarat, Mizoram and Manipur. When applying for your visa you can ask for an All India Liquor Permit. Foreigners can also get the permit from any Govt of India Tourist Office in Delhi or the state capitals. Instant 'spot' permits are issued by some hotels.

Exchange rates

	Rs		Rs
Australian $	30	New Zealand $	29
Euro	50	United Kingdom £	80
Japanese Yen	0.40	United States $	45

What to take → *See also Checklist on page 71.*

Travel light. Most essentials are available in the larger cities, items are cheap and laundry services are generally speedy. Here are some items you might find particularly helpful:

Loose-fitting, light cotton **clothes** are good for travelling almost anywhere at any time of year, being cool and comfortable with the added advantage of being quick drying. Pale colours may give some protection against mosquitoes. Sarongs are useful - they can be used as a skirt, scarf, towel etc. Women should dress modestly. Brief shorts and tight vest tops are best avoided, though on the beach 'modest' swimwear is fine. Locally bought, inexpensive and cool *kurta pyjama* for men, and *shalwar kameez* for women are excellent options on the plains but it can be cold in the north between December and February and also everywhere at heights above 1,500 m, where some heavier clothing is essential. Comfortable shoes, sandals or trainers are essential. Take high-factor sun screen and a sun hat.

It is best to take a sufficient supply of personal **medicines** from home, including inhalers and anti-malarial drugs (Proguanil is not available from pharmacists). Most **toiletries**, contact lens cleaners, tampons and barrier contraceptives are available in the larger cities. Contact lens wearers may be affected by pollution in some large cities, so carry spectacles and a spare set plus your prescription.

Photocopies of essential **documents**, passport identification and visa pages, and spare photos are useful when applying for permits or in case of loss or theft.

The wealth of **photographic** opportunity justifies good equipment. The following is recommended: a single reflex camera with interchangeable lenses; wide angle (28-35 mm), tele-photo (70-200), macro lens (for good close-ups); ultra-violet and a polarising filter for dusty conditions and high altitudes; plenty of film and extra batteries (they are affected by very low temperatures); waterproof covering for all equipment. Although good quality films are available in all major cities and tourist centres, it is best to take rolls of films from home and certainly any specialist camera batteries. In India, only buy films from a reputable shop since hawkers and roadside stalls may not be reliable; check the carton carefully as well as the expiry date. Whilst on the subject, many monuments now charge a camera fee ranging from Rs 20-50 for still cameras, and as much as Rs 500 for video cameras (more for professionals). Special permits are needed from the Archaeological Survey of India, Delhi for using tripods and artificial lights.

Budget travellers Nets are rarely provided in cheap hotels so try to take an impregnated mosquito net. A wedge-shaped one (for single-point fixing) is preferable. Earplugs come in handy when a hotel room is particularly noisy, especially during festivals when loudspeakers playing Hindi film music tend to work overtime. On overnight journeys, blocking out the perpetual light is effective with eyemasks (given away by some airlines). Take a good padlock to secure your budget room too. Those with a secret combination number are recommended. A cotton, sheet sleeping bag which can cover a pillow; these are cheap and easy to get made at any tailor's shop. Toilet paper, soap, towel and the washbasin plug may all be missing so be prepared.

Money

Prices in the handbook are quoted in Rupees, although top hotels often quote rates in US$. Very few people are familiar with international currencies apart from currency touts on city street corners. Visitors do best to think in Rupee terms.

Currency

→ *Always check the security features carefully and avoid changing with unlicensed dealers.*

Indian currency is the Indian Rupee (Re/Rs). It is **not** possible to purchase these before you leave. If you want cash on arrival it is best to get it at the airport bank. Rupee notes are printed in denominations of Rs 1000 (rarely seen), 500, 100, 50, 20, 10. The Rupee is divided into 100 Paise. Coins are minted in denominations of Rs 5, 2, 1, and 50, 25, 20, 10 and 5 Paise, though coins below 50 paise are rarely seen. Carry money, mostly as travellers' cheques, in a money belt worn under clothing. Have enough for daily requirements in an easily accessible place. The Rs 500 note is difficult to change outside the big cities, and it has also encouraged a wave of convincing forged copies.

Exchange

Travellers' cheques (TCs) issued by **American Express** and **Thomas Cook** are accepted without difficulty in the major towns and tourist centres. Most banks, but not all, will accept US$ or £ sterling TCs, so it is a good idea to carry some of each. Other major currency TCs are also accepted in some larger cities. Euro currency notes may not be accepted in Indian banking for some time, so do not rely on them alone. TCs can be exchanged in banks, hotels or a growing number of private dealers, the latter often offering a faster service at a higher rate. They can be used directly for payment in the more expensive hotels and souvenir shops, as well as for purchasing airline tickets and foreign quota train tickets. Otherwise, ensure that you have enough cash to cover your needs. Your passport and visa must be shown. In banks, encashing any form of currency nearly always takes up to 30 minutes or longer, so it is worth taking larger denomination TCs and changing enough money to last for some days. If you are travelling to remote areas it can be worth buying Indian Rupee TCs from a major bank, as these are more widely accepted than foreign currency ones. If stolen, you must get a police report and be prepared to contact the issuing company with the numbers of the stolen cheques, your receipt and a plausible story! For some, the wait for replacement cheques can take weeks, so take great care of them!

Credit cards and debit cards Major credit cards are increasingly acceptable in the main centres, but with exceptions (eg Chennai does not give cash against **Amex**). In smaller cities and towns it is still rare to be able to pay by credit card. Payment by credit card can sometimes be more expensive than payment by cash, whilst some credit card companies charge a premium on cash withdrawals. **Visa** and **Mastercard** have a growing number of **ATMs** in major cities; try *ICICI*, *HDFC* and *Centurion Banks*. This is by the far easiest way to obtain cash against either a credit or debit card. Railway Reservation centres in 17 major cities are now taking payment for train tickets by Visa card which can be very quick as the queue is very short, although they cannot generally be used for Tourist Quota tickets! Websites that list locations of ATMs that are http://international.visa.com, www.mastercard.com and www.americanexpress.com.

Changing money If you cash sterling, make certain you have not been given Rupees at the dollar rate. The *State Bank of India* and several others in major towns are authorized to deal in foreign exchange. Some give cash against **Visa/Master cards** (eg *Standard Chartered Grindlays*, *Bank of Baroda* who print a list of their

Money matters

It can be difficult to use torn or very worn currency notes. Check notes when you are given them and refuse any that are damaged.

Request some Rs 100 and 50 notes. Rs 500 (can be mistaken for Rs 100) notes can reduce 'wallet bulge' but be difficult to change.

A good supply of small denomination notes always comes in handy for bus tickets, cheap meals and tipping. Remember that if offered a large note, the recipient will never have any change!

It can be worth carrying a few clean, new sterling or dollar notes for use where travellers' cheques and credit cards are not accepted. It is likely to be quite a while before Euro notes are widely accepted.

participating branches, *Andhra Bank*). **American Express** cardholders can use their cards to get either cash or TCs in the four major cities. They also have offices in Ahmadabad, Coimbatore, Goa, Guwahati, Hyderabad, Pune, Thiruvananthapuram and Vadodara. The larger cities and tourist centres have **licensed money changers** with offices usually in the commercial sector. Changing money through unauthorized dealers is illegal. There is virtually no currency black market now. Premiums on the street corner are very small and highly risky, especially with the influx of fake Rs 500 notes. Large **hotels** change money 24 hours a day for guests, but banks often give a substantially better rate of exchange than hotels.

It is best to get exchange on arrival at the airport bank or the *Thomas Cook* counter. Thomas Cook has a high reputation for excellent service and have branches across the country. Many international flights arrive during the night, and it is generally far easier and less time consuming to change money at the airport than in the city.

You should be given a foreign currency **encashment certificate** when you change money through a bank or authorized dealer. Ask for one if it is not automatically given. It allows you to change Indian Rupees back to your own currency on departure, so ensure that you have a valid one at this time. It also enables you to use Rupees to pay hotel bills or buy air or train tickets for which payment in foreign exchange may be required although in practice, those using mid-range or cheaper hotels rarely have to produce them. The certificates are only valid for three months.

Transferring money to India

Thomas Cook, *American Express* and *Standard Chartered Grindlays* and others can make 'instant' transfers to their offices in India but charge a high fee (about US$30 or 15%). Sending a bank draft (up to US$1,000) by post (4-7 days by Speedpost) is the cheapest option. **Western Union** have a growing number of agents (check www.westernunion.com), while Thomas Cook, operates through international Moneygram, www.moneygram.com.

Cost of living

The cost of living in India remains well below that in the West. The average wage is about Rs 12,000 per month (US$240) for government employees according to government statistics - manual workers and unskilled labourers expect to earn at least Rs 100 per day; women are often paid less than men, and in some parts of rural India earn as little as Rs 30.

Cost of travelling

Most food, accommodation and public transport, especially rail and bus, are exceptionally cheap. There is a widening range of moderately priced but clean hotels and restaurants outside the big cities, making it possible to get a great deal for your money. Budget travellers sharing a room, eating in local restaurants, and using the cheapest means of travel can expect to spend around Rs 450-500 (about US$10-12) a day, though you can each get by on less in the south. Those looking for the comfort of the occasional night in a simple a/c room, and using reserved seats on trains and luxury buses, should budget for about US$25-30 a day. However, if you travel alone and are looking for reasonably comfortable a/c rooms, use taxis and second class a/c train berths, expect to spend around US$70 a day. When shopping or hiring an unmetered vehicle, bargaining is expected, and essential.

Getting there

Air

India is accessible by air from virtually every continent. Most international flights arrive in Delhi, Mumbai,Chennai or Kolkata. There are also international airports in several other cities (eg Ahmadabad, Ludhiana, Thiruvananthapuram, Goa), some of which allow customs formalities to be completed there although the flight may be routed through a principal airport. Some carriers permit 'open-jaw' travel, arriving in, and departing from, different cities in India. Some (eg **Air India, British Airways**) have convenient non-stop flights from Europe, eg from London to Delhi, takes only nine hours.

Charter flights
Several tour operators from Europe, especially from Britain (eg *First Choice,* T0870-7500001, www.firstchoice.co.uk; *JMC,* T0870-7580203, www.holidays.jmc.com, *Jewel in the Crown,* T01293-533338, www.jewelholidays.com, *Manos,* T01273-427333, www.manos.co.uk, *Somak,* T020-84233000, F84237700, www.somak.co.uk, *Tropical Places,* T01342-330710, www.tropical.co.uk) flying from Gatwick and Manchester, offer package holidays between October and April to Goa and Kerala. They are often exceptional value (especially in November and from mid-January to mid-March).

The following rules apply:
1 They are not available to Indian nationals.
2 The deal must include accommodation. If you take the cheap 'dorm house' option, it may be necessary to change to a more comfortable room. It may be difficult to find a room during the peak Christmas and New Year period so it is worth paying a little extra on booking, to ensure accommodation of a reasonable standard.
3 Officially, charter passengers can only stay for a maximum of 45 days, although this restriction can be bent somewhat if you have a valid visa to cover the duration of your proposed extension. You may not travel on a non-charter international flight (eg to Sri Lanka) while in India.

Stop-overs and Round-the-World tickets
You can arrange several stop-overs in India on Round-the-World and long distance tickets. RTW tickets allow you to fly in to one and out from another international aiport. You may be able to arrange some internal flights using international carriers eg **Air India,** www.airindia.com, sometimes allows stop-overs within India for a small extra charge.

Discounts
The cheapest fares from Europe tend to be with Central European, Central Asian or Middle Eastern airlines. With these airlines it pays to confirm your return flight as early as possible. You can also get good discounts from Australasia, Southeast Asia and Japan.

If you plan to visit two or more South Asian countries within three weeks, you may qualify for a 30% discount on your international tickets. Ask your National Tourist office. International air tickets can be bought in India though payment must be made in foreign exchange.

Ticket agents

Companies dealing in volume and taking reduced commissions for ticket sales can offer better deals than the airlines themselves. The national press carry their advertisements. *Trailfinders* of London, T020-79383939, worldwide agencies; *STA*, in London, T0870-1606070, www.statravel.co.uk, with over 100 offices worldwide, offers special deals for under-26s; *Travelbag*, T01420-80828, www.travelbag. adventures.co.uk, quotes competitive fares. **General Sales Agents** (GSAs) for specific airlines can sometimes offer attractive deals: *Jet Air*, 188 Hammersmith Rd, London W6 7DJ, T020-89701555, for *Gulf Air*, *Kuwait Airways* etc and **Welcome Travels**, 58 Wells St, London W1P 3RA, T020-74363011, for *Air India*.

Airline security

International airlines vary in their arrangements and requirements for security, in particular the carrying of equipment like radios, tape-recorders, lap-top computers and batteries. It is advisable to ring the airline in advance to confirm what their current regulations are. **Internal airlines often have different rules from the international carriers**. You are strongly advised not to pack valuables in your luggage. Avoid repacking at the airport.

From the UK, Continental Europe and the Middle East

➔ *Expect to pay anything from £300 to £500 from London.*
The best deals are offered from the UK (try www.cheapflights.com, which also provides additional useful information). You can pick up attractive deals on *Air India* which flies direct to Delhi and Mumbai throughout the year. A few European airlines (eg *Lufthansa*, *KLM*) and several from the Middle East (eg *Emirates*, *Gulf Air*, *Kuwait Airways*, *Royal Jordanian*) offer good discounts to Mumbai and other Indian regional capitals from London, but fly via their hub cities, so adding to the journey time. *Virgin Atlantic* www.virgin-atlantic.com, now offer a three times weekly London-Delhi-London service. Good deals can be offered by General Sales Agents (GSAs), see above. Consolidators in UK quote competitive fares: *Bridge the World*, T0870-4447474, www.b-t-w.co.uk. *Flight bookers*, T087-0107000 from UK, 020-77572626 from elsewhere, www.ebookers.com. *North South Travel*, T01245- 608291 (profits to charity).

From Australasia via the Far East

Qantas, *Singapore Airlines*, *Thai Airways*, *Malaysian Airlines*, *Cathay Pacific* and *Air India* are the principal airlines connecting the continents. They fly to one of the Indian regional capitals. *STA* and *Flight Centres* offer discounted tickets from their branches in major cities in Australia and New Zealand. *Abercrombie & Kent*, *Adventure World*, *Peregrine*, and *Travel Corporation of India*, organize tours.

From North America

From the east coast, it is best to fly direct to India from New York via London by *Air India* (18 hours), or pick up a direct charter from UK to Goa or Thiruvananthapuram but this will usually involve a stopover in London. Discounted tickets on *British Airways*, *KLM*, *Lufthansa*, *Gulf Air* and *Kuwait Airways* are sold through agents although they will invariably fly via their country's capital cities. From the west coast, it is best to fly via Hong Kong, Singapore or Bangkok to Delhi, Kolkata or Mumbai using one of those countries' national carriers. *Air Brokers International*, www.airbrokers.com, are competitive and reputable. *Hari World Travels*, www.hariworld.com, and *STA*, www.statravel.co.uk, have offices in many US cities, Toronto and Ontario. Student fares are also available from *Council Travel*, www.counciltravel.com, with several offices in the USA and *Travel Cuts*, T0800-6672887, www.travelcuts.com, in Canada.

Road

Crossings between India and its neighbours are affected by the political relations between them. Get your Indian visa in advance, before arriving at the border. Several road border crossings are open periodically, but permission to cross cannot be guaranteed. Those listed below are the main crossings which are normally open throughout the year to tourists. New direct 'friendship' **buses** have been introduced between Lahore and Delhi, and between Dhaka and Kolkata. Note also that you are not allowed to take any Indian currency from India into Pakistan. Indian Rupees can be changed on a 1:1 basis at the border.

From Bangladesh

To Kolkata from Dhaka and Jessore. The Bangaon-Benapol crossing is the most reliable. On the Bangladesh side rickshaws are available from Benapol, while buses and minibuses go to Bangaon railway station from the border. **To Tripura** from Dhaka is only four hours by road from the border crossing just 2 km from the centre of Agartala, which has flights to Kolkata. The border post is efficient when open but arrive there before 1500, as the formalities often take time. Regulations are subject to change so find out in advance. In London, Bangladesh High Commission, T020-75840081, F72252130.

From Bhutan

To Bagdogra, the nearest airport is three to four hours' drive from Jaigaon, the rather untidy and unkempt Indian border town. The Indian Immigration checkpost is on the main street, about a kilometre from the 'Bhutan Gate' at the border town of Phuntsholing where it is possible to spend a night. Accommodation ranges from the simple *Central Hotel* to the moderate government run *Druk Hotel*. To enter Bhutan you need an Entry Permit and a Visa.

From Nepal

➔ *Four crossings are in common use: enquire from the Nepal Embassy, T020-72291594, F72299861, London.*
To Delhi via Banbassa is the shortest direct route between Kathmandu and Delhi, via the Nepali town of Mahendranagar and Banbassa.

To Varanasi via Gorakhpur you must go to the **Sonauli-Bhairawa** crossing, the shortest and fastest route to Varanasi; many continue to Delhi from there. From Kathmandu or Pokhara you can get to Bhairawa, 6 km inside the Nepal border, Sonauli on the border itself, and Nautanwa on the Indian side. From there, buses take 3½ hours to Gorakhpur, with train connections for Delhi, or 5½ hours by bus to Varanasi, see page 203.

To Patna via Raxaul-Birganj several buses run daily from Raxaul to Patna (5-7 hours) but timings are unreliable and the buses are crowded and uncomfortable. Night buses from Patna reach the border in the early morning; morning buses from Patna connect with the night bus to Kathmandu. Either way you have to have at least one night bus journey unless you stay overnight at Birganj or Raxaul, which is not recommended. The bus journey between Kathmandu or Pokhara and the border takes about 11-12 hours. Even Express buses are slow and packed. 'Tourist' minibuses are the only moderately comfortable option. For details see Patna, page 737.

Kakarbhitta (Kakarvita) is on the Nepalese side of a wide river which forms the border here between India and Nepal. A kilometre long road bridge links it to the Indian town of Raniganj on the east bank. Cycle rickshaws run between the two. A small notice and an Indian flag are all that mark the Indian Immigration checkpost which is in a shady grove of trees by the road. The larger Indian town of Bagdogra is 15 km away. For details see under Siliguri, page 611.

From Pakistan

Wagha border, 23 km from Lahore, is the only crossing open. Vans from central Lahore take you to the border where you walk across through Pakistani and Indian immigration and customs. There are taxis and rickshaws on the Indian side to take you to Attari; buses from there go to **Amritsar** (see page 457). The only **train crossing** is an uncertain one. The Lahore to Amritsar train via the Wagha border post is scheduled to run twice weekly but it can take five hours to clear customs. It is normally much slower than the bus and is not recommended.

From Europe

The reopening of Iran to travellers of most nationalities has reinstated the Istanbul-Teheran- Quetta route when the political situation in the region is stable. We highly recommend Footprint's *Pakistan Handbook* for anyone contemplating the journey.

Touching down

Airport information

Duty free allowance

→ *Some airports have duty free shops though the range of goods is very limited.*

Tourists are allowed to bring in all personal effects 'which may reasonably be required', without charge. The official customs allowance includes 200 cigarettes or 50 cigars, 0.95 litres of alcohol, a camera with five rolls of film and a pair of binoculars. Valuable personal effects or professional equipment must be registered on a Tourist Baggage Re Export Form (TBRE), including jewellery, special camera equipment and lenses, lap-top computers, sound and video recorders. These forms require the serial numbers of such equipment. It saves considerable frustration if you know the numbers in advance and are ready to show the serial numbers on the equipment. In addition to the forms, details of imported equipment may be entered into your passport. Save time by completing the formalities while waiting for your baggage. **It is essential to keep these forms** for showing to the customs when leaving India, otherwise considerable delays are very likely at the time of departure.

Currency regulations

There are no restrictions on the amount of foreign currency or travellers' cheques a tourist may bring into India. If you were carrying more than US$10,000 or its equivalent in cash or travellers' cheques you need to fill in a currency declaration form.

Prohibited items

The import of dangerous drugs, live plants, gold coins, gold and silver bullion and silver coins not in current use are either banned or subject to strict regulation. It is illegal to import firearms into India without special permission. Enquire at consular offices abroad for details.

Export restrictions

Export of gold jewellery purchased in India is allowed up to a value of Rs 2,000 and other jewellery (including settings with precious stones) up to a value of Rs 10,000.

Touching down

Electricity 220-240 volts AC. Some top hotels have transformers. There may be pronounced variations in the voltage, and power cuts are common. During power cuts, diesel generators are often used to provide power for essential equipment but this may not always cover air-conditioning. India uses round-pin plugs and socket sizes vary so you are advised to take a universal adaptor (available at most airports). Many hotels don't have electric razor sockets.

Hours of business Banks: 1030-1430, Monday-Friday; 1030-1230, Saturday. Top hotels sometimes have a 24-hour service. **Post offices**: Usually 1000-1700, Monday-Friday; Saturday mornings.

Government offices: 0930-1700, Monday- Friday; 0930-1300, Saturday (some open on alternate Saturday). **Shops**: 0930-1800, Monday-Saturday. Bazars keep longer hours. There are regional variations.

IDD 91. A double ring repeated regularly means it is ringing. Equal tones with equal pauses means engaged.

Official time GMT +5½ hours throughout the year (USA, EST +10½ hours).

Weights and measures Metric system has come into universal use in the cities. In remote areas local measures are sometimes used. One lakh is 100,000 and 1 core is 10 million.

Export of antiquities and art objects over 100 years old is restricted. Ivory, skins of all animals, *toosh* wool, snake skin and articles made from them are banned, unless you get permission for export. For further information enquire at the Indian High Commission or consulate, or access the Government of India at www.indiagov.org, or the customs at www.konark.ncst.ernet.in/ customs/.

Documentation

The formalities on arrival in India have been increasingly streamlined during the last five years and the facilities at the major international airports greatly improved. However, arrival can still be a slow process. Disembarkation cards, with an attached customs declaration, are handed out to passengers during the inward flight. The immigration form should be handed in at the immigration counter on arrival. The customs slip will be returned, for handing over to the customs on leaving the baggage collection hall. The immigration formalities at both Delhi and Mumbai can be very slow. You may well find that there are delays of over an hour in processing passengers passing through immigration who need help with filling forms.

Departure tax

Rs 500 is payable for all international departures other than those to neighbouring SAARC countries, when the tax is Rs 150. This must be paid in Rupees in India unless it is included in your international ticket; check when buying. Look for 'FT' in the tax column of your ticket. A domestic departure tax is payable on internal flights when the ticket has been paid for in Rupees. 'Security Check' your baggage for the hold before checking-in at Departure and identify them again outside the departure lounge. Cabin baggage should have a luggage tag for stamping after it has been security checked. Regulations are extra strict in sensitive border areas and at military airports (eg Leh, Ladakh and Dabolim, Goa).

⁝ First impressions

On arrival at any of India's major cities the first impressions can take you aback. The exciting images of an ancient and richly diverse culture which draw many visitors to India can be overwhelmed by the immediate sensations which first greet you...

Pollution All the cities seriously suffer.

Noise Many people also find India incredibly noisy, as radios, videos and loudspeakers seem to blare in unlikely places at **all** times.

Smells India has an almost baffling mixture of smells, from the richly pungent and unpleasant to the delicately subtle.

Pressure From stepping out of your hotel everybody seems to clamour to sell you their services. Taxi and rickshaw drivers are always there when you don't want them, much less often when you do. There often seems to be no sense of personal space or privacy. Young women are often stared at.

Public hygiene – or lack of it. It is common to see people urinating in public places and defecating in the open countryside. These can all be daunting and make early adjustment to India difficult. Even on a short visit give yourself time and space to adjust.

Essentials Touching down

Public transport to and from airport
→ *See detailed advice under international airports.*

Most major international airports have special **bus** services into the town centre from early morning to around midnight. **Pre-paid taxis** to the city are available at all major airports. Some airports have up to three categories, 'limousine', 'luxury' and ordinary. The first two usually have prominent counters, so you may have to insist if you want to use the standard service. Insist on being taken to your chosen destination even if the driver claims the city is unsafe, or there is a major festival and everywhere is full, or the hotel has closed down, etc...

Local customs and laws

Most travellers experience great warmth and hospitality in India. You may however, be surprised that with the warm welcome comes an open curiosity about personal matters. Total strangers on a train, for example, may ask for details about your job, income and family circumstances, or discuss politics and religion.

Conduct
Respect for the foreign visitor should be reciprocated by a sensitivity towards local customs and culture. How you dress is mostly how people judge you. Clean, modest clothes and a smile go a long way. Scanty, tight clothing draws unwanted attention. Nudity is not permitted on beaches in India and although there are some places where this ban is ignored, it causes much offence. Displays of intimacy are not considered suitable in public. You may at times be justifiably frustrated by delays, bureaucracy and inefficiency, but displays of anger and rudeness will not achieve anything positive, and often make things worse. The concept of time and punctuality is also rather vague so be prepared to be kept waiting.

Courtesy
It takes little effort to learn common gestures of courtesy and they are greatly appreciated. The **greeting** when meeting or parting, used universally among the Hindus across India,

is the palms joined together as in prayer, sometimes accompanied with the word *namaste* (North and West), *namoshkar* (East) or *vanakkam* in Tamil. Muslims use the greeting *assalām aleikum*, with the response *waleikum assalām*, meaning 'peace be with you'; '**please**' is *mehrbani-se*; '**thank you**' is often expressed by a smile, or with the somewhat formal *dhannyabad*, *shukriya* (Urdu), and *nandri* in Tamil.

⁝ No smoking please

Several state governments have passed a law banning smoking in all public buildings and transport but exempting 'open spaces'. To avoid fines, check for notices.

Hands and eating

Traditionally, Indians use the right hand for eating, cutlery being alien at the table although westernized restaurants will always provide these. In rural India, don't expect table knives and forks though you might find small spoons. Use your right hand for giving, receiving, eating or shaking hands as the left is considered to be unclean since it is associated with washing after using the toilet.

Women

Indian women in urban and rural areas differ in their social interactions with men. Certainly, to the westerner, Indian women may seem to remain in the background and appear shy when approached, often hiding their face and avoiding eye contact. Yet you will see them working in public, often in jobs traditionally associated with men in the West, in the fields, in construction sites or in the market place. Even from a distance, men should not photograph women without their consent.

Women do not, in general, shake hands with men since physical contact is not traditionally acceptable between acquaintances of the opposite sex. A westernized city woman, however, may feel free to shake hands with a foreign visitor. In traditional rural circles, it is still the custom for men to be offered food first, separately, so don't be surprised if you, as foreign guest (man or woman), are awarded this special status when invited to an Indian home, and never set eyes on your hostess.

Visiting religious sites → *Walk clockwise around a shrine (keeping it to your right).*
Visitors to all religious places should be dressed in clean, modest clothes; shorts and vests are inappropriate. Always remove shoes before entering a temple or mosque (and all leather items in Jain temples). Sun-baked stone floors often call for thick socks to protect against the heat. Menstruating women are considered 'unclean' and should not enter places of worship. It is discourteous to sit with one's back to a temple or shrine. You will be expected to sit cross-legged on the floor - avoid pointing your feet at others when attending prayers at a temple.

Non-Hindus are sometimes excluded from the inner sanctum of **Hindu** temples and occasionally even from the temple itself. Look for signs or ask. In certain temples, and on special occasions, men may only enter if they wear unstitched clothing such as a *dhoti*.

In **Buddhist** shrines, turn prayer wheels in a clockwise direction. In **Sikh** gurudwaras, everyone should cover their head, even if it is with a handkerchief. Tobacco and cigarettes should not be taken in. In **Muslim** mosques, visitors should only have their face, hands and feet exposed; women should also cover their heads. Mosques may be closed to non-Muslims shortly before formal prayers.

Some temples have a register or a receipt book for **donations** which works like an obligatory entry fee. The money is normally used for the upkeep and services of the temple or monastery. In some pilgrimage centres, as at Pushkar, priests can become unpleasantly persistent. In general, if you wish to leave a donation, put money in the donation box; some priests and Buddhist monks do not handle money. It is not customary to shake hands with a priest or monk. **Alms** *Sanyasis* (holy men), and some pilgrims, depend on gifts of money.

Guide fees

Guides at tourist sites vary considerably in their knowledge and ability. Government trained and l1icensed guides are covered by specified fees. Local temple and site guides should charge less. Approximate charges: for four people for half a day, Rs 280, for a full day, Rs 400; for five to 15 people for half a day Rs 400, for a full day, Rs 530. Rs 125 for a language other than English.

Begging

Beggars are often found in busy street corners in large Indian cities, as well as at bus and train stations where they often target foreigners for special attention. Visitors usually find this very distressing, especially the sight of severely undernourished children or those displaying physical deformity. You may be particularly affected when some persist on making physical contact. You might find a firm "*Jaao*" (go away) works. In the larger cities, beggars are often exploited by syndicates which cream off most of their takings. Yet those seeking alms near religious sites are another matter, and you may see Indian worshippers giving freely to those less fortunate than themselves, since this is tied up with gaining 'merit'. How you deal with begging is a matter of personal choice but it is perhaps better to give to a recognized charity than to make largely ineffectual handouts to individuals. It is not helpful to hand out sweets, 'school pens' and money indiscriminately to open-palmed children who tag on to any foreigner. Some visitors prefer to give food to beggars.

Young people occasionally follow travellers around and attempt to exchange words in English. When you find this tiring, say "bye bye". If you wish to avoid shaking hands, use the Indian greeting and say *namaste*.

Charitable giving → www.IndianOs.com, www.Indiacharitynet.com.

Some visitors like to support self-help co-operatives, orphanages, disabled or disadvantaged groups, or international charities which work with local partners, by either making a donation or by buying their products. Some of these are listed under the appropriate towns. A few (which also welcome volunteers) are listed here.

Concern India Foundation, 6K Dubash Marg, Mumbai, T022-2029707, www.concernindia.org, is an umbrella organization working with local charities. **Oxfam**, Sushil Bhawan, 210 Shahpur Jat, New Delhi 110049, T011-6491774; 274 Banbury Rd, Oxford OX2 7D2, UK (400 grassroots projects). **SOS Children's Villages**, A-7 Nizamuddin (W), New Delhi 110013, T011-4647835, (over 30 poor and orphaned children's projects in India. **Trek-Aid**, 2 Somerset Cottages, Stoke Villages, Plymouth, Devon, PL3 4AZ, (health, education etc through self-help schemes for displaced Tibetan refugees). **Save the Children India**, 4C Swapnalok, 47 LJ Mard, Mumbai 400036, www.savethechildrenindia.org. **Urmul Trust**, Urmul Dairy, Ganganagar Rd, Bikaner, Rajasthan, T523093 (health care, education and rural crafts in Rajasthani villages). **Very Special Arts India**, C 418 Defence Colony, New Delhi, T4615243, verdi@ del2.vsnl.net.in, promotes the creative power in people with disabilities and works to enrich their lives through remedial therapies.

Tipping

A tip of Rs 10 to a bell-boy carrying luggage in a modest **hotel** (Rs 20 in a higher category) would be appropriate. In up-market **restaurants**, a 10% tip is acceptable when 'Service' is not already included, while in places serving very cheap meals, round off the bill with small change. Indians don't normally tip **taxi drivers** but a small extra amount over the fare is welcomed. **Porters** at airports and railway stations often have a fixed rate displayed but will usually press for more. Rs 10 per item carried would be fair. For tour guides, a tip of Rs 50 per day from each member of a coach group (or Rs 100 per person in a car) can safely be regarded as generous.

Photography

When photographing people, it is polite to first ask - they will usually respond warmly with smiles, although the 'moment' may have been lost as they line up, military style! Visitors often promise to send copies of the photos - don't, unless you really mean to do so. Photography of airports, military installations, bridges and in tribal and 'sensitive border areas', is not permitted.

Safety

Personal security

In general the threats to personal security for travellers in India are remarkably small. In most areas it is possible to travel either individually or in groups without any risk of personal violence. However, care is necessary in some places, and basic common sense needs to be used with respect to looking after valuables.

Some parts of India are subject to political violence. The Vale of Kashmir and Jammu remains under tight military control. Even when the border area is relatively quiet, very few hotels are open in Srinagar and the army is massively deployed and on constant alert. Despite the promises of travel touts that Kashmir is completely safe, tourists who visit, do so at considerable risk and are subjected to regular curfews. There is no prospect of an early solution to the political problem or of a quick return to normality. Some areas have long been noted for banditry. However in the great majority of places visited by tourists, violent crime and personal attacks are extremely rare.

Theft

Theft is not uncommon. It is best to keep travellers' cheques, passports and valuables with you at all times since you can't regard hotel rooms as automatically safe; even hotel safes don't guarantee secure storage. Avoid leaving valuables near open windows even when you are in the room. Use your own padlock in a budget hotel when you go out. Pickpockets and other thieves operate in the big cities. Crowded areas are particularly high risk. Take special care of your belongings when getting on or off public transport. **Never** accept food or drink from casual acquaintances; travellers have reported being drugged and then robbed.

Confidence tricksters

These are particularly common where people are on the move, notably around railway stations or places where budget tourists gather. A common plea is some sudden and desperate calamity; sometimes a letter will be produced in English to back up the claim. The demands are likely to increase sharply if sympathy is shown. See also page 62.

Security on trains

It can be difficult to keep an eye on your belongings when travelling. Nothing of value should be left close to open train windows. First class a/c compartments are self-contained and normally completely secure. Second class a/c compartments are larger, allowing more movement of passengers but are not so secure so luggage should be chained to a seat for security overnight. Locks and chains are easily available at main stations and bazaars but they are better brought from home. Some travellers prefer to reserve upper berths which offer some added protection against theft and also have the benefit of allowing daytime sleeping.

Police → *Some towns have introduced special Tourist Police to help the foreign traveller.*

If you have items stolen, they should be reported to the police as soon as possible. Keep a separate record of vital documents, including passport details and travellers' cheques numbers. Larger hotels will be able to assist in contacting and dealing with the police.

Dealings with the police can be very difficult and in the worst regions such as Bihar even dangerous. The paperwork involved in reporting losses can be time consuming and irritating, and your own documentation (eg passport and visas) may be demanded. In some states the police themselves sometimes demand bribes, though tourists should not assume, however, that if procedures move slowly they are automatically being expected to offer a bribe. If you face really serious problems, for example in connection with a driving accident, you should contact your consular office as quickly as possible. You should ensure you always have your International driving licence and motorbike or car documentation with you.

Drugs

Certain areas have become associated with foreigners taking drugs such as Manali and Manikaran (Himachal), Puri (Orissa), Kovalam (Kerala), Gokarna and Hampi (Karnataka) and the beaches in Goa. Be aware that the government takes the misuse of drugs very seriously. Anyone charged with the illegal possession of drugs risks facing a fine of Rs 100,000 and a minimum 10 years' imprisonment.

Women travellers → *See also page 26.*

There are some simple precautions to take, particularly when travelling alone, to avoid both personal harassment and giving offence. Modest dress is always advisable; loose-fitting non-see-through clothes, covering the shoulders, and skirts, dresses or shorts of a decent length attract less attention. Many find the *shalwar-kameez*-scarf ideal. In mosques women should be covered from head to ankle. In Sikh temples everyone should cover their heads. Unaccompanied women are most vulnerable in major cities, crowded bazars, beach resorts and tourist centres where men may follow them and touch them. "Eve teasing" is the euphemism for physical harassment; some buses have seats reserved for women. If you are harassed, it can be effective to make a scene. Avoid travelling alone by rickshaw or taxi late at night. It is best to be accompanied by a friend while being measured for clothing in tailors' shops or when having an ayurvedic massage.

Be firm and clear if you don't wish to speak to someone. To deal with unwanted advances from men, one tip is to say that you are married (wearing a 'wedding' ring may help); having children also raises your level of respect.

Advice

It Is better to seek advice on security from your own embassy than from travel agencies. Before you travel you can contact:

Australian Department of Foreign Affairs, Canberra, Australia, T06-62613305, www.dfat.gov.au/consular/advice.html. Canadian official advice is on www.dfait-maeci.gc.ca/travelreport/menu_e.html.
British Foreign and Commonwealth Office, Travel Advice Unit, Consular Division, 1 Palace St, London SW1E 5HE, UK, T020-72384503, F72384545, www.fco.gov.uk/travel.
US State Department's Bureau of Consular Affairs, Overseas Citizens Services, Room 4800, Department of State, Washington, DC 20520-4818, USA, T0202-6474225, F6473000, www.travel.state.gov/travel_warnings.html.

Getting around

Air

India has a comprehensive network linking the major cities of the different states. In addition to **Indian Airlines** (the nationalized carrier), www.indian-airlines.nic.in, and its subsidiary **Alliance Air**, there are a few private airlines such as **Jet Airways**, www.jetairways.com, and **Sahara**, www.saharaairline.com, which provide supplementary flights on several routes as well as filling gaps in a particular area, as with **Jagson**. Competition from the efficiently run private sector has, in general, improved the quality of services provided by the nationalized airlines. The Airports Authorities too have made efforts to improve handling on the ground. Although flying is expensive, for covering vast distances or awkward links on a route, it is an option worth considering, though delays and re-routing can be irritating. For short distances, and on some routes (eg Delhi-Agra-Delhi), it makes more sense to travel by train.

Air tickets → *See table on page 43 for approximate prices.*

All the major airlines are connected to the central reservation system and there are local travel agents who will book your tickets for a fee if you don't want to spend precious time waiting in a queue. Remember that tickets are in great demand in the peak season on some sectors (eg Delhi-Leh-Delhi) so it is essential to get them months ahead. If you are able to pre-plan your trip, it is even possible to ask if the internal flights can be booked at the time you buy your international air ticket at home through an agent (eg **Trailfinders**, **SD Enterprises**, London) or direct (eg **Jet Airways**). You can also book internal flights on the internet, www.welcomtravel.com, and collect and pay for them on your arrival in India.

Payment

Non-resident, foreign passport holders buying air tickets in India must pay the 'US dollar rate' (higher than published Rupee rates) and pay in foreign exchange (major credit cards, travellers' cheques accepted), or in rupees against an encashment certificate which will be endorsed accordingly. There is very little difference in prices quoted by competing airlines.

Special fares

Indian Airlines, www.indian-airlines.nic.in, and **Jet Airways**, www.jetairways.com, offer special seven, 15 and 21 day unlimited travel, deals from around US$300-750 (some are limited to one sector) which represent good savings. **Youth fares** 25% discount is given on US$ fares for anyone between 12 and 30 years. **Night savers** 25% discount fares are being introduced on late night flights between some metropolitan cities.

Delays

Be prepared for delays, especially in North India during the winter. Nearly all northern routes originate in Delhi, where from early December through to February, smog has become an increasingly common morning hazard, sometimes delaying departures by several hours.

Air travel tips

Security Indian airlines don't permit batteries in cabin baggage, and once confiscated, you may never see your batteries again. You may need to identify your baggage after they have been checked in and just before they are loaded onto the

Approximate economy airfares on popular routes

Sector	US$	Sector	US$	Sector	US$
From Agra to:		From Bhubaneshwar to:		From Goa to:	
Delhi	60	Kolkata[4]	90	Mumbai	100
Khajuraho	90	Chennai	205	From Hyderabad to:	
Varanasi	110	Delhi	220	Mumbai	125
From Ahmedabad to:		Varanasi	130	Nagpur	115
Bangalore	225	From Bhuj to:		From Jaipur to:	
Kolkata[4]	235	Mumbai	105	Jodhpur	85
Chennai	250	From Calicut[2] to:		Mumbai	160
Delhi	140	Chennai	95	Udaipur	85
Hyderabad	170	Mumbai	145	From Jammu to:	
Jaipur	110	From Chandigarh to:		Leh	75
Mumbai	90	Delhi	80	From Jodhpur to:	
Vadodara	40	Leh	75	Mumbai	155
From Amritsar to:		From Chennai to:		From Khajuraho:	
Delhi	105	Cochin[3]	125	Varanasi	85
From Aurangabad to:		Coimbatore	95	From Kolkata[4] to:	
Delhi	170	Delhi	265	Chennai	225
Mumbai	80	Goa	145	Delhi	205
From Bagdogra for Darjeeling to:		Hyderabad	110	Guwahati	75
		Madurai	95	Jaipur	225
Kolkata[4]	85	Mangalore	110	Lucknow	160
Delhi	190	Mumbai	165	Mumbai	235
Guwahati	55	Port Blair	200	Patna	105
From Bangalore to:		Trichy	85	Port Blair	200
Kolkata[4]	270	Trivandrum[1]	110	Visakhapatnam	150
Chennai	70	From Cochin[3] to:		From Mangalore to:	
Cochin[3]	85	Goa	130	Mumbai	125
Delhi	260	Mumbai	160	From Mumbai to:	
Goa	110	From Delhi to:		Trivandrum[1]	200
Hyderabad	110	Goa	240		
Mumbai	145	Jodhpur	110		
Pune	150	Khajuraho	105		
Trivandrum[1]	125	Leh	110		
From Bhopal to:		Mumbai	180		
Delhi	125	Trivandrum[1]	365		
Mumbai	135	Udaipur	110		

Alternative names:
[1] Thiruvananthapuram
[2] Kozhikode
[3] Kochi
[4] Calcutta

Essentials Getting around

plane. All baggage destined for the hold must be X-rayed by security before checking in, so do this first on arrival at the airport.

Telephone There is a free telephone service at major airports (occasionally through the tourist office counter), to contact any hotel of your choice.

Wait-lists If you don't have a confirmed booking and are 'wait-listed' it pays to arrive early at the airport and be persistent in enquiring about your position.

Rail → www.indianrail.gov.in.

Trains can still be the cheapest and most comfortable means of travelling long distances saving you hotel expenses on overnight journeys. It gives access to

⁝ Riding the rails

High class, comfortable, and by Indian standards quick new Express trains have brought many journeys within daytime reach. But while they offer an increasingly functional means of covering long distances in comfort, it is the overnight trips which still retain something of the early feel of Indian train travel. The bedding carefully prepared – and now available on a/c Second Class trains – the early morning light illuminating another stretch of hazy Indian landscape, the spontaneous conversations with fellow travellers – these are still on offer, giving a value far beyond the still modest prices. Furthermore, India still has a complete guide to its rail timetables.

booking station Retiring Rooms, which can be useful from time to time. Above all, you have an ideal opportunity to meet local travellers and catch a glimpse of life on the ground. Remember the dark glass fitted on a/c coaches does restrict vision.

High-speed trains

There are over 170 air-conditioned 'high-speed' **Shatabdi** for day travel, and **Rajdhani Express** ('Capital City') for overnight journeys. These cover large sections of the network but as they are in high demand you need to book them up to 60 days ahead. Meals and drinks are usually included.

Royal trains

You can travel like a maharaja on the **Palace on Wheels** which gives visitors an opportunity to see some of the 'royal' cities in Rajasthan during the winter months for around US$250 a day (see page 330). A similar tour which also includes a part of Gujarat is **The Royal Orient** which uses the old royal carriages. The **Bauddha Parikrama Express** which runs from Kolkata, covers some important Buddhist locations. The introduction of a further 'royal' route in Andhra Pradesh is expected.

Steam

For rail enthusiasts, the steam-hauled narrow-gauge trains between Kurseong and Darjeeling in North Bengal (a World Heritage Site), and between Mettupalayam and Coonoor, and a special one between Ooty and Runnymede in the Nilgiris, are an attraction. **SD Enterprises** (address below) is recommended for tailor-made trips. The oldest working steam engine, *Fairy Queen*, built in 1855, runs a weekend tour to Sariska from Delhi in the winter. See page 330.

Classes

A/c First Class, available only on main routes and cheaper than flying, is very comfortable (bedding provided). It will also be possible for tourists to reserve special coaches (some a/c) which are normally allocated to senior railway officials only. **A/c Sleeper**, two and three-tier, are clean and comfortable and good value. **A/c Executive Class**, with wide reclining seats, are available on many *Shatabdi* trains at double the price of the ordinary **a/c Chair Car** which are equally comfortable. **1st Class** (non-a/c) is gradually being phased out (now rather run-down but still pleasant if you like open windows). **Sleeper Class** provides basic upholstered seats and is a 'Reserved' class though tickets are sometimes 'subject to available accomodation'. **2nd Class** (non-a/c) two and three-tier, provides exceptionally cheap travel but can be crowded and uncomfortable, and toilet facilities can be unpleasant. It is nearly always better to use the Indian style toilets as they are better maintained.

Train touts

Many railway stations – and some bus stations and major tourist sites – are heavily populated with touts. Self-styled 'agents' will board trains before they enter the station and seek out tourists, often picking up their luggage and setting off with words such as "Madam!/Sir! Come with me madam/sir! You need top class hotel ...". They will even select porters to take your luggage without giving you any say. If you have succeeded in getting off the train or even in obtaining a trolley you will find hands eager to push it for you. For a first time visitor such touts can be more than a nuisance. You need to keep calm and firm. Decide in advance where you want to stay. If you need a porter on trains, select one yourself and agree a price **before** the porter sets off with your baggage. If travelling with a companion one can stay guarding the luggage while the other gets hold of a taxi and negotiates the price to the hotel. It sounds complicated, and sometimes it feels it. The most important thing is to behave as if you know what you are doing!

Essentials Getting around

Indrail passes

These allow travel across the network without having to pay extra reservation fees and sleeper charges but you have to spend a high proportion of your time on the train to make it worthwhile. However, the advantages of pre-arranged reservations and automatic access to 'Tourist Quotas' can tip the balance in their favour for some travellers.

Tourists (foreigners and Indians resident abroad) may buy these passes for periods ranging from seven to 90 days from the tourist sections of principal railway booking offices, and pay in foreign currency, major credit cards, travellers' cheques or rupees with encashment certificates. Rail-cum-air tickets are also to be made available.

Indrail passes can also conveniently be bought abroad from special agents. For most people contemplating a single long journey soon after arriving in India, the Half or One day Pass with a confirmed reservation is worth the peace of mind, two or four day passes are also sold. A White Pass allows first class a/c travel; a Green, a/c two-tier Sleepers and Chair Cars; and the Yellow, only second class travel. Passes for up to four days' duration are only sold abroad.

Cost A/c first class costs about double the rate for two-tier shown below, and non a/c second class about half. Children (five-12) travel at half the adult fare. The young (12-30) and senior citizens (65+) are allowed a 30% discount on journeys over 500 km (just show passport).

Period	US$ A/c 2-tier	Period	US$ A/c 2-tier
½ day	26	21 days	198
1 day	43	30 days	248
7 days	135	60 days	400
15 days	185	90 days	530

Fares for individual journeys are based on distance covered and reflect both the class and the type of train. Higher rates apply on the Mail and Express trains and the air conditioned *Shatabdi* and *Rajdhani Expresses*.

Rail travel tips → *For long journeys reserve a berth well in advance.*
Food and drink: it is best to carry some though tea and snacks are sold on the platforms (through the windows). Carry plenty of small notes and coins on long

journeys. Rs 50 and Rs 100 notes can be difficult to change when purchasing small food items. On long distance trains, the 'pantry' car is often near the upper class carriages (bogies).

Timetables Regional timetables are available cheaply from station bookstalls; the monthly 'Indian Bradshaw' is sold in principal stations. The handy 'Trains at a Glance' (Rs 25) lists popular trains likely to be used by most foreign travellers and is available in UK from SD Enterprises Ltd (see Indrail).

Delays Always allow plenty of time for booking and for making connections. Delays are common on all types of transport. The special **Shatabdi** and **Rajdhani Express** are generally quite reliable. Ordinary Express and Mail trains have priority over local services and occasionally surprise by being punctual, but generally the longer the journey time, the greater the delay. Delays on the rail network are cumulative, so arrivals and departures from mid-stations are often several hours behind schedule. Allow at least two hours for connections, more if the first part of the journey is long distance.

Tickets By asking a travel agent to get yours for a small fee, usually around Rs 50, saves much time and effort. Non-Indrail Pass tickets can be bought over the counter. It is always best to book as far in advance as possible (usually up to 60 days). Avoid touts at the station offering tickets, hotels or money changing. Only 'General Quota' (ie 2nd Class) tickets are sold on the day of travel. All others must be reserved in advance. For last minute trips, buy a 2nd Class ticket and request and pay for an upgrade from the Travelling Ticket Inspector (TTE) on board.

Ladies' queues Separate (much shorter) ticket queues may be available for women.

Credit cards Some main stations now have separate credit card booking queues - even shorter than women's queues! A service charge of Rs 30 is levied.

Quotas A large number of seats are technically reserved as 'quotas' for various groups of travellers (civil servants, military personnel, foreign tourists etc). In addition, many stations have their own quota for particular trains so that a train may be 'fully booked' when there are still some tickets available from the special quota of other stations. These are only sold on the day of departure so wait-listed passengers are often able to travel at the last minute. Ask the Superintendent on duty to try the 'Special' or 'VIP Quota'. The 'Tatkal' system realeases a small percentage of seats at 0800 on the day before a train departs; you pay an extra Rs 50 to get on an otherwise heavily booked train.

Reservations Ask for the separate Tourist Quota counter at main stations, and while queuing fill up the Reservation Form which requires the number and name of the train, preferred class of travel, and the passenger's name, age and sex (for Tourist Quota you may need to mention the passport number and nationality); you can use one form for up to six passengers. If you don't have a reservation for a particular train but carry an Indrail Pass, you may get one by arriving about three hours early. Tourist Quota tickets must be paid for in foreign exchange, so have an exchange certificate handy if yu use Rupees. It is possible to buy tickets for trains on most routes countrywide at many of the 520 computerised reservation centres across India. A short cut is to buy an ordinary 2nd class ticket and try upgrading to a/c by paying the conductor.

Porters They can carry prodigious amounts of luggage. Rates vary from station to station but around Rs 10 per item of luggage (check board on the station platform) is fair. They can be quite aggressive particularly on the main tourist routes: be firm but polite and remember that they will always leave the train when it pulls out of the station!

Getting a seat It is usually impossible to make seat reservations at small 'intermediate' stations as they don't have an allocation. You can sometimes use a porter to get you a seat in a second class carriage. For about Rs 20 he will take the luggage and ensure that you get a seat.

Berths It is worth asking for upper berths, especially in second class three-tier sleepers, as they can also be used during the day time when the lower berths are used as seats, and which may only be used for lying down after 2100.

Overbooking Passengers with valid tickets but no berth reservations are sometimes permitted to travel overnight, causing great discomfort to travellers occupying lower berths. Wait-listed passengers should confirm the status of their ticket in advance by calling enquiries at the nearest computerised reservation office. At the station, check the reservation charts (usually on the relevant platform) and contact the Station Manager or Ticket Collector.

Bedding Travelling at night in the winter can be very cold in North India and in a/c coaches. Bedding is provided on second class a/c sleepers. On others it can be hired for Rs 20 from the Station Manager for first class.

Ladies' compartments A woman travelling alone, overnight, on an unreserved second class train can ask if there is one of these.

Security Keep valuables close to you, securely locked, and away from windows. For security, carry a good lock and chain to attach your luggage. There are usually metal loops under the lower berth for this purpose.

Left-luggage Bags left in station cloakrooms must be lockable. Don't leave any food in them. These are especially useful when there is time to sight-see before an evening train, although luggage can be left for up to 30 days.

Pre-paid taxis Many main stations have a pre-paid taxi (or rickshaw) service which offers a reliable, fair-price service. Give your receipt to the driver upon reaching the destination.

Road

Road travel is often the only choice for reaching many of the places of outstanding interest in which India is so rich. For the uninitiated, travel by road can also be a worrying experience because of the apparent absence of conventional traffic regulations and also in the mountains, especially during the rainy season when landslides are possible. Vehicles drive on the left - in theory. Routes around the major cities are usually crowded with lorry traffic, especially at night, and the main roads are often poor and slow. There are a few motorway- style expressways, but most main roads are single track. Some district roads are quiet, and although they are not fast they can be a good way of seeing the country and village life if you have the time.

Bus

Buses now reach virtually every part of India, offering a cheap, if often uncomfortable, means of visiting places off the rail network. Very few villages are now more than 2 or 3 km from a bus stop. Services are run by the State Corporation from the State Bus Stand (and private companies which often have offices nearby). The latter allow advance reservation and though tickets prices are a little higher, they have fewer stops and are a bit more comfortable.

There are three categories. **A/c luxury coaches**: though comfortable for sight-seeing trips, apart from the very best 'sleeper coaches', even these can be very uncomfortable for really long journeys. Often the air conditioning is very cold, so wrap up. Journeys over 10 hours can be extremely tiring so it is better to go by train if there is a choice. **Express buses**: run over long distances (frequently overnight), these are often called 'video coaches' and can be an appalling experience unless you appreciate loud film music blasting through the night. Ear plugs and eye masks may ease the pain. They rarely average more than 45 km per hour. **Local buses**: these are often very crowded, quite bumpy and slow and usually poorly maintained. However, over short distances, they can be a very cheap, friendly and easy way of getting about. Even where signboards are not in English someone will usually give you directions. Many larger towns have **minibus** services which charge a little more than the buses and pick up and drop passengers on request. Again very crowded, and with restricted headroom, they are the fastest way of getting about many of the larger towns.

⫶ The hazards of road travel

On most routes it is impossible to average more than 50-60 kph in a car. Journeys are often very long, and can seem an endless succession of horn blowing, unexpected dangers, and unforeseen delays. Villages are often congested – beware of the concealed spine-breaking speed bumps – and cattle, sheep and goats may wander at will across the road. Directions can also be difficult to find. Drivers frequently don't know the way, maps are often hopelessly inaccurate and map reading is an almost entirely unknown skill. Training in driving is negligible and the test often a farce. You will note a characteristic side-saddle posture, one hand constantly on the horn, but there can be real dangers from poor judgement, irresponsible overtaking and a general philosophy of 'might is right'.

Bus travel tips Some towns have different bus stations for different destinations. Booking on major long-distance routes is now computerized. Book in advance where possible and avoid the back of the bus where it can be very bumpy. If your destination is only served by a local bus you may do better to take the Express bus and 'persuade' the driver, with a tip in advance, to stop where you want to get off. You will have to pay the full fare to the first stop beyond your destination but you will get there faster and more comfortably. When an unreserved bus pulls into a bus station, there is usually an unholy scramble for seats, whilst those arriving have to struggle to get off! In many areas there is an unwritten 'rule of reservation' using handkerchiefs or bags thrust through the windows to reserve seats. Some visitors may feel a more justified right to a seat having fought their way through the crowd, but it is generally best to do as local people do and be prepared with a handkerchief or 'sarong'. As soon as it touches the seat, it is yours!

Car

A car provides a chance to travel off the beaten track, and gives unrivalled opportunities for seeing something of India's great variety of villages and small towns. Until recently, the most widely used hire car was the Hindustan Ambassador. However, except for the newest model, they are often very unreliable, and although they still have their devotees, many find them uncomfortable for long journeys. For a similar price, Maruti cars and vans (Omni) are much more reliable and are now the preferred choice in many areas. Gypsy 4WDs and Jeeps are also available, especially in the hills, where larger Sumos have made an appearance. Maruti Esteems and Toyota Qualis are comfortable and have optional reliable a/c. A specialist operator can be very helpful in arranging itineraries and car hire in advance.

Car hire, with a driver, is generally cheaper than in the West. A car shared by three or four can be very good value. Be sure to check carefully the mileage at the beginning and end of the trip. Two or three-day trips from main towns can also give excellent opportunities for sightseeing off the beaten track in reasonable comfort. Local drivers often know their way much better than drivers from other states, so where possible it is a good idea to get a local driver who speaks the state language, in addition to being able to communicate with you. In the mountains, it is better to use a driver who knows the roads. Drivers may sleep in the car overnight, though hotels sometimes provide a bed for them. They are responsible for all their expenses, including their meals. Car (and auto) drivers increase their earnings by taking you to hotels and shops where they get a handsome commission (which you will pay for!). If you feel inclined, a tip at the end of the tour of Rs 100 per day in addition to their daily allowance is perfectly acceptable. Check beforehand if fuel and inter-state taxes are included in the hire charge.

Cars can be hired through private companies. International companies such as **Hertz, Europcar** and **Budget** operate in some major cities and offer reliable cars; their rates are generally higher than those of local firms (eg **Sai Service, Wheels**). The price of an imported car can be three times that of the Ambassador.

Car with Driver Ambassador	Economy Maruti 800 Contessa	Regular A/C Maruti 800 Opel etc	Premium A/C Maruti 1000 Qualis	Luxury A/C Esteem
8 hrs/80 km	Rs 800	Rs 1,000	Rs 1,400	Rs 1,800+
Extra km	Rs 4-7	Rs 9	Rs 13	Rs 18
Extra hour	Rs 40	Rs 50	Rs 70	Rs 100
Out of town				
Per km	Rs 7	Rs 9	Rs 13	Rs 18
Night halt	Rs 100	Rs 200	Rs 250	Rs 250

Importing a car Tourists may import their own vehicles into India with a Carnet de Passage (Triptyques) issued by any recognized automobile association or club affiliated to the Alliance Internationale de Tourisme in Geneva.

Self-drive car hire is still in its infancy and many visitors may find the road conditions difficult and sometimes dangerous. If you drive yourself it is essential to take great care. Pedestrians, cattle and a wide range of other animals roam at will. This can be particularly dangerous when driving after dark especially as even other vehicles often carry no lights.

Car travel tips When booking emphasize the importance of good tyres and general roadworthiness. **Fuel**: on main roads across India petrol stations are reasonably frequent, but some areas are poorly served. Some service stations only have diesel pumps though they may have small reserves of petrol. Always carry a spare can. Diesel is widely available and normally much cheaper than petrol. Petrol is rarely above 92 octane. **Insurance**: drivers must have third party insurance. This may have to be with an Indian insurer, or with a foreign insurer who has a national guarantor. You must also be in possession of an 'International Driving Permit', issued by a recognised driving authority in your home country (eg the AA in the UK, apply at least six weeks before leaving). **Asking the way**: can be very frustrating as you are likely to get widely conflicting advice each time you stop to ask. On the main roads, 'mile' posts periodically appear in English and can help. Elsewhere, it is best to ask directions often and follow the 'average direction'! **Accidents**: often produce large and angry crowds very quickly. It is best to leave the scene of the accident and report it to the police as quickly as possible thereafter. **Provisions**: ensure that you have adequate food and drink, and a basic tool set in the car.

Taxi

'Yellow-top' taxis in cities and large towns are metered, although tariffs change frequently. These changes are shown on a fare chart which should be read in conjunction with the meter reading. Increased night time rates apply in some cities, and there is a small charge for luggage, insist on the taxi meter being 'flagged' in your presence. If the driver refuses, the official advice is to call the police. This may not work, but it is worth trying. When a taxi doesn't have a meter, you will need to fix the fare before starting the journey. Ask at the hotel desk for a guide price.

At stations and airports it is often possible to share taxis to a central point. It is worth looking for fellow passengers who may be travelling in your direction and get a pre-paid taxi. At night, always have a clear idea of where you want to go and insist on being taken there. Taxi drivers may try to convince you that the hotel you have chosen 'closed three years ago', is 'completely full' or is an 'unsafe den'. Say that you have an advance reservation.

Rickshaw

Auto-rickshaws ('autos') are almost universally available in towns across India and are the cheapest convenient way of getting about. It is best to walk a short distance away from a hotel gate before picking up an auto to avoid paying an inflated rate. In addition to using them for short journeys it is often possible to hire them by the hour, or for a half or full day's sight-seeing. In some areas younger drivers who speak some English and know their local area well, may want to show you around. However, rickshaw drivers are often paid a commission by hotels, restaurants and gift shops, so advice is not always impartial. Drivers sometimes refuse to use a meter, quote a ridiculous price or attempt to stop short of your destination. If you have real problems it can help to threaten to go to the police. Beware of some rickshaw drivers who show the fare chart for taxis, especially in Mumbai.

Cycle-rickshaws and horse-drawn tongas are more common in the more rustic setting of a small town or the outskirts of a large one. You will need to fix a price by bargaining. The animal attached to a tonga usually looks too undernourished to have the strength to pull the driver, leave alone passengers. Beware of some rickshaw drivers who show the fare chart for taxis, especially in Mumbai.

Cycling → *You are usually not far from a 'puncture wallah' who can make minor repairs cheaply.*

Cycling is an excellent way of seeing the quiet by-ways of India. It is easy to hire bikes in most small towns for about Rs 15-20 per day. Indian bikes are heavy and without gears, but on the flat they offer a good way of exploring comparatively short distances outside towns. In the more prosperous tourist resorts, mountain bikes are now becoming available, but at a higher hire charge. It is also quite possible to tour more extensively and you may then want to buy a cycle.

There are shops in every town and the local Raleighs are considered the best, with Atlas and BSA good alternatives; expect to pay around Rs 1,200-1,500 for a second-hand Indian bike but remember to bargain. At the end of your trip you can usually sell it quite easily at half that price. Imported bikes have the advantage of lighter weight and gears, but are more difficult to get repaired, and carry the much greater risk of being stolen or damaged. If you wish to take your own, it is quite easy if you dismantle it and pack it in its original shipping carton; be sure to take all essential spares including a pump. It is possible to get Indian spares for 26" wheel cycles. All cyclists should take bungy cords (to strap down a backpack) and good lights from home, although cycling at night is not recommended; take care not to leave your machine parked anywhere with your belongings though. Bike repair shops are universal and charges are nominal.

It is possible to cover 50 to 80 km a day quite comfortably - "the National Highways are manic but country roads, especially along the coast, can be idyllic, if rather dusty and bumpy". You can even put your bike on a boat for the backwater trip or on top of a bus. Should you wish to take your bike on the train, allow plenty of time for booking it in on the brake van at the Parcels office, and for filling in forms.

It is best to start a journey early in the morning, stop at midday and resume cycling in the late afternoon. Night-riding, though cooler, can be hazardous because of lack of lighting and poor road surfaces. Try to avoid the major highways as far as possible. Fortunately foreign cyclists are usually greeted with cheers, waves and smiles and truck drivers are sometimes happy to give lifts to cyclists (and their bikes). This is a good way of taking some of the hardship out of cycling round India.

⦙ On the road on a motorbike

An experienced motorbiker writes: unless you bring your own bike (Carnet de passage, huge deposit) the only acceptable machine is the legendary Enfield Bullet 350 or 500 cc. Humming along the Indian roads or tracks this lovely four stroke classic machine is a must. Also available in diesel version (1.5 litres per 100 km and much cheaper fuel) the 500 cc is much better for travelling with luggage and easier to take home as brakes and 12v lights conform with EC regulations.

Expect a cruising speed of around 50 kph. Riding above 70 gets very tiring due to the lack of silent blocks and the nerve-wracking Indian roads. A good average distance is 200 km per day. Riding at night furthers the excitement – practise at home on a death race video first, but bear in mind that accidents can turn into a first-hand lynching experience! If you stop, prepare to settle quickly in cash, but while third party insurance is cheap (Rs 53 per year!) refunds are less than guaranteed.

Buying In Delhi, Karol Bagh is the biker's den, where you can have your second hand bike assembled to order. It's also good for arranging shipping (Rs 13,000 to Europe), and for spares and gear. You can now find good helmets at a fraction of the European price (Studds Rs 300-Rs 2,000 for a full

face type), also goggles, sturdy panniers and extras. A Bullet will cost from Rs 25,000 to Rs 40,000 second hand, or Rs 50,000-Rs 60,000 new. Allow plenty of time to shop around.

Papers Many Indians and tourists don't bother changing the name on the ownership papers. If you are driving through more than one state this is rash, as it is essential to have the papers in your name, plus the NOC (No Objection Certificate) from the Motor Vehicles Department if you intend to export the vehicle home. Regardless of the dealer's assertions to the contrary, demand the NOC as otherwise you will have to apply for it in the state of origin. You have to allow 15 days.

Spares Before buying, negotiate the essential extras: mirrors, luggage carriers, better saddle, battery. Spares are cheap and readily available for the 350cc model. Take along a spare throttle and clutch cable, a handful of nuts and bolts, puncture repair kit and pump or emergency canister so you don't have to leave the bike unattended while hitching a lift to the nearest puncture wallah – and of course a full set of tools. Check the oil level daily. Finally, remember that for long distances you can load your bike on a night train (Rs 100 per 100 km). Just turn up at the parcel office with an empty petrol tank at least two hours before departure.

Essentials Getting around

Motorcycling → See under Car and Cycling above for general advice.

Motorcycling across India is particularly attractive for bike enthusiasts. It is easy to buy new Indian-made motorcycles including the Enfield Bullet and several 100cc Japanese models, including Suzukis and Hondas made in collaboration with Indian firms. Buying new ensures greater reliability and fixed price - (Indian Rajdoots are less expensive but have a poor reputation for reliability). Buying second hand in Rupees takes more time but is quite possible; expect to get a 30-40% discount. You can get a broker to help with the paperwork involved (certificate of ownership, insurance etc) for a fee. They charge about Rs 5,000 for a 'No Objection Certificate' (NOC) which is essential for reselling; it is easier to have the bike in your name. When selling, don't be in a hurry, and only negotiate with "ready cash" buyers. A black bike is easier to sell than a coloured one! Repairs are usually easy to arrange and quite cheap. Bring your own helmet and an International Driving Permit.

Adventuremoto, www.aventuremoto.com, for biking in Rajasthan and Garhwal Himalaya.
Chandertal Tours & Himalayan Folkways, based in the UK, organizes Royal Enfield tours of the high Himalaya (Himachal and Ladakh) and Rajasthan. Contact: 20 The Fridays, East Dean, Eastbourne, East Sussex, BN20 0DH, UK, T0091-1323-422213, www.steali.co.uk/india.
Peter and Friends Classic Adventures, an Indo-German company based in Goa at Casa Tres Amigos, Socol Vado 425, Assagao (4 km east on Anjuna road), T0832-2682411, F262076, www.classic-bike-india.de, runs organized motorbike tours in Goa and the Himalaya with good back up. They are well organized, friendly and popular with Germans. They also hire out Enfield motorbikes in Goa (US$120-165/week).
Royal Enfield Motors, Chennai, T0445-43300, F543253. Tours with full back up. You can choose between Rajasthan, Himachal/Ladakh and South India (about US$1,200-1,600 for 14 days).

Hitchhiking

Hitchhiking is uncommon in India, partly because public transport is so cheap. If you try, you are likely to spend a very long time on the roadside. However, getting a lift on motorbikes/scooters and on trucks in areas with little public transport can be worthwhile, whilst those riding motorbikes or scooters in Goa can be expected to pick up the occasional hitchhiking policeman! It is not recommended for women on their own.

Maps → *The export of large scale maps from India is prohibited. For trekking maps, see page 69.*

For anyone interested in the geography of India, or even simply getting around, trying to buy good maps is a depressing experience. For security reasons it is illegal to sell large scale maps of areas within 80 km of the coast or national borders.

The **Bartholomew** 1:4 m map sheet of India is the most authoritative, detailed and easy to use map available. It can be bought worldwide. **GeoCenter World Map** 1:2 m, covers India in three regional sections and are clearly printed. **Nelles'** regional maps of India at the scale of 1:1.5 m offer generally clear route maps, though neither the road classifications nor alignments are wholly reliable. The same criticism applies to the attractively produced and easy to read **Lonely Planet Travel Atlas of India and Bangladesh** (1995, 162 pp).

State and town plans are published by the **TT Company**. These are often the best available though they are not wholly reliable. For the larger cities they provide the most compact yet clear map sheets (generally 50 mm x 75 mm format). **Indian Map Service** publishes a limited number of maps of Rajasthan and Maharashtra.

The Survey of India publishes large scale 1:10,000 town plans of approximately 70 cities. These detailed plans are the only surveyed town maps in India, and some are over 20 years old. The Survey also has topographic maps at the scale of 1:25,000 and 1:50,000 in addition to its 1:250,000 scale coverage, some of which are as recent as the late 1980s. However, maps are regarded as highly sensitive and it is only possible to buy these from main agents of the Survey of India.

Stanfords, 12-14 Long Acre, London, WC2, T020 78361321, www.stanfords.co.uk, offer a mail order service.

Sleeping

India has an enormously wide range of accommodation. You can stay safely and very cheaply by western standards right across the country. In all the major cities there are also high quality hotels, offering a full range of facilities. In small centres even the best hotels are far more variable. In Rajasthan and Gujarat, old Maharajas' palaces

A bed for the night

LL (US$250+) and L (US$150-250) These are exceptional hotels. They are in the metropolitan cities or in exclusive locations such as a commanding coastal promontory, a lake island or a scenic hilltop, with virtually nothing to fault them. They have high class business facilities, specialist restaurants and well-stocked bars, several pools, sports.

AL (US$100-150) and A (US$50-100) Most major towns have at least some in these categories which too reach high international standards but are less exclusive. Many quote an inflated 'dollar price' to foreigners.

B (US$25-50) Comfortable but not plush, choice of restaurants, pool, some have a gym. These are often aimed at the business client.

C (Rs 750-1200) In many small towns the best hotel is in this category, but they are not necessarily the best value. Some charge higher prices for a flash reception area, usually central a/c, restaurant, satellite TV, foreign exchange and travel desk.

D (Rs 400-750) These hotels often offer very good value though quality and cleanliness can vary widely. Most have some a/c rooms with bath, satellite TV, restaurants. They may have some rooms in the E price range, so if you are looking for good but cheap accommodation, start here!

E (Rs 200-400) Simple room with fan (occasionally air-cooler or a/c), often shared toilet and shower. May not have a restaurant or provide bed linen, towel etc.

F (Under Rs 200) Very basic, shared toilet (often 'squat'), bucket and tap, variable cleanliness and hygiene. E and F category hotels are often in busy parts of town. They may have some rooms for under Rs 100, and dormitory beds for under Rs 50. (Some only have four or six beds.)

Essentials Sleeping

and forts have been privately converted into comfortable, unusual hotels. Hotels in beach resorts and hill-stations, because of their location and special appeal, often deviate from the description of our different categories. In the peak season (October to April for most of India) bookings can be extremely heavy in popular destinations. It is sometimes possible to book in advance by phone, fax or e-mail, but double check your reservation, and always try to arrive as early as possible in the day.

Price categories → *The categories are based on prices of double rooms excluding taxes.*

They are **not** star ratings and individual facilities vary widely. Modest hotels may not have their own restaurant but will often offer 'room service', bringing in food from outside. In South and West India, and in 'temple towns', the restaurants may only serve vegetarian food. Many hotels operate a '24 hour check-out' system. Make sure that this means that you can stay 24 hours from the time of check-in. Expect to pay more in Delhi, Mumbai, and to a lesser extent in Chennai and Kolkata for all categories. Prices away from large cities tend to be lower for comparable hotels. Away from the metropolitan cities, in South India, room rates tend to be lower than the North, and the standard of cleanliness is higher.

Large reductions are made by hotels in all categories **out-of-season** in many resorts. Always ask if any is available. You may also request the 10-15% agent's commission to be deducted from your bill if you book direct. Clarify whether the agreed figure includes all taxes.

In general most hotel rooms rated at Rs 1,200 or above are subject to an expenditure tax of 10%. Many states levy an additional luxury tax of between 10 and 25%, and some hotels add a service charge of 10%. Taxes are not necessarily payable on meals, so it is worth settling the meals bill separately from the room bill. Most hotels in the **C** category and above accept payment by credit card. Check your final bill carefully. Visitors have complained of **incorrect bills**, even in the most expensive hotels. The problem particularly afflicts groups, when last-minute extras appear mysteriously on some guests' bills. Check the evening before departure, and keep all receipts.

Hotel facilities

You have to be prepared for difficulties which are uncommon in the West. It is best to inspect the room and check that all equipment (a/c, TV, water heater, flush) works before checking in at a modest hotel.

In some states **power cuts** are common, or hot water may be restricted to certain times of day. The largest hotels have their own generators but it is best to carry a good torch.

Usually, only category **B** and above have **central a/c**. Elsewhere a/c rooms are cooled by individual units and occasionally by large 'air-coolers' which can be noisy and unreliable. When they fail to operate tell the management as it is often possible to get a rapid repair done, or to transfer to a room where the unit is working. During power cuts generators may not be able to cope with providing air-conditioning. Fans are provided in all but the cheapest of hotels.

Apart from those in the **A** category and above, 'attached bath' does not necessarily refer to a bathroom with a bathtub. Most will provide a **bathroom** with a toilet, basin and a shower. In the lower priced hotels and outside large towns, a bucket and tap may replace the shower, and an Indian 'squat' toilet instead of a Western WC (squat toilets often cleaner). Mid-price hotels, which are clean and pleasant, don't always provide towels, soap and toilet paper.

In some regions **water supply** is rationed periodically. Keep a bucket filled to use for flushing the toilet during water cuts. Occasionally, tap water may be discoloured due to rusty tanks. During the cold weather and in hill stations, hot water will be available at certain times of the day, sometimes in buckets, but is usually very restricted in quantity. Electric water heaters may provide enough for a shower but not enough to fill a bath tub! For details on drinking water, see page 56.

Laundry can be arranged very cheaply (eg a shirt washed and pressed for Rs 15-20 in **C-D** category; but Rs 50 or more in luxury hotels) and quickly (in 12-24 hours). It is best not to risk delicate fibres, though luxury hotels can usually handle these and also dry-clean items.

At some times of the year and in some places **mosquitoes** can be a real problem, and not all hotels have mosquito-proof rooms or mosquito nets. In cheap hotels you need to be prepared for a wider range of insect life, including flies, cockroaches and ants. Poisonous insects are extremely rare in towns. Hotel managements are nearly always prepared with insecticide sprays. Few small hotels in mosquito-prone areas supply nets so it is best for budget travellers to take one from home. An impregnated, wedge-shaped one (for single-point fixing) is preferable, available in all good camping/outdoor shops. Remember to shut windows and doors at dusk. Electrical devices are now widely available, as are mosquito coils which burn slowly. Dusk and early evening are the worst times for mosquitoes so trousers and long-sleeved shirts are advisable, especially out of doors. At night, fans can be very effective in keeping mosquitoes off, and remember to tuck the net under the mattress all round. As well as insects, expect to find spiders larger and hairier than those you see at home; they are mostly harmless and more frightened of you than you are of them! You will be lucky to come across a scorpion in rural areas (always check shoes/boots before putting them on). You are more likely to have a resident gecko (a harmless house lizard) in your room. They are your friends as they keep the number of mosquitoes down.

Hotels close to temples can be very **noisy**, especially during festivals. Music blares from loudspeakers late at night and from very early in the morning, often making sleep impossible. Mosques call the faithful to prayers at dawn. Some find earplugs helpful.

Tourist 'Bungalows'
The different State Tourism Development Corporations run their own hotels and hostels which are often located in places of special interest. These are very reasonably priced, though they may be rather dated, restaurant menus may be limited and service is often slow. Upkeep varies and in some states it is sadly well below standard.

Railway and airport retiring rooms
Railway stations often have 'Retiring Rooms' or 'Rest Rooms' which may be hired for periods of between one and 24 hours by anyone holding an onward train ticket. They are cheap and simple though some stations have a couple of a/c rooms, which are often heavily booked. In general, you must contact the Ticket Collector on duty for available rooms/beds. They are convenient for short stops, though some can be very noisy. Some major airports (eg Delhi, Mumbai) have similar facilities.

Government rest houses
Rest house may sometimes be available for overnight stays, particularly in remote areas. They are usually extremely basic, with a caretaker who can sometimes provide a simple meal, given sufficient notice. Check the room rate in advance as foreigners are sometimes overcharged. Government officials always take precedence, even over-booked guests.

Indian style hotels
These, catering for Indian businessmen, are springing up fast in or on the outskirts of many small and medium sized towns. Most have some air-conditioned rooms and attached showers. They are variable in quality but it is increasingly possible to find excellent value accommodation even in remote areas.

Hostels
The Department of Tourism runs 16 hostels, each with about 50 beds, usually organized into dormitory accommodation. The YHA have a few sites all over India. Travellers may also stay in religious hostels (*dharamshalas*) for up to three days. These are primarily intended for pilgrims, and are sometimes free of charge though voluntary offerings are always welcome. Usually only vegetarian food is permitted; smoking and alcohol are not.

Camping
Mid-price hotels with large grounds are sometimes willing to allow camping. Regional tourist offices have details of new developments. For information on YMCA camping facilities contact: **YMCA**, The National General Secretary, National Council of YMCAs of India, PB No 14, Massey Hall, Jai Singh Rd, New Delhi 1.

Eating

Food

→ See page 1241 for a food glossary. Regional cuisine is covered in the introduction to each state.
You find just as much variety in dishes and presentation crossing India as you would on an equivalent journey across Europe. Combinations of spices give each region its distinctive flavour.

The larger hotels, open to non-residents, often offer **buffet** lunches with Indian, Western and sometimes Chinese dishes. These can be good value (Rs 250-300; but around Rs 450 in the top grades), and can provide a welcome, comfortable break in the cool. The health risks, however, of food kept warm for long periods in metal containers are considerable, especially if turnover at the buffet is slow. This can be the case even in five star hotels.

It is essential to be very careful since food hygiene may be poor, flies abound and refrigeration in the hot weather may be inadequate and intermittent because of power cuts. It is best to eat only freshly prepared food by ordering from the menu (especially meat and fish dishes); avoid salads and cut fruit.

If you are unused to spicy food, go slow! Stick to Western or mild Chinese meals in good restaurants, and try the odd Indian dish to test your reaction. Those used to Indian spices may choose to be more adventurous. Popular local restaurants are obvious from the number of people eating in them. Try a traditional thali, which is a complete meal served on a large stainless steel plate (or very occasionally on a banana leaf). Several preparations, placed in small bowls, surround the central serving of wholewheat chapati and rice. A vegetarian thali would include *daal* (lentils), two or three curries (which can be quite hot), and crisp poppadums, although there are regional variations. A variety of pickles are offered - mango and lime are two of the most popular. These can be exceptionally hot, and are designed to be taken in minute quantities alongside the main dishes. Plain *dahi* (yoghurt) in the south, or *raita* in the north, usually acts as a bland 'cooler'. Simple *dhabas* (rustic roadside eateries) are an alternative experience for sampling authentic local dishes.

Many city restaurants offer some so-called **European options** such as toasted sandwiches, stuffed pancakes, apple pies, crumbles and cheese cakes. Italian favourites (pizzas, pastas) can be very different from what you are used to. Western confectionery, in general, is disappointing. Ice creams, on the other hand, can be exceptionally good (there are excellent Indian ones as well as international brands such as Cadbury's and *Walls*).

India has many delicious tropical **fruits**. Some are highly seasonal (eg mangoes, pineapples and lychees), while others (eg bananas, grapes, oranges) are available throughout the year. It is safe to eat the ones you can wash and peel.

Drink

Drinking water used to be regarded as one of India's biggest hazards. It is still true that water from the tap or a well should never be considered safe to drink since public water supplies are often polluted. Bottled water is now widely available (Rs 10-12 per litre) although not all bottled water is mineral water; some is simply purified water from an urban supply. Buy from a shop or stall, check the seal carefully (some companies now add a second clear plastic seal around the bottle top) and avoid street hawkers; when disposing bottles, crush to prevent misuse. There is growing

⁝ Two masala dosai and a pot of tea!

One traveller to Ooty reported that a hotel bar had closed, apparently permanently. He found however that it was still possible to obtain alcoholic drinks from the restaurant. Having ordered and been served a beer, he was intrigued that when the bill came it was made out for "2 masala dosai". The price was, of course, correct for the beer!

Another traveller found that a well-known hotel in the heart of New Delhi also appeared to have been forced to adapt its attitude to serving alcohol to the prevailing laws. Asked in the early evening for a double whisky the barman was very happy to comply until he was asked to serve it in the garden. On being told that he could only drink it in the bar the visitor expressed great disappointment, on which the barman relented, whispering that if the visitor really wanted to drink it outside he would serve it to him in a tea pot!

If you are thirsting for alcohol in a prohibitionist area perhaps you need to order two masala dosai and a pot of tea.

concern over the mountains of plastic bottles that are collecting and the waste of resources to produce them, so travellers are encouraged to use alternative methods of getting safe drinking water. In some towns (eg Dharamshala, Leh) purified water is now sold for refilling your own container. Travellers may wish to purify water themselves (see page 71). A portable water filter is a good option, carrying the drinking water in a plastic bottle in an insulated carrier. Always carry enough drinking water with you when travelling. It is important to use pure water for cleaning teeth.

Tea and **coffee** are safe and widely available. Both are normally served sweet, and with milk. If you wish, say 'no sugar' (*chini nahin*), 'no milk' (*dudh nahin*) when ordering. Alternatively, ask for a pot of tea, and milk and sugar to be brought separately. Freshly brewed coffee is a common drink in South India, but in the North, ordinary city restaurants will usually serve the instant variety.

Bottled **carbonated drinks** such as 'Coke', 'Pepsi', 'Teem' and 'Gold Spot' are universally available but always check the seal when you buy from a street stall. There are also several brands of fruit **juice** sold in cartons, including mango, pineapple and apple. Don't add ice cubes as the water source may be contaminated. Take care with fresh fruit juices or *lassis* as ice is often added.

Indians rarely drink **alcohol** with a meal, water being on hand. In the past wines and spirits were generally either imported and extremely expensive, or local and of poor quality. Now, the best Indian whisky, rum and brandy are widely accepted, as are good Champagnoise and other wines from Maharashtra. If you hanker after a bottle of imported wine, you will only find it in the top restaurants and have to pay Rs 800-1,000 at least. For the urban elite, cooling Indian beers are popular when eating out and so are widely available, though you may need to check the 'chill' value. The 'English Pub' has appeared in major cities, where the foreign traveller too would feel comfortable. Elsewhere, seedy, all male drinking dens in the larger cities are best avoided. Head for the better hotel bar instead. In rural India, local rice, palm, cashew or date juice *toddy* and *arak* should be treated with great caution. However, the Sikkimese *chhang* makes a pleasant change drunk out of a wooden tankard through a bamboo straw! Most states have alcohol free 'dry' days; a few enforce degrees of Prohibition. Some up-market restaurants may serve beer even if it's not listed so it's worth asking. For 'dry' states and Liquor Permits, see page 28.

Entertainment

Despite an economic boom in cities like Delhi and Mumbai and the rapid growth of a young business class, India's nightlife remains meagre, focused on club discos in the biggest hotels. In Goa, beach raves and parties (associated with Goa Trance and the drug scene), which usually take place in make-shift venues, continue to attract large groups of foreigners particularly during Christmas and the New Year. More traditional, popular entertainment is widespread across Indian villages in the form of folk drama, dance and music, each region having its own styles, and open air village performance being common. The hugely popular Hindi film industry comes largely out of this tradition. It's always easy to find a cinema, but prepare for a long sitting with a standard story line and set of characters and lots of action. See also pages 70 for spectator sports and for cinema.

Festivals and events

India has an extraordinary wealth of festivals with many celebrated nationwide, while others are specific to a particular state or community or even a particular temple. Many festivals fall on different dates each year depending on the Hindu lunar calendar so check with the tourist office.

The Hindu Calendar → *See further page 1338.*
Hindus follow two distinct eras: The *Vikrama Samvat* which began in 57 BC and the *Salivahan Saka* which dates from 78 AD and has been the official Indian calendar since 1957. The *Saka* new year starts on 22 March and has the same length as the Gregorian calendar. The 29½ day lunar month with its 'dark' and 'bright' halves based on the new and full moons, are named after 12 constellations, and total a 354 day year. The calendar cleverly has an extra month (*adhik maas*) every 2½-3 years, to bring it in line with the solar year of 365 days coinciding with the Gregorian calendar of the West.

Some major national and regional festivals are listed below; details of these and others appear under the particular state or town. A few count as national holidays: **26 January**: *Republic Day*; **15 August**: *Independence Day*; **2 October**: *Mahatma Gandhi's Birthday*; **25 December**: *Christmas Day*.

Major festivals and fairs
1 January *New Year's Day* is accepted officially when following the Gregorian calendar but there are regional variations which fall on different dates, often coinciding with spring/harvest time in March and April: *Losar* in Ladakh, *Naba Barsha* in Bengal (14 April), *Goru* in Assam, *Ugadi* in Andhra, *Vishu* in Kerala and *Jamshed Navroj* for the Parsi community. **January 14** *Makar Sankranti* marks the end of winter and is celebrated with kite flying, especially in Gujarat. *Pongal* is Tamil Nadu's harvest festival. **26** *Republic Day Parade* in New Delhi. Communist-style display of military strength.

February *Vasant Panchami*, the Spring festival when people wear bright yellow clothes to mark the advent of the season with singing, dancing and feasting. In Bengal it is also *Saraswati Puja* when the goddess of learning is worshipped. *Desert Festival* - Jaisalmer, Rajasthan. *Nagaur Camel Fair* - Rajasthan. *Surajkund Crafts Mela* - Haryana. *International Yoga Festival* - Rishikesh, Uttaranchal. *Elephanta Festival* - Maharashtra. *Konark Festival* - Orissa.

⋮ Purnima (Full Moon)

Many religious festivals depend on the phases of the moon. Full moon days are particularly significant and can mean extra crowding and merrymaking in temple towns throughout India, and are sometimes public holidays.

February-March *Maha Sivaratri* marks the night when Siva danced his celestial dance of destruction (*Tandava*) celebrated with feasting and fairs at Siva temples, but preceded by a night of devotional readings and hymn singing. *Carnival* - Goa. Spectacular costumes, music and dance, float processions and feasting mark the three day event.

March *Ellora Festival of Classical Dance and Music* - Maharashtra. *Khajuraho Dance Festival* - Madhya Pradesh. *Gangaur Mela* - Rajasthan. *Holi*, the festival of colours, marks the climax of spring. The previous night bonfires are lit in parts of North India symbolizing the end of winter (and conquering of evil). People have fun throwing coloured powder and water at each other and in the evening some gamble with friends. If you don't mind getting covered in colours, you can risk going out but celebrations can sometimes get very rowdy (and unpleasant). Some worship Krishna who defeated the demon Putana.

April *Mahavir Jayanti. Baisakhi* - North India.

April/May *Buddha Jayanti*, the first full moon night in April/May marks the birth of the Buddha. *Pooram* - Thrissur, Kerala.

June/July *Rath Yatra* - Puri, Orissa. *Hemis Festival* - Leh, Ladakh. *Teej* - Jaipur, Rajasthan.

July/August *Raksha (or Rakhi) Bandhan*symbolizes the bond between brother and sister, celebrated mainly in North India at full-moon. A sister says special prayers for her brother and ties colouredthreads around his wrist to remind him of the special bond. He in turn gives a gift and promises to protect and care for her. Sometimes *rakshas* are exchanged as a mark of friendship. *Narial Purnima* on the same full moon. Hindus, particularly in coastal areas of West and South India, make offerings of *narial* (coconuts) to the Vedic god Varuna (Lord of the waters) by throwing them into the sea. **15 August** *Independence Day*, a national secular holiday is marked by special events, and in Delhi there is an impressive flag hoisting ceremony at the Red Fort. *Ganesh Chaturthi*, was established just over 100 years ago by the Indian nationalist leader Tilak. The elephant-headed God of good omen is shown special reverence. On the last of the five-day festival after harvest, clay images of Ganesh are taken in procession with dancers and musicians, and are immersed in the sea, river or pond.

August/September *Janmashtami*, the birth of Krishna is celebrated at midnight at Krishna temples. Special festivities are held in Mathura his birth place and nearby at Vrindavan where Rasalilas (dance dramas) are performed through the night.

September/October *Dasara* has many local variations. In North India, celebrations for the nine nights *(navaratri)* are marked with *Ramlila*, various episodes of the Ramayana story (see page 1329) are enacted with particular reference to the battle between the forces of good and evil. In some parts of India it celebrates *Rama*'s victory over the Demon king *Ravana* of Lanka with the help of loyal *Hanuman* (Monkey). Huge effigies of *Ravana* made of bamboo and paper are burnt on the 10th day (*Vijaya dasami*) of *Dasara* in public open spaces. In other regions the focus is on Durga's victory over the demon *Mahishasura*. Bengal celebrates *Durga* puja. *Onam* - Kerala.

Essentials Festivals & events

October/November 2 October *Gandhi Jayanti*, Mahatma Gandhi's birthday, is remembered with prayer meetings and devotional singing. *Diwali/Deepavali* (Sanskrit *ideepa* lamp), the festival of lights, is celebrated particularly in North India. Some Hindus celebrate Krishna's victory over the demon *Narakasura*, some Rama's return after his 14 years' exile in the forest when citizens lit his way with oil lamps, see also page 1343. The festival falls on the dark *chaturdasi* (14th) night (the one preceding the new moon), when rows of lamps or candles are lit in remembrance, and *rangolis* are painted on the floor as a sign of welcome. Fireworks have become an integral part of the celebration which are often set off days before Diwali. Equally, Lakshmi, the Goddess of Wealth (as well as Ganesh) is worshipped by merchants and the business community who open the new financial year's account on the day. Most people wear new clothes; some play games of chance. In Bengal *Kali Puja* is celebrated the day before Diwali but is a wholly distinct festival. *Pushkar Fair* - Rajasthan. *Guru Nanak Jayanti* commemorates the birth of Guru Nanak. *Akhand Pat* (unbroken reading of the holy book) takes place and the book itself (*Granth*) is taken out in procession. *Sonepur Fair* - Bihar.

25 December *Christmas Day*, Indian Christians celebrate the birth of Christ in much the same way as in the West; many churches hold services/mass at midnight. There is an air of festivity in city markets which are specially decorated and illuminated. **31 December** *New Year's Eve* Each year hotel prices peak during this period and large supplements are added for meals and entertainment in the upper category hotels. Some churches mark the night with a *Midnight Mass*. *Shekhavati Festival* - Rajasthan. *Hampi-Vijaynagar Festival* - Karnataka.

Muslim holy days

These are fixed according to the lunar calendar, see page 1340. According to the Gregorian calendar, they tend to fall 11 days earlier each year, dependent on the sighting of the new moon.

Ramadan is the start of the month of fasting when all Muslims (except young children, the very elderly, the sick, pregnant women and travellers) must abstain from food and drink, from sunrise to sunset.

Id ul Fitr is the three-day festival that marks the end of Ramadan.

Id-ul-Zuha/Bakr-Id is when Muslims commemorate Ibrahim's sacrifice of his son according to God's commandment; the main time of pilgrimage to Mecca (the Hajj). It is marked by the sacrifice of a goat, feasting and alms giving.

Muharram is when the killing of the Prophet's grandson, Hussain, is commemorated by Shi'a Muslims. Decorated *tazias* (replicas of the martyr's tomb) are carried in procession by devout wailing followers who beat their chests to express their grief. Hyderabad and Lucknow are famous for their grand *tazias*. Shi'as fast for the 10 days.

Shopping

India excels in producing fine crafts at affordable prices through the tradition of passing down of ancestral skills. You can get handicrafts of different states from the government emporia in the major cities which guarantee quality at fixed prices (no bargaining), but many are poorly displayed, not helped by reluctant and unenthusiastic staff. Private upmarket shops and top hotel arcades offer better quality, choice and service but at a price. Vibrant and colourful local bazars are often a great experience but you must be prepared to bargain.

Bargaining can be fun and quite satisfying. It is best to get an idea of prices being asked by different stalls for items you are interested in, before taking the plunge. Some shopkeepers will happily quote twice the actual price to a foreigner showing interest, so you might well start by halving the asking price. On the other hand it would be inappropriate to do the same in an established shop with price-tags, though a plea for the "best price" or a "special discount" might reap results even here. Remain good humoured throughout. Walking away slowly might be the test to ascertain whether your custom is sought and you are called back!

The country is a vast market place but there are **regional specializations**. If you are planning to travel widely, wait to find the best places to buy specific items. Export of certain items is controlled or banned, see page 35.

What to buy

Carpets and dhurries The superb hand-knotted carpets of Kashmir, using old Persian designs woven in wool or silk or both, are hard to beat for their beauty and quality. Kashmiri traders can now be found throughout India, wherever there is hint of foreign tourism. Agra too has a long tradition of producing wool carpets and welcomes visitors to their factories. Tibetan refugees in Darjeeling and Gangtok produce excellent carpets which are less expensive but of very high quality. They will make carpets to order and parcel post them safely. Flat woven cotton dhurries in subtle colours are best seen in Rajasthan,

Jewellery Whether it is chunky tribal necklaces from the Himalaya, heavy 'silver' bangles from Rajasthan, fine Orissan filigree, legendary pearls from Hyderabad, Jaipuri uncut gems set in gold or semi-precious stones in silver, or glass bangles from Varanasi, the visitor is drawn to the arcade shop window as much as the way-side stall. It is best to buy from reputable shops as street stalls often pass off fake ivory, silver, gems, stones and coral as real. Make sure your knowledge is up to scratch if considering investing in gems or jewellery, and never be persuaded to buy for an unknown third-party.

Metal work The choice is vast - from brass, copper and white-metal plates and bowls in the North, with ornate patterns or plain polished surfaces, exquisite Jaipuri enamelled silver pill boxes, tribal lost-wax *dhokra* toys from Orissa, Bihar and Bengal, Nawabi silver-on-gun metal Bidri pieces from around Hyderabad, to exceptional copies of Chola bronzes cast near Thanjavur.

Paintings Coveted contemporary Indian art is exhibited in modern galleries in the state capitals often at a fraction of London or New York prices. Traditional 'Mughal' miniatures, sometimes using natural pigments on old paper (don't be fooled) and new silk, are reaching mass production levels in Rajasthan's back alleys. Fine examples can still be found in good crafts shops.

Stoneware Artisans in Agra inspired by the Taj Mahal continue the tradition of inlaying tiny pieces of gem stones on fine white marble, to produce something for every pocket, from a small coaster to a large table top. Softer soap stone is cheaper. Stone temple carvings are produced for sale in Tamil Nadu (try Mahabalipuram), Orissa (Puri, Konark) and Uttar Pradesh (near Hamirpur).

Textiles Handlooms produce rich shot silk from Kanchipuram, skillful *ikat* from Gujarat, Orissa and Andhra, brocades from Varanasi, golden *muga* from Assam, printed silks and batiks from Bengal or opulent *Himroo* shawls from Aurangabad. Sober handspun *khadi*, colourful Rajasthani block-printed cottons using vegetable dyes, tribal weaving from remote Himalayan villages, and tie-and-dye Gujarati *bandhni* are easier on the pocket. Kashmiri embroidery on wool, Lucknowi *chickan* shadow work on fine voil or *zari* (gold/silver thread) work on silk, produce unique pieces. The *pashmina* shawl and scarf from Kashmir have travelled to every continent and are available in dozens of colours at less inflated prices. They come in various widths and quality (often mixed with silk). See page 535. All trade in tush (toosh) wool is banned.

Wood craft Each region has its special wood - walnut in Kashmir, sandalwood in Mysore, rosewood in the South, sheesham in the North. Carving, inlay and lacquer work are specialities. The southern states produce fine carved wooden panels and images which are sold through the state emporia (they offer a posting service).

Pitfalls
Taxi/rickshaw/hire car drivers and tour guides sometimes insist on recommending certain shops where they expect a commission, but prices there are invariably inflated. Some shops offer to pack and post your purchases but small private shops can't always be trusted. Unless you have a specific recommendation from a person you know, only make such arrangements in government emporia or a large store. Don't enter into any arrangement to help 'export' marble items, jewellery etc which a shopkeeper may propose by making tempting promises of passing on some of the profits to you. Several have been cheated through misuse of their credit card accounts, and being left with unwanted purchases. Make sure that credit cards are not 'run off' more than once when making a purchase.

Sport and activities

Opportunities in adventure sports are now being offered. Such thrills can be combined with more conventional sightseeing. Apart from the activities listed here, you can also try ballooning, heli-skiing, hang-gliding, mountain or rock climbing and even motor rallying. There are skiing resorts in Himachal Pradesh, namely Manali and Narkanda, but they do not compare with western resorts.

Participation sports

Biking
For those keen on moving faster along the road, discover the joys of travelling on the two wheels of a motorbike. The 350cc Enfield Bullets are particularly attractive. Vespa, Kinetic Honda and other makes of scooters in India are slower than motorbikes but comfortable for short hauls of less than 100 km and have the advantage of a 'dicky' for spares, and a spare tyre. See page 51.

Bird watching
The country's diverse and rich natural habitats harbour over 1,200 species of birds of which around 150 are endemic. Visitors to all parts of the country can enjoy spotting Oriental species whether it is in towns and cities, in the country side or more abundantly in the national parks and sanctuaries. On the plains, the cooler months (November to March) are the most comfortable for a chance to see migratory birds from the hills, but the highlands themselves are ideal between May and June and again after the monsoons when visibility improves in October and November. Water bodies large and small draw visiting water fowl from other continents during the winter.

Keoladeo Ghana (Bharatpur) in Rajasthan, Sultanpur in Haryana, Chilika, in Orissa, Pulicat and Vedanthangal in Tamil Nadu, Ranganathittoo in Karnataka, Tadoba, in Maharashtra and Nal Sarovar in Gujarat. *A Birdwatcher's Guide to India* by Krys Kazmierczak and Raj Singh, published by Prion Ltd, Sandy, Bedfordshire, UK, 1998, is well researched and comprehensive with helpful practical information and maps.

The government's **Salim Ali Centre for Ornithology and Natural History** (SACON) is in Coimbatore. Useful websites include www.orientalbirdclub.org, and biks@giasdlo1.vsnl.net.in, for *Bird Link*, concerned with conservation of birds and their habitat.

Camel safaris

Today's camel safaris try to recreate something of the atmosphere of the early camel trains. The Thar desert, in Rajasthan, with its vast stretches of sand, dotted with dunes and its own specially adapted shrubs and wildlife is ideal territory. The guides are expert navigators and the villages on the way add colour to an unforgettable experience, if you are prepared to sit out the somewhat uncomfortable ride, see page 423.

Cycling

Cycling offers a peaceful - not to mention healthy - alternative to cars, buses or trains. Touring on locally hired bicycles is possible along country roads in Rajasthan, Uttaranchal and South India - ideal if you want to see village life in India and the lesser known wildlife parks. Consult a good Indian agent for advice. For example, a week's cycling trip could cover about 250 km in the Garhwal foothills, starting in Rishikesh, passing through the Corbett and Rajaji National Parks over easy gradients, to finish in Ramnagar. Expert guides, cycles and support vehicle, accommodation in simple resthouses or tents, are included.

Horse safaris

Gaining in popularity they are offered in Rajasthan, particularly in the Shekhawati area, and south of Jodhpur around Sodawas and Kumbhalgarh. Conditions are similar to camel safaris with grooms (and often the horse owner) accompanying. The best months are November to March when it is cooler in the day (and often cold at night). The trails chosen usually enable you to visit small villages, old forts and temples, and take you through a variety of terrain and vegetation including scrub covered arid plains to forested hills. The charges can be a lot higher than for a camel safari but the night stays are often in comfortable palaces, forts or *havelis*.

Snooker

Invented in the hill station clubs of British India, snooker has become increasingly popular in major cities across the country. Snooker halls have tables available for hire by the hour, and are often crowded with young people. They can be dimly lit and have loud music, but they also attract young families. Arcade games, sometimes harking back to those popular in the West in the early 90s, have their own devotees among the young.

Watersports

Sun, sand and warm waters for safe swimming are not the only attractions along the long stretches of unspoilt coastal India. Select beaches in Goa, and the crystal clear waters around the Andamans and the Laccadive islands, are excellent for diving. Snorkelling is possible more widely, as well as parasailing, wind surfing and water skiing. The scuba diving centres are on Miramar Beach and Bogmalo in Goa, on Havelock Island and the Marine National Park in the Andamans, and on Bangaram in the Lakshadweeps. Courses are well-run and cost around US$75 for an introductory dive, US$350 for four days, or US$600 for a two-week Dive Master course. To check details of approved courses contact *PADI International*, Head Office, Unit 6, Unicorn Park, Whitby Road, Bristol, BS4 4EX, T0117-9711717, F9721821, general@Tadi.co.uk or *PADI Europe*, Oberwilerstrasse 3, CH-8442, Hettlingen, Switzerland, T052-3041414, F3041499, admin@Tadi.ch In addition, coastal resorts in Kerala and Goa offer fishing trips and dolphin viewing during the season, sometimes combining these with a beach barbecue.

White water rafting

The snow-fed rivers which flow through Kashmir, Himachal, Uttaranchal and Sikkim offer excellent white water rafting. The popular waters range from grades II-III for amateurs (Zanskar, Indus) to the greater challenges of grades IV-VI for the experienced (eg Chenab, Beas, Sutlej, Rangit, Tons). The options range from a half-day trip to one lasting several days, and again allows a chance to see scenery, places and people off the beaten track. The trips are organized and managed by professional teams who have trained abroad. The rivers can sometimes be dangerous in August and September.

Yoga and meditation

There has been a growing Western interest in the ancient life-disciplines in search of physical and spiritual wellbeing, as practised in ancient India. Yoga is supposed to regulate the nervous system and aims to attain perfect equilibrium through the practice of *asanas* (body postures), breath control, discipline, cleansing, contemplation and awareness. It seeks to achieve moral purification through abstinence and restraint (dietary and sexual). Meditation which complements yoga to relieve stress, increase awareness and bring inner peace prescribes *dhyana* (purposeful concentration) by withdrawing oneself from external distractions and focusing ones attention to consciousness itself. This leads ultimately to *samadhi* (release from worldly bonds). At the practical level *Hatha Yoga* has captured the Western imagination as it promises good health through postural exercises, while the search for inner peace and calm drive others to learn meditation techniques.

Centres across the country offer courses for beginners and practitioners. Some are at special resort hotels which offer all inclusive packages in idyllic locations, some advocate simple communal living in an ashram while others may require rigorous discipline in austere monastic surroundings. Whether you wish to embark on a serious study of yoga or sample an hour's introductory meditation session, India offers opportunities for all, though you may need to apply in advance for some popular courses. Popular centres in places frequented by travellers are listed thoughout the book. The *International Yoga Festival* is held in Rishikesh in the Himalayan foothills, each February.

Trekking

The Himalaya offers unlimited opportunities to view not only the natural beauty of mountains and the unique flora and fauna, but also the diverse groups of people who live in the ranges and valleys, many of whom have retained unique cultural identities because of their isolation. The treks described in this Handbook are only for guidance. They try to give you a flavour of an area or a destination. Some trails fall within the 'Inner Line' for which special **permits** are required. Other parts of India offer attractive options for hikers. For more detailed information, see Footprint's Indian Himalaya Handbook. See also Books, page 1366.

Himalayan environment trust code of practice

Deforestation Make no open fires and discourage others making one for you. Limit use of firewood and heated water and use only permitted dead wood. Choose accommodation where kerosene or fuel-efficient wood burning stoves are used.

Litter Remove it. Burn or bury paper and carry away non-degradable litter. If you find other people's litter, remove their's too! Pack food in biodegradable containers.

Water Keep local water clean. Do not use detergents and pollutants in streams and springs. Where there are no toilets be sure you are at least 30 m away from water source and bury or cover. Do not allow cooks or porters to throw rubbish in nearby streams and rivers.

Plants Do not take cuttings, seeds and roots – it is illegal in all parts of the Himalaya.

Begging Giving to children can encourage begging. Donations to a project, health centre or school may be more constructive.

Be aware of **local traditions** and **cultures**; respect their **privacy**, and ask permission before taking photographs; respect their **holy places**, never touching or removing religious objects, and removing shoes before entering temples; be aware of local **etiquette**, dressing modestly particularly when visiting temples and shrines and while walking through villages avoiding shorts, skimpy tops and tight-fitting outfits. Do not hold hands and kiss in public.

Essentials Sport & activities

Types of trekking

Independent trekking There are some outstandingly beautiful treks, though they are often not through the 'wilderness' sometimes conjured up. However, trekking alone is not recommended as you will be in unfamiliar territory where you may not be able to communicate with the local people and if injured you may not have help at hand. Independent trekkers should get a specialist publication with detailed route descriptions and a good map. Remember, mountain topography is subject to constant change, and tracks and crossings can be affected very rapidly. Speak to those who know the area well and have been trekking to the places you intend visiting.

Backpacking camping Hundreds of people arrive each year with a pack and some personal equipment, buy some food and set off trekking, carrying their own gear and choosing their own campsites or places to stay. Serious trekkers will need a framed backpack. Supplies of fuel wood are scarce and flat ground suitable for camping rare. It is not always easy to find isolated and 'private' campsites.

Trekking without a tent Although common in Nepal, only a few trails in India offer the ease and comfort of this option. Exceptions are the Singalila Ridge trail in the Darjeeling area, the Sikkim Kanchenjunga trek, the Markha Valley trek in Ladakh and some lower elevation trails around Shimla and Manali. On these, it is often possible to stay in 'trekking huts' or in simple village homes. You carry clothes and bedding, as with youth hostelling, and for a few rupees a night you get a space on the floor, a wooden pallet or a camp bed, or in the more luxurious inns, a room and shower. The food is simple, usually vegetable curry, rice and *daal* which although repetitive, is healthy and can be tasty. This approach brings you into more contact with the local population, the limiting factor being the routes where accommodation is available.

Locally organized treks Porters can usually be hired through an agent in the town or village at the start of a trek. Porters hired in the bazar may be cheaper than agency porters but may be unreliable. Make sure they are experienced in carrying loads over distances at high altitude. They will help carry your baggage, sometimes cook for you, and communicate with the local people. A good porter will know the area and some can tell you about local customs and point out interesting details en route. Away from roads, the footpath is the principal line of communication between villages. Tracks tend to be very good, well graded and in good condition. In remoter areas away from all habitation, tracks may be indistinct and a local guide is recommended. Although some porters speak a little English (or another foreign language) you may have communication problems and misunderstandings. Remember, you may be expected to provide your porter's warm clothing and protective wear including shoes, gloves and goggles on high altitude treks.

Hiring a *sardar* and crew is more expensive but well worthwhile since he will speak some English, act as a guide, take care of engaging porters and cooks, arrange for provisions and sort out all logistical problems. A *sardar* will cost more and although he may be prepared to carry a load, his principal function will be as a guide and overseer for the porters. Make sure your *sardar* is experienced in the area you will be travelling in and can show good references which are his own and not borrowed.

Using a trekking agent Trekking agents based in Delhi or at hill stations (eg Dehradun, Shimla, Manali, Dharamshala, Leh, Darjeeling, Gangtok) will organize treks for a fee and provide a *sardar*, porters, cooks, food and equipment, but it requires effort and careful thought on your part. This method can be excellent and is recommended for a group, preferably with some experience, that wants to follow a specific itinerary.

You have to follow a pre-arranged itinerary in some areas, as required by the government, and also as porters expect to arrive at certain points on schedule. You can make arrangements from abroad in advance; often a protracted business with faxes and emails. Alternatively, wait until you get to India but allow at least a week to make arrangements.

Fully organized and escorted trek A company or individual with local knowledge and expertise organizes a trip and sells it. Some or all camp equipment, food, cooking, planning the stages, decision-making based on progress and weather conditions, liaison with porters, shopkeepers etc are all taken care of. When operating abroad, the agency may take care of all travel arrangements, ticketing, visas and permits. Make sure that both you and the trekking company understand exactly who is to provide what equipment. This has the advantage of being a good, safe introduction to the country. You will be able to travel with limited knowledge of the region and its culture and get to places more easily which as an individual you might not reach, without the expense of completely kitting yourself out. You should read and follow any advice in the preparatory material you are sent, as your enjoyment greatly depends on it.

An escorted trek involves going with a group; you will camp together but not necessarily all walk together. If you are willing to trade some of your independence for careful, efficient organization and make the effort to ensure the group works well together, the experience can be very rewarding. Ideally there should be no more than 20 trekkers (preferably around 12). Companies have reputations to maintain and try to comply with western concepts of hygiene. Before booking, check the itinerary (is it too demanding, or not adventurous enough?), whether the leader is qualified and is familiar with the route, and what exactly is provided by way of equipment.

Local agents

Tourist offices and government approved trekking agents in **Delhi** and the hill stations will organize fairly inexpensive treks (on some routes, it is compulsory to trek in this way). Tour operators and travel agents are listed in each town. The following are recommended:
Ibex, G-66 East of Kailash, T6912641, F6846403, www.ibexexpeditions.com.
Mercury Himalayan Explorations, Jeevan Tara Building, Parliament St, T3732866.
NEI (Nature Expedition India), B-966 Ansals Palam Vihar, Gurgaon, New Delhi Suburb, T0124-6368601, F6368604, neiindia@del3.vsnl.net.in.
Peak Adventure Tours, T-305 DAV Building, DDA Shopping Complex, Magur Vihar Phase-1, T2711284, F2711292, peakadv@nde.vsnl.net.in.
Snow Leaopard Adventures, slaindia@vsnl.com.
Wanderlust, M 51-52 Palika Bhawan, opposite *Hyatt Regency*, T6883397, T6885188, www.wanderlustindia.com.
  The following government organizations can advise and organize treks:
Garhwal Mandal Vikas Nigam, Kailash Gate, By Pass Rd, Rishikesh, T430372, F481783.
Himalayan Mountaineering Institutes, in hill stations in Uttaranchal and Himachal and Darjeeling, West Bengal.
Kumaon Mandal Vikas Nigam, Secretariat, Mallital, Nainital, T/F36209.

Foreign operators

These, having contacts with agents in India, offer relatively expensive trips to include food, porters, cooks, *sardar* (guide), mess and toilet tents.

Australia and New Zealand
Adventure World, Sydney, T99567766; Auckland, T5245118.
Himalayan Travellers, Wellington, T863325.
Peregrine Adventures, Melbourne, T96638661.

UK
Exodus, T020-87723822, www. Exodus.co.uk.
Explore Worldwide, T01252-760100, info@explore.co.uk.
High Places, T0114-2757500, www.highplaces.co.uk.
Himalayan Kingdoms, T01453-8444400, www.himalayankingdom.co.uk.
KE Adventure, T01768-773966, www.keadventure.com.
Snow Lion Expeditions, T0800-5258735, www.snowlion.com.

USA
High Adventure Travel, T800-3500612, www.airtreks.com.
Himalayan Travel, T800-2252380. www.gorp.com/himtravel.htm/.
Mercury, T0800-2231474.
Mountain Travel Sobek, T800-2272384, www.mtsobek.com.

Essentials Sport & activities

Trekking seasons

These vary with the area you plan to visit and the elevation. Autumn is best in most parts of the Himalaya though March to May can be pleasant. The monsoons (mid-June to end-September) can obviously be very wet and localized thunderstorms can occur at any time, particularly in the spring and summer. Start your trek early in the morning as the monsoon approaches. It often continues to rain heavily up to mid-October in the eastern Himalaya. The Kullu valley is unsuitable for trekking during the monsoons but areas beyond the central Himalayan range, eg Ladakh, Zanskar, Lahul and Spiti are largely unaffected. Be prepared for extremes in temperatures in all seasons so come prepared with light clothing as well as enough waterproof protection. Winters can be exceptionally cold; high passes can be closed and you need more equipment. Winter treks on all but a few low-altitude ones (up to 3,200 m) are only recommended for the experienced trekker accompanied by a knowledgeable local guide.

West Himalaya: Garhwal and Kumaon Himalaya Uttaranchal (pages 236-239) This area is an all-season trekking destination because of its variety of climate and terrain. It is perhaps best in May-June when days are cool and clear. Even with the onset of the monsoons when mist covers the mountains you may get breaks in the rain of three or four days. Clouds can lift to give you some good mountain views but equipment may feel a little damp. The mountains are best for flowers in July-August. Late September to mid-November is again good for trekking.

Himachal (pages 522-528) The best times are as in Garhwal and Kumaon. The monsoon (mid-July to mid-September) is generally very wet and offer no mountain views. Trekking is usually possible from May to October when most passes are open (the Parvati Pass may be blocked until early July). In July-September high altitude flowers are in bloom including summer rhododendrons.

Kashmir (Kashmir, currently risky because of the political situation, Ladakh, page 554 and Zanskar, page 556) Trekking is ideal between April-November. In Ladakh (the area open to trekkers), the motorable road from Manali to Leh is normally open from mid-June to October though flights to Leh from Delhi operate all year round. Most treks cross passes above 4,500 m and are passable from early July to September.

East Himalaya: Darjeeling area (pages 606-609) April-May has a chance of occasional showers but the rhododendrons and magnolias are in full bloom; October-November is usually dry with excellent visibility. Early December is possible but very cold.

Sikkim (pages 635-635) Mid-February to late May and again October-early December are possible; April-May, October-November are best.

Away from the Himalaya Some hill stations offer opportunities for short treks. Generally, November to March is best.

Satpura (Madhya Pradesh) Pachmarhi to Mahadeo and Dhupgarh peaks.

Aravallis (Rajasthan) Mount Abu to Shikhar, Achalgarh and Gaumukh.

Western Ghats Karnataka Madikere, Tala Cauvery, Igutappa, Tadiandamole, Virajpet, Ponnampet, Srimangala, Nagarhole. **Kerala** On the Ghats, from Munnar and Ponmudi.

Nilgiris Udhagamandalam (Ooty), Coonoor, Pollachi, Topslip, Monamboli, Valparai, Grass Hills, Vaguvarai, Chanduvarai, Kilavarai, Kodaikkanal. The hills can be damp during November-December and are best from January to May.

Trekking permits → *Always carry your passport. Without one you can be turned back or, if in a restricted area, be deported at one of the regular trekking permit inspection points.*

Trekking is permitted in all areas other than those described as Restricted or Protected and within the **'Inner Line'**, so that you may not go close to the international boundary in many places. Often, destinations falling within these 'sensitive' zones which have recently been opened for trekking, require treks to be organized by a recognized Indian Travel Agent for groups of at least four, travelling on a specified route, accompanied by a representative/liaison officer. Sometimes there are restrictions on the maximum number of days, season and type of transport used. The 'Inner Line' runs parallel and 40 km inside the international boundary; Kaza (Himachal Pradesh), however, is now open to group trekkers though overnight stay is not allowed at Puh, Khabo or Sumdo. Other areas now open to tourists include Kalindi Khal (Garhwal), Milam Glacier (Kumaon), Khardung La, Tso Moriri and Pangong (Ladakh), Tsangu Lake, Lachung and Yumthang (Sikkim) and Kameng Valley (Arunachal Pradesh). On arrival in India, Government approved trekking agencies can obtain permits relatively easily, usually within three or four days. It can be much slower applying for trekking permits from abroad and may also slow down your visa application.Some restricted areas are still totally closed to foreigners. For other restricted areas, permits are issued at the Foreigners' Regional Registration Offices in Delhi, Mumbai, Kolkata and Chennai (and sometimes at a local FRRO), from Immigration officers at some points of entry, and sometimes at the District Magistrate's. There are also entrance fees for the various national parks and conservation areas which can be as much as Rs 350 for foreigners.

Mountaineering courses

Information on mountaineering is available from: **Indian Mountaineering Federation**, Benito Juarez Marg, New Delhi.

Courses in mountaineering, skiing, high altitude trekking and mountain-rescue are offered by:
Garhwal Mandal Vikas Nigam (GMVN), Muni-ki-Reti, Rishikesh.

Himalayan Mountaineering Institute, Nehru Hill, Darjeeling.
Mountaineering Institute and Allied Sports Complex, 1½ km out of Manali.
The Nehru Institute of Mountaineering, Uttarkashi.

Equipment and clothing

If you have good equipment, it is worth taking it, especially your own boots. Mountaineering and trekking equipment can sometimes be hired from various hill stations. Ask the *Institutes of Mountaineering* and tourist offices there. Guard against cold, wet, sudden changes of temperature, strong sun and wind! Waterproof jacket with hood and over-trousers (windproof, waterproof and 'breather' type); warm sweater; 'fleece' jacket; tracksuit; hiking trousers or shorts (knee length but not cycling); cotton T shirts; cotton underwear; thermal underwear (vests, longjohns); gloves; balaclava or ski toque; sun hat; swimwear. Try to carry lightweight, quick-drying fabrics that can be easily washed in cold water streams. (After the trek, you might consider offering clothes you can part with to your porter.) Good lightweight walking boots with ankle support should be comfortable and well worn in, as blisters can ruin a trek; spare laces, good trainers (for resting the feet; also suitable for many low-level treks except in snow and off-the-trails); polypropylene undersocks, heavy walking socks. Sunglasses (with UV filter), snow glasses if you are planning to go above the snow line, high-factor sun block (15+), lip cream, a good sleeping bag (cheap ones from a local market are unsuitable above 4,000 m) plus cotton liner, a Thermarest pad or a double thickness foam sleeping mat, 2 m square plastic sheet (sold locally), torch (flashlight) with replacement batteries or a Petzl headtorch, a compass, binoculars, insulated bag water-bottle (to also take to bed!), a day pack, a tent (in certain areas). Those expecting to climb high, cross glaciers etc may need to hire crampons, ice axes, snow gaiters, ropes etc as well as a silver survival blanket and a reinforced plastic 'bivouac bag'. A kerosene stove and strong fuel container suitable for high altitudes (kerosene is widely available); water filter and containers; nesting cooking pots (at least two); enamel mug and spoon and bags for provisions. Be sure to eat a balanced diet. Local foods will be available along the trail, and in fact the porters' meal of *chapati* or rice, vegetables, daal and sweet milky tea is quite nutritious. Some shops stock limited amounts of dry goods for trekkers (noodles, chocolate bars, canned foods, fruit, nuts, porridge oats etc). You might prefer to take some freeze-dried packs of favourites from home. Remember to thoroughly boil the fresh (unpasteurized) local milk.

Maps

Survey of India has started producing trekking maps, Scale 1:250,000; a few only are available covering the Himachal and Uttaranchal areas. For details see page 52. **Leomann** Indian Himalaya maps (1:200,000) cover Uttaranchal, Himachal Pradesh and Jammu and Kashmir in eight sheets (1987-1994), and give descriptive itineraries of trekking routes. The **US Army Series (AMS)** U502 at the scale of 1:250,000 are available from selected booksellers in the United States and Europe. Showing contours at 250 or 500 ft, the series was completed before 1960, so some features, notably roads, are out of date. However, they provide good topographic information.

Essentials Sport & activities

Spectator sports

Cricket

India's greatest popular entertainment has become sport, with cricket in particular having a fanatical following across the country. Reinforced by satellite TV and radio, and a national side that enjoys high world rankings and much outstanding individual talent, stars have cult status, and you can see children trying to model themselves on their game on any and every open space. The national side's greatest moment was, arguably, winning the 1983 World Cup. When foreign national sides tour India, tickets are remarkably easy to come by (for Test matches at least), and are considerably cheaper than for corresponding fixtures back home. Tickets are often sold through local bank branches.

Football (Soccer)

Football is increasing in popularity across India, notably in the professional leagues of Goa and West Bengal. The crowds generate tremendous fervour for the big matches, and standards are improving. African players are now featuring more frequently with Indian teams and monthly salaries have risen to over Rs 40,000 per month, a very good wage by Indian standards.

Health

It should be no surprise that since parts of India remain poor that health services are basic and that communicable diseases are an ever-present threat. However, there is a thriving private sector - up to 70% of all health care. Health care in the region is varied: there are some decent private and government clinics/hospitals, which more often than not follow the more aggressive American style of medicine (where you will be referred straight to a specialist) but as with all medical care, first impressions count.

Before you go

Ideally, you should see your GP or travel clinic at least six weeks before your departure for general advice on travel risks, malaria and vaccinations. Make sure you have travel insurance, get a dental check (especially if you are going to be away for more than a month), know your own blood group and if you suffer a long-term condition such as diabetes or epilepsy make sure someone knows or that you have a Medic Alert bracelet/necklace with this information on it.

Vaccination	Obligatory	Recommended
Polio		Yes if nil in last 10 years
Tetanus		Yes if nil in last 10 years (but after 5 doses you have had enough for life)
Typhoid		Yes if nil in last three years
Rabies		Yes for most areas
Hepatitis A		Yes - the disease can be caught easily from food/water
BCG		Yes if staying for more than one month

Yellow Fever does not exist in the country and the Indians want to keep it that way, and so require evidence of vaccination if you have recently travelled from Africa or South America.

Malaria India is a real medical advice conundrum for malaria. Malaria risk is mainly of the P.vivax type and exists throughout the year even in the major cities of Delhi,

⦂ Water purification

There are various ways of purifying water in order to make it safe to drink. Dirty water should first be strained through a filter bag, and then boiled or treated.

Bringing water to a rolling **boil** at sea level is sufficient to make water safe for drinking, but at higher altitudes you have to boil the water for longer to ensure that all the microbes are killed.

Various sterilizing methods can be used and there are propriety preparations containing **chlorine** (eg 'Puritabs') or **iodine** (eg 'Pota Aqua') compounds. Chlorine compounds generally do not kill protozoa (eg giardia). Prolonged usage of iodine compounds may lead to thyroid problems, although this is rare if used for less than a year.

There are a number of **water filters** now on the market, available both in personal and expedition size. There are two types of water filter, **mechanical** and **chemical**. Mechanical filters are usually a combination of carbon, ceramic and paper, although they can be difficult to use. Although cheaper, the disadvantage of mechanical filters is that they do not always remove viruses or protozoa. Chemical filters use a combination of an iodine resin filter and a mechanical filter. The advantage is that according to the manufacturers' claims, everything in the water will be killed. The disadvantage is that the filters need replacing, adding a third to the price.

Essentials Health

Mumbai and Kolkata. The deadly P.falciparum malaria also exists. Areas currently free of malaria include Kashmir, Sikkim, Jammu and Himachal Pradesh. The choice of malaria drug depends on where you will travel, which type of malaria you may be exposed to, and your medical/psychological history. However, it should be noted that the British and the US have different views of the level of resistance to chloroquine. The US believe the resistance is too high to recommend chloroquine but we still recommend it - this advice may change. Some countries advise early treatment rather than drug prophylaxis. Always check with your doctor or travel clinic for the most up to date advice.

What to take

Mosquito repellents: remember that DEET (Di-ethyltoluamide) is the gold standard. Apply the repellent every four to six hours but more often if you are sweating heavily. If a non-DEET product is used check who tested it. Validated products (tested at the London School of Hygiene and Tropical Medicine) include Mosiguard, Non-DEET Jungle formula and non-DEET Autan. If you want to use citronella remember that it must be applied very frequently (ie hourly) to be effective. If you are popular target for insect bites or develop lumps quite soon after being bitten, carry an Aspivenin kit. This syringe suction device is available from many chemists and draws out some of the allergic materials and provides quick relief. **Sun block: Pain killers:** Remember that more than eight paracemol a day can lead to liver failure. **Ciproxin (Ciprofloxacin):** a useful antibiotic for some forms of travellers diarrhoea (see below). **Anti-malarials:** start times for the anti-malarials vary in that if you have never taken Lariam (Mefloquine) before it is advised to start it at least two to three weeks before the entry to a malarial zone (to help identify serious side-effects early). Chloroquine and Paludrine are often started a week before the trip to establish a pattern but Doxycycline and Malarone can be started only one-two days before entry to the malarial area. **Immodium (Pepto-Bismol** is similar and used a lot in USA): a great standby for those diarrhoeas that occur at awkward times (ie before a long

Health insurance scandal

"The auto-rickshaw drivers want you to fill in your health insurance forms and give them the payments, and meantime they'll arrange free food, lodgings and guides around the city. Two drivers suggested this to me and I was there for three hours or so".

Some hospitals claiming insurance payment for 'extra days' will even suggest you get a share of the proceeds. Steer clear.

There have also been cases of deliberate 'food-poisoning' reported in some cheap restaurants in main tourist centres such as the Taj Ganj in Agra, Jaipur and Varanasi. These scams involve tours and private 'hospitals' who present highly inflated bills.

coach/train journey or on a trek). It helps stop the flow of diarrhoea and in my view is of more benefit than harm. It was believed that letting the bacteria or viruses flow out had to be more beneficial. However, with Immodium they still come out, just in a more solid form. For longer trips involving jungle treks taking a clean **needle pack,** clean **dental pack** and **water filtration devices** are common-sense measures.

An A-Z of health risks

The greater disease risk in India is caused by the greater volume of disease carriers in the shape of mosquitoes and sandflies. The key viral disease is Dengue fever, which is transmitted by a mosquito that bites during the day. The disease is like a very nasty form of the 'flu with two-three days of illness, followed by a short period of recovery, then a second attack of illness. Westerners very rarely get the worst haemorrhagic form of the disease. Bacterial diseases include tuberculosis (TB) and some causes of the more common traveller's diarrhoea. The parasitic diseases are many but the two key ones are malaria and Indian trypanosomiasis (known as Chagas Disease).

Altitude Sickness
Symptoms This can creep up on you as just a mild headache with nausea or lethargy during your visit to the Himalayas. The more serious disease is caused by fluid collecting in the brain in the enclosed space of the skull and can lead to coma and death. There is also a lung disease version with breathlessness and fluid infiltration of the lungs.
Cures The best cure is to descend as soon as possible.
Prevention Get acclimatized. Do not try to reach the highest levels on your first few days of arrival. Try to avoid flying directly into the cities of highest altitude. Climbers like to take treatment drugs as protective measures but this can lead to macho idiocy and death. The peaks are still there and so are the trails, whether it takes you a bit longer than someone else does not matter as long as you come back down alive.

Dengue fever
Symptoms This disease can be contracted throughout India and is an increasing problem. In travellers this can cause a severe 'flu-like illness which includes symptoms of fever, lethargy, enlarged lymph glands and muscle pains. It starts suddenly, lasts for two to three days, seems to get better for two to three days and then kicks in again for another two to three days. It is usually all over in an unpleasant week. The local children are prone to the much nastier haemorrhagic form of the disease, which causes them to bleed from internal organs, mucous membranes and often leads to their death.
Cures Traveller's version of the disease is self limiting and forces rest and recuperation.

Prevention The mosquitoes that carry the Dengue virus bite during the day unlike the malaria mosquitoes. Which sadly means that repellent application and covered limbs are a 24 hour issue. Check your accommodation for flower pots and shallow pools of water since these are where the dengue-carrying mosquitoes breed.

Diarrhoea

Symptoms Diarrhoea can refer either to loose stools or an increased frequency; both of these can be a nuisance. It should be short lasting but persistence beyond two weeks, with blood or pain, require specialist medical attention.

Cures Ciproxin (Ciprofloxacin) is a useful antibiotic for bacterial traveller's diarrhoea. It can be obtained by private prescription in the UK which is expensive, or bought over the counter in Indian pharmacies. You need to take one 500 mg tablet when the diarrhoea starts and if you do not feel better in 24 hours, the diarrhoea is likely to have a non-bacterial cause and may be viral (in which case there is little you can do apart from keep yourself rehydrated and wait for it to settle on its own). The key treatment with all diarrhoeas is rehydration. Try to keep hydrated by taking the right mixture of salt and water. This is available as Oral Rehydration Salts (ORS) in ready-made sachets or can be made up by adding a teaspoon of sugar and a half teaspoon of salt to a litre of clean water. Drink at least one large cup of this drink for each loose stool. You can also use flat carbonated drinks as an alternative. Immodium and Pepto-Bismol provide symptomatic relief.

Prevention The standard advice is to be careful with water and ice for drinking. Ask yourself where the water came from. If you have any doubts then boil it or filter and treat it. There are many filter/treatment devices now available on the market. Food can also transmit disease. Be wary of salads (what were they washed in, who handled them), re-heated foods or food that has been left out in the sun having been cooked earlier in the day. There is a simple adage that says wash it, peel it, boil it or forget it. Also be wary of unpasteurised dairy products, these can transmit a range of diseases from brucellosis (fevers and constipation), to listeria (meningitis) and tuberculosis of the gut (obstruction, constipation, fevers and weight loss).

Hepatitis

Symptoms Hepatitis means inflammation of the liver. Viral causes of the disease can be acquired anywhere in South America. The most obvious symptom is a yellowing of your skin or the whites of your eyes. However, prior to this all that you may notice is itching and tiredness.

Cures Early on, depending on the type of hepatitis, a vaccine or immunoglobulin may reduce the duration of the illness.

Prevention Pre-travel hepatitis A vaccine is the best bet. Hepatitis B (for which there is a vaccine) is spread through blood and unprotected sexual intercourse, both of these can be avoided. Unfortunately there is no vaccine for hepatitis C or the increasing alphabetical list of other Hepatitis viruses.

Leishmaniasis

Symptoms A skin and a liver/kidney form of this disease occurs in India. If infected, you may notice a raised lump, which leads to a purplish discoloration on white skin and a possible ulcer. The parasite is transmitted by the bite of a sandfly. Sandflies do not fly very far and the greatest risk is at ground levels, so if you can avoid sleeping on the jungle floor, do so. There is another rarer form which is caused by a sub species of the parasite, this affects the musocal tissues such as lips and nose. Treatment and mode of transmission are the same.

Cures Several weeks treatment is required under specialist supervision.

Prevention Sleep above ground, under a permethrin treated net, use insect repellent and get a specialist opinion on any unusual skin lesions as soon as you can.

Malaria and insect bite prevention

Symptoms Malaria can cause death within 24 hours. It can start as something just resembling an attack of flu. You may feel tired, lethargic, headachy; or worse, develop fits, followed by coma and then death. Have a low index of suspicion because it is very easy to write off vague symptoms, which may actually be malaria. Whilst abroad and on return get tested as soon as possible, the test could save your life.

Cures Treatment is with drugs and may be oral or into a vein depending on the seriousness of the infection. Remember ABCD: Awareness (of whether the disease is present in the area you are travelling in), Bite avoidance, Chemoprohylaxis, Diagnosis.

Prevention This is best summarized by the B and C of the ABCD, bite avoidance and chemoprophylaxis. Wear clothes that cover arms and legs and use effective insect repellents in areas with known risks of insect-spread disease. Use a mosquito net dipped in permethrin as both a physical and chemical barrier at night in the same areas. Guard against the contraction of malaria with the correct anti-malarials (see above). Some would prefer to take test kits for malaria with them and have standby treatment available. However, the field tests of the blood kits have had poor results: when you have malaria you are usually too ill to be able to do the tests correctly enough to make the right diagnosis. Standby treatment (treatment that you carry and take yourself for malaria) should still ideally be supervised by a doctor since the drugs themselves can be toxic if taken incorrectly. The Royal Homeopathic Hospital in the UK does not advocate homeopathic options for malaria prevention or treatment.

Rabies

Symptoms Most of you will know when you have been bitten. It may take days or weeks before odd tingling sensations occur in the affected part, followed by a fear of drinking water and spasms which lead to death.

Cures There is no cure for rabies once it has hold of the Central Nervous System.

Prevention Avoid getting bitten. Dog lovers have to remember that this is a whole new ball game. A full course of rabies vaccine is 100% effective. If you get bitten you will need more vaccine and if you had no pre-exposure vaccine or an inadequate amount you will also need to be injected with something called immunoglobulin. It is always wise to wash the wound but animal bites should ideally not be stitched up in the early stages.

Sexual health

The range of visible and invisible diseases is awesome. Unprotected sex can spread HIV, Hepatitis B and C, Gonorrhea (green discharge), chlamydia (nothing to see but may cause painful urination and later female infertility), painful recurrent herpes, syphilis and warts, just to name a few. You can cut down the risk by using condoms, a femidom or avoiding sex altogether.Keeping in touch

Sun protection

Symptoms White Britons are notorious for becoming red in hot countries because they like to stay out longer than everyone else and do not use adequate sun protection. Long-term sun damage leads to a loss of elasticity of skin and the development of pre-cancerous lesions. Many years later a mild or a very malignant form of cancer may develop. The milder basal cell carcinoma, if detected early, can be treated by cutting it out or freezing it. The much nastier malignant melanoma may have already spread to bone and brain at the time that it is first noticed.

Prevention Sun screen. SPF stands for Sun Protection Factor. It is measured by determining how long a given person takes to 'burn' with and without the sunscreen product on. So, if it takes 10 times longer to burn with the sunscreen product applied, then that product has an SPF of 10. However, do not just use higher factors just to stay out in the sun longer. 'Flash frying' (desperate bursts of excessive exposure), is known to increase the risks of skin cancer. Aloe vera gel is a good pain reliever for sunburn.

Tuberculosis (TB)

Symptoms Cough, blood in spit, weight loss, fever. If you drink unpasteurised milk you can get gut or pelvic TB which can lead to intestinal obstruction and infertility.
Cures At least three drugs are required and the treatment period is at least 6 months.
Prevention If staying for over one month have a skin test for TB followed by the BCG vaccine. Try to avoid people coughing on your face and if you have an unexplained illness on your return ask your doctor to think about TB.

Underwater health

Symptoms If you go diving make sure that you are fit do so. **The British Scuba Association** (BSAC), Telford's Quay, South Pier Road, Ellesmere Port, Cheshire CH65 4FL, United Kingdom, T01513-506200, F506215, www.bsac.com, can put you in touch with doctors who do medical examinations. Protect your feet from cuts, beach dog parasites (larva migrans) and sea urchins. The latter are almost impossible to remove but can be dissolved with lime or vinegar. Keep an eye out for secondary infection.
Cures Antibiotics for secondary infections. Serious diving injuries may need time in a decompression chamber.
Prevention Check that the dive company know what they are doing, have appropriate certification from BSAC or Professional Association of Diving Instructors (PADI), Unit 7, St Philips Central, Albert Road, St Philips, Bristol, BS2 0TD, T0117-3007234, www.padi.com, and that the equipment is well maintained.

Further information

Centers for Disease Control and Prevention (USA) www.cdc.gov This site from the US Government gives excellent advice on travel health, has useful disease maps and details of disease outbreaks.
Department of Health Travel Advice (UK) www.doh.gov.uk/traveladvice This excellent site is also available as a free booklet, the T6, from post offices. It lists the vaccine advice requirements for each country.
Medic Alert (UK) www.medicalalert.co.uk This is the website of the foundation that produces bracelets and necklaces for those with existing medical problems. Once you have ordered your bracelet/necklace you write your key medical details on paper inside it, so that if you collapse, a medical person can identify you as someone with epilepsy or allergy to peanuts etc.
NetDoctor (UK) www.Netdoctor.co.uk This general health advice site has a useful section on travel and has an 'ask the expert', interactive chat forum.
Public Health Laboratory Service (UK) www.phls.org.uk This site has up-to-date malaria advice guidelines for travel around the world. It gives specific advice about the right drugs for each location. It also has useful information for those who are pregnant, suffering from epilepsy or planning to travel with children.
Travel Screening Services (UK) www.travelscreening.co.uk A private clinic dedicated to integrated travel health. The clinic gives vaccine, travel health advice, email and SMS text vaccine reminders and screens returned travellers for tropical diseases.
Websites Foreign and Commonwealth Office (FCO) (UK) www.fco.gov.uk This is a key travel advice site, with useful information on the country, people, climate and lists the UK embassies/consulates. The site also promotes the concept of 'Know Before You Go' and encourages travel insurance and appropriate travel health advice.

Books

Expedition Medicine (The Royal Geographic Society), editors David Warrell and Sarah Anderson ISBN 1 86197 040-4.
International Travel & Health World Health Organisation, Geneva ISBN 92 4 158026 7.
The Travellers Good Health Guide by Dr Ted Lankester by ISBN 0-85969-827-0.
The World's Most Dangerous Places by Robert Young Pelton, Coskun Aral and Wink Dulles ISBN 1-566952-140-9.

Keeping in touch

Communications

Internet

Access is becoming increasingly available in major cities and tourist centres as cyber cafés mushroom and PCOs (Public Call Office) are beginning to offer the service, but in small towns the machines can be woefully slow. The web is spreading wider to reach remote areas, and is becoming faster year by year. As access improves, surfing charges fall (now around Rs 130 per hour). Alternatively, you can ask a hotel or a travel agent if they will allow you to use their system but hotel rates tend to be much higher.

Post

The post is frequently unreliable, and delays are common. It is advisable to use a post office where it is possible to hand over mail for franking across the counter, or a top hotel post box. Valuable items should only be sent by **Registered Mail**. Government Emporia or shops in the larger hotels will send purchases home if the items are difficult to carry. **Airmail** service to Europe, Africa and Australia takes at least a week and a little longer for the Americas. **Speed post** (which takes about four days to the UK) is available from major towns. Specialist shippers deal with larger items, normally approximately US$150 per cubic metre. **Courier services** (eg *DHL, ATS*) are available in the larger towns. At some main post offices you can send small packages under 2 kg as Letter Post (rather than parcel post) which is much cheaper at Rs 220. 'Book Post' (for printed paper) is cheaper still, approximately Rs 170 for 5 kg. Book parcels must be sewn in cloth (best over see-through plastic) with a small open 'window' slit for contents to be seen.

Sending a **parcel** can take up to two hours. Check that the post office holds necessary customs declaration forms (two/three copies needed). Write 'No commercial value' if returning used clothes, books etc. Air mail is expensive; sea mail slow but reasonable (10 kg, Rs 800). 'Packers' outside post offices will do all necessary cloth covering, sealing etc for Rs 20-50; you address the parcel, obtain stamps from a separate counter; stick stamps and one customs form to the parcel with glue available (the other form/s must be partially sewn on). Post at the Parcels Counter and obtain a Registration slip. **Maximum dimensions:** height 1 m, width 0.8 m, circumference 1.8 m. Cost: sea mail Rs 775 for first kilogram, Rs 70 each extra kilogram. Air mail also Rs 775 first kilogram, Rs 200 each subsequent kilogram. Many people complain that private shops offering a postal service actually send cheap substitutes. It is usually too late to complain when the buyer finds out. It is best to buy your item and then get it packed and posted yourself.

Poste restante facilities are widely available in even quite small towns at the GPO where mail is held for one month. Ask for mail to be addressed to you with your surname in capitals and underlined. When asking for mail at Poste Restante check under surname as well as Christian name. Any special issue foreign stamps are likely to be stolen from envelopes in the Indian postal service and letters may be thrown away. Advise people who are sending you mail to India to use only definitive stamps (without pictures).

The email explosion

As the internet shrinks the world, travellers are increasingly using emails to keep in touch with home. Their free accounts are invariably with **hotmail.com**, **yahoo.com**, **email.com** or **backpackers.com**; usually the less common the provider, the quicker the access.

India has its own set of problems which can be frustrating: very few machines which may also be out-dated; untrained staff and poor technical support; the server may be unreliable; the system may be clogged with users, especially during day; there may be frequent power cuts ... There are exceptions, of course.

New offices are opening weekly and new towns are getting connected. To track down the most reliable and best value internet service, ask other travellers. The length of the queue can be a good indicator. On the web, you can get a list from **www.netcafe guide.com** Don't always head for the cheapest since they may also have the oldest and slowest equipment. Rates vary, but in mid-2001, it cost between Rs 20-50 for an hour.

Hot tips

1 Use the folder facility to save mail
2 Keep your in-box clear to reduce loading time
3 Avoid junk mail by not giving your address to on-line companies
4 Avoid downloading and using scanned pictures and documents
5 Save files and back up regularly

The system can be efficient and satisfying but it can also become an expensive habit with more than its fair share of frustrations. As one sending an email to us mused, "many a hard-up traveller will wax lyrical about 'getting away from it all' and escaping 'the pressure of western society'. They will then spend hours and several hundred rupees a week slaving over a computer keyboard in some hot and sticky back street office".

Essentials Keeping in touch

Telephone → *International code: 00 91. Phone codes for towns are printed after the town name or in the listings of smaller towns*

International Direct Dialling is now widely available in privately run call 'booths', usually labelled on yellow boards with the letters 'PCO-STD-ISD'. You dial the call yourself, and the time and cost are displayed on a computer screen. They are by far the best places from which to telephone abroad. Cheap rate (2100-0600) means long queues may form outside booths. Telephone calls from hotels are usually much more expensive (check price before calling). Major global **mobile phone** companies have partner servers in India, but coverage remains uneven. You can buy a local "pay as you go card" if you are going to make heavy local use of the mobile. **Ringing tone**: double ring, repeated regularly; **Engaged**: equal length, on and off. Both are similar to UK ringing and engaged tones.

One disadvantage of the tremendous pace of the telecommunications revolution is the fact that millions of telephone numbers go out of date every year. Current telephone directories themselves are often out of date and some of the numbers given in the Handbook will have been changed even as we go to press. Directory enquiries, **197**, can be helpful but works only for the local area code.

Fax services are available from many PCOs and larger hotels, who charge either by the minute or per page.

● *India is running out of phone numbers. The answer is to put an additional "2" on the front of existing numbers. Unfortunately some states seem to have implemented this, others not and some have reverted to the existing number. Our best advice is if the number in the text does not work, add a "2".*

⁞ Best short-wave frequencies

BBC World service Signal strength varies throughout the day, with lower frequencies better during the night. The nightly "South Asia Report" offers up to the minute reports. Try 15310, 17790 or 1413, 5975, 11955, 17630, 17705. Also www.bbc.uk/worldservice/sasia

Voice of America 1400-1800 GMT; 1575, 6110, 7125, 9645, 9700, 9760, 15255,15395 Mhz. www.voa.gov/sasia
Deutsche Welle: 0600-1800 GMT; 6075, 9545, 17845; other frequencies include 17560, 12000 and 21640.

Media

Newspapers and magazine

International newspapers (mainly English language) are sold in the bookshops of top hotels in major cities, and occasionally by booksellers elsewhere. India has a large English language press. They all have extensive analysis of contemporary Indian and some international issues. The major papers now have internet sites which are excellent for keeping daily track on events, news and weather. The best known are: **The Hindu** (www.thehindu.com), **The Hindustan Times** (www.hindustantimes.com), **The Independent, The Times of India** (www.timesofindia.com/) and **The Statesman** (www.thestatesman.org/). **The Economic Times** is possibly the best for independent reporting and world coverage. **The Telegraph** (www.telegraphindia.com/) has good foreign coverage. **The Indian Express** (www.expressindia.com/) has stood out as being consistently critical of the Congress Party and Government. **The Asian Age** gives good coverage of Indian and international affairs. Of the fortnightly magazines, some of the most widely read are **Sunday, India Today** and **Frontline**, all of which are current affairs journals on the model of Time or Newsweek.

Television and radio

India's national radio and television network, **Doordarshan**, broadcasts in national and regional languages but things have moved on. The advent of satellite TV has hit even remote rural areas. The 'Dish' can help travellers keep in touch through **Star TV** from Hong Kong (accessing **BBC World, CNN** etc), **VTV** (music) and **Sport,** now available even in some modest hotels in the smallest of towns. The decision by the government to issue more licences to satellite broadcasters has resulted in up to 50 available channels from **MTV** to **Maharishi Veda Vision!**

North India

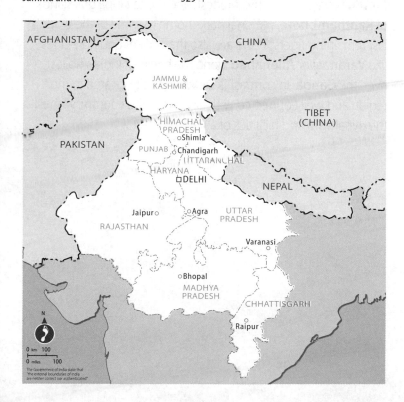

Introduction

India's northern region has some of the greatest sights for travellers in the world. Agra, with its ethereal **Taj Mahal**, Rajasthan's **royal palaces**, and the astonishing temples of **Khajuraho** and the **Sikh Golden Temple** of Amritsar, have awed and charmed visitors from all over the globe.

But North India's well-known sights are just the beginning. Some of the **Himalaya's** most beautiful yet little known mountains are found north of Delhi in Hinduism's 'home of the gods', the Garhwal Himalaya. Still further north are former British hill stations like **Shimla** and **Mussoorie**, while beyond are the high altitude deserts of the Tibetan borderlands, **Spiti** and **Ladakh**.

Then there are the lush green forests of **Kanha** and **Bandhavgarh** in Madhya Pradesh and the savanna grasslands of **Ranthambhore**, national parks home to some of the world's last remaining tigers. There are also the ancient and holy cities like **Varanasi** or **Allahabad** along the banks of India's holiest river, the **Ganga**. In contrast is **Delhi**, centrally located in the region and well connected with all parts of the country, with all the dynamism and facilities of a modern capital.

Delhi

● Footprint features

Introduction

Delhi can take you aback with its vibrancy and growth. Less than 60 years ago the spacious, quiet and planned city of **New Delhi** was still the pride of late colonial British India, while immediately to its north the crowded lanes of **Old Delhi** resonated with the sounds of a bustling medieval market. Today both worlds have been overtaken by the brash rush of modernisation. As Delhi's population surges towards 13 million its tentacles spread in all directions from both the ancient core of Shahjahan's city in the north and the late British capital of New Delhi to its south.

A daytime drive from the airport gives something of the feel of this dynamism, the roads often crowded with traffic, new highrise buildings transforming the spacious outlines of Lutyens' New Delhi with its broad tree lined avenues, into a humming commercial hub centred around **Connaught Place**. Close to New Delhi Railway station, the hub of New Delhi's network to the rest of India, the cheap hotels and guesthouses of **Paharganj**, heart of backpackerland, squeeze between cloth merchants and wholesalers, cheek by jowl in the narrow lanes. In Old Delhi, further north, with the **Red Fort** and **Jama Masjid**, the old city is still a dense network of narrow alleys and tightly packed markets and houses. Your senses are bombarded by noise, bustle, smells and apparent chaos. A 'third city' comprises the remorselessly growing squatter settlements (jhuggies) which provide the only shelter for at least one-third of Delhi's total population. To the south is yet another, newer, chrome and glass city, the city of the modern suburbs and urban 'farms', where the rural areas of Gurgaon have become the preserve of the prosperous, with shopping malls, banks and private housing estates. Old and new, simple and sophisticated, traditional and modern, East and West are all juxtaposed.

★ Don't miss...

❶ Stand at the **India Gate** and look west along Rajpath Hill and the Secretariats, page 89.

❷ Travel back to the 12th century at the **Qutb Minar** complex with its impressive tower and even older gupta pillar, page 96.

❸ No visit to Delhi would be complete without visiting **Raj Ghat** where there's a prominent memorial to Mahatma Gandi, page 92.

❹ Take a bicycle rickshaw down **Chandni Chowk** to the spice market and back through the bazar to finish at **Jama Masjid**, page 107.

❺ If you can't get to the Taj Mahal in Agra, make sure you visit **Humayun's tomb** in a lovely garden setting, page 94.

❻ Visit the **Red Fort** at night for a spectacular son et lumière show, page 100.

Delhi

Ins and outs

Getting there

→ *Phone code: 011. Dial 1952, then old number, to get new phone number. Colour map 2, grid A6.*
Population: 12.8 million. Area: 434 sq km. Scheduled castes: 19%.

Delhi is served by the **Indira Gandhi (IGI) Airport** to the southwest of the city. The Domestic Terminal 1 is 15 km from Connaught Circus, the central hub of activity and the main hotel area in New Delhi. It handles flights from 2 separate sections: 'A' (exclusively for **Indian Airlines**) and 'B' (for others). The International Terminal 2 is 23 km from the centre. During the day, the journey to Connaught Circus can take from 30 to 45 mins from the Domestic Terminal and 45 mins to 1 hr from the International Terminal. A free shuttle runs between the terminals. To get to town take a pre-paid taxi or an airport coach or consider asking your hotel to collect.

The principal **Inter State Bus Terminus (ISBT)** is at Kashmir Gate (near the Red Fort) about 30 mins by bus from Connaught Place. Services connect it to the other ISBTs.

There are three main railway stations. The busy **New Delhi** station, a 10-min walk north of Connaught Place, can be maddeningly chaotic; you need to have all your wits about you. The quieter **Hazrat Nizamuddin** (which has some south-bound trains) is 5 km southeast of Connaught Place. The overpoweringly crowded **Old Delhi (Main) Station** (2 km north of Connaught Place) has a few important trains.

Getting around

Auto-rickshaws and taxis are widely available, though few are prepared to use their meters, especially for foreigners - use the pre-paid stand at the junction of Radial Road 1 and Connaught Place. They offer the only realistic choice for getting about the city, which is much too spread out to walk, as city buses are usually packed and have long queues. Be on your guard around New Delhi station. A road (State Entry Rd, but the name is well concealed) runs from the southern end of platform 1 to Connaught Place. This is a hassle-free alternative to the main Chelmsford Rd during the day (gate closed at night). See Transport, page 126, for further details.

Orientation

Connaught Place, the main commercial centre of New Delhi, is about 1 km south of New Delhi railway station and the main backpackers' area, Paharganj. Running due south of Connaught Place is Janpath with small shops selling a variety of craft products and hotels like the *Imperial* and *Le Meridien*. Running east west across Janpath is Rajpath with all the major state buildings at its western end. Immediately beyond them is the diplomatic enclave, Chanakyapuri. Most of the upmarket hotels are scattered across the wide area between Connaught Place and the airport to the southwest. As Delhi has spread southwards a series of new markets has grown up to serve extensive housing colonies such as South Extension, Greater Kailash and Safdarjang Enclave. This development has brought one of the major historic sites, the Qutb Minar, within the limits of the southern city, about half an hour by taxi from Connaught Place. About 2 km northeast of Connaught Place are the Jama Masjid and the Red Fort, the heart of Shah Jahanabad, or Old Delhi. It too has a thriving commercial centre, focused on Chandni Chowk, but set in a far more traditional complex of crowded winding lanes and small shops.

Climate

October-March are the best months, but December and January can get quite cold at night. Pollution can affect asthma sufferers. Monsoon lasts from mid-June to mid-September. May and June are very hot and dry.

⦂ Taxi tips

The first-time visitor can be vulnerable to exploitation by taxi drivers at the airport.

If arriving at night, you are very strongly advised to have a destination in mind and get a **pre-paid taxi**. Be firm about being dropped at the hotel of your choice and insist that you have a reservation; you can always change hotels the next day if you are unhappy. **Don't admit to being a first-time visitor**.

If you don't take a pre-paid taxi, the driver will demand an inflated fare. He may insist that the hotel you want to go to has closed or is full and will suggest one where he will get a commission (and you will be overcharged).

Sadly, some travellers have been told that the city was unsafe with street fighting, police barricades (which do exist) and curfews and have then been taken to Agra or Jaipur.

In the city always check that **auto-rickshaw** and **taxi** meters are cleared and try to insist on the meter being used. If you wish to travel a short distance, eg from Janpath to the New Delhi Railway Station, often auto-rickshaws may ask Rs 50 or more, three or four times the proper rate. Similarly, if you are staying away from the centre, it may be difficult to get an auto-rickshaw or taxi late at night; get the hotel doorman to call you one and pay him a small tip. Carry plenty of coins and small notes. As a last resort you can threaten drivers with police action if they prove to be particularly difficult (T3737300); drivers can lose their permits if they attempt to cheat. Since, it is common that with fare revisions, meters are not always changed, drivers must carry a card with the revised fares (six times the meter reading).

History

The cities of Delhi

Modern Delhi spreads over the remains of nearly a dozen earlier centres which once occupied this vital strategic site. **Old Delhi** or **Shah Jahanabad** (the '7th City') was built by the Mughal Emperor Shah Jahan in the first half of the 17th century. Focusing on his great Red Fort and Jama Masjid, this old city is still a dense network of narrow alleys and tightly packed markets and houses, with Muslims, Sikhs and Hindus living side by side, but separated in their own defined quarters.

Immediately to the south is the British-built capital of **New Delhi**, a self-conscious attempt to match the imperial grandeur of the Mughal capital, while post-Independence Delhi has dramatically accelerated its suburban expansion. There is also a 'third city', often scarcely seen, its squatter settlements which provide the only shelter for at least one-third of Delhi's total population.

New Delhi: the origins

New Delhi's present position as capital was only confirmed on 12 December 1911, when King George V announced at the Delhi Durbar that the capital of India was to move from Calcutta to Delhi. The new city, planned under the leadership of British architect Edwin Lutyens, was inaugurated on 9 February 1931.

Delhi is now very spread out. In fact it has pushed across the state border into Gurgaon District of Haryana.

New Delhi

Related maps
A Central New Delhi, page 90
B Old Delhi, page 104
C Paharganj, page 112

N

0 metres 700
0 yards 700

■ Sleeping	6 Diplomat	12 Manor	17 Siddharth
1 27 Jorbagh	7 Hyatt Regency	13 Master Paying	18 Surya (Crown Plaza)
2 Ambassador	8 Jukaso Inn	Guest House	19 Taj Mahal
3 Ashok & Samrat	9 Kailash Nath	14 Maurya Sheraton	20 Taj Palace
4 Bajaj & Clark	10 La Sagrita	15 Oberoi	21 Vasant Continental
5 Claridges	11 Legend Inn	16 Rajdoot & Karim	22 Youth Hostel & Moti Mehal Delux

Lutyens and Baker For an architect, the project was a dream. The new city was to cover 26 sq km and to be a dramatic statement of British imperial ambitions. Edwin Lutyens decided that he would design the palatial Viceroy's House and his friend Herbert Baker would design the nearby Government Secretariat and Imperial Legislative Assembly. Between them they would style the symbolically important approach to these magnificent structures.

The King favoured something in form and flavour similar to the Mughal masterpieces but fretted over the horrendous expense that this would incur. A petition signed by eminent public figures such as Bernard Shaw and Thomas Hardy advocated an Indian style and an Indian master builder. Herbert Baker had made known his own views even before his appointment when he wrote "first and foremost it is the spirit of British sovereignty which must be imprisoned in its stone and bronze". Lord Hardinge, the Viceroy, suggested "western architecture with an Oriental motif". As Tillotson has shown, Lutyens was appalled by the political pressure to adopt Indian styles. For one thing, he despised Indian architecture. "Even before he had seen any examples of it", writes Tillotson, "he pronounced Mughal architecture to be 'piffle', and seeing it did not disturb that conviction". Yet in the end, Lutyens was forced to settle for the compromise.

Choice of site The city was to accommodate 70,000 people and have boundless possibilities for future expansion. A foundation stone was hastily cut and laid by King George V at the Durbar, but when Lutyens and his team arrived and toured the site on elephant back they decided that it was unsuitable. The Viceroy decided on another site in South Delhi. So in 1913 the foundation stone was uplifted and moved on a bullock cart to **Raisina Hill**.

Land was levelled, roads were built, water and electricity connected to the site, and the same red sandstone employed that Akbar and Shah Jahan

⁞ Capital Chaos?

Delhi's transport has long been severely criticised. With its first metro only now under construction, a fleet of decaying buses and auto-rickshaws pumping out a noxious mixture of black fumes into the city's air. In July 1998 the Indian Supreme Court took the unprecedented step of ordering a complete switch of buses and autos from burning diesel and two stroke fuel to Compressed Natural Gas (CNG), to be completed by April 2001. By early April when the deadline for the transfer arrived, but only 2,000 of Delhi's fleet of 14,000 buses, most of them privately operated, had been converted. Converted eco-friendly vehicles sport a green line and by 2002 the transistion was almost complete.

had used in their magnificent forts and tombs, with marble lavished on the interiors. In the busiest year, 29,000 people were working on the site and buildings took shape. The Viceroy's House, the centre-piece of imperial proportions, was 1 km around the foundations, bigger than Louis XIV's palace at Versailles. It had a colossal dome surmounting a long colonnade and 340 rooms in all. It took nearly 20 years to complete, similar to the time it took to build the Taj Mahal.

Indian touches to a classical style The project was surrounded by controversy from beginning to end. Opting for a fundamentally classical structure, both Baker and Lutyens sought to incorporate Indian motifs, many entirely superficial. While some claim that Lutyens achieved a unique synthesis of the two traditions, Tillotson asks whether "the sprinkling of a few simplified and classicized Indian details (especially *chhattris*) over a classical palace" could be called a synthesis. The chief exception was the dome of the Viceroy's House, which though based on the Buddhist stupa at Sanchi, is an essentially classical form, see page 270. A striking irony in the overall design resulted from the late requirement to build a council chamber for the representative assembly which was created by political reforms in 1919. This now houses the Lok Sabha, but its centrality to the current Indian constitution is belied by Baker's design which tucks it away almost invisibly to the north of the northern Secretariat.

The Raisina crossing (see page 90) The grand design was for an approach to all the Government buildings along the King's Way (Rajpath). This was to be 2.4 km long, would lead to the Great Palace where ceremonial parades could be held, then up Raisina Hill between the Secretariat buildings, up to the entrance to the Viceroy's House. The palace was intended to be in view at all times, increasingly impressive as one got nearer. There was much debate over the gradient of Raisina Hill and eventually just over 5% was agreed upon.

In the event the effect was not what was intended. Only when the Viceroy's House was nearing completion was it realized that as you progress from the bottom of the King's Way up Raisina Hill, the Viceroy's House sinks down over the horizon like the setting sun so that only the top part of the palace is visible. Lutyens recognized the mistake too late to make any change, and called this effect his 'Bakerloo'. Baker and Lutyens blamed each other and did not speak to one another for the next five years.

Delhi since Independence Government Ministries and Departments have spread across South Delhi but it also has many trees and attractive parks. Beyond the range of New Delhi's broad avenues are other urban worlds. New satellite towns and housing colonies such as Ghaziabad and NOIDA on the east bank of the River

Yamuna have sprung up, while at least one-third of the city's population continue to live in 'jhuggies' (squatter huts). High quality housing has spread southwards from the airport into the neighbouring state of Haryana, where the former rural fields of Gurgaon District have taken on the character of a rapidly commercialising high value suburb, with shopping malls, banks and private housing estates.

Current politics

Delhi has its own Assembly, though its political powers as the government of National Capital Territory of about 14 million people are very limited. Right wing Hindu parties have always been a force in Delhi politics but in the December 1998 Assembly elections the Congress (I) party recaptured Delhi from the BJP, a victory re-inforced by the municipal elections in 2002 when the Congress swept the BJP from power. There has been a long running debate over the question of statehood for the Delhi capital region but no real sign of change in its present status.

Sights

The sites of interest are grouped in three main areas. In the centre is the British built capital of **New Delhi**, with its government buildings and wide avenues. **Shah Jahanabad** (Old Delhi) is about 7 km north of Connaught Circus. Ten kilometres to the south is the **Qutb Minar** complex, with the old fortress city of **Tughluqabad** 8 km to its east. You can visit each separately, or link routes together into a day-tour to include the most interesting sites. This description starts near the centre of the modern political and administrative centre of Indian government. The second section describes sites in the south and the third, Old Delhi. See page 124 for tour details.

Central New Delhi

India Gate A tour of New Delhi will usually start with a visit to India Gate. This war memorial is situated at the eastern end of **Rajpath**. Designed by Lutyens, it commemorates more than 70,000 Indian soldiers who died in the First World War. Some 13,516 names of British and Indian soldiers killed on the Northwest Frontier and in the Afghan War of 1919 are engraved on the arch and foundations. Under the arch is the Amar Jawan Jyoti, commemorating Indian armed forces' losses in the Indo-Pakistan War of 1971. The arch (43 m high) stands on a base of Bharatpur stone and rises in stages. Below the cornice are Imperial Suns and on both sides of the arch is inscribed INDIA flanked by the dates MCMXIV (1914 left) and MCMXIX (1919). Facing the arch is an open cupola which once contained a statue of King George V, now removed to an almost unvisited site on the banks of the Yamuna in the Civil Lines. Similar to the Hindu *chhattri* signifying regality, it is decorated with nautilus shells symbolizing British maritime power.

To the northwest of India Gate are two impressive buildings, **Hyderabad House** and **Baroda House**, built as residences for the Nizam of Hyderabad and the Gaekwar of Baroda. Now used as offices, both were carefully placed to indicate the paramountcy of the British Raj over the Princely States. The *Nizam*, reputed to be the richest man in the world, ruled over an area equal to that of France. The *Gaekwar* belonged to the top level of Indian Princes and both, along with the Maharajas of Mysore, Jammu and Kashmir and Gwalior were entitled to receive 21-gun salutes.

Rajpath leads west from India Gate towards **Janpath**. To the north are the **National Archives**. Formerly the Imperial Record Office, and designed by Lutyens, this was intended to be a part of a much more ambitious complex of public buildings. To the south is the **National Museum** (see under Museums). The foundation stone was laid by Jawarharlal Nehru in 1955 and the building completed in 1960. Rajpath continues to the foot of Raisina Hill, now called Vijay Chowk.

★ **The Secretariats** At the Secretariat and Rashtrapati Bhavan gates, the mounted and unmounted troops parade in full uniform on Saturdays at 1030 and are worth attending. Standing on either side of Raisina Hill, **North Block** houses the Home and Finance Ministries, **South Block** the Ministry of Foreign Affairs. These long classical buildings, topped by Baroque domes, designed by Baker, are similar to his Government Buildings of Pretoria, and were derived from Wren's Royal Naval College at Greenwich. The towers were originally designed to be twice the height of the buildings and to act as beacons guarding the way to the inner sanctum. Their height was reduced and with it their impact. The domes are decorated with lotus motifs and elephants, while the north and south gateways are Mughal in design. On the northern Secretariat building is the imperialistic inscription "Liberty will not descend to a people: a people must raise themselves to liberty. It is a blessing which must be earned before it can be enjoyed".

In the **Great Court** between the Secretariats are the four **Dominion Columns**, donated by the governments of Australia, Canada, New Zealand and South Africa - ironically, as it turned out. The resemblance of Baker's domes to his work in Pretoria is also striking and ironic! Each is crowned by a bronze ship sailing east, symbolizing the maritime and mercantile supremacy of the British Empire. In the centre of the court is the Jaipur column of red sandstone topped with a white egg, bronze lotus and six-pointed glass star of India (which has evolved into today's five-pointed star). Across the entrance to the Great Court is a 205 m wrought iron screen.

Central New Delhi

Related map
A Connaught Place,
page 110

Sleeping ■
1 Grand Inter-Continental
2 Indraprastha
3 Janpath
4 Le Meridien

Eating ●
1 Nathu's
2 Triveni Café & Gallery

★ **Rashtrapati Bhavan** Once the Viceroy's House, Rashtrapati Bhavan is the official
residence of the President of India. Designed by **Lutyens**, it combines western and eastern styles. Philip Davies describes it as a masterpiece of symmetry, discipline, silhouette and harmony. The Durbar Hall inside, 23 m in diameter, has coloured marble from all parts of India.

To the south is Flagstaff House, formerly the residence of the Commander-in-Chief. Re-named **Teen Murti Bhawan** it now houses the Nehru Memorial Museum. Designed by **Robert Tor Russell**, in 1948 it became the Prime Minister's residence. The **Martyr's Memorial**, at the junction of Sardar Patel Marg and Willingdon Crescent, is a magnificent 26-m long, 3-m high bronze sculpture by DP Roy Chowdhury. The 11 statues of national heroes are headed by Mahatma Gandhi.

Parliament House ⓘ *No photography.* Northeast of the Viceroy's House is the **Council House**, now **Sansad Bhavan**. Baker designed this and Lutyens suggested that it be circular (173 m diameter). Originally, it was intended to have a dome but this plan was dropped. Inside is the library and chambers for the Council of State, Chamber of Princes and Legislative Assembly - the **Lok Sabha**.

Just opposite the Council House is the **Rakabganj Gurudwara** in Pandit Pant Marg. This 20th-century white marble shrine, which integrates the late Mughal and Rajasthani styles, marks the spot where the headless body of **Guru Tegh Bahadur**, the ninth Sikh Guru (see page 1346), was cremated in 1657. West of the Council House is the Cathedral **Church of the Redemption** (1927-35) and to its north the Italianate Roman Catholic **Church of the Sacred Heart** (1930-34), both conceived by Henry Medd whose designs won architectural competitions.

Connaught Place and its outer ring, **Connaught Circus**, comprise two-storeyed arcaded buildings, arranged radially. In 1995 they were re-named **Rajiv Chowk** and **Indira Chowk** respectively, but are still widely known by their original names. Designed by **Robert Tor Russell**, they have become the main commercial centre of Delhi. Vendors of all sorts gather in the area; an unusual service rendered is ear cleaning with very dubious looking equipment, claiming to improve hearing! Sadly, the area also attracts bands of aggressive touts ready to take advantage of the unwary traveller by getting them into spurious 'official' or 'government' shops and travel agencies. The area (and Palika Bazar) is renowned for its shoe-shine tricksters. Large wadges of slime appear mysteriously on shoes and are then pointed out eagerly by attendant boys or men who offer to clean them off at a price. This can just be the start of 'necessary repairs' to the shoes for which bills of over Rs 300 are not unknown. If caught, insist politely but firmly that the dirt is cleaned off free of charge.

To the south in **Janpath** (the People's Way), the east and west Courts were hostels for the members of the newly convened Legislative Assembly. With their long colonnaded verandahs, these are Tuscan in character.

Lakshmi Narayan Mandir To the west of Connaught Circus is the Lakshmi Narayan **Birla Temple** in Mandir Marg. Financed by the prominent industrialist **Raja Baldeo Birla** in 1938, this is one of the most popular Hindu shrines in the city and one of Delhi's few striking examples of Hindu architecture. Dedicated to Lakshmi, the goddess of well-being, it is commonly referred to as **Birla Mandir**. The design is in the Orissan style with tall curved towers (*sikhara*) capped by large *amalakas*. The exterior is faced with red and ochre stone and white marble. Built around a central courtyard, the main shrine has images of Narayan and his consort Lakshmi while two separate cells have icons of Siva (the Destroyer) and his consort Durga (the 10-armed destroyer of demons). The temple is flanked by a *dharamshala* (rest house) and a Buddhist *vihara* (monastery).

East from the Birla Temple, down Kali Bari Marg to Baba Kharak Singh Marg (Irwin Rd), is the **Hanuman Mandir**. This small temple (circa 1724) was built by Maharaja Jai Singh II of Jaipur. Of no great architectural interest, the temple is increasingly popular with devotees. **Mangal haat** (Tuesday Fair) is a popular market.

★ **Jantar Mantar** Just to the east of the Hanuman Mandir in Sansad Marg (Parliament St) is **Jai Singh's observatory** ('Jantar Mantar'). The Mughal Emperor Mohammad Shah (ruled 1719-48) entrusted the renowned astronomer **Maharaja Jai Singh II** with the task of revising the calendar and correcting the astronomical tables used by contemporary priests, see page 336. Daily astral observations were made for years before construction began and plastered brick structures were favoured for the site instead of brass instruments. Built in 1725 it is slightly smaller than the later observatory at Jaipur.

Memorial Ghats Beyond Delhi Gate lies the **Yamuna**, marked by a series of memorials to India's leaders. The river itself, a kilometre away, is invisible from the road, protected by a low rise and banks of trees. The most prominent memorial, immediately opposite the end of Jawaharlal Nehru Road, is that of **Mahatma Gandhi** at ★ **Raj Ghat**. To its north is **Shanti Vana** ('forest of peace'), landscaped gardens where Prime Minister Jawaharlal Nehru was cremated in 1964, and subsequently his grandson Sanjay Gandhi in 1980, daughter **Indira Gandhi** in 1984 and elder grandson, Rajiv, in 1991. To the north again is **Vijay Ghat** ('Victory bank') where Prime Minister Lal Bahadur Shastri was cremated in 1965.

Kotla Firoz Shah Immediately to the south of Raj Ghat is the **Indraprastha Stadium**, one of India's biggest sports stadiums. Between that and the Mathura Rd is Kotla Firoz Shah, the citadel of Firozabad, built by **Firoz Shah Tughluq** (ruled 1351-88) in 1351. At its height it stretched from Hauz Khas in the south, to north of the Delhi ridge, and east to the Yamuna River, but little remains as the stone was extensively used for the later cities of Shergarh and Shahjhanabad.

From Bahadurshah Zafar Marg you enter the central enclosure, the largest of the three originals (covered for the most part by modern buildings). The most striking feature is the tapering 14-m high monolithic polished sandstone Asoka pillar (third century BC). Firoz Shah was deeply interested in antiquities and had it brought from Topra (Haryana), 100 km away, wrapped in silk and muslin, on a 42-wheeled carriage drawn apparently by 200 men at each wheel. The Brahmi inscription carries the Emperor Asoka's message of goodwill to his subjects. Nearby is a circular *baoli* (well) and a ruined mosque. In its original state it is said to have accommodated over 10,000 worshippers and was where the Mongol Timur prayed during his sacking of Delhi in 1398. Apparently, he was so impressed by it that the Samarkand mosque was modelled on it. It is said that three secret passages lead from the Kush-ki-Firoz

the Qutb Minar. Immediately to its south is the **Pragati Maidan**, a permanent
exhibition centre, and further south is the Purana Qila.

Purana Qila (Old Fort) ① *0800-1830, US$2 (foreigners), sound and light show
(evenings) Rs 25, entrance by west gate, guidebooks and postcards, clean toilets.*
Purana Qila, now an attractive and quiet park, witnessed the crucial struggle between
the Mughal **Emperor Humayun** and his formidable Afghan rival **Sher Shah Suri**. The
massive gateways and walls were probably built by Humayun, who laid the first brick of
his new capital Dinpanah in 1534. The few surviving buildings within this roughly
octagonal fort were the work of Sher Shah, who defeated Humayun in 1540, razed
Dinpanah to the ground and started to build his own capital **Shergarh** on the same site.
Humayun regained his throne in 1555 and destroyed Shergarh, but he died a year later.

The massive double-storeyed **Bara Darwaza** (Great Gate) is the main entrance to
the fort. The two bay-deep cells on the inside of the enclosure were used after the
Partition of India in 1947 to provide shelter for refugees from Pakistan. The south gate,
the **Humayun Darwaza**, bears an ink inscription mentioning Sher Shah and the date
950 AH (1543-44 AD), while the north gate is known as the **Talaqi Darwaza** (Forbidden
Gate). The **Qila-i-Kuhna Masjid** (mosque of the Old Fort) was built by Sher Shah and is
considered one of the finest examples of Indo-Afghan architecture. The arches,
tessellations and rich ornamentation in black and white marble against red
sandstone became very popular during the Mughal period. Though the fort is in ruins,
the mosque is in good condition.

Sher Mandal, a small octagonal tower south of the mosque, was probably built
by Sher Shah as a pleasure pavilion from which to view the river. In the last year of his
life Humayun used it as a library, spending hours poring over his cherished collection
of miniatures and manuscripts. It is said that when he heard the *muezzin's* call to
prayer he hurried down the steps of the building and slipped. The fall proved fatal.
Grey Ware pottery found south of Sher Mandal in 1955 provided evidence suggesting
that this was also the site of the legendary Indraprasth.

South Delhi

The spacious layout of New Delhi has been preserved despite the building on empty
sites and the sub-division of previously large gardens. Still close to the centre, there
are several attractive high-class residential areas such as Jor Bagh near the Lodi
Gardens, while beyond the Ring Road are sprawling estates of flats and larger
apartments and huge shopping and commercial centres.

The Lodi Gardens The Lodi Gardens and Tombs are 1 km to the southwest of the
Purana Qila. The beautiful gardens, with mellow stone tombs of the 15th- and
16th-century Lodi rulers, are popular for gentle strolls as much as for jogging. In the
middle of the garden facing the east entrance from Max Mueller Rd is **Bara Gumbad**
(Big Dome), a mosque built in 1494. The raised courtyard is provided with an
imposing gateway and *mehman khana* (guest rooms). The platform in the centre
appears to have had a tank for ritual ablutions.

The Sheesh (Shish) **Gumbad** (Glass Dome, late 15th-century) is built on a raised
incline a few metres north of the Bara Gumbad and was once decorated with glazed
blue tiles, painted floral designs and Koranic inscriptions. The façade gives the
impression of a two-storeyed building, typical of Lodi architecture. **Mohammad
Shah's tomb** (1450) is that of the third Sayyid ruler. It has sloping buttresses, an
octagonal plan, projecting eaves and lotus patterns on the ceiling. **Sikander Lodi's
tomb**, built by his son in 1517, is also an octagonal structure decorated with Hindu

motifs. A structural innovation is the double dome which was later refined under the Mughals. The 16th-century **Athpula** (Bridge of Eight Piers) nearby, near the northeastern entrance, is attributed to Nawab Bahadur, a nobleman at Akbar's court.

Safdarjang's tomb ① *Open sunrise to sunset*. Relatively little visited, Safdarjang's tomb was built by Nawab Shuja-ud-Daulah for his father Mirza Mukhim Abdul Khan, entitled Safdarjang, who was Governor of Oudh (1719-48), and Wazir of his successor (1748-54). Safdarjang died in 1754. With its high enclosure walls, *char bagh* layout of gardens, fountain and central domed mausoleum, it follows the tradition of Humayun's tomb. Typically, the real tomb is just below ground level. Flanking the mausoleum are pavilions used by Shuja-ud-Daulah as his family residence. Immediately to its south is the battlefield where Timur and his Mongol horde crushed Mahmud Shah Tughluq on 12 December 1398.

★ **Hazrat Nizamuddin** ① *Dress ultra-modestly if you don't want to feel uncomfortable*. At the east end of the Lodi Road is Hazrat Nizamuddin Dargah. Nizamuddin 'village', now tucked away behind the residential suburb of Nizamuddin West, off Mathura Road, grew up around the shrine of Sheikh Nizamuddin Aulia (1236-1325), a Chishti saint. *Qawwalis* are sung at sunset after *namaaz* (prayers).

West of the central shrine is the **Jama-at-khana Mosque** (1325). Its decorated arches are typical of the Khalji design also seen at the Ala'i Darwaza at the Qutb Minar. South of the main tomb and behind finely crafted screens is the grave of princess Jahanara, Shah Jahan's eldest and favourite daughter. She shared the emperor's last years when he was imprisoned at Agra Fort. The grave, open to the sky, is in accordance with the epitaph written by her "Let naught cover my grave save the green grass, for grass suffices as the covering of the lowly". Pilgrims congregate at the shrine twice a year for the *Urs* (fair) held to mark the anniversaries of Hazrat Nizamuddin Aulia and his disciple **Amir Khusrau**, whose tomb is nearby.

★ **Humayun's tomb** ① *Open daily, sunrise to sunset, US$5 foreigners, Rs 10 Indians, video cameras Rs 25, located in Nizamuddin, 15 mins by taxi from Connaught Circus, allow 45 mins, soft drinks, guide books and postcards available*. Eclipsed later by the Taj Mahal and the Jama Masjid, Humayun's tomb is the best example in Delhi of the early Mughal style of tomb. Superbly maintained, it is well worth a visit, preferably before visiting the Taj Mahal in Agra. **Humayun**, the second Mughal Emperor, was forced into exile in Persia after being heavily defeated by the Afghan Sher Shah in 1540. He returned to India in 1545, finally recapturing Delhi in 1555. The tomb was designed and built by his senior widow and mother of his son Akbar, Hamida Begum. A Persian from Khurasan, after her pilgrimage to Mecca she was known as **Haji Begum**. She supervised the entire construction of the tomb (1564-73), camping on the site.

The plan The tomb has an octagonal plan, lofty arches, pillared kiosks and the double dome of Central Asian origin, which appears here for the first time in India. Outside Gujarat, Hindu temples make no use of the dome, but the Indian Muslim dome had until now, been of a flatter shape as opposed to the tall Persian dome rising on a more slender neck. Here also is the first standard example of the garden tomb concept: the **char bagh** (garden divided into quadrants), water channels and fountains. This form culminated in the gardens of the Taj Mahal. However, the tomb also shows a number of distinctively Hindu motifs. Tillotson has pointed out that in Humayun's tomb, Hindu *chhattris* (small domed kiosks), complete with temple columns and *chajjas* (broad eaves), surround the central dome. The bulbous finial on top of the dome and the star motif in the spandrels of the main arches are also Hindu, the latter being a solar symbol.

The approach The tomb enclosure has two high double-storeyed gateways: the entrance to the west and the other to the south. A *baradari* occupies the centre of the east wall, and a bath chamber that of the north wall. Several Moghul princes, princesses and Haji Begum herself lie buried here. During the 1857 Mutiny **Bahadur Shah II**, the last Moghul Emperor of Delhi, took shelter here with his three sons. Over 80, he was seen as a figurehead by Muslims opposing the British. When captured he was transported to Yangon (Rangoon) for the remaining four years of his life.

The dome (38-m high) does not have the swell of the Taj Mahal and the decoration of the whole edifice is much simpler. It is of red sandstone with some white marble to highlight the lines of the building. There is some attractive inlay work, and some *jalis* in the balcony fence and on some of the recessed keel arch windows. **The interior** is austere and consists of three storeys of arches rising up to the dome. The Emperor's tomb is of white marble and quite plain without any inscription. The overall impression is that of a much bulkier, more squat building than the Taj Mahal. The cavernous space under the main tombs is an ideal home for great colonies of bats.

Minor sites south of the tomb An **Asokan Rock Edict**, at Okhla, lies 3 km south and 500 m to the west of the Mathura Road. Discovered in 1966, this is one of Asoka's (272-232 BC) minor Rock Edicts. It confirms that ancient Delhi was an important town on a trunk route connecting commercial centres with provincial capitals. The 18th-century **Kalkaji temple** is close by and is dedicated to the goddess Kali who, having killed all the demons who terrorized the neighbourhood, installed herself on the hill nearby to be worshipped.

From here it is possible either to continue on an outer circuit of Delhi by going south to **Tughluqabad** (see page 99), or travelling west on a shorter inner circuit of the southern city. **Begumpuri Masjid**, a 14th-century mosque built by Khan-i- Jahan, lies just off Aurobindo Marg, south of its junction with Panscheel Marg.

About 1 km to the north is **Bijai Mandal** (Victory Palace), an unusual octagonal building with sloping sides and a doorway at each cardinal point. It is not clear whether it was the bastion of Muhammad-bin Tughluq's Jahanpanah or a tower from which to review his troops. It is said that an **underground passage** links it with Tughluqabad (south) and Kotla Firoz Shah (north); 1 km to the southeast is the **Khirki Masjid**, built in 1380 by the *Wazir* of Firoz Shah Tughluq. The upper storey wall is broken with *khirkis* (windows), hence its name.

★ **Hauz Khas** ① *1 hr cultural show, daily, 1845, Rs 100 (check with Delhi Tourism), upmarket restaurants and shops have opened.* Immediately to the north again, and entered off either Aurobindo Marg on the east side or Africa Avenue on the west side, is Hauz Khas. Ala-ud-din Khalji (ruled 1296-1313) created a large tank here for the use of the inhabitants of **Siri**, the second capital city of Delhi founded by him. Fifty years later **Firoz Shah Tughluq** cleaned up the silted tank and raised several buildings on its east and south banks which are known as Hauz Khas or Royal Tank.

Firoz Shah's austere tomb is found here. The multi-storeyed wings, on the north and west of Firoz Shah's tomb, were built by him in 1354 as a *madrasa* (college). The octagonal and square *chhattris* were built as tombs, possibly to the teachers at the college. Hauz Khas is now widely used as a park for early morning recreation - walking, running and yoga exercises. Classical music concerts, dance performances and a *son et lumière* show are held in the evenings when monuments are illuminated by thousands of earthen lamps and torches.

The courts of the Delhi Lawn Tennis Association, where Indian Davis Cup matches are played when held in Delhi, are just to the north of the gardens on Africa Avenue. To the northeast of Hauz Khas is the **Moth ki Masjid**. **Sikander Lodi** (ruled 1488-1517) is said to have picked up a grain of *moth* (lentil) from a mosque and given it to his *Wazir*

(Prime Minister), Miyan Bhuwa. The grain was sown and it multiplied until enough had been earned to build this mosque. Possibly the finest example of Lodi architecture, the design shows innovation in the decoration of its *mihrab* and arches special treatment of the central arch and the construction of domes over the prayer hall. In these it anticipates several features of later Mughal architecture.

★ The Qutb Minar Complex

Muhammad Ghuri conquered northwest India at the very end of the 12th century. The conquest of the Gangetic plain down to Benares (Varanasi) was undertaken by Muhammad's Turkish slave and chief general, **Qutb-ud-din-Aibak**, whilst another general took Bihar and Bengal. In the process, temples were reduced to rubble, the remaining Buddhist centres were dealt their death blow and their monks slaughtered. When Muhammad was assassinated in 1206, his gains passed to the loyal Qutb-ud-din-Aibak. Thus the first sultans or Muslim kings of Delhi became known as the **Slave Dynasty** (1026-1290). For the next three centuries the Slave Dynasty and the succeeding Khalji (1290-1320), Tughluq (1320-1414), Sayyid (1414-45) and Lodi (1451-1526) dynasties provided Delhi with fluctuating authority. The legacy of their ambitions survives in the tombs, forts and palaces that litter Delhi Ridge and the surrounding plain. **Qutb-ud-din-Aibak** died after only four years in power, but he left his mark with the **Qutb Minar** and his **citadel**. Qutb Minar, built to proclaim the victory of Islam over the infidel (unbeliever), dominates the countryside for miles around. Visit the Minar first.

Qutb Minar (1) In 1199 work began on what was intended to be the most glorious tower of victory in the world and was to be the prototype of all *minars* (towers) in India. Qutb-ud-din-Aibak had probably seen and been influenced by the brick victory pillars

Qutb Minar complex

Gupta Pillar: the magic of iron

In the courtyard of the Quwwat-ul-Islam Mosque (2) is the fourth-century iron pillar. The Sanskrit inscription states that it was erected as a flagstaff in honour of Vishnu and in memory of the Gupta King Chandragupta II (375-413). Originally the pillar was topped by an image of Vishnu's vahana (carrier or vehicle) Garuda, the mythical half bird of prey, half man, and probably stood facing a Vishnu temple. The purity of its wrought iron (98%) is extraordinary, and it has survived 1,600 years virtually without blemish. A local tradition regards the pillar as having magical qualities. Anyone who can encircle it with their hands behind their back will have good fortune. This is difficult as the pillar is now fenced off!

in Ghazni in Afghanistan, but this one was also intended to serve as the minaret attached to the Might of Islam Mosque. From here the muezzin could call the faithful to prayer. Later every mosque would incorporate its minaret.

As a mighty reminder of the importance of the ruler as Allah's representative on earth, the Qutb Minar (literally 'axis minaret') stood at the centre of the community. A pivot of Faith, Justice and Righteousness, its name also carried the message of Qutb-ud-din's ('Axis of the Faith') own achievements. The inscriptions carved in Kufi script tell that "the tower was erected to cast the shadow of God over both east and west". For Qutb-ud-din-Aibak it marked the eastern limit of the empire of the One God. Its western counterpart is the **Giralda Tower** built by Yusuf in Seville.

The Qutb Minar is 73 m high and consists of five storeys. The diameter of the base is 14.4 m and 2.7 m at the top. Qutb-ud-din built the first three and his son-in-law Iltutmish embellished these and added a fourth. This is indicated in some of the Persian and Nagari (North Indian) inscriptions which also record that it was twice damaged by lightning in 1326 and 1368. While repairing the damage caused by the second, Firoz Shah Tughluq added a fifth storey and used marble to face the red and buff sandstone. This was the first time contrasting colours were used decoratively, later to become such a feature of Mughal buildings. Firoz's fifth storey was topped by a graceful cupola but this fell down during an earthquake in 1803. A new one was added by a Major Robert Smith in 1829 but was so out of keeping that it was removed in 1848 and now stands in the gardens.

The original storeys are heavily indented with different styles of fluting, alternately round and angular on the bottom, round on the second and angular on the third. The beautifully carved honeycomb detail beneath the balconies is reminiscent of the Alhambra Palace in Spain. The calligraphy bands are verses from the Koran and praises to its patron builder.

Quwwat-ul-Islam Mosque (2) The Quwwat-ul-Islam Mosque (The Might of Islam Mosque), the earliest surviving mosque in India, is to the northwest of the Qutb Minar. It was begun in 1192, immediately after Qutb-ud-din's conquest of Delhi and completed in 1198, using the remains of no fewer than 27 local Hindu and Jain temples.

The architectural style contained elements that Muslims brought from Arabia, including buildings made of mud and brick and decorated with glazed tiles, *squinches* (arches set diagonally across the corners of a square chamber to facilitate the raising of a dome and to effect a transition from a square to a round structure), the pointed arch and the true dome. Finally, Muslim buildings came alive through ornamental calligraphy and geometric patterning. This was in marked contrast to indigenous Indian styles of architecture. Hindu, Buddhist and Jain buildings relied on the post-and-beam system in which spaces were traversed by corbelling, ie shaping

flat-laid stones to create all arch. The arched screen that runs along the western end of the courtyard beautifully illustrates the fact that it was Hindu methods that still prevailed at this stage, for the 16-m high arch uses Indian corbelling, the corners being smoothed off to form the curved line.

Screens (4) Qutb-ud-din's screen formed the façade of the mosque and, facing in the direction of Mecca, became the focal point. The sandstone screen is carved in the Indo-Islamic style, lotuses mingling with Koranic calligraphy. The later screenwork and other extensions (1230) are fundamentally Islamic in style, the flowers and leaves having been replaced by more arabesque patterns.

Indian builders mainly used stone, which from the fourth century AD had been intricately carved with representations of the gods. In their first buildings in India the Muslim architects designed the buildings and local Indian craftsmen built them and decorated them with typical motifs such as the vase and foliage, tasselled ropes, bells and cows.

Iltutmish's extension The mosque was enlarged twice. In 1230 Qutb-ud-din's son-in-law and successor **Shamsuddin Iltutmish** doubled its size by extending the colonnades and prayer hall - 'Iltutmish's extension'. This accommodated a larger congregation, and in the more stable conditions of Iltutmish's reign, Islam was obviously gaining ground. The arches of the extension are nearer to the true arch and are similar to the Gothic arch that appeared in Europe at this time. The decoration is Islamic.

Almost 100 years after Iltutmish's death, the mosque was enlarged again, by **Ala-ud-din Khalji**. The conductor of tireless and bloody military campaigns, Ala-ud-din proclaimed himself 'God's representative on earth'. His architectural ambitions, however, were not fully realized, because on his death in 1316 only part of the north and east extensions were completed.

Ala'i Minar (8) and the Ala'i Darwaza (9) To the north of the Qutb complex is the 26-m **Ala'i Minar**, intended to surpass the tower of the Qutb, but not completed beyond the first storey. Ala-ud-din did complete the south gateway to the building, the **Ala'i Darwaza**; inscriptions testify that it was built in 1311 (Muslim 710 AH). He benefited from events in Central Asia. Since the early 13th century, Mongol hordes from Central Asia fanned out east and west, destroying the civilization of the Seljuk Turks in West Asia, and refugee artists, architects, craftsmen and poets fled east. They brought to India features and techniques that had developed in Byzantine Turkey, some of which can be seen in the Ala'i Darwaza.

The gate-house is a large sandstone cuboid, into which are set small cusped arches with carved *jali* screens. The lavish ornamentation of geometric and floral designs in red sandstone and white marble produced a dramatic effect when viewed against the surrounding buildings.

The inner chamber, 11 m sq has doorways and, for the first time in India, true arches. Above each doorway is an Arabic inscription with its creator's name and one of his self-assumed titles - 'The Second Alexander'. The north doorway, which is the main entrance, is the most elaborately carved. The dome, raised on squinched arches, is flat and shallow. Of the effects employed, the arches with their 'lotus-bud' fringes are Seljuk, as is the dome with the rounded finial and the façade. These now became trademarks of the **Khalji style**, remaining virtually unchanged until their further development in Humayun's tomb.

Iltutmish's Tomb (3) Built in 1235, Iltutmish's Tomb lies in the northwest of the compound, midway along the west wall of the mosque. It is the first surviving tomb of a Muslim ruler in India. Two other tombs also stand within the extended Might of Islam Mosque.

The idea of a tomb was quite alien to Hindus, who had been practising cremation since around 400 BC. Blending Hindu and Muslim styles, the outside is relatively plain with three arched and decorated doorways. The interior carries reminders of the nomadic origins of the first Muslim rulers. Like a Central Asian *yurt* (tent) in its decoration, it combines the familiar Indian motifs of the wheel, bell, chain and lotus with the equally familiar geometric arabesque patterning. The west wall is inset with three *mihrabs* that indicate the direction of Mecca.

The tomb originally supported a dome resting on *squinches* which you can still see. The dome collapsed (witness the slabs of stone lying around) suggesting that the technique was as yet unrefined. From the corbelled squinches it may be assumed that the dome was corbelled too, as found in contemporary Gujarat and Rajput temples. The blocks of masonry were fixed together using the Indian technology of iron dowels. In later Indo-Islamic buildings lime plaster was used for bonding.

Other tombs ⓘ *Open from sunrise to sunset, US$5 foreigners, Rs 10 Indians; no longer free on Fri, Bus 505 from New Delhi Rly station (Ajmeri Gate), Super Bazar (east of Connaught Circus) and Cottage Industries Emporium, Janpath*. To the southwest of this uncompleted mosque, an L-shaped ruin marks the site of **Ala-ud-din Khalji's tomb (6)** within the confines of a **madrasa** (college) **(7)**. This is the first time in India that a tomb and *madrasa* are found together, another custom inherited from the Seljuks.

Immediately to the east of the Ala'i Darwaza stands the **tomb of Imam Zamin**, an early 16th-century *sufi* 'saint' from Turkestan. It is an octagonal structure with a plastered sandstone dome and has *jali* screens, a characteristic of the Lodi style of decoration.

★ **Tughluqabad** ⓘ *Sunrise-1700, free, allow 1 hr, very deserted so don't go alone, take plenty of water, for return rickshaws, turn right at entrance and walk 200 m*. Tughluqabad's ruins, 7½ km east from Qutb Minar, still convey a sense of the power and energy of the newly arrived Muslims in India. From the walls you get a magnificent impression of the strategic advantages of the site. **Ghiyas'ud-Din Tughluq** (ruled 1321-25), after ascending the throne of Delhi, selected this site for his capital. He built a massive fort around his capital city which stands high on a rocky outcrop of the Delhi Ridge. The fort is roughly octagonal in plan with a circumference of 6½ km. The vast size, strength and obvious solidity of the whole give it an air of massive grandeur. It was not until Babur (ruled 1526-30) that dynamite was used in warfare, so this is a very defensible site.

East of the main entrance is the rectangular **citadel**. A wider area immediately to the west and bounded by walls contained the **palaces**. Beyond this to the north lay the **city**. Now marked by the ruins of houses, the streets were laid out in a grid fashion. Inside the citadel enclosure is the **Vijay Mandal** tower and the remains of several halls including a long underground passage. The fort also contained seven tanks.

A causeway connects the fort with the tomb of Ghiyas'ud-Din Tughluq, while a wide embankment near its southeast corner gave access to the fortresses of **Adilabad** about 1 km away, built a little later by Ghiyas'ud-Din's son Muhammad. The tomb is very well preserved and has red sandstone walls with a pronounced slope (the first Muslim building in India to have sloping walls), crowned with a white marble dome. This dome, like that of the Ala'i Darwaza at the Qutb, is crowned by an *amalaka*, a feature of Hindu architecture. Also Hindu is the trabeate arch at the tomb's fortress wall entrance. Inside are three cenotaphs belonging to Ghiyas'ud-Din, his wife and son Muhammad.

Ghiyas'ud-Din Tughluq quickly found that military victories were no guarantee of lengthy rule. When he returned home after a victorious campaign the welcoming pavilion erected by his son and successor, **Muhammad-bin Tughluq**, was deliberately collapsed over him. Tughluqabad was abandoned shortly afterwards and was thus only inhabited for five years. The Tughluq dynasty continued to hold Delhi until Timur sacked it and slaughtered its Inhabitants. For a brief period Tughluq power shifted to Jaunpur near Varanasi, where the Tughluq architectural traditions were carried forward in some superb mosques. See page 192.

★ **Baha'i Temple (Lotus Temple)** ⓘ *1 Apr-30 Sep 0900-1900, 1 Oct-31 Mar 0930-1730, closed Mon, visitors are welcome to services, and at other times the temple is open for silent meditation and prayer. Audio visual presentations about the faith in English are at 1100, 1200, 1400 and 1530, remove your shoes before entering. Taxi or auto-rickshaw though Bus 433 from the centre (Jantar Mantar) goes to Nehru Place, within walking distance (1½ km) of the temple at Kalkaji.* Architecturally the Baha'i Temple is a remarkably striking building. Constructed in 1980-81, it is built out of white marble and in the characteristic Baha'i temple shape of a lotus flower - 45 lotus petals form the walls - which internally creates a feeling of light and space (34-m high, 70 m in diameter). It is a simple design, brilliantly executed and very elegant in form. All Baha'i temples are nine sided, symbolizing 'comprehensiveness, oneness and unity'. The Delhi temple which seats 1,300, is surrounded by nine pools, an attractive feature also helping to keep the building cool. It is particularly attractive when flood-lit. Baha'i temples are "dedicated to the worship of God, for peoples of all races, religions or castes. Only the Holy Scriptures of the Baha'i Faith and earlier revelations are read or recited". The **Baha'i faith** was founded by a Persian, Baha'u'llah (meaning 'glory of God'; 1817-92), who is believed to be the manifestation of God for this age. His teachings were directed towards the unification of the human race, the establishment of a permanent universal peace.

Old Delhi

Shah Jahan (ruled 1628-58) decided to move back from Agra to Delhi in 1638. Within 10 years the huge city of **Shah-jahanabad**, now known as Old Delhi, was built. Much of the building material was taken from the ruins of Firozabad and Shergarh. See further Books, on page 1362.

Shah-jahanabad was laid out in blocks with wide roads, residential quarters, bazars and mosques. Its principal street, **Chandni Chowk**, had a tree-lined canal flowing down its centre which quickly became renowned throughout Asia. The jumble of shops, labyrinthine alleys running off a main thoroughfare with craftsmen's workshops, hotels, mosques and temples, cause it to retain some of its magic. A cycle rickshaw ride gives you a good feel of the place.

The impressive red sandstone façade of the **Diagambar Jain Mandir** (temple) standing at the eastern end of Chandni Chowk, faces the Red Fort. Built in 1656, it contains an image of Adinath. The bird hospital within this compound releases the birds on recovery (instead of returning them to their owners); many remain within the temple precincts.

The city of Shah Jahanabad was protected by rubble-built walls, some of which still survive. These walls were pierced by 14 main gates. The **Ajmeri Gate**, **Turkman Gate** (often referred to by auto-rickshaw wallahs as 'Truckman Gate'!), **Kashmir Gate** and **Delhi Gate** still survive. Between this new city and the river Yamuna, Shah Jahan built a fort. Most of it was built out of red (*lal*) sandstone, hence the name **Lal Qila** (Red Fort), the same as that at Agra on which the Delhi fort is modelled. Begun in 1639 and completed in 1648, it is said to have cost Rs 10 million, much of which was spent on the opulent marble palaces within.

★ The Red Fort (Lal Qila)

ⓘ *Closed Mon, daily sunrise to sunset, US$2 foreigners, Rs 10 Indians, no longer free on Fri, allow 1 hr. The entrance is through the Lahore Gate (nearest the car park) with*

the admission kiosk opposite. Keep your ticket as you will need to show it at the Drum **101**
House. The toilets are in Chatta Chowk (near Art Corner shop through archway) and
near Asad Burj but are best avoided.

Visitors may be saddened by the neglected state of the once imposing fort - coloured marble-inlay is missing and the gardens are bare. Even from a distance the walls of the fort towered massively above the flat banks of the Yamuna on which it was built. Despite the modern development of roads and shops and the never ending traffic, that dominating impression is still immensely powerful. In front of the fort is a massive *maidan* (open space). From the Lahore Gate, the Prime Minister addresses enormous crowds on 15 August, Independence Day.

The plan of Shah Jahan's new city symbolized the link between religious authority enshrined in the Jama Masjid to the west, and political authority represented by the Diwan-i-Am in the Fort, joined by Chandni Chowk, the route used by the Emperor. Sadly, parts of the fort are poorly maintained.

The approach The entrance is by the Lahore Gate (make this clear to the rickshaw driver). The defensive barbican that juts out in front of the Lahore Gate was built by Aurangzeb, see page 1304. A common story suggests that Aurangzeb built the curtain wall at the entrance to save his nobles and visiting dignitaries from having to walk - and bow - the whole length of Chandni Chowk, for no one was allowed to ride in the presence of the Emperor. When the Emperor sat in the Diwan-i-Am he could see all the

Delhi Sights Old Delhi

Red Fort, Delhi

N

0 metres (approx) 100
0 yards (approx) 100

1 Sawan	4 Hammam	7 Tasbih Khana &
2 Bhadon	5 Diwan-i-Khas	Mussaman Burj
3 Nahr-i-Bihisht	6 Khas Mahal	

⋮ A gift from Florence?

There are 318 Florentine pietra dura plaques in the niche behind the throne, showing flowers, birds and lions, as well as the central figure of Orpheus, playing to the beasts. In between these Italian panels are Mughal pietra dura works with flowery arabesques and birds. Ebba Koch argues that the techniques employed by the Mughal artisans are exactly the same as the Italian ones, so there must have been a direct connection.

This is not to say that there was no independent development of Mughal inlay craftsmanship. Such a view has been described by Tillotson as the result of wishful thinking by Europeans, eager to claim a stake in the superb work. In fact the Mughals had an equally fine tradition of stone carving and of inlay work on which to draw as the Florentine princes, as can be seen from the work in the Jami Masjid in Ahmadabad, built in 1414.

way down the Chowk, so the addition must have been greatly welcomed by his courtiers. The new entrance arrangement also made an attacking army more vulnerable to the defenders on the walls.

Chatta Chowk Inside is the 'Covered Bazar', quite exceptional in the 17th century. In Shah Jahan's time there were shops on both upper and lower levels. Originally they catered for the Imperial household and carried stocks of silks, brocades, velvets, gold and silverware, jewellery and gems. There were coffee shops too for nobles and courtiers. Walk through the left-hand archway and you will see a small building on your right near the Art Corner shop.

The Naubat Khana (Naqqar Khana) The Naubat Khana (**Drum House** or music gallery), immediately beyond the bazar, marked the entrance to the inner apartments of the fort. Here everyone except the princes of the royal family had to dismount and leave their horses or elephants (*hathi*), hence its other name of **Hathi Pol** (Elephant Gate). Five times a day ceremonial music was played on the kettle drum, shahnais (a kind of oboe) and cymbals, glorifying the emperor. In 1754 the Emperor Ahmad Shah was murdered here. The gateway with four floors is decorated with floral designs. You can still see traces of the original panels painted in gold or other colours on the interior of the gateway.

Diwan-i-Am Between the first inner court and the royal palaces at the heart of the fort, stood the Diwan-i-Am (Hall of Public Audience), the farthest point the normal visitor would reach. It has seen many dramatic events - the destructive whirlwind of the Persian Nadir Shah in 1739 and of Ahmad Shah the Afghan in 1756, and the trial of the last 'King of Delhi', **Bahadur Shah II** in 1858.

The well-proportioned hall was both a functional building and a showpiece intended to hint at the opulence of the palace itself. In Shah Jahan's time the sandstone was hidden behind a very thin layer of white polished plaster, *chunam*. This was decorated with floral motifs in many colours, especially gilt. Silk carpets and heavy curtains hung from the canopy rings outside the building, such interiors reminders of the Mughals' nomadic origins in Central Asia, where royal durbars were held in tents.

The throne surround At the back of the hall is a platform for the emperor's throne. Around this was a gold railing, within which stood the princes and great nobles separated from the lesser nobles (inside the hall) and minor officials from the general public in the courtyard (now the lawn). Behind the throne canopy are 12 marble inlaid panels. Figurative workmanship is very unusual in Islamic buildings, and this one

⁞ The peacock throne: a glittering prize

In the centre of the Diwan-i-Khas (5) is a marble pedestal on which stood the Peacock Throne which Shah Jahan commissioned on his accession in 1627. It took seven years to make. The throne was designed with two peacocks standing behind with a parrot carved out of a single emerald between them. It was inlaid with a vast number of precious stones – sapphires, rubies, emeralds, pearls and diamonds. Over the top was a gem encrusted gold canopy edged with pearls, supported by 12 pillars.

The throne was carried off by Nadir Shah, a Turk, who after conquering Persia sacked Delhi in 1739. Soon after his occupation of Delhi a riot broke out in which 900 of his soldiers were killed. Nadir Shah himself rode through the streets of Delhi to assess the situation when some residents were rash enough to throw stones at him. Enraged, Nadir Shah ordered the entire population of Delhi to be massacred, resulting in 30,000 dead. In the evening the 'Great' Mughal (Mohammad Shah) begged for mercy, and such was Nadir Shah's control over his troops that he was able immediately to halt the carnage. The invaders took with them as much as they could extort from all the nobles. Bahadur Shah later replaced the throne with a poor copy. The Peacock Throne itself was broken up by Nadir Shah's assassins in 1747; some of the jewels are believed to have been incorporated into the late Shah of Iran's throne.

panel is the only example in the Red Fort. Wherever you stand in the hall (everyone except the Emperor's favourite son had to stand), there is an uninterrupted view of the throne - a powerful psychological effect.

Shah Jahan used to spend about two hours a day in the Diwan-i-Am. According to Bernier, the French traveller, the emperor would enter to a fanfare and mount the throne by a flight of movable steps. The business comprised official and domestic administration, reports from the provinces, tax and revenue matters and official appointments. On the personal side, Shah Jahan would listen to accounts of illness, dream interpretations and anecdotes from his ministers and nobles. He usually retired to bed at around 2200 and liked to be read to, his particular favourite being the *Babur-i-nama*, the autobiography of his great great-grandfather.

Wednesday was the day of judgement. Sentences were often brutal but swift and sometimes the punishment of dismemberment, beating or death was carried out on the spot. The executioners were close at hand with axes and whips. On Friday, the Muslim holy day, there would be no business.

Inner palace buildings Behind the Diwan-i-Am is the private enclosure of the fort. Along the east wall, overlooking the river Yamuna, Shah Jahan set six small palaces (five survive). Also within this compound are the Harem, the Life-Bestowing Garden and the Nahr-i-Bihisht (Stream of Paradise). Leave the throne canopy area by the steps to your left, follow the path and carry on until you reach the white marble garden pavilion.

Life-Bestowing Gardens (Hayat Baksh Bagh) The original gardens were landscaped according to the Islamic principles of the Persian *char bagh*, with pavilions, fountains and water courses dividing the garden into various but regular beds. The two pavilions **Sawan (1)** and **Bhadon (2)**, named after the first two months of the rainy season (July-August), reveal something of the character of the garden. The garden used to create the effect of the monsoon and contemporary accounts tell us that in the pavilions, some of which were especially erected for the *Teej*

Delhi Sights Old Delhi

Old Delhi

To New Tibetan Colony & Wongdhen House

Metcalfe House

Indraprastha College

Northern Ridge

Pir Ghaib

Hindu Rao Hospital

Asokan Pillar

Mutiny Memorial

To Roshanara Gardens

Ridge Rd

Chauburja Marg

Rajpur Rd

Underhill Rd

Shamnath Marg

Shri Ram Rd

M Gandhi Rd

Mother Teresa's

Ladakh Buddha Vihara

Hindu Rao Marg

Rai Niwas Marg

Raj Narain Marg

5

CIVIL LINES

Yamuna Marg

Trans Yamuna Bridge

Rani Jhansi Rd

Rajpur Rd

Court Rd

Qudsia Gardens

Tourist Camp

Ring Rd

NH 1

To Delhi Sarai Rohilla Station

MOTIA BAGH

Christ Church (Boulevard Rd)

Grand Trunk Rd

Qudsia Marg

New Courts

Tis Hazari

Gokhale Marg

Inter State Bus Terminal

Kashmir Gate

Nigambodh Ghat

St James

Lothian Marg

Mahatma Gandhi Marg

Gurudwara

Zorawar Singh Rd

Old Delhi Station

(Hamilton Rd)

7

Azad

S P Mukherji Marg

Lajpat Rai Bazar

Naya Bazar

Mission Rd

Church Rd

Related map
A Paharganj, page 112

Sadar Bazar

Spice

Khari Baoli

Lahori Gate

Fatehpuri Masjid

Town Hall

M G Park

Chandni Chowk

1

Sisganj Gurudwara

Diagambar Jain Temple

Birla Hospital

Idgah Rd

Hoshiar Singh Rd

Jhande Walan Rd

Qutb Rd

Shraddhanand Marg

Lal Kuan Bazar

Nai Sarak

Dariba Kalan

Meena Bazar

Jama Masjid

Netaji Subhash

Chawri Bazar

Kasturba Hospital

1

MULTANI DHANDA

RAMNAGAR

Chauk Hauz Qazi

Sita Ram Bazar

Churi Walan Chauk

A

Ajmeri Gate

Ajmeri Gate Rd

Desh Bandhu Gupta Rd

Kamla

Asaf Ali Rd

Ramila Grounds

Turkman Gate

To Karol Bagh & Clark & White House Hotels

PAHARGANJ

New Delhi Station

Bhavbhuti Marg

J Nehru Marg

G B Pant

Main Bazar

Ramdwara Rd

Basant Rd

Chelmsford Rd

State Entry Rd

Vivekanand Marg (Minto Rd)

Tagore Marg

Nur Jahan Rd

Jahangir Rd

Press Rd

Turkman Marg

M Ranjit Singh Rd

6

Basant La

Stadium

Panchkuin Marg

Minto Bridge

D Dayal Upadhay Marg

CONNAUGHT PLACE

N

0 metres 200
0 yards 200

■ **Sleeping**
1 Bhagiruth Palace
2 Broadway

3 Flora
4 Neeru
5 Oberoi Maidens

6 Ranjit
7 Tera

● **Eating**
1 Karim's
2 Motimahal

3 Peshawari

festival which marks the arrival of the monsoon, the royal ladies would sit in silver swings and watch the rains. Water flowed from the back wall of the pavilion through a slit above the marble shelf and over the niches in the wall. Gold and silver pots of flowers were placed in these alcoves during the day whilst at night candles were lit to create a glistening and colourful effect. To the west is **Mehtab Bagh** which has a *baoli* (step well) to its northwest.

Shahi Burj From the pavilion next to the Shahi Burj ('Royal Tower') the canal known as the **Nahr-i-Bihisht (3)** (Stream of Paradise) began its journey along the Royal Terrace. The three-storey octagonal Tower, seriously damaged in 1857, is still unsafe. The lower storey contained a tank from which water was raised to flow into the garden. In Shah Jahan's time the Yamuna lapped the walls. Shah Jahan used the tower as his most private office and only his sons and a few senior ministers were allowed with him.

Moti Masjid To the right are the three marble domes of Aurangzeb's 'Pearl Mosque' (shoes must be removed). Bar the cupolas, it is completely hidden behind a wall of red sandstone, now painted white. Built in 1662 of polished white marble, it has some exquisite decoration. All the surfaces are highly decorated in a fashion similar to rococo, which was developed at the same time in Europe. Unusually the prayer hall is on a raised platform with inlaid outlines of individual 'prayer mats' (*musallas*) in black marble. While the outer walls were aligned to the cardinal points like all the other fort buildings, the inner walls were positioned so that the mosque would correctly face Mecca.

Hammam (4) The Royal Baths have three apartments separated by corridors with canals to carry water to each room. The two flanking the entrance, for the royal children, had hot and cold baths. The room furthest away from the door has three basins for rose water fountains.

Diwan-i-Khas (5) Beyond is the single-storeyed 'Hall of Private Audience', topped by four Hindu-style *chhattris* and built completely of white marble. The *dado* (lower part of the wall) on the interior was richly decorated with inlaid precious and semi-precious stones. The ceiling was silver but was removed by the Marathas in 1760 - see page 1306. Outside, the hall used to have a marble pavement and an arcaded court. Both have gone.

This was the Mughal office of state. Shah Jahan spent two hours here before retiring for a meal, siesta and prayers. In the evening he would return to the Hall for more work before going to the harem. The hall's splendour moved the 14th-century poet **Amir Khusrau** to write the lines inscribed above the corner arches of the north and south walls: *"Agar Firdaus bar rue Zamin-ast/Hamin ast o Hamin ast o Hamin ast"* (If there be a paradise on earth, it is here, it is here, it is here).

Royal palaces Next to the Diwan-i-Khas is the three-roomed **Khas Mahal (6)** (Private Palace). Nearest the Diwan-i-Khas is the **Tasbih Khana (7)** (Chamber for the Telling of Rosaries) where the emperor would worship privately with his rosary of 99 beads, one for each of the mystical names of Allah. In the centre is the Khwabgah (*'Palace of Dreams'*) which gives on to the octagonal **Mussaman Burj** tower. Here Shah Jahan would be seen each morning. A balcony was added to the tower in 1809 and here George V and Queen Mary appeared in their Coronation Durbar of 1911. The **Tosh Khana** (*Robe Room*), to the south, has a beautiful marble screen at its north end, carved with the scales of justice above the filigree grille. If you are standing with your back to the Diwan-i-Khas you will see a host of circulating suns (a symbol of royalty), but if your back is to the next building (the Rang Mahal), you will see moons surrounding the scales. All these rooms were sumptuously decorated with fine silk carpets, rich silk brocade curtains and lavishly decorated walls. After 1857 the British used the Khas Mahal as an officer's mess and sadly it was defaced.

Beneath the Khas Mahal is the **Khirzi Gate**. This is neglected now, but was an important and convenient private entrance for the Emperor and his most senior nobles.

The **Rang Mahal** (Palace of Colours), the residence of the chief *sultana*, was also the place where the Emperor ate most of his meals. To protect the rich carpets, calico-covered leather sheets were spread out. It was divided into six apartments. Privacy and coolness were ensured by the use of marble *jali* screens. Like the other palaces it was beautifully decorated with a silver ceiling ornamented with golden flowers to reflect the water in the channel running through the building. The north and south apartments were both known as **Sheesh Mahal** (Palace of Mirrors) since into the ceiling were set hundreds of small mirrors. In the evening when candles were lit a starlit effect would be produced. This type of decoration was a favourite in Rajasthan before the Mughals arrived (see page 340 - Amber Fort). In the summer the ladies went to the water-cooled cellars underground (not accessible now).

Through the palace ran the **Life-bestowing Stream** and at its centre is a lotus shaped marble basin which had an ivory fountain. As might be expected in such a cloistered and cossetted environment, the ladies sometimes got bored. In the 18th century the **Empress of Jahandar Shah** sat gazing out at the river and remarked that she had never seen a boat sink. Shortly afterwards a boat was deliberately capsized so that she could be entertained by the sight of people bobbing up and down in the water crying for help.

Museums The southernmost of the palaces, the **Mumtaz Mahal** (Palace of Jewels) ① *daily except Fri, 0900-1700*, was also used by the harem. The lower half of its walls are of marble and it contains six apartments. After the Mutiny of 1857 it was used as a guardroom and since 1912 it has been a museum with exhibits of textiles, weapons, carpets, jade and metalwork as well as works depicting life in the court. It should not be missed.

Spice market Outside of the Red Fort, cycle rickshaws offer a trip to the Spice Market, Jama Masjid and back through the bazar. You travel slowly westwards down Chandni Chowk passing the town hall. Dismount at Church Road and follow your guide into the heart of the market on Khari Baoli where wholesalers sell every conceivable spice. Ask to go to the roof for an excellent view over the market and back towards the Red Fort. The ride back through the bazar is equally fascinating - look up at the amazing electricity system. The final excitement is getting back across Netaji Subhash Marg. Panic not, the rickshaw wallahs know what they are doing. Negotiate for one hour and expect to pay about Rs 40. The spice laden air may irritate your throat.

★ Jama Masjid (The Friday Mosque)

① *Visitors welcome from 30 mins after sunrise until 1200; and from 1345 until 30 mins before sunset, free.*

The magnificent Jama Masjid is the largest mosque in India and the last great architectural work of Shah Jahan, intended to dwarf all mosques that had gone before it. With the fort, it dominates Old Delhi.The mosque is much simpler in its ornamentation than Shah Jahan's secular buildings - a judicious blend of red sandstone and white marble, which are interspersed in the domes, minarets and cusped arches.

The gateways Symbolizing the separation of the sacred and the secular, the threshold is a place of great importance where the worshipper steps to a higher plane. There are three huge gateways, the largest being to the east. This was reserved for the royal family who gathered in a private gallery in its upper storey. Today, the faithful enter through the east gate on Fridays and for *Id-ul-Fitr* and *Id-ul-Adha*. The latter commemorates Abraham's (Ibrahim's) sacrificial offering of his son Ishmael (Ismail). Islam (unlike the Jewish and Christian tradition) believes that Abraham offered to sacrifice Ishmael, Isaac's brother. The general public enter by the north gate. You must remove shoes and cover your head.

The courtyard The façade has the main arch (*iwan*), five smaller arches on each side with two flanking minarets and three bulbous domes behind, all perfectly proportioned. The *iwan* draws the worshippers' attention into the building. The minarets have great views from the top; well worth the climb for Rs 10 (woman may not be allowed to climb alone). **Hauz** In the centre of the courtyard, is an ablution tank placed as usual between the inner and outer parts of the building to remind the worshipper that it is through the ritual of baptism that one first enters the community of believers. **Dikka** In front of the ablution tank, stands a raised platform. Muslim communities grew so rapidly that by the eighth century it sometimes became necessary to introduce a second *muballigh* (prayer leader) who stood on this platform and copied the postures and chants of the *imam* inside to relay them to a much larger congregation. With the introduction of the loudspeaker and amplification, the dikka and the muballigh became redundant. In the northwest corner of the masjid there is a small shed. For a small fee, the faithful are shown a hair from the beard of the prophet, as well as his sandal and his footprint in rock.

The Kawthar Inscription Set up in 1766, the inscription commemorates the place where a worshipper had a vision of the Prophet standing by the celestial tank in paradise. It is here that the Prophet will stand on Judgment Day. In most Islamic buildings, the inscriptions are passages from the Koran or Sayings of the Prophet. Shah Jahan, however, preferred to have sayings extolling the virtues of the builder and architect as well. The 10 detailed panels on the façade indicate the date of construction (1650-56), the cost (10 lakhs - one million rupees), the history of the building, the architect (Ustad Khalil) and the builder (Nur Allah Ahmed, probably the son of the man who did most of the work on the Taj Mahal).

North of the Red Fort

Delhi's centre of gravity has shifted steadily south since 1947. The old Civil Lines area to the north of Kashmir Gate is now often by-passed but there are several sites of interest. Going north past the Old Delhi Post Office, just before Kashmir Gate (now by-passed by the main road), is **St James' Church**, completed in 1836. It was built by Colonel James Skinner, who had a great military reputation in the Punjab.

Kashmir Gate was built by the British, along with other bastions in Shah Jahan's original city walls, in 1835. It was blown up in the Mutiny of 1857. Immediately to the north of the gate today is the main Inter-State Bus Terminus. On the opposite side of the road are the **Qudsia Gardens**, named after the wife of the Mughal Emperor Muhammad Shah, who laid out the gardens in 1748. Mother Teresa's Orphanage is nearby at 12 Raj Narain Road. Volunteers should write in advance to Shishu Bhavan, 12 Commisioner's Lane, Delhi 110054 (T2518457). The *Oberoi Maidens Hotel*, 1 km further north, is at the heart of the **Civil Lines** which was the centre of British Administration until New Delhi was completed. Further north again is a mound on which Tamerlane camped when he attacked Delhi.

Running north to south is the **Delhi Ridge**. At the southern end of the Ridge is the President's Estate in New Delhi. However, it was on the northern end that the major monuments of British India, before New Delhi itself was thought of, were built. To reach the crest of the Ridge, still covered in low scrub, go down Raj Niwas Rd, just south of the *Oberoi Maidens Hotel*. At the end of Raj Niwas Marg turn left and then right into Hindu Rao Marg, named after Hindu Rao, whose house (now a hospital on the west facing the Ridge) played a vital role in the British troops' defence after the Mutiny. The road makes the short but quite steep climb up the Ridge. Turning left at the top of the ridge, an **Asokan pillar** is just off to the left. Further down the road is the Gothic **Mutiny Memorial**. There are excellent views over the old city. To the southwest is **Sabzi Mandi**, the old city's vegetable market, to the southeast the Jama Masjid. Running north from the Mutiny Memorial, the Ridge Rd (now Rani Jhansi Marg) goes to the University.

Trans-Yamuna

Once simply the barren floodplain of the Yamuna River, since the early 1960s the eastern bank of the Yamuna has become a sprawling city in its own right. Bridges now connect it with the main city from the old Civil Lines in the north to Nizamuddin in the south. It stretches from Ghaziabad in the east to NOIDA in the south. Although there is little of tourist interest in what was once largely a sprawling slum, new business centres have sprung up, and there is a hotels and restaurants.

Museums

Field Museum ① *Purana Qila, Mathura Rd, closed Mon, 1000-1700.* Archaeological finds of excavations at this site, below which lies the legendary city of Indraprastha, including coins from the early Sunga period (200-100 BC), red earthenware from the Kushan period (100 BC-300 AD), seals and figurines from the Gupta period (200-600 AD) and stone sculptures (700-800 AD). Later artefacts include Rajput coins (900-1200 AD), glazed ware and coins from the Sultanate period (1206-1526 AD).

National Gallery of Modern Art ① *Jaipur House, near India Gate, T3384640, closed Mon, 1000-1700, foreigners Rs 150, Indians Rs 10.* The excellent collection is housed in a former residence of the Maharaja of Jaipur. Some of the best exhibits are on the ground floor which is devoted to post-1930 works. To view the collections chronologically, begin on the first floor. Artists include: Amrita Shergil (ground floor): over 100 exhibits, synthesizing the flat treatment of Indian painting with a realistic tone; Rabindranath Tagore (ground floor): examples from a brief but intense spell in the 1930s; The Bombay School or Company School (first floor): includes Western painters who documented their visits to India, the British painter Thomas Daniell whose style seems to anticipate the camera. Realism is reflected in Indian painting of the early 19th century represented by the schools of Avadh, Patna, Sikkim and Thanjavur; The Bengal School (the late 19th-century Revivalist Movement): artists such as Abanindranath Tagore and Nandalal Bose have their works exhibited here. Western influence was discarded in response to the nationalist movement. Inspiration derived from Indian folk art is evident in the works of Jamini Roy and YD Shukla. The Japanese influence can be seen in the use of wash techniques and a miniature style. Labelling could be better. Postcards, booklets and prints are available at the reception.

★ **National Museum** ① *Janpath, T3019272, closed Mon, 1000-1700, foreigners Rs 150, Indians Rs 10, camera Rs 300; free guided tours 1030, 1130, 1200, 1400, films are screened every day (1430), marble squat toilets, but dirty.* The collection was formed from the nucleus of the Exhibition of Indian Art, London (1947). Now merged with the Asian Antiquities Museum it displays a rich collection of the artistic treasure of Central Asia and India including ethnological objects from prehistoric archaeological finds to the late Medieval period. Replicas of exhibits and books on Indian culture and art are on sale. There is a research library.

Ground Floor Prehistoric: seals, figurines, toy animals and jewellery from the Harappan civilization (2400-1500 BC). Maurya Period: terracottas and stone heads from the Sunga period (third century BC) include the *chaturmukha* (four-faced) *lingam*. Gandhara School: stucco heads showing the Graeco Roman influence. Gupta terracottas (circa 400 AD): include two life size images of the river goddesses Ganga and Yamuna and the four-armed bust of Vishnu from a temple near Lal Kot. South Indian sculpture: from Pallava and early Chola temples and relief panels from Mysore. Tenth-century AD sculptures. Bronzes from the Buddhist monastery at Nalanda. Some of Buddha's relics were placed in the Thai pavilion in 1997.

First floor Illustrated manuscripts: include the *Babur-i-nama* in the Emperor's own handwriting and an autographed copy of Jahangir's memoirs. Miniature paintings: Include the 16th-century Jain School, the 18th-century Rajasthani School and the Pahari Schools of Garhwal, Basoli and Kangra. The Aurel Stein Collection consists of antiquities recovered by him during his explorations of Central Asia and the western borders of China at the turn of the century.

Second floor Pre-Columbian and Mayan artefacts: anthropological section devoted to tribal artefacts and folk arts. Sharad Rani Bakkiwal Gallery of Musical Instruments: displays over 300 instruments collected by the famous *sarod* player.

Natural History Museum ① *FICCI Building, Barakhamba Rd, closed Mon, 1000-1700.* A small but well-assembled introduction to India's natural heritage. A Discovery Room offers children the opportunity to handle specimens and take part in creative activities such as animal modelling. Daily filmshow (1130-1530), regular lectures and exhibitions organized in conjunction with other natural history organizations.

★ **Nehru Memorial Museum and Library** ① *Teen Murti Bhavan, closed Mon, museum 1000-1500 and Planetarium 1130-1500, Library closed Sun, 0900-1900, free.* The official residence of India's first Prime Minister, Jawaharlal Nehru, converted after his death (1964) into a national memorial. The reception, study and bedroom are intact. Note his extensive reading and wide interests. A *Jyoti Jawahar* (torch) symbolizes the eternal values he inspired, and a granite rock is carved with extracts from his historic speech at midnight 14-15 August 1947. Films and *son et lumière*. Very informative and vivid history of the Independence Movement.

★ **Craft Museum** ① *Bhairon Rd, closed Mon, 1000-1700, café recommended (excellent dosas).* The large 'Village Complex' recreated here with rural huts has over 20,000 pieces of traditional crafts from all over India - a rich collection of 18th-20th century objects including terracottas, bronzes, enamel work, wood painting and carving, brocades and jewellery. Good crafts for sale from the shop or from the craftsmen who can be seen at work. Interesting, evocative and highly recommended.

Connaught Place

7 Marina & Chemists *A1*
8 Nirula's, Ice Creams & Potpouri Restaurant *A3*
9 Park *C1*
10 Ringo Guest House & Don't Pass Me By Restaurant *C2*
11 YMCA Tourist Hostel *D1*
12 York *A3*

13 YWCA International Guest House *D1*

● **Eating**
1 Amber *C2*
2 DVB *C2*
3 Delhi Darbar *A3*
4 Fridays *B2*
5 Kwality *C2*
6 Wengers & Rodeo *B2*
7 Wimpy & Pizza King *C2*
8 Zen *A2*

○ **Shopping**
1 Bookworm *A2*
2 Central Cottage Industries Emporium *D2*
3 Hidesign *B1*
4 Jain's Bookshop *A2*
5 Khadi Gramodyog *B1*
6 Map Sales Office *C2*
7 Oxford Book & Stationery *C2*
8 The Shop *C1*

■ **Sleeping**
1 Central Court
2 Centrepoint *D3*
3 Hans Plaza *C3*
4 Hotel 55 *A2*
5 Imperial *D2*
6 Jain's Guest House *C2*

0 metres 100
0 yards 100

Rabindra Bhavan ⓘ*Copernicus Marg*. Housing the national academies of literature (Sahitya Akademi), fine arts and sculpture (Lalit Kala Akademi), and the performing arts (Sangeet Natak Akademi) in separate wings. All have libraries and display galleries. Postcards and reproductions on sale.

★ **Rail Transport Museum** ⓘ*closed Mon and public holidays, Apr-Sep 0930-1230, 1330-1930; Oct-Mar 0930-1230, 1330-1730, Rs 5, camera Rs 10, good booklet, Rs 30, poor toilets, auto from centre Rs 35, Chanakyapuri, southwest of Connaught Place.* The museum preserves a memorable account of 144 years of the history of Indian Railways with 26 vintage locomotives, 17 carriages and saloons including a four-wheeled saloon used by Edward VII in 1876 and the Maharaja of Mysore's saloon.

Red Fort Museum ⓘ*Mumtaz Mahal, Lal Qila, closed Mon, 1000-1700.* On display are the swords, hookahs, chess sets, armoury, carpets etc of the Mughal Emperors from Babur to Bahadurshah Zafar. Miniatures depict life at the court, maps and monuments of Delhi and portraits.

Gandhi Museums Gandhi Museum ⓘ*Birla House, Tees, Jan Marg (near* Claridges Hotel)*,closed Mon and 2nd Sat, 0930-1730, free, film at 1500,* contains photos and memorabilia including his few possessions during his final days in the house. A monument marks where he fell. Worth a visit. **Gandhi Darshan** ⓘ*opposite Raj Ghat, closed Mon, 1000-1700,* has five pavilions - sculpture, photographs and paintings of Gandhi and the history of the *Satyagraha* movement, the philosophy of non-violence. **Gandhi Smarak Sangrahalaya** ⓘ*Raj Ghat, T3011480, closed Thu, 0930-1730, film (English and Hindi, normally 1600),* displays some of Gandhi's personal belongings. Small library includes recordings of speeches. **Indira Gandhi Museum** ⓘ*1 Safdarjang Rd, T3010094, 0930-1700, free,* charts the phases of her life from childhood up to the moment of her death (preserved in her sari with blood stains when she was struck down at her own garden gate).

Other museums Airforce Museum ⓘ*Palam Marg, T3035684, closed Mon and Tue, 1000-1700,* contains guns, bullets, uniforms and photographs recording the history of the Indian Air Force. Excellent aircraft which include a Westland 'Wapiti'. **Dolls Museum** ⓘ*Nehru House, Bahadur Shah Zafar Marg, closed Mon, 1000-1800, films for members (under 16s only) on 2nd Sat,* has over 6,000 dolls. **Pragati Maidan** ⓘ*Mathura Rd, 1000-1700, Sun and public holidays 1000-2000,* has five permanent exhibitions including the 'Nehru Pavilion' which is small but comprehensive. 'The Son of India' features the life of Sanjay Gandhi. 'Atomic Energy' and 'Defence' pavilions demonstrate India's technological and industrial achievements.

Parks and zoos

Delhi has many very well-kept parks, ideal places to relax. They are also good places for casual birdwatching. Delhi's Birdwatching Society has listed over 350 species seen in the city. Peacocks, weaver-birds, spotted owlets, kingfishers and the koel are relatively common. The arrival of the pied-crested cuckoo heralds the monsoon. Visit Sultanpur and Bharatpur if you are a serious birdwatcher. The parks usually open 0600-2000.

Buddha Jayanti Park, Sardar Patel Marg, opposite Assam House, see page 86, commemorates the 2,500th anniversary of Gautama Buddha's attainment of nirvana. A sapling of the original Bodhi tree taken to Sri Lanka by Emperor Asoka's daughter in the third century BC is planted here. Rockeries, streams, bridges and the sloping terrain create an atmosphere of peace and tranquillity.

Lodi Gardens on the Lodi Estate, see map page 86, is a very popular and pleasant park set around the 14th- and 15th-century Lodi and Sayyid tombs. Nearby is the ornamental pool behind Safdarjang's Tomb attracts white-fronted and common kingfishers.

The **Mughal Gardens** are very carefully tended to in the classic *char bagh* style. They are open to the public in February to March when the flowers are in full bloom. For an entry permit at other times contact the India Tourist Office. Rashtrapati Bhavan Estate.

Nehru Park at Chanakyapuri, see map page 86, is a landscaped garden. Sayings of the late Jawaharlal Nehru are inscribed on the rocks. There is a swimming pool and snack bar to the south.

Qudsia Bagh, near Kashmir Gate, see map page 104, has an imposing gateway with pavilions at each end overlooking the river. Peacocks are common here. The gardens were laid out in 1748 by Qudsia Begum, a slave who became the favourite mistress of the Mughal Emperor Mohammad Shah. From here the British opened fire on Kashmir Gate during the Mutiny of 1857.

Roshanara Gardens in Gulabi Bagh, see map page 104, were laid out in 1640 by Princess Roshanara, Shah Jahan's younger daughter, shortly after the completion of Shah Jahanabad. In recent years the garden has been landscaped in Japanese style.

Zoological Gardens house over 1,000 animals, reptiles and birds. The most popular attractions are the white tiger from Rewa and the elephant which plays the harmonica! Well laid out. Worth visiting. They are situated at Purana Qila, see map page 86.

Paharganj

Related map
A Connaught Place,
page 110

■ **Sleeping**
1 Ajay's Ankur & Bholenath Travel
2 Anoop Appetite & Hare Krishna

3 Chanakya
4 City Palace
5 Gold Regency & Temptations Restaurant
6 Hare Rama & Rooftop Restaurant
7 Major Den's & India International
8 Mohak Palace
9 My Hotel

10 Namaskar
11 Navrang
12 Rail Yatri Nivas
13 Relax
14 Saina International
15 Shree Lodge
16 Sri Lanka Buddhist Rest House
17 Star Palace
18 Star Paradise

19 Starview
20 The Nest
21 Vishal

● **Eating**
1 Madan's
2 Malhotra

⬤ Sleeping → *Phone code Delhi: 011*

Avoid hotel touts. Airport taxis may pretend not to know the location of your chosen hotel so give full details. Insist to be taken there.

Hotel prices in Delhi are significantly higher than in most other parts of the country. Smaller **C, D** guesthouses away from the centre in South Delhi (eg Kailash, Safdarjang) or in Sunder Nagar, are quieter and often good value but may not provide food. Cheaper **E, F** accommodation is concentrated around Janpath and Paharganj (New Delhi), and Chandni Chowk (Old Delhi)- well patronized but basic and usually cramped yet good for meeting other budget travellers. Some have dormitory beds for under Rs 100. Youth hostels are listed under 'New Delhi' below, campsites under 'Old Delhi'. Hotels in New Delhi centre are grouped under 'Centra New Delhi', 'Connaught Place' and 'Paharganj'.

NB Added to your bill will be 10% Luxury Tax, 10% Service Charge, 20% Expenditure Tax (where rooms are over Rs 1,200 per night). See page 53 for price categories. Signs in some hotels warn against taking drugs as this is becoming a serious cause for concern. Police raids are frequent.

Airport *p84*

Avoid **AL-A** Centaur near airport.
LL Radisson, Mahipalpur, next to International Airport, T6129191, F6129090, www.radisson.com. 260 rooms, all facilities, large and shiny, pool, squash, pleasant and relaxed.
A-B Shanti Palace, A67 Mahipalpur Extn, NH8, T6781271, F6781274, shantipalace@mantramail.com. 20 very clean rooms, ask for room with a view of the runway, "5 star hotel for 3 star price"!
B-C International Inn A78, NH8, T6784665, F6784664. Basic rooms .
B-C Star, A288, T6784092, NH8. Basic rooms (avoid basement).
D Tara Inn, A55, Gurgaon Rd, Mahipalpur, T6783677. Comfortable and good value rooms, restaurant.
E Airport Retiring Rooms, left side when entering Departure hall, contact Airport

Manager. Double room, Rs 650 or Rs 450 per person. Simple, allocated 'first come, first served' to confirmed ticket holders but often full. Dormitory: Rs 90.

Central New Delhi *p89, map p90*

Airports 15-23 km. Railway about 1-3 km. Some city centre hotel rooms are windowless.
LL-L Grand Inter-Continental, Barakhamba Ave, T3411001, F3411234, www.interconti.com. 444 rooms, 25-storey hotel some find impersonal, others among best in its class, good patisserie.
LL-L Le Meridien, Windsor Pl, Janpath, T3710101, F3714545, www.lemeridien-newdelhi.com. 355 rooms, visually striking, "too American, no soul", unusual pool.
LL-L Metropolitan Hotel Nikko, Bangla Sahib Rd, T3342000, F3343000, www.hotelnikko delhi.com. 178 room Japanese chain hotel.
A-B Janpath (ITDC), Janpath, T3340070, F3347083. 213 rooms, no pool, indifferent service experienced.

Connaught Place *p91, map p110*
LL-L Park, 15 Sansad Marg, T3743000, F3744000, www.theparkhotels.com. 230 rooms, good views, friendly, exclusive Bengali cuisine, Spanish restaurant, very comfortable hotel.
L-AL Imperial, Janpath, T3341234, F3342255, www.theimperialindia.com. 255 rooms, colonial feel, well-tended gardens, good pool, flashier and more expensive since rebuilding, new *Daniell's* bar and *Spice Route* restaurant. Recommended.
AL The Hans Plaza, 15 Barakhamba Rd (on 16th-20th floor), T3316861, F3314830, www.hansgroup.com. 70 rooms, 'boutique hotel', clean, quiet, superb views. Recommended (if you like heights).
A Centrepoint, 13 Kasturba Gandhi Marg, T3324805, F3329138, cpoint@del2.vsnl.net.in. Well-located, old charming building in a small park, 60 large clean rooms, bath tubs, though smarter road side rooms can be noisy,

Delhi Listings Sleeping

restaurant lacks variety but reasonable breakfasts (included), reception "willing but pushed", good exchange rate.

AMarina, G-59 Connaught Circus, T3324658, F3328609, marina@nde.vsnl.net.in. 93 clean rooms (**A**suites), bath with tubs, some large, others cramped but refurbished, attractive reception, good coffee shop, travel agent recommended, pleasant.

A-B Nirula's, L-Block, Connaught Circus, T3322419, F3353957, www.nirulas.com. 29 rooms, most are comfortable and pleasant, good Potpourri restaurant, ice cream and pastry shops, internet, very central, clean, peaceful suites, efficient and good value. Recommended.

BCentral Court, N-Block, T3315013, F3317582. Simple hotel with basic 60s furniture, clean, very large doubles/suites with bath (small singles), windows in doors only, coffee shop, friendly staff.

BFifty Five, H-55 Connaught Pl, T3321244, F3320769, hotelfiftyfive@hotmail.com. 15 small, clean, simple rooms (some windowless), darkish decor, central a/c, road can be a bit noisy, roof terrace for breakfast, helpful, very friendly staff.

B-CYWCA International Guest House, Sansad Marg (near Jantar Mantar), T3361561, www.ywcaindia.org. 24 clean, upgraded a/c rooms, centre 1 km, open to both sexes, restaurant (see below), handy internet in foyer, peaceful garden, convenient location, good value.

B-CYMCA Tourist Hostel, Jai Singh Rd, T3361915, F3746032. 120 rooms, for both sexes, a/c rooms with bath (B-Block, non a/c and shared bath), some reported dirty, restaurant (breakfast included but disappointing), travel, peaceful gardens, tennis, good pool (Rs 100 extra), luggage stored (Rs 5 per day), pay in advance but check bill, reserve ahead.

CIndraprastha (ITDC), 19 Ashoka Rd, T3344511, F3368153, www.theashok group.com. 547 rooms (few 'superior' rooms, 71 are 4-bedded), renovated, excellent a/c *Coconut Grove* south Indian restaurant, maximum 7 days, good value.

EJain's Guest House, 7 Pratap Singh Building, Janpath Lane. Clean rooms without bath, quiet.

EMrs Colack's Guest House, Janpath Lane, T3328758. Small simple rooms, adequate but very basic.

Off Kasturba Gandhi Marg:
E-F Ringo Guest House, 17 Scindia House (upstairs), T3310605. Tiny rooms (some windowless) but no bugs, cheap crowded dorm (beds 15 cm apart) or beds on rooftop, no hot showers, basic toilets, lockers, good restaurant (0700-2300), courtyard, friendly staff, backpackers' haunt (other hotel touts waylay travellers).

Paharganj *map p112*
Rooms tend to be cheap, usually with shared baths, and the street-side rooms can be noisy. Though the packed bazars and crowded lanes are often filthy, Parharganj is popular with backpackers. There are plenty of shops selling 'souvenirs', travel agents, hotels and cafés, and despite the fact that most of the facilities are mediocre the area is reasonably convenient, sandwiched between the main sights and near the main railway station. For a more sedate, 'authentic' experience, stay elsewhere.

BGold Regency, 4350 Main Bazar, T3540101, F3540202, www.goldregency.com. 40 good, clean, smallish a/c rooms, moderately priced restaurant, disco, Cyber Café, good facilities but some power problems.

BTourist Deluxe, 7361 Qutb Rd, Ramnagar, T3670985, F3648416, touristdeluxe@vsnl.net. 59 comfortable a/c rooms, few **C**suites with tubs, vegetarian restaurant, on busy main road.

CIndia International, 2485 Nalwa St, behind Imperial Cinema, T/F3677229, hindiandx@vsnl.com. Clean rooms, central a/c, indoor pool, sauna, friendly.

CRelax, 4970, Randwara Rd, Nehru Bazar, T3681030, F3679398, vidur109@ hotmail.com. Attractive hotel on busy market street with 2 large terraces, a/c doubles, sadly not too friendly.

CTourist, T3610334, F3559418, tourist@ schand.com. 65 rooms, 33 a/c, cleaner than Tourist Deluxe (and uncarpeted), vegetarian restaurant, rooms at rear quieter.

DBaba Deluxe, 7795 Arakashan Rd, Ramnagar, T3548334, F3559858. 52 clean rooms, generator.

DChanakya, Rajguru Rd, T3618824. Very basic rooms, noisy on road, good restaurant.

D-E City Palace, 2014, Street 7, Chuna Mandi, T3542678 hotelcity@rediff.com. Newish hotel, rooms (some windowless) with clean tiled baths, some a/c, round beds and sofas, 2 suites, restaurant on top. Peaceful, very friendly.

D-E Hare Rama Guest House, 298 Main Bazar, T3629293, F3632795, www.harerama huesthouse.com. 65 clean rooms, 24-hr hot water, has Jewish prayer room.

D-E Major Den's, 2314 Laksh16 ci Narain St, behind Imperial Cinema, T3629599, majorsden@hotmail.com. Clean rooms in family home (front rooms with windows best), friendly personal service, quiet, safe storage, good value (up to Rs 450). Recommended.

D-E My Hotel, 901 Gali Chandi Wali, T3616215. 42 pleasant rooms in a new, quiet hotel, some a/c (up to Rs 675), restaurant on top, cyber café.

D-E Rly Retiring Rooms, New (and Old) Delhi Rly Station. For 12 and 24 hrs, dorm beds (10 rooms, 6 a/c are usually pre-booked), only for train ticket-holders, basic, noisy, but convenient.

D-E Saina International, 2324 Chuna Mandi, near Imperial Cinema, T3529144, F7520879. Clean rooms, some a/c, hot water, open-air restaurant serves beer (avoid travel desk), friendly, quiet for area.

D Starview, 5136 Main Bazar, T3556300, F3554220. Rooms vary, some a/c, rates negotiable, a bit noisy.

E Ajay's, 5084a Main Bazar, T3543125, F3540656, ajay5084@hotmail.com. 48 fairly clean (windowless) rooms with bath (1 a/c), dorm, good bakery, restaurant, friendly, but antisocial guests can be noisy.

E Ankur, next door, good internet, exchange, laundry.

E Anoop, 1566 Main Bazar. Rooms with bath, some with air-cooler, very clean though basic, noisy at times, safe, good 24-hr rooftop restaurant shared with *Hare Krishna* (waiters can 'forget' to give change).

E Hare Krishna, 1572 Main Bazar, T3529186, F3632942, harekrishnagh@hotmail.com. Very clean rooms with bath (some windowless, stuffy), friendly, travel, great rooftop restaurant.

E Om Palace, 8126 Arakashan Rd, Ramnagar, T3527121. Basic rooms, clean linen.

E Shree Lodge, 2012-2015 Chuna Mandi, T3526864. Clean rooms, quiet, good value.

E Star Palace, 4590 Dal Mandi, off Main Bazar (lane opposite Khalsa Boots), T3628584, www.stargroupofhotels.com. Clean well kept rooms with "fantastic showers", a/c extra, quiet, friendly but "feel a bit like a battery hen".

Some hotels, even cheaper, may suffer from noise (noticeable at night, use good ear-plugs).

E-F Rail Yatri Nivas, behind New Delhi Rly Station (3 min walk from Ajmeri Gate, 8-storey building). 36 rooms with shower (Rs 300, a/c Rs 500), 172 dorm beds (Rs 70), 12 hr option, restaurant, reserve in advance through ITB (see Rail Transport below) or New Delhi Rly Station, Gate 2, quoting ticket number and send money order for room and 'key deposit', check carefully before signing 'check-in' list, max stay 3 nights, check-out 1000 (try your luck then, if you haven't pre-booked).

E-F Vishal, 1575/80 Main Bazar, T3527629. Some rooms with bath, fairly clean, avoid restaurants (pestering 'trinket' sellers).

F Mohak Palace, Multani Dhanda. Clean, friendly, safe to leave luggage.

F Namaskar, 917 Chandiwalan, Main Bazar, T3621234, F7522233, namaskarhotel@ yahoo.com. Small basic rooms (2-4 beds) with bath (bucket hot water), clean but some windowless, newer **D** a/c rooms (Rs 500) in extension, generator, safe, friendly service, good atmosphere, quiet at night, stores luggage, reserve ahead, unreliable travel information.

F Navrang, Mohalla Baoli, 644/c 6 Tooti Chowk. Very small rooms (Rs 70), shared facilities, no hot water, friendly, pricey luggage store.

Outer New Delhi *map p86*

Airports 9-17 km. Railway 5-9 km. Centre 5 km.

LL Taj Mahal, 1 Mansingh Rd, T3016162, F3026070, www.tajhotels.com. 300 rooms, excellent restaurants and service (*Haveli* offers wide choice and explanations for the newcomer, *Ming House's* spicing varies), coffee shop pokey and disappointing, good *Khazana* shop, lavishly finished, good city views but lacks atmosphere.

LL Taj Palace, 2 Sardar Patel Marg, T6110202, F6110808, www.tajhotels.com. 421 rooms, purpose-built for business travellers, generally excellent, *Orient Express* restaurant highly recommended (haute French), "service outstanding, food superb".

LL-L Maurya Sheraton Hotel and **Towers**, Sardar Patel Marg, T6112233, F6113333, www.welcomgroup.com. 440 rooms, excellent décor and service, splendid pool (solar heated), disco (noisy late at night, so avoid rooms nearby), good restaurants (see page 117).

LL-L Oberoi, Dr Zakir Hussain Marg, T4363030, F4364084, www.oberoihotels.com. 287 rooms, overlooking golf club, immaculate, quietly efficient, excellent all round but expensive Chinese restaurant disappointing.

L Claridges, 12 Aurangzeb Rd, T3010211, F3010625, claridges.hotel@gems.vsnl.net.in. 164 rooms, colonial atmosphere, attractive restaurants (good *Jade Garden* Chinese), impeccable service.

L Siddharth, 3 Rajendra Pl, T5762501, F5781016, jhl@del2.vsnl.net.in. 98 good rooms.

AL Ambassador (Taj), Sujan Singh Park, T4632600, F4632252, www.tajhotels.com. 81 rooms, no pool but garden.

AL Ashok (ITDC), 50-B Chanakyapuri, T6110101, F6873216, www.theashok group.com. 571 large rooms (some upgraded), sunny coffee shop, 24-hr bank, quiet but overpriced.

AL Diplomat, 9 Sardar Patel Marg, T3010204, F3018605, diplomat@nda.vsnl.net.in. 25 rooms, no pool, quietly located, very popular.

Hotels in residential districts are worth considering. Avoid *Singh Palace*, Karol Bagh. **B Bajaj Indian Homestay**, 8A/34 WEA, Karol Bagh, T5736509, F5812905, www.indianhomestay.com. Newish, Indian decor, mod cons, breakfast included.

B LaSagrita, 14 Sunder Nagar, T4358572, F4356956, lasagrit@del3.vsnl.net.in. 24 recently refurbished a/c rooms, modern bathrooms, phone, restaurant, helpful staff, quiet location.

B Nirula's, C-135 Sector 2, NOIDA (15 km east of centre), T85-526512, F85-551069, www.nirulas.com (also in Connaught Circus). Comfortable, friendly and helpful, pleasant atmosphere, good *Potpourri* restaurant and bar. **B Orchid**, G4 S Extn 1, T4643529, F4626924, hotelorchid@yahoo.com. 18 a/c rooms, restaurants nearby, pleasant, helpful staff.

B Patel Continental, 8/10 E Patel Nagar, T5740107. 24 rooms, no restaurant but some nearby (try *Malika*, for good food and beer), room service, no commission to autos.

B Rajdoot, Mathura Rd, T4316666, F4647442. 55 rooms, near Nizammuddin Railway, pool.

B-C Jukaso Inn, 50 Sunder Nagar, T4690308, F4694402, jukaso@vsnl.com. 50 a/c rooms, garden, pleasant, quiet, friendly.

C Pal's Inn, E Patel Nagar, Karol Bagh, www.indiamart.com/pals-inn. 16 rooms in new guest house, marble baths, clean, well kept, lobby café facing park (full breakfast included), good car hire (Rs 600 for 8 hrs), friendly and caring owner, attentive staff.

C Yatri Paying Guest House, corner of Panchkuin and Mandir Margs, T7525563. Large clean rooms (some a/c), cold in winter, garden, mosquito problem, quiet, "peaceful oasis", friendly, welcoming but can't stay long.

C-D Master Paying Guesthouse, R-500 New Rajendra Nagar (Shankar & GR Hospital Rds crossing), T5850914, urvashi@del2.vsnl.net.in. Clean rooms (some Ba/c), spotless shared facilities, rooftop for breakfast, evening thalis, warm welcome, personal attention, secure.

Youth hostels

F Youth Hostel, 5 Naya Marg, Chanakyapuri, T3016285. Basic dorm (Rs 30), breakfast, prefer International YHA members, popular.

Old Delhi *p100, map p104*

Airports 17-25 km. Old and New Delhi Railway 1-3 km.

AL Oberoi Maidens, 7 Sham Nath Marg, T3975464, F3980771, www.oberoihotels.com. 54 rooms, many large well-appointed rooms, restaurant (slow), barbecue nights are excellent, coffee shop, old-style bar, attractive colonial style in quiet area, spacious gardens with excellent pool, friendly welcome, personal attention. Recommended.

B Broadway, 4/15A Asaf Ali Rd, T3273821, F3269966, broadway@vsnl.net.in. Indian business hotel, 32 clean but gloomy rooms, good but overpriced. *Chor Bizarre* restaurant and bar (see below).

B-C Ranjit, Maharaja Ranjit Singh Rd, T3231256, F3233166, www.theashok group.com. 186 rooms, about half a/c, veg restaurant, pool, well located for sights.

C Flora, Dayanand Rd, Daryaganj, T3273634, F3280887. 63 small but clean rooms, 24 a/c, centre 2 km, good restaurant.

D Bhagirath Palace, opposite Red Fort, Chandni Chowk, T3866223, F3955274, hotbha@del3.vsnl.net.in. 18 rooms, some a/c, 1 km Old Delhi Railway, bar.

E Noor, 421 Matia Mahal, Jama Masjid (first left after *Flora's Restaurant*, then 3rd left), T3267791. 34 clean, quiet rooms, shared facilities (Indian WC), fans, rooftop views of Jama Masjid and fort, experience of Old Delhi.

E Tera, 2802a Bazar, Kashmir Gate, T3911532, F3959660. 42 rooms, some a/c, 500 m Old Delhi Railway, restaurant, coffee shop, TV.

E Wongdhen House, 15A New Tibetan Colony, Manju-ka-Tilla, T3916689, F3945962, wongdhenhouse@hotmail.com. Very clean rooms, some with TV, safe, homely, good breakfast and Tibetan meals, an insight into Tibetan culture, peacefully located by the Yamuna River yet 15 mins by auto-rickshaw north from Old Delhi station..

Camping

F New Delhi Tourist Camp, Nehru Marg, opposite JP Narayan Hospital. 130 tiny rooms (deluxe **E** rooms, cooler/TV Rs 35 extra) plus cheaper dorm beds, hot water, refurbished restaurant, exchange, travel, pleasant gardens, EATS bus to airport (Rs 50 plus Rs 10 for luggage), friendly atmosphere, secure, helpful, popular (groups should book in advance).

F Tourist Camp, Qudsia Gardens, opposite Inter-State Bus Terminus. Camping and huts, food available.

South Delhi *p93*

Airports 9-17 km. Railway 12 km. Centre 10 km. Several 20 mins' drive from airport.

LL-L Grand Hyatt Delhi, Nelson Mandela Rd, Vasant Kunj Phase II, T6121234, F6895891, www.hyatt.com. 390 rooms, 25 suites in new, luxury hotel, choice of good restaurants, health club, tennis, golf (20 mins drive). Recommended.

LL-L Hyatt Regency, Bhikaiji Cama Pl, Ring Rd, T6181234, F6186833, www.delhi.hyatt.com. 518 rooms, rooms tiny for price, restaurants good but expensive (*La Piazza* buffet Rs 550).

L Manor, 77 Friends Colony, T6925151, F6922299, www.themanordelhi.com. Boutique hotel with 16 stylish rooms, heavenly beds, polished stone surfaces and chrome, relaxing garden, a haven.

L Surya (*Crown Plaza*), New Friends Colony, T6835070, F6837758, www.suryadelhicrown plaza.com. 195 rooms, isolated, good views, good service but mediocre restaurants.

L Vasant Continental, Vasant Vihar, T6148800, F6873842, www.jaypeehotels.com. 110 rooms, convenient for airports (free transfer), more personal, 'Indian' atmosphere, large pool and gardens near Basant Lok Market, good service, but overpriced (lacks many 'A' facilities).

B '27' Jorbagh, 27 Jorbagh (2 mins from Lodi tombs), T4698647, F4698475, www.guesthouse27@hotmail.com. 20 a/c rooms, car hire, not plush but very quiet (Western food nearby), hassle free, book ahead. Highly recommended.

B Kailash Nath, 39 Prithviraj Rd, T4694523, F4635706. 15 a/c rooms in private guesthouse in a bungalow, free airport pick-up/drop, full services, used by NGOs and foreign consultants.

B Legend Inn, E-4 East of Kailash, T6210111, F6483351, www.thelegendinn.com. Comfortable a/c rooms, no restaurant, homely.

⊘ Eating

The larger **hotel restaurants** are often the best for cuisine, décor and ambience. **Buffets** (lunch or dinner) cost Rs 500 or more, eg Le Meridien's *La Brasserie*, Rs 550. Others may only open around 1930 for dinner; some close on Sun. **Alcohol** is served in most top hotels, but only in some non-hotel restaurants eg *Amber, Ginza, Kwality*.

Central New Delhi *p89, map p90*

See also Connaught Place and Paharganj below.

ⵯ **Bukhara**, at *Maurya Sheraton*, T6112233. Stylish Northwest Frontier cuisine. Amidst rugged walls draped with rich rugs (but seating not too comfortable), worth every rupee.

ⵯ **Chinese**, does great soups, "waiters treat beer bottles as fine wines!".

ⵯ **Corbett's**, *Claridge's Hotel*, T3010211. Authentic North Indian. Animal park theme outdoor, straw huts, jungle soundtrack, hidden animals delight children, good value.

ⵯ **Dum Phukt**, *Maurya Sheraton*, T6112233. North Indian. Slowly steam- cooked in sealed *handis* produces excellent melt-in-the-mouth Nawabi dishes. High quality service and decor. Expensive and a bit pretentious.

₹₹₹ **La Rochelle**, *Oberoi*, T4364084. French.

₹₹₹ **Lodi**, Lodi Gardens, T4655054. Excellent lunchtime continental, dinner Indian.

₹₹₹ **Parikrama**, 'Antriksh', Kasturba Gandhi Marg, T3721616. International. Savour the rich food and the views as it revolves slowly!

₹₹₹ **Spice Route**, *Imperial Hotel*. Excellent Kerala, Thai, Vietnamese cuisines.

₹₹ **Basil and Thyme**, Santushti Complex, Chanakyapuri, T4673322. Continental. Pleasant setting, simple décor, a/c, modestly priced Western snacks at lunch, fashionable meeting place (busy 1300-1400).

₹₹ **Moti Mahal Deluxe**, Malcha Marg, Chanakyapuri (near *Diplomat*), T6118698. Excellent Mughlai, closed Tue.

₹₹ **Ten (YWCA International GH)**, Sansad Marg. Indian, Western. Good meals and snacks. New management, clean, modern, well run.

₹ **Andhra Bhavan**, near India Gate. South Indian (Chettinad).

₹ **Karim's Nemat Kada**, Nizamuddin West. Mughlai. Good value.

Connaught Place *p91, map p110*

₹₹₹ **Rodeo**, 12a, T3713780. Excellent Mexican (3-course and beer, Rs 350), Italian, continental. "Heavenly", fast service.

₹₹₹ **Zen**, T3724458. Stylish, impersonal but popular, generous portions for Chinese, more expensive Japanese and seafood.

₹₹ **Amber**, N-Block, T3312092. Lightly spiced.

₹₹ **Berco's**, L-Block, T3318134. Chinese, Japanese. Generous helpings, fast service, very popular, quieter for dinner.

₹₹ **DVB**, 13 Regal Building with smart and cosy pub below. Round the world meals, good buffet (Rs 250), á la carte (Rs 150+), good music, great Espresso coffee.

₹₹ **Embassy**, D-11. International. Mirrored, very popular, good food, but waiters 'demand' 10% tip.

₹₹ **Fridays**, F-16. Western meals, Texmex, great decor with 50s objects on walls, TV, Western music, 'Happy Hour' (1700-1930).

₹₹ **Gaylord**, 14 Regal Building. International.

₹₹ **Kwality**, Parliament St. International. Try spicy Punjabi dishes with various breads.

₹₹ **Pizza Express**, D Inner Circle. Pizzas from Rs 165, coke Rs 35, glass of wine Rs 165, but good, closes 2300.

₹₹ **Potpourri**, *Nirula's*, L-Block. Indian and continental. Bright, clean and very popular - tasty light meals, snacks, ice creams, salad bar (safe!) Rs 143, beers, several branches including N-Block, Defence Colony Flyover.

₹ **Delhi Darbar**, 49 Connaught Circus. North Indian. Good mutton dishes, bar.

₹ **Don't Pass Me By**, by *Ringos*, 17 Scindia House. Chinese. Bit dingy, but good basic food and plenty of it, prompt, cooler upstairs (is also tour agent).

₹ **Kake's**, H-block, Plaza Building. Famous Punjabi *dhaba*. *Handi* dishes and delicious green masala fish, very cheap.

₹ **Nathu's**, Bengali Market (east of Connaught Pl). Sweet shops serving mainly vegetarian food. Good *dosa, idli, utthapam* and North Indian *chana bathura*, clean, functional canteen.

₹ **Nizam's Kathi Kebabs**, H-5 Plaza. Very good, tasty filled *parathas*, good value, clean, excellent '3-D toilets' (note emergency button!).

Paharganj *map p112*

Rooftop restaurants are great locations.

Appetite, 1575 Main Bazar, T7532079. Chinese, Nepali, Italian. mouth-watering bakery, good lassis.

Madan's, 1601 Main Bazar. International. Egg and chips to *thalis*, not special but friendly, popular, good value.

Malhotra's, 1833 Laxmi Narayan St. Good Indian and Chinese, wide choice, a/c section; also take-away.

Temptation, at *Chanakya*, 4350 Main Bazar. Pleasant. Good western (veg burgers, cakes), internet, disco and bar.

Old Delhi and the North
p100, map p104

₹₹₹ **Chor Bizarre**, *Broadway Hotel*, Asaf Ali Rd, T3273821. Noted *tandoori* and *Kashmiri* cuisine (*Wazwan*, Rs 500). Comfortable though quirky décor.

₹ **Flora**, Daryaganj. North Indian. Excellent *kalmi* chicken kebab, *biryani* and breads, dark and gloomy but good food, very popular.

₹ **Karim's**, Gali Kababiyan (south of Jama Masjid). Mughlai. Authentic, busy, plenty of local colour; "a tourist landmark - and a must!".

₹ **Peshawari**, 3707 Subhash Marg, Daryaganj. Tiny, with tiled walls, serves delicious chicken, closed Tue.

▮▮▮ La Piazza, Hyatt Regency, Bhikaji Cama Pl, T6181234. Authentic Italian. Mon-Sat lunch buffet Rs 550, try pizzas from wood-fired oven, good atmosphere and surroundings.

▮▮▮ Orient Express, *Taj Palace Hotel*, T6110202. Continental. Recreated luxury of the famous train carriages.

▮▮▮ TK's, Japanese, Teppanyaki - very visual!

Hauz Khas Village

▮▮▮ Park Baluchi. Highly praised cuisine.

▮▮▮ Suko Thai. Authentic Thai, pleasant décor, view of ruins from rooftop.

Asiad Village

▮▮ Angeethi, Siri Fort Marg. Tandoori.

▮▮ Ankur, Siri Fort Marg.Mughlai and Italian. Good food, bar.

▮▮ The Big Chill, F-38 East of Kailash (off Lala Lajpat Rai Path near Spring Meadows Hospital), T6481020. 1230 till late. A bright, new café with a difference. Wide range of carefully prepared, wholesome light meals of grills, bakes, fresh pasta and salads, spectacularly successful homemade desserts. Great atmosphere (choose your own music), good prices.

▮▮ Chopsticks, Siri Fort Marg, T6493628. Chinese, Thai. Good value, pleasant ambience, bar, weekend buffet lunches.

▮▮ Diva, M8A Gt Kailash II, T6215673. Stylish Italian, innovative menu, great ambience.

▮▮ Golden Dragon, C Block, Vasant Vihar. Very reliable Chinese, reasonably priced.

▮▮ Imperial Garden, Gt Kailash II, T6477798. Excellent Oriental.

▮▮ M-Block Market, Greater Kailash, Pt I. Has *McDonald's, Pizza Express, Baskin Robbins* etc.

▮▮ Mini Mahal, C-25A Vasant Vihar. North Indian. Popular with diplomats.

▮▮ Miyako, N-Block, Gt Kailash I, T6281553. Japanese. Authentic. Teppanyaki, some Japanese seating.

▮▮ Priya Cinema Complex, Basant Lok Market, Vasant Vihar. Has *McDonald's, Pizza Express, Baskin Robbins* etc.

▮ Aalis, Panchsheel Enclave. Good *Kathis*.

▮ Colonelz Kebabz, Defence Colony Market. Tandoori. Excellent tikkas and kebabs. Several others, including RK Puram. and delicious, safe 'street food' 1000-2200.

▮ Keraleeyam, Yusuf Sarai, next to Indian Oil. Malabar. Spicy unusual non-vegetarian dishes.

▮ Moti Mahal, S Extn II (branch at M-13 GKI). Tandoori. Noisy and now very average food, more pleasant tented section outside.

Vegetarian

Naivedyam, Haus Khas Village, T6960426. Very good south Indian, clean and cheap.

Sagar, 18 Defence Colony Market. Excellent South Indian. Cheap and "amazing!" *thalis* and coffee, very hectic (frequent queues). (Others in Vasant Kunj, Malviya Nagar and NOIDA).

Sona Rupa, 46 Janpath. Recommended for snacks (1030-2400).

Tea lounges, coffee bars, confectioners

The old fashioned 'tea on the lawns' still served at the *Imperial* and in the *Claridges'* courtyard or a/c inside if you prefer.

Aapki Pasand, 15 Netaji Subhash Marg. Unique tea-tasting.

Baristas, smart new chain of coffee shops.

Confectioners outside top hotels include:

Chocolate Wheel, 55 Jorbagh.

Hot Breads, N-Block, Gt Kailash I, Connaught Pl. Good cakes, quiches, salads, rolls, espresso and cappuccino, limited seating.

Nirula's Pastry Shop, L-Block, Connaught Pl. Very good choice.

Wengers, A-Block, Connaught Pl. Good choice.

✪ Bars and clubs

1st and 7th of month and national holidays are 'dry' days. Normally hotel restaurants, bars and clubs serve alcohol. All top hotels have bars.

Djinn's at *Hyatt Regency*, the place to be seen, Rs 750 minimum, live band, pool table, food.

Patiala Peg at *Imperial Hotel*, trendy.

Pegasus at *Nirula's*, N-Connaught Circus. English-style pub, very friendly.

Radisson, near the airport, has a sports bar with snooker and bowling and good cocktails.

Discos

CJ's, *Le Meridien*. Selective entry, cover charge.

Ghungroo, *Maurya Sheraton* (residents only).

My kind of place, *Taj Palace*, T6110202.

Oasis, *Hyatt Regency*. Popular (2200-early hrs).

🎵 Entertainment

First City monthly (Rs 20) with reviews, the free fortnightly weekly Delhi City Info, and the weekly Delhi Diary, from hotels and other outlets, carry listings of what's on.

Cinemas

PVR Anupam, Community Centre, Saket, T6865999. Good choice, phone reservations before 2000.
Priya (the 'young spot'), Vasant Vihar, T6140048. Usual action movies.
Satyam, Patel Nagar, T5797385.
Around Connaught Place, Regal, Plaza etc usually screen Hindi movies. It can be an entertaining experience in itself simply to watch the audience interaction - they know the plot, the songs - but unaccompanied women may find it unpleasant.

Clubs

Some have reciprocal membership facilities with foreign clubs.

Chelmsford Club, Raisina Rd, T3714694.
Delhi Gymkhana Club, 2 Safdarjang Rd, T3015533. Mostly for government and defence personnel, squash, tennis, swimming, bar and restaurant.
Habitat Centre, Lodi Rd, T4682222, with good programme of lectures, exhibitions, excellent restaurant.

Son et Lumière

Except during the monsoon:
Hauz Khas: 1 hr cultural show in illuminated ruins, daily, 1845, Rs 100.
Nehru Pavilion, Pragati Maidan: Jawaharlal and his vision, daily except Mon, 1600.
Red Fort: Oct-Mar 1800-1900 (Hindi), 1930-2030 (English), 1 hr later Apr-Sep. Entry Rs 10 and Rs 20. Tickets available after 1700. (Be sure to take mosquito cream.)
Teen Murti House: 'A Tryst with Destiny': 1800-1900 (Hindi), 1915-2015 (English). Rs 5. Enquiries T3015026.

☸ Festivals and events

Consult the weekly *Delhi Diary* available at hotels and many shops and offices around town for exact dates. The following list gives an approximate indication of the dates.

January

Lohri (**13th**), the climax of winter is celebrated with bonfires and singing. Republic Day Parade (**26th**), Rajpath. A spectacular fly-past and military march-past, with colourful pageants and tableaux from every state, dances and music. Tickets through travel agents and most hotels, approximately Rs 100. You can see the full dress preview free, usually 2 days before (see under Secretariats); week-long celebrations during which government buildings are illuminated. Beating the Retreat (**29th**), Vijay Chowk, a stirring display by the armed forces' bands marks the end of the Republic Day celebrations. Martyr's Day (**30th**),

marks Mahatma Gandhi's death anniversary; devotional *bhajans* and Guard of Honour at Raj Ghat. Shankarlal Sangeet Sammelan (movable), North Indian music festival. Kite Flying Festival on Makar Sankranti above Palika Bazar, Connaught Pl.

February

Vasant Panchami (**2nd**), celebrates the first day of spring. The Mughal Gardens are opened to the public for a month. Delhi Flower Show, Purana Qila. Thyagaraja Festival, South Indian music and dance, Vaikunthnath Temple, opposite J Nehru University.

March

Basant Ritu Sammelan, North Indian music festival.

April

Amir Khusrau's Birth Anniversary, a fair in Nizamuddin celebrates this with prayers and *qawwali* singing.

May

Buddha Jayanti, the **first full moon night** in May marks the birth of the Buddha and prayer meetings are held at Ladakh Buddha Vihara, Ring Rd and Buddha Vihara, Mandir Marg.

August

Janmashtami celebrates the birth of the Hindu god Krishna. Special *puja*, Lakshmi Narayan Mandir. **Independence Day (15th),** impressive flag hoisting ceremony and Prime Ministerial address at the Red Fort. **Vishnu Digambar Sammelan,** North Indian music and dance festival.

October

Gandhi Jayanti (**2nd**), Mahatma Gandhi's birthday; devotional singing at Raj Ghat.

Dasara, with over 200 Ramlila performances all over the city recounting the Ramayana story (see introduction on Hinduism, page 1324). **The Ramlila Ballet** at Delhi Gate (south of Red Fort) and Ramlila Ground, is performed for a month and is most spectacular. Huge effigies of Ravana are burnt on the **9th night**; noisy and flamboyant. **National Drama Festival,** Shri Ram Centre. **Diwali,** the festival of lights; lighting of earthen lamps, candles and firework displays. **National Drama Festival,** Rabindra Bhavan.

December

Christmas (25th). Special Christmas Eve entertainments at all major hotels and restaurants; midnight mass and services at all churches. **Ayyappa Temple Festival,** Ayyappa Swami Temple, Ramakrishnapuram; South Indian music. **New Year's Eve (31st),** celebrated in most hotels and restaurants offering special food and entertainment. Muslim festivals of **Ramadan, Id-ul-Fitr, Id-ul-Zuha** and **Muharram** celebrated according to lunar calendar (see page 1340).

○ Shopping

Weekly 'Free Ads' (Rs 5, Thu) lists 2nd-hand cameras, binoculars, etc (T3737777 to place ad free, 24 hrs).

Shops generally open from 1000-1930 (Winter 1000-1900). Food stores, chemists stay open later. Most shopping areas are closed on **Sun**. Exceptions include: **Mon** closing at Defence Colony, INA, Jangpura, Karol Bagh, Lajpat Nagar, Nizamuddin, Sarojini Nagar, South Extension; **Tue** closing at Aurobindo Pl, Greater Kailash (GK), Green Park, Hauz Khas, RK Puram, Safdarjang, Vasant Vihar, Yusuf Sarai Markets. Banks tend to follow the same pattern.

Art

Galleries exhibiting contemporary art are listed in *Delhi Diary*, eg:
Delhi Art Gallery, Hauz Khas Village, newly expanded, good mid-range contemporary art. **Espace,** 16 Community Centre, New Friends Colony, T6830499, group and solo shows; artists from all over India.

Books

Many booksellers will pack and post books abroad but they may need to confirm the cost of postage, so a return visit may be necessary.

Connaught Place *p91, map p110*
Bookworm, B-29. Wide selection, including art, Indology, fiction.
Central News Agency, P 23/90. Carries national and foreign newspapers and journals.
ED Galgotia, 17B. Highly recommended.
Jain's Bookshop C-Block, the government book agency.
New Book Depot, 18B. Highly recommended.
Oxford Book and Stationery, Scindia House. Wide selection, including art, Indology, fiction.
People Tree, 8 Regal Building, Parliament St. Ecology oriented.

Janpath has a line of small bookshops.
Jacksons, 5106, Main Bazar, opposite
Medikos Opticians, Paharganj, T3520801.
Selection in many languages.
Manohar, 4753/23 Ansar Rd, Daryaganj, Old
Delhi. A real treasure trove for books on
South Asia and India in particular, published
worldwide, most helpful and knowledgeable
staff. Highly recommended.
Motilal Banarsidass, Nai Sarak, Chandni
Chowk. Have books on Indology.
Munshiram Manoharlal, Nai Sarak, Chandni
Chowk. Have books on Indology.

Khan Market
Bahri & Sons, opposite Main Gate. Has a
wide choice.
The Bookshop, has a wide choice (also at
Jor Bagh Market).
MI, 15a. Has a wide choice.

South extensions
Crossword, Ebony, 2nd Floor, D-4, Part 2, very
good selection in modern, spacious shop.
Timeless, 46 The Housing Society, 3rd floor
and basement, Part 1, full of coffee tables, art
books and novels.

Hotel booksellers often carry a good
selection of imported books about India,
though some charge inflated prices. Among
those with specialist academic and art books
focusing on India are: **Jainson's**, *Janpath
Hotel*; **Krishan**, *Claridges*; **Khazana**, *Taj Mahal*
and *Taj Palace hotels* (0900-2000; daily).

Antiquarian/second-hand books
Prabhu & Sons, Hauz Khas Village, well-
hidden on 1st floor balcony down side street.
Vintage, next door.

Clothing

For **inexpensive** (Western and Indian)
clothes, try shops along Janpath and
between Sansad Marg and Janpath; you can
bargain down 50%.
Main Bazar, Paharganj, often passes off very
poor quality items.
Palika Bazar, Connaught Circus,
underground, a/c, can be a hassle but has
decent salwar kameez, leather jackets and
trousers (bargain very hard).

Top quality clothes in the latest
Western styles and fashionable fabrics are
almost unobtainable.
Archana, Gt Kailash I has several boutiques.
Fab India, 14N-Gt Kailash I (4 outlets in N
Block and also in Vasant Kunj). Excellent
shirts, Nehru jackets, *salwar kameez*, linen,
furnishing fabrics and now furniture.
The Shop, Regal Building, Connaught Pl.
Modest selection.
Hauz Khas Village and **Sunder Nagar Market**
have some designer wear.

For Indian style, try shops in Janpath:
Khadi shop, near the Regal building. Also try
Chandni Chowk shops. Regional styles at the
state emporia on Baba Kharak Singh Marg.
Sari shops abound.
Central Cottage Industries Emporium,
good selection, also sells fabrics.

Tailoring at small shops charge around
Rs 70-100 to copy a dress or shirt; trousers Rs
100-150. Nearly all big hotels have
up-market boutiques and also fabric/tailor's
shops (some may allow fabric purchased
elsewhere); allow 24 hrs for stitching.
Delhi Cloth House, fabric.
Grover, fabric.
Khan Market, several tailors and cloth stores.
Shankar Market near Connaught Pl, has
good suiting, corduroys, denim etc, and will
suggest tailors.

Food

For **groceries** try shops along Janpath,
Gt Kailash Market (Pt I-M), Jorbagh and
Khan Markets.
Assam, excellent Indian teas.
Bhim Sen's, Bengali Market (end of Tansen
Marg near Connaught Pl). Some of the best,
freshest (hence safest) Indian sweets sold here.
Central Cottage Industries Emporium,
Janpath. Excellent Indian teas.
Darjeeling Tea Bureau, Kaka Nagar Market
(opposite Delhi Golf Club), T4622442,
F6843737, nathmulls@goldentipstea.com.
Charming, reliable and good selection.
Highly recommended.
Evergreen, Green Park. Fresh *jelabies*.
Khari Baoli, Chandni Chowk, lined with
colourful shops. Spices and dried fruit etc.
Modern Bazar, Vasant Vihar Market. Cold
meats, cheeses, yoghurts, tea.

Steak House, Jorbagh Market. Cold meats, cheeses, yoghurts.
Super Bazar, Outer Circle, Connaught Circus. Groceries.
Tea City outlets are widely advertised.
W Bengal Emporia, excellent Indian teas.

Handicrafts

Carpets
Carpets can be found in shops in most top hotels and a number round Connaught Pl, not necessarily fixed-price. If you are visiting Agra, check out the prices here first.

Earthenware
Unglazed earthenware *khumba matkas* (water pots) are sold round New Delhi Rly Station (workshops behind the main road).

Emporia
Government run, fixed price emporia are often dull with reluctant sales staff, but give a newcomer an idea of fair prices. Most open 1000-1800 (close for lunch, 1330-1400).
Central Cottage Industries Emporium, corner of Janpath and Tolstoy Marg, offers hassle-free shopping, exchange counter (spend at least 50% of amount to be cashed, take bills to till and use travellers' cheques/ credit card to pay and get exchange), gift wrapping, will pack and post overseas; the best one if you are short of time.
Dilli Haat opposite INA Market, is a well-designed open-air complex with rows of brick alcoves for craft stalls from different states, changed periodically; local craftsmen's outlets (bargaining possible), occasional fairs (tribal art, textiles etc). (Also good regional food - hygienic, safe 'street food'!) Very pleasant, quiet, clean (no smoking) and uncrowded, no hassle. Entry Rs 10, open 1000-2230.
Khadi Gramodyog Bhawan, Regal Building, for inexpensive homespun cotton *kurta pajama* (loose shirt and trousers), cotton/silk waistcoats, fabrics and Jaipuri paintings.
Several state emporia are along Baba Kharak Singh Marg; convenient, but prices are higher than in the states locally.
Among them **W Bengal** (tea), **Delhi** (silk), **Bihar** (excellent Madhubani paintings, gems), **Gujarat** (good quilts, bedspreads), **Kashmir** (papier-mâché, shawls, carpets, wood carving), **Maharashtra** (bedspreads), **Assam** (blankets,

silk, tea), **Rajasthan** (printed cotton, miniature paintings, jewellery), **Tripura** (wood sculptures, cane work), **Orissa** (silk *ikat*, stoneware, silver filigree), **UP**, **Andhra Pradesh** (dolls, printed fabric, cotton *ikat*), **Kerala** (sandalwood), **MP**.
Small stalls along Janpath can be fun to explore but bargain hard.
Khazana, *Taj Mahal* and *Taj Palace hotels* (0900-2000; daily) is high class.
Santushti, Chanakyapuri, opposite *Hotel Samrat* has attractive a/c units in a garden setting, hassle free. Shops sell good quality clothes, crafts, linen, saris, silver etc (1000-1800, except Sun, some close for lunch), **Basil and Thyme** serves trendy western snacks (busy 1300-1400); **Anokhi**, near the entrance, has good household gifts and clothes; **IK** sells high quality silver gifts, jewellery and paintings.
See also **Craft Village**, page 110, and **Dilli Haat**, above.

Handmade paper
Handpaper World, 78 Scindia House, Janpath.
Khadi Gramudyog, Connaught Pl.

Jewellery
Traditional silver and goldsmiths in Dariba Kalan, off Chandni Chowk (north of Jama Masjid). Cheap bangles and along Janpath; also at Hanuman Mandir, Gt Kailash I, N-Block, where you can get *henna* painted on the hand.
Jewel Mine, 12A Palika Bazar, has silver, beads and semi-precious stones, fair prices, pleasant.
Sundar Nagar market (see below).

Leather
Cheap sandals from Janpath (Rs 100).
Baluja, Connaught Pl. Shoes.
Bata, Connaught Pl. Shoes and bags.
Bharat, Connaught Pl, opposite *Nirula's*.
Central Cottage Industries Emporium, Janpath.
Hidesign, G49, Connaught Pl.
Khan Market, leather goods and shoes.
South Extension, leather goods and shoes.

Marble
For inlay work, Agra is the place (some are alabaster or soapstone, not marble).

Markets and shopping centres

See also Handicrafts and Emporia above.
Beware of pick pockets.

Ansal Plaza, HUDCO, Khelgaon Marg (S of South Extension) is Delhi's first European style shopping mall. Very smart, lots of chains.
Basant Lok, Vasant Vihar, has a few up-market shops attracting the young.
Green Park has a handy supermarket and a South Indian *Woodlands* restaurant.
Hauz Khas village authentic, old village houses converted into designer shops selling handicrafts, ceramics, antiques and furniture in addition to luxury wear. Many shops are expensive, but some are good value. You will also find art galleries and restaurants.
Jorbagh, Gt Kailash Pt I-M, Western travellers hankering for the familiar, and prepared to pay the price, will find a good range of eatables and toiletries.
Khan Market, good for book, food, clothes.
Main Bazar, Paharganj. Western travellers hankering for the familiar, and prepared to pay the price, will find a good range of eatables and toiletries.
Santushti, Chanakyapuri (see Handicrafts).
Sarojini Nagar sells daily necessities as well as cheap fabric and clothing.
South Extension, is good for clothes, shoes, jewellery, music etc.
Sunder Nagar has a few shops selling Indian handicrafts and jewellery (precious and semi-precious); some quite original.
Tibetan Market stalls along Janpath have plenty of curios - most are new but rapidly aged to look authentic.

Maps

Eicher Delhi map and City Guide are excellent.
The Survey of India Map in Janpath Lane, off Janpath, has a selection (cities, areas, states), some out-of-date. Typical government office! See page 52. Open 1000-1700.

Music

Berco's Melody House, E-8, Connaught Pl, good value Cds.
Godin, 1 Regal Building, for instruments (sitar, tabla etc).

Photography

Delhi Photo Co, 78 Janpath. 24-hr service, good quality prints, sometimes carelessly cut.
Kodak, A-22 Janpath.
Kinsey Bros, A-2 Connaught Pl. Good quality, good value, next day service.
Quick Colour Lab, Kanishka Shopping Plaza.
Radiant, B-45 Connaught Circus (near Plaza Cinema). Very good service and quality.
Rama Color, Khan Market. Modern, Western style, photos in 24 hrs.

▲ Activities and tours

Bowling

The **Qutab Hotel** has a 4-lane semi-automatic bowling alley, T6521010.

Cricket

Matches at Kotla stadium, Rs 300 (no food/drink, cameras, cigarettes/matches, or knives).

Golf

Delhi Golf Club, Dr Zakir Hussein Marg, T4362768. 18 and 9-hole courses in a sanctuary attracting over 300 species of birds. Open 0500-1900. Clubs for hire.
NOIDA Golf Club, Sector 38, T91572753, 18-hole. Open 0500-1900, closed Tue.

Riding

Delhi Riding Club, Safdarjang Rd, T3011891. Phone the day before. Rides 0630-0930, 1430-1900.

Swimming

Many hotels empty their pools over the winter (Dec-Feb). The *Maurya Sheraton's* is solar heated and open all year. When open, the *Taj Mahal, Le Meridien, Maurya, Ashok* and *Imperial* charge non-residents around Rs 500, *Claridges* and *YWCA Tourist Hostel* charge less.
NMDC Pools, at Nehru Park near *Hotel Ashok*. Public pool.

Tennis

Delhi Lawn Tennis Association, Africa Ave, T6515899.

Tour operators

www.fhrai.com. Avoid **Visit India Tours**.
There are agents in all the major hotels. Many are around Connaught Circus, Paharganj, Rajendra Place and Nehru Place; some send a rep to your hotel to discuss. Most belong to special associations (IATA, PATA, TAAI) which you can approach with complaints if you are dissatisfied. We list some of the best. Some will get air and rail tickets/reservations for about Rs 50 eg **Outbound**, **Peak Adventures**, **Wanderlust**, **Y's**. American Express, A-Block, Connaught Pl, T3324119. Reliable, efficient, particularly for cardholders.
Cox and Kings, H Block, Connaught Circus, T3736032, F3312849.
Creative Travel, 27-30 Creative Plaza, Nanak Pura, Moti Bagh, T4679192, F6889764, www.travel2india.com. Efficient, reliable, helpful, good reps. Recommended.
Highland, N-29 Middle Circle, Connaught Pl, T3318236, F3329121, highlandtravels@usa.net. Friendly, competent, reasonably priced.
Ibex, G66 East of Kailash, T6912641, F6846403, www.Ibexexpeditions.com. Adventure tours.
International Trade Towers, Nehru Pl, T6423035.
Mahendra Travels, 2 Scindia House, Janpath, T3737861, F3737862, Friendly, reliable, professional.
Outbound, 216-A/11 Gautam Nagar, 3rd floor, T6521308, F6522617, outbound@vsnl.com. Air/train bookings, reliable.
Oriental Travels, *Marina Hotel,* Connaught Pl, New Delhi 110001, T3327214, F332 7127 Tours, car rentals, ticketing, etc.
Paradise Holidays, 20-B Basant Lok, Community centre, Vasant Vihar, T6145116, F614 5112, www.paradiseholidays.com.in. Experienced, professional, reliable drivers and cars, ticketing. Peak Adventure, T-305, DAV Complex, DDA Shopping Complex, Mayur Vihar Phase-1, T2711284, F2711292, peakadv@nde.vsnl.net.in. Treks, special interest, good cars and guides. Recommended.
Potala Tours & Travels, 101 Antriksh Bhavan, 22 K Ghandi Marg, T3722552, F3713309, www.potatatours.com. Excellent

staff, car tours, ticketing, etc. Highly recommended for not just Tibetan India.
Razdan Holidays, 308 Magnum House No 1, Karampura Commercial Complex, T5156460, F5459190, www.razdanholidays.com.
Royal Expeditions, R-184, Gt Kailash I, T6238545, F6475954, www.royal expeditions.com. 'Unique experience' in North India. STIC, 36 Janpath, T3320239. Student specialists.
Sita Inbound, 4 Malcha Marg Shopping Centre, Diplomatic Enclave, New Delhi 110 021, www.sitaindia.com. Tours throughout India.
Thomas Cook, *Hotel Imperial,* Janpath, T3342171; 85A Panchkuin Marg, T3747404. *Indebo*, 116-117 Aurobindo Pl, Hauz Klas, New Delhi 110016, T6861722, F6862122, indebo.india@vsnl.com. Specialise in individual and group tours.
Tiger Camp, B-9, Sector 27, Noida 201, T9154874, F91524878. Wildlife, angling, elephant and jeep safaris.
Travel Corp of India, C35 Connaught Circus, T3315181, F3316705.
Wanderlust, M51/52 Palika Bhawan, opposite *Hyatt Regency*, T4102180, F6885188, www.wanderlustindia.com. Adventure, forts and palaces, efficient.
Welcome Travels, 209 Skipper Corner, 88 Nehru Pl, T6424638, F6443037, welcometravel @vsnl.com. Recommended for trekking in Ladakh and Garwhal. See also page 21.
Y's, YMCA Tourist Hostel, Jaisingh Rd, T3361915. Discounted tickets.

Tours

Guided sightseeing tours can be arranged through approved travel agents and tour operators. Many small agents, eg opposite New Delhi Rly Station, seemingly offer unusual itineraries, but their standards can't be guaranteed and their rates are not significantly lower. **India Tourism Development Corporation** (ITDC) and **Delhi Tourism** both run city sightseeing tours. Combining Old and New Delhi tours on the same day can be very tiring. A/c coaches are particularly recommended during the summer months. The price includes transport and guide services, but all are whistle-stop tours. Check whether the recently raised entrance fees to many sights are still included in the price of the tour. A group of 3 or 4 people could consider hiring a car and doing the tour at their own pace. Another alternative is to hire an auto-rickshaw for the day (around Rs 200). It will entail visiting gift shops for the driver to get a commission, but you don't have to buy. **Chor Bizarre**, *Hotel Broadway*, T3273821 (see page 118) offer special walking tours of Old Delhi, with good lunch, 0930-1330, 1300-1630, Rs 350 each, Rs 400 for both.

For **approved tourist guides** contact India Tourist Office and travel agents. Rates: Delhi only, half day Rs 90, full day Rs 160.

Many companies offer coach tours to **Agra** (eg ITDC, from L1 Connaught Circus, 0630-2200 except Fri, Rs 600, a/c coach). However, travelling by road is slow and uncomfortable; by car, allow at least four hours each way. Train is a better option; take either the *Shatabdi*, or *Taj Express*.

Delhi Tourism Tours
Check time, T3314229. Book day in advance.
Departure point: Delhi Tourism, Bombay Life Building, N-Block, Connaught Pl.
New Delhi Tour (0800-1400): Jantar Mantar, Qutb Minar, Lakshmi Narayan Temple, Safdarjang's Tomb, Diplomatic Enclave, India Gate.
Old Delhi Tour (1400-1700): Jama Masjid, Red Fort, Shanit Vana, Raj Ghat, Kotla Firoz Shah.
Evening Tour (1800-2200): Lakshmi Narayan Temple (evening prayer), India Gate, Purana Qila, son et lumière (Red Fort), Jama Masjid (dinner at a Mughlai restaurant). Both Rs 150.
Museum Tour (Sun only, check time): Air Force, Rail and Transport, and National Museums, Indira Gandhi Memorial, Nehru Planetarium, Museum of Natural History and Dolls Museum.

ITDC Tours
Guides are generally good but tours are rushed, T3320331. Tickets can be booked from *Hotel Indraprastha*, T3344511.
New Delhi Tour departs from L-1 Connaught Circus and *Hotel Indraprastha* (0800-1330), Rs 125 (a/c coach): Jantar Mantar, Lakshmi Narayan Temple, India Gate, Nehru Pavilion, Pragati Maidan (closed Monday), Humayun's Tomb, Qutb Minar.
Old Delhi Tour: departs from *Hotel Indraprastha*. (1400-1700), Rs 100: Kotla Firoz Shah, Raj Ghat, Shantivana, Jama Masjid and Red Fort.

Yoga and meditation

Shri Aurobindo Ashram, Aurobindo Marg near IIT, T6567863.
Sivananda Yoga Centre, 41 Kailash Colony, T6480869.
Tushita Mahayana Meditation Centre, 9 Padmini Enclave, Hauz Khas, T6513400.

⊖ Transport

Air

International flights arrive at the **Indira Gandhi International Terminal**. Enquiries T5622011; pre-recorded arrivals and departures, T144/5; reservations, T146. Money changing; Thomas Cook accepts only their own Tcs. Watch out for inflated prices for food and drink.

The **Palam Domestic Terminal**; enquiries T3295121; pre-recorded arrivals and departures, T142/3, private airlines, T149, **Indian Airlines** reservations, T141.

Fog in winter can cause major **delays** with early morning departures, which sets up a chain reaction and affects many subsequent flights in North India. It is best to phone before leaving for the airport.

Delhi has daily connections (many direct) with the following domestic destinations. The number of flights, if more than 1, is shown in brackets.

Airlines: IC = Indian Airlines, CD Alliance, JA Jagson, S2 Sahara, 9W Jet Air, AI Air India, BG Bangladesh Biman, RA Royal Nepal, TBA Trans Bharat Aviation.

Daily flights: **Agra** (IC); **Ahmadabad** (IC 2, 9W); **Bagdogra** (for Darjeeling) (9W); **Bangalore** (IC 2, 9W); **Bhopal** (IC 2); **Bhubaneshwar**; **Kolkata** (IC 2, 9W); **Chandigarh** (9W); **Chennai (Madras)** (IC 2, 9W); **Cochin** (CD, IC, S2); **Goa** (CD, IC, S2);

Guwahati (IC, 9W); **Hyderabad** (IC 2, S2, 9W); **Jaipur** (9W); **Jammu** (IC, 9W), **Kathmandu** (IC, RA); **Khajuraho** (IC, 9W); **Kullu** (JA, TBA); **Lucknow** (S2, 9W); **Mumbai (Bombay)** (CD, IC 9, 9W 8, S2 3, AI); **Nagpur** (IC); **Patna** (IC); **Pune** (IC, 9W); **Raipur** (CD); **Rajkot**; **Ranchi** (IC); **Srinagar** (CD, 9W); **Trivandrum** (IC, 9W); **Udaipur** (IC, 9W); **Vadodara** (CD); **Varanasi** (IC, S2, 9W).

Non-daily flights: Amritsar (IC 3, AI 2); **Aurangabad** (IC 4); **Bagdogra** (for Darjiling) (IC 3, 9W 3); **Chandigarh** (IC, CD, JA); **Chennai (Madras)** (AI 3); **Dhaka** (BG 2); **Dibrugarh** (S2 3); **Guwahati** (IC 2, S2 2); **Gwalior** (CD 3, IC 4); **Indore** (CD 6, IC 6, 9W 6); **Imphal** (IC 2); **Jaipur** (CD 4, IC 8); **Jaisalmer** (CD, JA 3); **Jodhpur** (CD 3, JA 2); **Leh** (CD 4, CD 7); **Lucknow** (CD 3, IC 5); **Paro** (KP 2); **Shimla** (JA 3); **Srinagar** (IC 6); **Udaipur** (CD 6).

Transport to and from the airport
Bus: run by Ex-Servicemen's Airlink Transport Service (EATS) , F Block Connaught Pl, T3316530, **Delhi Transport Corp (DTC)** and Airports Authority of India (AAI) from the 2 terminals go to Connaught Place, New Delhi Railway Station and ISBT (Kashmir Gate) via some hotels. One leaves from IA office, Connaught Place, goes to the Domestic and then the International terminal, 0400, 0530, 0730, 1000, 1400, 1530, 1800, 1900, 2200, 2330; Rs 50; Rs 10 luggage. There is a booth just outside 'Arrivals' at the International and Domestic terminals. A bus is a safe, economical option, particularly for the first-time visitor on a budget. At night, take a pre-paid taxi to a pre-booked hotel (see below). There is a Travellers' Lounge above the Arrival Hall, Rs 25 per seat (very noisy TV). **Free shuttle** between the 2 terminals every 30 mins during the day. Some hotel buses leave from the Domestic terminal. **Bus 780** runs between the airport and New Delhi Railway station.

Taxi: the International and Domestic terminals have **pre-paid taxi** counters outside the baggage hall (3 price categories) which ensure that you pay the right amount (give your name, exact destination and number of all items of luggage). Most expensive are white 'DLZ' **limousines** and then white 'DLY' **luxury taxis**. Cheapest are 'DLT' **ordinary Delhi taxis** (black with yellow top Ambassador/Fiat cars, often very old). 'DLY'

charge 3 times the DLT price, see page 37. A 'Welcome' desk by the baggage reclamation offers **expensive** taxis only. Take your receipt to the ticket counter outside to find your taxi and give it to the driver when you reach the destination; you don't need to tip (although they will ask!). From the International terminal **DLT taxis** charge about Rs 200 for the town-centre (Connaught Place area); night charges, double, 2300-0500. Rates from the Domestic terminal are slightly lower.

The Government **Tourist Information** desk is usually very helpful and efficient. They will book a hotel but not in the 'budget' category. **Indian Railways Counter**, beyond pre-paid taxi kiosks. Helpful computerized booking; easier and quicker than at a station.

Auto-rickshaw

Local
Widely available at about half the cost of taxis (Rs 4 per km). Normal capacity for foreigners is 2 people! (3rd person extra); insist on using the metre or agree fare in advance. Expect to pay Rs 10 for the shortest journeys. Pre-paid auto kiosks at Palika Bazar and New Delhi station give you an idea of a fair charge. Allow Rs 50 for 2 hrs' sight-seeing/shopping. It is best to walk away from tourist centres to look for an auto. When using the meter, you pay 2½ times the reading plus Rs 3; another 100% from 2300 to 0500. Ask to see tariff card and follow a map. **Cycle-rickshaws** and **tongas** (horse drawn traps) are available in the Old City. Be prepared to bargain, remembering that it should be cheaper than motorized transport, eg New Delhi station to Jama Masjid Rs 15-20. They are not allowed into Connaught Place.

Bicycle

Cycle hire
Shops are near Minto Bridge, off Connaught Place, on Mohan Singh Place near *Rivoli* cinema and in Paharganj; about Rs 5 per hour to Rs 25 per day plus a refundable deposit.

Bus

Local
The city bus service run by the **Delhi Transport Corporation (DTC)** connects all important points in the city. There are over

300 routes. Information is available at DTC assistance booths and at all major bus stops. Don't be afraid to ask conductors or fellow passengers. Buses are often hopelessly overcrowded so only use at off-peak.

Directional route classification: 1st digit of bus route number (1-9) determines the direction in which it travels and also indicates the terminal depot: **1** Azadpur (northwest); **2** Kashmir Gate (northeast); **3** ITO (Income Tax Office) and Indraprastha (Central); **4** Lajpat Nagar (southeast); **5** All-India Medical School (south); **6** Sarojini Nagar (southwest); **7**, **8**, **9** Dhaula Khan, Raja Garden and Punjabi Bagh respectively (west).

Night services: a skeletal service 2300-0130. These can also take extremely roundabout routes. Tickets are Rs 1, 2 and 3. DTC Head Office, T3315085. Local enquiries T3319847. ISBT Office T2518836.

Private buses and mini buses: also operate on DTC routes. Tickets are Rs 1-7.

Long distance
Delhi is linked to most major centres in North India. Services are provided by Delhi Transport Corp (DTC) and State Roadways of neighbouring states from various **Inter-State Bus Termini (ISBT)**; these have bus services between them. Allow at least 30 mins for buying a ticket and finding the right bus.

Kashmir Gate, T2968709, has a restaurant, left luggage (Rs 5 per day), bank (1000-1400 Mon-Fri; 1000-1200 Sat), Post Office (0800-1700 Mon-Sat) and telephones (includes International calls). DTC, T2968836. For Manali: Himachal Roadways T2966725 (or Himachal Tourism which operate from various pick-up points), are better maintained than unregistered private buses.

Ajmeri Gate: UP Roadways, T2968709; to Almora (5 hrs), Dehradun, Haridwar, Mussoorie.

Kingsway Camp: Haryana Roadways, T2961262; daily to Agra (5-6 hrs, Rs 80, quicker by rail), Chandigarh (5 hrs), Jaipur (Rs 150, 6½ hrs), Mathura etc.

Rajpur Rd: Himachal Roadways, T2966725; twice daily to Dharamshala (12 hrs), Manali (15 hrs), Shimla (10 hrs) etc. Jammu and Kashmir RTC, *Hotel Kanishka*, T3324511; to Jammu; *Yatri Niwas Hotel* to Srinagar. Punjab Roadways, T2967842, to Amritsar, Chandigarh, Jammu, Pathankot. **Sarai Kale Khan Ring Rd** (near Nizamuddin Rly

station): Terminal, T4638092. (Auto-rickshaws to Paharganj, Rs 50.) **Rajasthan Roadways**, T2961246, for Agra, 5-6 hrs (quicker by rail), Rs 58; via Mathura and Vrindavan, Ajmer, Alwar, Bharatpur (5 hrs), Bikaner (11 hrs), Gwalior, Jodhpur, Pushkar (10 hrs), Udaipur etc. **Anand Vihar**, Yamuna Bundh Rd, T2152431: **UP Roadways**, T2149089, to Dehradun (259 km, 6 hrs via Roorkee); Haridwar (5 hrs), Gorakhpur, Kanpur, Jhansi, Lucknow, Nainital, Varanasi. From **Bikaner House**, Pandara Rd (south of India Gate), T3383469; for several 'Deluxe' buses to Jaipur, 6 hrs, Rs 230 (a/c); ask for 'direct' bus (some buses stop at Amber for a tour of the fort). To Udaipur (via Ajmer), 1900; to Jodhpur (2120, 2200).

To Nepal Direct private buses run to Kathmandu, though the 36 hr journey is quite exhausting. A much shorter route to Nepal is to the Indian border town of **Banbassa** (see page 136) via Tanakpur and crossing to the western Nepal border town of Mahendranagar which has the Sukla Phanta Wildlife Reserve nearby. The onward journey to Kathmandu is about 20 hrs (the first section is over the very bumpy Mahindra Highway). It is best done in shorter stages via Royal Bardia National Park (5 hrs), or Nepalganj which has buses to Kathmandu and Pokhara (14 hrs). **UP Roadways** buses for Banbassa leave daily around 0730 from the **Tis-Hazari** Bus terminal and take under 8 hrs (but check details carefully).

To Pakistan A direct luxury 'Friendship' bus to Lahore runs on Tue, Wed, Sat and Sun, departing at 0600 from Ambedkar Stadium terminal, Old Delhi (reserve ahead, Rs 800, 14 hrs), for Indians with valid visas and relations in Pakistan, and for Pakistanis.

Car

All road journeys in India are slow. Main roads out of Delhi are very heavily congested. Best time to leave is very early morning.

Delhi is well connected by road with major cities: by **NH2** to **Agra** (200 km), **Ajmer** (399 km); by **NH1** to **Amritsar** (446 km), **Bhopal** (741 km), **Chandigarh** (249 km), **Gwalior** (319 km); by **NH8** to **Jaipur** (261 km), **Jammu** (586 km), **Jodhpur** (604 km), **Kanpur** (490 km), **Kota** (505 km); by **NH24** to **Lucknow** (569 km), **Pathankot** (478 km), **Shimla** (368 km), **Srinagar** (876 km), **Udaipur** (635 km) and **Varanasi** (765 km).

Car hire

An excellent way of getting about town either for sightseeing or if you have several journeys to make during the day.

Full day local use with driver (non a/c) is about Rs 700-800, 80 km/8 hrs, driver overnight *bata* Rs 150 per day; self-drive 24 hrs/150 km Rs 1,200. Airport to city centre Rs 400-500. To Jaipur, about Rs 3,000; return Rs 5,400. The Tourist Office, 88 Janpath, has a list of approved agents.

Cozy Travels, N1 BMC House, Middle Circle, Connaught Place, T3311593, F37113869, cozytravels@vsnl.net.com, for Ambassador or similar, Rs 650 non-a/c, Rs 850 a/c.

Ex-Soldiers Tourist Taxis, opposite 16 Dr Rajendra Prasad Marg.

Metropole Tourist Service, 244 Defence Flyover Market, T4312212, F4311819, metropole@vsnl.com, car/jeep (US$30-40 per day), reliable and recommended.

Mohindra Tourist Taxis, corner of Poorvi/Paschimi Margs, Vasant Vihar, T6143188, "excellent service, safe driving".

Western Court Tourist Taxis, 36 Janpath, outside *Hotel Imperial*, T3321236. Helpful.

International companies charge higher prices but provide dependable service:

Budget, 78/3 Janpath, T3715657, F3739182; G3 Arunachal Building, Barakhamba Rd, T3318600; 82 Nehru Pl, T6452634.

Europcar, 14 Basant Lok, Vasant Vihar, T6140373, F6145383; M-3 Connaught Circus, T6862248.

Hertz, Barakhamba Rd, T3318695; GF29 Ansal Chamber, Bhikaji Cama Pl, T6197188, F6197206.

Motorcycle

Karol Bagh has specialist shops. Avoid **Madaan Motors**, Karol Bagh.

Chawla Motorcycles, 1770, Shri Kissan Dass Marg, Naiwali Gali, is very reliable, trustworthy, highly recommended for restoring classic bikes.

Ess Aar Motors, Jhandewalan Extn, west of Paharganj. Recommended for buying Enfields, very helpful.

Inder Motors, 1744 Hari Singh Nalwa Gali, Abdul Aziz Rd, T5725879.

Nanna Motors, 112 Press Rd (east of Connaught Circus), T3351769. Recommended for buying Enfields, very helpful.

Environment friendly taxis and autos with a green stripe run on compressed natural gas.

Yellow-top taxis: are easily available at taxi stands or you can hail one on the road. Meter: multiply the final reading by 6 and add Rs 3.50 (eg Rs 4 will be Rs 27.50). You can ask for the conversion card. Add 25% night charge (2300-0500) plus 50p for each piece of heavy luggage (over 20 kg). These extras apply to auto-rickshaws as well. For complaints, ring special police cell, T3737300.

Private: **1629**. Ring for a taxi, anywhere in Delhi. Reliable but expensive, Rs 15 per km.

Train

'Trains at a glance' (Rs 25) lists important trains across India.

Delhi Tourism, Connaught Circus issues tickets on the spot

Local

The Delhi suburban railway is neither very popular nor convenient. A ring route operates 3 times a day - 0755, 1625, 1725, starting from Hazrat Nizamuddin station.

Long distance

New Delhi Railway Station and **Hazrat Nizamuddin Station** (just north, and 5 km southeast of Connaught Place, respectively) connect Delhi with most major destinations. The latter has many important south-bound trains. **Old Delhi (Main) Station**, 6 km north of the centre, has broad and metre gauge trains. **Delhi Sarai Rohilla**, serves Rajasthan.

Enquiries T131, T3366177. **Waiting Rooms**, and **Rest Rooms**, are for those 'in transit' (tickets are likely to be checked). Authorized **porters** (*coolies*), wear red shirts and white *dhotis;* the number on the brass badge identifies each so it is best to make a note of it, and agree the charge, before engaging one. For **left luggage**, you need a secure lock and chain.

Reservations T1330 or 3348686, Old Delhi T3975357, though generally for **Northern Railway only** (not all-India). Allow time (1-2 hrs) and be prepared to be very patient as it can be a nightmare, but don't be tempted to go to an unauthorized agent (see below).The Central Booking Office has counters for paying by

⁞ Tricksters

Beware of travel agents' touts at New Delhi Rly Station, offering 'adventure tours' and other services. These are often over-priced and poor.

Another ploy: taxis call at a 'Tourist Office' opposite the station to "confirm your pre-booked hotel reservation" only to report that "the hotel is full". To reserve a hotel make your own phone call. Always insist on being taken direct to a hotel of your choice. The same 'Tourist Office' will tell you trains are full (when they are not) and offer private taxis to Jaipur or Agra at US$75 each, which is not good value.

credit cards (although these cannot be used for booking tickets on the tourist quota). **Computerized reservation offices** (in separate building in Connaught Circus); 0745-2100, Sun 0745-1400; fee Rs 20. May be quicker than ITB, but no advice offered. The Sarojini Nagar office is quick, hassle free (especially the credit card counter) and is well worth the detour. Alternatively, you can use a recommended travel agent for tickets/reservations and pay Rs 30-50 fee.

At **New Delhi Station**: International Tourist Bureau (ITB), 1st Floor, Main Building, T3734164, F3343050, for foreigners, Mon-Fri 0930-1630; Sat 0930-1430; efficient and helpful if slow. You need your passport and visa; pay in US$, or rupees (with an encashment certificate). Those with **Indrail passes**, should confirm bookings. There is also a counter for foreigners and NRIs at Delhi Tourism, N-36 Connaught Pl, 1000-1700, Mon-Sat. The *Airport* counter (when open) is quick and efficient for air tickets and reservations. **Exchange**: Thomas Cook, near Platform 12, New Delhi Station, by VIP Parking, Ajmeri Gate, open 24 hrs. The **pre-paid taxi** and **auto-rickshaw** kiosks are next to the taxi rank as you come out of the station. Queue at the appropriate window, give your name, exact destination (hotel/street), number of pieces of luggage over 20 kg; collect your slip on payment and go to the head of the taxi/auto-rickshaw rank (you are not supposed to hire one 'privately'). Hand the slip to the driver at your destination; you don't need to tip. An auto to Connaught Place costs around Rs 15, Old Delhi Station Rs 25. Rickshaw drivers/touts may say the ITB is closed/has moved and then offer fake Rail Passes, or falsely insist that you need a hotel reservation slip before leaving the station; you don't. Some take you to a travel agent, others insist that you

need a rickshaw to Paharganj. Avoid *Kashmir Holiday Tours and Travels*, opposite the station. Arriving very early or late in the day can be an added problem.

Stations from which trains originate have codes: **OD** - Old Delhi, **ND** - New Delhi, **HN** - Hazrat Nizamuddin, **DSR** - Delhi Sarai Rohilla.

Some principal services are: **Agra**: *Shatabdi Exp, 2002*, ND 0600, 2 hrs; *Taj Exp, 2180*, HN, 0715, 2¾ hrs. **Ahmadabad**: *Rajdhani Exp, 2958, ND, 1935*, Tue, Thu, Sat, 14½ hrs. **Amritsar**: *Shatabdi Exp, 2013*, ND, 1630, 6 hrs; *New Delhi-Amritsar Exp, 4659*, ND, 1320, 8½ hrs; *Shane Punjab Exp, 2497*, ND, 0650, 7½ hrs. **Bangalore**: *Rajdhani Exp, 2430*, Mon, Tue, Fri, Sat, HN, 2050, 34 hrs; **Bhubaneswar**: *Rajdhani Exp, 2422*, ND, 1715, 24 hrs. **Bhopal**: *Shatabdi Exp, 2002*, ND, 0600, 8¾ hrs. **Bikaner**: *Bikaner Exp, 4789*, DSR, 0835, 10¼ hrs; *Bikaner Mail, 4791*, DSR, 2125, 11 hrs. **Kolkata**: *Rajdhani Exp, 2302*, ND, 1715, 17½ hrs (via Varanasi and Gaya; except Tue and Fri, *2306* via Patna, 19½ hrs); *Kalka-Howrah Mail, 2312*, OD, 0730, 23½ hrs. **Chandigarh**: *Shatabdi Exp, 2011*, ND, 0740, 3 hrs; *Shatabdi Exp, 2005*, ND, 1715, 3 hrs. **Chennai**: *Rajdhani Exp, 2434*, Wed, Fri, HN, 1530, 29 hrs; *GT Exp, 2616*, ND, 1840, 36¼ hrs; *Tamil Nadu Exp, 2622*, ND, 2230, 33¼ hrs; **Dehradun**: *Shatabdi Exp, 2017*, ND, 0700, 5¾ hrs. **Goa**: see Margao. **Guwahati**: *Rajdhani Exp, 2424*, ND, Tue, Wed, Sat, 1700, 28 hrs; *Rajdhani Exp, 2436, ND, Mon, Fri, 1240, 32 hrs*. **Gwalior**: *Shatabdi Exp, 2002*, ND, 0600, 3¼ hrs. **Haridwar**: *Shatabdi Exp, 2017*, ND, 0700, 4¼ hrs; *Mussoorie Exp, 4041*, OD, 2215, 7¾ hrs. **Jabalpur**: *Mahakoshal Exp, 1450*, HN, 1620, 18¼ hrs. **Jaipur**: *Shatabdi Exp, 2015*, daily except Sun, ND, 0615, 4¾ hrs; *Delhi-Jodhpur Exp, 4859*, OD, 1655, 5½ hrs. **Jammu**: *Malwa Exp, 9367*, ND, 0810, 10 hrs. *Rajdhani Exp, 2425*, ND, Fri, 2100, 9½ hrs. **Jhansi**: *Shatabdi Exp, 2002*, ND,

0600, 4½ hrs; *Lakshadweep Exp, 2618,* HN, 0955, 6 hrs. **Jodhpur**: *Mandore Exp, 2461,* OD, 2100, 11 hrs. **Kalka (for Shimla)**: *Shatabdi Exp, 2005,* ND, 1715, 4¾ hrs. **Kanpur**: *Shatabdi Exp, 2004,* ND, 0620, 5 hrs. **Lucknow**: *Shatabdi Exp, 2004,* ND, 0620, 6½ hrs. **Margao** (Goa): *Rajdhani Exp,* Wed, Thu, HN, 1100, 26 hrs. **Mathura**: *Taj Exp, 2180,* HN, 0715, 2 hrs. **Mumbai** (Central): *Rajdhani Exp, 2952,* ND, 1600, 17 hrs; *Paschim Exp, 2926,* ND, 1700, 22 hrs; *Golden Temple Mail, 2904,* ND, 0755, 22 hrs. **New Jalpaiguri** (for Darjeeling): *Rajdhani Exp, 2424,* Tue, Wed, Sat, ND, 1700, 21½ hrs. **Patna**: *NE Exp, 5622,* ND, 0645, 17 hrs. **Shimla**: *Howrah-Kalka Mail, 2311,* DSR, 2245 (change at **Kalka** to *101 railcar*), total 11 hrs (book sleeper ahead). From ND: *Himalayan Queen, 4095,* 0600 to

Kalka, 5¼ hrs, change to narrow gauge *255,* 1105, total 13¼ hrs or *Shatabdi Exp, 2011,* 0740 to Chandigarh, 3¼ hrs leaving you an hour to reach Kalka for the narrow guage *255,* 1105, total 11 ½ hrs (see Shimla and Kalka, page 473). **Secunderabad** *Rajdhani Exp, 2430,* Mon, Tue, Fri, Sat, HN, 2050, 22 hrs. **Thiruvananantapuram**: *Rajdhani Exp,* HN, 0930, 31 hrs. **Udaipur**: *Chetak Exp, 9615,* DSR, 1410, 20¼ hrs; *Ahamadabad Exp, 9943,* DSR, 2100, 21 hrs. **Varanasi**: *Poorva Exp, 2382,* Mon, Tue, Fri, ND, 1615, 12¼ hrs; *Vishwanath Exp, 4258,* ND, 1330, 16 hrs.

For special steam *Fairy Queen* and the diesel *Palace on Wheels* tours see page 44 under Rajasthan. The latter departs from Delhi Cantonment every Wed Sep-Apr, US$270-325 each per night with 2 sharing a cabin.

❶ Directory

Airline offices

Abbreviations used: **A** = Airport phone no. **KG Marg** = Kasturba Gandhi Marg

Domestic: check in for all **Indian Airlines** flights at terminal 1-A. For J class Tele Check-in T5665166. Check in for all other domestic airlines Terminal 1-B. Arrivals for all domestic flights Terminal 1-C. **Indian Airlines**, Safdarjang Airport, Aurobindo Marg, 24-hr daily (to avoid delays be there at 0830), T141, T4620566 (2100-0700), F4624322, closed Sun; pre-recorded flight information (English) T142; Reservations also 1000-1700, Mon-Sat, at *Ashok Hotel,* T6110101; A 5665121 (and F-block, Connaught Pl). **Alliance Air** is a subsidiary, Safdarjang Airport, T4621267, A 5665854.

Private: Jagson Airways, 12 E Vandana Building, 11 Tolstoy Marg, T3328580, A 5665375. **Jet Airways**, 13 Community Centre, Yusuf Sarai, T6853700, A 5675404; G-12 Connaught Pl, T3320961, A 5665404, Tele Check-in T6562266. **Sahara**, 7th floor, 14 KG Marg, T3326851, A 5675234.

International: Aeroflot, 1517 Tolstoy Marg, off Janpath, T3312843. **Air Canada**, Janpath, T3737263, A 5652850. **Air France**, 6 Scindia House, KG Marg, T3738004, A 5652294. **Air India**, 124 Connaught Circus, T3731225, A 5652050, and 23 Himalaya House, KG Marg, T3311502. **Alitalia**, 3rd floor,

16 Barakhamba Rd, T3311019, A 5652348. **Biman**, WTC, Up Gr Fl, Babar Rd, T3414401, A 5652943. **British Airways**, DLF Plaza Tower, Gurgaon, T916-359911; Gopal Das Building, Barakhamba Rd, T3327139, A 5652077. **Cathay Pacific**, 809 Ashoka Estate, Barakhamba Rd, T3321286. **Delta**, DLF Centre, Gurgaon T916-388977; Sansad Marg, T3730197. **Druk Air**, 36 Janpath, T3310990, A 5653207. **El-Al**, 911 Prakash Deep, 7 Tolstoy Marg, T3357965. **Emirates**, 18 Barakhamba Rd, T3316044, A 5696861. **Gulf Air**, G-12 Connaught Circus, T3324293, A 5652065. **Japan Airlines**, Chandralok Building, Janpath, 13327104, A 5653942. **KLM**, 7 Tolstoy Marg, T3357747, A 5652715. **Kuwait**, Ansal Bhawan, KG Marg, T3354373. **Lufthansa**, 56 Janpath, T3323207, A 5652064. **Malaysian**, Ashoka Building, 24 Barakhamba Rd, 10th floor, T3359711, A 5652395. **Nepal Airlines**, 44 Janpath, T3320817, A 5696876. **PIA**, 26 KG Marg, T3737791, A 5652841. **Philippine**, N-40 Connaught Circus, T3314978. **Qantas**, 13 Tolstoy Marg, T3355284. **Royal Jordanian** G-56 Connaught Circus, T3327418. **Saudia**, 16 Barakhamba Rd, T3310464. **SAS**, 14 KG Marg, T3352299. **Singapore Airlines**, Ashoka Estate, 24 Barakhamba Rd, T3326373, A 5653072. **Sri Lanka**, Janpath Hotel, Janpath, T3731473, A 5652349. **Swissair**, Gurgaon 1916-388911; 1 Sansad Marg, T3325511, A 5652531. **Thai**, *Park Royal Hotel,* Nehru Pl

T6239988, A 5652796. **United Airlines**, 14 KG Marg, T3357004, A 5653910. **US Air**, 24 Barakhamba Rd, T3311362. **Virgin**, Janpath Hotel, T3343302.

Banks

To open an account with a student or tourist visa, try Canara Bank or Union Bank. Open Mon-Fri 1000-1400, Sat 1000-1200 (extended hours becoming more common). Localities in Delhi, including banks, close in rotation on different days of the week. Cash against Visa can take up to 1 hr; it is usually quicker to change foreign cash and TCs at hotels, though the rate may be slightly poorer.

ATMs: for International Visa/Plus cardholders using usual PIN at HDFC, HSBC, Standard Chartered and Citibanks all over Delhi (check free *Delhi Diary*).

Foreign banks and money changers: include American Express, A-Block Connaught Pl, excellent for changing money (closed Sun); small branch in Paharganj. Standard Chartered Grindlays, 15 KG Marg (Tolstoy Marg); Sita, F-12 Connaught Pl. Thomas Cook *Hotel Imperial*, Janpath; New Delhi Railway station (24 hrs).

Indian banks (dealing in foreign exchange) **open 24 hrs**: Central Bank of India, *Ashok Hotel*. State Bank of India, Palam Airport.

Transfer from overseas: Western Union, SITA, F-12, Connaught Pl; for fast money transfer.

Chemists

(24 hrs) in many hospitals, eg **Hindu Rao Hospital**, Sabzi Mandi; **Ram Manohar Lohia Hospital**, Willingdon Crescent; **S Kripalani Hospital**, Panchkuin Rd. In Connaught Pl: **Nath Brothers**, G-2, off Marina Arcade; **Chemico**, H-45.

Cultural centres

Alliance Française, M-5 NDSE Part II, T6258128. Classes, library, films. 1000-1700, closed Sun. **American Centre** (US Information Service), 24 Kasturba Gandhi Marg, T3316841. Large library (20,000 books). 0830-1730, closed Wed. **British Council**, 17 Kasturba Gandhi Marg, T3711401, 0900-1700, Mon-Fri.

Library with excellent reference section, 1000-1800, closed Sun and Mon. **Japan Cultural Centre**, 32 Feroze Shah Rd, T3329803. Classes, films, exhibitions. 0900-1300 and Tue-Fri 1400-1700, closed Sun. **Max Mueller Bhawan**, 3 Kasturba Gandhi Marg, T3329506. Classes, library, cultural programmes. 0900-1800, closed Sun.

Embassies

Visas are easy (photo needed), collect passport next day. **Afghanistan**, 5/50-F Shantipath, T6886625. **Australia**, 1/50-G Shantipath, T6888223. **Austria**, EP 13 Chandragupta Marg, T6889037. **Bangladesh**, 56 MG Rd (Ring Rd), Lajpat Nagar III, T6834065. **Belgium**, 50-N Shantipath, T6889851. **Bhutan**, Chandragupta Marg, T6889809. **Canada**, 7-8 Shantipath, T6876500. **China**, 50-D Shantipath, T6871585, Visa applications Mon, Wed, Fri, 0900-1200 (4 days). **Czech**, 50-M Niti Marg, T6110205. **Denmark**, 11 Aurangzeb Rd, T3010900. **Finland**, E-3 Nyaya Marg, T6115258. **France**, 2/50-E Shantipath, T6118790. **Germany**, 6/50-G Shantipath, T6871831. **Hungary**, 2/50 Niti Marg, T6114737. **Indonesia**, 50-A Chanakyapuri, T6118642. **Ireland**, 13 Jor Bagh, T4626733. **Israel**, 3 Aurangzeb Rd, T3013238. **Italy**, 50E Chandragupta Marg, T6114355. **Japan**, 50-G Shantipath, T6876581. **Korea** (Republic), 9 Chandragupta Marg, T6884840. **Malaysia**, 50-M Satya Marg, T6111291. **Myanmar**, 3/50-F Nyaya Marg, T6889007. **Nepal**, Barakhamba Rd, T3328191. **Netherlands**, 6/50 Shantipath, T6884951. **New Zealand**, 50-N Nyaya Marg, T6883170. **Norway**, 50-C Shantipath, T6873532. **Pakistan**, 2/50-G Shantipath, T4676004. Visas in 24 hrs, pay by bank draft (cash not accepted). **Portugal**, 13 Sunder Nagar, T4601262. **Russian Federation**, Shantipath, T6873799. **Singapore**, E 6 Chandragupta Marg, T6877939. **South Africa**, B-18 Vasant Marg, T6149411. **Spain**, 12 Prithviraj Rd, T3792085. **Sri Lanka**, 27 Kautilya Marg, T3010201. **Sweden**, Nyaya Marg, T4197100. **Switzerland**, Nyaya Marg, T6878372. **Thailand**, 56-N Nyaya Marg, T6118103, visa applications 0900-1200, collect next day. **UK**, Shantipath, T6872161. **USA**, Shantipath, T4198000.

Hospitals

Embassies and High Commissions have lists of recommended doctors and dentists. Doctors approved by IAMAT (International Association for Medical Assistance to Travellers) are listed in a directory. Casualty and emergency wards in both private and government hospitals are open 24 hrs. **All India Institute of Medical Sciences (AIIMS)**, Ansari Nagar, T6864851. **Escorts Heart Institute**, Okhla Rd, T6825000. **Ram Manohar Lohia**, Willingdon Crescent, T3365525, 24 hr A&E. **Hindu Rao**, Sabzi Mandi, T2513355. **JP Narain**, J Nehru Marg, Delhi Gate, T3311621. **Safdarjang General**, Sri Aurobindo Marg, T6165060. **S Kripalani**, Panchkuin Rd, T3363788. **Swedish Clinic**, C118 Defence Colony, T4642179. 24-hr dental emergencies.

Post office

Post offices throughout the city. Stamps are often available from the Reception in the larger hotels. **Speedpost** from 36 centres. Head post offices at **Sansad Marg**, 1000-1830 Mon-Sat, **Eastern Court**, Janpath, 24 hrs, **Connaught Place**, A-Block, 1000-1700 Mon-Sat (parcel packing service outside). New Delhi GPO at **Ashoka Place** (in the middle of a very busy roundabout on Baba Kharak Singh Mark, southwest of Connaught Pl), 24 hrs.

Poste restante: here and make sure senders specify 'New Delhi 110001'; collect from counter behind sorting office, 0900-1700, until 1300, Sat. Take passport. (GPO at Kashmir Gate, Old Delhi, T2960639, is less convenient.) **Kashmir Gate**, 1000-1900 Mon-Fri, 1000-1230 Sat. **Safdarjang**, Sorting Office, open 24 hrs.

Tourist offices

Most are open 1000-1800, Mon-Fri.

Information offices: Govt of India Tourist Office, 88 Janpath, T3320008 (0900-1800, closed Sun). Helpful; issues permits for visits to Rashtrapati Bhavan and gardens. Also at International Airport. **Delhi Tourism**, N-36 Connaught Pl, T3315322, F3313637. For hotel, transport and tours: 18, DDA SCO Complex, Defence Colony, T4623782, Coffee Home

Annexe, Baba Kharak Singh Marg, T3363607 (0700-2100); also at Airport Terminals; Maharana Pratap Inter-State Bus Terminal, T2962181; New Delhi Rly Station, T3732374; Old Delhi Railway Station, T2511083. **ITDC**, L-1 Connaught Circus, T3320331.

State tourist offices: each state has a tourist office in Delhi. Some have useful information but don't expect too much. On Baba Kharak Singh Marg: **Assam**, T3345897. **Gujarat**, A-6, T3340305. **Karnataka**, C-4, T3363862. **Maharashtra**, A-8, T3363773. **Manipur**, 2nd floor, C-7, T3344026, F3361520. Helpful information, and at 2 Sardar Patel Marg, Chanakyapuri, T3013311. **Orissa**, B-4, T3365515. **Tamil Nadu**, C-1, T3735427. **West Bengal**, A-2, T3732640. In the Chandralok Building (opp *Imperial Hotel*), 36 Janpath: **Haryana**, T3324911; **Himachal Pradesh**, T3325320; **Uttar Pradesh**, T3322251. In the Kanishka Shopping Plaza, 19 Ashoka Rd: **Bihar**, T3368371. **Jammu and Kashmir**, T3345373. **Kerala**, T3368541. **Madhya Pradesh**, T3341187. **Punjab**, T3323055. Others: **Andaman and Nicobar Islands**, 12 Chanakyapuri, T6871443 (open 1500-1700). **Andhra Pradesh**, 1 Ashoka Rd, T3382013. **Arunachal Pradesh**, Kautiliya Marg, Chanakyapuri, T3017909. **Goa**, 18 Amrita Shergil Marg, T4629967. **Meghalaya** 9 Aurangzeb Rd, T3014417. Very helpful and friendly. **Nagaland**, 29 Aurangzeb Rd, T3015038. **Rajasthan**, Bikaner House, Pandara Rd, south of India Gate, T3381884. **Sikkim**, 14 Panchsheel Marg, T61153466. **Tripura**, Kautliya Marg, T3014607.

Useful addresses

Ambulance (24 hrs): T102. **Fire**: T101. **Foreigners' Registration Office**: 1st floor, Hans Bhawan, Tilak Bridge, T3319489. **Police**: 1100. Traffic police are identified by their blue and white uniforms and white helmets. All police stations register losses and complaints, can be a very lengthy process. Police Assistance kiosks are at important junctions; Connaught Pl one is geared to assist foreign travellers.

Leaving Delhi

Going south

Surajkund

Surajkund (meaning sun pool) is a perennial lake surrounded by rock-cut steps, built by the Rajput king Surajpal Tomar. According to tradition this is where the Rajputs first settled near Delhi in the 11th century AD. At the head of the reservoir, to the east, are the ruins of what is believed to have been a sun temple. A little south is Siddha Kund, a pool of fresh water trickling from a rock crevice which is said to have healing properties.

The annual *Craft Mela*, held in February in the village complex, draws crafts people from all over India - potters, weavers, metal and stone workers, painters, printers, wood carvers, embroiderers.

Sultanpur Bird Sanctuary

→ *Best time to visit: Nov-Feb when there are northern migratory birds.*

ⓘ *Take a blue Haryana bus to Gurgaon from Delhi (every 10 mins from Dhaula Khan). At Gurgaon take a Chandu bus (3-4 daily) and get off at Sultanpur.*

Beyond Gurgaon, 46 km from Delhi, is a small bird sanctuary with a *jheel* (shallow lake) with reeds and other waterside plants growing round the rim. The large and handsome Sarus, the only indigenous Indian crane, breed in the reed beds. The migratory demoiselle, the smallest member of the crane family, comes to the lakeside in huge flights late in the winter evenings. The greylag and bar-headed geese and most of the migratory duck species visit the jheel including the ruddy shelduck, mallard, teal and gadwall. Coots are common as are white (rosy) pelicans, flamingos and a variety of waders. Of the indigenous birds visiting Sultanpur, the grey pelican, cormorant, painted stork, grey and pond heron and egret, are all to be seen plus a few white ibis and the blacknecked stork.

The Grand Trunk Road south

The main road route from Delhi to Agra follows the grand trunk road through the big industrial estates of Faridabad and then across agricultural land watered by the Yamuna River. Rice and wheat are the principal crops, the former during the rainy and the latter during the winter season. The landscape is flat, though there are some low hills at places like Radha Kund and Gobardhan on the west side towards Rajasthan.

The Delhi Jaipur Road

The NH8 is the main route between Delhi and Jaipur but although it is very busy there are some attractive stops en route, notably at Neemrana, which allows an overnight stay between Delhi and Jaipur. **Tikli**, 8 km off the Sonah road (turn off at Badshapur), about an hour's drive from Delhi towards the Aravalli hills, is a gem of a rural escape lovingly conceived by an English couple who have architecturally combined the best of East and West, following Lutyens. The exclusive "farmhouse" stands in a flower and bird filled garden, has an inviting pool and is a place to spoil yourself. Ask for Manender Farm, Gairatpur Bass village. **Rewari**, 83 km from Delhi, was founded in 1000 AD by Raja Rawat but there are the ruins of a still older town east of the 'modern' walls. It has been a prosperous centre for the manufacture of iron and brass vessels. On a rocky outcrop just above an unspoilt village, is the beautiful **Neemrana Fort** built in 1464 by Prithvi Raj Chauhan III and converted into an exceptional hotel. The village with a step well, and the fort ruins above, are worth exploring.

Going north

Meerut → *Phone code: 0121. Population: 850,000.*
ⓘ *The Inter-city bus stand is near Sadr Bazar in the centre which has buses from Delhi ISBT, Kashmir Gate, 2 hrs. Trains to/from New Delhi take 1½ hrs. The railway stations are to the west and the City bus stand nearly 2 km to the southeast.*

Meerut, known to this day as the place where the Indian Mutiny broke out in 1857, is a busy marketing, commercial and administrative town. It reputedly produces 80% of the world's cricket equipment, although Sialkot (in Pakistan) makes the same claim! Although the old city is compact, the cantonment to the north is typically spaced out with some attractive broad tree-lined streets.

On 10 May 1857 the first revolt that was to end the East India Company's rule and usher in the era of the British Indian Empire rocked the streets of Meerut. However, the town's history goes back as early as Asoka's time: the modern town contains various Hindu and Muslim buildings from the 11th century onwards.

The British cantonment has a particularly fine Mall. The cemetery of St John's, the old garrison Church (1821) contains interesting memorials. The Baleshwar Nath Temple and several old Hindu shrines surround the Suraj Kund tank (1714) which is fed by a canal from the Ganga. The mausolea and mosques indicate strong Mughal influence. The Jama Masjid (1019, later restored by Humayun), is one of the oldest in India. The red sandstone Shah Pir Maqbara (1628) on Hapur Road was built by the Empress Nur Jahan and further west on Delhi Road is the Abu Maqbara, with a large tank. Qutb-ud-din Aibak is believed to have built the Maqbara of Salar Masa-ud Ghazi (1194). The Nauchandi Mela is held in March.

Going to Nepal

The road east from Delhi to the Nepal border gives access to some popular hill stations of the Uttaranchal Himalaya and to the Corbett National Park.

Ghaziabad

This is a modern satellite town for Delhi, with a population of 520,000, comprising tall blocks, low-rise buildings and low-cost housing, all made of brick or reinforced concrete, with little or no aesthetic appeal. Beyond Ghaziabad is countryside, an area where two crops are cultivated each year, mostly rice in the monsoon and wheat in winter, but also sugarcane. Countless bullock carts trundle along the highway and line up outside the refineries.

Garmukhteswar

The small town, with some typical North Indian temples, stands on the west bank of the Ganga, with riverside ghats. According to the Mahabharata, this is where King Santanu met the Goddess Ganga in human form. Each year at the full moon in October and November, thousands of pilgrims converge to bathe in the holy waters. From the road bridge you may see turtles swimming around in the waters below.

Moradabad

A large provincial town, noted for its inlaid tin, brass and bell metal, is a traffic bottleneck. Founded in 1625, it was named after Prince Murad, Shah Jahan's son. The Jama Masjid (1634) is north of the ruined fort on the Ramganga River. There are a few basic, clean places to stay here.

Founded in 1623 by two Afghan Rohillas who served under the Mughals. Subsequently, the Rohillas united and expanded their empire (Rohilkhand, see page 147), but in 1772 the region was invaded by the Marathas. The Nawab of Rampur remained loyal to the British during the Mutiny and supported them in the second Afghan War. There is an extensive palace and fort here. The State library has oriental manuscripts and an excellent collection of 16th- to 18th-century portraits, including a contemporary painting of Babur and a small book of Turkish verse with notes by both Babur and Shah Jahan.

Banbassa

The small town on the India-Nepal border with a large Nepali population has a friendly feel. It is the shortest route from Delhi to Nepal. About 2 km south of town, the small Good Shepherd Mission has an orphanage, school, farm and a leprosy colony. They welcome visitors. Nepal border officials may demand payment to 'validate' visas, but can be put off if you request a receipt. It is best to take a rickshaw or tonga to the border and checkpoints. Under eight hours from Delhi.

Listings: Leaving Delhi

● Sleeping

Surajkund p134
B **Raj Hans**, T252318, F252842, 75 a/c, clean rooms, restaurant, bar.
B-C **Sunbird**, T251357, set in landscaped lawns, deer park, nine-hole golf, boating, open to non-residents.
C-D **Hermitage**, T252312, 108 (mostly a/c) in hut clusters, restaurant, lawns.
C-E **Shama**, T320683. Ssome a/c rooms, restaurant, bar.

Sultanpur Bird Sanctuary p134
D **Rosy Pelican Complex**, T0124-71242. A/c rooms, camper huts, camping and restaurant.

Tikli p134
B **Tikli Bottom**, T11-3351272, honiwala@vsnl.com. 3 immaculate, uniquely furnished guest bedrooms, promises imaginative cuisine (own garden produce) and a peaceful place to unwind outside Delhi in the middle or at the end of an Indian tour. A memorable en-famille experience. Advance reservations only.

Rewari p134
AL-A **Neemrana Fort Palace**, T01494-6007, F6005, sales@neemrana.com. There are 42 rooms quiet and peaceful (occasional loud chanting from village below!), full of character and beautifully furnished with collectors'

pieces (particularly recommended: Baag, Dakshin, Jharoka, Surya Mahals, though some (eg Moonga) are a testing climb up to the seventh level. Superb Rajasthani and French cuisine (non-residents Rs 350 which allows looking around), other visitors must pay Rs 100, magical atmosphere, part-day rates, reservations essential. Highly recommended.
D **Sandpiper Motel**, T5224. Restaurant, bar.

Meerut p135
D **Navin Deluxe Abu Lane**, 3 km from train centre in city centre.
D **Quality**, Begum Bridge area.
D **Shaleen**, Begum Bridge area.

Rampur p136
D **Modipur**, 22 a/c rooms, and a restaurant.

● Transport

Surajkund p134
It is 11 km from the Qutb Minar, on the Badarpur-Mehrauli road. You reach Surajkund by driving south on NH2 then turning right halfway to Faridabad. This road will bring you back to NH8 at Gurgaon. Special buses run during the Mela from Delhi (every 30 mins, 0830-1730, from Haryana Emporium, Baba Kharak Singh Marg).

Uttar Pradesh

❂ Footprint features

Introduction

Among the **high peaks** to the north of Uttar Pradesh, Himalayan springs provide the source of the sacred **River Ganga** – regarded by Hindus as the physical and spiritual life source of the country – which subsequently cuts a wide swathe through the state. The Garhwal and Kumaon Himalaya, as well as the 'holy abodes' of the Gods in the mountain shrines of the great Yatra pilgrimage route, no longer belong to Uttar Pradesh following the creation in late 2000 of the new state of Uttaranchal. However, Uttar Pradesh remains at the heart of much of India's religious and cultural life: the cradle of Hinduism and the cultural heartland of Indian Islam, a double identity symbolized by the presence of such contrasting sites as the **Taj Mahal** and the **Mughal fort** at Delhi and Agra, and the bathing ghats at **Varanasi** and **Allahabad** which attract millions of pilgrims. In the plains, historic cities such as Allahabad, Varanasi, **Lucknow** and **Mathura** are surrounded by a land transformed by great irrigation schemes.

★ Don't miss...

1 No visit to India is complete without going to **Agra**. The show sites, Taj Mahal and the Red Fort, won't disappoint but spare time to visit the baby Taj, I'timad-ud-Daulah, across the river, page 165.

2 Looking for souvenirs? How about chikan, zari or attar from the good craftsmen of **Lucknow**? You can also see one of the key battlegrounds of the 1857 Uprising here, page 145.

3 Get up really early to visit the Ghats at **Varanasi** to watch pilgrims bathe in the sacred Ganga or hire a boat at sunset to watch leaf-boat lamps floating downstream, page 186.

4 Many find peace at the deer park at **Sarnath**, although the rest of the site maybe disappointing, page 190.

5 Climb the **Panch Mahal** at Fatehpur Sikri for fine views over Akbar's short-lived capital or marvel at the lattice work in the **Tomb of Sheikh Salim Chishti**, page 175.

6 **Jaunpur**, with it's fine regional Islamic architecture, is well worth a visit, page 192.

UTTARANCHAL

DELHI

HARYANA

RAJASTHAN

Meerut

Moradabad

Vrindavan

Mathura

Fatehpur Sikri **5**

Agra **1**

Etawah

Gwalior

Jhansi

Orchha

MADHYA PRADESH

Khajuraho

Bareilly

Shahjahanpur

Dudhwa National Park

Lucknow **2**

Kanpur

Allahabad

Ayodhya

Faizabad

Gorakhpur

Nautanwa

Kusinagara

Jaunpur **6**

Sarnath **4**

Varanasi **3**

BIHAR

JHARKHAND

N

0 km 50
0 miles 50

Background → *Population: 166 million. Area: 238,155 sq km. Languages: Hindi.*

The land

The landscapes of Uttar Pradesh ('Northern Province') are dominated by the flat alluvial plains of the Ganges and its tributaries. The north of the state runs along the southern margins of the **Shiwalik Hills**, which parallel the Himalaya, succeeded on their south by the often marshy **Terai**, which, until they were cleared for cultivation in the 1950s, formed a belt of jungle 65-km wide from the Ganga gorge at Haridwar to Bihar. The **Gangetic Plain** occupies most of the state, almost featureless and flat, stiflingly hot, dry and dusty in summer. To the south again are the northern margins of the Peninsula, including the outer slopes of the Vindhyan Mountains in the southeast which in places rise to more than 600 m.

Climate

Although winter nights are cold everywhere in Uttar Pradesh, daytime temperatures can reach 25°C on the plains even in December and January. Between April and June temperatures soar and can reach 50°C. A desiccating hot wind, known as the Loo, often blows from the west. Despite a drop of temperature between June and September humidity increases, making it a very uncomfortable season.

Culture

The majority of the population are Hindu but nearly one fifth are Muslim, concentrated between Aligarh and Faizabad in what is called 'The Muslim Belt'. Today, adherents of Buddhism, Jainism, Christianity and Sikhism together constitute less than 3% of the state's population. Ethnically, the great majority of people on the plains are of Indo-Aryan stock. Most people speak Hindi, but Urdu is still quite widely used among Muslims. There are numerous local dialects. A broad division can be made between those on the plains and the *Pahari* (hill) dialects- one of the reasons given by the residents for the creation of the separate state of Uttaranchal in what was the Himalayan region of Uttar Pradesh (see following chapter).

Modern Uttar Pradesh

Uttar Pradesh has produced most of India's prime ministers since Independence, including Jawaharlal Nehru, his daughter Indira Gandhi and grandson Rajiv Gandhi. However, after three decades of Congress dominance, Uttar Pradesh politics has become like a frequently shaken kaleidoscope. Lower caste groups have become increasingly effectively mobilized, and have transferred their votes from the Congress to alternatives, mainly the Janata Party and the Bahujan Samaj Party. The rout of the Congress was completed by the emergence in the state of the BJP. Changing alliances, uncertainty and confusion have characterized much of the last five years. The state legislative assembly meets at Lucknow, the capital. Including those who now represent constituencies in Uttaranchal, but where there have not yet been new Parliamentary elections, UP has 85 seats in the Lok Sabha (Lower House) and 34 seats in the Rajya Sabha (Upper House), more than any other state. The BJP suffered a major reverse in the Assembly elections of 2002, with the the Samajwadi Party (SP) and the Bahujan Samaj Party (BSP) re-emerging as major forces in the State's legislative assembly. However, none had an overall majority and the Governor imposed President's rule in mid-2002, with the possibility of new elections to follow.

Central Uttar Pradesh

★ Lucknow

→ *Phone code: 0522. Colour map 3, grid A2. Population: 2,300,000. Allow 3 days to do the city's sights some justice.*
In Kipling's *Kim* "no city – except Bombay, the queen of all – was more beautiful in her garish style than Lucknow". The capital of the state sprawls along the banks of the Gomti River in the heart of Uttar Pradesh. The ordered Cantonment area contrasts with the saffron-washed buildings of the congested city centre, dotted with decaying mansions and historic monuments. In the heart of the old city traditional craftsmen continue to produce the rich gold zari work, delicate chikan embroidery and strong attar perfume. The arts still flourish and the bookshops do brisk trade in serious reading. Veils have largely disappeared as progressive college girls speed along on their scooters weaving between cows, cars and rickshaws. ▶ *For Sleeping, Eating and other listings, see pages 151-157.*

Ins and outs

Getting there The modern airport, connected by direct flights to Delhi, Kolkata, Mumbai and Patna, is 14 km south of the city, about half an hour by taxi. Lucknow is well connected by train and road to other major cities of the north. The City Railway

Lucknow

Related maps
A Lucknow Hussainabad, page 142
B Lucknow centre, page 144

■ Sleeping	2 Asha Deep	4 Dharamshalas	6 Railway
1 Amarpreet & Vishwanath	3 Deep Avadh	5 Kohinoor	Retiring Rooms

Uttar Pradesh Central Uttar Pradesh Lucknow

Station is in the southeast corner of the Husainabad area, close to the historic sights, while the Charbagh Railway Station is to the south. The Kaiserbagh Bus Stand near the centre is for long-distance services, while local buses terminate at the Charbagh Station Bus Stand.

Getting around The main sites are close enough to the centre to visit by cycle-rickshaw, or by hopping on a cheap shared tempo which run on fixed routes. However, the city is quite spread out and for extended sight-seeing it is worth hiring a taxi. See Transport, page 154, for further details.

Climate Temperatures: can reach 45°C in May lowering to 10°C in Jan. Rainfall: 300 mm in Jul and Aug with very little from Oct-May. Best time to visit: Oct-early Apr.

Background

Today Lucknow is a major administrative centre and market city, growing rapidly on both sides of the Gomti River from its historic core along the river's right bank. Although the discovery of **Painted Grey Ware** and **Northern Black** pottery demonstrates the long period over which the site has been occupied, its main claim to fame is as the capital of the cultured Nawabs of **Oudh** (*Avadh*), and later the scene of one of the most remarkable episodes in the 'Uprising' of 1857.

Lucknow developed rapidly under the Mughal Emperor Akbar's patronage in the 16th century. In the early 18th century, Nawab Saadat Khan Burhan-ul-Mulk, a Persian courtier founded the Oudh Dynasty. The city's growing reputation as a cultural centre attracted many others from Persia, leaving an indelible Shi'a imprint on the city's life. The builder of 'modern' Lucknow was Nawab Asaf-ud-Daula who shifted his capital here from Faizabad in 1775. In the attempt to build a wonderful city he emptied the regal coffers.

In the mid-1850s under **Lord Dalhousie**, the British annexed a number of Indian states. Percival Spear suggested that Dalhousie considered British rule so superior to Indian that the more territory directly administered by the British the better it would be for Indians. He evolved a policy of lapse whereby the states of Indian princes without direct heirs could be taken over on the ruler's death. Chronic mismanagement was also deemed just cause for takeover, the

Lucknow Hussainabad

Jobs for the boys?

In 1784 Lucknow and its region suffered an appalling famine, and thousands of starving people flocked into the city. In a spectacular example of 'food for work' – pre-Keynes Keynesian economics – Asaf-ud-Daula decided to build the Great Imambara. He offered work night and day, reputedly employing 22,000 men, women and children. However, in order to ensure that the task was not finished too quickly, he divided it into two parts. During the day, normal building proceeded. At night the workmen destroyed one quarter of what had been built the previous day. Nobles were allowed to work at night to spare them the embarrassment of being seen as having to labour to survive. To the labourers this was a life-saving act of charity, even if the building itself is widely reported as something of a monstrosity.

justification given for the annexation of Oudh. The novelist Premchand in the *Chess Players* attributes the fall of Oudh to the fact that "small and big, rich and poor, were dedicated alike to sensual joys ... song, dance and opium". History suggests that Nawab Wajid Ali Shah continued with his game of chess even as British soldiers occupied his capital. A strong British presence was established in the city as it became a key administrative and military centre. **Satyajit Ray's** film *'Satranj Ki Khilari (The Chess Players)'* is excellent.

When the **'Uprising'** (previously referred to as the Mutiny) broke in 1857, Sir Henry Lawrence gathered the British community into the Residency which rapidly became a fortress. The ensuing siege lasted for 87 days. When the relieving force under Sir Colin Campbell finally broke through, the once splendid Residency was a blackened ruin, its walls pockmarked and gaping with cannonball holes. Today it is a mute witness to a desperate struggle.

Under the **Nawabs**, Lucknow evolved specialized styles of dance, poetry, music and calligraphy. The Lucknowi *gharana* (house) of music and the exquisite crafts are reminders of its splendid past as it remains the regional cultural capital. Today, of the vintage modes of travel, only the *ekka* (one-horse carriage) has survived. To trace its Muslim heritage, visit the Bara and Chhota Imambaras, Shah Najaf Imambara and take a look at the Rumi Darwaza, Clock Tower and Chattar Manzil. Among the Colonial monuments, the Residency and Constantia (La Martinière College) are the most rewarding.

Parivartan Chowk and the black **Mayawati monument** which faces *Clarks Avadh Hotel* symbolize the spirit of 'change' (parivartan) which the 1997-98 government of the fiery Chief Minister Mayawati hoped to encourage by giving increasing power to the scheduled castes. Recently Lucknow has been through periods of violent communal tension which is partly explained by the important BJP presence here. It is the Lok Sabha seat of the Prime Minister, Mr Atal Behari Vajpayee. See Books, page 1363, for further reading.

Sights

The original centre of the city is believed to be the high ground crowned by the Mosque of Aurangzeb on the right bank of the Gomti. Tillotson, an architectural historian, suggests that the major buildings of Asaf-ud-Daula, built after 1775 – the **Bara Imambara**, the **Rumi Darwaza** (Turkish Gate) and the **mosque** between them dramatically illustrate the 'debased Mughal' style of 'Indo-European' architecture in decline. The monuments have been divided into three main groups. They usually open between 0600 and 1700.

North West and Hussainabad Just south of the Hardinge Bridge was the **Machhi Bhavan** ('Fish House') enclosure Safdarjang, Governor of Oudh (1719-48), was permitted to use the fish insignia (a royal/Imperial symbol/crest) by the Mughal Emperor Akbar. The Machhi Bhavan itself, once a fort, was blown up by the British in 1857, the only surviving part being the *baoli* which escaped because it was sunk into the hillside. Allow 2-3 hours for the Hussainabad tour.

★ **Bara Imambara**① *Rs 10 for all buildings on the site*, on the western slope of the enclosure, is a huge vaulted hall which, like all *imambaras*, serves as the starting point for the Muharram procession, see page 60. The vast hall (50-m long and 15-m high), built by Asaf-ud-Daula to provide employment during a famine, is one of the largest in the world, unsupported by pillars. Note: "Spiting (sic), smoking and call of nature strictly prohibited"! The remarkable *bhul-bhulaya*, a maze of interconnecting passages above, is reached by stairs; a delightful diversion. One visitor spent over an hour trying to find his way out, though others have managed in less! Notice: "No gent with a lady visitor allowed... without a Trust employee/guide.". The five-storeyed *baoli* is connected directly with the River Gomti. Legends suggest that secret tunnels connect the lower steps, which are always under water, with a treasure stored beneath the Imambara itself.

At the end of the avenue leading up to the *imambara* from the river is the **Rumi Darwaza** (1784). Further along is the 19th-century gothic 67-m high Hussainabad **Clocktower** (1880s) designed by Roskell Payne, which contains the largest clock in India though three of the four faces have been smashed. Next to it is the attractive octagonal Hussainabad Tank (1837-42), around which is the Taluqdar's Hall and the incomplete Satkhanda (1840) seven-storeyed watchtower. There are excellent views of Lucknow from the top.

Lucknow centre

N

0 metres 500
0 yards 500

■ Sleeping		● Eating
1 Airlines	5 Clarks Avadh, Indian	8 Grand
2 Arif Castles	Airlines & Oberoi	9 NRK
3 Capoor's &	6 Empire	10 Ranjana
Nowab's Restaurant	7 Gomti Tourist	11 Tourist
4 Chowdhuri Lodge	Bungalow	12 Vaishali

● Eating
1 Kwality
2 Mu Man's Royal Café
3 Ritz Continental,
Moments & Vyanjan
4 Spicy Bite

★ **Hussainabad Imambara** (Chhota Imambara), with its golden dome and
elaborate calligraphy and containing beautiful chandeliers, gilt edged mirrors and a
silver throne (1837), is illuminated during Muharram. Further west is the **Jami Masjid**
begun by Muhammad Shah and finished by his wife in the mid-1840s. **Victoria Park**
(1890) with several British tombs is nearby. South of the park is the Chowk, the Old
City bazar where there are some interesting old buildings including the **Dargah of
Hazrat Abbas** which contains a relic, a metal crest from the battle at Kerbala. Nearby
is **Nadan Mahal** (circa 1600), with the tomb of Shaikh Abdur Rahim, Akbar's Governor
of Oudh, and son of Ibrahim Chishti. This is a fine building, built in the Mughal style
and faced with red sandstone.

★ **Residency and Hazratganj area** The Residency's 3,000 mostly European
occupants, hastily brought there by **Sir Henry Lawrence**, came under siege on the
evening of 30 June 1857. Two days later Lawrence was fatally injured. After 90 days,
Generals Sir Henry Havelock and Sir James Outram appeared through the battered
walls with a column of Highlanders. However, the siege was intensified and sepoy
engineers began tunnelling to lay mines to blow the place up. From quite early on,
there was a shortage of food and disease spread. As rations dwindled, smallpox,
cholera and scurvy set in. Havelock was slowly dying of dysentery. The heroic
Irishman, Henry Kavanagh, had sat in the tunnels and shot mutineers as they
wriggled forward to lay more mines. He then volunteered to run the gauntlet through
the enemy lines to find Sir Colin Campbell's relieving force, which he did by swimming
the Gomti. On 17 November, Lucknow was finally relieved. Of the 2,994 men, women
and children who had taken refuge in the Residency, only 1,000 marched out.

The **Residency Compound**, inside the Residency's scarred walls, is now a
historic monument. You enter through the Bailey Guard gate. The **Treasury** on your
right served as an arsenal while the grand Banquet Hall next door housed the
wounded during the 'Uprising'. On the lawn of **Doctor Fayrer's House** to your left,
stands a marble cross to Sir Henry Lawrence. **Begum Kothi**, which belonged to Mrs
Walters who married the Nawab of Oudh, can be reached through the long grass
(popular with Indian courting couples!), but the old officers' mess has made way for
flats and apartments.

The **Residency** (1800) ① Rs 5, foreigners Rs 100, cameras free, to the northeast,
built by Saadat Ali Khan, has tykhunas (cool underground rooms for summer use)
where there is a museum. At the time of the 'Uprising' the Residency was overlooked
by high houses, now all destroyed, which gave cover to snipers firing into the
compound. There are many etchings and records including Tennyson's "Relief of
Lucknow". Suggestions of a wooden staircase for officers, an underground passage
to the palace, a secret room hidden in the wall behind false doors, all conjure up
images of the past. The graves of Lawrence, Neill and others are in the church
cemetery. Women visitors should not visit the cemetery alone. Just outside the
Residency on the banks of the Gomti is a white obelisk commemorating the
'Nationalist Insurgents' who lost their lives in 1857.

Southeast of the Residency, near the Hanuman Setu, is the Chattar Manzil
(Umbrella Palace) now the Central Drug Research Institute, where the submerged
basement provided natural air-conditioning. There are also the sad remains of the
Kaisarbagh Palace (1850) conceived as a grand château. Better preserved are the
almost twin **Tombs** of Saadat Ali Khan (1814) and Khurshid Begum and the restored
Baradari housing a **Picture Gallery** (see below). To its east again are **Nur Bakhsh Kothi**
and Tarawali Kothi (circa 1832), the observatory of the royal astronomer Colonel
Wilcox, which is now the *State Bank of India*.

Eastern Group ★ **Shah Najaf Imambara** (1814-27), near the Gomti, has the tombs of
Nawab Ghazi-ud-Din Haidar and his three wives, with its white dome and elaborate

interior decorations. It was used by sepoy mutineers as a stronghold in 1857. Wajid Ali Shah's (ruled 1847-56) pleasure garden Sikandar Bagh to its east is now the Botanical Gardens.

To the south of these are **Wingfield Park**, laid out in the 1860s, which contains a marble pavilion and some statues. **Christchurch** (1860), a memorial to the British killed during the 'Uprising', is nearby, along with the imposing Legislative Council Chamber (1928) and **Raj Bhawan** (Government House), enlarged in 1907.

To the east is ★ **Constantia**, now **La Martinière College**, planned as the country residence of Major-General Claude Martin (1735-1800), a French soldier of fortune who is buried in the crypt. He ran highly successful indigo and money-lending businesses. The red-brick wedding cake of a building was completed after Martin's death from the endowment set aside by him for a school here and at Kolkata for 'Anglo-Indians' (Kipling's *Kim* being one of them). For the students' bravery during the siege of the Residency, the school was unique in being awarded Battle Honours. The chapel, historical photos and the crypt are interesting. You may ask to look around both outside and within. The office is at the east end.

Further south, **Dilkusha** (Heart's Delight), once a royal shooting lodge in what was a large deer park, is being restored. There are graves of soldiers who died here during the 'Uprising'. General Havelock died here; his grave obelisk is in Alam Bagh, 100 m northeast of the garden's main gateway (3 km southwest of Char Bagh station).

Museums The **State Museum** ① *Banarsi Bagh, T235542, closed Mon, 1030-1630*, is the oldest in Uttar Pradesh and one of the richest in India, now housing all archaeological material. First to 11th-century exhibits of Hindu, Buddhist and Jain works including stone sculptures from Mathura, busts and friezes from Allahabad and Garhwal. Also marble sculptures, paintings, natural history and anthropology (an Egyptian mummy). Relics of the British Raj, removed at the time of Independence, are in the backyard. **Gandhi Museum and Library** ① *Gandhi Bhawan, Kaisarbagh, free*, has numerous photos though few are labelled in English. **Motilal Nehru Children's Museum** ① *Balvidya Mandir, Motilal Marg, closed Mon, 1030-1730*, has a collection of dolls. **Picture Gallery** *Hussainabad, closed Sun, 0800-1730*, has portraits of the Nawabs. MG Marg refers to Mahatma Gandhi Marg.

Parks and zoos Botanical Gardens are at Shah Najaf Imambara. **Zoo** (Prince of Wales) ① *0500-1900, closed Sat and Sun, Rs 5, car Rs 100*.

Dudhwa National Park → *Colour map 3, grid A2. 220 km north of Lucknow.*

A reserve since 1879, Dudhwa was designated a national park in 1977 and Project Tiger Reserve in 1988 by adding 200 sq km of the Kishanpur Sanctuary, 30 km away. Bordering the Sarda River in the Terai, it is very similar to the Corbett National Park. It has sal forest (in addition to sheesham, asna, khair and sagaun), tall savannah grasslands and large marshy areas watered by the Neora and Sohel rivers.

Ins and outs Getting around Jeep hire or minibus, Rs 20-30 per km, from park office at Dudhwa. Elephants are recommended, available at Dudhwa only. Each carries 4, Rs 50 per person for 2½ hrs (minimum charge Rs 200). Book elephant ride on arrival at park. See Transport for further details. **Entry** For 3 days, Rs 100, extra Rs 50 per day. Indians and students pay reduced rates. Camera fee Rs 50, video Rs 500. Road fees for light/heavy vehicles, Rs 50/100 per day. Night driving is not allowed in the park so arrive before sunset. **Climate** Feb-Apr (open mid-Nov to mid-Jun); in Apr-Jun it becomes very hot, dry and dusty, but is good for viewing big game. Temperature: Summer: maximum 35°C, minimum 10°C. Winter: maximum 30°C, minimum 4°C. Annual rainfall: 1,500 mm; most Jun-Sep.

Wildlife The swamps are the ideal habitat of the **barasingha** (swamp deer with 12 tined antlers, *Cervus duvanceli*), now numbering about 2,000, which are best seen in the Sathiana and Kakraha blocks. The tiger population is believed to be about 30 though they are rarely spotted. Dudhwa also has sambar, nilgai, some sloth bears (*Melursus ursinus*), the endangered hispid hare, fishing cats and a few leopards. The one-horned rhino was reintroduced from northeast India in 1985 but visitors are not allowed into the enclosure. The 400 species of avifauna includes Bengal floricans, pied and Great Indian hornbills, owls and king vultures. It also attracts a great variety of water birds (swamp partridge, eastern white stork) in addition to birds of prey (osprey, hawks, fishing eagles). Banke Tal is good for bird watching.

Bareilly → *Phone code: 0581. Colour map 3, grid A2.*
Bareilly, the capital of Rohilkhand (see page136), was founded in 1537 by the Bas Deo and Barel Deo brothers (hence Bareilly) and traces of their fortress remain. It was ceded to the British in 1801 and later contributed to the drama of the 'Uprising'. There are three 17th-century mosques and two churches in town. Bareilly is known for its iron industry and its gold *zari* work. It is an important rail junction and its population numbers 700,000.

Faizabad → *Phone code: 05278. Colour map 3, grid A3. Population: 160,000.*
Faizabad, 124 km east of Lucknow, is handy for visiting Ayodhya. It was once the capital of Oudh. Shuja-ud-Daula (1754-75), the third Nawab of Oudh, built Fort Calcutta here after his defeat by the British at Buxar in 1764. The 42-m high white marble **Mausoleum of Bahu Begum** (circa 1816), his widow, is particularly fine. Gulab Bari (Mausoleum of Shuja-ud-Daula, circa 1775) nearby, contains the tombs of his mother and father.

Ayodhya → *Phone code: 05276 .Colour map 3, grid A3. Population: 50,000.*
Ayodhya, 9 km from Faizabad and meaning 'a place where battles cannot take place', also on the banks of the **Ghaghara River**, is one of the seven holy Hindu cities (others are Mathura, Haridwar, Varanasi, Ujjain, Dwarka and Kanchipuram). It is regarded by many Hindus as the birthplace of Rama and where he once reigned, though the historian Romila Thapar stresses that there is no evidence for such a belief. Jains regard it as the birthplace of the first and fourth Tirthankars, and the Buddha is also thought to have stayed here.

The Archaeological Survey of India and the Indian Institute of Advanced Study began excavation in 1978. The ruins have a circumference of between 4 and 5 km, rising at some places to 10 m above the ground. According to Professor BB Lal, the site was occupied from at least the seventh century BC if not earlier, when both iron and copper were in use. Later finds include a Jain figure from the fourth to third century BC, possibly the earliest Jain figure found in India. Houses during this period were built in kiln-baked brick, and various coins have been found from periods up to the fourth century AD, some indicating extensive trade with East India. BB Lal goes on: "many of the now standing temples having been erected during the past two centuries only".

In accordance with Muslim practice elsewhere, a number of temples were razed and mosques were built on the site, often using the same building material. In recent years Ayodhya has become the focus of intense political activity by the *Vishwa Hindu Parishad*, an organization asserting a form of militant Hinduism, and the BJP, its leading political ally. They claim that Ayodhya was **'Ramajanambhumi'** (Rama's birthplace) and that this holy site is beneath the remains of the **Babri Mosque** built by **Babur**, deserted now for many years. On 6 December 1992, the mosque was destroyed by militant Hindus. This was followed by widespread disturbances resulting in over 2,500 deaths across the country. Ayodhya remains a potential

Rama's birth

Rama's father, Dasaratha, unable to have children by any of his wives, was instructed to perform a great sacrifice in order that his wives might conceive. At the same time there was great trouble in the home of the gods, for Ravana, the king of the demons, had been assured by Brahma that he could never be harmed by a human, or by "devas and other supernatural beings". When the gods learned of this promise they turned to Vishnu and begged him to be born as a man so that he could put an end to Ravana. Vishnu agreed that he would be born as four sons of Dasaratha, who was then performing his sacrifice.

The sacred fire was lit and ghee poured on. Out of the flames emerged a startling figure. He held out a bowl of payasam (a milk dessert) to Dasaratha and said: "The gods are pleased with your sacrifice. If your wives drink this payasam they will be blessed with sons".

Dasaratha was overjoyed. He immediately gave the payasam to his wives. In due course all three became pregnant. Kausalya gave birth to Rama and Kaikeyi gave birth to Bharata. Sumitra, having taken two portions of the divine payasam, gave birth to the twins, Lakshmana and Satrughuna.

flashpoint, so check conditions first if you plan to visit. The massacre of young Hindu activists returning from Ayodhya to Gujarat in February 2002 resulted in over 1,000 deaths in the following months. See further, page 1224.

Other sites include **Lakshmana Ghat** (3 km from the station) where Rama's brother committed suicide. **Hanumangarh** takes its name from the Hanuman and Sita temple and the massive walls surrounding it.

Gorakhpur → *Phone code: 0551. Colour map 3, grid A4. Population: 625,000.*

Gorakhpur, at the confluence of the Rapti and Rohini rivers, is the last major Indian town travellers bound for Nepal pass through. The British and the Gurkha armies clashed nearby in the early 18th century. Later it became the recruitment centre for Gurkha soldiers enlisting into the British and Indian armies. The **Gorakhnath Temple** attracts Hindu pilgrims, particularly *Kanfata sadhus* who have part of their ears cut. Unusual terracotta pottery figures and animals are made here.

Kusinagara → *Colour map 3, grid A4. 50 km east of Gorakhpur.*

Kusinagara is celebrated as the place where the Buddha died and was cremated and passed into *parinirvana*; the actual site is unknown. Originally known as Kushinara, it is one of four major Buddhist pilgrimage sites. See page 1341. Monasteries established after the Buddha's death flourished here until the 13th century.

In the main site, the core of the **Main Stupa** possibly dates from Asoka's time with the **Parinirvana Temple**. The restored 6-m recumbent sandstone figure of the dying Buddha in a shrine in front may have been brought from Mathura by the monk Haribala during King Kumargupta's reign (413-455 AD). The stupas, chaityas and viharas, however, were 'lost' for centuries. The Chinese pilgrims Fa Hien, Hiuen Tsang, and I Tsing, all recorded the decay and ruins of Kusinagara between 900 and 1,000 years after the Buddha's death. The stupa and the temple were rediscovered only in the 1880s. The **Mathakuar shrine** to the southwest has a large Buddha in the *bhumisparsha mudra* and marks the place where the Buddha last drank water. **Rambahar stupa** (Mukutabandhana), 1 km east, was built by the Malla Dynasty to house the Buddha's relics after the cremation. Some of the bricks (which have holes for easier firing) were calved to form figures.

149
following clues left by the Chinese travellers. A shaft was driven through the centre of
the Nirvana stupa "which brought to light a copper plate placed on the mouth of a
relic casket in the form of a copper vessel with charcoal, cowries, precious stones and
a gold coin of Kumaragupta I". The whole area was occupied until the 11th century. In
all there are eight groups of monasteries, stupas and images, indicating that
Kusinagara was a substantial community.

Kanpur → *Phone code: 0512. Colour map 3, grid B2.*

With a population of over 2½ million people, Kanpur is the largest city of Uttar
Pradesh and the most important industrial centre in the state. Cotton mills were first
established in 1869, some of the first in India. It is now one of the major industrial
cities in India with aviation, woollen and leather industries, cotton, flour and
vegetable oil mills, sugar refineries and chemical works.

Background Despite this industrial boom the UP Gazetteer 1908 description could
have been written today. "The fields are never bare except in the hot months, after the
spring harvest has been gathered. Even the grass withers, and hardly a green thing is
visible except a few patches of garden crops near the village sites, and the carefully
watered fields of sugar cane. With the breaking of the monsoon the scene changes as
if by magic; the turf is renewed, and tall grasses begin to shoot in the small patches of
jungle. A month later, the autumn crops – rice, the millets and maize – have begun to
clothe the naked fields till late in the year, and are succeeded by the spring crops –
wheat, barley and gram. In March they ripen and the great plain is then a rolling sea of
golden corn, in which appear islands of trees and villages".

Kanpur

Sleeping		4 Landmark, Gaurav	7 Pandit	● Eating
1	Atithi	& Geet	8 Saurabh	1 Fast Food
2	Attic & Little Chef	5 Meera Inn	9 Vaishali	
3	Ganges	6 Orient & Kwality Restaurant		

0 metres 200
0 yards 200

To Calcutta

Kanpur was one of the most important British garrisons on the Ganga. During the 'Uprising' the insurgents rallied under Nana Sahib, who bore a grievance against the British because he had received only a small pension. They laid siege to the British community of around 400 men, women and children who had been gathered together under General Sir Hugh Wheeler. Inadequately protected and without enough food, after 18 days the defenders were severely reduced through gunshot wounds, starvation and disease. Nana Sahib then offered a truce and arranged for boats to take the survivors downstream to Allahabad. When they were boarding at Satichaura Ghat, they were raked with fire and hacked down by horsemen. One boat escaped. The survivors were either butchered and thrown down a well or died of cholera and dysentery. The reprisals were as horrible. General Sir James Neill "was seized with an Old Testamental vision of revenge" (Moorhouse). To break a man's religion and caste, pork and beef were stuffed down his throat, thus condemning him to eternal damnation. More often than not, suspected mutineers were bayoneted on sight. Nana Sahib escaped after pretending to commit suicide in the Ganga and is believed to have died in Nepal in 1859. See Further reading, page 1363, for recommended reading.

Sights The principal British monuments are in the southeast of the city in the old cantonment area. Stone posts mark the lines of the trenches near **All Soul's Memorial Church** (1862-75), a handsome Gothic style building designed by Walter Granville. A tiled pavement outside marks the graves of those executed on 1 July 1857, soon after the Satichaura Ghat massacre. To the east, the **Memorial Garden** has a statue by Marochetti and a screen designed by Sir Henry Yule which were brought here after Independence. The infamous **Satichaura Ghat**, 1 km northeast of the church by the Ganga, has a small Siva temple. You can walk along the river from the Lucknow Road bridge (about 200 m, but very dirty) which leads to the site of the boat massacre just upstream of the temple, where cannons were stationed on the high banks. The temple is altered but the landing ghats are still used by fishermen's boats and for washing clothes.

At the siege site, remains of the walls are still visible – as is the privy drain system and the well. The Massacre House was north of the canal about 250 m from the Ganga, and north of the Arms Factory, now marked by a statue of Nana Sahib. In the city centre there is the King Edward VII **Memorial (KEM) Hall** and **Christ Church** (1848). The higher grade hotels are along the Mall, some within reach of Meston Road with its interesting, faded, colonial architecture and cheap leather goods shops.

Nana Sahib's home town, **Bithur**, 20 km north of Kanpur, has pleasant ghats by the Ganga. His opulent palace was destroyed by the British in 1857 and is now marked by a memorial bust. Ruins of a few large well heads survive in a park west of the main road into town from Kanpur. 'Trainspotters' should allow two hours.

Kannauj was **Harsha's** capital in the seventh century and later that of the Tomar and Rathor Rajputs. There is little of interest in the town today except for the **Archaeological Museum** (sculptures dating from the first and second centuries AD), the **Shrine of Raja Ajaipal** (1021) and the **Jama Masjid** (between the town and the station) which was converted from a Hindu temple by Ibrahim Shah of Jaunpur (early 15th century).

Bhitargaon ① *the nearest station is Ghatampur; from there take an auto-rickshaw, from Kanpur Central, Banda Pass, 1528, 0655, 1½ hrs, but no convenient return train, alternatively, visit the site from Pokhrayan Station, Chhapra. Gwalior Mail, 1144, 0915, 1¼ hrs; Gwalior Mail, 1143, 1620, 2 hrs, is half way between Kanpur and Hamirpur.* Its large brick-built Gupta temple, dating from the late fifth century and the sole survivor of its type, has been restored. The relief panels have disappeared, though the *makaras* (water monsters) and gargoyle-type faces remain.

● Sleeping

Lucknow *p141, maps p141 and p144*
L-ALTaj Mahal, Vipin Khand, Gomti Nagar, 5 km east of railway station, T393939, F392282, tmhghm.14c@tajgroup.sprintrpg.ems.vsnl.net.in. 110 rooms, excellent restaurant, good pool, attractive gardens (transplanted mature palms!), city's most luxurious hotel and the only really quiet one.
AClarks Avadh, 8 MG Marg, T220131, F216507. 98 rooms, good restaurants (see below), modern, clean, comfortable, efficient, attentive service. Recommended.
BArif Castle, 4 Rana Pratap Marg, Hazratganj, T211313, F211360. 52 rooms (a/c or boiler may not work), good location, moderately efficient.
CKohinoor, 6 Station Rd, T217693, F218586. 52 rooms, restaurant, clean, good service.
C-DCapoor's, 52 Hazratganj, T213958, F234023. 24 rooms, some a/c, good restaurant, old world charm but rather neglected.
C-DGomti (UP Tourism), 6 Sapru Marg, T220624, F212659. 80 rooms, some a/c, restaurant, bar, clean, attentive service.
C-EAmarpreet, Subhash Marg, Charbagh, T456626, F456602, hotelap@sancharnet.in. Modern, comfortable (Rs 400-2,000).
C-EVishwanath, Subhash Marg, Charbagh, T450879, F458779, markanday201@hotmail.com. Similar rooms but better value than Amarpreet, also has restaurant.
DDeep Avadh, 133/273 Aminabad Rd, T216521, F228832. 79 rooms, some a/c with TV, restaurant, travel desk.
DGrand, 4 Lalbagh, T231307. 22 modern a/c rooms, restaurant, revamped and aiming high, good discounts.
DNRK, 17/2 Ashok Marg, Hazratganj, T280380. Clean rooms with bath with hot water, some a/c, restaurant.
D-EAsha Deep, near DAV College, Aishabagh Rd, T201056. 55 clean rooms, 21 a/c (5 deluxe), TV, no restaurant but room service, helpful staff, 24-hr checkout.
E-FChowdhuri Lodge, 3 Vidhan Sabha Marg, down an alley opposite the GPO, Hazratganj, T221911. 20 rooms, some with bath and cooler, very drab and boxlike, poor nets but safe and cheap. This place is dirty and mosquito-infested.

Dudhwa National Park *p146*
All hotels are basic and foreigners pay more. Advance booking (15 days), and full payment (bank draft/postal order) is needed. Bedding is available at Dudhwa and Sathiana which have electricity; electricity generators on request at Sathiana, Sonaripur and Belrayan, at extra charge.

Dudhwa
DForest Resthouse, 5 suites (1 a/c).
ETharu huts, 12.
ELog huts, 2.

Sathiana
DForest Resthouse, 2 suites.
ELog huts, 6.

Bankatti
EForest Resthouse, 4 suites. Reservations: Chief Conservator of Forests, UP, 17 Rana Pratap Marg, Lucknow, T0522-283902, for rest houses and Dy Director, Dudhwa Project Tiger, Palia, Lakhimpur Kheri, T05871-33485, for others.

Sonaripur, Belrayan and Kila
EForest Resthouses; and 25 Fdorm beds at Dudhwa. Reserve with Field Director, Dudhwa Project Tiger, Lakhimpur Kheri, T05872-52106.

Palia
D-ETiger Haven, T05871-33912. Lodges.
Only Dudhwa has a canteen serving meals and snacks. Other places have cooking facilities (crockery and utensils). Provisions must be brought in. Palia (10 km) has eating places.

Bareilly *p147*
B-DSwarn Towers, Station Rd, 5-min walk from station, T473143, swarntowers@netsewa.com. 29 rooms, clean, modern, friendly 'Cheers' bar for drinks and snacks.

D-E Uberoi Anand and Annexe, 46 Civil Lines, T570838, F476111. 100 rooms, some a/c or air-cooled, restaurant, exchange, terrace garden.
E-F Civil and Military, Station Rd, T475879. 22 air-cooled rooms, dorm beds (Rs 50), central, restaurant, bar.
F Railway Retiring Rooms, 2 rooms, clean, hot and cold water, secure.

Faizabad p147
E Shan-e-Avadh, T23586, F26545. Next door to *Tirupati*, 52 rooms with bath, hot water, good restaurant, clean.
E Tirupati, Main Rd, T23231. Near Civil Lines Bus Stand, 45 rooms with bath (bucket hot water), some a/c, best upstairs at rear, good restaurant, modern.
F Railway Retiring Rooms. 2 rooms, dorm.

Ayodhya p147
Better hotels in Faizabad.
E-F Pathik Niwas Saket (UP Tourism), turn right from railway station, T2007. Very clean, basic rooms, 1 a/c, simple restaurant, tourist information, friendly.

Gorakhpur p148
Budget hotels opposite the railway station can be noisy.
C-D Ganges Delux, Cinema Rd, T336330. Comfortable a/c rooms.
D Avantika, Mohaddipur, Airport Rd (NH28), beyond crossroads 3 km from railway station, T338765. Good rooms and restaurant, modern.
D Ganges, Tarang Crossing, T333530. Some a/c rooms, good restaurant and ice cream parlour, well managed. Recommended.
D President, next door, T337654. Best rooms, a/c with TV, 2 restaurants include pure veg.
D Upvan, Nepal Rd, T336503. (Ask rickshaw for *Bobina* next door). Some a/c or good air-cooled rooms, Indian restaurant, clean, efficient room-service. Recommended.
E Kailash, Nepal Rd, 1 km from railway station, T336404. All air-cooled rooms, clean linen and bath, good management, no restaurants nearby.
E Railway Retiring Rooms, upstairs from Platform 1. Some a/c (best deluxe) and 3 dorms, restaurant, quiet. Recommended.

Kusinagara p148
E Pathik Niwas (UP Tourism), near ASI office, T7138. 8 rooms, tourist office.
Dharamshalas, the Chinese temple's new block, is recommended.

Kanpur p149, map p149
Some budget hotels are reluctant to take foreigners as it means filling up forms. Pools in hotels Meghdoot and Grand Trunk.
A Landmark, Som Datta Plaza, 10th The Mall, T317601, F315291, landmark@lwi.vsnl.net.in. 89 rooms, smart restaurants, casual coffee lounge, station/airport pickup, well kept. Good but pricey.
C Swagat, 80 Feet Rd, Brahmnagar, T541923.
D Attic, 15/198 V Singh Rd, Civil Lines, T311691. 7 a/c rooms, some with TV in colonial house, garden.
D Gaurav, 18/54 The Mall, T368616. 33 a/c rooms, restaurant, pleasant garden.
D Geet, 18/174-5 The Mall, T311024, 40 a/c rooms, restaurant recommended, exchange. Slightly cheaper
D Meera Inn, 37/19H The Mall, T319972. Some a/c rooms, restaurant (Indian snacks, drinks), clean, good value.
D Orient, The Mall, T366130. Some a/c (in summer), basic Indian restaurant, once popular, colonial guesthouse, now a bit shabby but run by charming family, well located.
D Saurabh, 24/54 Birhana Rd, T367712. 22 a/c rooms, good restaurant.
D-E Ganges, 51/50 Nayaganj, T352965, F311356. 80 rooms, some a/c and with bath, restaurant.
E Pandit, 49/7 General Ganj, T318413, F313492. 25 rooms, some a/c, restaurant (Indian veg, Chinese).
F Vaishali, Meston Rd (Tilak Hall Lane), T353404, F311356. Decent rooms, small baths.

---

❼ Eating

Lucknow p141, maps p141 and p144
1st and 7th of month and public holidays are 'dry' days.
The better hotels serve good Lucknowi food – rich *biryanis*, *roomali roti* and *kebabs* and *kulfis* to end the meal. Special *Dum Phukt* (steam cooked) dishes are worth trying.

● **Phone codes** *Lucknow: 0522; Bareilly: 0581; Faizabad: 05278; Ayodhya: 05276;*
● *Gorakhpur: 0551; Kanpur: 0512*

♥ Clark's Avadh: **Gulfam café**, downstairs of hotel. International. One notch down, but good value light meals, friendly service, plusher and more formal, rooftoop.
♥ Falaknuma, T220131. In hotel, serves tasty, spicy Nawabi cuisine by candle light, good views, pricey beer (Rs 125).
♥ Sahib Café, international, more casual, good choice, pleasing bright décor, the smart place to meet for business or pleasure.
♥ Taj Residency: **Oudhyana**, T39393. In hotel, special Avadhi food, lovely surroundings.
♥ Chung Fa, S-7 Gole Market, Mahanagar, T373550. Good Chinese.
♥ Kwality, Mayfair Building, Hazratganj, T223331. International. Cool, typical fare.
♥ Mu Man's Royal Café, 51 Hazratganj, T227070. Excellent Chinese. Live Indian music some nights. Recommended.
♥ Nowab's at *Capoor's Hotel*. Clean, good breakfasts, attentive service.
♥ Ritz Continental, Ashok Marg, opposite Jawahar Bhavan, Gole Market. Good vegetarian but "dismally slow".
♥ Spicy Bite, 12 Rani Laxmi Bai Marg, T22550. Snacks and bakery.
♥ Vyanjan, Vinay Palace, Ashok Marg, T280537. Good a/c vegetarian.
♥ Chowdhuri Annexe, off Vidhan Sabha Marg (opposite GPO). Good Indian in basic eatery.
♥ Moments, corner of Ashok/Sapru Margs. Very good north Indian meat dishes.
♥ Tundey's, Aminabad Chowk. Kebabs (named after one-armed ancestor) are sought after locally.

Faizabad *p147*
Gulnar, Main Rd 'T' junction. Good curries.

Gorakhpur *p148*
Ganesh, pure vegetarian South Indian.
Hotel restaurants recommended including *Avantika, Ganges* and *President*. Also fast food outlets near Indira Children's Park.

Kanpur *p149, map p149*
Fast Food, outlet at Nai Sarak crossing.
Fu-Tu, The Mall. For Chinese.
Hot Trak, The Mall, near *Landmark*. Fast food.
Kabab Corner, Sarvodaya Nagar. North Indian.
Kwality, The Mall, International, with bar.
Little Chef, near *Attic Hotel*.
Sarovar, Sarvodaya Nagar. For North Indian.
Shalaka, in shopping arcade opposite

Landmark. For pizzas and South Indian snacks.
Shanghai, The Mall. Chinese.

153

⊛ Festivals and events

Lucknow *p141, maps p141 and p144*
Oct-Nov: National Kite Flying Competition at the Patang Park, MG Marg the day after *Diwali*. **25 Nov-5 Dec**: Mahotsav Festival with emphasis on Indian classical music – song, drama and dance, processions, boating and *ekka* races, crafts and cuisine.

Kusinagara *p148*
Buddha Jayanti (first full moon in **Apr/May**) marks the Buddha's birth. A huge fair is held when his relics (on public display at this time only) are taken out in procession.

⊙ Shopping

Lucknow *p141, maps p141 and p144*
Shops usually open 1000- 1930, markets up to 2000. Hazratganj, Janpath closed on Sun; Aminabad, Chowk, Sadar, Super Bazar on Thu.
Lucknow is famous for fine floral *chikan* or 'shadow' embroidery in pastel colours, produced around the Chowk. You will also find gold *zari* and sequin work and prized *attar*.

Hazratganj
Gangotri, 31/29, handloom and crafts, and other Government emporia.

Chikan
Asghar Ali, near Chowk, for *attar* perfume.
Bhagwat Das, Kusum Deep, Chowk, T268459. Pay about Rs 600-900 for ladies 'Punjabi' outfits, or soft saris (5 m of fabric for dress making).
Khazana, at *Taj Mahal*, has high class handicrafts (0900-2200, daily).
Lal Behari Tandon, 17 Ashok Marg.
Ram Advani, Mayfair Cinema Building, next to British Council, Hazratganj. Outstanding book shop; highly knowledgeable owner.
Sewa, Sri Ram Market, Cantt.
Universal Booksellers, Hazratganj. Large stock covering all subjects.

Kanpur *p149, map p149*
Main shopping areas are The Mall, Birhana Rd and Navin Market. Kanpur is famous for cotton and leather products (along Meston Rd).
UPICA, Phulkari, Tantuja emporia, The Mall.

Uttar Pradesh Listings: Central Uttar Pradesh

▲ Activities and tours

Lucknow *p141, maps p141 and p144*
Golf
Golf course at La Martinière Boys College, open to the public. The only golf course in India where one of the hazards is a tomb – that of Augustus Nayne, a British officer who fell in the 'Uprising' and was reputedly buried with his monocle still in place.

Racing
Race course at Cantonment.

Swimming
Pools at KD Singh Baba Stadium and *Hotel Clarks Avadh*.

Tour companies
Garhwal, 432/4 New Civil Lines, T387349.
Kumaon, 2 Gopal Khera House, Sarojini Naidu Marg, T215903.
Reception centre, and guides: (English, German, Russian) 4 hrs, Rs 400 or 8 hrs, Rs 750. Charbagh Railway Station, Main Hall, 0700-2000, T452533.
Regional, 10/4 Station Rd, T226205.
Sita, 29/9 Rana Pratap Marg, T/F273839.
State Information, Hazratganj, T224728.
Tornos, C-2016 Indira Nagar, T380610. Very reliable, reasonable prices.
Tourist offices UP, 3 Nawal Kishore Rd, Chitrahar Building, opposite Prince Complex, T228349, F221776.
UP Tours, 6 Sapru Marg, T/F212659. For tours, car hire, air/rail tickets. **Tours**: Shah Najaf Imambara, Picture Gallery, Rumi Darwaza, Shaheed Smarak (Martyrs' Memorial), Residency, Bara Imambara. Enjoyable and good value. Pick-up from Charbagh station 0830, *Gomti Hotel*, 0915, return 1335. Rs 55.

Kanpur *p149, map p149*
Tour companies
Jet Air, 24/1, LIC Building, 1st floor, The Mall, T212787 (GSA for several foreign airlines). Very efficient. Recommended.
Sita, 18/53, T352980, F311458. For *Indian Airlines*.

⊖ Transport

Lucknow *p141, maps p141 and p144*
Air
Amausi airport, 14 km; pre-paid taxis available, Rs 160-200 to hotel. **Indian Airlines**, *Hotel Clarks*, T240927 (1000-1730, ticketing 1000-1300,1400-1630); airport T436327. Flights to **Delhi**, **Kolkata**, **Patna**, **Mumbai**. Jet Airways, 5 Park Rd, T239612, Airport T434009, to Delhi. **Sahara**, 7 Kapoorthala Complex, T377675, airport T437771; flies to Delhi. **Air India** T226171.

Bus
Local Extensive network and cheap. UP Roadways bus stands are mostly local and some out-of-town from Char Bagh (opposite railway station), T242066.
Long distance Out-of-town: UP Roadways, **Charbagh Bus Stand**, T450988 (24-hr left luggage), 0600-2200, Rs 2-5 per piece. Bus to **Kanpur**, 2½ hrs. Kaisarbagh Bus Stand, T222503. Bus to **Delhi**, 10-12 hrs.

Rickshaw
Tempo-rickshaws on fixed routes are cheap (Rs 3 minimum), and easy to use (from station, cross the road and ask for a landmark nearby, eg GPO). Cycle-rickshaws and horse tongas are widely available; Rs 10 for 2 km.

Taxi
Unmetered. Private taxis from **Lucknow Car Taxi Owners Assoc**, Station Rd, and hotels and agencies. Full day a/c (8 hrs; 80 km), non-a/c Rs 500, a/c Rs 1,000.

Train
Take special care of belongings at the railway station. Theft is common.
Lucknow is on the Northern and Northeastern railway. **Charbagh (Lucknow Junction)** Station is 3 km southwest of town centre. Computerized reservation is nearby (turn right from station; it is on the first street corner on the left). 24-hr left luggage across the road. Rest room, dormitory bed and locker (use your own lock), Rs 30 for 12 hrs.
Northern Railway: enquiries T131 (Arrival T1331, Departures T1332); reservations Charbagh T259932. **NE Rly**: enquiries T251433. City Station: T242411; weekdays 0830-1530, 1600-1930, Sun 0830-1530.

Agra Fort: *Lucknow Agra Fort Exp, 5313,*
1820, 15½ hrs. **Allahabad**: *Nauchandi Exp,*
4512, 0600, 4¾ hrs; *Ganga-Gomti Exp, 4216,*
1820, 3¼ hrs; *Kathgodham Mughalsarai Exp,*
5016, 2225, 8½ hrs. **Bhopal**: *Pushpak Exp,*
2134, 1920, 10½ hrs; *Lucknow Bhopal Exp,*
1274, 2235, Wed, Sat, 11½ hrs. **Gorakhpur**
(for Nepal): Several, best are *Kathdogam*
Howrah Bagh Exp, 3020, 0615, 7 hrs; *Lucknow*
Gorakhpur Exp, 5008, 2300, 6¾ hrs. **Jabalpur**
(for Kanha): *Chitrakoot Exp, 5010,* 1730,
15½ hrs. **Jhansi**: *Kushinagar Exp, 1016,* 0040,
6½ hrs; *Pushpak Exp, 2134,* 1920, 6½ hrs.
Kanpur: *Gomti Exp, 2419,* 0535, except Sun,
1½ hrs; *Shatabdi Exp*, 2003, 1520, 1½ hrs;
Kolkata (H): *Amritsar-Howrah Mail, 3006,*
1055, 20¾ hrs; *Doon Exp, 3010,* 0845,
22¼ hrs. **Lalkuan (for Nainital)**: *Nainital Exp,*
5308, 2120, 9¼ hrs. **New Delhi**: *Gomti Exp,*
2419, 0535, not Sun, 8 hrs; *Shatabdi Exp,*
2003, 1520, 6¼ hrs; *Lucknow New Delhi Mail,*
4229, 2200, 9¼ hrs. **Varanasi**: *Kashi*
Vishwanath Exp, 4258, 2315, 6¼ hrs; *Varuna*
Exp, 4228, 1800, 5¾ hrs.

Dudhwa National Park *p146*
Air
Nearest airports are Lucknow (219 km) and
Bareilly (260 km) in India, and Dhangari
(35 km) in Nepal.

Bus
UP Roadways and private buses connect
Palia with **Lakhimpur Kheri** and **Lucknow**
(219 km), **Shahjahanpur** (107 km), **Bareilly**
(260 km) and **Delhi** (420 km).

Train
Dudhwa is on the **Northeast Railway**, metre
gauge line, and is connected with Lucknow
and Moradabad, via Mailani (45 km from
the park). A branch line from Mailani links
places in the park. Transport is not always
available at **Dudhwa Station**; best to get off
at Palia (10 km) and take the hourly bus or
taxi. The accommodation is 4 km from
Dudhwa rly station, 10 km from Palia and
37 km from Mailani.

Bareilly *p147*
Bus
Extensive connections with all major cities
on the plains.

Train
The station is 3 km from the centre with
frequent tempo transfer, Rs 5. **Dehra Dun**:
Doon Exp, 3009, 2350, 7½ hrs; *Varanasi Dehra*
Dun Exp, 4265, 0033, 8½ hrs. **Delhi (OD)**:
Avadh-Assam Exp, 5609, 0923, 6½ hrs; *Bareilly*
Delhi Exp, 4555, 1415, 7 hrs. **Delhi (ND)**:
Shramjeevi Exp, 2401, 0010, 5½ hrs;
Kashi-Viswanath Exp, 4257, 0100, 5¾ hrs;
Lucknow New Delhi Mail, 4229, 0150, 5½ hrs.
Lucknow: *Rohelkhand Exp, 5309,* 0800, 7¾ hrs.
Varanasi: *Shramjeevi Exp, 2402,* 1745, 9 hrs;
Kashi-Viswanath Exp, 4258, 1840, 10¾ hrs.

Faizabad *p147*
Bus Bus Stand, T22964, bus to **Lucknow**, 3
hrs, Rs 47; **Varanasi**, 0630, 6 hrs, Rs 156.

Train Railway station, T22984.

Ayodhya *p147*
Bus T2067.

Train
T2032. **Jodhpur, via Agra and Jaipur**:
Marudhar Exp, 4853, 2040 (Mon, Wed, Sat),
9¼ hrs (Agra), 17½ hrs (Jaipur), 20¼ hrs
(Jodhpur). **Varanasi**: *Marudhar Exp, 4854,*
0549 (Tue, Fri, Sun), 3¾ hrs.

Gorakhpur *p148*
Air (and bus)
To Nepal Connections by **Nepal Airways**,
Sidhartha Nagar (near bus stop), Bhairawa,
T20667. Recommended for good value.
Flights to **Kathmandu** (US$75), **Pokhara**
(US$35), **Nepalganj** (US$77).

Bus
Long distance The bus station is a 3-min
walk from the railway station. City buses
meet most main trains. Services to **Lucknow**
(6-7 hrs), **Varanasi**, 205 km (from Katchari
Stand, 6 hrs), **Patna** (10 hrs), **Kusinagara**
(55 km, on the hour) and others.
　The usual route by bus is to go north to
Nautanwa via Pharenda, crossing the Nepal
border at Sonauli. You can visit **Lumbini**
(130 km) just across the Nepal border, the
birthplace of the Buddha. The bus stand is
near the railway station. UP Govt buses (green
and yellow) are 'Express' and depart close to
schedule. Other private buses (sometimes
deluxe a/c up to Kathmandu and Pokhara)

leave from opposite the railway station. Services from 0500, for **Nautanwa** (95 km; 2½ hrs) or **Sonauli**, just beyond, on the border (102 km; Rs 40; 3 hrs). Buses to **Kathmandu** (Rs 100; 12 hrs), **Pokhara** (Rs 80; 10 hrs), **Nepalganj** (Rs 120) or **Narayanghat** (Rs 35 for National Park). Most depart at 0700. Local buses every 30 mins to **Lumbini** (Rs 10 for day trip) and **Butwal** (Rs 9). There are different bus stands depending on the destination. Beware of ticket touts in Gorakhpur (private buses opposite railway station) and Nepal border. Some overcharge and others demand excessive 'luggage charge'. When buying a ticket, make absolutely sure which bus, what is included in ticket (meals, overnight accommodation), when and from where it departs (may be 2 hrs delay). Avoid *International Tourism Agency* opposite railway station; their buses are very poorly maintained. Nepalese buses from Sonauli are alright.

At Sonauli you need to fill in a small blue form and get your Exit Visa stamp at the Indian Immigration office. You then proceed to the Nepalese Immigration counter to get your Entrance Visa stamp (starting date of visa noted); the counter is open from 0530-2100. If you leave Gorakhpur after 1400 you will arrive at Sonauli after 1700 and will probably do better to stay overnight on the Indian side (mosquito problem) and walk across or get a rickshaw for Rs 5 in the morning to maximize visa days. From there you can take a bus/jeep (Rs 5) to **Bhairawa** in Nepal (6 km) where onward buses to Kathmandu 235 km (0630, 0730, 0830, Rs 75) and flights are available. Indian rupees are exchanged on the Nepal side.

Train
Local Gorakhpur Junc, NE Rly HQ station, has tourist information, left luggage (only with padlocks, Rs 15 per piece) and computerized reservations; good waiting rooms. **Delhi**: *Barauni-Katihar Amritsar Exp, 5207*, 1245, 15½ hrs; *Assam Exp, 5609*, 2359, 16 hrs. **New Delhi**: *Vaishali Exp, 2553*, 1715, 13½ hrs (often longer, up to 20 hrs); several others. **Kolkata** (H): *Howrah Bagh Exp, 3020*, 1315, 22½ hrs. **Lucknow**: *Lucknow Exp, 5007*, 2300, 6¼ hrs. **Varanasi**: *Krishak Exp, 5001*, 0630, 5¾ hrs; *Manduadih Exp, 5103*, 1650, 5½ hrs; *Chauri Chaura Exp, 5004*, 2210, 6½ hrs.

Long distance Metre gauge from Gorakhpur Junction. Nautanwa: the most convenient are 2 *Fast Passenger* trains, *95*, 0615, 2½ hrs (return departs Nautanwa, *96*, 0910); *93*, 1230, 3¼ hrs (return *94*, 1700). No need to book ahead (1st class, Rs 100; 2nd class, Rs 35). See above for bus services to Kathmandu and Pokhara from Nautanwa.

Kusinagara *p148*
Buses and taxis from Gorakhpur (30 mins).

Kanpur *p149, map p149*
Air
Chakeri airport, T42642; flights suspended. **Indian Airlines**, opposite MG College, Civil Lines, T211430.

TUP Roadways Bus Stand, Collectorganj, T253014 (for Lucknow, Allahabad etc); Chunniganj, T210646 (for Delhi, Agra).

Bus
Local City Bus Service has extensive network.

Rickshaw
Rickshaw and tonga: tempos, auto-rickshaws, cycle-rickshaws and horse tongas are available.

Taxi
Private taxis from Canal Rd taxi stand, hotels and agencies. Full day (8 hrs) about Rs 250.

Train
Kanpur is on the main broad gauge Delhi-Kolkata line and also has lines from Lucknow, Agra and Central India. **Central Station**, T131, T212181; Anwarganj, T245488. **Agra**: *Toofan Exp, 3007*, 0815, 7 hrs (Agra Cantt); *Link Exp, 5313A*, 2200, 11½ hrs (Agra Fort). **Kolkata (H)**: *Rajdhani Exp* (via Gaya), *2302/2422*, 2210, 12½ hrs; *Kalka-Howrah Mail, 2312*, 1440, 16¼ hrs. **Lucknow**: *Shatabdi Exp, 2004*, 1120, 1¼ hrs; *Pratapgarh Exp, 4124*, 1735, 1½ hrs. **New Delhi**: *Shatabdi Exp, 2003*, 1640, 5 hrs; *Rajdhani Exp, 2301/2305*, 0448, 5 hrs. **Patna**: *Rajdhani Exp, 2306/2310/2424*, 2155, 8 hrs; *Poorva Exp, 2304*, 2315, Wed, Thu, Sat, Sun, 8½ hrs; *Northeast Exp, 5622*, 1310, 9¼ hrs. **Varanasi**: *Lichhavi Exp 5206*, 2330, 6 hrs; *Farakka Exp, 3484/3414*, 0540, 9¾ hrs.

Directory

Lucknow *p141, maps p141 and p144*
Banks Weekdays 1030-1430, Sat 1030-1230.
State Bank, Hazratganj, and Punjab National
Bank, Ashok Marg change money. **Cultural
centres** British Library, Hazratganj,
T222144, opposite a most intriguing modern
Roman Catholic Cathedral, where you can call
in and read the papers. 1000-1800, closed Sun
and Mon. **Hospitals** Dufferin (Women's),
Golaganj, T244050. King George's, Chowk,
T265175. Sanjay Gandhi, Rai Bareli Rd,
T440007. **Internet** 30 Hazratganj. Rs 3 per
hr, clean, fairly fast. **Post office** GPO: Vidhan
Sabha Marg, 0930-1730. Head post offices: in
Chowk and Mahanagar. **Useful
addresses** Ambulance: T244040. Fire: T101.
Police: T100. Archaeological Survey of India:
Amirud Daula Kothi, Kaisarbagh, T245719.
Foreigners' Registration Office: 5th floor,
Jawahar Bhavan, Ashok Marg. Passport Office:
Nav Chetna Building, Ashok Marg, T223003.
Wildlife Office: 17 Rana Pratap Marg, T283902.

Dudhwa National Park *p146*
Tourist offices Reception Centre, Dudhwa
National Park, Lakhimpur Kheri, near Dist
Magistrate's house, T5872-52106. Wildlife
Warden, Dudhwa National Park, Palia,
T05871-33485. Tours available in season.
Useful addresses Palia has a bank, a
basic health centre and a post office.
Dudhwa has a dispensary.

Gorakhpur *p148*
Useful addresses Telephone: ISD and fax
services from Door Sanchar, The Target,
opposite Vijay Cinema. UP Tourist offices,
Park Rd, Civil Lines, T335450; counter on
Platform 1, railway station. Travel Bureau,
opposite railway station, *Hotel Elora
Building*, T202233.

Kanpur *p149, map p149*
Banks Usually open 1030-1430. Standard
Chartered Grindlays, 16 MG Rd. Changes
TCs. Allahabad Bank, MG Rd.
Hospitals Cantonment General,
T368876. Dufferin, T311510. KPM, T60351.
JLRS, Sarvodaya Nagar, T297247. **Post
office** Head GPO: Bara Chauraha, The Mall,
T60324 (open 24 hrs). **Tourist offices** UP,
26/51 Birhana Rd, opposite Post office,
T358186. Useful addresses Ambulance:
T62500, Police: T100.

Southern Uttar Pradesh

Agra → *Phone code: 0562. Colour map 3, grid A1. Population: 1.3 million.*

The romance of the world's most famous building still astonishes in its power and
beauty. In addition to the Taj Mahal, Agra houses the great monuments of the Red Fort
and the I'timad-ud-Daulah, but to experience their beauty you have to endure the less
attractive sides of one of India's least prepossessing towns. Like Delhi, Agra stands on
the right bank of the River Yamuna. The polluted condition of the river is a reminder of
the fact that Agra today is one of Uttar Pradesh's largest and most industrialized cities.
Numerous crafts and service industries have flourished, associated with the large
tourist traffic - hotels and transport, carpets, *pietra dura* in marble, zari embroidery and
leather - but there are also many small-scale engineering industries. Visitors are
subjected to a barrage of high power selling. Despite it all, the experience is still
unmissable. You can avoid some of the hassle by staying at Bharatpur or Fatehpur Sikri
and visit Agra for the day. ** For Sleeping, Eating and other listings, see pages 177-183.*

Ins and outs
Getting there By far the best way to see Agra on a day trip from Delhi is by using
the *Shatabdi Express* train, which gives you 12 hrs in the city. Considering waiting
time and delays, it is often faster than flying, and infinitely more comfortable than
bus or car. Book – it is a popular service. It is also the best train if travelling from

Bhopal, Jhansi and Gwalior to the south. Alternatively you can fly to Agra from Delhi, Varanasi and Khajuraho, and get a transfer to town quite easily. There are frequent 'express' buses from Delhi and Jaipur, but it can take 4 tiring hours of often nightmare driving by bus or car.

Getting around Buses run a regular service between the station, bus stands and the main sites and up to 2 km of the Taj Mahal. See Entrances on page 166. Cycle-rickshaws and taxis can be hired to go further afield, or a bike if it's not too hot. See Transport, page 181 for further details.

Agra

Related maps
A Red Fort, page 160
B Taj Mahal, page 166

Sleeping	5 Clarks Shiraz , TCI &	9 Mayur Tourist	12 Taj View E6
1 Agra D3	Mercury Travels E4	Complex E6	13 Tourist Bungalow
2 Amar E5	6 Holiday Inn E6	10 Mughal Sheraton E6	& UP Tourist Office A1
3 Ashok E2	7 Howard Park Plaza E6	11 Railway Retiring	14 Tourist Rest House D3
4 Atithi E5	8 Mansingh Palace E5	Rooms C3/E1	15 Youth Hostel A2

0 metres 300
0 yards 300

Rainfall: 250 mm in Aug to very little between Oct-May. Best time to visit: Nov-Mar.

History

With minor interruptions Agra alternated with Delhi as the capital of the Mughal Empire. **Sikander Lodi** seized it from a rebellious governor and made it his capital in 1501. He died in Agra but is buried in Delhi (see page 93). Agra was Babur's capital. He is believed to have laid out a pleasure garden on the east bank of the River Yamuna and his son Humayun built a mosque here in 1530. **Akbar** lived in Agra in the early years of his reign. Ralph Fitch, the English Elizabethan traveller, described a "magnificent city, with broad streets and tall buildings". He also saw Akbar's new capital at Fatehpur Sikri, 40 km west, describing a route lined all the way with stalls and markets. Akbar moved his capital again to Lahore, before returning to Agra in 1599, where he spent the last six years of his life. **Jahangir** left Agra for Kashmir in 1618 and never returned. Despite modifying the Red Fort and building the Taj Mahal, **Shah Jahan** too moved away in 1638 to his new city Shah Jahanabad in Delhi, though he returned in 1650 to spend his last days in Agra as his son Aurangzeb's prisoner. **Aurangzeb**, the last of the Great Mughals, moved the seat of government permanently to Delhi. In the 18th century it suffered at the hands of the Jats, was taken, lost and retaken by the Marathas who, in turn, were ousted by the British in 1803. It was the centre of much fighting in the 'Uprising' and was the administrative centre of the Northwest Provinces and Oudh until that too was transferred to Allahabad in 1877. See page 1304 for further details.

★ Agra Fort (Red Fort)

On the west bank of the River Yamuna, Akbar's magnificent fort dominates the centre of the city. Akbar erected the walls and gates and the first buildings inside. **Shah Jahan** built the impressive imperial quarters and mosque, while Aurangzeb added the outer ramparts.

The outer walls, just over 20 m high and faced with red sandstone, tower above the outer moat. The fort is crescent-shaped with a long, nearly straight wall facing the river, punctuated at regular intervals by bastions. The

Eating
1 Daawat *E6*
2 Maya *E6*
3 Only *E4*
4 PAC *E5*
5 Petals *E3*
6 Priya *D3*
7 Sonam *E5*
8 Zorba the Buddha *E2*

Uttar Pradesh Southern Uttar Pradesh *Agra Fort*

‼ Ins and outs

1 Don't rush. Soak up the atmosphere.
2 Try to allow time for the fort and the little gem, the I'timad-ud-Daulah.
3 In late winter and spring, wild bees often nest in the outer walls of some of Agra's major buildings. While there is no cause for alarm, they can sometimes be a nuisance.

4 You don't need a guide. They are generally more interested in getting you to a carpet or marble factory.
5 Many unofficial guides at the Taj will try to get money by showing you the 'best' place to photograph or 'yodeling' inside the tomb. Don't pay.

Agra Fort

N

0 metres 50
0 yards 50

1 Jahangiri Mahal
2 Jodh Bai's Palace
3 Anguri Bagh
4 Golden Pavilions
5 Khas Mahal
6 Mussaman Burj
7 Sheesh Mahal & Hammams
8 Diwan-i-Khas
9 Terrace
10 Black Marble Throne
11 Machhi Bhavan
12 Diwan-i-Am
13 Nagina Masjid

main entrance used to be in the centre of the west wall, the Delhi Gate, facing the
bazar. It led to the Jami Masjid in the city but is now permanently closed. You can only
enter now from the Amar Singh gate in the south. Although only the southern third of
the fort is open to the public, this includes nearly all the buildings of interest.

You enter through the **Amar Singh Gate** having had to contend with vendors of
cheap soapstone boxes and knick-knacks. If you want to buy something, bargain hard.
Guides will offer their services – most are not particularly good. Rs 500 Development
Authority 'tax' covers visits to all Agra and Fatehpur Sikri sites on the same day.

Fortifications

These tower above the 9-m wide, 10-m deep moat (still evident but containing
stagnant water) formerly filled with water from the Yamuna. There is an outer wall on
the riverside and an imposing 22 m high inner, main wall, giving a feeling of great
defensive power. Although it served as a model for Shah Jahan's
Red Fort in Delhi, its own model was the Rajput fort built by Raja
Man Singh Tomar of Gwalior in 1500, see page 277. If an
aggressor managed to get through the outer gate they would
have to make a right hand turn and thereby expose their flank to

❖ The best route round is to start with the building on your right before going through the gate.

the defenders on the inner wall. The inner gate is solidly powerful but has been
attractively decorated with tiles. The similarities with Islamic patterns of the tilework
are obvious, though the Persian blue was also used in the Gwalior Fort and may well
have been imitated from that example. The incline up to this point and beyond was
suitable for elephants and as you walk past the last gate and up the broad brick-lined
ramp with ridged slabs, it is easy to imagine arriving on elephant back. At the top of
this 100-m ramp is a **gate** with a map and description board on your left.

Jahangiri Mahal (1) Despite its name, this was built by Akbar (circa 1570) as women's
quarters. It is all that survives of his original palace buildings. In front is a large **stone
bowl** with steps both inside and outside, which was probably filled with fragrant rose
water for bathing. Almost 75 m sq, the palace has a simple stone exterior. Tillotson
has pointed out that the blind arcade of pointed arches inlaid with white marble
which decorate the façade is copied from 14th-century monuments of the Khaljis and
Tughluqs in Delhi. He notes that they are complemented by some features derived
from Hindu architecture, including the balconies (*jarokhas*) protruding from the
central section, the sloping dripstone in place of eaves (*chajja*) along the top of the
façade, and the domed *chhattris* at its ends. The presence of distinctively Hindu
features does not indicate a synthesis of architectural styles at this early stage of
Mughal architecture, as can be seen much more clearly from inside the Jahangiri
Mahal. Here most of the features are straightforwardly Hindu; square headed arches
and extraordinarily carved capitals and brackets illustrate the vivid work of local
Hindu craftsmen employed by Akbar without any attempt either to curb their
enthusiasm for florid decoration and mythical animals nor to produce a fusion of
Hindu and Islamic ideas. Tillotson argues that the central courtyard is essentially
Hindu, in significant contrast with most earlier Indo-Islamic buildings. In these, an
Islamic scheme was modified by Hindu touches. He suggests, therefore, that the
Jahangiri Mahal marks the start of a more fundamental kind of Hinduization, typical of
several projects during Akbar's middle period of rule, including the palace complex in
Fatehpur Sikri. However, it did not represent a real fusion of ideas – something that
only came under Shah Jahan – simply a juxtaposition of sharply contrasting styles.

Jodh Bai's Palace (2) On the south side, this is named after one of Jahangir's wives.
On the east the hall court leads onto a more open yard by the inner wall of the fort. In
contrast to other palaces in the fort, this is quite simple. Through the slits in the wall
you can see the Taj.

Turn left through to Shah Jahan's Khas Mahal (1636). The open tower allows you to view the walls and see to your left the decorated Mussaman Burj tower. The use of white marble transforms the atmosphere, contributing to the new sense of grace and light.

Anguri Bagh (3) (Vine Garden) The formal, 85 m sq, geometric gardens are on the left. In Shah Jahan's time the geometric patterns were enhanced by decorative flower beds. In the middle of the white marble platform wall in front is a decorative water slide. From the pool with its bays for seating and its fountains, water would drain off along channels decorated to mimic a stream. The surface was scalloped to produce a rippling waterfall, or inlaid to create a shimmering stream bed. Behind vertical water drops, there are little cusped arch niches into which flowers would be placed during the day and lamps at night. The effect was magical.

> ❉ The open pavilion on your right has a superb view across to the Taj.

Golden Pavilions (4) The curved *chala* roofs of the small pavilions by the Khas Mahal are based on the roof shape of Bengali village huts constructed out of curved bamboo, designed to keep off heavy rain. The shape was first expressed in stone by the Sultans of Bengal. Originally gilded, these were probably ladies' bedrooms, with hiding places for jewellery in the walls. These pavilions are traditionally associated with Shah Jahan's daughters, Roshanara and Jahanara.

Khas Mahal (5) This was the model for the Diwan-i-Khas at the Red Fort in Delhi. Some of the original interior decoration has been restored (1895) and gives an impression of how splendid the painted ceiling must have been. The metal rings were probably used for *punkhas*. Underneath are cool rooms used to escape the summer heat. The Khas Mahal illustrates Shahs' original architectural contribution.

These buildings retain some distinctively Islamic Persian features – the geometrical planning of the pavilions and the formal layout of the gardens, for example. Tillotson points out that here "Hindu motifs are treated in a new manner, which is less directly imitative of the Hindu antecedents. The temple columns and corbel capitals have been stripped of their rich carving and turned into simpler, smoother forms ... the *chhattris* have Islamic domes. Through these subtle changes the indigenous motifs have lost their specifically Hindu identity; they therefore contrast less strongly with the Islamic components, and are bound with them into a new style. The unity is assisted by the use of the cusped arch and the *Bangladar* roof". Seen in this light, the Khas Mahal achieves a true synthesis which eluded Akbar's designs.

Mussaman Burj (6) On the left of the Khas Mahal is the Mussaman Burj (*Octagonal Tower*, though sometimes corrupted into Saman Burj, then translated as *Jasmine Tower*). It is a beautiful octagonal tower with an open pavilion. With its openness, elevation and the benefit of cooling evening breezes blowing in off the River Yamuna, this could well have been used as the emperor's bedroom. It has been suggested that this is where Shah Jahan lay on his deathbed, gazing at the Taj. Access to this tower is through a magnificently decorated and intimate apartment with a scalloped fountain in the centre. The inlay work here is exquisite, especially above the pillars. In front of the fountain is a sunken courtyard which could be filled by water carriers, to work the fountains in the pool.

Sheesh Mahal (7) (Mirror Palace) Here are further examples of decorative water engineering in the *hammams*; the water here may have been warmed by lamps. The mirrors which were more precious than marble were set into the walls, often specially chiselled to accommodate their crooked shape. The defensive qualities of the site and the fortifications are obvious. In the area between the outer rampart and the inner was the emperor's grandstand seat.

Diwan-i-Khas (8) (Hall of Private Audience, 1637) This is next to the Mussaman Burj, approached on this route by a staircase which brings you out at the side. The interior of the Diwan-i-Khas, a three-sided pavilion with a terrace of fine proportions, would have been richly decorated with tapestries and carpets. The double columns in marble inlaid with semi-precious stones in delightful floral patterns in *pietra dura* have finely carved capitals.

Terrace and Machhi Bhavan

ⓘ *Closed Fri, 0700-1800, foreigners US$5, Indians Rs 25, tax Rs 50, allow minimum of 1½ hrs for a visit.*

In front of the Diwan-i-Khas are two throne 'platforms' on a **terrace (9)**. Gascoigne recounts how Shah Jahan tried to trick a haughty Persian ambassador into bowing low as he approached the throne by erecting a fence with a small wicket gate so that his visitor would have to enter on hands and knees. The ambassador did so, but entered backwards, thus presenting his bottom first to the Emperor. The **black marble throne (10)** at the rear of the terrace was used by Jahangir when claiming to be Emperor at Allahabad. The emperor sat on the white marble platform facing the **Machhi Bhavan (11)** (Fish Enclosure), which once contained pools and fountains, waiting to meet visiting dignitaries.

Diwan-i-Am (12) Go down an internal staircase and you enter the Diwan-i-Am from the side. The clever positioning of the pillars gives the visitor arriving through the gates in the right and left hand walls of the courtyard an uninterrupted view of the throne. On the back wall of the pavilion are *jali* screens to enable the women of the court to watch without being seen. The open-sided, cusped arched hall built of plaster on red stone, is very impressive. The throne alcove of richly decorated white marble completed after seven years' work in 1634 used to house the Peacock Throne. Its decoration made it extraordinary: "the canopy was carved in enamel work and studded with individual gems, its interior was thickly encrusted with rubies, garnets and diamonds, and it was supported on 12 emerald covered columns" writes Tillotson. When Shah Jahan moved his capital to Delhi he took the throne with him to the Red Fort, only for it to be taken back to Persia as loot by Nadir Shah in 1739.

Nagina Masjid (13) From the corner opposite the Diwan-i-Khas two doorways lead to a view over the small courtyards of the *zenana* (harem). Further round in the next corner is the Nagina Masjid. Shoes must be removed at the doorway. Built by Shah Jahan, this was the private mosque of the ladies of the court. Beneath it was a *mina* bazar for the ladies to make purchases from the marble balcony above.

Looking out of the Diwan-i-Am you can see the domes of the **Moti Masjid** (Pearl Mosque, 1646-53), an extremely fine building closed to visitors because of structural problems. Opposite the Diwan-i-Am are the barracks and **Mina Bazar**, also closed to the public. In the paved area in front of the Diwan-i-Am is a large well and the tomb of **Mr John Russell Colvin**, the Lieutenant Governor of the Northwest Provinces who died here during the 1857 'Uprising'. Stylistically it is sadly out of place. The yellow buildings date from the British period.

Jama Masjid

The mosque built in 1648, near the Fort railway, no longer connected to the Fort, is attributed to Shah Jahan's dutiful elder daughter Jahanara. Though in need of repair and not comparable to buildings within the fort, its symmetry has suffered since a small minaret fell in the 1980s. The fine marble steps and bold geometric patterns on the domes are quite striking. The large gardens have deer, black buck and monkeys.

★ I'timad-ud-Daulah and the east bank

Sometimes called 'Baby Taj', this is the least visited of Agra's three great monuments and relatively free of trinket sellers. It set a startling precedent as the first Mughal building to be faced with white marble inlaid with contrasting stones. New stone inlay repairs may be in progress which is very interesting to watch. Unlike the Taj it is small, intimate and has a gentle serenity. Beware, the monkeys here are aggressive and may attack without provocation.

History

The tomb was built for **Ghiyas Beg**, a Persian who had obtained service in Akbar's court, and his wife, see page 1304. On Jahangir's succession in 1605 he became *Wazir* (Chief Minister) and received the title of I'timad-ud-Daulah ('Pillar of Government'). Jahangir fell in love with his daughter, **Mehrunissa**, who at the time was married to a Persian. When her husband died in 1607 (and it has been said, without substantiation, that Jahangir had a hand in his death), she entered Jahangir's court as a lady-in-waiting. Four years later Jahangir married her. Thereafter she was known first as **Nur Mahal** ('Light of the Palace'), later being promoted to **Nur Jahan** ('Light of the World'), see page 1304.

Nur Jahan's family was almost an extension of the royal family. Her father was *Wazir* and her brother, Asaf Khan, was Jahangir's second most trusted adviser and later Shah Jahan's (ruled 1627-58) *Wazir*. Her niece Mumtaz married Shah Jahan (ruled 1627-58). Asaf Khan's son, Shaishta Khan, became Aurangzeb's (ruled 1658-1707) *Wazir*. In short, her family provided two successive first ladies and three successive chief ministers, and as the Mughal historian Bamber Gascoigne noted, the two most perfect Mughal tombs, I'timad-ud-Daulah and the Taj Mahal, belong to the Persian adventurer and his granddaughter rather than to the great Mughal Emperors themselves.

The tomb

ⓘ *0700-1800, Indians Rs 10, foreigners US$2 plus Rs 10 tax, video camera Rs 25.*

Nur Jahan built the tomb for her father in the *Char Bagh* that he himself had laid out, in the six years after her father died in 1622; some 4 km upstream from the Taj Mahal and on the opposite bank of the River Yamuna, it is beautifully conceived in white marble, mosaic and lattice and there is a good view from the roof of the entrance. The enclosure is approached from the east through a red sandstone gateway embellished with marble mosaics. A sandstone pathway leads to the main tomb which stands on a low platform (4 m high and 45 m sq) inlaid with marble decoration. The tomb itself is a low building (21 m sq) with a dome-roofed octagonal minaret (12-m high) at each corner and a central rooftop pavilion in marble tracery. If it has a shortcoming it is that the minarets rather dwarf the central pavilion, making it appear squat, though the decoration is superb.

Marble screens of geometric lattice work permit soft lighting of the inner chamber. The yellow marble caskets appear to have been carved out of wood. On the top of the woman's tomb is a replica of a slate (as if to imply "here is my heart, clear as a slate, write on it what you will"). On the engraved walls of the chamber is the recurring theme of a wine flask with snakes as handles – perhaps a reference by Nur Jahan, the tomb's creator, to her husband Jahangir's excessive drinking. The flanking chambers contain the tombs of other family members. Stylistically, the tomb marks a change from the sturdy and manly buildings of Akbar's reign to softer, more feminine lines. The curved

66 99 The white marble of the Taj is extraordinarily luminescent and even on dull days seems bright: the whole building appears to change its hue according to the light in the sky.

roof with broad eaves retains a distinctive Hindu influence. In the rooftop pavilion there are replica tombs – this became a popular feature throughout North India.

The main chamber, richly decorated with mosaics and semi-precious stones inlaid in the white marble, contains the tomb of I'timad-ud-Daulah. Some have argued that the concept and skill must have travelled from its European home of 16th-century Florence to India (see page 102). However, there are differences between the two. Florentine *pietra dura* is figurative whereas the Indian version is essentially decorative and can be seen as a refinement of its Indian predecessor, the patterned mosaic.

Chini ka Rauza
① *Open sunrise to sunset, free.*

The Persian Afzal Khan, who was a minister under Shah Jahan, is buried here, 1 km north of the I'timad-ud-Daulah. He died in Lahore in 1639 but was buried in this tomb which had been constructed during his lifetime. The chamber has been severely damaged. The outside is decorated with glazed (*chini*) tiles, as were many Mughal buildings in Lahore showing strong Persian influence. The glazed surface exfoliated in the Indian monsoon climate. A visit to the roof of the Chini ka Rauza shows how the false dome is carried on a drum base over the true dome, to aggrandize it.

Ram Bagh
① *Open sunrise to sunset, Rs 2.*

At 3 km upstream from I'timad-ud-Daulah, Ram Bagh is believed to be the first Mughal garden in India. Its name is a corruption of the original 'Arambagh' – literally 'garden of rest'. Reputed to have been laid out by Babur (ruled 1526-30) as a pleasure garden, it was the resting place of his body before its interment at Kabul.

★ Taj Mahal

History
When the Taj Mahal was constructed, the Mughal Empire was already past its prime. The Taj, despite its unquestionable beauty, was an extravagance which the Empire could not afford. Because of his profligate overspending of State funds, for the last eight years of his life Shah Jahan was imprisoned by his son Aurangzeb and confined to his marble palace at the Agra Fort.

The state of the Taj declined with the fortunes of the Mughal Empire, the gardens becoming overgrown. In the 19th century the Taj was a favourite place for courting couples and open air balls were held by the British outside the tomb itself. Lord Bentinck, Governor General 1828-35, planned to have the Taj dismantled and sold off in pieces by auction in England. Cranes were even erected in the garden. The plan was only abandoned when a pilot auction of part of Agra Fort failed to attract enough interest. Fortunately, Lord Curzon, one of Bentinck's successors (1899-1905), repaired much of the damage done over the centuries, reset the marble platform around the Taj, and cleaned up the gardens.

Viewing

The best way of viewing the Taj is to do so at different times of the day and year. The white marble of the Taj is extraordinarily luminescent and even on dull days seems bright: the whole building appears to change its hue according to the light in the sky. It may be possible to view it by moonlight in the winter months; at other times see it from outside the compound. In winter (December-February), it is worth being there at sunrise. Then the mists that often lie over the River Yamuna lift as the sun rises and casts its golden rays over the pearl white tomb. Beautifully lit in the soft light, the Taj appears to float on air. At sunset, the view from across the river is equally attractive; take an auto-rickshaw through the agricultural area south of the I'timad-ud-Daulah to a small Hindu temple (small donation expected). The Archaeological Survey of India explicitly asks visitors not to make donations to anyone including the custodians in the tomb who often ask for money. **No photo inside the tomb (instant fines charged). See also page 16.**

Entrances

You can approach the Taj from three directions. The southern entrance is from the township that sprang up during the construction of the Taj and the western entrance, where there are State Government emporia selling souvenirs and handicrafts, is usually used by those arriving from the fort. At the Eastern entrance, autos, rickshaws and camel drivers offer to take visitors to the gate for up to Rs 100 each; however, an official free shuttle 'battery bus' regularly ferries visitors from the car park to the gate (though hawkers may insist that it is not running). On the eastern approach, the flanking buildings were stables and accommodation for visitors to the Taj. To reduce damage to the marble by the polluted atmosphere, strict rules prohibit vehicles emitting noxious fumes within 2 km of the monument.

The approach

In the unique beauty of the Taj, subtlety is blended with grandeur and a massive overall design is matched with immaculately intricate execution. All contribute to the breathtaking first impression as you pass through the arch of the entrance gateway. You will already have seen the dome of the tomb in the distance, looking almost like a miniature, but as you go into the open square before the main entrance the Taj itself is so well hidden that you almost wonder where it can be. The glorious surprise is kept until the last moment, for wholly concealing it is the massive red sandstone gateway of the entrance, guarding the enormous wealth inside and symbolizing the divide between the secular world and paradise. Although the present entrance is to the side of the gateway, you can still get something of the effect by going from the present entrance straight to what is now the exit.

Taj Mahal & Taj Ganj

■ **Sleeping**
1 Gulshan
2 Host
3 India Guest House
4 Shah Jahan
5 Sheela
6 Sidhartha
7 Sikander
8 Taj Khema & Tours
9 Taj View Lodge

● **Eating**
1 Honey
2 Lucky
3 Shankar Vegis
4 Taj Cafeteria

⋮ Charbagh: The Mughal garden

In the Koran, the garden is repeatedly seen as a symbol for paradise. Islam was born in the deserts of Arabia. Muslims venerate water, without which plants will not grow - the old Persian word pairidaeza means 'garden'. It is no coincidence then that green is the colour of Islam.

Four main rivers of paradise are also specified: water, milk, wine and purified honey. This is the origin of the quartered garden (charbagh). The watercourses divided the garden into quadrats and all was enclosed behind a private wall. To the Muslim the beauty of creation and of the garden was held to be a reflection of God. The great Sufi poet **Rumi** used much garden imagery: "The trees are engaged in ritual prayer and the birds in singing the litany". Thus, the garden becomes as important as the tomb.

The gateway, completed in 1648, stands 30 m high. The small domed pavilions (*chhattris*) on top are Hindu in style and signify regality. The huge brass door is recent. The original doors were solid silver and decorated with 1,100 nails whose heads were contemporary silver coins. Along with some other treasures, they were plundered by the Jats who ravaged the Mughal Empire after its collapse. A final feature of the gateway is that the lettering appears to be the same size. The engravers skilfully enlarged and lengthened the letters as their distance from the ground increased, creating the illusion of uniformity. Although the gateway is remarkable in itself, one of its functions is to prevent you getting any glimpse of the tomb inside until you are right in the doorway itself. From here only the tomb is visible, stunning in its nearness, but as you move forward the minarets come into view. From here, see how the people walking around the tomb are dwarfed by the 70-m high dome. Stone masons can be seen at work near the entrance.

The garden

The Taj garden, well kept though it is nowadays, is nothing compared with its former glory. The whole of the Taj complex means 580 by 300 m and the garden 300 by 300 m and you may see bullocks pulling the lawnmowers around! The guiding principle is one of symmetry. The *char bagh*, separated by the watercourses (rivers of heaven) originating from the central, raised pool, were divided into 16 flower beds, making a total of 64. Each bed was planted with 400 plants. The trees, all carefully planted to maintain the symmetry, were either cypress (signifying death) or fruit trees (life). The channels were stocked with colourful fish and the gardens with beautiful birds. Royal visitors were invited to the tomb – hence the stables and guesthouses. It is well worth wandering along the side avenues for not only is it much more peaceful but also good for framing photos of the tomb with foliage. Guards expect tips when you take waterfront photos.

The mosque and its jawab

On the east and west sides of the tomb are identical red sandstone buildings. On the west (left hand side) is a mosque. It is common in Islam to build one next to a tomb. It sanctifies the area and provides a place for worship. The replica on the other side is known as the **Jawab** (answer). This cannot be used for prayer as it faces away from Mecca.

The tomb

① *Daily except Fri, 0600-1900, Rs 25 (Indians), foreigners US$5, plus Rs 500 Agra Development Authority 'tax' (which covers all Agra and Fatehpur Sikri sites on the same day), includes a still camera (video cameras may not be allowed). A torch is very useful for the crypt, though officially they are not allowed in (nor are knives, cigarettes, matches, lighters and food but free lockers available), allow at least 1 hr.*

The four **minarets**, 41.6-m high, at each corner of the plinth provide balance to the tomb. Minarets used in this way first appeared in India with Akbar's tomb at Sikandra. They were used again at I'timad-ud-Daulah and are refined still further here. Each has a deliberate slant outwards – the southwest by 20 cm, the others by five centimetres. Familiar with the disastrous effects of earthquakes on mosques in Gujarat to the south, the architects designed the minarets so they would fall away from the tomb, not onto it. On each pillar is written a letter (R, H, M, N) which together spell the word ar-Rahman (The All Merciful), one of the 99 names of Allah.

The **plinth** is 6.7-m high and 95 m sq and leads to the tomb. Here, shoes must be removed or cloth overshoes worn which are Rs 2, though strictly free.

The **tomb** is square with bevelled corners. Each side is 56.6-m long with a large central arch flanked by two pointed arches. At each corner smaller domes rise while in the centre is the main dome topped by a brass finial. The dome is actually a double dome and this device, Central Asian in origin, was used to gain height. With the Taj, the Mughals brought to fruition an experiment first tried in Humayun's tomb in Delhi, 90 years earlier. The resemblance of the dome to a huge pearl is not coincidental. There is a saying of the Prophet that describes the throne of God as a dome of white pearl supported by four pillars. The exterior ornamentation is calligraphy (verses of the Koran), beautifully carved panels in bas relief and superb inlay work. The last, in the form of large floral sweeps and chevrons, is immaculately proportioned. The **interior** of the mausoleum comprises a lofty central chamber, a crypt (*maqbara*) immediately below this, and four octagonal corner rooms originally intended to house the graves of other family members. Shah Jahan's son and usurper, Aurangzeb (ruled 1658-1707), failed to honour this wish. The central chamber contains replica tombs, the real ones being in the crypt. It was customary to have a public tomb and a private one. The public tomb was originally surrounded by a jewel encrusted silver screen. Aurangzeb removed this, fearing it might be stolen, and replaced it with an octagonal screen of marble and inlaid precious stones, then costing Rs 50,000. It is a stupendous piece of workmanship. The lattice (*jali*) screens are each carved from one block of marble. Even these curved surfaces have been inlaid. If you examine the flowers by placing a flashlight on the surface you can see how luminescent the marble is and the intricacy of the inlay work. Some flowers have as many as 64 pieces making up the petals sometimes achieving a 3D effect. This chamber is open at sunrise, but may close during the day. Above the tombs is a **Cairene lamp** whose flame is supposed to never go out. This one was given by Lord Curzon, Governor General of India (1899-1905), to replace the original which was stolen by Jats. The tomb of Mumtaz with the 'female' slate, rests immediately beneath the dome. If you look from behind it, you can see how it lines up centrally with the main entrance. Shah Jahan's tomb is larger and to the side, marked by a 'male' pen-box, the sign of a cultured or noble person. Not originally intended to be placed there but squeezed in by Aurangzeb, this flaws the otherwise perfect symmetry of the whole complex. Both tombs are exquisitely inlaid with semi-precious stones. Finally, the **acoustics** of the building are superb, the domed ceiling being designed to echo chants from the Koran and musicians' melodies. Walk round the outside of the tomb before retrieving your shoes to appreciate it from all sides.

The **museum** ① *closed Fri, 1000-1700, Rs 5*, housed in a building to the west has a small collection of Mughal memorabilia, photographs and miniatures of the Taj through the ages but has no textual information.

★ Sikandra

Akbar's tomb

① *Sunrise to sunset, Rs 15 (Indians), foreigners US$2, includes still camera, video Rs 25. Parking by main entrance, local buses from Fort; autos demand Rs 100 for return trip. Morning is the best time to visit when few others are likely to be around.*

Following the Timurid tradition, Akbar (ruled 1556-1605) had started to build his own tomb at Sikandra, 4 km northwest. He died during its construction and his son **Jahangir** completed it in 1613, after he had considerably modified the design and had much of the earlier work pulled down. The result is an impressive, large but architecturally confused tomb. A huge gateway, the **Buland Darwaza**, in the style of the massive Victory Gate at Fatehpur Sikri, leads to the great garden enclosure. The decoration on the gateway is strikingly bold, with its large mosaic patterns, a forerunner of the *pietra dura* technique whereby recesses were cut into the bedding stone of marble or sandstone and pieces set into it. The white minarets atop the entrance were an innovation which reappear, almost unchanged, at the Taj Mahal. The walled garden enclosure is laid out in the *char bagh* style, with the mausoleum at the centre.

A broad paved path leads to the 22.5-m high tomb with four storeys. The first three storeys of red sandstone are in the style of Fatehpur Sikri. On top of them sits a white marble courtyard containing a finely carved replica sepulchre (the real tomb is below ground level). This fourth storey makes extensive use of white marble, later seen at the I'timad-ud-Daulah and the Taj Mahal. Visitors are not allowed up to this level.

The lowest storey, nearly 100 m sq and 9-m high, contains massive cloisters. The entrance on the south side leads to the tomb chamber. The vaulted ceiling of the vestibule was ornately frescoed in gold and blue of which a section has been restored; a chapter from the Koran runs under the cornice. A gentle ramp leads down through a narrow arched passage to the tomb chamber. Sealed bays, off the main chamber, contain other tombs (shoes must be removed or cloth overshoes worn; hire Rs 2). In a niche opposite the entrance is an alabaster tablet inscribed with the 99 divine names of Allah. The sepulchre is in the centre of the room, whose velvety darkness is pierced by a single slanting shaft of light from a high window. The custodian, in expectation of a donation, makes 'Akbaaarrrr' echo around the chamber.

Four kilometres south of Sikandra, nearly opposite the high gateway of the ancient **Kach ki sarai** building, is a sculptured horse, believed to mark the spot where Akbar's favourite horse died. There are also *kos minars* (marking a *kos*, about 4 km) and several other tombs on the way.

Mathura → *Phone code. 0565. Colour map 2, grid A0. Population: 300,000. 50 km from Agra.*

Mathura, on the west bank of the Yamuna, is one of the most sacred cities of Hinduism dating back to 600 BC. For Vaishnavites it is perhaps the supremely sacred city of India, being the reputed birthplace of **Krishna**, the most human aspect of Vishnu. Krishna is widely seen as the embodiment of the ideal lover, soldier, statesman, as well as the adorable baby, or wayward child. Many places are associated with episodes in his life (see Excursions below). Mathura's ancient structures were mostly destroyed by Muslims but its religious association draws thousands of pilgrims.

Today, Mathura is an important industrial city with much evidence of modernizing on the approach from the highway. The opening of a big oil refinery on the outskirts of the city in 1975 caused great concern among environmentalists that atmospheric pollution would irreversibly damage the Taj Mahal only 50 km away.

History Ptolemy mentioned the town and it assumed the importance of a capital city during the first to second century **Kushan Empire**. When the Chinese traveller Hiuen Tsang visited it in 634 AD it was an important Buddhist centre with several monasteries. However, **Mahmud of Ghazni** sacked the city and desecrated its temples in 1017, followed by **Sikander Lodi** in 1500, whilst the Mughal **Emperor Aurangzeb** used a local revolt in which his governor was killed as an excuse to destroy the main temples. Jats and Marathas fought over the city as the Mughal Empire declined, but at the beginning of the 19th century it came under British control. They laid out a cantonment in the south and left a cemetery and the Roman Catholic **Sacred Heart Cathedral** (1870).

Sights There are no pre-Muslim monuments of any significance, and some of the finest buildings have been badly scarred by decay, neglect and misuse. You enter Mathura by the finely carved **Holi Gate** and in the centre is the **Jami Masjid** (1660-61) with four minarets, which was built by Abd-un-Nadi, Aurangzeb's governor. It has a raised courtyard and above the façade which was once covered with brightly coloured enamel tiles, are the 99 names of Allah.

The **Katra** (500 m) contains a mosque built by Aurangzeb. This stands over the ruins of one of Mathura's most famous temples, the **Kesava Deo Mandir** which, in turn had been built on the ruins of a Buddhist monastery of the Kushan period. This is considered to be **Sri Krishna Janmabhumi** (Krishna's birthplace). The main statues are particularly serene and attractive but there may be difficulty in entering due to extra security at times since there is a mosque next to it. At the rear of this enclosure is a newer **Temple of Kesava**, built by Bir Singh of Orchha, see page 283. Nearby is the **Potara Kund**, a stepped tank in which Krishna's baby clothes were washed. It is faced in the familiar local red sandstone with access for cattle and horses.

The river and its ghats are the focal point for Hindu pilgrims – a paved street runs their length. **Vishram Ghat** (rebuilt in 1814) is where Krishna rested after killing Kamsa. Cows, monkeys and turtles are fed when the *Arati* ceremony is performed, morning and evening which is best seen from a boat.

Mathura

Sleeping ■
1 Agra
2 International Guest House
3 Kwality
4 Madhuvan
5 Modern

The **Sati Burj** (late 16th century), on the river, is a square, four-storey red sandstone tower with a plastered dome said to commemorate the *sati* by the wife of Rajbihari Mal of Amber. The **Kans Qila** fort was built by Raja Man Singh of Amber and was rebuilt by Akbar but only the foundations remain. Nothing survives of Maharaja Jai Singh's, see page 336, observatory.

★ **Archaeological museum** ① *Dampier Nagar, T403191, in an octagonal red sandstone building, 1 Jul-30 Apr, 1000-1700, 1 May-30 Jun, 0730-1230, closed Sun, Mon, 2nd Sat every month, Rs 25 (foreigners), Rs 5 (Indians), camera Rs 20.* Here is an extensive and impressive collection of sculptures, terracottas, bronzes and coins; also the fifth-century 'Standing Buddha', numerous Gupta figures, a first-century headless Buddha, Kushana sculptures and Gandhara pieces.

Excursions **Gokul**, 2 km away, is approached by a long flight of steps from the river. It is associated with very early Hindu legends, where Vishnu first appeared as Krishna. It is the headquarters of the Vallabhacharya Sect who built some large temples.

Mahaban, 9 km southeast of Mathura on the east bank of the Yamuna, means 'a great forest'. There is no forest now but in 1634 Shah Jahan is recorded as having killed four tigers in a hunt here. The town was sacked by Mahmud of Ghazni in the 11th century. Each year in August Vaishnavite pilgrims come to the Nanda Krishna **Palace** where Krishna was believed to have been secretly raised. His cradle stands in the hall, the hole in the wall is where the *gopis* hid his flute, and the place where his mother stood churning butter is marked by a polished pillar.

Baradari of Sikander Lodi, 28 km south of Mathura, is the 12 pillared pavilion of Sikander Lodi, one time King of Delhi, built in 1495, and the 1611 **Tomb of Mariam uz Zamani**, Akbar's Hindu Rajput wife who is said to have been converted to Christianity, though there is little supporting evidence. There are beautiful carvings on the red sandstone structure.

Govardhan, 26 km west of Mathura on the Deeg road, lies in the narrow range of the Girraj Hills. In legend, when Indra caused a tremendous flood, Krishna raised these hills up above the flood for seven days so that people could escape. The **Harideva Temple**, by the Manasi Ganga River, was built by Raja Bhagwan Das in the reign of Akbar. On the opposite bank are the *chhattris* of Ranjit Singh and Balwant Singh, both rulers of Bharatpur. There are stone ghats on all sides, built in 1817. Krishna is believed to have ritually bathed at the temple to purify himself after killing the demon bull Arishta.

Vrindavan

→ *Phone code: 0571. Colour map 2, grid A6. The temples are open morning and evening usually between 0900 and 1200 and 0800 and 2100 when you can attend worship*

Vrindavan – 'Forest of Tulsi (basil) Plants' – is the most famous of the holy sites around Mathura. In Vrindavan, Krishna played with the *gopis* (cowgirls), stealing their clothes while they bathed. You are entering perhaps the most sacred region of India for Vaishnavite Hindus, where many of the stories surrounding **Krishna** are set, see page 1328).

At the entrance to the town is the 16th-century temple of **Gobind Dev** (1590), the 'Divine Cowherd', Krishna. Built by Man Singh of Jaipur during Akbar's reign, it was severely damaged by the less tolerant Aurangzeb. Nearby there is a Dravidian style temple dedicated to **Sri Ranganathji** (Vishnu), with three *gopura*, each nearly 30 m high. There is an annual 10-day *Rath* (car) festival in March/April. The 16th-century **Madan Mohan** temple stands above a ghat on an arm of the river; there is a pavilion decorated with cobra carvings. Siva is believed to have struck Devi here and made it a place for curing snake bites. The octagonal tower is similar to the one on the 16th-century **Jagat Krishna** temple.

Other temples include **Jugal Kishor** (reputedly 1027) near Kesi Ghat, **Banke Behari** near Purana Bazar where great excitement builds up each time the curtain before the deity is opened for *darshan* and **Radha Ballabh,** partly demolished by Aurangzeb, close by. **ISKCON** (International Society for Krishna Consciousness) with the Shri Krishna Balaram Temple, has a modern marble memorial. The centre runs yoga and meditation courses.

Aligarh Originally a Rajput stronghold from 1194, Aligarh ('high fort'), about 35 km northeast of Mathura, was administered by Muslim Governors appointed by the King of Delhi. The fort built in 1524 was subsequently reinforced by French and then British engineers. After the Mughals, it fell into Jat, Maratha and Rohilla hands before being taken by the British under Lord Lake in 1803. The 'Uprising' of 1857 quickly spread from Meerut when the ninth Native Infantry left to join the rebels at Delhi. The British regained control five months later. There are several **mosques** and the **Aligarh Muslim University**, founded by Sir Saiyad Ahmad Khan in 1875 as the Anglo-Oriental College, modelled on the Oxford and Cambridge collegiate system.

★ Fatehpur Sikri→ *Phone code: 05619. Colour map 2, grid A6. Population: 29,000.*

The red sandstone capital of Emperor Akbar, one of his architectural achievements, spreads along a ridge. The great mosque and palace buildings, deserted after only 14 years are still a vivid reminder of his power and vision. Perfectly preserved, it conjures up the lifestyle of the Mughals at the height of their glory.

History
The first two Great Mughals, Babur (ruled 1526-30) and his son Humayun (ruled 1530-40, 1555-56) both won (in Humayun's case, won back) Hindustan at the end of their lives, and they left an essentially alien rule. Akbar, the third and greatest of the Mughals changed that. By marrying a Hindu princess, forging alliances with the Rajput leaders and making the administration of India a partnership with Hindu nobles and princes rather than armed foreign minority rule, Akbar consolidated his ancestors' gains, and won

widespread loyalty and respect. Akbar had enormous personal magnetism. Though illiterate, he had great wisdom and learning as well as undoubted administrative and military skills. Fatehpur Sikri is testimony to this remarkable character.

Although he had many wives, the 26-year-old Akbar had no living heir; the children born to him had all died in infancy. He visited holy men to enlist their prayers for a son and heir. **Sheikh Salim Chishti**, living at Sikri, a village 37 km southwest of Agra, told the emperor that he would have three sons. Soon after, one of his wives, the daughter of the Raja of Amber, became pregnant, so Akbar sent her to live near the sage. A son Salim was born, later to be known as **Jahangir**. The prophecy was fulfilled when in 1570 another wife gave birth to Murad and in 1572, to Daniyal. Salim Chishti's tomb is here.

Akbar, so impressed by this sequence of events, resolved to build an entirely new capital at Sikri in honour of the saint. The holy man had set up his hermitage on a low hill of hard reddish sandstone, an ideal building material, easy to work and yet very durable. The building techniques used imitated carvings in wood, as well as canvas from the Mughal camp (eg awnings). During the next 14 years a new city appeared on this hill – 'Fatehpur' (town of victory) added to the name of the old village, 'Sikri'. Later additions and alterations were made and debate continues over the function and dates of the various buildings. It is over 400 years old and yet perfectly preserved, thanks to careful conservation work carried out by the Archaeological Survey of India at the turn of the century. There are three sections to the City: 'The Royal Palace', 'Outside the Royal Palace' and the 'Jami Masjid'.

When Akbar left, it was slowly abandoned to become ruined and deserted by the early 1600s. Some believe the emperor's decision was precipitated by the failure of the water supply, whilst local folklore claims the decision was due to the loss of the court singer Tansen, one of the "nine gems" of Akbar's court. However, there may well have been political and strategic motives. Akbar's change in attitude towards orthodox Islam and his earlier veneration of the Chishti saints supplanted by a new imperial ideology, may have influenced his decision. In 1585 he moved his court to Lahore and when he returned south again, it was to Agra. But it was at Fatehpur Sikri that Akbar spent the richest and most productive years of his 49-year reign.

The entrance

You enter Fatehpur Sikri through the **Agra Gate**. The straight road from Agra was laid out in Akbar's time. If approaching from Bharatpur you will pass the site of a lake (32-km circumference) which provided one defensive barrier. On the other sides was a massive defensive wall with nine gates: Clockwise – Delhi, Lal, Agra, Bir or Suraj (Sun), Chandar (Moon), Gwaliori, Tehra (Crooked), Chor (Thief's) and Ajmeri. Sadly there are men with 'performing' bears along this road – they should be discouraged – avoid stopping to photograph and tip.

✱ Official guides can be good: Rs 100; Rs 30 off-season. Avoid main entrance (lots of hawkers); take right hand fork after passing through Agra gate to hassle-free 2nd entrance.

From the Agra Gate you pass the sandstone **Tansen's Baradari** on your right and go through the triple arched **Chahar Suq** with a gallery with two *chhattris* above which may have been a **Nakkar khana** (Drum House). The road inside the main city wall leading to the entrance would have been lined with bazars. Next on your right is the square, shallow-domed **Mint** with artisans' workshops or animal shelters, around a courtyard. Workmen still chip away at blocks of stone in the dimly lit interior.

The Royal Palace

The **Diwan-i-Am** (Hall of Public Audience) was also used for celebrations and public prayers. It has cloisters on three sides of a rectangular courtyard and to the west, a pavilion with the emperor's throne, with *jali* screens on either side separating the court ladies. Some scholars suggest that the west orientation may have had the added significance of Akbar's vision of himself playing a semi-divine role.

This backed onto the private palace. In the centre of the courtyard behind the throne is the **Pachisi Board (1)** or Chaupar. It is said that Akbar had slave girls dressed in yellow, blue and red, moved around as 'pieces'!

The **Diwan-i-Khas** (Hall of Private Audience) to your right, is a two-storey building with corner kiosks. It is a single room with a unique circular throne platform. Here Akbar would spend long hours in discussion with Christians, Jains, Buddhists, Hindus and Parsis. They would sit along the walls of the balcony connected to the **Throne Pillar** by screened 'bridges', while courtiers could listen to the discussions from the ground floor. Decorative techniques and metaphysical labels are incorporated here – the pillar is lotus shaped (a Hindu and Buddhist motif), the Royal Umbrella (*chhattri*) is Hindu, and the Tree of Life, Islamic. The bottom of the pillar is carved in four tiers; Muslim, Hindu, Christian and Buddhist designs. The Throne Pillar can be approached by steps from the outside although there is no access to the upper floor. The design of the Hall deliberately followed the archaic universal pattern of establishing a hallowed spot from which spiritual influence could radiate. In his later years, Akbar developed a mystical cult around himself that saw him as being semi-divine.

An Archaeological Survey of India team recently discovered an "airconditioned palace" built for Akbar, while digging up steps leading down to a water tank set in the middle of the main palace complex. The subterranean chambers were found under the small quadrangle in sandstone, set in the middle of a water tank and connected on all four sides by narrow corridors. It's not yet open to the public.

In the **Treasury** in the northwest corner of the courtyard is the **Ankh Michauli** (Blind Man's Buff), possibly used for playing the game, comprising three rooms each protected by a narrow corridor with guards. The *makaras* on brackets are mythical sea creatures who guard the treasures under the sea. Just in front of the Treasury is **The Astrologer's Seat**, a small kiosk with elaborate carvings on the Gujarati 'caterpillar' struts which may have been used by the court astrologer or treasurer.

Fatehpur Sikri

■ **Sleeping**	5 Maurya	1 Pachisi Board	6 Jodh Bai's Palace
1 Ajay Palace &		2 Turkish Sultana's	7 Hawa Mahal
Restaurant	● **Eating**	House	8 Nagina Masjid
2 Dak Bungalow	1 Shree Café	3 Dawlatkhana-i-Khas	9 Raja Birbal's Palace
3 Goverdhan		4 Sunahra Makan	10 Tomb of Sheikh
4 Gulistan Tourist Complex		5 Panch Mahal	Salim Chishti

0 metres 100
0 yards 100

The **Turkish Sultana's House (2)** or Anup Talao Pavilion is directly opposite, beyond the Pachisi Board. Sultana Ruqayya Begum was Akbar's favourite and her 'house', with a balcony on each side, is exquisitely carved with Islamic decorations. Scholars suggest this may have been a pleasure pavilion. The geometrical pattern on the ceiling is reminiscent of Central Asian carvings in wood while the walls may have been set originally with reflecting glass to create a Sheesh Mahal (Mirror Palace). In the centre of this smaller south courtyard is the **Anup Talao** where the Emperor may have sat on the platform, surrounded by perfumed water. The *Akbarnama* mentions the emperor's show of charity when he filled the Talao with copper, silver and gold coins and distributed them over three years.

Dawlatkhana-i-Khas (3) The emperor's private chambers are next to the rose-water fountain in the corner. There are two main rooms on the ground floor. One housed his library – the recesses in the walls were for manuscripts. Although unable to read or write himself, Akbar enjoyed having books read to him. Wherever he went, his library of 50,000 manuscripts accompanied him. The larger room behind was his resting area. On the first floor is the **Khwabgah** ('Palace of Dreams') which would have had rich carpets, hangings and cushions. This too was decorated with gold and ultramarine paintings. The southern window known as the Jharokha Darshan was where the Emperor showed himself to his people every morning.

Sunahra Makan (4) or the Christian wife **Maryam's** House. Leaving the Dawlatkhana-i-Khas you enter another courtyard which contained the **Ladies' garden** for the *zenana*, and the two-storeyed house for the Emperor's mother, which was embellished with golden murals in the Persian style. The inscriptions on the beams are verses by **Fazl**, Akbar's poet laureate, one of the '*Navaratna*' (Nine Jewels) of the Court. Toilets in the corner of the garden are quite clean.

The **Panch Mahal (5)** is an elegant, airy five-storeyed pavilion just north of this, each floor smaller than the one below, rising to a single domed kiosk on top. The horizontal line of this terraced building is emphasized by wide overhanging eaves (for providing shade), parapets broken by the supporting pillars of which there are 84 on the ground floor (the magic number of seven planets multiplied by 12 signs of the zodiac). The 56 carved column on the second floor and all different and know Hindu influence. Originally dampened scented grass screens (*khuss*) which were hung in the open spaces, provided protection from the heat and sun, as well as privacy for the women who used the pavilion.

> **:** *From the upper storeys there is a fine view of the rest of Fatehpur Sikri and the adjoining countryside. The impression is that of an encampment in red stone.*

Jodh Bai's Palace (6) Jodh Bai, the daughter of the Maharaja of Amber, lived in Raniwas, the spacious palace in the centre, assured of privacy and security by high walls and a 9-m high guarded gate to the east. Outside the north wall is the 'hanging' **Hawa Mahal (7)** (Palace of Winds) with beautiful *jali* screens facing the *zenana* garden which was once enclosed, and the bridge (a later addition) led to the Hathipol. Through the arch is the small **Nagina Masjid (8)**, the mosque for the ladies of the court. The *hammams* (baths) are to the south of the palace. The centre of the building is a quadrangle around which were the harem quarters, each section self-contained with roof terraces. The style, a blend of Hindu and Muslim (the lotus, chain and bell designs being Hindu, the black domes Muslim), is strongly reminiscent oAf Gujarati temples, possibly owing to the craftsmen brought in (see *jarokha* windows, niches, pillars and brackets). The upper pavilions north and south have interesting ceiling structure (imitating the bamboo and thatch roof of huts), here covered with blue glazed tiles, adding colour to the buildings of red sandstone favoured by Akbar. Jodh Bai's vegetarian kitchen opposite the Palace has attractive chevron patterns.

Raja Birbal's Palace (9) Birbal, Akbar's Hindu Prime Minister, was the brightest of Akbar's 'Nine Jewels'. This highly ornamented house to the northwest of Jodh Bai's Palace has two storeys – four rooms and two porches with pyramidal roofs below, and two rooms with cupolas and screened terraces above. Again the building combines

Hindu and Islamic elements (note the brackets, eaves, *jarokhas*). Of particular interest is the insulating effect of the double-domed structure of the roofs and cupolas which allowed the rooms to remain cool, and the diagonal positioning of the upper rooms which ensured a shady terrace. Some scholars believe that this building, *Mahal-i-Ilahi*, was not for Birbal, but for Akbar's senior queens.

South of the Raja's house are the **stables**, a long courtyard surrounded by cells which probably housed zenana servants rather than the emperor's camels and horses, though the rings suggest animals may have been tied there.

Jami Masjid

Leaving the Royal Palace you proceed across a car park to the Jami Masjid and the sacred section of Fatehpur Sikri. The oldest place of worship here was the **Stone Cutters' Mosque** (circa 1565) to the west of the Jami Masjid. It was built near Sheikh Salim Chishti's cell which was later incorporated into it by stonecutters who settled on the ridge when quarrying for the Agra Fort began. It has carved monolithic 'S' brackets to support the wide sloping eaves.

The **King's Gate** (Badshahi Darwaza) is the entrance Akbar used. Shoes must be left at the gate but there are strips of carpet cross the courtyard to save burning your feet. The porch is packed with aggressive salesmen. The two other gates on the south and north walls were altered by subsequent additions. Built in 1571-72, this is one of the largest mosques in India. Inside is the congregational courtyard (132 x 111 m). To your right in the corner is the **Jamaat Khana Hall** and next to this the **Tomb of the Royal Ladies** on the north wall. The square nave carries the principal dome painted in the Persian style, with pillared aisles leading to side chapels carrying subsidiary domes. The **mihrab** in the centre of the west wall orientates worshippers towards Mecca. The sanctuary is adorned with carving, inlay work and painting.

The **Tomb of Sheikh Salim Chishti (10)**, a masterpiece in brilliant white marble, dominates the northern half of the courtyard. The Gujarati-style serpentine 'S' struts, infilled with *jali*, are highly decorative while the carved pillar bases and lattice screens are stunning pieces of craftsmanship. The canopy over the tomb is inlaid with mother of pearl. On the cenotaph is the date of the saint's death (1571) and the date of the building's completion (1580); the superb marble screens enclosing the verandah were added by Jahangir's foster brother in 1606. Around the entrance are inscribed the names of God, the Prophet and the four Caliphs of Islam. The shrine inside, on the spot of the saint's hermitage, originally had a red sandstone dome, which was marble veneered around 1806. Both Hindu and Muslim women pray at the shrine, tying cotton threads, hoping for the miracle of parenthood that Akbar was blessed with.

Next to it, in the courtyard, is the larger, red, sandstone tomb of **Nawab Islam Khan**, Sheikh Salim's grandson, and other members of the family.

Buland Darwaza (Triumphal Gate) dominates the south wall but it is a bit out of place. Built to celebrate Akbar's brilliant conquest of Gujarat (circa 1576), it sets the style for later gateways. The high gate is approached from the outside by a flight of steps which adds to its grandeur. The decoration shows Hindu influence, but is severe and restrained, emphasizing the lines of its arches with plain surfaces. You see an inscription on the right of a verse from the Qur'an:

> *Said Jesus Son of Mary (on whom be peace):*
> *The world is but a bridge;*
> *pass over it but build no houses on it. He*
> *who hopes for an hour, hopes for*
> *Eternity. The world is an hour. Spend it*
> *in prayer, for the rest is unseen.*

① *Sunrise to sunset, Rs 5 Indians, foreigners US$5. It is best to visit early, before the crowds. Official guides are good (about Rs 100; Rs 30 off season) but avoid others. Allow 3 hrs and carry plenty of drinking water.*

Between the Royal Palace and the Jami Masjid, a paved pathway to the northwest leads to the **Hathipol** (Elephant Gate). This was the ceremonial entrance to the palace quarters, guarded by stone elephants, with its *nakkar khana* and bazar alongside. Nearby are the **waterworks**, with a deep well which had an ingenious mechanism for raising water to the aqueducts above ridge height. The **caravanserai** around a large courtyard fits on the ridge side, and was probably one of a series built to accommodate travellers, tradesmen and guards. Down a ramp immediately beyond is the **Hiran Minar**, an unusual tower studded with stone tusks, thought to commemorate Akbar's favourite elephant, Hiran. However, it was probably an *Akash Diya* ('lamp to light the sky') or the 'zero point' for marking road distances in *kos*. You can climb up the spiral staircase inside it but take care as the top has no guard rail. This part of Fatehpur Sikri is off the main tourist track, and though less well preserved it is worth the detour to get the 'lost city' feeling, away from the crowds.

Listings: Southern Uttar Pradesh

⊕ Sleeping

Agra *p157, maps p158 and p166*
Most hotels are 5-10 km from the airport and 2-5 km from Agra Cantt Railway. Top hotels offer discounts May-Sep.
LL-L Amar Vilas (Oberoi), near Taj East Gate. New, ultra-luxurious hotel in prime location.
LL-L Mughal Sheraton (Welcomgroup), Fatehabad Rd, 1 km from Taj, T331701, F331730. 285 rooms, those with Taj view not worth the extra. *Nauratna* restaurant (bland Mughlai), good live Indian music, beautifully designed in the Mughal tradition (Aga Khan Award for architecture), rooftop observatory offers good views of the Taj.
L Clarks Shiraz, 54 Taj Rd, T361421, F361428, clarkraj@nda.vsnl.net.in. 237 rooms (bit tired), often full with groups, good rooftop restaurant with live music, distant view of the Taj from top floor, good shops, pleasant gardens (needing attention) and pool.
L Mansingh Palace, 181/2 Fatehabad Rd, T331771, F330202. 50 comfortable rooms, many with view of the Taj a kilometre away, Indian food good.
L Taj View (Taj Group), Fatehabad Rd, T232400, F232420, tajagra@tajhotels.com. 100 rooms, superior (even nos) have very

distant Taj view, lacks character, good pool (Rs 250 for non-residents), *Khazana* shop.
L-AL Trident (Oberoi), Fatehabad Rd, T331818, F331827, reservations@ tridentag.com. 143 very comfortable rooms, lowrise, immaculately clean but characterless, good pool, beautiful gardens, polite, friendly staff, restaurant disappointing (poolside BBQ better, but expensive).
AL Holiday Inn, Sanjay Place, Hariparwat Chowk, MG Rd, 8 km from Taj, T357642, F357625, hinnagra@sancharnet.in. New location, 94 rooms, restaurant, business centre, can arrange golf and tennis (10 km away).
A Great Value Agra, Bansal Nagar, Fatehabad Rd, T330225, F352645. Modern, comfortable, good value.
A Howard Park Plaza, Fatehabad Rd, T331870, F330408, howard@nda.vsnl.net.in. 85 comfortable rooms, good buffet breakfast (Indian/western), service can be slow.
A-B Ashok (ITDC), 6B Mall Rd, 3 km Taj, T361225, F361620, itdcagra@ sancharnet.com. 55 comfortable a/c rooms, good restaurant but a little dated, pool (non-resident foreigners Rs 200), pleasant, helpful staff, good value.
B Amar, Tourist Complex area, Fatehabad Rd, T331885, F330299, amaragra@sancharnet.in

---

● *For an explanation of the sleeping and eating price codes used in this guide, see inside the*
● *front cover. Other relevant information is found in Essentials pages 52-57.*

68 functional, comfortable a/c rooms (standard better value), bright a/c restaurant, pool, but can be noisy and lacks personality, rates negotiable (taxis get commission).
B Atithi, Fatehabad Rd, T330879, F330878, hotelatithi@hotmail.com. 44 adequate a/c rooms (some bath tubs dirty), extra bed Rs 200, restaurant, clean pool, welcoming staff.
C-D Mayur Tourist Complex, Fatehabad Rd, T332302, F332907. 30 rooms (most a/c) in pleasant bungalows, could be better maintained, restaurant, bar (pricey beer), pool (Rs 125), garden setting, good value.
D Jaiwal, 3 Taj Rd, next to *Kwality*, T363716. 17 cleanish rooms (front better), some a/c.
D-E Agra, 165 Gen Cariappa Rd, 500 m from fort, T363312, F361146. 18 large rooms (some air-cooled), could be cleaner, intermittent hot water, cheap meals, pleasant garden and patio, basic, old fashioned but helpful staff.
D-E Akbar, 196 Gen Cariappa Rd, near fort, T363312, F361146. Rooms vary, some have bath, others tiny, small garden, very friendly and helpful staff.
D-E Safari, Shamsabad Rd, T360013. Clean, small rooms, simple rooftop restaurant, away from hectic Taj Ganj area. Recommended.
D-E Sheela, East Gate, 2-min walk from Taj, T331194. 20 clean, comfortable rooms with bath, fan, mosquito-proof (some **E** air-cooled with hot shower), pleasant garden, camping Rs 20, good restaurant, very quiet, reliable laundry, secure (ask for gates to be unlocked for sunrise!), excellent value (no commission to rickshaws) but check bills carefully, reserve ahead. Recommended.
D-E Tourist Bungalow (UP Tourism), Station Rd opposite Raja-ki-Mandi station, T350120. Some a/c rooms, dorm and camping, clean but far from centre.
E Gypsy, Shamsabad Rd, near Radio Station, south of Taj Ganj, T36040. Clean rooms, friendly but overpriced.
E New Bakshi House, 5 Laxman Nagar, towards airport, T368035. Best room has a/c, good food, free pick-up, clean, well run, helpful owners.
E Tourist Rest House, Balugunj, Kachcheri Rd, T363961, F366910. Western toilet, hot showers, air-cooling inadequate in summer, a/c, pure-vegetarian restaurant, fairly basic, a bit dog-eared but friendly, helpful and

knowledgeable manager, travel agent, relaxing garden, good value, often full.
F Railway Retiring Rooms at Agra Fort, T364163, and Cantt Stations, T131. For passengers, advance reservations with money order/draft to Rly Supt, Agra Cantt. Some a/c rooms and dorm.

Taj Ganj

Several cheap guesthouses include:
E-F Host, West Gate, T331010. Clean rooms with bath and hot water, some a/c with bath and balcony, rooftop restaurant with good views but food unpredictable.
E-F Sidhartha, 250 m south from Taj West Gate, T331238, 264711. Rooms with bath and hot water (could be cleaner), good restaurant, pleasant courtyard and rooftop.
F Gulshan, South Gate. Mediocre rooms with bath, good, cheap food but slow service (no commission to rickshaws).
F India Guest House, South Gate, T330909. 8 simple, clean rooms, some with coolers, shared toilets, average food, lovely family atmosphere. Recommended.
F Shah Jahan, T331159. Room with a view of the Taj, hot shower, simple, cheap, north Indian food, Taj view.
F Sikander, near South Gate. Few clean rooms, basic food.
F Taj View Lodge, off Taj Rd. Few rooms, no views, noisy.

Camping

C Mayur, hotel.
D Grand, hotel.
D Lauries, hotel.
E Agra, hotel.
E Taj Khema hotels.
E Tourist Bungalow, hotel.
E-F Akbar Inn.

Mathura *p169, map p170*
Hotels serve vegetarian food only. No alcohol.
B-C Madhuvan, Krishna Nagar, T420064, F420684. 28 rooms, some a/c with bath, restaurant, exchange, travel, pool.
B-C Radha Ashok (Best Western), Masani By-pass Rd, Chatikara, 4 km north from centre, T530395, F530396, bwra@vsnl.com. 21 comfortable rooms (freezing a/c) in modern hotel, good restaurant, pool.

● **Phone codes** *Agra: 0562; Mathura: 0565; Vrindavan: 0571; Fatehpur Sikri: 05619*

C-D **Mansarovar Palace**, State Bank Crossing, T408686, F401611. 22 rooms, most a/c, restaurant.
E **Agra**, near Bengali Ghat, T403318. Some aircooled rooms, traditional, friendly.
E **Tourist Bungalow** (UP Tourism), Civil Lines, Bypass Rd, T407822. 14 rooms, restaurant, bar.
F **International Guest House**, Katra Keshav Deo, T405888. Some air-cooled rooms.
Dwaper Resorts, at 162 km marker, NH2, 17 km south of Mathura on the Agra Rd, T0565-480092. Restaurant, attractive gardens, convenient rest stop.
Gokul (UP Tourism), Delhi Bypass Rd. Indian, open-air.
Modern, T404747. Near Old Bus Stand.
Quality, T406195. Near Old Bus Stand. With a restaurant.
Radha Ashok, recommended.
Railway Retiring Rooms, at Cantt and Junc Stations.

Vrindavan *p171, map p172*
C-D **Geet Govind Tourist Complex**, Nandanvan, T442517. 10 rooms (some a/c), veg restaurant (no alcohol).
D-E **International Rest House** (ISKCON), Raman Reti, T442478. Clean rooms, good, reasonably priced veg restaurant, very popular, book well ahead.

Fatehpur Sikri *p172, map p174*
It is worth spending a night here to make an early start.
D **Gulistan Tourist Complex** (UP Tourism), Agra Rd, 1 km from Bus Stand, T882490. Good rooms with modern facilities, some C a/c, restaurant, quiet, pleasant grounds, mixed reports on food and service.
E-F **Govardhan**, Buland Darwaza Rd Crossing, T882643. Rooms with clean common bath, air-cooled suites with fridge, summer camping (Rs 20), 40% university student discount, garden restaurant, pool, well maintained, lively and conscientious owner. Recommended.
E-F **Maurya**, near Buland Darwaza, T882348. Very basic rooms (rock hard bed), some with bath (bucket hot water), snacks.
  North Indian food available at **Sher-e-Punjab**, By-Pass Rd (with rooms), T882238. North Indian food available.

● Eating

Agra *p157, maps p158 and p166*
The top hotels are the most comfortable.
₹₹₹ **PAC** opposite *Amar*. Chinese and Indian. Newish, quite up-market, large outdoor seating, clean, good food and service, breakfast to dinner, no beer.
₹₹₹ **Petals**, 19A Taj Rd, Sadar Bazar, T363087. Mughlai specially. Comfortable, modern, a/c, good food and service.
₹₹₹ **Priya**, 4/17 Baluganj, behind *Ratan Deep Hotel*. Indian, Chinese, a/c, very good Indian, friendly, live *sitar* music, nice garden.
₹₹₹ **Taj Khema**, near Taj East Gate, T330140. Indian. Good food (after ordering, ask to sit out and view the Taj by moonlight while you wait).
₹₹ **Dasaprakash**, 1 Gwalior Rd. South Indian. A/c, modern, very good but a bit overpriced.
₹₹ **Maya**, Fatehabad Rd, Purani Mandi, Taj Ganj. Mixed. Good Punjabi *thalis* (Rs 120), garlic naan, pasta, "special tea", friendly, prompt service, hygienic, tasty. Recommended.
₹₹ **Only**, 45 Taj Rd (Phool Sayed Crossing). International. A/c indoor, or on large lawns (usual mosquitoes), pleasant atmosphere, tourist oriented food all day.
₹₹ **Sonam**, 51 Taj Rd. Indian, Chinese. A/c, good food, clean, bar, cheaper *thalis*, pleasant garden. Recommended.
₹₹ **Tin Tin**, near Taj. Chinese. Friendly owners, good escape from hawkers.
₹₹ **Zorba the Buddha** (Osho), behind Tourist Office, E13 Shopping Arcade, GC Shivhare Rd. A/c, no artificial colours, good cooking (spicy on request), "fantastic *daal* and fruit *lassis*", pleasant, very clean, not cheap, 1200-1500, 1800-2100.
₹ **Gulati**, MG Rd. Good Indian.

Near the Taj
₹ **Daawat**, Fatehabad Rd, 5-min walk from Taj. Indian. Pleasant garden area, beer.
₹ **Honey**, Taj South Gate. Best banana *lassis*.
₹ **Lucky**, good food, seasoned to your taste, pleasant, friendly.

Vegetarian
Deviram, Ajmer Rd. Good sweets despite appalling exterior.
Shankar Vegis, Chowk Kaghzi, 150 m south of Taj Gate. Occasional barbecues on rooftop, 'special tea' (beer in teapots), all to loud music!

Fatehpur Sikri *p172, map p174*
Ajay, North Indian, does good *thalis*, Rs 50.

▲ Festivals and events

Agra *p157, maps p158 and p166*
18-27 Feb: Taj Mahotsav is a celebration of
the region's arts, crafts, culture and cuisine.
Aug/Sep: A fair at Kailash (14 km). A temple
marks the place where Siva is believed to
have appeared in the form of a stone lingam.

Mathura *p169, map p170*
Mar: Rang Gulal, the colourful *Holi* festival.
Similar festivities at Janmashtami. Banjatra
(Forest Pilgrimage). During the monsoon,
episodes from Krishna's life are enacted.

○ Shopping

Agra *p157, maps p158 and p166*
Never agree to any export 'deals' (you might
not be sent what you ordered) and take great
care with credit card slips (fiddles reported).
    The handicrafts Agra specializes in are mostly
related to the court eg jewellery, inlaid and
carved marble, carpets and clothes. The main
shopping areas for everyday items as well as
handicrafts are Sadar Bazar (closed Tue), Kinari
Bazar, Gwalior Rd, Mahatma Gandhi Rd and
Pratap Pura. Many rickshaws, taxi drivers and
guides earn up to 40% commission by taking
tourists to marble/curio/carpet shops. Insist on
not being rushed away from sights. To shop, go
independently. To get a good price you have to
bargain hard anyway.

Books
Modern Book Depot, Sadar Bazar. *Hotel Taj
View* shop.

Carpets
Silk/cotton/wool mix hand knotted carpets
and woven *dhurries* are all made in Agra.
High quality and cheaper than in Delhi.
Mughal Arts Emporium, Shamshabad Rd.
Also has marble. Artificial silk is sometimes
passed off as pure silk.

Clothes
Boutiques on Taj Rd, Sadar Bazar.
East & West Design, 18/184 Purani Mandi,
Fatehabad Rd. German-run, good clothes
and crafts.

Handlooms and handicrafts
State Govt emporia in arcade at Taj entrance.
Also **UP Handlooms** and **UPICA** at Sanjay
Place, Hari Parbat.
Sweety Musicals, 869/1 Gwalior Rd, Naulakha,
T363595. Indian classical musical instruments.

Jewellery
Never agree to have jewellery posted.
    (If you are not visiting Jaipur) try:
Jewel House Kohinoor, 41 MG Rd.
Munshi Lal next to UP Handicrafts Palace.
Sunrise Jeweller, 796 Sadar Bazar.

Marble
Delicately inlaid marble work is a speciality.
Sometimes cheaper alabaster and fake
stones for inlay are used and quality varies.
Akbar International, Fatehabad Rd. Good
selection, inlay demonstration, fair prices.
Handicrafts Inn, 3 Gorg Niketan, Fatehabad
Rd, Taj Ganj. Recommended.
Krafts Palace, 506 The Mall. Watch
craftsmen working here. Recommended.
New Fine Art Marble, Taj South gate.
Oswal, 30 Munro Rd, Sadar Bazar, T363240.
Watch craftsmen working here.
Subhash 18/1 Gwalior Rd. Recommended.
UP Handicrafts Palace, 49 Bansal Nagar. Very
wide selection from table tops to coasters,
high quality and good value. Recommended.
    Avoid **Unique Handicrafts**, Taj Rd.
Travellers sold fakes.

Photography
Agra Colour Lab, E6-7 Shopping Arcade,
Sadar Bazar. For 1-hr processing.
    Many others including in Taj complex and
Sadar Bazar.

▲ Activities and tours

Agra *p157, maps p158 and p166*
Swimming
Swimming pools in most **A** and **AL** hotels are
open to non-residents.

Tour companies
ATS, 48 MMIG, Shaheed Nagar, T333357,
atsagr@nde.vsnl.net.in. Tours to Khajuraho.
Aargee, Fatehabad Rd, T360529, F360456.
Mercury, *Hotel Clarks Shiraz*, 54 Taj Rd,
T/F360282. Helpful and reliable.
Sita, Sadar Bazar, T361429.

TCI, *Hotel Clarks Shiraz*, T361121.
Touraids, 46 G Shivahare Rd, Sadar Bazar,
T363138.
Travel Bureau, near *Taj View Hotel*, T330219.
UP, 64 Taj Rd, T360517, and at Tourist
Bungalow, Raja-ki-Mandi, T350120, Agra
Cantonment; T368598. Rajasthan, T360017
and Haryana, at Taj Mahal Shopping Arcade.
UP Tourism, *Taj Khema*, east Gate, Taj Mahal,
T330140.
UP Tours, T351720. Tourist offices Govt of
India, 191 The Mall, T363377. Guides
available (about Rs 100), helpful and friendly
Director and staff. Kheria (Agra) Airport
counter, during flight times.

  Coach tours: Fatehpur Sikri-Taj
Mahal-Agra Fort (full day) 1000-1800, Rs 100
(including guide but not entry);
Sikandra-Fatehpur Sikri (half day) 0930-1400,
Rs 100 (excludes entry fees); Sikandra-
Fatehpur Sikri-Taj Mahal-Agra Fort (full day),
0930-1800; Fatehpur Sikri (half day)
1030-1430 which only gives 45 mins at the
site; not worthwhile, better take a taxi if you
can afford it. Some tours start and finish at
Agra Cantt Rly Station, T368598.

⊙ Transport

Agra *p157, maps p158 and p166*
Air
Kheria airport is 7 km from city centre.
Transport to town: airport bus to/from major
hotels; auto-rickshaws charge about Rs 50
and taxis, Rs 75. **Indian Airlines**, Clarks Shiraz,
T361180, airport T361241. Daily flights to
Delhi, and to **Varanasi** via Khajuraho. Long
delays in flight departures and arrivals
possible especially in winter when Agra and
Delhi airports close for periods due to fog.

Bicycle
Bike hire: Sadar Bazar, near Police station
and near *Tourist Rest House*, Rs 15 per day.

Bus
Local City Bus Service covers most areas.
Plenty leave from the Taj Mahal area and the
Fort Bus Stand. Buses also go to the main sites.
Long distance Most buses from Jaipur
go on to a 2nd stop near Hotel Sakura:
closer to most hotels and where there is
less hassle from touts; auto from first stop
to Taj Ganj, Rs 25.

UPSRTC Roadways Bus Stand, Idgah,
enquiry T367543; **Fort Bus Station** (opposite
Power House), T364557; Ram Bagh Crossing
(across River Yamuna). *Deluxe* buses from
Hotel Sheetal, T369420. **Delhi** from tourist
office, 0700, 1445, *Deluxe*, 4 hrs. Most long
distance services leave from the **Idgah Bus
Stand**; *Deluxe* recommended. Daily *Express*
buses to: **Fatehpur Sikri** (Rs 16-28, 1 hr),
very bumpy; **Gwalior** (119 km via Dholpur
and Morena); **Jaipur** (240 km via Bharatpur
and Mahua, 5-6 hrs); government bus
recommended (problems reported on
private buses), Rs 103, hourly; **Khajuraho**
(400 km via Jhansi, 0500, 12 hrs), direct 0500,
10 hrs; **Lucknow** (357 km via Shikohabad,
Etawah and Kanpur), 0700, 11 hrs, Rs 150;
Nainital (376 km via Tundla, Etah, Bareilly
and Haldwani, 10 hrs).

Rickshaw
Auto rickshaw: eg Idgah Bus Stand to Taj
Ganj, Rs 25. Cycle rickshaw: Rs 10-15 for short
trips (pay more to avoid visiting shops!); Taj
Ganj to fort Rs 10; Rs 75-100 for visiting
sights, PO, bank etc; Rs 150 for 12 hrs.

Taxi/car hire
Tourist taxis from travel agents, remarkably
good value for visiting nearby sights.
Non-a/c car Rs 3.5 per km, full day Rs 350
(100 km), half day Rs 175 (45 km), a/c rates
approximately double. **Budget** Rent-a-car,
T361771; **UP Tours**, T351720.

Train
Train travel from Delhi is quicker and more
reliable. Thieves operate at the station so
watch your bags.
  Agra has 7 railway stations – the most
important are **Agra Cantonment** on the main
Delhi-Mumbai line, and **Agra Fort**. Agra
Cantonment, enquiries T131, reservations
T364519, open 0800-2000. Foreigners' queue
at Window 1. Good 1st class waiting room.
Pre-paid taxi/auto rickshaw kiosk outside
the station. Avoid hotel touts. Railway stations:
Agra Fort, T132, T364163; **Raja-ki-Mandi**,
T133; **Tundla**, T345646. Unless stated
otherwise, trains mentioned arrive and depart
from Agra Cantt in the southwest of the city,
about 5 km from the Taj Mahal. From **New
Delhi**: best is *Shatabdi Exp, 2002*, 0600, 2 hrs
(meal included); *Kerala Exp, 2626*, 1130,

Power to pedal

To achieve a 'Greener', cleaner Agra by reducing pollution by vehicle emissions, a new model of cycle rickshaw has been developed by the Institute for Transportation and Development Policy, an Indian NGO, with help from the US Agency for International Development, after consulting local organizations and the men who will be pedalling them. The much lighter (and easier to operate), more comfortable and faster transport for two, is an attractive alternative to fume emitting engines. The concerned visitor can opt to hire one from outside a top hotel for around Rs 150, to be wheeled around the city to see the Taj, the Fort, sample local cuisine and also reduce approaches by hawkers and beggars.

2¼ hrs; from **New Delhi (HN)**: *Taj Exp, 2180,* 0705, 2½ hrs; *Lakshadweep Exp, 2618,* 0955, 2½ hrs; *Goa Exp, 2780,* 1500, 2½ hrs.To **New Delhi**: *Shatabdi Exp, 2001,* 2018, 2 hrs; to **New Delhi (HN)**: *Taj Exp, 2179,* 1835, 3½ hrs. To **Bhopal**: *Shatabdi Exp, 2002,* 0800, 6¼ hrs; **Gwalior**: *Taj Exp, 2180,* 0955, 2 hrs; *Shatabdi Exp, 2002,* 0800, 1¼ hrs; *Punjab Mail, 2138,* 0830, 1¾ hrs. **Jaipur** *Marudhar Exp, 4853/63,* 1505, 6¾ hrs. **Jhansi**: *Shatabdi Exp, 2002,* 0800, 2½ hrs (to catch bus to Khajuraho, last at 1315); *Punjab Mail, 2138,* 0830, 3¼ hrs; *Lakshadweep Exp, 2618,* 1235, 3 hrs. **Lalkuan (for Nainital)**: *Kumaon Exp, 5311,* 2200, 11¾ hrs. **Ernakulam/Kochi**: *Mangla Lakshadweep Exp 2618,* 1235, 52 hrs. **Kolkata (H)**: *Jodhpur- Howrah Exp, 2308,* 0635, 22¼ hrs (from Fort). **Lucknow** (from Fort): *Marudhar Exp, 4854/4864,* 2105, 5¾ hrs; *Agra Lucknow Exp, 5314,* 1730, 15½ hrs. **Mathura**: *Marudhar Exp, 4853/4863,* 0715, 1¼ hrs; *Taj Exp,* 2179, 1835, 50 mins. **Mumbai** (CST): *Punjab Mail, 2138,* 0830, 23¼ hrs. **Varanasi** via **Lucknow**: *Marudhar Exp, 4854/4864,* 2105, 11-12 hrs (book ahead); from Tundla (30 mins by taxi from Agra) *Lichchavi Exp, 5206,* 2015, 9 hrs; or go to Mughal Sarai (16 km from Varanasi) 13-14 hrs.

Mathura *p169, map p170*
Bus
Long distance Frequent service to **Delhi**, **Jaipur** and neighbouring towns from the New Bus Stand opposite *Hotel Nepal*. Buses to **Govardhan** and **Agra** from Old Bus Stand near the rly station, T4064680.

Taxi
From opposite District Hospital. Also, buses, auto and cycle rickshaws.

Train
Mathura Junc is the main station, T405830. Cantt Station is at Bahadurganj (metre gauge). Sri Krishna Janmabhumi is at Bhuteshwar. For Delhi and Agra, the best is to **Agra Cantt**: *Taj Exp, 2180,* 0900, 47 mins. **New Delhi (HN)**: *Taj Exp, 2179,* 1930, 2¼ hrs. **Sawai Madhopur**: *Golden Temple Mail, 2904,* 1025, 3 hrs; *Bandra Exp, 9020,* 0140, 3½ hrs; *Janata Exp, 9024,* 1735, 4 hrs. **Vrindavan**: see below.

Vrindavan *p171, map p172*
To and from **Mathura**: buses, tempos and auto-rickshaws.

Train
Service from Mathura Junction at 0627, 0850, 1457, 1655, 1925, takes 35 mins; returns from **Vrindavan** at 0725, 0940, 1610, 1740, 2015.

Fatehpur Sikri *p172, map p174*
Bus
Frequent buses from Agra Idgah Bus Stand (1 hr) Rs 16.

Taxi
From Agra include the trip in a day's sightseeing (about Rs 650 return).

Train
To **Sawai Madhopore** (for Ranthambore), departs 0600, 0900, 1800.

Phone codes *Agra: 0562; Mathura: 0565; Vrindavan: 0571; Fatehpur Sikri: 05619*

Agra *p157, maps p158 and p166*

Banks Andhra Bank, Taj Rd, opposite *Kwality's* gives cash against card. **Canara**, Sadar Bazar and Sanjay Place, and others. **Hospitals** District, Chhipitola Rd/MG Rd, T363043. **Lady Lyall**, S Bhagat Singh Rd, T267987. **SN**, Hospital Rd, T361314. **Amit Jaggi Hospital**, Vibhav Nagar, T330600. Clean, safe but "Pays commission to rickshaws, presents extortionate bills, keeps

you in longer than necessary". **Post office** The Mall (24 hrs). GPO: opposite India Tourist Office, with Poste Restante. **Useful addresses** Ambulance: T202. Fire: T201. Police: T200. Foreigners' Registration Office: 16 Idgah Colony, T367563.

Mathura *p169, map p170*

Hospitals District Hospital, near Agra Rd, T406315. Methodist Hospital, Vrindavan Rd, T406032. **Tourist offices UP**, near Old Bus Stand, T405351.

Eastern Uttar Pradesh

★ Varanasi → *Phone code: 0542. Colour map 3, grid B4. Population: over a million.*

Perhaps the holiest of India's cities, Varanasi defies easy description. A highly congested maze of narrow alleys winding behind its waterfront ghats, at once highly sacred yet physically often far from clean. As an image, an idea and a symbol of Hinduism's central realities, the city draws pilgrims from around the world, to worship, to meditate, and above all to bathe. It is a place to be born and a place to die. In the cold mists of a winter's dawn, you can see life and death laid bare. For an outside observer it can be an uncomfortable experience, juxtaposing the inner philosophical mysteries of Hinduism with the practical complications of living literally and metaphorically on the edge.

The city's focus extends from Raj Ghat in the north, to Assi Ghat in the south. At dawn the riverbank's stone steps begin to hum with activity. Early risers immerse themselves in the water as they face the rising sun, boatmen wait expectantly on the waterside, pilgrims flock to the temples, flower sellers do brisk business, astrologers prepare to read palms and horoscopes while families carry the dead to their last rites by the holy river. A few steps away from the ghats, motor-bikers speed through the lanes narrowly missing a motley band of wandering sadhus, hopeful beggars, curious visitors and wandering cows, while packs of stray dogs scavenge among the piles of rubbish.

▶▶ *For Sleeping, Eating and other listings, see pages 197-204.*

Ins and outs

Getting there Several airlines link Varanasi with Delhi, Lucknow, Khajuraho, Kathmandu, Mumbai and other cities. From Babatpur airport (22 km away) there is an airport bus which goes as far as the *Indian Airlines* office in the Cantonment area but not into the city centre. Alternatively you can take a taxi. Most long-distance buses arrive at the bus stand near the cross-roads 500 m northeast of the Junction Station. Most trains stop at the Junction Station near the Cantonment, about 3 km northwest of the Old City and the budget hotels. Some trains (eg, Delhi-Kolkata *Rajdhani* and *Expresses* to New Jalpaiguri and Guwahati) do not pass through Varanasi itself but stop at Mughal Sarai, 16 km away, which is easily accessible by rail or road from Varanasi. A rickshaw from Mughal Sarai to Assi Ghat costs around Rs 100.

Getting around The only way really to see the heart of the Old City is on foot, though no visit is complete without an early morning boat trip along the Ghats. Yet Varanasi is quite spread out: the university to the south is nearly 7 km from the spacious Cantonment area and the Junction Station to the north. Around town, cycle-rickshaws are common, while autos are usually shared. Buses are hopelessly crowded so you might consider hiring a bike if you are staying a few days. Unmetered taxis are best for longer sightseeing trips. The city has some of the disadvantages of pilgrimage centres, notably rickshaw drivers who seem determined to extort as much as possible from unsuspecting visitors. See Transport, page 202, for further details.

Varanasi

Related map
A Varanasi Ghats, page 188

	5 Dak Bungalow	13 Sita
	6 Diamond	14 Sun Shiv
	7 Garden View	15 Surya, Hilarious
	8 GM Guest House	Restaurant, Music
	9 Hindustan	India & Air India
	International	16 Taj Ganges
■ Sleeping	& Eats & Bites	& Burger King
1 Ashok	10 India & Vaibhav	17 Temple on Ganges
2 Baba & Shiva	11 Malti	& Ganges View
3 Buddha	12 Pradeep & Poonam	18 UP Tourist Bungalow
4 Clarks Hotels, Air India		

19 Varanasi Ashok	
● Eating	
1 Ashiana	
2 Bread of Life	
3 Gudiya	
4 Kwality	
5 Mandarin & El Parador	
6 Pizzeria Café Vaatika	
7 Sindhi	

300 mm. Dry during other months. Best time to visit: Nov-Mar.

Background

Varanasi derives its name from two streams, the Varuna to the north and the Assi, a small trickle, on the south. **Banaras** is a corruption of Varanasi but it is also called **Kashi** ('The City of Light') by Hindus. As one of the seven sacred cities of Hinduism (see page 1326) it attracts well over one million pilgrims while about 30,000 Brahmins are permanant residents. The Jains too consider it holy because three *tirthankars* (seventh Suarsvanath, 11th Shyeyanshnath, 23th Parsvanath) were born here.

Varanasi is said to combine all the virtues of all other places of pilgrimage, and anyone dying within the area marked by the **Panch Kosi Road** is transported straight to heaven. Some devout Hindus move to Varanasi to end their days and have their ashes scattered in the holy Ganga. Every pilgrim, in addition to visiting the holy sites, must make a circuit of the Panch Kosi Road which runs outside and round the sacred territory of Varanasi. This starts at Manikarnika Ghat, runs along the waterfront to Assi Ghat, then round the outskirts in a large semi-circle to Barna Ghat. The 58-km route is lined with trees and shrines and the pilgrimage is supposed to take six days, each day's walk finishing in a small village, equipped with temples and *dharamshalas*.

Varanasi was probably already an important town by the seventh century BC when Babylon and Nineveh were at the peak of their power. The Buddha visited it in 500 BC and it was mentioned in both the *Mahabharata* and the *Ramayana*. It became a centre of culture, education, commerce and craftsmanship but was raided by **Mahmud of Ghazni's** army in 1033 and by Qutb-ud-din Ghuri in 1194. **Ala-ud-din Khalji**, the King of Delhi (1294-1316), destroyed temples and built mosques on their sites. The Muslim influence was strong so even in the 18th century the city, for a brief period, was known as Mohammadabad. Despite its early foundation hardly any building dates before the 17th century, and few are more than 200 years old.

The city stands as the chief centre of **Sanskrit learning** in North India. Sanskrit, the oldest of the Indo-European languages, used for Hindu ritual has been sustained here long after it ceased to be a living language elsewhere. The Banaras Hindu **University** has over 150,000 rare manuscripts. Hindu devotional movements flourished here, especially in the 15th century under Ramananda, and **Kabir**, one of India's greatest poets, lived in the city. It was here that **Tulsi Das** translated the Ramayana from Sanskrit into Hindi.

Sights

★ **Old Centre Visvanath Temple** (1777) has been the main Siva temple in Varanasi for over 1,000 years. The original temple, destroyed in the 12th century, was replaced by a mosque. It was rebuilt in the 16th, and again destroyed within a century. The present **'Golden' temple** was built in 1777 by Ahilya Bai of Indore. The gold plating on the roof was provided by Maharaja Ranjit Singh in 1835. Its pointed spires are typically North Indian in style and the exterior is finely carved. Only Hindus are allowed inside. There are good views and photos from second floor of a silk shop across the road (pay about Rs 5) though 'guards' may object if you are seen taking photos. The 18th-century **Annapurna Temple** (*anna* food; *purna* filled) nearby, built by Baji Rao I, has shrines dedicated to Siva, Ganesh, Hanuman and Surya. Ask for directions as you make your way through the maze of alleys around the temples.

The **Gyan Kup** (Well of Knowledge) next door is said to contain the Siva lingam from the original temple – the well is protected by a stone screen and canopy. The **Gyanvapi Mosque** (Great Mosque of Aurangzeb) with 71-m high minarets shows evidence of the original Hindu temple, in the foundations, the columns and at the rear.

The 17th-century **Alamgir Mosque** (Beni Madhav ka Darera), on Panchganga Ghat, was Aurangzeb's smaller mosque. It was built on the original Vishnu temple of

⁝ Polluted Ganga purifies itself

All along the Ganga, the major problem of waste disposal (of human effluent and industrial toxins) has defied the best efforts of the Ganga Action Plan set up in 1986 to solve it. The diversion and treatment of raw sewage in seven main cities was planned. In Varanasi however, the 17th-century sewers, the inadequate capacity of the sewage works, the increased waterflow during the monsoons and the erratic electricity supply (essential for pumping) have all remained problems. In addition, although most Hindus are cremated, an estimated 45,000 uncremated or partially cremated bodies are put in the Ganga each year. A breed of scavenger turtles which dispose of rotting flesh was introduced down river but the turtles disappeared.

The Uttar Pradesh Water Board (Jal Nigam) has put forward a Ganga Action Plan II, but critics of the first failed scheme are proposing an alternative under the guidance of a Banaras Hindu University engineering professor Veer Bhadra Mishra. It remains to be seen whether his proposal of a massive educational programme backed by advanced engineering will help Varanasi purify the tide of filth that enters it every day.

Although the Ganga may be one of the world's most polluted rivers, like many tropical rivers it can cleanse itself quickly. Scientists had discovered the river's exceptional property in the last century. The cholera microbe did not survive three hours in Ganga water whereas in distilled water it survived 24 hours!

the Marathas, parts of which were used in its construction. You can climb on to the top for fantastic views (donation expected). Two minarets are missing – one fell and killed some people and the other was taken down by the government as a precaution.

Back lanes The maze of narrow lanes, or *galis*, along the ghats through the old quarters exude the smells and sounds of this holy city. They are fascinating to stroll through though easy to get lost in! Some find it all too over-powering. Near the Town Hall (1845) built by the Maharaja of Vizianagram, is the **Kotwali** (Police Station) with the Temple of **Bhaironath**, built by Baji Rao II in 1825. The image inside is believed to be of the Kotwal (Superintendent) who rides on a ghostly dog. Stalls sell sugar dogs to be offered to the image. In the temple garden of **Gopal Mandir** near the Kotwali is a small hut in which Tulsi Das is said to have composed the *Binaya Patrika* poem.

The **Bhelupura Temple** with a museum marks the birthplace of the 23rd Jain Tirthankar **Parsvanath** who preached non-violence. The **Durga Temple** (18th-century) to the south along Durga Kund Road, was built in the Nagara style. It is painted red with ochre and has the typical five spires (symbolizing the elements) merging into one (Brahma). Non-Hindus may view from rooftop nearby. Next door in a peaceful garden, the **Tulsi Manas Temple** (1964) in white marble commemorates the medieval poet Tulsi Das. It has walls engraved with verses and scenes from the *Ramcharitmanas*, composed in a Hindi dialect, instead of the conventional Sanskrit, and is open to all (closed 1130-1530). Good views from the second floor of 'Disneyland style' animated show. **Bharat Mata Temple**, south of Cantt Station, has a relief map of 'Mother India' in marble. Good bookshop, but not worth a detour.

★ **River front** The hundred and more **ghats** on the river are the main attraction for visitors to Varanasi. Visit them at first light before sunrise, 0430 in summer, 0600 in winter when Hindu pilgrims come to bathe in the sacred Ganga, facing the rising sun, or at dusk when leaf-boat lamps are floated down the river, usually from 1800 (try Mir

or Assi Ghat). Start the river trip at Dasasvamedha Ghat where you can hire a boat
quite cheaply especially if you can share, bargain to about Rs 60-120 per hour for two
to eight at dawn. You may go either upstream (south) towards
Harishchandra Ghat or downstream to Manikarnika Ghat. You
may prefer to have a boat on the river at sunset and watch the
lamps floated on the river, or go in the afternoon at a fraction of
the price quoted at dawn.For photographs, visit the riverside
between 0700-0900. The foggy sunshine early in the morning
often clears to produce a beautiful light.

‖ Photography is not permitted at the burning ghats but travellers are told that it is allowed and then a large fine is demanded. Other scams involve conmen collecting 'donations' to provide wood for burning the poor.

Kite flying is a popular pastime, as elsewhere in India, especially all along the river bank. The serious competitors endeavour to bring down other flyers' kites and so fortify their twine by coating it with a mix of crushed light bulbs and flour paste to make it razor sharp! The quieter ghats, eg Panchganga, are good for watching the fun – boys in their boats on the river scramble to retrieve downed kites as trophies that can be re-used even though the kites themselves are very cheap.

Dasasvamedha Ghat Named as the 'Place of Ten Horse Sacrifices' performed here by **Brahma,** God of Creation. Some believe that in the age of the gods when the world was in chaos, **Divodasa** was appointed King of Kashi by Brahma. He accepted, on condition that all the gods would leave Varanasi. Even **Siva** was forced to leave but Brahma set the test for Divodasa, confident that he would get the complex ceremony wrong, allowing the gods back into the city. However, the ritual was performed flawlessly, and the ghat has thus become one of the holiest, especially at eclipses. Bathing here is regarded as being almost as meritorious as making the sacrifice.

Going south You will pass **Munshi Ghat**, where some of the city's sizeable Muslim population (25%) come to bathe. The river has no religious significance for them. Close by is **Darbhanga Ghat** where the mansion had a hand-operated cable lift. Professional washermen work at the **Dhobi Ghat;** there is religious merit in having your clothes washed in the Ganga. Brahmins have their own washermen to avoid caste pollution. The municipality has built separate washing facilities away from the ghat.

Narad and **Chauki Ghats** are held sacred since the **Buddha** received enlightenment here under a *peepul* tree. Those who bathe together at Narad, supposedly go home and quarrel! The pink water tower here is for storing Ganga water. High water levels are recorded at **Raj Ghat**. The flood levels are difficult to imagine when the river is at its lowest in January/February. **Mansarovar Ghat** leads to ruins of several temples around a lake. **Kedar Ghat** is named after Kedarnath, a pilgrimage site in the Uttaranchal, with a Bengali temple nearby.

The **Harishchandra Ghat** is particularly holy and is dedicated to King Harishchandra. It is now the most sacred *smashan* or cremation ghat although Manikarnika is more popular. Behind the ghat is a *gopuram* of a Dravidian style temple. The **Karnataka Ghat** is one of many regional ghats which are attended by priests who know the local languages, castes, customs and festivals.

The **Hanuman Ghat** is where Vallabha, the leader of a revivalist Krishna bhakti cult was born in the late 15th century. **Shivala Ghat** (Kali Ghat) is privately owned by the ex-ruler of Varanasi. **Chet Singh's Fort**, Shivala, stands behind the ghat. The fort, the old palace of the Maharajas, is where the British imprisoned him but he escaped by climbing down to the river and swimming away. **Anandamayi Ghat** is named after the Bengali saint Anandamayi Ma (died 1982) who received 'enlightenment' at 17 and spent her life teaching and in charitable work. **Jain Ghat** is near the birthplace of Tirthankar Shyeyanshnath. **Tulsi Ghat** commemorates the great saint-poet **Tulsi Das** who lived here (see Tulsi Manas Temple above). Furthest upstream is the **Assi Ghat**, where the river Assi meets the Ganga, one of the five that pilgrims should bathe from in a day. The order is Assi, Dasasvamedha, Barnasangam, Panchganga and Manikarnika. Upstream on the east bank is the Ramnagar Fort, the Maharaja of Varanasi's residence (see below). Here the boat will turn to take you back to Dasasvamedha Ghat.

Going north This way you will pass the following: **Man Mandir Ghat** ① *normally 0930-1730 but if you enquire locally you may be able to get in at dawn or dusk*, built by Maharajah Man Singh of Amber in 1600 and one of the oldest in Varanasi. The palace was restored in the last century with brick and plaster. The beautiful stone balcony on the northeast corner gives an indication of how the original looked. Maharaja Jai Singh of Jaipur converted the palace into an **observatory** in 1710, see also Jaipur (page 336). Like its counterparts in Delhi, Jaipur and Ujjain, the observatory contains a fascinating collection of instruments built of brick, cement and stone. The most striking of these, at the entrance, is the Bhittiyantra, or wall quadrant, over 3 m high and just under 3 m broad and in the same plane as the line of longitude. Similarly placed is the Samratyantra which is designed to slope upwards pointing at the Pole Star. From the top of the Chakra Yantra there is a superb view of the ghats and the town. Near the entrance to the observatory is a small **Siva Temple** whose shrine is a lingam immersed in water. During droughts, water is added to the cistern to make it overflow for good luck.

The **Dom Raja's House** is next door, flanked by painted tigers. The **doms** are the 'Untouchables' of Varanasi who are integral to the cremation ceremony. As Untouchables they can handle the corpse, a ritually polluting act for Hindus. They also supply the flame from the temple for the funeral pyre. Their presence is essential

Varanasi Ghats

Sleeping	7 Lara	13 Tandon House Lodge	● Eating
1 Alka	8 Mishra	& Street View	1 Garden &
2 Barahdari	9 Puja	Restaurant	Universal Books
3 Ganga Fuji	10 River View	14 Trimurti Lodge	2 Jalayog Café
4 Ganges	11 Scindia Guest House	15 Yogi & Golden	3 Keshari
5 Gautam	12 Shanti & Puja	Lodges, Fagins & Blue	
6 Kumiko	Guest House	Moon Restaurants	

and also lucrative since there are fees for the various services they provide. The Dom
Raja is the hereditary title of the leader of these Untouchables. You can climb up
through the astronomical observatory (which is overrun by monkeys) to the Raja
Dom's Palace – a guide will take you round the court room, and on to the roof which
has the best view of the river.

Mir Ghat leads to a sacred well; widows who dedicate themselves to prayer, are
fed and clothed here. Then comes **Lalita Ghat** with the distinctive Nepalese style
temple with a golden roof above and a Ganga mandir at water level.

Above **Manikarnika Ghat** is a well into which Siva's dead wife Sati's earring is
supposed to have fallen when Siva was carrying her after she committed suicide –
see page 219. The Brahmins managed to find the jewel from the earring (*manikarnika*)
and returned it to Siva who blessed the place. Offerings of *bilva* flowers, milk,
sandalwood and sweetmeats are thrown into the tank where pilgrims come to bathe.
Between the well and the ghat is *Charanpaduka*, a stone slab with Vishnu's footprint.
Boatmen may pursuade you to leave a 'private' offering to perform a puja (a ploy to
increasing their earnings)!

The adjoining **Jalasayin Ghat** is the principal burning ghat of the city. The
expensive scented sandalwood which the rich alone can afford is used sparingly;
usually not more than two kilos. You may see floating bundles covered in white cloth;
children, and those dying of 'high fever', or smallpox in the past, are not cremated but
put into the river. This avoids injuring *Sitala* the goddess of smallpox.

Scindia Ghat, originally built in 1830, was so large that it collapsed. **Ram Ghat**
was built by the Maharaja of Jaipur. Five rivers are supposed to meet at the
magnificent **Panchganga Ghat** – the Ganga, Sarasvati, Gyana, Kirana and Dhutpapa.
The stone column can hold around 1,000 lamps at festivals. The impressive flights of
stone steps run up to the Alamgir Mosque (see above). At **Gai Ghat** there is a statue of
a sacred cow whilst at **Trilochana Ghat** there is a temple to Siva in his form as the
'Three-eyed' (*Trilochana*); two turrets stand out of the water. **Raj Ghat** is the last on the
boat journey. Excavations have revealed an eighth century BC site of a city on a grassy
mound nearby. Raj Ghat was where the river was forded until bridges were built.

Other sights

Varanasi is famous for ornamental brasswork, silk weaving and for its glass beads,
exported all over the world. *Zari* work, whether embroidered or woven, once used
silver or gold thread but is now done with gilded copper or brass. Visit the
Governmentt Weaving Centre at Chauka Ghat to watch weavers at work. The
significance of **silk** in India's traditional life is deep-rooted. Silk was considered a
pure fabric, most appropriate for use on ceremonial and religious occasions. Its
lustre, softness and richness of natural colour gave it precedence over all other
fabrics. White or natural coloured silk was worn by the Brahmins and others who were
'twice born'. Women wore bright colours and the darker hues were reserved for the
lowest caste in the formal hierarchy, few of whom could afford it. Silk garments were
worn for ceremonials like births and marriages, and offerings of finely woven silks
were made to deities in temples. This concept of purity may have given impetus to the
growth of silk-weaving centres around ancient temple towns like Kanchipuram,
Varanasi, Bhubaneswar and Ujjain, a tradition that is kept alive today, see page 570.

Banaras Hindu University (BHU) is one of the largest campus universities in India to
the south of the city and enjoys a pleasant, relaxed atmosphere. Founded at the turn of
the nineteenth century, it was originally intended for the study of Sanskrit, Indian art,
music and culture and has the Bharat Kala Bhavan Museum (see below). The **New
Visvanath Temple** (1966), one of the tallest in India, is in the university semi circle and
was financed by the Birla family. It was planned by Madan Mohan Malaviya (1862-1942),
Chancellor of the university, who believed in Hinduism without caste distinctions. The
marble Shiva temple modelled on the old Visvanath Temple, is open to all.

The 17th-century **Ramnagar Fort** ⓘ *ferry Rs 6 return, rickshaws from centre, across a crumbling double-decker bridge, Rs 75, ask to wait or take a boat back or walk over the pontoon bridge*, across the river, was the home of the Maharaja of Varanasi; the Durbar Hall houses a **museum** (see below). Beautiful situation, surrounded by narrow, crowded streets, but the Fort is run down. *Ramlila* performances during Dasara.

Museums

Bharat Kala Bhavan ⓘ *BHU, May-Jun 0730-1230, rest of year: 1100-1630, closed Sun and holidays, Rs 40 for foreigners, Rs 5 Indians, Rs 10 camera (lockers at entrance)*, exhibits include sculptures from Mathura and Sarnath, excellent Mughal miniature paintings and Benarasi brocades. The **Ramnagar Fort Museum** ⓘ *across the river, summer 0900-1200, 1400-1700, winter 1000-1300, 1400-1700, Rs 7 (includes Fort)*, has palanquins, elephant *howdahs*, costumes, arms and furniture gathering dust. See the amazing locally made astrological clock and single cylinder steam driven fan!

★ **Sarnath** → *Phone code: 0542. Colour map 3, grid B4. 10 km northeast of Varanasi.*
Sarnath is one of Buddhism's major centres in India. Given its great historic importance visitors may be disappointed to find the stupas neglected and the very limited collection in the museum, although it houses some superb pieces. Nevertheless, many find the deer park a place of peace and reflection despite distractions of loud transistor radios and young monks running around or playing cricket!

Sarnath

```
0 metres    50
0 yards     50
```

■ **Sleeping**   2 Tourist Bungalow
1 Birla Rest House   & Restaurant

When he had gained enlightenment at Bodh Gaya, the **Buddha** came to the deer park at Sarnath and delivered his first sermon (circa 528 BC), usually referred to as *Dharmachakra* (The Wheel of Law). Since then, the site has been revered. The Chinese traveller Hiuen Tsang described the *sangharama* (monastery) in 640 AD as having 1,500 monks, a 65-m high *vihara*, a figure of the Buddha represented by a wheel, a 22-m high stone stupa built by Asoka, a larger 90-m high stupa and three lakes. The remains here and the sculptures now at the Indian Museum, Kolkata and the National Museum, Delhi reveal that Sarnath was a centre of religious activity, learning and art, continuously from the fourth century BC until its abandonment in the ninth century AD and ultimate destruction by Muslim armies in 1197.

In May, on first full-moon, *Buddha Jayanti* marks the Buddha's birthday. A fair is held and relics which are not on public display at any other time are taken out in procession.

Enclosure A separate entrance leads to the enclosure on the far right. The statue on the right is of **Anagarika Dharmapala**, the founder of the Mahabodhi Society which has assumed responsibility for the upkeep of Sarnath and Bodh Gaya. The modern **Mulagandhakuti Vihara** (1929-31) contains frescoes by the Japanese artist Kosetsu Nosu depicting scenes from the Buddha's life. An urn in the ground is supposed to hold a Buddha relic obtained from Taxila (Pakistan). The **Bodhi tree** (*pipal, Ficus religiosa*) planted in 1931 is a sapling of the one in Sri Lanka which was grown from a cutting taken there circa 236 BC by Mahinda's sister Princess Sanghamitta.

Here is the **Dhamekh Stupa** (fifth to sixth century AD) ① *Rs 5, foreigners US$2, video camera Rs 25*, or Dharma Chakra, the most imposing monument at Sarnath, built where the Buddha delivered his first sermon to his five disciples. Along with his birth, enlightenment and death, this incident is one of the four most significant. The stupa consists of a 28-m diameter stone plinth which rises to a height of 13 m. Each of the eight faces has an arched recess for an image. Above this base rises a 31-m high cylindrical tower. The upper part was probably unfinished. The central section has elaborate Gupta designs eg luxuriant foliation, geometric patterns, birds and flowers. The Brahmi script dates from sixth to ninth centuries. The stupa was enlarged six times and the well-known figures of a standing Boddhisattva and the Buddha teaching were found nearby.

Other sights The **deer park** is holy to Jains because **Shyeyanshnath**, the 11th Tirthankar, was born near the Dhamekh stupa. The temple to your left as you move between the stupas commemorates him, 'Sarnath' may be derived from his name. The monastery (fifth century onwards) in the southwest corner is one of four in the Deer Park. The others are along the north edge. All are of brick with cells off a central courtyard which are in ruins.

Dharmarajika Stupa was built by the Emperor Asoka to contain relics of the Buddha. It was enlarged on several occasions but was destroyed by Jagat Singh, Dewan of the Maharaja of Benares, in 1794, when a green marble casket containing human bones and pearls was found. The British Resident at the Maharaja's court published an account of the discovery thereby drawing the attention of scholars to the site.

The **Main shrine** is a rectangular building, 29 m by 27 m, with doubly recessed corners and is 5½-m high. The building, marking the place of the Buddha's meditation, is attributed to Asoka and the later Guptas. The concrete path and interior brick walls were added later to reinforce the building. To the rear is the 5 m lower portion of a polished sandstone **Asokan Column** (third century BC). The original was about 15 m high with a lion capital which is now in the Archaeological Museum. The four lions sitting back to back with the wheel of law below them is now the symbol of the Indian Union. The column was one of many erected by Asoka to promulgate the faith and this contained a message to the monks and nuns not to create any schisms and to spread the word.

The modern **Burmese monastery** is worth the short detour from the road. It is very colourful and peaceful with no hawkers and hardly any tourists. Tibetan, Thai and Chinese monasteries have also been built around the old complex. The Central Institute of Higher Tibetan Studies, near the ruins, runs courses and carries out research. The library has a good collection of texts and manuscripts.

The **museum** ① *closed Fri, 0930-1700*, has a well-displayed collection of pieces from the site, including the famous lion capital (Asokan Column), a Sunga Period (first century BC) stone railing, Kushana Period (second century AD) Boddhisattvas, Gupta Period (fifth century AD) figures, including the magnificent seated Buddha. Allow about one hour. Tickets are Rs 5 from across the road where Archaeological Survey booklets are for sale. Cameras and bags are not normally allowed.

Chaukhandi, 500 m south, has a fifth-century Stupa. On top of this is an octagonal brick tower built by Akbar in 1588 to commemorate the visit his father Humayun made to the site. The inscription above the doorway reads 'As Humayun, king of the Seven Climes, now residing in paradise, deigned to come and sit here one day, thereby increasing the splendour of the sun, so Akbar, his son and humble servant, resolved to build on this spot a lofty tower reaching to the blue sky'.

★ Jaunpur

→ *Phone code: 05452. Colour map 3, grid B4. Population: 160,000. 58 km northwest of Varanasi.*

Jaunpur is a uniquely important centre of 14th- and 15th-century regional Islamic architecture. Once the short-lived capital of the Sharqi Dynasty, today only the ruins of some magnificent mosques and its famous Akbari Bridge distinguish it from hundreds of other dusty, modest Uttar Pradesh towns. The buildings that remain remind us of its brief period as one of India's main centres of political, architectural and artistic development and so is well worth a visit if you can spare the time.

History Located at a strategic crossing point of the Gomti River, Jaunpur was established by Feroz Shah Tughluq in 1360 as part of his drive to the East. Earlier Hindu and Jain structures were destroyed to provide material for the mosques with which the Sharqi Dynasty rapidly embellished their capital. The Sharqi kings – named 'Kings of

Jaunpur

To Shahganj (32 km)
To Lucknow
To Lal Darwaza Masjid
Malhni Marg
Char Ungli Masjid
Nawab Yusuf Marg
Water Tower
Jami Masjid
Atala Masjid
Gomti River
Qila Rd
Stone Lion
Old Shahi Fort
Kalichkhan's Tomb
Akbari Bridge
Sultanpur Rd
Turkish Baths
Feroz Shah's Tomb
Sharqi Tomb
Cemetery of the 7 Sharqi Kings
To Azamgarh
To Varanasi
Jamakhan's Tomb
Jhanjhri Masjid
To Varanasi (53 km)
Tilakdhari College Rd
Mirzapur Rd
Allahabad Rd
Bypass
Dindayal Upadhya Rd
To Jaunpur City Railway Station (1 km)
N
0 metres 500
0 yards 500

■ **Sleeping**
1 Chandra Continental
2 Railway Retiring Rooms

● **Eating**
1 Surya

the East' by Feroz Shah – established effective independence from the Tughluqs who
had been crushed in Timur's sack of Delhi in 1398. They maintained it until 1479, when Husain Shah, the last Sharqi king, was violently deposed by Ibrahim Lodi. Although all the secular buildings, including palaces and courts, were razed to the ground, Ibrahim Lodi spared at least some of the mosques. Some of the city's destruction visible today can be put down to much later events – floods in 1773 and 1871 and an earthquake in 1934. According to Rushbrook Williams this last catastrophe destroyed seven of the 15 arches in the great 200-m long Akbari Bridge, designed by the Afghan architect Afzal Ali and built between 1564-68. The stone lion above an elephant at the end of the bridge marks the point from which distances from the city were measured.

Sights The **bridge** emphasized Jaunpur's role as the centre of a pre-Mughal trading network. In the 17th century the Gomti allowed ships up to 18 tons to navigate over 200 km upstream. Under the great king Shams-ud-din-Ibrahim (1402-36) Jaunpur became a centre of the arts and university education. Today, however, it is the remains of the fort and the mosques which are most worth visiting.

The **Old Shahi Fort**, just north of the Akbari Bridge, is an irregular grassy quadrangle enclosed by ruined stone walls. It shelters the oldest **mosque** in Jaunpur (1377), a narrow arcade (40 m by 7 m) supported by carved pillars, named after its builder, Ibrahim Naib Barbak, Feroz Shah Tughluq's brother. In the mid-19th century Fergusson described some distinctive yellow and blue enamelled bricks on the fine 15 m high stone gateway, and an inscribed monolith (1766) at the entrance, still visible today. Of particular interest is the almost perfect model of a **hammam** (Turkish bath) which you can wander around. ① *Rs 2*.

Perhaps the most striking of the surviving mosques, the **Atala**, stands less than 400 m to the north of the fort. Built in 1408 on the site of the Hindu Atala Devi temple, it marks the triumphant beginning of Shams-ud-din-Ibrahim's reign and introduces unique features of Jaunpuri style. An arched gateway or 'pylon' fronts the sanctuary on the west side of the 50-m square court; the remaining three sides are spacious cloisters, two-storeyed and five aisles deep. The pylon has sloping sides, as in other Tughluq building, and its central arch is over 22 m high – along with the arch of the great Jami Masjid nearby, the highest in India. Other features borrowed from the Tughluq style are a recessed arch with its ornamented fringe, and tapering turrets on the west wall. Although artisans were brought in from Delhi, Jaunpur builders soon articulated their Tughluq traditions in a highly distinctive way. Note the beautiful sanctuary interior with its decorated nave and transepts, and the perforated stone screens. At the far end, the transepts are two-storeyed, with the upper section screened off for the zenana.

The same weakness applies to the 'most ambitious' of Jaunpur's mosques, the **Jami Masjid**, about 1 km north of the fort. Begun by Shah Ibrahim in 1438 it was completed by Husain Shah, the last Sharqi king, in 1470. Raised about 6 m on an artificial platform, the worshipper is forced to climb a steep flight of steps to enter the 60-m square courtyard. Built on an even grander scale than the Atala Mosque, the 25 m high central pylon dominates the sanctuary. Note the unsupported transept halls which create a remarkable clear covered open space. Despite the lack of pillars they have survived earthquakes as well as normal ageing. Allow three hours on foot for the main sights.

Allahabad → *Phone code: 0532. Colour map 3, grid B3. Population: 1,015,000.*

The narrow spit of land at the confluence of the Ganges and Yamuna rivers, normally an almost deserted river beach of fine sand, becomes home for two weeks once every 12 years to the Kumbh Mela, when over 12 million pilgrims converge to bathe in the holy waters. The 2001 Kumbh Mela has been described as "the most spectacular ever", with live pictures shown on the internet! Allahabad has grown around this spot and is today a rapidly growing commercial and administrative city. It is particularly sacred for Hindus because it is at the confluence of the Ganga and the Jamuna. For the Muslims and the British too, this became a strategically vital centre; they have left their imprint on the landmarks of the city. ▸▸ *For Sleeping, Eating and other listings, see pages 197-204.*

Ins and outs

Getting there Bamrauli airport is 18 km west of town. The Civil Lines (MG Marg) Bus stand and the Leader Rd stand, near Junction station, are used by buses arriving from the north and west, while Zero Rd bus stand, half way between the Junction and City railway stations, serves local and southern routes, including Khajuraho. Just south of the Civil Lines, Allahabad Junction station is the main stop for Delhi and Kolkata trains. There are also direct trains from Mumbai and key cities of South India.

Getting around Many of the city's hotels are in Civil Lines, within easy reach of the Junction station (rear exit) and the bus stands. Although this centre is quite compact you need an auto-rickshaw to get to some of the main sights, including the Fort and the Sangam. Metered taxis and cycle-rickshaws are also easily available. See Transport, page 203, for further details.

History

Ancient sites here point to Allahabad's early history. Draupadi Ghat has revealed signs of extensive habitation and quantities of pottery, Northern Black Polished Ware, dated between 1100 and 800 BC. Remains of the **The Kushans** were found on the Bharadwaj Ashram site. The Muslims first conquered it in 1194 and renamed it

Allahabad

■ **Sleeping**
1 Allahabad Regency
2 Funara
3 Kanha Shyam
4 Prayagraj
5 Presidency
6 Royal
7 Santosh Palace
8 Tourist Bungalow & Tourist Office
9 Yatrik

Allahabad in 1584. It later became the HQ of the British Government of the Northwest Provinces and Oudh, and here the transfer of government from the East India Company to the crown was announced by Lord Canning in 1858.

Sights

Prayag (The confluence) The purifying power of a sacred river is strongest at a confluence. In addition, the mythical underground river **Sarasvati** is also said to surface here. Bathing here is auspicious at all times of the year, more so at *Magh Mela* which occurs every year for 15 days (January/February) and longer at the ★ **Kumbh Mela** when pilgrims bathe at prayag to wash away a lifetime's sins. In legend, Hindu gods and demons vied for the pot (*kumbha*) that held the nectar of immortality (*amrit*). During the 12-day fight for possession, Vishnu spilt four drops of *amrit* which fell to earth, making four sacred places: Allahabad, Haridwar (Uttaranchal), Ujjain (MP) and Nasik (Maharashtra). Holiest of all is Allahabad, the site of the Maha (great) Kumbh Mela. This festival moves every three years returning to Allahabad every 12th year (last in 2001). **Boats** leave from nearby ghats, the nearest being the one by the fort.

Mughal Period Allahabad has few monuments pre-dating the Muslim period. The **Fort**, begun in 1583, was the largest of **Akbar's** forts. It has three massive gateways and 7 m high walls, seen to advantage from across the river. The Marathas held it from 1739 to 1750, then the Pathans, and finally the British from 1801. Most of the fort is closed to visitors, including the third-century BC Asoka pillar, moved there from Kausambi under Akbar's orders. Under the fort's east wall is the **Undying Banyan Tree** (*Akshaivata*), an underground temple from which pilgrims threw themselves to achieve salvation in death. To see, ask for a permit at the Tourist Office.

Khusrau Bagh The typical Mughal garden enclosure houses the handsome tomb of **Prince Khusrau**. After staging an unsuccessful rebellion against his father **Jahangir** in 1607, Khusrau spent the next year in chains. When freed, he encouraged a plot to assassinate his father but was discovered. Partially blinded and kept a captive, he was murdered in 1615 by his own brother, later the **Emperor Shah Jahan** (ruled 1627-58). The burial chamber is underground with decorative plasterwork. The tomb to the west is thought to be his sister's. Further west is the two-storey tomb of his Rajput mother.

Buildings from the British Period Canning Town, opposite Junction Railway Station, was laid out on a grid in the 1860s. Within it are the Old High Court and Public Offices, classical style buildings from the late 19th century including the Gothic style **All Saint's** Cathedral. At the east end of the Civil Lines is Alfred Park (now Chandra Sekhar Azad Park), north of which stands **Muir College**, a fine example of 'Indo-

Eating
& India Coffee House
1 El Chico
4 Kwality
2 Hot Stuff
3 Jade Garden, Kwality

Saracenic' architecture. It was later established as the University of Allahabad. West of this is **Mayo Hall** with **St Joseph's Roman Catholic Cathedral** (1879) to its south. ★ **Holy Trinity Church** (early 19th century) on J Nehru Marg, contains memorials from the Gwalior Campaign (1843) and the 'Uprising' (1857).

Museums

The Allahabad Museum ① *Chandra Sekhar Azad Park, Kamla Nehru Rd, closed Mon, 1030-1730, foreigners charged Rs100, 18 galleries.* Contains a wide range of stone sculptures (second century BC from Bharhut and Kausambi, first century AD Kushana from Mathura, fourth to sixth century Gupta and 11th-century carvings from Khajuraho). Also a fine collection of Rajasthani miniatures, terracotta figurines, coins and paintings by Nicholas Roerich. ★ **Anand Bhavan** is the former Nehru family home contains many interesting items relating to **Motilal Nehru** (1861-1931), active in the Independence movement, **Jawaharlal Nehru** (1889-1964), Independent India's first Prime Minister, **Indira Gandhi** (1917-84) (Prime Minister 1966-77, 1980-84) and her sons **Sanjay Gandhi** who died 1980 and **Rajiv Gandhi** (Prime Minister 1984-89) who was assassinated in 1991. The garden (free) is pleasant to relax in. Next to it stands **Swaraj Bhawan** (where Indira Gandhi was born) ① *closed Mon, 1100-1300, 1600-1730, Rs 5,* which is interesting to wander through.

Chunar (35 km southwest of Varanasi. Colour map 3, grid B4) ① *Buses from City Station, Varanasi take 1½ hrs, Rs 75 return.* Chunar sandstone is famous as the material of the Asoka pillars, highly polished in a technique said to be Persian. The town is also noted for its **fort** built on a spur of the Kaimur Hills, 53 m above the surrounding plain. It was of obvious strategic importance and changed hands a number of times. The army occupies the fort today, but you can look around. There is an impressive well with steps leading down to a water gate; watch out for snakes. The British Cemetery below the fort overlooks the Ganga. Islamic tombs of Shah Kasim Suleiman and his son here, feature in paintings by Daniells and others.

Kausambi (Colour map 3, grid B3. 44 km southwest of Allahabad). According to the epics, Kausam was founded by a descendant of the *Pandavas* who left Hastinapur when it was destroyed by floods from the Ganga. It is one of the earliest historical cities of the region. According to Hiuen Tsang the Buddha preached here and two *viharas* (monasteries) were built to commemorate the event.The enormous ruins are spread through several villages.

The ramparts form an approximate rectangle over 6 km in perimeter with bastions that tower up to nearly 23 m. Originally made of mud they were later surfaced with bricks. The town was occupied continuously from the eighth century BC to sixth century AD. In the southwest corner are possibly the remains of a palace. The main **stupa** (fifth century BC) measured 25 m in diameter and 25 m in height. There is also the damaged shaft of a sandstone column, probably erected during the rule of the Mauryan Emperor Asoka. GR Sharma of the University of Allahabad has now worked at four main areas on the site. The earliest excavations made near the Asokan pillar suggested that the first of the three periods of settlement of the site came immediately before the **Northern Black Polished Ware** period. The second period dated back to 300 BC and included the first brick building, a road and finds of coins with the typical Kausambi 'lanky bull' motifs. In the third period of occupation (175 BC-325 AD), the coins found testify to a succession of rulers; Mitras, followed by Kushan kings and then by Maghas. The road evidently continued in use up to about 300 AD and the site itself was occupied until about 400 AD. Many of the coins and terracottas discovered here are now on display in the Allahabad City Museum and Kausambi Museum at the University of Allahabad.

Listings: Eastern Uttar Pradesh

⊜ Sleeping

Varanasi *p183, maps p184 and p188*
Discounts in off-season (Jun-Jul). Be prepared for power cuts and carry a torch at night. Be aware that some insist on taking you to hotels where they get a commission. Hotels on the river front can be difficult to locate, particularly at night. Local people will often show you the way but may expect a commission from the hotel, thus increasing the rate you pay.

L-AL Taj Ganges, Nadesar Palace Ground, T345100, F348067, ganges.varanasi@tajhotels.com. 130 rooms, good restaurants, pool (closed in winter), top class facilities, busy, but efficient service, taxis from here overcharge.

AL Clarks Varanasi, The Mall, T348501, F348186, clarkvns@satyam.net.in. 113 rooms, pool (non-residents, Rs 200), large, bustling, quiet location, good facilities, good restaurant (adventurous Indian nouvelle cuisine!) but expensive drinks.

A Best Western Kashika (Clarks), was *Ideal*, The Mall (connected to *Clarks Tower* by enclosed bridge), 5 km from centre, T348501, F348186, clarksvns@satyam.net.in. 40 very clean, well furnished rooms, limited Indian restaurant, friendly and helpful, plenty of light creates pleasant atmosphere, good value, share facilities with other 2 Clarks hotels here.

A Clarks Tower, The Mall, T348250, F348685, clarksvns@satyam.net.in. 58 decent rooms, pool, restaurant (beer Rs 170), some reports of unfriendly service.

A Hindustan International, C 21/3 Maldahiya, T351484, F350931, hhivns@lw1.vsnl.net.in. 108 rooms, modern, with the look of a multi-storeyed car park, pool (non-residents, Rs 200), clean and comfortable, good views from higher rooms, but food and laundry not recommended.

A Hotel Palace, converted old palace, the best hotel on the banks of the Ganga.

A-B Varanasi Ashok (ITDC), The Mall, T346020, F348089. 84 comfortable but uninspiring rooms, central a/c, good restaurant, good bookshop, large well-kept gardens, pool could be cleaner.

B-C Ganges View, Assi Ghat, T368640, F368703, www.hoteltemple.com. Old patrician home converted into welcoming guest house with a tastefully decorated range of small rooms (noisy fan), very pleasant atmosphere, interesting clientele (artists, academics), lovely riverside verandas, vegetarian food, free yoga lessons, book ahead.

C India, 59 Patel Nagar, Cantt, T343009, mathur/varanasi@dartmail.dartnet. 83 rooms, some a/c, better in renovated building, restaurant (popular so service can be slow), bar, good garden, very clean (mosquitoes, however), good value.

C-D Diamond, Bhelupura, T310696, F310703, diamotel@lw1.vsnl.net.in. 40 rooms, most a/c though regular rooms are just as good, restaurant, exchange, gardens, reasonable value.

C-D Pradeep, Jagatganj, T204963, F204898. 45 clean rooms, most a/c, near noisy junction, excellent *Poonam* restaurant (see below), very attractive roof top bar/restaurant with real lawn, friendly staff (nearby, a therapist offers 'Delusion Removal Conversation'!).

C-D Vaibhav, 56 Patel Nagar, Cantt, T346477, F346466. 60 clean rooms with bath (some excellent a/c), no mosquitoes, modern, restaurant good but dark, bar good service and value though a bit soulless, discount deal offered at airport. Recommended (rickshaws "don't know hotel").

C-E Surya, behind *Clarks*, Varuna Bridge Rd, Cantt, T343014, F348330. 60 rooms, modern and clean, some a/c rooms, internet, restaurant (unexciting but good food and filling), large relaxing garden, reasonable value.

Most **D** hotels have rooms with TV and attached baths.

D Barahdari, near GPO, Maidagin, T/F330581. 16 large rooms, some a/c (check unit and water heater), veg restaurant, exchange, garden, simple, clean.

D Malti, 31/3 Vidyapith Rd, T223878. 47 simple rooms, some a/c with balcony, restaurant, modern hotel. avoids early morning heat and includes transport to/from ghat north of Alamgir mosque. Recommended.

For an explanation of the sleeping and eating price codes used in this guide, see inside the front cover. Other relevant information is found in Essentials pages 52-57.

Uttar Pradesh Listings: Eastern Uttar Pradesh

D-E Gautam, Ramkatora, Kabir Chaura Rd, T206239, F206450. 37 good, clean a/c rooms with phone, some a/c, some with TV, good restaurant, efficient service.

D-E Lara, Dasaswamedha Rd, T320323, F450739. 28 comfortable rooms, some a/c, bit grubby, good Indian veg restaurant.

Riverside

Rooms with river view are worth the extra.
D-E Alka, Mirghat, T328445, F328474, hotelalka@hotmail.com. 16 rooms, some deluxe, some shared bath, clean, spacious, with great views over the ghats, friendly atmosphere, good restaurant. Recommended, book ahead.

D-E Temple on Ganges, near Assi Ghat, T312340, F312740. 26 spartan rooms with bath (western toilets), views of sunrise over Ganga, **F** dorm, friendly, peaceful, clean, average rooftop veg restaurant (no alcohol), free yoga lessons, rail ticketing (Rs 50), boat rides (Rs 60, 2 hrs), mixed reports (poor laundry, little boys employed).

D-F Scindia Guest House, Scindia Ghat, T320319, F327317. 21 small rooms, some with bath and balcony (river facing rooms much better), dorm, clean, poor food (very slow), superb rooftop views, staff friendly but small boys employed.

D-F Sita Guest House, D22/16 Chausatti Ghat, T450061, F314606, sita_guest_house@yahoo.com. 20 rooms with river views, most with balconies, clean, rooftop restaurant, internet, good value.

E Ganges, Dasasvamedha Rd, T/F321097, F391565, bhataksun@yahoo.com. 24 rooms (1-6 bed), some with bath (**D** a/c), discounts given, cleanliness varies (inspect first), pleasant restaurant on 1st floor overlooks bazar, exchange, email air/rail tickets, popular.

E Mishra, near Manikarnika Ghat, T/F327761. 37 rooms with bath in newish hotel, most with balcony, best with river view.

E Sandhya Guest House, near Shivala Ghat PO. Not too clean, rooftop restaurant with good views, homemade brown bread, helpful.

E-F Puja Guest House, D1/45 Lalita Ghat (near Nepali Temple), T326102. Cheap rooftop restaurant, help with air, bus, train tickets, not recommended for single women.

E-F River View, Brahma Ghat by Gai Ghat (approach from R Tagore Rd, inaccessible to rickshaws), T334565, hotelriverview@hotmail.com. 15 rooms, most with hot bath, good view (watch the dawn from front rooms and dolphins from rooftop!), rooftop restaurant planned, very helpful, safe, good family atmosphere. Recommended.

E-F Shanti Guest House, 8/129 Garwasi Tola, near Manikarnika Ghat (well-signposted), T320956, info@visitvaranasi.com (discount on e-mail bookings). 31 rooms vary, some **D** a/c, open-air dorm, 24-hr rooftop restaurant serving tasty food, backpackers' haunt.

F Ajay, near Munshi Ghat. Rooms on several levels, clean, rooftop restaurant with great views, good service, tasty food.

F Baba Guest House, D20/15 Munshi Ghat, T328672, babaguesthouse@yahoo.com. 20 basic rooms (Rs 100-150), some bath, rooftop restaurant.

F Ganga Fuji Home, D7/21 Shakar Kand Gali, near Golden Temple, T327979, F320676. 10 small, clean rooms, common bath, friendly.

F Golden Lodge, D8/35 Kalika Gali, near Golden Temple, T393832, F328567. 14 cell-like clean rooms, some with bath (hot water), enthusiastic proprietor, a/c restaurant (*Fagin's*), some character, check-out 1030, not the best.

F Kumiko, riverside near Dasasvamedha Ghat. Rooms and dorm, breakfast and dinner, Japanese spoken, very clean, friendly owner, if a bit paranoid (2000 curfew). Recommended.

F Shiva Guest House, D20/14 Munshi Ghat, T452108, shiva_guest_house@hotmail.com. 17 simple, clean rooms, some with hot bath, rooftop restaurant (good food), family run, friendly. Recommended.

F Tandon House Lodge, Badri Narayan Ghat, T331223, F334717. 15 basic rooms (bed bugs), with bath, peaceful riverside location with good views, good roof, away from tourist area.

F Trimurti Guest House Lodge, next to Golden Temple, T393554. Reasonably clean small rooms (Rs 80-120), some air-cooled with bath, some top floor rooms have good views, friendly, good food.

F Yogi Lodge, D8/29 Kalika Gali, near Golden Temple, T392588, yogilodge@yahoo.com. 15 simple rooms (Rs 100), shared bath, dorm (Rs 50), meals on roof terrace, congested area, internet, small rooms now poorer but still popular with backpackers. Rickshaws don't get commission, so may take you to *Yogi* hotels which are poorer (take a non-English speaking rickshaw to Godoulia, then phone).

Elsewhere
D Ashok, Vidyapeeth Rd, T221391. 25 rooms in modern hotel, hot water in mornings, restaurant, reasonable value.

E Blue Star, S14/84 G Maldahiya (fairly close to railway station), T343137. Small garden, rooms and dorm, front noisy, very basic but good value, friendly welcome, reasonable food.

E Buddha, C26/35 Lahurabir (behind hotel *Ayaya*), T343686, F514020. 22 large clean rooms (2 **D** a/c), hot showers, pleasant restaurant on veranda in the garden, friendly, helpful, safe, good choice. Recommended.

E Dak Bungalow, Caravan Park, The Mall, near TV Tower, T345685. 142 bare rooms (cheaper without hot water), dorm (Rs 16), good food (especially breakfasts) but slow service, occasional dancing and sitar music (evenings), large garden, quiet, pleasant atmosphere (friendly manager with amazing beard!), out-of-town, camping.

E GM Guest House, Chandrika Colony, Sigra behind Church, T221292. 21 large clean rooms, some with balcony (some **C** a/c), bath with constant hot water, excellent room service providing good inexpensive food.

E Garden View, Sigra Crossing, 64/129 Vidyapith Rd, T221093. 12 air-cooled rooms with bath, good restaurant, simple but clean, good service. Recommended.

E Park Villa, Rathayatra Crossing, T357050. 14 rooms, atmospheric, decaying, interesting and friendly, food poor.

E Radiant YMCA Tourist Hostel, 28A Sampoornanand Nagar, Sigra, T363928, radiant/varanasi@dartmail.dartnet.com. Internet, exchange.

E Sun Shiv, D 54/16-D Ravi Niketan, Jaddumandi Rd (off Aurangabad Rd), T350468, F350699, hotelsunshiv@usa.net. Modest rooms with balconies, room service, quiet, no commission to rickshaws.

E Tourist Bungalow (UP Tourism), off Parade Kothi, opposite rly station, T343413. 39 rooms, some **D** a/c, with bath, 'deluxe suites' and dorm (Rs 75) in barrack-style 2-storey building, restaurant, bar, shady verandah, pleasant garden, simple, clean and efficient, very helpful Tourist Office. Auto-rickshaws may take you to the inferior private 'Tourist Bungalow' nearby which has no garden.

E-F International Guest House, C32/4 (opposite BHU), T360912. Rooms, dorm, camping in garden.

F Railway Retiring Rooms at Varanasi Cantt, some a/c rooms and dorm.

Sarnath *p190, map p190*
D-E Tourist Bungalow (UP Tourism), T586965. Rooms and dorm (Rs 70), Indian restaurant, tourist office, tours.

F Birla Rest House, near Mulagandhakuti Vihara. Dorm (Rs 50).

Jaunpur *p192, map p192*
E Chandra Continental, Tilakdhari College Rd, Olandganj, T64388. 12 clean rooms.

F Railway Retiring Rooms, 2 rooms (Rs 35).

Surya, Qila Rd, for snacks, clean.

Allahabad *p193, map p194*
MG Marg is Mahatma Gandhi Marg.

B Kanha Shyam, Civil Lines, T420290. 85 rooms, pool, the most comfortable.

C Allahabad Regency, 16 Tashkent Marg, T601519, F600450. 13 a/c rooms, restaurant, pool (closed in winter), pleasant garden.

C Presidency, 19D Sarojini Naidu Marg, T623308, F623897. 11 comfortable a/c rooms, restaurant, pool, peaceful street.

C Yatrik, 33 Sardar Patel Marg, 1 km railway station, T601713, F601509. 37 a/c rooms, smartened entrance, restaurant, lovely garden, good value, clean and comfortable, good service, pool (closed in winter).

D Finaro, 8 Hastings Rd, opposite High Court, T622452, F622218, imtindia@sancharnet.in. 95 simple rooms with bath (geyser), pleasant small garden, near railway station and Civil Lines shopping, excellent home cooking, very helpful proprietor. Recommended.

D Tourist Bungalow (UP Tourism), 35 MG Marg, T601440. Rooms vary, some clean, good size a/c with bath and hot water, restaurant, bar, pleasant garden but can be noisy.

D-E Santosh Palace, 100 Katju Rd, T654773. Good, clean, quiet rooms with bath and hot water (aircooled or a/c).

E Prayagraj, 51/104 Katju Rd, air-cooled rooms with bath, TV, good beds, clean, but prayer calls at mosque opposite.

F Railway Retiring Rooms and dorm.

F Royal, Smith Rd, T623285. Large house with big rooms, restaurant, friendly.

❶ Eating

Varanasi *p183, maps p184 and p188*
Restaurants outside hotels tend to be vegetarian and are not allowed to serve alcohol. Dry days on the 1st and 7th of each month, and some public holidays. The locally made *Melody* chocolate ice-cream is reputed to taste like the best Belgian double chocolate!

Top hotels have expensive restaurants.
ⅲ Varanasi Ashok, does good Indian. Lacks ambience, but try chicken *Kebab-e-Kalni*, *Paneer Capsium Bhujia*, stuffed *Paratha*, and *Puri-Bhaji* for breakfast.

The Old Centre
ⅱ Fagin's (Golden Lodge), Kalika Gali. International. A/c, in a rather dark basement.
ⅱ Ganga Fuji, Kalika Gali. International. Reasonable, safe food, tempered down for western palate, live classical music in the evenings, helpful and friendly owner, popular. Recommended for ambiance and hospitality.
ⅱ Keshari, near *Ganges Hotel*, off Dasasvamedha Ghat. Excellent vegetarian *thalis*, "the longest menu in town", quick efficient service. Highly recommended.
ⅱ Monalisa, Western favourites.
ⅱ Spicy Bites. Western snacks are good. *Nachos* are a treat, friendly service, travellers' notice board and newspapers. Recommended.
ⅱ Shivan's Magna, 5/15 Tripura Bhairavi, T321945. Clean, plush, good value.
ⅰ Alka, Mir Ghat. Very good vegetarian, clean kitchen, friendly management.
ⅰ Babla, Yadav Katra, Godoulia. Vegetarian, excellent spring rolls.
ⅰ Garden, opposite Sushil Cinema, Godoulia. Indian, Chinese and continental. Excellent food (if a bit slow), pleasant rooftop, friendly.
ⅰ Jalayog, Godoulia. Good, traditional veg breakfast, cheap Indian snacks and sweets.
ⅰ Shanti, Manikarnika Ghat, is open 24 hrs, but reports of 'bad food'.
ⅰ Sona Rupa, Indian veg and Chinese. Large tables, quiet, good prices and service, but 'too much chilli in everything' for some.
ⅰ Street View, Gai Ghat. Good breakfast, 'Ayurvedic tea' recommended, friendly owners.

Elsewhere
ⅱ Burger King, Nai Bazar, Cantt (next to *Taj Ganges*) Veg only! Good cheese burger, ice creams, also chow miens, soups etc, no seating but recommended, worth detour if you have a long wait for the train.
ⅱ Bread of Life, B 3/322 Shivala, near Ratnakar Park. Great cakes, also burritos, pizza, pasta, but no local dishes, small portions and poor service.

Near Assi Ghat:
ⅱ Gudiya, 43 Cantonment (next to India Tourist Office). Chinese. Food OK but pricey.
ⅱ Haifa, good Middle East dishes, great atmosphere.
ⅱ Pizza Place, a bit grubby but oven fresh pizzas, lasagnas.
ⅱ Pizzeria Café Vaatika, wonderful terrace on the Ganga, friendly staff, Italian and Indian food, excellent coffee.
ⅱ Poonam, in *Pradeep Hotel*. Indian. Good variety, clean, smart professional staff, ignore drab décor and order banana lassi, *masala* dishes and finish with *Shahi tukra* (poor toilet).
ⅰ Ashiana, Clark Rd, Varuna Bridge. Indian and Chinese.
ⅰ Coffee House, Bhelapura. Decent South Indian.
ⅰ Eats & Bites, C21/4 Shri Ram Complex, Maldahiya, next to *Hindustan International Hotel*. International. Great food, excellent service, moderate prices.
ⅰ Kerala, Bhelapura. Good vegetarian.
$ Mandarin, near *Tourist Bungalow* and railway station. Chinese. Lacks flavour.
ⅰ Sindhi, Bhelapura, next to Lalita Cinema. Excellent Indian vegetarian, difficult for foreigners to get fully-sugared Indian chai.

Allahabad *p193, map p194*
ⅱ El Chico, 24 MG Marg. Good quality and wide choice, with bakery next door.
ⅱ Jade Garden, *Tepso Hotel*, MG Marg. For Chinese.
ⅱ Kwality, MG Marg. New upmarket café.
ⅰ Hot Stuff, 15 Elgin Rd. Smart, fast food, also good ices.
ⅰ Tripti, Katju Rd. Indian.

❷ Entertainment

Varanasi *p183, maps p184 and p188*
Clarks Cultural Centre, Peshwa Palace, Raj Ghat, in an old Brahmin refectory. Enquire at *Clarks Varanasi*, The Mall, T348501 or at travel agents. Evening entertainment begins at sunset with *Ganga aarti* with floating of lamps, performance of music and dance;

US$20 including pick-up from hotels 1730, return 2030. At dawn, witness prayers with chanting and singing; provides a vantage point for photographs. A funfair with big-wheel etc (safety not up to international standards) near GPO by the roundabout.

Allahabad *p193, map p194*
Prayag Sangeet Samiti presents music and dance programmes in the evenings.

✪ Festivals and events

Varanasi *p183, maps p184 and p188*
Jan: Parswanath Jayanti has an elephant drawn *rath* from Belunala to Bhelupura. **Feb**: Ganga Water Rally, organized by UP Tourism, is an international and national kayak get-together from Allahabad to Chunar Fort. A 40-km race from Chunar to Varanasi takes place on the final day (6-8 Feb 2005). **Late Feb/ Early Mar**: 3 days at Sivaratri, festival of Dhrupad music attracts performers from near and far, beginners and stars, in a very congenial atmosphere, a wonderful experience. **Mar/Apr**: Holi is celebrated with great fervour. **Apr**: pilgrims walk around 'Kashi', as laid down in the scriptures. Jain *Mahavir Jayanti*. **Apr/May**: Sankat Mochan Music Festival, Sankat Mochan Mandir. Non-stop temple music, open to all (28 Apr-2 May 2005). **May**: Ganga Dasara celebrates the day the waters of the Ganga reached Haridwar. **Oct/Nov**: Dasara Ramlila at Ramnagar. Ganga Festival is organized by UP Tourism alongside a 10 day craft fair (22-26 Nov 2004, 12-15 Nov 2005). Nagnathaiya draws up to 50,000 worshippers to Tulsi Ghat, re-enacting the story of Krishna jumping into the Yamuna to overcome *Kalija*, the King of the Serpents (16 Nov 2004, 5 Nov 2005). Nakkataiya A fair at Chetganj recalling Rama's brother, Lakshmana, cutting off Ravana's sister's nose when she attempted to force him into a marriage! At Nati Imli, **Bharat Milap**, the meeting of Rama and Bharat after 14 years' separation is celebrated – the Maharaja of Varanasi attends in full regalia on elephant back. **Dec-Feb**: Music festivals.

Allahabad *p193, map p194*
Jan/Feb: Magh and Kumbh Mela in 2013.

◎ Shopping

Varanasi *p183, maps p184 and p188*
Main shopping areas are Chowk, Godoulia, Visvanath Gali, Gyanvapi and Thatheri Bazar Varanasi is famous for silks including brocades (Temple Bazar, Visvanath Gali), brassware, gold jewellery, *sitar* making and hand block printed goods.

Books
Ashok Hotel has new and secondhand (especially 'coffee-table') books.
City Bookshop, opposite *Indica Books*, sells new and secondhand, will also buy, good value and very helpful.
Harmony, B1/100 Assi Ghat. Good selection including travel guides.
Indica Books, D 40/18 Godoulia, near crossing, T321640. Specialist Indological bookshop.
Universal Book Co, D40/60 Godoulia, nearby. Wide range of English language books.

Handloom and handicrafts
Ali Handicrafts (Workers Village), C 19/19 A-5 Lallapura (between Varuna Hospital and Muslim School), T355676. Wholesale shop for silk scarves, saris, excellent and much cheaper than most, personal callers welcome.
Bhagwan Stores, in Visvanath Gali and K37/32 Golghar. Recommended.
Brijraman Das, in Visvanath Gali and K37/32 Golghar. Recommended.
Ganga Handlooms, D10/18 Kohli Katra, off Viswanath Gali, near Golden Temple (ask locally). 1100-2000. Large selection of beautiful cotton fabrics, *ikats*, vegetable dyes, good tailors, great patterns (western).
Mohan Silks, in Visvanath Gali and K37/32 Golghar. Recommended.
Muslim Silk Weaving Centre is next door.
Oriental Arts Emporium, 10/252 Maqbool Alam Rd, Chauki Ghat.

▲▲ Activities and tours

Varanasi *p183, maps p184 and p188*
Swimming
Pools at hotels *Taj Ganges*, *Varanasi Ashok*, *Hindustan* and *Clarks Varanasi* (Rs 150-200 for non-residents).

Tour companies
Sita, 53 The Mall, T/F348445.
TCI, *Ideal Hotel*, The Mall, T342866, F346209.
Highly recommended.
Touraids, *Hotel India*, 59 Patel Nagar, T342598.
Travel Bureau, *Ideal Hotel*, The Mall, Cantt,
T344347. Highly recommended.
UP Roadways Tour I: River trip, temples,
Benaras Hindu University. **Tour II**: Sarnath
and Ramnagar Fort. Daily, summer
1430-1825, winter 1400-1755. Starts from
Tourist Bungalow, picking up from Govt of
India Tourist Office, The Mall. Tickets on bus.
Varuna, Pandey Haveli, near Bank of India
(Old City), T393568. All ticketing (Rs 200 for
reconfirmation!); also tours.

Yoga and meditation
Vag Yoga Consciousness Society, B3/13A
Shivala, T311706.
Yoga Institute, BHU, T310290.

Allahabad *p193, map p194*
Mayo Hall Complex, one of the largest
training centres in India for table tennis,
basketball, badminton and volleyball.

Tour operators
Ankita, 15A S Patel Marg, T603308.
Varuna, Civil Lines, T624323.

⊖ Transport

Varanasi *p183, maps p184 and p188*
Air
Transport to town by bus to *Indian Airlines*,
Tourist Office, top hotels and railway station.
Tickets for bus from Arrival Hall, Rs 20, or from
Indian Airlines, T346588. Departs from tourist
office 1030, 1200, 1430; from airport, 30-45
mins after each flight. Transfer by taxi, a/c Rs
300, non-a/c Rs 200. Some taxis offer free
transfer and claima commission from hotel on
arrival. **Indian Airlines**, 52 Yadunath Marg,
Cantt, T345959, airport, T343742, flies daily to
Delhi via **Khajuraho** and **Agra**; to
Bhubaneswar, Tue, Thu, Sat, Sun; to **Mumbai**
via **Lucknow**, Mon, Wed, Fri. **Kathmandu**,
daily. **Indian Airlines** flights originating in Delhi
are subject to severe delays in Jan and Feb
because of fog. Try to get a direct flight from
Delhi. **Jet Airways**, S20/56D Kennedy Rd, The
Mall, T511444 (airport T622795), flies to Delhi
daily. **Sahara**, Mint House, opposite Taj Ganges,

T343094 (airport T622334), flies to/from **Delhi**,
Lucknow and **Mumbai**, daily except Sun.

Bicycle
Cycle and motorcycle hire: near *Hotel
Hindustan International*, Maldahiya.

Bus
Local Cover most of Varanasi but crowded.
Long distance UP Roadways Bus Stand,
Sher Shah Suri Marg, near raily station, Cantt,
open 24 hrs, T343746. Reservations for deluxe
buses to Allahabad. Buses to **Sarnath**, 9 km,
Rs 2 (see Excursions below). Frequent services
to **Allahabad**, 122 km, 4 hrs; **Gorakhpur**,
7 hrs; **Jaunpur**, 1 hr, Rs 22. Also to **Delhi**, daily,
via **Khajuraho and Agra**; **Lucknow** 286 km
(0745, 1515), 9 hrs. Private buses stop
opposite the railway station. **Khajuraho**:
565 km, 1600 bus to Rewa (night stop); next
day change bus at Satna. **Gaya**: better by rail.

Ferry
This is the best way to enjoy Varanasi. It is
necessary to bargain especially for the early
morning ghats visit (1 hr): shared boat: Rs 50
per hr is the official rate for a small boat carrying
up to 4 people, larger boats Rs 75. Ask around
for others to share boat; river crossing about Rs
5. A boat ride at dusk is also recommended.

Rickshaw
Tempos and auto-rickshaws usually run on
fixed routes; those near hotel gates overcharge
(fix the fare before hiring). They are not allowed
in the narrow streets of the old city but will go
to Godoulia in the centre or to Dasasvamedha
Ghat, Rs 15-20 from station. Cycle-rickshaws,
day hire, about Rs 100.

Taxi
Unmetered taxis. Private taxis from agents
and hotels. Full day (90 km; 8 hrs), a/c Rs
1000, non a/c Rs 600-800; basic rate per km
about a/c Rs 86, non a/c Rs 64.

Train
Beware: the large 'Tourist Information
Counter' at Junction station run by travel
agents adds large commissions to rail tickets.
 Most trains stop at the Junction (or
Cantonment) **Station**, T348031 with 24 hr
left luggage; to reach a *Cantt hotel* on foot,
use the back exit. Can be very crowded; use a

retiring room if you have a long wait. **Mughal Sarai** station has the Delhi/Kolkata *Rajdhani Exp* (though some go via Patna); see below. Get your tickets (preferably a day in advance) from the **Foreign Tourist Assistance** inside the main hall which is very helpful and efficient, passport required (0800-2200, Sun 0800-1400). When it is closed use the computerized railway reservations (0800-1400, 1430-2000). **Agra Fort**: *Marudhar Exp, 4853/4863*, 1725/1835, 12½ /11¼ hrs (book ahead); or go to Tundla from Mughal Sarai (see below). **Allahabad**: *Mahanagari Exp, 1094*, 1130, 3½ hrs; *Sarnath Exp, 4260*, 1230, 2¾ hrs; *Kamayani Exp, 1072*, 1550, 3¾ hrs. **Chennai**: *Ganga-Kaveri Exp, 6040*, 1745, Mon, Wed, 41 hrs, reserve early. **Dehra Dun**: *Varanasi Dehra Dun Exp, 4265*, 0840, 24¼ hrs. **Gaya**: *Dehra Dun Exp, 3010*, 1615, 5¼ hrs. **Gorakhpur** (for Nepal): *Krishak Exp, 5002*, 1630, 5½ hrs; *Manduadih Gorakhpur Exp, 5104A, 0550, 5¼ hrs; **Jaunpur**: *Sutlej Doon Exp 3307*, 0640 1¼ hr; *Farakka Exp, 3483*, 1230, 50 mins. **Kanpur**: *Neelachal Exp, 8475*, 0742, Mon, Wed, Sat, 7¼ hrs; **Kolkata** (**H**): *Amritsar-Howrah Mail, 3006*, 1650, 14¾ hrs; *Doon Exp, 3010*, 1615, 14¾ hrs. **Lucknow**: *Varuna Exp, 4227*, 0510, 4¾ hrs; *Kashi-Visvanath Exp, 4257*, 1410, 6½ hrs. **Mahoba** (for *Khajuraho*): *Bundelkhand Exp, 1108*, 1330, 12¼ hrs (onward bus, 0600). **Satna** (for *Khajuraho*): *Satna Mahanagari Exp, 1094*, 1130, 6½ hrs (from Satna, bumpy bus next day, 4 hrs). **Mumbai** (CST): *Varanasi Lokmanya Tilak Exp, 1066*, 2025, Tue, Thu, Sun, 25¾ hrs. **New Delhi**: *Lichchavi Exp, 5205*, 1500, 13½ hrs; *Shramjeevi Exp, 2401*, 1520, 14¼ hrs. **Mughal Sarai** station (with retiring rooms and left luggage), T925703. Take a connecting train from Varanasi (45 mins), or allow plenty of time as you need to cross the Ganga and there are huge jams. Best to take a taxi from Varanasi as buses are not dependable and a rickshaw would feel very vulnerable next to the speeding juggernauts. **Agra**: *Marudhar Exp*, 1725, 13 hrs. **Kolkata** (**H**): *Rajdhani Exp, 2302/2422*, 0235, 8-10 hrs; *Kalka Howrah Mail, 2312*, 2030, 10½ hrs. **New Delhi**: *Poorva Exp, 2381/2303*, 1910/2045, Wed, Thu, Sun, 13/11½ hrs; *Neelanchal Exp, 8475*, 0655, Mon, Wed, Sat, 14½ hrs; *Rajdhani Exp, 2301/5*, 0050, 9¼ hrs. **New Jalpaiguri** (for

Darjeeling): *Mahananda Exp, 4084*, 2120, 18½ hrs; *NE Exp, 5622*, 1835, 16 hrs and to **Guwahati**, 24¼ hrs.

Transport to Nepal

Payment for Nepalese visa at border in cash only (Indian or Nepalese); TCs are not accepted.

To Kathmandu, the journey requires an overnight stay near the border plus about 20 hrs on the road so can be tiring. UP Roadways buses go via **Gorakhpur** to **Sonauli**, depart 4 or 5 times per day, check for timings (usually early morning or night), 0300, 0400, 0930, 2130 (9-10 hrs), Rs 110; from Sonauli, 0600; (Lumbini is 386 km). Private buses (agents near UP *Tourist Bungalow*), often demand inclusive fares for hotel stay; you may prefer to opt for their deluxe buses to the border. Well organized bus service by **Paul Travels**, near *Tourist Bungalow*, Rs 400; departs 0800, overnight in basic hotel (breakfast); next morning, departs 0830 (10-11 hrs). See page 34.

Sarnath *p190, map p190*

Infrequent bus service; also included in coach tours. From Varanasi, bus from opposite railway station (Rs 5), sometimes stops opposite *Taj Hotel*. Auto-rickshaws (Rs 50), tempo seat (Rs 10). The road is bumpy; cycling is not recommended as trucks travel along it at great speed. Taxis take 30 mins (Rs 400 including wait).

Jaunpur *p192, map p192*
Bus

Frequent service along NH56 to/from **Varanasi** and **Lucknow** including *Express* (under 2 hrs). Ask to be dropped at the Akbari Bridge (crossroads north of the bus stand) where you can pick up a cycle rickshaw.

Taxi

From Varanasi, Rs 800 return.

Train

To **Varanasi** *Sutlej Exp, 3308*, 1820, 2 hrs; *Varuna Exp, 4228*, 2200.

Allahabad *p193, map p194*

Allahabad is on the major broad gauge route from Delhi to Kolkata but also has metre gauge trains.

UP Roadways and other state RTCs link Allahabad with **Delhi** (643 km), **Gwalior**, **Jaunpur**, **Jhansi** (375 km), **Kanpur**, **Lucknow** (204 km), **Meerut**, **Patna** (368 km), **Rewa**, **Sasaram** and **Varanasi** (122 km). Roadways Bus Stands: Civil Lines, T601257; Zero Rd, T50192; Leader Rd (south gate of Junction station), T601224. Private bus stands at Ram Bagh and Leader Rd for luxury coaches to **Lucknow** and **Varanasi**.

Train

Allahabad Junction, T604256, to avoid long queues use ticket booth on the north side. Prayag (broad gauge trains for Kanpur and Lucknow) with Left Luggage; **Allahabad City** (mostly for Varanasi); **Daraganj** (metre gauge). **Jabalpur**: *Patna Lokmanya Tilak Exp*, *3201*, 0830, 6½ hrs; *Varanasi Lokmanya Tilak Exp*, *2166*, 2330, Tue, Fri, Sun, 5½ hrs. **Jhansi**: *Bundelkhand Exp*, *1108*, 1830, 12½ hrs. **Lucknow**: *Ganga-Gomti Exp*, *2415*, 0600, 3½ hrs (2nd class only); *Nauchandi/Link Exp*, *4011/4511*, 1730, 5 hrs. **Kolkata**: *Kalka-Howrah Mail*, *2312*, 1730, 13¼ hrs; *Rajdhani Exp*, *2302*, 0023, 10¼ hrs. **Mumbai** (CST): *Bombay Mail*, *3003*, 1110, 24¼ hrs; *Mahanagiri Exp*, *1094*, 1505, 24¼ hrs. (Lokmanya Tilak). **New Delhi**: *Prayagraj Exp*, *2417*, 2130, 10½ hrs; *Poorva Exp*, *2303/2381*, 2255, 9¼ hrs. **Patna**: *Magadh Exp*, *2392*, 0500, 6¼ hrs; *Udyan Abha-Toofan Exp*, *3008*, 2230, 7 hrs; *Howrah Quila Exp*, *3112*, 1025, 8½ hrs. **Varanasi**: *Varanasi Kashi Exp*, *1027*, 0845, 4 hrs; *Sarnath Exp*, *4259*, 1305, 3 hrs; *Bundelkhand Exp*, *1107*, 0640, 3¼ hrs.

✪ Directory

Varanasi *p183, maps p184 and p188*
Airline offices Air India, *Sri Das Foundation, The Mall*, T340192. **Banks** Most banks refuse to change money. Travellers are often stopped and asked for 'change'. State Bank of India at *Hotel Best Western Kashika* (Mon-Fri 1000-1400), and Godoulia (near *Indica Books*), takes approximately 1 hr, changes Visa, TCs. Also at *Clarks Varanasi* and at airport. Radiant Services, D48/139A Misir Pokhra (by Mazda Cinema), Luxa Road,

Godoulia, T358852. Open daily 0700-2200, changes TCs and 36 currencies, "long-winded but faster than a bank". They also have a 24-hr counter at *Shanti Guest House*, T392017, and Cantt Office, above *Union Bank of India*, on the Mall, T511052. Shops changing money offer a poor rate. **Hospitals** Chemists: near hospitals. Heritage Hospital, Lanka, T313977. Private hospital, out-patients 0830-2000. BHU Hospital, T312542. RK Mission Hospital, Luxa, T321727. SSPG Hospital, Kabir Chaura Rd, T333723. **Internet** In lane near Dasasvamedha Ghat, well signed. Several others, **The Messenger**, Temple Kashi Karvat, in the lanes. 7 terminals, Rs 30 per hr is recommended. Astro Travel, B1/108 Assi Ghat, for STD/ISD and email. **Post office** Head Post Office: Bisheshwarganj (parcel packing outside). Post office in Cantt, post Mon-Sat 1000-1800, telegraph 0930-1630. A man offers to 'help' get a parcel posted for a fee (Rs 100), but you can do this yourself! A convenient PO is in an alley opposite *Garden Restaurant* in Godoulia. Couriers: City Airlinkers, Cantt, T344214. First Flight, Jagatganj. **Tourist offices** UP, Tourist Bungalow, Parade Kothi, T/F511638. 1000-1700, closed Sun, very helpful, Japanese spoken. Counter, Cantt Railway Station, near 'Enquiry', T346370. 0600-2000, very helpful information and map. Govt of India, 15B The Mall, Cantt, T/F343744. 0900-18001000-1700, closed Sun, well run, very helpful manager and staff; guides available, about Rs 250 (half day), Rs 380 (full day) depending on group size. Counter, Babatpur Airport. Bihar, Englishiya Market, Cantt, T343821. 0800-2000. **Useful addresses** Ambulance: T333723. Fire: T101, T322888. Police: T100. Foreigners' Registration Office: Sidh Giri Bagh (not easy to find), T353968. Local Intelligence Office, T351968. Language courses: week long 'Tourist Hindi' courses, next to *Shanti Guest House*, Manikarnika Ghat.

Allahabad *p193, map p194*
Banks Bank of Baroda, 61 MG Marg. **Hospitals** Dufferin, Hospital Chowk, T651822. Motilal Nehru, Colvin, T652141.

✦ Footprint features

Introduction

Uttaranchal, India's 27th state, comprises thirteen Himalayan districts sandwiched between Himachal Pradesh to the west and Nepal to the east. The region, also known as Uttarkhand, has some of India's most magnificent mountain scenery, but it also has a highly distinctive **hill culture**, and its own Pahari dialects. For years there has been an undercurrent of popular demand for the creation of a new state, many hoping that it would enable the region to break free of the dominant Uttar Pradesh power brokers. The new state stretches from the densely populated foothills up to the heights of the **Nanda Devi range**, containing outstandingly beautiful yet relatively little-known trekking routes.

★ Don't miss...

1. Escape the heat of the plains by heading to a hill station: Dehra Dun, Mussoorie or, better still, **Landour**, with its fresh, clean, pine-scented air, page 213.

2. Watch priests performing spectacular Ganga aarti at sunset in **Haridwar**, said to be one of the oldest cities in the world, page 218.

3. Chill out in an ashram at **Rishikesh** and follow in the tracks of the Beatles and the Maharishi Mahesh Yogi, page 222.

4. If you have a spare 10 days, walk the **Curzon Trail**, an incomparably beautiful trek, which crosses the **Kuari Pass**, said to be one of the finest vantage points in the Himalaya, page 240.

5. If time is tight, trek the **Valley of the Flowers**, page 233.

6. Have a few days rest at **Nainital**, a charming hill station, to visit the atmospheric British cemetery, page 245.

7. Unquestionably, the highlight of the area is **Corbett National Park**: try and spot a tiger, page 253.

Uttaranchal

Background → *Population: 8½ million. Area: 53,480 sq km.*

The land

The extraordinarily contorted geology of the Garhwal and Kumaon Himalaya reflects the fierce uplifting and the complex movements which have taken place since the Himalaya began to be formed. The outer ranges of the Siwaliks, generally less than 2500 m high, are a jumble of deeply dissected sediments. In places these are separated from the Lesser Himalayan ranges by great longitudinal valleys, or *duns*, such as Dehra Dun, while in the Lesser Himalaya immediately to their north, towns such as Mussoorie, Almora and Nainital offered coolness in the summer from the overpowering heat of the plains. Immediately to their north again the high peaks are surrounded by deep valleys, at their heads still some of the world's largest glaciers. Some meteorologists predict that the Himalaya will be glacier-free within 30 years or so. This is not the result of recent global warming, but the latest phase in the 10,000 year retreat of the latest northern hemisphere Ice Age. Glaciers such as the Milam, still several kilometres long, are covered in boulders, and float over the masses of material which have been dropped by glaciers too shrunk to move it any further. Forming a massive barrier to their north are the permanent snows and high peaks such as **Nanda Devi** (7,816 m), **Shivling** and other peaks over 6,000 m.

Climate

The climate of Uttaranchal is dominated by the monsoon, with over three quarters of the rainfall coming between June and September, but temperature is controlled both by height and by season. In the lower valleys, such as Dehra Dun, summers are hot and sticky and maximum temperatures can go up to 45°C. Towns on the ridges up to 2,000 m high, such as Almora and Ranikhet, experience maximum temperatures in the summer of up to 34°C. Yet in winter these same towns experience snow fall, and temperatures even in the outer valleys are as low as 3°C or 4°C. Despite a drop of temperature between June and September humidity increases, making it a very uncomfortable season in the foothills. The high peaks are under permanent snow. In the higher hills the air is always fresh but can be very cold. Late April to early June and September-October are generally the best times for trekking.

Culture

Ethnically, on the plains the inhabitants are largely of Indo-Aryan origin, northwards giving way to strong Mongoloid influences on the border with Tibet. Most people **speak** Hindi, but Urdu is still quite widely used among Muslims. There are numerous local dialects. In Uttaranchal Garhwali and Kumaoni (hill) dialects predominate, one of the reasons given by the residents for the creation of a separate state of Uttaranchal in the Himalayan region of Uttar Pradesh.

History

Up until the 14th century Garhwal (Land of the Forts) comprised a number of petty principalities. Ajai Pal (1358-70) consolidated these and became the Raja of Garhwal. The region was a popular plundering ground for Sikh brigands – see Rampur, page 136. The **Gurkhas** overran it in 1803, taking men, women and children into slavery and conscripting males into their army. Gurkha encroachments on the territory around Gorakhpur led the British to expel them from Garhwal and Kumaon in 1814. They took the eastern part of Garhwal as British Garhwal and returned the western part, Tehri Garhwal, to the deposed Raja. It has been suggested that the hillsmen of this region have always been resentful of their political domination by the plainsmen of Uttar Pradesh, and hence the creation of Uttaranchal on ninth November 2000 is the fulfillment of a long cherished dream. However, many of those who fought for the new state feel short-changed and see little prospect of real power being transferred to the hills people. Having realised their ambition for a separate 'Uttarakhand', the new state's name of Uttaranchal was a political decision by the ruling BJP party. The new State Assembly has been formed initially by the transfer of Members of the Uttar Pradesh Legislative Assembly who represent Uttaranchal constituencies. In the first state elections, held in February 2002, the Congress swept the BJP from power, and the veteran Congress leader ND Tiwari became Chief Minister.

The question of the capital is still contentious. Dehra Dun has initially been given the status of 'interim capital', but there are still demands that it should be transferred to Gairsain, a hill town in the heart of the new state.

Economy

Scattered farming villages among picturesque terraces present the skill with which Uttaranchal's mountain people have adapted to their hill environment. Agriculture is still by far the most important economic activity for people throughout the hills, often carried out with apparent simplicity but considerable sophistication, both of engineering and of cropping types. On many of the cultivated hillsides terracing is essential and wonderfully intricate, and a wide variety of crops – paddy, wheat, barley and lentils on the low lying irrigated terraces, sugar cane, chillies, buckwheat and millets higher up. Market gardening and potato cultivation have spread around all the townships. Rotation of crops is widely practised and intensive use of animal manure helps to fertilise the soil. The terraces themselves, sometimes as high as 6-m, may have as many as 500 flights, and some villages have up to 6,000 individual terraces. Given that it takes one man a day to build a wall a 1-m high and 2-m long, it is easy to see what vast amounts of labour have gone into their construction, and how much care is lavished on their maintenance, for they are the peoples' security.

The forests also supply vital wealth. Apart from the timber itself resin is often a valuable export, and wood carving is a widely practised skill. Today tourism is an increasingly important source of income. Indian visitors from the plains and foreigners seeking to experience something of the high Himalayan ranges. Tourism is believed to bring in approximately US$50 million a year, and horticulture, fruit cultivation and the production of medicinal plants are potentially of great value, though transport remains a huge problem. While the new state has massive hydroelectric potential its development is highly controversial. The Tehri Dam has been the focus of intense opposition from environmental campaigners for over 20 years, and while that project is now nearing completion other schemes may be very difficult to promote, despite the rapidly growing demand for electricity on the plains.

Dehra Dun → Phone code: 0135. Colour map 1, grid B4. Population: 370,000.

Dehra Dun (dera – camp; dun – valley, pronounced 'doon'), lies in a wooded valley in the Shiwalik Hills. In Hindu legend the Dun Valley was part of Siva's stamping ground. Rama and his brother are said to have done penance for killing Ravana, and the five Pandavas stopped here on their way to the mountains. It makes a pleasant and relaxing stop on the way to the hills, and its mild climate has made it a popular retirement town. The cantonment, across the seasonal Bindal Rao River, is spacious and well wooded, while the Mussoorie road is lined with very attractive houses.
▸▸ *For Sleeping, Eating and other listings, see pages 211-213.*

Getting there The railway station, off Haridwar Rd to the south of town, has trains from Delhi, Varanasi and Kolkata. Buses heading for the Mussoorie and the Garhwal hills use the Mussoorie Bus Stand outside the station, while those bound for the plains and the Kumaon hills use the Delhi Bus Stand near *Hotel Drona*, 500 m away. Share taxis operate services to the hills from the stand outside the railway station.

Getting around The City Bus Stand, also used by private buses, is just north of the Clock Tower in the busy town centre, about 10 mins on foot from the railway station. Although the town centre is compact it is best to get a taxi or auto-rickshaw for visiting the various sights which are between 4-8 km (10-20 mins ride) away. See Transport, page 212, for further details.

History

A third-century BC Asoka rock inscription found near Kalsi suggests that the area was ruled by the emperor. During the 17th and 18th centuries Dehra Dun changed hands several times. The Gurkhas overran it on the westward expansion from Kumaon to Kangra, finally ceding it to the British in 1815 who developed it as a centre of education and research. It is still a major centre for government institutions like the

Dehra Dun

To Robber's Cave (6 km)
To Mussoorie
To Tapkesvar Cave Temple (1 km)
Archaeological Survey of India
Survey of India
Map Sales
Raipur Rd
GMVN
Dilaram Bazar
Memorial Arch
New Cantonment Rd
Kalidas Rd
St Thomas
Doon School
Bindal Rao
Kaulagarh Rd
Ch Bihari Lal Marg
Raipur Rd
Subhash Rd
President Travels
Astley Hall
Bookshops
PNB
Dun Club
Ugrasain Rd
Survey Office
Cinema
Cinema
Clock Tower
City Bus Stand
Subhash Park
Pant Rd
Convent Rd
Rajaji National Park Office
Ansari Marg
Cross Rd
RC
Thalt Rd
Mori Bazar
Paltan Bazar
Gandhi Rd
Paramount
Delhi Bus Stand
Amritkaur Rd
Subhash Rd
SBI
Eastern Canal Rd
Shivaji Marg
Saharanpur Rd
Mussoorie Bus Stand
Doon's Tours
Tyagi Rd
Haridwar Rd
To Wadia Institute of Himalayan Geology
To Nainital
To Lakshman Sidh, Airport (24 km) & Rishikesh
To Shahasradhara (13 km)
Rispana Rao
To Forest Research Institute, Botanical Gardens & Indian Military Academy

N

0 metres 200
0 yards 200

■ **Sleeping**
1 Ajanta Continental
2 Deepshikha
3 Drona
4 Great Value
5 Kwality
6 Madhuban
7 Osho Resorts
8 President
9 Relax
10 Victoria

● **Eating**
1 Bossa Nova, Daddy's & Vegetarian
2 Dominos
3 Kumar

Uttaranchal Dehra Dun

Survey of India and for the Indian Army, and in November 2000 it became the provisional state capital of Uttaranchal though many hill-dwellers consider it too close to sea-level to reflect the mountainous nature of the new state.

Sights

The **Survey of India**, founded in 1767, has its headquarters on Rajpur Road, about 4 km from the Clock Tower. The **Doon School**, off Kaulagarh Road, India's first public school, is still one of its most prestigious. Further along, the highly regarded **Forest Research Institute** (1914), an impressive red-brick building which was designed by Lutyens, is surrounded by the fine lawns of the Botanical Gardens and forests. It has excellent museums which are open from 0900 to 1730 on weekdays. The **Royal Indian Military College** (1922), in quaint mock Tudor style and the Indian Military Academy (1932), which opened with 40 cadets now takes 1,200.

The **Tapkesvar Cave Temple** ① *open sunrise to sunset, buses stop 500 m from the temple*, 5 km northwest, is in a pleasant setting with cool sulphur springs for bathing. There is a simple Indian café nearby.

Robber's Cave (8 km), **Lakshman Sidh** (12 km), the snows at **Chakrata** (9 km) and sulphur springs at **Shahasradhara** (14 km) are also within easy reach. The springs were threatened by limestone quarrying on the hills around until the High Court forced their closure. Replanting of the deforested hills has been allowing the water table and the springs to recover.

Saharanpur → *67 km south of Dehra Dun.*

Saharanpur, actually in Uttar Pradesh, is famous for carved wood furniture. It was founded in 1340 as a summer retreat for the Mughals. During the British period it became an important military base but the Government also set out **Botanical Gardens** in 1817. The **Eastern Yamuna Canal**, one of the first great 19th-century canals to irrigate the Ganga-Yamuna doab, transformed the landscape of what had been a heavily overpopulated region. It has become a particularly important source of fruit trees for the whole of India. The *Mango Festival* is held in June/July when hundreds of varieties are displayed. Watch woodcarvers at work in Lakdi Bazar and the old market place.

Listings: Dehra Dun

Sleeping

Dehra Dun *p209, map p210*

There are good discounts out-of-season (Aug-Feb). The cheaper hotels are near the station and the Clock Tower; the upmarket ones are north, along Rajpur Rd.

A Madhuban (Best Western), 97 Rajpur Rd, T749990, F746496, hotel_madhuban@ nde.vsnl.net.in. 45 rooms, good restaurants, pleasant garden, comfortable though rather characterless, but friendly staff, excellent views.

B Ajanta Continental, 101 Rajpur Rd, T749595, F747722. 29 rooms, good restaurant and bar, pool, pleasant ambience.

B-C Great Value Dehradun (Clarks), 74C Rajpur Rd, 4 km from the railway station, T746094, F746058, www.greatvaluehotel.com. 53 pleasant a/c rooms (some upgraded),

restaurant (Indian classical singing, evenings), business centre, modern, clean, good service, lives up to its name. Recommended.

B-C President, 6 Astley Hall, Rajpur Rd, T657386, F658883. 17 a/c rooms, good restaurant, bar, coffee shop, exchange, travel, golf and riding arranged, pleasant service.

B-D Osho Resorts, 111 Rajpur Rd, T749544, F748535, satish2@nde.vsnl.net.in. 20 clean, cottage rooms attached to the ashram.

C Relax, 7 Court Rd, T657776, F656406, htl@ nde.vsnl.net.in. 32 clean a/c or air-cooled rooms, restaurant, bar, overpriced.

C-D Drona (GMVN), 45 Gandhi Rd, T654371. 68 rooms, some a/c, dorm (Rs 70, men only), restaurants (good Indian), bar, large, busy and good value, tourist office in compound.

D Deepshikha, 57/1 Rajpur Rd, T659888. 22 rooms (some a/c), pleasant, modern.

D **Kwality**, 19 Rajpur Rd, T657001. 17 large rooms, some a/c, some singles, a bit ragged around the edges but OK, reasonable restaurant, bar.

E-F **Victoria**, opposite station, T623486. 32 simple rooms, some with bath, clean linen, 24 hr check out, safe, friendly.

Saharanpur *p211*
C-D **Taj**, near Clock Tower Chowk.
D **Swagat**, near Clock Tower Chowk, a modest business hotel.

⊘ Eating

Dehra Dun *p209, map p210*
♥ **Domino's**, Rajpur Rd, T746501. Pizza delivery.
♥♥ **Kumar**, 15B Rajpur Rd (towards *Kwality*). Tasty Punjabi dishes, friendly staff.
Outside hotels:
♥ **Bossa Nova**, Astley Hall. Ice creams and western snacks.
♥ **Daddy's** above *The Vegetarian*, serves travellers' favourites.
♥ **Osho**, 111 Rajpur Rd. Good snacks in roadside café 'Rajneesh' atmosphere.
♥ **The Vegetarian**, 3 Astley Plaza, Rajpur Rd. Non-veg.
Sheetal Restaurant, west of town on canal bank, is in an attractive setting.

Bakeries
Ellora, Rajpur Rd, Paltan Bazar. Fresh bread, biscuits and local sticky toffees!
Grand, Rajpur Rd, Paltan Bazar. Fresh bread, biscuits and local toffees.

⊙ Shopping

Dehra Dun *p209, map p210*
Shops around the Clock Tower, in Rajpur Rd, Paltan Bazar and Astley Hall, sell handwoven woollens, brassware and jewellery. For trekking equipment, try **Paramount**, 16 Moti Bazar (west of Paltan Bazar). For books, particularly natural history and related topics, try **The Green Bookshop**, on Rajpur Rd. Also **English Book Depot**, 15 Rajpur Rd, T655192, www.englishbookdepot.com. Extensive collection of English fiction and non-fiction.

▲▲ Activities and tours

Dehra Dun *p209, map p210*
Tour companies
For tours to *Chandrapuri Tent Camp* and *Auli Ski Resort*, see page 243.
GMVN, Old Survey Chowk, 74/1 Rajpur Rd, T656817, F654408.
Garhwal Adventure Tour, 151 Araghar, T/F627769, gtt@nde.vsnl.net.in. For trekking in Garhwal and Kumaon, experienced and knowledgeable.
President Travel, T6551116. Ticketing.

⊙ Transport

Dehra Dun *p209, map p210*
Air
Jolly Grant air strip (24 km), enquiry T682052; limited flights to/from **Delhi**.

Bus
Local From Rajpur Rd, near clocktower.
Long distance Delhi Bus Stand, Gandhi Rd, T653797, for most hill destinations and the plains; Mussoorie Bus Stand, outside the railway station, T623435. Half hourly to **Mussoorie**, 0600-2000, tickets from counter number 1, Rs 22. Private buses from City Bus Stand, Parade Ground. Regular services to **Mussoorie**, 1½ hrs; **Nainital**, 12 hrs; **Kullu**, 14 hrs; **Haridwar**, 1hrs. **From Shimla**: HP Roadways to Dehra Dun; deluxe buses, depart 0700, 0900, Rs 180; ordinary, last depart 1030 (10 hrs), Rs 140.

Car
Car hire: from **Drona Travels** (GMVN), T656894, or **Ventures**, BMS Business Centre, 87 Rajpur Rd, T652724.Try also **Doon Tours & Travels**, 16 Bhatt Shopping Complex, 1 Haridwar Rd, T624520. Rs 800 per day.

Taxi
Taxi (T627877) and **auto-rickshaw**: the cheaper crowded Vikrams are easily available.

Train
Railway Station, T622131. Reservations opposite, 0800-2000, Sun 0800-1400; book early for Haridwar. **New Delhi**: *Shatabdi Exp, 2018*, 1700, 5¾ hrs; **Delhi**: *Dehradun Bandra*

Exp, 9020, 1035, 10 hrs; Mussoorie Exp, 4042, 2115, 9¾ hrs. **Allahabad**: Link Exp, 4114, 1315, 18¾ hrs. **Kolkata**: Doon Exp, 3010, 1945, 34½ hrs (via **Varanasi**, 19½ hrs). **Varanasi**: Dehra Dun-Varanasi Exp, 4266, 1815, 24 hrs.

⊙ Directory

Dehra Dun p209, map p210
Banks Punjab National Bank, Ashley Hall, Ugrasain Rd. Exchange on 1st floor, 1000-1400, 1500-1600, Sat 1000-1230;

State Bank of India, Convent Rd, 1st floor. President Travels, 45 Rajpur Rd, changes TCs. **Hospital** Doon Hospital, Amrit Kaur Rd, T659355. **Tourist offices** GMVN, 74/1 Rajpur Rd, T746817; Hill Tourism, 3/3 Industrial Area, Patel Nagar, T627405623585. Uttaranchal, 45 Gandhi Rd, next to Drona Hotel, T653217. Mon-Sat, 1000-1700. **Useful addresses** Rajaji National Park office, 5/1 Ansari Marg, T621669. The only office issuing permits for Rajaji. Wildlife Institute of India, PO Box 18, Chandrabani, T620912, wii@giasdloi.vsnl.net.in.

Mussoorie

→ Phone code: 01362. Colour map 1, grid B4. Population: 30,000 .Altitude: 1,970 m.
Mussoorie, named after the Himalayan shrub mansoor, has commanding views over the Doon Valley to the south and towards the High Himalaya to the north. It is spread out over 16 km along a horseshoe-shaped ridge up to which run a series of buttress-like subsidiaries. Being the nearest hill station to Delhi, it is very popular with Indian tourists though no longer as clean as it was once, and it is nothing over other hill stations. Landour, another 300 m higher and away from the crowds, by contrast has fresh, clean, pine scented air. ➤➤ For Sleeping, Eating and other listings, see pages 214-217.

Ins and outs

Getting there Other than trekking in 7 km, the 30 km road from Dehra Dun (just under 1¾ hrs away by bus) is the only way to the town, arriving at the library (west end of the long Mall) or the Masonic Lodge bus stand (east end). Buses from Delhi take 6-7 hrs.

Getting around Taxis are available for longer journeys, including the steep climb up to Landour but for local trips cycle rickshaws are available or you can hire a bike. See Transport, page 217, for further details.

Climate Summer: maximum 32°C, minimum 7°C. Winter: maximum 7°C, minimum 1°C. Monsoons end Jun-Sep. Winter showers and snowfalls in Dec/Jan.

Sights

Captain Young 'discovered' Mussoorie in 1826 and it developed as an escape from the heat of the plains for the British troops. **Landour**, at 2,270 m, to the east has the old barracks area. The first British residence was built here which was followed by The Mall, Club, Christ Church (1837) and the library. It makes a really nice walk up through the woods and away from the pressing crowds of The Mall. There are good views, though the weather changes very quickly. 'Char Dukan' is a small junction in the cantonment area with two snack bar /shops and a very reliable post office; the road to the right leads to the **International Language School** and the one to the left to **Lal Tibba** – a nice view point with binoculars. The Woodstock School and the Language School are in a magnificent location, and some of the guest houses have stunning views. To the west are Convent Hill, **Happy Valley** where Tibetan refugees have settled (the school there may welcome volunteers to teach English), and the pleasant **Municipal Garden**. Mall Road connects Kulri and Library Bazars. Camel's Back and Cart Roads also connect the two, but more circuitously.

From the tourist office, **Lal Tibba** and nearby **Childe's Lodge** on the highest hill, are 5 km away. **Gun Hill**, where before Independence a midday gun fire enabled residents to set their watches, with a 400 m ropeway costing Rs 30 return, open from 0900-1900, can be reached by a bridle path in 20 minutes on horse back from the Kutchery on The Mall; the view of the snow-capped peaks is stunning and best at sunrise, although the mess of souvenir stalls, cafés and photographers later in the day may not appeal to all. The **Camel's Back Road**, from Kulri to the library, is a very pleasant 3-km walk.

Excursions

Kempty Falls, 15 km on the Chakrata Road, is pretty and a popular picnic spot. A taxi is about Rs 250 with a one hour stop. Heading to **Dhanolti**, 25 km away, you can go on a further 3 km to find the **Surkhanda Devi Temple** at 3,030 m. There are superb views of several high peaks over 6,500 m. A taxi is Rs 600 with a 2-3 hour stop. Buses between Mussoorie and Chamba take you within 2 km of the hill top.

Listings: Mussoorie

☉ Sleeping

Mussoorie *p213, map below and p216*
Most hotels check out at 1000.

Some are old-fashioned but full of character. The Mall is closed to cars and buses in the high season. You may have to walk to your hotel; porters are available at the bus stands. Prices are based on high-season tariffs, which are often quite ridiculous; most offer big off-season discounts, offering more realistic value for money.

L-AL Residency Manor (Jaypee), Barlow Ganj, 4 km southeast of town, a long walk, T631800, F631022, jaypee.residency@ smt.spritrpg.ems.vsnl.net.in. 90 rooms, smart, large and impressive (US$145-240 includes meals).

Mussoorie

Related map
A Mussoorie centre, page 216

N
Not to scale

■ **Sleeping**
1 Carlton's Plaisance
2 Golden Heaven
3 Kasamanda Lodge
4 Padmini Nivas
5 Shipra

● **Eating**
1 Coffee House
2 Tavern

AL-A Nabha Resort (Claridge's), Airfield, Barlow Ganj Rd, 2 km town centre, T631426, F631425. 22 rooms with verandah arranged around attractive garden in converted hill 'palace', superb views, excellent management, single storey, Raj style but with all modern comforts. Highly recommended.

A-B Connaught Castle, The Mall, T632210, F632538. 29 comfortable rooms, restaurant, 50% off-season discount.

B Kasamanda Palace Hotel (Heritage), near The Mall, T632424, F630007, kasmanda@ vsnl.com. 14 comfortable rooms, once Basset Hall of the Christ Church complex (built 1836), a British sanatorium, then royal guesthouse from 1915, interesting furnishings (hunting trophies, bric-a-brac), 2 dining rooms, peaceful, spacious grounds (putting green, croquet), one of the better options but small off-season discount Steep climb from Mall Rd so call for jeep transfer.

B Mall Palace, The Mall, T632097, F632297. 25 reasonable rooms with views, some tubs, clean, comfortable.

B Padmini Nivas, Library, The Mall, T631093, F632793, harshada@nde.vsnl.net.in. 27 rooms in former palace with character, some with good views, also (**A**) cottages,

not grand but pleasant ambience, good restaurant (pure veg Gujarati).

B Shipra, The Mall, T632662, F632941. 80 comfortable rooms in modern hotel, some with views, lift, restaurant.

B-C Cloud End Forest Resort, 7 km from town, T632242, F630822. 7 rooms with bath in colonial period lodge. Home-cooked meals, rustic (bucket water), fabulous views.

B-C Great Value (Clarks), Camel's Back Rd, Kulri, T632088, F631442. 35 modern comfortable rooms, good value (but not quite great!).

B-C Golden Heaven, near clock tower, Landour, T633319. 12 rooms plus a cottage, reasonably clean, TV, hot water, good value off-season.

C Filigree, Camel's Back Rd, Kulri, T632380, F632360, mustimes@nde.vsnl.net.in. 18 rooms, some well equipped, good restaurant, terrace with views. Uninspiring exterior but recommended.

C Holiday Inn, The Mall, T632794. 19 reasonable rooms, no restaurant, modern, clean, best with views.

C Uday, Camel's Back Rd, T631016. 10 rooms, TV, hot water, friendly, good views.

C-D Garhwal Terrace (GMVN), The Mall near Ropeway, T632682. 24 simple but clean rooms, dorm (Rs 130), restaurant, reasonable maintenance, excellent views.

D Carlton's Plaisance, Charleville Rd, T632800. 12 rooms (some with fine views), good restaurant (includes Tibetan), very Victorian with period furniture, peaceful orchard, spacious, charming and attentive service.

D Valley View, The Mall (Kulri) near Ropeway, T632324. 14 clean rooms (some with kitchenette), restaurant, bakery, garden, friendly, good service.

E Shalimar, Charleville Rd, T632410. 10 rooms, pleasant atmosphere.

E-F Broadway, Camel's Back Rd (next to rink), T632243. 10 rooms with bath (bucket hot water), best with views and geyser, Indian meals, old hotel.

There are also a string of modern **B-C** hotels to the west of Gandhi Chowk on The Mall and Motilal Nehru Rd.

Surkhanda Devi Temple *p214*
C Dhanolti Breeze, Rauslikhal, Kanatal, 5 km from the temple. Comfortable rooms.

Uttaranchal Listings: Mussoorie

3 Whispering Windows, Swiss Café & City Point

C-D **The Hermitage**, on a ridge, 16 comfortable rooms, pleasant lawns and restaurant, nightly bonfire with music.

Cafés

Swiss Café and City Point, Gandhi Chowk. Reasonable fast food.

⑨ Eating

Mussoorie *p213, map below and p214*
Restaurants may be closed out-of-season, and to non-residents.
  Carlton's **Plaisance, Roselynn, Savoy** and **Valley View** have good restaurants. Some have a bar.
🍴 **Prakash**, Landour (above Woodstock School). Really good sandwiches, omelettes etc; also beer and cheese but at a silly price.
🍴 **Bhelpuri**, chaat, kababs, ice cream, also chicken curry with pulao, kulchas, dosas.
🍴 **Char Dukan**, Landour (above Woodstock School). Snacks. Really good sandwiches, omelettes etc.
🍴 **Coffee House**, Library, towards Happy Valley.
🍴 **Kwality**, above *Bank of Baroda*, Kulri. International. Dependable quality.
🍴 **Tavern**, Kulri. Dancing some nights.
🍴 **Whispering Windows**, Library. International. With a popular bar.
🍴 **Madras Café**, Kulri. Very good South Indian, friendly staff.
🍴 **Rice Bowl**, The Mall. Tibetan and Chinese.

ⓞ Shopping

Mussoorie *p213, map below p214*
The main areas are Library, Kulri and Landour Bazars and Shawfield Rd near Padmini Niwas.

Crafts
Banaras House, The Mall. Silks.
Baru Mal Janki Dass, tribal silver jewellery.
Inder Singh, The Mall. Handcrafted sticks.
Nirankari Cottage Industries, The Mall. Handcrafted sticks.
Star Walking Sticks, The Mall. Handcrafted sticks.

Photography
Computerised Colour Lab, The Mall.
Mela Ram, The Mall.

Woollens
Anand Gift Emporium, near GPO.
Garwhal Wool House, near GPO.
Natraj, Picture Palace.
Tibetan outdoor market, near Padmini Nivas.

Mussoorie centre

GUN HILL

Sleeping		
1 Broadway	4 Garhwal Terrace	8 Sheela
2 Connaught Castle	5 Great Value	9 Uday
3 Filigree	6 Holiday Inn	10 Valley View
	7 Mall Palace & Hill Queen	

Eating	
1 Kwality	
2 Madras Café	
3 Rice Bowl	

0 metres 100
0 yards 100

▲ Activities and tours

Mussoorie *p213, maps p214 and p216*
Fishing
In the Aglar and Yamuna rivers for mahseer and hill trout. Permit from Division Forest Officer, Yamuna Division, T632535, is required.

Horse-riding
1-hr ride (7 km) around Camel's Back Rd, Rs 250. Off-season, Rs 100.

Paragliding
Through **Snowbird Flying Club** near the lake, T632366; 1000-1700.

Tour companies
Garhwal Alpine Tours, Masonic Lodge, T632507.
Kulwant Travels, Masonic Lodge Bus Stand, T632717.
   Tours Operated by **GMVN**. Kempty Falls: Rs 50, season: 0900, 1200, 1500; off-season: 1000, 1300. Dhanolti, Surkhanda Devi Temple, Mussoorie Lake: full day (0900), Rs 130, season only. Tickets from KMVN and Uttaranchal Tourism.

⊖ Transport

Mussoorie *p213, maps p214 and p216*
Air
Jolly Grant air strip, 60 km, limited flights to/from **Delhi** (see Dehra Dun above). 0800-1100, 1200-1500, Mon-Sat; 0800-1400, Sun.

Bicycle
Bike hire: near Picture Palace.

Bus
Long distance Stands Kincraig T632691; Library (Gandhi Chowk), T632258, Masonic Lodge (Kulri), T632259. Frequent service to **Chamba**, scenic trip via Dhanolti, 3 hrs; **Dehra Dun** through Ghat roads, Rs 22,

1¾ hrs. From **Delhi** ISBT, dep 0515, 2230, 6-7 hrs, about Rs 90; stop for snacks at *Cheetal Grand*. Also buses from **Saharanpur Rly** and **Tehri**. Private buses to **Delhi**, are Rs 200-250 depending on a/c facility.

Car
Pay Rs 60 to drive on The Mall.

Rickshaw
Cycle-rickshaw: for the Mall, fixed fare chart from tourist office.

Taxi
Stand at Library, T632115; Stand at Masonic Lodge, T631407; **Kulwant Travels**, Masonic Lodge Bus Stand, T632717. To Dehra Dun, Rs 350, Delhi Rs 2,200.

Train
See above for trains from Dehra Dun.
Railway Out Agency (computerised all-India reservations), Kulri, T632846.

❶ Directory

Mussoorie *p213, maps p214 and p216*
Banks Exchange can be difficult. Bank of Baroda, Kulri; or try Dehradun.
Hospitals Civil Hospital at Landour, T632053. **Community**, South Rd, T632891. St Mary's, Gun Hill Rd, T632845. GPO: Kulri. **Language schools** Landour, T631487, F631917. Have their own textbooks. Individual lessons, Rs 100 per hr (less if sharing); maximum 4 lessons per day. Standard of teachers varies dramatically so try a few till you are happy. **Library** Gandhi Chowk, small fee. **Tourist offices** GMVN, Library Bus Stand and *Tourist Bungalow*, The Mall, T632948. UP Tourism, The Mall, T632863. **Useful addresses** Ambulance: T632829. **Fire**: T632100. **Police**: Kotwali, T632003. **Foreigners' Registration**: Kotwali, next to Courts, opposite Hakmans, T632205.

For an explanation of the sleeping and eating price codes used in this guide, see inside the front cover. Other relevant information is found in Essentials pages 52-57.

Haridwar → *Phone code: 0133. Colour map 1, grid C4. Population: 175,000.*

Haridwar, said to be one of the oldest cities in the world, lies at the base of the Shiwalik Hills where the River Ganga passes through its last gorge and begins a 2,000-km journey across the plains. Legend has sanctified it by placing Vishnu's footprint on the river bank, making Haridwar ('Vishnu's gate') one of the seven holy cities of Hinduism – see Hindu Holy Sites, page 1326. From sunrise, pilgrims come to bathe at the ghat to cleanse themselves of their sins. You will notice holy men in their huts dispensing wisdom to the willing, and wandering sadhus who have made make-shift shelters under trees. Here too, you can watch priests performing spectacular Ganga arati at sunset. Despite local opposition, Haridwar was included in the new state of Uttaranchal. ▶▶ For Sleeping, Eating and other listings, see pages 220-222.

History

Various episodes from the *Mahabharata* are set in this ancient town which was mentioned by the Chinese traveller Hiuen Tsang. It attracted the attention of **Timur** who sacked it in 1399, see page 1300. The town, on the west bank of the river, centres on **Hari-ki-Pairi**, where **Vishnu** is believed to have left his footprint. At this point part of the Ganga has been diverted as irrigation water is drawn off for the Upper Ganga Canal system and for a hydro-electric power station.

Haridwar

■ **Sleeping**	5 Gangotree	9 Rahi
1 Alaknanda	6 Mansorovar	10 Sahni
2 Ashwani	International	11 Suvidha Deluxe
3 Dharamshalas	7 Midtown	12 Teerth
4 Ganga Azure	8 Panama	

● **Eating**
1 Ahaar & Chotiwala
2 Bestee

0 metres 200
0 yards 200

Uttaranchal Haridwar

Near the steps at Hari-ki-Pairi is a modern clocktower and some temples, none particularly old. Further down, foodstalls and shrines line alleyways leading off into the bazar. There are six bridges to take you across the river, where it is quieter. A new footbridge leads directly to Hari-ki-Pairi. Foreign visitors are likely to be approached for donations for its construction and upkeep! There are many *ashrams* here like Shatikunj, Ananda Mayee Ma and Premnagar. Many have herb gardens producing ayurvedic medicines.

Moti (Lower) bazar, parallel to the Jawalapur-Haridwar Road, is interesting, colourful, invariably crowded and surprisingly clean and tidy. Stalls sell coloured powder piled high in carefully made cones (for *tikas*). Others sell saris, jewellery, brass and aluminium pots, sweets and snacks.

Mansa Devi Temple is worth visiting for the view. Set on the southernmost hill of the Shiwaliks, it is accessible on foot or by the crowded cable car, from 0630 to 2030 for Rs 31 return. A package ticket including Chandi Devi temple on the other side of the Ganga, 4 km away costs Rs 100. Towards Rishikesh, 5 km from Haridwar, are the newer temples: **Pawan Dham** with a Hanuman temple, its spectacular glittering glass interior and the seven-storey **Bharat Mata Mandir** to Mother India.

Kankhal, 3 km downstream, with the **Temple of Dakseshwara** is where Siva's wife, Sati, is believed to have burnt herself to death. Professor Wendy Doniger vividly summarizes the story as told in the *Puranas*: "**Daksa**, a son of Brahma, gave his daughter Sati in marriage to Siva, but he did not invite Siva to his grand sacrifice. Sati, in anger, burnt herself to death. Siva destroyed the sacrifice and beheaded Daksa, but when the gods praised Siva he restored the sacrifice and gave Daksa the head of a goat. When Siva learned that Sati had killed herself, he took up her body and danced in grief, troubling the world with his dance and his tears until the gods cut the corpse into pieces. When the *yoni* fell, Siva took the form of a *linga*, and peace was re-established in the universe". See also page 575.

Rajaji National Park → *Colour map 1, grid B4. Altitude: 302-1,000 m.*

Uttaranchal's largest park, 820 sq km, is named after C Rajagopalachari, the only Indian to hold the post of Governor General. The Shiwaliks are rugged and dangerously steep slopes. The parks vegetation ranges from rich *sal, bhabbar* tracts, broad-leaf mixed forest to *Chir* pine forests interspersed with areas of scrub and pasture which provide a home for a wide variety of wildlife including over 23 mammal and 438 species of bird. On foot, however you are likely to see very little. Even by car or jeep many are disappointed as few animals are spotted.

Ins and outs

The park is accessible from Haridwar, Rishikesh and Dehra Dun. Permits from Haridwar office, *Mohan's Adventure* or at Chilla Park. Open 15 Nov-15 Jun, daily, between sunrise and sunset. Entry first 3 days Rs 350 (foreigners), Rs 30 (Indians). Additional day; Rs 175 and Rs 20. Camera, Rs 50; video, Rs 500. Elephant rides from Chilla, Rs 400 (foreigners), Rs 200 (Indians), 2 hrs. Chilla, 7 km from Haridwar, is the best here for viewing. Car permit Rs 100. Jeep hire from Haridwar, Rishikesh or Dehradun.

Wildlife

A large number of **elephants**, together with the rarely-seen **tiger**, are at the northwest limit of their range in India. The elephants move up into the hills when the water holes are dry. A census taken in 2001 recorded 453 elephants, 30 tigers and 236 **leopards** in the park. Other animals include spotted deer, sambar, muntjac, nilgai and ghoral. Along the tracks, you may spot wild boar, langur and macaque; the Himalayan yellow-throated marten and civet are rare. Peacocks, jungle fowl and kaleej pheasants can be spotted in the drier areas, while waterbirds attracted by the Ganga and the Song rivers include many kinds of geese, ducks, cormorant, teal and spoonbill among others.

Listings: Haridwar

● Sleeping

Haridwar *p218, map p218*
There are over a 100 places to stay. Many offer off-season discounts outside Jun and Jul, up to 50% Nov-Feb.
B-C Alaknanda (UP Tourism), Belwala (east bank), By-pass Rd, T426379, F423787. 32 rooms, best a/c with bath, dorm (Rs 100), restaurant (simple veg), small garden, on river bank, quiet.
C Classic Residency, Delhi-Haridwar Rd, Jwalapur Rd, 1.5 km south of town, T428005, F420374, www.newagehotelsandresorts.com. 44 a/c rooms, all facilities, shuttles to Hari-ki-Pairi, activity tours arranged.
C Teerth, Subhash Ghat, Hari-ki-Pairi, T425211. 36 reasonable rooms, some air-cooled, excellent central location with great views over ghats, high quality cooking, friendly and helpful staff, good value.
C-D Gautam Siddhartha, Haridwar-Delhi Rd, Singh Dwar, T424206. 14 rooms in a new comfortable hotel near the Ganga.
C-D Mansarovar International, Upper Rd, towards Hari-ki-Pairi, T426501. 56 clean, simple rooms, dorm (Rs 100), restaurant.
C-D Suvidha Deluxe, SN Nagar, T427423, F629033, suvidha@aakashdeepgroup.com. 28 reasonably good rooms, some a/c, restaurant, modern, clean, central but quiet.
D Gangotree, Upper Rd, T424407. 14 simple rooms, attached bath, bucket hot water.
D Midtown, Railway Rd, T427507, F426001. 23 rooms, some a/c, modern, reasonably clean, fairly quiet.
D Rahi (Uttaranchal Tourism), opposite railway station, T426430. 19 rooms (some a/c), dorm beds (Rs 50), restaurant, tourist information.
D-E Ganga Azure, Railway Rd, T427101, F425407, shyamco@vsnl.com. 32 adequate rooms, TV, hot water, some (**B**) a/c, decent restaurant.

D-E Samrat, Sadhubela Rd, T427380. 14 good rooms with bath.
E Deep, Sadhubela Rd,T427609. 10 clean rooms. Recommended.
E Sahni, Niranjani Akhara Rd, SN Nagar, T427906. 42 fairly clean, basic rooms, some with bath, some air-cooled (extra charge), hot water in buckets, helpful service.
    Some **F** around the bazar and station.

Rajaji National Park *p219*
For reservation of a guesthouse, contact Rajaji National Park, 5/1 Ansari Marg, Dehra Dun, T621669, www.rajajinationalpark.com.
D-E Forest Rest Houses near all the gates.All have at least 2 suites. Those at Chilla and Motichur cost Rs 450. Others at Asarodi, Beribara, Kansrao, Kunnao, Phandowala, Ranipur and Satyanarain are Rs 225. All have electricity and water supply except Beribara and Kansrao. Very basic, self-catering (utensils provided), not good value, 'concrete boxes'.
D-E Tourist Bungalow, Chilla. With rooms, dorm (Rs 100) and tents. To stay in a tribal village, contact **Mohan's Adventure**, T420910, see Haridwar.

● Eating

Haridwar *p218, map p218*
Only vegetarian food is available in town and there is no alcohol.
 Aahar, Railway Rd. Punjabi. Chinese and continental. Excellent meals.
 Big Ben, at *Ganga Azure*. Decent, large range of Indian, Chinese and continental.
 Bestee, Railway Rd. Mughlai and South Indian. "Excellent stuffed *parathas*".
 Chotiwalas, several (including on Railway Rd, opposite Tourist Office) of varying quality.
 Mohan's Fast Food, Chitra Cinema, has been recommended. Cheap stalls on Railway Rd provide simple food for pilgrims.

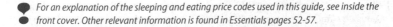
For an explanation of the sleeping and eating price codes used in this guide, see inside the front cover. Other relevant information is found in Essentials pages 52-57.

⊛ Festivals and events

Haridwar *p218, map p218*
Thousands of pilgrims visit the city, especially when the birth of the river (*Dikhanti*) is celebrated in spring. **Kumbh Mela**, held here every 12th year (next in Apr 2010), and **Ardha Kumbh** every 6 years (next in 2004), attract millions of devotees who come to bathe in the confined area near Hari-ki-Pairi, see page 193.

▲ Activities and tours

Haridwar *p218, map p218*
Tour companies
Ashwani Travels, 3 Railway Rd, T424581, F423656, ashwanitravels@hotmail.com. Official agent of GMVN, specializing in pilgrimage tours, also trekking.
Mohan's Adventure, next to Chitra Cinema, Railway Rd, T420910, F425594, mohansadventure@vsnl.com. Very reliable trips run by the experienced Sanjeev Mehta. Trekking, jeep safaris, rafting. Jungle trips into Rajaji National Park, with night stay in tribal village. Highly recommended.
   Tours   Daily, same day tours of Haridwar-Rishikesh, 0930, Rs 50; Dehra dun-Mussoorie, 0800, Rs 140; Rajaji National Park, 1000, 1430.

⊖ Transport

Haridwar *p218, map p218*
Bus
Long distance   Roadways Bus Stand, Railway Station, T427037; **Garhwal Motor Owners Union**, T426886, also has buses.
Rishikesh share taxis and buses (Rs 15 from bus stand, 45 mins). Share tempos from Bhimgoda tank (Rs 15-20, more for Lakshman Jhula); autos from across the river. Taxis, Rs 330. Buses to/from **Delhi**, hourly (4-5 hrs); **Dehra Dun** (1¼ hr); **Mathura** and **Vrindavan**, 10 hrs. **Rajasthan State Transport**, booth just inside bus station entrance, run deluxe buses to **Jaipur**, 0430, 0730, 1630, 1645, 1730, 1830, Rs 366, 12 hrs; also to **Udaipur** and **Pushkar**; several private buses to **Delhi**, Rs 120-150; **Ajmer/Pushkar**, 1300, 1500, 1600, 1700, Rs 270, 15 hrs; **Jaipur (via Delhi)**, same times as Ajmer, Rs 220, 15 hrs; **Jodhpur**, same timings, Rs 350, 15 hrs; **Nainital** (season only), 2000, Rs 220, 9 hrs; **Agra/Mathura**, 2000, Rs 180, 10-11 hrs.

Rickshaw
Stands near railway station, fares negotiable. Taxi Union, T427738.

Taxi
Stands near railway station, fares negotiable. Taxi Union, T427738.
   Rates for visiting the mountains are competitive; 4 day round trip, about Rs 4000.

Train
Railway Station, T131. Reservation office 0800-2000. Three trains per day to **Rishikesh**, 0515, 0845, 1715 ("train will arrive exactly at 8:45, on approximately platform two!"), better to take road transport; **Allahabad**: *Link Exp, 4114,* 1445, 17¼ hrs. **Delhi (OD)**: *Dehra Dun Bandra Exp, 9020,* 1310, 7 hrs; *Mussoorie Exp, 4042,* 2300, 8 hrs (beware of thieves). **Delhi (ND)**: *Shatabdi Exp, 2018,* 1810, 4½ hrs. **Dehra Dun**: *Doon Exp, 3009,* 0535, 1¾ hrs; *Varanasi Dehra Dun Exp, 4265,* 0640, 2¼ hrs. hrs. **Varanasi**: *Dehra Dun Varanasi Exp, 4266,* 2010, 22 hrs. For **Nainital**: *Dehradun-Kathgodam Exp 4320,* 2230, 9 hrs. For **Shimla**, travel via Ambala and Kalka (trains better than bus).

Rajaji National Park *p219*
The park has 8 entry gates.
   From **Dehra Dun**: Mohan (25 km on Delhi-Dehra Dun highway, 5 hr drive from Delhi), Ramgarh (14 km, Delhi-Dehra Dun highway, via Clement Town) and **Lachhiwala** (18 km, Dehra Dun-Hardwar route, right turn before Doiwala). From **Haridwar**: Chilla (7 km, via private bus route to Rishikesh), Motichur (9 km, Haridwar-Rishikesh or Dehra Dun-Haridwar highways) and **Ranipur** (9 km, Haridwar-BHEL-Mohand Road). From **Rishikesh**: Kunnao (6 km, via private bus route on Rishikesh-Pashulok route). From **Kotdwara**: Laldhang (25 km, via private bus route to Kotdwara to Chilla).

⊕ Directory

Haridwar *p218, map p218*
Banks   All close from Sat pm to Mon am. State Bank of India, Station Rd, 1030-1430. £ and $ cash only. Bank of Baroda, Upper Rd. Cash on Visa cards only. Canara Bank, Upper Rd. Changes TCs. **Hospitals**   District, Upper Rd, T426060. RK Mission, Kankhal, T427141.

Chemists: on Railway and Upper Rd. **Post office** Railway Rd. 1000-1630. **Tourist offices** Uttaranchal, Motel Rahi, T427370. 1000-1700 (Mon-Sat). **Lalta Rao Bridge**, T424240 (1000-1700). Counter at railway station, T427817 (0500-1200, Mon-Sat). **Ganga Sabha**, near Hari-ki Pairi, T427925. **Useful addresses** Police: T425160. **Rajaji National Park office**: Balkeshwar, T425193.

Rishikesh → *Phone code: 01350. Colour map 1, grid B4. Population: 72,000.*

The Ganga, at this point still an astonishingly clear water river, links all the holy places of one of Hinduism's most sacred regions. Rishikesh stands tight-packed on the banks of the river as it runs swiftly through the southernmost ranges of the Shiwaliks on its way to the Plains. At Rishikesh the river begins to cut through the low foothills,

☛ *A vegetarian temple town: meat and alcohol are prohibited; eggs are only eaten in private*

which were once more densely forested than today. Those forests offered the prospect of quiet retreat, the original basis of the ashram ideal. Maharishi Mahesh Yogi had his ashram here and captured the imagination and attention of the Beatles in the 1960s. Today, however, the town has become heavily commercialized, full of ashrams, sadhus and visitors attending courses in yoga and meditation. Some find it disappointing and lacking in atmosphere, others thoroughly enjoy and stay for weeks. It is surrounded by wonderful birdwatching territory.
▸▸ *For Sleeping, Eating and other listings, see pages 223-226.*

Rishikesh

To Tehri & Gangotri
To Deoprayag
Lakshman Temple
Badrinath Rd
To Tehri & Gangotri
Taxis & Tempos
Sivananda Ashram
Lakshman Jhula
By Pass Rd
Yoga Niketan
Ram (Sivananda Jhula)
Sant Sevak
To Hotel Shipra, Airport (16 km) & Dehra Dun
Clock Tower
Swargashram
Pauri Forest
Chandrabhaga River
MUNI-KI-RETI
Kailash Ashram
Geeta Bhavan
Parmarth Niketan
Banprasth
Dehra Dun Rd
Kailash Gate
Ved Niketan
Hatha Yoga Centre
Nehru Rd
Yatra (Local)
Pushkar Temple
Dayanand Ashram
Shankacharya Ashram
Ganga River
Lakshmanjhula Rd
Maharishi Mahesh Yogi Ashram
Railway Rd
Main
Tilak Rd
Ghat Rd
Main Bazar
Railway Booking
Hanuman Temple
Agarwal Rd
Main Rd
Taxis
Raghunath Mandir
Triveni Ghat
Ferry (Sep-May)
Forest
To Haridwar
Haridwar Rd
Gohri Reserve Forest
To Virbhadra Temple

N

0 metres 500
0 yards 500

■ **Sleeping**
1 Ashoka
2 Bombay
3 Brijwasi Palace
4 Forest Guest House
5 Ganga Kinare
6 GMVN Rishilok
7 Gurudev
8 Inderlok
9 Natraj
10 Suruchi

● **Eating**
1 Al Kwality & Apex
2 Chotiwalas
3 East-West
4 Madras Café
5 Neelam
6 Rasoi Garden
7 Rishiraj

Ins and outs

Getting there From Haridwar, buses are both quicker and far more frequent than trains. Buses from Delhi and Dehra Dun arrive at the main bus stand in the town centre and also stop south of Ram Jhula.

Getting around The centre near the bus stands and station is compact and is an easy walk to the river, less than a kilometre away. The ashrams are to the north. You can take a cycle-rickshaw or shared tempo (Rs 5-10) from the Bazar to the two suspension bridges and then walk across to the east side. You can also cross the river on a boat near Ram Jhula (Rs 4). See Transport, page 225, for further details.

Climate Summer: maximum 41°C, minimum 37°C. Winter: maximum 32°C, minimum 18°C. Average annual rainfall: 1,524 mm, mostly Jun to Sep.

Sights

Rishikesh ('Hair of Sages') has a large number of ashrams. It is worth walking down to the river bank where pilgrims purify themselves by bathing in the Ganga at **Triveni Ghat** (which has some striking statues of Siva), offering milk and feeding the fish at dawn, and floating lamps after sunset for evening *aarati*. Many ashrams which offer the seeker a spiritual haven are on the east bank of the river at **Swargashram**. Some of them are bizarrely colourful, architectural curiosities leading Geoffrey Moorhouse to describe it as a cross between Blackpool and Lourdes. Several ashrams are seats of spiritual learning and meditation and offer courses (see below). **Muni-ki-Reti** is the area along the Chandrabhaga River which also has some temples. Be aware that not all in saffron/orange clothing are sadhus; some are con-men. If you walk northeast up the river you will find some secluded **beaches**.

There are two suspension bridges over the Geanga – **Ram (Sivananda) Jhula**, between Sivananda Ashram and Swargashram, and **Lakshman Jhula**. Music concerts are held in the Ram Jhula area on Sunday evenings but women should be careful. The Lakshman Jhula area is very picturesque with the best views though you may be troubled by rhesus monkeys.

Rishikesh is the base for several pilgrimages and treks, including the **Char Dham Pilgrimage**, see box on page 231, or going to the Garhwal hills and Hemkund Sahib.

Listings: Rishikesh

⊜ Sleeping

Rishikesh *p222, map p222*
Most people prefer the peace across the river to the noisy, polluted atmosphere in town.
AL Ananda in theHimllayas, I he Palace, Narendranagar, T27500, F27550. Exclusive heatlh resort with 75 rooms (some have original furniture), superb location and views. Place to spoil yourself.
B Ganga Banks, Shivpuri, is a 'green' resort with 28 comfortable, eco-friendly cottages with bath, built with local raw materials, restaurant, pool, health spa, in natural surroundings employing recycling techniques (no plastics), solar heating, well placed for trekking, rafting, etc.

B Ganga Kinare, 16 Virbhadra Rd, on quiet riverside 2 km from centre, T431658, F435243. 36 rooms (best face river), central a/c (heating inadequate in winter), pleasant restaurant, exchange, meditation, yoga (1-3 week courses), treks, boating (Sep-Mar), rafting.
B Natraj, Dehra Dun Rd, T431099, F433355, natraj@nde.vsnl.net.in. 49 a/c rooms, restaurant (veg), large gardens, pool (Rs 250 for non-residents), modern, free airport transfer.
C Camp with 35 Swiss tents with beds facing the 'private' riverside beach. Contact *Wanderlust*, T011-4102180, F6885188, www.wanderlustindia.com.
C-D Inderlok, Railway Rd, T430555, F432855, inderlok@nde.vsnl.net.in. 25 clean rooms, some a/c, with balconies, restaurant (veg), terrace

lawn, older hotel but well kept and with pleasant ambience and mountain views.
D Shikar. Good clean a/c rooms, some with bath (order hot water), very good restaurant and superb views from rooftop.
D Shipra, Dehra Dun Rd, T430533. 24 rooms in modern hotel, restaurant.
D Suruchi, T432269. Comfortable rooms (some air-cooled) and recommended restaurant.
D-F Rishilok (GMVN), Badrinath Rd, Muni-ki-Reti, T430373, F430372. 46 clean rooms, some with bath in new cottages and 2-storey blocks, dorm (Rs 80), restaurant, pleasant garden, efficient service, above and away from Main Rd, peaceful.

Across the river
E-F Brijwasi Palace, 1st right after Ram Jhula, 2nd left before Ved Niketan, T435181, F435918, hotelbrijwasipalace@vsnl.com. 22 standard doubles with hot shower, some with geyser, clean, peaceful garden restaurant, yoga in basement, pleasant staff. Good value. Recommended.

Lakshman Jhula
E Phool Shanti, 6 km on Neelkanth Rd (north of Lakshman Jhula), T433174. Pleasant, quiet retreat by the Ganga.
E-F Divya, T434938, www.laxmanjhula.com. 22 clean, but small rooms, attached hot bath, restaurant with travellers' favourites.
E-F Om, T433272. 12 clean rooms, hot water.
F Bombay Kshetra, 20 basic rooms around a courtyard (all less than Rs 100), clean common bath, popular.
F Gurudev, opposite Rishiraj. 7 clean rooms, some attached, roof terrace with good views, yoga, massage, ayurvedic meals.

In town
Several **F** hotels near Main Bus Stand.
F Ashoka, away from noise of bus stand, T433111. 30 simple rooms, some attached.
  Ashrams are mostly on the east bank of the *jhulas*. Catering mainly for pilgrims; foreigners may need special permission. Some can be filthy; inspect first. They are always simple, rated **E-F** and hot water comes in buckets.

Ram (Sivananda) Jhula
E Hatha Yoga Centre, 2 lanes beyond *Green Hotel*, very clean, tranquil and excellent value, occasional evening concert with local musicians on roof, yoga optional!
Banprasth, next door, has clean rooms with bath in pleasant surroundings.

Lakshman Jhula
Adanyanda, is very clean, with marble floors and tiled bathrooms.
Eagles' Nest Retreat, T9837100215. Popular for spiritual healing, yoga, reiki, sauna etc.
Sant Sevak, near Lakshman Jhula, has fairly modern rooms.

● Eating

Rishikesh *p222, map p222*
♥♥ **A1 Kwality**, near GMVN *Rishilok*. Varied.
♥♥ **Ganga View**, Lakshman Jhula. Western lunch, thali dinner (1800-2000), snacks, pleasant location.
♥♥ **Midway**, 'resort' towards Haridwar (Rs 10 by tempo). For those desperate to replenish their protein intake, good tandoori and curries, washed down with chilled beer.

Near Ram Jhula
♥ **Chotiwalas**, Swargashram, east bank. Crowded, plenty of atmosphere, inexpensive; one closer to the river is a bit cleaner, more spacious, nicer rooftop.

On the west bank
♥ **East-West**. Italian. Good breads and olive 'pizzas', but suspect hygiene.
♥ **Hill Top**, Lakshman Jhula. Wide choice with good views.
♥ **Madras Café** by boat jetty. Mainly South Indian. Excellent service, cheese on brown toast to masala dosas.
♥ **Neelam** near Yatra Bus Stand. Indian, Continental. Very good value.
♥ **Rasoi Garden**, Swargashram, 2-min walk behind *Green Hotel*. Excellent coffee, pizzas, pittas and hummus, peaceful.
♥ **Rishiraj**, near Lakshman Jhula. Italian.
  Safe drinking water is sold to refill bottles near the Ram Jhula.

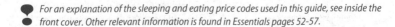

For an explanation of the sleeping and eating price codes used in this guide, see inside the front cover. Other relevant information is found in Essentials pages 52-57.

❀ Festivals and events

Rishikesh *p222, map p222*
Feb: International Yoga week, an opportunity to learn yoga on the banks of the Ganga. T434300 for details of dates etc.

◘ Shopping

Rishikesh *p222, map p222*
Dehra Dun Rd, Haridwar Rd, Ghat Rd and Railway Rd have markets and curio shops. The latter are limited for choice and overpriced.
Gandhi Ashram Khadi Bhandar, Haridwar Rd.
Ganga Emporium, by Ram Jhula at the head of the bridge, especially spiritual texts, café attached – read, relax and sip a cool drink!
Garhwal Wool and Craft (opposite Yatra Office), Muni-ki-Reti.
Photo Centre, Dehra Dun Rd.
UP Handlooms, Dehra Dun Rd.

▲ Activities and tours

Rishikesh *p222, map p222*
Boat rides
On the Ganga from Swargashram Ghat. Fix rates with local boatmen.

Music
Sivananda Ramesh towards Muni-ki-Reti Taxi Stand, T437581. Lessons in tabla, sitar, santoor, singing etc.

Rafting
Several whitewater rafting outfits on the Ganga, north of town. Best to book ahead
Himalayan River Runners. Highly recommended, operate from Mar to May, Sep to Oct, www.hrr.india.com, with an office in Delhi (188A Jorbagh).
Shivpuri, 18 km upstream, has a GMVN.
Rafting Beach Camp: double tent, Rs 400; meals Rs 80-100.
    Mohan's Ganga River Camps and **Garhwal Himalayan Exploration** offer rafting from Shivpuri: Rs 580 including lunch. *Mohan's* 5-day Ganga Expedition includes whitewater, Rs 1,200 per day covers food and camping.
Kaudiyala Resort, 38 km away, has tents at Rs 100, beds at Rs 65, meals Rs 150. Rafting Rs 350 per day. Birdwatching. Contact **GMVN** Yatra Office, T431793. See also **Ganga Banks** under 'Sleeping' above.

Swimming
Hotel Natraj pool (non-residents, Rs 250).

Tour companies
GMVN (see below).
Garhwal Himalayan Exploration, PO Box 29, T431654, F431501.
Triveni, Haridwar Rd, T430989. Recommended for rafting and trekking (see Sports and activities).

Trekking
With guides, transport, camping; meals cost about Rs 1,500 per day through local agents.

Yoga
Meditation courses and instruction in Vedanta. Most hotels can put you in touch.
Onkarananda Ashram (Durga Mandir) above Yoga Niketan, T430883, good Iyengar yoga courses, also offers music and classical dance.
Parmarth Niketan and Swargashram, T430252, are vast, and can be impersonal.
Sivananda Ashram (Divine Life Society), T430040: short to 3 month courses (apply 1 month ahead); holds music classes and produces herbal medicines.
Ved Niketan. Flexible programme of yoga; also Hindi, Sanskrit, music and dance classes.

⊖ Transport

Rishikesh *p222, map p222*
Pilgrim centres of Badrinath (301 km); Gangotri (258 km); Kedarnath (228 km); Uttarkashi (154 km); Yamunotri (288 km)

Bus
Long distance Roadways or **Main Bus Stand**, Haridwar Rd, T430066. Buses from Delhi finally stop by the Govind-Radha Mandir south of Ram Jhula, 15-min walk from the bridge. Reserve tickets at the Local (Yatra) Bus Stand from around 1600, the day before (especially during Yatra season, May-Nov); open 0400-1900. Various State Government bus services (DTC, Haryana Roadways, Himachal RTC, UP Roadways).
Major destinations: Chandigarh (252 km), **Dehra Dun** (42 km), **Delhi** (238 km, 6 hrs, taxi 5 hrs). **Haridwar** (24 km); also share taxis from bus stand or auto rickshaws from Ram Jhula. **Mussoorie** (77 km), Patiala,

Saharanpur. For **Shimla**: best to go to Dehra Dun and stay overnight and catch 0600 bus; or get a bus from Haridwar (0600, 1000, 1600, 2200) but it's a long hot journey (see 'Train' under Haridwar). From **Yatra (Local) Bus Stand**, Dehra Dun Rd, during the Yatra season, to **Char Dhams**: buses leave early for the very long routes to Hanuman Chatti (for Yamunotri), **Badrinath, Gangotri, Gaurikund** (for Kedarnath); best to take a 'Luxury' bus, and break your journey. For **Badrinath** and **Hemkund** stop overnight at Joshimath (after 1630 road to Govindghat is southbound only). Although the **Yatra season** ends in late Oct (Yamunotri, Gangotri, Kedarnath) to mid-Nov (Badrinath), bus frequency drops drastically during Oct. Even light rains can cause severe road blocks, mainly due to landslides. Bus for Badrinath dep from Private Bus Stand (100 m right from station), Rs 180, but noisy, crowded and uncomfortable. **Garhwal Motor Owners Union**, T430076; **Tehri Garhwal MOU, Triveni**, Haridwar Rd, T430989. From **Delhi**, best to get a bus to Haridwar and train from there (2nd class sleeper recommended) to Haridwar: *Shatabdi Exp, 2017*, 0700 (ND), 4½ hrs; *Mussoorie, 4042*, 2215 (OD) 2220, 7½ hrs. See Haridwar for departing trains. Reservations office, 0800-1800. For **travelling north**, cheapest are 'Newspaper taxis', eg Joshimath, Rs 140 per person; ask at **Sanjay News Agency**, Main Rd (before turn-off to Ghat Rd) or travel agent.

Ferry
Ferry boat from near Ram Jhula for river crossing, Rs 4; Rs 6 return.

Jeep
Jeep hire for Badrinath (1-way), 1500-2000, is the best option. Book the evening before, for all.

Motorbike
Motorbike (Bullet) **mechanic**: Bila, opposite *Ganga View Hotel*, Lakshman Jhula.

Rickshaw
Cycle-rickshaw: rates negotiable. Constant shuttle between town centre and Lakshman Jhula.

Taxi
(Unmetered) from **Garhwal Mandal TCS**, Haridwar Rd or tour operators.

Tempo
Mostly fixed routes. From Ram Jhula shared, to Rishikesh Bazar Rs 3; from Lakshman Jhula Rs 5; to Haridwar Rs 15, 50 mins. Foreigners will probably be asked for more.

Train
There is a branch line from Haridwar to Rishikesh but the bus is quicker.

⊙ Directory

Rishikesh *p222, map p222*
Banks Bank of Baroda, Dehra Dun Rd, T430653. Accepts Visa and Master Card. **State Bank of India**, Railway Rd. Mon-Fri 1000-1400, Sat 1000-1200. **Hospital** Govt Hospital, Dehra Dun Rd, T430402. **Nirmal Ashram**, T432215. **Sivananda**, Muni-ki-Reti, T430040. **Internet** Several in town. **Blue Hills Travels** has best facilities in Ram Jhula area (Rs 50/hr), but queueing often necessary. Try **Rana Tele Point** at *Jhula Restaurant*, near taxi stand, Lakshman Jhula (Rs 30/hr) or several on the other bank. Connections are generally unreliable, better in the morning. **Post office** Open 0700-2200. GPO: at Harilal Marg, Lakshman Jhula and Muni-ki-Reti. Ghat Rd. Swargashram GPO by *Chotiwalas*. **Tourist offices** Garhwal Mandal Vikas Nigam (GMVN) & Yatra Office, Kailash Gate, By Pass Rd, T430372, F431783. Organizes trekking, mountaineering, rafting and Char Dham tour (12 days). **Uttaranchal**, 162 Rly Rd, T430209. Helpful. Plans to move to the Tourist Bungalow. During Yatra season, only at Yatra Bus Stand. **Useful addresses** Ambulance: T102. **Fire**: T101. **Police**: T100.

Garhwal and the Pilgrimage (Yatra)

The shrines of Kedarnath, Yamunotri, Gangotri and Badrinath are visited by hundreds of thousands of Hindu pilgrims each summer. They come from all corners of the subcontinent to engage in, what Dalrymple calls, a modern-day Indian Canterbury Tales.
» *For Sleeping, Eating and other listings, see pages 243-244.*

Ins and outs
Temples and trekking routes open from the end of April to mid-November (October for Badrinath). For trekking see page 234. June is very crowded; heavy rains July to mid-September may trigger landslips. Best in May, mid-September to mid-October. Yatra tourists on public buses are required to register with the Yatra Office at the Yatra (Local) Bus Stand, Rishikesh (open 0600-2200). A current certificate covering immunization against cholera and typhoid is needed. In practice, 'Registration' is often waived, but the immunization certificate is checked. Accommodation prices are higher in this area.

Background
Garhwal's fragmented political history gives no clue as to the region's religious significance. The sources of the Yamuna and the Ganga and some of Hinduism's holiest mountains lie in the heart of the region. Since the seventh-century Tamil saint **Sankaracharya** travelled north on his mission to reinvigorate Hinduism's northern heartland, some have been watched over permanently by South Indian priests. The most famous is the Rawal – head priest – at the Badrinath temple, who to this day comes from Kerala. Badrinath is one of the four *dhams* **'holiest abodes'** of the gods. Along with **Dwarka**, **Puri** and **Ramesvaram**, they mark the cardinal points of Hinduism's cultural geography.

After a ritual purificatory bathe in the Ganga at Haridwar and, preferably, Rishikesh, the pilgrim begins the 301-km journey from Haridwar to Badrinath. The purpose is to worship, purify and acquire merit. Roads go all the way to Gangotri and Badrinath, and to within 14 km of Yamunotri and Kedarnath. The correct order for pilgrims is to visit the holy places from west to east: Yamunotri, Gangotri, Kedarnath and Badrinath.

Yamunotri and Gangotri

Yamunotri can be reached from Rishikesh or from Dehra Dun via Yamuna Bridge and Barkot. The former is the more popular. From Rishikesh it is 83 km to Tehri (or 165 km via Deoprayag). **Tehri**, northeast of Rishikesh, the capital of the former princely state, will eventually be submerged by the waters behind the controversial and still unfinished Tehri Dam. **New Tehri**, 24 km from the original town, is a 'planned' town and the new district headquarters.

Yamunotri → *Colour map 1, grid B4. Altitude: 3,291 m.*
Dominated by **Banderpunch** (6,316 m), Yamunotri, the source of the Yamuna, is believed to be the daughter of Surya, the sun, and the twin sister of Yama, the Lord of Death. Anyone who bathes in her waters will be spared an agonizing death.

To begin the trek to reach the temple take a jeep from **Hanuman Chatti** (large vehicles stop here and pick up) to **Janki Chatti**, 8 km further up which is pleasanter and where you can leave luggage.

The trek along the riverbank is exhilarating with the mountains rising up on each side, the last 5 km somewhat steeper. The source itself is a difficult 1-km climb from the 19th-century **Yamunotri Temple** ① *0600-1200, 1400-2100*, with a black marble deity. The modern temple was rebuilt this century after floods and snow destroyed it. There are **hot springs** nearby (the most sacred being Surya Kund) in which pilgrims cook potatoes and rice tied in a piece of cloth. The meal, which takes only a few mins to cook is first offered to the deity and then distributed as *prasad*. On the return to Hanuman Chatti, you can visit the **Someshwar Temple** at **Kharsali**, 3 km across the river from Janki Chatti. The temple is one of the oldest and finest in the region and there are excellent views of the mountains.

Uttarkashi → *Colour map 2, grid A2. Altitude: 3,140 m. 240 km from Rishikesh.*
The busy town en route to Gangotri has several places to stay but are full during the season. The *Nehru Institute of Mountaineering* here offers courses and from here you can trek to **Dodital**. Porters can be hired locally and there are also tour operators, see below. The bazaar is near the bus stand and from here you can buy provisions. If you are in town on 14 January you will witness the *Makar Sankranti Garhwal* festival of music and dance.

Gangotri → *Colour map 2, grid A2. Altitude: 3,140 m. 240 km from Rishikesh.*
Gangotri is the second of the major shrines in the Garhwal Himalaya. A high bridge now takes the road across the Jad Ganga River joining the Bhagirathi which rushes through narrow gorges, so buses travel all the way. The 18th-century granite **temple** is

Garhwal & Kumaon treks

dedicated to the Goddess **Ganga**, where she is believed to have descended to earth. It was built by a Gurkha commander, Amar Singh Thapa, in the early 18th century and later rebuilt by the Maharaja of Jaipur.

Hindus believe that Ganga (here **Bhagirathi**) came down from heaven after **King Bhagirath's** centuries-long penance. He wanted to ensure his dead relatives' ascent to heaven by having their ashes washed by the sacred waters of the Ganga. When the tempestuous river arrived on earth, the force of her flow had to be checked by **Siva** who received her in the coils of his hair, lest she sweep all away. A submerged lingam is visible in the winter months.

Rishikund, 55 km from Uttarkashi, has hot sulphur springs near **Gangnani** suitable for bathing, and a 15th-century temple above. The **Gaurikund waterfall** here is one of the most beautiful in the Himalaya. Below Gangotri are **Bhojbasa** and **Gaumukh**, which are on a gradual but nevertheless scenically stunning trek. You can continue to trek another 6 km to Nandanvan (4,400 m), base camp for Bhagirathi peak, and continue 4 km to Tapovan (4,463 m), known for its meadows that encircle the base of Shivling peak. See page 236.

From Rishikesh to Kedarnath

From Rishikesh the road follows the west bank of the Ganga and quickly enters forest. At the 23rd milestone, at **Gular-dogi** village, is the old orchard and garden of the Maharaja of Tehri Garhwal which is close to a white sand and rock beach.

The section up to **Deoprayag** (68 km) is astonishingly beautiful. The folding and erosion of the hills can be clearly seen on the mainly uninhabited steep scarps on the opposite bank. Luxuriant forest runs down to the water's edge which in many places is fringed with silver sand beaches. In places the river rushes over gentle rapids. A few kilometres before Byasi is Vashisht Gufa (the cave where the saint meditated) which has an Ashram. About 5 km after **Byasi** the road makes a gradual ascent to round an important bluff. At the top, there are fine views down to the river. Villages now become more common. The way that small pocket handkerchief-sized fields have been created by terracing is marvellous. Jeep hire from here is easy, to Badrinath or Rishikesh.

Deoprayag is the most important of the hill *prayags* because it is at the junction of the Bhagirathi and Alaknanda rivers, Gangotri is the source of the Bhagirathi and Badrinath is near the source of the Alaknanda. Below Deoprayag, the river becomes the Ganga. The town tumbles down the precipitous hillside in the deeply cut 'V' between the junction of the two rivers, with houses almost on top of one another. Where the rivers meet is a pilgrims' bathing ghat, artificially made into the shape of India. From Deoprayag, the road is relatively flat as far as Srinagar (35 km) and for much of the way you pass through well-cultivated land. The Siva and Raghunath temples here attract pilgrims.

The old capital of Tehri Garhwal, **Srinagar** was devastated when the Gohna Lake dam was destroyed by an earthquake in the mid-19th century. The most attractive part of Srinagar, which is a university town, runs from the square down towards the river. There are some typical hill houses with elaborately carved door jambs. The 35-km route from Srinagar to **Rudraprayag**, at the confluence of the Mandakini and Alaknanda, is again mostly through cultivated areas. Roughly half way an enormous landslip indicates the fragility of the mountains. Approximately 5 km before reaching Rudrapayag, in a grove of trees by a village, is a tablet marking the spot where the 'man-eating leopard of Rudraprayag' was finally killed by Jim Corbett, see page 253. Rudraprayag with its temples is strung out along a fairly narrow part of the Alaknanda Valley.

It is an offence to photograph sensitive installations, troop movements and bridges on most routes. Offenders can be treated very severely

Kedarnath → *Colour map 1, grid B5.*

① *Buses from Rishikesh to Rudraprayag and Gaurikund.*

For Kedarnath, leave the Pilgrim road at Rudraprayag, cross the Alaknanda River, and go through a tunnel before following the Mandakini Valley (the tributary) through terraced cultivation and green fields. The road goes past the first town Tilwara, 9 km, then Kund, to **Guptakashi** where Siva proposed to Parvati. If time permits and you have hired a jeep from Guptakachi, stop at **Sonprayag**, 26 km, a small village at the confluence of the Mandakini and Son Ganga rivers, to visit the Triyuginarayan Temple where the gods were married. Find the viewpoint here before continuing to **Gaurikund**, 4 km away, where the motorable road ends. The *Rest House* at Gaurikund, has 10 rooms; at Guptakashi, six rooms. Hundreds of pilgrims bathe in the hot sulphur springs in season.

From here you either trek – early start recommended – or ride a mule to Kedarnath. It is 14 km away. The ascent, which is fairly steep at first, is through forests and green valleys to Jungle Ghatti and Rambara (over 1,500 m); the latter part goes through dense vegetation, ravines and passes beautiful waterfalls. Beyond Rambara the path is steep again. At intervals tea stalls sell refreshments.

Kedarnath Temple
→ *Altitude: 3,584 m. 77 km from Rudraprayag. Pujas are held at 0600 and 1800.*
The area around Kedarnath is known as Kedarkhand, the *Abode of Siva*. Kedarnath has one of the 12 *jyotirlingas* – see page 305. In the *Mahabharata*, the **Pandavas** built the temple to atone for their sins after the battle at Kurukshetra – see page 443. The Kedarnath Temple is older and more impressive than Badrinath. Some claim it is originally over 800 years old. Built of stone, unpainted but carved outside, it comprises a simple, squat, curved tower and a wooden roofed *mandapa*. Set against an impressive backdrop of snow-capped peaks, the principal one being the Kedarnath peak (6,970 m), the view from the forecourt is ruined by ugly 'tube' lights. At the entrance to the temple is a large Nandi statue.

Vasuki Tal → *A guide is necessary. Altitude: 4,235 m.*
Vasuki Tal, about 6 km away, the source of Son Ganga, is to the west up along a goat track. It has superb views of the Chaukhamba Peak (7,164 m). A short distance northwest is the beautiful Painya Tal where through the clear water you can see the rectangular rocks which form the lake bottom.

⁝ Pilgrimage: purification and piety

Bad karma (see page 1325), the impurity caused by bad actions in previous births, and death itself, are the focus of some of Hinduism's most important rituals. Rivers are believed to have great purifying power, stronger at the source, at their confluence, and at the mouth. There are five 'Prayags' (confluences) in the Himalayan section of the Ganga – Deoprayag, Rudraprayag, Karnaprayag, Nandaprayag and Vishnuprayag, called Trayagraj (King of Prayags). On the plains, Allahabad is the most important confluence of all, where the Yamuna, the Ganga and the mythical underground river, the Sarasvati, all meet.

Piety Hardship enhances the rewards of the yatra pilgrims. The really devout prostrate themselves either for the whole distance or around the temple, lying face down, stretching the arms forwards, standing up, moving up to where their fingertips reached and then repeating the exercise, each one accompanied by a chant. Most pilgrims today prefer to make the journey by bus or by car.

Kedarnath Musk Deer Sanctuary

The area bounded by the Mandal-Ukhimath road and the high peaks to the north, the Kedarnath Temple is just outside, was set aside in 1972 principally to protect the endangered Himalayan musk deer – the male carries the prized musk pod. There is a breeding centre at Khanchula Kharak about 10 km from Chopta. The diversity of the park's flora and fauna are particular attractions. Dense forested hills of chir pine, oak, birch and rhododendron and alpine meadows with the presence of numerous Himalayan flowering plants, reflect the diverse climate and topography of the area while 40% of the rocky heights remain under permanent snow. Wildlife includes jackal, black bear, leopard, snow leopard, sambar, *bharal* and Himalayan tarh, as well as 146 species of bird. A 2-km trek from Sari village near Chopta leads to Deoriatal, at 2,438 m, overlooking Chaukhamba Peak.

The Panch Kedars

There are five temples visited by pilgrims: Kedarnath, Madhmaheswar, Tungnath, Rudranath and Kalpeshwar. These vary in altitude from 1,500-3,680 m in the Rudra Himalaya and is an arduous circuit. Kedarnath and Badrinath are only 41 km apart with a tiring *yatra* (pilgrim route) between the two; most pilgrims take the longer but easier way round by bus or car. The myth of the 'five Sivas' relates how parts of the shattered Nandi Bull fell in the five places – the humped back at Kedarnath, the stomach at Madhmaheswar, the legs at Tungnath, the face at Rudranath and the hair at Kalpeshwar. Since all but Kalpeshwar and Tungnath are inaccessible in the winter, each deity has a winter seat in a temple at Ukhimath where the images are brought down in the autumn. They are returned to their principal temples in the spring.

Panch Kedar trek

If you wish to undertake the 170 km, 14-day trek, start at Rishikesh, visiting Kedarnath first (see above). Return to Guptakashi and proceed to Kalimath to start the 24 km trek to **Madhmaheswar** from Mansuna village. You can stop overnight at Ransi, 1 km southwest of Madhmaheswar, and continue following the Ganga through the Kedarnath Musk Deer Sanctuary (see above). From near the temple at 3,030 m which has three streams flowing by it, you can see Chaukhamba Peak (7,164 m).

Tungnath, at 3,680 m, the highest temple, is surrounded by the picturesque Nanda Devi, Neelkanth and Kedarnath mountains. You reach it by a 3-km trek from Chopta, on a driving route from Ukhimath to Gopeshwar, passing through villages, fields and wooded hills before reaching meadows with rhododendrons. The two-hour climb, though steep, is not difficult since it is along a good rocky path with occasional benches.

For **Rudranath**, at 3,030 m, get to Gopeshwar by road and then on to Sagar (5 km) for the 24-km trek covering stony, slippery ground through tall grass, thick oak and rhododendron forests. Landslides are quite common. The grey stone Rudranth temple has the Rudraganga flowing by it. The views of the Nandadevi, Trisul and Hathi Parbat peaks and down to the small lakes glistening in the surroundings are fantastic.

Kalpeshwar, at 2,100 m, near Joshimath, is the only one of the Panch Kedars accessible throughout the year. Its position overlooking the Urgam Valley offers beautiful views of the Garhwal's most fertile region with its terraced cultivation of rice, wheat and vegetables. Trekking across the Mandakini starts from Tangni.

Rudraprayag to Badrinath

Along the Pilgrim Road, about midway between Rudraprayag and Karnaprayag, you pass **Gauchar**, famous locally for its annual cattle fair. The valley is wider here providing the local population with very good agricultural land. The beautiful Pindar River joins the Alaknanda at **Karnaprayag**, 17 km, while **Nandaprayag** is the confluence with the Mandakini River. All these places have GMVN accommodation. **Chamoli**, 40 km further on, is the principal market for the Chamoli district though the HQ is Gopeshwar on the hillside opposite. The valley walls are now much higher and steeper and the road twists and turns more. Troop movements up to the border with Tibet/China are common and military establishments are a frequent sight on the Pilgrim road. From Chamoli onwards the road is an impressive feat of engineering.

Joshimath → *Phone code: 01389. Colour map 2, grid B3. Altitude: 1,875 m.*

Joshimath is at the junction of two formerly important trans-Himalayan trading routes. Travellers to Govindghat and beyond may be forced to spend a night here as the road closes to northbound traffic at 1630.

Joshimath is now the base for India's longest and highest cable car route to Auli Ski Resort, with beautiful views of Nanda Devi, Kamet, Mana Parvat and Dunagiri peaks, all above 7,000 m. There is a restaurant in the meadow, see below.

Vishnuprayag

Vishnuprayag is at the bottom of the gorge at the confluence of the Alaknanda and Dhauliganga rivers. Some 12 km and a steep downhill stretch brings the road from Joshimath to the winter headquarters of the Rawal of Badrinath.

Buses for Badrinath, along the narrow hair-raising route start around 0600, the one-way flow regulated by police. You travel through precipitous gorges, past another Hanuman Chatti with a temple and climb above the treeline to reach the most colourful of the *Char Dhams*, in the valley.

The Bhotias (Bhutias), a border people with Mongoloid features and strong ties with Tibet live along these passes – see page 625. The women wear distinctive Arab-like headdress. Like their counterparts in the eastern Himalaya, they used to combine high altitude cultivation with animal husbandry and trading, taking manufactured goods from India to Tibet and returning with salt and borax. When the border closed following the 1962 Indo-Chinese War, they were forced to seek alternative income and some were resettled by the government.

Auli → *Colour map 2, grid B3. Altitude: 2,519 m. By road it is16 km from Joshimath, or a 5-km trek.*

The extensive meadows at Auli on the way to the Kauri Pass had been used for cattle grazing by the local herders. After the Indo-Chinese War (1962), a road was built from Joshimath to Auli and a Winter Craft Centre set up for the Border Police in the 1970s. With panoramic views of mountains, particularly Nanda Devi and others in the sanctuary, and Mana and Kamet on the Indo-Tibet border, and good slopes, Auli has been developed as a **ski** resort by GMVN and Uttaranchal Tourism operating from January to early March. There is a 500-m ski lift and 800-m chair lift. You can stay at *Tourist Rest House.*① *Getting there: a modern 25-seater cable car carries people from Joshimath, Rs 225 return per person. Jeeps/taxis: between Joshimath and Auli. Regular buses from Rishikesh (253 km), Haridwar (276 km) up to Joshimath.*

Badrinath → *Phone code: 01389. Colour map 1, grid B5. Altitude: 3,150 m.*

① *See Transport, page 225, for getting there details.*

According to Hindu *Shastras*, no pilgrimage is complete without a visit to Badrinath, the abode of Vishnu. Along with Ramesvaram, Dwarka and Puri, it is one of the four holiest places in India, see page 1326. Guarding it are the Nar and Narayan ranges and in the distance towers the magnificent pyramid-shaped peak of **Neelkanth**, at 6,558 m; a hike to its base takes two hours. *Badri* is derived from a wild fruit that Vishnu was said to have lived on when he did penance at Badrivan, the area which covers all five important temples including Kedarnath. Shankaracharya, the monist philosopher from South India, is credited with establishing the four great pilgrimage centres in the early ninth century AD, see page 1326.

The main **Badrinath Temple** is small and brightly painted in green, blue, pink, yellow, white, silver and red. The shrine is usually crowded with worshippers. The *Rawal* (Head Priest) always comes from a Namboodri village in Kerala, the birthplace of Shankaracharya. Badrinath is snowbound over winter, when the images are transferred to Pandukeshwar, and open from late April to October. Along with worshipping in the temple and dispensing alms to the official (sometimes wealthy) temple beggars outside, it is customary to bathe in **Tapt Kund**, a hot pool nearby below the temple. This is fed by a hot sulphurous spring in which Agni (the god of fire) resides by kind permission of Vishnu. The temperature is around 45°C. *Badrinath Festival* takes place from 3 to 10 June.

Hemkund and the Valley of Flowers → *Colour map 1, grid B5.*

① *Permits to enter the national park are issued at the police post at the road head of Govindghat, Rs 350, plus camera fee, Rs 50; may be negotiable in the off-season. Camping overnight in the valley or taking back plants or flowers is prohibited.*

Govindghat, 20 km from Joshimath, is on the road to Badrinath. A bridle track leads to Ghangharia, for the Valley of Flowers, 19 km further on, and Hemkund Sahib. This trailhead is very crowded in the peak season (May-June). You can trek or hire mules for the two-day journey; there are several **tea-stalls** along the route.

Ghangharia, at 3,048 m, is a 14-km walk from Govindghat. May to June are very busy. Those arriving late without a reservation may only find floor space in the Gurudwara or must sleep in a field.

To reach **Hemkund** (6 km further on at 4,329 m) after 1 km from Ghangharia leave the main Valley of Flowers track, up a path to the right. **Guru Gobind Singh** is believed to have sat here in meditation during a previous incarnation, see page 1345. It is an important Sikh pilgrimage site. On the shore of the lake where pilgrims bathe in the icy cold waters, is a modern *gurudwara*; well worth the long trek though some may suffer from the high altitude. Hemkund is also a Hindu pilgrimage site, referred to as

Lokpal. Lakshman, the younger brother of Rama, meditated by the lake and regained his health after being severely wounded by Ravana's son, Meghnath. A small Lakshman temple stands near the *gurudwara*. Despite its ancient connections, Hemkund/Lokpal was 'discovered' by a Sikh *Havildar*, Solan Singh, and only became a major pilgrimage centre after 1930.

The 14-km long trail from Govindghat to Ghangharia runs along a narrow forested valley past the villages of Pulna and Bhiyundar. **The Valley of Flowers** ① *best season Jul-Aug 3,000-3,600 m*, is a further 5 km. Hathi Parbat (Elephant Peak), at 6,700 m, rises dramatically at the head of the narrow side valley. Close views of mountains can be seen from Bhiyundar. The trek has beautifully varied scenery. After crossing the Alaknanda River by suspension bridge the winding path follows the Laxman Ganga as its constant companion, passing dense forests and commanding panoramic views of the lovely Kak Bhusundi Valley on its way to the hamlet of Ghangaria (Govind Dham), the base for the Valley of Flowers, nestling amidst giant deodars. As the path from Ghangaria gradually climbs to the Valley of Flowers, glaciers, snow bridges, alpine flowers and wildlife appear at intervals. The 6-km long and 2-km wide 'U' shaped valley is laced by waterfalls. The River Pushpati and many other small streams wind across it, and its floor, carpeted with alpine flowers during the monsoons, is particularly beautiful. It is especially popular because of its accessibility. The Valley was popularized by **Frank Smythe**, the well-known mountaineer, in 1931. Local people had always kept clear of the Valley because of the belief that it was haunted, and any who entered it would be spirited away. A memorial stone to Margaret Legge, an Edinburgh botanist, who slipped and fell to her death in 1939 reads, "I will lift up mine eyes unto the hills from whence cometh my strength".

Satopanth → *25 km from Badrinath. Take a guide.*

Satopanth, a glacial lake, takes a day to reach from Badrinath. You follow the track along the Alaknanda Valley, a gentle climb up to **Mana** village (6 km north) near the border, inhabited by Bhotias. Foreigners need to register here and sometimes deposit their cameras since they are not permitted to take photographs. Nearby is the cave where **Vyasa** is said to have written the epic *Mahabharata*. The track disappears and you cross a snowbridge, trek across flower-filled meadows before catching sight of the impressive 144-m **Vasudhara Falls**. The ascent becomes more difficult as you approach the source of the Alaknanda near where the Satopanth and Bhagirathi Kharak glaciers meet. The remaining trek takes you across the **Chakra Tirth** meadow and over the steep ridge of the glacier till you see the striking green Satopanth Lake. According to legend its three corners mark the seats of Brahma, Vishnu and Siva. The peaks of **Satopanth** (7,084 m) from which the glacier flows, **Neelkanth** (6,558 m) and **Chaukhamba** (7,164 m) make a spectacular sight.

Trekking in the Garhwal and the Kumaon Himalaya

This region contains some of the finest mountains in the Himalaya and is highly accessible and yet surprisingly very few westerners visit it, many preferring to go to Nepal. Of the many treks available, eight routes are included here. The scenic splendour of these mountains lies partly in the fact that the forests around the big peaks are still in wonderfully untouched and the local population unaffected by the ravages of mass tourism. Also in Garhwal and Kumaon there are ranges that you can easily get among, enabling a greater feeling of intimacy with the alpine giants. The mountains have been described as "a series of rugged ranges tossed about in the most intricate confusion" (Walton, 1910). ▸▸ *For Sleeping, Eating and other listings, see pages 243-244.*

66 99 Famous mountaineers of the 1930s like Bill Tilman, Eric Shipton and Frank Smythe all marvelled at the beauty of the region and Edmund Hillary's first Himalayan peak was Mukut Parbat in Garhwal.

Ins and outs

See previous section for transport details. Reliable local agents who will make all arrangements including accommodation and porters, are in Haridwar, Dehra Dun and Rishikesh (see pages 213, 221 and 66). Porter agents in Uttarkashi, Joshimath, Munsiyari etc who act as trekking agents may not be as reliable; negotiate rates for specific services and insist on reliable porters. Time to visit: Feb and Mar: at lower altitudes for the spectacular rhododendrons. Apr and May: at higher altitudes, though it can get very hot and views can be restricted due to large scale burning. Jul and Aug: the monsoon is good for alpine flowers but wet, humid and cloudy for much, though not all, of the time. If the monsoon is heavy, roads and tracks can become impassable. Sep: the air is beautifully rainwashed, but early morning clear skies can give way by 1000 to cloud, and the views may completely disappear. Oct and Nov: when temperatures are lower, the skies clearer and the vegetation greener following the monsoon.

Background

This region had been open since the British took over in 1815 but it was closed in 1960 due to political troubles with China, and during this period Nepal became popular with climbers and trekkers. Garhwal and Kumaon Himalaya have gradually been opened to explorers since 1975, though parts bordering Tibet remain closed.

Much of the early Himalayan exploration was undertaken here. **Trisul**, 7,120 m, after it had been climbed by Doctor Tom Longstaff in 1906, remained the highest mountain climbed for the next 30 years. Famous mountaineers of the 1930s like Bill Tilman, Eric Shipton and Frank Smythe all marvelled at the beauty of the region and Edmund Hillary's first Himalayan peak was Mukut Parbat in Garhwal. Later climbers like Chris Bonington, Peter Boardman, Joe Tasker and Dick Renshaw used alpine techniques to conquer Changabang and Dunagiri.

Trekking

Trekking in this region is not highly organized so you need to be well prepared. A good map for the area is Leomann's, Indian Himalya Sheet 8, Kumaon Garhwal. On most treks you need a tent (though not The Pindari Glacier trek, for example). Very few villagers speak English, but the rewards for the well-equipped trekker who has planned carefully are great, especially the feeling of being far from the madding crowd. If you are travelling in small groups of three to four persons it is often possible to get overnight accommodation in villagers' houses but despite their hospitality, this is uncomfortable. GMVN and KMVN lodges where available, provide rustic but clean rooms and some have deluxe rooms with bath. Caretakers cook simple meals. If you would like to leave logistics to someone else, hire a government recognized specialist tour operator (see page 1157).

Around **Gangotri** and **Yamunotri** in Garhwal there are a number of good treks, some suitable for the independent or 'go-it-alone' trekker. **Nanda Devi** is the other area and this forms a ring that includes both Garhwal and Kumaon. There are many more treks than those indicated here. The lower part of the Niti Valley, and the Darma Valley, are open to groups of four with requisite permits. You are not allowed to go beyond Badrinath.

Gangotri to Gaumukh

The best known trek here is to Gaumukh (The Cow's Mouth) and, if desired, beyond onto the Gangotri Glacier. Gaumukh can easily be managed in three days with minimal equipment but carry provisions.

From Gangotri, at 3,046 m, follow the well-defined, gradually ascending path for 14 km to **Bhojbasa** at 3,792 m. It takes about five hours.

The 4 km to **Gaumukh**, the last kilometres across boulder scree and moraine, takes about one hour so it is quite feasible to go from Bhojbasa to Gaumukh, spend some time there, then return the same day. There are plenty of tea houses en route. Gaumukh, the present source of the Bhagirathi (Ganga) River, is at the mouth of the Gangotri Glacier where blocks of glacier ice fall into the river and pilgrims cleanse themselves in freezing water. There are breathtaking views. There is basic tent accommodation.

Beyond Gaumukh more care and camping equipment is required. The **Gangotri Glacier** is situated in an amphitheatre of 6,500-7,000 m peaks which include Satopanth (7,084 m), Vasuki (6,792 m), Bhagirathi (6,556 m), Kedar Dome and the prominent trio of Bhagirathi I, II and III; Shivling (6,543 m), standing alone, is one of the most spectacular peaks in the entire Himalaya.

Tapovan → *Altitude: 4,463 m.*

In a breathtaking setting in a grassy meadow on the east bank of the Gangotri Glacier, this is the base camp for climbing expeditions to the stunningly beautiful **Shivling** (6,543 m), Siva's lingam and the 'Matterhorn of the Himalaya'. You can either return the same way or make a round trip by crossing over the glacier for 3 km to **Nandanvan**, at 4,400 m, and continuing upwards for a further 6 km to Vasuki Tal beneath **Vasuki** peak (6,792 m). Since the glacier crossing is fairly risky, it is recommended only for the experienced trekker. The return is via Nandanvan, the west bank of the Gangotri Glacier crossing the Raktvarn Glacier to Gaumukh-Raktvarn, so called because of the rust coloured boulders in its moraine.

Gangotri to Kedartal

This is an excellent short trek with scenic variety and spectacular views but be aware of the problems associated with altitude and allow time for acclimatization. It requires a tent, stove and food. It is 17 km to Kedartal (5,000 m), a small glacial lake surrounded by **Meru** (6,672 m), Pithwara (6,904 m) and Bhrigupanth (6,772 m).

Leaving Gangotri you proceed up the gorge of the Kedar Ganga (Siva's contribution to the Bhagirathi River). It is 8 km to Bhoj Kharak and then a further 4 km to Kedar Kharak, passing through some beautiful Himalayan birch forest en route. The bark from the trees (*bhoj* in Garhwali) was used by sages and hermits for manuscripts. From Kedar Kharak, where you can camp, it is a laborious 5-km ascent to Kedartal. Besides the peaks surrounding the lake you can also see the Gangotri range.

You return to Gangotri the same way. **Rudugaira Kharak** is the base camp for the peaks at the head of the Rudugaira Valley. Coming down towards Gangotri you must cross to the opposite bank near Patangnidhar to avoid the cliffs on the west bank. Nearer Gangotri cross back to the west bank.

Gangori to Yamunotri via Dodital

This is a beautiful trek between Kalyani and Hanuman Chatti, a distance of 49 km. You can do a round trip from either end. It takes five days.

From **Uttarkashi** take a local bus to Kalyani via **Gangori**, 3 km away, or walk it. At **Kalyani**, 1,829 m, the recognized starting point of the trek, you take a track to the right. From here it gets steeper as the path climbs through forest to **Agoda** 5 km away.

There is a suitable camping or halting place 2 km beyond Agoda. The next day carry on to **Dodital**, 16 km away at 3,024 m, picturesquely set in a forest of pine, deodar and oak. This is the source of the Asi Ganga and is stocked with trout. There is a dilapidated *Forest Rest House* and several cheap lodges. Above the lake there are fine views of Bandar Punch (Monkey's Tail, 6,387 m). To reach **Hanuman Chatti** at 2,400 m, walk for 6 km up to the Aineha Pass, 3,667 m, which also has splendid views. Then it is a 22-km walk down to Hanuman Chatti, the roadhead for Yamunotri.

Har-ki-Dun Trek

Har-ki-Dun (God's Valley) nestles in the northwest corner of Garhwal near the Sutlej-Yamuna watershed. The people of the area have the distinction of worshipping **Duryodhana**, head of the crafty royal family in the *Mahabharata*, rather than siding with the pious Pandavas (see page 1318). The valley is dominated by Swargarohini (6,096 m) and Kalanag. From **Nowgaon**, 9 km south of Barkot, take a bus to the roadhead of **Sankri**. From here it is a gradual ascent over 12 km to **Taluka**, and **Osla** (2,559 m), 11 km further. Another 8 km and 1,000 m higher is **Har-ki-Dun** (3,565 m), an ideal base for exploring the valley. Allow three days to Har-ki-Dun. There are *Forest* and *Tourist Rest Houses* at all these places.

You can return to Nowgaon or, if properly equipped and provisioned, trek for 29 km on to **Yamunotri** via the Yamunotri Pass (5,172 m). You will need to allow time for acclimatization. The views from the pass are well worth the effort.

Nanda Devi area

Nanda Devi (7,816 m), named after the all-encompassing form of the female deity, dominates the Garhwal and Kumaon Himalaya. With its two peaks separated by a 4-km long ridge, the second highest mountain in India is incredibly beautiful. She is also the most important of Garhwal's deities, protected by a ring of mountains, 112 km in circumference, containing 12 peaks over 6,400 m high. In only one place is this defensive ring lower than 5,500 m, at the **Rishi Gorge**, one of the deepest in the world. It is the place of ascetic sages (*rishis*). The Nanda Devi Sanctuary is a World Biosphere Reserve.

Background

For half a century the problems which engaged the attention of many experienced explorers and mountaineers was not so much how to climb the mountain but how to get to it. Various attempts were made from a number of places to gain entry into what became known as the Nanda Devi Sanctuary. The riddle was finally solved by the 'Terrible Twins', Bill Tillman and Eric Shipton in a characteristically lightweight expedition (these two great mountaineers would agonize over whether to take one shirt or two on an expedition lasting a few months!). The way they discovered was up the Rishiganga and through the difficult Rishi Gorge. They made two trips into the Sanctuary during their five month expedition in the Garhwal Himalaya in 1934. Bill Tillman returned in 1936 (Shipton was on Hugh Rutledge's Everest Expedition) with a small climbing party and climbed the mountain with little real difficulty. See Books, page 1362, for recommended reading.

Pindari Glacier Trek

This trek along the southern edge of the Sanctuary is an 'out and back' trek, ie you return by the same route. KMVN *Tourist Lodges* (some with only four beds) are dotted along the route so this trek can be done with little equipment, although a sleeping bag is essential. Book accommodation early or take your own tent. The trek is 66 km from Song, which has the last bus terminus.

From **Bageshwar**, see page 249, get a local bus to **Bharari** at 1,524 m which has a PWD *Rest House* and a cheap hotel. From here you can walk 16 km along the Sarju Valley to **Song** or take another bus. It is just over 1½ km further to **Loharkhet**, at 1,829 m, which also has a PWD *Bungalow* in the village and a basic KMVN *Tourist Rest House* overlooking it. Good views of the hillside opposite and the head of the Sarju Valley. It is 11 km from Loharkhet to **Dhakuri** via the Dhakuri Pass (2,835 m) which has a wonderful view of the south of the Nanda Devi Sanctuary including Panwali Dhar (6,683 m) and Maiktoli (6,803 m). The walk to the pass is mostly through forest on a well graded path. About 100 m below the pass on the north side is a clearing with a PWD *Bungalow* and a KMVN *Tourist Rest House*. Great views, especially at sunrise and sunset.

In the Pindar Valley you descend to **Khati** 8 km away at 2,194 m, first through rhododendron, then mixed forests dominated by stunted oak. Khati is a village with over 50 households situated on a spur that runs down to the river, some 200 m below.

Nanda Devi area treks

There is a PWD *Bungalow*, KMVN *Tourist Rest House* and a village hotel. You can buy biscuits, eggs and chocolate, brought in by mule from Bharari.

From Khati follow the Pindar 8 km to **Dwali**, 2,580 m, which is at the confluence of the Pindar and the Kaphini rivers. Here there is a KMVN *Travellers' Lodge* and a run down PWD *Bungalow*. If you have a tent, camp in front. The next halt 6 km on is **Phurkiya**, 3,260 m, which also has a KMVN *Travellers' Lodge*. This can be used as a base for going up to Zero Point (4,000 m), a view point from where the steep falling glacier can be seen (it is difficult for trekkers to go up to the snout of the glacier itself). On either side there are impressive peaks, including Panwali Dwar (6,683 m) and Nanda Kot (6,876 m). Return to Bharari the same way.

From Dwali, however, a side trip to the **Kaphini Glacier** is worthwhile. Alternatively, you could trek up to **Sundar Dhunga Glacier** from Khati. Including either of these, the trek can be accomplished in a week but for comfort allow nine days.

Roopkund Trek → *Altitude: 4,800 m.*

Kund means lake in Garhwali.

A legend relates Nanda Devi, the wife of Siva, to this small lake. When her sister Balpa accompanied her husband King Jasidhwal of the medieval Kingdom of Kanauj on a pilgrimage to Kailash (Mount Trisul), she delivered a child at Balpa de Sulera (adjoining Bhagwabasa), thus polluting the entire mountain. Nanda Devi's herald Latu (who has a temple at Wan), at the command of the Goddess, hurled the royal pilgrimage party into the small tarn called Roopkund; hence the remains of the 300 bodies found in the lake. Thirty years ago the Indian anthropologist DN Majumdar discovered a number of frozen bodies around this small mountain tarn, the remains of a party of pilgrims on a *yatra* who died when bad weather closed in. Carbon-dating suggests the bones are 600 years old.

This is a highly varied and scenic trek which can be undertaken by a suitably equipped party. A week is sufficient – nine days if you want to take it more comfortably with a rest day for acclimatization. The trek can start in Debal where you can pick up provisions, or at Bagrigarh (see below). You can usually get porters at Gwaldam or Debal.

Gwaldam

→ *Colour map 2, grid B3. Altitude: 1,950 m.*

Gwaldam is a small market strung out along a ridge surrounded by orchards. The British established tea plantations which have since been abandoned. GMVN *Tourist Bungalow* has splendid views from the garden, especially at dawn and dusk, of Trisul (7,120 m) and Nanda Ghunti (6,310 m). Gwaldam, one of the starting points for the trek to Roopkund, see page 239, overlooks the beautiful Pindar River which the road follows down to its confluence with the Alaknanda River at **Karnaprayag**. The road jins the Pilgrim road which runs from **Rishikesh** and **Haridwar** to **Badrinath**, see page 232.

From Gwaldam, at 1,950 m, walk down through attractive pine forest, cross the River Pindar and continue 8 km to **Debal**, at 1,350 m, where there is a KMVN *Tourist Rest House*, a *Forest Rest House* and *dharamshalas*. From here you can either walk 12 km along a dirt road through villages with views of Trishul (6,855 m), or go by cramped jeep-taxi to **Bagrigad** which is 500 m below the **Lohajung Pass** (2,350 m) where there is an attractive GMVN *Travellers' Lodge* and two cheap lodges, right on the ridge beside a pretty shrine. The best option is *Patwal Tourist Lodge*, PO Mundoli, Chamoli, T246427, which has spotless, comfortable rooms, immaculate toiltet and showers (bucket hot water), and treks arranged by a retired Army officer. Good views here of Nanda Ghunti. and Trisul from the terrace. If time is at a premium, you can save a day by going by bus from Gwaldam to Tharali, taking another bus to Debal, catching the jeep-taxi to Bagrigadh and walking up to Lohajung in one long day.

From **Lohajung** you walk down through stunted oak forest and along the *Wan Gad* (river) 12 km to the village of **Wan**, 2,400 m, which has a *Forest Rest House* and GMVN *Travellers' Lodge*. From Wan it is essentially wilderness travel as you make the ascent to Roopkund, first walking through thick forest to **Bedni Bugyal** (*bugyal –* meadow) which is used as summer pasture. This is at 3,550 m and has good views of Trisul, Nandaghunti and the Badrinath range to the north. There are some shepherds' stone huts which you may be able to use but it is better to take a tent.

From Bedni it is a gradual 7-km climb along a well defined path over the 4,500 m **Kalwa Vinayak** to more shepherds' huts at Bhagwabasa, at 4,000 m, the base for the final walk up to Roopkund. A stove is necessary for cooking and it can be very cold at night, but water is available about 150 m northeast and up the slope from the campsite. From here, it is two to three hours up to **Roopkund**. Immediately after the monsoon the views can disappear in cloud by 1000, so it is best to leave early. In the final steep part the ground can be icy. Roopkund Lake itself is small and unimpressive, but from the 4,900 m ridge approximately 50 m above Roopkund there is a magnificent view of the west face of Trisul rising over 3,500 m from the floor of the intervening hanging valley to the summit. Return to Gwaldam by the same route or via **Ali Bugyal** and village Didina which by-passes Wan.

Curzon Trail

The Curzon Trail is an incomparably beautiful trek. However, rapid ascent follows equally steep descent from one valley to the next, and at no point does the trek get close to the high snow-covered peaks. It was the route followed by Tilman and Shipton on their way to the Rishi Gorge, and by other mountaineers en route to the peaks on the Indo-Tibetan border. The crossing of the Kuari Pass is a fitting conclusion to a trek that takes in three lesser passes and five major rivers – the Pindar, Kaliganga, Nandakini, Birehiganga and Dhauliganga. The trail was named after Lord Curzon, a keen trekker, and the path may have been specially improved for him. After 1947 it was officially renamed the 'Nehru Trail'. Take camping equipment. Some stopping off places have no suitable accommodation.

This trek begins at **Joshimath** via Auli, or at **Gwaldam** and ends at **Tapovan** in the Dhauliganga Valley on the Joshimath-Niti Pass road. It crosses the **Kuari Pass** (4,268 m), one of the finest vantage points in the Himalaya.

From Gwaldam proceed to **Wan** as in the previous trek. Then, go over the Kokinkhal Pass to **Kanol** (2,900 m) through thick mixed forest for 10 km to **Sutol**, at 2,100 m, in the Nandakini Valley. There is a good campsite by the river. The next two stages follow the Nandakini downstream 10 km to Padergaon, 2,500 m, via Ala. The

Conquering Nanda Devi on apricot brandy

For half a century, the problem facing many experienced explorers and mountaineers was not so much how to climb the mountain but how to get to what became known as the Nanda Devi Sanctuary. The riddle was finally solved by Bill Tilman and Eric Shipton in a characteristically lightweight expedition. They discovered the way up the Rishiganga and through the difficult Rishi Gorge and made two trips into the sanctuary during their five month expedition in 1934. Bill Tilman returned in 1936 with a small party and climbed the mountain with little real difficulty.

Tilman, a purist, wrote "mountaineering is in danger of becoming mechanized. It is therefore pleasing to record that in climbing Nanda Devi no climbing aids were used, apart, that is, from the apricot brandy we took. Our solitary oxygen apparatus was fortunately drowned, pitons were forgotten at base camp and crampons were solemnly carried up only to be abandoned" (The Ascent of Nanda Devi).

In 1936 the monsoon was particularly heavy. The Pindar River rose dramatically. In the village of Tharali 40 lives were lost on 29 August, the day that Tilman's party reached the summit. Some say the anger of the Goddess was provoked by the violation of her sanctuary.

trail to Tapovan leads up over the rhododendron forest clad **Ramni Pass** (3,100 m) with a good view of the Kuari Pass. The trail southwest of Ramni goes to the nearby road head at **Ghat**, from where you can also start the trek. To reach Tapovan from Ramni is a good three days' walk, down through lush forest to cross the Birehiganga River by an impressive suspension bridge, up around the horseshoe-shaped hanging valley around Pana Village, over an intervening spur and into the forested tributary valley of the Kuari nallah. There is no settlement in this area; *bharal* (mountain goats) and the rarely seen Himalayan black bear inhabit the rich forest. Waterfalls tumble down over steep crags. There is a camp and a cave (about one hour) before the Kuari pass at **Dhakwani** (3,200 m).

I leave early to get the full effect of sunrise over the peaks on the Indo-Tibetan border. Some of the peaks seen are Kamet, Badrinath (7,040 m), Dunagiri (7,066 m) and Changabang (6,863 m). There is a wonderful wooded campsite with marvellous views about 300 m below the pass. From here the trail drops down over 2,000 m to **Tapovan** and the Joshimath-Niti road. There is a hot sulpher spring (90°C) here and a bus service to **Joshimath**. Allow 10 days for the trek. A shorter trail leads from the campsite along a scenic ridge to Auli and a further 4 km down to Joshimath.

Nanda Devi and Milam Glacier Trek
Much of this area was only reopened to trekkers in 1993 after more than 30 years of seclusion. The Milam Valley, incised by the 36-km long Gori Ganga gorge, was part of the old trade route between Kumaon and Tibet, only interrupted by the Indian-Chinese War of 1962. Milam, which once had 500 households, many occupied by wealthy traders and surrounded by barley and potato fields, has been reduced to a handful of occupied cottages. The trek is moderate, with some sustained steady walking but no really steep gradients or altitude problems. The route is through some of the remotest regions of the Himalaya with spectacular scenery and rich wildlife.

Day 1 From **Munsiari** a 10-hour drive from Almora, takes you down to Selapani where the trail up the Milam Valley begins. **Lilam** (1,800 m) is an easy 7-km walk (2½ hours) where the tiny *Rest House* offers a convenient halt or camping ground for the first night. See page 249 for details about Munsiari.

Day 2 (14 km; seven hours) From Lilam the trail enters the spectacular 25-km long gorge. Etched into the cliff face above the Gori Ganga the hillsides above are covered in dense bamboo thickets and mixed rain forest. After the junction of the Ralam and Gori Ganga rivers the track climbs to a tea shop at Radgari, then goes on to a small *Rest House* at **Bugdiar** (2,700 m). A memorial commemorates villagers and army personnel lost in the avalanche of 1989. Only a few houses remain on the edge of a wasteland.

Day 3 (16 km; six hours) The valley opens up after climbing quite steeply to a huge overhanging cliff, which shelters a local deity. The route enters progressively drier terrain, but there are two waterfalls of about 100 m, one opposite a tea shop at Mapang. The track climbs to **Rilkote** (3,200 m).

Day 4 (13 km; six hours) Passing deserted villages in the now almost arid landscape the track goes through the large village of **Burphu**, backed by the Burphu Peak (6,300 m). Nanda Devi East comes into view before reaching **Ganghar** village (3,300 m) where only three of the former 60 families remain. Some of the houses have beautiful carved wooden door and window frames; the carefully walled fields below are deserted.

Day 5 (7 km; three hours) A steep narrow track leads into the **Pachhu Valley**, dominated by the northeast face of Nanda Devi East 3,800 m above the Pachhu Glacier. Dwarf rhododendron and birch, with anemones and primulas below, line the first section of the track before it emerges into alpine meadows below the debris of the glacier itself. **Tom Longstaff** came through this valley in his unsuccessful attempt to climb Nanda Devi East in 1905 before trying the parallel valley to the south of Pachhu via what is now known as Longstaff's Col. There is a campsite (3,900 m), 3 km from the base of Nanda Devi East, with both the col and the summit clearly visible in good weather.

Day 6 Side treks are possible up to the Pachhu Glacier and along its edge to the glacial lake **Nanda Kund**.

Day 7 (17 km; six hours) Returning via Ghanghar at Burfu, the track crosses the Gori Ganga on a wooden bridge then climbs to the former staging post of **Milam** (3,300 m).

Day 8 Another 'excursion' (10 km; eight hours) is possible from Milam to the **Milam Glacier** (4,100 m). There are superb views of the clean ice uncovered by debris from the track which runs along the left bank of the Milam Glacier. Three tributary glaciers join the main Milam Glacier.

Day 9 (13 km; five hours) The track runs along the left bank of the river via Tola village to the base of the 4,750 m Brijganga Pass, outside **Sumdu** village (3,400 m).

Day 10 (12 km; seven hours) Superb views characterize this steady climb to the top of the pass. The razor sharp Panchulis dominate the south while the twin peaks of Nanda Devi are straight ahead. **Ralam** village is a steep drop below the pass (3,700 m).

Day 11 (10 km; six hours) This can be a rest day or a day trek up to the Shankalpa Glacier along the watershed between the rarely visited Ralam and Darma valleys.

Day 12-14 (six hours each day) The trek runs steadily down through the thickly forested Ralam valley, passing Marjhali, Bhujani, Buria, Sarpa and Besani villages.

Day 15 (11 km; four hours) Return from Lilam to Munsiari via a number of villages.

Darma Valley Trek

The easternmost of the Kumaon valleys, the Darma Valley is now also open to trekkers but you need permission. Separated from western Nepal by the Kaliganga River and with Tibet to the north the valley is one of the least explored in the Himalaya. From the roadhead at **Dharchula** (on the India/Nepal border) it is possible to trek for four or five days up to Sipu and also to spend time exploring the numerous side valleys. Buses are available from Pithorgarh, see page 249, and Almora up to Dharchula from where it is often possible to get local transport for a further 32 km up to **Sobala**. Then it is a three to four days' trek up to Sipu, the northernmost point allowed under present regulations.

Listings: Garhwal

🛏 Sleeping

Yatra *p227*
D-E Rest Houses, GMVN, have some 'deluxe' rooms which are still basic, with toilet and hot water, dorm (Rs 60-100).

Also simple guesthouses in places. Reserve ahead; during Yatra season, GMVN places may only be available if you book their organized tour. Carry some bottled water and take a good torch.

Tehri *p227*
E hotel with a pleasant 'delux' room with bath, but there are no appealing eateries.

Yamunotri *p227*
Hanuman Chatti
E Tourist Rest House, by the river. GMVN, clean, simple rooms, dorm (Rs 100), hot water in buckets, the only decent place.

Janki Chatti
Rest House, GMVN.

Other lodges and places to eat. At Yamunotri, the GMVN **Rest House**, is on a hill. Also dharamshalas and basic lodges.

Dodital *p228*
D-E Akash Ganga.
D-E Shivam, T2525, have some a/c rooms.
E Ceeway short walk from bazar. Decent.
E GMVN Tourist Bungalow, near bridge, T2236. 33 rooms with bath, few a/c, vegetarian meals. Small.

E-F hotels are clustered near the bus stand.

Gangotri *p228*
C Shikhar Nature Resort, 5 km out of town, by the Bhagirathi River, T011-331244, F3323660, www.shikhar.com. Luxury tents with mod cons in scenic setting.
E Birla Niketan, nearby, has rooms with bath. Other lodges have rooms without bath and electricity for under Rs 100.
E Ganga Niketan, across road bridge. Decent rooms and a simple terrace restaurant.

E Monal is on the road to Gangotri.
E Tourist Rest House, across footbridge. 20 rooms and dorm, meals.

Gular-dogi *p229*
B The Glasshouse on the Ganges (Neemrana Hotels), in idyllic setting, T013548-9218, sales@ neemrana.com. Rooms with views in 3 cottages, very helpful and willing staff, good food, ideal for total relaxation.

Deoprayag *p229*
E Tourist Bungalow, 1½ km from main bazar and bus stand on a hillside. 16 rooms, some with bath, meals.

Srinagar *p230*
D-E Tourist Rest House, near bus stop in central square, T2110, has 90 rooms, deluxe with bath, cheaper cabins and dorm, restaurant, tourist office, clean and quiet.
E Alka and **Menka**, opposite *Tourist Rest House*, among others in town.

Rudraprayag *p230*
D New Tourist Bungalow, on a hill. Has 25 rooms, deluxe with bath and dorm.
E Chandrapuri Camp, north of town, by the river, has 10 safari type tents for 4.

Kedarnath Temple *p230*
E Tourist Rest House, has 16 rooms, some with bath, and dorm.

Joshimath *p232*
Hotel prices rise in high season.
D-E Neelkantha Motel, Upper Mall, by bus stand, T22226. 15 comfortable rooms, some deluxe with bath, dorm, restaurant (acceptable though limited menu), helpful staff (arrange jeep, porter), often full.

Older **Dronagiri**, near Ropeway, is dark and less pleasant.
E Kamet, by Ropeway, Lower Mall. Rooms not great value but cheaper rooms in annexe facing main road.
F Auli Paying Guest House, opposite the police station, has an 8-bed dorm (Rs 100).

Uttaranchal Listings: Garhwal

 For an explanation of the sleeping and eating price codes used in this guide, see inside the front cover. Other relevant information is found in Essentials pages 52-57.

F **Nanda Devi** between Upper and Lower Mall, in the bazar, T22170. Basic, cheap, porter agents.

F **Shailja**, behind *Neelkanth Motel*, is basic but friendly, good food but check bill.

F **Shivlok**, has basic doubles.

Badrinath *p233*

E **Devlok** (GMVN), near Bus Stand, T85212, has 30 large rooms, a restaurant, and the best in the trekking area.

For pilgrims: *dharamshalas* and *chattis* (resthouses), T85204.

Govindghat *p233*

E **Bharat Lodge**, at the far end of town, with bucket hot water.

Forest Rest House and **Govind Singh Gurudwara**, free accommodation and food to all (donations accepted) and reliable cloakroom service for trekkers.

Ghangharia *p233*

D-F **Tourist Lodge**, overpriced rooms, dorm (Rs 100), tent (Rs 60).

E **Merry Lodge**, rooms with bath.

F **Krishna**, cheap rooms with bath.

Free *Gurudwara* (Sikh religious complex).

Bhojbasa *p236*

A **Tourist Rest House**, has 4 rooms and a dorm without bedding. This, however, is often full.

You may hire good value 2-person tents for Rs 160 a night.

There is also an *ashram* where trekkers and pilgrims can stay.

Chirbasa

Tented accommodation (5 km before Bhojbasa).

● Eating

Dodital *p228*

In the bazar serve vegetarian *thalis*.

Gangotri *p228*

Numerous tea and food stalls near the temple.

Joshimath *p232*

Several places serve veg meals.

Pindari, serves delicious *thalis*, "light years ahead of the competition".

Paradise, near *Pindari*.

▲▲ Activities and tours

Dodital *p228*

Tour companies

Crystal Adventure, *Hotel Tapovan*, near Tourist Bungalow, T2566.

Mount Support, Nautial Bhawan, Bhatwari Rd, near bus stand.

● Transport

Yamunotri *p227*

Bus

Early bus (0600) best from Rishikesh to Hanuman Chatti (210 km, 9 hrs).

Dodital *p228*

Frequent buses to Rishikesh (140 km) and Gangotri (100 km) during the *yatra* season. For a return trip in a taxi to Gangotri, Rs 1,300.

Joshimath *p232*

Bus

Frequent to Badrinath, 4 hrs, via Govindghat, 1 hr, Rs 7; to Kedarprayag, 1300, 4 hrs; Rishikesh, 0400, 0600, 10 hrs; Rudraprayag, 1100, 5 hrs.

● Directory

Joshimath *p232*

Tourist office In annexe above *Neekanth Motel*, T22181, helpful. **Useful addresses** Trekking agents at *Nanda Devi hotel*: **Great Himalayan Expeditions**. Highly recommended for "local knowledge, good humour, high spirits and reliability". **Garhwal Mountain Services**, T22288. For porters. **Eskimo Travels**, next to GMVN, has also been recommended for trekking, climbing and skiing.

Nainital

→ *Phone code: 05942. Colour map 1, grid C5. Population: 40,000. Altitude: 1,938 m.*
Set around a small lake, the charming hill station of Nainital has many villas, bungalows and fine houses with their well-kept lawns on the fairly steep tree covered hillsides. Overcrowded in summer, the resort is pleasanter out of season, with some attractive walks and only a few foreign tourists. ▸▸ *For Sleeping, Eating and other listings, see pages 249-253.*

Ins and outs

Getting there The nearest railway station is 1¾ hrs away at Kathgodam, linked to Nainital by frequent buses. The climb from Kathgodam to Nainital is dramatic, rising 1,300 m over 30 km. The road follows the valley of the Balaya stream then winds up the hillsides through forests and small villages. After the long drive the town around the *tal* (lake) appears suddenly; the land south and on the plains-side fall away quite steeply so you only see the lake when you are at its edge. Buses from Delhi and the surrounding hill stations use the Tallital bus stand at the southern end of the lake, while some buses from Ramnagar (and Corbett National Park) use the Mallital bus stand at the northern end.

Getting around The Mall, pedestrianized at peak times, is the hub of Nainital's life. You can hire a cycle-rickshaw if the walk feels too much, or take a taxi for travelling further afield. See Transport, page 252, for further details.

Climate Temperature: summer max 26°C, min 16°C, winter max 10°C, min 3°C. Rainfall: Jul 769 mm to 5 mm in Dec. Best season: Apr to May and Oct to Nov though May and Jun are busy.

Background

In 1839 the small hamlet of Nainital was 'discovered' by a Mr P Barron, a sugar manufacturer from Saharanpur. He was so impressed by the 1½ km long and 500 m wide lake that he returned with a sailing boat a year later, carried up in sections from the plains. In due course Nainital became the summer capital of the then United Provinces. An old legend of Siva and Sati (see page 219) associates the place as where Sati's eyes fell (hence *naini*). The *tal* (lake) is surrounded by seven hills, the *Sapta-Shring*.

On 18 September 1880 disaster struck the town. At the north end of the lake, known now as Mallital (the southern part is Tallital) stood the *Victoria Hotel*. In two days nearly 1,000 mm of rain fell leading to a landslip which crushed some outhouses, burying several people. The cliff overhanging the hotel collapsed, burying the soldiers and civilians engaged in rescue work and making it impossible to save the 150 buried. Later the area was levelled, became known as The Flats, and was used for public meetings and impromptu games of football and cricket. Today it is more a bus park in the tourist season, although sports tournaments are held here in June, August and December.

Nainital is popular as an Indian family holiday centre, especially in the summer season, when hotels are full, prices soar and there is little peace and quiet. Congestion and pollution is taking its toll; the *tal*, now much reduced in size, is unable to cope with the increased tourist traffic. The pony riders, curio-sellers and snack stalls increase in number while the lake water becomes dirty and unable to support fish. Concerns that the lake contains excess amounts of toxic metals are exasperated by the fact that it is the only source of the town's drinking water. It is best to drink bottled water here. It can be very cold in winter, and depressions sometimes bring cloud and rain which obscures the views of the mountains.

Sights

There is little of architectural interest other than the colonial style villas overlooking the lake (walking is the major attraction of this town). The **Church of St John in the Wilderness** (1846), one of the earliest buildings, is beyond Mallital, below the Nainital Club. The most distinctive building is **Government House** (1899, now the

Nainital

To Naina Peak

Upper China Mall

Waverly Rd — 12

Secretariat

The Mall

3

16

Display Garden

St John in the Wilderness

Nainital Club

19

7

MALLITAL

4

3

Ropeway

18

Sukha Tal (dry)

Sukhatal Bus Stand

8

Mallital Bazar

Bank of Baroda

SBI

15

Cyberia

Flatties Rock

Rickshaws

Boat Club

2

THE FLATS

6

Nainital Yacht Club

1

Bookshop

Kumaon Woolens

Nanda Devi Mandir

Kaladhungi Rd

9

Naini Tai

East

Laggan Rd

South Mall

Ayarpatha Rd

AYARPATHA

Middle Ayarpatha Mall

Tiffin Tops

Sherwood College

Polo Ground

To Raj Bhawan

N

0 metres 200

0 yards 200

■	**Sleeping**	5	Classic	10	Prince	15	Tourist Home
1	Alka	6	Grand	11	Sarovar Rest House	16	Vikram Vantage
2	Alka Annexe	7	Manu Maharani	12	Shervani Hilltop Inn		Inn
3	Balrampur House	8	Mount View Naina	13	Silverton	17	YMCA
4	Belvedere	9	Naina Retreat	14	Snow View	18	Youth Hostel

Uttaranchal Nainital

Secretariat) which was designed in stone by FW Stephens who was also responsible for VT (now CST) and Churchgate Stations in Mumbai (Bombay). Early in the season it is pleasant to walk round (the Lower Mall is pedestrianized) or take a boat across the lake; remember it can still be very cold in March.

Naina (Cheena) **Peak** (2,610 m) is a 5-km walk from the lake. From the top, there are stunning views of the Himalaya including **Nanda Devi** (7,816 m) and the mountains on the Tibetan border. In season there is a 'gondola' (Ropeway) which runs from the Mallital end of the lake to **Snow View** (2,270 m), another good vantage point for viewing the snow-capped peaks. It is also possible to make the 2-km steep climb up to the viewpoint from the north end of the lake, passing the small Tibetan gompa which has fluttering prayer flags marking it.

Hanumangarh with a small temple off Haldwani Road, and the **Observatory** (open evenings) further along the path (3 km from the lake), have lookouts for watching the sun set over the plains. The opposite side has only a few cottages and much higher up near the ridge are two private boys' schools – Sherwood College and St Joseph's. The atmospheric **British Cemetery** with its crumbling graves is about 3 km southeast of town. Take the minor road at the south end of the lake (not the Rampur Road); on the right side, the remains of the entrance gate are just visible behind some trees.

Excursions

Sat Tal, 24 km away, has seven lakes including the jade green Garud Tal, the olive green Rama Tal and Sita Tal.

Naukuchiyatal, 26 km away, is a lake with nine corners, hence the name. It is beautifully unspoilt, and quiet paddling round the lake allows you to see lots of birds; boats for hire. Tour buses stop around 1630.

Pangot, 15 km from Nainital via Kilbury, is in ideal birding territory where over 580 species have been recorded.

Jeolikote, a small hamlet on the main road up from Ranpur, 18 km south of Nainital, is known for its health centre and butterflies, honey and mushrooms. It offers a peaceful weekend retreat.

Snow View (2,270m)
14
Upper China Mall
Tibetan Monastery
6
i 5
The Mall
2 Library
4
SHER-KA-DANDA
13
17
1
St Francis
10
Pashan Devi Mandir
Parvat Tours
Tallital
11 Railway Booking Office
Bus Stand
TALLITAL
Haldwani Rd
Bhowali Rd
Ramsay Rd
St Joseph's College
To Hanumoungarh & Observatory

19 YWCA

● Eating
1 Kwality

2 Purohit, Machan
   & Nanak
3 Sakley
4 Sher-e-Punjab

Uttaranchal Nainital

Almora → Phone code: 05962. Colour map 1, grid C5. Population: 32,500. Altitude: 1,646 m.

Like many hill towns, Almora occupies a picturesque horseshoe-shaped ridge. The Mall runs about 100 m below the ridge line, while the pedestrianized bazar above is jostling and colourful. Almora was founded in 1560 by the Chand Dynasty who ruled over most of Kumaon, which comprises the present districts of Nainital, Almora and Pithoragarh. Overrun by the Gurkhas in 1798, it was heavily bombed by the British as they tried to expel them in the Gurkha Wars of 1814-15. Traces of an old Chand fort, stone-paved roads, wooden houses with beautifully carved façades and homes decorated with traditional murals, reflect its heritage. Today it is an important market town and administrative centre and is also regarded as the cultural capital of the area.

Ins and outs
Getting there Buses and jeeps from neighbouring hill towns use the bus stands on the Mall. There are also daily buses to Kathgodam the rail head, and also to Nepal.

Getting around The Mall and the bazar are within walking distance of several hotels. Almora also has a few viewpoints which call for a pleasant stroll. For others further afield, you can get a taxi near the Mall bus stand. See Transport, page 253, for further details.

Sights
Swami Vivekenanda came to Almora and gained enlightenment in a small cave at **Kasar Devi** on Kalimatiya Hill, 7 km northeast of town. This makes a pleasant walk and there are good views from the hill. Another vantage point for sunrise and sunset is Bright End Corner, 2½ km southwest of Mall Road, near All India Radio. The stone **Udyotchandesvar Temple**, above Mall Road, houses Kumaon's presiding deity, Nanda Devi, whose festival is in August/September. Almora's *Tamta* artisans still use traditional methods to work with copper. Copper metallurgy was known to the people here as early as the second century BC and is associated with the Kuninda Dynasty who traded in copper articles. The handbeaten copper pots are 'silver plated' in the traditional way (*kalhai*).

Excursions
Jageswar, 34 km, in a serene wooded gorge famous for the 164 ornamented temples built by the Chand rajas, has one of the 12 *jyotirlingas*. The temples here and in nearby Gandeswar are very fine examples of early medieval hill temple architecture but are rarely visited by outsiders. The one dedicated to Jogeswar with finely carved pillars has a small museum; 6 km before Jageswar, a roadside sign points to stone-age **cave paintings** (about 50 m off the road). These are in red, white and black, depicting human figures, trees, animals and possibly water courses. Though several paintings were damaged by storage of cement bags during bridge building work nearby, many can be seen and are worth the short stop.

Once the capital of the Chand rajas, **Binsar** has a bird sanctuary sited at 2,410 m with superb views of valleys around and panoramic mountain views. It is 28 km away.

Kausani → Altitude: 1,892 m. 50 km north of Almora.
① *Buses from Almora and Ranikhet (2½-3½ hrs). Joshimath is a tough but spectacular 10-hr journey.*

Kausani sits on a narrow ridge among pine forests with wonderfully wide views of the **Nanda Devi** group of mountains stretching over 300 km along the horizon. The view is particularly stunning at sunrise. You may trek from here to Bageswar, Gwaldam and the Pindari Glacier. In 1929 **Mahatma Gandhi** spent 12 days at what is now Anashakti Ashram.

From Kausani, the road descends to Garur and Baijnath. The small town of Baijnath on the banks of the Gomti River has distinctively carved 12th- and 13th- century Katyuri temples. They are now mostly ruined, but its houses have intricately carved wooden doors and windows – see also page 487. The main 10th-century temple houses a beautiful image of **Parvati**. Siva and Parvati are believed to have married at the confluence of the Gomti and Garur Ganga. The Katyur Dynasty, which ruled the valley for 500 years, took their name from Siva and Parvati's mythical son, **Karttikeya**. **Garur** has plenty of buses/taxis northwards. Just north of Garur a road runs northwest to Gwaldam, see Roopkund trek, page 239, and another east to Bageshwar.

Bageshwar

Bageshwar, meaning Siva as 'Lord of Eloquent Speech', stands at the confluence of the Gomti and Sarju rivers. It is Kumaon's most important pilgrimage centre and has several temples and two sacred pools.

Munsiari → *Altitude: 2,300 m.*

ⓘ *Buses from Almora, change at Thal; from Haldwani or Nainital, take bus to Pithorgarh and change. To Almora (11 hrs) and Pithorgarh (8 hrs), 0500 and another for Pithorgarh in the afternoon.*

This is a quiet hill town overlooked by the majestic five peaks of **Panchuli** which, in legend, served as the five *chulis* (stoves) used to cook the last meal of the five Pandava brothers before they ascended to heaven. Munsiari is a base for treks into the Milam, Ralam and Namik glaciers, and towards Panchuli. It is also the start of an easy trek (three to four days) via Namik to Dwali in the Pindar Valley.

Pithorgarh

Sitting in a small valley with some fine temples built by the Chands, it is overlooked by a hill fort, 7 km away, dating from times when the town was at the crossroads of trade routes. The district, separated from Almora in 1962, borders Nepal and Tibet and has a number of high peaks such as Nanda Devi East (7,434 m) and West (7,816 m), and offers trekking to many glaciers including **Milam, Namik Ralam** and **Panchuli**. See page 237 (no permit needed). There are good views from Chandak Hill 7 km away at 1,890 m. It is on the Pilgrim road to **Mount Kailash** and **Mansarovar Lake**. The Mount Kailash trek (Indian nationals only) starts from Askot. *Saur Adventure Club* is in Simalgher Bazar. The place is known for its fine gold and silver jewellery and bowls carved out of *sal* wood.

Listings: Nainital

◉ Sleeping

Nainital *p245, map p246*
Peak rates (given here) can be high. Good off-season discounts are usual but may mean inadequate heating.
AL-A Manu Maharani, Grasmere, near Display Garden, T37341, F37350, vivekb@ nde.vsnl.net.in. 66 modern rooms, good views.
A Naini Retreat (Claridges), Ayarpattha Slopes, 2 km from Mallital Bazar, T35105, F35103. 34 rooms, good restaurant, "excellent quality, service and location".

A Shervani Hilltop Inn, Waverly Rd, T36304. 21 rooms in old royal home, some in cottages, peaceful, lovely garden, free jeep to centre.
A-B Balarampur House, Mallital, T36236, travcon.holidays@vsnl.com. 10 well-furnished rooms in a royal summer retreat converted to a luxury hotel, pleasant location.
A-B Vikram Vintage Inn, near ATI, Mallital, T36179, F36117. 36 large, comfortable rooms, quiet wooded area but not all facilities (no pool).
B Belvedere (WelcomHeritage), above *Bank of Baroda*, Mallital, T37434, F35082,

www.welcomheritage.com. 22 comfortable large rooms (good value family suite) with good lake views, in former Raja's summer palace – a colonial building with pleasant garden, restaurant, well located, quiet, friendly owners, helpful staff.

B-D Classic, The Mall, T45173, F37704, www.newagehotelsandresorts.com. 25 pleasant rooms some with balcony, good restaurant, yoga.

C Alka, The Mall, Tallital, T35220, F36629, www.alkahotel.com, and separate **Annexe** (closed in winter) nearby. 72 well-appointed, lake facing rooms, central heating, jungle theme, seasonal floating restaurant (good Indian). Recommended.

C Grand, The Mall, near Flatties Rock, T35406. 31 basic but clean rooms, colonial style but faded, good food served on lake-facing verandah (order 3 hrs in advance), family run, friendly, good service. Recommended.

C-D Prince, The Mall, T36817. 18 small, but comfortable rooms, decent room service.

C-F Sarovar, near Tallital Bus Stand, T35570. 30 (**C**) rooms, 8-bed dorms (Rs 40), hot water, good value.

D Silverton, Sher-ka-Danda, 2½ km centre, T35249. 27 rooms in 'chalets', some with good views, peaceful, veg restaurant.

D-E KMVN Rest Houses are good value outside May to mid-Jul.

E-F Mount View Naina, near Sukhatal Bus Stand, T35400. 42 small, grubby rooms with bath, some with TV, restaurant, dorm (Rs 20), gardens, good value.

F Youth Hostel, west of Mallital Bazar, T36353. 5 and 8-bed dorms, open to non-members (Rs 25), cheap meals, quiet, good, book 15 days ahead.

Ropeway Rest House, Snow View, T35772. Rooms with bath.

Sat Tal *p247*

C Sat Tal Camp, with pyramid tents, kayaking, mountain biking, rock climbing.
E Damayanti, with 4 rooms.

Naukuchiyatal *p247*

B-C Lake Side, T47138. Well maintained and attractive. Rooms and dorm (Rs 46-60).

Pangot *p247*

B-C Jungle Lore Lodge, has a cottage and hut with baths, 2 tents with shared facilities, meals included (from home-grown produce), library. Contact *Asian Adventures*, T0120-4524874, www.asianadventures.com.

Jeolikote *p247*

B Cottage, nestled on the hillside, T44413. Swiss chalet-style, has 3 beautiful spacious rooms with good valley views, meals included. Highly recommended.

Almora *p248*

Most hotels give off-season discount of 50%.
B-E Shikhar, Mall Rd, near bus stand, T30253, F31734, jsbisht@nde.vsnl.net.in. 55 rooms (vary widely), some with hot bath, good restaurant, fairly clean.

C-D Himsagar, Mall Rd, T30711, F30439. 18 comfortable rooms, best with view, hot water, TV, friendly.

D Savoy, above the GPO, T30329. 17 good sized but basic rooms, some with hot bath, restaurant, pleasant terrace and quiet garden.

D Snow View. 15 rooms, some in cottages.

D-E Holiday Home (KMVN), 2 km southwest of bus stand, T30250. 14 simple cottages and 18 rooms with hot bath, dorm (Rs 60), restaurant, garden, good mountain views.

D-E Konark, Mall Rd, T31217. 13 clean rooms, TV, hot water in mornings, good views.

E Shyam, L R Shah Road, T35467, F34113, shyam2@nde.vsnl.net.in. 18 small but clean rooms, good terrace views.

F Kailas, up path opposite GPO, Mall Rd, T30624, F30100, jawaharlalsah@India.com. 24 rooms all under Rs 100. "Weird and wonderful décor" of Mr Shah. Gloomy, dirty and poor food.

Jageswar *p248*

D-E Jagnath (KMVN) at Jageswar, has rooms, dorm (Rs 60) and a restaurant.

Binsar *p248*

B Binsar Valley Resort, T0177-480169, just outside the sanctuary, with 9 rooms in cottages, pleasant, clean, in spacious grounds, good food, exceptional service, good riding, river fishing and trekking, family run.

⬤ *For an explanation of the sleeping and eating price codes used in this guide, see inside the*
⬤ *front cover. Other relevant information is found in Essentials pages 52-57.*

D Nanda Devi, in the heart of the sanctuary, T51110. Only filtered rainwater, electricity from solar batteries for few hours each evening.
Forest Rest House, on a thickly wooded spur near *Nanda Devi*, 1920s with 1930s cutlery and table linen lists still hanging on the walls! The furniture and décor are evocative of the Raj, and the caretaker may occasionally be persuaded to open the house for a few hours or for viewing.

Anashakti Ashram *p248*
B-D Krishna Mountview, near Gandhi Ashram, with 30 smart rooms, some with good views, fine location, credit cards accepted.
D-F Trishul, 2 km from town, with 6 basic cottages and dorm, restaurant, compass on the lawn to spot the peaks.
F Uttarkhand Tourist Lodge (View Point), near bus stand. Excellent value.

Baijnath *p249*
E Tourist Bungalow and Inspection House.

Bageshwar *p249*
C Wayfarer Retreat, 13 km before Chaukori
E Bagnath, 20 rooms, where you can hire trekking equipment, restaurant.

Munsiari *p249*
C Wayfarer Mountain Resort, 1 km beyond town. Comfortable Swiss tents, toilets, electricity, phone, Rs 1,200 including meals, forest walks, treks, trout fishing jeeps, professionally run, contact *Asian Adventures*, T011-8524874, wildtours@vsnl.com.
D Tourist Rest House, main road just before the town. Comfortable, welcome hot showers, good value; also 2 other cheap lodges.

Pithorgarh *p249*
C Rhythm Camp, spacious tents with baths, meals included, views of valleys and peaks, T/F011-626292.
D-E Ulka Devi, T22434, with restaurant. Others near the bus station are very basic.

Eating

Nainital *p245, map p246*
Most restaurants are at the north of the lake, on the Mall. Some have a limited off-season menu.

Kwality, on the lake. Western and good Indian. Ideally located.
Machan, The Mall. Good Indian/Chinese and pizzas.
Sakley, The Mall, near GPO. Western dishes and confectionery.
Sher-e-Punjab, Mallital Bazar. Tasty, North Indian. Another half way to Tallital, with one serving very good local Kumaon dishes.

Vegetarian
Kumaon Farm Products, towards Ropeway, is good for snacks.
Nanak serves Western fast food.
Purohit, The Mall, opposite Kwality. Recommended for *thalis*.

Almora *p248*
Plenty of choice along the busy Mall Rd.
$$ Glory, good North Indian, but a bit pricey.
$ Madras Café, beyond the bus stand. Good Indian meals and snacks.

Anashakti Ashram *p248*
Hill Queen, above *Uttarkhand Tourist Lodge*, serves reasonably priced meals.

Festivals and events

Almora *p248*
Dasara is celebrated with colourful Ramlila pageants. Kumaon Festival of Arts.

Shopping

Nainital *p245, map p246*
Bazars sell local woollens and candles at Tallital and Mallital. Also souvenir shops on the Mall, Mallital, including **UP Handlooms**, Gandhi Ashram. Along the far edges of the Flats, Tibetan refugees sell wool and acrylic shawls; you can try steaming *momos* at a stall!
Kumaon Woollens, Mallital Bazar has locally made tweed – see also Almora, below.
Narain's Bookshop, The Mall (below *Grand Hotel*). A good selection.

Almora *p248*
Ashok Traders, LR Shah Rd, sells local copper articles.
Kumaon Woollens, just above the *KMVN Holiday Home*. Produces and sells 'Harris'

type tweed. Locally knitted jumpers and the traditional Panchmarhi shawls ('five weave') in soft wool are popular.

Photography
Sangam, Mall Road, opposite GPO. Slide, black and white films, lithium batteries available.

▲▲ Activities and tours

Nainital *p245, map p246*
Boating
Boat hire: peddle or sail on the lake, Rs 80 per hr; up and down Rs 60; pedal boat Rs 40.

Fishing
Permits for Nainital Lake from Executive Officer, Nagar Palika. For other lakes Fisheries Officer, Bhimtal. Boat hire from Boat Club, Mallital.

Mountaineering and trekking
Equipment can be hired from **Nainital Mountaineering Club**, T2051, and **KMVN**, Tourist Office, Mallital. The Club organizes rock climbing at Barapathar, 3 km away.

Pony hire
Snow View, Rs 40; Tiffin Top Rs 60; Naina (Chinna) Peak, Rs 150 (2½-3 hrs; can leave at 0500 to see sunrise from the top, but dress warmly); Naina Devi, Rs 30; horses are generally fit and well cared for. Horse Stand in Mallital, opposite *State Bank of India*.

Tour companies
Parvat Tours & Information (KMVN), Dandi House, Tallital, near Rickshaw Stand, T35656, among others on the Mall. Charges about Rs 80 per day; Bhimtal, half day. Day tours: Sat tal; Ranikhet; Mukteshwar (with the Veterinary Research Centre); Kaladhungi. 2-day trips: Kausani; Ranikhet/Almora; Corbett.
Vibgyor, 56 Tallital Bazar, T/F35806.

Munsiari *p249*
The *Nanda Devi Mountaineering Institution*, is in the SBI Building.
   In the main bazar is *Panchuli Trekking* and *Nanda Devi Trekking*, the former run by an elderly Milam tribal villager who has vast and accurate knowledge of the area.

Almora *p248*
Tour companies
High Adventure, Mall Rd opposite Post Office, T32277, F31734. Organizes treks, cave tours, bus tickets.

⊖ Transport

Nainital *p245, map p246*
Wherever possible, avoid night driving. The hill roads can be dangerous. Flat, straight stretches are rare, road lighting does not exist and villagers frequently drive their animals along them or graze them at the kerbside. During the monsoon (Jun-Sep) landslips are fairly common. Usually these are cleared promptly but in the case of severe slips requiring days to clear, bus passengers are transferred.
   Mall Road: Access toll Rs 50. Access barred, May, Jun, Oct: heavy vehicles, 0800-1130, 1430-2230; light vehicles, 1800-2200; Nov-Apr: all vehicles, 1800-2000.

Air
The nearest airport is Pantnagar (71 km) on the plains (flights suspended). **Parvat Tours** transfer coaches to Nainital (2 hrs). Open 1000-1600.

Bus
Long distance **UP Roadways**, Tallital, for major inter-city services, T35518, 0930-1200, 1230-1700; **DTC**, *Hotel Ashok*, Tallital, T35180. **Kumaon Motor Owners' Union** (KMOU), bus stand near Tourist Office, Sukhatal, Mallital, T35451; used by private operators. Regular services to **Almora** (66 km, 3 hrs); **Dehra Dun** (390 km); **Delhi** (322 km), a/c night coach, 2100 (Rs 250, 8-9 hrs), or via Haldwani. **Haridwar** (390 km, 8 hrs); **Kausani** (120 km, 5 hrs); **Ranikhet** (60 km, 3 hrs) and **Ramnagar** for Corbett (66 km, 3½ hrs plus 3½ hrs)

Rickshaw
Cycle-rickshaw and **dandi**: about Rs 5-10 along The Mall.

Ropeway
Cable-car/gondola, T35772, from 'Poplars', Mallital (near GB Pant Statue) to Snow View, summer 0700-1900 in theory, but usually opens at 1000, winter 1000-1600, return fare Rs 50, advance booking recommended in season, tickets valid for a 1-hr halt at the top. Some claim its anchorage is weak.

Taxi
From **Parvat Tours**, Tallital, T35656. Full day Rs 650 (120 km).

Train
All India computerised reservation office, Tallital Bus Stand, T35518. Mon-Fri, 0900-1200, 1400-1700, Sat, 0900-1200. The nearest railhead is **Kathgodam** (35 km), taxi, Rs 350 (peak season). **Delhi (OD)**: *Ranikhet Exp, 5014*, 2040, 8 hrs. Towards **Dehradun and Haridwar (OD)**: *Dehradun-Kathgodam Exp, 4321*, 2230, 9 hrs. **Kolkata (H) via Lucknow and Gorakhpur**, *Howrah Bagh Exp, 3020*, 1930, 64½ hrs. An alternative for **Lucknow** is the *Nainital Exp, 5307*, 2050, 9¼ hrs from **Lalkuan**, south of Kathgodam.

Almora *p248*
Bus
Connect Almora with **Kathgodam** (90 km, 3 hrs) for **rail** links, and with **Nainital** (3 hrs) and **Ranikhet** (2½ hrs). Hourly buses to **Kausani** (3 hrs). Direct buses go to **Banbassa** and the Nepal border, depart 0730 (6 hrs).

Jeep
Share jeeps to **Ranikhet**, Rs 35. For **Nainital**, take **Haldwani** jeep as far as **Bhowali**, then bus or jeep to Nainital.

❶ Directory

Nainital *p245, map p246*
Banks In Mallital: Bank of Baroda, below *Belvedere Hotel*. For cash against Visa card. State Bank of India for exchange.
Hospital BD Pande Govt Hospital, Mallital, T35012350. **Internet** Not much choice. Try Cyberia, The Mall, near ropeway. Reasonably reliable connection if a bit pricy at Rs 2/min.
Library The Library, The Mall, by the lake. Open weekdays (closed mid-morning to mid-afternoon). Pleasant for dropping in.
Post office Mallital. Branch at Tallital.
Tourist offices KMVN: Information Centre, at *Parvat Tours*; at Secretariat, Mallital, T/F36209. Uttaranchal, Mall Rd, Mallital, T35337. Tourist Bungalow, T35400. **Useful addresses** Ambulance: T35022. Fire: T35626. Police: T35424 (Mallital), T35525 (Tallital).

Almora *p248*
Banks State Bank of India, Mall Road. May change Amex TCs, but don't rely on this. Best to change in advance. **Hospitals** District Hospital, Chowk Bazar, T30322. **Post office** GPO on Mall Rd. **Tourist offices** KMVN, at Holiday Home, and **Uttaranchal**, opposite GPO, T30180. 1000-1700.

(right margin, vertical) Uttaranchal Corbett National Park

★ Corbett National Park

→ *Phone code: 05945. Colour map 1, grid C5. Altitude: 400-1,200 m*
The journey from Delhi to one of the finest wildlife parks in India offers excellent views of the almost flat, fertile and densely populated Ganga-Yamuna doab, one of the most prosperous agricultural regions of North India. Corbett is India's first national park and one of its finest. It is notable not only for its rich and varied wildlife and birdlife but also for its scenic charm and magnificent sub-montane and riverain views.
▸ *For Sleeping, Eating and other listings, see pages 256-258.*

Entry

Foreigners Rs 350, Indians Rs 30. Entrance permit for Dhikala is valid for 3 days (2 nights), each additional day, Rs 175, Indians Rs 20. Otherwise permit is valid for a single visit each time the park is entered. Entrance permits are not transferable between gates (eg a morning visit to Bijrani and a night halt at Dhikala will entail payment of all entrance fees on both occasions). Car/jeep Rs 100 plus Rs 30 for driver. All visitors in cars or jeeps must have a guide, Rs 100 for the first 4 hrs plus Rs 20 for each additional hour at Dhikala. In Bijrani, these fees are Rs 75 and Rs 15 respectively. Camera and video fees have been dropped. See Transport, page 258, for further details.

Access

Day visits are allowed by entry at the Amdanda and Laldhang Gates for Bijrani and Jhirna respectively. A limit of 40 vehicles per day at each entrance is applied. Prior reservation to enter is recommended for day visits, although not always necessary at dawn, when entry is determined on a first-come-first-served basis. You may be refused entry when the quota is filled. The main gate at Dhangarhi (for Dhikala) is approximately 16 km north of Ramnagar on the Ranikhet road. There is no entry to the park from the Kalagarh side. From 1 Mar until the monsoon all roads around Dhikala, except the main approach road, are closed between 1100-1500 when visitors are not allowed to move about the forest. A reservation at the Bijrani or Dhela *Forest Rest Houses* does not entitle visitors to enter by the Dhangari gate. Only visitors who are staying overnight may enter Dhikala. Closed 15 June-15 November.

Climate

Rainfall is heavier in the higher hills, on average the valley receives 1,550 mm, the bulk from Jul to mid-Sep. Summer days are hot but the nights quite pleasant. Winter nights can get very cold and there is often a frost and freezing fog in the low lying tracts. Jan to mid-Jun; for birdwatching, Dec-Feb. Summer is the best time for seeing the larger mammals which are bolder in leaving the forest cover to come to the river and water holes; early summer for scenic charm and floral interest. Closed 15 Jun-15 Nov.

Wildlife

The park has always been noted for its **tigers**; there are around 80 but they are not easily spotted. About 10% of visitors see one – usually entering at the Bijrani gate. There are leopards too but they are seldom seen. Sambar, chital, para (hog deer) and muntjac (barking deer) are the main prey of the big cats and their population fluctuates around 20,000. Some like the chital are highly gregarious whilst the large sambar, visually very impressive with its antlers, is usually solitary. The two commonly seen monkeys of North India are the rhesus (a macaque – reddish face and brownish body) and the common langur (black face and silvery coat). Elephants are now permanent inhabitants since the Ramganga Dam has flooded their old trekking routes. There are now a few hundred and they are seen quite often. Other animals include porcupine, wild boar (often seen around Dhikala) – some can be quite dangerous, attacking unsuspecting visitors who have food with them. In total there are over 50 species of mammal alone, though the dam appears to have caused significant losses. The last Swamp deer was seen in March 1978, and the loss of habitat has been keenly felt by the cheetal, hog deer and porcupine, all of which appear to be declining.

There are 26 species of reptiles and seven of amphibians. In certain stretches of the river and in the Ramganga Lake are the common mugger crocodile, notice prohibits swimming – "Survivors will be prosecuted"!), the fish eating gharial, soft shelled tortoises in the streams, otters and river fish. The python is quite common.

The birdlife is especially impressive with over 600 species and this includes a wide range of water birds, birds of prey such as the crested serpent eagle, harriers, Pallas' fishing eagle, osprey, buzzards and vultures. Woodland birds include: Indian and Great Pied hornbills, parakeets, laughing thrushes, babblers and cuckoos. Doves, bee-eaters, rollers, bulbuls, warblers, finches, robins and chats are to be seen in the open scrub from the viewing towers. The rarer ibis bill is one of the main attractions for serious twitchers.

Vegetation

There are 110 species of trees, 51 species of shrubs, three species of bamboos and 27 species of climbers. The valley floor is covered with tall elephant grass (*Nall* in the local terminology), lantana bushes and patches of *sal* and *sheesham* (*Dalbergia*

☷ Tiger, tiger, burning bright ...

Jim Corbett was born in 1875 into the large family of the postmaster at Nainital. From childhood he was fascinated by the jungles around Nainital. This developed into a considerable knowledge of the ecosystem's workings. He became a superb shot, killing his first leopard when he was eight. Tigers were his most sought after prey, followed by leopards which were difficult to sight, let alone shoot.

He continued to hunt during his working life in the Bengal Northeast Railway and later as an advisor to the army. But from the mid-1920s he turned to photography, tracking and killing only the man-eating leopards and tigers that terrorized the Kumaon hills from time to time. Later in life he recounted his exploits in a series of books about man-eaters and the jungle: *The Man-Eating Leopard of Rudrapayag*, *The Man-eaters of Kumaon* and *Jungle Lore*. For a biography of Corbett see *Carpet Sahib: The life of Jim Corbett* by Martin Booth.

Jim Corbett has always been an inspiration to India's conservationists. On 1 April 1973 Project Tiger was inaugurated in nine parks, the aim being to preserve the rapidly dwindling population of tigers in India. The scheme was later extended to over 18 reserves.

sissoo) forest, whilst the enclosing hills on both sides are completely forest covered, with *sal*, *bakli*, *khair*, *jhingan*, *tendu*, *pula* and *sain*. *Charas* grows wild in the fields. Nullahs and ravines running deep into the forests are dry for much of the year, but there are swift torrents during the monsoon. These hold brakes of bamboo and thick scrub growth.

Viewing

Elephant rides are available from Dhikala where there are about five animals, and three at Bijrani. Each elephant can carry four people. This is the best way to see the jungle and the wildlife. Morning and evening, two hours, Rs 200 per person (foreigner), Rs 100 (Indian); book at Dhikala or Bijrani Reception (whichever is relevant). Book as early as possible on arrival since these rides are very popular. **Cars** and **jeeps** may drive round part of the park. Check with Reception. Jeep safari (up to six persons), two to four hours, Rs 500; day hire Rs 800-1000 (negotiable) from Ramnagar. Apart from the immediate area within the complex at Dhikala, **don't go walking in the park**. Tiger and elephant attacks are not unknown. The two watch towers are good vantage points for spotting wildlife. Night driving is not allowed in the park.

Ramnagar

Ramnagar, with a railway station, 134 km from Moradabad, is 18 km from the Park boundary and 50 km from **Dhikala**. It is a noisy town with the Project Tiger for Corbett reservations, and provides a night halt. They will receive faxes and hold them.

Kaladhungi

At Kaladhungi visit **Jim Corbett's house**, now a small museum, Rs 10. The area is an extension of the Tiger Reserve with equally good wildlife but minus the restrictions, and is also excellent for bird watching. If you turn up the road opposite and continue up into the hills, travelling along a delightful, metalled road that winds its way up the hillsides through *chir* pine forest and the occasional village, with impressive views of the plains. You enter Nainital at the north end of the lake.

Ranikhet → *Phone code: 05966. Colour map 1, grid C5.*

Rani Padmadevi, the queen of Raja Sudhardev is believed to have chosen this scenic place, hence Ranikhet (The Queen's Field). In 1869 the land was bought from local villagers and the British established a summer rest and recreation settlement for their troops, made it a cantonment town and developed it as a quiet hill station. Set along a 1,800 m high ridge, Ranikhet sprawls out through the surrounding forest without having a proper centre. This is one of its attractions and there are many enjoyable walks. The views from the ridge are magnificent and the twin peaks of Nanda Devi (7,816 m and 7,434 m) can be clearly seen. At **Upat**, 6 km away, there is a beautifully located nine-hole golf course and a Kali temple.

Listings: Corbett National Park

🛌 Sleeping

Corbett National Park *p253*

If you are travelling to the park without reserved accommodation, you must go to Ramnagar first to make a booking, see page 255. Dhikala is the park centre and has accommodation. Remember to get a clearance card from Dhikala from the office here before leaving in the morning. There is a decent restaurant (big portions). Also a small *dhaba* with cheaper food and basic necessities (biscuits, chocolate, soap etc).

Within the park

Reservations for all accommodation, except

Corbett National Park

Sleeping ■
1 Cabins, Forest Rest Houses, Tourist
2 Corbett Hideaway (Claridge's)
3 Corbett Jungle
Hutments & Loghuts
Resort (Quality Inn)
4 Corbett Ramganga Resort
5 Corbett Riverside Resort
5 Govind
6 KMVN Lodge

Annexe and Cabin 3 at Dhikala, can be booked at the Reception Centre in Ramnagar. The exceptions can at present only be booked in the UP/Uttaranchal Tourist Office in Delhi. Small quotas are also available from the Park office in Dehra Dun. Enquiries: The Director, Corbett Tiger Reserve Reception Centre, T05947-51489, F51376. Open 7 days a week, 0830-1300, 1500-1700. Foreigners pay about 3 times more than Indians. Entry permits and vehicle charges are payable at the respective gate. However, early booking is recommended in season and at weekends and holidays as the park is very popular and easily accessible from Delhi.

Dhikala:
B Old Forest Rest House, 5 suites (Rs 1500).
C Annexe, 7 rooms (Rs 900) (Rs 900) can only be reserved at UP Tourist Office, Delhi, T3322251 (see above).
C Cabin 1 and 4, 3 suites each (Rs 900).
C Cabin 3 with 2 suites (Rs 900) can only be reserved at UP Tourist Office, Delhi, T3322251 (see above).
C New Forest Rest House, 4 suites (Rs 900).
D Tourist Hutment, 6 3-bed suites (Rs 700).
F Loghuts, 24 bunks (Rs 100), separated into Indian and foreigner sections, but not noise-proof! Bedding is available, Rs 25. The restaurant is good with wonderful views, is reasonably priced but has limited choice.

A small dhaba provides a cheaper option.

Outside the park
In top resorts, meals and guided visits are included in the price.
AL Tiger Tops Corbett Lodge (Infinity Resorts), T05947-51279, F85280, 8 km north of Ramnagar. 24 rooms, pool, lawns, mango orchards, good food, "unreconstructed, old world feel", charming staff.
A Call of the Wild, Betal Ghat (40 km from Ramnagar), T05942-35972. 16 rooms in four cottages in Shikar style, pool.
A Corbett Hideaway (Claridges), Garjia, above the river (10-min drive from gate), T87932, F87933. 30 upmarket lodges in orchard on riverside, 20 luxury tents, jeep transfer to park, good food, very good naturalist in Imran Khan, well run, own elephant for viewing, pool.
A Corbett Jungle Resort, Kumeria Reserve Forest, Mohan, T/F05947-51219, about 13 km from the Dhangarhi entrance, among mango and sal trees. 18 small cottages, imaginatively designed and built of natural materials, restaurant, elephant rides, jeeps, jungle walks, swimming in Kosi River, eco-friendly resort.
A Corbett Ramganga Resort, Jhamaria, 17 km from Dhangarhi, T011-4620981, F4640325, on the river. 10 well-appointed rooms in cottages, 8 Swiss cottage tents, safe spring water, river rafting, riding, rockclimbing and gliding, fishing (fighting fish in the river pools below), excellent pool and ground, friendly service, very picturesque position on the river edge.
A Tiger Camp, Dhikuli, T87901. 10 clean cottages (with 10 more to come) in Kumaoni Village style but modern interiors, rooms with fan and bath (**E**), tents (shared bath), electricity (plus generator), good food, lovely garden, jeep, hiking, friendly owner, recommended, contact *Asian Adventures*, Delhi, T0120-4524874, F4524878, tigercamp@indianwildlife.com.

Ramnagar detail
To Corbett
Reception Centre
STD/Fax
To Ranikhet
KUMERIA
Mohan
Main Park Entrance
Sultan
Dhangarhi
Café
Garjia
River Kosi
Bijrani
Amdanda Gate
Forest Rest House
Watch Tower
Ramnagar
To Haldwani
To Moradabad

Ramnagar *p255*
B-C Corbett Inn.
C-D KMVN Lodge.
E Govind, and 100 m down the road.
 Also cheap, basic **F** guest houses in town.

Kaladhungi *p255*
B Camp Corbett, 25 km east of Corbett, T42277, F35493. Cottages and tents, wonderful meals, an outstanding resort run by the hospitable Anand family, relaxing and totally hassle free, pick-up from Haldwani station arranged. Highly recommended.

Ranikhet *p256*
B Chevron Rosemount, The Mall (2 km centre), T20191. Refurbished old colonial building, stylish, croquet lawn, tennis.
B-D Parwati Inn, above bus stand, T20631, F20403. Good choice from 32 large rooms, restaurant, friendly staff, credit cards accepted, best in the town itself.
C-D Moon, Sadar Bazar, T20382. 14 clean rooms plus 2 (**B**) cottages, TV, restaurant.
C-D West View, MG Rd (5 km centre), T20261. 19 rooms in old fashioned hotel, restaurant, exchange, large grounds, golf club nearby.
D-E Himadri, Chilia naula, 7 km west, T205882. New unit next to the temple complex, rooms, dorm (Rs 50), restaurant.
D-E Kalika, T202972. Pleasant rooms with bath, some 'super deluxe', restaurant (mostly Indian), attractive location in the upper cantonment with good views.

▲ Activities and tours

Corbett National Park *p253, map p256*
Conducted tours
GMVN run 3-day tours from Delhi departing every Fri in season. Reservations: Uttar Pradesh Tourist Office, Chandralok Building, 36 Janpath, New Delhi, T3322251.

Tour operators
Mohit Agarwal, T011-91524874, wildindiatours@vsnl.com. Arranges jeep transfer, accommodation etc.
Tigerland Safaris, T05947-82122, www.tigerlandsafaris.com. Well-organised safaris, professional service. Recommended.

Wild Encounters, T011-6212720, wildencounters@rediffmail.com.

◉ Transport

Corbett National Park *p253, map p256*
Air
Phoolbagh airport at Pantnagar (130 km) has no flights at present.

Bus
The Delhi-Dhikala road (260 km) passes through Moradabad (turn left after Moradabad, towards Kashipur and Ramnagar), 5½-6 hrs – strewn with bus/lorry/car crashes.
 Bus to **Ramnagar**, 1000 from Dhikala (after elephant ride), from Ramnagar, 1530, Rs 43, not reliable; several from Kumeria, Rs 12; several to **Moradabad** and **Ranikhet** (wait outside Dhangarhi gate, no need to return to Ramnagar). Also buses to **Delhi** (6½-7 hrs), and Lucknow.

Jeep
From near Ramnagar Park office; to Dhikala (return), Rs 500 one way; Rs 600-800 return, plus driver fee (Rs 30).

Train
Nearest station is at Ramnagar (50 km), for **Moradabad** and **Delhi**. From Old Delhi railway station, *Corbett Park Link Exp*, *5016A*, 2245, 6 hrs; from Ramnagar, *5014A*, 2110, 7¼ hrs.

Ranikhet *p256*
Bus
Regular buses to **Ramnagar**, **Almora** and **Nainital** operated by KMOU, T20214, and UP Roadways (may change), T20516, with bus stands at each end of the Mall.

◉ Directory

Ranikhet *p256*
Banks State Bank of India, at the top end of The Mall. Changes Amex and Thomas Cook TCs only. **Hospital** Civil Hospital, near Bus Stand, T20422. **Post office** On The Mall. **Tourist office** Uttaranchal, The Mall, T20227. 1000-1700.

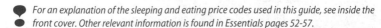
For an explanation of the sleeping and eating price codes used in this guide, see inside the front cover. Other relevant information is found in Essentials pages 52-57.

❖ Footprint features

Introduction

Madhya Pradesh and Chhattisgarh are at the heart of India. They contain many of the **tribal groups** least touched by modernization and most of India's remaining genuine forest. The magnificent paintings made in rock shelters at **Bhimbetka** illustrate the continuity of settlement for over half a million years, while Buddhism left a still visible mark in the glories of **Sanchi**'s 2,000-year old stupas. The magnificent palaces of **Orchha** and temples of **Khajuraho** testify to the power of Rajput dynasties for over a 1,000 years. Flowing westwards along the southern edge of the great Vindhyan ranges runs the **Narmada**, the site of one of the largest - and most controversial - dam development programmes in the world. Yet Madhya Pradesh remains largely unindustrialized and little visited, allowing the still dense forests and grasslands of the east to house two of India's best national parks at **Kanha** and **Bandhavgarh**.

On 1 November 2000 sixteen districts in the southeast of Madhya Pradesh were carved out to create the new state of Chhattisgarh. One of the least accessible areas of peninsular India, it is a largely tribal state.

★ Don't miss...

❶ Cross the river at **Orchha** and watch the sun go down behind the Royal Chhattris, page 286.

❷ Fancy the life of Reilly? Then imagine stopping the 'drinks' train on the Maharaja's dining table to fill your glass in the **Jai Vilas Palace**, Gwalior, page 280.

❸ Stay with the **Maharaja Vishwaraj Singh**, a real alternative to Rajasthan's palace circuit in the largely tribal state of Chhattisgarh, page 320.

❹ Relax and unwind at little visited **Sanchi**, one of the most important Buddhist sites in India, page 270.

❺ For something a little different at a temple, admire the erotic sculptures at **Khajuraho**, page 288.

❻ Marvel at the sheer size of **Mandu Fort**, with its 45 km parapet wall overlooking the sheer drop towards the Namar plains, page 306.

❼ If you've read *The Jungle Book*, the **Kanha National Park** is a must-visit destination, as the source of inspiration for Kipling, page 311.

Background → *Population: 60.39 million. Area: 308,000 sq km.*

The land

Madhya Pradesh has some magnificent scenery. The dominating **Vindhyan** mountains run diagonally across the heart of Madhya Pradesh while the Kaimur range runs to the north and east, overlooking the Gangetic plain around Varanasi and Allahabad. Both rise to 600 m but are frequently cut by deep forest-clad ravines. Behind the Kaimur range is the **Baghelkhand plateau** while the Hazaribagh range juts into the state in the east. The **Narmada** rising in the east, flows west to the Arabian Sea, along with the Tapti to its south. Black volcanic soils are often visible across the state, but in some places the land is stony and inhospitable. Between Gwalior and Jhansi the Chambal River has dug deep gorges, creating a *badlands* area which **dacoits** have enjoyed as hideouts.

Climate Most rainfall comes between June and September, increasing from about 1,000 mm in the west to 2,000 mm in the east. March-May is hot and dry, average maximum temperatures exceeding 33°C and often reaching 44°C. The average daily maximum during the monsoon is 30°C and the minimum 19°C, when the landscape turns green and places like Mandu are particularly attractive. Winters are dry and pleasant. The average daily maximum temperature from November to February is 27°C and the minimum 10°C.

History

Rock paintings and stone artefacts prove the existence of Stone Age cultures. Although the region was incorporated into successive states from the empire of Asoka to that of the Mughals, it was rarely the centre of a major power.

In the 10th century a number of dynasties controlled different parts of the region, most notably the Chandelas at Khajuraho. Gwalior was conquered by the Muslims in the 11th century, whose influence spread southeast under the Khaljis into Malwa during the 13th century. Akbar annexed this into his empire in the mid-16th century. The Scindia and Holkar Dynasties of Marathas ruled independently at Gwalior and Indore respectively during the 18th century.

Under the British the region became known as the Central Provinces and under the state re-organization after independence the modern state of Madhya Pradesh was created.

Culture

Even though the majority of the former state of Madhya Pradesh's tribal people now have their own state of Chhattisgarh, MP remains the home of many tribals, including Bhils, Gonds and Baigas. Many have been painfully absorbed into the mainstream of Indian life. Hindi is the most widely spoken language. On each of the borders the languages of neighbouring states – particularly Marathi and Gujarati in the west – are quite commonly used. The Bhils speak **Bhili** and the Gonds **Gondi**, independent in origin to the Indo-European and Dravidian language groups.

Textiles are important but Madhya Pradesh also has a strong traditional village handicraft industry. Handloom *Chanderi* and *Maheshwar* silks are especially sought after. The tribal population produce attractive handicrafts.

Modern Madhya Pradesh

With the exception of 1977 and 1989, the Congress Party has held a comfortable majority of the Assembly seats, though the **BJP** and its predecessors have always been strong. In the last Lok Sabha elections in 1998 MP elected 40 members to the Lok Sabha. The BJP won 30 seats to the Congress Party's 10, but the Congress

⁝ Tribal traditions

In the last hundred years the Baigas of Central India have been forced to abandon shifting cultivation in favour of settled agriculture. Traditionally semi-nomadic, most tribals have now been settled but liquor and drug dependency are said to be common among the men. Over the centuries, tribal territory has gradually been nibbled away, and everywhere their way of life is under threat.

The Gonds, the largest of the tribes, managed to maintain their independence until the last century. From 1200 AD there were as many as four Gond Kingdoms. Some tribal traditions, mythology and folklore have been preserved, though they have been exposed to outside cultural influences. Today one of the biggest threats to the tribals comes from the dams across the Narmada River which will flood vast tracts of tribal forest land.

retained its hold on the state legislature of 320 seats in elections at the end of 1998 with Digvijay Singh returning as Chief Minister. With the formation of Chhattisgarh the state legislative assembly lost 90 of its seats to the new state, reducing the total to 230, but the Congress retained a secure majority. 11 of Madhya Pradesh's members of the Lok Sabha now represent constituencies in Chhattisgarh, and these will represent the new state until the next Lok Sabha elections.

Under Digvijay Singh's leadership Madhya Pradesh has been one of the first states to tackle its huge Government overspend problem. His cut backs on government jobs produced a strong reaction from the opposition, but by June 2002 the policy had led MP to being one of the first states to return to financial surplus.

Central Madhya Pradesh

Bhopal → *Phone code: 0755. Colour map 2, grid C6. Population: 1,450,000.*

Situated round two artificial lakes and on gently rolling hills, parts of Bhopal, the state capital of Madhya Pradesh, have a spacious feel with some pleasant parks, ambitious royal palaces and modern public buildings. The busy and rather dirty core of the Old City with its large mosques, as well as the crowded commercial centre in the New Market area of TT Nagar beyond the lakes to the southwest, is less attractive.
▸▸ *For Sleeping, Eating and other listings, see pages 273-276.*

Ins and outs

Getting there Only 7 hrs by the *Shatabdi Express* train from Delhi, Bhopal is on the main line to South India. There are direct flights from Delhi, Gwalior and Bombay, and an extensive network of long distance buses. The long distance bus stand is on Hamidia Rd, the main hotel area. The airport is about 20 mins by bus from the town centre.

Getting around The town is quite spread out, and even from the Old City centre it takes about 15 mins to walk from the railway station to the bus station. Local buses go to all parts of town but the best bet is an auto-rickshaw. A surcharge will be charged to go to the Shamla Hills or other points on the edge of town. See Transport, page 275, for details.

History

Legend suggests that Bhopal stands on an 11th-century site created by Raja Bhoja, who is believed to have built a *pal* (dam) which created the lakes. The modern city was developed by **Dost Mohammad Khan**, one of Aurangzeb's Afghan governors, who planned to set out wide roads, adorn it with monuments and replant the gardens. After his death Bhopal remained almost an island state in Malwa. Loyal to the British throughout the 18th century, from 1857 until 1926, Bhopal was ruled by two Muslim women. It still retains a strong Muslim character. In 1984, the city hit international news headlines with the **Union Carbide** disaster when a poisonous gas escape killed and injured thousands of people.

Sights

In 1878 Shah Jahan Begum (ruled 1868-1901), began work on the pink **Taj-ul Masjid**, one of the largest mosques in India, but it was left unfinished for over a century. It is a striking sight, with three white domes, two massive minarets and an impressive hall with attractive pillars. Today it is used as a religious school (madrassa). The main Chote Talao entrance, which has steps, is closed, so enter by the Lall Market gate. The smaller **Jama Masjid** (1837) in the bazar, with its minarets topped by gold spikes, was built by Qudsia Begum and the **Moti Masjid** (1860, based on the Jama Masjid in Delhi), was built by her daughter, Sikander Begum. At the entrance to the Chowk in the old city area is **Shaukat Mahal**, designed by a Frenchman, combining Post-Renaissance and Gothic styles. Nearby is the **Sadar Manzil**, the Hall of Public Audience of the former rulers of Bhopal. South of the Lower Lake is the modern

Bhopal

To Islamnagar & Sanchi   To Delhi

To Indore & Airport

Idgah Hills

Berasia Rd

Chinola Rd

Taj-ul Masjid

Hamidia Rd

Graveyard

Hamidia Rd

A

Sadar Manzil

Mangalwar Rd

OLD CITY

Stadium

To Raisen

Imam Square

Chowk

Pol

Pulbogda Rd

Sultania Rd

Central Library

Upper Lake

Moti Masjid

Sultania Rd

Bhadbadha Rd

Bharat Bhavan & Café

Lower Lake

JAHANGIR ABAD

2

State Archaeological Museum

Sports Ground

Obaidullaganj Rd

Kamla Park Rd

Rabindra Bhavan, Apsara & Amaltha Restaurants

Jail Rd

Lake Drive Rd

1

Raj Bhavan

Arera Hill

T T NAGAR

Air India

Lakshmi Narayan Temple

5

To Boats

3

British Library

4

Main Rd No. 1

Vallabh Bhavan & Birla Museum

M P NAGAR

NEW MARKET

Shamla Hills

S

i

T T NAGAR

T T Nagar Rd

SHASTRI NAGAR

Main Rd No 2

CHAR IMLI

N

To Tribal Habitat Museum of Man

Main Rd No 3

To Bhojpur, Bhimbetka & Itarsi

Related map
A Hamidia Road, page 265

0 metres 700
0 yards 700

■ **Sleeping**
1 Jehan Numa Palace
2 Lake View Ashok

3 Palash (MP Tourism)
4 Panchanan (MP Tourism)
5 Residency & Amer Palace

Lakshmi Narayan (Birla) **Temple** (Vaishnavite), Arera Hills. There are good views from here and in the evening from Shamla Hills. There are pedalo and sailing boats for hire on the Upper Lake.

Museums

State Archaeological Museum ① *Banganga Rd, opposite Ravindra Bhawan, south of the Lower Lake, closed Mon, 1000-1700, camera Rs 2*, houses sculptures, antiquities and tribal handicrafts, stone sculptures in gallery grounds and an interesting collection of 87 small Jain bronzes of the Paramar period (12th century) from a single site in Dhar District. **Birla Museum** ① *closed Mon, 0900-1200, 1400-1700, Rs 3*, by the Lakshmi Narayan Temple, complements the former. Small collection of well-displayed rare sculptures (seventh to 12th centuries) in Siva, Vishnu and Devi galleries. **Bharat Bhawan** ① *1400-2000 Feb-Oct, 1300-1900 Nov-Jan, closed Mon, Rs 5*, a centre for creative and performing arts, is in the Shamla Hills. Designed by the Indian architect Charles Correa in unobtrusive low-rise buildings, it houses an impressive collection of rural and tribal arts, a modern art gallery, crafts gallery, print maker's studio, library and theatre for performing arts, and a café. **Tribal Habitat (Museum of Man)** ① *closed Mon, 1000-1800*, south of Shamla Hills, is an open-air permanent exhibition of tribal huts in typical settings from different parts of India showing details of interiors. A shop sells good tribal crafts.

Excursions

Islamnagar, 11 km from the town centre on a drive north past the former Union Carbide factory, is an attractive little oasis of calm in a tiny village. The palace at the heart of the gardens was built by Dost Mohammad Khan, the early Afghan ruler of Bhopal. The pavilion pillars are decorated with floral patterns. The two-storeyed Rani Mahal and the baths (*hammam*) of the Chaman Mahal can also still be seen. The gardens are lovingly tended by the elderly chowkidar who, despite his limited English, is a very helpful guide. The gate is normally locked but as the village is very small it is usually easy to find him.

> ⚑ *If you just have a day to spare, hire a car and visit Bhimbetka in the morning and Sanchi in the afternoon.*

A cluster of sites to the northeast of Bhopal – **Sanchi, Vidisha, Gyaraspur, the Udaygiri caves** and **Udaypur** – can be visited on a day trip, see page 270. Equally, **Bhimbetka** to the south can be combined with **Bhojpur** 28 km from Bhopal; see below.

Hamidia Road

→ *Colour map 2, grid C6. A 4-hr excursion by taxi from Bhopal to Bhojpur and Bhimbetka will cost Rs 500 round trip.*

Bhojpur is famous for its Siva temple, sometimes referred to as the 'Somnath of the North', and for its dams, a testimony to the crucial importance of irrigation water for agriculture in this region. Both the religious and civil functions implicit in these buildings owed their origin to the 11th-century Paramar king of Dhar, **Raja Bhoj** (1010-53), who was noted not only as a great builder but also as a scholar.

Bhojeshwar Temple is a simple square with sides of just over 20 m. Surmounted by a corbelled dome the lower doorposts are plain while the columns and upper sections inside are richly carved. Two ornamental figures guard the entrance. On a striking three-tiered sandstone platform over 6 m sq is a polished stone lingam 2.35-m high and nearly 6 m in circumference, the largest in India. The temple was never completed but the traditional medieval means of building the towering structures of great Hindu temples are still visible in the earth ramp, built as a temporary expedient to enable large stones to be raised to the height of the wall, yet in this case never cleared away. The gigantic patterns engraved on surrounding rocks, which are now protected by rails, suggest that the temple was part of a grand plan (note one of a Siva temple with pilgrims' footprints). Equally interesting are over 1,300 masons' marks that appear on and around the temple which would have been erased on completion. Stone masons can be seen working on site.

There is a white-washed **Jain shrine** nearby, behind a modern community centre, which encloses a 6-m high black statue of a Tirthankara flanked by two smaller ones. The inscription on the pedestal uses 11th-century script. A caretaker holds the keys.

The huge lake to the west once created by two massive stone and earth dams, has now disappeared. Built between two hills, the Cyclopean dams were up to 100 m wide at the base and retained a lake of over 700 sq km, but in 1430 Hoshang Shah of Malwa demolished the dams. The Gonds believe that it took three years to drain, and that the local climate underwent a major change as a result of its drying out.

★ Bhimbetka Hill

→ *Colour map 2, grid C6. Enthusiasts and some visitors have found the site disappointing.*
ⓘ *From Bhopal, take the Hoshangabad bus and ask to be dropped at the Bhimbetka turning (the caves are a 3-km walk). You may get a lift from a truck along the main road to Bhojpur. Alternatively, from Bhopal take a bus to Obaidullaganj, 7 km north of the Bhimbetka turning, and hire a bicycle there. There is no obvious signpost in English to Bhimbetka on the main road. At a Hindi sign (on the left), a lane turns right with a railway crossing immediately after the turn. The caves are to the right, off this lane. A taxi from Bhopal is the easiest way to visit the caves and Bhojpur temple.*

Bhimbetka has South Asia's richest collection of prehistoric paintings and many other archaeological discoveries. The site was discovered by VS Wakanker of the Vikram University, Ujjain, in 1957. In the middle of a dense deciduous forest, there are over 30 species of trees with edible fruit, flower seeds and tubers – a vital food for tribal people even today. You may notice teak and *tendu*, the latter harvested in May and June to make *bidis* for smoking. The area is also rich in wildlife including several species of deer, wild boar, sloth bear, antelope, leopard, jackal, scaly anteater and many birds. Perennial springs provide the essential year-round water supply. This is the setting for a total of more than 1,000 shelters which were occupied from the early Stone Age to the late Stone Age perhaps less than 2,000 years ago.

Dating of the occupation is far from complete. In the bottom layers of the settlement sequence were a few pebble tools. There was a thin layer of bare material above this, followed by a thick layer of **Acheulian deposits**. Over 2½ m of accumulated material were excavated in Cave III F-23 for example, bringing to light successive floors paved with stone

and large quantities of stone implements that were clearly being made in the cave.
This period is dominated by flake tools – blades, scrapers, cleavers and handaxes.
Some of the core tools, often beautifully executed, were found to weigh up to 40 kg.

This level is followed in many caves by **Middle Palaeolithic** materials (approximately
40,000-12,000 BC), suggesting that this culture developed on the same site out of the
preceding Acheulian culture. The same raw materials are used, although the tools are
generally smaller. The **Upper Palaeolithic** period (approximately 12,000-5500 BC) was
even shorter than the Middle, again growing out of it. Short thin blades made their
appearance for the first time. It was in the **Mesolithic period**, immediately following the
Upper Palaeolithic, that the largest number of caves were occupied. A Ghosh suggests
that during this period there was a huge increase in population and some of the cave
paintings can be correlated with this period. There may have been improvement in the
climate, although there is evidence for climatic change even within the Mesolithic
period, which at Bhimbetka has been Carbon-14 dated as running from 5500-1000 BC.
A brand new technology was introduced. Tiny stone tools – microliths – were made:
knives, arrow heads, spearheads and sickles. Hard, fine-grained rocks like chert and
chalcedony were the basic material. The raw materials for the new industry had to be
brought in – the nearest source is near Barkhera, 7 km to the southeast. The dead were
buried in caves still occupied by the living, usually, though not always, in a crouched
position with the head to the east. Grave goods like antlers and stone tools were buried
alongside them. In the middle level of the deposits are copper tools and pottery. The
site seems to have been largely deserted by the end of the first millennium BC. Several
circular structures on the hills around have been interpreted as much later stupas, a
view supported by Asokan inscription, found 20 km west of Bhimbetka.

The caves By far the most striking remains today, however, are the paintings
covering walls and ceilings in over 500 shelters and in rocky hollows. Some are quite
small, while some are as much as 10 m long. Red and white are the dominant colours
used, but green and occasionally yellow are also found. These were obtained from
manganese, haematite, soft red stone and charcoal, sometimes combined with
animal fat and leaf extract. The site has been enclosed to allow visitors to be taken
around nine representative caves by Archaeological Survey guides during daylight
hours. The tour along a well-made path linking the major
shelters takes about 45 minutes; allow longer if you wish to
explore independently (there are about 130 caves along 4 km).
The caretaker will expect a small tip. There are plans to provide a
proper car park, picnic area and water supply with UNCF help.
The **paintings** belong to three periods. The Upper Palaeolithic
paintings, usually in white, dark red and green lines, depict large
animals, eg bison, rhinoceros and tiger. The Mesolithic figures

*Take water if hot; there
are no facilities. The area is
often virtually deserted
and it is not easy to find
specific caves with
worthwhile paintings
outside the enclosure.*

and animals, usually in red, are smaller but they lose their proportions and
naturalism. Hunting is a common theme - 'stick men' appear; they are shown
grazing, riding and hunting animals, dancing in groups. Women are sometimes seen
with a child or appear pregnant. The later period, probably dating from the early
centuries AD when green and yellow colours are also used, is quite different, showing
battle scenes with men riding on elephants and horses, holding spears, shields,
bows and arrows. Religious symbols, Ganesh and Siva, trees and flowers also
appear. Some shelters were used over several periods and you can spot interesting
details: Auditorium 3 has deer, peacock, leopard, old men and dancers; Rock Shelter
1 shows two elephants and a nilgai; No 8 has a garlanded king on horseback with
hunters and a cheetah; No 9 has a flower pot, elephant and an old man; No 10 shows
Ganesh, Siva lingam and a tree; No 7, stylized hunters on horseback based on simple
crosses; No 6, drummer, group dancers, tree roots and branches, bisons.

Barkhera 7 km southeast of Bhimbetka, Barkhera is one of the richest open air Stone Age sites in South Asia. On the southern edge of the road there are thousands of Acheulian tools scattered in the thick teak forest, and fields to the north of the road are equally rich in tools. Today there is little of interest to see around the tiny market town.

★ Pachmarhi

→ *Phone code: 07578. Colour map 3, grid C1. Population: 11,300. Altitude: 1,100 m.*

Pachmarhi is one of the most beautiful and friendly hill stations in Central India and rarely sees Western visitors. Except at the height of summer, the air remains pleasantly fresh and cool. The massive iron-rich sandstones which rise steeply from the trough of the Narmada Valley floor to form the Satpura Ranges offer plenty of scope for quiet, wooded walks, with several view points, waterfalls, rock pools and hills to climb within easy reach. The Gondwana series, known locally as Pachmarhi sandstones, are rich in plant fossils, notably of ferns. The area is also known for its ancient cave paintings.

Ins and outs Getting there Pachmarhi can easily be reached by bus in about 6 hrs. It is similarly accessible from Nagpur. Piparia (see below), between Jabalpur and Itarsi, is the nearest railway station. **Getting around** The town is pleasant to walk around, most hotels being either near the bus stand or in the bazar. You can share a jeep to the major points of interest. See Transport, page 276, for further details.

History In 1857 Captain Forsyth of the Bengal Lancers 'discovered' the spot on which Pachmarhi came to be built. He was said to have headed a column of troops but in fact was accompanied by just two others. The beautiful landscape of the plateau of the Satpura range impressed him with its tranquil forests of wild bamboo, *sal*, *yamun*, *amla* and *gular* trees, interspersed with deep pools fed by the streams that ran across the iron-stained sandstone hills. Later, the British developed Pachmarhi as a military sanatorium and hot weather resort.

Pachmarhi

Related map
A Pachmarhi centre, page 269

N

0 km   1
0 miles   1

■ **Sleeping**
1 Holiday Homes
2 Nandan Van
3 Nilambar
4 Panchvati Cottages
5 Rock End Manor
6 Satpura Retreat

The **Panch Pandav** 'caves', walking south from the bus stand beyond the
Cantonment, are believed to have sheltered Buddhist monks in the first century BC; a
fact confirmed by the recent discovery of the remains of a stupa from this period (6 m
in circumference) at the caves. There are several delightful spots nearby. The small
natural bathing pool **Apsara Vihar** is along a path to the left. The pool has a broad
shallow edge, suitable for children to paddle. There is a short scramble from there to
the top of **Rajat Pratap**, the 'big fall', over 110 m high.

There are other falls on the river which make attractive outings, including
Jalwataran (Duchess Fall), 3 km along the path from Belle Vue. It is a strenuous 4-km
walk to the base of the first cascade, perhaps the most attractive in Pachmarhi.

The square-topped hill at **Chauragarh**, on the southern edge of the Pachmarhi
plateau, is 10 km away. You follow the road past *Satpura Retreat* and head south.
Priyadarshini Point, on the way, from which Captain Forsyth is said to have first set
eyes on the Pachmarhi region, still gives a commanding view over the town and the
region. You can look back at the **Handi Khoh** ravine from this vantage point. The
ridge-top temple draws crowds of tribals and pilgrims for *Sivaratri* in February-March.
It may owe its sanctity to the remarkable spring which flows out of the Cave of
Mahadeo nearly 100 m inside the hillside. The temple is reached by 1,300 steps, and
there are superb views from the top. It helps to have a bike to get there.

To the north of the bazar, a 3-km hike past some ancient rock shelters leads to
the **Jatashankar Cave** where the Siva lingam bears the likeness of the god's coiled
matted hair.

Pachmarhi centre

To Jatashankar Cave (2.5km)

To Piparia (47 km)

Piparia Rd

Bazar

To Nandan Van (1 km), Rock End Manor,
Nilambar & Panchvati Cottages (3 km)

Arvind Marg

Shubhash Marg

Patel Marg

Chemist

Vegetable

Bike Hire

Gandhi Statue

Gandhi
Chowk

N

To Cantonment

After Kim Clark

0 metres   100
0 yards   100

■ **Sleeping**
1 Abhilasha
2 Kachnar
3 Manjushri
4 Misty Meadows

● **Eating**
1 Bomaby
2 Mahfil

A peaceful hill crowned by a group of stupas and abandoned monasteries are together one of the most important Buddhist sites in India. Although the Buddha himself never came to Sanchi it has a quiet stillness now, lost at many of the other famous places of religious pilgrimage, yet in keeping with the Buddhist faith. It was included on the World Heritage list in 1989. The imposing hilltop site has commanding views. Sitting under the trees in the bright sunshine, it is easy to be moved by the surroundings. Comparatively few people venture here so it is a good place to relax, unwind and explore the countryside.

Ins and outs Getting there Some 47 km northeast of Bhopal, Sanchi can easily be visited by car for a ½-day trip from Bhopal. The road out of Bhopal runs along the railway. Once in the countryside the Vindhya Hills lie to your right – the higher ground all covered in low scrub jungle, the flat lowland cultivated. **Getting around** Entrance at Main Gate (bottom of hill). Museum 1000-1700, site open until sunset (usually 1800 in winter). Allow at least 1½ hours. If in a hurry, visit Stupas 1, 2 and 3, Gupta Temple (17), Temple 18, and Monasteries 45 and 51. The Stupa is within walking distance from the railway station. See Transport, page 276, for further details.

Background The first stupa was built during **Asoka's** reign in the third century BC, using bricks and mud mortar. Just over a century later it was doubled in size; a balcony/walkway and a railing were added. The gateways were built 75 years later. Finally in 450 AD four images of the Buddha (belonging to the later period), were placed facing each of the gateways. The entrances are staggered because it was

Sanchi

Sleeping		
■ **Sleeping**	3 Tourist Cafeteria &	1 Gupta Temple
1 Buddhist Guest House	Rest House	2 Temple 31 (7th C)
2 Circuit House	4 Travellers' Lodge	3 Monastery 46 & 47

4 Monastery & Temple 45
5 Monastery Structure 43
6 Temple 44

commonly believed that evil spirits could only travel in a straight line. The wall was built for the same purpose. The **Great Stupa**, one of the largest in India (37 m in diameter, 16 m high), does not compare with the one at Anuradhapura in Sri Lanka. In India they became taller in proportion to their bases, in other countries the shape was modified further. Around the great stupas were lesser ones, often containing the ashes of monks famous for their piety and learning, plus a whole complex of buildings, eg monasteries, dining rooms, shrine-rooms, preaching halls and rest-houses for pilgrims. These can be seen at Sanchi.

From the 14th century Sanchi lay half buried, virtually forgotten and deserted until 'rediscovered' by General Taylor in 1818, the year before the Ajanta caves were found. Amateur archaeologists and treasure hunters caused considerable damage. Some say a local landholder, others say General Taylor, used the Asoka Pillar to build a sugarcane press, breaking it up in the process. Sir John Marshall, Director General of Archaeology from 1912-19, ordered the jungle to be cut back and extensive restoration to be effected, restoring it to its present condition.

Originally, the brick and mortar domes were plastered and shone brilliant white in the tropical sun. The earliest decorative carving was done on wood and ivory but the craftsmen at Sanchi readily transferred their skills to the yellow sandstone here, which lends itself to intricate carving. The **carvings** illustrate scenes from the life of Buddha, events in the history of Buddhism and the *Jataka* stories (legends about the Buddha's previous lives). See Books, page 1364, for further reading.

The site The Gateways The basic model consists of two pillars joined by three architraves (cross beams), sculpted as if they actually passed through the upright posts. They are regarded as the finest of all Buddhist toranas. The **East Gate** shows the young prince Siddhartha Gautama, leaving his father's palace and setting off on his journey towards enlightenment, and the dream his mother had before Gautama's birth. The **West Gate** portrays the seven incarnations of the Buddha. The **North Gate**, crowned by a wheel of law, illustrates the miracles associated with the Buddha as told in the *Jatakas*. The **South Gate** reveals the birth of Gautama in a series of dramatically rich carvings. Just to the right of the south gate is the stump of the pillar erected by Asoka in the third century BC. The capital, with its four lion heads, is in the local museum. It recalls the one in the Sarnath Museum, of superior workmanship that was adopted as the national symbol of Independent India.

Monastery 51 is reached by steps opposite the west gateway of the Great Stupa. It is well preserved with thick stone walls faced with flat bricks and is typical in plan. A raised, pillared verandah with 22 monastic cells behind, surrounds a brick-paved courtyard. The discovery of charred wood suggested that roofs and pillars may have been constructed with wood. There was possibly a chapel at the centre of the west side; the massive 'bowl' beyond the west gate was caused by removal of a large boulder which you can see on your way to Stupa 2.

Stupa 2 stands on a terrace down the slope. The original balustrade has been dated to the second century BC with later additions. The decoration, though interesting, is much simpler than on Stupa 1, especially when dealing with the human form. The relic chamber of the stupa contained valuable relics of 10 saints belonging to three generations after the Buddha's immediate disciples, which may explain the choice of this site, below the main terrace.

The **Gupta Temple** (fifth century) is one of the early structural temples of India, built of stone slabs with a flat roof. It has a square sanctuary and a pillared portico and shows the sombre decoration and symmetry typical of its style. **Temple 18** (seventh century), built on the site of an earlier apsidal temple, has only nine of its 12 pillars still standing which resemble those found in the Buddhist cave temples of western India. **Monastery and Temple 45** (seventh-11th centuries) ① *closed Mon, 0900-1700, foreigners US $5*, on the eastern edge shows a more developed style of a North Indian temple. The monastery is built around a courtyard with a ruined temple of which only the core of the carved spire remains. The ornamental doorway and the Buddha image in the sanctuary with a decorative oval halo, are still visible.

Museum Archaeological Museum ① *closed Fri, 0900-1700, foreigners US$5*, near entrance to monument. Exhibits include finds from the site (caskets, pottery, parts of gateway, images), dating from the Asokan period. Archaeological Survey guide books to the site and museum are available.

Gupta sites near Sanchi
① *Car from Bhopal add on Rs 125 to the car hire to Sanchi to include Vidisha and Udaygiri. Bus from Sanchi regular service (Bhopal-Vidisha and Raisen-Vidisha), Rs 5. Cycle (see below). The train to Sanchi is 20 mins by local train.* Bhopal Dadar Exp, 1058, 0950, 1½ hrs; Punjab Mail 2138, 1533, 1½ hrs (convenient for Jalgaon for Ajanta, 8 hrs, or Mumbai, 16 hrs).

Vidisha In the fifth to sixth centuries BC Vidisha (known as **Besnagar** in Pali), located at the junction of the Betwa and Bes rivers, was an important trade centre of the Sunga Dynasty where Asoka was governor in the third century BC. The use of lime mortar in the construction of a shrine dedicated to Vishnu, dating from the second century BC, suggests this was one of the first structures in India to use 'cement'. The citizens of Vidisha were patrons of the monuments at Sanchi. Deserted after the sixth century AD, it came into prominence again as Bhilsa between the ninth to 12th centuries. It later passed on to the Malwa Sultans, the Mughals and the Scindias. The ruins of the Bijamandal Mosque and Gumbaz-ka Makbara both date from the Muslim period with remains of votive pillars nearby. The small museum contains some of Vidisha's earliest antiquities.

Heliodorus Pillar, the 'Khambha Baba', is a free-standing monolithic column, similar to Asokan pillars but much smaller, dated to 140 BC. It is 3 km after crossing the Betwa River. The inscription demonstrates that relations existed between the Greeks in the Punjab and the kings of this area and that Heliodorus had become a follower of Vishnu.

Udaygiri Caves ① *From Vidisha take a tonga or auto-rickshaw (about Rs 40, includes waiting, or cycle from Bhopal and visit Vidisha and Udaygiri (an enjoyable 20 km each way). The group of rock-cut sanctuaries, 4 km north of Vidisha, are carved into the sandstone hillside, an inscription in one indicating that they were produced during the reign of Chandragupta II (382-401 AD). The caves possess all the distinctive features that gave Gupta art its unique vitality, vigour and richness of expression: the beautifully moulded capitals, the design of the entrance, and the system of continuing the architrave as a string-course around the structure. The caves have been numbered, probably in the sequence in which they were excavated.*

Cave 1 has a frontage created out of a natural ledge of rock. The row of four pillars bear the 'vase and foliage' pattern about which Percy Brown wrote: "the Gupta capital typifies a renewal of faith, the water nourishing the plant trailing from its brim, an allegory which has produced the vase and flower motif". The shrines become progressively more ornate. **Cave 5** depicts Vishnu in a massive carving in his Varaha (Boar) incarnation holding the earth goddess Prithvi aloft on one tusk. Another large sculpture is of the reclining Vishnu. Both reflect the grand vision and aspirations of the carvers. **Cave 19** is notable for its high pillars, its long portico and pillared hall.

Udaypur (60 km north from Udaygiri) ① *From Bhopal: Pathankot Exp (1530) train to Basoda (1830; the station is Ganjbasoda), then bus (Rs 6) or tonga (Rs 25) to Udaypur.* The colossal **Neelkantheswara Temple**, the centrepiece here, is an outstanding example of 11th-century Paramara architecture. Built of red sandstone, it stands on a high platform and has a delicately carved, beautifully proportioned spire. **Basoda** is 24 km away and has accommodation, see listings page 274.

Gyaraspur 64 km northeast of Bhopal, Gyaraspur is an attractive and important site of medieval Jain and Hindu activity. The late ninth-century **Maladevi Temple**, on the hill above the village, is the most striking of the remains with the ruins of a stupa to its west. Partly rock cut (the sanctum conveniently set in a cave at the back), it has served as both a Hindu and a Jain shrine. There are ruins of an eight-pillared temple, *Athakhambe*, and a four-pillared *Chaukhambe*.

Eran Eran, north of Gyaraspur, has the only extant standing Gupta column (485 AD) near today's small village (once the fortified **Airikina**) which is reached by dusty tracks. The large (5-m long) late fifth-century Vishnu Varaha here (represented wholly as a boar) is carved with tiny figures of *sadhus* who are believed to have sheltered in its bristles during the Flood.

Listings: Central Madhya Pradesh

⬤ Sleeping

Bhopal *p263, maps p264 and p265*
Mid-price hotels are in Hamidia Rd and Berasia Rd (15-min walk from bus and train station). Better hotels: in the quiet Shamla Hills (5 km from railway, 2 km from centre).
A Jehan Numa Palace, 157 Shamla Hill, T661100, F661720, www.hoteljehanuma palace.com. 60 pleasant rooms with verandah around courtyards, some in annexe, good restaurants, gardens, internet café, good position but no lake view, friendly and efficient, pleasant atmosphere, "pricey but wonderful".
A Noor-us-Sabah (WelcomHeritage), VIP Rd, Koh-e-Fiza, T/49101, F749110, welcomheritage @bigfoot.com. 70 comfortable modernized rooms in a 1920s palace, best in town.
B Lake View Ashok (ITDC), Shamla Hills, opposite TV Tower, T541600, F541607. Modern hotel, 45 comfortable but slightly shabby rooms (hot water erratic), good restaurant, competitive car hire, helpful staff, quiet location with views of Upper Lake.
B-C Amer Palace, 209 Zone 1, MP Nagar, T557127, F573309. 60 a/c rooms, good restaurant, "best pastry shop in town", pleasant modern hotel.

B-C Nisarga, 211 Zone 1, MP Nagar, T555701, F558948. 41 rooms, very good restaurant (Chinese recommended), comfortable business style hotel.
B-C Residency, 208 MP Nagar, T556001, F557637, 48 a/c rooms, modern, clean rooms, excellent restaurant, pool.
C-D Palash, near '45 Bungalows', TT Nagar, T/F553006. 33 rooms (17 a/c, 1 R).
D Motel Shiraz, Hamidia Rd, T552513. 22 rooms, some a/c in cottages, basic.
D Panchanan, New Market, T551647, F553076. 5 a/c rooms, restaurant, bar, breakfast included, often full.
D President International, Berasia Rd, T557291. Some comfortable a/c rooms, restaurant, bar.
D-E Shrimaya, No 3 Hamidia Rd, T535454, F532711. 27 modern rooms, some a/c.
    Most budget hotels are dire and infested with mosquitoes. Many refuse to take foreigners. There are cheap hotels on Station Rd (best avoided).
E Rama International, Radha Cinema Complex, T543281. 12 rooms, some a/c, little place tucked back, simple, rather dark but quiet.
E Sonali, near Radha Talkies, Hamidia Rd, T533880, F510337, clean rooms (best a/c),

⬤ *For an explanation of the sleeping and eating price codes used in this guide, see inside the*
⬤ *front cover. Other relevant information is found in Essentials pages 52-57.*

good food (room service), professional and courteous staff. Recommended.
F Ranjit's, Hamidia Rd, T533511. Clean, simple rooms, attached bath (bucket hot water), TV, good restaurant.

Pachmarhi *p268, maps p268 and p269*
High season is May-Jun and Nov-Dec.
   Off-season discounts: 25% at MPT and SADA; 40-60% at private hotels.
B Rock End Manor, T52079. 6 deluxe rooms, 3 a/c, some with 6-m high ceilings in restored colonial building, lovely views of old golf course and polo fields. Recommended.
B-D Satpura Retreat, Mahadeo Rd (2 km from centre), T52097. 6 rooms, 2 a/c, attractive old bungalow with verandah, in pleasant setting.
D Kachnar, Arvind Marg, T52323. 12 spacious, clean, comfortable rooms with bath (bucket hot water), very friendly, helpful. Recommended.
D Nilambar, T52004. 2-bed attractive cottages (hot water) with good views.
D Panchvati Cottages, T52096.
Five 2-bedroom cottages, 5 huts, all with TV and hot water, reasonably priced restaurant, bar, quiet, well-maintained.
D-E Manjushri, Shubhash Marg, T52016. 26 rooms (bucket hot water), clean, friendly.
E Misty Meadows, Patel Marg, T52136. Decent rooms, bucket hot water, beautiful garden, pleasant hotel.
E Nandan Van (SADA), T52018. 12 cottages (hot water), in spacious peaceful gardens.
E-F Natraj, opposite Bus Stand, T52151. 16 rooms, friendly.
F Abhilasha, near Vegetable Market, T52203. 10 rooms, bucket hot water, 24-hr check-out.
F Panchali, Main Rd, T52223. 8 rooms, good restaurant.
F Sapna, Main Rd, T52209. 7 rooms, clean.

Sanchi *p270, map p270*
E Tourist Cafeteria, by the museum, T62743. 2 basic but clean rooms.
E Travellers' Lodge, T62723. 8 clean, comfortable rooms, 2 a/c, restaurant, pleasant garden, at foot of stupa hill.
F Buddhist Guest House, near railway station, T62739. 20 clean, spartan but pleasant rooms (Rs 50), also dorm, contact Bhikku-in-charge, Mahabodhi Society, often full.

F Railway Retiring Rooms, 2 large rooms with shower and dressing room (Rs 100), busy line.
Rest House, near Circuit House, eerie and run down, hospitable, Rs 130 each including breakfast and good veg dinner, "the caretaker is brilliant!".

Basoda *p273*
F Hotel Kumud Palace, at Kala Bag, Bareth Road, T07594-22223, with 16 clean air-cooled or a/c rooms, hot water, TV and a restaurant.

◐ Eating

Bhopal *p263, maps p264 and p265*
▼▼▼ **Jehan Numa Palace**, International, 3 restaurants, garden barbecues, 24-hr coffee shop with western snacks, excellent Indian. Very pleasant.
▼▼▼ **Lakeview Ashok**. International. Some excellent dishes, pleasant ambience but service can be slow.
▼▼ **Bagicha**, 3 Hamidia Rd. Mughlai. 'Garden' restaurant and bar, good food, but pricey, and sometimes abysmal service.
▼▼ **Kwality**, Hamidia Rd and New Market. Indian, Chinese, continental. Dark but cool and comfortable.
▼ **Indian Coffee Houses** are in Hamidia Rd, Sivaji Nagar and New Market. Indian. Good *thalis* but poor *dosas*.
▼ **Jyoti**, 53 Hamidia Rd. Indian. Spartan but excellent cheap vegetarian *thalis*.
▼ **Taj**, 52 Hamidia Rd. Indian. Good food, pleasant roof garden.

Cafés and fast food
Manohar Place (sign in Hindi), 6 Hamidia Rd. *Dosas* and snacks (fantastic *pakoras*), very reasonable, excellent sweets, delicious fresh fruit juices, an Indian café.

Pachmarhi *p268, maps p268 and p269*
MP Tourism hotels (some listed above) have bland restaurants serving Indian and a few Chinese dishes:
▼▼ **Bombay**, Gandhi Chowk, serves excellent chicken and mutton.
▼▼ **Satpura Retreat**, most pleasant.
   Several basic places near the Bus Stand:
▼ **Mahfil** good.

Sanchi *p270, map p270*

🍴 **Kapil**, New Bus Stand. Good, cheap vegetarian food.

🍴 **Tourist Cafeteria** by the museum. Clean, pricey average meals, bit oily (suspicious shortage of change), small tidy garden.

🍴 **Travellers' Lodge**. Indian and Chinese. Non-residents with advance notice.

❀ Festivals and events

Bhopal *p263, maps p264 and p265*
Jan 26-28: Lok Rang features local crafts and cultural performances. **Feb**: Bhopal Mahotsav is similar. **Summer Festival**, Bharat Bhawan centre stages art exhibitions, theatre and music.

O Shopping

Bhopal *p263, maps p264 and p265*
Most shops open 0930-2000 and close on Sun (some Mon). **Chowk** and **New Market** are the main shopping centres.
Handicrafts Emporium, Hamidia Rd. Stock souvenirs and local handicrafts.
MP State Emporium, GTB Complex, TT Nagar. Specializes in local *chanderi* (cotton/silk mix, so sheer that Aurangzeb insisted that his daughter wear 7 layers of it!) as well as tussar and other raw silks.
Mrignayanee Emporium, 23 New Shopping Centre. Stock souvenirs and local handicrafts.

Books
Landmark, Arera Colony, T565238. Also near water tower in the Old City.
Variety Bookhouse, GTB Complex, New Market, has an extensive choice in English.

▲ Activities and tours

Bhopal *p263, maps p264 and p265*
Tours
MP Tourism *Bhopal Tours* on Sun, Tue and Thu, 0900-1600.

⊖ Transport

Bhopal *p263, maps p264 and p265*
Air
The airport is 11 km from centre. Transport to town: by taxi, about Rs 200-250. *Indian Airlines* bus to the airport from City Office, 0700.
Air India, GTB Complex, TT Nagar, T553468;

Indian Airlines, Bhad Bhada Rd, T778434, airport T646123, flies to Mumbai daily via Indore; also Delhi (2 via Gwalior). **Jet Airways**, T275990, airport T645676, to Mumbai.

Bus
Local Re 1-Rs 8.
Long distance **Gwalior** 422 km, 0600, 1900; **Indore** 187 km, frequent, good a/c coach 0845, 1430, 4 hrs; **Sanchi** 45 km, 1½ hrs, hourly from Hamidia Rd Bus Stand. Nadara (State) Bus Stand, T540841, services include: **Agra** 541 km; **Jaipur** 572 km; **Khajuraho** 387 km, from Jhansi, bus 4½ hrs. **Mandu** 290 km, go to Indore and change; **Nagpur** 345 km; **Pachmarhi** 0230-1615; **Shivpuri**, 1130-1500. **Ujjain** bus to Devas (about 3 hrs; then jeep or bus to Ujjain).

Car
Car hire tends to be more expensive than in other states; MP Tourism (Transport) a/c and non a/c cars; local hire Rs 1,000-1,800 for 125 km. Out of town: Rs 5-8 per km, plus night halt charge, Rs 250.

Rickshaw
Auto-rickshaw: minimum Rs 5, but some demand extra to Shamla Hills area, agree fare in advance.

Taxi
(Unmetered). **Bhojpur** and **Bhimbetka** will cost around Rs 500 by taxi, 4 hrs round trip. **Kanha** (540 km) is better visited from Jabalpur or Satna.

Train
City Booking T553399. Railway Station, enquiry T131, reservation T540170. Booking office and tourist information on Platform 1. **Agra Cantt**: see Delhi, and deduct 4-5 hrs. **Amritsar**: *Dadar Amritsar Exp, 1057*, 1510, 24¾ hrs. **Bangalore**: *Rajdhani Exp, 2430*, 0450, Mon, Tue, Fri, Sat, 26 hrs. **Chennai**: *Tamil Nadu Exp, 2622*, 0805, 23 hrs. **Delhi (ND)**: *Chhattisgarh Exp, 8237*, 0645, 13¾ hrs; *Punjab Mail, 2137*, 0920, 11 hrs; *Dadar Amritsar Exp, 1057*, 1510, 13¾ hrs; *GT Exp, 2615*, 1740, 11½ hrs; *AP Exp, 2723*, 2235, 10 hrs. **Gwalior**: *Punjab Mail, 2137*, 0920, 5½ hrs; *Dadar Amritsar Exp, 1057*, 1510, 6½ hrs. **Jabalpur**: *Narmada Exp Pass, 8233*, 2300, 7 hrs; *Amarkantak Exp, 8254*, 1600, Tue, Thu, Fri, Sat, 6 hrs. **Jalgaon (for Aurangabad)**: *Karnataka*

Exp, 2628, 0705, 6½ hrs. **Kolkata:** *Shipru Exp,* 9305, 0225, Mon, Thu, Fri, 28 hrs. **Lucknow:** *Pushpak Exp, 2133,* 2205, 11½ hrs; *Kushi Nagar Exp, 1015,* 1420, 11½ hrs. **Mumbai (CST):** *Punjab Mail, 2138,* 1650, 15 hrs; *Pushpak Exp, 2134,* 0605, 14½ hrs. **Ujjain:** *Narmada Exp, 8234,* 0535, 5½ hrs, continues to **Indore.**

Pachmarhi *p268, maps p268 and p269*
4WD
Most hotels can arrange 4WD Gypsys, Rs 900-1,000 per day.

Bus
Long distance Bus Stand, T52029. Daily services to **Bhopal** 0530, 1500, 6 hrs; **Indore** 0630; **Khargon** 1830; **Nagpur** 0700, 1000, 12 hrs; **Piparia** 0700, 1000, 1300, 1½ hrs.

Motorbike
Bike from Shubhash Marg, Rs 20.

Train
The nearest station is Piparia, 47 km.

Sanchi *p270, map p270*
Bus
Long distance Frequent service from Bhopal, Hamidia Rd, 0630-1930, 1½ hrs direct or over 2 hrs via Raisen; the latter is more attractive; also to **Vidisha.**

Taxi
Hire in Bhopal (or book in advance in Delhi); allow Rs 500 for visit and 1½ hrs each way.

Train
English timetable. Trains on the Jhansi-Itarsi section of the Central Railway, stop in Sanchi. *Pathankot Exp,* depart from Bhopal, 1530, 1 hr. The *Shatabdi Exp* does not stop at Sanchi; 1st class passengers travelling over 161 km and 2nd class passengers (minimum group of 10) travelling over 400 km may request a stop at Sanchi on the *Punjab Mail.* Enquire and arrange this in advance. For **Bhopal**, depart 0645, very slow; **Vidisha,** local train, 20 mins.

● Directory

Bhopal *p263, maps p264 and p265*
Banks Indian Overseas Bank, near *Surya Hotel* for foreign exchange. **Cultural centres** British Council Library, GTB Complex, Roshanpura Naka, New Market, Tue-Sat, 1100-1900. English periodicals and newspapers in cool reading room. **Hospitals** Carewell, Mahadev Mandir Rd, T543983. **Mayo,** Shahjanabad, T535584. **Internet** Jehan Numa Palace Hotel (Rs 100 per hr). **Post office** Central GPO: TT Nagar; Sultania Rd for Poste Restante. **Tourist offices** MP Tourism, Gangotri, 4th floor, TT Nagar, T774340, F772384, www.mptourism.com. Railway Station, T646827. **Useful addresses** Ambulance: T552222. **Fire:** T553333. Travel agents: **Radiant,** 24 Ahmadabad Rd, T7057403, F554773. **Travel Bureau,** 2 Van Vihar Rd, T/F739997.

Northern Madhya Pradesh

★ Gwalior → *Phone code: 0751. Colour map 3, grid B1. Population: 827,000.*

Surrounded by attractive open plateau country immediately to the north of the Vindhyas, Gwalior is set in one of the state's driest regions. The majestic hill fort, formerly the key to control of the Central Provinces, dominates a ridge overlooking the town spread out below. Here the Jai Vilas Palace bears testimony to the idiosyncratic tastes of the Scindia Maharajas. Much of the town, which sees few tourists, is very busy, noisy and crowded. ▶▶ *For Sleeping, Eating and other listings, see pages 295-302.*

Ins and outs
Getting there There are a few flights from Delhi and Mumbai, but the *Shatabdi Express* gives Gwalior excellent train connections with Agra and Delhi to the north and

Jhansi and Bhopal to the south. The railway station and MP State Bus Stand are southeast of the fort. From there, it is 6 km along the dusty MLB Road to the Jayaji Chowk area of Lashkar, the New Town.

Getting around In addition to a tempo stand near the station there are unmetered autos and taxis. Gwalior is quite spread out and the fort is a stiff climb. See Transport, page 299, for further details.

Climate Best time to visit is Nov-Mar.

History

In legend, Gwalior's history goes back to 8 AD when the chieftain **Suraj Sen** was cured of leprosy by a hermit saint, Gwalipa. In gratitude he founded and named the city after him. An inscription in the fort records that during the fifth-century reign of Mihiragula the Hun, a temple of the sun was erected here. Later, Rajput clans took and held the fort. Muslim invaders like **Qutb-ud-din-Aibak** (12th century) ruled Gwalior before it passed through a succession of Tomar Rajput, Mughal, Afghan and Maratha hands. During the 1857 **Mutiny**, the Maharaja remained loyal to the British but 6,500 of his troops mutinied on 14 June. The next year, there was fierce fighting round Gwalior, the rebels being led by Tantia Topi and the **Rani of Jhansi**. When the fort was taken by the British, the Rani was found, dressed in men's clothes, among the slain.

Gwalior Fort

0 metres 300
0 yards 300

1 Hindola Gate
2 Gujari Mahal Palace & Archaeological Museum
3 Ganesh Gate
4 Lakshman Gate, Chaturbhuja Temple & Jain Sculptures
5 Hathia Paur
6 Man Mandir Palace
7 Vikramaditya & Karan Mandir Palaces

Sights

The fort contains awe-inspiring Jain sculptures, Jain and Hindu temples and the charming sandstone palace. In the town are the palaces, the Moti Mahal and the 19th-century Jai Vilas. The Maharaja (Scindia) of Gwalior was one of five Maharajas awarded a 21-gun salute by the British.

★ **The fort** ① *1000-1700; US$5 for foreigners, though some have reported getting in for 25 paise at the Urwahi Gate; allow 2-3 hrs, English speaking guides here expect Rs 200 (hotel guides charge more).* The fort stands on a sandstone precipice 91 m above the surrounding plain, 2.8-km long and 200-850-m wide. In places the cliff overhangs, elsewhere it has been steepened to make it unscaleable. The main entrance to the north comprised a twisting, easily defended approach. On the west is the **Urwahi Gorge** and another well guarded entrance. The fort's size is impressive but the eye cannot capture all of it at once. Apart from its natural defences, Gwalior had the advantage of an unlimited water supply with many tanks on the plateau.

Approach The fort is a long way to walk from the town. You may enter from the northeast by the Gwalior or Alamgiri Gate but it is quite a steep climb (and don't forget the interesting Jain sculptures on the west side). Mineral water is sold at the ticket counter; decline the booklet. Alternatively, take a taxi or an auto-rickshaw (cycle rickshaws often refuse to take you) and enter from the west by the Urwahi Gate. After visiting the temples and palaces, you can descend to the Gujari Mahal in the northeast and pick up an auto from the Gwalior Gate. Visitors to the fort (particularly young women) are sometimes hassled by boys who can be quite unpleasant.

Western entrance Above the **Urwahi Gate** there are 21 Jain sculptures dating from the seventh to 15th centuries, some up to 20 m tall. An offended Babur ordered their faces and genitalia to be destroyed. Modern restorers have only repaired the faces. There is a paved terrace along one side (ask to be dropped near the steps to view the sculptures since vehicles may not park along the road).

Northeast entrance A 1-km steep, rough ramp, with good views, leads to the main palace buildings. You first pass through the **Gwalior Gate** (1660), the first of several gates, mostly built between 1486 and 1516. Next is the Badalgarh or **Hindola (1)** named because of the swing which was once here. It is (unusually) a true structural arch, flanked by two circular towers. Note the use of material from older buildings.

At the base of the ramp the **Gujari Mahal Palace** (circa 1510) containing the **Archaeological Museum (2)** is to the right (see museums below). Some distance from the fort above, this palace was built by Raja Man Singh for his Gujar queen Mrignayani. The exterior is well preserved. The 'Bhairon' gate no longer exists and the fourth is the simple **Ganesh (3)** with a *kabutar khana* (pigeon house) and a small tank nearby. The

Gwalior

Banda Dhura Mata

To Agra (NH 3)

Gwalior
Fort

To Tombs of Tansen & Ghaus
Muhammad

To Airport
& Delhi

To Agra

New MP
Bus Stand

To Morar

Narrow Gauge

Rani Jhansi
Memorial

Indian
Airlines

Tansen Rd

Station Rd

Link Rd

Tempo
Stand

Gandhi Marg

Roop
Singh
Stadium

Phool
Bagh

Zoo

Moti Mahal
& Museum

Luxmiganj New Rd

Nai Sarak

MLB Rd

Jayaji
Chowk

Sarafa
Bazar

Falkar
Bazar

Bookshop

Scindia
Museum

Jai Vilas Palace

Jhansi Rd

Tempo Stand

Daulatganj

Lohiya Bazar Marg

Jayendraganj

High
Court

Inderganj
Chowk

Hari Singh Marg

LASHKAR

Private
Bus Stand

Madhavganj Marg

Bus Stand Rd

Chhattris

Palase Rd

Related map
A Gwalior Fort, page 277

N

To Shivpuri

To Khajuraho

0 metres 500
0 yards 500

Sleeping		Eating
1 DM Motel	5 Tansen, Circuit	1 Indian Coffee
2 Fort View	House & Tourist Office	Houses
3 Gwalior	6 Usha Kiran Palace	2 Kwality
4 Shelter	7 Vivek Continental	3 Volga

mosque beyond stands on the site of an old shrine to the hermit Gwalipa, the present temple having been built later with some of the original material. Before the **Lakshman Gate** (circa 14th century) is the ninth-century Vishnu **Chaturbhuja Temple (4)**, with later additions, in a deep gap. A Muslim tomb and the northeast group of Jain sculptures are nearby. **Hathia Paur (5)** (Elephant Gate, 1516), the last, is the entrance to the main Man Mandir palace which also had a Hawa gate, now demolished.

★ **Man Mandir Palace (6)** (1486-1516), built by Raja Man Singh, is the most impressive building in the fort. The 30-m high eastern retaining wall is a vast rock face on the cliff-side interrupted by large rounded bastions. The palace had ornamental parapets and cupolas, once brightly gilded, while blue, green and yellow tile-work with patterns of elephants, human figures, ducks, parrots, banana plants and flowers covered the exterior walls. The remarkable tiles, and the style of their inlay are probably derived from Chanderi (200 km south) or Mandu. The beautifully decorated little rooms arranged round two inner courts have small entrances, suggesting they were built for the royal ladies. The iron rings here were used for swings and decorative wall hangings.

Interestingly, in addition to the two storeys above ground there are two underground floors which provided refuge from hot weather and acted as circular dungeons when required; these should not be missed. **Guru Har Gobind** who was once detained here was freed at the behest of Nur Jahan – he was permitted to take out any others who could touch his shawl so he attached eight tassels which enabled 56 prisoners to be freed with him! On 24 June 1658 **Emperor Aurangzeb** took his elder brother **Murad** captive en route to Delhi and then transferred him to Gwalior fort to be imprisoned. In December of the same year Aurangzeb ordered his execution.

Angled ventilation ducts allowed in fresh air while pipes in the walls were used as 'speaking tubes'. You will find an octagonal bath which would have been filled with perfumed water – the water welled up through inlet holes in the floor which have now been blocked. The south wall which incorporates the arched Hathia Paur with its guardroom above is particularly ornate with moulded and colourfully tiled friezes. *Son et Lumière* each evening. A small **museum** ① *closed Fri, 0800-1800, guides are around, especially for the underground floors (if you don't have a torch); give a small tip*, opposite the façade has interesting archaeological pieces of Hindu deities.

> ‖ *A torch is essential to explore the lower floors: there are holes in the floor, some of which are quite deep. Underground levels are infested with bats (easily disturbed) and so there is a revolting smell.*

Vikramaditya Palace (7) (1516) ① *Tue-Sun 0800-1700 (1 Apr-30 Sep, 0700-1000, 1500-1800), free*, is located between Man Mandir and Karan Mandir, connected with them by narrow galleries. Inside is an open hall (*baradari*) with a domed roof. Opposite the Dhonda Gate is the **Karan Mandir (7)** (1454-79), more properly called the Kirtti Mandir after its builder Raja Kirtti Singh. It is a long, two-storeyed building with a large, pillared hall and fine plaster moulding on ceilings of adjacent rooms. Just northwest is the **Jauhar Tank** where the Rajput women performed *jauhar* (mass suicide) just before the fort was taken by Iltutmish in 1232 (see page 1299), and also at Chittaurgarh (see page 386). The two unremarkable Muslim palaces, Jahangiri and Shah Jahan Mahals are further north. Moving south from Hathia Paur, towards the east wall, are the **Sas Bahu Mandirs**. Dedicated to Vishnu, the 11th-century 'Mother and Daughter- in-law' pair of temples built by Mahipala Kachhawaha (1093) still preserve fine carvings in places. The larger 12-sided is more interesting although only the *Mahamandapa* (Assembly Hall) remains. The smaller has an ornately carved base with a frieze of elephants, and a vaulted ceiling under the pyramidal roof. The wide ridged stone 'awning' is well preserved. An impressive modern marble **gurudwara** (1970) in memory of Sikh Guru Har Gobind (1595-1644), who had been imprisoned in the fort, is to its south. The Guru Granth Sahib is read right through the day while it provides a haven of cool respite for visitors. To its west is **Suraj Kund**, a large tank, first referred to in the fifth century, where Suraj Sen's leprosy was cured, though the water is now green and stagnant.

★ **Teli-ka Mandir** probably means 'oil man's temple'. It is the earliest temple in Gwalior, and architecturally has more in common with some early Orissan temples than those in the south (though sometimes guides suggest a link with Telangana in modern Andhra Pradesh suggesting the fusion of Dravidian and North Indian architectural styles). This unique 25-m high Pratihara (mid-eighth century) Vishnu Temple is essentially a sanctuary with a *garuda* at the entrance. The oblong vaulted roof rather resembles a Buddhist *chaitya* and the Vaital Deul (Bhubaneswar). Tillotson records how after the 'Mutiny' "this great medieval temple, for example, was put to service as a soda-water factory and coffee shop. By such acts of desecration the British showed Indian rulers how the ancient Hindu heritage was then regarded by those who laid claim to power and authority". It was reconstructed in 1881-83. The Katora Tal behind was excavated when the fort was built, like many others here. The Ek-khamba Tal has a single stone column standing in it. **Rani Tal (12)** further south was supposedly intended for the royal ladies; it is connected underground to the neighbouring **Chedi Tal**!

Jain sculptures in the southeast corner can be seen from a path below the wall.

The town After Daulat Rao Scindia acquired Gwalior in 1809 he pitched camp to the south of the fort. The new city that arose was **Lashkar** (The Camp) with palaces, King George Park (now Gandhi Park) and the *chhattris* of the Maharajas. **Jayaji Chowk**, once an elegant square, dominated by late 19th- and early 20th-century buildings, notably the Regal Cinema, and the Chowk bazar can still be a pleasant place to watch people going about their business from one of the good little restaurants.

★ **Jai Vilas Palace** (1872-74) ① *closed Wed, 0930-1700, tickets at gate: Rs 25, foreigners Rs 175, camera Rs 25, video Rs 75, guided tours (1 hr) sometimes compulsory*, designed by Lt-Col Sir Michael Filose, resembles an Italian palazzo in places, using painted sandstone to imitate marble. Part of the palace is the present Maharaja's residence but 35 rooms house the **Scindia Museum**, an idiosyncratic collection of royal possessions, curiosities (eg 3-D mirror portraits), carpets (note the Persian rug with royal portraits) and interesting memorabilia.

In a separate building opposite (show ticket) is the extraordinary **Durbar Hall**. It is approached by a crystal staircase and in it hang two of the world's largest chandeliers each weighing 3½ tons; the ceiling was tested beforehand by getting 10 elephants to climb up a 2 km ramp! The gilding used 56 kilos of gold. Underneath is the dining room. The battery operated silver train set transported cigars, dry fruit and drinks round the table, after dinner. The lifting of a container or bottle would automatically reduce pressure on the track, and so stop the train! Southeast of the fort is the spot where **Rani Lakshmi Bai** of Jhansi was cremated, marked by a stirring statue.

The Royal **Chhattris**, south of town, are each dedicated to a Gwalior Maharaja. These ghostly pavilions are in various stages of neglect. The lighted images are still clothed and 'fed' daily. Be there at 1600 when they are shown again by the guardians after their afternoon nap.

In the crowded Hazira in the **Old Town**, northeast of the fort, is the **Tomb of Ghaus Muhammad**, a 16th-century Afghan prince who helped Babur to win the fort. It is in an early Mughal style with finely carved *jali* screens. Hindus and Muslims both make pilgrimage to the tomb. Nearby, in an attractive garden setting, is the **Tomb of Tansen**, the most famous musician of Akbar's court. It is the venue for the annual music festival (November/December). The present tamarind tree replaces the old one which was believed to have magical properties. Tansen was an exponent of the *dhrupad* style, and laid the foundations for what in the 19th century became the Gwalior *ghurana* style, noted for its stress on composition and forceful performance. One of the best known contemporary exponents is Amjad Ali Khan, a renowned sarod player. A recently built **Sun Temple** similar in style to Konark is at Morar, a few kilometres east of the tombs.

Museums

Gujari Mahal Archaeological Museum ① *closed Mon, 1000-1700*, inside Hindola Gate (northeast), Fort. Pretty palace with interesting collection including sculptures and archaeological pieces (second and first century BC), terracottas (Vidisha, Ujjain), coins and paintings, copies of frescoes from the Bagh caves. Ask curator to see the beautiful 10th-century Shalbhanjika (Tree Goddess) miniature. Some museums and palaces are closed on Monday (Sound and Light show daily).

Shivpuri National Park

➔ *Phone code: 07492. Colour map 3, grid B1. 114 km southwest of Gwalior. Best season: Jan-Mar.*

The dense forests of the Shivpuri or Madhav National Park were the hunting grounds of the Mughal Emperors, when great herds of elephants were captured for Emperor Akbar. Now mainly a deer park in forested hill territory, this was also where Maharajas of Gwalior once hunted.

The park is a 156-sq km dry deciduous forest, with Sakhya Sagar, a large perennial lake attracting a large number of migratory birds in the winter. Stop where the forest track crosses the stream from the Waste Wier. **George Castle** on high ground, once the Scindias' hunting lodge, and **Burah Koh** watchtower have good views over the lake at sunset. Animals include nilgai, chinkara, chowsingha, sambar, cheetal and wild pig. Chandpata Lake attracts numerous waterbirds including migratory pochard, pintail, teal, mallard, demoiselle crane and bar-headed geese which remain until May.

Near the Tourist Village, the pink **Madhav Vilas summer palace** ① *1500-2000 (can be viewed from the boundary wall at other times), the palace is not open to visitors, evening prayers (arati) and concert of quality classical singing around 1900*, is now a government building. The impressive marble *chhattris* of the **Scindia** rulers, with fine *pietra dura* inlay and *jali* work, are set in formal Mughal gardens with flowering trees. They synthesize Hindu and Islamic styles with their *sikharas* and Mughal pavilions. Curiously, meals are still prepared for the past rulers! **Bhadaiya Kund** nearby has a spring rich in minerals.

Jhansi ➔ *Phone code: 0517. Colour map 3, grid B1. Population: 405,000.*

Jhansi, in Uttar Pradesh, is best known for its fort and the involvement in the 1857 Mutiny of its queen Rani Lakshmi Bai. Today it is a useful stop on the train from Delhi en route to visiting Khajuraho by road. There is plenty to explore nearby, though this is equally easily done from peaceful Orchha which offers a happy escape from the busy small town atmosphere.

History Jhansi was a small village until taken by the Marathas in 1742 who extended the old Fort. In 1853 it 'lapsed' (see page 142) to the British when the Raja died without leaving a male heir. The fort was seized in 1857 by mutineers and most of the occupants slaughtered. The young Rani, who had been denied rule by the British, joined the rebels but had to retire to Gwalior. She continued her attempts to return after the British regained control of Jhansi. She was killed in action on 18 June 1858 at Kotah-ki-Sarai "dressed like a man ... holding her sword two-handed and the reins of her horse in her teeth ..." (Hibbert), see page 280. The British ceded the fort to the Maharaja of Scindia and exchanged it for Gwalior in 1866.

Sights Shankar Fort ① *0800-1700*, was built by Bir Singh Deo in 1613. The nucleus of the fort, which has concentric walls up to 9 m high with 10 gates, was breached by the British in 1858. There are good views from the walls. Rani Mahal, once Lakshmi

Bai's home, is an **archaeological museum** (ninth-12th century). **Retribution Hill** ⓘ *closed Mon, 2nd Sun each month, 1030-1630 (6 Apr-30 Jun, 0730-1230), foreigners US$2*, marks the last stand of the Mutineers in 1858. The **State Museum** near the fort in a vast modern building has a good collection of stone sculptures in addition to weapons and ethnography.

Excursion Barua Sagar ⓘ *from Jhansi Railway Station, buses for Khajuraho (0600, 0700, 1100) will stop here (1 hr) on request; a 5-min walk along a narrow tree-lined canal leads to the fort; ask locally for keys, to return, wave down any bus to Jhansi (frequent service)*, 24 km east along the Khajuraho road, has the ruins of a historic fort where the Maratha Peshwas fought the Bundelas. The deserted sandstone fort has excellent views over the Sagar (lake) created by a dam across the Betwa river. The ninth-century early Pratihara temple, Jarai-ka-Math to Siva and Parvati, of red sandstone here is highly ornamented. Yet the place is rarely visited and is wonderfully peaceful; you can swim in the lake.

Jhansi

Sleeping		5 Raj Palace	Eating
1 Central		6 Samrat	1 Holiday & Indian
2 Chanda		7 Sita	Sweetshop
3 Jhansi & Restaurant		8 Veerangana (UPTDC)	2 Nav Bharat
4 Prakash			

0 metres 300
0 yards 300

★ Orchha → *Phone code: 07680. Colour map 3, grid B1. Population: 8,500.*

Highly picturesque, in the middle of nowhere, abandoned and somewhat neglected, Orchha pays rich rewards to the visitor and is an ideal stop between Gwalior and Khajuraho. Set on an island on a bend in the Betwa River, the fort palace from a bygone era is raised on a rocky promontory above the surrounding wooded countryside. This largely untouched island of peace and calm is approached by a remarkable early 17th-century granite bridge built by Bir Singh Deo, while all around, the forest encroaches on the tombs and monuments. ▸▸ *For Sleeping, Eating and other listings, see pages 295-302.*

Ins and outs

Getting there Orchha is quite easily reached by road from Jhansi. After travelling 9 km southeast along the Khajuraho Rd, a minor road turns south for the remaining 7 km to Orchha. There are taxis, tempos or buses from Jhansi station, but it is best to travel during daylight hours, and book and enquire about return transport well ahead.

Getting around The fort palace complex and the village are all easily seen on foot. The riverside is a 10-min stroll away. If you are laden with luggage you can get a rickshaw from the village centre to your hotel. See Jhansi above for further details Women are advised not to wander around the site alone.

History

The Bundela chief **Raja Rudra Pratap** (1501-31) chose an easily defended and beautiful site for his capital. In the 11th century, a Rajput prince is said to have offered himself as a sacrifice to the mountain goddess Vrindavasini; she prevented his death and named him '*Bundela*' (one who offered blood). The dynasty ruled over the area between the Yamuna and Narmada rivers, having stepped into the vacuum left by the Tughlaqs and extended their power, moving their base to Orchha (meaning hidden). Raja Rudra Pratap threw a wall around the existing settlement and began work on the palace building (circa 1525-31) and an arched bridge to it. This was completed by his successor Bharti Chand (1531-54) who was installed in the Raj Mahal with great ceremony.

The continuing fortunes of the dynasty may have stemmed from the rulers' diplomatic skills. Though the third ruler, the religious **Madhukar Shah**, was defeated in battle by Akbar and was exiled in 1578 (died 1592), he nevertheless won the Mughal Emperor's friendship. Later Bir Singh Deo (1605-27, see **Datia** below), while opposing Akbar, aligned himself with Prince Salim (Jahangir), who later rewarded him with the throne of Orchha, thus ensuring its ongoing prosperity. The Jahangir Mahal was built to commemorate the Emperor's visit to Orchha. However, Bir Singh's first son, Jhujan, ran foul of Shah Jahan and, ignoring orders, treacherously killed the neighbouring chief of Chauragarh. The imperial army routed Jhujan and Orchha was pillaged. In 1783 the Bundela capital was moved to Tikamgarh, leaving Orchha to the *dhak* forests, the Betwa River and its guardian eagles.

The site

ⓘ *Entry to whole complex and other sites in Orchha, Rs 30 (Indians Rs 5); camera (no flash) Rs 20, video Rs 50; only available from ticket office at Palace entrance. Allow about 2 hrs. Highly recommended.*

Orchha is a wonderful example of a medieval fort palace. Within the turreted walls are gardens, gateways, pavilions and temples, near the Betwa and Jamni rivers. On a moonlit night, the view across the palaces with their *chhattris* and ornamented battlements is enchanting. A suggested route is to visit the Raj Mahal with its Hall of Private Audience then go through the doorway to the Hall of Public Audience. From here go down the ramp and follow the path to the Rai Praveen Mahal. Continue along the path to the Jahangir Mahal, arriving back at the courtyard of the Sheesh Mahal.

The Raj Mahal (1), to the right of the quadrangle, exemplifies Bundela Rajput architecture. There are two rectangular courtyards around which the floors rise in tiers (inspired by the Koshak Mahal in Chanderi, built a century earlier); typically there are cool chambers below ground and a fountain. Some of the original blue tile decoration remains on the upper outer walls. To the left of the first courtyard is the Hall of Private Audience which would have been covered with rich carpets and cushions (note floor-level windows). The Hall of the Public Audience has two quarter-size plaster

✸ *The buildings are in a bad state of repair. If you go to the top take extra care. Carry a torch.*

elephants. Despite the neglected appearance of the royal chambers off the second courtyard, some have beautiful murals on the ceilings and walls. Representing both religious and secular themes, one series is devoted to the *Ramayana*, another to Vishnu's incarnations, others to scenes of court life – musicians, hunters, river excursions, fairground. Normally locked, but the caretaker will unlock some ground floor rooms. Don't miss Rooms 5 and 6 which have the best paintings but you will need a torch. There is a *Sheesh Mahal* upstairs as well as good views of other palaces and temples from the very top; watch your step though, especially in strong winds. In mid-2002, the Raj Mahal was being repaired.

Rai Praveen Mahal (2) was probably named after the musician-courtesan who was a favourite at the princely court of Indrajit, brother of Ram Shah (1592-1604). The low two-storey brick palace with cool underground chambers and beautifully carved

Orchha

To Jhansi

To Lakshminarayan Temple (1 km)

Vanvasi Temple

Radhika Vihari Temple

Yagya Shala

Panchnukhi Mahadevi

Wheat Fields

Betwa River

Canara

Anand Mahal Gardens

Wheat Fields

Bazar

Bus & Tempo Stand

Daujikothi

Kanchana Ghat

Royal Chhattris

Betwa River

N
Not to Scale

■ Sleeping	5 Orchha Resorts	1 Raj Mahal	7 Ram Raja Temple
1 Amar Mahal	6 Sheesh Mahal	2 Rai Praveen Mahal	8 Chaturbhuj Temple
2 Betwa Cottages		3 Hamaam	9 Phool Bagh
3 Deep Regency & Rukmani	● Eating	4 Royal Gate	10 Radhika Raman Temple
4 Fort View & Ganpati	1 Betwa Tarang	5 Camel Stables	
	2 Bhola	6 Jahangir Mahal	

66 99 You can climb up any of the corner staircases (steep and uneven so a torch is helpful), which lead up, by stages, to the very top of the temple. On the roof are langurs, wild bee hives and vultures nesting in corner towers.

stone niches is built to scale with surrounding trees and the Anand Mandal gardens. To get to the underground rooms, turn left down steps on exiting the main rooms.

The octagonal flowerbeds are ingeniously watered from two wells. A new path bypasses the **Royal Gate (4)**, and takes you via the **hamaam (3)** and past the **camel stables (5)** to the most impressive of the three palaces.

Jahangir Mahal (6), built in the 17th century by Raja Bir Singh Deo to commemorate the Emperor's visit, synthesizes Hindu and Muslim styles as a tribute to his benefactor. The 70-m sq palace, which is best entered from the east, the original main entrance flanked by elephants, can also be entered from the south. It has a large square interior courtyard around which are the apartments in three storeys. The guided tour goes to the top of these up narrow and dark stairways. Each corner bastion and the projection in the middle of each side is topped by a dome. These contain apartments with intervening terraces – hanging balconies with balustrades and wide eaves create strong lines set off by attractive arches and brackets, decorative cobalt and turquoise blue tiles, *chhattris* and *jali* screens giving this huge palace a delicate and airy feel. There is a small **museum** ① *closed Fri, 1000-1700, shop*, with a rundown assortment of photos, sculptures and *sati* stones; Hindi labels.

Just south of the crossroads is the **Ram Raja Temple (7)** ① *0800-1230, 1900-2130 (1 hr later on summer evenings), cameras and leather articles must be left outside*, which forms a focus for village life. The temple courtyard and the narrow lane leading to it have stalls selling souvenirs and the area occasionally swells with pilgrims and sanyasis. The pink and cream paint is not in keeping with the other temples. It is interesting to visit during *arati*; otherwise there is little to see inside. Following the appearance of Rama in a dream, the pious Madhukar Shah brought an image of the god from Ayodhya and placed it in this palace prior to its installation in a temple. However, when the temple was ready it proved impossible to shift the image and the king remembered, only too late, the divine instruction that the deity must remain in the place where it was first installed. It is the only palace-turned-temple in the country where Rama is worshipped as king.

Chaturbhuj Temple (8) ① *usually open 0800-1700*, up the steps from the Ram Raja Temple courtyard, was built by King Madhukar Shah for his Queen Kunwari to house the image of Rama brought from Ayodhya. Laid out in the form of a cross, a symbolic representation of the four-armed god Krishna, there is a triple-arched gate with attractive *jharokas* on the exterior. The tallest *sikhara* is over the *Garbagriha* shrine, to the left of which you will see a Ganesh and a set of kettle drums. The high arches and ceilings with vaulting and lotus domes painted in a rich red in places, are particularly striking. You can climb up any of the corner staircases (steep and uneven so a torch is helpful), which lead up, by stages, to the very top of the temple. The second level gives access to tiny decorated balconies which provided privileged seating. There are good views of the nine palaces from the top, reached by the mini labyrinth of narrow corridors and steps (take a torch). On the roof are langurs, wild bee hives and vultures nesting in corner towers.

A 1-km paved path links the Ram Raja with Bir Singh Deo's early 17th-century **Lakshminarayan Temple** ① *0900-1700, 15-min walk, auto-rickshaws charge Rs 30 return, ticket attendant gives 'tour', naming characters illustrated, go up the tower-steep steps but very good views of entire area,* on a low hill, which incorporates elements of fort architecture. The typical village houses along the path are freshly white-washed at *Diwali*. The diagonal plan enclosing the central square temple structure is most unusual. The excellent murals (religious and secular), on the interior walls and ceilings of the four cool galleries around the temple here, are well-preserved examples of the Bundela school. The paintings in red, black, yellow, grey and turquoise portray Hindu deities, scenes from the epics, historical events including the early British period (note the interesting details of Lakshmi Bai's battle against the British), as well as giving an insight into the domestic pleasures of royalty.

Phool Bagh (9) is a formal garden and an eight-pillared pavilion which has a cool underground apartment. Well worth a visit.

Of the 15 **Royal Chhattris**, to former rulers grouped by the Kanchana Ghat by the river, about half are neglected and overgrown but pleasant for walking around in the late afternoon. A few are well-preserved; ask the watchman if you want to look inside. He will take you to the upper levels by some very narrow, dark stairs: good fun but take a torch and be careful. He will expect a small tip. The chhattris are best photographed from the opposite bank: take a stick as dogs can be a problem.

Village bazar

The small but busy village bazar, with some interesting temples nearby, is about 10 minutes walk from the riverside where a series of royal *chhattris* still stand as sentinels. The riverside is ideal for lazing under a shady tree. Cross the bridge and head upstream for better spots for swimming (watch out for currents).

Datia

Datia itself is not nearly as attractive as Orchha but is interesting to visit nevertheless, particularly as there is hardly a tourist in sight. The forgotten palace lies on the edge of the lively town with a significant Muslim population.

Govind Mandir Palace ① *0800-1700, caretaker 'guide' (speaks little English but holds keys), expects Rs 50 for a tour.* Bir Singh Deo's Govind Mandir Palace (circa 1620), unlike other Bundelkhand palaces, was conceived as an integrated whole, its form and decoration blending Mughal and Rajput styles. Standing on an uneven rocky ridge, the palace has five storeys visible, while several cool underground floors excavated out of the rock, remain hidden. (Lower floors are very dark - carry a torch). Dilapidated and deserted, it is still imposing and atmospheric. The Bundela chief Bir Singh Deo supported Salim (later Jahangir) against his father Akbar, and may have been responsible for robbing and killing Abul Fazl in an ambush. His successors, however, were loyal to the Mughals.

The main entrance is on the east side, approached through very narrow crowded streets, while the south overlooks the lake Karna Sagar. There is a profusion of arches, *chhattris*, ornamental *jali* screens, coloured tiling, balconies and oriel windows which open up delightful views. Within the square plan which surrounds the central courtyard, a separate five-storey 'tower' houses the royal apartments which itself is connected with the surrounding palace by four colonnaded flying bridges, completing this unusual architectural marvel. Strangely it was occupied only intermittently (possibly never by the royal family). The paintings – in deep red, orange and green – though few, are lovely. The first floor has a Dancing Room with stucco figures, the second floor the Queen's Room and a Dancing Room with beautiful wall and ceiling paintings of peacocks, elephants and kings, while the third floor has bridges and the Diwan-i-khas, for private audience (note the Mughal tomb in the corner). Keys are needed to go above this level. The King's Room on the fourth floor with its shallow dome has a beautifully sculpted ceiling with geometric designs of flower petals and stars while the roof parapet has remains of green and blue tiles. There are excellent views all round.

Sonagiri A few kilometres north of Datia, just off the main road, Sonagiri has 77 white Jain temples on a hill reached by a paved path. Some date from the 17th century, the one to Chatranatha is the best. It is a pilgrim site for *Digambara* Jains (see page 1344) many of whom attend the evening *arati* between 1800-2100.

★ Deogarh → *Colour map 3, grid B1. 23 km southwest of Lalitpur.*

On the Uttar Pradesh side of the Betwa River, the small village of Deogarh (Fort of the Gods) offers the chance to rest and enjoy cliff-top views of the Betwa River, go hiking and wildlife watching in the forest, and visit numerous temples. Impressive cliffs overlook the river with shrines and reliefs carved into the cliff walls. On the southern fringes of the great Gupta Empire (fourth to sixth century AD), its relative isolation has meant that some fine temples survive.

Sights The temples were built of local stone (and occasionally granite), rather than the more easily destroyed brick. The sixth-century red sandstone, partly ruined but otherwise well preserved, **Dasavatara Temple** is the finest here. The central sanctum had four flat-roofed entrance porticoes in place of the normal one, and the first northern pyramidal temple *sikhara*, though little of it remains. There are fine sculptures on the three walls, of Vishnu legends and a doorway with carvings of Ganga and Yamuna. The remarkable Anantashayi Vishnu, in Harle's phrase, lies "dreaming another aeon into existence". While Lakshmi gently holds Vishnu, the sacred lotus with Brahma rises from his navel.

The dramatic **hilltop fort** encloses 31 Jain temples dating from the ninth to 10th centuries with sculpted panels, images and 'thousand image pillars'; the best examples are in temples 11 and 12. Nearby, the Sahu Jain Sangrahalaya has some fine 10th- to 11th-century carvings. A well marked path from the parking lot here leads to the river and the shrines; it is a fairly long walk.

Chanderi The road climbs steeply to approach Chanderi, 37 km west of Lalitpur, an important town under the Mandu sultans, which was dominated by a hill fort. It is attractively placed in an embayment in the hills overlooking the Betwa River and contains the 15th-century Koshak Mahal and other ruined palaces, market places, mosques and tombs. The old town, 8 km north and buried in jungle, has Jain temples dating from the 10th century. Chanderi is famous for very fine saris and brocades. There is a *Dak Bungalow*.

From Jhansi to Khajuraho The route along the edge of the mainly agricultural hill region of Bundelkhand is on the northern edge of the Peninsula. The forested hill slopes are quite evident as you cross a number of rivers such as the Betwa and Dhasan as they flow off the plateau. Before Independence it was a land of small Rajput and Muslim states, struggling to maintain and expand their power against the greater forces from the plains to the north. Much is now open farmland with occasional scrub or forest, with outcropping rocks and hills. This very attractive route has very little traffic. For a stop-off, the Tourist Cafeteria in Nowgong, has a pleasant breezy restaurant in a pretty garden.

★ Khajuraho → *Phone code: 07686. Colour map 3, grid B2. Population: 6,500.*

Khajuraho, home to what are now perhaps the most famous of India's temples on account of their remarkable erotic sculptures, lies in a rich, well-watered plain. Set miles from the nearest town in an open forested and cultivated landscape with the striking Vindhyan Hills as a backdrop, it is listed as a World Heritage Site. Sadly, this breeds very aggressive touts. The small village away from the tourist areas has a pleasant laid back feel. ➤➤ *For Sleeping, Eating and other listings, see pages 295-302.*

Ins and outs

Getting there Daily flights connect Khajuraho with Delhi, Agra and Varanasi. The airport is only 5 km from most hotels, with cycle-rickshaws and taxis available for transfer. Alternatively travel by bus or car from Jhansi across the open rolling northern plains of Madhya Pradesh, or come from the Varanasi direction via Satna or Mahoba. There are buses from other major cities in the north which come into the Main Bus Stand.

Getting around Khajuraho is still a small village though the temples are scattered over 8 sq km. Although some are within walking distance, hiring a bike is a good alternative to getting a cycle-rickshaw to visit the temples to the east and south. See Transport, page 301, for further details.

Climate Summer: maximum 47°C, minimum 21°C. Winter: maximum 32°C, minimum 4°C. Annual rainfall: 1,120 mm; monsoon Jul-Aug. Best time to visit is between Oct and Mar. In Apr-Jun it becomes very hot, dry and dusty.

Background

Khajuraho was formerly the capital of the old kingdom of Jajhauti, the region now known as **Bundelkhand**. The name Khajuraho may be derived from *khajura* (date palm), which grows freely in the area and perhaps because there were two golden *khajura* trees on a carved gate here. The old name was Kharjuravahaka (scorpion bearer), the scorpion symbolizing poisonous lust.

Khajuraho's temples were built under later Chandela kings between 950 and 1050 AD in a truly inspired burst of creativity, but were 'lost' for centuries until they were accidentally 'discovered' by a British army engineer in 1839. Of the original 85 temples, the 20 surviving are among the finest in India.

Basham suggested that India's art came from secular craftsmen who, although they worked to instructions, loved the world they knew, their inspiration not so much a ceaseless quest for the absolute as a delight in the world as they saw it.

The Gods and demi-gods in temples all over India are young and handsome, their bodies rounded, often richly jewelled. They are often smiling and sorrow is rarely portrayed. Temple sculpture makes full use of the female form as a decorative motif. Goddesses and female attendants are often shown naked from the waist up, with tiny waists and large, rounded breasts, posing languidly – a picture of well-being and relaxation. See Books, page 1363, for further reading.

Shakti worship and erotic sculptures Although each temple here is dedicated to a different deity, each expresses its own nature through the creative energy of Shakti. Tantric beliefs within Hinduism led to the development of Shakti cults which stressed that the male could be activated only by being united with the female in which sexual expression and spiritual desire were intermingled. Since this could not be suppressed it was given a priestly blessing and incorporated into the regular ritual. Romila Thapar traces its origin to the persisting worship of the Mother Goddess (from the Indus Valley civilization, third millennium BC), which has remained a feature of religion in India. Until this century, many temples kept *devadasis* (literally, servants of God), women whose duty included being the female partner in these rituals.

The presence of erotic temple sculptures, even though they account for less than 10% of the total carvings, have sometimes been viewed as the work of a degenerate society obsessed with sex. Some believe they illustrate the Kama Sutra, the sensuality outside the temple contrasting with the serenity within. Yet others argue that they illustrate ritual symbolism of sexual intercourse in **Tantric belief**, see page 1331. The Chandelas were followers of the Tantric cult which believes that gratification of earthly desires is a step towards attaining the ultimate liberation or *moksha*.

Whatever the explanation, the sculptures are remarkable and show great sensitivity and warmth, reflecting society in an age free from inhibitions. They express the celebration of all human activity, displaying one aspect of the nature of Hinduism itself, a genuine love of life.

Chandela Rajputs The Chandela Rajputs claimed descent from the moon. **Hemwati**, the lovely young daughter of a Brahmin priest, was seduced by the Moon God while bathing in a forest pool. The child born of this union was **Chandravarman**, the founder of the

Khajuraho

Sleeping
1 Casa di William
2 Clarks Bundela, Touraids & Indian Airlines
3 Harmony
4 Holiday Inn
5 Jass Trident
6 Khajuraho Ashok
7 Lakeside (MP Tourism)
8 Marble Palace & Yadav Guest House
9 New Bharat Lodge & Lakshmi
10 Payal (MP Tourism)
11 Rahil (MP Tourism)
12 Sunset View & Chandela Emporium
13 Surya
14 Tourist Bungalow (MP Tourism) & Travellers Lodge
15 Yogi Lodge
16 Zen

Eating
1 La Terrazza
2 Lovely & Agarwal
3 Madras Coffee House
4 Mediterraneo
5 Paradise
6 Rimjhun & Raja Cafe
7 Safari & State Bank of India

Temples
1 Chitragupta
2 Jagadambi
3 Kandariya Mahadeva
4 Lakshmana
5 Matangesvara
6 Parvati
7 Varaha
8 Vishvanatha
9 Adinatha
10 Parsvanatha
11 Santinatha

0 metres 300
0 yards 300

dynasty. Brought up in the forests by his mother who sought refuge from a censorious society, Chandravarman, when established as ruler of the local area, had a dream visitation from his mother. She implored him to build temples that would reveal human passions and in doing so bring about a realization of the emptiness of desire.

The Chandelas, whose symbol recalls the 16-year-old king who slayed a lion bare-handed, developed into a strong regional power in the early 10th century. Under their patronage Jajhauti became prosperous, and the rulers decorated their kingdom with forts, palaces, tanks and temples, mainly concentrated in their strongholds of Mahoba, Kalinjar, Ajaigarh and also Dudhai, Chandpur, Madanpur and Deogarh (Jhansi District).

With the fading of Chandela fortunes, the importance of Khajuraho waned but temple building continued until the 12th century at a much reduced pace. Far removed from the political centres of the kingdom, the location of Khajuraho minimized the danger of external attack and symbolized its role as a celestial refuge.

The temples

ⓘ *Daily, sunrise to sunset. The entrance is opposite the car park, flanked by curio shops and restaurants. The ticket office is to the left; foreigners US $5, camera Rs 25 (sometimes). Guides charge around Rs 250 for a small group (enquire at Raja's Café or Tourist Office). Some guides are best avoided ("obsessed with sex!"); some push the new Cultural Centre, souvenir shop and puppet show (overpriced at Rs 250). Free guided tours are sometimes available in the peak season 0900-1430, except Fri and holidays, audio tours from 0900. Avoid the toilets. Son et lumière Rs 200.*

The temples, built mostly of a fine sandstone from Panna and Ajaigarh – although granite was used in a few – can be conveniently divided into three groups: the **Western** (opposite bazar), **Eastern** (30 minutes away on foot) and **Southern**. The Western Group, which dominates the village, are the most impressive and the gardens the best kept. The temples in the other two groups are remarkable and pleasing in their own right but if you feel that temple fatigue is likely to set in, then the Western Group are the ones to see, especially the Lakshmana Temple. Allow a day (minimum five hours) for sightseeing.

The temples here are compact and tall, raised on a high platform with an ambulatory path around, but with no enclosure wall. Each follows an east-west axis and has the essential *garbha-griha* (sanctum) containing the chief image, joined to the hall for *mandapa* (worshippers) by a *antarala* (vestibule). The hall is approached through an ardha mandapa (porch); both have pyramidal towers. Larger temples have lateral transepts and balconied windows, an internal ambulatory and subsidiary shrines. The sanctuary is surmounted by a tall *sikhara* (tower), while smaller towers rise from other parts of the temple, imitating mountain peaks culminating in the highest. The sanctum is usually *sapta-ratha* (seven projections in plan and elevation), while the cubical section below the *sikhara* repeats the number, having seven bands, *sapta-bada*. The whole, studded with sculptured statues with clear lines of projections and recesses, makes most effective use of light and shade. The sculptures themselves are in the round or in high or medium relief depicting cult images, deities, celestial nymphs, secular figures and animals or mythical beasts.

In India's medieval period of temple building, simple stonework techniques replaced previous wooden and brick work. Temples were heavily and ornately decorated. Heavy cornices, strong, broad pillars and the wide base of the tower (*sikhara*) give them the feeling of strength and solidity, only partly counteracted by the ornate friezes.

Western Group Varaha Temple (circa 900-25), a shrine dedicated to Vishnu in his third incarnation as **Varaha**, the boar (**Vishnu**, The Preserver), is usually depicted resting on a bed of serpents, until summoned to save the world from disaster. The rat-demon **Hiranyaksha** stole the earth and dragged it down to his underwater home.

66 99 The details differentiate between an Officer (beard), General (beard and belly) and Priest (beard, belly and stick). An ordinary soldier has none of these. You might spot the occasional error...

The Gods begged for Vishnu's help. The demon created 1,000 replicas of himself to confuse any pursuer, but Vishnu incarnated himself as a boar and was able to dig deep and seek out the real demon. Thus, Hiranyaksha was destroyed and the world saved. The 2.6-m long Varaha is of highly polished sandstone covered with 674 deities. He is the Lord of the Three Worlds – water, earth and heaven, and under him is the serpent *Sesha* and the feet of the broken figure of *Prithvi*, the earth goddess. The lotus ceiling shows superb relief carving.

The temples are in a peaceful setting of a beautiful park. The area covered by the Western Group was originally a sacred lake – perhaps a reason for the high plinths.

Lakshmana Temple (circa 950 AD) is the earliest and best preserves the architectural features that typify the larger temples here. The **platform** has friezes of hunting and battle scenes with soldiers, elephants and horses as well as scenes from daily life including the erotic. The **basement** again has bands of carvings – processional friezes showing animals, soldiers, acrobats, musicians, dancers, domestic scenes, festivities, ceremonies, loving couples and deities. The details differentiate between an Officer (beard), General (beard and belly) and Priest (beard, belly and stick). An ordinary soldier has none of these. You might spot the occasional error – a camel has legs jointed like a horse! Note the beautifully carved elephants at shoulder height, each one different.

On the **walls** are the major sculptures of gods and goddesses in two rows, with *sura-sundaris* or *apsaras* in attendance on the raised sections and loving couples in the recesses. All the figures are relaxed, resting their weight on one leg, thus accentuating their curves. The bands are broken by ornate balconied windows with carved pillars and overhanging eaves. The nymphs shown attending to their toilet, bearing offerings, dancing, playing musical instruments or as sensual lovers, are executed with great skill. They are graceful and fluid (note the taut muscle or creased skin), with expressive faces and gestures. The best examples are seen in the recesses below the main tower.

The **façades** are covered in superb sculpture. On the south façade are a couple of minstrels, their faces expressing devotional ecstasy, a dancing Ganesh, ladies attending to their toilet, and groups of lovers. Moving to the southwest, a *sura-sundari* applies vermilion while another plays with a ball. In the northwest corner is a nymph after her bath in her wet clothes. The south face of the northwest shrine has a fine Ganesh panel. On the north face, returning towards the porch, there is a group of *apsaras* accomplished in art and music (one plays the flute, another paints, yet another writes a letter). The east face of the subsidiary shrine in the southeast corner has a master architect with his apprentices.

Leave shoes at the entrance and enter **the interior** through a simple *makara-torana* flanked by gladiators. The circular ceiling of the porch (*ardha mandapa*) is a superbly carved open lotus blossom. In the hall (*mandapa*) is a raised platform possibly used for dancing and tantric rituals. At each corner of the platform are pillars with carved brackets with *apsaras* which are among the finest sculptures at Khajuraho. There are eight figures on each column, representing the eight sects of Tantra. The sanctum (*garba-griha*) doorway has a panel showing incarnations of Vishnu while the lintel has

Lakshmi with Brahma and Siva on either side. A frieze above depicts the nine planets including *Rahu*, while Krishna legends and innumerable carvings of animals, birds and humans, appear on the wall. The *pancha-ratha* sanctum has a three-headed Vishnu as Vaikuntha, and around it are 10 incarnations and 14 forms of Vishnu.

Kandariya Mahadeva Temple (circa 1025-50) is the most developed, the largest and tallest of the Khajuraho temples. Dedicated to **Siva**, the elaborately carved *makara torana* doorway leads to a porch with an ornate ceiling and a dark inner sanctum with a marble linga. The temple roof rises in a series of seven bands of peaks to the summit of the central, 31 m high *sikhara*. There are 84 smaller, subsidiary towers which are replicas. The architectural and sculptural genius of Khajuraho reaches its peak in this temple where every element is richly endowed. The platform is unique in the way it projects to the sides and rear, reflecting the plan of the transepts. It also has the highest and most ornamental basement with intricately carved processional friezes. Leaving the temple, walk to the rear of the delightful gardens to the other two temples.

Along the same platform, to Kandariya's north is the **Jagadambi Temple** (early 11th century), which is similar in layout and predates the next temple, the Chitragupta. It has a standing Parvati image in the sanctum but was originally dedicated to Vishnu. The outer walls have no projecting balconies but the lavish decorations include some of the best carvings of deities – several of Vishnu, a particularly fine *Yama*, numerous nymphs and amorous couples. In between is the ruined **Mahadeva shrine** (11th century). Little remains except a porch, under which *Sardula*, a mythical lion, towers over a half-kneeling woman.

Chitragupta Temple (early 11th century) is the only one here dedicated to Surya, the Sun God. Longer and lower than its companions, it has been much restored (platform, steps, entrance porch, northeast façade). Unlike the simple basement mouldings of the Jagadambi, here there are processional friezes; the *maha-mandapa* ceiling too has progressed from the simple square in the former to an ornate octagonal ceiling. The *garbha griha* has Surya driving his chariot of seven horses, while on the south façade is a statue of Vishnu with 11 heads signifying his 10 incarnations, see page 1328.

Vishvanatha Temple (1002) is dedicated to Siva. According to the longer inscription on the wall, it originally had an emerald linga in addition to the stone one present today. Built before the Kandariya Mahadeva, they are similar in design and plan. The high, moulded basement has fine scrollwork and carvings of processions of men and animals as well as loving couples. On the nine principal basement niches of both are the *Sapta-matrikas* (seven 'Mothers') with *Ganesha* and *Virabhadra*. The excellent carvings include a fine musician with a flute and amorous couples inside the temple, and divinities attended by enchanting nymphs in innumerable poses (one removing a thorn from her foot), on the south façade. Only two subsidiary shrines of the original four remain. Sharing the same raised platform and facing the temple is the **Nandi Pavilion** with a fine elephant frieze on the basement. It houses a 2.2-m polished sandstone Nandi bull (Siva's vehicle). Before coming down the steps note the sleeping *mahout* on an elephant!

Outside this garden complex of temples and next to the Lakshmana temple is the **Matangesvara Temple** (900-25 AD), simpler in form and decoration than its neighbour and unlike all the others, still in everyday use. It has an interesting circular interior which contains a large Siva linga.

Chausath Yogini (late ninth century) is a ruined Jain temple in coarse granite on a platform. It stands apart from the rest of the Western Group beyond the tank. Only 35 of the original *chausath* (64) shrines to the *yoginis* (attendants of Kali), of the 'open-air' temple, remain.

Eastern Group South of the village is the ruined **'Ghantai' Temple** (late 10th century). The fine carvings of chains-and-bells (*ghanta*) on the pillars, the richly ornamented doorway and ceiling of the entrance porch can only be seen from the road. Walk through Khajuraho village to the small **Javari Temple** (late 11th century), with its tall, slender *sikhara*. It has a highly decorative doorway and finely sculpted figures on the walls. About 200 m north is the **Vamana Temple** (late 11th century), with a four-armed Vamana incarnation of Vishnu in the sanctum. This is in the fully developed Chandela style and has a single tower and no ambulatory. The walls are adorned with sensuous *sura-sundaris*. Returning to the modern part of Khajuraho, you pass the early 10th-century so-called **Brahma Temple** on the bank of Ninora-tal. A Vishnu temple, wrongly attributed to Brahma, it has a sandstone *sikhara* on a granite structure.

Three **Jain temples** stand within an enclosure about 500 m southeast of the Ghantai Temple; others are scattered around the village. The **Parsvanatha Temple** (mid-10th century), is the largest and one of the finest. The curvilinear tower dominates the structure and is beautifully carved. There are no balconies but light enters through fretted windows. Although a Jain temple, there are numerous Vaishnav deities, many of them excellently carved on the three wall panels. Some of the best known non-erotic sculptures too are found here, particularly the graceful *sura-sundaris* (one applying kohl and another removing a thorn, on the south façade; one tying ankle-bells on the north façade), as well as the fine *Dikpalas* in the corners. The interior is richly carved with elephants, lions, sea goddesses and Jain figures. The temple was originally dedicated to Adinatha, but the modern black marble image of Parsvanatha was placed in the sanctum in 1860. Next, is the smaller and simpler **Adinatha Temple** (late 11th century), where only the sanctum (containing a modern image) and vestibule have survived – the porch is modern. The sculptures on three bands again depict attractive *sura-sundaris*, the niches have *yakshis*, the corners, *Dikpalas*. **Santinatha Temple** with its 4½-m statue of Adinatha is the main place of Jain worship. An inscription dating it at 1027-28 is covered with plaster – the thoroughly renovated temple retains its ancient heart and medieval sculptures. The small sand coloured structures around the temples are reconstructions around remains of old shrines. There is also a small Jain museum and picture gallery here.

Southern Group The two temples stand on open land. The setting, attractive at sunset, lacks the overall ambience of the Western Group but the backdrop of the Vindhyas is impressive. **Duladeo Temple**, 800 m southwest of the Jain temples down a path off the road, is the last the Chandelas built here, when temple building was already in decline. There are 20 *apsara* brackets but the figures are often repetitive and appear to lack the quality of carving found in earlier temples. The shrine door and *mandapa* ceiling have some fine carving while the linga has 11 rows of 100 lingas. **Chaturbhuja Temple** (circa 1100), 3 km south of the village, anticipates the Duladeo but lacks erotic sculptures. The sanctum contains an exceptional 2.7 m four-armed *Dakshina-murti* Vishnu image while outside there are some fine *Dikpalas*, nymphs and mythical beasts in niches.

Excursions

At **Rajgarh**, 5 km south, is the imposing ruined 19th-century hilltop fort-palace of the Maharaja which the Oberoi Group will convert to a heritage hotel. It is particularly interesting when villagers congregate for the Tuesday Market. Get there by auto-rickshaw or car. The **Panna National Park** is accessed along the Satna Road with attractive waterfalls on the way. Alternatively, you can visit the diamond mines at **Majhgawan** (0900-1100) and return via ancient **Kalinjar** and **Ajaigarh** (see page 294). **Ranegh Falls**, 17 km south of Khajuraho, on the Ken River are splendid after the monsoons, with lovely pools. It is 1½ hours by bike but is hard work. A better bet may be to hire a jeep.

Panna National Park ① *Nov to May, foreigners Rs 100 (with guide), camera Rs 100. Getting there: easiest from Madla (27 km from Khajuraho). Gypsy or*

Madhya Pradesh & Chhattsgarh Northern Madhya Pradesh Khajuraho motorbike hire from Khajuraho, or bus, tour of park can be arranged in Madla. The **Ken River**, parts of which have been declared a sanctuary for fish eating *gharials*, flows across the Panna National Park, which is a Project Tiger Reserve. The park, rich in biodiversity, covers dense forest, open meadows, plateaus and gorge with waterfalls (particularly the attractive Pandav Falls to the east), and supports chinkara, sambar, nilgai and the big cats. Although tiger sightings are rare, it is pleasant to visit in winter. There is little wildlife to be seen in the dry season (when the gharials are removed for their own protection).

Satna The main junction for rail travel to/from Varanasi and Khajuraho, Satna sprawls along the railway line. The impressive gateways and railings from the Buddhist stupa (180 BC), which can be seen at the Allahabad and Kolkata museums, once stood nearby at **Bharhut**.

Chandela Forts

The Chandela kings' main defensive bases were Mahoba and Kalinjar, but as the kingdom expanded these were complemented by other forts at Ajaigarh, Orchha, Datia, Deogarh and Chanderi. Like other kings, they donated villages to maintain the families of soldiers who had died in war. Heroic virtues were instilled into a child from birth and women admired men who fought well; *sati* became common practice throughout the region. After the mid-10th century the independent Chandelas joined a Hindu confederacy to repel Afghan invasions. **Mahmud of Ghazni**, the 'Idol Breaker', made at least 17 of his plunder raids into India between 1000-27, ultimately taking the title, albeit briefly, Lord of Kalinjar.

The forts suffered varied fortunes until the British took them over in the early 19th century. Now the area is being invaded by forests of teak and ebony but offer an insight into totally unspoilt territory. Ajaigarh and Kalinjar are quite 'primitive' but a visit, particularly to the former, is worthwhile. A tour of these and Chitrakoot is really worthwhile. Enlist a local guide to show you the best spots if you travel independently; Ajay Singh (see Khajuraho, Directory) is very knowledgeable and can organize jeep/motorbike. Carry water. Several Chandela forts are linked by a road which runs along the UP-MP border.

Ajaigarh Ajaigarh, 36 km north of Panna, surrounded by dense forest, stands on a granite outcrop crowned by a 15-m perpendicular scarp. Ajaigarh was a self-contained hill fort, intended to withstand long sieges and to house the entire population of the region, which accounts for its great size. Despite its inaccessibility and the difficult 250 m climb involved (allow about 40 minutes on the way up), the fort is worth visiting for its peaceful atmosphere and wonderful views. Two of the original five gates are accessible; the large stone steps here once helped elephants in their steep ascent. Encircling the hill, the fort wall encloses part-ruined temples; only four of the original 22 temples remain. Rock carvings, pillars and sculptures from Hindu and Jain temples, some later used by Muslims to reinforce the fortifications, today lie scattered amongst woodland. The old stone quarry now filled by a lake is said to have provided stone for Khajuraho.

> ✱ *Some believe it is auspicious to eat here, hence the remains of bonfires and presence of picnickers.*

Kalinjar Some 20 km from Ajaigarh this fort stands on the last spur of the Vindhya hills overlooking the Gangetic plains, a plateau with a steep scarp on all sides. One of the most ancient sites in Bundelkhand (Ptolemy's Kanagora), it combines the sanctity of remote hilltops with natural defensive strength. One legend names Kalinjar after Siva, the Lord of Destruction (*kal* = death, *jar* = decay). The ancient hill has long been a place of pilgrimage and worship for Hindu sadhus, rishis and pilgrims. It is rarely visited by other travellers.

The design of the fort has a mystical significance. The only approach is from the north and entry is through **seven gates** with barbicans corresponding to the seven known planets and stations through which the soul must pass before being absorbed into Brahma. At the crest, crumbling Hindu and Muslim monuments stand side by side on the 1½-km long plateau. Beyond the last gate, a drop of about 3.6 m leads to **Sita Sej**, a stone couch set in a rock-cut chamber (fourth century). Beyond, a passage leads to Patalganga (underground Ganga), believed to run through Kalinjar. Koth Tirth at the centre of the fort is a 90-m long tank with ghats leading down to it.

Numerous stone relics are scattered about the site; a dancing Ganesh, Nandi bulls, a model temple complete with figures like a miniature Khajuraho, a reclining Siva, Sati pillars and several *lingams* and *yonis* (fertility symbols).

Mahoba *The station is 3 km from the Bus Stand. To Jhansi: 4 hrs; to Varanasi via Allahabad: 11 hrs.* 63 km north of Khajuraho, Mahoba was reputedly founded by Raja Chandravarman, in 800 AD. Today, it is a small town with a fort on a low hill, several ancient tanks and a thriving 'Dariba' or betel market. The vines are grown under traditional shelters to produce high quality *paan* (betel leaf) for which the area is famous.

After winning Bundelkhand, the Chandela kings dedicated themselves not only to building temples for their gods, but also to bringing water to the land. They created large tanks by damming shallow valleys. Mahoba's oldest tank, **Rahila Sagar** (circa 900) has impressive ruins of a ninth-century granite Sun Temple. The 12th-century **Madan Sagar** has a granite Siva temple nearby and a ruined Vishnu temple on one of its rocky islets. Along its embankment is the old fort, **Qila Mismar** with ruins of palaces, Hindu temples and a tomb. In the fields, remains of Buddhist and Jain sculptures lie abandoned. Gokhar Hill, near Madan Sagar, with 24 Jain Tirthankaras figures carved out of sheer rock, is worth exploring. Two pools, Ram and Suraj Kund, lined with granite slabs, were originally intended for sacrificial fires. There is a *Tourist Bungalow* here with a restaurant and bar.

Chitrakoot On the north flank of the Vindhyas where they dip gently beneath the Ganges Plains,175 km from Khajuraho, Chitrakoot's forests and peaceful rivers were home to Rama and Sita in 11 of their 14 years of exile. **Ramghat**, the principal bathing ghat on the banks of the beautiful Mandakini River, is widely revered in India and the site of countless pilgrimages, though scarcely known to foreigners. Like the much more famous waters of the Yamuna at Allahabad or the Ganga at Varanasi, the River Mandakini is lined with temples. A good way to see the ghats is to hire a boat. Upstream from Ramghat the Mandakini passes through a particularly beautiful stretch of wooded valley.

Listings: Northern Madhya Pradesh

● Sleeping

Gwalior *p276, map p278*
There are several basic hotels with acceptable rooms, but some can be noisy.
A Usha Kiran Palace (Welcomgroup), Jayendraganj, T323993, F321103. 28 a/c rooms (some vast suites), refurbished rooms particularly good, beautiful gardens, good restaurant, billiards, retains character of charming royal guesthouse ("elegant and subdued"), friendly. Recommended.

B-C Gwalior Regency, Link Rd, near New Bus Stand, T340670, F343520. 51 modern rooms (some a/c), few **D**, restaurant, pool.
B-C Shelter, Padav (off Tansen Rd), 200 m railway station and bus stand, T326209, F326212. Modern clean rooms (some a/c), few **D**, good restaurant, bar, pool.
C-D Tansen, 6A Gandhi Rd, T340370, F340371. 36 rooms, 24 a/c, impressive reception but rooms drab and grubby, restaurant, bar, garden, car hire, tourist information, camping, quiet, but old circuit house with draughty (cold in winter) open corridors.

D-E Vivek Continental, Topi Bazar, T329016. 30 rooms, some air-cooled with bath (check for cleanliness), restaurant, pool.
E DM, Link Rd, near New Bus Stand, T342038. Rooms with bath (hot water), could be cleaner but good value and reasonably quiet.

Shivpuri National Park p281

D Delhi Hotel, Madhav Chowk, A-B Rd, T33093. Simple rooms with bath, some a/c, vegetarian restaurant.
D Tourist Village (MP Tourism), Jhansi Rd, 5 km east of town, Bhadaiya Kund, T23760, F34166. 19 rooms in cottages, 5 a/c, 2 4-bed, pleasant restaurant, attractive location overlooking lake, jeep hire, close to the park.
D-E Chinkara Motel, NH3, 4 km south of Shivpuri, T21297. 4 clean rooms, restaurant.

Jhansi p281, map p282

It is best to stay at Orchha.
B Chanda, 365/1A Civil Lines, opposite Laxmi Bai Park, T450014, F450027. 24 comfortable a/c or air cooled rooms with bath, restaurant.
B Sita, Shivpuri Rd, T444690, F444691. 23 smart, clean a/c rooms with bath, good restaurant, car hire, exchange.
C Jhansi, Shastri Marg, 3 km railway, T470360. 28 overpriced rooms, restaurant, bar, exchange, very faded colonial feel, desperately needing overhaul yet garden well kept.
D Prakash, Sardari Lal Market, south of fort, T444133, F441946. 28 clean, decent rooms with bath, some air-cooled, restaurant, bar, pool.
D-E Raj Palace, Shastri Marg, T470544. 14 simple clean rooms with bath, a/c, air cooled, but over-priced.
D-E Veerangana, Shivpuri Rd, 1 km railway, Numaish Maidan, T442402. 20 rooms, 4 a/c, dorm (Rs 50), reasonable restaurant, bar, pleasant garden, mosquito infested.
E Samrat, Chitra Chauraha near railway station, T444943. Rooms with fan, mosquito mesh, rooftop preferable (No 210 best with shower, others have bucket), food brought to room, very friendly. Recommended.
E-F Central, 701 Civil Lines (500 m rly), T440509, F445141. 39 rooms (some 4-bed), some air-cooled, with bath, Indian meals.
F Railway Retiring Rooms and 6-bed dorm. Other hotels near the station are dirty.

Orchha p282, map p284

Hotels are best on the idyllic riverside.
A Amar Mahal, T52102, F52203, www.alsisar. com. Built in 2003, looks like a Maharaja palace, comfortable, friendly staff and management. Excellent but expensive restaurant.
B Orchha Resort, Kanchanghat, on riverside, T/F452759. 32 immaculate a/c rooms, 12 luxury a/c tents around tennis court, high standard, interesting décor (wall paintings, marble inlay), excellent restaurant (strict veg), friendly and attentive staff, exchange, gym, excellent outdoor pool (high wall along river for privacy), well tended gardens, taxi to Khajuraho Rs 1600.
MP Tourism's 2 units should be reserved in advance:
B-D Sheesh Mahal inside Fort, uphill from Bus Stand, T52624. 8 rooms (2 **B** includes Royal Suite with terrace, antique fittings and furniture, huge marble tub (for shower), panoramic view from toilet too), modernized within limits, restaurant, full of character, atmospheric, magnificent views, friendly staff, **D** rooms (no TV or a/c) great value.
C-D Betwa Cottages, overlooking river, 10-min walk from Bus Stand, T52618. 10 clean rooms in cottages, some a/c, well designed with rustic paintings, spacious well-kept gardens with scattered ruins, average restaurant.
Several new guesthouses on the main road 2 mins' walk from the temples charge around Rs 250 for a small double room with bath; some have no window. Best of these is:
E Ganpati, T52765. 8 airy rooms hot shower, clean sheets, small courtyard, parking.
E Fort View, just north of crossroads, T52701. Retired school teacher's clean and friendly guesthouse, hot water in buckets, new dorm.
E-F Deep Regency, T52076.
E-F Rukmani, T52184, have tiny rooms off a narrow corridor, some with bath.

Datia p286

E Datia Motel (MP Tourism), 2 km from town on Gwalior Rd, T38125, opened in Dec 2001, overlooks the palace and lake. There are 4 spotless, airy, bright rooms and a restaurant.
F Shri Raghunath Ganga Hotel, Station Rd, opposite Pitambara Peeth Temple, T36754. 9 air-cooled rooms, baths, clean, secure (Rs 200). Owners helpful and very welcoming.

For an explanation of the sleeping and eating price codes used in this guide, see inside the front cover. Other relevant information is found in Essentials pages 52-57.

Deogarh *p287*

E Tourist Bungalow, across the street from Dasavatara Temple. Clean air cooled rooms, water from nearby pump, kitchen. The caretaker, Mr Yadev, will prepare meals and escort you on hikes to half a dozen temples, 5 to 10 km away in the woods.

Khajuraho *p288, map p289*

Most hotels are within 1 km of the western temples, notably along Jain Temple Rd. They are subject to frequent power cuts but top hotels have generators.

A Chandela (Taj), Airport Rd, T72355, F72366. 102 rooms (singles good value), some not spotless, expensive restaurants (slow service, ordinary food), best bookshop in town though pricey, predatory shopkeepers, small temple in pleasant garden.

A Clarks Khajuraho, modern, 104 rooms, large grounds, pool and tennis.

A Holiday Inn, Airport Rd, T72301, F72304. Plush 50 rooms, all facilities, bookshop.

A Jass Trident, By-pass Rd, T72344, F72385. 94 rooms, quieter away from reception, pleasant atmosphere, attractive, good food, pool (non-residents Rs 150) and gardens, cultural programmes "too routine", friendly, pick-up from airport, excellent service.

A-B Clarks Bundela, Airport Rd, T72386, F72385. Comfortable rooms, well-managed.

B Khajuraho Ashok (ITDC), well located near Western temples, T74024, F72239. 38 rooms, some with temple view, restaurant (good Indian; reduced menu off-season), attractive pool (non-residents Rs 100), pleasant garden, shop sells good value curios and clothes (helpful tailor), friendly, attentive service.

D Casa di William, 100 m north, opposite pond, T74244, F72252. 15 pleasant rooms with bath, some a/c, roof restaurant.

D Lakeside, by Sib Sagar Lake, T74120. 18 functional rooms and dorm, clean but noisy, beautiful evening views.

D Payal, 10-min walk from centre, T74076. 25 decent rooms with bath, some a/c, restaurant (good breakfast and tea), bar, very quiet garden, helpful staff, good value.

D-E Surya, Jain Temple Rd, T74145. 20 small, clean and basic rooms, some a/c, veg restaurant, pleasant garden, helpful staff.

297

D-F Marble Palace, opposite Gole Market, Jain Temples Rd, T74353. 9 spacious rooms, dorm beds, interesting features – marble tiles, modern baths (tubs).

E Rahil, T74062. 12 rooms and dorm (Rs 60), restaurant, large gardens.

E Tourist Bungalow, T74221. 6 rooms, good food but lacks ambience.

E Tourist Village, T74128. 13 well-equipped attractive 2-room 'ethnic' huts, some with bath, outdoor restaurant, quiet, good value, bike useful, campsite nearby.

E-F Sunset View, south of Bazar, alongside Chandela Emporium, T74077. Well located near Lake, 'unfinished' look with unimposing entrance, 20 simple rooms (6 air-cooled with tubs), fairly clean, pleasant terrace and garden, good value.

E-F Zen, Jain Temple Rd, T74228. 12 large and bright rooms, air cooler, clean attached bath (some tubs), *Ristorante Italiano* in garden.

F New Bharat Lodge, near *Payal*, T74082. 12 refurbished rooms, some with small patio.

F Yadav Guest House, just east of *New Bharat Lodge*. Very cheap and basic but clean.

F Yogi Lodge, near Bazar, T74158. With terrace, very well run, clean.

Panna National Park *p293*

B Ken River Lodge, T011-91524874, F91524878. In a beautiful location, www.indiamart.com/ken. Cottages, 'Swiss' tents, tree-top restaurant, fishing, boating, swimming, park tours.

D-E Giles' Treehouse, T07732-25135; 3 km from Madla, serves food (chilled beers are sent 20 m up a tree by a pulley system!). Camping possible, contact *Raja's Café*, Khajuraho.

E Rest Houses, ask at gate or park office, Panna. Carry provisions.

Satna *p294*

Most **D** hotels have some a/c rooms with bath.

D Bharhut, over Railway Bridge in Civil Lines, T07672-26071. 8 rooms (2 a/c), restaurant.

D USA, on the edge of town, towards Khajuraho. Reasonably clean.

E Rajdeep, Rewa Rd, 300 m to right from bus station, T07672-23045. Big clean rooms with fan, net, dorm (Rs 60), good Indian food, very friendly.

Madhya Pradesh & Chhattisgarh Listings: Northern Madhya Pradesh

F Tourist Bungalow, near Bus Stand, T07670-65326. 8 rooms, restaurant (order in advance).

F Pitri Smriti Visram Grih, Ramghat, Hathi Darwaza, T07670-65314. 16 basic rooms with bath (could be cleaner), very friendly manager, pleasant place. All vegetarian; no alcohol.

● Eating

Gwalior *p276, map p278*

₸₸₸ Usha Kiran Palace, International. Good snacks, average meals, occasional classical music, bar, attentive service, pleasant ambience.

₸₸ Kwality south of the Fort. Mainly Indian and snacks. Rather dark but helpful staff.

₸ Indian Coffee House near the station, in *India Hotel*; also one just off Jayaji Chowk (upstairs in bazar). Recommended for South Indian breakfasts and snacks.

₸ Volga, near Inderganj Chowk. Indian. Popular locally.

Jhansi *p281, map p282*

₸₸ Holiday, Shastri Marg. Indian and western. Clean, a/c, reasonably priced (good Indian sweetshop next door). *Hotels Sita* and *Samrat* are recommended.

₸ Nav Bharat, Shastri Marg. Indian snacks.

Orchha *p282, map p284*

₸₸₸ Orchha Resorts, vegetarian. Pleasant décor, à la carte or buffet (breakfast Rs 200, lunch/dinner Rs 400).

₸₸ Betwa Tarang, near Fort bridge (upstairs). Good food, pleasant roof terrace or indoor, clean toilets. Also 'picnic' meals by the riverside.

₸₸ Sheesh Mahal. International, non-vegetarian served in a large foyer. Great north Indian, chilled beer, good service.

₸ Bhola, opposite post office. Basic but serves freshly cooked simple meals.

Khajuraho *p288, map p289*

Top hotels have very comfortable seating and good bars. Beer is expensive everywhere; Rs 100 minimum in hotels.

₸₸₸ Ashok. Indian fish dishes particularly recommended. Try grilled mutton, Goan fish, Indian breakfast (puri, aloo).

₸₸₸ Jass Trident is good all round.

₸₸₸ Mediterraneo, opposite *Surya Hotel*. Italian. Good bruschetta, fresh pasta dishes, Indian/Italian owned.

₸₸ Paradise, Main Rd, opposite Shiv Sagar Lake, T72349. Western, Indian. Good meals reasonably priced (excellent banana pancakes), family run, friendly and inviting.

₸₸ Raja Café, opposite Western Group. Western, Indian. Shady terrace with good view from top, bland food, pricey, often unfriendly service, undeservedly popular.

₸₸ Rimjhun, opposite Vishvanatha Temple. International. Good food, attentive service, generous portions. Nearby liquor stall has beer.

₸₸ La Terrazza near *Yogi Lodge*. Continental. Clean, good food, interesting trips to forts nearby (see below).

₸ Agarwal, nearby, does good Indian.

₸ Lovely, opposite museum. North Indian. Special *thali* (Rs 20), good curd, cheap, friendly.

₸ Madras Coffee House, Jain Temple Rd, does good *dosas*.

₸ Ristorante Italiano, *Zen Hotel,* has been recommended.

₸ Safari, bizarre array of menus, very good food, large helpings (Rs 35-40 dish), good lassi, amazing Indian muesli but slow service (breakfast can take 1 hr).

Satna *p294*

New India Coffee House, with *Rajdeep*. Good breakfasts.

Savera, restaurant near station. Wide choice, reasonably priced 'take aways'.

Chitrakoot *p295*

Digbeah, near bridge on Ramghat. Lunchtime *thalis* recommended.

● Entertainment

Gwalior *p276, map p278*

Winter evenings are chilly. Take a torch (seating on stepped terrace covered with mats).

Son et Lumière in front of Man Mandir Palace, Gwalior Fort, 45 min, 1830 in Hindi, 1930 in English (1 hr later in summer). Colourful spectacle tracing the history of the site with interesting anecdotes. No bus; there is unlikely to be any transport available at the end of the show. Taxis, Rs 250 for return trip from hotels. Alternatively, visit the Fort last when hiring a car for the day in the summer (day hire covers only a single fort visit).

⊕ Festivals and events

Orchha *p282, map p284*
Several annual events are celebrated including Ram Vivah (Rama's marriage) in late **Nov/Dec** when colourful processions draw crowds particularly as superbly trained horses perform extraordinary feats where one removes a horseman's eye make-up with a hoof!

Khajuraho *p288, map p289*
Dance Festival, **Feb-Mar**. Many of the country's most accomplished dancers perform in the spectacular setting of the Western Group of Temples. Contact Tourist Office.

O Shopping

Gwalior *p276, map p278*
Kothari, Sarafa Bazar. Brocade, *chanderi* (light and flimsy cotton and silk material), silk saris.
Ganpatlal Krishna Lal, Sarafa Bazar. Jewellery and antiques. These close on Tue.
MP Emporium, Sarafa Bazar. Handlooms.
MP Khadi Sangh, Sarafa Bazar. Handlooms.
MD Fine Arts, Subhash Market. Paintings and objets d'art.
Mrignayani's (an MP State Emporium) in Patankar Bazar also recommended.

Books
Loyal, near High Court, Nai Sarak.

Photography
Goyal Studio, Daulat Ganj.

Khajuraho *p288, map p289*
Gift shops sell cheap stone and bronze sculptures, handicrafts and gems in the bazar near the Western Group (**Panna diamond mines**, the largest in the country, are nearby).
Chandela Emporium, near Sibsagar, has a large selection of gifts, crafts and jewellery.
Ganesh Garments, Jain Temples Rd. Reasonable western clothes (quick alterations).
Karan Jewellers for diamonds. Tuesday Market at Rajgarh (see Excursions above).
MP Emporium for fixed prices; small craft shops on way to Javeri temple cheaper than the bazar.

Photography
Dosaj and **Bajpai**, in market opposite the Western Group.

▲▲ Activities and tours

Gwalior *p276, map p278*
Tour companies
SS Travels, Usha Kiran Palace.
Travel Bureau, near Madhoganj Police, Lashkar, T/F331765.

Tours
To **Orchha** and **Shivpuri**, Rs 1,200 (car for 5), same day return. City sights, Rs 400.

Jhansi *p281, map p282*
Tour companies
Touraids, Jai Complex, Civil Lines, T443490, helpful and reliable manager with a fleet of cars for hire.
Travel Bureau, 197 Chand Gate, Nai Basti, T443076.

Khajuraho *p288, map p289*
Tour companies
ATS Tours, Sevagram, T74242, F72385, also Agra office.
Ajay Singh, *La Terazza Restaurant*, opposite Western Group of Temples (or near Old Palace, Ajaigarh), recommended for tours, including Chandela forts and Chitrakoot (see below).
Bhavan Travel, Raja Market, near Western Group, T74275. Good guides.
Touraids, near *Clarks Bundela*, reliable cars with drivers.
Travel Bureau, 84 Sevagram.

⊖ Transport

Gwalior *p276, map p278*
On the NH3, Gwalior is 114 km from Shivpuri and 119 km from Agra

Air
The airport is 9 km from town. Indian Airlines, T326872, airport T470124, flies to **Delhi** and **Mumbai** via Bhopal and Indore, 3 weekly. Taxi to town, about Rs 120.

Bicycle
Cycle hire from a couple of small shops near Jayaji Chowk.

Rickshaw
Unmetered "Wacky-Racer" **tempos** and **auto-rickshaw** available. **Cycle rickshaw**: charge around Rs 25 from the centre to the fort.

Madhya Pradesh & Chhattisgarh Listings: Northern Madhya Pradesh

Taxi

Charge about Rs 450 for 80 km per 8 hrs visiting all sights, once only; best to visit fort last and stay on for *Son et Lumière*. Evening visit to fort, Rs 250.

Train

Tickets for the Shatabdi Express are usually sold in the separate, 'non- computerised' queue. Gwalior is on the Central Railways main Delhi-Mumbai and Chennai-Delhi lines. Rly station: enquiries T22544, reservations T25306. **Agra Cantt**: *Lakshadweep Exp, 2617,* 1010, 1¾ hrs; *Punjab Mail, 2137,* 1500, 1¾ hrs; *Dadar Amritsar Exp, 1057,* 2150, 1¾ hrs. **Bhopal**: *Shatabdi Exp, 2002,* 0918, 5 hrs; *Punjab Mail, 2138,* 1025, 6¼ hrs; *Lakshadweep Exp, 2618,* 1415, 6 hrs. **Delhi**: *Lakshadweep Exp, 2617,* 1010, 6 hrs (HN); *Punjab Mail, 2137,* 1500, 5½ hrs (ND); *Taj Exp, 2179,* 1655, 5 hrs (HN). **Jabalpur (for Kanha)**: *Gondwana Exp, 2412,* 1838, 11 hrs; *Mahakoshal Exp, 1450,* 2110, 13¼ hrs. **Jhansi**: *Shatabdi Exp, 2002,* 0918, 1 hr; *Punjab Mail, 2138,* 1025, 1½ hrs; *Lakshadweep Exp, 2618,* 1415, 1½ hrs. **Lucknow**: *Gwalior Barauni Mail, 5224,* 1115, 9 hrs. **Mumbai (CST)**: *Punjab Mail, 2138,* 1025, 21¼ hrs, plus others to Dadar. **Varanasi**: *Bundelkhand Exp, 1107,* 1725, 17 hrs (calling at **Allahabad** 4 hrs earlier).

Shivpuri National Park *p281*
Air

Nearest airport is at Gwalior (112 km).

Bus

Regular bus services from Bhopal, Chanderi, Indore, Jhansi (101 km, 3 hrs by car) and Ujjain.

Rickshaw

Auto-rickshaws available at Bus Stand.

Train

Nearest stations are at Jhansi and Gwalior.

Jhansi *p281, map p282*
Bus

Long distance To major North Indian cities from **Kanpur Rd Bus Stand**, 3 km east of railway station: **Gwalior** 0645-1800 via Datia; **Khajuraho**, so-called 'Deluxe' from railway station (fairly direct, bumpy but through attractive countryside), 1100 (tickets from booth on Platform 1, or on bus; Rs 85, plus luggage Rs 5, 5 hrs) picks up from bus stand around 1130, other buses 1700, 1800; **Lalitpur** 0730, 1025, 2100, 2300. **Shivpuri** 0500-1800. **Orchha**: buses from Kanpur Rd Bus Stand, half-hourly during daylight, take about 30 mins, Rs 5; quicker by **auto-rickshaw** from Jhansi railway station, Rs 125-175; return after sightseeing Rs 275-340; **taxis**: equally overpriced, about Rs 300-350; **tempos**: from bus stand 30 mins, Rs 10.

Car

Car hire with driver: about Rs 5 per km, minimum 200 km per day; night halt Rs 150. To **Khajuraho**, *Hotel Sit*a; *Touraids*, Rs 2,100.

Rickshaw

Auto-rickshaws, Rs 20 from the railway station to hotel or bus stand; tempo, Rs 3 each from the station to main bus stand.

Train

Train porters are expensive here: agree a price in advance.
Agra Cantt: see Delhi. **Bhopal**: *Shatabdi Exp, 2002,* 1032, 3¾ hrs; *Punjab Mail, 2138,* 1215, 4½ hrs; *Lakshadweep Exp, 2618,* 1547, 4¼ hrs. **Delhi**: *Lakshadweep Exp, 2617,* 0850, 7¼ hrs (HN); *Punjab Mail, 2137,* 1340, 6¾ hrs (ND); *Shatabdi Exp, 2001,* 1755, 5 hrs (HN). **Jabalpur (for Kanha)**: *Godwana Exp, 2412,* 2012, 9½ hrs. **Jalgaon (for Aurangabad)**: *Amritsar Dadar Exp, 1058,* 0545, 14¼ hrs; *Punjab Mail, 2138,* 1215, 11¾ hrs. **Lucknow**: *Kushi Nagar Exp, 1015,* 2000, 7 hrs (continues to **Gorakhpur**, 5¼ hrs); *Gwailor Barauni Mail, 5224,* 1315, 7 hrs, plus several non-daily services. **Mumbai**: *Punjab Mail, 2138,* 1215, 19½ hrs, plus several to Dadar. **Varanasi**: *Bundelkhand Exp, 1107,* 1920, 15 hrs.

Datia *p286*

75 km south of Gwalior; 34 km from Jhansi.

Bus

Frequent from Jhansi (1 hr, Rs 10), and Gwalior (Rs 30).

Rickshaw

Tempos and cycle-rickshaws run the 2 km between Datia station and the fort/palace (10 mins, Rs 20), and the 5 km between Sonagiri station and the temples.

Train
Both are on the Delhi-Mumbai main line.
From Gwalior: *Bundelkhand Exp, 1107, 1725,*
1¼ hrs. From Jhansi: *Bundelkhand Exp, 1108,*
0730, 21 mins; *Chappra-Gwalior Mail, 1144,*
1435, 21 mins. For return to **Jhansi**,
Chhattisgarh Exp, 8238, depart Sonagiri
1210, Datia 1225.

Deogarh *p287*
Jakhlaun (13 km) is the nearest station, with
buses to **Deogarh** and **Lalitpur**. Lalitpur
(30 km away) has auto-rickshaws for transfer
to Deogarh (1 hr, Rs 200). It also has trains to
Jhansi: *Kushinagar Exp, 1015,* 1840, 1½ hrs;
Jhelum Exp, 1077, 1230, 1½ hrs; *Amritsar Exp,*
1457, 1818, 1½ hrs. **Bina-Etawa**, south of
Deogarh, is an important railway junction.

Khajuraho *p288, map p289*
Most places are within walking distance;
temple groups are easily reached on a bike.

Air
Flights are heavily booked in season, confirm
onward flight on arrival. The airport is 5 km
south of the village centre. Transport to
town: Taxi Rs 100, occasional auto-rickshaw
Rs 50 (overpriced; difficult to bargain). **Indian
Airlines**: *Clarks Bundela*, T74035, Airport
T74036; credit cards not accepted. Flies daily
from **Delhi** to Khajuraho (2½ hrs) via **Agra**,
returning the same route; also to **Varanasi**.
Jet Airways: T74406 (airport), daily to **Delhi**
via **Varanasi**.

Bicycle
Cycle hire behind museum, Jain Temples Rd;
Rs 25 per day, recommended mode though
not allowed in temple complex.

Bus
Long distance buses arrive at a newish
bus stand 1½ km south of the main bazar on
Airport Rd (which offers computerized
reservations on buses and trains elsewhere).
Daily buses to **Agra** 391 km, 0900
(10-12 hrs); **Bhopal** 350 km, 0600, 0730;
Gwalior 280 km (9 hrs); **Indore** 480 km,
0600; **Jabalpur** 210 km, 0730 via Satna; this
bus connects with trains to Jabalpur, better
than travelling all the way by bus – see
Satna, 2100 (via Damoh); **Jhansi** 176 km,
0530- 1645 (4½-5 hrs), semi-deluxe via

Orchha 1115; **Mahoba** (stops 3 km from the
railway station), several 0700-1900 (3 hrs)
and **Satna**, 0830, 0930, 1430, 1530, 4 hrs
(very uncomfortable), Rs 55. UP Roadways
runs a service to **Agra** via Gwalior, a long and
tiring journey.

Car
Car hire with driver to **Jhansi**, Rs 2,000
through **Touraids**, 3½ hrs. **Agra** or **Varanasi**,
Rs 5,000, 8-9 hrs.

Rickshaw
Cycle-rickshaws are expensive (Rs 30 for
shortest journey), negotiate fare; Rs 75 per
half day.

Taxi
From **MP Tourism** or **Touraids** near *Clarks
Hotel*, but overpriced.

Train
Railheads are **Jhansi** (176 km, for Agra,
Delhi, Bhopal); **Satna** (117 km, best for
Varanasi, see below); **Mahoba** (51 km,
alternative for Varanasi, but few slow trains
daily, small quota).

Satna *p294*
Bus
To **Amarkantak** 0750; for **Bandhavgarh**: daily
bus to **Tala**, 0800, 4 hrs (Rs 28); **Chitrakoot**
0500, 1200, 1530; **Khajuraho**: very
uncomfortable MPSRTC bus depart
0630-1530, 4 hrs (Rs 27); you can buy fruit
from market towns en route. In Satna, it stops
at the railway bridge which is a 2-km walk
from the station (rickshaws charge Rs 10).

Train
Reservations from office on right, outside
main entrance. **Jabalpur-Katni**: there are
good connections with 0730 bus from
Khajuraho (get off Khajuraho bus at railway
bridge); bus also connects with Allahabad
(4 hrs), Jabalpur, Lucknow, Chennai and
Patna. **Kolkata** *Howrah Mumbai Mail, 3004,*
1705, 20¼ hrs. **Mumbai (CST)** *Howrah
Mumbai Mail, 3003,* 1415, 21¼ hrs;
Mahanagri Exp, 1094, 1800, 21¼ hrs.
Varanasi *Sarnath Exp, 5159,* 0840, 7½ hrs;
5217/5219, 0705, 7½ hrs; *Mahanagri Exp,*
1093, 2000, 8¼ hrs; plus many at awkward
times, or certain days only.

Chitrakoot *p295*

Bus

Regular services to **Jhansi**, **Mahoba**, **Satna** and **Chhattarpur**.

Train

The nearest station is Karwi (Chitrakoot Dham) with trains between **Delhi (HN)** and **Jabalpur** and to **Lucknow**, then tempo to **Chitrakoot**, 30 mins, Rs 10. **Delhi (HN)** via Agra: *Nizamuddin Mahakosal Exp*, 2033, 14 hrs (for Agra deduct 4½ hrs).

⊙ Directory

Gwalior *p276, map p278*

Post office GPO: Jayaji Chowk, Birla Nagar, Morar and Residency. **Tourist offices** MP Tourism, *Motel Tansen*, 6A Gandhi Marg, T340370, F340371; Railway station, T540777. Tourist Taxis, available from *MP Tourism*.

Jhansi *p281, map p282*

Banks State Bank of India, Jayaji Chowk week 1030-1430, Sat 1030-1230; also *Sita* and *Jhansi* hotels. **Tourist offices** MP Tourism at railway station, T442622, will book Orchha hotels. UP Tourism, *Hotel Veerangana*, T441267.

Orchha *p282, map p284*

Banks Orchha Resorts for residents; Canara Bank, main street, changes TCs.

Khajuraho *p288, map p289*

Banks State Bank of India, opposite Western Group, foreign exchange facilities, can be busy. **Post office** Bus Stand, 0900-1700. "Beware. Parcel contents disappear!". **Tourist offices** Govt of India, opposite W Group, 0900-1730, Sat 0800-1230. Counter at bus stand. Guides Rs 100 per day. **MP**, Chandela Cultural Centre, north of Western Group, T74051, F72330. **Useful addresses** Police: T72032.

Indore

To Airport · To Dhar · To Annapurna Temple (1km) · To Manik Bagh Palace

Subhash Marg · Bara Ganapati · MG Rd · Kejari Bazar · Cloth · Khejuri Mandir · New Palace · Rajwada · Jawahar Marg · Ada Bazar · Gangwal (Dharnaka) · Chattri Bagh · Biya Bani Rd · Saraswati River · Lal Bagh Palace · Rajwada Chowk · Rail Rd · MG Rd · Gandhi Hall · Rupayana Bookshop · Maharani Rd · Shastri Bridge · Gandhi Statue · High Court · Shiva Shakti Travels · University · Patel Bridge · Patel Statue · Nehru Statue · Sarwate · Nehru Park · Dentist · Chandra Bhaga · Manik Bagh Rd · Bhanwar Kila Rd · Sanyogita · Khan River · Navlakha Rd · RNT

N

0 metres 300
0 yards 300

Sleeping
1 Amaltas International
2 Ashoka
3 Balwas
4 Embassy
5 Indotels Manor House & Bookworld
6 Kanchan
7 MP Tourist Bungalow & Tourist Office, Ravindra Natyagrih & Apsara Restaurant
8 Payal
9 President & Landmark Restaurants
10 Shreemaya

Western Madhya Pradesh

Indore → *Phone code: 0731. Colour map 2, grid C5. Population: 1,600,000.*

A rapidly growing and rather characterless industrial city, Indore is on the banks of the rivers Sarasvati and Khan. A major centre for cotton textiles and the automobile industry, but the city is notable for Hindustani classical music. ▶▶ *For Sleeping, Eating and other listings, see pages 313-319.*

Ins and outs

Getting there Indore has direct flights to Bhopal, Delhi, Gwalior and Mumbai. It is under 5 hrs by the fastest train from Bhopal. The railway station and the Sarwate Bus Stand are near the town centre, but buses to Mandu go from the Gangwal Bus Stand, 10-min auto ride away.

Getting around Indore is quite spread out so it is best to take an auto to visit the sights away from the centre. Some prefer to hire a bike. See Transport, page 317, for further details.

● Eating
1 Café Udupi & Prithvilok
2 Ding Ding
3 Gypsy
4 Indian Coffee House
5 Statue

Climate Temperature: Summer: maximum 40°C, minimum 22°C; Winter: maximum 29°C, minimum 10°C. Annual rainfall: 1,050 mm, mostly July-September. The best time to visit is October-March, or June-September, if also visiting Mandu.

History

The land on which Indore was built was given to **Malhar Rao Holkar** in 1733 by the Maratha Peshwas, see page 1066, in appreciation of his help in many of their battles. Malhar Rao left much of the statecraft in the highly gifted hands of his widowed daughter-in-law who succeeded him to the throne. The city was destroyed in 1801 but recovered and was the British headquarters of their Central India Agency. The ruling family of Indore, the **Holkars**, took the British side during the Mutiny in 1857. Indore was one of the first states to open temples, schools and public wells to *Harijans* (Untouchables), in support of Gandhi's campaign against untouchability.

Sights

The **Rajwada** (Old Palace) with its seven-storeyed gateway, faces the main square. A third fire in 1984 destroyed most of it; now only the façade remains.

On the north side is the **New Palace** and garden. In the streets are some good timber houses with deep recessed verandahs and carved pillars.

Kanch Mandir① *1000, allow 30 mins, shoes to be left at door*, is on Jawahar Marg next to *Hotel Sheesh Mahal*. Inside this Jain temple thousands of mirrors adorn the walls, floor and ceilings, supplemented by brightly patterned ceramic tiles, Chinese lantern-type glass lamps and cut glass chandeliers, all exquisitely crafted. There are about 50 murals depicting scenes of conversion to Jainism and 19th-century courtly life. The use of glass beads and raised figures produces a pleasing 3D effect. The image of the Mahavir is in plain black onyx. This mirrored palace is at variance with the austerity and simplicity of the Mahavira's supposed existence and teachings.

Chhattri Bagh, on the banks of the Khan River, has seven memorials of the Holkar kings but the sanctums are locked. Although in a peaceful setting, the place is overgrown and unkempt and hardly worth a special detour.

Lal Bagh (The Nehru Centre) ① *closed Mon, 1100-1800, small entry fee*, southwest of town, once the residence of the Maharaja, built and decorated in a confusion of styles, is now a museum and cultural centre. The rooms have been restored and furnished to pleasing effect. Queen Victoria looks on to the main 'entrance portico' (you leave through this and enter through a side entrance). There are a number of sporting trophies including stuffed tigers. The Maharaja, a keen sportsman, is seen in photographs rowing on a lake, and flying in an early aeroplane. Both these are in fact 'backdrop paintings' with a hole for him to stand in to be photographed! There are also good prints of the Old Palace. The entrance hall is in marble and gilt rococo with a display of prehistoric artefacts. Two attractive rooms are predominantly 'Indian' and include Mughal exhibits. On the first floor is the coin collection which dates mostly from the Muslim period. Exhibits include miniatures, contemporary Indian sculptures and paintings, Italian sculptures and intricately inlaid boxes. The garden, though maintained, is dry and dusty.

> ‡ *If time is precious, visit this museum instead of the Cental Museum – riotously varied and fascinating.*

Central Museum ① *Agra-Mumbai Rd, near GPO, closed Mon, 1100-1800, free, guides available, allow 30 mins*, has two main galleries: **Gallery I** with artefacts from circa 50,000-4000 BC, some from west Malwa including stone tools, quartz sickles, ornaments. Also a model of the first Hindu temple at Bharhut (another is at Lal Bagh). **Gallery II** contains Hindu mythological carvings. Sculptures stand in the grounds, which were possibly a battlefield during the Mutiny.

Dewas **EM Forster** 'worked' here in the court of the Raja of Dewas Senior in 1921, having visited it earlier in 1912. Forster came to regard his stay in this dusty town as the 'great opportunity' of his life and used this experience to good effect with the autobiographical *The Hill of Devi* and his most famous novel, *A Passage to India*. It is worth going up the 'Hill of Devi' overlooking the town for the views; you can drive all the way to the temple at the top. Dewas today is an important industrial centre.

Ujjain → *Phone code: 0734. Colour map 2, grid C5. Population: 430,000.*

Ujjain, one of the best known cities of ancient India and one of Hinduism's seven sacred cities, see page 1326, is one of the four centres of the Kumbh Mela, see page 195, attracting about three million pilgrims every 12 years. At other times, a constant stream come to bathe in the river Shipra and worship at the temples. Despite its sanctity and its age, it has few remarkable buildings. In its heyday, Ujjain was on a flourishing trade route to Mesopotamia and Egypt. Nowadays, it is little more than a provincial town.

Ins and outs Getting there The airport in Indore has good connections with major surrounding cities, as does the train. There are direct buses from surrounding cities. If you prefer better hotels and have a car, visit Ujjain from Indore. **Getting around** The temples are some distance away so you'll need transport, but there are basic hotels and restaurants near the bus and railway stations. See Transport, page 317, for further details. **Climate** Best time to visit is Oct-Mar.

Background Many dynasties ruled over this prosperous city and it is said to have been the seat of the viceroyalty of Asoka in 275 BC. His sons were born here, and it was from here that they set out to preach Buddhism. The poet **Kalidasa**, one of the *Nava Ratna* (Nine Gems) of Hindu literature, wrote some of his works here.

Ujjain stands on the **first meridian** of longitude for Hindu astronomers, who believed that the **Tropic of Cancer** also passed through the site. This explains the presence of the **Vedha Shala** observatory, southwest of town, built by Raja Jai Singh II of Jaipur around 1730 when he was the Governor of Malwa under the Mughals. Small, compared to the Jantar Mantars, it has only five instruments. Even today the *Ephemeris* tables (predicted positions of the planets), are published here.

Sights **Mahakaleshwar Temple**, dedicated to Siva, was rebuilt by Marathas in the 18th century. The temple lingam is one of the 12 *jyotirlingas* (in India, believed to be *swayambhu* – born of itself). The myths surrounding the 'linga of light' go back to the second century BC and were developed to explain and justify linga worship, see page 1331. The Chaubis Khambha Darwaza (circa 11th century) has 24 carved pillars which probably belonged to the medieval temple.

Close to the tank near Mahakaleshwar is a large sculpted image of Ganesh in the **Bade Ganeshji-ka Mandir**. A rock covered with turmeric is worshipped as the head of a legendary king Vikramaditya in the centre of the **Harsiddhi Mandir**. **Gopal Mandir** in the bazar contains a silver image of Krishna and an ornamental silver door. The **Bina-Niv-ki-Masjid** in Anantpeth, originally a Jain temple (see entrance porch), was converted to a mosque (circa 1400), by the first independent Sultan of Malwa. The

Ujjain

To Gada Kalika Temples
To Bhartham Temple & Kaliadeh Palace
Chousath Yogini
Tilke Twar Marg
Gautam Marg
Ankpat Marg
Govardhan Sagar
Chakra Teertha
Veer Durgadas Marg
Patel Marg
Water Tower
Lala Lajpat Rai Marg
Udayan Marg
Heera Mill Marg
Shipra River
Sidhasen Marg
Gopal Temple
Sharma Marg
Mandir Marg
Nazar Ali Marg
Ksheer Sagar
Ashtok Marg
To Bhopal
Chattri Chowk
Ramghat
Ram Ghat Marg
Norozee Marg
Tilak Marg
Arya Samaj Marg
Laxmi Bai Marg
Gandhi Statue
Sakhya Raja Marg
Harsiddhi Mandir
Duje Ganeshji-ka Mandir
Chaubis Khamba Darwaza
Mahakaleshwar Marg
Mahakaleshwar Temple
Harsiddhi Marg
Chardham Temple
To Chintamani Ganesh Temple
Ahilya Bai Marg
Subhash Marg
Footbridge
Madhar Chowk Clock Tower
Kalidas Marg
Khawajahan Marg
University Rd
To Veda Shala Observatory
To Yatri Niwas & Dewas
N
0 metres 500
0 yards 500

	Sleeping			Eating	
1	Ajay	3	Girnar	● Eating	3 Kwality Ice Creams
2	Ayodhya Lodge	4	Ramkrishna	1 5 Star Restaurant	4 Sudama
		5	Shipra (MP Tourism)	2 Ashnol	

Chintamani Ganesh Temple across the river is believed to have ancient medieval origins. There are other smaller temples and shrines along the river and the atmosphere at these is generally very restful and relaxed.

★ Mandu (Mandav)

→ *Phone code: 07292. Colour map 2, grid C5. Population: 5,000.*

Architecturally, Mandu represents the best in a provincial Islamic style, restrained and lacking in elaborate external ornamentation. Fine buildings are spread over the naturally defensible plateau with a sheer drop towards the Namar plains to the south and waterfalls flowing into the Kakra Khoh gorge. You can visit Mandu from Indore on a long day excursion, but it is better to have a peaceful break here for a couple of days.

▸▸ *For Sleeping, Eating and other listings, see pages 313-319.*

Ins and outs

Getting there Indore is the nearest centre for air, bus and train connections.

Getting around Everything worth visiting, spread across a few kilometres, can be reached on foot, bike or rickshaw. See Transport, page 317, for further details.

Climate Temperature: Summer: maximum 36°C, minimum 28°C. Winter: maximum 22°C, minimum 7°C. Rainfall: 1,050 mm. Best time to visit: during the monsoon when the tanks are full and the rain turns the countryside a verdant green. Good Oct-Feb.

History

Perched along the **Vindhya ranges**, Mandu was fortified as early as the sixth century. By 1261, King Jayavaram transferred the Paramara capital from Dhar to Mandu itself. The whole area fell to the Muslims in 1293, though Mandu remained under Hindu rule until 1305, when it came under the Khaljis in Delhi. The first of these Pathan sultans re-named **Mandu, Shadiabad** (City of Joy). Hoshang Shah (1405-35) made it his capital and as Mandu's strategic importance grew he embellished it with its most important civic buildings. Under his successor, the liberal Mahmud Khalji, a resurgence of art and literature followed, fostering Hindu, Jain as well as Muslim development. Mandu remained a prosperous centre of peace and stability under his son Ghiyasuddin until 1500. Several early Mughal rulers enjoyed visiting Mandu, but by the end of the Mughal period it had effectively been abandoned, and in 1732 it passed into Maratha hands.

Sights

Most of the buildings date from 1401 to 1526 – some have stones salvaged from desecrated local Hindu temples. There are six groups of buildings at Mandu, the first three being the most important. The return trip taking in Roopmati's Pavilion is about 14 km. The 45-km parapet wall with 12 gates was built from rubble and boulders. Most notable is **Delhi Gate** (1405-7), the main entrance to the city. The approach is through a series of well fortified subsidiary gates such as Alamgir and Bhangi Darwaza (the only one now open). The present road is along this route.

Royal Enclave Mosque of Dilwar Khan (1405) ① *entry Rs 2*, is the earliest Islamic building, comprising a central colonnaded courtyard. There are Hindu influences in the main entrances. **Hathi Pol** (Elephant Gate) is the main entrance to the royal enclosure. **Hindola Mahal** (Swing Palace, circa 1425), built on a 'T' plan, was the audience hall, acquiring its name from its inward sloping walls which give the impression of swaying. Behind and to the west of the Hindola Mahal is a jumble of ruins which was once the palace of the Malwa Sultans.

Here is the 6½-m deep **Champa Baoli**, an underground well (its water is said to have smelt like the *champak* flower), cool vaulted *tyhkhanas* (rooms for summer use), a *hammam* (hot bath) and a water pavilion.

The late 15th-century **Jahaz Mahal** (Ship Palace), reflects the spirit of romantic beauty characteristic of the palace life of the Muslim rulers of India. Built between two artificial lakes, Munj and Kapur Talaos, it is 122 m long and only 15 m wide. Its shape and kiosks give it the impression of a stately ship. Built to house Ghiyas'ud-Din's increasing *harem*, it was 'crewed' entirely by women, some from as far off places as Turkey and Abyssinia, and consists of three great halls with a beautiful bath at the north end.

Other places of interest in this enclave are **Taveli Mahal (2)** (stables and guardhouse), from which there is a wonderful panorama of the ruins of Mandu; it has a small **museum**. Two large wells – the *Ujala* (bright) and *Andheri* (dark) **baolis**, and **Gada Shah's House and Shop (3)**, Kesar Kasturi Mahal are nearby. The last, in ruins, retains the romance of its second name – Gada Shah taking pity on a group of gypsies trying to sell their perfumed *kesar* and *kasturi* which had been ruined by a downpour, bought their wares and then had to use it all in his palace since it was unsaleable.

Central Group Hoshang Shah's Tomb (4) (circa 1440) ① *US$5 for foreigners*, in Mandu Bazar, is India's first marble monument, a refined example of Afghan architecture. It has a well-proportioned dome, delicate marble latticework and porticoed courts and towers. The square base of the interior changes to an octagon through being raised by arches to the next level, and then becomes 16-sided further up. Shah Jahan sent four of his architects, including Ustad Ahmed, who is associated with the Taj Mahal, to study it for inspiration. The adjoining **Jama Masjid (4)** (1454), which took three generations to complete, was inspired by the great mosque at Damascus. Conceived by Hoshang Shah on a grand scale, it is on a high plinth

Mandu Fort

Sleeping
1 Maharaja
2 MP Tourism Tourist Cottages
3 MP Tourism Travellers' Lodge
4 Roopmati

1 Chishti Khan's Palace
2 Taveli Mahal & Museum
3 Gada Shah's House & Baolis
4 Hoshang Shah's Tomb & Jama Masjid

5 Ashrafi Mahal
6 Chaapan Mahal & Ek-Khamba
7 Nilkanth Palace
8 Malik Mughith Mosque & Caravansarai

0 metres 800
0 yards 800

(4.6 m), with a large domed porch ornamented with jali screens and bands of blue enamel tiles set as stars. The courtyard is flanked by colonnades. The western one is the Prayer Hall and is the most imposing of all with numerous rows of arches and pillars which support the ceilings of the three great domes and the 58 smaller ones. The central niche (*mihrab*) is beautifully designed and ornamented along its sides with a scroll of interwoven Arabic letters containing quotations from the Koran.

Ashrafi Mahal (5) (Palace of gold coins, circa 1436-40), now a ruin, was conceived as the first *madrassa* of Persian studies. Its builder Mahmud Shah Khilji (1436-69) built the seven-storeyed tower to celebrate his victory over Rana Khumba of Mewar (Udaipur). Only one storey has survived. Also in ruins is the tomb, intended to be the largest building in Mandu.

Sagar Talao Group To the east of the road between the village and Sagar Talao is the **Hathi Mahal** (Elephant Palace). It takes its names from its stumpy pillars supporting the dome and was probably a *baradari* (pleasure pavilion), turned into a tomb with a mosque by it. The **Tomb of Darya Khan** (circa 1526), a red masonry mausoleum once embellished with rich enamel patterns, is nearby.

In the large group of monuments around the picturesque **Sagar Talao** (lake) is the **Malik Mughith Mosque (8)** built in 1432. It has a west wall retaining blue tile decoration in carved niches. In front is the **caravanserai** (also 1432), an open courtyard with two halls with rooms at both ends, probably for storage of goods while the halls provided living accommodation. The **Dai-ka-Mahal (9)** (Gumbad) to the south is a tomb which may first have been a house belonging to the wet-nurse of a Mandu Prince, and was later converted to her tomb. Alongside, the ruins of a pretty mosque has a fine octagonal base to the dome, decorated with small kiosks.

Rewa Kund Group Rewa Kund , 3.2 km south of the village, is a sacred tank whose waters were lifted to supply the **Palace of Baz Bahadur** (1508-09), the musician prince, on the rising ground above. The palace was built before Baz Bahadur, the last Sultan of Malwa (1555), came to occupy it. The main portion of the palace consists of a spacious open court with halls and rooms on all sides and a beautiful cistern in its centre. On the terrace above are two *baradaris* (pavilions) from which there are lovely views.

On higher ground at the southern edge of the plateau is **Roopmati's Pavilion (10)**, originally built as a military observation post but later modified and added to as a palace, so that Baz Bahadur's mistress could have her *darshan* (view) of the sacred **Narmada River**, seen 305 m below winding like a white serpent across the plains. The shepherdess **Roopmati**, the story goes, so impressed Baz Bahadur with her singing that he captured her. She agreed to go to Mandu with Baz Bahadur when he promised that she would live in a palace within sight of her beloved river! He built the Rewa Kund so that she could practise her Hindu rites. The pavilions, square with hemispherical domes, are the latest additions.

Other palaces On the edge of the plateau is the **Lal Mahal** (Red/Ruby Palace) or Lal Bungalow, once used as a royal summer retreat. **Chishti Khan's Palace (1)**, used during the monsoon, is now in ruins but offers good views. West of Sagar Talao the Islamic **Nilkanth Palace (7)**, built for Akbar's Hindu wife, contains the Nilkanth (Siva) shrine. On the scarp of one of the great ravines, reached by steps and commanding a magnificent view of the valleys below, it was used by the Mughals as a water palace. On one of the outer room walls is an inscription recording Akbar's expeditions into the Deccan and the futility of temporal riches.

The **Lohani Caves** and temple ruins are near Hoshang Shah's Tomb. Approached by steep rock-cut steps, they are a maze of dark and damp caverns in the hillside. Panoramic views of the surroundings from **Sunset Point** in front of the caves.

ⓘ *Regular bus services from Barwaha, Khandwa, Dhar and Dhamnod. The nearest railhead is Barwaha (39 km) on the Western Railway.*

On the north bank of the Narmada, Maheshwar has been identified as **Mahishmati**, the ancient capital of King Kartivirarjun, a spectacular temple city mentioned in the *Ramayana* and *Mahabharata* epics. The Holkar queen **Rani Ahilyabai of Indore** who died in 1795 was responsible for revitalizing the city by building temples and a fort complex. According to Sir John Malcolm, the queen was widely revered. She had "an almost sacred respect for native rights ... she heard every complaint in person". The palace inside the fort contains exhibits of the Holkar family treasures and memorabilia including the small shrine on a palanquin which is carried down from the fort during the annual *Dasara* ceremony. There is also a statue of the Rani seated on her throne.

The town is renowned for its *Maheshwar* saris woven in a unique way for over 200 years. Woven in cotton and silk, the 'body' of the sari may be plain, checked or striped. The **Ghats** on the river bank are interesting to visit and watch the daily rituals of ordinary villagers. Lining the banks are stone memorials to the *satis*. The temples to see are Kaleshwara, Rajarajeshwara, Vithaleshwara and Ahileshwar.

Omkareshwar (Mandhata)

ⓘ *Omkareshwar is connected to Indore, Ujjain, Khandhwa and Omkareshwar Rd railway station (12 km) by regular bus services. The railhead is on the Ratlam-Khandwa section of the Western Railway.*

A sacred island shaped like the holy Hindu symbol 'Om' at the confluence of the Narmada and the Kaveri, Omkareshwar has drawn pilgrims for centuries. Over 2 km long and 1 km wide the island is divided north to south by a deep gully. The ground slopes gently along the north edge but in the south and east there are cliffs over 150 m high forming a gorge. The village spreads to the south bank from the island, now linked by a bridge. The river is reputedly very deep and has crocodiles.

Sri Omkareshwar Mahadeo Temple has one of the 12 *jyotirlingas* in India, natural rock features that are believed to be representations of Siva. The oldest temple is at the east end of the island, **Siddhnath Temple** on the hill is a fine example of early medieval temple architecture, its main feature being a frieze of elephants over 1½-m high carved on a stone slab at its outer perimeter. Craftsmen have carved elaborate figures on the upper portion of the temple and its roof. Encircling the shrine are verandahs with columns carved in circles, polygons and squares. A gigantic Nandi bull is carved in the hillside opposite the temple to **Gauri Somnath** at the west end of the island.

The temples were severely damaged after the Muslim invasions of **Mahmud of Ghazni**. Every dome was overturned and the sculptured figures mutilated. They became completely overgrown, and *Murray's Guide* records that when the Peshwa Baji Rao II wanted to repair the temple it could not be found, so he built a new one. Subsequently repairs were carried out to the part that was discovered.

Jabalpur → *Phone code: 0761. Colour map 3, grid C2. Population: 952,000.*

On the upper reaches of the River Narmada in the heart of India's forested tribal belt, Jabalpur is remarkably little visited. It serves as the main gateway to two of India's finest wildlife reserves, Kanha and Bandhavgarh. Jabalpur town was the capital and pleasure resort of the Gond kings during the 12th century. It was later the seat of the Kalchuri Dynasty until it fell to the Marathas. The British took it in 1817 and left their mark with the cantonment residences and barracks.

Getting there Although there are long distance buses to Jabalpur from the surrounding large cities, it is most comfortable to travel here by train. Under 8 hrs from Bhopal or Allahabad, there are also good connections to Nagpur and South India. The main station is on the edge of the Civil Lines, under 2 km from the town centre. The cheaper hotels are easily reached from the main bus stand. Hotel touts are very active round the station and bus stand so it is best to have a hotel in mind.

Getting around The town is too spread out to cover on foot easily but there are plenty of taxis, unmetered autos and cheap shared tempos. See Transport, page 318, for further details. Warning: rickshaws offer cheap fares to hotel and then charge a commission.

Sights

Madan Mahal Fort (1116) ① *closed Mon and holidays, 1000-1700, free, take tempo from stand near the Krishna Hotel to Sharda Chowk, Rs 2, then walk up the left-hand hill, built by the Gond ruler Madan Shah on a hill just to the west of the city, has superb views. Rani Durgavati Museum and Memorial houses a collection of sculptures and prehistoric relics, and the Tilwara Ghat where Mahatma Gandhi's ashes were immersed in the Narmada, are all places of interest. There are also Jain temples.*

Excursions

The **Marble Rocks** are 22 km west of Jabalpur ① *take a tempo from the stand near* Hotel Krishna *to Bhedaghat, Rs 8, which takes you right to the Marble Rocks Car Park, a taxi from Jabalpur costs around Rs 500 return, walk up to see the waterfalls, or go past the Mandir to the town and follow steps down for boat trips (30 min, Rs 10, recommended, though if alone it costs Rs 200 to hire the whole boat), snacks, drinks and mineral water are available.* Captain J Forsyth wrote of them: "The eye never wearies of the effect produced by the broken and reflected sunlight, glancing from a pinnacle of snow-white marble reared against the deep blue of the sky and again losing itself in the soft bluish greys of their recesses". These white rocks, with views of black/dark green volcanic seams, rise to 30 m on either side of the Narmada River and in moonlight produce a magical effect; floodlights have been added, though boating may not be possible. Stalls sell cheap soap-stone carvings. There is accommodation if you need to stay, in Bhedaghat nearby.

Jabalpur

Sleeping ■
1 Ambassador
2 Anand
3 Jackson's, Chadha Travels & Bookshop
4 Kalchuri
5 Krishna & Satyam Shivam Sundaram Restaurant
6 Rishi Regency
7 Samadariya & Woodlands Restaurant
8 Sidharth & Arihant Palace
9 Utsav

Eating ●
1 Indian Coffee House

0 metres 500
0 yards 500
N

Other sights nearby are the **Dhuandhar Falls** ('smoke cascade'), where the Narmada plunges through a narrow chasm, **Hathi-ka-paon** (Elephant's Foot Rock) and **Monkey's Leap** ledge. Nearby is the **Chausath Yogini Mandir**, a 10th-century temple with stone carvings. Legend suggests that it is connected to the Gond queen Durgavati's palace by an **underground passage**. Approached by a long flight of steps, there is an excellent view of the Narmada from the top. The British era **Pariyat tank**, 12 km from Jabalpur, is a popular picnic and fishing spot for locals, Rs 200 return by taxi.

Mandla → *Colour map 3, grid C2. Kanha National Park is about 40 km from Mandla.*

The capital of the ancient Gond Kingdom of Garha-Mandla early in the Christian era, Mandla is of great historical significance to the Gond tribal peoples. The Gond Queen Rani Durgavati took her life here when her army was cornered by Mughal forces under Asaf Khan in 1564. The **fort** was built in the 17th century and is surrounded on three sides by the Narmada River. It passed to the Marathas and then to the British in 1818. The jungle has since taken over the ruins (only a few towers remain), though there are some temples and ghats in the town. The Gond Raja Hirde Shah built a large **palace** in a commanding site nearby in **Ramnagar** (15 km), of which little remains.

★ Kanha National Park

→ *Colour map 3, grid C2. Area: 1,945 sq km. Altitude: 450-950 m.*

This is the country about which Kipling wrote so vividly in his Jungle Books. The area was famed as a hunter's paradise but now the valley has been well developed as a national park. Lying in the Maikal hills in the eastern part of the Satpura Range, the park has deciduous hardwoods, rolling grasslands and meandering streams of the Banjar River.

The park forms the core of the Kanha Tiger Reserve. It was created in 1974 and also protects the rare hardground-adapted barasingha (swamp deer). George Schaller, the zoologist, conducted the first ever scientific study of the tiger here and research is also being done on deer and langur habitat. ▶▶ *For Sleeping, Eating and other listings, see pages 313-319.*

Ins and outs

Getting there The journey by car takes about 5 hrs from Jabalpur on a poor road. The main gates are at Kisli and Mukki. If arriving in the evening stop overnight at Khatia or Kisli as vehicles are not allowed into the park after dark. From Nagpur or Raipur enter via Mukki Gate. Diesel vehicles, motorcycles and bicycles are not allowed in the park.

Entry Rs 200 (foreigners), Rs 20 (Indians). Movie cameras Rs 25-250. Visitor centres at Khatia and Mukki gates and at Kanha, the one at Kanha is the largest. 0700-1030, 1600-1800. Recommended: informative for displays, short films, audio-visual shows and books for sale. Recommended minimum stay: two nights.

Getting around Visitors may not walk around inside the park, you can walk in the peaceful forest between the gate at Kanha and the park itself. See also Viewing. See Transport, page 318, for further details.

Climate It can get very cold on winter nights. Summer: maximum 43°C, minimum 11°C; Winter: maximum 29°C, minimum 2°C. Annual rainfall: 1,250 mm; monsoon Jul-Sep. Best time to visit is Jan to Jun. Closed 1 Jul-31 Oct.

Wildlife

Kanha has 22 species of mammal and the most easily spotted are the three-striped palm squirrel, common langur monkey, jackal, wild boar, cheetal, sambar, Branden barasingha and blackbuck. Less commonly seen are Indian hare, *dhole* (Indian wild dog) and gaur. Rarely seen are Indian fox, sloth bear, striped hyena, tiger (estimated at about 100), leopard, *nilgai* (blue bull), Indian porcupine, wolf (outside park proper) and the Indian pangolin (sometimes called a scaly anteater).

As for birds, Kanha has 230 species recorded. Good vantage points are in the hills where the mixed and bamboo forest harbours many species. Commonly seen species are: leaf warblers, minivets, black ibis, common peafowl, racket-tailed drongo, hawk eagle, red-wattled lapwing, various species of flycatcher, woodpecker, pigeon, dove, parakeet, babbler, mynah, Indian roller, white breasted kingfisher and grey hornbill.

Viewing

Forest Department guides accompany visitors around the park on mapped-out circuits to see a cross-section of wildlife from a jeep (about Rs 400 or Rs 9 per km); tours start at Kisli 0600, 1800. Reserve seats on arrival and share with others for economy. However, a traveller comments: "vehicles chase each other round, their paths crossing and re-crossing and their noisy engines presumably driving the more timid wildlife way back from the tracks". It is better to stop the vehicle on the forest track and in front of the grasslands.

The *sal* forests do not normally allow good viewing. The best areas are the meadows around Kanha. **Bamni Dadar** (Sunset Point) affords a view of the dense jungle and animals typical of the mixed forest zone: sambar, barking deer and chausingha (four-horned antelope). Early morning and late afternoon are ideal times and binoculars are invaluable. *Machans* (viewing platforms/observation towers), are available for use during daylight; those above waterholes (eg *Sravanta*), are recommended.

Elephants, once used for tiger tracking, are now only available for 'joy rides' outside the park at Kisli. MP Tourism vehicle hire: Gypsy four-wheel-drives and jeeps from the Baghira Log Huts, Kisli in the park (for maximum six), Rs 9 per km. Petrol is often not available at Kisli; nearest pumps at Mandla. Book previous day.

Kanha National Park

★ Bandhavgarh National Park

→ *Phone code: 07653. Altitude: 800 m.*

The park is set in extremely rugged terrain with many hills. The marshes which used to be perennial now support a vast grassland savanna. Though it involves quite a journey you may be rewarded with sighting one of the few tigers; a three-day stay gives you a 90% chance of seeing one! There are also interesting cave shrines scattered around the park, with Brahmi inscriptions dating from the first century BC. You can visit the remains of a fort believed to be 2,000 years old where you may spot crag martins and brown rock thrush.

Bandhavgarh (pronounced Bandogarh) is not very far from Rewa, famous as the original home of the white tiger, now only found in zoos. Before becoming a national park in 1968, it was the game reserve of the Maharajas of Rewa. The conservation programme helps to protect wildlife from disease, fire, grazing and poaching.

Ins and outs

This compact park is in the Vindhya hills with a core area of 105 sq km and a buffer zone of 437 sq km. The main entrance and park office is at Tala to the north of the park. Rs 200 (foreigners), Rs 20 (Indians), still camera Rs 10, video Rs 100 per day, so retain receipt. See Viewing for Getting around information. See Transport, page 318, for further details. Best time to visit: Feb-Jun. Closed 1 Jul-31 Oct. Temperature range: 42°C to 2°C. Rainfall: 1,500 mm.

Wildlife

The park has a wide variety of game and has a longer 'season' than Kanha. Its main wild beasts are tiger, leopard, sloth bear, gaur, sambar, chital, muntjac, *nilgai*, chinkara and wild pigs. There are over 60 tigers, but they remain very elusive. The flowering and fruit trees attract woodland birds which include green pigeon, Jerdon's leaf bird, crested serpent eagle and variable hawk eagle.

Viewing

Jeeps are available from dawn to 1000 and 1600 until dusk when the animals are most active; compulsory Forest Department guide, Rs 50. The short way round is 18 km, the long, 37 km. The fort, 18 km away, requires a four-wheel drive vehicle; ask at the *White Tiger Forest Lodge* about MP Tourism Jeeps (Rs 9 per km). Jeep Tours (up to 6 passengers), Rs 550; private hire from Talu Rs 400 (each entry) after bargaining; vehicle entry Rs 25 per day.

Forest Department elephants (two-seater), Rs 200 plus Rs 50 per person per hour, are recommended. 'Tiger Show' (visitors are rushed by jeep to an elephant which has tracked a tiger) costs Rs 50 but this may be stopped. Some feel the constant traffic of elephants and jeeps is affecting wildlife – "a bit like a circus". Viewing *machans* are available during the day; Bhadrashila Watch Tower attracts gaur.

Listings: Western Madhya Pradesh

💬 Sleeping

Indore *p303, map p302*
AM Rd, Agra-Mumbai Rd;
RNT Marg is RN Tagore Marg.
L-AL Taj Residency, Meghdoot Gardens,
T557700, F555355. 80 very comfortable

rooms, very good coffee shop.
B Indotels Manor House, A-M Rd, T537301.
66 a/c rooms (odd numbers at back are quieter), restaurant (bar with noisy TV), pool, comfortable but not central and overpriced.
B President, 163 RNT Marg, T528866
F512230. 65 comfortable a/c rooms, good

south Indian restaurant, modern, friendly, good travel desk.

B-C Mashal, Jhoomerghat, Rasalpura, A-M Rd, T856230, F856138. 36 comfortable a/c rooms, gardens, pool, squash.

C Shreemaya, 12/1 RNT Marg (near railway), T514081, krishna@bom4.vsnl.net.in. 61 a/c rooms with bath, very good popular cafeteria (South Indian), exchange, Indian style hotel, 0900 check-out.

C-D Kanchan Tilak, 585/2 MG Rd, Palasia, T538606. 39 rooms, good restaurant, garden, clean, modern, family atmosphere, pleasant lobby, good service and value but noisy.

D Amaltas International, A-M Rd, 2 RK Puram, T432631, F554358. 30 small rooms, some a/c, restaurant claustrophobic but good value, bar, garden, far from centre.

D Balwas, 30/2 S Tukoganj, T434934. 38 rooms, some a/c, good restaurant, popular with tours from Gulf, quiet, good value.

D Kanchan, Kanchan Bagh, T270871. 28 comfortable rooms, some a/c with bath, restaurant, bar, good value. Recommended.

D Tourist Bungalow, behind Ravindra Natya Griha, RNT Marg, T521818. 6 rooms, 2 a/c with bath, Nos 4 and 5 larger, breakfast only, Tourist Office, safe, peaceful.

E Ashoka, T46591. Clean rooms (hot water).

E Embassy, 9/1/3 MG Rd, T436574. 30 rooms, some a/c, small, no frills.

E Payal, Chhoti Gwaltoli, near Patel Bridge, opposite Sarawate bus station, T463202. Neat rooms with bath, some aircooled with TV.

Ujjain *p304, map p305*

C Surana Palace, 23 GDC Rd (southeast of Madhav Chowk), T513045. Comfortable rooms, good restaurant.

C-D Shipra (MP Tourism), University Rd, T551495. 30 rooms (10 a/c), restaurant, beer bar, travel, garden, quiet but run down and major mosquito menace.

E Girnar Subhash Marg, about 1 km west of station, T555873. Good value, clean rooms, some with bath.

E-F Ajay, opposite railway station. Some rooms air-cooled with bath.

E-F Yatri Niwas (MP Tourism), LB Shastri Marg, 2½ km south of station, T511398. 4 rooms, 60 dorm beds, canteen, clean, quiet.

F Ayodhya Lodge, Laxmi Bai Marg, is similar (need to bargain).

F Ramkrishna, Subhash Marg, T557012. Basic rooms, some with bath (check first), veg restaurant.

F Railway Retiring Rooms.

Mandu *p306, map p307*

Severe water shortage is likely before the monsoon - buckets are provided.

C-D Roopmati (500 m beyond entrance), T63270. 10 a/c rooms with balcony, decent showers, restaurant, beer.

D Maharaja, 500 m before Jahaz Mahal, T63288. Well-kept rooms with bath (bucket hot water), courtyard, limited menu restaurant.

D Tourist Cottages (MP Tourism), Roopmati Rd, 20-min walk from Bus Stand, T63235. 20 rooms (6 **C** a/c), spacious cottages with small lounge, No 16 best a/c, No 18 best non-a/c (avoid 1, 2, 7 and 8), good restaurant, gardens, peaceful setting by Sagar Talao Lake.

E Travellers' Lodge (MP Tourism), near SADA barrier (ask to be dropped before reaching bus stand), T63221. 8 rooms, restaurant (order ahead), bright and cheerful, very pleasant, excellent view of plateau. Reserve ahead at MP Tourism, Bhopal or Indore. Some non-vegetarian food is served in MPTDC hotels.

Tourist Cottages, good veg dishes, bar closed "because people kept sitting around and drinking, all the time!".

The fruit and vegetable market is opposite Jama Masjid.

Maheshwar *p309*

E Narmada Cottages, T07283-42055. With 6 rooms, and *dharamshalas*.

Omkareshwar *p309*

For an overnight stay there is **Holkar Guest House** and **dharamshalas**.

Jabalpur *p309, map p310*

Hotels have some a/c rooms with bath and TV.

C-D Ashok, Wright Town, T414101, F504151, ashoka_hotel@hotmail.com. 45 rooms, 22 a/c, some deluxe (**B**), restaurant, bar, garden, tours. Recommended.

C-D Jackson's, Civil Lines, T323412, F322066. 44 dated rooms, disappointing restaurant,

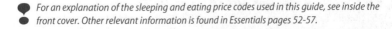

For an explanation of the sleeping and eating price codes used in this guide, see inside the front cover. Other relevant information is found in Essentials pages 52-57.

exchange, pleasant garden, deteriorating a/c and all rather run down.

C-D Kalchuri (MP Tourism), Wright Town, near railway, T321491. 30 clean rooms (14 a/c), good restaurant, bar, good value but close to noisy temple.

C-D Rishi Regency, opposite *State Bank of India*, T321804. 32 rooms, a/c or air-cooled, restaurant, bar, exchange.

C-D Samadariya, off Russell Chowk, T316800. Modern, quiet, with a/c rooms (some cheaper), good *Woodlands* South Indian restaurant.

C-D Utsav, Russel Chowk, T414038. Comfortable rooms, some a/c with tubs, disappointing food.

D Arihant Palace, Russell Chowk, T372311. Modern, pleasant and quiet, poor restaurant.

D Krishna, near Rani Durgavati Museum, Napier Town, T310318, F315153. 25 rooms, some a/c, restaurant, garden, pool.

D Sidharth, Russell Chowk, T409247. Some a/c rooms, modern.

F Anand, near Nassdera Bridge. Clean rooms with bath though noisy, helpful staff.

Kanha National Park *p311, map p312*
Some hotels will arrange pick-up from Jabalpur. Meals may be included.
    Reserve rooms in advance; most are open 1 Nov-30 Jun. Private lodges are outside the park and usually offer good discounts in May-Jun when the park is closed.

AL Kanha Jungle Lodge, Dulaylat-Raipur Rd, just south of Mukki, T07632-56323, www.adventure-india.com. 12 km from Baihar and main road. 19 simple clean, comfortable rooms with hot shower, restaurant, bar, meals included (only Indian but excellent), surrounded by *sal* forest, good bird-watching, park tours with good guides, contact *Tiger Resorts*, T011-6853760, F6865212.

AL Royal Tiger Resort, Mukki Gate, T011-6140091, F6140903, www.royaltiger.com. 18 comfortable suites, good baths.

B Kipling Camp, near Khatia. Chalets, pleasant ambience and well run, all-inclusive package though breakfast boxes "on the stingy side", contact Bob Wright, *Tollygunge Club*, 120 Deshapran Sasmal Rd, Kolkata, T033-4733306, or *Sita Travels* in major cities.

B Wild Chalet Resort, Mocha Village, T0761-332178. Cottages with shower overlooking river, good food and park tours, helpful and efficient manager, recommended, contact *Indian Adventures*, T022-6408742, www.indianwildlife.com.

C Krishna Jungle Lodge, near Kipling Camp. 30 rooms, good food, pool, contact *Hotel Krishna*, Jabalpur, T0761-310318, F315153.

Inside the park
D Baghira Log Huts, Kisli, T07649-77227. 16 rooms, restaurant, cheaper canteen, restaurant. Reservations, MP Tourism, Bhopal, T554340, F552384.

F Tourist Hostel, Kisli, opposite bus stand. 24 dorm beds (roof may leak), no nets (mosquito ridden), Rs 240 includes uninspiring veg meals in a grim canteen. Reservations, MP Tourism, Bhopal, T554340, F552384.

Bandhavgarh National Park *p313*
AL Bandhavgarh Jungle Lodge, within walking distance of the Park gates, T65317, F65320, www.adventure-india.com. 10 comfortable cottages and 2 4-room houses with modern facilities (hot and cold showers and toilets), resident naturalist, jeep and animal excursions, reserve through *Tiger Resorts*, T011-6853760, F6865212. There are dhabas opposite the Jungle Lodge which serve good snacks, breakfasts and thalis.

B Tiger Trails, east of Tala Gate, T0761-322178. Brick cottages in large estate with a lake and stream, separate dining hall, library, experienced naturalist, jungle visits, contact *Indian Adventures*, T022-6408742, F6432622.

C Jungle Camp, west of Tala gate, reservations: *Tiger Tops Mountain Travel*, 1/1 Rani Jhansi Rd, New Delhi. Specializes in upmarket tours.

C-D Patel Lodge near *Natural Heritage Lodge*. Rooms with bath, and 3 meals, pleasant location, good food.

C-D White Tiger Forest Lodge (MP Tourism), Tala, overlooking river, T65308. 26 rooms (8 a/c), restaurant (expensive, tiny portions, but good), bar, jeep hire (for residents), modest but good value, the best rooms are in detached cottages by the river, "in need of a good sweep". Reservations: *MP Tourism*, Bhopal, T554340, F552384. Also **Forest Rest House**.

D V Patel Resort, off Umaria Rd, T65323. 4 clean rooms with bath (hot water), meals in garden; also complete packages.
E Kum-kum opposite *White Tiger*, T65324. 4 very basic, large, clean rooms with fan, hot water, excellent veg food (Rs 25 for 'all you can eat'), friendly, helpful, well-run, jeep driver Saleem is expert tiger spotter. Recommended.

● Eating

Indore *p303, map p302*
♥♥♥ **Taj Residency**, in hotel.
♥♥♥ **Indotels Manor House**, in hotel, with bars, have International menus.
♥♥ **Colonel's Fast Foods**, 2 MG Rd.
♥♥ **Ding Ding**, 18/5 MG Marg. Open air eating.
♥♥ **Gypsy**, 17 MG Rd. Fast food. Good Western snacks, cakes and ices.
♥♥ **Landmark**, RNT Marg, by *President*. Indian, Continental. Good ambience, unusual offerings.
♥♥ **Pizza Hut**, 8B Silver Arcade, 56 Chhapan Dukan, New Palasia. Excellent pizzas, for free delivery T432625.
♥♥ **Woodlands**, at *President*, 163 RNT Marg. Vegetarian. South Indian. A/c, bar, good food.
  Several restaurants near bus stand and railway station serve Indian meals.
♥ **Apsara**, RNT Marg. Indian vegetarian. A/c and outdoors (evening).
♥ **Café Udupi**, Cloth Market. Indian.
♥ **Indian Coffee House**, off MG Rd. Indian. Light snacks, dated décor.
♥ **Prithvilok**, Cloth Market. Indian.
♥ **Statue**, 565 MG Rd. Indian veg. Large *thalis*.

Ujjain *p304, map p305*
♥♥ **Ashnol**, University Rd. Indian vegetarian in pleasant a/c surroundings.
♥♥ **Surana Palace**. Indian, some Chinese. Pleasant outdoor seating option, best in town.
♥ **5 Star**, 1st floor, by Madhav Chowk Clock Tower. Mainly South Indian. Tasty snacks and meals, roof top pleasanter.
♥ **Kwality Ice Creams**, further south.
♥ **Sudama**, next to Ramkrishna, Subhash Marg. Good Indian meals.
  Many others opposite the railway station.

Jabalpur *p309, map p310*
♥♥ **Samadariya**. International. Smart décor, meals or snacks.
♥ **Indian Coffee House**, near Clock Tower. South Indian, good breakfasts, snacks, coffee.

♥ **Satyam Shivam Sundaram**, 1st floor (air-cooled) near Jyoti Cinema. Vegetarian Indian. Very good value, tasty thalis.

Kanha National Park *p311, map p312*
Most lodges include meals.
Baghira Log huts, Kisli, have a restaurant and bar (see above). Ask for boiled water specifically; water served at the private lodges is generally filtered. Cold drinks are usually available but fresh fruit is not.

⊛ Festivals and events

Ujjain *p304, map p305*
Kumbh Mela takes place here every 12 years, see page 195. The next one is in 2005.
Feb/Mar: Mahasivaratri Fair is held at the Mahakaleshwar Temple. **Nov**: Kartik Mela, the month-long fair, draws large crowds from surrounding villages.

● Shopping

Indore *p303, map p302*
Cheap Jack, Prince Yashwant Rd. Antiques.
The Gallery, 2-C Tukoganj. Antiques, curios.
Kejari Bazar in metalware.
Sarafa Market specializes in savoury snacks and antique jewellery.

On MG Rd
Gift House, handicrafts.
Mrignayani Emporium, handicrafts.
Rupmati, sell handloom cloth and Chanderi and Maheshwari saris.
Sweet House, handicrafts.

Books
Bookworld A-M Rd.
Rupayana, MG Rd.

Jabalpur *p309, map p310*
Books
Universal Book Service, opposite *India Coffee House*. Interesting stock. Recommended.

▲ Activities and tours

Indore *p303, map p302*
Tour companies
MP Tourism, tours Jul-Sep: Mandu Wed, Fri, Sat and Sun, Rs 100; Omkareshwar and Maheshwar Mon and Thu, Rs 75. Both

depart from *Tourist Bungalow*, 0730, return 1900. Tours of **Mandu** from *Vijayant*, 165 RNT Marg, T430771, every Sun.
Travel Bureau, T491521.
Shiv Shakti, opposite Shabna Tower, RNT Marg, T523696.

Ujjain *p304, map p305*
Tours
MP Tourism *Ujjain Darshan* bus covers 11 temples and sights, Rs 100, 3½ hrs.

Jabalpur *p309, map p310*
Tour companies
Chadha Travels, *Jackson's Hotel*, T322178, F322066. Reliable service. Recommended.

⊖ Transport

Indore *p303, map p302*
Unmetered **taxis**, tempos, metered **autos** and **cycle rickshaws** are available. Transport to town: ask *Indian Airlines* officer or police to fix rickshaw or taxi rate with driver (about Rs 70-90).

Air
The airport is 9 km west of town; taxis charge Rs 150. **Indian Airlines** (*Alliance Air*), Race Course Rd, T431595; airport T411758, flies to **Bhopal**, **Mumbai**, **Delhi** daily, and **Gwalior** (Mon, Fri). **Jet Airways**, G2 Vidyapathi, Race Course Rd, T544590, airport T620819, to **Delhi** and **Mumbai**. **Sahara**, to **Delhi**, **Bhopal**.

Bus
Long distance Timetables in Hindi only. Sarwate Bus Stand (south of railway station, through Exit 1), helpful enquiry desk, T465688. Gangwal Bus Stand (3 km west of town), T480688, has easy transfer by local bus or rickshaw to town centre. Private bus companies operate from east of the railway station. From **Sarwate**: (some return buses terminate at Gangwal): to **Bhopal** (187 km) 0800-2300, **Gwalior** 0500-1830 and **Ujjain** (55 km). For **Jhansi** 2100; **Khajuraho** 1700; **Omkareshwar** hourly; change at Omkareshwar Rd (6 hrs). **Pachmarhi** 2145; **Satna** 1415. From **Gangwal**: to **Ahmadabad**; **Aurangabad** (for Ajanta and Ellora caves) and **Amrawati**; **Dhar** (hourly) then **Mandu** (149 km, 6 hrs), 1 direct bus daily to Mandu from Indore at 1515.

Train
Indore is on a spur of the Mumbai-Delhi line to Ujjain. Station has pre-paid rickshaws. Enquiries, T131, Reservations, opposite, in front of Rly Hospital, T430275. **Bhopal**: *Malwa Exp, 9367*, 1230, 5¼ hrs. **Kolkata** (H): *Shipra Exp, 9305*, 2030, Mon, Thu, Fri, 36½ hrs. **Delhi** (ND): *Malwa Exp, 9367*, 1230, 19¼ hrs; *Indore Nizamuddin Exp, 2415*, 1610, 14 hrs (HN). **Jaipur**: *Purna-Jaipur Exp, 9770*, 2200, 16 hrs. **Mumbai** (Central): *Avantika Exp, 2962*, 1550, 14¾ hrs. **Ujjain**: *Intercity Exp, 9303*, 0600, not Sun, 1¾ hrs; *Narmada Exp, 8233*, 1415, 1½ hrs; *Malwa Exp, 9367*, 1230, 1½ hrs.

Ujjain *p304, map p305*
Sights by **taxi** (Rs 500-700), **auto-rickshaw** (Rs 200-300), **tempos** and **cycle-rickshaws**.

Air
Nearest airport is at Indore (53 km), connected by regular flights with Delhi, Gwalior, Bhopal and Mumbai.

Bicycle
There are plenty of cycles to hire.

Bus
Long distance Hindi timetables only. Direct to **Bhopal**; regular to: **Dhar**, **Indore** (53 km, 1½ hrs), **Gwalior**, **Mandu** (149 km, 6 hrs), **Omkareshwar**.

Train
Pre-paid rickshaws. **Ahmadabad**: *Bhopal-Rajkot Exp, 1270*, 2315, 9 hrs; *Sabarmati Exp, 9166*, 2050, 10½ hrs. **Bhopal**: *Narmada Exp, 8233*, 1700, 5½ hrs; *Malwa Exp, 9367*, 1435, 4¾ hrs. **Indore**: *Narmada Exp, 8234*, 1130, 2¾ hrs; *Malwa Exp, 9368*, 1140, 1¾ hrs. **Mumbai** (Central): *Avantika Exp, 2962*, 1735, 13¼ hrs. **New Delhi**: *Malwa Exp, 9367*, 1435, 17¼ hrs; *Indore-Nizamuddin Exp, 2415*, 1755, 12¼ hrs (HN).

Mandu *p306, map p307*
Just off NH3, Mandu is most accessible from Indore. **Cycle-rickshaws** (Rs 20 for 'sights') and **bicycles** are available. No taxis.

Air
Nearest airport is at **Indore** with Indian Airlines connections to Bhopal, Gwalior, Jaipur, Mumbai and Delhi.

Long distance Regular services to **Dhar** (35 km, 1½ hrs), first depart 0530; change there for **Indore** (99 km, 4-5 hrs) and **Ujjain**. There is one direct bus per day to Indore at 0720 (3½ hrs). Indore has better choice for other destinations. Also to **Bhopal** (286 km), **Ratlam** (124 km), **Ujjain** (152 km).

Train

Most convenient railheads are **Ratlam** (124 km) on Mumbai-Delhi line, and **Indore** (99 km) on branch route. Ratlam has connections from Vadodara, Bhopal, Kanpur.

Jabalpur *p309, map p310*
Air

Indian Airlines, T322178, flies 3 times a week to **Delhi** via **Gwalior** (though airport regularly closed, making Bhopal the nearest airport).

Bus

Services for Kanha via Mandla; MP Tourism bus from their railway station office at 0800 (6 hrs, Rs 100), is much faster than 1100, Rs 50 (see Kanha Transport below). **Khajuraho**, 0900. Also to Allahabad, Bhopal, Nagpur, Varanasi and other main centres by private coach.

Train

Jabalpur is on the Mumbai-Allahabad-Kolkata railway line. **Allahabad**: *Mumbai Howrah Mail, 3004,* 1400, 6½ hrs. **Bhopal**: *Narmada Exp, 8234,* 2215, 8 hrs. **Delhi** (HN): *Mahakosal Exp, 1449,* 1500, 19¾ hrs; *Gondwana Exp, 2411,* 1540, 15¾ hrs (both stopping at **Agra Cantt** 4-4½ hrs earlier). **Lucknow**: *Chitrakoot Exp, 5009,* 1900, 15 hrs. **Kolkata**: *Shakipunj Exp, 1448,* 1900, 19½ hrs.

Kanha National Park *p311, map p312*
Air

Indian Airlines flies to Nagpur (226 km) from **Mumbai**, **Kolkata** and **Bhubaneswar**, **Hyderabad**, **Delhi** and **Bhopal**.

Bus

Kanha connected with **Jabalpur**, **Nagpur** and **Bilaspur** by motorable, but often poor roads. Buses daily, from Jabalpur to **Kisli** (0800, 1100) via Mandla and Chiraidongri; faster 0800 (MP Tourism, railway station) takes 6 hrs (Rs 100) arriving in time for park transport; 0900 goes to Mukki. To Jabalpur, 0800 (slow), 1200 (faster).

Jeep

Private hire to **Jabalpur** around US$55.

Train

Jabalpur (173 km) on the **Mumbai-Allahabad-Kolkata**, **Delhi-Jabalpur** and **Chennai-Varanasi** main lines; or via **Raipur**, 230 km. A wonderful narrow gauge (diesel) train runs between Mandla and Jabalpur.

Bandhavgarh National Park *p313*
Air

Not possible at present through Jabalpur (see Kanha above). Khajuraho airport nearest, then by road (see below).

Bus

From **Tala**, buses to **Rewa** and others; from **Satna**, 5 hrs, and Katni Rail Junction.

Jeep

From Tala possible to get a jeep seat (Rs 50) to Satna (insist on your full seat!); poor road, bumpy and dusty 3-hr ride. From **Umaria**: jeep to Tala for park, Rs 200, good for sharing, or rickshaw (Rs 10) from Umaria rly station to bus station and get a local bus to Tala. From **Jabalpur** drive to Shajpura (144 km) then take a country road (fairly hilly) to Umaria. From **Khajuraho** (237 km) 5 hrs. Taxis available from **Satna** (129 km) 3 hrs, Katni and Umaria.

Train

Umaria (35 km) is the nearest station on the Katni-Bilaspur sector (1 hr by road), where you can get a bus to Tala. Direct train from Umaria to **Delhi**: *Utkal Express, 8477,* 2010, 17¼ hrs. To **Bhubaneswar**, *Utkal Express, 8478,* 0641, 28¼ hrs. To **Jabalpur**, *Mahakosal Exp, 1450,* 0855, 1½ hrs. **Varanasi**, *Sarnath Exp, 4259,* 0700, 9 hrs (book well ahead for a berth). From Satna to **Katni**, 0815. From Katni to **Umaria**, 0955, 2 hrs, Rs 9.

⊙ Directory

Indore *p303, map p302*
Banks State Bank of India, 13 Ranade Complex, Old Palasia. **Hospitals** Lifeline, Meghdoot Gdns, T553878. Choithram Hospital, Manikbagh Rd. Recommended. **Chemists**: on Maharani Rd. **Post office** CTO: K Nehru Park, Fax, 0700-2000. GPO: AB Rd. **Tourist offices** MP, behind Ravindra

Natyagrih, T528653. **Useful addresses**
Ambulance: T102. **Fire:** T101. **Police:** T100.

Ujjain *p304, map p305*
Banks State Bank, Budhwariya off Udayan Marg, near Water Tower, changes cash (not TCs); after 1030. **Tourist offices** MP, railway station, T559648.

Mandu *p306, map p307*
Bank State Bank of India (no exchange), 1100-1500, closed Thu and Sun. **Tourist offices** *Travellers' Lodge*, T63221. *Tourist Cottages* runs tours from Bhopal and Indore.

Jabalpur *p309, map p310*
Banks State Bank of India, *Jackson's Hotel* advise on getting cash against credit cards.

Tourist offices MP Tourism, railway station, T322111, F321490, car hire, runs daily bus to Kanha, dep 0800, return 1900.

Kanha National Park *p311, map p312*
Banks You can't cash TCs at Kanha, Kisli, Mukki or Mandla, nor at any of the lodges. The nearest bank for exchange is in Jabalpur.
Hospitals Basic hospitals are Mandla Civil Hospital and Katra Mission Hospital. Only basic first aid at Mukki, Mocha and Baihar.
Photography Films from Baghira Log Huts, Kisli. **Post office** At Mocha and Mukki. **Telephone** At Khatia (non-STD). Nearest STD at Mandla. **Tourist offices** MP, Jabalpur Railway Station, T322111. For car hire and and accommodation, contact Bhopal, T778383, F774289.

Chhattisgarh → *Population: under 21 million. Area: 135,000 sq km.*

The land
The hilly and forested region of Chhattisgarh ('36 forts'), one of the least densely populated and urbanised regions of peninsular India, retains a strongly rural character. The ancient granites, gneisses and sedimentaries which comprise the major geological formations of the state contain an abundance of minerals, from gold and diamonds to coal and iron ore, dolomite and bauxite. Chhattisgarh is estimated to have reserves of nearly 27 billion tonnes of coal and nearly 200 million tonnes of top quality iron ore. Yet there is also fertile agricultural land, and where the brown forest soils have been converted to agricultural land they yield good rice harvests, lending the state the reputation of being India's 'rice bowl'. Forest cover extends up to 40% of the state's area, with 70% of India's *tendu* leaf production, used for making *bidis*.

Industry
Despite the poverty which still characterises much of Chhattisgarh, the new state already has a wide range of mineral based industries. It earns approximately US$400 mn a year from mining alone and the state has over 75 large or medium scale plants producing such goods as cement, steel, iron and rails. The new Chief Minister, Ajit Jogi, has been pushing for large scale multinational investment in the mining industry. Chhattisgarh is also a significant power surplus state, and is continuing to develop its thermal electricity capacity to export to other states.

Modern Chhattisgarh
Chhattisgarh became an independent state on 1st November 2000, though the first demand for the creation of a state for the region can be traced back to 1925. It comprises the largely tribal districts of the southeast corner of Madhya Pradesh. Some suggested that the long-standing tribal demand for a separate state was finally ceded by Madhya Pradesh because of the difficulty of controlling the violent Naxalites, groups of revolutionary guerrillas. While that may be an exaggeration - the violent-death rate is far lower than in many American cities, for example – it was one of the least developed parts of Madhya Pradesh, and the political and economic challenge facing the new state government is huge.

The challenge is particularly obvious in terms of social and economic development. Literacy rates are among the lowest in India, with 46% literate across the state as a whole, and Bastar District having over 80% still illiterate. Half the households have no drinking water, only one third have any electricity connection, over 40% of girls are married before they are 20 and infant mortality is still 84%.

Raipur → *Phone code: 0771. Colour map 6, grid A3. Population: 605,000.*

Raipur is the rapidly growing new state capital of Chhattisgarh, and also the regional transport centre. Water tanks and a temple date from the 17th and 18th centuries. Jai Stambh Chowk (Chhattisgarh Circle) is generally regarded to be the centre of town with the Head Post Office, State Bank and several hotels close by.

Durg

Durg, west of Raipur on the NH6, is now joined to the Hindustan steel works town at **Bhilainagar**. Durg is the only place with reasonable accommodation in the area.

★ Kawardha → *Season: Sep-Apr*

Kawardha is a small town in the Rajnandgaon region of Chhattisgarh. In this remote area Maharaja Vishwaraj Singh welcomes visitors to his late 1930s palace. It provides a delightfully quiet unspoiled contrast with India's big cities and with the much busier tourist route of Rajasthan's 'palace circuit'. The Radha Krishna family temple with underground rooms is nearby. You can visit the 11th-century Chandela style temples at nearby Bhoramdev with beautiful carvings, stepwells, enjoy excellent bird-watching or explore the area's natural beauty on foot with the Yuvraj. The Gonds and the gentle Baiga tribe continue to follow a primitive lifestyle in the surrounding forests; ecologically sensitive visits are arranged.

Bilaspur

ⓘ *Services to main towns in Chhattisgarh and neighbouring states from New Bus Stand (1 km from listed hotels). There is a train from New Delhi: Chhattisgarh Exp, 8237, taking 31½ hrs (via Bhopal, 17½ hrs).*

Unless you have a passionate interest in cement production, or have chosen a particularly circuitous train routing to reach a cricket match, there is little reason to stop here. However, if forced to stay overnight there are a number of reasonable hotels and an excellent restaurant (at *Shyama* hotel) about 2 km from the railway station.

Kanker

Some 140 km south of Raipur, Kanker is a district headquarters town, with some fine century-old colonial buildings. It nestles by a tributary of the Mahanadi river, amidst unspoilt forests and hills, the home of several tribal groups who continue to practise age old crafts and traditions. Kanker's royal family, who trace their ancestors back to the 12th century, welcomes guests to their palace to share their region's culture and history.

Bastar District

ⓘ *See Kawardha above for connections via Raipur. Car hire is Rs 3000 per day from Kanker Palace.*

Lying in the southern tip of Chhattisgarh, Bastar district is home to several indigenous tribal groups in one of the state's more densely forested areas. There are two national parks within driving distance of Jagdalpur, the district headquarters, which also serves as a useful base for visiting the region's tribal areas.

Jagdalpur, 160 km south of Kanker, is the centre of the tribal heartland of Bastar where you can see the Gond, Halba, Muriya, Madia, Dhurwa and Bhattra people.

Mrignayani emporium collects and sells their arts and crafts. There is a small **tribal** 321
museum maintained by the Anthropological Society of India.

Situated 35 km south west of Jagdalpur, in the transition zone marking the natural southern limit of *sal* and the northern limit of teak, **Kanger Valley National Park** is a narrow stretch of mixed virgin forest, playing host to tiger, panther, sambhar, wild pig, flying squirrel as well as a wide range of reptiles and birds. Within the park the **Kailash** and **Kutumsar Gupha** are attractive limestone caves which are popular with visitors. Forest guides are available. The 100-ft **Tirathgarh Falls**, 39 km south west of Jagdalpur, sees the Kanger River descend the valley in a series of steps. Overnight stay is possible in basic forest rest houses at Kutumsar, Netanar and Teerathgarh. Contact Director Kangerghati NP, Jagdalpur, T07782-22261.

Indravati National Park

This park along the Indravati River was designated a Project Tiger reserve in 1982. The dense monsoon forest interspersed with grassy glades is known as ancient Dandakaranya, cited in the *Ramayana* as the place where Rama was exiled. Apart from increasing tiger protection, the park is seen as the best reserve for the wild buffalo (*Bubalus amee*) and an ideal alternative home for the endangered Branden barasingha (hardground swamp deer), which is only found in Kanha further north. The NH43 is a good, scenic road, ideal for seeing the Bastar tribal area. Following the Indravati west from Jagdalpur, the popular waterfalls at **Chitrakote** (38 km) drop some 30 m in a horseshoe curve and provide an attractive diversion.

Barnawapara Sanctuary

① *Best season: Nov-Apr. Permission to enter from DFO, Wildlife Division, Old Chhattisgarh College Campus, Raipur, T0771-425064. You can stay in forest rest houses on the outskirts of the sanctuary or inside at Barnawapara which has 2 basic rooms.*

Occupying 245 sq km in the northern part of Mahasamund district, near Sirpur, this Sanctuary offers the chance to see several species of deer in the hilly *sal* forest as well as sloth bear and bison; tigers and panthers are present though rarely seen. Migratory birds are attracted by artificial waterholes in the winter. *Dev Travels* organize tours.

Listings: Chhattisgarh

● Sleeping

Raipur *p320*
B Mayura, GE Rd, near Raj Talkies, 2 km from stations, T536001, F536004, hotelmayura@ rediffmail.com. 60 good rooms, central a/c, TV, excellent *Kapri* restaurant, airport pick up.
B Piccadily, Mohaba Bazar, 5 km from town towards Durg, T323002, F323040, www.hotel piccadily.com. 54 comfortable rooms, central a/c, attached bath with tubs, TV, airport/ station pick up, pool (roadside), friendly staff, well-run, out of town location only drawback.
B-C Aditya, KK Rd, near Jai Stambh Chowk, T/F223281. 34 decent rooms, central a/c, TV.
D-E Chhattisgarh, Teli Bandha, 4 km from centre towards airport, T427906. 30 rooms,

some a/c, hot bath, TV, restaurant.
D-E Radhika, Jai Stambh Chowk, T233806, www.hotelradhika.com. Rather scruffy rooms with TV and bath, some a/c, those at front suffer from road noise, good restaurant.
Several **E-F** hotels near railway station. Earplugs may be needed for a good sleep.

Durg *p320*
D-E Sagar, opposite railway station, T0788-321120, has 60 clean rooms with bath (some a/c), a/c restaurant, friendly. Recommended but often full.
D-E Sheela, Indira Market, with clean, well-furnished rooms (some a/c), good a/c restaurant, bar, friendly. Cycle-rickshaws offer free transfer from station (paid by hotel).

Kawardha *p320*
A Palace Kawardha, T07741-32085, F32088,
www.pant.co.uk/travel/kawardha. 5 large
suites with pleasant verandahs, western baths,
imposing Durbar Hall, attractive gardens, a
unique experience visiting tribal settlements,
temples, wildlife Kanha, jeep excursions, short
treks nearby into surrounding hills (5-8 km,
2½-5 hrs), longer treks into the jungle with
advance notice, very warm hospitality.
US$108 includes meals, reservations essential.

Kanker *p320*
A The Royal Palace, in a garden setting,
T07868-22005, kankerpalace@rediffmail.com.
Once residency of British Agent, has 3 modern
suites but aims to retain "earthy flavour".
Maharajkumar Surya Pratap Deo arranges
interesting excursions to explore both the
natural surroundings as well as the area's rich
tribal heritage. Reserve a month ahead.

Jagdalpur *p320*
D- E Hotel Akansha Deluxe, T25336, has
rooms and a restaurant. Cheaper options
include *Akash, Anand and Athithi*.
   In a nearby village, the Kanker family's **Bastar
Village Farm** has 3 comfortable cottages for
visitors who wish to experience rural living with
a difference (advance notice needed).

▲ Activities and tours

Raipur *p320*
Tour operators
Dev Travels, behind Netaji Subhash
Stadium, Ahmedji Colony, T651000,
F650213, www.devtravel.com. Professional
agency, can arrange cars for visiting tribal
areas, wildlife sanctuaries etc.
Oberoi Tours & Travels, KK Rd, opp *Aditya*,
T539988, F632577. Efficient air ticketing office.

⊖ Transport

Raipur *p320*
Air
Mana airport, 15 km southeast of town. Taxis
take around 30 mins to the centre; the better
hotels provide free pick up with advance
notice. **Indian Airlines**, T583072, airport

1424201. Daily flights to **Delhi** via **Jabalpur**
(Tue, Sat) or **Nagpur** (other days). Also
3 flights per week to **Mumbai** via
Bhubaneswar.

Bus
New Bus Stand, 3 km from the railway
station has services to all towns in
Chhattisgarh and Madhya Pradesh.

Train
Enquiry, T528130. **Ahmedabad**: *Howrah
Ahmedabad Exp, 8034*, 1155, 27½ hrs.
Allahabad: *Sarnath Exp, 5159*, 2055, 16½ hrs
(to **Varanasi**, 20½ hrs). **Kolkata (H)**: *Gitanjali
Exp, 2859*, 0055, 14 hrs; *Mumbai Howrah Mail,
2809*, 1640, 15 hrs. **Mumbai (CST)**: *Gitanjali
Exp, 2860*, 0200, 19½ hrs; *Howrah Mumbai
Mail, 2810*, 0940, 21½ hrs. **New Delhi**:
Chhattisgarh Exp, 8237, 1440, 30½ hrs (via
Bhopal, 16 hrs).

Kawardha *p320*
Bus
Express buses run from Raipur and Bilaspur,
where cars can also be hired, or ask for pick
up from either city (4½ hrs) or **Kanha
National Park** (5½ hrs; US$65 for 3).

Jeep
Ask at *Palace Kawardha*, Raipur US$40,
Kanha US$50.

Train
From Raipur (140 km) and Bilaspur (124 km).

⊙ Directory

Raipur *p320*
Banks ICICI, opposite Raj Kumar College,
GE Rd. Exchanges cash and TCs, also ATM.
State Bank of India, Jai Stambh Chowk. Cash
and Tcs. **Hospitals** Government Medical
College Hospital, T511101. Private MMI,
T412310. **Internet** At Planet Café, opposite
Old Bus Stand, has good connection. **Post
office** Head Post Office, Jai Stambh Chowk.
Tourist office Chhattisgarh, at
Chhattisgarh Hotel, Teli Bandha (4 km),
T442706. Minimal information.

*For an explanation of the sleeping and eating price codes used in this guide, see inside the
front cover. Other relevant information is found in Essentials pages 52-57.*

Rajasthan

⁑ Footprint features

Introduction

Rajasthan has long been regarded as the real home of the traditional Maharajas. **Jaipur**, **Udaipur**, **Jodhpur** and **Jaisalmer** have become some of India's most popular tourist destinations. However, as **palaces**, **forts** and **country estates** are steadily being converted into hotels even Rajasthan's most romantically inaccessible outposts are opening up. From the richly painted **havelis** of **Shekhawati** in the north to the magnificent **Jain temples** of **Mount Abu** or **Ranakpur** in the south, the state's wealth of history and art provides a unique opportunity to see something of a disappearing world.

Yet as celebrations at festivals throughout the year, or camel and cattle fairs such as that at **Pushkar** demonstrate, traditional ways of life continue to flourish through all the external changes.

★ Don't miss...

❶ Get caught up in the excitement of **Pushkar's cattle and camel fair** held each November, page 354.

❷ Take a rickshaw from Amber to **Jaigarh Fort** and see the Jai Ban cannon. At 50 tonnes, it's reputedly the largest ever built, page 340.

❸ **Ranthambhore National Park** is the place where you are most likely to spot a tiger - but you'll have to get up early in the morning, page 372.

❹ **Bundi**, in a beautiful narrow valley, is little visited and is especially atmospheric during Gangaur in April, page 374.

❺ Udaipur is undeniably romantic but, for a change, go to the **Monsoon Palace**, 15 km to the west, and watch the swifts return to their nests at sunset, page 385.

❻ Cool down at Mount Abu and explore the **Dilwara Jain Temples**. There are also some pleasant walks here, page 393.

❼ Head for the desert with **Jaisalmer** as your target and watch the city emerge like a mirage. Then take a camel safari, page 423.

Rajasthan

Background → *Population: 56.47 million. Area: 342,000 sq km.*

The land

Running like a spine through Rajasthan the **Aravalli Hills** are some of the oldest mountains in the world. A series of jagged, heavily folded ranges, they stretch from **Mount Abu** in the southwest (1,720 m) to Kota and Bundi in the east. Mount Abu is granite but the range has a mixture of rocks, and Rajasthan is the source of the glittering white Makrana marble used in the Taj Mahal.

In the northwest is the arid and forbidding **Thar Desert**, with its shifting sand dunes and crushingly high summer temperatures. James Tod, the first British emissary to the region, was constantly reminded that "the names for the region - *Marwar, Maroosthali,* or *Maru-desh,* mean 'the land of death'". Before Parition from Pakistan **Jaisalmer** and **Bikaner** dominated the overland routes to the west. **Jodhpur** lies on the edge of this arid tract, the link between the true desert and the semi arid but cultivable regions to the east.

Around Jaipur and Bharatpur, cultivated land is interspersed with rocky outcrops such as those at Amber. In the south the average elevation is higher (330-1,150 m). **Mewar**, the southeast region of modern Rajasthan, with **Udaipur** and **Chittaurgarh** as two of the region's former capitals, is hilly, while around **Bharatpur** in the northeast the landscape forms part of the nearly flat Yamuna drainage basin. The **Kota** and **Bundi plateau** has good, black, deep and well drained soils, intensively cultivated.

Climate Rajasthan is one of the driest regions of India. Its location on the margins of pure desert has made much of it particularly susceptible to climatic change, and fossil sand dunes found as far east as Delhi testify to the advance and retreat of the desert over the last 5,000 years. Except in the hills the summer temperatures are very high with a maximum of 46°C and an average from May to August of 38°C. In winter the daily maximum in most low lying areas is 22°C-28°C and the minimum 8°C-14°C. January nights in the desert can feel very cold. Over three quarters of the rainfall comes between July and September.

Wildlife The scrub jungle thins westwards to desert. Tamarisk and arid zone plants are found in the west. The natural jungle is ideal territory for tigers, leopards, sloth bear, sambhar (large brown deer) and chital (smaller spotted deer) now normally restricted to game reserves. Nilgai (blue bulls), blackbuck and ravine deer are fairly numerous on the plains. There is a great variety of birds. Bikaner is famous for its sand grouse, whilst Bharatpur and other low-lying swampy places in the southeast are popular winter grounds for migratory birds from Siberia and Northern Europe.

History

Early Origins Humans lived along the **Banas River** 100,000 years ago. **Harappan** and post-Harappan (third-second millennium BC) cultures have been discovered, as at Kalibangan where pottery has been dated to 2700 BC. The Mauryan Emperor Asoka controlled this part of the state in the 3rd century BC, to be succeeded by the Bactrian Greeks (second century BC), the Sakas (Scythians, second to fourth centuries AD), the Guptas (fourth to sixth centuries) and the Huns (sixth century). Rajput dynasties rose from the seventh to the 11th centuries and until the end of the 12th century they controlled much of North India.

Rajputs Rajputs claimed to be the original *kshatriyas* (warriors) of the ancient *varna* system, born out of the fire offering of the Gods on Mount Abu. They were probably descended from the Huns and Scythians who had entered India in the sixth century, and they modelled themselves on Rama, the hero of the *Ramayana* epic, seeing themselves as protectors of the Hindu *dharma* against invaders. The Brahmins made considerable efforts to give them royal lineages and accorded them *kshatriya* status. They were provided with genealogies which connected them with either the solar or lunar race. The Rajputs went to great lengths to insist on their *kshatriya* status, a means of demonstrating to their subjects that not only was it foolhardy, but also sacrilegious to oppose their authority. Associated with this was promotion of those qualities or attributes ascribed to the martial castes, for example chivalry, bravery and unquestioning loyalty.

The Mughals and the Rajputs Rather than engage in costly campaigns to crush the Rajputs, the Mughal Emperor **Akbar** (ruled 1556-1605) sought conciliation. Many Rajput princes were given high office in return for loyalty and Akbar sealed this important strategic alliance by marrying a Rajput princess, **Jodha Bai**, the daughter of the Maharaja of Amber. The relationship between the Rajput princes and the Mughals did not always remain so close, and in the later Mughal period several Rajput princes sought to secure their autonomy from Mughal rule. Such autonomy was brought to an end by the spread of British colonial power. With the settlement that followed the defeat of the Marathas in 1818, the Rajput princes were confirmed in their status. However, there continued to be rivalries, and attitudes to British rule varied. After the quelling of the Mutiny in 1858 and the establishment of the British Indian Empire, the Rajput Princely States gained in appearance and show of power, with 21 gun salutes, royal polo matches and durbars, just as they lost its reality.

Culture

Today **tribals** constitute 12% of the state population, nearly double the national average. The Bhils and Minas are the largest groups, but Sahariyas, Damariyas, Garasias and Gaduliya Lohars are all important. The tribes share many common traits but differences in their costumes and jewellery, their gods, fairs and festivals also set them apart from one another.

The **Bhils** comprise nearly 40% of Rajasthan's tribal population with their stronghold in Baneshwar. *Bhil* (bow) describes their original skill at hunting. Today, the accepted head of all the Rajput Clans of Rajasthan – the Maharana of Udaipur – is crowned by anointing his forehead with blood drawn from the palm of a Bhil chieftain, affirming the alliance and loyalty of his tribe. Rajput rulers came to value the guerrilla tactics of the Bhils. Physically short, stocky and dark with broad noses and thick lips, the Bhils once lived off roots, leaves and fruits of the forest and the increasingly scarce game. Most now farm land and keep cattle, goats and sheep, or as day labourers. Thousands congregate near the confluence of the Mahi and Som rivers in Dungarpur district for the *Baneshwar fair* in January and February.

The **Minas** are Rajasthan's largest and most widely spread tribal group. The Minas are tall, with an athletic build, light brown complexion and sharp features. The men wear a loincloth round the waist, a waistcoat and a brightly coloured turban while the women wear a long gathered skirt (*ghaghra*), a small blouse (*kurti-kanchali*) and a large scarf. Most Minas are cultivators who measure their wealth in cattle and other livestock. Like other tribal groups they have a tradition of giving grain, clothes, animals and jewellery to the needy. Though their marriage ceremony, performed round a fire, is similar to a Hindu one, divorce is not uncommon.

The **Gaduliya Lohars**, named after their beautiful bullock carts (*gadis*), are nomadic blacksmiths, said to have wandered from their homeland of Mewar because of their promise to their 'lord' Maharana Pratap, who was ousted from Chittaurgarh by Akbar. This clan of warring Rajputs vowed to re-enter the city only with a victorious Maharana Pratap. Unfortunately the Maharana was killed on the battlefield, so even today many of them prefer a nomadic life.

The **Sahariyas** are jungle dwellers, their name possibly deriving from the Persian *sehr* (jungle). They are regarded as the most backward tribe in Rajasthan and eke out a living as shifting cultivators and by hunting and fishing. More recently they have also undertaken menial and manual work on daily wages.

The **Sidhis** from the area bordering Gujarat are believed to have originally come from Africa in the 13th century; they retain some elements of African dress and custom such as breaking coconuts with their heads and fire-walking.

Religion Hindus predominate, with Muslims making up the largest minority. Jains, numerically tiny, are a significant influence through their role as merchants and traders. Islam extended into Rajasthan with the conquest of Ajmer in the 12th century. The saint Khwajah Mu'inuddin Chishti had his refuge at Ajmer, now a popular pilgrimage place. Sikhs and Christians form a very small minority. The Aryan invaders were often in conflict with tribal groups and gradually forced most of them back into the remote craggy and forested Aravallis.

Language The principal language is Rajasthani, a close relative of Hindi, the four most important dialects being Marwari in the west, Jaipuri in the east, Malwi in the southeast and Mewati in the northeast.

Crafts Bandhani is an ancient technique of tie-dyeing common throughout Rajasthan. The fabric is pinched together in selected places, tied round with twine or thread and then dyed. Afterwards, the cords are removed to reveal a pattern in the original or preceding colour; the process is often repeated, the dyeing sequence going from light to dark.

Block-printing Hand-held wood blocks are carefully cut to enable patterns in different colours to be printed; up to five blocks may be used for an elaborate design. Traditionally colours were based on vegetable pigments though now many use chemical dyes. Printing is done in a long shed and after the block printing is complete, the fabric is boiled to make the dye fast. Sanganer, just south of the city, is still well known for block-printing, see page 341.

Miniature paintings using old paper or silk, using natural colours derived from minerals, rocks and vegetables following old techniques are produced in varying degrees of quality. The princely states were important patrons of medieval miniature painting and various schools developed in different areas drawing from local traditions and combining them with Mughal art. The tradition continues to draw from Rajput court culture, Hindu and Jain traditions, and folk lore.

Pottery 'Jaipur Blue Pottery' uses a coarse grey clay that is quite brittle even when fired. It is then decorated with floral and geometric patterns along Persian lines utilizing rich ultramarines, turquoise and lapis colours on a plain off-white/grey background. In the villages, the common pot is thrown on a simple stone wheel, partially dried, then finished with a hammer before being decorated, glazed and fired.

Modern Rajasthan

After Independence the region's 18 princely states were ultimately absorbed into the new state of Rajasthan on 1 November 1956. The successors of royal families have lost power but still retain considerable political influence. The palaces, many of them converted to hotels with varying degrees of success, maintain the memory of princely India. Rajasthan now sends 25 members to the Lok Sabha. The Congress dominated politics until the 1989 elections, when it was defeated by the BJP. However, in the 1998 Lok Sabha elections the BJP retained only five of the state's 25 seats, 18 of the remainder going to the Congress, and the BJP also lost power in the state assembly elections at the end of 1998.

Economy Rajasthan is one of the least densely populated and poorest states in India. Primarily an agricultural and pastoral economy, it does have good mineral resources. Tourism makes a large contribution to the regional economy.

Elopement marriages

The Garasias (under 3% of Rajasthan's tribals) have an interesting custom of marriage through elopement, which usually takes place at the annual Gaur fair in March. After the elopement, which can be spontaneous or pre-arranged, a bride price is paid to the bride's father. Once the couple have 'disappeared' they have to remain hidden in the jungle for three days while the rest of the tribe hunts for them. If caught during that period they are severely beaten and forcibly separated. However, if they have proved their skills in survival and in remaining hidden, their marriage is recognized and they return to live with the rest of the tribe. Should the arrangement not work out, the woman returns home. Widows are forced to remarry, since their children – and not they – are given a share in the husband's property.

Rajasthan's low and erratic rainfall puts irrigation at a premium, but most of the crops are rainfed: wheat, hardy *bajra* (pearl millet) in the more arid areas; *jowar* (sorghum), maize and pulses elsewhere. Cotton is important in the north and south of the state. Rajasthan shares waters from the Bhakra Dam project with Punjab, and the Chambal Valley project with Madhya Pradesh. With improved management techniques over 30% of the sown area could be brought under irrigation. The enormously ambitious Rajasthan canal is working much less efficiently than had originally been planned. Rajasthan has a very large livestock population and is the largest wool producing state. It also breeds camels.

Rajasthan is rich in minerals though, accounting for India's entire output of zinc concentrates, emeralds and garnets, 94% of its gypsum, 76% of silver ore, 84% of asbestos, 68% of feldspar and 12% of mica. It has rich salt deposits at Sambhar and elsewhere, and copper mines at Khetri and Dariba. The white marble favoured by the Mughal builders is mined at Makrana north of Ajmer.

The main industries are textiles, the manufacture of rugs and woollen goods, vegetable oil and dyes. Heavy industry includes the construction of railway rolling stock, copper and zinc smelting. The chemical industry also produces caustic soda, calcium carbides and sulphuric acid, fertilizer, pesticides and insecticides. There is a rapidly expanding light industry which includes precision instrument manufacture at Kota and television assembly. Traditional handicrafts such as pottery, jewellery, marble work, embossed brass, block printing, embroidery and decorative painting are now very good foreign exchange earners.

Ins and outs

Tours The half-day and full day village tours offered are very variable and tend to go on well-worn paths. In many villages you can see traditional housing, often simply but beautifully decorated, rural handicrafts and farming. Contact Ramesh Jangid, *Alternative Travels*, T015974-22239, for experiencing rural life with homestays in villages. Several cities, including Jaipur, Jodhpur, Mount Abu, operate a 'paying guest' scheme through the local tourist office. Some tour companies specialize in arranging unusual historic destinations: *North West Safaris*, Ahmedabad, T079-6302019, F6300962, ssibal@ad1.vsnl.net.in, is recommended. It is certainly worth organizing your own tour to see something of rural Rajasthan.

Camel and horse safaris Rajasthan is unique in offering the opportunity to see typical desert landscape and rural life on camel or horse back. These are mainly offered in the areas around Jodhpur, Jaisalmer, Bikaner, Shekhawati and around Kotri and Kumbhalgarh to the south.

Railways The diesel *Palace on Wheels* has been widely publicized. Weekly departures (Wed) from Delhi, from Oct to mid-Apr cost about US$200 per night. The itinerary includes Jaipur and Amber Fort, followed by overnight travel to Chittaurgarh, Udaipur (*Lake Palace Hotel*), Jaisalmer, Jodhpur (*Umaid Bhawan Palace*) and Bharatpur ending with visits to Fatehpur Sikri, Agra and Delhi. It is a well packaged but rather compressed taster for some of the key sites. The *Royal Orient* which does a similar journey through Rajasthan and Gujarat also starts in Dehli. See page 44. The oldest working steam engine, *Fairy Queen* built in 1855, has been commissioned to run a weekend tour for 50, to Sariska Tiger Sanctuary (via Alwar; transfer by road) from Delhi, twice a month in the winter. It costs Rs 8,000. Contact in New Delhi: National Rail Museum, T6881816, F6880804, www.icindia.com/fairy. Travelling by night means that you don't see much of the countryside.

Heritage hotels Some of the converted palaces, forts and *havelis* offer good facilities in charming buildings. However, even in the most expensive of the conversions, while some rooms may have excellent views others have little or none. Some places, especially in more remote rural areas, remain very simple; facilities may be rudimentary (eg hot water may come in buckets), and despite efforts at their control, pests like rats are sometimes found. The *Heritage Hotels Assoc*, Jaipur, T371194, F372084, can supply a list of member hotels which are particularly attractive. For *Historic Resort Hotels (HRH)* in former palaces (good discounts for single rooms and off season), contact City Palace, Udaipur, T0294-419023, F419020, www.hrhindia.com. *WelcomHeritage*, T11-6868992, F6868994, www.welcomheritage.com. The Taj Group too owns some former royal lodges, F022-2837272, www.tajhotels.com. Reserve these hotels in advance.

Festivals Rajasthan celebrates a number of festivals of its own as well as the main Hindu festivals.

January For Urs, in Ajmer, Muslim pilgrims congregate at the mosques. **Kite flying festival** in Jaipur, spectacular. **Camel Festival** at **Bikaner**, features camel polo, races and dancing camels.

February Shivratri. **Desert Festival** in Jaisalmer is a tourist festival with camel races, camel polo and desert music and dance. This coincides with the *tribal fair* at Baneshwar. Week-long *Cattle Fair* starts at **Karauli**.

March Holi. **Elephant Festival** is marked with colourful processions in Jaipur.

April Gangaur Festival, is in honour of Gangaur (Parvati), the consort of Siva (see Jaipur festivals). This coincides with the **Mewar Festival** at Udaipur.

August Teej, a fertility festival celebrates the reunion of Siva and Parvati at the onset of the monsoon. In Jaipur, there is a big procession with ornately dressed elephants on the first day. In the villages women wear bright clothes and green striped veils, and sit on swings decorated with flowers, singing songs to welcome the rains; *Nag Panchami*, Manasa is worshipped as the snake goddess; Jodhpur honours the serpent king Naga and women visit snake charmers.

October Marwar Festival at Jodhpur.

November-February Cattle and camel fairs at Pushkar and Kolayat, Nagaur and Tilwara, are famous.

Northern Rajasthan

★ **Jaipur** → *Phone code: 0141. Colour map 2, grid B5. Population: 2,325,000.*

Jaipur, the colourful capital of a richly colourful state, is a highly distinctive planned city, made all the more attractive by the pink wash that most buildings are periodically given. It is deservedly included on the popular tourist 'Golden Triangle' of Delhi-Jaipur-Agra. It has some fine museums in the atmospheric Old City with its bazars, palaces and havelis, as well as a couple of forts and Amber nearby which are well worth exploring. Its downside includes traffic jams, terrible pollution, over-zealous rickshaw drivers and persistent hotel touts. ▶▶ *For Sleeping, Eating and other listings see pages 355-370.*

Ins and outs

Getting there Sanganer airport, 15 km south of town, has flights from Ahmadabad, Aurangabad, Delhi, Jodhpur, Mumbai, Rajkot and Udaipur. Airport buses, taxis and autos take about 30 mins to the centre. The railway station to the west of town, now has improved broad gauge links with major cities. The new NH8 from Delhi has cut the road journey to under 4 hrs. Long distance buses arrive at the Sindhi Camp Bus Terminal, a 15-min walk east of the station. Most hotels are a short auto-rickshaw ride away from the station and bus terminal.

Getting around The Old City, to the northeast of town, holds most of the sights and the colourful bazar within its walls, and is best explored on foot, though to get there you can hire a rickshaw. The city buses are overcrowded. See Transport, page 367, for further details. MG Rd is Mahatma Gandhi Road, MI Rd is Mirza Ismail Road.

Climate Temperature: Summer: max 42°C, min 26°C; Winter maximum 22°C, minimum 8°C. Rainfall 220 mm in Aug. Best time to visit: Nov to Mar

History

Jaipur (City of Victory) was founded in 1727 by **Maharaja Jai Singh II**, a Kachhawaha Rajput, who ruled from 1699-1744. He had inherited a kingdom under threat not only from the last great Mughal Emperor Aurangzeb but also from the Maratha armies of Gujarat and Maharashtra. Victories over the Marathas and diplomacy with Aurangzeb won back the favour of the ageing Mughal so that the political stability Maharaja Jai Singh was instrumental in creating was protected, allowing him to pursue his scientific and cultural interests. Jaipur is very much a product of his intellect and talent. A charming story relates an encounter between the Emperor Aurangzeb and the 10-year-old Rajput prince. When asked what punishment he deserved for his family's hostility and resistance to the Mughals, the boy answered "Your Majesty, when the groom takes the bride's hand, he confers lifelong protection. Now that the Emperor has taken my hand, what have I to fear?". Impressed by his tact and intelligence, Aurangzeb bestowed the title of *Sawai* (one and a quarter) on him, signifying that he would be a leader.

Jai Singh loved **mathematics** and **science**. A brilliant Brahmin scholar, Vidyadhar Bhattacharya from Bengal, helped him to design the city. Jai Singh also studied ancient texts on astronomy, had the works of Ptolemy and Euclid translated into Sanskrit. Work began in 1727 and it took four years to build the main palaces, central square and principal roads. The layout of streets was based on a mathematical grid of nine squares representing the ancient Hindu map of the universe, with the sacred

Mount Meru, home of Siva, occupying the central square. In Jaipur the royal palace is at the centre. The three by three square grid was modified by relocating the northwest square in the southeast, allowing the hill fort of Nahargar to overlook and protect the capital. The surrounding hills also provided good defence. At the southeast and southwest corners of the city were squares with pavilions and ornamental fountains. Water for these was provided by an underground aqueduct with outlets for public use along the streets. The main streets are 33-yards wide (33 is auspicious in Hinduism); the lesser ones are graded in width down to 4 m, all being in proportion to one another. The sidewalks were deliberately wide to allow free flow of pedestrian traffic. In Jai Singh's day, the buildings were painted in a variety of colours, including grey with white borders. Pink, a traditional colour of welcome, was used in 1853 in honour of the visit by Prince Albert, and the colour is still used.

★ The City Palace (1728-32)

ⓘ *Rs 150, Indians Rs 35 (includes Sawai Man Singh II Museum and Jaigarh Fort, valid for 2 days). Camera: still, free; video (unnecessary) Rs 100; doorkeepers expect tips when photographed. Photography in galleries prohibited, only of façades allowed. Guide books, post cards and maps available. 0930-1700 (last entry 1630).*

The City Palace occupies the centre of Jaipur, covers one seventh of its area and is surrounded by a high wall – the *Sarahad*. It differs from conventional Rajput fort palaces in its separation of the palace from its fortifications. In contrast the Jaipur Palace has much more in common with Mughal models, with its main buildings scattered in a fortified campus. To find the main **entrance**, from the Hawa Mahal go north about 250 m along the Sireh Deori Bazar past the Town Hall (Vidhan Sabha) and turn left through an arch – the *Sireh Deori* (boundary gate). Pass under a second arch – the *Naqqar Darwaza* (drum gate) – into **Jaleb Chowk**, the courtyard which formerly housed the Palace guard. Today it is where coaches park. A gateway to the south leads to the Jantar Mantar, the main palace buildings and museum and the Hawa Mahal.

Mubarak Mahal The main entrance leads into a large courtyard at the centre of which is the Mubarak Mahal, faced in white marble. Built in 1890, originally as a guesthouse for the Maharaja, the Mubarak Mahal is a small but immaculately conceived two-storeyed building, designed on the same cosmological plan in miniature as the

Jaipur City Palace

Havelis of Jaipur

Jaipur's formal planning recognized the importance of the joint family as the traditional social unit around which the houses should be built. The normal building was the *haveli* (Persian for 'enclosed space'), a three to five-storeyed house built around a shaded communal courtyard. To counter the heat and glare, the shops and houses were deep rather than wide. Large eaves and awnings provided shade. An outer gate and walls provided security and privacy.

A number of *havelis* usually formed a *mohalla* (district) and about 400 of these a *chokra* (section). Each district housed a particular trade. Muslim jewel cutters still live in Johari Bazar, marble workers in Chandpol Bazar and Hindu cloth merchants in Nehru Bazar.

city itself – a square divided into a 3x3 square grid (see page 331). Tillotson describes the cantilevered balconies, the roof parapet, the pierced balustrade and the open arcade of the upper gallery – "The open space above each arch in the gallery... make the building's roof appear to float weightlessly above it. The lightness and the depth are typically Rajput features".

The **Textile and Costume Museum** on the first floor has fine examples of fabrics and costumes from all over India as well as musical instruments and toys from the royal nursery. In the northwest corner of the courtyard is the **Armoury Museum** containing an impressive array of weaponry. Just outside the armour museum is **Rajendra Pol**, a gate flanked by two elephants, each carved from a single block of marble, which leads to the inner courtyard. There are beautifully carved alcoves with delicate arches and *jali* screens and a fine pair of patterned brass doors.

Diwan-i-Khas (Sarbato Bhadra) The gateway leads to the courtyard known variously as the Diwan-i-Am, the Sarbato Bhadra or the Diwan-i-Khas Chowk. Today the building in its centre is known as the Diwan-i-Khas (circa 1730). Originally the Diwan-i-Am, it was reduced to the hall of private audience (Diwan-i-Khas) when the new Diwan-i-Am was built to its southeast at the end of the 18th century. The courtyard itself reflects the overwhelming influence of Mughal style, despite the presence of some Hindu designs. In the Diwan-i-Khas (in Sanskrit, Sarbato Bhadra) are two huge silver urns used by Sawai Madho Singh for carrying Ganga water to England, see box on page 337.

Diwan-i-Am (Diwan Khana) Art gallery The 'new' Hall of Public Audience built by Maharaja Sawai Pratap Singh (1778-1803) today houses a fine collection of Persian and Indian miniatures, some of the carpets the Maharajas had made for them and an equally fine collection of manuscripts. To its north is the Carriage Museum. In the middle of the west wall of the Diwan-i-Am courtyard, opposite the art gallery, is the **Ganesh Pol**, which leads via a narrow passage and the Peacock Gate into **Pritam Niwas Chowk**. This courtyard has the original palace building 'Chandra Mahal' to its north, the zenana on its northwest, and the Anand Mahal to its south. Several extremely attractive doors, rich and vivid in their peacock blue, aquamarine and amber colours, have a small marble Hindu god watching over them.

Chandra Mahal ⓘ *Not always open to visitors.* Built between 1727 and 1734 the Moon Palace is the earliest building of the palace complex. Externally it appears to have seven storeys, though inside the first and second floors are actually one high-ceilinged hall. On the ground floor (north) a wide verandah – the **Pritam Niwas** (House of the beloved) – with Italian wall paintings, faces the formal Jai Niwas garden. The main section of the ground floor is an Audience Hall.

The hall on the first (and second) floors, the **Sukh Niwas** (House of pleasure), underwent a Victorian reconstruction, above which are the **Rang Mandir** and the **Sobha Niwas**, built to the same plan. The two top storeys are much smaller, with the mirror palace of the **Chavi Niwas** succeeded by the small open marble pavilion which crowns the structure, the **Mukat Niwas**. This gives superb views of the city and Tiger Fort.

Jaipur

Related map
A Jaipur City Palace, page 332

N

0 metres 200
0 yards 200

■ Sleeping

1	Achrol Lodge *D1*	7	Diggi Palace *C4*
2	Alsisar *B3*	8	Evergreen *C3*
3	Arya Niwas *B3*	9	Gangaur *B2*
4	Bissau Palace *A4*	10	Jai Mahal Palace *C1*
5	Chirmi Palace *C2*	11	Jaipur Ashok *B2*
6	City Centre &	12	Jaipur Inn *A2*
	Maharani Palace *B2*	13	Kanchandeep *B2*
		14	Karni Niwas *B2*

15	Lakshmi Vilas *E4*
16	Madhuban *A1*
17	Mansingh Tower *C3*
18	Megh Niwas & Jas Vilas *A1*
19	Meru Palace *D4*
20	Nana-Ki-Haveli *D5*
21	Natraj *B2*

In the northeast corner of the Pritam Niwas Chowk, leading into the *zenana*, is the **Krishna door**, its surface embossed with scenes of the deity's life. The door is sealed in the traditional way with a rope sealed with wax over the lock.

North of the Chandra Mahal, the early 18th-century **Govind Deo Temple**, which was probably built as a residence, has been restored by an ancient technique using

22 Rajputana Palace Sheraton *B1*	
23 Rambagh Palace *E3*	
24 Santha Bagh *E4*	
25 Shivam *B2*	
26 Teej Tourist Bungalow *B2*	
27 Umaid Bhawan *A2*	
28 Youth Hostel *E2*	

● **Eating**
1 Chaitanya *B3*
2 Chanakya *C4*
3 Copper Chimney & Handi *C3*
4 Indian Coffee House *C4*
5 Indiana *C4*
6 LMB *B5*
7 Niros & Book Corner *C4*

8 Pizza Hut, Swaad & Rajasthan Travels *B2*
9 Rainbow *C2*
10 Surya Mahal & Bookshop *C4*

molasses, curd, coconut water, fenugreek, rope fibres and lime. The furniture is European – Bohemian glass chandeliers – the decoration Indian. Following the steps around you will see a *mandala* (circular diagram of the cosmos), made from rifles around the royal crest of Jaipur. The ceiling of this hall is in finely worked gold. Further on are the beautiful Mughal style fountains and the **Jai Niwas gardens** (1727), laid out as a *charbagh*, the **Badal Mahal** (circa 1750) and the **Tal Katora** tank. The view extends beyond the compound walls to the Nahargarh (Tiger Fort) on the hills beyond.

Sights

★ **Hawa Mahal (Palace of the Winds)** ⓘ *closed Fri, 1000-1630, Rs 5, cameras Rs 30, enter from Tripolia Bazar (west of the GPO); for best views accept invitation from shop owners on upper floors across the street.* The 'Palace of the Winds' (circa 1799) forms part of the east wall of the City Palace complex and is best seen from the street outside. Possibly Jaipur's most famous building, it is the pink sandstone eastern façade of a palace built for the ladies of the harem by Sawai Pratap Singh. The five storeys stand on a high podium with an entrance from the west. The elaborate façade contains 953 small casements in a huge curve, each with a balcony and crowning arch. The windows enabled cool air (*hawa*) to circulate and allowed the ladies who were secluded in the *zenana* to watch processions below without being seen.

★ **Jantar Mantar (Observatory)** ⓘ *0930-1630, Rs 5 (Mon free), camera Rs 50, video Rs 100, guide, Rs 10, very worthwhile, it gets extremely hot in the middle of the day and there is no shade.* Literally 'Instruments for measuring the harmony of the heavens', the Jantar Mantar was built between 1728 and 1734. Jai Singh wanted things on a grand scale and chose stone with a marble facing on the important planes. Each instrument serves a particular function and each gives an accurate reading. For Hindus the matching of horoscopes still plays an essential part in the selection of marriage partners, and astrologers are consulted in making all important decisions.

Moving clockwise you will see the following instruments or **yantras: 1 Small 'Samrat'** is a large sundial (the triangular structure) with flanking quadrants marked off in hours and minutes. The arc on your left shows the time from sunrise to midday, the one on the right midday to sundown. Read the time where the shadow is sharpest. The dial gives solar time so to adjust it to Indian Standard Time, between one minute 15 seconds and 32 minutes must be added according to the time of year and solar position as shown on the board.
2 'Dhruva' locates the position of the Pole Star at night and those of the 12 zodiac signs. The graduation and lettering in Hindi follows the traditional unit of measurement based on the human breath calculated to last six seconds. Thus: four breaths = one *pala* (24 seconds), 60 palas = one *gati* (24 minutes), 60 gatis = one day (24 hours).
3 'Narivalya' has two dials: south facing for when the sun is in the southern hemisphere (21 September-21 March) and north facing for the rest of the year. At noon the sun falls on the north-south line.
4 The Observer's Seat was intended for Jai Singh.
5 Small 'Kranti' is used to measure the longitude and latitude of celestial bodies.
6 'Raj' (King of Instruments) is used once a year to calculate the Hindu calendar, which is based on the Jaipur Standard as it has been for 270 years. A telescope is attached over the central hole. The bar at the back is used for sighting, while the plain disk is used as a blackboard to record observations.
7 'Unnathamsa' is used for finding the altitudes of the celestial bodies. Round-the-clock observations can be made and the sunken steps allow any part of the dial to be read.
8 'Disha' points to the north.
9 'Dakshina', a wall aligned north-south, is used for observing the position and movement of heavenly bodies when passing over the meridian.

Sawai Madho Singh: devotion across the oceans

The present Maharaja's grandfather was an extremely devout Hindu. Any physical contact with a non-Hindu was deemed to be ritually defiling, so any contact with the British carried awkward ritual problems. Whenever required to meet a British official, including the Viceroy, the Maharaja would wear white gloves, and after any meeting would ritually purify himself in a bath of Ganga water and have the clothes he wore burnt. When he went to England to celebrate Queen Victoria's Diamond Jubilee Sawai Madho Singh had a P&O liner refitted to include a Krishna temple and carried sufficient Ganga water with him in two 309 kg silver urns to last the trip.

10 Large 'Samrat' Similar to the small one (1) but ten times larger and thus accurate to two seconds instead of 20 seconds. The sundial is 27.4 m high. It is used on a particularly holy full moon in July/August, to predict the length and heaviness of the monsoon for the local area.

11 'Rashivalayas' has 12 sundials for the signs of the zodiac and is similar to the Samrat yantras. The five at the back (north to south), are Gemini, Taurus, Cancer, Virgo and Leo. In front of them are Aries and Libra, and then in the front, again (north-south), Aquarius, Pisces, Capricorn, Scorpio and Sagittarius. The instruments enable readings to be made at the instant each zodiacal sign crosses the meridian.

12 'Jai Prakash' acts as a double check on all the other instruments. It measures the rotation of the sun, and the two hemispheres together form a map of the heavens. The small iron plate strung between crosswires shows the sun's longitude and latitude and which zodiacal sign it is passing through.

13 Small 'Ram' is a smaller version of the Jai Prakash Yantra (12).

14 Large 'Ram Yantra' Similarly, this finds the altitude and the azimuth (arc of the celestial circle from Zenith to horizon).

15 'Diganta' also measures the azimuth of any celestial body.

16 Large 'Kranti' is similar to the smaller Kranti (5).

★ **Nahargarh (Tiger Fort, 1734)** ① *1000-1630, Rs 2, camera Rs 30.* The small fort with its immense walls and bastions stands on a sheer rock face. The city at its foot was designed to give access to the fort in case of attack. You have to walk first through some quiet and attractive streets at the base of the hill, then 2 km up a steep, rough winding path to reach the top. Beautifully floodlit at night. Much of the original fort is in ruins but the walls and 19th-century additions survive, including rooms furnished for maharajas. This is a 'real fort', quiet and unrushed, with breathtaking views from the and interesting buildingsbattlements. *Durg Café* has good views and sells quite reasonable snacks, drinks and chilled beer but service is slow for meals.

You can combine this visit with the **Jaigarh Fort**, see page 340, 7 km away (part of the same defensive network), along the flat-topped hill. Women alone have been taken advantage of so you are urged to join a group.

Birla Mandir Something of an architectural curiosity, the modern temple built by the Birla family in the southeast of the city is impressive in scale and in the eclecticism of its religious art.

Surya Mandir ① *Galta Pol can be reached by taking a bus, or by walking the 2 km from the Hawa Mahal. It is about 600 m uphill and then downhill.* From Galta Pol take a walk to the 'Valley of the Monkeys', east of Jaipur, to get a view of the city from the

The Jaipur foot

The 'Jaipur foot' may sound like an affliction, but for thousands it represents a miraculous answer to the problem of living with an amputated leg.

Artificial feet were available long before orthopaedic surgeons in Jaipur began to work on a local solution to a specifically Indian problem. For while the surgeons had been fitting high quality western-designed artificial feet for some time, they found that patients would frequently give them up and return to crutches. They couldn't use the rigid wooden foot supplied, which had been designed to fit inside shoes and failed to meet the needs for flexibility essential for sitting cross-legged or for walking across fields and village tracks.

The answer was to adapt the foot with local skills and technology and a highly resilient, flexible and lightweight foot was developed. The work has been one of the many social service projects undertaken by the Bhagwan Mahaveer Viklang Sahayata Samiti voluntary body to help people irrespective of caste, religion or politics. (Those interested may contact SMS Hospital, Jaipur.) Patients arrive at Jaipur from all over India, but the society now organizes camps in many parts of the country. The Rotary Jaipur Limb Project, started in UK in 1984 raises money to help establish Limb Camps in India and elsewhere.

Surya Mandir (Sun Temple). Walk down the steps to the five old temples dedicated to Rama-Sita and Radha-Krishna, with some nice wall paintings. You can watch hundreds of monkeys that play in the water of the tank below.

Museums, parks and zoos Central Museum ① *Albert Hall, Ram Niwas Gardens (see above), closed Fri, 1000-1630, Rs 3 (Mon free),* has mainly excellent decorative metalware, miniature portraits and other art pieces. Also Rajasthani costumes, pottery, woodwork, brassware etc (some dusty and poorly labelled). **Sawai Man Singh II Museum** ① *0930-1700, Rs 150 (Indians Rs 35),* part of City Palace. Excellent display of paintings, miniatures, textiles, costumes, armoury, maps, objects from royal court (16th-19th centuries), see above. **Modern Art Gallery** ① *Ravindra Rang Manch, Ram Niwas Gardens, closed Fri, 1000-1630,* has a collection of contemporary Rajasthani art. **Zoological Garden** ① *Ram Niwas Gardens, Rs 2,* has a crocodile farm.

★ Amber (Amer) → *Colour map 2, grid A5. 11 km north of Jaipur.*

As you take the winding road from modern Jaipur between the barren hills immediately to the north there is little hint of the magnificent fort and palace which once dominated the narrow valley. Today there is little hint of the city that once was, just the palace clinging to the side of the rocky hill, overlooked by the fort above, with a small town at its base. In the high season this is one of India's most popular tourist sites, with a continuous train of colourfully decorated elephants walking up and down the ramp. One penalty of its popularity is the persistence of the vendors.

Background Amber was the site of a Hindu temple built by the Mina tribes as early as the 10th century. Two centuries later the Kachhawaha Rajputs made it their capital, which it remained until Sawai Jai Singh II moved to his newly planned city of Jaipur in 1727. Its location made Amber strategically crucial for the Mughal emperors as they moved south, and the Maharajahs of Amber took care to establish close relations with successive Mughal rulers. The building of the fort palace was begun by Raja Man Singh, a noted Rajput General in Akbar's army, in 1600.

The palace ⓘ *Tickets in the Chowk, just below the steps up to Shila Mata. Rs 50; still camera Rs75, video Rs 150. 0900-1630. Son et lumière is planned. Take the green bus from the Hawa Mahal (Palace of the Winds), Rs 5 (buses originate at Ajmeri Gate), or auto-rickshaw Rs 60 (Rs 150 for return, including the wait). Tourist information is at the new Elephant Stand, T530264. Guides, about Rs 250 for a half day (group of 4).* You can reach the palace either by foot, jeep or elephant. The walk is quite easy and mainly on a separate path. Jeeps charge Rs 100 each way, or Rs 10 per seat. The elephants carry up to four persons on a padded seat. The ride can be somewhat unnerving when the elephant comes close to the edge of the road, but it is perfectly safe. You have to buy a 'return ticket' even if you wish to walk down later (elephants get bad tempered as the day wears on). It costs Rs 400 per elephant carrying four (sometimes discounted).

After passing through a series of five defensive gates, you reach the first courtyard of the **Raj Mahal** built by Man Singh I in 1600, entered through the **Suraj Pol** (Sun Gate). Here you can get a short ride around the courtyard on an elephant, but bargain very hard. There are some toilets near the dismounting platform. On the south side of this Jaleb Chowk with the flower beds, is a flight of steps leading up to the **Singh Pol** (Lion Gate) entrance to the upper courtyard of the palace.

> ⚑ *A stroll uphill just before sunset avoids crowds and captures the magic of the place. The monkeys here will try to steal any food you have visible.*

On your right after climbing the steps is the green marble-pillared **Shila Mata Temple** (to Kali as Goddess of War) which contains a black marble image of the goddess Man Singh I brought back from Jessore (now in Bangladesh; the chief priest has always been Bengali). The silver doors with images of Durga and Saraswati were added by his successor. The temple only opens at certain times of the day and then, only allows a limited number of visitors at a time so ask before joining the queue!

In the left hand corner of the courtyard, the **Diwan-i-Am** (Hall of Public Audience) was built by Raja Jai Singh I in 1639. Originally, it was an open pavilion with cream marble pillars supporting an unusual striped canopy-shaped ceiling, with a portico with double red sandstone columns. The room on the east was added by Sawai Ram Singh II. The **Ganesh Pol** (circa 1700-25), colourfully painted and with mosaic decoration separates the private from the public areas.

This leads onto the **Jai Singh I court** with a formal garden. To the east is the two-storeyed cream coloured marble pavilion – **Jai Mandir** (Diwan-i-Khas or Hall of Private Audience) below and **Jas Mandir** (1635-40) with a curved Bengali roof, on the terrace above. The former, with its marble columns and painted ceiling, has lovely views across the lake.

Amber Palace

1 Shila Mata
2 Diwan-i-Am
  (Daftar Khana above)
3 Jai Singh I Garden
4 Jai Mandir
  (Jas Mandir, 1st floor)
5 Sohag Mandir
  (1st floor)
6 Palace of Man
  Singh I (1st floor)
7 Zenana

Not to scale

The latter has colourful mosaics, mirrors and marble *jali* screens which let in cooling breezes. Both have **Shish Mahals** (Mirror Palaces) faced with mirrors, seen to full effect when lit by a match. To the west of the chowk is the **Sukh Niwas**, a pleasure palace with a marble water course to cool the air, and doors inlaid with ivory and sandalwood. The Mughal influence is quite apparent in this chowk.

Above the Ganesh Pol is the **Sohag Mandir**, a rectangular chamber with beautiful latticed windows and octagonal rooms to each side. From the rooftop there are stunning views over the palace across the town of Amber, the long curtain wall surrounding the town and further north, through the 'V' shaped entrance in the hills, to the plains beyond (particularly good for photographs). Beyond this courtyard is the **Palace of Man Singh I**. A high wall separates it from the Jai Singh Palace. In the centre of the chowk which was once open is a **baradari** (12-arched pavilion), combining Mughal and Hindu influences. The surrounding palace, a complex warren of passages and staircases, was turned into *zenana* quarters when the newer palaces were built by Jai Singh.

The Old Palace The palace at the base of the hill, to the north, started in the early 13th century, is of little interest today. The temples nearby include the **Jagatsiromani Temple** dedicated to Krishna, with carvings and paintings. Close by is the old temple to Narasinghji and *Panna Mian-ki-Baoli* (step well). A stone path from the Chand Pol in the first courtyard of Amber Palace leads to the ruins.

★ **Jaigarh Fort** ⓘ *1000-1630, Rs 20, still camera Rs 20, vehicle entry Rs 50. Jeeps (Rs 50 per person) are available in Amber if you do not wish to walk (see above). It is also a pleasant rickshaw journey; tell the driver if you want to go to the bottom of the footpath or to take the road to the top (much further and more expensive). Above the Palace on*

Around Amber

1 Mohan Bari
2 Dal Ram Bagh
3 Parian Ka Bagh
4 Elephant Route
5 Jaleb Chowk

0 metres 200
0 yards 200

the hill top stands the gigantic bulk of Jaigarh, impressively lit at night, a testimony of
the power of the Jaipur rulers. Visit strongly recommended.

From Amber Palace, turn right out of the Suraj Pol and follow a stone road past the old elephant quarters. This is the start of a steady climb of about 25 minutes. The road is protected throughout its length by a strong wall which zigzags up the hill to the fort's main gate. What appears at first to be two adjoining forts is in fact all part of the same structure which follows the contour of the hilltop. From Nahargarh to Jaigarh is an 8-km walk.

The forbidding medieval fort was never captured and so has survived virtually intact which makes it particularly interesting. In the 16th century well-planned **cannon foundry** you can see the pit where the barrels were cast, the capstan-powered lathe which bored out the cannon and the iron-workers' drills, taps and dies. The **armoury** has a large collection of swords and small arms. There is a small *café* outside the armoury.

There are gardens, a granary, open and closed reservoirs; the ancient temples of Ram Harihar (10th century) and Kal Bhairava (12th century) are within the fort. You can explore a warren of complicated dark passageways among the palaces. Many of the apartments are open and you can see the collections of coins and puppets (shows on demand).

The other part of the fort, at a slightly higher elevation, has a tall watch tower. From here there are tremendous views of the surrounding hills. The massive 50 tonne **Jai Ban cannon** stands on top of one tower. Allegedly the largest cannon on wheels in the world, with an 8 m barrel, it had a range of around 20 km, but it was never used; only tested once. Some 7 km further along the top of the hill is the smaller Nahargarh Fort overlooking Jaipur itself. See page 337.

Sanganer (12 km southwest of Jaipur) ⓘ *Hourly buses from Jaipur.* The airport road gives access to this small town through two ruined triple gateways beyond which is the ruined palace and old Jain temples. The greater attractions of Sanganer are block-printing and paper-making. The latter uses waste cotton and silk rags which are pulped, sieved, strained and dried. *Salim's Paper Factory* offers tours to visitors. Screen and block-printing is done in *Chipa Basti* where you can watch the printers in workshops and purchase samples, usually at a fraction of the price asked in Jaipur. *The Village Restaurant* is near the airport. There is a *Donkey Fair* in October at Looniyabas nearby, when thousands of animals are traded.

Jal Mahal & Gaitore (8 km north of Amber). The **Man Sarobar** lake has the attractive, Rajput style **Jal Mahal** (Water Palace, 1735) at its centre. Though often dry in the summer, during the monsoon the lake is transformed from a huge grassy field into a beautiful water hyacinth-filled lake. Opposite the lake at **Gaitore** are the marble and sandstone *chhatris* of the rulers of Jaipur, built by Jai Singh II and set in landscaped gardens.

Sisodia Ranika Bagh ⓘ *8 km east on the Agra Rd, 0800-1800, Rs 10.* These are among the many landscaped gardens laid out by kings and courtiers in the 18th and 19th centuries. Sisodia Ranika Bagh was built for Jai Singh's second wife, with attractive tiered gardens with fountains, watercourses and pavilions with murals. **Vidyadhar Bagh** ⓘ *Agra Rd, 0800-1800, Re 1,* is a beautiful garden laid out in honour of Jai Singh's friend and city planner Vidyadhar Bhattacharya.

Ramgarh Lake (30 km northeast from Jaipur (45 minutes drive)). This 15 sq km lake of Jamwa Ramgarh, which attracts large flocks of waterfowl in winter, lies within a game sanctuary with good boating and bird watching. It is being developed as a watersports resort. Built to supply Jaipur with water it now provides less than 1% of the city's needs and in years of severe drought it may dry up completely. The 300-sq km Jamwa Sanctuary which once provided the Jaipur royal family with game still has some panthers, nilgai and small game.

★ Samode → *Phone code: 01423. Colour map 2, grid A5. 42 km north of Jaipur.*

At the head of the enclosed valley in the dry rugged hills of the northern Aravallis, Samode stands on a former caravan route. Today, the sleepy village, with its local artisans producing printed cloth and glass bangles, nestles within its old walls. A stay at the Bagh or the Palace is a wonderful way to relax and refresh away from the chaos and pollution of Indian cities. Samode is well worth the short visit from Jaipur or en route to the painted towns of Shekhawati.

The Palace, which dominates the village, is fabulously decorated with 300-year old wall paintings (hunting scenes, floral motifs etc) which still look almost new. Around the first floor of the Darbar Hall are magnificent alcoves, decorated with mirrors like *shish mahal* and *jali* screens through which the royal ladies would have looked down into the grand jewel-like Darbar Hall.

Towering immediately above the palace is **Samode Fort**, the Maharajah's former residence, reached in times of trouble by an underground passage. The old stone zig-zag path has been replaced by 300 steps. Though dilapidated, there are excellent views from the ramparts; a caretaker has the keys. The main fort gate is the starting point of some enticing **walks** into the Aravallis. A paved path leads to a shrine about 3 km away. There are two other powerful forts you can walk to, forming a circular walk ending back in Samode. Allow three hours, wear good shoes and a hat, and carry water. There is a small artists' colony in the village that produces good quality miniature **paintings** on old paper.

Samode Bagh, a large 400-year old Mughal-style formal garden with fountains and pavilions, has been beautifully restored. It is 3 km southeast of Samode (towards the main Jaipur-Agra road).

★ Shekhawati

Covering an area of about 300 sq km on the often arid and rock studded plains to the northeast of the Aravalli mountain range, Shekhawati, is the homeland of the Marwari community. The painted havelis in Sikar and Jhunjhunun dsitricts form an open-air art gallery dating from the mid-19th century.

Although a day trip gives you an idea of its treasures, it is better to spend a couple of nights in Shekhawati to see some good examples of temples, frescoed forts, chhatris and step-wells at leisure. The *havelis* are often occupied by the family or retainers who will happily show you around but many charge a fee of about Rs 20. Many havelis are in a poor state of repair with fading paintings which may appear monotonously alike. ▸▸ *For Sleeping, Eating and other listings see pages 355-370.*

Ins and outs

Getting there You can get to the principal Shekhawati towns by train (overnight from Delhi; day trains from Jaipur) but road access is easier. A car comes in handy to see the area, though there are crowded buses from Delhi, Jaipur and Bikaner to some towns. Buses leave every 30 mins from 0500-2000 from Jaipur's Main Bus Station and take about 3 hrs.

Getting around Within each town it is best to enlist the help of a local person (possibly from the hotels listed below) to direct you to the best *havelis*. Local buses run between towns every 15 to 20 mins and take about an hour. *Castle Mandawa*, *Dundlod Fort* and *Roop Niwas* at Nawalgarh offer 1 week safaris with nights in royal tents (occasionally in castles or heritage hotels). You can expect folk music concerts,

⁞ Shekhawati havelis

The *havelis* in Shekhawati were usually built around two courtyards - one for general use, and the other a zenana courtyard for the women. They were made from brick and local stone, and plastered. Murals were either painted on dry surfaces or on wet plaster. Mineral colours were derived from indigo, ochre, lead, copper, lapis lazuli, lime, and even gold. The subject of the paintings varied. The 10 avatars of Vishnu, Krishna Lila, the Ramayana and Mahabharata, folk tales, historic events and the daily life in Shekhawati were popular themes, together with a fascination for portraying the British and their curious ways.

campfires, and spend time visiting eco-farms, rural communities and *havelis* en route, all with jeep support. Power cuts can cause real problems in hotels bringing to a halt cooling in summer, heating (and hot water) in winter and lighting at night – always have a torch handy.

History

The 'garden of Shekha' was named after Rao Shekhaji of Amarsar (1433-88) who challenged the Kachhawahas, refusing to pay tribute to the rulers at Amber. These Rajput barons made inroads into Muslim territory even during Mughal rule, and declared Shekhawati independent from the Jaipur suzerainty until 1738. During this period the merchants lavishly decorated their houses with paintings on religious, folk and historical themes. As Mughal power collapsed Shekhawati became a region of lawless banditry. In the early 19th century the British East India Company brought it under their control, bringing peace but also imposing taxes and tolls on trade which the Marwaris resented. Many of the merchants migrated to other parts of the country to seek their fortune and those who flourished returned their wealth to their homeland and took over as patrons of the artists.

Sikar District → *Phone code: 01572. Colour map 2, grid A5. Population: 184,900.*
Occupying the southwestern flank of the Shekhawati region, Sikar district has a number of picturesque towns including Ramgarh which has the highest concentration of painted havelis. Since 1947, 29 cases of sati have been recorded in the Sikar and its two neighbouring districts.

Sikar The late 17th-century fort was built when Sikar was an important trading centre and the wealthiest *thikana* (feudatory) under Jaipur. You can visit the old quarter and see the Wedgwood blue 'Biyani' (1920) and 'Mahal' (1845), Murarka and Somani *havelis* and murals and carvings in Gopinath, Raghunath and Madan Mohan temples.

Lachhmangarh Founded early 19th century, the town plan was based on Jaipur's model; this can be seen by climbing up to the old fort which has now been renovated by the Jhunjhunwala family. The fine *havelis* include one of the area's grandest – Ganeriwala with *char chowks* (four courtyards), the 'Rathi' *haveli* near the Clock Tower in the market, and others in the Chowkhani.

Fatehpur Fatehpur, founded in the mid-15th century by a Kayamkhani Nawab, has very attractive *havelis* along the Churu-Sikar road. Visit in particular the Devra (1005), Singhania (circa 1880), Goenka (circa 1880) and Saraogi. Later amusing frescoes showing European influence can be seen in the Jalan and Bharthia (1929) *havelis.* The town also produces good tic and-dye fabrics.There are a few places to eat and sleep here. Just before Ratangarh, 40 km along the NH11, on the Bikaner road, is the *Midway Kurja* restaurant, with a pleasant garden, a good craft and book shop.

Jhunjhunun District → *Colour map 2, grid A5. Population: 72,000.*
Jhunjhunun district occupies the northwestern section of the region and has some of the more popularly visited towns in Shekhawati.

Mandawa (Phone code: 015972). At Fatehpur, a country road to the east takes you to Mandawa (22 km), a small, rather dirty bustling town. Founded in the mid-18th century, it has interesting murals in the large rugged fort (circa 1755) built by Thakur Nawal Singh, which is now a hotel. The *havelis* are past their prime; the Goenka *havelis* (Ladhuram Tarkesvar 1878, and Dedraj Turmal, 1898); the *Ladia havelis* – Gulab Rai (1870) and Sneh Ram (1906), Nandlal Murmuria (1935), Bansidhar Newatia (1910) and the Mohanlal Saraf (1870) *havelis* are interesting. The Siva temple here has a rock crystal lingam. The *Mandawa Haveli* near Sonthaliya Gate (northeast of town) displays local crafts, 0600-2200 daily. If you stay overnight in Mandawa you can visit the Harlalka *baoli* (a working step well) early in the morning to watch oxen at work on the ramp to raise water. *Desert Music Festival*, October to November. There are some reasonably priced, good quality miniatures on 'silk' at the *Mandawa Art School* at the castle gate, and fabrics and carpets at *CM Souvenirs*, Main Market.

Nawalgarh (Phone code: 015974. 25 km southeast of Mandawa). Nawalgarh was founded in 1737 by Thakur Nawal Singh. The town has a colourful bazar and two forts (circa 1730). The Bala Kila which has a kiosk with beautiful ceiling paintings is approached via the fruit market in the town centre and entered through the *Hotel Radha*. It also has the *Roop Niwas Palace* (now a hotel) and some 18th-century temples with 19th- and early 20th-century paintings.

There are numerous fine *havelis* worth visiting. They are perhaps the best restored haveli of Shekhawati. The ground floor of **Anandilal Poddar haveli** ① *Rs 40 (foreigners) includes camera and guide*, is now converted to a museum. The 1920s haveli has around 700 frescoes remarkably restored in the courtyard and displays tribal costumes (a bit unsophisticated), miniature paintings, household utensils and scale models of musical instruments.

Also try to visit the 19th-century **Kesardev Murarka** ① *most charge Rs 15-20 for viewing*, which has a finely painted façade, and the Radheshyam Murarka (early-20th century). These are being converted to museums. The owners organize the *Shekhawati Festival* in January displaying the arts and crafts of the region. The paintings here depict anything from European women having a bath to Hindu religious themes and Jesus Christ. There are also interesting temples in town including Ganga Mai near Nansa Gate.

Dundlod West of Nawalgarh, Dundlod fort (1750), which stands in the middle of the village, is now a Heritage Hotel. The gateways lead to a grassy court where steps lead up to the Diwan Khana furnished with period furniture, portraits and hangings; there is a library with a collection of rare books of Indian history and the *duchatta* above, which allowed the ladies in *purdah* to watch court ceremonies unobserved. ① *Darbar Hall: Rs 20 for non-residents*. The Goenka haveli near the fort has three painted courtyards, and the Satyanarayan temple has religious paintings but both these may be closed in the low season.

Jhunjhunun (Phone code: 015972. Colour map 2, grid A5). Jhunjhunun was a stronghold of the Kayamkhani Nawabs until defeated by the Hindu Sardul Singh in 1730. The Mohanlal Iswardas Modi (1896), Tibriwala (1883) and the Muslim Nuruddin

⁞ The love story of Dhola and Maru

There are numerous versions of this romantic legend of the separation of a young couple and their subsequent reunion.

Prince Dhola of Narvar is married in infancy to Princess Maruni (Maru) of Pugal in Marwar. However, the child bride returns home with her parents and only wakens to a longing for her husband when she reaches adolescence but learns that Dhola has remarried. Although, the prince longs to find his first wife, Malvani of Malwa his new bride uses every means to hold him back. Dhola finally escapes when Malvani sleeps, having found a camel that will speed him to Pugal within a single day. He surmounts the many obstacles that are conjured up by Malvani, and the couple are reunited. On the return journey, Maru is bitten by a venomous snake but Dhola remains with her. His prayers are answered when a passing yogi performs a miracle and brings her back to life. The tale ends happily - Maru assumes her rightful place and is adored by the people of Narvar.

Farooqi *havelis* (which is devoid of figures) and the maqbara are all worth seeing. The *Chhe* (6) *Haveli* complex, Khetri Mahal (1760) and the Biharilal temple (1776), which has attractive frescoes (closed during lunch time), are also interesting. The Rani Sati temple commemorates Narayana Devi who is believed to have become a sati; her stone is venerated by many of the wealthy *bania* community and an annual Marwari fair is held (protesting women's groups feel it glorifies the practice of *sati*).

Alwar → *Phone code: 0144. Colour map 2, grid A6. Population: 261,000.*

As Mughal power crumbled Rao Pratap Singhji of Macheri founded Alwar as his capital in 1771. He shook off Jat power over the region and rebelled against Jaipur suzerainty making Alwar an independent state. His successors lent military assistance to the British in their battles against the Marathas in 1803 AD, and in consequence gained the support of the colonial power. Today, visitors to Sariska may consider stopping here

Sights Alwar is protected by the hilltop **Bala Quilla** which has the remains of palaces, temples and 10 tanks built by the first rulers of Alwar. It stands 308 m above the town, to the northwest, and is reached by a steep four-wheel drive track (with permission from the Police Station). There are splendid views but little else to see.

The **Vinai Vilas Mahal** ① *closed Fri, 1030-1630, Rs 3*, the City Palace (1840), with intricate *jali* work, ornate *jarokha* balconies and courtyards, houses government offices on the ground floor, and a fine museum upstairs. The palace is impressive but poorly maintained and the Darbar Room is closed. The museum houses miniature paintings, armoury, sandalwood carvings, ivory objects, jade art, musical instruments and princely relics. There are over 7,000 manuscripts in various Asian languages. Next to the city palace are the lake and royal cenotaphs. To the right of the main entrance to the palace is a two-storey processional elephant carriage designed to carry 50 people and be pulled by four elephants.

The **Yeshwant Niwas** was built by Maharaja Jai Singh in the Italianate style but he never lived in it. Instead he built the **Vijay Mandir** ① *closed Fri, 1000-1630, Rs 3*, beside Vijay Sagar in 1918. It is a 105-room palace with a façade resembling an anchored ship, 10 km from Alwar. Part of it is open to the public with prior permission from the royal family or their secretary.

Excursion Kesroli, 10 km northeast, has a seven-turreted 16th-century fort atop a rocky hillock, now sympathetically (though modestly) restored by the owners of

Neemrana. An escape from Delhi (three hours' drive) and convenient for an overnight halt; turn left off NH8 at Dharuhera for Alwar road.

Sariska Tiger Reserve → *Phone code: 0144. Colour map 2, grid A6.*

The 480-sq km sanctuary comprises dry deciduous forest of *ber, dhok* and *tendu*, set in a valley surrounded by the barren Aravalli hills. The princely shooting reserve of the Maharajah of Alwar in the Aravallis was declared a sanctuary in 1955 and is a tiger reserve under **Project Tiger**.

Ins and outs Early morning jeep trips from *Sariska Palace Hotel* or *Tiger Den* go into the park as far as the Monkey Temple, where you can get a cup of tea and watch monkeys and peacocks. Jeep-hire for non-standard trips in the reserve, Rs 750-850 for three hours, excluding entry fees. Rs 200 (foreigners); vehicle Rs 125 per trip. Open all year. During the monsoon travel through the forest may be difficult. Best season to visit is between Novovember and April.

Wildlife The main rhesus monkey population live at Talvriksh near Kushalgarh, whilst at Bhartri-Hari you will see many langurs. The chowsingha, or **four-horned antelope**, is found here. Other deer include chital and sambar. You may see nilgai, wild boar, jackals, hyenas, hares and porcupines, though tigers and leopards are rarely seen, since the reserve is closed at night to visitors. During the monsoons the place is alive with birds but many animals move to higher ground. There are ground birds such as peafowl, jungle fowl, spur fowl and the grey partridge. Babblers, bulbuls and tree pies are common round the lodges. In the dry season, when the streams disappear, the animals become dependant on man-made water holes at Kalighatti, Salopka and Pandhupol.

Sights Kankwari Fort, where Emperor Aurangzeb is believed to have imprisoned his brother Dara Shikoh, the rightful heir to the Mughal throne, is within the park. The old **Bhartrihari Temple** has a fair and six hour dance-drama in September/October. **Neelkanth** has a complex of sixth to 10th-century carved temples. These forts and temples are quite spread out. You can hire jeeps in Sariska. **Sariska**, the gateway for the Sariska National Park, is a pleasant, quiet place to stay and relax. **Bhangarh**, 55 km away, on the outskirts of the reserve, is a deserted city of some 10,000 dwellings established in 1631. It was abandoned 300 years ago, supposedly after it was cursed by a magician.

Kanota From Jaipur the road east along the NH11 runs to Kanota, 14 km away. The 200-year-old castle surrounded by orchards and gardens, has been converted into a distinctive hotel.

Bhandarej Some 62 km from Jaipur, south of Dausa, has accommodation.

Karauli Noted for its pale red sandstone, widely used for building, Karauli, founded in 1348, was the seat of a small princely state which played a prominent part in support of the Mughal Emperors. The impressive **City Palace** has some fine wall paintings, stone carvings and a fine Darbar Hall. Fairs are held at nearby temples lasting a week to a fortnight: *Sivaratri, Kaila Devi* (October). The market sells good local crafts.

Deeg → *Phone code: 05641. Colour map 2, grid A6. Population: 41,000.*

Between Alwar and Mathura, Deeg, a dusty north Indian town, was the summer resort of the Bharatpur maharajas who built the fort, and 'Monsoon' pleasure palace with pavilions, reservoirs and ingenious fountains to take full advantage of the cooling long-awaited monsoon rains. Accommodation is very poor so avoid spending a night here.

History Badan Singh (1722-56), a Sinsini Jat, began the development of the town as capital of his newly founded Jat Kingdom. The central citadel was built by his son **Suraj Mal** in 1730. In the late 18th century the town reverted to the Raja of Bharatpur. The British stormed the fort in December 1804, after which the fortifications were dismantled.

Sights The rubble and mud walls of the square **fort** are strengthened by 12 bastions and a wide, shallow moat. The entrance is over a narrow bridge across the moat, through a gate studded with anti-elephant spikes. Negotiating the thorny undergrowth, you can climb the ramparts which rise 20 m above the moat. You can walk right around along the wide path on top of the walls and climb the stairs to the roof of the citadel for good views all round.

The palaces are flanked by two reservoirs, and set around a central square formal garden in the style of a Mughal *char bagh*. The main entrance is from the north, through the ornamental, Singh (Lion) Pol. The impressive main palace **Gopal Bhavan** (1763), bordering Gopal Sagar, is flanked by Sawon and Bhadon pavilions (1760). Water was directed over the roof lines to create the effect of sheets of monsoon rain. Outside, overlooking the formal garden, is a beautiful white marble *hindola* (swing).

To the south, bordering the central garden, is the single-storey marble **Suraj Bhavan** (circa 1760), a temple and **Kishan Bhavan** with its decorated façade. The water reservoir to its west was built at a height to operate the fountains and cascades effectively; it held enough water to work all the fountains for a few hours though it took a week to fill from four wells with bullocks drawing water up in leather buckets. Now, the 500 or so fountains are turned on once a year for the *Monsoon festival* in August. All these are gravity fed from huge holding tanks on the Palace roof. Coloured dyes are inserted into individual pipes to create a spectacular effect. The (old) **Purana Mahal** beyond, with a curved roof and some fine architectural points now houses government offices but the wall paintings in the entrance chamber of the inner court, though simple, are worth seeing.

Keshav Bhavan, a *baradari* or garden pavilion, stands between the central garden and Rup Sagar with the **Sheesh Mahal** (Mirror Palace, 1725) in the southeast corner. **Nand Bhavan** (circa 1760), north of the central garden, is a large hall with frescoes inside but it has a deserted feel. The pavilion took the monsoon theme further; the double-roof was ingeniously used to create the effect of thunder above - water channelled through hollow pillars rotated heavy stone balls which made the sound! On a sunny day the fountains are believed to have produced a rainbow. The **'Monsoon' Pleasure Palaces** ① *0800-1200 and 1300-1900, free*, to the west of the fort were begun by Suraj Mal.

Bharatpur → *Phone code: 05644. Colour map 2, grid A6. Population: 157,000.*

A popular halting place on the 'Golden Triangle', Bharatpur, 40 km south, at the confluence of the Ruparel and Banganga rivers, is known for its **Keoladeo Ghana Bird Sanctuary**. The old fort is rarely visited by foreign travellers but is worthwhile. The Bharatpur ruling family was Jat and constantly harassed the later Mughals. Under Badan Singh they controlled a large tract between Delhi and Agra, then led by Suraj Mal they seized Agra and marched on to Delhi in 1763.

Built by Suraj Mal, the **Lohagarh** fort appears impregnable. The British initially repulsed in 1803 took it in 1825. There are double ramparts, a wide moat and an inner moat around the palace. Inside the fort are three palaces (circa 1730) and Jewel House and Court to their north. The **museum** ① *closed Fri, 1000-1630, Rs 3*, in the Kachhari Kalan exhibits archaeological finds from villages nearby, dating from the first to 19th centuries as well as paintings and artefacts. **Peharsar** ① *Rs 30 to 'headman' secures a tour*, 5 km from centre, with a carpet weaving community, is very interesting to visit.

★ Bharatpur-Keoladeo Ghana National Park

Once the hunting estate of the Maharajas of Bharatpur, with daily shoots recorded of up to 4,000 birds, the 29 sq km piece of marshland, with over 360 species, is one of the finest bird sanctuaries in the world. It has been designated a World Heritage site. The late Maharaja Brajendra Singh converted his hunting estate into a bird sanctuary in 1956 and devoted many of his retired years to establishing it. He had inherited both his title and an interest in wildlife from his deposed father, Kishan Singh, who grossly overspent his budget – 30 Rolls Royces, private jazz band and extremely costly wild animals including "dozens of lions, elephants, leopards and tigers" for Bharatpur's jungles.

Keoladeo Ghana National Park

■ Sleeping			● Eating
1 Bharatpur Forest Lodge	5 Pelican & Sunbird		1 Bambinoo
2 Eagle's Nest	6 Pratap Palace & Moon		2 Snack Bar
3 Falcon Guest House &	Dance Restaurant		
Jungle Lodge	7 Shanti Kutir Rest House		
4 Nightingale	8 Spoonhill		
	9 Tourist Guest House		

❝❞ Kishan Singh, grossly overspent his budget – 30 Rolls Royces, private jazz band and extremely costly wild animals including "dozens of lions, elephants, leopards and tigers" for Bharatpur's jungles.

Ins and outs Getting there The park is 4 km south of Bharatpur town. Buses from Agra take about an hour to the park entrance. From there rickshaws charge Rs 10 to a lodge (even for 200 m!). **Getting around** Good naturalist guides: Rs 85 per hr per group; Rs 40 per hr per person at entrance, or contact *Nature Bureau, Haveli SVP Shastri*, Neemda Gate, T/F25498. Official cycle-rickshaws at the entrance are numbered and work in rotation, Rs 30 per hr for 2 (drivers may be reluctant to take more than one). Well worthwhile; some rickshaw-wallahs can help identify birds (and know their location); a small tip is appropriate. It is best to carry your own pair of binoculars. The narrower paths are not recommended as the rough surface make them too noisy. It is equally feasible to just walk or hire a bike (best option). A boat ride is highly recommended for viewing; boatmen are equally knowledgeable; from the *Rest House* near the jetty. Rs 100 (foreigners); payable each time you enter, professional video camera Rs 1,500, car Rs 75. See Bharatput for further transport details. Allow a full day, though you can spot many species in just two hours. **Climate** Winters can be cold and foggy, especially in the early morning. It is especially good Nov-Feb when it is frequented by Northern hemisphere migratory birds.

Wildlife A handful of rare Siberian Crane visit annually. The ancient migratory system, some 1,500 years old, is in danger of being lost since young cranes must learn the route from older birds (it is not instinctive). These cranes are disappearing – eaten by Afghans and sometimes employed as fashionable 'guards' to protect Pakistani homes (they call out when strangers approach). September to October is the breeding season but it's worth visiting any time of the year.

Among other birds to be seen are egrets, ducks, coots, storks, kingfishers, spoonbills, Sarus cranes, birds of prey including Laggar falcon, greater spotted eagle, marsh harrier, Scops owl and Pallas' eagle. Shortage of water may result in migrants failing to arrive. There are also chital deer, sambar, nilgai, feral cattle, wild cats, hyenas, wild boar and monitor lizards, whilst near Python Point, there are usually some very large rock pythons.

Birds can be watched from a short distance from the road between the boat jetty and Keoladeo temple, especially Sapan Mori crossing, since they have got accustomed to visitors. Dawn (which can be very cold) and dusk are the best times; trees around Keoladeo temple are favoured by birds for sleeping in, so are particularly rewarding at dawn. Midday may prove too hot so take a book and find a shady spot. Carry a sun hat, binoculars and plenty of drinking water.

Jaipur to Ajmer → *Colour map 2, grid A5 and B5.*

It is a very pleasant drive along the NH8 from Jaipur to Ajmer. After crossing relatively low lying land to Kishangarh the road enters the Aravallis. The direct railway line from Jaipur to Jodhpur passes by the Sambhar salt lake, a site of special wetland interest identified by the Slimbridge Waterfowl Trust, and Makrana, where the white marble used in the Taj Mahal was quarried.

Kuchaman is a large village with temples and relics. It is a popular tea and snacks stop for travellers between Shekhawati and Ajmer. Here Gurjar Pratiharas built a massive clifftop fort with 10 gates. The Chauhans drove the Pratiharas out of the area and for some time it was ruled by the Gaurs. From 1400, it has been in the hands of the Rathores who embellished it with mirrors, murals and gilding in superb palaces and pavilions. The fort has been restored at an enormous cost and is a unique experience. Cars have to be parked in the courtyard after the first couple of gates, and a four-wheel drive jeep takes guests to their rooms after checking in at the Reception. You can visit the Krishna temple with a 2,000 year old image, and the Kalimata ka Mandir which has an eighth-century black stone deity, shop in the Meena Bazar or watch local village craftspeople.

Kishangarh ① *An important railway junction between Jaipur and Ajmer.* Kishangarh was a small princely state, founded by Kishan Singh in 1603. Local artists known for their depiction of the Krishna legend and other Hindu themes were given refuge here by the royal family when fleeing religious persecution during the reign of the overzealous Mughal Emperor Aurangzeb. Under their patronage the artists reached a high standard of excellence and they continue the tradition of painting Kishangarh miniatures here. Most of those available are cheap copies on old paper using watercolours instead of the mineral pigments of the originals. You can also watch marble carving and polishing.

The fort palace which has been converted to a hotel stands on the shores of a lake. Its Hathi Pol (Elephant Gate) has walls decorated with fine murals, and, though partly in ruins, you can see battlements, courtyards with gardens, shady balconies, brass doors and windows with coloured panes of glass. The temple has a fine collection of miniatures. India's best marble is quarried at nearby Makrana.

Roopangarh About 20 km from Kishangarh, Roopangarh was an important fort founded in 1649 AD on the old caravan route along the Sambhar Lake. The village is a centre for craft industries – leather embroidery, block printing, pottery and handloom weaving can all be seen. The Sunday market features at least 100 cobblers making and repairing *mojdi* footwear. You can stay at

Ajmer → *Phone code: 0145. Colour map 2, grid B5. Population: 401,000.*

Situated in a basin at the foot of Taragarh Hill, Ajmer is surrounded by a stone wall with five gateways. Renowned throughout the Muslim world as the burial place of Mu'inuddin Chishti who claimed descent from the son-in-law of Mohammad, seven pilgrimages to Ajmer are believed to equal one to Mecca. Every year, especially at the annual Islamic festivals of Id and Muharram, thousands of pilgrims converge on this ancient town on the banks of the Ana Sagar Lake. The tomb of the Sufi saint is considered the second holiest site after Mecca. ▸▸ *For Sleeping, Eating and other listings see pages 355-370.*

Ins and outs
Getting there Visitors come to Ajmer for its own sake and also en route to Pushkar. The railway station has several cheap hotels and eating places just across the busy main road. Buses for Pushkar use the stand nearby; the main State and Private Bus Stands are chaotic and dirty, and are about 2 km away.

Getting around The main sights and congested bazars, which can be seen in a day, are within 15-20-mins walk of the railway station, but to get to Ana Sagar, hail an auto-rickshaw. Shuttle buses run between the main bus stand and the railway station. See Transport, page 369, for further details.

History

According to tradition, Ajmer was founded in 145 AD by Raja Ajaipal, one of the Chauhan kings. In the 11th and 12th centuries it was attacked by Mahmud of Ghazni and Muhammad Ghuri. Born in Afghanistan, Mu'inuddin Chishti visited Ajmer in 1192 and died here in 1235 and his tomb became a place of pilgrimage.

The houses of Mewar, Malwa and Jodhpur each ruled for a time until Akbar annexed it in 1556 and made the dargah a place of pilgrimage. He built a palace, later occupied by Jahangir who laid out the beautiful Daulat Bagh garden by the artificial lake Ana Sagar, which dates from circa 1135. Jahangir also received the first British ambassador from King James I in the Daulat Bagh in 1616. Shah Jahan, Aurangzeb's successor, embellished the garden with five fine marble pavilions.

After the Mughals, Ajmer returned to the House of Jodhpur and later to the Marathas. The British annexed it in 1818 and brought it under their direct rule.

Ajmer

Sleeping

1 Aaram
2 Aravalli Resort
3 Bhola
4 Dak Bungalow
5 Haveli Heritage Inn
6 Hilltop Cottage & Mamata Fast Food
7 Khadim Tourist Bungalow
8 Mansingh Palace
9 Nagpal
10 Regency

Eating

1 Honey Dew
2 Jai Hind & Amba

0 metres 500
0 yards 500

N

⁝ A saint of the people

Khwaja Mu'inuddin Chishti probably came to India before the Turkish conquests which brought Islam sweeping across northern India. A sufi, unlike the Muslim invaders, he came in peace. He devoted his life to the poor people of Ajmer and its region. He was strongly influenced by the *Upanishads*; some reports claim that he married the daughter of a Hindu Raja.

His influence during his lifetime was enormous, but continued through the establishment of the *Chishti* school or *silsila*, which flourished 'because it produced respected spiritualists and propounded Catholic doctrines'. Hindus were attracted to the movement but did not have to renounce their faith, and *Sufi khanqah* (a form of hospice) were accessible to all.

Almost immediately after his death Khwaja Mu'innuddin Chishti's followers carried on his mission. The present structure was built by Ghiyasuddin Khalji of Malwa, but the embellishment of the shrine to its present ornate character is still seen as far less important than the spiritual nature of the Saint it commemorates.

Sights

Dargah of Khwaja Mu'inuddin Chishti The Dargah of Khwaja Mu'inuddin Chishti (1143-1235) is the tomb of the Sufi saint which was begun by Iltutmish and completed by Humayun. Set in the heart of the old town, the entrance is through the bazar. Access to the main gate is on foot or by tonga or auto. The Emperor Akbar first made a pilgrimage to the shrine to give thanks for conquering Chittor in 1567, and the second for the birth of his son Prince Salim. From 1570 to 1580, Akbar made almost annual pilgrimages to Ajmer on foot from Agra, and the *kos* minars (brick marking pillars at about two-mile intervals) along the road from Agra are witness of the popularity of the pilgrimage route. On their first visit, rich Muslims pay for a feast of rice, ghee, sugar, almonds, raisins and spices to be cooked in one of the large pots in the courtyard inside. In the inner courtyard is the white marble **Shah Jahan Masjid** (circa 1650), with 11 arches and a carved balustrade on three sides. In the inner court is the **Dargah** (tomb), also white marble, square with a domed roof and two entrances. The ceiling is gold-embossed velvet, and silver rails and gates enclose the tomb. At festival times the tomb is packed with pilgrims, and the crush of people can be overpowering. Nearby is the **Mazar** (tomb) of Bibi Hafiz Jamal, daughter of the saint, a small enclosure with marble latticework. Close by is that of Chimni Begum, daughter of Shah Jahan. She never married, refusing to leave her father during the seven years he was held captive by Aurangzeb in Agra Fort.

Arhai-din-ka Jhonpra Mosque The Arhai-din-ka Jhonpra Mosque ('The Hut of two and a half days') lies beyond the Dargah in a narrow valley. Originally a Jain college built in 1153, it was partially destroyed by Muhammad of Ghori in 1192, and in 1210 turned into a mosque by Qutb-ud-din-Aibak who built a massive screen of seven arches in front of the pillared halls, allegedly in two and a half days (hence its name). The temple pillars which were incorporated in the building are all different.

Akbar's Palace (Government museum) ⓘ *closed Fri, 1000-1630, Rs 3, no photography*, is in the city centre near the east wall. It is a large rectangular building with a fine gate. Today it houses the Government museum and contains fine sculpture from sixth to 17th centuries, paintings and old Rajput and Mughal armour.

Nasiyan Jain Temple ⓘ *0800-1700, Rs 5, a visit here is recommended*. The ornate Nasiyan Jain Temple (Red Temple) on Prithviraj Marg has a remarkable museum alongside the Jain shrine, which itself is open only to Jains. Ajmer has a large Jain population (about 25% of the city's total). The Shri Siddhkut Chaityalaya was founded in 1864 in honour of the first Jain Tirthankar, Rishabdeo, by a Jain diamond merchant, Raj Bahadur Seth Moolchand Nemichand Soni (hence its alternative name, the Soni temple). The opening was celebrated in 1895. Behind a wholly unimposing exterior, on its first floor the Svarna Nagari Hall houses an astonishing reconstruction of the Jain conception of the Universe, with gold plated replicas of every Jain shrine in India. Over 1,000 kg of gold is estimated to have been used, and at one end of the gallery diamonds have also been placed behind decorative coloured glass to give an appearance of backlighting. Encased in a huge room behind glass, the whole can be seen from different external galleries. The holy mountain, Sumeru, is at the centre of the continent, and around it are a remarkable collection of model temples. Suspended from the ceiling are *vimanas* and silver balls.

Taragarh Taragarh (Star Fort), built by Ajaipal Chauhan in 1100 with massive 4½-m thick walls, stands on the hilltop overlooking the town. The views of the city are good but the walk up the winding bridle path, tiring. A jeepable road, however, has reduced the climb on foot and made access easier. Jeeps charge Rs 500 for the trip. Along the way is a graveyard of Muslim 'martyrs' who died storming the fort.

Pushkar → *Phone code: 0145. Colour map 2, grid B5. Population: 11,500.*

Pushkar lies in a narrow dry valley overshadowed by impressive rocky hills which offer spectacular views of the desert at sunset. The lake at its heart, almost magically

Pushkar

Sleeping
1 Everest Guest House
2 Lake View
3 Navratan Palace
4 Oasis
5 Paramount
6 Peacock Holiday Resort
7 Purnima
8 Pushkar Inn, Sunset Café & Bro-Sis Restaurant
9 Pushkar Palace
10 Raj Palace
11 RTDC Tourist Village
12 Sarovar
13 Venus & Restaurant
14 VK & Om Shiva Restaurant
15 White House

Eating
1 Juice Centre
2 Moondance
3 Rainbow
4 RS Restaurant
5 Siva & Bharatpur House
6 Sun & Moon
≡ Ghat (steps)

0 metres (approx) 300
0 yards (approx) 300

N

⁝ Persistent Pandas

Pandas – priests with responsibility for particular families or local communities – meet pilgrim buses and arrange the necessary rituals, keeping records of who has attended. If you receive a 'blessing', temple priests may charge for a coconut they use; they may also ask for a minimum 'donation' and then try to increase this ("Is that all you can give for your dead family member?"). Once a donation has been paid, a red braid (a **Pushkar passport**) is tied round the wrist which then protects you from further demands. Since it is difficult to escape this 'ceremony', it is perhaps best not to resist. Go along and enjoy it though your 'donation' may never reach the temple. Pay a modest Rs 15-20 even when the figure suggested may well be Rs 500-1,000!

beautiful in the really early morning or late evening light, is one of India's most sacred. The celebrated Pushkar Fair transforms the quiet village to a colourful week of heightened activity. The once peaceful lakeside village on the edge of the desert has been markedly changed by the year-round presence of large numbers of foreigners who were originally drawn by the famous fair. Some travellers fail to see its attraction now because of the continuous hassle from beggars, shopkeepers, holy men and millions of flies.

Ins and outs

Getting there Most visitors arrive by bus which heads for the Central (Marwar) Bus Stand overrun by aggressive hotel touts and porters, but you can ask to be dropped beforehand on entering the town from Ajmer. The road from Ajmer passes the village of Nausar and a striking 2-km long pass through the Nag Pahar (Snake Hill) which divides Pushkar from Ajmer.

Getting around Pushkar is small enough to explore on foot. Hire a bike to venture further. See Transport, page 369, for further details.

Sights

Pushkar lake is believed to mark the spot where a lotus thrown by Brahma landed. Ghats lead down to the water to enable pilgrims to bathe. Fa Hien, the Chinese traveller who visited Pushkar in the fifth century AD commented on the number of pilgrims. Though several of the older temples were subsequently destroyed by Aurangzeb, many remain.

There are 52 ghats around the lake and dozens of other temples, most of which are closed from 1200 to 1600. The **Brahma temple**, at the farther end of the lake, is a particularly holy shrine and draws pilgrims throughout the year. Although not the only Brahma temple in India, as people claim, it is the only major pilgrim place for followers of the Hindu God of Creation. The **Mahadev temple** is said to date from 12th century while the **Julelal temple** is modern and jazzy. A steep 3-km climb up the hill leads to the **Savitri temple** dedicated to Brahma's first wife. Excellent views.

Kartik Purnima is marked by a vast **cattle and camel fair** (November), see box on page 355. Pilgrims bathe in the lake, the night of the full moon being the most auspicious time, and float 'boats' of marigold and rose petals in the moonlight. Camel traders often arrive a few days early to engage in the serious business of buying and selling and most of the animals disappear before the official starting date. Arrive three days ahead if you don't want to miss this part of the fair. The all-night drumming and singing in this Tent City can get very tiring. Travellers warn of pickpockets and purse slashers.

⦂ The pull of cattle and camels

The huge *Mela* is Pushkar's biggest draw. Over 200,000 visitors and pilgrims and hordes of cattle and camels with their semi-nomadic tribal drivers, crowd into the town. Farmers, breeders and camel traders buy and sell. Sales in leather whips, shoes, embroidered animal covers soar while women bargain over clay pots, bangles, necklaces and printed cloth.

Events begin four to five days before the full moon in November.

There are horse and camel races and betting is heavy. In the *Ladhu Umt* race teams of up to 10 men cling to camels and one another, in a hilarious and often chaotic spectacle. The Tug-of-War between Rajasthanis and foreigners is usually won by the local favourites. There are also sideshows with jugglers, acrobats, magicians and folk dancers. At nightfall there is music and dancing outside the tents, around friendly fires – an unforgettable experience.

Listings: Northern Rajasthan

⊜ Sleeping

Jaipur *p331, map p334*
Jaipur's popularity has meant that foreigners are being targeted by hotel and shop touts, so you need to be on your guard.
LL-L Jai Mahal Palace (Taj), Jacob Rd, Civil Lines, T223636, F223660. 102 rooms (6 unique suites), imaginative, plush, good solar heated pool, gardens especially lovely, geared to package tours.
LL-L Rajvilas (Oberoi), Agra Road, on the outskirts, T680101, F680202, reservations@ rajvilas.com. 72 beautifully furnished a/c rooms (pricey villas with private pools, courtyard groups, 14 luxury a/c 'tents' with bath), ayurvedic 'spa' in restored *haveli*, re-created fort-palace architecture in large gardens, orchards, pools and fountains, award winner. Exceptional hotel.
LL-L Rambagh Palace (Taj), Bhawani Singh Rd, T381919, F381098. 106 rooms, Maharaja Ram Singh's (1835-80) hunting lodge, extensively modified by Madho Singh II (1880-1922), some excellent rooms, others disappointing, pleasant relaxing atmosphere, good food and service, superb gardens, indoor pool, good shops, not-residents pay Rs 400 to visi.
L Raj Palace (GKV Heritage), *Chomu Haveli*, Zorwar Singh Gate, Amer Rd, T634077, F630489 (office T/F373119). 25 spacious suites with modern baths (extra bed US$15), 5-storeyed *haveli* (1728) with character,

carefully restored, garden, well managed, friendly service.
L Rajputana Palace Sheraton (Welcomgroup), Palace Rd, T401140, F401122, rajputana@welcomgroup.com. Ultra modern *haveli*-style, 216 rooms, lush garden and open courtyard for live entertainment, excellent bookshop, rather impersonal.
L Trident (Oberoi), Amber Road, opposite Jal Mahal, T670101, F670303. 138 a/c rooms, attractive overlooking lake or hills, fully equipped, excellent service. Recommended.
A Clarks Amer, JL Nehru Marg, T549437, F550013, clkamer@jp1.dot.net.in. 202 rooms (a/c erratic), 8 km centre, less 'exotic' than 'palace hotels', friendly, good shops, garden, food occasionally inspired.
A-B Holiday Inn, Amer Rd (just northeast of city), T672000, F672335. Comfortable, well managed, friendly and helpful.
A-B Mansingh Tower, Sansar Chandra Rd, T378771, F377582, mansinghjaipur@ mailcity.com. 91 rooms, no garden or pool (older *Mansingh* has had poor reports).
B Bissau Palace (Heritage Hotel), outside Chandpol (access through busy Old City), T304371, F304628, bissau@sancharnet.in. 45 a/c rooms, some charming, in home of the Rawal of Bissau (built 1919) with library, interesting 'memorabilia', dining in "sheesh mahal", excellent camel safaris, exchange etc from *Karwan Tours*. Recommended for delightful atmosphere, charming hosts.

B Jaipur Ashok (ITDC), Jai Singh Circle, Bani Park, T204491, F204498. 97 rooms, comfortable but unimaginative, good food, pool (Rs 150 non-residents).

B Jas Vilas, next to *Megh Niwas*, C-9 Sawai Jai Singh Highway, Bani Park, T204638, www.jasvilas.com. An excellent small hotel with 8 a/c rooms with bath (tub, power shower), internet, delicious home-cooked meals, lawns, fine pool, friendly family.

B Karauli House, New Sanganer Rd, Sodala (towards the airport), T290763, F292633, www.karauli.com. 6 rooms in a family 'retreat', large garden, pool, personal attention, home-cooked meals.

B Maharani Palace (Best Western), Station Rd, opposite Polo Victory, T2947028, F202112. Modern 60 room hotel with roof-top pool.

B Samode Haveli, Gangapol, Old City, T632407, F632370, reservations@samode.com. 20 lovely rooms, charming 19th-century *haveli* with beautiful decorations (more personal in scale than Samode Palace), magnificent dining room (lunch/dinner, Rs 325/400), midday snacks, friendly atmosphere, good rooftop views over city. Highly recommended. Reservations essential.

B-C Alsisar Haveli, Sansar Chandra Rd, T364685, F364652. 30 comfortable a/c rooms, modern frescoes, excellent conversion of 1890s character home, attractive courtyards, average food (try *Chaitanya* nearby, listed below), beautiful pool, village safaris, "super-quiet", friendly, very attentive and courteous service. Highly recommended.

C Chirmi Palace (Heritage Hotel), Dhuleshwar Garden, Sardar Patel Marg, T365063, F364462, chirmi@vsnl.com. 150-year-old *haveli* conversion, 15 spacious a/c rooms, traditional Rajasthani decor, attractive dining room, lawns, pool, e-mail, gentle staff.

C Megh Niwas, C-9 Jai Singh Hwy, Bani Park, T202034, F201420. Comfortable rooms, impeccably clean and tastefully decorated, in former royal home (some air-cooled), average buffets, family run, good pool, helpful staff.

C Meru Palace, Sawai Ram Singh Rd, T371111, F378882, kotawaha@jp1.dot.net.in. 48 rooms (some **B** suites), good veg restaurant, bar, exchange, marble building, not a palace but pleasant.

C Nana-ki-Haveli, Fateh Tiba, Moti Dungri Rd, near Old City (ask for directions), T615502, F605481. 7 spacious a/c rooms in modernised 1918 garden house, very hospitable, friendly family, excellent home cooking. Highly recommended.

C Shahar Palace, Ajmer Rd, Barwada Colony, Civil Lines, T221861, F214356. Lovely house in beautiful garden, a/c rooms, verandah restaurant, also camping (vans, tents), safe and quiet, friendly helpful family.

C Umaid Bhawan, D1-2A Bani Park, T316184, www.umaidbhawan.com. 24 immaculate a/c rooms with bath, hot shower, 2 larger **B** suites, home-cooked food, pleasant pool, small lawn, very quiet lane, free pick-up service, friendly and helpful. Recommended.

C-D Atithi, 1 Park House Scheme, MI Rd, T378679. Very clean rooms, wonderful hot showers, relaxing roof terrace, internet, good veg food, helpful, friendly staff.

C-D General's Retreat, Sardar Patel Rd, T377134, F367518. 10 rooms with bath, some with kitchenettes, attractive bungalow of a retired general, pleasant gardens, restaurant.

C-D Kanchandeep, Vanasthali Marg (south of Central Bus Stand), T364507, F364518. 56 reasonable a/c rooms (prices vary) in modern 5-storey pink building, slightly brash, varied veg restaurant, attentive service.

C Madhuban, D237 Behari Marg, Bani Park, T205427, F202344, www.madhuban.net. Clean, quiet rooms in friendly cluster of bungalows around small courtyards, **B** suite, pleasant garden, helpful staff, restaurant (good food). Recommended.

C-D Royal Castle, A70 Jai Ambey Nagar, Tonk Rd, south of Jaipur, T551425, F721655, delta@jp1.dot.net.in. Spacious rooms (some a/c), hot water, safe and quiet, family run, delicious home cooking, ask for free pick-up from airport/station.

C-D Santha Bagh, Kalyan Path, Narain Singh Rd, T566790, F560332. 10 comfortable rooms (a/c or air-cooled), very friendly and helpful staff, excellent meals, lawn.

D Arya Niwas, Sansar Chandra Rd, T372456, F361871, tarun@aryaniwas.com. 50 very clean rooms but not always quiet, modernized and smart, good very cheap veg food, pleasant lounge, book shop, good travel desk, tranquil

● *For an explanation of the sleeping and eating price codes used in this guide, see inside the*
● *front cover. Other relevant information is found in Essentials pages 52-57.*

lawn, friendly, helpful (arrive by 1800), good yoga lessons, great value. Recommended.

D Gangaur (RTDC), MI Rd, T371641, F371647. 63 rooms, some a/c, restaurant.

D Lakshmi Vilas, Sawai Ram Singh Marg, T381567. 21 rooms, some a/c, Indian veg restaurant, quiet, large open grassy court.

D Natraj, 20 Motilal Atal Rd, T361348, F371796. 17 clean rooms, some very pleasant, large, a/c, good veg restaurant.

D Teej (RTDC), Jai Singh Hwy, T374373. 48 bland, clean rooms, some a/c, **F** dorm (Rs 50).

D-E Diggi Palace, Shivaji Marg, T373091, F370359. Pleasant rooms, some with shower, some have no windows, good restaurant, peaceful garden, good value.

D-E Jaipur Inn, B17 Shiv Marg, Bani Park, T201121, F204796, jaipurin@sancharnet.in. 18 rooms (shared bath), mosquito problem, some a/c (Rs 750), **F** dorm (Rs 80), secure, very clean, spacious, food varies (good veg buffet), pleasant rooftop for chilled beer and snacks, use of kitchen, internet, camping (see below), often full.

D-E Karni Niwas, C-5 Motilal Rd, T365433, F375034. Spotless rooms with hot shower, some large a/c, some with balconies, breakfast and snacks, internet (Rs 2 per min), very friendly and helpful owners.

Several hotels have dormitory beds (Rs 50-80).

E City Centre, near Central Bus Stand, T368320. Good size, clean room, western toilet, hot showers, good value, rickshaws reluctant (no commission).

E Evergreen, Chameliwala Market, opposite GPO, MI Rd, T363446. 96 rooms (quality and prices vary), clean on 1st floor with showers (Rs 200), **F** dorm, good restaurant, efficient bus ticketing, peaceful garden, small pleasant pool, cyber café, full of cliquey backpackers, foreigners only, often full.

F Tourist Hotel (RTDC), MI Rd, T360238. 47 simple rooms with bath, dorm (Rs 50), little atmosphere, beer bar, tours.

F Shivam, A26, C1, Bharatia Path, Kanti Chandra Rd, Bani Park (behind *Ashok*), T201008. Some rooms with hot shower, dorm in converted garage (Rs 60), mosquito menace, hop over fence and use *Ashok's* pool (Rs 150)!

F Youth Hostel, T373311, near the Stadium, out of town. Discounts for YHA members.

The tourist office has a list of families.

Paying guests: Mostly **D-E** (some have dorm beds); good home cooked meals are a bonus.

E Mandap Homestays, Bhilwa Garden, Moti Dungri Rd. 5 rooms with baths, bungalow of a former ruling family, large gardens.

E Shri Sai Nath, 1233 Mali Colony, outside Chandpol, T304975, shreesainath@indya.com. 8 clean, quiet rooms (though in an unimpressive area), meals on request, very hospitable family, warm welcome, "a real delight and very helpful".

Camping

D-E Jaipur Inn, in pleasant garden, own tent/van Rs 50 each.

F Youth Hostel.

Amber *p338*

B-C Chokhi Dhani, T225001, F225007. 31 attractive standard and 34 'executive' huts (the 'Shekhavati haveli' with carved doors, open courtyard and frescoes, has 6 suites), very modern inside with a/c, TV, comfortable beds, marble bathrooms with hot showers/tubs, pool, gym, exchange.

Ramgarh Lake *p341*

A-B Ramgarh Lodge, overlooking the lake, has 17 rooms (two enormous suites) in the royal hunting lodge with a museum and library, plenty of hunting trophies, limited restaurant, delightful walks, ruins of old Kachhawaha fort nearby.

D Jheel Tourist Village, 10 rustic huts (Rs 400).

Samode *p342*

AL-A Samode Palace, T141-632407, F631397, www.samode.com. 40 a/c rooms, tastefully modernized, courtyard restaurant ("coffee shop menu at lunch"), buffets, gardens, attractive new pool, shop with good textiles, remarkable setting and atmosphere, attentive service, Rs 100 entry for non-residents. *Samode Haveli,* Jaipur can reserve rooms and arrange taxi.

B Samode Bagh, 3 km away. 50 luxury tents equipped as colourful hotel rooms with fan, sit-out, and new, marble bathrooms in the old walls, *Darbar* tent, al fresco meals, beautiful pool, tennis, lovely setting in peaceful walled Mughal gardens (see above), plenty of birdwatching, "amazing". Recommended. Reserve ahead.

Mandawa *p344*
B **Castle Mandawa**, T23124, F23171, www.castlemandawa.com. 70 a/c rooms in wonderfully atmospheric castle, each unique and tastefully furnished, modern baths, special tower suite complete with swing, many with 4-posters and period trappings, immaculately clean, excellent views.
B **Desert Resort**, T23151, 1 km south, isolated setting. 60 rooms in a walled, purpose built 'village' complex, attractively laid out and well maintained, pricey restaurant (Rs 250-450; buffets for groups), pool, good ayurvedic massage, shady garden, good views of countryside, camel rides. Contact Mandawa House, Jaipur, T0141-371194, F372084.
C **Mandawa Haveli**, near Sonthaliya Gate, T23088 hotelmandawahaveli@yahoo.com. 7 rooms with modernized baths in a 3-storeyed, *haveli* with impressive original 19th-century frescoes in courtyard, Rajasthani meals.
C-D **Heritage Mandawa**, off Mukundgarh Rd, T23742, F23743, 200 m from the main bazar street and the bus stand. 13 rooms with local 'ethnic' furnishings in an old *haveli*, attached baths (hot water), dining hall (set menu Rs 125-250), clean and pleasant, quite quiet, very friendly, camel rides, taxis. Camping possible in grounds.

Nawalgarh *p344*
Lone tourists have been harassed in the bazar.
C **Apani Dhani**, Jhunjhunun Rd, 1 km from railway station, 500 m north of Bus Stand, T22239, www.apanidhani.com. 10 'environmentally friendly' thatched huts of mud and straw (Indian toilets) in an 'ecological farm' run by Ramesh Jangid (helpful and very knowledgeable), attractive, comfortable home-grown veg, pleasant atmosphere (see also *Tourist Pension*).
C **Roop Niwas Palace**, T22008, F23388, 1 km northeast of town. 35 rooms (older ones are large, air-cooled and simply furnished with old fashioned bathrooms, the newer are a/c but smaller), most are in 3 storeys around courtyards, good food, large gardens (peacocks), pool, stables (camels, 35 horses), 'safaris', attractive, small 90-year old palace, warm and hospitable Rajput family run, pleasant. Simple but recommended.
D **Shekhawati Guest House**, 500 m from *Roop Niwas*, T22058, 24658, www.shek hawatirestaurant.com. 10 clean rooms with bath (hot water), Rs 400, very pleasant garden restaurant, excellent homecooked traditional dishes (spotless kitchen, own garden produce, meals Rs 150-200), charming hosts, peaceful (out of town), internet. Recommended.
D-E **DS Guest House**, next door to *Shekhawati Guest House*, T22703, has similar rooms in a large family home next door.
E **Jangid Tourist Pension**, behind Maur hospital, T24060. Rooms with bath, good veg meals, tours, jeep/cycle hire, camel rides, cultural shows, quiet, clean, welcoming.

Dunlod *p344*
Carry a torch for power cuts.
B **Dundlod Fort** (*Heritage Hotel*), in village centre, T015974-52180 (or T/F0141-213224), www.dundlod.com. 42 varied rooms, some opening on to terraces with lovely views, some period furniture and original decor, most with modernized bathrooms, full of atmosphere, jeep tours, camel/horse rides, interesting, hospitable host.

Jhunjhunun *p344*
B-C **Jamuna Resort**, outside town, T30871, F32603. 4 air-cooled cottage rooms with attractive mirror work and murals, over priced 'Golden Room' with painted ceiling, open-air Rajasthani restaurant, gardens, pool (open to hotel/restaurant guests only), pleasant and clean.
C-D **Shiv Shekhawati**, Muni Ashram, T32651, F34070. 18 simple clean rooms, 8 a/c, all with bath and hot water, good veg restaurant, tourist office (guides). The owner of both, LK Jangid, is very knowledgeable.
D-F **Neelam**, opposite Kethan Hospital (off the highway), T38415. A/c and air-cooled rooms with bath and TV, others with shared facilities, restaurant serving snacks.

E-F Sangam, near bus stand, T32544, F34063. Clean rooms, better with bath at rear, veg meals.

Alwar *p345*

D Alwar, 26 Manu Marg, T20012, F332250, ukrustagi@hotmail.com. Set on the main road with an attractive garden, 10 rooms (some a/c) with baths (hot showers), TV, fridge and phone, restaurant (closed on Mon), arranges swimming at nearby club, efficient service.
D Meenal (RTDC), near Circuit House, T347352. 6 rooms with bath, 2 a/c, restaurant, bar.

A cluster of hotels belonging to the same family are 500 m east of the bus stand:
D-E Ankur, T333025. 9 rooms (Rs 150-600).
D-E Ashoka, T21780. 35 rooms, clean and comfortable, deluxe rooms have TV, running hot water and western toilets, cheaper rooms have Indian toilets (hot water in buckets), restaurant.
D-E Atlantic, T343181. 11 rooms with baths.
D-E Imperial Guest House, T21430. Air-cooled rooms (a/c rooms with colour TV), vegetarian restaurant (south Indian snacks).
E Aravali, Nehru Marg, 500 m south of the station, T332883, F332011. Some air-cooled rooms, **F** dorm, reasonable restaurant, bar, swimming arranged.
E Saroop Vilas Palace, near Moti Doongri, T331218. Renovated royal mansion, 5 rooms with bath (western toilets), vegetarian restaurant (non veg to order).

Kesroli *p345*

B Hill Fort Kesroli, Alwar Rd, T0144-89352, sales@neemrana.com. Around a courtyard are 22 comfortable, if eccentric, airy rooms, reasonable restaurant and service, relaxing, and in a lovely isolated rural location.

Sariska Tiger Reserve *p346*

B Sariska Palace, T41322, sariska@ del2.vsnl.net.in (40 km from Alwar railway). 101 refurbished a/c rooms (annexe lacks the charm of the Lodge), restaurant and bar, gym, pool, ayurvedic and yoga centre, tours, converted royal hunting lodge full of photographs and stuffed tigers.
C-D Tiger Haven, Viratnagar Rd, T841314. 10 clean comfortable a/c or air-cooled rooms in stone built cottages, resident naturalist, peaceful spot, pleasant staff, mixed reports on meals.

C-D Tiger Resort, near Park check post, T86268. 8 rooms (some a/c) with baths (hot showers), TV, phones, some rooms with shared bath, dorm beds (Rs 250), run by retired army officer's family, restaurant, fishing, horse/camel riding arranged, 4WD jeep safaris in park and to fort.
D Forest Rest House, Main Rd, opposite turning to Kushalgarh. Simple rooms.

Kanota *p346*

C Royal Castle, 12 clean, well-decorated, comfortable rooms, good restaurant, collection of arms and carriages, library of rare books, manuscripts and paintings, horse and camel rides. Recommended. Contact T0141-561291, F561045.

Bhandarej *p346*

B Bhadrawati Palace, T0141-372919. 35 rooms with bath in converted palace, gardens, pool, wide choice in restaurant; also orchard with camping facilities, 5 km from palace.

Karauli *p346*

B Bhanwar Vilas Palace (Heritage Hotel), T07464-20024, F21035, www.karauli.com, has 21 comfortable rooms in converted 1938 palace whichhas a faded but fascinating interior. Most rooms are air-cooled (cheaper in cottage), restaurant, tours, camping

Bharatpur *p347*

A Moti Mahal Palace-Golbagh (Taj), being renovated, 86 rooms, no pool but squash.
C Chandra Mahal, Peharsar, Jaipur-Agra Rd, Nadbai, T05643-3238. Simply furnished, 19th-century *haveli* with character, quality set meals (from Rs 250), jeep-hire, good service, rupee payment only.
E Welcome, Golhagh Palace Rd, off Agra Rd, T23077. Basic, clean, good food, friendly.

Keoladeo Ghana National Park
p347, map p348
Some budget hotels have tented accommodation.

Inside the park
B Bharatpur Forest Lodge (ITDC), 2.5 km from gate, T22760, F22064, book in advance. 17 comfortable a/c rooms, 10 with balconies, extra bed Rs 300, restaurant,

grotty bar, very friendly staff, peaceful, boats for bird watching, animals (eg wild boar) wander into the compound. Entry fee each time you enter park.
E Shanti Kutir Rest House, near boat jetty, T22265. 5 clean rooms in old hunting lodge.

Outside the park

B Laxmi Vilas Palace (Heritage Hotel), Kakaji ki Kothi, Agra Rd, 2.5 km from town (auto-rickshaws outside), T23523, F25259. 22 good rooms around a pleasant courtyard, good food and service, attractive 19th-century hunting lodge, pleasantly old fashioned, welcoming friendly staff, craft shop, park tours, no credit cards/TCs.

C-D Pratap Palace, near Park Gate, T24245, F25093. 24 rooms (8 a/c) with bath, 4 **F** with clean shared bath (Rs 150), mediocre restaurant, helpful management, good value.

D Falcon Guest House, off NH11, T23815. Very clean well-kept rooms, some a/c with bath, owned by naturalist, good information, bike hire, quiet, very helpful, warm welcome, off-season discount. Recommended.

D Nightingale, near Park gate, T27022. Deluxe 2-bed tents with bath, others with shared bath, good food, contact *Asian Adventures* T/F011-8525014 or *North West Safaris*, T/F079-6302019, F6300962, ssibal@ad1.vsnl.net.in.

D-E Sunbird, near Park gate, T25701. Simple clean rooms with hot shower, better on 1st floor, pleasant restaurant but slow service, bike hire, good value.

E Jungle Lodge, Shankar Colony (next to *Falcon*), T25622. 6 clean rooms (but lots of mosquitoes), excellent meals for residents, quiet, friendly family, 'no Indians' policy.

E Kiran Guest House, 364 Rajendra Nagar, 300 m northeast of park gate, T23845. 5 clean rooms, excellent meals, peaceful, safe, homely, helpful, knowledgeable family.

E Pelican, near Park gate, T24221. 9 clean rooms with fan, best No 8 with hot shower, quite modern with tiny balcony, restaurant, friendly, bike hire (Rs 40 per day), good info.

E Spoonbill, near *Saras*, T23571. Good value rooms with shared facility (hot water in buckets), dorm (Rs 60), run by charming ex-Army officer, courteous and friendly service, good food, bike hire. Recommended.

F Tourist Guest House, behind *Moondance*. 2 rooms with bath, 1 shared, dorm (Rs 30), basic but acceptable.

Kuchaman *p350*

A-B Kuchaman Fort (Heritage Hotel), 12 km from Bikaner, T01586-20882, F20476, sariska@del2.vsnl.net.in, with 36 comfortable a/c rooms in a part of the fort, attractively furnished, jacuzzi, gym, unusual 200-year old cavernous underground pool, camel/horse riding, royal hospitality

Kishangarh *p350*

B-C Phool Mahal Palace, Kishangarh Old City, T/F01463-47405. A 19th-century garden palace set next to the fort's medieval moat. Patios face Gundalao lake where there are plenty of water birds. 14 beautifully decorated a/c rooms, good food, attentive manager.

Roopangarh *p350*

B Roopangarh Fort (Heritage Hotel), T01497-20217. There are 20 large, high-ceilinged rooms, rich in character, Marwar decor and great cuisine. Excursions to Makrana and Sambhar salt lake, friendly staff.

Ajmer *p350, map p351*

Prices rise sharply, as much as 10 times, during Pushkar mela. Hotels are booked well in advance.

A Mansingh Palace, Ana Sagar Circular Rd, Vaishali Nagar, away from centre, T425702. 60 rooms, modern and the most comfortable in town. Allows short-stay rates. Useful if waiting for a night train.

C-D Aaram off Ana Sagar Circular Rd, opposite *Mansingh*, T425272. 22 rooms, a/c, restaurant, small garden, decent, modern.

C-D Khadim (RTDC), Savitri Girls' College Rd, near bus station, T627490. 49 rooms, 11 a/c (**C** suites), dorm (Rs 50), good restaurant, bar, Tourist Information, car hire, pleasant setting, popular and good value.

C-E Nagpal, opposite railway station, T429603. 16 rooms vary widely, some with bath (a/c up to Rs 1000).

D Hilltop Cottage, 164 Shastri Nagar (hard to find), near shopping centre, T623984. Neither a cottage nor on a hilltop but a family home taking guests, clean, comfortable rooms some with bath and hot water, meals, good situation in residential area with hills nearby for walks.

D New Park, Panch Kund Rd, T72464. 32 clean and comfortable rooms, attached baths, a/c or air-cooled, simple decor, superb views of hills and dunes, outdoor dining area, own farm produce, pool.

D Regency, Delhi Gate, near Dargah, T620296, F621750, bahulbali@jp1.dot.net.in. 20 clean, comfortable, air-cooled or a/c rooms (Rs 400-750), TV, phone, a/c restaurant, bar, travel, in very crowded area but set back from road.

D-E Haveli Heritage Inn, Kutchery Rd, T621607. 12 rooms in century old *haveli* (Rs 350-600), clean, comfortable, family run, good home cooking, historic associations with Gandhi, Nehru etc, located on busy main road but with a pleasant courtyard.

E Aravalli Resort, near bus stand (next to RTDC), T627089. 4 rooms (Rs 300), clean and comfortable.

E Bhola, Prithviraj Marg, T423844. Simple clean rooms, good vegetarian restaurant. The tourist office, T52426, has a list of Paying Guest accommodation.

Pushkar *p353, map p353*

During the fair, charges rocket. Booking is essential. Light sleepers should bring ear plugs.

A-B Pushkar Palace (Heritage Hotel), T772001, F772226, www.hotelpushkarpalace.com. A renovated old palace, 44 rooms, best on lakeside with a/c and bath on 1st and 2nd floors, pleasant terrace and garden overlooking lake, good restaurant, camel and horse safaris, safe, "refreshingly civilized, if plain", cash only, US$200-300 during Fair.

B Jagat Niwas Palace, Ajmer Rd, T772953, F772952. 36 rooms, 5-storeys with brash decor.

B-C Pushkar Resorts, Motisar Rd, Ganhera (3 km away), T772017, F772946, pushres@ datainfosys.net. Pushkar's up-market resort, 40 individual cottages with TV, phone, large garden, delicious meals (home-grown produce), pool, sports (putting green, golf practice tees), book/handicraft shop, unique camel *kufila* (caravan) tours, desert jeep safaris, great location, enthusiastic staff.

C Jagat Singh Palace, Ajmer Rd, T772953, F772952, hppalace@datainfosys.com. 36 a/c rooms in new building imitating a Rajput fort, impressive, colourful interiors, attractive vegetarian restaurant, exchange, garden, gym, pool planned.

C-D JP's Tourist Resort, Ganhera, T772067, F772026. 28 clean 'traditional' thatched cottage rooms to suites (Rs 400-1000), colourfully decorated with sculptures,

mandapa paintings, bathrooms need improving, al fresco meals, garden and orchards among dunes.

C-D Oasis, near Ajmer Bus Stand, T772100. 35 rooms with bath, some a/c (Rs 500-1050), 24-hr coffee shop, exchange, garden with shady trees and potted plants, pool.

C-D Peacock Holiday Resort, 1 km centre, near Ajmer Bus Stand, T772093, F772516. 40 rooms, some a/c (Rs 450-1100), pleasant shady courtyard and small clean pool, exchange, jacuzzi, friendly staff, adequate food, travel, camel safaris, less than immaculate but very popular, crowded during camel fair despite price rise, year round camp site for overlanders and campers with facilities Rs 50 (see also below).

D Navratan Palace, near Brahma temple, T772145, F772225. 15 clean rooms, some a/c with hot showers, comfortable though not particularly attractive, pool, small garden with views.

D Pushkar Inns, on the lake. Aircooled rooms with bath, some shared, could be cleaner, popular Sunset café and German bakery, lake and hill views, camping /trailer parking.

D Sunset Café by *Pushkar Palace*, overlooking lake. 10 rooms (some with tubs) but their cakes have deteriorated.

D-E Sarovar, on lakeside, T772040. 38 clean rooms (best with lake view, in old part), some a/c with bath and cheap 6-bed dorm, set around courtyard in former lakeside palace, some rooms have splendid views, indifferent vegetarian restaurant, attractive gardens.

D-F Paramount, Bari Basti, T772428, F772244. 16 clean, comfortable rooms, some with bath, better with balcony Rs 600, 3 new a/c, elevated site with splendid views.

Rooms with shared facilities often around Rs 80 but can soar to Rs 400 during mela.

Some budget hotels offer views of the lake from communal rooftops; to escape the noise of the Main Bazar, choose one in a back street of Bari Basti or near Ajmer Bus Stand.

E Everest Guest House, short walk from Marwar Bus Stand, T772080. Some rooms with bath and **F** dorm, quiet, clean.

E Holiday Resort, Ajmer bus station, T772130. 8 rooms with bath, fairly clean, marble floors, pleasant garden, *Mansarovar thali* restaurant.

F-F Lake View, Main Bazar, well-placed by the ghat, T/F772106, www.pusharraj.com. Rooms with shared facilities, some have no window, 3 with bath, bit shabby, arrive at 1000 for better room.

E-F VK, near *Pushkar Palace*, T772174. Clean, decent rooms (Rs 100), some with bath and 24-hr hot water (power shower!), excellent *Om Shiva* garden restaurant nearby, friendly and helpful. Recommended.

E-F White House, in narrow alley near Marwar Bus Stand, T/ F772950, hotelwhitehouse@usa.net. Rooms with hot showers, small with shared facilities, larger with balcony, good views from terrace and upstairs, orchards, home grown vegetables, restaurant, internet, gym, yoga, billiards, travel desk, clean and well run, friendly.

F Poonam Palace, Shiv Chowk, near Marwar Bus Stand (away from lake). Clean rooms with bath, roof terrace (fire lit on chilly nights), nice garden, peaceful, friendly.

F Raj Palace, opposite Old Rangnath Temple, Chhoti Basti, clean rooms with cupboard size baths (free hot buckets), good beds, average restaurant, enthusiastic young staff.

F Shyam Krishna Guest House, Chhoti Basti, T772461. Part of 200 year old temple complex with 10 rooms around a courtyard, some with *jali* work on upper floor, more being added, family run, popular with artists and those keen to learn Indian music etc.

F Venus, Main Market, Ajmer road T772323. 15 simple rooms with bath and hot shower, clean, very popular roof restaurant, meals in the garden, see Eating.

During the fair

It is best to visit early in this week when toilets are still reasonably clean. RTDC erects a remarkable **Tourist Village** for 100,000 people – conveniently placed, deluxe/super deluxe tents (Rs 2,000-3,500 with meals), ordinary/dorm tents (Rs 200 per bed), 30 'cottages', some deluxe (Rs 4000; Rs 350-850 off-season). Beds and blankets, some running water, Indian toilets are standard. Meals are served in a separate tent (or eat delicious cheap, local food at the tribal tented villages near the show ground "with interesting company to match"). Reservation with payment, essential (open 12 months ahead); contact RTDC, Chandralok Building, 36 Jan Path, New Delhi 110001, or at Jaipur.

Others, privately run, charge about US$150-250 including meals for Regular and 'Swiss' double tent (US$30 extra bed):

Colonel's Desert Camp, T772407, Motisar Rd, Ghanera. Tents with toilet and shower, contact *Wanderlust*, T011-6875200, F6885188.

Peacock International Camp Resort, T772093, F772516. Among orchards with pool at Devnagar (2 km from Mela Ground), free transport.

Pushkar Palace, T772001, F772226. Sets up 180 'Swiss' cottages and 50 Deluxe tents, flush toilets.

Royal Tents Camp (WelcomHeritage) comfortable tents with verandah, flush toilet, hot water in buckets or "shower of sorts", Rajasthani cuisine, very well organized. Reservations: T011-6868992, F6868994.

Wanderlust Desert Camp, T011-4102180, F6885188, www.wanderlustindia.com. 120 Swiss tents with bath, electricity, varied meals. Some private camps are some distance from fair ground and may lack security.

✪ Eating

Jaipur *p331, map p334*

YYY Jaimahal Palace, in top hotel. International. Beautiful surroundings, buffets recommended.

YYY Rambagh Palace, in top hotel. International. Smart restaurant, attractive decor, pricey but generous.

YY Chaitanya, Sansar Ch Rd (100 m from Alsisar, in shopping complex on opposite side of road). Excellent vegetarian.

YY Chanakya, MI Rd. Indian vegetarian. Good food and service, pleasant atmosphere, very clean, huge tasty *thalis* (Rs 150).

YY Copper Chimney, MI Rd. International. A/c, part open-air, open for lunch and dinner only, quality food, generous helpings, dimly lit.

YYY Indiana, J2-34 Mahaveer Marg. Garden restaurant. "Great food". Half open-air, cane chairs and decor, music some evenings.

YY LMB, Johari Bazar, Old City. Rajasthani vegetarian. A/c (50s fairground decor), but generous tasty *thalis;* sweets and *kulfis.*

YY Mehfil, Anukampa Mansion-II, off MI Rd, T367272. Superb range of good quality dishes, friendly service, great ambience.

YY Natraj, MI Rd. Rajasthani, some Chinese. A/c, veg snacks and silver-leaf sweets.

YY Niros, MI Rd, T374493. International. A/c, pleasant decor, wide choice.

YY Rainbow, MI Rd. International. Good food, clean, some drinks pricey.

Ϋ Surya Mahal MI Rd. Indian. Try *paneer butter masala* (good ices next door).
Ϋ Swaad, B Ganpati Plaza, Motilal Atal Rd, T360749. International. A/c, wide choice, good meals and snacks, excellent service, beer downstairs.

Several good value pure veg restaurants on Station Rd (near the Bus Station).
Ϋ Handi, back of Maya Mansion. Indian. Partly open-air, simple canteen style.
Ϋ Laxmi, Johari Bazar. Indian vegetarian. Good food and sweets.
Ϋ Shri Shanker, with lively atmosphere, grubby looking but freshly cooked (Rs 30); also on the Gaitor road towards Amber, serve large helpings for Rs 60.
Ϋ Sun City, Gangapol. Good value meals in an eccentric environment.

Cafés and fast food
BBs, Bhandari Chambers, MI Rd. Western. A/c, clean, swanky, main courses Rs 50.
Jai Mangal Palace, opposite Central Bus Stand. Snacks. A/c, "tasty *pakoras* and huge pot of wonderful real coffee", bar.
MacDonalds, outside *LMB*, branches on MI Rd near Raj Mandir Cinema and in Gurav Towers near *Clarke's Amerhotel*.
Pizza Hut, 109 Ganpati Plaza, MI Rd, T388627. A/c, great pizzas.
Rendezvous, C-84 Prithviraj Rd, T410377. New, spotless a/c coffee bar, newspapers, message board, book exchange. Real coffee, excellent cakes, sandwiches.
Royal Fast Food, Johari Bazar. South Indian. Air-cooled, good snacks.

Amber *p338*
Chokhi Dhani Restaurant, a/c, interesting decor though very dimly lit. Buffet lunch, à la carte or multi-course Rajasthani meals from leaf platters and pottery. Occasionally you can watch puppeteers, folk dancers, *nats* (acrobatics) and artisans at work on pottery, block printing, rolling lac into bangles and metal work. Camel, horse and boat rides for Rs 10. A craft bazaar sells various handicrafts.
Highway Dhaba, decorated with truck tyres everywhere, serves typical Punjabi food enlivened by *ghazals* and Punjabi music.

There are a number of restaurants and beer bars on Jaipur-Sanganer highway.
Amrapalli Village Resort serves veg food in pleasant environment.

Alwar *p345*
Baba, Hope Circle, near the clock tower. Popular for 'milk cake' (*kalakand*) and other Rajasthani sweets.
Narulas, Kashiram Circle near Ganesh Cinema. A/c restaurant, popular for Punjabi non veg and veg dishes, "best in town".

Keoladeo Ghana National Park
p347, map p348
Outside the park
All offer some Indian and Western dishes.
Ϋ Eagle's Nest, 100-seater restaurant serving good north Indian (a/c promised).
Ϋ Moon Dance tent, near *Pratap Palace*. Good food, lively atmosphere, beer.
Ϋ Bambino, near Park Gate. Open-air in garden.
Ϋ Pelican. Good choice, chicken, vegetarian, Israeli dishes, 'westernized'.
Ϋ Spoonbill. Good food, obliging (beer and special *kheer* on request). Recommended.

Ajmer *p350, map p351*
Ϋ Amba, opposite station. Good snacks, *idli-wada*, pizza.
Ϋ Honey Dew, Station Rd. Indian, Continental. Pleasant shady garden, good Indian snacks all day, disappointing Western.
Ϋ Jai Hind in alley by clock tower, opposite rly station. Best for Indian vegetarian. Delicious, cheap meals.
Ϋ Mamata, Shastri Nagar Shopping Centre. Fast food, snacks.
Ϋ Regency, Delhi Gate. Indian, Continental. Bright, decent surroundings, good food.
Ϋ Tandoor, Jaipur Rd, 1 km from bus station. Dinner in the garden with log fires, a/c section for lunch, good food (try *paneer butter masala* and *tandoori* chicken), cake shop, ice creams, also snacks to take away, cyber café. Recommended.

Son halwa, a local sweet speciality, is sold near the dargah and at the market near Station Road (try **Azad**).

Pushkar *p353, map p353*
No meat, fish or eggs are served in this temple town. Alcohol and 'narcotics' are banned. Take special care during the fair: eat only freshly cooked food and drink bottled water.

Long stay budget travellers have encouraged western and Israeli favourites like falafel and apple pie, while Nepali and Tibetan immigrants have brought their own

⦂ Gangaur – Prayer for a good husband

Ishar and Gangaur are the mythical man and wife who embody marital harmony. Colourfully dressed young women carrying brass pitchers on their heads make their way through the streets to the temple of Gauri (another name for Parvati). Here they ceremonially bathe the deity who is then decked with flowers. Young women pray for good husbands, and the long life of their husbands (if they are already married). The festival ends with singing and rejoicing as it is believed that if a woman is unhappy while she sings she will be landed with an ill-tempered husband! The festivities end when Siva arrives, accompanied by elephants, to escort his bride Gauri home.

specialities. Roadside vendors offer a variety of filling *thalis* for under Rs 15.

♛ **Bro-Sis**, Pushkar Palace Road. Western snacks. Good value service and surroundings, fruit juice, veg burrito, burgers.

♛ **Moondance**, just by the turning to *Pushkar Palace*. Adventurous Western menu, good Italian.

♛ **Halwai ki gali** and other sweet shops sell *malpura* (syrupy pancake), as well as usual Rajasthani/Bengali sweets.

♛ **Karmima**, and other small places opposite *Ashish-Manish Riding*, offer home cooked *thalis* (Rs 15/20) and excellent fresh, pure orange/sweet lime juice.

♛ **Om Shiva**, 20 m from *VK Hotel*, open air rooftop. Good breakfasts (brown bread, garlic cheese, pancakes, fruit), buffets (Rs 45) or à-la-carte, well presented and hygienic. Another *Om Shiva* opposite *State Bank of Bikaner & Jaipur*, which is inferior.

♛ **RS**, near Brahma Temple. Good Indian, some Chinese and western.

♛ **Rainbow** (above *Krishna*), Brahma Chowk. Wide choice: pizzas, jacket potatoes, enchiladas, hummus, falafel, Indian dishes.

♛ **Sun and Moon**, Brahma Temple Rd. Very good food, friendly, great garden to relax in (hammocks).

♛ **Sunset Café** by *Pushkar Palace* overlooking lake. Breakfasts, snacks.

♛ **Venus**, Ajmer Rd. Mixed menu. À-la-carte (good sizzlers) in the garden, also *thalis* (Rs 35), on the rooftop.

⦿ Entertainment

Jaipur *p331, map p334*
Raj Mandir Cinema, MI Rd. 'Experience' a Hindi film in shell pink interior.
Ravindra Rang Manch, Ram Niwas Garden. Sometimes hosts cultural programmes and music shows. Also 'shows' at Theme Villages on the outskirts – see below.

⦿ Festivals and events

Jaipur *p331, map p334*
All the Hindu festivals are celebrated (see page 187 and above).
14 Jan: Makar Sankranti The kite flying festival is spectacular. Everything closes down in the afternoon and kites are flown from every rooftop, street and even from bicycles! The object is to bring down other kites, attempted to the deafening cheers of huge crowds. **Elephant Festival**, **Mar**, at Chaugan stadium, procession, elephant polo etc; **Gangaur Festival**, **Apr**, about a fortnight after *Holi*, when a colourful procession of women start from the City Palace with the idol of Goddess Gauri. They travel from the Tripolia gate to Talkatora, and these areas of the city are closed to traffic during the festival. **Jul/Aug** Teej, **Aug**, the special celebrations in Jaipur have elephants, camels and dancers joining in the processions.

Ajmer p350, map p351

The **Urs** festival commemorating *Khwaja Mu'inuddin Chishti's* death in 1235 is celebrated with 6 days of almost continuous music, starting on sighting the new moon in the 7th month of the Islamic year. Devotees from all over India and the Middle East make the pilgrimage. *Qawwalis* and other Urdu music developed in the courts of rulers can be heard. On the final day, women wash the tomb with their hair, then squeeze the rose water into bottles as medicine for the sick. A **Jain festival** with colourful processions is held on **23 Nov**.

O Shopping

Jaipur p331, map p334

You may find better bargains in other cities in Rajasthan, especially Jodhpur.

Jaipur's popularity has meant that foreigners are being targeted by hotel and shop touts, so you need to be on your guard.

The traditional bazars and small shops are well worth a visit; cheaper than MI Rd shops but may not accept credit cards. Most open 1030-1930; closed on Sun.

Antiques and art

Bapu Bazar, specializes in printed cloth.
Chaupar, for textiles.
Chomu Haveli Art Palace specializes in 'ageing' newly crafted items.
Hawa Mahal, opposite Ramganj Bazar, you will find the famous featherweight Jaipuri *razais* (quilts).
Johari Bazar for jewellery.
Khajanewalon-ka-Rasta, off Chandpol bazar, for marble and stoneware.
Manglam Arts, Amer Rd. Sells modern miniature paintings and silver.
Maniharon-ka-Rasta for lac bangles which the city is famous for.
Nehru Bazars, for textiles.
Ramganj Bazar has leather footwear.
Tripolia Bazar (3 gates). Inexpensive jewellery.

Books

Book Corner, MI Rd by *Niro's Restaurant*. Good selection.
Book Wise, *Rajputana Sheraton Hotel*. Vast range, fair price.

Carpets

Art Age, Plot 2, Bhawani Singh Rd. Watch *durrie* weavers.
Channi Carpets and Textiles, Mount Rd, opposite Ramgarh Rd. Factory shop, watch carpets being handknotted, then washed, cut and quality checked with a blow lamp!
Kashmiri Carpet Museum, 327 Old Amer Rd, near Zorawar Singh Gate. Excellent stock.
Maharaja, Chandpol (near *Samode Haveli*). Watch carpet weavers and craftsmen, good value carpets and printed cotton.
The Reject Shop, Bhawani Singh Rd. For 'Shyam Ahuja' *durrie* collections.

Handicrafts

Jaipur specializes in printed cotton, handicrafts, carpets and *durries*; also embroidered leather footwear and blue pottery.
Anokhi, 2 Tilak Marg, opposite Udyog Bhawan, T381247, sam@anokhi.com. Well-crafted, attractive block-printed clothing, linen etc. Recommended (commendable enterprise; visit their workshop/farm outside Jaipur).
Gems & Silver Palace, G11 Amber Tower, Sansar Ch Rd. Good choice of 'old' textiles, reasonable prices, helpful owners.
Handloom Haveli, Lalpura House, Sansar Ch Rd.
Handloom House, Rituraj Building, MI Rd (near *Tourist Hostel*).
Rajasthali, Govt Handicrafts, MI Rd, 50 m west of Ajmeri Gate.
Rajasthan Fabrics & Arts, near City Palace gate. Exquisite textiles.

Jewellery

Jaipur is famous for gold, jewellery and gem stones (particularly emeralds, rubies, sapphires and diamonds, but the last requires special certification for export). For about Rs 40 you can have gems valued. Semi-precious stones set in silver are more affordable (but check for loose settings, catches and cracked stones); sterling silver items are rare in India and the content varies widely. Bargaining is easier on your own so avoid being taken by a 'guide'.
Bhuramal Rajmal Surana, 1st floor, between nos 264 and 268, Haldiyon-ka-Rasta.
Dwarka's, H20 Bhagat Singh Marg, T360301.

Gem Testing Laboratory off MI Rd near New Gate (reputable jewellers should not object). Check for members of 'Gems and Jewellery Association of Rajasthan'.
Johari Bazar, you may be able to see craftsmen at work especially in Gopalji-ki-Rasta.
NK Meghraj, 239-240 Johari Bazar.
Ornaments, 32 Sudharma Arcade, Chameliwala Market, opposite GPO (turn left, first right and right again), T365051. for stones and silver (wholesale prices; made up in 24 hrs).

Warning Never agree to 'help to export' jewellery. Report of misuse of credit card accounts at **Monopoli Gems** opposite Sarga Sooli, Kishore Niwas Tripolia Bazar, **Apache Indian Jewellers** (also operating as **Krishna Gems** or **Ashirwad Gems & Art**) opposite Samodia Complex, Loha Mandi, SC Rd. **Do not use credit cards** to buy these goods.

Photography
Shops on MI Rd and Chaura Rasta.

Pottery
Kripal Kumbha, B-18, Shiv Marg, Bani Park.
Blue Pottery Art Centre, Amer Rd, near Jain Mandir. For unusual pots.

Silverware
Amrapali Silver Shop, Chameliwala Market, opposite GPO, MI Rd.
Arun's Emporium, MI Rd.
Balaji's, Sireh Deori Bazar (off *Johari Bazar*).
Silver and Art Palace, Amer Rd.

Amber *p338*
At Amber near the *baoli* and temples, are demonstrations of block printing etc. Shops sell gems, jewellery, textiles, handicrafts and 'antiques' (objects up to 90 years old; genuine 100-year old antiques may not be exported). Travellers warn that the privately owned *Rajasthan Small Scale Cottage Industries*, Jagat Shiromani Temple Rd, looks like a government fixed price shop but charges very high prices.

Ajmer *p350, map p351*
Fine local silver jewellery, tie-and-dye textiles and camel hide articles are best buys. The shopping areas are Madar Gate, Station Rd, Purani Mandi, Naya Bazar and Kaisarganj. Some of the alleys in the old town have good shopping.
Arts and Art's, Bhojan Shala, near Jain Temple.

Pushkar *p353, map p353*
There is plenty to attract the western eye; check quality and bargain hard.

Books
Several have second-hand copies; shop around as prices vary.

Cloth
Essar, Shop 6, Sadar Bazar, opposite Narad Kunj. Excellent tailoring (jacket Rs 250-300 including fabric).
Harish, Brahma Temple Rd, for lightweight *razai* quilts, bedsheets, cloth bags.

Hairdressing and massage
Many hotels now offer health clubs, barbers, massages, yoga.
Shri Ram Janta, Chhoti Basti Ghat, No 12, offers "bone crack", with "turbo-powered hands"! (Rs 50) – also henna, haircuts, hand painting.

Paintings
Miniatures on silk and old paper everywhere.
JP Dhabai's, opposite Shiva Cloth Store near *Payal Guest House*, Main Bazar. Offers fine quality (painted with a single squirrel hair!) at a price. Recommended.

▲ Activities and tours

Jaipur *p331, map p334*
Some hotels will arrange golf, tennis or squash.

Polo
Ground near Rambagh Palace. *Ashok Hotel* and *Khetri House*.

Tour companies
Aravalli Safari, opposite *Rajputana Palace Hotel*, Palace Rd, T373124. Very professional.
Forts & Palaces Tours, A-110 Bhan Nagar, Queens Rd, T351117, www.palaces-tours.com. Dependable tours, including camel safaris; friendly, knowledgeable and enthusiastic.
Karwan Tours, *Hotel Bissau Palace*, outside Chandpol, T/F308103, www.karwantours.com. For camel safaris, tours, taxis, ticketing, exchange, very helpful.
Marudhar Tours, H-20 Bhagat Singh Marg, C-scheme, T371768, marudhar@ datainfosys.net.in. Car hire, air/train tickets.
Rajasthan Travel, 52 Ganpati Plaza, MI Rd, T365408. Ticketing, reliable guides.

RTDC Tours City Sightseeing, half day: 0800-1300, 1130-1630, 1330-1830, Rs 90; Central Museum, City Palace, Amber Fort and Palace, Gaitore, *Nawab ki Haveli*, Jantar Mantar, Jal Mahal, Hawa Mahal; City Sightseeing, full day: 0900-1800, Rs 1350; including places above plus Nahargarh Fort, Indology Museum, Dolls Museum, Galta, Birla Planetarium. Jaigarh Fort. Nahargarh evening tour, 1800-2200, includes non-veg meal, folk dances. Book at Railway station, Gangaur or *Tourist Hotel*. Other operators also offer city sightseeing: half/ full day, Rs 100-150. The tours are worthwhile, but may miss out promised sights and claim that they are closed. Some may find the guides' English difficult to follow and the obligatory trip to shops, tedious.
Sita, Station Rd, T361404, ticketing, money transfer.

Yoga and meditation
Vipasana Centre, Dhammathali, Galta (3 km east of centre) runs courses for new and experienced students, T641520.

Alwar *p345*
Tours
Rajasthan, Tourist Reception Centre, Nehru Marg, opposite railway station, T347348.

Keoladeo Ghana National Park
p347, map p348
Tour operator
GTA, near Tourist Lodge, Golbagh Rd, T28188, F25259, vfauzdar@yahoo.com. Knowledgeable English speaking guides, Rs 300 for 2 hrs.

Pushkar *p353, map p353*
Riding
Horses Rs 150-200 per hr, camel Rs 30-50 per hr, at most hotels and near Brahma temple. Lessons: Rs 150 per hr (minimum 10 hr over 5 days) from *Ashish- Manish*, opposite Brahma temple, *Sunset Café* and others.

Swimming
Sarovar, Oasis, Peacock hotels, non-residents pay Rs 40-50.

Tour companies
Pushkar Travels, *Pushkar Palace Hotel*, excellent service, good buses, ticketing Rs 50. Avoid Shiva Travel, near *Om Hotel*.

Jaipur *p331, map p334*
Air
Sanganer airport now 'international' with flights to Dubai via Delhi, has good facilities. Transport to town: taxi, 30 mins, Rs 250; auto rickshaw Rs 120, bus Rs 30. Indian Airlines, Nehru Pl, Tonk Rd, T514500. Indian Airlines flights to Aurangabad; Delhi; Jaisalmer; Jodhpur; Mumbai; Udaipur. Jet Airways, T412222, airport T551352: Delhi, Mumbai, Udaipur.

Bus
Local City buses are cheap.
To Amber originate from Ajmeri Gate, junction with MI Rd so get on there if you want a seat.
Long distance Central Bus Stand, Sindhi Camp, Station Rd. Enquiries: Deluxe, T375834, Express, T363277 (24 hrs), Narain Singh Circle, T564016. The better 'Deluxe' buses are very popular so book 2 days in advance. Deluxe buses depart from Platform 3 which has the Reservation counter. Journeys can be very bumpy and tiring. Left luggage, Rs 10 per item per day. Avoid hotel touts and use the pre-paid auto rickshaw counter to get to your hotel. To Agra about hourly; (230 km, 5 hrs, via Bharatpur, Rs 120); Ajmer (131 km, ½ hourly, 3 hrs, Rs 75); Bharatpur Rs 90; Delhi (261 km, ½ hourly, 5 hrs, Rs 200); Jaisalmer (654 km, 2200, 15 hrs via Jodhpur, Rs 320). Jodhpur (332 km, frequent, 7 hrs, Rs 190); Udaipur (374 km, 12 hrs, Rs 230). *Jai Ambay*, MI Rd, T214777, runs coaches on major routes, including Pushkar (3½ hrs, Rs 85).

Rickshaw
Auto rickshaw: station to city centre hotel, about Rs 25; Sightseeing, 8 hrs, Rs 235 for 2-seater; Rs 370 for 4-seater. From railway and bus stations, drivers (who expect to take you to shops for commission) offer whole day hire including Amber for Rs 150; have your list of sights planned and refuse to go to shops. Cycle rickshaws: (often rickety) station to central hotels, Rs 15; full day Rs 100.

Taxi
Unmetered taxis; 4 hrs Rs 350 (40 km), 8 hrs Rs 550 (city and Amber) Out of city Rs 5 per km, *Marudhar Tours* (see Tour companies above); RTDC, T315714.

Train

Enquiry, T131, T133, reservation T135. Computerized booking office in separate building to front and left of station; separate queue for foreigners. Persistent auto-rickshaw drivers, may quote Rs 10 to anywhere in town, then overcharge for city tour. Use the pre-paid rickshaw counter. **Abu Rd (for Mount Abu)** *Aravali Exp, 9708,* 0700, 9 hrs. **Agra Cantt**: *Marudhar Exp, 4854/4864,* 1505, 7 hrs. **Ahmadabad**: *Ashram* Exp, 2916, 2050, 11 hrs. *Rajdhani Exp, 2958,* Tue, Thu, Sat, 0045, 9 hrs. **Ajmer**: *Shatabdi Exp, 2015,* not Sun, 1045, 2 hrs; *Aravali Exp, 9708,* 0700, 2 hrs; **Bikaner**: *Intercity Exp, 2468,* 1500, 7 hrs. **Chittaurgarh**: *Jaipur-Purna Exp, 9769,* 1220, 7½ hrs; *Chetak Exp, 9615,* 2050, 8½ hrs. **Delhi**: *Shatabdi Exp, 2016,* not Sun, 1755, 4¾ hrs; *Jaipur Delhi Exp, 2414,* 1620, 5¾ hrs. **Jodhpur**: *Jodhpur Delhi Exp, 4859,* 2330, 6 hrs. **Mumbai (C)**: *Jaipur Mumbai Exp 2956,* 1330, 18 hrs. **Udaipur** *Chetak Exp, 9615,* 2220, 12 hrs.

Samode *p342*
Samode is a 1-hr drive from Jaipur. **Buses** from Chandpol go to **Chomu** where you can pick up a local bus to **Samode**. Taxis charge Rs 800.

Jhunjhunun *p344*
Bicycle
Apani Dhani, Nawalgarh, arranges cycle tours in Shekhawati.

Bus
To **Nawalgarh**: from Delhi, best from ISBT daily at 0800, 2200 and 2300, 8 hrs. From Jaipur frequent buses from 0630-1830 (Express in the morning), 3½ hrs. Also to **Sikar** from Jaipur and Bikaner.

Jeep
For hire in Samode, Nawalgarh, Mandawa and Dundlod, about Rs 1,200 per day.

Taxi
From Jaipur, diesel Ambassador, Rs 1,200 for day tour of parts of Shekhawati; with detours, up to Rs 1,500; Rs 1,700 including 1 night. A/c cars can be twice as much. Local hire is possible in Mandawa, Mukundgarh and Nawalgarh.

Train
From Jaipur, 3 trains run daily to stations in Shekhawati. *Shekhawati Exp* (Delhi-Jaipur):

To **Mukundgarh**: from Delhi, 2315, 7½ hrs; from Jaipur, 1015, 1330, 1805, 4 hrs. To **Nawalgarh**: from Delhi, 2230, 8½ hrs. To **Jhunjhunun**: from Delhi, dep 2315, 7½ hrs, arriving in Sikar after 2 hrs; from Jaipur, dep 1805, 5 hrs, continues to Delhi, 6 hrs. To **Sikar** from Bikaner, depart 2025, 7 hrs.

Alwar *p345*
Bus
There are regular buses to/from **Delhi** (4-5 hrs) and **Jaipur**. Frequent service to **Bharatpur** (2¾ hrs), **Deeg** (1¾ hrs) and **Sariska** (1 hr).

Train
New Delhi: *Shatabdi Exp, 2016,* not Sun, 1941, 2¾ hrs. **Delhi**: *Jodhpur Delhi Exp, 4860,* 0835, 3 hrs; *Jaipur-Delhi Exp, 2414,* 1845, 3 hrs.

Sariska Tiger Reserve *p346*
Air
Nearest airport at Jaipur (110 km).

Train
Nearest at Alwar (36 km), buses to sanctuary.

Bharatpur *p347*
Buses tend to get very crowded but give an insight into Indian rural life.
Auto-rickshaw from railway station (6 km) to park Rs 60; from bus stand (4 km), Rs 30.

Air
Nearest airport is at Agra (55 km).

Bus
From **Agra** (55 km, 1½ hrs, Rs 28), **Deeg** Rs 20; **Delhi** (185 km, 6 hrs, Rs 90) and **Jaipur** (175 km, 5 hrs, Rs 70) arrive at Anah Gate just off NH11 (east of town).

Train
Delhi (ND): *Paschim Exp, 2925,* 0630, 4 hrs; *Golden Temple Mail, 2903,* 1540, 3½ hrs; *Mumbai-Firozepur Janata Exp, 9023,* 0800, 5½ hrs. **Sawai Madhopur**: *Paschim Exp, 2926,* 1955, 2½ hrs; *Golden Temple Mail, 2904,* 1055, 2½ hrs.

Keoladeo Ghana National Park
p347, map p348
Bicycle
Bicycle hire: near *Saras* or ask your hotel; Rs 40 per day; hire on previous evening for

an early start next day. See Bharatpur, above, for transport details.

Ajmer *p350, map p351*
Ajmer Station is seemingly overrun with rats - not a pleasant place to wait for a night train.

Bus
Enquiries, T427603. Buses every 30 mins to **Agra**, **Delhi**, **Jaipur**, 3 hrs; **Jodhpur**, 5 hrs; **Bikaner**, 7 hrs; **Chittaurgarh** (190 km); **Udaipur** (302 km) via Chittaurgarh; **Kota** via Bundi. Buses for **Pushkar** (Rs 4) which leave from near the station, are very crowded. Jeep: better but difficult to get.

Rickshaw
Auto rickshaw: to **Pushkar**, Rs 60 after bargaining.

Train
Reservations, T431965, 0830-1330, 1400-1630, enquiries, T131. **Ahmadabad**: *Ahmadabad Mail, 9106*, 0735, 10 hrs; *Ashram Exp, 2916*, 2325, 8½ hrs, last 3 via **Beawar**, 1 hr. **Chittaurgarh**: *Ahmadabad Exp, 9943*, 0750, 5 hrs. **Delhi**: *Ahmadabad Delhi Mail, 9105*, 2033, 9 hrs; *Shatabdi Exp, 2016* not Sun, 1530, 6¾ hrs; (OD) *Ashram Exp, 2915*, 0215, 8 hrs. **Jaipur**: *AjmerJaipur Exp, 9652*, 0640, 3 hrs; *Aravali Exp, 9707*, 1733, 2½ hrs; *Shatabdi Exp, 2016*, 1530, not Sun, 2 hrs. **Jodhpur**: *Jodhpur Mail, 4893*, 0545, 6 hrs. **Udaipur**: *Ahmadabad Exp, 9943*, 0750, 0½ hrs.

Pushkar *p353, map p353*
Bicycle/motorbike
Cycle/motorbike hire: **Michael Cycle, SL Cycles**, Ajmer Bus Stand Rd, very helpful, Rs 3 per hr, Rs 25 per day; also from the market. **Hotel Oasis** has Vespa scooters, Rs 300 per day.

Bus
Long distance Frequent service to/from **Ajmer** Rs 4. Direct buses to **Jodhpur** via Merta (8 hrs) but it is quicker to return to Ajmer and take an express bus (4-5 hrs) from there ('First class' passengers travel on the roof!). **Pushkar Travels**, good minibuses; avoid **Shrinath Travels**, overcrowded, often late, charges last minute premiums.

Car
Rs 10 entry 'tax' per vehicle. **Delhi**: 10 hrs; **Jaipur**: 3 hrs.

Rickshaw
Auto-rickshaw: to Ajmer Rs 60 after bargaining.

⊙ Directory

Jaipur *p331, map p334*
Airlines offices Air India, MI Rd (opposite All India Rd), T368569. Lufthansa, T561360; others at Jaipur Tower, MI Rd, T377051.
Banks Several on MI Rd. Open 1030-1430, 1530-1630. For Visa: **Indus Bank**, C-Scheme; **SBBJ**. **Thomas Cook**, Jaipur Towers, 1st floor, MI Rd (500 m from railway station, T360801, 0930-1730, open Sun). No commission on own TCs, Rs 20 for others. Recommended. Also hotels, eg *Rambagh Palace* (0700-2000). Travellers report misuse of credit cards at some jewellers opposite Hawa Mahal.
Hospitals Santokba Durlabhji, Bhawani Singh Rd, T566251. **SMS**, Sawai Ram Singh Marg, T560291. **Bani Park**, D9 Kabir Marg, T203864. **Internet** At Ganpati Plaza basement, Rs 40 per hr. Cyber Café, 15 Nandisha Inn, Sivaji Rd. Reliable. Interphase C-Scheme. At hotels: **Mewar**, near Central Bus Stand, T206042 and **Jaipur Inn**. **Post office** GPO, MI Rd. Excellent parcel service. **Tourist offices** Department of Tourism, Government Hostel Campus, MI Rd, Jaipur, 302 001, T410595, F201045, www.rajasthantourism india.com, palaceonwheelsindia.com. RTDC, *Hotel Swagatam Campus*, T202586, F204065. Counters at railway station, T315714 and Central Bus Stand. Guides for 4-8 hrs, about Rs 250-400 (Rs 100 extra for French, German, Japanese, Spanish). Gujarat, *Tourist Hotel*, opposite GPO, T362017. **Useful addresses** Ambulance: T102. Fire: T101. Police: T100.

Dunlod *p344*
Banks UCO Bank, changes currency.

Alwar *p345*
Internet Near the bus and railway station and on Manu Marg

Deeg *p346*
Banks SBBJ near Binarayan Gate, may ask to see proof of purchase, or refuse to change TCs.

Keoladeo Ghana National Park
p347, map p348
Tourist offices Rajasthan, *Hotel Saras*, T22542. **Wildlife office**, Forest Rest House, T22777. Guides available.

Ajmer *p350, map p351*
Banks Bank of Baroda, opposite GPO, accepts Visa, Mastercard; **State Bank of India** near Bus Stand, changes cash, TCs. **Tourist**

offices Alongside *Khadim Hotel*, T52426. 0800-1200, 1500-1800, closed Sun, very helpful. Approved guide (4-8 hrs, about Rs 250-400) and tourist taxi hire. Counter at railway station, near 1st class main gate, entrance on right from car park.

Pushkar *p353, map p353*
Banks SBBJ changes TCs; Hotels **Peacock** and **Oasis** offer exchange for a small commission.
Hospital Shyama, Heloj Rd, T772087. **Post office** At the Chowk with a very helpful Postmaster, east end of Main Bazar.

Southeastern Rajasthan

Kota → *Phone code: 0744. Colour map 2, grid B5. Population: 537,000.*

Kota, below a deep gorge of the Chambal River, was once on a major trade route from Delhi to Gujarat. Off the beaten track for most visitors, it still retains some parks, gardens, wide tree-lined streets and princely architecture, and is a good base for visits to the historic monuments of Hadoti in Jhalawar, Bundi and Baran. An army headquarter town, it is now a rapidly expanding industrial area for processing chemicals, with hydro-electric and nuclear power plants nearby. ▸▸ *For Sleeping, Eating and other listings see pages 377-380.*

Ins and outs
Getting there Trains link Kota Junction station with Jaipur, Delhi (via Sawai Madhopur) and Mumbai. The station is 4 km north of the bus station at the town centre; shuttle buses run between the two. Regular buses run to Bundi and Jhalawar.

Getting around Autos, cycle rickshaws and fixed-route tempos ferry passengers around town. Parts of the palace in the old fortified town, including the Museum, are worth exploring on foot. See Transport, page 379, for further details.

History
Cave paintings date the occupation of the area along the Chambal River to prehistoric times. It was ruled by Bhil chieftains until the 13th century, when Jait Singh of Bundi, a Hada Chauhan, usurped their territory. Kota became an independent state from Bundi when Rao Madho Singh was installed as ruler in 1631 with the blessings of the Mughal Emperor Shah Jahan.

Sights
At the south end of the town, near the barrage, is the vast, strongly fortified **City Palace** (1625) which you enter by the south gate. There are some striking buildings with delicate ornamental stonework on the balconies and façade, though parts are decaying. The **Hathi Pol** (Elephant Gate 1625-48), decorated with more recent murals, shows a royal wedding procession. The **Bhim Mahal**, an early 18th-century Darbar Hall, is covered with Rajput miniatures documenting the town's history and local legends, as well as intricate mirror work and ivory inlaid doors. The best preserved murals and carved marble panels are in the chambers upstairs and in the Arjun

Mahal. These murals feature motifs characteristic of the Kota School of art, including portraiture (especially profiles), hunting scenes, festivals and the Krishna Lila. The **Madho Singh Museum** ① *daily except Fri, 1000-1630, Rs 50 for foreigners, Rs 50 (upstairs), camera Rs 50, video Rs 75*, has an impressive collection of arms and armour, as well as china, silver objects, sculpture and princely relics.

The 15th-century **Kishore Sagar** tank between the station and the palace occasionally has boats for hire. The **Jag Mandir** Island Palace (closed to visitors) is in the centre of the lake. The **Chattra Vlas Park**, near the *Chambal Tourist Bungalow*, has a good view of the lake and the island palace, besides *chhatris* which are attractive though somewhat neglected. The government **Brij Vilas Palace Museum** ① *1000-1700, Rs 3, no photography*, near the park, has architectural fragments and individual sculptures salvaged from the ruins of medieval temples of southeastern Rajasthan (some poorly labelled), besides pre-historic rock inscriptions, coins, weapons, Bundi school miniatures, manuscripts (13th-century Bhagvad Gita on one page!) and costumes.

The **Chambal Gardens** by *Amar Niwas*, south of the fort, is a pleasant place for a view of the river. The pond is stocked with fish-eating gharial crocodiles which have become rare in Rajasthan. A variety of birds, including occasionally flamingos, can be seen at the river and in nearby ponds. Upstream at **Bharatiya Kund** is a popular swimming spot whilst the Kota barrage controls the river level and is the headworks for an irrigation system downstream. Photography of the barrage gates is prohibited but you can photograph the view from the bridge. **Boat rides** ① *ask at Tourist Office,*

Kota

To Bundi & Jaipur
To Junction Station, Umed Bhavan (4 km) & Delhi

Circuit House
Collectorate Circle
SBBJ
Station Rd
CIVIL LINES
NAYAPURA
Bundi Rd
Nayapura Circle
Stadium
Ladpura Gate
Chhattri
Club
Wild Life Office
Zoo
Chambal River
Sarovar Rd
Rampura Rd
Brij Vilas Palace Museum
Umaid Vilas Garden
Kishore Sagar
Clock Tower
Jag Mandir
To Kota Dam
Barrage Rd
Patan Pol
Naya Darwaza Entrance
Suraj Pol
Ghumanpura
Kotri Tank
Kota Barrage
Fort
City Palace & Museum
Chambal Gardens
Right Main Canal
Mela Ground
Shopping Centre
Jhalawar Rd
To Airport & Jhalarapatan (85 km)

N
0 metres   500
0 yards   500

■ Sleeping
1 Brijraj Bhawan Palace
2 Chambal
3 Navrang
4 Palkiya Haveli
5 Phul Plaza
6 Sukhdam

Rs 400 per hr, for bird and crocodile watching.

The **Umed Bhawan** (1904), 4 km north of town, was built for the Maharao Umaid Singh II and designed by Sir Samuel Swinton Jacob in collaboration with Indian designers. The buff-coloured stone exterior with a stucco finish has typical Rajput detail. The interior, however, is Edwardian with a fine drawing-room, banquet hall and garden.

Khaitoon (pronounced Khetun), about 12 km from Kota, is famous for *Doria* saris with a distinctive checked pattern which are woven on traditional pit handlooms using silk and cotton threads and pure gold *zari*. Prices range from Rs 500 for simple cotton ones, to Rs 25,000 for silk with a high gold content in the zari. About 2000-2500 men and women work at home on weaving Doria saris.

Bardoli → *50 km south of Kota.*

Bardoli (Barolli) has some of the finest examples of 10th-century Pratihara temples in India, just east of the bus stand. The restored **Ghatesvara Temple** has an elaborately carved *sikhara* over the sanctuary and a columned porch. Inside are sculptures of Siva dancing flanked by Brahma and Vishnu with river goddesses and dancing maidens beneath. One of the sanctuary's five stone lingas resembles an upturned pot or *ghata*.

★ Ranthambhore National Park

→ *Phone code: 07462. Colour map 2, grid B6.*
The park is one of the finest tiger reserves in the country where most visitors spending a couple of nights are likely to spot one of these majestic animals. Once the private tiger reserve of the Maharaja of Jaipur, in 1972 the sanctuary came under the **Project Tiger** scheme. It covers 410 sq km and runs from the easternmost spur of the Aravallis to the Vindhya range. It has both the old fort and the wildlife sanctuary,

Ranthambhore National Park

Sleeping	4 Hammir	8 Sawai Madhopur
1 Ankur Resorts	5 Oberoi	Lodge
2 Anurag Resort	6 Ranthambhore Bagh	9 Sher Bagh
3 Castle Jhoomar Baori	7 Regency	10 Tiger Moon Resort

also known as **Sawai Madhopur**, after the town which has some Jain temples with
gilded paintings. The national park is 10 km east of Sawai Madhopur town with the
approach along a narrow valley; the main gate is 4 km from the boundary. Set in dry
deciduous forest, the area covers rocky hills and open valleys dotted with small
pools and fruit trees. The fort dominates the landscape. The path to it zig-zags up
the steep outcrop in a series of ramps and through two impressive gateways.
▶▶ For Sleeping, Eating and other listings see pages 377-380.

Ins and outs

The park has good roads and tracks. Entry is by park jeep or open bus (Canter) on 3 hr
tours; 14 jeeps (or Gypsys) and 8 Canters are allowed in at any one time to minimize
disturbance. Jeeps are better but can be difficult to get in the peak season so request
one at the time of booking your lodge. Visitors are picked up from their hotels. It can
be very cold at dawn in winter so go well prepared. Open Oct-Jun. Tours: 0700-1000,
1500-1800; summer 0630-0930, 1500-1800. Jeep hire: Rs 750 for up to 5 passengers;
jeep entry Rs 125; guide Rs 350; plus individual entry fee Rs 25 (Indians), Rs 200
(foreigners). Camera free, video Rs 50. Seat in a Canter, Rs 105. Bookings start at 0600
and 1330 for same day tours; advance bookings from1000-1330. Climate 49°C-28°C.
Best time to visit: Nov-Apr (vegetation dies down in Apr exposing tigers). The Forest
Dept Project Tiger Office, T20223, is behind the railway station. Avoid weekends when
there are larger numbers of noisy visitors.

Wildlife

Tiger sightings are reported almost daily, usually in the early morning, especially from
November to April. Travellers see them "totally unconcerned, amble past only 30 ft
(10 m) away"! Sadly, poaching is prevalent, and the tiger population has been
depleted to around 30. The lakeside woods and grassland provide an ideal habitat for
herds of chital and sambar deer and sounders of wild boar. Nilgai antelope and
chinkara gazelles prefer the drier areas of the park. Langur, mongoose and hare are
prolific. There are also sloth bear, a few leopards, and the occasional rare caracal.
Crocodiles bask by the lakes, and some rocky ponds have fresh water
turtles.Extensive birdlife include spurfowl, jungle fowl, partridges, quails, crested
serpent eagle, woodpeckers, flycatchers etc. There are also water birds like storks,
ducks and geese at the lakes and waterholes. Padam Talao by the Jogi Mahal is the
park's favourite water source; there are also water holes at Raj Bagh and Milak.

Sawai Madhopur

To Chemist (200m)

To Tonk & Jaipur — To Jaipur

To Kota & Mumbai

GPO

SBI

SBI

Main Bazar

Sawai Madhopur Junction

Project Tiger Office

To Delhi

To Ranthambhore National Park & Hotels

To Sawai Madhopur 'City'

N

0 metres 100
0 yards 100

■ Sleeping
1 Swagath
2 Vishal

● Eating
1 Agarwal
2 Asha

① *Free. The entrance to the fort is before the gate to the park. Open dawn to dusk, though the Park Interpretation Centre near the small car park may not be open.*

There is believed to have been a settlement here in the eighth century. The earliest historic record is of it being wrested by the Chauhans in the 10th century. In the 11th century, after Ajmer was lost to Ghori, the Chauhans made it their capital. Hamir Chauhan, the ruler of Ranthambhore in the 14th century gave shelter to enemies of the Delhi sultanate, resulting in a massive siege and the Afghan conquest of the fort. The fort was later surrendered to Emperor Akbar in the 16th century when Ranthambhore's commander saw resistance was useless, finally passing to the rulers of Jaipur. The forests of Ranthambhore historically guarded the fort from invasions but with peace under the Raj they became a hunting preserve of the Jaipur royal family. The fort wall runs round the summit and has a number of semi-circular bastions, some with sheer drops of over 65 m and stunning views. Inside the fort you can see a Siva temple – where Rana Hamir beheaded himself rather than face being humiliated by the conquering Delhi army – ruined palaces, pavilions and tanks. Mineral water, tea and soft drinks are sold at the foot of the climb to the fort and next to the Ganesh temple near the tanks.

★ Bundi → *Phone code: 0747. Colour map 2, grid B5. Population: 65,000.*

Bundi, in a beautiful narrow valley above which towers the Taragarh Fort, can easily be visited on a day trip from Kota. The drive into the town is particularly pleasing as the road runs along the hillside overlooking the valley opposite the fort. Completely unspoilt and rarely visited, it is still worth spending a day or two here to soak in the atmosphere. Bundi is especially colourful and interesting during the festivals, *Gangaur,* and *Kalji Teej Fair.*▸▸ *For Sleeping, Eating and other listings see pages 377-380.*

Ins and outs
Getting there Bundi is best reached by bus or car from Kota, Chittaurgarh, Ajmer or Sawai Madhopur.

Getting around The town itself has a compact, if crowded, centre. From the bus stand to the south, a few mins' walk through the interesting bazar brings you to the start of the climb to the hillside palace and the fort beyond. For visiting sights around Bundi, autos and cycle-rickshaws are available or you can hire a bike from town. See Transport, page 380, for further details.

History
Formerly a small state founded in 1342, Bundi's fortunes varied inversely with those of its more powerful neighbours. Neither wealthy nor powerful, it nevertheless ranked high in the Rajput hierarchy since the founding family belonged to the specially blessed Hada Chauhan clan. After Prithviraj Chauhan was defeated by Muhammad Ghuri in 1193, the rulers sought refuge in Mewar. However, adventurous clan members overran the Bhils and Minas in the Chambal valley and established the kingdom of Hadavati or **Hadoti** which covers the area around Bundi, Kota and Jhalawar in southeastern Rajasthan. It prospered under the guidance of the able 19th-century ruler Zalim Singh, but then declined on his death. The British reunited the territory in 1894.

Sights
Taragrh Fort The fort (1342) stands in sombre contrast to the beauty of the town and the lakes below. There are excellent views but it is a 20-minute difficult climb; good

shoes help. The eastern wall is crenellated with high ramparts while the main gate to the west is flanked by octagonal towers. The **Bhim Burj** tower dominates the fort and provided the platform for the Garbh Ganjam, a huge cannon. A pit to the side once provided shelter for the artillery men, and there are several stepped water tanks inside. Cars can go as far as the TV tower then it is 600 m along a rough track.

The palace The palace complex below Taragarh which was begun around 1600 is at the northern end of the bazar. The buildings, on various levels, follow the shape of the hill. A steep, rough stone ramp leads up through the **Hazari Darwaza** (Gate of the Thousand) where the garrison lived; you may need to enter through a small door within the darwaza. The palace entrance is through the **Hathi Pol** (Elephant Gate, 1607-31), which has two carved elephants with a water clock. Steps lead up to **Ratan Daulat** above the stables, the unusually small Diwan-i-Am which was intended to accommodate a select few at public audience. A delicate marble balcony overhangs the courtyard giving a view of the throne to the less privileged, who stood below. The **Chattar Mahal** (1660), the newer palace of green serpentine rock, is pure Rajput in style and contains private apartments decorated with wall paintings, glass and mirrors. The **Badal Mahal** bedroom has finely decorated ceilings. Rooms of the Chattar Mahal are kept locked but you may ask for permission at the Rawla office

Bundi

Sleeping
1 Haveli Braj Bhushanjee
2 Kasera & Roof Café
3 Kishan Niwas
4 Kothi Ishwari Niwas
5 Lake View
6 Royal Retreat
7 Windavali

Eating
1 Diamond & Sher-e-Punjab

0 metres 200
0 yards 200

To Chittaurgarh
To Train Station
To 84-Pillared Chhatri & Kota

⦂ Opium poppies

Crossing the high plateau between Bundi and Chittaurgarh the landscape suddenly becomes dotted with tiny patches of papery white flowers. These two Rajasthani districts, along with the neighbouring districts of Madhya Pradesh, are India's opium poppy growing belt, accounting for over 90% of production. As early as the fifteenth century this region produced opium for trade with China. Today the whole process is tightly monitored by the Government. Licences to grow are hard won and easily lost. No farmer can grow more than half a bigha of opium poppy (less than one twentieth of a hectare), and each must produce at least 6 kg of opium for sale to the Government. Failure to reach this tough target results in the loss of the licence to grow. Laying out the field, actual cultivation and sale are all government controlled. Between late February and early April the farmers harvest the crop by incising fine lines in one quarter of each poppy head in the evening, and collecting the sap first thing in the morning. The harvesting has to be so precise that each evening a different quarter of the seed head will be cut on a different face - north, south, east or west. Finally the Government announces the collection point for the harvested opium just two or three days in advance, and farmers have to travel miles to the centre selected for weighing and final payment.

behind the Ayurvedic Hospital below the palace. The **Chitrashali**, a cloistered courtyard (open to the public, free entry) with a gallery running around a garden of fountains, has a splendid collection of miniatures showing scenes from the Radha Krishna story. Turquoise, blues and greens dominate (other pigments may have faded with exposure to sunlight) though the elephant panels on the dado are in a contrasting red. The murals (circa 1800) are some of the finest examples of Rajput art but are not properly maintained. There is supposed to be a labyrinth of catacombs in which the state treasures are believed to have been stored. Each ruler was allowed one visit but when the last guide died in the 1940s the secret of its location was lost! At night, the palace is lit up and the bazar comes alive. To see Badal and Chattar Mahals, ask at Rawla office behind Ayurvedic Hospital.

Other sights There are several 16th-17th-century stepwells and 'tanks' (*kunds*) in town. The 46-m deep **Raniji-ki-baori**① *closed Sun, 2nd Sat each month, 1000-1700, free, caretaker unlocks the gate*, with beautiful pillars and bas relief sculpture panels of Vishnu's 10 *avatars*, is the most impressive. No longer in use, the water is stagnant.

Sukh Niwas (Mahal), a summer pleasure palace, faces the **Jait Sagar** lake where Kipling spent a night in the original pavilion. Further out are the 66 royal memorials at the rarely visited **Sar Bagh**, some of which have beautiful carvings. The caretaker expects Rs 10 tip.

The square artificial **Naval Sagar** lake has in its centre a half-submerged temple to Varuna, the god of water. The lake surface beautifully reflects the entire town and palace. West of the Naval Sagar, 10 km away, is **Phool Sagar Palace**, which was started in 1945 but was left unfinished. Prior permission is needed to view.

Excursions On the road to Chittaurgarh **Menal**, 96 km, has a cluster of Siva temples believed to date from the time of the Guptas. They are associated with the Chauhans and other Rajput dynasties. Though neglected the temples have some fine carvings

Pradesh. Behind is a deep, wooded ravine with a seasonal waterfall.

Jhalawar Jhalawar, 85 km southeast of Kota, was the capital of the princely state of the Jhalas which was separated from Kota by the British in 1838. It lies in a thickly forested area on the edge of the Malwa plateau with some interesting local forts, temples and ancient cave sites nearby.

The **Garh Palace** in the town centre, now housing government offices, has some fine wall paintings which can be seen with permission. The **museum** ① *closed Fri, 1000-1630, Rs 3*, here, established in 1915, has a worthwhile collection of sculptures, paintings and manuscripts. **Bhawani Natyashala** (1921) was known for its performances ranging from Shakespearean plays to Shakuntala dramas. The stage with a subterranean driveway allowed horses and chariots to be brought on stage during performances.

Jhalarapatan ① *Buses from Kota to Jhalawar; then auto-rickshaw or local bus for sights. The Ujjain-Jhalawar road is appalling.* The small walled town, 7 km south of Jhalawar, has several fine 11th-century Hindu temples, the **Padmanath Sun Temple** on the main road being the best. The **Shantinath Jain temple** has an entrance flanked by marble elephants. There are some fine carvings on the rear façade and silver polished idols inside the shrines.

Chandrabhaga Fair is a cattle and camel fair with all the colour and authenticity of Pushkar without its commercialization. Animals are traded in large numbers in the fields, pilgrims come to bathe in the river as the temples become the centre of religious activity and the town is abuzz with all manner of vendors.

Seven kilometres away, **Chandrawati**, on the banks of the Chandrabhaga River, has the ruins of some seventh-century Hindu temples with fragments of fine sculpture.

Listings: Southeastern Rajasthan

● Sleeping

Kota *p370, map p371*
B Brijraj Bhawan Palace, Civil Lines, T450529, F450057. 6 spacious a/c rooms with verandahs, fixed Indian meals, old British Residency with character, stately drawing and dining rooms (regal memorabilia), superb location, immaculate gardens by river, croquet, tennis.
B Umed Bhavan (WelcomHeritage), Palace Rd (see above), T325262, F451110. 24 large, comfortable rooms (12 refurbished), sympathetic conversion, interesting memoribilia and state rooms, sunny terraces, behind woods (langurs, deer, parakeets, peacocks), billiards, tennis, attentive staff.
C Palkiya Haveli, Mokha Para (in walled city), near Suraj Pol, T328797, F327275. 10 a/c rooms with bath (tubs), 2 **B**, well restored,

carved wood furniture, exquisite murals at entrance, very good fixed meals, very peaceful courtyard garden (full of birds), family run.
C Sukhdham, Civil Lines, T320081, F327781, sukhdham@datainfosys.net. 14 rooms (size varies), 8 a/c, in a 19th-century British residence with sandstone balconies and screens, fixed meals, large garden, family run.
D Navrang, Collectorate Circle, Civil Lines, T323294, F450044. 25 decent, clean rooms, aircooled or a/c, TV, **C** suites, new a/c vegetarian restaurant, well managed.
D-E Surya Royal, Jhalawar Rd, T324240. 35 rooms, most air cooled or a/c with hot showers, **C** suites, restaurant, popular, fairly modern, business hotel.
D-E Vandana, Jhalawar Rd, T326841, F329605. Good value, aircooled and a/c (some **D**).
F budget hotels near the bus stand and station can be noisy and dirty.

● *For an explanation of the sleeping and eating price codes used in this guide, see inside the* ● *front cover. Other relevant information is found in Essentials pages 52-57.*

Book well ahead. Hotels tend to be overpriced – rooms can be dusty and electricity erratic. Carry a torch. Most down to **B** category are geared for tour groups so may neglect independent travellers.

L **Vaniyavilas** (Oberoi), T23999, F23988. Large garden resort set around a re-created *haveli* with frescoes. 25 a/c luxury tents (wood floor, TV, marble baths), pool, billiards, elephant rides, "fabulous spa". Exceptional.

AL **Sawai Madhopur Lodge** (Taj), Ranthambhore Rd, T20541, F20718. 20-min drive from park, 16 a/c rooms (6 tents Oct-Mar), dated hunting lodge but comfortable, good buffet watched over by tigers' heads, pool unusable (green algae), front desk lacks sparkle, park tour by jeep Rs 1420 each.

AL **Sherbagh Tented Camp**, Sherpur, T52120. Luxury tents with hot showers, award winning eco-camp, bar, dinner around fire, lake trips for birders, jungle ambience. well organized.

B **Tiger Den Resort**, Khilchipur-Ranthambhore Rd, T52070, F20702. 20 rooms (some a/c) in brick cottages around a lawn, evening meals (Indian buffet) seated around braziers, surrounded by farmland near guava groves, 6 km from park.

B **Tiger Moon Resort**, near Sherpur on the edge of the park (12 km railway), T52042. 32 stone, and 5 simple bamboo 'cottages', all with modern fittings, hot water, some tents are added in the peak season, buffet meals, bar, library, pool, expensive safaris, pleasant "jungle ambience".

B-C **Ranthambhore Regency**, T21176. A/c rooms in cottages.

C-D **Ankur Resorts**, 2 km railway, T20792, F20697. 15 simple rooms and 10 cottages with bath, tents in high season, in garden setting, fairly clean, fixed meals, friendly, helpful.

C-D **Hill View**, T22173, F21212. Attractive, large garden complex set in hills with great views, 20 cottage rooms (claustrophobic, but plans for a/c when prices will rise), attached baths, fixed meals.

D **Anurag Resort**, T20451, F20697. Single-storey bungalow with a garden has 17 tired, aircooled rooms with bath (poorly maintained), dorm beds (Rs 75), camping,

restaurant, large lawns, log fires, naturalist, jungle visits, helpful owner.

D **Hammir**, T20562, F21842. 6 newer rooms (rest are a bit shabby), restaurant (beer served), wildlife videos, friendly and cheerful.

D-E **Tiger Safari**, T21137. Rooms with fan (and hard beds), better a/c rooms, very clean baths (hot shower), quiet, arranges park jeep/bus.

Sawai Madhopur: the small hotels in the noisy market areas are rather seedy.

E-F **Rajeev Resort**, 16 Indira Colony, Civil Lines, T21413. 11 fairly decent rooms (some with western toilets), and larger 4-bedded rooms, simple meals to order.

F **Swagath**, T20601, 13 rooms in a rather ordinary guesthouse, 5 with bath (Western toilets, hot showers), singles with shared bath, Rs 50.

F **Vishal**, Main Bazar, opposite SBI, T20504. 7 passable rooms some with bath (hot water in buckets).

Bundi *p374, map p375*

B-C **Haveli Braj Bhushanjee**, below Fort, opposite Ayurvedic Hospital (entrance in alley), T442322, F442142, res@ kiplingsbundi.com. 18 quaint rooms (each different) with clean bath (hot showers), in 19th-century 4-storey *haveli* with plenty of atmosphere and interesting memorabilia, home-cooked Brahmin vegetarian meals (no alcohol), pleasant terrace, good fort views, pick-up from station on request, good craft shop below. Recommended.

B-C **Ishwari Niwas Palace**, opposite Circuit House, 1 Civil Lines, T443541, F442486, www.ishwariniwas.com. 20 simple air-cooled rooms (period furnishings) with bath, around a courtyard, tired looking old Rajput family home, traditional meals (Rs 250), friendly, peaceful, good local tours.

D **Royal Retreat**, below Fort, T444426, F443278, jpbundi@yahoo.com. Looks run down but quite clean and well kept inside, open courts, 5 largish rooms most with bath (others **E**), family run, good veg restaurant, café, rooftop dining with views, good craft shop, internet.

D-E **Vrindavati** (RTDC), 300 m from Sukh Mahal, on Jait Sagar Lake, T442473. 7 rooms in old bungalow in attractive garden with

🔊 *Phone codes* Kota: 0744; Ranthambhore: 07462; Bundi: 0747 beautiful views, tents, simple meals to order, helpful staff.

E Lake View Paying Guest House, Bohra Meghwan ji ki Haveli, Balchand Para, just below the palace, by Nawal Sagar, T442326, lakeview@yahoo.com. 4 simple clean rooms (shared bath) in 150-year old *haveli* with some wall paintings, private terrace shared with monkeys and peacocks, lovely views from rooftop, warm welcome, very friendly hosts.

E-F Kasera, Haveli Dev Baxjiki, Nagadi Bazar (old part of town), T444679. 14 rooms, some with air-cooler and hot shower, other singles (Rs 50), good vegetarian meals in rooftop restaurant, special lassi and cane juice, 350-year-old *haveli*, pleasant family.

E-F Kishan Niwas, near Laxmi Nath Temple, Nahar ka Chohtta, by Moti Mahal, T445807, F443278. Spartan, clean rooms with bath (hot water), good home cooking, Mr Singh is very friendly and helpful.

Menal *p376*
E Menal Motel, has 1 simple room – handy for a cup of tea or a simple meal.

Jhalawar *p377*
D Purvaj, in the town centre, a delightful old *haveli*, owned by an interesting family, delicious and simple homecooked meals.

🍴 Eating

Kota *p370, map p371*
Good kulfis and homemade ices in Sindhi shops.

♬ **Payal**, Nayapura. Good Indian. Also some Chinese, and Indianized Continental.
♬ **Venue**, Civil Lines. A/c, good Indian but very spicy, disappointing western.
♬ **Hariyali**, Bundi Rd. Good Punjabi, some Chinese/Continental. Pleasant garden restaurant, outdoors or under a small shelter, very popular but transport can be difficult.
♬ **Priya**, Nayapura. Popular for Indian veg.
♬ **Maheswari**, Nayapura. Indian veg.

Snacks and drinks
Palace View, outdoor meals/snacks. Handy for visitors to the City Palace.
Jodhpur Sweets, Ghumanpura Market. Saffron *lassis* and flavoured milks (pista, almonds etc).

p372, map p372
♬ **Asha**, next to bus stand and **Agrawal**. Otherwise, try hotels.

Bundi *p374, map p375*
Diamond, Suryamahal Chowk, in hotel. Very popular locally for cheap vegetarian meals, handy when visiting stepwells.
Sher-e-Punjab, in hotel, near *Diamond*, serves non-vegetarian.
Sathi Cold Drinks, Palace Rd, in hotel. Excellent *lassis* (try saffron, spices, pistachio and fruit), pleasant seating.

✹ Festivals and events

Kota *p370, map p371*
Colourful **Gangaur** (**Apr**) and Teej (**Aug**).
Dasara Mela (**Oct**). Great atmosphere, with shows in lit up Palace grounds.

▲ Activities and tours

Ranthambhore National Park
p372, map p372
Tour operator
Forts & Palaces, Dang walon ka mohalla, Sawai Madhopur, T34042, jaipur@palaces-tours.com.

⊖ Transport

Kota *p370, map p371*
Air
No flights at present.

Bus
At least hourly bus to **Bundi** (45 mins) and a few daily to **Ajmer**, **Chittaurgarh**, **Jhalarapatan** (2½ hrs); also to **Gwalior**, **Sawai Madhopur** and Ujjain.

Train
From Kota Junction: **Bharatpur**: *Golden Temple Mail, 2903*, 1130, 4 hrs (and Mathura, 5 hrs). **Mumbai** (Central): *Rajdhani Exp, 2952*, 2050, 11¾ hrs; *Paschim Exp, 2926*, 2355, 15½ hrs; *Golden Temple Mail, 2904*, 1455, 15¼ hrs. **New Delhi**: *Rajdhani Exp, 2951*, 0430, 5½ hrs; *Golden Temple Mail, 2903*, 1130, 7½ hrs; *Dehra Dun Exp, 9019*, 1955, 10½ hrs – all via **Sawai Madhopur**, 1½ hrs.

p372, map p372

Bus

Bus Stand is 500 m from railway station. Road from Sawai Madhopur to Bundi via **Lakheri** is appalling and best avoided (3½ hrs).

To **Sawai Madhopur** from Kota and Jaipur are slow (4 hrs); trains are better.

Train

Sawai Madhopur Junction, T20222. It is on the main Delhi-Mumbai line. From **Jaipur**: *Jaipur-Mumbai, 2956,* 1350, 2 hrs. **Jaipur**: *Mumbai-Jaipur Exp, 2955,* 1035, 2 hrs. **Jodhpur**: *Sawai Madhopur-Jodhpur Intercity Exp, 2465,* 1710. **Kota**: *Golden Temple Mail, 2904,* 1320, 1¼ hrs; *Mumbai Exp, 2956,* 1550, 1½ hrs. **Mumbai**: *Jaipur Mumbai Exp, 2956,* 1550, 16 hrs; *Paschim Exp, 2926,* 2220, 17¼ hrs; *Golden Temple Mail, 2904,* 1320, 15 hrs. **New Delhi** (via Bharatpur and Mathura) *Golden Temple Mail, 2903,* 1300, 6 hrs; *Dehra Dun Exp, 9019,* 2140, 8 hrs.

Bundi *p374, map p375*

Bus

To **Ajmer** (165 km), 5 hrs; **Kota** (37 km), 45 mins; **Chittaurgarh** (157 km), 5 hrs; **Udaipur** (120 km), 3 hrs.

Train

T22582. The station south of town has a train each way between Kota and Neemuch via Chittaurgarh.

⊙ Directory

Kota *p370, map p371*
Hospitals MBS Hospital, T450241.
Internet Acme, 2nd floor, Kalawati Paliwal Market, Gumantpura. **Tourist office** Rajasthan, Nayapura Bagh, T327695.
Police T450066.

Ranthambhore National Park
p372, map p372
Conservation group Tiger Watch, T20811. **Internet** Cyber Café on Ranthambhore Rd near entrance to *Ankur Resort* entrance.

Bundi *p374, map p375*
Banks Exchange can be a problem; try Bank of Baroda. **Hospitals** T32833, City, T32827. SS Nursing Home, T32333.
Internet At Royal Retreat. **Tourist office** At Circuit House, T22697, has a list of paying guest accommodation.

Southern Rajasthan

Udaipur → *Phone code: 0294. Colour map 2, grid B4. Population: 308,000.*

Set in the Girwa valley amidst the Aravalli hills of south Rajasthan, Udaipur is a beautiful city, regarded by many as one of the most romantic in India. In contrast to some of its desert neighbours it presents an enchanting image of white marble palaces, placid blue lakes, attractive gardens and green hills that keep the wilderness at bay. High above the lake towers the massive palace of the Maharanas. From its rooftop gardens and balconies, you can look over Lake Pichola, at the summer palace, 'adrift like a snowflake' in its centre. Around the lake, the houses and temples of the old city stretch out in a pale honeycomb making Udaipur an oasis of colour in a stark and arid region. ⋙ *For Sleeping, Eating and other listings see pages 397-408.*

Ins and outs

Getting there The airport, about 30-45 mins by taxi or City Bus from town, has flights from several cities. The main Bus Stand is east of Udai Pol, 2-3 km from most hotels, while Udaipur City Railway Station is another 1 km south. Both have auto-rickshaw stands outside as well as pushy hotel touts. Udaipur station to the north, is inconvenient.

To Ajmer & Mount Abu

To Shilpigram (8 km)

To Nathdwara & Jaipur

Udaipur Bari Rd

Fateh Sagar

Sahelion Ki Bari
Moti Magri Rd

Sukhadia Circle

Related map
A Jagdish Mandir area,
page 383

Moti Magri (640m)
Pratap Smarak
Rock Garden

Pedalos

To Rani Village Hotel & Shilpigram (8 km)

Nehru Island

Fateh Sagar Rd

Apollo Arts

Mohta Park
Bharatiya Lok Kala Museum

Saheli Marg

Pancholi

Stadium

Gem Arts

Chetak Circle
Hospital Rd

Laxmi Vilas Rd

Hathi Pol Rd

Residency Rd

Ashok Nagar Rd

Indian Airlines

Shastri Circle

To Ahar & Mahasati (3 km)

Sanjay Park

Rani Rd

(643m)

Swaroop Sagar

Amba Pol Rd

Hathi Pol

Ashwani Rd

Delhi Gate

Rang Sagar

Bari Badi Rd

Town Hall

Brahma Pol Rd

Shakti Vari Rd

Moti Chowta

Dhan Mandi Rd

Bapu Bazaar

To Pratap Country Inn (6 km), Airport (25 km) & Chittaurgarh

To Monsoo Palace, Sarijangarh (15 km)

Amba Pol

Lake Rd

Chand Pol

Bara Bazar
Oswal Bhawan Rd

Clock Tower

Suraj Pol

Bansi Ghat

City Palace

Jagdish Mandir

Rajika M Chotta

Bhatiyani Chotta

Gulab Bagh

Main State Bus Stand

Udai Pol

Jag Niwas Island

Vijay Cycles

Lake Palace Rd

Jag Mandir Island

Lake Pichola

Sajjan Niwas Garden

Regional Library

City Station Rd

Dud h

Kishan Pol

Sunset Point (640m)

Jal Burj

Udaipur City Station

NH8

To Ahmadabad & Shikarbadi Hotel (3 km)

Meera Kala Mandir

N

0 metres 300
0 yards 300

Sleeping
1 Chandra Prakash & Gulmohar D3
2 Dream Haven D2
3 Fateh Prakash & Shiv Niwas D2
4 Haveli D2
5 Hilltop Palace C2
6 Kajri C3
7 Lake Palace D2
8 Lakend C1
9 Lake Shore, Wonder View & Bharti Restaurant D2
10 Laxmi Vilas Palace C2
11 Mahendra Prakash D2
12 Mewar Inn B3
13 Natural C2
14 Pratap Palace C1
15 Queen's Café & Udai Kothi D1
16 Raj Palace, Kumbha Palace & Mona Lisa D2
17 Rajdarshan & Delhi Darbar Restaurant C2
18 Rang Niwas Palace & Palace View Restaurant D2
19 Ranjit Niwas D2
20 Sarovar D2
21 Yatri Guest House D3

Eating
1 Berrys C2
2 Chief D3
3 Garden Hotel & Haryali D3
4 Park View & Natraj D3
5 Sunset Terrace D2

Getting around The touristy area around the Jagdish temple and the City Palace, the main focus of interest, is best explored on foot but there are several sights further afield. City buses and unmetered auto-rickshaws cover the whole city and surrounding area. There are taxis too though some travellers prefer to hire a scooter or bike. It is best to reserve a hotel ahead or ask for a particular street or area of town. See Transport, page 406, for further details.

❧ Be prepared for the crowds, dirt and pollution and the persistent hotel touts who descend on new arrivals.

Climate Temperature: Summer, maximum 38°C, minimum 25°C. Monsoon Jun to Sep, average 175 mm. Best time to visit: Nov to Mar.

History

The **Ranas of Mewar** who traced their ancestry back to the Sun, first ruled the region from their seventh-century stronghold Chittaurgarh. In 1568, **Maharana Udai Singh**, founded a new capital on the shores of Lake Pichola and named it Udaipur ('The city of sunrise'), having selected the spot in 1559. On the advice of an ascetic who interrupted his rabbit hunt, Udai Singh had a temple built above the lake and then his palace around it. In contrast to the house of Jaipur, the rulers of Udaipur prided themselves on being independent from other more powerful regional neighbours, particularly the Mughals. In a piece of local princely one-upmanship, **Maharana Pratap Singh**, heir apparent to the throne of Udaipur, invited Raja Man Singh of Jaipur to a lakeside picnic. Afterwards he had the ground on which his guest had trodden washed with sacred Ganga water, and insisted that his generals take purificatory baths. Man Singh reaped appropriate revenge by preventing Pratap Singh from acceding to his throne. Udaipur, for all its individuality, remained one of the poorer princely states in Rajasthan, a consequence of being almost constantly at war. In 1818, Mewar, the kingdom of the Udaipur Maharanas, came under British political control but still managed to avoid almost all British cultural influence.

Sights

The Old City Udaipur is a traditionally planned fortified city. Its bastioned rampart walls are pierced by massive gates, each studded with iron spikes as protection against enemy war elephants. The five remaining gates are: **Hathi Pol** (Elephant Gate – north), **Chand Pol** (Moon Gate – west), **Kishan Pol** (south), the main entrance **Suraj Pol** (Sun Gate-east) and **Delhi Gate** (northeast). On the west side, the City is bounded by the beautiful Pichola Lake and to the east and north, by moats. To the south is the fortified hill of Eklingigarh. The main street leads from the Hathi Pol to the massive City Palace on the lake side.

The walled city is a maze of narrow winding lanes flanked by tall whitewashed houses with doorways decorated with Mewar folk art, windows with stained glass or jali screens, majestic *havelis* with spacious inner courtyards and shops. Many of the houses here were given by the Maharana to retainers – barbers, priests, traders and artisans while many rural landholders (titled *jagirdars*), had a *haveli* (townhouse) conveniently located near the palace.

The 18th to 19th-century **Bagore-ki-haveli** with 130 rooms was built as a miniature of the city palace with cool shady courtyards containing some peacock mosaic and fretwork, carved pillars made from granite, marble and the local blueish grey stone, and lime plastered walls. The museum (see below) has a beautiful collection of folk costumes, turbans, hookahs, local art and utensils. See also, Entertainment.

The **Jagdish Mandir**, 150 m north of the palace (1651), was built by Maharana Jagat Singh. The temple, currently being renovated, is a fine example of the Nagari style. A shrine with a brass *Garuda* stands outside and stone elephants flank the entrance steps; within is a black stone image of Vishnu as Jagannath, the Lord of the Universe.

★ **City Palace** ① *0920-1730, last entry 1630, from Ganesh Deori Gate: Rs 60 (more from near Lake Palace Ghat), camera Rs 75, video Rs 300; from 'Maharajah's gallery', you can get a pass for Fateh Prakash Palace, Shiv Niwas and Shambu Niwas, Rs 75. Guided tour takes about 1 hr, Rs 100 each. Crystal Gallery is open to guests only at lunch and dinner.* The impressive complex of several palaces is a blend of Rajput and Mughal influences. Half of it, with a great plaster façade, is still occupied by the royal family. Between the **Bari Pol** (Great Gate, 1600) to the north, and the **Tripolia Gate** (1713), are eight *toranas* (arches), under which the rulers were weighed against gold and silver on their birthdays, which was then distributed to the poor. Beyond the Tripolia the **Ganesh Deori Gate** leads south to the fine **Rai Angan** (Royal Courtyard, 1571), with the Jewel Room. From here you can wander through a number of picturesque palace enclosures of the *Mardana*, some beautifully decorated.

The attractive **Mor Chowk** court, intended for ceremonial *darbars*, was added in the mid-17th century, which has beautiful late 19th-century peacock mosaics. The throne room to its south, the **Surya Chopar**, from which the Rana (who claimed descent from the Sun), paid homage to his divine ancestor. To the Chowk's north, the **Chhoti Chitra Shali** has interesting blue tiles while the **Manak Mahal** (Ruby Palace) was filled with figures of porcelain and glass in the mid-19th century. The **Moti Mahal** (Pearl Palace) is a *sheesh mahal* decorated with mirrors which was added on the third level and has the small prayer room with illustrations of the Krishna legend. On either side of the Chowk are the women's quarters with shuttered windows which allowed the ladies to view the proceedings below. At the top level the breezy pavilions which open out to superb views, is the **Chini ki Chitra Mahal** (1711-34) which has fine ornamentation of Dutch and Chinese-made tiles counterpointed with mirror work. To the north, the **Bari Mahal** or Amar Vilas (1699-1711) was added on top of a low hill. It has a pleasant garden with full grown trees around a square water tank in the central court. The cloisters with cusped arches have wide eaves and is raised above the ground to protect the covered spaces from heavy monsoon rain. This was an intimate 'playground' where the royal family amused themselves and were entertained.

At the far end is the **Queen's Palace**, now exhibiting palanquins, howdahs and photos of British Residents. An exhibition traces the progress of a project to record the history of the Udaipur dynasty.

On the west side of the Tripolia are the **Karan Vilas** (1620-28) and **Khush Mahal**, a rather grotesque pleasure palace for European guests, whilst to the south lies the **Shambhu Niwas Palace** the present residence of the Maharana.

Maharana Fateh Singh added to this the opulent **Shiv Niwas** with a beautiful courtyard and public rooms, and the **Fateh Prakash Palace**. Here the **Darbar Hall**'s royal portrait gallery displays swords still oiled and sharp. The Bohemian

Jagdish Mandir area

Chand Pol
Gangor Ghat Rd
Moti Chotta
Bara Bazar
Clock Tower
Ganesh Chowk
Shreeji Sari Centre
Jagdish Mandir
Kilash Marg
Gangor Ghat
Motorbike Hire
Rang Niwas ki-Haveli Museum
Mewar International
Bhatiyani Chotta
Lake Pichola
Sai Books
Lal Ghat
To City Palace
To City Palace

N
0 metres 100
0 yards 100

Sleeping
1 Badi Haveli
2 Caravanserai
3 Evergreen & Lalghat Guest House
4 Gokul
5 Gyaneshwar Lodge
6 Jagat Niwas & Kankarwa Haveli
7 Jheel
8 Lake Ghat
9 Nukkad
10 Pratap Bhavan
11 Ratan Palace & Sai Niwas
12 Relish

Eating
1 Heaven
2 King Roof Café
3 Mayur

chandeliers (1880s) are reflected by Venetian mirrors, the larger ones made in India of lead crystal. Both, now exclusive hotels (see below), are worth visiting.

The **Crystal Gallery** on the first floor has an extensive collection of cut-crystal furniture, vases etc, made in Birmingham, England in the 1870s, supplemented by velvet, rich 'zardozi' brocade, objects in gold and silver and a precious stone-studded throne. See below for opening times.

Part of the City palace is a **government museum** with second century BC inscriptions, fifth to eighth-century sculpture and 9,000 miniature paintings of 17th- and 19th-century Mewar schools of art, but also a stuffed kangaroo and Siamese twin deer.

Fringed with hills, gardens, *havelis*, ghats and temples, Lake Pichola is the scenic focus of Udaipur though parts get covered periodically with vegetation. Set in it are the **Jag Niwas**, see below, and the **Jag Mandir Palaces**. The Jag Mandir in the south is notable for the Gul Mahal, a domed pavilion started by Karan Singh (1620-28) and completed by Jagat Singh (1628-52). It is built of yellow sandstone inlaid with marble around an attractive courtyard. Maharajah Karan Singh gave the young Prince Khurram (later Shah Jahan), refuge here when he was in revolt against his father Jahangir in 1623, cementing a friendly relationship between the Mewar Maharaja and the future Mughal Emperor. Refugee European ladies and children were also given sanctuary here by Maharana Sarap Singh during the Mutiny. There is a lovely pavilion with four stone elephants on each side (some of the broken trunks have been replaced with polystyrene!). You get superb views from the balconies.

An enjoyable **boat trip** ① *1-hr, on the hour, Rs 200, lands on Jag Mandir (worthwhile especially in the late afternoon light), or 30-min boat ride, Rs 100, not landing, Rs 25 for entering hotel complex!*, around the lake including a visit to Jag Mandir island, operates from Bansi Ghat (City Palace) Jetty.

★ **The Lake Palace** The **Jag Niwas** ① *visiting for non-residents: boat ticket from Bansi Ghat jetty with buffet meal, Rs 500-625 (see 'Eating'), some have found the meals disappointing, tour operators make block bookings so book in advance or try your luck at the jetty*, island has the Dilaram and Bari Mahal Palaces. They were built by Maharana Jagat Singh II in 1746 and cover the whole island. Once the royal summer residences (now a hotel), they seem to float like a dream ship on the blue waters of the lake. The courtly atmosphere, elegance and opulence of princely times, the painted ceilings, antique furniture combined with the truly magical setting make it one of the most romantic in India. Superb views.

The **Jal Burj** ① *auto from Jagdish Mandir to Sunset Point, Rs 20*, is on the water's edge, south of the town. A pleasant two-hour walk to the south of the city takes you to the Sunset Point which has excellent views. From the small **Dudh Talai** (Milk Lake) ① *Rs 5 day time, Rs 10 evening*, nearby, there is an attractive walk to the main lake, especially pleasant in the evening when large fruit bats can often be seen. A left turn up a new road leads to Manikya Lal Verma Park which has a 'musical fountain' which is switched on in the evening.

Other sights in the city Overlooking the Fateh Sagar is the **Moti Magri** (Pearl Hill) ① *Rs 10, camera free*. There are several statues of local heroes in the attractive rock gardens including one of Maharana Pratap on his horse Chetak, to which he owed his life. Local guides claim that Chetak jumped an abyss of extraordinary width in the heat of the battle of Haldighati (1576) even after losing one leg. See *Hero of Haldighati*, for further details.

Sahelion ki Bari (Garden of the Maids of Honour) ① *0900-1800, Rs 2, plus Rs 2 for 'fountain show'*, north of the city. Attractive and restful, this ornamental pleasure garden is a very pleasant spot. In a pavilion in the first courtyard opposite the entrance, a children's museum has curious exhibits including a pickled scorpion, a

human skeleton, and busts of Einstein and Archimedes! Beautiful black marble 385
kiosks decorate the corners of a square pool. An elegant round lotus pond has four
marble elephants spouting water.To the north is a rose garden with over 100 varieties.

Museums The 18th-19th-century **Bagore-Ki-Haveli** ① *Gangor Ghat, T523858, daily,
1000-1900, Rs 10*, has been superbly restored by the West Zone Cultural Centre.
Several rooms display typical furnishings, utensils, costumes, musical instruments
with interesting informative general notes. Examples of contemporary art and
exquisite marble carving are also displayed. Well maintained, interesting; worth a
visit. **Bharatiya Lok Kala Museum** ① *north of Chetak Circle, T529296, 0900-1800, Rs
10, camera Rs 50*, responsible for preservation of Rajasthani folk arts.

Excursions
Monsoon Palace ① *park, Rs 90 each plus rickshaw entry Rs 20, taxis minimum Rs
300 (tourist taxis Rs 450 including road toll), auto-rickshaws Rs 150 return, including
road toll at the foot of the hill (start from Udaipur by 1700 for sunset), allow about 3 hrs
for the round trip*. The deserted hilltop Monsoon Palace is 15 km west of Udaipur. The
unfinished building on **Sajjangarh**, which looks picturesque from the west facing
battlements, was named after Sajjan Singh (1874-84) and was planned to be high
enough to see his ancestral home, Chittaurgarh. Normally, you need a permit from the
police in town to enter though many find a tip to the gateman suffices ("huge doors
open at the sight of rupee notes!"). The palace itself is very run down but the views of
Udaipur from the hill top are just as good (though the highest roof is spoilt by radio
antennas). A visit in the late afternoon is recommended; take binoculars. Watch the
swifts return magically to their nests in the roof at the stroke of sunset.

Shilipgram ① *Rani Rd, northwest, near Havala (5 km) beyond Fateh Sagar, T31304,
daily, 1000-1800 in season, Rs 10, take a taxi or auto-rickshaw, if you cycle, you can
have a break and cold drink at the boat jetty on Nehru Island*. At this 'Crafts Village'
there are about 30 traditional huts from Rajasthan, Gujarat, Maharashtra and Goa,
faithfully replicated. The collection of colourful folk art, folk music and dancing makes
for an interesting outing. Crafts demonstrations (pottery, blockprinting, puppet
making, painting, sculpting etc) are held mostly at weekends and you can buy quality
items direct from the rural craftspeople. There are also outdoor performances by
dancers, musicians and puppeteers. *Utsav* (festival) is held from 24 December to 2
January when a visit is particularly rewarding. *Shilpi Café and Beer Bar* is good for
snacks. There is a spotless, well managed swimming pool where you can swim for Rs
100 (loungers, Rs 50). Short camel rides offered but are not recommended for women
alone ("camel driver may climb up behind you and behave most unpleasantly").
Allow two hours for a visit at weekends. **Bari Lake**, 12 km northwest, past Shilipgram,
is a clean lake in a quiet spot. A good place for a swim and picnic.

Jaisamand Lake (52 km southeast of Udaipur). Before the building of huge modern
dams in India, Jaisamand was the second largest artificial lake in Asia, 15 km by 10 km.
Dating from the late 17th century, it is surrounded by the summer palaces of the Ranis of
Udaipur. The highest two of the surrounding hills are topped by the **Hawa Mahal** and **Ruti
Rani** palaces, now empty but worth visiting for the architecture and the view. A small
sanctuary nearby has deer, antelope and panther. Tribals still inhabit some islands on
the lake. Crocodiles, keelback water snakes and turtles bask on other islands.

Bambora ① *From Udaipur go 12 km east along the airport road and take the right
turn towards Jaisamand Lake*. The imposing 18th-century hilltop fortress of Bambora,
45-minutes' drive south of Udaipur, has been converted at an enormous restoration
cost by the royal family of Sodawas, yet retaining its ancient character.

Rajasthan Southern Rajasthan Bambora

★ **Kumbhalgarh**, 64 km, and the superb Jain temples at ★ **Ranakpur**, 90 km, to the northwest can be visited allowing a whole day, see pages 389 and 391. This trip is highly recommended. Good value tours are available during the season. They are also en route to Deogarh and Jodhpur with interesting places to stay overnight.

South of Udaipur

Rishabdeo Rishabdeo, 63 km south of Udaipur off the NH8, has a remarkable 14th-century Jain temple with fine white marble carving and black marble statuary. Dedicated to the first Jain Tirthankar, Adinath or Rishabdev, Hindus, Bhils as well as Jains worship there; a small donation (Rs 10-20) is appreciated.

★ **Dungarpur** (Phone code: 02964. Colour map 2, grid C4. Population 50,000). Dungarpur (the 'City of Hills') dates from the 13th century. The district is the main home of the Bhil tribal people, see page 327. It is also renowned for its stone masons. The attractive and friendly village has one of the most richly decorated palaces in Rajasthan, the Juna Mahal. Surrounded on three sides by Lake Gaibsagar and backed by picturesque hills, the more recent **Udai Bilas Palace** (now a heritage hotel) was built by Maharawal Udai Singhji in the 19th century and extended in 1943. The huge courtyard surrounds a 'pleasure pool' with a four-storeyed carved pavilion in its centre.

The **Juna Mahal** ① *open to guests staying at Udai Bilas and by ticket (from Palace) for non residents, Rs 100, keep your own transport if not staying overnight, if the entrance half way up the hill is closed, try one at the top*, 2 km above the village, dates from the 13th century when members of the Mewar clan at Chittaur moved south to found a new kingdom after a family split. The seven-storeyed fortress-like structure with turrets, narrow entrances and tiny windows has colourful and vibrant rooms. There are some fine *jarokha* balconies and sculpted panels illustrating musicians and dancers in the local green-grey parava stone. The interior is profusely decorated with fine miniature wall paintings. There is a jewel of a *Sheesh Mahal* with glass and mirror inlay work while the Maharawal's bedroom on the top floor has a cupboard with scenes from the *Kama Sutra*. The fort ruins on the hilltop above the palace make an ideal picnic spot, offering panoramic views over the town.

Dungarpur is a **birdwatchers' paradise** with lots of ducks, moorhens, waders, ibises at the lake, and tropical green pigeons and grey hornbills in the woodlands. Some interesting **temples** nearby include the 12th-century Siva temple at **Deo Somnath**, 12 km away, and the splendid complex of temple ruins profusely decorated with stone sculptures.

Chittaurgarh (Chittor)

→ *Phone code: 01472. Colour map 2, grid B5. Population: 72,000.*

Chittaurgarh fort stands on a 152-m high rocky hill, rising abruptly above the surrounding plain. The walls, 5 km long, enclose the deserted ruins while the slopes are covered with scrub jungle. The modern town lies at the foot of the hill with access across a limestone bridge of 10 arches over the Gambheri River. ⤳ *For Sleeping, Eating and other listings see pages 397-408.*

History

One of the oldest cities in Rajasthan, Chittaurgarh was founded formally in 728 by Bappu Rawal, who according to legend was reared by the Bhil tribe. However, two sites near the River Berach have shown stone tools dating from half a million years ago and Buddhist relics from a few centuries BC. From the 12th century it became the centre of Mewar. Excavations in the **Mahasati** area of the fort have shown four shrines with ashes and charred bones, the earliest dating from about the 11th century AD.

Sights

The fort ① *Rs 100 from the Archaeological Survey Office, opposite Rana Kumbha's Palace, guide books are not always available so ask at* Panna Hotel, *visiting the fort on foot means a circuit of 7 km, allow 4 hrs, views from the battlements and towers are worth the effort,* dominates the city. Until 1568 the town was situated within the walls. Today the lower town sprawls to the west of the fort. The winding 1½-km ascent is defended by seven impressive gates: the Padal Pol (1) is where Rawat Bagh Singh, the Rajput leader, fell during the second siege; the Bhairon or Tuta (broken) Pol (2) where Jaimal, one of the heroes of the third siege, was killed by Akbar in 1567 (*chhatris* to Jaimal and Patta); the Hanuman Pol and Ganesh Pol; the Jorla or Joined Gate whose upper arch is connected to the Lakshman Pol; finally the Ram Pol (1459) which is the main gate. Inside the walls is a village and ruined palaces, towers and temples. This is where the young **Udai Singh** was saved by his nurse **Panna Dai**; she sacrificed her own son by substituting him for the baby prince when, as heir to the throne, Udai Singh's life was threatened.

On the right immediately inside the fort are the ruins of **Rana Kumbha's Palace (3)** (1433-68), originally built of dressed stone with a stucco covering. It is approached by

Chittaurgarh

Rajasthan Southern Rajasthan Chittaurgarh

0 metres 500
0 yards 500

N

■ Sleeping
1 Birla Rest House
2 Chetak
3 Janta Avas Grih
4 Meera
5 Natraj

6 Panna
7 Pratap Palace
8 Railway Retiring Rooms

○ Sights
1 Padal Pol
2 Bhairon Pol
3 Rana Kumbha's Palace, Nau Lakha Bandar & Archaeological Office

4 Khumbha Shyama & Mira Bai Temples
5 Sat Bis Deori Temple
6 Shringara Chauri Temple
7 Rana Ratan Singh's Palace
8 Fateh Prakash Palace & Museum
9 Vijay Stambha & Mahasati

10 Samadhishvara Temple
11 Palaces of Jaimal & Patta
12 Kalika Mata Temple & Chonda's House
13 Padmini's Palace
14 Adbhutanatha Temple
15 Kirti Stambha

⁚ The Jauhar – Rajput Chivalry

On three occasions during Chittaurgarh's history its inhabitants preferred death to surrender, the women marching en masse into the flames of a funeral pyre in a form of ritual suicide known as jauhar before the men threw open the gates and charged towards an overwhelming enemy and annihilation. The first was in 1303 when Ala-ud-din Khalji, the King of Delhi, laid claim to the beautiful Padmini, wife of the Rana's uncle. When she refused, he laid siege to the fort. The women committed jauhar, Padmini entering last, and over 50,000 men were killed in battle. The fort was retaken in 1313.

In 1535 Bahadur Shah of Gujarat laid claim to Chittaurgarh. Every Rajput clan lost its leader in the battle in which over 32,000 lives were lost, and 13,000 women and children died in the sacred jauhar which preceded the final charge.

The third and final sack of Chittaurgarh occurred only 32 years later when Akbar stormed the fort. Again, the women and children committed themselves to the flames, and again all the clans lost their chiefs as 8,000 defenders burst out of the gates. When Akbar entered the city and saw that it had been transformed into a mass grave, he ordered the destruction of the buildings.

In 1567, after this bloody episode in Chittaurgarh's history, it was abandoned and the capital of Mewar was moved to Udaipur. In 1615 Jahangir restored the city to the Rajputs.

two gateways, the large **Badi Pol** and the three-bay deep **Tripolia**. Once there were elephant and horse stables, zenanas (recognized by the jali screen), and a Siva temple. The jauhar committed by Padmini and her followers is believed to have taken place beneath the courtyard. The north frontage of the palace contains an attractive combination of canopied balconies. Across from the palace is the archaeological office and the **Nau Lakha Bhandar** (The Treasury; nau lakha – 900,000). The **temple** to Rana Kumbha's wife **Mira Bai (4)** who was a renowned poetess is visible from the Palace and stands close to the Kumbha Shyama Temple (both circa 1440). The older 11th-century Jain **Sat Bis Deori (5)** with its 27 shrines, is nearby. The **Shringara Chauri Temple (6)** (circa 1456), near the fort entrance, has sculptured panels of musicians, warriors and Jain deities.

Rana Ratan Singh's Palace (7) is to the north by the Ratneshwar Lake. Built in stone around 1530 it too had stucco covering. Originally rectangular in plan and enclosed within a high wall, it was subsequently much altered. The main gate to the south still stands as an example of the style employed.

The early 20th-century **Fateh Prakash Palace (8)** built by Maharana Fateh Singh (died 1930) houses a disappointing museum. To the south is the **Vijay Stambha (9)** (1458-68), one of the most interesting buildings in the fort, built by Rana Kumbha to celebrate his victory over Mahmud Khilji of Malwa in 1440. Visible for miles around, it stands on a base 14 m sq and 3 m high, and rises 37 m. The nine-storeyed sandstone tower has been restored; the upper section retains some of the original sculpture. For Re 0.50 you can climb to the top. Nearby is the **Mahasati** terrace where the ranas were cremated when Chittaurgarh was the capital of Mewar. There are also numerous sati stones. Just to the south is the **Samadhishvara Temple (10)** to Siva (11th and 15th centuries) with some good sculptured friezes. Steps down lead to the deep **Gomukh Kund**, where the sacred spring water enters through a stone carved as a cow's mouth (hence its name).

Of the two **Palaces of Jaimal and Patta (11)**, renowned for their actions during the siege of 1567, the latter, based on the zenana building of Rana Kumbha's Palace, is

more interesting. You then pass the **Bhimtal** before seeing the **Kalika Mata Temple**
(originally an eighth-century Surya temple, rebuilt mid-16th) with exterior carvings
and the ruins of **Chonda's House** with its three-storey domed tower. Chonda did not
claim the title when his father, Rana Lakha, died in 1421.

Padmini's Palace (late 13th century, rebuilt at the end of the 19th) is sited in the
middle of the lake surrounded by pretty gardens. Ala-ud-din Khilji is said to have seen
Padmini's beautiful reflection in the water through a mirror on the palace wall. This
striking vision convinced him that she had to be his.

You pass the deer park on your way round to the **Suraj Pol** (Sun Gate) and pass
the **Adbhutanatha Temple** to Siva **(12)** before reaching the second tower, the **Kirti
Stambha**, a Tower of Fame (13th, 15th centuries). Smaller than the Vijay Stambha (23
m) with only seven storeys, it is dedicated to Adinath, the first Jain Tirthankar. Naked
figures of Tirthankars are repeated several hundred times on the face of the tower. A
narrow internal staircase goes to the top.

Of particular interest are the number of tanks and wells in the fort that have
survived the centuries. Water, from both natural and artificial sources, was harnessed
to provide an uninterrupted supply to the people.

Bijaipur Bijaipur is a feudal village about 40 km northeast of Chittaurgarh. The
16th-century castle, set among the Vindhya hills, has a splendid location near the
Bassi-Bijaipur wildlife sanctuary which is home to panther, antelope and other
wildlife. The forests are interspersed with lakes, reservoirs, streams and waterfalls
with good birdlife in the winter months. The ruined Pannagarh Fort facing a lily
covered lake is believed to be one of the oldest in Rajasthan.

Rajsamand Lake At **Kankroli**, 56 km north of Udaipur on the NH8, is the Rajsamand
Lake. The Nauchoki Bund (embankment) has ornamental pavilions and toranas, all of
marble and exquisitely carved. On the southeast side of the lake is a beautiful temple.

★ **Deogarh** (Colour map 2, grid B4. Altitude: 700 m). Deogarh is an excellent place
to break journey between Jaipur and Udaipur to visit sights nearby. Some 2 km off the
NH8 about half way between Ajmer and Udaipur, it is a very pleasant, little frequented
town with a dusty but interesting bazar. Its elevation makes it relatively cool and the
countryside and surrounding hills are good for gentle treks. There is an old fort on a
hill as well as the Deogarh Mahal palace on a hillock in the centre with interesting
murals and mirror work. Raghosagar lake, which is very pleasant to walk around, has
an island with a romantic ruined temple and tombs. It attracts numerous migratory
birds and is an attractive setting for the charming 200-year-old palace, *Gokal Vilas*,
the private home of the present Rawat Saheb Nahar Singhji (a knowledgeable
historian and art connoisseur) and the Ranisahiba. Their two sons have opened the
renovated 17th-century Deogarh Mahal Palace to guests.

Kumbhalgarh and its surroundings

→ *Colour map 2, grid B4. 63 km from Udaipur.*
Little-known Kumbhalgarh is one of the finest examples of defensive fortification in
Rajasthan. You can wander round the palace, the many temples and along the walls to
savour the great panoramic views. It is two hours north of Udaipur through the attractive
Rajasthani countryside. The small fields are well kept, wherever possible irrigated from
the streams, Persian wheels and 'tanks' that are dotted across the landscape. A round
trip from Udaipur could also take in Eklingji and Nathdwara, or be extended to
Ghanerao and Ranakpur. ➤➤ *For Sleeping, Eating and other listings see pages 397-408.*

Eklingji ① *occasional buses go from Udaipur to Eklingji (22 km)*, is set in a deep ravine containing the Eklingji lake. *RTDC* run tours from Udaipur, 1400-1900. The white marble **Eklingji Temple** ① *0500-0700, 1000-1300 and 1700-1900, evenings draw crowds of worshippers (few tourists), no photography*, has a two-storey *mandapa* to Siva, the family deity of the Mewars. It dates from 734 AD but was rebuilt in the 15th century. Back street shops sell miniature paintings. Lots of waterbirds – and very quiet.

Delwara (25 km north of Udaipur). There is a 10th-century Jain temple with carved marble columns and sculpted ceilings here. A seven-storey fort palace has been converted to a heritage hotel,

Nathdwara ① *Several buses from Udaipur from early morning*. This is a centre of the Krishna worshipping community of Gujarati merchants who are followers of Vallabhacharya (15th century). Non-Hindus are not allowed inside the temple, but the outside has interesting paintings. The **Shrinathji temple** is one of the richest Hindu temples in India. At one time only high caste Hindus (Brahmins, Kshatriyas) were allowed inside, and the **pichhwais** (temple hangings) were placed outside, for those castes and communities who were not allowed into the sanctum to experience the events in the temple courtyard and learn about the life of Lord Krishna. You can watch the 400-year old tradition of pichchwais painting which originated here. The Bazar sells pichchwai painted on homespun cloth.

★ Kumbhalgarh Fort

Built mostly by Maharana Kumbha (circa 1485), it is situated on a west facing ridge of the Aravallis, commanding a great strategic position on the border between the Rajput kingdoms of Udaipur (Mewar) and Jodhpur (Marwar).It gives superb views over the lower land to the northwest, standing over 200 m above the pass leading via Ghanerao towards Udaipur. Though off the beaten tourist track, it is accessible enough to make a visit practicable passing though charming villages and hilly terrain. The final dramatic approach is across deep ravines and through thick scrub jungle. Kumbhalgarh Fort was the second most important fort of the Mewar Kingdom after Chittaurgarh.

The approaches Seven gates guarded the approaches while seven ramparts were reinforced by semicircular bastions and towers. The 36 km-long walls with curious bulbous towers exude a feeling of power as they snake their way up and down impossibly steep terrain.The walls enclose a large plateau containing the smaller Katargarh Fort with the decaying palace of Fateh Singh, a garrison, 365 temples and shrines, and a village. The occupants, reputedly 30,000, could be self-sufficient in food and water, with enough storage to last a year. Kumbhalgarh is believed to have been taken only once; and that too because the water in the ponds was poisoned by enemy Mughals during the reign of Rana Pratap.

The first gate **Arait Pol** is some distance from the main fort; the area was once thick jungle harbouring tigers and wild boar. Signals would be flashed by mirror in times of emergency. **Hulla Pol** (Gate of Disturbance) is named after the point reached by invading Mughal armies in 1567. **Hanuman Pol** contains a shrine and temple. The **Bhairava Pol** records the 19th-century Chief Minister who was exiled. The fifth gate, the **Paghra** (Stirrup) **Pol**, is where the cavalry assembled; the Star tower nearby has walls 8 m thick. The **Top-Khana** (Cannon Gate) is alleged to have a secret escape tunnel. The last, **Nimbu** (Lemon) **Pol** has the Chamundi temple beside it.

The palace It is a 30-minute walk, fairly steep in parts, from the car park to the roof of the Maharana's darbar hall. Tiers of inner ramparts rise to the summit like a fairytale castle, up to the appropriately named **Badal Mahal** (19th century) or Palace in the Clouds, with the interior painted in pastel colours. Most of the empty palace is usually unlocked (a *chaukidar* holds the keys). The views over the walls to the jungle-covered hillsides (now a wildlife reserve) and across the deserts of Marwar towards Jodhpur, are stunning. The palace rooms are decorated in a 19th-century style and some have attractive coloured friezes, but are unfurnished. After the maze-like palace at Udaipur, this is very compact. The **Maharana's palace** ① *US$2*, has a remarkable blue darbar hall with floral motifs on the ceiling. Polished chunar – lime – is used on walls and window sills, but the steel ceiling girders give away its late 19th-century age. A gap separated the *mardana* (men's) palace from the *zenana* (women's) palace. Some of the rooms in the zenana have an attractive painted frieze with elephants, crocodiles and camels. A circular Ganesh temple is in the corner of the *zenana* courtyard. A striking feature of the toilets was the ventilation system which allowed fresh air into the room while the toilet was in use.

Temples The Neelkantha, Kumbhaswami temples and Raimal's *chhatri* nearby, are worth visiting. The Mahadeva Temple (1458) in a gorge below contains black marble slabs inscribed with the history of Mewar.

Kumbhalgarh Wildlife Sanctuary The sanctuary to the west of the fort covering about 600 sq km has a sizeable wildlife population but you have to be extremely lucky to spot any big game in the thick undergrowth. Some visitors have seen bear, panther, wolf and hyena but most have to be contented with seeing nilgai, sambhar deer, wild boar, jackal, jungle cat and birds. Crocodiles and water fowl can be seen at Thandi Beri lake. Jeep and horse safaris can be organized from several hotels in the vicinity including *Aodhi*, Ranakpur, Ghanerao, Narlai.The rides can be quite demanding as the tracks are very rough. There is a four-wheel drive jeep track, and a trekking trail through the safari area (see *Shivika Lake Hotel*, Ranakpur, listed below). The tribal Bhils and Garasias (the latter found only in this belt) can be seen here, living in their traditional huts.

Ghanerao Ghanerao with its red sandstone *havelis* has a number of old temples, *baolis* and marble *chhatris*, 5 km beyond the reserve, was founded in 1606 by Gopal Das Rathore of the Mertia clan. The village lay at the entrance to one of the few passes through the Aravallis between the territories held by the Rajput princes of Jodhpur and Udaipur. The beautiful 1606 castle has marble pavilions, courtyards, faded paintings, wells, elephant stables and walls marked with canon balls. The present Thakur Sajjan Singh who has opened his castle to guests, organizes two to three day treks to Kumbhalgarh Fort, 18 km (50 km by jeepable road) and Ranakpur temples.The Mahavir Jain Temple, 5 km away, is a beautiful little 10th-century temple.

Rawla Narlai About 25 km from Kumbhalgarh Fort and one-hour's drive from Ranakpur, this Hindu and Jain religious centre has a 17th-century fort with interesting architecture, right in the heart of the village, which is ideal for a stop over.

★ Ranakpur

→ *90 km from Udaipur. 25 km southwest of Kumbhalgarh. Public transport or tours from Udaipur or Kumbhalgarh.* ① *Daily; closes for lunch about 1300 when you can get a good thali, Rs 15, in the dining hall. Non-Jains may visit the Adinatha only between 1100 and 1700 except lunchtime. Shoes and socks must be removed at the entrance. Black clothing is not permitted. The head priest helps to show people around, then asks for a donation. Photos (1200-1700) with permission from Kalyanji Anandji Trust office next to the temple, camera Rs 40, video Rs 150; photography of the principal Adinatha image is prohibited.*

You can approach Ranakpur through the wildlife reserve in 1½ hours. One of five holy Jain sites and a popular pilgrimage centre, it has one of the best known Jain temple complexes in the country. Though not comparable to the Dilwara temples in Mount

Abu, it has very fine ornamentation and is in a wonderful setting with peacocks, langurs and numerous birds. A visit is highly recommended.

The **Adinatha** (1439), the most noteworthy of the three main temples here, is dedicated to the first Tirthankar. The sanctuary is symmetrically planned around the central shrine and is within a 100 m sq raised terrace enclosed in a high wall with 66 subsidiary shrines lining it, each with a spire; the gateways consist of triple-storey porches. The sanctuary with a clustered centre tower contains a *chaumukha* (four-fold) marble image of Adinatha. The whole, including the extraordinary array of engraved pillars (1,144, and all different), carved ceilings and arches are intricately decorated, often with images of Jain saints, friezes of scenes from their lives and holy sites. The beautiful lace-like interiors of the corbelled domes are a superb example of western Indian temple style. The **Parsvanatha** and **Neminath** are two smaller Jain temples facing this, the former with a black image of Parsvanatha in the sanctuary and erotic carvings outside. The star-shaped **Surya Narayana Temple** (mid-15th century) is nearby.

The semi-enclosed deer park with spotted deer, nilgai and good birdlife next to the temple, attracts the odd panther!

★ Mount Abu

→ *Phone code: 02974. Colour map 2, grid B3. Population: 15,600. Altitude: 1,720 m.*

Mount Abu, Rajasthan's only hill resort, away from the congestion and traffic of the tourist centres on the plains, stretches along a 20-km long plateau. Many of the rulers from surrounding princely states had summer houses built here. Today, it draws visitors from Rajasthan who come to escape the searing heat of summer and also to see the exquisite Dilwara Jain temples. There is attractive countryside to explore as it is well wooded with flowering trees and numerous orchids during the monsoon, a good variety of birdlife but the town itself is tacky and unappealing. ⇥ *For Sleeping, Eating and other listings see pages 397-408.*

Ins and outs

Getting there The nearest railway station is at Abu Rd, 27 km away. It is often quicker to take a bus that will go all the way to Mount Abu, instead of going to Abu Rd by train and then taking a bus up the hill.

Getting around The compact area by Nakki Lake with several hotels, restaurants and shops, is pedestrianized. Taxis available at a stand nearby to get you to more distant hotels and to visit the Dilwara Temples if you don't feel up to the uphill hike. See Transport, page 407, for further details.

Background

Mount Abu was the home of the legendary sage **Vasishtha**. One day Nandini, his precious wish-fulfilling cow, fell into a great lake. Vasishtha requested the gods in the Himalaya to save her so they sent *Arbuda*, a cobra, who carried a rock on his head and dropped it into the lake, displacing the water, and so saved Nandini. The place became known as *Arbudachala*, the 'Hill of Arbuda'. Vasishtha also created the four powerful 'fire-born' Rajput tribes, including the houses of Jaipur and Udaipur at a ritual fire ceremony on the mount. **Nakki Talao** (Lake), sacred to Hindus, was, in legend, scooped out by fingernails (*nakki*) of gods attempting to escape the wrath of a demon.

Abu was leased by the British Government from the Maharao of Sirohi and was used as the HQ for the Resident of Rajputana until 1947, and as a sanatorium for troops. There are rowing boats for hire and a pleasant walk around the lake past the Raghunath Temple. The Toad Rock is here too; the other rock formations (Nandi and

Camel) are not as obvious. A local curiosity is a *baba gari* (a sort of pram), which is used as a small cart to transport goods, and occasionally children!

Sights

★ **Dilwara Jain Temples** ① *1200-1800 for non-Jains, free, no photography, some guides are excellent, shoes and cameras, leather items and backpacks (against tokens, Re 1 per item) are left outside, tip expected. It is 1-hr's uphill walk from town, or share a jeep, Rs 5 each, good* masala chai *available nearby.* Set in beautiful surroundings of mango trees and wooded hills, 5 km from town centre, the temples have superb marble carvings. The complex of five principal temples is surrounded by a high wall, dazzling white in the sunlight. There is a resthouse for pilgrims on the approach road. A notice warns "Any lady in monthly cycle if enters any of the temples she may suffer"!

Chaumukha temple, the grey sandstone three-storey building, is approached through the entrance on your left. Combining 13th- and 15th-century styles, it is generally regarded as inferior to the two main temples. The colonnaded hall (ground floor) contains four-faced images of the Tirthankar Parsvanatha (hence *chaumukha*), and figures of *dikpalas* and *yakshis*. Along the entrance avenue on the right is a statue of Ganesh.

Mount Abu

Sleeping
1 Aravalli
2 Cama Rajputana Club Resort
3 Ganesh
4 Hillock
5 Kashiva's Lake Residency
6 Palace (Bikaner House)
7 Sheraton & Veena Restaurant
8 Shikhar Tourist Bungalow
9 Sunrise Palace
10 Sunset Inn

Related map
A Mount Abu centre, page 396

Adinatha Temple (Vimala Shah Temple) lies directly ahead; the oldest and most famous of the Dilwara group. Immediately outside the entrance to the temple is a small portico known as the *Hastishala* (elephant hall), built by Prithvipal in 1147-59 which contains a figure of the patron, Vimala Shah, the Chief Minister of the Solanki King, on horseback. Vimala Shah commissioned the temple dedicated to Adinatha in 1031-32. The riders on the 10 beautifully carved elephants that surround him were removed during Alauddin Khilji's reign. Dilwara belonged to Saivite Hindus who were unwilling to part with it until Vimala Shah could prove that it had once belonged to a Jain community. In a dream, the goddess Ambika (Ambadevi or Durga) instructed him to dig under a *champak* tree where he found a huge image of Adinatha and so won the land. To the southwest, behind the hall, is a small shrine to *Ambika*, once the premier deity.

In common with many Jain temples the plain exterior conceals a wonderfully ornately carved interior. It is an early example of the Jain style in West India, set within a rectangular court lined with small shrines and a double colonnade. The white marble of which the entire temple is built was brought not from Makrana, as some guide books suggest, but from the relatively nearby marble quarries of Ambaji in Gujarat, 25 km south of Abu Road. Hardly a surface is left unadorned. *Makaras* guard the entrance, and below them are conches. The cusped arches and ornate capitals are beautifully designed and superbly made.

Lining the walls of the main hall are 52 shrines. Although the carvings themselves are simple, the ceiling panels in front of the saints' cells are very ornate. Going clockwise round the cells, the more important ceiling sculptures illustrate: **Cell 1** lions, dancers and musicians; **2-7** people bringing offerings, birds, music making; **8** Jain teacher preaching; **9** the major auspicious events in the life of the Tirthankars; and **10** Neminath's life, including his marriage, and playing with Krishna and the gopis. In the southeast corner of the temple between cells **22** and **23** is a large black idol of Adinath, reputedly installed by Vimal Shah in 1031. By cell **32** Krishna is shown subduing Kaliya Nag, half human and half snake, and other Krishna scenes; **38** the 16 armed goddess Vidyadevi (goddess of knowledge); **46-48** 16 armed goddesses, including the goddess of smallpox, Shitala Mata; and **49** Narasimha, the 'man-lion' tearing open the stomach of the demon Hiranya-Kashyapa, surrounded by an opening lotus.

Dilwara Temples, Mount Abu

Neminatha (Luna Vasahi) Temple

Digambara Temple

Risah Deo (Adinatha) Temple

Adinatha (Vimala Shah) Temple

Entrance

Chaumukha (Parsvanatha) Temple

N

0 metres 20
0 yards 20

1 Ganesh
2 Office & Guidebooks
3 Hastishala (Elephant Portico)
4 Ambika Shrine
5 Adinatha Shrine

66 99 If you have another 1½ hours, walk up to Jai Gurudev's meditation eyrie – gurus always choose good views!

As in Gujarati Hindu temples, the main hall focuses on the sanctum which contains the 2½-m image of Adinatha, the first Tirthankar. To its east is the *Mandapa*, a form of octagonal nave nearly 8 m in diameter. Its dome is supported by eight slender columns; the exquisite lotus ceiling carved from a single block of marble rises in 11 concentric circles, carved with elaborately repeated figures. Superimposed across the lower rings are 16 brackets carved in the form of the goddesses of knowledge.

Risah Deo Temple, opposite the Vimala Visahi, is unfinished. It encloses a huge brass Tirthankar image weighing 4.3 tonnes and made of *panchadhatu* (five metals) – gold, silver, copper, brass and zinc. The temple was commenced in the late 13th century but building activity was curtailed by war with Gujarat and never completed.

Luna Visahi or **Neminatha Temple** (1231) to the north of the Adinatha Temple, was erected by two wealthy merchants and dedicated to the 22nd Tirthankar. The niches on either side of the sanctum's entrance were for their wives. The decorative carving and *jali* work here are excellent. The small domes in front of the shrine containing the bejewelled Neminatha figure, the exquisitely carved lotus on the *sabhamandapa* ceiling and the sculptures on the colonnades are noteworthy.

There is a fifth temple for the **Digambar** ('sky-clad') Jains which is far more austere.

Walks **Trevor's Tank** ① *Rs 5, Rs 80 (foreigners), car/jeep taken up to the lake Rs 125*, 500 m beyond the Dilwara Jain temples, is the small wildlife sanctuary covering 289 sq km with the lake which acts as a watering hole for animals including sloth bear, sambhar, wild boar and panther. Most of these are nocturnal but on your walk you are quite likely to see a crocodile basking on the rocks. The bird life is extensive with eagles, kites, grey jungle fowl, red spurfowl, francolin, flycatchers, bulbuls etc seen during walks on the trails in the sanctuary. There are superb views from the trails that lead through the park.

Adhar Devi, 3 km from town, is a 15th-century Durga temple carved out of a rock and approached by 220 steep steps. There are steep treks to Anandra point or to a Mahadev temple nearby for great views.

Around **Nakki Lake** Honeymoon Point, and Sunset Point to the west, give superb views across the plains. They can both be reached by a pleasant walk from the bus stand (about 2 km). You can continue from Honeymoon Point to Limbdi House. If you have another 1½ hours, walk up to Jai Gurudev's meditation eyrie – gurus always choose good views! If you want to avoid the crowds at Sunset Point, take the Bailey's Walk from the Hanuman Temple near Honeymoon Point to Valley View Point which joins up with the Sunset Point walk. You can also walk from the Ganesh temple to the Crags for some great views.

The headquarters of the Spiritual University movement of the **Brahma kumaris** is **Om Shanti Bhavan**, T38268, with its ostentatious entrance on Subhash Road. You may notice many residents dressed in white taking a walk around the lake in the evening. It is possible to stay in simple but comfortable rooms with attached baths and attend discourses, meditation sessions, yoga lessons etc; good vegetarian meals are provided. The **Spiritual Museum** ① *0800-2000*, near the pony stand by the lake, also offers meditation and Raja yoga courses. The charitable trust runs several worthy institutions including a really good hospital.

The **Aravalli Hills**, part of the subcontinent's oldest mountain range, look more like rocky outcrops, in places quite barren save for date palms and thorny acacias. From Mount Abu it is possible to make day-treks to nearby spots.

Achalgarh, 11 km away, has superb views. The picturesque **Achaleshwar Temple** (ninth century) is believed to have Siva's toeprint, a brass Nandi and a deep hole claimed to reach into the underworld. On the side of Mandakini tank near the car park is an image of Adi Pal, the Paramara king and three large stone buffaloes pierced with arrows. In legend, the tank was once filled with *ghee* and the buffaloes, really demons in disguise, came every night to drink from it until they were shot by Adi Pal. A 10-minute climb up a path leads up to a group of carved Jain temples.

Guru Shikhar(1,720 m) is the highest peak in the area and there is a road almost to the top. Taxis from Mount Abu take about an hour. To get to the small Vishnu temple you need to climb 300 steps or hire a palanquin. There are good views especially at dawn.

Gaumukh (Cow's Mouth), 8 km southeast, on the way to Abu Road, has a small stream flowing from the mouth of a marble cow. There is also a Nandi bull, and the tank is believed to be the site of Vasishtha's fire from which the four great Rajput clans were created. An image of the sage is flanked by ones of Rama and Krishna.

The **Arbuda Devi Temple**, carved out of the rocky hillside, is also worth walking to for the superb views over the hills.

Bera ⓘ *Trains from Mumbai and Ajmer via Abu Rd (Aravalli and Ranakpur Exp) stop at Jawai Dam and Mori Bera*. About 34 km from Sirohi, the large panther population in the surrounding hills and the Jawai river area draws wildlife photographers; there are also antelopes and jackals. Visit the **Jawai Dam**, 150 km from Mount Abu towards Jodhpur, to see historic embankments, numerous birds and basking marsh crocodiles.

Mount Abu centre

Sleeping ■	5 Lake Palace	10 Samrat International	2 Kanak
1 Abu International	6 Maharaja International	& Navjivan	3 King's Food
2 Connaught House	& Restaurant	11 Suruchi	4 Madras Café
3 Hilltone Madhuban &	7 Maharana Pratap		5 Neelam
Tourist Guest House	8 Mount	**Eating** ●	6 Sher-e-Punjab
4 Kesar Bhavan Palace	9 Rajendra	1 Haveli	7 Veena

0 metres 100
0 yards 100

Jalor ① *Trains from Jodhpur and Ahmadabad.* Some 160 km north of Mount Abu, Jalor is an historic citadel. In the early 14th century, the Afghani Diwan of Marwar, Alauddin Khilji, took over the town and set up his own kingdom. Later, the Mughal Emperor Akbar captured it and returned the principality to his allies, the Rathores of Marwar. The medieval fort straddles a hill near the main bazar and encloses some shrines. It is a steep climb up but the views from the fort are rewarding. Jalor bazar is good for handicrafts, silver jewellery and textiles.

Bhenswada ① *Trains and buses from Abu Rd.* Bhenswada, a small, colourful village on the Jawai River, 16 km east of Jalor, has another Rajput country estate whose 'castle' with a Hawa Mahal, Zenana Chowk and Sirai Mahal, has been converted into an attractive hotel. The jungles and hills nearby have panther, nilgai, chinkara, blackbuck, jungle cat, jackal, porcupines and spiny tailed lizards.

Listings: Southern Rajasthan

● Sleeping

Udaipur *p380, maps p381 and p383*
Travellers gravitate towards Lalghat and the Jagdish Mandir area for best views of the lake.
LL-L Fateh Prakash (HRH), City Palace, T528016, F528006, sales@hrhindia.com. 9 rooms (US$150) and 7 suites (US$300), period furniture, restaurant (see below), facilities of *Shiv Niwas*, good service (residents may ask for a 'Pass' at entrance of City Palace, for a short cut to hotel).
LL-L Lake Palace (Taj), Pichola Lake, T528800, F528700, jaideep.khanna@tajhotels.com. 84 rooms, most with lake view, superb situation (see Sights above), an experience, excellent suites and service (see Eating).
L Shiv Niwas (HRH), City Palace (right after entrance), T528016, F528006, sales@hrhindia. com. 19 rooms (US$125), 17 suites (US$300-600), some with superb lake views, very comfortable, good restaurant, pleasant outdoor seating for all meals around a lovely marble pool (non-residents pay Rs 300 to swim), tennis, squash, excellent service, beautiful surroundings, reserve ahead in season.
L-AL Trident (Oberoi), overlooking Lake Pichola, peaceful far side, T432200, F432211, www.oberoihotels.com. Tastefully decorated, all facilities, good pool, varied restaurants, polite but friendly, lush gardens, un-pretentious, relaxing, own ferry to City Palace.
AL Laxmi Vilas Palace (ITDC), T529711 F526273, on hillock above Fateh Sagar, 5 km station. 54 rooms (45 a/c), built as royal guesthouse, still atmospheric, good pool (non-residents, Rs 175), tennis.

A-B Hilltop Palace, 5 Ambavgarh near Fateh Sagar, T432245, F432136. 55 rooms (large rooms upstairs with balcony), restaurant (visit for a view from the roof!), bar, exchange, pool, good food, friendly and efficient service.
B Rajdarshan, 18 Pannabai Marg, inside Hathi Pol against the walls, by the lake edge, T526601, F524588. 52 rooms, very good restaurant, bar, exchange, pool, good views from balconies, pleasant service.
B Shikarbadi (HRH), Govardhan Vilas, Ahmadabad Rd (5 km from centre), T583201, F584841. 26 good, re-furbished a/c rooms, 9 (C) deluxe tents, pool, horse riding (Rs 150 per 40 mins), 100-year old royal hunting lodge and stud farm with lake, lovely gardens, deer park.
B-C Jagat Niwas, 24-25 Lalghat (on the lake), T415547, F560414. 21 individual, very clean rooms, most with bath (some rooms are tiny "windowless cupboards"), beautifully restored 17th-century "fairy tale" *haveli*, very good restaurant, helpful staff, good travel desk, excellent service. Recommended.
  Equally comfortable rooms in the neighbouring *Hotel Jagat Niwas Palace.*
B-C Udai Kothi, Hanuman Ghat, outside Chandpol, T432180, F430412, udaikothi@ yahoo.com. Elegant, comfortable rooms, fabulous roof top with pool and restaurant.
C Kankarwa Haveli, 26 Lalghat, T411457, F521403. 3 mins from bazar, quiet, impressive views from terrace, 14 rooms with baths in renovated 250-year old *haveli* on lake shore, breakfast and snacks on the roof terrace, meals on request, family run.
C Pratap Palace, on Fateh Sagar, T431701, F431700. Good rooms, some a/c, most with

lake views, attractive hotel, lawns, peaceful, very friendly.

C Sarovar, 1 Panchdevri Marg, Hanuman Ghat, T432801, F431732, www.hotelsarovar.com. 21 rooms on 3 floors in a new hotel, 13 overlook Lake Pichola (3 **B** are a/c), clean and comfortable, rooftop restaurant, sunbathing terrace, free use of good pool near Shilipgram.

C-D Caravanserai (*Jaiwana Haveli*, part mid-18th century), 14 Lal Ghat (wrought iron gates lead into small garden), T411103, F521252. 24 rooms, some cramped, better in rear of main building (larger and with views), average food, bar, lots of stairs.

C-D Lakend, Alkapuri, Fateh Sagar, T431400, F431406. 85 rooms, some a/c, pool, modern with large lakeside garden, reasonably attractive rooms with balconies, very peaceful, excellent views (plans to extend into luxury hotel).

C-D Vinayak, 39-40 Kalaji Goraji, T522166, near Gulab Bagh. Very central, beautiful gardens, quiet, big rooms, friendly management, popular with Indian guests.

C-D Wonder View, 6 Panchdevri Marg, T522996, F415287. 8 rooms on 4 floors (newish matchbox-like building) but with good views especially from rooftop with restaurant (food arrives slowly from ground floor kitchen!), friendly, peaceful and relaxed part of town.

D Fountain, Sukhadia Circle, T560290, F527549. 30 rooms, most a/c with TV, lawn, very popular.

D Kajri (RTDC), Shastri Circle, T410501. 53 rooms, some a/c and dorm, deluxe overlooking garden best, dull restaurant, Tourist Reception Centre.

D Pratap Bhawan, 12 Lal Ghat, T560566, F415015, pratapbhawan@usa.net. 8 large, clean rooms with baths in lovely guesthouse, lake-facing terrace restaurant, excellent, home-cooked meals, warm welcome from retired army colonel and his wife.

On Lake Palace Rd

B-C Rang Niwas Palace, T523891, F520294. 24 well-renovated rooms with bath, some a/c, and some in annexe, restaurant, very pleasant pool (non-residents, Rs 100), gardens, very helpful staff, old-world and charming but near busy road junction.

D-E Haveli, T528294. Some rooms with bath tub, courtyard, clean, very helpful manager.

D-E Mahendra Prakash, T529370. 15 large, spotless but simple rooms (hot water), some a/c, pleasant patio garden, excellent pool, friendly, excellent service.

Paying guest accommodation list at Tourist Reception Centre, Fateh Memorial.

Budget hotels Lal Ghat area
(Narrow, quiet streets)

D Sai Niwas, 75 Navghat, T421586, F450009, www.hotelsainivas.com. Redecorated in Rajasthani style, rooms with bath and hot water, beautiful roof-terrace with good views.

D-E Jheel Guest House, 56 Gangor Ghat (behind temple), T28321. Pleasant rooms, dearer in new extension with bath and hot water and some views, best view rooms Rs 400 (No 1 has enormous mirrors!), good rooftop restaurant.

D-E Mughal Palace, T417954, shanu_21@ yahoo.com. Clean rooms with bath, Indian terrace restaurant, solar power, internet, specially for artists, exhibitions.

D-E Ratan Palace, 21 Lal Ghat (down alley going south past *Lalghat GH*), T561153. Spotless rooms with bath (size varies), constant hot water, 'unfinished' feel, rooftop restaurant (lacks ambience), very helpful, friendly manager, efficient travel bookings, "attracts more mature travellers", good value.

E Evergreen, 32 Lal Ghat. 7 rooms, good rooftop restaurant, clean, quiet and relaxed, western visitors only, "bit of a 'scene'", avoid tours and safaris.

E Lake Ghat, 4/13 Lalghat, 150 m behind Jagdish Mandir T521636. Some good rooms, clean, friendly, superb view from terraces, good food.

E Relish, 60 Gadiya Devra, excellent rooftop restaurant with 6 clean rooms with bath.

E-F Badi Haveli, near Jagdish Temple, T412588. 8 rooms with bath, some good, restaurant, travel (Ranakpur and Kumbhalgarh, 0800-1900, Rs 250), terraces with lake view, pleasant atmosphere, very friendly owner.

E-F Lalghat Guest House, 33 Lal Ghat, T525301. Best rooms with marble bath recommended, cheaper have no window, **F** dorm (Rs 80) good clean beds with curtains(!), spotless baths, breakfast, snacks,

Rajasthan Listings: Southern Rajasthan

good views from terraces, very relaxed, good travel desk.

F Gyaneshwar Lodge, Gangor Ghat Rd, Lalghat Corner. Friendly with cheap veg food at *Namaste* restaurant.

F Nukkad Guest House, 56 Ganesh Ghat (signposted from Jagdish Temple). 9 small, simple rooms (from Rs 50), some with bath, in typical family house, home cooked meals, rooftop, very friendly and helpful, clean.

Bhatiyani Chotta

D-E Raj Palace, at 103, T527092. Clean rooms with bath (best **C**) and dorm, restaurant, garden, comfortable beds, excellent service, city tour, Rs 120.

E Kumbha Palace, at 104, T422702. 8 rooms, clean, good linen, quiet, very good rooftop restaurant (see below), atmospheric, good views, attractive, riding (Rs 600).

F Mona Lisa, at 104, T561562. Some rooms air-cooled, with bath, good breakfast, garden, pleasant and quiet, family run, good value.

Lake Palace Rd area

E Gulmohar, 9 Sheetla Marg, T422857. 16 rooms, pleasant and obliging staff, near Gulab Bagh but can be noisy.

E Ranjit Niwas, Kalaji Goraji Temple Rd, T525774. 14 rooms some with hot shower, some cheaper and **F** dorm, in quiet residential area, small garden, good views from rooftop, village safaris organized, friendly atmosphere

F Chandra Prakash (near Sajjan Niwas Garden), T422909. Some rooms with bath, clean, quiet, food good value, helpful manager.

Elsewhere

E Dream Haven, 22 Bhim Parmeshvar Marg, just over Chandpol, on the edge of the lake. 6 clean, simple rooms with bath, family run, no frills but excellent rooftop restaurant.

E Dream Palace, Saheliyon ki Bari Rd, T527227. Decent rooms (some **D** a/c), modern facilities, restaurant, small garden but pleasant hotel.

E Lake Star, 80 Naga Nagri, outside Chand Pol. Clean comfortable rooms with shower, breathtaking views, rooftop restaurant, super friendly and helpful family.

E-F Island Tower, 10 Nag Marg, outside Chand Pol. 14 clean rooms (avoid street side Rs 200 with shower), roof restaurant with brilliant views, quiet, peaceful, friendly, helpful, geared to tourist needs.

E-F Natural, 55 Rang Sagar (between New and Chand Pol bridges), T431979, hotelnatural@yahoo.co.in. 15 rooms with hot showers, sunny balconies facing lake, good restaurant (see below), good puppet show (1930), peaceful, "a home from home".

F Mewar Inn, 42 Residency Rd (pleasantly away from centre), T522090, F525002, mewarinn@hotmail.com. Rooms vary, some with (brief!) hot shower best (Rs 99), very clean but street side incredibly noisy, no commission to rickshaws (if they refuse to go; try a horse carriage!), *Osho* veg restaurant, bike hire, rickshaw to town Rs 10-20, very friendly, YHA discounts.

F Queens Café,14 Bajrang Marg (first left after Chand Pol), T430875. 2 decent rooms, shared bath, roof terrace with good views, tasty home cooked meals (Indian, continental), welcoming family, homely.

Near the bus stand

D-E Pathik, City Station Rd, T483080. 17 rooms most a/c, with bath (hot water), TV, phone, restaurant, travel desk, crowded area, lots of bus traffic.

E Yatri Guest House, 3/4 Panchkuin Rd, Udaipol, T27251. Simple rooms, helpful, knowledgeable owner.

Jaisamand Lake *p385*

B Jaisamand Island Resort, Baba Island, T02906 2222. 40 well-equipped a/c rooms, pool and garden. Excellent location with great views but mixed reports on food and service.

Bambora *p385*

B Karni Fort, Heritage Hotel, T512101, F512105, www.karnihotels.com. Beautifully decorated rooms, marble bathrooms, impressive modernized interiors, courtyards, fountains, friendly manager, exceptional marble swimming pool, idyllic "in the middle of nowhere". Reservations on T0291-433320, F433495, welcome@ndf.vsnl.net.in.

Dungarpur *p386*

B Udai Bilas Palace, 2 km from town, T30808, F31008, www.udaibilaspalace.com. 19 unique a/c rooms (3 suites are vast), some with mirror mosaics and art deco furniture, others in old guesthouse, all with lake or garden view, beautiful swimming pool, boating, idyllic setting, very peaceful and relaxing.

E-F Vaibhav, Saghwara Rd, T30244. Simple rooms, tea stall style restaurant, owner very friendly and helpful.

Chittaurgarh *p386, map p387*
Chittaurgarh has few hotels and changing money can be a problem. Udaipur has a better choice.

C-D Padmini, Chanderiya Rd, near Sainik School on the outskirts, T41718, F40072, hotel_padmini@rediff.mail 45 clean rooms, 15 a/c, good Indian restaurant, large grounds, horse riding.

C-D Pratap Palace, Sri Gurukul Rd, near Head Post Office, T/F40099, hpratap@ hotmail.com. Pleasant, dated but fairly clean rooms, some a/c, good food in restaurant or in pleasant garden.

D-E Meera, near the railway station, T41427, F40466. 26 rooms, 8 a/c (some **C** with tubs) with TV and phone, restaurant (Gujarati/north Indian) and dimly lit, well-stocked bar, shoe-shine and barber on the landing!

D-E Panna (RTDC), Udaipur Rd, near railway station, T40842, F43942. 31 simple rooms, a/c best with fort view (4 with Western toilets), dorm, veg dining hall, run down but attentive service.

D-F Chetak, opposite railway station (a short walk past transport offices), T41588. Modern hotel, 23 clean, fairly pleasant rooms (various categories), only 'deluxe' have Western toilets and hot showers.

E Janta Avas Grih (RTDC), Station Rd, T41089. 4 simple, rooms with bath, restaurant.
Best places to eat are in hotels.

Bijaipur *p389*
B Castle Bijaipur, is a Heritage Hotel, T/F01472-40099, www.castlebijaipur.com, with 24 rooms decorated in traditional style – comfortable furniture and modern bathrooms in the new wing, small rooms in the original castle – pleasant garden, hill views from breezy terrace, Rajasthani meals, jeep/horse safaris with camping.

Deogarh *p389*
A-B Deogarh Mahal, T02951-52777, F52555, www.deogarhmahal.com. In superb old fort, 36 rooms, atmospheric suites furnished in traditional style with good views (Royal and Honeymoon suites – "like sleeping in a jewel box" – and a railway carriage!), attached

baths, excellent lotus shaped pool, Mewari meals in the courtyard, home grown produce, bar, folk entertainment, boating, bird watching, jeep safaris, nostalgic local railway journeys, hospitable and delightful hosts, well run. Outstanding hotel, highly recommended, reserve ahead.

E Deogarh Motel, T52011. 4 clean rooms with bath, reasonable refreshments.

Eklingji *p390*
B Heritage Resort, T0294-440382, is in a fabulous location by lake ringed by hills, excellent a/c rooms, contemporary building in traditional design, good food, pool, boating, riding, good walking and cycling, pleasanter to stay here for seeing Udaipur.

F Guest House, very basic.

Delwara *p390*
AL Devigarh, T02953-89211, F89357, www.deviresorts.com. 23 unique suites, ultra- modern interiors, restrained minimalist decor, comfortable but unconventional for Rajasthan and devoid of local colour (literally!), good heated pool and health spa.

Nathdwara *p390*
C-D Pratap Palace (Heritage Resort), 5 km from temple, rooms and suites with hot water and Western toilets in a restored *haveli*, carved balconies, pool, gym, camel/jeep/horse safaris, treks.

D-E Gokul (RTDC), near Lalbagh, 2 km from bus stand, T02953-30917. 6 rooms and dorm (Rs 50), restaurant.

Kumbhalgarh Fort *p389*
Government Rest Houses and school hostels nearby may have rooms available.

A Aodhi (HRH), isolated, 2 km from fort gate, T02954-42341, F42349. 26 renovated rooms, modern stone "cottages" (hot water bottles in bed), heaters in winter, Room 19 recommended (long climb), good restaurant ("sumptuous meal when Udaipur Maharana is in residence"), pool for the really hardy only in winter, disastrous laundry, very helpful staff, TCs exchanged, fabulous views, very quiet, superb horse safaris (US$200 per night), trekking, tribal village tours.

B Kumbhalgarh Fort, en route Kelwara to Kumbhalgarh, T02954-42057. 24 rooms with modern facilities, superb location with hill,

lake and valley views, garden, tented dining area, bar, exchange, pool, cycle hire, riding.
C Ratnadeep, Kelwara, in the middle of a bustling village, T02954-42217, F42340. 8 clean rooms, some a/c, modern with TV, western toilets, small lawn, camel, horse and jeep safaris.

Ghanerao *p391*
C Royal Castle, Ghanerao, Dist Pali, T02934-84035. Decidedly rustic 'castle', 20 simple rooms with renovated baths (geysers), pricey **B** suites, restaurant (simple food), a bit run down but has nostalgic appeal of faded glory, charming hosts, jeeps and camping arranged.
E Bagha-ka-Bagh (Tiger's Den), 4 km from castle. Spartan hunting lodge among tall grass jungle near wildlife sanctuary gate, 10 very basic rooms, 5 with bucket hot water, dorm, generator for electricity, breathtaking location, wildlife (including panther, nilgai), rich birdlife, treks to Kumbhalgarh, Ranakpur. Contact *North West Safaris*, T/F079-6302019, F6300962, ssibal@ad1.vsnl.net.in.

Rawla Narlai *p391*
C Fort Rawla Narlai, T82425. Has 12 rooms individually decorated with antiques in the renovated fort, new showers, good simple meals under the stars, helpful, friendly staff (in need of new uniforms), attractive garden setting, good riding, contact *Ajit Bhawan*, T0291-511410, F510674.

Ranakpur *p391*
B Maharani Bagh (WelcomHeritage), Ranakpur Rd (4 km north), Sadri, T02934-3705, www.welcomheritage.com. 19 well-furnished modern cottages in lovely 19th-century walled orchard of Jodhpur royal family, outdoor restaurant (traditional Marwari buffets Rs 325), pool.
C Shivika Lake Hotel, near the lake in pleasant jungle setting. 10 modest but clean rooms with baths, hot water, 2 tents with shared bath, delicious Rajasthani food (limited veg; power cuts pose problems despite generators), treks, jeep safaris with spotter guide in Kumbhalgarh sanctuary; personal attention, friendly hosts. Reservations: *North West Safaris* T079-6302019, F6300962, nwsafaris@hotmail.com.
D-E Hotel Castle, cottage rooms in jungle setting, moderately priced lunch stop en route.

D-E Shilpi (RTDC), on a hillock, T02934-3674. 12 clean rooms, best with hot water, dorm (dirty), veg meals.
F Dharamshala, some comfortable rooms, simple and extremely cheap veg meals.

Mount Abu *p392, maps p393 and p396*
Prices (as given) shoot up during *Diwali*, Christmas week and summer (20 Apr to 20 Jun) when many **D-F** hotels triple their rates; meals, ponies and jeeps too cost a lot more. Off-season discounts vary between 30-70%. Touts can be a nuisance to travellers at the Bus Stand.
A-B Cama Rajputana Club Resort (Heritage), T38205, F38412. Refurbished old club house (1895) for Mount Abu's royal and British residents, guests become temporary members, 40 rooms in split level cottages with views, 2 period suites, average restaurant, eco-friendly (recycled water, alternative energy), beautifully landscaped gardens, billiards, tennis etc, efficient service.
A-B Hillock, opposite petrol pump, T38463, F38467. 36 rooms, restaurant (excellent *kebabs*), exchange, garden, modern, small pool, efficient, clean and well presented if slightly anonymous, pleasant setting.
A-B Hilltone, set back from road near *Hillock*, T38391, F38395. 68 rooms (some a/c, heaters), good *Handi* restaurant, exchange, pool, garden, quiet.
B Connaught House (WelcomHeritage), Rajendra Marg, uphill opposite bus stand, T38560. British Resident of Jodhpur's colonial bungalow, 14 pleasantly old-fashioned rooms (royal memorabilia), modern rooms in quieter new cottage, restaurant (average à la carte, good Rajasthani meals on order for Rs 250), trekking with guide, gardens filled with birds, managed by royal family, reservations www.welcomheritage.com.
B Palace Hotel (Heritage), Bikaner House, Dilwara Rd, 3 km from centre, T38673, F38674. 38 large rooms with period and reproduction furniture in Swinton Jacob's imposing 1894 hunting lodge, also new annexe, atmospheric public rooms, characterful dining room (good, expensive set menu, unsatisfactory service), tennis etc, very quiet, set in sprawling (overgrown) grounds (bears come searching for honeycombs at night!).
B-C Sunrise Palace, Bharatpur Kothi, near petrol pump, T43573, F38775. 16 large

rooms in a grand building though a bit musty (could do with a clean), good small restaurant, elevated with excellent views over town.

C Aravalli, opposite RTDC's *Shikhar*, T43316. 40 rooms (12 in cottages, 10 in newer wing) on different levels with hill views, restaurant, very well maintained, landscaped terraced garden, pool, gym, good off-season discount.

C Chacha Inn, Main Rd, T43374, F38624. Attractive though a bit brash with lots of artefacts on display, 22 good rooms with modern facilities, 6 a/c, some with balconies, restaurant, bar, exchange, garden, parking, 'free' puppet show evenings.

C Kesar Bhavan Palace, Sunset Rd, facing polo ground, T43173, F38467. 19th-century residence of the Sirohi royal family (Mt Abu's oldest royal property), renovated rooms in main palace and 10 attractive rooms with period furniture in stable wing, comfortable, modernized, balconies good views, western breakfast, meals brought in to order, family run, environment friendly (energy saving devices), T079-6560962, F02712-23729.

C Madhuban, near the bus stand, T38822, F38900, hotmadhuban@yahoo.com. 10 spacious, clean rooms with tiny marble baths, room service food.

C Sunset Inn, Sunset Rd, 1 km centre, T43194, F43515. 40 spacious rooms, some a/c, modern facilities, veg restaurant, outdoor dining, garden, wooded site, pleasant atmosphere.

C Suruchi Hill Resort, opposite Polo ground, T43577, F38573. 43 good rooms (some a/c), attached baths, simple and clean with TV and phone, vegetarian restaurant, 70% off-peak discount.

C-D Shikhar (RTDC), elevated above the petrol pump, T38129. 82 simple rooms with bath (Rs 400-1200), some 'deluxe' in annexe and good value cottages (avoid old rooms), dorm, Indian restaurant, bar, garden, pretty views but stiff climb up.

There is a list of families taking paying guests from Tourist Information, or ask at Connaught House, above.

D Abu International, opposite Polo Ground, T38177. 43 rooms, simple, clean, restaurant.

D Lake Palace, facing lake, T37254, F38817. 13 dirty a/c rooms, garden restaurant, beautifully situated with great lake views from terrace.

D Maharaja International, near Bus Stand, T43161, F38637. 53 comfortable rooms with hot shower, good restaurant, galleries with views, friendly staff.

D Maharana Pratap, tucked away off the main road near Polo ground, T38667. Rooms with baths, modern facilities.

D Navjivan, T38153.

D Samrat International, near Bus Stand, T43173, F38467. 50 rooms, *Takshila* veg restaurant, exchange, travel, shares reception area with cheaper

D-E Sheratone, near Bus Stand, T43544. 40 rooms, modern, clean, characterless, but enthusiastic owner.

E Ganesh, west of the polo ground, uphill behind Brahma Kumari, T43591. Simple rooms, plenty of hot water, very quiet, helpful owner.

E Kashiva's Lake Residency, opposite *Lake Palace*, T43209, F43107. Beautiful location on a slope facing the Lake. Cottage-style, some lake facing, hot water, breakfast and snacks.

E Mamta Palace, Sunset Rd, T43356, F37110. Rooms on several floors in an uninspiring building but clean and comfortable with baths (hot showers), TV and phone, excellent value.

F Arbuda, Nakki Lake Rd, T43358. Rooms with Indian wc, fairly clean but musty smelling, restaurant.

F Rajendra, Rajendra Rd (from bus stand, turn right at Post Office), T38174. Well-designed, clean rooms with bath (bucket hot water), thalis, huge balcony, friendly.

Bera *p396*

A Leopard's Lair, in colourful Raika village near the lake and jungle, T02933-43478. 7 a/c rooms in well-designed stone cottages, modern amenities, delicious meals included, bar, pool, garden, horse and camel riding, birdwatching, panther viewing 'safaris' with owner.

Jalor *p397*

C-D Geetco, T02973-34011, F34015, geetco @yahoo.com. Comfortable rooms and good veg restaurant, large new hotel a few mins' walk from the bus station.

Bhenswada *p397*

B Rawla Bhenswada, T02978-22080. 12 comfortable rooms with bath, unique interiors (swings and silver settees for beds), inspired decor, delicious Marwari meals, parakeet-filled orchards, courtyard lawns, pool, interesting visits to Rabari herdsmen and Bhil tribal hamlets, hospitable family.

Highly recommended. Reservations: *North West Safaris*, T079-6302019, F6300962, ssibal@ad1.vsnl.net.in.

● Eating

Udaipur *p380, maps p381 and p383*
Try the local daal, bhati, choorma. The larger hotels have bars and there are restaurants in plush *Heritage* hotels (see above) – worth simply for the visit but remember non-vegetarian buffet food kept warm for long periods can be risky.

♥♥♥ Darbar Hall (see above).

♥♥♥ Fateh Prakash's beautiful *Gallery Restaurant*. Superb views "but bland continental food", English cream teas (Rs 125, nice brownies, good scones minus cream).

♥♥♥ Lake Palace. At *Jarokha*: good buffet lunch 1230-1430 (Rs 650), dinner 1930-2030 (Rs 770) often preceded by puppet show at 1800, expensive drinks (check bill).

♥♥♥ Shiv Niwas. "Exemplary à la carte", buffet (Rs 650), disappointing desserts, dine in luxury by the pool listening to live Indian classical music (Rs 1,000); bar expensive but the grand surroundings are worth a drink.

Lal Ghat area
♥♥ Jagat Niwas, 24-25 Lalghat, T415547. Mainly Indian. *Jarokha* rooftop restaurant with fabulous lake views, excellent meals, breakfast, teas, ices.

♥♥ Sai Niwas, 75 Navghat. International. Excellent views from roof terrace, good evening meal, freshly cooked, attentive service.

Elsewhere
♥♥ Berrys, near Chetak Circle. International. Standard menu, comfortable, open 1000-2300.

♥♥ Bharti, Bhim Prameshwar Marg, Lake Pichola Hotel Rd. International (including Swiss, Mexican). Good food, friendly. Another at Suraj Pol, T561771. Indian breakfast, dinner. Beautiful gardens, clean, recommended.

♥♥ Kumbha Palace, 104 Bhatiyani Chotta, T422702. Excellent Indian and western food. Rooftop, simple seating under awning (chocolate cake, baked potato, pizzas), friendly.

♥♥ Natural, 55 Rang Sagar, T431983. International including Tibetan, Italian and Mexican. Good buffet breakfasts, home-baking, peaceful rooftop.

♥♥ Park View, City Station Rd. Good.

Lal Ghat area
No alcohol near the temple; "usual fare" includes pancakes, macaroni etc for the homesick westerner; some still show the locally shot Octopussy!

♥ Gokul, Gadiya Devra. Good, cheap breakfasts.

♥ Heaven, street corner near Lal Ghat. International. A long climb up to rooftop, stunning uninterrupted lake views, usual fare.

♥ King Roof Café, Gangor Ghat. North Indian. Delicious spicy dishes, comfy chairs, usual rickety bamboo and matting for shade, most hospitable owner.

♥ Maxim's, nearby, is part art gallery (silk paintings). Slow service but good food.

♥ Mayur, Mothi Chowtha, opposite Jagdish Temple. Mainly Indian. Pleasant for veg thali (Rs 35), snacks and Octopussy, but slow service, also exchange after hours (good rate if you walk away!), internet.

♥ Purohit, Anand Plaza. Good *dosas*.

Avoid **Blue Shore**.

City Palace and Lake Palace Rd area
Garden Hotel, opposite Gulab Bagh, Gujarati/Rajasthani. Air-cooled, excellent veg *thalis*, Rs 45 (try *khadhi, khaman, makkhan buda*), busy at lunch but not for dinner, interesting building, elderly waiters (will show you around kitchen).

Hariyali, near Gulab Bagh. Good North Indian. In a pleasant garden setting.

Samor Bagh, pleasant garden, friendly staff, good butter chicken, dance performance.

Sunset Terrace, Bansi Ghat, Lake Pichola. Very pleasant, superb views of City Palace Complex.

Elsewhere
Abrais, Panch Devri Marg. Good food, friendly and attentive service, great views from 'the other side'.

Delhi Darbar, Hathi Pol. Good Mughlai.

Dream Haven, 22 Bhim Parmeshver Marg, across Chandpol. Excellent, never-ending *thalis* (Rs 25) on rooftop.

Natraj near Town Hall. Rajasthani. Excellent *thalis* in family run simple dining hall, very welcoming and efficient.

Chittaurgarh *p386, map p387*
RTDC Café, near the Vijay Stambha is handy for visitors to the fort.

Ƭ Aodhi, thatched restaurant with central barbecue area. Good Indian (try *laal maas*, a mutton dish), wide choice, authentic 7-course Mewari meal but service can be very slow.
Ƭ Ratnadeep, à la carte veg menu. A shack makes tea and sells chocolates, mineral water, biscuits near the fort gate.

Ranakpur *p391*
No restaurants near the temple, only tea stall, but decent, cheap meals (Rs 10-15), around noon and lunch, before sunset.
Roopam, Ranakpur-Maharani Bagh road, near *Shivika*. Good Rajasthani food. Pleasant village theme setting, modern facilities, popular.
Shivika Lake, part open-air restaurant by lake with hill views. Delicious Rajasthani lunches (Rs 150-250), non-spicy curries possible, barbecued chicken, excellent breakfasts, tea by the lake, family run, shabby but clean.
      The **temple** serves decent meals (Rs 15) around noon and just before sunset.

Mount Abu *p392, maps p393 and p396*
Gujaratis visit Mount Abu in large numbers, some come to escape the state's prohibition on alcohol.
Ƭ Handi at *Hilltone Hotel*. Gujarati, Punjabi, Western. Plenty of choice, very comfortable, open 0900-2300. This, and other large hotels have bars.
Ƭ Neelam, near bus stand. Indian meals (Rs 50-75), Chinese dishes, Western snacks.
Ƭ Shere-e-Punjab. Among the best in town for veg/non veg Indian (also some Chinese/western).
Ƭ Bhavani, by the Bus Stand. Good for *daal-bhatti-choorma*, Rajasthani snacks and *rabri* (sweet).
Ƭ Kanak near Bus Stand. Great Gujarati *thalis* and South Indian snacks (Rs 30-50). Quick service, popular.
Ƭ King's Food, near *MK*, Nakki Lake Rd. Very popular for North Indian veg meal (Rs 40); also Chinese and South Indian, western snacks.
Ƭ Madras Café, Nakki Lake Rd. Indian. Veg 'hot dog', thalis, juices, real coffee and milk shakes in a garden, meals indoors.
Ƭ Maharaja, near Bus Stand. Gujarati. Simple, clean, excellent value thalis at breakneck speed.
Ƭ Purohit, near Bus Stand. Great Gujarati *thalis* and South Indian snacks (Rs 30-50). Quick service, popular.

Ƭ Uncle Fast Food, Raj Bhawan Rd. Fresh and cheap snacks, immaculately clean.
Ƭ Veena, near Taxi Stand. Brews real coffee, serves traditional Indian meals and a few Western favourites, very clean, outdoors, loud music.

⦿ Entertainment

Udaipur *p380, maps p381 and p383*
Bharatiya Lok Kala Museum, T529296. Good puppet show and folk dancing, 1200-1300, 1800-1900, Sep-Mar, Rs 50, camera Rs 50. Recommended.
Meera Kala Mandir, south of railway station, T583176. Daily except Sun, 1900-2000, Rs 60; cultural programme, a bit touristy and amateurish. See 'Shilipgram' above.

⦿ Festivals and events

Udaipur *p380, maps p381 and p383*
Mewar Festival, **Apr**.

Dungarpur *p386*
Baneshwar Fair, **Feb**, a tribal festival at the Baneshwar Temple, 70 km southeast of Dungarpur which draws- large crowds. Bhils gather at the temple for ritual bathing at the confluence of rivers. Direct buses run from Dungarpur to Baneshwar during the fair; avoid staying at the camp. **Vagad Festival** during this period offers an insight into local tribal culture. Both festivals are uncommercialized and really authentic. Details from *Udai Bilas*.

Mount Abu *p392, maps p393 and p396*
An annual **Summer Festival** features folk music, dancing, fireworks etc. (**1-3 Jun**). Diwali is especially colourful.

⦿ Shopping

Udaipur *p380, maps p381 and p383*
Bandhani tie-and-dye fabrics, embroidery and paintings are widely available. Paintings are of 3 types: miniatures in the classical style of courtly Mewar; *phads* or folk art; and *pichchwais* or religious art (see Nathdwara below). The more expensive ones are 'old' – 20-30 years – and are in beautiful dusky colours; the cheaper ones are brighter.

Books

Mewar International, 35 Lalghat. 'One-Stop-Shop' for wide selection of English books, exchange, films.
Sai, 168 City Palace Rd, 100 m from City Palace gate. Good English books, internet, exchange, travel services.

Clothing

Good in Hathi Pol but shop around.
Ganpati, inside Chandpol, T417136. Good value, ready in 24 hrs.
Monsoon Collection, 55 Bhatiyani Chotta, quick, quality, tailoring.
Udaipur New Tailors, inside Hathi Pol. Gents tailoring, reasonably priced, excellent service.

Handicrafts and paintings

Some shops pass off recent work as antique.
Gangour, Mothi Chowtha. Quality miniature paintings.
KK Kasara opposite Nami Gali, 139 Mothi Chowtha. Good religious statues, jewellery.
Mangalam, near Sahelioyon ki Bari.
Mayur Arts, Moti Magri, T528931. Silver furniture, miniatures etc for serious collectors.
Sisodia Handicrafts, entrance of Shiv Niwas Palace. Miniature 'needle paintings' of high quality – see artist at work, no hard sell.

Opticians

Bharat Opticals, 106 Bapu Bazar, T561197. Good spectacles (including frames) from Rs 800, 3 hrs.

Photography

Deluxe Camera, 109 Bapu Bazar, 3rd floor. Good repairs.

Mount Abu *p392, maps p393 and p396*
Shopping is less hassle here than in the tourist towns; most are open 0900-2100 daily. Readymade Indian clothing and silver jewellery are particularly good value.
Chacha Museum. Good metal, wood, stone crafts, paintings and odd curios (fixed price but may give a discount).
Khadi Gramudyog, opposite pony hire. Handloom fabric, carved agate boxes, marble figures.
Rajasthan emporia, Raj Bhavan Rd, opposite the bus stand.

Roopali, near Nakki Lake. Silver jewellery.
For *Garasia* tribal jewellery try stalls near the GPO.
Saurashtra, emporia, Raj Bhavan Rd, opposite the bus stand.

▲ Activities and tours

Udaipur *p380, maps p381 and p383*
Riding
On elephant, camel or horse: travel agencies (eg *Namaskar, Parul* in Lalghat) arrange elephant and camel rides, Rs 200 per hr but need sufficient notice. Horse riding through hotels (Shikarbadi, Pratap Country Inn and some castles around Udaipur).

Swimming

Some hotel pools are open to non-residents: *Lakshmi Vilas* (Rs 175); *Rang Niwas* (Rs 100); *Shiv Niwas* (Rs 300). Also at Shilipgram Craft Village, Rs 100.

Tour companies

Aravalli Safari, 1 Sheetla Marg, Lake Palace Rd, T420282, F420121. Very professional.
Forts & Palaces, 34-35 Shrimal Bhavan, Garden Rd, T417359, jaipur@palaces-tours.com.
Parul, *Jagat Niwas Hotel*, Lalghat, T522990, parul@ad.vsnl.net.in. Air/train, palace hotels, car hire, exchange.
Rajasthan Travels. Excellent service, **Srinath Travel**, T529391. Direct buses to Mount Abu, Mumbai etc.
    Tours Rickshaw tours may mean lots of shop stops.
Rajasthan Tourism, *Hotel Kajri*, Shastri Circle, T410501. **City sightseeing: half day** (0800- 1300) Rs 70. Reported poor.
Excursion: half day (1400-1900), Haldighati, Nathdwara, Eklingji, Rs 100. Chittaurgarh (0800-1800), Rs 250 (with lunch); Ranakpur, Kumbhalgarh (0800- 1900) Rs 250; Jagat-Jaisamand-Chavand-Rishabdeo (0800-1900) Rs 250 (with lunch).

Vintage and classic cars

Once the royal garage with petrol pumps still in the forecourt, the *Garden Hotel* opposite Gulab Bagh displays 19 interesting models. Guided tour, Rs 100.

Rajasthan Listings: Southern Rajasthan

● *Phone codes* Udaipur: 0294; Dungarpur: 02964; Chittaurgarh: 01472; Mount Abu: 02974

Tours

Rajasthan Tourism, Station Rd, T41089, run 2 daily tours, 0800-1130, 1500-1830. Summer (May-Jun), 0700-1030, 1600-1930. Tours start from *Panna*, Udaipur Rd. Guide fees: Rs 250 for half day; Rs 450 for full day including surrounding excursions.

Mount Abu *p392, maps p393 and p396*
Mountain sports

For rock climbing, rapelling, contact Mountaineering Institute, near *Gujarat Bhawan Hostel*; equipment and guide/instructors are available.

Swimming, tennis, billiards

Non-residents can pay to use facilities at the *Cama Rajputana* and *Bikaner House Palace* hotels.

Tours

Rajasthan Tourism and **Rajasthan SRTC** run daily tours to Dilwara, Achalgarh, Guru Shikhar, Nakki Lake, Sunset Point, Adhar Devi and Om Shanti Bhavan, 0830-1300, 1330-1900, Rs 100.
Gujarat, Maharajah and Green Travels also offer similar tours; Ambaji-Kumbhairyaji tours Rs 50.

⊖Transport

Udaipur *p380, maps p381 and p383*
Air

Dabok airport is 25 km east, T655453. Security check is thorough; no batteries or knives allowed in hand luggage. Transport to town: taxis Rs 200; auto Rs 180. **Indian Airlines**, Delhi Gate, T410999, 1000-1315, 1400-1700. Airport, T655453, Enquiry T142. Reserve well ahead. **Indian Airlines** flights to **Aurangabad**; **Delhi**, US$ 90; **Jaipur, Jaisalmer, Jodhpur, Mumbai**. Jet Airways, T561105, airport T656192: **Delhi** via **Jaipur, Mumbai**. UP Air, daily to **Delhi, Jaipur, Mumbai, Rajkot**.

Bicycle

Bicycle hire: Rs 30 per day, well maintained, from **Vijay Cycles** half way down Bhatiyani Chotta; also shops near *Kajri Hotel*, Lalghat and Gangor Ghat area, which also have scooters (Rs 150 per day).

Bus

Long distance Main State Bus Stand, near railway line opposite Udai Pol, T484191; reservations 0700-2100. State RTC buses to **Agra** 15 hrs; **Ahmadabad** 252 km, 7 hrs; **Bhopal** 765 km, 15 hrs; **Bikaner** 13 hrs; **Delhi** 635 km, 17 hrs; **Indore** 635 km; **Jaipur** 405 km, 10 hrs; **Jaisalmer** 14 hrs; **Jodhpur** 8 hrs; **Mount Abu** 270 km, 0800, 1030 and 1500, 7 hrs, Rs 60 (Tourist bus, Rs 85, not much faster); **Mumbai** 802 km, very tiring, 16 hrs; **Pushkar** (Tourist bus, 7 hrs, Rs 100); **Ujjain** (7 hrs). Private buses and Luxury coaches run mostly at night. **Ahmadabad** *Bonney Travels*, Paldi, Ahmedabad, has a/c coaches with reclining seats (contact *Shobha Travels*, City Station Rd), depart 1400 (6½ hrs), Rs 250, with drink/snack stops every 2 hrs. Highly recommended. *Shrinath* and *Punjab Travels* have non a/c buses to **Ahmedabad** and **Mount Abu**. **Jaipur**: several 'deluxe' buses (computerized booking) with reclining seats, Rs 230, more expensive but better. **Jaisalmer**: change at Jodhpur, Rs 180. **Jodhpur**: several options but best to book a good seat a day ahead, Rs 90. Tour operators have **taxis** for Kumbhalgarh and Ranakpur.

Motorbike

Motorbike hire: scooters and bikes can be hired from a small courtyard behind *Badi Haveli* (Jagdish Temple area).

Rickshaw

Auto-rickshaw: pre-paid stands at the bus and railway stations; expect to pay Rs 25 to Lalghat and Jagdish Mandir. Sample fares: Jagdish Mandir to Sunset Pt Rs 20, Monsoon Palace (return) Rs 120, airport Rs 180. Tempos: large rickshaws for 8-10 on fixed routes but will stop anywhere, Rs 3-5.

Taxi

RTDC taxis from Fath Memorial, Suraj Pol. Private taxis from airport, rly station, bus stands and major hotels; negotiate rates. **Taxi Stand**, Chetak Circle, T525112. **Tourist Taxi Service**, Lake Palace Rd, T524169.

Train

Udaipur City station, 4 km southeast of centre, T131. Pre-paid rickshaw to Jagdish Mandir, Rs 25. **Ahmadabad**: *Ahmadabad Exp, 9012*, 2115, 9 hrs (change for Mumbai,

0705). **Ajmer**: *Delhi SR Exp, 9944*, 0825,
11½ hrs; *Chetak Exp, 9616*, 1815, 8½ hrs.
Delhi (SR): *Chetak Exp, 9616*, 1815, 19 hrs
(best to change at Jaipur at 0715 to faster
Intercity for Delhi Junction station). **Jalgaon**:
(day and night trains) to visit Ajanta etc.
Jaipur: *Delhi SR Exp, 9944*, 0830, 15 hrs;
Chetak Exp, 9616, 1810, 11¼ hrs.

Dungarpur *p386*
Buses to/from **Udaipur** (110 km), 3 hrs.
Ahmadabad (170 km), 4 hrs by car.

Chittaurgarh *p386, map p387*
Bicycle
For hire opposite railway station, Rs 2 per hr.

Bus
Long distance Enquiries, T41177. Roads
are poor and even the relatively short ride
to Udaipur can be excruciatingly
uncomfortable. Daily buses to **Bundi**
(4 hrs), **Kota** (5 hrs), **Ajmer** (5 hrs) and
Udaipur (2½ hrs) along a picturesque route
passing fields of pink and white poppies,
grown legally for opium.

Rickshaw
Auto and cycle-rickshaw: negotiate fares.

Train
The fort is over 6 km from station.
   Bottled water at Chittaurgarh station is
often tampered with.
   Enquiries, T41009. A 117 km branch line
runs from **Chittaurgarh** to **Udaipur**. At
Mavli Junction (72 km) another branch runs
down the Aravalli scarp to **Marwar Junction**
(150 km). The views along this line are very
picturesque. By taking this route you can visit
Udaipur, Ajmer and Jodhpur in a circular
journey. **Ajmer**: *Purna-Jaipur Exp, 9770*, 0550,
4¼ hrs; *Ahmadabad DSR Exp, 9944*, 1500,
6 hrs. **Indore**: *Jaipur-Purna Exp, 9769*, 2015,
7¼ hrs. **Jaipur**: *Purna Jaipur Exp, 9770*, 0550,
8¼ hrs; *Chetak Exp, 9616*, 2200, 8¾ hrs; both
continue to **Delhi** 15-16 hrs. **Udaipur**:
Chetak Exp, 9615, 0650, 3¾ hrs; *DSR
Ahmadabad Exp, 9943*, 1345 4¼ hrs
(continues to Ahmadabad, 17 hrs).

Deogarh *p389*
There is a direct bus service from Ajmer but
most visitors use private transport.

Kumbhalgarh Fort *p389*
Bus
For the fort: buses (irregular times) from
Chetak Circle, Udaipur go to **Kelwara**, Rs 20,
3 hrs (cars take 2 hrs); from there a local bus
(Rs 2) can take you a further 4 km up to a car
park; the final 2-km climb is on foot; the
return is a pleasant downhill walk of 1 hr.

Taxi
From Udaipur, a taxi for 4, Rs 900, can cover the
fort and Ranakpur in 11 hrs; very worthwhile.
   Jeep taxis charge Rs 50-100 from Kelwara to
the fort (and say there are no buses). Return
buses to Jaipur from Kelwara until 1730.

Ranakpur *p391*
Bus
From **Udaipur**, 6 daily (0530-1600), slow,
4 hrs from **Jodhpur** (doesn't stop long
enough to see the temples so break your
journey here) and **Mount Abu**.

Train
Palna Junction on the Ajmer-Mount Abu line
is 39 km away.

Mount Abu *p392, maps p393 and p396*
Toll on entering town, Rs 5 per head.
Frequent rockfalls during the monsoon
makes the road from Mount Abu hazardous;
avoid night journeys

Air
The nearest airport is at Udaipur.

Bus
Local For Dilwara and/or Achalgarh.
Long distance State Bus Stand, Main Rd
(opposite Tourist Office); Private Bus Stand,
north of Polo Ground (towards lake). To **Abu
Rd**: hourly bus (45 mins-1 hr) Rs 12.
Ahmadabad: several (7 hrs, Rs 130) via
Palanpur for Bhuj (3 hrs). **Delhi**: overnight.
Jaipur (overnight, 9 hrs). **Jodhpur** am and
pm (6 hrs). **Mumbai, Pune**: early morning
(18 hrs). **Udaipur**: 0830, 1500, 2200 (6 hrs,
Rs 90). **Vadodara**: 0930, 1930 (5 hrs). *Shobha*
and *Gujarat Travels* run private buses.

Pony
Pony hire: Short rides from Rs 5.

Taxi and jeep
With posted fares for sightseeing; about Rs 700 per day; anywhere in town Rs 30; to Sunset Point Rs 50. Taxi: (for sharing) **Abu Rd** Rs 300; **Dilwara** stand is near the bazar.

Train
Western Rly Out Agency near petrol pump has a small reservation quota, 0900-1600, Sun 0900-1230. Book onward reservations well in advance; you may have to wait 2-3 days even in the off-season. Abu Rd is the railhead with frequent buses to Mount Abu. To **Ahmadabad**: *Ashram Exp, 2916,* 0423, 3½ hrs; *Ahmadabad Mail, 9106,* 1305, 4½ hrs; *Aravali Exp, 9708,* 1615, 4¾ hrs (continues to Mumbai, further 8½ hrs). **Delhi**: *Ahmadabad Delhi Mail, 9105,* 1430, 15¾ hrs; *Ashram Exp, 2915,* 2123, 13¾ hrs. **Jaipur**: *Aravalli Exp, 9707,* 1110, 9 hrs; *Ahmadabad-Delhi Mail, 9105,* 1430, 9 hrs. **Jodhpur**: *Ranakpur Exp, 4708,* 0440, 5¼ hrs; *Surya Nagri Exp, 4846,* 0150, 5½ hrs.

ⓘDirectory

Udaipur *p380, maps p381 and p383*
Banks 1000-1430 (Sat 1000-1230). Foreign exchange at: **Amex**, *TGS Tours*, Chetak Circle. Bank of Baroda, opposite Town Hall, Bapu Bazar. For Amex, *TGS Tours*, Chetak Circle, 0930-1930. **Thomas Cook**, inside City Palace. 24 hr ATM at **HDFC**, Chetak Circle; **ICICI**,

Madhuban, near GPO. **Hospitals** Private: Aravali Hospital, 332 Ambamata Main Rd, opposite *Charak Hostel*, T430222, very clean, professional. Udaipur Hospital, Gulab Bagh Rd, T421900. Both recommended. **Chemists**: on Hospital Rd. **Internet** Mayur, Mothi Chowtha. **Mewar**, *Raj Palace Hotel*, Bhatiyani Chotta, T410364. One Stop Shop, near *Lal Ghat Guest House*. Sai, 168 City Palace Rd. Thomas Cook, City Palace Courtyard. Cyber café near *Jagat Niwas*. **Post office** GPO: Chetak Circle. Parcelling service at *Chetak Global Services*, opposite, Rs 150. Poste Restante: c/o The Postmaster, Shastri Circle, 313001, Udaipur. **Tourist offices** Rajasthan, Tourist Reception Centre, Fath Memorial, Suraj Pol, T411535. 1000-1700. Guides 4-8 hrs, about Rs 250-400. Also from Tourist Assistance Centre. Counters at City Railway Station, T412984. 0800-1200 and at Dabok Airport at flight times, T655433. **Useful addresses** Ambulance: T23333. Fire: T27111. Police: T3000.

Mount Abu *p392, maps p393 and p396*
Banks Poor place for exchange; Union Bank of India, best. **Post office** GPO: is on Raj Bhavan Rd. **Tourist offices** Rajasthan Tourism, opposite Bus Stand, T38151. 0800-1100, 1600-2000 (1000-1330, 1400-1700 off-season), Guides 4-8 hrs, about Rs 250-400. Shobha Travels, T38302, and Gujarat Travels, Main Bazar.

Western Rajasthan

★ **Jodhpur** → *Phone code: 0291. Colour map 2, grid B3. Population: 847,000.*

The second city of Rajasthan, once the capital of Marwar, Jodhpur sprawls around the massively impressive clifftop Meherangarh Fort, one of the most rewarding in the state. The outer city, covering a large area, has the added bonus of the vast Umaid Bhavan Palace with its art deco interior. The old city centre is very busy with a lot of action but heavily choked. However, Jodhpur is well worth visiting.▶▶ *For Sleeping, Eating and other listings see pages 424-434.*

Ins and outs
Getting there Jodhpur has air links with Delhi, Jaipur, Mumbai and Udaipur, and is also an essential stop for most visitors to Jaisalmer and western Rajasthan. The airport is 5 km south of town. Be prepared for beggars and hordes of rickshaw drivers on arrival at the station; rickshaw to old town Rs10-15, fort Rs 20-25.

Getting around A pleasant way to explore the Old City is by hiring a bike. If you are really fit you can attempt cycling up to see Meherangarh – worth it for the free-wheel back down! See Transport, page 432, for further details.

Climate Summer: maximum 42°C, minimum 29°C. Rainfall: 120 mm in Jul and Aug. Best time to visit: Nov to Mar.

History

The **Rathore** Rajputs had moved to **Marwar** – the 'region of death' – in 1211, after their defeat at Kanauj by Muhammad Ghori. In 1459 Rao Jodha, forced to leave the Rathore capital at Mandore, 8 km to the north, chose this place as his capital because of its strategic location on the edge of the Thar Desert. The Rathores subsequently controlled wide areas of Rajasthan. Rao Udai Singh of Jodhpur (died 1581) received

Jodhpur

Related map
A Meherangarh Fort, page 411

4 Chauhan's	13 Newton's Manor
5 Cosy Guest House	14 Rajwada
6 Devi Bhawan	15 Raman Guest House
7 Durag Niwas	16 Ratanada Polo Palace
& Durag Vilas	17 Rawat
8 Durjan Niwas	18 Royal Palace
9 Fort View	19 Taj Hari Mahal
10 Ghoomar	20 Umaid Bhawan Palace
11 Govind	21 Umang International
12 Karni Bhawan	22 Youth Hostel

Sleeping
1 Abhay Days
2 Ajit Bhawan, Ranbanka & Tandoori Nights
3 Akshey

● **Eating**
1 Agra Sweet Home & Uttam
2 Jodhpur Coffee House & Poonam Vegetarian
3 Kalinga
4 Mishrilal
5 Rawat Mishtan Bhandar
6 Shandar

Rajasthan Western Rajasthan Jodhpur

the title of Raja from Akbar and Sawai Raja Sur Singh (died 1595), conquered Gujarat and part of the Deccan for the Emperor. Maharaja Jaswant Singh (died 1678), having supported Shah Jahan in the Mughal struggle for succession in 1658, had a problematic relationship with the subsequent Mughal rule of Aurangzeb, and Ajit Singh was only able to succeed him after Aurangzeb's own death in 1707. In addition to driving the Mughals out of Ajmer he added substantially to the Meherangarh Fort in Jodhpur. His successor, Maharaja Abhai Singh (died 1749) captured Ahmadabad, and the State came into treaty relations with the British in 1818.

Jodhpur lies on the once strategic Delhi-Gujarat trading route and the Marwaris managed and benefited from the traffic of opium, copper, silk, sandalwood, dates, coffee and much more besides.

Sights

The **Old City** is surrounded by a huge 9½-km long wall which has 101 bastions and seven gates, above which are inscribed the name of the place to which the road leads. It comprises a labyrinthine maze of narrow streets. Some of the houses and temples are of richly carved stone, in particular the red sandstone buildings of the Siré (Sardar) Bazar. Here the **Taleti Mahal** (early 17th century), one of three concubines' palaces in Jodhpur, has the unique feature of *jarokhas* decorated with temple columns.

The **new city** beyond the walls is of interest too. Overlooking the Umaid Sagar is the **Umaid Bhawan Palace** on Chittar Hill. Building started in 1929 as a famine relief exercise when the monsoon failed for the third year running. Over 3,000 people worked for 14 years, building this vast 347 room palace of sandstone and marble. The hand hewn blocks which are interlocked into position, use no mortar. It was designed by HV Lanchester, with the most modern furnishing and facilities in mind, and completed in 1943. The interior decoration was left to the artist JS Norblin, a refugee from Poland; he painted the frescoes in the Throne Room (East Wing). For Tillotson, an architectural historian, it is "the finest example of Indo-Deco. The forms are crisp and precise, and the bland monochrome of the stone makes the eye concentrate on their carved shapes.".

If you can spare no more than a day, try to see Meherangarh Fort and Museum, the nearby Jaswant Thada (cenotaphs) and Umaid Bhavan Palace.

The royal family still occupy part of the palace. Part is a museum and part a luxury hotel (see below), and the interior produces a remarkable sensation of separation from the Indian environment in which it is set. There is a subterranean swimming pool decorated with signs of the zodiac; the murals are Norblin's. The murals are in the hotel section, Rs 330 cover charge to be spent in the coffee shop.

Just southeast of Raikabagh Station are the **Raikabagh Palace** and the **Jubilee Buildings**, public offices designed by Sir Samuel Swinton Jacob in the Indo-Saracenic style. On the Mandore Road, 2 km to the north, is the large **Mahamandir** temple.

★ Meherangarh

ⓘ *1000-1700 (museum only, closed 1300-1430), foreigners Rs 50, Indians Rs 20, guide Rs 50, camera Rs 50, video Rs 100, you are requested not to tip guides, but contribute to the Staff Welfare Fund at the booking office if you wish, allow at least 2 hrs, near the ticket office on the terrace there is a pleasant restaurant.*

The 'Majestic Fort' sprawls along the top of a steep escarpment with a sheer drop to the south. Originally started by Rao Jodha in 1459, it has walls up to 36 m high and 21 m wide, towering above the plains. Most of what stands today is from the period of Maharajah Jaswant Singh (1638-78). On his death in 1678, Aurangzeb occupied the fort. However, after Aurangzeb's death Meherangarh returned to Jaswant Singh's son Ajit Singh and remained the royal residence until the Umaid Bhavan was completed in 1943.

The summit has three areas: the Palace (northwest), a wide terrace to the east of the Palace, and the strongly fortified area to the south. There are extensive views from the top. One approach is by a winding path up the west side, possible by rickshaw, but the main approach and car park is from the east. The climb is quite stiff; the disabled may use the elevator.

The gateways There were originally seven gateways. The first, the **Fateh** Gate, is heavily fortified with spikes and a barbican that forces a 45° turn. The smaller **Gopal** Gate is followed by the **Bhairon** Gate, with large guardrooms. The fourth, **Toati** Gate, is now missing but the fifth, **Dodhkangra** Gate, marked with cannon shots, stands over a turn in the path and has loopholed battlements for easy defence. Next is the **Marti** Gate, a long passage flanked by guardrooms. The last, **Loha** (Iron) Gate, controls the final turn into the fort and has handprints (31 on one side and five on the other) of royal *satis*, the wives of Maharajas, see page 1318. It is said that six queens and 58 concubines became *satis* on Ajit Singh's funeral pyre in 1724. *Satis* carried the Bhagavad Gita with them into the flames and legend has it that the holy book would never perish. The main entrance is through the **Jay** (Victory) **Pol**.

The Old Palaces From the **Loha Gate** the ramp leads up to the **Suraj** (Sun) **Pol**, which opens onto the **Singar Choki Chowk**. This is the main entrance to the museum, and a guide takes visitors round the inner buildings.

Meherangarh Fort

After Tillotson

Used for royal ceremonies such as the anointing of rajas, the north, west and southwest sides of the Singar Choki Chowk date from the period immediately before the Mughal occupation in 1678. The upper storeys of the chowk were part of the *zenana*, and from the **Jhanki Mahal** ('glimpse palace') on the upper floor of the north wing the women could look down on the activities of the courtyard. Thus the chowk below has the features characteristic of much of the rest of the *zenana*, *jarokhas* surmounted by the distinctive Bengali style eaves, and beautifully ornate *jali* screens. These allowed cooling breezes to ventilate rooms and corridors in the often stiflingly hot desert summers.

Also typical of Mughal buildings was the use of material hung from rings below the eaves to provide roof covering, as in the columned halls of the **Daulat Khana** and the **Sileh Khana** (armoury), which date from Ajit Singh's reign. The collection of Indian weapons in the armoury is unequalled, with remarkable swords and daggers, often beautifully decorated with calligraphy. Along the ramparts antique cannonry can be seen. Shah Jahan's red silk and velvet tent lavishly embroidered with gold thread, used in the Imperial Mughal campaign, is in the **Tent Room**. The **Jewel House** has a wonderful collection of jewellery, including diamond eyebrows held by hooks over the ears. There are also palanquins, howdahs and ornate royal cradles, all marvellously preserved.

The **Phool Mahal** (Flower Palace), above the Sileh Khana, was built by Abhai Singh (1724-49) as a hall of private audience. The stone jali screens are original and there are striking portraits of former rulers, a lavishly gilded ceiling and the Jodhpur coat of arms displayed above the royal couch; the murals of the 36 musical modes are a late 19th-century addition.

The **Umaid Vilas**, which houses Rajput miniatures, is linked to the **Sheesh Mahal** (Mirror Palace), built by Ajit Singh between 1707 and 1724. The room has characteristic large and regularly sized mirror work, unlike Mughal 'mirror palaces'. Immediately to its south, and above the Sardar Vilas, is the **Takhat Vilas**. Added by Maharajah Takhat Singh (1843-73), it has wall murals of dancing girls, love legends and Krishna Lila, while its ceiling has two unusual features: massive wooden beams to provide support and the curious use of colourful Belgian Christmas tree balls.

The **Ajit Vilas** has a fascinating collection of musical instruments and costumes. On the ground floor of the Takhat Vilas is **Sardar Vilas**, and to its south the **Khabka** and **Chandan Mahals** (sleeping quarters). The **Moti Vilas**, wings to the north, east and south of the Moti Mahal Chowk, date from Jaswant Singh's reign. The women could watch proceedings in the courtyard below through the *jali* screens of the surrounding wings. Tillotson suggests that the **Moti Mahal** (Pearl Palace) ① *15 mins for Rs 150, reported as uncannily accurate about the past!*, to the west, although placed in the *zenana* of the fort, was such a magnificent building that it could only have served the purpose of a Diwan-i-Am (Hall of Public Audience). The Moti Mahal is fronted by excellently carved 19th-century woodwork, while inside waist-level niches housed oil lamps whose light would have shimmered from the mirrored ceiling. A palmist reads your fortune at Moti Mahal Chowk (museum area).

Jaswant Thada ① *1000-1300, 1400-1700, Rs 10.* This is the cremation ground of the former rulers with distinctive memorials in white marble which commemorate Jaswant Singh II (1899) and successive rulers of Marwar.

Museums ★ Mehrangarh Fort Palace Museum is in a series of palaces with beautifully designed and decorated windows and walls. It has a magnificent collection of the Maharajas' memorabilia – superbly maintained and presented (see above).

The **Old Fort Museum** ① *summer 0800-1800, winter 0900-1700, closed 1230-1430, so be there by 1100 if visiting in the morning, tours with English speaking* guides provided, is fascinating. Palanquins, royal howdahs lavishly upholstered and one of silver, a golden throne, shoes with pearls, paintings, mirrors, cribs, weapons and a magnificently embroidered royal desert tent, among the exhibits.

Umaid Bhawan Palace Museum ① *0900-1700, Rs 50 (Indians Rs 10)*, includes the Darbar Hall with its murals; good collection of miniatures, armour and old clocks. Some are disappointed.

Government Museum ① *Umaid Park, closed Fri, 1000-1630, Rs 3*, is a time-capsule from the British Raj, little added since Independence, with some moth-eaten stuffed animals and featherless birds, images of Jain Tirthankars, miniature portraits and antiquities. A small **zoo** in the gardens has a few rare exotic species.

Excursions

Village safaris A village safari visiting a Bishnoi village is recommended. Most tours include the hamlets of Guda, Khejarali, Raika cameleers' settlement and Salawas (see below). Tours by *Ajit Bhawan, Madho Niwas* (T434486), *Jhalamandgarh* and *Rohetgarh*. About Rs 450 for four hours.

Mandore ① *Frequent local/city bus, 100 m from the station and Paota Bus Stand.* Some 8 km north of Jodhpur, the old 14th-century capital of Marwar is set on a plateau. Set around the old cremation ground with the red sandstone *chhatris* of the Rathore rulers, the gardens are usually crowded with Indian tourists at weekends. The **Shrine of the 33 Crore Gods** is a hall containing huge painted rock-cut figures of heroes and gods. The largest *deval*, a combination of temple and cenotaph, is Ajit Singh's (died 1724); worth a closer look but is unkempt. A small **museum** ① *closed Fri, 1000-1630*, in the Janana Mahal contains some fine sculpture and miniature paintings. The remains of an eighth century Hindu temple is on a hilltop nearby.

Bal Samand Lake The oldest artificial lake in Rajasthan, is 5 km north. Dating from 1159, it is surrounded by parkland laid out in 1936 where the 19th-century *Hawa Mahal* was turned into a royal summer palace. Although the interior is European in style, it has entirely traditional red sandstone filigree windows and beautifully carved balconies.

Around Jodhpur

Salawas ① *Buses from Jodhpur.* Salawas, about 30-minutes' drive south from Jodhpur, is well known for its pit loom weaving. The village produces *durries*, carpets, rugs, bed covers and tents using camel hair, goat hair, wool and cotton in colourful and interesting patterns. You can visit the weavers' co-operative *Roopraj Durrie Udyog,* where you can buy authentic village crafts, but watch out for high prices and pushy salesmen.

Luni ① *Trains and buses from Jodhpur (40 km).* The tiny bustling village of Luni sits in the shadow of the 19th-century red sandstone Fort Chanwa which has been converted to a hotel. With its complex of courtyards, water wheels, and intricately carved façades, the fort and its village offer an attractive and peaceful alternative to the crowds of Jodhpur.

Rohet ① *Frequent buses from Jodhpur (50 km north).* Rohet, once a picturesque hamlet settled by the Bishnoi community, is now a busy highway village. At the end of the village a lake attracts numerous winter migrants in addition to resident birds. Rohetgarh, a small 'castle' beside the lake, has a collection of antique hunting weapons.

Sardar Samand (60 km southeast of Jodhpur). The lake nearby is a beautiful setting for the royal 1933 art deco hunting lodge, Sardar Samand Palace, see listings page

425. The lake attracts pelicans, flamingos, cranes, egrets and kingfishers and the wildlife sanctuary has blackbuck, gazelle and nilgai.

Balotra The small textile town, 60 km southwest of Jodhpur, is known for its traditional weaving using pit looms and block prints. Nearby is the beautiful Jain temple with elephant murals at **Nakoda**, which also hosts a remarkable **camel and cattle fair** which takes place on the river bed in March/April. Kanana, near Balotra, celebrates *Holi* with stage shows and other entertainment. There is a *dharamshala* at Nakoda and guesthouses at Balotra.

Tilwara (127 km from Jodhpur). The Mallinathji **cattle fair** is a major event. Over 80,000 animals are brought making it Rajasthan's largest, including Kapila (Krishna's) cows and Kathiawari horses.

Osian ⓘ *Jodhpur-Jaisalmer train stops at Osian, also, 4 daily buses from Jodhpur, 2 hrs, worth visiting; allow 1 hr there.* Surrounded by sand dunes, this ancient town north of Jodhpur in the Thar desert contains the largest group of eighth to 10th-century Hindu and Jain temples in Rajasthan. The typical Pratihara Dynasty **temple complex** is set on a terrace whose walls are finely decorated with mouldings and miniatures. The sanctuary walls have central projections with carved panels and above these rise curved towers. The doorways are usually decorated with river goddesses, serpents and scrollwork. The 23 temples are grouped in several sites north, west and south of the town. The western group contains a mixture of Hindu temples, including the **Surya Temple** (early eighth century) with beautifully carved pillars. The Jain **Mahavira Temple** (eighth to 10th centuries) the best preserved, 200 m further on a hillock, rises above the town. The **Sachiya Mata Temple** (11th-12th century) is a living temple of the Golden Durga.

Khimsar On the edge of the desert, 80 km northeast of Jodhpur (60 km from Osian), Khimsar was founded by the Jain saint Mahavir 2,500 years ago. The isolated, battle scarred, 16th-century moated castle of which a section remains, had a *zenana* added in the mid-18th century and a regal wing added in the 1940s.

Nagaur (Colour map 2, grid A4. 137 km north of Jodhpur) Nagaur, which was a centre of Chishti Sufis, has attracted interest as it preserves some fine examples of pre-Mughal and Mughal architecture. The dull stretch of desert is enlivened by Nagaur's fort palace, temples and *havelis*. The walls are said to date from the 11th-12th century Chauhan period. Akbar built the mosque here and there is a shrine of the disciple of Mu'inuddin Chishti of Ajmer (see page 352). The fort which has palaces of the Mughal emperors and of the Marwars being restored with help from the Paul Getty Foundation, has excellent wall paintings and interesting ancient systems of rainwater conservation and storage, ably explained by a very knowledgeable curator. The popular *Cattle and Camel Fair* (February) is held just outside the town during which there are camel races, cock fights, folk dancing and music. The fields become full of encampments of pastoral communities, tribal people and livestock dealers with their cattle, camels, sheep, goat and other animals.

Bikaner → *Phone code: 0151. Colour map 2, grid A4. Population: 530,000 million.*

Bikaner is an oasis town among scrub and sand dunes. The rocky outcrop in a barren landscape provides a dramatic setting for the Junagarh Fort, one of the finest in western Rajasthan. The old walled city retains a medieval air, while outside the walls, palaces and mansions survive. Well off the usual tourist route, Bikaner is en route to Jaisalmer from Jaipur or Shekhawati. ▶▶ *For Sleeping, Eating and other listings see pages 424-434.*

Ins and outs

Getting there Bikaner is a full day's drive from Jaipur but it may be worth stopping a night in Samode or the Shekhawati region (see page 342). The railway station is central and has services from Delhi (Sarai Rohilla), Jaipur and Jodhpur. The New Bus Stand is 3 km to the north but you can ask to be dropped in town (unless you arrive from the north).

Getting around The fort and the Old City are within easy walking distance from the station. Autos and cycle-rickshaws transfer passengers between the station and the New Bus Stand. Women on their own have complained of unpleasant experiences. See Transport, page 433, for further details. Taxis can be difficult to get from the Lalgarh Palace area in the evening.

Background

Bikaner was set up as an independent kingdom in 1488 by Rao Bikaji, the younger son of Jodhpur's founder, Rao Jodha. Protected by the harsh desert countryside and by the military rulers who even humbled Aurangzeb's powerful Mughal army, it developed as a major centre in the cross-desert caravan trade. Even today, Bikaner's Marwari traders are noted throughout North India for their business acumen.

Like other desert trading cities, Bikaner would have decayed into a small town of little significance with the development of the sea ports but for the foresight of **Maharajah Ganga Singhji** who introduced wide ranging economic reforms which ensured the survival of the city. Among his greatest achievements was the 1927-28 **Bikaner Gang Canal** which turned 285,000 ha of arid scrub into cultivable land.

Sights

There is enough of interest in Bikaner to make it worth spending at least a couple of days exploring. The atmospheric Old City enclosed within high walls, with its merchant *havelis*, temples and bazars, is worth seeking out. Enter through the Kote gate and you will still see camels, bullocks and donkeys pulling carts through narrow winding lanes. Some visitors are disappointed by the dirt and smell.

Junagarh Fort (1588-93) ① *1000-1630 (last entry), Rs 50 (Indians Rs 10); camera Rs 30, video Rs 100 (limited permission), guided tours in Hindi and English, private guides near the gate offer better 'in-depth' tours; Rs 100 for 4, 2 hrs*, is one of the finest examples in Rajasthan of the paradox between medieval military architecture and beautiful interior decoration. Started in 1588 by Raja Rai Singh (1571-1611), a strong ally of the Mughal Empire, who led Akbar's army in numerous battles, it had palaces added for the next three centuries.

You enter the superbly preserved fort by the yellow sandstone **Suraj Prole** (Sun Gate, 1593) to the east. The pale red sandstone perimeter wall is surrounded by a moat (the lake no longer exists) while the Chowks have beautifully designed palaces with balconies, kiosks and fine *jali* screens. The interiors are beautifully decorated with shell-work, lime plaster, mirror-and-glass inlays, gold leaf, carving, carpets and lacquer work. The ramparts offer good views of the elephant and horse stables and temples, the old city with the desert beyond, and the relatively more recent city areas around the medieval walls.

The walls of the **Lal Niwas**, which are the oldest, are elaborately decorated in red and gold. Karan Singh commemorated a victory over Aurangzeb by building the **Karan Mahal** (1631-39) across the Chowk. Successive rulers added the **Gaj Mandir** (1745-87) with its mirrored Shish Mahal, and the **Chattra Niwas** (1872-87) with its pitched roof and English 'field sport' plates decorating the walls.

The magnificent Coronation Hall, adorned with plaster work, lacquer, mirror and glass, is in Maharaja Surat Singh's **Anup Mahal** (1788-1828). The decorative façades around the Anup Mahal Chowk, though painted white, are in fact of stone. The fort also includes the **Chetar Mahal** and **Chini Burj** of Dungar Singh (1872-87) and **Ganga Niwas** of Ganga Singh (1898-1943), who did much to modernize his state and also built the Lalgarh Palace to the north. Mirror work, carving and marble decorate the ornate **Chandra Mahal** (Moon Palace) and the **Phul Mahal** (Flower Palace), built by Maharaja Gaj Singh. These last two are shown to foreigners at the end as a 'special tour' when the guide expects an extra tip! The royal chamber in the Chandra Mahal has strategically placed mirrors so that any intruder entering could be seen by the Maharaja from his bed.

The fort **museum** has Sanskrit and Persian manuscripts, miniature paintings, jewels, enamelware, silver, weapons, palanquins, howdahs, and war drums. During the Second World War, Ganga Singhji was a signatory to the Versailles treaty, and pictures of his life and rule, the bi-plane he received as a war memento, and other princely relics of the period can be seen in the fort. **Har Mandir**, the royal temple where birth and wedding ceremonies were celebrated, is still used for Gangaur and other festivities. The well nearby is reputedly over 130 m deep.

Prachina Museum ① *Rs 25 (guided tour), shop, small clean café outside is open air but shady*, in the grounds exhibits beautifully crafted costumes and objects.

Lalgarh Palace ① *palace closed Wed, museum closed Sun, 1000-1700, Rs 40 (museum extra Rs 20)*. The red sandstone Lalgarh Palace stands in huge grounds to the north of the city, surrounded by rocks and sand dunes. Designed by Sir Swinton Jacob in 1902, the palace complex, with extensions over the next few decades, has attractive courtyards overlooked by intricate *zenana* screen windows and *jarokha* balconies, columned corridors and period furnishings. The banquet hall is full of hunting trophies and photographs.His Highness Doctor Karni Singh of Bikaner was well known for his

Bikaner

Sleeping		5 Dhola Maru	9 Marudhar	12 Sagar	● Eating
1 Bhairon Vilas	6 Harasar Haveli	10 Meghsar Castle	13 Shanti Niwas &	1 Amber
2 Bhanwar Niwas	7 Inder Restaurant	& Kishan Palace	Adarsh	2 Chhotu
3 Bharat Niwas	8 Lalgarh, Laxmi	11 Palace View,	14 Shri Ram	Motoo
4 Desert Wind	Niwas, Maan Vilas	Kalinga	15 Thar	3 Kesria

shooting expertise - both with a camera and with a gun. The bougainvillaea, parakeets and peacocks add to the attraction of the gardens in which the Bikaner State Railway Carriage is preserved. The Lalgarh complex now has several hotels (see Sleeping below). You can visit Lalgarh for a meal and to see the **Sadul Museum** which houses old maps, photos and royal memorabilia. Plenty of interest and well displayed.

Havelis There are some exquisite havelis in Bikaner belonging to the Rampuria, Kothari, Vaid and Daga merchant families. The sandstone carvings combine traditional Rajasthani haveli architecture with colonial influence. Ask for Rampuria Street and the Purana Bazar and wander through lanes lined with fine façades. Among them is Bhanwar Niwas which has been converted into a heritage hotel.

Ganga Golden Jubilee Museum ① *Public Park, closed Sun, 1000-1630, Rs 3*, has a fine small collection of pottery, paintings and weapons. There are excellent examples of Bikaner miniature paintings which are specially prized because of their very fine quality. You can also see petrified wood fossils from the desert.

Excursions

Bhand Sagar ① *free but caretakers may charge Rs 10 for cameras*, 5 km southwest, has a group of Hindu and Jain temples which are believed to be the oldest extant structures of Bikaner, dating from the days when it was just a desert trading out-post of Jodhpur. The white painted sandstone Bandeshwar Temple with a towering *shikhara* roof and painted sculptures, murals, mirrorwork inside, is the most interesting. The Sandeshwar Temple, dedicated to Neminath, has gold leaf painting, *meenakari* work and marble sculptures. They are hard to find and difficult to approach by car but rickshaw wallahs know the way. There are numerous steps but wonderful views. A longer excursion to Kalibangan to the north, is described on page 418.

Gajner National Park, 30 km west Bikaner, now a part of a palace hotel, was a private preserve which once provided the royal family of Bikaner with game. This birder's paradise is surrounded by 13,000 ha of scrub forest which harbours large colonies of nilgai, chinkara, blackbuck, wild boar and desert reptiles. Throughout the day, a train of antelope, gazelle and pigs can be seen arriving to drink at the lake. Winter migratory birds include the Imperial black-bellied sand grouse, cranes and migratory ducks. Some visitors have spotted Great Indian bustard at the water's edge. There is a picnic spot by the lake from where visitors can view the birds. It is worth stopping for an hour's mini-safari if you are in the vicinity.

Kolayat ① *by car or rail*, 50 km southwest via Gajner road, is an important Hindu pilgrimage centre around a sacred lake with 52 ghats and a group of five temples built by Ganga Singhji (none of which is architecturally significant). The oasis village comes alive at the November full moon when a three-day festival draws thousands of pilgrims who take part in ritual bathing. The *Cattle and Camel Fair* (November) is very colourful and authentic but it can get quite riotous after dark. Since facilities are minimal, it is best to arrive before the festival to find a local family with space to spare, or ask a travel agent in Bikaner.

Karni Mata Mandir ① *closed 1200-1600, free, camera Rs 40, the train leaves Bikaner, 1000, returns 1230, buses from Bikaner New Bus Stand or Ganga Shahar Rd, hourly, Rs 7 (share auto-rickshaw from Station Rd to Bus, Rs 3), on return journey, for Station Rd, get off at* Thar Hotel *and walk or take auto-rickshaw, taxi about Rs 200 return*, 33 km south at Deshnoke, is a 17th-century temple. The massive silver gates and beautiful white marble carvings on the façade were added by Ganga Singh (1898-1943) who dedicated the temple to a 15th-century female mystic Karniji, worshipped as an incarnation of Durga. A gallery describes her life. Mice and rats, revered and fed with sweets and milk in the belief that they are reincarnated saints, swarm over the temple around your feet; spotting the white rat is supposed to bring good luck! Take socks as the floor is dirty.

Kakoo is about 75 km south of Bikaner. The picturesque village with attractive huts and surrounded by sand dunes is the starting point for desert camel safaris costing Rs 1500 per day with tented facilities. It is less commercialized than safaris near Jaisalmer.

Camel Research Farm ① *closed Sun, 1500-1700, photography "prohibited" but camel drivers ask to be photographed! A pleasant cycle ride along a very quiet road, or hire a rickshaw, 9 km southeast*, claims to be the only one in Asia. Rides may be available but no refreshments. Good views from the top of the tower.

Kalibangan & Harappan sites ① *Local buses to Kalibangan from Suratgarh, which can be reached by bus from Bikaner, Hanumangarh, Sirsa (Haryana) or Mandi Dabwali (Punjab). The broad gauge train line connects Suratgarh with Anupgarh, about 15 km from the Pakistan border, where it terminates. Kalibangan is about half way to Anupgarh. The nearest station is Raghunathgarh, but travel from there to Kalibangan is difficult (check at Suratgarh or Anupgarh). From Suratgarh to Anupgarh: Passenger, 0755, 2¼ hrs. Trains from Suratgarh: Bikaner (Lalgarh Junction): Chandigarh Exp, 4887, 0835, 3¼ hrs. Bhatinda: Chandigarh Exp, 4888, 1955, 3¼ hrs.* One of North India's most important early settlement regions stretches from the Shimla hills down past the important Harappan sites of Hanumangarh and Kalibangan, north of Bikaner.

Late Harappan sites have been explored by archaeologists, notably A Ghosh, since 1962. They were identified in the upper part of the valley, the easternmost region of the Indus Valley civilization. Across the border in Pakistan are the premier sites of Harappa (200 km) and Moenjo Daro (450 km). Here, the most impressive of the sites today is that of **Kalibangan** (west off the NH15 at Suratgarh). On the south bank of the Ghaggar River it was a heavily fortified citadel mound, rising about 10 m above the level of the plain. There were several pre-Harappan phases. Allchin and Allchin record that the bricks of the early phase were already standardized, though not to the same size as later Harappan bricks. The ramparts were made of mud brick and a range of pottery and ornaments have been found. The early pottery is especially interesting, predominantly red or pink with black painting.

Khichan Four kilometres from Phalodi, southwest of Bikaner, just off the NH15, is a lovely village with superb red sandstone havelis of the Oswal Jains. Beyond the village are sand dunes and mustard fields, and a lake which attracts ducks and other waterfowl. The once small quiet village has grown into a bustling agricultural centre and a prominent bird feeding station. Jain villagers put out grain behind the village for winter visitors; up to 8,000 demoiselle cranes and occasionally Common eastern cranes can be seen in December and January on the feeding grounds.

Pokaran Pokaran, between Jaisalmer and Jodhpur, stands on the edge of the great desert with dunes stretching 100 km west to the Pakistan border. It provides a mid-way stopover between Bikaner/Jodhpur and Jaisalmer for tourists as it did for royal and merchant caravans in the past. The impressive 16th-century yellow sandstone Pokaran fort, overlooking a confusion of streets in the town below, has a small museum with an interesting collection of medieval weapons, costumes and paintings. There are good views from the ramparts. Pokaran is also well known for its potters who make red-and-white pottery and terracotta horses/elephants. **Ramdeora**, the Hindu and Jain pilgrim centre nearby, has Bishnoi hamlets and a preserve for blackbuck antelope, Indian gazelle, bustards and sand grouse.

Ramdeora Fair is an important religious event (September). **Khetolai**, about 25 km northwest of Pokaran, is the site of India's first nuclear test explosion held underground on 18 March 1974, and of further tests in May 1998.

★ Jaisalmer

→ *Phone code: 02992. Colour map 2, grid A2. Population: 58,300. 275 km from Jodhpur.*

The approach to Jaisalmer across the hot barren desert is magical as the city shimmers like a mirage. With the crenellated golden sandstone town walls and narrow streets lined with exquisitely carved buildings, through which camel carts trundle leisurely, it has an extraordinarily medieval feel and an incredible atmosphere. The fort inside, perched on its hilltop, contains some gems of Jain temple building, while beautifully decorated merchants' havelis are scattered through the town. Jaisalmer gives convenient access to the surrounding desert wilderness, sand dunes and oasis villages ideal for camel rides and safaris. A few travellers find the town is overrated and the people unfriendly. Parts are decaying and wear an air of neglect but efforts are being made – all, including new structures, must be built out of the local honey-coloured sandstone. ➤➤ *For Sleeping, Eating and other listings see pages 424-434.*

Ins and outs

Getting there The nearest airport is at Jodhpur. Trains from Jodhpur arrive at Jaisalmer railway station, to the east of town. Phone ahead and ask your hotel if they offer a pick-up. Most long-distance buses arrive at the station bus stand and then go to Amar Sagar Pol which is about a 15-min walk from the fort gate.

Getting around Unmetered jeeps and auto-rickshaws can be hired at the station (and in the walled town) but they are no help inside the fort so you may have to carry your luggage some distance uphill if you choose a fort hotel. You can hire a bike for the day from Gopa Chowk (Rs 25) though the whole town is really best explored on foot. Most of the hotels and restaurants are clustered around the 2 chowks and inside the fort. See Transport, page 434, for further details.

Climate Temperature: Summer 42°C, minimum 27°C. Winter: maximum 25°C, minimum 8°C. Rainfall: 100 mm during Jul and Aug. Best time to visit is Nov-Mar.

Background

Founded by Prince Jaisal in 1156, Jaisalmer grew to be a major staging post on the trade route across the forbidding Thar desert from India to the West. The merchants prospered and invested part of their wealth in building beautiful houses and temples with the local sandstone. The growth of maritime trade between India and the West caused a decline in trade across the desert which ceased altogether in 1947. However, the wars with Pakistan (1965 and 1971) resulted in the Indian government developing the transport facilities to the border to improve troop movement. This has also helped visitors to gain access. Today, the army and tourism are mainstays of the local economy but the town is relatively free of hassle from hawkers.

Sights

The fort On the roughly triangular-shaped Trikuta Hill, the fort stands 76 m above the town, enclosed by a 9-m wall with 99 bastions (mostly 1633-1647). You enter the fort from the east from Gopa Chowk. The inner, higher fort wall and the old gates up the ramp (Suraj, Ganesh, Hawa and Rang Pols) provided further defences. The Suraj Pol (1594), once an outer gate, is flanked by heavy bastions and has bands of decoration which imitate local textile designs. Take a walk through the narrow streets within the fort, often blocked by the odd goat or cow, and see how even today about a 1,000 of the town's people live in tiny houses inside the fort often with beautiful carvings on doors and balconies. It is not difficult to get lost.

As with many other Rajput forts, within the massive defences are a series of palaces, the product of successive generations of rulers' flights of fancy. Often called the Golden Fort because of the colour of the sandstone, it dominates the town. The stone is relatively easy to carve and the dry climate has meant that the fineness of detail has been preserved through the centuries. The *jali* work and delicately ornamented balconies and windows with wide eaves break the solidity of the thick walls which gives protection from the heat, while the high plinths of the buildings keep off the sand.

Rajmahal Palace ① *0800-1300, 1500-1700, Rs 20 (Indians Rs 10), camera Rs 50*. The Juna Mahal (circa 1500) of the seven-storey palace with its *jali* screens is one of the oldest Rajasthani palaces. The rather plain *zenana* block to its west, facing the *chauhata* (square) is decorated with false *jalis*. Next to it is the *mardana* (men's quarters) including the Rang Mahal above the Hawa Pol, built during the reign of Mulraj II (1762-1820), which has highly detailed murals and mirror decoration. Sarvotam Vilas built by Akhai Singh (1722-62) is ornamented with blue tiles and glass mosaics. The adjacent Gaj Vilas (1884) stands on a high plinth. Mulraj II's Moti Mahal has floral decoration and carved doors.

The open square beyond the gates has a platform reached by climbing some steps; this is where court was held or royal visitors entertained. There are also fascinating **Jain temples** (12th-16th centuries) ① *0700-1200, camera Rs 50, leather shoes not permitted*. Whilst the Rajputs were devout Hindus they permitted Jainism to be practised. The **Parsvanatha** (1417) has a fine gateway, an ornate porch and 52 subsidiary shrines surrounding the main structure. The brackets are elaborately carved as maidens and dancers. The exterior of the **Rishbhanatha** (1479) has more

Jaisalmer

Related map
A Jaisalmer Fort, page 422

A Jaisalmer Fort, page 422

0 metres 200
0 yards 200

N

■ **Sleeping**
1 Gorbandh Palace
2 Heritage Inn
3 Jaisal Palace
   & Kalpana Restaurant

4 Jawahar Niwas
5 Mandir Palace
6 Moomal
7 Nachana Haveli
8 Narayan Niwas &

Narayan Vilas
9 Pooja
10 Ringo
11 Rajdhani
12 Renuka

Shantinatha built at the same time. The **Ashtapadi** (16th century) incorporates the Hindu deities of Vishnu, Kali and Lakshmi into its decoration. The **Mahavir** Temple ① *view 1000-1100*, has an emerald statue. The **Sambhavanatha** (1431) ① *1000-1100*, has vaults beneath it that were used for document storage. The *Gyan Bhandar* here is famous for its ancient manuscripts.

> ⚑ *'Sunset Point', just north of the fort, is popular at sundown for views over Jaisalmer. The best light for photography is in the late afternoon.*

Havelis Time and tourism have taken their toll and many havelis are threatened. **JiJ**, a charity, are working to repair and stabilise the houses. Visit www.jaisalmer-in-jeoprdy.org, to find out more. There are many exceptional *havelis* (mansions of rich merchants) both in the fort and the walled town. Many have beautifully carved façades, *jali* screens and oriel windows overhanging the streets below. The ground floor is raised above the dusty streets and each has an inner courtyard surrounded by richly decorated apartments. An unofficial 'guide' will usually show you the way to them for about Rs 20. Inside Amar Sagar Pol, the former ruler's 20th-century palace **Badal Mahal** with a five-storeyed tower, has fine carvings. **Salim Singh-ki haveli** (17th century) ① *good carvings but being poorly restored, over-long guided tour*, near the fort entrance is especially attractive with peacock brackets and because of its distinctive and decorative upper portion is often referred to as the Ship Palace. **Nathumal-ki haveli** (1885) ① *when the havelis are occupied, you may be allowed in on a polite request, otherwise, your 'guide' will help you gain access for a small fee*, nearer Gandhi Chowk, was built for the Prime Minister. Partly carved out of rock by two craftsmen, each undertaking one half of the house, it has a highly decorative façade with an attractive front door guarded by two elephants. Inside is a wealth of decoration; notice the tiny horse-drawn carriage and a locomotive showing European influence!

Patwon-ki haveli (1805) ① *best 1030-1700, Rs 2 to view the gold ceilings and enjoy the view from the rooftop*, further east, is a group of five built for five brothers. Possibly the finest in town, they have beautiful murals and carved pillars. A profusion of balconies cover the front wall and the inner courtyard is surrounded by richly decorated apartments; parts well-restored. The main courtyard and some roofs are now used as shops.

Gadi Sagar tank The Gadi Sagar (Gadisar or Gharisar) tank, southeast of the city walls, was the oasis which led Prince Jaisal to settle here. Now connected by a pipe to the Indira Gandhi Canal, it has water all year. It attracts migratory birds and has many small shrines around it and is well worth visiting, especially in the late afternoon (see museums below). The delightful archway is said to have been built by a distinguished courtesan who built a temple on top to prevent the king destroying the gate.

To Mohangarh (NH15)

Kishanghat Pol

To Rawalkot Hotel (10 km) & Jodhpur

State Bus Stand

Auto Stand

Barmer Rd

Gadi Sagar Pol

Desert National Park Office

To Rajwada & Wood Fossil Park

Folklore Museum

Tilon-ki Pol

Gadi Sagar

To Rajwada & Wood Fossil Park (17 km)

13 Rama Guest House
   Golden City
14 Samrat & Karam
   Palace
15 Swastika

● Eating
1 Natraj
2 3ky, Trio
  & Thar Safari
3 Treat

Bada (Barra) **Bagh**ⓘ *Rs 10, auto-rickshaws, Rs 40 return*, 6 km north of Jaisalmer, is an attractive oasis with mango trees and other vegetation not normally seen in the desert. The reservoir and interesting systems of sanitary drainage may interest some but the cenotaphs are unexciting. There is a viewpoint from the royal *chhatris* (memorials) here but the intrusive tall army watch posts spoil sunset views.

The pleasant **Amar Sagar**ⓘ *camera Rs 50, video Rs 100*, 5 km northwest, was once a formal garden with a pleasure palace of Amar Singh (1661-1703) on the bank of a lake which dries up during the hot season. The Jain temple there has been restored.

Lodurva ⓘ *camera Rs 50*, 15 km northwest of Jaisalmer, contains a number of Jain temples that are the only remains of a once flourishing Marwar capital. Rising honey-coloured out of the desert, they are beautifully carved with *jali* outside and are well maintained. Worth visiting. The road beyond Lodurva is unsealed.

Sam dunes (or *Sain*) ⓘ *Rs 2, car Rs 10 (camera fees may be introduced), camel rates usually start at Rs 50 per hr but can be bargained down*, 40 km west of Jaisalmer, is popular for sunset camel rides. It is not really a remote spot in the middle of the desert but the only real large stretch of sand near town; the dunes proper only covering a small area, yet quite impressive. Right in the middle of the dunes, "Sunset view" is like a fairground, slightly tacky with lots of day-trippers; the only escape from this and the camel men is to walk quite a way away!

Khuriⓘ *best months Nov-Feb, Rs 3 (may be increased in line with Desert National Park), car Rs 10, buses from Jaisalmer take 1½ hrs, jeep for 4, Rs 450 for sunset tour*, 40 km southwest, of Jaisalmer is a small picturesque desert village of decorated mud thatched buildings which was ruled by the Sodha clan for four centuries. Visitors are attracted by shifting sand dunes, some 80 m high, but the peace of the village has been spoilt by the growing number of huts, tents and guesthouses which have opened along the road and near the dunes. Persistent hotel and camel agents board all buses bound for Khuri.

Thar Desert National Park is near Khuri, the core being about 60 km from Jaisalmer (the road between Sam and Khuri is motorable with a high clearance vehicle). The park was created to protect 3,000 sq km of the Thar Desert, the habitat for drought resistant, endangered and rare species which have adjusted to the unique and inhospitable conditions of extreme temperatures. The desert has undulating dunes and vast expanses of flat land where the trees are leafless, thorny and have long roots. Fascinating for birdwatching, it is one of the few places in India where the **Great Indian bustard** is proliferating (it can weigh up to 14 kg and reach a height of 40 cm). In winter it also attracts the migratory **houbara bustard**. You can see imperial black-bellied and common

Jaisalmer Fort

5 Laxmi Niwas &
  Surya Restaurant
6 Paradise
7 Sandrella
8 Simla
9 Sri Nath Palace
10 Suraj

N

0 metres   100
0 yards   100

■ **Sleeping**
1 Deepak
2 Fort View & Kanchan
  Shree Restaurant
3 Jaisal Castle
4 Laxmi Niwas (New)

● **Eating**
1 8th July
2 Little Tibet
3 Purezza
4 Vyas

On a camel's back

Camel safaris draw many to Jaisalmer. They give an insight into otherwise inaccessible desert interiors and a chance to see rural life, desert flora and fauna. The 'safari' is not a major expedition in the middle of nowhere. Instead, it is often along tracks, stopping off for sightseeing at temples and villages along the way. The camel driver/owner usually drives the camel or rides alongside (avoid one sharing your camel), usually for two hours in the morning and three hours in the afternoon, with a long lunch stop in between. There is usually jeep or camel cart backup with tents and 'kitchen' close by, though thankfully out of sight. It can be fun, especially if you are with companions and have a knowledgeable camel driver.

The tour lasting three days and two nights circuits around Jaisalmer via Mool Sagar, the Sam sand dunes and Lodruva. En route you pass through a few Muslim, Rajput and tribal villages, occupied and abandoned. You see fields of hardy millet and come across flocks of sheep and goats with their tinkling bells. Supper is around a fire (a home-cooked meal is sometimes simply warmed up) before spending the first night on a mattress under the stars. Next morning, after breakfast (tea, toast and boiled egg or sometimes porridge, pakoras, toast and jam, the safari proper begins, starting with a gentle walk working up to a fast trot (make sure you have proper stirrups fitted). Midday meal (chapati and daal) will be cooked by the camel driver on an open fire. When you stop to camp for the night, you may be joined by a member of the travel company from Jaisalmer. He will have brought out another meal on a motorbike to be warmed up over the camp fire. Next morning after breakfast you resume the gentle journey back to town. A leisurely stop for a freshly prepared lunch around midday allows you to return to base around 1600 – just two days after you started.

Carry biscuits and bottled water, though hawkers selling soft drinks, water, beer and chocolate materialize in the desert at contrived drink stops. Hygiene conditions are far from ideal – 'washing up' is in sand – and travellers often return feeling unwell.

Indian sand grouse, five species of vultures, six of eagle, falcons, and flocks of larks at Sudasari, in the core of the park, 60 km from Jaisalmer. Chinkaras are a common sight, as are Desert and Indian foxes. Blackbuck and Desert cat can be seen at times. Closer to sunset, you can spot desert hare in the bushes.

While most hotels will try to sell you a tour by four-wheel drive vehicle, this is no longer necessary. You can hire any jeep or high clearance car (Ambassador, Sumo) for the trip to the park. Off-the-road journeys are by camel or camel cart (park tour Rs 50 and Rs 150 respectively).

Barmer (Phone code: 02982. Colour map 2, grid B2) ① *A hot and dusty bus journey to Jaisalmer, 4 hrs; Mount Abu, 6 hrs.* This dusty desert town, 153 km south of Jaisalmer, is surrounded by sand dunes and scrublands. It is a major centre for wood carving, *durrie* rug weaving, embroidery and block printing (you can watch printers in Khatriyon ki galli). The 10th- to 11th-century Kiradu temples, though badly damaged, are interesting. Someshvara (1020), the most intact, has some intricate carving but the dome and the tower have collapsed

Dhorimmana The area further south of Barmer, has some of the most colourful and traditional Bishnoi villages and a large population of chinkaras and desert fauna. The village women wear a lot of attractive jewellery but may be reluctant to be photographed so it is best to ask first. PWD Rest house has clean and comfortable rooms.

Listings: Western Rajasthan

● Sleeping

Jodhpur *p408, map p409*
Hotel reductions from Apr to Oct. See also page 413 for out of town alternatives.
LL-L Umaid Bhawan Palace (Welcome Heritage), 5 km centre (car to town Rs 250; rickshaw Rs 30), T510101, F510100. 95 a/c rooms (suites up to US$990), unusual pool, luxurious ambience, expensive bufffet and meals in impressive dining hall, snacks in pleasant *Pillars* overlooking lovely garden, non-residents' pay Rs 330 'cover charge' adjusted against meals.
L Taj Hari Mahal, 5 Residency Rd, T439700, F614451. 93 plush rooms blending traditional and modern, imaginatively designed, good restaurants, excellent pool, the epitome of comfort.
B Ajit Bhawan (Heritage Hotel), Airport Rd, near Circuit House, T510410, F510674. 30 air-cooled rooms with bath, best in cottages in 'village' complex (a real farmyard), few cheaper small rooms, good pool (non-residents Rs 250), good Indian buffets, well-kept garden, 'village safari' (see Excursions above), group-oriented.
B Durjan Niwas, Daspan Vihar, off Loco Shed Rd, Ratanada, T649546, F616991.15 comfortable rooms (20 more planned) with balcony, pool, old house of Thakur family in a quiet location, friendly and helpful.
B Ranbanka, T512801, F512800. 30 renovated rooms, pool, garden.
B Royal Palace, Bhatia Circle, Ratanada, T515429, F515449, hrpalaceindia@ yahoo.com. 22 a/c rooms, 2 suites, extra bed Rs 200, modern 4-storey building, restaurant (meals Rs 150), helpful family and staff.
B-C Ratanada Polo Palace, Residency Rd, T431910, F433360, serena@ndf.vsnl.net.in. 50 spacious, well-equipped rooms, poolside dinners with folk music, large clean pool, tennis.
C Abhay Days, Mandore Rd, off Paota Circle,

T542988, F542978, www.daysindia.com. New hotel with western standards, excellent reasonably priced vegetarian restaurant.
C Karni Bhawan (Heritage Hotel), Palace Rd, Ratanada, T512101, F512105, www.karni hotels.com. 30 rooms, some a/c (**B** suites), festival theme decor and period furniture to match, in 1940s red sandstone building, village theme restaurant, peaceful lawns, clean pool, unhurried helpful staff.
C Madho Niwas, New Airport Rd, Ratanada, T512486, F512086, www.indiaoverland.com. Renovated rooms, Marwari meals in garden, pool, village safaris.
C-D Devi Bhavan, 1 Ratanada Rd, T511067, F512215. 8 rooms with bath (a/c erratic), delightful suburban garden, excellent Indian dinner, Rajput family home.
C-D Jug Villa, Shikargarh on the outskirts. Pleasant a/c cottages, good Gujarati *thalis* around fire in the garden at night, large lawn, good views of fort at sunset, book through North West Safaris, T079-6302019, F6300962, ssibal@ad1.vsnl.net.in.
C-D Newton's Manor, 86 Jawahar Colony, opposite Ratanada Polo Palace, Central School Rd, T430686, F610603. Renovated a/c rooms, touches of Victoriana, breakfast and dinner on request, exchange.
C-E Haveli Guest House, Makaran Mohalla, opposite Turji ka Jhalra, T614615, havelighj@ sify.com. Sandstone building with 7 balconies, 22 simple, clean rooms, cheerful decor, breezy rood terrace with veg restaurant, quiet, helpful owner.
    Guesthouses and cheaper **E** and **F** hotels often have shared baths.
D Akshey, behind station, opposite Raikabagh Palace (quick access to centre through rear door), T510327, F619562. Some modern a/c rooms, cheap dorm, poorly run restaurant, pleasant garden, peaceful, good value.
D-E Durag Vilas, 1 Old Public Park, near

● *For an explanation of the sleeping and eating price codes used in this guide, see inside the*
● *front cover. Other relevant information is found in Essentials pages 52-57.*

Circuit House, T621300. 6 very clean, quiet, air-cooled rooms with shower, 1 **C** a/c, travel bookings, desert safaris, family run, friendly, helpful, free lift from station/ airport.

D-E Blue House (R), Sumer Bhawan, Moti Chowk, T/F619133, bluehouse36@ hotmail.com. 7 clean rooms, 5 with bath (hot water all day), home cooked meals, great views from roof top restaurant.

D-F Chauhan's Guest House, Fort Rd, inside Nagori Gate, T541497. Rooms vary (some a/c with hot shower), relaxing café, family run, shop, book exchange.

E Govind, Station Rd, 200 m to right from station, opposite GPO, T622758. 14 clean rooms but bathrooms have ant problem, some **D** a/c, good rooftop veg restaurant with fort views (breakfast from 0530!), camel safaris, bus and rail ticketing, internet, friendly, very helpful owner but noisy location.

E Rawat, north of Umaid Public Park, T545622. Very quiet, large clean rooms, some a/c, but poor food and slow service.

E-F Raman Guest House, opposite Kesar Bagh, Shiv Rd, T513980. Clean though simply furnished rooms with bath (hot water), family atmosphere, traditional meals, quiet area.

F Cosy Guest House (was *Joshi's Blue House*), Novechokiya Rd (north from Jalori Gate), Brahm Puri, Chuna ki Choki, just west of the fort, T612066. 6 simple clean rooms, 3-bed dorm (Rs 40), all day bucket hot water, good home-cooked meals (other restaurants 15-min walk), bus bookings, rooftop views of fort and old city, quiet, very friendly and homely, no commission to rickshaws.

F Fort View, Lakshmi Bhavan, near Jalori Gate, T439923. Simple rooms from Rs 70 some with bath (best on roof), good Indian veg meals to order, pleasant though dusty rooftop, friendly welcoming owner. Recommended.

F Youth Hostel, Ratanada, T5110160. Dorms (Rs 25, non-members Rs 45), rooms with shared bath, canteen meals.

Durag Niwas, 1 Old Public Park, next to *Durag Vilas* (cheaper and longer established), T639092, duragniwas@usa.net. 10-min walk from bus station (phone for free lift). Pleasant rooms (may need to bargain), good cheap food, very quiet, clean and friendly.

Bal Samand Lake *p413*

A Bal Samand Palace, is in extensive grounds, on lakeside, T0291-545991. There are 6 attractively furnished suites in the separate atmospheric palace and 30 rooms in the imaginatiively renovated stables, restaurant (mainly buffet), pool, boating, pleasant orchards which attract nilgai, jackals, peacocks. Excellent alternative to staying in Jodhpur. Reservations T011-6868992, F6868994.

Luni *p413*

C Fort Chanwa, T0291-432460. Has 30 good rooms, not large but well furnished, individually designed (best in the keep), excellent Rajasthani meals in impressive dining room (Rs 300), pleasant lawn for drinks, pool, well managed but a bit impersonal. Recommended. You can visit craft villages (eg Salawas), watch good handloom weaving and bargain to buy.

Rohet *p413*

B Rohetgarh, T02936-68231, rohetgarh@wilnetonline.net. 29 rooms, attached baths (avoid rooms near outdoor restaurant), excellent Rajasthani food, ordinary architecture but in beautiful environment, pleasant lake view terraces, pool, riding and safaris to Bishnoi, Raika and artisans' villages, boating.

Sardar Samand *p413*

B Sardar Samand Palace, T011-6868992, F6868994. An annexe has 19 comfortable rooms. There is a Rajasthani restaurant, pool, extensive grounds, lovely walks, tennis, squash, riding and boating.

Osian *p414*

AL Camel Camp, on the highest sand dunes at Osian, T0291-37023. A complex of 10 double bedded luxury tents with modern conveniences (attached baths, hot showers), restaurant, bar, US$100 per tent inclusive of meals and camel safaris, ask in advance for jeep/camel transfers from the main road or station to avoid a steep climb up the dunes.

Also some **E** and **F** guesthouses in town.

Rajasthan Listings: Western Rajasthan

● *Phone codes Jodhpur: 0291; Bikaner: 0151; Jaisalmer: 02992; Barmer: 02982*

Khimsar *p414*

A Khimsar Fort, T01585-62345, F62228. 48 large, comfortable a/c rooms good restaurant on breezy roof top with lovely views, pool, yoga, gym, beautiful large gardens, "fire dances at the illuminated medieval fort ruins really captivating".

Nagaur *p414*

A Royal Camp, T011-6868992, F6868994, during the camel fair (and usually October to March). Delightful deluxe two-bed furnished tents (hot water bottles, heaters etc), Western flush toilets, hot water in buckets, dining tent for buffets.

Several **D-E** guesthouses in town have Indian toilets and provide hot water. Places serve good but extremely spicy north Indian vegetarian food. Tourists staying in town may find the early morning (0400) prayer calls from the mosque and *bhajan* singing at dawn at the temples a major detraction.

Bikaner *p414, map p416*

AL Lalgarh Palace (WelcomHeritage), 3 km from the railway, T540201, F522253, www.welcomheritage.com. 38 large a/c rooms, attractive red sandstone façade, built in 1902, beautiful decorations (see above), sports, good pool, mixed reports on food.

AL-B Laxmi Niwas, Lalgarh Complex, T202777, F525219, laxminiwaspalace@ 123india.com. 31 large, tastefully furnished rooms and suites with fabulous carvings, beautifully painted ceilings, gardens, courtyard with fountains, lattice work balconies, splendid restaurant, pool, gym, billiards, attentive staff.

A Heritage Resort, along the Jaipur highway, '9 Km' post, T752234, F207674. 36 cottage rooms, pleasant location, sprawling garden, bar, restaurant, outdoor coffee shop, pool, sports.

A-B Bhanwar Niwas, Rampuria St, Old City (500 m from Kote Gate), ask for *Rampuria Haveli*, T529323, F200880. 20 rooms around a courtyard (more being converted), early 20th-century *haveli*, Indian kitsch decor, excellent vegetarian dinner, bar in an old *baori* (reconfirm booking).

A-B Karni Bhawan Palace (HRH), Gandhi Colony behind Lalgarh Palace, T524701, F522408, www.hrhindia.com. 12 comfortable a/c rooms and spacious suites retaining plenty

of art deco features, good restaurant, internet, large garden, peaceful, pleasant staff, attentive service.

B Bhairon Vilas, near fort, T544751, F523642. Restored 1800s aristocratic *haveli*, great atmosphere, 18 attractive rooms, some with period furniture, excellent rooftop restaurant (Rajasthani, some Punjabi, Chinese, western) with live entertainment (musicians, dancers), good views, lawn, warm hospitality. Recommended.

B Maan Bilas (HRH), Lalgarh Complex, T540220, F522408, www.hrhindia.com. 9 comfortable garden facing rooms in a renovated outhouse, lawns, internet.

C Basant Vihar Palace, Ganganagore Rd, T528288, F528299. Rooms in attractive early-20th century palatial sandstone mansion built by Maharajah Ganga Sinhji, magnificent darbar hall, pool, large gardens, old lily ponds.

C Meghsar Castle, 9 Gajner Rd, T527315. 10 aircooled rooms in modern hotel but in traditional Rajput sandstone style, very attractive garden, friendly manager.

C Sagar, next to Lalgarh Palace, T520677, F201877. 32 good a/c rooms in modern building, few round huts, popular restaurant, exchange, internet.

C-D Bharat Niwas, near PBM Hospital, Sadul Colony, T523025, F523674. 24 rooms, a/c or air-cooled, good food, internet, clean, pleasant atmosphere, friendly.

C-D Palace View, near Lalgarh Palace, T527072. 16 clean, comfortable rooms (some a/c), good views of palace and gardens, restaurant (good 'unlimited' breakfast, wide choice), pleasant small garden, courteous, hospitable family. Recommended.

C-E Harasar Haveli, opposite Stadium, T209891, F523150, harasar-haveli@ yahoo.com. 16 rooms in converted mansion, some with verandahs and good views (Rs 250-850), dining room with period memorabilia, garden, exchange, internet, clean and friendly.

C-E Marudhar Heritage, Bhagwan Mahaveer Marg, near Station Rd, T522524. Good rooms, aircooled or a/c, bath with hot showers (am), TV, very clean and comfortable, generous *thalis* (Rs 50), friendly owner.

Budget hotel rooms usually have shared bath; often serve Indian veg food only. Tourist office has list of Paying Guest hotels.

D Shivam, Sadulganj, T203112, F525150.

Good rooms in nice bungalow in residential locality, restaurant, small garden, friendly.
D Thar, Hospital Rd, Ambedkar Circle (up a flight of steps from shopping complex), T543050, F525150. 35 clean rooms with bath (7 a/c) most with balconies, also dorm, Indian restaurant, coffee shop, good service, desert camping possible.
D-E Desert Winds, by MN Hospital, near Karni Stadium, 1 km Bus Stand, T542202. 6 clean, comfortable rooms, good food, pleasant balcony and garden, friendly family.
D-E Dhola Maru (RTDC), near Puran Singh Circle, T529621. 25 rooms with bath, dorm (Rs 50), some a/c, restaurant, bar, adequate.
E Kishan Palace, 8 Gajner Rd, T527762, F522041. Good value clean rooms, pleasant garden but on a noisy road.
E-F Kalinga, near Lalgarh Palace, T209751. Rooms for Rs 150-250, small baths, hot water and western toilets, meals from *Sagar* hotel.
F Railway Retiring Rooms and dorm are good value, reservations T524660.
F Vijay Guest House, Jaipur Rd, T231244, F525150. 3 clean rooms with shower, 3 with shared bath, use of fridge, delicious home cooked thali/set meals, travel information, camping (Rs 50) and caravan, pleasant garden, quiet very hospitable and knowledgeable host, great value. Recommended. Vijay's camel safaris also highly recommended.

Gajner National Park *p417*
A Gajner Palace, beautifully set by a lake, T01534-55063, F55060, www.hrhindia.com. With 40 renovated a/c rooms in the palace and its wings, most with brass beds and fireplaces, full of character (Edwardian Raj nostalgia), billiards, tennis, jeeps to scrub forest (Rs 1000), cycle hire (Rs 200), horse and camel rides, boating, good walking (great views from *Shabnam Cottage* on a hilltop), attractive red sandstone façades, latticework, pleasantly unfrequented and atmospheric, friendly manager and staff. Visitors are welcome from 0800 to 1730, Rs 100.

Karni Mata Mandir *p417*
F Yatri Niwas, nearby has simple rooms. Rajasthani food is sold by the temple.

Kakoo *p418*
E Dr Karni Singh's Rest House, adjoining the home of his forefathers, T01532-33006. Has

simple rooms and 3 rustic huts with attached baths, hot water in buckets for overnight stay.

Khichan *p418*
E-F Hotel Sunrise, halfway to Phalodi. Few basic rooms (mostly with Indian toilets). This is the only hotel.

Pokaran *p418*
C Fort Pokaran, T02994-22274, F22279. 14 quaint rooms with bath (need improving), old 4-posters, some carved columns, warm hospitality, good hot lunches Rs 200-250 (order ahead if passing through town).
D Godavan, on NH15, T22275. 2 rooms and 2 huts, mediocre restaurant (slow service), clean toilet, pool. Pick up fresh *pakoras* from highway stalls on the outskirts or delicious *gulab jamuns* from the local *halwai* (sweet shop).

In Manwar
10 km south of Dechhu, 61 km from Pokaran:
B-C Manwar Desert Camp, beautifully designed cottages with attractive interiors, some a/c, restaurant (a good lunch stop), book shop, handicrafts.
   Tented Resort, 2½ km on a sand dune off the road, has very good 2-bed tents with attached hot showers and flush toilets, meals, camel and jeep safaris and visits to Bishnoi villages. Reservations T02928-66137.

Jaisalmer *p419, maps p420 and p422*
Some hotels close in Apr-Jun. Very low room prices may be conditional on taking the hotel's camel safari (check beforehand); refusal may mean having to move out. Hot water morning and night.
A Fort Rajwada, 1 Hotel Complex, Jodhpur-Barmer Link Rd, T53533, F53733, www.fort rajwada.com. 65 top class rooms and 4 suites conceived by an opera set designer, luxury hotel with many stylish traditional features.
A Heritage Inn, 43 Sam Rd, T50901, F51638, channicarpets@vsnl.com. 55 good-sized rooms, single-storey sandstone desert architecture, restaurant, bar, pleasant interior, garden, pool, well-managed.
A Rawal-Kot (WelcomHeritage), Jodhpur Rd, 8 km from town. 31 large, comfortable, a/c or air-cooled rooms, attractively furnished, good restaurants, no pool, modern yet medieval atmosphere, good views of fort, friendly. Reservations: T011-6868992, F6868994.

A-B Rang Mahal, 5 Sam Rd, 2 km from fort, T50907, F51305, www.hotelrangmahal.com. 53 spacious rooms with balconies, desert architecture, extensive à la carte, largest pool in town (free to restaurant guests).

B Dhola Maru,15 km northeast of fort, T52863, F52761. 42 a/c rooms in attractive sandstone building but standards slipping and mixed reports of unhelpful staff, informative lectures by owner though.

B Gorbandh Palace (HRH), Sam Rd, 2½ km from town, T53801, F53811, www.hrh india.com. 67 rooms around courtyard in plush hotel, traditional decor, central a/c, also luxury tents, good but pricey set meals, noisy entertainment, pleasant pool, book/handicrafts shop, airport, station transfer.

B Himmatgarh Palace, 1 Ramgarh Rd, 2½ km from town, T52002, F52005. 40 a/c rooms (slow to cool), in attractive sandstone building, deluxe rooms with fridge, pool, great views from garden.

B Narayan Niwas Palace, opposite Jain Temple, Malka Rd, T52753, F52101. A converted caravanserai with 43 rooms, some a/c, modernized with bath (good hot showers, tubs), others spartan and windowless and overpriced, simple interiors, good Indian food in dining hall, pleasant courtyards.

B Rajwada, Jodhpur-Barmer Link Rd, T53233, F53733. 69 a/c rooms in large modern fort-like hotel with carved balconies, traditional 18th-century décor, swimming pool, billiards, gardens.

B-C Jawahar Niwas, Bada Bagh Rd, T52208, F52611. Small but attractive carved *haveli*, 11 renovated period furnished, large rooms in the main palace, 7 cheaper rooms in annexe, garden tented restaurant (overpriced), exorbitant phone calls, superb views, quiet, friendly helpful staff.

C Nachna Haveli, Gandhi Chowk (just up from *Trio*), T52110, F52778. Converted 18th-century Rajput *haveli* with carved balconies and period artefacts, 7 huge aircooled rooms with small attached baths, around courtyard, better **B** rooms, rather crowded area of town, rooftop restaurant.

C-D Jaisal Palace, near Gandhi Chowk, behind SBI, T52717, F50257, hoteljaisalpalace @yahoo.com. Simple, clean rooms with bath, 6 a/c, 8 aircooled, 1st floor balconies with views, Rajasthani food on roof terrace, train/bus bookings.

C-D Moomal (RTDC), Amar Sagar Rd, T52392. 51 rooms, a/c, some cheaper in round huts and dorm, mediocre restaurant, bar, tours, friendly and helpful.

C-D Suraj, behind Jain Temple, T51623. 5 basic but clean rooms with bath (some large, painted) in beautiful 530-year old *haveli*, some with view, atmospheric.

D Rama Guest House, Salim Singh-ki Haveli Marg, Dibba Para, T52570. 12 rooms, Indian restaurant, good views from rooftop, pleasant, relaxed.

D Rawal Kot, Fort Rd, T/F50444. 31 rooms in modern hotel built like a *haveli* with pleasant courtyards, a/c restaurant, rooftop restaurant with barbecue, good views from terrace.

D Saroj Palace, opp Collector's office, T53575, F52575. 16 clean, comfortable rooms (6 a/c, rest aircooled), attached bath, friendly owner, rooftop restaurant with good views.

There are several budget hotels around the fort and near **Amar Sagar Pol** – check rooms first. Some allow travellers to sleep on the roof for Rs 30-50. The tourist office has a Paying Guest accommodation list.

In and around the fort

D-F Paradise, opposite Royal Palace, T52674. 24 basic rooms, best **C** with hot showers, most with balcony and views, camping on roof terrace - Rs 60 for tent, Rs 40 for bed, "pleasant and cheap way to stay in Fort", safe lockers, limited room-service, good value camel safaris, some reports of being hassled.

D-F Simla, 5 clean rooms in old *haveli*, attractive wall hangings, 1 large with bath, others minute with bath downstairs, no safari pressure.

E Sri Nath Palace, *haveli* opposite Jain Temple, T52907. Avoid top floor (no toilet), restaurant, helpful, friendly owners, good camel safaris.

E Swastika, opposite *SBI*, near Amar Sagar Pol, T52483. 9 clean, well-kept rooms, most with bath, dorm, internet, bus/train bookings, family run.

E-F Deepak, behind Fort Jain temples, T52665. 25 rooms (most with hot showers, western toilets), best 8, 9 and 12, good vegetarian food (Brahmin), beds on rooftop, superb views, internet, travel ticketing, helpful owners, mixed reports about camel safaris.

E-F Laxmi Niwas, T52758, in Fort (signposted). 6 simple but clean rooms with bath in newer section at east end of fort,

better upstairs, with good views from terrace, good breakfast; also cheaper 5 homely rooms with common bath in older section (west of fort), warm welcome.
F Raj Palace, near Fort, T53264. 12 clean rooms, restaurant serves snacks, restored 18th-century building, cheerful, young manager, very helpful.
F Sandrella, Main Bazar. Free hot water in buckets, free jeep from bus or railway station, very friendly, good away-from-the-crowd 2-day safaris Rs 750, Indian/Australian venture. Avoid Peacock.

Elsewhere
E-F Golden City, Dibba Para, near first fort gate, T51664, hotelgoldencity@hotmail.com. Clean comfortable air cooled rooms with hot shower, 3 **D** a/c, rooftop restaurant with good views, free station transfer, exchange, internet, family atmosphere.
E-F Ringo Guesthouse, Mainpura St, Gandhi Chowk, T51627, bhatinarendra@hotmail.com. Comfortable rooms in family home, most with hot showers, some with tubs and a/c, rooftop restaurant, superb views over town from upper storeys, good camel safaris.
F Rajdhani, towards *Patwon-ki Haveli*, T52746. Clean rooms with hot shower, rooftop snacks, reliable safari, friendly.
F Renuka, opposite *SBI*, Chainpura St, T52757, F40323. 15 rooms (upstairs better), 8 with hot showers (Rs 80-200), roof-top restaurant with good views, friendly, helpful, clean, peaceful, free station pick up (call ahead), popular, safaris (no hard sell).
F Samrat, south of *Salim Singh-ki-Haveli*, T51498. 9 pleasantly furnished clean rooms, some with bath and balcony (Rs 30 to 200 with a/c), dorm (Rs 10), rooftop restaurant, helpful, family run, travel tickets, cycle hire.

Bada Bagh *p422*
Suman Motel, with rooms and vegetarian restaurant nearby.

Sam dunes *p422*
D-E RTDC Huts, Mr Sodha's. Facing the dunes, very busy in late afternoon and sunset but very pleasant at night and early morning.

Khuri *p422*
D-E Khuri Guest House. Recommended.
D-E Mama's Recommended.

Thar Desert National Park *p422*
E Rest Huts, facing the park are adequate. Permission is needed from the Collector as well as the Director, DNP, Barmer Road, Jaisalmer for a fee (Rs 100 per person, likely to increase soon).

Barmer *p423*
D-E Kailash Sarovar, Station Rd, a few minutes' walk from station, T22104. The best in town with decent rooms, some a/c, rooftop restaurant.

❷ Eating

Jodhpur *p408, map p409*
Best restaurants are in hotels (reserve ahead).
ŤŤŤ Ajit Bhawan, T510410, evening buffet (Rs 250), excellent meal in garden on a warm evening with entertainment, but poor atmosphere if eating indoors in winter.
ŤŤŤ Umaid Bhavan's, T633316, palatial, formal *Marwar Hall* (Rs 325 entrance refunded against bill). Beautiful coffee shop on terrace overlooking lovely garden.
ŤŤ Kalinga, below *Adarsh Niwas*, opposite station. Western and Indian. A/c, good food (try butter chicken and aubergine dishes), friendly service, music may not please.
ŤŤ On the Rocks, near *Ajit Bhavan*, good Indian and Continental. Lovely gardens.
Daal-bhatti, lassi and *kachoris* are sold around Jalori and Sojati Gates.
Ť Jodhpur Coffee House, Sojati Gate. Good South Indian snacks, good *thalis* Rs 18.
Ť Poonam, High Court Rd. Pure veg Indian. "Gorgeous 4-foot masala dosas".
Ť Shandar, Jalori Gate. Indian vegetarian. Good food and sweets.
Ť Tandoori Nights, next to Ajit Bhawan. Mughlai. Excellent meals, braziers at table for winter nights outdoors.
Ť Uttam, High Court Rd, near Sojati Gate. Good a/c *thali* restaurant friendly, fast service.

Sweets and drinks
Agra Sweet Home, near Sojati Gate.
Janata, Nai Sarak. Recommended.
Mishrilal, main entrance to Sardar Bazar. Splendid creamy and saffron flavoured *makhania lassi* – the best in town!
Rawat Mishtan Bhandar, near railway station. Tempting Indian sweets and drinks.

Veg restaurants on Station Rd. You can dine in style at the first 4 hotels listed.

Amber, Indian, some western dishes. Most popular, but reports of falling standards.

Bhairon Vilas's breezy roof top, for Rajasthani meals, order ahead.

Bhanwar Niwas.

Harasar Haveli.

Kesria, Jaipur Rd. Pleasant countryside location, popular on breezy summer evenings but disappointing food.

Niroj, near government bus stand. Popular for Indian-Chinese-Continental food, bar.

Teja Garden, Jaipur Rd. Pleasant outdoor garden restaurant, average food.

Vijay Guest House, delicious home-cooked veg *thalis*, non-veg set menu (Rs 60-100).

Fast food

Try the local specialities – *Bikaneri bhujia/sev/ namkeen* – savoury snacks made from dough. Sweets (including Rajasthani *ghevar* and Bengali *rasgulla*) are best at **Bikharam Chandiram**, **Aggarwal**, **Girdharalal** and **Haldiram**, all in Station Rd, Kote Gate area. **Chhotu Motoo** at *Joshi*. Fresh Rajasthani sweets and snacks. Visit Purana Bazar for ice-cold lassis by day, hot milk (milk, sugar, cream, whipped up with a flourish) at night. **Jamani Doodh Bhandar**, Vaidya Chowk.

Jaisalmer *p419, maps p420 and p422*
In and around the fort

8th Jul, just inside fort (another opposite Fort Gate). Vegetarian. Pleasant rooftop seating – popular for breakfast, pizzas, food average, pleasant for evening drink, mixed reports on service.

Little Tibet, beyond the palace chowk. Momos and much more of travellers' choice, generous, hygienic, enthusiastic staff, popular.

Natraj, next to *Salim Singh-ki-Haveli*. Mixed. Spacious rooftop with good views and a/c room, beer bar, wide choice (meat dishes Rs 80-100), average Indian and Chinese, clean toilet.

Purezza, Vyas Para. Excellent salads, Italian cheese veggies.

Surya, near Laxmi Niwas. Mixed. Good food, colourful, atmospheric, sit on cushions overlooking the city.

Vyas, Fort. Simple, good veg *thalis* (Rs 20-30), pleasant staff.

Gandhi Chowk

Sky, mainly Indian, 'English' breakfasts and some Italian. On rooftop, Rajasthani dancers and musicians, colourful and noisy!

Top Deck, good meat dishes (lamb steaks, southern fried chicken, Rs 60).

Trio, partly open-air, tented restaurant with small terrace, choice of cushions or chairs, excellent 'proper' tea, good atmosphere and creative food (try safari soup), musicians at dinner expect tips, view of Mandir Palace and fort illuminated, usually crowded.

Ringo Rooftop (separate from hotel), good north Indian including meat dishes. Superb views of fort.

Snacks and drinks

Chai stalls at Gopa Chowk make good 'Indian' tea before 1730. Hot and crisp kachoris and samosas opposite Jain temples near Narayan Niwas, are great for breakfast or high tea. **Dhanraj Bhatia**. Scrumptious Indian sweets including Jaisalmeri delights (try *godwa*). **Doodh bhandars** in Hanuman Chauraya sell a delicious mix of creamy milk, cardamom and sugar, whipped up with a flourish, between sunset and mid-night. **Kanchan Shree**, Gopa Chowk, 250 m from Salim Singh ki Haveli. Still among the best for drinks. *Lassis* (19 varieties) and ice cream floats. **Mohan Juice Centre**, near *Sunil Bhatia Rest House*. Delicious lassis, good breakfasts.

⊕ Bars and clubs

Jodhpur *p408, map p409*
In **Umaid Palace**, **Ashok** and in **Kalinga Restaurant** (see above).

Bikaner *p414, map p416*
Niroj is near the government bus stand.

Jaisalmer *p419, maps p420 and p422*
Gorbandh Palace, has a well stocked bar, **Jawahar Niwas**, **Naryan Niwas** and other **B** hotels.

⊕ Entertainment

Jaisalmer *p419, map p*
Cultural Centre off the Jaisalmer-Barra Bagh Rd. Evening music and dances Rs 10.

Systems

⊕ Festivals and events

Jodhpur p408, map p409
Several are special to Rajasthan (see page 330). **Jul/Aug**, Nag Panchami, when *Naga* (*naag*), the cobra, is worshipped. The day is dedicated to *Sesha*, the thousand-headed god or *Anant* ('infinite') *Vishnu*, who is often depicted reclining on a bed of serpents. In Jodhpur, snake charmers gather for a colourful fair in Mandore. **Marwar Festival** (**Oct**), held at full moon, includes music, puppet shows, turban tying competitions, camel polo and ends with a fire dance on the dunes at Osian.

Bikaner p414, map p416
Jan Camel Fair and Diwali (**Oct/Nov**) are especially spectacular in Junagarh Fort, in the Old City near Kote Gate and some smaller palaces.

Jaisalmer p419, maps p420 and p422
Feb 3-day Desert Festival with *Son et Lumière* amid the sand dunes at Sam, folk dancing, puppet shows and camel races, camel polo and camel acrobatics, Mr Desert competition. You can also watch craftsmen at work. Rail and hotel reservations can be difficult.
Royal Camp (WelcomHeritage), T011-6868992, F6868994, and *Gorbandh Palace* (see Sleeping above) in its courtyard, offer comfortable tents, flush toilet, hot water in buckets, Rajasthani meals, entertainment. **Feb/Mar** Holi is especially colourful but gets riotous.

Barmer p423
Thar Festival in **Mar** highlights desert culture and handicrafts.

◎ Shopping

Jodhpur p408, map p409
Export of items over 100-years-old is prohibited. Jodhpur is famous for its once popular *jodhpurs* (riding breeches), tie-and-dye fabrics, lacquer work and leather shoes. The main areas are: **Sojati Gate** for gifts, **Station Rd** for jewellery, **Tripolia Bazar** for handicrafts, **Khanda Falsa** for tie-and-dye, **Lakhara Bazar** for lac bangles. Shoes are made in **Mochi Bazar**, **Sardarpura** and **Clock Tower**,

bandhanas in **Bambamola**, and around **Siwanchi** and **Jalori Gates**. *Durries* are woven at **Salavas** village, 18 km away.

Antiques
Shops on road between Umaid and Ajit Bhawans, flourishing trade though pricey.

Books
John's Good Books, Bhati Circle, Circuit House Rd, T437638, small but quite good selection. **Khazana**, at Taj *Hari Mahal*, has books on India, and English fiction.

Handloom and handicrafts
Khadi Sangh, Station Rd. Quality, fair prices. **Marasthaly**, High Court Rd. Quality, fair prices. **Rajasthan Khadi Sangathan**, BK ka Bagh.

Photography
Shops in High Court Rd, Sojati Gate and in Jalori Gate. **Kala Colour Lab**, opposite MG Hospital, is recommended.

Spices
Mohanlal Verhomal, 209B, Kirana Merchant (from Clock Tower enter veg market, then turn right), T/F615846, www.mvspices.com. Sought after for hand mixed spices.

Bikaner p414, map p416
Bikaner is famous for *Usta* work which includes footwear, purses and cushions. You can also get local carpets and woodwork. The main shopping centres are on KEM (MG) Rd (from near the fort) and around Kote Gate in the Old City, Modern Market.
Cottage Industries Institute, Junagarh Fort. **Rajasthali**, counter at Information Centre.

Photography
Shops on MG Rd.

Pokaran p418
Kashida, just outside town, Jaisalmer-Bikaner Rd. Excellent handwoven crafts from the desert region, clean, well laid out, reasonably priced, profits help local self-help projects.

Jaisalmer p419, maps p420 and p422
Shops spen 1000-1330 and 1500-1900. Jaisalmer is famous for its handicrafts – stone-carved statues, leather ware, brass enamel engraving, shawls, tie-and-dye work,

embroidered and block printed fabrics, but garments are often poorly finished. Traders are more relaxed and welcoming here, and expect you to bargain. Look in **Siré Bazar,** Sonaron-ka- Bas and the narrow lanes of the old city including **Kamal Handicrafts,** and **Damodar** in the Fort. In Gandhi Chowk: **Rajasthali** (closed Tue); good **Khadi Emporium** at the end of the courtyard just above *Narayan Niwas Hotel.* **Jaisalmer Art Export,** behind *Patwon-ki Haveli* has high quality textiles.

Books
Bhatia News Agency, Court Rd. Good selection including travel guides; second hand books bought and sold.

Tailors
Mr Durga, small shop near fort entrance (between *New Tourist* and *Srilekha Hotels*). Excellent western style tailoring. Shirts made to measure, around Rs 200.
Nagpur, Koba Chowk. Western style tailoring.
Raju, Kachari Rd, outside Amar Sagar Pol. Western style tailoring.

▲▲ Activities and tours

Jodhpur *p408, map p409*
Tour companies
Aravali Safari, 4 Kuchaman House Area, Airport Rd, T626799.
Forts & Palaces, 15 Old Public Park, T511207, www.palaces-tours.com.
Poly Travels, 10D Bus Stand, Paota, T545210, F547642, poly@nda.vsnl.net.in.
   Tour City sightseeing: half day (0830-1300, 1400-1800). Fort and palaces, Jaswant Thada, Mandore Gardens, Govt Museum, bazar around Old City clock tower.

Bikaner *p414, map p416*
Camel safaris
You have to arrange these through private operators. A popular route is Raiser to Katriasar sand dunes on the Jaipur road, facing a fire dancers' village.
Aravalli Tours, Rs 1600 per person (toilet tent between 5 2-person tents).
Camel Man (see Tour companies), arranges excellent camel safaris, jeep tours and cycling, light weight 'igloo' tents, clean mattresses and sheets, good food and guidance. Camel safaris

to see antelopes, colourful villages and potters at work; vary from 1-2 hr rides to those lasting 5 days; Rs 500-800 per person per day.
Fata Mogana, T200561, professional, 20 years experience.
Gorbandh Safari, T540123, F524806.
Virendra Singh Tanwar, T0151-525594, offers up-market camel safaris from Bikaner towards Jaisalmer.

Tour companies
Aravalli Tours, opposite Municipal Council Hall, Junagarh Rd, T571124. Efficient.
Camel Man, *Vijay Guest House,* opposite Sophia School, Jaipur Rd, T231244, F525150. Offers good value, reliable, friendly and professional safaris (see above) and tourist guides.
Forts & Palaces, Jodhasar House, Hanuman Hatha, T205985, jaipur@palaces-tours.com. Experienced, efficient.
Travel Plan, Bhanwar Niwas, Rampuria St, T529323.

Jaisalmer *p419, maps p420 and p422*
Swimming
Gorbandh Palace (non-residents Rs 350); also *Heritage Inn* and *Fort Rajwada.*

Tour companies
Aravali Safari, near Patwon-ki Gali, T52632. Professional. Recommended.
Forts & Palaces, *Nachna Haveli,* Gandhi Chowk, T52538, jaipur@palaces-tours.com. Experienced, efficient.
Rajasthan Tourism, T52406. City sightseeing: half day, 0900-1200. Fort, *havelis,* Gadisagar Lake. Sam sand dunes: half day, 1500-1900.
Safari Tours, Gandhi Chowk, T/F51058.
Sahara Travels, Gopa Chowk, right of the 1st Fort gate, T52609. Mr (Desert) Bissa's reliable camel safaris with good food.
Thar Safari, Gandhi Chowk, near *Trio,* T52722, F53214. Reliable tours.
   Avoid: Adventure Travel, near Fort 1st Gate; Travellers Agency (of *Puskhar Palace*), near *Skyroom* restaurant; Adventure Tours (at *New Tourist Hotel*).

⊖ Transport

Jodhpur *p408, map p409*
Air
Transport to town: by taxi, Rs 200; auto-rickshaw, Rs 120. **Indian Airlines,** near

Bhati Cross Roads, T510757. 1000-1300, 1400-1700; airport, T512617. **Indian Airlines** flies to **Delhi, Jaipur, Mumbai, Udaipur**. Jet Airways, T302222, airport T331331: **Delhi**.

Bicycle
Bike hire: shops on the road opposite the station (near *Kalinga Restaurant*).

Bus
Local Mini-buses cover most of the city except Fort and *Umaid Bhavan Palace*.
Long distance Earplugs are recommended on video coaches. Allow time to find the correct bus; match number on ticket with bus registration plate.

A convenient bus route links Jodhpur with Ghanerao and Ranakpur, Kumbhalgar and Udaipur. RST Bus Stand, near Raikabagh rly station, T544989. 1000-1700; bookings also at tourist office. **Ahmadabad**, 11 hrs; **Jaipur**, frequent, 8 hrs; **Mt Abu Rd**, 6½ hrs; **Ajmer**, 4½ hrs; **Jaisalmer**, 0630 (depart Jaisalmer, 1400), 5-6 hrs, Rs 90; faster than train but scenically tedious; **Pali**, 4 hrs, Rs 30; **Udaipur**, 8-9 hrs, best to book a good seat a day ahead. Private operators: *HR Travels, Sun City Tours*, and *Sethi Yatra*, opposite Main Railway Station. **Private Buses**: ask at *Govind Hotel*, opposite Railway Station. Deluxe video coaches and Express buses between Jodhpur and **Delhi, Ahmadabad, Bikaner, Bhilwara**: most depart 0600 and 2200. **Jaipur** 5 hrs; **Jaisalmer**: about hourly from 0600 ('when full'), 4-5 hrs, Rs 100 (tickets from travel agents); comfortable buses on good road, but beware of touts on arrival at Jaisalmer, decide on hotel in advance.

Car
Car hire: from tourist office, *Ghoomer Hotel*, whole day about Rs 550; half day Rs 300.

Rickshaw
Railway station to fort should be about Rs 25 (may demand Rs 50; try walking away).

Taxi
T620238.

Train
Jodhpur Station enquiries: T131. Open 0800-2400. Reservations: T636407. Open 0900-1300, 1330-1600. Advance reservations, next to GPO. Tourist Bureau, T545083 (0500-2300). **International Tourist Waiting Room** for passengers in transit (ground floor), with big sofas and showers; clean Indian toilets in 2nd Class Waiting Room on the 1st floor of the Station Foyer. To **Abu Rd (Mount Abu)**: *Ranakpur Exp, 4707*, 1515, 5½ hrs. **Agra**: *Marudhar Exp, 4854/4864*, 0700, 14 hrs *Jodhpur-Howrah Exp, 2308*, 1715, 12¾ hrs. **Ahmadabad**: *Surya Nagri Exp, 4845*, 1855, 9½ hrs. **Barmer**: *Barmer Exp, 4807*, 0805, 4½ hrs. **Delhi** (no 1st class): *Mandore Exp, 2462*, 1930, 11 hrs (OD); *Jodhpur Delhi Exp, 4860*, 2300, 12½ hrs (OD) **Jaipur**: *Inter-City Exp, 2467*, 0545, 6 hrs; *Mandore Exp, 2462*, 1930, 5 hrs; *Marudhar Exp, 4854/4864*, 0700, 5 hrs. **Jaisalmer**: *Jodhpur Jaisalmer Exp*, and *4810 Exp*, 2315, 6½ hrs. **Varanasi** via Lucknow: *Marudhar Exp, 4854/4864*, 0700, 19 hrs (Lucknow), 26 hrs (Varanasi).

Bikaner *p414, map p416*
From **Delhi** (435 km); **Jaipur** (330 km); **Jodhpur** (250 km); **Jaisalmer** (320 km); **Ajmer** (280 km); **Mumbai** (1,250 km).

Bus
Long distance The New Bus Stand is 3 km north of town. Private buses leave from south of the Fort. Rajasthan Roadways, enquiries, T523800; daily deluxe buses to **Ajmer, Jodhpur, Jaisalmer** (8 hrs), **Udaipur**. 2 daily to **Delhi** via Hissar (12 hrs). Rajasthan Tourism, T27445, deluxe coach to **Jaipur**, 7 hrs.

Rickshaw
Auto-rickshaw: between station and Bus Stand or Lalgarh Palace, Rs 25.

Taxi
Unmetered, at station, bus stand or through hotels.

Train
Enquiries, T61131, reservations, 0800-1400, 1415-2000, Sun 0800-1400. For tourist quota (when trains are full) apply to Manager's Office by Radio Tower near *Jaswant Bhawan Hotel*. **Delhi**: *Bikaner-DSR Exp, 4790*, 0830, 10 ½ hrs; *Bikaner-DSRi Mail, 4792*, 1945, 10 hrs. From Delhi (SR), the overnight train (*DSR Bikaner Mail*,

4791, 2125, best 2nd Class sleeper), gives very good sunrise views. **Jaipur**: *Intercity Exp, 2466,* 0540, 5 hrs. **Jodhpur**: *KJC Exp, 4667,* 1230, 5½ hrs; *Ranakpur Exp, 4707,* 0935, 5½ hrs (continues to Ahmadabad, further 10 hrs) and Mumbai (Bandra), another 10½ hrs.

Jaisalmer *p419, maps p420 and p422*
Jaisalmer is on NH15 (Pathankot-Samakhiali). Transport to town from train and bus station is by autorickshaws or jeeps; police are on duty so less harassment but ask to be taken as close to your hotel as possible.

Air
No flights from the nearest airport at Jodhpur. **Alliance Air** from Delhi, 1030, via Jaipur; to Delhi, 1330. Check with **Crown Travels**, Sam Rd, T51912.

Bus
Long distance State (Roadways) buses, from near the station, T53141 and near Amar Sagar Pol. Services to Ajmer, Barmer, Bikaner (330 km on poor road, 9 hrs, Rs 100), Jaipur (638 km); Abu Rd for Mount Abu. **Jodhpur** (285 km) hourly service, 5½ hrs, Rs 80, RTDC coach, depart Jaisalmer, 1400 (depart Jodhpur 0630). **Udaipur**: (663 km), tiring 14 hrs. Private deluxe coaches from outside Amar Sagar Pol, to Jodhpur and Bikaner. Operators: **Marudhara Travels**, Station Rd, T52351. **National Tours**, Hanuman Choraha, T52348. Touts may board buses outside town to press you to take their jeep; it is better to walk 10-15 min from Amar Sagar Pol and choose a hotel.

Train
Foreign Tourist Bureau with waiting room, T52354. **Jodhpur**: *Jaisalmer Jodhpur Exp, 4609, 4809 Exp,* 2225, 7 hrs, sleeper, Rs 510, Can get very cold (and dusty) so take sleeping bag, or book bedding. (From Jodhpur, *4810,* depart 2315, 6½ hrs).

● Directory

Jodhpur *p408, map p409*
Banks 1030-1400. For Visa. **Punjab National Bank**, Ratanada. For TCs. **State Bank of India**, High Court Rd (inside High Court complex). Currency and TCs. **Hospital** MG Hospital, T636437. **Dispensary**: Paota, Residency. Open 0800-1200, 1700-1900, Sun 0800-1200. **Internet** Amardeep, Sardarpura, 3 km southwest of railway station, above *Marudhar Jewellers*, **Ghoomer Hotel**. **Post office** GPO: south of Jodhpur station, 1000-2000, Sat 1000-1600. **Tourist offices** Rajasthan, by *Ghoomar Hotel*, High Court Rd, T544010. 0800-1200, 1500-1800. International Tourist Bureau, railway station, T439052. **Useful addresses** Ambulance: T102. **Fire**: T101. **Police**: T100.

Bikaner *p414, map p416*
Banks Bank of Baroda, Ambedkar Circle, cash against Visa; **State Bank of Bikaner & Jaipur**, Ambedkar Circle; also near fort's Suraj Pol. Changes TCs but may charge up to 10% commission! Harasar Haveli Hotel charges 1%. **Hospital** PBM Hospital, Hospital Rd, T524175. **Internet** Meghsar Castle, **Hotel Sagar** and **Harasar Haveli**, Rs 2 per min; others at Sadulganj, Sagar Rd, Jaipur Rd and Gajner Rd, and near the fort. **Post office** GPO: behind Junagarh Fort. **Tourist offices** Rajasthan, *Dhola-Maru Tourist Bungalow*, Poonam Singh Circle, T527445. 0800-1800, Oct-Mar, car-hire. **Useful addresses** Ambulance: T61902. Police: T100.

Jaisalmer *p419, maps p420 and p422*
Banks 1030-1430, Mon-Fri, 1030-1230, Sat, closed Sun. On Gandhi Chowk: Bank of Baroda and SBBJ, TCs and cash against credit cards; **State of Bank of India**, *Nachna Haveli*, currency only. **Hospitals** SJHospital, Gandhi Marg, T52343. **Internet** Joshi Travel, opposite PO, Central Market, Gopa Chowk, T/F50455 joshitravel@hotmail.com. Cyber café, modern equipment, also STD, fax etc. Others may have problems connecting. **Post office** GPO: near Police Station, T52407. With Poste Restante. **Tourist offices** Rajasthan, near TRC, Station Rd, Gadi Sagar Pol, T52406, 0800-1200, 1500-1800. Counter at railway station. **Useful addresses** Collector/magistrate: T52201; Fire: T52352. **Police**: T53322.

Haryana and Punjab

Introduction

The flat, open and richly cultivated plains of Haryana and Punjab witnessed some of ancient India's most significant battles. Kurukshetra, Krishna's battlefield in the Mahabharata, and Panipat, where Muslim power was established, lie in Haryana just north of Delhi. **Amritsar's Golden Temple**, one of the great treasures of North India, is the holiest centre of worship for the Sikhs, whose roots lie in the soil of the Punjab. Le Corbusier's specially designed capital, **Chandigarh**, modernist in conception and secular in spirit, could scarcely stand in greater contrast. Ironically many now seem to visit Chandigarh more for the quixotic delights of **Nek Chand's "Rock Garden"** than for its European architect's alien buildings.

Through extensive irrigation Haryana and Punjab have become the most productive states of India. Most of the major towns and cities of the region are close to the Grand Trunk Road, the great highway from Peshawar to Calcutta which Rudyard Kipling described as "the backbone of all Hind". Today it is still the route from Delhi into the Himalayan states of Himachal Pradesh and Kashmir.

★ Don't miss...

❶ The stunning Golden Temple at **Amritsar** is a haven of peace and best seen at dawn, page 452.

❷ Catch the ceremonial changing of the guards at the **Wagha Border** crossing between India and Pakistan, page 457.

❸ The area around Ludhiana was fiercely fought over in the 1st Sikh War. The British finally broke the spirit of the magnificent Sikh army at **Sobraon** on the banks of the Sutlej River, page 447.

❹ After Le Courbusier's modernist buildings, Nek Chand's '**Rock Garden**' in Chandigarh offers much light relief, page 443.

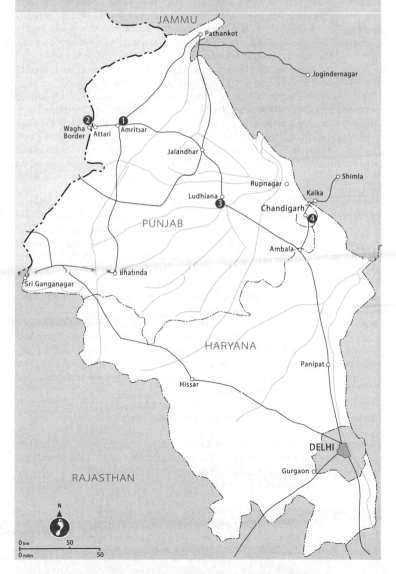

Haryana & Punjab

Background → *Haryana Population: 21.1 million. Area: 44,200 sq km. 20%.*
Punjab Population: 24.29 million. Area: 50,300 sq km.

The land
Punjab and Haryana occupy the strategic borderlands between the Indus and Yamuna-Ganga river systems. Well over 1000 km from the sea, their gently sloping plains are less than 275 m above sea level. In the southwest, on the arid borders of Rajasthan, sand dunes form gentle undulations in the plain.

History
Before independence The **Ghaggar Valley**, running from the Shiwaliks down to the Rajasthan desert, was the home of fortified urban settlements before 3000 BC and the rise of the Harappan civilization. The rising tide of Aryan influence steadily became the dominant force. It was here that the **Vedas** took shape. The region became vital for the Muslim kings of the Delhi Sultanate 1,500 years later and was part of the Mughals' core region of power.

Sikhism became an increasingly powerful force after Guru Nanak, who lived in the Punjab from 1469 to 1539, first established his community of 'seekers'. See page 1346. Aurangzeb tried to put down Sikhism by force, encouraging the Sikhs to become militant. In 1799 **Ranjit Singh** set up a Sikh confederacy which governed until the late 1830s. Two wars with the British ended in 1849, after which the Sikh community played an important role in British India, see page 1345. In 1857 they took the British side in the Mutiny, and were given prominent positions in the Indian armed services throughout the later period of British rule. However, many Sikhs also joined the struggle for Independence, and suffered grievously at the **Jallianwala Bagh** massacre in 1919, see page 454.

In 1947 Punjab was torn apart by the massacres which accompanied **Partition**. In the atmosphere of increasing communal violence, the Punjab was divided in two, leaving over five million Sikhs and Hindus in Muslim West Pakistan and 40 million Muslims in predominantly Hindu India. Many people, terrified by the prospect of losing all that they had worked for, turned on each other. **Amritsar**, 24 km from the border and the main railway station between Delhi and Lahore, witnessed some of the worst carnage. In six terrible weeks from August to mid-September at least half a million people died, and over 13 million people crossed the new borders of India and Pakistan.

After independence Sikh political opinion in Punjab continued to stress the need for a measure of autonomy within India's federal constitution. The creation of linguistic states in 1956 encouraged the Sikh Akali Dal to press for the further division of Punjab. Religious identity in itself was inadmissable under the Indian Constitution as a basis for separate statehood, and the Akalis therefore argued the distinctiveness of Punjabi from Hindi. Punjabi agitation in 1966 succeeded in achieving the further sub-division of the Punjab into the present states of Punjab (predominantly Sikh), Haryana (predominantly Hindu) and Himachal Pradesh (a purely mountain state, 96% Hindu).

Government In 1947, the Indian government built Chandigarh as the modern administrative capital for the Punjab. When Haryana was created in 1966 Chandigarh became the capital for both states. Arbitration was promised to decide its ultimate allocation, but its future remains undecided.

Recent political developments **Punjab** has 13 seats in the Lok Sabha (Lower House) and seven seats in the Rajya Sabha (Upper House) in the national parliament in New Delhi. In recent years Punjab has had several periods of direct rule from New Delhi. After the decade of political turmoil in the 1980s, marked by widespread violence surrounding the emergence of an Independence movement in Punjab, normality has returned. In the February 2002 elections the Congress recaptured power from the Akali Dal and the BJP combine which had governed since 1997, and the Party President, Captain Amarinder Singh, became the State's 21st Chief Minister.

Haryana has five seats in the Rajya Sabha and 10 seats in the Lok Sabha in New Delhi. Following a trend seen in many states recent assembly elections have seen regional parties gain increasing strength at the expense of national parties like the Congress. In the February 2000 Assembly elections the Indian National Lok Dal (a party which, despite its name, is almost entirely restricted to Haryana) won 47 of the 90 seats, Congress being the runner up with 21.

Culture

Despite the strong influence of Hinduism and to a much lesser extent Islam, Sikhism displays a distinctive character of its own. Its literature has strong connections with Sufism. Guru Nanak used the Punjabi language as a medium for poetry. Typically Hindu celebrations and festivals such as *Dasara* and *Diwali* are enthusiastically observed as are the birth and death anniversaries of the gurus and saints. Sikh music, much of it like the Mughal *ghazal* and *qawwali* is immensely popular.

The long *kurta* (shirt) and baggy trousers drawn in at the ankle are traditional and popular forms of dress with Punjabi men. Women usually wear a similar *salwar kamiz* with a *dupatta* (long scarf). Sikh men are distinctive for their turbans and beards. See page 1345.

The Sikhs are often thought of as enterprising and practical people, using machines from tractors to tubewells, threshing machines to grinders. They are now found driving buses, taxis, and hire cars. They were the drivers in the Indian army and have maintained this role ever since.

Two-thirds of the 21 million people in Punjab speak **Punjabi**, a close relative of Hindi, while the remainder speak **Hindi**.

Chandigarh→ *Phone code: 0172. Colour map 1, grid B3. Population: 900,900.*

In 1947 when Lahore, Punjab's former capital, was allocated to Pakistan, the Indian government decided to build a new capital for the Indian state of the Punjab. The result is Chandigarh, a planned city in the post-war modernist style, acting as the dual capital of Punjab and Haryana states. Some critics describe Chandigarh as soulless. Not quite the garden city it was dreamt to be, it is nevertheless a convenient stop en route to Himachal Pradesh, or before flying to Leh. ►► For Sleeping, Eating and other listings, see pages 446-449.

Ins and outs

Getting there The airport and railway stations are some distance from the centre with pre-paid auto rickshaws to town. From the large bus terminus in the busy Sector 17, you can walk across to several budget hotels and restaurants.

Getting around Buses serve the different sectors but if you are only here for a few hours, it is best to hire transport as there are long distances to cover in this widely spread out city and it is not always easy to find a taxi or auto-rickshaws for single journeys. See Transport, page 448, for further details.

Climate Temperature: summer, maximum 39°C, minimum 25°C; winter, maximum 20°C, minimum 7°C. Rainfall: over 250 mm from Jun-Aug. Best time to visit: Nov-Mar.

The initial plans for the creation of the city were drawn in New York by Mayer and Novicki. When the latter died in 1950 the work was entrusted to the internationally renowned architect **Le Corbusier** who supervised the layout and was responsible for the grand buildings. Fry and Drew designed the residential and commercial areas.

Jawaharlal Nehru said of Chandigarh "Let this be a new town symbolic of the freedom of India, unfettered by the traditions of the past, an expression of the nation's faith in the future". Its detractors describe it as a concrete prairie, the product of 'the ivory tower school of architecture' and despite its planning many regard Chandigarh as a characterless failure. Today there is a growing scarcity of land, despite the complete ban on industrial activity, a ban which has had the advantage of greatly limiting air pollution.

Sights

Chandigarh's major centres are: the **Capitol Complex** consisting of the Secretariat, Legislative Assembly and High Court in the northeast with the Shiwalik Hills as a backdrop; **Sector 17**, the central business district with administrative and state government offices, shopping areas and banks; a **Cultural Zone** in Sector 14, for education which includes a museum and a campus university with institutions for engineering, architecture, Asian studies and medicine. A vast new colonnaded **Shopping Mall** has opened in Sector 35, with hotels, restaurants, banks, a well-stocked supermarket, internet/international phones etc.

The multi-pillared **High Court** stands nearby with a reflective pool in front. Primary colour panels break up the vast expanses of grey concrete but this classic work of modernist architecture looks stark and bleak. The **Legislative Assembly** has a removable dome and a mural by Le Corbusier that symbolizes evolution. In the same sector is the **Open Hand Monument**. The insignia of the Chandigarh Administration, it

Chandigarh

Related map
A Sectors 17 &22, page 441

Sleeping
1 Kapil
2 Maya Palace
3 Mountview
4 President

Eating
1 Ginza

0 metres 400
0 yards 400

symbolizes 'the hand to give and the hand to take; peace and prosperity, and the unity of humankind'. The metal monument rotates in the wind, 14 m high and weighing 50 tonnes, sometimes resembling a bird in flight. The geometrical hill nearby, known as the **Tower of Shadows** ① *tours 1030-1230 and 1420-1630, ask at Secretariat reception desk (you may need special permission to enter)*, was designed to beautify the complex, breaking its symmetrical lines.

Government Museum and Art Gallery ① *closed Mon, 1000-1630, S10*, has a collection of stone sculptures dating back to the Gandhara period, miniature paintings and modern art. Also prehistoric fossils and artefacts. **Museum of Evolution of Life** ① *closed Mon, 1000-1630, S10*, has exhibits covering 5,000 years from the Indus Valley Civilization to the present day. **Fine Arts Museum**, Punjab University, S14. All the faculties of the university are in Gandhi Bhavan, S14; the university specializes in Gandhi studies.

Rose Gardens ① *rose show in early March, till sunset, S16*, one of the largest in Asia (25 ha), contains over 1,500 varieties of roses; well worth visiting in spring.

★ **Rock Garden** or *Garden of Nek Chand.* ① *Apr-Sep, 0900-1300, 1500-1900, (1400-1800, Oct-Mar), S1, allow 3 hrs to do this unique and imaginative place some justice, highly recommended.* The creation of Nek Chand, a road inspector in the Capitol City project, the 'garden' comprises an extraordinary collection of stones from the nearby Shiwaliks (carried on his bike) and domestic rubbish transformed into sculptures. Nek Chand dreamed of 'creating a temple to Gods and Goddesses' out of discarded items of everyday use, for example bottle tops, fluorescent lights, mud guards, tin cans, and by highly imaginative re-assembling made models of people and animals. These have been set out along a maze of paths, creating an often amusing and enjoyable park. First opened in 1976 the park is still being extended. The low archways make visitors bow to the gods who have blessed the park.

Just below the rock garden is **Sukhna Lake**, an artificial lake, the venue of the Asian rowing championships and circled by a walk. Crowded on holidays and Sunday. There are cafeterías, boating and fishing (permits).

Zoological Park ① *Rs 100 per car, Rs 10 per person*, Chaat Bir, a few kilometres out of the city centre, also has a lion and deer safari park.

Chandigarh – Sectors 17 & 22

	Sleeping		4 Pankaj & Restaurant		Eating		3 Hot Millions, Bar &
	1 Aroma		5 Piccadily		1 Bhoj Vegetarian,		Universal Bookshop
	2 Divyadeep & Bhoj		6 Shivalik View		Chopsticks & Tasty Bite		4 Kwality
	3 Jullunder		7 Siva		2 Ghazal		5 Mehfil

0 metres 200
0 yards 200

Chandigarh to Himachal Pradesh → *Colour map 1, grid B3.*

Kalka, beyond Pinjore, is the starting point for the scenic mountain railway to Shimla; see page 466. The quickest route to **Dharamshala** is via Ropar and Anandpur Sahib, and past Govindsagar, created by the vast Bhakra-Nangal Dam.

Pinjore (Pinjaur)

The **Yadavindra Gardens**, at Pinjore, 20 km on Kalka Road, were laid out by Aurangzeb's foster brother Fidai Khan, who also designed the Badshahi Mosque in Lahore. Within the Mughal *charbagh* gardens are a number of palaces in a Mughal-Rajasthani style: Shish Mahal, which has mirror-encased ceiling and is cooled by water flowing underneath (remove a slab to see!); the Rang Mahal, a highly decorated pavilion; the Jal Mahal, set among fountains, cool and delightful; camel rides and fairground attractions to tempt city dwellers. Keep a close eye on your luggage at all times; thefts reported.

Anandpur Sahib

ⓘ *Bus from Chandigarh and Ropar. Train to Ambala: Himachal Exp, 4544, 2210, 3½ hrs. To Nangal Dam Express, 4553, 0620, 30 mins.*

Anandpur Sahib (City of Divine Bliss), in a picturesque setting at the foot of the Shiwaliks by the river Sutlej, was established by the ninth Guru, Tegh Bahadur, in 1664, when the Sikhs had been forced into the foothills of the Himalaya by increasing Mughal opposition. Guru Tegh Bahadur himself was executed in Delhi, and his severed head was brought to Anandpur Sahib to be cremated. The event added to the determination of his son, Guru Gobind Singh, to forge a new body to protect the Sikh Community. The Khalsa Panth was thus created on Baisakhi Day in 1699. Anandpur Sahib became both a fortress and a centre of Sikh learning. *Hola Mohalla* is celebrated the day after Holi when battles are re-enacted by nihangs (Guru Gobind Singh's army) on horseback, dressed in blue and huge turbans, carrying old weapons. There is a small museum recounting the history of the Sikhs in a series of paintings.

Patiala

Patiala, a neatly kept town southwest of Chandigarh, was once the capital of an independent state, along with Jind and Nabha, whose ruling houses were all Sikh. The Maharaja of Patiala's treaty with the British in 1809 kept Ranjit Singh out. In due course the Maharaja became a premier Sikh prince and remained so until 1947.

Surrounded by a moat, the huge concentric **Bahadurgarh fort** was built by **Maharaja Ala Singh** in the late 18th century. It is a good example of a *nara durg*, a large fort built on a plain, housing a garrison large enough to repulse strong attacks such as the fierce Maratha attempt in 1794. Now a Police Commando Training School, it is closed to visitors but you may request the guards at the back gate to allow you to sign in and look around. The Sikh Palace is almost in ruins and the Moghul Mosque survives through the amateur conservation efforts of the Fort Commandant. ⓘ *Getting there: take Rajpura bus from Platform 19.*

The **Old Motibagh Palace** (late 19th century) is about 3 km to the south, at the end of Mall Road. It is one of the largest residences in Asia with 15 dining halls. The grotesquely oversized rambling central building is surrounded by lawns and trees. A combination of European, Rajput and Mughal styles, part of it is now the National Institute for Sports. The Sheesh Mahal has a **Museum and Art Gallery** housing ethnography, arms, natural history and miniature paintings. There is an unusual sunken lake and a curious 19th-century suspension bridge.

Chandigarh to Delhi → *Colour map 1, grid B3 and C3.*

From December to March the fields are green with wheat, though towards Delhi many are now planted with vegetables for the Delhi market. If travelling by train through this area at harvest time, expect to find your nostrils, clothes and luggage filled with dust and chaff! The Grand Trunk Road through Haryana is one of the busiest in India. It has long stretches lined with magnificent trees, and villagers have to buy rights to the leaves and wood.

Ambala

Ambala, now the district headquarters, became a large British cantonment, laid out from 1843 onwards in grid fashion. The famous Gupta iron pillar now at the Qutb Minar in Delhi was originally on the hill just outside town.

Kurukshetra

The battlefield where Arjuna learned the meaning of *dharma* has left no trace. See page 1318. The flat plain around Kurukshetra is described in Sanskrit literature as 'Brahmavarta' (Land of Brahma). Like many other sacred sites it becomes the special focus of pilgrimage at the time of exceptional astronomical events. In Kurukshetra, eclipses of the sun are marked by special pilgrimages, when over one million people come to the tank. It is believed that the waters of all India's sacred tanks meet together at the moment of eclipse, giving extra merit to anyone who can bathe in it at that moment.

Brahmasar Lake, 1 km west, a pilgrim site, is visited by a wide range of wildfowl, particularly from December to February. Temples and ghats surround the tank. The modern temple can best be described as kitsch, a reproduction of earlier temple styles. But the site is important for its influence on the development of Hindu ideas, not Hindu architecture. There are also the remains of a **Muslim Fort**, including the **Tomb of Shaikh Chilli Jalal** (died 1582) and **Lal Masjid**, a small red sandstone mosque. The carving on the domes is similar to that at Fatehpur Sikri.

Karnal

Karnal was taken by the British in 1797 who established a cantonment here in 1811. At Uchana, 3 km north, Haryana Tourism has created an artificial lake.

Panipat

Panipat is the site of three great battles which mark the rise and fall of the Mughal Empire. It stands on the higher ground made up of the debris of earlier settlements near the old bank of the River Yamuna. Today it is an important textile town with over 30,000 looms. A high proportion of the products, carpets, curtains and tablewear, is exported.

In the first battle of Panipat on 21 April 1526 Babur, the first Mughal Emperor, fought Ibrahim Lodi, the Sultan of Delhi, reputedly resulting in the death of 20,000 of the sultan's army, including Ibrahim Lodi. The second battle, on 5 November 1556, changed the course of India's history, as it secured Mughal power. **Akbar**, who had just succeeded his father Humayun, and his general, defeated Hemu, the nephew of the Afghan Sher Shah. There was a mass slaughter of the captives, and in the gruesome tradition of Genghis Khan, a victory pillar was built with their heads plastered in. The third battle took place on 13 January 1761. The once great Mughal Empire was threatened from the west by the resurgent **Rajputs** and from the northwest by the Afghans. The distracted Mughal minister called in the Marathas. Despite their numbers, the Marathas lost and their soldiers fled. However, the Afghan leader **Ahmad Shah Durrani** was unable to take advantage of his victory as his followers mutinied for the two-years' arrears of pay he owed them. North India was thus left in a political vacuum which adventurers tried to fill during the next 40 years.

The main old building in Panipat is a shrine to the Muslim saint Abu Ali Kalandar.

Southwestern Haryana → *Colour map 2, grid A5 and A6.*

Road and rail criss-cross the largely flat plain where irrigation sustains lushly cultivated fields. Further west dry land predominates, shading into the deserts of Rajasthan. The NH10 gives access to several remote archaeological sites and India's most important early settlement region but it is rarely visited.

Rohtak → *77 km from Delhi.*
The archaeological sites at **Khokhra Kot** and **Ramala Ala** have revealed pottery from pre-Harappan and early historical times after 1500 BC. Coin moulds from the first century have thrown valuable light on the processes of minting coins. Today, it is well known for its turbans, interwoven with gold and silver thread.

Hissar
Hissar was founded in 1354 by Firuz Shah Tughlaq who constructed a canal to bring water to his hunting ground. This was renovated in the 19th century and incorporated into the West Yamuna Canal. The Gujari Mahal in the old fort was built from the remains of a Jain temple. The citadel contains the Mosque of Firuz Shah (late 14th century) and the Jahaz (ship) east of the city, which takes its name from its shape (reminiscent of that at Mandu – see page 307). Hissar exports cattle all over India and is widely known for its twice yearly **cattle fairs**.

Sirsa
Sirsa was settled from around 1500 BC with pottery known as Rang Mahal Ware. Thus it was clearly occupied long before the traditional date of its founding – the sixth century AD – when it was known as Sarasvati. Just north of **Sirsa** the road crosses the usually dry bed of the Ghaggar River, one of North India's most important early settlement regions. The **Kalibangan** Harappan site is just beyond Suratgarh to the west, see page 418. There is a large cattle fair here in August to September.

Chandigarh to Amritsar → *Colour map 1, grid B2 and B3.*

Many of the small towns along this route show signs of Punjab's rapid industrialization; steel rolling, textiles, sugar mills, food processing and a whole range of small industrial services from computers to advertizing.

Sirhind
Mahmud of Ghazni extended his control to the town in the early 11th century when it became the border town for Muslim possessions in India, hence Sar-i-Hind ('Frontier of India'). Later it became Sher Shah Suri's capital, whose army was defeated by Humayun in 1555.

The town's period of greatest splendour was between 1556 and 1707. The stone-built Tomb of Mir Miran is an octagon topped by a dome. Another octagonal tomb, ornately decorated with painted flowers, is that of Pirbandi Nakshwala, with its pear shaped dome covered in glazed tiles. Salabat Beg Haveli is a large and well-preserved Mughal house whilst the Sarai of the Mughal emperors, in the southeast of the town, is now a public hall. For the Sikhs, Sirhind is associated with the brutal execution of the two younger sons of the 10th Guru, who were bricked up alive in the fort in 1705 for refusing to convert to Islam.

Ludhiana

A rapidly growing town on the bank of the Sutlej River, Ludhiana is a major textile (hosiery) and light engineering centre. Here you can get good quality fabric from the market and garments copied cheaply by expert tailors. The rich agricultural area around it supports a large grain market. Founded in 1480 by Lodi princes from Delhi (hence its name), Ludhiana subsequently passed through a number of hands. The surrounding area was fiercely fought over during the First Sikh War with the British in 1845-46. The three major battlefields at **Mudki, Firozshah** and **Sobraon** all have commemorative obelisks. The town is also the home of the **Christian Medical College Hospital**, which is in partnership with the CMC hospital in Vellore. The world famous **Punjab Agricultural University**, on the edge of town, has a good museum. In Februrary, a show of *Rural Games* of Punjab is organized at Kila Raipur nearby.

Jalandhar

Jalandhar (Jullundur) is an ancient city of which very little survives. It was sacked by Mahmud of Ghazni and under the Mughals it was an important administrative centre. Today, it is a major road and rail junction with a busy market, the Rainik Bazar, a network of narrow alleys full of shops which only cycle rickshaws and scooters can negotiate. The cantonment area to the southeast was established in 1846 to house army units after the treaties signed in Lahore in March and December 1846 which ended the First Sikh War.

Kapurthala

① *On the train line to Firozpur and can be reached by changing at Jalandhar. Daily bus services from Jalandhar and Amritsar.*

Kapurthala is the capital of the former Sikh princely state and the home town of the **Ahluwalia** family who conquered it in 1747. Its army fought against the British at Aliwal in the First Sikh War but took the British side during the Second Sikh War (1848) and the Mutiny (1857).

Later governed as a model city-state, the French-educated ruler Jagajit Singh, who ascended the throne in 1890, tried to make his capital city a Parisian replica. His palace, the **Jalaukhana**, might have come straight out of the French Renaissance, except that the red sandstone with which it was started had to give way to pink stucco when funds ran out. The palace is now a boys' school. The Maharaja's international preferences changed when he married a Spanish dancer, however, and the **Villa Buena Vista** (1894) has an Iberian flavour.

Firozpur

① *Train from Firozpur Cantt: Jalandhar, Tawi Exp, 4806, 1010, 2¾ hrs. From Firozpur City: New Delhi, Punjab Mail, 2138, 2150, 7¼ hrs; Janata Exp, 9024, 0430, 9¼ hrs.*

Firozpur, southwest of Jalandhar and close to the Pakistan border, was founded during the rule of Firoz Shah Tughluq in the mid-14th century, passed to the Sikhs, and then the British in 1835. There is a British cemetery on the GT Road link to Ludhiana. The extension of the Sirhind Canal in the 1880s transformed the previously poverty-stricken agricultural region into a prosperous canal colony and is intensively cultivated today.

Goindwal and Tarn Taran

On the way from Jalandhar to Amritsar there are important *gurudwaras* where Sikhs on pilgrimage traditionally stop. There are separate bathing places for men and women at Goindwal, with a small market place outside the temple. The *gurudwara* at Taran Tarn is surrounded by a busy bazar. It is quite impressive, with a water tank all around and cloisters providing welcome shade.

⊜ Sleeping

Chandigarh *p439, maps p440 and p441*
Rickshaw drivers act as hotel touts.
B Mountview, S10, T740544, F742220,
citco10@ch1.dot.net.in. 69 rooms, pool,
good business hotel.
B North Park, out of town at Pachkula, near
Ghaggar Bridge, T561959, F566959.
43 comfortable rooms.
C Classic, S35-C, T/F663275. Comfortable
modern hotel (buffet breakfast included),
bar, reasonable value.
C Piccadily, Himalaya Marg, S 22, 500 m
from ISBT, T07571, F705692. 48 a/c rooms,
smart restaurant, bar.
C President, Madhya Marg, S26, near
railway station, T771737. 20 rooms,
restaurant, bar, bookshop.
C Shivalik View, S17, T700001, F701094,
citco17@ch1.dot.net.in. 102 rooms, business
centre, good Chinese restaurant, friendly.
C-D Maya Palace, 325-28, S35-B, T600547,
F660555. 28 a/c rooms.
C-D Pankaj, S22-A, T709891, F706480,
colharsharam@hotmail.com. 14 comfortable
rooms, some a/c rooms with bath, good
restaurant, exchange.
D Aroma, S22, T700045, T700051. 27 clean
rooms, some a/c.
D Divyadeep, S22, T703103. 15 rooms, some
a/c, neat and clean, good *Bhoj* restaurant.
D Jullunder, S22, opposite ISBT, T706777. 16
cleanish rooms, hot water, Indian restaurant.
D Kapil, 303 S35-B, T603163. 13 rooms,
central a/c, restaurant (Chinese, Indian), bar.
E Siva, half way along Udyog Path, 1st floor,
S22, few clean rooms, hot shower, meals.

Pinjore *p442*
D Budgerigar, provides a place for the night.

Anandpur Sahib *p442*
E Champa Tourist Huts, on road between
Gurudwara Keshgarh Sahib and Anandgarh
Fort has 4-room huts with kitchenette.

Patiala *p442*
D Green's, Mall Rd, T0175-213070. 15 rooms,
most a/c, restaurant, bar, pleasant. Cheaper
hotels are near the bus station.

Ambala *p443*
D Batra Palace, Lawrence Rd, behind Bus
Station, T0171-640159. Comfortable rooms
with 'proper' bathroom (hot water), friendly
room service with good food. Recommended.
D Kingfisher (Haryana Tourism), 5 km north
of town (near junction of Amritsar-
Chandigarh roads), T0171-443732. 13 rooms,
2 a/c, restaurant, attractive gardens and pool.

Kurukshetra *p443*
D-E Neelkanthi Krishna Dham, has simple
rooms, dorm beds, Rs 75-100, restaurant,
lockers and camping.

Karnal *p443*
C Jewel, Kunjpura Rd, T/F0184-255340.
21 comfortable rooms, restaurant, exchange
(not bank rates), modern business hotel.
C-E Karna Lake, just off the NH1
(signposted Chakravarti Lake), T0184-
255264. A/c huts, cheap rooms, restaurant,
boating, pleasant setting.
  Avoid **Imperial Bar** and hotels nearby.

Panipat *p443*
C Gold, GT Rd, south of town, T01742-22284,
F20079. 29 a/c rooms, restaurants, bar, pool.
C-D Skylark, GT Rd, T01742-21051. Some a/c
rooms and dorm (Rs 100), restaurant, fast food
D Midtown, GT Rd, town centre, T01742-
30769, F32676. 28 a/c rooms, restaurant.

Rohtak *p444*
C-D Tilyar, T01262-43119, has some a/c rooms
and dorms (Rs 100), restaurant and boating.

Hissar *p444*
E Flamingo, T01662-2606, guesthouse and
camper huts, a/c rooms, restaurant.
  Also eating places at the bus stand.

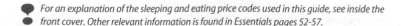
For an explanation of the sleeping and eating price codes used in this guide, see inside the front cover. Other relevant information is found in Essentials pages 52-57.

Sirhind *p444*

E Bougainvillea Tourist Complex, GT Rd towards Mandi Gobindgarh, outside town. 8 rooms, some a/c, floating restaurant, camping and showers for non-residents.
E Mulsari Tourist Complex, Aam Khas Baghz. Old caravanserai conversion, 4 rooms, restaurant, beer bar, Mughal garden, archaeological ruins nearby.
E Queens Flower Tourist Resort, on Sirhind canal at Neelon. 6 rooms, some a/c, restaurant, bar, garden.

Ludhiana *p445*

A Majestic Park Plaza.
B-C City Heart, near Clock Tower, GT Rd, T0161-740235, F740243. 44 rooms, excellent restaurant.
C Grewals, 148 Ferozepur Rd, T0161-400465, F402674. 40 rooms, restaurant.
C Gulmor, Ferozepur Rd, T0161-401742. 28 rooms, central a/c, restaurant, exchange.
D Shiraz, Ferozepur Rd, T0161-25252. 21 rooms, some with TV, near railway and centre, central a/c, restaurant.

Jalandhar *p445*

B-C Green Park, 36 Green Park, 5 km centre, T0181-2341. 15 a/c rooms.
C Kamal Palace, EH-192, Civil Lines, T0181-58462. 41 very comfortable rooms, central a/c, modern and well-presented.
D Plaza, Old Court Rd, New Plaza Chowk, T0181-225833, F2344400. 23 rooms, some a/c rooms with bath, restaurant, bar.
D Sky Lark, Circuit House Rd, T0181-225221, F225063. 72 rooms with bath, half a/c, near bus stand, restaurant, bar.
E Ramji Dass, Model Town Rd, T0181-3252. 10 rooms, some a/c with bath, restaurant.

Kapurthala *p445*

Magnolia Tourist Complex, on western edge of town, T01822-2322. 4 rooms, restaurant, bar, garden, very pleasant for a break or an overnight stop.

⊘ Eating

Chandigarh *p439, maps p440 and p441*
♥♥♥ Aroma, in hotel, 24-hr coffee shop.

♥♥♥ Mehfil, in hotel, 183, S17, T703539. International. Upmarket, a/c, comfortable seating, spicy meals.
♥♥♥ Mountview, in hotel, 24-hr coffee shop.
♥♥♥ Shivalik View, in hotel, 24-hr coffee shop.
♥♥ Bhoj at Divyadeep, S22, Himalaya Marg. Indian Vegetarian. Good *thalis,* pleasant, clean, busy at lunch.
♥♥ Chopsticks, Himalaya Marg. Chinese. Smart, cool, reasonable food.
♥♥ Ghazal, 189, S17. International. Comfortable, good Indian.
♥♥ Kwality, 20, S17. International. Usual fare, good ices. Others nearby do good spicy chicken dishes.
♥♥ Pankaj, S22. North Indian. Well presented, excellent tandoori, chilled beer.
♥♥ Pizza Hut, 51, S26, Madhya Marg.
♥ Ginza, 40, S14 (University Campus). Chinese.

Fast food

Hot Millions, S17, wide choice. 3 places.
Tasty Bite, Himalaya Marg. Good South Indian eats and burgers.
Down Under 183-4, S17, is a pleasant bar.

Ambala *p443*

Puran Singh Ka Vishal Mashoor, near the station, excellent, reasonably priced chicken, mutton and veg dishes, also icecreams.

Ludhiana *p445*

Cafe 33, 33 SCF, Sarabha Nagar Market. Indian.
Chicken Plaza, Ghumar Mandi. "Fantastic" chicken with nan, try haryali chicken.
City Heart Hotel. International. Wide choice, well prepared, generous portions, chilled beer, genial, helpful and reasonably prompt service.
Domino's Pizza, 11-C Sarabha Nagar Market, T453784. For those western food cravings, delivery service, branch on Mall.
Gazebo, 15 Bhadaur House Market. International menu in a/c comfort.
Hot Breads, 32-C Sarabha Nagar. Kabab Corner, 186 Rani Jhansi Rd, Civil Lines.
Larks, City Market. Punjabi. Typical *dhaba*, but clean, chicken dishes recommended.

Jalandhar *p445*

Food available in hotels.
Clock Tower, Nehru Garden. Also has a bar.

Haryana & Punjab Listings: Chandigarh

🎭 Entertainment

Chandigarh *p439, maps p440 and p441*
Theatre
Tagore Theatre, S18. Varied programme.

🎪 Festivals and events

Chandigarh *p439, maps p440 and p441*
All the Hindu festivals are celebrated especially **Baisakhi**, celebrated by both Hindus and Sikhs as **New Year's Day** (**13/14 Apr**). Bhangra dancers perform.

🛍 Shopping

Chandigarh *p439, maps p440 and p441*
Most shops are open 1000-1330, 1530-1945; closed Sun. Small shops in S19 and S22 are open on Sun. A large new Mall in S35. S17 and 22 have **State Govt Emporia**.

Bookshops
In S17 including **Universal**, near *Hot Millions*, Main Square, recommended. Also good **University Bookshop**.

Photography
A-One Studio, S22.
Batra Colour Lab, S27.

Patiala *p442*
Lacquerware at 94 Bichittar Nagar, New Patiala.

🏔 Activities and tours

Chandigarh *p439, maps p440 and p441*
Swimming
Pool, S23, 14 (Univ).
Lake Pool Complex, S23, temporary membership available.

Tour companies
Chandigarh Tourism, Chandigarh Emporium, S17. Local tours and further afield to Pinjore Gardens, Bhakra dam, Shimla, Kullu and Manali and Amritsar (minimum 20 persons). Also from Chandigarh Tourism Office, ISBT.Local tour departs at 1130, Rs 50, 4 hrs; visit the Rock Garden independently for a more leisurely visit. **Cozy Tours**, SCF I Sector 10, T740850.

Yoga
Yoga centre, S23, near nursery.

🚗 Transport

Chandigarh *p439, maps p440 and p441*
Air
Airport, 11 km. Taxis charge Rs 275 to centre. **Indian Airlines**: reservations, S17, T704539, airport, T656029 1000-1630. To **Amritsar, Delhi** Thu, Sat; **Leh** Wed (highly weather dependent), US$75. **Jet Airways**, 14 S 9D Madhya Marg, T740550, airport T658935, daily to **Delhi**. **Air India**: T704834.

Bicycle
Cycles hired free to CITCO hotel guests.

Bus
Local CTU run reasonably good city service. **Long distance** It is easier to get a seat on the Shimla bus from Chandigarh than from Kalka. Many buses daily from ISBT, S17, with a post office and tourist office. Transport offices: ISBT, S17 (0900-1300, 1400-1600), Chandigarh, T704005; Haryana, T704014; Himachal, T704015; Punjab, T704023. Buy bus tickets from the designated booths next to platforms before boarding. Seat numbers (written on the back of tickets) are often assigned. Shimla buses (via Kalka) leave from platform 10. To **Amritsar**, 6 hrs (from *Aroma Hotel*, T708686); **Pathankot**, 7 hrs; **Dharamshala**, 10 hrs; **Kalka** (from Platform 10), Rs 11-28. Buses to Shimla also stop at Kalka; **Kullu** 12 hrs. Also Himachal Tourism coaches during the season, to **Delhi**, 5 hrs, Rs 150; **Manali**, 0800, 10 hrs, Rs 250; **Shimla**, 5 hrs, Rs 80.

Rickshaw
Auto-rickshaw: Metered with a minimum fare, but you can bargain. Stands at Bus Station, Railway Station and the Rock Garden. **Cycle rickshaw**: are unmetered.

Taxi
Local Private taxi stands in S22, S17, S35. Chandigarh Tourism (CITCO), S17, T703839. **Long distance** To Kalka, up to Rs 400.

Train
The station (8 km) has a clean waiting room but a poor bus service to the city. **Prepaid auto-rickshaws**, Rs 45 to S22; to bus stand Rs 34; to Kalka (for the brave) Rs 200. Enquiries, T704131, reservations, T704382,

1000-1700; City Booking Office, 1st floor, Inter-State Bus Terminal (ISBT), S17, T704382, Mon-Sat 0800-1345, 1445-2000, Sun 0800-1400. Tourist office, 0600-2030. No train to Amritsar. **New Delhi**: *Shatabdi Exp, 2006*, 0650, 3¼ hrs; *Shatabdi Exp, 2012*, 1220, 3¼ hrs; *Himalayan Queen, 4096*, 1738, 4½ hrs. **Old Delhi**: *Kalka-Howrah Mail, 2312*, 0100, 5½ hrs. **Shimla**: *Amritsar Kalka Exp, 4536*, 0700, 1¼ hrs to **Kalka**, then 3 hr wait for *Exp 255* to Shimla (1105, 6 hrs).

Patiala *p442*

The railway and bus stations are at the north end of Mall Road, 1 km from the centre.

Bus

Daily services to Delhi, other towns in Punjab and neighbouring states.

Train

Patiala is on the branch line to Bhatinda and Firozpur.

Ambala *p443*
Train

New Delhi: *Shatabdi Exp, 2006,* 0723, 2½ hrs. *Shatabdi Exp, 2012,* 1302, 2½ hrs. Frequent trains to **Chandigarh**. Northern Railway connects **Shimla** trains with those from **Jammu Tawi** and **Lucknow**.

Ludhiana *p445*
Air

Jet Airways T406231, airport T846159: Delhi flights suspended.

Bus

Long distance Daily services connect Ludhiana with Delhi and towns in Punjab and neighbouring states.

Train

To Amritsar: *Shatabdi Exp, 2013,* 2021, 1¾ hrs; *Katihar Amritsar Exp, 5705,* 1010, 2½ hrs; *Paschim Exp, 2925,* 1645, 2½ hrs; *New Delhi-Amritsar Exp, 4659,* 1930, 2½ hrs. **To Delhi**: *Shatabdi Exp, 2014,* 0703, 3¾ hrs; *Paschim Exp, 2926,* 1100, 5½ hrs; *Golden Temple Mail, 2904,* 0025, 7 hrs.

Jalandhar *p445*
Bus

A/c coach connects with **Air India** flights from Delhi airport to London, 1700 (9 hrs), return 0400; Rs 350.

Train

The City and Cantt stations are on the same line, though not all trains stop at both. There are many trains to Amritsar and Ludhiana. From City station: **Amritsar**: *Katihar Amritsar Exp, 5705,* 1110, 1½ hrs; *Shatabdi Exp, 2013,* 2105, 1 hr; *Dadar-Amritsar Exp, 1057,* 1515, 1½ hr; *Paschim Exp, 2925,* 1810, 1 hr. **Kolkata**: via Ludhiana and Varanasi, *Amritsar-Howrah Mail, 3006,* 1955, 34 hrs. **Delhi**: via Ludhiana and Meerut, *Shatabdi Exp, 2014,* 0614, 4½ hrs; *Paschim Exp, 2926,* 0908, 7 hrs; *Golden Temple Mail, 2904,* 2255, 8½ hrs.

● Directory

Chandigarh *p439, maps p440 and p441*
Banks Exchange: **Paul's Merchants**, S22, speedy, efficient, good rates, will send rep to hotel. Recommended. **American Express** TCs only. **Hospitals** (with 24-hr chemists): General Hospital, S16, T780756; PG Institute, S12, T541005. **Tourist offices** at ISBT, S17; Chandigarh, 1st floor, ISBT (Main Bus Terminal), T704614, Mon-Fri 0900-1700, Sat 0900-1300. **Himachal**, 1st floor, ISBT, T708569. **Useful addresses** Ambulance: T102. Fire: T101. Police: T100. **Foreigners' Registration Office**: Town Hall Bldg, S17 (weekdays 1000-1700), T741100.

Patiala *p442*
Bank State Bank of Patiala, in the centre, changes money reasonably quickly.

Jalandhar *p445*
Useful address Thomas Cook, for exchange, 2 Alpha Estate, 39 GT Rd, T238790.

449

Haryana & Punjab Listings: Chandigarh

Northern Punjab

Amritsar → *Phone code: 0183. Colour map 1, grid B2. Population: 976,000.*

Amritsar (Pool of the Nectar of Immortality) is named after the sacred pool in the Golden Temple, the holiest of Sikh sites. It is pleasantly friendly and noticeably free of persistent hawkers and rickshaw wallahs. The temple itself, the city's singular attraction, is a haven of peace amidst an essentially congested city. The atmosphere is particularly powerful from before dawn to early light, when the surrounding glistening white marble pavement is still cold under foot and the gold begins to shimmer on the lightening water. You cannot help but be touched by the sanctity of the place. ▶▶ *For Sleeping, Eating and other listings, see pages 456-458.*

Ins and outs

Getting there Rajasansi airport is 11 km away with taxi or auto-rickshaw transfers. The railway is central but the bus station is 2 km east; both are a 15-min auto-rickshaw ride from the Golden Temple to the south. If you have a couple of hours to spare between connections, you can a fit in a visit. Overland coaches go through Amritsar for the only land crossing open between India and Pakistan only 35 km away.

Getting around The city is quite spread out. Cycle-rickshaws squeeze through the crowded lanes. Auto-rickshaws are handy for longer journeys unless you get a bike. See Transport, page 457, for further details.

Background

The original site for the city was granted by the Mughal Emperor Akbar (ruled 1556-1605) who also visited the temple and it has been sacred to the Sikhs since the time of the fourth guru, Ram Das (Guru 1574-1581). He insisted on paying its value to the local Jats who owned it, thereby eliminating the possibility of future disputes on ownership. Ram Das then invited local merchants to live and trade in the immediate vicinity. In 1577 he heard that a cripple had been miraculously cured while bathing in the pool here. The pool was enlarged and named Amrit Sarovar ('Immortality'). Arjan Dev (Guru 1581-1601), Ram Das' son and successor, enlarged the tank further and built the original temple at its centre from 1589-1601. The Afghan Ahmad Shah Durrani, desecrated the Golden Temple in 1757. The Sikhs united and drove him out, but four years later he defeated the Sikh armies, sacking the town and blowing up the temple. Later, the Sikhs re-conquered the Punjab and restored the temple and tank. Under their greatest secular leader, Maharaja **Ranjit Singh**, the temple was rebuilt in 1764. In 1830 he donated 100 kg (220 lbs) of gold which was applied to the copper sheets on the roof and much of the exterior of the building, giving rise to the name 'The Golden Temple'. Now Punjab's second largest town, Amritsar was a traditional junction of trade routes. The different peoples, Yarkandis, Turkomans, Kashmiris, Tibetans and Iranians, indicate its connections with the Old Silk Road.

★ The Golden Temple

The spiritual nerve centre of the Sikh faith, every Sikh tries to make a visit and bathe in the holy water. It is immensely powerful, spiritual and welcoming to all.

Visiting the temple Shoes, socks, sticks and umbrellas are left outside at the cloakroom at no charge. Visitors should wash their feet outside the entrance. It is best to go early as for much of the year the marble gets too hot by noon. Dress appropriately and cover your head in the temple precincts. Head scarves are available during the day but not at night; a handkerchief suffices. Avoid sitting with back towards the temple. Tobacco, narcotics and intoxicants are not permitted. You may wish to visit the community kitchen for breakfast (dawn to 0900) before visiting the temple. The Information Office near the main entrance is very helpful.

Worship Singing is central to Sikh worship. After building the temple, Arjan Dev compiled a collection of hymns of the great medieval saints and this became the *Adi Granth* (Original Holy book). It was installed in the temple as the focus of devotion and teaching. Gobind Singh, the 10th and last Guru (1675-1708) revised the book and also refused to name a successor saying that the book itself would be the Sikh guru. It thus became known as the *Granth Sahib* (The Holy Book as Guru).

The temple compound Entering the temple compound through the main entrance or Clock Tower you see the Harmandir (also spelt *Harimandir*, and known by Hindus as the Durbar Sahib), the Golden Temple itself, beautifully reflected in the stunning expanse of water which surrounds it. Each morning (0400 summer, 0500 winter) the Guru Granth Sahib is brought in a vivid procession from the **Akal Takht** at the east end to the **Harmandir**, to be returned at night (2200 summer, 2100 winter). The former represents temporal power, the latter spiritual – and so they do not quite face each other. Some like to attend Palki Sahib (night ceremony).

Amritsar

5 Gurudwara Baba
   Deep Singh
6 Guru Ram Das Rest
   House
7 Kishore Castle
8 MK Hotel, Domino's,
   Nexus & Bowling Alley
9 Mohan International
10 Palace & Pegasus

11 Quin's Land
12 Ritz
13 Royal Castle
14 Sita Niwas
15 Sundew

● **Eating**
1 Bharawan
2 Burger King

3 Curd Stall
4 Kesars
5 Kwality & Salads Plus
6 Kundan
7 Natraj
8 Neelam
9 Sheetal

■ **Sleeping**
1 Airlines
2 Golden Tower
3 Grand
4 Gurudwara Baba Attal

0 metres 500
0 yards 500

N

66 99 Voluntary service, which continues to be a feature of modern Sikhism, extends to the kitchen staff and workers. The Amritsar kitchen may feed up to 10,000 people a day, with 3,000 at a sitting. It is free of charge and vegetarian, though Sikhs are not banned from eating meat. Lunch is 1100-1500 and dinner 1900 onwards.

All pilgrims walk clockwise round the tank, stopping at shrines and bathing in the tank on the way round to the Harmandir itself. The tank is surrounded by an 8-m wide white marble pavement, banded with black and brown Jaipur marble.

East End To the left of the entrance steps are the bathing ghats and an area screened off from public view for ladies. Also on this side are the **68 Holy Places** representing 68 Hindu pilgrimage sites. When the tank was built, Arjan Dev told his followers that rather than visit all the orthodox Hindu places of pilgrimage, they should just bathe here thus acquiring equivalent merit.

A shrine contains a copy of the **Granth Sahib**. Here and at other booths round the tank the Holy Book is read for devotees. Sikhs can arrange with the temple authorities to have the book read in their name in exchange for a donation. The *granthi* (reader) is a temple employee and a standard reading lasts for three hours, while a complete reading takes 48 hours. The tree in the centre at the east end of the tank is popularly associated with a healing miracle.

Dining Hall, Kitchen, Assembly Hall and **Guesthouses** The surrounding white arcade of buildings (*bunghas*), are hostels for visitors. Through the archway a path leads to the Guru Ram Das Langar (kitchen and dining hall) immediately on the left, while two tall octagonal minarets, the 18th-century Ramgarhia Minars, provide a vantage point over the temple and inner city. At the far end of the path are the Guru Ram Das Sarai and the Guru Nanak Niwas, where pilgrims can stay free for up to three nights. Sikhs

Golden Temple

have a community kitchen where all temple visitors, regardless of their religious
belief, can eat together. The third Guru, **Amar Das** (1552-74), abolished the custom of
eating only with others of the same caste, and Amar Das even refused to bless the
Mughal Emperor Akbar unless he was prepared to eat with everyone else who was
present. Voluntary service, which continues to be a feature of modern Sikhism,
extends to the kitchen staff and workers. The Amritsar kitchen may feed up to 10,000
people a day, with 3,000 at a sitting. It is free of charge and vegetarian, though Sikhs
are not banned from eating meat. Lunch is 1100-1500 and dinner 1900 onwards. Next
to the Amar Das Langar is the residence of Baba **Kharak Singh** who is hailed by Sikhs
as a saint. His followers are distinguished by their orange turbans while temple
employees and members of the militant Akali sect wear blue or black turbans.

Returning to the temple tank, the shrine on the south side is to Baba **Deep Singh**.
When Ahmad Shah Durrani attacked Amritsar in 1758, Baba Deep Singh was copying
out the Granth Sahib. He went out to fight with his followers, vowing to defend the
temple with his life. He was mortally wounded, 6 km from town; some say that his
head was hacked from his body. Grimly determined and holding his head on with one
hand he fought on. On his way back to the temple he died on this spot. The story is
recounted in the picture behind glass.

West end The complex to the west has the Akal Takht, the flagstaffs, and the Shrine
of Guru Gobind Singh. The **flagstaffs** symbolize religion and politics, in the Sikh case
intertwined. They are joined in the middle by the emblem of the Sikh nation, the two
swords of Hargobind, representing spiritual and temporal authority. The circle is
inscribed with the Sikh rallying call *Ek Omkar* (God is One).

Started when Arjan Dev was Guru (1581-1605), and completed by Guru
Hargobind in 1609, the **Akal Takht** is the seat of the Sikh's religious committee. It is
largely a mixture of 18th- and early 19th-century building, the upper storeys being
the work of Ranjit Singh. It has a first floor room with a low balcony which houses a
gilt covered ark, central to the initiation of new members of the **Khalsa** brotherhood.

To the side of the flagstaffs is a **shrine** dedicated to the 10th and last guru,
Gobind Singh (Guru 1675-1708). In front of the entrance to the temple causeway is a
square, a gathering place for visitors.

Sometimes you may see **Nihang** (meaning 'crocodile') Sikhs, followers of the
militant Gobind Singh, dressed in blue and armed with swords, lances, curved daggers.

At the centre of the tank stands the most holy of all Sikh shrines, the **Harmandir**
(The Golden Temple). Worshippers obtain the sweet *prasad* after crossing the
causeway to the temple where they make an offering. The 60-m long bridge, usually
crowded with worshippers, is built out of white marble like the lower floor of the
temple. The rest of the temple is covered in copper gilt. On the doorways verses
from the Guru Granth Sahib are inscribed in Gurumukhi script while rich floral
paintings decorate the walls and excellent silver work marks the doors. The roof has
the modified onion-shaped dome, or inverted lotus, characteristic of Sikh temples,
but in this case it is covered in the gold that Ranjit Singh added for embellishment.

The ground floor of the three-storey temple contains the Holy Book placed on a
platform under a jewel encrusted canopy. The **Guru Granth Sahib** contains
approximately 3,500 hymns. Professional singers and musicians sing verses from the
book continuously from 0400-2200 in the summer and 0500-2200 in winter. An
excited crowd of worshippers attempts to touch the serpent horn. Each evening the
holy book is taken ceremoniously to the Akal Takht and brought back the next
morning; visitors are welcome. The palanquin used for this, set with emeralds, rubies
and diamonds with silver poles and a golden canopy, can be seen in the treasury on
the first floor of the entrance to the temple. Through the day, pilgrims place offerings
of flowers or money around the book. There is no ritual in the worship or pressure
from temple officials to donate money. The marble walls are decorated with

mirrorwork, gold leaf and designs of birds, animals and flowers in semiprecious stones in the Mughal style.

On the first floor is a balcony on which three respected Sikhs always perform the **Akhand Path** (Unbroken Reading). In order to preserve unity and maintain continuity, there must always be someone practising devotions. The top floor is where the gurus used to sit and here again someone performs the *Akhand Path*.

On the edge of the tank just west of the entrance is the **Tree Shrine**, a gnarled, 450-years old *jubi* tree, is reputed to have been the favourite resting place of the first chief priest of the temple. Women tie strings to the ingeniously supported branches, hoping to be blessed with a son by the primaeval fertility spirits that choose such places as their home. It is also a favourite spot to arrange and sanctify marriages, despite the protests of the temple authorities. The **Sikh Museum** at the main entrance to the temple (just before steps leading down to the *parikrama*) is somewhat martial, reflecting the struggles against the Mughals, the British and the Indian Army. The **Sikh Library** in the Guru Nanak Building has a good selection of books in English (as well as current national newspapers); closed on Sundays.

The town

The old city is south of the railway station encircled by a ring road which traces the line of the city walls built during the reign of Ranjit Singh. **Jallianwala Bagh**, noted for the most notorious massacre under British rule, is 400 m north of the Golden Temple.

Relations with the British had soured in 1919. *Hartals* became a common form of demonstration. The Punjab which had supplied 60% of Indian troops committed to the First World War was one of the hardest hit economically in 1918 and tension was high. The Lieutenant Governor of the province decided on a 'fist force' to repulse the essentially non-violent but vigorous demonstrations. Some looting occurred in Amritsar and the British called in reinforcements. These arrived under the command of **General Dyer**.

Dyer banned all meetings but people were reported to be gathering on Sunday 13 April 1919 as pilgrims poured into Amritsar to celebrate *Baisakhi*, the Sikh New Year and the anniversary of the founding of the *khalsa* in 1699. That afternoon thousands were crammed into Jallianwala Bagh, a piece of waste ground popular with travellers, surrounded on all sides by high walls with only a narrow alley for access. Dyer personally led some troops to the place, gave the crowd no warning and ordered his men to open fire leaving 379 dead and 1,200 wounded. Other brutal acts followed.

The Jallianwala Bagh massacre was hushed up and the British Government in London was only aware of it six months later at which time the Hunter Committee was set up to investigate the incident. It did not accept Dyer's excuse that he acted as he did to prevent another insurrection throughout India on the scale of the Mutiny of 1857. He was asked to resign and returned to England where he died in 1927. However, he was not universally condemned. A debate in the House of Lords produced a majority of 126 to 86 in his favour and the *Morning Post* newspaper launched a fund for 'The Man who Saved India'. Over £26,000 was raised to comfort the dying General.

India was outraged by Dyer's massacre. Gandhi, who had called the nationwide *hartal* in March, started the Non Co-operation Movement, which was to be a vital feature of the struggle for Independence. This was not the end of the affair. O'Dwyer, the Governor of the Province, was shot dead at a meeting in Caxton Hall, London, by a survivor of Jallianwala Bagh who was hanged for the offence.

Today the gardens are a pleasant enclosed park. They are entered by a narrow path between the houses, opening out over lawns. A memorial plaque recounts the history at the entrance, and a large memorial dominates the east end of the garden. On the north side is a well in which many who tried to escape the bullets were drowned, and remnants of walls have been preserved to show the bullet holes.

The old town has a number of mosques and Hindu temples – the **Durgiana Temple** (16th century), and the new **Vaishnodevi Temple** which imitates the difficult access to the famous Himalayan original in requiring the worshipper to wade awkwardly through water. Northeast of the railway station are the **Ram Bagh** gardens, the Mall and Lawrence Road shopping areas.

Border crossing to Pakistan → *Pakistan time is 30 mins behind IST.*

The road continues west to the Pakistan border. Despite the easing in the political situation in Punjab there are numerous police check posts so motor bikes and cars may be stopped several times. It is better to take Pakistani rupees into Pakistan to avoid being hassled. You can change money in Amritsar (Link Road/Albert Road) or just across the border. The **road** crossing for foreigners is currently through the Wagha check post, 35 km from Amritsar along the attractive and tree-lined GT Rd to **Attari**, the last town before the border, just 2 km from Wagha. From **Amritsar**, frequent minibuses take about one hour to Attari, where you get a rickshaw to Wagha; Taxis Rs 500 (Rs 550 return, to see *flag ceremony*) take 30 minutes; auto-rickshaw Rs 250 (Rs 350 return). The **train** goes from India (Amritsar) to Pakistan (Lahore) on Monday and Thursday (*Amritsar Lahore Exp, 4607*) at 0700, arrives at Atari (on the border) at 0740, and with four hours scheduled for the border crossing, it's not due to arrive in Lahore until 1615. The train (*Lahore Amritsar Exp, 4608*) returns on Tuesday and Friday at 0800. This train is seriously affected by the state of political relations between India and Pakistan. At the end of November when Sikhs visit shrines in Pakistan the train may be restricted to Sikh pilgrims.When running, it can be a very slow journey with sometimes protracted customs and immigration formalities. Crossing the border by road is more convenient than by train. We highly recommend the Footprint 'Pakistan Handbook'.

Wagha

The changing of the guards and the ceremonial lowering of the flags ceremony at sundown carried out with great show and rivalry, is quite a spectacle. There is much synchronized foot stamping, gate slamming and displays of scorn by colourful soldiers! New viewing galleries have been built but crowds still clamour to get the best view. Women are allowed to get to the front, and there is a VIP section (open to foreign visitors) next to the gate. It is best to get there near closing time though photography is difficult with the setting sun.

It is best to cross in the morning; allow an hour for formalities though it can take longer especially for a bus load (five different passport and customs checks on the Indian side; three on the Pakistan side taking nearly three hours to process 15 travellers). The border check post is nominally open from 1000-1500, Indian time, but is subject to change. Unless you have your own vehicle or are on the new through-coach from Delhi to Lahore, you have to walk from the Indian check post to the Pakistani check post. Indian porters can carry your luggage to the border line, where it is transferred to a Pakistani porter; expect to pay Rs 25-50 after bargaining (Indian side) and Rs 30-50 (Pakistani) respectively. There is a bank within the customs area with foreign currency exchange facilities. Beyond Pakistani immigration and customs, there is a taxi and minicab park; you can usually share one to Lahore (30 km). Amritsar to Lahore usually takes three to five hours though there can be unexpected delays.

A luxury coach runs between Delhi and Lahore, see page 128. At the border: *Niagra Falls Restaurant* has four air-cooled rooms, restaurant and a beer bar.

Pathankot

Pathankot, a crossroads town and trading centre on the border with Himachal Pradesh, is the gateway to Jammu Kashmir and western Himachal. It is also the starting point for the Kangra Valley Railway but has little else to offer. **Shapur Kandi Fort** (16th century), 13 km to the north, is on the banks of the Ravi River, once the stronghold of the Rajas of Pathan and now no more than a ruin, has a hydro electricity power station at Ranjit Sagar Dam.

Listings: Northern Punjab

◉ Sleeping

Amritsar *p450, map p451*

B MK, Dist Shopping Centre, Ranjit Ave, T504610. New central hotel with 75 rooms, restaurant, pool on 2nd floor.

B Mohan International, Albert Rd, T227801, F226520, hotel@jla.vsnl.net.in. 38 rooms, good restaurants (authentic Punjabi), pool (non-residents Rs 100).

B Ritz, Plaza 45 The Mall, T562836, F566027, ritz@del3.vsnl.net.in. Well located, recently renovated, but characterless, dark restaurant (need a torch!), bar, large grounds.

C Mrs Bhandari's Guest House, 10 Cantonment, northwest of town, T228509, F222390, payal@mol.net.in. 9 a/c rooms with bath, no TV, has character – Heath Robinson baths, fire places, hot water bottles, sepia prints, 'English' meals (residents only), pool (Mar-Nov), large grounds, quiet, attractive, camping (Rs 150), expensive car hire, no credit cards, attentive service, run by Mrs Bhandari and her family. Recommended.

C Royal Castle, 309 Albert Rd (corner of Court Rd), T225562, F225563. 28 modern a/c rooms, very smart restaurant, bar, coffee shop.

C Sun City Towers, Queens Rd, T229636, F222117. 24 modern a/c rooms.

C-D Golden Tower, Chowk Fuwara, T534446. 20 rooms (15 a/c) with hot showers.

D Airlines, Cooper Rd, T213697. 25 rooms, some a/c, restaurants, rooftop garden, Ayurvedic clinic for grey hair and baldness!

D Grand, Queens Rd, opposite railway station, T62977, F229677. 25 rooms, some a/c, gloomy restaurant but good food, beer, nice garden for tea, very friendly management. Recommended.

D Kishore Castle, 10 Queens Rd, T402818. 25 rooms.

D-E Mayur, GT Rd, outside Model Town, 1 km railway station. 15 rooms with hot shower, room service for meals, helpful manager.

D-E Quin's Land, 3 Queen's Rd, T224052. 15 clean rooms with air cooler, 3 a/c, a little dark but reasonable and friendly.

D-E Sundew, off Queens Rd (left out of station, then 100 m left through an arch, down narrow lane). Range of rooms, spotless, breakfast by room service, very helpful.

D-F Sita Niwas, east of Golden Temple, T543092. Rooms vary, fans or a/c, hot water in buckets, a bit run down, room service (cheap Indian meals), can be noisy at dawn (pilgrims), very helpful and friendly manager, taxi for Wagha Rs 350 return. Recommended.

E Palace and Pegasus, Queens Rd, opposite railway station, T65111. Comfortable rooms (some a/c), bucket hot water, don't risk the food here.

F Rest houses in /near the Golden Temple. Some free (up to 3 nights), very simple food; please leave a donation. Tobacco, alcohol and drugs are prohibited. Local Sikh families welcome guests, Rs 1500 for two including meals. Contact *Time Travels* (see Directory) or *Munjeeta Travels*, 12 Cavendish Rd, Woking, UK, T01483-773331.

◉ Eating

Amritsar *p450, map p451*

Eating with pilgrims can be a great experience.

♥♥♥ **MK, Mohan**, International. Smart, comfortable, good food.

♥♥♥ **Mrs Bhandari's**, T228509. For unexpected Raj tones (see above), ring ahead for a table.

♥♥♥ **Royal Castle**, International. Smart, comfortable, good food.

♥♥ **Burger King**, near *Salads Plus*.

♥♥ **Domino's Pizza**, 50 Dist Shopping Centre, Ranjit Ave, T508091.

♥♥ **Kwality**, The Mall. International. Cool, good Indian.

♥♥ **Salads Plus**, also South Indian snacks under canopy outside.

♥♥ **Sheetal**, Queens Rd. Good food, excellent service, pleasant ambience.

The corner of the Mall and Malaviya Rd comes alive with ice cream and fast-food stalls in the evening. *Dhabas* near the station

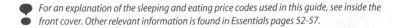
For an explanation of the sleeping and eating price codes used in this guide, see inside the front cover. Other relevant information is found in Essentials pages 52-57.

and temple sell local *daal, saag paneer* and mouth-watering *stuffed parathas*.

🍴 **Bharawan's**, near Town Hall (excellent lunch *thalis*), for good vegetarian.

🍴 **Curd stall** (opposite *Ashar Guest House*) sells excellent, safe *lassis*.

🍴 **Gagan**, 34 Sita Niwas Rd, near the Golden Temple. Simple, good Indian, not spicey.

🍴 **Kesars**, Passian Darwaza, near Durgiana Temple (and elsewhere).

🍴 **Kundan**, near Chitra Cinema, Hall Gate.

🍴 **Neelam**, near Jallianwalla Bagh. Indian, Chinese. Cheap, plentiful and really tasty.

Cakes

Newish patisseries on Link and Queens Rds including:

Bakewell, Cooper Rd. Good for cakes and fruit puddings.

La Patisserie, though not brilliant, offer good choice.

Popular Bakery, Queen's Rd.

⚅ Festivals and events

Amritsar *p450, map p451*

Apr Baisakhi, for Sikhs, the Hindu New Year marks the day in 1699 Guru Gobind Singh organized the Sikhs into the Khalsa, see page 1345. The vigorous *bhangra* dance is a common sight in the villages. The birth anniversaries of the 10 gurus are observed as holy days and those of Guru Nanak (Oct/Nov), and Guru Gobind Singh (Dec/Jan), are celebrated as festivals with *Akhand Path* and processions.

Oct/Nov Diwali Illumination of the Golden Temple, fireworks.

▲▲ Activities and tours

Amritsar *p450, map p451*

Tour operators

Link Travels, outside Golden Temple Clock Tower Car Parking, T559635.

Time Travels, 14 Kapoor Plaza, Crystal Sq, T400131, www.travelamritsar.com. Organizes tours to Dharamshala, Manali, Shimla etc, local villages, as well as to important Gurudwaras in the state. Very efficient, helpful. Recommended.

⊖ Transport

Amritsar *p450, map p451*

Air

Rajsansi Airport, T500911; taxi (Rs 250) or auto-rickshaw (Rs 70) to town. **Indian Airlines**, 39A Court Rd, T213393, airport T500911. **New Delhi**: Tue, Thu, Sat. Also weekly flights to/from London and Birmingham on Uzbek and Turkmenistan Airways. Contact in UK T0207-9354775. **Air India**, T546122.

Bicycle

Cycle hire: worthwhile; from Hide Market.

Bus

Long distance Daily (from **OD Swarna Shatabdi**, 2029, 0630, 5½ hrs) services to **Delhi** (tiring 10 hrs); **Dharamshala** (change at Pathankot, 7 hrs); **Dalhousie** (8 hrs), **Jammu** (5 hrs); **Pathankot** (3 hrs); **Chandigarh** (5 hrs); **Shimla** 0530 and 0730, 10 hrs. *Link Travels* luxury coach to Delhi, Jammu (overnight); Jammu, Chandigarh 0600, 1400.

Rickshaw

Auto-rickshaw/tonga: full day, Rs 500, half day Rs 300.

Taxi

Local Non-a/c car from *Time Travels* and *Link Travels* (see Directory): full day, Rs 800, half day Rs 550, Wagha Rs 600. *Link Travels,* outside Golden Temple Clock Tower Car Parking.

Long distance To **Delhi** Rs 5,200, **Dharamshala** Rs 2,700.

Train

Some trains to and from Jammu don't stop at Pathankot Junction but at Chakki Bank. There is a tempo service between the two stations. T131. Computerized reservations in the Golden Temple Complex (far right of the office), open until 2000 on weekdays. No train to Chandigarh. **Kolkata**: via Lucknow (16½ hrs) and Varanasi (22¼ hrs); *Amritsar-Howrah Mail, 3006,* 1745, 37¼ hrs. **Mumbai (Central)**: *Golden Temple Mail, 2904,* 2130, 32½ hrs; *Paschim Exp, 2926,* 0755, 31½ hrs. **New Delhi**: *Shatabdi Exp, 2014,*

0515, 5¾ hrs; *Flying Mail, 4648,* 1130, 9 hrs (OD); *Amritsar Shatabdi, 2032,* 1705, 5¾ hrs. **Pathankot**: *Ravi Exp, 4633,* 0915, 2¼ hrs ; *Muri Exp, 8101,* 0555, 2¾ hrs. See 'Border crossing' below for details of train to Lahore (Pakistan).

Pathankot *p455*
Bus
Bus and railway stations are 100 m apart. Buses to all important towns nearby.

Taxi
Shared taxis available at the railway station if the prospect of a hill bus journey fails to thrill.

Train
For main connections see page 457. A spectacular narrow gauge Kangra Valley Railway, built in 1928, runs to Jogindernagar, 56 km northwest of Mandi in HP. See page 510. **Baijnath Paprola**: *3PB Passenger,* 0835, 5½ hrs. **Baijnath and Jogindernagar**: *3PBJ Passenger,* 0920, 6½ and 8¾ hrs. **Amritsar**: *Hatia Exp* 8102, 1645, 2¾ hrs and to **Delhi**: 12 hrs.

❶ Directory

Amritsar *p450, map p451*
Bank Punjab Bank, next door to Golden Temple, quick.

✷ Footprint features

Introduction

Himachal Pradesh is dominated by successive ridges of snow covered peaks, the outer ranges of the Himalaya themselves. Known across India for its early summer climate, its deliciously cool mountain streams and its seemingly endless supplies of temperate fruit, Himachal also has excellent trekking.

Shimla, famous as a British Hill Station, **Dharamshala**, the Indian home of the Dalai Lama, and **Kullu** and **Manali** have been favourite destinations for over a decade.

Today, however, it is possible to visit the far more remote and until recently closed regions. Himachal has become the main access route to Ladakh. The road to Leh crosses the **Rohtang Pass** just north of Manali and has opened up the side routes for trekking. Sarahan's **Bhimakali temple**, the moraine-filled **Baspa Valley**, and Spiti's spectacular **Tabo monastery** more than justify the journey along the dangerously precipitous and landslide-ridden **Hindustan-Tibet Road**.

The beautiful landscape is also the setting for a rich interweaving of **Hindu** and **Buddhist** traditions, while in the foothills of **Kangra** the Mughal miniature artistic heritage was subtly modified to develop a distinctive regional art form.

★ Don't miss...

❶ Stroll around the faded streets of **Shimla** and imagine the 'poodle fakers' living it up in the time of the Raj, page 463.

❷ Climb behind **Bhimakali Temple** in Sarahan for a picturesque view, page 469.

❸ For an immense sense of the spiritual, the **Chos Khor Gompa** at Tabo is unsurpassed in this region, page 478.

❹ Travel through the apple orchards in the Kullu Valley to reach **Naggar** with its interesting castle, page 490.

❺ If you have a head for heights, take the Manali to Leh road and stop at **Rohtang Pass** for spectacular views of precipitous cliffs, page 503.

❻ Many head for **Dharamshala**, now the home of the Dalai Lama. This is a good place to consider a trek or a ride on the mountain railway, page 507.

❼ Try **Pragpur**, a medieval 'Heritage' Village, for a few days of complete relaxation, page 513.

Himachal Pradesh

Background → *Population: over 6 million. Area: 55,673 sq km. See also the Footprint 'Indian Himalaya Handbook'.*

The land

Himachal Pradesh (Himalayan Province) is wholly mountainous, with peaks rising to over 6,700 m. The **Dhaula Dhar** range runs from the northwest to the Kullu Valley. The **Pir Panjal** is farther north and parallel to it. High, remote, arid and starkly beautiful, Lahul and Spiti are sparsely populated. They contrast strongly with the well-wooded lushness of those areas to the south of the Himalayan axis.

Climate At lower altitudes the summers can be very hot and humid whereas the higher mountains are permanently under snow. In Shimla, the Kangra Valley, Chamba and the Kullu Valley, the monsoon arrives in mid-June and lasts until mid-September, giving periods of very heavy rain; in the Kullu Valley there can be sudden downpours in March and early April. As in many hill stations there are often sharp contrasts between sun and shade temperatures, particularly noticeable in spring and autumn when the average temperatures are lower, but the sun can be very warm. To the north, Lahul and Spiti are beyond the influence of the monsoon. Consequently they share the high altitude desert climatic characteristics of Ladakh.

History

Originally the region was inhabited by a tribe called the Dasas who were later assimilated by the Aryans. From the 10th-century parts were occupied by the Muslims. Kangra, for example, submitted to Mahmud of Ghazni and later became a Mughal Province. The Gurkhas of Nepal invaded Himachal in the early 19th century and incorporated it into their kingdom as did the Sikhs some years later. The British finally took over the princely states in the middle of the 19th century.

Culture

Religion Although the statistics suggest that Himachal is one of the most Hindu states in India, its culture reflects the strong influence of Buddhism, notably in the border regions with Tibet and in the hill stations where many Tibetan refugees have made their homes. In the villages many of the festivals are shared by Hindus and Buddhists alike. There are also small minorities of Sikhs, Muslims and Christians.

People Hill tribes such as the Gaddis, Gujars, Kinnaurs, Lahaulis and Pangwalas have all been assimilated into the dominant Hindu culture though the caste system is simpler and less rigid than elsewhere. The tribal peoples in Lahul and Spiti follow a form of Buddhism while Kinnauris mix Buddhism with Hinduism in their rituals. Their folklore has the common theme of heroism and legends of love and Natti, the attractive folk dance of the high hills, is widely performed.

Language The dominant local language is Pahari, a Hindi dialect derived from Sanskrit and Prakrit but largely unintelligible to plains dwellers. Hindi is the medium for instruction in schools and is widely spoken.

Handicrafts Handicrafts include wood carving, spinning wool, leather tanning, pottery and bamboo crafts. Wool products are the most abundant and it is a common sight in the hills to see men spinning wool by hand as they watch over their flocks or as they are walking along. Good quality shawls made from the fine hair from pashmina goats, particularly in Kullu, are highly sought after. *Namdas* (rugs) and rich pile carpets in Tibetan designs are also produced. Buddhist *thangkas*, silverware and chunky tribal silver jewellery are popular with tourists and are sold in bazars.

Himachal Pradesh was granted full statehood in 1970. There are 68 seats in the State Assembly, but as one of India's smallest states Himachal Pradesh elects four members of the Lok Sabha and three representatives to the Rajya Sabha. Since 1966 Shimla has been the state capital. Dharamshala has been the home of the Dalai Lama since 1959, following the Chinese takeover of Tibet.

Current political developments Even though Himachal is quite close to Delhi, it still has the feel of a political backwater. News from the state rarely makes the national newspapers, and while the contest for representation in the Lok Sabha and in the Assembly is intense, the two-horse race between Congress and the BJP rarely attracts much attention. The BJP took power in the last State Assembly elections under the Chief Ministership of Professor Prem Kumar Dhumal, although in the 1998 Lok Sabha Elections the Congress and the BJP shared four Lok Sabha seats between them.

Southern Himachal

★ Shimla

→ *Phone code: 0177. Colour map 1, grid B3. Population: approx 142,200. Altitude: 2,213 m.*

Once a charming hill station and the summer capital of the British, an air of decay hangs over many of Shimla's Raj buildings, strung out for about 3 km along the ridgeline. Below them a maze of narrow streets, bazars and shabby 'local' houses with corrugated iron roofs cling to the hillside. Some find it delightfully quaint and less spoilt than other Himalayan hill stations. There are still some lovely walks, lined with magnificent pines and cedars giving a beautifully fresh scent to the air. ⇥ *For Sleeping, Eating and other listings, see pages 470-474.*

Ins and outs

Getting there Despite the romance of the narrow gauge railway from Kalka, see page 466, most people get to Shimla by bus or taxi as it is so much quicker. The bus stand and the station are on Cart Rd, where porters jostle to take your luggage up the steep hill to a hotel. If you are staying on the western side of town it is worth getting off the bus at the railway station. Buses from the east, including Rampur and Kinnaur, stop at the Rivoli bus stand. Shimla (Jabbarhatti) airport has a coach (Rs 50) in season, and taxis (Rs 350) for transfer.

Getting around The Mall can only be seen on foot, it takes about half an hour to walk from the Viceroy's Lodge to Christ Church. The main traffic artery is Cart Rd which continues past the station to the Main Bus Stand, taxi rank and the two-stage lift which goes to the Mall above (Rs 5). The Victory Tunnel cuts through from the Cart Rd to the north side of the hill. See Transport, page 473, for further details. As in colonial times, vehicles are generally not allowed on the Mall and The Ridge.

Climate Oct-Nov are very pleasant, with warm days and cool nights. Dec-Feb is cold and there are snowfalls. Mar-Apr are changeable, storms are not infrequent and the air can feel very chilly. Avoid May-Jun, the height of the Indian tourist season prior to the monsoon.

Himachal Pradesh Southern Himachal Shimla

Shimla is strung out on a long crescent-shaped ridge which connects a number of hilltops from which there are good views of the snow-capped peaks to the north: Jakhu (2,453 m), Prospect Hill (2,176 m), Observatory Hill (2,148 m), Elysium Hill (2,255 m) and Summer Hill (2,103 m). For the British, the only way of beating the hot weather on the plains in May and June was to move to hill stations which they endowed with mock Tudor houses, churches, clubs, parks with bandstands of English county towns, and a main street invariably called the Mall.

Christ Church (1844), on the open area of The Ridge, dominates the eastern end of town. Consecrated in 1857 a clock and porch were added later. The original chancel window, designed by Lockwood Kipling, Rudyards father, is no longer there. The mock tudor **library** building (circa 1910) is next door. The Mall joins The Ridge at Kipling's **"Scandal Point"**, where today groups gather to exchange gossip. Originally the name referred to the stir caused by the supposed 'elopement' of a lady from the Viceregal Lodge and a dashing Patiala prince after they arranged a rendezvous here.

The **Gaiety Theatre** (1887) and the **Town Hall** (circa 1910) are reminiscent of the 'Arts and Crafts' style, as well as the timbered **General Post Office** (1886). Beyond, to the west, is the *Grand Hotel*. Further down you pass the sinister looking **Gorton Castle**, designed by **Sir Samuel Swinton Jacob**, which was once the Civil Secretariat. A road to the left leads to the railway station, while one to the right goes to Annandale, the racecourse and cricket ground. The Mall leads to the rebuilt *Cecil Hotel*. On Observatory Hill (the watershed), the **Viceregal Lodge** (1888) was built for Lord Dufferin in the Elizabethan style but with an indoor tennis court. Now the **Rashtrapati Niwas** ⓘ *1000-1630, a small entry fee to the house includes a very brief guided tour*, it houses the Indian Institute of Advanced Study (IIAS) and stands in large grounds with good

Shimla

To The Glen
To Airport
To Chadwick Falls (1 km)

Himachal University

KAITHU BAZAR

SUMMER HILL

GLEN FOREST

Annandale Race Course

Tara Hall (Loreto Convent)

Summer Hill Station

Annandale Club

GLEN URQUHART

State Bank of India

Circular Rd

TV Tower

Observatory
Gate
The Mall

CHAURA MAIDAN

Victory Tunnel

The Mall

Cart Rd

Taxis

The

Viceregal Lodge (IIAS)

Gorton Castle

Taxis

Bazar

Gopal Mandir

OBSERVATORY HILL

Taxis

Main Shimla Station

Shimla Extension

A

Shimla Club

To Prospect Hill (1 km)

To Kalka

Shimla Kalka Rd

Bypass

FOREST NURSERY

Kamla Nehru

To Asia the Dawn Hotel, Tara Devi & Airport

KHILLINI

Cart Rd

N

To Springfield & Eastbourne Hotels

0 metres 200
0 yards 200

■ Sleeping	3 Harsha	6 Shingar
1 Chapslee House	4 Oberoi Cecil	7 Tashkent
2 Dalziel	5 Oberoi Clarkes	8 Woodville Palace

views of the mountains. Reminders of its British origins include a gatehouse, a chapel and the meticulously polished brass fire hydrants imported from Manchester. Inside, you may only visit the main reception rooms and the library which are lined from floor to ceiling with impressive teak panelling. It is a long uphill walk from the gate.

Walks

There are several pleasant walks in and around Shimla. **Jakhu Temple** on a hill with excellent views (2,455 m), dedicated to Hanuman the monkey god, is 2 km from Christ Church. Walking sticks (handy for warding off monkeys, which can be vicious – keep your distance and all food out of sight and reach) are available at *chai* shops at the start of the ascent.

The Glen (1,830 m), to the northwest, is a 4-km walk from the centre past the *Cecil Hotel*. **Summer Hill** (1,983 m), a pleasant 'suburb' 5 km from town, is a stop on the Shimla-Kalka railway. **Chadwick Falls** (1,586 m), 3 km further, drops 67 m during the monsoons.

Prospect Hill (2,175 m) is 5 km from The Ridge and a 20-minute walk from Boileauganj to the west. **Tara Devi** (1,851 m), with a hilltop temple, 11 km southwest from the railway station, can also be reached by car or train.

Museums

The **State Museum** ⓘ *closed Mon, 1000-1330, 1400-1700, free*, near Chaura Maidan. A 30-minute walk west from the GPO along the Mall; then a short climb from the *Harsha Hotel*. Small, with a good sculpture collection and miniatures from the Kangra School; also contemporary art including work by Roerich, costumes, jewellery, bronzes and textiles. Well labelled.

Kufri About 16 km from Shimla, at 2,500 m, Kufri hosts a winter sports festival. However, don't expect European or American resort slopes or facilities. There are some attractions around and about the town. At **Danes Folly** (2,330 m), 5 km away, is a government run orchard. A 10-minute walk uphill takes you to a mini zoo of Himalayan wildlife. **Mahasu peak** ⓘ *bus, Rs 15*, 20 minutes from a path behind the Kufri Resort cottages, offers fabulous mountain views on a clear day and there is a small but interesting temple at the start of the walk. The best time to visit is in January and February.

Chharabra Chharabra is an enjoyable 3-km forest walk down from Kufri. The Wildflower Hall which once stood here was the residence of **Lord Kitchener**, Commander-in-Chief of the Indian Army. The original building was replaced; its successor was converted into a hotel which burnt down in 1993. Oberoi has opened a new luxury hotel, see listings page 471.

Related map
A Shimla Mall & The Ridge, page 466

Himachal Pradesh Southern Himachal Shimla

Naldera Off the Hindusthan-Tibet road, 26 km north of Shimla, Naldera has a nine-hole golf course, possibly the oldest in India and the beautiful Mahung temple. The colourful *Sipi Fair* in June attracts crowds from surrounding villages who sell handicrafts.

Tattapani, 18 km north across the Sutlej River, has a hot spring flowing from the banks of the Sutlej River. *Tourist Inn*, T0177-485949, has three rooms and very basic dorm (Rs 30), meals.

Chail ⓘ *from Shimla, bus at 0830 takes 2½ hrs; you can return by a different route.* In a superb forest setting with fine snow views (45 km southeast of Shimla; off the NH22), Chail was once the Maharaja of Patiala's summer capital. Built on three adjacent hills, it is claimed to have the country's highest cricket ground at 2,444 m, a 2-km walk from the bus stand! The old palace on Rajgarh Hill has been converted to a hotel while the old residency 'Snow view' and a Sikh temple stand on the other two hills. The **Chail Sanctuary**, once a private hunting reserve, is popular with birdwatchers. A cheer pheasant breeding programme was started here in 1988. It is an idyllic spot but not when the weekend day-trippers descend on the tiny resort.

Kalka Kalka is the terminus for the narrow gauge railway from Shimla. The Kalka-Shimla line (0.76 m), completed in 1903, runs 97 km from Kalka in the foothills to Shimla at over 2,000 m. The magnificent journey takes just over five hours. The steepest gradient is 1 in 33; there are 107 tunnels covering 8 km and bridges over 3 km. Order a meal in advance at Kalka or Shimla station. See below.

Nalagarh ⓘ *On request the Nalagarh Resort hotel pick-up from Ropar (20 km) or Kalka (40 km). Car from Chandigarh, 45 mins; Delhi, about 5 hrs (drivers accommodated).* The area around Nalagarh was once ruled by the Chandela Rajputs. The fort has wonderful

Shimla Mall & The Ridge

■ Sleeping	5 Samrat	**● Eating**	6 Himani
1 Combermere	6 Vikrant	1 Alfa	7 Indian Coffee
2 Dreamland	7 White	2 Baljee's	House
& Ashoka	8 Woodland	3 Choice Chinese	8 Naaz
3 Mayur	9 YMCA	4 Devico	9 New Plaza
4 Mehman	10 YWCA	5 Goofa	10 Park

⠿ The seasonal move of government

So beneficial were the effects of the cooler mountain air that Shimla, 'discovered' by the British in 1819, became the summer seat of government from 1865 to 1939. The capital was shifted there from Calcutta and later from Delhi (1912 onwards) and all business was transacted from this cool mountain retreat.

Huge baggage trains were needed to transport the mountains of files and the whole operation cost thousands of rupees. At the end of the season back they would all leave.

Women heavily outnumbered men, as wives of many British men who ran the empire escaped to the hills for long periods. Army officers spent their leave there. Social life in hill stations became a round of parties, balls, formal promenades along the Mall and brief flirtations.

views above an estate of forests and orchards and is built on five levels around manicured grassy courts. Originally built in the 15th century; the Diwan-i-Khas (1618) is now the Banquet Hall. The present Raja has opened his home to guests.

Shimla to Kinnaur and Spiti

★ Old Hindustan Tibet Road

➔ *Colour map 1, grid B3 and 4. The road may be severely damaged in the rains.*

The Old Hindustan Tibet road runs east from Shimla to the Tibetan border through a landscape of lush tropical valleys, snow clad peaks and precipitous gorges. Connecting a string of prosperous looking farms, villages and towns, it passes through terraced slopes covered with orchards before entering the high altitude deserts of Spiti. As the narrow road winds even deeper towards the Tibetan border its unprotected sides plunge hundreds of metres to the roaring monsoon-swollen River Sutlej below, grasping at huge boulders brought down by thundering landslides into the gloomy gorges. By bus or jeep, this road is not for the faint-hearted.

Inner Line Permits (ILP) Inner Line Permits are needed for travel close to the Tibetan border but are easy to get. The 'Inner Line' runs parallel to and 40 km inside the border; all visitors are barred, except from places like Kaza which are specifically exempt. Overnight stay is not permitted in Puh, Khabo and Sumdo. Rules may be further relaxed, so check with the tourist office. Permits are issued free to individuals, for 7 days from the date (easily renewable for 3 days at Kaza or Recong Peo). Take 3 passport photos, valid passport, 2 copies of the front page of passport and Indian Visa and complete the form from Sub-Divisional Magistrate's office (SDM) In Shimla (T257009), Recong Peo (T22452) or Kaza (T2212) (difficult in the last). Permits also available (in theory) from: Resident Comissioner of Himachal Pradesh, Himachal Bhavan, 27 Sikandra Road, New Delhi, T3716574 and other magistrates officers. Permits say "no overnight halts and no photography" though rules have been relaxed considerably. In Shimla, travel agents charge Rs 150. In Kaza, you need the additional 'No Objection' certificate from the Chief of Police – a mere formality of a stamp and signature. In Recong Peo, the whole process takes about an hour (which may include 'chai' or breakfast with the SDM). Accommodation is limited to simple rest houses, lodges or tents. In some places enterprising local families are opening their modest homes to paying guests. Local village shops often stock canned food and bottled water, and you may be surprised by the advent of television even in remote villages. It is virtually impossible to get foreign exchange in this area.

Narkanda The small market town at 2,700 m occupies a superb position on the col. The town offers a base from which to ski however the skiing does not compare with that found in western resorts. Enquire at Marketing Office in Shimla for skiing excursions in winter and seven day beginners course (Rs 4,500-5,000).

Nirath The road drops sharply through woodland interspersed with apple orchards from Narkanda, down to Kingel from where it zig-zags down to Sainj. The seasonal route is best by 4WD though buses cover this route very carefully. Some 5 km beyond Sainj there are superb views across the valley, and of a wall of eroded outwash deposits at least 50 m thick. The main road passes through Nirath where there is a **Surya Temple** believed to date from the eighth century which still has some fine carving preserved on the outer walls and has carved wooden panels within. At an altitude of between 800-900 m the Sutlej Valley towards Rampur has a subtropical summer climate, with mango trees and bananas replacing apples.

Rampur Bushahr This is one of Himachal's most important market towns. Padam Palace (1920s), opposite the bus stand, once the residence of the Raja, has interesting carved wooden panels and wall murals, but is difficult to enter. The Sat Narain Temple in the main bazar (1926) has a beautiful but decaying façade. The *Lavi Fair* (11-14 November) draws large crowds of colourful hill people who bring their produce – handicrafts, carpets, rugs, fruit and nuts and animals – to the special market. There are sporting competitions in the day, and dancing and making music around bonfires after dark.

Rampur to Sarahan From Rampur the highway enters one of the most exciting, and geologically active, stretches of road in the region. During the rains the Sutlej River is a surging torrent of muddy water, dropping over 450 m in under 30 km and passing through gorges and deeply incised valleys. Although an ancient trade route, the road is comparatively recent and is constantly being upgraded particularly in connection with the Nathpa-Jhakhri HEP scheme, with a 28 km long tunnel from Nathpa, near Wangtu, to Jhakhri, about 10 km beyond Rampur. When completed this will be one of the largest Hydel schemes in the world. The blasting both for the shafts and for road widening has further destabilized the already landslide-prone hillsides and during the rains the road may be blocked. Blockages are usually cleared within hours,

Around Shimla

⁞ Human sacrifice in the Himalaya

Human sacrifice was practised for centuries in the original Bhimakali temple in Sarahan. During the 16th and 17th centuries this was carried out with elaborate rituals. The sacrificial victim would be kept in the adjoining Narasimha Temple. After the ritual offering his blood would be placed on Bhimakali's tongue for her to 'drink' and would then be used to wash the feet of a second deity Ushadevi. The priest would also place a mark of blood on the forehead of each worshipper. The sacrificed head would finally be thrown into the Sutlej river and the body into the well in the courtyard which is now blocked.

though travelling times are wholly unpredictable. You also need a strong stomach, both for the main road and for diversions, especially up the Baspa Valley to Sangla. Some 9 km west of Jeori the river passes through a dramatic gorge. On the north side of the river isolated tiny pockets of cultivated land cling to the hillside. **Jeori** is the junction for Sarahan, 21 km South, an hour away. There are several provisions stores to pick up the basics here since Sarahan has very limited supplies.

★ **Sarahan** → *Phone code: 01782. Colour map 1, grid B3. Population: 1,200. Altitude: 1,850 m.*

An important market for traders of neighbouring regions. It is an attractive town, surrounded by high peaks, with a pheasant breeding centre nearby. The bazar is interesting: friendly villagers greet travellers, shops sell flowers, bright red and gold scarves and other offerings for worshippers among local produce, fancy goods, clothes and jewellery. It is also a stop on the trekkers' route.

Sights Sarahan was the old capital of the local Rampur Bushahr rulers and has a palace complex containing the strikingly carved wood-bonded **Bhimakali Temple** (rebuilt circa 1927), in a mixture of Hindu and Buddhist styles. The two temples stand on a slope among apple and apricot orchards behind the bazar. The Bhimakali is dedicated to Durga as the destroyer of the *asuras* (demons) and has a Brahmin priest in attendance. Plan for an early morning visit to the temple to see morning prayers; evening prayers are around 1900. Leave shoes and leather objects with the attendant and wear the saffron cap offered to you before entering. You may only photograph the outside of the temples. It is worth climbing around the back of the complex for a picturesque view.

According to some sources the ancient temple on the right (closed for safety reasons) is many centuries old (see box). Built in traditional timber-bonded style it has white-washed dry stone and rubble masonry alternating with horizontal deodar or spruce beams to withstand earthquakes. The upper floors have balconies and windows with superb ornamental woodcarving; the silver repoussée work doors are also impressive. The first floor has a 200-year-old gold image of goddess Bhimkali which is actively worshipped only during the *Dasara* festival when animals and birds are sacrificed in the courtyard, while on the second floor daily early morning *puja* is carried out to a second image. The sacrificial altar and the old well are in the courtyard with three other shrines. The palace of the Rampur rajas behind the temple has a drawing room with ornate furniture and a painted ceiling; the caretaker may let you in.

The **Pheasant Breeding Centre** ① *summer 0830-1830, winter 0930-1630, free*, on a hill, a 1-km strenuous walk from the main road, on a wooded trail, has Monal, Khalij, Western Tragopan and other varities in cages.

A pilgrimage route encircles **Shrikhand Mahadev** peak (5,227 m), which takes pilgrims seven days to go round. On a clear day you get fantastic panoramic views of the snow covered peaks.

Listings: Southern Himachal

🛏 Sleeping

Shimla *p463, maps p464 and p466*
Prices soar in May and Jun when modest accommodation can be difficult to find especially if you arrive after midday, so book ahead. Some close off-season, whilst those below **B** that remain open offer discounts of 30-50%. Don't leave windows open unattended; an open invitation for mischievous monkeys! From the railway or bus station it is a stiff climb up to hotels on or near the Ridge. Porters available (agree about Rs 20 per heavy bag). Also, ask for his metal token (to ensure safe delivery) and return it on reaching your destination! They often get a large commission to take you to selected hotels.

AL Oberoi Cecil, Chaura Maidan (quiet end of the Mall), T204848, F211024, reservations@ thececil.com. 79 rooms, colonial grandeur on the edge of town, with superb views, beautifully renovated, stylishly furnished, good restaurant, special ultramodern pool, full-board. Recommended.

AL Oberoi Clarkes, The Mall, near Lift, T251010, F211321, clarkes@nde.vsnl.net.in. 39 large, comfortable rooms, those with mountain views at rear may suffer from traffic noise at night, front rooms with town views quieter, impressive dining room (good buffets), pleasant bar, has character, well run but lacks some **A** facilities, no pool, front has had a facelift, full-board only.

A Chapslee House (Heritage), Lakkar Bazar, T202542, F258633, www.chapslee.com. 6 suites only, charming, full of character, large grounds, exquisite interior, good views, excellent meals (disappointing *thali* though) and excellent service, if you can get in.

A-B Combermere, 2 entrances, next to the Lift at top and bottom, T252242, F252251, hot_comb@hotmail.com. 40 excellent rooms (including some **AL** penthouses) on 9 levels (partly served by lift), well located, friendly, efficient, very helpful, pleasant terrace and bar, games room, central heating.

A-B Springfields (Quality Inn), opposite Tibetan School, Chhota Shimla, T221297, F221298, information@ ushashriramhotels.com. 11 "shabby genteel suites still decorated in 1920s style", in old

Maharaja's bungalow "where staff refused to be tipped"! Superb views, lawns, restaurant.

A-B Woodville Palace (Heritage), Raj Bhavan Rd, The Mall, T223919, F223098. 14 rooms (variable), some good **A** suites with period furniture (freezing in winter), dining hall worth visiting for eclectic mixture of portraits, weapons and hunting trophies! (non-residents onadvance notice), owned by Raja of Jubbal's family and featured in "Jewel in the Crown", good views, spacious, large grounds,, one of the quietest.

B Eastbourne, Khillini, near Bishop Cotton School, 5 km from bus stand, T223665, F223890, eastbourne@vacationvalue.com. 24 rooms (noisy near reception), good restaurant, flower-filled gardens in wooded setting, well furnished, friendly.

B-C Harsha, The Mall, Chaura Maidan, next to State Museum, T258441, F212868, hotelharsha@hotmail.com. 21 rooms, restaurant, rather uninspired but friendly service, pleasant and quiet location.

C Mehman, above Christ Church, T213692. 21 rooms (some with mirrored ceilings!), plumbing a bit suspect, modern, very clean, great views from the front, very helpful staff.

C Shingar, The Mall, T252881, F252998. 34 clean rooms, restaurant, TV.

C-D Samrat, Cambermere Bridge, The Mall, T258572, F208767. 20 small rooms, restaurant (Indian, Chinese), helpful.

C-E Mayur, above Christ Church, T252392, F254919, hotel_mayur@vsnl.com. 28 rooms, some with mountain views, some with tub, good restaurant but check bill, modern, clean, lift, helpful staff.

C-E White, Lakkar Bazar, T/F255276. 28 clean rooms with bath, TV, some with good views and balcony.

D-E Dalziel, The Mall, above Station, T252691, F206725. 25 clean enough rooms with bath (hot water), Indian meals, not bad value, prices depend on size of TV!

D-E Woodland, T211002, Daisy Bank, The Ridge, beyond *Mehman*. 17 rooms, some **C** wood-panelled, downstairs with views, some with bath (even tubs), avoid noisy downstairs rooms near Reception, friendly, good room service, safe luggage storage, off-season bargain.

E YMCA, The Ridge, above Christ Church, T252375, F211016. 40 rooms (**D** in annexe best with bath), clean linen, hot water in mornings, clean bathrooms on 2nd floor, avoid west side near noisy cinema, main and top floors reported dirty, mediocre meals (breakfast included), quiet, relaxed, popular but very institutionalized, gym and billiards.
E-F Tashkent, lane down off Mall, above Victory Tunnel. Very basic, rooms vary, some with bath and TV (possible to bargain down), views from balcony overhanging long drop.
E-F Vikrant, near the bus terminal, T255334. 23 clean rooms, shared bath (bucket hot water), some attached, TV, efficient.
E-F YWCA, Constantia, behind Telegraph Office, T203081. 20 clean rooms for both sexes, heavily booked May-Jun, off-season discounts, water at certain times of day, superb position, safe and very good value.

Kufri *p465*
B Kufri Holiday Resort, T0177-280300. 22 rooms and 8 modern cottages (2 and 3 bedrooms), limited hot water, cold in winter, but attractive design and setting with flower-filled gardens, outstanding views from cottages above and good walks.

Chharabra *p465*
L Wildflower Hall, T0177-480808, www.oberoihotels.com. Plush and modern with a period exterior, mountain views from rooms at rear, good restaurants and lovely gardens surrounded by deodar forest with beautifully peaceful walks.

Naldera *p466*
A-C Log Huts, T0177-487739. 6 rooms.
C Golf Glade, T0177-287739. 5 rooms, restaurant and bar.

Chail *p466*
A-B Chail Palace, T01792-48141, F48142. 19 rooms and 3 suites in old stone-built mansion; avoid basement rooms 21, 22, 23 and dark, dingy wooden chalets but others OK, billiards, tennis, orchards.
C Banjara Camp, www.banjaracamps.com. Deluxe 2-bed tents, bath tent, all meals, well organized. Recommended.
D Himneel, 16 rooms, restaurant, modest but full of character. *Kailash* restaurant serves good value breakfasts and lunches.

Kalka *p466*
F Retiring Rooms, good for early morning departures, can be in demand in season so reserve ahead at Kalka or Shimla.

If using your own transport, there are many hotels, guesthouses and *dhabas* along the Kalka-Shimla road. Kasauli is an attractive hill resort a 16 km hike away with a few hotels.

Nalagarh *p466*
B Nalagarh Resort (WelcomHeritage), T01795-23009, F23021. 15 comfortable rooms (some suites), with modern baths, traditional furniture, good food but buffets only, small pool, tennis, rural surroundings, run by Raja's family who meet guests, friendly and welcoming, plenty of atmosphere. Recommended. Reserve ahead.

Narkanda *p468*
C-D Hatu, T01782-8430. 16 rooms, restaurant, commanding views, skiing equipment for hire. A small restaurant down lane near bazar has limited menu.

Rampur Bushahr *p468*
B-D Bushehar Regency, T01782-34103. 20 rooms, some a/c, well positioned, restaurant, bar nearby.
E-F Bhagwati, below bus stand near river, T01782-33117. Clean rooms with bath (hot water), TV, restaurant, friendly.
E-F Narendra, Indira Market near bus stand on the river, T01782-33155, F34055. 15 rooms, with bath, TV, restaurant, bar. Others with shared bath.
F Bodh, near bus stand, T01782-33302. 5 rooms, dorm, Tibetan/Chinese restaurant, friendly, helpful owner.
Sutlej View, on main road overlooking river, 1 km west of town centre. Clean, limited menu but good food, attractive terrace, open 0900-2200.

Sarahan *p469*
C-D Srikhand (HPTDC), T74234, on a superb hilltop site, overlooking the Sutlej valley, Srikhand peak and the range beyond. 19 rooms with bath and hot water (3 large with balcony, 8 smaller with views, 4 in annexe cheaper), dorm (Rs 75), 2-bedroom royal cottage, restaurant but limited menu.
E Sangrika, near Police Assistance, T74491, F78243. 8 rooms with Indian toilets,

6 planned with western toilets on 1st floor, family run, homecooked meals.

E-F Temple rooms, Rs 100-300, dorm Rs 25. New guesthouses opening. *Dhabas* in town have basic food (rice, daal and snacks).

❼ Eating

Shimla *p463, maps p464 and p466*
Top hotels have pleasant bars; not so good in town. Take special care with food hygiene.

Top hotels with international menus, specially recommended are:
₸₸₸ **Cecil**, atmospheric, plush, modernized.
₸₸₸ **Chapslee**, old-fashioned.
₸₸₸ **Clarke's**, good set lunch but plays painful classical music at dinner.
₸₸₸ **Woodville Palace**, intimate.
₸₸ **Dominos**, The Mall. Pizzas.
₸₸ **Guptajee's Vaishnav Bhojanalaya**, 62 Middle Bezar. Excellent vegetarian Indian.
₸₸ **Himani**, The Mall. Indian. Restaurant above, tasty Mughlai, bar below.
₸₸ **Nalini**, The Mall, T207892. International. Pleasant, good service, 0830-2200; also ice creams and sweets counters.

Below the Mall, towards Lower Bazar, good cheap *dhabas* sell snacks (eg *tikki channa*).
₸ **Choice**, Middle Bazar, down steps from Fire Station. Chinese. Wide choice.
₸ **Indian Coffee House**, The Mall. International. South Indian snacks, excellent coffee, some western dishes, old world feel, uniformed waiters, spartan and dim.
₸ **Malook's** opposite Gaiety Theatre, down steps. Good Tibetan dishes (excellent *thukpas* and noodles).
₸ **New Plaza**, 60/61 Middle Bazar, down steps, T255438. Excellent value, friendly, simple but clean, serves a variety of western dishes.

Cafés and fast food
Baljees, 26 The Mall, opposite Town Hall. Good snacks, justifiably packed, cakes and sweets from takeaway counter.
Goofa (below Ashiana), The Ridge. Veg, dull, dimly lit but decent pizzas and *thalis*.
Park just above Mall, beyond Scandal Point. Indian, Continental. Very popular traveller hangout (great pizzas, excellent espresso coffee). Recommended.

◉ Entertainment

Shimla *p463, maps p464 and p466*
Cinema
Bollywood films are shown at the *Ritz* and the *Rivoli*.

✦ Festivals and events

Shimla *p463, maps p464 and p466*
In **Jun** the **Summer Festival** includes cultural programmes from Himachal and neighbouring states, and art and handicrafts exhibitions.

◯ Shopping

Shimla *p463, maps p464 and p466*
The main shopping areas are The Mall, Lower Bazar and Lakkar Bazar
Himachal Emporium, The Mall, opposite Telegraph Office, for local woollen items.
Tibetan Self-Help Handicrafts Centre, near Kusumpti, 6 km, produces carpets and woven goods, keeping Tibetan traditions alive, sold through other outlets in town.

Books
Maria Brothers, 78 The Mall, good selection of antiquarian books, maps and prints, 1030-1300, 1700-2000.
Minerva, 46 The Mall, opposite Gaiety Theatre for books and maps, good range.

▲▲ Activities and tours

Shimla *p463, maps p464 and p466*
Golf
Naldera, 9-hole. Casual members: green fee and equipment, about Rs 100, see page 466.

Ice skating
Skating rink: below *Rivoli*, on ice in winter, day's membership Rs 50 to skate to loud Indian film hits.

Skiing
Early Jan to mid-Mar. Ski courses at Narkanda (64 km) organized by Himachal Tourism, 7 and 15-day courses, Jan-Mar, Rs 1,700-3,000; see page 468 and also Manali.

● *For an explanation of the sleeping and eating price codes used in this guide, see inside the*
● *front cover. Other relevant information is found in Essentials pages 52-57.*

Tour companies

Band Box, 9 The Mall, T258157, F203055, bboxhv@satyam.net.in. Jeep safaris (around Rs 1600 per day), helpful advice.
Hi-Lander, 62 The Mall, T201565, F204026 for adventure tours and treks.
HPTDC's various tours during the season are well run, usually 1000-1700 (Rs 150). All start from Rivoli, enquire when booking for other pick up points. Return drop at Lift or Victory Tunnel. Two tours visit Kufri, Chini Bungalow and Nature Park; one returns to Shimla via Fagu, Naldehra and Mashobra, the other by Chail and Kairighat. A further tour visits Fagu, Theog, Matiana and Narkanda. Book in advance at the HPTDC marketing office on The Mall. Tour companies charge Rs 700-800 per car for 5.

○ Transport

Shimla *p463, maps p464 and p466*
Air
Shimla (Jabbarhatti) airport has daily flights from Delhi, Kullu and Ludhiana by *Jagsons*, 58 The Mall, T/F225177. Flights can be badly disrupted by the weather especially during the monsoon. Taxis charge Rs 300 to town.

Bus
Local From Cart Rd. Lift: 2-stage lift from the Taxi Stand on Cart Rd and near *Hotel Samrat* on The Mall, takes passengers to and from The Mall, 0800-2200, Rs 5.
Long distance From **Main Bus Stand**, Cart Rd. Buy tickets from counter before boarding bus (signs in Hindi so ask for help) some long-distance buses can be reserved in advance: *HPTDC* coaches during the season are good value and reliable: to **Chandigarh** 4 hrs, Rs 80, **Dehra Dun** 9 hrs, **Delhi** 10-12 hrs, Rs 339, overnight to **Dharamshala** 10 hrs, Rs 135. **Manali** dep outside the 'Tunnel', 8-10 hrs, Rs 338, tickets from Main Bus Stand.. HPRTC deluxe buses between Shimla and Delhi in the summer (9 hrs).
From **Rivoli** (Lakkar Bazaar): **Rampur** hourly from 0530, 8 hrs, and **Chitkul**, 2 daily; **Jeori** for Sarahan (8 hrs).

Taxi
Local Near lift on Cart Rd, T257645; fixed fares.
Long distance Union Stands near the lift, T205164, and by the Main Bus Stand on Cart Road. **Chandigarh**, Rs 1,000; **Kalka** (90 km), Rs 800; **Mussoorie**, Rs2,500, 8 hrs, including stops; **Rekong-Peo**, Rs 2,500 (11 hrs).

Train
Enquiry T254289. The main station has computerized reservations (T252915), 1000-1330, 1400-1700, Sun 1000-1400. The newer extension station, where some trains start and terminate, is just below the Main bus stand. Travel to/from Shimla involves a change of gauge at Kalka (see Box and Kalka below). It is quicker by bus but requires a stronger stomach. **To Chandigarh** via Kalka: Shimla to Kalka on *Shimla-Kalka Exp, 256*, 1035, 5½ hrs, then Kalka to Chandigarh on *Himalayan Queen, 4096*, 1650, 40 mins.
To New Delhi via Kalka: Shimla to Kalka on *Shimla-Kalka Exp, 256*, 1035, 5½ hrs, then Kalka to New Delhi on *Himalayan Queen, 4096*, 1650, 5½ hrs. **To Old Delhi**: Shimla to Kalka on *Shimla-Kalka Mail, 252*, 1745, 5 hrs, then Kalka to Old Delhi on *Kalka-Howrah Mail, 2312*, 2345, 6¾ hrs. The day train to Delhi is recommended. **From Delhi to Kalka**: *Himalayan Queen, 4095*, ND, 0600, 5¼ hrs; *Howrah-Kalka Mail, 2311*, OD, 2250, 6¼ hrs, then change to narrow gauge to Shimla (see Kalka). **By narrow gauge**: To Kalka: *Exp 258* (Season), 0925, 6 hrs; *Exp 256*, 1035 (1000 from Shimla Ext), 3½ hrs; *Rail Car102* (Season, for minimum 6), 1130, 5 hrs; *2KS Passenger*, 1425 (1400 from Shimla Ext), 6 hrs; *Exp 254* (Season), 1550, 5¼ hrs; *Sivalik Deluxe Exp 242*, 1730, 4¾ hrs; *Mail 252*, 1745, 5½ hrs.

Kalka *p466*
Easily reached from Shimla, by bus or taxi (Rs 800), and from **Chandigarh** by taxi (Rs 400).

Train
The train often arrives on the Kalka platform already full of locals who board it while it waits in the siding! Worth paying Rs 150-170 plus reservation fee of Rs 20 to guarantee a seat on 1st class.
    1st class waiting room for ticket holders only. It is essential (especially during the

'season') to have an advance reservation for the narrow gauge train. The quicker 16-seater glass top *Rail Car* can only be booked at Kalka. Season (for *254/257*): 1 May-15 Jul (school holidays start at end-May); 15 Sep-30 Oct; 15 Dec-1 Jan. The daily *Sivalik Deluxe Express* (No *241/242*), the line's pride and joy boasts "Toilet fittings of latest variety" and "Curtains of latest design"! The pricier ticket (Rs 305) includes tea and breakfast/dinner at Barog. **To Chandigarh**: *Shatabdi Exp, 2006,* 0600, 45 mins (to New Delhi, 4 hrs); *Himalayan Queen, 4096,* 1650, 45 mins (to New Delhi, 5½ hrs). **To Old Delhi**: *Kalka-Howrah Mail, 2312,* 2345, 5½ hrs. **From Delhi to Kalka**: *Himalayan Queen, 4095,* ND, 0600, 5¼ hrs; *Howrah-Kalka Mail, 2311,* OD, 2250, 5¼ hrs. **By narrow gauge**: **To Shimla**: *1KS Passenger,* 0400, 5½ hrs; *Sivalik Exp Deluxe 241,* 0530, 4¾ hrs; *Exp 253* (Season), 0600, 5 hrs; *Mail 251,* 0630, 5½ hrs; *Rail Car 101* (Season), 1135, 4 hrs; *Exp 255,*1155, 5½ hrs; *Exp 257* (Season), 1230, 6 hrs. A further service is also in place.

Rampur Bushahr *p468*
Bus
Often late and overcrowded. To **Chandigarh**; **Delhi**; **Mandi** (9 hrs); **Recong Peo** (5 hrs) and **Puh**; **Sarahan** (2-3 hrs), better to change at Jeori; **Shimla**, several (5-6 hrs); **Tapri** (and Kalpa) 0545 (3¾ hrs), change at Karchham for Sangla and Chitkul.

Sarahan *p469*
Bus
Daily between **Shimla** (Rivoli Bus Stand) and **Jeori** on the Highway (6 hrs), quicker by car. Local buses between Jeori and the army cantonment below Sarahan.

✪ Directory

Shimla *p463, maps p464 and p466*
Banks Changing foreign currency outside Shimla is not easy except in Manali or McLeodganj. Do not depend on credit cards for cash. Exchange procedure is awkward; photocopies of passport and visa needed. Grindlays, The Mall, and UCO quick and efficient. **Hospital** Snowdon Hospital: Dr Puri, Mehghana Complex, The Mall, T201936, speaks fluent English, is efficient, and very reasonable. **Internet** Tourist office, The Mall, 2 machines, Rs 50 per hr, also 2 at Telegraph Office. **Post office** GPO, The Mall (near Scandal Point). Open 1000-1600 Sun. Poste Restante: Counter 10 (separate entrance), chaotic, 0800-1700, Sun 1000-1600. CTO nearby. **Tourist offices** Himachal (HPTDC), The Mall, T258302, F252557, hptdc@nde.vsnl.net.in. 0900-1800, in season, 0900-1900, very helpful. Victory Tunnel, Cart Rd, T254589, 1000-1700. Directorate, 28 SDA Complex, Kasumpti Complex, T225924. **Himachal Tourism** has a/c and non-a/c cars. **Corporate Office**, Ritz Annexe, T252704, F252206.

Kinnaur and Spiti

The regions of Kinnaur and Spiti lie in the rainshadow of the outer Himalayan ranges. The climate in Spiti is much drier than in the Kullu Valley and is similar to that of Ladakh. The temperatures are more extreme both in summer and winter and most of the landscape is barren and bleak. The wind can be bitingly cold even when the sun is hot. The annual rainfall is very low so cultivation is restricted to the ribbons of land that fringe rivers with irrigation potential. The crops include potatoes, wheat, barley and millet. The people are of Mongol origin and almost everyone follows a Tibetan form of Buddhism.

Kinnaur and Spiti can only be seen by following the circular route (the southern part of which is the Old Hindustan Tibet Road which follows the Sutlej River). The Baspa valley is a side route up a dead end valley via Sangla to Chitkul, recommended for its views and landscapes, villages, pagodas and culture. Kinnaur is the only route in to Spiti, which has the evocative Tibetan. Buddhist sites of Tabo and Kaza, set against the backdrop of a rugged landscape. The road then goes on round to the Rohtang Pass and Manali, or on up to Ladakh. See page 1366 for books about the area. ▸▸ For Sleeping, Eating and other listings, see pages 483-486.

Kinnaur

An exciting mountain road runs through cliffside cuttings along the left bank of the Sutlej – frequently blocked by rockfalls and landslides during the monsoons. At **Choling** the Sutlej roars through a narrow force, and at **Wangtu** the road re-crosses the river where vehicle details are checked. Immediately after crossing the Wangtu bridge a narrow side road goes to **Kafnoo village** (2,427 m), in the Bhabha Valley (a camping site and the start for an attractive 10-day trek to the Pin Valley). From Wangtu the road route runs to **Tapri** (1,870 m) and **Karchham** (1,899 m) both of which have hot springs. Here the

> ☃ *Most Kinnauri Buddhist temples only accept visitors at around 0700 and 1900. You must wear a hat and a special belt available locally.*

Baspa River joins the Sutlej from the south. A hair-raising excursion by a precipitous winding rough road leads 16 km up the Baspa Valley to Sangla; buses take approximately 1½ hrs.

★ Baspa Valley → *Colour map 1, grid B4.*

The valley carries the marks of a succession of glacial events which have shaped it, although the glaciers which formed the valley have now retreated to the high slopes above Chitkul at over 4,500 m. All villages in Baspa are characterized by exaggerated

Kinnaur & Spiti

The stuff of epics

The **bhoj patra**, found distinctively in the Sangla Valley, is a revered product. The extraordinarily fine waterproof layers just beneath the bark of the bhoj patra tree were used for writing centuries ago, particularly where palm leaves were not available. Renowned for its suppleness, strength and apparent indestructibility, bark from this valley was used for some of Hinduism's most ancient writings, including the epics, and it is still highly valued for copying sacred texts. Genealogies which trace the descent of some families in the Sangla Valley to the legendary Pandavas are still widely accepted, and connections between the residents of the valley and the early roots of Hinduism are treasured.

steeply sloping slate roofs, rich wood carving and elaborate pagoda temples. Although Kinner Kailash (sacred to Hindus and Buddhists) is not visible from here, the valley is on the circumambulating *Parikrama/Kora* route which encircles the massif. Fields of the pink coloured *ogla*, a small flower seed grown specifically in the Baspa Valley for grinding into grain, add a beautiful colouring in the season.

Sangla Sangla, at 2,680 m, is built on the massive buttress of a terminal moraine which marked one of the major glacial advances about 50,000 years ago. The Baspa River has cut a deep trench on its south flank. Immediately above is the flat valley floor, formed on the lake bed which was once dammed behind the moraine. Sangla village has excellent carving and is full of character. No foreign exchange is available but there are telephone facilities. There is a **saffron** farm just north of Sangla, claimed to be better than at Pampore in Kashmir, and it is famous for its apples. The climate is ideal, especially as there is no hail damage.

The old seven-storey **Killa** (Fort) ① *0800-0900, 1800-1900*, where the Kinnaur rajas were once crowned, is 1 km north of new Sangla just before the road enters the village. It was occupied by the local rulers for centuries. It now has a temple to Kamakshi where the idol is from Guwahati, Assam646.

Barseri Barseri, 8 km from Sangla, is situated on an outwash cone which has engulfed part of the Baspa's valley floor. This well-kept "green village" is happy to show visitors its solar heaters, *chakkis* (water mills) and water driven prayer wheels. The Buddha Mandir with *Shakyamuni* and other images and a large prayer wheel is beautiful inside. Villagers weave shawls and do woodcarving.

The Rakcham pagoda-style temple with beautiful wood carving is to Shamshir Debta, Devi and Naga, combining Buddhist and Hindu deities. The ibex horns on the roof are ancient male fertility symbols. There is also a pre-Buddist, animist Bon cho shrine and a Siva temple.

Chitkul (18 km from Barseri, altitude: 3,450 m), with its typical houses, Buddhist temple and a small tower, is the furthest point foreigners can travel without special permits. The Kagyupa (Oral Transmission School), has a highly valued, old image of the Shakyamuni Buddha. There are four directional kings on either side of the door as well as a Wheel of Life. You can walk along the Baspa River which has paths on both sides. The rough path along the tributary starting at the bridge across the river, below the bus stand, is very steep in places with loose stones. Do not attempt alone. One basic shop sells a few provisions.

66 99 "At last they entered a world within a world – a valley of leagues where the high hills were fashioned of the mere rubble and refuse from off the knees of the mountains .... Surely the gods live here." Rudyard Kipling

Recong Peo Also called 'Peo', at 2,290 m, the District HQ is a busy little market town. The Sub-Divisional Magistrate's office in a three-storey building below the bus stand deals with Inner Line Permits (see page 467). A short walk above the town takes you to the Kalachakra Temple with a large Buddha statue outside – good views of Kinner Kailash. A shop here sells provisions, medicines and has a telephone but there aren't any exchange facilities.

Kothi village, reached by a path from the Kalachakra Temple, has ancient Hindu temples associated with the Pandavas. One has a tank of sacred fish, 30 minutes' walk from the bazar.

Kalpa Kalpa (Chini), 12 km from Recong Peo at 2,960 m, is reached after a stiff climb. It has an interesting temple complex and Budh mandir and is surrounded by apple, *bemi* (wild apricot) and plum orchards and chilgoza pine forests.

Pangi A high road from Kalpa/Recong Peo with little traffic passes through Chilgoza pine forests, north to the hamlet of Pangi, 10 km away. Pangi is surrounded by apple orchards. The colourful Sheshri Nag temple at the top of the village has an inscription in a strange script above the entrance and standing stones in the courtyard. Apart from two Buddhist temples, the carved pagoda temple to Sheshri's mother encloses a huge boulder representing the Devi. The road then goes over bare and rugged hills beyond to **Morang** which has impressive monasteries with wood carvings and sculptures.

Jangi At Jangi there is a check post and to Puh, just south of Kah which is a steep climb with hairpin bends. The road follows the Spiti while the Sutlej valley disappears to the east towards the Tibet border.

★ Spiti

"At last they entered a world within a world – a valley of leagues where the high hills were fashioned of the mere rubble and refuse from off the knees of the mountains .... Surely the gods live here."
Rudyard Kipling

Khabo (2,831 m), a morning's drive from Kalpa, is at the confluence of the Sutlej and Spiti rivers. The entry into the Spiti valley at Khabo is a rare example of crossing from the Himalaya to the Trans-Himalaya without going over a major pass. The 180 km State Highway 30, which joins Sumdo with Batal (Sumdo is the last village of Kinnau – has a Border Police check post and a tea shop), passes through an arid valley with small patches of cultivation of peas and barley near the snow melt streams. It is 31 km to Tabo from Sumdo.

At the crossroads of two ancient trade routes, Tabo was one of the great centres of Buddhist learning and culture. Founded in 996, the monastery is the oldest living Buddhist establishment in this part of the world. Today, the small town is rapidly being modernized with paved streets and electric lights. Government offices have appeared alongside traditional mud homes and the local shops stock basic provisions for trekkers. There is a post office.

★ **Chos Khor Gompa** Founded in 996 as a scholastic institution, the Gompa's original layout was planned as a *mandala* centred around a **Du khang** (Assembly Hall). The deodar wood used was imported from Kullu, Kinnaur, Chamba and Kashmir while the lack of quality structural stone resulted in the extensive use of earth, strengthened with gypsum for the high walls. Today the gompa houses 60 lamas and has a good collection of scriptures, *thangkas* and art pieces. It is most important and has an immense sense of the spiritual. Carry a torch. No photography allowed.

Many of the **colourful murals** come close to the pure Indian style identified with Ajanta. The technique required the surface to be coated with several thin layers of lime and yak-skin glue and burnished vigorously to provide the 'ground' which was then smoothed and freshened with animal fat and butter. Natural vegetable dyes and powdered stone colours were mixed with *dzo* milk and yak urine for painting. The early Indian style murals used a profusion of reds and yellows with little stress on landscaping, the area around the principal figures being filled with small divinities. These images wear seraphic smiles and have half-shut dreamy eyes depicting introspective meditation. The later 17th-century paintings illustrate the Central Tibetan/ Chinese art form where ultramarine takes over from the earlier dominance of reds and yellows, and landscapes become lively and vivid with the appearance of cliffs, swirling clouds, stylized flames, flora and fauna. Here the twists and turns of the limbs and the flowing elaborate drapery show great fluency. This is one of the few gompas in the Tibetan Buddhist influenced areas of Ladakh, Lahaul and Spiti where the highly structured art of painting the complex Tibetan religious iconography is taught. What appears outwardly as a free art form is taught on lined grid paper where each shape and form is closely measured.

Nine temples Tsuglhakhang ('academy') The 'resplendent' central *Mahavairochana* – a composite of four figures, each facing a cardinal direction, represents the unity of all Buddhas. On the walls inside are stucco figures of different Buddhas and Bodhisattvas. The floral ceiling decorations are in the Ajanta style.

Dri Tsang khang (Inner Sanctum) and **Kora** (Circumambulatory Path) At the centre of the 'mandala', the five *Dhyani* Buddhas escorted by four Bodhisattvas here, emerge from the darkness lit by a shaft of sunlight.

Masks, weapons and ritual costumes are stored in the **Gon Khang** which is closed to visitors. **Zhalma** (Picture Hall) has a 17th-century entrance temple where the murals are recent and in pure Tibetan style.

Dromton Lhakhang Chenpo (17th century) Dominated by Medicine Buddhas. The ceiling, in high Tibetan style, is exceptional, depicting *nagas*, titans, peacocks and parrots amongst rainbows.

Ser Khang (Golden Temple) The walls were believed to have been coated with a layer of gold dust as thick as a yak's skin for painting the numerous larger-than-life figures. They were renewed in 16-17th centuries.

Chamba Chenpo La Khang Dedicated to the Maitreya (Future) Buddha, this temple has a 6-m high seated statue. The murals of the eight Buddhas may be some of the earliest in Tabo.

To the north, the small **natural caves** above the road were an integral part of the monastic complex. Pho Gompa, the only surviving, with early murals showing pure Indian influence, has been restored. These post Ajantan paintings, however, are already fading. On open ground to the east, on both sides of a dyke, there are pre-Buddhist rock carvings on metamorphosed igneous rocks showing ibex, swastikas, *yonis*, horses, panthers and human figures.

A large *Mala* (sacrificial wood) **tree** at the northwest corner of the enclave, the only one of four to survive, is held sacred by the villagers, while the monastery courtyard has *Ganday* trees which bear yellow, sweetly-scented flowers in the spring.

Dankar Once the capital of Spiti, Dankar is a tiny village. The early 16th-century fort/monastery **Dankar Gompa** (3,890 m), which once served as a jail, stands on an impressive overhang, perched on crumbling towers. Today it has over 160 lamas in residence. The 'highest temple' has a collection of Bhotia Buddhist scriptures, a four-in-one *Dhyani Buddha* and interesting murals of Medicine Buddhas and protector deities. The gompa is a two-hour very steep climb from a point 2 km away, beyond Shichling on the main road. The jeepable road from the SH30, about 1 km west of Shichling, winds up 8 km to Dankar (a two-hour walk) and is easier. A beautiful large pond at just under 4,100 m is reached by a 2½ km track.

Lalung Gompa, known for its carved wood panelling, is off the SH30, 22 km from Kaza, reached by 8-km narrow, motorable track. From Dankar Gompa this is a two-hour trek. Carry plenty of water as there are no streams and it can get very hot.

Pin Valley About 5 km from Dankar is a sign for the Pin Valley National Park which is on the other side of the river. The Pin River joins the Spiti at Attargo. Above Attargo, 10 km along the Pin Valley, is the **Kungri Gompa** (circa 1330), which though not old is in an established monastic site with old-carved wooden sculptures and is commonly understood to be a Bon monastery still practising elements of the pre Buddhist Bon religion. The trek from the Bhabha Valley ends at the road head at Kungri, see page 525. One bus a day departs from Kaza at 1200, goes along the Pin Valley as far as Mikkim and turns straight back at 1400, not allowing enough time to visit the Gompa. You therefore face a long walk unless you can hitch a lift on a passing tractor or truck.

At the confluence of the Pin River and one of its tributaries, 1 km from Mikkim, **Sangam** can be reached by one of two pulley systems. The one nearest the bus stop, across a bridge, requires your own rope harness. The other, 750 m west along the river has a person-size bucket. Both require a reasonable degree of fitness to negotiate, especially if crossing alone. The local greeting is *joolay, joolay*!

Pin Valley National Park is described as the 'land of ibex and snow leopard' and was created to conserve the flora and fauna of the cold desert. It adjoins the Great Himalayan National Park (southwest), and Rupi Bhabha Sanctuary (south) with the Bara Shigri Glacier forming its north boundary. The park covers 675 sq km with a buffer zone of 1,150 sq km mainly to its east where there are villages, and varies in altitude from 3,600 m to 6,630 m. The **wildlife** includes Siberian ibex, snow leopard, red fox, pika, weasels, lammergeier, Himalayan griffon, golden eagle, Chakor partridge, Himalayan snow cock and a variety of rose finches. The Siberian ibex can be sighted at high altitudes, beyond Hikim and Thango village. From July to September the young ibex kids need protection and so the females move up to the higher pastures near cliffs while the adult males concentrate on feeding lower down. The 60-km long Lingti Valley is famous for its fossils.

Although rugged, the summer brings more rain here than the rest of Spiti resulting in a profusion of wild flowers.

Kaza Kaza, at 3,600 m, is 13 km from Lingti village. Old Kaza has village homes while New Kaza sports government offices. It is a busy bus terminus with a small market, a basic health centre and jeeps for hire. Inner Line Permits are issued by the SDM's office. Tourist facilities are open May to October. No foreign exchange is available. If you are in need of supplies, Kibber, 19 km away, has a school, post office, a bank and several provisions stores for trekkers.

There is an attractive one-day circular trek from here to **Hikim** and **Komik** villages visiting the monastery midway. Hikim gompa (early 14th century), modelled on a Chinese castle, was built under Mongol patronage.

Kibber-Gete Wildlife Sanctuary ⓘ *Bus from Kaza (about 1 hr)*. One of the world's highest wildlife sanctuaries covering an area 98 sq km, it has **Mount Gya** (6,754 m) to the north and **Kamelong** (5,867 m) to the south. On the drive from Kibber to Tashigang, you may spot musk deer and bharal sheep but to see larger mammals (bear, wolf and the rare snow leopard) you would need to trek. Also to be seen are Himalayan birds of prey as well as snowcock and other high-altitude birds.

Tashigang, 18 km away, is one of the highest villages in the world connected by road. **Ki Monastery** on the way is the largest in Spiti and houses 300 lamas. Although it has suffered from wars, fires and earthquakes it still has a good collection of *thangkas* and *kangyurs* (scriptures). Although no permit is needed, the monks have instituted their private 'entrance fee' system which, by all accounts, appears quite flexible and linked to the visitors perceived ability to pay. There are a few cheap guest houses and camping is possible. If you cannot stay take a bus up and walk down via the Ki Monastery, 11 km from Kaza.

To Lahul Losar, at 4,079 m, is the last village in Spiti reached after driving through fields growing peas and cabbage among poplars, willows and apple orchards. There is a rest house and guesthouse and a couple of cafes serving Tibetan/Spitian food.

The road continues up for 18 km to the **Kunzum La** (Pass) at 4,551 m. It means 'meeting place for ibex' and gives access to Lahul and good views of some of the highest peaks of the Chandrabhaga (CB) group notably CB 14, 16 and 17 that lie immediately opposite the Kunzum La to the west. To the southeast is the Karcha Peak (6,271 m). The pass has an ancient chorten marker. The temple to **Gyephang**, the presiding deity, is circumambulated by those crossing the pass; the giver of any offering in cash which sticks to the stone image receives special blessing.

The road does 19 hairpin bends to descend down the rock strewn terrain to the valley of the river Chandra to **Batal** where the tea shop serves noodles and sells biscuits and bottled water, and on to **Chhota Dhara** and **Chhatru**, with rest houses and eateries, and then **Gramphoo** joining the Manali-Keylong-Leh highway (three hours journey from the pass). Gramphoo is 62 km from Manali.

Shimla to Kullu Valley

Bilaspur Bilaspur used to be the centre of a district in which the tribal Daora peoples panned in the silts of the Beas and Sutlej for gold. Their main source, the Seer Khud, has now been flooded by the Bhakra Nangal Lake and they have shifted their area of search upstream. For a bite to eat visit the *Lake View Café*.

Bhakra-Nangal Dam The dam on the river **Sutlej** is one of the highest dams in the world at 225 m and was built as part of the Indus Waters Treaty between India and Pakistan (1960). The Treaty allocated the water of the rivers Sutlej, Beas and Ravi to India. The dam provides electricity for Punjab, Haryana and Delhi. It is also the source for the Rajasthan Canal project, which takes water over 1,500 km south to the Thar desert. There is accommodation should you wish to stay.

Una to Mandi Having passed through Una, along the main bus route, **Ghanahatti**, a further 18 km on, has the adequate *Monal Restaurant*. There are some magnificent views, sometimes across intensively cultivated land, sometimes through plantations of chilgoza, khir and other species. In **Shalaghat**, further on, accommodation is available. The road descends into a deep valley before climbing again to the small market town of **Bhararighat**. A jeep can take over two hours for this part of the journey. In **Brahmpukar** the road to Beri and Mandi is a very attractive country lane. The more heavily used though still quiet road to the main Bilaspur-Manali road joins it at **Ghaghas**. During the monsoons landslides on the NH21 may result in very long delays. Carry plenty of water and some food.

The tree-lined and attractive approach to **Sundernagar** from the south gives some indication of the town's rapid growth and prosperity.

Mandi (Sahor)

→ *Phone code: 01905. Colour map 1, grid B3. Population: 26,900. Altitude: 760 m.*
ⓘ *Daily bus to Kataula (20 km, with an attractive pagoda temple), and onto Bagi (8 km). Follow a steep trail through the forest of rhododendron, oak, deodar and kail (3 hrs). After arriving at a group of large shepherd huts the trail to the left goes to the temple, the right to the Forest Rest House.*

Founded by a Rajput prince in circa 1520, Mandi is held sacred by both Hindus and Buddhists. The old town with the main (Indira) bazar is huddled on the left bank of the Beas at the southern end of the Kullu Valley, just below its junction with the Uhl River. The Beas bridge (claimed to be the world's longest non-pillar bridge) is across Sukheti Khad at the east end of town. The main bus station is across the river, just above the open sports ground. It is worth stopping a night in this quaint town with 81 temples, a 17th-century palace and a colourful bazar.

Sights Triloknath Temple (1520) on the river bank, built in the Nagari style with a tiled roof, has a life-size three-faced Siva image (Lord of three worlds), riding a bull with Parvati on his lap. It is at the centre of a group of 13th to 16th-century sculpted stone shrines. The Kali Devi statue which emphasizes the natural shape of the stone, illustrates the ancient Himalayan practice of stone worship.

Panchavaktra Temple, at the confluence of the Beas and a tributary with views of the Trilokinath, has a five-faced image (*Panchanana*) of Siva. The image is unusually conceived like a temple *shikhara* on an altar plinth. Note the interesting frieze of yogis on a small temple alongside.

Bhutnath Temple (circa 1520) by the river in the town centre is the focus at *Sivaratri* festival (see below). The modern shrines nearby are brightly painted.

In lower Sumkhetar, west of the main bazar, is the 16th-century **Ardhanarishvara Temple** where the Siva image is a composite male/female form combining the passive Siva (right) and the activating energy of Parvati (left). Although the *mandapa* is ruined, the carvings on the *shikhara* tower and above the inner sanctum door, are particularly fine.

From the old suspension bridge on the Dharamshala road, if you follow a narrow lane up into the main market, you will see the slate roof over a deep spring which is the **Mata Kuan Rani Temple**, dedicated to the 'Princess of the Well'. The story of this Princess of Sahor (Mandi) and her consort **Padmasambhava**, who introduced Mahayana Buddhism in Tibet, describes how the angry king condemned the two to die in a fire which raged for seven days and when the smoke cleared a lake appeared with a lotus – Rewalsar or *Tso Pema* (Tibetan 'Lotus Lake').

Excursions The small dark **Rewalsar Lake** ⓘ *many buses from Mandi, originating from bus stand with pick up from below the palace, Indira Bazar, 1 hr, Rs 14,* 24 km southeast, with its floating reed islands, is a popular pilgrimage centre. The colourful

Tibetan Buddhist monastery was founded in the 14th century though the pagoda-like structure is late 19th century. The Gurudwara commemorates Guru Gobind Singh's stay here. Start early for the hilltop temples by the transmission tower as it is a steep and hot climb. The *Sisu* fair is held in February/March.

At **Prashar,** the three-tiered pagoda Rishi temple by a sacred lake is in a basin surrounded by high mountains with fantastic views of the Pir Panjal range. The rich woodcarvings here suggest a date earlier than the Manali Dhungri Temple (1553) which is not as fine. No smoking, alcohol or leather items are allowed near the temple or lake. There are basic Pilgrim Rest Houses. A forest rest house is 1 km west of temple.

You can walk to Aut, see further, page 482, from Prashar in six to seven hours. A level trail east crosses a col in under a kilometre. Take the good path down to the right side of the *nullah* (valley) and cross the stream on a clear path. Climb a little and then follow a broad path on the left bank to the road. Turn right and down to Peon village in the Chir nullah and continue to Aut.

Tirthan Valley and Jalori Pass

From Mandi the NH21 runs east then south along the left bank of the Beas, much diminished in size by the dam at **Pandoh**, 19 km from Mandi, from which water is channelled to the Sutlej. The dam site is on a spectacular meander of the Beas (photography strictly prohibited). The NH21 crosses over the dam to the right bank of the Beas then follows the superb **Larji Gorge**, in which the Beas now forms a lake for a large part of the way upstream to Aut. A large Hydro-Electric project is being constructed along this stretch. At **Aut,** pronounced 'out', there is trout fishing (season March to October, best in March and April). Permits issued by the Fishery Office in Largi, Rs 100 per day. The main bazar road has a few cheap hotels and eating places. It is also a good place to stop and stock up with trekking supplies such as dried apricots and nuts. From Aut, a road branches off across the Beas into the **Tirthan Valley** climbing through beautiful wooded scenery with deodar and larch up to the Jalori Pass. Allow at least 1½ hours by jeep to **Shoja**, 42 km from Mandi, and another 30 minutes to Jalori. Contact tourist office in Kullu or *Doli Guest House* for trekking routes. One suggested trek is Banjar-Laisa- Paldi-Dhaugi/Banogi-Sainj, total 30 km, two days.

Banjar ① *taxis to Jalori Pass, Rs 600 (Rs 900 return), Jibhi/Ghayaghi, Rs 200, Kullu, Rs 600, Manali, Rs 1200, Mandi, Rs 700, Shimla, Rs 3000, buses are rare,* with attractive wood fronted shops lining the narrow street, has the best examples in the area of timber bonded Himalayan architecture in the fort-like rectangular temple of Murlidhar (Krishna). Half way to **Chaini**, 3 km away, the large Shring Rishi temple to the deified local sage is very colourful with beautiful wooden balconies and an impressive 45-m tall tower which was damaged in the last earthquake. The entrance, 7 m above ground, is reached by climbing a notched tree trunk. Such free standing temple towers found in eastern Tibet, were sometimes used for defence and incorporated into Thakur's castles in the western Himalaya. The fortified villages here even have farmhouses like towers.

Jibhi and Ghayaghi ① *The last few kilometres above Jibhi are extremely steep and narrow, though astonishingly, local buses ply the route. Bus to Jalori can take 1 hr (Rs 5). Some go via Ghayaghi (approximate times): Kulla-Bagipul, 0800; Manali-Rampur, 1000; Kullu-Dalash, 1100; Manali-Ani, 1100. If heading for Shimla or Kinnaur, change buses at Sainj on NH22.* From Banjar the road climbs increasingly steeply to Jibhi, 9 km away, where there is also accommodation and trekking. Contact Mr BS Rana at *Doli Guest House* or *Seraj Himalayan Tours* who also arrange safaris. Two kilometres beyond is Ghayaghi, also with some accommadation.

Shoja Shoja, a Rajput village in the heart of the forest, offers a base for treks in the Great Himalayan National Park.

Jalori Pass *Bus from Ani and Khanag to the south, runs to the Pass and back. 4 buses daily traverse the pass in each direction when it is open (8-9 months). See Ghayaghi above. Bus to Sainj, 3½ hrs, and on to Shimla, 5 hrs. You may wish to take the bus up to the Pass and walk down, or even camp a night at the Pass. Check road conditions before travelling. Pass only open in good weather from mid-April* (Altitude: 3,350 m). The new Jalori pass which links Inner and Outer Seraj (150 m lower than the old pass) is 76 km from Kullu. A ruined fort, Raghupur Garh, sits high to the west of the pass and from the meadows there are fantastic views, especially of the Pir Panjal range. Take the path straight from the first hairpin after the pass and head upwards, for about 30 to 40 minutes. The road is most suitable for four-wheel drive vehicles.

There is a very pleasant, gradual walk, 5 km east, through woodland (one hour), starting at the path to the right of the temple. It is easy to follow. **Sereuil Sar** ('Pure Water') is where local women worship Burhi Nagini Devi, the snake goddess, and walk around the lake pouring a line of *ghee*. The lake is perpetually clean. It is claimed that leaves are cleared in the mornings by a pair of resident birds! *Dhabas* provide simple refreshments and one has two very basic cheap rooms at the Pass.

Great Himalayan National Park & Tirthan Sanctuary ① *Rs 4, still camera Rs 4, video Rs 2000, filming Rs 20,000.* The park (60,561 ha, altitude: 1,500-5,800 m, access is easiest from April to June and September to October) and sanctuary (6,825 ha) lie southeast of Kullu town in the Seraj Forest Division, an area bounded by mountain ridges (except to the west) and watered by the upper reaches of the rivers Jiwa, Sainj and Tirthan. The national park was created in 1948 and has its headquarters in Shamshi.The hills are covered in part by dense forest of blue pine, deciduous broadleaved and fir trees and also shrubs and grassland; thickets of bamboo make it impenetrable in places. Attractive species of iris, frittilaria, gagea and primula are found in the high altitude meadows. Wildlife include the panther, Himalayan black bear, brown bear, tahr, musk deer, red fox, goral and bharal. The rich birdlife includes six species of pheasant.

Goshiani is the base for treks into the park. The first 3 km is fairly gentle and runs along the river before rising to harder rocky terrain, allowing plenty of opportunity to see birds and butterflies. The trout farm here sells fresh fish at Rs 150 per kg. Fishing permits, Rs 100, are obtainable from the Fisheries Department.

Listings: Kinnaur and Spiti

⊜ Sleeping

Sangla *p476*
B-C Banjara Camps, Barseri, via Sangla, superb riverside site 8 km beyond Sangla. 18 twin bed and some 4-bed deluxe tents, separate (or attached) bath tents, varied meals included, friendly staff, excellent site, mountain biking, trekking, Lahul, Spiti, Ladakh tours. Highly recommended. Buses stop 2 km from the campsite (6 km out of Sangla), where road drops down to right, car park at foot of hill is 500-m walk from camp (horn will summon porters!), reservations: 1A

Hauz Khas Village, New Delhi T011-6861397, F6855152, www.banjaracamps.com.
D Kinner Camp, Barseri, 017864-T2382. Small tents with beds/ sleeping bags, shared baths, bird watching, trekking, jeep safaris, meals, cafeteria for day visitors, superb location.
E-F Mount Kailash, T017864-22227. Clean pleasant rooms (hot shower).
F Sangla Guest House, near shops. Clean rooms with bath (hot water), restaurant.
F Trekker's Lodge, going out of town towards Chitkul. Run by a veteran mountaineer.

● *For an explanation of the sleeping and eating price codes used in this guide, see inside the* ● *front cover. Other relevant information is found in Essentials pages 52-57.*

Barseri *p476*
E **Rupin**, guesthouse, faces the river.

Chitkul *p476*
E-F **Thakur Guest House**, 4 rooms with
bath, 3 with shared bath, varied meals.
F **Amar Guest House**, clean double rooms
(Rs 100), hot water, friendly family
atmosphere. Recommended.
F **PWD Rest House**. 4 rooms, lawns, attractive.

Recong Peo *p477*
E **Shivling Guest House**, near bus Stand,
T017852-22421. 4 rooms with bath,
restaurant, good view of Shivling peak.
Vijay, good *parathas*, quick service.
Vikas, good views.

Kalpa *p477*
Most hotels have superb views.
C **Kinner Villa**, Delhi T011-6982903, F6980746.
circuits@vsnl.net.in. 11 rooms with bath, in new
building, attractively located, seasonal tents.
C-E **Kinner Kailash Cottage** (open
May-Nov) T01786-26159. Commanding
position, 5 rooms (with bath tub, Rs 1100),
limited menu, camping.
E **Forest Rest House** (2 km), caretaker can
prepare meals, modern building, camping
overnight (with permission) in school
grounds from 1600-1000.
F **Aucktong Guest House ("Aunties")**, near
Circuit House, 1 km north on Pangi road,
T01786-26019. 4 clean spacious rooms, large
windows, restaurant, pleasant, very friendly
("arrived for one night and stayed a week!").

Tabo *p478*
C **Banjara Camp**, 11 deluxe 2-bed tents, bath
tent, all meals, well organized.
Recommended. Contact Delhi T011-6861397,
F6855152, www.banjaracamps.com.
D-E **Millennium Guest House**, run by
monks in the complex, 13 colourful rooms
(rats for conmpany), shared dirty toilets, hot
water on request, meals.
    Also cheaper guesthouses in the village,
many allowing camping.
Tanzin, near monastery. Tibetan food,
friendly, family run, best in village.

Dankar *p479*
Sleeping is limited here. The Gompa has
2 rooms; only one has a bed.

Pin Valley *p479*
Norzang Guest House, rooms for Rs 100. PWD
Rest House. Sub-post office but no provisions.

Kaza *p479*
C-D **Pomodoro Country**, Kaza-Rangrik Rd
(8 km northwest of town). 6 rooms (hot
showers) in Italian family run farmhouse,
excellent restaurant (homemade pasta and
breads etc), 4 Teepee style tents, riding, treks.
D-E **Kunpen Gakyith**, near Post Office.
Newish building, restaurant, lawn.
E **Kaycee Lodge**, simple rooms, good service.
E **Tourist Lodge**, 4 rooms, tents, catering.
F **Mahabhadra**, basic but large room, shared
bath, very clean, meals. Recommended.
    Kaza is also ideal for **camping**.

Shalaghat *p481*
D **Mehman**, and restaurant occupies an
extraordinarily bold setting.

Sundernagar *p481*
D **Relax Inn**, on Mandi side of town, modern,
clean and **Chinar Restaurant**, on NH21,
south of centre, is modern and decent.

Mandi *p481*
C **Visco Resorts**, just outside Mandi, T25057.
Large rooms (some for 4) in modern resort,
clean, lovely setting, good cheap restaurant.
C-D **Mayfair**, corner of Indira Bazar, T22777.
14 a/c rooms with bath, good restaurant (see
eating below), clean, well-kept.
D **Mandav** (HPTDC), above Main Bus Stand,
T35503, F35551. 13 clean rooms with bath
(cheaper **E** in annexe), 2 **C** a/c, restaurant,
beer, friendly, helpful, good value.
D **Munish Resorts**, on hillside 3 km above
New Beas Bridge (Rs 30 by auto from bus
stand), T35035, F35036. 15 clean rooms with
bath, restaurant, lovely views, colourful
garden with tempting fruit (Rs 100 fine for
each fruit/flower picked!), friendly family.
D-E **Evening Plaza**, Indira Bazar, T25123.
14 reasonable rooms, some a/c, TV, changes
cash and TCs at a good rate (1% commission).
E **Ashoka Holiday Inn**, near Chohatta Bazar,
Gandhi Chowk, T23832. 6 grubby rooms.
E-F **Raj Mahal**, lane to right of Palace, Indira
Bazar, T22401, F23737. 12 rooms, deluxe
rooms with bath (sharpened sword in one
might be mistaken for a towel rail!), 4 'special'
rooms, period furniture and paintings, others

F, former 'Palace' has character but in need of attention, restaurant, bar, garden temple, a fine example of Pahari art – "like staying at a great aunt's", run by the polite 'raja'.
F Vyas, 5-min walk from bus stand, past sports ground (signs), T35556. 6 small rooms, 4-bedded dorm (Rs 40), clean enough, quiet overlooking Beas, good value.

Rewalsar Lake p481
E Rawalsar Inn, above the lake, T01905-80252. It has 12 reasonable rooms with bath, some with TV and balcony, dorm (Rs 75).

Banjar p482
C Guest House.
E Meena, beyond bus stand.
E Shivani, beyond bus stand.

Shoja p482
D Shoja Retreat, wooden lodge with fantastic views, good food and trekking information.
F Forest Rest House, enjoys a spectacular and isolated position just below the Jalori Pass.

Goshiani p483
Raju's Place, is a family-run river-facing guesthouse, three rooms with bath. They offer meals, treks and safaris.

❼ Eating

Kaza p479
Layul, a restaurant, does Chinese, Tibetan and Indian dishes, and cold beer.
Also several bakeries and cafés.

Mandi p481
Café Shiraz, HPTDC, Gandhi Chowk, near Bhutnath Temple. Snacks only, dim, bus ticketing available.
Mayfair, efficient and tasty North Indian, some continental and Chinese. Best in town.
Raj Mahal, quiet, peaceful (interesting photos and antiques), pleasant garden, good value but limited menu and surly waiters.

Rewalsar Lake p481
Gomush Tibetan Restaurant, near Gompa, does excellent momos.
Some dhabas are by the bus terminal.

❀ Festivals and events

Mandi p481
Feb/Mar Sivaratri Fair, a week of dance, music and drama as temple deities from surrounding hills are taken in procession with chariots and palanquins to visit the Madho Rai and Bhutnath Temples.

◎ Shopping

Mandi p481
Indira Bazar, below the palace is a modern shopping centre, claimed to be the largest in North India with 340 shops.

Handicrafts
Near Bhutnath Temple with colourful tailors' shops.

◓ Transport

Sangla p476
Bus
To Chitkul (often 2-3 hrs late); Shimla via Tapri (10 hrs); Recong Peo, 0630; from Tapri, 0930. 4WD recommended between Karchham and Chitkul in bad weather.

Chitkul p476
Bus
Two buses a day to/from Karchham (0930) via Sangla (1100) and Rakcham; from Tapri, 0930; from Recong Peo 0600 (prompt).

Recong Peo p477
Bus
Reserve ticket from booth shortly before departure. Bus to Chandigarh; Delhi 1030; Kalpa, occasional; Kaza (9 hrs), gets very crowded so reserve seat before 0700; Puh; Rampur, frequent (5 hrs); Sangla/Chitkul (4 hrs); Shimla; Tabo, via Kaza (9-10 hrs), Rs 65.

Kalpa p477
Bus
To Shimla, 0730; Chitkul, 1300. To get to Peo for Kaza bus at 0730, walk down (40 mins) or arrange taxi from Peo. Travellers may not be allowed beyond Jangi without an 'Inner Line' permit. Contact SDM in Recong Peo a day ahead, see page 467.

Bus

To **Chandigarh** via Kinnaur, 0900; **Kaza**, 1000.

Kaza *p479*

Bus

Reserve a seat at least 1 hr ahead or night before. The road via Kunzum-La and Rhotang Pass can be blocked well into Jul.

New Bus Stand, bottom end of village. In summer: from **Manali** (201 km), 12 hrs via Rohtang Pass and Kunzum La; **Shimla** (412 km) on the route described, 2 days. Approximate times shown: daily to **Chango**, 1400; **Kibber** 0900, **Losar** 0900; **Mikkim** (19 km from Attargo), in the Pin Valley, 1200 (2 hrs); returns 1400. Long distance buses to **Kullu**, 0400; **Manali** (from Tabo), 0500; **Chandigarh** 0630. The last 3 are heavily used.

Mandi *p481*

Bus

Chandigarh (203 km, 5 hrs). **Dharamshala** 0830, 1200, 1830, Rs 80, 6 hrs; **Kullu/Manali** every ½ hr, 3 hrs, Rs 44 (Kullu), 4 hrs, Rs 68 (Manali); **Shimla** (5½ hrs, Rs 100). Book private buses in town or opposite the bus stand at least **one day in advance**; they do not originate in Mandi. **Dharamshala**, 5 hrs, Rs 250. Kullu/Manali, 2 hrs (Kullu), 3½ hrs (Manali), Rs 150.

Taxi

Rs 600 to **Kullu**; Rs 1000 to **Manali**; Rs 1200 to **Dharamshala**.

Train

Jogindernagar (55 km) is on the narrow gauge from Pathankot.

◐ Directory

Mandi *p481*

Banks Bank of Baroda, Hospital Rd, in the old town centre, can take over an hour to change Visa; **Indian Overseas Bank** changes TCs. **Evening Plaza Hotel** is the only place to change cash (see above). Mandi has one of the few banks in Himachal able to give cash on Visa cards.

★ Kullu Valley: valley of the Gods → *Colour map 1, grid B3 and 4. See also the trekking map on page 524.*

The Beas Valley was the gateway to Lahul for the Central Asian trade in wool and borax. It is enclosed to the north by the Pir Panjal range, to the west by the Bara Bangahal and to the east by the Parvati range. The approach is through a narrow funnel or gorge but in the upper part it extends outwards. The name Kullu is derived from Kulantpith 'the end of the habitable world'. It is steeped in Hindu religious tradition, every stream, rock and blade of grass seemingly imbued with some religious significance. ➤ *For Sleeping, Eating and other listings, see pages 494-501.*

History For a long time the **Kullu Kingdom** was restricted to the upper Beas Valley. The original capital was at Jagatsukh, 5 km to the south of Manali. In the 15th century it was extended south to Mandi. In the 17th century the capital was shifted to Kullu and the kingdom's boundaries extended into Lahul and Spiti and as far east as the Sutlej. In 1847, Kullu came under British control and was governed from Dharamshala.

Kullu → *Phone code: 01902. Colour map 1, grid B3. Population: 18,300. Altitude: 1,219 m.*

Sprawling along the grassy west bank of the Beas, Kullu, the district headquarters, hosts the dramatically colourful Dasara festival. Less commercialized than its neighbour Manali, it is known across India as the home of apple growing and the locally woven woollen shawls. There is little to occupy you here as a tourist. ➤ *For Sleeping, Eating and other listings, see pages 494-501.*

Ins and outs

Getting there Kullu-Manali (Bhuntar) airport, 10 km south, has flights from Delhi, Shimla and Ludhiana; transfer by bus or taxi (Rs 150), to Manali (Rs 650), Manikaran (Rs 500). For buses from the south, get off at Dhalpur Bus Stand if you choose a nearby hotel.

Getting around The Main Bus Stand and Dhalpur with ample hotels and restaurants are close enough for walking. Buses and taxis go to nearby sights. See Transport, page 500, for further details.

Climate: Mid-Sep-mid-Nov are the best seasons. May and Jun are hot but offer good trekking options. Mar-mid-Apr can be cold with occasional heavy rain.

Sights

The bulky curvilinear temples seem to resemble the huge boulders found in river beds and on hillsides. A peculiar feature of the Nagari temples is the umbrella- shaped covering made of wood or zinc sheets placed over and around the *amalaka* stone at the top of the spire.

The **Raghunathji Temple** is the temple of the principal god of the Dasara festival. The shrine houses an image of Shri Raghunath (brought here from Ayodhya in circa 1657), in his chariot. **Bhekhli**, a 3-km climb away, has excellent views from the

Kullu

Sleeping		3 Kullu Valley	5 Ramneek	Eating		3 Monal Café
1 Aaditya	4 Madhu	6 Sarwari	1 Ashiyana	Food Junction
2 Bijleshwar	Chandrika	7 Shobla	2 Hot Stuff	4 Rohtang

To Silver Moon, Vaishali & Apple Valley Resort

To Bijli Mahadev, Mandi & Bhuntar Airport (10 km)

⦂ Dasara in Kullu

Dasara celebrates Rama's victory over the demon Ravana. From their various high mountain homes about 360 gods come to Kullu, drawn in their raths (chariots) by villagers to pay homage to Raghunathji who is ceremoniously brought from his temple in Kullu.

The goddess Hadimba, patron deity of the Kullu Rajas has to come before any other lesser deities are allowed near. Her chariot is the fastest and her departure marks the end of the festivities. All converge on the maidan on the first evening of the festival in a long procession accompanied by shrill trumpeters. Thereafter there are dances, music and a market. During the high point of the fair a buffalo is sacrificed in front of a jostling crowd. Jamlu, the village God of Malana, high up in the hills, follows an old tradition. He watches the festivities from across the river, but refuses to take part! (see page 527). On the last day Raghunathji's rath is taken to the river bank where a small bonfire is lit to symbolize the burning of Ravana, before Ragunathji is returned to his temple in a wooden palanquin.

Jagannathi Temple. The copper 16th-17th-century mask of the Devi inside has local Gaddi tribal features. The wall painting of Durga is in traditional folk style. There are also superb views on the steep but poorly marked climb to the tiny **Vaishno Devi Temple**, 4 km north, on Kullu-Manali road.

Excursions

Bijli Mahadev① *several buses until late afternoon from Left Bank Bus Stand, the road to Bijli is rough and the buses are in a poor state*, 11 km from Kullu at 2,435 m, is connected by road most of the way with a 2-km walk up steps from the road head. The temple on a steep hill has a 20-m rod on top which is reputedly struck by *bijli* (lightning) regularly, shattering the stone *lingam* inside. The priests put the lingam together each time with *ghee* (clarified butter) and a grain mixture until the next strike breaks it apart again.

Bajaura Temple, on the banks of the Beas River, about 200 m off the NH21 at **Hat** (Hatta), is one of the oldest in the valley. The massive pyramidal structure is magnificently decorated with stone images of Vishnu, Ganesh and Mahishasuramardini (Durga as the Slayer of the Buffalo Demon, see page 1331) in the outer shrines. The slender bodies, elongated faces and limbs suggest East Indian Pala influence. Floriated scrollwork decorate the exterior walls.

★ Parvati Valley

→ *Phone code: 01902. Colour map 1, grid B3 and B4. See also the trekking map on page 524.*
The Parvati (Parbati) Valley runs northeast from Bhuntar. Attractive orchards and the fresh green of terraced rice cultivation line the route. Known for its hot springs at Manikaran, more recently the valley has become infamous for the droves of chillum-smoking Israelis and Europeans who decamp here in the summer months attracted by the intensive cultivation of narcotics.➤➤ *For Sleeping, Eating and other listings, see pages 494-501.*

Ins and outs Several local buses (and jeep taxis) travel daily to the valley from Kullu via Bhuntar, taking about 2 hrs to Manikaran, which also has buses from Manali. See page 526 for trekking information. The area is prone to landslides and flash floods – take extra special care. See individual Transport sections for details.

⁞ Disappearances in the valley

Cases of Western travellers going missing in recent years continue to be reported. They seem to have occurred mostly when trekking alone or camping. Some suggest that there have beeen genuine accidents in the mountains or that some drug users have "opted out" and chosen to sever their ties and remain with sadhus in remote caves.

On the other hand, in the summer of 2000 three trekkers were found dead, victims of two savage attacks. The threat to personal safety is very real so if you are trekking beyond Manikaran, or from Naggar across the Chandrakhani Pass to the Malana Valley, you should not walk alone. Only use registered guides through local trekking agents. treasured.

Jari is the point where the deep Malana Nala joins the Parvati River. It is a popular resting place for trekkers but also for drug users. The guesthouses vary; a few away from the village centre have better views.

Kasol Kasol is the next village enroute to Manikaran. The quiet little village has spread on both sides of the road bridge which crosses a tributary that flows into the Parvati, not far from the village itself. About half a kilometre beyond the village, a narrow side road leads to the river and the location of a fine hot spring on the river bank. Kasol is the main destination for long stay visitors, many of whom sit in a haze of charas smoke by day, repeating the process by night! **Chhalal** is a 20-minute walk from Kasol. It is a quiet village where families take in guests. A couple of guesthouses have also sprung up here.

Manikaran ① *frequent buses from Bhuntar airport (which has buses to Kullu/Manali 1 hr 50 mins, Rs 20)*, 45 km from Kullu, is at the bottom of a dark gorge with **hot sulphur springs** emerging from the rock strewn banks of the Parvati. The local legend describes how while Parvati bathed in the river, Naga, the serpent god stole her *manikaran* (earrings). At Siva's command Naga angrily blew them back from underground causing a spring to flow. Hindu and Sikh pilgrims come to the Rama temple and the gurdwara and gather to cook their food by the springs, purportedly the hottest in the world. There are separate baths for men and women. Manikaran, though not attractive in itself, provides a brief halt for trekkers. Short treks go to Pulga and Khirganga beyond while a footpath (affected by landslips in places), leads to the Pin Valley in Spiti. If trekking this route, go with a registered guide. Do not attempt alone. A road goes on for 15 km to **Barseni**. It has also become a popular place for dropouts.

Pulga, a noisy village, seemingly overrun by giggling children, is in a beautiful location with some cheap guesthouses. It is a good four-hour walk east of Manikaran. Some longstay travellers prefer the basic airy guesthouses outside the village which offer meals.

Khirganga is along the trek which winds through the lush Parvati Valley, east of Pulga. It is known for its sacred ancient hot springs marking the place where Siva is thought to have meditated for 2,000 years. There is an open bathing pool for men and an enclosed pool for women, next to the humble shrine at the source. A few tents may be hired. *Dhabas* sell vegetarian food. This is the last village in this valley.

Kullu to Manali → *Colour map 1, grid B3.*

The NH21 continues north along the west side of the Beas. The older road to the east of the river goes through terraced rice fields and endless apple orchards, and is

Himachal Pradesh Kullu Valley Parvati

rougher and more circuitous but more interesting. Sections of both roads can be washed away during the monsoon. As you wind out the centre of Kullu along the right bank you'll pass the Sitaramata Temple embedded in the conglomerate cliff and Raison, a grassy meadow favoured by trekkers. Then on to Katrain and Naggar before reaching Manali. ▸▸ *For Sleeping, Eating and other listings, see pages 494-501.*

Katrain, in the widest part of the Kullu Valley, mid-way between Kullu and Manali, is overlooked by Baragarh Peak (3,325 m). There are plenty of options for an overnight stay. Across the bridge at **Patli Kuhl**, the road climbs through apple orchards to Naggar.

★ Naggar → *Phone code: 01902. Colour map 1, grid B3.*

Naggar's (Nagar) interesting castle sits high above Katrain. Built in the early 16th century, it withstood the earthquake of 1905 and is a fine example of timber-bonded building of West Himalaya. It was built around a courtyard with verandahs, from where there are enchanting views over the valley. With a pleasant, unhurried atmosphere, it is a good place to stop a while. It is also an entry for treks to Malana, see page 527.

The **castle**, probably built by Raja Sidh Singh, was used as a royal residence and state headquarters until the 17th century when the capital was transferred to Sultanpur (see Kullu). It continued as a summer palace until the British arrived in 1846, when it was sold to Major Hay, the first Assistant Commissioner, who Europeanized part of it, fitting staircases, fireplaces et cetera. Extensive renovations have produced fine results, especially in the intricately carved woodwork. In the first courtyard are several black *barselas* (sati stones) with primitive carvings. Beyond the courtyard and overlooking the valley the **Jagti Pat temple** houses a cracked stone slab measuring 2½ m by 1½ m by 2 m believed to be a piece of Deo Tibba which represents the deity in 'the celestial seat of all the gods'. A priest visits the slab every day.

The small **museum** ① *Rs 10*, has some interesting exhibits, including examples of local women's dress and headdress (*pattu* and *thippu*) and folk dance costumes (*chola*). There are also local implements for butter and tea making, and musical instruments like the broad bell horn (*karnal*) and long curled horn (*singa*).

Roerich Art Gallery ① *closed Mon, 0900-1300 (winter from 1000), 1400-1700, Rs 10*, a 2-km climb from the castle, is Nicholas Roerich's old home in a peaceful garden with excellent views. The small museum downstairs has a collection of photos and his distinctive stylized paintings of the Himalayas using striking colours.

Uruswati Institute ① *Rs 15*, uphill from the main house, was set up in 1993. The Himalayan Folk and Tribal Art Museum is well presented, with contemporary art upstairs. One room upstairs is devoted to a charming collection of Russian traditional costumes, dolls, musical instruments.

There are a number of **temples** around the castle including the 11th-century Gauri Shankar Siva near the bazar, with some fine stone carving. Facing the castle is the Chaturbhuj to Vishnu. Higher up, the wooden Tripura Sundari with a multi-level pagoda roof in the Himachal style celebrates its fair around mid-May. Above that is the Murlidhar Krishna at Thawa, claimed as the oldest in the area which has a beautifully carved stone base. Damaged in the 1905 earthquake, it is now well restored. There are fine mountain views from here.

★ Manali → *Phone code: 01902. Colour map 1, grid B3. Population: 6,300. Altitude: 1,926 m.*

Manali occupies the valley with the once unspoilt Old Village to the north and Vashisht, up on the opposite hillside across the river. Set amidst picturesque apple orchards, Manali is packed with Pahari-speaking Kullus, Lahaulis, Nepali labourers and enterprising Tibetan refugees who have opened guesthouses, restaurants and craft shops. The town has become increasingly built-up with dozens of new hotel

Manali

To Monal & Shiv Shakti, Surya & Manu Temple

To Himalaya & Rockway

F Guest Houses

To Keylong & Leh

OLD MANALI

To Vashisht

Club House

HPTDC Hot Baths & Pyramid Centre

Mall Rd

Club House

Deodar Forest Reserve

CHADIARI

Manalsu Nala

Dhungri Deodar Forest

Hadimba Devi Temple

The Mall

DHUNGRI

Related map
A Manali centre, page 492

To Ambassador Resort

Gurudwara Rd (School Rd)

Taxi

MODEL TOWN

Mission Rd

Shiali Mahadev Rd

Hadimba Rd

Model Town Rd

SBI

Gompa Rd

Tibetan Monastery

Tibetan Monastery

Beas River

Naggar Rd

ALEO VILLAGE

Mountaineering Institute

To Kullu & Bhuntar Airport

To Holiday Inn (2.5 km),
Sterling Himalaya, Manali
Resorts (5 km) & Naggar

Himachal Pradesh Kullu Valley Manali

N

0 metres 100
0 yards 100

Sleeping
1 Apple View &
  Upcountry Lodge
2 Ambika & Mountview
3 Ashok Mayur

4 Bridge View
5 Cairn Lodge
6 Chetna
7 Dragon
8 Highland
9 John Banon's
  Guesthouse
10 Jungal Bungalow
11 Krishna
12 Leela Huts
13 Log Huts

14 Manali Heights
15 Mayflower
16 Piccadily
17 Pinewood
18 Riverside Cottage
19 Rohtang Manalsu
20 Sita
21 Snowcrest Manor
22 Sunshine
23 Surabhi
24 Tourist Lodge

25 Vishranti

● **Eating**
1 German Bakery
2 Il Forno
3 Ish
4 Moondance
5 Nirvana
6 Rohtang Café
7 Shiva
8 Tibetan Kitchen

blocks. It is also a major tourist destination for Indian holidaymakers. Others, together with adventure seeking foreigners, are attracted by the culturally different hill people and the scenic treks this part of the Himalaya offers. It is the start of the recommended two-day road route to Leh in the summer months. ▸▸ *For Sleeping, Eating and other listings, see pages 494-501.*

Ins and outs

Getting there   Kullu-Manali (Bhuntar) airport (near Kullu) is 50 km away with bus and taxi transfers. The Bus and Taxi Stands are right in the centre of Manali town (although many private buses stop short of the centre) within easy reach of some budget hotels – the upmarket ones are a taxi ride away.

Getting around   Manali and around, though hilly, is ideal for walking. For journeys outside taxi rates are high, so it is worth hiring a motorcycle to explore. See Transport, page 500, for further details.

Climate   Best season is Mar-Apr but can have occasional heavy rain and be cold with snow in the villages. May-Jun offer better trekking; also post monsoon mid-Sep-mid-Nov.

Sights

The **Tibetan Monastery**, built by refugees, is not old but is attractive and is the centre of a small carpet making industry. Rugs and other handicrafts are for sale. The colourful **bazar** sells Kullu shawls, caps and Tibetan souvenirs.

Old Manali is 3 km away, across Manalsu Nala. Manali is named after Manu, the Law Giver, who legend tells arrived here by boat when fleeing from a great flood centuries ago. The road from newer Manali crosses Manalsu Nala and climbs uphill and through some unspoilt villages continuing to the modern Manu Mandir – visitors may have to abandon their aged rickshaws and walk up part of the hill. The last few years have seen continuing building work in the lower reaches of the village, where the buildings close to the bridge wear a look of fatigue. Higher up, newer guesthouses mingle with attractive old farmsteads with wooden balconies and thick stone tiled roofs. While out of season Old Manali retains a quiet charm, this can be diminished during the tourist season by the arrival of techno music and the drug scene.

Vashisht is a small hillside village that can be reached by road or a footpath, a 30-40-minute walk from tourist office. Note the carvings on the houses of the wealthy farmers. Below the

Manali centre

Not to scale

■ Sleeping
1 Ashiana & Vibhutis
2 Beas
3 Rohtang Inn

● Eating
1 Adarsh & Palan Sher-e-Punjab
2 Chopsticks & Mountview
3 German Bakery

4 Juniper
5 Manali Sweets
6 Mayur
7 Monalisa
8 Peter & Sadhana's Garden Café
9 Sa Ba
10 Tibetan Dhaba
11 Tibetan Friends' Corner
12 Superbake

: Freedom walking

'Freedom' walking, popular in Nepal, is not really feasible here and porters and/or horses are required. These are not always easily available and prices fluctuate considerably. A good arrangement is to go on an organized trek with a group. You can do it independently but it requires greater planning. The trek into or from Zanskar is only recommended for the vigorously fit.

village, there is a temple to Rama and Vashisht, with sulphur springs; remove shoes at the entrance (small fee). **Hot springs** at the top of the hill lead to free communal baths in the village centre.They can get dirty - best in the morning.Clean well-maintained baths are lower down but they were closed in 2001. The village, with its messy jumble of old village houses and newer buildings, has cheap places to stay which attract a new generation of young travellers. A two-hour walk past the village up the hillside leads to a **waterfall**.

Dhungri Village is at the top of Hadimba Road. Follow the road uphill, past the gates leading to the temple and take the path 50 m further to arrive at the village centre. The village houses have cedar wood carving and balconies with superb views across the valley. Travellers are welcomed into family homes and traditional village life carries on around the guests.

★ **Hadimba Devi Temple** The Dhungri temple (1553), in a clearing among ancient deodars, is an enjoyable 2-km walk from the tourist office. Built by Maharaja Bahadur Singh, the 27-m high pagoda temple has a three-tier roof and some fine naturalistic wood carving of animals and plants, especially around the doorway. The structure itself is relatively crude, and the pagoda is far from perfectly perpendicular. Massive deodar planks form the roof but in contrast to the scale of the structure the brass image of the goddess Hadimba inside, is tiny. A legend tells how the God Bhima fell in love with **Hadimba**, the sister of the demon Tandi. Bhima killed Tandi in battle and married Hadimba, whose spirituality, coupled with her marriage to a god, led to her being worshipped as a goddess. Today she is seen as an incarnation of Kali.

The small doorway, less than 1 m high, is surrounded by wood-carved panels of animals, mythical beasts, scrolls, a row of foot soldiers and deities, while inside against a natural rock is the small black image of the Devi. To the left is a natural rock shelter where legend has it that Hadimba took refuge and prayed before she was deified. The greatly enlarged footprints imprinted on a black rock are believed to be hers. Hadimba Devi plays a central part in the annual festival in May, at both Kullu and Manali.

To prevent the **master craftsman** producing another temple to equal this elsewhere, the king ordered his right hand to be cut off. The artist is believed to have mastered the technique with his left hand and reproduced a similar work of excellence at Trilokinath in the Pattan Valley. Unfortunately, his new master became equally jealous and had his head cut off (see page 505)!

A **feast and sacrifice** is held in mid-July when the image from the new temple in Old Manali is carried to the Hadimba temple where 18 ritual blood sacrifices are performed. Sacrifices include a fish and a vegetable (!), but ends with the beheading of an ox in front of a frenzied crowd. This ceremony is not for the faint-hearted. Pickpockets are rife, and known to take advantage of awestruck tourists, so take care.

★ Walks

Manali is the trail head for a number of interesting and popular treks. There are also the following short hikes. Beyond Old Manali, the **shepherd trail**, which winds its way up

Himachal Pradesh Kullu Valley Manali

and down the hillside, allows you to capture a picture of Himalayan life as well as see some superb birdlife. The path starts at some concrete steps (after *Ish* restaurant) on the first hairpin bend along the paved road to Old Manali (or you can pick it up where the road ends and taxis turn around at the top of the hill) and continues along the cemented path, which turns into a dirt trail. Return the same way four to five hours.

This walk takes you towards Solang. In Old Manali Village take the right fork and then turn left in front of the new temple. This trail is a classic, following the right bank of the Beas River up towards the Solang Valley passing the villages of **Goshal**, **Shanag**, **Buruwa** to **Solang** (2,480 m), a small ski resort with all of 2½ km of runs! Solang is 14 km (5 hours). You can get tea, biscuits and nuts along the walk and even be tempted by steaming spicy noodles. To return to Manali it is a steady walk down the valley side to the main Rohtang Pass-Manali Highway where you can pick up a bus (Rs 5) or shared jeep (Rs 10).

Go prepared for cold for this walk as it takes you through woodland shading you from the sun. Keeping the **Hadimba Temple** on your right follow the contour of the hill and bear right to pick up a clear pack-horse trail which heads up the steep valley. This is a steady uphill climb through woodland giving superb views of the river below, abundant Himalayan birdlife and a chance to see all manner of activity in the woods, chopping, cutting and burning. An enjoyable 3 to 4 hour walk.

This walk takes you to the village of **Sethan** (12 km). Take a local bus to the *Holiday Inn* on the Naggar road. With the hotel behind you, cross the road and pass through the orchard and fields which have low mud walls all round which can be walked on. Bear east till you come to a disused track and then bear right and follow it to the once untouched village of **Prini** which now has several five-star hotels! If you are lucky the *chai* shop will be open. Further east, the trail to Sethan village becomes somewhat indistinct, though local people are at hand to point you in the right direction. It is a superb three-hour hike up a wooded valley to Sethan (3,000 m), which is well off the tourist trail.

Listings: Kullu Valley

● Sleeping

Kullu *p486, map p487*
The choice of hotels is widening, some good hotels in all ranges, though very full during Dasara. Large off-season discounts (30-50%).
A Apple Valley Resorts, Mohal, NH21, on the Beas River, 6 km from airport, T22310, F24116. 36 comfortable, very well-designed modern chalets in landscaped grounds, excellent food, friendly reception, rafting nearby.
C Silver Moon (HPTDC), perched on a hill, 2 km south of centre, T22488 (taxis Rs 50 from Kullu centre, buses stop at gate if requested – ask for the last barrier south out of Kullu). 6 rooms with bath and heaters, each with small sitting room in traditional style, very clean, good food, has character (possibly enhanced because Mahatma Gandhi stayed here).
C Vaishali, Gandhinagar, 1 km south of bus stand No 2, T24225, F23073. 33 rooms, excellent restaurant, modern immaculate kitchen, pleasant small garden running down to river, rafting 4 km south.
C-D Sarwari, 10-min walk south of Dhalpur Bus Stand, T22471. 16 rooms (10 in more spacious new wing), 8-bed dorm (Rs 75), good value restaurant, beer, pleasant gardens, elevated with good views, peaceful.
C-D Shobla, T22800. 25 rooms, central, clean, pleasant atmosphere, airy restaurant, overlooking river.

● *For an explanation of the sleeping and eating price codes used in this guide, see inside the*
● *front cover. Other relevant information is found in Essentials pages 52-57.*

D-E Aaditya, Lower Dhalpur, T24263. Decently furnished rooms with bath (hot shower), some with river-facing balcony, others cheaper, smart, room service meals, bar.

D-E Ramneek, Dhalpur, T24449. 21 clean rooms with bath (hot water), TV, decently maintained.

E Bijleshwar View, T22857. Rooms with fireplace, TV, bath (hot water), only moderately clean, restaurant, peaceful garden, friendly.

E Madhu Chandrika, near Lower Dhalpur Bazar, T24395, F22720. Rooms and dorm, quiet area.

E Rohtang, Dhalpur, T22303. 12 rooms with bath, restaurant (Indian, Chinese), simple, clean and good value.

E-F Kullu Valley Hotel, Akhara Bazar, T22223. Rooms with TV, phone, bath tub, restaurant.

Jari *p489*

F Village Guest House, follow signs, a 10-min walk up, through and beyond village. There are 5 simple rooms with clean, shared hot bath and a restaurant in an excellent location on the edge of a traditional farming village, very friendly, good value.

Chhalal *p489*

C-D Kasol Resorts, with a good choice of 17 rooms including 1 **B** suite, hot water, TV, rooftop restaurant.

There are now about 30 cheap **F** guesthouses and family houses which take in paying guests in this expanding village.

Manikaran *p489*

D Parvati, near the temple, T01902-73735. 10 simple rooms, sulphur baths, restaurant.

A cheaper guest house on the square has clean rooms. There are several **E** and **F** guesthouses in the lower part of the village, some with baths fed by the hot springs. However, prices in season rise to unbelievable rates given that most rooms are of the basic to very basic variety, at best. Some obviously cater for the drug-induced end of the market, so choose carefully. Local families also take paying guests.

Pulga *p489*

F Trimurti, is recommended.

Avoid **Rama Guest House** where some rooms are dark and cramped.

Katrain *p490*

A Span Resort, 8 attractive stone cottages with 25 rooms overlooking the river, sports, riding, good views, trout hatchery nearby ensures good river fishing, very comfortable, but some **C** category facilities.

C River Bank, attractive décor, comfortable.

C-D Orchard Resorts, 2 km south of Katrain, with 16 attractive wood-panelled 'cottages', with hot water, TV, heaters, good off season discount.

E Anglers' Bungalow, spartan but has superb views. Katrain and Naggar, are on opposite sides of the river.

Naggar *p490*

C-D Castle, T47816. A guesthouse and then a hotel since 1978, 13 rooms (vary), stylish but traditional decor and furniture, comfortable beds, fireplaces, modernized baths, best **B** overlook valley, some share bath (**E**), very basic dorm (Rs 75), "beautifully renovated, enchanting", restaurant, good service.

D-E Poonam Mountain Lodge, T47747. 6 spotless rooms, constant hot water, very good food, but avoid insistence on booking treks.

D-E Sheetal, Roerich Marg near Castle, T47750. 14 very pleasant rooms with bath, overlooking valley, clean and spacious, hot water (some tubs), TV, use of kitchen.

F Ragini, T/F47793. 9 smart rooms with modernized baths (hot water), lick of paint required, large windows, good views from rooftop restaurant, good value.

E-F Snow View, down steps past Tripura Sundari Temple, T47735, rooms and restaurant, weaving co-op outlet.

F Alliance, 200 m above Castle, T47763. 6 rooms, hot water, meals, clean, simple, homely, very good value.

F Chand Kulvi, near Bus Stand, T47713. 8 rooms, some with bath, away from road, lovely garden.

F Uttam, near bus stand. Pleasant clean rooms with hot shower.

Himachal Pradesh Listings: Kullu Valley

● *Phone codes Kullu, Parvati Valley, Naggar and Manali: 01902;*

Hotels continue to be built for the heavy demand in season. Hotels are often full, in May and Jun, so better to visit off-season when most offer discounts. Winter heating is a definite bonus. (Helpful Private Hoteliers' Information Centre is near the Taxi Stand).

AL Holiday Inn, 2.5 km south of Manali on Naggar Rd, T52262, F52562. Luxury hotel.

AL Manali Resorts, 5 km south of Manali on Kullu Rd, T52274, F52174. 50 rooms, a luxury base for winter sports, lovely position with landscaped gardens by Beas River.

AL Snowcrest Manor (was *Panchratan*) beyond *Log Huts*, T53354, F53188. 30 rooms, modern hotel, on steep hillside, great views.

A Ambassador Resort, Sunny Side, Chadiari, overlooking Old Manali, T52235, F52173. 40 rooms, interesting design, good views.

A Leela Huts, Sunshine Orchards, The Mall (N), T52464. Luxury huts, sitting room, kitchen.

A Log Huts (HPTDC), top of Circuit House Rd high above Manalsu Nala, T52407, F52325. 2-bedroom cottages, 12 newer and modern, 6 spacious though dated, kitchen, attractive views, cafeteria nearby and room service.

A Sterling Himalayan Continental, Prini, Naggar Rd, T53011, F52494. 35 immaculate, very comfortable rooms, airport transfer, taxi Rs 50 from centre, 2½ km.

B Hadimba Cottage, T52334. 12 deluxe cottages consisting of a bedroom, drawing-cum-dining room and kitchen.

B Manali Heights, near Log Huts, T52621, F52618. 27 centrally heated rooms, bath tubs, direct dialling, all comforts, stylish décor.

B Piccadily, The Mall, T52152, F52113. 44 rooms, clean, modern though signs of wear, welcoming reception, good restaurant but very slow service.

B-C John Banon's Hotel, Manali Orchards, T52335, F52392. 12 rooms with snow views (6 newer **B**), full board (good Continental), garden, peaceful, simple, rustic but pleasant.

C Mayflower, The Mall, opposite Circuit House, T52104, F53923. 18 rooms, spacious, tastefully decorated wood-panelled suites (cold in winter but log fires fill the room with smoke), no TV, no restaurant, great value.

Many cheap hotels on School Rd. Model Town offer modest rooms, often shared baths, some have restaurants, some room service. May only provide hot water in buckets.

D Ashiana, T52232. Clean, comfortable rooms with hot shower, good restaurant.

D Chetna, near *Log Huts*, T52245. 13 comfortable rooms with balconies, hot water, good open-air restaurant, lawns, elevated, with beautiful views.

D Highland, near *Log Huts*, T52399. 36 rooms (22 new centrally heated), some with balcony, hot showers, restaurant (mainly Chinese), pleasant garden, stone building with bright, clean, comfortable rooms.

D Pinewood, The Mall, T52518. 10 heated rooms, restaurant, gardens, attractive rooms (best upstairs), good views, quiet.

D Rohtang Inn, opposite Bus Stand, The Mall, T52441. 12 modern rooms, bath tubs, meals.

D Rohtang Manalsu, near Circuit House, The Mall, T52332. 27 large rooms, good restaurant, garden, superb views.

D Sunshine, The Mall, T52320. 9 rooms in old traditional house, others in newer cottage, log fires, lot of character, restaurant, lovely garden, peaceful, family atmosphere, friendly, good value.

D-E Beas, near Tourist Office, T52832. 31 rooms with bath, TV, breakfast, room service meals, magnificent river views.

D-E Johnson's Lodge, The Mall, T53023. Fully furnished, kitchen, full of character, old but clean, orchard gardens, restaurant; also new hotel in the complex.

E Ambika, Model Town, T52203, F53993, large and airy rooms with clean bath, mountain views, average meals, use of kitchen, excellent value.

E Mountview, end of Model Town Rd, T52465. Large rooms, shower and western toilet, some with great views, heater Rs 50, discounts off-season when restaurant is closed (breakfast and *thalis* only), very secure, friendly and helpful, excellent value.

Dhungri Village

Many families offer rooms with basic facilities (Rs 50-70). Several are in traditional houses, clean rooms, covered in wood carving, basic bedding, small stove (fuel can be bought), some have balconies with fantastic views.

F Freedom Café takes guests.

F Scenic Cottage, some rooms with baths.

Old Manali

In general, the further you walk, the greater the reward. Club House side (turn right after Manalsu Bridge):

D-E Ashok Mayur, about 300 m from bridge (opposite *Shiva Café*). Few comfortable rooms, terrace, restaurant.

D-E Dragon, T52790, F52769, dragontours@ hotmail.com. 16 comfortable rooms with bath, traditional construction, internet, fine mountain views, garden, apple orchard, café.

E Cairn Lodge, above Club House, T52861. 3 pleasant, comfortable, wood-panelled rooms, attached hot bath, good café.

E-F Upcountry Lodge, above Club House, T52257. 9 clean rooms, attached hot bath, quiet location in orchards, pleasant garden.

F Apple View, above Club House in orchard, T53899. 4 clean rooms with shared hot bath in quiet location.

F Jungal Bungalow, above Club House, T52278. 7 clean rooms, common hot shower, good service, friendly, pleasant atmosphere.

Uphill on the village outskirts:

F Krishna, T53071. Well established, 8 basic rooms, common bath (hot water), verandah with great views of snowy peaks.

F Surya Cottage, above village, beyond Manu Temple, T54362. 6 simple rooms with shared hot bath, friendly, good value.

Beyond the village, along the cemented path are the last 2 before the wilderness:

E-F Monal, a little further, up steep cemented steps, T53848. 9 rooms, some with hot showers, others shared, café, pretty garden, superb views all round.

E-F Shiv Shakti, T54170. 4 pleasant rooms and café attached hot bath, friendly farming family, fine views across valley and mountains beyond.

Upriver, taking the path up the steps by *Ish*:

F Himalaya Cottage. 8 simple rooms, restaurant, fine location by the river.

F Rockway Cottage, the last one, a 10-min walk from the road, T54328.10 well crafted, but simple rooms, most with local heaters, clean common bath, very friendly, excellent location. Recommended.

Vashisht

D Bhrigu, just above HPTDC Baths, T53414. Comfortable, if dated rooms with bath, some with good views, restaurant.

D Sita, near HPTDC Baths, T52164. Good rooms and restaurant.

D Surabhi below the village, T52796. Clean, attractive rooms, modern bath fittings (real tubs!), big windows facing mountains, cable TV, restaurant, exchange, exceptional value off-season.

E Vishranti, on path to HPTDC Baths, T53421. Clean, light rooms with bath, pleasant garden.

E-F Bodh, Village Centre, T54165, bunteee23@hotmail.com. 5 clean, tidy rooms, shared bath (hot shower), good views from terrace.

Solang *p494*

E Friendship Guest House, run by a friendly family, has rooms.

🍴 Eating

Kullu *p486, map p487*

Ashiyana, in hotel, Sarvari Bazar. Clean, good south Indian.

Hot Stuff Food Junction, near tourist information. Good for snacks, light meals, outdoor seating.

Monal Café, simple meals.

Shobla, in hotel. Has pleasant restaurant. *Vaishali's* a/c restaurant is excellent.

Chhalal *p489*

Evergreen Restaurant, is the most popular with a wide choice of Indian and western food including all the travellers' favourites plus more. A major meeting place in season.

Manikaran *p489*

Sikh Gurudwara, does excellent meals, steam cooked at the springs (donation only).

Wayside stalls serve local food, while some near the springs cater for westerners.

Holy Palace, in bazar, look for the finely carved doors.

There is a classier sister concern of *Evergreen* in Kasol, similar menu.

Pulga *p489*

Paradise Restaurant, in the village, does great vegetarian dishes. Also has information on guides and equipment for treks up the valley and over the Pin-Parvati Pass (5,300 m). If you are lucky, you may be able to persuade the watchman of the old *Forest Rest House* to let you in. The 'visitors' registration book' contains entries that date back to the 1930's and include several well known mountaineers who have passed by.

Chandrakhani Himalayan Health Food, Roerich Marg, above Tripura Sundari temple. Serves local food – millet, brown rice, tofu, fresh pasta and cheese.
Nightingale 200 m above bus stand. Trout.
Ristorante Italiano, bus stand. Open in season, Fri-Sun.

Manali *p490, maps p491 and p492*
Hotels may need advance notice from non-residents. Some close in the off-season.
♥♥♥**Chopsticks**, The Mall, opposite Bus Stand, T52539. Tibetan, Chinese, Japanese. Very good food, large helpings, very good curd and pancakes, also good breakfast (porridge), friendly, warm (wood-burning stoves), welcoming.
♥♥♥**Johnson's Café**, Circuit House Rd. Western (varied menu). Elegant restaurant in a large garden, specializes in trout, excellent home made pasta, good filter coffee, delicious icecreams. Recommended.
♥♥♥**Mayur**, Mission Rd. Vast international menu. Excellent food, smart, efficient service, subdued decor, very pleasant with linen table cloths and candles on tables, Indian classical music, great ambience, cosy with wood-burning stove and generator.
♥♥**Adarsh**, The Mall (opposite Kunzam). One of many Punjabi places, but has more style and better menu than others.
♥♥**Juniper**. Good Indian, Chinese.
♥♥**Il Forno**, Hadimba Rd. Italian. Attractive pizzeria, half way up hill.
♥♥**Italiano**, corner of Mall and Circuit House Rd, 1st floor. Well cooked selection of pizza, pasta and fish, good value.
♥♥**Monalisa** in Bazar. International. Friendly, smallish, good choice, popular.
♥♥**Mountview**, The Mall, opposite Bus Stand. Good Tibetan, Japanese, some Chinese. Unpretentious, pleasant, warm (wood-burning stove), friendly amiable owner.
♥♥**Sa Ba**, Nehru Park. Mixed. Excellent Indian, snacks, pizzas, cakes, some outdoor seating to people-watch, recommended (no toilet).
♥♥**Vibhuti's**, The Mall, corner of Model Town Rd, up short flight of steps. South Indian vegetarian. Delicious *masala dosas*.
♥**Manali Sweets**, Shiali Mahadev Rd. Excellent Indian sweets (superb *gulab jamuns*!), also good *thalis* (Rs 40).
♥**Mountview**, end of Model Town Rd. Italian,

Indian. Good pizzas, spaghetti, opens 0600 for breakfast.
♥**Palan Sher-e-Punjab**, near Taxis, The Mall. Good Punjabi vegetarian.
♥**Tibet Kitchen**, across Manalsu bridge, Club House Rd. Tasty momos, pleasant ambience, friendly service.
♥**Tibetan Dhaba**, back of bus station. Very small and cosy, great *momos*, bring your own container for "take- away"!
♥**Tibetan Friends' Corner**, behind the post office. Shop with café above. Excellent *momos* and Tibetan dishes, good value.

Cafés and fast food
German Bakery, opposite Nehru Park, good cakes, breads, real coffee, not cheap, popular.
Peter and Sadhana's Garden Café, behind German Bakery. Quiches, fresh bread, cakes (try French toast with honey), excellent muesli, good filter coffee, home made jams and peanut butter sold, garden.

Dhungri Village
There is a bakery and restaurant opposite the temple. Stalls sell snacks, drinks and bare necessities.
Green Forest, Dhungri Village, on the forest path, past temple down towards Old Manali, just after leaving the forest. Vegetarian. Excellent breakfasts and meals.

Old Manali
Plenty of Israeli dishes and music which can range from techno to Tibetan.
Ish, on left past shops going uphill (before road swings to right). Fruit muesli, pizzas.
Moondance, opposite *Pizza Olive*. Good choice of western favourites. Recommended.
Pizza Olive, next door, lives up to its name.
Rasta Café, above village, near *Surya*. Popular, modern, with ubiquitous Bob Marley !
River Music, by bridge. Popular hangout, travellers' staples plus Israeli.
Shiva Garden Café, 100 m further uphill. Good food with an adventurous international flavour plus 'German bakery', delightful spot, pleasant ambience with open-air seating, restful music (Tibetan enterprise) good views over Manalsu Nala, very reasonable.
Tibetan Kitchen, **German Bakery**, over-the-counter branch, just beyond Manalsu bridge, and left. Reasonably priced cakes, breads, real coffee, trekkers' supplies.

Yangkhor, past *Moondance*. Tibetan and western favourites.

Vashisht
Lhasa Café, in village centre, above *Vashisht Video Hall* (which shows 2-3 films daily).
Pyramid Centre, path below HPTDC Baths. Western. Set in beautiful relaxing garden with wonderful views across valley, hot/cold drinks, cakes, 0700-2200; glassed-in section offers tasty and varied veg dishes (Italian manager), massage, London trained hairdresser in summer, local information on activities.
Superbake, has some good bread, cakes, biscuits and chilled drinks.
Zodiac Café, village centre, for food, music and wonderful cinnamon *chai*, great for meeting other travellers.

✸ Festivals and events

Kullu *p486, map p487*
End-Apr Colourful 3-day **Cattle Fair** attracts villagers from the surrounding area. Numerous cultural events accompany. **Dasara** is sacred to the goddess Durga which, elsewhere in India, tends to be overshadowed by **Diwali** which follows a few weeks later. In this part of the Himalaya it is a great social event and a get-together of the Gods..

Manali *p490, maps p491 and p492*
Mid-Feb Week-long **Winter Sports Carnival. May** 3-day colourful **Dhungri** Forest festival at Hadimba Devi Temple, celebrated by hill women.

○ Shopping

Kullu *p486, map p487*
Best buys are shawls, caps, *gadmas*.
The state weaving co-operative, **Bhutti Weavers Colony**, 6 km south, has retail outlets, **Bhuttico**; 1 store 2 km south of *Apple Valley Resorts*.
Akhara Bazar has a **Govt Handicrafts Emporium**, **Himachal Khadi Emporium** and **Khadi Gramudyog**. **Charm Shilp** is good for sandals.

Manali *p490, maps p491 and p492*
Books
Bookworm, NAC Market, behind Bus Station. Huge stock of quality paperbacks, reasonably

priced. Highly recommended. New branch near Manali Post Office, 1000-1800.

Crafts and local curios
Bhutico Bodh, along the Hindu Temple in bazaar, T52269, has a good range of shawls.
Charitable Trust Tibetan Handicrafts, the Mall, government shop.
Manushi, in the market, women's co-op producing good quality shawls, hats, socks.
Om Collection, good Tibetan T-shirts, dresses, jewellery, jumpers.
Shree-la Crafts, friendly owner, good value silver jewellery. Tibetan Bazar and Tibetan Carpet Centre.

Tailors
Gulati Traders, Gulati Complex, Sikh tailors, quick, good quality, copies and originals (caps to order, ready in hrs, Rs 75).

▲▲ Activities and tours

Kullu *p486, map p487*
Tour companies
Look East, c/o Bajaj Autos, Manikaran Chowk, Shamshi, T65771. Recommended for river rafting and bike hire.

Naggar *p490*
Trekking
For Malana, it is best to employ a local guide. Pawan, from the old *chai* shop in the main village, is recommended. Avoid *Poonam's*.

Manali *p490, maps p491 and p492*
Skiing and mountaineering
Mountaineering and Allied Sports Institute, 1.5 km out of town, organizes courses in mountaineering, skiing, watersports, high altitude trekking and mountain-rescue courses; 5 and 7-day ski courses, Rs 3,000 for the latter, Jan-Mar. There is a hostel, an exhibition of equipment and an auditorium.

Tour companies
Valleycon, NAC Market. Friendly and helpful.
Himalayan Adventurers, opposite *Kunzam*, T52750, F52182. Recommended. **Swagatam**, opposite *Kunzam*, The Mall, T52990, F54290. Long distance buses, trekking, rafting, very efficient. Recommended.

HPTDC, T53531 or 52116. Daily, in season by luxury coach (or car for five): to Nehru Kund, Rahla Falls, Marhi, Rohtang Pass, 1000-1700, Rs 150 (car Rs 1,000); to Solang, Jagatsukh and Naggar; 1000-1600, Rs 170 (car Rs 1,100); to Manikaran, 0900-1800, Rs 175 (car Rs 900).

Club House, HPTDC, on river bank, has snooker, billiard, badminton, table tennis, well-appointed restaurant and bar, Rs 5 plus table/court fees. Also a small museum on Himachali culture. A gym and steam bath are planned. Primarily in place for domestic visitors.

Trekking

Clarify details and number of trekkers involved. **Himalayan Journeys**, near *German Bakery*, T52365, F53065, www.himalayanjourneys india.com.

Monal Himalayan Travels, opposite Bus Stand, T52715.

Shambala, NAC Market, Shop 40 (opposite *Bookworm*), T52760, F52690. Excellent guide, horses and food.

Shangri-la Adventures, Tibetan Colony, Rohtang Rd, T52734, F52404, shang-adv@ hotmail.com. Treks to Zanskar, Ladakh, Spiti, fishing, rafting, experienced Tibetan guides, competitive pricing for small groups, excellent service from Jigme, honest, friendly.

WH Adventure Travel, opposite Rambagh Taxi Stand, The Mall, T98170-69096, whadventure@yahoo.com. Mr Ghosh is very knowledgeable, advises on routes; organizes treks, jeep safaris, mountaineering in Lahul, Spiti, Zanskar and Ladakh.

⊖ Transport

Kullu *p486, map p487*
Air

Transport to town: buses and taxis at the airport. **Jagson**, Dhalpur Maidan, T66187, Apt T65303, to **Delhi, Shimla**, flights often cancelled.

Bus

Most buses coming to Kullu continue to Manali.

Main Bus Stand, Sarvari Khad with a booking office: for long distance and to **Manali**; Left Bank Bus Stand across the bridge: buses for **Naggar** (half hourly in summer) and **Bijli Mahadev**; some go to **Manali**; Dhalpur Bus Stand for buses to the south but board these at the Main Bus Stand to be sure of a seat. HPTDC deluxe bus to **Chandigarh** (270 km), 0800, 8 hrs, Rs 320; **Delhi** (512 km) 15 hrs (extra buses during season), government and *HPTDC buses* are better than some private ones, leaves Delhi 1600, Rs 400 (a/c Rs 600); **Dharamshala**, 0800-0900, 8 hrs, Rs 250; **Shimla** (235 km), 0900, 8 hrs, Rs 250. Tickets from Tourist Office.

Taxi
Opposite Dhalpur Bus Stand.

Naggar *p490*
Bus

The bus stop is in the Bazar, below the castle. Daily bus between **Kullu** and **Manali** via Naggar by the scenic east bank route; Kullu and Manali (1½ hrs each, Rs 5). Manali to **Patli Kuhl** (6 km from Naggar, 45 mins, Rs 10); where you can get a local bus (half hourly in summer), rickshaw (Rs 60).

Manali *p490, maps p491 and p492*
Air

Flights connect Bhuntar near Kullu, with Delhi, Shimla and Ludhiana. **Jagsons**, T52843. Transport to town: taxi to Manali, Rs 650 for 4 persons. Himachal Transport (green) bus, every 15 mins, Rs 25 (allow 2½ hrs travel time from Manali).

Bus

Long distance See page 128. HPTDC coaches in season (fewer in winter); Deluxe have 2 seats on either side: **Harisons** and **Swagatam** (see directory), run own buses. **Chandigarh** 0700, 10 hrs, Rs 225; **Delhi** a/c 1530, 15 hrs, Rs 550; non a/c 1700, Rs 375. **Dharamshala** 0530, 0810, Rs 160, Private coach 1900, 2230, 10-11 hrs, Rs 275, year round; **Keylong** 0600, 6 hrs, Rs 85. **Kullu** via **Naggar**: 2 daily, Rs 25, 1 hr; other Kullu buses via NH stop at **Patli Kuhl** (see Naggar above). **Mandi**, Rs 85. **Rohtang Pass** 0900, day trip with photo-stops, striking scenery (take sweater/jacket), 1½ hrs at pass, Rs 120. **Shimla** (280 km), 0900, 1900, 9 hrs, Rs 225. **To Leh** HPTDC and private coaches run ordinary and luxury buses during the season (mid-Jun to end-Sep), but not always daily; usually based on demand. Seats should be reserved ahead. Front seats are best though the cab gets filled by locals wanting a 'lift'. Those joining the bus in Keylong must reserve from Manali to be certain of a seat. Rs 400-850

(Rs 1,200 including tent and meals); usual overnight stop is at Sarchu where other cheaper tents may be available (some choose to sleep on the bus). The 530 km takes about 24-28 hrs on the road, 0600, arrive Leh next afternoon. Various State RTCs offer direct services to major towns. HRTC Bus Stand, The Mall, reservations, 1000-1200, 1400-1600. Reports of some drivers getting drunk, hence unsafe.

Motorbike

Enfields and Hondas for hire; reasonable charges at *Enfield Club,* Vashisht Rd, T54090 or *Nirvana,* Circuit House Rd, T53222. Choice of bikes in good condition (on-site mechanic), Enfield Rs 6,000 per month, others Rs 5,000, daily rate Rs 300, 3rd party insurance, helmets, professional service. Recommended. Passport or air ticket must be left as a deposit; reserve ahead in high season. The uncrowded Kullu-Manali road via Naggar is ideal.

Taxi

Local The local union is very strong, office near tourist office, T52450. Fares tend to be high; from bus stand: Rs 50 for hotels (2-3 km). To Vashisht or top of Old Manali Rd, Rs 60; auto-rickshaws Rs 30.

Long distance **Aut**, Rs 900, Rs 1,200 (return); **Darcha**, Rs 3,000; **Keylong**, Rs 2,400; **Kullu**, Rs 550 (Rs 800 return); **Mandi**, Rs 1,200 (Rs 1,500 return); **Naggar**, Rs 350 (Rs 400 return); **Rohtang Pass**, Rs 900, Rs 1,100.

Train

From Delhi, up to **Chandigarh** or **Shimla**, or via Pathankot to **Jogindernagar**, and then bus transfers, see page 128

❻ Directory

Kullu *p486, map p487*
Banks State Bank of Patiala (1100-1400), Akhara Bazar (north of town) for foreign exchange (cash and TCs only); **State Bank of India**, off NH21, south of town. Nearest Visa exchange at Mandi. **Internet** Internet facilities are growing. **Tourist offices** Himachal, T22349, near Maidan, 1000-1700, local maps available, advises on exchange, trekking in the Tirthan Valley etc.

Manali *p490, maps p491 and p492*
Banks State Bank of India, The Mall, 100 m above *Picadilly Hotel.* Only changes AmEx TCs. **UCO Bank**, The Mall, opposite Nehru Park (1000-1430, closed Tue), changes TCs, quicker and more polite than the *SBI.* Signs indicate exchanges on The Mall; try **Swagatam** opposite Kunzam, changes major TCs, cash against Visa. **Hospitals** Mission Hospital, T52379. **Men Tsee Khang**, Gompa Rd, highly recommended for Tibetan herbal/mineral treatments. **Chemists:** opposite NAC Market. **Internet** Nirvana Café, Circuit House Rd, Old Manali. 9 machines, well run. Several others in town and Old Manali. **Post office** GPO, off Model Town Rd. 0900-1700, Mon-Sat. Very efficient. **Telephone** Telecom office, south of Shiali Mahadev Rd. Gopal Travels, opposite temple in bazar. Friendly, ISD phone, receives faxes, photocopies. **Tourist offices** HPTDC, next to *Kunzam Hotel,* The Mall, T53531, F52325, helpful for bus and hotel bookings, T52116.

Lahul and the Manali-Leh road

→ *Colour map 1, grid A3 and B3.*
Lying between the green alpine slopes of the Kullu and Chamba valleys to the south and the dry, arid plateau of Ladakh, the mountainous arid landscapes of Lahul manage to get enough rain during the monsoon months to allow extensive cultivation, particularly on terraces, of potatoes, green peas and hops (for beer making). Lahul potatoes are some of the best in the country and are used as seed for propagation. These and rare herbs have brought wealth to the area. Most people follow a curious blend of both Hindu and Buddhist customs though there are a few who belong wholly to one or the other religion. ▶▶ *For Sleeping, Eating and other listings, see pages 506-506.*

⦂ Only for the determined

Streams cross the road at several places. These may be impassable during heavy rain, and those fed by snow-melt swell significantly during the day as meltwater increases, so travel in the late afternoon can be more difficult than in the early morning when the flow is at its lowest. Rockfalls are also a common hazard.

Ins and outs The whole region can be approached by road from 3 directions: from Shimla via the Spiti Valley; from Manali over the Rohtang Pass (3,985 m), into Upper Lahul; and from Zanskar and Ladakh over the Shingo La and Baralacha La (passes). The Shingo La gives access to Lahul from Zanskar (see page 557), while the Baralacha La (4,880 m) on the Leh-Manali road provides access from Ladakh. There is a trekking route from Manali to Zanskar. See individual Transport sections for details.

History Historically there are similarities between this region and Ladakh since in the 10th century Lahul, Spiti and Zanskar were part of the Ladakh Kingdom. The Hindu Rajas in Kullu paid tribute to Ladakh. In the 17th century Ladakh was defeated by a combined Mongol-Tibetan force. Later Lahul was separated into Upper Lahul which fell under the control of Kullu, and Lower Lahul which came under the Chamba Rajas. The whole region came under the Sikhs as their empire expanded, whilst under the British Lahul and Kullu were part of the administrative area centred on Kangra.

Manali to Leh

This stunningly beautiful road, one of the highest in the world, is currently the main route for foreigners into the region of Lahul and on to Leh. The 530-km highway is usually open from July to September, depending on snow fall; most buses stop in mid-September. The first 52 km runs up the Kullu valley, then climbs through the Rohtang Pass. The Pass itself normally opens at the end of May and is the only way into Lahul until the new tunnel is completed (2005). No permits are necessary.

Leaving Manali From Manali the NH21 goes through the village of Palchan and then begins a sharp climb to **Kothi**, at 2,530 m, set below towering cliffs. Beautiful views of coniferous hillsides and meadows unwind as the road climbs through 2,800 m, conifers giving way to poplars and then banks of flowers. The 70-m high **Rohalla Falls**, 19 km from Manali at an altitude of 3,500 m, are a spectacular sight.

Himachal Pradesh Lahul & the Manali-Leh road

⁝ Motorcycling from Manali to Leh

Allow four days on the way up, to help acclimatize as the 500 km road will take you from 2,000 m to 5,420 m and down to 3,500 m (Leh). The last petrol station is in Tandi, 7 km before Keylong, A full tank plus five to 10 litres of spare petrol will take you to Leh. Above 3,500 m, you should open the air intake on your carb to compensate for the loss of power.

Apart from Keylong, there are no hotels, only a few tented camps, providing basic food and shelter from mid-June to mid-September. Some will be noisy and drafty. The lack of toilet facilities leads to pollution near the camps (don't forget your lighter for waste paper). A tent and mini stove plus pot, soups, tea, biscuits, muesli, will add extra comfort, allowing you to camp in the wild expanses of the Moray Plains (4,700 m).

Unless you plan to sleep in the camp there, you must reach Pang before 1300 on the way up, 1500 on the way down, as the police will not allow you to proceed beyond the checkpoint after these times. The army camp in Pang has helpful officers and some medical facilities.

The landscape, covered in snow for up to eight months of the year, becomes totally devoid of trees above Marrhi, a seasonal settlement and restaurant stop, as the road climbs through a series of tight hairpins to the Rohtang Pass.

★ **Rohtang Pass** From the pass you get spectacular views of precipitous cliffs, deep ravines, large glaciers and moraines. Buses stop for photos. From June until mid October, when Himachal Tourism runs a daily bus tour from Manali, the pass becomes the temporary home to a dozen or more noisy roadside 'cafes'.

The descent to **Gramphoo** (Gramphu), which is no more than a couple of houses at the junction of the road from Tabo and Kaza, offers superb views of the glaciated valley of the Chandra River, source of the Chenab. To the north and east rise the peaks of Lahul, averaging around 6,000 m and with the highest, Mulkila, reaching 6,520 m. As the road descends towards Khoksar there is an excellent view of the Lumphu Nala coming down from the Tempo La glacier. An earlier glacial maximum is indicated by the huge terminal moraine visible half way up the valley.

There is a police check post in **Khoksar**, at 3,140 m, where you may be required to show your passport and sign a register. This can take some time if more than one bus arrives at once. About 8 km west of Khoksar work has started on the proposed Rohtang tunnel to link the Solang Valley with the Chandra Valley. If you cross the bridge here you find an attractive waterfall.

Gondhla It is worth stopping here to see the 'castle' belonging to the local *thakur* (ruler), built around 1700. The seven-storey house with staircases made of wooden logs has a verandah running around the top and numerous apartments on the various floors. The fourth floor was for private prayer, while the Thakur held court from the verandah. There is much to see in this neglected, ramshackle house, particularly old weapons, statues, costumes and furniture. The 'sword of wisdom' believed to be a gift from the Dalai Lama some time ago, is of special interest. On close inspection you will notice thin wires have been hammered together to form the blade, a technique from Toledo, Spain! The huge rock near the Government School, which some claim to be of ancient origin, has larger-than-life figures of *Bodhisattvas* carved on it.

Route As the road turns north approaching **Tandi** the Chandra rushes through a gorge, giving a superb view of the massively contorted, folded and faulted rocks of the Himalaya. Tandi itself is at the confluence of the Chandra and Bhaga rivers, forming the Chandrabhaga or Chenab. **Keylong** is 8 km from here, see page 505. At Tandi you can take a left turn and visit the Pattan Valley before heading to Keylong to continue on the journey.

Pattan Valley → *Colour map 1, grid A3 and B3.*

The Pattan Vally has a highly distinctive agricultural system which despite its isolated situation is closely tied in to the Indian market. Pollarded willows are crowded together all around the villages, offering roofing material for the flat-roofed houses and fodder for the cattle during the six-month winter. Introduced by a British missionary in the 19th century to try and help stabilize the deeply eroded slopes, willows have become a vital part of the valley's village life, with the additional benefit of offering shade from the hot summer sun along the roads and family compounds. Equally important are the three commercial crops which dominate farming; hops, potatoes and peas, all exported from the valley, while wheat and barley are the most common subsistence grain crops.

Ins and outs Just out of Tandi after crossing the Bhaga River on the Keylong road, the Udeypur road doubles back along the right bank of the Chenab running close to but high above the river. The road passes through Ruding, Shansha, 15 km from Tandi, Jahlma, 6 km and Thirot, another 11 km on (rest house here). A bridge at Jhooling crosses the Chenab. Some 6 km further on, the road enters a striking gorge where a bridge crosses the river before taking the road up to Trilokinath, 6 km away.

★ **Trilokinath** Trilokinath, at 2,760 m, is approached by a very attractive road which climbs up the left bank of the Chenab. The glitteringly white-painted Trilokinath temple stands at the end of the village street on top of a cliff.

The Siva **temple** has been restored by Tibetan Buddhists, whose influence is far stronger than the Hindu. Tibetan prayer-flags decorate the entrance to the temple which is in the ancient wooden pagoda style. In the courtyard is a tiny stone Nandi and a granite lingam, Saivite symbols which are dwarfed in significance by the Buddhist symbols of the sanctuary; typical prayer-wheels constantly being turned by pilgrims, and a 12th-century six-armed white marble Avalokiteshwara image (Bodhisattva) in the shrine along with other Buddhist images. The original columns date from Lalitaditya's reign in the eighth century, but there has been considerable modernization as well as restoration, with the installation of bright electric lights including a strikingly garish and flickering *chakra* on the ceiling. Hindus and Buddhists celebrate the three-day *Pauri Festival* in August.

Udeypur Ten kilometres from the junction with the Trilokinath road is Udeypur (Udaipur). Visited in the summer it is difficult to imagine that the area is completely isolated by sometimes over 2 m of snow during the six winter months. It is supplied by weekly helicopter flights (weather permitting). The helipad is at the entrance to the village. Trekking routes cross the valley here and further west, see page 523.

The unique **Mrikula** (Markula) **Devi temple** (AD1028-63) is above the bazar. The temple dedicated to Kali looks wholly unimposing from the outside with a battered looking wood-tiled 'conical' roof and crude outside walls. However, inside are some beautiful, intricate deodar-wood carvings belonging to two periods. The façade of the shrine, the *mandapa* (hall) ceiling and the pillars supporting it are earlier than those beside the window, the architraves and two western pillars. Scenes from the *Mahabharata* and the *Ramayana* epics decorate the architraves, while the two door guardians (*dvarapalas*), which are relatively crude, are stained with the blood of sacrificed goats and rams. The wood carvings here closely resemble those of the Hadimba Temple at Manali and some believe it was the work of the same

16th-century craftsman. See page 493. The silver image of Kali (*Mahisha-shurmardini*) 1570, inside, is a strange mixture of Rajasthani and Tibetan styles (note the Lama-like headcovering), with an oddly proportioned body.

Keylong → *Phone code: 019002. Colour map 1, grid B3. Altitude: 3,350 m.*

The principal town of the district of Lahul, Keylong is set amidst fields of barley and buckwheat surrounded by brown hills and snowy peaks and was once the home of Moravian missionaries. Only traders and trekkers can negotiate the pass out of season. Keylong is an increasingly widely used stopping point for people en route to Leh or trekking in the Lahul/Spiti area. Landslides on the Leh-Manali road can cause quite long delays and the town can be an unintended rest halt for a couple of days. It has little to offer, though the views are very attractive and there are pleasant walks. There is a pleasant circuit of the town by road which can be done comfortably in under two hours. ▶▶ *For Sleeping, Eating and other listings, see pages 506-506.*

Sights
The bus stand with a few tea stalls alongside is on the NH21 which by-passes the town. Tracks run down into the town centre. The **local deity** 'Kelang Wazir' is kept in Shri Nawang Dorje's home which you are welcome to visit. There is a **Tibetan Centre for Performing Arts**. A statue in the centre of Keylong commemorates the Indian nationalist **Rash Behari Bose** (born 15 May 1886 near Kolkata).

Excursions
Khardong Monastery, 3½ km away across the Chandra River up a steep tree-shaded path, is the most important in the area. It is believed to have been founded 900 years ago and was renovated in 1912. Nuns and monks enjoy equality; married lamas spend the summer months at home cultivating their fields and return to the monastery in winter. The monastery, with its four temples, contains a huge barrel drum, a valuable library and collections of *thangkas*, Buddha statues, musical instruments, costumes and ancient weapons.

    Sha-Shur Monastery, a kilometre away, was in legend reputedly founded as early as 17 AD by a Buddhist missionary from Zanskar, Lama Deva Tyatsho who was sent by the Bhutanese king. It has ancient connections with Bhutan and contains numerous wall paintings and a 4½-m *thangka*. The annual festival is held in June/July.

    Tayul Monastery, above Satingri village, has a 4-m high statue of Padma Sambhava, wall paintings and a library containing valuable scriptures and *thangkas*. The *mani* wheel here is supposed to turn on its own marking specially auspicious occasions, the last time having been in 1986.

To Leh From Keylong the road passes through very altitude desert with extraordinary mountain views. **Jespa** (21 km; 3,200 m), has a campsite, a few tea stalls and a mountaineering institute. Himachal Tourism's concrete '*Lodge*' with three basic rooms with toilets, cheap camping in the yard. About 2 km beyond Jespa is **Teh** which has accommodation.

    All vehicles must stop for passport checks at **Darcha** check post where the Bhaga River is bridged. Tents appear on the grassy river bank in the summer to provide a halt for trekkers to Zanskar. The road climbs to **Patseo** where you can get a view back of Darcha. A little further is **Zingzingbar**. Icy streams flow across the road while grey and red-brown scree reach down from the bare mountainside to the road edge. The road then goes over the **Baralacha La** (54 km; 4,880 m), 107 km from Keylong, at the crossroads of Lahul, Zanskar, Spiti and Ladakh regions before dropping to **Sarchu** (HP border). *NEI* (Nature Expeditions India) sets up 15 double Alpine tents with beds and linen for Rs 1200, with electricity generator, toilet and shower tents. Contact T011-6368601, F6368604, neisales@mantraonline.com. There is also *Tented Camp* (Himachal Tourism), mostly with two-bed tents (sometimes reported dirty), communal toilet tents, late night Indian meal and breakfast; private bus passengers without reservations are accommodated whenever possible (Rs 150 per person); open mid-June to mid-September.

The road runs beyond Brandy Nala by the Tsarap River before negotiating 22 spectacular hairpin bends to climb up to the **Nakli La** (4,950 m) and **Lachalung La** (5,065 m). It then descends past tall earth and rock pillars to **Pang**, a summer settlement in a narrow valley where you can stop for an expensive 'breakfast' (usually roti, vegetables and omelettes to order). The camp remains open beyond 15 September; overnight stop is possible in communal tents. The 40 km wide Moray plains (4,400 m) provide a change from the slower mountain road. The road then climbs to **Taglang La** (5,370 m), the highest motorable pass along this route and the second highest in the world; the altitude is likely to affect many travellers at this point. You descend slowly towards the valley, passing small villages, before entering a narrow gorge with purple coloured cliffs. The road turns left to continue along the Indus basin passing **Upshi** with a sheep farm and a check post, and then **Thikse**, before reaching **Leh**.

Listings: Lahul

● Sleeping

Udeypur *p504*
E **Forest Rest House**, off the road in a pleasant raised position, 2 rooms with bath, very basic, bring your own sleeping bag. Camping is possible in an attractive site abut 4 km beyond the town (permission from Forest Officer) but since there is no water supply, nearby water has to be carried in from a spring about 300 m further up the road. Carry provisions as there is little in the bazar.

Keylong *p505*
D **Dekyid**, below police station. 3-storey hotel, friendly, helpful reception, decent sized rooms with bath, quiet, excellent views over fields, good restaurant but service very slow.
D **Snowland**, above Circuit House, T2219. 15 rooms with bath, modest but adequate, friendly reception. Recommended.
E **Tourist Bungalow** (HPTDC), T22247. 3 rooms with bath, 2-bed tents, dorm (Rs 50), meals to order, solar heated pool, reserve ahead, open mid-Jun to mid-Oct.
F **Gyespa**, in bazar close to footpath from bus stand. Small rooms, basic but adequate, good restaurant.

Several local restaurants on main road including **Vikrant**, recommended.

Teh *p505*
C **Ibex Hotel**, glass and cement block, comfortable rooms, ISD, reserve (Manali) T01901-2480.

● Transport

Keylong *p505*
Bus
State and private luxury buses are most comfortable but charge more than double the 'B' class fare (see below). To **Manali** (6-8 hrs); to **Leh** (18 hrs, Rs 300-375). To board deluxe buses to Leh in Keylong, reserve ahead and pay full fare from Manali (Rs 700, plus Rs 300 for tent and meals in Sarchu).

Jeep
To **Manali** by jeep, 4 hrs, weather permitting; **Sarchu** 6 hrs, **Leh** 14 hrs.

● Directory

Keylong *p505*
Banks State Bank of India; no foreign exchange.

● *For an explanation of the sleeping and eating price codes used in this guide, see inside the* ● *front cover. Other relevant information is found in Essentials pages 52-57.*

Northern Himachal

★ Dharamshala

→ *Phone code: 01892. Colour map 1, grid B3. Population: 8,600. Altitude: 1,250-1,980 m.*

Dharamshala has a spectacular setting along a spur of the Dhauladhar range, varying in height from 1,250 m at the 'Lower Town' bazar to McLeodganj, 1,768 m at the pleasanter McLeodganj. It is this 'Upper' and more attractive part of town that attracts the bulk of visitors. Surrounded by forests of chir pine, rhododendron and Himalayan Oak, it is set against a backdrop of high peaks on three sides, with superb views over the Kangra Valley and Shiwaliks, and of the great granite mountains that almost overhang the town. ▸▸ *For Sleeping, Eating and other listings, see pages 515-522.*

Ins and outs

Getting there Flights to Gaggal Airport (13 km). Lower Dharamshala is well connected by bus with towns near and far. You can travel from Shimla to the southeast or from Hoshiarpur to the southwest along the fastest route from Delhi. The nearest station on the scenic mountain railway is at Kangra while Pathankot to the west is on the broad gauge.

Dharamshala

To Dharamkot (2 km)
To Bhagsu Temple & Waterfall
To Tushita, Triund & Dharamkot
☐ TIPA
Mountaineering Institute ☐
Niyngmapa Monastery
Related map
A McLeodganj, page 510
Tipa Rd
Bhagsu Rd
To TCV, Dal Lake, Himgiri Hotel & Naddi
Mall Rd *M 1 Rd*
FORSYTHGANJ   McLEODGANJ
Charan Khad
Mall (Cantonment) Rd
St John in the Wilderness
Geden Choeling Nunnery
Jogibara Rd
Bus Route to Dharamshala
Dip Tse-Chok Ling Monastery
Tsuglagkhang, Namgyal Monastery & Tibet Museum
Dhauladhar Travels
Dalai Lama's Residence
Delek Hospital
Cantonment Rd
Men Tse Khang
Nechung
Central Tibetan Administration & Library
To Khanyiara & Tol (4km)
GANGCHEN KYISHONG
Bus Route to McLeodganj & Cantonment
Kotwali Bazar
Metal Craft Centre
Taxis ☐
Cinema Rd
Lower TCV
Heartbeat Communications
LOWER DHARAMSHALA
Museum of Kangra Art
District Hospital
BOB
Foreigners' Registration Office
CIVIL LINES
To Pathankot
To Kangra

N
0 metres 200
0 yards 200

■ Sleeping
1 Chonor House
2 Clouds End Villa
3 Deyki Palbor
4 Dhauladhar
5 Dhauladhar View
6 Jaldhara Cottage
7 Kashmir House
8 Rainbow
9 Shanti
10 Shimla
11 Sun & Snow
12 Surbhi GH
13 Tara

● Eating
1 Midtown
2 Rising Moon

❗ Fight over the flight of the living Buddha

Rival claims by two boy-gods to the position of the 17th Karmapa, the head of the Kagyu Buddhist sect and the inheritor of the coveted black hat 'woven from the hair of 10,000 angels', has created a rift in high Buddhist clerical circles. The Indian headquarters of the powerful and affluent Kagyu sect is in Rumtek in Sikkim. On 5 January 2000, the dramatic appearance of the 14 year old Urgyen Thinley in Dharamshala after a strenuous mountain crossing after escaping from captivity in Tibet, has put the cat among the pigeons. The older claimant, Thaye Dorje now 19, who escaped from Tibet as the 17th incarnation of a 12th-century spiritual leader in 1994, is being groomed in the quiet backwaters of Kalimpong, away from the warring monks of Rumtek, for the third highest position (after the Dalai Lama and the Panchen Lama) in Tibetan Buddhism. Thaye Dorje's supporters are ready to oppose any move by the Karmapa to usurp the 'throne' they feel rightfully belongs to their earlier find.

Getting around From Dharamshala, it is almost 10 km by the bus route to McLeodganj but a shorter, steeper path (3 km), takes about 45 mins on foot. Local jeeps use this bumpy, potholed shortcut. Compact McLeodganj itself, and its surroundings, are ideal for walking. For trekking in Northern Himachal, see page 528

Background

The hill station was established by the British between 1815 and 1847, but remained a minor town until the **Dalai Lama** settled here after Chinese invasion of Tibet in October 1959. There is an obvious Tibetan influence in McLeodganj. The Tibetan community has tended to take over the hospitality business, sometimes a cause of friction with the local population. Now many westerners come here because they are particularly interested in Buddhism, meditation or the Tibetan cause. A visitor's attempt to use a few phrases in Tibetan is always warmly responded to: *tashi delek* (hello, good luck), *thukje-chey* (thank you), *thukje-sik* (please), *gong-thag* (sorry), *shoo-den-jaa-go* (goodbye) and reply *chipgyu nang-go*! **Foreign volunteers** are often accepted at the hospital and other units here. Also ask at *Hotel Tibet, Green Shop* or *Khana Nirvana* for the free monthly '*Contact*' which carries news of opportunities. English language teachers are in high demand to teach newly-arrived refugees, for short or long term.

Sights

The **Church of St John-in-the-Wilderness** (1860) ⓘ *1000-1700*, with attractive stained glass windows, is a short distance below McLeodganj. Along with other buildings in the area, it was destroyed by the earthquake of 1905 but has been rebuilt. In April 1998 thieves tried to steal the old bell, cast in London, which was installed in 1915, but could only move it 300 m. The Eighth **Lord Elgin**, one of the few Viceroys to die in office, is buried here according to his wish as it reminded him of his native Scotland.

The **Namgyal Monastery** at McLeodganj, with the Buddhist School of Dialectics, mostly attended by small groups of animated 'debating' monks, is known as Little Lhasa. This Tsuglagkhang ('cathedral') opposite the Dalai Lama's residence resembles the centre of the one in Lhasa and is five minutes' walk from the main bazar. It contains large gilded bronzes of the Buddha, Avalokiteshvara and Padmasambhava. To the left of the Tsuglagkhang is the **Kalachakra Temple** with very good modern murals of *mandalas*, protectors of the Dharma, and Buddhist masters of different lineages of Tibetan Buddhism, with the central image of Shakyamuni. Sand mandalas (which can be viewed on completion), are constructed throughout the year, accompanied by ceremonies. The temple is very important as the practice of Kalachakra Tantra is instrumental in bringing about world peace and harmony.

The **Dalai Lama** usually leads the prayers on special occasions – 10 days for *Monlam Chenmo* following *Losar*, *Saga Dawa* (May) and his own birthday (6th July). If you wish to have an audience with him, you need to sign up in advance at the Security Office (go upstairs) by *Hotel Tibet*. On the day, arrive early with your passport. Cameras, bags and rucksacks are not permitted. His Holiness is a Head of State and the incarnation of Avalokitesvara, the Bodhisattva of Love and Great Compassion; show respect by dressing appropriately (no shorts, sleeveless tops, dirty or torn clothes); monks may 'monitor' visitors. See page 38. **Dip Tse-Chok Ling Monastery**,with its golden roof in a wooded valley, can be seen from above. See sleeping below. Further down the 3-km steep motorable road to Dharamshala is the Nechung Monastery in **Gangchen Kyishong** with the Central Tibetan Administration (CTA) which began work in 1988.

The **Norbulingka Institute** ① *T22664, F24982, www.norbulingkainstitute.org*, is becoming a major centre for Buddhist teaching and practical work. Named after the summer residence of the Seventh Dalai Lama built in 1754, it was set up to ensure the survival of Tibetan Buddhism's cultural heritage. Up to 100 students and 300 Tibetan employees are engaged in a variety of crafts in wood, metal, silk and metal, *thangka* painting (some excellent) and Tibetan Language. The temple has a 4.5-m high gilded statue of the Buddha and over 1,000 painted images. There is a small **museum** of traditional 'dolls' made by monks and a **Tibetan Library** with a good range of books and magazines. You can attend lectures and classes on Tibetan culture and language and Buddhism or attend two **meditation** classes, free but a donation is appreciated. Those attending regularly pay Rs 100 per meditation session.

The **Museum of Kangra Art** ① *Main Rd*, closed Mon, *1000-1700 (closed 1330-1400), free, allow ½ hr*, near the bus stand in Lower Dharamshala, includes regional jewellery, paintings, carvings, a reminder of the rich local heritage contrasted with the celebrated Tibetan presence. Copies of Roerich paintings will be of interest to those not planning to visit Naggar.

Located near Namgyal Monastery in McLeodganj, the **Tibetan Museum** ① *www.thetibetmuseum.org, Tue-Sun, 0900-1300, 1400-1700, Rs 5*, has an interesting collection of documents and photographs detailing Tibetan history, the Chinese occupation of Tibet and visions of the future for the country. It is an essential visit for those interested in the Tibetan cause.

Walks around McLeodganj

Bhagsu, an easy 2-km stroll east, or Rs 30-40 auto ride, has a temple to Bhagsunath (Siva). Outside the rainy season lovely walks are possible. The mountain stream here, feeds a small pool for pilgrims, while there is an attractive waterfall 1 km beyond. It is a relaxing place with great views, and so attracts some to stay here. Unfortunately this has resulted in it becoming very touristy, with increasing building activity up the valley towards Dharamkot and an influx of noisy day-trippers.

Dharamkot, 3 km away, has very fine views and you can continue on towards the snowline. In September, a fair is held at **Dal Lake** (1,837 m), 3 km from McLeodganj bus stand; it is a pleasant walk but the 'lake', no more than a small pond, is disappointing.

Naddi Gaon ① *buses from Dharamshala, 0800-1900*, 1½ km further uphill from the bridge by Dal Lake, has superb views of the Dhauladhar Range. **Kareri Lake** is further on. The TCV (Tibetan Childrens' Village) nearby educates and trains children in traditional handicrafts. Big hotels are rapidly appearing next to the traditional Naddi village. Most enjoy excellent views.

It is an 8-km trek to **Triund**, 2,827 m, at the foot of the Dhauladhar where there is a *Forest Lodge* on a hill top. Some trekkers pitch tents, whilst others make use of caves or shepherds' huts. Take provisions and warm sleeping gear if planning to stay overnight. Well worth the effort. A further 5 km, one-hour walk, brings you to **Ilaka**.

Jogindernagar ① *train from Pathankot, enquiry T52279*, is the terminus of the beautiful journey by narrow gauge rail from Pathankot via Kangra. The hydro power scheme here and at nearby Bassi channels water from the River Uhl. Paragliding and hang gliding is possible at Bir (19 km) and Billing (33 km).

Baijnath ① *Train from Pathankot or Jogindernagar and bus to/from Mandi, 3½ hrs, Rs 40*. The temples are old by hill standards, dating from at least 1204. Note the Lakshmi/Vishnu figure and the graceful balcony window on the north wall. The **Vaidyanatha Temple** (originally circa 800), which contains one of 12 *jyotirlingas*

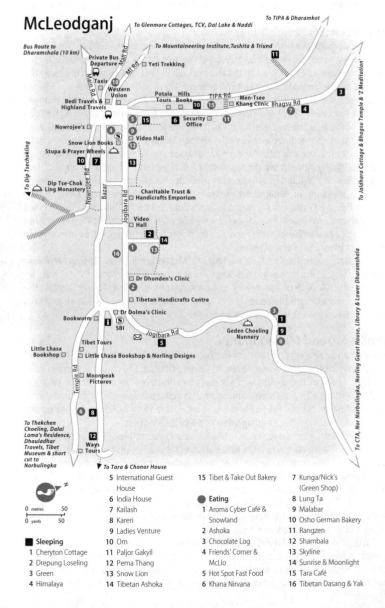

McLeodganj

Sleeping
1 Cheryton Cottage
2 Drepung Loseling
3 Green
4 Himalaya
5 International Guest House
6 India House
7 Kailash
8 Kareri
9 Ladies Venture
10 Om
11 Paljor Gakyil
12 Pema Thang
13 Snow Lion
14 Tibetan Ashoka
15 Tibet & Take Out Bakery

Eating
1 Aroma Cyber Café & Snowland
2 Ashoka
3 Chocolate Log
4 Friends' Corner & McLlo
5 Hot Spot Fast Food
6 Khana Nirvana
7 Kunga/Nick's (Green Shop)
8 Lung Ta
9 Malabar
10 Osho German Bakery
11 Rangzen
12 Shambala
13 Skyline
14 Sunrise & Moonlight
15 Tara Café
16 Tibetan Dasang & Yak

‏⁞‏ The little-known 'mountain' railway

A superb narrow gauge railway links Pathankot in the west with Jogindernagar via Kangra (near Dharamshala) and Baijnath. The views of the Kangra Valley are quite spectacular. This is very much a working service and not a 'relic' (this train can be packed with ordinary users). Sadly, it is often very late as it is incredibly slow, and very uncomfortable because of the hard seats. 'Tourists' would do better to sample short sections of the line, and allow for delays – any purposeful journey is better done by bus. See page 521 for an optimistic timetable.

stands by the roadside on the Mandi-Palampur road, within a vast rectangular enclosure. Originally known as **Kirangama**, its name was changed after the temple was dedicated to **Siva** in his form as the Lord of Physicians. It is a good example of the Nagari style; the walls have the characteristic niches enshrining images of Chamunda, Surya and Karttikeya and the *sikhara* tower is topped with an *amalaka* and pot. A life-size stone Nandi stands at the entrance.

Palampur This is a pleasant little town for walking, 16 km from Baijnath, 40 km from Dharamshala (via Yol), with beautiful snow views, surrounded by old British tea plantations, thriving on horticulture. It is a popular stop with trekkers; see page 528. The Neugal Khad, a 300-m wide chasm through which the Bandla flows is very impressive when the river swells during the monsoons. It holds a record for rainfall in the area!

Andretta ⓘ *Panchruki (3 km) is a stop on the Kangra Valley Railway (where there are cheap guesthouses).* An attractive village surrounded by orchards and tea gardens, 13 km from Palampur, Andretta is associated with **Norah Richards**, a follower of Mahatma Gandhi, who popularized rural theatre, and with the artist **Sardar Sobha Singh** who revived the Kangra School of painting. His paintings are big, brightly coloured, ultra-realistic and often devotional incorporating Sikh, Christian and Hindu images. There is an art gallery dedicated to his work and memory; prints, books, soft drinks are sold in the shop. The Andretta Pottery (signposted from the main road), is charming. It is run by an artist couple (Indian/English), who combine village pottery with 'slipware'. The Sikh partner is the son of Gurcharan Singh (of Delhi Blue Pottery fame) and is furthering the tradition of studio pottery; works are for sale. There is a Writers' Retreat run by the University of Punjab.

Kangra Valley

The Kangra Valley, between the Dhaula Dhar and the Shiwalik foothills, starts near Mandi and runs northwest to Pathankot. It is named after the town of Kangra but now the largest and main centre is Dharamshala. Chamba State, to its north, occupies part of the Ravi River valley and some of the Chenab Valley. ›› *For Sleeping, Eating and other listings, see pages 515-522.*

History

In 1620 Shah Jahan captured Kangra fort for his father Jahangir, and Kangra became a Mughal province. Many of the court artists fled to neighbouring Chamba and Kullu as the Rajas submitted to Mughal rule. When Mughal power weakened, the 16 year-old **Sansar Chand Katoch II** (1775-1823) recaptured the fort and the Rajas reasserted their independence. Under his powerful leadership, Kangra sought to extend its boundaries into the Chamba and Kullu Valleys but this was forestalled by the powerful Gurkhas from Nepal who conquered what is now the hill region of Uttaranchal and HP. With the rise of the Sikh Empire, the valley was occupied until the Treaty of Amritsar. Then under the British, Dharamshala was made the administrative capital of the region which led to the decline of Kangra.

Kangra School of Painting Raja Goverdhan Singh (1744-1773) of Guler gave shelter to many artists who had fled from the Mughals, and during the mid-18th century a new style of miniature painting developed. Based on Mughal miniature style, the subject matter derived from Radha/Krishna legends, the rajas and gods being depicted in a local setting. Under Sansar Chand II the region prospered and the Kangra School flourished. Kangra fort where he held court for nearly 25 years was adorned with paintings and attracted art lovers from great distances. Later he moved his capital to Nadaun and finally to **Sujanpur Tira** (80 km) and at each place the temples and palaces were enriched by artists. The 1905 earthquake damaged many of these buildings though you can still see some miniature wall paintings.

Kangra → *Phone code: 01892. Colour map 1, grid B3. Altitude: 615 m.*

Kangra, 18 km south of Dharamshala, was once the second most important kingdom in the West Himalaya after Kashmir. Kangra town, the capital, was also known as Bhawan or Nagarkot, and overlooks the Banganga River. It claims to have existed since the Vedic period with historical reference in Alexander's war records.

Sights Kangra fort *US$2, Indians Rs 5, auto Rs 70 return, taxi Rs 100*, stands on a steep rock dominating the valley. A narrow path leads up to the fort which was once protected by several gates and had the palace of the Katoch kings at the top. The fort, 5 km from the road bridge, is worth the effort. At its foot is a large modern Jain temple which has pilgrim accommodation (worth considering for its peaceful location). There is also a British Cemetery nearby. Inside the fort itself is an old Jain temple which is still in use. At the very top, the remains of Sansar Chand's palace offer commanding views.

Brajesvari Devi Temple, in Kangra Town, achieved a reputation for gold, pearls and diamonds and attracted many Muslim invaders from the 11th century including Mahmud of Ghazni, the Tughlaqs and the Lodis who periodically plundered its treasures and destroyed the idols. In the intervening years the temple was rebuilt and refurbished several times but in the great earthquake of 1905 both the temple and the fort were badly damaged. The Devi received unusual offerings from devotees. According to Abul Fazal, the pilgrims "cut out their tongues which grew again in the course of two or three days and sometimes in a few hours"! The present temple in which the deity sits under a silver dome with silver *chhatras* (umbrellas) was built in 1920 and stands behind the crowded, colourful bazar. The State Government maintains the temple; the priests are expected to receive gifts in kind only. The area is busy and quite dirty, with mostly pilgrim-oriented stalls. Above these is St Paul's Church and a Christian community. Along the river between Old Kangra and Kangra Mandir is a pleasant trail, mostly following long-disused roads past ruined houses and temples which evidence a once sizeable town.

Excursions A sandstone ridge to the northeast of the village, **Masrur** ① *buses from Kangra* (34 km southwest of Dharamshala, altitude: 800 m), has 15, 9th-10th century *sikhara* temples excavated out of solid rock. They are badly eroded and partly ruined. Even in this state they have been compared with the larger rock cut temples at Ellora in Maharashtra and at Mamallapuram south of Chennai. Their ridge-top position commands a superb view over the surrounding fertile countryside, but few of the original *shikharas* stand, and some of the most beautifully carved panels are now in the State Museum, Shimla.

Jawalamukhi ① *buses from Kangra*, is one of the most popular Hindu pilgrimage sites in Himachal and is recognized as one of 51 *Shakti pitha*. The **Devi temple**, tended by the followers of Gorakhnath, is set against a cliff and from a fissure comes a natural inflammable gas which accounts for the blue 'Eternal Flame'. Natural springs feed the two small pools of water; one appears to boil, the other with the flame flaring above the surface contains surprisingly cold water. Emperor Akbar's gift of gold leaf cover of the dome. In March/April there are colourful celebrations during the *Shakti Festival*; another in mid-October. There is accommodation here.

Pragpur, across the river Beas, 20 km southwest of Jawalamukhi, is a medieval 'Heritage' village with cobbled streets and slate-roofed houses. The fine 'Judges Court' (1918) nearby has been carefully restored using traditional techniques. A 3-4 day stay is recommended here and it is advisable to reserve ahead.

Chamba Valley

Dalhousie→ *Phone code: 01899. Colour map 1, grid B2. Population: 7,400. Altitude: 2,030 m.*
Dalhousie, named after the Governor-General (1848-56), was developed on land purchased by the British in 1853 from the Raja of Chamba. It sprawls out over five hills ranging from 1,600-2,400 m, just east of the Ravi River. By 1867 it was a sanatorium and reached its zenith in the 1920s and 30s as a cheaper alternative to Shimla. Rabindranath Tagore wrote his first poem in Dalhousie as a boy and Subhash Chandra Bose came secretly to plan his strategies during the Second World War, see page 756. Its popularity declined after 1947 and it became a quiet hill station with old colonial bungalows, surrounded by thick pine forests interspersed with oak and rhododendron. It remains a popular bolt hole for tourists from the plains but its importance today is due to the number of good schools and the presence of the army.

Sights The three Malls laid out for level walks are around Moti Tibba, Potreyn Hill and Upper Bakrota. The last, the finest, is about 330 m above **Gandhi Chowk** around which the town centres. From there two rounds of the Mall lead to Subhash Chowk. Tibetans make and sell handicrafts, woollens, jackets, cardigans and rugs. Their paintings and rock carvings can be seen along Garam Sarak Mall.

Just over 2 km from Gandhi Chowk is **Martyr's Memorial** at Panchpulla (five bridges), which commemorates Ajit Singh, a supporter of Subhash Bose and the

Dalhousie

Sleeping	4 Glory	Eating
1 Aroma-n-Claire	5 Grand View & Snow	1 Kwality
2 Crags	Lion Restaurant	2 Milan
3 Geetanjali	6 Youth Hostel	3 Moti Mahal

N Not to scale

Indian National Army during the Second World War. On the way you can see the **Satdhara** (seven springs), said to contain mica and medicinal properties. **Subhash Baoli** (1½ km from the square), is another spring. It is an easy climb and offers good views of the snows. Half a kilometre away **Jhandri Ghat**, the old palace of Chamba rulers, is set among tall pine trees. For a longer walk try the Bakrota Round (5 km), which gives good views of the mountains and takes you through the Tibetan settlement.

Excursions **Kalatope**, 9 km away, with good mountain views, is a level walk through a forest sanctuary with accommodation. The road is jeepable. **Khajjiar** ① *buses from Dalhousie, 0930, return 1530, 1 hr, Rs 13*, 22 km further along the motorable road, is a long, wide glade ringed by cedars with a small lake. You can explore the area in a pleasant three-day walk. Alternatively you can extend the day's walk to Khajjiar into a short trek to Dharamshala over two days. A 30-km path through dense deodar forest leads to Chamba.

★ Chamba → *Phone code: 01899. Colour map 1, grid B2. Altitude: 996 m.*

Picturesque Chamba is on the south bank of the Iravati (Ravi), its stone houses clinging to the hillside. Some see the medieval town as having an almost Italian feel, surrounded by lush forests and with its Chaugan or grassy meadow in the centre. Most hotels, temples and palaces are within walking distance of the bus stand.

Background Founded in the 10th century, **Chamba State** was on an important trade route from Lahul to Kashmir and was known as 'The Middle Kingdom'. Though Mughal suzerainty was accepted by the local Rajas, the kingdom remained autonomous though it came under Sikh rule from 1810-46. Its relative isolation led to the nurturing of the arts – painting, temple sculpture, handicrafts and unique rumal. The pieces of silk/cotton with fine embroidery imitate miniature paintings; the reverse is as good as the front.

Chamba is the centre of the **Gaddis**, shepherds who move their flocks of sheep and goats, numbering from a couple of hundred to a thousand, from lower pastures at around 1,500 m during winter to higher slopes at over 3,500 m, after snowmelt. They are usually only found in the Dhaula Dhar range which separates Kangra from Chamba. Some believe that these herdsmen first arrived in this part of Himachal in the 10th century though some moved from the area around Lahore (Pakistan) in the 18th century, during the Mughal period. Their religious belief combines animism with the worship of Siva; Bahrmaur with its distinctive Manimahesh temple is their principal centre of worship (see below).

In the winter the Gaddis can be seen round Kangra, Mandi and Bilaspur and in the small villages between Baijnath and Palampur. The men traditionally wear a *chola* (a loose white woollen garment), tied at the waist with a black wool rope and a white embroidered cap.

Sights The **Chaugan**, under a kilometre long, is the central hub of the town but sadly, over the last two decades, shops have encroached into the open space.

There are several ancient Pahari temples with attractive curvilinear stone towers. The **Lakshmi Narayana** Temple Complex (ninth to 11th centuries) contains six *sikhara* temples with deep wooden eaves, several smaller shrines and a tank. These are dedicated to Vishnu and Siva, with some of the brass images inlaid with copper and silver. The **Hari Rai Temple** (14th century) contains a fine 11th-century bronze Chaturmurti (four-armed Vishnu), rarely visible as it is usually 'dressed'. The 10th-century wooden **Chamunda Devi Temple**, 1 km north uphill from the bus stand, has some interesting wood carvings and stands over the river with commanding views. Others of note are the Bajreshwari, Bansigopal and Champavati.

The Akhand Chandi, the Chamba Maharajas' palace, beyond the Lakshmi Narayan complex, is now a college. The old **Rang Mahal** (Painted Palace) in the Surara

Mohalla, was built by Raja Umed Singh in the mid 18th-century. A prisoner of the 515
Mughals for 16 years, he was influenced by their architectural style. The wall paintings
in one room are splendid. The theme is usually religious, Krishna stories being
particularly popular. Some of these were removed to the Bhuri Singh Museum after a
fire, together with wood carvings and manuscripts.

The **Bhuri Singh Museum** ① *daily except Sun, 1000-1700*, near the Chaugan, in a
three-storey building houses a heritage collection, craft items including some
excellent *rumals*, carvings and fine examples of Chamba, Kangra and Basholi schools
of miniature paintings.

Listings: Northern Himachal

⊜ Sleeping

Dharamshala *p507, maps p507 and p510*
Most visitors stay in McLeodganj. In Mar, May
and early Jun accommodation may be difficult
to find. A 40% seasonal discount is usually
given from mid-Jun to Aug. Check out time is
mostly 1200. Check what time gate closes at
night to avoid being locked out.

Dharamshala
B Clouds End Villa, steep approach off
Jogibara Rd, T22109. 2 rooms and 1 bungalow
in Raja of Lambagraon's bungalow (Raj
period), not luxurious but very clean, annexe
has excellent valley views, authentic local
cuisine (everything home-made), tours,
peaceful, very friendly, excellent service.
B Norling Guest House, Norbulingka
Institute, Gangchen Kyishong, T22664,
F24982, norling@vsnl.com. Clean, comfortable
rooms, in modern facilities in a Tibetan style
house. Café accepts Master/Visa cards.
C-D Dhauladhar, Kotwali Bazar, T24926,
F24212. 23 rooms (2 **B** suites, cheaper in
annexe), clean, large rooms, restaurant, bar,
pleasant garden, billiard table, terrace for meals.
D Kashmir House, T22977. 10 large rooms
(1 **C** suite), hot water, TV, good value.
D-E Dhauladhar View, near Museum,
T22889. With 18 decent rooms.
E Dream, Pathankot Rd (9 km from town).
3 very clean rooms with bath, quiet, idyllic
spot beside river Gaj.
E Surbhi, T24677. 7 clean rooms in newish
hotel, hot water, some with view.
E-F Rainbow Lodge, Old Charri Rd, Kotwali
Bazar, T22647. 8 rooms, some with bath, TV.

E-F Shanti, Khanyara Rd, T25615. 6 rooms
including 2 singles, good views, hot water.
F Danubemiami, a block up from bus station.
Rooms with bath (bucket), fan, simple meals
(Rs 50), courteous and friendly staff, pleasant.
F Sun and Snow, past steps, near bank,
T22423. 12 clean rooms, hot water, some
with good views.

McLeodganj
B Chonor House, Thekchen Choeling Rd,
T21077, F21006, chonorhs@vsnl.com.
11 very comfortable rooms furnished in
Tibetan style (murals of lost monasteries and
mythical beasts), good restaurant, clean, well
managed, popular with foreign diplomats, a
quiet and lovely place. Book ahead. Accepts
credit cards. Recommended.
B Glenmore Cottages, off Mall Rd, T21010,
F21528. 5 'cottages' with bedroom, kitchen,
verandah, secluded old colonial house
surrounded by forest, good valley views,
great walks from doorstep.

South of the Bazar
B Pema Thang, opposite *Hotel Bhagsu*, T21612.
15 rooms with view, quiet, friendly, cooking
facilities possible, hot water, restaurant.
B Surya, T21418, F21868. 53 large rooms,
comfortable, quiet, good views, good
restaurant with bar, exchange, friendly.
B-C India House, Bhagsu Road, T21457,
F21144. 18 comfortable rooms in modern
hotel, TV, hot water, good restaurant, better
away from road with views.
C-D Tibet behind Bus Stand, T21587,
F21425. 20 renovated rooms with bath and
TV, not much difference between standard

*For an explanation of the sleeping and eating price codes used in this guide, see inside the
front cover. Other relevant information is found in Essentials pages 52-57.*

Himachal Pradesh Listings: Northern Himachal

and deluxe, those on roadside can be noisy, good restaurant, credit cards.
D Kareri, T21132, F21528, karerihl@ hotmail.com. 5 rooms with bath (tub), phone, TV, best with own balcony, good value.
D-E Cheryton Cottage, Jogibara Rd, enquire at *Chocolate Log*, T21237, 4 very smart rooms with bath, garden.
E Ladies Venture, Jogibara Rd, T21559. 13 clean rooms, some with bath, good dorm (Rs 50), peaceful, small restaurant (good Chinese and Western), terrace, very friendly.
E Om, western edge of bazar, T21313. 10 smart rooms, excellent shower, very good restaurant, internet, great views at sunset.
E Snow Lion, near prayer wheels, T21289. 8 rooms with bath, good restaurant (excellent cakes), friendly.
E Tara, near Bhagsu, T21181, tamdintara@ hotmail.com. 12 large, clean rooms, comfortable and safe, bath and 24-hr hot water, lovely views, warm friendly family, home cooked snacks, internet.
E-F Dip Tse-Chok Ling Monastery, below McLeodganj, climb down 300 steps, T21726, F21404. 20 clean rooms, 3 attached, some singles, hot showers, breakfast and dinner at set times, "wonderfully peaceful".
E-F Drepung Loseling, Jogibara Rd, T21087. 17 clean rooms with bath (some with hot water), dorm (Rs 30), terrace, friendly.
E-F Green Hotel, T21200. 19 variable rooms (avoid ones near the noisy courtyard), restaurant, popular with backpackers.
E-F Himalaya, Bhagsu Rd, T21337. 8 rooms, one with bath (hot shower), restaurant (good Tibetan brown bread, muesli, pancakes).
E-F Paljor Gakyil, T23143, TIPA Rd, up steps. 14 clean rooms with bath (hot shower), dorm (Rs 30), very friendly, excellent views.
E-F Tibetan Ashoka, T21763. 41 very clean rooms, some with hot shower and good views (cheapest with shared shower, bucket hot water extra Rs 10, no views), strict on check-out time, nice owners. Recommended.
F International Guest House, Jogibara Rd, just below PO, T21476. 8 fairly clean rooms with hot shower, friendly.
F Kailash, Jogibara Rd, T21044. 8 rooms, shared bath, good restaurant (one of the oldest in town), popular with Tibetans.

Bhagsu *p509*
C Meghawan, 15 rooms, TV, hot water, and restaurant, overpriced.
E Oak View, 6 new rooms with balcony, TV, hot water, restaurant, friendly.
E-F Pink and White, 16 rooms, some with bath, meals, friendly, clean, TV, ISD.
F Omni, above the village, five simple rooms (Rs 150), common bath, restaurant.

Dharamkot *p509*
C-D Dev Cottages, off McLeodganj to Dharamkot Rd (well signed), T21558. 12 comfortable rooms in 2-storey 'cottages', attached hot bath, TV, friendly.

Naddi Gaon *p509*
C-D Him Giri, T22998. Has cottages, an Indian and Chinese restaurant, friendly, good value.
C-D Nishaad Resorts, Cantt area, T21707, is modern, smart, wood-panelled units with bath, some apartments with kitchen, TV room, treks, family run, good value.
C-D Udechee Huts, above Dal Lake, T24781. Eight pleasantly furnished circular huts with bath (hot water), blending in with local style, restaurant, well kept, friendly hosts.
E-F Annapurna, T21336. 8 rooms, bath, TV.

Jogindernagar *p510*
D-E Uhl, on hill out of town, T01908-22002. 16 rooms with bath, best upstairs with balcony, simple, clean and peaceful, restaurant.

Baijnath *p510*
F Standard, T63714, behind bus station. 5 fairly clean and surprisingly tidy rooms with bath and hot water.

Palampur *p511*
Taxis are needed for first 3 hotels from bus or train station.
B-C Taragarh Palace (WelcomHeritage), in Al-hilal, 11 km southeast, T01894-63034, taragarh@vsnl.com. 12 rooms in 1930s summer resort, period furniture, atmospheric, tastefully decorated, good restaurant, tennis, pool, lovely gardens and mango orchards, luxury Swiss tents in summer.
C Masand Nayar Rentals, Neugal, 2 km bus stand, T01894-30623, F30931. 8 rooms, restaurant, clean, on hill away from bazar.

● *Phone codes Dharamshala and Kangra: 01892; Dalhousie and Chamba: 01899*

C Silver Oaks, Bandla Tea Estate, 1 km past *Masand*, T01894-30747, F30530. 14 large rooms, dorm for budget travellers, welcoming, quiet, scenic location with views of Dhaula Dhar peaks.
C-D T-Bud, 1 km from bus stand, T01894-31298. Beautiful setting, 23 adequate rooms (some big, airy), hot water, restaurant, pleasant lawn, clean, quiet, good service.
C-E Yamini, Ghaggar Rd, in town, T30631. 25 rooms with bath, quality varies, 8-bed dorm.

Kangra *p512*

Most hotels on the busy main road are noisy – even at night.
D-E Maurya, Dharamshala Rd, T25244. Clean but characterless rooms with bath, dorm, no restaurant or room service, disappointing.
E Anand, Nehru Bazar, above shops, T25243. 10 rooms, dining hall.
E Jannai, Chamunda Road, T65479. 5 rooms, restaurant, TV, hot water, closest to Kangra Mandir railway station.
E-F Dilraj Guest House, near Tehsil Chowk (taxi stand), T65362. 5 simple rooms in friendly family house, meals available. Recommended.
F Gupt Ganga Dharamshala, 30 rooms and 3 halls, please leave a donation.

Pragpur *p513*

B Judge's Court (Heritage), set in a large orchard, T01970-45035, F011-6885970, www.judgescourt.comeries@del2.vsnl.net.in. 7 tastefully decorated rooms in a fine mansion, one in annexe, 1 large private modernized suite in the '300 year old Kuthiala ancestral courtyard house, a few mins' walk away' with verandah overlooking the Dhauladhar, family hospitality, home-grown vegetables and fruit, fresh river fish, traditional meals, tours of Kangra Fort and other sights included (a ride on a part of the narrow-gauge mountain railway is possible) friendly, efficient management.

Dalhousie *p513, map p513*

Unfortunately some hotels look neglected and rundown, often because the cost of maintaining the Raj-built structures is prohibitive. Nearly all however have good mountain views and offer discounts out-of-season.
B-C Manimahesh (HPTDC), T42155. 18 rooms, restaurant.

B-C Silverton, near Circuit House, The Mall (Thandi Sarak), T42329. Old colonial building in large grounds, rooms with phone, TV.
C Alps Holiday Resort, Khajjiar Rd, Bakrota Hills, T40775, F40721, vacations@ valvalue.dhl.sml. 16 smart rooms in modern hotel, 2 km climb from centre.
C Grand View, near Bus Stand, T42823, F40609. 26 spacious rooms, restaurant, rather run down but better than some.
C-D Aroma-n-Claire, Court Rd, T42199. 20 rooms with bath, large but spartan, some with good views, restaurant, exchange, library, rather dated.
D Geetanjali (HPTDC), Thandi Sarak, near Bus Stand, T42155. 10 rooms (some 4-bed) with bath, simple restaurant.
E-F Crags, off The Mall (Garam Sarak), T42124. Tired but large, clean rooms with bath (hot water), meals, good views down valley, friendly, but check bill carefully.
E-F Glory, near Bus Stand, T42533. 5 rooms with bath, good restaurant,
F Youth Hostel, T42159. Good discounts for YHAI Members, reservations: tourist office, T42136.

Kalatope *p514*

E Tourist Lodge.

Khajjiar *p514*

C Devdar, T018992-36333. Has 12 clean rooms, dorm and beds in cottage, simple restaurant, horse riding, beautiful setting.
C Mini Swiss, T018992-36365. Comfortable, very clean rooms, great views, good restaurant.

Chamba *p514*

C-D Iravati (HPTDC), Court Rd, near Bus Stand, T22671, F22565. 19, mostly clean rooms with bath and hot water, restaurant (very slow, surly service but reasonably priced).
E Akhand Chandi, College Rd, Dogra Bazar, T24071. 9 rooms, some a/c, restaurant.
E The Orchard Hut, 8 km out of town (book through *Mani Manesh Travels* next to Lakshmi Narayana Temple, T22607), prakashd@nde.vsnl.net.in. Idyllic location (20 mins from nearest road), 4 rooms in guesthouse set in delightful garden, clean shared shower and toilets, pitch a tent in garden for Rs 100, superb home cooking (great all-inclusive deal), very friendly family, book at office in town first. Recommended.

E Rishi, opposite Lakshmi Narayana Temple, T24343. Rooms with bath (hot water), colour TV, good value meals, friendly owner.

● Eating

Dharamshala *p507, maps p507 and p510*
Enterprising Tibetans in the upper town offer good traveller favourites for those tired of curries; some serve beer. Be adventurous and try Tibetan soups (*thukpa*), noodle dishes, steamed or fried *momos* and *shabakleb*. Consider refilling your bottles with safe filtered, boiled water at the eco-friendly **Green shop** on Bhagsu Rd, Rs 5 per litre, also give used batteries here for recycling.
Midtown, Kotwali Bazar. Indian and Chinese, some continental, best in town.
Rising Moon, Tibetan, Chinese.

McLeodganj
McLlo, near Bus Stand. Indian, Western. Glassed in, 1st floor, beer, good value.
⛾ **Amdo Chachung**, Jogibara Rd. Good Tibetan. Nice terrace, cable TV.
⛾ **Ashoka**, Jogibara Rd. Varied. Pleasant atmosphere, very good curry.
⛾ **Friends Corner**, near Bus Stand. Good breakfasts, dim but popular.
⛾ **Hotel Tibet**, good Tibetan/Japanese restaurant and '*Take Out*' bakery.
⛾ **Khana Nirvana**, Temple Rd. International. Well-prepared Mexican/Italian dishes 'smoothies' (fruit juices), organic coffee, herb teas, American run, excellent ambience, good service, talks on Sun (1800) from Tibetan prisoners of conscience, music/poetry on Mon evening. Sun-Fri, orders taken between 0909-2047! Highly recommended.
⛾ **Lung-Ta**, Jogibara Rd. Classy Japanese veg restaurant, non-profit making concern, daily set menu or à la carte, good breads and cakes. Mon-Sat 1200-2030. Highly recommended.
⛾ **Om**, west end of bazar. Indian. Very good meals from Rs 35.
⛾ **Pema Thang**. Good vegetarian buffet brunch (Rs 150) on Sun 1000-1400.
⛾ **Shambala**, excellent breakfasts, western cakes and pancakes, try apple pie and lemon curd, good portions, very good value, pleasant atmosphere (records on request), quick and friendly. Recommended.
⛾ **Shangrila**, near prayer-wheels. Meal (Rs 25), delicious cakes.

⛾ **Snow Lion** offers good Tibetan and western meals, excellent cakes.
⛾ **Snowland** Jogibara Rd. Tibetan. Highly recommended for cheese momos.
⛾ **Tibetan Dasang/Lhoka**, Jogibara Rd. Tibetan plus. Also excellent porridge, fruit muesli.
⛾ **Yak**, Jogibara Rd. Tibetan.

Cafés and fast food
⛾ **Chocolate Log**, Jogibara Rd. International. Log-shaped, pleasant surprise, excellent cakes and snacks, clean, terrace or indoor seating below (closed Mon). Recommended.
⛾ **German Bakery**, MI Rd (steep road to Dharamkot), best bread and brown rice, open till 0100.
⛾ **Hot Spot**, near Bus Stand, for fast food.
⛾ **Kunga's/Nick's Italian Kitchen**, Bhagsu Rd. Good veg Italian. Quiches, pies etc, but some small portions.
⛾ **Moonlight** and **Sunrise**, opposite Tibetan Welfare Office, Bhagsu Rd. Small chai shops adjacent to each other with basic food. Excellent for meeting other travellers, especially in the evenings when overspill occupies benches opposite.
⛾ **Rangzen** (Freedom), Bhagsu Rd. Good health food, cakes.
⛾ **Tara Café**, Bhagsu Rd. Huge pancakes, friendly. Recommended.

Tibetan cookery
Sangye, at *Dreamland Hotel*, ssangye@hotmail.com. Runs 3 courses (soups, bread, momos), 1000-1200, 1700-1900, Rs 200 each. Friendly, fun, eat what you cook!

Bhagsu *p509*
Sri Guru Kirpa Restaurant, recommended for veg Indian and Chinese meals, or pizzas, though the spices can make you hit the roof.
The bakeries are really good.

Dharamkot *p509*
Pizza House, on the east side of the village. Pizzas and cakes.
Unity, towards Bhagsu. English owner creates amazing food, presented with style.

Kangra *p512*
Chicken Corner, Dharamshala Rd near the main bazar, an eccentric though fairly clean little hut does chicken dinners and acceptable breakfasts.

Dalhousie *p513, map p513*
Kwality, near GPO. Good Indian and Chinese if a bit pricey. Pleasant place with TV.
Milan, near GPO. Similar to *Kwality*. Very friendly, serves large portions.
Moti Mahal, on Subhash Chowk, north Indian.
New Metro, on Subhash Chowk, do good north Indian.
Snow Lion, near *Grand View*, Tibetan dishes.

Chamba *p514*
Several tea shops and **Ravi View Café**.

⊚ Entertainment

Dharamshala *p507, maps p507 and p510*
'Contact' is a monthly, free publication from *Hotel Tibet*, *Green shop* and *Khana Nirvana* listing details of courses, events etc.

Music and dance
TIPA (*Tibetan Institute of Performing Arts*), McLeodganj, stages occasional music and dance performances; details at Tourist Office.

Video halls
Two on Jogibara Rd, show western films; also documentaries on Tibet (look for posters/blackboards).

⊛ Festivals and events

Chamba *p514*
Gaddis and Gujjars take part in many cultural events to mark the start of harvesting.
Apr: Suhi Mela lasts 3 days. **Jul-Aug**: Minjar, 7-day harvest festival when people offer thanks to Varuna the rain god. Decorated horses and banners are taken out in procession through the streets to mark its start. Sri Raghuvira is followed by other images of gods in palanquins and the festival ends at the river Irawati where people float *minjars* (tassels of corn and coconut).

◯ Shopping

Dharamshala *p507, maps p507 and p510*
It is pleasantly relaxed to shop here. You are usually quoted a fair price from the start by the Tibetans. McLeodganj Bazar is good for Tibetan handicrafts (carpets, metalware, jewellery, jackets, handknitted cardigans, gloves); special Sunday market.

Green shop, Bhagsu Rd, sells recycled and handmade goods including cards and paper.
Tibetan Children's Villages (TCVs) outlets.
Tibetan Handicrafts Centre, ask at office for permission to watch artisans working on carpets, *thangkas* etc, reasonable prices.

Books and film
Bookworm, near *Surya Resort*, has a good selection of paperbacks, some second-hand.
Charitable Trust Bookshop, cards, books on Tibet and Buddhism.
DIIR, cards, books on Tibet and Buddhism.
Little Lhasa Bookshop, Temple Rd. Modern, computerized, same day service.
Moonpeak Pictures, Temple Rd. Modern, computerized, same day service.

Chamba *p514*
Handicrafts Centre, Rang Mahal. Rumal embroidery and leather goods.

⛰ Activities and tours

Dharamshala *p507, maps p507 and p510*
Meditation
Asho Spiritual Healing Institute, Bhagsu, T25320, hardeshsood@hotmail.com. Offers 10-day course on healing, 2 hrs per day, US$100 in season, less off season, maximum 6 people per course. Also Hindi lessons, Rs 100 per hr.
Himachal Vipassana Centre, Dhamma Sikhara, next to Tushita, T21309, info@sikhara. dhamma.org. 10-day retreat, meditation in silence, donations only, reserve in advance, information and registration Mon-Sat 1600-1700. Interesting **"Z Meditation"** course including yoga and meditation. Retreats offered in silence with separate discussion sessions, 5 days (starting Mon 1600 until Sat 1100), Rs 3500 includes a 'humble' breakfast, highly recommended for beginners, run by friendly couple in peaceful location with beautiful views. Information and registration at 1230 only, past post office, down stairs of Yongling School, follow "ZM" signs.
Himalayan Iyengar Yoga Centre, Dharamkot. Offers 5-day course in Hatha yoga, starting every Thu at 0830. Information and registration Mon, 1330.
Tushita Meditation Centre, T21366, quietly located in Dharamkot village 2 km north of McLeodganj, offers individual and group

meditation; 10-day 'Introduction to Buddishm' including lectures and meditation (residential courses get fully subscribed), enquiries Mon-Sat, 0930-1130, 1300-1630, simple accommodation on site.

See also **Tibetan Library** above and **Tibet travel agent** below.

Horse trekking
Contact **Highpoint Adventures** at *Sagar Book Shop*, Bhagsu Rd. Half or full day round trips, Rs 500-800.

Tour companies
In McLeodganj:
Dhauladhar Travels, Temple Rd, T21158, F21246 dhauladhar@hotmail.com. Agents for *Indian Airlines*.
Bedi Travels, Mall Rd, T21359. For long distance buses.
Bhagsu, Bazar, STD/ISD, fax.
HPTDC luxury coach in season: Dharamshala to McLeodganj, Kangra Temple and Fort, Jawalamukhi, 1000-1900, Rs 200; Dharamshala to McLeodganj, Bhagsunath, Dal Lake, Talnu, Tapovan, Chamunda, 0900-1700, Rs 200. Tickets from HPTDC Marketing Office in Dharamshala.
Potala, Bhagsu Rd, T21378, helpful staff.
Tibet Tours, Temple Rd, T21539, F21528, pilgrimage tours, with lectures by eminent Buddhist lamas. Recommended.
Ways Tours & Travels, Temple Rd, T21910, F21775, waystour@vsnl.net. Most reliable, Mr Gupta is very experienced, professional service.

Trekking
Best season Apr-Jun and Sep-Oct.
Highland Trekkers, opposite Taxi Union, T21740. Organize treks for smaller groups.
Himalayan Trekkers, Dharamkot, T21260. Organize treks reliably for smaller groups.
Mountaineering Institute on Ml Rd, T21787. Invaluable advice on routes, equipment, accommodation and camp sites etc. Equipment and porters can be hired for groups of eight or more, reasonable charges. The Deputy Director (SR Saini) has described many routes in *'Treks and Passes of Dhauladhar and Pir Pinjal'*, (Rs 150) although the scale of maps can be misleading. Consult the author for detailed guidance. Mon-Sat, 1000-1700.
Yeti Trekking, Ml Rd, T21032. Organize treks reliably for smaller groups.

Dalhousie *p513, map p513*
Tours
HPTDC have daily tours during the tourist season to Khajjiar, 0900-1500, Rs 600 (car for 5) or Rs 85 by luxury coach; to Chamba, 1000-1900, Rs 120 by luxury coach; to Pathankot (one way) by luxury coach, Rs 120.

⊖ Transport

Dharamshala *p507, maps p507 and p510*
It is dangerous to drive at night in the hills. The roads are not lit and the risks of running off the edge are great.

Air
Nearest airport at Gaggal, 13 km (taxi Rs 250-300). **Indian Airlines** from Delhi (Mon, Wed, Fri), 1315, 1½ hrs (return to Delhi at 1500). Airport is due for expansion in 2001, which will allow larger 50-seater planes to land in place of 18-seaters used presently. It may also allow for further connections.

Bus
Local Between Dharamshala and McLeodganj, 10 km, 30 mins' bus ride, Rs 6.
Long distance Most originate in Dharamshala, but some super and semi-deluxe buses leave from below the taxi stand in McLeodganj. HPTDC luxury coach (in season): to **Dalhousie** and **Chamba**: 0730, Rs150, 9 hrs; **Manali**: 0900, Rs 250, 8 hrs. HRTC buses to **Baijnath**: 2½ hrs, Rs 25; **Chandigarh**: (248 km), 9 hrs, via Una (overnight stop possible); **Delhi** (Kashmir Gate, 521 km), Deluxe coach departs McLeodganj 1630, 1815, 1930, 14 hrs, Rs 250; departs Delhi at same times. 1930, arrives Lower Dharamshala 1000, recommended for best morning views of the foothills (stops en route); Super Deluxe Coach to Connaught Place, 1900, Rs 350. Also deluxe buses to **Dehra Dun**: 2000, Rs 260 and **Shimla**, 2130 (from Dharamshala), Rs 230. **Kangra**: 50 mins, Rs 11; **Kullu** (214 km) 10 hrs; **Manali** (253 km) 11 hrs, Rs 130 (private Rs 250); best to travel by day (0800), fabulous views but bus gets overcrowded; avoid sitting by door where people start to sit on your lap! Always keep baggage with you; **Pathankot** (90 km) 4 hrs, connection for Amritsar, 3 hrs; **Shimla** (317 km, via Hamirpur/Bilaspur) 10 hrs. **Private buses** service **Dalhousie**: 0740, 6 hrs, Rs 125; **Delhi (Connaught Place)**: 1800,

1900, 11 hrs, Rs 350; **Dehra Dun**: 1900, 12 hrs, Rs 350; **Manali**: 0900, 2100, 8 hrs, Rs 250. Several private agents, although **Bedi Travels** have buses in the best condition (just!).

Taxi
Local Shared by 4, pick up shuttle taxi at Kotwali Bazar on its way down before it turns around at the bus stand, as it is usually full when it passes the taxi stand.
Long distance Can be hired from near the bus stands. Full day (80 km), Rs 800; between Dharamshala and McLeodganj, Rs 90.

Train
Nearest broad gauge railhead is at Pathankot; booking office at bus stand, 1000-1100 (no computer). For narrow gauge, see page 511.

Palampur p511
Air
The nearest airport is at Gaggal, 28 km with flights from Delhi (Mon, Wed, Fri).

Bus
Chandigarh, 265 km (via Nangal, Una, Kangra), 5½ hrs; Delhi, 535 km, 10 hrs. From **Delhi ISBT**, overnight deluxe bus. To **Andretta** (Private) from the bus station. **Dharamshala**, State buses from near the Nehru statue at the top of the main street.

Train
The town is 5 km from the railway station (taxi Rs 50). From Pathankot (narrow gauge) *Kangra Queen*, 0820, 4½ hrs, return departs Palampur 1345, via Kangra and Jawalamukhi, Rs 330 or Rs 190; see box above.

Kangra p512
Air
Gaggal airport 7 km away, has flights from Delhi (Mon, Wed, Fri).

Bus
Dharamshala: Rs 10, bus stand about 1 km to temple; you can cross the railway track and follow the path all the way down to the road bridge, way below; stop the bus to Dharamshala on the opposite side of the bridge (under 1 hr).

Taxi
Dharamshala Rs 400.

Train
Avoid arriving at either of the train stations after dark as they are isolated.
   Narrow gauge: to **Pathankot**: 0540, 0907, 1136, 1608, 1755, 1928, 4½ hrs; to **Baijnath**: 0807, 1038, 1817, 2027; to **Jogindernagar**: 0628, 1508; from **Pathankot**: 0435, 0835, 0921, 1300, 1600, 1800, 5 hrs (often 1 hr late!); continues to **Baijnath**, 2¼ hrs. The faster *Kangra Queen* from Pathankot, 0820, goes to Palampur. Kangra station serves Old Kangra with the fort, near the main road, while Kangra Mandir station is near the temple, bazar and most of the hotels. During the day there are regular rickshaw shuttles between Kangra Mandir station and Tehsil Chowk, Rs 3.

Dalhousie p513, map p513
Dalhousie is on NH1A. From: **Delhi** (559 km); **Chandigarh** (336 km); **Shimla** (414 km).

Bus
Long distance Chamba (56 km via Khajjiar) 1½ hrs; **Dharamshala** (180 km, 7 hrs via Gaggal on the Shimla bus, change at Gaggal, 30 mins from Dharamshala); **Pathankot** 120 km, 3 hrs.

Jeep
From bus stand, up to Gandhi Chowk, Rs 50, Bakrota Rs 90.

Train
Nearest station is at Pathankot, 2 hrs by taxi.

Chamba p514
Bus
Arrive at the north end of the Chaugan. **Dalhousie** (2 hrs plus stop in Khajjiar); direct to **Amritsar**, 0745, 8 hrs.

Jeep
Hire is relatively expensive. Special service during Manimahesh Yatra (see below).

● Directory

Dharamshala p507, maps p507 and p510
Banks Bank of Baroda, Kotwali Bazar. For Visa/Mastercard cash advances, order or ring T23175 with details, collect on next working day (Rs 100, plus 1% commission). State Bank of India,

Dharamshala and McLeodganj, changes TCs, 1000-1400, Sat 1000-1200. **Western Union**, near bus stand, McLeodganj, T704279, F707652. For money transfer and exchange, 1000-1930. **Hospitals** Delek Hospital, above Gangchen Kyishong, T21626, often foreign volunteer doctors, good for dentistry. District Hospital, Dharamshala, T22333. Men Tse Khang (Tibetan Medical Inst) T22484, Gangchen Kyishong, for Tibetan herbal medicine. Dr Dolma's and Dr Dhonden's clinics, near McLeodganj Bazar for Tibetan treatment. **Internet** Those with several machines are normally more reliable but power cuts and disconnections are not uncommon. **Post office** GPO, 1 km below tourist office on Main Rd, Mon-Sat, 1000-1630, another in Kotwali Bazar. In McLeodganj, the post office, Jogibara Rd, has poste restante (0900-1700, Sat 0900-1500). **Tourist offices** HPTDC Marketing Office, Kotwali Bazar, near Bus Stand, T24212, F24928. Mon-Sat, summer 0830-2100, winter 0900-2000, lunch 1330-1400, helpful. **Hotel Tibet** also has good information. In McLeodganj: HPTDC Tourist Information, behind post office. Mon-Sat, 1000-1700, not very useful. **Useful addresses** Foreigners' Registration Office: Civil Lines, Dharamshala, beyond GPO, near petrol pump. **Police:** T22150.

Palampur *p511*
Bank None changes money. **Tour operator** Golden Oriole, Nachhir, T/F32151, for treks.

Dalhousie *p513, map p513*
Banks Punjab Bank, Court Rd, changes TCs. **Hospital** Civil Hospital, T42126. **Post office** GPO: Gandhi Chowk. **Tourist offices** HP, near Bus Stand, T42136, 1000-1700, but opening irregular.

Chamba *p514*
Bank State Bank of India, Court Rd, Punjab Bank, Hospital Rd, change Amex TCs. **District commissioner** T22221. **Tourist office** *Hotel Iravati*, T22671. **Travel agents** Manimahesh, Lakshminarayan Temple Lane, T22507. Offers treks. **Thakur Taxis**, near Bus Stand, T22755, for sightseeing and touring.

★ Trekking in Himachal

Trekking from Shimla

From Shimla on the Hindustan-Tibet Highway, there are opportunities for short and long treks. These include **Chharabra**, 13 km beyond Shimla at 2,593 m and **Naldera**, 23 km from Shimla, which was Curzon's summer retreat, see page 466.

Still further on at **Narkanda**, 64 km from Shimla, is another trek with very good walks, especially up Hattu Peak. From Narkanda the road runs down to the Sutlej valley and enters Kinnaur and Spiti. Foreigners are allowed into Spiti with permits.

From just beyond Narkanda you can trek northwest over the **Jalori Pass** (3,350 m) in the **Seraj** region. Starting from Ani village reached by bus/jeep from Luhri in the Sutlej Valley below Narkanda, you trek into the lower part of the Kullu Valley, joining the Kullu-Manali road at Aut. There is a jeepable road over much of this route. An alternative is to proceed 65 km from Narkanda to **Rampur** and then trek into the Kullu Valley via the **Bashleo Pass** (3,600 m). There are forest rest houses en route so a tent is not essential. The pass is crossed on the third day of this five-day trek. Both treks end at **Banjar** in the Tirthan Valley from where there are buses to Kullu.

Trekking in Lahul, Kinnaur and Spiti

The border areas are being opened to trekkers with permits. At the same time the local tribal people are being exposed to outside influences which started with the introduction of television in these valleys. Now enterprising families open their homes to paying guests, youths offer their services as guides and muleteers and shops stock bottled drinks and canned food. However, anyone trekking in this region is advised to carry food, tents and all essentials.

Lahul

Lahul (and Zanskar and Ladakh) are ideal trekking destinations during the monsoon as they are not nearly as wet as most other regions. The best time to go is from mid-June to mid-October but some passes, eg Shingo-La, Parvati Pass, may remain snow bound until mid-July or even later.

You can take a trek from **Darcha**, see page 505, up the valley over the **Shingo La** and on to **Padum**, the capital of the Zanskar region. Padum is linked with Leh. Shingo La is over 5,000 m so some acclimatization is desirable. The route is well marked.

An alternative route to Zanskar is up the Chandra valley and over **Baralacha La**. From here a trail leads over a high pass to Phuktal, where you join the main trail coming from Darcha. Most travellers drive into Darcha; however, a fine trek past the 'Lake of the Moon' or Chandratal makes a nice and less known addition for those with a little more time. The route taken from **Manali** is over the **Hamta Pass** with good views of Deo Tibba (6,001 m), weather permitting, to **Chhatru** village in the Chandra Valley where a rest house has camping in the grounds and local families accommodate visitors in very basic homes. It is four days' trek from Manali. Two days along the dirt road brings you to **Batal** (to save time you can take the bus from Manali over the Rohtang Pass). The next stage of both variations is to Chandratal.

Chandratal (4,270 m) is 18 km from Batal. The first section up to Kunzum Pass is on the bus route. The remaining 8½-km trail is open June-October and brings you to the beautiful clear blue water lake, about a kilometre long and half a kilometre wide which lies on a glacial bowl. Carry your own tent and provisions. The lake can also be reached on a lower 14-km trail that directly runs from Batal (no regular buses from Manali).

From Chandratal the route crosses several fast flowing stream before reaching the Baralacha La (usually three days). You need to be very careful and take adequate safety precautions while negotiating these stream crossings. It then goes over another pass along the same ridge as the Shingo La, to join the main Darcha-Padum trail. From here you can continue on to **Padum** or return to Darcha in Lahul. This second option makes for a very good circular trek.

A third possibility is to trek down the Chenab Valley and either cross the Pir Panjal by one of a number of passes into the Ravi Valley via Bahrmaur, to Chamba or carry on to Kishtwar.

Lower Lahul You can trek from the district town of **Udeypur** at the base of the Miyar Nullah, the upper section of which is glaciated. To the east, high passes give access to the Bhaga valley and to the west to the Saichu Nala (Chenab tributary). The Trilokinath Temple nearby is well worth a visit, see page 504.

Trails run into the Miyar Nullah, renowned for flowers, then over the 5,100 m Kang La pass to Padum. Alternatively, you can follow the Chandrabhaga River to the scarcely visited Pangi valley with its rugged scenery and then over the 4,240 m Sach Pass leading to Chamba District.

Pangi Valley The Chandrabhaga flows at over 2,400 m after the two rivers meet in this desolate and craggy region. The cheerful and good-looking Pangiwals keep their unique heritage alive through their singing and dancing. The Mindhal temple to Devi is their focus of worship. **Kilar** is the HQ which has a rest house and the Detnag Temple nearby. From Kilar a wide trail follows the steep slopes above the Chandrabhaga (Chenab) River to Dharwas on the Himachal/Kashmir border and then onwards to **Atholi** in the Paddar region of Kishtwar, known for its sapphire mines.

Close to the Tibetan border on its east, Kinnaur has the Sutlej flowing through it. Garhwal is to the south, Spiti Valley to the north and Kullu to the west. See page 475. The rugged mountains and sparse rainfall makes Kinnaur resemble Lahul. The Kinners are Hindu but the Tibetan Buddhist influence is evident in the numerous gompas that can be seen alongside the temples. The *Phulaich* (*Festival of Flowers*) takes place in September when some villagers leave for the mountains for two days and nights to collect scented blossoms, then return on the third day to celebrate with singing and dancing. Kinnaur, including the lovely side valleys of **Sangla** and **Bhabha**, is now open with permits easily available from the District Magistrates in Shimla, Kullu or Keylong. These treks are immensely enjoyable; although there are stone huts and the occasional rest house, always carry a tent in this area.

Baspa Valley Starting from **Sangla** (2,680 m), you can take a fairly level forest walk up to Batrseri (5 km), then along the road up to Rakcham (8 km; 3,130 m) and climb gradually to reach **Chitkul** (18 km; 3,450 m), passing through Mastrang. Another option is to start at **Morang**, see page 477, which has a bus from Kalpa. The trail follows the Sutlej River bank for a short distance until the Tirung Gad meets it. Here it turns southeast and after going through a narrow valley reaches **Thangi**, a village connected to Morang by jeepable road where mules are available for hire. The track

Kullu Valley treks

Principal Trekking Routes

a Manali - Hamta Pass - Chhatru - Batal - Chandratal Lake - Baralacha La - Darcha - Shingola - Padum. (21 Days - 240 km)

b Manali - Sagordug Thach - Bara Bangahal - Holi - Chanaota Khas - (detour to Brahmaur) - Indrahar Pass - Triund - Dharamshala. (18 Days - 180 km)

c Manali - Solang - Tentu La - Manali Pass - Manali. (8 Days - 75 km)

0 km 5

0 miles 5

continues along barren hills to Rahtak (camping possible), before rising steeply to Charang Pass (5,266 m), then drops down following a mountain stream to Chitkul.

Bhabha Valley Another beautiful valley to trek, starting from **Kafnoo** (2,427 m), 22 km from Wangtu. Permit details have to be entered and stamped at the police post 1 km before Kafnoo reservoir. They are checked at Tabo.

There is level ground at the end of the road by the reservoir suitable for camping, but it can get flooded. Local guides available. From Kafnoo, the trail follows the right bank of the river for about a kilometre before crossing over to the left bank over a new bridge. From here, the trail gradually ascends to **Chokhapani** (known locally as Sholti), about a five-hour walk away. The riverside trail is slippery and not recommended. The upper trail climbs past Yangpa II then through fields around Musrang hamlet. There is an adequate campsite at Chokhapani (10 km, 3,000 m).

From Chokhapani to **Upper Mulling** (3,470 m) is a beautiful 8 km, four hours' walk (include lunch stop), following the left bank of the Bhabha stream. Initially going through forests the track then crosses open meadows. At the far end of the meadows is an ideal camping site by the river. The trail from Mulling enters a forested section leading to a snow bridge across the stream. Cross the stream and follow the steeply rising trail to the **Kara** meadows where the Government Animal Husbandry Department has a Merino sheep breeding centre. Ford the Bhabha River with care (either on horseback or by wading across with support from a fixed line), to the campsite at Pasha. This section takes three hours, so you can continue to the **Kara-Taria Pass Base**. The 5-km walk up a steep trail along the right fork of the Bhabha stream takes another four hours. Taria Base Pass (4,290 m) camp is below the steep slope leading to the Pass. Camp well away from the slope as it is prone to rock falls.

Pin Valley There is a steep descent over scree for the first kilometre from **Taria Pass**, followed by a five-hour 15-km walk along a narrow but clear trail to the first camp in the Pin Valley. None of the apparently promising campsites on the way has a good water source. The **Bara Boulder** site has a stream and good grazing for horses.

The 11-km stretch from Bara Boulder to **Mudh** (3,925 m) takes four hours. It is the highest permanently inhabited village in the Pin Valley and is surrounded by summer cultivation. Log bridges cross several streams feeding into the Pin River. There are places to stay and food is available but some villagers charge up to Rs 200-300 for a room. It is possible to camp outside the village. One campsite is on the flat plateau overlooking the river near the summer hut of the lay *lama* (before crossing the narrow foot bridge on the river), another is near the fields

d Manali - Naggar - Malana -
Manikaran - Kasol - Jari - Bijli
Mahadev - Naggar - Manali.
(9 Days - 140 km)

immediately below the village about the place where a side stream runs below the old monastery into the Pin. It is worth visiting the old gompas in the village.

From Mudh to **Gulling** is a gentle five-hour trek (15 km) along the right bank of the Pin. A single log bridge takes the path into Tilling village, followed by a gentle climb to the big village of **Sangam** on the opposite bank, see page 479. The track crosses a rocky spur and descends steeply to some small fields beside the river. Descend to the sandy river bed and cross diagonally to the single wire rope strung across the river. A makeshift pulley and harness crossing has to be rigged up here unless a suitable shallow spot can be found further downstream. Camp can be set up in the fields just below the road immediately above the crossing point.

From this point arrange to be picked up to drive to Spiti. You can visit the small but locally important Nyingmapa Gompa of Kungri (Ghungri), just above the road, and if you have an extra day based here you can walk up the short stretch of dirt road towards Sangam, then turn right into the virtually unknown Parahio River valley, an important tributary of the Pin.

Spiti

Meaning literally 'the place of Mani', Spiti is a high altitude desert, bare, rugged and inhospitable, with the Spiti River running from the slopes of Kunzum La (4,551 m) to Sumdo (3,230 m). Kunzum La offers seasonal access by road to Kullu from the valley, and it is also directly connected with Shimla via the NH22 and the SH30. Like neighbouring Lahul, Spiti is famous for its *gompas*. Foreigners are now allowed to trek in this region up to Kibber with permits, see page 467.

At **Tabo**, the Buddhist monastery is one of the region's most famous, see page 478. There is a dispensary and two adequate teashops. Foreigners are now allowed to stay overnight in Tabo. There are other important gompas at Dankar, Ki, Kungri and Lalung. Trekkers interested in **fossils** choose a trail starting at **Kaza** and travel to **Langza** (8½ km), which has a narrow motorable track. The trek goes to Hikim, the Tangyut monastery, Komik (8 km) and returns to Kaza (6 km). From Kibber (4,205 m) there is a 6-km track through alpine meadows to **Gete** (4,520 m) which claims to be one of the highest permanent settlements in the world only reached on foot.

Trekking in the Kullu and Parvati Valleys

Treks here vary in duration and degree of difficulty. There are pleasant walks up the subsidiary valleys from Aut and Katrain with the opportunity to camp in spectacular and high locations without having to spend very long getting there. An option is to take the bus up to the Rohtang Pass, 51 km from Manali, which is very spectacular and then walk down. There is a path, and it only takes a few hours.

The post-monsoon period (September to mid-November) is the most reliable **season**. Longer treks with crossings of high passes can be undertaken then, before the winter snows arrive. During the monsoon (June to September) it is wet but the rain is not continuous. It may rain all day or for only an hour or two. Visibility is affected and glimpses of mountains through the clouds are more likely than broad clear panoramic views. However, many flowering plants are at their best. There is trekking in the spring, that is April to May, but the weather is more unsettled and the higher passes may still have quite a lot of snow on them. There can be very good spells of fine weather during this period and it can get quite hot in May.

You will need to take your own **equipment** since that hired out by local agencies is often of an inferior quality. Kullu now has pony unions with fixed rates for guides, porters and horses. Ask at the Tourist Office and the Mountaineering Institute for information and assistance.

The valley of the Gods

No one knows the origin of the village of Malana. People believe that a band of renegade soldiers who deserted Alexander's army in the 4th century BC settled here (some wooden houses have soldiers carved on them); it is more probable that their antecedents were from the Indian plains. Their language, Kanashi, has no script but is linked to Tibetan. The villagers are directly involved in taking decisions on important matters affecting them, thus operating as an ancient democratic 'city state'. Language,

customs and religious practices too differ from neighbouring hill tribes, polygamy being permitted.

A charming myth is associated with Jamlu, the principal deity in the valley. Jamlu, possibly of pre-Aryan origin, was carrying a casket containing all the important deities of Hinduism and while crossing the mountains through the Chandrakhani Pass into Kullu, a strong gust of wind blew open the box and spread the deities all over the valley. Since then Malana has been known as 'The Valley of the Gods'.

Routes

From **Manali** you can go north into **Lahul** (Map trek **a**) and **Spiti** Valleys by crossing the Rohtang (3,985 m) or the Hampta Pass (4,270 m). Once over the great divide of the Pir Panjal the treks are as briefly described – see Trekking in Lahul, Kinnaur and Spiti above. West of Manali there are routes into the **Chamba** and **Kangra** Valleys (Map trek **b**).

Malana Valley The trek to Malana Valley offers an opportunity to see a relatively isolated and comparatively unspoilt hill community. From Manali you go to Naggar (28 km, which can also be reached by bus) and stay at **Rumsu** (2,377 m) which is higher. The Chandrakhani Pass (3,500 m) takes you into the Malana Valley at the head of which is the glacier. On the third day you can reach **Malana** (2,650 m, 20 km from Naggar), which has two guest houses. In the past you could only enter with permission from the villagers but this is no longer needed. On the fourth day you trek to **Jari** (1,500 m) where you can catch a bus to Kullu. The road from Jari to Malana may destroy the uniqueness of the community. The whole of the Malana Valley is dominated by **Deo Tibba** peak in the north.

Parvati Valley

To extend the trek from Malana it is possible to continue to **Manikaran** and onwards to Pulga and beyond in the scenic Parvati Valley. You can also get to Manikaran by bus from Kullu, see page 488. Up to **Khirganga** the trail is fairly clear but take care since the area is prone to heavy rain and land slips. Beyond Khirganga, the trek follows the valley up-river passing the tree line to Pandav Bridge and eventually arriving at the sacred lake and shrine at **Mantalai**. Here it splits leading up and over the Pin-Parvati Pass, and down into the dry Pin Valley.

Alternatively, you can explore the lower Parvati Valley by walking to **Kasol**, and then to Jari and Naggar via the temple of Bijli Mahadev (Map trek **d**).

Pin Valley

The difference between the Parvati and the Pin Valley is striking. Immense glaciers and bizarre moonscape rock formations here contrast with the verdant pastures and evergreen forests of the Parvati valley behind. The trek leads down to the traditional village of **Mudh**, see page 526. The road to Mudh is still incomplete so it takes about five hours to walk to Sangam and Chatral, leading to Kinnaur and Spiti. There are buses from Chatral to Kaza, see page 479. The trek from Manikaran to Kaza with passes over 5,300 m, can take 10-14 days. Guides and porters are necessary.

Trekking in Kangra

Baijnath, **Palampur** and **Dharamshala** are popular starting points. See page 508. From here you go over the **Dhaula Dhar** at passes such as the Indrahar and Minkiani (both from Dharamshala) and the Waru (from Palampur), then enter a feeder of the Upper Ravi Valley.

Midway up the valley which lies between the Manimahesh Dhar and Dhaula Dhar ranges is Bara Bangahal. From there you can go downstream to **Chamba** or upstream which offers the choice of at least three passes for crossing into the Kullu Valley. The northernmost of these is the Solang Pass which passes Beas Kund beneath Hanuman Tibba. In the middle is the Manali Pass whilst the southernmost is Sagar Pass. A good trip which includes the upper part of this valley is the round trip trek from Manali, see page 527.

> ‡ *There are very pleasant day walks throughout the Kangra Valley. Longer, more arduous treks are north over the Dhaula Dhar to Chamba or the Kullu Valley.*

Trekking from Chamba

The Chamba region receives less rain than the Kangra Valley to the south. A trek, particularly over the Pir Panjal into Lahul is possible during the monsoon months (June-September). The ideal season, though, is just after the monsoon. There are several short and longer treks from Chamba and Bahrmaur in the Upper Ravi Valley.

Pir Panjal To the north there are three main passes over the Pir Panjal into Lahul: the Kalicho, Kugti and Chobia Passes. At least five days should be allowed for crossing them as their heights are around 5,000 m and acclimatization is highly desirable. All the first stages of the walks are along the Budhil River. After the first two days, the services of a guide or porters are recommended for picking the right trail. Views from the passes are very good both of the Himalaya to the north and the Chenab Valley to the south. The descent from the passes is very steep. On reaching the road you can take a bus from **Udeypur** or **Trilokinath** in the Pattan Valley, to the Kullu Valley over Rohtang Pass. Several trails cross the high passes over the Pir Panjal range to give access to the Pattan valley of Lahaul. The semi nomadic Gaddi shepherds regularly use these to take their flocks across to the summer grazing grounds located in the high side valleys of Lahaul.

Bahrmaur (1,981 m) Also spelt Brahmaur or Bharmaur is 65 km from Chamba and can be reached by bus. It was the original capital Brahmapura for four centuries and has 8th-10th-century *Pahari* style temples. The best known are the Lakshminarayan group which is the centre of worship for the semi-nomadic Gaddi tribe. From Bahrmaur a three-day trek is possible to **Manimahesh Lake** (3,950 m), 34 km, in the Manimahesh Kailash (5,575 m), a spur running off the Pir Panjal. The **Manimahesh Yatra** begins in Chamba and ends at the lake, revered by local people as a resting place of Siva. Pilgrims arrive at the Manimahesh temple here and take a holy bath a fortnight after *Janmashtami* (September/October). The temple has a brass *Mahisasuramardini* image. During the *yatra* period buses, minibuses and taxis are laid on from Chamba to Bahrmaur. Many pilgrims trek the next 12 km to Hadsar although jeeps are available. From here it is a two-day climb to the lake with a night halt at Dhanchho. Himachal Tourism tents available at Bahmaur and there is also a rest house, Hadsar, Dhanchho and Manimahesh; contact tourist office, Dalhousie, T2136. Ponies and porters can be hired at each place. The nine-day trek starting from Chamba includes **Rakh** (20 km) on Day 1, **Bahrmaur** on Day 2, a rest stop there, then continuing to **Hadsar** (12 km), **Dhanchho** (7 km) and **Manimahesh** (7½ km) with a brief halt at **Bhairon Ghati**. The return is by the same route.

Jammu and Kashmir

Introduction

Jammu and Kashmir, the contested jewel of South Asia's northernmost region, has seen its astonishingly beautiful valleys and mountains repeatedly scarred by political dispute. Its **lakes**, fertile **valleys** and remote, **snow-covered peaks** have drawn rulers, pilgrims and ordinary travellers from the Mughals onwards.

Tragically, the beauty of the Vale of Kashmir has been effectively out of bounds for over fifteen years. However, the state has other fascinating and accessible regions, set in some of the world's most beautiful scenery. The spectacular high altitude deserts of **Ladakh** and **Zanskar** provide the setting for a hardy **Buddhist culture**, whose villages and monasteries retain strong links with Tibet. **Alchi**, **Hemis** and **Thikse** are just three of the most striking of the many **monasteries** clinging to mountainsides, and some of the highest altitude passes in the world allow entry to one of India's least known regions.

Sadly, although the major pilgrimage to **Amarnath** is massively guarded by the army, treks in the region cannot be regarded as safe. It is currently almost impossible to **trek** in Jammu and Kashmir, though it is still possible to get into Ladakh.

All foreigners entering the Vale of Kashmir and Ladakh are required to register their arrival. Despite the fact that visitors still go to the Vale of Kashmir there is a very obvious military presence and frequent acts of violence. Do not believe those touts and 'travel agents' in Delhi and elsewhere who will try to persuade you that everything is normal and perfectly safe in the Vale. It is not.

★ **Don't miss...**

1. The **Manali to Leh road** is a must for adrenalin junkies with some interesting monasteries to visit, page 547.
2. If it's safe, go to **Vaishno Devi**. Many visitors find the yatra very moving, page 539.
3. Mysterious dust-covered **Leh** is fascinating. Don't miss out on the bazar but remember to bargin hard, page 560.
4. Stay overnight and attend morning prayers at **Hemis**, the largest of the Ladakh monasteries, page 548.
5. **Alchi** is another important monastery that's well worth a visit, page 550.
6. If you have the time (and energy), trek from **Spituk** to **Hemis**, page 553.

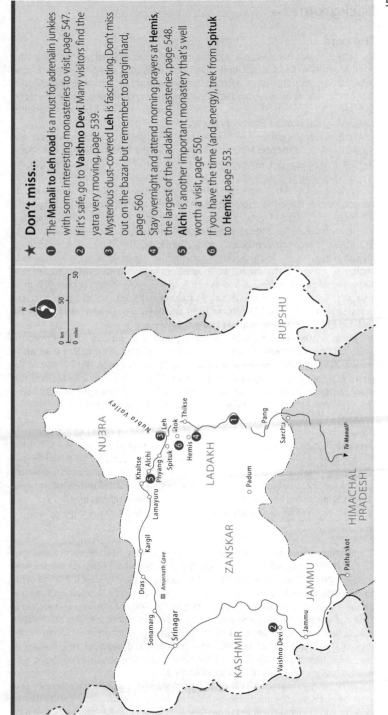

Jammu & Kashmir

Background → *Population: 10.1 million. Area: 222,000 sq km.*

The land

The largest of India's Himalayan states comprises three regions: Jammu, the mainly Hindu foothills in the south, the borderland with the Punjab and the transitional zone between the plains and the mountains; the **Vale of Kashmir**, overwhelmingly Muslim in the centre, lying between the Pir Panjal and the High Himalaya, where the Nagin and Dal lakes dominate Srinagar; **Ladakh** and **Zanskar**, the predominantly Buddhist western highlands of the great Himalayan axis.

Four mountain ranges cross Ladakh – Gt Himalaya, Zanskar, Ladakh and Karakoram – as do the river Indus and its tributaries the Zanskar, Shingo and Shyok. The Zanskar runs its course of 120 km before joining the Indus at Nimmu near Leh, the capital of Ladakh. During the winter months the frozen Zanskar provides the only access for Zanskaris into Ladakh. Ladakh also has the world's largest glaciers outside the polar regions, and the large and beautiful lake Pangong Tso, 150 km long and 4 km wide, at a height of over 4,000 m, predominantly Buddhist. Zanskar has two subsidiary valleys, the Stod (Doda Chu) and the Lung-Nak – Valley of darkness (Tsarap Chu) which converge below Padum, the capital. The Zanskar River flows along the valley from Padum to Zangla, then cuts through the Zanskar range in a series of impressive gorges to join the Indus. The main valley is approximately 300 km long and is ringed by mountains so access to it is over one of the high passes. The most important are the Pensi La connecting Zanskar with the Suru Valley in the west, the Umasi La with the Chenab Valley in the south and the Shingo La with Lahul in the east. This makes for very spectacular trekking country.

Jammu is the borderland with the **Punjab**, and the transitional zone between the plains and the mountains. To the north the Shiwaliks give onto the Pir Panjal which attain heights of 5,000 m. The Vale of Kashmir, lies between the Pir Panjal and the High Himalaya, at an average altitude of 1,580 m. Rising behind the Vale are the Great Himalaya which culminate in the west with Nanga Parbat ('Naked Mount' – 8,125 m). The Nagin and Dal lakes dominate Srinagar. Nearby is Anchar Lake.

Climate Even in the Vale, the air in summer is fresh and at night can even be quite brisk. The highest daytime temperatures in July rarely exceed 35°C but may fall as low as -11°C in winter. A short climb quickly reduces these tempertures. In Ladakh the sun cuts through the thin atmosphere, and daily and seasonal temperature variations are even wider. The rain-bearing clouds drifting in from the Arabian Sea never reach Ladakh. Srinagar receives over 650 mm per annum whereas Leh has only 85 mm, much as snow. Over half Srinagar's rain comes with westerly depressions in the winter.

History

Ruled for many years by Scythian and then Tartar princes, **Kashmir** was captured by Shams ud Din in 1341 who spread Islam across the Vale which subsequently became popular with the Mughals. Babur longed for the streams and cool mountain air of the Hindu Kush. In 1588 the Mughal Emperor Akbar conquered Kashmir and his son Jahangir (1605-27), captivated by the beauty of the Vale of Kashmir, planted chenar trees and constructed pleasure gardens. At the close of the first Sikh War in 1846 Jammu, the Vale of Kashmir, Ladakh, Baltistan and Gilgit were assigned to the Maharaja Gulab Singh of Jammu, who founded a dynasty of Dogra Rajputs, descended from the Katoch branch of the lunar race of Rajputs. Thus, Hindus ruled a mainly Muslim population of the Vale of Kashmir.

Rock carvings in Ladakh indicate that the region has been used for thousands of years by nomadic tribesmen who include the Mons of North India, the Dards, the Mongols and Changpa shepherds from Tibet. In Roman times Kashmir and Ladakh lay on a feeder of the great Silk Road that ran from China to the Mediterranean. By the end of the 10th century, Ladakh was controlled by the Thi Dynasty which founded a capital at Shey and built many forts. Tibetan Lamaistic Buddhism took hold at the same time and over 100 gompas were built. In 1533 Soyang Namgyal united the whole region up to the outskirts of Lhasa and made his capital at Leh. The Namgyal Dynasty still exists today and the Rani (Queen) of Stok was elected to the Indian Parliament. During the reigns of Senge Namgyal (circa 1570-1620) and Deldan Namgyal (circa 1620-60) Ladakh was threatened from the south and west by the Baltis, who had enlisted the assistance of the Mughals. They were beaten back and the Namgyals extended Ladakhi power. The expansionist era came to an end when the fifth Dalai Lama of Tibet, Nawang Lobsang Gyatso (1617-82) persuaded the Mongols, whom he had converted to Buddhism, to enter a military campaign against West Tibet and Ladakh. The Ladakhis were unable to repel the invading Mongol forces and in desperation Delegs Namgyal turned to Kashmir for help. The Mughal Governor of Kashmir sent troops to help the King of Leh regain his throne but in return he had to pay regular tribute and build a mosque. From then on the country became an extension of the Mughal Empire. In 1834 Zorwar Singh, an Army General, conquered Ladakh and brought the area under the control of the Dogra Maharajah of Kashmir. The dethroned royal family received the Stok Palace where they still live today.

Zanskar became an administrative part of Ladakh under Senge Namgyal whose three sons became the rulers of Ladakh, Guge and Zanskar/Spiti. This arrangement collapsed after Ladakh's war with Tibet and the Zanskar royal house divided, one part administering Padum, the other Zangla. Under the Dogras, the rulers were reduced to puppets as the marauding army wreaked havoc on the villages, monasteries and population.

Independence Kashmir's future remained unresolved at Independence. Eighteen months of fighting in 1948-49 left the state split by a UN monitored ceasefire line, much of which remains the de facto border between India and Pakistan. Of the total area of the pre-Independence State, over which India continues to claim the legitimate right to govern, 78,000 sq km are currently controlled by Pakistan and a further 42,600 sq km by China. Kashmir has remained the single most important cause of conflict between the two countries ever since 1949, while arguments for autonomy within the Kashmir Valley have periodically dominated the political agenda. Since 1989 the Indian army has struggled to keep control against a Pakistan-backed militia.

Following India's independence and partition in 1947 Ladakh, like Kashmir, was divided. Indian and Chinese troops have been stationed on the eastern border since the Chinese invasion of Tibet in 1950-51. From the early 1950s Chinese troops were stationed in the Aksai Chin, which India also claimed, and without Indian knowledge built a road linking Tibet with Xinjiang. This was one of the two fronts in China's war with India in 1962, which confirmed China's de facto hold on the territory. India still disputes its legality. Since the 1962 war the Indian army has maintained a very strong presence in Ladakh. The strategic requirements of better links with the rest of India were primarily responsible for Ladakh being 'opened up' to some influences from outside.

In May 2002 tension between India and Pakistan over Kashmir nearly boiled over into war. A terrorist attack on the Indian Parliament in December 2001 led India to move over half a million troops to the border, and many in India demanded military strikes in response to what they claimed was continuing Pakistan support for cross-border terrorism. A further attack on a bus and an army post in Jammu in May raised worldwide fears of a full-scale war, possibly escalating to nuclear conflict. Following huge diplomatic pressure, the tension was beginning to ease and there are encouraging signs following the "cricket diplomacy" in the spring of 2004. However Jammu and and the Vale of Kashmir seem set to remain completely out of bounds for the foreseeable future.

Culture

Culturally the people of Jammu, Kashmir and Ladakh could scarcely be more different from each other. The tennine million people are unevenly scattered. The Vale of Kashmir has over half, whilst Ladakh is the most sparsely populated. Jammu was traditionally the seat of Dogra power and serves a largely Hindu population with its affinities more with the Punjab than the Vale. Kashmir marks the northernmost advance of Islam in the Himalaya while Ladakh is aptly named 'Little Tibet'. Ethnically the Ladakhis are of Tibetan stock. Indeed, it was once a province of Tibet and was governed in secular matters by an independent prince and in spiritual affairs by the Dalai Lama. Tibetan Changpas form the bulk of the population in central and eastern Ladakh. These nomadic herdsmen can be seen living in black yak-hair tents on the mountains with their yaks, goats and sheep. They still provide the fine pashm goat wool. The Mons, nomads of Aryan stock, introduced Buddhism and established settlements in the valleys. The Droks or Dards from the Gilgit area settled along the Indus valley and introduced irrigation; many converted to Islam 300 years ago. Most are cultivators speaking a language based on Sanskrit. The Baltis with Central Asian origins mostly live in the Kargil region. The Zanskaris are of the same stock as the Ladakhis and because of the sheer isolation of their homeland were able to preserve their Buddhist culture against the onslaughts of Islam. The majority of Zanskaris are Buddhist, though there are Muslim families in Padum, the capital, dating from the Dogra invasion.

Kashmiri is influenced by Sanskrit and belongs to the Dardic branch of the Indo-Aryan languages. Linguistically and physically Kashmiris are similar to the tribes around Gilgit in Pakistan. The Ladakhis physically reveal Tibetan- Mongolian and Indo-Aryan origins while their language belongs to the Tibetan-Burmese group.

Religion

In the Vale of Kashmir, 95% of the people are **Muslim**, the majority being Sunnis, while in Jammu over 65% are **Hindu**. In Ladakh, 52% are Lamaistic **Buddhists**. Most follow Mahayana Buddhism of theVajrayana sect with a mixture of Bon animism and Tantric practices. The Red Hat Drukpa (or Kagyupa) sect of Tibetan monastic Buddhists enjoy royal patronage. The reformist Yellow Hat sect are Gelugpa Buddhists, and like the Dalai Lama, wear a yellow head-dress with their maroon robes. The more ancient Nyingmapa Buddhist have their seat in Tak-thok. Ladakhi lamas may also be physicians, teachers and astrologers; they also work in the fields, as do the *chomos* (nuns). Nearly every family has a member who chooses to become a lama (often the third son) or a chomo. The most important in the Tibetan tradition are recognized reincarnate *lamas* (Trulku), who are born to the position. The Buddhist *gompas* (monasteries) are places of worship, meditation and religious instruction and the structures, often sited on spectacular mountain ridges, add to the attraction of the landscape while remaining a central part of Ladakhi life. Ladakh also has a large number of Shi'a Muslims, mainly in Kargil District, many being immigrant

⁝ Surviving in a harsh climate

An almost total lack of precipitation has meant that cultivation must rely on irrigation. The rivers have been harnessed but with difficulty as the deep gorges presented a problem. In Ladakh it is restricted to the areas immediately around streams and rivers, and altitude and topography determine the choice of crop. Barley forms the staple food while peas are the most common vegetable and apples and apricots the most popular fruits. Because of the harshness of the climate and lack of rain, the cropping season usually lasts from April to October. Apple and apricots grow well, with the latter being dried for the winter, the kernel yielding oil for burning in prayer-lamps. At lower altitudes, grape, mulberry and walnut are grown. Travellers venturing out of Leh are likely to see villagers using traditional methods of cultivation with the help of *dzos* and donkeys and implements that have not changed for centuries.

Livestock is precious, especially the yak which provides meat, milk for butter, hair and hide for tents, boots, ropes and dung for fuel. Goats, especially in the eastern region, produce fine *pashm* for export. The Zanskar pony is fast and strong and therefore used for transport – and for the special game of Ladakhi polo!

Kashmiris and Dards. Their mosques and imambaras, influenced by Persian architecture, can be found in Leh proper and villages nearby.

The foundation of Sani in the 11th century is recognized as the first monastery in Zanskar. Phugtal and Karsha date from the same period. The sects developed alongside those in Ladakh. The Gelugpa (Yellow Hat) order was established in the 15th century and monasteries at Karsha, Lingshet and Mune belong to this. The Drukpa sect set up monasteries at Bardan and Zangla and 'occupied' that at Sani. These have links with Stakna near Leh and the Gelugpa is associated with the Lekir monastery. Traditional Ladakhi and Zanskari life, even today, comes close to Gandhi's idealized vision of life in ancient India.

Handicrafts

Kashmir is renowned for its distinctive and fine **handicrafts**. Many of these developed when Srinagar was an entrepôt on the ancient trans-Himalayan trade route. High quality craftsmanship in India initially owed much to the patronage of the court and Kashmir was no exception. From the 15th century onwards, carpet making, shawl weaving and embroidery and decorative techniques were actively encouraged and the tradition grew to demands made at home and abroad. Since tourism has been severely affected in the Vale since 1989, Kashmiri tradesmen have sought markets in other parts of India.

Kashmir **shawls** are world renowned for their softness and warmth. The best are pashmina and shahtush, the latter being the warmest, the rarest and, consequently, the most expensive. Prized by Moghuls and Maharajas they found their way to Europe and through Napoleon's Egyptian campaign became an item of fashion in France. The craft was possibly introduced from Persia in the 15th century. Originally a fine shawl would take months to complete especially if up to 100 colours were used. The soft fleece of the pashmina goat or the fine under hairs of the Tibetan antelope were used, the former for pashmina (cashmere) shawls, the latter for shahtush. The very best were soft and warm and yet so fine that they could be drawn through a finger ring. The designs changed over the years from floral patterns in the 17th century to Paisley in the 19th century. The Mughals, especially Akbar, used them as gifts. However, with

Ladakhi dress

Ladakhis dress in *gonchas*, loose woollen robes tied at the waist with a wide coloured band. Buddhists usually wear dark red while Muslims and nomadic tribes often use undyed material. The head dress varies from the simple Balti woollen cap with a rolled brim and the traditional *gonda* (a high embroidered hat) to the snake-shaped ornate black lambskin *perak* worn by some women. Studded with turquoise and lapis lazuli these are precious enough to be handed down as heirlooms.

the introduction of the Jacquard loom, cheap imitations were mass produced at a fraction of the price but shawl weaving. The Kashmir shawls thus became luxury items, their manufacture remaining an important source of employment in the Vale, but they ceased to be the major export.

All trade in Shahtush and articles made from the wool of the Chiru is banned, hence buying and exporting an article is illegal.

Hand knotted **carpets** are available in pure wool and mixed with cotton or silk. The patterns tend to the traditional, the Persian and Bukhara styles being common, though figurative designs such as The Tree of Life are becoming increasingly popular. Young boys work with a master and it is common to hear them calling out the colour changes in a chant. Child labour in carpet making across North India is increasingly widely criticized. Government attempts to insist on limiting hours of work and the provision of schooling often seem to be ignored. A large carpet will take months to complete, the price depending on the density of knots and the material used, silk being by far the most expensive. The salesmen usually claim that only vegetable dyes are used and whilst this is true in some instances, more readily available and cheaper chemical dyes are commonplace. After knotting, the pile is trimmed with scissors, loose threads burnt off and the carpet washed and dried. Look for the rug mark awarded when no child labour is used.

Papier mâché boxes, trays, coasters make ideal gifts. Paper is soaked, dried in a mould, then painted and lacquered. Traditionally, natural colouring was used (lapis lazuli for blue, gold leaf for gold, charcoal for black) but this is unlikely today. The patterns can be highly intricate and the finish exquisite.

Other crafts include crewel work (chain stitching) on fabric, fur coats and 'Kashmiri silver' jewellery, silk and fine woodcarving, particularly on walnut wood.

Modern government

The state enjoys a special status within the union. As defined in Article 370 of the constitution, since 1956 Jammu and Kashmir has had its own constitution affirming its integrity. The central government has direct control over defence, external affairs and communications within the state and indirect influence over citizenship, Supreme Court jurisdiction and emergency powers. In normal times the state sends six representatives to the Lok Sabha and two members who are nominated by the governor to the Rajya Sabha.

In Ladakh, the local government body, the Ladakh Hill Council, has once again put forth a demand to the Indian Government to separate the district from the rest of the state of Jammu and Kashmir. Citing reasons of cultural uniqueness and the fact that they do not wish to be part of any separatist movement in Kashmir, the Ladakhis demand being made into an 'Union Territory' directly funded by the central government.

Srinagar → *Colour map 1, grid A2. Population: 894,900. Altitude: 1,730 m.*

Founded by Raja Pravarasen in the sixth century and beautifully located around a number of lakes, Srinagar, 'the beautiful city', is divided in two by the river Jhelum which is crossed by a number of bridges (*kadal*). Despite the name, the beauty of Kashmir has never been reflected in that of its main town. The city's daily life revolves around the river and Dal and Nagin lakes but the lack of tourists has led to neglect. In view of the present political situation this edition of the Handbook does not carry details of places to visit outside Srinagar. ▶▶ *For Sleeping, Eating and other listings see pages 540-542.*

Ins and outs

Getting there Srinagar has daily flights from Delhi via Jammu and weekly flights from Leh. The taxi transfer takes 45 mins. Buses from Delhi and Jammu arrive after a tediously slow trip with army escorts. This journey must be undertaken in daylight. See Transport, page 541, for further details.

Security A few travellers continue to visit Srinagar, some using the road to Leh to enter Ladakh. It is essential to be extremely careful. Moving around the town can be hazardous, especially after dark – only a few suitable hotels and houseboats are open; there are no bars, beer shops or cinemas and phone links with the rest of India, let alone overseas, are poor. Dusk-to-dawn curfews are not uncommon. It still may not be possible to visit some of the sites outlined below.

Climate Temperatures: Summer maximum 32°C, minimum 18°C. Heaviest rainfall in Mar (100 mm), lightest in Nov (10 mm). Best time to visit: May-Sep.

Sights

The **Jama Masjid** (1674) is notable for the wooden pillars supporting the roof, each made from a single *deodar* tree. To the southeast is the **Rozabal mosque**, which has the 'tomb of Jesus' (Holger Kersten's *Jesus Lived in India* recounts the legend). Across the river is the **Pattar Masjid** (1623) built for the Empress Nur Jahan and renamed Shahi Mosque. **Shankaracharya Hill** is behind the Boulevard. The temple was built during Jahangir's reign but is said to be over a second-century BC temple built by Asoka's son. The hill was known as Takht-i-Sulaiman – The Throne of Solomon.

Dal Lake is 6.4 km long and 4 km wide and is divided into three parts by manmade causeways. The small islands are willow covered, while round the lake are groves of *chinar*, poplar and willow. The Mihrbahri people have lived around the lakes for centuries and are market gardeners, tending the floating beds of vegetables and flowers that they have made and cleverly shielded with weeds to make them unobtrusive. Set in front of a triangle of the lake created by the intersecting causeways with a slender bridge at the centre lies the famous **Nishat Bagh** (Garden of Gladness). Sandwiched between the hills and the lake, it was laid out by Asaf Khan, Nur Jahan's brother, in 1632, see page 164.

Shalimar Bagh is about 4 km away and set back from the lake. A channel extends up to their edge. Built by Jahangir for his wife, Nur Jahan, the gardens are distinguished by a series of terraces linked by a water channel. These are surrounded by decorative pools which can only be reached by stepping stones. The uppermost pavilion has elegant black marble pillars and niches in the walls for flowers during the day and candles or lamps at night. **Chashma Shahi** (Royal Spring, 1632) is a much smaller garden built around the course of a renowned spring and is attributed to Shah Jahan though it has been altered over the centuries.

Hazratbal (Majestic Place) is on the western shore of the lake and commands excellent views. The modern mosque has a special sanctity as a hair of the **prophet**

⁝ The most expensive spice in the world

Pampore, 16 km from Srinagar, is the centre of Kashmir's saffron industry. Saffron, a species of crocus (Crocus sativus), grows here in abundance, and in a few other places in the world, and is harvested by hand. Within each purple bloom, the three orange-red anthers yield pure saffron. Over 4,500 blooms make one ounce (28 g) of the spice, so the price of this delicate flavouring and colouring in cooking is high (once far more valuable than gold). Its value has led the Indian Government to set up a saffron research farm at Sangla in Himachal Pradesh.

The precious orange coloured dye was used by royalty and the colour saffron was chosen by monks for their robes after the Buddha's death.

Mohammad is preserved here. Just beyond is the **Nazim Bagh** (Garden of the Morning Breeze), one of the earliest Mughal Gardens and attributed to Akbar.

Jammu → *Phone code: 0191. Colour map 1, grid A2. Population: 378,400.*

Jammu, the second largest city in the state, is the winter capital of government and main entry point for Kashmir by rail. Not an attractive city, with few open spaces and too much traffic, it is chaotic with little to recommend it.

Ins and outs **Getting there** There are flights from Delhi and Srinagar. The railway station is in the New Town, across the Tawi River, and a few kilometres from the old hilltop town where most of the budget hotels are located. The General Bus Stand where inter-state buses come in, is at the foot of the steps off the Srinagar Road in the Old Town. **Getting around** The frequent, cheap city bus service or an auto-rickshaw comes in handy as the 2 parts of the town and some sights, are far apart. See Transport, page 541, for further details. **Climate** Temperature: Summer, maximum 40°C, minimum 28°C. Rainfall: Jul-Aug 310 mm, other months average 40 mm. Best time to visit: Nov-Mar.

Sights The **Raghunath Temple** (1857) in the old centre is one of the largest temple complexes in North India. The temple has seven shrines, with gold plated interiors. The most important houses the Dogras' patron deity, Rama, Vishnu's eighth incarnation. The arches and architectural details show Mughal influence. Morning and evening *aartis* are ritually attended.

The **Rambiresvar Temple** (1883), centrally located about 500 m from the Dogra Art Gallery on the Shalimar Road, is dedicated to Siva. It has a 75-m tower and extraordinary crystal lingams and is the largest Siva temple in North India.

The **Bahu Fort** with its ruined ramparts stands on a rock face overlooking the river south of the city, the oldest remaining building in the region. The original structure was improved and

Jammu

Sleeping ■
1 Cosmopolitan
2 Jammu Ashok
3 Jewel & Cultural Academy
4 KC Residency
5 Mansar & Tawi View
6 Picnic
7 Premier & Chinese Room Restaurant

N
Not to scale

rebuilt as the Mondi Palace (circa 1880) by the Dogra rulers. Bagh-e-Bahu gardens around the fort has a cafetería. The Old Palace is now the **High Court**.

Amar Mahal Museum ① *winter 0900-1230, 1330-1700, summer 0900-1230, 1330-1800, Sun 1000-1200, closed Mon, Rs 5, fine views of the river but no photography, Rs 25 by auto-rickshaw,* superbly sited on the bend of the Tawi, is just off Srinagar Road. There is a portrait gallery, Pahari paintings of *Mahabharata* scenes and royal memorabilia. The early 20th-century palace is a curiosity; its French designer gave it château-like sloping roofs and turrets. Four rooms are open but you can look into others through the windows.

Vaishno Devi

→ *Colour map 1, grid A2. 61 km north of Jammu. Visitors joining the yatra find it a very moving experience.*
The Vaishno Devi cave is one of the region's most important pilgrim sites. As the temple draws near you hear cries of 'Jai Matadi' (Victory to the Mother Goddess). Then at the shrine entrance, pilgrims walk in batches through cold ankle-deep water to the low and narrow cave entrance to get a glimpse of the deity.

The main pilgrimage season is March to July. The arduous climb along the 13-km track to the cave temple has been re-laid, widened and tiled, and railings provided. Another road from Lower Sanjichat to the Darbar brings you 2 km closer with 300 m less to climb. Ponies, *dandies* and porters are available from Katra at fixed rates. Auto-rickshaws and taxis can go as far as the Banganga. Yatra slips issued by the Shrine Board in Katra must be presented at Banganga checkpoint within six hours. Tea, drinks and snacks are available on the route.

Visitors should leave all leather items in a cloakroom at Vaishno Devi before entering the cave; carry bottled water and waterproofs. If you are on your own or in a small group, to avoid a wait for a group allocation, present yourself at Gates 1 or 2, and smile. **Katra** is an attractive town at the foot of the Trikuta Hills where visitors to the Vaisho Devi cave can stay.

Srinagar to Leh Road

The road to Leh from Srinagar must be one of the most fascinating journeys in the world as it negotiates high passes and fragile mountainsides. There are dramatic scenic and cultural changes as you go from Muslim, verdant Kashmir to Buddhist, ascetic Ladakh. Because of political unrest in Kashmir, the route, which runs very close to the Line of Control, may be closed to travellers. The alternative route to Leh from Manali is equally fascinating, see page 502.

Sonamarg, 'Path of Gold', 84 km from Srinagar at an altitude of 2,740 m, is the last major town in Kashmir before the Zoji La and Ladakh. From Zoji La the road descends to **Minamarg** meadow and Dras. The winter temperatures go down to -50°C, and heavy snow and strong winds cut off the town. The broad Kargil basin and its wide terraces are separated from the Mulbekh valley by the 12-km long **Wakha Gorge**.

On the bank of the River Suru, **Kargil**, at 2,740 m, was an important trading post on two routes, from Srinagar to Leh, and to Gilgit and the lower Indus Valley. Before 1990 it was the overnight stop on the Srinagar-Leh highway, and in 1999 the Pakistan army took control briefly of the heights surrounding the town before being forced to retreat.

From Kargil the road goes on 30 km to **Shergol**, the cultural boundary between Muslim and Buddhist areas and then passes **Mulbekh** after another 9 km and **Namika La**, at 3,720 m, known as the Pillar in the Sky. It climbs to **Photu La** at 4,093 m, the highest pass on the route. From here you can catch sight of the monastery at Lamayuru. The road does a series of loops to descend to **Khaltse** where it meets the milky green Indus River.

In **Lamayuru**, the monastery, 10 km from Khaltse, is perched on a crag overlooking the Indus in a striking setting between a drained lake and high mountains. The complex, which includes a library, thought to be the oldest in the region, was founded in the 11th century and belongs to the Tibetan Kagyupa sect. The present monastery dating from the 16th century was partly destroyed in the 19th. You can still see some of the murals, the 11-headed and 1,000-armed Avalokiteshvara image, along with the redecorated *Du-khang* (assembly hall). There are caves carved out of the mountain wall and some of the rooms are richly furnished with carpets, Tibetan tables and butter lamps. Festivals are in February/March and July. There are daily buses from Leh. Sleeping at *Monastery Hotel* or a few guesthouses. They do meals too. Camping near the stream in a willow grove.

Rizong, 53 km away, has a monastery and nunnery, which may accommodate visitors. **Saspul** village marks the wide valley from which you can reach **Alchi** by taking a branch road across the Indus after passing some caves. **Lekir** is off the main road, 8 km after Saspul. Further along the road you catch sight of the ruins of **Basgo** before it crosses the Chargyal Thang plain with chortens and *mani* walls and enters **Nimmu**. The road rejoins the Indus valley and rises to another bare plateau to give you the first glimpse of Leh, 30 km away. **Phyang** is on a hill and finally **Spituk** is reached, see page 547 for details of monasteries.

There are check points on some routes and foreigners will need to register at Upshi (Manali-Leh) or Khaltse (Srinagar-Leh). Visitors from Leh approach Lamayaru along this road.

Listings: Srinagar

Sleeping

Srinagar *p537*
Since the clampdown in Kashmir many hotels are occupied by military personnel. It is impossible to give reliable information.
A-L Grand Palace, Gupkar Rd, T470101, F453794. 60 rooms in re-opened palace.
A Shah Abbas, Boulevard Rd, T479334, F476553, www.shahabbashotel.com. 84 rooms facing lake or mountains.
D Tourist Reception Centre, Maulana Azad and Sherwani Rds, T474060, F476107. Rooms and dorm in Hostel.
E Cathay, Khonkhun, Dal Gate, T474014.
E Shabnam, Khonkhun, Dal Gate, T451813.

Houseboats are peculiar to Srinagar and are moored along the shores of the Dal Lake, the quieter and distant Nagin Lake and along the busy Jhelum. In the valley's hey day the boats were well kept and delightfully cosy. Still mostly family run, they usually include all meals. It is best to see the boat and make sure what services are included before hiring.
Bambri Palace, Dal Lake, Gate 2, F475774, immaculate, Md Yusuf Khankashi takes excellent care, well-furnished.
Garden of Eden, Dal Lake, T475407, owned by a reliable family.
Gurkha Houseboats, Nagin Lake, T421001, F420655, gurkhahb@ndf.vsnl.net.in. Very comfortable with 4 bedrooms, excursions.

Jammu *p538, map p538*
B Asia Jammu-Tawi, Nehru Market, north of town, T535757, F535756. 44 rooms, good restaurant, exchange, pool, clean, comfortable.
C Hari Niwas Palace, 3.5 km from centre, T543303. 18 a/c rooms.
C Jammu Ashok, opposite Amar Mahal. 48 rooms, restaurant, pool.
C KC Residency, Vir Marg, T542773, F542779. 61 a/c rooms, excellent restaurant, exchange, pool.
D Cosmopolitan, Vir Marg, T547561. 28 rooms, some a/c, good restaurant, bar.
D Jewel, Jewel Chowk, T547630. 18 rooms, some air-cooled, restaurant (mainly fast food).
D Premier, Vir Marg, T543234. 21 rooms, some a/c, restaurants, bar.
D-E Tourist Reception Centre, Vir Marg, T549554. 128 rooms with bath, a few air-cooled, good value with best in Blocks NA and A, poor dorm restaurant.
E Tawi View, below Gummat, T543752. Few air-cooled rooms.

Vaishno Devi *p539*
This is a selection of over 50 places, in Kalva unless stated.
B Country Inn, modern.
C Asia Vaishnodevi, T01991-32061,

F33344. 37 rooms, some a/c, restaurant, transport to Banganga.

C-D Ambica, T01991-32062. 50 rooms, a/c.
D Durga, 30 rooms, restaurant.
E Prem, Main Bazaar, T32014. Rooms with hot water and a fire, adequate.
E Tourist Bungalow, T32009. 42 rooms.
E-F Retiring Centre, T32309. Rooms and dorm, near the bus stand.
F Dormitories, at the half-way point to Vaishno Devi. Simple rooms provide sheets and blankets. Excellent vegetarian food is available – curd and *panir* (curd cheese) dishes are especially good. For non-*dhaba* food try the 2 vegetarian fast food places on the main street. Both clean and good. No alcohol.

● Eating

Jammu p538, map p538
∀∀∀ KC Residency, in hotel. International. Bizarre revolving restaurant, trundles round with an occasional jolt but serves excellent food, good views.
∀∀ Cosmopolitan, in hotel. Good Chinese and Kashmiri.
∀ Amritsarian, in Raghunath Bazar. Veg.
∀ India Coffee House, Exhibition Ground.
∀ Kailash, in Raghunath Bazar. Veg.

O Shopping

Jammu p538, map p538
Wool tunics (*pherans*), fine pashmina shawls and woodcarvings are good, as well as dried fruit and nuts. Main shopping areas: Raghunath Bazar, Hari Bazar, Upper Gummat.

● Transport

Srinagar *p537*
Srinagar is on NH1A linked to the rest of India by all-weather roads, some through superb scenery.

Air
Srinagar Airport, 14 km, T430334. Taxi to town: Rs 300. Stringent security checks so arrive at least 2 hrs ahead for departure. **Indian Airlines** T450257, airport T431696, flies to **Delhi**, and **Jammu** daily (same flight); **Leh**, daily. **Jet Airways** T400001, airport T433035: **Delhi** via **Jammu** daily.

Bus
To **Jammu** (293 km), by a narrow mountain road, often full of lorries and military convoys, takes 12 hrs; few stops for food and facilities.
Long distance State Roadways buses run to **Jammu** from Delhi, Chandigarh and Amritsar; some continue to **Srinagar**. J&KSRTC, TRC, Srinagar, T72698. Summer 0600-1800, winter 0700-1700. Bus to **Kargil** (alternate days in summer, Rs 120-200), **Leh** (434 km, Rs 200-360).

Ferry
Shikaras (boats): Rs 30 per hr but some ask for Rs 60.

Train
The nearest railhead is Jammu Tawi with coach (12 hrs) and taxi transfer (9 hrs). Govt TRC, 0700-1900. T72698 for reservation of 2nd-Class Sleeper and a/c only. Summer 0830-1900, winter 1000-1800.

Jammu *p538, map p538*
Air
Rambagh Airport, 6 km. **Transport to town**: taxis (Rs 200) and auto-rickshaws. **Indian Airlines**, TRC, Vir Marg, T542735, Apt T430449, flies to **Delhi** and **Srinagar** daily; **Leh** (Mon, Fri). **Jet Airways**, *KC Residency Hotel*, T574312, T453999; to **Delhi** and **Srinagar** daily.

Bus
Sumos run to Katra from the station. J&K SRTC, TRC, Vir Marg, T546851 (1000-1700), General Bus Stand, T542666 (0400-2000) direct buses to **Srinagar** (293 km), **Katra (for Vaishno Devi), Pathankot** and **Kishtwar**. Punjab Roadways T542782. To **Delhi** (586 km), daily. **Srinagar** buses leave from the railway station, usually 0600- 0700.

Taxi
Un-metered, T533485. Tourist taxis, T542231.

Train
Station, T531085. To **Delhi (OD)**: *Jammu Tawi Mail*, 4034, 1535, 14¼ hrs; *Jammu Tawi Delhi Exp, 2404*, 1800, 10½ hrs. **Delhi (ND)**: *Jammu Tawi Indore Malwa Exp, 9368*, 0815, 10½ hrs; *Jhelum Exp, 1078*, 2135, 12¼ hrs; *Shalimar Exp, 4646/6700*, 2050, 14¼ hrs; *Rajdhani Exp, 2426*, Sat, 2030, 9 hrs. **Kolkata (Sealdah)**: *Jammu Tawi Exp, 3152*, 1850, 45 hrs.

Air
Pawan Hans may resume helicopter service
to Sanjichat.

Bus/taxi
Buses and taxis leave from General Bus
Stand, Jammu (or the railway station at peak
season) and go to Katra (48 km); Rs 25, a/c
Rs 55; taxi Rs 500 for 4.

☉ Directory

Srinagar *p537*
Travel agent Sita, *Hotel Broadway*,
Maulana Azad Rd, T477186, F452600.

Tourist office J&K, TRC, T452690,
F479548. **Useful addresses** Ambulance:
T474591. **Fire**: T472222. **Police**: T100.

Jammu *p538, map p538*
Banks State Bank of India, Hari Market,
among several. **Post office** GPO: Pacca
Danga. Post Offices in Old Palaces, near
Dogra Art Gallery and Raghunath Temple.
Tourist offices J&K Tourism, Tourist
Reception Centre, Vir Marg, T548172. **Jammu
Tawi**, Railway Station, T544842. JKTDC,
T546412. **Useful addresses** Fire: T101.
Hospital: T547637. Police: T100. **Foreigners'
Registration Office**: Supt of Police, Canal Rd,
T542676. Foreigners must register.

Ladakh

→ *Colour map 1, grid A3. Population: 175,000. Altitude: 2,500-4,500 m, passes at 4,000-6,000 m, peaks up to 7,500 m.*
*The mountains of Ladakh – literally 'many passes' – may not be as spectacular as
some parts of the high Himalaya, for as even the valleys are at an altitude of 3,500 m
the summits are only 3,000 m higher. Because it is desert there is little snow on them
and they look like big brown hills, dry and dusty, with clusters of willows and desert
roses along the streams. Yet for thousands of visitors Ladakh is a completely magical
place, remote, with delightful, gentle, ungrasping people.* ›› *For Sleeping, Eating and
other listings see pages 557-562.*

Ins and outs
Entry Permits For the recently opened areas of Nubra and Shyok Valleys and Drokhpa,
Khardung La, Tso-moriri and Pangong Tso, the permit costs US$20, while trekkers in the
Hemis High Altitude Park must pay Rs 25 (Indians Rs 10) per day. As a matter of course
you should carry your passport with you since Ladakh is a sensitive border region.

Inner Line Permits Areas which would normally be restricted but are open to tourists
include Rizong, Likir, Phyang, Shey, Thikse, Chemrey and Tak-thok gompas. A permit
is needed to visit the newly opened areas. Permits are available from the DC office in
Leh. Almost all monasteries in Ladakh now charge foreigners Rs 25 entry fee. The area
is virtually **cut off** for 6 months when roads become impassable; the only link with the
outside world is by air. The frozen Zanskar River, the 'Tchadar', links Padum with
Nimmu near Leh. Animal transport is provided by yaks, ponies, Bactrian camels and
the broad backed *hunia* sheep.

Climate The temperature can go down to -30°C in Leh and Kargil and -50°C in Dras,
remaining sub-zero from Dec to Feb. Yet on clear sunny days in the summer, it can be
scorching hot and you can easily get sunburnt. Rainfall is only 50 mm annually and
there are even occasional dust storms. Take plenty of sun cream.

Background
Until very recently Ladakhi society has generally been very introverted and the
economy surprisingly self-sufficient. Ladakh also developed a very distinct culture.
Polyandry (where a woman has more than one husband) was common but many men

⁙ Conversation to construction

If you are interested in **voluntary work**, get in touch with the different organizations in Leh (SECMOL, LEDeG). There is a range of possibilities around Leh for potential volunteers – from teaching English to construction work. Alternatively, contact Ladakh Project, Apple Barn, Week, Dartington, Devon TQ9 6JP, UK, or 850 Talbot Ave, Albany, CA 94796, USA. Farm volunteers with the Ladakh Project are welcome from May-October, for a minimum of a one-month to stay and work with a Ladakh farming family. A contribution of about US$200 plus a nominal amount for daily lodging is expected.

became *lamas* (monks) and a few women *chomos* (nuns). Most people depended on subsistence agriculture but the harsh climate contributed to very high death rates and a stable population. That is rapidly changing. Imported goods are increasingly widely available and more and more people are taking part in the monetary economy. Ladakh and its capital Leh have only been open to tourists since 1974 but some argue that already there are too many.

★ Leh → *Phone code: 01982. Colour map 1, grid A3. Population: 27,500. Altitude: 3,500 m.*

Mysterious dust-covered Leh sits in a fertile side valley of the Indus, about 10 km from the river. Encircled by stark awe-inspiring mountains with the cold desert beyond, it is the nearest experience of Tibet in India.

The old Palace sits precariously on the hill to the north and looms over Leh. The wide Main Bazar Street (circa 1840s), which once accommodated caravans, with two old gates at each end has a colourful vegetable market where remarkably unpushy Ladakhi women sell local produce on the street side while they knit or chat. Makeshift craft and jewellery stalls line parts of Fort Road to the east to attract summer visitors along with Kashmiri shopkeepers who have come in search of greener pastures. The Old Village, mainly to the east of the Main Street, with its maze of narrow lanes, sits on the hillside below the Palace and is worth exploring. ▸▸ *For Sleeping, Eating and other listings see pages 557-562.*

Ins and outs

Getting there For 7-8 months in the year Leh's sole link with the outside world is by air. Tickets are in heavy demand so it is essential to book well ahead (you can do this from home on the internet). From mid-Jun to end-Sep (weather permitting), in addition to air passengers and trekkers, the Manali-Leh Highway opens to traffic bringing travellers to the New Bus Stand, south of town. There are jeeps from here as well as from the airport.

Getting around Most hotels are within a few mins' walk of the Main Bazar St around which Leh's activities are concentrated. All the places of interest in Leh itself can also be tackled on foot by most visitors though those arriving by air are urged to acclimatize for 48 hrs before exerting themselves. For visiting monasteries and spots out-of-town arrange a jeep or taxi. See Transport, page 561, for further details.

⁙ *Given the darkness of many buildings even at midday it is well worth taking a torch wherever you go; a must at night.*

Jammu & Kashmir Ladakh Leh

Climate Temperatures: Summer maximum 25°C, min 10°C; Winter maximum -3°C, minimum -14°C. Rainfall is minimal all year, highest is 8 mm in Aug. Best time to visit: May-Sep.

History

The city developed as a trading post and market, attracting a wide variety of merchants – from Yarkand, Kashgar, Kashmir, Tibet and North India. Tea, salt, household articles, wool and semi-precious stones were all traded in the market. Buddhism travelled along the Silk Road and the Kashmir and Ladakh feeder, which has also seen the passage of soldiers, explorers and pilgrims, forerunners of the tourists who today contribute most to the urban economy.

Leh orientation

Related map
A Leh centre, page 546

0 metres (approx) 400
0 yards (approx) 400

■ **Sleeping**	6 Lhung-Se-Jung	11 Padma	17 Silver Cloud
1 Hills View	7 Lung Snon	12 Padmaling	18 Snow View
2 Himalayan	8 New Antelope	13 Rafica	19 Tsemo La
3 K-Sar Palace	Guest House	14 Rainbow	
4 Kangla	9 Omasila	15 Remo	● **Eating**
5 Lharimo	10 Oriental	16 Ri-Rab	1 Mona Lisa

⁚ Prepare for a different lifestyle in Leh

The whitewashed sun-dried brick walls of a typical two-storey, flat-roofed Ladakhi house, often with decorative woodwork around doors and windows and a carefully nurtured garden, look inviting to a traveller after a very long hard journey, whether by road or air. Local families are opening their homes to provide for the increasing demand for accommodation for a very short peak season and new hotels are springing up. These are listed by the Tourism Department as A-D class hotels or as guesthouses and must charge fixed rates. However, prices do not reflect the type of furniture, furnishings and plumbing you might expect elsewhere in India although on the whole the rooms are kept clean. There is usually a space for sitting out – a 'garden' with a tree or two, some flower beds and some grass struggling to establish itself.

Electricity is limited, so expect power cuts which are random and unpredictable. Some hotels have generators. Those without may run out of tap water but buckets are always at hand. Hot water is a luxury, available only during mornings and evenings. Plumbing allows for flush WCs in at least D category hotels but the water from the basin disappears down the plughole only to emerge around your feet as there is only one drain in a corner of the bathroom!

Guests are encouraged to economize on water and electricity – you will notice the low-power bulbs and scarcity of lights in rooms and public areas, so put away your reading until sunrise.

Sights

Leh Palace ① *Summer 0700-0930, and also sometimes 1500-1800, Rs 25*. Leh Palace has been described as a miniature version of Lhasa's Potala Palace. Built in the mid-16th century, the Palace was partly in ruins by the 19th century. It has nine storeys, sloping buttresses and projecting wooden balconies. From the town below it is dazzling in the morning sun and ghostly at night. Built by King Singe Namgyal and still owned by the royal family, it is now unoccupied – they live in the palace at Stok. Visible damage was caused during Zorawar Singh's invasion from Kashmir in the last century. Be careful of the hazardous holes in the floor. After a steep climb some find the Palace disappointing, but the views from the roof are exceptional.

A part of the palace is a **museum**. Like the Lhasa Potala Palace it has numerous rooms, steps and narrow passages lined with old *thangkas*, paintings and arms. The central prayer room (not in use), usually locked but opened on request, has religious texts lining the walls. The Archaeological Survey of India is responsible for restoration and you may be able to watch work in progress. There are many painted scrolls, murals and old manuscripts in the ruined palace

Gomptas The 15th-century **Tsemo Gompa** (*tsemo* – red) ① *0700-0900, Rs 25*, is a strenuous walk north of the city and has a colossal two-storey high image of *Maitreya*, flanked by figures of *Avalokitesvara* (right) and *Manjusri* (left). It was founded by the Namgyal rulers and a portrait of Tashi Namgyal hangs on the left at the entrance. Of the monasteries, the **Soma Gompa** or the New Monastery (1957) in the main street of the Old Village was built to commemorate the 2,500th anniversary of the birth of Buddha. The remains of the **Leh Gompa** houses a large golden Buddha. **Sankar Gompa** (17th-18th centuries) ① *0700-1000, 1700-1900, prayers at 1830 (before visiting, check at the Tourist Office) with chanting, drums and cymbals, Rs 25*, of the Yellow Hat Sect, is one of the few gompas built in the valley bottom. It is an enjoyable 3-km walk past the *Himalayan Hotel* through fields. It houses the chief lama of Spituk and 20 others. The newer monks' quarters are on three sides of the courtyard with steps leading up to the *Du-Khang* (Assembly Hall). There are a number of gold statues, numerous wall paintings and sculptures including a large one of the 11 headed, 1,000-armed *Avalokitesvara*.

Shanti Stupa On the Changspa Lane across the stream, you reach the start of the stiff climb up to the white Japanese Shanti Stupa (1989). This is one of a series of 'Peace Pagodas' built by the Japanese around the world. There are good views from the top where a tea room offers a welcome sight after the climb. There is also a jeepable road.

Leh Mosque The architecturally striking Leh Mosque in the main bazar is worth visiting – the inner section is not open to woman visitors. The Sunni Muslim mosque is believed to stand on land granted by King Deldan Namgyal in the 1660s; his grandmother was the Muslim Queen of Ladakh.

★ **Ecological Centre & other centres of learning** ⓘ *T3585, Mon-Sat, 1400-1800*. Visit the **Ecological Centre of LEDeG** (Ladakh Ecological Development Group) and the Craft Shop, next to *Tsemo La Hotel*, which opened in 1984 to spread awareness of Ladakhi environmental issues, encourage self-help and use of alternative technology. It has a library of books on Ladakhi culture, Buddhism and the environment. The full 'Appropriate Technology' display is at the **New Ecology Centre** below the Shanti Stupa. There is also a handicrafts centre, a technical workshop and an organic vegetable garden there.

Leh centre

(After Katherine Ainger)

Not to scale

The non-profit making **SECMOL** (Students' Educational and Cultural Movement in Ladakh) is in Karzoo with an office in the Old Leh Road. It encourages the teaching of Ladakhi history, culture and crafts.

Women's Alliance of Ladakh Centre ⓘ *Off Sankar Rd, video shown daily except Sun, 1630 (min. 10 people), highly recommended*, is an alliance of 3,500 Ladakhi women, concerned with raising the status of traditional agriculture, preserving the traditionally high status of women which is being eroded in the modern sector, and creating an alternative development model based on self-reliance for Ladakh. The centre has a restaurant selling local and organic foods, and a craft shop. They hold spectacular festivals, cultural shows, dances etc which are advertised around Leh; mainly aimed at local people, but others are welcome. WAL, in conjunction with the Ladakh Project, runs a Farm Volunteer Scheme. Western volunteers live and work on a Ladakhi farm, helping to boost the status of traditional agriculture. An interesting video 'Ancient Futures' tracing ecologically sensitive Ladakh's changing face over two decades.

■ **Sleeping**
1 Bijoo
2 Bimla Guest House
3 Dehlux
4 Galdan Continental
5 Indus
6 Kang-lha Chen
7 Kangri & Exchange
8 Old Ladakh
9 Ti-Sei Guest House
10 Tourist Lodge
11 Yak Tail

● **Eating**
1 Amdo II
2 Budshah Inn & Tailors
3 Devi Tibetan
4 Dreamland
5 In-Style & Bakery
6 Kokonor
7 Kyishong
8 La Montessori
9 Nepali
10 Pumpernickel German Bakery
11 Summer Harvest
12 Tibetan Friend's Corner
13 Wok Tibetan Kitchen

Spectator sports   Polo, the 'national' sport, is popular in the summer and is played in the polo ground beyond the main Bus Stand. The local version which is fast and rough appears to follow no rules! The **Archery** Stadium is nearby where winter competitions attract large crowds; the target is a hanging white clay tablet.

Mani walls From the radio station there are two long mani walls. *Rongo Tajng* is in the centre of the open plain and was built as a memorial to Queen Skalzang Dolma by her son Dalden Namgyal. It is about 500 m long and was built in 1635. The stones have been meticulously carved. The other, a 350-m wall down the hill, is believed to have been built by Tsetan Namgyal in 1785 as a memorial to his father the king.

Monasteries along the Leh Manali Highway → *Colour map 1, grid A3.*
If you are short of time, try to see Thikse and Hemis, at least. On all trips go with a local Ladakhi guide as the Lamas can refuse admission if unaccompanied. Camera flash is usually not allowed in monasteries to reduce damage to wall paintings and *thangkas*. If you hire a car or jeep, which is good value when shared by four, you can visit the places below in a day. Carry a torch. Most expect a donation of Rs 25. The same advice applies to the monasteries along the Srinagar Road.

Choglamsar ① *Hourly buses, 0800-1800.* Choglamsar, south of Leh on the east bank of the Indus, is a green oasis with poplars and willows where there are golf links and a polo ground as well as horticultural nurseries. Some village houses use solar energy. The Central Institute of Buddhist Studies is here with a specialist library. Past the Tibetan Refugee Camps, Children's Village and the Arts and Crafts Centre, the Choglamsar Bridge crosses the Indus. The Chochot Yugma Imambara, a few minutes' walk from the bridge, is worth a visit.

★ Stok ① *Buses to Stok 0730, 1700, taxis from the Leh central taxi stand are available at fixed rates at any time.* Across Choglamsar Bridge, 16 km south of Leh, is the royal palace dating from the 1840s when the King of Ladakh was deposed by the invading Dogra forces. The last king died in 1974 but his widow continues to live here. His son continues the royal line and ascended the throne in July 1993. The palace is a rambling building where only a dozen of the 80 rooms are used. The small **Palace Museum** ① *May-Oct, 0800-1900, Rs 25*, with three rooms, is worth visiting. It is a showpiece for the royal *thangkas*, many 400 years old, crown jewels, dresses, coins, *peraks* (headdresses) encrusted with turquoise and lapis lazuli as well as religious objects.

There is an **archery** contest in July. The **gompa**, a short distance away, has some ritual dance masks. *Tsechu* is in February. A three-hour **walk** up the valley behind Stok takes you to some extraordinary mountain scenery dominated by the 6,121-m high Stok Kangri. Below the museum there is a clean hotel with good views.

Shey ① *All day; try to be there 0700-0900, 1700-1800 when prayers are chanted, Rs 15, hourly buses, 0800-1800.* Until the 16th century, Shey was the royal residence, located at an important vantage point in the Indus Valley. Kings of Leh were supposed to be born in the monastery. The royal family moved to Stok in order to escape advancing Dogra forces from Kashmir who came to exploit the trade in pashmina wool. Shey, along with Thikse, is also regarded as an auspicious place for cremation.

Much of the palace and the fort high above it have fallen into disrepair and is dirty though the soot covered wall paintings in the palace have now been restored. The palace gompa with its 17.5-m high blue-haired Maitreya Buddha, imitating the one at Tsemo Gumpa, is attended by Drukpa monks from Hemis. It is made of copper and brass but splendidly gilded and studded with precious gem stones. The large victory *stupa* is topped with gold. There are extensive grounds to the east (which once was a lake) with a large number of *chortens* in which cremated ashes of important monks, members of the royal family and the devout were buried. A newer temple houses another old giant Buddha statue. There are several rock carvings; particularly noteworthy is that of five *dhyani* Buddhas (circa eighth century) at the bottom of the hill. The small hotel below the gompa has spartan but clean rooms. It is 15 km southeast of Leh on the Indus River or can be reached along a stone path from Thikse.

★ **Thikse** ① *Rs 15 (mostly for restoration and maintenance), hourly buses, 0800-1800.* Situated 25 km south of Leh on a crag overlooking the flood plain on the east bank of the Indus, this is one of the most imposing monasteries in Ladakh and was part of the original Gelugpa order in the 15th century. The 12-storey monastery painted deep red, ochre and white, with typical tapering walls has 10 temples, a nunnery and 60 lamas in residence whose houses cling to the hillside below. The complex contains numerous stupas, statues, *thangkas*, wall paintings – note the fresco of the 84 *Mahasiddhas*, high above – swords and a large pillar engraved with the Buddha's teachings.

The new temple interior is dominated by a giant 15 m-high Buddha figure near the entrance. The principal *Dukhang* (assembly hall) right at the top of the building has holes in the wall for storing religious texts; good views from roof. The temple with the Guardian Deities, which in other monasteries may be closed to women, is open to all since parts of the offending figures are covered. The *Dukhang* lower down has Tibetan style wall paintings.

Thikse is a good place to watch religious ceremonies, usually at 0630 or 1200. An early start by taxi makes even the first possible. They are preceded by the playing of large standing drums and long horns similar to *alpenstock*. Masked dances are performed during special festivals.

Stakna Across the valley on a hill is the earliest Drukpa monastery which was built before Hemis, though its decorations are not as ancient. It is also called 'Tiger's nose' because of the shape of the hill site. This small but well-kept monastery has a beautiful silver-gilt *chorten* in the Assembly Hall which was installed around 1955 and some interesting paintings in the dark temple at the back. No need for a local guide as the lamas are always willing to open the doors. There are excellent views of the Indus valley and the Zanskar range.

★ **Hemis** ① *Bus services have improved making a day trip possible.* On the west bank of the Indus, 45 km south of Leh, the monastery, built on a green hillside surrounded by spectacular mountain scenery, is hidden in a gorge. It is the biggest and wealthiest in Ladakh and is a 'must' for visitors. You walk past *chortens* and sections of *mani* walls to enter the complex through the east gate which leads into a large 40 m x 20 m courtyard where sacred dances are performed during the *Hemis Tsechu*, end of June to early July. It commemorates the birth of Guru Padmasambhava who is believed to have fought local demons to protect the people. Young and old of both sexes, and lamas take part in masked dance-dramas while stalls sell handicrafts. The Drukpa monastery was founded by Stagsang Raspa during the reign of Senge Namgyal (circa 1630). Colourful flags flutter in the breeze from the four posts against the white walls of the buildings. On the north side are two assembly halls approached by a flight of steep stone steps. The large *Dukhang* to the right used for ceremonies is rather plain; the smaller *Tshogskhang* (the main temple) contains some silver gilt *chortens* and a Kashmiri lacquered-wood throne. The murals in the verandas depicting guardian deities, the *kalachakra* (wheel of life) and 'Lords of the four quarters' are well preserved. A staircase alongside the *Tshogskhang* leads to a roof terrace where there are a number of shrines including a bust of the founder. The *Lakhang* (chapel) has ancient Kashmiri bronzes and silver *chortens*, an important library of Tibetan style books and an impressive collection of *thangkas*, the largest of which is displayed every 12 years (next 2004). The heavy silk *thangka* is beautifully embroidered in bright coloured threads and pearls.

There is a pleasant 3-km walk uphill to another gompa. A stay in Hemis overnight enables you to attend early morning prayers, a moving experience and strongly recommended.

Monasteries along the Srinagar Road → *Colour map 1, grid A3.*

The Srinagar road out of Leh passes through a flat dusty basin mostly occupied by Army encampments with mile after mile of wire fencing.

Spituk (8 km from Leh) The monastery standing on a conical hill with three chapels was founded in the 11th century but the buildings, in a series of tiers with courtyards and steps, date from the 15th century. The newest is electrified. The Yellow-Hat Gelugpa monks created the precedent in Ladakh of building on mountain tops rather than valley floors. You can get good views of the countryside around.

The long 16th- to 17th-century **Du-khang** is the largest building and has two rows of seats along the length of the walls to a throne at the far end. Sculptures and miniature *chortens* are displayed on the altar. Spituk has a collection of ancient Jelbagh masks, icons and arms including some rescued from the Potala Palace in Lhasa.

The 16th- to 17th-century **Mahakal Temple** ① *Srinagar buses drop you on the highway, 4 daily, 20 mins*, higher up the hill contains a shrine of Vajrabhairava, often mistaken for the goddess Kali. The terrifying face is only unveiled in January, during the Gustor festival.

★ Phyang ① *Three buses daily, 1 hr; the morning bus allows you to explore the valley and walk back to Leh, but the afternoon bus only allows 20 mins for visit (last return, around 1700).* This gompa, 16 km from Leh, dominates a side valley with a village close by. It belongs to the Red Hat Kagyupa sect, with its 16th-century Gouon monastery built by the founder of the Namgyal Dynasty which is marked by a flagstaff at the entrance. It houses hundreds of statues including some Kashmiri bronzes (circa 14th century), *thangkas* and manuscript copies of the Kangyur and Tengyur. The temple walls have colourful paintings centering on the eight emblems of happiness which have been restored. It is the setting for a spectacular July *Tseruk festival* with masked dancing.

Phyang to Nimmu About 2 km before Nimmu the Indus enters an impressive canyon before the Zanskar joins it, a good photo opportunity. As the road bends, a lush green oasis with lines of poplars comes into view. The mud brick houses of Nimmu have grass drying on the flat rooftops to provide fodder for the winter. A dry stone *mani* wall runs along the road; beyond Nimmu the walls become 2 m wide in places with innumerable *chortens* alongside. The rocky outcrops on the hills to the right appear like a natural fortress.

Basgo ① *See Alchi below on how to get there.* The road passes through Basgo village with the ruins of a Buddhist citadel impressively sited on a spur overlooking the Indus Valley. It served as a royal residence for several periods between the 15th and 17th centuries. The Fort Palace was once considered almost impregnable having survived a three-year siege by Tibetan and Mongol armies in the 17th century.

Among the ruins only two temples have survived. The higher Maitreya Temple (mid-16th century) built by Tashi Namgyal's son contains a very fine Maitreya statue at the rear of the hall, flanked by *bodhisattvas*. Some murals from the early period illustrating the Tibetan Buddhist style have also survived on the walls and ceiling; among the Buddhas and *bodhisattvas* infilled with details of animals, birds and mermaids, appear images of Hindu divinities. The 17th-century Serzang (Gold and

Copper) Temple, with a carved doorway, is the other and contains another large Maitreya image whose head rises through the ceiling into a windowed box-like structure which can be seen by climbing up to the gallery above. The murals look faded and have been damaged by water.

Lekir (Likir) Some 5½ km from Basgo, a road on the right leads to Lekir by a scenic route. The picturesque white-washed monastery buildings rise in different levels on the hillside across the Lekir River. A huge saffron coloured Maitreya Buddha towers over the fields below. Lekir was built during the reign of Lachen Gyalpo who installed 600 monks here, headed by Lhawang Chosje (circa 1088). The gompa was invested with a collection of fine images, *thangkas* and murals to vie with those at Alchi. The present buildings date mainly from the 18th century since the original were destroyed by fire. A rough path up leads to the courtyard where a board explains the origin of the name: Klu-Khyil (snake coil) refers to the *nagas* here, reflected in the shape of the hill. Lekir was converted to the Gelugpa sect in the 15th century. The head lama, the younger brother of the Dalai Lama, has his apartments here, which were extended in the mid 1990s.

The **Du-khang** ⓘ *bus from Leh each afternoon, return each morning; see Alchi*, contains huge clay images of the Buddhas (past, present and future) and Kangyur and Tengyur manuscripts, the Kangyur having been first compiled in Ladakh during Lachen Gyalpo's reign. The **Nyenes-Khang** contains beautiful murals of the 35 confessional Buddhas and 16 arahats. The **Gon-Khang** houses a statue of the guardian deity here. A small but very interesting **museum**, ⓘ *Rs 15, opened on request (climb up to a hall above, up steep wooden stairs),* displays *thangkas*, old religious and domestic implements, costumes et cetera which are labelled in English.

Village craftsmen produce *thangkas*, carved wooden folding seats and clay pottery. If you wish to overnight, *Norbu Spon Guest House*, 3 km off main road towards Lekir, also allows camping and the two-storeyed white-washed *Lhankay Guest House* stands in fields.

★ **Alchi** The road enters Saspul, 8 km from the Lekir turn-off. About 2 km beyond the village, a link road with a suspension bridge over the river leads to Alchi which is hidden from view as you approach. A patchwork of cultivated fields surround the complex. A narrow path from the car park winds past village houses, donkeys and apricot trees to lead to the Dharma Chakra monastery. You will be expected to buy a ticket from one of the lamas on duty. The whole complex, about 100 m long and 60 m wide, is enclosed by a white-washed mud and straw wall. Alchi's large temple complex is regarded as one of the most important Buddhist centres in Ladakh and a jewel of monastic skill. A path on the right past two large prayer wheels and a row of smaller ones leads to the river which attracts deer down to the opposite bank

Alchi Choskor

To Indus River ↑

Jampang (Manjusri) Temple

Lotsawa (Translator's) Temple

Maitreya

Du-khang   Courtyard   Prayer Wheels

Wall

Vairacona

Large Prayer Wheels

Manjusri

Sum-stek (3-Tier) Temple   Wooden Porch

Maitreya

Entrance Chortens

Avalokitesvara

Kanjyur Lhakhang

Lhakhang Soma

N

Sculptures

0 metres 10
0 yards 10

them, line the wall. From here, you get a beautiful view of the Indus River with
mountains as a backdrop.

Founded in the 11th century by Rinchen Zangpo, the 'Great Translator', it was
richly decorated by artists from Kashmir and Tibet. Paintings of the mandalas which
have deep Tantric significance are particularly fine; some decorations are reminiscent
of Byzantine art. The monastery is maintained by monks from Lekir and is no longer a
place for active worship.

The temple complex The three **entrance chortens** are worth looking in to. Each has
vividly coloured paintings within, both along the interior walls as well as in the small
chorten-like openings on the ceilings. The first and largest of these has a portrait of the
founder Rinchen Zangpo. Some of the paintings here are being restored by researchers.

The **Du-khang** is the oldest temple, which has a courtyard (partially open to the
sky) with wooden pillars and painted walls; the left wall shows two rowing boats with
fluttering flags, a reminder perhaps of the presence in ancient times of lakes in this
desert. The brightly painted door to the Du-khang, about 1½ m high, and the entrance
archway has some fine woodcarving; note the dozen or so blue pottery Buddhas
stuck to the wall! The subsidiary shrines on either side of the doorway contain
Avalokitesvaras and *bodhisattvas* including a giant four-armed Maitreya figure to the
extreme right. This main Assembly Hall which was the principal place of worship
suffers from having very little natural light so visitors need a good torch. The 'shrine'
holds the principal gilded *Vairocana* (Resplendent) Buddha (traditionally white,
accompanied by the lion) with ornate decorations behind, flanked by four important
Buddha postures among others. The walls on either side are devoted to fine *Mandala*
paintings illustrating the four principal manifestations of the *Sarvavid* (Omniscient)
Buddha – *Vairocana*, *Sakyamuni* (the Preacher), *Manjusri* (Lord of Wisdom) and as
Prajna Paramita (Perfection of Wisdom) described in detail by Snellgrove and
Skorupski. There are interesting subsidiary panels, friezes and inscriptions. Note the
terrifying figure of *Mahakala* the guardian deity above the door with miniature panels
of royal and military scenes. The one portraying a drinking scene shows the royal pair
sanctified with haloes with wine-cups in hand, accompanied by the prince and
attendants – the detail of the clothing clearly shows Persian influence.

The **Lotsawa** (Translator's) and **Jampang** (Manjusri) Lhakhangs were built later and
probably neglected for some time. The former contains a portrait of Rinchen Zangpo
along with a seated Buddha while the latter has *Manjusri* where each directional face is
painted in the colour associated with the cardinal directions of north (dark green),
south (yellow), east (blue) and west (red). There are two small temples beyond.

Sum-stek, the three-tier temple with a carved wooden gallery on the façade, has
triple arches. Inside are three giant four-armed, garlanded stucco figures of *bodhisattvas*:
the white *Avalokitesvara* on the left, the principal terracotta-red *Maitreya* in the centre at
the back, and the ochre-yellow *Manjusri* on the right; their heads project to the upper
storey which is reached by a rustic ladder. The remarkable features here are the brightly
painted and gilded decorations on the clothing of the figures which include historical
incidents, musicians, palaces and places of pilgrimage. Quite incongruous court scenes
and Persian features appear on *Avalokitesvara* while the figures on *Maitreya* have Tantric
connotations illustrating the very different styles of ornamentation on the three figures.
The walls have numerous *mandalas* and inscriptions.

Lhakhang Soma (New temple) is a square hall with a *chorten* within; its walls are
totally covered with *mandalas* and paintings portraying incidents from the Buddha's
life and historic figures; the main figure here is the preaching Buddha. There is an
interesting panel of warriors on horseback near the door. **Kanjyur Lhakhang** in front of
the Lhakhang Soma houses the scriptures.

These once restricted areas are now open to visitors. Permits are freely issued by the District Magistrate (District Development Commissioner) in Leh to groups of four or more travelling together by jeep, for a maximum of seven days. Allow a day to get a permit which costs Rs 250. A lot of ground can be covered in the period but it is necessary to consult a Leh-based trekking and travel agent. You need to go fully equipped with tents, food and sleeping bags although there are a few rest houses and temporary lakeside tented camps are occasionally set up by tour companies.

★ **Tso-Moriri** (220 km from Leh) ① *get a jeep from Leh.* The Rupshu area, a dry, high altitude plateau to the east of the Leh-Manali Highway, is where the nomadic Changpas live, see page 534, in the bleak and windswept Chamathang highlands bordering Tibet. The route to the beautiful Tso-Moriri (*tso* – lake), the only nesting place of the bar-headed geese on the Indus is open to visitors. To the south of the 27-km long lake is the land of the Tibetan wild ass.

You can travel either via **Chhumathang**, 140 km, visiting the hot spring there or by crossing the high pass at Taglang La, leaving the Manali-Leh Highway at Debring. The route takes you past **Tsokar** basin, 154 km, where salt cakes the edges. A campsite along the lake with access to fresh water is opposite **Thukje** village which has a gompa and a 'wolf catching trap'! The road then reaches the hot sulphur springs at **Puga** before reaching the beautiful Tso-Moriri, about four hours drive from Tsokar. You can follow the lake bank and visit the solitary village of **Karzog**, at 4,500 m, north of the lake, which has a gompa. There are some rest houses and guest houses at Chhumathang and Karzog and camping at Tsokar and Karzog as well as a tent camp at Chhumathang.

★ **Pangong- Tso** From Leh you can also get a permit to visit the narrow 130-km long Pangong-Tso, at 4,250 m, the greater part of which lies in Tibet. The road, which is only suitable with four-wheel drive in places, is via **Karu** on the Manali-Leh Highway, where the road east goes through **Zingral** and over the Chang La pass. Beyond are **Durbuk**, a small village with low-roofed houses, and **Tangste**, the 'abode of Chishul warriors' with a Lotswa Temple, which is also an army base with a small bank. The rough jeep track takes you through an impressive rocky gorge which opens out to a valley which has camping by a fresh water stream in the hamlet of **Mugleb** and then on to **Lukung**, the last check-point and finally **Spangmik**, 153 km from Leh. On the way you will be able to see some Himalayan birds including *chikhor* (quail) which may end up in the cooking pot.

An overnight stop on the lake shore allows you to see the lake in different lights. You can walk between Lukung and Spangmik, 7 km, on this second day, passing small settlements growing barley and peas along the lake shore. Both villages have yaks which you can experience a ride on! You return to Leh on the third day. Tented camps at Durbuk, Tangtse, Lukung and Spangmik. ① *Getting there: jeep from Leh.*

★ **Nubra Valley** ① *From Leh there are 2 buses per week Jun-Sep (8 hrs); a few have tried by bike, which can be put on the roof of the bus for the outward journey (for those who can't face the hard pedalling!).* For an exhilarating high-altitude experience over possibly the highest motorable pass in the world travel across the Ladakh range over the 5,600 m **Khardung La**. North of Leh, this is along the old Silk Route to the lush green Nubra valley up to **Panamik**, 140 km from Leh, which has reddish, sulphurous hot springs nearby. It is best to visit this region after mid-June

Once camel caravans transported Chinese goods for exchanging with Indian produce. Camels which are now rare and prized can occasionally be seen on the sand dunes near Nubra, see also page 555. The relatively gentler climate here allows crops, fruit and nuts to grow, so some call it 'Ldumra' (orchard). You can visit the **Samstanling**, **Sumur** and **Deskit** gompas. There are rest houses at **Deskit, Panamik** and **Khardung** village with permission from the Executive Engineer, PWD, in Deskit. Local families take in guests and tented camps are sometimes set up by tour companies (double tents Rs 800 including food) during the season. Should you need medical help, there is a health centre at Deskit and a dispensary at Panamik.

Drokhpa area Dah and **Biama**(Bema) are two Drokhpa villages where the so-called pure Aryan tribe speaking a distinct dialect live in a fair degree of isolation; Buddhism here is mixed with animist practices. You may reach these Indus valley villages from **Khaltse** on the Leh-Srinagar road via Dumkhar, Tirit, Skurbuchan and Hanudo. There is a rest house at Biama and guest houses and a campsite.

Trekking in Ladakh

Some treks in the Indus Valley and the Nubra and Shyok Valleys are described here in brief. Make sure your trekking guide is experienced and competent. See page 64 for general advice and see Books, page 1366, for recommended reading. Some treks, eg Spituk to Hemis and Hemis High Altitude National Park, charge a fee of Rs 25 per person per day or Rs 10 for Indians.

Trekking in the Indus Valley Leh is the major town in this valley. For trekking, July and August are pleasant months. Go earlier and you will be trudging through snow much of the time. September and October are also good months, though colder at night.

★ **Spituk to Hemis** Both places are in the Indus Valley, just 30 km apart. A very satisfying nine to 10 days can be undertaken by traversing the Stok range to the Markha Valley, walking up the valley and then back over the Zanskar range to Hemis. The daily walking time on this trek is 5-6 hours so you must be fit.

There is an interesting monastery at **Spituk**, a short drive from Leh, see page 549. From Spituk proceed southwest of the Indus along a trail passing through barren countryside. After about 7 km you reach the **Jinchan Valley** and in a further five hours, the beautiful Rumbak village. Camp below the settlement. You can also trek here from Stok which takes two days and a steep ascent of the **Namlung La** (4,570 m).

From Rumbak it is a five-hour walk to Utse village. The camp is two hours further on at the base of the bleak **Gandha La** (4,700 m), open, bare and windswept. To go over the pass takes about three hours, then the same time again to negotiate the wooded ravine to Skiu. Here the path meets the Markha Valley. You can make a half day round trip from Skiu to see the impressive gorges on the Zanskar River. The stage to Markha where there is an impressive fort, is a six-hour walk. The monastery, which is not particularly impressive from the outside, has some superb wall paintings and *thangkas*, some dating from the 13th century. You need to take a torch.

The next destination is **Hankar** village, whose ruined fort forms an astonishing extension of the natural rock face, an extremely impressive ruin. From here the path climbs quite steeply to a plateau. There are good views of Nimaling Peak (6,000 m) and a number of *mani* walls en route. From **Nimaling** it is a two-hour climb to **Gongmaru La** (5,030 m) with views of the Stok range and the Indus Valley. The descent is arduous and involves stream crossings. There is a lovely campsite at **Shogdu** and another at **Sumda** village, 3 km further on. The final stage is down the valley to Martselang from where you can walk down 5 km to **Karu** village on the Leh-Manali road or take a 2 km diversion to visit Hemis monastery.

Hemis High Altitude National Park Set up in 1981, the park adjoining the monastery covers 600 sq km, comprising the catchments of Markha, Rumbak and Sumda nalas, with plans to extend across another 1,670 sq km. The rugged terrain with valleys often littered with rocks and rimmed by high peaks (some over 6,000 m), supports limited vegetation but contains some rare species of flora and fauna. For example the ibex,

Pallas's cat, *bharal* and *shapu* inhabit the area and a reserve to protect the endangered snow leopard is planned. It is hoped to restrict the activities of local villagers who graze livestock within the park, to a buffer zone so that their animals can be kept safe from attack by wolves and snow leopards.

There are camping sites which you can reserve through the Wildlife Warden, Leh. Since most of the park lies within 'Restricted' areas, you need a special Group Permit for entry, also issued in Leh. Contact a local travel agent for advice.

Lamayaru to Alchi This is a shorter trek of 5-6 days, however, the average daily walking time is 6½ hours so don't think that the shortness of the trek means less effort. Three passes, the **Printiki La** (3,500 m), **Konke La** (4,570 m) and **Stapski La** (5,200 m) are crossed rewarding the exertion of reaching them with excellent views.

The first stage involves walking from the usual campsite just below the monastery down the valley for 2 km then over the **Printiki La**. You then descend the Shillakong Valley and climb to **Phangi** village, passing huge boulders brought down by a landslide, and impressive irrigation in such a forbidding landscape. From Phangi you walk up the Ripchar Valley to **Khaltse**, crossing the river a number of times. There are a number of small settlements until you reach the summer grazing ground a few kilometres below the pass. The **Konke La** is a steep two-hour climb. From here you will see the Zanskar River and gorge and the Stok range.

Ladakh & Zanskar treks

The fourth stage should be with a guide since the trail splits, one leading to **Chillung** on the Zanskar River, the other to **Sumdahchenmo**, the latter being quite treacherous as it involves many river crossings (about three hours below Sumdahchenmo there is a path which climbs the ridge above the river; it is quite easy to miss this, hence the guide). There is a monastery here with an impressive statue of the Buddha and some attractive wall paintings. A camping site lies just beyond the village. The last stage of the trek is long, about eight hours walking, and takes you over the **Stapski La** to **Alchi**. The views from the top are superb. From Alchi you can get a bus to Leh.

Trekking in the Nubra & Shyok Valleys The gradual easing up of controls to visit the Nubra-Shyok valleys has now made possible treks that start from points in the Indus valley not far from Leh, cross the Ladakh Range to enter the Shyok River valley and then recross the Ladakh range further to the west to re-enter the Indus valley near Phyang monastery. Ask a good local trekking agent for advice on how to get required 'Restricted Area Permits'.

Day 1 Drive from Leh south along the Manali road to Karu, near Hemis, where you turn left and drive about 10 km to the roadhead at the village of Sakti, just past **Takthak monastery**. Trek about 90 minutes to **Chumchar** and camp.
Day 2 Cross the Ladakh range at the **Wari La** (4,400 m) and descend to Junlez on the northern flank.
Day 3 Walk downhill to **Tangyar** (3,700 m) with a nice gompa.
Days 4, 5, 6 A level walk along the **Shyok River** valley takes you to **Khalsar** from where you follow the military road west to the confluence of the Shyok and Nubra rivers at **Deskit**. On a hill above the village is a Gelugpa sect **monastery** (the largest in Nubra) built by the Ladakhi king Sohrab Zangpo in the early 1700's. There is large statue of Tsongkhapa and the Rimpoche of Thikse monastery south of Leh oversees this monastery also. The Rimpoche was nominated to the Rajya Sabha in 1998. The next biggest monastery in Nubra is near **Tiggur** halfway along the road north of Deskit to **Panamik** in the Nubra Valley. Called the **Samtanling** gompa, it was founded in 1842 and belongs to the Gelugpa sect. The Permit allows travel only up to the village of Panamik (see Nubra Valley above).
Days 7, 8, 9 Three days to gradually ascend the northern flanks of the Ladakh Range passing the hamlets of **Hundar, Wachan** and **Hundar Dok** to the high pastures of **Thanglasgo** (4,700 m).
Days 10, 11 Trek back over the Ladakh Range via the Lasermo La pass (5,150 m) to a campsite on the southern base of the pass.
Day 12 Camp at Phyang village about 1 km above Phyang monastery before driving back to Leh.

Zanskar → *Colour map 1, grid A2 and A3.*

Zanskar is a remote area of Ladakh contained by the Zanskar range to the north and the Himalaya to the south. It can be cut off by snow for as much as seven months each year when access is solely along the frozen Zanskar River. This isolation has helped Zanskar to preserve its cultural identity, though this is now being steadily eroded. Traditional values include a strong belief in Buddhism, frugal use of resources and population control. Values, which for centuries, have enabled Zanskaris to live in harmony with their hostile yet fragile environment. The long Zanskar Valley was 'opened' up for tourism even later than the rest of Ladakh and quickly became popular with trekkers. There is now river rafting on the Zanskar River ▶ *For Sleeping, Eating and other listings see pages 557-562.*

Zanskar became an administrative part of Ladakh under Senge Namgyal whose three sons became the rulers of Ladakh, Guge and Zanskar/Spiti. This arrangement collapsed after Ladakh's war with Tibet and the Zanskar royal house divided, one part administering Padum, the other Zangla. Under the Dogras, the rulers were reduced to puppets as the marauding army wreaked havoc on the villages, monasteries and population.

Padum → *Colour map 1, grid A3. No permit needed.*

Padum, the capital, has a population of about 1,000 of whom about 40% are Sunni Muslim. The present king of the Zanskar valley, Punchok Dawa who lives in his modest home in Padum, is held in high regard. On arrival you must report to the Tourist Officer. Access is either by the jeep road over the **Pensi La**, generally open from mid-June to mid-October with an alternate days' bus service from Kargil, 18 hours. The alternative method is to trek in.

Trekking in Zanskar

Trekking in Zanskar is not easy. The paths are often rough and steep, the passes high and the climate extreme. Provisions, fuel and camping equipment should be taken along from Kishtwar, Manali or Leh. You may get necessities such as dried milk, biscuits and sugar from Padum, though probably not at the beginning of the season. In Padum the Tourism Officer and Govt Development Officer will be able to advise and maybe even assist in hiring horses. Porters can be hired at **Sani** village for the traverse of the **Umasi La** into Kishtwar. Horses cannot use this pass. In Padum you may be able to hire porters with whom you can cover rougher terrain. It is best to contact a trekking agent in advance. See page 67. *Ibex* and *NEI* in Delhi organize special trekking and rafting in Zanskar and Ladakh. Otherwise try *Zanskar Tours and Travels*, T01983-45064, in Padum.

Pensi La to Padum You can trek this three-day route before the road opens (June-October) when it is free of vehicles.

Karsha to Lamayaru This is a demanding nine-day trek which includes seven passes, five of which are over 4,500 m. The highest is the Singi La (5,060 m). It is essential to be very fit before starting the trek. Each day's walking should take under six hours, but with time for rests and lunch this adds up to a full day. An extra day allows for flexibility.

The 16th-century monastery of the Tibetan Gelugpa (Yellow Hat) sect at **Karsha** is the largest and wealthiest in the Zanskar Valley and is occupied by nearly 200 monks. Karsha has an inn with dormitory beds and a vegetarian canteen.

Padum to Leh This is another demanding trek which also takes about 10 days. Some are through the spectacular gorges between Markha and Zangla. A local guide is recommended as this is truly a wilderness area. The trek involves walking along stream beds and in July there is still too much snow melt to allow safe crossings. Recommended only for August/September.

It is seven hours walking from Padum to Zangla and this includes crossing the Zanskar River by a string and twig bridge that spans over 40 m. Ponies are not allowed on it and if it is windy sensible humans don't cross! At **Zangla** you can see the King's palace, which has a collection of *thangkas* painted by the king's son (who was once a monk). The third stage takes you over the **Charcha La** (5,200 m). On the next stage river crossings are again necessary. This is time consuming and if you are travelling in mid-summer, an extra day may be called for.

You then follow the **Khurna River** to a narrow gorge that marks the ancient border between Zanskar and Ladakh, and end up below the **Rubarung La**. When you cross this you get good views of the Stok range. You then descend into the Markha valley and from here you can reach Leh in six stages by heading west into the heart of the valley and then crossing the Ganda La to Spituk, or in three stages by crossing the Gongmaru La and descending to Martselang and nearby Hemis.

★ **Padum to Darcha** This is a week long trek and starts with a walk along the Tsarap Chu to **Bardan**, which has stupas and interesting idols, and **Reru**.

After two stages you reach **Purni** (with a couple of shops and a popular campsite), where you can stay two nights and make a side trip to the impressive 11th-century **Phugtal monastery** (a two-hour walk). On a spectacular site, it has been carved out of the mountainside round a limestone cave. Usually there are about 50 monks in attendance. From Purni you continue on to Kargya, the last village before the **Shingo La**. It's another day's walk to the camp below this high pass (5,200 m).

The mountain scenery is stunning with 6,000 m plus peaks all around. Once over the pass you can stop at **Rumjack** where there is a campsite used by shepherds or you can go further to the confluence of the **Shingo River** and the **Barai River** where there is now a bridge. From here the trail passes through grazing land and it is about 15 km from the river to Darcha, the end of the trek. Keen trekkers can combine this with a trek from **Darcha** to **Manali**. The average daily walking time of the Padum-Darcha trek is six hours so you have to be very fit.

Listings: Ladakh

● Sleeping

Leh *p543, maps p544 and p546*
Advance reservations in **B** and **C** grade hotels may not be honoured in the peak season (mid-Jul to end-Aug) since they cater for tour/trekking groups whose arrival and departure can be unpredictable. Hotel touts can be a nuisance during the 14-day Ladakh festival. Outside the peak period expect discounts though few places remain open in the winter, eg *Siachen*, and *Kangri*. Many traditional Ladakhi homes offer rooms during the summer. Those in Karzoo and Changspa (some way from the bus stand) are quieter and preferable to those near the bazar. Top hotels often include meals in the room rate.
A-B Caravan Centre, Skara, T52282, F53779. 21 comfortable rooms, 10 suites under development, all with views, attractive gardens, "oasis in the desert", friendly staff, restaurant.
A-B Galdan Continental, off Fort Rd, T52173. 25 comfortable rooms, some with bath tub, around a grassy quad.
A-B K-Sar Palace, T/F52348. Large rooms with pleasant views, exchange.
B Bijoo, near Library, 100 m from Bazar, T52131. 2-storey white building hidden by wall,

18 good rooms with bath, good restaurant, pleasant flower-filled garden and shady seating, treks and tours, very helpful staff.
B Kang-lha Chen, T52144. 25 rooms, most with baths, good restaurant, pleasant shaded inner courtyard garden, own spring, quiet and peaceful, old fashioned but well maintained, open May-Oct.
B Kangri, Nehru Park, T52051. 22 rooms with bath, restaurant, loud generator nearby a nuisance until 2300, indifferent service.
B Lharimo, T52101. 30 simple but comfortable rooms with baths, good views from balconies, restaurant, attractive, central.
B Shambala, Skara, T52607. 24 large airy rooms, good restaurant (often caters for German packages), meals included, very pleasant, friendly staff, peaceful away from crowds, attractive garden with hammocks, free transport to centre.
C Omasila, Changspa, T52119. 26 rooms, restaurant (fresh garden vegetables), pleasant quiet location, own spring water.
C Yak Tail, Fort Rd, T52218. 14 rooms (newer have balconies), nice courtyard garden restaurant (good, reasonably priced Indian), exchange, open Apr-Sep, pleasant atmosphere.

● For an explanation of the sleeping and eating price codes used in this guide, see inside the front cover. Other relevant information is found in Essentials pages 52-57.

C-D **Rafica**, off Fort Rd, T52258. 74 very, comfortable rooms (no TV), some large, pleasant outdoor restaurant recommended (worth 1 hr wait for fresh food), friendly, exceptional staff, quiet (except front rooms), among fields, treks and tours, good value.
C-D **Snow View**, Karzoo, past Ecological Centre, T52336. 10 rooms (upstairs with good views), peaceful, far from bazar.
D **Dragon**, T52139. 16 rooms with bath, improved, almost always filled with trekking parties (porters camp in garden!).
D **Himalayan**, Sankar Gompa Rd, T52104. 26 rooms, most with bath, old building in a quiet, shady willow grove by a stream, restaurant, camping.
D **Lhung-Se-Jung**, Fort Rd, T52193. 18 smallish rooms with bath, 2-storey old building and small annexe, upstairs better, restaurant, small garden, quiet location, student discount, good service.
D **Padmaling**, Changspa, T52933. 10 clean rooms with bath, hot water morning and evening, helpful manager, *Mona Lisa* restaurant next door, pleasant garden, good views over Stok Kangri.
D **Ri-Rab**, Changspa, T52239. 10 clean simple rooms with baths, restaurant (own fresh garden vegetables).
D-E **Silver Cloud**, on the road opposite Sankar Gompa, 15 mins walk from centre, T53128, F52572. 15 very clean rooms, 9 with bath (1 **C**), in Ladakhi guesthouse, excellent food, large garden, friendly, helpful family.
D-E **Wisdom**, opposite *Rainbow*. Good rooms, excellent hot showers, very friendly Ladakhi family.

Fleas and bed bugs can be a problem; use your own sleeping bag if possible.

There is some budget accommodation along the Old Rd and in the Changspa area; some are very basic with cold water only.
E **Bimla Guest House**, Suku, T52754. 18 rooms, sitting area, welcoming.
E **Dehlux**, Suku, 9 rooms (hot water in buckets), garden, quiet.
E **Hills View**, T52058. 12 clean rooms (sharing bath between 2 rooms) some with good views, breakfast and snacks, pleasant staff, pretty garden, relaxing, safe, stores luggage.
E **Indus**, Suku, 17 large rooms some with bath (hot water in buckets), better upstairs, food.
E **Kangla**, Airport Rd, T52670. 14 rooms, very friendly, helpful, organize treks.

E **New Antelope Guest House**, Main St, T52086. 11 simple, clean rooms, some with bath, good food, quiet, shady garden.
E **Old Ladakh**, in the Old Town. 8 rooms, varying in comfort, has character, pleasant atmosphere, good place to meet others.
E **Oriental**, below Shanti Stupa. Very clean rooms in traditional family home, good home cooking, great views across the valley, friendly.
E **Padmaling**, Changspa, T52933. 10 clean rooms with bath, hot water morning and evening, nice garden and good views over Stok Kangri, friendly manager.
E **Rainbow**, Karzoo. Big, clean rooms with wonderful views of mountains and Shanti Stupa, hot water in buckets, great hospitality, good breakfasts. Recommended.
E **Shanti Guest House**, below Shanti Stupa, T53084. 9 well-heated rooms, most with great views, very good food, summer/winter treks arranged with guide, friendly Ladakhi family.
F **Lung Snon**, Sheynam Chulli Chan. 8 rooms, delightful guesthouse in peaceful countryside, clean and friendly, but simple, earth toilet.
F **Padma**, off Fort Rd. 6 clean rooms, upstairs has mountain views, earth toilets, peaceful garden, cheap meals to order.
F **Remo**, Fort Rd, T53336. Clean, quiet, simple rooms, shared toilets, bucket hot water (no charge), very kind family.
F **Ti-Sei Guest House**, Suku. Good value rooms in peaceful location, 'glass room' (**E**), meals, terrace.

Thikse *p548*
E **Shalzang Chamba Hotel**, with outdoor restaurant.

Hemis *p548*
Many householders take in guests.
F **Tourist**, camp or sleep on the floor, own sleeping bag, Rs 25. The tented restaurant is basic and grubby.

Alchi *p550*
Near Alchi car/bus park there are tea stalls and a few guesthouses.
E-F **Lotsava** on the path, simple.
Zimskhang, very basic rooms, walled-in open-air restaurant for light meals and snacks, camping.
Uley Tokpo Camp is a few kilometres before Alchi.

🍴 Unlucky in Leh

The supply of clean water and the sewage system can come under heavy pressure in the tourist season. Drink pressure boiled water from Dzomsa (see map) only or use water purification tablets. Bottled water can sometimes be more than a year old and doesn't always conform to safety standards. Meat is sometimes brought in unrefrigerated lorries having travelled two days, so is best avoided.

Saspul
Carefree Travels Camp, Worldroof Camping Resort and Restaurant.

Padum *p556*
Places to stay are limited, being mostly dormitory style. There is a Tourist complex with basic rooms, meals, you can camp. **Elbex**, has the best rooms and a restaurant.

🍴 Eating

Leh *p543, maps p544 and p546*
🍴🍴🍴 **Mona Lisa**, Changspa, T52687. International. Good atmosphere, quiet garden with shady trees, hanging lanterns, excellent food (try pizzas, momos, garlic cheese with bread), scrawny chickens, no desserts, service can be indifferent.
🍴🍴 **Dreamland** (separate from hotel). International. Good atmosphere and food especially Chinese, excellent breakfasts.
🍴🍴 **In-Style**, Fort Rd. International. Al fresco at back, popular for breakfast, takeaway snacks, also Chinese menu. Both have 'notice boards'.
🍴🍴 **Kokonor**, entrance on alley off Main St, 2nd floor. "Chinese and Tibetan specialities and western encouragements served with generosity and flair", very popular.
🍴🍴 **La Montessori**, Main St Bazar. Excellent Tibetan and Chinese. Filling soups, interesting local clientele.
🍴🍴 **Summer Harvest**, Fort Rd, 1st floor, next to *Dreamland*. Mainly Indian, also Chinese, Tibetan. Extensive menu of local and 'tourist' dishes from mutton *thukpa* (Rs 30) to tandoori chicken (Rs 160).
🍴 **Amdo II**, Main Bazar. Tibetan. Good fried momos, Rs 25-35 per dish, friendly (better than *Amdo Café* opposite).
🍴 **Budshah Inn**, Lal Chowk, top floor. North Indian. Lacks ambience but excellent Kashmiri (Rs 45, dish).

🍴 **Devi Tibetan**. Traditional meals, refreshing spiced teas.
🍴 **Nepali**. Nepali, Tibetan. Excellent veg *momos*.
🍴 **Tibetan Friend's Corner**. Clean, simple, delicious *kothay* (fried *momos*) Rs 25, huge pancakes, friendly, locally popular.

Confectionery
Four **German bakeries** sell good bread (trekking bread keeps for a week) and excellent cakes and muesli.
In Style similar fare to *Pumpernickel*.
Mona Lisa, similar fare to *Pumpernickel*.
Pumpernickel, Main St Bazar, the original German bakery is the best and friendliest, indoor/outdoor seating, excellent apricot and apple crumble/pie, message board for trekkers.

🎭 Entertainment

Leh *p543, maps p544 and p546*
The Ecological Centre shows occasional films, see page 546. Ladakhi dancing and singing, below entrance to Palace, 1800 (1 hr), Rs 50. Disappointing.

🎉 Festivals and events

Leh *p543, maps p544 and p546*
Dates vary depending on the lunar calendar. **Losar** which originated in the 15th century to protect people before going to battle is celebrated in **Dec**. The main events of the **Ladakh Festival** (1-15 Sep) are held in the Leh Polo grounds with smaller events arranged in other districts. Arranged by the State Government usually during the 1st week in Sep, there are 4 days of dances, displays of traditional costumes, Ladakhi plays and polo matches. **Buddha Purnima** (**Apr-May** full moon) marks the Buddha's birth

Gomptas and festivals

Buddhist festivals usually take place in the bleak winter months when villagers gather together, stalls spring up around the gompas and colourful dance dramas and masked dances are performed in the courtyards. Musical instruments, weapons and religious objects are brought out during these dance performances. The *Kushak* (high priest) is accompanied by monks in monotonous recitation while others play large cymbals, trumpets and drums. The serious theme of victory of Good over Evil is lightened by comic interludes. A few monasteries celebrate their festivals in the summer months for example Lamayuru, Hemis and Phyang.

O Shopping

Leh *p543, maps p544 and p546*
Please use your own bags. Plastic bags are not allowed in the bazar as they are not bio-degradable and were finding their way into streams when not piled on unsightly heaps.

Leh Bazar is full of shops selling curios, clothes and knick-knacks. Tea and *chang* (local barley brew) vessels, cups, butter churns, knitted carpets with Tibetan designs, Tibetan jewellery, prayer flags, musical bowls, are all available. Prices are high especially in Kashmiri shops so bargain vigorously. It is usually better to buy Ladakhi jewellery and souvenirs from Ladakhis who generally ask a fair price. There are tight restrictions on the export of anything over 100 years old. Baggage is checked at the airport partly for this reason. However, even though most items are antique looking, they are, in fact, fresh from the backstreet workshops. If you walk down the narrow lanes, you will probably find an artisan at work from whom you can buy direct.

Books
Artou Books, opposite Post Office, Zangsti and in Main Bazar has a good selection, especially on trekking in the region, also fax and international phone.
Book Worm, near *Galdan Hotel*, second-hand.

Crafts
Cottage Emporium, opposite *Dreamland Hotel*, large selection of carpets and pashminas.
Chan Gali, worth exploring for curios.
LEDeG Craft Shop at the Ecology Centre, and opposite the *State Bank* in the Main Bazar.
Ladakh Arts & Craft House, top of Fort Rd, opposite PO has a few interesting bric-a-brac.

Ladakhi Village Curios, selection of *thangkas*, inlaid bowls, baubles, bangles and beads.
Group of Ladakhis have stalls off the Fort Rd.
Sonam Bongo, top of Main Bazar St, has local costumes.
Tibetan Arts, selection of *thangkas*, inlaid bowls, baubles, bangles and beads.

Fruit and nuts
Available in season. Dried apricots can be bought along any roadside in Aug-Sep. Bottled juice is sold by the *Dzomsa* Laundry.

Photography
Syed Ali Shah's Postcard Shop, Choterantag St, is worth a visit. An authentic photographer's studio; collection of old photocopies sold, postcards, camera films.

Tailor
Next to *Budshah Inn* near mosque, excellent shirt maker, made-to-measure. Also several in Nowshara Gali.

▲ Activities and tours

Leh *p543, maps p544 and p546*
Mountaineering
Local tour companies offer treks and mountain climbing.

Polo
The Polo Club (the highest in the world); worth a visit.

Tours
Women on their own should take special care when arranging a tour with a driver/guide.
Explore Himalayas, PO Box 45, Main Bazar (opp *SBI*), T/F53354, wangchuks@hotmail.com.

"highly recommended, excellent crew, friendly, good to animals, environment conscious, food incredible!".
K2, Main Bazar, T53532, good rates for treks (Markha Valley), "very friendly, really care about ponies and the environment".
Rimo Expeditions, *Kang-lha Chen Hotel*, T53644, treks and rafting.

White-water rafting and kayaking
Possible on the Tsarap Chu and Zanskar rivers from mid-Jun; the upper reaches of the former (grade 4 rapids) are suitable for professionals only, though the remaining stretch can be enjoyed by the inexperienced. Along the Indus: Hemis to Choglamsar (easy, very scenic); Phey-Nimmu (grade 3); Nimmu-Khaltse (professional). Ensure the trip is organized by a well-experienced rafter and that life jackets and wet suits are provided. Half to full day, including transport and lunch, Rs 800-1,400. See Tour companies above.

⊙ Transport

Leh p543, maps p544 and p546
Air
The small airport is 5 km away on Srinagar Rd. It is surrounded by hills on 3 sides and the flight over the mountain ranges is spectacular. Transport to town: buses, and jeep-taxis (Rs 150), for sharing. Weather conditions may deteriorate rapidly even in the summer resulting in flight cancellations (especially outside Jul and Aug) so always be prepared for a delay or to take alternative road transport out of Ladakh. Furthermore, the airlines fly quite full planes into Leh but can take fewer passengers out because of the high altitude take-off. This adds to the difficulty of getting a flight out.
Book your tickets as soon as possible (several months ahead for Jul and Aug). You can book on the internet before you depart for India (eg www.welcometravel.com).

Flights are often cancelled. Tickets bought in Leh may not be 'confirmed'. The **Indian Airlines** office is near *Shambala Hotel* and is often chaotic. Avoid connecting with an onward flight or train immediately after your visit to Ladakh. If you fail to get on the outward flight, you do not get an immediate refund from the airline but have to reclaim it from the travel agent. It is therefore essential to have enough money to travel out by road

if your return is imperative; remember, a taxi to Manali takes 2 days and to Delhi, up to 4 days. Despite the difficulties, even if you do not have a firm outward booking and have been 'wait-listed' you may sometimes get on a flight at short notice, if weather conditions improve. It is worth asking. Check-in early to stand a better chance. **Indian Airlines**, T52255, F52155, airport T52255, flies from **Delhi**, 0620, Mon, Wed, Fri, Sun in season (Jul-Sep), with an additional 7 flights per week offered through its subsidiary **Alliance Air**, returns 1110 same days (in winter, this is the only link between Ladakh and the outside world); to **Jammu**, Mon, Fri; **Chandigarh**, Wed; **Srinagar**, Sun. Jet Airways, T50999, airport T53754, to **Delhi**.

Bus
Local The New Bus Stand is near the cemetery. The vehicles are ramshackle but the fares are low. See under monasteries for details. Enquiries J&KSRTC, T52285.
Long distance Himachal Tourism runs regular (not daily) Deluxe and Ordinary buses between Manali and Leh, usually mid-Jun to end-Sep, 2 days. To **Manali**, 530 km, 'Deluxe', booked at HPTDC, Fort Rd, or at travel agents, Rs 800 (Rs 1,100 includes camp bed and meals in Sarchu). Ordinary (Private) booked at bus stand, 'A' Rs 500, and 'B', Rs 350, stop overnight at Keylong. J&KSRTC bus **Kargil**, 230 km (alternate days in summer) Rs 110-180, **Srinagar** 434 km, Rs 200-360.

Road
If you have travelled by road you may already be better acclimatized, but a mild headache is common and can be treated with aspirin or paracetamol. Drink non-alcoholic fluids on journeys.

Leh is connected to Manali via Keylong (closed Oct to mid-Jun or longer) and to Srinagar, via Kargil, by a State Highway. Both can be seriously affected by landslides, causing long delays. The Leh-Srinagar Road is also often blocked by army convoys. Information on road conditions from the Traffic Police HQ, Maulana Azad Rd, Srinagar.

The road to **Manali**, crossing some very high passes, is open mid-Jun or early Jul, until end-Sep (depending on the weather) and takes 2 days. Road conditions may be poor in places. Departure from Leh can be

Jammu & Kashmir Listings: Ladakh

⁞ To fly or not to fly

Travel by road gives you an advantage over flying into Leh as it enables you to acclimatize to a high altitude plateau and if you are able to hire a jeep or car it will give you the flexibility of stopping to see the several sights on the way. However, some people find the bus journey from Manali (or Srinagar) terrifying and very uncomfortable, and most healthy people find that if they relax completely for two days after flying in, they acclimatize without difficulty. If you have a heart condition, consult your doctor on the advisability of your going to Leh.

early (0400) with overnight stop in Keylong; next day to Manali. Alternatively, camp in Sarchu (10 hrs from Leh), or Jespa; next day 14 hrs to Manali (Rs 150 each in Sarchu, camp). Roadside tents provide food *en route* during the tourist season; carry snacks, water and a good sleeping bag when planning to camp. Many travellers find the mountain roads extremely frightening and they are comparatively dangerous. Some are cut out of extremely unstable hillsides, usually with nothing between the road's edge and the nearly vertical drop below; parts remain rough and pot-holed and during the monsoons, landslides and rivers can make it impassable for 2-3 days. It is also a long and uncomfortable journey, but there is some spectacular scenery.

Taxi
4WD between Leh and Manali are expensive but recommended if you want to stop en route to visit monasteries. 2-day trip, about Rs 13,000. Taxis often return empty to Manali (some visitors choose to fly out of Leh) so may agree a much reduced fare for the return leg. Officially, Manali (or Srinagar) taxis are allowed to carry their passengers to and from Leh but are not permitted to do local tours, a rule fiercely monitored by the Leh Taxi Operators' Union.

Tourist taxi and jeep: Ladakh Taxi Operators' Union, Fort Rd. Fixed fares point to-point. From the airport to Main Bazar, about Rs 80; from Bus Stand Rs 60. A day's taxi hire to visit nearby *gompas* costs about Rs 1,000-1,200; Nubra Rs 6,000.

Alchi *p550*
Bus
Srinagar bound buses stop at Saspul; from there it is a 2½-km walk across the bridge. Buses depart for Leh for Alchi, around 0630, 1500, nearly 3 hrs.

❶ Directory

Leh *p543, maps p544 and p546*
Banks It is not possible to get money on credit cards. J&K Bank, Main Bazar; State Bank of India, exchange only next to tourist office, but slow. Large hotels and Amex (1030-1430, Sat 1030-1230) in Kangri and *Yak Tail*, charge a steep commission.
Hospitals SNM Hospital, T52014, 0900-1700 (also for advice on mountain sickness), after hours, T52360. During the day, doctors have little time; better at clinics in evenings. Soway Clinic, in Bazar; Kunfan Octsnang Clinic; Ladakh Medicate, behind post office (ask for Dr Norbu, Old Leh Rd).
Internet Email very erratic. Phone connections with the rest of India are unpredictable. On Fort Rd. **Post office** Head Post Office and Telegraph Office: Airport Rd, 3 km from Leh centre (1000-1500); parcels often disappear. Mail may be sent via Gypsy's World, Fort Rd, T52935 (not fail safe); make sure addressed c/o Gypsy's World, PO Box 160, Leh, Ladakh 194101, India. **Telephone** Pick up faxes here for a small fee; **Tourist offices** J&K, 2 km south, on Airport Rd, T5229.
Useful addresses Ambulance: T52014. Police: T52018. Foreigners' Registration Office: T52200.

Introduction

East India is the least visited region of India, yet it contains some of the country's most beautiful scenery, remarkable religious monuments and vibrant cultural centres. In **Kolkata** (Calcutta) it has India's second largest city, famous for its cultural contribution to the national life, yet at the same time notorious for its poverty. The Orissan temples of **Puri**, **Bhubaneswar** and **Konark** are among the most striking architectural monuments of any period of India's religious building, while in the interior of **Orissa**, **Bihar** and **Jharkhand**, as well as in the **Northeastern Hill States** and the **Andaman** and **Nicobar Islands**, some tribal societies are only just being brought into contact with the modern world. Forming the most impressive mountain frontier in the world, the **Himalaya** to the north have some of their most magnificent peaks in East India, with **Kangchendzonga** towering over **Sikkim** and the northern **hill stations** of West Bengal.

West Bengal

🍴 Footprint features

Introduction

The northern foothills of West Bengal's **Himalaya** are one of the great tea growing regions of the world. They can still be reached by the romantic steam-pulled 'toy train', now a World Heritage Site. **Darjeeling**, one of the picturesque hill stations imprinted with images of the colonial inheritance, is overlooked by the everlasting snows of the great **Kanchendzonga Range**.

To the south, in one of the world's most densely populated agricultural regions, **Kolkata** dominates the political, economic and cultural life of much of eastern India, a city that has fascinated, shocked and entranced, in almost equal measure, generations of visitors. The villages and towns which are scattered across the intensively cultivated rural landscape surrounding the city also have much to offer. In the border regions of **Bangladesh** are the remains of Muslim capitals of medieval eastern India and the remarkable terracotta temples of Bishnupur.

To the far south the humid mangroves of the **Sunderbans**, whose mudflats fade almost imperceptibly into the **Bay of Bengal**, are still home to a sizeable, though elusive, tiger population.

★ Don't miss...

❶ In **Kolkata**, contrast Lord Curzon's Victoria Memorial with the South Park Street cemetery, the last resting place of many of the Raj's servants, pages 575 and 577.

❷ Pamper your taste buds with some King Prawn cutlets followed by *mishti* (sweetmeats) at Kolkata's **Bengali restaurants**, page 587.

❸ After the bustle and noise of Kolkata, spend a peaceful day at the university town of **Santiniketan**, with its quiet, rural charm, page 596.

❹ There is a great Wednesday and Sunday market at **Kalimpong** with lots of unusual goods on sale, page 609.

❺ Visit a tea-growing estate in **Darjeeling** and trek through the flowering magnolias and rhododendrons bushes in the spring, page 607.

❻ If it is too cold in the hills, head down to the coast and see if you can spot a tiger swimming in the **Sunderban mangrove swamps**, page 619.

West Bengal

Background → *Population: 80.2 million. Area: 88,752 sq km. 6%. www.wbtourism.com.*

The land

Graphically described as being made up of "new mud, old mud and marsh", most of West Bengal lies on the western delta of the Ganga. Its limited higher ground, the basalt **Rajmahal Hills** just west of Murshidabad, are an extension of the ancient rocks of the peninsula. All that remains of the dense forests that once covered the state are the mangrove swamps of the **Sunderbans** in the far south and a narrow wooded belt along the southern slopes of the Himalaya.

The apparently unchanging face of the Bengali countryside is highly misleading. Rivers have constantly changed their courses, and over the last 300 years the Ganga has shifted progressively east, leaving the Hugli as a relatively minor channel. Minor variations in height make enormous differences to the quality of land for farming. Houses cluster along old river banks and any slightly higher ground that gives protection against floods. But the chief variety in the landscape of the plains of Bengal comes from the contrasting greens of the different varieties of rice and the clusters of tree-shaded hamlets, often producing startlingly attractive countryside.

The dominating mountains to the north and the plateau and hills of the southwest provide far greater scenic contrasts than the plains. The gently rising slopes which lead from the delta to the peninsular rocks of Bihar and Orissa, are the home of some of India's most primitive tribal peoples, although their forest habitat has been severely degraded.

Climate Hot and oppressively humid summers are followed by much cooler and clearer winters. Heavy storms occur in late March and April. These electric storms are marked by massive cloud formations, strong winds and heavy rain. Occasionally tropical cyclones also strike coastal areas at this time of year, though they are far more common between October and December.

History

In **prehistoric times** Bengal was home to Dravidian hunter-gatherers. In the first millennium BC, the Aryans from Central Asia, who had learned the agricultural techniques of the Indus Valley civilization and the art of weaving and pottery, arrived in Bengal, bringing with them the Sanskrit language. From about the fifth century BC trade in cotton, silk and coral from Ganga Nagar flourished. In the third century BC Bengal was part of the Mauryan Empire, but it remained densely forested and comparatively sparsely populated.

The **Guptas** conquered Bengal in the fourth century AD and trade with the Mediterranean expanded for the next 200 years, particularly with Rome. The fall of the Roman Empire in the fifth century led to a decline in Bengal's fortunes. Only with the founding of the **Pala Dynasty** in AD 750 was the region united once again. Bengal became a centre of Buddhism, and art and learning flourished. The **Senas** followed. They were great patrons of the arts and ruled for 50 years until deposed by the invading Turks, who began a century of Muslim rule under the Khaljis of the Delhi Sultanate. The birth of **Sri Chaitanya** in 1486, believed by many to be an incarnation of Lord Krishna, brought a revival of interest in Vedic literature. However, political power remained with the Muslims. The most notable of the Pathan kings who followed the Khaljis was Sher Shah, who extended his territory from Bihar into Bengal, which was ultimately taken back by the Mughal emperor Akbar, anxious to obtain the rich resources of rice, silk and saltpetre, between 1574 and 1576.

The increasing power of the Muslims spurred the **Portuguese** towards the subcontinent and they began trading with Bengal in the mid-16th century. Before long they faced competition from the Dutch and the British and in 1632 an attack on their port near Kolkata by Emperor Shah Jahan reduced their merchant power.

In 1690 the purchase of the three villages which grew into Calcutta, enabled the British to build a fort and consolidate their power. In 1700, Bengal became an independent Presidency and Calcutta prospered. The *firmans* (permits) granted were for trading from the ports but the British took the opportunity of gaining a monopoly over internal trade as well. The internal waterways gave them access to rich resources and to the other commodities was added the export of saltpetre to fuel the wars in Europe. After the death of the Emperor Aurangzeb, the authority of Delhi slowly crumbled. In 1756, Siraj-ud-Daula, the then Nawab of Bengal, began to take note of Kolkata's growing wealth. Finding the British strengthening the fortifications he attacked Fort William, finding little difficulty in capturing the city. Within a year, however, Clive took the city back and then defeated the Nawab at Plassey – a turning point for the British in India. Through the 19th century West Bengal became the economic and political centre of **British India**. Indigo and opium in the first half of the century, jute in the second, became staples of trade, along with engineering industries which grew with Kolkata's port activities and focus as a railway centre.

Calcutta developed as the major centre of **cultural and political activity** in modern India. Bengali literature, drama, art and music flourished. Religious reform movements such as the **Brahmo Samaj**, under the leadership of **Raja Ram Mohan Roy** in the 1830s, grew out of the juxtaposition of traditional Hinduism with Christian missionary activity in the early 19th century. Later, one of India's greatest poets, Nobel Prize winner **Rabindranath Tagore** (1861-1941), dominated India's cultural world, breathing moral and spiritual life into the political movement for independence.

Until 1905 Bengal had included much of modern Bihar and Orissa, as well as the whole of Bengal. Lord Curzon's short-lived Partition of Bengal in 1905 roused fierce opposition, and also encouraged the split between Muslims and Hindus which finally resulted in Bengali Muslim support for the creation of Pakistan in 1947. The division into the two new states was accompanied by the migration of over five million people and appalling massacres as Hindus and Muslims fled. West Bengal was again directly affected by the struggle to create Bangladesh, when about 10 million refugees arrived from East Pakistan after 25 March 1971. Most of them returned after Bangladesh gained its independence in December 1971.

Culture

The majority of the people are Bengalis. Tribal groups include Santals, Oraons and Mundas in the plains and the borders of Chota Nagpur, and Lepchas and Bhotias in the Himalaya. Over 85% of the population speak Bengali. Hindi, Urdu and tribal languages account for most of the remainder.

Bengalis are said to be obsessed about what they eat. The men often take a keen interest in buying the most important elements of the day's meal, namely fresh fish from the bazar. Typically, it is river fish, the most popular being *hilsa* and *bekti* or the widely available shellfish, especially king prawns. *Bekti* is grilled or fried and is tastier than the 'fried fish' of the west as it has often been marinated in mild spices first. The prized smoked hilsa, although delicious, has thousands of fine bones. *Maachh* (fish) comes in many forms as *jhol* (in a thin gravy), *jhal* (spicy and hot), *malai curry* (in coconut milk, mildly spiced), 'chop' (in a covering of mashed potato and crumbs) or *chingri maachher* 'cutlet' (flattened king prawn 'fillets', crumbed and fried). 'Chop' and 'cutlet' are hangovers, in name only, from the days of the Raj! Bengali cooking

You will only find the true flavour of Bengali cooking in someone's home, or at a couple of special Bengali restaurants.

uses mustard oil and mustard which grows in abundance, and a subtle mixture of spices. *Panch Phoron*, a mixture of five spices (cumin, mustard, fennel, onion seed and fenugreek) is used in some vegetable preparations. *Mishti* (sweetmeats) are another distinctive feature. Many are milk based and the famous *sandesh*, *roshogolla, roshomalai, pantua* and *Ladycaney* (named after Lady Canning, the wife of the first Viceroy of India!) are prepared with a kind of cottage cheese, in dozens of different textures, shapes, colours and tastes. Nearly all, though delicious, are very sweet. Pale pinkish brown, *mishti doi*, is an excellent sweet yoghurt eaten as a dessert, typically sold in hand-thrown clay pots.

Crafts

Silk has been woven in India for more than 3,500 years. The tradition continues with the weaving of the natural coloured wild silk called *tassar*. Bengal silk, commonly found as block-printed saris, has had a revival in the exquisite brocade weaving of *baluchari*, produced in the past under royal patronage, and is carried out today in Bankura. The saris are woven in traditional style with untwisted silk and have beautiful borders and *pallu* (the end section), which often depict horses, peacocks, flowers and human figures. **Fine cotton** is woven into saris, fabrics and articles for everyday use.

The **Bankura horse** has become a symbol of **pottery** in West Bengal which still flourishes in the districts of Bankura, see page 595, Midnapore and Birbhum. Soft **soap-stone** is used for carving copies of temple images, while **shell** bangles are considered auspicious. **Ivory** carvers once produced superb decorative items, a skill developed in the Mughal period. Today, bone and plastic have largely replaced ivory in inlay work. **Metal** workers produce brass and bell-metal ware while the tribal *dhokra* casters still follow the ancient *cire perdue* or lost-wax method, see page 689. The Kalighat *pat* paintings, too, are in a primitive style using bold colours and mythological themes. *Pats* go back to a time when travelling painter-storytellers went from village to village entertaining people with their tales, using illustrated scrolls.

Modern West Bengal

Since the mid-1960s political life has been dominated by the confrontation between the Communist Party of India Marxist (the CPM) and the Congress Party. The CPM has held power in the State Assembly continuously since June 1977. The Congress, the second largest party, has performed consistently better in the Lok Sabha parliamentary elections. Although the CPM retained power in the 1996 Assembly elections, its share of the urban vote, especially in Kolkata, dropped sharply, but Jyoti Basu, its octogenarian Chief Minister, remained one of India's most respected politicians. Jyoti Basu's retirement led some to expect an upset for the Communists. However, the Assembly elections in 2001 were won convincingly by the CPM-led Left Front under the new Chief Minister Buddhadeb Bhattacharjee.

★ Kolkata (Calcutta)

→ *Phone code: 033. Colour map 4, grid C2. Population: 13.22 million. www.wbtourism.com.*
To Bengalis Kolkata is the proud intellectual capital of India, with an outstanding contribution to the arts, services, medicine and social reform in its past, and a rich contemporary cultural life. As the former Imperial capital, Kolkata retains some of the country's most striking colonial buildings, yet at the same time it is truly an Indian city. Unique in India in retaining trams and in its underground metro, you take your life in your hands each time you cross Kolkata's streets. Hugely crowded, Kolkata's maidan, the parkland, give lungs to a city packed with some of the most densely populated slums, or bustees, anywhere in the world. ⟩⟩ *For Sleeping, Eating and other listings, see pages 585-595.*

Ins and outs

Getting there The Subhas Chandra Bose airport at Dum Dum serves both international and domestic flights with a taxi or coach transfer to the city centre taking 30-45 mins. **Haora (Howrah) station,** on the west bank of the Hugli, can be daunting and the taxi rank outside is often chaotic. Long distance buses arrive at Esplanade, within 15-20 mins' walk of most budget hotels.

Getting around You can cover much of Central Kolkata on foot but crossing a busy road can be a nightmare. For the rest you need transport. You may not fancy using hand-pulled rickshaws (unique to Kolkata), but they become indispensable when the streets are flooded. Buses and minibuses are often jam-packed and are best avoided. The electric trams can be slightly better outside peak periods. The city's showpiece Metro, though on a limited route, is worth a try. Taxis are relatively cheap but allow plenty of time to get through very congested traffic. Note that despite the footpath, it is not permitted to walk across the Vidyasagar Bridge (fine enforced). Taxi drivers expect passengers to pay the Rs 7 toll. See Transport, page 592 for further details.

Climate Temperature: summer, maximum 36°C, minimum 25°C; winter maximum 26°C, minimum 12°C. Rainfall: Jun-Sep 275 mm to Nov-Mar 10 mm. Best time to visit: Nov-Mar.

The city

Calcutta, as it came to be named, was founded by the remarkable English merchant trader **Job Charnock** in 1690. He was in charge of the East India Company factory (ie warehouse) in Hugli, then the centre of British trade from eastern India. Attacks from the local Muslim ruler forced him to flee - first down river to Sutanuti and then 1,500 km south to Chennai. However, in 1690 he selected three villages – Kalikata, Sutanuti and Govindpur – where Armenian and Portuguese traders had already settled, leased them from Emperor Aurangzeb and returned to what was to become the capital of British India.

The first fort here, named after King William III (completed 1707), was on the site of the present BBD Bagh. A deep defensive moat was dug in 1742 to strengthen the fort – the Maratha ditch. The Maratha threat never materialized but the city was captured easily by the 20-year-old **Siraj-ud-Daula**, the new Nawab of Bengal, in 1756. The 146 British residents who failed to escape by the fort's river gate were imprisoned

West Bengal Kolkata The City

Rabindra Bharati University & Museum

Rabindra Setu

Haora Bridge
Armenian Ghat
Motiseal Ghat

Haora Station

GT Rd
Church Rd
Rishi Ban Km Ch Rd

JORASANKO

Mahatma Gandhi Rd
M M Burman St
Rabindra

Sikh Gurudwara
BARA-BAZAR
Roman Catholic Cathedral

Armenian Church
Jewish Synagogue
Parsi Temple
Kolutola St
Nakhoda

HAORA

Teikal Ghat
Ramkrishnapur Ghat

Strand Rd
N Subhas Rd
Brabourne Rd

TIRETTA BAZAR

Foreshore Rd

Related maps
A *Central Kokata, page 574*
B *Around Sudder Street, page 576*
C *Park Street, page 578*

BBD BAGH

W Bengal Tourist Office
Old Court House St
Govt Place West

BOW BAZAR

Chandpal Ghat
St John's Church

Industrial Museum

Babu Ghat

Raj Bhavan
Govt Place East
Tipu Sultan's Mosque

GT Rd

Sibpur Rd

Eden Gardens
Eden Gardens Rd

Esplanade

To Botanical Gardens

Hugli River

Outram Ghat
Ranji Stadium

Lenin

Strand Rd

6

MAIDAN
G Nanak Sarani
Red Rd

New Market

B

Princep Ghat
Vidyasagar Setu

Sudder St

Dufferin Rd
JL Nehru Rd

6

Fort William

C

Napier Rd

St George's Gate

Castaviria Av
(Chowringhee)
Russell St
Park St

HASTINGS

Khidirpur Rd

7

Ho Chi Minh Sarani
Shakespeare Sarani
Cathedral Rd

US Consulate
CIS Consulate

Munshiganj Rd

Queens Way
Victoria Memorial & Museum

Planetarium

Laudon

Hospital Rd

St Paul's Cathedral
Air India
Nehru Children's Museum
Bengal Home Industries & Aeroflot

Pretoria St
Camac St

ISKCON
La Martiniere School
Kala Mandir

Race Course

Rabindra Sadan

Bhutan Consulate

Polo Ground

AJC Bose Rd

Central Plaza

Tolly's Nullah

Woodlands Nursing Home

AJC Bose Rd

Calcutta Club
8
Foreigners Registration Office

South Club

Max Muller Bhavan
AAEI

KHIDIRPUR

Belvedere Rd

4
Zoo

1
7

Netaji Bhavan
4
Elgin Rd
Heysham Rd

Bhowanipur Rd
Harish Mukharji Rd

BHAWANIPUR
Sanat Bose Rd

National Library

9

Paddopukur Rd

P Barua Sarani

Diamond Harbour Rd
Alipur Rd

Nepal Consulate

Calcutta Hospital

Horticultural Gardens

Kalighat Rd
Ashutosh Mukherjee Rd

Ramesh Ch Mitter Rd
Landsdowne Market

Motilal Nehru Rd
Ritchie Rd

2

German Consulate

Behala Rd

ALIPUR

Judges Court Rd

10

To IIM & Behala

To Kali Temple

To Tolly Club & Rabindra Sarobar

N

0 metres 300
0 yards 300

■ Sleeping	● Eating	
1 Hindusthan International	1 Aqua Java	5 Mainland China
2 New Haven	2 China Valley & Hot Breads	6 Scoop
3 Railway Retiring Rooms	3 Coffee House	7 Tibetan
4 Taj Bengal	4 Kewpie's Kitchen	8 Wimpy

for a night in a small guard room about 6 **573**
m by 5 m with only one window – the infamous **'Black Hole of Calcutta'**. Some records suggest 64 were imprisoned and only 23 survived.

The following year **Robert Clive** re-took the city. The new Fort William was built and in 1772 Calcutta became the capital of British administration in India with Warren Hastings as the first Governor of Bengal, see page 1306. Some of Calcutta's most impressive colonial buildings were built in the years that followed, when it became the first city of British India. It was also a time of Hindu and Muslim resurgence.

Kolkata: Independence & after

Colonial Calcutta grew as new traders, soldiers, administrators and their wives arrived, establishing their exclusive social and sports clubs. Trade in cloth, silk, lac, indigo, rice, areca nut and tobacco had originally attracted the Portuguese and British to Bengal. Later Calcutta's hinterland producing jute, iron ore, tea and coal led to large British firms establishing their headquarters in the city. Calcutta prospered as the commercial and political capital of British India up to 1911, when the capital was transferred to Delhi.

Independence and after

Kolkata had to absorb huge numbers of migrants immediately after Partition in 1947. When Pakistan ceased trading with India in 1949, Kolkata's economy suffered a massive blow as it lost its supplies of raw jute, and its failure to attract new investment created critical economic problems.

In the late 1960s the election of the Communist Party of India Marxist (**CPM**) led to a period of stability. As the party of Government the CPM has become committed to a mixed economy and has actively sought foreign private investment.

Ⓜ Metro Stations

1 Girish Park	6 Park St
2 MG Rd	7 Maidan
3 Central	8 Rabindra Sadan
4 Chandni Chowk	9 Dhawalipur
5 Esplanade	10 Jatindas Park

West Bengal Kolkata The City

Sights

Central Kolkata

★ **BBD Bagh (Dalhousie Sq)** Many historic Raj buildings surround the square which is quietest before 0900. Re-named Benoy Badal Dinesh (BBD) Bagh after three Bengali martyrs, the square has a small artificial lake, fed by natural springs. On Strand Road North is the dilapidated **Silver Mint** (1824-31).

The **Writers' Building** (1780), designed by Thomas Lyon as the trading HQ of the East India Company, was refaced in 1880. It is now the state Government Secretariat. The classical block with 57 sets of identical windows was built like barracks inside. **Mission Row** (now RN Mukharji Road) is Kolkata's oldest street,

Central Kolkata

■ Sleeping	● Eating	
1 Oberoi Grand	1 Amber	3 Nizam's
2 Peerless Inn	2 Eau Chew	4 Sagar

▪ Kolkata's place in the cosmic dance

Kolkata's site was particularly holy to Hindus. According to one myth, **King Daksa** was enraged when his daughter **Sati** married **Siva**. He organized a **Yajna** (grand sacrifice) to which he invited everyone in the kingdom – except his son-in-law. Distraught, **Kali** (Sati) threw herself on the sacrificial flames. Siva in turn arrived on the scene to find his wife's body already burnt. Tearing it from the flames, he started his dance of cosmic destruction. All the other gods, witnessing the devastation that Siva was causing in his anguish, pleaded with Vishnu to step in and end the chaos. **Vishnu** intercepted him with his *chakra* (discus-like weapon) and, in order to dislodge Kali's body from Siva's shoulder, chopped it into 51 pieces, which were flung far and wide. The place where each one fell became a place of pilgrimage – a *pithasthana*. Kali's little toe fell at Kali Ghat. The place, Kalikshetra or Kalikata, gave the city its name.

and contains the **Old Mission Church** (consecrated 1770), built by the Swedish missionary Johann Kiernander.

South of BBD Bagh The imposing **Raj Bhavan** (1799- 1802) is the residence of the Governor of West Bengal, formerly Government House. It was modelled on Kedleston Hall in Derbyshire, England (later Lord Curzon's home), and designed by **Charles Wyatt**, one of many Bengal engineers who based their designs on famous British buildings. Entry is restricted. The **Town Hall** (1813) has been converted into a museum. The **High Court** (1872) was modelled on the medieval cloth merchants' hall at Ypres in Flanders.

▪ *Sightseeing takes time, and Kolkata can be very hot and humid outside Nov -early Mar. Asthma sufferers find the traffic pollution very trying.*

The **Ochterlony Monument** (1828), re-named Shahid Minar (Martyrs' Memorial) in 1969, was built as a memorial to **Sir David Ochterlony**, who led East India Company troops against the Nepalese in 1814-16. The 46-m tall Greek Doric column has an Egyptian base and is topped by a Turkish cupola.

★ **St John's Church** (1787) (0900-1200, 1700-1800), like the later St Andrew's Kirk (1818), was modelled partially on St Martin-in-the-Fields, London. The soft sub-soil did not allow it to have a tall spire and architecturally it was thought to be 'full of blunders'. Verandahs were added to the north and south in 1811 to reduce the glare of the sun. Inside are Warren Hastings's desk and chair and the tomb of Bishop Middleton, first Bishop of Calcutta. 'The Last Supper', by **Johann Zoffany** in the south aisle, shows the city's residents dressed as the Apostles. Job Charnock is buried in the old cemetery. His octagonal mausoleum, the oldest piece of masonry in the city, is of Pallavaram granite (from Madras Presidency), which is named charnockite after him. The monument to the **Black Hole of Calcutta** was brought here from Dalhousie Square (BBD Bagh) in 1940.

Park Street ★ **South Park St Cemetery** The cemetery was opened in 1767 to accommodate the large number of the British who died serving their country. The heavily inscribed, decaying headstones, obelisks, pyramids and urns have been somewhat restored. A good booklet is available. Allow about 30 minutes. If alone, avoid going when it is deserted. A security guard opens the gate for foreigners, and will expect you to sign the visitors' book.

The cemetery is a quiet space on the south side of one of Kolkata's busiest streets. Gardners are actively trying to beautify the grounds. Several of the inscriptions make interesting reading. Death, often untimely, came from tropical diseases or other hazards such as battles, childbirth and even melancholia. More uncommonly, it was an excess of alcohol, or as for Sir Thomas D'Oyly, through "an inordinate use of the hokkah". Rose Aylmer died after eating too many pineapples! Tombs include those of **Col Kyd**, founder of the Botanical Gardens, and the great oriental scholar **Sir William Jones**.

Around Sudder Street Conveniently close to Chowringhee and the vast shopping arcade, New Market, Sudder Street is the focus for Kolkata's **backpackers** but it attracts very persistent touts and drug pushers. Beggars on Chowringhee and Park Street, often belong to organized syndicates who have to pay a large percentage of their 'earnings' for the privilege of working that area.

Around Sudder Street

N

0 metres 100
0 yards 100

■ **Sleeping**
1 Afraa, Delux, Paramount & Shabnam
2 Biman
3 Centre Point

4 Classic
5 Continental & Super Guest House
6 Crystal
7 Diplomat
8 Eagle Palace
9 Fairlawn
10 Galaxy
11 Green Star
12 Gujral Guest House
13 Lytton

14 Maria
15 Modern Lodge
16 Oberoi Grand
17 Paragon
18 Presidency Inn
19 Red Shield Guest House
20 Shilton
21 Sonali Resort
22 Timestar
23 Tourist Inn

● **Eating**
1 Blue Sky & Curd Corner
2 Jimmy's
3 Jo-Jo's
4 Kathleen's Bakery
5 Kathi Kebabs
6 Khalsa
7 Nahoum Bakery
8 Prince
9 Zaranj
10 Zurich

⁝ Changing street names

Although many of the city's streets have been renamed over the last three decades, the old names still survive in popular use and are more easily recognized by the public at large.

Bowbazar Street Bepin Beharii Ganguly Street
Chowringhee JL Nehru Road
Free School Street Mirza Ghalib Street
Harrington Street Ho-Chi-Minh Sarani
Harrison Road Mahatma Gandhi Road
Kyd Street Dr M Ishaque Road
Landsdowne Road Sarat Bose Road
Lindsay Street Nelly Sengupta Sarani
Lower Chitpur Road Rabindra Sarani
Lower Circular Road Acharya JC Bose Road
Theatre Road Shakespeare Sarani
Wellesley Street Rafi Ahmed Kidwai Road

The Maidan This area, 200 years ago, was covered in dense jungle. Often called the 'lungs' of the city, it is a unique 'green', covering over 400 ha along Chowringhee (JL Nehru Road). Larger than New York's Central Park, it is perhaps the largest urban park in the world! In it stands Fort William and several club houses providing tennis, football, rugby, cricket and even crown green bowls. Thousands each day pursue a hundred different interests – from early morning yogis, model plane enthusiasts, weekend cricketers and performers earning their living, to vast political gatherings.

Chowringhee You can still see some of the old imposing structures with pillared verandahs (designed by Italian architects as residences of prominent Englishmen) though modern high rise buildings have transformed the skyline of this ancient pilgrim route to Kalighat.

St Paul's Cathedral ① *0900-1200, 1500-1800, 5 services on Sun*, is the original metropolitan church of British India. Completed in 1847, its Gothic tower (dedicated in 1938) was designed to replace the earlier steeples which were destroyed by earthquakes. The cathedral has a fine altar piece, three 'Gothic' stained glass windows, two Florentine frescoes and the great West window by **Burne-Jones**. The original stained glass East window, intended for St George's Windsor, was destroyed by a cyclone in 1964 and was replaced by the present one four years later.

★ **Victoria Memorial** ① *Mar-Oct 1000-1630, Nov-Feb 1000-1530; Museum closed Mon (very crowded on Sun), 1000-1530, Rs 5 (foreigners Rs 150), guided tours at 1030 (allow at least 1 hr), cameras not permitted. Sound & Light show, summer 1945, winter 1915, 45 mins, Rs 20 front seats, Rs 10 elsewhere.* Lord Curzon's white marble monument to Queen Victoria and the Raj (1906-21) designed in Italian Renaissance-Mughal style stands in large, well-kept grounds with ornamental pools. A seated bronze Queen Victoria dominates the approach, while a marble statue stands in the main hall where visitors sometimes leave flowers at her feet! The building is illuminated in the evening; the 'musical fountain' is a special draw. The statues over the entrance porches (including Motherhood, Prudence and Learning), and around the central dome (of Art, Architecture, Justice, Charity) came from Italy. The impressive weather vane, a 5-m tall bronze winged figure of Victory weighing three tons, looks tiny from below. The principal gallery, covering the history of the city, includes a wealth of Raj memorabilia. There are fine miniatures, a rare collection of Persian manuscripts, and paintings by **Zoffany**, the two **Daniells**, and Samuel **Davis**.

Fort William After the defeat in 1756, see page 568, the British built a new massive fort on the site of the village of Govindapur. Designed to be impregnable, it was roughly octagonal and large enough to house all the Europeans in the city in case of an attack. Water from the river Hugli was channelled to fill the wide moat and the jungle around it was cleared to give a clear field of fire, which later became the Maidan. The barracks, stables, arsenal, prison and St Peter's Church are still there. Today the fort is the Eastern Region's Military Headquarters so you need permission to enter.

Park Street

Sleeping		
1	Astor	
2	Golden Park	
3	Gulsham International	
4	Kenilworth	
5	Middleton Inn	
6	Park	
7	VIP International	

8 YWCA

Eating
1 Big Max & Gangaur
2 Blue Fox & Bar-B-Q
3 Floriana
4 Flury's, Silver Grill
5 Golden Dragon

6 Gupta Brothers
7 Kwality
8 Mocambo
9 Moulin Rouge
10 Peter Cat
11 Pure Milk Centre
12 Upper Crust Bakery
   & A/c Market

0 metres 100
0 yards 100

West Bengal Kolkata Sights

☷ Worship of the clay goddess

Durga Puja, the 17th-century festival in honour of the 'clay goddess', precedes the full moon in late September/early October, when all offices and institutions close down and the Metro only operates from the late afternoon.

Images of the 10-armed, three-eyed goddess, a form of Shakti or Kali (see page 1331) astride her 'vehicle' the lion, portray Durga slaying Mahisasura, the evil 'buffalo' demon. Durga, shown with her four children Lakshmi, Sarasvati, Ganesh and Kartik, is worshipped in hundreds of brightly illuminated and beautifully decorated pandals (marquees) made of bamboo and coloured cloth. The priests perform prayers at appointed times in the morning and evening. On the fourth and last day of festivities, huge and often emotionally charged processions follow devotees who

carry the clay figures to be immersed in the river at many points along the banks. The potters return to collect clay from the river bank once again for the following year.

You can see the imagemakers in Kumartuli (see page 579) a few days earlier and visit the *pandals* early in the evening, before they become crowded. Local communities are immensely proud of their *pandals* and no effort is spared to put on the most impressive display. The images are decorated with intricate silver, golden or *shola* (white pith) ornaments, there are 'moving' electric light displays and huge structures are built (sometimes resembling a temple) in order to win competitions. The WB Tourist Bureau offers an all-night bus tour (Rs 50) as well as a two-hour launch trip on the Hugli to watch the immersion ceremony on the last night.

North Kolkata

On the opposite side of the river from Belur Math, the **Dakshineshwar Kali temple** ① *open to all; often crowded, buses from BBD Bagh*, was built in 1847 by Rani Rashmoni. The 12 smaller temples in the courtyard are dedicated to Siva, Radha and Krishna. Because of the Rani's low caste, no priest would serve there until Ramakrishna's elder brother agreed and was succeeded by Ramakrishna himself. Here, **Ramakrishna** achieved his spiritual vision of the unity of all religions.

South of the temple is Chitpur and **Kumartuli**. Off Chitpur Road, the *kumars* or potters work all year, preparing clay images around cores of bamboo and straw. For generations they have been making life-size idols for the *pujas* or festivals, particularly of Goddess Durga on a lion, slaying the demon. The images are usually unbaked since they are immersed in the holy river at the end of the festival. As the time of the *pujas* approaches, you will see thousands of images, often very brightly painted and gaudily dressed, awaiting the final finishing touch by the master painter. There are also *shola* artists, who make decorations for festivals and weddings .

Just north of the Belgachia metro station is the ornate Digambar Jain **Paresnath Temple** ① *0600-1200, 1500-1900, no leather*, dedicated to the 10th Tirthankara. Consecrated around 1867, it is richly decorated with mirrors and Venetian glass mosaics.

College Street This is the heart of intellectual Kolkata with the **university** and several academic institutions, including the old **Sanskrit College** and the élite **Presidency College**. Europeans and Indian benefactors established the Hindu College (1817) to provide a "liberal education". In 1855, this became the Presidency College. A centre for 19th-century Bengali writers, artists and reformers, it spawned the early 20th-century Swadeshi Movement. The famous **'Coffee House'** (opened in 1944), the

West Bengal Kolkata Sights

smoke-filled, cavernous haunt of the city's intelligentsia, still sells a good cup of coffee. Along the pavements are interesting second-hand book stalls.

Marble Palace ⓘ *closed Mon and Thu, 1000-1600, free pass from WB Tourist Bureau, 3/2 BBD Bagh, 24 hrs ahead, shoes must be removed, photography restricted.* The 'Palace' is in *Chor Bagan* (Thieves' Garden) at 46 Muktaram Babu Street. The one-man collection of Raja Rajendra Mullick is in his ornate home (1835) with an Italianate courtyard, classical columns, a large tank and Egyptian sphinxes. Six sleeping marble lions and statuary grace the lawns. The long galleries are crammed with statues, pottery, mirrors, chandeliers and English, Dutch and Italian paintings, disorganized and gathering dust. Allow 45 minutes. The rambling museum on two floors has curiosity appeal.

Jorasanko and Haora Bridge area Jorasanko, north of the Marble Palace, is the family home of Rabindranath Tagore, see page 597. This is also the **Rabindra Bharati University** (see also museums below). Further north on Baghbazar Street is the **Girish Mancha**, the Government theatre complex. The gorgeously well-kept **Armenian Church** of Holy Nazareth (1724) reminds us of the important trading role the small Armenian community who mostly came from Iran, played from the 17th century. Though the church is locked on weekdays you may ask to look around as the vestry is open during office hours. The 200 or so Armenians in the city still hold a service in Armenian in one of their two churches here every Sunday. Their college in Mirza Ghalib Street only has about half-a-dozen pupils since it admits only those of Armenian descent. On its east side is the **Roman Catholic Cathedral** (1797), built by the Portuguese. The **Jewish** community, mostly Sephardic, of Baghdadi origin, was also once very prominent in commerce. Their two cavernous synagogues, the grander in Canning Street, are well maintained and still used for services on alternate Saturdays. There are only around 50 Jews left in the city who continue to congregate at Nahoum's bakery in the New Market; the Jewish Girls School in Park Street has no pupils from the community.

    Haora Bridge (pronounced How-ra), or 'Rabindra Setu', was opened in 1943. This single-span cantilever bridge, a prominent landmark, replaced the old pontoon bridge, which joined the city with Haora and the railway station. To avoid affecting river currents and silting, the two 80-m high piers rise from road level; the 450-m span expands by a metre on a hot day. Best avoided in rush hour, but enjoy the sight of wrestlers underneath the bridge. The 1993 **Vidyasagar Setu**, further south, has eased the burden (no pedestrians).

South Kolkata

Kali Temple ⓘ *0500-2000, priests demand donations after involving foreigners in 'puja'.* The temple to Kali (1809), the patron goddess of Kolkata, usually seen in her blood-thirsty form garlanded with skulls. There was an older temple here, where the goddess's little toe is said to have fallen when **Siva** carried her charred corpse in a frenzied dance of mourning, and she was cut into pieces by Vishnu's *chakra*, see page 575. Non-Hindus have limited access to this important Hindu pilgrimage centre. Where once human sacrifices were made, only goats are offered daily on two wooden blocks to the south of the temple.

Mother Teresa's Homes Mother Teresa, an Albanian by birth, came to India to teach as a Loreto nun in 1931. She started her Order of the Missionaries of Charity in Kalighat to serve the destitute and dying 19 years later. You may see nuns in their white cotton saris with blue borders busy working in the many homes, clinics and orphanages in the city. *Nirmal Hriday* ('Pure Heart'), near the Kali Temple, the first 'home' for the dying was opened in 1952. Mother Teresa died on 5 September 1997 but her work continues. Anyone interested in **voluntary work** should write in advance to the office at 54A AJC Bose (Lower Circular) Road, T2497115. The Mother House here has a **museum** ⓘ *Charity Office, T2449267, closed Thu, 0800-1200, 1500-1800.*

National Library ⓘ *Weekdays, 1000-1800.* The former winter residence of the Lieutenant Governors of Bengal is on Belvedere Road in Alipur. Warren Hastings was given the site on which he built an "ordinary Anglo-Indian building", which later additions made more impressive. Built in the Renaissance Italian style, it stands in large wooded grounds. There are 15 km of closed stacks while the reading room has 10,000 reference books. There is a Rare Books Section and the **Asutosh Mookerjee** collection.

Haora (Howrah) and the West Bank → *Colour map 4, grid C1*

North of the city, some 16 km across the Ganga, is **Belur Math** ⓘ *winter, 0630-1100, 1600-1930; 1530-1900*, the international headquarters of the **Ramakrishna Mission**, founded in 1899 by **Swami Vivekananda**, a disciple of the 19th-century Hindu saint Ramakrishna (see page 873). He preached the unity of all religions and to symbolize this the *Math* ('monastery') synthesizes Hindu, Christian and Islamic architectural styles in a peaceful and meditative atmosphere.

The **Botanical Gardens** ⓘ *0700-1700, avoid Sun and public holidays when it is very crowded. 'Enquiry' inside Haora Gate, near the bus stand. Getting there: a white/orange CTC bus from Esplanade "goes like the wind" across the 'new' bridge (15 mins). Avoid Bus 55 and minibuses which may take an hour negotiating the old bridge; a very slow, hot and bumpy journey. The gardens are known locally as "B (bee) Gardens"*, on the west bank of the Hugli, 20 km south from BBD Bagh, were founded in 1787 by the East India Company. The flourishing 250-year-old **banyan tree**, with a circumference of over 300 m, is perhaps the largest in the world. The original trunk was destroyed by lightning in 1919 but over 1,500 offshoots form an impressive sight. The Orchid Houses and Palm House are closed on Sunday. The **National Herbarium** ⓘ *closed Sun and 2nd Sat, 1015-1600*, has 1½ million specimens of dried plants, the largest collection in South and South East Asia. The gardens are sadly neglected (dirty, rubbish heaps, no waste bins, tree labels missing) but can still make a welcome change from the city.

Museums

Academy of Fine Arts ⓘ *Cathedral Rd, closed Mon, 1500-1800*, was founded in 1933. The collection includes miniature paintings, textiles, works of Jamini Roy, Tagore and Desmond Doig and modern Indian sculpture in the gardens. Galleries exhibit works of local artists. Guide service and occasional films.

The **Asiatic Society** ⓘ *1 Park St, weekdays 1000-2000 , weekends 1000-1700*, the oldest institution of Oriental studies in the world, was founded in 1784 by the great Orientalist, Sir William Jones. It is a treasure house of 150,000 books and 60,000 ancient manuscripts in most Asian languages. The museum includes an Asokan edict, rare coins and paintings.

The **Asutosh Museum** ⓘ *University Centenary Building, College St, closed Sun and University holidays, weekdays 1030-1630, Sat 1030-1500*, of eastern Indian art and antiquity includes textiles, terracotta figures and Bengali folk art, but is poorly maintained with large sections frequently closed off. Good booklet.

★ **Birla Academy of Art and Culture** ⓘ *108/109 Southern Ave, T4662843, closed Mon, 1600-2000*, concentrates on medieval and contemporary paintings and sculpture. Worth visiting.

Birla Industrial and Technological Museum ⓘ *19A Gurusaday Rd, Tue Sun, 1000-1700, Rs 7; Rs 2 for coal mine etc.* Has some interesting models and displays. Try the mock coal mine tour; give the robots a miss.

★ **Indian Museum** ⓘ *27 JL Nehru Rd, T2499902, Mar-Nov 1000-1700, Dec-Feb 1000-1630; closed Mon, Rs 10, foreigners Rs 150, cameras Rs 50, guidebook.* Possibly Asia's largest, the '*Jadu Ghar*' (House of Magic) founded in 1814, has a worthwhile collection. The colonnaded Italianate building facing the Maidan has 36 galleries (though large sections are often closed off). Parts are poorly lit and gathering dust so it is best to be selective: geological collection including Siwalik fossils, good natural history and anthropology, outstanding exhibits from the Harappa and Moenjodaro periods, prized collection of Buddhist art, miniature paintings, 'Art and Textile' with ivory, glass and silverware, 'Theme Gallery' with rare paintings and 200-year-old hand-drawn maps, and many more. You need permission to see the exceptional collection of over 50,000 coins. Allow at least two hours.

Rabindra Bharati University Museum ⓘ *6/4 Dwarakanath Tagore Lane (red walls visible down lane opposite 263 Rabindra Sarani), 1000-1700, Sat 1000-1330, Sun and holidays 1100-1400,* houses the life and works of Rabindranath Tagore, who won the Nobel prize for Literature in 1913, and the 19th-century Renaissance movement in Bengal, in his family home.

Eden Gardens

ⓘ *Usually open for matches only, a small tip at Gate 14 gains entry on other days.* These gardens, which are situated in the northwest corner of the Maidan, were named after Lord Auckland's sisters Emily and Fanny Eden. There are pleasant walks, a lake and a small Burmese pagoda (typical of this type of Pyatthat). Laid out in 1834, part forms the Ranji Stadium where the first cricket match was played in 1864. Today, Test matches (November-February), international tennis championships and other sports fixtures attract crowds of 100,000.

Excursions from Kolkata

There are several interesting places within reach of a day's outing. Road travel is very slow so leave central Kolkata well before 0800 to avoid the worst traffic. For visiting the Sunderbans, see page 619.

Barrackpur and Hugli District → *25 km away.*
The riverside Gandhi Ghat has a museum and there is a pleasant garden in memory of Jawaharlal Nehru. The bronze Raj statues which were removed from their pedestals in Central Kolkata after Independence have found their way to the gardens of the bungalow of the former Governor (now a hospital) in Barrackpur. The tower in the garden was part of the river signalling system.

Many European nations had outposts along the River Hugli. Hugli District has a rich history. When the Mughals lost power, several of the ancient seats of earlier rulers of Bengal became centres of foreign trade. The Portuguese and British settled at Hugli, the Dutch chose Chinsura, the French Chandernagore, the Danes Serampore, the Greeks had an outpost at Rishra and the Germans and Austrians one at Bhadreswar!

Srirampur (Serampore) → *24 km north of Kolkata*
Founded by the Danes in 1616 as Fredricnagore, 'Serampore', a garden city, became a Danish colony in 1755. From the early 19th century it was the centre of missionary activity, until sold to the East India Company in 1845. The Government House, two churches and a Danish cemetery remain. **College of Textile Technology** ⓘ *12 Carey Rd, 1000-1630 (Sat 1000-1300).*

The Baptist missionaries **Carey, Marshman** and **Ward** came to Serampore since they were not welcomed by the English administrators in Calcutta. They set up the Baptist Mission Press, which by 1805 was printing in seven Indian languages. **Serampore College** (1818) ① *visit Mon-Fri 1000-1600, Sat 1000-1300, with permission from the Principal*, India's first Christian Theological college, was allowed to award degrees by the Danish king in 1829. The library has rare Sanskrit, Pali and Tibetan manuscripts and the Bible in over 40 Asian languages.

Chandernagore

The former French colony, which dates back to 1673, was one of the tiny pockets of non-British India that did not gain independence in 1947, but was handed over to India after a referendum in 1950. The churches, convents and cemeteries of the French are still there, although the old French street names have been replaced by Bengali. The former Quai de Dupleix, with its riverfront benches, still has a somewhat Gallic air. The Bhubanesvari and Nandadulal **temples** are worth visiting, especially during *Jagaddhatri Puja*. The **'Institute Chandernagar'** ① *weekdays 1600-1830, Sun 1100-11700, closed Thu*, at the **Residency** has interesting documents and relics of the French in India. The orange-painted Italian missionary **church** (1726) also stands witness to Chandernagore's European past.

Chinsura and Hugli

The Dutch acquired Chinsura from the Nawab of Murshidabad in 1628 and built the **Fort Gustavus**, but it was exchanged with Sumatra (Indonesia) and became British in 1825. The octagonal **Dutch church** (1678) with its cemetery nearby, a 17th-century Armenian church and three East India Company barracks remain. The Dutch are still remembered at the **Shandesvar Siva temple** on special occasions, when the lingam is bizarrely decked in Western clothes and a Dutch sword!

The Portuguese set up a 'factory' in Hugli in 1537 but Emperor Shah Jahan took the important trading post in 1632. The East India Company built their 'factory' in 1651, destroyed in skirmishes which marked the following six years, but Clive regained Hugli for the Company in 1757.

The Shi'a **Imambara** of Hazi Mohammed Mohasin (1836-76) has fine marble inlay decoration, a silver pulpit and elaborate lanterns. In **Chota Pandua** nearby, interesting Muslim buildings include the ruins of the 14th-century Bari Masjid which has elements of Buddhist sculpture. The **Amulya Pratnasala Museum** ① *closed 2nd and 4th Tue, Wed, 1400-2100*, in Rajbalhat has sculpture, coins, terracottas and manuscripts.

Bandel

Bandel (Portuguese *bandar* - 'wharf') ① *trains from Kolkata, rickshaws locally*, is now a railway junction town. The

Kolkata excursions

To Berhampur
Nabadwip
Hugli River
Kalna
To Pandua (20 km)
Krishnanagar
Shantipur
NH 34
Tribeni
5
Bandel
Bansberia
3
Hugli
1
Chinsura
2
Naihati
Chandernagore
To Tarakeswar
7
Sheorapuli
To Barddhaman
3
Barrackpur
Serampore
25
NH 2
24
To Pandua (Hugli District) & Barddhaman
Bali
Dakshineshwar
To Barasat & Bongaon
Belur
NH 34
To Kharagpur
Haora
Dum Dum
NH 6
KOLKATA
To Kharagpur
Diamond Harbour
Kakdwip
To Ganga Sagar (135 km)

66 99 The seafaring Portuguese believed that the statue of Our Lady of Happy Voyages in the bell tower could work miracles. Lost in the river, while being carried to save it from Shah Jahan's soldiers, it miraculously 'reappeared' two centuries later.

Portuguese built **Bandel Church** to Our Lady of the Rosary around 1660, on the site of an older Augustinian monastery. The keystone of the original church (1599), perhaps the earliest in Bengal, is on the riverside gate. Destroyed in 1640 by Shah Jahan, the church was reinstated 20 years later. The seafaring Portuguese believed that the statue of Our Lady of Happy Voyages in the bell tower could work miracles. Lost in the river, while being carried to save it from Shah Jahan's soldiers, it miraculously 'reappeared' two centuries later. The 18th-century stone and terracotta **Hanseswari Temple** is 4 km away.

Tribeni and Pandua

Originally '*Saptagram*' (seven villages), Tribeni (three rivers) is particularly holy, being at the confluence of the Ganga, Saraswati and Kunti. It has many Hindu **temples** and 11th to 12th-century Vaishnavite and Buddhist structures. The remains of the **Mazar of Zafarkhan Ghazi** (1313), the earliest mausoleum in eastern India, shows how black basalt sculpture and columns of earlier Hindu temples and palaces were incorporated into Muslim buildings.

Pandua (Hugli District) has several remains of the Pala and Sena periods. Shah Sufi-ud-din is thought to have built the 39-m **Victory Tower** after defeating the local Hindu ruler in 1340. Its circular base had a court house. Outside, a staircase spirals up the fluted surface, while inside there is enamelled decoration. Hoards of Kushana and Gupta Dynasty gold coins have been found in nearby **Mahanad**.

Kalna

ⓘ *Kalna has trains from Kolkata and rickshaws at the station, 3 km from the temples.*

The town north of Pandua, centred on the Maharaja of Burdwan's palace, has several fine 18th-century terracotta temples. Look for the Ramayana scenes on the large Lalji (1739), Krishna panels on the Krishnachandra (1752), assorted friezes on the Ananta Vasudeva (1754) and the later Pratapesvara (1849). Across the way is the unusual circular Siva temple (1809) with 108 small double-vaulted shrines.

Nabadwip

ⓘ *Getting there: from Krishnanagar to Mayapur; and Nabadwip across Gauranga Bridge. Nabadwip has trains from Sealdah and Haora, and ferries across to Mayapur.*

The birthplace of Sri Chaitanya, see page 568, is a pilgrimage centre for his followers and the river ghats are lined with temples where devotees worship by singing *keertans* and *bhajans*. **ISKCON** (International Society for Krishna Consciousness) has its Chandrodaya Mandir at **Mayapur** ⓘ *until 1300,* across the river.

⊜ Sleeping

Kolkata *p571, maps p572, p574, p576, p578*

Watch out for 10% luxury tax, 10% service charge and 20% expenditure tax. For usual facilities in different categories, see page 53. Most hotels listed are about 15 km from the airport. Medium price and budget hotels attracting foreigners are concentrated in the Sudder St area about 5 km from Haora station. **Telephone number changes** T1952 (dial old number to get new). "Ask Me" T4746363, advises on local affairs/numbers/addresses etc.

Airport
AL Airport Ashok, T5119111, F5119137, airportel@cal.vsnl.net.in. 149 rooms, modern, soundproofed, restaurant, unexciting though convenient for the airport (free transfer).
D Rest House III. Some a/c, doubles, and cheaper dorm beds.
E Airport Rest Rooms, Old Terminal Building.

Around the city
LL Oberoi Grand, 15 JL Nehru, T2492323, F2493229. 218 rooms and suites, atmospheric Victorian building opposite the Maidan exquisitely restored, suites have giant 4-posters, tea lounge (own blend of tea recommended), excellent restaurants including French, lovely pool (residents only).
LL Park, 17 Park St, T2493121, F2497343, www.theparkhotels.com. 150 rooms, good Chinese restaurant, health club, service not always up to décor, entrance themed on underground car park.
LL Taj Bengal, 34B Belvedere Rd, Alipore, T2483939, F2481766. 250 rooms, railway 10 km, opulent and modern, restaurants are plush, imaginative, intimate, with good food (ground floor Indian cheaper than 5th floor), leisurely service (unusual Bengali breakfast), *Khazana* shop for excellent textiles, *Baluchari* saris, *kantha* embroidery etc.
L Hindusthan International, 235/1 AJC Bose Rd, T2472394, F2472824. 212 rooms on 8 floors, railway 10 km, good buffet lunches and coffee shop, pool (non-residents Rs 250).
AL Kenilworth, 1 & 2 Little Russell St, T2823939, F2825136, www.kenilworth hotels.com, 105 well appointed rooms with good buffet breakfast and coffee shop

(excellent lunch buffet), English style pub (members and residents only), quiet location. Recommended.
AL-A Golden Park, 13 Ho Chi Minh Sarani, T2883939, F2889600. 78 rooms 'boutique hotel' with all facilities including pool and health club, restaurants, London-style pub (residents and members only).
B Astor, 15 Shakespeare Sarani, T2829950, F2827430, www.astorcalcutta.com. 35 comfortable a/c rooms with bath tubs (inferior annexe), open-air restaurant.
B Gulshan International, 21B Royd St, T2294227, F2290566, alambhai12@ hotmail.com. 16 clean, comfortable rooms, complimentary breakfast, efficient staff.
B Middleton Inn, 10 Middleton St, T2160449, F2468520, mi_inn@yahoo.com. 19 pleasantly furnished a/c rooms with hot bath (fridge, TV), not particularly spacious though spotlessly clean, original art, quiet and convenient. Recommended.
B Peerless Inn, 12 JL Nehru Rd, T2430301, F2486650, www.peerlessinn.com. 123 decent rooms, modern business hotel but drab exterior, excellent *Aaheli* restaurant.

Mid-priced hotels often have a few a/c rooms but may not have a generator and so have power cuts, especially in summer.
C-D New Haven Guest House, 19B Ritchie Rd (near junction of Ballygunge Circular Rd), T4754097. Simply furnished, cleanish rooms with bath, small front garden, only breakfast, residential area with good *dhaba* and Chinese restaurants within 10 mins' walk.
D YMCA, 25 JL Nehru Rd, T2492192, F2492234. 17 rooms, including 2 a/c, with bath, in large, rambling colonial building, run down but clean linen, check room first, some repainted are better, helpful staff, maximum stay 7 days, dorms (3, 4 and 7-bedded, Rs 260 per head), rates include meals (tiny gym next door, Rs 25).
D YWCA, 1 Middleton Row, T2297033. 30 rooms some with bath, dorm, everyone welcome, rates include breakfast and dinner, a pleasant oasis in the city.
E Udayachal Tourist Lodge (WBTDC), DG Block Sector II, Salt Lake, T3378246. Centre 20 km, 19 simple rooms, 5 a/c, dorm (Rs 80), meal included.

A-B Lytton, 14 Sudder St, T2491872, F2491747, www.lyttonhotelindia.com. 74 comfortable, tastefully furnished rooms, better in new block, good restaurants, bar, efficient, good value.

B Fairlawn, 13A Sudder St, T2451510, F2441835, www.fairlawnhotel.com. 20 a/c old- fashioned rooms (US$50 full board), semi- formal meals at set times, bric-à-brac everywhere.

B VIP International, 51 Mirza Ghalib St, T2290345, F2293715, hvipcal@hotmail.com. 33 a/c rooms, clean and comfortable, hot bath, friendly efficient staff.

B-C Presidency Inn, 2/1 Marquis St, T2520057, F2170800, hotelpresidency innpvtltd@rediff mail.com. 36 spotless a/c rooms in new hotel (2002), restaurant, chaotic reception.

C Eagle Palace, 12/2 Lindsay St, T2524259, F2816549, taran_eagle@yahoo.com. 18 good-sized, clean rooms with hot bath and TV, OK but a bit pricey.

C-E Crystal, 11/1 Kyd St, T2266400, F2465019, hcrystal@vsnl.net. 29 good, clean rooms (mostly a/c), those on top floor are light and airy (and cheaper), a bit pricey but OK.

C-E Gujral Guest House, 8-B Lindsay St, 2nd floor, T2526006, F2455109. 12 decent rooms, clean, varying sizes, some large but pricey.

Popular with backpackers, most hotels have cheaper singles and dormitories.

D Biman, 8/1B Chowringhee Lane, 2nd floor, T2461379. 25 clean rooms (10 a/c) with TV, bath, a bit pricey but friendly.

D Galaxy, 3 Stuart Lane, T2464565. 4 good rooms with attached bath and TV, decent choice but often full.

D Super Guest House, 30A Mirza Ghalib St, T2454241. 4 very clean a/c rooms with hot bath. The only spotless rooms in the area!

D-E Classic, 6/1A Kyd St, T2290256. 18 clean rooms (some a/c), some with bath (and cockroaches!), singles with common bath.

D-E Diplomat, 10 Sudder St, T2468434, F2468434. 18 rooms, some a/c with hot bath, others with common cold bucket bath, a bit run-down, air ticketing, exchange.

D-E Green Star, 33 Mirza Ghalib St, T2170607. 22 decent, clean rooms with bath, some a/c, some deluxe with TV, but staff pester for tips.

E Afraa, B/33/H/3 Mirza Ghalib St, 3rd floor, T2170087. 21 clean but small rooms, TV.

E Centrepoint, 20 Mirza Ghalib St, T2528184. 22 decent enough small rooms, some a/c, clean sheets and bath, grubby carpet.

E Continental Guest House, 30A Mirza Ghalib St, T2450663, continental-cal@hotmail.com. 19 clean rooms with decent tiled baths, cheaper rooms with clean common bath.

E Delux, B/33/H/4 Mirza Ghalib St, 3rd Floor, T2292703. 8 small but clean rooms with bath.

E Maria, 5/1 Sudder St, T2450860. 24 clean, basic rooms (hard beds), some with bath, dorm (Rs 70), internet, renovated early 2002.

E Paramount, 33/4 Mirza Ghalib St, T2290066. 40 clean rooms with bath and TV, helpful staff.

E Shabnam, B/33/H/4 Mirza Ghalib St, T2296061. 20 small, clean rooms, bath and TV.

E Shilton, 5A Sudder St, T2451512. 27 decent-sized rooms with bath, some triples, clean.

E Sonali Resort, 21A Mirza Ghalib St, T2451844. 13 good, clean rooms with bath, good choice.

E Timestar, 2 Tottee lane, T2450028. 30 reasonable rooms with bath from singles to 4-bedded, TV optional.

E Tourist Inn, 4/1 Sudder St, T2449818. 9 small, clean rooms with common bath.

E-F Paragon, 2 Stuart Lane, T2442445. 45 tiny cleanish rooms and dorms, new water heater to fill buckets, popular with backpackers. Salvation Army's

E-F Red Shield Guest House, 2 Sudder St, T2450599. 7 modest rooms, varying rates, some with bath, cramped bumper to bumper 6 and 10-bedded dorms (Rs 60/Rs 65), TV/sitting room, maximum stay 7 nights, lights out at 2200!

F Modern Lodge, 1 Stuart Lane, T2444960. 14 rooms, attached or common bath, pleasant lounge, very popular, almost permanently full, indifferent staff, no reservations so try at 1000.

Nabadwip p584

D-F ISKCON Guesthouse, some with bath, a/c, inexpensive 4-6 bed dorm, cheap meals.

E Indrajit, rooms with bath and restaurant.

E Trimurti rooms with bath and restaurant.

F Akintak Kutir is basic.

F Baishakhi, some rooms with bath.

● *For an explanation of the sleeping and eating price codes used in this guide, see inside the*
● *front cover. Other relevant information is found in Essentials pages 52-57.*

⑦ Eating

Kolkata *p571, maps p572, p574, p576, p578*

Thursdays are 'meatless' days but chicken and fish are available. Licensed restaurants serve alcohol (some are no longer pleasant places to eat in since the emphasis is on drink). Be prepared for a large surcharge for live (or even recorded) music. This, plus taxes, can double the price on the menu. Many restaurants, outside hotels, do not accept credit cards.

In hotels
♥♥♥ **Ban Thai**. Excellent, imaginative décor (Rs 600 each), reserve ahead.
♥♥♥ **China Valley**, *Ideal Plaza's*, Sarat Bose Rd. Chinese. Luxurious, with fountains.
♥♥♥ **Chinoiserie,** *Taj Bengal's*, T2233939.
♥♥♥ **Ming Room**, *Grand's*, T2492323. Chinese.

Outside hotels
♥♥♥ **Amber**, 11 Waterloo St, T2486520. North Indian. 3 floors of gourmet delights (try *tandoori*), generous helpings, fast service, bar, reservations essential. Highly recommended.
♥♥♥ **Bar-B-Q**, 43 Park St (closed Thu). Adjacent restaurants serve Indian and Chinese; bar.
♥♥♥ **Blue Fox**, 55 Park St, T2494165. Bar, popular, excellent sizzlers (lobster, crab and chicken *tetrazzini*). Recommended.
♥♥♥ **Zaranj**, 26 JL Nehru Rd. Tasteful, stylish, subdued décor, excellent food – try *pudina paratha, murgh makhani, tandoori* fish.

Elsewhere
♥♥♥ **Mainland China**, 3A Gurusaday Rd (south Kolkata), T2872006. Excellent Chinese. Unusual offerings, especially fish and seafood, tastefully decorated with burnished ceiling and evocative wall mural, pleasant ambience, courteous.

Around Sudder St
♥♥ **Badshah**, New Market. Well known for *kebab rolls*, bar (non a/c).
♥♥ **Blue Sky Café**, 3 Sudder St. Western, Chinese, Continental. Good choice, very popular budget travellers' meeting place, always full, excellent food. Recommended.
♥♥ **Curd Corner**, Sudder St. Very small but popular, excellent snacks.

♥♥ **Elfin**, near New Market. Cheap *thalis* and Chinese lunches.
♥♥ **Gupta**, 53C Mirza Ghalib St. Good Indian and Chinese. Small, intimate, softly lit, low ceilings (beware of fans!).
♥♥ **Jimmy's**, 14D Lindsay St. Chinese. Small, a/c, good *momos*, Szechuan dishes and ice cream.
♥♥ **Jo-jo's**, 30 Mirza Ghalib St (6 Sudder St), next to *Shilton*. Good Indian snacks and meals. 1st floor, a/c. Pleasant decor, run by friendly Sikh.
♥♥ **Kathleen's**, 12 Mirza Ghalib St (closed Thu). Comfortable, pleasant, '*Princess*' for families.
♥♥ **Khalsa**, 4C Madge Lane. Punjabi (no smoking). Try *malai korma, veg tarka* and carrot trifle cake. Also western breakfasts, excellent service, cheap, long-standing favourite.
♥♥ **Prince**, 17 Mirza Ghalib St. Basic Indian. Limited menu but praiseworthy Bengali dishes (great *mishti doi*), clean.
♥♥ **Zurich**, 3 Sudder St. Snacks. Laid, back café atmosphere, excellent snacks, breakfasts, clean and friendly, often full. Recommended.

Around Park St
♥♥ **Don Giovannis**, 22 Park St. Pizza café, and other western.
♥♥ **Floriana**, 13-D Russell St. Pleasant, north Indian, Chinese, good portions.
♥♥ **Golden Dragon**, 40 Park Mansions, Park St. Standard Chinese (closed Wed).
♥♥ **Kwality**, 17 Park St (closed Thu) and 2 Gariahat Rd (closed Wed). Famous for ice creams but also for excellent Indian and continental, usually crowded.
♥♥ **Mocambo**, 25B Park St. International. A/c, pleasant, highly descriptive menu, outstanding grilled *hilsa* served on banana leaf.
♥♥ **Moulin Rouge**, 31 Park St. International. Comfortable, a/c, good menu, service slow.
♥♥ **Peter Cat**, 18A Park St (closed Thu). International. Good kebabs and sizzlers, cheap cocktails, pleasant ambience.
♥♥ **Silver Grill**, 18E Park St. Chinese. Extensive menu, specialities *Limkai* chicken, Thai prawns.

Bengali (no alcohol)
♥♥ **Aaheli** at Peerless Inn, T2430222. Excellent, unusual menu, comfortable a/c, fairly pricey.

📞 *Phone code* Kolkata: 033

West Bengal Kolkata Eating

¶ **Kewpie's**, 2 Elgin Lane (between Elgin and Heysham Rds), T4748962, closed Mon. Authentic Bengali, home-cooking at its best, add on special dishes to basic *thali* (Rs 200), unusual fish and vegetarian. Few tables in rooms in a residence, a/c, open for lunch and dinner, sells recipe book and pickles. Highly recommended, reserve.

¶ **Radhu's**, Lake Market. Superb fish fry and chicken or prawn cutlet.

¶ **Suruchi** (All Bengal Women's Union), 89 Eliot Rd. Simple surroundings but carefully prepared by self-help women's group at lunchtime.

Bengali sweets

See also Background, page 569.

Bhim Chandra Nag, 8 Vivekananda Rd.

Chappan Bhog, 28B Shakespeare Sarani. Recommended for *chandrakala*, almond *pista barfi*, mango *roshogolla*, *kheer mohan* (also savouries).

KC Das, 11 Esplanade E, and 1/433 Gariahat Rd.

Nepal Chandra, Landsdowne Rd.

Pure Milk Centre near Rafi Ahmed Kidwai St/Ripon St corner. Good sweet 'curd' (*mishti doi*), usually sold out by lunchtime. Excellent hot *roshogollas*.

Bengali snacks

Fresh every afternoon at most sweet shops (1600-1730): try *shingaras*, *kochuris* and *nimkis*.

Gangaur, Russell St/ AJC Bose Rd corner.

Krishna, Camac St.

Radhu's, Lake Market. Superb snacks, rich *Mughlai paratha* and *aloor domm*.

Cafés and fast food

Aqua-Java, 79 Sambhunath Pandit St (south of the cathedral). Smart set coffee bar with innovative concoctions and snacks.

Coffee House, College St (see page 579).

Garden Café, Alipore Rd. For pizzas and *dosas*, burgers and Chinese fast food.

Wimpy, Rawdon St corner.

Chinese

Connoisseurs of Chinese cuisine go to **South Tangra Rd** (off the E Metropolitan Bypass) - basic eateries (Formica-top tables, waiters in shirt sleeves) excellent food, however approach is unpleasant past tanneries and open drains.

¶ **Ka Fu Lok** and **Sin Fa** do excellent soups, jumbo prawns and honey chicken, best to go early (noon for lunch, 2000 for dinner).

¶ **Lily's Kitchen**, try garlic chicken, sweet and sour fish, chop suey, steamed fish (40 mins), very generous so order half-plates.

Elsewhere:

¶ **Eau Chew**, P32 Mission Row Extn, upstairs. Chinese. Unusual menu, try Hot Chimney soup.

¶ **Mayfair China Bowl**, 122A Meghnad Saha Sarani (South Kolkata). Chinese. Small and intimate, serving 'Indianized' spicy Chinese and other Oriental cuisine, prawns a speciality.

Other nationalities

¶ **Pemayangtse**, 1 Meher Ali Rd, Park Circus, serves Tibetan.

¶ **Tibetan**, near Elgin Rd corner of JL Nehru Rd. Excellent dishes under Rs 50.

Confectionery

Flury's, 18 Park St (closed Mon). Traditional English breakfasts, good afternoon teas, pastry counter, but slow service.

Hot Breads, Central Plaza, 2/6 Sarat Bose Rd. Excellent breads, pastries and cakes.

Kathleen's, several branches, including 12 Mirza Ghalib St and corner of Lord Sinha Rd/AJC Bose Rd.

Kookie Jar, Rawdon St. One of the best, though pricey.

Nahoum, F20, New Market. Good pastries, cakes, savouries.

Upper Crust 1/1 Camac St (and Judges Court Rd). A/c, clean, modern, delicious cakes, pastries (try strawberry tarts), brown bread and pizzas.

Ice creams

Look out for *Rollicks*, *Vadilal's* and *Walls* outlets.

Icescapades, Russell St.

Scoop, 71 Strand Rd, Man-o-War Jetty, on riverside with terrace.

Kathi-rolls

Kathi-rolls (tender kebabs wrapped in *parathas*) are hard to beat. Try mutton/ chicken egg roll (if you don't want raw onions and green chillis, order "*no piaaz e mirchi*").

Manjinder Singh's, Ballygunge Phari, always busy; excellent Mughlai.

Nizam's, off SN Bannerjee Rd (opposite Elite Cinema), and 22/25 New Market.

Rehmania, Park St/AJC Bose Rd corner.

Vegetarian

Anand, Chittaranjan Ave. Good South Indian.

Gokul, Lord Sinha Rd. Excellent Rajasthani meals and sweets.

Gupta Brothers, Mirza Ghalib St. *Thalis* and Indian sweets, stand-up vegetarian and Bengali confectionery, good value.

Bars and clubs

Kolkata *p571, maps p572, p574, p576, p578*

Bars
The larger hotels have pleasant bars and upmarket restaurants serve alcohol. The top hotels are well stocked, luxurious but pricey. In Sudder St, *Fairlawn's* pleasant garden terrace is popular at dusk attracting anyone seeking a chilled beer, while *Lyttons* is also open to thirsty travellers from neighbouring hotels. Independent bars, open usually until 2230, lack atmosphere; some are positively men only.

Clubs
Bengal Club, 1/1 Russell St, T2499443, the former house of Lord Macaulay, has an excellent dining room.
Tollygunge Club, 120 DP Sasmal Rd, T4732316. Built on old indigo plantation, 18-hole golf course, riding, tennis, swimming, away from centre, atmosphere and location compensate for average rooms and restaurant.
    Some are affiliated to a number of Indian and foreign clubs including Royal Overseas League, Travellers, St James's, National Liberal, Oxford and Cambridge Universities.

Entertainment

Kolkata *p571, maps p572, p574, p576, p578*

Contact www.tulleeho.com, for nightlife in metro cities. *Calcutta: This Fortnight* is distributed free by West Bengal Tourist Office. The *Sunday Telegraph* magazine and English language dailies (*Statesman, Times of India, Asian Age, Hindustan Times*) carry a comprehensive list.

Cinema
A/c and comfortable cinemas showing English language films are mostly off JL Nehru Rd near Esplanade. *Elite*, SN Banerjee Rd. *Globe*, Lindsay St. *Jumna*, Marquis St. *Lighthouse*, Humayun Place. *Metro*, JL Nehru Rd. *Minerva*, Chowringhee Place. *Nandan*, T2231210, has festivals and screens all-time greats.

Dance, music and theatre
Regular performances at *Rabindra Sadan*, Cathedral Rd. *Kala Mandir*, 48 Shakespeare Sarani. *Gorky Sadan*, Gorky Terrace, near Minto Park. *Sisir Mancha*, 1/1 AJC Bose Rd. Some of these also hold art exhibition as at *Academy of Fine Arts*, Cathedral Rd, and *Ramakrishna Mission*, Gol Park. You can see Bengali theatre of a high standard at

Biswaroopa, 2A Raja Raj Kissen St and *Star Theatre*, 79/34 Bidhan Sarani.

Discos and nightclubs
At hotels: *Anticlock* (*Hindustan International*). Good live band, young crowd, good sizzlers, pool tables, ocean-liner décor. *Incognito* (*Taj Bengal*). Understated, relaxed ambience, 30-plus crowd, good food, taped music, fussy dress codes. *Someplace Else* (*Park*). Pub, live bands favoured by the young. *Tantra* (*Park*). Live bands/taped music, large floor, young crowd, adjacent *Bodhi Bar* has good single malts and cigars; closed Mon.

Performing arts
English-language productions staged by *British Council* and theatre clubs. *Sangeet Research Academy*, near Tollygunge Metro station, a national centre for training in Indian Classical music, stages free concert on Wed evenings. *Rabindra Bharati University*, 6/4 Dwarakanath Tagore Lane, holds performances, particularly during the winter, including singing, dancing and *jatras*. *Jatra* is community theatre, highly colourful and exaggerated both in delivery and make-up, drawing for its subject romantic favourites from mythology or more up-to-date social, political and religious themes.

West Bengal Kolkata Entertainment

❀ Festivals and events

Kolkata *p571, maps p572, p574, p576, p578*

Jan Ganga Sagar Mela at Sagar, 105 km south of Kolkata, where the River Hugli joins the sea, draws thousands of Hindu pilgrims. See page 619. **Mar/Apr** Holi (Dol Purnima) is the spring festival. **Jun-Jul** The Ratha Yatra (**Jun-Jul**) at Mahesh, nearby. **Sep-Oct** Durga Puja, Bengal's celebration of the goddess during **Dasara**. See box. **Oct-Nov** Diwali (*Kali Puja* in Bengal) is the festival of lights. **Dec** Christmas. Numerous churches hold special services, including Midnight Mass, and the New Market takes on a new look in Dec as Barra Din (Big Day) approaches with temporary stalls selling trees and baubles. Other religious festivals are observed as elsewhere in India.

⊙ Shopping

Kolkata *p571, maps p572, p574, p576, p578*

Most shops open 1000-1730 or later (some break for lunch) weekdays and 1000-1300 on Sat.

Art
Centre Art Gallery, 87C Park St. Mainly works by Bengali artists.
Emerald Isle, 40A Park Mansion, 57 Park St (1400-1900).
Gallerie 88, 28B Shakespeare Sarani. Contemporary art (1200-2000).
Metropolitan, 7 JL Nehru Rd (2nd Floor). Old prints and 'antiques', with maps.
Saroj, 3B Camac St. Old prints and 'antiques'.

Books
Kolkata Book Fair, Maidan near Victoria Memorial. End of Jan for a fortnight, stalls sell paperback fiction to antiquarian books.
Modern Book Depot, 15a JL Nehru Rd, opposite Lighthouse Cinema, T2490933. Long tradition, will search out titles.
Oxford Book Shop, Park St. New English titles, postcards, tiny café upstairs.
  A wealth of second-hand pavement bookstalls along **College St** mainly cater for students but may reveal an interesting 1st edition for a keen collector (see under Sights).

Clothes and accessories
Allen Solly, Rawdon St/Shakespeare Sarani corner, for menswear.
Ananda, 13 Russell St.
Burlington, 43 Park Mansions, 57 Park St. Sells foreign labels.

Kali, Judges Court Rd. Eastern and Western wear.
Meera Basu, 8 Sarat Bose Rd. *Kurtas* and saris.
Metro, outside Grand Hotel. For pricey leather goods.
Mexx, Rawdon St/Shakespeare Sarani corner. Western clothes and shoes.
Monapali, 15 Louden St, sells designer *salwar, kurtas*.
Ogaan, P545 Lake Rd Extn. High quality clothes including swimwear and lingerie.
Ritu's Boutique, 46A Rafi Ahmed Kidwai Rd. *Kurtas* and saris.
Taj Bengal arcade. For pricey leather goods.
Zenon, 111 Park St is more affordable.

Government Emporia
Government Emporia are mainly in the town centre and are fixed price shops; **Assam**, 8 Russell St. **Bihar**, 145 Rashbehari Ave. **Cauvery** and **Central Cottage Industries**, 7 JL Nehru Rd. **Handloom House**, 2 Lindsay St. **Kashmir Art**, 12 JL Nehru Rd. **Khadi Gramodyog**, 28 Chittaranjan Ave. **Manipur**, 15L Lindsay St. **Manjusha**, 7/1D Lindsay St. **Meghalaya**, 9 Russell St. **Phulkari**, 26B Camac St. **Rajasthali**, 30E JL Nehru Rd. **Refugee Handicrafts**, 2A Gariahat Rd. **Tripura**, 58 JL Nehru Rd. **UP**, 12B Lindsay St. Several at **Dakshinapan**, near Dhakuria Bridge, Mon-Fri 1030-1930, Sat 1030-1300, convenient, excellent selection of handloom and handicrafts.

Handicrafts and handloom
Several in Park St and streets leading off it.
Bengal Home Industries, 11 Camac St. Good selection of printed cottons, relaxed.

Jete, 71 Park St.
Manjusha, 71 Park St.
Priyadarshini, 14C Lindsay St.

Jewellery

Bepin Behari Ganguly St (Bow Bazar) is lined with mirrored jewellers' shops; PC Chandra, BB Dutt, B Sirkar are well known.

Maps

Survey of India, Sales Office, 13 Wood St.

Markets

The New Market, Lindsay St, behind the original Hogg Market (largely rebuilt since a fire in 1985), has over 2,500 shops. It used to be said that you could buy anything from a needle to an elephant (on order) in one of its stalls. Today it is still worth a visit, preferably early in the morning, to watch it come alive. You will find mundane everyday necessities to exotic luxuries, from fragrant florists to gory meat stalls. Be prepared to deal with pestering porters.

For conventional shopping try A/c Market, Shakespeare Sarani, Park Centre, Park St, Vardaan Market, Camac St. Opposite the New Market, Shriram Arcade is "like shopping in Singapore"! Kolkata has a number of bazars, each with a character of its own.

In Bentinck St are Muslim tailors, Chinese shoemakers interspersed with Indian sweetmeat shops and tea stalls. Gariahat market early in the morning attracts a very diverse clientele (city businessmen,

academics, cooks) who come to select choice fresh fish. In Shyambazar the coconut market starts business at 0500 and you will miss it if you arrive 2 hrs later. The colourful flower market is on Jagannath Ghat on the river bank. The old China Bazar no longer exists although Tiretta Bazar area still retains its ethnic flavour; try an exceptional Chinese breakfast off street stall!

Photography

Bombay Photos and Narain's, on Park St.
Bourne & Shepherd, 141 SN Banerjee Rd.

Tailors

Garments can be copied skilfully around New Market at Mr Alibaba, 13 Sudder St (opposite), S. Charran Singh, 7/1/c on Lindsay St, T2443662, among many.

Women's self-help centre

Shops where you can watch handloom weaving, batik printing, embroidery, handblock printing being practised are recommended. Several are centrally located, providing unusual gifts.
All Bengal Women's Union, 89 Elliot Rd.
Good Companions, 13C Russell St.
Karma Kutir, 32 Ballygunge Place. Embroidery.
Nari Seva Sangha in Jodhpur Park.
Sasha, 27 Mirza Ghalib St (off the Rd). Tue-Sat 1000-1900, Sun, Mon 1000-1300, excellent handicrafts including cane, bamboo, dokra, kantha, leather and crafts.
Women's Friendly Society, 29 Park Lane. Good embroidery and linen.

▲ Activites and tours

Kolkata p571, maps p572, p574, p576, p578

Cricket

Occasional Test matches and One Day Internationals at Eden Gardens (see page 582), "great experience", 100,000 capacity; get tickets in advance.

Football

The season starts in May and continues through the monsoons. The club grounds are on the Maidan (try East Bengal Football Club, T2484642).

Golf

Several courses include the Royal Calcutta Golf Club, 18 Golf Club Rd, T4731352, founded in 1829, the oldest golf club in the world outside the UK; it moved to its present course in 1910 having taken the radical step of admitting women in 1886.
The Tollygunge Club, 120 Despran Sasmal Rd, T4735954, course is on land that was once an indigo plantation.

Horse racing

Royal Calcutta Turf Club, T2291104. Racing takes place in the cool season (Nov to early

Apr) and monsoon (Jun-Oct); tote, bookmakers available. The Derby is in the first week of Jan.

Swimming

Oberoi Grand and *Hindustan International* hotel pools are open to non-residents (Rs 250).

Tours

WBTDC Tours *Departure point*: Tourism Centre, 3/2 BBD Bagh E, 1st Floor, T2488271 (1000-1330, 1415-1530). Daily coach tours (except Mon). 0730-1140 and 1240-1700. Air conditioned: full day, Rs 100. **Morning tour**: 0730, Eden Gardens, High Court, Writers' Building, Botanical Gardens, Belur Math, Dakshineswar, Kali Temple, Jain Temple and Esplanade, Indian Museum, Nehru Children's Museum, Victoria Memorial, The Zoo. Entry fees not included. CRUTA, 67B Beadon Street, T544497, offers 2-hr walking tours of North Kolkata, through the old streets. Private tour operators also offer city tours. Approved guides from WBTDC Tourist Office: about Rs 75 for half day; Rs 150 for full day.

Long distance Tourist coaches to Digha, daily, Rs 60; Santiniketan-Bakreswar; Malda-Murshidabad-Gaur-Pandua; Antpur-Bishnupur-Mukutmanipur-Jairambati-Kamarpukur- Tarakeswar, Rs 415; Mayapur (ISKCON)-Krishnanagar-Bethuadari Deer Park; Sunderbans- Tiger and Crocodile projects (not Jul to mid-Sep). Rs 750. Approved guides from WBTDC Tourist Office.

Tour operators

Best deals in air tickets to/from the East (through Bangkok) are offered by agents in the Sudder St area (about US$120). **American Express**, 21 Old Court House St, T2486181. **Mercury**, 46c JL Nehru Rd, T2423535. **Thomas Cook**, Chitrakut (2nd floor), 230a AJC Bose Rd, T2475354. **TCI**, 46C JL Nehru Rd. **Travel Planners**, 7 Red Cross Place, T2488304, F2488394, leisure@ giascl01.vsnl.net.in. Recommended.

⊖ Transport

Kolkata *p571, maps p572, p574, p576, p578*

Kolkata is at the eastern end of the Grand Trunk Rd (NH2); AA (East India), 19 Ballygunge Circ Rd, T4755131. Many of the city centre roads become one-way between 1400 and 2100 so expect tortuous detours.

Air

Enquiries T5266233. The spacious and fairly new terminal buildings are well organized and spotless. There is adequate seating in the departure lounge as well as a bookshop, drink dispenser and clean toilets. A Reservation counter for rail (same day travel only) and one for hotels are in the arrivals hall. At the International terminal: **State Bank of India** (24 hrs, changes rupees into US$ only). **Transport to town**: the **pre-paid taxi** service (closes at 2200) from Dum Dum to the city centre is excellent value, Rs 135, about 40 mins (but Deluxe cars, Rs 400-650). Return from the city centre costs more - Rs 150 if you bargain. **A/c coach transfer** to Indian Airline's city office, approximately 2 hourly from 0530, Rs 75. The public bus is a nightmare; strongly not recommended. The nearest **Metro station** is at Dum Dum (Rs 5 to city centre); auto-rickshaws to there, about Rs 60; total 40 mins. **Transit passengers** with onward flights may use the *Airport Rest Rooms* (some a/c, doubles, dorm, all good value). **Domestic**: **Indian Airlines**, T2114433 (24 hrs), T2119096; 0900-1830, chaotic office, better to book through travel agent. Tele check-in (with hand baggage only), J class airbus flights T5119633, Y class T5118564. Airport, T5119433. **Indian Airlines**: flies to Agartala; Ahmadabad, Aizwal, Bangalore, Bagdogra, Bhubaneswar, Chennai, Delhi, Dibrugarh, Dimapur, Guwahati, Hyderabad, Imphal, Jaipur, Jorhat, Lucknow, Mumbai, Nagpur, Patna, Port Blair, Ranchi, Silchar, Tezpur, Visakhapatnam. **Jet Airways**: flies to Bagdogra, Bangalore, Bhubaneswar, Chennai, Delhi, Guwahati, Hyderabad, Imphal, Jorhat, Mumbai. **Sahara**: flies to several destinations also. **International**: Indian Airlines flies to Chittagong, Dhaka, Kathmandu, Yangon. **Air India**: to Bangkok, Singapore, Tokyo. **Biman**: to Chittagong, Dhaka. Druk to Paro. **RNAC**: to Kathmandu. For other **International flights**, see page 32.

Bicycle

Bike hire: not easy; ask at your hotel if a staff bike is free. Spares are sold along Bentinck St, north of Chowringhee.

Bus

Local State Transport services run throughout the city and suburbs from 0500-2030; usually overcrowded after 0830, but very cheap. Faster, private minibuses (little more expensive) cover major routes. South Bengal minibuses are bigger and will often stop on request.

Long distance An extensive hub and spoke bus operation from Kolkata allows cheap travel within West Bengal and beyond. The Tourist Office, 3/2 BBD Bagh, has timetables. Advance bookings at computerized office of Kolkata State Transport Corp (STC), Esplanade, T2481916. **Kolkata STC**: to Balurghat; Digha; Diamond Harbour; Farakka; Mayapur; Siliguri etc. **North Bengal STC**: T2481916; **Digha**; **Jalpaiguri**; **Cooch Behar**; **Malda**; **Siliguri**, 12 hrs. **South Bengal STC**, Bankura, Bishnupur and Purulia. **Orissa & Bihar STC**, T2487734. **Puri**, 11 hrs. **Gaya**; Bokaro. **Sikkim Govt**, Gangtok via Siliguri. **Bhutan Govt**, Phuntsholing via Siliguri. **Bangladesh**, *Syamoli Paribahan*, 8 Marquis St, runs buses to Dhaka from *VIP Hotel*.

Ferry

Local To cross the Hugli, eg from Haora station, except Sun.

Long distance Shipping Corp of India, 13 Strand Rd, T2484640 (recorded information T2485420), operates a steamer to **Port Blair** in the Andamans. Some 2 or 3 sailings a month (3-4 days) with tickets available from 1000, 7 days ahead (be there at 0830; huge queue for 'bunk class'). See page 763.

Rickshaw

Hand-pulled rickshaws are used by the local people especially along the narrow congested lanes. **auto-rickshaws** operate outside the city centre, especially as shuttle service to Metro stations.

Taxi

Private taxi: car hire with driver, from Rs 700-1,050 (a/c) for 8 hrs. **Gainwell**, 8 Ho Chi Minh Sarani, T2426607, **Mercury**, 46C JL Nehru Rd, T2423555; **Wenz**, at Oberoi Grand,

at Airport T2492323; **Wheels**, 150 Lenin Sarani, T273081. Tourist taxis from India and WB Tourist Offices.

Local Yellow-top and yellow: Old meters start at Rs 5; double the reading and add 20% (Rs 12 minimum). Drivers carry conversion charts. Computerized meters are being introduced.

Long distance At Sealdah ignore touts who quote Rs 100 for Sudder St; instead, join the queue for licensed cabs. At **Haora** there are prepaid taxis; or get the Ferry across the river to Chandpal/Babu Ghat and hire a taxi or walk from there. Buses and minibuses get very crowded.

Tram

Kolkata is the only Indian city to run a network from 0400-2300, min Rs 2. Often crowded except on Sun.

Train

The **Metro** (unique in India) is usually clean, efficient and punctual. The 16½ km route from Dum Dum to Tollygunge runs from 0800, Sun 1400-2000; fare Rs 3-5. Enquiries T2494750. Note that trains are not as long as the platforms!

Kolkata is served by 2 railway stations, **Haora** ('Howrah', still used on timetables) and **Sealdah**. Haora station has a separate complex for platforms 18-21. Enquiries, Haora, T6602581, 'New' Complex, T6602217, Sealdah, T3503535. Central Enquiry, T1331. Reservation, T135 (computerized).

Computerized Booking Office, Rabindra Sadan, 61 JL Nehru Rd, T2472143. Railway Reservations, 6 Fairlie Place, BBD Bagh, T135; 0900-1300, 1330-1600, Sun 0900-1400 (best to go early). At Fairlie Place, tourists are automatically told to go to the Foreign Tourist Counter, upstairs (very efficient). However, unless you have an Indrail Pass or are buying one, it is worth checking whether seats are available for the trains you want downstairs first, as this can often be much quicker. **Foreign Tourist Quota**: If the trains you want are listed as 'Full', try the Tourist Counter, upstairs. It usually takes at least 30 mins, though some reported a miracle in 5 mins! Check carefully which queue to join for the region you want to travel in, as there are separate queues for Northern and South Eastern Railways.

Trains listed depart from Haora (Howrah), unless marked 'S' for Sealdah (timings change every Apr and Oct). To **Allahabad**: see New Delhi. **Agra Fort**: *Bikaner Exp, 2307,* 2330, 20½ hrs. **Bhubaneswar**: *Dhauli Exp, 2821,* 0605, 7½ hrs; *Falaknuma Exp, 2703,* 0825, 7½ hrs; *Howrah Puri Exp, 8007,* 2155, 7½ hrs. **Chennai**: *Coromandel Exp, 2841,* 1325, 28½ hrs; *Howrah Chennai Mail, 6003,* 1935, 33½ hrs. **New Delhi** via **Patna** and **Allahabad**: *Rajdhani Exp, 2301,* 1700 (except Wed, Sun), 16½ hrs; *Rajdhani Exp, 2305,* 1345 (Wed, Sun), 20 hrs; (**S**) *Rajdhani Exp, 2313,* 1655 (Mon, Tue, Thu, Sat), 17½ hrs. **Mumbai (CST)** : *Gitanjali Exp, 2860,* 1255, 32½ hrs (via

Nagpur, 18½ hrs); *Howrah Mumbai Mail, 2810,* 2005, 35½ hrs (via **Nagpur**, 19½ hrs); *Howrah Mumbai Mail, 2321,* 2200, 38 hrs. **Mumbai (Lokmanya Tilak)** : *Jnaneswari SD Exp, 2102,* 2305 (Wed, Thu, Sun), 32½ hrs (via **Nagpur**, 19 hrs). **Nagpur**: See Mumbai trains plus *Howrah Ahmedabad Exp, 8034,* 2050, 22½ hrs. **New Jalpaiguri (NJP)**: (**S**) *Kanchenjunga Exp, 5657,* 0625, 11½ hrs; (**S**) *Darjeeling Mail, 3143,* 1915, 13 hrs; *Kamrup Exp, 5959,* 1525, 14 hrs. **Puri**: *Jagannath Exp, 8409,* 1805, 11 hrs; *Howrah Puri Exp, 8007,* 2155, 11 hrs. **Ranchi**: *Howrah Hatia Exp, 8615,* 2135, 10 hrs.

❶ Directory

Kolkata *p571, maps p572, p574, p576, p578*

Airline offices
International: Aeroflot, 58 JL Nehru Rd, T2821617. **American Airlines**, T4751272. **Air France**, 41 JL Nehru Rd, T2872239. **Bangladesh Biman**, 30C JL Nehru Rd, T2293709, airport T5118772. **British Airways**, 41 JL Nehru Rd, T2883451, airport T5118262. **Cathay Pacific**, 1 Middleton Row, T2403211. **Delta**, T2475008. **Druk Air**, 1/A Ballygunge Circular Rd, T2402419, airport T5119976. **Gulf Air**, 230A AJC Bose Rd, T2477783. **Japan Airlines**, 35A JL Nehru Rd, T2298370. **KLM**, 1 Middleton St, T2403151, airport T5118329. **Kuwait Airways**, 230A AJC Bose Rd, T2474697. **Lufthansa**, 30A/B JL Nehru Rd, T2399365, airport T5118528. **Qantas**, *Hotel Hindusthan International*, AJC Bose Rd, T2470718. **Royal Brunei**, T2297112. **Royal Jordanian**, 2/6 Sarat Bose Rd, T4751272. **Royal Nepal**, 41 JL Nehru Rd, T2468549. **SAS**, 2/7 Sarat Bose Rd, T4750286. **Singapore Airlines**, 18D Park St, T2809898. **Sri Lankan**, 230A AJC Bose Rd, T2477783. **Tarom**, 2/7 Sarat Bose Rd, T2405178, airport T5119031. **Thai Airways**, 229 AJC Bose Rd, 8th floor, T2801630. **National airlines**: Air India, 50 JL Nehru Rd, T2422356, Airport T5119031. **Indian Airlines**, 39 Chittaranjan Ave, T2822356, Reservations T141/2116869 and *Hotel Hindusthan International*, T2476606, airport T5119433, Tele check-in T5119633 (J class), T5118564 (Y class). **Private airlines**: Jet Airways, Stephen Court, 18D Park St, T2292227, airport

T5119894. **Sahara**, 2A Shakespeare Sarani, T2827686, airport T5119545.

Banks
Mon-Fri 1030-1430, Sat 1030-1230. **Foreign Banks**: cash on Mastercard/Visa from SC/Grindlay's, 19 Netaji Subhas Rd and 41 JL Nehru Rd, T2202546. **ATM** at HKSB, 8 Netaji Subhas Rd, T2201833, 3A Shakespeare Sarani, 31 BBD Bagh. **Thomas Cook**, 2nd floor, 230A AJC Bose Rd. **Travellers Express**, 20 Mirza Ghalib St.

Consulates and High Commissions
Bangladesh, 9 Circus Ave, T2475208. **Bhutan**, 48 Tivoli Court, P Barua Sarani (off AJC Bose Rd). **Denmark**, 3 Netaji Subhas Rd, T2487478. **France**, 26 Park Mansions, Park St. **Germany**, 11 Hastings Park Rd, T4791141. **Italy**, 3 Raja Santosh Rd, T4792414. **Israel**, T2800028. **Japan**, 12 Pretoria St, T2822241. **Nepal**, 19 Woodlands, Alipore, T4791103. **Netherlands**, 31 Netaji Subhas Rd, T4493105. **Norway**, 230A AJC Bose Rd, T2474757. **Spain**, 1 Taratolla Rd, T4695954. **Sri Lanka**, 2 Hare St, T2485102. **Sweden**, 5/2 Russell St, T2807136. **Switzerland** 113 Park St, T295557. **Thailand**, 18B Mandeville Gardens, T4407836. **UK**, 1 Ho-Chi-Minh Sarani, T2423435/2825171. **USA**, 5/1 Ho-Chi-Minh Sarani, T2422335.

Cultural centres and libraries
Alliance Française, 5C Sukh Sagar, 2/5 Sarat Bose Rd, T4757084, afcalcut@cal.vsnl.net. **British Council** Information Centre

(relocated), Larsen & Tubro Building, Camac St (near Shakespeare Sarani), T2825370. Good for UK newspapers and journals, reference books. Useful internet. Tue-Sat, 1100-1900. **Max Mueller Bhavan**, 8 Ballygunge Circular Rd.

Hospitals

Government: Medical College Hospital, 88 College St, T2443213. **SSKM Hospital**, 244 AJC Bose Rd, T2239654. Private: **Belle Vue**, 9 Dr UN Brahmachari St, T2472321. **Woodlands**, 8B Alipore Rd, T4567080.

Other medical services: Ambulance: Curewell, T2294202. **Dhanwantary Clinic**, 1 National Library Ave, T4493734. **Emergency Doctors' Service**, A 165 Lake Gardens, T466770. **Chemists: Angel**, 151 Park St (24-hr). **Dey's**, 6/2B Lindsay St. **Lawrence & Mayo**, 20F Park St (Opticians). **Moonlight**, 180 SP Mukherjee Rd (24-hr).

Internet

Many across the city; several in Sudder/Park St area. Some charge as little as Rs 25 per hr.

Post office

Poste Restante, 0700-2230. Closed Sun and holidays. **Speed Post** At major post offices including Airport, Esplanade and Park St. **Central Telegraph Office** 8 Red Cross Place is

Tourist offices

Govt of India, 4 Shakespeare Sarani, T2821402 (airport T5518299). **Govt of West Bengal**, 2 Brabourne Rd, T2254723; **WBTDC**, Netaji Indoor Stadium, T2487302, wbtdc@ cal2.vsnl.net.in. **Tourism Centre**, 3/2 BBD Bagh (E), T2485917, F2485168. Closed 1330-1415. **ITDC**, 46C, JL Nehru Rd, T2825254, F2820922. **State Governments**: *Andaman & Nicobar Islands*, 2nd floor, 3a Auckland Place, T2475084. *Arunachal Pradesh*, 4B Chowringhee Place, T2486500. *Assam*, 8 Russell St, T2295094. *Bihar*, 26B Camac St, T2803304. *Gujarat*, 1 RN Mukherjee Rd, T2481904. *Haryana*, 49 Muktaram Babu St. *Himachal Pradesh*, 1/1A Princep St, T2219072. *Jammu* and *Kashmir*, 12 JL Nehru Rd, T2485794. *Madhya Pradesh*, 230A AJC Bose Rd, T2478543. *Manipur*, 26 Rowland Rd, T4747087. *Meghalaya*, 9 Russell St, T2290797, T2467002. *Mizoram*, 24 Old Ballygunge Rd, T4757887. *Nagaland*, 11 Shakespeare Sarani, T2825269. *Orissa*, 41 Lenin Sarani, T2260556. *Punjab*, 1/425, Gariahat Rd. *Rajasthan*, 2 Ganesh Ch Ave, T2159740. *Sikkim*, 5/2 Russell St, T2267516. *Tamil Nadu*, G26 Dakshinapan Shopping Complex, Dhakuria, T4720432. *Tripura*, 1 Pretoria St, T2425703. *UP*, 12A Netaji Subhas Rd, T2207855.

Bishnupur and Santiniketan

★ **Bishnupur** → *Phone code: 03244. Colour map 4, grid C1. Population: 61,900.*

The warrior Malla Kings ruled this part of Bengal from Bishnupur for nearly two centuries. The British subsequently sold it to the Maharajah of Burdwan. The Mallas were great patrons of the arts and built uniquely ornamental terracotta temples. It is also where the Dhrupad style of classical Indian singing originated. Local handicrafts include silk, tassar, conch-shell and bell-metal ware and the famous terracotta 'Bankura horse', Dokhra, and also slate statues and artefacts. Bengali sweetmeats and flavoured tobacco are local specialities. ▶▶ *For Sleeping, Eating and other listings, see pages 598-600.*

Sights

There are more than two dozen temples in Bishnupur, mostly dedicated to Krishna and Radha. They are usually built of brick but sometimes of laterite and on a square plan with a gently curved roof imitating the Bengali thatched (*chala*) hut. The terracotta tiles depict episodes from the *Ramayana* and *Mahabharata*, and also scenes from daily life. Inside, there is a sanctuary (*thakurbari*) and a platform (*vedi*) for the image, on one side. The upper storey has a gallery topped by one, five or even nine towers.

Most of the temples are concentrated within the fort, which was built later by Muslim rulers. Distances given are from the Tourist Lodge. The **Rasmancha** (3 km) is a unique Vishnu shrine. The well-preserved cannons, in particular the 4-m long **Dalmadal** to the south of the Rasmancha, date back to the Mallas. The **Jor Mandir** (5 km), a pair of hut-shaped temples with a single *sikhara*, built in 1655 by Raghunath Singh, has attractively ornamented panels. He also built the **Shyam Rai Temple** (7 km), perhaps the earliest example of the *pancharatna* (five towers) and a fine *sikhara*. Each façade is triple arched and the terracotta panels show scenes from the *Ramayana* and Krishna's life.

> ‖ *The temples can be very difficult to find on foot in the maze of narrow streets. It is best to arrange a cycle-rickshaw for a tour, Rs 50 for 2½ hrs.*

The large **Madan Mohan Temple** (5 km), with a white façade, was built of brick with terracotta panels in 1694 by King Durjan, while the 17th-century **Lalji** and **Madan Gopal** are built of laterite.

The **Mrinmoyee Mandir** (3 km) has a clay idol of Durga dating from AD 997, and in the courtyard a curiosity of nine trees growing together. Little remains of the Malla Kings' **Fort** (3½ km). You can see the gate of laterite, with firing holes drilled in different directions and a 13th-century stone chariot. The water reservoirs are still there though the moat, once served by seven lakes, is partly dry.

Durgapur→ *Population: 493,000.*

Durgapur, a spacious planned city, was built in the mid-1950s within easy reach of the rich belt of coal and iron ore. The steel plant, 10 km away, was commissioned in 1957. Durgapur supplies domestic gas to Kolkata while the 692 m barrage controls the 2,500 km canal network in the region. Visitors should contact the PRO in person (1030-1230, 1430-1630 on weekdays, 0930-1215 on Saturday), T553611, ext 315. The tourist office is at city centre.

★ Santiniketan → *Phone code: 03463. Colour map 4, grid C1. Population: 65,700.*

Santiniketan, the 'Abode of Peace', is a welcome change from the hectic traffic, noise and dirt of Kolkata. Even a brief visit to the shady university campus with an imprint of its artistic heritage, and its quiet, rural charm makes a profound impression on most visitors. ▶▶ *For Sleeping, Eating and other listings, see pages 598-600.*

Ins and outs
Getting there The nearest railway station is Bolpur, which has trains from Kolkata's Haora and Sealdah stations (booking essential). Cycle-rickshaws charge Rs 15-20 to Santiniketan, 3 km away. Local buses use a stand near the station. The road journey from Kolkata on the congested NH2 takes longer (213 km) as it can be very slow.

Getting around The Visva Bharati campus and Santiniketan's residential area around are ideal for exploring on foot. To get further afield you will need a cycle-rickshaw. See Transport, page 599, for further details.

Climate Summer maximum 39°C, minimum 34°C; Winter maximum 16°C, minimum 12°C. Annual rainfall: 1,250 mm, mainly Jun-Sep.

Vishva Bharati University
① *Closed Wed and Tue afternoon, sightseeing is permitted only after university hours - summer 1430-1700, winter 1415-1630 and during vacations 0700-1200, Rs 5, photography is not permitted. Note that all the separate compounds are sub-divided by wire fences - effectively it is 3 km from the hotels in Bolpur.*

The Maharishi Debendranath Tagore, father of Rabindranath Tagore, the Nobel Laureate, started an *ashram* which was later named 'Santiniketan'. In 1901 Rabindranath started an experimental place of learning with a 'classroom' under the trees, and a group of five pupils. It went on to become the Vishva Bharati University in 1921. It now attracts students from all over the world and aspires to be a spiritual meeting ground in a serene, culturally rich and artistic environment. Open-air classes are still a feature of this unique university. Among the many *Bhavans* are those concentrating on fine art (Kala Bhavan), and music and dance (Sangit Bhavan). The **Uttarayan Complex** where the poet lived consists of several buildings in distinctive architectural styles. **Sadhana** Prayer Hall, where Brahmo prayers are held on Wednesday, was founded in 1863 (see page 1336). The unusual hall enclosed by stained glass panels has a polished marble floor which is usually decorated with fresh *alpana* designs. **Chhatimtala**, where Maharishi Debendranath sat and meditated, is the site of special prayers at Convocation time. In keeping with its simplicity, graduates are presented with a twig with five leaves from the locally widespread *Saptaparni* trees.

Museums

Rabindra Bhavan ⓘ *closed Tue afternoon, Wed, 1030-1300, 1400-1630, no photography, bags may not be permitted, shoes must be removed before entering each building*, is a museum and research centre in the Uttarayan complex, containing photographs, manuscripts and Tagore's personal belongings; the peripheral buildings contain photos too. Well documented and very informative so allow at least an hour to read the 'small print'. The garden is delightful, particularly when the roses are blooming. **Kala Bhavan Gallery** ⓘ *closed Wed, 1500-1700*, has a rich collection of 20th-century Indian art, particularly sculptures, murals and paintings by famous Bengali artists. **Nandan Museum** ⓘ *Bharati, closed Wed. 0730-1200, 1400-1600,* has a collection of terracotta, paintings and original tracings of Ajanta murals.

Surul (4 km), with its evocative village atmosphere and small terracotta temples with interesting panels on their façades, makes a pleasant trip. The *zamindari* 'Rajbari' with its durga shrine gives an impression of times past.

Santiniketan

Sleeping
1 International Guest Houses
2 Guest House
3 Purba Palli Guest House
● Raihkinkar Sculptures

Ballavpur Deer Park (3 km) ① *closed Wed, 1000-1600*, is an area of rapidly eroding laterite *khowai* which has been reclaimed and forms a wooded area with spotted deer and winter migratory birds.

Excursions
Bakresvar ① *allow 5 hrs and tip the local guide about Rs 25*, 58 km northwest of Santiniketan, is known for its medicinal sulphurous hot springs (separate bathing areas for men and women, though you may not fancy the tepid pools full of people doing laundry). There are seven important kunds (springs) where the temperature varies from 36°C to 67°C, the hottest being Agnikunda (fire spring). Temples to Siva, Sakti, Kali and Vishnu make it a Hindu pilgrimage centre. The temples are small, modern and white tiled though the Kali temple is old, painted red and set in a clean courtyard.

Listings: Bishnupur and Santiniketan

● Sleeping

Bishnupur *p595*
D-E **Tourist Lodge**, T52013, 10 rooms, 5 a/c, 4-bed dorm (Rs 80), restaurant, also serves beer.
F **Retiring Rooms. Guest 'n Rest**, near Tagore's statue, serves Bengali food only.

Durgapur *p596*
B-C **Peerless Inn**, city centre near railway station, T0343-546601, F546603. 49 a/c rooms (some "prestige"), modern business hotel, pleasant garden restaurant. WBTDC
C **Pathik Motel**, Gandhi More, T0343-546399. 12 a/c rooms, meals, beer, Tourism Centre, Kolkata, T0343-2488271, F2485168.
Kwality, near the Steel Plant.
Qaiser, Nachan Rd.

Santiniketan *p596, map p597*
Bolpur:
C-E **Santiniketan Tourist Lodge (WBTDC)**, off main road, T52699, F52398. 34 rooms, varying sized a/c rooms, small non-a/c (**E**), 13 bed dorm (Rs 80), pleasant garden, poor food.
D **Rangamati**, Prabhat Sarani, Bhubandanga, T52305. 22 decent rooms (6 a/c), dorm (Rs 75), restaurant (Indian and Chinese).
D-E **Sathi**, Bhubandanga Rd, T56576, F56555. Some a/c, 3, 4 and 5-bedded rooms, best on 1st floor terrace (front and back).
E **Manasi Lodge**, Santiniketan Rd, T54200. Clean rooms, attached bath, helpful staff, courtyard restaurant.

E-F **Bolpur Lodge**, off Tourist Lodge Rd (ask rickshaw drivers), T52662. Modern, functional, inexpensive rooms with bath (some a/c), dorm, reasonable meals, quiet.
F **Railway Retiring Rooms**, 1 a/c, restaurant.

Santiniketan and beyond:
B-C **Camelia Resort**, Prantik (3 km from campus), T55044 (or T033-277540, F270630, multiple@cal2.vsnl.net.in). Clean, though dull, rooms (some a/c) on 3 floors around a central courtyard, good restaurant, beautiful large garden, pool, well located in open countryside but you need transport (rickshaws available), car hire (Rs 300 for 4 hrs), free transport to/from Bolpur station (Santiniketan Express).
B-C **Unique Palace**, Baganpara, T54538. A/c rooms, good restaurant, taxi for sightseeing.
C-D **Chhuti**, 241 Charupalli, Jamboni T52692, chhuti@cal.vsnl.net.in. Comfortable 'thatched' rooms with bath, some a/c, good restaurant, innovative.
D **Mayurakshi**, Prantik, near station, T52958. Some a/c rooms, unimaginative modern block but comfortable.
E **Poushali**, near Kala Bhavan, Pearsonpalli. 3-7 bed rooms, home cooked meals in restaurant.
F **International Guest Houses** (old and new) with simple rooms, one a/c, dining hall, contact PRO, Vishva Bharati, T52751, ext 6.

Bakresvar *p598*
E **Tourist Lodge**.
F **Youth Hostel**.

 For an explanation of the sleeping and eating price codes used in this guide, see inside the front cover. Other relevant information is found in Essentials pages 52-57.

🍴 Eating

Santiniketan *p596, map p597*
Camelia Resort, Prantik. Good food, wide choice, well-priced.

Chhuti and *Poushali* have restaurants but may require advance notice.
Kalor Dokan, an 'institution', open all hours.
Maduram, on Santiniketan Rd, near the petrol station, next to *NIIT Centre*, has been highly recommended.

🎉 Festivals and events

Bishnupur *p595*
Aug: Jhapan, in honour of the serpent goddess *Manasa*, dates from the 17th century. This regional harvest festival is linked with the fertility cult and is unique. Venomous snakes (cobras, pythons, vipers, kraits, flying snakes) are brought in baskets by snake-charmers who display amazing tricks.

Santiniketan *p596, map p597*
★ Poush Mela (**23-25 Dec**), an important fair, coinciding with the village's Foundation Day. Folk performances include *Santals* dances and *baul* songs. Bauls are Bengal's wandering minstrels, who are worshippers of Vishnu. They travel from village to village singing their songs, accompanied by a single string instrument, *ektara*, and a tiny drum. Tribal silver and 'Dhokra' metal crafts make attractive buys. Magh Mela (**end of Jan**), an agricultural and rural crafts fair at Sriniketan, marks the anniversary of the founding of *Brahmo Samaj*. **Vasanta Utsav** coincides with *Holi*. Programmes of dance, music and singing are held throughout the year, particularly good during the various festivals.

🛍 Shopping

Bishnupur *p595*
Cottage industries flourish in the different *paras* (quarters) each devoted to a specialized craft - pottery in Kamarpara, *sankha* (conch-shell) cutting in Sankharipara, and weaving, particularly Baluchari silk saris, in Tantipara. **Silk Khadi Seva Mandal**, Boltala, and **Terracotta Crafts**, 500 m from the Tourist Lodge, are recommended.

The local embossed leather work is distinctive. *Suprabhat*, Prabhat Sarani, Bhuban Nagar, opposite *Tourist Lodge*, Bolpur, T53963. Excellent, creative embroidery (including *kantha*), ready-made or to order, crafted by local village women, interesting owner. Handicrafts at *Gramin* and *Sarvodaya Ashram* in Bolpur; also Vishva Bharati *Silpa Sadans* in Santiniketan and Sriniketan.

Books
Manisha Granthalaya, Sriniketan Rd, Bolpur and *Subarnarekha* in Santiniketan sell rare books.

🚌 Transport

Bishnupur *p595*
Bus
Long distance WBSTC buses from Esplanade, Kolkata. Cars take up to 5 hrs on appalling roads. **STC Super Express** buses from Durgapur, 1115 (1 hr).

Car
Car hire From *Tourist Lodge; Kiron Homeo Hall*, Matukgunge.

Rickshaw
Cycle rickshaws are widely available.

Train
From Kolkata (H) to Bankura:
Howrah-Purulia Exp, 8017, 1640, 4 hrs.

Durgapur *p596*
Bus
Frequent buses, both to **Kolkata** (176 km) and to neighbouring towns, including Santiniketan.

Train
On the main railway line to Kolkata (*Shaktipunj Exp, 1448*, 1430, 2¼ hrs).

Santiniketan *p596, map p597*
Mainly **cycle rickshaws** and **taxis** available.

Train
Bolpur to **Kolkata** (H): *Shanti Niketan Exp, 3016*, 1310, 2½ hrs; *Kanchenjunga Exp, 5658*, (**S**), 1629, 4 hrs, booking highly recommended (avoid station counter as the

West Bengal Listings: Bishnupur & Santiniketan

pleasanter University booking office, 1030-1530, has a daily quota of 50 reserved seats, Rs 60). Also trains to New Jalpaiguri (for Darjeeling) via Malda. From **Kolkata** (H): *Ganadevta Exp, 3017,* 0605, 2¾ hrs; *Shanti Niketan Exp, 3015,* 0955, 2½ hrs.

🛈 Directory

Bishnupur *p595*
Banks State Bank of India changes

foreign cash. **Hospital** Sub-Division Hospital, near the Court. **Vishnu Pharmacy** in Maruee Bazar.

Santiniketan *p596, map p597*
Banks State Bank of India, Bolpur and Santiniketan; foreign TCs cashed in Santiniketan only. **Hospital** *Pearson Memorial Hospital,* Santiniketan. **Tourist office** Tourist Lodge, Bolpur, T52398. PRO, Vishva Bharati Office, T52751. 1000-1700, closed Tue afternoon, Wed.

North of Kolkata

Murshidabad → *Phone code: 03482. Colour map 4, grid C1. Population: 36,900.*

Named after Nawab Murshid Kuli Khan, a Diwan under Emperor Aurangzeb, Murshidabad, 12 km from Baharampur, became the capital of Bengal in 1705 and remained so up to the time of the battle of Plassey.

The **Nizamat Kila** on the river bank, near the town centre, encloses the Nawabs' old **Hazarduari** (1,000 doors) **Palace** ① *closed Fri, 1000-1630, Rs 2, no photography,* built in the Italian style in 1837. It is now a splendid museum with a portrait gallery, a circular durbar hall and a library and contains a rare collection of old arms, curios, china and paintings. ▸▸ *For Sleeping, Eating and other listings, see pages 611-618.*

The large newer **Imambara** (1847), opposite the palace, is also Italianate in style. The domed, square pavilion (**Madina**) with a verandah nearby may be what remains of the original Imambara. There are numerous 18th-century monuments in the city. Mir Jafar and later his son Miran lived at **Jafaragunj Deorhi**, known as the traitor's gate. **Kat-gola**, the garden-house of a rich Jain merchant, has a collection of curios and an old Jain temple. The **Palace of Jagat Sett**, one of the richest financiers of the 18th century, is 2 km from the Jafargung Cemetery to the north of the palace. The **Katra Mosque** (1724), modelled on the great mosque at Mecca and an important centre of learning, is outside the city to the east. It was built by Murshid Kuli Khan who lies buried under the staircase.

Moti Jheel (pearl lake) and the ruins of **Begum Ghaseti's palace** are 3 km south of the city. Only a mosque and a room remain. **Khosbagh** (Garden of Delight) across the river has three walled enclosures.

Malda → *Phone code: 03512. Colour map 4, grid B1.*

Once the Dutch and French traded from Old Malda, which lies at the confluence of two rivers 4 km away. Around 1680, the English established a market town here when they bought the village from a local landlord, and then moved to nearby **Ingraz (English) Bazar** (Englezabad) in 1771 where they built a fort. Now it is famous only for its juicy large Fajli mangoes and gives access to Gaur and Pandua.

The **Jami Masjid** in Old Malda was built in 1596 out of decorated brick and stone and displays some good carving on the entrance pillars. The 17-m **Nimasarai tower** across the river dating from the same period has strange stones embedded on the outer surface, which may have once been used to display beheaded criminals.

Malda Museum (1937) has a collection of stone images, coins and inscriptions from Gaur and Pandua. The **market** behind the Tourist Lodge is fascinating. Malda has several banks, post offices and hospitals.

Gaur → *Colour map 4, grid B1*

Gaur's situation on the banks of the River Ganga, yet within easy reach of the Rajmahal hills with their fine black basalt, made it possible for gifted stonemasons to construct beautiful religious and secular buildings. Muslim monuments of the Sultanate period are strewn around the quiet, deserted city.

History

On the ancient site of Lakshanavati, Gaur was the capital of King Sasanka in the seventh century, followed by the Buddhist Pala kings. The city became famous as a centre of education and culture during the reign of the Hindu Sena kings in the 12th century. At the beginning of the 13th century it was invaded by Bhaktiar Khalji and then captured by the Afghan Fakhr-ud-din Dynasty in the 14th century. They plundered the temples to construct their own mosques and tombs. Gaur was sacked by Sher Shah Suri in 1537 and the city's population was wiped out by plague in 1575.

The site

① *From Malda, get a bus for Mohodipur from near the Tourist Lodge and ask to be dropped at Pyasbari (tea and snacks available). Stay on the narrow tarmac road and you won't get lost. Turn right from the NH34 for the site in which you can wander around free. To return to Malda, stop a bus or share a taxi.*

Gaur

The remains of the embankments of the fort are to the south on the bank of the Bhagirati. The great golden mosque, **Bari Sona Masjid** or Baroduari (12-door), was built in 1526 and is an enormous rectangular stone-faced brick structure with a large open square in front. Fine marble carving is still visible on the remains of the minarets. Note the small Kali temple at the entrance.

Bangladesh can be seen from the **Dakhil Darwaza** (early 15th century), the main fort gateway with its five-storeyed towers. It was built of small red bricks embossed with terracotta decorations. The turrets and circular bastions produce a striking contrast of light and shade with decorative motifs of suns, rosettes, lamps and fretted borders. During the 15th century, a number of mosques and mausoleums were built in the new architectural style.

The **Firuz Minar** (Victory Tower) built by Sultan Firuz Shah in 1486 has a spiral staircase. The lower storeys are 12 sided while the upper are circular, with striking blue and white glazed tiles, used in

West Bengal North of Kolkata *Gaur*

addition to the terracotta and brick. The builders of the **Chika Mosque** (Bat Mosque, early 15th century), near the Kadam Rasul, made free use of Hindu idols in its construction. The **Chamkati Mosque** (circa 1475) shows the vaulted ceiling of the verandah. Inside the southeast corner of the Fort is the massive **Baisgazi Wall** (height being '22 yard') which enclosed the Old Palace with its *darbar, harem* etc. **Kadam Rasul** (1513) is a domed building with a Bengali *chala* roof, which housed the relic of the Prophet, a footprint in stone. The two-storeyed **Lukochuri Darwaza** (Hide-and-Seek Gate, circa 1655) is in the later Mughal style.

The **Tantipara Mosque** (circa 1475; *tanti*, weaver) has superbly decorated red brick with five entrance arches and octagonal turrets, while the elegant **Lattan** (Painted) **Mosque** (1475), attributed to Yusuf Shah, was decorated with bands of blue, green, yellow and white glazed tiles. Some 2 km south, the ruined **Chhoti Sona Masjid**, has a carved gate. It is close to the border with Bangladesh.

Ramkeli, not far from the Bari Sona Masjid, has the Madan Mohan Jiu Mandir and is of particular religious significance for the followers of **Sri Chaitanya**, the 14th-century Bengali religious reformer. **Tamaltola** marks the place where he meditated under a tree and pilgrims come here to see a footprint in stone.

Pandua

① From the Tourist Lodge, Malda, get a Siliguri or Raiganj bus (Rs 5) and ask to be dropped at Pandua Bus Stand (tea and snacks are available). The narrow tarmac road to the site, off the NH34, is easy to follow and gives a fascinating 'behind-the-scenes' view of Bengali village life. Buses from Adina return to Malda.

Pandua alternated with Gaur as a capital of Bengal between 1338 and 1500, when it was abandoned. Some ruins show clearly how the Muslims made free use of material from Hindu temples near Malda. The old brick-paved road, nearly 4-m wide and about 10-km long, passes through the town and most of the monuments stand close to it.

The **Adina Masjid** (1364-74) *① entry free*, exemplifies Muslim architecture in medieval Bengal. Built by Sultan Sikander Shah and once comparable to the great eighth-century mosque at Damascus, it is sadly in a poor state of repair. The vast space enclosed by pillared aisles has an 88-arch screen around a quadrangle with the mosque. Influence of 12th-century Sena architecture is evident in the tall, ornate, tiered *sikhara* and trefoil arches and the remarkable absence of a large entrance gateway. Most of the substructure, and some pillars, was of basalt plundered from existing Hindu temples and palaces. A small doorway in the western back wall of the mosque, clearly taken from an earlier Vishnu temple, exhibits the stonemasons' skill and the exceptional metalwork of the time. The **Eklakhi Mausoleum**, built of brick (circa 1412), has a Hindu idol carved on its front lintel. The **Qutb Shahi Mosque** (also *Sona* or Golden Mosque) was built in 1582. Further along are the ruins of the 17th-century **Chhoti** and **Bari Dargahs**.

★ Darjeeling

→ *Phone code: 0354. Colour map 4, grid A1. Population: 107,500. Altitude: 2,134 m.*

For tens of thousands of visitors from the steamy summer heat of the plains Darjeeling (Darjiling) has been the place to get away from it all. It is the principal escape from Kolkata. The idyllic setting, the exhilarating air outside town and stunning views of the Kangchendzonga range when there are gaps in the clouds attract trekkers too. Built on a crescent-shaped ridge Darjeeling is surrounded by hills which are thickly covered with coniferous forests and terraced tea gardens. Between June and September the monsoons bring heavy downpours, sometimes causing landslides, but the air clears after mid-September. Winter evenings are cold enough to demand log fires and warm clothing. ►► *For Sleeping, Eating and other listings, see pages 611-618.*

Getting there **Bagdogra**, near Siliguri, is Darjeeling's nearest airport where jeeps and share-taxis tout for business since buses only run from Siliguri (see below). Trains connect New Jalpaiguri/Siliguri with Kolkata and other major cities. The diesel 'toy train' runs from Siliguri/NJP in season but it is very slow. Most people reach Darjeeling by bus or share-taxi and arrive at the Bazar Bus stand in the lower town, though some taxis go to 'Clubside' on the Mall, which is more convenient for most accommodation. Buses from Gangtok arrive near the GPO. Roads can get washed away during the monsoons and may remain in poor condition even in Oct.

Darjeeling

Sleeping
1 Alice Villa
2 Aliment
3 Andy's
4 Bellevue, Old Bellevue, Indian Airlines & South Indian Café
5 Broadway
6 Dekeling & Dekeva's Restaurant
7 Ivanhoe
8 Lewis Jubilee Complex
9 Mahakal Palace
10 Maple Tourist Lodge
11 Mayfair
12 New Elgin
13 Pagoda
14 Prestige
15 Shangrila & Chinese Restaurant
16 Sinclairs
17 Tourist Lodge
18 Tower View
19 Triveni
20 Valentino & Chinese Restaurant
21 Windamere

Eating
1 Amigos
2 Glenary's
3 Hasty-Tasty
4 Nathmull's Tees
5 New Dish & Lhasno
6 Park

N
Not to scale

⁞ Quali-tea brew

An ancient Chinese legend suggests that 'tay', tea, originated in India, although tea was known to have been grown in China around 2700 BC. It is a species of Camellia, Camellia thea. After 1833, when its monopoly on importing tea from China was abolished, the East India Company made attempts to grow tea in Assam using wild 'chai' plants found growing there and later introduced it in Darjeeling and in the Nilgiri hills in the South. Today India is the largest producer of tea in the world. Assam grows over half and Darjeeling about a quarter of the nation's output. Once drunk only by the tribal people, it has now become India's national drink.

The old 'orthodox' method of tea processing produces the aromatic lighter coloured liquor of the Golden Flowery Orange Pekoe in its most superior grade. The fresh leaves are dried by fans on 'withering troughs' to reduce the moisture content and then rolled and pressed to express the juices which coat the leaves. These are left to ferment in a controlled environment to produce the desired aroma. Finally the leaves are dried by passing them through a heated drying chamber and then graded – the unbroken being the best quality, down to the 'fannings' and 'dust'. The more common 'crushing, tearing, curling' (CTC) method produces tea which gives a much darker liquor.

Most of Darjeeling's tea is sold through auction houses, the largest centre being in Kolkata. Tea tasting and blending are skills which have developed over a long period of time and are highly prized. The industry provides vital employment in the hill areas and is an assured foreign exchange earner.

Getting around Darjeeling's roads slope quite gently so it is easy to walk around the town; the air quality is poor in the lower town due to diesel exhaust fumes. The railway station is in the lower part of town on Hill Cart Rd, with the taxi and bus stands. The lower and upper roads are linked by a series of connecting roads and steep steps. The Chowrasta is a focal point with the busy Nehru Rd and The Mall leading off it. The Shrubbery (Government House) is at the north end on Birch Hill with St Andrew's Church at the highest point. For sights away from the centre you need to hire a taxi. Clubside is the most convenient rank, but bargain, especially out of season. Be prepared for seasonal water shortages and frequent power cuts. After dark a torch is essential. See Transport, page 616, for further details.

Climate Temperature: summer, maximum 19°C, minimum 14°C; Rainfall: Jun-Aug 600 mm, Nov-Feb 10 mm.

History

Darjeeling (official but rarely used spelling - Darjiling) means 'region of the *dorje* - thunderbolt'. The surrounding area once belonged to Sikkim, although parts were annexed from time to time by the Bhutanese and Nepalese. The East India Company returned the territory's sovereignty to the Rajas of Sikkim, which led to the British obtaining permission to gain the site of the hill-station called Darjeeling in 1835, in return for an annual payment, see page 796. It was practically uninhabited and thickly forested but soon grew into a popular health resort after a road and several houses were built and tea-growing was introduced. The Bengal Government escaped from the Kolkata heat to take up its official summer residence here. The upper reaches were originally occupied by the Europeans, who built houses with commanding views. Down the hillside on terraces sprawled the humbler huts and bazars of the Indian town.

Sights

Observatory Hill, sacred to **Siva**, is pleasant for walks though the views of the mountains are obscured by tall trees. The pedestrianized **Mall** to the east of the hill offers good views near the Chowrasta. Beware of the monkeys; they bite.

Aloobari Monastery on Tenzing Norgay Rd is open to visitors. Tibetan and Sikkimese handicrafts made by the monks are for sale.

The **Tibetan Refugee Self-help Centre** ① *T53122, closed Sun, walk to viewpoint 500 m beyond Windamere hotel and then walk down for about 30 mins (ask around)*, with its temple, school and hospital is north of town. After the Chinese invasion, thousands of Tibetan refugees settled in Darjeeling (many having accompanied the Dalai Lama) and the rehabilitation centre was set up in 1959 to enable them to continue to practise their skills and provide a sales outlet. You can watch them at work (carpet weaving, spinning, dyeing, woodwork, etc) during the season, when it is well worth a visit (closes for lunch). The shop sells carpets (orders taken and posted), textiles, curios or jewellery, though not cheap to buy.

The closest tea gardens to Darjeeling is the **Happy Valley Tea Estate** ① *closed Sun, Mon, visitors 0800-1200, sometimes 1300-1630 (best in the morning), with good guide informative tours*, a 2-km walk from the Market, which uses the 'orthodox' method, see box, page 604.

Museums

Natural History Museum ① *off Mall Rd, closed Wed afternoons and Thu, 1000-1600, Rs 2*, has a large collection of fauna of the region. Visit recommended. **Himalayan Mountaineering Institute and Everest Museum** ① *T52438, closed Tue in winter, 0900-1300, 1400-1600, Rs 15 (includes Zoo), still camera Rs 10, video Rs 20, entrance is through the zoo on Jawahar Rd West*, was previously headed by the late Tenzing Norgay who shared the first climb of Everest in 1953. It traces the history of attempted climbs from 1857 and displays old mountaineering equipment including that used on that historic Tenzing-Hillary climb. Recommended. **Ava Art Gallery** ① *Ghoom, T52469, 0800-1200, 1230-1800*, has exceptional embroidered portraits.

Parks and zoos

Lloyds Botanical Gardens ① *closed Sun and bank holidays, 0600-1700*, near the market, was laid out in 1878 on land given by Mr W Lloyd, owner of the Lloyd's Bank. It has a modest collection of Himalayan and Alpine flora including banks of azaleas and rhododendrons, magnolias, a good orchid house and a herbarium. Pleasant and quiet spot. **Victoria Falls** which is only impressive in the monsoons provides added interest to a three-hour nature trail. The **zoo** ① *1000-1600, Rs 15 (includes Himalayan Mountaineering Institute)*, is next to the Mountaineering Institute. High-altitude wildlife includes Himalayan black bear, Siberian tiger, red pandas, yaks and llama. There are large enclosures over a section of the hillside though at feeding time and wet weather they retreat into their small cement enclosures giving the impression that they are restricted to their cells. There is a reasonably successful snow leopard breeding programme.

> **◦** *Visit the Shrubbery behind Raj Bhawan on Birch Hill for spectacular views of Kangchendzonga.*

Excursions

Ghoom Monastery, at an altitude of 2,550 m, is the important Yiga-Choling Gompa, a Yellow-hat Buddhist Monastery. Built in 1875, it houses famous Buddhist scriptures. You can visit Ghoom 8 km away, on the steam 'Tourist Train' April-June, October-November. There is an interesting Darjeeling Himalayan Railway museum at the station, Rs 5. A few spruced up carriages do the 'tourists only' ride in summer with a photo stop at Batasia, departing at 1030, returning at 1230 (check). Fare Rs 220 but limited to 40 persons so go early to join the queue; tickets go on sale at 0800. See

⦂ Darjeeling Himalayan Railway – a mini miracle

For many people the somewhat erratic narrow gauge Toy Train between New Jalpaiguri and Darjeeling, with its 0.6 m (2 ft) gauge track which used to be hauled by sparkling tank engines, is a rewarding experience. The brainchild of an East Bengal railway agent Franklyn Prestage, the train promised to open access to the hills from the sweltering humidity of the Kolkata plains in the summer. Following the line of an earlier steam tramway, the name was changed to the Darjeeling Himalayan Railway Company in 1881. It is a stunning achievement, winding its way up the hillside, often with brilliant views over the plains covering the 82 km with gradients of up to one in 19. At Ghoom, it reaches 2,438 m and then descends 305 m to Darjeeling. The DHR has been upgraded to a 'World Heritage Site' and has newly refurbished carriages with cushioned seats and window curtains for the steam 'Tourist trains'. It is a must for steam buffs – despite derailments which are "swiftly dealt with and you are lifted back on the tracks within 20 minutes".

also 'Toy Train' under Siliguri on page 618. Alternatively, go on the diesel train at 0900, Rs 25 (1st class); Rs 4 (2nd class) and return on foot or by bus.

Batasia Loop, 5 km away on the way to Ghoom, which allows the narrow-gauge rail to do a figure of eight loop, has a war memorial with a pleasant small park with good mountain views (Rs 3).

Chunnu Falls, 10 km down a steep switchback road, has turned an impressive waterfall into an artificial concrete park with flower beds, metal stairways and viewing platforms. Limited refreshments are served on a pleasant terrace.

The disused **Lebong Race Course**, 8 km away, was once the smallest and highest in the world and still pleasant for a walk.It was started as a parade ground in 1885.

It is worth rising as early as 0400 to make the one hour journey for a breathtaking view (weather permitting) of the sunrise on Kangchendzonga at **Tiger Hill** ① *jeeps from Darjeeling, Rs 400. You may wish to walk back from Tiger Hill (about 2 hrs, 11 km) or visit Ghoom on the way back* (altitude: 2,590 m). Mount Everest (8,846 m), 225 km away, is visible on a clear day. (The crowds at sunrise disappear by mid-morning).

Excursions from Darjeeling

Mirik → *49 km from Darjeeling. Altitude: 1,730 m.*

Mirik, with its forests of japonica, orange orchards, tea gardens and cardamom plantations, held the promise of an attractive resort but is sadly neglected. **Sumendu Lake**, with its 3½-km cobbled promenade, offers boating. You can visit the carpet weaving centre at Krishannagar, south of the lake, or trek to Kurseong and Sandakphu.

Kurseong → *Altitude: 1,458 m.*

The small, peaceful hill station ('Place of the White Orchid'), surrounded by tea gardens, has some popular boarding schools. Travellers suggest stopping here overnight on the Toy Train between Siliguri and Darjeeling. You can visit the Makaibari Tea Estate (4 km, closed Monday) and the Forest Museum on Dow Hill.

At **Tung** nearby, the St Alphonsus Social and Agricultural Centre, run by a Canadian Jesuit is working with the local community through education, housing, agricultural, forestry and marketing projects. They welcome **volunteers**, contact SASAC, Tung, Darjeeling, West Bengal, T42059.

Trekking

Walks lead in gentle stages along safe roads and through wooded hills up to altitudes of 3,660 m. The best trekking season is in April-May when the magnolias and rhododendrons are in full bloom, or October-November. In spring there may be the occasional shower. In the autumn the air is dry and the visibility excellent. In winter the lower altitude trails that link Rimbick with Jhepi (18 km) can be very attractive for birdwatchers. Ask in Darjeeling for trekking routes as there is an extensive network of varied trails that link the hillside towns and villages. The agents in Darjeeling can organize four-seven day programmes. For trek agents, see Darjeeling above.

The **Tourist Bureau** in Darjeeling will provide detailed information, plan the trek and book your accommodation and also obtain necessary equipment (sleeping bag, wind-jacket etc) and arrange a Sherpa guide. Trekking gear can also be hired from the **Youth Hostel** where there is a very useful book of suggestions from other trekkers. **Himalayan Mountaineering Institute**, see page 605, runs some courses for trekkers about Rs 250 for Indians, Rs 1,200 for foreigners.

Sandakphu

Most trekkers and visitors either walk or drive by jeep to Sandakphu, a small settlement located at 3,636 m on the Singalila Ridge, 57 km from Darjeeling. A good viewing point 100 m above Sandakphu offers fantastic views, including the famous northern face of Everest (8,846 m), Kangchendzonga (8,598 m), Chomolhari, the highest peak in Bhutan, and numerous peaks such as Pandim that lie in Sikkim. Everest is 140 km from Sandakphu as the crow flies. The entire area is a birdwatcher's paradise with over 600 species including orioles, minivets, flycatchers, finches, sunbirds, thrushes, piculets, falconets and Hoodson's Imperial pigeons. The mixed rhododendron, oak and conifer forests of the area are particularly well preserved.

Darjeeling treks

Phalut, 22 km from Sandakphu, along an undulating, partly jeepable track, is at the junction of Nepal, Sikkim and West Bengal. It offers even closer views of Kangchendzonga. It is best to avoid trekking here in May-June and mid-September to 25 October when large numbers of college trekking teams from West Bengal can descend on the area. March and November are highly recommended for clear mountain views.

Singalila trek

The 160-km Singalila trek starts from the small border town of **Manebhanjang**, 26 km from Darjeeling. The journey to and from Darjeeling can be done by bus or you can hire a Land Rover or jeep and be driven there early in the morning in 1½ hours. There is a frontier check post at **Sukiapokhri**, 7 km short of Manebhanjang, where you need to enter your passport details in the register. If you have not arranged for transport to meet you at a particular point then it is entirely possible to travel back to Darjeeling from every roadhead by public bus with services at least once daily, often three to four times daily.

Sleeping at Trekkers' Huts, mostly with 15-25 beds and costing Rs 25-50/bed have been built or refurbished in Tonglu, Sandakphu, Phalut, Gorkhey, Molle, Rammam, Rimbick and Siri Khola. Although usually available, it is wise to book in advance from the Deputy Commissioner, Improvement Fund Trust, Darjeeling, during May/June and October when these trails can be very busy. Any trek agent in Darjeeling will arrange these bookings for a small fee. Private lodges such as *Sherpa Lodge* in Rimbick and Rammam, and other trailside lodges in Meghma, Jaubari and Kalpokhri, are usually friendly, flexible and provide a reasonable but basic accommodation.

Day 1 To Tonglu (or Tumling) 1 km beyond Manebhanjang town you reach a rough stone paved track leading sharply up to the left. Tonglu (3,030 m) is 11 km from this point if you follow the jeep track, slightly less if you take the frequent but very steep short cuts. Alternatively, head for Tumling, just the other side of the peak of the hill from Tonglu (you take the alternative road from Meghma and rejoin the main route, 1 km after Tumling). Sleeping at **Tonglu**. A Trekkers' Hut has 24 beds and a fine view of the Kangchendzonga range. Also in **Tumling** where *Shikhar Lodge has* simple basic and clean rooms, very pleasant, local teacher's friendly family, "fabulous supper and breakfast", lovely garden. There are tea shops at **Chitre** and **Meghma**. Meghma has an interesting monastery noted for its large collection of Buddhist sculptures – 108 statues, according to locals. Ask at the teahouse opposite, to get in. *Hotel Indica,* Meghma, is a simple Tibetan home with homemade cheese hanging from ceiling, but it is unfortunately dirty.

Day 2 To Jaubari and Gairibans A level walk along the ridge takes you past the long 'mani' wall to the Nepalese village of Jaubari where the trail turns sharply to the right back into Indian territory and down to the village of Gairibans in a forest clearing. No visa necessary.

Day 3 To Sandakphu It is 14 km uphill to Sandakphu, with a lunch break in Kalpokhri with its attractive lake surrounded by fir trees, about midway. The last 3 km from Bhikebhanjang (tea shop) to Sandakphu are particularly steep but the views from the Singalila Ridge make it all worthwhile. Another viewpoint is 100 m above Sandakphu (see above). There are three *Trekkers' Huts* each with its own dining area, toilets and cookhouse - caretakers can arrange simple meals on extra payment. *Sherpa Chalet,* Sandakphu, is basic, clean and comfortable and provides good food. The drive back to Manebhanjang by pre-arranged four-wheel drive can take four hours along a very rough track.

Although Gorkhey, Phalut, Rammam and Rimbick lie just south of the border with Sikkim, entering Sikkim is not permitted on this route. To do a **circular walk** continue 21 km along the Singalila ridge to **Phalut** (3,600 m) where there is a *Trekkers' Hut.*

Alternatively you can retrace your steps 4 km back towards **Bhikebhanjang** and then take a 16-km long trail through fine forests of the Singalila National Park down to **Rimbick** from where there is a daily bus to Darjeeling. From Phalut continue northeast for 7 km down to the *Trekkers' Hut* at **Gorkhey** where you can stay the night, or walk 3 km to the village of **Samanden**, 'hidden' in a hanging valley and a further 6 km to **Rammam**. The clean, comfortable *Sherpa Lodge*, in a nice garden, recommended for friendly service (bus tickets and seats reserved) and good food. Alternatively, the *Trekkers' Hut* is about 1 km before Rammam village. From Rammam it is a two-hour walk down to the attractive *Trekkers' Hut* at Siri Khola and a further two hours to Rimbick. This entire area is particularly rich in birdlife.

An alternative quieter trail links Sabarkum (7 km before Phalut on the main Sandakphu-Phalut trail) with Rammam with a possible overnight halting place at the **Molley** Trekkers' Hut. Good *dahl bhat* and *rakshi/tongba:* share the kitchen fire with the family. Sherpas eat in a shack 200 m uphill from the *Youth Hostel*.

Those with five days to spare can return by the **Rammam-Rimbick-Jhepi-Bijanbari** route (153 km). From Rammam you can cross by a suspension bridge over the Siri Khola River and follow the path up the valley, which leads to Dentam in Sikkim (entry into Sikkim is not permitted). This less well-trodden valley has rich birdlife (particularly kingfishers), and excellent views of undisturbed forest. From **Bijanbari** (762 m) it is possible to return to Darjeeling, 36 km away, in a jeep or climb a further 2 km to Pulbazar and then return to Darjeeling 16 km away. Those wishing only to go to Rimbick may return to Manebhanjang via Palmajua and Batasi (180 km), which takes one day.

★ Kalimpong

→ *Phone code: 03552. Colour map 4, grid B2. Population: 43,000. Altitude: 1,250 m.*
Set in beautiful wooded mountain scenery, Kalimpong, a remote hill station, has been a meeting point of the once 'three Closed Lands' on the trade route to Tibet, Bhutan and Nepal. It has a relaxed and unhurried air about it. Away from the crowded and rather scruffy centre near the Motor Stand with the sports ground to one side, the town becomes more spaced out as mountain roads wind up and down the hillsides leading up to the monasteries, mission schools and orchid nurseries nearby. The name is said by some to be derived from pong *(stronghold) of* kalon *(king's minister)*, or from Kalibong, *a plant fibre.* ▸▸ *For Sleeping, Eating and other listings, see pages 611-618.*

Ins and outs

Getting there Bagdogra is the nearest airport and New Jalpaiguri the nearest railhead. Buses and shared taxis from there arrive at the bazar Motor Stand in about 3 hrs. From Darjeeling, the 51-km journey (2½ hrs) is through beautiful scenery. The road winds down through the Lopchu former Peshok tea estates and then descends to 250 m at Tista where it crosses the river on a 'new' concrete bridge. 'Lovers' Meet' and 'View Point' give superb views of the Rangit and Tista rivers.

Getting around The centre is compact enough to be seen comfortably on foot. The surroundings are ideal for walking, though some may prefer transport to visit nearby sights. See Transport, page 617, for further details.

Climate Best season is Mar-Jun, Sep-Feb. The gentle climate has warm summers (around 30°C) and cool winters (down to 7°C).

Sights

The traditional **market** at the 10th Mile has great atmosphere. The *haat* here every Wednesday and Saturday draws colourful villagers who come to sell fruit, unfamiliar vegetables, traditional medicines, woollen cloth, yarn and much more. It is remarkably clean and laid back, a delight to explore and find unusual merchandise - curly young fern tops, bamboo shoots, dried mushrooms, fragrant spices, musk, *chaang* paraphernalia, large chunks of brown soap, and tiny chickens in baskets alongside gaudy posters. The oldest, the **Thongsa Gompa Bhutanese monastery**, 10th Mile (1692) has been renovated. Further north, the Tibetan monastery (Yellow Hat) at Tirpai, the **Tharpa Choling** (1922) has a library of Tibetan manuscripts and *thangkas*, see page 534. The **Pedong Bhutanese monastery** (1837) near the old Bhutanese Damsang Fort at Algara (15 km) holds ceremonial dances every February. At Durpin Dara, the highest point in Kalimpong with superb views, stands the **Ringkinpong monastery** of Zang Dog Palri Phodrang. Unique outside Tibet, it has a school of Tibetan Medicine and is particularly interesting when prayers are being chanted. **Doctor Graham's Homes**, 3 km, was started by the missionary Doctor John Anderson Graham in 1900 when he admitted six needy children. Now there are 1,200 pupils. Volunteers able to spend at least six months should write in advance. There are pleasant **hikes** through Tista Road and rice fields to **Chitray Falls**, 9 km, a three-hour walk to **Bhalu Khop** and a 1½ hours' downhill walk from the Motor Stand to the Relli River. You can **trek** from **Lava** (32 km; monastery and weekly market on Tuesday), or **Lolaygaon** (56 km), which has spectacular views of Kangchendzonga, or picnic on the river beaches at Tista Bazar and Kalijhora.

Kalimpong

Sleeping ■
1 Bethlehem Lodge
2 Chimal
3 Crown & Chinmoy Lodges
4 Deki Lodge
5 Gompu's & Restaurant
6 Gurudangma House
7 Himalayan
8 Kalimpong Park & Cloud
9 Silver Oaks

Eating ●
1 Bakery
2 Glenary's
3 Vegetarian Snacketeria

0 metres 200
0 yards 200

There are a few nurseries as Kalimpong excels in producing orchids, amaryllis, roses, cacti, dahlias and gladioli. Ganesh Mani Pradhan on 12th Mile, Universal on 8th Mile, Shanti Kunj on BL Dikshit Road, Himalayan on East Main Road, are among many. The Takdah Orchid Centre (44 km) sells 110 varieties. Some are disappointed.

Siliguri → *Phone code: 0353. Colour map 4, grid A1. Population: 470,000.*

Surrounded by tea plantations, Siliguri is a largely unattractive transport junction with a vast truck park to the north and a busy main road lined with shops. The narrow-gauge steam 'Toy Train' to Darjeeling starts from here during the tourist season. It is also used as a base for travel into the hills and to the Jaldapara National Park.

Jaldapara Wildlife Sanctuary

ⓘ *160 km from Bagdogra airport, 224 km from Darjeeling. The best time to visit is from Nov to Apr when forest cover is thinner.*

The River Torsa flows through this sanctuary. The riverine forests of sal, khair, sheeshu harbour the one-horned rhino, elephants, wild boar, bison, deer, leopard, gaur and the occasional tiger. It covers an area of 116 sq km and is situated close to Phuntsoling in Bhutan. Trained elephants are available to take visitors around.

Listings: North of Kolkata

⊜ Sleeping

Murshidabad *p600*
F Youth Hostels at Lalbagh and Murhsidabad, reserve through Youth Services, 32/1 BBD Bagh S, Kolkata, T280626. The *Tea shop* to the left of Hazarduari gate is recommended for quality.

Malda *p600*
D Chanakya, NH34, town centre, T66620. 17 rooms, some a/c, restaurant, clean, modern.
D-F Tourist Lodge, Ingraz Bazar, just northeast of bridge over NH34, T66123. 13 rooms around courtyard (4 a/c) some with bath, a/c bar, restaurant. Tourist information, reservations: Kolkata, T2488271, F2485168.
E Purbanchal, 500 m north of *Chanakya*, T66183 (or reservations on Kolkata, T224278), 30 rooms, restaurant, bar, car hire.
E Railway Retiring Rooms. A/c rooms and dorm, modernized, helpful staff (South Indian platform snacks recommended).
F Continental Lodge, 22 KJ Sanyal Rd, by State Bus Stand, T52388. 42 rooms, restaurant, friendly, clean, recommended.

Darjeeling *p602, map p603*
Most hotels are within 1 km from the station. Several include all meals in season (Mar-Jun, Sep-Nov) and offer discounts off-season. Some charge extra for Christmas and New Year.

AL-A Mayfair, The Mall, opposite Raj Bhavan gate, T56376, F52674. Superb location, among terrace gardens, 21 rooms (5 attractive wooden attics), 11 cottages on hillside below Mall, good Tiffany's restaurant.
A New Elgin, 32 HD Lama Rd, T54114, F54267. 25 rooms in character rambling bungalow, top floor rooms in annexe refurbished (shut windows against monkeys!), good food, pleasant terrace, some adverse reports on facilities, billing and cleanliness, overpriced.
A Windamere, Observatory Hill, T54041, F54043. 27 spacious rooms (no phone or TV), dated bathrooms (limited hot water), enviable position with good views (when clear), sun terraces, charming, plenty of character, a 'Raj' experience - memorabilia, coal fires ("fill room with smoke"), 'hotties' in bed, pre-war piano favourites to accompany 'tea', US$110 includes disappointing meals.
B Darjeeling Gymkhana Resort, The Mall, T54391, F54390. 12 modern rooms, Indian veg restaurant, club on doorstep, wooded location.
B Sinclairs, 18/1 Gandhi Rd, T56431, F54355. 54 rooms (central heating), restaurant, bar.
B-C Central, Robertson Rd, T54480, F56050. 52 rooms, re-opened after renovation.
C Dekeling Resort at Hawk's Nest, 2 AJC Bose Rd (15 min walk from centre), T53347, F53298, www.dekeling.com. 4 spacious suites with fireplaces in restored old wooden

Raj retreat, charming Tibetan hospitality, superb isolated position with mountain views, delicious food.

C Tourist Lodge, Bhanu Sarani, behind Gymkhana Club, T54411. 15 rooms (some **B**) rather dilapidated, poor service.

C Valentino, 6 Rockville Rd, T52228. 17 clean rooms with mountain views, central heating, Chinese restaurant recommended, bar.

D Bellevue, Chowrasta, T54075, F54330, www.darjeeling4you.com. 43 simple rooms with bath and hot water (mornings), some large, bright and airy (eg Rooms 35, 49), some a bit dated (musty in the monsoons), so inspect first, limited snacks, convenient location, good K'dzonga view from roof at sunrise.

C-D Dekeling, 51 Gandhi Rd (the Mall), T54159, F53289, www.dekeling.com. 11 rooms with bath on upper floors, 4 attic (D), front rooms with views (noisy when jeeps depart at 0400 for Tiger Hill with lots of hooting!), good *Dekeva's* restaurant, charming family, 'brilliant hosts', reserve ahead, 40% low-season discount.

C-D Main Old Bellevue Hotel, Chowrasta, T54178, www.darjeelinghotels.com (above the newer section). Rooms with character in the Heritage building in a pleasant garden.

Some budget hotels offer 3/4 bedded rooms; most have limited menu in restaurants.

D Alice Villa, 41 HD Lama Rd near DGHC Tourist Office, Chowrasta, T54181, 21 large clean rooms (fireplace in some, bucket of coal Rs 75), cosy bungalow, good value but food disappointing.

D Shangrila, 5 Nehru Rd, near Chowrasta, T54149, 10 rooms, some with good views, good restaurant, exchange.

E Andy's, 102 Zakir Hussain Rd, 5 mins from Chowrasta past pony sheds, T53125, 10 very clean, airy rooms, some with Indian WC, upper floors with small hot shower, bird's eye views from rooftop, kitchenette, storage for trekkers, friendly Gurung family. Recommended.

E Prestige, Laden La Rd (up steps, above GPO), T53199, rooms with bath, hot water, no heating so sunny side recommended (others can be damp), some with good views, clean, friendly, good but busy and very noisy, popular with Indian tourists.

E-F Pagoda, 1 Upper Beechwood Rd, very friendly, clean but basic rooms, some with bath (limited bucket hot water), central yet quite peaceful, good value.

F Aliment at 84, 100 m below *Hostel*, small, clean, bright rooms, hot shower, cheap food, internet, packed with travellers, good atmosphere, 'library', quiet, friendly owner.

F Broadway, 3 Coochbehar Rd, 29 rooms, good location with rooftop views.

F Lewis Jubilee Complex (DGHC), Dr SK Pal Rd, T56395, 30 rooms, 6-bed dorm (Rs 30), indifferent service.

F Tower View at 8/1, beyond TV Tower, pleasant, clean rooms with toilet, shared hot shower, dorm, good food, internet, homely, friendly family. Recommended;

F Youth Hostel (WB), Dr Zakir Hussain Rd, T52290, mainly dorm (Rs 25) being renovated, superb position, no restaurant, trekking info, out of town but popular.

Other guest houses on Dr Zakir Hussain Rd on the way up to the *Hostel*, include:

F Triveni, opposite, at 85, T53114. Well-kept rooms, home-cooked meals.

Mirik *p606*

D Jagjeet, T43206, good rooms, restaurant, bar.

E-F Tourist Lodge & Cottages (DGHC), T43237, modern rooms (Rs 350), dorm (Rs 30), pleasant cottages above lake (Rs 750), good restaurant.

At **Dudhia** (on Siliguri Rd): Gakul Wayside Inn, Rs 450.

Kurseong *p606*

D Tourist Lodge, Hill Cart Rd, T03554-44409. 16 rooms, fast food restaurant, bar, good views.

E Amarjeet, 12 Hill Cart Rd, T03554-44678, 14 rooms, restaurant.

Jaubari *p608*

F Teacher's Lodge, excellent value.

There is a large **Trekkers' Hut** at Gairibans with about 20 beds.

Bijanbari *p609*

C Karmi Farm, a haven of rural peace at Kolbong, which you may choose to use as a base, north of Bijanbari (access via Kaijali, four-wheel drives stop 20 mins walk away, or it is 2-3 hrs by pony from Pulbazar). 7 double rooms with bath, simple but spotless, superb

West Bengal Listings: North of Kolkata

For an explanation of the sleeping and eating price codes used in this guide, see inside the front cover. Other relevant information is found in Essentials pages 52-57.

food, run by Andrew Pulger-Frame, US$20 includes food, porters etc. Contact *Samsara Travel* in Darjeeling, T56370, samsara@ dte.vsnl.net.in, or in UK T/F01303-253803.

Kalimpong *p609, map p610*

Hotels open all year may offer discounts from Nov to Mar; not all accept credit cards.
B Himalayan (Heritage Hotel), Upper Cart Rd (10-min walk town centre), T55248, F55122. 20 rooms, 8 spacious suites in newer imaginatively designed 'cottages', rest in stone-built characterful family home of the MacDonalds (rooms better upstairs), lovely verandah, mountain views, attractive gardens, set menu meals at set times, helpful management.
B Morgan House, Singamari, Durpin Dara Hill, T55384, 3 km centre. 7 rooms with bath (good views from upstairs), restaurant, bar, beautiful location, gardens.
B Orchid Retreat, Ganesh Villa (longish walk from town), T/F55389, thakro@cal2.vsnl.net.in. In interesting orchid nursery, 6 rooms in traditional thatched cottages (built with local materials), hot water (no TV or phone), home-cooked meals (Rs 100-150), lovely terrace garden with special palm collection, personal attention, peaceful.
B Silver Oaks, Main Rd, T55296, F55368. 25 rooms, some with good views, good restaurant (own fruit and vegetables), pleasant garden;
B-C Gurudongma House, Hill Top Rd, T55204, F55290. Rooms in charming family house and cottage with meals, Alpine tents, gardens, personal service (collect from motor stand), book ahead. Also restored farmhouse at Samthar where you can enjoy country pleasures and wonderful food; contact Gurudongma Tours and Treks, gurutt@ satyam.net.in, who organize tours to Sikkim.
C Kalimpong Park, Ringkingpong Rd, T55304, F55982. 19 simply furnished, good-sized, airy rooms, **B** suites (some in older 2-storeyed house), good restaurant, bar, exchange, garden, pleasant peaceful location, knowledgeable owner. WB Tourism lodges are clean and simple, breakfast and dinner usually included.
C-D Cloud 9, Ringkingpong Rd, T57304. Clean attractive rooms, good restaurant.
D Crown Lodge, off Bag Dhara Rd, near Motor Stand, T55846. 21 clean well-maintained rooms with bath, hot water, generator, very friendly and helpful, pleasant.
E Bethlehem Lodge, Rishi Rd (5-min walk from Motor Stand), T55185. Decent rooms with bath, newish and quite clean.
E Chinmoy Lodge, near Motor Stand, T56264. Newish rooms with bath.
E Deki Lodge, Tirpai Rd, uphill from Motor Stand, T55095. Clean, basic rooms, good meals, very friendly Tibetan family, good value.
E-F Gompu's, off Main Rd, T55818. Clean rooms, good restaurant, questionable reports.

At Singamari

B Tashiding Tourist Lodge, T55929, 5 large rooms (Rs 1400-1600), 1 **D** single.
D Hill Top Tourist Lodge, T55654, off Ringkingpong Rd, 2 km from centre. 7 rooms, dorm (Rs 275).
D-E Aashiana, KD Pradhan Rd, T56717. Finds visitors rooms in comfortable homes, simple apartments or humble huts (Rs 200-800).
D-E Chimal, Ringkingpong Rd, 1 km from Bus Stand, T55776. 10 clean, sparse rooms with bath, some with hot water (Rs 250-500), restaurant, pleasant location, terrace, views.

Siliguri *p611*

Hill Cart Rd is officially Tenzing Norgay Rd.
B Cindrella, Sevoke Rd, '3rd mile' (out of town), T547136, F531173, www.cindrellahotels.com. 50 comfortable rooms, some a/c, competent vegetarian restaurant, pool, internet, car hire, pick-up from airport, efficient, best in Siliguri.
B Sinclairs, Mallaguri (Airport Rd), T522674, F522743, pressman india@hotmail.com. 54 comfortable rooms, good restaurants, pool, attentive service.
C-D Embassy, Sevoke More (near Hill Cart Rd), T435251. Comfortable rooms with bath.
C-D Mainak (WBTDC), Hill Cart Rd (near railway station; auto from NJP Rs 170), T432830, F432859, maitd@dte.vsnl.net.in. 38 comfortable rooms, 14 a/c (rooms vary), well-kept gardens, restaurant and bar, helpful staff (can book *Madarihat Lodge*, Jaldapara, see page 614).
D-E Chancellor, Sevoke More, T432360. 7 small clean rooms with bath (hot water), restaurant, pleasant Tibetan management.
D-E Ranjit, Hill Cart Rd, T431680. 60 clean but variable rooms, few a/c, good restaurant, bar.

D-E **Vinayak**, Hill Cart Rd, T431130. 29 clean rooms with bath, some a/c, good restaurant.

E **Mount View**, Hill Cart Rd, opposite Junc Station, T425919. Pleasant rooms, good restaurant (wide choice).

E **Siliguri Lodge**, Hill Cart Rd (near railway station), T533290. 10 rooms with bath, dorm.

E **Tourist Services Agency**, a quiet street opposite Central Bus Terminus, T430872. Some newer rooms upstairs, relaxed and popular.

F **Railway Retiring Rooms**, at Siliguri Junc, and New Jalpaiguri. 4 rooms and 6 dorm beds in each, vegetarian snacks.

F **Youth Hostel**, Kangchendzonga Stadium, 130 beds.

Jaldapara Wildlife Sanctuary *p611*
At **Baradabri**:

F **Youth Hostel and Lodge**, 4 km from Hasimara railway station, 18 km from Madarihat. 3 rooms, 14 beds in 4 dorms, poor catering, reserve through DFO, Jalpaiguri, T838, Coochbehar, T247, Tourism Centre, Jalpaiguri, T183 or Kolkata, T2488271, F2485168.

At **Hasimara**:

F **Nilpara Forest Bungalow**. 2 rooms, very basic, caretaker will prepare a simple meal if requested but take all provisions.

At **Hollong**:

C **Forest Lodge**, built of timber on stilts deep inside the sanctuary, 6 km from Madarihat. 7 rooms (all meals), the lodge is very popular and is en route to Phuntsholing in Bhutan, book well in advance through Tourist Bureau, Siliguri or DFO, Kolkata, T222774.

At **Madarihat**:

C **Travellers' Haven Tourist Lodge**, on park fringe, T62230, 8 rooms and restaurant (1 meal obligatory).

❶ Eating

Darjeeling *p602, map p603*
Hotels with restaurants will usually serve non-residents. Several have bars.

₮₮₮ **New Elgin**. Charming dining room with character, good meals, very pleasant service.

₮₮ **Dekeva's**, 52 Gandhi Rd. International. Charming, cosy, local meals, also fast food.

₮₮ **Glenary's**, Nehru Rd, tea-room with excellent confectionery, friendly, 1st class breakfast, Kalimpong cheese and wholemeal bread sold, licensed restaurant upstairs pricier, smart internet café (Rs 60 per hr).

₮₮ **New Dish** JP Sharma Rd (below Lhasoo). Chinese. Adventurous menu, excellent chicken entrées, friendly staff.

₮₮ **Park**, 41 Laden La Rd, opposite *State Bank of India*. Clean, pleasant atmosphere, very good Indian; also Chinese.

₮₮ **Valentino**, Chinese and Continental.

₮ **Amigos**, good Chinese.

₮ **Gol Ghar**, Main Bazar. Indian. Excellent meat dishes with *chapatis*, *naan* and *rotis*.

₮ **Lhasoo**, JP Sharma Rd. Tibetan. Friendly.

₮ **South Indian Café**, Chowrasta. Indian. Very good vegetarian meals.

Cafés
Hasty Tasty, Laden La Rd. Very good Indian fast food, not the cheapest but worth it.

Kalimpong *p609, map p610*
Most restaurants shut at 2000.

Cloud, very good food.

Glenary's, opposite Arts Centre and on Main Rd. Bakery sells good bread etc, with tables.

Gompu's, rear of hotel, informal, good views, friendly, very good food, including Chinese.

Vegetarian Snacketeria, Main Rd, opposite Main Bazar. Very good Indian snacks.

✦ Festivals and events

Darjeeling *p602, map p603*
Buddha Jayanti in **Apr-May** celebrates the birth of the Buddha in the monasteries.

◯ Shopping

Murshidabad *p600*
Woven and handblock-printed silk saris and bell-metal ware are the main local industries. Murshidabad also produces excellent mangoes.

Darjeeling *p602, map p603*
The markets are colourful and worth visiting.

Books
Greenland, Laden La Rd, up some steps near entrance to *Prestige Hotel*. Book swap.

Oxford Bookshop, Chowrasta, good stock especially local interest, amiable staff.

Photography
Das Studios on Nehru Rd, stationery, postcards, interesting black-and-white prints from Raj days; order from album (1-2 days).

Handicrafts

The local handicrafts sold widely including Buddhist *tankhas* which are hand painted scrolls surrounded by Chinese brocade, good wood carving, carpets, hand-woven cloth, jewellery, copper, brass and white metal religious curios such as prayer wheels, bowls and statues. The Chowrasta shops are closed on Sun and Chowk Bazar on Thu.

Dorjee, Laden La Rd.

Eastern Arts, Nehru Rd.

Gram Shilpa, for *khadi* cotton and silk, well stocked and very helpful.

H Mullick, curios from Chowrasta, a cut above the rest.

Hayden Hall, 42 Laden La Rd, colourful woollen goods made by local women's co-op.

Nepal Curios, Laden La Rd.

Tibetan Refugee Self-Help Centre, Gandhi Rd. See under 'Sights'.

Tea

Nathmull's, Laden La Rd (above GPO), nathmulls@goldentipstea.com. An institution, vast selection (Rs 90-3,000 a kg), avoid fancy packs, knowledgeable owner.

Kalimpong *p609, map p610*
Handicrafts

Tibetan and Nepalese handicrafts and woven fabrics are particularly good

Arts & Crafts Centre, near Motor Stand, embroidered clothes, fire-screens

Soni Emporium, near Motor Stand, Mani Link Rd, specializes in Himalayan handicrafts.

Paper

Gangjong, Puritam Rd (near Sports ground). Interesting hand-made paper factory.

Tailors

Lotus, Main Rd, for cloth and tailoring.

Naseem's in market, good *sulwar kameez*.

▲▲ Activities and tours

Darjeeling *p602, map p603*
Clubs

The old **Gymkhana Club** has 3 good **snooker** tables (Rs 20 per hr), **badminton**, **squash**, **tennis** and **roller skating**. Temporary membership Rs 30 per day, staff excellent. **Darjeeling Club**, Nehru Rd, T54348, the old Planters' Club, a relic of the Raj, membership

(Rs 50 per day), allows use of pleasant colonial restaurant (Rs 200 buffet), bar, **billiards**, a bit run down, but log fires, warm and friendly.

Riding

Pony rides are popular on the Mall starting at Chowrasta; also possible to do a scenic half-day ride to Ghoom – agree price, in writing!

River rafting

On the Tista, 2-day all-inclusive tented trips covering 25-65 km, Rs 450-1200, contact DGHC Tourism.

Tour operators

Clubside Tours & Travels, T16 JP Sharma Rd, T54646, F54123, hotel, tours/treks, good jeep hire, air tickets. **Juniper Tours**, behind police island, New Car Park, Laden La Rd, T52095, also *Indian Airlines*, *Jet Airways* agent; **Pineridge Travels**, Chowrasta, T53912.

DGHC, from Tourist Office (minimum 8). **Tour 1**: Tiger Hill, Senchal Lake, Ghoom Monastery, Batasia Loop. 0400-0730. Rs 60. **Tour 2**: Local sightseeing. Ava Gallery, Manjusha Emporium, Dhirdham Temple, Himalayan Mountaineering Institute, Zoo, Ropeway, Lebong Racecourse, Tibetan Refugee Self-help Centre. 0930-1230, 1330-1630. Rs 60. **Tour 3**: Mirik. 0800-1730. Rs 95. **Road tours**: Clubside Tours, JP Sharma Rd, T54646; Darjeeling Transport Corp, 30 Laden La Rd, T52074. Maruti vans, jeeps, Land Rovers and a few Sumos are available. Prices vary according to the season so negotiate rates.

Trekking agents

Himalayan Adventures, Das Studios, Nehru Rd, T54090, dastrek@aussiemail.com.au. **Himalayan Travels**, at *Sinclairs*, Gandhi Rd, T54544, long established; **Himalayan Nature Foundation**, opposite Dirdham Temple, T52237, experienced trekking agent, for Singalila, Sikkim etc. **Trek-Mate**, Singalila Arcade, Nehru Rd, T74092. Well-equipped.

Kalimpong *p609, map p610*
Tour operators

Kalimpong Tours & Travels, T55545. **Kalimtrek**, Main Market, Himalayan Stores, T55448, F55290, organizes treks, arranges paying-guest accommodation. **Mintry Transport**, Main Rd, T55741.

⊖ Transport

Murshidabad *p600*
Bus

From Baharampur local bus stand to Lalbagh, 1 hr, Rs 3; or shared auto-rickshaw, 30 mins, Rs 6. Then cycle-rickshaw to Hazarduari gate, Rs 8.

Train

Lalgola Passenger from Kolkata (S).

Malda *p600*
Bus

Local Buses are cheap and rickshaws are common. For **Gaur and Pandua**, buses and tongas; **Murshidabad** has a bus service.
Long distance N Bengal STC: regular Express services to Kolkata, 8 hrs. Reservations: Esplanade Terminus, Kolkata or at KJ Sanyal Rd, Malda, T52465.

Taxi

For **Gaur and Pandua**, about Rs 300.

Train

Kolkata (S): *Kanchenjunga, 5658* (AC/II), 1242, 8 hrs.

Darjeeling *p602, map p603*
Air

Nearest airport, **Bagdogra** (90 km), see page 617. Transfer by car or coach is 3-3½ hrs. Pre-paid taxi counter to left of exit, Rs 750 (sharing possible); the W Bengal Tourism Coach costs Rs 80 each. *Indian Airlines, Belle Vue Hotel*, Chowrasta, T52355, or T54230. Weekdays 1000-1700, Sun 1000-1300. Tourist Information counter.

Bus

NH31 connects Darjeeling with other parts of India.
Local Bus operators: N Bengal STC, T3133; Gurkha PAKU, Chowk Bazar Bus Stand, T53487; Darjeeling Siliguri Syndicate, Motor Stand; Singamari Syndicate, Main Taxi Stand, T52820; *Sikkim SNT agent*, T52101.
Long distance Fast bus services between Kolkata and Siliguri with connections to Darjeeling (see Siliguri, page 618). North Bengal STC, Darjeeling, T35133. **Darjeeling to/from Siliguri and Bagdogra**: During the 'season', W Bengal STC bus from Bazar Bus Stand, or more comfortable Tourist Coach (min 6 passengers),

leaving from *Tourist Lodge* and the traffic island near Keventers (3-3½ hrs) - tickets from tourist office, *Bellvue Hotel*. One visitor felt "for thrills and spills, no fairground attraction can rival the narrow hairpinned, switchback road that climbs the Himalayan foothills to Darjeeling".
Gangtok: SNT bus from near post office. Darjeeling Motor Service, Laden La Rd, T52101. **Kalimpong**: Jeeps and buses from the Bazar Motor stand: direct Jeep (2 hrs) and DGHC minibus; buses are infrequent, slower and not much cheaper. In winter, Kalimpong Motor Syndicate, small office tucked away under the bazar, Rs 60. **Nepal**: Land Rovers between 0600 and 0900 for journey to the border (Panitanki-Kakarbhitta). Private buses have connections from Siliguri (see above), through ticket (Rs 450). Alternatively, Pashupati Fatak on the border (Mirik Rd) has buses to Kathmandu.

Jeep

Share jeep to **Siliguri**, Rs 82 (2½ hrs via short cut); bus Rs 50 (3½-4 hrs). Jeep (for 5) **Kalimpong or Bagdogra**, Rs 900; **Siliguri**, Rs 600; **Gangtok**, Rs 1,500.

Ropeway Cable Car

Starts from North Point, 3 km from Chowk Bazar (share taxi Rs 5) connects Top Station with Takver in Singla Valley on the Little Rangit River. In season, 0930-1600 (15 mins each way) Rs 60 return.

Taxi

Private taxis charge approximately Rs 7 for Nehru Rd to Top Station. Stand, Robertson Rd/Laden La Rd.

Train

Darjeeling station has some old steam engines. Computerized Reservation allows nationwide booking; 0800-1400. Diesel service to **Siliguri** (narrow gauge), which is 80 km away, and **New Jalpaiguri Junction** (broad gauge), see page 618. At 0900 (8 hrs). The narrow gauge steam 'Tourist' train to Ghoom departs 1030, stops at Batasia Loop, Rs 220 (see Ghoom above).

Mirik *p606*
Road

Access from Bagdogra airport (55 km), Darjeeling (50 km) and Siliguri (52 km). To/from Darjeeling: buses, 0630 to 1500; Jeep, 1200, 1330.

Kurseong p606
Road

51 km from Siliguri, off the main Darjeeling road, or via Pankhabari. Buses and taxis from Siliguri, 3 hrs, Darjeeling, 2 hrs.

Train

The 'Toy Train' stops here; passenger service from 0645 to Darjeeling most of the year, Rs 10, 3½ hrs. The refurbished steam train runs a 'School' service between Darjeeling and Kurseong on weekdays in term time.

Kalimpong p609, map p610
Air

Nearest airport is at Bagdogra. A new airport is planned which will allow flights to Paro, Kathmandu and Dhaka, 80 km, 3-3½ hrs by car, Rs 700 (see Siliguri); also taxi seat or bus Rs 75. *Indian Airlines* information, T55741.

Bus

Kalimpong is off the NH31A to Gangtok. Taxis to Siliguri and Bagdogra, last depart 1500.

State and private buses use the Motor Stand. Several to **Siliguri**, 3 hrs; **Darjeeling**, 3½ hrs; **Gangtok**: 3½ hrs (very scenic), Rs 37. N Bengal STC sells tickets, Motor Stand, T55719, SNT, Bus Stand, T55319. **Kolkata**: fast 'Rocket' buses. **Darjeeling**: DGHC **minibus** (contact *Kalimpong Tours & Travels*).

Jeep

Faster, every 30 mins, 2-3 hrs, Rs 600; ask for pick-up point in Darjeeling for return trip.

Train

The nearest railhead is New Jalpaiguri/ Siliguri station, 67 km. Tickets from **Rly Out Agency**, Kalimpong Motor Stand.

Siliguri p611

Try to arrive in Siliguri or New Jalpaiguri In daylight (before 1900).

Air

Nearest airport, **Bagdogra**, 14 km away, with tourist information counter and little else; security checks can be rigorous. Daily flights to **Kolkata**, Delhi via Guwahati. *Indian Airlines, Mainak Tourist Lodge*, T431495, airport T450666; *Jet Airways*, Vinayak Bldg, Hill Cart Rd, T435876, airport T551588, daily. **Helicopter** daily in fine weather to Sikkim

(see page 632). Transfer: STC buses to Darjeeling and Gangtok. Taxis (for sharing) to Darjeeling (Rs 700), Gangtok (Rs 1,200), Kalimpong and Siliguri (Rs 160).

Bus

Siliguri is on NH31; Darjeeling (80 km), Gangtok (114 km) and Kalimpong (54 km) and served by State buses from WB, Bihar, Sikkim and Bhutan.
Tenzing Norgay Central Bus Terminus (CBT) next to the Junction Railway Station; **SNT Bus Station**, is across the Hill Cart Rd. Buses to N Bengal go from the **Dooars Bus Stand** at the junction of Sevoke and Bidhan Rds. The overnight North Bengal STC's 'Rocket' bus service between **Kolkata and Siliguri** depart 2100 from Hill Cart Rd, 12 hrs, Rs 180, a/c Rs 350. Reserve seats in Kolkata, or in Burdwan Rd, Siliguri, T20531. They can be very full and noisy. **Darjeeling** State buses (4 hrs, Rs 50) from CBT and Sevoke Rd, or more comfortable Tourist Bus (for minimum 6), Rs 80. **Kalimpong** 2-3 hrs. N Bengal STC, Sevoke Rd. **Madarihat** (for Jaldapara) leave from bus station on Hill Cart Rd. **Gangtok** SNT buses, 5 hrs; reserve near Mahananda Bridge, Hill Cart Rd, T21496. Deluxe private buses from CBT, Junction Station (separate ticket window), Rs 100.
Bhutan: *Bhutan Transport*, Hill Cart Rd (0900-1130, 1330-1630). To **Phuntsholing**: few buses daily, Rs 100, 3-4 hrs.
Nepal: to **Kathmandu** buses (or more conveniently taxi or Land Rover), to Panitanki on the border (35 km, 1 hr); transfer to Kakarbhitta by cycle-rickshaw. **Kakarbhitta**, the Nepalese border town has only basic accommodation. **Visa** US$1 per day (15-60 days) and 1 photo. Buses depart at 0400, 0500 to arrive at Kathmandu (or Pokhra) via W Nepal Highway (595 km), same evening (15-16 hrs); the journey can be very tiring. Tickets from *Tourist Services Agency*, Pradhan Nagar, Siliguri, T531219; Siliguri to Kakarbhitta (Rs 120); Kakarbhitta to Kathmandu/Pokhra (Nep Rs 320); also through tickets. From Kakarbhitta it is also possible to **fly** (seasonal) from Bhadrapur (34 km, with free transfer to airstrip) to Kathmandu (1 hr) by **RNAC** or **Everest Air** (Nep Rs 1400); agent *Sharma Travels*. Alternatively, get a taxi to Biratnagar in Nepal (150 km) and fly from there to Kathmandu (US$99).

Opposite *Air View Hotel*, Hill Cart Rd and on Sevoke Rd, and railway stations to connect with most trains. To **Darjeeling**, share jeep (Rs 82) for 5-7 passengers, 3-3½ hrs.

Train

Siliguri Junction (narrow gauge, T20017) and **New Jalpaiguri** ('NJP' broad gauge, T561371), 5 km away, both for **Toy Train**, with tourist information. There are buses, cycle-rickshaws (Rs 25), trains and taxis (Rs 40) between the two. NJP has good connections to other important centres in India. For long distance rail journeys from NJP, first buy tickets at Siliguri (Computerized Reservations, Bidhan Rd near Stadium), 1000-1300, 1330-1700 (for 1st class tickets, avoid queue; go to Chief Reservations Officer at side of building), then to NJP station for train. Porters demand Rs 50 for 2 cases. **Darjeeling**: from **Kolkata** to NJP by train, then bus or narrow-gauge **'Toy Train'** from **NJP** station (see page 606), also stops at **Siliguri Junc**. Steam 'Tourist' trains operate in the summer between Darjeeling and Ghoom but the daily service is diesel (Rs 20, dep 0830, 8 hrs). Services are often disrupted by landslides during the rains, though the upper section from Kurseong (accessible by bus/jeep) continues to run; check beforehand. Take special care of luggage; thefts reported. From NJP to **Kolkata (S)**: *Darjeeling Mail, 3144* (AC/CC&AC/II), 1920, 14 hrs. **Kolkata (H)**: *Kamrup Exp, 5960* (AC/II), 1645, 13½ hrs; *Kanchenjunga Exp, 5658* (AC/II), 0800, 12 hrs. **New Delhi**: *NE Exp, 5621*, 1725, 27 hrs; *Rajdhani Exp* (Mon, Wed, Thu, Fri), 2423, 1240, 21 hrs. From **Kolkata (S)**: *Darjeeling Mail, 3143*, 1900, 13 hrs, connects with the Toy Train from NJP.

Jaldapara Wildlife Sanctuary *p611*
Air

Indian Airlines has daily flights from Kolkata to Bagdogra (½ hr) and also from Guwahati and Delhi. From airport, bus to Siliguri; then 4 hrs' scenic drive through tea gardens to Jaldapara (155 km). There is an airfield at Hasimara.

Bus

Express buses from Kolkata to Madarihat or Siliguri to Park (128 km). Forest Department transport to Hollong inside the sanctuary.

Train

Hasimara Station (4 km from park) has trains from Siliguri Junction.

❶ Directory

Darjeeling *p602, map p603*
Banks (Limited hrs) Grindlays for Visa/Mastercard (£/$, 1130-1330), Rs 250 commission (less for next day collection). **Hospitals** *Planters' Hospital*, Nehru Rd, T54327. *Sadar Hospital*, T54218. *Mariam Nursing Home*, below Gymkhana Club, T54328, has been recommended for its medical facilities. Tibetan *Men Tse Khang*, 26 HD Lama Rd (Mon-Fri 0900-1200, 1400-1600). Other medical services Chemists: Frank Ross, Nehru Rd, Puri, Nehru Rd, above Keventer's. **Post office** GPO, Laden La Rd. Telegraph office: Gandhi Rd. **Tourist offices** W Bengal, 'Belle Vue', 1st floor, 1 Nehru Rd, T54050. 0930-1730, off-season 1030-1630, not much info available. Also at railway station, and at New Car Park, Laden La Rd. Darjeeling, Gorkha Hill Council (DGHC), Silver Fir (below *Windamere*), The Mall, T/F54214. Sikkim, T25277, issues permits free of charge. **Useful addresses** Foreigners' Registration Office: Laden La Rd, T54260; for Sikkim permits: go to District Magistrate, Lebong Cart Rd (north of centre), then get form stamped at FRO, and return to DM; 2 hrs.

Kalimpong *p609, map p610*
Banks Banks don't change money; Emporium, Mani Link Rd, accepts Visa and Mastercard. Most arrange car/jeep hire. **Useful addresses** There is a **hospital** and a **post office** near the police station.

Siliguri *p611*
Banks State Bank of India, Hill Cart Rd. Amex TCs. **Hospital** T430150; North Bengal Clinic, T420441. Recommended. Other medical services: Chemists on College Rd. **Internet** Moulik, behind *Vinayak*, Hill Cart Rd, T432312. **Tourist offices** Bhutan, near railway station. Sikkim, Hill Cart Rd; W Bengal, 1st floor, M4 Hill Cart Rd, T511974; also at *Mainak*, NJP Station and airport. **Travel agent** Help Tourism (Assoc of Conservation & Tourism), 143 Hill Cart Rd (1st floor), T535893, F433683, helptour@shivanet.com. Recommended for eastern Himalaya.

South of Kolkata

To the south of Kolkata lie the tidal estuary of the Hugli and the mangrove forests of the Sundarbans. Famous for their population of Bengal tigers, the Sundarbans stretch across into Bangladesh, but it is possible to take a day trip right down to the mouth of the Hugli or boat trips into the Sundarbans themselves. ▸▸ *For Sleeping, Eating and other listings, see page 620.*

Sagardwip

ⓘ *Bus/taxi to Harwood Point, Kakdwip, ferry across to Kochuberia Ghat (Sagardwip), then 30 mins bus across island to where the Ganga meets the sea.*

The *Ganga Sagar Mela* is held in mid-January, attracting over half a million pilgrims each year who come to bathe and then visit the **Kapil Muni Temple**. The island has been devastated many times by cyclones.

Sunderbans Tiger Reserve → *Colour map 6, grid A6.*

Sunderbans (pronounced Soonder-buns) or 'beautiful forests', is named after the 'Sunderi' trees. The mangrove swamps are said to be the largest estuarine forests in the world. Improved management is battling to halt the loss of mangrove cover as it is exploited for fuel. Most villagers depend on fishing and forestry, while local honey gatherers who are active in April and May, are said to wear masks on the backs of their heads to frighten away tigers, which they believe only attack from the rear! You will notice large areas of *bheries* for aquaculture. Prawn fisheries are the most lucrative and co-operative efforts are being encouraged by the government.

Wildlife

The biosphere reserve, a World Heritage Site, still preserves the natural habitat of about 300 **Bengal tigers** (*Panthera tigris*). They are bigger and richer in colour than elsewhere in South Asia and are thought to survive on salt water; rainwater is the only source of fresh water in the park. Tigers here have become strong swimmers, and are known to attack fishermen. Methods of improved management include providing permanent sources of fresh water for tigers by digging deep, monsoon-fed ponds, and solar-powered lighting to scare them away from villages, and electrifying dummy woodcutters! Spotted deer, wild boar, monkeys, snakes, fishing cats, water monitors, Olive Ridley sea turtles and a few large estuarine crocodiles are the other wildlife here, particularly on Lothian Island and Chamta block. You may see deer, boar, macaque and some birds but are very unlikely to see a tiger. However, it is wonderfully peaceful.

The **best season** is from November to March. Heavy rains and occasional severe cyclones in April to May and November to December can make a visit impossible, so best in December-February. Carry bottled water, torch, mosquito repellent and be prepared for cool nights in winter. You must always be accompanied by armed Forest Rangers. Motor launches can be hired from Canning, Basanti, Namkhana and Raidighi but it is better to go down the narrow creeks in country boats. Occasionally you can go ashore on bamboo-and-palm jetties to walk in the fenced-in areas of the forest which have watch towers (open, dawn to dusk only). Contact: Field Director, Sunderbans Tiger Reserve, Canning, 24 Parganas, T03218-55280.

You need a **permit** (valid four to five days) from Secretary, Department of Forests, Writers Building, T2215999, or contact WB Tourist Office, BBD Bagh, Kolkata where you can book a package tour; take your passport.

WBTDC Tours: Two-day, one night (not during monsoons, ie July-September) by coach and launch (crowds of other visitors may scare wildlife away, though), staying at *Sajnekhali Lodge*. Three-day cruise by launch – accommodation varies; 'Luxury' launch has decent facilities (fridge and TV), Rs 1,800 (four person cubicle with comfortable beds), Rs 2,900, meals included. Acceptable food, helpful staff. **Pugmarks** ① *10 Meher Ali Rd, Kolkata, T2873307, www.pugmarks@vsnl.in*, specialize in adventure tours in the area and have their own launch.

Sajnekhali has a **sanctuary** for water birds which you get to from Canning or Basanti. There is a small Forest Department Visitor Centre with a turtle hatchery, a crocodile tank and a mangrove nursery.

★ Digha → 185 km from Kolkata.

Digha was described by Warren Hastings visiting over 200 years ago as the 'Brighton of the East', though there is not a pebble for at least 2,000 km! The casuarina-lined, firm wide beach, is very popular with Bengalis. The small Chandaneswar Temple (10 km away in Orissa) is an important Siva temple which can be reached by bus.

Listings: South of Kolkata

⊜ Sleeping

Sagardwip *p619*
WBTDC organizes 2-day boat trips with accommodation on board or you can stay at **F Youth Hostel**. *Dharamshala*, free for 3 days.

Sunderbans Tiger Reserve *p619*
D Tourist Lodge, Sajnekhali, T03219-52560, raised on pillars and fenced from wildlife, solar power, 30 small, basic rooms with mosquito nets (ask for linen), 14 with Western toilets, hot water in buckets, 20-bed dorm (Rs 200), simple meals (poor choice but if you buy local fish, restaurant will cook it), no alcohol. Reserve in advance and carry your **permit**.

Digha *p620*
C Sea Coast, T03220-66305. Some a/c rooms.
C-E Tourist Lodge, T03220-66255. Rooms on 3 floors, 4 a/c, 5-bed dorm (Rs 80), meals, bar.
D Sea Hawk. Comfortable rooms, some a/c, cottages and cheaper dorm, T03220-66235.

⊜ Transport

Sunderbans Tiger Reserve *p619*
Road
By car from Kolkata or **Bus**: from Babu Ghat, Strand Rd, to **Basanti** via Sonakhali (first depart 0600, Rs 20, 3 hrs; last return to Kolkata,

1600), then hire a **boat** to the *Lodge* (Rs 250-300, 3 hrs). Alternatively, from Basanti, take public ferry to **Gosaba**, then travel across the island by 'van (flat-bed) rickshaw' (5 km) which enables you to see interesting village life, and finally take a boat to Sajnekhali (3 hrs from Basanti); recommended for at least one way. Ask *Lodge* staff to arrange boat hire with park guide. Since these are tidal waterways, boats are not always able to moor near the ghats. Enquire about timing.

Train
Kolkata (Sealdah) to **Canning** (105 km) and then **boat** to Docghat where you can get autos (shared) or a bus to Basanti where you get another boat. From Canning you can get a private boat direct to Sajnekhali *Lodge* (Rs 450-500 per day).

Digha *p620*
Bus
Express buses and WBTDC luxury buses from Kolkata take 6 hrs, the route having been shortened by the Norghat Bridge. Kolkata-Digha depart 0700 from Esplanade, Rs 35.

Train
The nearest railway halts are at Kharagpur (116 km) and Contai Rd (151 km) stations on the Southeast Rly.

⬤ *For an explanation of the sleeping and eating price codes used in this guide, see inside the front cover. Other relevant information is found in Essentials pages 52-57.*

❖ Footprint features

Introduction

Kangchendzonga, the third highest mountain in the world, dominates the skyline of Sikkim. Renowned for its rich flora and fauna as for its ethnically varied population, Sikkim's original inhabitants, the Lepchas, call the region Nye-mae-el ('Paradise'). To the later Bhutias it is Beymul Denjong ('The Hidden Valley of Rice'). The name Sikkim itself is commonly attributed to the Tsong word Su-khim, meaning New or Happy House.

With 660 species of **orchids**, some found at altitudes as high as 3,000 m, Sikkim is an orchid-lovers' paradise. Tourism is still in its infancy, with the monasteries of **Rumtek** and **Pemayangtse** just two of the fascinating centres of Buddhism in the state, which is attracting growing numbers of visitors. Sikkim is beginning to attract ramblers and trekkers too.

★ Don't miss...

1. Get up early and go to the **Tashi Viewpoint** just outside Gangtok to watch the sun rise over the Kangchendzonga range, page 628.
2. If orchids are your thing, then head for **Saramsa Gardens** where there are over 500 species, page 629.
3. **Rumtek Monastery**, a faithful reproduction of Chhofuk in Tibet is very impressive, page 629.
4. Stay overnight at the awe-inspiring **Pemayangtse Monastery** and take an early morning walk to see a breathtaking sunrise in perfect peace, page 633.
5. Trek to **Khechopari Lake** and watch leaflamps float on the clear water during evening prayers, page 634.

Sikkim

Background → *Population: 540,500. Area: 7,298 sq km.*

The land

Sikkim nestles between the peaks of the eastern Himalaya, stretching only 112 km from south to north and 64 km from east to west. Flat land is a rarity and the state encompasses the upper valley of the Tista River, a tributary of the Brahmaputra, while the watershed forms the borders with Tibet and Nepal. In the east the Chumbi valley lies between Sikkim and Bhutan, a tongue of Tibetan land that gives Sikkim its strategic and political sensitivity.

The Sikkimese believe Kangchendzonga (8,586 m, *Kanchenjunga*), the 'Five Treasures of the Great Snows', to be the repository of minerals, grains, salt, weapons and holy scriptures. On its west is the massive 31-km long Zemu glacier. Various explorers and mountaineers have claimed to have seen **yeti** or their prints in the vicinity of the mountain and its glacier, and in common with other regions of the Himalaya and Karakoram the 'abominable snowman' has its place in folklore.

Climate In the lower valleys Sikkim's climate is sub-tropical. Above 1,000 m, it is temperate, while the tops of the higher mountains are permanently under snow. Sikkim is one of the wettest regions of the Himalaya, most rain falling between mid-May and September.

History

From the 13th century Tibetans immigrated into Sikkim, including the Namgyal clan. In 1642 Phuntsog Namgyal (1604-70) became the **Chogyal** (king). Presided over a social system based on Tibetan Lamaistic Buddhism, and divided the land into 12 *Dzongs* (fortified districts).

In the 18th century Sikkim lost land to Nepal, Bhutan and the British. When the Gurkhas of Nepal launched a campaign into Tibet and were defeated by the Chinese in 1791-92, Sikkim won back its northern territories. The narrow Chumbi valley that separates Sikkim from Bhutan remained with Tibet.

When the British defeated Nepal in 1815, the southern part of the country was given back to Sikkim. However, in the next conflict with Nepal, Darjeeling was handed over to the British in return for their assistance. In 1848 the Terai region at the foot of the mountains was annexed by the British.

Nepalis migrated into Sikkim from the beginning of the 19th century, eventually becoming more numerous than the local inhabitants. This led to internal conflict also involving the British and the Tibetans. The British won the ensuing battles and declared Sikkim a Protectorate in 1890. The state was controlled by a British Political Officer who effectively stripped the *Gyalpos*, of executive power. It was many years before the Sikkimese regained control.

Culture

The Naong, Chang and Mon are believed to have inhabited Sikkim in prehistoric times. Each ethnic group has an impressive repertoire of folk songs and dances. The **Lepchas**, who call themselves Rongpas and claim to be the original inhabitants of Sikkim, may have come from Tibet well before the eighth century and brought Lamaistic Buddhism, which is still practised. They are now regarded as the indigenous peoples. They are deeply religious, peace loving and shy but cheerful. The government has reserved the **Dzongu** area in North and Central Sikkim for Lepchas, now making up less than 10% of the population. For a long time, the Lepchas' main contact with the outside world was the market-place at Mangan, where they bartered oranges and cardamom. Their alphabet was only devised in the 18th century by the king. The **Magar**, a minority group, are

● Permits

Free Inter Line Permits (ILPs) are issued to foreigners to enter Sikkim for up to 15 days (renewable twice). These allow visits to Gangtok, Rumtek, Phodong, Mangan, Gezing, Pemayangtse, Namchi, Pakyong, Rabangla and Soreng. Contact an Indian mission abroad when applying for an Indian visa (enclosing two extra photos), or at any FRO (Foreigners' Registration Office) or the Sikkim Tourism Office in New Delhi, Kolkata or Siliguri. Rangpo can issue a 15-day permit extendable in Gangtok or any District headquarter or by the Superintendent of Police, namchi

and Mangan. Certain areas in north and west Sikkim (Chumthang, Yumthang, Lachen, Chhangu, Dzongri) have been opened to groups of two to 20 trekkers and for mountain biking and water sports. Protected Areas Permits (PAP) can be arranged by some local travel agents; apply with a photocopies of passport (Indian visa, personal details), ILP and two photos.

To get your permit extended at the Foreigners' Registration Office at Gangtok, first visit the Magistrate's Office at the Secretariat on the ridge overlooking town to get a "No Objection" endorsement.

renowned as warriors and were involved in the coronation of Phuntsog Namgyal, the first Chogyal of Sikkim in 1642.

The **Bhotias** (meaning 'of Bhot/Tibet') or Bhutias entered Sikkim in the 13th century from Kham in Tibet. Many adapted to sedentary farming from pastoral nomadism and displaced the Lepchas. Some, however, retained their older lifestyle, and combined animal husbandry with trading over the Trans-Himalayan passes: Nathula (4,392 m), Jelepla (4,388 m), Donkiala (5,520 m) and Kongrala (4,809 m). Over the years the Bhotia have come into increased contact with the Lepcha and intermarried with them. Nearly every Bhotia family has one member who becomes a monk. Monasteries remain the repositories of Bhotia culture and festivals there are the principle social events. However, those who have visited Ladakh or Zanskar may find them architecturally and artistically a little disappointing. The Bhotias are famous for their weaving and are also skilled wood carvers.

The **Newars** entered Sikkim in large numbers from Nepal in the 19th century. Skilled in metal and woodwork, they were granted the right by the Chogyal to mine copper and mint the Sikkimese coinage. Other Nepali groups followed. With high altitude farming skills, they settled new lands and built houses directly on the ground unlike the Lepcha custom of building on stilts. The Newars were followed by the Chettris and other Nepali clans who introduced Hinduism, which became more popular as their numbers swelled.

Religion In Sikkim, as in Nepal, Hinduism and Buddhism have interacted and amalgamated so Himalayan Hinduism includes a pantheon of Buddhist *bodhisattvas* as well as Hindu deities. The animist tradition also retains a belief in evil spirits.

Buddhist **prayer flags** flutter in the breeze everywhere. The different types (wind, luck, victory etc) are printed with texts and symbols on coloured pieces of cloth and are tied to bamboo poles or trees. **Prayer wheels** carrying inscriptions (which should be turned clockwise) vary in size from small hand-held ones to vast drums which are installed by a monastery or stupa. Whitewashed masonry **chortens** (stupas) but usually commemorate the Buddha or Bodhisattva; the structure symbolizing the elements (earth, water, fire, air, ether). The eight **lucky signs** appear as parasol, pot or vase, conch shell, banner, two fishes, lotus, knot of eternity and the wheel of law

(Dharma Chakra). Bowls of water (Thing Duen Tsar) are offered in prayer from left to right during Buddhist worship. The gift of water from one who is free from greed and meanness is offered to quench thirsty spirits and to wash the feet, and represents flower (or welcome), incense, lamp, perfume and food.

Festivals Since the 22 major festivals are dictated by the agricultural cycle and the Hindu-Buddhist calendar, it is best to check dates with the Tourist Office.

February *Losar* Tibetan New Year – preceded by Lama dances in Rumtek. *Bumche* at Tashiding.

June *Saga Dawn* A Buddhist festival with huge religious processions round Gangtok. *Rumtek Chaams* Dance festival in commemoration of the eight manifestations of Guru Padmasambhava, who established Buddhism in Tibet.

August/September *Pang Lhabsol* commemorates the consecration of Kangchendzonga as Sikkim's guardian deity; the Lepchas believe that the mountain is their birthplace. The masked warrior dance is especially spectacular – Kangchendzonga appears in a red mask, her commander in a black one, while warriors wear traditional armour of helmets, swords and shields. Special celebrations are held in Pemayangtse.

September/October *Dasain*, one of the most important Nepali festivals, coincides with *Dasara* in North India, see page 59. On the first day barley seeds are planted in prayer rooms, invocations are made to Durga, and on the eighth day buffalo and goats are ritually sacrificed. *Diwali* (the Festival of Lights) follows *Dasain*.

December *Kagyat Dances* performed by monks (especially at Enchey), accompanied by religious music and chanting, enact themes from Buddhist mythology and end with the burning of effigies made of flour, wood and paper. This symbolizes the exorcism of evil spirits and the ushering in of prosperity for the coming year. *Losoog* (*Namsoong* for Lepchas at Gangtok) is the Sikkimese New Year, also called *Sonam Losar*. Farmers celebrate their harvest and beginning of their new cropping calendar.

Modern Sikkim → *www.sikkiminfo.net.*

Government In 1950, Sikkim became a Protectorate of India. In 1973 demands for accession to India by the local population consisting mainly of Nepalis grew, and Sikkim was formally made an associate state. The Gyalpos lost their power as a result of the new democratic constitution and Sikkim became the 22nd state in the Union in 1975. Although there is no separatist movement, India's takeover and the abolition of the monarchy, supported by many of those of Nepali origin, is still resented by many Sikkimese who don't really regard themselves as 'Indians'. The state enjoys special tax and other privileges, partly because of its highly sensitive geopolitical location on the disputed border with China.

★ Gangtok

→ *Phone code: 03592. Colour map 4, grid A2. Population: 29,200 Altitude: 1,547 m.*

Gangtok or 'High Hill', the capital, sits on a ridge overlooking the Ranipul River. The setting is spectacular with fine views of the Kangchendzonga range but the town appears to have lost some of its quaint charm with the mushrooming of concrete buildings along the national highway and the main road. The crowded New Market (Naya Bazar) on Mahatma Gandhi Marg and the colourful Lall Bazar are where all the town's commercial activity is concentrated. Away from the bustle, there are many serene areas and quiet back alleys which remain virtually untouched. ▶▶ *For Sleeping, Eating and other listings, see pages 629-632.*

Ins and outs

Getting there There are tentative plans to have an airport near Gangtok in 2 yrs. Most visitors arrive by the very attractive road from North Bengal (NH31A) which is motorable throughout the year except in very wet weather (mid-Jun to Sep), when there may be landslips. The old Teesta suspension bridge was taken down (pillars and wires can still be seen) and a new bridge was built further down in 1996. Permits and passports are checked at Rangpo where 15-day permits (extendable in Gangtok or district headquarters for up to 45 days) are available. SNT buses terminate at the Paljor Stadium Road stand while private buses stop short of the main bazar. Ask to be dropped near the Tourist Office which has some hotels and restaurants within easy reach. If you hire a jeep to Gangtok ask to be taken to your hotel since the taxi/jeep stand is 2 km short of the centre.

Getting around The busy hub around MG Marg is about a 20-min walk from end to end. Away from the bazars, the town is very pleasant for walking around (get map *Gangtok, an Artist's Impression*, Rs 50). For venturing further you will need to hire a jeep or taxi. See Transport, page 632, for further details.

Climate Temperature: summer, max 22°C, min 16°C; winter, max 14°C, min 4°C. Rainfall: heavy May-Sep (ave 575 mm). Best time to visit: Mar-Apr and Oct-Nov. Clothing: summer, light woollens and cotton; winter, heavy woollens.

Related map
A Gangtok centre, page 628

Gangtok

To Tashi View Point (9 km), Lachen & Phodong

♨ Saibaba Mandir

TV Tower ☐

Government Institute of Cottage Industries

☐ Himalayan Nursery

Zero ☐ Point

☐ Council House

Enchey Monastery ☐

Helipad ☐

Yak & Yeti ☐

Tashi Namgyal Academy ☐

4

S Nikhim Highway

Hanuman ♨ Mandir

To Natu La

SNT & Booking Office ☐

Paljor Stadium Rd

✚ Catholic Centre ■

Paljor Stadium

2

1

A

✝ CNI Church

♫

White Hall

Bhanu Path

The Ridge

Private Bus Stand ☐
Taxis ii ☐

Ⓢ

Tibet Rd

Taxis iii ☐

Palace of the Chogyal

3

Foreigners' Reg Office ☐

Tsuklakhang (Royal Chapel)

Supermarket ☐

1

MG Marg

Kazi Rd

Taxis i ☐
Lall Bazar

☐ Secretariat

NH31A

5

Naya Bazar

Deer Park

Government Press

Research Institute of Tibetology ☐

Deorali Orchid Sanctuary ☐

△ Do-drul Chorten

N

To Orchidarium, Rongpu, Rumtek & Darjeeling

Mile to June

■ Sleeping
1 Denzong Inn
2 Norkhill

3 Orchid
4 Siniolchu Lodge
5 Tashi Delek

You can stay a few days in **Gangtok**, making day trips to **Rumtek** and **Phodong** then move to **Gezing** or **Pelling**. From there you can walk up to **Pemayangtse** and perhaps visit **Khechopari Lake** before continuing to **Kalimpong** or **Darjeeling** in West Bengal. Numerous hairpin bends make road journeys extremely slow so expect to cover 30 to 40 km per hour. Conditions deteriorate considerably during the monsoon and can sometimes make travel impossible.

Sights

At the north end of the town the **Government Institute of Cottage Industries** ① *closed Sun and 2nd Sat of month, daily, 0900-1230, 1330-1530*, produces a wide range of local handicrafts, eg woollen carpets, jackets, dolls, handmade paper, carved and painted wooden tables. Good quality and prices but no parcel service.

Enchey Monastery is 3 km northeast of the main bazar, a pleasant walk. Built by the eighth Chogyal in the 1840s the present building dates from 1909. Religious dances are held in August and December; see Festivals above.

The **Palace of the Chogyal** is only open once a year in the last week of December for the *Pang Lhabsol* festival. Below this is the **Tsuklakhang** or Royal Chapel, standing on a high ridge where coronations and royal marriages took place. This is the major place of worship and has a large and impressive collection of scriptures. The interior is lavishly decorated with woodcarving and murals and houses a number of Buddha images. Visitors are welcome during Tibetan New Year but may not be permitted at other times; photography prohibited.

⚡ *MG Marg is Mahatma Gandhi Marg.*
PS Rd is Paljor Stadium Rd.

Moving south along the road you pass the **Secretariat** complex on your left. Beyond this is the **Deer Park**, loosely modelled on the famous one at Sarnath, see page 190, with a statue of the Buddha.

To the south, the important **Do-drul Chorten** with a golden top, contains relics and a complete set of holy texts. The surrounding 108 prayer wheels should be turned clockwise only. Nearby is a monastery for young lamas with large statues of the Buddha and Guru Padmasambhava.

The unique **Research Institute of Tibetology** ① *daily except Sun, 1000-1600*, on a hilltop was established in 1958 to promote research on Tibet and Mahayana Buddhism. The library maintains a large and important Buddhist collection with many fine *thangkas*, icons and art treasures on display.

For orchid lovers the small Flower show near Whitehall has a good display, Rs 5, from mid-March. The **Deorali Orchid Sanctuary**, south of town, has 200 species.

There are pleasant **walks** around Gangtok. **Tashi Viewpoint** via Enchey Monastery is 9 km. Go early to watch the sun rise over the Kangchendzonga range. **Hanuman Tok**, a hill with a small temple (8 km), is another viewpoint.

Gangtok centre

Potala Tours
Footbridge
Yak & Yeti Travels
Sikkim Tours & Travels
CNI
Footbridge
Private Bus Stand
Taxis ii
State Bank of India
Tashila Tours
Taxis iii
Thakurbari Temple & Dharamsala
Children's Park
Bank of Sikkim

Not to scale

■ **Sleeping**
1 Chumbi Residency
2 Green
3 Jopuno & Mist Tree Mountain
4 Lhakpa
5 Mayur
6 Modern Central
7 Netuk House
8 Sonam Delek
9 Sunny Guest House
10 Tibet

● **Eating**
1 Blue Sheep
2 House of Bamboo

★ Rumtek Monastery

➜ *Phone code: 03592. Colour map 4, grid A2. Altitude: 1,550 m. 24 km southwest of Gangtok.*

Standing in one of the attractive lower valleys southwest of Gangtok with fluttering prayer flags, the monastery is the headquarters of the Kagyu ('Black Hat') order of Tibetan Lamaistic Buddhism. The monks fled Tibet after the Chinese invasion, bringing with them whatever statues, *thangkas* and scriptures they could carry. At the invitation of the Chogyal they settled in Rumtek. The new monastery was built in the 1960s in the traditional style as a faithful copy of the Kagyu headquarters in Chhofuk, Tibet, with typical monastic paintings and intricate woodwork. The **Dharma Chakra Centre** with the unique **golden reliquary** of the 16th Gyalwa Karmapa, who died in 1981, is here.

Visitors are dropped at the gate at the bottom of a gentle uphill path; passports may be checked. A 20-minute walk past local houses and a couple of typical curio shops leads to the monastery. Outside, you may see pairs of monks chanting prayers in their quarters or catch some younger ones playing football in the field! The main hall is very impressive but lacks the atmosphere of Pemayangtse. Visitors are welcome are requested not to disturb the monks during prayers (usually 0400, 1800). In the adjacent building you can watch the wood-block printing of texts on handmade paper. The peace is broken when hordes of tourists arrive.

Saramsa Gardens and Rangpo

The gardens, 14 km south of Gangtok, contain over 500 indigenous species in what is more like a botanical garden with large orchidariums. Best season is March-early May, you may be disappointed at other times. The road to Saramsa forks east off the NH31a a few kilometres south of **Tadong** which has a couple of places with rooms and refreshments including the fairly modern *Tashi Tadong* and the *Daragaon*.

Further south, near the West Bengal border, Rangpo has a small bazar. Entry Permits are issued and checked here.

Listings: Gangtok

🌙 Sleeping

Gangtok *p627, maps p627 and p628*
Heating is essential in winter. Dogs bark at night, so take ear plugs. Expect discounts in Jul and Aug, Dec and Jan.
A Norkhill, above Paljor Stadium, T23186, F23187. 30 clean rooms in old palace, meals included, spacious public rooms, good views and gardens, exchange, curio shop, once excellent but standards slipping.
A-B Netuk House (Heritage Hotel), Tibet Rd (follow road up hill and ask), T22374, F24802, netuk@sikkim.org 8 comfortable, clean rooms with modern shower in an extension to a traditional family home, excellent Sikkimese meals, bar, quiet location, mountain views, friendly, excellent service. (Reservations: also Darjeeling T0354-54041, F54043); also excellent hotel in Pelling.

B Tashi Delek, MG Marg, T22991, F22362, tashi.delek@sikkim.org 60 ordinary rooms and **A** suites (better on upper floors), excellent restaurant, bar, exchange, airlines counter, terrace garden with enthralling views, friendly service, owner has great stories to tell of Sikkim's past. Pricey but recommended.
B-C Chumbi Residency, Tibet Rd, T26618, F22707, chumbires@sikkim.org Tall modern hotel, 25 good rooms on 2nd-4th floors (no lift), **B** suites, clean and quiet, coffee shop (Indian, Chinese), dynamic manager.
B-C Golden Nest, Nam Gang, below Assembly Building, T27008, nest_golden@hotmail.com. Clean, well furnished, 'superior' rooms very comfortable, restaurant (limited menu, beer), good service, mainly groups (big off-season discounts).
B-C Tibet (Dalai Lama Trust), PS Rd, T22523, F26223, htltibet@sancharnet.in. 30 rooms.

● For an explanation of the sleeping and eating price codes used in this guide, see inside the front cover. Other relevant information is found in Essentials pages 52-57.

Sikkim Listings: Gangtok

Good views from rooms at rear, restaurant (see below), bar, exchange, Tibetan books and crafts for sale, very pleasant, peaceful and charming (but some critical reports).
C-D Denzong Inn, near Lall Bazar, T22692, F22362. 24 rooms, good suites, restaurant.
C-D Sonam Delek, Tibet Rd, T22566, F23197, www.hotelsonamdelek.com. 15 rooms with bath best for views, pleasant restaurant (great local food), terrace garden, good service.
D Jopuno PS Rd, T23502, F22707 (at Institute of Hotel Management). 12 rooms (4 **C** deluxe), good restaurant and service, eager young staff.
D Mayur (Sikkim Tourism), PS Rd, T22825. 27 rooms with bath (rooms vary), restaurant, bar.
D Mist Tree Mountain, PS Rd, Pradhan Towers, T23827, F26339. Newish, good value rooms (Rs 400-500) 7-bed dorm (Rs 100), restaurant.
D Orchid, NH31A, T23151. 21 rooms, some with bath, front rooms better, restaurant (good Chinese) and bar, clean, good value.
Some budget hotels charge extra for heaters.
D-E Green, MG Marg, T/F23354, greenhotel@gokulnet.com. 45 rooms, some with bath but no views (Rs 250-475), good restaurant (Indian/Chinese).
D-E Siniolchu Lodge (Sikkim Tourism), above town, near Enchey Monastery, T22074. 24 rooms on 3 floors up a hillside, some with bath and heating, good views, restaurant, bar, tours.
E Lhakpa, Tibet Rd, T23002. 3 clean rooms in traditional house, some with bath, cheaper dorm, restaurant/ bar (very good Chinese, try noodle soups), roof terrace, views, good value.
E Modern Central Lodge, Tibet Rd, T23417. Clean rooms with toilets, some with bath, hot showers, best in front on upper floors, a bit noisy, basic but good restaurant, friendly bar, good value jeep tours (eg Chhangu US$12 with permit, Yuksom US$50 per day), very friendly and helpful, backpackers' choice.
E Sunny Guest House, next to Private Bus Stand, T22179. Some rooms with bath in pleasant hotel, super K'dzonga views from top floor.
F Primula Lodge, Church Rd, T23599. Clean, basic with shared bath.

Rumtek Monastery p629
B Shamhbala Mountain Resort, T52240, F530020, parekh.house@gems.net.in. In a large estate, 500 m before the monastery.

31 cottages in traditional tribal styles spread around grounds, or comfortable rooms in main building, most with good views from balconies, vegetarian restaurant (wide choice), bar, exchange, pick-up from Siliguri arranged.
C Martam Village Resort, Gangkha, Upper Martam, 5 km from the monastery.
11 thatched cottages built in traditional style with large picture windows overlooking the valley, good meals, pleasant, contact Gangtok T23314, F24391. Recommended.
D-E Jharna, T22714. Some rooms with hot water, restaurant, bar.
F Sangay, near monastery gate. Basic rooms in old guesthouse, fairly clean shared toilet, friendly.

Rangpo p629
D Tourist Lodge, 7 rooms, a simple restaurant and basic toilets. You can also stop here for a snack and drink.

❼ Eating

Gangtok p627, maps p627 and p628
Lightly spiced Sikkimese meat and vegetable dishes are usually eaten with noodles or rice. 'Churpi' is a local yak milk curd cheese. For 'Chimney Soup' order a day ahead.

In hotels
₩₩₩ **Blue Poppy**, *Tashi Delek*. International. Good meals from Rs 300 (Sikkimese recommended, order in advance).
₩₩₩ **Netuk House**, T22374. Excellent Sikkimese (order ahead). Unusual, delicately flavoured authentic home cooking, charming service, try the *chhang*.
₩₩₩ **Snow Lion**, *Hotel Tibet*, T22523. Very good Sikkimese and Tibetan but some poor reports on service, "flat beer, noisy and crowded".
₩₩ **Mayur** hotel. Good Tandoori.

Outside hotels
₩₩ **Tibet**, below High Court, MG Rd (also Kazi Rd). Westernized café menu, very clean.
₩ **Blue Sheep**, Tourist Office Building. Indian, Continental, Sikkimese at lunchtime, fast food on ground floor. Traditional, very clean, bar.
₩ **China Pilot**, Star Cinema Building, MG Rd. Very good-value Chinese.
₩ **House of Bamboo**, MG Rd. Indian veg.

¶Porkey's, Supermarket, MG Rd. Fast food, sausages etc, young crowd.

◐ Bars and clubs

Gangtok *p627, maps p627 and p628*
Bars
Bars in most restaurants serve local spirits distilled at Rangpo – brandy, rum, whiskey and liqueurs. *Chhang* is the unofficial national drink. A bamboo mug (*thungba*) is filled with fermented millet through which boiled water is allowed to percolate; the drink is sipped through a bamboo straw. You can enjoy this mildly intoxicating pleasant drink for over an hour simply by adding hot water.

◈ Festivals and events

Rumtek Monastery *p629*
Feb Special colourful **Losar** dances are held 2 days before the Tibetan New Year (check date). Arrive 3 days earlier to see rehearsals without masks, *pujas* and ceremonies are held during this period. **Jun** The important Rumtek *chaam* is performed on the 10th day of the 5th month of the Tibetan calendar; masked dancers present eight manifestations of the Guru Rimpoche. Tours in Jul-Aug from Gangtok.

◯ Shopping

Gangtok *p627, maps p627 and p628*
Books
Good Books, MG Marg, below Gandhi statue, small but interesting.

Handicrafts
Traditional crafts include carpets, *thangkas*, traditional jewellery, shirts, boots and fur caps and wood carving.
Handcrafts Centre, Zero Point, Mon-Sat 0930-1230, 1300-1530 where you can watch artisans. **Charitrust Handicrafts**, *Tibet Hotel* modest collection, good quality and prices; also books on Tibet.
Rural Development Agency, MG Marg and Naya Bazar.
The **markets** are interesting; **Lall Bazar** (*Haat* on Sun, closed Thu) sells some unusual local fruit and vegetables and yak's milk cheese fresh and dried (skewered on string).

▲ Activities and tours

Gangtok *p627, maps p627 and p628*
For trekking contact tourist offices or tour companies.

Mountaineering
Himalayan Mountaineering Institute based in Yuksom offers climbing courses in stunning surroundings.

River rafting
On rivers Tista (from Dikchu or Singtam, 1 hr drive from Gangtok) and Rangit (from **Melli Bazar**, 4 km from Teesta Bridge, which has a *Wayside Inn* for refreshments, or **Rishi**) arranged by Tourism Department and private travel agents, eg *Tashila*, 1 day US$45, 2-day US$70, some Grade 2-3 rapids. A 2-hr ride en route to Pemayangtse is ideal for the beginner; wonderful scenery.

Tour operators
Members of *TAAS* Travel agents Association of Sikkim, can organise permits for trekkers. Contact them in advance by email or fax. **Namgyal Treks and Tours**, 75 Tibet Rd, T23701, www.namgyaltreks.com. Experienced, well organized, expedition experience, "amazing trekking food; all rubbish carried out". **Sikkim Tours**, PO Box 155, GPO, Church Rd, T22188, F27191, sikkimtours@sikkim.org For treks and birdwatching. **Singalila**, NH31A opposite petrol pump, T21556, F20878. Arranges coach tours and river rafting. **Yak & Yeti**, *Hotel Superview Himalchuli*, NH31A, Zero Point, T21670, F20878, www.yakandyeti travels.com. Adventure tours and trekking (US$35-40 per day), efficient, "added luxury of eating tent". **Yuksom Tours and Treks**, Borong House, above Telephone Exchange, T23473, F22707, www.yuksom.com. Professional, well-equipped treks, good food, all inclusive US$55 per day.
Tours
Gangtok From Tourist Information Centre. **Morning tour** – Government Institute of Cottage Industries, Deer Park, Chorten, Research Institute of Tibetology, Orchid Sanctuary and Enchey Monastery. In season daily 0930-1230. Rs 45. **Afternoon tour** – Orchidarium and Rumtek Monastery, 1400/1430-1700. Rs 55. **Outside**

Gangtok Phodong tour – Rs 70 (more expensive by car). **West Sikkim** (minimum 16) Fri at 1030 returning Sun 1600 (2 nights), Rs 600. **Treks in West Sikkim**. Private tour companies offer similar tours and treks.

⊜ Transport

Gangtok *p627, maps p627 and p628*
Air
Nearest airport is **Bagdogra** (124 km); see page 616, under Siliguri. **Indian Airlines**, Tibet Rd, T23099. 1000-1300, 1400-1600; **Jet Airways**, MG Marg, T435876 (airport T551588). To Gangtok: shared taxi, 4-5 hrs, Rs 250 each, or *Snow-Lion* mini-bus; or get an SNT bus to Siliguri where bus/taxi to Gangtok is available. A daily government 4-seater **helicopter** runs between Bagdogra and Gangtok; unreliable since heavy cloud or rain prevents flights – but is an excellent option (Rs 1,500 each way, 45 mins, 10 kg luggage) with mesmerizing views. Tickets from Bagdogra airport counter or through a Gangtok travel agent.

Bus
SNT (Sikkim Nationalized Transport) Bus Stand, NH31A, T22016, 0900-1300, 1400-1600. Private buses from West Point Taxi Stand, NH31A, T22858. Some only operate in the high season. Buy tickets 24 hrs in advance; hotels can help. Long distance journeys about Rs 60. To **Rumtek** 1600 (1500 holidays) 1 hr; **Namchi**, which has a Govt 80-bed *Youth Hostel*, 0800, 1500 (4½ hrs); **Namok, Phodong, Chungthang, Mangan**, 0800, 1300 (return 1500); **Gezing**, 0700, 1300 (5 hrs); **Jorethang (then Pelling)**, 0800. For North Bengal: **Bagdogra** (about 5 hrs); **Darjeeling**, 94 km, between 0700-1330; from Darjeeling 0730-1400 (6-7 hrs); to **Kalimpong**, 75 km, 0830-1930 (4-4½ hrs), from Kalimpong 0700-1315; to **NJP/Siliguri** (115 km), 0700-1415 (4½-5 hrs); from Siliguri 0630-1300, 5 hrs. To **Kolkata** 1300; from Kolkata 1700; a/c bus Rs 280.

Taxi/jeep
Taxis charge exhorbitant rates to ferry passengers arriving at the taxi stand; from there it is a stiff 2-km climb to the centre

(For sharing): Stands (i) Lall Bazar (East Sikkim) (ii), Private Bus Stand (for North Bengal) and (iii) Children's Park (West Sikkim). Fixed rate charts within Gangtok, but negotiable for sightseeing. Rs 1,200 per day for travel outside Sikkim, Rs 1,000 within Sikkim; plus night halt Rs 200. **Chhangu**, Rs 400 return; **Rumtek**, shared, from 1030, Rs 25; **Yoksum**, Rs 800.

Train
Nearest railway stations are at **Siliguri/New Jalpaiguri**, Computerized Bookings, SNT Compound, for tickets (no tourist quota), 0800-1400.

Rumtek Monastery *p629*
Bus
From Gangtok about 1600 (1 hr) along a steep narrow road, return depart about 0800.

Jeep
Shared jeep: Rs 25 each; last return to Gangtok 1300. **Rumtek** to **Pemayangtse**, 4 hrs.

Taxi
From Gangtok, Rs 300 (return Rs 500, 1½ hr wait).

⊕ Directory

Gangtok *p627, maps p627 and p628*
Banks Open 1000-1400, Sat 1000-1200 (difficult to get exchange; poor rates on TCs from trek agents)). **State Bank of India**, MG Marg. **State Bank of Sikkim**, Tibet Rd. **Hospitals** On Stadium Rd: STNM Hospital, opposite *Hotel Mayur*, T22059. Other medical facilities: Unique Chemists. **Internet** Green Hotel on request. **Post office** GPO, Stadium Rd and PO in Gangtok Bazar. **Tourist offices** Sikkim, MG Marg, Gangtok Bazar, T22064. Open in season Mon-Sat 0900-1900, off season 1000-1600. Apply for permits here. Department of Tourism, T23425. **Useful addresses** Ambulance: T22059. Fire: T22001. Police: T22033.

Sikkim Listings: Gangtok

Sikkim regions

East Sikkim

Chhangu (Tsomgo) Lake → *36 km from Gangtok. Altitude: 3,774 m.*
ⓘ *Getting there: organized tour or by jeep through travel agents (permit needed; apply with photo and passport a day ahea). Allow 6 hrs for the return trip, Rs 800 for minivan.*

The lake is on the Nathu La Highway, the old trade route to Lhasa which until 1962 saw regular mule trains leave and return to Gangtok. The precipitous road passes through the Kyongnosla Sanctuary and leads to the holy lake which is completely frozen in winter, up to mid-May. It is best to visit March to May, September to mid-December. There are excellent views of Kangchendzonga from the nearby ridge and superb sunsets. On the way there is the **Shiv Gufa**, a few minutes' walk from the road. You have to enter the tiny cave on your hands and knees to see a small Siva image and several tridents embedded in the soft floor. The drive there is scenic but the lake area is overcrowded and spoilt by snack kiosks and loud Hindi music. Allow an hour to walk around the 1-km long lake. ►► *For Sleeping, Eating and other listings, see pages 639-640.*

Kyongnosla Alpine Sanctuary → *Altitude: 3,200 m- 4,100 m.*
The sanctuary, 31 km from Gangtok, extends from the '15th Mile' check post to the ridges bordering Rongchu and Chhangu Lake. Among the junipers and silver firs the sanctuary harbours some rare ground orchids and rhododendrons and numerous medicinal plants including the *Panax pseudo-ginseng*. The best season is from April to August, October to November. The Himalayan marmot has been reintroduced here. Other mammals include goral, serow, red panda, Himalayan black bear, Tibetan fox and yellow-throated martens, together with very colourful pheasants.

Two easy treks lead to the Shiv Gufa (1 km away) and Kheding (4 km) while longer and more difficult ones to Simulakha, Namnang Lakha and Nakcho are very scenic. Trekkers with permits for Chhangu may return from Nakcho via the lake.

West Sikkim

Gezing → *105 km west of Gangtok.*
ⓘ *An early bus or jeep from Gangtok allows you to see Tashiding, then stop overnight at Gezing or Pelling.*

Gezing (Gyalshing) is at the crossroads of bus routes and has a busy market with food stalls and shops selling provisions.

★ Pemayangtse → *112 km west of Gangtok. 72 km from Darjeeling. Altitude: 2,085 m.*
A full day trip by car from Gangtok, along a very scenic road, Pemayangste 'Perfect Sublime Lotus' was built during the reign of the third Chogyal Chador Namgyal in 1705. It is about 7 km from Gezing, above the main road to Pelling.

The awe-inspiring **monastery** ⓘ *0700-1600, Rs 10, good guided tours, 0700- 1000 and 1400-1600 (if closed, ask for key), no photography inside. Norma Lama, in charge of the monastery, plans to restore the roof and murals,* Sikkim's second oldest, is near the start of the Dzongri trek. For many, the monastery is the highlight of their visit to Sikkim – it has a certain aura about it. Take an early morning walk to the rear of the monastery to see a breathtaking sunrise in perfect peace. The walls and ceiling of the large *Dukhang* (prayer hall) have numerous *thangkas* and wall paintings, and there is an exceptional collection of religious artworks including an exquisite wooden sculpture on the top floor depicting the heavenly palace of Guru Rimpoche – the *Santhokpalri*, which was believed to have been revealed in a dream. The old stone and wood buildings to the side are the monks' quarters. According to tradition the monks have been recruited from the leading families in Sikkim as this is the headquarters of the Nyingmapa sect. Annual *chaam* dances are held at the end of February, and in September.

The **Denjong Padma Choeling Academy** (DPCA) here, set up to educate needy children, has several ancillary projects – crafts, weaving, dairy – and welcomes volunteers who can at the same time learn about Buddhism and local culture. The Meditation Centre offers courses and can accommodate visitors for a small charge and volunteers for free at the new hostel (see below). It can be a very rewarding experience. Volunteers spend a maximum of six weeks, between March and December. Contact Jules Stewart, London, T0207-229 4774, jjulesstewart@cs.com.

Rabdanste ① *from the main road, turn left just before the white sign "Gezing 6 km", cross the archery field and turn right behind the hill (road branches off just below Pemanyangtse). Follow the narrow rocky track for 500 m to reach the palace*, the ruined palace of the 17th- to 18th-century capital of Sikkim, is along the Gezing-bound track from the monastery, 3 km from Pelling.

Pelling → *2 km from the monastery and 9 km by road from Gezing.*
Pelling sits on a ridge with good views of the mountains. The small town has three areas linked by a winding road: Upper and Middle with views and hotels, and Lower Pelling with banks and other services. Upper Pelling is expanding rapidly with new hotels springing up to accommodate honeymooners from Kolkata.

You can visit the **Sanga Choelling Monastery** (circa 1697), possibly the oldest in Sikkim, which has some colourful mural paintings. The hilltop monastery is about 3 km along a fairly steep track through thick woods (about 30 minutes). The area is excellent for **walking**.

Khechopari Lake, Tashiding and Yuksom
A three-day gentle **trek** to this 'wishing' lake, Yuksom and back to Pelling is possible without a permit. A road west of the Pelling-Yuksom road leads to this tranquil lake where the clear waters reflect the surrounding densely wooded slopes of the hills with a monastery above – Lepchas believe that birds remove any leaf that floats down. Prayer flags flutter around the lake and it is particularly moving when leaflamps are floated with special prayers at dusk. The sanctity of the lake may be attributed to its shape in the form of a foot (symbolizing the Buddha's footprint), which can be seen from the surrounding hills.

The gold-topped **monastery**, 40 km from Gezing, built in 1716, stands on a conical hill between the Rathong and Rangit rivers on a spot consecrated by Guru Rimpoche. The gompa has been refurbished and all the frescos repainted. The most sacred *chorten* in Sikkim is here so even the sight of Tashiding is thought to bring blessing. You will see numerous stones with high-class carvings of *mantras* around the monastery. Pilgrims attend the *Bumchu* festival in February/March to drink water from the sacred pot which has never run dry for over 300 years. Below the monastery is the small Tshchu Phur cave where Guru Rinpoche meditated; follow the trail on the left of the entrance to Tashiding until you see a small house opposite and the painting on the rocks. Carry a torch if you plan to crawl into the cave.

Yuksom, 42 km north from Pelling by jeepable road, is where the first Chogyal was crowned in 1641. The wooden altar and stone throne above the Kathok lake are below the Norbu Gang chorten in a beautifully peaceful pine forest. The simple **Hermit's retreat** at **Dhubdi** (circa 1700) is up on a hill, 45 minutes' walk away. Yuksom is quiet and relaxing.

North Sikkim

Phodong → *Colour map 4, grid B1.*

The renovated early 18th-century monastery is 1 km above the north Sikkim Highway, about 2 km before Phodong village. It is a pleasant walk up to the little-visited gompa where friendly monks show you around; the track is jeepable. A further hike of 2 km takes you to the **Labrang** monastery of the Nyingmapa sect. Below the track nearby is the ruined palace of **Tumlong**, which was the capital of Sikkim for most of the 19th century.

Shingba Forest Reserve and Yumthang

→ *Colour map 4, grid A2. 135 km north of Gangtok. Altitude: 3,700 m.*

The road to Yumthang enters the Shingba Forest Reserve, which is lined with rhododendrons which harbouring civets and blood pheasants. The Rhododendron Sanctuary has 24 of the 40 species found in Sikkim and has attractive ground cover of aconites, gentians, poppies, saxifrages, potentillas and primulas.

The attractive high valley of **Yumthang** ① *jeep hire from Gangtok or tour organized by a travel agent*, is surrounded by mountains. The alpine meadow near the tree-line is a seasonal grazing ground for yaks. A few minutes' walk from the main road beyond a log bridge over the river Lachung are some sulphur hot springs. There is also a *Log House* with two rooms (no electricity); contact Forest Department. Permit needed. Yumesamdung above Yumthang is now accessible.

Trekking in Sikkim

→ *Best time to visit: Mar- late May, Oct-early Dec. Apr best for flowers.*

Trekking is in its infancy and many of the routes are through areas that seldom see foreigners. Consequently, facilities are poorly developed though the paths are usually clear. You do not need previous experience since most treks are between 2,000-3,800 m. An added attraction is that dzos (cross between a cow and a yak) will carry your gear instead of porters but they are slower. The trekking routes also pass through villages that give an insight into the tribal people's lifestyle. ➤ *For Sleeping, Eating and other listings, see pages 639-640.*

Ins and outs

Further reading & maps A Guide to Sikkim, Darjeeling Area and Bhutan by **Rajesh Verma**, 1995, for a brief introduction to the state and descriptions of treks in the area, with trekking profiles. The U 502 sheets for Sikkim are NG 45-3 and NG 45-4. PP Karan published a map at the scale of 1:150,000 in 1969. Price US$3, available from the Program Director of Geography, George Mason University, Fairfax, VA 22030, US. Sikkim Himalaya (Swiss Alpine Club) – Huber 1:50,000. Very detailed, £16. See page 64 for trekking advice.

Practicalities Foreigners must be in a group of two at least before applying for a **permit** to trek (approved agents can assist). Lachung and Yumthang valleys in North Sikkim (5 days) and Chhangu in East Sikkim (1 day) are now open to foreigners. **Trekking agents** are listed under Gangtok (above) and Darjeeling, see page 615. Tourist Information Centre, Gangtok has tents for Rs 25 per night. Yuksom can arrange guides Rs 300-400, cook Rs 250, porter Rs 100 and yak/pony Rs 150; book trekkers' huts (Rs 50 per head). **Leeches** can be a particular problem in the wet season, below 2,000 m.

Maenam Sanctuary Rabongla, at an altitude of 2,155 m, 24 km east of Legship, has *Hotel Maenam* with simple, clean rooms, and excellent food. *Mount Narsing Village Resort,* 15th Mile, 3 km from Rabongla, has bungalow rooms and safari tents. The trek from there through the sanctuary to Maenam peak (3,260 m) which dominates the town, takes about three hours. The sanctuary harbours red panda, civet, blood pheasant and black eagle and is most beautiful when the magnolia and rhododendron are in bloom in April-May. Bhaledunga, another 30-minute hike along the ridge, on the steep cliff edge above the Teesta, juts out in the shape of a cock's head.

Kangchendzonga National Park ① *Daily, park entry fee for trekkers (foreigners), Rs 180 (5 days) plus Rs 50 for each extra day, camera Rs 10, porter Rs 5, pack animal Rs 5, camping Rs 25 per tent, trekkers' hut Rs 50 per person (poor condition), Tsokha Hut Rs 75 per bed.* The park offers **trekking** routes through picturesque terraced fields of barley, past fruit orchards to lush green forests of pines, oak, chestnut, rhododendrons, giant magnolias, then to high passes crossing fast mountain streams and rugged terrain.

Animals in the park include Himalayan brown bear, black bear, the endangered musk deer, flying squirrel, Tibetan antelope, wild asses and Himalayan wild goats. The red panda, found between 3,000-4,000 m, lives mostly on treetops. There are about 600 species of birds.

The Kangchendzonga trek now falls wholly within the newly designated Kangchendzonga National Park. The park office in **Yuksom**, about 100 m below the

Sikkim treks

trekkers' huts, housed in a shiny new building has interesting exhibits – stuffed birds, posters about the local wildlife and a couple of locally found musk deer in an enclosure in the wooded yard. Helpful staff.

A local non-governmental organization has done a great deal to **clean up** the camp sites on the Kangchendzonga trail, which were increasingly becoming filthy and polluted with the larger numbers of trekkers going in. Toilets have been rebuilt and waste is now carefully channelled away from streams. Garbage is disposed of by burying in large pits, and seminars and discussions are held regularly among the village folk of Yuksom and Tsokha to educate them on more sustainable methods of forest exploitation. The example set has been very encouraging and it is hoped that this programme is transplanted to other trekking areas.

Fambong Lho Wildlife Reserve The reserve, a little beyond Rumtek, is 25 km from Gangtok across the Ranipool Valley. There are serene junglewalks in the hills, leading to waterfalls, mountain views, jungles with orchids, birds and wildlife (marten, fox, red panda, boar – even wolf and sloth bear). You are free to go on your own (though this is not advisable on some stretches) and can climb or walk for anything from one to six days. The entry fee is Rs 5 and there are log huts at Golitar and Tumin, Rs 50.

Gangtok- Pemayangtse- Yuksom- Dzongri It is possible to trek from **Pemayangtse** (eight to 15 days) or **Naya Bazar** (seven to eight days). From Darjeeling, a shorter trek goes to Singla and Pemayangtse. See also Darjeeling Treks, page 607.

To Lachen & Lachung
Mangan
Murmu Chu
Rani Chu
Phodong
Dik Chu
Dikchu
Fambong Lho Wildlife Sanctuary   GANGTOK
Lingmo
Tadong
Mangjing
Rumtek   Ranipul
Martam
Yangang Chu
Singtam
Rangpo   Rangpo Chu
Tistar River

The route is from Gangtok to Pemayangtse via Rumtek, then on to Yuksom, Bakhim and Dzongri (described briefly below). Although it is not a long trek there are excellent views throughout as you travel up the Ratong Chu River to the amphitheatre of peaks at the head of the valley. These include Kokthang (6,150 m), Ratong (6,683 m), Kabru Dume (6,604 m), Forked Peak (6,116 m) and the pyramid of Pandim (6,720 m) past which the trail runs.

From Pemayangtse the route passes through terraced fields of rice, barley and corn. After crossing the Rimbi Khola River on a narrow suspension bridge, the road gradually rises to Yuksom.

Yuksom – Thangshing – Gocha La Yuksom, 28 km from Pemayangtse – a two-hour drive, is the base for a trek to the Gocha La. This eight to nine day trek includes some magnificent scenery around Kangchendzonga.

Day 1 Yuksom to Tsokha An eight- hour climb to the growing village of Tsokha, settled by Lepcha yak herders and Tibetan refugees. The first half of the climb passes through dense semi-tropical forests and across the Prek

66 99 From the exposed and windswept hillsides nearby you can get a good panoramic view of the surrounding mountains and see a spectacular sunrise or sunset on Kangchendzonga.

Chu on a suspension bridge. A steep climb of six hours leads first to **Bakhim** (2,740 m) which has a tea stall and a Forest Bungalow. There are good views back down the trail. The track then goes on through silver fir and cypress to Tsokha (2,950 m), the last village (which is very Tibetan) on the trek. *Trekkers' hut*, camping ground and good *Mountain Hut* private lodge at Tsokha.

Day 2 Tsokha to Dzongri Mixed temperate forests gradually give way to rhododendron. **Phodang** is less than three hours up the track. Pandim, Narsingh and Joponu peaks are clearly visible, and a further one-hour climb takes the track above the rhododendron to a ridge. A gentle descent leads to Dzongri (4,030 m, 8 km from Bakhim), where nomadic yak herders stay in huts. There is a *Trekkers' hut* and camping ground. Dzongri attracts occasional pilgrims to its *chortens* containing Buddhist relics. From the exposed and windswept hillsides nearby you can get a good panoramic view of the surrounding mountains and see a spectacular sunrise or sunset on Kangchendzonga.

Day 3 Dzongri to Thangshing A trail through dwarf rhododendron and juniper climbs the ridge for 5 km. Pandim is immediately ahead. A steep drop descends to the Prek Chu again, crossed by a bridge, followed by a gentle climb to Thangshing (3,900 m). The southern ridge of Kangchendzonga is ahead. There is a *Trekkers' hut* and *camping ground*.

Day 4 Thangshing to Samity Lake The track leads through juniper scrub to a steeper section up a lateral moraine, followed by the drop down to the glacial – and holy – Samity Lake. The surrounding moraines give superb views of Kangchendzonga and other major peaks. You can camp here at 4,250 m or stay at a *Trekkers' hut* with two rooms and a kitchen.

Day 5 To Chemathang and Gocha La and return The climb up to Chemathang (4,800 m) and Gocha La (4,900 m) gives views up to the sheer face of the eastern wall of Kangchendzonga itself. Tibetans collect sprigs of the scrub juniper that grow in abundance here to use in religious rites. It is a vigorous walk to reach the pass, but almost equally impressive views can be gained from nearby slopes. Much of the walk is on the rough moraine.

Day 6 Samity Lake to Thangshing Return to Thangshing. This is only a two-hour walk, so it is possible to take it gently and make a diversion to the yak grazing grounds of Lam Pokhari Lake (3,900 m) above Thangshing. You may see some rare high altitude birds and blue sheep.

Day 7 Thangshing to Tsokha The return route can be made by a lower track, avoiding Dzongri. Dense rhododendron forests flank the right bank of the Prek Chu, rich in birdlife. The day ends in Tsokha village.

Listings: Sikkim regions

🛏 Sleeping

Kyongnosla Alpine Sanctuary *p633*
FLog Huts, with 2 rooms in each at
Kyongnosla and Lamnang Lakha. You must
apply for a permit (Rs 5) to Chief Wildlife
Warden, Sikkim Forest Department, Deorali,
Sikkim 737102, to enter the sanctuary.

Gezing *p633*
Most accommodation is above the main
square including **D-EAtri** and
E-FKanchendzonga.

Pemayangtse *p633*
DMount Pandim (15-min walk, below
monastery), T03593-50756. 25 large rooms
with bath (barely OK), some with beautiful
views, Indian and Chinese meals (non-
residents order in advance), very slow service
(get there early for breakfast), peaceful but run
down, reservations, Tourist Office, Gangtok.
FDPCA Hostel, half-way to Pelling, 9 decent
dorms, geysers and vegetarian meals.

Pelling *p634*
Power and water cuts can last 4 hrs or more
and dogs are prone to bark through the
night! With over 30 places to choose from,
the following are recommended.
C-DTouristo, nice rooms.
DNorbu Gang, Main Rd, T50566. Rooms with
bath, better views from those away from road,
restaurant. Superb views from terrace.
DPhamrong, near Garuda, Upper Pelling,
T58218, F58281. Clean, reasonable rooms,
good service, but poor breakfast, email.
DSikkim Tourist Centre, Upper Pelling,
near Jeep Stand, T50855 (Siliguri,
T/F433683). Simple rooms, some with views,
cheaper on roadside, rooftop restaurant
(cooking excellent but service limited; only
snacks after 1400), tours.
D-EHaven, Khechopari Rd, Middle Pelling.
Clean doubles with running hot water.
EGaruda, Upper Pelling, near bus stop,
T58319. Rooms in basic lodge with bath, hot

water (heaters Rs 35), dorm, restaurant
(breakfast on rooftop with mountain views),
backpackers favourite (interesting info).
FSisters Family Guest House, near *Garuda*,
T50569. 8 simple clean rooms, shared bath
(bucket hot water), great food, very friendly.

Khechopari Lake *p634*
FPilgrims' Lodge, on edge of lake.
Renovated, transformed, cleaner (Rs 140),
enterprising Mr Tenang provides Sikkimese
porridge and millet bread (and much more),
short hikes (circular) that bring guests back
to the lodge for another night's stay! A small
shop sells food.
   Families also offer to take in guests
(further 25 mins' walk up the hill).

Tashiding *p634*
FLaxmi, cheap rooms OK. Common bath
very smelly.
FSiniolchu, 5 clean rooms (3 on upper floor
are big and beautiful). Dorm beds, shared
bath, hot water, meals, friendly.
FTrekkers' Hut.

Yuksom *p634*
CTashigang, Main Road, T03595-41202,
tashigang2@yahoo.com. 21 good, clean
rooms with lovely views, own vegetable
garden, tennis, quiet, very welcoming.
   Also simple lodges near the bus stop.
Local meals available in the village.

Phodong *p635*
FYak and Yeti. Quiet and clean. Some rooms
with toilet, hot water in buckets, but meals are
pricey and take ages. Recommended.

Yuksom, Tsokha and Dzongri *p637*
ETrekkers' Huts, with rooms and dorm for
overnight stops, are fairly clean although the
toilets are basic. Bring sleeping bags; meals
are cooked by a caretaker. The huts are in
picturesque locations at Pemayangtse,
Yuksom, Tsokha and Dzongri.

 For an explanation of the sleeping and eating price codes used in this guide, see inside the
front cover. Other relevant information is found in Essentials pages 52-57.

❷ Eating

Pelling *p634*
Don't miss local **chhang** brewed in the area.
Alpine, Khechopari Rd (below Garuda).
Chinese, Kashmiri especially good. Wooden
cottage, painted yellow, run by friendly
Ladakhi lady.

Phodong *p635*
Northway, serves excellent Indian food, and
is friendly, relaxed, efficient and good value.

▲ Activities and tours

Pelling *p634*
Tour operators
Help Tourism, Sikkim Tourist Centre,
T50855, good information and tours.

❸ Transport

Bus
Buses can be crowded, especially during *Pujas*
and *Diwali*; get ticket on bus if ticket counter is
busy. There are SNT buses to Gangtok (0800,
1300), 5 hrs, Rs 50 (or go via Pelling and
Jorethang); Yuksom via Tashiding (1300),
4 hrs; Siliguri (0630, 1300), 5 hrs.

Jeep
Shared jeep to Darjeeling, Rs 60.

Pemayangtse *p633*
Bus/jeep
From Gezing: bus to monastery, 1000-1430,
Rs 15. Shared jeep, Rs 60.

Pelling *p634*
Bus/jeep
To **Gezing** bus or walk along steep downhill
track, 1 hr. To **Khechopari Lake**: last bus dep
1400, or you can walk 5 hrs (part very steep;
last 3 hrs follows road). Buses and
share-jeeps to **Yuksom, Damthang,
Gangtok** (4 hrs), **Darjeeling** via Jorethang,

tickets from *Father Travels* opposite Hotel
Garuda, Rs 180. **Siliguri**: SNT bus 0700;
tickets sold at provision store next to *Hotel
Pelling* where bus starts, and stops uphill at
Garuda at the jeep stand.

Khechopari Lake *p634*
Bus/jeep
From **Pelling**: jeep share, 1½ hrs; **Tashiding**
(3 options): (i) 0700 bus to Gezing, then jeep.
(ii) Bus to Yuksom 1500 (irregular) from
'junction', 10 km from lake; overnight in
Yuksom, then bus at 0700 (or jeep) to
Tashiding, 1 hr. (iii) Hitching a lift on the
Pelling to Tashiding jeep, which passes the
'junction' at about 1400; try sitting on top of
jeep to enjoy the beautiful scenery!

Tashiding *p634*
Bus/jeep
From Yuksom or Gezing: bus or jeep via
Legship; or climb 6 km (2 hrs). From
Pemayangtse: a day's walk.

Yuksom *p634*
Bus/jeep
Bus: to **Gezing and Tashiding**, 0700. Shared
jeep: to **Pelling**, 0600, 2 hrs, Rs 70 each, from
market place; buy ticket a day ahead.
Gangtok, Rs 120 each; sightseeing Rs 800;
guide Rs 110.

Phodong *p635*
Bus/jeep
From Gangtok bus to start of jeep track, 0800
(2 hrs), Rs 35; return bus, 1500. Jeeps travel
up to **Labrang**.

❶ Directory

Pelling *p634*
Bank State Bank of India, exchange rates
unavailable daily so unable to help! **Tourist
offices** Sikkim, Upper Pelling, near *Garuda*,
T50855. Helpful.

Northeastern Hill States

🍴 Footprint features

Introduction

The Northeast is a true frontier region. It has over 2,000 km of border with Bhutan, China, Myanmar (Burma) and Bangladesh, and is connected to the rest of India by a narrow 20-km wide corridor of land. One of the most ethnically and linguistically diverse regions in Asia, each of the seven Northeastern Hill states has its distinct culture and tradition.

Deep forests cover the sparsely populated foothills of the Himalaya, which comprise **Arunachal Pradesh**, only recently opened to visitors. To its south, **Assam**, which occupies the lush lowlands of the **Brahmaputra Valley**, is the most densely populated and largest of the states. **Meghalaya**'s beautiful hills have the dubious distinction of being the wettest region in the world. The little-visited four southeastern states of the region, **Nagaland**, **Manipur**, **Mizoram** and **Tripura**, make up a fascinating area, hilly, remote, and a zone where the **tribal cultures** of South and South East Asia intertwine.

Permits are needed to enter Arunachal Pradesh, Mizoram, Nagaland and Manipur. See under each state.

★ Don't miss...

1. Place a bet at the daily **Archery Stakes** in Shillong, page 662.
2. **Kaziranga National Park** is the place to see the Indian greater one-horned rhino (from the back of an elephant), page 648.
3. Stay at the Eco camp in **Nameri National Park** and go rafting or fishing, page 650.
4. Visit the wettest place in the world at **Mawsynram** near Cherrapunji, which has over 11 metres of rain every year, page 662.
5. Embark on the spectacular four-day journey to remote **Tawang Monastery**, page 668.
6. The start of the 'Road to Manadalay' is at Ledo in Assam but be sure to stop at the cemetery at **Kohima**, where the British stopped the Japanese invasion of India in April 1944, page 671.

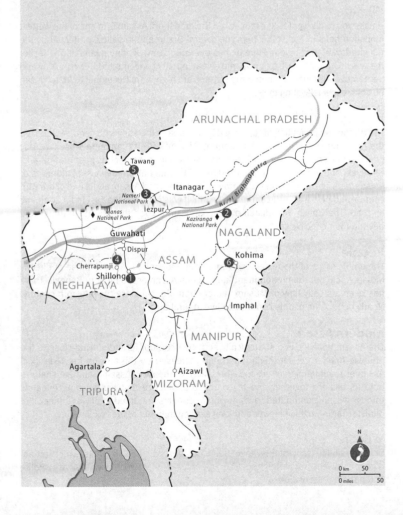

Assam → Population: 26.6 million. Area: 78,438 sq km. www.assamtourism.com.

The lush valley of the Brahmaputra, one of the world's great rivers, provides the setting for Assam's culturally rich and diverse communities. Although it is tea that has given the state a world name, the fertile river valley has been the home to generations of rice farmers, and tribal populations continue to have a significant presence in parts of the state.

The land

Assam stretches nearly 800 km from east to west, the length of the narrow floor of the Brahmaputra Valley. The Himalaya to the north and the Shillong Plateau to the south can be clearly seen. The state is dominated by the Brahmaputra, one of the great rivers of the world, which has a fertile alluvial plain for growing rice and is also famous for tea. Earthquakes are common, the one in 1950 was estimated as the fifth biggest earthquake ever recorded.

Climate

Unless you really want to see rain, avoid the monsoon! Assam is in one of the wettest monsoon belts in the world. Even the central Brahmaputra valley, protected by the rainshadow of the Shillong Plateau, has over 1,600 mm of annual rainfall. The rest of the Assam Valley has up to 3,200 mm a year, mostly concentrated between May and September. Although summer temperatures are high, from December to March it can be cold, especially at night.

History

The Ahoms, a Shan ruling tribe, arrived in the area in the early 13th century, deposed the ruler and established the kingdom of 'Assam' with its capital in Sibsagar. They later intermixed with Aryan stock and also with existing indigenous peoples (Morans, Chutiyas) and most converted to Hinduism. The Mughals made several attempts to invade without success, but the Burmese finally invaded Assam at the end of the 18th century and held it almost continuously until it was ceded to the East India Company in 1826. The British administered it in name until 1947 though many areas were beyond their effective control.

People

The ethnic origin of the Assamese varies from Mongoloid tribes to those of directly Indian stock, but the predominant language is Assamese, similar to Bengali. There has been a steady flow of Muslim settlers from Bengal since the late 19th century. Nearly 90% of the people continue to live in rural areas.

Modern Assam

The Assam Valley is in a strategically sensitive corridor for India, lying close to the Chinese frontier. Its sensitivity has been increased by the tension between local Assamese and immigrant groups. The failure of the AGP (Assam Gana Parishad) to hold its alliance together and to control the violence that has become endemic through Assam contributed to its downfall. Congress returned to power under Chief Minister Tarun Gogoi, a lawyer and long serving member of the Lok Sabha.

Wildlife

Several wildlife sanctuaries have been designated national parks which attract higher entry fees from foreigners (Rs 175), only a part of which goes towards wildlife and habitat preservation.

⦂ Visiting the Northeast

The Northeast has been a politically sensitive region since Independence. Insurgency in places continues to surface making travel in some areas unsafe. Arunachal Pradesh, most of Assam, Meghalaya and Mizoram are largely free of problems. Nevertheless, advice on travel to these and the other states should be taken locally.

Permits Visitors to Assam, Meghalaya and Tripura do not need permits but may need to register on arrival and departure. **Foreigners** visiting Arunachal Pradesh, Nagaland, Manipur and Mizoram may obtain Restricted Area Permits from the Ministry of Home Affairs, Foreigners Division, Lok Nayak Bhavan, Khan Market, New Delhi 110003. Send two photos and allow up to six weeks. **Indians** require Inner Line Permits from the Ministry of Home Affairs. Groups of four should travel together to get a permit; the State Tourist Offices can usually help.

Check the political situation and rules as they are subject to change.

★ Guwahati→ *Phone code: 0361. Colour map 4, grid B4. Population: 808,000.*

Despite its commanding position on the south bank of the mighty Brahmaputra, it is easy to forget that Guwahati is a riverside town, the waterside having little impact on people's lives. The main entrance point for visitors to the Northeastern states, the city retains a relaxed and friendly atmosphere. Paltan Bazar, where most visitors arrive, is very busy and crowded. North of the railway it is much quieter and has a rural feel. ▶▶ *For Sleeping, Eating and other listings, see pages 653-659.*

Ins and outs

Getting there Borjhar airport (23 km) has flights to Kolkata, Delhi, Bagdogra and airports throughout the Northeast. Flights to Bangkok were inaugurated in 2002. 1,151 km from Kolkata. Well connected by road to all major centres of the northeast region; at the junction of NH31, 37 and 40. It has occasional coaches, shared taxis and auto-rickshaws for transfer to town. The railway station is in the central Paltan Bazar, while most state and private buses arrive immediately to its south.

Getting around It is easy to walk around the two main commercial areas of Paltan and Pan (pronounced *Paan*) Bazars, which have most of the hotels and restaurants. Red minibuses or 'canters' are cheap and very efficient around the city (conductors call out the stops), whereas auto-rickshaws need hard bargaining. Political incidents in the city are rare so military presence usually remains discreet and low-key. Carry a torch when walking at night - large holes in pavements in places lead straight down into sewer channels. See Transport, page 656, for further details.

Climate Temperature: summer, maximum 32°C, minimum 25°C; winter, maximum 23°C, minimum 10°C. Rainfall: May-Aug 310 mm, minimal Nov-Feb.

History

Guwahati, on the site of the ancient capital of a succession of local chieftains, was once known as *Pragjyotishpur* ('the city of astrology'). The **Navagrah** (nine planets) **Temple** on a hill here was the ancient centre of astronomy and astrology. It was also a centre of learning and a place of Hindu pilgrimage. In the seventh century, Hiuen Tsang described its beautiful mountains, forests and wildlife. Today it is the business capital while **Dispur,** the 'Capital Area', is just to the south.

The **Janardhan Temple** (10th century) in the heart of the city, was rebuilt in the 17th century. The Buddha image here uniquely blends Hindu and Buddhist features. The **Umananda** (Siva) **Temple**, on Peacock Island in the Brahmaputra, can be reached by ferry. An Ahom king built the temple in 1594, believing Uma, Siva's consort, had stayed there. Ask the priests about the few rare golden langurs here.

Kamakhya Temple ① *0830-1300, 1500-1600 (Sun 0830-1200), buses from MG Rd (towards Adabari Bus Stand) can drop you near Kamakhya, take a 'canter' from AT Rd to the temple or walk up the steep and slippery rocky path at the back of the hill*, 8 km southwest, is believed to be an old Khasi sacrificial site on Nilachal Hill. It has been a centre for Tantric Hinduism and Sakti worship. Rebuilt in 1665 after the 10th-century temple was destroyed by a Brahmin convert to Islam, it typifies Assamese temple architecture with its distinctive beehive-shape *sikhara* (spire), the nymph motifs and the long turtleback hall. The dark sanctum contains the creative part of the goddess which is said to have fallen here, see page 580, and pilgrims enter to touch the wet *yoni* of Kamakhya (Sakti). Western visitors may be allowed into the sanctum but should be prepared for the charged atmosphere and to walk barefoot on a floor sprinkled with the sacrificial blood of a goat. Ask for Hemen Sarma, a knowledgeable resident Brahmin, on entering the complex. Further up the hill is a smaller temple and a Viewpoint with panoramic views of the Brahmaputra. See Festivals below.

Guwahati

■ Sleeping	7 Orchid &	● Eating
1 Ananda	Magnolia Restaurant	1 Apple Pie
2 Bellevue	8 Prag Continental	2 Jantosh
3 Brahmaputra Ashok	9 Rajmahal, Starline &	3 Magic Mushroom
4 Chilarai Regency	Woodlands Restaurant	4 Paradise
5 Dynasty & Nova	10 Tourist Lodge &	5 Woodlands
6 Nandan & Air India	Tourist Information	

⁝ Plantation labour

Today Assam produces most of India's tea. Old colonial tea planters' bungalows surrounded by neat rows of emerald green tea bushes dominate the landscape, particularly in Upper Assam. After an early experiment using imported Chinese labourers ended in near mutiny, the British began the mass recruitment of Adivasis from the Choto Nagpur plateau, Andhra Pradesh and Orissa. They have now been assimilated into Assamese society. One of the largest groups of organized labour in India today, they enjoy benefits undreamed of by other workers including free health care, education and subsidized food. The lifestyle of the plantation, hardly changed since the days of the Raj, has been tarnished lately by the rise of insurgency, with tea companies being targeted for extortion and kidnapping.

Basistha Ashram,12 km away, is believed to be sage Basistha's (Vasistha) hermitage, it is a scenic spot with three mountain streams nearby. **North Guwahati** is a sleepy town across Saraighat Bridge, which can also be reached by any ferry from the ghat. The **Digheswari Temple** is worth a visit. Take a rickshaw from the other bank or an auto-rickshaw or shared four-wheeler.

Museums

Assam State Museum ① *closed Mon and 2nd, 4th Sat, 1000-1615 (Nov-Mar), 1000-1700 (Apr-Oct), Rs 2, photography with permission*, covers epigraphy, sculpture, natural history et cetera; sections on village life, crafts and ethnography are particularly interesting. A small museum, well lit, thoughtfully displayed with notes in English and informative on neighbouring cultures. **Commercial Museum** ① *Mon-Sat, closed Sun and University holidays, 1230-1830, no photography*, Guwahati University, has collections of art and craft, commercial products, minerals and rocks, coins etc. **Srimata Sankaradeva Kalakshetra** ① *in Panjabari, on road to Narangi, closed Mon, 0800-2200, bus 8,* is a cultural complex set up to serve as a centre for Assamese dance, drama, music, fine arts and literature ("a theme park of Assamese life"). It features a museum, theatre, artists' village and heritage park.

Zoo and Botanical Gardens

① *Closed Fri, Oct-Mar 0800-1600, Apr-Sep 0700-1630, Rs 5, cameras: still camera Rs 5, telephoto lens Rs 25, video Rs 250. Auto-rickshaw from town Rs 50. Alternatively take a local bus along GNB Rd to the flyover (Rs 2), climb steps up to the flyover; take a southbound bus to the zoo (Rs 2). A few direct buses go all the way.*

Largely an open enclosure zoo with landscaped gardens, it has swamp tapirs, rhinos, tigers, lions, panthers and rich birdlife; several species from Northeast India that are not often seen elsewhere. Restaurants and souvenir shops.

Excursions

Hajo ① *buses from Adabari Bus Stand, 1 hr, the last return bus departs around 1600 but may be very crowded – you may have to travel on the roof,* a friendly and peaceful town, 34 km across the river, produces bell-metal work and is sacred to three religions. The **Hayagriba Madhab** Hindu temple is said to contain a Buddhist relic. Some believe this is where the Buddha attained Nirvana. Its hilltop location is more spectacular than the temple itself. The 'main' street behind the tank stocked with fish leads to an old Ganesh temple after 2 km; a friendly priest might allow you in. Hajo is also sacred to Muslims since the **Pao Mecca Mosque** built by Pir Ghiasuddin Aulia is supposed to have 'quarter' (*pao*) of the sanctity of Mecca.

The small village of **Sualkuchi** ① *ferry service from Guwahati, also buses to/from Hajo, 20 mins*, on the north bank of the Brahmaputra, is famous for silk production from non mulberry leaf-fed worms, hence its unique natural colour. Every household is involved with weaving of *muga*, *endi* or *pat* silk; prices are 30% cheaper than in Guwahati.

Pabitora is a small wildlife sanctuary a two-hour drive from Guwahati (60 km), on the border of Nagaon and Kamrup districts, has rhinos.

Madan Kamdev ① *buses from Guwahati go to Baihata on NH31 (5 km from the site); rickshaws run to the temples*, 45 km north of Guwahati, has been called Assam's Khajuraho. The temples which may date from the 11th-12th century, possibly reconstructed in the 18th, are believed to be associated with tantric practices. The principle shrine to Uma-Mahesvara or Siva-Parvati is still in use. The site museum has a collection of local finds. A Tourist Lodge is scheduled to open soon.

★ Kaziranga National Park

→ *Phone code: 03776. Colour map 4, grid B4. Altitude: 65 m.*

Kaziranga Reserve Forest was declared a game sanctuary in 1916 to save the Indian greater one-horned rhino and became a national park in 1974. It is now a World Heritage site. In a beautiful setting on the banks of the Brahmaputra, and with the Karbi Anglong Hills to the south, the 430 sq km park combines elephant grass mixed with thorny rattan cane, areas of semi-evergreen forest and shallow swamps.

Ins and outs

Getting there Guwahati is 215 km from Kohora, the entry point to Kaziranga on the NH37.

Getting around Park roads open 0800-1100, 1400-1630. Foreigners, Rs 175. Cameras (for each trip during any day): still, Rs 175, telephoto lens, Rs 210, video, Rs 525 (professional, Rs 7,000). 25% discount on fees after 3 consecutive days. See Transport, page 657, for further details.

Climate Summer maximum 35°C, minimum 18°C; Winter maximum 24°C, minimum 7°C. Annual rainfall 2,300 mm, heavy in summer. Best season: Mid-Nov to end-Apr (Dec, Jan best for birds); closed mid Apr-mid Oct during monsoons. Clothing: cottons and a warm jacket.

Kaziranga National Park

Sleeping ■
1 Aranya Tourist Lodge & Bank
2 Bonani Bonashree & Kunjaban
3 Wild Grass Resorts

Eating ●
1 Rhinorica Restaurant

Wildlife

The **rhino** population is about 1,200 here (1,500 in the country) but you can still easily see them in the marshes and grasslands. Poachers still kill the animal for its horn for its use in Chinese and Tibetan medicine. The park also has over 1,000 wild buffalo, sambar, swamp deer (over 500), hog deer, wild pig, hoolock gibbon, elephants (about 1,000) pythons and tiger (80 in 1997), the only predator of the docile rhino. There is a rich variety of shallow-water fowl including egrets, pond herons, river terns, black-necked stork, fishing eagles and adjutant storks, pelicans and the rare Bengal florican. There are otters and dolphins in the river.

Viewing

There are three **road routes** for visiting the park. **The Kaziranga Range** – Kohora, Daflang, Foliomari which is "full of big mammals"; the **Western Range** – Baguri, Monabeel, Bimoli, Kanchanjuri with tall elephant grass so visibility not great; and the **Eastern Range** – Agortoli, Sohola, Rangamatia, where you may see a lot of wildlife but at a distance. Keep receipts as fees are valid for several trips during one day.

Entry into the park is by own vehicle, hired jeep or trained elephants. Although elephants cover less ground than motor vehicles, they can get a lot closer to the wildlife, particularly rhinos and buffalo.However, the elephant rides get mixed reports (less enjoyable when demand is heavy and "other tourists get over-excited"!).They carry four and a seat may be booked through the Forest Range Officer, the night before the visit. **Elephant rides**, 0530-0630 or 0630-0730, Rs 525 foreigners (Indians Rs 120), plus jeep transfer between town and elephant pick-up, Rs 120. The viewing posts just inside the park may offer quieter viewing.

The Department of Tourism, Kaziranga and private agents hire out **jeeps** for five to six people. Government: Rs 400 for three hours; private: Rs 550 for 50 km or 2½ hours; *Wild Grass Resorts* charge Rs 10 per km, for example Eastern Range, Rs 700. A car or jeep must be accompanied by a Forest Department guide (free), who can give directions as well as spot wildlife. Cars and jeeps pay a road toll, Rs 150.

Panbari

Panbari Forest Reserve, 12 km from Kaziranga, has hoolock gibbons and a good variety of birdlife. Contact the Forest Office, Guwahati, for permission to visit.

★ Manas National Park

→ *Phone code: 03666. Colour map 4, grid A3. Altitude: 70 m.*

A World Heritage Site, and one of India's most beautiful sanctuaries, Manas lies in the Himalayan foothills, southeast of the river Manas, on the Assam-Bhutan border. Over half the area is covered with tall grass and scattered patches of woodland. This changes to dense semi-evergreen forest in the upper reaches and even to conifer on hills towards Bhutan.

Ins and outs

Permit It is essential to enter via Barpeta Rd by car or taxi. Permits are issued by the Field Director, Manas Project Tiger, Barpeta Rd, T32289, after he obtains confirmation of a police escort to accompany you. Pick up provisions. Use the Bansbari gate with a Forest Range Office (20 km, 30 mins) to get to Mathanguri inside the park (20 km, 30 mins). Do book a car/taxi for the return journey. If you travel during dawn (0500) and before sunset (0400) you may see some wildlife. Travel is not permitted after sunset.

Climate: summer maximum 35°C, minimum 18°C; winter maximum 24°C, minimum 7°C. Annual rainfall: 4,100 mm. Season: Nov-Mar. Clothing: heavy pullover/jacket for evenings, sun hat, shoes for wading through slippery streams essential (and several changes of clothing).

Background
The Manas, with a buffer zone 2,800 sq km (including two other far flung sanctuaries), and a core area of 391 sq km, was demarcated in 1977-78 when the preservation programme 'Project Tiger' was launched. At the last count there were over 80 tigers. UNESCO has released funds to help the national park recover from damage caused by Bodo rebels. Political troubles can lead to sudden closure of the park so get local advice before you plan to visit; contact *Wild Grass Tours*, Guwahati, T0361-546827, F630465.

Wildlife
The forests are home to most of the larger animals found in Kaziranga, most common being wild buffalo, swamp deer, hog deer, sambar and elephant. Some 22 of the animal and bird species are on the endangered list of the IUCN including the rare capped and golden langur which can be seen among the flowering trees, mostly on the Bhutan side. There are also pigmy hog, hispid hare, slow lorris, clouded leopard, rhino and tiger. The sanctuary is rich in birdlife (over 400 species), and attracts migratory flocks of redstarts, forktails, mergansers and ruddy shelduck. Otters are frequently seen in the Manas River.

Viewing
Occasionally boats, for two to eight, are for hire from the Forest Beat Officer, Mathanguri. To see the animals from close range, an elephant ride is best. These start from Mathanguri for one hour, 0900-1200, 1400-1700, Rs 525 for foreigners. Charges for entry and camera are similar to Kaziranga (see above).

Tezpur → *Phone code: 03712. Colour map 4, grid A4. 180 km northeast of Guwahati.*
Tezpur, on the north bank of the Brahmaputra, is the site of Assam's first tea plantations. Its ancient origins can be seen at Da Parbatia, west of town, which has the entrance gate of an early Gupta style temple.

An interesting excursion is to take a Guwahati-bound bus, get off at the bridge over the Brahmaputra, then negotiate with a boatman to take you to the river's confluence with the Bhoreli for some river **dolphin watching**. Some hotels, *Luit* for example, offer such trips. It involves a 30-minute rickshaw ride, Rs 150, followed by boat hire, Rs 800.

Around Tezpur
Nameri National Park ① *best time to visit is from Oct to Apr, viewing is on elephant back as there are no roads, you can trek within the park with a forest guide, entry and camera fees are similar to Kaziranga, see above,* a 210 sq km park on the Arunachal border, is on the river **Jia Bhoreli**, about 40 km north of Tezpur. There are tigers and elephants – 29 and 225 counted in 1997 – Indian bison, barking and hog deer. It is home to about 20 endangered white-winged wood ducks among 300 bird species, with evergreens, bamboo and some open grassland.

An **Eco camp** at Potasali organizes white-water rafting and mahseer fishing on the Bhoreli. Assam Anglers' Association, T02712-20004, rip.magdel@axcess-net.in, operate a strict 'catch-record-release' system to conserve the golden mahseer. Rafting, for fishing or nature watching, for two people on rubber rafts, Rs 650 per day, Rs 300 transport to/from raft.

Bhalukpong ① *taxi to/from Tezpur, 1 hr, Rs 250, bus from Balipura, change for Bhalukpong,* 20 km west of Nameri, just beyond the Arunachal Pradesh border, en route to Tawang, has a hot spring an orchid garden and good fishing. You can camp (own tent) on the picturesque bank of the River Jia Bhoreli.

ⓘ *Car is best from Tezpur (2 hrs), then from Orang to the park (15-km bumpy, dust track).*

Often called a miniature Kaziranga, the 76 sq km park, 66 km northwest of Tezpur, has similar flora and fauna, though viewing is not as rewarding. This is compensated by its peaceful and intimate atmosphere, especially if staying inside the park.

Jorhat → *Colour map 4, grid A5.*

Jorhat is one of Assam's major tea centres and is convenient for visiting Majuli Island to the north. The Tea festival is held in November.

Majuli Island

Majuli Island is possibly the largest river island in the world, though constantly changing an, reduced to around 700 sq km. The flooding of the Brahmaputra River means that that at times Majuli is reduced to a cluster of islands, some as small as a hut top. Roads keep shifting but villagers adapt to rerouting by building cost effective bamboo bridges. Cut off from the mainland to the south about 400 years ago, it is served by ferries from Jorhat and North Lakhimpur, but it can still be accessed from the north by road during summer. Majuli is also a birdwatchers' paradise. Foreigners must register on arrival and departure at the nearest police station.

At the forefront of Assamese Vaishnava culture, the island is an important centre for arts, crafts and science. Work is in progress to declare it a World Heritage Site. The *satras* (monasteries) here, inspired by the 15th-century saint Sankardeva and his disciple Madhavdeva, are worth visiting. They are essentially small, self-contained, self-sufficient villages where Vishnu is worshipped through regular performances of dance-dramas at the temples.

Some *satras* can be visited on foot in and around **Kamalabari** and **Garmur** but for others a rickshaw is handy. **Auniati**, a few kilometres west of Kamalabari, has an Angami tribal museum with old manuscripts, utensils, jewellery and handicrafts. **Bengenatti**, east of Uttar Kamalabari, is a centre for performing arts and tribal dance forms. Others worth visiting are at Nauten Kamalabari and Dekhinpat.

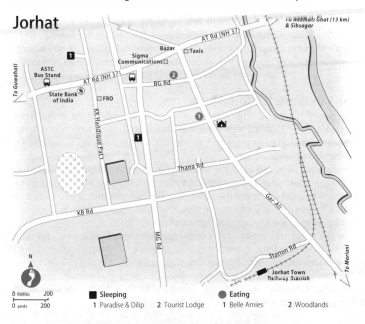

Jorhat

Sleeping		Eating	
1 Paradise & Dilip	2 Tourist Lodge	1 Belle Amies	2 Woodlands

Northeastern Hill States Assam Majuli Island

The sanctuary at **Bhalowguri**, 16 km away, was designated in 1998, but is scarcely visited by tourists. Viewing the wild elephants requires an overnight stay in the specially constructed hut on stilts. A "great experience". The current fee is a meagre Rs 20 per person (four hours' viewing), which includes an armed escort/guide, though the dense forest growth makes the gibbons hard to spot. Contact District Forest Officer in Jorhat, then Forest Range Officer at Mariani. Bus from the top of MG Road, Jorhat, go via **Mariani**, 18 km southeast.

Sibsagar and Digboi

District headquarters of the largest tea and oil producing area in the Northeast, **Sibsagar** was the Ahom capital for two centuries. There are several royal tanks. Daupadi (the Ahom King's wife) built the huge tank here in 1734. On the east bank there is birdwatching tower and a library. The tower of the Siva Dol on its bank is one of the tallest Siva temples in India. *Sivaratri* is celebrated in March.

The **Joysagar** at **Rangpur** ⓘ *local bus from BG Rd Bali Ghat, Rs 5, 20 mins; then cycle-rickshaw, Rs 10,* 5 km away, and the three temples on its bank date from 1697. **Talatal Ghar** (6 km), the seven-storeyed palace with three underground floors, was built between 1696-1714.

The oil fields of upper Assam were first exploited in 1879, the first wells came on stream here in 1892 and a refinery opened in 1900. Although **Digboi**'s own resources are drying up, the region has considerable potential. The surrounding forest is also a haven for birdlife. You may visit at your own risk with permission of OIL. There is an 18-hole golf course and a British Second World War cemetery nearby. For those wishing to visit Arunachal for Miao, Deban Valley, Namdapha Forest Reserve, be aware facilities are limited.

Dibrugarh and Tinsukia

Much of the old town of Dibrugarh was destroyed during the 1950 earthquake. The new town on the Brahmaputra is surrounded by tea estates.

Tinsukia, a major transport junction in the Northeast, is convenient for visiting the nearby Dibru-Saikhowa National Park and the small Borajan Reserve Forest.

Borajan Reserve Forest ⓘ *best to visit by car,* 5 km away, is a small (½ sq km) patch of forest which is home to five species of primate (Hoolock gibbon, capped langur, slow loris, stump tailed macaque and common macaque) but are not easy to spot.

Dibru-Saikhowa National Park

A national park since March 1999, on the southern flood plain of the Brahmaputra near Tinsukia, this is largely a semi-wet evergreen forest. The best time to visit is from November to March. Temperature ranges from 6°C to 36°C. Average annual rainfall ranges from 2,300 to 3,600 mm.

Entry points are at **Guijan** on the southern boundary and **Dhola** (near Saikhowa Ghat) at the northern edge, both accessible by bus from Tinsukia. From Guijan, a boat across the river takes you to the Range Office at the park entrance. If you cross from Dhola, the Range Office is 5 km into the park at Narbarmora; it is better to notify your arrival beforehand. See Kaziranga above for usual park fees.

The 340 sq km core area within a large bio-sphere reserve is a refuge for some endangered species – tiger, leopard, leopard cat, clouded leopard, elephant. The rich birdlife includes the very rare white-winged wood duck.

The Forest Department has one double-bedded room at Guijan, carry provisions. Contact DFO, Rangagora Rd, Tinsukia, T331472. The retired DFO, Mr Eunush Ali, knowledgeable about wildlife and the Northeast, T333079.

Margherita → *Colour map 4, grid A6.*

Margherita, the constituency of the present Chief Minister, is on Dihing river at the foot of the Patkoi Range, and was named by Italian railway engineers in the late 19th century after the Queen of Italy. The town is surrounded by tea estates and is the Northeast headquarters of Coal India Ltd. The last of the steam railway engines in Assam is still operating.

Ledo → *Colour map 4, grid A6.*

The small coal mining town of Ledo, 6 km northwest of Margherita, was the headquarters of Northern Combat Area Command during the Second World War and is the start of the 470 km Stilwell Road.

Named after General Joseph Stilwell, the road was the most ambitious and costliest engineering project of the war, US$137,000,000 at the time. Once a two lane, all-weather bitumen highway linking Ledo with Myitkyina in North Burma through the Pangso Pass and with Kunming in China (1,029 miles) it is now closed beyond Nampong in Arunachal Pradesh. A sign, 6 km west of Ledo, commemorates the Road to Mandalay but there is little else that remains of the massive Allied presence here.

Listings: Assam

☁ Sleeping

Guwahati *p645, map p646*

Hotel staff often speak little English. There are some budget hotels at Sadullah and M Nehru Rd crossing; those in Paltan Bazar are often full by the afternoon. You may need to complete 4 copies of the hotel registration slip and then register with the police (fairly quick). Most hotels outside Guwahati require photocopies of passport identification and the visa page.

B Brahmaputra Ashok, MG Rd, T541064, F540870, brahmaputra@satyam.net.in. 50 rooms (on riverside best), central a/c, TV, bamboo and cane furniture, good restaurant, credit cards, good travel agency.

B Dynasty, SS Rd, T510496, F522112. 68 comfortable rooms, good restaurants.

B-C Nandan, GS Rd, opposite *Indian Airlines*, T540855, F542634, nandan@gw1.vsnl.net.in. 55 rooms, some a/c, expensive suites, restaurants, *Upavan* for snacks, bar.

B-C Rajmahal, Paltan Bazar (near bus stand), T522478, F521559. 80 rooms (good value), excellent restaurant, all services, pool in summer (non-residents Rs 75, 45 mins).

C Bellevue, MG Rd, on river front opposite Raj Bhawan, T540847. 45 rooms, restaurant (Continental recommended), elevated woodland setting, quiet.

D Chilarai Regency, HP Brahmachari Rd, Paltan Bazar, T541530, F547917. 44 large rooms (some a/c), bar, exchange.

D Nova, SS Rd, T523464. Clean rooms (some a/c) in 4-storey block, reasonable restaurant (Indian, Chinese) but slow service (room service quicker), pleasant, friendly and helpful.

C Prag Continental, M Nehru Rd, Pan Bazar, T543785, F524554. 62 rooms, some a/c, terrace restaurants, *Continental Café*.

Most medium priced hotels have some a/c rooms and tend to serve Indian meals only.

D-E Starline, Md Shah Rd, Paltan Bazar, T542450. 74 clean rooms, 12 a/c with hot water 24 hrs, Indian/Chinese restaurant, polite and helpful staff.

E-F Ananda, M Nehru Rd, T544832. Small dark rooms but pleasant, vegetarian dining hall.

E-F Orchid, B Barua Rd, opposite stadium, T544471. 23 clean rooms, 5 a/c, hot water in buckets, set back from road in own compound with excellent *Magnolia* restaurant.

F Tourist Lodge (Assam Tourism), opposite railway station, T544475. 21 fairly clean simple rooms with nets, toilets and balcony, canteen, staff speak little English but are friendly, tourist information, good value.

F Railway Retiring Rooms, rooms (some a/c), small dorm, book at Enquiry Counter.

● *For an explanation of the sleeping and eating price codes used in this guide, see inside the*
● *front cover. Other relevant information is found in Essentials pages 52-57.*

Kaziranga National Park *p648, map p648*
C Wild Grass Resorts, lovely location, 1.5 km from NH37, 5.5 km from Kohora (ask for Kaziranga IB Bus Stop, 400 m north of resort), T62011 (Guwahati T0361-546827, F630465). 19 rooms, wood floors, cane furniture, deluxe camping (4 tents, common bath), can get very cold in winter, very good buffet lunch (Rs 50/65), huge pool, excellent service, spotless, relaxing, beautiful walks through forests and tea plantations, tours, pick up from Guwahati for groups, occasional cultural shows.
D Aranya Tourist Lodge, 1 km south of Kohora, T62429. 24 rooms with bath and balcony, some a/c, simple garden, restaurant and bar (slow service, order ahead), friendly.
D-E Bonani, near *Aranya Tourist Lodge*, T62423. 5 a/c rooms, limited menu.
F Bonashree, still cheaper, 9 rooms, a large verandah, pleasant garden, but often full.
Kunjaban Dormitory, linen optional, 5 or 12-bed (Rs 30-50), no cupboards. Reservations: Deputy Director, Tourism, Bonani, Kaziranga, T62423.

Dhansri and **Green Reed**, off the main road. **Rhinorica Restaurant** is at the bus stop on the main road.

Manas National Park *p649*
The town has medical facilities, a Tourist Information Office, banks and a post office.
E Doli, 200 m from station, 18 rooms with fan, net, bath, abundant food, helpful staff.
F Mathanguri Forest Lodge, built on hill overlooking Manas River is in a poor state but has the advantage of being within the park.

Forest Deparment's **Forest Lodge**, and **Bhutan Tourist Lodge**, Mathanguri are very simple but clean and well maintained, cook available but bring provisions (from Barpeta Rd), camping possible, book well in advance.

Prefabricated **Rest House** provides linen but no electricity, open Nov-Apr. Contact Field Director, Manas Tiger Reserve, PO Barpeta Rd, T33413. If you arrive late at Barpeta Rd you will need to spend the night there.

Tezpur *p650*
C-D Luit, Ranu Singh Rd, 100 m bus stand, T22083, F21220. 38 clean rooms, some a/c, best in new wing, restaurant, bar, travel.

E Basanth, Main Rd, T30831. Good, clean, well-maintained rooms (Rs 250).
E Durba, KK Rd, T22605. Clean rooms with TV, **Appayam** restaurant.
F Tourist Lodge, opposite Chitralekha Udyan, T21016. 6 large rooms with bath and dorm, very quiet and peaceful, tourist information.

Nameri National Park *p650*
C-D Eco Camp, T24246. Swiss cottage tents with thatched cover, some with bath, 6-bed dorm (Rs 125), wash block, meals. Contact *Wild Grass Tours*, T0361-546827.
F Forest Lodge, contact Range Officer.

Orang National Park *p651*
F Bungalows, 2 at park entrance, 2 1½ km inside the park, overlooking river. Bring own provisions – the cook/guide will prepare your food. Reservations, Divisional Forest Officer, Mangal Doi, T03713-22065.

Jorhat *p651, map p651*
D Paradise, Solicitor's Rd (off AT Rd), T0376-321521, F323512. 31 rooms, 9 a/c, hot water, restaurant, bar, exchange.
F Tourist Lodge, MG Rd, T0376-321579. Large, mosquito-filled rooms, poor tourist info.
Other **F** hotels are along Gar-Ali.
Dilip, near *Paradise Hotel*, T0376-321610. Clean, friendly, one of few places to accept foreigners.

Majuli Island *p651*
Circuit House, Garmur (Rs 100), contact SDO, Majuli, T03775-74424, ahead but often booked.

At Kamalabari:
Uttar Kamalabari Satra, very basic, bring own bedding and leave a donation, usually booked through **Wild Grass** but you may try to reserve on T03775-73392, ask to call Dulal Saikia (the head priest) to the phone, then ring back after 10 mins.
Guest House, at Nauten Kamalabari (8 km from Garmur), spartan, no hot water (Rs 30).

Sibsagar *p652*
E Siddhartha, BG Rd, T03772-223276, F20430. 29 rooms, restaurant, bar, modern.
E-F Brahmaputra, BG Rd, T03772-22000. 48 rooms, restaurant, helpful, clean.

Phone codes *Guwahati: 0361; Kaziranga National Park: 03776; Tezpur: 03712; Manas National Park: 03666*

F **Tourist Lodge**, near Siva Dol, T03772-22394. 6 rooms (often full), very helpful Tourist Office.

Digboi *p652*
C **Guest House**, Indian Oil Corporation, 22 large, spacious rooms, hot water, TV, excellent location. Reservations, Mr SR Koneru, T03751-64715, F64470.

Dibrugarh *p652*
B **Chang Bungalow**, near town. A 'Heritage' Planter's bungalow, sparkling clean, fabulous food, excellent staff, car and guide included. Contact *Purvi Discovery*, T301166, csn@ purvidiscovery.com.
C-E **Mona Lisa**, Mancotta Rd, Chowkidinghee, T0373-21416. 19 rooms, some large and a/c, best in new wing, good restaurant, bar.
D-E **Goswami**, few doors from *Mona Lisa*, T0373-21250. 12 rooms, some a/c, dining hall, *Green Valley Tours* office and bus pick-up.
  F paying guest accommodation in Assamese home, about Rs 200 including breakfast, contact Binoy Dowerah, T0373-22289.

Tinsukia *p652*
D-E **Highway**, AT Rd, T0374-336383, F335455, 500 m from New Tinsukia station. 20 rooms, some a/c, vegetarian restaurant, modern.
D-E **Jyoti**, Rangagora Rd, T0374-333245, F332608. 20 rather grubby rooms, some a/c, hot water, restaurant.
F **President**, Station Rd, T0374-20789. 32 rooms, vegetarian restaurant, TV, basic, noisy.
F **Retiring Rooms**, very basic veg refreshments.

⊙ Eating

Guwahati *p645, map p646*
Assamese thalis including rice, fish and vegetable curry, often cooked with mustard. You might try vegetarian *Kharoli*, Omita *Khar* (papaya cooked with burnt 'hark' of the banana plant). Only larger hotels serve Continental food and have bars.
₸₸₸ **Bellevue** for Continental. Recommended.
₸₸₸ **Dynasty** for Chinese. Recommended.
₸₸₸ **Rajmahal**, recommended.
₸₸ **Ming Room**, Rajgarh Rd, near Chandmari Flyover. Very good Chinese.
₸ **Apple Pie**, MC Rd. Pastries, ice creams.
₸ **Hits Cafeteria**, near Central School, Khanapara, T300090. Out in the suburbs, offers great lunch and dinner.

₸ **Lantosh**. Assamese. Takeaway and ice cream, clean.
₸ **Magic Mushroom**, MC Rd. International. Clean, good quality, varied menu, psychedelic décor, very friendly and helpful owner.
₸ **Magnolia**, *Orchid Hotel*, B Barua Rd. "Food arrives hot and quickly."
₸ **Paradise**, GNB Rd, Chandmari, T546904. Assamese. Serves "perfect thalis" (Rs 55), very clean and friendly, closes 1530-1800 (cycle rickshaw from station, Rs 10).
₸ **Station restaurant**, good omelettes (Rs 7).
₸ **Woodlands**, AT Rd (older branch on GS Rd). Indian vegetarian. Clean, a/c, specializes in lunch and dinner thalis (Rs 40).

Nameri National Park *p650*
Eco Eats, has some tribal dishes.

Jorhat *p651, map p651*
Belle Amies Food & Fun Junction, Gar-Ali. Indian/Chinese. Colour-coded menu to indicate hotness!
Canteen at State Bus Stand. Cheap, does good *roti* breakfasts (toilets).
Rajhans, AT Rd. Indian snacks.
Woodlands, BG Rd (between MG Rd and Gar Ali). Indian. Good thalis.

Majuli Island *p651*
Food is available at simple eateries. Carry drinking water.

Tinsukia *p652*
Cakes & Bakes, opposite *Hotel Jyoti*. Burgers, pizzas and excellent cakes, good value.
New Leaf at *Hotel Highway*. Cheap vegetarian restaurant. Best in town.

⊙ Entertainment

Guwahati *p645, map p646*
Boating
Paddle boats on the Long Pond (Digholi Pukhuri near the Museum Bus Stop). Spend a pleasant hour with a coffee from the canteen.

Planetarium
Guwahati Planetarium, Uzan Bazar, daily 1700 English show (good equipment), Rs 10.

Swimming
Assam Swimming Club, Ambari and Pool in Nehru Stadium.

⊛ Festivals and events

Guwahati *p645, map p646*
Magh Bihu in **Jan** and **Rongali Bihu** in
mid-Apr, the week-long festivities are
celebrated with singing and dancing. **Jun**:
Ambubachi marks the end of Mother Earth's
menstrual cycle with a fair at Kamakhya
Temple. In **Sep** the Manasa Festival honours
the Snake goddess. You can watch devotees
dancing and entering into trances from
galleries on the hillside. **Assam Tea Festival**
is celebrated on **26-28 Dec** with events in
various places.

⊙ Shopping

Guwahati *p645, map p646*
Books
In Pan Bazar:
Lawyers Book Stall, one of the region's
oldest and largest.
Modern Book Depot, best collection on the
region at rear.

Silk and handicrafts
Muga, pat and *endi* silks, hats, bamboo and
cane baskets, flutes, drums and pipes are
typical of the area. Guide prices: silk per
metre: *muga* Rs 400+ (saris Rs 4,000+), *pat*
Rs 250 (saris Rs 2,000+), *endi* Rs 150-300. *Pat
mikhala* and *shador*, Rs 1,500, *endi* shawls Rs
300+. Bargain in Pan Bazar and Fancy Bazar.
Assam at Ambari, sells silks, bamboo, wood,
brass and ceramics.
Assam Co-op Silk House, HB Rd, Pan Bazar,
for pure silk items.
Khadi Gramudyog, near *Guwahati Emporium*.
Manipur, Paltan Bazar.
Purbashree, GNB Rd, has traditional crafts.
Tantuja, Ulubari, has Bengal handloom.

▲ Activities and tours

Guwahati *p645, map p646*
Tour operators
Assam Tourism, *Tourist Lodge*, Station Rd,
T547102. **City**: Basistha Ashram, Zoo, Museum,
Kamakhya Temple, Govt Sales Emporium.
0900-1500. Rs 90. Tue, Sun (minimum 10).
River Cruises, from near Janardhan Temple,
winter 1500, 1600; summer 1600, 1700, 1 hr,
Rs 50. **Kaziranga**: Nov-Apr, departs 0900, arrives
1600, return 1600 on following day, Rs 600,

foreigners Rs 1,250 (inclusive) allows only from
1500 to 1000 (on next day) in the park.
Separate morning buses, departs 0700, 5½ hrs.
Shillong: departs 0700, Rs 255 (tiring, since the
windy hill roads take 3½ hrs each way). Private
companies (see below) may be more reliable.
Hemanta Doley, Sankardeva Udyan,
Machkhowa, T512121, for river trips.
Network Travels, GS Rd, T522007, F522105.
Imaginative tours, *Indian Airlines* agent,
efficient and reliable.
Purvi Discovery, www.purvidiscovery.com,
for varied tours. Excellent service.
Rhino, M Nehru Rd, T540061. For visiting
game reserves and Shillong.
Traveland, 1st floor, *Brahmaputra Ashok*, MG
Rd, T541064, F520762, rchaliha@
hotmail.com. "Knowledgeable and helpful".
Wild Grass, Barua Bhavan, 107 MC Rd, Uzan
Bazar, T546827, F630465, wildgrss@
sancharnet.in. Very helpful, knowledgeable,
efficient. Highly recommended for good
value wildlife, tribal tours and Arunachal (can
get a permit in 5 days), free travel advice on
phone (Nov-Apr). See also bus operators.

Kaziranga National Park *p648, map p648*
Tour operators
Assam Tourism, offers a 2-day tour (see
under Guwahati above). Tour operators, see
below, may be more reliable.
Wildgrass, wildgrss@sancharnet.in.

⊙ Transport

Guwahati *p645, map p646*
Air
Information T84235. Transport to town:
Indian Airlines and **Rhino Travels** coaches
connect with Kolkata flights, Rs 40, 1 hr.
Taxi, Rs 300, share taxi, Rs 100, 45 mins.
Auto-rickshaw, Rs 150. **Indian Airlines**,
Ganeshguri, near Dispur, T564420, airport,
T84375; 0900-1600. **Kolkata**, 2 daily; some
weekly to **Agartala**, **Delhi**, **Imphal**,
Lilabari. Jet Airways, Panchvati, GNB Rd,
T522402, airport T840600: to **Bagdogra**,
Delhi, **Imphal**, **Kolkata**; Sahara, GS Rd,
T547808: to **Delhi**, **Dibrugarh**. **Helicopter**:
Meghalaya Transport Corp to **Shillong**,
Mon-Sat (am and pm), Rs 1,000, and on to
Tura; tickets at airport.

Bus

Between midnight and 0500 buses are not allowed to enter the city, but taxis are. **Local** (See below). Red **minibus** 'canters' or 'Omni taxis' cover main roads. These are prone to accidents.

Long distance Private coaches (and taxis) operate from Paltan Bazar, with waiting rooms, left-luggage, snack bars. Operators: **Assam Valley**, T546133, **Blue Hills**, T547911, **Green Valley**, T544636, and others have buses to all the Hill States. **Assam STC Stand**, Paltan Bazar, T547941. Left-luggage, Rs 3 per day. Reservations 0630-1230, 1330-1700. Meghalaya STC, T547668. Buses to: **Aizawl** (11 hrs); **Imphal** (579 km); **Itanagar** (11 hrs); **Jorhat via Kohora (for Kaziranga)** (6 hrs); **Kaziranga and Upper Assam**: bus for Tinsukia and Digboi (0700 a/c; 0730), halt at *Wild Grass Resorts* after 4 hrs. **Kohima** 2000, 2015, 2030 (13 hrs); **Shillong** (103 km) hourly, 0600-1700, Rs 40 (3½ hrs); **Silchar** 1730; **Siliguri; Tezpur** every 30 mins (3½ hrs). **City Bus Stand**, Station Rd (north end): to **Hajo**,(1½ hr). **Adabari Bus Stand**, AT Rd (4 km west of centre) reached by 'canters' from MG Rd, has buses to Hajo, Orang and Nalbari.

Ferry

To **North Guwahati** from MG Rd Ferry Ghat. To **Peacock Island**: Rs 6 each way. 0700-1700.

Rickshaw

Auto-rickshaw: Paltan Bazar to Fancy Bazar Rs 20, Fancy Bazar to Navagraha Temple Rs 25.

Taxi

Local Sightseeing Rs 100 per hr (excluding petrol); *Guwahati Taxis*, Paltan Bazar, near Police Station; *Green Valley*, Silpukhuri, T545289, cars/jeeps Rs 700 per day plus overnight Rs 150. *Traveland*, 1st floor, *Brahmaputra Ashok*, MG Rd, T541064, F520762. Reliable and efficient. *Chandana*, Goswami Villa, Zoo Narengi Rd, T557870, F522105, has Tata Sumo (a/c), Rs 1500 per day.

Long distance From Paltan Bazar: Shillong, Rs 625 (5 sharing, Rs 125 each, they fill up quickly when trains arrive).

Train

Station has snack bars, chemists, tourist information, left luggage (trunks and suitcases only), on showing ticket. Enquiries:

T540330. Reservations: 100 m north of the station on Station Rd, T541799, 0800-1330,1400-2000; Foreign Tourists, Counter 3, where great patience is needed! The new line from Guwahati, along the south bank of the Brahmaputra to Jogighopa, should cut delays and speed up journey times when fully operational. To **Kolkata (H)**: *Kanchenjunga Exp, 5658* (AC/II), 2200, 22½ hrs (via **New Jalpaiguri**, 10 hrs); *Kamrup Exp, 5960* (AC/II), 0700, 23½; *Saraighat Exp, 3026,* Mon, Thu, Fri, 1000, 18 hrs (via **New Jalpaiguri**, 8 hrs). To **Delhi (ND)**: *Rajdhani Exp, 2423,* via Patna and Kanpur, Mon, Thu, Fri, 0600, 28 hrs; *Rajdhani Exp, 2435,* via Lucknow, Wed, Sun, 32½ hrs. To **Dibrugarh** Via Dimapur: *Brahmaputra Mail, 4056,* 1430, 16 hrs; *Kamrup Exp, 5959,* 1630, 14½ hrs.

Kaziranga National Park *p648, map p648*

Air

Nearest airport is at Jorhat (88 km). See page 656. Foreign tourists must use Guwahati's Borjhar airport, see page 645.

Road

Best to ask *Wild Grass*, if they have a vehicle going from Guwahati, or confirm timings of private buses. **ASTC** buses between Guwahati and Jorhat via **Kohora** stopping at **Nagaon** (30 mins, where you can stop overnight); departs 0900, 1000, 1100, 1230, Rs 85, 5-6 hrs. **Private**. *Green Valley* (office behind bus station) coaches dep Guwahati for Tinsukia and Digboi, 0700 (non a/c, Rs 95), 0730 (a/c, Rs 135); lunch stop at *Wild Grass Resorts*, after 4 hrs. **Guwahati**: a/c bus from Dibrugarh stops at resort for lunch; leaves at 1330. *Kaziranga Forest Lodge* has 10 seats reserved on the Express coach between Golaghat and Guwahati. Assam Tourism bus, depart 0930 from *Bonashree Lodge*, arrive Guwahati 1600, Rs 85 (lunch Rs 40). It is a very bumpy ride. From **Shillong** get a Jorhat bus and switch at **Jorabat** for Kaziranga.

Train

Furkating (75 km) has the nearest station with trains from Guwahati; buses via Golaghat.

Manas National Park *p649*

Bus

On good fair weather road between Guwahati and Barpeta Rd but no buses beyond; taxis charge, Rs 450-600 per journey.

Train
Nearest station at Barpeta Road (40 km) with trains to **Guwahati** and **Kolkata**.

Tezpur *p650*
Air
Saloni airport is to the north: **Indian Airlines**, T20083, T20353. Flies to/from **Kolkata** via **Imphal** twice weekly, and also to **Dimapur** twice weekly.

Bus
Frequent buses to/from **Guwahati**; **Kaziranga** until 1400. Daily to **Itanagar** (4 hrs); **Tawang** (12 hrs).

Taxi
To **Orang/Nameri**, Rs 550 plus petrol.

Jorhat *p651, map p651*
Air
Jorhat has the main airport 7 km from town with airlines coach or autos for transfer. Private taxis Rs 100 to town or Rs 600 to Kaziranga. **Indian Airlines**, T320011, Airport, T340294, to **Kolkata** via **Dimapur**; Jet Airways, *Hotel Paradise*, T325652, Airport, T326920: **Kolkata**, Wed, Thu, Fri, Sun. **Imphal**, Wed, Thu, Fri, Sun.

Bus
ASTC Stand on AT Rd has a good canteen. Private buses leave from outside ASTC: to **Guwahati**, 0600-0730 and 2000-2130, 7 hrs; **Sibsagar** (55 km); **Dibrugarh** (131 km). Ticket booths are nearby.

Train
The station (3 km southeast of bus stand) has no toilets. To **Guwahati**: *Intercity Exp, 5606*, 2005, 10½ hrs, via Lumding with narrow gauge to **Haflong**: 0715, 4½ hrs (beautiful route but tourists are discouraged; Haflong Tourist Lodge is now occupied by the military).

Majuli Island *p651*
Bus
Buses from Jorhat (at junction of MG and AT Roads) to **Neemati** (13 km north); allow 1 hr.

Ferry
Government ferry from **Neemati**, 1000, 1600, return 1330 (confirm timings); crossing time varies seasonally as boats have to circumnavigate sand bars. Buses run from the ghat to **Kamalabari** (about 5 km) and **Garmur** (8.5 km). You can also arrange private boats at the jetty for transporting a car.

Sibsagar *p652*
Nearest airport: Jorhat (60 km). Nearest railway station: Simaluguri (20 km). Regular buses to Guwahati, Kaziranga, Simaluguri.

Dibrugarh *p652*
Air
The airport is 16 km from town. **Indian Airlines**, T300114, Airport, T301551, to **Kolkata**, Tue, Wed, Thu, Sun. **Sahara**, T31216. Delhi via **Guwahati**, daily.

Bus
Private stand on AT Rd. *Green Valley* bus to Guwahati (Rs 190), Kaziranga (Rs 150) pick up from Goswami Guest House at 0715.

Train
To **Guwahati**: *Brahamaputra Mail, 4055*, 2015, 15½ hrs; *Rajdhani Exp, 2423A*, Thu, 1615, 12 hrs (continues to **New Delhi** in further 28 hrs); *Kamrup Exp, 5660* (AC/II), 1415, 16½ hrs (continues to **NJP** and **Kolkata (H)** in further 24 hrs). Local *BG Pass* to Ledo (via Tinsukia), 0700, 1600 (not Sat).

Tinsukia *p652*
Bus
ASTC stand on AT Rd; private buses from top end of Rangagora Rd. To Jorhat, Rs 80.

Train
The 2 stations are 3 km apart. New Tinsukia has most of the long distance trains.

❶ Directory

Guwahati *p645, map p646*
Airlines Air India, GS Rd, T561881; BA, *Pelican Travels*, *Hotel Brahmaputra Ashok*, T630123, Jet, T520202 (airport T840130); Sahara, T547808, or try agents at *Rajmahal Hotel*. **Banks** United Bank of India, HB Rd, Pan Bazar. TCs, min Rs 50 commission. Grindlays Bank, Dighali Pukhari, GNB/Earl Rds, Mon-Fri 1000-1500, Sat 1000-1230. TC Commission 1% or Rs 100, but quick and efficient. **Hospitals** Christian Hospital, Chatribari, T540193. Good Health, GS Rd,

T566911. **Medical College**, Bhangagarh, T561477. With 24-hr chemists outside. MM **Choudhury Hospital**, Pan Bazar, T543998. **Internet** Sangita Communications, Anuradha Cinema Complex, GNB Rd, 0830-2000. **Post** GPO (entrance on Shillong Rd) with Speed Post (7 days). Counter 1 for evaluation and 14 for stamps, then basement for franking. **CTO**: in Pan Bazar. **Tourist offices** Assam, Directorate, Station Rd, T/F547102. **Tourism**, B Barua Rd, T454421, assamtourism@gw1.vsnl.net.in. Counters at airport and railway station. **Arunachal Pradesh**, RC Barua Rd, Bhaskar Nagar, T562859, F566720. **India**, BK Kakati Rd, Ulubari, T547407. Mon-Fri 0930-1730, Sat 1000-1300, airport counter, helpful for planning trips to other parts of India. **Manipur**, Rajgarh Rd, T540707. **Meghalaya**, Ulubari, GS Rd, T527276. 1000-1700 except Sun; Rehabari, AK Azad Rd, T544343. **Tripura**, GS Rd, Ulubari, T528761. **Useful**

Kaziranga National Park *p648, map p648*
Post office near the Tourist Lodge and at the park. **Useful addresses** The Wildlife Society has a **library** of books and magazines and may show wildlife films to groups. Range Officer, T62428. Divisional Forest Officer, Bokakhat, T68007. Kaziranga Safari, T037376-325468, F325782, can book accommodation.

Jorhat *p651, map p651*
Banks State Bank of India, AT Rd. Exchanges TCs (show proof of purchase). **Internet** Sigma, AT Rd (near Gar-Ali). **Tourist office** Station Rd.

Tinsukia *p652*
Internet Sygma Systems, near Railway Overbridge, AT Rd. **Travel agent** Classic Travels AT Rd, T786125.

Meghalaya

→ *Entry permits, see page 645. Population: 2.3 million. Area: 22,500 sq km.*
Meghalaya, the 'abode of the clouds', with its pine-clad hills, beautiful lakes, high waterfalls and huge caverns, has been called 'the Scotland of the East' because of the similarity of climate, terrain and scenery. The wettest region in the world, between May and September the rain comes down like waterfalls as the warm monsoon air is forced up over the hills. Home to the Garo, Khasi and Jaintia tribes, the hill state retains an untouched feel. There are traditional Khasi villages near Shillong with views into Bangladesh.

The land
Much of the plateau is made up of the same ancient granites as are found in peninsular India; its south facing slope, overlooking Bangladesh, is very steep. The hills rise to heights just under 2,000 m which makes it pleasantly cool but it is also one of the wettest places on the earth (Mawsynram has received more than 20 m of rainfall in one year). Much is still densely forested. Shillong is the only important town; 80% of the people live in villages. Compact and isolated, Meghalaya's rolling plateau lies in a severe **earthquake** belt. The entire town of Shillong was destroyed in an earthquake in 1897.

History
The Khasi, Jaintia and Garo tribes each had their own small kingdoms until the 19th century when the British annexed them. The Garos, originally from Tibet, were animists. The Khasis are believed to be Austro-Asiatic. Jaintias are Mongolian and similar to the Shans of Burma. They believed in the universal presence of god and so built no temples. The dead were commemorated by erecting **monoliths** and groups of these can be seen in Khasi villages in central Meghalaya between Shillong and Cherrapunji. In the 19th century many Jaintias were converted to Christianity by missionaries, although they continued many of their old traditions.

People

Meghalaya is divided into three distinct areas, the Garo, Khasi and Jaintia Hills, each with its own language, culture and particular customs. All three tribes are matrilineal, passing down wealth and property through the female line, with the youngest daughter taking the responsibility of caring for the parents.

Government

The hill-state was created on 21 January 1972. Since 1980 the Congress Party has dominated Lok Sabha elections, but it has never won more than 25 of the 60 State Assembly seats. The Hill Peoples Union, though a minority, has claimed the largest number of seats, but once again the Congress won both Lok Sabha seats in the 1998 elections.

★ Shillong → *Phone code: 0364. Colour map 4, grid B4. Population: 132,900. Altitude: 1,496 m.*

Shillong, among pine-clad hills and lakes, retains a measure of its colonial past especially around the Ward Lake. Unattractive newer buildings have encroached open spaces and an air of decay is beginning to set in. ▶▶ *For Sleeping, Eating and other listings, see pages 663-665.*

Ins and outs

Getting there Helicopters take just 25 mins to fly in from Guwahati. However, most people travel in to the central Police Bazar by bus.

Getting around Shillong is quite spread out though the centre is fairly compact. The steep hills make rickshaws unsuitable but it is easy to find taxis and the city buses are relatively cheap and efficient. Due to simmering ethnic tension it is unsafe to walk around in unfamiliar parts of town after dark, although it is all right to travel by car. See Transport, page 664, for further details.

Climate Temperature: summer, maximum 23°C, minimum 15°C; winter, maximum 16°C, minimum 4°C. Annual rainfall 2,030 mm, mostly Jun-Sep. Best season Oct-May. Clothing: rainwear essential. Summer: cottons, light woollens. Winter: woollens.

Sights

The horseshoe shaped **Ward Lake** set in a landscaped botanical garden and popular for boating is near Raj Bhavan, a two-minute walk from Police Bazar. The **Botanical Garden**① *0900-1700*, is behind it. The **Butterfly Museum** ① *1000-1600*, is in a private house between Police Bazar and Wahingdoh, where butterflies are bred for conservation and sale. The **golf course**, amidst pines, is ideal for an early morning walk. *Tee & Putt* provides good freshly brewed coffee. **Bara Bazar** is well worth a visit to see authentic local colour. It attracts tribal people, mainly women, who come to buy and sell produce – vegetables, spices, pots, baskets, chickens and even bows and arrows. Small stalls sell real Khasi food. Just over a kilometre away is **Lady Hydari Park** ① *0830-1630, Rs 2, cameras: still, Rs 10, video/movie, Rs 1,000*, designed like a Japanese garden, where you will see the pine native to the area – *Pinus khasiana*. It is well laid out with its **Forest Museum** and **Mini Zoo**. The nearby **Crinoline Waterfalls** has a swimming pool surrounded by orchids, potted bonsais and a rock pool with reeds and water lilies. At Lumparing, Laban, the Buddhist **Lamasery** near the Assam Club is interesting but be prepared for a steep climb.

Shillong Peak (10 km, 1,960 m) is 3 km from the Cherrapunji Road, commanding spectacular views, **Laitkor Peak** on the same ridge, 3 km from the Shillong-Jowai Road, is under Air Force control; visitors have to report at the barrier. Buses drop you at the appropriate junction. **Elephant Falls** (12 km), off the Cherrapunji Road, is a scenic spot with two high falls. You can walk down to the lowest pool and get a good view, though the falls themselves are less impressive between November and May. The attractive **Umiam Lake** (Barapani), 16 km, offers fishing and boating.

Rhino Memorial Museum, Hospital Road, in a striking building, has a good tribal collection with a bizarre mix of military paraphernalia!

Mawsynram → *55 km from Shillong.*

The **Mawjymbuin Cave** ① *from Shillong, bus from Bara Bazar at 1400, 3 hrs, Rs 20*, has water dripping from a breast-shaped stone on to what looks like a Siva lingam. The rainfall record in Mawsynram has beaten that of Cherrapunji with over 20 m in one year. **Jakrem** (64km) ① *bus at 1400, 3 hrs*, has hot springs.

Cherrapunji → *Colour map 4, grid B4. Altitude: 1,300 m.*

The old administrative headquarters of the Khasis, picturesque Cherrapunji is a pleasant, quiet town spread out along a ridge with gravestones dotting the surrounding hillocks. Best time to visit for spectacular views is October-January, the drier months. The heat and humidity can be oppressive much of the year. By March it

Shillong

■ Sleeping		● Eating
1 Pinewood	3 Shillong Club	1 Abba
2 Polo Towers	4 Summit	2 New World

⁝ The Archery Stakes

The Archery Stakes, unique to Shillong, take place every day except Sunday. Members of different clubs shoot 1,500 arrows at a cylindrical bamboo target for four minutes. The punters count the number that stick and anyone who has guessed the last two digits of the number of arrows that stick is rewarded with an 80:1 win. A second shoot takes place an hour later when the odds are 6:1 but if you correctly forecast both results the odds are as high as 4,500:1. Naturally, the bookies are the best-dressed men in town!

Start times of the event vary so ask locally in the morning, and to find the exact field, go to the Polo Ground and mime! There are bookies' shops all over town and elsewhere in the state; bets are even placed as far off as Kolkata and Mumbai! The Stakes were legalized only in 1983 when the state government realized that it could raise a hefty 40% tax on the daily money spinner.

is hazy most days and the odd torrential shower is not unusual. It once held the record as the wettest place on earth, but nearby **Mawsynram** has surpassed this. On average it still gets 11,500 mm annually.

The colourful weekly **Ka Iewbah Sohrarim market** is held every eight days. The local orange flower honey is sold from a house (clearly signed) just below Cherra Bazar (about 100 m on the road; avoid plastic bottles). Surprisingly, a variety of banana here actually contains seeds.

Nohkalikai Falls, reputedly the world's fourth highest, is 5 km away, near Sohrarim. A vendor sells good orange flower honey. Montana Tourism, Cherra Bazar, arranges group tours (US$10). Limestone **caves** nearby include Krem Mawmluh (4,503 m) with a five river passage and Krem Phyllut (1,003 m) at **Mawsmai**, with a large fossil passage and two stream ways. Mawsmai also has high waterfalls in the wet season.

Jowai
ⓘ *From Shillong cars take 2½ hrs, buses a little longer.*

Jowai, 64 km southeast of Shillong on NH44, is the headquarters of the **Jaintia Hills**, circled by the Myntdu River. The market, full of tribal women, is particularly colourful.

Syndai, 40 km further south, has many caves used by ancient warriors as hide-outs including 'Krem Sweep' which has a vast chamber. India's longest (6,381 m) and deepest (106.8 m) Eocene Age cave with several cataracts and waterfalls is **Krem Um-Lawan**, 60 km southeast of Jowai near **Lumshnong**.

Tura → *220 km southwest of Guwahati.*
The headquarters of the **West Garo Hills** District, Tura sits at the foot of the jungle-clad 1,457 m Nokrek Peak. It is a spread-out town with a slow pace of life.

Shillong centre

N

0 metres 50
0 yards 50

3 Centre Point
4 Monsoon
5 Pine Borough

● **Eating**
1 Abba
2 Bakery
3 Eecee
4 Jadoh Stall

■ **Sleeping**
1 Alpine Continental
2 Baba Tourist Lodge

Tura Bazar is dominated by the new supermarket, a three-storey red-and-white, mini shopping mall and underground car park. The small fruit and vegetable market in the basement is well organized. A Museum-cum-Cultural Complex is planned 200 m west of Orchid Lodge. Weekly tribal markets are held in surrounding villages.

Nokrek Peak can be reached by a 5-km trek, but involves rock climbing, so is best not attempted alone. **Nokrek National Park** ① *jeeps from Tura Bazar: Rs 1,150-1,500 for the round trip (daily rate)*, is 55 km away. Ask the tourist office for a guide. **Naphak Lake**, 112 km, near the Simsang River is good for fishing and birdwatching.

Siju → *Colour map 4, grid B3.*
① *Bus to Baghmara, 45 km, 1½ hrs; from there to Tura, leaves at 0900.*

Southeast of Tura just below the town, with others nearby, is one of India's longest caves (4.8 km) with a fine river passage. Groups of at least four are needed for going caving so look out on noticeboards. It is more enjoyable and cheaper to travel this way.

Listings: Meghalaya

⊜ Sleeping

Shillong *p660, maps p661 and p662*
GS Rd is now U Tirot Sing Rd; Jail Rd is Pa Togan Sangma Rd; Jowai Rd is Rev Nichols Roy Rd; Kutchery Rd is Mahatma Gandhi (MG) Rd. Despite the change, old names continue to be used.
B-C Polo Towers, Polo Grounds, Oakland Rd, T222341, F220090, deval@cal.vsnl.net.in. 50 well-appointed rooms, exchange (cash), modern and efficient.
C Alpine Continental, Thana-Quinton Rd, T220991, F220996, alpineshillong@ hotmail.com. 41 comfortable rooms and suites, hot water (0730-1030), reasonable restaurant, small cosy bar, exchange (cash, TCs), terrace garden, prompt room service.
C Centre Point, GS Rd, Police Bazar, T225210, F225239. 24 comfortable modern rooms with views, good restaurant (Indian, Chinese).
C Pinewood, Rita Rd, near Raj Bhavan, T223116, F224176. 40 old-fashioned rooms (crying out for a coat of paint), **B** suites, a Raj relic, best in nostalgic old bungalow, spacious grounds, restaurants, bar, exchange, golf, well located, otherwise disappointing.
C-D Shillong Club, MG Rd (near Ward Lake), T226938. 18 rooms in 'colonial' club, Indian restaurant, bar, tennis, billiards.

C-D Summit, Sikandra, 23 Lachaumiere (south of NH between Dhankheti and Malki), T226216, fmh_sikandra@hotmail.com. Well-furnished, comfortable rooms, good food, family atmosphere. Recommended.
D-E Monsoon, GS Rd, T227106, F221840. 25 a/c rooms with bath, hot water (noisy on road side), Indian meals.
E Baba Tourist Lodge, GS Rd, T211285. 27 rooms, restaurant, basic, friendly, clean.
E Pine Borough, Police Bazar Rd, T227523. 20 rooms with bath, restaurant, bar.
E Yalana, Main Rd, Laitumkrah (near *Don Bosco*), T211240. 17 rooms in comfortable hotel, good restaurant, very friendly.

Umiam Lake *p661*
D Orchid Lake Resort, T64258, 18 rooms.

Tura *p662*
E Orchid Lodge (MTDC), New Tura (4 km from Tura Bazar), city bus to Dakopgre stops outside, or auto-rickshaw (Rs 50; Rs 70 at night), T03651-22568. 7 rooms, dorm (Rs 70), TV (variable reception despite a giant satellite dish), dining hall meals at set times, Tourist Office (tours of Siju, Balpakram).
E Rikman Continental, Tura Bazar, T03651-20744. 16 clean rooms, attached bath, restaurant. **Santi Hotel**, Rikman Shopping Point, Tura Bazar. Popular for thali lunches.

● *For an explanation of the sleeping and eating price codes used in this guide, see inside the front cover. Other relevant information is found in Essentials pages 52-57.*

Tourist Lodge (MTDC). Take own provisions, a chowkidar will cook for you. Another at Baghmara.

🍴 Eating

Shillong *p660, maps p661 and p662*
You can try a local pork dish, *dohkhleh* (minced brains with onion and spices) with *jadoh* (rice flavoured with turmeric or pig's blood!) and *saag* (greens) with spicy *tung tap* (hot chutney made with dried fish) at small restaurants in Bara Bazar and a stall behind *Centre Point*.

For variety try hotels **Centre Point** or **Pinewood**.
🍴 **Abba**, Malki Point and GS Rd. Delicious Chinese, closed Sun.
🍴 **Bakery** opposite, with pizzas and fast food. Recommended.
🍴 **Eecee**, near Bus Stand, Police Bazar. Western. Good restaurant and great cakes.
🍴 **Elektra Café Hits**, by Nazareth Hospital, Laitumkhra. International. Excellent for breakfast and lunch, delicious chocolate cake.
🍴 **New World**, GS Rd. Good Chinese.

Cherrapunji *p661*
The UFO-like **Orchid Restaurant**, opposite the falls, serves good food. **Cherra Bazar** has a few basic eateries.

🍸 Bars and clubs

Shillong *p660, maps p661 and p662*
Better bars at **Pinewood**, **Polo Towers** and **Shillong Club** for more atmosphere. *Kiad*, the local rice wine, is popular in roadside bars.

🛍 Shopping

Shillong *p660, maps p661 and p662*
You can get handwoven shawls, canework, Khasi jewellery, handicrafts, orange flower honey. Govt Emporia are on Jail Rd and GS Rd. In Bara Bazar, tribal women sell attractive Khasi silver, gold and amber jewellery.

Books
Modern Book Depot, GS Rd near *Monsoon*. Shop opposite is bigger and better!

Photography
Jai Studio Keating Rd. For films, photo-postcards.

⛰ Activities and tours

Shillong *p660, maps p661 and p662*
Golf
19-hole course at the Golf Club; clubs for hire; the wettest, and also one of the most beautiful 'natural' courses in the world.

Swimming
Club near Crinoline Waterfalls, 0600-1630 (ladies 1100-1200, 1400-1500).

Tour operators
Blue Hill Travels, Police Bazar. Very helpful.
Cultural Pursuits, Mawlai, Nongpdeng, T229016, F227282. Organize 'eco-adventure' tours of Assam, Meghalaya, and promise an unusual adventure.
Jais, Ray's Mansion, MG Rd, T222777, F224654.
Meghalaya Adventures, *Hotel Centre Point*, T225210 (office T224465). Offers cave tours. Visitors may contact Patricia Mukkim, a local teacher-cum-journalist, T230593, patria@technologist.com. She is well informed about local culture, history etc.
Meghalaya Tourism, T226220, departs from MTDC, Jail Rd: **Local sightseeing** (a few minutes at most sights, 2½ hrs at Umiam Lake). 0830-1530. Rs 85. Cherrapunji, Nohkalikai Falls, Mawsmai cave (torch essential!) and Falls: 0800-1600 (15-20 mins at each place). Rs 110. Recommended.

Watersports
Umiam Lake (16 km) for water-skiing, boating and fishing.

🚌 Transport

Shillong *p660, maps p661 and p662*
Air
Helicopter: **Meghalaya Helicopter** at Meghalaya Transport Corporation (MTC), T223200, flies from Guwahati (Mon-Sat) and Tura. Tickets from MTC Bus Stand, Jail Rd. Transport to **Guwahati airport** (127 km): taxi, Rs 850 (3 hrs), nearly double for dep after 1100, or hourly bus, Rs 50.

Bus

Long distance Meghalaya TC, Jail Rd. To
Guwahati, frequent, 0600-1700, 3½ hrs;
Silchar, 2100, 11½ hrs. Also from stands near
Anjali Cinema, Bara Bazar to towns in
Meghalaya. Private bus companies have
offices/booths around Police Bazar for
long-distance connections in the Northeast.

Taxi
Local Metered, yellow-top taxis cruise the
town picking up passengers to share rides.
Flag one down and hop in if he is going your
way; short hops, eg Police Bazar to
Laitumkhrah, Rs 10. MTDC taxis at *Pinewood
Ashok* or the Tourist Office. Sightseeing, Rs
1,400 (8 hrs, 100 km).
Long distance Tourist Taxi Association,
Police Bazar, share taxi to Guwahati, Rs 150
each, 3 hrs.

Train
Guwahati (103 km) the nearest railhead.
Tickets from MTC Bus Stand, T223200.
0600-1100, 1300-1600.

Cherrapunji *p661*
Bus
Long distance From Shillong (Bara Bazar),
to Cherrapunji, 1½ hrs; Mawmluh, 2 hrs.

Taxi
From Cherra Bazar for Nohkalikai Falls, Krem
Mawmluh and a view over the plains of
Bangladesh (on a clear day), Rs 300 with
bargaining; also share taxis to both.
Meghalaya Tourism, Shillong, runs **tours**
which visits several sights nearby.

Tura *p662*
Air
Helicopter services to/from **Shillong**
and **Guwahati**

Bus
To **Baghmara** 106 km (for Siju, none direct),
1300, 4-5 hrs, along the Bangladesh border.
Buy a ticket a day ahead from the booth near
the MTC Bus Stand, Tura Bazar; to avoid a
rugby scrum, ask your hotel to buy your
ticket for a small fee. Private buses to
Guwahati (8 hrs), **Shillong** (12 hrs, night bus
arrives at 0400), **Siliguri** from Tura Bazar.
Booking offices are easy to find.

❶ Directory

Shillong *p660, maps p661 and p662*
Airlines Jet Airways, Ray's Mansion, MG
(Kutchery) Rd. **Sheba Travels**, Police Bazar,
T227222. Indian Airlines agent, and airport
coach. **Banks** State Bank of India, MG
(Kutchery Rd), 1st Floor. Mon-Fri 1130-1400.
Indian Overseas Bank, GS Rd (Police Bazar
end). Both change currency and Tcs.
Hospitals Civil Hospital, GS Rd, T226381.
Nazareth Hospital, Laitumukhrah, T224052.
Ambulance, T224100. **Chemists** in Police
Bazar. **Internet** On GS Rd and Police Bazar
Rd. **Post office** GPO GS Rd, Police Bazar.
Tourist offices India, GS Rd, Police Bazar,
T225632. 1000-1700, free Shillong map.
Meghalaya, opposite Meghalaya Bus Stand,
Jail Rd, T226220. **Directorate of Tourism**,
Nokrek Building, 3rd Meghalaya Secretariat,
Lower Lachaumiere, T226054, tourism@
meghalaya.ren.nic.in. 0700-1800. Very helpful.
MTDC, Orchid Hotel, T224933, F224176,
mtdc@meghalaya.ren.nic.in. 1030-1630.
Useful addresses Foreigners' Registration
Office, Lachumiere near State Museum.

Arunachal Pradesh

→ *Area: 84,000 sq km. Population: 1.1 million.*
*This is Northeast India's largest and most remote state with a population of just over
one million. The Tawang Monastery, birthplace of the sixth Dalai Lama and home to
countless Buddhist treasures, is a major attraction, along with the state's rich tribal
heritage and its wonderful variety of orchids.* ▸▸ *For Sleeping, Eating and other listings,
see pages 669-670.*

⁝ Entering Arunachal

Permits may be given by the Resident Commissioner, Govt of Arunachal Pradesh, Nyaya Marg, Delhi, T3013956 or Liaison Officer, Roxi Cinema, JL Nehru Road, Kolkata, or Arunachal State Government (ask Wild Grass, Guwahati). Foreigners must book a group tour through an approved Indian travel agent. Independent travel is not encouraged. Itanagar, Ziro, Along, Pasighat, Miao, Namdapha, Tipi and Bhalukpong are open to tourists. The daily tariff requirement is US$150 (US$50 to the state government and US$100 to cover the costs of the travel agent). See page 645.

The land

On the Northeast frontier of India, Arunachal Pradesh is India's least densely populated state with just 13 people per sq km. It stretches from the foothills of the eastern Himalaya to their permanently snow-capped peaks to the north. The Brahmaputra, known here as the Siang River, enters the state from China and flows through a deeply cut valley. Stretching from the Himalaya to the steamy plains of the Brahmaputra valley, Arunachal Pradesh has an extraordinary range of forests from the Alpine to the subtropical – from rhododendrons to orchids, reeds and bamboo. It is an orchid lover's paradise with over 550 species identified. The wildlife includes elephants, clouded leopard, snow leopard, tiger, sloth bear, Himalayan black bear, red panda and musk deer. The Namdapha National Park is near Miao.

History

The entire region had remained isolated since 1873 when the British stopped free movement. After 1947 Arunachal became part of the North East Frontier Agency (NEFA). Its strategic significance was demonstrated by the Chinese invasion in 1962, and the Indian government subsequently broke up the Agency giving statehood to all the territories surrounding Assam. Arunachal became the 24th state in 1987, though China continues to argue that until the international border between it and India are agreed some of the territory remains disputed. At the same time the state is disputing its southern border with Assam, and in April 2001 the state government lodged a petition with India's Supreme Court against the government of Assam for "large scale encroachment" on its territory. Having long borders with China and Myanmar, it is a truly Frontier State. The state was opened to tourists in 1995 with the first foreigners being given permission to trek only as recently as 1998.

Culture

The Arunachali **people** are the state's greatest attraction. In the capital Itanagar you may even see Nishi warriors wearing hornbill feathers in their caps, carrying bearskin bags and their knives in monkey-skin scabbards.

A great diversity of the tribal people speak over 60 different dialects. Most have an oral tradition of recording their historic and cultural past by memorizing verses handed down through generations. Some Buddhist tribes have, however, maintained written records, largely recording their religious history. Some tribes worship Donyi and Polo, the Sun and Moon gods.

★ Itanagar-Naharlagun

→ *Phone code: 0360. Colour map 4, grid A5. Population: 61,900.*

Itanagar, the new capital and Naharlagun, the old town 10 km away, together provide the capital's administrative offices. Itanagar, sited between two hills, has the Governor's Residence on one and a new Buddhist temple on the other, with shops, bazar, traditional huts and more recent earthquake-proof wooden-framed buildings in between. The capital has been identified as Mayapur, the 11th-century capital of the Jitari Dynasty.

Ins and outs

Getting there Visitors arriving at Lilabari or North Lakhimpur in Assam take 2 hrs by bus (or a little less by taxi) to Itanagar, calling at Naharalagun Bus Station before climbing up along a scenic road to the new capital. Regular buses from Guwahati and Shillong.

Getting around Frequent buses run between Itanagar and Naharalagun from 0600-2000. Cycle-rickshaws only available in Naharlagun. See Transport, page 670, for further details.

Climate Rainfall: 2,660 mm. Best season: Oct-Mar.

Sights

The yellow-roofed **Buddhist Temple** stands in well-kept gardens on a hilltop with good views. The **Gyaker Sinyi** (Ganga Sekhi Lake), 6 km, is reached by a rough road through forests of bamboo and tree ferns. On reaching the foot of the hill, walk across a bamboo bridge, up steps cut on the hillside to reach a ridge overlooking the forest lake. The brick fort (14th-15th century) is believed to have been built by King Ramachandra. In Naharlagun, the **Polo Park** is on top of a ridge with interesting botanical specimens including the cane thicket, which looks like palm, as well as a small **zoo**.

Jawaharlal Nehru Museum ① *daily, except Mon*, has good coverage of tribal people – collection of art, wood carvings, musical instruments and religious objects. The first floor has archaeological finds from Malinthan, Itafort, Noksaparbat and others.

Bomdila and Tawang Monastery → *Colour map 4, grid A4.*

The whole journey, to reach Tawang from Tezpur in Assam – the nearest airport – is spectacular, passing waterfalls, terraced paddy fields, alpine forests and mountain streams. The road north crosses the border at **Bhalukpong**, see page 650, and continues towards Bomdila passing through low wooded slopes for about 60 km. On the bank of the Bhoreli River in the upper plains is **Tipl**, with the Orchid Research Centre and a glasshouse with 500 species of orchids. From there the road rises sharply to reach Bomdila.

Bomdila → *Altitude: 2,530 m.*

① *Buses from the main bus stand. Lower Town Tezpur and Tawang, 8 hrs. Private buses from Himalayan Holidays to Tezpur, 7 hrs.*

Bomdila has marvellous views of the snow-capped mountains. It has a craft centre, apple and cherry orchards and Buddhist *gompas*.

To Tawang

For the next 180 km the route passes through the pretty Dirang Valley shrouded in pine woods, then climbs to the **Sela Pass** at 4,215 m which presents a far starker view.

The successor to Lama Guru Rimpoche has been found in a village nearby. Stop a while here, along one of the highest motorable roads in the world. **Jaswantpur,** 4 km from the pass, has the *samadhi* to the brave Jawan (soldier) Jaswant Singh which commemorates how he, his fiancée and her friend valiantly held up the advancing Chinese army in 1962 for three days before laying down their lives. Drivers along this road, many of them ex-army personnel, stop to pay their respects at the poignant memorial. You see a high-altitude lake and the trout hatchery at Nuranang just below the pass before reaching Tawang.

★ Tawang Monastery → *Phone code: 03794. Population: 4,600.*
① *Regular buses and Tata Sumo services from Bomdila and Tezpur. Cars take nearly 2 days from Guwahati (400 km) through rough terrain. Foreigners should to travel in a small group in a hired vehicle from Tezpur (12 hrs). Check feasibility locally and don't travel after dark – visibility on the narrow mountain roads can be very poor at night.*

Set in breathtakingly beautiful scenery at over 3,000 m, the monastery, one of the largest in India, is the birthplace of the sixth Dalai Lama. Dating originally from 1642, it is the second oldest Buddhist monastery in the world (after Lhasa), and houses over 500 *lamas* belonging to the Gelugpa (Reformed) Sect of Mahayana Buddhist monks. Buddhism arrived in the area with Padmasambhava in the eighth century but the local Monpas were converted to the Tantric Buddhist cult only after the establishment of the monastery here in the 17th century. During renovations, the main building was completely rebuilt. Treasures include a 5½-m high Buddha, numerous sculptures, *thangkas* and priceless manuscripts. Tawang also has the 350-year old Tawang Gompa among dense forest which is the only Lady Lamasery (Buddhist Monastery for nuns) in Asia. The three-day annual *Losar festival* is usually in early January. Prayers are held every morning and afternoon. A craft centre produces woollen carpets.

Near Tawang
The **Lake District** ① *hire a jeep and guide, carry snacks and drinks, and be prepared for steep, treacherous mountain roads but it is worth it for the breathtaking mountain scenery,* just above Tawang beyond the monastery, is an exceptionally beautiful area with about 30 high altitude lakes. After a fork and an army outpost, the road continues towards **Klemta**, just a few kilometres from the Indian border. There are a few scattered monasteries and a shrine to all faiths at the spot where Guru Nanak rested as he trekked into Tibet, 500 years ago. **Ptso**, 25 km from Tawang, has a small cabin by a lake.

Ziro → *150 km north of Itanagar. Altitude: 1,475 m.*
① *Daily buses from Itanagar (200 km) and Lilabari (100 km).*

Ziro lies in a very picturesque level valley of the Apatani plateau, surrounded by pine-covered mountains. The **Apatani tribals** who live in small, densely populated villages, have evolved a sophisticated system of irrigated paddy cultivation. You can also visit Nisi tribal settlements.

Parasuram Kund
① *From Tinsukia, launch along the Brahmaputra (1½ hrs) to Sadiya Ghat, which has buses to Parasuram Kund.*

This lake, in Eastern Arunachal, attracts thousands of pilgrims at *Makar Sankranti* (mid-January) who come to the fair and to take a holy bath. Spartan Government *Tourist Lodge*; contact Dy Commissioner, Tezu, well in advance.

① *Entry Permit from Field Director, Miao; also accommodation at Deban 25 km away. Dibrugarh (140 km) has the nearest airport. State buses from there go to Miao, the entry point, via Margherita (64 km), the nearest railhead where you can also hire taxis.*

This park, at an altitude of 200-4,500 m, is close to the Myanmar border and can be approached from Deban. It is unique as it is home to four particular members of the cat family – tiger, leopard, snow leopard and clouded leopard. There are also elephants, sambhar, deer, gaur, goral and wild hogs, and rich birdlife. Best season is from October to April. The variety of vegetation is fascinating.

Listings: Arunachal Pradesh

● Sleeping

Itanagar-Naharlagun *p667*
Reserve hotels at least a month in advance.
In Itanagar:
B **Donyi-Polo Ashok**, Sector C, T212626, F212611. 20 rooms, 2 a/c suites, restaurant.
D **Arun Subansiri**, T212806. 30 rooms, restaurant.
E **Bomdila**, T212664.
In Naharlagun:
E **Arunachal**, T244439. 15 a/c rooms (some deluxe).
E **Hornbill**, T244419. 14 rooms, some deluxe.
F **Lakshmi**, 19 rooms (1st floor better).
F **Youth Hostel**, 60 beds.

Bomdila *p667*
C-F places to say including: Siphiyanq, Phong, Tourist Lodge and La. Tours are provided by *Himalayan Holidays*, ABC Buildings, Main Market, T22016, F22656, www.Himalayan-holidays.com.

Tawang Monastery *p668*
D-E **Tourist Lodge**, T22359. 20 well-furnished but poorly maintained rooms, contact Deputy Commissioner, T22222.
Private lodges include·
D-E **Paradise**, Old Bazar, T22063, 22307. Pleasant, clean, spacious rooms with bath, some deluxe, small dining room serving simple, freshly cooked meals. The manager also arranges jeep hire and takes guided tours. *Himalayan Holidays*, T23151, organize tours and jeep hire.

Ziro *p668*
E **Blue Pine** and other guest houses.
F **Inspection Bungalow** and **Circuit House**, 8 rooms. Reservations Dy Comm, Lower Subansiri District.

Namdapha National Park *p669*
E **Camp Namdapha**, bamboo huts, log cabins and tented accommodation.
F **Deban Forest Bungalow**, overlooking the Noa Dihing River.

● Shopping

Itanagar-Naharlagun *p667*
The cotton textiles are colourful and are beautifully patterned. You can also get wooden masks and figures, cane belts and caps. **Handicrafts Centres** have shawls, *thangkas*, handloom, wood carvings, cane and bamboo work and carpets; you can watch tribal craftsmen trimming, cutting and weaving cane.

▲ Activities and tours

Itanagar-Naharlagun *p667*
Tour operators
Arunachal Travels, Itanagar, agents for *Indian Airlines*.
Himalayan Holiday, Naharlagun, T246232, F243051.
Nature Expeditions India, Gurgaon, T0124-6368601, neiindia@del3.vsnl.net.in.
Purvi Discovery, www.purvidiscovery.com.

Northeastern Hill States Listings: Arunachal Pradesh

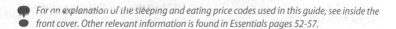
For an explanation of the sleeping and eating price codes used in this guide, see inside the front cover. Other relevant information is found in Essentials pages 52-57.

⊖ **Transport**

Itanagar-Naharlagun *p667*

Air
Nearest airport is Lilabari in Assam, 57 km from Naharlagun, 67 km from Itanagar, which has twice weekly flights from Guwahati. Transfer by bus. Indian Airlines; T212760. From Kolkata access is best through **Dibrugarh** (1½ hrs) by Indian Airlines, Mon, Wed, Fri, Sun.

Bus
APST from Naharlagun Bus Station. **Guwahati**, 381 km, 8 hrs, Rs 135; **Shillong**, 481 km, Rs 170. Ziro, 6 hrs, **North Lakhimpur**; **Bomdila**, Mon, Thu, 12 hrs. *Blue Hills* overnight coach to Guwahati, 11½ hrs. Enquiries: T244221.

Taxi
Naharlagun/Itanagar, Rs 170 plus fuel; Rs 25 (shared taxi).

Train
The nearest railhead is North Lakhimpur in Assam, 50 km from Naharlagun and 60 km from Itanagar; Harmoti station is 23 km from Naharlagun. Railway Out Agency, Naharlagun bus station, T244209. Nearest railheads for the bigger towns: **Along**: Silapathar; **Tezu**: Tinsukia; **Namdapha**: Margherita.

❶ **Directory**

Itanagar-Naharlagun *p667*
There are **banks** and **post offices**. **Hospitals** Itanagar, Naharlagun. **Tourist offices** India, Sector 'C', Naharlagun, T244328. **Arunachal Pradesh**, Naharlagun.

Nagaland

→ *Entry permits, see page 645. Population: 2 million. Area: 16,579 sq km. Altitude: 900-1,200 m. Languages: Angami, Ao, Chang and many other tribal languages.*
Nagaland, the narrow strip of mountain territory, has a long border with Myanmar (Burma) to the east. There are green valleys with meandering streams, high mountains with deep gorges and a rich variety of flora and fauna.▸▸ *For Sleeping, Eating and other listings, see pages 672-673.*

History
The British reached peace with the Nagas at the end of the 19th century and found them useful allies in the war against the Japanese, who advanced as far as Kohima before finally retreating from the region. After Indian independence, Nagaland became a separate state on 1 December 1963. A separatist movement for full independence continues, as the 1975 Shillong Accord was rejected. A series of month- to-month cease fires have been in effect during the 1990s with a year-long extension (the longest yet) being agreed since the present BJP government came to power.

Culture
Nagaland is almost entirely inhabited by 15 groups of the Tibeto-Burmese tribes – among them are the Angamis, Aos, Konyaks, Kukis, Lothas, Semas and Wanchus, collectively known as the **Nagas**. The Nagas were once head hunters and have been known for their fierceness and the regular raids they made on Assam and Burma. The warring tribes believed that since the enemy's animated soul (*yaha* in Wanchu dialect) was to be found at the nape of the neck, it could only be set free once beheaded. However, since the spiritual soul, *mio*, resided in the head and brought good fortune, enemy heads (and those of dead comrades) were prized as they could add to a community's own store of dead ancestors. The hilltop villages are protected by stone walls. The *morung*, a meeting house, acts as a boys' dormitory, and is used for storing weapons and once displayed the prizes of war (enemy heads). The huge sacred drum stands by each *morung* is a hollowed-out tree trunk carved to resemble

a buffalo head. Some believe that the Nagas' ancestors came from the seafaring nation of Sumatra and retain their link with their island past in their legends, village drums and ceremonial jewellery, which uses shells.

Religion Today 90% of the Nagas are Christians. Originally, although they revered natural 'spirits', the Nagas believed in a single overseeing but unknown superforce, and hence accepted the Christian Gospel quite readily. The Bible was translated into many of the Naga dialects (nearly every village has a church), yet the people have retained many of their old customs. There are also remains of the Hindu Kingdom of the Kacharis at Dimapur near the present capital Kohima, which was destroyed by the Assamese Ahoms in the 16th century.

The ancient **craft** of weaving on portable looms is still practised by the women. The strips of colourful cloth are stitched together to produce shawls in different patterns which distinguish each tribe. Ao warriors wear the red and black striped shawl with a central white band embroidered with symbols.

★ Kohima → *Phone code: 0370. Colour map 4, grid B5. Population: 78,600. Altitude: 1,500 m.*

The British-built town of Kohima lies in the valley between higher hills, alongside the immaculately kept war cemetery. Kohima attracted world attention during the Second World War because it was here that the Japanese advance was halted by the British and Indian forces. The original Angami Kohima Village is set on a hill above overlooking the Main Bazar.

Ins and outs

Getting there Dimapur has the nearest airport and railhead; buses (Rs 50) and taxis take about 3 hrs to Kohima centre. There are also buses from Guwahati and Imphal.

Getting around The central market area is compact enough; otherwise hire a taxi or use a minibus. There may be a strong military presence in town. See Transport, page 673, for further details.

Climate Best time to visit. Nov-Apr.

Sights

The **Second World War Cemetery** is in a beautiful setting, with well maintained lawns where rose bushes bloom in season. Two tall crosses stand out at the lowest and highest points. The stone markers each have a polished bronze plaque with epitaphs commemorating the men who fell here, to halt "the invasion of India by the forces of Japan in April 1944" by the British 14th Army under General William Slim. The flowering cherry tree which was used by Japanese soldiers as a snipers' post was destroyed; what grew from the old stump marks the limit of the enemy advance. At the base of the 2nd Division lower cross, near the main entrance, are the lines:

> When you go home
> Tell them of us and say
> For your tomorrow
> We gave our today.

The striking red-roofed **Cathedral of Reconciliation** (1995) on a hill overlooks the cemetery. Part funded by the Japanese government, representatives from both sides of the conflict attended the inauguration.

The **Main Bazar** attracts colourful tribal women who come to buy and sell their produce. The vast **Kohima Village** (Bara Basti) has a traditional Naga ceremonial gateway carved with motifs of guns, warriors and symbols of prosperity, though the 20th century has had its impact. The traditional Naga house here has crossed 'horns' on the gables, carved heads to signify the status of the family, huge baskets to hold the grain in front of the house and a trough where rice beer is made for the community.

Nagaland State Museum ⓘ *closed Sun and 2nd Sat, 0930-1430. At Bayavu Hill Colony, 1.5 km from centre,* has a collection of anthropological exhibits of the different Naga tribes. The basement has birds and animals of the Northeastern Hill states.

Excursions

Khonoma is an authentic tribal village, 20 km southwest, with a proud past surrounded by extensive terraces for rice cultivation. Another 20 km along the same road takes you to **Dzulekie**, at 2,134 m, with attractive waterfalls and trout streams in a deep rocky gorge. There is a Tourist Rest House and Cottages.

Trek to **Jopfu Peak**, at 3,043 m, 15 km south, between November and March for clear mountain views. **Dzukou Valley**, at 2,438 m, 15 km further south, is best from June to September, for its colourful rhododendrons, lilies and meadow flowers. A new campsite should be ready on the Jakhama route.

Dimapur

Dimapur, on the edge of the plains northwest of Kohima, is the railhead and has Nagaland's only airport. Busy and crowded, it is the state's main trading and commercial centre.

This was the old capital of the Kacharis (13th-16th century) and the **Kachari relics**, including a huge brick-built arch, are 1 km from the NST Bus Station. Nearby are 30 huge mushroom-shaped carved megaliths believed to represent the fertility cult. Visit **Chumukedima** old village on a hill above town, or trek to the **Triple Falls** at Seithekima.

Listings: Nagaland

🛌 Sleeping

Kohima *p671*
C Japfü (ITDC), PR Hill, T222721. 27 large heated rooms, restaurants.
E Ambassador, D Block, T222444. 12 rooms.
E Pine, Phool Bazar, T222234. 7 rooms with bath, 7 rooms.
E Valley View, Old Bus Station, T22738. 16 rooms.
F Tourist Lodge, New Minister's Hill, T22417. 17 rooms.

Dimapur *p672*
C-E Tragopan, Circular Rd near Overbridge, T03862-21416. 22 rooms, some a/c, restaurant.
D Tourist Lodge, near Nagaland Bus Station, T03862-20147. Double rooms, tourist office.

🍴 Eating

Kohima *p671*
Local dishes are simple but may include the unusual: zongtak beans, water snails, eels and fermented fish! Most places offer Indian and Chinese dishes.
𝖄 Dimori Cove, 6 km along NH39 towards Manipur. Small swimming pool, good views.
𝖄 Naga, Secretariat, also offers Japanese. Pleasant, lively.

✹ Festivals and events

Kohima *p671*
The different tribes celebrate their special festivals when priests perform ceremonies followed by dancing, singing and drinking.
Feb: Sekrenyi is celebrated by Angamis for 10 days when all work in the fields ceases.
Apr: Konyak Aoling, a 6-day 'New Year'

● *For an explanation of the sleeping and eating price codes used in this guide, see inside the*
● *front cover. Other relevant information is found in Essentials pages 52-57.*

festival marking the beginning of spring.
May: Ao Moatsu, 6-day festival marking the beginning of the growing season. **Tourism Cultural Festivals** in **May** and **Oct**.

◯ Shopping

Kohima *p671*
Warm and colourful Naga shawls are excellent. You can also get beads, shoulder bags, decorative spears, table mats, wood carvings and bamboo baskets.
Gürttel is recommended.

▲ Activities and tours

Kohima *p671*
Nagaland Tourism, offers 4 and 5-day group cultural, and adventure (trekking, tribal) tours.

◉ Transport

Kohima *p671*
Air and train
See Dimapur below.

Bus
Blue Hills luxury coaches go to other capitals in the Northeast; Green Hills, Taxi Stand, for coaches and flight bookings.

Taxi
Taxis from Dimapur, Rs 500, shared, Rs 100.
Nagaland State Transport (NST), T222265.

Dimapur *p672*
Air
The airport is 5 km from town. Indian Airlines, T29366. Airport, T24441. To **Kolkata** via **Guwahati**, Tue, Thu, Sat, Sun.

Bus
SNT and private buses from Golaghat Rd to **Guwahati** 292 km (10-11 hrs), **Imphal** 142 km (5-6 hrs); from Nagaland Bus Stand to **Kohima**, 3 hrs.

Train
To **Delhi (OD)**: *Brahmaputra Mail, 4055,* 0510, 48 hrs. **Dibrugarh**: *Kamrup Exp, 5959,* 2225, 8½ hrs. *Brahmaputra Mail, 4056,* 2005, 9½ hrs. **Guwahati**: *Rajdhani, 2423A,* Thu, 2315, 5½ hrs; *Kamrup Exp, 5960,* 2235, 8 hrs.

❶ Directory

Kohima *p671*
There are **banks**, a **post office** and a **hospital**, T222916. **Tourist offices**, T222214.

Manipur

→ *Entry permits, see page 645. Five-day permits can be issued by all missions abroad, all FRROs, Home Commissioner, Imphal.*

The former princely state of Manipur, the 'land of jewels' bordering Myanmar, has a low-lying basin in its centre surrounded by hills that rise to over 2,000 m. The reedy Lake Loktak, the largest freshwater lake in the Northeast, and the flat-bottomed basin and river valleys that drain into it, add to the beauty of the land. It is the land of graceful Rasa dances, of the famous Women's market in Imphal, of rare orchids, and the endangered thamin, the brow-antlered deer. ▶▶ *For Sleeping, Eating and other listings, see pages 676-677.*

History

Manipur has always been quite independent of its neighbouring tribal areas. It was often invaded from Burma but also enjoyed long periods of relatively stable government. At the end of the Indo-Burmese War in 1826 it was brought into India by the Treaty of Yandabo, British sovereignty being recognized in 1891. In 1939 a remarkable women's social revolt ('Nupilan' from 'nupi' – women and 'lan' – war) led to government action against monopolistic traders. The contemporary party *Nisha Bundh* consists of an all-women patrol that seeks to keep the streets safe at night. The role of women traders can be seen most colourfully in the women's market.

During the Second World War Imphal was occupied by the Japanese. After Indian independence Manipur became a Union Territory and achieved statehood in 1972.

People → *Population: 2.4 million. Area: 22,327 sq km.*

The majority of the population are Vaishnavite Hindus. They belong to the *Meithe* tribe and are related to the *Shans* of Burma, who live in the valleys. The 20 or so hill-tribes who constitute about a third of the population are Christian.

Like the Nagas, the Manipuris have a reputation for being great warriors, still practising their skills of wrestling, sword fighting and martial arts. Most of wars were fought across the border in Burma. They are also keen on sport, and polo, which is said to have originated in Manipur, is the principal sport.

Dance, drama and music

The ancient musical forms of the valley dwellers are closely connected to the worship of Vishnu, expressed in **Manipuri dancing**. The *Rasa* dances performed at every ceremony are characterized by graceful and restrained movements and delicate hand gestures. The ornate costumes worn by the veiled women are glittering and colourful; the stiff, heavy skirts barely move. The *Sankirtana* dance often precedes the *Rasa*. It is usually performed by men and is vigorous, rhythmic and athletic, and they play on the *pung* (drums) and cymbals while they dance. The tribal ritual dances, some of which are performed by priests and priestesses before deities, may end in a trance. Others can last several days, observing a strict form and accompanied by the drone of a bowed instrument, *pana*. *Thang-ta* is a skilful martial art performed to beating drums, and is practised by both sexes dressed in black.

Political developments

Troubled by a variety of internal conflicts since the late 1980s and with separatist movements voicing open dissent with rule from New Delhi, Manipur's State Assembly has had an unsettled recent history. Although democracy is highly popular, with over 90% of the 1.3 million electorate turning out to vote in the election held in February 2000, instability has continued. While the Congress party won the largest number of seats in the 60-strong Assembly the government was formed by an alliance of minority parties, led by the Samata Party, which was a partner of the BJP in India's central government. In May 2001 the coalition broke down. In the face of continuing political violence, on 2 June 2001 the Central Government imposed President's Rule, despite the pleas of a new five party alliance, the People's Democratic Alliance, to try and form a government including the BJP at its core.

Imphal → *Phone code: 0385. Colour map 4, grid B5. Population: 217,300.*

The capital Imphal (from *yumpham*, homestead) lies in the heart of an oval-shaped valley cut through by narrow rivers and surrounded by forested hills. The city has the large open space of the Polo Ground but is otherwise not particularly attractive. Because of its location it has become a principal export route for Myanmar's illegal drugs.

Ins and outs

Getting there The airport is 8 km south of the city with taxis and autos for transfer. Bus travel is tiring because of the long distances involved.

Getting around The dusty centre and the 'Ima Market' are easy to cover on foot. Auto and cycle-rickshaws can take you to places beyond the centre. See Transport, page 676, for further details.

Sights

The **Shri Govindaji Temple** to Krishna with two golden domes adjoins the royal palace. This Vaishnavite centre with shrines to Vishnu, Balaram, Krishna and Jagannath has regular performances of ceremonial dancing (Manipuri dancing originated here). Overlooking the University (8 km), the historic palace of **Langthaband**, with its ceremonial houses and temples, stands on the hills among formally planted pine and jackfruit trees, 8 km along the Indo-Burma road.

Khwairamband Bazar ('Ima Market') ① *0700-1900*, in the town centre is the largest women's bazar perhaps anywhere in the country. It is an excellent place for handicrafts and handloom goods, as well as vegetables, fish and other foodstuffs, jewellery and cosmetics. As many as 3,000 women gather here every day. It represents a form of family work-sharing, for while younger mothers stay at home to look after children, the older women and grandmothers come to market. The women do not bargain and will be offended if you try to pick through fruit or vegetables, as they take great pride in serving only the best quality at a fair price. Their own union helps to maintain the bazar and is a potent political force.

The **War Cemeteries** are managed by the Commonwealth War Graves Commission, one on the Imphal-Dimapur NH39 and the other on the Imphal-Ukhrul Road. They are beautifully maintained and serenely peaceful sites.

The **Konghampat Orchidarium** ① *best season Apr-May*, 12 km along the NH39, set up by the Forest Department, has over 120 species of orchids including some rare ones.

Manipur State Museum ① *near Polo Ground, T220709, closed Mon, 1000-1630*, has a collection of art, archaeology, natural history, geology and textiles, and also costumes, portraits and old arms. **Matua Museum** is a private collection of art, textiles and manuscripts to preserve the identity of Manipuri culture.

Excursions

Moirang, 45 km from Imphal, on Loktak Lake, is noted for its early Manipuri folk-culture and the traditional folk dance form. The temple to the forest god, *Thankgjing*, has robes of the 12th-century Moirang kings and holds a ritual dance festival each summer. During the Second World War Moirang was the HQ of the Indian National Army (INA) for a short time, and their flag was raised in the palace grounds as a symbol of national independence for the first time on 12 April 1944. There is an INA memorial and a war museum. You can stay on **Sendra Island** in Loktak Lake (see Listings page 676).

Imphal

Sleeping
1 Eastern Star
2 Imphal

Eating
1 Sangam
2 Welcome

3 White Palace

Not to scale

Keibul Lamjao National Park

① *The nearest airport and railway are at Dimapur, 32 km from Imphal. Best time to visit: Dec-May. Temperature range: 41°C to 0°C. Rainfall: 1,280 mm.*

The park, covering 25 sq km, is the only floating sanctuary of its kind. It has a small population of thamin (Sangai), the endangered brow-antlered deer. The Sanctuary was set up in 1977 on Loktak Lake when the swamps, the natural habitat of the thamin, were reclaimed for cultivation resulting in the near extinction of this 'dancing deer'. The thamin feed on mats of floating humus covered with grass and *phumdi* reeds until the rainy season when they move to the hills. You can travel through the creeks on small boats. There is also a viewing tower on Babel Ching hillock. Other wildlife include hog deer, wild boar, panther, fishing cat and water birds. *Forest Lodges* at Phubala and Sendra. Travel restrictions for foreigners as elsewhere in the Northeast.

Listings: Manipur

● Sleeping

Imphal *p674, map p675*
D Anand Continental, Khoyathong Rd, T220459. Good rooms with bath and TV.
D Imphal, Dimapur Rd, North AOC, T220459, F320339, manipur@x400.nicgw.nic.in. 60 large rooms, some a/c, modern facilities, restaurant.
D White Palace, 113 MG Ave, T220599. 26 rooms.
D-E Excellency, Airport Rd, T225401, F222936. Varied rooms, some a/c , restaurant.
F Youth Hostel, Khuman Lampak, dorm (Rs 30). Govindaji Temple prepares local dishes with advance notice.

Sendra Island *p675*
F Sendra Tourist Home, cheap beds, small restaurant, contact Department of Tourism, T20802 (Imphal). A very peaceful spot with lovely views of the lake where fishermen, who live on islands of floating weeds, use nets to farm fish and water chestnut (*singhara*).

● Eating

Imphal *p674, map p675*
Manipur is a 'dry' state. In hotel restaurants, try *iromba*, the Manipuri savoury dish of fish, vegetables and bamboo shoots and the sweet *Kabok* made with molasses and rice.
Sangam and **Welcome** are inexpensive.

● Entertainment

Imphal *p674, map p675*
Cultural shows with Manipuri dancing at **Rupmahal**, BT Rd and at **Kala Academy**.

● Festivals and events

Imphal *p674, map p675*
Feb-Mar: Yaosang on full-moon night, boys and girls dance the Thabal Chongba and sing in a circle in the moonlight. A festival in **May-Jun** is held in honour of forest gods. **Sep**: Heikru Hitongba is mainly non-religious, when there are boat races along a 16 m wide moat in narrow boats with large numbers of rowers.

▲▲ Activities and tours

Imphal *p674, map p675*
Manipur Tourism tours to Sri Govindaji Temple, Bishnupur, INA Memorial, Moirang, KL National Park and the Loktak Lake, depart *Hotel Imphal*, Sun 0800.

● Transport

Imphal *p674, map p675*
Air
Taxi to town, Rs 150. **Indian Airlines**, MG Ave, T220999, airport T220888: **Kolkata**, daily (some via **Aizwal**); **Delhi**, **Guwahati**, **Jorhat**, **Silchar**, 2-3 weekly. **Sahara**, T330834. **Jet Airways**, *Hotel Nirmala*, MG Ave, T230831, airport T227499: **Guwahati**, Tue, Wed; **Kolkata** (via Guwahati), Tue, Wed (via Jorhat), Thu, Sun.

Bus
Long distance Buses connect Dimapur (215 km) the nearest railhead, with **Imphal** (8 hrs), Rs 45; share taxi Rs 100. Daily private buses (some a/c) for **Guwahati** (579 km), 24 hrs, via Silchar (198 km) to Shillong, through: **Blue Hills**, MG Ave, T226443. **Manipur Golden Travels**, MG Ave, T221332. **Kangleipak**, T222131.

Rickshaw
Auto and cycle-rickshaws are available locally.

Taxi
Tourist taxis from Tourist Information Centre. Rest unmetered.

❶ Directory

Imphal *p674, map p675*
Banks Banks in Bazar, Thangal Bazar and MG Ave. **Hospital** Hospitals at Porompat and Lamphalpat. **Post office** There is a GPO. **Tourist companies** Seven Sisters,

North AOC, T228778, F222936. For touring the region. **Manipur**, Hotel Imphal, T220802, F224354, manipur@x400.nicgw.nic.in. 0900-1630, closed Sun, 2nd Sat. **Meghalaya**, Hotel Imphal, T220459. **India**, Old Lambulane, Jail Rd, T221131. Closed Sat, Sun, airport desk opens for flights.

Mizoram

→ *Entry permits, see page 645. The state government can also issue permits. Population: 891,100. Area: 21,000 sq km.*
The southernmost of the Northeastern Hill States, Mizoram lies between Myanmar (Burma) and Bangladesh. Until 1972 it was known as the 'Lushai Hills', a district of Assam. The half a dozen or so parallel north-south ranges of hills rising to over 2,000 m are covered in dense forests of bamboo and wild banana. At the bottom of the deep gorges the rivers run in narrow ribbons. ▸▸ *For Sleeping, Eating and other listings, see pages 678-679.*

Culture

Mizo is derived from *mi* (man) and *zo* (highland), a collective name given by their neighbours to a number of tribes that settled in the area. The different groups of tribal people are thought to have originally come from Northwest China in the seventh century, gradually travelled southwards and reached this area less than 300 years ago. The Mizos were animists, believing in good and evil spirits of the woodland. Mizo villages perch on top of the ridges with the chief's house and the *zawlbuk* (bachelors' dormitory) in the centre. Built on steep slopes, houses often have front doors at street level while the backs stand precariously on stilts. Every home proudly displays orchids and pots of geranium, begonia and balsam. Over a thousand varieties of medicinal plants grow wild.

Religion The raiding of British tea plantations up until the end of the 19th century led to the introduction of Inner Line permits which restricted movement of people but gave free access to missionaries, who carried out their religious duties and introduced literacy, which is exceptionally high in this state, the language having adopted the Roman script. Most Mizos are Christian converts and have a strong tradition of Western choral singing. The mainly nomadic Chakmas along the western border practise a religion which combines Hinduism, Buddhism and animism. Some even claim descent from one of the lost tribes of Israel. A few **Kukis** who were once headhunters, and **Chins**, have converted to Judaism.

Economy

Rice and maize, supplemented by shifting cultivation, supports 75% of the population. There are no mineral resources exploited yet and no large-scale industries though the government has sponsored some light industrial development in Aizawl. Handicrafts and handwoven textiles predominate.

Aizawl→ *Phone code: 0389. Map 4, grid B5 and C5. Population: 229,700. Altitude: 1,132 m.*

The road from Silchar comes upon the isolated capital Aizawl (pronounced Eye-jull), built along a central ridge and several surrounding spurs. White-painted churches stand out above the residential buildings that cling precariously to the hillsides.

Getting there Flights connect Aizawl with Kolkata, Guwahati and Imphal. Travellers from the rest of the Northeast usually arrive by bus via Silchar to the north.

Getting around From the central market area and Treasury Square, it is a steep 2 km uphill climb to Chandmari and Chaltlang Hill, further up. Minibuses and taxis cover most areas of town.

Climate Temperature: summer, maximum 29°C, minimum 20°C. Winter, maximum 21°C, minimum 11°C. Annual rainfall: 3,000 mm.

Sights

Bara Bazar, the main shopping centre, is on the other side of the central ridge. The steep Zion Street is lined with stalls selling garments and Mizo music cassettes. In the main market people gather in their traditional costumes to sell produce from farms and homesteads including river crab in little wicker baskets. At the **Weaving Centre** you can watch women at their looms weaving traditional shawls which are for sale. **Luangmual Handicrafts Centre**, 7 km away, has a *khumbeu* ceremonial bamboo hat made using waterproof wild *hnahthial* leaves.

Mizoram State Museum ⓘ *McDonald's Hill in town centre, Tue-Fri 0930-1600, Mon 1200-1600*, is small but has an interesting collection of historical relics, ancient costumes and traditional implements.

Listings: Mizoram

◉ Sleeping

Mizoram *p677*
In **downtown Zarkawt**:
D **Ahimsa**, T341133. Comfortable rooms, restaurant.
In **Chaltlang**, high above town:
D-E **Ritz**, Bara Bazar, T326247. Comfortable rooms, some with bath, good restaurant.
E **Tourist Lodge**, T341083. 14 large but tired rooms, good restaurant, good views.

◑ Eating

Mizoram *p677*
Labyrinth, Chandmari. Serves cheap Chinese and Indian food.
You can find cheap local Mizo food around Bara Bazar.

⊛ Festivals and events

Mizoram *p677*
Early Mar: Chapchar Kut, a traditional spring festival marking the end of *Jhumming* is

celebrated with singing, dancing and feasting. **Cheraw** is performed by nimble-footed girls who dance in and out of bamboo poles, clapped together by teams of young men. Similar dances are performed in Myanmar, Thailand and the Philippines.

⊖ Transport

Mizoram *p677*
Air
New Langpui Airport (37 km north); for tickets and bus transfer *Quality Travels*, Chandmari, T341265. *Indian Airlines* flies to **Kolkata** and **Guwahati**, Mon, Wed, Fri, with some flights via Imphal.

Bus
Mizoram State Transport. Buses to **Silchar**, 180 km (9 hrs), Rs 150, the nearest railhead; 4-WD Sumos are quicker. Private buses to **Guwahati** via Silchar and Shillong, Rs 280.

Taxi
About Rs 200 for 2 hrs' sightseeing in town.

● *For an explanation of the sleeping and eating price codes used in this guide, see inside the* ● *front cover. Other relevant information is found in Essentials pages 52-57.*

❶ Directory

Mizoram *p677*
Bank State Bank of India. **Post** office GPO, Treasury Square.

Hospital Civil Hospital, T342318, Presbyterian Hospital, Durtland (7 km).
Tourist office Mizoram, Treasury Square, T341227; apply to Mizoram House elsewhere for permits.

Tripura

→ *Permits are no longer necessary but visitors must 'Register' at Agartala airport. Population: 3.19 million. Area: 10,492 sq km.*

Still extensively forested, the tiny former Hindu Princely State of Tripura managed to retain a large degree of independence through much of the last millennium. Extensively forested, its predominantly tribal people retain centuries-old practices, though Agartala begins to show signs of modern development. ▸▸ *For Sleeping, Eating and other listings, see pages 681-682.*

The land

Covering just under 10,500 sq km, Tripura is almost surrounded on the north, west and south by Bangladesh. The north falls into four valleys, separated by hills rising to just under 1,000 m. The more open land of the south is still forested. Indian hardwoods include sal (*Shorea robusta*), which is economically important. Parts of the state get over 4,000 mm of annual rainfall.

History

Tripura is believed to have existed in the times of the epic *Mahabharata*. Historically, it was ruled by the **Manikyas** of Indo-Mongolian origin from the 14th century. Since Tripura was constantly feuding with her neighbours, particularly the Nawabs of Bengal, the British offered help to the Maharaja and established a protectorate, separating the princely state from tribal lands outside the control of the Hindu rajas. The Manikyas ruled continuously right up to 15 October 1949 when Tripura acceded to India. It became a full state in 1972. In the 1930s, Maharaja Bir Bikram made his kingdom more accessible by opening an airport. **Rabindranath Tagore** based his play *Visarjan* and novel *Rajasri* on the legends of the Manikyas.

Culture

Tripura remains predominantly tribal, with distinctive customs. A typical tribal welcome involves building a bamboo arch, garlanding the honoured guest while wafting incense. An egg, believed to absorb evil spirits, is rubbed in paddy, dipped in water and then symbolically thrown away. You may notice brightly coloured parasols in the village pond which are put there in honour of dead ancestors.

Modern Tripura

Rice is the main crop while rubber has gained importance (now second only to Kerala in production). Jute, cotton, tea and fruit are important cash crops. Sugarcane, mustard and potatoes are also grown. In the last 10 years the Indian Government has encouraged small industries. Weaving, carpentry, pottery and basket making are common. Tripura suffers from the continuing failure of Bangladesh and India to agree a trade and travel treaty, which would allow goods to be taken in transit across Bangladesh. This adds hugely to the time and cost of transport to Kolkata, still a major market for Tripura goods, and lorries can take two weeks to make a journey that could take two days by the direct route.

The **democratic process** in the state operates under severe constraints. Politically motivated killings and kidnaps are common. The Disturbed Areas Act operates in the majority of the 45 police station areas. Reang refugees continue to flood in from Mizoram and the temporary camps in the north are full. Election to the Tripura Hill Areas Autonomous District Council held on 3 May 2000 were won by the newly formed Indigenous Peoples Front of Tripura who defeated the Left Front, but there were widespread threats and intimidation.

There is a high degree of **literacy** in the state, in 2001 total literacy reaching nearly 75%, and despite its small size it has has no less than 17 daily newspapers (two in English and 15 in Bengali)!

Agartala → *Phone code: 0381. Colour map 4, grid C4. Population: 189,300. Altitude: 1,280 m.*

Once a pleasant city, Agartala has mushroomed unchecked and the growth in population has far outstripped the essential services. The city's redbrick official buildings contrast with the British preference for white paint, still obvious on some important structures, notably the Maharaja's palace. While there are some pleasant suburbs, the centre's open drains with wooden covers are prone to flooding in the monsoons.

Ins and outs

Getting there The most convenient way to get to Agartala is by air but tickets are in short supply. Travellers must register their arrival and departure. Transfer from the airport is by taxi or bus which arrive at the Motor stand to the southeast of the palace.

Getting around The centre is compact enough to cover on foot; otherwise you can get a rickshaw. There may be a strong military presence in town. Travelling outside Agartala is hazardous because of tribal insurgents who have taken to kidnapping for ransom. Some sections of the Agartala-Assam Highway are closed except to vehicles travelling in convoy; there are usually 3 or 4 each day. See Transport, page 681, for further details.

Climate Summer maximum 35°C, minimum 24°C. Winter maximum 27°C, minimum 13°C. Annual rainfall: 2,240 mm, Jun-Aug. Best season: Sep-Mar. Clothing: cottons in summer, woollens in winter.

Sights

The airport road from the north of town leads to the **Ujjayanta Palace**. Built by Maharaja Radha Kishore Manikya in 1901, it stands amidst large well-kept 'Mughal' gardens with pools and floodlit musical fountains. The vast palace has magnificent tiled floors, a carved wooden ceiling in the Chinese room, and beautifully crafted front doors. Now the State Legislature, it is normally closed to visitors, but you may ask to look around when the Assembly is not in session. The late 19th-century **Jagannath temple** across an artificial lake in front of the palace, rises to a striking orange four-storeyed *sikhara*.

The **Temple of Chaturdasa Devata**, 8 km east, near Old Agartala, is dedicated to 14 gods and goddesses, represented by their heads only. It combines the Bengali Bankura style with a Buddhist *stupa* type structure. In July, *Kharchi Puja,* which has evolved from a tribal festival, attracts worshippers from all over Tripura.

Tripura Government Museum ① *HG Basak Rd, weekdays 1000-1700*, has a small but well-displayed collection of rare stone images, old coins, Bengal *kantha* embroidery and archaeological finds from the region including 8th- to 10th-century Buddhist sculptures from Pilak.

Excursions

Sipahijala ① *0700-1600, hourly buses from Agartala*, a botanical garden with a small zoo (elephant rides) and a boating lake, is well worth a visit. It is 33 km away. The zoo is beautifully kept (Mr Bhowmik, in charge, was trained in London) and new enclosures provide a more natural habitat. There are tigers, lions, cheetahs, bears and a rhino; the spectacle monkeys live in the trees above while the lake attracts migrating birds. It may be possible to visit a rubber plantation and watch the processing on a trip.

Neermahal ① *tourist coaches from Agartala, once there, singing boatmen row you across the lake!* 53 km south, is a water-palace built in 1930 by the late Maharaja in the middle of **Rudrasagar Lake** attracting migrating birds. The striking white and red fairytale castle with towers, kiosks, pavilions and bridges is fun to explore. Now being restored, it is particularly beautiful illuminated at night. Accommodation at

Tripura Sundari Temple, 57 km away, in the ancient capital **Udaipur**, was built on Dhanisagar hill in the mid-16th century. The 'Matabari' is believed to be one of the 51 holy *pithasthans* mentioned in the *Tantras*, where the Mother Goddess is served by red-robed priests. The pond behind has huge turtles which are delighted to be fed. A large fair is held during *Diwali* in October/November. There is a good *Lodge*, and buses and jeeps from Agartala.

Northeastern Hill States Listings: Tripura

Listings: Tripura

● Sleeping

Agartala *p680*
Most **D-E** have some a/c rooms.
C-D Welcome Palace, HG Basak Rd, T224940, welcome_palace@usa.net. The newest and most comfortable hotel with some very clean a/c rooms, good restaurant.
D Rajdhani, BK Rd, near *Indian Airlines* (northeast of Palace), T225387. 27 clean rooms with bath, car hire, 'first lift in Tripura!'.
D Royal Guest House, Palace Compound, West Gate, T225652. Rooms with bath, restaurant.
D-E Brideway, Palace Ground, T207298. 12 rooms (some a/c wih bath), room service (Indian, Chinese).
D-E Meenakshi, Hawkers Corner, Khushbagan (near Museum), T225810. Indian meals.
D-F Ambar, Sakuntala Rd (south of Palace), T228439. Rooms with bath (some a/c), restaurant.
E-F New Sonali, GB Hospital Rd, Kunjaban, T225322. 12 rooms, Indian and Chinese food.

Sipahijala *p681*
F Forest Bungalow, in well-kept gardens

above the lake, meals provided. Contact Chief Conservator of Forests, Agartala, T223779.

Neermahal *p681*
E-F Sagarmahal Tourist Lodge, on the lake, with 44 comfortable rooms, restaurant.

● Eating

Agartala *p680*
Abhishek, LNB Rd. Seating out of doors and in.
Kurry Klub, at *Welcome Palace*. Comfortable a/c, good Indian and Chinese.

Neermahal *p681*
Superb Bengali snacks and sweets are sold along the road and simple clean restaurants serve good meals (Rs 25-40).

● Transport

Agartala *p680*
Air
Airport transfer, 13 km: taxi, Rs 135; auto-rickshaw, Rs 70. *Indian Airlines,* Palace Compound, T225470, Airport, T342020, to **Kolkata**, daily; **Guwahati**, Wed, Sat, Sun.

● *For an explanation of the sleeping and eating price codes used in this guide, see inside the*
● *front cover. Other relevant information is found in Essentials pages 52-57.*

Bus

Local Service in the city.
Long distance Travelling out of Agartala is difficult; see 'Ins & Outs'.

Tripura STC Bus Stand is on LN Bari Rd. To/from **Dharmanagar**, 8 hrs. Private bus to **Silchar** (317 km). **Bangladesh border** crossing, just 2 km from the centre, is convenient for anyone with a visa to get to Dhaka which is 4 hrs by road and 3 hrs by train. The Bangladesh Visa Office is by *Brideway Hotel*; fee for UK nationals: about US$46 for 6 months; US$23 for nationals of USA and Australia.

Rickshaw
Auto and cycle rickshaw. Sightseeing – about Rs 50 and Rs 30 per hr.

Taxi
Tourist taxi from Directorate of Information, about Rs 500 per day.

Train
Kumarghat, 140 km, is the nearest railhead. Bookings at State Bus Stand.

● Directory

Agartala *p680*
Bank State Bank of India, HG Basak Rd.
Hospital GB Hospital, Kunjaban. **Post office** GPO: Chowmohani. **Tour operator** Green Valley Travels. **Tourist office** Ujjayant Palace, East Wing, T225930.

‖ Footprint features

Introduction

The Sun Temple at **Konark** acted as a beacon for sailors for nearly a millennium, while the great and architecturally astonishing temples of **Bhubaneswar** and **Puri** have drawn pilgrims in their millions from across India. Meanwhile holidaymakers from Kolkata have enjoyed Puri's broad, sandy beaches.

Over 2,000 years ago the fertile delta on which **Bhubaneswar**, the modern capital, stands witnessed one of the most significant battles of India's history when the Emperor Asoka, having massacred his Kalingan opponents, converted to Buddhism and laid the foundations for one of the great empires of world history.

Inland, Orissa's beautiful hills, home to the tribal peoples, are among the least densely populated and most densely forested regions of India. Beneath them lie rich resources of iron ore, coal, bauxite and other minerals, but despite some mining activity much of the interior retains its remote charm.

Orissa

★ Don't miss...

❶ Visit a few of the 500 or so temples surrounding **Bindusagar Tank** in Bhubaneswar and then see a performance of the classical *Odissi* dance or some folk dancing, page 691.

❷ Visit the **Jain caves** at Udayagiri. The Rani Gumpha has some particularly fine carvings, page 698.

❸ Watch the Kolkata crowd enjoying themselves in **Puri** but try to be there at the end of June during the car festival when 500,000 celebrate in a riot of colour and noise, page 701.

❹ Check out the temple porch at the World Heritage site of **Konark**, which has some of the best sculptures in India, page 703.

❺ If you can cope with the pollution and the lack of accommodation, **Paradeep** at the mouth of the Mahanadi River is the place to watch giant Pacific Ridley turtles lay their eggs, page 712.

❻ There are some interesting and picturesque markets at **Nandapur** and **Ramgiri**, page 723.

CHHATTISGARH

JHARKHAND

○ Rourkela

○ Sundergarh

○ Khiching

Similipal National Park

○ Keonjhargarh

Usbakothi Wildlife Sanctuary

Sambalpur

Baragarh

Phulbani

○ Jaugada

Berhampur ○

○ Chandragiri

Taptpani

Gopalpur ○

Bay of Bengal

Udayagiri & Khandagiri

❷

Cuttack

Udayagiri ○ ○ Ratnagiri
○ Lalitgiri

Bhubaneswar ❶

Puri ○ ○ Konark ❹

❸

Chilika Lake

○ Chandipur

Paradeep ❺

N

0 km   50
0 miles   50

Jeypore ●

Koraput ● ❻

ANDHRA PRADESH

❻

Background → *Population: 36.7 million. Area: 156,000 sq km.*

The land

Near the coast it is easy to get the impression that Orissa is nothing but a flat alluvial plain with mile after mile of paddy fields along the coastal plains. **Chilika Lake** in the south, only a few metres deep, covers up to 1,100 sq km. The coastline has shifted significantly in the last 2,000 years as the land has risen relative to sea level along long stretches. Chiliika Lake itself had become cut off from the sea until a newly opened channel reconnected it, allowing sea water to replenish the declining salinity levels.

Inland it is a different story. Ninety per cent of Orissa is made up not of alluvium but of the ancient rocks of peninsular India, some with huge iron ore resources. Until recently the densely forested hills were made inhospitable both by the difficulty of clearing the forest and by the devastating prevalence of malaria. Dense deciduous *sal* forest, peopled only by tribal groups living in isolation with a 'stone age' culture, dominated the landscape, and shifting cultivation was widely practised. There are still rarely travelled roads and the scenic rewards for the slowness of parts of the journey are great. The lakes to the south of Koraput in the 3,000 million year old hills are particularly striking. Much of the forest has now been severely thinned and cultivation has spread up many of the valleys but there remain remote and sparsely populated areas, and an atmosphere of quiet stillness unimaginable when you are on the plains.

Climate Lying just south of the Tropic of Cancer, Orissa is very warm throughout the year, though the hills are sufficiently high to bring a welcome coolness. January and February are dry, but showers increase through the spring and the monsoon from June to September is one of the wettest in India. Coastal districts are particularly at risk from cyclones in October and November. The most recent of these was the catastrophic cyclone of October 1999 which caused the death of over 8,000 people, and an estimated three million cattle, as well as inflicting massive damage to villages, forests and agricultural land. It is best to avoid the monsoon season. Even in October-November cyclones may strike the coastal districts with devastating force.

History

Coastal Orissa, a part of the ancient kingdom of Kalinga, grew prosperous through trading, using its port of Kalinganagar as early as the fourth century BC. Their colonial influence extended as far as modern Indonesia. The Mauryan Emperor Asoka crushed the Kalingan Kingdom at Dhauligiri in 262 BC, but after experiencing the horrors of war and the accompanying bloodshed he converted to Buddhism. He preached the philosophy of peace, and while Buddhism flowered, his tolerance allowed Jainism and Hinduism to continue. After Asoka, the first century BC King Kharavela, a fervent Jain, built up a vast empire, recorded in the remarkable Udayagiri caves near Bhubaneswar. After Kharavela, separate political territories emerged in the north and centre of the region. Maritime trade flourished and Buddhism became a popular again.

The greatest period of temple building in Bhubaneswar coincided with the **Kesaris** (sixth-11th century), to be followed by the Ganga Dynasty (11th-15th century), who were responsible for the Jagannath Temple in Puri (circa 1100) and the Sun Temple at Konark (circa 1250).

Orissa resisted the annexation of her territory by **Muslims**. After a short period of Afghan rule, the powerful Mughals arrived as conquerors in 1592 and during their reign destroyed many of the Bhubaneswar temples. It was their violent disruption of temple life in Puri and Bhubaneswar that later led the Brahmin community to ban all non-Hindus from the precincts of the Lingaraj and Jagannath temples. The Mughals were followed by the Marathas in 1751.

In 1765 after Clive's win at Plassey, parts of Orissa, Bihar and Bengal were acquired by the **East India Company** with further gains in Cuttack and Puri at the beginning of the following century. Thus, by 1803, British rule extended over the whole region.

Culture

Orissa has the third highest concentration of tribals in India. The tribal **population**, nearly 25% of the total, live mainly in the Koraput, Kandhamal, Sundargarh and Mayurbhanj districts. Some 62 *Adivasi* ('ancient inhabitants') or tribal groups live in remote hill regions of the state, some virtually untouched by modern civilization, and so have kept their tribal traditions alive. Each has a distinct language and pattern of social and religious customs. They are not economically advanced and literacy is low. However, the tribal groups have highly developed artistic ability, as seen in their body paintings, ornaments, weaving and wall paintings. Music and dance also form an integral part of life-cycle ceremonies and seasonal festivals. They are remarkable in having maintained their distinct identities in a hostile and exploitative environment. There has been a new interest in their rich heritage and the Tourism Department is keen to promote visits to tribal areas, see below, page 722.

> ✷ *Suggested reading, Norman Lewis 'A Goddess in the Stones'*

The **Khonds**, the most numerous (about 100,000), live mainly in the west and speak Kuvi, a Dravidian language, and Kui. They used to practise human 'Meriah' sacrifice (now replaced by animal sacrifice), offering the blood to their supreme goddess represented by a piece of wood or stone, to ensure fertility of the soil. They use bows and arrows to protect themselves against wild animals.

The **Santals**, the second most numerous group, come from the northern districts of Mayurbhanj and Balasore. In the northwestern industrial belt, they have abandoned their aboriginal lifestyle to go and work in the steel mills. They belong to 12 patrilineal clans (*paris* or *sibs*) and speak Santali, one of the oldest languages in India. Santals believe that evil spirits in trees, forests and rivers have to be appeased by magic. The women carry out witchcraft while the *ojhas* are the medicine men. Music and dance are an integral part of their daily life, particularly during festivals in October-November and March-April.

In the southern districts, especially in Koraput, there are about 6,000 of the **Bondos** ('naked people') of Tibeto-Burmese origin. They live isolated on high hills, growing rice by shifting cultivation and keeping domesticated cows and goats, and can only be seen when they come to trade in local markets. Bondo women are noticeable for their striking bead, brass and silver necklaces, and their shaved heads, decorated with plaits of palmyra leaves.

The **Saoras**, another major tribe, mostly live in hilly areas of Parlakhemundi (Gajapati district) and Gunupur (Rayagada district). Saoras live in extended families (*birindas*), descended from a common ancestor, under a headman who is helped by a religious leader. The *shamans* are able to communicate with watchful deified ancestors. Village houses of mud and stone walls are raised on plinths with high wooden platforms inside to store grain. The walls are decorated with remarkable paintings; traditional designs now incorporate hunters on aeroplanes and bicycles!

The **Koya** who live in villages in clearings in the middle of dense forest are distinguished by their headgear made of bison horn.

Dance, drama and music The region's magnificent temple sculpture gave rise to a classical dance form, **Odissi**, which shadows the postures, expressions and lyrical qualities of the carved figures. The dance was a ritual offering performed in the *nata mandirs* by the *maharis* (temple dancers) resplendent in their costume and jewellery. The subject is often Jayadev's *Gita Govinda* (12th century), which explores the depths of Krishna's love for Radha, the dancer expressing the sensual and the devotional.

Orissan temples

Orissan temples are graced by a tall, curvilinear tower, the *deul* (pronounced *day-ool*) or *rekha deul*, and a much lower, more open structure or porch in front of the entrance to the tower, the *jagamohana*. The dark interior of the sanctuary is designed to allow only a glimpse of the presiding deity and to enable priests to conduct ritual worship. A dancing hall (*nata mandir*) and a hall of offering (*bhoga mandir*) were often added in later temples.

The square plan of the sanctuary tower and the porch are broken vertically by the inward curving form of the main tower. Each exterior face of the sanctuary tower is divided by vertical, flat-faced projections (*rathas*).

Some Orissan architects likened the structure of the temple to that of the human body, and the names given to the vertical sections correspond to main parts of the body.

1 The platform (*pishta*) Early temples had no platform. In contrast, in highly developed temples (eg Surya temple at Konark), the platform may be more than 3 m high.

2 The lower storey (*bada*) corresponds to the lower limbs. In early temples this was divided into three parts, the base (the foot), above which was a perpendicular section corresponding to the shin. This was topped by a set of mouldings. In some mature temples the scale of this section was greatly elongated and was itself then divided into five layers.

3 The upper storey (*gandi*, or human trunk) is a curvilinear spire in the case of the sanctuary, or a pyramidal roof in the case of the porch.

4 The head (*mastaka*) with crowning features. Divided into a series of elements, the 'head' or mastaka of the sanctuary developed over time. The 'neck' (*beki*) – a recessed cylindrical portion, is surmounted by the skull, amla. This is represented by a symbolic fruit, the amalaka. On the *amla* rests a 'water pot', an auspicious symbol, then on top of all comes the sacred weapon of the deity.

The **folk dances** usually performed during festivals take various forms – day-long *Danda Nata*, the traditional fishermen's dance, *Chaitighoda* which requires a horse dummy, the battle dance called *Paika Nritya*, and *Chhau*, the dance-drama reminiscent of Orissa's martial past. There are also tribal dances performed in colourful costumes with distinctive headgear made of animal horns and shells, to the accompaniment of string instruments, flutes and drums.

Food and drink Rice forms the staple food, wheat taking second place. Meals include lightly spiced side dishes of vegetables and pulses, chutneys and pickles. Fresh seafood, especially prawns and the flat *pomfret* fish, are common in coastal areas. Try *mahura* or *saga bhaja* (fried mustard or spinach leaves), *dahi baigono* (aubergines cooked with yoghurt) or the festive *besara* (vegetables cooked with mustard seed paste).

Orissa is particularly noted for its milk sweets – *rasamalai*, *khiramohan*, *rajbhoga*, *rabidi*, *chhenapodapitha* and *kalakanda*. *Khiri* is prepared with milk and rice, semolina or vermicelli while special *pithas* are often filled with sweetened coconut.

Art and architecture

The temples of Bhubaneswar, along with those of Puri and Konark, represent a remarkably full record of the development of Orissan architecture from the seventh to many are virtually intact and some are still in everyday use – centres of active pilgrimage, worship and faith.

Crafts

Stone carving has been highly developed in Orissa for over 2,000 years. The artistry that produced the early sculptures and the superb carvings on Orissan temples in Bhubaneswar, Puri and Konark is still kept alive by modern craftsmen. They produce beautiful figures, bowls or plates carved out of soft soapstone, hard *kochila* or multicoloured serpentine from Khiching. Orissa also has a tradition of **hornwork** in Parlakhemundi and Cuttack, buffalo horn being carved into the typical small flat figures of animals and birds.

Silver filigree is perhaps one of the most distinctive and exquisite works of the Cuttack jewellers who turn fine silver wire into beautiful, fragile objects with floral patterns. The metal used is close to sterling silver which is drawn through finer and finer holes to make the wire.

Metal work is popular. Craftsmen use brass (alloy of copper and zinc) and bell-metal (alloy of copper and tin) to produce small figurines, vases and plates. The tribal metal casting in the *dhokra* style by the lost-wax (*cire perdue*) process is found in Dhenkanal and Mayurbhanj districts. A clay core of the basic shape is covered by fine wax 'threads' before the whole is enclosed in a shell of straw and clay and then baked in a tiny charcoal fire. At the firing, molten metal is poured in, to displace the melting wax. Similar casting is done by tribal peoples in Bihar, Madhya Pradesh, Manipur and West Bengal.

Brightly coloured **wood carvings** of the deities in the Jagannath temple, and figures of animals and birds make attractive gifts. **Ivory** inlay (now replaced by plastic) was traditionally carried out for rich patrons of the Puri temple, and also for making illustrated wooden covers for palm leaf manuscripts. The tradition of using **papier-mâché** masks of deities and animal characters to tell stories from the epics also comes from Orissa.

Orissan temple

After Brown

The *chitrakars* (picture makers), particularly from the village of Raghurajpur, 12 km from Puri, **paint** the *pattachitras* on specially prepared cloth, coated with earth to stiffen it and finally finished with lacquer after painting, producing pictures and attractive playing cards. Old sets of *ganjapa* cards consisted of 96 discs. The vibrant colours traditionally came from earth, stone, leaves and flowers. The best *chitrakars* are those allowed the honour to paint the Puri temple deities and their 'cars' each year. They are also commissioned by the rich to produce fine temple murals and manuscripts on paper and palmleaf. However, what are usually available in the bazars are cruder examples for pilgrims to take home.

Finds of the 16th century reveal how illustrated manuscripts were produced by holding an iron stylus stationary while moving a **palm leaf** underneath. It was a technique that helped to give the Oriya script its rounded form. The leaves were first prepared by drying, boiling, drying again, and then flattening them before coating with powdered shell. After inscribing, the grooves were rubbed with soot or powdered charcoal, while colour was added with a brush. The leaves were then stacked and strung together and placed between decorative wooden covers. The *pattachitra* artists in Raghurajpur have also revived this art form.

Pipli, a small town about 20 km southwest of Bhubaneswar, is famous for its **appliqué** work using brightly coloured embroidered cloth, probably originally designed for use in the Jagannath temple. The roadside stalls sell items for the house and garden – parasols, cushion covers, wall-hangings – using striking animal, bird and flower patterns on a backcloth. Unfortunately, mass production has resulted in the loss of attention to detail of the original fine 'Pipli work' which picked out the motifs by cleverly stuffing sections of the pattern. The best pieces now tend to be sent away to the government emporia in Bhubaneswar, Delhi and Kolkata.

Textile weaving has been a traditional craft throughout Orissa for generations and thousands are still employed in this cottage industry. It is one of the few regions in India producing **ikat** – see also page 1025 – the technique of 'resist-dyeing' the warp or weft thread, or both, before weaving, so that the fabric that emerges from the loom has a delicate enmeshed pattern. The favourite designs include rows of flowers, birds and animals, using either tussar or cotton yarn. **Berhampur**, **Sambalpur**, **Mayurbhanj** and **Nuapatna** all produce silk and cotton ikat saris. Some also produce tapestry, bedspreads and embroidered fabric.

Crafts villages While some (for example Raghurajpur and Pipli) are used to passing tourists, others are rarely visited by foreigners. It is worth visiting to see craftsmen at work and perhaps buy their goods. In **Raghurajpur** (reached via Chandapur, 10 km from Puri on the Bhubaneswar road), you can watch artists painting *pattachitras* in bright folk-art style or etching palm leaves (see *chitrakars* above). Sadly, the village has now been reduced to a sales exercise: "more commerce than culture". **Pipli**, on the Bhubaneswar-Puri Road, specializes in appliqué work, **Balakati**, 10 km from Bhubaneswar, in bell-metal, while there is a community of Tibetan carpet weavers at **Chandragiri** near the Taptapani Hot Springs in tribal country. Adjacent to the Buddhist site of **Lalitgiri** is a stone-carvers' village. Master-weavers work at their looms in **Nuapatna** and **Maniabandha**, 100 km from Bhubaneswar, and in the narrow streets next to the temple at **Berhampur**. **Cuttack** remains famous for silver filigree work.

Modern Orissa

Political power in Orissa has alternated between the Congress and Opposition parties, most recently the BJD (the Biju Janata Dal – named after its former leader Biju Patnaik), which in alliance with the BJP won 16 of the 21 Lok Sabha seats in the 1998 election. The same combination won an overwhelming majority in the Assembly elections of February 2000. The Chief Minister is Naveen Patnaik, the son of Biju Patnaik, who has a strong reputation for integrity.

The Mahanadi Delta

★ Bhubaneswar

→ *Phone code: 0674. Colour map 6, grid A6. Population: 647,300. www.orissa-tourism.com.*
Set on the edge of the lush green rice fields of the Mahanadi Delta, the pleasantly broad streets of the planned town of Bhubaneswar offer a striking contrast to the architectural legacy of its period of greatness over one thousand years ago. Named after 'The Lord of the Universe', Bhubaneswar still has some 500 of the original '7,000' temples that once surrounded Bindusagar Tank. The graceful towers of those early temples, complemented by the extraordinary fineness of the stone carving, make Bhubaneswar one of the most rewarding destinations in East India.
▸▸ *For Sleeping, Eating and other listings, see pages 704-709 .*

Ins and outs
Getting there The airport is only 4 km from the town centre and several hotels are within 1 km of the railway station on the main Kolkata-Chennai line. Although the new bus stand is 6 km out of town long-distance buses stop at the Old Bus Stand in the town centre first. Buses for Konark and Puri can be boarded by the State Museum.

Getting around The temples are quite spread out so it is best to hire a rickshaw, though you can get round on foot if you have plenty of time. See Transport, page 708, for further details.

Climate Temperatures: summer maximum 38°C, minimum 26°C; winter maximum 29°C, minimum 16°C. Rainfall: Jun-Oct ave 250 mm, little during other months. Best time to visit: Nov-Mar.

History
Several sites testify to the importance of the Bhubaneswar region far earlier than the seventh to 11th centuries, when the Kalinga kings ruled over the area. Both Jain and Buddhist shrines give clear evidence of important settlements around Bhubaneswar in the first two centuries BC. The remains of a ruined moated city, Sisupalgarh (opposite the Dhauligiri battlefield and Asokan edicts), show that it was occupied from the beginning of the third century BC to the middle of the fourth century AD and the pottery shows Roman influence. Bhubaneswar is the capital of Orissa, chosen in 1948 in place of Cuttack partly because it was the ancient capital of the Kalinga Empire.

Sights
Parsuramesvara Temple The seventh-century temple, though small, is highly decorated, and is the best preserved of the early Bhubaneswar temples. The rectangular porch and the stepped roof indicate an early date. Even so, the porch was probably built after the sanctuary itself, as suggested by the rather crude junction between the two. In the early period the masonry was kept in place by weight and balance alone. Other features include the carving of a goddess and two sea-monsters on the lintel over the sanctuary door.

✦ Temple priests may approach you for donations; these are not compulsory

The temple marks an important stage in the development of Hindu power at the expense of Buddhism in seventh-century Orissa, illustrated by the frequent representation of **Lakulisa**, the seventh-century priest responsible for Hindu proselytism. He is sculpted In Buddha-like form, and often surrounded by disciples. Note also, the distinctive *chaitya* windows developed earlier in Buddhist *chaitya* halls, as at Ajanta. There are two on the front of the sanctuary tower.

The sanctuary is divided horizontally and vertically into three sections. The carvings show motifs and styles that were to reach their full flowering in later temples. The base, for example, has a top moulding (close to the ground) decorated with scrolls, birds, humans and floral motifs. At about eye level, the mouldings are distinctive. The recessed frieze (discarded in later designs) is embossed with early examples of the amorous couples which were to become such a prominent feature of the Konark temple, interspersed with *vyalas* (rampant lions) astride crouching

Bhubaneswar

Sleeping	7 Lingaraj	**Eating**	2 Svarnajalesvara
1 Bhubaneswar	8 Marrion	1 Atithi Bhavan	3 Muktesvara, Siddhesvara
& Upasana	9 Panthanivas &	2 Banjara	& Kedaresvara
2 Bicky Inn	Orissa Tourist Office	3 Hare Krishna	4 Satrughnesvara Group
3 Chandrakala	10 Sahara	4 Venus Inn	5 Makaresvara, Mitresvara
4 Ekamra	11 Shatabdi		& Chitrakarini
5 Kalinga Ashok	12 Sishmo	**Temples**	6 Lakshmanesvara,
6 Kamala	13 Swosti	1 Parsuramesvara	Bharatesvara, Satrughnesvara

0 metres 500
0 yards 500

side and four latticed windows. The vigorous and graceful sculptures of musicians and dancers he carvings on each side of the western doorway are outstanding.

The main accessory deities are placed in niches on each side of the sanctuary housing the principal deity. The Parsuramesvara Temple was dedicated to Siva; only two of the three original deities survive. On the south of the sanctuary, at eye level in the middle of the tower, is the four-armed elephant-headed Ganesh, his trunk curled towards a bowl of *laddus,* his favourite sweet. In the southern niche is Karttikeya (Subrahmanya) with a peacock, carrying a fruit in his right hand and a spear in his left. The lintel above Karttikeya illustrates the marriage of Siva and Parvati; to their right are Agni (Fire), the kneeling Brahma, and Surya (Sun).

Muktesvara Temple Beautifully decorated with outstanding carvings, this late 10th-century temple belongs to the end of the first phase of temple building. Although it still has the three-fold horizontal division of the lower storey, a feature of the early period, the plan of the sanctuary is now divided into the five-sectioned form. Also, the platform here consists of five mouldings, as in later temples.

New designs include graceful female figures and pilasters carved with *nagas* and *naginis* (snakes). Most strikingly, the porch has a new and more dramatic layered form. Ketu, too, is introduced as the ninth planet and Ganesh is joined by his mount, the mouse.

The Muktesvara displays the unique gateway arch (*torana*) dated at about AD 900; although the upper portion is restored, the original skill can still be seen in the graceful female figures. The rectangular tank at its east end, used by priests and devotees, and the well to the south, into which women still toss coins in the hope of curing infertility, symbolize the continued holiness of the site. On the door frame of the well is the figure of Lakulisa (see Parsuramesvara above).

The *chaitya* windows carved on the sanctuary tower show the finest examples of the *bho* motif – the grinning face of a lion with beaded tassels emerging from its mouth, flanked by two dwarves. Notice the monkey scenes on the outer frame of the diamond-shaped lattice windows on the north and south walls.

Siddhesvara Temple Immediately to the northwest of the Muktesvara is the later Siddhesvara Temple. It shows the mature Orissan temple form almost complete. The vertical lower section is divided into five parts and the *amla* on top of the sanctuary is supported by four squatting figures. However, the overall effect is comparatively plain, as sculptures marked out on the rock were never executed.

Gauri Temple The Gauri Temple to the south is probably of the late 10th century but it is built in the *khakhara* form (see Vaital Deul below), and has been substantially repaired. The porch was rebuilt in the early 20th century but still has a few original sculptures of real merit. Note the girl shown leaning against a post with a bird perched on it, on the south face of the eastern projection of the sanctuary. On the western projection is an equally beautiful sculpture of a girl removing her anklets.

Dikpalas: the Directional Guardians

Rajarani Temple ① *0600-1800, foreigners US$2, Indians Rs 5, video camera Rs 25.* The entrance to the Rajarani Temple (early 11th century) is about 300 m east of the main road, set back 200 m from the road. It no longer has an image of the deity in the sanctuary and is therefore out of use. The main tower is surrounded by four miniature copies, giving the sanctuary an almost circular appearance.

The porch (*jagmohana*) is comparatively plain even though it has the mature style of a pyramidal roof. Many of the carvings remain unfinished but give an insight into the method of cutting the stone into sections ('blocking out') followed by rough shaping ('boasted'), to be finished later by the master sculptor. The finished work in the main sanctuary is extremely fine.

Perhaps the best-preserved features of the temple are the *Dikpalas* (Guardians of the eight cardinal directions) who protect the central shrine from every quarter. They are placed in pairs about 3 m above ground level, in the lower section of the main sanctuary tower.

Starting from the left (south) of the porch they appear in the following order:

1 Facing east, **Indra**, the guardian of the east, holds a thunderbolt and an elephant goad, and his vehicle is the elephant.

2 At right angles to Indra, facing south, is the pot-bellied and bearded **Agni**, god of fire, riding a ram, guarding the southeast.

3 Moving a few metres along the wall, on the far side of the projection, is the south-facing **Yama**, holding a staff and a noose, with his vehicle the buffalo. The skull on his staff is a Tantric symbol.

4 Again at right angles to Yama is the west-facing **Nirritti**, guardian of the southwest. Nirritti, the god of misery, holds a severed head and a sword over the lying figure of a man.

5 Again facing west, but on the north side of the sanctuary's central projection, is the guardian of the west, **Varuna**. He holds the noose symbolizing fate in his left hand. His vehicle is the sea creature *makara*.

6 At right angles to Varuna, facing north, is **Vayu** (meaning 'wind'), guardian of the northwest. He holds a fluttering banner, and his vehicle is the deer.

7 The last pair of guardians are on the further side of the central projection, on the north and east facing sides respectively. First is **Kubera**, guardian of the north (pot-bellied to symbolize prosperity), placed above seven jars of precious stones. He has a horse.

8 **Ishana**, guardian of the northeast, symbolizing fecundity, is shown as was customary, with an erect phallus and accompanied by an emaciated figure.

Brahmesvara Temple The temple (built in 1060) is still in use today. As you enter from the north you pass through the two enclosure walls, the inner forming a compact surround for the temple complex, which is raised on a platform. Facing you is a well-oiled image of Lakshmi, covered in cloth, with incense sticks burning in front. The sanctuary itself houses a Siva *linga*. There are minor shrines in each corner of the compound.

The sanctuary tower has a five-fold vertical division, typical of the later temples. The base (*pabhaga*) and the top of the wall (*varanda*) have rich carvings. The lower section of the wall is decorated alternately by miniature *khakhara* style 'temples', sculptures of rampant lions, while the central niches of the miniature temple carvings at the corners of the lower section have *Dikpalas*. In the corresponding spaces of the upper section are miniatures of the normal temple sanctuary towers, and graceful secular figures, including erotic couples.

Satrughnes-vara Group Lakshmanesvara, Bharatesvara and **Satrughnesvara** temples are almost certainly the oldest in Bhubaneswar, dating from the late sixth century. The southernmost temple in the group has been rebuilt by the Archaeological Department of Orissa. Only the cores of these three temple are now visible.

Vaital Temple A significant feature of this small, late eighth-century temple is its form. Seen from the road the semi-cylindrical shape in section of the *deul* is immediately distinct. Its *khakhara* style derives, as Percy Brown says, from the shape of the *gopurams* of Dravida temples in South India, taken originally from the Buddhist *chaitya* halls.

Another striking feature is the temple's tantric associations, marked by its presiding deity, Chamunda (a terrible form of Durga). Durga herself appears on the north face of the *bada* as the eight-armed *Mahishasuramardini* (slayer of the buffalo demon) holding a snake, bow, shield, sword, trident, thunderbolt and an arrow, and she is piercing the neck of the demon.

Outside, on the east face of the *deul*, the lower of the two *chaitya* windows has a beautifully carved figure of the sun god Surya, with Usha (Dawn) and Pratyusha shooting arrows on either side of him while Aruna (also Dawn) drives a chariot in front. It has a certain incongruity in view of the image within the sanctum itself. The upper *chaitya*window has a 10-armed Nataraja, or dancing Siva.

Further evidence of the tantric basis of the temple comes from the stone post to which sacrifices were tethered, just in front of the *jagamohana*. The figure of Chamunda in the central niche is extremely difficult to see without artificial light, though very early morning sun penetrates the gloom of the interior. The most chilling of the other figures is that of a male on the north wall "rising from the ground after filling his skull-cup with the blood of a person whose severed head lies on the right; on the pedestal is an offering of two more heads".

Lingaraja Temple Along with the Jagannatha Temple at Puri the Lingaraja Temple (AD 1000), built 100 years earlier, represents the peak of achievement of the Orissan middle period. Non-Hindus are not allowed inside but you may get a view from a special platform outside the north perimeter wall; early morning and late afternoon are best for photography.

Even from a distance the sanctuary's 54-m high tower (the *Sri Mandir*) dominates the landscape. It is one of the four main buildings in the temple compound, with several subsidiary shrines. To the left of the tower is the *Jagamohana* (pillared porch), then the *Nata Mandir* (dancing hall) and finally the *Bhoga Mandir* (Hall of Offering). The latter two were added a century after the sanctuary and the porch.

The monumental tower which rises in a distinctive curve, is 17 m sq in plan with projecting faces. The *amla* head with a pot shaped pinnacle carrying the trident of Siva is supported by four mythical gryphons. The middle section has vertical lines of miniature towers sculpted in sharp relief on a background of horizontal mouldings. The massive protruding sculpture of a lion crushing an elephant on each side is a common symbol in Orissan architecture.

Ekamra Kanan The Government Regional Plant Resource Centre in Nayapally (north of town) has a large rose garden (Flower Show, December/January), woods, flowerbeds and a large lake which attracts migratory birds. It also boasts a Cactus Garden with over 550 species of cacti and succulents, one of the largest collections in India.

Nandan Kanan ① *0730-1730 (summer), 0800-1700 daily except Mon, Rs 5 (foreigners, Rs 40), camera Rs 5, video Rs 500, guide Rs 45 but unnecessary. Cable car across the lake, Rs 22, last return 1600. Safari Rs 12, closed 1130-1400.* The subsidiary road from Bhubaneswar to Cuttack, the medieval regional capital, passes Nandan Kanan after 20 km where the zoo and botanical garden are surrounded by dense forest. There are tigers, including rare white ones, lion and white tiger safaris, rhinos, panthers, leopards and a variety of wildfowl and reptiles, in their natural surroundings. It has also succeeded in breeding black panthers and *gharials* in captivity. The botanical gardens with its cactus house and rosarium are across the lake; much of it is derelict. The *Shradhanjali Restaurant*, near the entrance serves good thalis and snacks.

The **Orissa State Museum** ⓘ *Gautam Nagar, closed Mon and Govt holidays, 1000-1300, 1400-1700 (last entry 1600), Re 1, allow 1-2 hrs. Beware of the rats (not part of the exhibits)!*, collection includes archaeological exhibits, copper plates, coins, sculptures, musical instruments and rare palm leaf manuscripts; good anthropological section. The Tribal Research Institute's **Tribal Museum of Man** ⓘ *CRP Square, 1000-1700 except Sun, northwest of town, off NH5 on bus route*, has a collection of tribal dress, weapons and jewellery (enquire at Tourist Office about reopening after the cyclone damage). **Kalanagar** ⓘ *1000-1700 except Sun, on the Khandagiri Rd.* Display of traditional art and crafts, stone sculptures, *pattachitras*, brass casting, horn ware, terracotta and silver filigree.

★ Udayagiri and Khandagiri caves → *Colour map 6, grid A5.*

The caves on the two low hills of **Udayagiri** and **Khandagiri** date from the time of Jain occupation of the region, at least the second century BC. A narrow valley winds between the hills, the route of an early Buddhist pilgrim track leading to a stupa which probably stood on the present site of Bhubaneswar.

The coarse-grained sandstone which forms Khandagiri ('broken hill') and Udayagiri ('hill of the sunrise') rises nearly 40 m above the surrounding lateritic and infertile plain. The crumbling nature of the sandstone into which the caves were dug has exposed them to severe damage, moderately repaired by the Archaeological Survey of India.

Around Bhubaneswar & Cuttack

Ins and outs

Getting there 6 km from Bhubaneswar, the caves are very easy to visit by car, bus, rickshaw (Rs 120 return, includes waiting) or bicycle from Bhubaneswar, but the area can get very crowded.

Getting around You can take the path up towards Udayagiri to the right of the hills as you face them, and follow the route indicated to visit the caves in order. Some with sculptures are protected by wire-meshed gates. The most significant are described below. Foreigners US$2, video Rs 25 for Udayagiri. Khandagiri is free. 0800-1800; allow 2-3 hrs.

History

The **Jain caves** are among the earliest in India. Furthermore, some of the rock inscriptions found above the *Hati Gumpha* (Elephant Cave, No 14) and elsewhere, speak of the Chedi Dynasty who ruled over Kalinga from their capital, probably at Sisupalgarh, 9 km southeast of Khandagiri.

Kharavela, according to his own record, extended his rule across a large part of North, Central and South India. At home he made great efforts to improve canals, rebuild his capital city of Kalinganagara, and also to excavate some of the caves at Udayagiri-Khandagiri. Probably all the caves now visible were constructed during the 150 years before Christ. Designed for the ascetic life of Jain monks, they simply

Udayagiri & Khandagiri Caves

Sleeping
1 Cave View Resort

provided dry shelter, with no concessions to any form of comfort. Too low to stand in, the cells are no more than cramped sleeping compartments.

Although the Jains did not enjoy royal patronage after the fall of Kharavela's Dynasty, Jain occupation was continuous throughout successive Buddhist and Hindu periods in the region. The Parsvanatha temple on top of Khandagiri was built in the early 19th century, while the Hindu temple dates from the 1970s.

Udayagiri

Cave 1 The **Rani Gumpha**, on the path to the right, is the largest and most impressive of the caves. It is a double-storeyed monastery cut on three sides of a quadrangle with fine wall friezes and some pillars that have been restored. The right wing of the lower storey is guarded by two sentries. The pilasters at the entrance to the cell and the arches are beautifully carved with religious and royal scenes while the main central wing celebrates the king's victory march. There are two small guard rooms with decorative outer walls. In the upper storey, the doorway arches to the cells are ornately carved; auspicious Jain symbols (snake and lotus) appear among vivid secular friezes of a woman's abduction, an elopement, and a duel between a man and a woman.

Cave 10 **Ganesh Gumpha** About 50 m from the top of the steps. Friezes illustrate the Sanskrit love story of Udayan and Bassavadatta. From Cave 10 go up the path to the right, where an **apsidal structure** was unearthed in 1958. Very similar to a Buddhist *chaitya* hall in plan, it was almost certainly a place of worship for Jain monks.

Cave 12 **Bagha Gumpha** is carved bizarrely into the shape of a tiger's open mouth, an inscription showing it to have been the cave of the town judge.

Cave 14 The last important cave on Udayagiri, the **Hati Gumpha** (Elephant Cave), has the most important inscription, that of King Kharavela. Protected by a masonry shelter since 1902, it is in the Magadhi script.

Khandagiri

Caves 1 and 2 Known as **Tatwa Gumpha** from the parrots carved on their door arches. Two sentries in *dhotis* guard Cave 1 which bears the name **Kusuma**. Modern steps lead up to the more elaborately carved Cave 2 on the left. On the back of the cell are Brahmi inscriptions in red pigment (first century BC to first century AD).

Cave 3 **Ananta Gumpha**, at the top of the flight of steps, named after the two serpents on the door arches, has some very interesting reliefs using unique motifs; note especially the sculpted façade. On the back wall of the cell, among the various symbols is the *svastika*, auspicious to the Jains.

Cave 7 **Navamuni Gumpha**, named after the nine Tirthankaras (*munis*) carved on the back and right walls, was originally a residential cell. On the back wall of the original right hand cell are seven Tirthankaras in high relief including Parsvanatha under a seven-hooded canopy, and Risabanatha with a halo, seated on a bull.

There are lovely carvings of Digambara Jains on the back wall of the shrine with a corrugated iron roof half way up to the Jain temple.

Bhubaneswar to Puri and Konark

The round trip to Puri, one of the four holiest pilgrimage centres for Hindus, and Konark, according to Mark Twain one of the wonders of the world, crosses the irrigated rice growing plains of the Mahanadi delta.

★ Dhauli

The horrors of the Kalinga war at Dhauli led Asoka to acknowledge the value of Buddhist teachings. The two 'Kalinga Edicts' differ from others which expound Buddhist principles. The rock edicts at the bottom of the hill (circa 260 BC) give detailed

"...You are in charge of many thousand living beings. You should gain the affection of men. All men are my children, and as I desire for my children that they obtain welfare and happiness both in this world and next, the same do I desire for all men ...". Above the inscription you can see the front of an elephant carved out of an enormous rock. Unfortunately, the edict is difficult to see clearly behind its protective cage.

Now the rock edicts are almost ignored by the bus loads of tourists who are taken on up the hill to the Buddhist **Peace Pagoda**. Known as the **ShantiStupa**, the Pagoda was built in the early 1970s by the Japan Buddha Sangha and Kalinga Nippon Buddha Sangha. The old Hindu temple of Lord Dhavaleswar which was reconstructed in 1972 is also on the hilltop here.

★ Puri → *Phone code: 06752. Colour map 6, grid A5. Population: 157,600.*

Puri's tourist guesthouses cater to the flocks of Kolkata holiday makers who take advantage of the highly revered Jagannath Temple and the good sandy beach to combine pilgrimage with relaxation. The massive curvilinear temple tower dominates the skyline, and the otherwise sleepy town seethes with life during the car festival (*Rath Yatra*). Yet for most of the year Puri feels like an out of season backwater with quiet shady lanes with prettily painted houses. ▸▸ *For Sleeping, Eating and other listings, see pages 704-709* .

Puri

Sleeping	7 Lotus & Harry's Café	15 Vijoya International
1 Arya Palace	8 Love & Life	16 Youth Hostel
2 BNR	9 Mayfair Beach Resort	17 Z
3 Derby	10 Nilachal Ashok	
4 Gandhara International	11 Panthanivas & OTDC	● Eating
& Sunset Row Cottages	Tourist Office	1 Chungwah
5 Holiday House & Kaoi's	12 Puri	2 Peace
Castle	13 Repose	3 Wild Grass
6 Holiday Resort	14 Shankar International	

N

0 metres 500
0 yards 500

Orissa The Mahanadi Delta Puri

Getting there The station is about 1 km from the main hotels and the bus stand, 500 m north of it, on Grand Rd. Cycle-rickshaws tout for business all across town.

Getting around It is well worth hiring a bike to visit the temple and bazar and explore along the coast if you don't wish to hire a rickshaw. See Transport, page 709, for further details.

Climate Temperature: maximum 32°C, minimum 18°C. Rainfall: mostly from Jun-Oct (ave 220 mm). Best time to visit: Nov-Mar.

History

The Sabaras, an *adivasi* tribal group who predated the Dravidians and Aryans, were believed to have inhabited the thickly wooded area around Puri. Some believe that this was **Dantapura**, which once held the holy Buddhist Tooth relic. According to Murray, in Japan and Sri Lanka, the *Tooth Festival* of Buddha was celebrated with three chariots and the similarity with the *Rath Yatra* at Puri further strengthens the theory that the deities here evolved from Buddhist symbols.

Sights

Jagannath Temple The Jagannath Temple is the major attraction of Puri and, for Hindus, to remain here for three days and three nights is considered particularly rewarding. The temple attracts thousands on feast days and particularly during Rath Yatra. Non-Hindus are not allowed inside this temple. The fact that in the eyes of Jagannath (Lord of the Universe), there are no caste distinctions, has made Puri a very popular destination with the devout. The wooden figures of the three deities, **Jagannath, Balabhadra** and **Subhadra** stand in the sanctuary garlanded and decorated by the priests. The extraordinary form that Jagannath takes is believed to be the unfinished work of the craftsman god Viswakarma, who in anger left this portrayal of Lord Vishnu incomplete. Small wooden replicas of the three images are available around the temple.

There are vantage points for viewing the temple, for example the roof of Raghunandan Library opposite the main entrance to the east or from the *Jaga Balia Lodge* nearby; a small donation is expected in return.

The temple is referred to by some as the 'white pagoda' (the Konark Temple being the 'black pagoda') and was completed at the end of the 12th century. The original temple built in the Kalinga style consisted of the **deul** (sanctuary) and the **jagamohan** (audience hall) in front of it. It was only in the 14th or 15th century that the '**nata mandir**' (dance hall) and the '*bhoga mandir*' (hall of offerings) were added in alignment in the style of other Orissan temples. The **nata mandir** is unusual in that it has 16 pillars in four rows to support the large ceiling. The site is a virtual 200 m sq enclosed within an outer wall 6-m high. Within is another concentric wall which may have acted as fortification, inside which stands the tallest temple in Orissa, 65 m high, crowned by the wheel of Vishnu and a flag. On the higher ground in the enclosure are 30 small shrines, much in the Buddhist stupa tradition. Pilgrims are expected to visit at least three of these smaller temples before proceeding to the main temple. The outer wall has the main **Lion entrance**. On this east side there is an intricately carved 10-m high free-standing stone pillar with a small figure of *Aruna*, the charioteer of the Sun. This once stood in front of the *Nata Mandir* at Konark, see page 702. To the left of the main entrance is the temple kitchen which daily prepares 56 varieties of food making up the *Bhogas* which are offered to the deities five times a day; the *mahaprasada* is then distributed from the *Ananda Bazar* to thousands. At festival times as many as 250,000 are served daily. The temple is supposed to be a self-sufficient community, served by 6,000 priests and over 10,000 others who depend on it for their livelihood. The four sacred *tanks* in Puri

☃ Rath Yatra

Lord Jagannath's 'car' festival commemorates Krishna's journey from Gokul to Mathura in an extraordinary riot of colour and noise. Shaped like a temple sanctuary and brightly decorated, Lord Jagannath's 13-m tall 'car', the largest, has 16 wheels each 2 m in diameter. Loud gongs announce the boarding of the deities onto the chariots with the arrival of the Raja of Puri accompanied by bedecked elephants. With a golden broom and sprinkling holy water, the Raja fulfils his role as the 'sweeper of the gods', symbolizing that all castes are equal before God. The procession is led by Balabhadra's car, followed by Subhadra's with Lord **Jagannath's**

bringing up the rear, about 4,000 people being needed to draw each chariot.

During the week away, the deities are daily dressed in new garments and treated to special rice cakes (*podapitha*), before they return with a similar procession. Jagannath has to implore Lakshmi (his consort) who had to remain behind and now bars his way, to allow him in! The ceremonies and the fairs attract more than 500,000 devotees to Puri each year. In the past some were said to have thrown themselves under a massive wheel to die a blessed death. The short journey may take as much as 24 hours. After the festival, the raths are broken up and bits are sold to pilgrims as relics.

provide thousands of pilgrims with the opportunity to take a holy dip. The **Narendra Tank** is particularly famous since the deities are taken there during the Snana Yatra.

Gundicha Ghar The terminus of the Rath Yatra, where the deities from the Jagannath Temple spend a week, is open to Hindus only. It shows the unique and ingenious way wrought-iron framework supported the laterite lintels of the massive temples.

The beach The long stretch of Puri's golden beach is shallow enough to walk out a long distance. Sunrise is particularly striking. The currents can be treacherous at times. Take great care and avoid swimming out too far. The best hotels have a stretch of fairly clean sand. The customary *nolia*, fisherman turned life-saver in a distinctive conical hat, may be hired for either half or a full day, at a small price. The fishing villages along the coast are worth visiting, but be prepared to pick your way carefully!

★ Konark → *Phone code: 06758 .Colour map 6, grid A6.*

Konark (Konarak) is one of the most vivid architectural treasures of Hindu India and is a World Heritage Site. It no longer stands as a landmark on the sea shore since the land has risen and the sea is now 2 km away. Though much of it now lies in ruins, the porch is still magnificent. ▶▶ *For Sleeping, Eating and other listings, see pages 704-709 .*

Ins and outs

Getting there The 35 km drive from Puri (small toll charged) through attractive scenery passes a Turtle Research Centre off the Marine Drive after 10 km, and through coastal villages with beautifully decorated houses including Chaitan, a stone carvers' hamlet. The energetic can cycle to Konark and bring the bike back on the bus.

Getting around The site is very compact and can only be seen on foot. See Transport, page 709, for further details.

The Sun Temple was built by King Langula Narasimha Deva in the 13th century, although there may have been an older ninth-century temple on the same site. Built of *khondalite*, it is said to have taken 1,200 masons 16 years to complete. It was only in 1901 that the first tentative steps were taken to reclaim the ruins of the temple from the encroaching sand. By that stage not only had the sanctuary or *deul* collapsed but a number of the statues had been removed, many in the 1830s by the Hindu Raja of Khurda, who wanted them to decorate temples he was building in his own fort, 100 km away, and at Puri. There has been substantial renovation, some of it protective and some replacing fallen stonework and sculptures.

The site

The **Surya Temple** is set back 180 m from the road and is reached by a wide laterite path. The sanctuary has no deity for worship, so shoes may be worn. The exception is the small structure in the northeast corner of the site which houses the old *Navagraha* (nine planets) doorway arch, removed from the temple. The path to the temple is lined with beggars, as in major centres of Hindu pilgrimage.

Archaeological Survey and Government approved **guides** conduct tours of under an hour. Unofficial guides will press their services, but can be unreliable.

The temple compound

At the eastern entrance is the *bhoga mandira* (refectory), an isolated hall with pillars raised on a richly decorated platform; some believe this may have been a *nata mandira* (dancing hall). To its west is an open space leading to the porch (*jagamohana*) which rises magnificently to its original height of 39 m. To its east is the massive lower section of the original sanctuary (*deul*), once over 60 m tall.

From the south wall you can see that the temple was built in the form of a war chariot. Twelve pairs of great wheels were sculpted on either side of the temple platform. In front of the eastern entrance a team of seven horses were shown straining to pull the chariot towards the dawn. In Hindu mythology the Sun god traverses the

Konark

sky in a chariot drawn by seven horses, each representing a day of the week. The 12 pairs of wheels may have symbolized the 12 months (24 fortnights) of the year, and the eight spokes in each wheel, the divisions of the day into eight *prahars*. Each wheel also functions as a working sundial!

The sculptures

The walls of the *bhoga mandir* are covered by carvings, but as Debala Mitra writes, there are of "mediocre quality". The platform gives an excellent view of the whole east front of the main temple with its porch doorway, and the large, remarkably vivid carvings on the terraces of its pyramidal roof, unique in Orissan architecture, see page 688.

The sculptures draw for their subject from every aspect of life – dancers, musicians, figures from mythology, scenes of love and war, of court life, hunting, elephant fights. Since the temple was conceived to reflect a rounded picture of life and since *mithuna* or union in love is a part of that, a significant section of the sculpture is erotic art. Konark is unusual in that the carvings are found both on the outer and inner surfaces.

The porch roof is divided into three tiers, separated by terraces. Above the bottom and middle tiers is a series of musicians vividly captured in a variety of rhythmic poses playing drums, cymbals and *vinas*. On the bottom tier at either end of the central segments are dramatic sculptures of Siva as the awe-inspiring Bhairava. The top of the porch is crowned with the flattened spheres typical of Orissan temples.

The plinth (*upana*), a few centimetres high, runs right round the base of the temple, and is decorated with a variety of friezes – elephants (estimated at over 1,700, and each different!), including wild elephants being trapped, military marches, hunting, journeys, and a variety of other animals including crocodiles and a giraffe.

The platform is divided into the same five horizontal layers that characterize the temple itself. These are richly decorated with creepers and scrolls, and end with tiny motifs of *chaitya* windows. Along the lower mouldings are spaced miniature temple-like façades – *khakhara-mundis* – which contain niches. Set into these are figures, often of young women – caressing a bird, washing hair, playing the *vina*. The slabs between have a variety of carvings – some are erotic, some are *nagas* or *naginis*, each with a human head but with the tail of a snake.

The middle of the platform has three horizontal mouldings at about eye level. Above this, the *upper jangha* is richly sculpted, sometimes with religious scenes such as *Mahishasuramardini* (Durga as the Goddess of destruction) and *Jagannatha*, enshrined in a temple. Other sculptures show royal courts or simple family scenes. Along the top of the platform is the verandah, consisting of two mouldings separated by a narrow recess. Though severely damaged, these are decorated with friezes.

From the platform you will see the intricately carved eight-spoked wheels, each shown with its axle, a decorated hub and an axle pin. Floral motifs, creepers and the widely shown *chaitya* windows cover the stonework. Medallions with gods such as Surya and Vishnu, erotic figures, noblemen and animals – all add immense life to the structure.

The sanctum sanctorum

Although the *jagmohana* is now the dominant building of the complex, the scale of the sanctuary is still evident. The climb up the outer walls and then down into the sanctuary itself, which is possible for the reasonably agile, allows you to see at close quarters the remarkable chlorite statues of Surya on the outer south wall and offers an almost unique opportunity to see the inside of a temple sanctuary in full light.

It is best to climb up the main eastern steps of the porch and to walk round it to the left (south) side. The east door of the porch is the best preserved. Each door jamb is divided into eight facets, all carved with a variety of reliefs. The larger than life-sized grey-green chlorite statue of Surya is in sharp contrast with the surrounding yellowish-orange *khondalite* stone. He stands on a chariot drawn by his seven horses, lashed by Aruna, the charioteer, surrounded by two four-armed gods, a pot-bellied Brahma on the right and possibly Vishnu on the left. Below them are possibly four wives of Surya.

The original approach was through the porch. Now, a flight of steps from the west end of the temple leads down into the inner sanctum. The main feature inside is the chlorite platform at the western end of the 10 m sq room intended for the presiding deity. This image from the pedestal was moved to the Jagannath Temple complex in Puri. The platform that remains is nonetheless outstanding; some carvings almost certainly show the King, the donor of the temple, accompanied by priests. The hollows on top of the platform's eastern edge resulted from the placing of pots over a long period.

The temple grounds: the colossi

① *0600-1800, foreigners, US$5, video camera Rs 25. Official guides, Rs 75-100 per hr.*

Originally each of the three staircases to the porch was guarded by a pair of colossi – rampant lions on top of a crouching elephant to the east, decorated elephants to the north, and war horses to the south. The last two pairs have been remounted a short distance from their original sites. The lions have been put in front of the eastern steps up to the *Bhoga mandira* near the entrance.

Museum

Archaeological Museum ① *closed Fri, 0900-1700, Rs 5, near Travellers' Lodge.* Small collection including many important pieces from the Sun Temple complex. Occasional lectures and film shows. Archaeological Survey publications for sale.

Listings: The Mahanadi Delta

● Sleeping

Bhubaneswar *p691, map p692*
AL Oberoi Bhubaneswar, CBI, Nayapalli, off NH5, T301010, F300333, reservations@ oberoibh.com. 70 well-furnished a/c rooms in sparse site, uninspiring architecture, good à la carte but disappointing buffets; small rooms, small pool, large price tag!
AL-A Mayfair Lagoon, 8B Jaydev Vihar, Nayapalli, 5 km from centre, T557701, F557702, mayfairlagoon@hotmail.com. Modern, low-level 'palace' style hotel with 63 attractive cottages set around lagoon, all facilities, very stylish, friendly efficient staff. Best of the 5-stars. Recommended.
A Quality Inn Crown, IRC Village, Nayapalli on NH5, 5 km from town, T555500, F550001, www.qualityinncrown.com. 68 comfortable a/c rooms with hot bath (tubs), double-glazed, so quiet, good pool, bar, efficient, friendly staff.
A Sishmo, 86/A1 Gautam Nagar, T433600, F433351, www.orissaindia.com/sishmo. 72 comfortable a/c rooms, all facilities including health club and pool, good restaurant, well-run hotel, best in town centre.
A Swosti, 103 Janpath, T535771, F535784, www.swosti.com. 60 central a/c rooms, restaurant, bar, overpriced compared to those out of town, good discounts when business is slack.
A Swosti Plaza, P-1 jaydev Vihar, 5 km from centre, T301936, F301880, www.swosti.com. 106 a/c rooms in distinctive hotel based on Orissan temple design, fair-sized rooms though some road noise, 3 restaurants, Scottish theme bar.
A-B Marrion, 6 Janpath, opposite Sri Ram Mandir, T502328, F503287, themarrion@

● *For an explanation of the sleeping and eating price codes used in this guide, see inside the*
● *front cover. Other relevant information is found in Essentials pages 52-57.*

hotmail.com. 60 a/c rooms, very spongy carpets in standard class (like moon-walking!), restaurant, bar, pool exposed to dust from road, pleasant garden being sacrificed for larger bar.

B Kalinga Ashok, Gautam Nagar, T431055, F432066. 32 clean rooms (4 **A** suites), all a/c, TV, hot bath, restaurant, coffee shop, bar, exchange.

B-D Bicky Inn, 61 Janpath, T536435. Range of 26 small, but well-kept rooms, mostly a/c, Indian-style hotel, roof-top restaurant.

C-E Sahara, 76 Buddha Nagar, T311081, F311995, hotelsahara@rediffmail.com. 25 decent, good-sized rooms with hot bath, some a/c, quiet, reasonable restaurant, friendly helpful staff. Recommended.

D Kamala, Old Station Bazar, T570132. Decent sized clean rooms with bath, TV, some a/c but noisy from railway station next door.

D Upasana, Cuttack Rd, behind *Bhubaneswar*, T314144, F310044, upanasa_bbsr@yahoo.co.in. 20 good clean rooms with hot bath, TV, away from main road so quieter, friendly. Recommended.

D-E Bhubaneswar, Cuttack Rd, T313245, www.orissaindia.com/bhubaneswarhotel. 42 rooms with bath, some a/c, clean, good value though staff could be more helpful.

D-E Chandrakala, 74 Ashok Nagar, T532411. 31 small but clean rooms with bath, TV, veg food (room service), handy for station.

D-E Panthanivas, Jaydev Marg, T432515. Clean, spacious rooms, hot bath, some a/c, restaurant, 0800 check out, tourist office.

E Ekamra, Kalpana Square, T311732. Simple, grubby rooms, though clean linen, cheap singles, restaurant, good internet café below.

E-F Lingaraj, Old Station Bazar, T313565. Basic clean rooms, dorm.

Udayagiri and Khandagiri caves
p696, map p697
E-F Cave View Resort.

Puri *p699, map p699*
Avoid arriving at your hotel by rickshaw as commission will be added to the room rate. Instead, get down nearby and walk.

Most backpackers stay in hotels on CT Rd towards the fishing village at the eastern end. Domestic visitors prefer the seaside resorts along Marine Drive. Most check out at 0800 and several have a 2200 curfew. Check before staying out late! Top hotels will arrange pick-up from the station.

A Hans Coco Palms, Swargdwar, just off New Marine Drive, T30038, F30165, contact@hansgroup.com. 40 good a/c rooms with sea facing balconies/terraces, palm-filled restaurant, pleasant garden, good pool, good discounts for single occupancy, friendly staff, knowledgeable manager, book ahead in season. Recommended.

A Mayfair Beach Resort, CT Rd, T27800, F24242, www.mayfair-resorts.com. 34 well-furnished a/c cottages and rooms, some with sea view, rampant tropical garden, good pool (residents only), clean section of beach, good restaurants, very well run, friendly staff. Recommended.

A-B Toshali Sands, Konark Marine Drive (8 km), T22888, F23899, www.toshali india.com. 104 rooms (mostly suites) in cottages and villas set in attractive and extensive gardens (butterflies' paradise!), all very comfortable, 2 km walk to beach, sports facilities though pool could be cleaner, pricey restaurant with little choice nearby.

B Nilachal Ashok (ITDC), next to Raj Bhavan, VIP Rd, T23639, F23676, nilaashok@satyam.net.in. 34 clean, good-sized a/c rooms, TV, some with sea view, beach access via scrubby back garden.

B Pearl Beach Club, Sipasurabali, next to *Sterling Resorts* (5 km), T30109. Large new resort, first of several destined to appear in this area. 224 comfortable a/c rooms with all facilities, boat service to cross river to beach.

B-C Asian Inn Beach Resort, New Marine Drive, T31307, F31348. New hotel with 31 rooms, some a/c and suites, smallish but clean and comfortable, TV, good restaurant, well run.

B-D Sterling Resorts, Sipasurabali Village (5 km west of Marine Parade by rough, sandy track), T30391, F30090, www.sterling chalo.com. 350 comfortable rooms with kitchenettes in the sprawling complex, refurbished in 2002, all facilities including decent pool, boat to beach, primarily for domestic holidaymakers.

C-D Arya Palace, CT Rd, T32688. 32 rooms (some a/c) in new hotel clean and airy, hot bath, TV, generous discounts when quiet.

Orissa Listings: The Mahanadi Delta

705

■ *Phone codes Bhubaneswar: 0674; Puri: 06752; Konark: 06758*

C-D BNR, CT Rd, T22063, F23005, bnrhotel@
hotmail.com. Recently revamped, 34 large,
clean rooms, some a/c, first floor better with
wide verandahs overlooking sea, siestas
encouraged (quiet hours 1400-1600!), an
old-world curiosity claiming to serve the best
continental food in Puri, billiards, croquet, a
unique choice.

C-D Samudra, CT Rd, T22705, F28654,
hsamudra@yahoo.co.in. 52 decent clean
rooms, all with breezy sea facing balconies,
better at front on higher floors with sea view,
TV, restaurant, friendly staff.

C-D Vijoya International, CT Rd, T22702,
F22881, hotelvijoya@ rediffmail.com. 44
clean but dark rooms, half a/c, large garden,
quiet, friendly staff, pool and health club.

D-E Holiday House, CT Rd, T23782, F24363.
45 reasonable, good-sized clean rooms, better
sea facing (prices rise with altitude!), restaurant.

D-E Panthanivas (OTDC), CT Rd, T22740.
48 rooms including 3 **B** suites, a few a/c,
rooms in old block run down, better in
newer block closer to sea, tour booking,
pleasant garden with beach access.

D-E Puri, Marine Parade, T22114, F22744,
purihotel@satyam.net.in. Huge hotel on
seafront with 127 rooms, including 9 and
10-bedded rooms! Popular Indian family
hotel so quieter during the week, wide
choice, clean, some a/c, veg restaurant
(Indian/Chinese).

D-F Gandhara, CT Rd, T24117, F25909. Clean,
comfortable rooms, some a/c, friendly, good
value, cheap dorms, restaurant, popular.

E Shankar International, CT Rd, T22696,
F23637. 30 rooms with beach views in
Indian-style hotel set around lawn, small but
clean, restaurant.

E-F Kasi's Castle, CT Rd, T24522. 9 spotless
rooms with attached bath in friendly family
house, good choice. Recommended,
though avoid arriving by rickshaw
(commission demanded).

E-F Lotus, CT Rd, T23852. 9 simple rooms
(mostly **F**), quite clean, good restaurant
(*Harry's Cafe*, see Eating below).

E-F Love & Life, CT Rd, T24433, F26093,
love&life@satyam.net.in. Good value rooms
in 3-storeyed, airy building with cottages at
rear, theoretical hot water, nets, dorm, very
clean, good choice.

E-F Sun Row Cottage, CT Rd, T23259.
10 simple rooms in double cottages set
around small, colourful garden, restaurant,
long-stay discounts.

E-F Z, CT Rd, T22554, www.zhotelindia.com.
12 spacious rooms plus dorm in old
mansion, best sea facing, terrace, some wirh
clean shared bath, good food, friendly,
solar-powered, pleasant garden, TV/games
room, popular. Recommended, book ahead.

F Derby, CT Rd, T23961. 10 sea facing rooms
with bath, garden, popular.

F Pink House, CT Rd, T22253. 15 rooms,
some 3-5 bedded, directly on beach, friendly,
popular with backpackers, beach shack
restaurant (suspect hygiene).

F Santana, CT Rd (at end of fishing village),
T23491. Simple rooms in friendly, secure
hotel, popular with Japanese.

F Youth Hostel, CT Rd, T22424. Separate,
though somewhat dishevelled male and
female dorms, some 2-3 bedded, camping,
good Indian meals.

Konark *p701, map p702*

E Panthanivas (OTDC), opposite temple,
T36831. 11 clean rooms with nets, 2 a/c with
hot bath, smaller rooms a bit dark, separate
Geetanjali restaurant.

E Travellers Lodge, T36820. 4 slightly
larger rooms.

E-F Yatri Nivas, T36820, F36821. 28 good
value, clean rooms with nets, some
4-bedded, 8 a/c with geyser and TV, pleasant
lawn and gardens, restaurant, dorm beds (Rs
30) in open-air auditorium except during
festival, free cultural programme on
weekend evenings during season.

F Bijaya Lodge, T36478. Basic rooms with
attached bath.

F Konark Lodge, T36502. 4 cheap, basic
rooms with attached bath.

F Labanya Lodge, away from temple,
T35824, F35860. Best of the budget lodges.
13 clean rooms, mostly with attached bath,
breakfast available, cycle hire, travel. There
are plenty of cheap eating places and stalls
lining the road opposite the temple
entrance, serving thalis and snacks such as
'idle' and the inevitable 'Sand Witch'!

---

❷ Eating

Bhubaneswar *p691, map p692*
🍴 Mayfair Lagoon, very pleasant
restaurants include outdoor truck-stop style.

Full marks for Western fast food and confectionery.

¶¶¶ **Quality Crown Inn**, 1970's Bollywood theme restaurant.

¶¶¶ **Sishmo**. International. Excellent food, pleasant décor.

¶¶¶ **Swosti**. Varied menu. Dimly lit, generous portions, local specialities to advance order.

¶¶ **Banjara**, Station Square. Good Indian for lunch and dinner.

¶¶ **Hare Krishna**, Lalchand Complex, Janpath, T503188. Strict vegetarian. Upstairs, a/c, smart, tasty food.

¶¶ **Panthanivas**, local specialities with advance notice.

¶ **Atithi Bhavan**, near Lingaraj Temple.

¶ **Green Park**, 74 Buddha Nagar. Excellent fresh food, popular with local people.

¶ **New Ganguram Sweets**, Brit Market, Station Square. Delicious Indian sweets and snacks.

¶ **Venus Inn**, 217 Bapuji Nagar (2nd Floor) near Ashok. Good South Indian vegetarian.

Puri *p699, map p699*
The abundance of fresh fish is worth taking advantageof although an unaccustomed stomach might well object to a daily intake of seafood. Ensure that ingredients are fresh and cooked thoroughly. Hotels expect advance notice from non-residents.

¶¶ **Chung Wah** at *Hotel Lee Garden*, VIP Rd has good Chinese.

¶¶ **Wild Grass**, VIP Rd. Pleasant open-air restaurant with rustic theme. Good North Indian veg and non-veg, some Orissan specialities, friendly. Recommended.

¶ **Harry's café**, CT Rd. Pure veg (no onion or garlic) South Indian. Good thalis and snacks.

¶ **Peace**, CT Rd. Friendly, good food.

☻ Entertainment

Bhubaneswar *p691, map p692*
Programmes of Odissi and folk dances and folk drama are staged regularly and worth seeking out. **Rabindra Mandap**, near GPO and **Suchana Bhavan** near Bus Stand.

Puri *p699, map p699*
Top hotels and resorts have **bars**. Classical *Odissi* dance, folk dances and drama which are always performed for festivals are also staged from time to time and are worth seeking out.

❋ Festivals and events

Bhubaneswar *p691, map p692*
End-Jan: Tribal Fair attended by groups from different regions – excellent performances and crafts exhibitions.
Mar/Apr: Asokashtami, the Lingaraja Car Festival. The image of Siva is drawn on a chariot from the Lingaraja Temple to visit the Ramesvara Temple for 4 days.

Puri *p699, map p699*
Feb/Mar: Beach Festival, 1 week of cultural shows, crafts and food stalls. **Mid-Apr**: 21-day **Chandan Yatra** coincides with the Hindu New Year when images of Jagannath, his brother and sister are taken out in boats on the Narendra Tank. *Chandan* is the sandal paste used to anoint the deities. **Snana Yatra**, which follows, marks the ritual bathing of the deities on a special barge. For 15 days the gods are kept out of sight, when worshippers may only pray before *pattachitras* (paintings). Every few years new images of the deities are carved from specially selected trees and the old ones are secretly buried by the temple priests.
Jun/Jul: Rath Yatra, see box on page 701.

Konark *p701, map p702*
Feb: Honouring the Sun god; pilgrims flock here from evening to sunrise. **1-5 Dec**: Classical dance festival at the open-air auditorium opposite *Yatri Nivas*.

⊙ Shopping

Bhubaneswar *p691, map p692*
Many shops close on Thu and take a long lunch break. Market Building shops have fixed prices.
Khadi Gramodoyag Bhavan, Kalpana Sq. Hand-spun cotton garments.
Orissa State Handloom (West Market) is recommended for saris and handloom fabrics.
Utkalika (East Tower) sells Orissa handloom and handicrafts.

Books
Modern Book Depot, Station Sq, good selection on the region's history and art, well run.

Orissa Listings: The Mahanadi Delta

Books

Loknath, CT Rd. Second-hand, sale/exchange, library (Rs 7 per day), postcards.

Hairdresser

Face Beauty Parlour, CT Rd, towards fishing village. Excellent service, including expert massage by woman owner.

Handicrafts

Stone carvings, papier-mâché masks, painted wood figures, paintings, appliqué, hornwork make good buys.

Akbar, CT Rd. Cheap painted cards.

Odissi, Dolamandap Sahi. Handlooms.

Sudarshan, Station Rd. Stone carving, where you can also watch masons at work carving out images of deities.

Sun Crafts in Tinikonia Bagicha.

Utkalika and **Crafts Complex**, Mochi Sahi Square.

Weavers' Co-op Society, Grand Rd. Handlooms.

Visit the vast **bazar** around the Jagannath Temple, along Bada Danda and Swargadwara, but you have to bargain. Pathuria Sahi is the stone carvers' quarter and Raghurajpur (12 km) produces *pattachitras* and etchings on palm leaf, see page 689. See also Craft Villages in Orissa Introduction.

▲▲ Activities and tours

Bhubaneswar *p691, map p692*
Tours

OTDC: by 'luxury' coach from Transport Unit, behind *Panthanivas*, T431515. Ask about special tours to **Chilika Lake**. Will pick up/drop from hotels. Daily tours to Nandankanan, Khandagiri, **Udaigiri**, Dhauli and **museum** with good guide. 0900-1730 (except Mon), Rs 130. **Pipli**, **Konark** and **Puri**. 0900-1800, Rs 125. **Puri** and **Satpada**. 0830-1800, Rs 175. **Barkul** and **Narayani**. 0830-1800, Rs 160. **OTDC** and private operators have a/c and non a/c cars for full and half day sightseeing. A round trip by car visiting Konark and Puri from Bhubaneswar takes 6 to 8 hrs. Allow at least 1 hr for Konark.

Discover Tours, 463 Lewis Rd, T430477, F430828, www.orissadiscover.com. For special interest tours (treks, wildlife parks, tribal and textile villages), US$250 for 5-day

tour. Sarat Acharya and Bijaya Pattnaik are excellent guides, very knowledgeable, US$20 per day. Can organize tours even at a day's notice, though ask ahead for full service. Highly recommended.

Swosti Travels, 103 Janpath, T535773, F534794, www.swosti.com. Good, but expensive, specialist tours (tribal, architectural, wildlife), though not the most welcoming.

Puri *p699, map p699*
Tour operators

Tourist Office has a list of government approved tour companies. Almost every hotel on CT Rd has a travel office.

Heritage Tours at *Mayfair Beach Resort*, T23656, F24595 are reliable and offer a good benchmark for comparing prices.

OTDC to Konark, Dhauli, Bhubaneswar, Khandagiri, Udayagiri and Nandankanan Zoo. It is a long day. 0630-1900, Rs 130 non a/c, Rs 160 a/c. Chilika Lake (Satpada), 0630-1930, Rs 110. Private operators offer similar tours at cheaper rates, including more leisurely Konark only tours and specialized cultural trips.

☉ Transport

Bhubaneswar *p691, map p692*
Air

Airport 4 km. Taxi transfer, Rs 100 through OTDC. From airport Rs 100-150. **Indian Airlines**, Rajpath, T530533, airport, T535743. Daily flights to **Delhi** and **Kolkata**. **Chennai** and **Visakhapatnam**, Mon, Wed, Fri, Sun. **Hyderabad** and **Mumbai**, Tue, Thu, Sat. **Jet Airways**, T535877. Daily flights to **Kolkata**, 3 flights weekly to **Bangalore**, 2 a week to **Chennai**.

Bus

Local City buses are cheap and cover major routes but avoid evening rush hour.

Long distance New Bus Stand is at Baramunda on the NH5 (6 km from centre) where there are auto rickshaws for transfer. Enquiries T550769. Some long-distance buses go through the city first, stopping at the Old Bus Stand, off Rajpath. Regular buses to **Puri** and **Konark** (both 1½-2 hrs) pick up passengers from outside the museum on Lewis Rd. Most are quite full thoughlocal people will often offer their seats to foreigners. If you choose to be noble and stand, these buses usually thin out at Pipli. Buses to **Cuttack** (1 hr) stop on the opposite side of the road.

Rickshaw
Negotiate rates in advance.

Tourist taxi
Unmetered, Rs 50 minimum. OTDC (Transport), T431515, cars, Rs 440, a/c, Rs 600, for 8 hrs or 80 km. Out-of-town rates are higher.

Train
Reservations, T502042, enquiries, T532233. Computerized booking hall is in separate building opposite the station. Auto and cycle-rickshaws for transfer. **Chennai**: *Coromandal Exp, 2841*, 2040, 21 hrs; *Howrah Chennai Mail, 6003*, 0320, 25½ hrs. **Kolkata (H)**: *Dhauli Exp, 2822*, 1355, 8 hrs; *Coromandal Exp, 2842*, 0520, 8½ hrs; *Falaknuma Exp, 2704*, 1110, 8½ hrs; *Chennai Howrah Mail, 6004*, 2215, 9 hrs; *Puri Howrah Exp, 8008*, 2100, 9½ hrs; *Jagannath Exp, 8410*, 2300, 9½ hrs; *East Coast Exp, 7046*, 0505, 10½ hrs; *Tirupati Howrah Exp, 7480*, 1510, 13 hrs. **Mumbai (CST)**: *Konark Exp, 1020*, 1350, 38½ hrs. **Secunderabad**: *Falaknuma Exp, 2703*, 1540, 20½ hrs; *Konark Exp, 1020*, 1350, 21 hrs; *East Coast Exp, 7045*, 1910, 24 hrs; *Visakha Exp, 7615*, 0725, 25 hrs.

Puri *p699, map p699*

Air
Bhubaneswar 60 km, is the nearest airport (see page 708). Taxi to Puri around Rs 450, 1-1½ hrs.

Bus
The huge, open bus stand on Grand Road runs regular buses to **Bhubaneswar** and **Konark**. Minibuses are faster. Also services to **Cuttack, Visakhapatnam** and **Kolkata**. OSRTC, T23786.

Cycle and motorcycle
Good option for exploring the coast. Several outlets on CT Rd. Cycles Rs 15 - Rs 25 per day, depending on condition. Motorbikes Rs 150 - Rs 250 per day.

Cycle rickshaw
Available all over town. Bus Stand to CT Rd, Rs 15; railway station Rs 10. To prevent commission being added to room price, get

dropped off at *BNR* and walk along CT Rd to desired hotel.

Taxi
Tourist taxis from larger hotels and from Taxi Stand (T22161); Rs 550 per 8 hrs or 80 km.

Train
Enquiry, T131. **Kolkata (H)**: *Puri Howrah Exp, 8008*, 1900, 11½ hrs; *Jagannath Exp, 8410*, 2115, 11½ hrs. **New Delhi**: *Purushottam Exp, 2801*, 2015, 32½ hrs.

Konark *p701, map p702*
OTDC by 'luxury' coach from Puri and Bhubaneswar (65 km), or you can hire a car.

❶ Directory

Bhubaneswar *p691, map p692*
Banks State Bank of India, Rajpath, by Police Station. Exchange on 1st floor, £ and US$ cash and TCs (closed Sun). Also at IDCO Towers, Janpath on the way to NH5. ICICI, near Shree Raj Talkies, Janpath for over the counter exchange. Separate **ICICI Centre** on Janpath has an ATM which can be used by Visa card holders. **Hospital** Capital Hospital, Unit 6, T401983. **Internet** At *Ekamra Hotel* and next to *Sahara*. **Post office** GPO, Sachivalaya Marg. **Tourist offices** Orissa, Jayadev Marg, behind *Panthanivas*, T431299 1030-1700, closed Sun. Airport counter, T534006. Rly station counter, T530715. **Govt of India**, B-21, BJB Nagar, T432203. **Useful addresses** Foreigners' Registration Office, Sahid Nagar, T540555.

Puri *p699, map p699*
Banks Allahabad Bank, Temple Rd is best for changing cash. **Andhra Bank**, near GPO gives cash on Visa cards. Other exchanges on CT Rd. **Hospital** District HQ Hospital, T22062. ID Hospital, Red Cross Rd, T22094. **Post office** GPO on Kutchery Rd. PCOs and internet on CT Rd. **Tourist office** Orissa, Station Rd, T22664 (1000-1700, closed Sun) with a **museum** above. Tourist counter, railway station, T23536.

Konark *p701, map p702*
Post office Sub Post Office, near *Panthanivas*. **Tourist office** Yatri Nivas, T/F36821.

The Northeast

Cuttack → *Phone code: 0671. Colour map 6, grid A6. Population: 535,100.*

Cuttack occupies an important strategic position in relation to the network of canals in the region. Situated at the head of the Mahanadi delta and surrounded by the great river and its tributary the Kathjuri, the town is almost an island, its crowded streets and bazars clustered up towards its western end. ›› *For Sleeping, Eating and other listings, see pages 713-714.*

Ins and outs

Getting there Long-distance buses stop at the Bus Stand in Link Rd, while the railway station is just to the east of the main town. The main hotel area is further west.

Getting around Cycle-rickshaws provide transport around town. Auto-rickshaws at the bus and railway stations, take you for a ride, financially as well as literally! See Transport, page 713, for further details.

History

Cuttack, one of Orissa's oldest cities and its medieval capital, was founded by Nrupat Kesari (ruled 920-935). It remained the administrative centre until the end of the British Raj and was the state capital until 1956.

Cuttack

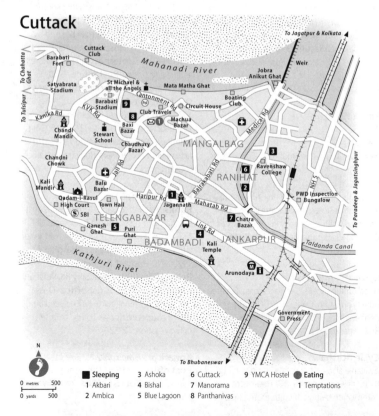

	Sleeping	3	Ashoka	6	Cuttack	9	YMCA Hostel	**Eating**
	1 Akbari	4	Bishal	7	Manorama			1 Temptations
	2 Ambica	5	Blue Lagoon	8	Panthanivas			

The ancient **stone embankment** to the south was built in the 11th century by the Kesari ruler to protect the town from flooding by the Kathjuri River. It still stands as a reminder of the engineering skills practised 900 years ago. The **Qadam-i-Rasul** (Kadam Rasul) in the centre of the old city, visited as a shrine by both Muslims and Hindus, has three 18th-century mosques with beautiful domes and a music gallery. The shrines contain relics of the Prophet Mohammad; the Prophet's footprint is carved on a circular stone. The famous silver filigree shops are nearby in Balu Bazar.

The blue granite 13th-century **Barabati Fort** to the northwest is being excavated by the Archaeological Survey. Its wide moat and a gateway are still there but the nine-storeyed palace has disappeared. Probably built by one of the Ganga rulers in the early 13th century, it was in Marhatta hands when it was taken by the British in 1803. Close to the fort is the vast **Barabati Stadium** where major sporting and cultural events are held. The **Church of St Michael and all the Angels** (CNI) by the river, typical of Raj-style church buildings, is worth a visit.

Ratnagiri, Udayagiri and Lalitgiri → *Colour map 6, grid A6.*

The beautiful hills and rice growing lands are home to remarkable Buddhist remains of the Vajrayana sect, set in an idyllic situation surrounded by green fields. The excavations at the three sites have revealed Buddhist structures, both stupas and monasteries, as well as sculptures and Buddha images.

Ins and outs

Getting there The sites can all be visited in a day from Cuttack or Bhubaneswar by car. If you go by bus you will need to stay overnight.

Getting around Rickshaws can be hired at Patharajpur. See Transport, page 711, for further details.

Ratnagiri → *Cuttack 70 km. Bhubaneswar 115 km.*

Ratnagiri ① *museums, Sat-Thu, 1000-1700, foreigners US$2*, the site of the 'Jewel Hill', on the bank of River Keluo, has produced the best finds. The extensive remains show excellent sculptural skill combining different coloured stones, from blue-green chlorite to the purple-red garnets encrusted in brownish silver khondalite. The finds include three monasteries (two quadrangular), eight temples and several stupas believed to date from the seventh-century. The largest monastery (No 1) is 55 m sq with a surrounding verandah with 60 pillars built around a courtyard entered through a carved gateway. At one end a shrine has a khondalite Buddha image and remnants of about two dozen cells for monks which were built of brick but had stone door frames. Look for the intricate carving on the doorway of the back porch wall: a dancer stamping her feet; a royal lady with her arm around a maid; a woman meditating. The seventh-century University of *Pushpagiri* may have flourished here; Hiuen Tsang, the Chinese traveller, after his visit in AD 639 described it as one of Orissa's two Buddhist centres of learning. Four galleries display fine sculptural figures dating from the ninth-10th centuries, terracotta and ivory objects, inscribed copper plates and miniature bronzes produced by the lost-wax process.

Udayagiri → *10 km south of Ratnagiri.*
① *Foreigners US$2.*

Excavations by the Archaeological Department (in progress in mid-2001) have unearthed better preserved carvings including the door jambs to the sanctum. The

Turtles in peril

Virtually every species of mangrove is found in the mangrove forests in the Bhitarkanika Wildlife Sanctuary, north of Paradeep, but their swamps are better known for their estuarine crocodiles, water monitors, cobras and above all Olive Ridley turtles (*Lepidochelys olivacea*), which have mysteriously arrived each year in vast numbers to lay eggs on a 10 km stretch of Gahirmatha beach.

Sea turtles are believed to return to nest where they hatched so the cycle continues. They arrive at night, for a fortnight around the full moon from October to May, with a spectacular arribadas (Portuguese 'the coming')

in February, when record numbers find their way from the Indian Ocean or from Australia, via the Pacific. They lay their eggs in nests excavated in the sand, a safe distance above the waterline and shed a salty "tear" afterwards. The eggs hatch about 2 months later, the incubation temperature deciding the sex; clutches are male around 24-26°C and female around 30-32°C, mixed when temperatures are in between.

The turtles compete for food with the fishermen and already thousands have met their death when trapped by their nets.

monastery, within a large compound, has 18 cells with a verandah arranged around a courtyard. The 3-m Lokesvar Buddha image here has an eighth - century inscription on it. Further up the hill, fragments of sculpture have been excavated among the ruins.

Lalitgiri
① *Foreigners US$2.*

The site about 3 km south of Bandareswar village was first excavated by the ASI in 1985. Large architectural remains including a 20-m high apsidal temple have been found together with sculptures and decorated door jambs. A stone platform with inscriptions dates this site closer to the second century although Kushana Brahmi inscriptions on an underlying brick stupa suggest Buddhist occupation around the first century BC. Three caskets were also found, two of which contained stone, silver and gold caskets with preserved relics inside. The caretaker will open the small museum. There is a stone-carvers' village at the base of Lalitgiri which traces its connections back to ancient times and produces excellent pieces of sculpture.

Paradeep → *94 km from Cuttack on the NH5A.*
① *Regular buses from Cuttack and Bhubaneswar.*

Paradeep is a port at the mouth of the Mahanadi River. Some 2,500 years ago Orissan sailors regularly set sail for Indonesia and mainland Southeast Asia from this point. Thousands of giant Pacific Ridley turtles migrate from as far afield as South America yearly to lay their eggs but now many face their death as they approach the shore, see box, page 712. Visitors today find they can't escape industrial pollution even here – "a layer of black dust settles on every surface in no time". There are a few overnight options.

Listings: The Northeast

◉ Sleeping

Cuttack *p710, map p710*
B-C Akbari Continental, Haripur Rd,
Dolmundai, T623251, F623254. 60 rooms,
central a/c, hot bath with tubs, balconies
view of garden obscured by ugly extension,
inefficient reception, all a bit tatty.
C Blue Lagoon, Ring Rd, near Puri Ghat,
T631884, F611936, www.hoteltheblue
lagoon.com. Central a/c, cramped singles,
river views, overpowering blue decor, decent
restaurant and fast food corner, overly helpful
staff, newish but showing signs of wear, plush
in design though not in execution.
C-D Manorama Plaza, Mahatab Rd, T331905,
F329139. 54 clean, reasonable though small
rooms, most a/c, restaurant, quiet area, travel
desk, bizarre 'birdsong' door bells.
C-E Ashoka, Ice Factory Rd, College Square,
T613508, F613091, ashok@dte.vsnl.net.in. 50
clean rooms, half a/c with hot bath, chaotic
reception but rooms OK once allocated!
Restaurant, taxi service, handy for trains.
D-E Panthanivas (OTDC), Buxi Bazar,
T306916. Not recommended.
D-F Ambica, Pilgrim Rd, College Sq,
T610137, F629038, hotelambica@
yahoo.com. Range of rooms from a/c to
cheap singles with shared bath, clean and
simple, friendly manager, veg restaurant,
close to railway.
E Bishal, Link Rd, Badambadi, T310752.
15 rooms (4a/c), quite comfortable and
clean, hot bath, TV, handy for bus station but
suffers from road noise.
E-F Railway Retiring Rooms. 4 rooms
(1 a/c), cheap dorm (Rs 25).
F Cuttack, College Rd, T610766. Basic, but
serviceable rooms, some with bath, restaurant.

Ratnagiri, Udayagiri and Lalitgiri *p711*
F Panthasala, Patharajpur (Cuttack
T312225), Simple rooms, caretaker may
provide a meal with advance notice.
A new **Tourist Complex** is under way.

◉ Eating

Cuttack *p710, map p710*
Outside the better hotels there is little to attract
the gourmet. In the evenings street stalls set up
around Buxi Bazar for a cheap bite.
Temptations, near Buxi Bazar has the best
and safest ice-creams in town, also
reasonable pizzas and snacks.

◉ Entertainment

Cuttack *p710, map p710*
You can try a makeshift pedalo on the
Mahanadi River. **Mahanadi Boating Club**
(2 men, a few chairs and an umbrella), on
Ring Rd, charge Rs 15 per person per half hr.
Also power boat at Rs 550 per hr.

◉ Shopping

Cuttack *p710, map p710*
Utkalika, Jail Rd, has a very good selection of
textiles and handicrafts including horn and
brass objects and jewellery. The famous silver
filigree shops are in Nayasarak and Balu Bazar.

▲▲ Activities and tours

Cuttack *p710, map p710*
Tour operators
Club Travels, Mani Sahu Chowk, Buxi
Bazar, T304999.
Tirupati, Chauliaganj, T642707. For local
sightseeing.

◉ Transport

Cuttack *p710, map p710*
Air
The nearest airport is at Bhubaneswar
(29 km). See page 708.

Bus
Services to all points in Orissa from the main
bus stand in Badambari. Regular services to
Bhubaneswar. Also state transport to major
towns in **Andhra Pradesh**, **Chhattisgarh**,

Orissa Listings: The Northeast

Madhya Pradesh and **West Bengal** (including Kolkata).

Cycle rickshaw
The best for short distances.

Taxi
At railway station and some hotels. Full day trip to **Lalitgiri**, **Ratnagiri** and **Udayagiri** (excluding entrance fees), Rs 600-Rs 800, depending on bargaining skills.

Train
Bhubaneswar and **Puri**: Several express and passenger trains, but timings can be unreliable, so quicker to take bus. **Chennai**: *Coromandal Exp, 2841*, 2000, 21½ hrs; *Howrah Chennai Mail, 1935*, 0230, 26½ hrs. **Kolkata (H)**: *Dhauli Exp, 2822*, 1425, 7½ hrs; *Coromandal Exp, 2842*, 0600, 7½ hrs; *Falaknuma Exp, 2704*, 1150, 8 hrs; *Jagannath Exp, 8410*, 2345, 9 hrs; *East Coast Exp, 7046*, 0550, 10 hrs. **New Delhi**: *Purushottam Exp, 2801*, 2225, 30½ hrs. **Secunderabad**: *Falaknuma Exp, 2703*, 1500, 21½ hrs; *East Coast Exp, 7045*, 1830, 24 hrs.

Ratnagiri, Udayagiri and Lalitgiri *p711*
It is possible to do a day excursion from Cuttack or Bhubaneswar by car (Rs 800). Get

to Chandikhol on NH5 (43 km), with some roadside eating places and turn right on NH5A (towards Paradeep) and then take the first turn left (at '12 km', before Patharajpur). Udayagiri is 1.5 km west of the road (8 km from NH5A) and Ratnagiri, 10 km further north. Return to the NH5A and continue towards Paradeep passing the Patharajpur *Panthasala* (Rest House) on the right. Turn right (south) at '20 km' for Lalitgiri which is 5 km away. Alternatively, buses from Cuttack stop at Chandikhol where you can hire a car for a 85 km return journey. Or take another bus towards Patharajpur hire a rickshaw and visit the first 2 sites.

❶ Directory

Cuttack *p710, map p710*
Banks State Bank of India, near High Court, exchanges £ and US$ TCs and cash. Forex on first floor. **Hospital** Christian Mission Hospital, recommended. Private clinics on Medical Rd. **Internet** 3 on Jail Rd next to Rajtarangiri Cinema. Decent connections, Rs 25 per hr. **Tourist office** Orissa, Arunodaya Market Building, Link Rd, T312225. Railway Station Counter, T610507. Both have helpful staff.

Northern Orissa→ *Colour map 6, grid A6.*

It is possible to visit several places of historic and religious interest in North and Northwest Orissa in three to seven days, as well as to see outstandingly beautiful scenery and the Similipal National Park. Some of the accommodation is excellent value (particularly at Chandipur), though in places it is very basic. ▸▸ *For Sleeping, Eating and other listings, see pages 716-718 .*

Baleshwar

Northeast from Bhubaneswar, this medieval maritime trading port was first established by the British in 1642 with subsequent competition from the French who called it *Farasidinga* and the Dutch *Dinamardinga*. Ruins of **Dutch tombs** can still be seen and traces of **canals**, up which ocean-going ships were hauled inland. The Khirachora Gopinath Temple is at Remuna (9 km) and Panchalingesvar Temple, 30 km away.

Chandipur

Chandipur, 16 km from Balashwar, on the coast has one of Orissa's finest beaches. The tide recedes 5 km daily and the dunes and casuarina groves make it particularly attractive and a pleasant, quiet stopping place. When the tide is in, scores of fisherfolk trawl for small fish along the coast. About 3 km north of *Panthanivas* is the fishing harbour at Balarama Gadi where fresh fish can be bought daily. The occasional explosions that can be heard come from the missile testing site nearby, on the road to Baleshwar.

Mayurbhanj District

The district is thickly forested with hills, waterfalls and streams and is the home of much of India's wildlife which can now be seen at Similipal. There are prehistoric sites at Kuchai and Kuliana. The historic sites are Khiching, Baripada and Haripur, where the Bhanja rulers have left their mark.

The area produces excellent tussar silk, carvings in multi-coloured translucent serpentine stone (from Khiching) and tribal metal casting of toys and cult images. The tribal people have enriched the culture of the district particularly with their traditional dances. Accommodation throughout the district is very basic.

Haripur → *16 km southeast of Baripada.*
ⓘ *There is a regular bus service.*

Haripur was founded by Maharaja Harihar in 1400 as the capital of the Bhanja Dynasty. A later king built the magnificent **Rasikaraya Temple** which, though now in ruins, is a unique example of a brick-built Orissan temple. The area is still fascinating as it has several other historic buildings nearby. The ruins of Ranihamsapur, the inner apartment of the queen, is to the north of the courtyard while the remains of the Durbar Hall with its beautiful sculptured stone columns and arches is to the east. The brick-built **Radhamohan Temple** and 14th-century **Jagannath Temple** are architecturally interesting although the deities were moved and are now worshipped in **Pratapapur** nearby.

Baripada

The district headquarters has a **museum** to the east of town with a small collection of stone sculpture, coins, seals, terracottas and inscriptions (summer 0700-1200, winter 1000-1700, closed Monday and holidays). *Chhau* dance festival, known as *Chaitra Parba*, in mid-April; the *Rath Yatra* in July is unique because the chariot carrying *Subhadra* is drawn by women.

Similipal National Park

→ *Colour map 3, grid A6. Malaria prophylaxis is strongly recommended.*
Similipal is Orissa's principal wildlife sanctuary covering 2,750 sq km at the heart of which is one of the country's earliest tiger reserves. The area has majestic sal forests interspersed with rosewood and flowering trees, expanses of grassland, waterfalls, gorges and river valleys.

Ins and outs

Spend 2-3 days to make the visit worthwhile. Foreigners entrance fee, Rs 100; vehicle charge, Rs 100; camera fee, Rs 50. Video cameras are only allowed with prior written permission from Chief Wildlife Warden, Bhubaneswar.

Getting there Entry is from Pithabata, near Baripada (NH5), or Jashipur (NH6), where there is a crocodile breeding centre. Entry permits from the Range Officer, Pithabata Check Gate or the Assistant Conservator of Forests, Khairi, Jashipur, T06797-32474. Some tour operators in Bhubaneswar can make all the arrangements (eg *Discover Tours*) but need 4 weeks notice - otherwise try for a permit on the day with a local agent (try *Ambika* in Baripada). Entrance for day visitors: 0600-1200, those with reservations 0600-1400. All visitors must leave before sunset.

Climate Best time to visit: Nov-Feb (park open from 1 Nov-15 Jun); May-Jun can be very hot. Temperature: 45°C to 5°C. Rainfall: 2,000 mm.

Wildlife

The 42 species of animals include tiger (99), elephant (449), leopard (119), wolf, chital, sambar, deer, gaur and flying squirrel. There are over 230 species of birds including mynahs, parakeet and peacocks.

Viewing

Open jeeps (Commanders) or more the comfortable, though enclosed, Tata Sumos are the usual choice of vehicle inside the park (Rs 1,200-1,500 for up to five). Jeep hire can be arranged through the Forest Office, Jashipur, Baripada Tourist Office or *Hotel Ambika* which can also help to arrange accommodation. However, logging disturbance and dense vegetation make viewing difficult and is further hindered by noisy visitors (who ignore the 'Silence' signs). and there is an increasing problem of littering in the park.

Visitors are allowed to go to the waterfalls, the *Chahala* woodland and *Nawana* valley, in the core area, on the dedicated forest road. The *Barehipani* waterfall with a drop of 400 m, and the *Joranda Falls*, 150 m, are both very impressive as are the Bachhurichara grassland where you might see a herd of elephants and the 1,158 m peak of Meghasani. However, most of the larger wildlife prefer to remain further inside the core area which does not allow visitors.

Khiching → *About 20 km west of Joshipur along the NH6.*

The capital of the **Bhanja** rulers in the 10th-11th century, a visit to Khiching can be combined with an excursion to Similipal from Chandipur (see above).

The local deity **Kichakesvari**, once the family goddess of the Mayurbhanj royal family, has a unique temple built entirely of chlorite slabs. The reconstructed 20th-century temple, which has fine carvings, is believed to have used the traditional temple building skills which date back to the eighth century. Nearby there are a number of other temples built in the Kalinga style, some of which are still in use.

Listings: Northern Orissa

● Sleeping

Baleshwar *p714*
B-C Torrento, Januganj, 4 km from centre near NH5, T06782-363481. 28 comfortable rooms, some a/c, recently renovated, good restaurant, exchange, pool and health club.
C-F Sahadevkhunta, close to bus stand (turn left), T06782-362657, F363660. Wide range of rooms with bath, some a/c, restaurant/bar.
E-F Railway Retiring Rooms. A/c and non a/c rooms, dorm (Rs 30).

Chandipur *p714*
Other hotels on the main road are reluctant to accept foreigners.

D-E Panthanivas (OTDC), on the beach, T06782-370051. 33 rooms, a few a/c, dorm (Rs 70), nets, ISD/internet facility, decent food, helpful staff, better in newer block, ample mosquitoes and cockroaches in old block closer to beach. Conducted tours including Similipal (minimum 10 people).
Others on road leading to *Panthanivas*.
D-E Shubnam, T06782-370025. 29 rooms (6 a/c), clean, friendly, nets, better maintained than *Panthanivas*.
E Chandipur, T06782-370030. Small, simple rooms with attached bath, clean linen, nets.
F Golden, opposite *Shubnam*. Basic rooms.

Baripada *p715*
D-F Ambika, Roxy Rd, T06792-52557. 20

reasonably clean rooms, some a/c, friendly and helpful staff, decent restaurant, tour of Similipal arranged, good value.

D-F Mohapatra, opposite Bus Stand, T06792-55226. 8 simple rooms, some a/c though a bit grubby, balconies overlook the bus stand.

D-F Sibapriya, Traffic Square, T06792-55138. 20 rooms, 'best in town' but non a/c rooms grubby, a/c better, restaurant.

F Ganesh Bhavan, Main Market, T06792-52784. 32 basic rooms, some with bath.

Similipal National Park *p715*
D Camp Polpola Retreat, inside the park, www.pugmarks.org, can be booked through Pugmarks, 10 Meher Ali Rd, Kolkata, T033-2873307, F2407737, who organize tours to Similpal. (OTDC),

E Forest Rest Houses, though the booking process is complicated and all food provisions should be taken with you. The caretaker at each will help you to cook a meal. Most rooms have several beds and average out at around Rs 200-400 per head for foreigners if full, otherwise it can work out quite expensive. Maximum stay is 3 nights. Those at **Chahala** (an old hunting lodge, 35 km from Jashipur), **Nawana** (60 km), **Joranda** (72 km) and **Barehpani** (with view of waterfall, 52 km) must be booked through Field Director, Similipal Tiger Reserve Office, PO Bhanjpur, Baripada, 757002 Orissa. Write enclosing a self addressed envelope (min 30 days and max 60 days before proposed date of stay) and include names of group members, sex, age, nationality, visa/passport details. You will hear about method of advance payment. Rest Houses at **Badampahar** (16 km from Jashipur), **Gudgudia** (25 km), and **Jamuani** (25 km), though not in the core area, are easier to reserve, in person, up to 10 days in advance from DFO, Karanjia, Jashipur, I06796-20226. Reservation counter open 1000-1330 every day.

E-F Aranyanivas (OTDC), at Lulung (3 km from Pithabata Gate). 8 double rooms, two 12-bed dorms, restaurant (only one inside park), completely run on solar power.

Panthasala, outside the park area, 35 km from Baripada towards Jashipur, has 4 double rooms. Reserve both through Tourist Officer, Baripada. Inside the core area there are some very spartan

Inspection Bungalow, contact Executive Engineer, PO Baripada.

Revenue Rest Shed, PO Khiching, contact Dist Magistrate, PO Baripada.

⊖ Transport

Baleshwar *p714*
Bus
Bus Stand is on Sahadevkhunta Rd with services to all major towns, though few to **Chandipur**.

Taxi
From railway staion to Chandipur demand Rs 150 before bargaining.

Train
Railway station is 500 m from Bus Stand, on the main Chennai-Kolkata line.
Bhubaneswar (spelt **Balasore** in timetables): best is *Dhauli Exp, 2821*, 0946, 3½ hrs. **Chennai**: *Coromandel Exp, 2841*, 1707, 24½ hrs; *Howrah Chennai Mail, 6003*, 2325, 29½ hrs. **Kolkata (H)**: *Coromandel Exp, 2842*, 0907, 4½ hrs; *Falakmuna Exp, 2704, 1457*, 4½ hrs; *East Coast Exp, 7046*, 1025, 5½ hrs. **New Delhi**: *Rajdhani Exp, 2421*, 1232 (Wed, Sun), 21½ hrs; *Purushottam Exp, 2801*, 0145, 27 hrs. **Puri**: *Jagannath Exp, 8409*, 2240, 6½ hrs. **Secunderabad**: *Falaknuma Exp, 2703*, 1202, 24½ hrs.

Chandipur *p714*
Bus
Only 4 or 5 per day to/from Baleshwar. Ask at *Panthanivas* for approximate timings.

Taxi
Ask for Rs 150 to/from Baleshwar.

Baripada *p715*
Bus
Private and government buses serve all major towns in the region.

Jeep
Jeeps available for hire to visit Similipal. Ask at *Hotel Ambika* or tourist office.

Train
Nearest stations at Baleshwar (Balasore) and
Tata Nagar.

Similipal National Park *p715*
Bus
The road from Baripada is via Lulung, 30 km
west, which has a regular bus service.

Train
The nearest stations on the Southeastern
Railways are at Tatanagar and Balasore.

Khiching *p716*
Bus
Regular buses from Baripada, 150 km.

Train
Nearest train station is 96 km away, but it is
better to get down at Balasore, 210 km, which
has a fast service on the Southeast Railway.

❻ Directory

Baleshwar *p714*
Bank State Bank of India, Branch, near ITT,
3 km from the railway station; the only bank
authorized to deal in foreign exchange
between Cuttack and Kolkata, so come
prepared! **Tourist offices** Orissa, SPA
Marketing Complex, Block B, Station Square
(at end of Station Rd, immediately opposite
to the left, 1st floor), T362048. Railway
Station Counter, platform 1. T363123.

Baripada *p715*
Banks Nearest foreign exchange is at
Baleshwar. (The Central Co-op Bank paints a
list of its top ten defaulters on the wall
outside!) **Tourist office** Baghra Rd, near Bus
Stand, T52710. **Tiger Reserve Office**, Bhanjpur
(2 km), T52593, F56705, simitig@dte.vsnl.
net.in. **Useful services** There is a District
Hospital, post office and shops selling local
handicrafts and handloom.

Western Orissa

*Settled in ancient times, Ptolemy's text of the second century refers to this area as a
diamond trading centre. In the eighth century King Indrabhuti became a Buddhist and
a preacher of the Vajrayana sect.* ▸▸ *For Sleeping, Eating and other listings, see page 720 .*

Sambalpur → *Phone code: 0663. Colour map 6, grid A5.*

Sambalpur is a pleasant, small town with a number of decent hotels and a few
restaurants grouped in the centre. The presiding deity Samalesvari to whom a temple
was built here by the Chauhans in the mid-16th century probably accounts for the
town's name. The district is famous for its **textiles**, particularly its tie-and-dye *ikat*
work. The villages and the countryside are pleasant in themselves and you might
consider visiting **Baragarh**, 1½ hours, and **Barpali**, three hours' drive, with a guide, if
you are interested in weaving. **Sonepur**, a lively small town with a colourful market
square and temple, is particularly rewarding. A scenic road from Sambalpur along the
Mahanadi River ends in a footpath down across the wide sandbank over half the river
in the dry season. Small boats ferry passengers across the remainder.

 Debjharan Sanctuary ① *taxis from Sambalpur cost Rs 300-400 for a return
day-trip,* has been recently created and developed as a picnic spot in forest situated
35 km south of Sambalpur, 5 km east of the NH6. There is a small waterfall and a dam
with waterhole at Chaura Asi Mal and a *Forest Rest House.*

Ushakothi → *48 km east of Sambalpur on the NH6.*
Ushakothi Wildlife Sanctuary is densely forested and covers 130 sq km. The sanctuary
has wild elephant, leopard, tiger, bison, wild boar and *chital* (barking deer). Best time

to visit is November-June, at night. Take a guide with search lights and see the wildlife from the watch-towers sited near watering points to which the animals come. Open hooded jeeps are recommended. Permits to visit, and guides, from the Forest Range Officer, PO Badrama. *Forest Rest House*, Badrama, 3 km away, is very basic (no electricity); on site ask for Choudhary Babu, Dealing Clerk, between 1000-1600.

Hirakud Dam

① *Regular buses from Sambalpur.*

The Mahanadi created enormous problems every year through devastating floods of the delta region and in order to combat these the Hirakud Dam was built about 20 km northwest of Sambalpur. The key section is a 1,100 m long masonry dam, with a further earth dam of over 3,500 m. One of the longest mainstream dams in the world, it is over 60 m high and drains an area twice the size of Sri Lanka. Since its completion in 1957 there have been no serious floods in the Mahanadi delta and allows the irrigation of vast areas of high quality land. You get an excellent view from the revolving tower, Gandhi Minar at one end of the dam. Contact the Deputy Superintendent of Police, Security Force, Hirakud before visiting.

Debrigarh Wildlife Sanctuary

① *Best season Oct-May. For permission and guides, contact DFO (Wildlife), Motijharan, T0663-402741. For information contact Chief Wildlife Warden (Orissa), Bhubaneswar, cwlwob@hotmail.com.*

This sanctuary adjoins Hirakud Lake around 50 km from Sambalpur. With an area of 347 sq km, the dry deciduous forest is home to tiger, leopard, sloth bear, chital, sambar, nilgai and a number of resident and migratory birds. Muggar crocodiles and freshwater turtles are amongst the reptiles present. Entry to the sanctuary is at Dhodrokusum, with a watchtower at Pathedurga. There are basic *Forest Rest Houses* at Dhodrokusum and Dechua, or a *Tourist Cottage* at Chaurasimal.

Huma → *About 32 km south of Sambalpur.*

Huma has a famous **Leaning Temple** ① *regular buses from Sambalpur to Huma Chowk, then walk 2 km to the temple*, on the bank of the Mahanadi, dedicated to Lord Siva. The temple leans southwards but the pinnacle is vertical. The colourful Kudo fish, easily seen from January to June, are believed to belong to Siva so are never caught by fishermen; visitors may feed them grain. Country boats are available for hire.

Sundargarh District

To the north of Sambalpur is Sundargarh District. In the tribal heartland, it is an area of undulating hills with the richest deposits of mineral wealth in the state. Cave paintings are evidence of the existence of early man. Once relatively untouched by modern civilization, the district was chosen for the siting of the first public sector steel plant at Rourkela. The route from Sambalpur to Rourkela runs north, 192 km, passing through some glorious scenery. The Brahmani flows along a wide rocky and sandy bed, a torrent in the monsoon, with forested hills on either side.

Rourkela → *Phone code: 0661. Colour map 3, grid C5. Population: 224,600.*

A large industrial town girdled by a range of hills and encircled by rivers, Rourkela was selected for its prime position as a steel plant in 1955 which has a Fertilizer Complex attached to it. The power for the steel plant comes from Hirakud. Both may be visited with permission from the PRO. There are banks, post offices, shops and hospitals.

Listings: Western Orissa

⊜ Sleeping

Sambalpur *p718*
C-D Saket, T402345, F401911. 30 decent, clean rooms with hot bath, TV, some a/c, restaurant.
C-D Sheela Towers, VSS Marg, T403117, F403456. 41 clean, comfortable though smallish rooms, TV, 2 restaurants.
D-E Panthanivas (OTDC), Brook's Hill, end of VSS Marg, T411282. 24 rooms (half a/c with TV), restaurant, bar, clean linen, all rooms with balconies but few with decent views.
D-E Uphar, T403078, F521440. Slightly cheaper sister concern of *Uphar Palace*.
D-E Uphar Palace, T400519, F522668. 29 good clean rooms with attached bath, some a/c, TV, 2 restaurants (good South Indian).
E-F Li-n-ja, near Ashoka Talkies, T521301. Clean rooms, grubby building, veg restaurant.
F Rani Lodge, next to *Uphar Palace*, T522173. Clean, simple rooms with attached bath, nets.

Hirakud Dam *p719*
E Ashok Nivas, good guesthouse at one end of the dam.

Rourkela *p719*
B Mayfair Garden, Panposh Rd (3 km), T502013. Touted as a 'farm resort', 18 comfortable rooms, decent restaurant, pool.
D Radhika, Bisra Rd, opposite railway station (1-min walk), T510795, F523196. 60 large rooms, reasonably clean, helpful staff.
D-E Panthanivas (OTDC), Sector 5 (2 km), T643280. 17 rooms, mostly a/c, restaurant/bar. Several other cheaper hotels on Bisra Rd within walking distance of bus and railway stations.

▲▲ Activities and tours

Sambalpur *p718*
Tour companies
Providing jeeps and taxis for sight-seeing.
Nalini Travels, Buddharaja, near flyover, T400407. **Swati Travels**, near Ashoka Talkies.

⊜ Transport

Sambalpur *p718*
Bus
Sambalpur has 2 bus stands, one for government buses, the other for private buses near Laxmi Talkies. Both are within a short cycle-rickshaw ride from VSS Marg, though the latter has more regular services to major towns in the area.

Jeep/taxi
Jeep/taxi hire: the easiest way to visit wildlife sanctuaries. See Directory for travel agents or contact tourist office. Return jeeps to **Debjharan**, Rs 300-400; to **Ushakothi** (1600-0400), Rs 500.

Train
Sambalpur has 2 stations, Khetrajpur and Sambalpur Rd. Both are between 2-3 km from the hotels on VSS Marg. **Kolkata (H)**: *Koraput Howrah Exp, 8006*, 1640, 13 hrs. **Puri** (via **Bhubaneswar**): *Tapaswini Exp, 8451*, 2220, 9½ hrs (6½ hrs).

Rourkela *p719*
Bus
New Bus Stand is within walking distance of hotels on Bisra Rd. Turn right and right again. Government and private buses to all major destinations in the region.

Train
Station is 1-min walk from Bisra Rd and hotels. **Kolkata (H)** : *Shatabdi Exp, 2022*, 1405, 7 hrs; *Ispat Exp, 8112*, 1240, 8 hrs. **Mumbai (CST)** : *Gitanjali Exp, 2860*, 1930, 26 hrs. **Patna**: *South Bihar Link Exp, 3287*, 1425, 18 hrs. **Puri** via **Bhubaneswar**: *Tapaswini Exp, 8451*, 1910, 12½ hrs (10 hrs); *Utkal Exp, 8478*, 1800, 16 hrs (12½ hrs).

❶ Directory

Sambalpur *p718*
Bank State Bank of India, near Collectorate, for foreign exchange. **Post office** Main post office, near Collectorate. Several internet cafes on VSS Marg (Rs 20-25 per hour). **Tourist offices** Orissa, at *Panthanivas*, T411118. Very helpful staff, worth a visit to plan excursions. Railway counter at *Khetrajpur*, T521661. Tours are often cancelled due to lack of passengers.

Southern Orissa

★ Chilika Lake → *Colour map 6, grid A5 and B5. Mosquitoes can be a problem.*

ⓘ *Boats, 1½ hrs, Rs 20. Nalabana bird watching trip, Rs 120, 4 hrs. Book 2000 night before, pay 0730 on day and wait until the boat is full.*

Chilika is the largest brackish water lake in Asia (1,100 sq km) stretching across the Khurdha, Puri and Ganjam districts, and forms an enormous lagoon as it is joined to the Bay of Bengal with a narrow mouth, a sandy ridge separating it from the sea.

The lake is the winter home of migratory birds, some flying great distances from Iran, Central Asia and Siberia. During the winter months (November-February) you can watch white bellied sea eagles, ospreys, golden plovers, sandpipers, flamingos, pelicans, shovellers and gulls. The lake attracts fishermen who come in search of prawn, mackerel and crab. Some ornithologists blame the growth in prawn farming, as well as the increasing discharge from rivers, silting and salinity for reduced bird numbers. The large Nalabana Island (Reed Island) sanctuary is often under water.

The **Kalijai Temple** stands on one of the tiny rock islands. Weekends get very crowded. **Satpada**, on the other side of the lake, has a Tourism Complex.
>> *For Sleeping, Eating and other listings, see pages 723-726 .*

Ganjam District→ *Colour map 6, grid B5.*

Ganjam District, south of Chilika Lake, takes its name from the Persian '*Ganj – Am*', meaning granary of the world, a testimony to its agricultural fertility. Still largely covered in dense forest, it was settled in prehistoric times and came under the influence of Emperor Asoka's rule. The handicrafts of the region include brass and bell-metal ware, hornwork, wood carvings, silks and carpets.

Ganjam
Ganjam was the District Headquarters, but the administration was moved to Chatrapur because of its unhealthy location. Its chief interest is the small East India Company fort and a Christian cemetery at the north end of town, near a large factory between the main road and the sea. An interesting excursion inland takes you to Aska (52 km) and Bhanjanagar (85 km).

Berhampur
A trading centre for silk fabric, Berhampur is the major commercial town of the District. The Thakurani, Jagannath and Nilakanthesvar Siva **temples** ⓘ *near DIG Residence, summer 0700-1400, winter 1000-1700, closed Mon and Government holidays*, are worth visiting. It is also a good place to shop for silks. The museum has a collection of sculpture, anthropological and natural history specimens; no photography.

Gopalpur → *Phone code: 0680.*
Gopalpur was an ancient sea port from which early settlers from Kalinga sailed as far as Java, Bali and Sumatra. Then it was a port for the export of Aska sugar and 'coolie' labour to the Assam tea gardens. Later still it became a popular seaside resort for the British offering a beautiful sandy beach. Today, however, it has a rather faded feeling and appearance. Sand dunes, groves of coconut and casuarinas separate the small town from the beach, while the backwaters, creeks and lagoons give some variety.

A red and white lighthouse opens to visitors briefly each afternoon; there are good views but photography is not allowed.

Taptapani
① *Direct bus from Berhampur, 50 km, Bhubaneswar, 240 km.*

Water from the very hot sulphur springs discovered at Taptapani in a forest setting, 50 km from Berhampur, is channelled to a pool for bathing. There is a shrine to goddess Kandhi inside the original *kund* (pool) as it is believed to cure infertility – tribal women come to the hot water pool near the *Panthanivas* hotel (D-E) to try to pick up a seed pod from the mud at the bottom.

Chandragiri
In the tribal hills, 32 km south of Taptapani, Tibetan carpet weavers have settled in a refugee colony at Chandragiri. The temple and Buddhist prayer flags lend a distinctive atmosphere. You can watch weavers and craftsmen at work; good prices.

Jaugada → *35 km north of Berhampur.*
① *Reached by a jeep road from Purusottampur which has buses from Berhampur.*

Jaugada in the Malati Hills is famous for one of **Asoka's 'Kalinga Edicts'** (see Dhauli above) which was discovered in the early 19th century, but the shelter was built only in 1975. Emperor Asoka's doctrine of conquest through love instead of the sword and his declaration "All men are my children" appear here. Sadly, some parts of the inscriptions have disappeared. The old fort (circa sixth century) contains stone images of the five *Pandavas* which are worshipped in the Guptesvar Temple.

Buguda, a few kilometres away, has the Viranchinarayan Temple with its beautifully carved wooden *Jagamohan* and murals depicting stories from the epic Ramayana. Also, close by, **Buddhakhol** has Buddhist sculptures and shrines to Siva.

Tribal areas→ *Colour map 6, grid B3. Best season is from Oct to Mar.*

Orissa's rich tribal heritage has survived among the hills and forests across the districts of Koraput, Kandhamal, Kalahandi, Ganjam, Keonjhar, Dhenkanal and Mayurbhanj. The state government is actively promoting tourism in some of these areas, see page 687. It is best to book a tour at least a month ahead to allow time to get permits to visit tribal territories. Without permits, tours are restricted to roadside villages where development programmes are already changing traditional values and in some cases the influx of tourism has created a disappointing 'circus' effect, with demands of money for photos, dances and sweets for the children. With permits and a guide it is possible to visit the more isolated villages. Individual visitors face difficulties from the local police, so it is best to take a guide in any instance. Always seek out the village chief for permission to enter a village. Photography is prohibited in Bondo and Dongariya territories. Permission should always be asked before taking photographs of tribal people. Respect their privacy should they decline. Walking around settlements with a video camera glued to the eye is not appreciated. Away from the main towns accommodation is very basic and some camping is necessary when trekking. Transport is usually by non-a/c car, jeep or minibus. Foreign exchange is only available in Sunubeda so it is best to change money in advance.

Tribal markets

Typical 'Social Interest' tours offered by travel agents include a number of tribal villages with a chance to attend interesting festivals and markets. Some of the tribes seen in these areas may include Dongariya Kondhs, Dhurubas, Parajas, Koyas, Bondos and Gadabas. In Koraput District: **Ramgiri**, 70 km southwest of Jeypore, has a very picturesque Tuesday market where Kondh people come to sell fresh vegetables and baskets and to buy salt. **Nandapur**, 44 km south of Koraput. Brings tribal ladies to the colourful Wednesday market where they sell beedi leaves and large almond-flavoured seeds. **Ankadeli**, 90 km southwest of Koraput, has a Thursday market where Bondo women, clad entirely in bead, come to sell handloom fabric, beads and exquisite woven grass headbands. **Rayagada** has some good accommodation. Sleeping and eating also available at **Laxmipur** and **Baliguda** (see listings page 723).

Jeypore → *Phone code: 06854.*

Jeypore itself is unspoilt by tourism and the scenery around is very beautiful. There are several monuments including a fort and palace. It is quite possible to organize your own tour from Jeypore and reportedly easier to get permits to visit tribal areas in Koraput rather than in Bhubaneswar.

Koraput

Koraput is a useful base for visiting the tribal areas. There is a small tribal **museum** ① *closed Wed, 1500-1700, Sun 1000-1600*, although you may need a guide to understand the exhibits. There are larged modern Jagannath Temples (Hindus only) where large galleries of images are reproduced from shrines. The Orissa Coffee Planters' Association, located around 20 km from Koraput, are happy to show visitors around the plantation which has fruits and spices as well as coffee.

Kotapad → *46 km northwest of Jeypore on N43.*

The clean area of weavers' houses in Kotapad has large pots of cotton and tussore silk soaking in natural dyes, while keins hang drying. Weavers are happy to show you work in progress. The Co-op ensures even pricing – Rs 350-600 buys a 3-m shawl. It is worth seeking out award winner Jagabandhu Samarth. As the word gets around, weavers will find you to show you their pieces but there is no pressure to buy.

Listings: Southern Orissa

🛏 Sleeping

Chilika Lake *p721*
D-E Panthanivas (OTDC), Barkul,
I06756-20488 (1 km from road end).
20 small rooms, some a/c, restaurant, bar, tourist office, boating complex, 0800 check out, busy at weekends and holidays.
D-E Panthanivas (OTDC), Rambha,
T06810-78346. 11 rooms, some a/c, half-rate for day visitors (0900-1700).
E Yatri Nivas, Satpada, north side of the lake, closest to Puri, T06752-62077. Attractive location, decent rooms. Best 1st floor foor views and balconies.
F Shree Khrishna Lodge, Barkul (500 m from *Panthanivas*), T06756-21195. Simple, clean rooms, some with bath.
Chilka Dhaba, immediately south of turn off for *Panthanivas* at Barkul, specialise in tiger prawns from the lake. Recommended.

Berhampur *p721*
Few visitors stay overnight, preferring to head on to Gopalpur. However, if arriving late, the following are adequate:

E **Hotel Radha**, near the Old Bus Stand.
E **Radha Hotel**, close to railway station.
E **Udipi**, near the Old Bus Stand.
F **Gitanjali**, close to railway station.
F **Puspa**, Gatekeeper's Square, 1½ km from the New Bus Stand. Basic.
F **Railway Retiring Rooms** and dorm.
F **Ranjan**, Gatekeeper's Square, 1½ km from the New Bus Stand. Basic.

Gopalpur *p721*

AL **Oberoi Palm Beach**, T242021, F242300, pbeach@sancharnet.in. 18 rooms around gardens, good restaurants, bar, private beach, sports facilities, run like a British country house, relaxing (until the bill comes!).
C-D **Sea Pearl**, T242556. Decent, albeit pricey rooms with bath and TV, all with balcony though some face the building next door.
D **Song of the Sea**, next to lighthouse, T242347. Clean, light and airy rooms in family run hotel, peaceful location, simple restaurant, best at front on first floor with sea view, pleasant though pricey.
D-E **Green Park**, T242016, greenpark016@ yahoo.com. Clean rooms (some a/c), simple Indian-style hotel, best with sea view, 24-hr check out.
D-E **Panthanivas** (OTDC), T242088. 15 stuffy rooms in run-down building, 2 a/c with TV, mosquito-infested dorm, restaurant.
E **Holiday Home**, T242049. Simple rooms, some with TV, clean bath and linen, small singles, restaurant, large terrace overlooking sea.
E **Mermaid**, T282050. Good, clean breezy rooms, better on 1st floor with sea facing balconies, good restaurant (order ahead), one of the best.
E **Sea Side Breeze**, T242075. Only hotel right on the beach, 14 clean rooms, food on order, ideal for backpackers.
F **Heaven Spot**, Rewu St. 5 small, basic but new and clean (2002) rooms with attached bath, away from beach, serves as a base but little else.
F **Nataraj**, T242340. 10 simple rooms, away from beach, attached bath, food available.
F **Rosalin**, T242071. 9 very basic rooms, some with attached bath, small garden, food on order, friendly but prepare for mosquitoes!
F **Sai Tourist Lodge**, T242041. 6 basic rooms in family house with attached or shared bath.

F **Youth Hostel**. Members only, very basic, dreary dorms in building which should be condemned.

Rayagada *p723*

D **Sai International**, JK Rd, T06856-25555, F23396, has 40 good, comfortable rooms, several a/c, TV, hot bath, restaurant, bar, staff still learning how to deal with foreigners but excellent value.
E-F **Jyoti Mahal**, Convent Rd, T06856-23015, has 25 reasonably sized rooms with bath, a bit grubby but friendly, decent restaurant.
E-F **Swagath**, New Colony, T06856-22208, has 44 clean rooms, good local style restaurant.

Laxmipur *p723*

Hotel Konark, the green building by Ambedkar Chowk. Good thalis and a friendly young English speaking owner. Good lunch stop.

Baliguda *p723*

Baliguda is basically a one-street town, a quiet, friendly place with a slow pace of life.
F **Santosh**, off Main Road, with 16 rooms, best on the first floor with attached bath, the only place with experience of foreigners.

Jeypore *p723*

C-D **Hello Jeypore**, East Octroi Check Post, NH43 (2 km centre), T31127, F30601, hellojeypore@yours.com. Best in town though noisy area, 30 comfortable, well-furnished a/c rooms overlooking lovely garden, hot power shower in mornings, TV, efficient service, excellent restaurant (try *alu raita*). Recommended.
E-F **Madhumati**, NKT Rd, T40307. 30 large rooms, some a/c, TV, mosquito problem, restaurant, bar, very helpful manager.
E-F **Princess**, near Bus Stand, NH43 (corner of Main Rd), T30027, princessco@vsnl.com. 40 reasonable rooms (some **D** a/c), hot bath, TV, cheaper singles, good restaurant, accommodating staff, well run.
F **Roseland Lodge**. Very cheap rooms, common bath, basic but friendly. Excellent restaurant at *Hello Jeypore* and reasonable food (though dark restaurant) at *Princess*.
Girija, Main Rd. Good for chicken and Chinese dishes.
Kasturi, thalis.

Koraput p723

F **Ambica Heavens**. Decent rooms with bath, TV, quieter at the back.
F **Athithi Bhavan**. Managed by the Jagannath Temple Trust, simple rooms with bath, TV, temple food, can be noisy.
Dolphin's Plaza, below *Ambica Heavens*, is worth a try for meals.

▲ Activities and tours

Jeypore p723
Tour operators
Discover Tours, see Bhubaneswar. Highly recommended. Perfect Travels, Rajmahal Chowk, T41856. Car and driver, Rs 850 per day. **Travel Care**, Sardar Patel Marg, T22291, F23286. For tours write to Mr Pujari 4-6 weeks in advance with a photocopy of the relevant passport pages.

⊜ Transport

Chilika Lake p721
Chilika Lake is easiest to reach by road (NH5) from Barkul, 6 km south of Balugaon or Rambha at the south end of the lake.

Bus
Buses from **Bhubaneswar** and **Berhampur**. Satpada at the northern end can only be reached via **Puri** from where there are plenty of day trips offering 'dolphin safaris'.

Ferry
OTDC motor launches are available from Barkul, Rambha and Satpada although during the week it may not be cost effective. **Dolphin watching** is the main focus of boats from Satpada. Private country boats are also available at Barkul and Rambha.

Train
Slow passenger trains on the Chennai-Kolkata line stop at **Balugaon**, **Chilika**, **Khallikote** and **Rambha**.

Berhampur p721
Bus
The Old and New Bus Stands are about 3 km from the railway station, 2 km from each other. Government buses use the Old Bus Stand, private buses (which are more regular and reliable) the New Bus Stand and cover major towns in Orissa and neighbouring states.

Taxi
Available from Old Bus Stand.

Train
On the main Chennai-Kolkata line. Berhampur is referred to as **Brahmapur** in time-tables.
Chennai: *Coromandel Exp, 2841*, 2340, 18 hrs; *Howrah Chennai Mail, 6003*, 0645, 22½ hrs.
Kolkata (H) via **Bhubaneswar**: *Coromandel Exp, 2842*, 0230, 11½ hrs; *Falaknuma Exp, 2704*, 0805, 11½ hrs; *Chennai Howrah Mail, 6004*, 1855, 12½ hrs; *East Coast Exp, 7046*, 0140, 14½ hrs; *Tirupati Howrah Exp, 7480*, 1115, 16½ hrs. **Secunderabad**: *Falaknuma Exp, 2703*, 1850, 17½ hrs; *Konark Exp, 1020*, 1645, 18 hrs; *East Coast Exp, 7045*, 2240, 20 hrs; *Visakha Exp, 7615*, 1025, 21½ hrs.

Gopalpur p721
Regular private buses from New Bus Stand, Berhampur (30 min).

Jeypore p723
Bus
Night buses from Berhampur.

Car
If travelling by car from the coast, make sure the car can manage the hill roads and the driver is not worried about entering tribal areas.

Train
The station is 7 km away. A daily train connects with Vishakhapatnam. From Vizag, *Kirandol Exp*, 0745, 8 hrs. Superb views for first 3 hrs uphill then down to Araku Valley; 2nd class is full of firewood and farm produce and so best avoided. From the north, travel to Vizianagaram station, and from there by bus (or taxi).

Koraput p723
Train
Bhubaneswar: *Hirakhand Exp, 8447*, 1130, 10 hrs. From Bhubaneswar, *Hirakhand Exp, 8447*, 2120, 14½ hrs. **Kolkata (H)**: *Koraput Howrah Exp, 8006*, 0415, 25 hrs.

Chilika Lake *p721*
A **post office**, a Govt **dispensary** and a **tourist office** at Barkul, T20855.

Berhampur *p721*
Bank State Bank of India, Main Branch, State Bank Rd, changes foreign cash and TCs.

Tourist office New Bus Stand, 1st floor, T250226. Railway station counter, T203870. **Useful services** Christian Mission Hospital, **post offices** and **shops**.

Koraput *p723*
Bank Sunabeda, 18 km away. State Bank of India, the only one in the area. **Tourist office** Orissa, Koraput Club, T06852-50318.

Bihar and Jharkhand

❃ Footprint features

Introduction

Bihar, which takes its name from the word 'vihara', or monastery, was the early home of Buddhism and the birthplace of one of India's most revered emperors, Asoka. His Buddhist legacy has left its imprint in some of the state's most visited pilgrimage sites, for while it may be on the outskirts of modern Patna, **Kumrahar** still has fragmentary remains of the early Mauryan capital, in **Bodh Gaya** and **Nalanda**, Buddhism's tradition is powerfully visible.

After the creation of the new state of Jharkhand modern Bihar is confined to the densely populated, and desperately poor, **Ganges plains**. The state has a chequered recent political history. Separated from Bengal in 1912, in 1936 another partition led to the creation of Orissa. After Independence the reorganization of Indian states saw the transfer of territory from Bihar to West Bengal, while the tribal groups had already begun to campaign for a separate state for the tribal areas of the Chota Nagpur plateau in South Bihar. On 15 November 2000 this dream was finally achieved with the division of Bihar into two, the Chota Nagpur plateau becoming the new state of Jharkhand.

★ Don't miss...

❶ **Sonepur Fair** is the scene of one of Asia's most remarkable cattle fairs in November, page 736.

❷ Take the very pleasant 5km walk at Vaishali to the **Kolhua Asoka Pillar**, page 736.

❸ Visit the impressive ruins at **Nalanda**, possibly the site of the world's oldest university, page 739.

❹ **Bodh Gaya** can resemble a medieval encampment as pilgrims from all over the world visit one of the holiest Buddhist pilgrimage centres, page 743.

❺ **Sher Shah's mausoleum** at Sasaram appears to float in an artifical tank. It is a great place for a relaxing break, page 745.

❻ Join pilgrims at 0400 and climb **Parsnath Hill** to catch superb views of the sunrise and the surrounding countryside, page 750.

Background → *Population: Bihar 82.88 million, Jharkhand 26.9 million.*
Area: Bihar 174,000 sq km, Jharkhand 65,000 sq km.

The land

Bihar and Jharkhand form a region of transition. The wet lowlands to the east give way to the much drier and now more prosperous alluvial plains to the west. From north to south, the two states stretch 600 km from the foothills of the Himalaya across the flat plains to the forested and mineral-rich hills of Chota Nagpur (now in Jharkhand). The River Ganga runs through the heart of the plains, joined by its tributaries from the Nepal Himalaya to the north and from the Vindhyan Hills of the Peninsula to the south. To the north of the Ganga are the scars of old river beds which often form chains of lakes during the monsoon and provide a vital source of fish. North Bihar is India's biggest producer of freshwater fish, over half of which is sold to Kolkata. Torrential rain in the Himalayan foothills and the flatness of the Ganga valley floor cause some of the rivers, like the Kosi, to flood catastrophically. Over a period of 130 years the Kosi has moved over 110 km westwards.

History

The name Bihar is derived from *vihara* (monastery), suggesting its wealth of religious monuments. All the major religions of India have left a mark, most notably Buddhism and Jainism. The world's first university of Buddhist learning was founded at Nalanda, southeast of Patna.

Bihar was settled from the west as Aryan tribes moved down the Ganga valley, clearing the forest and developing cultivation. Agriculture provided the base for the Magadhan kings who ruled from the sixth to the fourth centuries BC. The early Magadhan kings had their capital at **Rajgir**, 100 km southeast of modern Patna. It was surrounded by 40 km of stone walls which can still be seen. Later they moved their capital to **Pataliputra**, the site of modern Patna.

The Guptas, who played a central role in the flowering of Hindu culture of the classical period, rescued Magadha in the fourth to fifth centuries AD from more than 600 years of obscurity. They were followed by the Palas of Bengal who ruled until defeated by the Muslims in 1197. The Delhi sultans and a succession of independent Muslim rulers controlled the region until the arrival of the Mughals who retained it until the British won the Battle of Buxar in 1764. Subsequently Bihar was separated from Bengal and became a province under British rule until India's independence in 1947.

Culture

There is a sharp division between the agricultural plains of north Bihar, with three-quarters of the combined population total, and the Chota Nagpur plateau to the south, where a high proportion of India's mineral resources are concentrated. The plains are peopled largely by Hindus but five centuries of Muslim political dominance have resulted in a significant Muslim population (14% today). Aboriginal **tribal peoples** in Jharkhand, include Santal, Oraon, Munda Kharia and Ho tribes. Some have converted to Christianity in large numbers.

Hindi is dominant throughout the plains, with related dialects elsewhere (eg Maithili, Bhojpuri, Magahi). Urdu is spoken by many Muslims, and tribal languages by nearly 10% of the population (eg Austro-Asiatic Santali and Dravidian Oraon).

Local festivals

In **April/May** is *Buddha Jayanti* celebrating the Buddha's birth when Bodh Gaya and Rajgir attract Buddhists from all over the world, while *Mahavira Jayanti* brings Jains to the sacred Parsnath Hill. In **June** a unique 14-day *marriage market* takes place in a large mango grove in Saurath where the nation's Mithila Brahmins gather. Parents

Bihar's plains: gift of the Himalaya?

Severe flooding of Bihar's rivers has prompted some environmentalists to blame deforestation in Nepal. Rising population, commercial logging and bad agricultural practices have been held responsible for widespread damage on Bihar's plains. But recent research sheds doubt on this apparently simple cause and effect. For one thing, the River Kosi has been shifting its course for decades, and floods have washed down silt from the Himalaya for centuries. Without them the plains would not exist. To limit damage from the Kosi, a protective embankment along the southern flank of the Himalaya was built in 1960 to limit the flooding and westward movement of the river, and to protect agricultural land. Attempts to control the Kosi by building dams in Nepal are still under consideration, but the very large amounts of silt, plus the fact that the Himalayan foothills are a zone of major earthquakes, makes projects extremely difficult to implement effectively. To the south of the Ganga is another stretch of alluvium, much shallower than that to the north of the river and about 150 km wide. When the Ganga is in full flow it is higher than the tributaries which join it from the south, so it is also subject to severe floods between July and October. The alluvium barely covers the ancient rocks of peninsular India which form the Chota Nagpur plateau, emerging in broken hills to the south. There is beautiful open parkland scenery in Chota Nagpur itself, much of the original forest having been cleared.

come with horoscopes to arrange marriages of their sons and daughters. **October/November** has *Pataliputra Festival* starting with *Dasara* in October and ends with the Sonepur Fair. *Durga puja*, *Dasara* and *Diwali* are celebrated. *Chhath* or *Surya Puja* takes place six days after *Diwali*. To mark the harvest, fresh paddy, sweets and fruit are offered by devotees in procession; women, waist deep in the Ganga, offer homage at sunrise and sunset. *Sonepur Fair* is the scene of one of Asia's most remarkable cattle fairs in November.

Food and drink
The typical Bihari meal consists of boiled rice, unleavened bread, lentils and vegetables cooked with hot spices. *Sattoo*, a combination of grains, is made into a dough and eaten either as a savoury, or a sweet when mixed with sugar or jaggery. The mixture can also be taken as a drink when mixed with milk or water and flavoured with cardamoms and cloves. *Puri-aloo*, deep fried Indian bread with potatoes cooked with onions and garlic, and *kachoris* made with wheat and lentil flour and served with *kala chana* (black gram), are tasty snacks.

Modern Bihar
From its pre-eminent position in the culture and politics of early and classical India, Bihar has declined today to one of India's poorest and most badly administered states. There are periodic outbreaks of caste-based violence in the countryside, notably in Jharkhand. Many of the tribal peoples have been under pressure from agricultural settlers from the plains. Often in desperation the poor have moved to cities like Kolkata and Mumbai, or to work on tea estates.

Bihar is one of the most troubled political administrations of modern India. Successive governments have been charged with corruption and maladministration, and it is widely regarded across India as the most lawless state in the country. Since the mid 1990s the state government has been run by Laloo Prasad Yadav and his wife Rabri Devi, currently at the head of the Rabri Janata Dal (RJD).

In the State Assembly elections in February 2000 the RJD (124 seats) won the narrowest of victories over the BJP and its allies (123 seats, a victory gained by welding together a powerful alliance of the poor (*dalits*) and Muslims. It was able to re-take power by securing the support of the Congress, which initially had threatened to boycott the RJD. Laloo Prasad had been forced out of office in 1997 as a result of corruption charges, to be replaced as Chief Minister by his wife Rabri Devi, who is now serving her third term as Chief Minister.

Patna → *Phone code: 0612. Colour map 3, grid B5. Population: 1.4 million.*

Despite its size, Patna, Bihar's straggling capital, in its more attractive areas has the air more of a semi-rural provincial town. However, it is one of India's poorest cities, stretching along the south bank of the Ganga for about 15 km. Divided in two by the large open Maidan, the central city is crowded, dusty and has little of architectural interest. Scant evidence remains of its earlier wealth and political supremacy. Thousands sleep on the streets and there are few street lights at night. However, around the station food stalls are neatly set out and illuminated, and it can be interesting to take a cycle-rickshaw round by day or night. Many tribal people come into the town, often working on roads or building sites. ▸▸ For Sleeping , Eating and other listings, see pages 736-738.

Patna City

To Rajendra Smriti
Museum &
Sadaquat Ashram

Related map
A Patna centre, page 734

Sleeping ■
1 Kautilya Vihar, Amrali Restaurant & Paryatan Bhavan Tourist Office
2 Pataliputra Ashok

Eating ●
1 Jayasarmin

0 metres 500
0 yards 500

Ins and outs

Getting there **Patna airport**, 7 km from town, has coaches and taxis for transfer. Long distance State buses arrive at the Gandhi Square Bus Stand, which is between 15-25 mins' walk from most budget hotels. These are strung out down Fraser Rd towards Patna Junction railway station and Vir Kunwar Singh (Hardinge) Bus Stand (serving Gaya, Varanasi and Nepal).

Getting around The centre of Patna is compact enough to walk around, though autos and cycle rickshaws are easily available. For longer distance trips you can hire unmetered taxis from major hotels. See Transport, page 737, for further details.

History

At the confluence of the rivers Son, Punpun, Gandak and Ganga, Patna's history can be traced back 2,500 years. Ajatasatru, the second Magadha king who ruled from Rajgir, built a small fort at Pataligrama. Later Chandragupta Maurya founded the Mauryan Empire with Pataliputra as its capital. Buddhist histories suggest that it was here that Asoka usurped the throne of his father, Bindusara, murdering all his rivals and starting a reign of terror, before a conversion eight years later. It marked the beginning of perhaps the greatest reforming kingship the world has known. The Greek ambassador Megasthenes was deeply impressed y the efficiency of the Chandragupta administration and the splendour of the city. Ruins can be seen at Kumrahar, Bhiknapahari and Bulandhi Bagh with its 75 m wooden passage. Excavations date the site back to the pre-Mauryan times of 600 BC. In the 16th century the Pathan Sher Shah Suri established the foundations of a new Patna, building a majestic mosque in 1540 which dominates the skyline.

Bihar & Jharkhand Patna

Patna's buildings reflect its administrative and educational functions. The Collectorate, Court and educational institutions are all close to the river bank in the western part of the city as are the Raj Bhavan, the High Court and the better residential quarters. To the east is Old Patna with its bazars, old mosques, Har Mandir and St Mary's Church.

St Mary's or Padri-ki-Haveli (Priest's House, circa 1775), is the oldest Christian church in Bihar. The fine 'Raj' cemetery alongside has gravestones dating back to 1760; some were connected with the opium trade. Now overgrown, it can still be worth exploring.

Golghar The *Gola* (round house), an extraordinary ovoid dome between the Maidan and the Ganga, was built of stone slabs in 1786 by Captain John Garstin of the Bengal Engineers, who planned this grain store for the army in case of a repeat of the 1770 famine. It has a base 125 m wide, where the wall is 3.6 m thick, with two brick staircases that spiral up the outside; the workforce were to carry the grain up at one end and descend by the other. It was never completed so the last line of the inscription "First filled and publicly closed by …" remains unfinished. Sometimes, it is possible to go inside and listen to the remarkable echo. It is well worth climbing the steps for an excellent view of the city and the Ganga. Between July and September the river can be over 5 km wide at this point.

Har Mandir is in the Chowk area of old Patna. The *gurudwara* built by Maharaja Ranjit Singh is the second of the four great *takhts* (thrones) of the Sikhs and consecrates the birthplace of the 10th Guru, Gobind Singh, in 1660. The shrine of white marble with kiosks on the terrace above has a museum on the third floor.

Kumrahar Excavations at the site of the ancient capital of Pataliputra have revealed ruins enclosed within a high brick wall. These date back to 600 BC, the first of four distinct periods of settlement over the following 1,200 years. The buildings, mainly of wood, were devastated by a fire and lay hidden in the silt. The more recent fifth phase dates from the beginning of the 17th century.

The most important finds are rare wooden ramparts and a large Mauryan three-storeyed assembly hall, that was 77 m square, with 15 rows of five highly polished sandstone pillars dating back to 400-300 BC. The garden site has little to show today other than the single 6 m intact pillar. The tiny museum has its small collection of valuable finds almost invisibly shut away in a dark room.

At **Gulzaribagh**, about 8 km east of the Golghar near Kumrahar, are the former East India Company's principal **opium**

Patna centre

Ganga River

Buddha Ghat

Golgha

Ashok Raj Path

To Rajendra Smriti Museum (2 km)

Angus Girls

British Library

(Fazal Ali Rd)   Bank Rd

Dr T N Banerjee Rd

Mahatma Gandhi Maidan

To Khuda Baksh Oriental Library

Indian Airlines

Buddha Marg

(SP Verma Rd)

(Brajkishore Path)

Patna State Museum

Indira Gandhi Science Complex

Fraser Rd

Dak Bungalow Rd

Exhibition Rd

To Kadam Kuan

To Pataliputra Ashok

Jamal Rd

To Secretariat

Buddha Marg

Fraser Rd

(Kranti Marg)

Rajendra Path

To Kolkata

Station Rd

Patna Junction

To Airport & Varanasi

N

0 metres   300
0 yards   300

◼ Sleeping
1 AAEI
2 Maurya Patna
3 Mayur
4 Rajasthan
5 Republic
6 Satkar International
7 Sheodar

⬤ Eating
1 Ashok
2 Chef
3 Marwari
4 Mayfair

godowns (warehouses), now a Government printing press. The three long buildings with porticoes on each side were strategically placed by the river for boats to carry the opium down to Kolkata. The old *godowns*, ballroom and hall are open to visitors.

Museums

Indira Gandhi Science Complex, corner of Buddha Marg and Bailey Road, includes a planetarium. **Jalan Museum** in **Quila House** ① *get prior permission from the owner, Mr BM Jalan, Hira Pl, Dak Bungalow Rd, Patna 1, T225070, F235777, quilahouse@ hotmail.com*, is across the road from Har Mandir. The private house was built over the ruins of Sher Shah's fort and is a museum containing Chinese paintings and a valuable collection of jade and silver filigree work of the Mughal period. **Saif Khan's Mosque** (Pathar-ki- Masjid) on the river bank was built in 1621 by Parwez Shah, the son of the Mughal Emperor Jahangir. **Khuda Baksh Oriental Public Library** (1900) has one of the largest private collections of books and rare Persian and Arabic manuscripts, Rajput paintings and the only books rescued from the Moorish University of Cordoba, Spain. It is now a national library. **State Museum** ① *closed Mon, 1030-1630, (avoid toilets), Buddha Marg*, has a collection of coins, paintings, terracotta, bronze and stone sculptures including the famous Mauryan Didarganji Yakshi (circa 200 BC), Jain sculptures (second, third centuries) and finds from Bodh Gaya, Nalanda et cetera. The presentation is uneven, with scarcely any labels and some moth-eaten exhibits. However, the first floor gallery is well lit with a collection of terracotta heads from the third century BC; the mezzanine floor has an interesting collection of Tibetan *thangkas*.

Around Patna

→ *Colour map 6, grid A4. You can visit both Sonepur and Vaishali in a comfortable day's excursion.*

Near its confluence with the Gandak, 22 km across the Ganga, Sonepur has a station on the Northeast Railway. Sonepur witnesses Asia's biggest cattle market which begins on the full moon of *Kartik Purnima* (November). The month-long fair draws thousands to the magic shows, folk dances, contests of skill and stalls selling handicrafts and handlooms. Mark Shand's *Travels on my Elephant* gives a colourful account of the fair. Elephants – as well as camels, horses and birds – are still bought and sold at this fair but numbers are dwindling. Bihar Tourism sets up a Tourist Village a week before the Fair and Swiss Cottage Tents are furnished and have attached baths.

Vaishali → *Colour map 3, grid B5.*
ⓘ *BSTDC tour (Rs 70); buses; taxis (Rs 750).*

Vaishali – derived from King Visala, from the *Ramayana* – dates back to the sixth century BC when it was a flourishing city of the Lichchavis, reputedly one of the first cities in the world to adopt a republican form of government. This is where the Buddha preached his last sermon and announced his approaching Nirvana. A century later, in 383 BC, it was the venue of the second Buddhist Council, when two stupas were erected. Jains of the Svetambara sect believe that Mahavir was born in Vaishali in 599 BC. Today the district is part of the Mithila region famous for Madhubani paintings on the walls of village houses.

The **Asoka Pillar** at **Kolhua**, also known as Bhimsen-ki-Lathi (stick), is a single 18 m piece of very highly polished red sandstone with a bell-shaped inverted lotus capital and a life-sized lion carved on top. Asoka pillars (*stambhas*) were unornamented, with a circular section that tapered like the trunk of a palm tree. They may have been forerunners of temples developed from the ancient form of worshipping in the forest. This is one of two Asoka pillars that remain in situ. The 'Wheel of Law' which tops many of the pillars – and appears on the Indian flag – is the mark of the social and political order laid down by the Emperor.

Ramkund is also known as Monkey Tank since it was thought to have been dug by monkeys who offered the Buddha a bowl of honey. The two Buddhist **stupas** are said to hold urns containing the Buddha's ashes; the second was only excavated in 1958. The ancient **Coronation Tank** (*Kharauna Pokhar*) contains holy water which was used for anointing the ruler of Vaisali at his coronation. The **Lotus Tank** nearby is thought to be a picnic spot of the sixth century BC.

A very pleasant, easy 5-km **walk** from the *Tourist Bungalow* to the Asoka Pillar takes you through picturesque villages, passing the Japanese stupa, the museum and an old small stupa.

Listings: Patna

🛏 Sleeping

Patna *p732, maps p732 and p734*
Some streets have been renamed – Bir Chand Patel Path (or Marg) has replaced Gardiner Rd. Some old names continue to be used, eg Bailey Rd (J Nehru Marg), Fraser Rd (Nazharul Huque Path), Exhibition Rd (Braj Kishore Path).
A-B Maurya Patna, Fraser Rd, S Gandhi Maidan, T222060, F222069. 80 rooms and suites, modern and best. Pool (Rs 150 per day non-residents).
B Pataliputra Ashok (ITDC), Bir Chand Patel Path, T226270, F223467. 45 rooms (half-day rates), good restaurant, travel, tourist office.
C-D Rajasthan, Fraser Rd, T225102. 20 rooms some a/c, good veg meals, welcoming.
C-D Republic, Lauriya Bagh, Exhibition Rd, T655021, F655024. 35 a/c rooms, dining hall (very good veg meals), exchange, roof garden.

C-D **Satkar International**, Fraser Rd, T220551, F220556. 50 rooms, central a/c, minimal maintenance, good restaurant.

D **Jayasarmin**, Kankarbagh Rd (5-min walk Patna Junction station), T354281. Large, clean rooms, a/c or air-cooled, good room service, good restaurant (slow service).

D **Mayur**, Fraser Rd, T224149. Basic, clean rooms, some with bath, restaurant.

D-E **Kautiliya Vihar** (Bihar Tourism), Bir Chand Patel Path, T225411. 44 rooms, some a/c, dorm beds (Rs 50), restaurant, exchange, travel.

E **Sheodar**, Fraser Rd, T227210. Fairly clean rooms, some a/c.

F **AAEI**, Dak Bungalow Rd. 1 room with bath, good value, worth trying even if you are not a member.

Avoid **Railway Retiring Rooms**.

🍴 Eating

Patna p732, maps p732 and p734
Hotels on Fraser Rd and Ashok Rajpath usually have a restaurant.

🍴🍴🍴 **Pataliputra Ashok**. International. Good food, excellent kebabs, poolside barbecue, but slow service.

🍴🍴 **Amrali**, Bir Chand Patel Path (Kautilya Vihar building). Indian vegetarian. Excellent dishes, quick service. Dimly lit but recommended.

🍴🍴 **Ashok** (1st floor). Rather dark but good Indian. Good Chinese.

🍴🍴 **Nalanda** at Satkar International. Indian. Pleasant atmosphere, good food.

🍴 **Marwari Awas Griha**. Small, busy dining hall serving excellent vegetarian thalis.

🍴 **Mayfair**, inexpensive snacks and ice creams.

🛍 Shopping

Patna p732, maps p732 and p734
Patna and its surrounding villages are known for **wooden toys** and **inlay work**, silver jewellery in beaten rustic style, tussar silk, lacquerware, leather shoes and Madhubani paintings. Govt emporia at **Bihar** on E Gandhi Maidan, **Khadi Gramudyog** and shops at Patna Market, New Market, Maurya Lok Complex and Boring Canal Rd. Govt **Lacquerware**, Maghalpura for lacquer on wood.

Books
South end of Fraser Rd.
Reader's Corner also has old books.

▲▲ Activities and tours

Patna p732, maps p732 and p734
Tour companies
Ashok, Hotel Pataliputra Ashok, T223238.
TCI, Maurya Hotel, T221699.
Bihar Tourism (BSTDC), Ashok Travels & Tours and Patna Tours. **City sight-seeing** Oct-Mar, Rajgir, Nalanda and Pawapuri, usually 0800-2200, Rs 80-100. **Longer tours** To Vaishali, Bodh Gaya, Buxar and Sasaram. Buses can be slow and uncomfortable.

⊖ Transport

Patna p732, maps p732 and p734
Air
Transport to town, taxis, or Indian Airlines. Coach to City Office via some hotels, Rs 30; Tourist taxi transfers, about Rs 120 (Rs 350 deluxe). Airport enquiry, T223199. **Indian Airlines**, Gandhi Maidan, T226433, Airport T223199. Daily to **Kolkata**, **Delhi**, **Lucknow**, **Mumbai** and **Ranchi**. **Sahara**, Raj Towers, Boring Canal Rd, T661109, **Delhi** and **Mumbai**.

Bus
Long distance Luxury and Express bus services between Patna and regional centres including **Kolkata**, **Siliguri**, **Bhagalpur**, **Ranchi**, **Hazaribagh**, **Monghyr** and **Gumra**. Bihar SRTC, Gandhi Maidan, opposite GPO, T651862; Reservations: 1030-1800; at Junction railway Station, T221475. Private bus stand opposite Vir Kunwar Singh (Harding) Park.
To Nepal STRCs and private buses run daily from Harding Park Bus Stand to Raxaul (5-7 hrs, Rs 60). However, timings are difficult and the buses extremely crowded and uncomfortable. Night buses reach the border early in the morning. Morning buses from Patna connect with the night bus to Kathmandu. Either way you have an overnight bus journey, unless you stay at Birganj – an unenviable option, though there are two modest hotels. Raxaul has little to offer; Ajanta, Ashram Rd, has rooms with

Bihar & Jharkhand Listings: Patna

● For an explanation of the sleeping and eating price codes used in this guide, see inside the
● front cover. Other relevant information is found in Essentials pages 52-57.

bath. In **Raxaul** the tempo stand is south of the railway line and the Immigration and Customs office. You can cross the border to **Birganj** by rickshaw/tempo (15-20 mins). In Birganj the tempo stand and Bus Park are in Adarsh Nagar, to the south of town. In the morning, buses depart from the Bus Stand east of the Clock Tower. To **Tandi Bazar** (4 hrs, for Chitwan, Rs 60), **Pokhara** (11-12 hrs, Rs 90) and **Kathmandu** (11-12 hrs, Rs 95). Even Express buses are slow and packed. 'Tourist' minibuses are the only moderately comfortable option. You need an Exit stamp in **Raxaul** from the Indian Immigration office (round the corner, and across the road from the Customs office) - a great hassle. You may need Customs clearance first. After crossing the border you need to get an Entry stamp from the Nepalese Immigration counter (usually open early morning to late evening). Occasionally an unjustified additional fee is demanded for 'extras', eg Registration card, or a 'Visa' fee in US$. **From Nepal** When travelling to India via Patna it is best to stay overnight in **Hetauda** and catch the 0530 bus to Birganj (3 hrs); go to the Bus Stand at 0500 to get a seat. At **Birganj**, walk or get a (pricey) horse-drawn rickshaw to the auto-tempo stand at the second crossroads. From there travel to Raxaul. Remember to get an Exit stamp from Nepalese Immigration before crossing the border and an Entry stamp from Indian Immigration in Raxaul.

Car

Car hire: tourist taxis, TCI, competitive rates, including longer tours; also **Ashok Travels and Tours**, about Rs 500 per 4 hrs to Rs 1,000 per 8 hrs for a/c. Out-of-town touring (600 km), eg Vaishali, Rs 1,200-1,700; Bodh Gaya, Rajgir, Nalanda, Rs 4,500 (a/c).

Taxi

Private unmetered taxis available from the airport, railway station, some hotels and important tourist sites. Fix rates beforehand. The same applies to **rickshaws** and tongas.

Train

Reservations on Northeast Railways, ie to Gorakpur, Raxaul, must be made at Sonepur station, not Patna.

Patna Junction railway Station, enquiries, T131, reservations, T230899. **Delhi (ND)**: *Vikramshila/Magadh Exp, 3467/2391*, 1900, 16½ hrs; *Rajdhani Exp, 2423/2309*, 2115, not Wed or Sun, 13 hrs. **Delhi (OD)**: *Brahmaputra Mail, 4055*, 1323, 15½ hrs. **Dhanbad**: *Damodar Exp, 3330*, 2245, 6½ hrs. **Gaya**: *Patna Hatia Exp, 8625*, 0950, 2½ hrs; *Palamau Exp, 3348*, 2000, 2½ hrs. **Guwahati**: *NE Exp, 5622*, 2220, 20½ hrs; *Rajdhani Exp, 2424*, 0555, Tue, Wed, Sat, 16 hrs. **Kolkata**: *Toofan Exp, 3008*, 0542, 12½ hrs; *Rajdhani Exp, 2306*, 0555, Mon, Fri, 7½ hrs; *Poorva Exp, 2304*, 0800, Wed, Thu, Sat, Sun, 8½ hrs. **Mumbai (Dadar)**: *Guwahati Dadar Exp, 5646/5648*, 1515, Tue, Wed, Sun, 32 hrs. **Varanasi**: *Farraka Exp, 3413/3483*, 0610, 6 hrs; *Sharmjevvi Exp, 2401*, 1105, 4 hrs.

❶ Directory

Patna *p732, maps p732 and p734*
Banks State Bank of India, Gandhi Maidan, may refuse to cash Amex TCs. **Trade Wings**, Hotel Maurya complex. Efficient, good rate. **Hospitals** Patna Medical College Hospital, Ashok Rajpath E, T652301. **Nalanda Medical College Hospital**, T641159, By-Pass Rd. **Post office** GPO: Station Rd. **Central Telegraph Office**, Buddha Marg. Cultural centres and library British Library, Bank Rd, near Gandhi Maidan. 1030-1830 Tue-Sat. Very good collection and helpful staff. **Tourist offices** India, Room 151, Paryatan Bhawan, Bir Chand Patel Path, T226721. 1000-1700, excellent service, arranges local tours and excursions. Also there, **Bihar**, T225411, F236218. Counters at Pataliputra Ashok, T225295, Airport and Patna Junction Railway Station. **ITDC**, Pataliputra Ashok, T226270. **Tourism Department**, Government of Bihar, 9D Hutment, Secretariat, T/F224531.

Patna to Bodh Gaya → *Colour map 3, grid B5 and B6.*

The area to the south of Patna has many major Buddhist sites, and also some Muslim and Hindu places of pilgrimage. This circular route to the southwest of Patna visits the ruins of Nalanda, one of the world's oldest universities, Rajgir, royal capital of the Magadh Empire, the Barabar Caves and Bodh Gaya. On the return journey to Patna, you can take a longer route via the immense tombs of Sher Shah at Sasaram. It is preferable to take at least two days even for the shorter trip. Once out of Patna the countryside is often very attractive, the early morning being particularly crisp and inviting. From March through to the monsoon it gets extremely hot during the day.

Biharsharif → *13 km from Nalanda.*
Biharsharif remained an Islamic cultural centre up to the 16th century. The *dargahs* (tombs) of Mukhdoom Shah, a 13th-century saint and Malik Ibrahim Baya, draw large numbers of Muslims, particularly during the annual Urs fair.

Pawapuri → *Also Apapuri - 'sinless town'.*
Pawapuri is particularly sacred to the Jains since Mahavir, the founder of Jainism, gained enlightenment here. The lotus pond where he bathed and on whose bank he was cremated has a white marble temple, the *Jalamandir*, in its centre and Samosharan Temple.

★ Nalanda → *Colour map 3, grid B6. Site open 0900-1750.*

Nalanda has the ruins of one of the world's oldest universities, founded in the fifth century AD on an ancient site of pilgrimage and teaching which had been visited by the Buddha and Mahavir (who spent '14 rainy seasons' in the area). According to Ghosh, Hiuen Tsang ascribed its name, which means 'charity without intermission', to the Buddha's liberality in an earlier birth. ⁕ *For Sleeping , Eating and other listings, see pages 743-747.*

History
Nalanda was hidden under a vast mound for centuries. Its archaeological importance was only established in the 1860s with most of the excavation taking place over about 20 years from 1916. The monasteries went through varying periods of occupation, and in one case nine different levels of building have been discovered. The Buddhist monastic movement resulted in large communities withdrawing into retreats. Even in the seventh century, according to Hiuen-Tsang, Buddhism was declining except in Bihar and Bengal where it enjoyed royal patronage and the support of the laity. The sanctuaries were often vast, as is the one here (500 m x 250 m).

The site
The remains of 11 monasteries and several *chaityas* (temples) built mainly in red brick, have been found as well as a large stairway, a library, lecture halls, dormitories, cells, ovens and wells. The buildings are in several storeys and tiers on massive terraces of solid brick, with stucco decorations of the Buddha as well as Hindu deities, and secular figures. Several of the monasteries have a guarded entrance on the western wall; the monks' cells are around a central courtyard with a wide verandah (or a high wall in some cases). Opposite the entrance, the centre of the eastern wall has a shrine which must have contained an impressive image. Remains of drains which carried sewage to the east, and staircases giving access to the different storeys can be seen.

The monasteries are numbered one to 11, from south to north. The path from the gate enters the complex between one and four and goes across an open space to **Temple No 3**, the largest here. Almost certainly this was originally built by Asoka. The

🔖 *Nalanda by A Ghosh, 6th ed, 1986, gives excellent detailed descriptions of the site and the Museum*

earliest temples were small structures, completely incorporated into the successively larger mounds. The north facing shrine chamber on top may have once contained an enormous Buddha image. The highest point gives a commanding view over the site as a whole, particularly impressive in the evening light.

Returning east, **Monasteries 1, 1A** and **1B** are the most important of the monastery group. Ghosh suggests that the lower monastery was built by a Sumatran king in the reign of the third Pala king, Devapala, between AD 810-850. There was an earlier monastery underneath, which had been substantially damaged. It is possible to walk around all three of these southern monasteries.

There are several interesting features in the other monasteries: double rows of cells in **Monastery 5**, brick courtyards and two sets of double ovens in the upper courtyard of **6**, and evidence of three successive monasteries built on the same site at **7**. There is an imposing shrine and unique doorway in **8**, striking drains in **9** and arched doorways in **10**. The fragments of 25 stone pillars were recovered from the ruins of **11**, which stood 1 m apart and 2 m high. Ghosh suggests that fire was a recurrent hazard, and that every monastery was deserted and reoccupied.

In addition to the monasteries and the main temple, four other temples have been excavated. **Temples 12, 13** and **14** are in a line stretching north from the main temple. They all have a square outline and originally had large Buddha images, now destroyed. On the north of Temple **13** a brick smelting furnace was discovered, while the niches of the image's pedestal in Temple **14** contain the only example of mural painting in Nalanda. Little remains.

Temple site 2, east of monasteries seven and eight and reached by a path between them, has a sculpted dado with over 200 panels showing a wide variety of scenes depicting Hindu deities.

Apart from the monasteries and temples there are several images, including the Buddha and Marachi (the Buddhist goddess of dawn).

Excavations to the northeast in **Sarai Mound** show evidence of a brick temple with frescoes of elephants and horses. The villages of **Bargaon** and **Begampur** to the north and **Jagadishpur** to the southwest contain impressive Buddhist and Hindu images.

Nava Nalanda Mahavihar

About 2 km from the principal site is a post-graduate Institute for Research into Buddhism and Pali literature set up by the Govt of Bihar, which has many rare manuscripts; it is now the site of the Indira Gandhi Open University. There is a

Nalanda

⁑ Monastic University for the Buddhist world

It is assumed that the Gupta emperors were responsible for Nalanda's first monasteries. In the seventh century Hiuen-Tsang spent 12 years, both as a student and a teacher, at Nalanda which once had over 3,000 teachers and philosophers. The monks were supported by 200 villages, and a library of nine million manuscripts attracted men from countries as far flung as Java, Sumatra, Korea, Japan and China. Great honour was attached to a Nalanda student and admission was restricted with seven or eight out of 10 applicants failing to gain a place.

I-Tsing, another Chinese scholar, arrived here in AD 673 and also kept detailed records, describing the severe lifestyle of the monks. The divisions of the day were measured by a water-clock, and the syllabus involved the study of Buddhist and Brahmanical scriptures, logic, metaphysics, medicine and Sanskrit grammar.

The University flourished until 1199 when the Afghan Bhaktiar Khalji sacked it, burning, pillaging and driving the surviving residents into hiding. It was the end of living Buddhism in India until the modern revival.

colourful **Thai Temple** built in the 1980s. **Kundalpur**, 1.6 km north of Nalanda, is believed by the Digambara sect of Jains to be the birthplace of Mahavir.

★ Rajgir → *Phone code: 6119. Colour map 3, grid B6. Population: 33,700.*

Encircled by rugged forested hills, Rajgir is held sacred by both Buddhists and Jains for its association with Mahavir, who taught here for many years, and the Buddha. You can still see parts of the 40-km cyclopean drystone wall that once enclosed the ancient city and fort. Today, the *kund* (hot springs) with large open-air baths are a special attraction. Non-Hindus are not allowed into the Surya Temple. The Kund Market nearby, where buses stop, has chops, stalls and local eating places with basic rooms.

The site

Gridhrakuta, the 'Hill of Vultures', was one of the Buddha's favourite places where he delivered many important sermons, and was where he is believed to have converted the Magadhan King **Bimbisara**, who had built the old stone road leading up the hill. It was used by Hiuen-Tsang in the seventh century and still provides the best access. Rock-cut steps lead to the two natural caves; plaques and Buddhist shrines were found in the area (now in Nalanda Museum). The first Buddhist Council was held in the **Saptaparni Cave** on Vaibhara Hill, six months after the Buddha's death, and his teachings were written down for the first time. On the way to the cave is the large, 7-m high **Pippala stone house**, an extraordinary 'watchtower' built of blocks of stone. On all sides there are small cells for guards which were later used by monks.

⁑ *Rajgir by Md Hamid Kuraishi, 5th ed, 1987, describes the site with maps*

Little survives of the fifth-century BC **Ajatasatru Fort**. The outer wall was built with blocks of stone up to 1½ m long, with smaller boulders in its core. In places it was 4 m high and over 5 m wide. Of the 32 large gates (and 64 small ones) mentioned in ancient texts, only one to the north has survived. Of the inner city wall, which was about 5 km long and roughly pentagonal, only a section to the south remains, with three gaps through which the old roads ran. A part of the deep moat which was cut into the rock can also be seen. In the valley, a 6-m high circular brick structure, decorated with stucco figures, had an old Jain shrine called **Maniyar Math**.

Nearby **Venuvana,** the bamboo grove where the Buddha spent some time, where excavations revealed a room, some stupas and the Karanda Tank, is now a deer park with a small zoo. To the south of Venuvana there are Jain and Hindu temples. Ruins of Buddha's favourite retreat within the valley, the **Jivakamarvana Monastery** (fourth to third century BC), have been found with four halls and several rooms.

The **Visva Santi Stupa** ① *cable car (600 m) for access, usually 0900-1300, 1500-1700, good for the views,* built by the Japanese on top of Ratnagiri is dedicated to world peace. The large white Nipponzan Myohoji stupa has four golden statues of the Buddha representing his birth, enlightenment, preaching and death.

Mahavir spent "14 rainy seasons" in Rajgir and the 20th Tirthankara was born here so it is a major Jain pilgrimage centre, with temples on most of the hilltops.

Gaya → *Phone code: 0631 .Colour map 3, grid B5. Population: 383,200.*

Gaya, on slightly raised ground in the valley between two hills, was blessed by Vishnu with the power to absolve all temporal sins. Its many sacred shrines attract Hindus at Pitrapaksh Tarpan (September-October), when prayers are offered for the dead before pilgrims take a dip in the seasonal holy River Phalgu. Cremations take place on funeral pyres in the burning ghats along the river.

Sights

There are several old Buddhist temples and monastery remains around Gaya. In the centre of the town is the **Vishnupad Temple,** supposed to have been built over Vishnu's footprint, which is imprinted on a rock set in a silver basin. The 30-m high temple has eight rows of beautifully carved pillars supporting the *mandapa* (pavilion), which were refurbished in 1787. Only Hindus are permitted into the sanctum and temple grounds which has the *Akshayabat* (the immortal banyan tree under which the Buddha is believed to have meditated for six years), where the final puja for the dead takes place. Brahmayoni Hill, 1 km southwest, with its 1,000 stone steps, which lead to a vantage point for viewing both Gaya and Bodh Gaya.

Gaya

The **Surya Temple** at **Deo,** 20 km away, dedicated to the Sun God, attracts large crowds in November when *Chhatt* Puja is celebrated.

Excursions

Barabar Caves is 35 km north. The 22-km rough track leading to the caves in the impressive granite hill turns east off the main road to Patna at **Belagunj** (30 minutes from Gaya, two hours from Patna) where buses stop. From here allow four hours to walk up (45 km by four-wheel drive, "a real challenge"). It is

■ Sleeping
1 Ajatshatru & Sujata Restaurant
2 Pal Rest House
3 Siddharth International
4 Surya

The whale-backed quartzite gneiss hill stands in wild and rugged country. Inscriptions reveal that, on instructions from Asoka, four chambers were excavated, cut and chiselled to a high polish by the stonemasons, as retreats for ascetics who belonged to a sect related to Jainism. Percy Brown pointed out that the extraordinary caves, particularly the *Lomas Rishi* and the *Sudama*, are exact copies of ordinary beehive shaped huts built with bamboo, wood and thatch. The barrel-vaulted chamber inside the *Sudama* is 10 m long, 6 m wide and 3½ m high which through a doorway leads to a circular cell of 6 m diameter. The most impressive craftsmanship is seen on the façade of the *Lomas Rishi* which replicates the horseshoe shaped gable end of a wooden structure with two lunettes which have very fine carvings of lattice-work and rows of elephants paying homage to Buddhist stupas. Excavation is incomplete as there was a possibility of the cave collapsing. There is also a Siva temple on the Siddheshwar peak.

The caves inspired the setting of EM Forster's A Passage to India. They date from the 3rd century BC and are the earliest examples of rock-cut sanctuaries.

At **Nagarjuna Hill** there are three further rock-cut sanctuaries, 1 km northeast from Barabar. The *Gopi* (Milkmaid's) cave having the largest chamber. Inscriptions date these to about 50 years after the excavations at Barabar.

★ Bodh Gaya → *Phone code: 0631. Colour map 3, grid B5. Population: 30,900.*

Bodh Gaya, a quiet village near the river Niranjana (Phalgu), is one of the holiest Buddhist pilgrimage centres. It was under the Bo tree here that Gautama, the prince, attained enlightenment to become the Buddha. ⇥ *For Sleeping , Eating and other listings, see pages 745-747.*

Ins and outs
Getting there Travel in daylight only, for your own safety. Buses run from Gaya, Patna, Nalanda and Rajgir.

Getting around Hotels, temple and monasteries are a few mins' walk from the bus stand. See Transport, page 747, for further details.

Climate Summer, maximum, 47°C, minimum, 28°C; winter, maximum, 28°C, minimum, 4°C. Annual rainfall: 1,860 mm.

The site
Bodh Gaya was 'lost' for centuries until rediscovered by Burmese Buddhists in 1877 which led to restoration work by the British. UNESCO has recently given its preliminary approval to declare Bodh Gaya as a World Heritage site, with the event to be marked by the arrival of a 152 m high bronze statue (made in the UK).

Lamas, Rimpoches and Buddhists from all over the world assemble here during the *monlam* when the area north of the bus station resembles a medieval encampment with tents serving as informal restaurants and accommodation. The food is smoky and there are long waits, but it is atmospheric and full of colour. The 'tourist season' draws to a close at the end of February when many restaurants close and meditation courses stop running. Unfortunately the air can get heavily polluted, partly due to badly serviced buses, making a walk along the road rather unpleasant.

Mahabodhi Temple
① *Temple Office T400620, cameras, Rs 5, access is by a road alongside the* Birla Dharamshala *and* Tibetan Guest House.

❝❞ The red sandstone slab, the Vajrasila, under the tree marks the place where Gautama sat in meditation. Today, pilgrims tie pieces of coloured cloth on its branches when they come to pray.

Asoka's original shrine near the Bodhi tree was replaced by this temple in the second century, which in turn went through several alterations. The temple on a high and broad plinth, with a soaring 54-m high pyramidal spire with a square cross-section and four smaller spires, houses a gilded image of the Enlightened Buddha. The smaller spires may have been added when Burmese Buddhists attempted extensive rebuilding in the 14th century. An ornately carved stone railing in bas relief surrounds the temple on three sides and several carved Buddhist stupas depict tales from the Buddha's early life. Unlike earlier circular railings this had to conform to the quadrangle of the temple structure. Its height of 2 m, its lighter proportions and the quality of the carving dates it to the Sunga period (early first century BC). The *entrancetorana* (ornamental archway) is on the east side. The lotus pond where the Buddha may have bathed is to the south. To the north is the *Chankramana*, a raised platform (first century) with lotus flowers carved on it, which marks the consecrated promenade used by the Buddha while meditating. Numerous attempts to restore the temple have obscured the original. The candle-lit evening ceremony is worth attending.

The original Bodhi tree (pipal or *Ficus religiosa*) was supposedly destroyed by Asoka before he was converted, and others which replaced it also died. The present tree behind the temple is believed to come from the original stock – Prince Mahinda carried a sapling from the sacred Bo tree to Sri Lanka when he went to spread Buddhism there. This in turn produced a sapling which was brought back to Bodh Gaya. The red sandstone slab, the **Vajrasila**, under the tree marks the place where Gautama sat in meditation. Today, pilgrims tie pieces of coloured cloth on its branches when they come to pray.

Bodh Gaya

	Sleeping		4 Shashi		● Eating
	1 Bodh Gaya Ashok		5 Shivan House		1 Café Om
	2 Buddha International		6 Sujata		2 Gautam, Pole Pole
	3 Mahabodhi Society Rest		7 Tourist Bungalow (Siddharth		& New Pole Pole
	House & Restaurant		& Buddha Vihars), Youth		3 Shiva
	(Sri Lanka Guest House)		Hostel & State Bank of India		

0 metres 300
0 yards 300

Animeshlochana is another sacred spot where the Buddha stood to gaze in gratitude at the Bodhi tree for a week, after his Enlightenment. The temple also attracts Hindu pilgrims since the Buddha is considered to be one of the *avatars* or incarnations of Vishnu.

Other temples
Pilgrims from many lands have built their own temples. You can start at the giant 20-m stone **Buddha statue** which was installed at the end of the road in 1989. The modern two-storey, spotless **Japanese Temple** ⓘ *0700-1200, 1400-1800*, next door with beautiful polished marble floors has gold images of the Buddha. The **Tibetan Temple** and **Monastery** next to this (1938) is ornately painted and has a *Dharma Chakra* (Wheel of Law) which must be turned three times when praying for forgiveness of sins. A large 2-m metal ceremonial drum in red and gold is also on display. Opposite is the **Nipponji Temple** complex with a free clinic, monastery and a Peace Bell (rung from 0600-1200 and at 1700). Returning to the Mahabodhi Temple you will pass the colourful **Bhutan Temple** protected by carved Himalayan deities, a glittering pagoda-style **Thai Temple** and a **Bangladesh Temple**. The **Chinese Temple** houses an enormous, revolving ceremonial prayer drum.

Teaching centres
Magadha University, an international centre for studies in history, culture and philosophy, is about 3 km from the Mahabodhi Temple. The **Tibetan Medical and Astro Institute** carries out research and gives advice. **Meditation courses** varying from a week to a month during the winter, follow both the Mahayana and Hinanyana traditions; enquire at the Burmese, Tibetan and Thai monasteries. The **International Meditation Centre** ⓘ *enquiries to Woodland Rd, Denbury, Devon, England, TQ12 6DY, opposite the Thai monastery, T400707*, also holds courses. The **Root Institute**, off the Magadha University Road which is involved in community self-help schemes, also runs popular short introductory courses.

Muslim sites → *Colour map 3, grid B5.*
★ **Sasaram Sher Shah Suri**, who was responsible for the tombs, asked the master builder Aliwal Khan to build a tomb for his father **Hasan Khan** around 1535. This later inspired the building of the impressive second tomb for Sher Shah himself. The first imitated the octagonal structure and walled enclosure of the earlier Lodi tombs but was rather plain. What followed, however, was extraordinary not only in scale, but also in its conception. **Sher Shah's mausoleum** ⓘ *Mar-Jul 0700-1800, Aug-Feb 0800-1700, Rs 2, 500 m away*, was set in a large artificial lake so it appears to float. A modern redbrick gateway opposite the Dak Bungalow leads down to the tombs. You enter it by a causeway after going through a guard room on the north bank (originally visitors approached by barge from the ghat on the east side). The pleasant grounds and the lake provide a relaxing break.

> ⚑ *This Muslim site, between Gaya and Varanasi, is well worth a visit. The tombs are a short rickshaw ride from the railway station.*

Listings: Patna to Bodh Gaya

◉ Sleeping

Nalanda *p739*
D **Gautam Vihar**, Bihar Tourism, Some a/c and dorm, simple but the best.
E **Tathaghat Vihar**. Modest rooms.

F **Ajatashatru Vihar**. Very basic, dorm only.
F **Burmese Rest House**, beyond museum.
F **Inspection Bungalow**, meals to order, contact Supt, Archaeological Survey of India, Patna.
F **Youth Hostel**.

Several Jain Dharamshalas near the station.
A Centaur Hokke, 2 km from Kund Market, T25245, F25231. 24 comfortable rooms (few Western style), primarily for Japanese pilgrims, excellent Japanese restaurant (fresh ingredients daily), open Nov-Mar, reserve well ahead (guarantees 'beds' not 'rooms' in high season).
D Gautam Vihar, T25273, 12 rooms (some a/c) with bath and verandah.
D-E Siddharth, near Kund Market, T25216, has good rooms with bath, and decent food.
D-E Tathagat Vihar, T25176. 32 simple rooms (some a/c), dorm, Indian restaurant, open Nov-Mar.

Gaya *p742, map p742*

Mostly very basic with non a/c rooms.
B-C Siddharth International, off Station Rd, T426243. Some a/c rooms, modern, "food is probably the best in Gaya", exchange, but noisy and overpriced.
D-E Ajatshatru, opposite railway station, T434584. Range of rooms with bath (hot water), some gloomy and noisy, but popular ground floor restaurant has large menu, cheap but good basic food.
E Surya, Swarajpuri Rd, between *Samrat Hotel* and bus stand, T424004. Some rooms with bath and hot water, cleanest of the cheap hotels, and quieter being away from extremely noisy railway station.
F Pal Rest House, off Station Rd, T436753. Some rooms with bath, quieter at rear.
Railway Retiring Rooms, at Gaya Junction. 6 rooms, 2 a/c.

Bodh Gaya *p743, map p744*

Simple budget hotels often quote higher rates so bargain.
B Bodh Gaya Ashok (ITDC), near museum, T400790, F400788. 32 rooms, 24 a/c, 48-bed Japanese-style dorm with special hot water bath, good restaurant, pleasant but not luxurious, large garden.

B Sujata, Buddha Marg, past the Bangladesh Temple, T400761, F400515. 27 rooms, some Japanese baths, restaurant, exchange.
C Shashi, next door, T400459. Small, clean rooms, restaurant.
D-E New Mahayana, Main Rd. Good value clean rooms.
D-E Siddharth Vihar, near Thai Temple, T400445. 7 large rooms, meals to order, poor service.
E Root Institute, Magadha University Rd, T400714. Rooms in traditional local huts in a peaceful, shared bath, rural setting (Rs 360 double including breakfast), excellent food.
F Buddha Vihar, next door to *Siddharth Vihar*, T400445, 3 to 6 bed dorms (Rs 75), very basic.
F Shivan, near temple. Clean rooms, some with bath, hot water, friendly.

Monasteries

Some monasteries provide spartan accommodation primarily for pilgrims; contact the monk in charge. They expect guests to conform to certain rules of conduct.
D Japanese Monastery, near Buddha Statue, T400747. Comfortable spotless rooms sometimes available, good Japanese meals.
E-F Mahabodhi Soc. 6 rooms, 3 dorms, vegetarian canteen.
F Bhutan Monastery (Druk Do Nagcholing). 18 rooms in guesthouses, shared facilities.
F Burmese Vihar, Gaya Rd. Simple rooms (some newer) with nets, dorm, no fan, garden (eat at *Pole Pole* opposite).

Sasaram *p745*

Try to avoid staying overnight.
F Shilpa Deluxe, GT Rd, T06184-23305. 15 rooms, dirty, staff have TV on loud non-stop.
F Youth Hostel. Station *Refreshment Room* for breakfast and simple thalis, fairly clean, "nice waiters at least try to chase the rats"!

Eating

Rajgir *p741*

Green, Kund market near Bus Stop. Basic, cheap, simple Indian – tables in verandah.

Bodh Gaya *p743, map p744*

Most tent restaurants operate in winter only.
The Ashok has a good a/c restaurant.
Café Om, best Tibetan *thukpa*. Also excellent fresh cakes, cheesecakes and a stall with cheap attractive items.

For an explanation of the sleeping and eating price codes used in this guide, see inside the front cover. Other relevant information is found in Essentials pages 52-57.

Gautam's, tent nearby for apple strudel and cinnamon rolls.

Pole Pole, tent opposite Burmese Vihar. Clean, excellent management, good though not exceptional food.

Shiva, diagonally opposite entrance to temple. Some Japanese and simple Western.

Sri Lanka Guest House does Chinese.

▲ Activities and tours

Gaya *p742, map p742*
Tour companies
Sakun, Shyam Bazar, Ramna Rd.

☉ Transport

Nalanda *p739*
Bus
Regular bus services from Patna (90 km north), Rajgir (15 km) with the nearest railway station.

Rickshaw
Cycle-rickshaw and **tonga**; outside the Tourist Information Centre.

Rajgir *p741*
Bus
To **Patna** (105 km), 4 hrs; and **Gaya** 3 hrs.

Rickshaw/taxi
Auto-rickshaw or share-taxi to visit the sites, and Nalanda.

Gaya *p742, map p742*
Bus
Local To **Bodh Gaya**: buses from the station; from **Zila School Bus Stand**, mini-buses and autos, but always very crowded; rickshaws (6-seater), Rs 8 per seat, better value. Try to persuade a cycle-rickshaw driver to take you; worth it for the relative peace and comfort. None after 1800.
Long distance From **Stand across the river**: to Rajgir; from **Gandhi Maidan Bus Stand**: Patna, Ranchi and Hazaribagh.

Rickshaw
Auto and cycle-rickshaws: easily available.

Train

Gaya is on the Grand Chord line of the Delhi-Kolkata section of Eastern Railway. Gaya Junction railway Station, enquiries and reservations: T32031, 0900-1600. **Delhi (ND)**: *Rajdhani Exp, 2301/2421*, 2211, 12 hrs; *Purushottam Exp, 2801*, 1338, 15 hrs;. **Kolkata (H)**: *Howrah Exp, 2308*, 2043, 8 hrs; *Kalka-Howrah Mail, 2312*, 2320, 7½ hrs; *Rajdhani Exp, 2302/2422*, 0433, 6½ hrs; plus others. **Patna**: *Palamau Exp, 3347*, 0217, 2½ hrs; *Hatia Patna Exp, 8626*, 1415, 2½ hrs. **Varanasi**: *Doon Exp, 3009*, 0547, 5½ hrs; *AC Exp, 2381*, Wed, Thu, Sun, 1600, 3½ hrs. *Poorva Exp, 2381*, 1600, Wed, Thu, Sun, 3½ hrs; plus lots that arrive/ depart in middle of night.

Bodh Gaya *p743, map p744*
Patna has the nearest airport, while Gaya (16 km) has the nearest railway station. The main bus stand is opposite the Mahabodhi Temple. Auto-rickshaws and overcrowded buses take about 30 mins from Gaya.

Sasaram *p745*
Train
To Gaya, *Doon Exp, 3009*, 1908, 2 hrs.
From Gaya, 0607, 1½ hrs; **to Varanasi**, 0755, 3½ hrs; **from Varanasi**: 1620, 2½ hrs.

❶ Directory

Gaya *p742, map p742*
Post office Station Rd. Warning from travellers whose mail/parcels were pilfered here. **Tourist office** Bihar, Gaya Junction railway Station Main Hall, T432155, 0600-2100.

Bodh Gaya *p743, map p744*
Banks Bank of India in *Embassy Hotel* changes cash (up to US$100), State Bank of India in *New Mahayana Hotel*. Changes cash, TCs, Mon-Fri 1030-1430, Sat 1030-1230.
Post office T400742. Mon-Sat 1000-1700.
Tourist office Bihar, 34-35 Mahabodhi Temple Market Complex. 1000-1700.

Jharkhand

Background

The land Jharkhand lies on the once densely forested northern edge of the Indian Peninsula. The rolling plateau, lying at an altitude of between 300-400 m, with occasional outcrops rising to nearly 1,000 m, is largely comprised of the granites and gneisses of ancient Gondwanaland. On the north it drops quite sharply to the plains of the Ganges, while a great fault has created the valley of the mineral rich Damodar. The plateau still has an open feel, forest being interspersed by agricultural land, except where coal and iron ore mining have created a scarred industrial landscape of mines and soil tips. To the south of the Damodar valley are the Ranchi plateaus, broken up by remarkable looking flat-topped hillocks or *mesas*. Up to 20% is still under forest, though exploitation of the forest continues apace. The soils are often poor, sometimes lateritic, and easily eroded if proper conservation measures are not adopted.

Recent political developments The inauguration of the state in the early hours of 15 November 2000 was set symbolically on the birth anniversary of Birsa Munda, leader of the Santhal rebellion in 1831-32. The origins of the present state can be traced to the formation of the Chota Nagpur Unnati Samaj in 1921, which proposed the creation of a separate Jharkhand state in 1928. The State Assembly (81 seats) is currently dominated by the National Democratic Alliance (NDA) which hold 45 of the seats, 33 of them from the BJP, which provided the first and current Chief Minister Babulal Marandi. The opposition focuses on the Jharkhand Mukti Morcha, led by their President and long-time activist Sibu Soren. Jharkhand's future is heavily dependent upon the exploitation of its mineral wealth, targeted to contribute annually Rs 1,500 crore to the state's coffers.

Ranchi → *Phone code: 0651. Colour map 3, grid C6. Population: 846,500.*

Once the summer capital of Bihar state, Ranchi still attracts holiday makers for its location on higher ground in the heart of the **Chota Nagpur** tribal country. An industrial town and a major educational centre, Ranchi is also known for its mental asylum at Kanke, 9 km north. The town is surrounded by rolling forested land with waterfalls and lakes and is in the heart of one of India's great tribal belts. The Ranchi district has been the recent scene of violently suppressed demonstrations, opposed to Koel-Karo dam project. ⏵ *For Sleeping, Eating and other listings, see pages 750-752.*

Sights

The 17th-century **Jagannath Temple** on a hillock at **Jagannathpur** (10 km southwest) is in the style of the great temple in Puri (annual *Ratha Yatra* in June/July). **Ranchi Museum** (4 km) ① *Tribal Research Institute Bldg, Morabadi Rd, closed Sun, 1030-1700, free.* Collection of stone sculpture, terracottas and arms as well as ethnological objects at the Institute itself. **Ranchi University** ① *1100-1700,* has ethnographic collections of central Indian states and Andaman and Nicobar Islands.

Ranchi Lake is popular for local people to relax, while the adjacent **Ranchi Hill** offers good views of the town and surrounding countryside. **Tagore Hill** (3 km) is named after Rabindranath Tagore who wrote several books and poems here.

Excursions

The Subhanarekha River, which rises southeast of the town, is interrupted by several impressive waterfalls, within easy range of Ranchi. **Hundru Falls**, 45 km east, are

formed by the 100 m drop of the river, particularly impressive just after the monsoons.
You can picnic and bathe in the pools at the bottom. Others in the area include **Johna**, 40 km east on the Purulia Road, and **Dassamghagh Falls** (34 km) which has a tea house. It is dangerous to bathe at Dassamghagh; several people have drowned. Mundas believe that the god of the Falls demands sacrifices.

Wildlife sanctuaries → *Colour map 3, grid B5 and C5.*

There are game reserves set in often stunningly beautiful and remote scenery on the **Chota Nagpur plateau,** which can be easily reached from Ranchi. This is one of the poorest areas of India, with extensive missionary activity.

Palamau (Betla) National Park

Palamau's vegetation is mainly *sal* and bamboo, though it is now considerably degraded. Once the home of the extinct Indian **cheetah**, the world's first tiger census was taken in this Project Tiger Reserve in 1932. The wildlife also includes leopard, gaur, sambar, muntjac and nilgai, Indian wolf and many species of birds. The North Koel River and its tributary run through the park but in the summer animals become dependent on waterholes. The Flame of the Forest (*Butea monosperma*) and *mahua* flowers also attract wildlife. The **Hathibajwa** wooden tower and **Madhuchuhan** hide, 'Tree Top' and 'hides' at **Kamaladah** are good vantage points. Elephants can be seen after the monsoons and until the waterholes begin to dry up in March. Over 200 species of water and woodland birds, the remains of two 16th-century **forts** of Chero kings who once ruled from here, and hot springs add to the interest. Jeeps for viewing the animals can be hired from the Forest Dept.

> **‡** *The National Park is open throughout the year, though the best time to visit is from Oct to Apr.*

Hazaribagh Wildlife Sanctuary

ⓘ *Evening park tour from Divisional Forest Office, Hazaribagh, 1700-2200, Rs 50.*

Hazaribagh ('thousand gardens') town is close to the wildlife sanctuary, waterfalls, Tilaiya Dam (55 km) and Konar Dam (51 km). Set in hilly terrain but slightly lower than the town at 550 m, the park, a Project Tiger Reserve, is a part of the Chota Nagpur plateau in forested tribal territory, interspersed with grass meadows and some deep waterways. The park supports sambar, nilgai, deer, chital, leopard, tiger, wild boar and wild cat. There are 10 watchtowers and hides for viewing. Roads allow easy access; the NH33 takes you to the Pokharia gate, 16 km from Hazaribagh. The best time to visit is from February to April.

Eastern Jharkhand

Jamshedpur → *Phone code: 0657. Population: 570,300.*

This flourishing steel town lies 130 km southeast of Ranchi, established as a planned township by the Parsi industrialist Jamshedji Tata in 1908. Located close to rich iron and coal deposits, there are also limestone quarries and some magnesite. The town has retained much of its natural attraction, with its lakes and rivers enclosed by the Dolma hills, in spite of the pollution from its heavy plants. The town is split in two by the steel plant and rail sidings. **Keenan Stadium** in Bistupur, north of town, is the venue for international cricket matches. **Dalma Wildlife Sanctuary**, a few kilometres out of Jamshedpur, on the Ranchi Road is noted for its elephant population.

Other centres have emerged along the Damodar Valley which cuts through the Chota Nagpur plateau through rocky, thickly wooded areas which are the home of the many aboriginal tribal people of Jharkhand. The Santals, Bedia, Khond, Munda and Oraon were the original inhabitants and though a few still live in isolated villages, most have joined the workforce in the industrial townships. The river valley has a number of hydro-electric power stations and with them large dams. The activities in this valley are coal in Dhanbad, locomotives in Chittaranjan and in Bokaro.

Parsnath Hill → *Colour map 3, grid B6. Altitude: 1,366 m.*

ⓘ *From Dhanbad, the nearest large town with hotels (see above): Train Asansol-Varanasi Pass, 129, 0805, then minibus from Parsnath station to Madhuban, Rs 15, 40 minutes, or taxi, Rs 200. Buses also from Dhanbad, 0545, to Isri; then taxi (if you want to return that day) or another bus to Madhuban at 1000, and stay overnight in a dharamshala. Return bus from Madhuban at 1530. Madhuban's dharamshalas and lodges may be full during holidays and festivals.*

About 150 km along the Kolkata Road from Bodh Gaya, near Dumri and Madhuban, is the holy hill of Parsnath. Particularly sacred to the Jains, a track winds up through Parsnath's forested slopes to the 24 shrines which crown the hilly northern outcrops of the Indian Peninsula. The shrines are rarely visited by foreigners but are a regular pilgrimage site for thousands of devout Jains and Hindus. The highest shrine is dedicated to the last forerunner of Mahavir himself, Lord Parsvanatha, see page 1344, who is believed to have achieved enlightenment while meditating in the cave, now enshrined in the temple. Leather items are not allowed on the hill.

Most pilgrims start climbing at 0400, the best time to catch superb views of sunrise and the surrounding countryside. It is a three-hour climb but *dhoolis* are available; allow eight hours in all. The super-fit can manage a climb in just over two hours and run down much faster. A visit is highly recommended.

Listings: Jharkhand

● Sleeping

Ranchi *p748*
Finding accommodation in Ranchi can be difficult, most hotels are generally full.
B Yuvraj Palace, Doranda, T500326, F500328. Best in town, 25 central a/c rooms, multi-cuisine restaurant, bar; sister hotel *Yuvraj*.
B-C Kwality Inns, T460469, F304038. 36 rooms, mostly a/c, reasonable, clean, restaurant, though lack-lustre staff.
B-D BNR, Station Rd, T208048. 22 rooms in cottages in old station building, some a/c, restaurant, lawns, tennis, old-world feel.
C Hindustan, Main Rd, T206032, F205565. 32 reasonable rooms with TV, some a/c, decent restaurant, overpriced but likely to have vacancies.
C Yuvraj, Doranda, T502842, 500328. 35 rooms, some a/c, restaurant/bar.
E-F Birsa Vihar, Main Rd, T314826. 30 simple rooms, dorm, tourist office.
Other **E-F** hotels on Station Rd, plus a few mid-range choices on Main Rd, often claim to be full.

Palamau National Park *p749*
D-F Van Vihar, inside Reserve, Betla, T06562-56513. 25 rooms, fairly comfortable a/c, good deer viewing, Tourist Information, but reports of no electricity or food.
E Debjani, food available.
E Forest Rest Houses, inside Reserve. 20 basic rooms.

● *For an explanation of the sleeping and eating price codes used in this guide, see inside the front cover. Other relevant information is found in Essentials pages 52-57.*

E **Forest Rest Houses**, Kehr and Kechki. Reservations: Field Director, Project Tiger, Palamau, Daltonganj.
E **Rest Houses** at Mundu, Garu, Chhipadohar and Baresand, contact Div Forest Officer, S Forest Div, Daltonganj.
E **Tourist Lodge**, near Reserve. 10 rooms.

Hazaribagh Wildlife Sanctuary p749
D-E **Tourist Lodge**, T06546-24337. 9 rooms, some a/c, Tourist information (T835218).
Govt Guest House, 12 rooms, are near Bus Stand.

Inexpensive Indian style hotels with restaurants in the town centre near the bazar: **Ashok**, **Magadh** and **Standard**.
Forest Rest Houses at Rajdewra and Harhad within the sanctuary area are very spartan.

Jamshedpur p749
Budget hotels are close to Tata Nagar railway station. Mid-range hotels are 2-3 km from bus and train stations in Bistupur.
C **Darshan**, opposite Ram Mandir, Main Rd, T424317, F439939. 26 decent, clean a/c rooms, restaurant.
C-D **Boulevard**, Main Rd, Bistupur, T435321, F427743. 36 large, sparse rooms, TV, hot bath, clean, friendly. Recommended.
C-D **South Park**, Q Rd, Bistupur, T435001, F428506, www.hotelsouthpark.com. Comfortable rooms, some a/c, clean hot bath, good restaurant, helpful staff. Recommended.
The Host, L Rd, Bistupur is similar to *Kwality*.
Kwality, Main Rd, Bistupur, is a good licensed restaurant. It also sells confectionery.

▲ Activities and tours

Jamshedpur p749
Tour operators
Akash, Ranchi Club Complex, Main Rd, T5076495.
Pal Travels, Main Rd, T208312.

☉ Transport

Ranchi p748
Air
The airport is 13 km away. **Indian Airlines**, Main Rd, T203042, airport, T141, T501554.

Daily to **Delhi**, **Mumbai** and **Patna**. 4 flights a week to **Kolkata** and **Lucknow**.

Bus
Private bus stand at Kantatoli, 2 km from Main Rd, T308907; serves major towns in Jharkhand and surrounding states. Government bus stand, Station Rd, T304328. Also Ratu Rd bus stand (4 km) for buses towards Madhya Pradesh (eg Daltonganj).

Train
Enquiries, T131. Reservations, T135. Computerized Reservation Centre, G-41 Sainak Market, Main Rd, T301097. **Dhanbad**: *Maurya Exp, 5027*, 1700, 4½ hrs. **Gaya**: *Hatia Patna Exp, 8626*, 0625, 7½ hrs; *Hatia Patna Exp, 8624*, 1840, 8½ hrs. Both continue to **Patna**, 10 hrs and 11½ hrs. **Kolkata (H)**: *Hatia Howrah Exp, 8616*, 2005, 12½ hrs. **New Delhi**: *Rajdhani Exp, 2439*, 1640 (Wed), 18 hrs.

Palamau National Park p749
Air
Through Ranchi (140 km).

Car
Take the road west north west out of Ranchi for **Kuru** (57 km), in Kuru fork right to Tori, then towards Daltonganj.

Train
From Daltonganj (25 km), or Chhipadohar (80 km).

Hazaribagh Wildlife Sanctuary p749
Car
North from Ranchi on the NH33 through Ramgarh to Hazaribagh (91 km) and to the main gate at Pokharia.

Train
Hazaribagh Rd Station (66 km).

Jamshedpur p749
Bus
Jamshedpur Bus Stand is situated at Mango, 4 km from Bistupur, with regular services to the main centres in the region.

Bihar & Jharkhand Jharkhand

Rickshaw

Auto-rickshaws (unmetered) run on a shared basis along the main routes. Otherwise you are at the mercy of a 'reserved rickshaw', expect to bargain. Tata Nagar to Bistupur should be no more than Rs 30.

Train

Tata Nagar station is on the SE railway on the Kolkata (Howrah)-Mumbai line. Enquiries, T131. To **New Delhi**: *Purushottam Exp, 2801*, 0625, 22½ hrs. **Kolkata (H)**: *Shatabdi Exp, 2022*, 1650 (not Sat), 4½ hrs; *Steel Exp, 8014*, 0600, 4½ hrs; *Gitanjali Exp,* 2859, 1030, 4½ hrs. **Puri** via **Bhubaneswar**: *Purushottam, 2802*, 2025, 10½ hrs; *Utkal Exp, 8478*, 2130, 12½ hrs. **Ranchi**: *Howrah Hatia Exp, 8615*, 0220, 5½ hrs.

⊙ Directory

Jamshedpur *p749*
Banks Bank of Baroda, Main Rd, Bistupur; for cash on credit cards. ICICI, K Rd, Bistupur; ATM for Visa withdrawals.
Tourist office Jharkhand, near United Club, Bistupur, T835218.

Andaman and Nicobar

❧ Footprint features

Introduction

The Andaman and Nicobar Islands have brilliant tropical plants and are thickly forested with rainforest and tropical trees, with mangrove swamps on the water's edge. Hilly in parts, they have superb palm-fringed, white-sand beaches and coral reefs. The sparkling clear water is excellent for **snorkelling** with increasing opportunity for fabulous **scuba diving** for beginners and the experienced. The Andamans are also a **birdwatcher's paradise** with 242 species recorded, and the **wildlife** includes 58 species of mammals and 83 reptiles, many endemic as the islands are isolated. It is now, in theory, possible to visit some of the newly opened remoter islands. The islands' **aboriginal tribal people** are of special interest to anthropologists. Some, like the Jarawas and Sentinelese in the Andamans, have remained isolated and hostile to outsiders even up to the end of the 20th century. Others (eg the Great Andamanese) have interacted with non-tribal settlers for decades and now there are very few left. The Government of India keeps the Primitive Tribal Reserve Areas out of bounds.

Andaman & Nicobar Islands

Coco Channel
Landfall Is
North Andaman
Smith Is
Ross Is
Diglipur
Narcondam Is
Interview Is
Sound Is
Mayabunder
Middle Andaman
Rangat
Long Is
Baratang Is
South Andaman
Barran Is
Havelock Is
Ritchie's Archipelago
Neil Is
Gandhi Marine Park
PORT BLAIR
Ross Is
Rutland Is
Cinque Is
Brothers & Sisters Is
Duncan Passage
Little Andaman
Andaman Sea
Bay of Bengal
Ten Degree Channel
Car Nicobar
Tillanchang Dwip
Tarasa Dwip
Camorta
Trinkat
Nancowry
Nicobar Islands
Katchal
Sombrero Channel
Little Nicobar
Great Nicobar
Indira Point
N
0 km   50
0 miles   50

Background → *Population: 356,300. Area: 8,249 sq km.*

Entry regulations

Foreigners with tourist visas for India are allowed a maximum stay of 30 days on arrival at Port Blair, the capital, by air or sea, but may not visit tribal areas or restricted islands including Nicobar. Foreign tourists may now apply and get a Restricted Area Permit after Registration at Immigration (two extra photos with your passport sometimes needed), at a cost of US$30 (payable in dollars or rupees, but must be cash). It is no longer necessary to get a permit in advance. CID will extend your permit up to a maximum stay of 15 days without difficulty, but only when your initial period of approval is about to expire. Any extension is only valid for stay ing in Port Blair.

Officially, permits allow foreigners to visit and stay overnight in Port Blair, Havelock, Long Island, Neil Island, entire islands of South and Middle Andaman (excluding tribal reserve), Baratang, Rangat, Mayabunder, Diglipur, North Passage Island, Little Andaman Island (excluding tribal reserve), and all islands in Mahatma Gandhi Marine National Park except Boat, Hobay, Twin Island, Tarmugli, Malay and Pluto Island. You can also visit Jolly Buoy, Red Skin (may reopen after crocodile infestation), South Cinque, Mount Harriet and Madhuban, Ross Island, Narcondam, Interview, Brother, Sister and Barren Island during the daytime. In practice, requests to visit remote islands such as Barren, North Passage and Narcondam, which have recently been opened to tourists, are often refused even though ships sail to them. Some dive companies arrange overnight stays on courses.

Indians may visit the Andamans and Nicobars without a permit but must obtain a permit for restricted areas on arrival at Car Nicobar or from the Duty Commissioner (Nicobar) at Port Blair.

Foreigners working in the Andamans can get a four-month visa but to extend the stay, the person must leave India (not simply the islands) and re-enter with a new visa and permit.

The land

The Andaman and Nicobar group comprises about 300 islands formed by a submarine mountain range which divides the Bay of Bengal from the Andaman Sea. The islands lie between latitudes 6° to 14° north (about level with Chennai and longitudes 92°-94° east, a span of 725 km). The land rises to 730 m (Saddle Peak), formed mainly of limestones, sandstones and clays. The Andamans are separated from the Nicobars by a 90-m deep 150 km strait. The Andamans group has 204 islands (26 inhabited) with its three main islands of North, Middle and South, which are separated by mangrove-fringed islets and are together called **Great Andaman**. The **Nicobar Islands** comprise 12 inhabited and seven uninhabited islands including the three groups, Car Nicobar in the north, Camorta and Nancowry in the middle and the largest, Great Nicobar in the south.

The canopied rainforests harbour 3,000 species of **plants** including mangroves, epiphytes (130 ferns, 100 orchids), palms, woody climbers, valuable timbers (teak, mahogany, Andaman *paduk*, resistant to termites) and a wide variety of tropical fruit. Marine **fauna** is particularly diverse including rare species (dugong, grey teal, Estuarine crocodile and marine turtles) and a variety of tropical fish and coral (see MG National Marine Park on page 765).

The **climate** is tropical. Temperature: 20°C to 32°C. Annual rainfall: 2,540 mm. Monsoons – usually May to mid-September, and November to mid-December (though the first may arrive as early as mid-April, bringing heavy rain on most days). Best season is end-November to mid-April. The island climate has no extremes, the main contrasts coming with the arrival of the monsoons, and tropical storms in late summer can cause damage.

Lying on the trade route between Burma and India the islands appeared on Ptolemy's second century map and were also recorded by the Chinese traveller I-Tsing in the seventh century. At the end of the 17th century the Marathas established a base there to attack the trading British, Dutch and Portuguese ships. Dutch pirates and French Jesuits had made contact with the islands before the Danish East India Company made attempts to evangelize the islands in the mid-18th century. The reputation of ferocity attributed to the Nicobarese may have been partly due to Malay pirates who attacked and killed sailors of any trading vessel that came ashore (some anthropologists believe that in spite of common belief, the aboriginals themselves were not cannibals). The first British attempt to occupy the islands was made in 1788 when the Governor General of India sent Lt Blair (whose name was given to the first port) and, although the first convicts were sent there in 1794, it was abandoned within a couple of years.

After the 'First War of Independence' (the 'Mutiny') in 1857 the British gained control of most of the islands and used them as a penal colony for its prisoners (who until then had been sent to Sumatra) right up to Indian Independence, with a short break from 1942-45 when the Japanese occupied Port Blair, Ross Island and the Nicobar Islands. However, political prisoners were sent in large numbers only after the completion of the **Cellular Jail** in 1906. Each revolt on the mainland resulted in the transportation of people from various parts of India, hence the presence of Bengalis, Malayans and Burmese among others. Subhas Chandra Bose, the Indian Nationalist, first raised the Indian tricolour here in 1943.

Culture

Sir Arthur Conan Doyle in 1890 described the islanders as "perhaps ... the smallest race upon this earth... fierce, morose and intractable". In the mid-19th century, the British guessed the **tribal population** was around 5,000 but the number has been steadily dwindling. Today most of the inhabitants are Indians, Burmese and Malays – some, descendants of the criminals who were transported there. Since the 1950s, refugees from East Pakistan (now Bangladesh), Burma and Indian emigrants from Guyana have settled on the main islands to be followed more recently by Tamils from Sri Lanka. The largest concentration is around the capital, Port Blair, with the majority of the tribal people (about 15% of the population) living in the Nicobars.

Hindi, Bengali, Tamil, Malayalam and English are spoken. The **Andamanese language**, which bears no resemblance to any other language, uses prefixes and suffixes to indicate the function of a word and is extraordinary in using simply two concepts of number, 'one' and 'greater than one'.

Modern Andaman and Nicobar

Economy Tourism is rapidly becoming the Andamans' most important industry and the runway at the airport was extended in 2003. Forests represent an important resource. The government has divided 40% of the forests into Primitive Tribal Reserve areas which are only open to Indian visitors with permits, and the remaining 60% as Protected Areas set aside for timber for export as plywoods, hardwoods and matchwoods (a Swedish multinational owns extensive logging rights). Rubber and mahogany have been planted in addition to teak and rosewood which are commercially in demand. Fishing – lobsters, prawns and sea fish – and agriculture are also important, with rice a staple food crop.

Government As a Union Territory the Andamans and Nicobar Islands have a Lieutenant Governor, Shri Nagendra Nath Jha, a retired member of the Indian Foreign Service and member of the BJP's National Executive since 1994. The islands also have one MP, Shri Bishnu Pada Ray (BJP).

🔹 Tribals of Andaman and Nicobar

One story goes that the monkey god Hanuman stopped in the Andamans on his way to Lanka in search of Sita (see page 1319), giving the islands his name. They have been inhabited by Aboriginal tribes (some Negrito) for thousands of years but remained unexplored because anyone attempting to land would be attacked. Today there are only a few **Andamanese**, who once inhabited the Great Andamans, some **Onges** in Little Andaman who traditionally painted their naked bodies, the fierce **Jarawas** on South Andaman and the **Sentinelese** on North Sentinel. Car Nicobar (Carnic) is inhabited by the mongoloid **Nicobarese**, the most numerous groups, and **Shompens** who may have been of pre-Dravidian stock, live in Great Nicobar.

Hunting wild pigs, fishing with nets and catching turtles with harpoons from dug-out canoes, the islanders used iron for arrowheads and metal from wrecks for harpoons. Some tribes made pottery but the **Andamanese** particularly were exceptional since they had not discovered fire-making.

The Anthropological Survey of India and the Andaman Administration have been jointly trying to establish friendly contact with the Jarawas and Sentinelese since the 1960s. They consistently repelled groups of explorers with poisoned arrows. More recently, some **Sentinelese** have picked up coconuts (which do not grow on their island) that were left on the beach as a gesture of friendship by anthropologists. In January 1991, Indian anthropologists succeeded in landing on North Sentinel and in February, a few Sentinelese boarded a lifeboat to accept gifts of coconuts. Study groups have made regular visits, removing most of their clothes in order to be accepted. The 400 or so Sentinelese do not appear to have a hierarchical social structure; they are naked, painting their bodies with chalk and ochre and wearing bead and bone ornaments. The **Jarawas** remain in the Tribal Reserve set aside to the west of the Andaman Trunk Road, all along the South and Middle Andamans.

Port Blair → *Phone code: 03192. Colour map 6. Population: 100,200.*

Port Blair, the capital, about 1,200 km from Kolkata and Chennai, has only a handful of sights. The small town has changed in the last three decades from one which saw a ship from the mainland once a month if the weather permitted, to a place connected by flights from Chennai and Kolkata several times a week. It now has a hospital, shops, schools and colleges and a few museums, in addition to resort hotels and watersports facilities. ▶▶ *For Sleeping, Eating and other listings, see pages 759-764.*

Ins and outs

Getting there **Lamba Line airport**, 3 km south of Port Blair, has flights from Kolkata and Chennai. You can get a bus or taxi to town. Ships from the mainland dock at Haddo jetty where you can get taxis but they invariably overcharge.

Getting around As Port Blair is very small, you can easily see the sights in a couple of days. Aberdeen Village with the Bazar in the town centre has most of the budget hotels, the bus station, shops and offices. Hiring a motorbike or scooter can help you to get around as bicycles can be hard work on the hills. Further afield, buses cover sights and towns on the limited road network. Inter-island ferries sail to coastal towns and islands which are far more relaxing than the capital. See Transport, page 763, for further details.

Sights

The **Cellular Jail** (north of Aberdeen Jetty, 1886-1906) ① *closed Mon, 0900-1200, 1400-1700, Rs 5, camera, Rs 10, video camera, Rs 50, allow 1 hr*, was originally built by the British to house dangerous criminals. Subsequently it was used to place Indian freedom fighters until 1938; it could hold 698 solitary prisoners in small narrow cells. The Japanese used it for their prisoners of war during their occupation from 1942-45. Three of the original seven wings which extended from the central guard tower survive; the jail was renovated in 1998. There is a site **museum**, photographs and lists of 'convicts' held, a 'death house' and the gallows, where you can get an impression

Port Blair

Related map
A Port Blair centre, page 760

N

0 metres 500
0 yards 500

■ **Sleeping**
1 Andaman Teal House
2 ANIIDCO Tourist Home, Megapode Nest & Nicobari Cottages
3 Holiday Resort & Daawath Restaurant
4 Hornbill Nest
5 Peerless Resort & Andaman Divers
6 Sinclairs Bay View & Samudra Divers

● **Eating**
1 Anurod Bakery

of the conditions within the prison in the early 1900s and the implements used in torture. A well-presented 45-minute **Sound and Light** show on prison life in English is shown daily at 1915, Rs 10. Highly recommended.

Chatham Saw Mill ① *except Sun, 0630-1430 (0830 is a good time to arrive to avoid the lunch break), allow about 1½ hrs*, is one of the oldest in Asia, employing 1,000 workers. Tours take you through the different processes of turning logs into 'seasoned' planks. For tours, report to the Security Office just outside the main gate. Photography is not allowed. The **museum** is listed below.

The **Mini Zoo** ① *closed Mon, 0800-1700*, has a small, uninspiring collection in some very old wooden cages with a few specimens of unusual island fauna including a sea crocodile farm **Zoological Survey of India Museum and Research Library**, near Andaman Teal House, Delanipur, has information on butterflies, corals, sponges etc.

At **Sippighat Farm** ① *daily except Mon, 0600-1100, 1200-1600*, 14 km away, you can see cash crops such as spices and other plants being propagated. A watersports complex has been developed nearby (see Entertainment below).

Viper Island, near Haddo Wharf, is at the mouth of Port Blair harbour where convicts were interned before the Cellular Jail was built.

Museums

Anthropological Museum ① *closed Mon, 1000-1230, 1400-1600*, has a small but interesting collection of photographs and artefacts, and records of exploratory expeditions. Worth a visit.

Marine Museum ① *opposite Andaman Teal House, closed Mon, 0830-1200, 1400-1700, Rs 10, camera, Rs 20, video camera, Rs 40, allow 30 mins*, has a collection of corals and shells and a display of 350 species of marine life.

Forest Museum ① *Haddo near the Saw Mill, 0800-1200, 1430-1700*, has unusual local woods including red paduk, satin and marble woods and shows the use of different woods in the timber industry and methods of lumbering and finishing.

Listings: Port Blair p757, maps p758 and p760

◉ Sleeping

Many hotels offer discounts in low season (Apr-Sep).
A Bay Island, Marine Hill, 2 km, T34101, F33389. 48 a/c rooms, some small, imitating local huts (not all have sea view), cool open lounge and restaurant, good gardens but poor tennis court, sea water pool, keen on conservation (discounts to students of "ecology and conservation"!), far from beach but excellent view across harbour entrance.
A Peerless Resort, Corbyn's Cove (4 km), set back from beach, T33462, F33463. 48 rooms, 4 cottages, good *Snack Bar* (see Corbyn's Cove on page 765), pleasant and airy, well-kept mature gardens, tennis, beach nearby (take own snorkelling equipment), dive centre, excellent service, warm atmosphere, free airport transfer but need taxis to town (in daytime, best to wait on beach for one passing).
B Sinclairs Bay View, South Pt, T32937, F31824. Refurbished resort hotel in elevated location overlooking Ross Island, no beach, 24 rooms, some a/c, restaurant, excellent and popular bar, pool, dive centre.
C-D Shompen, 2 Middle Pt, T32360, F32425. 40 rooms (noisy in front, windowless and very hot in centre), 15 a/c overpriced, rooftop restaurant, free airport transfer, tours, popular with backpackers, friendly, helpful staff, off-season/long stay discounts.
D-E Abhishek, Goalghar, T33565, inconvenient location. Friendly, helpful management, good restaurant and bar, snorkel equipment for hire, free transfer (usually meets flights).
E Andaman Teal House, Delanipur, T32642. 27 cleanish rooms with bath, some a/c, comfortable wicker furniture, good views, spacious lounge-restaurant.

E **Holiday Resort**, Prem Nagar, T30516. Large clean rooms with bath, bucket hot water, good restaurant, TV in lounge, helpful manager, stores luggage, internet.

E **Hornbill Nest**, 10 mins' walk from Corbyn's Cove, T32018. 20 clean rooms, 2-6 beds on hillside overlooking sea, central open-air lounge and restaurant, transport difficult (stop a 'returning empty' taxi), best for those wanting cheapish shared room near beach but thefts reported. Reservations: Tourist Office, near Secretariat, T32933, F3265.

E **Jagannath**, Moulana Azad Rd, 7 mins from bazar, T33140. 15 clean rooms, some with bath and balcony in newer block but no hot water, filtered water, helpful staff.

E **NK International**, Fore Shore Rd, T33066. 31 very simple rooms, some a/c with bath, few with good view across Phoenix Jetty, functional grey concrete block.

E **Shah and Shah**, near Aberdeen Bazar, T33696. 23 excellent large clean rooms, huge first floor balcony. Recommended.

F **Central Lodge** Middle Point, Goalghar, set back, T33634. One of the cheapest, some rooms with bath but often full, camping.

F **Jaimathi**, 78 Moulana Azad Rd, T33457. Large rooms, generally clean but variable standard, bucket hot water, very good cheap food (try ginger fish, prawn *biriyani*), bar, helpful staff.

F **Kavita**, Aberdeen Bazar, opposite CID, T33742. 24 rooms, often has room when all others full (at time of ship arrive/depart), 1 night only.

Haddo Hill

Tourist Home Complex, ANIIDCO, T32380, F21227. Has a central restaurant, bar and gardens with superb views to the port and Phoenix Bay.

C **Megapode Nest**. 25 good a/c rooms off central lounge area (no view), short walk from restaurant, large terrace, very peaceful, very good but no food or drink outside mealtimes.

C **Nicobari Cottages**, T32207. 2 a/c rondavels, mainly for officials.

D **Tourist Home**, 18 refurbished rooms attached to the reception area, restaurant, very good value. Reservations: New Marine Dry Docks, T32376.

Port Blair centre

■ Sleeping
1 Abishek
2 Bay Island
3 Central Lodge
4 Jaamathi & New India Café
5 Jagganath

Guest House
6 Kavita & Kwality Ice Cream
7 NK International
8 Shah & Shah
9 Shompen & Shompen Travels

10 Youth Hostel

● Eating
1 Annapoorna Café
2 China Room
3 Islet
4 New Lighthouse

0 metres (approx) 100
0 yards (approx) 100

❼ Eating

Good seafood is now widely available and even the cheapest hotels offer prawn and crab curries. Larger hotels have a wider selection, but meals (most ingredients imported from the mainland) and drinks can be expensive. **Government Guest Houses** are open to non-residents. All Indian restaurants have excellent fish fry (spiced tuna or mackerel chunks) for under Rs 15. Highly recommended, especially for trips out of Port Blair.

₮₮₮ **Bay Island**, Marine Hill. International. Luxurious surroundings, seafood recommended, lunch buffet Rs 350.

₮₮ **China Room**, Aberdeen Village. Chinese. Owned by Burmese/Punjabi couple. Eat in pleasant shady outdoor yard, dinner by candlelight (but mosquito problem), freshly prepared with home-grown veg, not drenched in oil, soya or tomato sauce, order your own seafood 'specials' the day before, beer.

₮₮ **Islet**, 1st floor, GB Pant Rd (takeaway downstairs). Indian, Chinese. Relax with a cool beer on the narrow balcony with views across stadium, generous portions but quality overrated.

₮₮ **New India Café**, next to *Hotel Jaimathi*. Good Indian, some Western dishes. Great food and prices, Continental breakfast, lobster and other specials on request, but very slow service (wait an hour for dinner).

₮₮ **New Lighthouse**, opposite *Municipal Guest House*, Indian, Chinese. Wide choice in small open-air café, evening BBQ, closes 2145.

₮₮ **Shompen Rooftop**. Indian, Continental. Limited menu (try *aloo jeera* and *daal*), fish dishes a bit hit-and-miss.

₮ **Annapurna Café**, Aberdeen Bazar. International. Wide selection, try their different *dosas* and Indian sweets, best place for European style breakfast, a/c rooms, very popular. Recommended.

₮ **Anurod Bakery**, towards Teal House. Sell good cakes, snacks and corn flakes.

₮ **Daawath**, below *Holiday Resort*. Mainly Indian. Good breakfasts and curries, avoid Western.

₮ **Kwality** ice cream next door to *Kavita*.

₮ **Teal Bakery** behind bus stand. Good fruit cakes.

₮ **Tourist Home Complex**, Haddo. Indian. Excellent thali lunches, try the chicken dishes in the evening.

There are several juice bars between the bus stand and clock tower.

❶ Bars and clubs

Peerless Beach Resort, Sinclairs Bay View, Tourist Home Complex, **Abishek** and **Shompen** have bars.

Beers and spirits from bar below **Shalimar Hotel**, Delanipur.

❻ Entertainment

Occasional dance performances for tourists. **Film of islands' tribal life** at government hotels at 1730.

❋ Festivals and events

End-Feb: Island Tourism Festival for 10 days, with music and dancing from all over India and focusing on local crafts, culture and food.

❍ Shopping

Local curio shops are by the clocktower and opposite the post office. Tailors sell hammocks. **Sagarika Cottage Emporium** next to tourist office. Open 0900-1800, closed Sun. Selection of souvenirs in wood and shell (the government limits for collection of shells).

Wine shops

1 behind *Hotel Shah and Shah*, 1 opposite the Syrian Christian church (open until 1930).

▲ Activities and tours

Scuba diving

Andaman Divers, Peerless Resort, Corbyn's Cove, T33461/35771.

Samudra, *Sinclairs Bay View Hote*, T33159.

Swimming

Swimming is excellent. The best spot is the crescent shaped Corbyn's Cove or 1 of the uninhabited islands which tourists may visit for the day.

 For an explanation of the sleeping and eating price codes used in this guide, see inside the front cover. Other relevant information is found in Essentials pages 52-57.

Island Travel, Aberdeen Bazar, T33358. *Indian Airlines/Alliance Air*, *Jet Airways* agents, good for excursions, car hire, postcards and exchange.
Sagar Tours, 7 Krishna Building, Haddo, T33704, F33318.
Shompen Travels, 2 Middle Pt, T32644, F32425. Local tours, Wandoor to Jolly Buoy/ Red Skin ferry.

Tours City Tour, 0830, 1200, Rs 40. Corbyn's Cove, 0830, 1700, Rs 40. Chiriya Tapu, 0900, Rs 75.

Bus excursions to **Wandoor** for Marine National Park, 0830, Rs 75; via sights, Tue-Sun, 0900, Rs 75.

Boat from Wandoor Beach to **Red Skin**, 1000, Rs 55 and to **Jolly Buoy**, Rs 85; also to **Car Nicobar** (closed to foreigners at present). **Cinque Island** can be visited on an organized tour.

Watersports

At **Andaman Water Sports Complex**, next to Fisheries Museum, Sippighat, T30769. 0700-1100, 1500-2000. Sailing, paddle boats, wind surfing, paragliding.

Resort hotels have limited equipment. **Andaman Adventure**, near *Holiday Inn*, has good snorkelling equipment for hire, Rs 60/day, US$100 deposit.

⊙ Transport

Make sure you confirm reservations. Problems can occur from mid-Apr to mid-May and during the Tourism Festival.

Air

Alliance Air flights from Kolkata and Chennai, 5 times a week and **Jet Airways** daily from Chennai. The new extended runway may permit flights to/from Delhi. Transport to town: most buses pass the airport entrance. Taxis should charge Rs 30 per person; fix fare first. Some hotels send taxis. Flights are always fully booked at least a month ahead (earlier for Apr-May). However, because of the strict enforcement of the 30-day stay regulations, officials may find you a seat to fly out even at the last moment. If stuck, try for tickets from Island Travel or from **Jet Airways**, or **Indian Airlines/Alliance Air**, and ask the office manager to be placed on the priority waiting list. Book well ahead. You may request your international carrier to get Andaman's tickets, preferably 6 months ahead. Reconfirm on arrival in India, and after you get to Port Blair. Avoid mid-Apr when the summer holiday rush starts. **Indian Airlines**, G55 Middle Pt, behind PO, T34744, F31483. Airport T32983. **Jet Airways**, 189 Main Rd, Junglighat, T36922, airport T35911.

Bicycle

Hire from shop between Aberdeen Bazar and the Bus Stop (about Rs 5 per hr) but you need to be very fit to manage the hilly island.

Bus

Long distance Central Bus Station near Aberdeen Bazar serves state and private buses, T32278. Regular service to villages and districts. Bus stops at *Shompen Hotel* and near the airport. A few private buses run between Chatham jetty and the Cellular Jail. To **Rangat**, 2 private buses daily (6-7 hrs), 1 via Mayabunder at 0420. **Mayabunder** daily departs 0530-0630, Rs 70 (deluxe, Rs 120); often noisy video bus. Buy tickets a day ahead from agents around the bus stand. **For state buses**: Transport office opposite entrance to Phoenix jetty; numbered tickets go on sale at 1400. Long queues, plenty of touts. The *Diglipur Express* is the quickest to the far north, and the only way of reaching Diglipur (which involves crossing 3 creeks) the same night. Depart 0530, arrive 1930 (Rs 90). Others to Mayabunder miss the last ferry to Kalighat (1630) which connects to Diglipur.

Ferry

Sailings between **Haddo Jetty**, Port Blair and Kolkata (66 hrs) and Chennai (60 hrs) run to a schedule of sorts 3 to 4 times a month. Also Vishakapatnam (56 hrs) once a month. For immigration formalities, see page 755. Tentative schedules for the month are usually available at the end of the previous month; times of departure and arrival appear about a week before in the local papers. Last minute changes are made depending on weather conditions and tides. Tickets are issued 7 days

⁑ Into the deep

There are many excellent locations for snorkelling. The most popular site for a day trip is MG National Marine Park (Wandoor); Chiriya Tapu is very easy to reach from Port Blair. It is best to bring your own mask and snorkel. You may need to pay up to Rs 5,000 as deposit when hiring equipment. Most close from early May during the monsoons.

Scuba diving is a boom business in the Andamans and the number of diving schools is growing. It is difficult to find a cheaper and more beautiful location to learn to dive in the world. For fanatics, longer dive trips can be organized to unexplored sites around the Andamans providing enough people are interested. The best dive sites for a day trip are in the vicinity of Cinque Island though the Government tax of Rs 1,000 for dives makes it pricey.

Samudra based at *Sinclairs Bay View Hotel*, Port Blair, run by Sri Manavi Tukker ("tough instructor!"), and **Andaman Divers** with Swiss instructors, at *Peerless Resort*, Corbyn's Cove, charge around Rs 16,000 for a four-day PADI affiliated Open Water course and certificates. Very well organized. You can also get two Open Water dives for Rs 3,200 at the latter.

The experienced Swiss divers of **Andaman Scuba Club** operate from *Café del Mar* on Beach No 3, Havelock Island.

Please do not remove **dead coral** even if you find pieces on the beach.

ahead but are not sold on the day of sailing. They can be difficult to get. Apply with 3 photos to **Shipping Corporation of India**, 2 Supply Rd, near Mosque, T33347, for tickets. Sailing schedules are also available opposite *Lakshmi Narayan Hotel*, Aberdeen Bazar. The Directorate of Tourism (see above) has a **tourist quota** of 12 bunk class berths for each sailing from Port Blair to Kolkata and Chennai. Put your name down well in advance. A few days before sailing, collect a form which entitles you to claim a berth from the Shipping Corporation of India a day or 2 before tickets go on public sale.
SCI. Chennai: Port Trust, near Customs House, Jawahar Bldg, Rajaji Salai, T5231401, F5231218, and Dy Director of Shipping Services, A & N, 6 Rajaji Salai, T5220841. **Kolkata**: 1st floor, 18 Strand Rd, T2482354, F2482435. **Mumbai**: Apeejay House, 4th floor, Dinsa Wacha Rd, T2822101, F2022438. **Port Blair**: (for Chennai sector) Phoenix Bay Jetty, T32528, F30480.
Vishakapatnam, opposite Port main gate, Banojirow and Pattabhirmayya, T565597, F566507. Ships vary but prices are approximately: Deluxe Cabin (2 beds, shower), Rs 3,900 each; 1st/A Class (4 bunks, shower), Rs 2,400; B Class (4/8 berth), Rs 2,800; 2nd Class (for 6), Rs 2,700; a/c dormitory, Rs 1,800 (on MV

Akbar only); Bunk Class, Rs 1,150. The ships are 25 to 65 years old! **Facilities**: meals cost Rs 120 (cabin), Rs 60 (bunk) per day but some may not find them suitable. It is best to carry some snacks. A kiosk sells biscuits, cigarettes, mineral water, soft drinks. **Arrival**: disembarkation can be chaotic and a free-for-all. Taxis demand Rs 50 to go anywhere.

In addition to the mainland service, a bewildering range of inter-island and harbour ferries operate from Port Blair.
Inter-island ferry most ferries operate from Phoenix Bay Jetty. Details from Directorate of Shipping Services, Port Blair, T32426. Passengers may feel sea-sick! Regular sailings to **Havelock, Neil** and **Long Islands, Rangat Bay, Mayabunder** and **Aerial Bay** appear in the *Daily Telegrams* newspaper (or ring Shipping Corp of India for times, T33347). There are 2 decks and hawkers sell snacks on board. **Diglipur** via Aerial Bay Jetty, Tue evening and Fri morning, Rs 90, 14 hrs. **Havelock**, Rs 25, 4 hrs, direct. **Neil**, Wed and Fri, 4 hrs. **Rangat**, 4 a week, 7 hrs. There are also less frequent services to the 2 volcanic islands of Narcondam and Barren. **Little Andaman** (Hut Bay), once a week, Rs 25-70, 8 hrs. Fares are often doubled if tickets are not bought in

advance. **Harbour ferry**: from Phoenix Jetty (vehicular only) to Hope Town, Bamboo Flats, Ross Island daily except Wed, 0830, 1000,1230, Rs 20; Cholunga Wharf, Phoenix Bay: Harbour Cruise, Rs 25, 1500-1700, including Viper Island. From Chatham Jetty to Bamboo Flats and Dundas Pt, about hourly, 0600-2025 (2 hrs).

Motorbike
Motorbike and scooter hire: Prashant Travels, Phoenix Bay, and next to *Jagannath Hotel*. Newish fleet of motorbikes, Rs 150 per day (Rs 1,000 deposit) return by 1900; scooters, Rs 120; **TSG** (TS Guruswamy), Moulana Azad Rd, near Anthropology Museum, T32894. **GDM**, further up the same road, has good Kinetic Hondas, Rs 200 per day (very good condition, start first time!). Check insurance papers. Recommended for trips to Wandoor, Chiriya Tapu, Mt Harriet and Corbyn's Cove.

Rickshaw and taxi
Please use pre-paid **Traffic Complaint Cards** to report taxi and rickshaw drivers who refuse to use a meter to take you to your destination etc. In time, this may lead to positive action. Available from the Inspector, Traffic Branch, Police Station, Aberdeen (opposite Bus Stand), T34472, ext 309.

Central Taxi Stand, opposite bus station and by clocktower, Aberdeen Bazar, charge Rs 20 about town, Rs 50 for Corbyn's Bay and Haddo Jetty. They generally refuse to use meters and are overpriced.

Train
Railway Reservations Office, near Secretariat, T33042, open 0800-1230, 1300-1400. Supposedly separate queues for Kolkata and Chennai, but a total free-for-all in a small building – a sad sight of a crowd behaving badly. Best avoided. Buy tickets in advance on the mainland if possible.

⊙ Directory

Banks Credit cards are not accepted anywhere in the Andamans. TCs are only changed at Island Travels, Aberdeen Bazar, Port Blair. **Island Travels** change currency and TCs. Hotels **Shompen** and **Bay Island** will change TCs if you spend foreign currency there. **State Bank of India** opp bus station. Open 0900-1300, Sat 0900-1100.

Laundry Near Bazar Taxi stand recommended. **Libraries** State Library, near *Annapoorna Café*, has a small collection of reference books on the Andamans, useful for identification of corals and fish. Open 1230-1945. **Post office** GPO, near centre, by Indian Airlines office. 0700-2200 weekdays, 0800-1800 weekends. **CTO**, for international calls and Fax service. Also several private STD and ISD booths. Make your important international calls in Port Blair since links from elsewhere on the islands are unreliable. **Tent hire** from Andaman Teal House, good condition (deposit, Rs 2,500, Rs 50-70 per day).

Tourist offices Govt of India, 2nd floor (above Super Shoppe), 189 Junglighat Main Rd (VIP Rd), T33006. Enthusiastic, knowledgeable officer (printout of local information). **Director of Tourism**, opposite Indian Airlines, T32694, F30933. Register on the Tourist Quota for boats to Kolkata and Chennai. Unhelpful reception desk (notice "Your time is precious, do not waste it here" sums it up!). Poor postcards. Airport counter open at flight times, T32414. **ANIIDCO** (Andaman and Nicobar Islands Integrated Dev Corp), New Marine Dry Docks (first gate after entrance to Phoenix jetty), T32098/33695. Airport counter T32414. Runs *Tourist Home Complex*, Haddo. Screens occasional films about the islands. **Useful addresses** Fire, T32101. Hospital, T32102. Police, T33077. **Chief Conservator of Forests**, T33321; Deputy, T32816. Helpful. **PWD Office**, between *Shompen Hotel* and *Lighthouse Cinema*, T33050.

South Andaman and the Marine National Park

Chiriya Tapu

Chiriya Tapu, 28 km from Port Blair, at the southern tip of South Andaman, is only an hour by road. Popular for birdwatching, it has excellent beaches with good snorkelling. From the bus stop, which has some tea shops, a track past the *Forest Guest House* (not possible to stay here), leads to the first beach. Continue along the trail through the forest for 20 minutes (several smaller trails are ideal for birdwatching), until you reach a second beach with very good corals 50 m out; at low tide you can walk a long way. The corals are not so spectacular along the coastline, but there is a large range of fish. ▸▸ *For Sleeping, Eating and other listings, see page 768.*

Corbyn's Cove → *5 km from Port Blair.*

Although the only beach close to Port Blair, the cove is only busy at weekends. The water is warm with gentle surf and the white-sand beach is clean and palm fringed. A government Eco-friendly Tourist Village is under way 1½ km north of the Cove.

Mount Harriet

The hill is good for either a morning or a whole day trip but make an early start to avoid the heat. A path through the forest starts by the derelict water viaduct in Hope Town, which joins the surfaced road near the top (excellent vines for would-be-Tarzans here!). Allow 1½ hours to the top. Alternatively, the bus from the jetty stops in Hope Town near the viaduct, or will drop you at the start of the road up the hill with a 4-km walk from here. Near the top of the road lie the ruins of the Chief Commissioner's bungalow, abandoned in 1942. Signs show where the rooms were.

It is also possible to ride a scooter to the top but you will pass the **Forest Check Post** ① *Rs 10, scooter Rs 10, camera Rs 25, video camera Rs 1,500,* where national park fees are charged. Taking the forest path on foot avoids the check post and fees.

Black Rocks

Black Rocks (Kalapathar) is 2 km from Mount Harriet and **Madhuban** via Mount Carpenter, 16 km. A signpost marks the start of the nature trail from Mount Harriet which is easy to follow as far as the Black Rocks, the spot where prisoners were pushed to their death. After Black Rocks, the trail is unclear; it is easy to get lost so take a guide if you plan to walk the whole route. The walk back along the rocky coast is uninteresting; you can get a bus 5 km after the lighthouse. **Madhuban Beach** is on the east side where young elephants are trained for forestry; at **Burma Nalla**, 3 km away, they are used for lumbering.

Ross Island

Ross Island was originally developed under the British as the Residence of the Chief Commissioner, and the administrative headquarters. During the Second World War, it was occupied by the Japanese whose legacy is an ugly complex of concrete bunkers which are still intact. The rest of the buildings on the island are ruins with spotted deer living peacefully among them. In many cases the walls are only still standing because of the climbing trees. However, the church in the centre and the Subalterns' club are impressive. The small **museum** ① *open dawn to dusk, except Wed, Rs 10 on arrival; foreigners must sign a registration book, allow 2 hrs, boat charter Rs 1,000 (no tourist boat),* by the cafeteria has interesting old photos. The Island is officially still under the jurisdiction of the Indian Navy and swimming is not allowed despite the clear enticing waters by the jetty.

Marine National Park and the Off Islands

About 30 km southwest of Port Blair, the Mahatma Gandhi Marine National Park is well worth visiting. The coral beds and underwater life are exceptional off some of these uninhabited islands.

Ins and outs

From Port Blair there are frequent public buses to Wandoor, where from the wooden jetty by the Park Reception Centre, tour boats leave daily at 1000 and return about 1430. Bus, Rs 8 (tour operators charge Rs 100 return!); 0830 bus connects with the 1000 tour. Advance booking is unnecessary. Tickets (boat and entry) are sold at the small kiosk by the bus stop. Jolly Buoy, Rs 150 (return), 50 mins; Red Skin, Rs 85, 30 mins.

Background

Covering an area of 280 sq km, the park is a group of 15 islands with blue waters separating them. It includes Grub, Redskin, Jolly Buoy, Pluto, Boat Island, with Tarmugli to the west, Kalapahar or Rutland to the east and the Twins to the south. It is very rich, not only in marine life but also in the variety of tropical flowers and birds. The dense forests come down to the beach where the mangrove thrives on the water's edge.

South Andaman & Marine National Park

Near **Wandoor**, some white-sand beaches strewn with driftwood, provide good snorkelling at high tide for those who miss the tour. The Diving Society, 1 km from the jetty, runs courses, see box, page 763. **Alexander Island**, opposite Wandoor jetty, is uninhabited and is covered in dense rain forest. Permission to visit is given to students and for scientific research by the Chief Wildlife Warden, Haddo, Port Blair.

Wildlife

There is a rich variety of tropical fauna, including angelfish, green parrot, yellow butterfly, black surgeon and blue damsel fish. There are also silver jacks, squirrel, clown fish and sweetlips as well as sea cucumbers, sea anemones, starfish and a variety of shells – cowries, turbots, conches and the rarer giant clam, up to a metre wide (coral and shell collecting is strictly forbidden). It offers excellent opportunities for **watersports**, including snorkelling and scuba diving. There are turtles, sharks and barracudas on the outer reefs and many beautiful corals including brain, finger, mushroom and antler, the colours derived from the algae that thrive in the living coral.

Viewing

① *Park entry Rs 10.*

In the park only **Jolly Buoy** and **Red Skin** islands are open to tourists, as well as **Cinque**, further south. It is forbidden to land on any other island or stop overnight within the park. Mask and snorkel hire available here and in Port Blair.

Tours depend on demand, minimum 10 people; ask your hotel to enquire. The cost, around Rs 1,000, covers transport to/from any hotel in Port Blair, park entry fee, simple packed lunch, soft drinks and bottled water. You will be picked up around 0530 and taken to Wandoor Village by boat (3½-4 hours, depending on the tide) allowing a maximum of four hours on the island since boats must return before dark. There are plans to introduce faster boats, starting from Chiriya Tapu.

Park information

Jolly Buoy ① *by glass-bottomed boat, allowing 2-4 hrs on the island, boats from Wandoor Jetty at 1030 (check), Jolly Buoy, Rs 150, Red Skin, Rs 85,* is a small island at the centre of the park; at low tide you can walk round it in less than one hour. Beach palm umbrellas provide shade while toilets and a changing room are set back from the beach. Jolly Buoy is good for first-time snorkellers. You can view coral and the marine life while still standing or kneeling. For the more experienced, there is a wall 10 m off the beach. When the tide is going out there are very strong currents around the island. There are also scorpion fish. All rubbish should be placed in the bin provided and returned to the mainland.

When open to tourists, **Red Skin** has a limited beach coastline, mostly to the west, with caves to the rocky north and mangrove swamps to the south and east. However, the conditions are ideal for snorkelling; near low tide you can go out 150 m and still be in shallow waters. There are a couple of forest trails and a small freshwater spring; you may occasionally see spotted deer.

Cinque Island ① *you may only visit Cinque on a trip organized by a tour company (ask any major hotel in town), boat Rs 1,500, Brothers and Sisters Islands, a part of the Cinque Group, can only be visited as part of a diving trip,* is really two hilly islands joined by a permanent sand bar. The sheltered bay here, with very clear water, makes it the best place for snorkelling in the park. It is a long day trip and expensive to visit, but very worthwhile. If you walk along the beach to the right of where you land, a forest trail leads you to another excellent beach on the other side of the island where there is a tremendous range of coral. Only suitable for the experienced since there is no supervision or help at hand on this side.

Listings: South Andaman and the Marine National Park

● Sleeping

Chiriya Tapu *p765*
There are excellent camping spots here, with fresh water, in the village set back from the Munda Pahar Beach. The trail continues through the forest to a couple of smaller beaches.

Mount Harriet *p765*
Forest Guest House (with permission). You can get water and tea from the caretaker. There is an octagonal viewing platform at the top with good views of Ross Island, and a small garden for picnics.

● Eating

Corbyn's Cove *p765*
Snack Bar at *Peerless Beach Resort* serves reasonable food (fish and chips), open all day, friendly staff, quick service, good toilets at resort with lockers and changing rooms.

Ross Island *p765*
A small cafeteria sells cold drinks and biscuits. Take a picnic if you plan to spend the day, and if the cafeteria is shut, try cracking open a fallen coconut. Delicious!

● Transport

Chiriya Tapu *p765*
Buses leave from Port Blair stand at 0500, 0730, 1030, 1200 (1 hr) but often late; returns 10 mins after arrivals; last at 1900. It is an easy journey by hired scooter but beware of oncoming traffic; the single-track road has many blind bends. Taxi Rs 120 one way.

Corbyn's Cove *p765*
Easiest by taxi (Rs 60); plenty available for return journey.

Mount Harriet *p765*
Tours are operated by the Directorate of Shipping from Phoenix Bay Jetty, T32725. Vehicles must take a ferry from Phoenix Bay to Bamboo Flats. Chatham to Hope Town or Bamboo Flats carry foot passengers only; from Bamboo Flats it is a 20- min walk along the coast to Hope Town. A bus (0600, 0800) runs along this road. For return from Hope Town jetty: 1315, 1415 to Bamboo Flats and 1500 to Phoenix Bay; Bamboo Flats to Chatham Jetty: 1520, 1615, 1735, 1830. Taxis charge Rs 350 return to the top from Bamboo Flats jetty. By road alone it is 45 km instead of 15 km.

Ross Island *p765*
Boats (daily except Wed) from Phoenix Jetty, 0830, 1030, 1230, 1400, 1500. Take early boat as later ones get crowded, especially at weekends. Return boat at 0840, 1040, 1240, 1410, 1640.

Ritchie's Archipelago

The archipelago lies between 20 and 40 km off the east coast of south Andaman and Baratang Islands. Most are inhabited, but only three are open to foreign visitors: Havelock (the most popular), Neil and Long Island. They are the focus of the government's tourist effort and can be reached by the regular ferry service between Port Blair (Phoenix Jetty) and Rangat Bay (Nimbutala Jetty). ▶▶ *For Sleeping, Eating and other listings, see pages 769-771.*

Havelock Island

This beautiful island with pristine white beaches is the government's principal centre for tourist development outside Port Blair. It is the island chosen by most visitors as an escape from Port Blair. Despite its popularity, you can (as anywhere in the Andamans) escape from other visitors and find your private bit of beach for the day. You can cycle along the road to **Radhnagar** beach (No 7), 11 km to the southwest of the Jetty (No 1), and one of the best in the Andamans. Beach No 3 is 3 km from the jetty, while No 5 is further south. A week-long *Mela* marking the birth of Subhas Chandra Bose is held in January with special Bengali cultural programmes. On arrival passports and permits are checked at the jetty where guesthouse touts pester new arrivals. There is a rather confusing (and illogical) system of referring to beaches and settlements on the island by numbers. Sand flies can be a real nuisance.

Neil Island
ⓘ *To/from Port Blair takes 4 hrs, Rs 9; to Havelock, 2½ hrs, Rs 6.*

Neil is the smallest island in the Andamans you can stay on. It is very relaxed and attracts fewer visitors than Havelock. The best beach is close to the jetty and you will find shops sell provisions and basic camping gear (except tents, hammocks).

Long Island
ⓘ *From Rangat it is possible to get a lumber boat from the mangrove jetty to Long Island (if taking a bus, ask for 'Long Island jetty'). Ask at jetty for ferry to Port Blair via Havelock; usually 2 boats a week.*

The settlement is dominated by the plywood factory. Outside the port area are concrete walkways.

Listings: Ritchie's Archipelago

🛏 Sleeping

Havelock Island *p769*
Beach camping is not allowed.
At **Beach No 7**:
B-F Jungle Resort, T37656, F37657, susheeldixit@yahoo.com. Remote and deeply shaded, small, bamboo, Nicobari 'Eco huts' on stilts, nets, 10 deluxe with wash block, excellent but expensive (Rs 2,600); also basic open huts with nets (overpriced), common bath not too clean, pricey food, beer, postcards, promoting 'eco-friendly tourism'.
At **Beach No 5**:
B-E Dolphin Resort, public bus stops 100 m from the entrance, then walk down a sandy track to campsite, T82411, www.andaman. nic.in. 18 huts on stilts, very thin walls (Rs 300–

1,500), pleasant gardens, limited restaurant, no good beach nearby as it is a dumping ground for felled trees cleared for the resort, popular with Indian tourists so reserve ahead.
F Tented Camp, rather neglected, tents, limited lunch and dinner thalis (order ahead), popular and cheap, very peaceful, closes at first rainfall. Reservation Secretariat, Director of Tourism, Port Blair, T32694. There is a permanent naval base near this beach.
At **Beach No 3**:
C Wild Orchid, T33358, F30109, islandtravel@ yahoo.com. 6 Thai-style bungalows with fan, bath and verandah, garden.
E Café del Mar, on the beach, www.andaman scubaclub.com. 6 simple but comfortable bungalows, good restaurant, spacious 'resort', diving run by 2 experienced Swiss.

● *For an explanation of the sleeping and eating price codes used in this guide, see inside the*
● *front cover. Other relevant information is found in Essentials pages 52-57.*

E Pristine Beach, next door, T82344. 6 simeple huts, licensed bar.

Near the **Jetty (No 1)**:

E MS, T82439, rooms with bath and open-sided thatched huts with floor mattress, net, good food.

E Maya Sea View, T82367, 8 rooms vary, some with bath and sea view, shabby but good meeting place.

Neil Island *p769*

Camping allowed. Beach No 1 is unspoilt and peaceful though visitors often leave litter behind. Ask to get water from a farm well.

E Hawabill Nest, T82630, simple, clean

rooms (Rs 400-800 if a/c works) with hot shower, dorm (Rs 75), cook (buy provisions in the market and ask him to prepare meal), snorkel hire. Reservation, Secretariat, Director of Tourism, Port Blair, T32694.

Long Island *p769*

At Lalaji Beach, a 2-hr walk through woods or by boat, Rs 200, there is camping by a small coconut plantation. The beach is lined with coconut trees and cattle steal any food left lying about. The drinking water quality from the well near the beach is suspect.

F Forest Dept Guest House, on path uphill to

South Andaman & Ritchie's Archipelago

the left from jetty, simple but only Rs 20.
Must book ahead in Port Blair or Rangat. The
baker is helpful and sells good coconut
croissants.

🍴 Eating

Havelock Island *p769*
Near the **Jetty, No 1**:
There are several basic places serving
reasonable fish, vegetable and rice dishes.
Das is the friendliest and best.
MS, wonderful garlic fish (pick your own!).
Women's Co-op Café does good thalis.
At **Beach No 7**:
Harmony, near the beach, excellent
lunch/dinner, Rs 60 (delicately spiced huge
fish steak, spicy vegetables, chips, dessert)
but order before owner's market visit, pots of
tea all day (books, cassettes to accompany),
great atmosphere, packed in the evening,
may have to wait 2 hrs in season so friendly
and enterprising Ashok has set up chess,
backgammon and carom.

Neil Island *p769*
Chand, in the village, does great chick pea
daal, egg rolls and *vadais*.
Shanti, next door, is good too. Bottled water
is in short supply.

🛍 Shopping

Havelock Island *p769*
Village **No 3** has a good market.
General Stores, varied camping equipment.

⛰ Activities and tours

Havelock Island *p769*
Andaman Scuba Club, Beach No 3 at *Café del
Mar*, www.andamanscubaclub.com (better
areas and prices than from Port Blair), Swiss run,
professional and friendly, digital equipment,
PADI course, 2-dive trip with dive master.

⊖ Transport

Havelock Island *p769*
Two taxis and a jeep drive from the jetty to
Beach Nos 3, 5 and 7, Rs 10-30.

Bikes
Bikes and scooters: for hire at Jetty (ask at
hotel) or at the *paan* shop under Susmita
Electronics. Also outside Dolphin Resort.
Bikes, Rs 35; scooters, Rs 125.

Bus
Local   Regular service from Jetty (No 1) all
the way to Radhnagar Beach (No 7), via Village
No 3 and *Dolphin Resort* (No 5); 2 hourly,
0700-1100, 1500-1900; from No 7, 0600-1000,
1400-1800. Avoid being swamped by school
children at 0800 and 1500.

Ferry
Inter-island, from Phoenix Jetty to Havelock,
daily, 0600, 4-6 hrs depending on boat; new
faster service on *Rangat* 0600, 1200 (not
daily, usually weekends), 2 hrs (buy ticket at
Phoenix Jetty the day before 0900-1100).

ⓘ Directory

Havelock Island *p769*
Bank for exchange. **Medical centre** at No
3. **Internet** at No 7.

Middle and North Andamans

The Andaman Trunk Road is the only road to the north from Port Blair. Since it passes
through the restricted Jarawa tribal reserve, it is not possible to drive along this
yourself. There are daily buses to Rangat and Mayabunder. Occasionally the more
adventurous Jarawas hitch a lift on the bus to the edge of the reserve. The route runs
through some spectacular forest but sadly, despite controls, there has already been a
lot of selective clearance of hardwoods.

Although the government has lifted restrictions on where you can visit, until
new *Yatri Niwases* are built, accommodation is limited. PWD *Rest Houses*, usually

on the outskirts of a village, provide the best accommodation. Ones at Rangat, Mayabunder, Kalighat, Diglipur, Aerial Bay, Kalipur and Long Island are open to tourists when rooms are available. They are clean, often the best place to eat and excellent value (rates are uniform and clearly posted). Government and local officials have priority, and they are often full. The housekeeper requires permission from the local PWD officer to release a room. Patience, politeness and a clean appearance help! Reserve in advance at PWD Office between *Shompen Hotel* and Lighthouse Cinema, Port Blair, but bookings are not always honoured. ▶▶ *For Sleeping, Eating and other listings, see pages 774-776.*

Middle Andaman

Rangat

It is the only place with a choice of private accommodation for at least 20 visitors. **Amkunj Beach**, 8 km, has little shade left but there is good snorkelling off the rocks at the top end of the beach: from Rangat, take any bus heading for Nimbutala or Mayabunder up to the fork for Rangat Bay, then walk 1 km along track to right just after the heli-pad.

There is a good sandy beach across the road from *Hawksbill Nest*. Ideal for swimming but it is a Wildlife Sanctuary where turtles nest between November-April. In order to step onto the beach permission is needed from the Forest Department at Rangat, Mayabunder or the Beat Officer at Betapur, 4 km north of *Hawksbill Nest*; entrance fee Rs 10 per day. Those caught on the beach without permission are promised "an unpleasant experience".

Mayabunder → *157 km by sea from Port Blair.*

Mayabunder is the administrative centre for Middle and North Andaman. All amenities are situated along a single road which runs along the brow of a ridge sticking out into the bay; the port is at the north end.

You can visit **Karmateng Beach**, 25 minutes away by bus. A shallow sandy slope over 1 km long, with a few rocks at the north end, it is not so good for snorkelling or swimming, as it is exposed and the sea is choppy. A short distance from Karmateng is another idyllic beach popular with foreign tourists at **Gujinala**. You need permission from DFO in Mayabunder or from Beat Officer at Karmateng.

There are several islands in the bay opposite the jetty which can be reached by *dunghy*; ask fishermen and expect to pay Rs 120 for a boat charter for several hours. All offer safe beaches for swimming but there is no good coral. **Avis Island** is a private coconut plantation. Again you need permission from the Forestry Department to visit.

Avis Island

This tiny island is just east of Mayabunder but its ownership is disputed between the Forestry Department and The Coconut Society of Mayabunder. To visit, get permission from DCF, Mayabunder, and charter a *dunghy*.

Foreign tourists are also permitted to visit (with permission from DCF, Mayabunder) **Curlew Island**, **Rayhill Island**, **Sound Island**, **Interview Island** and **Mohanpur** on the eastern coast of North Andaman. Tourists are encouraged to destroy illegal deer traps they find.

Interview Island

ⓘ *Can only be visited in a private boat.*

The island which has wild elephants now has a Protected Forest. Day visits can in overnight at the Forest Department *Guest House* with three rooms; contact DCF, Mayabunder.

Barren Islands

Across to the east from Middle Andaman, Barren has India's only active volcano which erupted in 1991 causing widespread destruction of the island's ecosystem. Smoky fire belches from the side of the crater. It is only possible to visit on a day trip with no landings permitted. Sailings are infrequent and it is essential to get a permit from the tourist office in Port Blair.

North Andaman

Kalighat

It is a small settlement at the point where the creek becomes too shallow for the ferry to go any further. Of no particular interest, it still makes a very pleasant and peaceful stopover between Port Blair and the north. You can cross the river by the mangrove footbridge and follow the path up into the forest which is good for birdwatching. Sadly you also get a good impression of how many hardwoods are being logged.

North Andaman

You can (with some effort; little English spoken) take a bus to the beach at Ramnagar (11 km). Better still, hire a cycle for Rs 5 per hour and enjoy a very pleasant push, ride, free-wheel, with a refreshing swim at the end as a reward.

Diglipur

Previously known as Port Cornwallis, Diglipur is the most northerly commercial centre which foreigners can visit. There is a good market and shops; a special *Mela* is held in January/February which attracts traders.

Aerial Bay

The small fishing village is the last peaceful location before returning to Port Blair. Most of the fish is taken to the market in Diglipur.

Smith and Ross Islands

From Aerial Bay, you can visit the islands just north where it is possible to camp on pleasant forested beaches (though there are plans to build bungalows here, in which case free camping may be banned). You need permission from the Range Officer ① *opposite Jetty entrance, Mon-Sat, 0700-1400, ferry 0600, 1400, Rs 5; or hire a* dunghy, he doesn't issue permits for Lamia Bay.

Saddle Peak National Park

Theoretically 'Lamia Bay Permits' for Saddle Peak and Lamia Bay are available from the Beat Officer in Lamia Bay. However, the path from Lamia Bay to Saddle Peak is very overgrown. **Kalipur** is a small group of farm houses on both sides of the road with a shop and a *Yatri Niwas* a few kilometres south of Aerial Bay. There is a very interesting beach at Kalipur with Saddle Peak as an impressive backdrop, accessible via a small path almost opposite the *Turtle Resort*.

Lamia Bay has a pebble beach south of Kalipur which you can walk to. From the bus stop the road leads straight ahead onto a path which is easy to follow (30 minutes). It is possible to camp under a small, round palm-leaf shelter. To the north, there are small bays strewn with large eroded boulders, whilst the beaches to the south lead towards Saddle Peak (730 m), 4½ km away.

Despite the relatively short distance to **Saddle Peak**, the rocky beach, the steep climb, the thick forest and the heat, mean that you need a whole day for the trek, starting early in the morning after camping in Lamia Bay. Don't attempt the whole trip in a day from Aerial Bay.

Narcondam Island

East of North Andaman, this is the most remote island in the group. An extinct craterless volcano, it is covered in luxuriant forest that is the home of the unique Narcondam hornbill was declared a sanctuary in 1977. It is a birdwatchers' paradise though permission to visit is very hard to get and only 24-hour stops are allowed. There are occasional sailings from Aerial Bay.

Little Andaman Island

This large island lies 120 km (eight hours) south of Port Blair across the Duncan Passage. Note that Malaria is rife here. The main village, **Hut Bay** to the southeast, is 2 km away from the jetty. Heavily deforested during the 1960s and 70s, much of the island has become virtually treeless. Betel, red palm and banana plantations dominate the scenery. It is possible to camp on the large beach in the north of the island, 22 km from the jetty, but tourist facilities are virtually non-existent, with only one restaurant next to the *GM Lodge*, and no bottled water so you need to carry everything with you.

Listings: Middle and North Andamans

Sleeping

Rangat *p772*

E Hawksbill Nest, Cuthbert Bay, 18 km from Rangat (buses to Mayabunder go past all day, ask for 'Yatri Niwas'). 8 clean sea-facing rooms (Rs 250, better views on 1st floor), 2 a/c (Rs 400) 4-bed dorms (Rs 75). Book ahead at Secretariat, Dir. of Tourism, Port Blair, T32694.

F Chandra Mohan Lodge, blue wooden building on outskirts of town, rundown, but friendly staff.

Avoid **Krishna**.

Mayabunder *p772*

E Swiftlet Nest, 10 km from Mayabunder, away from the beach, T73211, overlooking paddy fields (forest not cleared at the beach). 10 good rooms (Rs 250), 4 a/c (Rs 400), dorm (Rs 75), 'manager absent' but good food, helpful staff.

F Dhanalakshmi and **Lakshmi Narayan** have small, dirty rooms.

As a last resort, Jetty **Waiting Rooms** provide some shelter and canteen food.

Kalighat *p773*

There are a few hotels near the jetty.

F PWD **Rest House**, on a hill, 2 mins' walk

from jetty (book ahed in Port Blair). 3 rooms (1 for VIPs only), friendly housekeeper, excellent vegetable thalis, generous portions.

Diglipur *p773*
E Drua, 15 rooms (Rs 200), unhelpful manager. **F Laxmi**, 4 clean rooms with common bath (Rs 120), friendly, helpful. Recommended. **Sports Stadium**, with clean, spacious, guarded area for travellers with immaculate toilets and showers. Recommended.

Aerial Bay *p773*
F PWD **Rest House** high up on a hill (book ahead in Port Blair). 2 rooms, often full.

Also an unmarked wooden hotel on the left, coming into town from Diglipur.

Saddle Peak National Park *p774*
E-F Turtle Resort Yatri Niwas, 8 rooms, Rs 250 (4 a/c, Rs 400), dorm (Rs 75), poor food, dirty public areas, unhelpful staff. Very peaceful, on a hillock overlooking paddy fields with thick forests leading up to the Saddle Peak National Park to the south. Though called '*Turtle Resort*', the rooms are named after birds like Ostrich and Penguin! Contact T32747.

Little Andaman Island *p774*
F GM Lodge, tiny singles, 1 double. **F PWD Rest House** (book ahead in Port Blair), excellent clean double rooms, no food, rather hostile staff insist on waking guests at 0600.

ⓕ Eating

Rangat *p772*
Annapurna, on corner of vegetable market (from bus stand, turn left opposite *Krishna Lodge*, then right and left again). Good food. **Darbar Bakery**, near bus stand (on right, at start of road leading to PWD *Rest House*). Good selection.

Kalighat *p773*
Bakery next door to *Viji*. **Viji** has reasonable food.

Diglipur *p773*
Plenty of snack bars, tea houses and fresh fruit in the market.

Aerial Bay *p773*
Excellent fish is sold near harbour gates; larger fish (tuna and barracuda) in the afternoon (Rs 20-30 per kg).

A few shops sell basic provisions and there is a small market by the bus stand. **Mohan**, owner speaks some English and is helpful, will prepare excellent fish dishes for you, good thalis, selection of drinks.

ⓞ Transport

Rangat *p772*
Bus
To **Mayabunder** 0600, connects with ferry to Kalighat at 0930, later bus at 1145; to **Port Blair** *Exp* (B), daily, 0800, 0900 (Rs 33). From **Port Blair** by bus to Rangat there are 2 ferry crossings (Nilambur and Gandhi Ghat). Takes up to 8 hrs to Rangat town, depending on bus connections, ie whether your bus goes on this ferry and/or if bus is waiting on other side at Nilambur.

Ferry
The jetty is at Rangat Bay (Nimbutala), 7 km from town. To **Port Blair** 0600, 7 hrs, buy tickets (Rs 30) on board. There is an 'Inner' (Creek) and an 'Outer' route, the latter via Strait, Havelock (30-min stop) and Neil islands (see Transport under Port Blair). Lumber boats from Mangrove Jetty go to **Long Island**; **Mayabunder**, 3 per week, 3 hrs.

Mayabunder *p772*
Bus
Port Blair *Exp* (A) and (C), depart 0600, tickets sold from 1500 the day before, at bus station (2 km from jetty). **Rangat** local bus, 0830-1700. Also some private buses. **Karmateng** many for beach, 0715-1700 (return bus approximately 35 mins after these times). **Diglipur** the road is still under construction.

Ferry
For **Diglipur** take local ferry to Kalighat, or wait for the inter-island ferry from Port Blair which calls here en route to Aerial Bay every 11-12 days. **Kalighat** small sea ferry daily, 0930, 1445, 2½ hrs (Rs 3), is very crowded, with little shade. Private *dunghies* leave at dawn; they can carry 20 people (Rs 25 each) and the occasional scooter; a

charter costs Rs 400. **Port Blair** Check outside Asst Commissioner's office near police station for schedules.

Kalighat *p773*
Bus

To **Diglipur** Regular local service (45 mins), 0630, 0800, 1030, 1130, 1400, connect with ferry from Mayabunder.

Ferry

To **Mayabunder** daily, 0500, 1230, 2 hrs (Rs 3), can get very crowded and virtually no shade; also *Dunghy*, 0600, 2 hrs (Rs 15); or charter a *dunghy* at any time for about Rs 300 (the rate for a full boat).

Diglipur *p773*
Bus

To all the surrounding villages and beaches. Regular service to Kalighat, 45 mins (last at 1900) and Aerial Bay (30 mins) which has the occasional boat to Port Blair.

Aerial Bay *p773*
Bus

It is not possible to reach Port Blair by bus in 1 day, the furthest you can hope to get is Rangat. Private and public buses to **Diglipur** and **Kalipur**, approximately every hour.

Ferry

To **Mayabunder** and **Port Blair** (2 sailings a month). The jetty ticket office is not always sure when the next boat is due; better to contact the coastguard tower who have radio contact with Port Blair (no telephone connection with South Andaman). Fare: bunk Rs 47, deck Rs 27 (cabins for Govt officials only); Indian canteen meals. Tickets go on sale the day before departure at the Tehsildar's office, next to Diglipur *Rest House*; to avoid a long wait there, buy on the boat, though you may sometimes have to pay more, and only get a deck ticket.

Saddle Peak National Park *p774*
Bus

Buses between Diglipur and Kalipur, via Aerial Bay. From Kalipur: departs 1230, 1330, 1530, 1740, 2015; to Aerial Bay, 25 mins, Rs 2.

❶ Directory

Rangat *p772*
Banks State Bank of India, by the bus stand.
Post Office opposite the Police Station.

Nicobar Islands

The names given by travellers and sailors from the east and the west all referred to these islands as the Land of the Naked - Nicobar is derived from the Tamil word *nakkavaram*. The islands which lay on the trade route to the Far East were visited in the 11th century by the seafaring Cholas during the rule of King Rajendra I who attempted to extend his rule here. Before the British used the Nicobars as a penal territory in the late 19th century, European missionaries (particularly the Danish) made converts during the 17th and 18th centuries but few survived the difficulties of the climate and most died of fever within a year.

The islands, including **Katchal** with a large rubber plantation, **Nancowry** harbour, **Indira Point**, India's southernmost tip and **Campbell Bay** (Great Nicobar), are closed to foreign visitors; Car Nicobar to the north can be visited by Indians with a permit. The significant tribal population live in distinctive huts, which look like large thatched domes that are raised on stilts about 2 m high and are entered through the floor. The Nicobarese enjoy wrestling, fishing, swimming and canoeing but are best known for their love of music. Villages still participate in competitions of traditional unaccompanied singing and dancing which mark every festivity.

South India

Introduction

Despite the continuous flow of people and ideas between North and South India over the last 4,000 years and more, the four states of South India - Andhra Pradesh, Karnataka, Kerala and Tamil Nadu - have a distinct identity. Each has its own major language, and the region has its own cultural traditions of literature, art, architecture and music. Some of Hinduism's most important schools of philosophy have had their origin in the far south, yet here Christianity pre-dates many of them, and in Kerala and Tamil Nadu makes a far more visible contribution to life than in most other parts of India.

As a backdrop to this cultural diversity is a great range of often beautiful scenery. **The Nilgiris** ('blue hills') may be thought of as only hills in comparison with the Himalaya, but soaring to over 2,500 metres they often present a dramatic wall overlooking the **plains of Tamil Nadu** to the east or the narrow coastal strip of **Kerala** and **Karnataka** to the west. Delightful hill stations – **Kodaikkanal**, **Coonoor**, **Munnar** and the more popular **Ooty** – enjoy the best of a low latitude, high altitude climate. On the plains below are some of India's greatest cultural treasures, including the distinctive southern temples at **Madurai**, **Thanjavur** and **Mamallapuram** among many, while **forts** and **palaces** add another dimension to the visitor's choices.

Tamil Nadu

⁞ Footprint features

Introduction

Tamil Nadu, once known as the Coromandel coast, has a language and poetic literature over 2,000 years old. It also boasts some of the most remarkable **temple architecture** in India, and, with an extraordinarily rich, living tradition of **music** and **dance**. Temple towns and historic sites are dotted across the plains, especially in the fertile Thanjavur delta, while the **hill stations** of the Western Ghats are within easy reach. The former French territory of **Pondicherry**, a coastal enclave on the eastern seaboard of central Tamil Nadu, has its own distinctive colonial inheritance,

The wealth of its culture, the open friendliness of the Tamil people, and the wide range of beautiful landscapes make Tamil Nadu one of India's most rewarding states to visit.

★ Don't miss...

❶ Meditation enthusiasts head for **Sri Aurobindo Ashram** at futuristic Auroville. Nearby **Pondicherry** still has a hint of its French heritage, pages 817 and 814

❷ Thanjavur's **Brihadisvara Temple** is one of the great monuments of South India and has a captivating atmosphere, especially in the evening, page 837

❸ Attend the memorable evening puja at **Nataraja Temple**, Chidambaram, page 842

❹ Head for the cool of the hill stations. There are many lovely ghat roads but the **Blue Mountain Railway**, which ends up at Ooty, is the best means of transport, page 852

❺ Tea time at the elephant camp in the **Mudumalai Wildlife Sanctuary** is worth watching but you need to get up at dawn to see the wildlife, page 853

❻ The crowds at the **Minakshi Temple**, Madurai can be overpowering but the experience is unforgettable, page 863

❼ The Bay of Bengal, the Indian Ocean and the Arabian sea all meet at **Kanniyakumari**, the most southerly point of India. Go in April to see the sun and moon on the same horizon, page 873

Tamil Nadu

Background → *Population: 62.1 million. Area: 130,000 sq km.*

The land

Tamil Nadu rises from the flat coastal plains in the east to the magnificent Western Ghats – the Nilgiris in the north and the Palani, Cardamom and Anamalai hills in the south. The Nilgiris – 'blue mountains' – rise like a wall above the haze of the plains to heights of over 2,500 m. The plains are hot, often dry and dusty, with isolated blocks of granite forming often bizarre shapes on the ancient eroded surface. The coast itself is a flat alluvial plain, with deltas at the mouths of major rivers. The medieval rulers in Tamil Nadu often created tanks which now add a beautiful touch to the landscape.

Climate Most rain falls between October and December and is the worst time to travel. The best time to visit is from mid-December to early March when the dry sunny weather sets in and before the heat gets too crushing. The hills can then be really cold, especially at night. In the rain shadow of the Western Ghats, temperatures never fall much below 21°C except in the hills, but although humidity is often high maximum temperatures rarely exceed 42°C.

History

Tamil Nadu's cultural identity has been shaped by the Dravidians, who have inhabited the south since at least the fourth millennium BC. Tamil, India's oldest living language, developed from the earlier languages of people who were probably displaced from the north by Aryan-based culture from 2000 BC to 1500 BC.

By the fourth century BC Tamil Nadu was under the rule of three dynasties. The **Cholas** occupied the coastal area east of Thanjavur and inland to the head of the Kaveri Delta at Tiruchi. The south – Madurai, Tirunelveli and a part of southern Kerala were under the **Pandiyas** while the **Cheras** controlled much of what is now Kerala on the west coast of the peninsula.

The **Pandiyas** returned to power in the Tamil area after the decline of the Cholas and ruled from 1175 to 1300. In the 13th century, international trade flourished under their control and was only superseded by the rise of Vijayanagar (Hampi, see page 1002. The **Pallavas** of Kanchi came to power in the fourth century AD and were dominant between AD 550-869. Possibly of northern origin, under their control Mahabalipuram (Mamallapuram) became an important port in the seventh century. The **Cholas** returned to power in 850 and were a dominant political force until 1173. During the 11th-century, Rajendra Chola (1013-44) extended Chola power to the River Ganga in Bengal. His naval expeditions to the Malayan Peninsula resulted in Chola domination over the trade routes of the Indian Ocean to Java, Sumatra and China until the resumption of Pandiya power for a further century.

The defeat of the great Vijayanagar Empire by a confederacy of Muslim states in 1565 forced their leaders south. As the Nayaka kings they continued to rule from as far south as Madurai well into the 17th century. Ultimately when Muslim political control finally reached Tamil Nadu it was as brief as it was tenuous.

It was more than 150 years after their founding of Fort St George at Madras in 1639 before the **East India Company** could claim political supremacy in South India. Haidar Ali, who mounted the throne of Mysore in 1761, and his son Tipu Sultan, allied with the French, won many battles against the English. The Treaty of Versailles in 1783 brought the French and English together and Tipu was forced to make peace. The English took Malabar in 1792, and in 1801 Lord Wellesley brought together most of the south under the Madras Presidency, see page 981.

The French acquired land at Pondicherry in 1673. In 1742, Dupleix was named Governor of the French India Company and took up residence at **Pondicherry**. He seized Madras within a few years but in 1751 Clive attacked Arcot. His victory was the

⁝ The terrifying guardian deities

Many Hindu villagers in Tamil Nadu believe in guardian deities of the village – Ayyanar, Muneeswaram, Kaliamman, Mariamman and many more. Groups of larger than life images built of brick, wood or stone and covered in brightly painted lime plaster (chunam) guard the outskirts of several villages. They are deliberately terrifying, designed to frighten away evil spirits from village homes, but villagers themselves are also very frightened of these gods and try to keep away from them.

The deities are supposed to prevent epidemics, but if an epidemic does strike special sacrifices are offered, mainly of rice. Firewalking, often undertaken in fulfilment of a vow, is a feature of the special festivals at these shrines. Disease is also believed to be held at bay by other ceremonies, including piercing the cheeks and tongue with wire and the carrying of kavadis (special carriages or boxes, sometimes designed like a coffin).

beginning of the end of French ambitions in India. The Treaty of Paris brought their Empire to a close in 1763 although they retained five counting houses.

Culture

The great majority of Tamilians are Dravidians with Mediterranean ethnic origins. They have been settled in Tamil Nadu for several thousand years. Tamil, the main language of the State, is spoken by over 85% of the population. Hindus make up nearly 90% of the population, and over 5% are Christian, a group especially strong in the south where Roman Catholic and Protestant missions have been active for over 500 years. There are a small but significant minorities of Muslims, Jains and Parsis.

There are isolated groups of as many as 18 different types of **tribal people** who live in the Nilgiri Hills. Some of them are of aboriginal stock although local archaeological discoveries suggest that an extinct race preceded them. The **Todas'** life and religion revolve around their long-horned buffalo which are a measure of their wealth. Their small villages are called *munds* with half a dozen or so igloo- like, windowless bamboo and dried grass huts. The animist temples and 'cathedrals' or *boa*, which only men are allowed to enter, are of similar construction but larger. Their chief goddess 'Tiekirzi', the creator of the indispensable buffalo, and her brother 'On', rule the world of the dead and the living. There are only about 1,000 Todas left. The **Badagas** are the main tribal group and probably came from Karnataka. Like the Kotas and Kurumbas, they speak a mixture of Kannada and Tamil and their oral tradition is rich in folktales, poetry, songs and chants. Agriculturalists, their villages are mainly in the upper plateau, with rows of three-roomed houses. They worship Siva and observe special tribal festivals including an unusual fire feast In honour of the gods of harvest. Progressive and adaptable, they are being absorbed into the local community faster than the others.

Cuisine Many Tamilians are vegetarian and the strict Brahmins among them avoid the use of garlic and onion and in some cases even tomatoes. Favourites for breakfast or *'tiffin'* (snack) include *dosai* (thin crisp pancakes, plain or *masala* when stuffed with mildly spiced potato and onion), *idli* (steamed, fermented rice cakes), delicious rice-based *pongal* (worth searching out) and *vadai* (savoury lentil doughnuts), all served with a coconut chutney and *sambar* (a spicy lentil and vegetable broth). A *thali* here centres around boiled rice with a selection of vegetable preparations served in

 The south excels in vegetarian food reflecting what grows in abundance in the region – particularly coconut, chillies, tamarind and bananas.

Tamil Nadu Background

small steel containers, as well as pickles, *papadum*, *rasam* (a clear, peppery lentil 'soup'), plain curd. The food from Chettinad tends to be particularly hot and spicy. The dessert is usually *payasam* (similar to creamy rice pudding) to round off the meal. South Indian coffee is a treat. It is freshly ground and filtered, mixed with hot milk and sugar, and traditionally served frothed up in small stainless steel tumblers.

Literature Tamil is the oldest of India's living languages, with a literature stretching back to the early centuries before Christ. The poet and thinker Thiruvalluvar, author of the 'Thirukkural' (first century BC-second century AD) is still revered today. From around the second century AD a poets' academy known as the **Sangam** was established in Madurai. Sangam literature suggests that life in Tamil society had a social hierarchy with the sages at the top, followed by peasants, hunters, artisans, soldiers, fishermen and scavengers – quite different from the caste system that existed in the rest of the subcontinent. From the beginning of the Christian era Tamil religious thinkers began to transform the image of Krishna from the remote and heroic figure of the epics into the focus of a new and passionate devotional worship – *bhakti*. From the seventh to the 10th century there was a surge of writing new hymns of praise, sometimes referred to as 'the Tamil *Veda*'. Attention focused on the 'marvels of Krishna's birth and infancy and his heroic and amorous exploits as a youth among the cowherds and cowherdesses of Gokula'. In the ninth century Vaishnavite Brahmans produced the *Bhagavata Purana*, which, through frequent translation into all India's major languages, became the vehicle for the new worship of Krishna. Its 10th book has been called "one of the truly great books of Hinduism". There are over forty translations into Bengali alone.

Music Changes constantly occurred in different schools of music within the basic framework of **raga-tala-prabandha** which was well established by the seventh century. From the 13th century the division between the *Hindustani* or the northern system (which included the western and eastern regions as well) and the *Carnatic* or the southern system, became pronounced. The southern school has a more scale-based structure of *raga* whereas the northern school has greater flexibility and thus continued to develop through the centuries. The *tala* too is much more precise. It is also nearly always devotional or didactic whereas the northern system also includes non-religious, everyday themes which are sometimes sensuous. The language that lends itself naturally to the southern system is Telugu and the only bowed instrument that is used to accompany vocal music is the violin, imported from the West but played rather differently.

The fundamental form in Carnatic music is the **varnam**. This is like an étude which conforms to phrases and melodic movements of a particular *raga*. They all have lyrics. The complex structure reaches its height in the *kritis* which are usually devotional. Unlike some North Indian musical forms in which the melody became more important than the lyric, *kriti* restored the balance between words and music.

Dance and drama **Bharata Natyam** is thought to be the oldest form of classical dance in India. Originating in Tamil Nadu, it is essentially a highly stylized solo feminine dance which combines movement, music and mime with *nritta* (pure dance) and *nritya* (expression), usually on the theme of spiritual love. The two related dance forms, the *Bhagavata Mela*, performed by men in some important temples and the *Kuravanji*, a dance-opera for women for certain temple festivals also come from Tamil Nadu.

Temple architecture Temple building was a comparatively late development in Hindu worship, see page 688. Long before the first temple was built, shrines were dotted across the land, each with its own mythology. Even the most majestic of South Indian temples have basic features in common with these original shrines, and many of them have simply grown by a process of accretion.

Temple worship

David Shulman gives an excellent idea of the way in which a pilgrim approaches the temple. He writes: "There is often to begin with, the long, uncomfortable journey to the shrine, which may be defined as a form of asceticism, tapas... Once the pilgrim arrives at the shrine, he sees before him the towering gopurams or gates set in the walls that enclose the sacred area. He leaves his shoes outside the gate; he will also usually undergo an initial purification by bathing. Once the pilgrim goes through the gopuram the real journey begins... The tall gopurams of the South Indian temple create a sense of dynamism, of movement away from the gate and towards the centre, which is locked inside the stone heart of the main shrine...".

What do pilgrims hope to achieve by their pilgrimage? Usually there is a practical aim – the worshipper comes into contact with a power that helps him in his ordinary life. By offering his own sacrifice to the god, he hopes that the god will reward him by meeting his wishes – for good health, for a suitable husband or wife, for the birth of a child, for prosperity. As Shulman says: "It is important to realize that no one in Tamil Nadu goes on pilgrimage in order to attain release from this *moksha* (world). What has happened in the Tamil tradition is that the world-renouncing goal of the ascetic has been redefined as equivalent to *bhakti* (worship and praise). Pilgrimage came to be a substitute for sannyasa". The Hindu bhakti movements which developed personal worship and praise of a personal Lord, directed the worshipper back to the world in which they live rather than to seek release from it, see also page 1326.

The **Dravida** or Dravidian style underwent several changes under the different dynasties that ruled for about 1,000 years from the time of the Pallavas who laid its foundations. In Mahabalipuram, rock-cut cave temples, *mandapas* (small excavated columned halls), and *rathas* (monoliths in the shape of temple chariots) were carved out by the early Pallavas. These were followed by structural temples and *bas relief* sculptures on giant rocks. The Ekambaresvara Temple in Kanchipuram shows the evolution of the Dravidian style – the shrine with its pyramidal tower and the separate *mandapa* all within the courtyard with its high enclosure wall made up of cells. Six centuries later the two separate structures were joined by the covered hall (*antarala*). A large subsidiary shrine there, which took the place of an entrance gateway, also hinted at the later *gopuram*.

The **Cholas** did away with the rampant lion pilasters, introducing high relief, half-size sculptures of deities and the gryphon motifs. Their greatest architectural achievements are seen in the early 11th-century temples at Gangaikondacholapuram and at Thanjavur where they built huge pyramidal towers on high vertical bases with exquisitely carved figures in niches on the walls.

The **Pandiyas** introduced the practice of building prominent watch towers, the *gopurams* and concentric, often battlemented fortress walls which enclosed the courtyards with shrines. The *gopuram* took its name from the 'cow gate' of the Vedic village, which later became the city gate and finally the monumental temple entrance. Although the first two storeys are usually built solidly of stone masonry, the rest is of lighter material, usually brick and plaster. You can see examples of Pandiya *gopurams* at Jambukesvara near Tiruchirappalli and in Chidambaram and Tirumalai, see page 842. In the Ramesvaram region on the coast in southern Tamil Nadu, open courtyards, trefoil arches and chariot forms became distinguishing features.

From the 13th century Muslim conquerors penetrated ever deeper into the south, bringing a halt to large scale temple building for 200 years. However by the 15th century the **Vijayanagar** kings established their Empire across much of South India, building their fortressed city at Hampi. Their temples were carved out in harmony with the rock, the flat-roofed halls having numerous distinctive highly sculpted pillars. There was a proliferation of special purpose buildings within the temple enclosure. Around the central temple, a subsidiary shrine was built – usually to the northwest – to house the consort of the main deity and to celebrate their marriage anniversary; a many-pillared open hall with a central altar, or *kalyana mandapa*, made its appearance close to the east entrance. The development of the temple complex with several shrines to different deities in the courtyard, the tradition of building *gopurams* in each of the four enclosure walls and the remarkable use of the horse motif, sometimes lions or dragons, mark the Vijayanagara period. The *kalyana mandapas* of the temples at Vellore and Kanchipuram make particular use of hippogryphs in their pillars.

After the defeat of Vijayanagar by the Muslim sultans of the Deccan, the Hindu rulers were pushed further south. The **Nayakas** emerged in the 17th century with their capital at Madurai and continued to build temple complexes with tall *gopurams*. These increased in height to become dominating structures covered profusely with plaster decorations. The tall *gopurams* of Vijayanagar and Nayaka periods may have served a strategic purpose, but they moved away from the earlier *Chola* practice of giving the central shrine the tallest tower. The *kalyana mandapa* or marriage hall with a 'hundred' or 'thousand' pillars, and the temple tank with steps on all four sides, were introduced in some southern temples, along with the *Nandi* bull, Siva's 'vehicle', which occupies a prominent position at the entrance to the main Saivite shrine.

Modern Tamil Nadu

Tamil Nadu took its present form as a result of the States Reorganization Act of 1956. Until 1967 the Assembly was dominated by the Indian National Congress, but after an attempt by the central government to impose Hindi as the national language the Congress Party was routed in 1967 by a regional party, the Dravida Munnetra Kazhagam (the DMK) under its leader CN Annadurai. After his death the party split and since then either the **DMK**, or the splinter party, the **All India Anna DMK**, has been in power in the State.

Neither party has any constituency beyond Tamil Nadu and thus at the all India level each has been forced to seek alliances with national parties. From the late 1960s the AIADMK, which controlled the State Assembly for most of the time, has been led by two film stars. The first, **MG Ramachandran**, known lovingly by his initials MGR, was a charismatic figure who even after a stroke which left him paralysed remained the Chief Minister until his death. **Jayalalitha**, his successor and a film actress who had starred in many of MGR's films, became a highly controversial Chief Minister. She and her party were ousted by the DMK in the May 1996 elections, but, cleared of a wide range of criminal charges, she re-entered the Legislative Assembly in March 2002, taking over once more as Chief Minister.

Economy Since Independence in 1947 Tamil Nadu has become one of India's leading industrial states. With a quarter of India's spinning capacity textiles are tremendously important and the state is famous both for handloom cottons and silks and for factory-made textiles. Leather and fabrics have also long been a vital export industry, but in recent years a range of new industries have developed using locally available raw materials like iron ore, bauxite and magnesite. Chennai has become home to the Ford car factory and the city also makes lorries, buses and trains.

Chennai (Madras)

→ *Phone code: 044. Colour map 7, grid A5. Population: 5.36 million*

Today the impression of relative quiet which once distinguished Madras from the other major colonial cities has been swept aside. Chennai has grown dramatically, and from its old core between Fort St George and the Harbour it has spread rapidly across the surrounding plain through its industrialized northern suburbs and affluent residential suburbs of the south and west. The State Government has made great efforts to house the rapidly growing population, but squatter settlements and informal housing continue to be scattered throughout the city, a reminder that alongside growing modernisation and prosperity poverty is still widespread.

▶▶ *For Sleeping, Eating and other listings, see pages 798-807.*

Ins and outs

Getting there Chennai's air terminals are about 12 km from the city centre. Airport buses run a circuit of the main hotels, and include Egmore station; otherwise get a pre-paid taxi or auto-rickshaw. Trains from the north and west come into the Central Station behind the port. Lines from the south terminate at Egmore, which has hotels nearby.

Getting around Chennai is very spread out and walking is usually uncomfortably hot so it's best to find an auto. Taxis are fairly rare and expensive. The bus service is extensive and frequent, but often very crowded. See Transport, page 803, for further details.

Climate Temperature: Summer, maximum 38°C, minimum 27°C; Winter, maximum 29°C, minimum 20°C. Rainfall: Aug-Dec, average 200 mm; Jun-Jul, average 3 mm. Best time to visit: Dec-Mar.

Background

Armenian and Portuguese traders had settled in the San Thome area before the arrival of the British. In 1639, **Francis Day**, a trader with the East India Company, negotiated the grant of a tiny plot of sandy land to the north of the Cooum River as the base for a warehouse or 'factory'. It was completed on 23 April 1640, St George's Day. Its choice was dictated partly by local politics – Francis Day's friendship with Dharmala Ayyappa Nayak provided a useful lever with the Vijayanagar Raja of Chandragiri – but more importantly by the favourable local price of cotton goods.

By 1654 Fort St George had a church and English residences – the 'White Town'. To its north was 'Black Town', referred to locally as Chennaipatnam, after Chennappa Nayak, Dharmala Ayyappa Nayak's father. The two towns merged and Madraspatnam grew with the acquisition of neighbouring villages of Tiru-alli-keni (Lily Tank) now Triplicane, in 1676. In 1693, Governor Yale (founder of Yale University in the USA) acquired Egmore, Purasawalkam and Tondiarpet from Emperor Aurangzeb, who had by that time extended Mughal power to the far south. In 1746 Madras was captured by the French, to be returned to British control as a result of the Treaty of Aix la Chapelle in 1748. By the middle of the 18th century many other villages such as Nungambakkam, Ennore, Perambur, San Thome and Mylapore (the 'city of the peacock') were added with the help of friendly Nawabs. In 1793 Calcutta became the chief centre of British administration in India, though Madras continued to be the centre of the **East India Company's** expanding power in South India.

The city is still growing although many services, including water supply and housing, are stretched beyond breaking point. Since Independence an increasing range of heavy and light goods industries have been added to long established cotton textiles and a leather industry. The opening of a new Ford Motor Company plant in Sriperumbudur, between Chennai and Kanchipuram, has led some in the city to claim it as "the Detroit of India".

Sights

Fort St George

The beginning of the city of Madras was marked by the building of the 'Factory House' with its fortifications on the beach. It was completed by the British in 1654 but was

Chennai city

Related maps
A George Town, page 790
B Central Chennai, page 794
C South Chennai, page 796

Bay of Bengal

Suburban railway
1 Madras Central
2 Egmore
3 Park
4 Fort
5 Beach
6 Roypuram
7 Washermanpet
8 Basin Bridge
9 Perambur
10 Chetput
11 Nungambakkam
12 Kodambakkam
13 Mambalam
14 Saidapet
15 Guindy
16 St Thomas Mount
17 Meenambakkam
18 Trisoolam

MRTS
1 Beach Junction
2 Fort
3 Park
4 Chintadripet
5 Chepauk
6 Triplicane
7 Lloyds Rd
8 Luz

Sleeping
1 Ramada Madras
2 Trident

Tamil Nadu Chennai Background

rebuilt several times. The present structure of Fort St George, a fine example of 17th-century British military architecture, was mostly built in 1666. The country's tallest flagstaff, thought to be over 300 years old, stood here. The 24 black **Charnockite**, see page 1350, pillars were reclaimed by the British in 1762 after the French had carried them off to Pondicherry in 1746. Today the Fort houses government offices.

The **State Legislative Hall** has fine woodwork and black and white stone paving. You can also see the old barracks and officers' quarters including Lord Clive's house, which he rented from an Armenian merchant. One room, Clive's Corner, has small exhibits. Arthur Wellesley's house is 100 m further along.

St Mary's church ① *an excellent booklet about the church is for sale inside*, was built between 1678 and 1680 by Streynsham Master in solid masonry to a simple plan of three aisles with semi-circular cannon-proof roofs and 1.3-m thick walls. In times of siege it was used as a military dormitory and store house. The first English church in India and the oldest British building to survive, it was almost entirely rebuilt in 1759 after being damaged in a siege. **Governor Elihu Yale** was associated with the church. An American (born to English parents) he worked as a writer for the East India Company from the age of 24, rising to become Governor. Perhaps the best monument in the church is that erected by the East India Company to the famous missionary **Schwartz**, at one time the intermediary between the British and Haidar Ali. The original black font, made from 3,000-million-year-old Charnockite from Pallavaram, has been in continuous use since the church was consecrated. Outside the west entrance, the tombstone of Elizabeth Baker is one of the oldest British inscriptions in India.

George Town

Renamed after the future King George V on the occasion of his visit to India in 1905, George Town has long been the centre of Madras's commercial activity. The lawyer Stephen Popham, who was in Madras from 1778-95 was particularly enthusiastic about improving the city's sanitation. Popham laid out what was to become Madras's main commercial street, still known as **Popham's Broadway**.

In Popham's Broadway (Prakasham Road) is the **Wesleyan Church** (1820). In **Armenian Street** to its east is the beautiful ★ **Armenian Church** of the Holy Virgin Mary (1772). Solid walls and massive 3 m high wooden doors conceal the spotless open courtyard inside. On the site of an ancient cemetery, the oldest Armenian tombstone in the courtyard dates from 1663. The East India Company valued the Armenian community for their 'sober, frugal and wise' style of life and they were given the same rights as English settlers in 1688.

Immediately to the north of the Armenian Church is the Roman Catholic Cathedral, **St Mary of the Angels** (1675). The date 1642, inscribed at the entrance to the Church, is when the Capuchin monks built their first church in Madras.

The **High Court** ① *1045-1345, 1430-1630, Mon-Sat, contact Registrar for visit and guide,* is in the Indo-Saracenic style of the late 19th century developed by architects such as **Henry Irwin**, see page 796, who was also responsible for the National Art Gallery. You are allowed to visit the courtrooms in the law courts by using the entrance on the left. A fine example is Court No 13 which has stained glass, fretted woodwork, carved furniture, silvered panels and a painted ceiling.

The huge red central tower, nearly 50-m tall, built like a domed minaret to serve as a **lighthouse**, can be seen 30 km out at sea. It was in use from 1894 until 1977. You can climb to the top of the lighthouse for a good view. The original **Esplanade Lighthouse**, southeast of the High Court, is in the form of a large Doric pillar which took over from the Fort lighthouse in 1841.

The 19th-century growth of Madras can be traced north from Parry's Corner. **First Line Beach** (North Beach Road), built on reclaimed land in 1814 fronted the beach itself. The **GPO** (1844-84) was designed by Chisholm. The completion of the harbour (1896), transformed the economy of the city.

In the 18th century major commercial expansion took place between First Line Beach and **Mint Street**. The Mint was first opened in 1640, and from the end of the 17th century minted gold coins under licence for the Mughals, though it did not move to Mint Street until 1841-42.

Central Chennai and the Marina

Triplicane and **Chepauk** contain some of the finest examples of late 19th-century Indo-Saracenic architecture in India, focused on the University of Madras. The Governor of Madras, Mountstuart Elphinstone Grant-Duff (1881-86), decided to develop the Marina, especially as a promenade. Ever since it has been a favourite place for thousands of city dwellers to walk on Sunday evenings.

Marina Beach and aquarium Until the harbour was built at the end of the 19th century the sea washed up close to the present road, but the north drifting current has progressively widened the beach. **Anna Park** is named after the founder of the DMK, CN Annadurai. The **MGR Samadhi**, commemorating **MG Ramachandran**, the film star and charismatic Chief Minister during the 1980s, has become a focus of pilgrimage. The Sunday afternoon **market** on the beach is worth visiting.

> ✷ *Swimming unattended along Marina beach is dangerous (3 km)*

Chepauk and Beach Road **Chepauk Palace**, 4½ km away, was the former residence of the Nawab of Carnatic. The original four-domed Khalsa Mahal and the Humayun Mahal with a grand *durbar* hall, had a tower added between them in 1855. The original building is now hidden from the road by the modern PWD building,

George Town

Sleeping		Eating	
1 Central Tower	2 Sornam	1 Ganga	2 Rama Krishna
	3 YMCA		3 Saravanas

Ezhilagam. Immediately behind is the Chepauk **cricket ground** where test matches are played. Lining the Kamaraj Salai (South Beach Road) is a succession of University buildings. Despite its unlikely appearance, **Vivekenanda House** was Madras' first 'ice house' for storing ice imported . On the other side of the beach is the sculpture 'the Triumph of Labour'.

Island and Anna Salai (Mount Road) South of Fort St George is the Island created between 1696 and 1705. First the grounds for a Governor's residence, it later became a military camp, and it has retained its military ownership ever since.

Near the Round Thana is the Banqueting Hall of the old Government House, now known as **Rajaji Hall** (1802). Built to mark the British victory over Tipu Sultan, it is in an attractive setting, designed in the Greek temple style.

Wallajah Mosque① *0600-1200, 1600-2200*, the 'Big Mosque', was built in 1795 by the Nawab of the Carnatic. There are two slender minarets with golden domes on either side. **Parthasarathi Temple**, near the tank, is the oldest temple structure in Chennai and was built by eighth-century Pallava kings, and later renovated in the 16th by Vijayanagara rulers. Dedicated to Krishna as the royal charioteer, it shows five of Vishnu's 10 incarnations and is the only one dedicated to Parthasarathi.

Egmore A bridge across the Cooum at Egmore was opened in 1700. In the late 18th century, the area around Pantheon Road, between the Poonamallee High Road and the Cooum, became the centre of Madras's social and cultural life. Egmore's development, which continued for a century, started with the building of Horden's 'garden house' in 1715. The original 'pantheon' (public assembly rooms) which stood here, on **Pantheon Road** was completely replaced by one of India's National Libraries. The origins of the **Connemara Library** (built 1896) go back to 1662, 'when a bale of calico from Madras was exchanged for books in London'. At the southwest corner of the site stands Irwin's Victoria Memorial Hall, now the ★ **Art Gallery**, which Tillotson describes as one of "the proudest expressions of the Indo-Saracenic movement". The museum here houses one of the world's finest collections of South Indian bronzes but very disappointingly displayed, lit and described but still remarkable. Egmore has a number of other reminders of the Indo-Saracenic period of the 19th and early 20th centuries, the station itself, built in the 1930s, being one of the last. To the northeast of Egmore station is the splendid ★ **St Andrew's Church**, standing in a spacious compound. Consecrated in 1821, the church still has an active congregation. Apart from the façade which resembles St Martin-in-the-Fields in London, it is essentially circular, 25 m in diameter, and has a magnificent shallow-domed ceiling. You may ask to be allowed to go up the tower. See map, page 792.

Thousand Lights and Nungam-bakkam In the 18th and 19th centuries, the part of town on either side of Anna Salai became the focus for high class residential European settlement. At the end of the 18th century, British administrators and merchants began to arrive in ever larger numbers, and many built splendid houses, including Arthur Wellesley, the future Duke of Wellington. Doveton House is one of Chennai's few remaining 'garden houses'.

★ **St George's Cathedral**, 1816, has a spire over 40 m high. Don't miss the colonial graveyard northeast of the cathedral where banyans grow out of mausoleums.

South Chennai

The present **Basilica of San Thome**, built in 1898, surrounded now by the tenement rehousing scheme of a fishermen's colony, is claimed as one of the very few churches to be built over an apostle's tomb. St Thomas Didymus (Doubting Thomas) is believed to have come to India in AD 52. According to one legend, having landed on the west coast, he travelled across the peninsula, arriving in **Mylapore** ('town of peacocks') where he lived and preached. To escape persecution he took shelter in Little Mount

Egmore

Sleeping
1 Abu Palace
2 Blue Diamond & Jewel Box Restaurant
3 Impala Continental
4 Imperial
5 Laharry Transit
6 Madras Ashoka
7 Masa & New Laxsmi Lodge
8 New Victoria & Raj Residency
9 Pandian & Regent
10 Salvation Army Guest House
11 Satkar
12 Tristar
13 World University Centre
14 YWCA International Guest House

Eating
1 Balaji Woodlands
2 Stardust
3 Udipi Home Mathsya
4 Vasantha Bhawan

N

0 metres 100
0 yards 100

(see below). An alternative story recalls how he was invited to visit the King Gondophernes in Taxila, where he converted the king and his court before moving to South India. Some claim that his body was ultimately buried in the Italian town of Ortona. See map, page 796.

★ **Kapaleeswarar Temple** ① *0600-1200, 1600-2200*, 4 km away, is a 16th-century Siva temple with a 40-m *gopuram*, built after the original was destroyed by the Portuguese in 1566. Sacred to Tamil Saivites, non-Hindus are only allowed in the outer courtyard where there are several bronze statues.

The **Luz Church**, 1547-82; the date of 1516 in the inscription is probably wrong, is probably the oldest church in Chennai. It was built by the Portuguese in honour of Our Lady of Light. The Tamil name for the church, *Kattu Kovil*, means 'jungle temple', and a story suggests that Portuguese sailors were rescued from a storm by following a light. They traced it on shore, where it disappeared, and on this spot they built the church.

The **Theosophical Society** ① *Sat morning only, closed Sun, 0830-1000, 1400-1600, entrance south of Elphinstone Bridge, bus 5 from Central Chennai, ask taxi for Ayappa Temple on San Thome High Rd,* is set in large and beautifully quiet gardens. There are several shrines of different faiths and a Serene Garden of Remembrance for Madam Blavatsky and Colonel Olcott who founded the society in New York in 1875 and moved its headquarters to Madras in 1882. The 400-year-old magnificent banyan tree is of particular interest; go past the Nursery (kitchen) garden and look on the left at the central circle. Buildings include the Adyar Library and a Hall of Meditation.The brackish river here attracts many waders and seabirds.

Little Mount is where **St Thomas** is believed to have spent some time. The older of the two churches (1551), with its small vaulted chapel, was built by the Portuguese. The modern circular church was built in 1971. St Thomas is believed to have been martyred and bled to death in AD 52 on the **Great Mount**, though others believe that he was accidentally killed by a hunter's arrow. On top of the 90 m high 'mount' is the **Church of Our Lady of Expectation**. The altar marks the spot where, according to legend, Thomas fell.

Some legends suggest that after St Thomas had been martyred on the Little Mount his body was brought back to the beach which had been his home and was buried there. The **Armenian Christians** who came from Persia are believed to have found St Thomas' grave and built a tomb and a church over it in AD 530. The village was called San Thome. Marco Polo in his travels in 1293 recorded the chapel on the seashore and a Nestorian monastery on a hill to the west where the apostle was put to death. In 1523, when the Portuguese started to rebuild the church they discovered the tomb containing the relics consisting of a few bones, a lance head and an earthen pot containing bloodstained earth. The church was replaced by the neo-Gothic structure which has two spires and was granted the status of a basilica in 1956. The relics are kept in the sacristy and can be seen on request. There are 13th-century wall plaques, a modern stained glass window, a 450-year-old Madonna brought from Portugal and a 16th-century stone sundial.

The **Snake Park** ① *0830-1730*, Rs 2, trains run from Egmore (No 23C, or Beach station or buses from town centre, there is also a deer park (see under parks and zoos below), at **Guindy** is in the grounds of the Guindy National Park in the Raj Bhavan Estate, and has quite a wide collection of snakes and other reptiles. There is an hourly display from 1000 near the entrance, with a nearly inaudible recording; still "good fun".

Central Chennai

N

0 metres 300
0 yards 300

Tamil Nadu Chennai South Chennai

Sleeping	6 Grand Oriental	13 Savera
1 Ambassador Pallava	7 Guru	14 Shrilekha Regency
2 Broadlands, Paradise	8 Harrisons	15 Silver Star
& Comfort	9 Himalaya	16 Taj Coromandel
3 Chola Sheraton	10 Krishna	17 WUS Hostel
4 Connemara	11 Nilgiris Nest	18 YMCA
5 Cristal	12 Ranjith	

Tamil Nadu Chennai – South Chennai

Related map
Egmore, page 792

● **Eating**
1 Aavin
2 Annalakshmi
3 Buhari's & Chungking
4 Cascade
5 Chinatown
6 Copper Chimney
  Hot Breads
7 Dasaprakash
8 Gem
9 Maharajah
10 Mathura
11 Saravanas
12 Woodlands
   Drive-in

⊜ **MRTS**
1 Fort
2 Park
3 Chintadripet
4 Chepauk
5 Triplicane
6 Lloyd's Rd

Museums

★ Government Museum and Art Gallery

The Pantheon had been a 'place of public entertainment and balls' in the late 18th century. The museum is a red-brick rotunda surrounded by an Italianate arcade. Look for the excellent collection of bronzes and the interesting exhibits of Stone and Iron Age hunting and cooking implements which have been excavated locally. There is also an excellent numismatic collection and sections on botany (500-year-old teak and engineering designs inspired by plants), zoology (18.5 m whale skeleton) and arms and armoury. Although in some need of maintenance, one of the largest and finest collection of bronzes but disappointingly lit and displayed in the Art Gallery. Among the most striking examples are an 11th-century Nataraja from Tiruvengadu, seated images of Siva and Parvati from Kilaiyur, and large standing figures of Rama, Lakshmana and Sita from Vadakkuppanaiyur. Buddhist bronzes from Nagapattinam have been assigned to Chola and later periods.

The National Art Gallery, in a superb building designed by Henry Irwin, has a good collection of old paintings and sculptures including Tanjore paintings on glass, Rajput and Mughal miniatures, 17th-century Deccan paintings, 11th- and 12th-century handicrafts, metalware and ivory carvings. Fine 13th- and 14th-century bronzes are housed in a separate building at the rear.

South Chennai

■ Sleeping	🚌 Buses	
1 Andhra Mahila Sabha	1 Adyar	6 Indira Nagar
2 Park Sheraton	2 Anakaputhur	7 Kotturpuram
3 Parthan	3 Dr Ambedkar Bridge	8 Mandaveli
4 Transit House	4 Foreshore Estate	9 Mylapore
5 TTDC Youth Hostel	5 Guindy Industrial Estate	

0 metres 500
0 yards 500

The Gallery of Modern Art ⓘ *Pantheon Rd, closed Fri, 0900-1700, Rs 3,* *foreigners US$5, camera Rs 20, video Rs 100,* has a permanent collection of contemporary art with temporary exhibitions on the first floor.

Fort Museum
ⓘ *Closed Fri, 1000-1700, US$2 (foreigners), photography prohibited.*

The 18th-century building houses (within Fort St George) exhibits from 300 years of British Indian history. It includes prints, documents, paintings, sculpture, arms (medieval weapons with instructions on their use) and uniforms. The Indo-French gallery has some Louis XIV furniture and clocks. Clive Corner, which includes letters and photographs, is particularly interesting. Labelling and display are very disappointing.

Excursions

Anna Zoological Park
ⓘ *Daily except Tue, 0800-1700, Vandalur, 32 km.*

The zoo attempts to provide a natural environment and breed some endangered species. There are 28 species of mammals including a nocturnal animal house, a lion and bison safari park, 61 species of birds and eight species of reptiles. For Pulicat Lake and the bird sanctuary (Andhra Pradesh).

Cholamandal Artists' village
On the coast road to Mahabalipuram, 19 km from Chennai, is this village. Started in 1969, the community of artists who live and work here exhibit and sell their paintings, graphics, sculptures, pottery and batik. Occasional **dance performances** ⓘ *0600-2000, T412892,* in small open-air theatre. Stop for a short visit.

Dakshinchitra
ⓘ *East Coast Rd, T954114-472603 (from Chennai), Rs 50, foreigners Rs 175, enquiries Muttukadu, 6 guest rooms (Rs 550, a/c Rs 800).*

Set up by the non-profit making Madras Craft Foundation. It presents the arts and crafts of the four southern states and performance of folk-arts (eg puppet shows) in a setting of traditional 19th- and early 20th-century architecture. This living museum has a crafts shop and restaurant. Recommended. *MGM* right on the beach nearby, offers clean, comfortable accommodation, with good food, and a pool.

10 Queen Mary Art College
11 Saidapet
12 Taramani
13 T Nagar

🚇 MRTS
1 Luz
2 Mandavalli (Planned)
3 Greenways Rd

Tamil Nadu Chennai Lakshinchitra

● Sleeping

Airport *p787, map p788*

These hotels offer free airport transfers. Other hotels are 12-15 km from the airport
L Trident, 1/24 GST Rd, T2344747, F2346699. 166 rooms, restaurants all recommended, elegant garden setting.
AL Le Royal Meridien, near the airport, www.royalmeridien-chennai.com. Plush new hotel with all facilities including good restaurants and bars.
B-C Mount Heera, 287 MKN, Alandur, T2335656, F2331236. New, modern facilities.

George Town *p789, map p790*

Good location for Central Station and State Bus Stands. Many cheap hotels are along VOC (Walltax) Rd.
E Great Hotel, 149 VOC Rd, T5331706. 44 rooms, 3 a/c, all with TV, spacious.
E Railway Retiring Rooms, Central Station, T5353337, some a/c rooms, cheaper dorm.
E Sornam International, 7 Stringer St, T5353060. 50 rooms with TV, balcony, hot water, rooftop vegetarian restaurant, pleasant.
E Youth Hostel (TTDC), EVR Park (near Central Railway Station), T5389132. Reasonably quiet.
F YMCA, NSC Bose Rd, T5383941, opposite City bus stand.

Central Chennai *p790, map p794*

Many hotels are strung out within 1 km either side of Anna Salai (Mount Rd). A-E hotels collect an extra 20-30% tax.
L Chola Sheraton, 10 Cathedral Rd, T8280101, F8278779. 80 rooms 'boutique hotel', good restaurants (including *Peshawari*), airport transfer.
L Connemara (Taj), Binny's Rd (off Anna Salai), T8520123, F8523361. 148 rooms, renovated retaining splendid art deco features, extremely comfortable, excellent restaurants, bar, good *Giggles* bookshop, heavily booked Dec-Mar.
L Taj Coromandel, 17 NH Rd, T8272827, F8257104. 201 rooms, excellent restaurants, good pool. Recommended. Western tour groups dominate.

AL Ambassador Pallava, 53 Montieth Rd, T8554476, F8554492. 120 rooms in modern hotel, good restaurants (especially Chinese), pool (open to non-residents), health club.
A-B Grand Orient, 693 Anna Salai, T8523411, F8523412. 66 rooms, half renovated but others very worn, clean (usual hazard of cockroaches), helpful staff, good location.
B Residency, 49 GN Chetty Rd (convenient for airport), T8253434, F8250085. 112 excellent rooms, 4th floor upwards have good views (9th floor, plush **A** suites), excellent *Ahaar* restaurant, exchange, good car hire with knowledgeable drivers, better rooms and service than some higher priced hotels, highly recommended, reserve ahead.
B Savera, 69 Dr Radhakrishnan Rd, T8114700, F8113475, hotsave@md2.vsnl.net.in. 125 comfortable rooms, good pool (non-residents, Rs 150), older hotel but smart and clean (standard rooms identical to superior!), disaster prone travel desk.
D Broadlands, 16 Vallabha Agraharam St, T8548131. 50 rooms, a few with shower, dorm (Rs 50), set around lovely shady courtyards, clean with good service, reasonably quiet and extremely popular though some find it over-rated and over-priced, helpful management but operate "no-Indians" policy.
D Comfort, 22 Vallabha Agraharam, T8587661, F849671. 40 rooms, some a/c, clean, friendly, 5 mins from Marina Beach.
D Guru, 69 Marshalls Rd, 500 m from Egmore rly, T/F8554067. Large hotel, fairly clean rooms, (Rs 450+), some a/c, good vegetarian restaurant, no credit cards.
D Harrisons, 154/5 Village Rd, T8275271. Some a/c rooms, restaurant, bar.
D Himalaya International, 54 Triplicane High Rd, T8547522. 45 rooms, nice baths, some a/c, modern, welcoming, clean, bright, no food but available from *Hotel Gandhi* next door.
D Paradise, 17/1 Vallabha Agraharam St, T8547542, F8530052. Spacious clean rooms with fans (some with 2!) with shower, good value, very friendly and helpful owners.
D Ranjith, 9 NH Rd, T8270521, F8277688. 51 rooms, some a/c, restaurant (good non-vegetarian continental), excellent and reasonable bar, cool, pleasant and relaxing.

E Sree Krishna, 159 Peters Rd, T8522897. 15 rooms, some a/c with bath.
E YMCA (1), 14 Westcott Rd, Royapettah, T8532158.

Egmore *p791, map p792*

Many hotels (including several good 'budget') are clustered around the station and the EVR Periyar (Poonamallee) High Rd, an auto-rickshaw ride away to the north of the railway line.

A-B New Victoria, 3 Kennet Lane (200 m from station), T8253638, F8250070, www.hotelnewvictoria,com. 51 a/c rooms, restaurant (excellent *Lido* breakfast), bar, spacious, quiet, ideal business hotel. Recommended.

B Tristar, 29 Whannels Rd, T8550006, F8550561. New hotel with good a/c rooms, all facilities.

C Abu Palace, 926 EVR Periyar High Rd, T6412222, F6428091. Plush, well insulated rooms, restaurant, bar, smart business style hotel, concrete fortress-like exterior, huge enclosed lobby.

C Breeze, 850 EVR Periyar High Rd, T6413334, F6413301. 75 rooms, modern, popular.

C-D Raj Residency, 2 Kennet Lane, T8212214, F8312364, www.rajresidency.net. 72 rooms with balcony, veg restaurant, bar, recently opened, spacious.

Some cheaper **D** hotels on the main road may have a problem with noise except at rear of the building. Many **D** hotels also have cheaper rooms.

D Blue Diamond, 934 EVR Periyar High Rd, T6412244, F6428903. 33 rooms, some a/c, quieter at rear, good a/c restaurant (crowded at peak times), exchange.

D Pandian, 9 Kennet Lane, T8252901, F8258459. 90 rooms, some a/c, a/c restaurant, bar, clean but spartan, helpful staff, expensive room service.

D YWCA International Guest House, 1086 EVR Periyar High Rd, T5324234. Restaurant (rate includes breakfast), 60 rooms, with bath, few a/c, for men and women, popular so book early, excellent value, also *camping ground*, reservations Secretary.

D-E Imperial, 6 Gandhi Irwin Rd, T825975, F8252030. 80 good size, average rooms, some a/c, best at rear, 4 restaurants, good food, reasonable price, bar, friendly.

Kennet Lane budget hotels are often full.

E Impala Continental, opposite station, T8250564. 50 very nice, clean rooms with TV, near *Vasanta Bhavan* restaurant, good service.

E Masa, 15/1 Kennet Lane, T8252966, F8251261. 88 clean a/c rooms, hot water.

E New Laxmi Lodge, 16 Kennet Lane, T8254576. 50 rooms around courtyard in old building, set back in garden.

E Regent, 8 Kennet Lane, T8253347. 45 renovated clean rooms set around courtyard, friendly. Recommended.

E Satkar, 65 Ormes Rd (Flowers and Millers Rd junction), T6426304. Spotless rooms with bath, some a/c, good vegetarian *Suryaprakash* restaurant, helpful staff, good value but noisy.

E Silver Star, 5 Purasawalkam High Rd, T6424414. 38 simple clean rooms set back from road, open air restaurant in courtyard, helpful and friendly staff.

E YMCA (1), 14 Westcott Rd, Royapettah, and **(2)** at 17 Ritherdon Rd, Vepery, T5322831, where there are **D** rooms with bath.

F Cristal, 34 CNK Rd, Triplicane, T8572721. Clean basic rooms with tiled bath, very helpful service, better and cheaper than some others in the area.

F Laharry Transit Hostel, for women under 30 only, very cheap and good value.

F Railway Retiring Rooms, T8252527.

F World University Service, East Spur Tank Rd, T8263991. Some rooms with bath, dorm, International Student cards needed, couples not allowed to share a room, cheap canteen for Indian snacks, good value, well located for Egmore and south central Chennai.

South Chennai *p792, map p796*

L-AL Holiday Inn Crowne Plaza, 1 GST Rd, T2348976, F4340429. 187 rooms.

L-AL Park Sheraton, 132 TTK Rd, 14994101, F4997201. 160 rooms, *Dakshin Chettinad* restaurant, good pool.

C Parthan, 75 GN Chetty Rd (near Panagal Park), T8241592, F8241591. 29 clean, large, comfortable and quiet rooms, restaurant (Chinese), exchange. Recommended.

D Transit House, 26 Venkataraman St, Nagar, T4341346. Some a/c rooms, dorm (Rs 60), snack bar, pleasant garden, no credit cards.

E Andhra Mahila Sabha, 12 D Deshmukh Rd, T4938311. Some **D** a/c rooms, veg restaurant.

🍴 Eating

Central Chennai *p790, map p794*

Most restaurants are in Central Chennai and are open 1200-1500, 1900-2400. Those serving non-vegetarian dishes are often more expensive.

Recommended in hotels
†††Chola Sheraton's, Chinese chef and food. Good rooftop restaurant, superb views.
†††Patio's: "Exquisite Continental", pricey.
Golden Dragon does excellent Chinese.
†††Connemara's: romantic outdoor **Raintree** with good food, atmosphere and ethnic entertainment but "cavalier service". Very good buffet dinner on Sat night.
†††Rooftop, excellent Kashmiri and Mughlai, good views.
†††Savera's (Ground Floor): excellent Indian, very friendly, helpful service, live Indian music in the evenings.
†††Coromandel's: Southern Spice offers very good South Indian, evening dance recitals, freezing a/c.
†††Trident's Executive lunch, Rs 450.

Outside
†††Copper Chimney opposite *Chola Sheraton*. International, a/c, good tandoori, very clean, pleasant seating.
†††Kabul's TTK Rd. Mughlai. Rustic décor, clean, licensed.

Chinese
††Cascade, 15 Khaderi Nawaz Khan Rd. Chinese, Thai, Japanese and Malay.
††Chungking, 67 Anna Salai (opposite PO) (1030-2200), Chinese, where lack of atmosphere (dim lighting) is compensated for by good food.
††China Town, 74 Cathedral Rd. Chinese, a/c.
††Dynasty at *Harrison's Hotel*. Recommended.
††Southern Chinese, 683 Anna Salai, Thousand Lights (next to Anand Theatre). Recommended.

Others
††Annalakshmi, Anna Salai (opposite LIC). Wholesome, health-restoring offerings, Southeast Asian specialities (profits to charity, run by volunteers). Recommended.

††Buhari's, 83 Anna Salai. Good Indian, terrace, dimly lit a/c restaurant, unusual décor, try crab curry, egg *rotis* and Muslim dishes; branch in Park Town near Central Station.
††Dasaprakash, Anna Salai, next to *Higginbotham's Bookshop* (1200-1445, 1900-2345), south Indian (buffets Rs 120), also excellent milk shakes.
††Gem, Triplicane High Rd (200 m south of *Broadlands*). Non-vegetarian. Tiny Muslim restaurant.
††Jewel Box in *Blue Diamond Hotel*. Cool a/c, good for breakfasts, snacks and main courses (also Chinese).
††Stardust, 5 Kennet Lane. Multi-cuisine and pizzas, dimly lit.
†Maharaja, Triplicane High Rd, 100 m from *Broadlands*. Indian vegetarian.
†Ritz, *Rivera Hotel*. Wide choice of tasty dishes in clean restaurant.
†Saravana branches (209 NSC Bose Rd), 2 floors. Extremely clean, excellent snacks, fruit juices (try pomegranate!), sweetmeats, all freshly made.
†Woodlands Drive-In Restaurant, 30 Cathedral Rd (0600-2100). Rows of tables, simple, busy, go for breakfast.
†Udipi, 8/9 Anna Salai (near *Higginbotham's*), good range of snacks.

Cafés and fast food
Pizza Corner, NH Rd (near *Taj Coromandel*). Good value eat-in, take-out or delivered, "just like home", Rs 79 'Lunch Munch' for pizza, potato wedges and bottomless coke!
Aavin, Anna Salai, near tourist office. Milk bar, ice creams (no seats).
Nala's, Cathedral Rd, and **Naga's**, Village Rd, do good Indian sweets and savoury snacks.

Edgmore *p791, map p792*

†Balaji Woodlands, *Vee Yes Hotel*, Egmore. Indian vegetarian.
†Udipi Home Mathsya, 1 Hall's Rd (corner of Police Commissioner's Rd), Egmore. A/c, excellent, wide range of food. Recommended.
†Vasanta Bhavan, 10 Gandhi Irwin Rd, opposite Egmore station, 1st Flr. Very clean, excellent food, friendly staff, downstairs bakery does delicious sweets.

◐ Bars and clubs

It is possible to obtain alcoholic drinks without any difficulty despite local restrictions on sale of alcohol. Regulations change periodically, however, and All India Liquor Permits are available from either an Indian mission or a Govt of India Tourist office abroad or in one of the regional capitals. Try *Hotel Connemara's* large, bright bar, offering huge tankards of beer, "exceptional 'side-snacks', huge TV; casual clothes accepted".

◐ Entertainment

Cinemas

Those which show foreign (usually English language) films are mostly in the centre of town on Anna Salai. They are a/c and quite comfortable and you may appreciate a break on a hot day!

Music and dance

Chennai Music Academy auditoria is the scene of numerous performances of Indian music, dance and theatre, not only during the prestigious 3 week Music Festival from mid-Dec but right through the year; **Sabhas** are membership societies that offer cultural programmes 4 times a month to its members, but occasionally tickets are available at the door. There are several other auditoria: **Raja Annamalai Hall, Mylapore Fine Arts Club, Narada, Brahma and Krishna Gana Sabhas** and the little **Sittraragam. Kishkinta**, Tambaram, 4 km, train and courtesy bus (but not worth it).

◐ Festivals and events

On **Jan 14 Pongal Makara Sankranti**, the harvest thanksgiving, is celebrated all over Tamil Nadu for 3 days (public holiday). After ritually discarding old clothes and clay pots, festivities begin with cooking the first harvest rice in a special way symbolizing good fortune, and offering it to the Sun god. The second day is devoted to honouring the valuable cattle; cows and bulls are offered special new-rice dishes prepared with jaggery or nuts and green lentils. You will see them decorated with garlands, bells and balloons (!), their long horns painted in bright colours, before being taken out in procession around villages. Often they will pull carts decorated with foliage and flowers and carrying children, accompanied by noisy bands of musicians. On the final day of feasting, it is the turn of the 'workers' to receive thanks (and bonuses) from their employers.

◐ Shopping

Parry's corner and Anna Salai are principal centres. Most shops open Mon-Sat 0900-2000, some close for lunch 1300-1500. Weekly holidays may differ for shops in the same locality. There are often discount sales during the festival seasons of *Pongal, Diwali* and Christmas. The weekly **Free Ads** (Rs 5, Thu) has listings for second hand cameras, binoculars etc which travellers might want to buy or sell.

Books

Most bookshops open 0900-1900. **Higginbotham**'s, 814 Anna Salai and F39

Anna Nagar East, near Chintamani Market.
Side Effects, G17 Eldorado, 112 NH Rd, closes 1430-1600.

Many publishing houses have bookselling departments:
Allied Publishers (off Anna Salai) and **Oxford Book House** in Cathedral Grounds (Anna Salai) have extensive collections.
Danai Bookshops, the *Hotels Adyar Gate*, *Sindoori* and *Taj Coromandel* have branches, open 0830-2400.
Giggles , *Hotel Connemara*, 0930-2100 daily, specializes in all things Indian, helpful, reliable postage service (Rs 100 fee). Highly recommended.

Cassettes/CDs

Music World, 1st Flr, Spencer Plaza, Anna Salai, best in town.

Crafts

Victoria Technical Institute, Anna Salai near *Connemara Hotel*. Government-backed. South Indian handicrafts (wood carving, inlaid work, sandalwood) at fixed prices.
Poompuhar, 818 Anna Salai, specializes in 1st class bronzes.

Other Govt Emporia are along Anna Salai.
Central Cottage Industries, opposite *Taj Coromandel*, is recommended.

Other recommended shops:
Cane & Bamboo, 26 C-in-C Rd.
Habitat, K Nawaz Khan Rd nearby, good for special, unusual gifts.
Jamal's, 44 Devraja Mudali St.
Kalakshetra at Thiruvanmiyur excels in *kalamkari* and traditional weaving, also good household linen.
Kalpa Druma, 61 Cathedral Rd (opposite

Chola Sheraton), has attractive selection of wooden toys and panels.
Khazana at *Taj Coromandel*, good for special, unusual gifts.
New Kashmir Arts, 111 Anna Salai, for good carpets.
Tiffany's, 2nd floor, Spencer Plaza (antiques, bric-à-brac).
Vatika, 5 Spur Tank Rd, good for special, unusual gifts.

Department stores

Most open 0900-2000.
Burma Bazar, Rajaji Salai, for imports, especially electronic goods, bargain hard.
Five Stars, 60 Pantheon Rd, Egmore.
Harringtons, 99 Harrington Rd, Chetput.
Spencers Plaza, Anna Salai near *Connemara*, offers excellent choice for shopping in comfort.
Supermarket, 112 Davidson St and TNHB Building, Annanagar (closed Fri).

Fabrics

Chennai was founded because of the excellent and cheaply priced local cotton.
Amrapali in Fountain Plaza, and Adyar.
Co-optex, stock handloom silks and cottons.
Khadi, specialize in handspun and handwoven cotton.
Shilpi; **Urvashi**, TTK Rd, are good for cottons.
Look out for excellent Kanchipuram **silk** and **saris**.
Recommended for quality and value:
Handloom House, 7 Rattan Bazar.
Nalli (opposite Panagal Park) with excellent selection, both in T Nagar.
Rupkala, 191 Anna Salai, good prices, helpful staff.

▲▲ Activities and tours

Clubs

Temporary membership is available at most clubs, sometimes for sports only.
Chennai Boat Club, Adyar. Bar.
Chennai Cricket Club, Chepauk. Tennis, swimming, cricket, billiards, bar.
Chennai Gymkhana Club, Anna Salai. Tennis, swimming, cricket, billiards, library, bar.

Chennai Riders Club, Race View, Race Course, Velachery Rd. Riding (including lessons) throughout the year except Jun. Facilities in clubs are for members only, but you may be allowed in on being recommended by a member. Some hotel facilities may be used on payment of a fee.
Cosmopolitan Club, Anna Salai. Tennis, billiards, golf, library, bar.

Golf

At Guindy Race Course.

Swimming

Hotel pools open to non-residents: *Ambassador*, *Savera*. *Chennai Cricket Club* has an excellent pool (less crowded before noon); you need an introduction. Others open to the public are at *Marina Beach* and the *YMCA* pool at Saidapet. Sea bathing is safe at Elliot's Beach, though not attractive.

Tennis

Clubs allowing members' guests and temporary members to use courts are **Chennai Club, Gymkhana Club, Cricket Club, Cosmopolitan Club, Presidency Club** and **Lady Willingdon Club**. YMCA at Saidapet also has courts.

Tours

The following are on deluxe coaches and accompanied by a guide:
Tamil Nadu Tourism (TTDC). Departure points and reservations: Sales Counters at 4 EVR Periyar High Rd (opposite Central Station), T5360294; Express Bus Stand near High Ct compound, T5341982 (0600-2100).

Welcome Tours (sales agents), 150 Anna Sali (Agarchand Mansions), T8520908.
City sightseeing half-day: daily 0800-1300, 1330-1830. Fort St George, Government Museum (closed on Fri), Valluvar Kottam, Snake Park, Kapaleeswarar Temple, Elliot's Beach, Marina Beach. Rs 105, a/c Rs 150.
Full-day: daily 0800-1900. Drive along Marina Beach, Kapaleeswarar Temple, Snake Park, Vallavur Kottam, Museum, Fort St George (US$2 entry), St Mary's Church, Birla Planetarium, Muttukadu Boat House and VGP Golden Beach. Rs 160 (a/c Rs 240). Visitors have found the tours disappointing. **Excursions**: Mahabalipuram and Kanchipuram, 0730-1900, Rs 200 (a/c Rs 350) and Tirupati, 0630-2200, Rs 375 (a/c Rs 600).

Tour operators

Cox & Kings, A15 Eldorado Building, NH Rd.
Mercury, 191 Anna Salai, T8522993, F8520988.
Sita, 26 C-in-C Rd, T8278861, F8273536.
STIC, 142 NH Rd, T8271195
Surya, 1st Flr, Spencers Plaza, Anna Salai, very efficient, friendly, personal service.
Thomas Cook, 45 Montieth Rd, opposite *Ambassador Pallava Hotel*.
Welcome, 150 Anna Salai, near India Tourist Office, T8520908, open 24 hrs.

⊖ Transport

Air

The **Aringar Anna International airport** (named after CN Annadurai) with 2 terminals and the **Kamaraj Domestic airport** are on one site at Trisoolam in Meenambakkam, 12 km from the centre. Enquiries, T140, arrivals and departures T142. **Pre-paid taxis** from both; to Chennai Central or Egmore, Rs 150-180 (yellow taxis are cheaper than private), 30 mins; Rs 450 to Mahabalipuram. Buses to centre Rs 75 (day), Rs 100 (night). Airport, T2346013.
Auto-rickshaws to Chennai Central, Rs 100.
Suburban Railway the cheapest way into town, from Trisoolam suburban line station to Egmore and Fort, but trains are often packed.
Free Fone in the main concourse, after collecting baggage in the international airport, you can use this phone to ring hotels. Railway Bookings 1000-1700. Watch out for International prices for food and drink.

Domestic

Indian Airlines, 19 Marshalls Rd, T8555200 (daily, 0800-2000). Reservations, all 24 hrs: T8555209. Mini Booking Offices: 57 Dr Radhakrishnan Rd, T8279799; Umpherson St (near Broadway); 9 South Bagh Rd, T Nagar, T4347555. Airport T2343131. Check-in T2348483. Bangalore, Bhubaneswar, Coimbatore, Delhi, Goa, Hyderabad; Kochi, Kolkata, Madurai, via Tiruchirappalli; Mumbai, Port Blair and Pune, Puttaparthy, Thiruvananthapuram, Visakhapatnam. **Jet Airways**: 43 Montieth Rd, Egmore, T8414141, airport T2561818. To Bangalore, Coimbatore, Delhi, Hyderabad, Kochi, Kolkata, Mumbai, Port Blair, Pune, Thiruvananthapuram.
Sahara, T8263661: Delhi.

International

Air India flies to New York, Kuwait, London, Paris, Bangkok, Kuala Lumpur and Singapore;

it is possible to air cargo a motorbike on Air India or MAS to Singapore for approximately US$400. **Air Mauritius** have recently introduced direct flights from Mauritius. **British Airways** flies to London, Singapore. **Sri Lankan Airways** to Malaysia. **Saudia**, to some Middle East capitals.

Auto-rickshaw

Three-wheeler scooter taxis take 2 adults and a child, extra passengers negotiable. Usual extra night charge of 25% between 2200-0500. Rs 7 for 1st km. Insist on using the meter. If they refuse or claim theirs doesn't work, walk away; there are plenty available. During the rush hour, however, prices get inflated as most drivers refuse to use the meter; you may be moved, on occasion, to put the meter down yourself! Some drivers take you 'for a ride' to a shop. **Cycle-rickshaws** are often no cheaper. Fix the fare first.

Bus

Local
The cheap and convenient bus service is not overcrowded and offers a realistic alternative to auto-rickshaws and taxis outside the rush hour (0800-1000, 1700-1900). Make sure you know route numbers as most bus signs are in Tamil (Timetables from major bookshops). Pallavan Transport Corp (PTC), Anna Salai, runs an excellent network of buses from 0500-2300 and a skeleton service through the night. 'M' service on mini-buses are good for the route between Central and Egmore stations and journeys to the suburban rly stations. The 'V' service operates fast buses with fewer stops and have a yellow board with the route number and LSS (Limited Stop Service). PTC has a ½ hourly 'luxury' mini-bus service between Egmore Station, **Indian Airlines**, Marshalls Rd office and the airports at Meenambakkam picking up passengers from certain hotels (inform time keeper at Egmore in advance, T5361284). The fare is about Rs 20.

Long distance
The state highways are reasonably well maintained but the condition of other roads varies. The new East Coast Road (ECR) for Express buses and cars only has helped to cut some journey times. Fast long-distance Korean air buses now run on some routes, giving a comfortable ride on air-cushioned suspension.

Tamil Nadu Govt Express Parry's, T5341835, offers good connections within the whole region and the service is efficient and inexpensive. Best to take a/c coaches or super deluxe a/c. Buses originate from Express Bus Stand, Esplanade, picking up from T Nagar, Egmore, Broadway and Basin Bridge. Bookings 0700-2100. Other state and private companies cover the region but you may wish to avoid their video coaches which make listening, if not viewing, compulsory as there are no headphones! Interstate Bus Depot, Broadway Bus Stand handles enquiries and reservations. Computer reservations are now made on long distance routes.

Pallavan Transport Corp (PTC) T5366063; Reservations: 0430-2100. Beware of children who 'help' you to find your bus in the expectation of a tip; they may not have a clue! Also reports of men in Company uniforms selling tickets which turn out to be invalid; best to buy on the bus. From Tamil Nadu State Bus Stand (Broadway). The listings given are for route number, distance and journey time. **Coimbatore** No *462*, 500 km; **Chidambaram** and **Nagapattinam** *326*; **Kanchipuram** *76B*; **Kanniyakumari** *282*, 700 km; **Kumbakonum** *305*, 289 km, 61/2 hrs; **Madurai** *137*, 447 km, 10 hrs; **Mahabalipuram** *109* (High Court bus stand), Rs 19, 11/2 hrs (*108B* goes via Meenambakkam airport, 21/2 hrs) can be very crowded, see page 823; **Nagercoil** *198*, 682 km, 14 hrs; **Ooty** *465*, 565 km, 13 hrs; **Pondicherry** *108*, 106 km, 3 hrs; **Thanjavur** *323*, 320 km, 8 hrs; Tiruchirappalli *123*, 320 km and Route *124*, 7 hrs; **Tiruvannamalai** 122, 5 hrs; **Yercaud** *434*, 360 km, 8 hrs; **Bangalore (via Vellore and Krishnagiri)** *831*, 360 km, 8 hrs; **Bangalore (via Kolar)** 350 km, 71/2 hrs; **Mysore via Bangalore** *863*, 497 km, 11 hrs; **Tirupati via Kalahasti** *802*, 150 km, 31/2 hrs. Also several **Andhra Pradesh STC** buses to Tirupati daily. APSTC runs daily buses to many other towns in the state. Bus Stand, Parry's Esplanade, Enquiries, T5340830.

Car

Car hire
A/c or ordinary cars with drivers are good value and convenient for sightseeing,

especially for short journeys out of the city when shared between 3 and 5 people. Large hotels can arrange, eg *Regency* (Rs 600 per 8 hrs; Rs 750 for Mahabalipuram). **Ganesh Travels**, 36 PCO Rd, T8250066; **Window to the World** (Trichy), T0431-436052, F430832, faithpandian@sify.com, for tours from Chennai (and other towns); **Hertz**, 426 Anna Salai, T4330684, F4330014; TTDC 4 EVR, Periyar Rd, T5360294.

Ferry

Visas are now also issued on arrival at Port Blair, see page 755. Regular passenger ships to the Andaman and Nicobar Islands take 3 days. The *Shipping Corporation of India*, Jawahar Building, Rajaji Salai, T5231401. Also, *Deputy Directorate of Shipping Services*, A & N, 6 Rajaji Salai, T5226873. **Tickets to the Andaman Islands** At 0900 pick a 'letter of intent' to visit the Andamans, and collect details of sailings from the Shipping Corporation of India office. Go to the Foreigners' Registration Office at Shastri Bhavan, 26 Haddows Rd, and complete an application form for a **permit** and submit it with 2 photos before 1230; pick up at 1700 on the same day (or a day later if the application is submitted after 1230). Next day, take photocopies of your passport identification/Indian Visa pages and also of the Andamans permit, to the SCI office. Pick up a **Ticket** "Order Form", fill it in and queue for a ticket, 1000-1300. Women have an advantage when queuing!

Motor bike hire or purchase

Southern Motors, 282 TTH Rd, T4990784, is a good modern garage with efficient service. The *YWCA* on EVR Periyar High Rd is a good hotel for bikers and has a big shaded garden to park bikes securely.

MRTS

The Mass Rapid Transit System (raised, above-ground railway) covers the Beach-Chepauk and Chepauk- Mylapore sections.

Taxi

Yellow-top taxis are increasingly hard to find. Ask a hotel bell-boy to call one and insist on

using the meter (ask to see a chart before paying). Some refuse to go a short distance, some a long distance after 2000, or demand a 20% surcharge between 2200-0500. Drivers may ask for 4 or 5 times the metered fare; expect Rs 60-100 for 5 to 7 km.

Train

Suburban railway
Inexpensive and handy, but very crowded at peak times. Stops between Beach Rly Station and **Tambaram** (every 5 mins in rush hour) include **Fort**, **Park**, **Egmore**, **Chetpet**, **Nungambakkam**, **Kodambakkam**, **Mambalam**, **Saidapet**, **Guindy**, **St Thomas Mt**. Also serves suburbs of **Perambur** and **Villivakkam**. Convenient stop at **Trisoolam** for the airports, 500 m walk from the terminals.

Long distance
Smoking is banned on trains, stations and railway offices. There is a penalty of Rs 100. Chennai has 2 main stations, **Chennai Central (MC)** for broad gauge trains to all parts of India and **Egmore (ME)** for metre gauge (and some sections converted to broad gauge). The 2 have a mini-bus link; taxis take 5 mins. 'Beach Station' is for suburban services. **Chennai Central** enquiry, T131, reservations, T132, arrivals and departures, T133, then dial train no. Advance Reservations Centre, Southern Rly, is in a separate building in front of suburban station, open 0800-1400, 1415-2000, Sun 0800-1400. You can also order bedding. Indrail Passes and booking facilities for foreigners and NRIs, on the 1st floor. **Egmore** enquiry, T135, arrivals and departures, T134. There are also Southern Railway Booking Offices in Mambalam, T4833755, Tambaram and Chennai Beach. Meenambakkam Airport has a Rail Booking Counter. You may reserve 30 days in advance. From **Chennai Central Bangalore** *Shatabdi Exp, 2007*, 0600, not Tue, 7 hrs; *Lalbagh Exp, 2607*, 1545, 5¾ hrs; *Brindavan Exp, 2639*, 0715, 6 hrs. **Coimbatore** *Kovai Exp, 2675*, 0615, 7¾ hrs; *West Coast Exp, 6627*, 1100, 8¾ hrs; *Cheran Exp, 2673*, 2145, 8 1/2 hrs. **Delhi (ND)** *Tamil Nadu Exp, 2621*, 2200, 33½ hrs; *G.T. Exp, 2615*, 1630, 37½ hrs. **Delhi (HN)** *Rajdhani Exp, 2431*, 1915, Tue, Thu, 29½ hrs. **Guntakal** (for Hospet). *Chennai Dadar Exp, 1064*, 0650, 8 hrs; *Chennai-Mumbai Mail, 6010*, 2220, 10 hrs.

Hyderabad *Charminar Exp, 2759*, 1810, 14½ hrs; *Chennai-Hyderabud Exp, 7053*, 1600, 15 hrs. **Kochi (Cochin)** *Chennai-Aleppey Exp, 6041*, 1945, 13¾ hrs; *Guwahati Cochin Exp, 5624*, 1210, Fri, 14¾ hrs. **Kolkata (H)** *Coromandel Exp, 2842*, 0905, 29 hrs; *Howrah Mail, 6004*, 2230, 32½ hrs. **Mettupalayam** *Nilgiri Exp, 6605*, 2015, 10 hrs. **Mumbai (CST)** *Chennai-Mumbai Mail, 6010*, 2155, 30 hrs; *Chennai-Mumbai Exp, 6012*, 1145, 27 hrs. **Mysore** *Shatabdi Exp, 2007*, 0600, daily not Tue, 7 hrs; *Chennai Mysore Exp, 6222*, 2245, 9¼ hrs. **Thiruvananthapuram** *Guwahati*

Trivandrum Exp, 5628, 1210, Wed, 19¼ hrs; *Howrah Trivandrum Exp, 6324*, 0440, Tue, Sun, 18½ hrs. From **Egmore Kanniyakumari** *Chennai-Kanniyakumari Exp, 6121*, 1900, 15 hrs. **Madurai** *Chennai-Kanniyakumari Exp, 6121*, 1815, 10 hrs; *Vaigai Exp, 2635*, 1225, 8 hrs; *Pandyan Exp, 6717*, 2100, 9½ hrs via Kodai Rd (this connects with the bus service at **Kodaikkanal** reaching at midday). **Tiruchirappalli** *Vaigai Exp, 2635*, 1225, 5½ hrs; *Pallavan Exp, 2606*, 1530, 5½ hrs.

🕔 Directory

Airline offices

For domestic airlines see Transport. Most are open 0930-1730 Mon-Fri, 0930-1300 Sat; **Air India**, 19 Marshalls Rd, T8554477 (0930-1730, avoid 1300-1400), airport T2344927. **Air France**, 43 Montieth Rd, T8554916. **Sri Lankan**, 73 Cathedral Rd, T8261535. **British Airways**, Khalili Centre, Montieth Rd, T8554680, Airport T2348282. **Cathay Pacific**, Spencers Plaza, 769 Anna Salai, T8522418. **Gulf Air**, 52 Montieth Rd, T8553091. **KLM**, *Hotel Connemara*, T8524437. **Kuwait Airways**, 43 Montieth Rd, T8553797. **Lufthansa**, 167 Anna Salai, T8525095. **Malaysian Airlines**, 498 Anna Salai, T4349651. **Qantas**, 112 NH Rd, T8278680. T8522871. **Sabena**, 47 White's Rd, T8514337. **Saudia**, 560 Anna Salai, T4349666. **Singapore Airlines**, 108 Dr Radhakrishna Rd, T8522871. **Saudia**, 560 Anna Salai, T4349666. **Swissair**, 47 Whites Rd, T8526560. **General Sales Agents (GSA)** Air Kenya, Garuda Airways, Japan Airlines, Global Travels, 703 Anna Salai, T8523957. **Alitalia**, 548 Anna Salai, T4349822. **American, Air Canada, Bangladesh Biman, Royal Jordanian** and **TWA**, Thapar House, 43 Montieth Rd, T8569232. **Delta**, *Aviation Travels*, 47 Whites Rd, T8259655. **Iberian** and **Royal Nepal Airlines**, *STIC Travels*, 142 NH Rd, T8271195. **Egypt Air** and **Yemen Air**, *BAP Travels*, 135 Anna Salai, T849913. **Maldive Airways**, *Crossworld Tours*, 7 Rosy Tower, NH Rd. **Thai International**, Inter Globe, 144 Kodambakkam High Rd, T8262294.

Banks

Most open either 0830-1230 or 1000-1400 on weekdays; am only on Sat. Closed Sun, national holidays and 30 Jun and 31 Dec (foreign exchange dealing may close an hr early). A few big hotels have 24-hr banks. **State Bank of India, Thomas Cook, TT Travels** at International Airport, 24 hrs. **American Express**, G17, Spencer Plaza, Anna Salai, T8523628, F8523615, 0930-1930, offers all foreign exchange and TC services. **Thomas Cook** branches at: 45 Montieth Rd, Egmore. 20 Rajaji Salai. 112 NH Rd, T8274941, Mon-Fri 0930-1830 (closed 1300-1400), Sat 0930-1200. Both recommended. **Madura Travels**, Kennet Lane (near corner of Gandhi Irwin Rd), Egmore, change TCs, good rate. Many banks have branches on Anna Salai, Cathedral, Dr Radhakrishnan and EVR Periyar High Rds. **State Bank of India**, 103 Anna Salai (Foreign Ex in Tower Block at rear, good rate but only encash some TCs). Some banks have extended hrs: Indian Overseas, 473 EVR Periyar High Rd (0830-1530, Sat 0830-1230); Indian, EVR Periyar High Rd (near *Hotel Picnic*) (0830-1230, 1600-1800, Sat 0830-1030, 1600-1800). **Visa ATMs** at: CitiBank, Anna Salai (24 hrs). Alsa Promenade, Door 149, AA Block, 3rd Ave, Anna Nagar. Pushpa Shoppe, Adyar. HSBC, 30 Rajaji Salai. Pushpa Shoppe No 1, Adyar. Standard Chartered Bank, 37 Royapettah High Rd. **Credit cards** in Spencer Plaza, Anna Salai: American Express, G17, and others. Diners Club, Greenmore, 16 Haddows Rd.

Embassies and consulates

Most open 0830-1330, Mon-Fri. **Austria** 115 NH Rd, T8276036. **Belgium** 97 Anna Salai, T2352336. **Denmark** 8 Cathedral Rd, T8273399. **Finland** 742 Anna Salai, T8524141. **France** 16

Haddows Rd, T8266561. **Germany** 22 C-in-C Rd, T8271747. **Greece** 72 Harrington Rd, T8269194. **Italy** 19 Rajaji Salai, T5342141. **Japan** 60 Spur Tank Rd, T8265594. **Malaysia** 6 Sri Ram Nagar, T4343048. **Mauritius** 145 Starling Rd, T8271841. **Netherlands** 64 Armenian St, T5384894. **Norway** 44-45 Rajaji Salai, T517950. **Singapore** 109 Habibulla Rd, T8276393. **Spain** 8 Nimmo Rd, San Thome. **Sri Lanka** 9D Nawab Habibulla Ave, off Anderson Rd, T8276751. **Sweden** 6 Cathedral Rd, T8275792. **UK** Deputy High Commission, 24 Anderson Rd, Nungambakkam, T8275130. **USA** 220 Anna Salai, T8273040.

Hospitals

Apollo Hospital, 21 Greams Rd, T8277447. CSI Rainey, GA Rd, T5951204. Deviki Hospital, 148 Luz Church Rd, Mylapore, T4992607. National Hospital, 2nd Line Beach Rd, T511405. **Ambulance services** Ambulance Government, T102; St John's Ambulance, T8264630, 24-hr. Dental hospital Govt, T5340411; All-in-One, 34 Nowroji Rd, T6411911, 0400-2000, 0900-1200 Sun.

Internet

Cybervision, off Anna Salai, 64k ISDN; Datamen's, 273 Pycrofts Rd, good access, Rs 90 per hr; serves soft drinks. SRIS, 1st floor, F22-A, Spencer Plaza, 769 Anna Salai.

Language schools

Bharatiya Vidya Bhavan, 38/39 R E Mada St, T4943450, for Sanskrit. Hindi Prachar Sabha, T Nagar, T441824. International Inst of Tamil Studies, Central Polytechnic, T412992. Some of the foreign cultural centres have libraries and arrange film shows. Alliance Française, 3/4A College Rd, Nungambakkam, T8272650. American Center, 561 Anna Salai, library 0930-1800, closed Sun, T8277825. British Library, 737 Anna Salai, 1000-1900, closed Mon, T852002. Soviet, 27 Kasturi Rangan Rd, T4990050. Max Müeller Bhawan, 0900-1900, closed Sun, 13 Khadar Nawaz Rd, T8261314.

Medical services

SS Day & Night Chemists, 106D, 1st Main Rd, Anna Nagar.

Post office

Poste restante at the GPO, Rajaji Salai, George Town; other major post offices which accept Speed Post Mail are in Anna Salai, Pondy Bazar, T Nagar, Meenambakkam, NH Rd, Flower Bazar and Adyar. Opening times vary, 1st 3 open 0800-2030; CTO, Rajaji Salai (near Parry's Corner). Computerized ISTD booths all over town, some open 24 hrs. **Courier services** DHL, 44/45 Pantheon Rd, Egmore, T8553755, 0930-1800; Skypak, 19 Rutland Gate, T8274237; 173 Kodambakkam High Rd, T8274271, 24 hrs.

Telephone

Directory enquiry (national) T183, only from Chennai city itself.

Tourist offices

Govt of India (GITO), 154 Anna Salai, T8524785, F8522193, Mon-Fri 0915-1745, Sat until 1300. Domestic Airport Counter, 24 hrs; International Airport Counter, at flight times. India Tourism Development Corporation (ITDC), 29 Victoria Crescent, C-in-C Rd, T8278884, 0600-2000, Sun 0600-1400. Tamil Nadu (TTDC), 4 EVR Rd (opposite Central Station), T5382916, F5361385, www.tamilnadutourism.com. Includes booking of TTDC hotels and tours; Express Bus Stand, T5341982. TTDC, 25 Radhakrishnan Rd, T8547335; Information centres at Central Railway, Gate 2 (Sales Counter on Sun), Egmore stations, and domestic airport terminal, T2340569, 0700-2300. Govt of Tamil Nadu, Pangal Building, Saidapet. State tourist offices usually open from 1030-1700 on weekdays (closed Sun and 2nd Sat). Andaman and Nicobar Islands, Andaman House, North Main Rd Ext, Anna Nagar West Ext, Padi Village, T6259295, F63580292.

Useful addresses

Foreigners Registration Office, ground floor, Shastri Bhavan Annexe, 26 Haddows Rd. T8278210, for visa extensions, Mon-Fri 0930-1800.

The Coromandel Coast

Early morning is an excellent time to travel in most places in India, but especially in the South. The air is fresh and cool, the light limpid. Southwards from Chennai on the road to Mahabalipuram, Pondicherry and Cuddalore there are alternating groves of casuarina trees, many recently planted, with coconut and palmyra palms. In January and February, at harvest time, there is also a delightful scent of fresh straw in the air. Paddy, groundnut and sugarcane grow in the fields and grain is often spread out across the road to dry or be threshed by passing traffic. ▶▶ *For Sleeping, Eating and other listings, see pages 818-824 .*

Mahabalipuram (Mamallapuram)

➔ *Phone code: 04114. Colour map 7, grid B5. Population: 12,050.*
Now one of South India's most visited historic sights, Mahabalipuram occupies a stunning position on a rocky outcrop between the beach and a lagoon. The expanding village alongside, with its inviting sandy beach, is a popular haunt of foreign backpackers and there are now plenty of budget hotels and breezy beachside cafés. Mahabalipuram's real claim to fame rests on its ancient history and magnificent rock temples and carvings.

Ins and outs

Getting there Several daily buses from Chennai take about 1½ hours to the bus stand in the centre of the small village. They may stop at hotels north of Mahabalipuram, on the way, otherwise autos from anywhere in the village will ferry you there for Rs 50. Arriving by car, you may have to pay a Rs 20 toll at the booth near the post office on Covelong Rd.

Getting around Hiring a bike can be fun to get further afield. Beware of con men with "I'm a Sri Lankan refugee" story. See Transport, page 823, for further details.

Background

The coastal temple town Mahabalipuram is officially known as Mamallapuram after 'Mamalla' (great wrestler), the name given to Narasimhavarman I Pallavamalla, (ruled 630-68). The Pallava ruler made the port famous in the seventh century and was largely responsible for the temples. There are 14 cave temples and nine monolithic *rathas* (shrines in the shape of chariots), three stone temples and four relief sculptured rock panels.

A characteristic feature of the temples here was the system of water channels and tanks, drawn from the **Palar River**, which made it particularly suitable as a site of religious worship. The *naga* or serpent cult associated with water worship can be seen given prominence at Bhagiratha's Penance.

Carving in stone is still a living art; stone masons can be heard chipping away from dawn to dusk along the dusty roadsides, while students at the **Government School of Sculpture** ① *closed Tue, 0900-1300, 1400-1830.* near the Bus Stand, continue to practise the skills which flourished centuries ago.

Sights

The best time to walk round the site is early morning, especially for the best light on Bhagiratha's Penance. Allow two hours for a circuit. The paths on the top of the rock are not always clear, but it is difficult to get really lost.

⁞ Coromandel

As Hobson-Jobson pointed out, the name Coromandel has been confusingly misinterpreted by many writers, a confusion deepened by early European visitors using the terms Malabar and Coromandel interchangeably! Links have been suggested with apparent authority to such a wide range of meanings as 'black sand', 'the hot country', the 'land of the Kurus', 'the country of cholam (a millet)' or even 'rice fort'. In fact it means 'the realm of the Cholas'. The Coromandel Coast, the plain between Chennai and the Kaveri delta, has been a part of the great heartland of South Indian culture, as several of its most important sites still testify.

★ **Bhagiratha's Penance** Descent of the Ganga, sometimes referred to as **Arjuna's Penance**, is a bas relief sculpted on the face of two enormous adjacent rocks, 29-m long and 7-m high. It shows realistic life-size figures of animals, gods and saints watching the descent of the river from the Himalaya. Bhagiratha, Rama's ancestor, is seen praying for Ganga. A contrived waterfall fed from a collecting chamber above, issues from the natural crack between the two rocks. Some see the figure of an ascetic (on the upper register of the left hand side rock, near the cleft) as representing Arjuna's penance when praying for powers from Siva, though some authorities dispute this. The two large elephants are remarkable and there are also scenes from the fables in the *Panchatantra* and a small shrine to Vishnu. The characteristic system of water channels and tanks, drawn from the Palar River made this a particularly suitable site of religious worship associated with the *naga* (serpent) *cult*. Look for the group of three monkeys to the right of the panel.

A path north from 'Bhagiratha's Penance' goes to the double-storeyed rectangular **Ganesh** *ratha* with a highly decorative roof, and two pillars with lions at their base – an architectural feature which was to become significant. The Ganesh image inside is mid-20th century. To the west are the **Valayankuttai** and twin **Pidari** *rathas*. The path continues past the extraordinary, curiously pulsed, isolated rock, '**Krishna's Butterball**', through some huge boulders at the north end of the hillock to the **Trimurti Temple** caves which have three shrines to Brahma, Vishnu and Siva, the last with a lingam.

Mandapas ⓘ *Foreigners US$5.* The 10 *mandapas* are fairly shallow pillared halls or porticos excavated out of the rocky hillside. They provide space for superbly executed sculptures to illustrate tales from mythology, and illustrate the development of the Dravidian (South Indian) temple style.

On the south is a **Durga niche** (AD 630-60), while next door is the '**Gopi's Churn**', a Pallava cistern. Walk back along the ridge, passing 'Krishna's Butterball' on your left and some boulders with evidence of incomplete work. The **Varaha Mandapa** (AD 640-74) on the left of the ridge, shows two incarnations of Vishnu – Varaha (boar) and Vamana (dwarf) among scenes with kings and queens. The base forms a narrow receptacle for water for pilgrims to use before entering the temple. From here you can walk to the top of 'Bhagiratha's Penance'.

★ **Krishna Mandapa**, mid-seventh century, has a bas relief scene of Krishna lifting Mount Govardhana to protect a crowd of his kinsmen from the anger of the Rain God, Indra. The realistic portrayal of a cow licking its calf while being milked, is quite remarkable.

Kotikal Mandapa, early seventh century, may be the earliest of the *mandapas*, roughly carved with a small shrine with no image inside. **Ramanuja Mandapa** was originally a triple-cell Siva temple, converted later into a Vaishnava temple.

South of the new lighthouse the simple **Dharmaraja cave** (early seventh century) contains three empty shrines. To its west is **Isvara Temple** (or Old Lighthouse), a truncated Siva temple still standing like a beacon on the highest summit, with a view for miles around. (To the south, across the 'Five Rathas', is the nuclear power station of Kalpakkam; to the west is the flat lagoon and the original port of Mahabalipuram.)

★ **Mahishasuramardini Mandapa**, mid-seventh century, is immediately below. It has fine bas relief and finely carved columns with lion bases. The main sculpture shows the goddess Durga slaying the buffalo demon Mahishasura while another relief shows Vishnu lying under Adishesha, the seven-hooded serpent.

★ **Rathas** These mid-seventh-century monolithic temples, 1½ km south of the Old Lighthouse were influenced by Buddhist architecture as they resemble the *vihara* (monastery) and *chaitya* temple hall. They imitate in granite, temple structures that were originally built of wood and are among the oldest examples of their type.

The five *rathas* to the south of the hill are named after the Pancha Pandava (five Pandava brothers) in the epic *Mahabharata* and their wife Draupadi. The largest is the domed **Dharmaraja** with numerous images including an interesting Ardhanarishvara

Mahabalipuram

Tamil Nadu The Coromandel Coast Mahabalipuram

■ Sleeping	8 Siva Guest House &	● Eating
1 Crystal Shore Palace	Vinodhara	1 Curiosity
2 Guru	9 Surya & Village Restaurant	2 Dreamland
3 Lakshmi Lodge	10 Temple Bay Ashok	3 Gazebo
& Hemnath Travels	11 Tina Blue View Lodge	4 Honey Falls
4 La Vie en Rose	& Sea Queen	5 Luna Magica
5 New Papillon	12 Veeras	6 Moonrakers
6 Ramkrishna Lodge &	13 Youth Hostel &	7 Sea Rock
German Bakery	Camping (TTDC)	8 Sunrise
7 Sea Breeze & Nautilus	14 Vinayak	

N

0 metres 200
0 yards 200

Tamil Nadu's Tank Country

The Coromandel plains have some spectacular tanks. Some of these shallow reservoirs date back to the Pallava period (sixth to eighth centuries), and many were added by the Chola kings. Built in the eighth century they are an invaluable source of irrigation water. Just south of Chengalpattu, bounded by the National Highway to its west, the ancient Chembarambakkam Tank is dammed by a 9 km embankment. It is one of South India's most beautiful tanks and the largest in the region but over half the stored water is lost through evaporation.

(Siva-Parvati) at the rear. The barrel-vaulted Bhima nearby has a roof suggestive of a thatched hut, while next to it the dome-shaped ratha **Arjuna** imitates the Dharmaraja. **Draupadi ratha**, is the smallest and simplest and is again in the form of a thatched hut. The base, now covered by sand, conceals a lion in front which appears to carry it, which suggests that it may be a replica of a portable shrine. Immediately east is a large unfinished Nandi. To its west is the apsidal **Nakula-Sahadeva ratha** with a free-standing elephant nearby. The Bhima and Nakula-Sahadeva follow the oblong plan of the Buddhist *chaitya* hall and are built to two or more storeys, a precursor to the *gopuram*, the elaborate entrance gateway of the Dravidian temple.

★ **Shore Temple** ⓘ *Foreigners US$5, includes Five Rathas.* The temple by the sea is surrounded by gardens designed according to descriptions of the original layout from ancient texts. The World Heritage Site is immensely popular with day-trippers and school groups. Built at the end of the seventh century by King Rajasimha, it is unusual for its shrines to both Siva and Vishnu. The sandstone temple has a granite base and a basalt *kalasa* at the very top. Its position on the water's edge, with an east-facing altar designed to catch the rising sun and a stone pillar to hold the beacon for sailors at night, meant that there was no space for a forecourt or entrance gateway. Two additional shrines were built to the west asymmetrically. The second smaller spire adds to the temple's unusual structure. The outer parapet wall has lines of *Nandi* (Siva's sacred bull) and lion pilasters.

Saluvan kuppam Five kilometres north of Mahabalipuram, on the coast, is the excavated temple at Saluvankuppam which has the **Tiger Cave** *mandapa* with carvings of tigers' heads. The cave is not signposted from the beach. Secluded and very peaceful – a lovely place for a picnic. On the way you will see the **Mukunda Nayar Temple**.

Beaches Check about safety of **swimming** in the sea. To avoid hassle and have an undisturbed day by the beach, pay Rs 100 to use the small pool at *Crystal Shore Palace, Temple Bay Ashok* or *Sea Breeze,* or the bigger pool, 1 km north at *Tamil Nadu Beach Resort*. The **beach** north of the temples towards the *Ashok* and the rocky area behind the Descent of the Ganga are open latrines for the village and badly fouled.

Excursions
Tirukkalukundram ⓘ *Buses from Mahabalipuram take 30 mins or you can hire a bike.* A small Siva temple dedicated to Vedagirishvara is on top of the 3,000 million year old rock 14 km west of Mahabalipuram. About 400 steps take you to the top of the 160 m hill which has good views and also money conscious priests and 'guides'. Be prepared for a hot barefoot climb, 'donations' at several shrines and Rs 10 for shoe custodian! At midday it is said that you will see two Neophran vultures (*Pharaoh's chickens*) fly down to be fed by the priests – but you may be disappointed. The

Bhaktavatsleesvara in town with its *gopuram* (gateway) stands out like a beacon. The tank is considered holy and believed to produce a conch every 12 years. Small shops in the village sell cold drinks.

Sriperumbudur The birthplace of the 11th-century Hindu philosopher **Ramanuja**, is the town where Rajiv Gandhi was assassinated on 21 May 1991. There is a memorial at the site with sculpted columns in a well-kept garden.

★ Kanchipuram

→ *Phone code: 04112. Colour map 7, grid A5. Population: 153,000*

One of Hinduism's seven most sacred cities (see page 1326), 'the golden city of a thousand temples', dates from the early Cholas in the second century. The main temples' complexes are very spacious and only a few of the 70 or so scattered temples can be seen in a day's visit. The town itself relatively quiet except for crowds of pilgrims. ➤➤ *For Sleeping, Eating and other listings, see pages 818-824 .*

History

Buddhism is believed to have reached the Kanchipuram area in the third century BC. Successive dynasties made it their capital and built over 100 temples, the first as early as the fourth century. In addition to being a pilgrimage centre, it was a centre of learning, culture and philosophy. Sankaracharya and the Buddhist monk Bodhidharma lived and worked here.

Sights

★ Ekambaresvara Temple ① *Small entry fee, cameras Rs 3, Hindus only are allowed into the inner sanctuary.* The temple has five enclosures and a 'Thousand-pillared Hall' (actually 540). Dedicated to **Siva** in his ascetic form it was begun by the Pallavas and developed by the Cholas. At the beginning of the 16th century the Vijayanagara king Krishna Deva Raya built the high stone wall which surrounds the temple and the 59-m tall *rajagopuram* (main tower) on which are sculpted several figures of him and his consort.

‼ Most temples open early and are closed 1200-1600. A rickshaw is recommended.

The main sanctuary has a *lingam* made of earth (Siva as one of the elements) and the story of its origin is told on a carved panel. The teasing Parvati is believed to have unthinkingly covered her husband Siva's eyes for a moment with her hands which resulted in the earth being enveloped in darkness for years. The enraged Siva ordered Parvati to do severe penance during which time she worshipped her husband in the form of an earth *lingam* which she created. When Siva sent a flood to test her, she clung to the lingam with her hands until the waters subsided. Some believe they can see her fingerprints on the *lingam* here. On 18 April each year the sun's rays enters the sanctum though a small square hole. The old mango tree in one of the enclosures is claimed to be 1,000 years old and still bears fruit.

The *Panguni Uthiram Festival* in March-April, see page 785, is the largest and possibly the most atmospheric of Kanchipuram's temples.

★ Kailasanatha Early seventh century, it is considered the most beautiful of the town's temples. It was built of sandstone by the Pallava king Narasimha Varman II with the front completed by his son Mahendra III. The outer wall has a dividing wall with a shrine and doorways, separating a large courtyard. The unusual enclosure wall has 58 small raised shrines with a *Nandi* in most pavilions; some frescoes have survived. The seven shrines in the temple complex have images of different forms of Siva. The intricately carved panels on the walls depict legends about Siva with accompanying text in ancient Grantha script. Extensively restored. The festival *Mahashivaratri* is held in February.

Vaikuntha Perumal Eighth century and dedicated to Vishnu, this temple was built by the Pallava king Nandivarman just after the Kailasanatha and illustrates the progress of Dravidian temple architecture. The sanctuary is separated from the *mandapa* by an open space. The cloisters are built out of lines of lion pillars. Panels of bas relief accompanied by lines in old Tamil, trace the history of the wars between the Pallavas and Chalukyas. There is an unusual *vimana* (tower) with shrines in three tiers with figures of Vishnu in each.

★ **Varadaraja (Devarajasvami)** ① *Re 1, camera Rs 5, Hindus only are allowed into the sanctum. Marriage Hall.* Built by the Vijayanagara kings (circa 16th century), 3 km southeast of town, it has superb sculpture in its marriage hall (96 pillars). Figures on horseback wear half north Indian/half south Indian costumes. Note the rings at each corner and the massive flexible chain supposedly carved out of one piece of granite although they are no longer in one piece. The main shrine is on an elephant shaped rock, Hastagiri. The *Float Festival* is in February and November, *Brahmotsavam* in May, and *Garuda Sevai* in June.

Kanchipuram

■ Sleeping	3 Sri Krishna Lodge	● Eating
1 Baboo Soorya	4 Sri Rama Lodge	1 Saravana
2 Sree Kusal Lodge	5 Tamil Nadu	

0 metres 200
0 yards 200

Weavers From the 16th-century silk weavers have used high quality mulberry silk from neighbouring Karnataka, and pure gold thread, to weave in beautiful colours and patterns on their handlooms. Nowadays, about 20,000 work with silk and another 10,000 with cotton. To watch them at work in their spotless huts, contact **Weavers' Service Centre** ① *20 Station Rd, T222530, Sun-Thu, 1000-1700, no sale.*

Excursions

Vedanthangal Bird Sanctuary On the Trichy Road, 87 km from Chennai and 60 km from Mahabalipuram, Vedanthangal Sanctuary and Karikili Tank are thought to have existed as a protected area for about 250 years. The marshy site attracts numerous water fowl and provides their main nesting site. Visitors and residents include crested cormorants, night herons, grey pelicans, sand pipers, grey wagtails, open-billed storks, white ibis, egrets, little grebe and purple moorhens. Best season is from November to February. Best time is dawn and 1500-1800. Avoid weekends and holidays.

★ Pondicherry (Puducherry)

→ *Phone code: 0413. Colour map 7, grid B5. Population: 220,700. www.pondicherry.net.*
Pondicherry still enjoys a hint of its French colonial atmosphere in the grid pattern streets, distinctive police uniforms and the occasional colonial building. Yet despite its invigorating seafront and relaxing atmosphere the town is visited above all for the Sri Aurobindo Ashram which draws visitors from all over the world.

The Ashram pervades much of the town's life as its numerous buildings, workshops and shops are very much in evidence, as are portraits of Sri Aurobindo and The Mother. The Ashram buildings can be recognized by the pale grey was highlighted with white. The focus of reverence in the Main Building is the stone Samadhi (memorial) of the founders which is under a tree within the complex. It is a very peaceful spot. ⏩ *For Sleeping, Eating and other listings, see pages 818-824.*

Ins and outs

Getting there Buses now take under 4 hrs from Chennai on the East Coast Rd. Both the State and private bus stands are just west of the town, within walking distance or a short auto-ride from the centre but arrival can be chaotic with hassle from rickshaw drivers. The station on a branch line from Villupuram, which has trains to major destinations, is a few mins' walk south of the centre.

Getting around Pondicherry is pleasant to explore on foot, but hiring a bike or moped gives you the freedom to venture further along the coast independently. See Transport, page 823, for further details.

Climate Temperature: maximum 36°C in Jun, minimum 21°C in Jan. Rainfall: Oct-Dec, average 290 mm; Jan-Aug 4 mm. Best time to visit: Dec-Mar.

Background

The site of the town has been identified as ancient Vedapuri where **Agastya Muni** (a sage) had his hermitage in 1500 BC. In the first century AD Romans traded from nearby Arikamedu. Colonized by the French (re-named Puducherry), it was voluntarily handed over to the Indian Government in 1954 and became the Union Territory of Pondicherry.

Today, many visitors are attracted by the **Ashram** founded by Sri Aurobindo and his chief disciple Mirra Alfassa. Sri Aurobindo Ghosh was an early 20th-century Bengali nationalist and philosopher who struggled for freedom from British colonial power, see page 1337. He started the Ashram here to put into practice his ideals of a peaceful community. In this aim he found a lifelong French companion in **Mirra Alfassa**, who became universally known as **the Mother**. After his death in 1950, she continued as the spiritual successor and charismatic figure of Pondicherry until her own death in 1973 at the age of 93. Auroville, 'City of Dawn', was set up in 1968 as a tribute to Sri Aurobindo.

Sights

Sri Aurobindo Ashram ① *0800-1200, 1400-1800, free. Meditation: Mon, Tue, Wed, Fri, 1925-1950; in the Playground: Thu, Sun, 1940-2015,* has its main centre in rue de la Marine. The Bureau Central on Ambur Salai is the Information Centre which has occasional films, lectures and other performances. The **library** is ① *open daily 0730-1130, 1400-1645.*

The **French Institute**, rue St Louis, was set up in 1955 for the study of Indian culture; the Scientific and Technical Section for ecological studies. Superb library overlooking the sea, many books in French and English. The colonial building is worth seeing. Another worth seeking out is the grand white-washed **Lycee Français**, rue Victor Simonel, wtih its shady courtyard, columns and balconies, which is interesting and well preserved.

The French Catholic influence is evident in a number of **churches**, notably the Jesuit Cathedral (*Notre Dame de la Conception*; 1691-1765). The Church of Our Lady of Angels (1855) is noted for an oil painting of Our Lady of Assumption given to the Church by King Louis Napoleon III.

The **Botanical Gardens**, south of City Bus Stand, opened in 1826 and are pleasant after some renovation. The **Government (Pondicherry) Park**, laid out with lawns, flower beds and fountains (one at the centre is of Napoleon III period), is in front of the Raj Niwas, the residence of the Lieutenant Governor. The park was originally the site of the first French garrison, Fort Louis, destroyed in 1761 by the British.

Museums

Pondicherry Museum ① *now next to the public Library, Rue St Louis, except Mon and public holidays, 1000-1700, free,* has a good sculpture gallery and a section of archaeological finds from the Roman settlement at Arikamedu. The French gallery charts the history of the colony; includes the four-poster bed in which Dupleix is believed to have slept. **Children's Museum**, next to the Botanical Gardens, has a superb collection of snail shells from the Pondicherry region. There is also the **Bharati** and **Bharatidasan Memorial Museums**. The former is in 20 Eswaran Koil Street where the famous Tamil poet-patriot lived after arriving in 1908 in search of refuge. The latter is in 95 Perumal Koil Street, the home of Kanakasubburatnam who adopted the name meaning disciple of Bharati which has become the second place of literary pilgrimage. **Jawahar Toy Museum** ① *1000-1700, free,* Goubert Salai, has a small collection of costume dolls (dancers, professions) from different states; a 15-minute diversion. **Maison Ananda Rangapillai** on Rangapillai Street has material on French India from 1736-60.

Boat trips

① *Feb-Sep, 0600-0800 (advance booking essential), 1000-1100, 1400-1500, Rs 800 per group of up to 15, Rs 600 for a family, Rs 50 per person (minimum 5 persons).*

Boat trips on a converted fishing boat to see dolphins can be booked through the *Seagulls* restaurant and the Tourist Information Centre. The boat leaves the commercial fishing harbour, 15 minutes' bike ride away; best in early morning for chance to see dolphins.

Pondicherry

■ Sleeping

1 Anandha Inn	8 Garden House
2 Balan Guest House	9 International
3 de l'Orient	Guest House
4 de Pondicherry	10 Mass
5 Excursion Centre	11 Park Guest Hotel
6 Executive Inn	12 Ram Guest House
7 Family Guest House	13 Sea Side Guest House
	14 Sugura

15 Tourist Bungalow
16 Villa Helena

● Eating

1 Ashram Dining Room
2 Au Feu de Bois
3 Blue Dragon

To Beach Cottages (5 km)

To New Pier & New Lighthouse

Auroville (Phone code: 041386. Colour map 7, grid B5). Futuristically designed, the layout of Auroville and its major buildings were to reflect the principles of Sri Aurobindo's philosophy. Far from fully complete, it is nonetheless a striking living experiment.

Background The Mother (see Pondicherry above) had hoped that Auroville would be a major focus for meditation and spiritual regeneration. The Charter says "To live in Auroville one must be a willing servitor of the Divine Consciousness" and describes it as belonging "to humanity as a whole... the place of an unending education, of constant progress... a bridge between the past and the future... a site of material and spiritual researches". Development since 1968 has been very slow. The 'city' itself is largely unfinished.

The community at Auroville welcomes visitors who have a genuine interest in the philosophical basis of the community. Visitor Centre has a map, leaflets and a café.

Sights The **Matrimandir** (started 1968) at the centre is a 30-m high globe with the lotus bud shaped foundation urn in the Meditation Room with 12 hollow pillars and the centrepiece crystal, said to be the largest in the world, are in place. Open to visitors 1600-1700 ("you get five seconds to see the crystal"), but to spend time in meditation (1700-1800) go independently.

Cuddalore There are few signs of the town's origins as an **East India Company** trading settlement in 1684, north of **Fort St David** which was built soon after but destroyed by the French General Lally in 1758. The oldest part of the town is the commercial centre. In the middle is an open maidan, referred to in old records as 'the lawn' or 'the green', and the old Collector's house (1733).

Listings: The Coromandel Coast

⊜ Sleeping

Mahabalipuram *p808, map p810*
Even modest hotels charge 20% luxury tax.
There are several new places in the
Othavadai Street area.
L-AL Fisherman's Cove (Taj), Covelong Rd, 8
km north, T044304-8253454. 80 rooms, some
a/c cottages with seaview, excellent seafood
at restaurant right on the beach ("very
special"), beautiful site, very good facilities, ask
Reception about seasonal "turtle walks".
C Ideal Beach Resort, Covelong Rd (3½ km
north), T42240, F42243, ideal@
md2.vsnl.net.in. 30 rooms in cottages, some
a/c (limited hours), good restaurant,
exchange, pool and gardens, clean,
comfortable. Poor service reported though.
C-D Sea Breeze, T43035, F43065,
seabreezehotel@hotmail.com. Clean, spacious,
well-furnished rooms (some a/c, Rs 700),
pleasant position, direct beach access (dubious
swimming), pool (non-residents Rs 100), good
food, Chennai airport pick-up Rs 600.
D Mamalla Bhavan Annexe, 104 East Raja St,
T42260, F42160, www.mamallahotels.com. 43
clean, pleasant rooms, 17 a/c, nice balconies,
excellent vegetarian restaurant, exchange,
travel, spotless, friendly, very good value.
Highly recommended.
D Tamil Nadu Beach Resort, T42361, F42268.
48 cottages, some a/c but neglected, damp,
restaurants, bar (limited hours), exchange,
good pool (gets deep suddenly!)
(non-residents Rs 75), beautiful setting.
D-E Surya, 1 Thirukula St, T42292, F42992. 12
cottages overlooking small lake (1st floor with
balcony dearer), very clean, some a/c, in quiet
shaded gardens, a/c restaurant, camping, very
knowledgeable, friendly manager.
D-E Veeras, East Raja St, T42288. 16 rooms (10
a/c), clean, well kept, good restaurant, bar.
D-E Vinayak, 68 East Raja St, next to bus stand,
T42445. 14 rooms with balcony overlooking
garden in new hotel, TV, phone, comfortable.
D-F Crystal Shore Palace, 15 Thirukulam St,
T42448, F42335. 16 rooms around pleasant
courtyard, restaurant, coffee shop, fast internet,

snooker, pool (non-residents Rs 25 half day, Rs
50 full day), friendly. Recommended.
E Lakshmi Lodge, Othavadai St, T42463. 26
clean rooms, upstairs small but light,
downstairs, dark and poor, restaurant with
beach view, friendly, popular with
backpackers, "notice prohibits drugs but staff
try to sell you hemp".
E-F Siva Guest House, 2 Othavadai Cross St,
T43234, F43534, sivaguesthouse@
hotmail.com. 11 very clean rooms in new
hotel, taxi hire, internet, friendly. Highly
recommended.
E-F Tina Blue View Lodge, 1 Othavadai St,
T42319, F42511. 25 rooms with bath and
balcony (Room 9 best), cottages for long term
rent, garden, very friendly. Recommended.
F La Vie en Rose, 9 Old College Rd, near bus
stand, T42522, Lavieenrose45@hotmail.com.
7 rooms overlooking garden, friendly,
internet, interesting 'backpacker restaurant'
with balcony, French spoken.
F New Papillon, off Beach Rd, towards
Sunrise. Clean but simple rooms, shower (Rs
70), good restaurant upstairs (try muesli).
F Ramakrishna Lodge, 8A Othavadai St,
T42431. 31 well-kept, clean rooms with fan,
shower, western toilets, no nets (Rs 125),
courtyard, good rooftop restaurant with
travellers' menu and music, friendly, good
value (contact Vijay for informal yoga
classes). Recommended.

Ashram guesthouses
These are mainly for official visitors; open to
others ('not to hippies'); no alcohol or
smoking. They close by 2230 (latecomers
may be locked out). Book well in advance,
with a day's rate.
D Park Guest House, near Children's Park,
T237495, parkgh@auro ville.org.in. 93
excellent sea-facing rooms (Rs 400),
breakfasts, clean, quiet, great garden, reading
room, ideal for long stay. Recommended.
D Sea Side Guest House, 14 Goubert Salai,
T331713, seaside@sriaurobindosociety.org.in.
25 excellent, large rooms, hot showers,
breakfast, spotless, sea views. Recommended.

⬤ *For an explanation of the sleeping and eating price codes used in this guide, see inside the
front cover. Other relevant information is found in Essentials pages 52-57.*

E-F International Guest House, Gingee Salai, T336699. 57 very clean and airy rooms, some a/c, huge for the price, very popular, often full.
F Garden House, 136 Akkasamy Madam St (north of town). Decent, clean rooms with bath (major bed bug problem and sewer nearby), quiet, gates locked at 2230.

Near Auroville
F Coco Beach Cottage, East Coast Main Rd, Kottakuppam, opposite turning for Auroville. 4 rooms, a very friendly, clean guesthouse with a popular restaurant.

Auroville *p817*
Food is available at most guesthouses and there are a number of restaurants and bakeries in Auroville
   Experience! Auroville guide, e-india@webstudio6.com, available from Pondicherry Tourism (PTDC) in Pondicherry, has an excellent breakdown of the accommodation options. Guests are accommodated in 5 settings (Central; Exurban; Beach; Farm and Forest; Pukka), each of which have their own characteristics (location, quietness, family-orientated, interaction with Aurovilians, language, etc). Costs vary from **C-F**, though some operate on a 'kibbutz' type arrangement.
D-E Centre Guest House, T622155, F622708. Most short-stay visitors are accommodated here ("welcomes those who wish to see and be in Auroville, but not to work there"), lovely setting, famous weekly pizza.
E-F New Creation, T622125.

Camping
Surya, 1 TKM Rd, T42292, F42492, allows camping. Tent Rs 100, vehicle Rs 200.

Kanchipuram *p812, map p813*
C-D Baboo Soorya, 85 East Raja St, T222555, set back off main road down palm fringed lane. 38 clean, spacious rooms, some a/c, restaurant, snack bar, glass 'bubble' lift, friendly staff, quiet.
E Sri Rama Lodge, 20 Nellukkara St, near Bus Stand, T222435. Fairly basic rooms, some a/c with TV, a/c restaurant, quite quiet, helpful staff.

F Sri Krishna Lodge, 68-A Nellukara St, T222831. 28 good, clean rooms, some with bath, helpful, friendly manager.
F SreeKusal Lodge, 68C Nellukara St, T223356. 25 clean and good value rooms, TV, veg restaurant.

Vedanthangal Sanctuary *p814*
A long day-trip from Chennai is possible; otherwise the very simple:
F Forest Rest House has suites of rooms with electricity, bath and running water. The cook will prepare an Indian meal to order. Reservations: Wildlife Warden, DMS Campus, Taynampet, Chennai, T4321471; advance payment expected.

Pondicherry *p814, map p816*
A Hotel de l'Orient, 17 Romain Rolland St, T343067, F227829, orient1804@satyam.net.in. Beautifully renovated old school now a small exclusive hotel, 10 tastefully decorated rooms in colonial style with objet d'art, good restaurant (pseudo-French/Creole) and service, very smart, spotlessly clean, book ahead. Highly recommended.
B Anandha Inn, 154 Sardar Patel Rd, T330711, F331241, checkin@anandhainn.com, 2 km north of Main Bus Stand. 70 very comfortable, spotless a/c rooms (quieter at rear), business centre, health club, 2 restaurants, short walk from bazar and sea front, very efficient, friendly and professional.
B Hotel de Pondicherry, 38 rue Dumas, T339745, F342204. 9 rooms behind *Le Club* (can get noisy), simple, clean, comfortable, tastefully decorated (some with no windows but private courtyard), very friendly and efficient staff.
B Villa Helena, 14 Suffren St, T226789, F227087, netindia.com.gallery. 5 rooms with antique furniture around large shady courtyard (1 1st floor suite), includes breakfast.
C Executive Inn, 1a Perumal Koil St, T330929, F343101, sumer@satyam.net.in. 11 a/c suites, TV, restaurant, internet, non smoking, no alcohol, quiet yet short walk from beach front and bazar, good value. Recommended.
C Mass, Maraimalai Adigal Salai, T337221, F333654, just off the NH45A, near Bus Stand. 111 clean a/c rooms, restaurants, pastry shop, bar, exchange, internet, helpful staff.

Tamil Nadu Listings: The Coromandel Coast

C-D **Suguru**, 104 Sardar Patel Rd, T339022, F334377. Good, clean rooms, some a/c, excellent South Indian restaurant, bit noisy.

D-E **Family Guest House**, 526 MG Rd. T340346, familyguesthouse@ pondicherry.everyone.net. 4 rooms, TV, hot water, bit cramped but very clean, roof terrace, hall, dining area, friendly.

D-E **Ram Guest House**, 546 MG Rd, T220072, F337734, ramguest@hotmail.com. Recently opened, 20 excellent rooms, maintained to European standards, spotless, good breakfast from clean kitchen. Recommended.

E **Tourist Bungalow**, Uppalam (Dr Ambedkar) Rd, T226376. 12 rooms, some a/c, and VIP suites, in a garden.

E-F **Balan Guest House**, 20 Vellaja St, 330634. 17 immaculate rooms with bath, clean linen.

F **Cottage Guest House**, Periarmudaliarchavadi, T338434, on beach, 6 km north of town. Rooms in cottages, French food, bike and motorcycle hire, peaceful, good beach under palm and casuarina trees, very popular.

F **Excursion Centre**, Uppalam Rd. Very cheap bunk-beds in dorm, suitable for groups, south of town, clean and quiet, very good value.

F **Palm Beach Cottages**, by Serenity beach, 5 km north of town. Clean huts (Rs 150), concrete beds with mattress, small garden, 5-min walk from beach, friendly staff, excellent food, especially fish, good for bikers but noisy from the highway.

F **Railway Retiring Rooms** for passengers, quieter than most stations! All about 20-30 mins' walk from centre, best to hire a bicycle.

F **Youth Hostel**, Solaithandavan Kuppam, T223495, north of town. Dorm beds (Rs 30); close to the sea among fishermen's huts. Bicycle or transport essential.

● Eating

Mahabalipuram *p808, map p810*
Beachside cafés are pleasant for a drink: Sea Rock and Luna Magica. In top hotels waterfront cafés are especially attractive in the evening.

♦♦ **Curiosity**, Othavadai St. Wide range, excellent food, very willing to please.

♦♦ **Gazebo**, East Raja St. Charcoal grilled fish, pleasant seating.

♦♦ **German Bakery**, selling good bread, great cakes, tasty pastas (try yak cheese and lasagne) and Chinese dishes, very friendly, relaxed atmosphere, Nepali run, open Dec-Apr. Recommended.

♦♦ **Honey Falls**, Shore Temple Rd. Few tables, served with delicious fish.

♦♦ **La Vie en Rose**, upstairs near the Archaeological Office. French. Very good food, 'special teas' (in absence of licence!), friendly French manager.

♦♦ **Moonrakers**, Othavadai St. Pleasant and friendly. Recommended.

♦♦ **Nautilus**, near *Sea Breeze*, fish, seafood.

♦♦ **Tina Blue View** breezy restaurant, mixed reports (sometimes slow, unfriendly service).

♦♦ **Uma Lodge**. International.

♦♦ **Village**, near *Surya*. Some outdoor seating in pleasant lakeside position, rustic design, average food, chilled beers.

♦ **Dreamland**, Othavadai St. Western favourites, very friendly, relaxed.

♦ **Mamalla Bhavan Annexe**. Good South Indian vegetarian. Try paper *dosa* and outstanding *palak* dishes. Indoors a/c, or outdoors evenings.

Kanchipuram *p812, map p813*
Baboo Surya, a/c, cheap Indian vegetarian, good *thalis*.

Sri Rama Lodge, a/c, and **Sri Vela**, Station Rd, good breakfasts.

Saravana Bhavan, next to *Jaybala International*, 504 Gandhi Rd (50 m off the road). "Best in town".

Bakery Park Place, Odai St, cakes and sweets.

Pondicherry *p814, map p816*
♦♦♦♦ **Le Club**, 38 rue Dumas, T339745. French and Continental. Smart, excellent cuisine (Rs 400 for a splurge), French wine (Rs 1000), opinions differ, "we could have been in a French Bistro!" to "dearest but not the best", (0830-1830, closed Mon).

♦♦♦ **Blue Dragon**, 30 rue Dumas near the New Pier (south end of Goubert Salai). Chinese. Excellent food, surrounded by antique furniture.

♦♦♦ **Paris**, 104 Ambur Salai. Vietnamese (closed Fri).

♦♦♦ **Rendezvous**, 30 Suffren St. French and Continental. Attractive, modern, reasonable food (dish Rs 100) but overpriced wine, nice roof terrace, pleasant atmosphere.

♦♦♦ **Satsanga**, 30 rue Mahe de Labourdonnais St, T225867. Closed Thu. Continental (quite expensive wine Rs 200), friendly, French atmosphere with art 'gallery', pleasant outdoor setting. Mixed reports on food.

♥♥ Seagulls, near Children's Park. Continental and others. Large 1st floor terrace overlooking sea, bit overpriced, bar.

♥♥ La Terrasse, 5 Subbaiyah Salai. Excellent Continental. Good value, huge salads, no alcohol (0830-2000, closed Wed).

♥ Ashram Dining Hall, north of Govt Place. Indian vegetarian. Simple, filling, meals (Rs 20 per day) in an unusual setting, seating on cushions at low tables, farm grown produce, non-spicy and non-greasy. 'Ticket' from Ashram guesthouses or Central Bureau; then turn up at 0640, 1115, 1745 or 2000. Recommended though staff can be off-hand.

♥ Au Feu de Bois, rue Bussy. Pizzas, salads, crêpes lunchtime.

♥ Hot Breads, Ambur Salai. Café. Good burgers, chicken puffs (Rs 35) pizzas, great sandwiches, pastries, shakes (Rs 18), 0700-2100.

♥ Indian Coffee House, 41 Nehru St. Real local vegetarian fare throughout the day from 0700.

♥ Picnic, Kamaraj Salai. Very good vegetarian.

♥ Le Café Pondicherry, Goubert Salai, by Gandhi statue. Short eats. Pleasant spot, but ordinary fare (daytime).

♥ Ramanas, 25 Nehru St, excellent Indian, tasty fast food, a/c section.

Bakeries
Green Connection, Nehru St. Sells health food.
Mass Classique, Bazar St Laurent.

◉ Entertainment

Pondicherry *p814, map p816*
Cinema
On Kamaraj Salai and Vallabhai Patel Salai. Ask at Ashram for programmes.
Alliance Française, 33 rue Dumas. Has a library, organizes French cultural programmes, private restaurant. Register as a temporary member.

◉ Festivals and events

Mahabalipuram *p808, map p810*
Dec-early Feb: 6-week Dance Festival starting on 25 Dec; at Bhagiratha's (Arjuna's) Penance, Classical 1800-2030, Folk 2030-2100, every Sat, Sun and holidays. Long speeches in Tamil on opening (full-moon) night! **Mar**:

Masi Magam attracts large crowds of pilgrims.
Apr-May: Brahmotsava lasts for 10 days.
Oct-Nov: the Palanquin Festival is held at the Stalasayana Perumal Temple.

Pondicherry *p814, map p816*
4th-7th Jan: International Yoga Festival held at Kamban Kalairangam, contact Pondicherry Tourism for full details. **Jan**: Pongal is a 3-day harvest, earth and sun festival, popular in rural areas. **Feb/Mar**: Masi Magam on the full moon day of the Tamil month of Masi, pilgrims bathe in the sea when deities from about 40 temples from the surrounding area are taken in colourful procession for a ceremonial immersion. 'Fire walking' sometimes accompanies festivals here. **14th Jul**: Bastille Day. **Aug**: Fete de Pondicherry is a cultural programme.

◉ Shopping

Mahabalipuram *p808, map p810*
Handicrafts shops sell small figures in soapstone and metal.
On East Raja St: **Himalayan Handicrafts**, at 21, also has 900 books for exchange.
Books and newspapers at **JK Books**, off the beach on Othavadai St.
Hidesign, at 138. Excellent Western style leather goods, very reasonable. Recommended.
Silver Star, at 51, T42936. Good tailor.

Kanchipuram *p812, map p813*
Photography
PhotoFast, Nellukara St.

Silk
Silk and cotton fabrics with designs of birds, animals and temples or in plain beautiful colours, sometimes 'shot', are sold by the metre in addition to saris. It is best to buy from Govt shops or Co-operative Society stores.
AS Babu Shah, along Gandhi Rd, has high quality silks.
BM Silks, 23G Yadothagari, Sannathi St.
Sreenivas, 135 Thirukatchi Nambi St (Gandhi Rd).

Pondicherry *p814, map p816*
The shopping areas are along Nehru Street and Mahatma Gandhi Road. The 'Experience! Pondicherry' booklet has a good shopping guide.

Dolls of papier-mâché, terracotta and plaster are made and sold at Kosapalayam. Local grass is woven into *Korai* mats. Craftsmen at the Ashram produce marbled silk, hand dyed cloths, rugs, perfumes and incense sticks.

Antiques
Heritage Art Gallery, Rue Romain Rolland.

Books
Focus, 204 Cathedral St, good selection of Indian writing in English, cards, stationery, CDs, very helpful.
Kailash French Bookshop, 87 Lal Bahadur Shastri St, large stock

Boutiques
Several Ashram outlets on Nehru St.
Aurosarjan, Rue Bussy. Auroville clothes, crafts.
Sri Aurobindo Handmade paper 'factory', 44 Sardar Patel Rd; shop sells attractive products.
Vasa, rue Mahe de Labourdonnais, next to *Hotel Qualité*, Smart ladies' clothes.

Crafts
In addition to handicrafts emporia:
Cluny Centre, 46 Romain Rolland St, T/F335668. Run by a French order in a lovely colonial house where nuns design and oversee high quality embroidery.
Curio Centre, 40 Romain Rolland St, has some fine antiques and good reproduction colonial furniture.
Kalki, 134 Cathedral St, T39166. Produces exceptional printed and painted silk.

Music
La Mode, Rue Bussy. Cassettes and Cds.

Others
Home World supermarket, 172 Kamaraj Salai. Good toiletries.
Market off MG Rd. Excellent, worth visiting any day but especially on Mon.

▲ Activities and tours

Mahabalipuram *p808, map p810*
Tours
TTDC: to Kanchipuram and Mahabalipuram. 0500-1900. Tiring, but good value if you don't mind being rushed. It also includes a stop at the appallingly garish Indian kitsch, *VGP Beach Resort*.

Tour operators include **Hi Tours**, 123 East Raja St, T43260, F42160, travexs@vsnl.com. Train/air tickets, tours, forex, Kerala house boats.

Kanchipuram *p812, map p813*
Tours
Tourist information at *Hotel Tamil Nadu*, T22461, 1000-1700.

Pondicherry *p814, map p816*
Fishing
Deep sea fishing trips booked through *Pondicherry Tourism (PTDC)* (see below), 6/12 hours, Rs 1,500/2,500.

Rugby
Ask for Maurice Saint-Jacques at Lycée Française.

Sports complex
South of the town near the Govt Tourist Home.

Swimming
Pools in *Hotel Blue Star* and *Calva Bungalow*, Kamaraj Salai open to non-residents for a fee.

Tour operators
Auro Travels, Karikar Building, Nehru St, efficient, quick service.
PTDC Sightseeing, Rs 45, Ashram, 0815-1300: Ashram and related departments. Auroville (Matrimandir), 1430.
Sita, 124 Cathedral St, T336860.

Yoga
Ananda Ashram, Yoga Sadhana Beach, 16 Mettu St, Chinamudaliarchavadi, Kottakuppam. They run 1, 3, 6 month courses starting from Jan, Apr, Jul and Oct; or book through Pondicherry Tourism (see below), Rs 1,500 for 10 lecture modules.

Auroville *p817*
Tours
0830-1100 from Ashram in Pondicherry, autocare@auroville.org.in, 1430-1745 from *Cottage Complex*, Ambur Salai, includes Auroville Visitors' Centre, Matri Mandir, a school in New Creation Village. Visitors recommend going independently. A 5-day residential introduction to Auroville is available through the *Centre Guest House*, T622155 (Rs 1,000).

Transport

Mahabalipuram p808, map p810

Bicycle hire

From tourist office and shops in East Raja St and hotels, Rs 25 per day. Recommended for Tirukkalukundram – from Dec-Feb a comfortable and very attractive ride.
VM Hire, Othavadai St (opposite *Uma Lodge*). Bicycle Rs 25, moped Rs 100.

Bus

From Chennai also go to Tirukkalukundram and Pondicherry. Nos 19C, 68, 119A.

Car hire

From tourist office.

Mopeds

At **Bala Lodge** and **Vinodhara**, 4 Othavadai Cross St, Rs 125.

Taxi

Charge Rs 700-1000 for 1-day excursion from Chennai; Rs 450 to airport. To Pondicherry, Rs 700 (bargain hard).

Train

The nearest station is Chengalpattu, 29 km away with buses to Mahabalipuram, 1 hr.

Kanchipuram p812, map p813

Bicycle

The town is flat and easy to negotiate so the best and cheapest way to get about is by hiring a bike from near the bus stand or off East Raja St. Cycle and **auto-rickshaws** are available for visiting temples.

Bus

Long distance The bus station in the middle of town with direct Govt Express to **Chennai** (No 828) 2½ hrs, **Bangalore** (No 828), **Kaniyakumari** (No 193), **Pondicherry** (109 km, No 804) 3½ hrs, and **Tiruchirappalli** (No 122). For **Mahabalipuram** (65 km) 2 hrs, direct bus or take a bus to Chengalpattu (35 km) and catch one from there. Very frequent buses to **Vellore**, other buses go to **Tirupati** and **Tiruttani**.

Train

The station, on a branch line, is under a kilometre to the northeast of the bus stand.

There is 1 direct train to **Chennai Egmore** and **Chennai Beach**: *Kanchipuram-Chennai Beach Pass, 172 (S)*, 0705, 2 hrs **Egmore**; 2½ hrs **Chennai Beach**. Also trains to Arakkonam on the Chennai-Bangalore line.

Vedanthangal Sanctuary p814

Car or bus

From Chennai by car or bus from the Broadway Bus Stand, Chennai (only weekends) or one from Mahabalipuram. It is also included in some coach tours.

Train

To Chengalpattu (28 km) and then bus or taxi, 30 km to sanctuary.

Pondicherry p814, map p816

Bicycle/scooter hire

Jaypal, Gingee Salai.
Super Snack, Nehru St opposite Information Centre.
Vijay Arya, 9 Aurobindo St. Daily: cycle, Rs 25, scooter, Rs 120. Well worthwhile as the streets are broad, flat and quiet.

Also a hire shop just off Subbaiyah Salai (South Blvd).

Motor bikes for travelling round South India, Rs 250 per day. Pondicherry Tourism (PTDC) (see below) and *Le Cafe*, Beach Rd, hire bicycles, Rs 5 per hour, Rs 40/400 per day/month.

Bus

Local Negotiate fare first; bus stands to centre, Rs 20. Also cycle-rickshaws and auto-rickshaws found here.
Long distance State Express Bus Stand, NH45A, just west of the traffic circle. T337464. Computerized Reservations: 0700-2100 (helpful staff).
Mofussil (New) Bus Stand, further west, serves all other bus companies.
Local Bus Stand, T336919, 0430-1230, 1330-2130. Pondicherry Tourism Corporation (PTC), T337008, 0600-2200, also runs long distance services. Check timings.
Bangalore: 7½ hrs; **Chennai**: frequent Express buses, under 3 hrs; **Chidambaram**: frequent buses by all companies, 1½ hrs; **Coimbatore via Salem and Erode**: 8½-9½ hrs; **Gingee**, infrequent, 2 hrs; **Kanniyakumari**: overnight service; **Kannur and Mahé**: 15 hrs; **Karaikal**: 4 hrs; **Madurai**

via **Tiruchirapalli**: 6½-8 hrs overnight; **Mahabalipuram**: several, about 4 hrs; **Tirupati**: 6½-7 hrs; **Tiruvannamalai (via Villupuram)**: 3-3½ hrs; **Kottakarai**, frequent service from Town Bus Stand.

Car
Car hire Round trips to many destinations can be arranged at reasonable rates, eg return to **Bangalore** (310 km) Rs 2,000; **Chidambaram** (74 km), Rs 550; **Chennai** (166 km), Rs 1000; **Mahabalipuram** (130 km), Rs 800.

Taxi
Particularly along the canal; 4 hrs (50 km) Rs 250, 8 hrs (100 km) Rs 500.
Jupiter Travels, 170A Anna Salai, luxury taxis.

Train
Reservations, T336684, 0800-1400, 1500-1900, Mon-Sat; 0800-1400, Sun. 4-m gauge trains (1 hr) daily to **Villupuram** which offer prompt main line connections to **Chennai**, **Madurai**, **Tiruchirappalli**. No *652*, 0745 for Chennai and Madurai; *654*, 1920 for Chennai; *646*, 1655 for Chennai and Tiruchirapalli; *656*, 0500 for *Pandyan Exp 6717* to Tiruchirapalli, Kodai Rd and Madurai; *Quilon Mail 6105* to Tiruchirapalli and Kollam. From **Villupuram**: 4 trains daily for Pondy departs 0610, 0900, 1745, 2025. The half hourly bus to Villupuram stops 100m from station and connects with trains. Railway station, enquiries: 0900-1200, 1500-1800. It is possible to make computerized reservations from Pondy station to any other station, and has a quota on major trains leaving from Chennai Central.

Auroville *p817*
Bicycle
Rent a bicycle (Rs 15 per day, though at some guesthouses they are free) and take advantage of the many cycle paths. **Centre Guest House** is one of several places renting bikes/mopeds.

Taxi
Mopeds and taxis cost Rs 60/100 per day.
Long distance Either of the 2 roads north from Pondicherry towards Chennai leads to Auroville. A rickshaw from Pondicherry will cost around Rs 100, a taxi not much more (or Rs 300 for a 3-hr wait-and-return).

● Directory

Mahabalipuram *p808, map p810*
Banks Cherry, Beach St, for exchange. LKP, 130 East Raja St. Good rate, speedy. **Prithvi Securities**, opposite Mamalla Bhavan Annexe, no commission, transfers money.
Libraries Has English language dailies. Book exchange at *Himalayan Handicrafts*.
Post office Post office on a back street off Covelong Rd. **Tourist offices** Tamil Nadu, Covelong Rd (300 m north of Othavadai St), T42232, 0945-1745, closed Sat, Sun. 2 guides available here; others from Chennai. Car and cycle hire possible.

Kanchipuram *p812, map p813*
Banks State Bank of India, Gandhi Rd. Amex TCs not accepted; **Indian Overseas Bank**, Gandhi Rd. **Post office** Head Post Office, 27 Gandhi Rd.

Pondicherry *p814, map p816*
Banks Andhra Bank, Cathedral St, cash against Visa. **State Bank of India**, 5 Suffren St, changes cash and TCs (Amex, Thomas Cook), 24 hr ATM. **UCO Bank**, rue Labourdonnais, opposite Government Park, quick and efficient. **LKP**, rue Labourdonnais. No commission. **Cultural centres** French Institute, rue St Louis, close to the north end of Goubert Salai, and **Alliance Française** at the southern end of Goubert Salai for cultural programmes, 0800-1230, 1500-1900, Mon-Fri, 0830-1200, Sat. **Embassies and consulates** French Consulate, 2 Marine St. **Hospitals** General Hospital, rue Victor Simone, T336389; **Jipmer**, T372381. Ashram Dispensary, Depuis St, near seaside. **Internet** Many centres Ohm Infotech, 11 Nehru St. High speed. **Post office** Head Post Office, northwest corner of Govt Place. CTO, Rangapillai St. **Tourist offices** Auroville Information Centre, Ambur Salai, 12 Nehru St, T339497. **Ashram Reception Service**, Main Building, rue de la Marine, T334836. Pondicherry Tourism, 40 Goubert Salai, T339497, F358389, www.tourismpondicherry.com, 0845-1300, 1400-1700, daily, town maps, brochures, tours, sea cruises, fishing, car/bicycle hire, well run. Information Bureau, 19 Goubert Salai. **Useful addresses** Foreigners' Regional Registration Office, Goubert Salai.

The Palar Valley

The broad flat bed of the River Palar runs between the steep-sided northern Tamilnad hill ranges, an intensively irrigated, fertile and densely populated valley cutting through the much poorer and sometimes wooded high land on either side. The whole valley became the scene of an Anglo-French-Indian contest at the end of the 18th century. Today it is the centre of South India's vitally important leather industry and of intensive agricultural development. ►► *For Sleeping, Eating and other listings, see pages 828-829 .*

Vellore → *Phone code: 0416. Colour map 7, grid A5. Population: 177,400.*

The once strategically important centre of Vellore, pleasantly ringed by hills, has the air of a busy market town, though its fort and temple are reminders of its historic importance.

The fort is a major attraction, but Vellore is now world famous for its **Christian Medical College Hospital,** founded by the American missionary Ida Scudder in 1900. Started as a one-room dispensary, it extended to a small hospital through American support. Today it is one of the country's largest hospitals with over 1,200 beds and

Vellore

Sleeping ■
1 India Lodge & Raj Café
2 Mohan Mansion & Srinivasa Lodge
3 Nagha International
4 VDM Lodge

Eating ●
1 Babarchees
2 Bombay Diamond & Karthik
3 Chinatown
4 Dawn Bakery & Restaurants
5 Kwality Ice Cream
6 Palace Café
7 Shimla

0 metres 200
0 yards 200

large out-patients' department which caters for over 2,000 patients daily. The college has built a reputation for research in a wide range of tropical diseases. One of its earliest and most lasting programmes has been concerned with leprosy work and there is a rehabilitation centre attached. In recent years it has undertaken a wide ranging programme of social and development work in villages outside the town to back up its medical programmes.

Sights

Vijayanagar architecture is beautifully illustrated in the temple at ★ **Vellore Fort**, a perfect example of military architecture and a *jala durga* or water fort. Believed to have been built by the Vijayanagara kings and dating from the 14th century, the fort has round towers and huge gateways along its double wall. The moat, still filled with water by a subterranean drain, followed ancient principles of defence, with a colony of crocodiles. A wooden drawbridge crosses the moat to the southeast. Vellore came under British control in 1768 who defended it against Haidar Ali in 1782. After the victory in Seringapatnam in 1799, Tipu Sultan's family was imprisoned here and a *sepoy* mutiny of 1806, in which many British and Indian mutineers were killed, left many scars. In the fort is a parade ground, the CSI church, the Temple and two-storeyed *mahals* which are used as Government offices.

> ‼ *The easiest way on to the battlements of the fort is to go up the ramp on your right just after passing through the gate. The turret in the northeast corner gives superb views*

Jalakantesvara Templeⓘ *bathing Rs 2*, with a 30-m high seven-storeyed granite *gopuram*, has undergone considerable restoration. Enter from the south and inside on the left, the *kalyana mandapa* (wedding hall), one of the most beautiful structures of its kind, has vivid sculptures of dragons and 'hippogryphs' on its pillars. The temple consists of a shrine to Nataraja in the north and a lingam shrine in the west.

There is a small **museum** ⓘ *closed 2nd Sat every month and Hindu festivals, 0930-1700, free*, in the fort with an interesting collection of wood and stone carvings, sections on anthropology, painting, handicrafts, coins and nature.

★ Gingee → *Phone code: 04145. Colour map 7, grid B5.*

Gingee (pronounced Senjee) has a remarkable 15th-century Vijayanagar fort with much to explore. It is well off the beaten track, very peaceful and in beautiful surroundings. Spend the night here if you can.

Ins and outs

Getting there Gingee is just off the NH45, between Chennai and Tiruvannamalai, with frequent buses from both, and occasional buses from Pondicherry.

Getting around Allow at least half a day if you intend to climb the fort, preferably in the morning when it is cooler and less hazy (only for the fit and healthy).

Sights

The **fort**ⓘ *0900-1700, allow 2½ hrs for Rajagiri, and 2 hrs for Krishnagiri (if you have time), Rs 5, foreigners Rs 100, includes both forts, the Archaeological Survey of India Office, just off the main road towards the fort, may have guides to accompany you to the fort, carry provisions, especially plenty of drinks, some refreshments are sold only at the bottom of the hill,* was intensely contested by successive powers before being captured by an East India Company force in 1762, but by the end of the century it had lost its importance. Although it had Chola foundations, the 'most famous fort in the Carnatic' was almost entirely rebuilt in 1442. It is set on three Charnockite hills, Krishnagiri, Chakklidrug and Rajagiri, all strongly fortified. In places the hills on which the fort stands are sheer cliffs over 150 m high. The highest, **Rajagiri** ('king's hill'), has a south facing overhanging cliff face, on top of which is the citadel.

The inner fort contains two temples and the **Kalyana Mahal**, a square court with a 27-m breezy tower topped by pyramidal roof, surrounded by apartments for the women of the Governor's household. On top of the citadel is a huge cannon and a smooth granite slab known as the **Raja's bathing stone**. An extraordinary stone about 7-m high and balanced precariously on a rock, surrounded by a low circular brick wall, is referred to as the Prisoner's Well. There are fine Vijaynagara temples, granary, barracks and stables and an 'elephant tank'. A caretaker may unlock a temple and then expect a tip.

★ Tiruvannamalai

→ *Phone code: 04175. Colour map 7, grid B5. Population: 130,300.*
In a striking setting at the foot of the rocky Arunachala Hill, Tiruvannamali is one of the holiest towns of Tamil Nadu, and locally considered the home of Siva and his consort Parvati. It is a major pilgrimage centre.

Sights

One of the largest temples in South India, **★Arunachala Temple** (16th and 17th centuries) ⓘ *may close 1230-1530, pay toilets adjacent to temple north wall.*, was built mainly under the patronage of the Vijayanagar kings: its massive *gopurams*, the tallest of which is 66 m high, dominate the centre of the town. It is dedicated to Siva as God incarnate of Fire.

The temple has three sets of walls forming nested rectangles. Built at different periods they illustrate the way in which many Dravidian temples grew by accretion. The east end of each is extended to make a court, and the main entrance is at the east end of the temple. The lower parts of the *gopurams*, built of granite, date from the late Vijayanagar period but have been added to subsequently. The upper 10 storeys and the decoration are of brick and plaster. There are some remarkable carvings on the *gopurams*. On the outer wall of the east *gopuram*, for example, *Siva* is shown in the

Tiruvannamalai

south corner dancing with an elephant's skin. Inside the east doorway of the first courtyard is the 1,000-pillared *mandapa* built late in the Vijayanagar period. To the south of the court is a small shrine dedicated to *Subrahmanya*. To the south again is a large tank. The pillars in the *mandapa* are carved with typically vigorous horses, riders and lion-like *yalis*. The middle court has four much earlier *gopurams* (mid-14th century), a large *columned* mandapa and a tank. The innermost court may date from as early as the 11th century and the main sanctuary with carvings of deities is certainly of Chola origin. In the south is *Dakshinamurti*, the west shows *Siva* appearing out of a lingam, and the north has *Brahma*. The outer porch has small shrines to *Ganesh* and *Subrahmanya*. In front of the main shrine are a brass column lamp and the *Nandi* bull.

Priests insist on guiding visitors (and expect payment)

Sleeping
1 Aakash
2 Arunachala
3 Aruna Lodge
4 Ramakrishna

Eating
1 Brindavan

0 metres 200
0 yards 200

To Katpadi Junction
To Vellore
To Gingee, Tindivanam & Chennai
To Ramana Maharshi Ashramam (2 km) & Salem
Arunachala Hill
Subrahmanya Temple
Durga Temple
Big St
Gandhi Statue
Arunachala Temple
Sannathi St
Indra Tirtha Tank
Kilathur Rd
Polur Rd
Main
Muthuvinayagar Kovil St
Mathalangulam St
Chinnakadai Vithi
Kosai madam St
Tindivanam Rd
CTO
KN Mudali St

Listings: The Palar Valley

⊜ Sleeping

Vellore *p825, map p825*
D Prince Manor, 41 Katpadi Rd, T27106.
Comfortable rooms, very good restaurant.
D River View, New Katpadi Rd, T25251,
F25672, 1 km north of town. 31 rooms, some
a/c, modern hotel, pleasant inner courtyard
with mature palms, 3 good restaurants.

Budget hotels
Many cheap hotels along Babu Rao St, Gandhi
Rd and KVS Chetty St cater for families with
relatives in the hospital but the area is noisy.
F India Lodge, inexpensive rooms and *Raj
Café*, good vegetarian restaurant downstairs.
F Mohan Mansion, 12 Beri Bakkali St, T27083,
15 mins' walk from bus stand. Small hotel, basic
and clean, quieter than others near hospital.
F Nagha International Lodge, 13/A KVS
Chetty St, T226731. Some **E** a/c deluxe rooms.
F Sri Krishna Residency, 6 GPH Rd, T221374.
Clean and quiet rooms,
F Srinivasa Lodge, Beri Bakkali St, T26389.
Simple and clean.
F VDM Lodge, T224008. Very cheap,
pleasant, helpful staff.

Gingee *p826*
E Shivasand, M Gandhi Rd, opposite bus
stand, T22218. 21 clean, adequate rooms with
bath, 1 dearer a/c, vegetarian restaurant, a/c
bar and non vegetarian meals, good views of
fort from roof, helpful manager.
Avoid **Aruna Lodge**, near bus stand.

Tiruvannamalai *p827, map p827*
At full-moon pilgrims arrive to walk around
Arunachala Hill and hotels are over-booked.
D-E Arunachala, 5 Vadasannathi St, T28300.
Fairly new hotel with 32 clean, rooms, 16 a/c,
TV, hot water, best away from temple end,
can get noisy during festivals, veg meals.
D-E Ramakrishna, 34F Polur Rd, T25004,
F25008, info@hotelramakrishna.com.
Recently opened, 42 rooms, 21 a/c, TV, hot
water, excellent veg *tandoori* restaurant,
parking, modern, helpful and friendly staff.

D-E Seshabhavan, T22983. Clean rooms,
immersion heater for hot water.
F Aakash, 9 Polur Rd, T22151. 22 rooms,
friendly but rather noisy.
F Aruna Lodge, 82 Kosamadam St, T23291.
24 clean, adequate rooms with bath.

◐ Eating

Vellore *p825, map p825*
 ¶ **Palace Café**, 21 Katpadi Rd. Indian.
 ¶ *Hotel Karthik's* veg restaurant recommended.

Ida Scudder Rd
 ¶ **Anand** for excellent breakfasts.
 ¶ **Babarchee**, Babu Rao St. Good fast food.
 ¶ **Best**, some meals very spicy, nice *parathas*,
open 0600 for excellent breakfast.
 ¶ **Geetha** and **Susil**, rooftop or inside, good
service and food.
 ¶ **Shimla**, tandoori, *nan* very good.

Gandhi Rd
 ¶ **Chinatown**, a/c, small, friendly (play your
own tapes) – good food and service.
 ¶ **Dawn Bakery**, fresh bread and biscuits,
cakes, also sardines, fruit juices.

Tiruvannamalai *p827, map p827*
A thali lovers paradise with plenty of 'meals'
restaurants including **Brindavan**, 57 A Car St;
about Rs 15 per meal.
   Cafés near the Ramana Maharshi
Asramam serving western food:
Auro Usha, varied menu, **Manna**, salads and
snacks, and **German Bakery**.

⊛ Festivals and events

Tiruvannamalai *p827, map p827*
Karthikai Deepam Full moon day in
Nov-Dec. A huge beacon is lit on top of the
hill behind the temple. The flames, which
can be seen for miles around, are thought of
as Siva's lingam of fire, joining the
immeasurable depths to the limitless skies. A
cattle market is held.

O Shopping

Vellore *p825, map p825*

Most shops are along Main Bazar Rd and Long Bazar St. There is a large covered market south of the bus station. Vellore specializes in making 'Karigari' glazed pottery in a range of traditional and modern designs. Vases, water jugs, ashtrays and dishes are usually coloured blue, green and yellow.

Tailors

Beauty, Ameer Complex, Gandhi Rd, cheapest good quality tailoring.
Mr Kanappan, Gandhi Rd, very friendly, good quality, a little more expensive.

▲ Activities and tours

Vellore *p825, map p825*
Swimming

At *Hillside Resort*, CHAD (Community Health and Development), south of town, excellent private pool, Rs 250 per day popular with CMC medical students. Open early morning to late evening, closed Mon and from 1200-1500.

◉ Transport

Vellore *p825, map p825*
Bus

The Bus Station is off Long Bazar St, east of the Fort. Buses to **Tiruchirappalli**, **Tiruvannamalai** (from Burma Market Bus Stand), **Bangalore**, **Chennai**, **Ooty**, **Thanjavur** and **Tirupathi**. The regional state bus company PATC runs frequent services to **Kanchipuram** and **Bangalore** from 0500 (2½ hrs) and **Chennai**.

Train

Katpadi Junction, the main station, 8 km north of town is on the broad gauge line between **Chennai** and **Bangalore**. Buses and rickshaws (Rs 35) into Vellore. **Chennai (C)**: *Cheran Exp, 2674*, 0505, 2¼ hrs; *West Coast Exp, 6628*, 1303, 2½ hrs; *Kovai Exp, 2676*, 1915, 2 hrs.
Bangalore (C): *Brindavan Exp, 2639*, 0903, 4¼ hrs; *Chennai-Bangalore Exp, 6023*, 1515, 4½ hrs; it is also on the metre gauge line to **Villupuram** to the south, with daily passenger trains to **Tirupathi**, **Tiruvannamalai** and **Pondicherry**. The Cantonment Station is

about 1 km south of the GPO, and has a daily train to **Tiruchchirappalli**, *Tirupati Tiruchchi Exp, 6801*, 1910, 10¾ hrs.

Gingee *p826*
Bus

To/from **Pondicherry**, infrequent direct buses (2 hrs); better via Tindivanam (45 mins). To/from **Tiruvannamalai**, 39 km: several buses (1 hr), Rs 13; Express buses will not stop at the fort. TPTC bus 122 to/from **Chennai**.

Cycle-rickshaw

To visit the fort take a cycle-rickshaw from the bus stand to the hills; about Rs 30 for the round trip, including 2-hr wait.

Tiruvannamalai *p827, map p827*
Bicycle

Bicycle hire from near the Bus Stand but not recommended; cycling can be hazardous in this very busy small town.

Bus

Long distance Buses to major cities in **Tamil Nadu**, **Kerala** and **Karnataka**. Local people will point out your bus at the bus stand; you can usually get a seat although they do get crowded. To **Gingee**, frequent, 1 hr; **Chennai**, 5 hrs, Rs 30; **Pondicherry**, 3-3½ hrs.

Train

To **Tirupati** via Vellore Cantt, Katpadi and Chittor: *Tiruchchi Tirupati Exp, 6802*, 2300, 6½ hrs. **Pondicherry**: *Tir upati-Pondicherry Fast Pass, 641 (S)*, 0640, 3½ hrs.

◉ Directory

Vellore *p825, map p825*
Banks Central Bank, Ida Scudder Rd, east of hospital exit, is at least 10 mins faster at changing TCs than the **State Bank**.
Hospital CMC, Ida Scudder Rd, T32102.
Internet Net Paradise, north of bus stand.
Post office CMC Hospital has PO, stamps, takes parcels.

Tiruvannamalai *p827, map p827*
Bank Vysya Bank, Sannathi St. Quick for cash and TCs. **Internet** TICS, 4 Kosamadam St. Also Western Union. **Post office** A Car St.

● *Phone codes* Vellore: 0416; Gingee: 04145; Tiruvannamalai: 04175

Tiruchirappalli and Chettinad

➔ *Phone code: 0431. Colour map 7, grid B4. Population: 746,000.*

Known as Trichy or Tiruchi for short, Tiruchirappalli is at the head of the fertile Kaveri delta. Its rock fort is visible for miles around, across the flat surrounding plain, but it is its position at the head of the Kaveri delta, and the holy site of Srirangam, which have given it its greatest significance for over 1,000 years. Today Trichy is a clean, lively and modern city.

Chettinad, with a reputation as home to South India's hottest food and made famous by its jewellery traders, lies within easy reach to the south of Trichy.
▶▶ *For Sleeping, Eating and other listings, see pages 834-836 .*

Tiruchirappalli

Ins and outs

Getting there Trichy airport about 8 km from the town centre, has flights to Madurai and Chennai and also to Colombo. Well connected by train to major towns, the Junction Railway Station and the two bus stations are right in the centre of the main hotel area, all within walking distance.

Getting around Much of Trichy is quite easy to see on foot, but plenty of autos and local buses run to the Rock Fort and Srirangam. See Transport, page 835, for further details.

Background

Trichy was mentioned by Ptolemy in the second century BC. A Chola fortification from the second century, it came to prominence under the Nayakas from Madurai who built the fort and the town, capitalizing on its strategic position. In legend its name is traced to a three-headed demon, Trisiras, who terrorized both men and the gods until Siva overpowered him in the place called Tiruchi. Cigar-making became important between the two World Wars, while the indigenous *bidis* continue to be made, following a tradition started in the 18th century. Trichy is the country's largest centre manufacturing artificial diamonds. Jaffersha Street is commonly known as 'Diamond Bazar'. The town is also noted for its high quality string instruments, particularly *veenas* and *violins*.

Sights

★ **Rock Fort**, 1660, stands on an 84-m high rock. **Vinayaka Temple** (or Ucchi Pillayar Koil) ① *0600-2000, Re 1, camera Rs 10, video Rs 50,* approached from Chinna Bazar, is at the highest point, from which you get marvellous views. It is a fairly easy climb up 437 rock cut steps to reach it. The temple itself is disappointing. On your way up you come to the main 11th-century defence line and the remains of a thousand-pillared hall, destroyed in 1772, at the top of the first flight of steps. Further up is a hundred-pillared hall where civic receptions are held. At the end of the last flight is the **Tayumanasvami Temple**, dedicated to Siva, which has a golden *vimana* and a lingam which is carved out of the rock itself. There are also other seventh-century Pallava cave temples which have beautifully carved pillars and panels.

It is worthwhile discovering the old city on foot, particularly **Big Bazar Street** and **Chinna Bazar**. The Gandhi Market is a colourful vegetable and fruit market.

Among the dozen or so mosques in the town, the **Nadir Shah Mosque** near the city railway station stands out with its white dome and metal steeple, said to have been built with material taken from a Hindu temple. **St Joseph's College Church** (Church of our Lady of Lourdes), one of several Catholic churches here, designed as a smaller version of the Basilica at Lourdes in France has an unusual sandalwood altar but is rather garish inside. The grounds are a peaceful spot. The 18th-century **Christ Church**, the first English church, is north of the Teppakulam, while the early 19th-century **St John's Church** has a memorial plaque to Bishop Heber, one of India's best known missionary bishops, who died in Trichy in 1826.

Government Museumⓘ *Bharatiyar Rd, Cantt, closed Fri, 0900-1230, 1400-1700, free,* has a display of sculpture, art, archaeology, handicrafts, numismatics, geology and science.

Tiruchirappalli

■ Sleeping	7 Gajapriya	14 Sevana
1 Abirami	8 Jenney's Residency	15 Tamil Nadu
2 Aristo	9 Kanjenaa Plaza	
3 Arun	10 Lalshmi	● Eating
4 ASG Lodge	11 Raja Sugam & New Kurinji	1 Baskin 31 Robbins
5 Ashby	12 Ramayas	2 Kavitha
6 Femina	13 Sangam	3 Vincent Garden

66 99 ...guides will greet you on arrival – their abilitites are highly variable, some tell you that the staircase to the viewpoint will close shortly – usually a scam to encourage you to use their services...

Excursions

★ **Srirangam** The temple town on the Kaveri, just north of Trichy, is surrounded by seven concentric walled courtyards, with magnificent gateways and several shrines. On the way to Srirangam, is an interesting river *ghat* where pilgrims take their ritual bath before entering the temple. The countryside to the west of the temple is an excellent place to sample rural Indian life; a good way to spend a couple of hours.

Sri Ranganathasvami Temple ① *0615-1300, 1515-2045, camera, Rs 20, video Rs 70 (Rs 10 for the rooftop viewing tower), allow about 2 hrs, guides will greet you on arrival – their abilitites are highly variable, some tell you that the staircase to the viewpoint will close shortly – usually a scam to encourage you to use their services,* is one of the largest in India and dedicated to Vishnu, it has some fine carvings and a good atmosphere. The fact that it faces south, unlike most other Hindu temples, is explained by the legend that Rama intended to present the image of Ranganatha to a temple in Sri Lanka but this was impossible since the deity became fixed here, but it still honours the original destination. The temple, where the Vaishnava reformer **Ramanuja** settled and worshipped, is famous for its superb sculpture, the 21 impressive *gopurams* and its rich collection of temple jewellery. The 'thousand' pillared hall (904 columns) stands beyond the fourth wall, and in the fifth enclosure there is the unusual shrine to Tulukka Nachiyar, the God's Muslim consort. Non-Hindus are not allowed into the sanctuary but can enter the fourth courtyard where the famous sculptures of *gopis* (*Radha's* milk maids) in the Venugopala shrine can be seen.

The **festival** of *Vaikunta Ekadasi* ① *bus No 1 (C or D) from Trichy or hire a rickshaw,* and associated temple car festival, in December/January draws thousands of pilgrims who witness the transfer of the image of the deity from the inner sanctum under the golden *vimana* to the *mandapa*.

Amma Mandapam Nearby, on the north bank of the Kaveri, this spot is a hive of activity. The *ghats*, where devotees wash, bathe, commit cremated ashes and pray – are interesting to visit, although some may find the dirt and smell overpowering.

Tiruvanaik-kaval So named because a legendary elephant worshipped the lingam, Tiruvanaikkaval is 3 km east of Srirangam. It has the architecturally finer **Jambukesvara Temple** with its five walls and seven splendid *gopurams*, one of the oldest and largest Siva temples in Tamil Nadu. The unusual lingam under a *jambu* tree always remains under water. There are special festivals in January and the spring. In August *Pancha Piraharam* is celebrated and in *Panguni* the images of Siva and his consort Akhilandesvari exchange their dress. It is a major Siva temple in the heart of Vaishnava territory. ① *0600-1300, 1600-2130 officially (though usually open all day), temple elephant gives blessings at 1600-1700, worship 1100-1200, camera Rs 10, 200 m east off the main Tiruchi-Chennai road, a short stroll from Srirangam or easily reached by bus, non-Hindus are not allowed into the sanctuary.*

Chettinad → *Colour map 7, grid B5 and C5.*

Chettinad, occupying the hot and often dusty coastal plain, south of Trichy, is home to some of South India's wealthiest merchant families. Many of the villages are now semi-deserted but they retain a charm and distinctive style that repays a visit. The triangle Pudukkottai-Kiranur-Kodumbalur has a number of early Chola and late Pallava monuments containing fine cave sculptures.

Sites around Trichy

Close to **Kiranur**, 28 km from Trichy, is the eighth-century Kunnandarkoil cave temple, with the later addition of a Vijayanagar *nritta mandapa* which contains some excellent bronzes. **Narthamalai**, west of the road 6 km further, has important Chola temples including the Vijayalaya Choleesvaram with its circular sanctum, of particular interest in tracing the development of southern temple architecture. In the hills near Narthamalai are some Jain caves.

Pudukkottai

Pudukkottai, 50 km south of Trichy, was the capital of the former princely state ruled by the Tondaiman Rajas, founded by Raghunatha Raya Tondaiman in 1686. At one entrance to the town is a ceremonial arch raised by the Raja in honour of Queen Victoria's jubilee celebrations. The town's broad streets suggest a planned history – the temple is at the centre, with the old palace and a tank. The new palace is now the District Collector's office. The rock-cut **Sri Kokarnesvarar Temple** ① *closed 1200-1600*, at Thirukokarnam, 5 km north of the railway station, dates from the Pallava period. The natural rock shelters, caves, stone circles, dolmens and Neolithic burial sites show that there was very early human occupation. The **museum** ① *Big St, Thirukokarnam 5 km away, except Fri, 2nd Sat, public holidays, 0930-1700, free, allow 40 mins, recommended*, has a wide range of exhibits, including sections on geology, zoology and the economy as well as sculptures and the arts. The archaeology section has some excellent sculptures from nearby temples. There is a notable carving of Siva as *Dakshinamurti* and some fine bronzes from Pudukkottai itself

Sittannavasal, 13km away, has a Jain cave temple (circa eighth century) with sculptures, where monks took shelter when they fled from persecution in North India. In a shrine and verandah there are some fine frescoes in the Ajanta style and bas-relief carvings. You can also see rock hewn beds of the monks. The *Brahmi* inscriptions date from the second century BC.

Karaikkudi

① *The temple is 12km southeast of Arantang; which is 30 km northeast of Karaikkudi.*

Karaikkudi is in the heart of Chettinad, and has several typical mansions, antique and textile shops. You can visit the local *santhat* (market), craftsmen working in wood and metal, and gold and silversmiths in their workshops. At **Avudayarkoil**, the Athmanathar temple, has one of the most renowned sites in Tamil cultural history. A legend tells that Manickavaskar, a Pandyan Prime Minister, re-directed money intended for the purchase of horses to build the temple. However, his real fame lies as author of the *Thiruvasakam* ('holy outpourings'), one of the most revered Tamil poetic texts. Completely off the beaten track, the temple has superb sculptures, and is noted for the absence of any images of Siva or Parvati, the main deities, whose empty pedestals are worshipped. The wood carvings on the temple car are notable too.

Kanadukathan, 5 km north of Karaikkudi, has a number of formerly magnificent mansions, some of them empty except for bats, monkeys – and antique dealers. It has been estimated that the Burma teak and satinwood pillars in just one of the village's Chettiar houses weighed 300 tonnes, often superbly carved. The plaster on the walls is made from a mixture of lime, eggwhite, powdered shells and myrobalan fruit (the astringent fruit of the tree *Phyllantles emblica*), mixed into a paste which, when dried, gave a gleaming finish. Traditionally in the jewellery and trading business, the **Chettiars** now own a variety of large companies.

Listings: Tiruchirappalli and Chettinad

● Sleeping

Tiruchirappalli and Chettinad
p830, map p831

Most hotels are within easy reach of the station.
A Jenney's Residency, 3/14 Macdonalds Rd, T414414, F461451, www.Jenneysresidency.com. 93 top quality a/c rooms, good restaurants, pool (non-residents Rs 100), excellent travel desk, exchange, good hair/beauty salon (ladies/gents).
B-D Femina, 14C Williams Rd, T414501, F410615, try_femina@sancharnet.in. 157 clean rooms, 140 a/c, vegetarian restaurants, bar, pool in new block, good value, modern, comfortable 4-storey hotel.
C Sangam, Collector's Office Rd, T464480, F461779. 58 comfortable a/c rooms and restaurants (great tandoori), good breakfast in coffee shop, pleasant bar, exchange, okay pool, spacious lawns, very friendly.
C-D Kanjenaa Plaza, 50 Williams Rd (2-min walk from bus stand), T401501, F400387, kanjenaaplaza@rediffmail.com. 90 spacious, comfortable rooms with bath, 26 a/c, restaurant, bar, travel agent, quiet and clean.
C-D Ramyas, 13D/2 Williams Rd, T415128, F414852, vatnaa@eth.net. 78 spotless rooms, 24 a/c, restaurants, bar.
D Abirami, 10 Macdonalds Rd, T415001, F412819. 55 rooms, some a/c with bath, good busy a/c restaurant (vegetarian), exchange, old fashioned, noisy location.
D-E Ashby, 17A Junction Rd, T460652. 20 large a/c rooms with bath set around courtyard, good restaurants, bar, oldest hotel in town, with Raj character, a bit noisy but excellent friendly staff, good value.
D-E Gajapriya, 5 Royal Rd, T414411, F466456. 66 good value rooms, 28 a/c (no twin-bedded), non-veg restaurant, bar, library, car parking, spacious hotel, quieter than most.

D-E Tamil Nadu (TTDC), Macdonalds Rd, Cantt, T414346, F460725. 36 rooms (run down), some a/c with bath, restaurant, bar and tourist office.
E-F Sevana, 5 Royal Rd, Cantt, T415201. 44 rooms, some a/c with bath, a/c restaurant (Indian), bar, quiet, friendly.
F Arun, 24 State Bank, Rd T415021. 40 rooms in garden setting, restaurant, bar, TV, excellent value. Recommended.
F Raja Sugam, 13b Royal Rd, T460636.
F ASG Lodge opposite. Very noisy but quite clean (from Rs 75).
F Railway Retiring Rooms, some a/c, reputed to be some of the best in India.

Pudukkottai *p833*

E Shivalaya, Thirumayam Rd by Maternity Hospital (on a side street, just south of town, 1 km east of the Bus Stand), T04322-21864. Basic but clean, good rooms (some a/c). Poor restaurant (no breakfast), bar.
F Lakshme Lodge, Thirumayam Rd, 24 clean rooms, veg restaurant, good value.

Karaikkudi *p833*
Senjai

Very few suitable places to stay in the area.
AL The Bangala, T04565-20221, (or Chennai T4934851, F4934543), bangala@vsnl.com. 8 bright and spacious a/c rooms with period colonial furniture, in restored 1916 bungalow, a 'heritage guest house' of character amidst orchards and palms invoking a privileged life style on the outskirts of town, authentic Chettinad meals (or Continental), rest stop facilities for day visitors (lunch US$15-20), full-board option.

Devakottai
F Nivaas 1st left from bus station coming from the north, (no sign in English), is basic (no electric sockets), no English spoken.

● *For an explanation of the sleeping and eating price codes used in this guide, see inside the*
● *front cover. Other relevant information is found in Essentials pages 52-57.*

🍴 Eating

Tiruchirappalli and Chettinad
p830, map p831
Hotels
¶ **Abirami's**, T460001. A/c *Vasantha Bhawan* at the back, serves excellent vegetarian; front section is a 'meals' type eatery.
¶ **Jenney's Residency**, T461301. Good Chinese, extensive menu, attentive service but freezing a/c. Also *Wild West* bar.
¶ **Sangam's**, T464480. Indian, Continental.

Outside hotels
¶ **Kavitha**, Lawsons Rd. A/c. Excellent breakfasts and generous vegetarian thalis.
¶ **Vincent Garden**, Dindigul Rd. Very pleasant garden restaurant and pastry shop, lots of coloured lights but on a busy road.
    Some good Indian vegetarian restaurants in Chinna Bazar include:
¶ **New Kurinji**, below *Hotel Guru*, Lawson's Rd. A/c vegetarian.
¶ **Vasantha Bhawan** and **Ragunath**, thalis, good service.

🎉 Festivals and events

Tiruchirappalli and Chettinad
p830, map p831
Mar: Festival of Floats on the Teppakulam when the temple deities are taken out onto the sacred lake on rafts. Several at Srirangam.

Pudukkottai *p833*
In **Jan and Feb** bullock races (*manju viruttu*) are held in the area.

🛍 Shopping

Tiruchirappalli and Chettinad
p830, map p831
Very 'Indian' with artificial diamonds, toys and bangles on offer.
Khadi Gramudyog, Chinna Bazar.
Khadi Kraft, Junction Rd, opposite railway station.
Poompuhar, near Main Guard Gate.

Books
Higginbothams, Nandi Koil St, ner tank. Towards Srirangam temple.

Heritage Arts, 5 Amma Mandapam Rd, T432113, good 'Chola' bronzes cast by lost wax process (staff happy to explain), tribal jewellery, silk selection, astute but not pushy; branches at *Jenney's Residency* and *Femina* hotels.

🏔 Activities and tours

Tiruchirappalli and Chettinad
p830, map p
Tour operators
Galaxy, Williams Rd (Kanjenaa Plaza), for air and train tickets.
Window to the World, 44A Royar Thoppu, Srirangam, T436052, F430832, windowtothe world@vsnl.com, for tours from Chennai, Bangalore, Kochi, Madurai and Thiruvananthapuram. Recommended for tours (good cars with drivers), ticketing, general advice.

🚌 Transport

Tiruchirappalli and Chettinad
p830, map p831
Air
The airport is 8 km from the centre (taxi Rs 75). **Indian Airlines**, Dindigul Rd, 2 km from Express Bus Stand, T481433, airport T420563; flies to **Chennai** daily except Mon and Fri. **Sri Lankan**, 14 Williams Rd, T414076 (0900-1730) to **Colombo**.

Bicycle
Bicycle hire From Junction Rd near the station.

Bus
Local Good City Bus service. From airport Nos 7, 63, 122, 128, take 30 mins. The Central State Bus Stand is across from the tourist office (No 1 Bus passes all the sights); 20 mins to Chatram Bus Stand.
Long distance The bus stands are 1 km from the railway station and are chaotic; TN Govt Express, T460992, Central, T460425. Frequent buses to **Coimbatore** 205 km (5½ hrs), **Kumbakonam** 92 km, **Chennai** (6 hrs), **Madurai** 161 km (3 hrs), **Palani** 152 km (3½ hrs), **Thanjavur** (1½ hrs). Also 2 to **Kanniyakumari** (9 hrs), **Kodai** (5½ hrs) and **Tirupati** (9½ hrs).

Unmetered taxis, and tourist taxis from *Kavria Travels*, *Hotel Sangam*, Collector's Office Rd, T464480. **Cycle-rickshaws** and **auto-rickshaws** (best avoided).

Train
Enquiries, T131. **Bangalore**: *Thanjavur Mysore Exp, 6231*, 2040, 9½ hrs, continues to **Mysore**, 3¼ hrs. **Chennai**: *Pallavan Exp, 2606*, 0630, 5½ hrs; *Vaigai Exp, 2636*, 0910, 5¼ hrs. **Kollam**: *Nagore-Quilon Exp, 6361*, 1615, 12½ hrs. **Madurai**: *Vaigai Exp, 2635*, 1745, 2¾ hrs. **Villupuram (for Pondicherry)**: *Tiruchchi Tirupati Exp, 6802*, 1400, 7 hrs; *Cholan Exp, 6854*, 0800, 6½ hrs, plus frequent bus to Pondicherry (1 hr) or another train (4 daily).

Pudukkottai *p833*
Bus
Buses go to Tiruchirappalli, Thanjavur, Madurai, Ramnad, Rameswaram, and Sittanavasal.

Train
The station is 2 km southwest of the bus stand. Trains for Egmore, change at Tambaram. **Trichy** 1¼ hrs. **Rameswaram** *Tambaram Rameswaram Exp, 6701*, 0833, 5¼ hrs.

Karaikkudi *p833*
Bus
Routes link town with every part of the state.

Train
The *Rameswaram* and *Sethu Exp* connect Tambaram and Rameswaram with Karaikkudi.

❻ Directory

Tiruchirappalli and Chettinad
p830, map p831

Banks Exchange is available at Western Union money transfer in Jenne Plaza, Cantonment. 0900-1730 Mon-Sat. Quick, good rates. **Internet** Mas Media, Main Rd, 6 terminals; Central Telegraph Office, Permanent Rd. **Tourist offices** At *Hotel Tamil Nadu Complex*, 1 Williams Rd, T460136. Mon-Fri, 0945-1745. Also counters at Airport and Junction Station, 0600-2000. **Useful addresses** State Bank of India, Dindigul Rd. Sri Lanka Airways, at *Femina Hotel* complex.

Pudukkottai *p833*
Banks State Bank of India, East Main St.

Chola Heartland and the Kaveri Delta

★ Thanjavur (Tanjore)

→ *Phone code: 04362. Colour map 7, grid B5. Population: 215,700.*

Thanjavur's Brihadisvara Temple, a *World Heritage Site*, is one of the great monuments of South India. In the heart of the lush, rice growing delta of the Kaveri, today the town feels much more like a throbbing rural market centre than a modern commercial or industrial city. ⟫ *For Sleeping, Eating and other listings, see pages 844-847.*

Ins and outs

Getting there Most long distance buses now stop at the New bus stand 4 km southwest of the centre, but there are frequent local buses and autos (Rs 25) to town and the railway station.

Getting around It is less than a 15-min walk from the hotels to the Brihadisvara Temple. See Transport, page 846 for further details.

Climate Summer: maximum 37°C, minimum 33°C; Winter: maximum 24°C, minimum 23°C. Annual rainfall: 940 mm.

History

The capital of the great Chola Empire and later of the *Thanjavur* Nayaka and Maratha rulers, the Chola kings built most of Thanjavur's 93 temples. The Cholas were great patrons of the arts and while they lavished their wealth to build temples, they encouraged the belief in the divine right of kings, and the practice of donating a part of one's wealth to the temple for spiritual gain.

Sights

★ **Brihadisvara Temple** ① *0600-2030; inner sanctum closed 1230-1600*. Known as the **'Big Temple'**, this is the achievement of the Chola king **Rajaraja I** (ruled AD 985-1012). The magnificent main temple has a 62-m high *vimana* (the tallest in India), topped by a dome carved from an 80 ton block of granite, which needed a 6.5 km ramp to raise it to the top. The attractive gardens, the clean surroundings and well-lit sanctuaries make a visit doubly rewarding; good atmosphere, especially in the evening.

The entrance is from the east. After crossing the moat you enter through two *gopurams*, the second guarded by two *dvarapalas* typical of the early Chola period, when the gopurams on the outer enclosure walls were dwarfed by the scale of the

Thanjavur

N

0 metres 200
0 yards 200

■ **Sleeping**
1 Ganash
2 Karthik & New Bombay Sweet
3 Iluxi
4 Lion City
5 Oriental Towers
6 Pandyar Residency
7 Parisutham
8 Tamil Nadu I
9 Yagappa

● **Eating**
1 Algappa
2 Sathars

vimana over the main shrine. An enormous *Nandi*, carved out of a single block of granite 6 m long, guards the entrance to the sanctuary. According to one of the many myths that revolve around the image of a wounded *Nandi*, the Thanjavur Nandi was growing larger and larger, threatening the temple, until a nail was driven in its back.

The temple, built mainly with large granite blocks, has superb inscriptions and sculptures of Siva, Vishnu and Durga on three sides of the massive plinth. Siva appears in three forms, the dancer with 10 arms, the seated figure with a sword and trident, and Siva bearing a spear. The carvings of dancers showing the 81 different Bharat Natyam poses are the first to record classical dance form in this manner.

The main shrine has a large *lingam*. In the inner courtyard are Chola frescoes on walls prepared with lime plaster, smoothed and polished, then painted while the surface was wet. These were hidden under later Nayaka paintings. Chambers 7 and 9 are well preserved and have fresco paintings of kings, queens and musicians.

The permanent exhibition in the temple complex ⓘ *0900-1200, 1600-2000*, has reproductions of the paintings and a record of the Archaeological Survey of India's conservation programme. Since music and dance were a vital part of temple life and dancing in the temple would accompany the chanting of the holy scriptures which the community attended, Rajaraja also built two housing colonies nearby to accommodate 400 *devadasis* (temple dancers). Subsidiary shrines were added to the main temple at different periods. The Vijayanagara kings built the Amman shrine, the Nayakas the Subrahmanya shrine and the Marathas the Ganesh shrine.

The Palace ⓘ *Closed Wed, 0900-1300, 1400-1700.* Built by the Nayakas in the mid-16th century and later completed by the Marathas, the palace is now partly in ruins. The evidence of its original splendour can be seen in the ornate Durbar Hall. The towers are worth climbing for a good view; one tower has a whale skeleton washed up in Chennai! The **art gallery** with bronze and granite sculptures (0900-1300, 1500-1800), **Sangeeta Mahal** with excellent acoustics, **Saraswati Mahal Library** and the **Tamil University Museum** are here, together with some Government offices.

Schwartz Church This church (1779) is dedicated to the Danish missionary FC Schwartz who died in 1798. There is a particularly striking marble bas-relief sculpture at the west end of the church by Flaxman of Schwartz on his deathbed, showing him surrounded by the family of Raja Serfoji to whom he was tutor, see page 789.

Museums and libraries
★ **Rajaraja Museum and Nayak Darbar Hall Art Gallery** ⓘ *Thanjavur Palace, daily, 0900-1200, 1500-1800, Rs 3, camera Rs 5, video Rs 100,* has a large and excellent collection of Chola bronzes and granite pieces. Look for Bhairava, Umasahita Siva, Kali, Somaskanda and the Rama Lakshmana group. **Saraswati Mahal Library** ⓘ *daily except Wed, 1000-1300, 1330-1730, free, scholars only,* in the palace is one of the country's major reference libraries, having over 40,000 rare books, several first editions and about 8,000 palm leaf manuscripts.

Excursions
Thiruvaiyaru ⓘ *Frequent buses from the old bus station, Thanjavur (30 mins, crowded).* A visit to Thiruvaiyaru, 13 km away, with the Panchanatheswara Siva temple, known for its *Thyagaraja Music Festival*, gives a glimpse of South Indian rural life. Hardly visited by tourists, music connoisseurs arrive in large numbers in January. Performances vary and the often subtle music is marred by loud amplification. The *Car Festival* is in March.

Kumbakonam → *Phone code: 0435. Colour map 7, grid B5. Population: 140,000.*

This very pleasant town, 54 km from Thanjavur, was named from the legend where Siva was said to have broken a *kumbh* (water pot) after it was brought here by a great flood. The water from the pot is reputed to have filled the Mahamakam Tank. High quality betel vines, used for chewing paan, are grown here.

Sights

There are 18 temples ⓘ *closed 1200-1630,* in the town centre and a monastery of the Kanchipuram Sankaracharya. The oldest is the **Nagesvara Swami Temple**, a Saivite temple begun in AD 886. The small Nataraja shrine on the right before you reach the main sanctum is designed to look like a chariot being pulled by horses and elephants. Superb statues decorate the outside walls of the inner shrine; Dakshinamurti (exterior south wall), Ardinarisvara (west facing) and Brahma (north) are in the central panels, described as among the best

> ⁑ *The temples in this region contain some exceptional pieces of jewellery – seen on payment of a small fee.*

works of sculpture of the Chola period. The temple has a special atmosphere and is definitely worth a visit. No photography inside.

Sarangapani is the largest of Kumbakonam's shrines. Dedicated to Vishnu, it is dominated by its 11-storey main *gopuram*, 44-m tall. The Nayaka *mandapa*, inside the first court, leads through a second, smaller *gopuram* to a further *mandapa*.

The **Kumbesvara Temple** dates mainly from the 17th century and is the largest Siva temple in the town. It has a long colonnaded *mandapa* and a magnificent collection of silver *vahanas* (vehicles) for carrying the deities during festivals. The **Ramasvami Temple** is another Nayaka period building, with beautiful carved rearing horses in its pillared *mandapa*. The frescoes on the walls depict events from the *Ramayana*. The Navaratri Festival is observed with great colour.

Kumbakonam

Sleeping		Eating
1 ARR & Restaurant	3 Femina	1 A & A
2 Chela	4 Pandiyan	
	5 Raya's	

The **Mahamakam Tank** is visited for a bathe by huge numbers of pilgrims every 12 years, when 'Jupiter passes over the sign of Leo'. It is believed that on the day of the festival nine of India's holiest rivers manifest themselves in the tank, including the Ganga, Yamuna and Narmada.

★ Darasuram

ⓘ *Open sunrise to sunset, there is a small museum in the northeast corner, but the nata mandapa in the northwest corner has an excellent collection of sculptures, immediately to the west, a group of large sculptures represents Siva as a beggar with a number of attendants.*

Five kilometres south of Kumbakonam, is Darasuram with the **Airavatesvara Temple**, after Thanjavur and Gangaikondacholapuram, the third of the great Chola temples, built during the reign of **Rajaraja II** between 1146-72.

The **entrance** is through two gateways. A small inner gateway leads to a court where the mainly granite temple stands in the centre. The *gopuram* is supported by beautifully carved *apsaras*. Inside, there are friezes of dancing figures and musicians. The *mandapa* is best entered from the south. Note the elephant, ridden by dwarfs, whose trunk is lost down the jaws of a crocodile. The pillars illustrate mythological stories for example 'the penance of Parvati'. The five gods Agni, Indra, Brahma, Vishnu and Vayu in the niches are all shown paying homage to Siva. The **main mandapa**, completely enclosed and joined to the central shrine, has figures carved in black basalt on the outside. The ceilings are also richly decorated and the pillars have the same flower emblems as in the outer *mandapa*. The main shrine has some outstanding sculptures; the guardians on the north are particularly fine. Sculpted door-keepers with massive clubs guard the entrance to the main shrine which has a *Nandi* at the entrance. Some of the niches inside contain superb early Chola sculptures of polished black basalt, including a unique sculpture of Ardhanarisvara with three faces and eight arms, a four-armed Nagaraja and a very unusual sculpture of Siva destroying Narasimha. The **outer walls** are also highly decorative. Siva as Dakshinamurti on the south wall, Brahma on the north wall and Siva appearing out of the linga on the west wall. The inner wall of the encircling walkway (*prakara*) is divided into cells, each originally to house a deity. The corners of the courtyard have been enlarged to make four mandapas, again with beautiful decoration.

❗ *You can spend a worthwhile afternoon visiting Darasuram first and then Gangaikonda-cholapuram (after 1600) by car*

Swamimalai

Swamimalai, 3 km from Darasuram, one of the abodes of Lord Murugan, is famous for its school of iconography and craftsmen producing Chola style bronzes using the 'lost wax' process.

★ Gangaikondacholapuram

ⓘ *Buses from Chidambaram or Kumbakonam.*

Once the capital of the Chola king Rajendra (1012-44), the town of Gangakondacholapuram (meaning 'The city of the Chola who conquered the Ganga') has now all but disappeared. The temple and the 5-km long 11th-century reservoir embankment survive.

The **temple** which Rajendra built was designed to rival the Brihadisvara temple built by Rajendra's father Rajaraja in Thanjavur. Unlike the *Nandi* in Thanjavur, the huge *Nandi* facing the *mandapa* and sanctuary inside the compound by the ruined east *gopuram* is not carved out of one block of stone. As in Thanjavur, the *mandapa* and sanctuary are raised on a high platform, orientated from west to east and climbed by steps. The whole building is over 100 m long and over 40 m wide. Two massive doorkeepers (*dvarapalas*) stand guard at the entrance to the long closed *mandapa* (the first of the many subsequent *mandapas* which expanded to 'halls of 1,000 pillars'); the plinth is original. A narrow colonnaded hall (*mukha-mandapa*) links this hall to the shrine. On the east side of this hall are various carvings of Siva such as bestowing grace on Vishnu, who worships him with his lotus-eye. On the northeast is a large panel, a masterpiece of Chola art, showing Siva blessing Chandikesvara, the steward. At the centre of the shrine is a huge *lingam* on a round stand. As in Thanjavur there is a magnificent eighth-tiered, pyramidal *vimana* (tower) above the sanctuary, nearly 55 m high. Unlike the austere straight line of the Thanjavur temple, however, here gentle curves are introduced. Ask the custodian to allow you to look inside (best for light in the morning). Immediately to the north of the *mandapa* is an excellently carved shrine dedicated to Chandikesvara. To north and south are two shrines dedicated to Kailasanatha with excellent wall sculptures. The small shrine in the southwest corner is to Ganesh.

★ Chidambaram → *Phone code: 04144. Colour map 7, grid B5. Population: 59,000.*

The capital of the Cholas from AD 907 to 1310, the temple town of Chidambaram is one of Tamil Nadu's most important holy towns. The town has lots of character and is rarely visited by foreigners.

Chidambaram

N

U metres 200
0 yards 200

■ **Sleeping**
1 Akshaya
2 Raja Rajan
3 Ramanathan Mansions
4 Ramayas Lodge
5 Ritz
6 Saradharam
7 Sri Nataraj
8 Star Lodge
9 Tamil Nadu & Youth Hostel

● **Eating**
1 Sree Ganesa Bhavan
2 Udupi

★ **Nataraja Temple** ① *0400-1200. 1630-2100, visitors may be asked for donations, entrance into the inner sanctum Rs 50, enter the temple by the East Gate, men must remove their shirts,* is dedicated to the dancing Lord Siva, a favourite deity of the Chola kings. One legend surrounding its construction suggests that it was built by 'the golden coloured Emperor', **Hiranya Varna Chakravarti**, who suffered from leprosy. He came to Chidambaram on a pilgrimage from Kashmir in about AD 500. After bathing in the temple tank he was reputed to have recovered from the disease, and as a thanks-offering rebuilt and enlarged the temple. The evening puja at 1800 is particularly interesting. At each shrine the visitor will be daubed with *vibhuti* (sacred ash) and paste. It is not easy to see some of the sculptures in the interior gloom. You may need patience and persuasive powers if you want to take your own time but it is worth the effort.

Chidambaram is a highly active temple, with Brahmins at every shrine – though they all belong to a local community, unrelated to the 3,000 Brahmins Hiranya Varna Chakravarti is reputed to have brought with him from Kashmir.

There are records of the temple's existence before the 10th century and inscriptions from the 11th century. On each side are four enormous gopurams, those on the north and south being about 45 m high. The east *gopuram* (AD 1250), through which you enter the temple, is the oldest. The north *gopuram* was built by the great Vijayanagar king **Krishna Deva Raya** (1509-30).

Immediately on entering the East Gate is the large **Sivaganga** tank, and the **Raja Sabha**, a 1,000 columned *mandapa* (1595-1685). In the northwest of the compound are temples dedicated to **Subrahmanya** (late 13th century), and to its south the 12th century shrine to Sivakumasundari or Parvati (circa 14th century). The ceiling paintings are 17th century.

Nataraja Temple, Chidambaram

Subrahmanya Temple

Navagraha Shrine

Sivakumasundari Temple

Sivaganga Tank

Raja Sabha

Mulasthana Shrine

Deva Sabha

Entrance

Govindaraja Shrine

Chit Sabha & Kanaka Sabha

Nritta Sabha

Nandi Pavilion

Ganesh Shrine

N

0 metres 50
0 yards 50

- - - Barrier

(After MICHELL)

Those who make oblations

"The Chidambaram temple has never had landed or other endowments, and it belongs to a group of Brahmans called Dikshitars ('those who make oblations') who are held in high regarded by the community, according to the South Arcot District Gazetteer. You may notice that they have the single Brahmin style tuft of hair at the front rather than the back of their heads. They marry only among themselves and ritual here is more like family worship.

Theoretically all the married males have a say in the running of the temple. They support it by going round the district asking for alms and offerings for themselves.

Each has his own particular clients, and in return for the alms he receives he undertakes to make offerings at the shrine of his benefactors. From time to time he will send them holy ash or an invitation to a special festival.

20 Dikshitars are always on duty at the temple, each male doing the work which is divided into 20-day rotas. The one on duty becomes the owner of the routine offerings of food made at the shrine. Large presents of food are divided among all the Dikshitars. The right to the other oblations is sold by auction every 20 days to one of the Dikshitars at a meeting of the community".

At the southern end of this outer compound is what is said to be the largest shrine to **Ganesh** in India. The next inner compound has been filled with colonnades and passageways. In the innermost shrine are two images of Siva, the Nataraja and the lingam. A later Vishnu shrine to Govindaraja was added by the Vijayanagar kings.

The **inner enclosure**, the most sacred, contains four important Sabhas (halls), the **deva sabha**, where the temple managers hold their meetings; the **chit sabha** or *chit ambalam* (from which the temple and the town get their names), meaning the hall of wisdom; the **kanakha sabha**, or golden hall; and the **nritta sabha**, or hall of dancing. Siva is worshipped in the *chit ambalam*, a plain wooden building standing on a stone base, in his form as Lord of the Dance, Nataraja. The area immediately over the deity's head is gold plated. Immediately behind the idol is the focus of the temple's power, the 'Akasa Lingam', representing the invisible element, 'space', and hence is itself invisible. Known as the 'Chidambaram secret'.

Excursions

Tranquebar ① *From Chidambaram most require a change at Sirkazhi. From Thanjavur, some direct buses; others involve change at Mayiladuthurai (24 km).* The Danish king Christian IV received permission from Raghunath Nayak of Thanjavur to build a fort here (at Tharangampadi) in 1620. The Danish Tranquebar Mission was founded in 1706 and the **Danesborg fort** and the old **church** still survive. The Danes set up the first Tamil printing press, altering the script to make the casting of type easier. The Danish connection resulted in the National Museum of Copenhagen today possessing a remarkable collection of 17th-century Thanjavur paintings and Chola bronzes. There is a **museum** and a good beach.

Point Calimere Wildlife and Bird Sanctuary ① *Open throughout the year, best season – mid-Dec to Feb, Rs 5, camera Rs 5, video Rs 50.* The coastal sanctuary, half of which is tidal swamp, is famous for its migratory water birds. The Great Vedaranayam Salt Swamp (or 'Great Swamp') attracts one of the largest colonies of **flamingos** in Asia (5-10,000) especially in December and January. Some 243 different bird species have been spotted here. In the spring the green pigeons, rosy pastors, koels, mynahs and barbets can be seen. In the winter vegetable food and insects attract paradise flycatchers, Indian pittas, shrikes, swallows, drongos, minivets, blue jays, woodpeckers and robins among others. Spotted deer, black buck, feral horses and wild boar are also found, as well as reptiles. The swamp supports a major commercial fishing industry. Jeeps can be booked at reception. Exploring on foot is a pleasant alternative to being 'bussed'; ask at reception for a guide.

Listings: Chola Heartland and the Kaveri Delta

Sleeping

Thanjavur *p836, map p837*
Even modest hotels charge 20% Luxury Tax.
A Parisutham, 55 GA Canal Rd, T331801, F330318, hotel.parisutham@vsnl.com. 52 clean a/c rooms in modern, quality hotel, good restaurants (live local music from 1945), lovely pool, exchange, friendly, helpful, good atmosphere (avoid smaller, noisy a/c ground floor rooms).
B Oriental Towers, 2889 South Pillai Rd, near railway station, T330724, F330770, www.hotelorientaltowers.com. 163 average-size, a/c rooms , though suites better, good restaurants, bar, pool on top floor (non-residents Rs 100), business centre, hotel decor rather tired.
B Sangam, Trichy Rd, T325151, F324895. 54 a/c upgraded rooms, modernized with pool, restaurant, garden.
D Ideal River View Resort, Vennar Bank, Palli Agraharam (6 km north of centre), T350533, F334933, ideal@md2.vsnl.net.in. Clean, comfortable cottages (some a/c) in large grounds, restaurant, boating, peaceful, shuttle to town. Recommended.
D Pandyar Residency, Kutchery Rd, near Big Temple, T330574. 63 rooms, some a/c, some overlook temple, restaurant, bar.
D Temple Tower, 20/1A SM Rd, near Flyover, T35125, F33727. Clean, spacious though slightly dingy rooms, some a/c, restaurants (poor breakfast), bar, "fantastic laundry".
D-E Lion City, 130 Gandhiji Rd, T375650, F331730, hotellioncity@hotmail.com. 25 well-appointed rooms in recently opened hotel, TV, hot water, clean, spacious, good service. Recommended.
D-E Tamil Nadu I (TTDC), Gandhiji Rd, 5 min walk from railway, T331421, F331930. 32 small rooms with bath, rather dark, some a/c, in pleasant setting around a cool inner courtyard, simple restaurant, bar, Tourist Office.
D-E Yagappa, off Trichy Rd, south of station, T30421. Good size, comfortable rooms with bath, restaurant, bar, good value.
E-F Karthik, 73 S Rampart St, T378662. 43 adequate rooms, 3 a/c, popular veg restaurant (eat off a banana leaf at lunch time), friendly.
E-F Kasi, 1494 S Rampart St, T331908. 42 nice, clean rooms (from Rs 115), some with TV, hot showers, 3 a/c. Recommended.
F Ganesh Lodge, next to railway station, T331113. 25 basic but clean rooms (delux overpriced), good veg restaurant.
F Youth Hostel, Medical College Rd, T23597. Dorm (Rs 40).

Kumbakonam *p839, map p839*
20% Luxury Tax is always added.
D Chela, 9 Ayekulam Rd, T430336, F431592, 30 rooms, 8 a/c, clean, restaurant, spacious. Recommended.
D Raya's, 18 Head PO Rd, near Tank, T432170, F422479. 43 clean rooms, some a/c with bath, TV, safes, mirrored VIP suite, good restaurant, bar, 24-hr check-out, exchanges cash.
E ARR, 21 TSR Big St, T421234. 50 good size, clean rooms, some a/c, with bath, TV, bar, room service meals.
E Femina, Head PO Rd (towards Tank), T420369. Clean and quiet rooms.
F Pandiyan, 52 Sarangapani East Sannadi St, T430397. 20 clean rooms with bath (vary, some dark), good restaurant, good value.
F Sri Abbirami, 3 John Selvaraj Nagar, T433276. Slightly grubby rooms but friendly.
A&A, Ayekulam Rd. Excellent veg restaurant opposite *Sri Abbirami*. Good, clean, north and south Indian vegetarian meals.

For an explanation of the sleeping and eating price codes used in this guide, see inside the front cover. Other relevant information is found in Essentials pages 52-57.

Swamimalai *p840*

A Sterling Swamimalai, Thimmakkudy, T0435-420044, shr.ibtmd@ elnet.ems.vsnl.net.in, in a restored 100-year-old 'heritage' home with inner courtyard, wood carving, traditional vegetarian meals, yoga, meditation.The rooms are simple with bath but cramped and dark. The Ayurveda Herbal Health Centre is recommended as a "complete experience" but US$100 each.

Chidambaram *p841, map p841*

Most hotels also do single room rates.
C-D Saradharam, 19 VGP St, T21336, F22656, hsrcdm@vsnl.com. 46 basic, tired, grubby overpriced rooms, 20 a/c, noisy bus station opposite, but very good restaurants, bar, internet.
D Ritz, 2 VGP (Venugopal Pillai) St, T23312, F21098.18 excellent a/c rooms very clean, modern hotel, rooftop restaurant. Highly recommended.
D-E Akshaya, 17-18 East Car St, T20192. 24 rooms, mostly non a/c, rooftop overlooks temple grounds, comfortable small hotel right in the centre (can be noisy).
F Raja Rajan, 162 West Car St, T22690. 14 pleasant rooms, 1 good a/c, friendly.
F Ramanathan Mansions, 127 Bazar St, T22411. 28 rooms with bath, spacious and airy (no power sockets), quieter than most, away from busy temple area, friendly.
F Ramayas Lodge, 120 South Car St, T23011. 24 clean rooms with bath in newish hotel, 2 a/c, TV, phone, good value.
F Star Lodge, 101 South Car St, T22743. 37 basic rooms set around open central landings, friendly.

Point Calimere (Kodikkarai) *p843*

November and December are busy; advance reservation is recommended from Wildlife Warden, 3 Main St, Thanjavur.
F Calimere Rest House, 4 derelict rooms.
F Poonarai llam, 14 simple rooms with bath and balcony (Rs 15 per person), caretaker may be able to arrange a meal with advance notice, intended for foreign visitors, rooms often available.
  Snacks are available from tea shops.

Vedaranyam

F PV Thevar Lodge, 40 North Main St, 50 m from bus station (English sign high up only visible in daylight), T50330. 37 basic rooms with bath and fan, can be mosquito-proofed, fairly clean, very friendly owners, good value. Indian vegetarian meals are available in the bazar near the bus stand.

🍴 Eating

Thanjavur *p836, map p837*
In hotels:
🍴 **Oriental Towers**, for quality food.
🍴 **Parisutham**, Good North Indian meat dishes, excellent vegetarian *thalis* ("best of 72 curries"!), service can be slow.
🍴 **Algappa**, Gandhiji Rd. A/c restaurant.
🍴 **New Bombay Sweets**, tasty Indian snacks.
🍴 **Sathars**, Tandoori recommended.
🍴 **Vasantha Vihar** on west side of Railway Station Rd between station and *Tamil Nadu hotel*. Good *thalis* and snacks.

Chidambaram *p841, map p841*
🍴 **Hotel Saradharam**, 10 VGP St. A/c. Excellent range of meals, pizzas and European dishes. Good variety and value, popular.
🍴 **Sree Ganesa Bhavan**, West Car St. South Indian vegetarian. Friendly, helpful staff.
🍴 **Udupi**, West Car St. Good veg, nice, clean.

➕ Entertainment

Thanjavur *p836, map p837*
Bharat Natyam, performances by Guru Herambanathan from a family of dancers, 1/2378 Krishanayar Lane, Ellaiyamman Koil St, T333759.
South Zone Cultural Centre Palace, T331272, organizes programmes in the Big Temple, 2nd and 4th Sat; free.

✻ Festivals and events

Chidambaram *p841, map p841*
Feb/Mar: Natyanjali dance festival for 5 days starting with *Maha Sivaratri*. **Jun/Jul**: Ani Tirumanjanam Festival. **Dec/Jan**: Markazhi Tiruvathirai Festival.

Tamil Nadu Listings: Chola Heartland & the Kaveri Delta

O Shopping

Thanjavur *p836, map p837*
You may not export any object over 100 years old. Thanjavur is known for its decorative copper plates with silver and brass relief (repoussé) work, raised "glass" painting, wood carving and bronze and brass casting. Granite carving is being revived by the Government through centres which produce superbly sculpted images. Crafts shops abound in Gandhiji Rd Bazar. **Jaising**, at hotel *Parisutham*, arranges free workshop visits.

'Antiques'
Govindarajan's, 31 Kuthirai Katti St, Karandhai (a few kilometres from town), T330282, is a treasure house of pricey old, and affordable new pieces; artists and craftsmen at work.

▲▲ Activities and tours

Thanjavur *p836, map p837*
Tours
TTDC *Temple tour* of Thanjavur and surroundings by a/c coach; enquire at Tourist Office. Mon-Fri, 1000-1745.

⊖ Transport

Thanjavur *p836, map p837*
Locally there are unmetered and tourist taxis, cycle-rickshaws and auto-rickshaws and a city bus service.

Air
Tiruchirapalli airport is about 1 hr by car.

Bus
Long distance Old State and Municipal Bus Stand, south of the fort, for local services. Buses from Kumbakonam stop at the corner before going out to the New Bus Stand, T333455. CRC (Cholan), T332455. New (Mofussil) Bus Stand is on Trichy Rd. Daily service to **Chidambaram** (4 hrs), **Kumbakonam** (1 hr), **Chennai** (8 hrs), **Madurai** (3½ hrs), **Pondicherry** (6 hrs), **Tirupathi**, **Tiruchirappalli** (1½ hrs). Also to **Vedaranyam** (100 km) for Point Calimere, about hourly, 4-4½ hrs.

Train
Long distance Reservations, T331131, 0800-1400, 1500-1700 Mon-Sat; 0800-1400 Sun. **Bangalore**: *Thanjavur Mysore Exp, 6231,* 1845, 11½ hrs, continues to **Mysore**, 3¼ hrs. **Chennai (ME)**: *Rockfort Exp, 6878,* 2000, 9 hrs. **Tiruchirappalli**: *Tambaram Rameswaram Exp, 6701,* 0520, 2 hrs; *Fast Passenger Exp, 6761,* 1300, 3 hrs; *Cholan Exp, 6853,* 1700, 1¾ hrs.

Kumbakonam *p839, map p839*
Bus
Long distance TN Govt Express buses to **Chennai**, No 305, several daily (7½ hrs); half hourly to Thanjavur.

Car hire Half day for excursions, Rs 400.

Train
Long distance Station 2 km from town centre. Trains to Chennai (Egmore), 1010-2110, change at Tambaram (8½-9 hrs), Chidambaram (2 hrs), Thanjavur (50 mins) and Tiruchirappalli, 0600-1555 (2½ hrs).

Chidambaram *p841, map p841*
Bike hire Along VGP St.

Bus
Chaotic bus station. Daily services to Chennai, Madurai, Thanjavur, and to Karaikal (2 hrs), Nagapattinam and Pondicherry (2 hrs).

Train
Reservations T22298, 0800-1200, 1400-1700; Sun 0800-1400. **Chennai (E)** (change at Tambaram): *Rameswaram Tambaram Exp, 6702,* 2307, 6¾ hrs; *Cholan Exp, 6854,* 1153, 6 hrs. **Kumbakonam**: *Sethu Exp, 6713,* 1832, 2 hrs, continues to **Thanjavur**, 3 hrs and **Tiruchirappalli**, 5 hrs; *Cholan Exp, 6853,* 1410, 2 hrs, continues to **Thanjavur**, 3 hrs, and **Tiruchirapalli**, 4¾ hrs.

Kodikkarai *p843*
Bus
Buses via Vedaranyam which has services to/from Thanjavur, Tiruchirapalli, Nagapattinam, Chennai etc. From Thanjavur buses leave the New Bus Stand for **Vedaranyam** (100 km) about hourly

(4-4½ hrs); buses and vans from there to Kodikkarai (11 km) which take about 30 mins. Avoid being dropped at 'Sri Rama's Feet' on the way, near a shrine which is of no special interest.

● Directory

Thanjavur *p836, map p837*
Banks Canara Bank, South Main St, changes TCs. **Hospital** Govt Hospital, Hospital Rd, south of the old town. **Post office** Head Post and Telegraph Office are off the Railway Station Rd. **Tourist offices** Tamil Nadu, Jawan Bhawan, T333017, 1000-1745, Mon-Fri, very helpful. **Useful addresses** Police,

south of the Big Temple between the canal and the railway, T332200.

Kumbakonam *p839, map p839*
Banks Changing money is difficult. State Bank of India, TSR Big St. **Internet** End of Kamaraj Rd, close to clock tower. **Post office** Post office near Mahamakam Tank.

Chidambaram *p841, map p841*
Banks Changing money can be difficult. City Union Bank, West Car St has exchange facilities. **Indian Bank**, 64 South Car St, changes cash. Post office Head Post Office, North Car St. **Tourist offices** At *Hotel Tamil Nadu*, Railway Feeder Rd, T22739.

Coimbatore and the Nilgiri Hills

Surrounded by rich agricultural land and within sight of the towering Nilgiri Hills, Coimbatore is high enough to be significantly cooler and pleasanter than the coastal plains. One of South India's most important industrial cities, the development of hydro-electricity from the Pykara Falls in the 1930s led to a cotton boom in Coimbatore. The centre of a rich agricultural area, Coimbatore has a noted agricultural university. There isn't much here in the way of tourist attractions.
▸▸ *For Sleeping, Eating and other listings, see pages 854-861.*

Coimbatore → *Phone code: 0422. Colour map 7, grid B3. Population: 923,000.*

Background

Coimbatore is at the heart of a region of great historical importance, an area of contact between the plains of Tamil Nadu to the east, the plateaus of Mysore to the north and the coastal plains of Kerala, reached through the Palakkad gap to the south. The frequency with which the word *palayam* ('encampment') occurs indicates the extent to which this was also a region of conflict between the *Cholas*, the *Pandiyas* and the *Cheras*. Sadly, the city has experienced outbreaks of violence, so enquire about the situation before visiting.

Sights

The Siva temple at Perur, 6 km west of the centre has outstanding ceiling decorations, including many paintings. Thirumalai Nayaka's outer buildings date from 1623-59 but the inner shrine is much older.

College Museum ① *closed Sun and Govt holidays, 0900-1200, 1400-1700, Tamil Nadu Agricultural Univ,* has special collections of minerals, rocks, insects, pests, fungal diseases, snakes, silver and gold medals. Guide service. **Gass Forest Museum** ① *closed Sun, 2nd Sat and public holidays, 1900-1300, 1400-1630, 3½ km north of town,* exhibits forestry and forest products. Worth visiting.

Salem → *Phone code: 0427. Colour map 7, grid B4. Population: 693,200.*

Salem, an important transport junction, is surrounded by hills with the Shevaroy and Nagaramalai Hills to the north. It is a busy, rapidly growing industrial town – particularly for textiles and metal based industries – with modern shopping centres. It has little to offer and it is more pleasant to move on to Yercaud.

The old town is on the east bank of the River Manimutheru. Along Bazar Street, each evening, cotton carpets made nearby. The **cemetery**, next to the Collector's office, has some interesting tombstones. To the southeast of the town on a ridge of the Jarugumalai Hills is a highly visible *Naman* painted in *chunam* and ochre. The temple on the nearby hill (1919), is particularly sacred to the weavers' community. Some 600 steps lead to the top which has excellent views over the town.

The **Government Museum** ① *closed Fri and 2nd Sat, 0900-1230, 1400-1700,* has a largely disappointing collection including a few Chola bronzes, a portrait of Gandhi by Ramalingam and a library.

Coimbatore

■ Sleeping	3 KK Residency & Indian	● Eating
1 Channma International	Coffee House	1 Dakshin
2 Heritage Inn, City	4 Meena	2 Pushpa Bakery
Tower & Cloud Nine	5 Niligris Nest	3 Royal Hindu
Restaurant	6 Tamil Nadu (Star)	4 Solai Drive-in

0 metres 300
0 yards 300

Yercaud and the Shevaroy Hills

→ *Phone code: 04281. Altitude: 1,515 m . Season: throughout the year, busy Apr-Jun and Christmas.*

The beautiful drive up the steep and sharply winding ghat road from Salem quickly brings a sharp freshness to the air as it climbs to over 1500 m. The minor 'resort' has a small artificial **lake** with Anna Park nearby. Some attractive though unsignposted walks start here. In May there is a special festival focused on the **Shevaroyan Temple**, on top of the third highest peak in the hill range. Many tribal people take part, but access is only possible on foot. Ask for details in the Tamil Nadu Tourist Office in Chennai.

Just outside the town is **Lady's Seat**, which overlooks the ghat road and gives wonderful views across the Salem plains. Near the old Norton Bungalow on the Shevaroyan Temple Road, is another well known local spot, **Bear's Cave**. Formed by two huge boulders, it is occupied by huge colonies of bats. The whole area is full of botanical interest. There is an **Orchidarium-cum-Nursery** and a **Horticultural Research Station**.

The Nilgiri Ghat Road → *Colour map 7, grid B3.*

The ghat journey up to Coonoor, 32 km away, is one of the most scenic in South India, giving superb views over the plains below. Between Mettupalayam and the start of the ghat road, there are magnificent groves of tall slender areca nut palms.

Mettupalayam

Mettupalayam has become the centre for the areca nut trade as well as producing synthetic gems. Areca palms are immensely valuable trees; the nut is used across India wrapped in betel vine leaves – two of the essential ingredients of India's universal after-meal digestive, *paan*. The town is the starting point of the ghat railway line up to Ooty, see page 852. If you take the early morning train you can continue to Mysore by bus from Ooty on the same day, making a very pleasant trip.

Coonoor → *Phone code: 0423. Colour map 7, grid B3. Population: 50,100. Altitude: 1,800 m.*

Coonor is smaller and much less developed than Ooty, and enjoys a milder climate. It is a pleasant place to relax, with an interesting market although hotel touts can be unpleasantly pushy on arrival. The picturesque hills around the town are covered in coffee and tea plantations and it is an ideal place for walking.

Ins and outs

Getting there When you arrive by train, or by bus, which doesn't always visit the main bus-stand if continuing to Ooty, the main town of Lower Coonoor will be to the east, across the river. Upper Coonoor, with the better hotels 2-3 km away, is further east.

Getting there See Transport, page 860, for further details.

Climate Summer: maximum 24°C, minimum 14°C; Winter: maximum 19°C, min 9°C. Annual rainfall: 130 cm. Best season: Apr-Jun, Sep-Oct. Clothing: Summer: light woollens, Winter: woollens.

Sights

Sim's Park ① *0800-1830, Rs 5, camera Rs 25, video Rs 250* (mid-19th century), named in 1874 after JD Sim, a secretary to the Madras Club, is a large park in Upper

Coonoor. On the slopes of a ravine this clean, well maintained park has been developed into a botanical garden partly in the Japanese style. It has over 330 varieties of roses and many gentle monkeys! The Fruit and Vegetable Show is held in May. Coonoor also has the **Pomological Station** where the State Agricultural Department researches on fruits including persimmon, apricot and pomegranates. The **Pasteur Institute** ① *opposite the main entrance to Sim's Park, guided tours on Sat between 1030 and 1115, or with permission of the Director,* established in 1907, researches into rabies and manufactures polio vaccine. Contact the United Planters' Association of South India (UPASI), Glenview, to visit tea and coffee plantations. The **Daily Market**, near the Bus Stand, is a fascinating warren of tiny stalls and shops. The **Wellington barracks**, 3 km northeast of Lower Coonoor, which are the raison d'être for the town, were built in 1852. It is now the Headquarters of the Indian Defence Services Staff College and also of the Madras Regiment, which is over 250 years old and the oldest in the Indian Army.

Walks

Lamb's Rock, on a high precipice, 9 km away, has good views over the Coimbatore plains and coffee and tea estates on the slopes. At **Dolphin's Nose** ① *several buses 0700-1615*, 12 km away, you can see Catherine Falls, a further 10 km away. Best early morning. **Droog** ① *buses 0900, 1345*, 13 km away, has ruins of a 16th-century fort used by Tipu Sultan, and requires a 3-km walk.

Udhagamandalam (Ooty)

→ *Phone code: 0423. Colour map 7, grid B3. Population: 93,900. Altitude: 2,286 m.*

Known as the 'Queen of the Blue Mountains', along with Kotagiri and Coonoor nearby, Ooty is famous for its rolling hills covered in pine and eucalyptus forests and its coffee and tea plantations. Developed as a hill station by the British, it is no longer the haven it once was; the centre of town has been heavily built up and can be quite unpleasant in the holiday months of April to June, and again around October. Stay in the outskirts which are still pleasant and quiet.

Ins and outs

Getting there The only way to arrive in Ooty in style is on the quaint rack and pinion train, when it is running. Alternatively, there are buses from all over the State and from Mysore. The bus stand is just south of the railway station, close to the bazar and many hotels.

Getting about Ooty is quite spread out and hilly, so autos and taxis are the most practical means of getting about. See Transport, page 860, for further details. Kodaikkanal is a better choice of hill station.

Climate: summer: maximum 25°C, minimum 10°C; winter: maximum 21°C, minimum 5°C. Best season: Apr-Jun.

History

Near the borders of three southern states, Udhagamandalam had been inhabited by *Toda* tribal people who lived in villages or 'munds' consisting of a handful of huts, see page 783. The British shortened the name to 'Ooty' and because of its climate developed it as a summer retreat. A Government House was built, and the British lifestyle developed with cottages and clubs – tennis, golf, riding – and teas on the lawn. Most of the buildings that survive are sadly very neglected.

At the **Botanical Gardens** ⓘ *0800-1800, Rs 25, camera, Rs 50, video Rs 500, 3 km northeast of railway station,* there are over 1,000 varieties of plants, shrubs and trees including orchids, ferns, alpines and medicinal plants among beautiful lawns and glass houses. To the east of the garden in a Toda *mund* is the Wood House made of logs. The Annual Flower Show is held in the third week of May.

The **Rose Garden** ⓘ *0800-1800, 750 m from Charing Cross,* has over 1,500 varieties of roses.

Ooty Lake ⓘ *0800-1800, Rs 3, camera Rs 10, video Rs 100,* 2½-km long, built in 1825 as a vast irrigation tank, is now more than half over-grown with water-hyacinth though it is still used enthusiastically for boating and pedallo hire.

Kandal Cross, 3 km west of the railway station, is a Roman Catholic shrine considered the 'Jerusalem of the East'. During the clearing of the area as a graveyard in 1927 an enormous 4-m high boulder was found and since then a cross was erected. Now a relic of the True Cross brought to India by an Apostolic delegate is shown to pilgrims every day. The annual feast is in May.

Udhagamandalam (Ooty)

Tamil Nadu Coimbatore & the Nilgiri Hills Udhagamandalam

■ Sleeping		● Eating	
1 Alkapuri	8 Sanjay	1 Blue Hills	
2 Chanderi, Restaurant	9 Savoy (Taj)	2 Hot Breads	
& Travel Agents	10 Southern Star	3 Kebab Corner	
3 Dasaprakesh	11 Sterling Resorts	4 Sharma's	
4 Durga	12 Tamil Nadu	5 Shinkow's Chinese	
5 Edassery's	13 YMCA	6 Sri Vijaya Vilas	
6 Garden View	14 YWCA	7 Top Café & New	
7 Geetha Lodge		Tandoor Mahal	

N

0 metres	300
0 yards	300

The Blue Mountain Railway

The delightful narrow gauge steam Mountain Railway, in its blue and cream livery, goes from Mettupalayam to Ooty via Coonoor negotiating 16 tunnels and 31 major bridges climbing from 326 m to 2,193 m. It was opened on 15 June 1899. The railway scenes of the 'Marabar Express' in the film of A Passage to India were shot here. The whole 4½-hour (46 km) journey through tea plantations and lush forests is highly recommended for the scenery (First Class front coach for best views). Hillgrove (17 km) a 'watering stop' in the past, and Coonoor (27 km) with its loco shed,

have refreshments and clean toilets.

The Blue Mountain train has limited First Class seating and can get very crowded in season, though some trains have a new, more spacious First Class carriage. See Mettupalayam, page 859. For enthusiasts, the more expensive Heritage Steam Chariot with special spacious carriages runs between Ooty and Runneymede picnic area, 23 km away, at weekends (more often in season).

The drawback is that you can be stranded for hours when the engine breaks down; some decide to scramble to the nearest road to flag down a bus.

St Stephen's Church was Ooty's first church, built in the 1820s. Much of the wood is said to be from Tipu Sultan's Lal Bagh Palace in Srirangapatnam. The inside of the church and the graveyard at the rear are worth seeing.

Dodabetta ① *buses from Ooty, 1000-1500, autos and taxis (Rs 200 round trip) go to the summit*, is 10 km east of the railway station off the Kotagiri road. The 'big mountain' reaches 2,638 m and is the second highest in the Western Ghats sheltering Coonoor from the southwest monsoons when Ooty gets heavy rains. The top is often shrouded in mist. There is a viewing platform at the summit, near where you can see a species of rhododendron growing in the wild.

Hiking or simply **walking** is excellent in the Nilgiris, undisturbed, quiet and interesting. Climbing Dodabetta or Mukurti is hardly a challenge. The longer walks through the sholas are best undertaken with a guide. It is possible to see characteristic features of Toda settlements such as *munds* and *boas*, see page 850. **Dodabetta-Snowdon-Ooty walk** starts at "Dodabetta Junction" directly opposite the 3-km road to the summit. It is a pleasant path which curves gently downhill through a variety of woodland – eucalyptus, conifer – back to Ooty and need take no more than a couple of hours. For longer treks, contact Nilgiris Trekking Association, Kavitha Nilayam, 31-D Bank Road, or R Seniappan, 137 Upper Bazar, T444449, sehiappan@yahoo.com

Excursions

In Ughaghamandalam Mukurti Peak ① *buses from Ooty every 30 mins from 0630 or you can take a tour, book early as they are popular*, is 36 km away, off the Gudalur road. After 26 km you reach the 6-km long Mukurti Lake. Mukurti Peak, not an easy climb, is to the west. The name suggests a severed nose to describe the peak. The Todas believe that the souls of the dead and the sacrificed buffaloes leap to the next world from this sacred peak. It is an excellent place to escape for walking and to view the occasional wildlife or to fish from the lake or go boating.

Avalanche ① *buses from Ooty, 1110*, a valley, is a beautiful part of the *shola*, 24 km from town, with plenty of rhododendrons, magnolias and orchids and a trout stream running through, and is excellent for walking and superb scenery. Forestry Department Guest House, clean with good food; Avalanche Top is 4 km from the bungalow.

The **River Pykara** ① *several buses from 0630-2030, or take a car or bicycle,* 19 km from Ooty, has a dam and power plant. There is breathtaking scenery. The Falls, about 6 km from the bridge on the main road, are best in July though it is very wet then, but they are also worth visiting from August to December.

Kotagiri ① *Frequent services from Coonoor, Mettupalayam Railway Station and Ooty.* Kotagiri has an altitude of 1,980 m and is 29 km from Ooty. It sits on the northeast crest of the plateau overlooking the plains. It has a milder climate than Ooty. The name comes from Kotar-Keri, the street of the *Kotas* who were one of the original hill tribes and have a village to the west of the town.

You can visit some **scenic spots** – St Catherine Falls (8 km) and Elk Falls (7 km), or one of the peaks – Kodanad Viewpoint (16 km) which you reach through the tea estates or one of the several buses running from 0610, or Rangaswamy Pillar which is an isolated rock and the conical Rangaswamy Peak.

★ Mudumalai Wildlife Sanctuary

→ *Phone code: 0423. Colour map 7, grid B3.*
The sanctuary adjoins Bandipur beyond the Moyar River, its hills (885-1,000 m), ravines, flats and valleys being an extension of the same environment. The park is one of the more popular and is trying to limit numbers of visitors to reduce disturbance to the elephants.

Ins and outs
There is a Range Office at Kargudi and a Reception Centre, 0630-1800, at Theppakadu where buses between Mysore anld Ooty stop. Open through the year, 0630-0900, 1600-1800. See Transport, page 860, for details. Best seasons: Sep-Oct, Mar-May when the undergrowth dies down, it is easier to see the animals, particularly when they are on the move at dawn. Entrance Rs 15 Indians, Rs 150 foreigners; still camera Rs 10.

Wildlife
The sanctuary has large herds of elephant, gaur, sambar, barking deer, wild dog, Nilgiri langur, bonnet monkey, wild boar, four-horned antelope and the rarer tiger and leopard, as well as smaller mammals and many birds and reptiles. **Elephant Camp**, south of Theppakadu. Wild elephants are tamed here. Some are bred in captivity and trained to work for the timber industry. You can watch the elephants being fed in the late afternoon, learn about each individual elephant's diet and the specially prepared 'cakes' of food.

Viewing
You can hire a jeep for about Rs 6 per kilmetre but must be accompanied by a guide. Most 'Night Safaris' are best avoided – "you go up and down the main road by jeep". Elephant rides at 0630 (Rs 100 per elephant for four for 45 minutes); check timing and book in advance at the Wildlife Office, Mahalingam Building, Coonoor Road, Ooty. They can be fun even though you may not see much wildlife. The 46-seater coach, first come, first served, Rs 25 each, can be noisy with shrieking children. There are *machans* near water holes and salt licks and along the Moyar River. With patience you can see a lot, especially rare and beautiful birds. Trekking in the remoter parts of the forest with guides can be arranged from some lodges. You can spend a day climbing the hill and bathe at the impressive waterfalls. The core area is not open to visitors

Listings: Coimbatore and the Nilgiri Hills

🔵 Sleeping

Coimbatore *p847, map p848*
There are many budget hotels in the area
around the bus stations,to the east of the
railway station, and in the Gandhipuram area.
B Heritage Inn, 38 Sivaswamy Rd, T231451,
F233223, www.hotelheritageinn.com. 63
modern, a/c rooms ('standard' good value),
good restaurants, internet, excellent service.
B Nilgiris Nest, 739-A Avanashi Rd, T217247,
F217131, nilgiris@md3.vsnl.net.in, 2 km rly. 38
a/c rooms, some small, restaurant, bar,
amazing supermarket downstairs (for Western
snackers!), business facilities, roof garden.
B-C City Tower, Sivaswamy Rd (just off Dr
Nanjappa Rd), Gandhipuram, near bus stand,
T230641, F230103, hotelcitytower@sify.com.
91 very good, re-decorated rooms, some a/c,
small balconies, 2 restaurants (rooftop
tandoori; ground floor), no alcohol, very
good service. Recommended.
D-E Tamil Nadu (TTDC), Dr Nanjappa Rd,
opposite Bus Station, T302176,F303511. 49
rooms, some a/c with TV (charge), restaurant,
bar, "nice and quiet, though rather run down".
D-F Channma International, 18/109 Big
Bazaar St, T396631, F396443. 36 spacious
clean rooms, tiny windows, in oldish hotel
with art-deco styling, restaurant, Internet,
health club and pool next door.
E-F KK Residency, 7 Shastri Rd, by Central
Bus Stand, Ramnagar, T232433, F236996.
42 smallish but clean rooms, 6 a/c, good
condition, restaurant, friendly service.
E-F Meena, 109 Kalingarayar St, T235420.
30 clean and pleasant rooms in small
family-hotel, veg restaurant.

Salem *p848*
It is advisable to choose rooms away from
the road side.
C Salem Castle, A-4 Bharati St, Swarnapuri,
T448702, F446996, 4 km railway. 64
comfortable, very clean a/c rooms,
restaurants (good Chinese but expensive),
coffee shop, bar, exchange, pool, rather
brash modern hotel. The rest are Indian style.

D-E City View, Omalur Main Rd, T449715.
Rooms with bath, some clean, large a/c,
meals, travel. *Shree Saravanabhavan* in the
same block does good south Indian veg food.
D-E Ganesh Mahal, 323 Omalur Rd, T332820,
F443098. 45 pleasant rooms, TV, good
restaurant, bar. Modern and comfortable.
D-E Raj Castle, 320 Omalur Rd, T333532.
21 nicley fitted rooms, 4 a/c, some with
balcony, TV, hotwater mornings, tourist car.
D-E Selvam, near *Raj Castle*, T449331. Clean
rooms with bath, some a/c, good restaurant.
F Railway Retiring Rooms, battered but
with olde-worlde feel.

Yercaud *p849*
Most hotels offer off- season discounts
Jan-Mar, Aug-Dec.
C Sterling Resort, near Lady's Seat, T22700,
F22537. 59 rooms (few **B** suites), modern,
excellent views.
D Shevaroys, Main (Hospital) Rd, near lake,
T22288, F22387. 32 rooms, 11 **C** cottages
with baths, restaurant, bar, good views.
D Tamil Nadu (TTDC), Salem-Yercaud Ghat
Rd, near lake, behind Panchayat Office,
T22273, F22745. 12 rooms, restaurant, garden.
E Kapilaksa, Arthur Seat Rd (10-min walk
from bus stand). Clean rooms, good views
from balcony and roof, quiet, no discount.
F Youth Hostel, dorm bed (Rs 125),
simple, reservations: Manager or Chennai
T830390, F830380.

Mettupalayam *p849*
D Saravana Bhavan, out of town on Ooty
road near gates to Black Thunder Water
theme park. New and finding its feet.
E-F Bharath Bharan, 200 m from railway
station. Very basic, some with bath and a/c,
could be cleaner, quiet surroundings.
F Surya International, town centre, fairly
clean rooms (Rs 150), rooftop restaurant,
often empty, quiet, but characterless.
D, 5 km outside, on the Ooty Rd, is an open
air restaurant, clean toilets.
Karna Hotel in bus station is good for *dosas*.

 *For an explanation of the sleeping and eating price codes used in this guide, see inside the
front cover. Other relevant information is found in Essentials pages 52-57.*

Coonoor p849

Most hotels are 3-5 km from the station and bus stand.

AL Garden Retreat (Taj), Church Rd, Upper Coonoor, T220021, F232775. 33 rooms, spacious cottage style and homely (**A** off-season), many with open fires, very well kept, good dining room though service can be slow, beautiful gardens, no pool.

B Velan Ritz, 14 Orange Grove Rd, Bedford, T230632, F230606. Completely rebuilt, 21 very comfortable rooms, good garden.

D La Barrier Inn, Coonoor Club Rd, T232561. 6 spacious, clean rooms with TV and hot water, breakfast only, quiet location, lovely views.

E Tamil Nadu (TTDC), Ooty Rd, Mt Pleasant (1 km north of station), T232813. Simple rooms, TV, restaurant, bar and *Youth Hostel* dorm.

E Vivek Tourist Home, Upasi Rd (near Bedford Circle), Upper Coonoor, T230658. 60 clean rooms with bath and balcony, some **D** with TV, restaurant. Recommended.

E 'Wyoming' Guest House (YWCA), near Hospital. Upper Coonoor (auto from bus stand Rs 25), T234426. 8 large rooms and 2 dorms (8-bedded), with character, excellent food (no alcohol) but check bill, garden, friendly, helpful, popular, "a great place to stay", manager qualified in alternative therapies (runs clinic and courses). Book ahead. For **paying guest accommodation** contact Ms Padmini at 'Sudharama', Mount Pleasant, T31933.

Udhagamandalam p850, map p851

Rates quoted are for the 'Season'. Good discounts Jul-Mar except during Puja and Christmas. Add 30% tax in upper categories.

Winter nights can be bitterly cold and hotel fireplaces are often inadequate.

AL Savoy (Taj), 77 Sylkes Rd, T444142, F443318. 40 rooms (**A** off-season) but rather dreary and overpriced. Worth visiting for its interesting history and lovely gardens.

A Holiday Inn (Gem Park), Sheddon Rd, T441761, F444302. 95 rooms, very modern, fine views, average restaurants.

A-B Aruna (Comfort Inn), Gorishola Rd, T444140, F444229. 88 comfortable rooms, 'Victorian' architecture in large landscaped grounds with superb views.

A-B Sullivan Court Selbourne Rd, T441416, F441417, wgsull@md5.vsnl.net.in. Very comfortable rooms in new smart hotel, very good restaurants, rate negotiable.

B Monarch, off Havelock Rd, T444408, F442455. Comfortable rooms, expensive suites, indoor heated pool.

B Southern Star (Merit Inn), 22 Havelock Rd, T443601. 67 rooms, some refurbished, restaurant (over-attentive service), tea garden, good, clean, comfortable, attracts filmstars, bar "closed" but drinks available.

C Glyngarth, Golf Club Rd, Fingerpost (2 km from centre), T445754, glyngarth@sify.com. 5 double rooms with period furniture, modern baths, in a colonial building (1853), varied meals (fresh garden produce), large grounds, characterful.

C-D Alkapuri, 36 Ettines Rd, T440648, F449468. 50 rooms set around courtyard, clinically-clean throughout, friendly.

C-D Durga, Ettines Rd, T443837. 27 well-appointed rooms, some very spacious, some with tubs, hot water mornings, cheaper (smaller) rooms good value.

D Dasaprakash, Ettines Rd, T442434. 100 rooms (no shower/bath), vegetarian restaurants, coffee shop, exchange, garden, comfortable, quiet location.

D Edassery's, Commercial Rd, T442239, F447185. 18 pleasant, well-furnished rooms, good, if a little small, hot water, TV, restaurant, friendly staff.

D Ooty Gate, Coonoor Rd, few mins' walk from Charing Cross, T441622, F444258. 85 very clean rooms with bath (some **C** suites), heaters (best at rear with views, quieter), good restaurant (limited off-season), bar, recommended for service and value.

D Tamil Nadu (TTDC), Charing Cross, up steps by Tourist Office, T444378, F444369. Rooms and penthouse with good views, restaurant, bar, exchange, pleasant hotel.

D YWCA Anandagiri, Ettines Rd, T442218. Some pleasant cottages, cheap dorm beds, popular with the young, not central, restaurant.

Most budget accommodation is centred around Commercial Rd and Ettines Rd; many are filthy and noisy flea pits. Avoid Youth Hostel.

E **Reflections**, North Lake Rd, T443834. 6 rooms (cheaper dorm beds), clean, homely guest house with good views, pleasant dining room serving good food, friendly owners but "not recommended for females travelling alone".
E **Sanjay**, Charing Cross, T443160. 55 rooms, some with small balcony, TV, dorm beds (Rs 30-50), restaurants, sometimes noisy at night, gloomy choice of paint but clean.
E-F **Garden View**, North Lake Rd, by Rly station, T443349. 26 good size rooms with bath, deluxe, with better views and hot tap, restaurant, a little tired but clean.
E-F **Geetha**, Commercial Rd, T444186. 13 very clean rooms, cheap dorm, shared Indian toilet, central but fairly quiet, good value.

Kotagiri *p853*

If you wish to stay overnight there is:
E **Top Hill Lodge**, near Police Station, with rooms, restaurant and bar.
F **Blue Star**, next to Bus Station, rooms with shower and toilet in modern building.

Mudumalai Wildlife Sanctuary *p853*

Advance booking is essential especially during season and at weekends. Better near Masinagudi which also has restaurants and shops. Some in **Bokkapuram**, 3 km further south. Ask private lodges for pick-up if arriving by bus at Theppakadu.
B **Bamboo Banks Farm Guest House**, Masinagudi, T526222, bambanks@hotmail.com. 6 clean rooms, 4 in cottages in a fine setting, attractive garden, good food, birdwatching, riding, jeep.
C **Jungle Retreat**, Bokkapuram, T/F526469, www.jungle-retreat.com. Large rooms with modern baths, private terrace, superb views, "wonderful quiet place", friendly relaxed owners (Mr and Mrs Mathias), high standards, good treks with local guides, elephant rides, TCs accepted. Highly recommended.
C **Monarch Safari Park**, Bokkapuram, on a hill side, T526326. 14 rooms in twin *machan* huts on stilts with bath (sadly rats enter at night), open-sided restaurant, cycles, birdwatching, good riding (Rs 150 per hour), some sporting facilities, meditation centre, large grounds, "lovely spot", management slack, friendly if slow service.
C-D **Blue Valley Resorts**, Bokkapuram, T526244. 8 comfortable huts (C suites), restaurants, scenic location, wildlife tours.

C-D **Jungle Hut**, near Bokkapuram, T526240. 12 clean, simple rooms with bath in 3 stone cottages in valley, good food – "lovely home cooking", pool, jeep hire, game viewing and treks, very friendly welcome. Recommended.
D **Forest Hills Farm**, 300 m from *Jungle Hut*, T526216. 6 modern rooms with bath and views, good food, friendly, game viewing. Recommended.
D **Jungle Trails**, 2 km off Sighur Ghat Rd (23 km from Ooty, ask bus to stop; flat walk, well marked), T526256. 3 clean rooms in a bungalow, rustic ("bamboo shutters propped open with poles"), dorm beds (Rs 100), and *machan* good for viewing the moving tapestry (4 trails and pool visible), meals Rs 200, dedicated to animal watching (quiet after dark; no candles on verandah, no sitting in the garden by moonlight), *Cheetal Walk*, 1997 by A Davidas, the owner's father. Recommended.
D-E **Mountania**, Masinagudi (500 m from bus stand), T526337. Rooms in cottages (prices vary), "nice but a bit overpriced", restaurant, jeep tour to waterfalls, easy animal spotting (evening better than morning).

Theppakadu

E **Tamil Nadu** (TTDC *Youth Hostel*), T526249. 3 rooms, 24 beds in dorm (Rs 45), restaurant, van for viewing. Several Government Forest Department huts charge Rs 80 for double rooms; reserve in advance through the Wildlife Warden, Mudumalai WLS, 1st floor, Mahalingam Building, Coonoor Rd, Ooty, T44098 or Wildlife Warden, Kargudi, T26.
Also near the river:
Log House, 2 rooms, 4 dorm beds (Rs 20).
Sylvan Lodge, 4 rooms, recommended.

Kargudi

Rest House and **Annexe**, ask for deluxe rooms.
Abhayaranyam Rest House, 2 rooms.
Annexe, 2 rooms, recommended.
F **Peacock**, dormitory, 50 beds, food excellent.
Minivet and **Morgan**, dormitory, 8 and 12 beds. All Rs 5 per bed

Masinagudi

Log House, 5 rooms.
Rest House, 3 rooms.

🍴 Eating

Coimbatore *p847, map p848*
♔♔♔ **Cloud Nine**, *City Tower Hotel*. International. Excellent views from rooftop of one of city's tallest buildings, good food (try asparagus soup) and service but puzzling menu, nice atmosphere (full of families on Sun evening).
♔♔ **China Restaurant**, 410 Trichy Rd.
♔♔ **Dakshin** in *Shree Annapoorna Hotel* Complex, 47 East Arokiasamy Rd, RS Puram. International. Very smart serving good food.
♔♔ **Dasa**. Vegetarian. A/c, good ice creams.
♔♔ **Solai Drive-in**, Nehru Stadium, near VOC Park. Chinese, Indian food and good ice creams.
♔ **Indian Coffee House**, Ramar Koil St. South Indian snacks.
♔ **Pushpa Bakery**, Nehru Rd.
♔ **Richy Rich**, DB Rd. Good milk shakes.
♔ **Royal Hindu**, opposite Junction station. Indian vegetarian.

Coonoor *p849*
The Only Place, Sim's Park Rd. Simple, homely, good food.
Sri Lakshmi, next to bus station. Freshly cooked, quality veg; try *paneer* butter masala and *Kashmiri naan*.

Udhagamandalam *p850, map p851*
There are usually bars in larger hotels. 'Southern Star' is recommended, though expensive
♔♔♔ **Savoy**, recommended for relaxed atmosphere and good, not-too-spicy food, buffets more affordable.
♔♔ **New Tandoor Mahal**, Commercial Rd. Smart, serving meat and chicken dishes, good vegetarian curries, beers, but over-zealous waiters.
♔♔ **Ritz**. Good food, excellent lemon sodas.
♔ **Blue Hills**, Charing Cross. Good value Indian and Continental, non-vegetarian.
♔ **Kabab Corner**, Commercial Rd. Indian. Good curries and naan, pleasing upmarket, western décor.
♔ **Kaveri**, Charing Cross. Good cakes and savoury snacks but atmosphere nil.
♔ **Sharma Bhojanalaya** 12C Lower Bazar. Upstairs, comfortable (padded banquettes!), overlooks race course, good vegetarian lunch *thali* (Rs 40).
♔ **Shinkow's**, 42 Commissioner's Rd (near Collector's Office). Authentic Chinese, popular, especially late evening.

♔ **Woodlands**, vegetarian (no alcohol) in pleasant character building.
♔ **Hot Breads**, Charing Cross. Tasty hot dogs, pizzas etc.
♔ **VK Bakery**, 148 Commercial Rd. Recommended for fresh meat and vegetarian patties, bread and cakes.
♔ **Nilgiri Dairy Farms** outlets sell quality milk products.

🎭 Entertainment

Coimbatore *p847, map p848*
Cinema
Central, Mettupalayam Rd, near Coimbatore North station, shows English films.

Udhagamandalam *p850, map p851*
The renovated 100-year-old 'Assembly Rooms' Garden Rd, T42250, shows films in English.

✺ Festivals and events

Udhagamandalam *p850, map p851*
Jan: Ooty celebrates **Pongal**. **May**: the Annual Flower and Dog Shows in the Botanical Gardens. *Summer Festival* of cultural programmes with stars from all over India.

🛍 Shopping

Coimbatore *p847, map p848*
Region famous for handlooms and handicrafts.
Poompuhar, 1239 Big Bazaar St. Good crafts, shipping service. Good handloom in Sukrawarpettai, Gandhipuram's lively bazaar, *Asoka Plaza*, Dr Nanjappa Rd, south of Central Bus Stand, *Lakshmi Complex*, Cross Cut Rd and *Cherran Towers*, Arts College Rd.

Books
Landmark, next to Lakshmi Mills, Avanashi Rd (2 km northeast of Junction station), new English titles. Secondhand stalls in Raja St.

Jewellery
Big Bazar St.

Music
Plenty of Hindi pop.

Salem *p848*
Handlooms and jewellery (silver and gold chains) are best buys at **Agrahram**. The VOC

market behind Chinnakadai St, with an entrance next to no 318, is interesting.

Coonoor *p849*
The bazar is full of colour and activity.
Mission Arts and Crafts, Figure of 8 Rd.
Shanthi Mahal near the Bus Stand.
Spencer's, Figure of 8 Rd.
Variety Hall, Jubilee Bridge.

Photography
Lawndays, Bedford Circle, 1 hr processing.

Udhagamandalam *p850, map p851*
Most shops open 0900- 1200, 1500-2000. The smaller shops keep longer hours. The main areas are Charing Cross, Municipal Market, Upper and Lower Bazar.
Toda Showroom, Charing Cross. Sells silver and tribal shawls.
Variety Hall, Silver Market. Old family firm (1890s). Good range of silk, helpful, credit cards.

Books
Higginbotham's, near Central Library or Charing Cross, 1000-1300, 1550-1930.

▲ Activities and tours

Coimbatore *p847, map p848*
Yoga
Integral Yoga Institute, 116 Bashyakaralu Rd (W) off DB Rd, RS Puram. Run by American couple, courses/classes in yoga and meditation; private lessons on request.

Yercaud *p849*
Tours
Tourist information at *Hotel Tamil Nadu*, T2273.

Coonoor *p849*
Tours
TTDC from Ooty (reserve in Ooty Tourist Office). Coonoor-Kotagiri Rs 120, 6 hrs; visiting Valley View, Sim's Park, Lamb's Rock, Dolphin's Nose, Kodadu view point.

Udhagamandalam *p850, map p851*
Boating and rowing
On Ooty Lake.

Horse riding
Gymkhana Club, T442254. Temporary membership; beautifully situated amidst superbly maintained 18-hole golf course. Riding from *Regency Villa*: Rs 500 for 2 hrs with 'guide'; good fun but no helmets.

Tour operators
Blue Mountain, Nahar Complex, Charing Cross, T443650, luxury coach bookings to neighbouring states.
George Hawkes, 52C Nahar Complex, T442756, for tourist taxis.
Sangeetha Travels, 13 Bharathiyar Complex, Charing Cross, T/F444782 for steam train.
TTDC, reservations *Hotel Tamil Nadu*, T444370. Ooty and Mudumalai: Ooty Lake, Dodabetta Peak, Botanical Gardens, Mudumalai Wildlife Sanctuary. Daily 0830-2000. Rs 150. **Kotagiri** and **Coonoor**: Kotagiri, Kodanad View Point, Lamb's Rock, Dolphin's Nose, Sim's Park. Daily 0830-1830. Rs 130.
Woodlands Tourism, Race Course Rd, T442551, offers Ooty and Coonoor: 0930-1730. Rs 130. Stunning views.

Yoga
Rajayoga Meditation Centre, 88 Victoria Hall, Ettines Rd.

◉ Transport

Coimbatore *p847, map p848*
Air
Peelamedu Airport (12 km centre). Transport to town: Cheran Transport airport coach to/from several hotels and the city, Rs 25; taxis Rs 150-200; auto-rickshaw Rs 85. On Trichy Rd: **Indian Airlines**, T399833, airport T574623, 1000-1300, 1345-1730. **Bangalore**; **Chennai**; **Delhi**; **Kochi**; **Kozhikode**; **Mumbai**. Jet Airways: 1055/1 Gowtham Centre, Avinashi Rd, T212034, airport T575375 to **Bangalore**; **Chennai**; **Mumbai** .

Auto-rickshaw
Minimum Rs 8.

Bus
Local City buses run a good service: several connect the bus stations in Gandhipuram with the Junction Rly Station 2 km south. No 20 goes to the airport (Rs 20).
Long distance 4 main bus stations, off Dr Nanjappa Rd. **City** or **'Town' Bus Stand** in Gandhipuram. **Thiruvallur Bus Stand**, Cross Cut Rd. Computerized reservations

0700-2100, T26700. Frequent Government Express buses to Madurai (5 hrs), Chennai (12 hrs), Mysore (6 hrs), Ooty (3 hrs), Tiruchirappalli (5½ hrs). 'Central' Bus Stand is further south, on corner of Shastri Rd. State buses to Bangalore and Mysore; Ooty via Mettupalayam (see below for train connection) and Coonoor every 20 mins, 0400-2400, 5 hrs. **Ukkadam Bus Stand**, south of the city, serves towns within the state (Pollachi, Madurai) and in northern Kerala (Pallakad, Thrissur, Munnar).

Taxi

Tourist taxis and yellow top taxis are available at the bus stations, rly station and taxi stands. Rs 2.50 per km; for out-station hill journeys, Rs 3 per km; minimum Rs 30.

Train

Junction Station, enquiries, T132, reservations, T131, 0700-1300, 1400-2030. **Bangalore**: *Tilak Exp, 1014,* 0515, 7¼ hrs; *Intercity Exp, 2678,* 1425, 7 hrs; *Kanniyakumari Bangalore Exp, 6525,* 1955, 9 hrs. **Chennai**: *West Coast Exp, 6628,* 0630, 9 hrs; *Kovai Exp, 2676,* 1340, 7½ hrs; *Nilgiri Exp, 6606,* 2040, 9¼ hrs. **Kochi (HT)**: *Tiruchirappalli-Kochi Exp, 6865,* 0045, 5½ hrs; *Hyderabad-Kochi Exp, 7030,* 0935, daily, 5½ hrs. Other trains: *W Coast Exp (Chennai – Coimbatore – Kozhikode – Bangalore),* daily to Kozhikode (4½ hrs) and Bangalore (9 hrs). For **Ooty**, train depart 0625 connects with narrow gauge steam train from Mettupalayam. Line to Coonoor is subject to landslides. Narrow gauge diesel from Coonoor to Ooty. There are two connecting trains daily: *Nilgiri Exp, 6605,* 0525, change to train 562 (S), 0710, arrive Ooty 1200; *Trichur-MettypalayamPass, 534 (S),* 1100, change to train *564 (S),* 1315 arrive Ooty 1745.

Salem *p848*

Air

Coimbatore is the nearest airport with commercial services.

Bus

The New Bus Stand, north of the Hospital, off Omalur Rd, has buses to Namakkal, 1¼ hrs. Salem is well connected by bus with all major towns in Tamil Nadu, Kerala and South Karnataka. TN Government Express buses, to **Dindigul**, 4 hrs.

Train

Junction is the main station. Enquiries, T132. Reservations, T131, 0700-1300, 1400-2030. **Bangalore**: *Tilak Exp, 1014,* 0750, 4½ hrs; *Intercity Exp, 2678,* 1705, 4 hrs. **Chennai (C)**: *Coimbator-Chennai Exp, 2680,* 0835, 5 hrs. **Kochi (HT) (Cochin)**: *Hyderabad Cochin Exp, 7030,* 0615, not Tue, 9 hrs; *Raptisagar Exp, 5012/5222,* 0830, Mon, Thu, Fri, Sun, 9¾ hrs. **Madurai**: *Mumbai-Nagercoil Exp, 6339,* not Tue, Wed, Sun, 1735, 6 hrs. **Ramesvaram**: no direct trains, change at Dindigul. For **Ooty**, *Nilgiri Exp, 6605,* 0135, connects with narrow gauge steam train from Mettupalayam; departs from **Mettupalayam** at 0745, arrives Ooty at 1200.

Yercaud *p849*

Bus

There are no local buses but some from Salem (1 hr) continue through town and connect with nearby villages.

Mettupalayam *p849*

Car to Ooty, 2 hrs.

Train

The *Nilgiri Exp* from Chennai via Coimbatore, connects with the *Blue Mountain Railway*. (This line is subject to landslides and washouts that can close the route for some months. Check before travelling.) From Chennai *6605,* 2015, 10 hrs; to Chennai, *6606,* 1925, 10½ hrs. For those coming from Coimbatore, it is better to arrive in advance at Mettupalayam by bus; this avoids a mad dash at the station from Platform 2 to 1 to catch the connecting train!

Blue Mountain Railway The first part from Mettupalayam to Coonoor is by **steam** when not disrupted by landslides (great to look around the engine sheds!); from there to Ooty by **diesel**. To Coonoor and **Ooty** 2 return trains daily; *562(S),* 0710, arrive Coonoor, 1030, Ooty, 1200 (5½ hrs); return from Ooty, *561(S),* 1500, arrive Coonoor, 1605, Mettupalayam 1835, 3½ hrs. Also *564(S),* 1315, arrive Coonoor, 1610, Ooty, 1745; return from Ooty next day *567(S),* 0915, arrive Coonoor, 1025, Mettupalayam 1245. The *Heritage Steam Chariot* runs from Ooty to Runneymede.

Coonoor *p849*

Bus

Frequent buses to **Ooty** (every 10 mins from 0530) some via Sim's Park and many via Wellington. Also regular services to **Kotagiri** and **Coimbatore** (every 30 mins) through Mettupalayam. Direct bus to **Mysore** (or change at Ooty).

Rickshaw

Rickshaws charge whatever they think they can get, pay Rs25 to Bedford from the station and bus stand.

Taxi

MB, Belmont, T236207.

Train

The *Blue Mountain Railway* runs from Mettupalayam to Coonoor (steam), 3 hrs; continues to Ooty (diesel), 1½ hrs. See Mettupalayam above. The *Heritage Steam Chariot* runs from Ooty to Runneymede beyond Coonoor. See Ooty.

Udhagamandalam *p850, map p851*

Arrive early for buses to ensure a seat. They often leave early if full.

Ghat roads have numerous hairpin bends which can have fairly heavy traffic and very bad surfaces at times. The Gudalur road passes through Mudumalai and Bandipur sanctuaries (see page 853). You might see an elephant herd and other wildlife – especially at night.

Air

Nearest airport, Coimbatore, 105 km. Taxis available.

Auto-rickshaw

Unmetered, minimum Rs 7.

Bike hire available.

Bus

Long distance *Cheran*, T443970. Frequent buses to **Coonoor** (every 10 mins, 0530-2045), **Coimbatore** (every 20 mins, 0530-2000, 3½ hrs) and **Mettupalayam** (0530-2100, 2 hrs). Also to **Bangalore** (0630-2000), **Mysore** (0800-1530, 3½-5 hrs) and **Kozhikode** (0630-1515), **Chennai** (1630-1830), **Palakkad** (0715-1515), **Palani** (0800-1800). Daily buses

to **Kannur** (0915, 2000), **Hassan** (1130, 1500), **Kanniyakumari** (1745), **Kodaikkanal** (0630, 9½ hrs via magnificent route through Palani, **Madikere** (0700, 1100), **Pondicherry** (1700), **Salem** (1300). Check timings. Several on the short route (36 km) to **Masinagudi/ Mudumalai**, Rs 7, 1½ hrs; a steep and windy but interesting road.

Taxi

Minimum charge, about Rs 12.

Train

Railway station, T442246. From Mettupalayam *Blue Mountain* (steam to Coonoor; then diesel to Ooty), 2 return-trains daily; *562(S)*, 0710, arrive **Coonoor** 1030, **Ooty** 1200, 5½ hrs; return from Ooty, *561(S)*, 1500, arrive Coonoor 1605, Mettupalayam 1835, 3½ hrs. Also, *564(S)*, 1315, arrive Coonoor 1610, Ooty 1745; return from Ooty next day, *567(S)*, 0915, arrive Coonoor 1025, Mettupalayam 1245.

Steam The *Heritage Steam Chariot* to Runneymede runs at weekends (more frequent in season). It departs Ooty 1000, returns 1600 (delayed when engine runs out of steam!). Highly recommended. Tickets include Indian packed lunch: Rs 280, or Rs 550 in Maharaja coach, from *Sangeetha* (listed above) or Ooty railway station.

Mudumalai Wildlife Sanctuary *p853*

Bus

Theppakadu is on the Mysore-Ooty bus route. From **Mysore**, services from 0615 (1½-2 hrs); last bus to Mysore around 2000. From **Ooty** via Gudalur on a very winding road (about 2½ hrs); direct 20 km steep road used by buses, under 1 hr. Few buses between Theppakadu and Masinagudi.

Jeep

Available at bus stands and from lodges.

❶ Directory

Coimbatore *p847, map p848*

Banks Several on Oppankara St. State Bank of India (exchange upstairs), and Bank of Baroda are on Bank Rd. **Hospitals** Government Hospital, Trichy Rd. **Post office** Near flyover, Railway Feeder Rd, fax. **Travel agents** Alooha, corner near *Heritage*

Inn, helpful. **Useful addresses** Automobile Association, 42 Trichy Rd, T222994.

Yercaud *p849*
Banks Banks with foreign exchange facilities are on Main Rd. **Hospitals** Govt Hospital, 1 km from Bus Stand; Providence Hospital, on road to Lady's Seat. **Post office** Post office is on the Main Rd.

Coonoor *p849*
Banks Travancore Bank, Upper Coonor, (Bedford Circle) changes cash.
Hospitals Lawley Hospital, Mt Rd, T231050.

Udhagamandalam *p850, map p851*
Banks State Bank of India, on Bank Rd, deals in foreign exchange. **Hospitals** Govt Hospital, Hospital Rd, T442212.
Internet Gateways, 8/9 Moosa Sait Complex, Commercial Rd. Excellent, fast, ISDN lines, Rs 30 per hr. **Post offfice** Head Post Office, Collectorate and Telegraph Office, Town W Circle. **Tourist offices** Tamil Nadu, 7/72 Commercial Rd, Super Market, Charing Cross, T443977, lacks efficiency. **Useful addresses** Police, T100. Wildlife Warden, 1st floor, Mahalingam Building, T44098, 1000-1300, 1400-1730.

The Vaigai Valley

★ Madurai → *Phone code: 0452. Colour map 7, grid C4 .Population: 922,900. Altitude 100 m.*

Spread along the banks of the rocky bed of the Vaigai River, the modern industrial city of Madurai's main claim to fame is as a temple town. It is one of Tamil culture's most vital centres. The temple and bazar at the heart of this very crowded and polluted city can feel quite uncomfortable and overpowering to a westerner, but despite its dirt and noise, it is an experience. Around the city the area of fertile agricultural land is dotted with exotically shaped granite mountain ranges such as Nagamalai ("snake hills") and Yanaimalai ("elephant hills"). ▶▶ *For Sleeping, Eating and other listings, see pages 875-882 .*

Ins and outs

Getting there The airport, 12 km from town, is linked by buses to the city centre, but there are also taxis and autos. The railway station is within easy walking distance of many budget hotels (predatory rickshaw drivers/hotel touts may tell you otherwise). Hire an auto to reach the few north of the river. The main express bus stand is next to the station though there are 2 others 3-6 km away, with bus links between them.

Getting around Although very spread out, the centre is compact and the temple is within easy walking distance of most budget hotels. See Transport, page 880, for further details. Prepare for hordes of touts.

Climate Temperature: Summer, maximum 37°C, minimum 26°C; winter maximum 30°C, minimum 21°C. Rainfall: Oct-Nov, average 190 mm. Dec-Jul, average 140 mm.

History

According to legend, drops of nectar fell from Siva's locks on this site, so it was named 'Madhuram' or Madurai, the nectar city. The city's history goes back to the sixth century BC. Ancient Madurai, which traded with Greece and Rome, was a centre of Tamil culture, famous for its writers and poets during the last of the three *'Sangam'* periods (Tamil 'Academies') nearly 2,000 years ago. The Pandiyans, a major power from the sixth to the beginning of the 10th century, made Madurai their capital. For the following 300 years, they remained here, although they were subservient to the Cholas who gained control over the area, after which the Pandiyans returned to power. For a short period it became a Sultanate after Malik Kafur completely destroyed the city in 1310. In

Tamil Nadu Vaigai Valley Madurai

1364 it was captured by Hindu Vijayanagar kings, who remained until 1565, after which their local governors the Nayakas asserted their independence.

The Nayakas have been seen essentially as warriors, given an official position by the Vijayanagar rulers; though in Sanskrit, the term applied to someone of prominence and leadership. Burton Stein comments, "the history of the Vijayanagara is essentially the history of the great Telugu Nayakas" from Madurai.

The Vijayanagar kings were great builders and preserved and enriched the architectural heritage of the town. The Nayakas laid out the old town in the pattern of a lotus with narrow streets surrounding the Minakshi Temple at the centre. The streets on the four sides of the central temple are named after the festivals which take place in them and give their relative direction, for example South 'Masi' Street, East 'Avanimoola' Street and East 'Chitrai' Street. The greatest of the Nayaka rulers, Thirumalai (ruled 1623-55), built the *gopurams* of the temple. After the Carnatic Wars the British destroyed the fort in 1840, filling in the surrounding moat (now followed by the four Veli streets).

Madurai

Sleeping
1 Madurai Ashok
2 Pandiyan
3 Tamil Nadu Star
4 Youth Hostel
5 YWCA

Transport
1 Central (Periyar) & Government (Express)

66 99 At 2110 an image of Sundareswarar is carried in procession from the shrine near the east gopuram to Minakshi, to 'sleep' by her side, which is returned the next morning; worth attending.

Sights

★ **Minakshi Temple** ⓘ *Inner Temple open 0500-1230, 1600-2130, camera fee Rs 30, video not allowed, at South Entrance (valid for multiple entry), the sanctuary is open only to Hindus. Art museum 0600-2000, Re 2, extra camera fee Rs 5 at the door, camera fee Rs 30 at the temple office near the South Tower – good views from the top of the South Gate when open.* This is an outstanding example of Vijayanagar temple architecture, exactly contemporary with the Taj Mahal in Agra. Minakshi, the 'fish-eyed goddess' and the consort of Siva, has a temple to the south, and Sundareswarar (Siva), a temple to the west. Since she is the presiding deity the daily ceremonies are first performed in her shrine, and unlike the practice at other temples, Sundareswarar plays a secondary role. The temple's nine towering *gopurams* stand out with their colourful stucco images of gods, goddesses and animals which are renewed and painted every 12 years. There are about 4,000 granite sculptures on the

Minakshi Temple

1 Killikootu (Parrot Cage) & Oonjal (Swing) Mandapams
2 Subrahmanya Shrine
3 Tamil Sangam College
4 Kambathadi Mandapam
5 Ayirakkal Mandapam, 'Thousand Pillared Hall' & Museum
6 Sabhapati Shrine
7 Musical Pillars
8 Nandi Pavillion
9 Kalyan Mandapam

lower levels. In addition to the Golden Lotus tank and various pillared halls there are five *vimanas* over the sanctuaries.

The temple is a hive of activity, with a colourful temple elephant, flower sellers and performances by musicians ① *1800-1930, 2100-2200*. At 2110 an image of Sundareswarar is carried in procession from the shrine near the east *gopuram* to Minakshi, to 'sleep' by her side, which is returned the next morning; worth attending. The procession around the temple is occasionally led by the elephant and a cow and is well worth watching. During the day the elephant is on continual duty, 'blessing' visitors with its trunk and then collecting a small offering. A banana pleases him enormously, but not his keeper! The flower and vegetable market, north end of East Chitrai Street, is colourful but watch out for the holes in the floor. You may be troubled by touts who suggest good vantage points for viewing which invariably turn out to be roofs of nearby shops.

The **main entrance** is through a small door of the *Ashta Sakthi Mandapa* (Porch of the eight goddesses) which projects from the wall, south of the eastern *gopuram*. Inside, to the left is the sacred *Tank of the Golden Lotus*, with a lamp in the centre, surrounded by pillared cloisters and steps down to the waters. The Sangam legend speaks of the test that ancient manuscripts had to undergo – they were thrown into the sacred tank, if they sank they were worthless, if they floated they were considered worthy! The north gallery has 17th-century murals, relating 64 miracles said to have been performed by Siva, and the southern has marble inscriptions of the 1,330 couplets of the *Tamil Book of Ethics*. To the west of the tank is the *Oonjal Mandapa,* the pavilion leading to the Meenakshi shrine. Here the pillars are carved in the form of the mythical beast *yali* which recurs in temples throughout the region. Golden images of Meenakshi and Sundareswarar are brought to the *oonjal* or swing each Friday evening where they are worshipped. Cages with parrots, Meenakshi's green bird

Madurai centre

Related map
A Minakshi Temple, page 863

N

0 metres 200
0 yards 200

■ Sleeping
1 Aarathy
2 Arima
3 Chentoor
4 Dhanamani
5 International
6 Park Plaza
7 Prem Nivas
8 Ravi Lodge
9 Ravi Towers
10 Sree Devi
11 Supreme & Thilaga
12 TM Lodge
13 Visakam
14 YMCA

● Eating
1 Amutham, Indo-Ceylon & Taj
2 Anna Meenakshi
3 Delhiwala Sweets
4 New Arya Bhavan

which brings luck, hung from the ceiling of the neighbouring *Kilikootu Mandapam* which is flanked by finely carved columns. The *Minakshi shrine* with the principal image of the goddess, stands in its own enclosure with smaller shrines around it.

To the north of the tank is another enclosure with smaller *gopurams* on four sides within which is the **Sundareswarar shrine** guarded by two tall *dwarapalas*. In the northeast corner, the superb sculptures of the divine marriage of Meenakshi and Sundareswarar being blessed by Vishnu and Brahma, and Siva in his 24 forms are in the 19th-century *Kambathadi Mandapa*, around the golden flagstaff.

The *thousand-pillared hall*, mid-16th century, is in the northeast corner of the complex. The 985 exquisitely carved columns include a lady playing the *veena*, a dancing Ganesh, and a gypsy leading a monkey. The **art museum** here exhibits temple art and architecture, fine brass and stone images, friezes and photos (the labelling could be improved). Just inside the museum to the right is a cluster of five musical pillars carved out of a single stone. Each pillar produces a different note which vibrates when tapped. Nayaka musicians could play these as an instrument.

The **Nandi pavilion** is to the east and is often occupied by flower sellers. The long *Pudu Mandapa* (New Mandapa), with its beautiful sculptures of *yalis* and Nayaka rulers and their ministers, is outside the enclosure wall, between the east tower and the base of the unfinished *Raya Gopuram* which was planned to be the tallest in the country.

Thirumalai Nayaka Palace ① *0900-1300, 1400-1700, bus 17, 17A, 11, 11A.* Built in 1636 in the Indo-Mughal style, its 15 domes and arches are adorned with stucco work while some of its 240 columns rise to 12 m. Its *Swarga Vilasam* (Celestial Pavilion), an arcaded octagonal structure, is curiously constructed in brick and mortar without any supporting rafters. Special artisans skilled in the use of traditional lime plaster and powdered seashell and quartz have renovated parts. The original complex had a shrine, an armoury, a theatre, royal quarters, a royal bandstand, a harem, a pond and a garden but only about a quarter survives since Thirumalai's grandson removed sections to build another palace in Tiruchirappalli, and the original Ranga Vilasam was destroyed by Muslim invaders. It is a bit run down.

Vandiyur Mariammam Teppakulam ① *Buses 4 and 44 take 10 mins from the Bus Stand and Railway Station.* To the southeast of town, this has a small shrine in its centre where the annual *Float Festival* takes place in January/February.

Museums

The best is the excellent **Gandhi Museum** ① *daily, 1000-1300, 1400-1730, free, excellent bookshop,* in the 300-year old Rani Mangammal Palace. It contains an art gallery, memorabilia (Gandhi's *dhoti* when he was shot), traces history of the Independence struggle from 1800, and the 'Quit India' movement. Informative, interesting and well laid out. Also has a Khadi and Village Industries Section and one of South Indian handicrafts. Yoga classes, offered daily, 0630. **Thirumalai Nayaka Palace Museum** concentrates on the history of Madurai with galleries on the famous Nayaka king and the art and architecture of Tamil Nadu. *Sound and Light* show (see Entertainment).

Dindigul

Now a large market town, Dindigul, north of Madurai, commands a strategic gap between the **Sirumalai Hills** to its east and the **Palani Hills** to the west. The market handles the produce of the Sirumalai Hills, including a renowned local variety of banana. Dindigul is particularly known for its cheroots (cigars).

The massive granite rock and **fort** ① *0730-1730, Rs 5, foreigners Rs 100, 2 km west of the bus stand, autos Rs 20,* towers over 90 m above the plain. The Mysore army captured it in 1745 and Haidar Ali was appointed Governor in 1755. It was ceded to the British under the Treaty of Seringapatam. There are magnificent views of the town, the valley and the hills on either side from the top of the rock fort. **Our Lady of Dolours Church**, one of several churches in the town, is over 250 years old and was rebuilt in 1970. The Old City is interesting to walk around; you can walk up to the fort from there. The station is 2 km south of the bus stand which has cheap lodges nearby.

★ Kodaikkanal and the Palani Hills

→ *Phone code: 04542. Colour map 7, grid C4. Population: 32,900. Altitude: 2,343 m.*
The climb up the Palanis is 47 km before Kodaikkanal (Kodai) and is one of the most rapid ascents anywhere across the ghats. The views are stunning. In the lower reaches of the climb you look down over the Kambam Valley, the Vaigai Lake and across to the Varushanad Hills beyond. Set high in the Palani Hills around a small artificial lake, the town has crisply fresh air even at the height of summer and the beautiful scent of pine and eucalyptus, making it a popular retreat from the southern plains. Today Kodai is a fast growing resort centre. ▶▶ *For Sleeping, Eating and other listings, see pages 875-882.*

Ins and outs
Getting there Buses make the long climb from Madurai and other cities to the central bus stand, which is within easy walking distance from most hotels. The nearest train station is Kodai Rd.

Kodaikkanal

Related map
A Kodaikkanal centre,
page 868

Sleeping ■
1 Greenlands Youth Hostel
2 Sterling Lake View
3 TTDC Tamil Nadu & Youth Hostal

Eating ●
1 Manna Bakery

it is worth getting an unmetered taxi. See Transport, page 881, for further details.

Climate Best time to visit is late Sep-early Oct. Apr-Jun are high season, avoid May when it is crowded and expensive. The mist can come down any time of the year, especially in the afternoon. Highs of 20°C in May dipping to 5°C in Jan.

Background

Kodai is the hill station to visit rather than Ooty. The lake, created in 1910 by the building of a dam just below the International School (established in 1901), acts as a focus for the town. The 5-km walk around its perimeter gives beautiful and contrasting views across the water and into the surrounding woods.

The **Palani Hills** were first surveyed by British administrators in 1821, but the surveyor's report was not published until 1837 – 10 years after Ooty had become the official 'sanitorium' for the British in South India. A proposal to build a sanitorium was made in 1861-62 by Colonel Hamilton, who noted the extremely healthy climate and the lack of disease. Despite the warmth of that recommendation the sanitorium was never built because the site was so difficult to get to. It was the freedom from malaria that was the greatest incentive to opening a hill station there. The American Mission in Madurai, established in 1834, had lost six of their early missionaries within a decade. It looked as if the Sirumalai Hills, at around 1,300 m, might provide a respite from the plains, but it was soon discovered that they were not high enough to eliminate malaria. The first two bungalows were built by June 1845. The major transformation came at the turn of the 20th century with the arrival of the car and the bus. In 1905 it was possible to do the whole journey from Kodai Road station to Kodai within the hours of daylight. The present road, up 'Law's Ghat' was opened to traffic in 1916.

Sights

Kodaikkanal Lake ① *Rs 5, toilets at south entrance*, covers 24 ha in a 'star' shape surrounded by wooded slopes. The walk around the lake takes about one hour. Boating is popular and fishing with permission. The lake, however, is polluted. The view over the plains from **Coaker's Walk**, built by Lieutenant Coaker in the 1870s, can be magnificent; on a clear day you can see Madurai. It is reached from a signposted path just above the bazar, 1 km from the Bus Stand.

Kurinji Andavar Temple, northeast of the town, past Chettiar Park, is dedicated to Murugan associated with the *kurinji* flower that blossoms once in 12 years. There are excellent views of the north and southern plains, including Palani and Vagai Dams. **St Peter's Church** (CSI) built in 1884, has a stained glass window dedicated to Bishop Caldwell. **The International School** has a commanding position on the lakeside, and provides education for children between the ages of 5 and 18 from India and abroad. There is also the Highclere School for Girls and the Bhavan's Gandhi Vidyasram School, founded in 1983, located on the way to Pillar Rocks.

Bear Shola Falls, named because it once attracted bears, is a favourite picnic spot about 2 km from the Bus Stand. These falls and others around Kodai have been reduced to a trickle. **Solar Physical Observatory** ① *during the season, Fri, 1000-1230, 1900-2100; 1000-1200, T40588, 4 km to the west from the Bus Stand*, was established in 1899 at a height of 2,347 m. **Pillar Rocks**, 7 km from the lake, is another striking viewpoint. There are three granite formations over 120 m high. There are over 100 *dolmens* and other megalithic remains that have been discovered in the Palanis, all datable to around the second century AD.

Shenbaganur Museum ① *1000-1130, 1500-1700*, is the local flora and fauna museum including 300 orchid species at the Sacred Heart College, a theological seminary founded in 1895. Small but interesting. It also has some archaeological remains. There is an attractive walk downhill from the town passing waterfalls.

A road runs west past the golf course and Pillar Rocks to **Berijam Lake**, 15 km away, which has beautiful views before running down to the lake. You can walk to Berijam in four hours and stay at the Forest Rest House, Rs 50. There is only a restaurant here. Continue the next day, by a short cut to **Top Station** in Kerala in 5-6 hours, where there is Forest Hut and shops and tea stalls selling snacks. There are then buses to **Munnar** 41 km away.

Palani ⓘ *Buses to Kodai and Madurai (3 hrs)*. The ghat road to Palani, passes through coffee, orange and banana smallholdings. Interplanting of crops such as pepper is further increasing the yields from what can be highly productive land, even on steep slopes. The hilltop shrine to **Murugan** (Subrahmanya) is an important site of pilgrimage. At full moon in January to February pilgrims walk from up to 80 km around and climb the 659 steps up to the shrine. Many carry shoulder-poles with elaborate bamboo or wooden structures on each end, living out the myth which surrounds the origin of the shrine.

Pollachi Pollachi has a population of 88,300 and is 61 km from Madurai. It has been an important trading centre for over 2,000 years, as is witnessed by the finds of Roman silver coins bearing the heads of the Emperors Augustus and Tiberias. Today it still occupies an important position on the route from east to west through the

Kodaikkanal centre

Sleeping
1 Anjay & Pakia Deepam Restaurant
2 Bala
3 Carlton
4 Garden Manor
5 Hilltop Towers
6 Jaya
7 JS Heritage, Econut, Hot Breads, Royal Tibet & Tibetan Brothers
8 Kay Pee Yem
9 Municipal New Rest House
10 Paradise Inn
11 R R Residency
12 Suhaag
13 Sunrise
14 Valley View
15 Villa Retreat & Kodai
16 Vignesh

Eating
1 Pastry Corner
2 Silver Inn
3 Tava & Hotel Jewell
4 Wang's Chinese

Palakkad Gap. It is also the gateway to the small but very attractive sanctuary. Sleeping at *Sakti*, newish, large and smart, rooms (Rs 300), veg restaurant.

Anamalai (Indira Gandhi) National Park ① *Open year round, best time to visit: Dec-Jun, avoid Sun, 0630-1830.* The park, near Pollachi, covers an area of 960 sq km in the western ghats. It is a beautiful, unspoilt forest, rarely visited, except Indian day-trippers. The Reception and Information Centre is at Top Slip. Written permission needed from District Forest Officer, Pollachi, T25356 (1½ km out of town towards Top Slip).

Wildlife includes Nilgiri langur, lion-tailed macaque, elephant, *gaur*, tiger, panther, sloth, wild boar, birds – including pied hornbill, drongo, red whiskered *bulbul*, black-headed oriole – and a large number of crocodiles in the Amaravathi reservoir. There is an elephant camp reached by a minibus ride through the forest, but rides can be disappointing. To view there are Forest Department vans, Rs 80. Restricted zone viewing, 0630-1900, 1700-1830. Birdwatching from Kariam Shola watch tower, 2 km from Topslip.

There are some trekking routes that vary from easy treks to Pandaravara (8 km), Kozhikamuthi (12 km) to Perunkundru peak (32 km) which is demanding. Permits from Range Officer, Topslip. Private guides charge Rs 50 for two.

To Ramesvaram

Seen from the air the plains of the Vaigai River form one of the most remarkable landscapes in India, for there are over 5,000 tanks, and irrigation has been so widely developed that scarcely a drop of water is wasted. The coastal districts of Ramnad have their own highly distinct economy and society. For the Hindus the sand banks barely concealed in the Palk Strait are like giant stepping stones linking India and Sri Lanka – Adam's Bridge. Both Hindu and Muslim communities have long established trading links across the Bay of Bengal – to Malaysia and Southeast Asia and to Sri Lanka. Small towns and villages along the coast such as Kilakkarai have long been associated with smuggling. The civil war in Sri Lanka has made it a sensitive region.

★ Ramesvaram → *Phone code: 04573. Colour map 7, grid C5. Population: 38,000.*

Ramesvaram is normally lapped by waters that are usually a limpid blue, but which can be whipped by cyclones into ferocious storm waves. This is where Rama is believed to have worshipped Siva, and so, a pilgrim to Varanasi is expected to visit Ramesvaram next. ▶ *For Sleeping, Eating and other listings, see pages 875-882 .*

Ins and outs

Getting there Ramesvaram is connected to Madurai and other centres by regular bus and train services. The bus stand is 2 km from the centre, the railway station 1 km further in and about 1 km southwest of the great temple.

Getting around Local buses go to the temple where there are a few places to stay. Avoid visiting on Mon; too crowded with pilgrims. See Transport, page 881, for further details.

Background

The *Ramayana* tells how the monkey king Hanuman built the bridges linking Ramnad to Pamban and Danushkodi (a spot where Rama is believed to have bathed) in order to help rescue Sita from the demon king Ravana. When he returned he was told by the *rishis* that he must purify himself after committing the sin of murdering a Brahmin, for *Ravana* was the son of a Brahmin. To do this he was advised to set up a *lingam* and worship Siva. The red image of Hanuman north of the main East Gate illustrates this story.

The original shrine long predates the present great Ramesvaram temple. It is one of India's most sacred shrines, being visited by pilgrims from all over India. The temple benefited from enormous donations from the 17th-century *Setupatis* ('guardians of the causeway'), who derived their wealth from the right to levy taxes on crossing to the island. The temple stands on slightly higher ground, surrounded by a freshwater lake.

Sights

The **Ramalingesvara (or Ramanathasvami) Temple** was founded by the Cholas but most of the temple was built in the Nayaka period (16th-17th centuries). It is a massive structure, enclosed by a huge rectangular wall with *gopurams* in the middle of three sides. Entrances through the east wall are approached through columned *mandapas* and the east *gopuram* is on the wall of the inner enclosure rather than the outer wall. Over 45 m high, it was begun in 1640 but left incomplete until recently. The west *gopuram* is comparatively new. In contrast the north and south *gopurams* were built by Keerana Rayar of the Deccan in about AD 1420. The most remarkable feature of the temple is its pillared *mandapas*. The longest corridor is over 200 m long. The pillars, nearly 4 m tall, are raised on moulded bases and the shafts decorated with scrollwork and lotus motifs. They give an impression of almost unending perspective, those on the north and south being particularly striking. There are two gateways on the east side which give access to the Parvati and Ramalinga shrines at the centre. The masonry shrine is probably the oldest building on the site, going back to 1173. On entering the East Gate you see the statue of Hanuman, then the *Nandi* flanked by statues of the Nayaka kings of Madurai, *Visvanatha* and *Krishnama*. The *Sphatikalinga Puja* is performed daily at 0500. Worshippers take a holy bath in the sea in a very calm bay 25 km away, where the waters are believed to wash away their sins. Fishermen occasionally offer to take visitors for a boat ride. The fishing village offers good views, but is extremely pungent.

> ❢ Non-Hindus are sometimes allowed beyond the first enclosure. Visitors should show respect and take photos with discretion. Place donations audibly in Hundi boxes which vary in size to accept cash, clothes, jewels, gold or silver!

Gandhamadana Parvatam, just over 2 km north of Ramesvaram takes, its name from the Sanskrit words *gandha* (fragrance) and *mad* (intoxicate), 'highly fragrant hill'. Dedicated to Rama's feet, this is the spot from which Hanuman is believed to have surveyed the area before taking his leap across the narrow Palk strait to Sri Lanka. You can get an excellent view from the top of the *mandapa*.

Dhanuskodi, at the tip of the peninsula, 20 km to the east of Ramesvaram island, is considered particularly holy. There is a good beach and excellent views. A trip is only recommended for the really hardy. Travel by bus, and then join a pilgrim group on a

Ramesvaram

0 metres (approx) 500
0 yards (approx) 500

■ Sleeping
1 Maharaja
2 Santhya Lodge
3 Swami Ramanatha Tourist Home
4 Tamil Nadu
5 Venkatesh

● Eating
1 Ashok Bhawan & Vasantha Vihar
2 Devasthanam Trust & Cycle Hire

🛕 Temple
1 Ramalingesvara

The Cardamom Hills→ *Colour map 7, grid C3 and C4.*

To the south of Madurai is a series of modest towns in the lee of the southern ranges of the Western Ghats. It is a comfortable day's drive from Madurai to Thiruvanathapuram, either via Tirunelveli or over the ghats, but there are several interesting places on the way if you wish to take your time.

Rajapalayam
① *To Sankaracoil, Rs 5, 30 mins; from there to Kalugumalai, Rs 3, 30 mins, buses to and from Tenkasi, Rs 10, 2 hrs.*

The town originated on the dispersal of the Vijayanagar families after 1565, see page 956. The Sankarankovil temple is worth visiting. The Western Ghats rise to heights of over 1,200 m and wild elephants still come down through the forests, devastating farmland.

Tenkasi
① *To Courtallam Falls frequent buses, Rs 3, to Courtallam Bus Stand, then walk through the grey arch to the 'Main Falls'. See Rajapalayam for transport to Tenkasi.*

Literally the Kashi (Varanasi) of the South, Tenkasi is the nearest town to the Kuttalam Falls, 6 km away. The impressive 16th-century Visvanatha Temple dedicated to Siva, has some fine carvings inside. The temple flagstaff is believed to be 400 years old. From Tenkasi the road goes through a low pass into the densely forested hills of Kerala.

Courtallam (Kuttalam)
Courtallam, with average temperatures of 22°-23°C, is a very popular health resort, especially during the monsoon. The 'Main Falls' is in town where the river Chittar cascades over 92 m. There is massage, toilets, special postal cancellations and other facilities available there. The waters, widely believed to have great curative powers, draw big crowds at the *Saral Festival* in July. To visit the 'Five Falls' bathing site above Courtallam, take an auto (Rs 60) or walk 4 km along Five Falls Road, which is a pleasant route through hill-station scenery. Alternatively, if you take the Tenkasi road (east), then turn south towards Ambasamudram (ignore Tiger Falls) and continue 4 km past a quarry, a right turn is signed to Old Kuttalam, with an idyllic falls for bathing. You will need transport. The Thirukutralanathar Temple contains old inscriptions while the small **Chitra Sabha Temple** nearby contains religious murals.

Virudhunagar
The name Virudhupatti (Hamlet of banners) was changed to Virudhunagar (City of banners) in 1915, and was upgraded to a full municipality in 1957, reflecting the upwardly mobile social status of the town's dominant local caste, the Nadars. Originally low caste toddy tappers, they have established a wide reputation as a dynamic and enterprising group. The powerful Congress leader, Kamaraj Nadar, was chiefly responsible for Mrs Gandhi's selection as Prime Minister.

Kalugumalai
Six kilometres south of Kovilpatti, Kalugumalai (Kazhugumalai) has a profusion of magnificent fifth-century bas-relief Jain figures on a huge rock which are well worth the detour. The Jain temple is to the north of the rock and is easily missed. There is also an unfinished monolithic cave temple to Siva (circa AD 950).

Tirunelveli and Palayamkottai

→ *Phone code: 0462. Colour map 7, grid C4. Population: 411,300.*

Located on the banks of the Tamraparni, the only perennial river of the south, Tirunelveli is an attractive market and educational centre surrounded by rice fields irrigated from the river's waters. Rising only 60 km to the east at an altitude of over 1,700 m, the river benefits from both the southwest and southeast monsoons. It tumbles down to the plains where it is bordered by a narrow strip of rich paddy growing land.

Tirunelveli is now joined with the twin settlement of Palayamkottai. It is a market town and one of the oldest Christian centres in Tamil Nadu. St Francis Xavier settled here to begin his ministry in India in the early 16th century, but it has also been a centre of Protestant missionary activity. In 1896 it became the head of an Anglican diocese, now Church of South India.

Kanthimathi Nellaiyappar Temple ① *Closed 1230-1600, no photography.* A twin temple with the north dedicated to Siva (Nellaiyappar) and the south to Parvati (Kanthi), is worth visiting. Each section has an enclosure over 150 m by 120 m. The temples have sculptures, musical pillars, valuable jewels, a golden lily tank and a 1,000-pillared *mandapa*. There is a large white *nandi* at the entrance. *Car festival* in June/July. The old town area around the temple is well worth a couple of hours of anyone's time, with the blue painted houses reminiscent of Jodhpur (but without the tourist crowds). **Palayamkottai** has **St John's Church** (Church Missionary Society) with a spire 35-m high, a landmark for miles around. The town produces palm-leaf articles.

Around Tirunelveli

Tiruchendur ① *Rs 50 for 'fast darshan', men must remove shirts.* The town, 50 km east of Tirunelveli, has a famous **shore temple** dedicated to Subrahmanya, see page 995. It is considered to be one of his six 'abodes'. It is a hive of activity during festivals. There are caves with rock-cut sculptures along the shore.

Manapad This is the predominantly Roman Catholic coastal village, 18 km south of Tiruchendur, where St Francis Xavier is said to have landed and lived in a cave near the headland. The Holy Cross Church (1581) close to the sea is believed to house a fragment of the True Cross from Jerusalem.

Tirunelveli

■ Sleeping	3 Sri Janakiram, Maruthi	● Eating
1 Aryaas	Restaurant & Barani	1 Central Café
2 Bluestar	4 Tamil Nadu	

0 metres 200
0 yards 200

★ Kanniyakumari → *Phone code: 04652. Colour map 7, grid C4. Population: 19,700.*

The southernmost point of mainland India and a site that captures the imagination of millions of Hindus, Kanniyakumari occupies a beautiful rocky headland site, though the town itself revolves largely around the pilgrim market selling tacky plastic knick-knacks. Associated with the Goddess Kumari, the virgin, Kanniyakumari (Cape Comorin) has become a busy pilgrimage centre. The memorial to Swami Vivekenanda, on a rocky promontory just over 400 m offshore, now dominates the view. The Bay of Bengal, the Indian Ocean and the Arabian Sea meet here giving spectacular sunrise, sunset and moonrise. In April the sun and the moon appear on the same horizon. The beach sands are of different colours, having been deposited from different directions. On the beach are the black monazite and red garnet sands.

Sights

The **Kanniyakumari Temple** ① *0400- 1200, 1700-2000, non-Hindus are not allowed into the sanctuary, shoes must be left outside and men must wear a dhoti to enter*, overlooks the shoreline. The legend tells of the Devi Kanya, one of the incarnations of Parvati, who sought to marry Siva by doing penance. When she was unsuccessful she vowed to remain an unmarried virgin. The deity who is the 'protector of India's shores' has an brilliant diamond on her nose ring which is supposed to shine out to sea. The East Gate is opened only on special occasions. Some of Mahatma Gandhi's ashes were placed in public view before immersion in the sea. The **Gandhi Mandapam** was built so that the sun shines on the spot where the ashes were placed, on his birthday, 2 October.

Vivekananda Memorial ① *daily except Tue, 0700-1100, 1400-1700, Rs 10, ferry Rs 20, 15 mins (see transport below), allow 1 hr for the visit, smoking and eating prohibited, take off shoes before entering, can be hot underfoot*, which stands on one of two rocks separated by about 70 m, is about 500 m from the mainland. The Bengali religious leader and philosopher Swami Vivekananda who came here as a simple monk and devotee of the Devi, swam out and sat in long and deep meditation on one of the rocks in 1892. He left inspired to speak on Hinduism at the Parliament of Religions in Chicago, preaching that "the Lord is one, but the sages describe Him differently". He looked on religion as the most powerful instrument of social regeneration and individual development. On his return, he founded the Ramakrishna Mission in Chennai, which now has spread across the world. The rock was renamed Vivekananda Rock and a memorial was built in 1970. The design of the *mandapa* incorporates different styles of temple architecture from all over India and now also houses a statue of Vivekananda. People also come to see Sri Pada Parai, the 'footprint' of the Devi where she did her penance on the rock – divine footprints are believed to be raised when enshrined on rock. A giant 40-m statue of the poet Thiruvalluvar is now installed on the rock nearby and work is progressing to allow visitors to land.

An informative photo exhibition, in **Vivekanandapuram**, 1 km north, can be reached by an easy walk along the beach though there is no access from that side. The Yoga Kendra there runs courses from June to December. Further north there is a pleasant sandy **beach**, 3½ km along Kovalam Road.

Around Kanniyakumari

★ **Suchindram** ① *Open to non-Hindus, priests acting as guides may expect donations.* The temple was founded during the Pandiyan period but was expanded under Thirumalai Nayaka in the 17th century. It was also used later as a sanctuary for the rulers of Travancore to the west and so contains treasures from many kingdoms. One of few temples dedicated to the Hindu Trinity, Brahma, Vishnu and Siva, it is in a rectangular enclosure which you enter through the massive ornate seven-storeyed *gopuram*. North of the temple is a large tank with a small shelter in the middle while round the walls is the typically broad street used for car festivals. Leading to the entrance is a long colonnade with musical pillars and with sculptures of Siva, Parvati, Ganesh and Subrahmanya on the front and a huge Hanuman statue inside. The main sanctuary, with a *lingam* dates from the ninth century but many of the other structures and sculptures date from the 13th century and after. There are special temple ceremonies at sunset on Friday.

Nagercoil ① *The railway station is 3 km from the bus station. Mumbai (CST): Nagercoil-Mumbai Exp, 6340, Mon, Tue, Wed, Sat, 0545, 39½ hrs; Kanniyakumari Mumbai Exp, 1082, 0520, 47 hrs. Frequent bus connections to Thiruvananthapuram, Kanniyakumari and Madurai.* Nagercoil is 19 km from Kanniyakumari and is set with a stunning backcloth of the Western Ghats, reflected from place to place in the broad tanks dotted with lotuses. The landscape begins to feel more like Kerala than Tamil Nadu. It is an important railway junction and bus terminal. It is often a bottleneck filled with lorries so be prepared for delays.

The old town of **Kottar**, now a suburb, was a centre of art, culture and pilgrimage. The **temple** ① *0630-0900, 1730-2000*, to Nagaraja, after which the town is named, is unique in that although the presiding deity is the Serpent God *Naga*, there are also shrines to Siva and Vishnu as well as images of Jain *Tirthankaras*, Mahavira and Parsvanatha on the pillars. The temple is alive with snakes during some festivals.

Christian missionaries played an important part in the town's development and have left their mark in schools, colleges, hospitals and of course churches of different denominations. There is also a prominent Muslim community in Kottar which is reflected in the closure of shops on Friday, remaining open on Sunday.

★ Padmanabhapuram

Padmanabhapuram, the old palace of the Rajas of Travancore, is beautifully kept and contains some fascinating architecture and paintings.

The palace
① *Closed Mon, 0900-1700, Rs 5 (accredited guide included, but expects 'donation' after tour), still camera Rs 5, video Rs 500. The museum directly opposite the ticket office contains some excellent wooden sculptures and copies of the murals.*

Padmanabhapuram's name (*Padma*, lotus; *nabha*, navel; *puram*, town) refers to the lotus emerging from the navel of Vishnu. From the ninth century this part of Tamil Nadu and neighbouring Kerala were governed by the Ay Dynasty, patrons both of Jainism and Hinduism. However, the land was always contested by the Cholas, the Pandiyas and the Cheras. By the late 11th century the new Venadu Dynasty emerged from the Chera rulers of Kerala and took control of Kanniyakumari District in AD 1125 under Raja Kodai Kerala Varman. Never a stable kingdom and with varying degrees of territorial control, Travancore State was governed from Padmanab- hapuram between 1590-1790, when the capital was shifted to Thiruvananthapuram. Although the Rajas of Travancore were Vaishnavite kings, they did not neglect Siva, as can be seen from various sculptures and paintings in the palace.

The King never officially married and the heir to the throne was his eldest sister's oldest son. This form of 'matrilineal descent' was characteristic of the earlier Chera Empire (who ruled for 200 years from the early 12th century). The palace shows the nice craftsmanship, especially in woodworking, that has been characteristic of Kerala's art and architecture. There are also some superb frescoes and excellent stone-sculpted figures. The outer cyclopean stone wall is fitted together without mortar. It encloses a total area of 75 ha, and the buildings of the palace cover 2 ha.

Listings: Vaigai Valley

◉ Sleeping

Madurai *p861, maps p862 and p864*
20% tax is added by even modest hotels.
Auto-rickshaws (about Rs 50) are available
from centre to hotels north of the river.
AL Garden Retreat (Taj), Pasumalai Hills,
7 TPK Rd, 5 km southwest of centre on NH7,
T601020, F604004. 30 rooms (some in old
colonial house), very attractive gardens
(labelled trees), outdoor dining but food
average, good bookshop, pool, great views.
A-B Ashok (ITDC), Alagarkoil Rd, T537531,
F537530. 43 musty rooms, pool (open to
non-residents), excellent restaurant.
A-B Pandiyan, Race Course, T537091,
F533424. 57 rooms, gloomy and not very
clean, pleasant garden, good restaurant
(delicious Nawabi Chicken).
B Days Inn Germanus, 28 By-Pass Rd,
T382001. Quiet, bright rooms, comfortable,
leafy views at rear, busy roundabout in front,
excellent food and service, no pool.
B-C Park Plaza, 114 W Perumal Maistry St,
T342112, F343654, www.hotelparkplaza.com.
55 smart, stylish a/c rooms, all facilities, comp
breakfast, excellent rooftop restaurant, bar.
B-C Supreme, 110 W Perumal Maistry St,
T343161, F342637, www.supremehotels.com.
69 modern clean rooms, 31 a/c on 7 floors,
good rooftop restaurant, bar, 24-hr travel,
exchange, internet, a bit noisy, bit overpriced.
C-D Chentoor, 106 W Perumal Maistry St,
T750490, F750499, www.hotelchentoor.com.
45 clean comfortable rooms (31 a/c) in
modern hotel, few with temple views, roof
top restaurant, friendly staff.
D Aarathy, 9 Perumalkoil, west of
Kundalalagar Temple, T731571. Decently
appointed rooms if a bit dingy, some a/c with
balcony, veg restaurant, quiet, very friendly.
D Tamil Nadu II (Star), Alagarkoil Rd,
T537462, F583203. 51 rooms, some a/c,
good restaurant, bar, exchange, quiet.
D YMCA International Guest House, Main
Guard Sq, near temple, T746649, F747950,
ymca@maduraionline.com. Simple a/c
double rooms, profits to worthwhile projects.
D-E International, 46 W Perumal Maistry St,
T341552, F340372, www.hotelinternational
ind.com. 34 clean rooms, views, TV, friendly.

D-E Prem Nivas, 102 W Perumal Maistry St,
T342532, F343618, premnivas@eth.net. Clean
rooms with bath, some **D** a/c, a/c restaurant
(ultra hot dishes!), basic but good value.
D-E Taj, 13a TPK Rd, T330783, F334876,
hoteltaj@maduraionline.com. Decent rooms
with bath (some noisy), some with a/c and TV.
E Arima, 4 TB Rd, T603261. 37 rooms, some
a/c, modern, simple, clean.
E Sree Devi, W Avani Moola St, T747431.
Rooms with bath, some **D** a/c, (avoid noisy
ground floor), good value, cleanish, modern
towerblock with views of temple gateway
from rooftop, changes TCs, friendly staff.
E TM Lodge, 50 W Perumal Maistry St,
T341651. 57 rooms (hot water), some a/c,
some with TV, balcony, very clean, bookings
for rail/bus journeys.
E-F Dhanamani, 20-22 Sunnamukara St,
T342703. Nice rooms (some with bath, fan,
TV), good roof terrace with temple views,
sitting area (8th floor).
E-F Ravi Lodge, 12 Mandayan Asari Lane,
Town Hall Rd, T343493. 30 clean rooms with
shower, fan, very quiet, good value.
F Thilaga, 111 W Perumal Maistry St,
T749762. 15 double clean rooms with TV, hot
water, friendly. Recommended.
F Tower View Lodge. Nice clean rooms with
toilet, shared clean hot shower, excellent
food, friendly and helpful family, internet.
F Visakam Lodge, 9 Kakathope St, T741241.
18 very clean rooms, excellent value.
F Youth Hostel, MGR Stadium, Race Course,
dorm (Rs 40-50).

Dindigul *p865*
C-D Maha Jyothi, Spencer Compound,
T0451-434313, F434317, hotelmaha jyothi@
rediffmail.com. Range of rooms, a/c, clean.
D Sukanya Lodge, by bus stand. Small,
rather dark a/c rooms, but very clean,
friendly staff, good value.
E-F Kurinji, 4 Spencer Compound, west of bus
stand (look for large antenna mast), T0451-
427017, 32 clean rooms, bit worn, adequate.
F Prakash, 9 Thiruvalluvar Salai, T0451-423577.
42 clean, spacious rooms. Recommended.
F Venkateshwar Lodge, near bus stand,
T0451-425881. 50 rooms, basic, clean, very
cheap; veg restaurant next door.

The more expensive hotels are some distance from the centre. Hotels are classified by off-season rates. From Apr-Jun prices rise by 30-50%; 20% tax and service charges apply. Most hotels have a restaurant, and rooms with attached bath down to **D** category.

A Carlton, Boat Club Rd, T40056, F41170, carlton@krahejahospitality.com. 91 excellent rooms, fully modernized colonial style hotel, excellent restaurant (try buffet lunch), billiards, tennis, golf and boating, superb position on lake, often full in season. Recommended.

A-B Lake View (Sterling), 44 Gymkhana Rd, T40313. Cottages, modern hotel/ apartment complex.

B Valley View (Sterling), Pallangi Rd, Vilpatti, T40635. 39 modern rooms but most without valley view, half-board in season, bit overpriced.

C RR Residency, Boathouse Rd, T44300, rrresidency@rediffmail.com. 7 well-furnished, top quality rooms in new hotel, though no views, veg restaurant next door.

C-D Bala, 11/49 Woodville Rd (opposite bus station), T41214, F41252, www.balacares.com. Classy, 57 rooms, good veg restaurant, friendly staff (entrance in private courtyard).

C-D Garden Manor, Lake Rd (10-min walk from bus), T40461. 7 rooms (including a 4-bed) with sit-out, restaurant (also tables outdoors), good location in gardens overlooking lake.

C-D J's Heritage, PT Rd, T41323, F40693, jaherit@md5.vsnl.net.in. 14 clean, comfortably furnished rooms, quiet, friendly and helpful management but rather over-priced.

C-D Tamil Nadu (TTDC), 47 Fern Hill Rd, T41336, F41340. 15 mins' walk from Bus Station (away from most interesting walks), restaurant and bar.

C-D Villa Retreat, Coaker's Walk, T40940, www.villaretreat.com. 8 deluxe rooms in an old house, 3 cottages (open fireplace), rustic, good service. Garden setting, excellent views, very clean but rather over-priced.

D Green Acres, 11/213 Lake Rd. T42384, F43813. Well appointed, clean rooms in pleasant colonial style home, quiet, peaceful.

D Hilltop Towers, Club Rd, T40413, F40415, httowers@md3.vsnl.net in. 26 modern comfortable rooms, can be noisy but very friendly management, good restaurant, bakery.

D Kodai, north end of Coaker's Walk, T40632, F42108, krh@pronet.net.in. 50 well-furnished 'cottages' with balcony, great views, restaurant. Clean, spacious, quiet setting.

D-E Suhaag, opposite Bus Stand, T41143. 20 comfortable rooms, TV, hot water; buses silent at night. Good value.

E Jewel, 7 Rd Junction, T40518. 9 clean, adequate rooms, 24-hr hot water, good value.

E Paradise Inn, Laws Ghat Rd, T41075. 40 comfortable spacious rooms now rather faded, but nice views, restaurant.

E Vignesh, Laws Ghat Rd, near lake, T44348. 6 spacious rooms (can inter-connect) in old period-style house, good views, garden setting. Recommended.

E-F Sunrise, PO Rd. Basic, but clean rooms with bath, front rooms best with excellent views, good value.

On **Anna Salai**: cheap basic lodges, mostly with shared bathroom can charge up to Rs 400 in season:

E Kay Pee Yem Lodge, T40555. 16 rooms.

E-F Anjay, T41080. 24 adequate rooms with balcony, popular.

F Railway Station, cheap rooms and dorm.

Youth hostels

F Greenlands, St Mary's Rd, Coaker's Walk end, T40899. 15 very basic, clean rooms (jug and bucket hot water 0700-0900), overpriced at Rs 225 but amazing views,a few new rooms, less atmospheric but have hot water on tap, pleasant gardens, 62-bed dorm (Rs 55-65), clean, but food poor and student groups can be noisy.

F Youth Hostel (TTDC), Fern Hill Rd, T41336, F41340. **D** rooms, dorm beds (Rs 60-1255), reservations: Manager, or Chennai, T830390.

Palani *p868*

F Forest Rest Houses, Top Slip, Mt Stuart, Varagaliar, Sethumadai and Amaravathinagar. May only allow 1 night stay. Reservations: District Forest Officer, Coimbatore S Div, Mahalingam Nagar, Pollachi, T04259-2508. Canteen serves good *dosa* and *thalis* for lunch.

Ramesvaram *p869, map p870*

D-E Hotel Tamil Nadu (TTDC), 14 East Car St, T21066, F21070. 53 rooms (2-6 beds), some

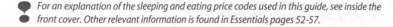

For an explanation of the sleeping and eating price codes used in this guide, see inside the front cover. Other relevant information is found in Essentials pages 52-57.

a/c, clean with sea-facing balconies, grubby restaurant (breakfast from 0700), bar, sea bathing possible nearby, exchange; very popular, book both well in advance.

D-E Maharaja, 7 Middle St, west of the Temple, T21271, F21247. 30 rooms, some a/c with bath, exchange, temple music broadcast on loudspeakers, otherwise recommended.

D-E Venkatesh, West Car St, T21296. Some a/c rooms, modern.

F Swami Ramanatha Tourist Home, between station and temple, opposite museum, T21217. Good clean rooms with bath, best budget option.

Other lodges and dharamsalas around the temple block include Star and Chola.

F Railway Retiring Rooms, T21226. 9 rooms.

Rajapalayam *p871*

F *Anandas Lodge*, 300 m left out of bus station. Clean, quiet rooms with vegetarian restaurant, courtyard design with views of the Ghats from roof, friendly, good value. Nearby, *Gandharva*, serves good non-veg.

Tenkasi *p871*

D-E Anantha, 116 Courtallam Rd. 31 rooms, hot water, a bit over-priced.

F Krishna, 2 Bus Stand Road, basic though fairly clean and spacious, excellent meals, noisy from being next to the bus station.

Others around bus stand but avoid *Vcl Tourist Home*. *Thavamani* and eateries around the bus stand serve good south Indian.

Courtallam *p871*

Over 30 lodges take in guests.

D Tamil Nadu (TTDC), opposite Parasakthi Women's College, T04633-22423. Adequate rooms, restaurant serves tasty veg meals.

F Sri Venkateswara (monkeys on building!), has rooms with Indian toilet, cold water.

Virudhunagar *p871*

F Amyon Lodge, 200 m from Bus Stand opposite Police Station. Clean, good value.

F Railway Retiring Rooms. Clean, veg meals.

Tirunelveli *p872, map p872*

Hotels are often full during the wedding season (Apr-Jun). Book ahead or arrive early

B-D Janakiram, 30 Madurai Rd, near Bus Stand, T331941, F331522. 70 clean, redecorated rooms, with hot shower, some a/c, lift, smart, brightly lit, outstanding veg rooftop restaurant. Highly recommended.

C-E Aryaas, 67 Madurai Rd, T339001, F339000, www.hotelaryaas.net. 69 rooms , 25 a/c, in dark 'bordello' style, non a/c better value, restaurants (separate vegetarian, but mosquito feast), bar. Excellent internet café opposite.

Several budget hotels are clustered near Junction Railway Station. Rooms usually with western toilet and shower.

C-E Barani, 29 Madurai Rd, T333234, F330170. 43 rooms, with hot shower, 10 a/c, clean, well maintained, vegetarian restaurant, in large, 4-storey modern block, lift, ample parking.

E Tamil Nadu, T324268. Has some dull rooms with bath and a restaurant, poorly maintained.

F Blue Star, 36 Madurai Rd, T334495. 50 rooms with cold shower, 10 a/c, good vegetarian restaurant, Indian style, modern. Good value.

F Railway Retiring Rooms. Clean, secure rooms and dorm. Excellent value.

Kanniyakumari *p873*

Hotels are in heavy demand; book well in advance. Better hotels have rooms with cold showers, hot tap and Western toilets.

B-C Maadhini, East Car St, T346787, F346657. Comfortable rooms with bath and fan (mosquito proof!), best with sea views (tell Reception if you don't want be woken early to watch the sun rise!), 'garden' restaurant in courtyard (evenings). Recommended.

B-C Seaview, East Car St, T347841, F347203. 61 excellent, large rooms, 30 a/c, in new hotel, all facilities, roof terrace. Highly recommended.

B-C Singaar, 5 Main Rd, T347992, F347991, singaar@sancharnet.in. 76 spacious, clean rooms, most a/c with balconies, modern hotel, well-maintained pool (non-residents Rs 100, 2 hrs), restaurant, extensive grounds, away from temple noise and crowds. Bit overpriced.

C-D Tamil Nadu Guest House, Beach Rd, T346257, F346030. 45 rooms, some with bath, 15 a/c, **B** twin cottages, good location, beautiful sunset views, but very slow service.

D Lakshmi, East Car St, T346333, F346627. 40 very clean rooms, some a/c with views, Indian WC, restaurant, 24-hr coffee shop.

friendly and helpful staff, but noisy 'when guests arrive at 0400-0500 to see sunrise from roof'. Excellent value.

D Shivas Residency, South Car St, T346150. 18 rooms, 3 a/c, in new hotel. Spacious, quiet, very clean. Recommended.

D-E Manickam, North Car St, T346387, F346657. 55 pleasant rooms, some with seaview and balcony, restaurant.

E Sankar Guest House, Main Rd, T346260, F346180. 36 large rooms, some delux with TV.

F Arunagiri, 59 Madurai Rd, T334553. 62 rooms with TV, some balconies, spacious, shady courtyard. very good value.

F Parvathi Nivas, West Car St, T346352. 22 basic, cool rooms in old-style lodge.

Nagercoil *p874*

D Rajam, MS Rd, Vadasery, 2 km rly, T04652-32581, F32589. 32 rooms, some a/c, restaurant, roof garden, exchange, good value.

D Parvathi, T33020. Is similar.

⊘ Eating

Madurai *p861, maps p862 and p864*
Hotels

▮▮▮ **Surya**, 7th floor rooftop (1700-2400) with good views.

▮▮▮ **Temple View** rooftop is excellent.

▮▮ **Supreme**, a/c restaurant (1700-2400), Excellent Andhra *thalis*, busy on Sun evenings.

▮ **Tamil Nadu II (Star)**, good Indian/Chinese.

Outside hotels

▮ **Anna Meenakshi**, W Perumal Maistry St. Popular South Indian.

▮ **Delhiwala Sweets**, W Tower St. Delicious Indian sweets and snacks.

▮ **Muniyandi Vilas**, at **Indo-Ceylon Restaurant**, and other outlets. Non-vegetarian. Try *paratha* and mutton curry.

▮ **New Arya Bhavan**. North and South Indian choices, ice cream.

▮ **Taj**, Town Hall Rd. Good value *thalis*, friendly.

Dindigul *p865*

Cascade Roof Garden at Sree Arya Bhavan, 19 KHF Building, near the bus stand, which serves very good vegetarian. West of the bus stand, Main Road is the shopping area.

Janakikarm, near new Roman Catholic Church. Pizzas, sweets and snacks, surprisingly good value – "*channa samosa* to die for!"

Kodaikkanal *p866, maps p866 and p868*
Hotels

▮▮▮ **Carlton**, set in very pleasant grounds overlooking lake and Garden Manor, good for tea and snacks.

▮▮▮ **Tava**, Hospital Rd, very good Indian.

▮▮ **Royal Tibet**, J's Heritage Complex, "try noodle soup and beef momos".

▮▮ **Silver Inn**, Hospital Rd. Traveller's breakfasts and Indian choices. Popular but slow service.

▮▮ **Tibetan Brothers**, J's Heritage Complex. 1200-2200 (closed 1600-1730) serves excellent Tibetan, homely atmosphere, good value. Highly recommended.

▮ **Apna Punjab** in 7 Rd. Indian.

Bakery and fast food

Eco-Nut, J's Heritage Complex, good whole foods, brown bread, jams, peanut butter etc (cheese, yoghurts, better and cheaper in **Dairy** across the road).

Hot Breads, J's Heritage Complex. Pastries.

Jacob, Main Bazar. Vasu, Lake Rd near Telephone Exchange.

Pastry Corner Anna Salai Bazar has brown bread and some pastries.

Philco's Cold Storage, opposite Kodai International School, J's Heritage Complex, for homemade choc, cakes, frozen foods, delicatessen. Also Internet.

Spencers Supermarket, Club Rd, has a wide range of local and foreign products (cheeses).

Tiny Manna Bakery on Bear Shola Rd, also serves pizzas and western vegetarian.

Rameswaram *p869, map p870*

Ashok Bhawan and **Vasantha Vihar** on West Car St and also at the Central Bus Stand, Indian vegetarian including Gujarati, but even poorer than *Hotel Tamil Nadu*.

Devasthanam Trust has a canteen opposite the east gate of the temple.

Tirunelveli *p872, map p872*

Central Café, near station. Good vegetarian.

MH Restaurant, opposite Aryaas. Western fast food, pizzas. Modern.

Kanniyakumari *p873*

Sangam, good *thalis*.

Sravanas, one near Jetty and one on Sannathi St, vegetarian. Recommended.

TTDC Restaurant. Looks like a barrack, but excellent non-vegetarian Indian meals.

◉ Entertainment

Madurai *p861, maps p862 and p864*
Minakshi Temple: 'Bed time of the God'
1930-45, not to be missed (see 'Sights' above).
Thirumalai Nayaka Palace: Sound and
Lightshow: English 1845-1930; Rs 5 (take
mosquito repellent), sadly, "poor, faded
tape"; during the day, dance drama and
concerts are held in the courtyard.

❈ Festivals and events

Madurai *p861, maps p862 and p864*
In **Jan/Feb** the annual Float Festival marks
the birth anniversary of Thirumalai Nayaka,
who originated it. Many temple deities in
silks and jewels, including Minakshi and
Sundareswarar, are taken out on a full moon
night on floats colourfully decorated with
hundreds of oil lamps and flowers. The floats
carry them to the central shrine to the
accompaniment of music and chanting.
Jallikattu Festival (Taming the Bull) is held in
Jan. Chitrai Festival in **Apr/May** is the most
important at the Minakshi Temple is the
10-day festival which celebrates the
marriage of Siva and Minakshi. In **Aug/Sep**
the **Avanimoolam** is the Coronation Festival
of Siva when the image of Lord
Sundareswarar is taken out to the riverbank
dressed as a worker.

Kodaikkanal *p866, maps p866 and p868*
May: Summer Tourist Festival: Boat race,
flower show, dog show etc.

Kanniyakumari *p873*
Chitra Purnima is a special full moon
celebration at the temple usually held in the
second week of **Apr**. Sunset and moonrise
can be seen together. In first week of **Oct**
Special **Navarathri** celebrations.

⦿ Shopping

Madurai *p861, maps p862 and p864*
Kashmiri 'emporia' pay 40-50% commission
to touts.
  Best buys are textiles, carvings in wood and
stone, brass images, jewellery and appliqué
work for temple chariots. Most shops are on
South Avani Moola St (for jewellery), Town
Hall Rd, Masi St and around the Temple.

Books
Higginbotham's Book Exchange, near temple.
New Century Book House, Town Hall Rd.

Handicrafts
Two good shops in North Chitrai St:
Handicrafts Emporium, 39-41 Town Hall Rd.
Khadi Gramodyog Bhandar and **Surabhi**
on W Veli St.

Textiles and tailors
Market near Pudu Mandapam, next to
Minakshi East Gate, sell fabric and is a
brilliant place to get clothes made.
Femina, 10 W Chitrai St. You can take
photos of Minakshi Temple from rooftop.
Hajee Moosa, 18 E Chitrai St, tailoring in 8
hrs; 'ready-mades' at **Shabnam**, at No 17.

Kodaikkanal *p866, maps p866 and p868*
For general **toiletries** and **food**, Anna Salai
Bazar Rd, near Pastry Corner. The town market,
off the bazar, has excellent vegetables.

Books
CLS and JJ, Anna Salai.

Handicrafts
Belgian Convent shop, east of town. Has
hand embroidered linen.
Cottage Crafts Shop, Anna Salai (Council for
Social Concerns in Kodai). Volunteer run,
0900-1230, 1400-1830, Mon-Sat.
Govt Sales Emporium near Township Bus
Stand. Only open in season.
Kashmir Handicrafts Centre, 2 North
Shopping Complex, Anna Salai. Shawls,
jewellery, brass and 'Numdah' rugs.
Khadi Emporium, Handloom Co-op,
Travancore Craft Works, Post Office Rd.

▲ Activities and tours

Madurai *p861, maps p862 and p864*
Tours
TTDC Temple tour of Madurai and
surroundings by a/c coach; half day, 0700-1200,
1500-2000. Rs 125. Recommended to get an
overview. Apr-Jun: **Courtallam** Rs 300.
Kodaikkanal 0700-2100, Rs 250. **Rameswaram**
Rs 275. Book at Hotel Tamil Nadu, West Veli St,
T337471. **Ex-Serviceman Travels** 1
Koodalalagar, Perumal Kovil St, T730571, **City**
half day, 0700, 1500, Rs 140; **Kodaikkanal** or

Ramesvaram 0700-1900, Rs 2750; overnight to **Kanniyakumari** 2200-1900, Rs 350.

Yoga
Gandhi Museum, T481060, 0630, daily classes.

Kodaikkanal *p866, maps p866 and p868*
Boating
Boat Club, T41315, allows daily membership with club facilities. Open 0900-1730.
TTDC Boathouse, next door. Open 0900-1730.

Golf
Club, T40323.

Riding
Ponies near the Boat House; officially Rs 100 per hr, doubled to include 'guide' (bargaining essential).

Tour operators
Sugam, PO Rd, Railway Out Agency.
Vijay Tours, near Tourist Information Centre, Anna Salai, T41137. Local sights, Rs 70-80.

☉ Transport

Madurai *p861, maps p862 and p864*
Air
Airport to city centre (12 km) by Pandiyan coach (calls at top hotels); taxi (Rs 375) or auto-rickshaw (Rs 80). **Indian Airlines**, 7A W Veli St, T741234. 1000-1300, 1400-1700; Airport, T670433. Flights to **Chennai** and **Mumbai**. Air India, opposite railway station, W Veli St.). **Jet Airways**, T526969; Airport T690771. To **Chennai**.

Auto-rickshaw
Rs 25, bargain first; very predatory.

Bus
Local There is a good network within the city and the suburbs.
Long distance Approaching from the south, to get to the centre, change to a city bus at Tirumangalam (15 km south). State and Private companies (MPTC, PRC, but check bus details carefully) run services to other cities. Most inter-city buses use the **New Central Bus Stand** (or Muttuthavani Bus Terminal), 6 km northeast of town, in open countryside, continuation of Alagar Koil Rd, on the toll Ring road (25 mins, Rs 40 by rickshaw, or city bus from town centre).

Buses for **Bangalore** (11 hrs), **Ernakulam** (**Kochi**), **Chennai** (10 hrs), **Pondicherry** (9 hrs), **Thiruvananthapuram** (8 hrs), **Kumbakonum**, **Rameshvaram** (under 4 hrs, every 15 mins), **Thanjavur** (4 hrs), **Tiruchirapalli** (2½ hrs), **Tirunelveli** (4 hrs, Rs 40). **Arapalayam Bus Stand**, 3 km northwest of centre (Bus route No 7A, auto-rickshaws Rs 20), T603740, for destinations to the north and northwest, including **Kodaikkanal**, buses (crowded in peak season, Apr-Jul); 3½ hrs (longer via Palani), Rs 150. Also buses to **Coimbatore** (5 hrs, change there for Mysore or Ooty), **Periyar/Kumili** (4 hrs), **Salem** (5½ hrs), **Dindigul. Central (Periyar) Bus Stands**, near W Veli St, are now used for buses around town and destinations in the immediate vicinity.

Car
To Kodaikkanal Rs 950 (Rs 1600 a/c), see local transport above.

Cycle-rickshaw
Can be persistent; offer Rs 20 around town.

Taxi/car hire
Unmetered; 10 hrs/225 km, Rs 450, Rs 675 (a/c); 6 hrs sightseeing, Rs 490 (Rs 750 a/c); 1 hr/10 km, Rs 65, Rs 100 (a/c). Janakiraman, 184 North Veli St; **Supreme**, 110 Perumal Maistry St, T743151.

Train
Madurai Junction is the main station: enquiries, T37597, reservations: 1st Class T23535, 2nd Class T33535. 0700-1300, 1330-2000. New Computer Reservation Centre to south of main entrance. Left luggage facilities. Pre-paid auto-rickshaw kiosk outside. **Chennai (ME)** via Villupuram for **Pondicherry**: *Vaigai Exp, 2636*, 0645, 8 hrs; *Pandiyan Exp, 6718*, 2020, 10 hrs. **Coimbatore**: *Fast Pass Exp, 6716*, 2135, 7 hrs; *Quillon Coimbatore Exp, 6782*, 0640, 5 hrs. **Kollam**: connect with trains from Virudhunagar (see page 1198). **Kanniyakumari**: *Chennai Egmore Kanniyakumari Exp, 6121*, 0415, 5¾ hrs. **Rameswaram**: *Coimbatore- Rameswaram Exp, 6715*, 0600, 4¾ hrs. **Thiruvananthapuram**: see Virudhunagar on page 871. **Tiruchirapalli**: several, *Vaigai Exp, 2636*, 0645, 2½ hrs (beautiful countryside); *Pandyan Exp, 6718*, 1925, 3½ hrs.

Dindigul *p865*
Bus
Good and frequent bus service to **Tiruchirappalli**, **Chennai**, **Salem** and **Coimbatore**. Also longer distance connections.

Train
Chennai (ME) *Vaigai Exp*, 2636 (AC/CC), 0745, 6¾ hrs via **Tiruchirappalli** 1½ hrs. **Madurai** *Vaigai Exp*, 2635 (AC/CC), 1905, 1¼ hrs. Broad gauge to **Karur** 2240, 1½ hrs.

Kodaikkanal *p866, maps p866 and p868*
Bicycle
Hire at the top of the Bazar. **JM Tea shop** and cycle hire, at Junction of Club Rd and Anna Salai, good bikes Rs 5 per hr, Rs 50 per day.

Bus
Long distance To **Bangalore**, overnight, 12 hrs; **Chennai** (497 km) 12 hrs, **Coimbatore** (171 km) 6 hrs; **Dindigul** (90 km) 3½ hrs, Kodai Rd, **Madurai** (120 km), 0730-1830, 4 hrs, about Rs 25; **Kumily** (Periyar), 1415, 5½ hrs, Rs 35 (packed!) change buses at Vatlgundu; **Palani** (65 km) 3 hrs; **Tiruchirappalli** (197 km) 5 hrs, during the season.

Taxi
Unmetered taxis available. Tourist taxis only from Madurai.

Train
Reservations, Jayaraj Hall, Coaker's Walk Rd. **Kodai Road**, 80 km away, is the nearest station.

Palani *p868*
Bus
From chaotic bus station at Pollachi (for Parambikulam) 0600, 1130, 1500 (check timings); ask for Top Slip, from **Perambikulam**, 0700, 1300.

Ramesvaram *p869, map p870*
Air
Madurai (154 km) has the nearest airport.

Bus
Local Marudhu Pandiyan Transport Corporation (MPTC) covers the town and the area around. The Bus Station is 2 km west of the town. You can get a bus from the Railway Station to the Ramalingesvara Temple, to Pamban or to Dhanuskodi (both via the temple). From the temple's east gate to Dhanuskodi roadhead and to Gandhamadana Parvatam, both about every 2 hrs. **Long distance** State, MPTC and private bus companies run regular services via Mandapam to several towns nearby. Central Bus Stand is 2 km from the main temple gate. **Govt Express Bus Reservations**, North Car St. 0700-2100. Frequent buses to **Madurai**, 173 km (4½ hrs); Tourist coach (hotel-to-hotel) is better.

Taxi
A few cars and jeeps are available from the railway station and hotels.

Train
Ramesvaram Railway Station, Enquiries and Reservations, T226. Open 0800-1300, 1330-1730. **Chennai**: *Sethu Exp*, 6714, 1510, 17¾ hrs via **Chengalpattu**, 16½ hrs. **Coimbatore**: *Coimbatore Fast Pass*, 6716, 1610, 12¼ hrs. **Madurai**: *Coimbatore Fast Pass*, 6716, 1610, 5 hrs. **Tiruchirappalli**: *Rameswaram Tambaram Exp*, 6702, 1200, 5½ hrs; *Sethu Exp*, 6714, 1510, 6¼ hrs.

Virudhunagar *p871*
Bus
Leave Madurai early morning for **Kollam** train; get off at police station and go to the end of the road opposite and turn left; the railway station is about 1 km on the right (take a rickshaw if carrying heavy luggage).

Train
To **Kollam** and **Thiruvananthapuram**, Platform 3 across the bridge. Kollam: *Fast Pass Exp*, 6761, 2150, 7 hrs.

Tirunelveli *p872, map p872*
Bus
Long distance Good bus connections to **Kanniyakumari**, **Thiruvananthapuram**, and to **Madurai** (faster to change buses at Tirumangalam), **Tiruchirappalli** and **Chennai**. For **Courtallam**, go to Tenkasi (Rs 12, 1½ hrs) and take bus to Courtallam (Rs 2, 20 mins).

Train
Chennai (ME): *Nellai Exp*, 6120 (AC/CC), 1900, 13¾ hrs. Broad gauge to **Chennai (MC)**: *Kanniyakumari Exp*, 6020, 1740, 15 hrs. Also to Madurai and Kanniyakumari.

Bus

Long distance Central Bus Station, west of town, about 15 mins walk from centre, T71285. It has a restaurant, waiting room and Retiring Rooms upstairs. There are frequent services to **Nagercoil** (½ hr), **Kovalam** and **Thiruvanan-thapuram** (2½ hrs) but the journey can be tiring and uncomfortable. Govt Express buses go to other major towns including **Chennai** (16 hrs), **Madurai** (6 hrs), **Rameswaram** (8½ hrs).

Ferry

To **Vivekananda Rock**, every 30 mins, 0700-1100, 1400-1700; sometimes 2 run continuously. Rs 10. Queues during festivals.

Train

Station to the north, off the Trivandrum Rd, large and well organized, T71247. **Chennai (ME)** (via Madurai): *Kanniyakumari Chennai Egmore Exp, 6122*, 1550, 15¾ hrs. **Delhi (ND)**: *Him Sagar Exp, 6317/6787*, Fri, 1245 (it does not stop in Chennai; it stops at Katpadi and then Gudur). **Madurai**: *Kanniyakumari Chennai Egmore Exp, 6122*, 1550, 5¼ hrs. **Mumbai (CST)**: *Kanniyakumari Mumbai Exp, 1082* (AC/II), 0445, 48 hrs. **Thiruvananthapuram**: *Kanniyakumari Mumbai Exp, 1082* (AC/II), 0445, 2¼ hrs.

Padmanabhapuram *p874*

Bus

Regular service to **Thiruvananthapuram** and **Kanniyakumari**. Less frequent buses to and from **Kovalam**. From Kovalam, depart approximately 0940 to Thuckalai. Rickshaw to Padmanabhapuram. Return buses from Thuckalai depart 1445, 1530.

Taxi

From Kovalam and Thiruvananthapuram including Padmanabhapuram, Suchindram and Kanniyakumari costs approximately Rs 800.

❶ Directory

Madurai *p861, maps p862 and p864*

Banks Several on East Avani Moola St. Andhra Bank, W Chitrai St, accepts credit cards; **Canara Bank**, W Veli St, cash Amex and sterling TCs. **Alagendran Finance**, 182D N Veli St. **Post office** GPO at north end of W Veli St (Scott Rd). In Tallakulam: Head Post Office and Central Telegraph Office, on Gokhale Rd. **Hospitals** Christian Mission Hospital, East Veli St; **Grace Kennet** Hospital, 34 Kennet Rd. **Internet** Dolphin, Madurai Junction station. Many west of temple and in budget hotel area charge Rs 20 per hr. **Tourist offices** W Veli St, T337471, 1000-1745, Mon-Fri; useful maps, tours arranged through agents, guides for hire. Madurai Junction Railway Station, Main Hall, 0630-2030. Airport counter, during flight times.

Kodaikkanal *p866, maps p866 and p868*

Banks Several on Anna Salai, 1000-1400 Mon to Fri, 1000-1200 Sat. **Indian Bank**, 15 min service. **Hotel Tamil Nadu**, exchange counter. **Hospitals** **Van Allan Hospital**, T41273, recommended. Consultations (non-emergency): 0930-1200, 1530-1630 Mon-Fri. 1000-1200 Sat. Clean and efficient, good doctors (not inclined to prescribe antibiotics). **Government Hospital**, T41292. **Post office** Head Post Office on Post Office Rd. Others in Main Bazar, Observatory, Lake View, Anantha Giri, Pambapuram and Shenbaganur. **Tourist offices** Tamil Nadu, *Rest House*, near Bus Stand, T41675. 1000-1745, except holidays. Helpful staff, maps available.

Ramesvaram *p869, map p870*

Post offices East of temple near Police Station and on Mela St towards Bus Station. 0930-1730. **Tourist offices** At 14 East Car St, T21371. 1000-1700. Railway Station, T21373, open (with breaks) 0700-2030. Temple Information, east side of the temple.

Tirunelveli *p872, map p872*

Banks Found on Trivandrum High Rd. **Hospital** In High Ground, Palayamkottai. **Post office** GPO, Trivandrum High Rd.

Kanniyakumari *p873*

Banks Branches of Canara Bank, Main Rd; State Bank of India; State Bank of Travancore, Beach Rd. **Post office** Head Post Office, Main Rd. Branches at Vivekandandapuram. 1100-1600 and Sannathi St, 1000-1400.

Kerala

⚑ Footprint features

Introduction

India's most densely populated region has a distinctive charm. Travellers are drawn to Kerala by its attractive palm-lined beaches – **Kovalam** and its quieter neighbouring resorts.

The **backwaters** beckon the visitor to catch a glimpse of Keralan village life, while festivals are marked by great **elephant marches**, **snake boat races** and colourful **Kathakali dances**. The **wildlife sanctuaries** and **national parks** offer the opportunity for seeing wild elephants and the endangered Nilgiri Tahr.

High levels of education and health care have given Kerala an enviable reputation elsewhere in India, and its unique balance of Hindu, Muslim and Christian, sets it apart even from its neighbours Tamil Nadu and Karnataka.

★ Don't miss...

❶ Kerala is the centre for ayurvedic medicine. Take part in a 'rejuvenation programme' at **Keraleeyamm** in Varkala, page 905.

❷ **Kovalam** has some of the best beaches in India; the Lighthouse Beach is still relatively quiet, page 894.

❸ If it is peace you are after then a trip on the **Backwaters** is a must. Watch waterside activities like coir making, toddy tapping and fishing from the quiet of a traditional dugout canoe or an exclusive kettuvallam-style houseboat, page 909.

❹ **Alappuzha** is the place to watch spectacular Snake Boat Races which are usually held in August, page 914.

❺ You stand a good chance of seeing lots of wildlife (as well as loads of fellow tourists) at **Periyar**, one of the best Nationbal Parks in the country, page 923.

❻ The **Pooram** in Thrissur is held at the end of April. The grand festival with elephants, parasols, drums and fireworks should not be missed, page 942.

❼ **Munnar**, surrounded by tea estates, is a genuine hill station and close to the highest peak in South India. There are some lovely bike rides in the surrounding hills, page 927.

Background → *Population: 32 million. Area: 39,000 sq km. www.kerala tourism.org.*

The land

Stretching from some of the highest mountains of the Western Ghats to the lush coastal plain, Kerala encapsulates the rich diversity of western India's coastal landscapes. Its narrow coastal fringe has been raised from the sea in the last one million years. Immediately inland are low, rolling hills of laterite, succeeded by the ancient rocks which form the backbone of the Western Ghats.

Dotted along the edge of the ghats from Ponmudi in the south to Sulthan Bathery in the north, Kerala's hill stations experience the full force of the southwest and northeast monsoons from May to November, but out of the monsoon season the hills offer lovely country for walks and treks.

The state's palm-fringed backwaters along the coastline are a special attraction. The Silent Valley National Park in the Western Ghats (restricted entry) has the only substantial area of tropical evergreen rain forest in the country. As forested land is increasingly under threat from soaring land values and growing population the Government has legislated to make all ecologically sensitive areas in Kerala the direct responsibility of the state.

Climate Kerala does not have an extended totally dry season characteristic of the rest of India, but is particularly wet from June to September. Maximum temperatures rarely rise above 32°C while minimum temperatures at sea level are never below 20°C.

History

The name Kerala is often widely explained today as meaning 'land of coconuts', derived from the Malayalam word 'kera' or coconut palm. However this is not its origin. '*Keralaputra*' – land of the sons of the Cheras – *putra*, son – was referred to in **Asoka's** edicts dating from between 273-236 BC, over a thousand years before the Malayalam language of contemporary Kerala took shape. To the Tamils the region was known for centuries as *Seranadu*, again meaning land of the Cheras.

Periodically the region had been under Tamil control. The Cheras, who established themselves in the Kuttanad region around Alappuzha as the first Kerala power, continued to use Tamil as the state language up to the seventh century. 200 years separated the ending of the first Chera Dynasty and the emergence of the powerful and prosperous second empire.

The Cheras developed a wide network of trade links in which both the long established Christian community and the Jewish community participated fully. Mahodayapuram (modern Kodangallur) traded from Cordoba in the west to Sumatra in the east. However, the neighbouring Cholas launched several successful attacks against Chera power from AD 985 onwards. When Chola power itself disintegrated at the end of the 11th century, minor principalities emerged, dominated by a new group, the Nambudiri Brahmans, and contested for control of the region's vital trade in spices – pepper, ginger, cardamom and cinnamon.

Calicut gradually became dominant under the **Zamorin** (literally *Lord of the Sea*), who had well-established contacts with the Arab world. By some accounts he was the wealthiest ruler in contemporary India. He was unable to use these advantages to unite Kerala, and during the 16th century the Portuguese exploited the rivalry of the Raja of Kolattiri with the Zamorin of Calicut, being granted permission to trade from Kochi in 1499. Over the following century there was fierce competition and sometimes open warfare between the Portuguese, bent on eliminating Arab trading competition, and the Zamorin, whose prosperity depended on that Arab trade. The competition was encouraged by the rulers of Kochi, in the hope that by keeping the hands of both tied in conflict their own independence would be strengthened.

After a century of hostility, the **Dutch** arrived on the west coast. The Zamorin seized the opportunity of gaining external support, and on 11 November 1614 concluded a Treaty giving the Dutch full trading rights. In 1615 the British East India Company was also given the right to trade by the Zamorin. By 1633 the Dutch had captured all the Portuguese forts of Kollam, Kodungallur, Purakkad, Kochi and Kannur. The ruler of Kochi rapidly made friends with the Dutch, in exchange having the new Mattancherry Palace built for him, and inevitably facing renewed conflict with Calicut as a result.

In the decade after 1740 Raja Marthanda Varma succeeded in uniting a number of petty states around Thiruvananthapuram and led them to a crushing victory over the Dutch in the Battle of Kolachel in 1741. By 1758 the Zamorin of Calicut was forced to withdraw from Kochi, but the **Travancore** ruler's reign was brief. In 1766 Haidar Ali had led his cavalry troops down onto the western coastal plain, and he and his son Tipu Sultan pushed further and further south with a violence that is still bitterly remembered. In 1789, as Tipu was preparing to launch a final assault on the south of Travancore, the British attacked him from the east. He withdrew his army from Kerala and the Zamorin and other Kerala leaders looked to the British to take control of the forts previously held by Tipu's officers. Tipu Sultan's first defeat at the hands of Lord Cornwallis led to the Treaty of Seringapatam in 1792, under which Tipu surrendered all his captured territory in the northern part of Kerala, to direct British rule. Travancore and Kochi became Princely states under ultimate British authority.

Culture

The distinctiveness of Kerala's cultural identity is reflected in the Brahmin myths of its origin. As Robin Jeffrey has put it, Parasurama, the sixth incarnation of Vishnu, having been banished from India, was given permission by Varuna, the Lord of the Sea, to reclaim all the land within the throw of his axe. When Parasaruma threw the axe it fell from Kanniyakumari to Gokarnam, and as the sea withdrew Kerala was formed. However, the new land had to be settled, so Parasurama introduced a special race of Brahmins, the **Nambudris**, to whom he gave all the land and unique customs. He then brought in Nairs – to act as servants and bodyguards for the Nambudris. "He gave them the matrilineal system of family, and stated that they should have no formal marriage, and that Nair women should always be available to satisfy the desires of Nambudri men."

Matriarchy may have originated in the 10th-century conflict with the Cholas, when the Nairs' vital role as soldiers allowed them to rise in status. The immigrant Nambudri Brahmins had far fewer women than men, so while the eldest sons married Nambudri women other sons married Kshatriya or Nair girls. Krishna Chaitanya suggests that as many Nair and Kshatriya men were slaughtered in the Chola wars there was a surplus of women in all three communities, encouraging the development of a **matrilineal system** in which women controlled family property. Nairs became numerically and politically the dominant force. In the mid 19th century the system was still dominant, as was slavery which was a widespread feature both socially and economically. From 1855, when European missionary pressure encouraged the Travancore government to abolish slavery, Nair dominance weakened. Education spread rapidly, contributing to the belief that qualifications rather than inherited status should determine economic opportunity, and by the beginning of the 20th century literacy in the towns was already higher than in Calcutta and there were over 20 daily newspapers.

Kerala is the first state in India to claim 100% **literacy** in some districts and women enjoy a high social status. The 2001 Census shows that overall literacy has reached 91%, and uniquely in India there are more women than men in the population.

The majority of the **population** is Hindu, but as much as a quarter of the population is Christian and there is also a large Muslim population. Religious communities have often lived amicably together. There is no conflict between the varying Hindu sects, and most temples have shrines to each of the major Hindu divinities. Christianity, which is thought to have been brought by St Thomas the Apostle to the coast of Kerala at Kodungallur in AD 52, has its own very long tradition. The equally large Muslim community traces its origins back to the spread of Islam across the Indian Ocean with Arab traders from the seventh century.

Cuisine Kerala's cuisine reflects its diverse religious traditions, its seaboard location and the ubiquitous presence of the coconut. Uniquely in India, for example, beef is widely eaten, although seafood is far more common. *Fish Moilee* is prepared with coconut milk and spices while for *Pollichathu* the fish is baked with chilli paste, curry leaves and spices. Coconut based dishes such as *thoran*, a dry dish of mixed vegetables chopped very small, herbs and a variety of curry leaves, with *avial*, similar to thoran but cooked in a sauce, are widely eaten. *Erisseri* is a thick curry of banana or yam and *kichadi* is beetroot or cucumber in coconut-curd paste. You can try these with the soft centred, lacy pancake *appam* or the soft noodle rice cakes *iddiappam*. Jack fruit, pineapples, custard apples and a seemingly endless variety of bananas – also play a vital part in many dishes. Rice is the staple cereal, around which in the typical Kerala *thali* will be a range of vegetables, served with *pappadum*, *rasam* (a thin clear pepper water or soup), spicy *sambar* made with lentils and vegetables, and *curd*. For dessert, you might get milk *payasam*, made with rice or vermicelli.

Language Malayalam, the state language, is the most recent of the Dravidian languages, developing from the 13th century with its origin in Sanskrit and the Proto-Dravidian language which also gave rise to Tamil.

Dance The special dance form of Kerala, **Kathakali**, has its origins in the *Theyyam*, a ritual tribal dance of North Kerala, and *kalaripayattu*, the martial arts practised by the high-caste Nayars, going back 1,000 years. In its present form of dance-drama, Kathakali has evolved over the last 400 years. The performance is usually out of doors, the stage is bare but for a large bronze oil-lamp, with the drummers on one side and the singers with cymbal and gong, who act as narrators, on the other. The art of mime reaches its peak in these highly stylized performances which always used to last through the night; now they often take just three to four hours. Kathakali is no longer strictly the preserve of the male dancer.

Putting on the elaborate make-up and costumes is very time consuming. The costume consists of a large, billowing skirt, a padded jacket, heavy ornaments and headgear. The make-up is all-important: *Thecha* (painted make-up) – *Pacha* (green) characterizing the Good and *Kathi* (knife, shape of a painted 'moustache'), the Villain; *Thadi* (bearded) – white for superhuman *hanumans*, black for the hunter and red for evil and fierce demons; *Kari* (black) signifying demonesses; *Minukku* (shining) 'simple' make-up representing the Gentle and Spiritual. The paints are natural pigments while the stiff 'mask' is created with rice paste and lime. The final application of a flower seed in the lower eyelid results in the red eyes you will see on stage.

This classical dance requires lengthy and hard training to make the body supple, the eyes expressive. The 24 *mudras* express the nine emotions of serenity, wonder, kindness, love, valour, fear, contempt, loathing and anger. The gods and mortals play out their roles amid the chaos brought about by human ambition, but the dance ends in peace and harmony restored by the gods.

Every 12 years the North Malabar village communities of Kannur and Kasaragod organize a **Theyyam** festival. The term itself is a corruption of *deivam*, or God. A

Traditional meals are eaten with the fingers, and on ceremonial occasions off banana leaves, though more commonly today off large stainless steel plates

⦂ Ayurvedic medicine

Ayurveda (science of life/health) is the ancient Hindu system of medicine – a naturalistic system depending on diagnosis of the body's 'humours' (wind, mucus, gall and sometimes, blood) to achieve a balance. In its early form, gods and demons were associated with cures and ailments; treatment was carried out by using herbs, minerals, formic acid (from ant hills) and water, and hence was limited in scope. Ayurveda classified substances and chemical compounds in the theory of panchabhutas or five 'elements'. It also noted the action of food and drugs on the human body. Ayurvedic massage using aromatic and medicinal oils to tone up the nervous system, has been practised in Kerala for centuries. Interest has been revived in this form of medicine and there are now several centres which include a 'rejuvenation programme'. There are Ayurvedic hospitals in the larger towns in Kerala and elsewhere.

combination of music and dance, the festival brings together all castes and religions, but is a development of a pre-Hindu cult. Many folk gods and goddesses continue to hold a place in the festival. Initial rituals invoke the deity while the drum beats, flaming torches and music and dance create a surreal atmosphere for the performance which is believed to ward of evil and bring prosperity.

The sensuous **Mohiniyattam**, performed by women, is known as the dance of the charmer or temptress. It evolved through the influence of Tamil dancers who brought Bharata Natyam to the Kerala royal courts. It is performed solo as in Bharata Natyam with a similar core repertoire and musical accompaniments but with the addition of *idakkai*, a percussion instrument. **Tullal**, again peculiar to Kerala, is another classical solo dance form which comes closer to contemporary life, and is marked for its simplicity, wit and humour.

Martial arts Kalaripayattu, possibly developed as a form of military training during the 11th century wars with the Cholas, is still practised in *kalaris* or gymnasia. The four disciplines give training in self-defence and attack. Kalaripayattu underlay the development of Kathakali and of other Kerala dance form. The folk dance *Valekali* common during temple festivals, and the Christian *Chavittu-Natakam*, in which dramatic pounding of the feet is a major feature, both derive from the martial art.

Handicrafts Temples and palaces have excellent carving, and rosewood is still inlaid with other woods, bone or plastics (to replace the traditional ivory). Wooden boxes with brass binding where plain or patterned strips of brass are used for decoration are also made, as are carved models of the 'snake boats'. Kerala produces astonishing *masks* and *theatrical ornaments*, particularly the Krishnattam masks which resemble the mask-like make up of the Kathakali dancers. Conch shells which are also available in great numbers are carved out in relief.

Modern Kerala

Government The reorganization of the Indian States in 1956 brought together the Malayalam language area of Kerala into one political unit. With the exception of some of the Kanniyakumari districts now in Tamil Nadu, it comprises all of Travancore, Kochi, Malabar and a part of South Kanara District from Karnataka.

 High Court of Kerala has issued a directive banning smoking in public places such as streets, bus stops, railway stations, buses, trains, restaurants etc

Kerala politics have often been unstable – even turbulent – since the first elections were held in March 1957. They have been dominated by the struggle between the Communist Party (Marxist), the Congress, and various minor parties, and the State government has often been formed by coalitions. Between 1957 and the middle 1980s President's Rule was imposed seven times. In the May 2001 Assembly elections the UDF swept back into power, reducing the Left Democratic Front to its lowest ever number of seats, and the veteran Congress leader A K Antony returned as Chief Minister.

Economy Traditionally Kerala's economy has depended heavily on agriculture. Estate crops, especially tea and rubber, make a major contribution to exports, while coconut and coconut products like coir, the coarse fibre used for matting and string and rope production, or copra, the oil-rich flesh of the coconut, continue to be vital to the state. Newer cash crops like pineapples have also begun to establish a national and international market. Rice production has been in long term decline, and between 1990 and 2000 production fell by 25% as farmers converted paddy land to other more profitable uses, stimulated by the rise of Kerala as a remittance economy, with large flows of money being repatriated by Malayali workers in the Gulf to invest in land, housing and small scale industries.

Festivals

Useful website www.kerala tourism.org, or pick up their annual 'Fairs and Festivals of Kerala'.

March-April (Meenam) and **October-November (Thulam)**: *Arattu* is the closing festival of the 10-day celebrations of the Padmanabhasvami Temple in Thiruvananthapuram in which the deity is processed around the temple inside the fort, and then down to the sea.

April-May: *Vishukani* celebrates the start of the rainy season. The fire crackers exploded to ward off evil spirits can be quite terrifyingly loud.

August-September: The biggest and most important festival is *Thiruvonam* (*Onam*), a harvest festival, celebrated throughout Kerala. *Onam Tourist Week* is a cultural feast of art and folk presentations at 20 venues in Thiruvananthapuram and other major Kerala towns. The four day festival is marked with elephant processions, Kathakali dances, fireworks, water carnivals and *vallam kalli*, the famous snake boat races, at Aranmula, Alappuzha, Kottayam, Kochi and Payipad; early September. *Nehru Trophy Boat Race* at Punnamadakayal, Alappuzha; August 2004: a ceremonial water procession followed by the famed snake boat race.

December-January: *Tiruvathira* is exclusively a festival for women, generally unmarried, and is associated with Kamadeva, the god of love. Swings are improvised from trees especially for the day.

The far south

Thiruvananthapuram (Trivandrum)

→ *Phone code 95471 (International: 04 71). Colour map 7, grid C3. Population: 744,700.*
The capital, a pleasant city built over gently rolling coastal land, retains a rural air away from the crowded centre. The imposing Secretariat stands apart from the busy bazar area along the central MG Road. The old fort and the large complex of the Padmanabhasvami Temple are to the south near the bustling bus stand, while the artistic and cultural heart, exemplified by the Museum building, is to the north.
▸▸ *For Sleeping, Eating and other listings, see pages 898-907.*

Ins and outs

Getting there The airport is only 15-mins' drive (outside the rush hour) from the town centre. You can hire a pre-paid taxi or auto into town, or wait for a local bus. The station and bus termini are at the southern end of town with buses to Kovalam using the stand opposite the fort entrance. Arrival is usually unpressurized.

Getting around The town is quite strung out, though the centre is compact. Buses are usually packed but very cheap. Autos, or more expensive taxis, are more convenient but bargain. See Transport, page 905, for further details.

Climate Temperature: highs of 33°C in Feb-Mar, dipping to 20°C for the rest of the year. Rainfall: Dec-Apr, average 50 mm; May-Nov, average 200 mm. Best time to visit: Dec-Mar.

History

Thiruvananthapuram became the capital of the Raja of Travancore in 1750 when the then Raja moved from Padmanabhapuram. The name is derived from *Tiru Ananta Puram*, the abode of the sacred serpent *Ananta* upon whose coils Vishnu lies in the main temple.

Sights

Sri Padma-nabhasvami Temple ① *0415-0515, 0645-0730, 0830-1030, 1130-1145, 1715-1915.* According to legend, the temple was built in stages to house the statue of Vishnu reclining on the sacred serpent *Ananta*, which was found in the forest. It was rebuilt in 1733 by Raja Marthanda Varma who dedicated the whole kingdom, including his rights and possessions, to the deity. Unusually for Kerala, it is in the Dravidian style with beautiful murals, sculptures and 368 carved granite pillars which support the main pavilion or *Kulashekhara Mandapa*. You can see the seven-storeyed *gopuram* with its sacred pool from outside; male visitors may wear a *dhoti* over their trousers to go inside, women a saree and blouse. Normally open only to Hindus but permission can sometimes be obtained if suitably dressed. Kerala Brahmins are often stricter than those in Tamil Nadu. They have rules of clothing even for male Hindus who must enter wearing only a white *dhoti*.

Christ Church ① *English service on Sun at 0730.* Built 1873, near Palayam opposite the stadium, and known locally as St Joseph's, this was the cantonment church and has some interesting gravestones.

Kanakakunnu Palace Some 800m northeast of the museum, the palace now belongs to the Government. It is well worth being taken around by the interesting and knowledgeable guide.

Related map
*A Thiruvananthapuram
centre, page 893*

To Kollam (NH 17)
To Ponmadi
Cosmopolitan Club
Sri Chitra Art Gallery
Zoo
Kanakunna Palace
PMG Circle
Air India
Indian Airlines
Vellayam-balam Palace
Museum of Science & Technology
LMS Junc
University Stadium
Napier Museum, Open Air Theatre & Natural History Museum
Observatory
Crafts Design Centre
New State Assembly
Christ
Public Library
Swimming Pool
VELLAYAMBALAM
Police Stadium
MLA's Hostel
Palayam Junction
St Joseph's Cathedral
Tagore Theatre
KUNNUKUZHI
University College
Town Hall
Connemara
VAZHUTAKKAD
Forest Museum
Central Survey Office
General Hospital Circle
Spencer Junction
A
Bakery Junction
Accountant General's Office
Air Lanka
Yoga Centre
Statue Rd
Statue Junction
Jaihind Travels
Foreigners' Registration Office
Secretariat
Central Stadium
Panavila Junction
GPO
Pulimudu Junc
Press Rd
Housing Board Junction
Children's Museum
THYCAUD
VANCHIYUR
Residency
(KITTS)
Ayurvedic College
A College Junction
Aristo Rd
Lab Supplies
6 3
THAMPANOOR
4
Mettukkada Mukku
Taikkad Junction
Chettikulangara Rd
KSRTC & TTC Bus Stand
2 8
Aristo Junction
9
VALIYASHALA
Overbridge
Central Station Rd
1
Thampanoor Junction
To Airport
Thakaraparambu Rd
Power House Junction
SRI VENKATESWARAM
Station & Railway Retiring Rooms
Power House Rd
Verma Travels
Padmavilasam Rd
Fort Bus Station
EAST FORT
Padmana-bhasvami Temple
FORT
Kuthiramalika Palace
To Airport
2
Buses to Kovalam
5 To Kovalam Beach (16 km)

N
0 metres 200
0 yards 200

■ Sleeping
1 Chaithram
2 Greenland
3 Highland
4 Horizon

5 Luciya
6 Manacaud
7 Mascot
8 Queens
9 Thamburu International

10 Wild Palms

● Eating
1 Indian Coffee House
2 Magnet

Botanical gardens and zoo ⓘ *Closed Mon, 0900-1645, Rs 2, video/cine cameras Rs* *5, entrance at southwest corner of park, 400 m east of Indian Airlines.* Set in wooded hilly parkland the zoo is spacious and offers delightful shaded walks. It has a wide collection of animals. The Botanical Gardens are here with many trees clearly labelled. Worth a visit. Other parks and gardens in the city – around the Secretariat, Gandhi Park, Waterworks Gardens and at Veli Tourist Village. The Aquarium near the beach has closed.

Museums

Arts and Crafts Museum (formerly **Napier**) ⓘ *closed Mon and public holidays, 1000-1700, Wed 1300-1645,* is north of city in the park grounds. A spectacular wooden building designed by RF Chisholm in traditional Kerala style and completed in 1872, it is a landmark. It has a famous collection of mainly eighth-18th-century South Indian bronzes, mostly from Chola, Vijayanagar and Nayaka periods; a few Jain and Buddhist sculptures and also excellent wood carvings. Ivory carvings and Kathakali costumes also displayed. Power cuts can be a hazard when visiting.

Sri Chitra Art Gallery ⓘ *closed Mon and Wed mornings, 1000-1700, Wed 1300-1645, Rs 5,* north of Napier Museum, has an excellent collection of Indian art with examples from early to modern schools. Paintings by Raja Ravi Verma and works from Java, Bali, China and Japan, Mughal and Rajput miniature paintings and Tanjore paintings embellished with semi-precious stones. Well worth a visit, as is the gallery devoted to modern art next door.

Kuthiramalika Palace Museum ⓘ *closed Mon, 0830-1230, 1530-1730, foreigners Rs 20, camera Rs 25, near Padmanabhaswami Temple,* is the palace of Maharajah Swathi Thirunal Balarama Varma, who was a musician, poet and social reformer, and is a good example of the Travancore style of architecture with some fine wood carving, and houses an interesting royal collection.

Thiruvananthapuram centre

To Kerala Tourist Office & Museums

N

0 metres 200
0 yards 200

■ **Sleeping**
1 Bhaskara Bhavan
  Tourist Paradise
2 Geeth & Kukies
3 Navaratna &
  Kalpakavadi Restaurant

4 Pravin
5 Regency
6 Residency Towers
7 South Park & Kerala
  Travels
8 Sundar

● **Eating**
1 Arul Jyoti
2 Indian Coffee House
3 Kalavara
4 Kerala House

Kerala The far south Thiruvananthapuram

★ Kovalam

→ *Phone code: 95471 (International: 0471). Colour map 7, grid C3. Population: 25,400.*
Once just a series of sandy bays separated by rocky promontories, deserted except for the scattered fishing villages under the coconut palms, Kovalam is becoming one of the Government's major tourist centres. For 20 years it catered largely for the western backpacker but now its superb beaches are the focus of package tours from Europe and visitors from all over India. ▸▸ *For Sleeping, Eating and other listings, see pages 898-907.*

Ins and outs

Getting there Taxis take 30 mins from the airport. Buses from Thiruvananthapuram stop at Waller Junction, just before Kovalam, just 5 mins walk from the Samudra Beach hotels. After 1½ km they turn off for the main bus stand at *Ashok Hotel* gate, 5-10 mins' walk from most southern hotels and cafés. Autos (and taxis) can also get to the beach end of the steep, narrow Lighthouse Rd.

Getting around You can walk the length of beach from the lighthouse end to the north of Samudra beach in about 20 mins. Carry a torch at night. See Transport, page 905, for further details.

Climate Best time to visit is Dec-Mar; even at the end of Mar it can get very hot around midday, though some beach umbrellas, chairs and recliners are available for hire.

Sights

There are four main stretches of beach, about 400 m long. A rocky promontory with the Charles Correa designed *Ashok Beach Resort* divides them into north and south sections. The beach immediately to the north of the promontory offers the most sheltered bathing and the clearest water. The southern beaches are much more populated. **Lighthouse Beach** is a long line of bars, cafés and very persistent vendors selling fruit, clothes, crafts, and unfortunately, drugs. It is still pleasant and quiet by some European holiday beach standards.

There are now lifeguard patrols but you still need to be careful when swimming. The sea can get rough, particularly between April and October with swells of up to 6 m. From May the sea-level rises removing the beach completely in places, and swimming becomes very dangerous.

Excursions

Vizhinjam, 6 km south, the capital of the later *Ay* rulers who dominated South Travancore in the ninth century AD. In the seventh century they had faced constant pressure from the Pandiyans who kept the Ay chieftains under firm control for long periods. Today Vizhinjam is the centre of the fishing industry and is being developed as a major container port. Scarcely visited by tourists, it is an easy walk from Kovalam. The traditional boats are rapidly being modernized and the catch is sold all over India, but you can still see the interest in the sale of fish, and women taking headloads to local markets.

Padmanabhapuram, the old palace of the Rajas of Travancore, makes an excellent day trip from town or from Kovalam. See page 874.

Neyyar Dam, Neyyar Wildlife Sanctuary At the foot of the Western Ghats, 30 km east of Thiruvananthapuram, the Neyyar Sanctuary occupies a beautiful, wooded and hilly landscape, dominated by the peak of Agasthya Malai (1,868 m). The vegetation ranges from grassland to tropical, wet evergreen. Wildlife includes gaur, sloth bear, Nilgiri Tahr, jungle cat, sambar deer, elephants and Nilgiri langur, but the most commonly seen animals are lion-tailed macaques and other monkeys. Tigers and

Kovalam

To Lagoona Beach Resort
Thiruvanan thapuram

Waller Junction

G V Raja Rd (Samudra Rd)

Samudra Beach

Kovalam Beach

Conference Centre
Coach Park

Gate

Western Travel

Elite Tours & Travel

Hawah Beach (Eve's Beach)

Taxis

Batik House

Kovalam Junction

Kovalam Junction

To Somatheeram, Surya Samudra Hotels & Kanniyakumari

Upasana Hospital

Lighthouse Beach

German Bakery

Lighthouse Rd

Lighthouse

VIZHINJAM

Rocks

N

0 metres 150
0 yards 150

Sleeping
1 Achutha
2 Al Italia
3 Aparna
4 Ashok
5 Blue Sea

6 Dwarka & Seashore
  Restaurant
7 Green Valley Cottages
8 Holiday Home Resort
9 Kadaloram
10 Maharaju Palace
11 Moonlight
12 Paradise Rock
13 Pink Flowers & Surya
  Niwas
14 Raja & Beach Castle
15 Rockholm

16 Samudra
17 Sea Face
18 Swagath
19 Swami Tourist Home
20 Wilson

Eating
1 Flamingo & Hawah
2 Garzia & Tailors
3 Island View
4 Lonely Planet
5 Neelkanth

6 Palm Beach
7 Santanas
8 Seaside
9 Sea View
10 Serenity
11 Shell's Bar
12 Siva's Moon
13 Velvet Moon

Kerala The far south Kovalam

leopards have also been reported. The Neyyar Dam supports a large population of crocodiles and otters; a crocodile farm was set up in 1977 near the administrative complex. To view you can take out a speed boat, for two Rs 100/150. Larger boats to view the forests enclosing the lake, Rs 20 each. Mini bus safari Rs 10. If you prefer to trek, best in December-April, get permission first. Details of access from the Chief Conservator of Forests (Wildlife), Forest HQ, Thiruvananthapuram, T322217, or the Assistant Wildlife Warden at Neyyar Dam, T0471-272182. See Agasthya Vanam Biological Park, below, for sleeping.

Agasthya Vanam Biological Park Immediately to the northeast of the Neyyar Wildlife sanctuary a section of dense forest, 'Agasthya Vanam', was set aside in 1992 to recreate biodiversity on a wide scale. The Sivananda *Yoga Vedanta Dhanwantari Ashram*, T290493, F451776, runs yoga and meditation course; highly intensive, only suitable for dedicated devotees of the school, others may find it hard going and heavy on Hinduism and Indian diet.

Ponmudi ⓘ *Several buses from Central Bus Stand from 0530 until 1630; return from Ponmudi, between 0615 and 1905 (2½ hrs).* Ponmudi is the nearest hill station to Thiruvananthapuram, 65 km away. In a spectacular and peaceful setting, the tourist complex, though basic, serves as a good base for trekking, birdwatching and visiting the nearby minimalist deer park.

★ Varkala

→ *Phone code: 95472 (International: 0472). Colour map 7, grid C3. Population: 42,300.*
Varkala attracts many visitors who find Kovalam "too developed", though it is rapidly becoming better known and touristy. The beach, backed by high reddish cliffs, is an excellent place to unwind, and the sea here is very enticing. There is a wide choice of accommodation options, along with a string of restaurants along the cliff top.
▶▶ *For Sleeping, Eating and other listings, see pages 898-907.*

Sights
Beaches Papanasam (Pavanacham) Beach has a fine strip of sand, with fewer and less persistant beach vendors than Kovalam. It is, however, a little more conservative than other popular beach destinations in India. The beach is popular with Indian families at weekends, especially the southerly end. The beach has lifeguards, and it is essential to swim in the designated flagged area.

For more **deserted beaches**, and interesting **fishing settlements**, either head north along the north cliff towards the **Alimood Mosque** in the middle distance, or scramble over the rocks at the bottom of Beach Road. Beach-wear is not appropriate when visiting these predominantly Muslim fishing villages. You will generally get a warm reception, though those taking a lot of photos of the fishermen pulling in their nets may be expected to share the workload! There are three steep paths down to the beach from the north cliff top – opposite *Johnny Cool* restaurant, *Doctors Ayurvedic Health Centre* and *Oottupura* restaurant – with the last being the least difficult. Alternatively, follow the less steep path/steps south from the Helipad, past *Marine Palace*, to access the beach from Beach Road. There is fencing along the cliff between the Helipad and *Clafouti* restaurant, but north of there great care must be taken (a torch is essential at night).

The village
In the village, a short distance inland, is the south Kerala style **Janardhanaswamy Temple**, a centre for pilgrimage. Largely re-built in the 13th century, the minor shrines

are older. The temple is primarily dedicated to Vishnu with subsidiary Saivite shrines outside the main precinct. The *Arattu* festival in March-April draws thousands of pilgrims. Non-Hindus are not permitted to enter. Opposite is the **Shree Rama Hanuman Temple**, with its busy temple tank. The main 'town' area (including the train station) is a further 2 km inland from 'Temple Junction'.

Varkala

Sleeping	
1 Ajantha Tourist Home	
2 Akshay	
3 Bamboo Village & Summer Land	
4 Clafouti	
5 Eden Garden	
6 Evergreen Beach Palace & Thiruvambadi Beach Resort	
7 Govt Rest House	
8 Gratitude Inn	
9 Hill Top Resort	
10 Mamma Chompos & Pizzeria	
11 Nikhil Beach Resort (new)	
12 Nikhil Beach Resort (old)	
13 Panchavadi	
14 Prasanth Garden	
15 Raja Park Beach Resort	
16 Red House annexe	
17 Red House	
18 Sea Pearl Chalets	
19 Suvarna Sangeetha Bhavanum	
20 Taj Garden Retreat	
21 White House	
Eating	
1 Cafe Italiano	
2 Chinnos	
3 Clafouti	
4 Kadaloram No 1	
5 Kerala	
6 Oottupura	
7 Sathram	
8 Sri Padman	
9 Sunrise	

On the cliff top to the north of the temple is the **Government Guest House**, formerly a palace of the Maharajah of Travancore. Behind this were buildings which housed the harems of the Maharajah, but these were sold off at Independence.

The **Nature Cure Hospital**, opened in 1983, treats patients entirely by diet and natural cures including hydrotherapy, chromotherapy (natural sunbath with different filters) and mud therapy, each treatment normally lasting 30 minutes. **Naturomission Yoga Ashram** near the Helipad, runs one, two and seven day courses in yoga, massage, meditation, and healing techniques. Payment by donation. There isn't any accommodation here.

Listings: The far south

⊜ Sleeping

Thiruvananthapuram *p891, map p892*
The centre and railway station area have many cheap hotels, some excellent value.
B Residency Tower, Press Rd, T331661, F331311, www.residencytower.com. 80 top quality rooms, 60 a/c with full facilities, good restaurants and bar, pool. Recommended.
B South Park, Spencer Junction, MG Rd, T333333, F331861, southpark@vsnl.com. Central a/c, 82 rooms, some dearer suites, good restaurants, bar, some business facilities, modern 'marble and glass hotel' but pricey, not named after the cartoon series.
B-C Chaithram (Kerala Tourism), Station Rd, T330977, F331446, chaitra@md3.vsnl.net.in. 80 rooms, 24 a/c, good a/c restaurant, bar, exchange, modern, clean, next to railway and bus stand, noisy area but good value, often full.
B-C Mascot (KTDC), Mascot Sq, T318990, F317745, ktdc@vsnl.com. 44 a/c rooms and suites, rather sombre inside, good restaurants, competent without being exciting.
C Horizon, Aristo Rd, T326888, F324444, horizon@md3.vsnl.net.in. 47 rooms, some **B** a/c, good restaurants (rooftop on weekend evenings), for breakfast opt for room service, bar, comfortable.
C Luciya, East Fort, T463443, F463347, sajluciya@md2.vsnl.net.in. 104 rooms, some a/c, large 'fantasy suites', others very small, good restaurant, exchange, pool.
C Wild Palms, Puthen Rd, 10-min walk Statue Junction (or ask for pick-up), T471175. 6 rooms in modern guesthouse (traditional design), some a/c, spacious, cool, welcoming.
C-D Highland, Manjalikulam Rd, T333200, F332645. 85 clean, comfortable rooms, some a/c in a tall block, sat TV.
C-D Regency, Manjalikulam Cross Rd, T330377, F331690, hotelregency@

satyam.net.in. 34 pleasant rooms, 24-hr hot water, daily change of sheets, friendly staff, acceptable restaurant, well maintained Indian business hotel, good value.
D Geeth, off MG Rd, near GPO, Pulimudu, T471987, F460278. 50 rooms, some a/c, rooftop restaurant recommended.
D Navaratna, YMCA Rd, T330473. 34 rooms, 2 a/c in modern tower block, restaurant, simple, clean, efficient and helpful.
D Thamburu International, Aristo Junction, opposite raillway station, T321974, F321987. Pleasant interior, comfortable rooms (some a/c), excellent value, sometimes full.
E-F Pravin, Manjalikulam Rd, 750 m from Thampanoor Rd, T330443. 36 basic but clean rooms, snacks only, friendly management, good value. Recommended.
F Bhaskara Bhavan Tourist Paradise, near Ayurvedic College, T330662. 40 rooms, sombre but clean, good value.
F Greenland, near Aristo Junction, T323485, short walk from station and bus. Rooms with bath, very safe, good value.
F Kukies Holiday Inn, Lukes Lane, T478530. Small, quiet, with a pleasant flower-filled courtyard, good value.
F Manacaud, Manjalikulam Rd, T330360. 46 basic rooms, some with bath, very friendly.
F Sundar, Manjalikulam Rd, T330532. 45 very basic rooms in old-style lodge, very cheap.
F Youth Hostel (KTDC), Veli (10 km from centre). Rooms and dorm (Rs 10), very cheap veg lunches, pretty lagoon separated from the sea by a sandbar, surrounded by coconut groves, clean beach, boating, some watersports, good views.

Airport
E Asha, 200m from Airport, T501050. Very handy for early departures, decent rooms with bath.

Kovalam *p894, map p895*

Long power cuts are common, so air-conditioners often do not work. Rooms open to the sea breeze can be an advantage though mosquito nets might be needed. The area behind the Lighthouse Beach is now full of hotels with a range of rooms from Rs 100 to an average of Rs 1,000 with all facilities. Rates shown here are for the High Season. Prices skyrocket in all hotels for the 2-week peak period (20 Dec-10 Jan), though it still pays to bargain. High season: 1-19 Dec, 11 Jan-28 Feb; Low season (especially May-Jul): expect discounts of 40-75%.

L Ashok Beach Resort, T480101, F481522, www.kovalamashok.com. 193 moderate size a/c rooms with sea view, pleasant peaceful grounds, impressive public areas, pool and tiny 'private' fenced beach (non-residents Rs 165), ayurvedic centre.

A Samudra, Samudra Beach, T480089, F480242, samudra@md3.vsnl.net.in. 50 improved rooms, best in newer wing facing sea, good pool in sea-facing landscaped garden, ayurvedic massage, unremarkable restaurant, mainly package tours, overpriced.

A Sea Face, Lighthouse Beach, T481591, F481320, www.seaface.com. 20 smallish rooms (best sea-facing), not mosquito proof, 14 a/c, excellent restaurant, lovely staff, right on beach, modern, pleasant pool and sundeck (non-residents Rs 200), ayurvedic massage. Recommended.

A Swayath, near Upasana Hospital, 5-min downhill to beach, T481148, F481150, swagathresorts.com. 20 spacious, modern rooms (most a/c) on 4 floors, 3 cheaper in 'Row House' much smaller, limited menu restaurant, pool (non-residents Rs 150), pleasant garden, good views, friendly and efficient.

A-B Abad Palm Shore, T481481, abad@vsnl.com. 35 a/c rooms, popular with groups, holiday-camp atmosphere but lovely pool and beach access.

B Aparna, Lighthouse Rd, uphill from beach, T480950. 8 excellent but smallish rooms in well-designed hotel, clean, very pleasant.

B Beach Castle, T480252, F480325, www.beachcastle.biz. 20 lovely sea-facing rooms in new hotel, some with tub, choose a/c or excellent suite, open-plan restaurant, great terrace views.

B Blue Sea, near Telegraph office, T481401, F480401, www.hotelbluesea.com. A most unusual hotel, 15 a/c rooms, in converted Kerala-style mansion with curious circular towers, large garden with good pool (non-residents Rs 150), very pleasant restaurant area, relaxing.

B Kadaloram Beach Resort, GV Raja Rd, T481116, F481115, info@kadaloram.com. 16 comfortable rooms (4 a/c), not a 'resort', 5 mins' walk to quiet beach, a bit isolated.

B Raja, T480355, F480455, www.rajahotel.com. 19 spacious, cool and calm rooms, 8 a/c, full facilities, bar, pool (non-residents Rs 150), fish pond containing your dinner!

B Rockholm, Lighthouse Rd, T480606, F480607, rockholm@techpark.net.in. 22 very good rooms and penthouse, wonderful position just above lighthouse, good terrace restaurant, clean, spacious, very pleasant hotel.

B-C Moonlight, inland from beach, T480375, F481078, moonlight@satyam.net.in. 10 clinically clean rooms (few with seaview), some with bath tub, fridge, locker, pool (non-residents Rs 100 half day), local backwater trips, good value. Recommended.

C Maharaju Palace, T485320, near the lighthouse, www.maharajupalace,com. 6 lovely rooms with balconies in beautiful, shady garden setting, very peaceful. Recommended.

C Wilson Tourist Home, up path behind Neelkantha, T/F480051, wilson@md3.vsnl.net.in. 24 pleasant and quiet rooms with bath, 14 a/c, open-air restaurant, balconies with fan, exchange, garden, clean, safe, friendly and helpful service. Recommended.

C-D Al Italia Beach Resort, Samudra Beach, T480042. 4 simple, modern rooms, secluded beach front (fishermen, early morning), quiet, breezy, shady restaurant, delicious food.

D-E Holiday Home Resort, Beach Rd (10 mins' walk from sea), T480497, homerest@md3.vsnl.net.in. Clean, pleasant rooms and cottages, some a/c, dorm (Rs 150), good food, beautiful flower garden, internet, quiet, friendly, excellent service. Recommended.

There are numerous budget cottages and rooms to let. Scouts greet arrivals at bus stand but you may pay considerably more if you use their services. You will find rooms to let, behind bars and restaurants, by walking from the *Sea Rock* towards the lighthouse, and on the Samudra Beach and GV Raja Rd (Samudra Rd).

E Achutha, Lighthouse Beach. With restaurant, recommended for good clean rooms, 'best bed in India' and good food.

E **Dwaraka Lodge**, Lighthouse Beach, T480411, marytambini@hotmail.com. 8 basic but clean rooms, some with bath, restaurant, quiet beach front location, art gallery, boat trips.
E **Green Valley Cottages**, T480636, indira_ravi@hotmail.com. 21 clean, fresh and quiet rooms with bath in lovely surroundings, restaurant. Recommended.
E **Paradise Rock**, Lighthouse Rd, T481069. 4 large rooms, hot showers, close to beach, good views and breeze.
E **White House**, T483388, whitehouse@vsnl.com. 12 clean and airy rooms, nets, use of common fridge and kitchen, close to beach, very good value. Recommended.
F **Pink Flowers**, Lighthouse Beach, behind *Neptune*. 4 immaculate rooms with bath, good location, friendly.
F **Surya Nivas**, Lighthouse Beach. 4 very clean rooms with bath, quiet, friendly.
F **Swami Tourist Home**, with good clean rooms, good food and friendly service.

Hotels near Kovalam
Pozhikkara Beach (5 km north):
A **Lagoona Beach Resort**, Pachalloor, T480049, off the highway, where the backwaters reach the sea, 'backwater' tours in country boats with excellent guide to see coir making, spice garden, tropical plants.
C-D **Backwater House**, T590155, bwhouse2001@hotmail.com. Simple but comfortable rooms.
Mulloor (6 km south):
B **Coconut Bay Beach Resort**, T480566, F343349, cocobay@vsnl.com. 13 spacious brick/stone cottages on beach, good restaurant, friendly, secluded location in traditional fishing village, next to *Siddharth Ayurvedic and Yoga Centre*. Recommended.
Pulinkudi (8 km south):
L-AL **Surya Samudra**, Mulloor PO, T480413, F481124. 15 large rooms in old Kerala houses re-assembled and modernized, bathrooms among banana plants (open-above!), no TV, 4 a/c (no sea view and no mosquitos!), very good food, exclusive (cut off from the country), secluded beach, stunning setting, popular with Germans. Recommended but overpriced; can book via *Toptour GMBH*, Piusallee 108, GD-48147 Münster, T251-235559, F235216.
Chowara (10 km south):
Beach has security staff on duty but hawkers filter through to pester sunbathers.

AL-A Somatheeram, T481600, F480600, soma@md2.vsnl.net.in. Ayurvedic health resort, 46 rooms, most in re-assembled Kerala houses with original antique wooden panels, carved doors etc, huge windows with sea views, inefficient restaurant ("one hour for cornflakes"!), some modern cottages, yoga by the beach. Low voltage (slow fans, dim lights), gloomy at night. Little too far from beach.
B **Manatheeram**, next door, T481610, F481611. 30 clean, breezy, beach-facing circular huts, grass screen windows, fans, good showers, good seafood on beach. Specialist ayurvedic treatments at both, massage (US$15 per hr).
Poovar Island:
(20 km south – approachable only by boat) taxis Rs 200.
AL **Poovar Island Resort** (Sarovar Park Plaza), stark@vsnl.com. Award winning boutique hotel with 'floating' cottages where the backwaters meet the sea.
A **Wilson Beach Resort**, T212063, F210019, www.wilsonresorts.com. Pleasant cottage-resort set amidst palms. A/c rooms, restaurant, pool, very quiet and secluded.

Agasthya *p896*
E **Agasthya House** (Kerala Tourism), opposite viewing tower, near Forest Information Centre, Kattakada, T272160, 6 rooms, on the edge of the reservoir, built like a concrete bunker ("hear the lions roaring at night in the Safari Park!"), disappointing restaurant, lunch Rs 20-50, beer, views, very helpful staff.

Ponmudi *p896*
F **Ponmudi Tourist Resort**, T890230, 24 rooms and 10 cottages, in attractive gardens surrounded by wooded hills, spartan facilities but spacious rooms, restaurant serves limited but reasonable vegetarian meals, beer available; also a post office and general stores.

Varkala *p896, map p897*
There are at least 50 guesthouses and "beach resorts", plus rooms in private houses. The cliff top area is fairly compact, so look around until you find what you want. None, however, is actually "on the beach". Almost all offer 'travel services'. Outside the high season of Nov-Mar, prices drop by up to 50%, though during the monsoon (Jun-Jul) many places close.

Beach Road area

AL-A Taj Garden Retreat, 500 m from the beach, T603000, F602296, retreat.varkala@tajhotel.com. 30 rooms, central a/c, excellent views, beautifully landscaped, pool, good but expensive restaurant, "absolutely lovely".

B-C Hill Top Beach Resort, north end, T601237, F607228, kutty@techpark.net. 25 rooms, 3 cottages set amongst palms, Internet, Ayurvedic treatments. Clean, pleasant and friendly.

B-D Akshay Beach Resort, Beach Rd (about 200 m from beach), T602668. 17 rooms, 4 spacious double a/c with bathtub and TV but singles very small, standard good value, bright, clean and smart, TV lounge, good restaurant.

B-E Nikhil Beach Resort, Beach Rd, T606122, F600583. 11 rooms, 4 a/c, exchange and money transfer. Clean, pleasant, good value.

C-D Eden Garden, T603910, edengarden2000@hotmail.com. 11 smallish but pleasant ethnic rooms, 1 suite, traditional-style buildings in beautiful garden-setting around a pond. Ayurvedic diets available, massage, quiet, family-run.

D Panchvadi, Beach Rd, T600200, F660400. 8 clean rooms (2 luxury) with bath (excellent showers), 24-hour check-in, laundry, Kerala style restaurant, good security, friendly helpful staff, close to beach. Recommended.

D Sea Pearl Chalets, Beach Rd, T605875, F605049, seapearlvarkala@hotmail.com. 10 circular thatched huts in breezy location on south cliff, great views, breakfasts.

D-E Marine Palace, Papanasam Beach, on path down from cliff, T603204. 12 rooms, some a/c in small bungalows (not a palace), good *Tandoori* restaurant very close to beach (but very slow service), simple, comfortable, friendly service, popular with the middle-aged!

E Gratitude Inn, Beach Rd (near Temple tank), T607841. 11 clean, spacious rooms, spring water in every tap, quiet, manager offers ayurvedic guidance, book shop, good value.

E Mamma Chompos, 100 m beyond *Akshay*, T603995. 7 large rooms in traditional Kerala style farmhouse above top quality pizza restaurant. Garden setting, friendly.

F Chinnus Home, nearby. Spacious rooms, clean baths, hammocks amoung palms.

North cliff

A-B Raja Park Beach Resort, near north cliff, T607060. Large a/c rooms with modern attached bath, TV, fridge, 150 year-old traditional Keralan wooden cottage with charming sitting terrace.

C-D Red House, near north cliff, T603239, mobile T9846074597, theredhouse@123india.com. 5 rooms in main house (**D**), 6 cottages (**C**), (1 luxury with fridge, cable TV) set in large private garden, plus large rooms with fridge and modern attached bath in annexe nearby. Very well run, excellent service. Recommended.

C-D Thiruvambadi Beach Resort, Thiruvambadi Beach Rd, Kurakkani, T601028, F604345, thiruvambadi@hotmail.com. 10 rooms, 7 with private balcony, hot water, rooftop restaurant, very quiet location.

D-E Clafouti, set back, T601414, F600494. 8 lovely rooms in new house (Rs 500), old house (Rs 200), all tiled baths, very clean, French run bakery for excellent pastries.

D-E Evergreen Beach Palace, Thiruvambadi Beach Rd, Kurakkanni, T603257. Large clean rooms with bath, a/c available, quite smart.

D-E Prasanth Garden, near north cliff. 3 very nice thatched cottages with verandahs in large, peaceful garden. Recommended.

D-E Summer Land, north cliff. 4 nice tiled roof cottages, verandah, quiet, breezy location.

D-E Suvarna Sangeetha Bhavanum, near north cliff. Rooms in large family house, popular with the "traveller" set.

E Bamboo Village, T610732, north cliff. 4 small very basic but charming thatched bamboo huts with wash-basin and toilet, private verandahs, among palms, very quiet with very great sea-views.

Inland

F Ajantha Tourist Home, Temple Junction, T603684. 16 very clean rooms with bath, very friendly and helpful staff, good restaurant next door.

F Anandan Tourist Home, opposite Railway station, T602135. 32 very cheap rooms, some a/c, restaurant, clean modern building, noisy in early mornings (temple next door), good value.

F Govt Guest House, towards *Taj hotel*, T602227. 8 rooms, former summer residence of Maharaja, charming appearance but bed bugs (and snoring caretaker!), meals (overpriced, no receipt), individual buildings are better, idyllic and quiet (wooden ceilings, marble floors, big baths, shaded porches, book in advance.

F JA Tourist Home, Temple Junction, T602453. 11 rooms, modern Indian hotel, good value, also excellent roof restaurant, delicious food, friendly but slow service.
F Sea Splendour, North Cliff end, Odayam Beach. Rooms with bath in retired teacher's guesthouse, excellent home cooking (unlimited and spoilt for choice), very quiet.

❼ Eating

Thiruvananthapuram *p891, map p892*
Café Magnet, Thycaud. Mixed menu. The 'in' place, boring décor but good food, "go early as it runs out, not yet spotted by westerners (no beer)".
Kalavara, Press Rd, T331362, Indian, Continental, Chinese fast food (burgers, shakes) takeaway. Food average, slow service but good value buffets in upstairs thatched section with a patch of garden – good ambience, limited views.
Kalpakavadi, YMCA Rd. Mixed menu. Modern and smart. Recommended.
Kerala House, near Statue Junction. Kerala cuisine. In basement of shopping complex, clean, slow for breakfast but newspaper provided; outside seating in the evening in roadside carpark area, cheaper, colourful and fun to pass the time, even if the food arrives cold; try *neem, kappa* and rice (delicious fish with tapioca), or inexpensive chicken dishes with coconut; bakery in the complex does excellent samosas and puffs.
Queen's, Aristo Junction. Indian non-veg. Chilli chicken and chicken fry recommended.
Arul Jyoti, MG Rd, opposite Secretariat. South Indian vegetarian. With a/c family room, clean, wide choice of good value dishes, try jumbo *dosas*.
Indian Coffee House, 2 on MG Rd (1 near YWCA, north of the Secretariat, another near KSRTC bus stand), the latter designed by the English architect Laurie Baker, spirals upwards – worth seeing, excellent value coffee and snacks.
Nalini, near *Spencer's supermarket*. Excellent Indian sweets.

Hotels
South Park. Good tandoori and buffet lunches.
Mascot. Excellent lunchtime buffet, pleasant, 24-hr coffee shop for all types of snacks, all good value, a cool haven at midday!

Pankaj, top floor. Good Indian buffet lunches, excellent views over city.
Orion, in *Residency*. Pepper steaks and cocktails recommended.
Coronet. Dark bar downstairs for refreshing cold beers, while you wait.
Luciya. Good buffet (outdoor barbecue) and southern dishes, poor service.

Kovalam *p894, map p895*
Most restaurants are along Lighthouse Beach.
Suisse. Stylish venue, unusual menu, very clean, generous portions, personal attention, good atmosphere, enjoyable though the music can get overpowering. Recommended.
Garzia Original fish dishes, sizzlers.
Rockholm. International. Very good food, pleasant terrace, beautiful views, especially early morning.
Santana Good atmosphere, music, backgammon, chess and good food (but very slow), open until late.
Sea Face. Breezy raised terrace on the beach by pleasant pool (coconuts above netted for safety!), varied choice, excellent food, versatile fish/ seafood (dearer), friendly and attentive. Recommended.

Towards the lighthouse, a few seafood places display the day's catch (some 1-m long) on metal-top tables for you to select from. Tiger prawns and lobsters are pricey; **avoid** fish on Sun evenings (unlikely to be very fresh). The order of the day is not to rush, service is often slow as tiny kitchens are unable to cope with large numbers!
Achutha, **Dwaraka** and **Swami** do good tandoori and snacks.
Krishna. Basic but good *thalis* (the 'cheapest in Kovalam').
Island View, good pastas, excellent seafood.
Lonely Planet, away from beach. Rare veg restaurant. Excellent Indian. Moderately spiced *thalis* recommended, good location overlooking paddy fields and coconut palms.
Palm Beach for good seafood.
Roy's, up from *Sea Rock*. Excellent local Kerala food, very clean, popular with local people.
Sea View, Hawah Beach, at foot of path from the bus stand. Excellent seafood tandoori.
Seashore, next to Dwaraka. Good à la carte variety (especially pizzas, fish, chicken and toffee dessert), friendly and popular.
Velvet Moon has fresh fish, good value, great hot apple 'cakes', real baked potatoes,

good snacks, friendly, relaxing top floor, getting a bit shabby.

Videos are shown free, nightly at some, often set against poorer food: **Neelkantha** with comfortable seats and a generator to overcome regular power cuts; **Shell's Bar** does excellent barbecue fish; **Siva** and **Flamingo** do good tandoori, especially barracuda.

Varkala *p896, map p897*
Many restaurants close out of season. Take extra care with drinking water. There are numerous restaurants along the north cliff, most with very similar menus (and excruciatingly slow service): **Chinnos, Kadaloram 1, Sunrise**. "Catch of the day" usually costs Rs 100-150 depending upon the type/size of fish, but make sure you don't get "catch of yesterday" (fresh fish keep their glassy eyes and bright silvery scales).

♔♔♔ **Taj Garden Retreat** (Rs 300, includes pool use), on Sun (1230-1530), good eat-all-you-want buffet.

♔ **Café Italiano**, has good Italian, but is pricey.

♔ **Clafouti** offers fresh pastries and cakes, but standards seem to drop when the French-Keralan owners are away.

♔ **Oottupura**, near helipad, excellent veg (masala dosa Rs 20, most dishes Rs 30-40).

♔ **Sathram**, Temple Junction, is excellent (daily changing *thalis* Rs 20), delicious small fish (Rs 10), popular with auto/bus drivers.

♔ **Sri Padman**, offers good food, Western breakfasts, and overlooks the temple tank.

♻ Bars and clubs

Thiruvananthapuram *p891, map p892*
Several of the hotels and the larger restaurants have bars though increased State govt taxes makes it difficult to get beer in non-govt run hotels.

Kovalam *p894, map p895*
Only a few hotels have licences; **Ashok** and **Samudra** open to non-residents. Beach restaurants often sell beer and some spirits.

☻ Entertainment

Thiruvananthapuram *p891, map p892*
Cinema
Several especially near Station and Overbridge Junction on MG Rd some showing English language films. **Kathakali** and other performances, through Tourist Office; **Kalaripayattu**: performances (0400-0700 and 1700-2000), **CVN Kalari**, East Fort, T474182, 0630-0830, watch from balcony, photography with permission only, free; also at Poojapura: **Veera Kerala Marma Kalari**, T330041.

Kovalam *p894, map p895*
Kathakali dance
Daily at Hotels *Ashok* and *Neptune,* Rs 100.

Varkala *p896, map p897*
There is a daily **Kathakali** demonstration at the *Kerala Kathakali Centre* by the helipad (Rs150, make-up 1700-1800, performance 1830-2000). The participants are generally students of the art rather than masters.

☻ Festivals and events

Thiruvananthapuram *p891, map p892*
Mar: **Chandanakuda** at Beemapalli, a shrine on Beach Rd 5 km southwest of the rly station, when local Muslims process to the mosque, holding incense sticks and pots. Marked by sword play, singing, dancing, elephant procession and fireworks. 10 day festival. **Mar -Apr** (Meenam) and **Oct -Nov** (Thulam): **Arattu** (see above). **Sep/Oct**: Navaratri at the special *mandapa* in Padmanabhasvami Temple. Several concerts which draw famous musicians. **Thiruvonam week** in **Sep**. **Nov-Mar**: Nishangandhi Dance Festival, at weekends when all important classical Indian dance forms are performed by leading artistes at Nishagandhi open-air auditorium, Kanakakkunnu Palace. **Oct**: A similar **Soorya Dance Festival** takes place from 1st-10th.

☼ Shopping

Thiruvananthapuram *p891, map p892*
Shopping areas include the Chalai Bazar, the Connemara market and the Main Rd from Palayam to the East Fort. Usually open 0900 to 2000 (some take a long lunch break). Although ivory goods have now been banned, inlay on wood carving and marquetry using other materials (bone, plastic) continue to flourish. *Kathakali* masks and traditional fabrics can be bought at a number of shops.

Books

DC, at Statue Junction India Book House, Pai & Co and Higginbotham's, on MG Rd among many. Modern Book Centre, Pulimudu Junction, excellent range.

Camping fuel

Laboratory Supplies, near Ayurvedic College Junction, methyl alcohol for *Trangia* camping stoves.

Clothing and fabric

Shopping centre opposite East Fort Bus stand has a large a/c shop with good selection of silks and saris but not cheap. Co-optex, Temple Rd. Good for fabrics and *lungis*. *Khadi* recommended from shops on MG Rd, south of Pulimudu Junction.

Handloom House, diagonally across from *Partha's* has an excellent range of fabrics, clothes and export quality *dhurries*. The other MG Rd branch near the Overbridge is not as good.

Partha's, towards East Fort. Recommended. Premier Stationers, MG Rd, opposite Post Office Rd, are best in town. Raymonds, Karal Kada, East Fort has good men's clothing.

Handicrafts

Gram Sree for excellent village crafts. Natesan Antique Arts and Gift Corner on MG Rd have high quality goods including old dowry boxes, carved wooden panels from old temple 'cars', miniature paintings and bronzes. Kairali has items of banana fibre, coconut, screw pine, mainly utilitarian, also sandalwood carvings and bell-metal lamps, utensils. Kalanjali, Palace Garden, across from the museum. Recommended. SMSM Handicrafts Emporium behind the Secretariat, Govt run, literally 'heaps' of items, wide range, reasonably priced.

Kovalam *p894, map p895*

Numerous craft shops, including Kashmiri and Tibetan shops sell a wide range of goods. The majority of shops are clustered around the bus stand at the gate of the *Ashok Hotel* with another group to the south around the lighthouse. Possible to get good quality paintings, metalwork, woodwork and carpets at reasonable prices. Gems and jewellery are widely available but notoriously difficult to be sure of quality. Zangsty Gems, Lighthouse Rd, good reputation for helpfulness and reliability.

Books

Several bookstalls sell, or 'hire' (Rs 10), English paperbacks. International Book Centre, 2nd Beach Rd.

Tailors

At short notice is very good value with fabrics available; better than ready mades; Brother Tailors, 2nd Beach Rd; Raja near hotel *Surya*; Suresh, next to restaurant *Garzia*. Charges vary, about Rs 50-80 per piece.

Varkala *p896, map p897*

Most of the handicraft shops are run by Kashmiris, who will tell you that everything (including the tie-dye t-shirts) is an "antique from Ladakh".

Elegance of India and Mushtaq, Beach Rd, sell Kashmiri handicrafts, carpets, jewellery etc, reported as honest, will safely air-freight carpets etc.

Suresh, on path south from helipad to *Marine Palace*, has handicrafts from Karnataka. There are several book exchange places along the north cliff, near *Marine Palace*, and on Beach Rd.

▲ Activities and tours

Thiruvananthapuram *p891, map p892*

Swimming

Waterworks, pool near museum, T318990, entry Rs 2, 0830-1200, 1400-1530, 1815-2000, closed Mon. Also at Mascot Hotel.

Tour operators

IATOn approved agencies include: Aries Travel, Press Rd, T330964, F470159, sivans@ giasmd2.vsnl.net.in. Jayasree, PO Box 5236 Pettah, T476603, F476803, www.jayasree travels.com. One-stop travel service, good coaches. Gt India Tour Co, Mullassery Towers, Vanross Junction, T331516, F330579, reliable but pricey; TourIndia, MG Rd, T330437, F331407, tourindia@ vsnl.com, run unique tours, eco-friendly tree house, backwater cruises, Periyar trek, sport fishing off Kochi; . *Vacation India*, Plamoodu Junc, T312028, F314561, runs tours throughout south India.

Kerala Tourism: (www.keralatourism.org) from *Hotel Chaithram*, T330031/695033. **1** City tour: 0800-1900, including Kovalam (125 km), Rs 190 including lunch, boating; half day, 1400-1900 including boating Rs 90. **2** Kanniyakumari: 0730-2100, including Kovalam, Padmanabhapuram and Kanniyakumari (200 km), Rs 210 daily; **3** Ponmudi: 0830-1900, daily, Golden Valley and Ponmudi (125 km), Rs 170. Long tours can be very exhausting, the stops at sites of interest are often very brief. Great India Tour Co, Mullassery Towers, Vanross Square, T331516, offers afternoon city tour among others.

Yoga
Institute of Yogic Culture, Vazhuthacaud. **Sivananda Ashram**, T290493.

Kovalam *p894, map p895*
Fishing
Can readily be arranged through the hotels, as can excursions on traditional catamarans or motor boats. Some near *Ashok Hotel* beach promise corals and beautiful fish just off-shore (do not expect to see very much).

Tour operators
East India Premier Tours, behind *Neelkantha Hotel*, T483246, F481994. Can suggest unusual hotels, **Visit India**, Lighthouse Rd, T481069, friendly and helpful, exchange, short country-boat backwater tours from Thiruvallam; **Great Indian Travel**, Lighthouse Rd, T481110, F480173, www.keralatours.com. Wide range, exchange, eco-friendly beach resort.

Varkala *p896, map p897*
Tour companies
Most hotels offer tours, air tickets, backwater trips, houseboats etc, as do the many agents along the north cliff and at Temple Junction.

Yoga
Scientific School of Yoga and Massage, Altharamoodu, Janardhana Temple, 10-day yoga and massage course (2 classes daily), Rs 500, professionally run by English speaking doctor, T695141. Also **shop** selling ayurvedic oils, soaps, shampoo etc. **Keraleeyamm**, north cliff, is one of the best of the many yoga/ayurvedic massage centres.

⊖ Transport

Thiruvananthapuram *p891, map p892*
Air
The airport is closed at night so you can't wait overnight, see Sleeping p898. The airport is near the beach, 6 km away. International flights via the Gulf states are very good value. Transport to town: by local bus No 14, pre-paid taxi (Rs 85) or auto-rickshaw (about Rs 30, 20 mins). Enquiry, T502323. Confirm international bookings and arrive in good time. Inflated prices at refreshments counter though cheap tea/coffee in the final lounge after 'Security' check. The banks at the airport are outside arrivals. *Johnson & Co* (travel agent) opposite Domestic Terminal, T503555.
International Indian Airlines, Mascot Sq, T318288, F501537 (and **Sri Lanka**, T501140): to **Colombo** and **Male**. Air India, Museum Rd, Velayambalam, T310310, A501426: flies to **London, New York, Frankfurt, Paris** and the Gulf; **Air Maldives**.
Domestic Indian Airlines: to **Bangalore**, **Chennai**, **Delhi**, **Mumbai**. Air India: **Mumbai**. Jet Airways, Akshay Towers, Shashtamangalam, T721018, airport 500710. **Chennai**, **Mumbai**.

Auto-rickshaw
Tell rickshaw drivers which Kovalam beach you want to get to in advance, otherwise they will charge much more when you get there. Charge minimum Rs 6.50 (will use meter if pressed); you may need to bargain for Kovalam, especially in the evening (Rs 70 is fair).

Bus
Local City Bus Station, fort, T463029. To **Kovalam**: from East Fort, No 888, 30 mins, Rs 7. **Long distance** Journeys through heavy traffic can be very uncomfortable and tiring. **Central Bus Station**, near railway station, Thampanoor, T323886. Buses to **Kanniyakumari via Nagercoil** or direct, frequent depart, 2½ hrs; **Kozhikode**, 10 hrs (*Exp*); **Madurai**, 1230, 6½ hrs; **Thrissur**, 7 hrs (Exp). Buses to **Ernakulam/Kochi** via Alappuzha and Kollam, start early, 5 hrs (*Exp*) or 6½ hrs. You can include a section of the backwaters on the way to Kochi by getting a boat from Kollam (shared taxis there cost Rs 60 each, see below). **TNSTC** to **Chennai,**

Coimbatore, Cuddalore, Erode, Kanniyakumari, Madurai from opposite the Central Railway station.

Car
Car hire From agents, Rs 700-800 per day; from *Vacation India,* Plamoodu Junction, T312028, F314561; *Southern Travel,* Shasthamangalam, T316850.

Motorcycle
Enfield rental: *Asian Trailblazers*, Marikar Buildings, MG Rd, T478211, asiantrailblazers@yahoo.com.

Taxi
From outside *Mascot Hotel* charge about Rs 7 per km; to Kovalam, Rs 175, return Rs 225 (waiting: extra Rs 50 per hr).

Train
Central Station, after 1800. Reservations in building adjoining station, T132. Advance, upstairs, open 0700-1300, 1330-1930, Sun 0900-1700; ask to see Chief Reservations Supervisor, Counter 8; surprisingly no "Foreigners' quota". To **Alappuzha**: *Intercity 6342*, 1630, 3 hrs. **Bangalore**: *Kanniyakumari-Bangalore Exp, 6525*, 0920, 19½ hrs; *Trivandrum Bangalore Exp, 6322*, 1505, Wed, 18¾ hrs. **Chennai**: *Trivandrum-Guwahati Exp, 6321* (AC/II), Thu, 1245, 18¼ hrs; *Trivandrum Chennai Mail, 6320* (AC/II), 1400, 18 hrs. **Delhi (HN)**, *Rajdhani Exp, 2431*, 1915, Tue, Thu, 31 hrs. **Ernakulam (Kochi)**: 10 trains daily between 0500-2145. *Trivandrum Ernakulam Exp, 6342*, 1630, 4¼ hrs; *Kerala Exp, 2625* (AC/II), 1110, 4¼ hrs, are two. **Kolkata (H)**: *Trivandrum-Guwahati Exp, 5627* (AC/II), 1245, Sun, 49 hrs; *Trivandrum-Howrah Exp, 6323*, 1245, Thu, Sat, 49 hrs. **Kanniyakumari**: *Bangalore Kanniyakumari Exp, 6526*, 1515, 2¼ hrs. **Kollam via Varkala**: 12 trains 0725-2035, 1¼ hrs.

Kovalam *p894, map p895*
There are 3 main points of access to Kovalam's beaches. Remember to specify which, when hiring an auto or taxi.

Auto-rickshaw
To Thiruvananthapuram, Rs 70-80, but need to bargain hard.

Bicycle
Bike hire: from *Voyager*, near Police Station, T4811993.

Bus
Local Frequent buses (0540-2100) into East Fort, Thiruvananthapuram, from bus stand outside *Ashok Hotel* gate (Kovalam beach), fast Rs 4.50, slow 3.30, (30 mins), also picks up from Waller Junction (Main Rd/Samudra beach). From East Fort bus station, auto-rickshaw to town centre, Rs 6, or walk. Green buses have limited stops; yellow/red buses continue through town up to museum.
Long distance To **Kanniyakumari**, **Kochi** via Kollam (Quilon) and via Kottayam, **Nagercoil**, **Padmanabhapuram**, **Varkala**, **Thodopuzha** via Kottayam.

Taxi
From taxi stand or through *Ashok* or *Samudra Hotels*. One-way to Thiruvananthapuram or airport, Rs 200; station Rs 175; city sights Rs 600; Kanniyakumari, Padmanabhapuram Rs 1,750 (8 hrs); Kochi Rs 2,250 (5 hrs); Kollam Rs 1100; Thekkady Rs 2,650 (6 hrs).

Varkala *p896, map p897*
Bus
Long distance To/from Temple Junction (not beach) for **Alappuzha** and **Kollam**, but often quicker to go to Paripally on NH47 and catch onward buses from there.

Motorcycle
Motorcycle hire Next door to *JA Tourist Home*, Temple Junction and *Mamma Chompo*, Beach Rd.

Rickshaw
From Beach Rd and Helipad (Rs 25 to station).

Taxi
From Beach Rd and Helipad (Rs 25 to station). To **Thiruvananthapuram**, Rs 350 (1¼ hrs).

Train
Several daily to coastal towns including **Thiruvananthapuram**, 0435, 0810, 0940, 1752 and 2103 (50 mins). Also to **Kanniyakumari**: 1107, 1400 (31/2 hrs); **Kollam**: 0550, 0640, 1710, 1834, 2150, 2232 (35 mins); **Mangalore**, 0640, 1834 (14 hrs).

● Directory

Thiruvananthapuram *p891, map p892*
Airline offices See Transport above for
domestic airlines. **Maldive Airways, Sri
Lankan,** Spencer Building, MG Rd, T322309,
and T475541. **Gulf Air,** T501205, and **Kuwait
Airways,** National Travel Service, Panavila
Junction, T321295 (airport T500437). **Saudi
Airways,** Arafath Travels, Pattom. **Banks** open
1000-1400, Mon to Fri, and 1000-1200, Sat.
State Bank of India, near Secretariat, with 24
hr ATM; **Canara Bank,** near Spencer Junction,
no hassle cash against Visa, friendly staff.
Andhra Bank, near *Canara Bank,* on opposite
side of road, Cash against Visa. The airport has
banks, including **Thomas Cook,** T502470.
Hospitals General Hospital, Vanchiyoor,
T443874. **Ramakrishna Ashrama Hospital,**
Sasthamangalam, T322123. **Ayurveda
Hospital,** T340938. **Homeopathy Hospital,**
T322125. **Other medical services:** Many
Chemists near hospitals; a few near Statue
Junction. **Opticians: Lens & Frames,** Pulimudu
Junc, T471354, up to date.
Internet Megabyte, CSI Building, 3rd and
4th floors, MG Rd, email: send Rs 15, receive Rs
10, friendly. **Tandem Communications,** Statue
Rd (MG Rd end), good telephone and fax
centre; colour photocopying, laser printing.
Central Telegraph office: Statue Rd, 200 m to
its north; open 24 hrs, best value internet.
Post office Poste Restante, Pulimudu
Junction, T473071, 0830-1800, efficient. PO:
north of Secretariat, off MG Rd, is better;
Speed Post (computerized; affected by power
failures); also PO at Thampanoor, opposite
Manjalikulam Rd. **Tourist offices** Tourist
offices are well supplied with leaflets and
information sheets and are very helpful.
**Department of Tourism, Goverment of
Kerala,** Main Office, Park View, opposite
museum, T322517, F322279,
www.keralatourism.org. 1000-1700, closed
Sun; and Thampanoor Central Bus Station
(T327224). **KTDC,** Central Reservations, Mascot
Sq, T318976, F314406, ktdc@vsnl.com. Tourist
Reception Centre, Thampanoor, near Bus
Station, T330031. **PRO,** near Press Secretariat
or Annexe, T468648. **India,** Airport, T451498.
Useful address Visa extension:
Foreigners' Regional Registration Office, City
Police Commissioner, Residency Rd, Thycaud,
T320486; allow up to a week, though it can

take less. Open 1000-1700, Mon-Sat. **Chief
Conservator of Forests,** T/F322217. **Wildlife
Warden,** PTP Nagar, Vattiyoorkavu, T360762.

Kovalam *p894, map p895*
Banks Central Bank, branch in *Ashok Hotel*
(around the corner near the bookshop)
changes money and TCs for non-residents
after 1045. Exchange at **Pournami
Handicrafts; Wilson's,** T480051, changes
money, any time, no hassle. Best rates (up to
3% higher), however, are at the airport.
Hospitals Emergency assistance either
through your hotel or from the **Govt Hospital**
in Thiruvananthapuram. **Upasana Hospital,**
near *Ashok Hotel* gate, has experienced
English speaking doctor; prompt, personal
attention. **Other medical services:** Ayurvedic
treatment offered by most upmarket resorts
(massage about Rs 700). Among many
Medicus, Lighthouse Rd, T480596, where Dr
Babu and his wife have clients returning year
after year; similarly, **Vasudeva,** T222510,
behind Neptune Hotel, is simple but with
experienced professionals. **Internet** Several
on Lighthouse Beach. **Post office** Inside
Ashok Hotel gate. **Telephone** Check
printed prices before paying for calls. Some
ISD booths near the bus stand. **Western
Travel,** opposite Bus Stand, until 2200. **Elite
Tours,** T481405, 2nd Beach Rd (30 m below
bus stand), 24-hr ISD from the *Batik House,*
Lighthouse Beach. **Tourist offices** Kerala
Tourism, T480085, inside *Ashok Hotel* gate,
helpful manager but erratic opening hours.

Varkala *p896, map p897*
Banks State Bank of Travancore changes
TCs, but will not change cash or accept Visa –
Bank of Baroda, next door, does. **Canara,** near
train station, gives advances on Visa cards (1%
commission). There are several
moneychangers: along the north cliff and
around Temple Junction (lower than $/£ rate
at Trivandrum airport), and most will give cash
advances on credit cards (at 5% commission!).
Internet at several places along north cliff,
helipad and Temple Junction (Rs 60 per hr).
Post office Next to *Sree Padman,* Temple
Junction, Mon-Sat 1000-1400; ISD phones
opposite; also at Maithalam and along north
cliff. **Tourist information** At the helipad,
Mon-Fri 1000-1700, Sat 1000-1500, will book
tours, backwater trips.

The Backwaters

Kollam (Quilon)

→ *Phone code: 95474 (International: 0474). Colour map 7, grid C3. Population: 361,400.*

Kollam is a shaded market town with a busy compact centre, on the side of the Ashtamudi Lake. At the south end of Kerala's backwaters, it is one of the main centres for boat trips up the canals. ➤➤ *For Sleeping, Eating and other listings, see pages 913-915.*

History

Known to Marco Polo (as *Koilum*) its port traded with Phoenicians, Persians, Greeks, Romans and Arabs as well as the Chinese. Kollam became the capital of the Venad Kingdom in the ninth century. The educated and accomplished king Raja Udaya Marthanda Varma convened a special council at Kollam to introduce a new era. After extensive astronomical calculations the new era was established to start on 15 August AD 825. The town was associated with the early history of Christianity.

Kollam

■ Sleeping		● Eating
1 Government Guest House	4 Mahalaxmi Lodge	1 Eat N Pack
2 Karthika	5 Shah International	2 India Coffee House
3 Lakshmi Tourist Home	6 Sudarshan	3 Suprabhatam
	7 Yatri Nivas	

Kerala The Backwaters Kollam

★ Kerala backwaters

The network of rivers, streams, lagoons, canals and tanks that occupies the alluvial plain between the Indian Ocean and the Western Ghats runs the length along the coast from Kollam to Kochi, the northern section known as Kuttanad. It gives an almost uniquely quiet view of Kerala village life, impossible to get simply from the road.

With only two permanent outlets to the sea, one at Kodungallur in the north and the other at Kochi, and a third opening during the southwest monsoon at Thottappally (where a cut was made to let the surplus stagnant freshwater out to sea), the lagoons are fed by a network of perennial rivers. These flush out the salts between May and September, but seawater rushes in at the end of the monsoon reaching up to 20 km inland. The backwaters become increasingly brackish through the dry season. The alternation between fresh and saltwater has been essential to the backwaters' aquatic life.

Reclamation for agriculture has reduced the surface water area, and the building of a barrier across the Vembanad Lake, north of Kumarakom, and other changes have altered the backwaters' ecology. Most of the original mangrove swamps have now been destroyed; a small residual patch at Kumarakom has limited protection. Many reclaimed areas (plots known as pokkali), are now used alternately for paddy, and fish and shrimp farming. In some parts of Vembanad the population density is four times that on the coastal zone.

On the backwaters' trip you can see how bunds have been built enclosing areas from the main lake. These bunds (often granite and cement) are strengthened by planting coconuts, while electric pumps are used to dry out the normally flooded land. Below the bund the lake is suffering excessive saline flooding, and the reduced exchange between the lakes and the sea has severely worsened pollution. Mass fish kills are reported, and water weed infestation has increased with the excessive use of fertilizers on agricultural land. The dramatic increase in the land value across Kerala has resulted in pressure to put every square centimetre to economic use.

Few of these problems are immediately visible on the backwaters' trip, which can be an idyllic experience. Waterside activities of coir making, toddy tapping, fishing, rice growing along the palm-lined banks and narrow strips of land that separate the waterways, and the constant quiet traffic of vallam (traditional dugouts) are typical. Advantage is taken of the comparatively long rainy season so while coconuts provide a vital economic resource, the land underneath is often intensively cultivated. From the boat you will see papaya, mangoes, jack fruit and cassava (*tapioca*) growing. Tapioca, only introduced to Kerala in 1920, is very popular since it gives remarkably high yields from lateritic soils that are about 'as fertile as railway ballast'.

Along the backwaters, traditional punted boats or motorized ferries provide one of the most delightful tours in India. The typical journey on a motor boat between Kollam and Alappuzha lasts over eight hours but some people find this too long. A shorter trip is possible, either by doing a round trip from Kollam, or by picking up or getting off the boat closer to Alappuzha (eg Changanacherry or Kottayam). Nearer Kochi too, a quiet half-day can be spent on a traditional dugout or you can have an exclusive upmarket overnight trip in a *kettuvallam* style houseboat.

Travel tip: even in the coolest times of year this journey during daytime can get very hot. Take a sun hat, sun block and plenty of water.

Kerala The Backwaters Kollam

Ashtamudi Lake ① *boats for hire for cruising from the Kollam Boat Club or from the DTPC, Guest House Compound, T742558, pedal or rowing boats for 2 or 4, Rs 20 per hr each*, with coconut palms on its banks and picturesque promontories extends north from the town. You might see some 'Chinese' fishing nets and in wider sections large-sailed dugouts carrying the local coir, copra and cashew.

Backwaters tours

Trips for groups of 10, or a 'cruise' for 20 to Alappuzha with a guide. Be aware that timings do alter See also Kumarakom and Alappuzha. **DTPC** (District Tourism Promotion Council) ① *Ashramam, T742558 dtpcqln@md3.vsnl.net, Tue and Sat, 1000, Rs 150 (ISIC Rs 100), halfway to Alumkadavu, Rs 100*, runs an eight hour 'Luxury' cruise from the jetty near slaughter house in season. En route, stops may include the longest snake boat in the world, Champakulam, an 11th-century black granite Buddha statue at Karumadi, and a coir processing village at Thrikkunnapuzha. However, some travellers say that the only stops are for meals, so check in advance. Some find the trip a little too long and 'samey'. The DTPC canal trip to **Munroe Island village**, ① *0900-1300, Rs 300*, is an alternative.

DTPC also has a more expensive alternative, the luxury *kettuvallam*, with two bedrooms, a bath and a kitchen hired out for Rs 4,500 for two (full day), traditional Kerala meals are served; overnight trips (24 hours) start at Rs 8,200. The 25 hp outboard engine does about 10 km per hour. You can also hire motor boats for a 'safari cruise' for eight people, Rs 200-300 per hour. Contact DTPC, T742558, or Soma, T477-261017. Further details on www.dtpc-quilontourism.com

Kollam to Alappuzha

Vallikkavu (Amrithapuri) Vallikkavu is 10 km north of Kollam. The ashram of Mata ('Mother') Amrithanandamayi, on the backwaters, is sandwiched between the sea and the river, accessible by boat or by road through Kayamkulam or Karungappally. *Darshan* is attended by large numbers of villagers and western visitors who come to receive a hud from 'Mother'. Spartan but spacious

Kollam to Alappuzha backwaters

accommodation is offered in a multi-storey block; Rs 150 includes very basic South Indian food. Western canteen (at extra cost) has a range of American-choice meals. Shops, bank, post office, library, Internet etc are available. Smoking, sex and alcohol are not allowed.

Mannarsala Mannarsala (32 km before Alappuzha) has a Nagaraja Temple in the forest. Traditionally Hindu *naga* (serpent) worshippers had temples in serpent groves. Mannarsala is the largest of these in Kerala with "30,000 images" of snake gods along the path and among the trees, and has many snakes living around the temple. Childless women come for special blessing and also return for a 'thanksgiving' ceremony afterwards when the child born to the couple is placed on special scales and gifts in kind equalling the weight are donated. The temple is unusual for its chief priestess.

Haripad Haripad has one of Kerala's oldest and most important Subrahmanya temples. The four armed idol is believed to have been found in a river, and the Snake Boat Race at **Payipad**, 3 km by bus, for three days commemorates its rescue and subsequent building of the temple (August). Boat processions on first two days followed by competitive races on third day; entry by ticket in August and November/December. There is a guesthouse on Mankotta Island on the backwaters, large comfortable rooms with bath, well kept, boating, squash.

Thottapally Squeezed between the backwaters and the sea, and 12 km from Haripad station, Thottapally makes a good stop on a backwaters trip, two hours from Alappuzha.

Aranmula Aranmula (10 km from Chengannur) has the Parthasarathi Temple and is known for its unique metal mirrors. The *Vallamkali* (or *Utthrittathi*) festival on the last day of Onam (August-September) is celebrated with the *Boat Race* (September). The festival celebrates the crossing of the river by Krishna, who is believed to be in all the boats simultaneously, so they are expected to arrive at the same time, not to race each other.

Alappuzha (Alleppey)

→ *Phone code: 95477 (International: 0477). Colour map 7, grid C3. Population: 177,100.*
Alappuzha (pronounced Alappoorra) has a large network of canals passing through the town and is a major centre for backwater cruises and the venue for the spectacular 'snake' boat races. There is little else of interest though the people are friendly.
▸▸ *For Sleeping, Eating and other listings, see pages 913-915.*

Sights
Alappuzha is the headquarters of Kerala's coir industry with some very old warehouses on the canal bank. It is also important for cashew nut processing. The centre of activity is the jetty with the bus stand nearby. Here, in places, the waterways are clogged and completely covered by the rampant water hyacinth with pretty blue flowers which remains a scourge. **St Thomas Church** is worth a look. There is a daily **Kathakali performance** ① *SD Pharmacy Buildings, near Iron Bridge, T241468, (1830, call ahead).*

Backwaters tours
Alappuzha is a starting point of backwater boat trips to Kollam, Changanacherry, Kottayam and Kochi. **DTPC** (District Tourism Promotion Council), Alappuzha, KSRTC Bus Station, T/253308. From August to May, eight-hour cruises depart at 1030, Monday, Wednesday, Friday, Rs 150, with stops for lunch and tea. Half-way cruise to

Alamkadavu, Rs 100 (ISIC gets reduction) on a local ferry, one-way (29 km) costs Rs 10, from 0500-2100, 2½ hours. Some visitors feel that this trip is so different from the Kollam-Alappuzha trip that it is worth doing both. Ferry to **Kottayam**, 1130, takes 2½ hours, Rs 8. Towards **Kochi** on a large canal is less interesting. The journeys in the daytime are more interesting for watching unspoilt village life of Kerala. **Private operators** offer similar trips, sometimes shorter (sometimes only stopping for a swim and lunch).

Casino Group runs a *Spice Boat Cruise* ① *contact Kochi T668221, F668001, casino@vsnl.com, US$325*, in modified *kettuvallams*, which are idyllic if not luxurious – shaded sit-outs, modern facilities including solar panels for electricity, two double rooms, limited menu. Also through *Soma* ① *opposite the boat jetty, 212 Raiban Annex, T0477-261017, soma@md2.vsnl.net.in*.

Around Alappuzha
Mararikulam On the coast, 15 km north of Alappuzha, this quiet, secluded beach until now was only known to the adjoining fishing village. The main village has a thriving cottage industry of coir and jute weaving.

Champakulam ① *Take the Alappuzha-Changanacherry bus (every 30 mins) to Moncombu (Rs 4), then rickshaw to Champakulam (4 km, Rs 12), Alappuzha-Edathna ferry leaves at 0615 and 1715 and stops at Champakulam. In Edathna you can visit the early Syrian St George's Church.* Sixteen kilometres southeast of Alappuzha, St Mary's Forane Church (Syrian) at this backwaters village dates only from 1870 but is on the site of one going back to AD 427. The English speaking priest is happy to show visitors round. Nearby the St Thomas Statuary makes wooden statues of Christ for export round the world. A 2-m statue of Jesus costs approximately US$450. Champakulam is particularly attractive because there is no traffic other than the occasional cycle, and the odd canoe. Visit recommended.

Alappuzha (Alleppey)

Sleeping ■	5 St George Lodge	4 Komala
1 Cherukara Nest		5 Saurashtra
2 Holiday Inn	Eating ●	6 Vijaya
3 Karthika Tourist Home	1 Aryas	
4 Narasimahapuram	2 Café Venice	
Lodge	3 Indian Coffee House	

Listings: The Backwaters

⊜ Sleeping

Kollam *p908, map p908*
Paying guests through Prof KRC Nair, Ambadi Lake Resorts, Ashramam, T744688.
A Aquaserene, Paravoor, 15 mins from town by road/boat, T512410, F512104. Splendid backwaters location, well-furnished chalets (some re-assembled Kerala houses) with TV, restaurant, Ayurvedic massage/treatment, boat rides.
B Ashtamudi Resorts, Chavara South (north of town), T882288, F882470, ashtamudi@md3.vsnl.net.in. 30 mins by car, 10 mins speed boat, 20 rms in 5 traditional chalets, dearer 'Queens Cottages' and 'King's Palace', all a/c with good views, catamaran trips, an ayurvedic resort.
C Palm Lagoon, Vellimon West, T523974, F533974, palmlagoon@mailroom.com. Delightful setting 18 km from town centre on north side of Ashtamudi Lake, can be reached from backwater cruise, attractive thatched cottages, including full board.
C-E Sudarsan, Hospital Rd, Parameswar Nagar, 5 mins from jetty, T744322, F740480, www.hotelsudarsan.com. 35 rooms, some a/c with bath, rear quieter, dim a/c restaurant, bar, exchange, backwater trips.
E Karthika, Chinnakada, T740106. 40 rooms with bath, some a/c, restaurant, bar, backwater trips arranged, mediocre.
E Lake View, Thoppikadavu, T794669, F795041. Near Thevally Bridge (5 km from station; 10 min walk from small Post Office northwest of town), beautiful position along lakeside, 4 clean, renovated rooms (2 have large balcony) (Rs 275+), lovely garden, good waterside restaurant, bar (occasionally noisy), friendly staff. Recommended.
E Shah International, TB Rd, Chinnakkada, T724362, F719435. 72 rooms, some **D** a/c, adequate restaurant, quiet, good value.
E-F Yatri Nivas, Guest House Compound by Ashtamudi Lake, Ashramam, T745538. 15 rooms and 2 6-bed dorms, great views from balconies, restaurant, beer (pricey), boating and free boat service from town jetty, ugly block building but clean and good value, cycles for hire, reservations at tourist office, Alappuzha.

F Govt Guest House, Ashramam, T743620. 8 large rooms, simple meals, fine 200-year-old building with garden on edge of lagoon, former British Residency, boating, small pool and park by the lake, full of character, often full.
F Lakshmi Tourist Home, Parry Junction, Main Rd, T740167. Some a/c, basic.
F Mahalaxmi Lodge, opposite Bus Station near Ashtamudi Lake, T749440. 7 very small rooms (Rs 90), shared outside toilet, adequate.

Thottapally *p911*
C-D Coconut Palms, Pandavapuram Heritage Village, T836251. Idyllic traditional house in shaded compound, on backwaters and 100 m from sea, package deals available including transport from *Aries Travel*, Trivandrum T0471-330964.

Alappuzha *p911, map p912*
Book ahead to avoid the scramble off the ferry. All hotels north of Vadai Canal are quieter.
A Kayaloram Lake Resort, Punnamada, on Vembanad Lake, 4 km; 15 mins by boat from jetty then 300 m walk or at 'Punchiri', Jetty Rd, T260573, F252918, kayaloram@satyam.net.in. 12 Kerala style wood and tile cottages around small inner 'courtyard' with 'open-to-sky' showers, pool, backwaters or lake trips, comfortable, very quiet and peaceful, restaurant (typical Kerala cuisine, Continental), ayurveda. Recommended.
B Emerald Isle Heritage Resort, on a backwater island, T703899, www.emerald islekerala.com. 4 rooms in a 150 year old traditional Kerala homestead, best with 'inside-outside' bathroom, meals included.
B Keraleeyam Ayurvedic Lake Resort, off the Thotampally main road (involves a short wooded walk), T241468, F251068, mail@keraleeyam.com. 1930s 'Heritage home', now attached to an ayurvedic pharmacy, 5 comfortable a/c rooms (hut better than house), pleasant courtyard lawn, great Kerala cuisine, excellent ayurvedic centre, boat rides on backwaters, view of races in season, homely atmosphere but uneven a/c.
C-D Alleppey Prince, AS Rd (NH47), 2 km north of centre, T243752, F243758. 30 good, clean rooms, central a/c, very dark bar, pool, luxury boats for backwaters.

D **Cherukara Nest**, just round the corner from bus station, T251509, F243782, zachs@md4.vsnl.net.in. Pleasant traditional home, clean rooms with bath, very helpful staff, Kerala meals on request.

E **Holiday Inn**, Vadai Canal North Bank, T242955. Clean, spacious rooms, good value.

E **Tharayil Tourist Home**, 750 m from boat jetty near lake, Thotampally, T/F243543. Some a/c rooms, clean, local furniture in family home.

F **Govt Rest House**, Beach Rd, 4 km Bus Stand, T243445. Excellent value, reasonable food (order in advance) but indifferent service, reservations: Dist Collector, Collectorate, Dist HQ, Alappuzha.

F **Karthika Tourist Home**, near Zilla Court, SDV Rd, north of canal, opposite Jetty, T245524. 39 clean, pleasant rooms, some large with baths (cockroaches), best No 31, helpful and friendly staff, good value.

F **Narasimhapuram Lodge**, Cullen Rd, T262662. Some a/c rooms, occasional weight-lifting competition with live commentary over loudspeakers!

F **St George Lodge**, CCNB Rd, A-5, T251620. 80 basic rooms, some with bath, good value, exchange, book ahead.

Mararikulam *p912*

A **Marari Beach**, T0478-863801, F863810, casino@vsnl.com. 40 well-furnished, comfortable, a/c, local style cottages among palm groves – some with private pool, good sea food, pool, ayurvedic treatment, yoga, bikes, very friendly staff, discounts April to September. Recommended.

Champakulam *p912*

D **Green Palace**, with Kerala meals and ayurvedic massage.

🍴 Eating

Kollam *p908, map p908*

Eat N Pack, near Taluk Office, Main St. Excellent value, clean, good choice of dishes, friendly. Recommended.

Indian Coffee House, Main Rd. For good coffee and non-vegetarian snacks, 0800-2030.

Suprabhatam, opposite Clock Tower, Main St. Adequate, vegetarian.

Alappuzha *p911, map p912*

🍴🍴 **Vemanad**, inside the *Prince Hotel*, International, comfortable a/c, reasonable food, alcohol in bar only.

🍴 **Annapoorna**, excellent vegetarian.

🍴 **Aryas**, south of Jetty, good for *idli, dosa, vadai*.

🍴 **Café Venice**, is just by the DTPC office.

🍴 **Indian Coffee House** does good value, tasty non-vegetarian snacks.

🍴 **Komala**, excellent South Indian thalis and some Chinese (poor rooms).

🍴 **Saurashtra**, vegetarian, ample helpings on banana leaf, locally popular.

🍴 **Vijaya**, good South Indian veg and Chinese.

☸ Festivals and events

Kollam *p908, map p908*

Jan: Kerala Tourism boat race on 19 Jan. **Apr**: colourful 10-day **Vishnu festival** in Asram Temple with procession and fireworks. **Aug-Sep**: Avadayattukotta Temple celebrates 5-day **Ashtami Rohani** festival. **Muharram** observed with processions at town mosque.

Alappuzha *p911, map p912*

For more details: www.keralatourism.org. **9-12 Jan**: Cheruppu celebrated in Mullakkal Devi Temple with procession of elephants, music and fireworks. **17-19 Jan**: Tourism Boat Race. **Jul**: DTPC Boat Race (3rd Sat) in backwaters. Champakulam Boat Race, Kerala's oldest, takes place 16 km ferry ride away on 'Moolam' day (check with tourist office) Jul 2004. The Nehru Trophy (14 Aug 2004), inaugurated in 1952, is largest **Snake Boat Race** in state. As many as 40 'snake boats' are rowed by several dozen oarsmen before huge crowds. Naval helicopters do mock rescue operations and stunt flying. Entry by ticket; Rs 125 recommended (avoid Rs 60/75 as it gets overcrowded and becomes dangerous and no fun). There are other snakeboat races held throughout the year.

🛍 Shopping

Kollam *p908, map p908*

The main areas are on the Main Rd. **Bishop Jaromnagar Shopping Mall** is modern and handy. **Kairali**, Beach Rd for crafts.

⬤ *For an explanation of the sleeping and eating price codes used in this guide, see inside the*
⬤ *front cover. Other relevant information is found in Essentials pages 52-57.*

▲ Activities and tours

Kollam *p908, map p908*
Tours
DTPC and others offer backwater cruises on big country boats (*kettuvallam*). An overnight tour from Rs 5,000 for two, includes meals. The gentle pace and quiet contribute to make this very worthwhile, but the heat and humidity may sometimes make it uncomfortable (no fans). **Tourindia** pioneered these house boat trips; contact at Karukapparambil, near Nehru Trophy Finishing Point, T0477-264961. **World Tours**, Tesson Arcade, T741249.

⊕ Transport

Kollam *p908, map p908*
Auto-rickshaw
Local auto-rickshaws are plentiful.

Bikes are available for hire.

Bus
Local Buses are plentiful.
Long distance KSRTC, T752008. Buses every 30 mins to Alappuzha (85 km, 2 hrs) and **Kochi** (140 km, 3½ hrs) and other towns on the coast. Daily bus to **Kumily** village for Periyar National Park (change at Kottayam), 1000, 7 hrs. Also buses to **Kanniyakumari**. Frequent services to **Kochi**, 3 hrs; **Thiruvananthapuram**, 2 hrs. For **Varkala** difficult by bus, take one to Kollambalam and change. However, all southbound trains stop at Varkala.

Train
The Junction railway station, T131, is about 3 km east of the boat jetty and bus station.
Chennai (MC): *Trivandrum Chennai Mail, 6320* (AC/II), 1520, 16¾ hrs. **Mumbai (CST)**: *Kanniyakumari Mumbai Exp, 1082*, 0845, 44 hrs. **Thiruvananthapuram**: *Vanchinad Exp, 6303*, 0853, 1½ hrs; *Parasuram Exp, 6350*, 1725, 1½ hrs; *Bangalore Kanniyakumari Exp, 6526*, 1335, 1¾ hrs, continues to **Kanniyakumari**, 2¼ hrs.

Alappuzha *p911, map p912*
Auto-rickshaws
Rickshaw drivers board incoming ferry and help you with luggage and offer to transport you to the Kochi/Ernakulam bus stand, but it is only a 5-min walk away.

Bus
Long distance T252501. Frequent buses to **Champakulam**; **Kochi**, 0630-2330, 1½ hrs; **Kollam** 2½ hrs; **Kottayam** 1½ hrs; **Thiruvananthapuram** 3½ hrs. Also to **Coimbatore**, 0615, 7 hrs.

Ferry
T252015. DTPC, ATDC, *Prince* and others: to **Champakulam** 9 trips from 0430-2300, 1½ hrs; **Changanacherry**, 3½ hrs; **Chengannur**, 5 hrs; **Kollam**, 8 hrs etc.

Train
Station, T253965, is 3 km from the Jetty with occasional buses from there. Trains to **Ernakulam (Junction)** depart 0600 to 1925 . To **Chennai**: *Alleppey Chennai Exp, 6042*, 1500, 15¾ hrs. **Thiruvananthapuram**: *Ernakulam Trivandrum Exp, 6341*, 0615, 3½ hrs.

⊕ Directory

Kollam *p908, map p908*
Hospitals District Hospital, T793409. **Post office** Head Post Office, Parameswara Nagar. Mon-Sat to 2000, Sun to 1800. Speed Post at Chinnakkada.**Tourist offices** DTPC, *Govt Guest House* Complex, T/F742558, dtpcqln@md3.vsnl.net.in. Offers cruises and coach tours, plus details of Kathakali performances; also, very helpful counter staff at Ferry jetty; KSRTC Bus station, T745625; Railway station, Platform 4. **Department of Tourism**, at *Guest House,* T743620. **KTDC**, *Yatri Nivas*, Ashramam, T748638.

Alappuzha *p911, map p912*
Bank Bank of Baroda, Mullakal Rd, Visa/Mastercard advances. **Canara**, opposite DTPC, changes most TCs but not cash. **Hospitals** District Hospital, 1253324. **Internet** Several on Mullakal Rd. **Post office** Off Mullakal Rd. **Tourist offices** KTDC, *Motel Aram*, T244460. ATDC (Alappuzha Tourism Dev Corp), Komala Rd, T/F243462, info@atdcaalleppey.com. DTPC, KSRTC Bus Station near jetty, T253308, F251720, 0830-2000 (7 days); helpful, good backwaters trips. Also *My Dream Tourist Service*, Cream Korner, Mullackal, T260005.

Kerala Listings: The Backwaters

Central Malabar

As with several other regional names the name 'Malabar' is an evocative combination of foreign and local elements. Hobson-Jobson has pointed out the Arab connection with the name 'Malabar', applied to the region which they also knew as the 'Pepper Coast'. 'Malai' is the Dravidian term for mountain, while 'bar' was applied by Arab sailors to a

Kochi (Cochin) & Ernakulam

Related maps
A *Ernakulam centre,*
page 918
B *Fort Kochi detail, page 920*

■ Sleeping	3 Casino & Maruthi	6 Island Inn
1 Abad	4 Fort House & Seagull	7 Presidency
2 Brunton Boat Yard	5 International	8 Seagull

number of the coastal regions with which they traded such as Zanzibar (the 'Country of the Blacks') and the Kalahbar (the Malay Coast). It is suggested that 'bar' indicates both a coast and kingdom. ▸▸ For Sleeping, Eating and other listings, see pages 933-949.

★ Kochi-Ernakulam → Phone code: 95484 (International: 0484).

Colour map 7, grid C2. Population: 1.15 million (Kochi 596,500, Ernakulam 558,000).

9 Taj Malabar
10 Trident

Eating
1 Bharat

Kochi (Cochin), one of South India's most interesting towns, still largely comprises low rise, picturesque buildings. Rich in history, despite rapid recent growth it retains a relaxed, quiet atmosphere once the majority of day-visitors leave. Narrow spits of land and coconut covered islands jut out into the wide, and almost enclosed, bay whose neck is lined with the famous Chinese fishing nets. Today, Kochi's twin town, Ernakulam, is busy and noisy by comparison, a dynamic city with soaring land prices and rapidly industrializing suburbs.

Ins and outs

Getting there The new Kochi International Airport is at Nedumbassery, 36 km away. Ernakulam Junction is the principal railway station, with the main long distance bus station close by. Both are within easy walking distance of some hotels, though pleasanter Fort Kochi is a bus or ferry ride away.

Getting around During the day, a good ferry service stops at major points around the bay. It is pleasant, cheap and quick. Once in Fort Kochi, the palace and the synagogue in 'Jew Town' are close enough to a jetty but some distance from the other sights eg St Francis Church. Autos and bikes can be hired. See Transport, page 944, for further details. Tourist Office produces a reasonable walking tour map of Fort Kochi.

Climate Temperature: unlike the rains, the temperature stays a consistent 25-30°C throughout the year. Rainfall: Dec-Mar, are 20 mm. Jun rises to over 700 mm. Best time to visit: Dec-Mar.

Background

From 1795 until India's Independence the long outer sand spit, with its narrow beach leading to the wide bay inland, was under British political control. The inner harbour was in Kochi State, while most of the hinterland was in the separate state of Travancore. The division of political authority delayed development of the harbour facilities until 1920-23, when the approach channel was dredged to allow any ship that could pass through the Suez Canal to dock safely, opening the harbour to modern shipping.

A trading port since at least Roman times, Kochi was on the main trade route between Europe and China. The town is in three main parts. **Fort Kochi** (Fort Cochin) occupies the southern promontory on the seaward side of the bay. **Willingdon Island** was created in the 1920s by dredging the bay to increase the depth of the entrance to the harbour to over 11 m. It is the HQ of the Southern Command of the Indian Navy, and has a naval airport and the railway terminus. Across the causeway from

Ernakulam centre

To Venduruthy Bridge, Willingdon Is, Airport & Fort Kochi

To Cochin Cultural Centre

N

Not to scale

■ **Sleeping**
1 Abad Plaza & Whizz
2 Avenue Regent
3 Bharat Tourist Home
4 Biju's Tourist Home & SAAS Tower
5 Dwaraka
6 Gaanam
7 Government Rest House
8 Hakoba
9 Luciya
10 Maple Tourist Home & New Colombia
11 Metropolitan
12 Modern Guesthouse
13 Paulson Park
14 Piazza Lodge
15 Sea Lord
16 Taj Residency
17 Yuvarani's Residency

● **Eating**
1 Bimbi's, Khyber & Yuvrani
2 Bimbi's Southern Star
3 Caravan
4 Chariot
5 Chinese Garden
6 Hot Breads
7 Indian Coffee House & City Park
8 Pandhal
9 Snowball
10 Woodlands

66 99 This gem of a synagogue dating from 1568 (rebuilt in 1662) is near Mattancherry Palace, at the heart of what is called locally Jew Town, now a fascinating mixture of shops (some selling antiques), warehouses and spice auction rooms.

Willingdon Island is **Ernakulam**. Immediately opposite the jetty at Ernakulam is **Bolghatty Island**, and beyond it **Vypeen Island**.

Sights
The historic buildings listed here are in **Fort Kochi**. A plaque in Vasco da Gama Square near the Customs Jetty commemorates the landing of **Vasco da Gama** in 1500. Next to it is the Stromberg Bastion, "one of the seven bastions of Fort Emanuel built in 1767", named after the Portuguese King. Little remains of the old Portuguese fort (founded 1503) except some ruins. Along the sea front are the Chinese fishing nets.

★ **Mattancherry Palace** ⓘ *closed Fri and National holidays, 1000-1700, Rs 2, photography not allowed*. The palace was built by the Portuguese (circa 1557) as a gift for the Raja of Kochi in exchange for trading rights. In 1663, it was largely rebuilt by the new occupants, the **Dutch**. Built on two floors round a quadrangle with a temple, the plan follows the traditional Kerala pattern known as *nalukettus* ('four buildings'), see page 893. Although the Palace has exhibits of the Rajas of Kochi (clothes, palanquins, weapons, furniture) the main feature is the series of murals painted on the wooden walls. These are remarkable, matched only by those in the Padmanabhapuram Palace, see page 874. The 'royal bedroom' has low wooden ceilings and walls covered in about 45 late 16th-century paintings illustrating the *Ramayana*, from the beginning to the point of Sita's return from captivity. Every available space is covered with rich red, yellow, black and white; blue and green are used sparingly. To the south of the Coronation Hall, the *kovinithilam* (staircase room) has six 18th-century, large murals including the coronation of Rama. The room to the north has a painting of Vishnu. Other rooms upstairs have more exhibits of the royal house. Two of the women's bedrooms downstairs have 19th century murals with greater detail. They relate Kalidasa's *Kumarasambava* and themes from the *Puranas*.

★ **Synagogue** ⓘ *closed Fri night, Sat and Jewish holidays (when a giant oil candelabra lights up the courtyard), 1000-1200 and 1500-1700, Rs 2, no video cameras, shoes must be removed, for information on other Kerala synagogues: www.isjm.org.jhr/llnos3-4/news/html.india*. For several centuries there were two Jewish communities. The earlier group (often referred to as 'black' Jews), who, according to one source, settled here in 587 BC. The earliest evidence of their presence is a copper inscription dated AD 388 (possibly as much as a century later) by the Prince of Malabar. Those referred to as 'white' Jews came much later, when, with Dutch and subsequently British patronage, they played a pivotal role as trading agents. Speaking fluent Malayalam, they made excellent go-betweens for foreigners seeking to establish contacts. This gem of a synagogue dating from 1568 (rebuilt in 1662) is near Mattancherry Palace, at the heart of what is called locally Jew Town, now a fascinating mixture of shops (some selling antiques), warehouses and spice auction rooms.

Stepping inside is an extraordinary experience of light and airlness, given partly by the flooring of 18th-century blue Cantonese ceramic tiles, hand painted and each one different. There are original glass oil lamps. The clock tower bears Roman, Hebrew and Malayalam characters. The community has shrunk to half a dozen families, with many now settled at Moshav Nevatim in Israel's Negev desert (see Footprint's Israel Handbook). The second Jewish synagogue (in Ernakulam) is deserted.

St Francis Church ① *Mon-Sat, Sun afternoon, Sun services in English 0800 (except 3rd Sun each month), visiting 0930-1730.* Originally dedicated to Santo Antonio, the patron saint of Portugal, St Francis Church is the first to reflect the new, European influenced tradition. In Fort Kochi, the original wooden structure (circa 1510) was replaced by the present stone building (there is no authority for the widely quoted date of 1546). Vasco da Gama died on the site in 1524 and was originally buried in the cemetery. Fourteen years later his body was removed to Portugal. The church was renamed St Francis in 1663, and the Dutch both converted it to a Protestant church and substantially modified it. They retained control until 1795, adding the impressive gable façade at the entrance. In 1804, it became an Anglican church. In 1949 the congregation joined the Church of South India. Note the old string-pulled *punkhas* (fans) and the Dutch and Portuguese grave stones that now line the walls.

Santa Cruz Cathedral Near St Francis Church, originally built in 1557 by the Portuguese, and used as a warehouse by the British in the 18th century, was rebuilt in the early 20th century. It has lovely carved wooden panels and pulpit, and an interesting graveyard.

Fort Kochi detail

To Vypeen

Chinese Fishing Nets
Kathakali Centre
River Rd
Fort Kochi Bus Stand
Fresh Fish Stalls
Rampath Rd
Children's Park
Princess St
Vasco da Gama Square
Tower Rd
Rose St
Burgher St
Bastion Rd
Indiom Books
Fosse Rd
Dutch Cemetery
St Francis
Cochin Club
Parade Ground
Port Office Rd
Quiros St
Dutch Cemetery Rd
Church St
Peter Celli St
+ Santa Cruz Cathedral
Beach Rd
Lily St
+ St Peter & Paul
Parade Rd
Napier St
KB Jacob Rd
Bishop's House
N
0 metres 200
0 yards 200

Sleeping ■
1 Adam's Old Inn
2 Chiramel Residency
3 Delight
4 Elite & Sabala Restaurant
5 Fort Heritage
6 Kapithan Inn
7 Malabar House
8 Old Courtyard
9 Oys
10 Park Avenue
11 Tharavadu Tourist Home

Eating ●
1 Chariot Fort
2 Kashi
3 Rendezvous Cyber Café

★ **Chinese fishing nets** Not unique to Kochi, but uniquely accessible to the short stay visitor, the cantilevered fishing nets line the entrance to the harbour mouth. Chinese traders are believed to have originally introduced them in the late 14th century although, today, parts of the nets are known by Portuguese names. They can best be seen either on the north end of the fort promontory, close to the Fort Kochi bus stand, or from a boat tour of the harbour.

Bolghatty Island has the 'palace' (circa 1745), set in large gardens and converted into a hotel. It was originally built by the Dutch and then became the home of the British Resident at the court of the Raja of Kochi after 1799. There is still some atmosphere of colonial decay which haunted the old building and gave it much of its charm.

Willingdon Island has become the hub of one of India's busiest ports. The Custom's House and the *Malabar Hotel* are to the north of the naval airport and the rail terminus. You can take a pleasant walk or an inexpensive ferry ride around the lake, though the docks warehouses and truck parks are not very picturesque.

Vypeen Island with the Portuguese Azhikotta Fort, built around 1503, stands by the police station. You can see cannon holes on the walls of the octagonal fort which was garrisoned by 20 soldiers when it guarded the entrance to the backwaters.

Museums

Parishith Thamburan Museum ① *Darbar Hall Rd, Ernakulam, T369047, closed Mon, 0930-1230 and 1500-1730, free.* In Old Durbar Hall with typical Kerala architecture. Nineteenth-century oil paintings, old coins, sculptures, items from Kochi royal family.

Museum of Kerala History ① *Edappally, Kochi, closed Mon and National holidays, 1000-1200, 1400-1600, Rs 2.* Starting with Neolithic man through St Thomas, Vasco da Gama and historical personalities of Kerala are represented with sound and light.

Indo-Portuguese Museum ① *Bishop's House, Napier St, Fort Kochi, closed Mon, 1000-1800, Rs 25.* Interesting collection of religious artefacts tracing the history of the Catholic church in South India.

Excursions

Our Lady's Convent, ① *Palluruthy, Thoppamnady, 14 km south of town, by appointment only, 1230508,* specializes in high quality needlework lace and embroidery. The sisters are very welcoming and it is an interesting tour with items for sale.

Raksha works with children with physical and mental disabilities. Interested volunteers should contact the Principal ① *Yasmin Manzil, VII/370 Darragh-es-Salaam Rd, Kochangadi, T227707.*

From the coast to Thekkadi

The foothills of the Ghats are intensively cultivated with cash crops, notably rubber, tea, coffee, cardamom and pepper, while the valley bottoms are given over to paddy. Despite very low yields when compared with Malayan rubber production, the area planted to rubber has grown dramatically. ▸▸ *For Sleeping, Eating and other listings, see pages 933-949.*

Kottayam → *Phone code: 95481 (International: 0481). Colour map 7, grid C3. Population: 60,700.*

Kottayam is surrounded by some of the most fertile and beautiful scenery in the state, with hills to its east and backwaters to the west. The compact town centre is noisy, busy and increasingly polluted but the outskirts are much pleasanter.

Background Kottayam is the main Christian centre in Kerala. The Christians in Kerala largely owed their allegiance to the Orthodox Syrian tradition until the arrival of the Portuguese. After the Inquisition was introduced in 1560 the Portuguese tried to encourage the conversion of Syrian Christians to Roman Catholicism. One of the cruder means was by intercepting ships carrying Syrian bishops and preventing them from joining their churches in Kerala. At the same time efforts were made to train Indian priests, and in 1599 the Thomas Christians were allowed to use the Syriac liturgy. A formal split occurred in the Syrian church in 1665 between the Roman Syrians from the Syrian Christians under their Bishop Mar Gregory. He was a Jacobite, hence the name Jacobite Christians being applied to his branch of the Syrian Church.

Subsequent divisions occurred in the 18th and 19th centuries, but several of the Protestant Syrian churches came back together when the Church of South India was formed in 1947. The town is the centre of Kerala's rubber industry.

Sights Two of the Syrian Orthodox churches, 50 m apart, are on a hillock about 2 km north of town. The 450-year-old **Cheria Palli** ('Small' St Mary's Church) has beautiful vegetable dye mural paintings over the altar. The **Valia Palli** ('Big' St Mary's Church) was built in 1550. Here, two 'Nestorian' crosses are carved on plaques inserted behind two side altars. One has a Pallavi inscription on it, the other a Syriac. The cross on the left of the altar is the original and may be the oldest Christian artefact in India; the one to the right is a copy. By the altar there is an unusual small triptych of an Indian St George slaying a dragon. Note the interesting Visitors Book 1898-1935 – a paper cutting reports that "the church has attracted many European and native gentlemen of high position". Mass at Valia Palli at 0900 on Sunday, and Cheria Palli at 0730 on Sunday and Wednesday. The Malankara Syrian Church has its headquarters at Devalokam.

Kumarakom→ *Phone code: 95481*
(International: 0481). 16 km from Kottayam.

An old rubber plantation set around the **Vembanad Lake** has been developed by the Tourism Department into a **bird sanctuary** ① *best season for birdlife Jun-Aug, 1000-1800, bus from Kottayam, 30 mins, goes to the Kumarakom Tourist Village, auto-rickshaws, Rs 125.* A path goes through the swamp to the main bird nesting area, while the island in the middle of the lake (*Pathiramanal* – 'midnight sands') can be reached by boat. It is worth hiring a guide for an early morning walk through the sanctuary. Ask at the entrance or at the hotels.

Kottayam to Kumily
→ *Colour map 7, grid C3*

The road to the hills rises from the plains, through tropical evergreen forests, rubber and spice plantations, pepper on the low land gives rise to tea and cardamom plantations. It is an interesting drive with superb views down the east side of the Ghats onto the Tamil Nadu plains. You may meet herds of Zebu cattle, buffalo and donkeys being driven from Tamil Nadu to market in Kerala. Above 1,000 m the air freshens and it can be cold. Be prepared for a rapid change in temperature.

Kottayam environs

To Ernakulam To Angamaly

Vaikom

Thaneer Mukkom Bund

To Cherthala

Vembanad Lake

Ettumanoor Kidangoor To Palai

Mannanam

Kumarakom Tourist Complex Manarkakad
Thirunakkara **5**
KK Rd **2** **1** KK Rd
Boat Jetty **3**
KOTTAYAM **6** **2** Puthupally **4**
Kodimatha Jetty Panachikad

To Thekkady & Sabarimala

MC Rd

Vazhapally Vazhoor
Changanacherry

Perunna

To Alappuzha
To Thiruvananthapuram

N

0 km 4
0 miles 4

■ **Sleeping**
1 Aida
2 Aiswarya
3 Ambassador & Anjali
4 Government Rest House
5 Green Park
6 Lake View & Vembanad Lake Resort

🚍 **Transport**
1 New Private
2 State

⦂ Sabarimala: a modern mass pilgrimage

Sabarimala pilgrims are readily visible in many parts of South India as they wear black dhotis as a symbol of the penance they must undergo for 41 days before they make the pilgrimage. In addition to the black dress, pilgrims must take two baths daily and only eat food at home during this period. The pilgrimage, which begins at Deepavali, is only for males and prepubescent and post-menstrual females, in order to avoid the defilement believed to be associated with menstruation.

The pilgrimage in January itself is deliberately hard, writes Vaidyanathan, because "the pilgrimage to the shrine symbolizes the struggle of the individual soul in its onward journey to the abode of bliss and beautitude. The path of the spiritual aspirant is always long, arduous and hazardous. And so is the pilgrimage to Sabarimala, what with the observance of severe austerities and trekking up forested mountains, risking attacks from wild animals".

Pelai Pelai, off the Kottayam-Thekady road, is known for its rubber estates belonging to the Dominic family and the beautiful 100-year old traditional Kerala plantation bungalow and a 50-year old estate mansion where hot Syrian-Catholic lunches are served. Plantation tours to watch latex collection and packing can be arranged through Casino Group.

Peermade (Peermed, Pirmed) ⓘ *Regular buses between Kottayam and Kumily, 3 hrs, Rs 45, several per day to/from Ernakulam.* Peermade is considerably lower than Thekkadi (Periyar). It is surrounded by tea, rubber and cardamom plantations and has a number of picturesque spots around the town. *Abraham's Spice Garden*, Kottayam-Kumily Rd (bus route), offers excellent tours with a family member (Rs 50 expected).

★ **Sabarimala** Many Hindu pilgrims make the journey to the forest shrine dedicated to Sri Aiyappan at Sabarimala (191 km north of Thiruvananthapuram) on a route through Kottayam. Aiyappan is a particularly favoured deity in Kerala and there are growing numbers of devotees. Donations to the shrine rose from Rs 2.4 million in 1970 to Rs 75 million in 1986. It is only open on specific occasions: *Mandalam*, 41 days from mid-November to end-December; *Makaravilakku*, mid-January, around Makara Sakranti; *Vishu*, mid-April; *Prathistha* day (May-June); and during the *Onam* festival (August-September). *The Sabarimala pilgrimage and the Ayyapan cults* by Radhika Sekar (M Banarsidass), and *Pilgrimage to Sabari* by KR Vaidyanathan, 1992 (Bharatiya Vidya Bhavan) makes good reading.

★ Thekkadi (Periyar National Park)
→ *Phone code: 954863 (International: 04863) .Colour map 7, grid C3. Area: 777 sq km.*
Set on an attractive Periyar lake side, significant wildlife sightings in Thekkadi are uncommon, but the beautiful setting attracts over 300,000 visitors a year. The small Kumily village with most of the guesthouses and eating places is 3 km above the lake.

Ins and outs Getting there Long distance buses reach Thekkadi lakeside via Kumily.
Getting around Local buses run between Kumily and the lake jetty, or you can hire a bike, share a jeep or take the pleasant walk. 'Cruises' at 0700, 0930, 1130, 1400, 1600. See Transport, page 946, for further details The park closes to traffic 1800-0600. **Climate** Temperature. summer, maximum29°C, minimum 18°C; winter, maximum 21°C, minimum 16°C. Annual rainfall: 2,600 mm. Season: Dec-May (best Mar-May), crowded around 14th Jan festival. Clothing: summer, cottons; winter, light woollens.

History In 1895 the lake was created by building a dam which covered 55 sq km of rich forest. A 180 m long tunnel led the water which had flowed into the Arabian Sea east into the *Suruli* and *Vaigai* rivers, irrigating extensive areas of Ramanathapuram and Madurai districts. The 780 sq km sanctuary was created by the old Travancore State government in 1934.

Wildlife Some visitors are disappointed, due to the small numbers seen. The sanctuary, near the border with Tamil Nadu, is in a beautiful setting and was designated a part of Project Tiger in 1973, though tigers are very rarely seen and it is better known for its elephants, which are very likely to be seen until March/April. Most bull elephants here are tuskless (*makhnas*). Bison, sambar, wild boar and barking deer are fairly common. In addition to 246 species of birds, there are 112 species of butterfly. Smaller animals include black Nilgiri langur, bonnet and lion tailed macaque, Giant and Flying squirrel and otter – "spectacular flight of 'flying foxes' (fruit bats) takes place over Spice Village each evening at about 1830".

Viewing Entry Rs 50 (foreigners) for 5 days. Video camera fees Rs 100. Ideal times are dawn and dusk so stay overnight (winter nights can get quite cold), and avoid weekends and holidays. A motor launch trip on the lake is recommended. Ask the Wildlife Preservation Officer, Thekkadi, T322027.

The forests have special viewing platforms which you can use if you prefer to walk with a Game Ranger who can act as guide. The three-hour **'trek'**, for only five people, 0700, Rs 60 you need to queue for about an hour outside the office. Much depends on your guide and your luck but not everybody comes face to face with a herd of elephants; some return very disappointed. Carry water and beware of leeches. Overnight stay in a watch tower (24-hour trek) for two, Rs 100, gives you a chance to see deer, bears, bisons and elephants. Guides arrange unofficial walking tours privately in the park periphery in the afternoon (not the best time for spotting wildlife); try to assess the guide before signing up. Tourindia, Thekkadi Rd, near Kerala Spices Centre, T323208, organizes treks and camping for one to two nights for "serious nature lovers". *Tiger Trails* is a commendable Eco Development project. Elephant rides have been suspended (contact Wildlife Information Counter, T322028). To see the dam, permission is needed from the

Periyar Wildlife Sanctuary

Sleeping		
1 Ambadi	5 Lissiya	9 St Michael's Inn
2 Claus Garden	6 Muckumal Regent	10 Taj Garden Retreat
3 Coffee Inn & Restaurant	Tower	
4 Lake Queen	7 Periyar House	
	8 Spice Village	

Kumily village is a good place to find spices, coffee and cashewnuts; check the PMCS outlet. The District Tourism Information Office, Thekkadi, T322620, runs plantation tours to the cardamon, rubber and coffee plantations of **Murikkady** (5 km); the tea, coffee and pepper plantations at **Vandiperiyer** (18 km); and the cardoman growing and auction centre at **Vandanmedu** (25 km).

Demonstrations of Indian classical dance are given daily at Natyagriham Theatre, Thamarakandom Road, near Ambady Junction, Thekkadi, T322941, (1730-1830, Rs 100).

Excursions There are a number of attractions that are within easy reach of Thekkadi. These include the traditional Keralan-style **Mangaladevi Temple**, situated amongst dense woodland on the peak of a 1,337 m hill, 15 km northeast of Thekkadi. Permission to visit the area must be obtained from the Wildlife Warden, Thekkadi, T322027, though the temple itself is only open during the *Chithra Pounami* holiday. Other picturesque spots around Thekkadi include **Pandikuzhi** (5 km) and **Chellarkovil** (15 km).

To Munnar and the Palanis → *Colour map 7, grid C3.*

There is a short drive across the undulating and richly cultivated, densely populated lowlands before climbing rapidly up one of South India's most attractive ghat roads.

Ettumanoor

Ettumanoor has possibly the wealthiest temple in Kerala. The present Mahadeva Temple was reconstructed in 1542, and is famous for its murals depicting scenes from the *Ramayana* and the Krishna legends, both inside and outside the *gopuram*. The typical circular shrine with a copper covered conical roof encloses a square sanctuary. The *Arattu* festival in March draws thousands of pilgrims when gold elephant statues are displayed.

Thattekad Bird Sanctuary

The Kochi-Munnar Road leads from Kothamangalam, to the bird sanctuary (20 km) with teak plantations, which is surrounded by the Periyar River which remains shallow most of the year. It attracts water birds and the indigenous Malabar grey hornbill, rose and blue-winged parakeet, egret, heron and mynah, while rarer birds like the Ceylon frog-mouth and rose-billed rollers are also found.

★ Munnar

→ *Phone code: 954865 (International: 04865). Colour map 7, grid C3. Altitude: 1,520 m.*

A major centre of Kerala's tea industry, and close to Anaimudi, at 2,695 m the highest peak in South India, Munnar is the nearest Kerala comes to a genuine hill station. It is surrounded by about 30 tea estates, among the highest in the world, and forest that is still rich in wildlife, including the reclusive Nilgiri Tahr, that continues to survive the increasing commercial use of the hills. The surrounding hills are home to the rare Neelakurunji orchid (*Strobilanthes*), which covers the hills in colour for a month once in 12 years (next due 2006). Despite the appearance of calm the town has witnessed catastrophes, notably the 1924 flood which destroyed the whole settlement. ▸▸ *For Sleeping, Eating and other listings, see pages 933-949.*

Ins and outs

Getting there The easiest access is by bus or taxi from Kochi, but there are daily buses to major towns in Kerala and Tamil Nadu. The state bus stands are in the centre of town but there is another in the bazar.

Getting around The town is small and pleasant for walking around, though there are autos. It is worth hiring a bike or a jeep for trips out of town. See Transport, page 946, for further details.

Climate The rains from Jun-Sep are very heavy (annual total 2700 mm).

Sights

It is possible to visit a working **tea factory** normally at Mattupetty. You can watch tea pickers at work and how tea is processed. Tea is also available for sale. Contact the Manager, Tata Regional Office, T530561, for information.

In the centre of Old Munnar, set on a hill immediately above the road in the centre of town, is **Christ Church**. Rather squat and now blackened by weathering, its exterior is unprepossessing, but inside it is a charming small church. Consecrated in 1910 it still contains its original 14 rows of wooden pews. Built to serve the tea estate managers and workers of the High Ranges, the last English language service was held in 1981. Its origins are suggested in several of the memorial plaques on the wall. Sunday services today are in Tamil (0800, when the church is always full) and Malayalam (1000). The Christmas service, which starts at 0430, is particularly special. A zig-zag path up the hill immediately behind the church leads to the small Pioneer cemetery, then through the Indian cemetery to the top.

Mount Carmel Roman Catholic church, the first Catholic Church in the High Ranges, is in Old Munnar on the road up to the Tata General Hospital. The first chapel on the site was founded in 1898 by Fr Alphonse who arrived in Munnar from Spain in 1854. The present church was built by the then Bishop of Vijayapuram in 1938.

Excursions

Mattupatty Lake ① *T530389, visits between 0900-1100, 1400-1530, Rs 5.* The lake, 13 km from Munnar and at an altitude of 1,700 m, is flanked by steep hills and woods. It was created by the small hydro-electricity dam. To its south is the Kerala Livestock

Munnar

4 Issac's Residency
5 Misha
6 Munnar Inn & Silver Spoon
7 Royal Retreat
8 Westwood
9 Zeena

0 metres 200
0 yards 200

■ **Sleeping**
1 Arafa
2 East End
3 Hill View

● **Eating**
1 Vegetarian

Development Board's research and cattle breeding centre – formerly the Indo-Swiss dairy project. In a beautiful semi-Alpine setting surrounded for much of the year by lush green fields, the centre offers interesting insights into the practical realities and achievements of cattle breeding in India today.

Top Station ⓘ *Buses from shelter north of Munnar post office, 0715, 0915, 1115, to Kovilor, passes Mattupetty Lake and Kundala Dam. Get off at Top Station, return bus after about 1 hr.* On the border with Tamil Nadu, 41 km from Munnar and at an altitude of 2,200 m, Top Station has some of the highest tea estates in India. It is an idyllic spot, with superb views over the Tamil Nadu plains and the edge of the Western Ghats. There are tea and soft drinks (check bottle seals) stalls in the hamlet. Top Station took its name from a ropeway that connected it via Middle Station to Lower Station at the valley bottom. The small town of Bodinayakkanur, which can be reached on the Devikulam road, lies in the valley.

★ **Eravikulam/Rajamalai National Park** ⓘ *Closed during the monsoons, Rs 50, plus Rs 100 per passenger for vehicles taken into the park, visitors are allowed in the Rajamala section of the park only.* The park (14 km northeast of Munnar) was set up in 1978 to preserve the endangered Nilgiri Tahr (Nilgiri Ibex). The conservation programme has resulted in the park now supporting the largest population of the species in the world, of nearly 2,000. The sure-footed wild goats live in herds on the steep black rocky slopes of the Anaimudi mountains. They are brownish, have short, flat horns with the male carrying a thick mane, and can be easily seen around the entrance. There are also elephants, sambars, gaurs, macaque and the occasional leopard and tiger. The scenery is magnificent, though the walks into the forest are steep and strenuous. There is an easier well made paved path from the park entrance following the road immediately below the bare granite outcrop of the Naikundi Hill to the Rajamalai Gap. From there it is a one-hour walk to the Forest Rest House. For those interested in **trekking** up to Anaimudi peak overnight visits can be arranged (Rs 200 per night) with permission from the Forest Ranger officer at Devikulam, T530487.

Cycling One ride goes up a gentle slope through a beautiful valley 8 km to the Letchmi Estate. There is a *chai* stall at the estate and the road continues to the head of the valley for views down to the forest beyond. A second ride (or walk) leaves Munnar by the south road for 3 km, turning left at the Head Works Dam, then takes a right turn past *Copper Castle*, then left to a tea-stall, sunset viewpoint, tea and cardamom plantations, again with spectacular views. Continue to the next tea-pickers' village for a further tea-stall. A shorter alternative to this route is to cross the dam and turn left, taking the quiet road north to the *High Range Club* and Munnar.

> There are some excellent cycle rides around Munnar, not all of them steep.

To Thrissur and Palakkad

One of South India's most important historically strategic routes, the road rises gently to the lowest pass through the Western Ghats along their entire length.

Kalady ⓘ *0530-1230, 1530-2000*, on the bank of the Periyar River, 45 km from Kochi, is the birthplace of one of India's most influential philosophers, **Sankaracharya**. Living in the eighth century, Sankaracharya founded the school of *advaita* philosophy, see page 1325, which spread widely across South India. There are now two shrines in his memory, one as *Dakshinamurti* and the other to the Goddess *Sarada*. The management of the shrines is in the hands of the Math at Sringeri in Karnataka, see page 995. The **Adi Sankara Kirti Stambha Mandapam** ⓘ *0700-1900, small entry fee. Kalady can easily be visited in an afternoon from Kochi or from Aluva by bus (40 mins).*, is a nine-storeyed octagonal tower, 46-m high, and details Sri Sankara's life and works and the Shan Maths, or six ways to worship. There are a couple of basic places to stay.

Thrissur (Trichur)

➔ *Phone code: 95487 (International: 0487). Colour map 7, grid B2. Population: 317,500.*
Thrissur (Tiru-siva-perur) is on the west end of the Palakkad gap which runs through the low pass between the Nilgiri and the Palani Hills. The route through the ghats is not scenic but it has been the most important link to the peninsular interior since Roman times. Thrissur has the unique Elephant Owners' Association and is particularly famous for its annual Pooram in April/May. Thrissur is built round a hill on which stands the Vadakkunnathan Temple and the open green. The town's bearings are given in cardinal directions from this raised 'Round'. ➤➤ *For Sleeping, Eating and other listings, see pages 933-949.*

History
Once the capital of Kochi State, Thrissur was captured by the Zamorin of Calicut and then by the Portuguese and the Dutch. In the 18th century it fell to Tipu Sultan before Raja Rama Varma, 'the architect of the town', came to the throne.

Sights
The **Vadakkunnathan Temple** ① *0400-1030, 1700-2030, non-Hindus are not permitted inside except during the Pooram festival, when restrictions are lifted*, a predominantly Siva temple, is also known as the Rishabhadri or Thenkailasam ('Kailash of the South'). At the shrine to the Jain Tirthankara Vrishabha, worshippers offer a thread from their clothing, symbolically to cover the saint's nakedness. The shrine to Sankara Narayana has superb murals depicting stories from the Mahabharata. It is a classic example of the Kerala style of architecture with its special pagoda-like roof richly decorated with fine wood carving. The temple plays a pivotal role in the *Pooram* celebrations (see festivals below). In September/October, there are live performances of Chakyarkothu, a classical art form. There is a small elephant compound attached to the temple.

The impressive **Lourdes Church** has an interesting underground shrine. The **Town Hall** is a striking building housing an art gallery with murals from other parts of the state.

Archaeological Museum, ask to see the royal chariot. ① *0900-1500, closed Mon. Town Hall Rd.* Next door, the **Art Museum**, has wood carvings, sculptures, an excellent collection of traditional lamps and old jewellery.

Thrissur Zoo ① *near the Art Museum, closed Mon, 1000-1700, small entry and camera fee, filming only with prior permission of the Director of Museums in Thiruvananthapuram*, is known for its snake collection.

Excursions
Cheruthuruthy ① *closed Sat, Sun, public holidays and in Apr and May, T0492-462418, frequent private buses from Thrissur northern bus stand (Vadakkechira Bus Stand) go straight to Kalamandalam, about 1 hr*, 29 km north of Thrissur near Shornur Junction, is famous for the Kerala Kalamandalam on the river bank, which led to a revival of *Kathakali* dancing. It is a centre for teaching music, drama, Mohiniyattam and Ottam Thullal in addition to Kathakali. You can watch training sessions from 0430-0630, 0830-1200 and 1530-1730. All night Kathakali performances: 26 January, 13 March, 15 August, 18 September, 9 November.

Palakkad (Palghat)
➔ *Phone code: 95491 (International: 0491. Colour map 7, grid B3. Population: 130,700.*
The strategically placed town marks a low point in the ghats (known as the Palakkad Gap). It is the road and rail route from Kerala to Coimbatore and Chennai. The area is

notable for tobacco and rice cultivation and processing, and its textile industry. Haidar Ali's old fort here was built in 1766, which the British took in 1790. The annual festival of *Chinakathoor Pooram* (end February to early March) held at the Sree Chinakathoor Bhagavathy Temple, Palappuram, features a 33 tusker procession, plus remarkable evening puppet shows. Bejewelled tuskers can also be seen at the 20-day *Nenmara-Vallangi Vela*, held at the Sree Nellikulangara Bhagavathy Temple, Kodakara (early April).

The coastal road north

Kodungallur (Cranganore) → *Colour map 7, grid C2 Population: 33,500*
At one time Kodungallur was the west coast's major port, and the capital of the Chera king Cheraman Perumal. **Kottapuram**, nearby, is where St Thomas is believed to have landed in AD 52. The commemorative shrine was built in 1952. Kodungallur is also associated by tradition with the arrival of the first Muslims to reach India by sea. Malik-ibn-Dinar is reputed to have built India's first **Juma Masjid**, 2 km from town. It is worth visiting the **Tiruvanchikulam Temple** and the **Portuguese fort**. The Syrian orthodox church in **Azikode** blends early Christian architecture in Kerala with surrounding Hindu traditions. Thus the images of Peter and Paul are placed where the *dvarapalas* (door-keepers) of Hindu temples would be found, and the portico in front of the church is for pilgrims.

Guruvayur → *Phone code: 95487 (International: 0487) Colour map 7, grid B2*
Guruvayur is a heaving pilgrimage centre, filled with stalls. The **Sri Krishna Temple** which probably dates from at least the 16th century makes it particulary important. In the outer enclosure there is a tall gold-plated flagpost and a pillar of lamps. The sanctum sanctorum is in the two-storeyed *srikoil*, with the image of the four-armed Krishna garlanded with pearls and marigolds. Photography of the tank is not allowed.

There are some pleasant beaches nearby which you can get to by rickshaw but they haven't any facilities.

An unusual feature of the temple at Guruvayur is the timing of the rituals. The sanctum opens at 0300 and closes at 2100. Except between 1300 and 1600, when it is closed, a continuous series of pujas and processions is performed. Non-Hindus are not allowed inside and are not made to feel welcome.

Punnathur Kotta ① *arrive early (opens 0900) to watch bathing and breakfasting (great photos), Rs 25, Mr Sathyapalan is knowledgeable and can show you around, take care; elephants can be dangerous*, a fort 4 km away, houses the 40 or so temple elephants and trains wild ones. Interesting insights into traditional animal training though not to everyone's taste. Though captive, the elephants are dedicated to Krishna and appear to be well cared for by seemingly attentive attendants.

Megalith trail: Guruvayur to Kunnamkulam
The Palakkad gap has been one of the few relatively easy routes through the ghats for 3,000 years and this area is noted for its wide range of megalithic monuments. Megalithic cultures spread from the Tamil Nadu plains down into Kerala, but developed their own local forms. The small villages of Eyyal, Chovvanur, Kakkad, Porkalam, Kattakampala and Kadamsseri, between Guruvayur and Kunnamkulam have hoodstones, hatstones, dolmens, burial urns and menhirs.

Kozhikode (Calicut)

→ *Phone code: 95495 (International: 0495) Colour map 7, grid B2 Population: 436,500*

Kozhikode (closest pronunciation korli-kodi) is a pleasant, if rather anonymous town and is no longer a port though there are still remnants of the trade in spices, copra and coconut oil in the Court Road/Big Bazar Road area. It offers a convenient break for travellers between coastal Kerala and southern towns inland.➤➤ *For Sleeping, Eating and other listings, see pages 933-949.*

Ins and outs

Getting there **Karipur airport**, 25 km south of the town centre, has connections with several major Indian cities. The station and main bus stand are near the town centre within easy reach of several hotels.

Getting around Autos are widely available and surprisingly cheap. See Transport, page 947, for further details.

Climate Temperature: summer, maximum 35°C, minimum 23°C; winter, maximum 32°C, minimum 22°C. Annual rainfall: 2,500 mm. Best season: Nov-Mar.

Kozhikode (Calicut)

	Sleeping ■	5	Malabar Palace &		Eating ●
	1 Alakapuri		Tom 'n' Jerry		1 Cochin Bakery
	2 Citizen Tourist Home	6	NCK Tourist Home		& Ice Cream
	3 Hyson Heritage &		& Indian Coffee House		2 Woodlands
	Metro Tourist Home	8	Sea Queen		
	4 Kalpakkai	9	Taj Residency		

0 metres (approx) 300
0 yards (approx) 300

Kerala Central Malabar Kozhikode

Background

In 1498 **Vasco da Gama** landed at Kappad nearby (see below), starting a turbulent, often violent, century and a half of contact with European powers. When the Portuguese arrived, Calicut was under the control of the Vijayanagar Empire, see page 1002. After a decade of violent raids the local Zamorin made peace with the Portuguese and gave them trading rights and the right to build a fort. They remained for over a century. In 1766 the city was threatened by the Muslim Raja from Mysore, Haidar Ali. The Zamorin offered peace but when the offer was rejected, barricaded himself and his family in the palace and burnt it to the ground. Although Haidar Ali soon left, his son Tipu Sultan returned 23 years later and devastated the entire region. British rule was imposed in 1792 by the Treaty of Seringapatam.

Today Kozhikode is a major commercial centre for northern Kerala with a strong Arab connection. Its main export today is not spices but workers to the Gulf (the airport has 21 direct flights a week to the area!). It is also a centre for Kerala's timber industry, boat building is important. There is nothing of Portuguese influence here and little of the former ruling family, the Zamorin Raja. The title however, survives and the current Raja, who succeeded to it in 1998, at the age of 87, lives in a nondescript suburban house. The matrilineal title passes to the oldest male in a vast extended family who is invariably extraordinarily aged!

Sights

A few interesting wooden mosques are to be found to the west of the town. For further details see www.calicut.org. **Pazhassiraja Museum** ① *closed Mon, 1000-1230, 1430-1700, 5 km on east Hill*, has exhibits including copies of original murals plus bronzes, old coins and models of the different types of megalithic monuments widespread in the area. The **Art Gallery** and **Krishna Menon Museum** ① *Mon, Wed afternoon only, 1000-1230, 1430-1700, free*, named after the Kerala politician who became a leading left-wing figure in India's post-Independence Congress Government, next door. Excellent collection of paintings by Indian artists; also wood and ivory carvings. A section of the museum is dedicated to VK Krishna Menon. Stay away from the town **beach** – mainly used as a loo.

Kappad, 16 km north, is where Vasco da Gama landed on 27th May 1498 with 170 men and erected a stone pillar to mark a discovery (his first landing) – an old plaque by the approach road to the beach commemorates the event. It is now the site of a small, poor, mainly Muslim, fishing village. Though it is a pleasant spot, the sea is unsuitable for swimming since pollution from Kozhikode filters down this far and the beach itself is used as a toilet by the fishermen.

Inland from Kozhikode: through Waynad → *Colour map 7, grid B2*

Waynad occupies some of Kerala's untouched, forest clad hills. The route from Kozhikode on the coast, across the Western Ghats to Mysore (214 km, 5½ hrs) or Ooty, is one of Kerala's most picturesque journeys. Many of the tea and coffee plantations now take in paying guests, and a number of imaginative accommodation options have recently opened. The road to Mysore passes through Vyittiri (65 km), and Kalpetta (9 km) before dividing. The more northerly route passes through Mananthavady (30 km), whilst the more southerly route to Mysore is via Sulthan Bathery (25 km) and Waynad Wildlife Sanctuary. The route to Ooty via Gudalur is marginally less scenic than the road to Mysore.

Kalpetta (phone code: 95493, International: 0493) lies at the heart of one of Kerala's most scenic regions, and provides a good base from which to explore the area. The rugged, wild Chembra Peak (2,100 m), 14 km west, the highest point in Waynad, is ideal for trekking. The hike south to **Pookot Lake** (10 km) is particularly rewarding. It is a popular destination for domestic tourists, making accommodation hard to come by during holiday periods. The *State Bank of Travancore* offers foreign exchange.

Sulthan Bathery (Sultan's Battery) ① *The road from Sulthan's Bathery to Gudalur (Tamil Nadu) is very rough, especially across the border and can take 2½ hrs by bus,* to the east of Kalpetta was formerly known as Ganapathivattom, 'the fields of Ganapathi'. In the 18th century, Tipu Sultan built a fort here in the heart of the Waynad coffee and cardamom growing region, but not much of it remains. Some 6 km east of the fort is a natural deep crack in the rock on which four inscriptions have been carved and some rough drawings.

Waynad Wildlife Sanctuary Waynad Wildlife Sanctuary is contiguous with Karnataka's Bandipur National Park and Tamil Nadu's Mudumalai National Park, although the latter two are far more developed in terms of accommodation and tours on offer. If you wish to visit the sanctuary, noted for its elephants, from the Kerala side, contact the Chief Conservator of Forests, Thiruvananthapuram, T0471-322217.

Coastal road from Kozhikode

Mahé (population 36,800), a tiny settlement of just 7 sq km with a very attractive harbour, is still a part of Pondicherry, hence once a 'colony of a colony'. Beautifully positioned on a slight hill overlooking the river, it was named after M Mahé de Labourdonnais, when he captured it for the French in 1725. Many still speak French and the very French Church of St Theresa celebrates her feast day on 14-15 October. From the neighbouring hill where the Basel Mission house was built are very attractive views of the Waynad hills inland. Mahé's 'tax haven' type status is evident in cheap beer, alcohol, gold jewellery and electrical goods; described by one as "a nightmare full of drunks". The beach to the south of town is dirty; to the north is better though neither is safe for bathing due to undercurrents.

Thalassery (Tellicherry) (Phone code: 95497, International: 0497, population 99,400). Once a pretty fishing village with a colourful bazar, some visitors today find it lacking atmosphere and rather dirty and crowded. The seashore is interesting when the fishermen unload their catch in large baskets and spread them out on mats to sell. It is a centre for training in gymnastics and circus acts so street performers and acrobats are not uncommon. You can see martial arts in local *kalaris.*

Thalassery was set up by the British East India Company in 1683 to export pepper and cardamom. The 300-acre Anjarkandy cinnamon plantation nearby was originally set up by the Company. In 1708 they obtained permission to build a **fort** which, having survived a siege laid by Haidar Ali, is still standing today on a rocky promontory about 15 m above sea level. Its proud little gateway, raised on a flight of steps, is flanked by colourful mustachioed figures. There are some attractive old buildings, some within the Citadel. The Armenian church is rather shabby now but the Catholic church still thrives though the population is largely *Moplah* (Kerala Muslims). The Odathil Mosque, believed to be 400 years old, is in the traditional Kerala style with a gabled roof and copper sheeting.

Muzhappilangad Beach (pronounced Murliplengarai), 5 km north, is an unspoilt, beautifully picturesque 4 km stretch of golden sand edged by palm trees at the northern end. *Beach Resort* is 10 minutes' walk west from the main road bus stand or rickshaw to the door along road behind the beach, T833471. Three double rooms with baths, food to order (ring in advance), beer, friendly owner.

Kannur (Cannanore)

→ *Phone code: 95497 (International: 0497) Colour map 7, grid B2*

Kannur stands on raised ground with cliffs at the sea face. The coconut fringed coastline has some attractive beaches nearby. Weavers' co-operatives and beedi factories provide employment but this is also the place to watch Theyyam dances.

Sights

Kannur, the centre of the Moplah community, a group of Arab descent, was also the capital of the North Kolathiri Rajas for several hundred years. Fort St Angelo was built out of laterite blocks by the Portuguese in 1505 and taken over by the British in 1790 as their most important military base in the south. At the end of the northwest promontory, in the old cantonmont area with its spacious colonial bungalows. The highly picturesque **Moplah town** is round the bay to the south of the fort. The attractive **Payyambalam Beach** is just 2 km away. Handloom weavers produce silk and cotton saris, shirts, *lungis* and soft furnishings sold through local co-operatives.

Bekal ① *From the south, trains get you to Kanhangad, just south of Bekal. From there buses go to a Palakunnu Junction, a few kilometres from the fort.* 16 km south of Kasaragod. En route, the road passes **Ezhimala**, 55 km, with a beach and a hill famous for its ayurvedic herbs. Bekal has an ancient **fort** on the sea, the largest and best preserved in Kerala, which gives superb views of the coastline. Originally built by the Kadamba kings, the fort passed under the control of Vijayanagar and of Tipu Sultan before being brought into the hands of the East India Company. Excavations have exposed some interesting structures. Just outside the fort is the Sri Mukhyaprana Temple. For *theyyam* and *yakshagana* performances contact the Bekal Tourist Office or Resorts Development Corporation, T736937. Bekal also has a beautiful and still undeveloped **beach** which Kerala Tourism talk of turning into a major resort.

Kasaragod This is the northernmost town in Kerala. From the bus stand, the walk to the sea through a sprawling residential area (mainly Moplah) takes about 30 minutes. The beach stretching northwards is magnificent and deserted. You can walk a long way before scrambling back to the main road, crossing paddy fields, backwaters, and the Konkan railway line.

Listings: Central Malabar

● Sleeping

Kochi-Ernakulam *p917, maps p916, 918, 920*
To capture the atmosphere, stay in Fort Kochi. Book well in advance for the Christmas period. Be prepared for a serious mosquito problem.

Bolghatty Island
B Bolghatty Palace, T355003, F354879, ktdc@vsnl.com, bolgatty@md3.vsnl.net.in. Former British Residency, built by Dutch in 1744, in once peaceful grounds (now a Municipal Park), partly refurbished, cottages open.

Ernakulam
AL Taj Residency, Marine Drive, T371471, F371401, residency.ernakulam@tajhotels.com. 109 rooms, good restaurants, pastry shop, all business facilities, commanding views over bay, immaculate, friendly, good value.
A-B Avenue Regent, 39/1796 MG Rd, 500 m from Junction station, T372662, F370129, www.avenueregent.com. 53 bright, modern, comfortable rooms, all facilities, excellent restaurants, business centre, avoid south side rooms (horrendous noise from water pump at 0300 and 1900). Recommended.
B-D Bharat (BTH), Durbar Hall Rd near Junction Rly, T353501, F370502, www.bharathotel.com.

92 clean rooms, some spacious a/c, best sea-facing, pleasant a/c restaurant, also excellent lunch *thalis,* exchange, efficient, excellent service, popular, good value.

C Abad Plaza (Best Western), MG Rd, T381122, F370729, abad@vsnl.com. 80 a/c rooms, fridge (free soft drinks), on busy main street, best rooms quieter on 5th floor (free breakfast and fitness club), restaurants recommended (no alcohol), good rooftop pool and jacuzzi, good value. Recommended.

C Metropolitan, Chavara Rd, near Juction Station, T352412, F382227, metropol@ md3.vsnl.net.in. 39 spotlessly clean modern a/c rooms, excellent restaurants and service, excellent value. Recommended.

C Yuvarani Residency, Jos Junction, MG Rd, T377040, F375780, www.yuvarani residency.com. 38 well-appointed rooms, mostly a/c, nicely furnished modern hotel, speciality seafood restaurant. Recommended.

C-E Dwaraka, MG Rd, T383238, F383244, www.dwaraka-hotel.com. 39 good-sized rooms with TV, some a/c, in established family run hotel, South Indian veg restaurant, good value.

D Gaanam, Chitoor Rd (behind *Sangeetha*), T367123, F354261, ganam@md3.vsnl.net.in. 40 rooms, modern, very clean, free breakfast, good restaurant.

D Paulson Park, Carrier Station Rd, T382179, F370072, paulsonpark@satyam.net.in. 55 clean, comfortable rooms in modern building, some good value a/c, restaurant, friendly staff. Recommended.

D Sealord, Shanmugham Rd, T382472, sealord@vsnl.com. 40 rooms, central a/c, rooftop restaurant.

D-E Biju's Tourist Home, Canon Shed Rd corner, near jetty, T38188128 good, renovated, large rooms with bath (hot water), few a/c, TV, room service meals, exchange, clean, comfortable, friendly, good value.

D-E SAAS Tower, Canon Shed Rd, T365319, F367365, saastower@yahoo.co.in. 32 good rooms, 23 a/c in modern hotel (beds rather short!), tasty Indian meals, good value.

D-E YMCA International House, 100 m from Central Bus Station, T353479, F364641, www.ymcaernakular.org. Simple rooms (some a/c), restaurant, welcoming.

E Luciya, Stadium Rd, near Bus Station,, T381177. 106 rooms with bath, some a/c, best with balcony, good restaurant and bar, friendly and helpful.

E Maple Tourist Home, opposite Main Boat Jetty, Canon Shed Rd, T355156, F371712. Clean rooms with bath, some **D** a/c, rear ones facing roof garden preferable, very quiet.

E Piazza Lodge, Kalathiparambu Rd, near south rly station, T367408, F370136. 33 good rooms, some a/c, clean, quiet, friendly.

F Hakoba Shanmugham Rd, T369839. 12 rooms, good sea views from some, clean, friendly, popular.

F Modern Guest House, Market Rd, T352130. Rooms with bath, clean, well-maintained, friendly staff. Recommended.

Fort Kochi

Far more atmospheric than Ernakulam.

L-AL Brunton Boatyard (Casino), T215461, F215562, casino@vsnl.com. Characterful rooms overlook the harbour (views – constantly changing tapestry), sympathetic new reconstruction of the original boatyard and a merchant's house around a giant raintree, interesting architecture and furniture (footstools to climb into bed!), good food (see Eating), discounts Apr-Sep.

A Malabar House Residency, 1/268 Parade Rd, near St Francis Church, T221199, malabarhouse@eth.net Comfortable rooms in characterful 18th-century colonial house, period furniture, dining pavilion (good Italian, south Indian), tandoori on terrace, minute pool in shaded grassy courtyard, stylish, German/Indian owners.

A-B Fort Heritage, near Britto School 1/283 Napier St, T225333. 10 beautiful, spacious rooms (a/c possible), bath tubs (but hot water unreliable), Kerala Christian cuisine and local dishes but very slow service, lovely lawn, sadly inefficient (bookings not honoured).

A-B Old Courtyard, 1/371, Princess Street, T226302, www.oldcourtyard.com. 8 beautiful, very comfortable rooms, superbly styled with old wooden furniture, overlooking sheltered courtyard, some with shared balconies, modern baths, no a/c or TV, attentive staff, breakfast included, average food but nice relaxed atmosphere.

● *For an explanation of the sleeping and eating price codes used in this guide, see inside the*
● *front cover. Other relevant information is found in Essentials pages 52-57.*

D Delight, Post Office Rd, opposite 'village green', T/F217658. 8 large rooms, spotless and stylish, breakfast served, very friendly family run ("can organize anything for you"). Highly recommended.

D Fort House, 2/6A Calvathy Rd, T226103, F222066. A few simple rooms within a walled courtyard with its own little jetty, lovely outlook, excellent food.

D-E Park Avenue, Princess St (marble-faced), T222671, F216670, hotel_parkavenue@ bplnet.com. 25 spotless rooms with bath, some a/c, pleasant and airy, roof restaurant, quiet location. Good value.

D-E Seagull, Calvathy Rd, between the ferry stops, T228128. 8 rooms, some a/c (some damp and dark), good restaurant, exchange, converted old warehouses on the waterside.

E Chiramel Residency, 1/296 Lily St opposite Parade Ground, T217310, F223902. Nice character house, 5 clean rooms, some with bath, friendly family.

E Elite, Princess St, T225733. Cheaper rooms long way from toilets, rooms at rear quieter, cheap restaurant.

E Kapithan Inn, Bernard Rd, 100m south of Cruz Cathedral, T226560. 7 rooms, clean and pleasant, family run.

E Oys Tourist Home, Burgher St, T215475. 6 peasant rooms in lamp-lit old building, lots of plants, good value.

E-F Adam's Old Inn, CC1/430 Burgher St, T/F217595. 10 rooms with bath (1 a/c), in restored old building, dorm beds, meals, helpful hosts.

Willingdon Island

L-AL Taj Malabar, T666811, F668297, mlbrbc.coc@tajhotels.com. 12 km centre. 97 well-furnished rooms, more character in old wing, good restaurants (veg lunch buffet recommended), excellent ambience, *Waterfront Café* for snacks, good pool, internet, very good service, superb setting with views across water, ferry from Ernakulam.

AL Trident (Oberoi), Bristow Rd, T669595, F669393, reservations@tridentcochin.com. 96 rooms overlook landscaped courtyard and pool, low-rise Kerala style building.

A-B Casino, T668221, F668001, casino@ vsnl.com. 70 well maintained rooms, lunch buffet (Rs 250), superb seafood in evening (best in town), character bar, outdoor pool in garden.

D Island Inn, Bristow Rd, near rly, T666816, F228013. 32 airy rooms, facing in to courtyard, pleasant atmosphere, very good food.

E-F Maruthi Tourist Home, next to *Casino*, T666365. 26 rooms, some a/c, Indian style, quite good value, bit shabby, good veg meals.

Bharat, restaurant, around the corner from *Maruthi* for excellent *thalis*, good service.

Kottayam *p921, map p922*

A Lake Village, near Kodimatha Jetty (next to *Vembanad Resort*), 3 km south of town, T303622. Comfortable bungalows with 'inside-outside' baths, excellent huge open-sided restaurant, very friendly staff.

B Vallikappen Home Stay XIII/179B Manganam, T572530, simtom@ satyam.net.in. A special alternative just outside town, 2 comfortable, clean guest rooms, interesting, cultured hosts, good Kerala/Western meals included, boats, heritage home and wildlife visits arranged.

C Anjali, KK Rd, 4 km from rly, T563661, F563669 27 rooms with bath, central a/c, good restaurants, exchange (limited).

C Vembanad Lake Resort, near Kodimatha Jetty (5 km centre, 2 km bus stand), T564866, F561633, www.vembanadresort.com. Simple rooms in 10 cottages (5 a/c), pleasant waterside garden, good houseboat restaurant.

D Aida, MC Rd, 2 km rly, T568391, F568399, aida@md3.vsnl.net.in. 40 rooms with bath, some a/c, back quieter, restaurant, bar, clean, pleasant. Recommended.

D Green Park, Kurian Uthup Rd, Nagampadam, T563311, F563312. 33 rooms with bath, 11 with noisy a/c, non-a/c at back intensely hot even at night, restaurant.

D-E Aiswarya (KTDC), near Thirunakkara Temple. 500 m from jetty, 2 km bus stand, T581254, F581253. 30 rooms, some a/c, restaurants, beer.

E Ambassador, KK Rd (set back), T563293. 18 rooms, some a/c, pleasant Indian style hotel and good restaurant, bar, exchange, friendly and helpful staff, very good value.

F Govt Rest House, on hill 2 km south of town, overlooking flat paddy land. Remarkable late 19th-century building with

Kerala Listings: Central Malabar

superb furniture and some original cutlery and tableware, reservations: District Collector, Kottayam or Executive Engineer, PWD Kottayam.
F Kaycees Lodge, off YMCA Rd, T563440. Good quality for the price and clean.
F Venad Tourist Complex, Ancheril Bldg, near State Bus Stand, T561383. Modern building, clean, restaurant. Recommended.

Kuarakom *p922*
26% taxes are added.
AL Houseboat (KTDC), unique, idyllic experience on the backwaters at a price. Kerala meals included, Rs 7,500 (day only), Rs 18,750 (1 night, 2 days). Contact Kumarakom Tourist Village, T0481-524258, F525862. Highly recommended.
AL-A Coconut Lagoon (Casino), T524491, F524495, casino@vsnl.com. 37 comfortable (some century-old) *tharawads* (traditional Kerala wooden cottages), some a/c, in Heritage Resort (discounts Apr-Sep), outdoor restaurant facing lagoon, good dinner buffet, good pool, very friendly, ayurvedic treatments, attractive waterside location, spectacular approach by boat (10 mins from road), some find 'sunset cruise' short and disappointing. Highly recommended.
AL-A Kumarakom Lake Resort, T524900, F524987, www.klresort.com. Individual villas with open-roofed showers set in delightful landscaped grounds. Recommended.
AL-A Taj Garden Retreat, 1/404 (14 km west of Kottayam), T524377, F524371. 19 a/c rooms, in attractive 120 year old 'Bakers' House', sympathetically renovated, newer cottages and a moored houseboat, good meals, an intimate hotel but packed (boosted by the Prime Minister's stay in early 2001?).
A Golden Waters (Tulip), T/F525826, alex@blr.vsnl.net.in. Among paddy fields and coconut groves, accessed by boat or paths and bridges, 28 well-furnished, Kerala ethnic cottages on the water, pool, specialist ayurvedic centre.

Pelai *p923*
B Estate mansion, 4 rooms with colonial period Kerala furniture, and a deluxe cottage room in the *Plantation Bungalow*. Contact Casino, T668221, F668001, casino@vsnl.com.

Peermade *p923*
C Wood Palace Resorts, www.woodpalaceresorts.com, has rooms with wonderful views in a renovated wooden building; good food and pleasant long hikes.

Thekkadi *p923, map p924*
Book all KTDC hotels well in advance.
L Lake Palace, T322024, F322282, aranyanivas@vsnl.com, ktdc@vsnl.com. 6 rooms in interesting building (US$198, meals included), restaurant (adequate, uninspired menu) access by free ferry (20 mins) from jetty (last trip 1600), idyllic island setting, superb views, wildlife spotting from lawn, relaxed and informal.
AL Spice Village (Casino), Thekkadi-Kumily Rd, T322315, F322317, casino@vsnl.com. 52 rooms in cottages with elephant grass thatch (cool and dark with wide eaves), labelled spice garden, good pool, very good restaurant though breakfast menu limited, buffet at lunch and dinner (Rs 350), chilled beer, excellent ayurvedic massage, forest walks to see smaller wildlife, luxurious, green, quiet, restful, friendly, excellent service (no individual tipping), discounts Apr-Sep. Recommended.
AL-A Taj Garden Retreat, Amalambika Rd, T322273, F322106, retreat.thekkady@tajhotels.com. 32 well-appointed rooms in thatched, a/c cottages, large windows open to good views, attractive pool, excellent facilities, attentive staff.
A Shalimar Spice Garden Murikkady, 4 km from Kumily, T322132, F323022, shalimar resort@vsnl.com. 12 rooms, Swiss-Italian run in inspired style, pool, ayurvedic flora therapy, water-massage, pricey.
A-B Carmelia Haven, Vandanmedu (20 km north on Puliyanmala Rd), on a tea, spice and coconut plantation, T870272, F870268. Exclusive and private, with a real tree house 6 m above ground, a cave house 3 m below, and a few discretely spaced cottages in a local style using lots of thatch, excellent open-air restaurant serves delicious Malabari food. Tours of tea factory, cardamon plantations, treks and boating. Factory fresh tea/cardamon for sale.
B Aranya Nivas (KTDC), by lake, T322023, F322282, aranyanivas@vsnl.com. 26 rooms (charges vary, generally overpriced),

Kerala Listings: Central Malabar

interesting old stone building – simple, pleasant restaurant ("very ordinary buffet"), pool but water too cold, poor service and maintenance reported ("sleepy, tenured staff'"), free boat trips twice a day on lake included, cycle hire, remember park is out-of-bounds after dark.

B Cardamom Country between Kumily and Thekkadi, T322806, F322807, cardamoncountry@vsnl.com. Spacious, comfortable cottages, good restaurant, nice pool, friendly staff (request off-season discount). Recommended.

B-C St Michael's Inn, near Tourist Information, T322355, F322356, bvlpala@md3.vsnl.net.in. Odd wedge-shaped rooms, some a/c.

B-E Lissiya International, near bus stand, T/F322288 www.thekkady.com/hotellissiya. Range of rooms and suites, some a/c with balconies, 8-bed dorm, restaurant.

C Periyar House, 5 min walk from lake, T322026, F322526. 48 rooms, some with bath (Rs 700 includes meals), simple, very pleasant, clean and comfortable, dorm, reasonable if slightly dingy, buffet meals, strong Goan beer available, pleasant place, good service.

D Ambadi, near Forest Check post (2 km), T322193, F322192. Some **C** a/c rooms and cottages, double-storey deluxe units with ornate wood decoration (but "uncomfortable, dangerous stairs, and rodents"), basic cottages good value, good restaurant, accepts Visa.

D-E Muckumkal Regent Tower, T322570, F323270, regenttower@hotmail.com. A/c and non-a/c rooms, plus budget rooms in *Muckumkal Tourist Home*, restaurant, parking.

E Manakala Forest Rest House, 7 km in the forest, T095486-322027 (book ahead). 3 rooms (sleep on wooden floor, bring sleeping bag, soft mat, net, mosquito cream, food and plenty of water), cook/guide accompanies, well placed for walks and watching animals close by at night. Rs 300 including boat transfer. Recommended.

In Kumily village, 3 km away:

E Mickey Cottage, T322196. Pleasant rooms, best with balcony, friendly family, excellent value. Highly recommended.

E-F Coffee Inn, 5 min walk from entrance gate and 3 km from Information centre, coffeeinn@satyam.net.in. 12 rooms in basic cottages, fan, nets (Rs 150-400), clean shared baths, lockers, lovely garden with hammocks, popular budget traveller 'hang-out' (no reservations; 'first come first served').

E-F Hill Park, Main St, T685509. 17 rooms with bath, fan, net, friendly helpful staff.

E-F Lake Queen, opposite Tourist Information, T322086, Lakequeen@Thekkady.com. Basic rooms, fan, nets, small bath, pleasanter upper floors (Rs 150-300), fairly clean, functional, run by Catholic Diocese (profits to charity).

F Claus Garden, Rosapukandam, 10 mins uphill from bus stand behind PO, 3rd turn right. Clean, simple rooms, shared toilet/shower, kitchenette, quiet, friendly.

Munnar *p925, map p926*

AM Rd is Alwaye-Munnar Rd. All hotels non a/c.

B Copper Castle, Kannan Devan Hills (out of town), T531201, F530438, copper@md4.vsnl.net.in. Delightfully perched on hillside with beautiful views of a cascading stream, good-sized comfortable rooms with baths (hot showers), restaurant (good sizzlers), friendly staff but slow service.

B Eastend, Temple Rd, T530452, F530227. 18 pleasant rooms and some cottages (solar heated water), good but expensive restaurant, attractively designed, quiet garden location, renovated 2002.

B Tall Trees, PO Box 40, Bison Valley Rd (out of town), www.thetalltreesmunnar.com. Very clean new cottages in beautiful location (many honeymooners!), excellent food, charming staff.

B Tea Country (KTDC), out of town, T530460, F530970, ktdc@vsnl.com. 43 rooms, good facilities, beautiful views, great walking, own transport essential.

B Westwood, T530884, F530886, www.hotelwestwood.com. 40 spacious, clean and modern rooms in new, wood-panelled hotel, lovely design, restaurant, quiet location, friendly service.

B-C Isaac's Residency, Top Station Rd, T530501, F530265. 32 very nice rooms with ultra-modern furnishings, 'Executive' rooms with great views, well maintained, 2 restaurants, bar, excellent quality.

B-C Munnar Inn, Telephone Office Junction, T530736, www.munnarinn.com. 12 well-appointed rooms with fridge, TV in brand new, centrally located hotel, trekking and travel desk, friendly service.

B-C Royal Retreat, Kannan Devan hills, near Bus Stand, T530240, F530440. 14 clean rooms with balcony (views now blocked by *Hill View* next door), colonial bungalow style but with marble and chrome (upstairs rooms in main building run down), pleasant garden but next to main road.

E Arafa Tourist Home, Upper Bazaar, T530302. 14 rooms with TV, phone in newly renovated lodge. Clean and excellent value.

E Misha Tourist Home, Old Bazar, T530376. Dull but clean rooms, 5-bed dorm in Christian guesthouse.

E Zeena Cottages, near *Hill View Hotel* in Tata tea plantation, T530560. Rooms in colonial house, good views, friendly people, simple, ask at Tourist Information Service.

Thrissur *p928*

Reserve ahead during Pooram – prices rocket.

B-D Luciya Palace, Marar Rd, T424731, F427290. 35 rooms, 15 a/c, 2 suites, large, clean, quiet rooms, TV, garden restaurant, internet next door, good service, pleasant.

C-D Surya, 15 km from town, 8 km from beach, T331347, sureshpr@md3.vsnl.net.in. 10 rooms (some a/c) in impressive old buildings, vegetarian meals, ayurvedic treatments, yoga, exchange, lawn.

D Mannapuram, Kuruppam Rd, T440933, F427692, www.mannapuram hotels.com. 46 well-appointed rooms, 16 a/c, in Indian business hotel, pleasant design and furnishings, good restaurant.

D Siddhartha Regency, Velliyanur/TB Rd, near railway and bus stations, Kokkalai, T424773, F425116. Decent a/c rooms, good restaurant.

D-E Bini Tourist Home, Round North, T335703, F332793. 24 rooms, TV, shower, 10 a/c, rather spartan but clean and spacious, restaurant, bar.

E Alukkas, Railway Station Rd, T424067, F424073. Clean, comfortable rooms, some a/c, good value.

F Railway Retiring Rooms. Well looked after and very good value.

F Yatri Nivas (KTDC), Stadium Rd, Chembukavu, T332333, F371481. 19 rooms (1 a/c, Rs 400), snacks. Several cheap hotels on Chembottil Lane and Railway Station Rd.

Cheruthuruthy *p928*

B-C River Retreat, T0488-462244, F462974. Set on the shores of the Bharatpuza, modernised colonial period royal mansion has a splendid river view, spacious a/c rooms with traditional furniture and modern baths

(few with river views), restaurant, sit-outs good for a chilled beer and snacks.

Palakkad *p928*

D Fort Palace, West Fort Rd, T534621, F534625. 19 rooms, some good a/c, restaurant, brash imitation turrets.

D Garden House (KTDC), Malampuzha, T815191. Mostly non a/c rooms, pleasant, a/c.

D Indraprastha, English Church Rd. T534641, F539531, F534641, www.hotelindraprastha.com. 30 rooms, some comfortable, a/c, restaurant, bar, modern, also some **A** rooms.

F Kalpaka, T534631.

F Kalyan, T534206, on GB Rd.

At Kodumbu

B Kairali Ayurvedic Health Resort, T322623, F324404, www.kairali.com. Excellent resort, beautifully landscaped grounds, own dairy and farm, extensive choice of treatments, competent and helpful staff, pool, tennis etc. Recommended.

Kodungallur *p929*

There are some **E** and **F** guesthouses in town.

Punnathur Kotta *p929*

D and **E** hotels have some a/c rooms and cheaper non-a/c; restaurants serve Indian vegetarian meals.

C Krishna Inn, T550777. Excellent hotel, worth the Rs 1000.

D RV Tower, East Nada, near Manjulal, T555225, F555427, near railway and bus stand. Smart, modern hotel.

D Vanamala Kusumam, South Nada, T556702, F555504. 30 rooms, some comfortable a/c, vegetarian restaurant.

D Vyshakh, near Temple pond, Ring Rd, East Nada, T556188. Comfortable rooms.

Several thali vegetarian restaurants near the temple. Also **Indian Coffee House**, East Nada for good snacks.

Kozhikode *p930, map p930*

Jail Rd is now Maulana Md Ali Rd, Mavoor Rd is Indira Gandhi Rd.

A Taj Residency, PT Usha Rd, near the sea, T765354, F766448, tajclt@md3.vsnl.net.in. 74 rooms, typical business hotel, gym, good pool, gaining importance as a heath spa offering ayurvedic treatment (Coimbatore school).

A-B Kadavu, on the river Chaliyar (14 km away), T080-5586861, www.trailsindia.com. 17 cottages and 57 rooms in a new backwaters resort, full facilities, beautifully landscaped,

B Fortune, Kannur Rd, T768888, fortunecalicut @vsnl.com. Business hotel, 63 rooms, Indian restaurant, gym, sauna, pool, massage.

B Malabar Palace, GH Rd, Manuelsons Junction, T721511, F721794, www.manuelsons.com. 52 a/c rooms (*Koran* in every room), excellent a/c restaurant, bar, very helpful Reception. Recommended.

B-D Hyson Heritage, 114 Bank Rd, T766423, F766518, www.hysonheritagekerala.com. 89 smallish rooms, 47 a/c, well-maintained, clean and smart with full facilities, friendly, efficient.

B-D Sea Queen, Beach Rd, T366604, F365854. 25 large, clean rooms, 12 comfortable a/c, well fitted though slightly faded, good restaurant, bar, good value.

D-E Alakapuri, Maulana Md Ali Rd, T723451, F720219. 40 rooms, some in cottage, some spacious a/c with traditional furniture and bath tubs, good South Indian restaurant, bar, exchange, old guesthouse with character in attractive garden.

D-E Kalpakka, Town Hall Rd, near railway station, T/F720222. 62 rooms (25 a/c), average restaurant, pool, gym, exchange, travel.

E Gayathri Internationali, T355367. 10 small cottage-like rooms with modern facilities, bar, restaurant.

E NCK Tourist Home, Mavoor Rd, above *India Coffee House*, T723530. 54 rooms, some stuffy, some a/c, with bath, good vegetarian restaurant, good value.

E-F Citizen Tourist Home, Mavoor Rd, T722352. 33 basic rooms, dark but good value, canteen.

E-F Metro Tourist Home, Mavoor Rd, T766029. 42 rather pleasing rooms in bustling hotel, some with TV, a bit noisy, south Indian restaurant.

F Railway Retiring Rooms. Very spacious, clean, good service.

Kappad *p931*

C Kappad Beach Resort, T95496-683760, F683706, moosa@kappadbeachresort.com. 16 rooms in 4 cottages, some a/c, superb views of the sea, restaurant upstairs serves unexciting food, pool, ayurvedic treatments, health club, yoga lessons, tours, helpful staff, relaxing.

Vyittiri *p931*

L Green Magic Nature Resort, T0471-331507, F331407, www.richsoft.com/ tourindia. Conceived by Babu Varghese, the pioneer of *kettuvallam* cruises on Kerala's backwaters, this eco-friendly resort has a luxury tree-house in the rainforest canopy, 26 m above ground. The open plan bedrooms accessible only by a hand-winched wicker cage have showers and flush toilets. Eco-lodges at ground level for vertigo-sufferers. Solar energy and *gober* gas (from cow dung) emphasise the resort's green credentials, and visitors are banned from bringing in plastics and cosmetics etc (jungle turmeric and burnt bark are provided as soap and toothpaste substitutes). Superb Keralan vegetarian meals included. Guests are collected from Kozhikode by 4WD, and are encouraged to follow the guide on foot through the forest for the last 30 mins. Highly recommended.

Kalpetta *p931*

B-C Green Gates, 2 km north, T602001, F603975, www .greengatehotel.com, is scenically located on a hillside amid woods within walking distance from town. Modern rooms with a/c, TV and baths (hot showers), disappointing restaurant, sit-outs with views, ayurvedic spa, helpful travel desk arranges trips to caves, wildlife sanctuaries and tribal colonies of Waynad, and fishing.

D-E Haritagiri, Padmanrabha Rd, T602070. A modern building in the heart of town just off the highway, some a/c rooms, clean and comfortable, restaurant "reasonable", good value but a rather noisy location.

D-E Pankaj, just off highway at south end of town, has a range of reasonable rooms, good cheap restaurant.

E Arun, next to southbound bus stand. Acceptable.

E-F PPS Tourist Home, Pinangode Rd, T603431, 25 rooms (Rs 150-275).

Sulthan Bathery *p932*

E-F guesthouses in town.

Mahe *p932*

E-F Arena, **E-F Sara** and **F Govt Guest House**, all simple and adequate.

Thalassery *p932*

B Ayisha Manzil, Court Rd, T231590, moosa@kappadbeachresort.com. A delightful

Kerala Listings:—entral Malabar

mid-19th century, colonial style heritage home overlooking the sea, family run, 6 massive a/c rooms with carved teak/rosewood furniture, huge baths, lots of British and Malabari memorabilia, fresh sea food, 'Moplah' mutton biryanis, 'temple pond' pool, superb views from terraces, excursions (weaving centre, Kannur fort, Theyyam dancing, plantations), can be hard to find so get directions.

D-E Paris Presidency, Logans Rd, T342666, F343666. 24 comfortable rooms with baths, TV, phone, restaurant (mixed reports), in busy shopping area.

E Residency, T324409. Cleanish rooms, some a/c, modern hotel, courteous service, good value.

F Pranam, AVK Nair Rd, Narangapuram. 14 cleanish rooms with bath.

Kannur p933

B Mascot Beach Resort, near Baby Beach, Burnassery (2 km from centre), T708445, F701102, mascot_beach_resort@vsnl.com. Good rooms and suites overlooking the sea, wide choice in restaurant, pool, friendly, excellent staff, beautifully located, quiet, perfect ayurvedic centre. Recommended.

B-C Kamala International, SM Rd, 500 m rly, T766910, F701819, www.thekamala.com. 36 renovated rooms, some a/c, 2 restaurants, roof garden, overpriced.

D-E Omar's Inn, opposite railway station, T706313. Some a/c.

D-E Yatri Nivas (KTDC), Thavakkara Rd, near Police Club T700717. Some a/c rooms, basic.

F Madan, Fort Rd, T768204. 28 spartan but clean rooms in very old Hindu hotel. Morning tea and lunch, good value.

The large pink **City Centre** complex has **Baskin Robbins** for ice-creams.

Bekal p933

D-E Bekal International, TB Rd, Hosdurg, south of Bekal, T702017, F704487, www.bekalinternational.com, has 45 rooms on four floors, some a/c with TV, phone, restaurant.

E-F Eeyem, Palakunnu junction, 10 min bus to fort, T736342 is an adequate Indian style hotel.

Kasaragod p933
Near Municipal Bus Stand
D-E City Tower, MG Rd, T430562, F430235. A/c rooms, Chinese and Indian restaurant.

E-F Enay Tourist Home, T421164. 32 rooms, attached bath, good value.

F Araam (KTDC), Thalappadi, Kunjathur, T872960. Basic rooms, tourist information. *Kafiya Restaurant*, MG Rd (west), modest, good.

🍴 Eating

Kochi-Ernakulam *p917, maps p916, 918, 920*
Ernakulam

🍴🍴🍴 **Taj Residency** plush, "Indian, too highly spiced".

🍴🍴 **Abad Plaza's Regency** for Chinese and seafood lunch buffet, and separate.

🍴🍴 **Avenue Regent**, excellent buffet lunch Rs 200.

🍴🍴 **Bimbi's Southern Star**, Shanmugam Rd. Excellent food, generous portions.

🍴🍴 **Canopy** coffee shop for snacks. Good food and service, no alcohol; good buffet breakfast.

🍴🍴 **Chinese Garden**, off MG Rd. A/c. Authentic Chinese cuisine.

🍴🍴 **Grand**, for Japanese dishes.

🍴🍴 **Khyber** serves North Indian meals upstairs.

🍴🍴 **Pandhal**, MG Rd. Keralan, Chinese, Continental. A/c, clean, serving tasty meals, excellent value. Recommended.

🍴🍴 **Sealord's**, rooftop for good fish dishes and Chinese.

🍴 **Bharat** for very good vegetarian *thalis* and Indian specialities in clean surroundings.

🍴 **City Park**, opposite *New Colombo*, for excellent Keralan meals.

🍴 **Malabar**, Market Rd. Excellent South Indian but rather gloomy.

🍴 **New Colombo**, Canon Shed Rd (next to Maple). Good snacks, fruit juices.

Cafés
Bimbi's, near Durbar Hall/MG Rd corner. Good fast food.

Caravan, Broadway (south), for ice creams and shakes.

Chariot, Convent Rd. Good café style meals.

Indian Coffee Houses, opposite *Bimbi's*; also Park Av and Canon Shed Rd corner. Good coffee and snacks but tediously slow.

Oven, Shanmugham Rd. Good pizzas and snacks (savoury and sweet).

Snow Ball, Rajaji Rd, near Muthoot Towers.

Fort Kochi
🍴🍴🍴 **Brunton Boatyard**, *History Restaurant* revives old recipes of Dutch, Portuguese,

Gujarati, British and Malabari merchants (interesting menu), *Terrace Grill* prepares freshly caught fish.

¶¶ **Malabar House Residency**. Excellent seafood, Mediterranean and local dishes.

¶ **Bhojana Shala**, Peter Celli St, T212494. Excellent lunch and evening eatery run by owners of *Kashi*.

¶ **Chariot Fort**, Children's Park/Princess Rd corner. Upmarket outdoor café feel, delicious cold coffees and cheese omelettes, expensive but popular.

¶ **Fort House** hotel. German/Indian run, in walled courtyard, "the best food ever".

¶ **Kashi**, Burgher St, T221769. Healthy salads, good lunches, delicious cakes, herbal teas at "Art café". Limited menu but changes daily, small (5+ tables), good atmosphere, 0830-1430, "run by expats, great ambience".

¶ **Rendezvous Cyber Café**, Burgher St, also serves traditional Kerala and continental.

¶ **Sabala** at *Elite* hotel, popular, pleasant atmosphere (good ice creams opposite).

¶ **Seagull**, Calvathy Rd. Good value (Rs 80 buffet lunch), pleasant verandah for drinks and dining overlooking harbour.

For really original fast food buy your own **fresh fish** when brought in by boat or from the nets, take it over to **Europa**, 'you buy, we cook' stalls on the sea front where they will be grilled or masala fried with chips (Rs 120).

Kottayam *p921, map p922*

¶ **Aida**. Large, uninspired menu, pleasantly cool (though 'chilled' drinks arrive warm!).

¶ **Green Park**. International. Reasonable but slow, beers, dinner in mosquito-ridden garden (or in own room for guests).

On TB Rd near the State bus station:

¶ **Black Stone**. Good vegetarian.

¶ **Indian Coffee House**. Dull.

¶ **Milkshake Bar**, opposite *Blackstone Hotel*, do 20 flavours, with or without ice cream.

Thekkadi *p923, map p924*

Hotel restaurants welcome non-residents.

¶¶ **Spice Village**. International. Excellent food and service, 'rustic' décor, fresh garden vegetables, "chef gives demonstration of a dish each night!"

¶ **Coffee Inn**. International (0700-2200), tables outside under the palms, bonfire in the evening, relaxed and peaceful, friendly, but very slow.

¶¶ **German Bakery**. Lake Rd. Delicious food, pleasant atmosphere, big set breakfast Rs 40.

¶¶ **Máchan Café**. Former Reuters photographer serves the "best coffee and cake here", good atmosphere, art on display.

Munnar *p925, map p926*

¶¶ **Eastend's**, The Greens. Very pleasant with glassed-in verandah serving good food, smart. Alternative: very cheap simple meals, if you join the drivers in the eatery 'below stairs' entered from the lower car park!

¶¶ **Royal Retreat**. International. Very pleasant, wide choice.

¶ **Silver Spoon**, near *Munnar Inn*, for good breakfast choices.

¶ **Vegetarian Restaurant** (next to *Misha*) Old Bazar, serves very good meals.

Thrissur *p928*

Most **D** hotels have good restaurants

¶¶ **City Centre**, next to Priya Tourist Home. Western snacks, bakery and good supermarket.

¶ **Elite Bharat**, Chembottil Lane, good South Indian breakfast and lunch.

¶ **Hot Breads**, Shopping Complex, West Round. Baked goodies and snacks.

¶ **Ming Palace**, opposite *Elite Bharat*, very good Chinese (upstairs).

¶ **Sapphire**, "for best chicken biriyani".

Kozhikode *p930, map p930*

¶¶ **Malabar Palace**, International, a/c, excellent food, efficient service.

¶ **India Coffee Houses** on Kallai and Mavoor Rd but breakfast not recommended.

¶ **Woodlands**, GH Rd (near Old Bus Stand). South Indian vegetarian.

◉ Entertainment

Kochi-Ernakulam *p917, maps p916, 918, 920*
Daily performances of **Kathakali** you can arrive early to watch the extraordinary make-up being applied.

Ernakulam Cochin Cultural Centre, Manikath Rd, off Ravipuram Rd, T368153, a/c 'theatre', authentic, English explanations; 1830-1930, make-up 1630, Rs 125. See India Foundation, Kalathil Parampil Lane (enter Chittoor Rd south) near Junction station, T369471, Dr Devan's 'interpreted' taste of Kathakali with esoteric English commentary; 1845-2000 (make-up from 1800), Rs 125.

Fort Kochi Kerala Kathakali Centre, River Rd, New Bus Stand, T221827. Rustic surroundings but lively performance, enjoyable; 1830-1930 (make-up 1700) but check timing, Rs 100; "main dancer does excellent ayurvedic massage"! **Draavidia**, 1/2001 YMCA Rd, T217025. Classical music with traditional instruments, in season 1800-1900, Rs 100 (take mosquito cream). **Kashi**, Burgher St, holds occasional sitar recitals. **Kalaripayattu** performances (0400-0700 and 1700-2000) at **ENS Kalari**, Nettoor, T809810. **Ayurveda: Sree Narayana Holistic Clinic**, Vypeen Island, T502362, ayurdara@sancharnet.in. 1-hr massage plus a Keralan thali on a rooftop with harbour views, Rs 500.

Munnar p925, map p926
Boating
Near DTPC Information, 0900-1800, Rs 80-180 for 30 mins.

Clubs
High Range Club, T530253, charming colonial-style planters' club, members only (or with reciprocal arrangements), visit by asking a planter to introduce you.
KDH Club, for Tata staff, also old-world, visit with permission, excellent pool table.

Confectionery and snacks
Mammas & Pappas, Beach Rd. French bakery.
Royal Cakes, Bank Rd. Recommended.
Cochin Bakery & Ice cream at CSI church. Serves hot snacks, fresh daily (1500).
Tom 'n' Jerry, Manuelsons Tower, GH Rd. For delicious ice creams.

Kannur p933, map p
Theyyam dance
At Parssinikadavu temple, 20 km north of Kannur, reached by bus. Performances (Dec-Mar) of ritual dance theatre at dawn (taxi essential) and often late-afternoon continuing to dusk. Pilgrims sometimes seek blessing from the principal dancer who may go into a trance after taking on the role of Mutthapan, a manifestation of Siva as Hunter.

⊛ Festivals and events

Kochi-Ernakulam p917, maps p916 and p918
Jan/Feb: Ulsavam at the Siva Temple in Ernakulam for eight days and at Tripunithura

Temple in **Nov/Dec**. There are elephant processions each day and folk dance and music performances. **Aug/Sep**: Onam.

Thrissur p928
Jan-Feb: Several temple festivals with elephants involved are held in the surrounding villages which can be as rewarding as the Pooram (eg Koorkancherry Thaippoya Mahotsavam, or Thaipooya Kavadiyattam, held at Sree Maheswara Temple, Koorkancherry, 2 km from Thrissur). Also held at the end of Feb is the **Uthralikavu Pooram**, at its most colourful at the Sree Ruthura Mahakalikavu Temple, Parithipra, Vodakancherry, on the route to Shornur Junction. **End-Mar**: 7-day Arratupuzha Festival at the Ayappa temple, 14 km from Thrissur. On the 5th day the deity processes with nine decorated elephants, while on the 6th day Pooram is celebrated with 61 elephants in the temple grounds on a grand scale. **Apr-May**: the magnificent 8-day Pooram, a grand festival with elephants, parasols, drums and fireworks, should not be missed. Several temples in town participate but particularly the Thiruvambady and Paramekkavu. It is marked by very noisy, colourful processions, joined by people of all religious communities irrespective of caste. The festivities are held from around 1300-1700 and again at night from around 2000. Elaborately bedecked elephants (each temple allowed up to 15) specially decorated with lamps and palm leaves, process to the Vadakkunnathan Temple carrying priests and deities to the accompaniment of extraordinary drumming. On the final day temple teams meet on the Tekkinkadu maidan for the drumming and Kudumattam competition; the festival terminates with a huge display of fireworks. **Aug/Sep**: the district also celebrates **Kamdassamkadavu Boat Races** at Onam. Also performances of **Pulikali**, unique to Thrissur, when mimers dressed as tigers dance to drumbeats.

Punnathur Kotta p929, map p
Feb/Mar: Utsavam, 10 days of festivities start with an elephant race and continue with colourful elephant processions and performances of Krishattam dances. Details from Kerala Tourist offices. **Nov-Dec**: 5-day Ekadasi with performances of Krishnanattom, a forerunner of Kathakali – an 8-day drama cycle.

Kozhikode *p930, map p930*
Feb: **Utsavam** at Srikantesvara Temple for 7 days during Sivaratri week. Elephant processions, exhibitions, fair and fireworks.

○ Shopping

Kochi-Ernakulam *p917, maps p916, 918, 920*
Coir products (eg mats), carvings on rosewood and buffalo horn and 'antiques'.
Ernakulam Several Govt Emporia on MG Rd, include **National Textiles** (another in Banerji Rd). Other shopping areas are in Broadway, Super Bazar, Anand Bazar, Prince St and New Rd. **Bhavi Books**, Convent Rd is recommended; **Paico**, Broadway, and Press Club Rd Ernakulam.
Fort Kochi Several in the last 25 years the narrow streets in Jew Town, towards the Synagogue have become popular for 'antique' hunters. About 25 shops have a similar range of both old and new curios. **Idiom Books**, VI/183 Synagogue Lane, Jew Town, T224028, very good range on India, travel, fiction, religion, philosophy etc. Another near St Francis Church, Princess St, extensive catalogue/postage worldwide. **Dhamdhere**, Pandithan Temple Rd, Mattancherry, T224481. Interesting to visit prefume manufacturers who confess many are synthetic (Rs 12), but the sandalwood oil is the real McCoy (Rs 100)!

Kottayam *p921, map p922*
Kottayam is a regional shopping centre. Camera services and repairs at **Camera Scan**, Edimariyil Bldg, near Kaycees Lodge, YMCA Rd, T566041.

Munnar *p925, map p926*
Munnar Supply Assoc (MSA), next to tourist information, established 1900, a bit of the old world, where you can get everything. Tailors in the bazar can copy your garments in 24 hrs. The newer Main Bazar is to the north.

Thrissur *p928*
Cotton spinning, weaving, textile industries, silk saris and brass lamps. Thrissur is also famous for its gold craftsmanship. Good handicrafts at **Khadi Gramodyog**, north of temple. **Cosmo Books**, west of temple. Excellent stock.

Kozhikode *p930, map p930*
Local handicrafts are rosewood and buffalo horn carvings and coir products.

Comtrust, South Manachira St, sells export quality, handwoven textiles; you may be able to watch dyeing and weaving in the factory next door; profits to charity. The area behind Malabar Mansion, SM St, has interesting shops.
Pai, Kallai Rd, for books.
TBS, next to *Malabar Palace Hotel*, good range of books, recommended.

▲▲ Activities and tours

Kochi-Ernakulam *p917, maps p916, 918, 920*
Tour companies
Clipper, 40/6531 Convent Rd, T364443, F381453, clipcol@md2.vsnl.net.in. **Olympus**, South end of MG Rd, near *Little Kingdom* shop, T373630. Very competent and helpful.
Pioneer Travels, Bristow Rd, T666148, F668490, pioneer@pner.com. Efficient and knowledgeable, can suggest unusual hotels/guesthouses. **VisitIndia**, Island Club House, 1st Main Rd, Willingdon Island, T668819, T98470-52030 (mob), F666959, www.visitindiatravel.com, for backwaters boat trips (see page 943), Kerala tours, health packages, car hire etc. **TCI**, T351286. **Weeks Tour**, T484-220168, F484-222632, w.e.e.k.s@usnl.com. offer tours in Goa, Karnataka, Kerala and Tamil Nadu. Good value.
   KTDC: Boat tours daily visiting Dutch Palace, Jewish Synagogue, Francis Church, Chinese Fishing Nets, Bolghatty Island. Depart from Sea Lord Jetty, Ernakulam. 0900-1230, 1400-1730; mornings cooler. Rs 70. Highly recommended.
Shorter Sunset Tour, 1730-1900, Rs 40.
Backwaters VisitIndia, Mr A Edassery, Island Club House, 1st Main Rd, Willingdon Island, T668819, F666959, www.visitindiatravel.com, organizes a delightful boat tour along Kochi's backwaters in a dugout, punted and engineless through very peaceful shady waterways passing unspoilt villages with toddy tappers, coir making, fishing et cetera; led by an excellent guide. Rs 350 for 4 hrs, depart 0830, 1430, 40-min drive to jetty. Highly recommended. They also have traditional *kettuvallams*; Rs 5000 (for couple) or Rs 8000 (2 bedroom); for 24 hrs, includes all meals. **Tourindia**, T0477-264961, www.richsoft.com/tourindia, also has *kettuvallams*; Ernakulam to Kuttanad backwaters and return. Rs 3,000 per head.
KTDC Backwater Village tours, T371761, daily from Kuthiathode, 0830-1300, afternoon

1430-1900 (40-min road transfer), country boat for 8-10, Rs 275. Special moonlight cruise on full moon. An alternative 'backwater' trip is to get a boat from High Court jetty to Mulavukadu Jetty, then ask for the Varapuzha boat. Get off at the last stop, Chetty Bhagam. Boat every 30 mins, 2 hr journey, Rs 5!

Kottayam *p921, map p922*
Tour operators
Concord, Manorama Junction, GS Rd, T560350.
Seeland, Padinjarekkara Chambers, KK Rd, T560337.

Thekkadi *p923, map p924*
Tour operators
Forest Park arranges jeep safaris and treks.

Munnar *p925, map p926*
Tours
DTPC, Old Munnar Bazar: Tea Valley, 1000-1800, Rs 250; Sandal Valley and Wildlife, 0900-1900, Rs 300.

Thrissur *p928*
Tour operators
VisitIndia, Island Club House, 1st Main Rd, Willingdon Island, T668819, F666959, www.visitindiatravel.com, offers 3-night *Pooram* packages (min 12) US$245.

Kozhikode *p930, map p930*
Tour operators
Safiya, Manuelsons Tower, GH Rd, T722770. Recommended. **Gt India Tours**, League House, Red Cross Rd, T723727.

Yoga
Kerala Yogasanam, New Rd. Others in Gandhigram and Maulana Md Ali Rd.

Kannur *p933*
Boating
Possible on the river behind the temple.

⊖ Transport

Kochi-Ernakulam *p917, maps p916, 918, 920*
Air
New international airport, 36 km northeast, is clean, hassle-free, T610113. *Classic* shop has a reasonable selection of 'coffee table' books. Transport to town: pre-paid taxis to Fort

Kochi, Rs 350-400. **Indian Airlines**, T360796, airport T610041 (domestic), T610101 (international): **Bangalore, Chennai, Mumbai, Delhi** via Goa, **Thiruvananthapuram**: daily; **Coimbatore, Hyderabad, Kozhikode** and **Tiruchirapalli**, all several flights per week. International flights to **Doha, Kuwait, Muscat, Sharjah**. **Jet Airways**, T369212, airport T610037: **Mumbai, Chennai, Bangalore**, daily.

Auto-rickshaw
On the whole rickshaw drivers have a reasonably good reputation here. If you have problems, ask police for help. If you are likely to arrive late at night, book a hotel in advance and insist on being taken as some rickshaw drivers take advantage of tourists. Within Fort Kochi, Rs 20.

Bus
Local Fairly frequent and cheap in Ernakulam. Journeys between Ernakulam, Willingdon and Fort Kochi useful after ferries stop running.
Long distance SRTCs run 'Express' and 'Fast' services from Ernakulam Terminus near Junction Railway station to major cities in the south; computerized reservations not always available. KSRTC T360531. To **Alappuzha**, every 20 mins, 1½ hrs, Rs 30; **Devikulam**, 6 hrs, Rs 42; **Kannur**, 7 hrs (Exp), 8½ hrs, Rs 85; **Kottayam**, 2½ hrs, Rs 38; **Kozhikode**, 5 hrs (Exp), Rs 72, 6½ hrs, Rs 65; **Munnar**, via Aluva, 4 hr, 0630; **Thekkadi** (Kumily) for Periyar, 0630, 6¾ hrs, Rs 80, or take later bus to Kottayam (frequent) which has several daily to Thekkadi; **Thiruvananthapuram**, 5 hrs (Exp), Rs 75, 6½ hrs, Rs 60; **Thrissur**, 1½ hrs (Exp), Rs 25. Interstate buses to: **Bangalore** via Kozhikode, Sulthan Bathery and Mysore, 0600-2100, night 12 hrs, day 15 hrs, Rs 175-210. **Mysore**, 2000, 10 hrs, Rs 190. TNSTC, T372616. To **Coimbatore** via Thrissur and Palakkad, 4¾ hrs (Exp), Rs 75; Kanniyakumari Exp, 8 hrs, Rs 110; **Chennai** via Coimbatore, Erode, Salem, 1530, 15 hrs, Rs 185; **Madurai**, via Kottayam, Kumly, Thekkadi 9 hrs (Exp), Rs 115; **Mysore**, 11 hrs, Rs 145. **Private operators**: from Kalloor and Ernakulam South Bus Stands including **Indira Travels**, DH Rd, T360693 and **SB Travels**, MG Rd, opposite Jos Annexe, T353080, **Princey Tours**, opposite *Sealord*

Hotel, T354712. Overnight coaches to **Bangalore**, 12 hrs, and **Mysore** 10 hrs. To **Kottayam**, every 30 mins, 2 hrs, **Munnar**, 4 hrs. Also to **Chennai** and **Coimbatore**.

Ferry

Ferries are the best way of getting about as they are faster, cheaper and much more comfortable than buses or autos. Enquiries, T371761. Ferry stops are clearly named.

Ernakulam Main Boat Jetty is 200 m from Junction railway station; High Court Jetty for ferries to Bolghatty.

Fort Kochi 'Customs' (main stop) with a separate one for Vypeen Island.

Willingdon Island 'Embarkation' (north) and 'Terminus' (west). From Ernakulam, to Bolghatty public ferry every 20 min, from High Court Jetty, 0600-2200. Ferries do not operate on Sun. Some take bikes/motor bikes. To Fort Kochi Customs 0600-2110 (30 mins). To Willingdon: ½-hourly from 0630 to 2110. To Vypeen Island via Willingdon Embarkation: ½-hourly, from 0530-2230, 30 mins. To Mattancherry: 6 from 0710-1740, 30 mins. From Bolghatty to Ernakulam and Fort Kochi, 1745-2000, Rs 50; speed boat hire from Bolghatty Palace, about Rs 200 to Fort Kochi. From Fort Kochi: customers to Malabar Hotel, ½-hourly to Vypeen Island, about 2 car ferries per hr. To Varapusha, 6 boats, 0740-1500, 2 hrs. Ferry hire: motor boat for up to 20, from Sea Lord jetty, book at KTDC office, Rs 200 per hr. You can do a harbour tour and visit Fort Kochi sights in 3 hrs; allow longer for a leisurely visit. KTDC Fort Kochi tour, 0900, 1400, 3½ hrs, Rs 60. Taxi boats are faster and more convenient – jetty closer to Bolghatty Palace, Rs 20 per head.

Taxi

Ernakulam Junc to Fort Kochi, Rs 150. On MG Rd, Ernakulam: Corp Taxi Stand, T361444. Private taxis: **Visit India**, Island Club House, 1st Main Rd, Willingdon Island, T668819, F666959, www.visitindiatravel.com. 8 hrs/80 km from Rs 650, Rs 800 (a/c); **Ceeyem**, Fort Kochi, T227281. KTDC, Shanmugham Rd.

Train

Service to Kochi Harbour Terminus remained suspended in 2000. Ernakulam/Kochi (Cochin) is on the broad gauge line joining Thiruvananthapuram to Mangalore,

Bangalore and Chennai. Most trains from major cities stop at Ernakulam Junction (the main station) although a few stop at Ernakulam town. Enquiries: Ernakulam Junction, T131. Trains stop at Ernakulam Town station, T390920, when incoming trains bypass Kochi. From Ernakulam Junction to: **Alappuzha**: several including Ernakulam Trivandrum Exp, 6341, 0615, 1 hr; Cannonare Ernakulam Alleppey Exp, 6308, 1130, not Thu or Sat, 1¼ hrs; Guruvayur Madurai Exp, 6726, 2350, 1 hr. **Chennai (MC)**: Alleppey Chennai Exp, 6042 (AC/II), 1500, 15¾ hrs; Trivandrum Chennai Mail, 6320, 1900, 13 hrs. **Delhi (HN)**: Ernakulam Nizamuddin Mangala Lakshadweep Exp, 2617, 1155, 40 hrs. **Thiruvananthapuram**: Vanchinad Exp, 6303, 0550, 4½ hrs; Venad Exp, 6301 (AC/CC), 1715, 5 hrs. From Ernakulam Town to: **Mangalore**: Parasuram Exp, 6349 (AC/CC), 1055, 10 hrs; Malabar Exp, 6329, 2305, 11¾ hrs. **Mumbai (CST)**: Kanniyakumari Mumbai Exp, 1082 (AC/II), 1230, 40½ hrs. **Thiruvananthapuram**: Parasuram Exp, 6350, 1355, 5 hrs; Cannanore Trivandrum Exp, 6348, 0040, 5¼ hrs.

Kottayam p921, map p922

Auto-rickshaw

To boat jetty, 2 km.

Bus

Long distance The New Private Bus Station is near the railway station. There are fast and frequent buses to **Thiruvananthapuram**, **Kochi**, **Thekkadi**; also 4 daily to **Madurai**, 7 hrs; 5 to **Munnar**, 5 hrs. State Bus Station, 2 km south, is especially chaotic with often a mad scramble to get on the Thekkadi/Periyar bus. Direct bus departs 0900, 4 hrs; otherwise buses every 2 hrs to **Kumily** between 0900-2250, change at Kumily. The route from Thekkadi to **Kottayam** takes 7 hrs over the Thekkadi pass.

Car

Car hire with driver to Thekkadi, Rs 850, 4 hrs.

Ferry

All year (in summer, backwater boats leave from Kodimatha Jetty; during the monsoons, use the Town Jetty, 3 km southwest of the railway station). Ferries to **Alappuzha**, 0715-1730, 3 hrs; interesting trip but very busy in peak season. **Champakulam**, 1530, 4 hrs; **Mannar**, 1430, 3 hrs (attractive backwaters up to Nedumudi Jetty). To **Champakulam**, 1600, 4 hrs. Alternatively, take ferry from Kumarakom to **Muhama** village (½-hourly from 0630-2100), 40 mins, and then go to Alappuzha by bus.

Train
Kollam: *Chennai Trivandrum Mail, 6319,* 0805, 2 hrs; *Bangalore Kanniyakumari Exp, 6526,* 1110, 2¼ hrs; *Vanchinad Exp, 6303,* 0655, 2 hrs (and on to **Thiruvananthapuram**, 3¼ hrs); also *Venad Exp, 6301* (AC/II), 1825, 3½ hrs.

Thekkadi *p923, map p924*
Bicycle
Bike hire From behind Bus Stand.

Bus
Local Minibuses hourly from Kumily go down to *Aranya Nivas* on the lakeside, Rs 2. At Kumily jeep drivers tell you there is no bus to Thekkadi and charge Rs 50 for the trip; autos charge Rs 25+.
Long distance State and private buses run between from Kumily: to **Alappuzha** 1115, 1345; **Kochi/Ernakulam** (6 hrs), 6 per day; **Kodaikkanal** (cancelled occasionally), 0630 (5½ hrs), or go to Vathalakundu and change; **Thiruvananthapuram**, 285 km (8 hrs), 3 per day. Buses also from Thekkadi (behind *Aranya Nivas*): to **Kottayam** (0600, 1430); several per hr to **Madurai**; late afternoon **Kollam** (4½ hrs). KTDC 2-day tours from Ernakulam, Sat depart 0730, return 2000, Rs 120.

Motor launches
On the lake 2-hr motor launch trips are inexpensive, scheduled every 2 hrs from 0700-1500; tickets sell out in peak season, Rs 50 (top deck Rs 90).

Munnar *p925, map p926*
Bicycle
Bike hire Raja, Rs 40 per day, Rs 20 per half day; from tourist information, Rs 50 per day. Joy Automobiles, GH Rd, car mechanics.

Bus
Long distance Frequent services to **Mattupetty** (30 mins), **Devikulam** (30 mins), **Adimali** (1 hr) and Top Station (1 hr). Daily to

Coimbatore (6 hrs); **Ernakulam/ Kochi** (4½ hrs); **Kodaikkanal** 0700 via Udumalpettai, change for Palani and Kodai. If the Palani-Kodai Rd is closed a further bus goes to Vatalakundu and then Kodai; **Kottayam** (5 hrs); **Madurai** via Theni (5 hrs); **Palani** (4½ hrs); **Thekkadi** (4½ hrs); **Thiruvanantha puram** (9 hrs); **Thrissur** via Perumbavoor (5 hrs).

Jeeps/taxis
Go to the Eravikulam National Park.

Thrissur *p928*
Auto-rickshaw
Yellow top local auto-rickshaws available.

Car
Car hire Francis, Round South, T323317.

Bus
Local Yellow top local buses available.
Long distance There are 3 bus stands. KSRTC, near railway station, southwest of 'Round' for long distance and interstate services including several to **Allapuzha** (3½ hrs), **Bangalore** (10 hrs), **Coimbatore** (3 hrs), **Guruvayur** (1 hr), **Kochi** (2 hrs), **Kozhikode**, **Chennai** (13 hrs), **Palakkad**, **Thiruvananthapuram** (7 hrs). North (Priyadarshini), just north of 'Round', buses to **Cheruthuruthy**, **Ottapalam**, **Palakkad**. Sakthan Thampuran, 2 km south of 'Round', for frequent private buses to **Guruvayur**, **Kannur**, **Kozhikode**.

Taxi
There are yellow top local taxis available.

Train
Kochi (Cochin): *Tiruchchirappalli Cochin Exp, 6865,* 0335, 2¾ hrs; *Hyderabad Cochin Exp, 7030,* 1245, not Tue, 2¼ hrs; *Raptisagar Exp, 5012/5222,* 1530, Mon, Thu, Fri, Sun, 2¾ hrs. **Chennai (MC)**: *Alleppey-Chennai Exp, 6042* (AC/II), 1810, 12½ hrs; *Trivandrum Chennai Mail, 6320,* 2045, 11¼ hrs; *Raptisagar Exp, 5011* (AC/II), 1110, Tue, Wed, Fri, Sat, 12¼ hrs.

Palakkad *p928*
Bus
KSRTC, for long distance; Municipal Bus Stand for **Kozhikode**, **Mannarghat** (Silent Valley), **Pollachi**.

Train

The main Junction station is 5 km northeast of town. Also Town Station. **Coimbatore:** *West Coast Exp, 6628,* 0500, 1½ hrs; *Cochin Hyderabad Exp, 7029,* 1405, 1¼ hrs; *Kerala Exp, 2625,* 1905, 1¼ hrs. **Chennai:** *West Coast Exp, 6628,* 0500, 10½ hrs; *Alleppey Chennai Exp, 6042,* 2025, 10¼ hrs. **Ernakulam Junction:** *Kerala Exp, 2626* (AC/II), 0720, 3 hrs; *Hyderabad Cochin Exp, 7030,* 1045, not Tue, 3½ hrs. **Kochi** (Cochin): *Hyderabad Cochin Exp, 7030,* 1045, not Tue, 4¼ hrs.

Punnathur Kotta *p929*
Bus

Bus station is east of the Sri Krishna Temple and several hotels. Buses to **Thrissur** (45 mins).

Kozhikode *p930, map p930*
Air

Airport, T712762. Transport to town: pre-paid taxi Rs 250; but from town Rs 35. **Indian Airlines,** Eroth Centre, Bank Rd, T766243, Airport T766056, flies to Mumbai, Coimbatore, Goa (Mon, Fri), Chennai, Tiruchirapalli (Wed, Sun) and Bahrain, Doha, Fujairah, Kuwait, Ras-Al-Khaimah and Sharjah. **Air India,** Bank Rd. Mumbai and Middle East (Abu Dhabi, Dubai, Muscat). **Jet Airways,** 29 Mavoor Rd, T740518, Airport T712375, to Mumbai.

Auto-rickshaw

From 'Old' bus stand, Maulana Md Ali (Jail) Rd

Bus

SKS Luxury buses from 'Old' bus stand, Maulana Md Ali (Jail) Rd.
Long distance KSRTC, T722771, from Mavoor Rd (near Bank Rd junction) to **Bangalore, Thiruvananthapuram** (via Thrissur, Ernakulam, Alappuzha, Kollam), 0630-2200 (10 hrs), **Ooty** (see Waynad below), etc. The New Bus Stand is further east on Mavoor Rd for private buses to the north including **Kannur.** Buses to the south go from the Old Bus Stand (Palayam).

Taxi

Tourist taxis, Palayam, T721854

Train

Trains to **Mangalore** (5 hrs), **Ernakulam** (4½ hrs), **Thiruvananthapuram** (9½-10 hrs). Also

to **Chennai** and **Coimbatore,** and **Goa** and **Mumbai** up the Konkan Railway line.

Kalpetta *p931*
Bus

Northeast-bound buses (Sulthan Bathery, etc) depart from main bus stand, whilst southwest-bound buses depart from stand on the opposite (east) side of main highway.

Kannur *p933*
Auto-rickshaw

Local auto-rickshaws in town.

Bus

Local Buses in town.
Long distance T707777. To **Kozhikode** (2½ hrs), **Mangalore** (4½ hrs), **Mercara** (6 hrs), **Mysore** (6 hrs).

Taxi

Taxis wait outside the bus stand.

Train

T705555. To **Mangalore:** *Chennai Mangalore Mail, 6601* (AC/II), 1045, 3¼ hrs; *Parasuram Exp, 6349* (AC/CC), 1820, 3¾ hrs. **Palakkad:** *Mangalore Tiruchchirappalli Exp, 6684,* 0920, 5½ hrs (continues to **Coimbatore,** add 1¼ hrs); *West Coast Exp, 6628,* 2315, 5¾ hrs (continues to **Chennai (MC),** add 10½ hrs); *Mangalore Chennai Mail, 6602,* 1420, 5 hrs (continues to **Chennai (MC),** add 10 hrs).

⊙ Directory

Kochi-Ernakulam *p917, maps p916, 918, 920*
Airline offices On MG Rd unless stated otherwise. **International:** Air India: T351260/380700, A610050. British Airways, T364867. Cathay Pacific and KLM, T362064. Lufthansa, T370776. Japan Airlines, T350544. Maldive Airlines, T351051. Singapore Airlines and Swissair, T367911. **Domestic:** Indian Airlines and Alliance Air, Durbar Hall Rd, near *Bharat Hotel,* T370242, A610101. Jet Airways, Elmar Sq Bldg, MG Rd, T369212, A610037. **Banks** Thomas Cook, Palal Towers, 1st floor, Right Wing, MG Rd, T369729, Mon-Sat, 0930-1800, exchange, TCs, very quick service. Union Bank, Panampilly Nagar, opens Sun. Most banks open till 1500, Several on MG Rd, Shanmugham Rd and on Broadway,

Ernakulam, and on Mattancherry Palace Rd, Fort Kochi. Ernakulam Head PO does Western Union money transfer. **Hospitals** General Hospital, Hospital Rd, Ernakulam, T360002 (nearby *Oriental Pharmacy*, Market Rd open 24 hrs). Govt Hospital, Fort Kochi, T224444. On MG Rd: City, T361809, and Medical Trust Hospital, T371852, have 24-hr pharmacies. City Dental Clinic T368164. **Internet** Net Point, near Junction Station. Fast connection Rs 30 per hr. **Post office** Ernakulam Head PO, Hospital Rd, 0830-2000, Sat 0930-1430, Sun 1000-1600, other holidays 1400-1700. Kochi Main PO, Mattancherry (for **Poste Restante**), 0800-2000, Sun 0930-1700; often empty. North End PO, Willingdon Island. CTO: (24 hrs) Jos Junction Building, 2nd floor, MG Rd, Ernakulam. **Tourist offices** Govt of India, next to *Malabar Hotel*, Willingdon Island, T668352, where you can pick up maps and small booklets, very helpful, 0900-1730, closed Sun. Guides. KTDC, Shanmugham Rd, Ernakulam, T353234, helpful accommodation officer, where you can get a small booklet 'Kerala Travel Facts' with useful listings, 0800-1800. Counter at Airport during flight hours, T667874. DTPC, Old Collectorate, Ernakulam, T381743. Tourist Desk, Main Boat Jetty, Ernakulam, T371761, touristdesk@satyam.net.in, 0900-1800. PJ Verghese helps tourists plan itineraries round Kerala on a voluntary basis, very helpful; maps, backwaters (country boat) tour, 0900, 1400, 3 hrs, Rs 300, tickets for Alappuzha-Kollam boat trip. **Useful addresses** AA: South India, MG Rd (opposite *Hotel Dwaraka*), T351369. Tourist Police: T666076, helps with information of all kinds. Visa extension: City Police Commissioner, High Court Ferry Station, Ernakulam, T360700. Foreigners' Regional Registration Office, T352454.

Kottayam *p921, map p922*

Post office MC Rd, 0800-2000, 1400-1730 on holidays. Kerala Tourist office, *Govt Guest House*, Nattakom, T562219. **Useful addresses** Bank of India, main branch, and Hotel Anjali change currency and Amex TCs.

Thekkadi *p923, map p924*

Hospital T322045, at Kumily. **Post office** State Bank of Travancore, by bus stand, quick TC exchange. **Tourist office** At *Aranya Nivas*, Thekkadi, T322023; at Thekkadi Junction, Kumily, T322620. **Useful information** Some travellers, particularly women on their own, found shopkeepers here aggressive and intimidating.

Munnar *p925, map p926*

Banks Federal Bank, near Tata Hospital Rd, very helpful; State Bank of India, 1000-1400, Sat 1000-1200. **Hospital** Excellent Tata General Hospital, T530270, on the north edge of town on the Rajamalai Rd. Good Chemist between Tata Regional Office and *Residency* hotel. **Internet** Next to *Misha hotel*, Rs 40/hr. Phone connections from Munnar are unreliable; alternative nearest ISD phone is in Kothamangalam. **Post office**: New Town centre. **Tourist offices** DTPC, Old Munnar Bazar, T531516, www.munnartourism.com, mainly for booking cycles, Rs 10 per hr, Rs 50 per day; see above for tours. Try the free Tourist Information Service, Main Bazar, opposite bus stop, T530349. Joseph Iype is a mine of invaluable information (small charge for photocopies); arranges accommodation, boats.

Thrissur *p928*

Banks State Bank of India, Town Hall Rd, Round East, near Paramekkavu Temple; State Bank of Travancore, (upstairs), opposite. **Hospital** Amala Cancer Hospital, Amalanagar (9 km, along the Guruvayur road), T211950. Recommended for general medicine, surgery etc. **Internet** Sruthy, north of temple ring. Good connections, Rs 30 per hr. **Tourist offices** In *Govt Guest House*, Palace Rd, T332300, and opposite Town Hall.

Palakkad *p928*

Bank State Bank of India, English Church Rd. **Tourist office** Near Children's Park, T538996.

Kozhikode *p930, map p930*

Airline office Air Maldives, T310181. **Banks** Exchange at SBI, Bank Rd. Good rates, no commission, friendly. Also Thomas Cook. **Hospital** Govt Hospital, T365367. Medical College Hospital, T421050. **Internet** Nidhi, near New Bus Stand or behind *Malabar Mansion*, SM St. Fast, Rs 30 per hr. **Post office** Near Mananchira. Central Telegraph Office: 24-hr ISD.

Tourist offices Kerala Tourism, *Govt Guest House* and Railway Station. KTDC, *Malabar Mansion*, SM St, T722391.

Sulthan Bathery *p932*
Banks There are several banks.

Thalassery *p932*
Bank State Bank of India changes money.

Kannur *p933*
Tourist offices Kerala Tourism, *Govt Guest House*, Payyambalam, T506366. KTDC, *Motel Araam*. DTPC, T506336.

Lakshadweep, Minicoy and Amindivi Islands

→ *Population: 60,600 225-450 km west of Kerala Area: 39,000 sq km Total land area: 32 sq km*

The islands, which make up the Lakshadweep ('100,000 islands'), have superb beaches and beautiful lagoons. There are, despite the name, only 11 inhabited and 11 uninhabited islands making up the group. Minicoy, the southernmost island, is 183 km from Kalpeni, its nearest neighbour. Geologically they are the northernmost extensions of the chain of coral islands that extends from the far south of the Maldives. The atolls are formed of belts of coral rocks almost surrounding semi-circular lagoons, with none more than 4 m above sea level. They are rich in guano, deposits of centuries of bird droppings. The wealth of coral formations (including black coral) attracts a variety of tropical fish – angel, clown, butterfly, surgeon, sweetlip, snappers and groupers. There are also manta and sting rays, harmless sharks and green and hawkbill turtles. At the right time of the year you may be able to watch them laying eggs, arriving on the beach at night, each laying 100 to 200 eggs in the holes they make in the sand. ▸▸ *For Sleeping, Eating and other listings, see pages 951-952.*

Ins and outs

Getting there You can only visit the islands on a package tour as individuals may not book independently. Lakshadweep Tourism's *Society for Promotion of Recreational Tourism and Sports* (SPORTS) and other tour operators organize package tours. These are listed below. See Transport, page 952, for further details

Climate Hottest: Mar-May. Summer, maximum 35°C, minimum 25°C; Winter, maximum 32°C, minimum 20°C. Annual rainfall: 1,600 mm, southwest monsoon mid-May to Sep. Best season: Oct-Mar when tours are conducted.

Permits Everyone needs a permit, for which you need to provide details of the place and date of birth, passport number, date and place of issue, expiry date (or copy relevant pages of your passport) and four photos; apply 2 months ahead. If you plan to dive, get a doctor's certificate to prove fitness.

The islands

Foreign tourists may only visit Bangaram and Kadmat Islands; Indians, Kadmat, Kavaratti, Kalpeni and Minicoy. Thinakkara and Cheriyam are being developed.

Kavaratti, the administrative capital, is in the centre of the archipelago. The Ajjara and Jamath mosques (of the 52 on the island) have the best woodcarvings and the former has a particularly good ceiling carved out of driftwood; a well within is believed to have medicinal water. The Aquarium with tropical fish and corals, the lake nearby and the tombs are the other sights. The woodcarving in the Ajjara is by superb local craftsmen and masons. *Duk Bungalow*, basic, with two rooms and a *Rest House* with four rooms may be reserved through the Administrator, Union Territory of Lakshadweep, Kozhikode 1. Local food from *dhabas*. There is a **bank** here.

Some of the other islands in the group are **Andratti**, one of the largest which was first to be converted to Islam, and **Agatti**, the only one with an airport (which neighbours Bangaram) and also has a beautiful lagoon and 20-bed *Tourist Complex*.

Barren, desolate and tiny, **Pitti** Island comprises a square reef and sand bank at its south end. It is a crucially important nesting place for terns and has now been listed as a wildlife sanctuary. Conservation groups are pressing for a ban on the planting of trees and the mining of coral, but the main risk to the birds is from local fishermen who collect shells and the terns' eggs for food. Nearby **Cheriam** and **Kalpeni** have suffered most from storm damage.

Bangaram is an uninhabited island where the Casino Group runs the *Island Resort* (see Sleepin below).

Kalpeni, with its group of three smaller uninhabited satellite islands, is surrounded by a lagoon rich in corals, which offers excellent watersport facilities including snorkelling and diving. The raised coral banks on the southeast and eastern shores are remains of a violent storm in 1847; the Moidin Mosque to the south has walls made of coral. The islands are reputedly free from crime – the women dress in wrap-around *lungis* (sarongs), wearing heavy gold ornaments here without any fear. Villagers entertain tourists with traditional dances, *Kolkali* and *Parichakkali*, illustrating themes drawn from folk and religious legends and accompanied by music and singing. On Koomel Bay overlooking Pitti and Tilakam islands, the *Dak Bungalow* and *Tourist Huts* provide accommodation.

Minicoy (Maliku), the southernmost and largest, is interesting because of its unique Maldivian character, having become a part of the archipelago more recently. The people speak *Mahl* similar to *Dhivehi* (the script is written right to left) and follow many of their customs; a few speak Hindi. The ancient seafaring people have been sailing long distances for centuries and the consequential dominance of women may have led Marco Polo to call this a 'female island'. Each of the nine closely knit matrilineal communities lives in an *athir* (village) and is headed by a *Moopan*. The village houses are colourfully furnished with carved wooden furniture. Tuna fishing is a major activity and the island has a cannery and ice storage. The superb lagoon of the palm-fringed crescent shaped island is enclosed by coral

Lakshadweep islands

reefs. Good views from the top of the 50 m lighthouse built by the British. You can stay at the *Tourist Huts*.

The **Amindivi** group consists of the northern islands of **Chetlat, Bitra** – the smallest (heavily populated by birds, for a long time a rich source of birds' eggs), **Kiltan** where ships from Aden called en route to Colombo, **Kadmat** and the densely populated **Amini**, rich in coconut palms, which was occupied by the Portuguese. **Kadmat**, an inhabited island 9 km long and only 200 m wide, has a beach and lagoon to the east and west, ideal for swimming and diving. The tourist huts shaded by palms are away from the local village. The Water Sports Institute has experienced qualified instructors. There are 10 executive and tourist *cottages* and a *Youth Hostel* with dorm for 40.

Listings: Lakshadweep, Minicoy & Amindivi Islands

● Sleeping

Lakshadweep, Minicoy and Amindivi Islands *p949*

Accommodation differs on the islands with Bangaram having special facilities. On Kavaratti and Kadmat, basic tourist cottages resemble local huts with tiled roofs and coconut palm matting walls. Each hut has 1 or 2 bedrooms, mosquito nets, fans and attached baths; electricity is wind or diesel generated. Meals are served on the beach and are similar to Keralan cuisine using plenty of coconut. Breakfast might be *idlis* or *pooris* with vegetables. Lunch and dinner might be rice and vegetable curry, *sambhar*, meat, chicken or fish curry. Vegetarian meals available on request. Bangaram offers an international menu.

AL Bangaram Island Resort: T0484-668221, F668001, casino@vsnl.com. 30 rooms with bath, in huts, simple despite the price with palm-matting walls and tiled floors, getting shabby, open-sided restaurant (local specialities often using fish and coconut can get repetitive), bar, "strong smell of sulphur when the water table is low".

● Bars and clubs

Lakshadweep, Minicoy and Amindivi Islands *p949*

Alcohol is available on board ship and on Bangaram Island (tourists requested not to carry alcohol).

▲ Activites and tours

Lakshadweep, Minicoy and Amindivi Islands *p949*

Windsurfing, scuba diving (Poseidon Neptune School), parasailing, waterskiing and snorkelling. Deep sea fishing (barracuda, sailfish, Yellow-fin, travelly) is possible on local boats with crew; serious anglers bring their own equipment; no diving or deep sea fishing Apr-Sep. The satellite islands of Tamakara, Parali I and II can be visited for the day. Package Rs 3,500-9,500 per head, ordinary and deluxe and depending on season. Reservation: *TCI*, MG Rd, Ernakulam, Kochi (opposite Kavitha Theatre), or in Mumbai office Chandu Mukhi, Nariman Point, or *Casino Hotel*, Willingdon Island, Kochi, T0484-666821, F668001, casino@vsnl.com.

Package tours Tourism is still in its infancy and facilities are limited on the islands you will be allowed to visit. The relatively expensive package tours (the only way to visit) operate from Oct-May. Schedules may change, so allow for extra days when booking onward travel. Most tours are monthly from end-Jan - mid-May. Lakshadweep Tourism (3 packages): Sports, Willingdon Is, Kochi, T0484-668141, F668155. 3 options cost Rs 6,000-10,000 per person (student discounts), including transport from Kochi. **Kadmat Water Sports**: 6 days (including 2-day sailing, stay in *Kadmat Cottages* or *hostel*). **Coral Reef**: 5 days to Kavaratti, Kalpeni and Minicoy Islands.

● For an explanation of the sleeping and eating price codes used in this guide, see inside the front cover. Other relevant information is found in Essentials pages 52-57.

Paradise Island Huts: 6 days to Kavaratti. **Casino Group:** Willingdon Is, Kochi For foreigners: for the resort only, US$250-350 (for 2), US$500-700 for 4, US$70 extra person (discounts Apr-Sep). **Bangaram** Kayaks, catamarans and sailing boats are free. For an extra charge each time: Scuba diving for beginners and the experienced (equipment for hire); deep sea big game fishing from 1 Oct-15 May – only minimal fishing equipment and boat crew; excursion to 3 neighbouring islands or snorkelling at ship wreck (for 8); glass-bottomed boat. Snorkelling in the lagoon can be disappointing due to poor visibility and dead corals. **Katmad Island Scuba Diving:** US$800, 1 Star CMAS Certificate US$30, Certified diver US$25 per dive; accompanying adult US$350, child (under 10) US$165. Travel by ship from Kochi (deck class) included; return air from Kochi or Goa to Agatti, US$300; return helicopter (Agatti-Kadmat), 15 mins, US$60, or local *pablo* boat.

Tour companies
Book at least 2 months ahead (see 'Permits' above). **Bangalore: Clipper Holidays**, 4 Magrath Rd, T/F5599032, clipper@ bangalore.wipro.net.in. **Kolkata: Ashok Travels**, T2423254, F2420922; **Mercury**, T2423555, F2423713, both in Everest Bldg, 46 JL Nehru Rd. **Chennai: Mercury**, 191 Mount Rd, T044-8522993, F8520988. **Kochi: SPORTS**, Indira Gandhi Rd, Willingdon Is, T0484-868387, F668647. **Kozhikode: Lakshadweep Travels**, 1 Gandhi Rd, T0495-767596. **Mangalore: Lakshadweep Foundation**, KSRM Bldg, Lighthouse Hill, T21969. **Mumbai: Lakshadweep Travelinks**, Jermahal 1st floor, Dhobitalo, T022-2054231, F2089282. **New Delhi: ITDC**, Kanishka Plaza, 19 Ashok Rd, T011-3325035, F332495; **SITA**, F-12 Connaught Place, T3311133, F3324652.

⊖ Transport

Lakshadweep, Minicoy and Amindivi Islands *p949*
Air
Agatti has a basic airport. **Indian Airlines** by 15-seater Dorniers (baggage allowance, 10 kg), unreliable service, "plane broke down": to/from Kochi, daily except Tue and Sun; to/from Goa: Tue, Sat. 1¼ hrs, US$300 return; transfer by *pablo* boat; helicopter May-Sep. Casino/Taneja by 5-seater P68C, 2 a week.

Ferry
MV *Tippu Sultan* sails from Kochi. 26 passengers in 1st and exec class have 2 and 4-berth a/c cabins with washbasins, shared toilets, Rs 5,000; 120 passengers in 2nd class in reclining seats in a/c halls, Rs 3,500. Ship anchors 30-45 mins away from each island; passengers are ferried from there. Total travel time from Kochi can take up to 30 hrs. **Inter-island transfers** are by helicopter (when available) during monsoons, 15 May-15 Sep (return US$60), or by *pablo* boats for 8.

ⓘ Directory

Lakshadweep, Minicoy and Amindivi Islands *p949*
Hospital Agatti has a medical centre; emergencies on the islands have helicopter back-up.

Karnataka

⦂ Footprint features

Introduction

Karnataka is the true meeting point of South and North India. The open plateau inland of the **Ghats** has witnessed a constant succession of influences from the north. Its northern districts saw the rise of architectural styles which shaped the distinctive traditions of **Chalukyan** and **Hoysala temples** seen at sites around **Pattadakal**, **Belur** and **Halebid** while the capital of the Vijaynagara kings, **Hampi**, remains as a haunting reminder of further refinement of temple building. Islam too spread its powerful influence to the southernmost towns and cities leaving its own stamp on Muslim architectural treasures. Today the state's capital, **Bangalore**, is one of the most rapidly developing cities in India.

★ Don't miss...

❶ **Jog Falls** are a spectacular site at the turn of year but watch out for leeches if you go to the foot of the falls, page 973.

❷ Go to Mysore at the end of September for the **Dasara** celebrations - the last day of the ten-day festival is especially good, page 979.

❸ Scholars of British history know that the Arthur Wellesley (Duke of Wellington) made his reputation in India defeating Tipu Sultan at **Srirangapatnam**. Don't miss Tipu's beautiful summer palace, page 981.

❹ The enormous **Hampi-Vijaynagara** ruins are hugely impressive, page 1002.

❺ End the day by watching the sun set from the eastern end of the tank at **Badami**, squeezed into a gorge between two high, red, sandstone hills, page 1011.

❻ **Bidar** has some of the finest example of Muslim architecture in the Deccan and it can be explored easily on foot, page 1013.

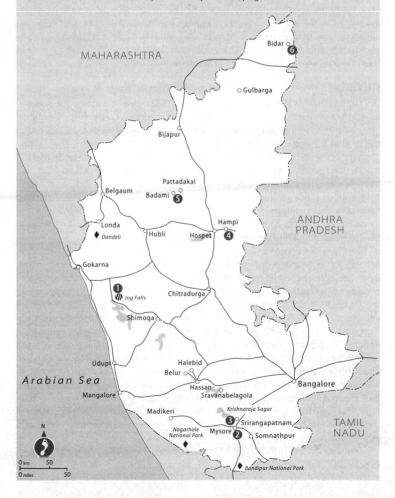

Karnataka

Background → *Population: 52.7 million. Area: 192,000 sq km.*

The land

The Western Ghats, called the Malnad or hill country, have beautiful forests with waterfalls and wildlife parks. To the east stretches the Mysore Plateau. Three great rivers originate in the Ghats – the Kaveri (or Cauvery, as it is still known in Karnataka), the Tungabhadra, and the Krishna. Some, like the short westward flowing Sharavati, have very impressive waterfalls, Jog Falls being one of the highest in the world. Parts of northern Karnataka are barren, rocky and covered with scrub, but the state has a lush coastline. From Coondapur to Karwar, the beautiful estuaries of the short fast-running rivers flowing west from the Ghats still have mangroves, some in uniquely good condition, although commercial exploitation seriously threatens their survival.

Climate The whole of the west coast is extremely wet from June to September, receiving about 1,500 mm in June and July alone. However, immediately to the east of the Western Ghats rainfall decreases dramatically. Temperatures rise to the low 30°C between February and June but fall slightly during and after the monsoon. On the plateaus of the south, especially around Bangalore and Mysore, temperatures are moderated by the altitude (generally around 1,000 m), and night temperatures are pleasantly cool through most of the year. The central and northern parts of the state get considerably hotter in April-May, often exceeding 40°C for days at a time. Humidity increases sharply during the monsoon.

History

The region between the Tungabhadra and the Krishna rivers, was home to some of the earliest settlements in peninsular India, over 500,000 years ago. By the Middle Stone Age there was already a regional division appearing between the black cotton soil area of the north and the granite-quartzite plateau of the south. The division appears between the Krishna and Tungabhadra rivers in the modern districts of Raichur and Bellary. In the north hunters used pebbles of jasper taken from river beds while quartz tools were developed to the south. The first agricultural communities of the peninsula have also been identified from what is now northern Karnataka. Radiocarbon datings put the earliest of these settlements at about 3,000 BC, and millets and gram were already widely grown by the first millennium BC. They have remained staple crops ever since.

Tradition in Karnataka states that Chandragupta Maurya, India's first emperor, became a Jain, renounced all worldly possessions and retired to Sravanabelagola. Dynasties, rising both from within the region and outside it, exercised varying degrees of control. The Western Gangas, from the third to 11th centuries, and the Banas (under the Pallavas), from fourth to ninth centuries, controlled large parts of modern Karnataka. The Chalukyas of central Karnataka took some of the lands between the Tungabhadra and Krishna rivers in the sixth century and built great temples in Badami. They and the Rashtrakutas tried to unite the plateau and the coastal areas while there were Tamil incursions in the south and east. The break-up of the Tamil Chola Empire allowed new powers in the neighbouring regions to take control. In Karnataka the Hoysalas (11th-14th centuries) took advantage of the opportunity, and built the magnificent temples at Belur, Halebid and Somnathpur, symbolizing both their power and their religious authority. Then came the Sangama and Tuluva kings of the Vijayanagara Empire, which reached its peak in the mid-16th century, with Hampi as their capital.

Muhammad bin Tughlaq had attacked northern Karnataka in the 13th century. Even during the Vijayanagar period the **Muslim sultanates** to the north were extending their influence. The Bidar period (1422-1526) of *Bahmani rule* was marked by wars with Gujarat and Malwa, continued campaigns against Vijayanagara, and expeditions against Orissa. **Mahmud Gawan,** the Wazir of the Bahmani sultanate, seized Karnataka between 1466 and 1481, and also took Goa, formerly guarded by Vijayanagar kings. By 1530 the kingdom had split into five independent sultanates: **Adil Shahis** of Bijapur, the **Qutb Shahi** of Golconda, the **Imad Shahi** of Ahmadnagar, the **Barid Shahi** of Bidar, and the **Imad Shahi** of Berar. From time to time they still came together to defend common interests, and in 1565 they co-operated to oust the Vijayanagar Raja, but Bijapur and Golconda gathered the lion's share of the spoils and they were rapidly succeeded by the Mughals and then the British. The south experienced a different succession of powers. While the Mughals were preoccupied fighting off the Marathas, the **Wodeyar** rulers of Mysore took Srirangapatnam and then Bangalore. They lost control to **Haidar Ali** in 1761, the opportunist commander-in-chief who with French help extended control and made Srirangapatnam his capital. The Mysore Wars followed and with Haidar Ali's, and then his son Tipu Sultan's death, the **British** re-established rule of the Wodeyars in 1799. The Hindu royal family was still administering Mysore up to the reorganization of the states in the 1950s when the Maharaja was appointed State Governor.

Art and architecture

Karnataka's role as a border territory was illustrated in the magnificent architecture of the Chalukyan Dynasty from AD 450 to 650. Here, notably in **Aihole**, were the first stirrings of *Brahman* temple design. A mixture of Jain temples illustrates the contact with the north of India which continued to influence the development of the Dravidian temples which grew alongside them. In Pattadakal alone it is possible to see examples of four temples built on North Indian '*Nagari*' principles and six built on South Indian '*Dravida*' lines. That contact was developed through the Hoysalas four centuries later. In **Belur**, **Halebid** and **Somnathpur**, the star-shaped plan of the base and the shrine, with the bell-shaped tower above and exquisitely crafted exterior and interior surfaces became a hallmark of their temples, a distinctive combination of the two traditions. The Vijayanagara kings advanced temple architecture to blend in with the rocky, boulder-ridden landscape at **Hampi**. Flat-roofed pavilions and intricately carved pillars characterized their style. **Bijapur** has some of the finest Muslim monuments on the Deccan, from the austere style of the Turkish rulers to the refinement in some of the pavilions and the world's second largest dome at the Gol Gumbaz.

Culture

While the **Lingayats** are the dominant caste group in northern Karnataka, a peasant caste, the **Vokkaligas**, is dominant in the south. Their rivalry still runs through Karnataka politics. Karnataka has its share of tribal people. The nomadic *Lambanis* in the north and west, are among several tribal peoples in the hill regions.

Try a typical Udupi **meal** which follows the pattern of a south Indian vegetarian thali, and is traditionally served on a green plantain leaf or on a stainless steel plate. The vegetable curries which accompany the rice may differ a little from those served in Tamil Nadu but are just as satisfying.

Most people speak the Dravidian **language** *Kannada* (Kanarese) although in the north there has been a lot of intermixture with speakers of Indo-Aryan languages. Kannada has the second oldest Dravidian **literary tradition**. The earliest classic known is *Kavirajamarga* which dates from the ninth century. A treatise on the writing of poetry, it refers to several earlier works which suggests that the language had been in existence for some centuries. Kannada inscriptions dating from fifth and sixth centuries support this view. Early writings in both Telugu and Kannada owe a lot to Jain influence. Kannada made a distinctive contribution in its very early development of prose writing. From the 10th to the 12th centuries a mixed poetry and prose form was developed by the writers *Pampa*, *Ponna* and *Ranna* - the 'three gems of Kannada literature'. Towards the end of the 12th century the Saivite saint **Basavanna** started a new Hindu renaissance and founded Virosivism. He disliked Brahmins and didn't believe in transmigration of souls; he didn't support child marriages or the veto on widow-remarriage. His sect, the reforming Lingayats, used simple rhythmic prose, the *vachanas*, to spread its teaching. The Hindu-Sanskrit tradition was greatly strengthened by the rise of the Vijayanagar Empire. One of their greatest kings, **Krishna Deva Raya** (ruled 1509-29), was also a poet in Telugu and Sanskrit. Later, Muslim power encouraged Hindu art forms almost to go underground, and expressions of Hindu devotion and faith became associated with song and dance for popular entertainment - the *Yakshagana* in Kannada, and the remarkable *Kathakali* in Kerala, see page 888.

Dance, drama and music

Open-air folk theatre or *Bayalata* of Karnataka has developed from religious ritual and is performed in honour of the local deity. The plays evolve and are improvised by the actors on an informal stage. The performances usually start at night and often last into the early hours. The famous *Yakshagana* or *Parijata* usually has a single narrator while the other forms of Bayalata have four or five, assisted by a jester. The plots of the *Dasarata* which enacts several stories and *Sannata* which elaborates one theme, are taken loosely from mythology but sometimes highlight real-life incidents and are performed by a company of actors and actresses. There is at least one star singer and dancer in each company and a troupe of dancers who perform in these dance-dramas and are also asked to perform at religious festivals and family celebrations.

The *Doddata* is less refined than the *Yakshagana* but both have much in common, beginning with a prayer to the god Ganesh, using verse and prose and drawing from the stories of the epics *Ramayana* and *Mahabharata*. The costumes are very elaborate with fantastic stage effects, loud noises and war cries and vigorous dances. It all amounts to a memorable experience but requires stamina as they continue all night!

Modern Karnataka

Government The 19 districts are grouped into four divisions – Bangalore, Mysore, Belgaum and Gulbarga. Assembly elections on 5 October 1999 saw the Congress return to power, under the leadership of S M Krishna, at the expense of the Janata Dal. Caste rivalry between Vokkaligas and Lingayats remains a powerful factor in the state's politics, and faction fighting within the parties has been a recurrent theme, so despite its large majority of over half the Assembly's seats there remains a question as to how long the Congress can hold together.

Economy Karnataka is now widely known as one of India's most rapidly modernising states. Along with Hyderabad in Andhra Pradesh, Bangalore is an undisputed leader in IT skills and industrial activity. Based on its early development of aeronautics and high precision machine tools, Bangalore has become a world centre for the computer industry, receiving a much-quoted seal of approval from Bill Gates. Outside the cities agriculture and forestry remain important. Demand for irrigation is growing rapidly, causing tension with neighbouring states like Tamil Nadu and Andhra Pradesh. Major food crops are rice, sorghum, millets and oilseeds.

The Maidan and Bangalore

→ *Phone code: 080. Colour map 7, grid A4. Population: 4.29 million.*

Bangalore takes many first time visitors by surprise. The state capital and India's sixth largest city, its reputation as a 'garden city' has survived the dynamic growth of computer and high-tech industries which have given it the reputation as an Indian Silicon Valley. The buzz around Brigade Road's shopping malls, cyber cafés and 'pubs' give it a more modern, open feel than many other Indian cities. Set at an altitude of over 1000 m, its climate adds to its attractions as a place for a relaxing break. ▶▶ *For Sleeping, Eating and other listings, see pages 964-969.*

Ins and outs

Getting there Bangalore's airport is 9 km from the Mahatma Gandhi/Brigade Rd area which has the bigger hotels. There are airport buses, autos and pre-paid taxis into town. About 5 km west of MG Road, the main City Station and the busy but well-organized bus stations are in Gandhi Nagar with most of the budget accommodation. For hotels in Sivaji Nagar and the MG Road area, it is best to get off at the Cantonment Station.

Getting around Bangalore is very spread out and you need transport to get around. In the Cubbon Park area in the centre, you will find the tourist office and museums, with MG Road to its east which is very pleasant to wander round with good shops and eating and drinking places. The Old City with its busy bazars is south of the City Station. See Transport, page 965, for further details.

Climate Temperature: summer maximum 36°C, minimum 22°C; winter maximum 27°C, minimum 15°C. Rainfall: May-Oct, average 150 mm; minimal for the rest of the year. Best time to visit: Nov-Mar.

Background

Kempe Gowda, a Magadi chieftain (1513-69) founded Bangalore (Bengaluru) in 1537, building a mud fort and marking the limits of the city by his four watch towers. His statue stands in front of the City Corporation buildings. It was extended and fortified by **Haidar Ali** and **Tipu Sultan**. When the British gained control after 1799 they installed the *Wodeyar* of Mysore as the ruler and the Rajas developed it into a major city. In 1831 the British took over the administration for a period of 50 years, making it a spacious garrison town, planting impressive avenues and creating parks, building comfortable bungalows surrounded by beautiful lawns with tennis courts, as well as churches and museums. When the Wodeyars returned they handed over the cantonment area to the British, and only after Independence were the city and cantonment areas amalgamated.

Sights

The **Bull Temple** at Basavanagudi in the southwest was built in the Kempe Gowda period in mid-16th century. The monolithic *Nandi* bull is believed to have grown in size and now measures nearly 5 m in height and over 6 m in length! It is made of grey granite polished with a mixture of groundnut oil and charcoal. Nearby is one of Kempe Gowda's four towers.

The **Kempe Gowda Fort** on Krishnarajendra Road, was built of mud in 1537 and was rebuilt in stone two centuries later by Tipu Sultan. It is not open to the public.

Tipu's Summer Palace① *0800-1800, Rs 5, foreigners US$2, video camera Rs 25,* to the south, was started by Haidar Ali and completed by his son Tipu Sultan in 1789. Based on the Daria Daulat Bagh in Srirangapatnam, the two-storeyed ornate structure

Bangalore city

N

0 metres 300
0 yards 300

Related map
A M G Road area, page 962

■ **Sleeping**
1 Ajantha
2 Ashok
3 Bangalore International
4 Central Park
5 Comfort Inn
6 Geo
7 Harsha
8 Janardhana
9 Kensington Terrace
10 Le Meridian
11 Mahaveer & Handicrafts
12 Oberoi
13 Pushpamala, Sukh Sagar & Kamat Café
14 Ramanashree & Noodles Restaurant
15 Sandhya Lodge
16 Shoba Lodge
17 Taj Residency
18 Taj Westend & Chalukma Restaurant
19 Vellara

has a substantial amount of wood with walls and ceilings painted in brilliant colours with beautiful carvings. A museum traces the period of Haidar Ali and Tipu Sultan. Some choose to view the façade from outside instead.

The **Venkataramanasvami Temple** is in the Dravida style which, when the Wodeyar Dynasty was restored at the end of the 18th century, the new Maharajah is believed to have worshipped in first, before entering the palace.

The grand **Bangalore Palace** ① *0700-1300, 1600-2030, free, frequent buses from the City Station and Sivaji Nagar*, of the Mysore Maharajahs, visibly but improbably inspired by Windsor Castle, is only open to the public for a week around 1 November.

The **ISKCON** temple, enshrining the deities Krishna-Balarama and Gaura Nitai, is located on 'Hare Krishna Hill', 1 R Block, Chord Road, Rajaji Nagar, northwest of town. It is a striking architectural blend of traditional and modern.

Museums

Government Museum ① *Kasturba Gandhi Rd, Cubbon Park, closed Mon, 1000-1700, Rs 4*. Opened in 1886, it is one of the oldest museums in the country. It has 18 galleries including Neolithic finds from the Chandravalli excavations, and from the Indus Valley, especially Moenjodaro antiquities. There is also antique jewellery, textiles, coins, art – especially miniature paintings – and geology. The **Venkatappa Art Gallery** ① *next door, closed Mon, 1000-1700*, displays the works of the painter Venkatappa, wood sculptor Rajaram, Hebbar and others. **Visveswaraya Industrial and Technological Museum** ① *Kasturba Gandhi Rd, next to Museum, closed Mon, 1000-1700, Rs 10*, includes vintage steam engine of Mahratha railways and India's oldest combat aircraft. The **Trade Centre** next door has a permanent exhibition of what the state produces. There are also plans to convert the 100-year old **Manikyavelu Mansion** on Palace Road into a **National Art Gallery**.

20 Vijay Residence
21 Windsor Manor
22 Woodlands

3 Pizza Hut
4 Sapna
5 Shezan

● **Bars**

● **Eating**
1 Amarvathi
2 Casa Piccola

6 Black Cadillac
7 Pub World
8 Purple Haze

Lalbagh Gardens ① *0900-1800, Rs 2, allow 2 hrs*, superb Botanical Gardens, were laid out by Haidar Ali in 1760. Tipu Sultan added a wealth of plants and trees from many countries – there are over 1,800 species of tropical, subtropical and medicinal plants and a Floral Clock. The Glass House holds temporary exhibitions. There is a Kempe Gowda Tower (1537) here. *Flower Shows* in Republic Day (26 January) and Independence Day (15 August) weeks.

Cubbon Park in the Cantonment dates from 1864. Fountains, a bandstand and statues were added, together with official buildings including the High Court,

M G Road area

	Sleeping		Eating		
	1 Algate & Imperial		1 Ballal Residence's Palmgrove	13	Rice Bowl
	2 Brindavan		2 Blue Nile	14	Roomalee
	3 Gateway		3 Chungwah	15	Tycoons
	4 Highgates		4 Coconut Grove	16	Ullas
	5 Ivory Tower		5 Continental Chinese	17	Wimpy's & Koshy's
	(Barton Centre)		6 Cosmo	18	Woody's Vegetarian
	6 Nahar Heritage		7 Earthen Oven		
	7 New Central Lodge		& Baskin Robbins		Bars
	8 Nilgiris Nest & Nilgiris		8 Koshy's	19	Downtown
	Upper Crust Café		9 Kwality	20	Nasa
	9 Rama		10 Lake View	21	Night Watchman
	10 St Marks		11 Mac's Fast Food	22	Peco's
			12 Prince's & Cyber Café	23	Pub World
				24	The Underground

N

0 metres 100
0 yards 100

Karnataka The Maidan & Bangalore

State Library and museums. The **Vidhan Soudha** is a post Independence granite building in the neo-Dravida style which houses the State Legislature and Secretariat; the Cabinet Room has a huge sandalwood door (get permission to see it after office hours). The **Aquarium** ① *Tue-Sat, 0900-1715, Sun 1000-1830, small fee,* on Kasturba Gandhi Road, has a good freshwater collection. Outside is a fish restaurant and fresh fish stalls.

Excursions

Whitefield, 16 km east of Bangalore on the airport road, is known for the Sai Baba Ashram at 'Brindavan'. It also has the International Technical Park, a modern self-contained community of high tech workers. **Ayurgram** is a Kerala theme resort with an ayurvedic centre and a vegetarian restaurant.

    Bannerghatta National Park ① *21 km south on Anekal Rd, closed Tue, 0900-1700, Rs 15, foreigners Rs 200 (some think too high to see "a few big cats in cages"), camera Rs15, video Rs 50, bus No 366 from City Market, 365 from City Bus Stand, 368 from Sivajinagar,* has a lion and tiger 'safari' in a caged area, a crocodile and snake farm and offers elephant rides. Picturesque scenery and a temple. The **'safari'** includes caged tiger, lion, bison, elephant and crocodiles. The park proper also harbours deer, wild boar, leopards (rarely spotted) and a good variety of birds. Viewing is by jeep or bus accompanied by guides; you may see little in 20 minutes and photograph even less through the windows.

    From Chikballapur, on the NH7 north of Bangalore, it is 10 km to the granite hill of **Nandidurg** ① *the hills can be visited as a day excursion from Bangalore's Central Bus Stand, KSRTC, ask for Nandi Hill bus not Nandidurga (another local destination), buses at 0730, 0830, 0930, return 1400, 1630, 1830,* from where there are superb views. Literally 'the fort of Nandi', the place was named after Siva's bull in the Nandi Hills. Regarded as a minor hill resort today, Nandidurg was once a summer retreat for Tipu Sultan, who thought it would be impossible to capture. Guarded on three sides by almost sheer cliffs, on one side over 300 m high, Tipu massively fortified the western approach. The **Bhoganandisvara Temple**, ninth and 16th centuries, at the foot of the hill is an important example of the Nolamba style which had later extensions built during the Vijayanagar period (eg *gopuram* at the entrance). The second gate leads to a colonnaded enclosure with twin Siva shrines. The early style is suggested by the plainness of the walls, but the stone windows have carvings of Nataraj and Durga. The main sanctuary has pyramidal towers and an octagonal roof.

To Mysore

The southern route to Mysore through Kanakapura and Malvalli is longer than the more northerly rail and road route. The southern route crosses the open parkland of the Maidan, rising to over 1,200 m. The ancient rocks of some of the oldest granites in India which give reddish or brown soils, often with extraordinary outcropping hills and boulders, provided David Lean and Richard Goodwin with the ideal filming location to capture the atmosphere of E M Forster's Barabar Cave for their film of 'A Passage to India' without the hazards of working in Bihar. The lower cave sequences were filmed at **Savandurga** ① *get BTS bus from Bangalore City bus stand 0700, 0900, or to Magadi, then auto-rickshaw, Rs 50, ask at the Lakshmi store for directions and guide to cave and spectacular climb up Kempi Gowda hill, there is also a small Forest Park, 0900-1700,* and the upper caves at **Rama Dhavara** ① *25 km south, 2 km from Ramanagaram, the caves are visible from the road, and easy to find,* though only false entrances were made for the film, with interior shots done in studio.

Karnataka The Maidan & Bangalore

963

State Library and museums. The **Vidhan Soudha** is a post Independence granite building in the neo-Dravida style which houses the State Legislature and Secretariat; the Cabinet Room has a huge sandalwood door (get permission to see it after office hours). The **Aquarium** ① *Tue-Sat, 0900-1715, Sun 1000-1830, small fee,* on Kasturba Gandhi Road, has a good freshwater collection. Outside is a fish restaurant and fresh fish stalls.

Excursions

Whitefield, 16 km east of Bangalore on the airport road, is known for the Sai Baba Ashram at 'Brindavan'. It also has the International Technical Park, a modern self-contained community of high tech workers. **Ayurgram** is a Kerala theme resort with an ayurvedic centre and a vegetarian restaurant.

    Bannerghatta National Park ① *21 km south on Anekal Rd, closed Tue, 0900-1700, Rs 15, foreigners Rs 200 (some think too high to see "a few big cats in cages"), camera Rs15, video Rs 50, bus No 366 from City Market, 365 from City Bus Stand, 368 from Sivajinagar,* has a lion and tiger 'safari' in a caged area, a crocodile and snake farm and offers elephant rides. Picturesque scenery and a temple. The **'safari'** includes caged tiger, lion, bison, elephant and crocodiles. The park proper also harbours deer, wild boar, leopards (rarely spotted) and a good variety of birds. Viewing is by jeep or bus accompanied by guides; you may see little in 20 minutes and photograph even less through the windows.

    From Chikballapur, on the NH7 north of Bangalore, it is 10 km to the granite hill of **Nandidurg** ① *the hills can be visited as a day excursion from Bangalore's Central Bus Stand, KSRTC, ask for Nandi Hill bus not Nandidurga (another local destination), buses at 0730, 0830, 0930, return 1400, 1630, 1830,* from where there are superb views. Literally 'the fort of Nandi', the place was named after Siva's bull in the Nandi Hills. Regarded as a minor hill resort today, Nandidurg was once a summer retreat for Tipu Sultan, who thought it would be impossible to capture. Guarded on three sides by almost sheer cliffs, on one side over 300 m high, Tipu massively fortified the western approach. The **Bhoganandisvara Temple**, ninth and 16th centuries, at the foot of the hill is an important example of the Nolamba style which had later extensions built during the Vijayanagar period (eg *gopuram* at the entrance). The second gate leads to a colonnaded enclosure with twin Siva shrines. The early style is suggested by the plainness of the walls, but the stone windows have carvings of Nataraj and Durga. The main sanctuary has pyramidal towers and an octagonal roof.

To Mysore

The southern route to Mysore through Kanakapura and Malvalli is longer than the more northerly rail and road route. The southern route crosses the open parkland of the Maidan, rising to over 1,200 m. The ancient rocks of some of the oldest granites in India which give reddish or brown soils, often with extraordinary outcropping hills and boulders, provided David Lean and Richard Goodwin with the ideal filming location to capture the atmosphere of E M Forster's Barabar Cave for their film of 'A Passage to India' without the hazards of working in Bihar. The lower cave sequences were filmed at **Savandurga** ① *get BTS bus from Bangalore City bus stand 0700, 0900, or to Magadi, then auto-rickshaw, Rs 50, ask at the Lakshmi store for directions and guide to cave and spectacular climb up Kempi Gowda hill, there is also a small Forest Park, 0900-1700,* and the upper caves at **Rama Dhavara** ① *25 km south, 2 km from Ramanagaram, the caves are visible from the road, and easy to find,* though only false entrances were made for the film, with interior shots done in studio.

Listings: The Maidan and Bangalore

● Sleeping

Bangalore *p959, maps p960 and p962*
Luxury hotels can add 25% in taxes and charge prohibitive rates for use of pools by non-residents. Several hotels are clustered around the MG Rd area near the centre with restaurants, cinemas and shops nearby.
Power cuts are common so carry a torch (flashlight). Ask for quiet rooms away from the street and not close to generators.
LL Oberoi, 37-39 MG Rd, T5585858, F5585960. 160 superb rooms and suites with private sit-outs, attractive Japanese gardens but disappointing food in garden restaurant.
LL-L Leela Palace, Airport Rd, T5211234, F5212323. New, impressive 254 room hotel, with pool, health club, ayurvedic centre.
LL-L The Park, MG Rd, T5594666, F5594029. 109 attractive, spacious rooms, all facilities (internet), restaurant, *Monsoon* for tropical cuisine inc southeast Asian, popular bar.
LL-L West End (Taj), Race Course Rd, near railway, T2255055, F2200010. 135 rooms, rooms around lawn better than in newer block, *Old World* rooms near entrance "dismal" so view first, superb lawns, excellent outdoor restaurants, pool (non-residents, Rs 500). Highly recommended.
LL-AL Le Meridien, 28 Sankey Rd, T2262233, F2267676. 201 luxury rooms, renovated and re-equipped, excellent service.
LL-AL Windsor Manor, 25 Sankey Rd, T2269898, F2264941, 8 km railway. 240 rooms, 100 in new Sheraton Tower (expensive suites), excellent restaurants (delicious Indian buffet, Chinese "perfect", superb atmosphere, faultless service). Highly recommended.
L-AL Taj Residency, 41/3 MG Rd (Trinity Circle), T5584444, F5584748. 162 rooms, balconies with bougainvilleas, good Indian restaurant, excellent Chinese lunch buffets, bookshop sells foreign newspapers.
AL Ashok (ITDC), Kumara Krupa High Grounds (get off at Cantt station if travelling by train), T2269462, F2250033. 187 comfortable rooms (baths could be better), spacious grounds, good pool (non-residents Rs 300).

AL-A Central Park, 47 Dickenson Rd, off MG Rd, T5584242, F5588594. 130 rooms, 'American style', very plush, creole and continental food, live jazz Wed-Sat.
AL-A Eagle Ridge (Orange County Resort), 16 km from MG Rd, T5536861, www.trailsindia.com. New wooded resort on the outskirts, comfortable, all facilities.
A Gateway (Taj), 66 Residency Rd, T5584545, F5584030. 96 a/c rooms, 6 km railway, excellent SouthIndian *Karavalli* restaurant, *Potluck café*.
A St Mark's, 4/1 St Mark's Rd, T2279090, F2275700, stmarks@vsnl.com. 94 a/c rooms, restaurants, no pool.
A-B Ivory Tower, Penthouse (12th) floor of Barton Centre, 84 MG Rd, T5589333, F5588697, ivoryhor@satyam.net.in. 22 comfortable, spacious rooms (huge beds!), Parsi cuisine, stunning views over city, excellent value if you like heights, friendly.
A-B Ramanashree Comfort, 16 Raja Rammohan Roy Rd, near Richmond Circle, T2235250 F2221214. 68 rooms (a/c not always effective), Chinese restaurant, friendly service (may give discounts).
A-B Vijay Residency (Comfort Inn), 18, III Main Rd, near railway and City Bus Station, T2203024, F2281065. 47 very comfortable rooms, good restaurant (no alcohol), friendly.
B Algate, 93 Residency (Brigade Rd crossing), T5594786, algate@blg.vsnl.net.in. 30 quiet, a/c rooms, modern.
B Bangalore International, 2A-2B Crescent Rd, T2268011. 72 renovated rooms, restaurant with live music, looks promising.
B Harsha, 11 Venkataswamy Naidu Rd (Park Rd), Shivajinagar, T2865566, F2865943. 80 clean rooms, 40 a/c, restaurants, bar, exchange, pool.
B Highgates, 33 Church St, T5597172, F5597799. 40 clean rooms, *Palms* restaurant (Malabari, Mangalorean, Chettinad seafood and Kerala fish curries), breakfast included, modern, light, airy atmosphere, friendly.
B Nahar Heritage, 14 St Mark's Rd, T2278731, F2278737. 48 rooms, friendly service, very good restaurant, good value. Recommended.

B Rama, 40/2, Lavelle Rd (off MG Rd) near Cubbon Park, T2273381, F2214587, hotelrama@vsnl.com. 55 a/c rooms, restaurant and bar on 1st Flr, good food but 'disco' music, shabby exterior though pleasant inside with good clean rooms, Indian business hotel, good value (breakfast included).
B-D Woodlands, 5 Raja Rammohan Roy Rd, T2225111, F2236963. 240 rooms, some a/c and cottages, with attached baths and fridge, good a/c restaurant, bar, coffee shop, exchange, large but pleasant Indian style hotel, good value.
C-D Geo, 11 Devganga Rd (near Richmond Circle), T2220494 F2221993. 71 rooms, modern bath, restaurant slow but reasonable food, clean business hotel.
C-D Nilgiris Nest, 171 Brigade Rd, T5588401, F5582853. 24 rooms, 5 a/c on upper floor, very central, restaurant, exchange, supermarket below, busy location, clean, comfortable, good value.
D Brindavan, 40 MG Rd, T5584000. 112 spacious rooms with shower, some **C** a/c, superb *thali* restaurant, fairly quiet, non a/c good value. Recommended.
D Casa Piccola, Devatha Plaza, 131 Residency Rd, T2270754, casapiccola@vsnl.com. 4 guest rooms with bath, breakfast, common living room and kitchen, excellent café (see below), Italian/Indian owners.
D Pulikeshi, 168/29 5th Cross, Gandhinagar, T2269727. 22 very clean rooms, some a/c, very quiet, friendly. Recommended.
D Vellara, 283 Brigade Rd, T5369116. 36 immaculate and spacious rooms with TV (top floor best), excellent value and location. Recommended.
D-E Ajantha, 22A MG Rd (7 km, City railway), T5584321. 62 spacious rooms some a/c and cottages with wc (no showers), restaurant (South Indian vegetarian), very helpful.
E Imperial, 93-94 Residency Rd. T5588391. 20 clean rooms with bath, good location, good value.
E Janardhana, Kumara Krupa High Grounds, T2254444. 58 good size rooms, spartan but clean, restaurant (South Indian), popular Indian business hotel.
E New Central Lodge, 56 Infantry Rd, at the Central St end, T5592395. 35 simple, clean enough rooms, some with bath, hot water (0500-1000).

In **Gandhi Nagar**: the '*Majestic*' Cinema area is good for budget accommodation. Hotels here are quieter and less likely to be full than on MG Rd.
E Mahaveer, 8/9 Tank Bund Rd, opposite bus station, near City railway station, T2873670, F2870735. 44 smallish rooms, 5 a/c, modern 5-storey hotel, clean, basic, front rooms can be very noisy, larger **D** deluxe rooms at back quieter.
E Pushpamala, 9, 2nd Cross, SC Rd (neon sign stands out above others), T2874010, opposite Bus Station, travel agent. Clean, good value and surprisingly quiet, cheap and cheerful.
E Railway Retiring Rooms, 23 rooms cheaper dorm for passengers in transit.
E Sandhya Lodge, 70 SC Rd. T2874065, F2874064. 100 good rooms, rooms with bath, train reservations.
E Vybhab, 60 SC Rd, T2873997. 29 clean rooms with bath (cold water), TV, opposite *Movie land Cinema*, great value.

Hostels
E YWCA, 40 Mission Rd, T2277334. Basic rooms with bath, open to both sexes.
E-F YMCA (City), Nrupathunga Rd, near Cubbon Park, T2211848. None too clean, but great atmosphere, excellent café.
F YHA Guest House and Programme Centre. Contact Mr Sridhara, KFC Bldg, 48 Church St, T5585417, F2261468.

Nandidurg *p963*
E Mayura Pine Top, T08156-78624, 2 rooms and the best food in town, contact Manager or KSTDC, Bangalore, T2212901.
F Rest Houses, reserve through Director of Horticulture, Lalbagh, Bangalore, T5602231.

⊘ Eating

Bangalore *p959, maps p960 and p962*
We recommend trying the local Kannada chicken and Maddur vada.
▼▼▼ **Ashok's**, Windsor Manor. Buffet lunches.
▼▼▼ **Cosmo**, Magrath Rd. Good "fusion" food, anything from burritos to lamb bourgignon to Pad Thai.

¶¶¶ **Mandarin Room** (for Chinese) and the barbecue at the *West End* are recommended.
¶¶¶ **Rice Bowl**, Lavelle Rd, T5587417, and Residency Rd. Chinese, Tibetan. Well cooked, large portions. Good steaks at
¶¶¶ **Shezan**, Brigade Rd and and at Lavelle Rd (behind *Airlines* Hotel).
¶¶¶ **Tycoons**, 83 Infantry Rd, T5591356. International, with garden seating.
¶¶ **Amarvathi**, 45/3 Residency Rd. Spicy South Indian.
¶¶ **Angan**, Lady Curzon Rd. North Indian in a re-created Punjabi *dhaba* setting.
¶¶ **Chungwah**, 43 Church St. Chinese.
¶¶ **Coconut Grove**, Church St. Varied and good southern menu (Chettinad, Keralan and Kodagan), beers, sit out under shade.
¶¶ **Earthen Oven**, 76, Residency Rd. Chicken tikka etc. Minimalist décor - room looks upside down but the food's good!.
¶¶ **Koshy's**, 39 St Mark's Rd. Pleasant, old-fashioned, atmospheric, licensed. Good grills and roasts, Syrian Christian fish curries and Sunday south Indian brunch.
¶¶ **Prince's**, 9 Brigade Rd, 1st Flr, with *Knock Out Disco* next door.
¶ **Ballal Residence** Hotel, 74/4 III Cross, Residency Rd, T5597277. Indian, a/c *Palmgrove* serves excellent giant lunch *thalis* Rs 75, "super atmosphere, surrounded by Indian families and businessmen".
¶ **Blue Nile**, Church St. Tasty north Indian and tandoori.
¶ **Gautam**, 17 Museum Rd. Excellent south Indian veg restaurant and juice bar. Spacious and comfortable.
¶ **Rock Garden**, Infantry Rd. Small range of lunches between 1230-1500, cheap.
¶ **Sapna**, Residency Rd. Good, quick, clean business lunches.
¶ **Sukh Sagar**, near Majestic Cinema, 6 SM Rd, 3 floors. Each serving different style of food, fresh fruit juice, excellent South Indian *thalis* and Chinese snacks, very clean, modern, a/c.
¶ **Tandoor**, 28 MG Rd. North Indian specialities.

Bakeries
At *Taj, West End, Windsor Manor* hotels.
Hot Breads, Infantry Rd, Residency Rd and 44 Brigade Rd. Good for pastries.
Nilgiri's Upper Crust Café, Brigade Rd. Sells snacks, breads, pastries and cheeses, slightly expensive but good, clean toilets.

Cafés and fast food
Casa Piccola. Pizzas, burgers, steaks, ice cream desserts, "excellent food, very good hygiene, European coffee house atmosphere". Highly recommended ('*Raga*' - good gift shop next door).
Indiana Fast Foods, 9 St Patrick's Complex, Brigade Rd. Serves American fast foods.
Kentucky Fried Chicken, Brigade Rd, "a great escape from Indian food!", serves vegetarian too, clean, safe ice creams, salads.
Lake View, MG Rd. Sandwiches, pizza, shakes, ice cream.
Mac's Fast Food, Church St. Separate section for women and families, disappointing food.
Pizza Hut, Cunningham Rd.
Spencer's Café, outside *Spencer's* supermarket, MG Rd. For varied pizzas.
Wimpy nearby, quite expensive but good (especially vegetarian).
YMCA, near Cubbon Park, has an excellent cheap a/c café.

Ice cream
Baskin 31 Robbins ice creams, Residency Rd, opposite *Gateway Hotel*. The city's best. Excellent fruit ices and shakes.

Vegetarian
Chalukma, Race Course Rd, by *West End Hotel*. Excellent vegetarian.
Darshini, many outlets for fresh, cheap south Indian snacks.
Indraprastha, 47 SC Rd, in *Hotel Adora*. Superb Indian, cheap, packed with Indians all day.
Ullas, MG Rd, 1st floor verandah restaurant. Very good Indian and Chinese vegetarian, snacks, sweets. Tasty, excellent service, inexpensive and very popular.

Bannerghatta National Park *p963*
Mayura Vanashree, KSTDC, T8428542.

◑ Bars and clubs

Bangalore *p959, maps p960 and p962*
Bars open from 1900-2300, but some open 1100-2300. Larger hotels have bars.
180 Proof, St Marks Rd. Trendy bar, with Thai food restaurant and dance floor.
Black Cadillac, 50 Residency Rd. American style.

Downtown, Residency Rd. Looks like a modern English pub, nice atmosphere, 2 crowded snooker tables.

Nasa, 1/4 Church St. Built like a space shuttle (beer from the Fuel Tank), laser show, latest western dance sounds, videos, loud, trendy (check bill).

Night Watchman, 46/1 Church St. Excellent nightspot, tequila slammers, superb music, "you can let your hair down here".

Pecos, Rest House Rd/Brigade Rd. Small and crowded, great music and vibe, best for Blues. Recommended.

Pub World, 65 Residency Rd. Draught beer, videos, loud music.

Purple Haze, 17/1 Residency, opp Black Cadillac. New style theme venue.

Windsor Manor, British colonial theme pub in new Sheraton Tower. 'Theme' pubs are popular: beer about Rs 40; lunches at some from Rs 90. Most open 1000-1430, 1730-2300.

◉ Entertainment

Bangalore *p959, maps p960 and p962*
Cinema
Galaxy, Residency Rd. A/c.
Rex, Brigade Rd. A/c.
Santosh, Brigade-Residency Rd corner and Kempe Gowda Rd. A/c.
Symphony, MG Rd (by Ullas). English films.

○ Shopping

Bangalore *p959, maps p960 and p962*
Shops and markets open early and close late (about 2000) though they remain closed from 1300-1600.

Local specialities These include brass, copper, soapstone statues, sandalwood and rosewood carvings and coloured wood inlay work. Sandalwood oils and soaps, incense sticks, lacquer work, ceramics, carpets. Also fabrics (silk, cotton, georgette), watches and silver jewellery.

Cauvery, MG Rd. Central Cottage Emporium, MG Rd. Central Cottage Industries, Cunningham Rd. Khadi Gramudyog, Silver Jubilee Park Rd, near City Market. Manjusha, MG Rd. Mota Shopping Complex, Brigade Rd. Raga, A-13, Devatha Plaza, 131 Residency Rd, for very attractive gifts. Shrungar, MG Rd. UP Handlooms, 8

Mahaveer Shopping Complex, Kempe Gowda Rd.

Art
Shakshi Gallery, Presidency, 82 St Marks Rd, for contemporary shows.

Books
Gangarams, 72 MG Rd, has a wide ranging and expanding collection.
International Book House, 97 Residency Rd.
Premier, 46/1 Church St (and Museum Rd), small, with a good selection of specialist and academic books (best Wodehouse collection anywhere!), helpful owner.

Markets
To see a colourful local market with plenty of atmosphere, selling fruit, vegetables and flowers, try City Market southeast of the station or Russell Market, Sivaji Nagar.

Silk and sarees
Deepam, MG Rd, reasonable prices, helpful.
Janardhana, Unity Building, JC Rd.
Karnataka Silks Industries, Gupta Market, Kempe Gowda Rd.
Mysore Silk Showroom, Leo Complex, MG Rd.
Vijayalakshmi, Kempe Gowda Rd, will also make shirts.

▲ Activities and tours

Bangalore *p959, maps p960 and p962*
Golf
Bangalore Golf Club, Sankey Rd, foreign visitors pay US$35. New International Championship Golf Course, near the airport. 0600-1800, closed Mon.
KGA Golf Club charges Rs 200 weekdays, Rs 400 weekends.

Horse racing
Bangalore is famous for racing and stud farms.
Bangalore Turf Club, Race Course Rd; season May-Jul and Nov-Mar. The favourite always wins!

Swimming
Expect to pay Rs 500 for pools in hotels (eg *Ashok, West End, Windsor Manor*). Pools at Corp Office, near Square, Kensington Park Rd, near Ulsoor Lake, Sankey Tank, Sadhiv Nagar, Jayanagar 3rd Block.

Tennis
Bangalore Tennis Club, Cubbon Park.

Tour operators

Clipper Holidays, 4 Magrath Rd, T5592023, F5599833, clipper@bangalore.wipro.net.in. Tours, treks (everything provided), Kerala backwaters etc. Very helpful and efficient.
Greenwood Adventures, 2080, 12th B Main, MIG 3rd Phase, Newtown, Yelhalanka, T8462354, greenwood_adventures@hotmail.com. Specializes in treks in Karnataka and Kerala.
Karnataka Tourism, tours from Badami House, NR Square, T2275883: **Bangalore City Sightseeing**: Tipu's Palace, Bull Temple, Lalbagh, Ulsoor Lake, Vidhan Soudha, Museums, also stops at Government Emporia. Half-day, 0730-1330 and 1400-1930. Rs 85. Recommended. **1-day** Sravanabelagola, Belur and Halebid, Fri, Sun (except monsoons), 0715-2200, Rs 340; **Mysore** daily, 0715-2300, Rs 240-300 including meals.
Regal Holidays, 105/17 8th Cross, RMV Extn, T3314566, F3340171, regal@giasbg01.vsnl.net.in. Royal connections, culture, wildlife, horse safaris (Rs 4000 a day).
Sita, St Mark's Rd, T2212826.
Thomas Cook, 55 MG Rd, T5594168 (foreign exchange and TCs), and 70 MG Rd (all services), T5586439, F5588036.

⊙ Transport

Bangalore *p959, maps p960 and p962*
Air
Transport to town: (9-14 km) taxi, 20 mins, Rs 150-200; auto-rickshaw, Rs 80. KSRTC coach from airport to major hotels, MG Rd and bus station, Rs 40. To airport: special bus leaves from Sivajinagar Stop (near *Hotel Harsha*).

Indian Airlines and Alliance Air, Cauvery Bhavan, Kempe Gowda Rd, T2211914, airport T5266233, Reservations T141, fly to **Chennai**, **Coimbatore**, **Delhi**, **Goa**, **Hyderabad**, **Kochi**, **Kolkata**, **Mangalore**, **Mumbai**, **Pune**, **Thiruvananthapuram**. Jet Airways, 1-4 M Block, Unity Bldg, JC Rd, T2276617, airport T5220688, fly to **Chennai**, **Coimbatore**, **Delhi**, **Goa**, **Hyderabad**, **Kochi**, **Kolkata**, **Mumbai**. Sahara, Church St, T5586976, airport T5262531. Flies twice daily to **Delhi** and **Mumbai**. Air India flies weekly to **Jakarta**.

Auto-rickshaw
Metered, widely available, surcharge 15%, ask for card.

Bus
Local City buses run a frequent and inexpensive service throughout the city.
Long distance Video coaches can be noisy and very tiring. **City Bus Station**, opposite the City Rly Station, is extremely busy but well organized. **Central (KSRTC) Bus Station** is just to the south, T2871261. Karnataka (KSRTC), **Andhra** (APSRTC) and Tamil Nadu (TTC) run efficient, frequent and inexpensive services to all major cities in South and Central India. Frequent service to **Mysore** (3 hrs); several to **Hassan** (4 hrs), **Hyderabad**, **Madikeri** (6 hrs), **Madurai** (9 hrs), **Mangalore** (9 hrs), **Ooty** (7 hrs), **Puttaparthi** (4-5 hrs, Rs 65), **Tirupati** (6½ hrs). Private operators' Deluxe or Ordinary coaches are usually more comfortable though a bit more expensive. They operate from the City and Kalasipalyam Bus Stations.

Car
Private car hire Firms for city and out-of-town sightseeing. Cab Service, Sabari Complex, Residency Rd, T5586121. **City Taxi**, T5539999. Use meters (min charge Rs30), or Rs400 for 4 hrs (40 km free then Rs 8 per km), call out service, reliable. Europcar, T2219502 F2225645. Hertz, T5599408, F5584759. Karnataka STDC (See Directory). About Rs 600-800 for 8 hrs or 80 km; extra km Rs 4-7. Out-of-town, Rs 1,200 (Rs 2,000 a/c).

Taxi
Taxis at railway stations, see below.

Train
Pre-paid taxi service available at City Station. **Pre-paid auto-rickshaw** to MG Rd, Rs 25-30. Enquiries and reservations, T132; arrival and departure, T133. City Railway Station, Computerized Advance Reservations in newer building on right of entrance; No 14 is Foreigners' Counter (also for disabled); the Chief Reservations Officer is on the ground floor. For Tourist Quota you need your passport and a "wait-listed" ticket number (Ticket Office is to the left of the station). If you are booking a ticket for a journey out of the Southern Region go to 1st floor booking

office and join the queue for your region; no special queue for foreigners on the 1st floor. Buying tickets here can be a complicated business! Cantt Station, T135. Disembark at Cantt Station for some hotels.
Bhopal: *Rajdhani Exp, 2429*, Mon, Wed, Thu, Sun, 1835, 27 hrs (reaches **Delhi (HN)** in 35 hrs). **Chennai**: *Shatabdi Exp, 2008*, daily except Tue, 1625, 5 hrs; *Lalbagh Exp, 2608*, 0630, 5½ hrs; *Brindavan Exp, 2640*, 1430, 5¼ hrs; *Bangalore-Chennai Exp, 6024* (AC/II), 0800, 6 hrs. **Delhi (ND)**: see Bhopal. **Goa** (Londa): *Chalukya Exp, 1018*, Mon, Tue, Fri, 0600, 10½ hrs; *Ranichennamma Express, 6589*, 2030, 11 hrs. **Hospet**: *Hampi Exp, 6592*, 2200, 10 hrs. **Kolkata (H)**: *Bangalore Guwahati Exp, 5625*, Wed, Fri, 2330, 38¼ hrs. **Mumbai (CST)**: *Udyan Exp, 6530*, 2030, 24 hrs; *Chalukya Exp, 1018*, Mon, Tue, Fri, 0600, 26 hrs. **Maddur** and **Mysore**: *Chamundi Exp, 6216,*1815, 2½ hrs;*Tipu Express, 6206*, 1415, 2½ hrs; or **Mysore**: *Tipu Express 6206*, 1415, 2½ hrs; *Shatabdi Exp, 2007,*daily except Tue, 1100, 2 hrs (for a/c, Rs 280). **Secunderabad**: *Bangalore Secunderabad Exp, 7006* (AC/II), 1705, 13½ hrs. **Thiruvananthapuram**: *Kanniyakumari Exp, 6526* (AC/II), 2100, 18 hrs.

⬤ Directory

Bangalore *p959, maps p960 and p962*
Airline offices Air India, Unity Building, JC Rd, T2277747. At Sunrise Chambers, 22 Ulsoor Rd: **Air France**, T5589397, **Gulf Air**, T5584702, **Kuwait**, T5594243, **Royal Jordanian**, T5594240, **Air Canada, American Airlines**, T5585394. **British Airways**, Sophia Complex, St Marks Rd, T2214034. **Cathay Pacific**, *West End Hotel*, T2259130. **JAL**, 9/1, 2 Residency Rd, T215416. **KLM**, *West End Hotel*, T2258703. **Lufthansa**, Dickenson Rd, T5588791. **Malaysian**, Richmond Circle, T2213030. **Singapore**, Richmond Rd, T2213833. **SwissAir**, Richmond Rd, T2211983. **Banks** Usually open 1000-1400, Mon-Fri. **Standard Chartered**, 26, MG Rd. For Visa, ATMs at **Citibank**, Nilgri's Complex, Brigade Rd. Many options for exchange.
Cultural centres Alliance Française,

Millers Tank Bund Rd, off Thimmaiah Rd, opposite station. **British Library**, St Mark's Rd/Church St corner (Koshy's Bldg), 1030-1830, Tue-Sat. **Max Mueller Bhavan**, 3 Lavalle Rd. **Palm Leaf Library**, Chamarajpet, 33, V Main Rd. An unusual collection of old leaves which one traveller found held his special leaf giving accurate details of his character, past, present, and yet to be tested, future; those arriving here simply out of curiosity may be disappointed since the custodian may not be able to trace the special leaf! **Hospitals** Bowring and Lady Curzon Hospital, Hospital Rd, T5591362, north of Cubbon Park. **Mallya Hospital**, Vittal Mallya Rd, south of Cubbon Park, T2277979, one of the best; **Baptist Hospital** Hebbal, T3330321. **Other medical services Chemists**: at hospitals. **Dentist**: Grace, 1 Dinnur Main Rd, RT Nagar, T3334638. Excellent. **Internet** Cyber Café on Brigade Rd (near Church St); very good, safe cold coffee. **Cyber Q**, Brigade Rd, near Vellara, with pool tables; **Trans World** 2 Magrath Rd, with coffee shop. **Post office** GPO, Cubbon Rd near Raj Bhawan, open 1000-1800. **Poste Restante** here, open Mon-Sat, 1030-1600. Brigade Rd and Museum Rd have post and telegraph offices; Museum Rd has a Foreign Post Office. **Tourist offices** Govt of India, KFC Building, 48 Church St, T/F5585417, 1000-1800 Mon-Sat. **Dept of Tourism**, F Block, 1st floor, Cauvery Bhavan, KG Rd, T2215489, F2272403, www.indiaseek.com/karnataka/tourism. **Himachal Pradesh**, Himachal Emporium, Ganesh Complex, 13 SC Rd, T286391. **Karnataka STDC**, 10/4 Kasturba Rd, 2nd floor, Queen's Circle (near MG Rd Corner), T2212901, www.nic.in/kstdc. Very helpful and efficient. Also at Badami House, NR Sq, T2275869, F2238016, where tours originate. City Railway Station Counter, T2870068. 0700-2100. Airport Counter, T5268012. 0700-2030. **Useful addresses Ambulance**: T102. **Visa extensions**: Commissioner of Police, Infantry Rd. **Chief Wildlife Warden**, Aranya Bhavan, 18th Cross, Malleswaram, T3341993.

The Western Plateau

The road from Bangalore crosses the open plains of the Western Plateau, intensively cultivated where irrigation is possible from tanks or the occasional well. It is the land of the Vokkaliga caste, the dominant agricultural community of southern Karnataka, longstanding rivals of the reformist Lingayats of the northern districts. Belur and Halebid can be seen in a very long day from Bangalore, but it is better to allow longer if you can and to stay in Hassan overnight. ▸▸ *For Sleeping, Eating and other listings, see pages 973-975.*

★ Sravanabelagola (Shravanabelgola)

→ *Phone code: 08176. Population: 4120.*

The statue of Gommateshwara, sacred to Jains, stands on Vindhyagiri (sometimes known as Indrabetta or Indragiri), rising 150 m above the plain while Chandragiri to the north (also known as Chikka Betta) is just under half that height.

History

The Gommateshwara statue was erected at some time between AD 980 and 983. Just over 17-m high, it represents the saintly prince *Bahubali*, son of the first Tirthankara, after he had gained enlightenment. Having fought a fierce war with his brother *Bharata* over the rights to succession, *Bahubali* accepted defeat when he had won the battle because he recognized its futility. Passing on his kingdom to his defeated brother, Bahubali adopted a life of meditation.

The site

Nearly 700 steps carved in the steep granite slope start near the village tank. The path up gives excellent views. Shoes must be removed, but be aware that the granite can get extremely hot, so thick socks are recommended. It can be quite tiring in the heat, so it is advisable to carry water. Dhoolis are available at the foot of Indragiri to carry visitors up the steps. There are several small shrines on the way to the statue on top. In order, these are the *Odeagal Basti*, the *Brahmadeva Mandapa*, the *Akhanda Bagilu* and the *Siddhara Basti*, all built in the 12th century except the *Brahmadeva Mandapa* which is 200 years older. Several are intricately carved. It is worth stopping at one about two-thirds of the way up.

The carved statue is nude (possibly as he is a *Digambara* or 'sky clad' Jain) and captures the tranquillity typical of much Buddhist and Jain art. The depth of the saint's meditation and withdrawal from the world is suggested by the spiralling creepers shown growing up his legs and arms, and by the ant hills and snakes at his feet. He is shown standing on a lotus. While the features are finely carved, the overall proportions are odd, with greatly enlarged shoulders, lengthened arms but shortened legs.

Sravanabelagola is often crowded with visitors. Every 12th year it is the focus for Jain pilgrims from across India to celebrate the *Mastakabhisheka* – the 'magnificent anointment', or sacred head-anointing ceremony. The night before the ceremony 1,008 pots – 'kalashas' – holding sacred water are sold by auction to devotees. The pots are left at the statue's feet overnight, and the following morning the water is poured over the statue's head from specially erected scaffolding. The water is followed by *ghee*, milk, coconut water, turmeric paste, honey and vermilion powder. Some even sprinkle gold dust. Unlike many festivals in India, the event is watched by the thousands of devotees in complete silence. The next celebration will be between 2006 and 2008.

In the town itself is the **Bhandari basti** (1159 and added to later), about 200 m to the left from the path leading up to the Gommatesvara statue. Inside are 24 images of Tirthankaras in a spacious sanctuary. There are 500 rock-cut steps to the top of the hill and it takes about 30 minutes to climb. It is safe to leave luggage at the Tourist Office branch at the entrance (closed 1300-1415).

There are 14 shrines on **Chandragiri** and the Mauryan emperor **Chandragupta**, who is believed by some to have become a Jain and left his empire to fast and meditate, is buried here. The temples are all in the Dravidian style, the Chamundaraya Basti, built in AD 982 being one of the most remarkable. There is a good example of a free-standing pillar or *mana-stambha* in front of the *Parsvanathasvami Basti*. These pillars, sometimes as high as 15 m, were placed at the temple entrance. Here, the stepped base with a square cross-section transforms to a circular section and the column is then topped by a capital.

Hassan → *Phone code: 08172. Colour map 7, grid A2. Population: 117,400.*

This pleasant, busy little town, is a good base from which to see Belur and Halebid. Buses pull in at the centre with most hotels within a short walking distance. The railway station is 2 km to the east. The collection in the **District Museum** ① *Maharaja Park, closed Mon and government holidays, 0900-1700, free*, includes sculpture, paintings, weapons, coins and inscriptions. An **aquarium** ① *1000-1300, 1500-1930, Rs 2,* has a small collection of tropical fish, well displayed.

Belur and Halebid → *Phone code: 08177. Colour map 7, grid A2.*

The Hoysalas who ruled a large kingdom between the rivers Krishna and the Kaveri, made Belur and Halebid their capital. Great warriors, they also patronized culture and art. The artisans were encouraged to rival each other and even sign their names on their work of art. Steatite gave the sculptors the opportunity to work with intricate detail since the rock is initially comparatively soft when quarried but hardens with

Hassan

N

0 metres 200
0 yards 200

■ Sleeping	
1 D R Karigowda	4 Southern Star
2 Hassan Ashok	5 Sri Krishna
3 Mahaveer, Abhiruchi	6 Suvarna Regency
& Suruchi Restaurant	7 Vaishnavi Lodge

● Eating
1 GRR

exposure to air. The temples, built as prayers for victory in battle, are small but superbly conceived.

★ Belur

On the banks of the Yagachi River, Belur was the first capital of the dynasty. The temples stand in a courtyard with the Chennakesavara (1116) near the centre. One of the earliest of its type it took a century to complete. It celebrated the Hoysala victory over the Cholas at Talakad. Dedicated to *Krishna* it stands in a courtyard surrounded by a rectangular wall, built on a star-shaped platform with an ambulatory. The figure of *Garuda*, Vishnu's carrier, guards the entrance, facing the temple with joined palms.

The temples ① *Temples close at 2030, search light charge for interiors Rs 10; carry a torch, ASI trained guides on site (often excellent), agree to Rs 60-75 for 4 visitors (though official rate is higher), vehicle parking Rs 15.* At first glance **the Chennakesava Temple** (see also Somnathpur, page 983) is unimpressive because the superstructure has been lost. However, exquisite sculptures cover the exterior with the friezes. The line of 644 elephants (each different) surround the base, with rows of figures and foliage above. The detail of the 38 female figures is perfect. Look at the young musicians and dancers on either side of the main door and the unusual perforated screens between the columns. Ten have typical bold geometrical patterns while the other 10 depict scenes from the *Puranas* in its tracery. Inside superb carving decorates the hand-lathe-turned pillars and the bracket-figures on the ceiling. Each round filigreed pillar is different and bears witness to individual sculptors producing a masterpiece in competition with each other. The unique Narasimha pillar at the centre of the hall is particularly fine and originally could be rotated. The detail is astounding. The jewellery on the figures is hollow and movable and the droplets of water seem to hang at the ends of the dancer's wet hair on a bracket above you. On the platform in front of the shrine is the figure of Santalesvara dancing in homage to Lord Krishna. The shrine containing a 3 m high black polished deity is occasionally opened for *darshan*. The annual *Car Festival* is held in March-April.

To the west is the **Viranarayana Temple** which has some fine sculpture and smaller shrines around it. It is worth visiting the **Jain Bastis** a few kilometres away although the decoration is incomplete on most.

★ Halebid

The ancient capital of the Hoysala Empire was founded in the early 11th century as *Dvarasamudra*. It was destroyed by the armies of the Delhi Sultanate in 1311 and 1327, after which it was deserted and later renamed Halebidu or Halebid (Old Capital). Fortunately the great Hoysalesvara Temple survived.

The temples The **Jain bastis** is worth first visiting the remarkably simple 12th-century Jain Bastis at Basthalli about 1 km south. With lathe-turned and multi-faceted columns, several bastis stand in a garden enclosure, which you can walk around and see the dark interiors with carved ceilings. The smaller **Kedaresvara Temple** with some highly polished columns is on a road going south. There are cycles for hourly hire so you can visit these quieter sites, untroubled by the crowds besieging the Hoysalesvara.

The Hoysalesvara Temple ① *Temples close at 2030, ASI trained guides on site (often excellent), agree to Rs 60-75 for 4 visitors (though official rate is higher), vehicle parking Rs 15,* set in lawns, has two shrines dedicated to *Siva* with a *Nandi* bull facing each. The largest of the Hoysala temples, it was started in 1121 but remains unfinished. In structure it is similar to the one at Belur, but its superstructure was never completed. There are extraordinary half life-size statues of Hindu deities with minute details, all around the temple. These, and the six bands of sculpture below, show the excellence of the artisans' craft. The lines of elephants at the base, followed by lions and then horsemen, a floral scroll and then most impressive of all, at eye level, stories from the epics and the *Bhagavata Purana*. This frieze relates incidents from the *Ramayana* and *Mahabharata*; among them Krishna lifting Mount Govardhana, Rama defeating the demon god Ravana. The friezes above show *yalis* and *hamsa* or geese. Of the original 84 female figures (like the ones at Belur) only 14 remain; over the years, 70 were stolen.

The **Archaeological Museum** 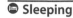 *closed Fri 1000-1700, Rs 2, no photography*, is on the lawn near the south entrance where the Archaeological Survey of India maintains a gallery of 12th-13th-century sculptures, wood carvings, idols, coins and inscriptions. Some sculptures are displayed outside. To the west is a small lake.

To Mangalore

The direct route from Hassan to Mangalore along the **NH48** is dramatic as it crosses the Western Ghats. There are stunning views. Alternatively, going via Belur a beautiful hill road runs south through the forest to **Sakleshpur** on the NH48. *Sri Durga Darshan* does good cheap Indian meals, cold drinks and coffee.

Chikmagalur and Shimoga

Chikmagalur, northeast of Belur, means 'younger daughter's town', and according to legend it was the dowry for the younger daughter of a local chieftain. In addition to the Hoysala style **Kodandarama Temple** there are mosques, the moated fort and the St Joseph's Roman Catholic Cathedral. The town is at the centre of one of India's major **coffee** growing areas. Coffee was first grown in the Baba Budan Hills, just to the north, in 1670. The Central Coffee Research Institute was set up in 1925. The district has curing works for the processing of raw coffee. **Shimoga** is useful for a night halt between Hampi to Hassan or Mysore.

★ Jog Falls

The falls are a magnificently spectacular sight in the wet season and the best time to visit is late November to early January. The 50-km long **Hirebhasgar Reservoir** now regulates the flow of the Sharavati River in order to generate hydro-electricity. The Mysore Power Corporation releases water to the falls every second Sunday from 1000-1800. Often during the monsoon the falls are shrouded in mist. Leeches are a hazard if you walk down to the base of the falls.

There are four falls. The highest is the *Raja*, with a fall of 250 m and a pool below 40 m deep. Next is the *Roarer*, while a short distance to the south is the *Rocket*, which spurts great shafts of water out into the air. In contrast the *Rani* (once called the White Lady) cascades over the rocks. The walk to the bottom of the falls is well worthwhile. A walk to the top (not in the monsoons) offering breathtaking views of the river cascading and the valley, is highly recommended. The Inspection Bungalow has excellent views.

Listings: The Western Plateau

⊖ Sleeping

Sravanabelagola *p970*
All facilities are very basic but it is worth staying overnight to see the statue early. A central bureau can arrange a decent room.
E Karnataka Bhavan, 50 rooms. Reserve at *Karnataka Tourism*, 9 St Mark's Rd, Bangalore, T579139.
F Vidyananda Nilaya Dharamshala, closest to the bus stand, rooms with toilet and fan,

"bucket shower", blanket but no sheets, courtyard, good value at Rs 60, reserve through SDJMI Committee.
F Yatri Niwas (SDJMI). Large rooms, good attached baths, clean (Rs 160).

Hassan *p971, map p971*
B Hassan Ashok (ITDC), BM Rd, opposite Race Course Rd, 500 m from bus stand, T68731, F67154, hsnashok@bgl.vsnl.net.in. 46 fading rooms, half a/c, good restaurant,

bar, exchange (poor rate), pleasant grounds, not good value.

B Hoysala Village Resort, Belur Rd, T56065 (6 km from town). 33 cottage rooms, restaurant, bar, attractive resort with gardens and pool.

B-C Southern Star, BM Rd, T51816, F68916, sshassan@vsnl.com. 48 very nice clean a/c rooms in modern hotel, TV, limited restaurant (good Indian across the road), bar, good views of countryside, excellent service.

D-E Cauvery Comforts, BM Rd, T63117. 35 simple non a/c rooms with TV, bath (hot water mornings).

D-E Sri Krishna, BM Rd, T63240, 40 a/c rooms with modern facilities, south Indian food, car hire, good value.

D-E Suvarna Regency, 97 BM Rd (500 m south of bus stand) T64006, F63822, www.htoelsuvarna.com. 70 brilliant rooms, clean and cool, some with tub, modern, swish, good veg restaurant, car hire. Very helpful, efficient, excellent value. Recommended.

E DR Karigowda, BM Rd (1 km railway), T64506. 30 modern, clean comfortable rooms, 2 a/c, quieter at back, restaurant (good choice), hospitable. Good value.

E-F Mahaveer, BM Rd, 250 m south of Bus Stand, T68885. 22 rooms, good restaurant, very clean, quiet, friendly.

F Vaishnavi Lodge, Harsha Mahal/Church Rd, T67413. 44 clean, spacious rooms, excellent value, friendly. Recommended.

Belur *p972*

E Mayura Velapuri (KSTDC), Temple Rd, T22209. 2 old rooms, 10 newer, clean, spacious with bath (Rs 200), 20-bed dorms (block book), reasonable restaurant (south Indian meals and egg curry quick service; non-veg slow), friendly and obliging staff make up for what it lacks in comfort.

E-F Annapoorna, Temple Rd, T22009. 8 cleanish rooms and restaurant.

E-F Vishnu Lodge, Main Rd, T22263, 27 rooms with bath, some with TV (Rs 50-200), vegetarian restaurant.

F Sri Raghavendra, right by temple. Cosy rooms (Rs 75-100), homely and friendly.

Halebid *p972*

F Mayura Shantala (KSTDC), T73224, Inspection Bungalow compound in nice garden overlooking temple. 4 rooms with fan, nets and bath (Rs 220, 2 better furnished), limited kitchen. Others, plainer but adequate (Rs 150).

Chikmagalur *p973*

AL Taj Garden Retreat, outside town, on a hill side, T08262-30217, with 29 luxury a/c rooms lined along the pool, good for visiting Belur and Halebid (40 km).

Several **F** lodges in town, along Indira Gandhi Rd, include **Quality Inn**, T31257, with 20 rooms, restaurant.

Shimogoa *p973*

C Jewel, smart modern hotel in town, clean comfortable a/c rooms (Rs 850, accepts Visa), restaurant.

D-E Ashoka Deluxe Lodge, large clean rooms, fairly quiet, unattractive restaurant.

D-E Navaratna International, Savarline Rd (1 km bus stand). Clean, small, dark rooms, cockroaches, some a/c, restaurants.

D-E Ramakrishna Lodge, off Main St (near Gopi Circle), with large modern clean rooms, some a/c, good veg restaurant.

Jog Falls *p973*

Hotels are very basic and there are no eating facilities available at night.

E-F Mayura Gerusoppa (KSTDC), T08186-44732. 10 rooms.

F Youth Hostel, Shimoga Rd. Empty rooms (no beds), some dorm beds with dirty bedding. Local families take in guests. Stalls near the falls serve reasonable breakfast and meals during the day.

🍴 Eating

Sravanabelagola *p970*

There are vegetarian **cafés** and cold drink **stalls** at the foot of the hill and a **canteen** at the bus station.

Hassan *p971, map p971*

🍴 **Hassan Ashok**, in hotel, International. Good food, prompt service.

● *For an explanation of the sleeping and eating price codes used in this guide, see inside the* ● *front cover. Other relevant information is found in Essentials pages 52-57.*

¶¶ **Suvarna Regency**, in hotel. Very good
South Indian vegetarian, excellent breakfasts,
popular *Golden Gate* bar and restaurant
downstairs, T60316.
¶ **Abhiruchi**, *Mahaveer's* (North Indian,
Chinese), scruffy surroundings, pleasant staff.
¶ **GRR**, opposite Bus Stand, for non-veg food
and friendly staff.
¶ **Suruchi**, below, for vegetarians.

Belur *p972*
Pooja Bakery, sells biscuits and hot snacks.

⊖ Transport

Sravanabelagola *p970*
Direct buses to/from **Mysore** and **Bangalore**
run in the morning; in the afternoon, change
at Channarayapatna. The morning express
buses to/from Mysore serve small villages
travelling over dusty, though interesting,
roads up to Krishnarajapet, then very few
stops between there and Mysore. There are
also tours from Bangalore.

Hassan *p971, map p971*
Bus
Local Bus Stand, T68418.
Long distance at least hourly to **Belur**
from about 0700 (35 km, 1 hr) and **Halebid**
from about 0800 (31 km, 1 hr); all very
crowded. Few direct to **Sravanabelagola** in
the morning (1 hr); alternatively travel to
Channarayapatna and change to bus for
Sravanabelagola. Also to **Bangalore** about
every 30 mins (4½ hrs), **Goa** (14 hrs), **Hampi**,
Mangalore (5 hrs), **Mysore** hourly (3 hrs).
You can reserve seats for the 0730 departure
to **Hospet** (9 hrs).

Taxi
Private Tourist Taxis, hired from **Cauvery
Tourist Centre**, Race Course Rd, T68026.

Tonga
Tongas are also available.

Train
Railway Station is 2 km east of centre. New
broad gauge line is now running. **Arsikere**:
1050, 2100, 1 hr. **Mysore**: 0605, 1830, 3 hrs.

Bus
The bus stand is about 1 km from the
temples. Half-hourly to **Hassan** (1 hr; last at
2030); to **Halebid** (30 mins). To **Shimoga** for
Hampi and Jog Falls (4 hrs), 0800, 0845
(check at bus stand); to **Mysore** (1½ hrs).

Halebid *p972*
Bus
The Bus Stand, where you can get good
meals, is near the temples. KSRTC buses,
half-hourly to Hassan (45 mins) and from
there to **Bangalore**, **Mangalore**, **Mysore**.
Also direct to **Belur** (12 km, 1 hr) and from
there to Hassan.

Shimogaa *p973*
Rickshaw
Rickshaws should charge Rs 10 around the
town centre.

Jog Falls *p973*
Bus
To/from **Karwar** daily, arriving evening, and
leaving Jog in the morning. Other
destinations include **Sagar**, **Shimoga** for
Belur or Hassan (4 hrs), **Slrsi** (2 hrs). A new
road connects Honavar with Jog. **Goa**: (8 hrs)
bus to Colva at 1100 is very crowded, 2300 is
easier to get a seat on.

Taxi
To **Panaji**, Rs 1,500 (6 hrs).

Train
Jog is 16 km from the railway at **Talguppa**.
Trains from Bangalore involve a change in
Shimoga town.

⊕ Directory

Hassan *p971, map p971*
Banks State Bank of Mysore and State
Bank of India, Narasimharaja Circle, change
US$, £ cash and TCs. **Hospital** General
Hospital, Hospital Rd, **Mission Hospital**, Race
Course Rd. **Internet** next to Suvarna and
Vaishnavi hotels. **Photo shop** Next door
to *Bank of Mysore*. **Post office** 100 m from
bus stand. **Tourist office** India, Vartha
Bhavan, BM Rd, T68862. Very helpful.

✿ Phone codes *Sravanabelagola: 08176; Hassan: 08172; Belur: 08177; Halebid: 08177*

The Central Maidan → *Colour map 7, grid A3.*

The NH4 runs from Bangalore to Hubli-Dharwad, Pune and Mumbai across the high open country east of the crest line of the Western Ghats, following one of the main routes for trade and military movement over centuries. ►► *For Sleeping, Eating and other listings, see pages 976-977.*

Chitradurga → *202 km northwest of Bangalore.*

Chitradurga is at the foot of a group of granite hills, rising to 1,175 m in the south. The **Fort of Seven Rounds** ① *closed public holidays, open sunrise to sunset, Indians Rs 5, foreigners Rs 100, allow 2 hrs, the fort is 2 km from bus stand, 4 km from railway station*, was built in the 17th century by Nayak Poligars, semi-independent landlords who fled south after the collapse of the Vijayanagar Empire in 1565. They were crushed by **Haidar Ali** in 1779 who replaced the Nayaka's mud fort with stone and **Tipu Sultan** built a palace, mosque, granaries and oilpits in it. There are four secret entrances in addition to the 19 gateways, and ingenious water tanks which collected rainwater. There are also 14 temples, including a cave temple to the west of the wall. They are placed in an extraordinary jumble of outcropping granite rocks, a similar setting to that of Hampi 300 km to the north. The Hidimbeshwara temple is the oldest temple on the site.

Belgaum → *Phone code: 0831. Colour map 5, grid C4. Population: 399,600.*

An important border town, Belgaum makes an interesting stop on the Mumbai-Bangalore road or as a trip from Goa. Easily accessible, the crowded market in the centre of town gives a glimpse of India untouched by tourism. With its strategic position in the Deccan plateau, the town had been ruled by many dynasties including the Chalukyas, Rattas, Vijaynagaras, Bahmanis and the Marathas. Most of the monuments date from the early 13th century.

The **fort**, immediately east of the town centre, currently being renovated, though pre-Muslim was rebuilt by Yusuf Adil Shah, the Sultan of Bijapur, in 1481. Inside the **Masjid-i-Sata** (1519), the best of the numerous mosques in Belgaum was built by a captain in the Bijapur army, Azad Khan. Belgaum is also noted for its Jain architecture and sculpture. The late Chalukyan **Kamala Basti** with typical beautifully lathe-turned pillars and a black stone Neminatha sculpture, stands within the fort walls. To the south of the fort and about 800 m north of the *Hotel Sanman* on the Mumbai-Bangalore by-pass, is a beautifully sculpted Jain temple, which according to an inscription, was built by Malikaryuna. Along the entrance wall are well carved sculptures of musicians.

Listings: The Central Maidan

⊜ Sleeping

Chitradurga *p976*
C-D Amogha International, Santhe Honda Rd, T08194-20762, F20760, is the best in town. Clean, spacious, modern rooms, some a/c suites, 2 restaurants, good vegetarian but service slow.
F Maurya, Santhe Bagilu (within city walls), T08194-24448. 12 acceptable rooms ("heaviest padlock and keyplate in India!"), bit noisy.

● *For an explanation of the sleeping and eating price codes used in this guide, see inside the front cover. Other relevant information is found in Essentials pages 52-57.*

Belgaum *p976*

C-D Adarsha Palace, College Rd, T435777, F431022. Small modern and 'personal', some a/c rooms, excellent *Angaan* veg restaurant (non-veg on rooftop), pleasant atomosphere, friendly staff, good value. Recommended.

C-D Sanman Deluxe, College St, T430777, F430790. Similar to *Adarsha Palace,* in a new building (much cheaper in old *Sanman*), 2 restaurants.

D Milan, Club Rd (4 km railway), T470555. 45 rooms with bath (hot shower), some a/c, vegetarian restaurant, good value.

D-E Keerthi, Poona-Bangalore Rd, short walk from Central Bus Stand, T46699, F423297. Large modern hotel, some a/c rooms, restaurant.

E-F Sheetal, Khade Bazar near bus station, T470222. Cleanish rooms with bath (prices vary), vegetarian restaurant, Indian style, noisy hotel in busy and quite entertaining bazar street.

F Mayura Malaprabha (KSTDC), Ashok Nagar, HUDCO Complex near lake, T470781. 6 simple clean rooms in modern cottages, dorm (Rs 40), restaurant, bar, Tourist Office.

☉ Transport

Chitradurga *p976*

Bus

To/from **Bangalore, Davangere, Hospet, Hubli** and **Mysore**.

Train

From **Arsikere, Bangalore, Guntakal, Hubli**.

Belgaum *p976*

Air

The airport is 10 km from the centre (no flights at present).

Bus

Central Bus Stand for long distance services. **Panaji** (0600-1715), **Margao** (0545-1500), **Mapusa** (0715-1715) take 5 hrs, Rs 45.

Train

The station is near the bus stand, 4 km south of the centre; autos available. **Bangalore**: *Ranichennamma Exp, 6590*, 1810, 13 hrs. **Mumbai (CST)** and **Pune**: change at Pune for Mumbai *Chalukya/Sharavathi Exp, 1018/1036*, Mon, Tue, Fri, Sat, 1805, 14 hrs. **Goa** via Londa 8 trains daily, 0135-2030, 1 hr.

(right margin, vertical) Karnataka Mysore & the southern Maidan

Mysore and the southern Maidan

→ *Phone code: 0821. Colour map 7, grid B3. Population: 742,300.*

The city of royal palaces, sandalwood and the manufacture of incense sticks, Mysore has a pleasant climate, some beautiful parks and wide, shady avenues, and though more relaxed in comparison with its dynamic neighbour Bangalore, it is lively. The former capital of the princely state, it is Karnataka's second largest city which some visitors find too noisy and busy to be pleasant. ➤➤ *For Sleeping, Eating and other listings, see pages 987-993.*

Ins and outs

Getting there The railway station is about 1 km to the northwest of the town centre while the 3 bus stands are all central within easy reach of hotels.

Getting around Mysore is comfortably compact for walking though there are plenty of autos and buses. See Transport, page 980, for further details.

Climate Summer maximum 28°C; winter maximum 22°C. Rainfall; 74 cm Best season to visit is Oct (*Dusara Festival*) to Mar, but much more pleasant than on the lower plains throughout the year.

ⓘ *Enter by south gate, 1030-1730, Rs 15, cameras must be left in lockers (free), you take the key, shoes left, allow about 1 hr, 2 if you wish to see everything (worth taking a guide), guidebook, Rs 10. Often very crowded, especially at weekends which can be overwhelming, visitors are channelled through rooms at the general pace, go early. Downstairs is fairly accessible to the disabled. On Sun nights, government holidays and during festivals, the palace is lit by 50,000 light bulbs; well worth seeing after 1900.*

The City Palace (Amber Vilas), was designed by Henry Irwin and built in 1897 after a fire which burnt down the old wooden palace. It is in the *Indo-Saracenic* style in grand proportions, with domes, arches and colonnades of carved pillars and shiny marble floors. One of the largest palaces in the country with some art treasures, it is beautifully restored and maintained. The stained glass, wall paintings, ivory inlaid doors and the ornate golden throne (now displayed during *Dasara*) are all remarkable. The fabulous collection of jewels, 'amazing in its extravagance', is only rarely on display.

Ground Floor Visitors are led through the 'Car Passage' with cannons and carriages to the *Gombe thotti* (Dolls' pavilion). This originally displayed dolls during *dasara* and today houses, in addition, a model of the old palace, European marble statues and the golden *howdah* (the battery-operated red and green bulbs on top of the canopy as 'Stop' and 'Go' signals to the *mahout*!). The last is still used during *dasara* but goddess Chamundeshwari rides on the elephant. The octagonal *Kalyana Mandap* (marriage hall), or Peacock Pavilion, south of the courtyard, has a

Mysore

Sleeping
1 Quality Inn Southern Star
2 Ramanashree Comfort, Amaravathi Restaurant, KSE & Seagull Travels
3 Siddharta
4 Sudarshan Lodge

Transport
1 Central Bus Stand (KSRTC)
2 City Bus Stand (incl Srirangapatnam)
3 Suburban & Private Bus Stand (incl Somnathpur)

Related map
A Mysore centre, page 980

● Medieval pageantry at Mysore

Dasara is celebrated with medieval pageantry for 10 days. Although the Dasara festival can be traced back to the Puranas and is widely observed across India, in the South it achieved its special prominence under the Vijayanagar kings. As the Mahanavami festival it has been celebrated every year since it was sponsored by Raja Wodeyar in September 1610 at Srirangapatnam. It symbolizes the victory of goddess Chamundeswari (Durga) over the demon Mahishasura. Today the festival is still enormously colourful. On the last day a colourfully bedecked elephant with a golden howdah carrying the statue of the goddess, processes from the palace through the city to Banni Mantap, about 5 km away, where the Banni tree is worshipped. The temple float festival takes place at a tank at the foot of Chamundi Hill and a car festival on top. In the evening there is a torchlight parade by the mounted guards who provide an exciting display of horse- manship and the night ends with a display of fireworks. A good time for cultural programmes particularly at the Palace Durbar Hall and Exhibition Grounds which along with other public buildings, are ablaze with illuminations.

beautiful stained glass ceiling and excellent paintings of scenes from the *dasara* and other festivities on 26 canvas panels. Note the exquisite details, especially of No 19. The Portrait Gallery and the Period Furniture Room lead off this pavilion.

1st Floor A marble staircase leads to the magnificent *Durbar Hall* (47 m x 13 m), a grand colonnaded hall with lavishly framed paintings by famous Indian artists. The asbestos-lined ceiling has paintings of Vishnu incarnations. A passage takes you past the beautifully inlaid wood-and-ivory door of the Ganesh Temple, to the *Amba* (Amber) *Vilas* for private audience (*Diwan-i-Khas*). This exquisitely decorated hall has three doors. The central silver door depicts Vishnu's 10 incarnations and the eight *dikpalas* (directional guardians), with Krishna figures on the reverse (see the tiny Krishna on a leaf, kissing his toes!), all done in *repoussé* on teak and rosewood. The stained glass (possibly Belgian, in Art Nouveau style), cast iron pillars from Glasgow, carved wood ceiling, chandeliers, etched glass windows, the *pietra dura* on the floors and the elegant colour scheme all add to its grandeur.

The jewel encrusted **Golden Throne** with its ornate steps, which some like to attribute to ancient Vedic times, was originally made of figwood decorated with ivory before it was embellished with gold, silver and jewels. Others trace its history to 1336 when the Vijaynagar kings 'found' it and they say, passed it on to the Wodeyars who continue to use it during *dasara*.

Other sights and musems

Maharaja's Residence ① *1000-1830, Rs 15.* Now a museum, the ground floor, with an enclosed courtyard, displays costumes, musical instruments, children's toys and numerous portraits. The upper floor has a small collection of weapons. Some find it disappointing.

Chamundi Hill ① *Vehicle toll Rs 10, City Bus No 185.* The hill immediately to the southeast of the town has a temple to Durga (Chamundeswari) celebrating her victory over the buffalo god. She became the guardian deity of the Wodeyars. Beautiful views on a clear day, otherwise there is little to see but a pleasant trip all the same. The giant *Nandi*, carved in 1659, is on the motorable road down so it is possible to walk to it along the trail from the top and be picked up by a car later or catch a return bus from the road. If you continue along the trail you will end up having to get a rickshaw back.

The Government **Sandalwood Oil Factory** ⓘ *T483651, Mon-Sat, 0800-1700, no photography inside, shop sells soap, incense sticks etc*, is where oil is extracted and incense made. **Silk Factory** ⓘ *Manathavadi Rd, T481803, Mon-Sat, 0930-1630, no photography, shop sells saris from Rs 3,000*, has weavers producing Mysore silk saris, often with gold *zari* work. Staff will often show you the process from thread winding to jacquard weaving, but speak little English. Good **walks** are possible in the Government House if the guard at the gate allows you in.

Chamarajendra Art Gallery ⓘ *0800-1700, Rs 5, no photography*, at Jaganmohan Palace (1861). Indian Miniature paintings and others, including Ravi Varma and Nicholas Roerich. Also exhibition of ceramics, stone, ivory, sandalwood, antique furniture and old musical instruments. No descriptions or guide book; many items randomly displayed ("an overgrown bric-a-brac collection") but pleasant atmosphere. **Folklore Museum** ⓘ *University of Mysore, Manasa Gangotri, closed 2nd Sat and Sun, 1030-1730, free*, has a collection including weapons, jewellery, folk toys, utensils. Photography with permission of Director. **Medical College Museum** ⓘ *0830-1730, Sun 0800-1300, free*, has botanical paintings, charts, models, weapons.

Excursion

Sri Mahalingeshwara Temple ⓘ *12 km away, is 1 km off the Bhogadi road (right turn after K Hemmanahalli, beyond Mysore University Campus), taxi or auto-rickshaw.*The 800-year old Hoysala Temple has been carefully restored by local villagers under the supervision of the Archaeological Survey of India. The structure is an authentic replica of the old temple – here, too, the low ceiling encourages humility by forcing the worshipper to bow before the shrine. The surrounding garden has been planted with

Mysore centre

Sleeping
1 Anugraha
2 Bombay Tiffanys
3 Dasaprakash & Veg Restaurant
4 Maurya Palace, Mayura Residency & Govardhan
5 Mayura Hoysala, Yatri Nivas & KSTDC Travels
6 Park Lane
7 Sangeeth
8 Viceroy & Palace Plaza

Eating
1 Bombay Tiffanys
2 Mysore Memories & Raintree (at King's Court)
3 Penguin Ice Creams
4 Raghu Niwas
5 Ritz
6 RRR
7 Shilpashri
8 Sri Rama & Ashok Books
9 SR Plantain Leaf

N

0 metres   200
0 yards   200

66 99 Darin Daulat Bagh is "an absolute jewel" with colourful frescoes of battle scenes between the French, British and Mysore armies, ornamental arches and gilded paintings on the teak walls and ceilings which are full of interesting detail.

herbs and saplings, including some rare medicinal trees, and provides a tranquil spot away from the city.

★ Srirangapatnam

→ *Phone code: 08236. Colour map 7, grid B3. Population: 21,900*

Srirangapatnam has played a crucial role in the region since its origins in the 10th century. Occupying an easily fortified island site in the Kaveri River, it has been home to religious reformers and military conquerors, and makes a fascinating day trip from Mysore, 12 km away. The island is over 3 km long and 1 km wide so it is best to hire a cycle from a shop on the main road to get around.

History

The name comes from the temple of Vishnu Sri Ranganathasvami, which is far older than the fort or the town. The site was a focal point in South India's political development. The fort was built under the Vijayanagar kings in 1454. 150 years later the last Vijayanagar king handed over authority to the Hindu Wodeyars of Mysore, who made it their capital. In the second half of the 18th century it became the capital of **Haidar Ali**, who defended it against the Marathas in 1759, laying the foundations of his expanding power. He was succeeded by his son **Tipu Sultan**, who also used the town as his headquarters.

Colonel Wellesley, the future **Duke of Wellington**, established his military reputation in the battle in which Tipu Sultan was finally killed on 4 May 1799, see page 1308 though victory should be more correctly attributed to his brother, the Governor General. Tipu died in exceptionally fierce fighting near the north gate of the fort; the place is marked by a very simple monument. Wellesley was immediately appointed Governor of Srirangapatnam, the start of a further five years of campaigning in India.

Sights

The fort had triple fortifications, but the British destroyed most of it. The **Jama Masjid** ① *0800-1300, 1600-2000*, built by Tipu Sultan, has minarets, and there are two Hindu **temples**, Narasimha (17th century) and Gangadharesvara (16th century). Daria Daulat Bagh and the Gumbaz are wonderful. The same cannot be said of the rickshaw drivers.

Daria Daulat Bagh (Splendour of the Sea), 1 km to the east of the fort, is Tipu's beautiful **summer palace** ① *closed Fri, 0900-1700, US$2 foreigners, Rs 2*, built in 1784, in its lovely garden. It is "an absolute jewel" with colourful frescoes of battle scenes between the French, British and Mysore armies, ornamental arches and gilded paintings on the teak walls and ceilings which are full of interesting detail. The west wall shows Haidar Ali and Tipu Sultan leading their elephant forces at the battle of Polilur (1780), inflicting a massive defeat on the British. As a result of the battle Colonel Baillie, the defeated British commander, was a prisoner in Srirangapatnam for many years. The murals on the east walls show Tipu offering hospitality to neighbouring princes at various palace durbars. The small museum upstairs has 19th-century European paintings and Tipu's belongings. Excellently maintained by the Archaeological Survey of India though the green sun screens make it look unpromising.

The Gumbaz ① *Closed Fri, 0900-1700, donation collected.* The family mausoleum (3 km), was built by Tipu in remembrance of his father. Approached through an avenue of cypresses, the ornate white domed Gumbaz contains beautiful ivory-on-wood inlay and Tipu's tiger stripe emblem. Some of his swords and shields are kept here. The tranquil atmosphere is a perfect setting for the elegant and quiet mausoleum which houses the tomb of Haider Ali in the centre, that of his wife on the east and of Tipu Sultan on the west.

On the banks of the Cauvery, just north of the Lalbagh Palace (Rs 2), is a jetty where six seater coracles are available for river rides. Great fun!

Ranganathittoo Bird Sanctuary

① *0600-0900, 1600-1800, Rs 15, Rs 150 for foreigners, still camera Rs 10. Boats (0830-1330, 1430-1830), Rs 10 each, minimum charge Rs 150. Kiosk sells snacks and postcards. Best season: Jun-Oct. Mysore City Bus 126, or auto from Srirangapatnam.*

Some 5 km upstream of Srirangapatnam is the riverine site of the Ranganathittoo Bird Sanctuary, established in 1975. Several rocky islands, some bare while the larger are well wooded, provide excellent habitat for waterbirds, including Black crowned night heron, Eurasian Spoonbill and cormorants. Fourteen species of waterbirds use the

Srirangapatnam

To Bangalore (120 km)

Delhi Bridge Ruins
Bathing Ghat
Water Gate
Wellesley Bridge
Dungeons
Ranganathasvami Temple
Gangadharesvara
Narasimha Temple
Dungeons
De Havilland's Arch
Jama Masjid
FORT
Bangalore Gate
Elephant Gate
Flagstaff
Kaveri River
Piriyapatna Bridge
Mysore Gate
Daria Daulat Bagh & Museum
Entrance
Garrison Cemetery
Catholic Cemetery
Abbé Dubois
Scott's Bungalow Tomb
Obelisk
SRIRANGAPATNAM ISLAND
To Mysore (11 km)
Abba Garden
Kaveri River
To Madikeri & Ranganathittoo Bird Sanctuary
To Mysore (11 km)

N

0 metres 500
0 yards 500

■ **Sleeping**
1 Amblee Palace
2 Balaji Garden Resort
3 Fort View
4 Mayura River View & PWD Rest House

● **Eating**
1 Sai Baba

sanctuary as a breeding ground, most of which begin to breed in June. There is a large colony of fruit bats in trees on the edge of the river and a number of marsh crocodiles between the small islands.It is a popular tourist site, receiving hundreds of visitors every day. It is possible to go round some of the islands on the river by boat, but not to land. Boat and guide can be hired from the jetty for 15-20 minute rides.

★ Somnathpur → *Phone code: 08227.*

This tiny village, east of Mysore, has one of the best preserved and the only complete one of approximately 80 Hoysala temples in the Mysore region. The drive from Srirangapatnam via Bannur is particularly lovely, passing a couple of lakes through beautiful country and pretty, clean villages.

The small but exquisite **Kesava Temple** (1268) ① *0900-1700, US$2 (foreigners), allow at least 1 hr, KSTDC Canteen in the garden, buses from Mysore take 1-1½ hrs; via Bannur (25 km, 45 mins) then to Somnathpur (3 km, 15 min by bus or a lovely walk or bike ride through attractive countryside)*, in its gardens, is maintained by the Archaeological Department. Excellent ceilings show the distinctive features of the late Hoysala style, and here the roof is intact where other famous temples have lost theirs. The temple has three sanctuaries with the *trikutachala* (triple roof) and stands in the middle of its rectangular courtyard (70 m long, 55 m wide) with cloisters containing 64 cells around it. From the east gateway there is a superb view of the temple with an ambulatory standing on its raised platform, in the form of a 16-pointed star. The pillared hall in the centre with the three shrines to the west give it the form of a cross in plan. Walk around the temple to see the bands of sculptured figures which are particularly fine. The lowest of the six shows a line of elephants, symbolizing strength and stability, then horsemen for speed, followed by a floral scroll. The next band of beautifully carved figures (at eye level) is the most fascinating and tells stories from the epics. Above is the *yali* frieze, the monsters and foliage possibly depicting the river Ganga and uppermost is a line of *hamsa*, the legendary goose.

★ Sivasamudram

→ *Best in July and August.*

Here, the Kaveri plunges over 100 m into a series of wild and inaccessible gorges. At the top of the falls the river divides around the island of Sivasamudram, the Barachukki channel on the east and the Gaganchukki on the west. The **hydro-electricity project** was completed in 1902, the first HEP scheme of any size in India. During the wet season the falls are an impressive sight, water cascading over a wide area in a series of leaps. Guest houses may be reserved through Executive Engineer, KEB and the PWD at Bluff, Malavalli Taluk, Mandya District.

Biligiri Rangaswamy

→ *Altitude: 1,000-1,600 m.*
① *From Mysore, via Nanjangud (23 km) and Chamrajnagar, Nagavalli and*

Nellore villages. The Ghat Rd starts at the Forest Check Post after passing 2 lakes. The camp (90 km from Mysore) is beyond the second check post.

This BR Hills wildlife sanctuary in a hilly area with moist deciduous and semi-evergreen forests interspersed with grassland, is southeast of Mysore. The best time for wildlife sighting is November to May. The Soliga tribals pay special respect to an ancient champak tree (*Dodda sampige mara*) believed to be 1,000 years old. The **wildlife** includes panther, sloth bear (better sightings here than at other southern sanctuaries), elephant, various deer, gaur and tiger (infrequent) as well as 270 species of birds.

Bandipur National Park

→ *Colour map 7, grid B3. Altitude: 780-1,455 m. Area: 874 sq km.*
ⓘ *0600-0900, 1600-1800, Rs 15, Rs 150 for foreigners, still camera Rs 10, best time: Nov-Feb avoiding the hot, dry months, temperature range: 30°C- 18°C, rainfall: 1,000 mm, buses stop at the main entrance.*

Bandipur was set up by the Mysore Maharajah in 1931. It has a mixture of subtropical moist and dry deciduous forests (predominantly teak and Anogeissus) and scrubland in the Nilgiri foothills. The wetter areas support rosewood, sandalwood, silk cotton and *jamun*. You should easily spot *gaur*, *chital* (spotted deer), elephant, sambar, flying squirrel and four-horned antelope, but tigers and leopards are rare. Also good variety of birdlife including crested hawk, serpent eagles and tiny-eared owl.

Private cars are not allowed. Jeeps and vans are available through Forestry Department; one hour coach rides (morning and afternoon, 0630-1630), Rs 10 each but other noisy visitors scare away wildlife. Viewing is best from *machans* (raised platforms) near watering places; ask to reserve ahead. Dull coloured clothes are recommended. No extended elephant rides in the park now; only 30-minute 'joy rides' at 0930.

Coorg (Kodagu) and Nagarhole

Coorg is one of the few areas in South India to have retained its original forests. The climate is not as cool as other 'hill-stations' but is still a pleasant change from the plains. With the introduction of three new states in India in 2000, local desire for statehood has been reawakened.The capital of Coorg District, Madikeri, is an attractive small town in a beautiful hilly setting surrounded by the forested slopes of the Western Ghats. It promises to become an attractive trekking destination.

Ins and outs

Getting there Coorg is only accessible by road at present although an airport and railway station are planned. Frequent local and express buses arrive at Madikeri's bus stand from the west coast after a journey through beautiful wooded hills passing small towns and a wildlife sanctuary. From Mysore and Coimbatore an equally pleasant route traverses the Maidan. In winter there is often hill fog at night, making after dark driving dangerous.

Getting around Madikeri is ideal for walking though you may need to hire an auto on arrival to reach the better hotels. See Transport, page 993, for further details.

Climate Maximum (May) 29°C, Minimum (Jan) 9°C. Annual rainfall: 3,250 mm.

Madikeri (Mercara)

→ *Phone code: 08272. Colour map 7, grid B2. Population: 32,300. Altitude: 1,150 m. www.madikeri.com.*
History Although there were references to the Kodaga people in the Tamil Sangam literature of the second century AD, the earliest Kodaga inscriptions date from the

many of their courtiers moved south, establishing regional kingdoms. One of these groups were the Haleri Rajas, members of the Lingayat caste whose leader Virarajendra set up the first Kodaga dynasty at Haleri, 10 km from the present district capital of Madikeri. The later Kodagu Rajas were noted for some bizarre behaviour. Dodda Vira (1780-1809) was reputed to have put most of his relatives to death, a pattern followed by the last king, Vira Raja, before he was forced to abdicate by the British in 1834. In 1852 the last Lingayat ruler of Kodagu, Chikkavirarajendra Wodeyar, became the first Indian prince to sail to England, and the economic character of the State was quickly transformed. Coffee was introduced, becoming the staple crop of the region. The forests of Kodagu are still home to wild elephants and other wildlife, while the Kodaga people are very proud of the martial traditions and their hospitality. Kodagu also has a highly distinctive cuisine, in which pork curry *(pandi curry)* and rice dumplings *(kadumbuttu)* are particular favourites.

Sights The **Omkareshwara Temple**, dedicated to both Vishnu and Siva, was built in 1820. The tiled roofs are typical of Kerala Hindu architecture, while the domes show Muslim influence. The **fort** with its three stone gateways, built between 1812-14 by Lingarajendra Wodeyar II, is on high ground dominating the town. It has a small **museum** ① *closed Mon and holidays, 0900-1700*, in St Mark's Church as well as the town prison, a temple and a chapel while the palace houses government offices. The **'Rajas' Tombs'** (Gaddige), built in 1820 to the north of the town, are the memorials of Virarajendra and his wife and of Lingarajendra. Although the rajas were Hindu, their commemorative monuments are Muslim in style; Kodagas both bury and cremate their dead. The Friday **Market** near the bus stand, is very colourful as all the local tribal people come to town to sell their produce. It is known locally as 'shandy', a British bastardisation of the Coorg word *shante*, meaning simply market. On Mahadevped Road, which leads to the Rajas' tombs, is a 250-year-old **Siva temple** with an interesting stone façade. Madikeri has an attractive nine-hole **golf** course.

Madikeri

	Sleeping	5 Hilltown	● Eating
	1 Amrita	6 Mayura Valley View	1 Choice
	2 Cauvery	7 Popular Residency	2 Rajdarshan
	3 Chitra	8 Travellers' Bungalow	3 Taj
	4 East End	9 Vinayaka Lodge	4 Udupi Veglands

Not to scale

Trekking Madikeri and the surrounding area makes for beautiful walking but if you want to venture further you'll need to take a guide as paths can soon become indistinct and confusing. **Abbi Falls** is a 30-minute rickshaw ride (9 km, Rs 150 round trip) through forests and coffee plantations. It is also an enjoyable walk along a fairly quiet road. The falls themselves are beautiful and well worth the visit. You can do a beautiful short trek down the valley and then up and around above the falls before rejoining the main road. Do not attempt it alone since there are no trails and you must depend on your sense of direction along forest paths.

Bhagamandala ① *Getting there: half-hourly service from Madikeri's private bus stand from 0630-2000. Also* Rama Motors *tour bus departs 0830, with 30-min stop.* The Triveni bathing ghat is 36 km southwest at the confluence of the three rivers, Kaveri, Kanike and Suiyothi. Among many small shrines the Bhandeshwara temple, standing in a large stone courtyard surrounded by Keralan-style buildings on all four sides, is particularly striking. You can stay at the temple for a very small charge.

Kakkabe ① *Getting there: from Madikeri to Kakkabe, bus at 0630; jeep 1 hr.* This small town, 35 km from Madikeri, gives access to the highest peak in Coorg, Thandiandamole (1,800 m). Padi Iggutappa nearby is the most important temple in Coorg.

Nisargadhama ① *0900-1800, Rs 15, Rs 150 for foreigners, still camera Rs 10.* The small island reserve in the Kaveri River, 2 km from Kushalnagar, is accessed over a hanging bridge. It consists mostly of bamboo thickets and trees, including sandalwood, and is very good for seeing parakeets, bee eaters and woodpeckers and a variety of butterflies. There is a deer park, pedalo boating, a resident elephant and tall bamboo tree houses for wildlife viewing. The park is very peaceful and pleasant, completely untouched by tourism.

Dubare Forest The reserve forest, 15 km from Kushalnagar, is notable for its wide variety of birdlife. There is a *Forest Rest House*, an elephant training camp and the possibility of fishing on the Cauvery. Contact Forestry Office in Madikeri, T25708.

Nagarhole (Rajiv Gandhi) National Park → *Colour map 7, grid B2.*

Nagarhole – meaning snake, streams– was once the Maharajas' reserved forest and became a national park in 1955. Covering gentle hills bordering Kerala, it includes swampland, streams, moist deciduous forest, stands of bamboo and valuable timber in teak and rosewood trees. The Kabini River, which is a tributary of the Kaveri, flows through the deciduous forest where the upper canopy reaches 30 m. The park is accessible both by road and river. A number of tribesmen, particularly Kurumbas (honey-gatherers) who still practise ancient skills, live amongst and care for the elephants.

Ins and outs Main entrance is near Hunsur on the northern side of the Park. Buses run between Hunsur and Kote-Hand Post (35 km). Indians Rs 15, foreigners Rs 150, camera Rs 10. The southern entrance is 5 km from Kabini River Lodge at Karapur. See Transport, page 987, for further details.

Wildlife In addition to elephants, the park also has *gaur* (Indian bison), *dhole* (Indian wild dogs), wild cats, four-horned antelopes, flying squirrels, sloth bears, monkeys and *sambar* deer- "better sightings than at Mudumalai". Tigers and leopards are sighted infrequently. Many varieties of birds include the rare Malabar *trogon*, great black woodpecker, Indian pitta, pied hornbill, whistling thrush and Green Imperial pigeon. Also waterfowl and reptiles. Savanna fires are common in the grassland areas of the Western Ghats, sometimes caused deliberately to improve grazing, sometimes accidental or natural.

Viewing The edge of the dam between March to June during the dry period, makes viewing easier. Jeeps, vans and guides through the Forest Department. One hour tour at 1715. Viewing from *machans* near waterholes. Trekking is possible with permission (enquire at Hunsur office, T08222-52041 well in advance). You can also visit the Government's Elephant Training Camp at Haballa. Organized one hour tours are available on 15 and 26 seater coaches – not very suitable for the purpose. Four-seater jeeps are far quieter.

Listings: Mysore and the southern Maidan

● Sleeping

Mysore *p977, maps p978 and p980*
JLB Rd is Jhansi Lakshmi Bai Rd,
B-N Rd is Bangalore- Nilgiri Rd

May is the most important wedding month and so hotels get booked in advance. In the expensive hotels sales tax on food, luxury tax on rooms and a service charge can increase the bill significantly.

AL-A Southern Star (Quality Inn), 13-14 Vinoba Rd, T426426, F421689, sstar@sancharnet.in. 72 luxurious rooms, great pool (non-residents Rs 150), helpful, friendly, top quality hotel. Recommended.

AL-B Lalitha Mahal Palace (ITDC), Narasipur Rd, T571265, F571770. 54 rooms (**A** rooms in turret disappointing), suites (US$230-740), built in 1931 for the Maharaja's non-vegetarian, foreign guests, grand setting, old-fashioned (some original baths with extraordinary spraying system), for nostalgia stay in the old wing, attractive pool, but disappointing restaurant.

B Indus Valley, near Lalitha Mahal, T473437, F473590 anita@bgl.vsnl.net.in. Splendidly located health resort, half-way up a hill, 22 rooms (in main building or in cottage), hot showers and western toilets, TV in lounge, ayurvedic massages and treatments, pleasant walks, veg restaurant (ayurvedic recipes!), herbal wines, friendly staff, family run by Dr Krishna and his wife; interesting experience.

B Kaynes Hotel, off Hunsur Rd, T402931. 22 rooms with bath, reasonable restaurant, pool, tennis, gym.

B Ramanashree Comfort (Best Western), L-43A Hardinge Circle, T522202, F565781, ramanmys@sancharnet.in. 68 a/c rooms, 2 good restaurants, spotlessly clean, spacious, airy and light, excellent, but no pool.

B-C Dasaprakash Paradise, 105 Vivekananda Rd, Yadavgiri, T515655, 2 km north of rly station. 90 rooms, 36 a/c with bath, very good restaurant (vegetarian), very clean, comfortable and quiet. Recommended.

B-C Green Hotel (Chittaranjan Palace), 2270 Vinoba Rd (near Mysore University) on a bus route, T512536, F516139, grenhotl@giasbg01.vsnl.net.in. 31 rooms, best are in the palace (unique sympathetic conversion), more comfortable than 24 in newer block (including 12 simple ground floor rooms), good meals (notify ahead) in cool verandah or on immaculate lawns but noisy road traffic, nice garden, solar heating, profits to charity, exemplary employment practices hence charming, enthusiastic staff. Recommended though away from centre.

B-C Metropole, 5 JLB Rd. Closed indefinitely.

B-C Viceroy, Sri Harsha Rd, T424001, F433391. 30 comfortable rooms with phone, some a/c (best have tubs), very clean and well appointed, good a/c restaurant, exchange, travel, but over-priced and bookings not always honoured.

The Gandhi Square area has some Indian style hotels which are clean and good value.

C-D Ganesh Palace Inn, L17 Chandragupta Rd (near CBS), T428985. Clean, spacious rooms, some a/c, friendly.

C-D Maurya Palace, Sri Harsha Rd, T435912, F429304. 27 rooms (6 a/c), very clean, well

Karnataka Listings: Mysore & the southern Maidan

furnished but no views, good value. **C** a/c rooms with bath tubs, hot water, some Indian toilets, back much quieter, very clean, modern, good **Dynasty** restaurant, friendly, good value, reserve ahead.

C-D Mayura Hoysala (KSTDC), 2 JLB Rd, T425349. 20 rooms in lovely Raj-style hotel, chintz throughout and spotless, 3 restaurants, bar, tourist desk.

C-D Siddharta, 73/1 Guest House Rd, Nazarabad, T522888, F520692. 105 rooms, some a/c, huge with tubs, good restaurant (Indian vegetarian), exchange, immaculate.

D Vyshak International, 19 Seebaiah Rd, T421777. New business hotel near the centre, good value, friendly.

D-E Bombay Tiffany's, 313 Sayaji Rao Rd, T435255, F433105, bombaytiffanys@ yahoo.co.in. 54 rooms, 12 a/c in new hotel, clean and in excellent condition. Regular rooms a little bare, but Delux and a/c very good value. Small courtyard dining-area.

D-E Dasaprakash, Gandhi Sq, T443456. 144 rooms, some with shower and western wc, few a/c, no frills but clean, fresh, well maintained, attractive courtyard, quite quiet, rather dark vegetarian restaurant, good service, attractive courtyard. Recommended.

D-E Govardhan, Sri Harsha Rd, T431960. 60 simple but clean lodge-style rooms, some with TV, excellent vegetarian restaurant, great value.

E MTR Yatrinivas, 2747 Chandragupta Rd. 21 nicely furnished, medium sized rooms with TV, in briand new hotel in busy bazar area.

E Rajmahal Deluxe, Jaganmohan Palace Sq. T421196. 26 light and airy rooms with bath, some with balcony, welcoming and helpful.

E Ritz, B-N Rd near Central Bus Station, T422668. Very dark rooms but pleasant open shaded courtyard, good restaurant, efficient service.

E Sudarshan Lodge, opposite Jaganmohan Palace, T426718. 44 clean rooms and dorm, quiet, friendly.

F Anugraha, Jus Complex, SR Rd (by S Patel Rd), T430768. Good sized standard, clean rooms, hot water 0600-1000, back rooms quieter, friendly and helpful. There are several cheap lodges north of the Central Bus Stand.

F Park Lane, 2720, Sri Harsha Rd, T430400. 8 basic, small, interesting rooms, bar, nicely shaded restaurant. Noisy music.

Srirangapatnam *p981, map p982*

B-C New Amblee Holiday Resort, on the Kaveri, T52326, F52358, ambleeresorts@ eth.net. 28 rather deteriorating rooms, billiards, overpriced.

C Fort View Resort, T52777, F53177. 12 upmarket rooms (4 with corner tub!), Rajasthani architecture, huge beds, shady landscaped gardens, gloomy restaurant (pricey), organic kitchen garden, pool, boating, fishing, efficient.

D Mayura River View, T52114. Beautifully situated on the river (has crocs!), 8 comfortable rooms with sit-outs, 2 a/c, good vegetarian restaurant (Indian, Chinese), most relaxing, really quiet. Next door,

D-E Balaji Garden Resort, Mysore Rd (1 km from Piriyapatna Bridge), T53297. 12 good value cottages (suites) and 28 smallish rooms built around a central courtyard, well furnished, tiled and comfortable, cottages are good value, pool, restaurant.

F PWD Rest House, charming former residence of George Harris, lovley, basic rooms (Rs 50), but clean and quiet. Book ahead at PWD office near Ranganathaswami Temple, T52051.

Bheemeshwari and Doddamakali

B Cauvery Fishing Camps are hidden amid steep hills on the banks of the Kaveri, south of Halagur. It is a peaceful place where mahseer attract anglers. Accommodation is in tents or huts with attached bath. Separate rates for anglers. Contact *Jungle Lodges*, T080-5597025, F5586163, www.junglelodges.com.

Biligiri Rangaswamy *p983*

B K Gudi Camp, Kyathadevara. 8 twin-bedded quality tents with modern toilets, simple meals in the open air or 4 4-bedded rooms at the royal hunting lodge, elephant ride, birding, trekking, comfortable experience despite remoteness, contact *Jungle Lodges and Resorts*, T5597025, F5586163.

Phone codes Belgaum: 0831; Mysore: 0821; Srirangapatnam: 08236; Samnathpur: 08227; Madikeri: 08272.

Karnataka Listings: Mysore & the southern Maidan

Bandipur National Park p984

It is important to reserve rooms well in advance; avoid weekends.

AL Bush Betta Wildlife Resort, 5 km from entrance. 2 dirty jungle huts, lack staff, highly overpriced (foreigners pay double, US$200).

B-C Tusker Trails, Mangla Village, 3 km from Bandipur campus. 6 rustic cottages with verandahs around pool with good views, bamboo hut on stilts, nearby 'dam' attracts wildlfe, includes meals, entry and park rides. Foreigners pay double.

D Jungle Trails, outside the park, a small guesthouse owned by wildlife enthusiast, simple meals, wildlife viewing from netted porch and *machans* on riverside.

E Mayura Prakruti (KSTDC), at Melkamanahalli nearby, T08229-33001. Simple rooms in cottages (Rs 400) and restaurant under shady trees.

F Forest Lodges, Guest Houses with attached baths, and 3 **Wooden Cottages** for 12 in Kakanhalla, Mulehole and Kalkere. A couple of **VIP lodges** - Rajendra I and II, and **Swiss Cottage tents**. Cooks prepare food to order (cooking in rooms prohibited).

F Venuvihar Lodge, in beautiful Gopalaswamy Hills (20 km) Meals available but take provisions. Book in advance through Forest Department, Woodyard, Mysore, T480110.

Madikeri p984, map p985

Power cuts are common. Carry a torch and keep candles handy. Finding hotels during holidays can be problematic.

B Coorg International, Convent Rd, T28071, F28073. 27 large and comfortable rooms, restaurant (poor), pool, tours and trekking, overpriced.

C Capitol Village, 5 km from town. 13 large, airy rooms, dorm (Rs 150), traditional Keralan building (tiled roof, wooden beams) set in a coffee, cardamom and pepper estate, very quiet, outdoor eating under shady trees (Rs 75-150), rickshaw from town centre Rs 40. Book 10 days in advance through *Hotel Cauvery*, Madikeri.

C-D Rajdarshan,116/2 MG Rd, T29142, F28367, hrdij@vsnl.net. 25 well laid-out, clean rooms (need renovating), excellent restaurant, friendly staff, modern, with views over town.

D-E Cauvery, School Rd, T25492. 26 clean, pleasant but basic rooms with fans, Indian

meals, bar, away from main road. Helpful management, info on trekking.

D-E Hilltown, Daswal Rd, T23801, hilltown@rediffmail.com. 38 modern, pleasant and airy rooms with TV in new hotel, marble-floored throughout, restaurant. Great value, highly recommended.

D-E Popular Residency, Kohinoor Rd. 10 clean and pleasant rooms in new hotel, well fitted-out, north Indian veg restaurant, good value.

E Amrita, T23607. Resembling something out of a Spanish soap opera, clean rooms with bath, restaurant, eager to please staff.

E Chitra, School Rd, T25372, F25191, near bus stand. 31 non-descript rooms with western toilets, hot shower, simple but clean, north Indian veg restaurant, bar, helpful and knowledgeable English speaking trekking guide (Mr Muktar).

E East End, Gen Thimaya Rd, T29996. Darkish rooms but good restaurant (excellent dosas).

E Mayura Valley View (KSTDC), Raja's Seat, T28387. Perched on clifftop, outstanding views over town and across rolling forests, 25 rooms but sadly very run down and semi-deserted, book direct or at Karnataka Tourism, Bangalore, 12212901.

E-F Vinayaka Lodge, 25 m from bus stand, T29830. 50 rooms with bath, hot water buckets, friendly staff, clean and quiet (bus stand noisy early morning), good value.

Kakkabe p986

D-E Palace Estate, 2 km south of Kakkabe along Palace Road (rickshaw from Kakkabe Rs 35), a small, traditional farm growing coffee, pepper, cardamom and bananas. Situated close to the late 18th-century Nalnad Palace, a summer hunting lodge of the kings of Coorg, isolated, ideal for walking. Also unique, interesting local recipes, English speaking guide Rs 150. Reserve ahead, T08272-38446 or book through *Cauvery Hotel*, Madikeri.

D-F Honey Valley Estate (a similar set-up just 3 km from *Palace Estate*), Yavakapadi, with jeep access up rough track; owner collects from bus stop. There are three rooms in better equipped modern home, singles in old house, home-cooked meals, very welcoming. Recommended. Contact T08272-38339, honeyvalley_2001@ yahoo.com.

D-E **Cauvery Nisargadhama**, 8 simple
cottages, built of bamboo/teak, some with
balconies on stilts over the water, electricity
(no fan), hot water, peaceful (despite
nocturnal rats), but poor food. Contact
Forestry Office, Madikeri T08272-26308.

Dubare Forest *p986*

B **Orange County Resort**, near Siddapur,
T/F08274-58481, www.trailsindia.com.
Luxury resort in 300 acres of coffee and spice
plantations, on banks of the Cauvery. 42
cottages, houseboat, full facilities, pool,
health spa, fishing at Valanoor (18 km).

Nagarhole *p986*

From Sep-Jun:

AL-A Kabini River Lodges (Karnataka
Tourism), at Karapur (75 km from Mysore) on
reservoir bank. 14 rooms in Mysore Maharajas'
18th-century hunting lodge and bungalow, 6
newer cabins overlooking lake, 5 tents, simple
but acceptable, good restaurant, bar,
exchange, package includes meals, sailing,
rides in coracles on the Kaveri, jeep/minibus at
Nagarhole and Murkal complex, park tour
with naturalist, very professionally run (some
feel "ordered around"). Recommended.
Foreigners pay double. Reservations:
Bangalore, *Jungle Lodges and Resorts*,
T5597025, F5586163, www.junglelodges.com,
or *Clipper Holidays*, T5592043, F5599833,
clipper@bangalore.wipro.net.in.

AL-A Waterwoods, 500 m away, surrounded
by the Kabini river, T08228-44421. 6 luxury
rooms with sit-outs in a ranchstyle house,
exquisitely furnished, beautiful gardens on
water's edge, delicious home-cooking, solar
power, friendly staff, boating, jeep, ayurvedic
massage, gym, swimming, walking,
charming, informal atmosphere, peaceful,
secluded. Highly recommended.

A **Jungle Inn**, Veeranahosahalli, main
entrance, T08222-46022. 7 well-appointed
rooms and 3 dorms, in colonial-style lodges,
varied meals, boating, elephant rides.
Hammock Leisure Holidays, T5307963. Forest
Dept Rest Houses in the Park:

B **Cauvery**, 2 rooms; book on T080-3341993.

B **Gangotri**, 3 rooms with bath, simple but
comfortable, dorm beds (Rs 40), services of
cook, book at least 15 days in advance on
T0821-480901.

● Eating

Mysore *p977, maps p978 and p980*
♔♔♔ **Ramanashree Comfort**, in hotel.
♔♔♔ **Southern Star**, in hotel. Recommended.
♔♔♔ **Green** - "superb cooking, colourful,
subtle, among the best" (see above).
♔♔ **King's Court's**, MG Square, *Mysore
Memories* and outdoor *Raintree* BBQ, popular.
♔♔ **Park Lane** hotel. Mixed menu. Carefully
prepared, good food, Indian classical music
at dinner, attractive shaded courtyard/
garden, pleasant atmosphere, bar, red lights
to call waiters! The place to be seen.
♔♔ **Shanghai**, Vinoba Rd. Superb Chinese,
shabby interior. 1100-1500, 1830-2300.
♔♔ **Shilpashri**, Gandhi Sq. Comfortable rooftop,
reasonably priced, tourist oriented, chilled
beers, friendly but service can be slow.
♔♔ **Siddharta**, great south Indian but crowded
non-a/c dining room facing car park.
♔ **Amaravathi** (*Roopa's*), Hardinge Circle.
Spicy hot Andhra meals on banana leaves.
♔ **Dasaprakash Hotel**, good breakfast, huge
southern *thali* (Rs 25).
♔ **Ganesh** opposite Central Bus Stand. Great
dosas, sweets.
♔ **Jewel Rock**, *Maurya Palace*, Sri Harsha Rd.
Great chicken tikka and spicy cashewnut
chicken, go early to avoid queueing.
♔ **Mylari** in *Hotel Mahadeshwara*, Nazarbad
Main Rd (ask rickshaw driver), the best *dosas*
in town served on a palm leaf, mornings
until 1100, "undiscovered by tourists", basic
surroundings, may have to queue.
♔ **RRR** Gandhi Sq. Part a/c, tasty non-veg on
plantain leaves, good for lunch.
♔ **SR Plantain Leaf** (*Chalukya's*), Rajkamal
Talkies Rd. Decent veg *thalis* on banana leaf;
also tandoori chicken.
♔ **Samrat**, next to *Indra Bhavan*, Dhanvantri
Rd, Range of tasty north Indian vegetarian.
♔ **Santosh**, near bus station. Excellent value
thalis (Rs 16).

Cafés and fast food

Indra Café, Sayaji Rd. Excellent bhel puri, sev
puri etc.
Penguin Ice-cream Parlour, comfortable
sofas shared with local teens into Hindi 'pop'.
Raghu Niwas, B-N Rd, opposite *Ritz*. Does
very good breakfasts.
Sri Rama Veg, 397 Dhanvantri Rd. Serves
fast food, good juices.

Sweets
Bombay Tiffanys, Devraja Market Building. Try the *Mysore Pak* here.

Madikeri *p984, map p985*
Capitol, near private bus stand. Despite its exterior, serves excellent veg meals.
Choice, School Rd (20 m from centre). Very good food, choice of ground floor or rooftop.
Udupi Veglands, opposite fort. Lovely, clean, spacious wooden eatery, delicious and cheap vegetarian *thalis*.
Taj, College Rd. 'Cheap and best', clean.

🍷 Bars and clubs

Mysore *p977, maps p978 and p980*
The best bars are in hotels: *Lalitha Mahal Palace* and *Lokranjan Mahal Palace*.

🎭 Entertainment

Mysore *p977, maps p978 and p980*
Cinema
Two cinemas show English language films.

🎉 Festivals and events

Mysore *p977, maps p978 and p980*
Mar-Apr: Temple car festival with 15 day fair, at the picturesque town of *Nanjangud*, 23 km south (Erode road); **Vairamudi** festival lasts 6 days when deities are adorned with 3 diamond crowns, at Melkote Temple, 52 km. **11 Aug**: Feast of St Philomena, statue of the saint is taken out in procession through city streets ending with a service at the cathedral. **End Sep-early-Oct**: Dasara, see box page 979.

🛍 Shopping

Mysore *p977, maps p978 and p980*
Books
Ashok, Dhanvantri Rd, T435533, excellent.

Clothing
Craft Emporium and cloth shops in the middle part of Vinoba Rd are recommended for good selection and good quality. Competent tailors will make up and deliver within a couple of hours.
Badshah's, 20 Devraj Urs Rd, T429799, beautifully finished salwar-kameez, Mr Yasin speaks good English.

For **silks** at reasonable prices, try Sayaji Rao Rd. Watch machine weaving at **Karnataka Silk Industry**'s factory shop, Mananthody Rd, 0730-1130, 1230-1630, Mon-Sat.

Handicrafts
Superb carved figures, sandalwood and rosewood items, silks, incense sticks, handicrafts. The main shopping area is Sayaji Rao Rd.
Cauvery Arts & Crafts Emporium for sandalwood and rosewood items, 1000-1330, 1500-1930, closed Thu (non-receipt of parcel reported by traveller).
Devaraja Market, lanes of stalls selling spices, perfumes and much more; good "antique" shop (fixed price) has excellent sandalwood and rosewood items. Worth visiting.
Sri Lakshmi Fine Arts & Crafts (opposite the zoo) also has a factory shop at 2226 Sawday Rd, Mandi Mohalla.
Also recommended are **Shankar** at 12, **Ganesh** at 532 Dhanvantri Rd, and **Khadi Vastralaya**.

Photography
Rekha, top quality. Others on Dhanvantri Rd.

🏞 Activities and tours

Mysore *p977, maps p978 and p980*
Horse racing
Can be fun – great location and lots of local colour.

Sports clubs
Chennai Sports Club, Lalitha Mahal Palace Rd, just before the hotel.

Swimming
Mysore University has an Olympic-size pool.

Tour operators
KSE, *Hotel Roopa*, B-N Rd, T446099, very competent, recommended.
Seagull, by 8 Ramanashree Complex, T529732, F520535, for cars/drivers, flights, wildlife tours etc, helpful.
Skyway International Travels, No 370/4 JLB Rd, T426642, F422762, www.skywaytour.com.
TCI, Gandhi Sq, T443023. Pleasant and helpful.
Yatri Nivas, KSTDC, 2 JLB Rd, T423492.
Mysore, daily 0715-2030, Rs115, local sights and Chamundi Hill, Kukkara Halli Lake,

Somanathapura, Srirangapatnam and Brindavan Gardens. **Belur, Halebid, Sravanabelagola**: Tue, Wed, Fri, Sun, 0715-2200, Rs 210 (long and tiring but worth it if you are not travelling to Hassan).

Yoga

Sri Patanjala Yogashala, Parakala Mutt, next to Jaganmohan Palace. Astanga Vinyasa yoga; daily instruction in English from BNS Iyengar, 0600-0900, 1600-1900, US$100 per month. Recommended.

Madikeri *p984, map p985*

Fishing

Coorg Wildlife Society, see page 993, can arrange a licence for fishing on the Kaveri river (Rs 500 per day, Rs 1000 weekend). The highlight is the prospect of pulling in a mahseer which can grow up to 45 kg in weight; all fish to be returned to the river. This is at Trust Land Estate,Valnoor, near Kushalnagar, where there is a lodge but you'll need to carry food. Mr Ponappa has the keys to the lodge and can also issue the licence. Contact Professor MB Madaiah, T0827-6 76443. **Orange County Resort** is in Dubare Forest, see page 986.

Tours

Friends' Tours and Travel, below *Bank of India*, College Rd. Recommended for their knowledge and enthusiasm. They do tailor-made treks at about Rs 275 per day per person to include guide, food and accommodation in temples, schools, huts etc. They have a 'basecamp' at Thalathmane, 4 km from Madikeri, which people can also stay at even if not trekking. Has basic huts and blankets for Rs 50 each, home cooking from nearby at little extra cost. Contact Mr Raja Shekar on T29974, T29102 (1000-1930) or T25672 (2100-0900).
Hotel Cauvery, will also arrange treks.

⊖ Transport

Mysore *p977, maps p978 and p980*

Air

No flights from Mysore at present. **Indian Airlines**, 2 JLB Rd, T421846.

Auto-rickshaw

Easily available.

Car

Car hire Travel companies and KSTDC, Rs 500 (4 hrs/40 km) for city sightseeing; Rs 850 to include Srirangapatnam and Brindavan. *KSE* charges Rs 700 for Somnathpur, Srirangapatnam and Bird Sanctuary.

Bus

Local City Bus Station, southeast of KR Circle, T425819. To **Silk Weaving Centre**, Nos 1, 2, 4 and 8; **Brindavan Gardens**, No 303; **Chamundi Hill**, No 201; **Srirangapatnam**, No 313. Central Bus Station, T529853. **Bandipur**, Platform 9, **Ooty** etc, Platform 11.
Long distance There are 3 bus stations: **Central**, mainly for long distance SRTC, T520853, **City** for local buses, and **B3 Suburban** and **Private** including Somnathpur. SRTC buses of Karnataka, Tamil Nadu and Kerala run regular daily services between Mysore and other major cities. Check timings. Many private companies near Gandhi Sq operate overnight sleepers and interstate buses which may be faster and marginally less uncomfortable. Book ahead for busy routes (eg Hassan). The bus station has a list of buses with reserved places.
Somnathpur: few from Surburban station, 1 hr direct, or longer via Bannur or via Narasipur. Several buses daily to many towns from **Central** Bus Station. **Bangalore**: every ¼ hr, from non-stop platform. Semi-deluxe, every ¼ hr. **Coimbatore**: 0845; **Hospet**: 1930 (10 hrs), very tiring; **Salem**: 1030 (7 hrs); **Thiruvananthapuram**: Super-deluxe, 14 hrs. Several to **Satyamangalam** where you can connect with buses to Tamil Nadu. The journey is through wilderness and forests with spectacular scenery as the road finally plunges from the plateau down to the plains.

Train

Advance Computerized Reservations in separate section; ask for foreigners' counter. T131. Enquiries T520103, 0800-2000 (closed 1330-1400); Sun 0800-1400. Left luggage 0600-2200, Rs 3-Rs 6 per day. Tourist Information, telephone and toilets on Platform 1. Taxi counter at entrance. To **Bangalore** (non-stop): *Tippu Exp, 6205*, 1120, 2½ hrs; *Shatabdi Exp, 2008*, daily except Tue, 1410, 2 hrs (continues to **Chennai** another 5 hrs). **Bangalore** via **Sriranga-patnam, Mandya** and **Maddur**: *Chamundi Exp 6215*,

0645, 3 hrs; *Kaveri Chennai Exp 6221*, 1805, 2¾ hrs. **Chennai**: *Chennai Exp 6221*, 1805, 10½ hrs; *Shatabdi Exp, 2008,* not Tue, 1410, 7 hrs. **Madurai**: change at Bangalore. **Mumbai**: *Sharavathi Exp, 1036*, Sat only, 0600, 26 hrs.

Srirangapatnam *p981, map p982*
Trains and buses between **Bangalore** and **Mysore** stop here but arrival can be tiresome with hassle from rickshaw dirvers, traders and beggars. Buses 313 and 316 from Mysore City Bus Stand (half-hourly) take 50 mins.

Bandipur National Park *p984*
Bandipur is in Karnataka while the neighbouring park, Mudumalai, is in Tamil Nadu, but they are extensions of the same forest reserve which also stretches west to include the undeveloped Kerala reserve of Waynad. They are on the Mysore to Ooty bus route, about 2½ hrs south from Mysore and 2½ hrs from Ooty. Buses go to and from **Mysore** (80 km) between 0615-1530.

Madikeri *p984, map p985*
Auto-rickshaw
From *Hotel Chitra* to Abbi Falls, Rs 150 including 1 hr wait there.

Bus
Frequent express buses to **Bangalore** Plat 4, from 0615 (6 hrs); **Chikmagalur**; **Hassan** (3½ hrs); **Kannur**; **Mangalore**, Plat 2, 0530-2400 (3½ hrs); **Mysore** Plat 3, half hourly 0600-2300 (3 hrs) via **Kushalnagar** (for Tibetan settlements) are very crowded during the rush hour ("cloth salesmen hold auctions on the bus!"); **Thalassery**. Daily to **Coimbatore**, **Kannur**, **Madurai** 1900, **Mumbai** 0930, **Ooty** 0730, 2030, **Virajpet**. **Private Bus Stand**: *Kamadenu Travels* above Bus Stand, T27024, for *Purnima Travels* bus to **Bangalore**. *Shakti Motor Service* to **Nagarhole** (4½ hrs); **Virajpet** .

Nisargadhama *p986*
Bus
The bus from Madikeri passes park gates 2 km before Kushalnagar.

Rickshaw
A rickshaw from Kushalnagar Rs 10.

Nagarhole *p986*
Bus
From Mysore, *Exp*, 3 hrs, Rs 35; Madikere, 4½ hrs. Bangalore, 6 hrs. For *Kabini River Lodge* and *Waterworlds*, be sure to get the Karapur (not the Nagarhole) bus; *Jungle Lodges* bus leaves Bangalore at 0730, stops in Mysore (around 0930), reaching Kabini around 1230; return bus departs 1315. State bus from Mysore to **Karapur**.

Train
Nearest, Mysore (96 km). See page 984.

ⓘ Directory

Mysore *p977, maps p978 and p980*
Banks State Bank of Mysore, corner of Sayaji Rao Rd and Sardar Patel Rd. and opposite GPO in city centre. LKP Forex, near Clock Tower. **Hospitals** Medical College, corner of Irwin and Sayaji Rao Rd. KR Hospital, T443300; Mission Hospital (Mary Holdsworth), Tilaknagar, in a striking building dating from 1906. **Internet** Coca Cola Cyber Space, 2 Madvesha Complex, Nazarabad, near Sri Harsha Rd. Cyber Net Corner, 2/3B Indira Bhavan, Dhanvantri Rd. Pal Net, Nehru Circle. Avoid *Internet World* near Ritz. **Post office** GPO, on corner of Ashoka Rd and Irwin Rd; Poste Restante here. **Tourist offices** Karnataka, Yatri Nivas, 2 JLB Rd, T423652, efficient, at Old Exhibition Building (corner of Irwin Rd), T422096. 1000-1730 (guides available). Counters at Railway Station, T440719 and Bus Stand. **Useful addresses** Forest Office, and Project Tiger, Forest Department, Woodyard, Ashokpuram, T480110 (City Bus No 61).

Madikeri *p984, map p985*
Banks Canara Bank, Main Rd, accepts some TCs and Visa. **Internet** Cyber Zone, next to *Chitra Hotel*. Rs 30 per hr, excellent. **Post office** Behind Private Bus Stand. **Tourist office** Next to *PWD Travellers' Bungalow*, Mangalore Rd, T25648. **Useful addresses** Community Centre, south of Fort, Main Rd, holds occasional shows. **Coorg Wildlife Society**, 2 km from GT Circle along Mysore Rd, then 1 km to left, T23505. Forestry Office, Aranya Bhavan, Mysore Rd, 3 km from town, T25708.

The West Coast and Mangalore

→ *Phone code: 0824. Colour map 7, grid A2. Population: 328,700.*
Capital of South Kanara District, the hilly town of Mangalore makes a pleasant,
relaxing stop between Goa and Kerala. Rarely visited by western tourists, it has some
interesting churches and decent accommodation. ➤➤ *For Sleeping, Eating and other listings,*
see pages 998-1001.

Ins and outs

Getting there Bajpe airport is 22 km from town. The Konkan railway has trains from
Goa and Mumbai while the old broad gauge goes down the coast to Kozhikode and
then inland to Coimbatore. The new Kankanadi station is 6 km northeast of the City
station which is just south of the centre at Hampankatta. The KSRTC Bus Station is 3
km north of the Private Bus Stand in the busy town centre.

Getting around Although the centre is compact enough to be covered on foot, autos are
handy but may refuse to use their meters. See Transport, page 991, for further details.

Background

In the 14th and 15th centuries Mangalore traded with Persian and Arab merchants and
was fought over by the Nayaka princes and the Portuguese. In the 18th century its
control was contested by Haidar Ali – who made it his centre for shipbuilding – and
Tipu Sultan on the one hand, and the British on the other.

The modern port, 10 km north of the town, is now India's ninth largest cargo
handling port. Mangalore's economy is dominated by agricultural processing and
port-related activities. Imports include tropical timber from Southeast Asia for
furniture making, a necessity since India placed major restrictions on its own teak
felling. The port handles 75% of India's coffee exports and the bulk of its cashew nuts.
The latter are brought from many coastal areas – notably from Kerala, where 90% of
India's cashews are grown; the National Cashew Research Centre is inland, at Puttur.
Mangalore's other claim to fame is that it produces Ganesh Bidis, the cheap
alternative to cigarettes that are a few pieces of tobacco wrapped in a leaf tied with
thread. The leaf used varies; one being from the Camel's Foot Tree (*Bauhinia*).
Mangalorean red clay roof tiles, used extensively in Southern India have been
manufactured here for 130 years. To visit, contact Mr Pai of Summer Sands Beach
Resort, T467690 (see Ullal).

Sights

St Aloysius College Chapel ① *on Lighthouse Hill, 0830-1000, 1200-1430,*
1530-1800, has remarkable 19th-century frescoes painted by the Italian trained Jesuit
priest Moscheni cover the walls and ceilings in a profusion of scenes. The town has a
sizeable Roman Catholic population (about 20%).

The tile-roofed low structure of the 10th-century **Mangaladevi Temple** is named
after a Malabar Princess, Mangala Devi, who may have given her name to Mangalore.
The 11th-century **Sri Manjunatha Temple** (with the Kadri Caves), 3 km from the centre
– a cycle rickshaw ride away – has a rough linga; its central image is a bronze
Lokeshwara (968 AD).

There are also lakes which have water with medicinal properties, and the Old
Lighthouse dating from the 18th century. It is generally believed to have been built by
Haider Ali, who built a naval dockyard in Mangalore.

You can take a trip out to the sand bar at the river mouth to watch fascinating
boat building and river traffic on the Netravathi River.

Shremmanti Bai Memorial Museum ① *0900-1700, free,* has a collection including archaeology, ethnology, porcelain and wood carvings. **Mahatma Gandhi Museum** ① *Canara High School, closed Sun and holidays, 0930-1230, 1400-1730, free,* collection includes zoology, anthropology, sculpture, art and manuscripts. Market Road, with an excellent range of shops, is good for browsing.

Religious sites in the Ghats

The forested hills of the Western Ghats are home to some wonderful examples of Jain and Hindu sculpture and architecture. The temples are often centres of pilgrimage, such as the **Subrahmanya Temple** at Sullia or the **Saivite Temple** at Dharamasthala. **Mudabidri**, the 'Jain Varanasi', has superbly carved *basti*. In Jain tradition, no two columns are alike, and many are elaborately carved with graceful figures and floral and knot patterns. **Karkala** has a giant monolithic Jain statue. The Hindu philosopher Sankaracharya was associated with the small town of **Sringeri**, near the source of the Tunga River. For full details see the South Indian Handbook.

Karnataka's Sapphire Coast → *Colour map 7, grid A2.*

Poor transport made the route up the Karnataka's 'sapphire coast' to Goa one of the least travelled scenic routes in India. This is now changing. The Western Ghats are never far away, while the road and the Konkan railway frequently skirt the Arabian Sea in the north passing some magnificent beaches. ➤➤ *For Sleeping, Eating and other listings, see pages 998-1001.*

Udupi (Udipi) → *Phone code: 08252. Population: 113,000.*

Udupi, one of Karnataka's most important pilgrimage sites, is the birthplace of the 12th-century saint Madhva, who set up eight sannyasi *maths* (monasteries) in the town, see page 1326. It is a pleasant town rarely visited by foreigners.

According to one legend the statue of *Krishna* once turned to give a low caste devotee *darshan*. The **Sri Krishna Math** (Car Street) in the heart of the town is set around a large tank, the *Madhva Sarovar*, into which devotees believe that the Ganga flows every 10 years. There are some attractive *math* buildings with colonnades and arches fronting the temple square, as well as huge wooden temple chariots. This Hindu temple, like many others, is of far greater religious than architectural importance, and receives a succession of highly placed political leaders. Visitors are 'blessed' by the temple elephant. The biennial *Paraya Mahotsava*, on 17/18 January of even-numbered years, when the temple management changes hands (the priest-in-charge heads each of the eight *maths* in turn). *Seven Day Festival,* 9-15 January, is marked by an extravagant opening ceremony complete with firecrackers, dancing elephants, brass band and "eccentric re-enactments of mythical scenes while towering wooden temple cars, illuminated by strip lights followed by noisy portable generators, totter around the square, pulled by dozens of pilgrims".

Sri Ananthasana Temple, where Madhva is believed to have de-materialized while teaching his followers, is in the centre of the temple square. The eight important *maths* are around Car Street: Sode, Puthige and Adamar (south); Pejawar and Palamar (west); Krishna and Shirur (north); and Kaniyur (east). Udupi is almost as well known today as the home of a family of Kanarese Brahmins who have established a chain of coffee houses/hotels across South India.

Manipal Five kilometres inland from Udupi, Manipal is famous throughout Karnataka as the centre of **Yakshagana** dance drama, which like Kathakali in Kerala is an all night spectacle. The Rashtrakavi Govind Pai **Museum**, MGM College, has a collection of sculpture, bronze, inscriptions and coins.

⦂ Udupi – home of 'Brahmin meals ready'

The name of Udupi is associated across South India with authentic Brahmin cooking – which means vegetarian food at its best. But what is authentic Udupi cuisine? Pamela Philipose, writing in the Indian Express, suggests that strictly it is food prepared for temple use prepared by Shivali Brahmins at the Krishna temple. It is therefore not only wholly vegetarian, but it never uses onions or garlic.

Pumpkins and gourds are the essential ingredients, while sambar, which must also contain ground coconut and coconut oil, is its base. Rasam, the spicy pepper water, is compulsory, as are the ingredients jackfruit, heart-shaped colocasia leaves, raw green bananas, mango pickle, red chilli and salt. *Adyes* (dumplings) *ajadinas* (dry curries) and chutneys, including one made of the skin of the ridge gourd, are specialities. Favourite dishes are Kosambiri with pickle, coconut chutney and appalam. At least two vegetables will be served, including runner beans, and rice. Sweets include payasa and holige.

Malpe Five kilometres west of Udupi, Malpe is one of the best port sites in southern Karnataka. Across the bay is the island of Darya Bahadurgarh and 5 km to the southwest is **St Mary's Isle**, composed of dramatic hexagonal basalt, where **Vasco da Gama** landed in 1498 and set up a cross. The fishing village at one end of the beach, and the fish market on the docks are very smelly; the beach too is used as a public toilet in places. If you are prepared for an unpleasant walk or cycle ride, you can reach a deserted sandy beach but there are no facilities so take your own food and water.

Bhatkal ⓘ *Getting there: direct bus to Jog Falls at 0600 from the bus station (2 hrs). Later buses take 3 hrs.* One of the many bullock cart tracks that used to be the chief means of access over the Western Ghats started from Bhatkal. Now only a small town with a predominantly Muslim population, in the 16th century it was the main port of the *Vijayanagar* Empire. It also has two interesting small temples. From the north the 17th-century Jain *Chandranatha Basti* with two buildings linked by a porch, is approached first. The use of stone tiling is a particularly striking reflection of local climatic conditions, and is a feature of the Hindu temple to its south, a 17th-century Vijayanagar temple with typical animal carvings. In the old cemetery of the church is possibly the oldest British memorial in India, inscribed: "Here lyeth the body of George Wye merchant dec. XXXI March Anno Dom NRT Christi Sal Mundi MDCXXXVII, 1637".

Gokarna → *Phone code: 08386. Colour map 7, grid A1.*

The narrow streets, traditional houses and temples together with its long wide expanse of beach, lure growing numbers of backpackers moving on from Goa who search for an alternative hideaway on the unspoilt beaches to the south. There is a somewhat curious mix of Hindu pilgrims and castaways from the hippy era here who are tolerated rather than welcome. Visitors should respect local sensibilities and dress suitably in town.

Sights Ganesh is believed to have tricked **Ravana** into putting down the famous Atmalinga on this spot now sanctified in the **Mahabalesvara temple**. As Ravana was unable to lift the linga up again, it is called *Mahabala* (the strong one). **Tambraparni Teertha** stream is particularly sacred for casting the ashes of the dead. Today Gokarna is also a centre of Sanskrit learning.

Most travellers head for the beaches to the south. The path from town passing **Kudle** (pronounced Koodlee) **Beach** is well sign-posted but quite rugged, especially south of the **Om Beach** (about 3 km), and should not be attempted with a full back-pack during the middle of the day. Also, though parts are lit at night, stretches are isolated; single women especially should take a companion. Boats from Gokarna to Om charge around Rs 200 one-way. Om Beach can now also be reached by a motorable track which can be accessed from near *Mayura Samudra* hotel. It is no longer quite the secluded paradise. As with Kudle, in season it can get extremely busy and the combination of too many people, shortage of fresh water and poor hygiene, results in the beaches getting rather dirty. **Half Moon** and **Paradise Beaches**, popular with log-stayers, can be reached by continuing to walk over the headlands and are another 2 km or so apart.

Karwar The administrative headquarters of North Kanara District on the banks of the Kalinadi River, Karwar has a deep-water Naval port protected by five islands. One of these was 'Anjedive' of old, known to seafarers centuries before **Vasco da Gama** called at the island in 1498, and the Portuguese built a fort there. It was later used as a Goan penal colony. Since it is now under the control of the Navy it is off-limits to all foreigners. From 1638 to 1752 there was an English settlement here, surviving on the pepper trade. The Portuguese held it for the next 50 years until the old town was destroyed in 1801. Today Karwar, strung out between the port and the estuary, has an unpleasant beach. However, the beaches a little to the south rival those of Goa but are still deserted. Of interest is the hill fort, an octagonal church, and a 300-year old temple.

Gokarna

After Shelley Malgarin & Kim Clark

Sleeping ■
1 Gokarna International
2 Green's Om
3 New Prasad Nileye
4 Nimmu
5 Ramdev Lodge
6 Shastri's Guest House
7 Vaibhav Nivas

Eating ●
1 Kinara
2 Pai
3 Prema
4 Vishwa

Karnataka The West Coast & Mangalore *Gokarna*

Listings: The West Coast and Mangalore

⏺ Sleeping

Mangalore p994

There is a 12½% luxury tax and the big hotels have bars.

A-B Manjarun (Taj), Old Port Rd, T420420, F420585, mangalore@tajhotels.com. 101 excellent rooms with tubs ('budget' rooms perfectly adequate), some with sea/river view, restaurant, all facilities, pool (non-residents half-day Rs 200), friendly service.

B-C Moti Mahal, Falnir Rd, T441411, F441011, motimahal.vasnet.com. 90 a/c rooms, restaurant and bar, coffee shop, pool and poolside BBQ.

B-C Poonja International, KS Rao Rd, T440171, F441081. 154 rooms, central a/c, wide range of facilities including exchange, spotlessly clean, excellent complimentary buffet breakfast, excellent value.

B-D Mangalore International, KS Rao Rd, T444860, F444859. 45 clean, well appointed rooms, 30 a/c, modern and airy, veg restaurant (no alcohol), excellent service.

C-D Pentagon, Kankanadi (6 km northeast), T439203. 41 rooms and suites, most a/c, restaurant, in modern highway-side hotel.

E Dhanyabad, Hampankatta Circle, T440066, F440069. 44 spacious rooms, good value, convenient (open late).

E Indraprastha, Lighthouse Hill Rd, T425750. Good value rooms with bath, helpful staff.

E Railway Retiring Rooms City Station, 3 good rooms, dorm beds, water cooler, shower, toilet, "outstanding value".

F Adarsh, Market Rd, T440878. 60 basic rooms, some with TV, well kept and friendly, excellent service, good value.

F Rupa, Balmatta Road. T421271. 69 tatty but airy rooms, friendly staff.

F Surya, Greens Compound, Balmatta Rd, T425736. 18 rooms with bath, vegetarian restaurant, internet (Rs 30) with good connection, set back from road, uninspiring exterior but worth considering for tranquility.

Ullal Beach (10 km south)

C-D Summer Sands Beach Resort, Chotamangalore, T467690, summer@ satyam.net.in. 85 rooms, 30 a/c, in simple but comfortable bungalows in the local style, superb Konkani meals, bar, good pool, ayurvedic treatments, yoga lessons, local trips arranged. (*Nirmala Convent* at Ullal produces intricate cutwork embroidery articles.)

Udupi p995

C-D Sriram Residency, opposite Post Office T530761 30 very nice rooms in top-quality new hotel, bar and 2 restaurants, travel desk, good service.

C-E Swadesh Heritage, MV Rd T529605 F520205, www.hotelswadesh.com. 34 spotlessly clean rooms, 14 a/c, in newish hotel (even basic rooms very good value), bar, 2 restaurants. Highly recommended.

D-E Udupi Residency, near Service Bus Stand, T530005. 33 excellent rooms, 11 a/c, clean and very well maintained, restaurant. Highly recommended new hotel.

F Kalpana Lodge, Upendra Bag, T20440, F71112. 62 rooms, some with bath, cheap.

Manipal p995

B-C Valley View International, on campus, has 70 good a/c rooms with upmarket facilities, pool, recommended.

D Green Park. 38 rooms, some a/c, restaurant.

Malpe p996

E Silver Sands, T22223, Thotham Beach, 1 km north, hard to find. 8 pleasant cottages, limited menu restaurant, friendly.

E Tourist Home, half way to Thotham Beach, four pleasant, seaside rooms. Indian breakfast at the top of the road.

Bhatkal p996

F Seema, very basic, airless rooms, noisy.

F Vaibhav Lodge, are very basic, airless rooms, noisy.

Gokarna p996, map p997
Town

D-E Gokarna International, T56622, F56848. 43 modern rooms (3 a/c) with bath

⏺ *For an explanation of the sleeping and eating price codes used in this guide, see inside the*
● *front cover. Other relevant information is found in Essentials pages 52-57.*

and tubs, back quieter and have balconies, restaurant,bar, friendly staff, and the first lift in Gokarna! Recommended.

E-F Green's 'Om', 2-minute walk from bus stand, T56445. 20 clean, airy, well maintained rooms with bath, 2 a/c, restaurant (Nepali, Indian, Western) and bar operates in peak season. Very good value.

E-F New Prasad Nilaya, near the Bus Stand, T57135. Spacious but very run-down rooms with shower, some balconies, upstairs slightly better, friendly staff.

E-F Shri Laxmi, Bus Stand Rd, T560365. Clean, spacious rooms in newly-converted family house. Small scale but friendly and good value.

F Mayura Samudra (KSTDC), 2 km north on hilltop facing the sea, T56236. 3 rooms, dining room, garden, helpful staff but quite a trek.

F Nimmu Guest House, near Temple, T56730.15 clean rooms with shared Indian toilets, 5 newest are better value as they are big, bright and catch the breeze, limited roof space for overspill, garden, laid-back and friendly, safe luggage storage. Recommended.

F Shastri's Guest House, Dasanamath, T56220. 24 rooms with bath, some 3-4 bedded, set back from road, quiet.

F Vaibhav Nivas, Ganjigadde off Main St (5 mins walk from bazar), T56714. Family guest house, small rooms, annexe with 10 rooms, some with bath (Indian and western WC), meals, luggage store.

Beaches

Mud and palm leaf huts with shared facilites charge Rs 30-60 (extra for a mattress). The lack of security in beach huts has prompted the guesthouses in town to offer to store luggage for a small charge.

The exceptions are at the southern end of **Kudle**:

F Shiva Prasad, with decent brick-built rooms with fan.

On Om:

F Namaste with acceptable rooms, though far from the best swimming areas.

F Nirvana, "one of nicest and cheapest" (Rs 40) but no beds so hammock or inflatable mattress recommended, shower, restaurant.

An upmarket hotel is to be built here.

D Bhadra, on NH17 (4 km north of Karwar), T08382-25212. 20 rooms, some a/c, lovely views over estuary, restaurant, a modern hotel. A roadside stall outside the hotel serves very good value vegetarian food.

F Anand Lodge, near bus stand, T26156. Rooms with Indian WC, basic but OK.

● Eating

Mangalore *p994*

▼▼▼ **Embers** for open-air dinners by the pool at *Manjarun Hotel*.

▼ **Lalith**, Balmatta Rd. T426793. Basement restaurant with excellent food, cold beer and friendly service.

▼ **Hao Hao** and ▼ **Hao Ming**, in Balmatta, good Chinese, a/c.

▼ **Surabhi**. Tandoori and cold beer, handy if waiting for a night bus.

▼ **Ting Hao** at *Hotel Sujatha*, KS Rao Rd. Dark a/c, does large portions of Chinese/Indian (opens 1800).

Udupi *p995*

Dwarike, Car St, facing Temple Sq. Immaculately clean, modern, good service, comfortable, western and South Indian food, excellent snacks, ice creams.

Gokul, opposite Swadeshi Heritage, Excellent vegetarian, good value.

Manipal *p995*

JJ's Fast Food, *Hotel Bhavani*, Parkala Rd. For western snacks.

Gokarna *p996, map p997*

Soft drinks can be wildly over-priced; check before ordering.

Cheap vegetarian *thalis* are available near the bus stand and along Main St while shacks at the entrance to the town beach serve up the usual disarray of travellers' favourites.

▼ **Kinara**, near Gokarna Beach, ice creams, Indian and some western food. Basic but clean and well-run.

▼ **Pai**, near Vegetable Market does good masala dosa.

▼ **Prema**, opposite Mahabalesvar temple, with a large room upstairs, does great fruit

Karnataka Listings: The West Coast & Mangalore

salads, ices, *gudbad* and its own delicious soft garlic cheese. Popularity has resulted in slow and surly service. Icecream parlours abound; try *gudbad* with nuts and fruit.

♥ **Vishwa**, on the beach. Nepali run, varied menu including Tibetan, large helpings. Standards are improving on the southern beaches with traveller food, drinks and internet access becoming available, though often only in the peak season.

Spanish Chai shop, Kudle, and **Hotel Look Sea** are popular.

Karwar *p997*

Fish Restaurant, along the street in *Sidvha Hotel*. Excellent bistro type restaurant.

⊖ Transport

Mangalore *p994*

Air

Bajpe airport is 22 km out of town. **Transport from town**: taxi, Rs 200; shared Rs 50 each; coach from **Indian Airlines**, Hathill Complex, Lalbag, T455259. Airport, T752433. **Chennai** via Bangalore, **Mumbai**. Jet Airways: Ram Bhavan Complex, Kodaibail, T441181, airport, T752709. **Bangalore** and **Mumbai**.

Autorickshaw

Minimum charge Rs 8; Rs 35 to the Kankanadi station from the centre, and Rs 25 from KSRTC Lalbag, Bus Station (higher than the meter charge because of the 'locality').

Car

Car hire Rs 4 per km, Rs 7 for a/c.

Bus

Long distance Numerous private bus companies around the *Taj Mahal* Restaurant, Falnir Rd (and a few opposite KSRTC) serve Bangalore, Bijapur, Goa, Ernakulam, Hampi, Gokarna, Kochi, Mumbai, Udupi etc. **KSRTC State bus stand**, Bajjai Rd, is well-organized. Booking hall at entrance has a computer printout of timetable in English; main indicator board shows different bus categories: red - ordinary; blue - semi-deluxe; green - super-deluxe. (*Exp* buses may be reserved 7 days ahead). For town centre and railway, leave bus stand, turn left 50 m to private bus shelter for bus 19 or 33. **Mysore** and **Bangalore**: 296 km, 7 hrs and 405 km, 9 hrs, ½ hrly from 0600 (route through Madikeri is the most pleasant); trains take 20 hrs. **Chennai** 717 km; **Madurai** 691 km, 16 hrs. **Mumbai**; **Panaji**, 10 hrs.

Train

Central Station has a computerized booking office. **Chennai**: *Mangalore Mail, 6602* (AC/II), 1115, 19 hrs; *West Coast Exp, 6628*, 2010, 19 hrs. **Kollam**: *Malabar Express, 6330*, dep 1630, 15 hrs, and to **Thiruvananthapuram**, 17 hrs: also *Parasuram Exp 6350*, 0345. **Madgaon**: *Matsyagandha Exp, 2620*, 1450, 4½ hrs (on to Thane and LT for Mumbai).**Palakkad**: *Mangalore-Tiruchirappalli Exp, 6684*, 0600, 8 hrs; *W Coast Exp, 6628*, 2010, 8½ hrs. From **Kankanadi Station**: **Mumbai** (Lokmanya Tilak) via Madgaon: *Nethravati Exp, 6346*,1450, 17½ hrs. **Madgaon**: *Lakshadeep Exp, 2617*, 2310, 4 hrs.

Udupi *p995*

Bicycle

Bicycles are available for hire.

Bus

Frequent service to **Mangalore** (11/2 hrs). Also mornings and evenings to **Bangalore** and **Mysore** from 0600; **Hubli** from 0900; **Dharmashala**, from 0600-0945, 1400-1830; **Mumbai** at 1120, 1520, 1700, 1920.

Train

The station is 5 km from the town centre; auto, Rs 35. **Madgaon**: *Netravati Exp, 6636*, 1608, 4 hrs, and on to Mumbai (LT).

Gokarna *p996, map p997*

Bus

KSRTC buses provide a good service: **Chaudi** 2 hrs; **Karwar** (via Ankola) frequent (1 hr); **Hospet** 0700, 1425 (10 hrs); **Jog Falls** 0700, 1130 (6 hrs); **Margao**, 0814 (4 hrs); **Mangalore via Udipi** 0645 (7 hrs); **Panaji** 0800 (5 hrs).

Train

Gokarna Road station is 10 km from the town, 2 km from the NH17; most trains are met by auto-rickshaws and a private bus. Rs 10 to Gokarna bus stand. State buses can be flagged down on the NH17. **Madgaon (Margao)**: *Mangalore-Madgaon Pass, KR2 (K)*, 1110, 2¼ hrs; **Mangalore**: *Madgaon-Mangalore Pass, KR1 (K)*, 1532, 5 hrs.

Bus

To **Jog Falls**, 0730 and 1500 (6 hrs). Frequent buses to **Palolem**, **Margao** (Madgaon) and **Panaji**, also direct buses to Colva. Buses often full – may have to fight to get on. The road crosses the Kali River (car toll, Rs 5) then reaches the Goa border and check post (8 km north).

☉ Directory

Mangalore p994
Airlines Cathay Pacific, *Manjarun Hotel*; Jet, Kuwait and Quatar at Rama Bhavan, near Bishop's Palace, KS Rao Rd. **Bank** Bank of Baroda, Balmatta Rd, exchange on credit cards. **Internet** Frontline, Ayesha Towers, KS Rao Rd, T441537, Rs 40 per hr. Internet World, City Light Building, Falnir Rd. Cheap, helpful. **Photography** Foto Flash, KS Rao Rd. **Post office** Panje Mangesh Rd (1st left after *Poonja Arcade*, by petrol station) has Speed Post. **Tourist offices** Karnataka, *Hotel Indraprashta* (incomplete building), Lighthouse Hill Rd opposite Kasturba

Hospital, Ground floor, T442926. Helpful, friendly if limited tourist information. Transport T421692. **Travel agents** Four Wings, 2-3 Ganesh Mahal, KS Rao Rd, T440531, F440536. Air tickets, tours, hotels, branches in Bangalore and Udipi, exchange (TCs, £, US$ cash), helpful. Recommended. **Trade Wings**, Lighthouse Hill Road, T426225, F422004. Exchange ticketing, tours etc.

Udupi p995
Bank State Bank of India, next to Service Bus Stand. **Travel agent** Four Wings, Vyavahar Complex, Anjuman Rd, near City Bus Stand, TR24222. Also exchange.

Gokarna p996, map p997
Exchange Pai STD, opposite *Ramdev Lodge*, and **Kiran's Internet**, change money. **Internet** Several in town and on Kudle and Om beaches. **Sriram**, near post office, is best.

Karwar p997
Bank State Bank of India changes money.

Northern Karnataka and Hampi

The combination of an extraordinary boulder strewn landscape and the ruins of the great Vijayanagar Empire make Hampi one of the most atmospheric historic sites of the Deccan. The remains at Hampi are very scattered and need at least one whole day, and two to see more fully. ►► *For Sleeping, Eating and other listings, see pages 1016-1020.*

Hospet ►► *Phone code: 00394. Colour map 5, grid C5. Population: 163,300.*
Hospet can be used as a base by visitors to Hampi since it offers a variety of accommodation and has the nearest railway station. However, it suffers from pollution. Hampi is a quieter and more convenient option.

Ins and outs Getting there The station, about 500 m north of the town centre, has connections with Hyderabad and Bangalore. The bus stand is right in the town centre and most hotels are within easy walking distance. **Getting around** There are buses and auto-rickshaws to Hampi. Hire a bicycle on arrival as the site is spread out. Some paths are too rough to ride on. See Transport, page 1018, for further details.

Sights The main bazaar in Hospet, with old houses and character, is interesting to walk around. There is a significant Muslim population and *Muharram* is celebrated with vigour with *firewalkers* walking across burning embers along with noisy celebrations, a custom which may go back to long before Islam arrived. Villagers still celebrate events such as the beginning or end of migrations to seasonal feeding grounds of livestock, with huge bonfires. Cattle are driven through such fires to protect them from disease. The archaeologists Allchin and Allchin suggest that Neolithic ash mounds around Hospet could have resulted from similar celebrations over 5,000 years ago.

Excursions The 2-km **Tungabhadra Dam** ⓘ *Rs 5, local bus takes 15 mins,* 6 km away, is 49 m high and offers panoramic views. One of the largest masonry dams in the country it was completed in 1953 to provide electricity for irrigation in the surrounding districts.

★ Hampi → *Phone code: 08394. Colour map 5, grid C5. Best season: Oct-Mar.*

The rocky outcrops surrounding Hampi provided the 14th-century Vijayanagar kings with an apparently impregnable hill fortress in which they built a stupendous range of palaces and temples. Although now largely in ruins the site is still hugely impressive and despite the hawkers still enjoys a very relaxed feel.

Ins and outs

You enter the area from the west at Hampi Bazaar or from the south at Kamalapuram. The tourist office is located here on the approach to Virupaksha Temple. US$5 for foreigners (Indians Rs 10) to enter the Vitthala temple. This also includes the Lotus Mahal (Royal Enclosure), same day only. The rest is free. A 4-hr guided tour of the site (but without going into the temples) costs around Rs 250. 0800-1230, 1500-1830. Before entering the precinct, foreigners are expected to register at the police office on the left. See Transport, page 1018, for details.

Background

Hampi was once the seat of the Vijayanagara Empire and a major centre of Hindu rule for 200 years from its foundation in 1336, although there may have been a settlement

Hospet

Sleeping
1 Inspection Bungalow
2 Karthik
3 Malligi & Restaurant
4 Nagarjuna Residency
5 Priyadarshini
6 Sandarshan
7 Shanbhag Towers
8 Sivananda
9 Vishwa & Shanthi Restaurant

Eating
1 SLV Yatri Nivas

in the area as early as 1,000 years before then. The city was enormously wealthy, 'greater than Rome', with a market full of jewels and palaces plated with gold, having held a monopoly of trade in spices and cotton. It was very well fortified and defended by a large army. With the defeat in 1565 at Talikota at the hands of the Deccan Sultans, the city was largely destroyed. Today the stark and barren area of 26 sq km on the right bank of the River Tungabhadra has the ruins of the great empire strewn across it.

The site for the capital was chosen for strategic reasons but the craftsmen adopted an ingenious style to blend in their architectural masterpieces with the barren and rocky landscape. Most of the site is early 16th century, built during the 20-year reign of Krishna Deva Raya (1509-29) with the citadel standing on the bank of the river. Excavations undertaken by the Archaeological Survey of India are still in progress.

Sacred Centre

The road from the west comes over Hemakuta Hill, overlooking the sacred centre of Vijayanagara (the 'Town of Victory', 13 km northeast of Hospet town), the Virupaksha Temple and the Tungabhadra River to its north. . On the hill are two large Ganesh monolithic sculptures and some small temples. Good views at sunset. Climb Matanga Parvat, over the road, early in the morning (around 0530) for a spectacular sunrise. Always climb Matanga in a group and don't carry valuables as muggings have been reported.

The road runs down to the village, the once world-famous **market place**. You can now only see the wide pathway running east from the towering **Virupaksha** (*Pampapati*) **Temple** with its nine-storey *gopuram*, to where the bazaar hummed with activity.The temple is still in use; note the interesting paintings on the *mandapam* ceiling. The monkeys here can be aggressive.

The Riverside

You can walk along the river bank (1,500 m) to the famous Vitthala Temple. The path is easy and passes several interesting ruins including small 'cave' temples – worthwhile with a guide.

Alternatively, a motorable road skirts the Royal Enclosure to the south, and goes all the way to the Vitthala Temple. On the way back you can visit the **Raghunatha Temple**, on a hill top, for its Dravidian style, quiet atmosphere and excellent view of the countryside from the rocks above, especially at sunset.

After passing **Achyuta Bazaar**, which leads to the Tiruvengalanatha Temple 400 m to the south, the riverside path goes near **Sugriva's Cave**, where it is said that Sita's jewels, dropped as she was abducted by the demon Ravana, were hidden by Sugriva. There are good views of the ancient ruined bridge to the east, and nearby the path continues past the only early period Vaishnavite shrine, the 14th-century **Narasimha Temple**. The **King's balance** is at the end of the path as it approaches the Vitthala Temple. It is said that the rulers were weighed against gold, jewels and food, which were then distributed to Brahmins.

The **Vitthala Temple** ① *foreigners US$5 (allows entry to Lotus Mahal on the same day 0800-1600)*, a World Heritage Monument, is dedicated to Vishnu. It stands in a rectangular courtyard, enclosed within high walls. Probably built in the mid-15th century, it is one of the oldest and most intricately carved, with its *gopurams* and *mandapas*. The *Dolotsava mandapa* has 56 superbly sculpted slender pillars which can be struck to produce different musical notes. It has elephants on the balustrades and horses at the entrance. The other two ceremonial *mandapas*, though less finely carved have some interesting carved pillars, eg Krishna hiding in a tree from the *gopis*, a woman using a serpent twisted around a stick to churn a pot of buttermilk. In the courtyard is a superb chariot carved out of granite, the wheels raised off the ground so that they could be revolved!

Krishnapura

On the road between the Virupaksha Bazar and the Citadel, you pass Krishnapura, Hampi's earliest Vaishnava township with a Chariot Street 50 m wide and 600 m long, which is now a cultivated field. The **Krishna temple** has a very impressive gateway to the east. Just southwest of the Krishna temple is the colossal monolithic **statue of Lakshmi Narasimha** in the form of a four-armed man-lion with fearsome bulging eyes sheltered under a seven-headed serpent, *Ananta*. It is over 6 m high but sadly damaged.

The road south, from the Sacred Centre towards the Royal Enclosure, passes the excavated **Prasanna Virupaksha** (misleadingly named 'underground') **Temple** and interesting watchtowers.

Royal Enclosure

At the heart of the Metropolis is the small **Hazara Rama Temple**, the Vaishanava 'chapel royal'. The outer enclosure wall to the north has five rows of carved friezes while the outer walls of the *mandapa* has three. The episodes from the epic *Ramayana* are told in great detail, starting with the bottom row of the north end of the west *mandapa* wall.

Hampi - Vijaynagara

■ **Sleeping**
1 Mayura Bhuvaneswari
2 Rahul
3 Shanti Shambhu & Raju
4 Vicky

Vijayanagar's Nava Ratri

It is not difficult to imagine the magnificence of the Vijayanagar court or of some of its special occasions. The Mahanavami festival, an annual royal ceremony of the 15th and 16th century was held from mid-September to mid-October. The festival lives on across South India today, often known as Navaratri. Many Persian and Portuguese travellers visited the court when all activity centred around the "House of victory" – the Mahanavami Dibba - and the King's Audience Hall. Now they are just vast granite platforms, which almost certainly carried wooden buildings. Through the festivities the King sometimes shared his throne, or sat at its foot while it was occupied by a richly decorated processional image of the god, while at other times he was alone.

Stein writes: "What was viewed was a combination of great durbar with its offerings of homage and wealth to the King and return of gifts from the King – exchanges of honours; the sacrificial re-consecration of the King's arms – his soldiers, horses, elephants – in which hundreds of thousands of animals were slaughtered; *darshana* and *puja* of the King's tutelary – the goddess – as well as his closest kinsmen; and a variety of athletic contests, dancing and singing processions involving the King's women and temple dancers from throughout the realm, and fireworks displays. The focus of these diverse and magnificent entertainments was always the King as glorious and conquering warrior, as the possessor of vast riches lavishly displayed by him and his women (queens and their maids of honour) and distributed to his followers."

The two-storeyed **Lotus Mahal** ⓘ *0600-1800, foreigners US$5 (allows same day entry to Vitthala Temple)*, is in the **Zenana** or ladies' quarter, screened off by its high walls. The watchtower is in ruins but you can see the domed **stables** for 10 elephants with a pavilion in the centre and the guardhouse. Each stable had a wooden beamed ceiling from which chains were attached to the elephants' backs and necks. In the **Durbar Enclosure** is the specially built decorated platform of the **Mahanavami Dibba**, from which the royal family watched the pageants and tournaments during the nine nights of *navaratri* festivities. The 8 m-high square platform originally had a covering of bricks, timber and metal but what remains still shows superb carvings of hunting and battle scenes, as well as dancers and musicians.

The exceptional skill of water engineering is displayed in the excavated system of aqueducts, tanks, sluices and canals, which could function today. The 22 m square **Pushkarini** is the attractive stepped tank at the centre of the enclosure. The road towards Kamalapuram passes the **Queen's Bath**, in the open air, surrounded by a narrow moat, which had scented water filling the bath from lotus shaped fountains. It measures about 15 m x 2 m and has interesting stucco work around it.

Museum

The **Archaeological Museum** ⓘ *closed Fri, 1000-1700*, at Kamalapuram has a collection of sculpture, paintings, copper plates and coins. The ASI booklet is on sale. There is a scale model of Hampi in the courtyard.

Gadag

Gadag is an important and typical cotton collection market. The **cotton market** is well worth a visit. The **fort** at Gadag has a Saivite temple of *Trimbakeshwar*, 'Lord of the Three Peaks', elaborately carved, and an enormous carved bull. An inscription dates the temple at AD 868. Gadag is a railway junction and so has tea stalls, cold drinks, simple restaurants and a *Dak Bungalow*.

Bijapur → *Phone code: 08352. Colour map 5, grid C5. Population: 245,900.*

Bijapur has the air of a northern Muslim city with its mausolea, mosques and palaces. It has some of the finest mosques in the Deccan and retains real character. The chowk between the bus station and MG Rd is quite atmospheric in the evening. Overall it is a provincial, grubby but unhurried town.

Ins and outs
Getting there The railway station is just outside the east wall of the fort under 1 km from the Gol Gumbaz while long distance buses draw in just west of the citadel. Both arrival points are close enough to several hotels.

Getting around It is easy to walk or cycle round the town. There are also autos and tongas; negotiate for '8 sight tour price'. See Transport, page 1000, for further details.

History
The Chalukyas who ruled over Bijapur were overthrown at the end of the 12th century. In the early years of the 14th century the Delhi Sultans took it for a time until the Bahmanis, with their capital in Gulbarga, ruled through a governor in Bijapur who declared independence in 1489 and founded the **Adil Shahi Dynasty**. Of Turkish origin, they held power until 1686.

Bijapur

N

0 metres 400
0 yards 400

■ **Sleeping**
1 Madhuvan &
 Restaurant
2 Samat & Kanishka
 International

3 Sanman
4 Santosh & Kapil
 Restaurant

● **Eating**
1 Priyadarshini
2 Shrinidhi

Sights

★ **The Jama Masjid** is one of the finest in the Deccan with a large shallow, onion-shaped dome and arcaded court. It was built by Ali Adil Shah I (ruled 1557-79) during Bijapur's rise to power and displays a classic restraint. The Emperor Aurangzeb added a grand entrance to the Masjid and also had a square painted for each of the 2,250 worshippers that it can accommodate. The **Citadel** with its own wall has few of its grand buildings intact. One is the Durbar Hall, **Gagan Mahal** (Sky Palace), open to the north so that the citizens outside were not excluded. It had royal residential quarters on either side with screened balconies for the women to remain unseen while they watched the court below. Another worth visiting is the **Jal Manzil**, or the water pavilion, a cool sanctuary.

★ **Ibrahim Rauza** ① *0600-1800, foreigners $2, Indians Rs 5, video camera Rs 25, early morning best to avoid crowds*, the palatial 17th-century tomb west of the city wall, is beautifully proportioned. It has slender minarets and carved decorative panels with lotus, wheel and cross patterns as well as bold Arabic calligraphy, bearing witness to the tolerance of the Adil Shahi Dynasty towards other religions. Built during the dynasty's most prosperous period when the arts and culture flourished, it also contains the tomb of Ibrahim Adil Shah II (ruled 1580-1626) who had it built for his wife but died first. Near the Rauza is a huge tank, the Taj Bauri, built by Ibrahim II in memory of his wife. The approach is through a giant gateway flanked by two octagonal towers.

Gol Gumbaz ① *0630-1730, foreigners US$2, Indians Rs 5, video camera Rs 25 (complaint book available!), some choose to just view it from the gate*, the vast whitewashed tomb of Mohammad Adil Shah buried here with his wife, daughter and favourite court dancer, has the world's second largest dome (unsupported by pillars), and one of its least attractive. Its extraordinary **whispering gallery** carries a message across 38 m which is repeated 11 times. However, noisy crowds make hearing a whisper quite impossible; quietest in early morning. Numerous narrow steps in one of the corner towers, lead to the 3 m wide gallery. The plaster here was made out of eggs, cowdung, grass and jaggery. There is an excellent view of the city with its walls from the base of the dome.

The **Nakkar Khana**, the gate house, is now a Museum. The **Asar Mahal** (circa 1646) was built with a tank watered by the old conduit system. It was used as a court house and has teak pillars and interesting frescoes in the upper floor. The **Mehtar Mahal** (1620) with its delicate minarets and carved stone trellises and brackets supporting the balconies which form a decorative gateway, was supposed to have been built for the palace sweepers.

To the west, **Sherza Burj** (Lion Gate) in the 10 km long fort wall, has the enormous 55 tonne, 4.3 m long, 1.5 m diameter cannon *Malik-i-Maidan* (Ruler of the Plains) on the west. To avoid being deafened the gunner is believed to have dived into the tank off the platform! It was cast in the mid-16th century in Ahmadnagar, and was brought back as a prize of war pulled by "400 bullocks, 10 elephants and hundreds of soldiers". Note the muzzle – a lion's head with open jaws with an elephant being crushed to death inside. Inside the city wall, close by, is **Upli Burj**, the 24 m high watch tower on high ground with its long guns and water tanks.

The **Bara Kaman** was possibly a 17th-century construction by Adil Shah III. Planned as a mammoth 12 storey building with the shadow of the uppermost storey designed to fall onto the tomb of the Gol Gumbaz, construction was ended after just 2 storeys with the death of the ruler. An impressive series of arches on a raised platform is all that remains.

The **Archaeological Museum** ① *1000-1700, Rs 2*, in the gatehouse of the Gol Gumbaz has an excellent collection of Chinese porcelain, parchments, paintings, armoury, miniatures, stone sculpture and old Bijapur carpets.

The cradle of Hindu Temple architecture

Although Bijapur became an important Muslim regional capital, its surrounding region has several villages which, nearly 1500 years ago, were centres of Chalukyan power and the hearth of new traditions in Indian temple building. At a major Indian crossroads, the temples at Aihole represent the first finely worked experiments in what were to become distinct North and South Indian temple styles. ▸▸ *For Sleeping, Eating and other listings, see pages 1016-1020.*

Ins and outs Since it takes a half day to see Badami, visiting the sites by bus doesn't allow time for Mahakuta. It is well worth hiring a car in Bijapur which allows you to see all the sites quite comfortably in a day. If travelling by bus it is best to visit Badami first, followed by Pattadakal and Aihole. By car it is best to start at Aihole and end at Badami.

★ Aihole→ *Phone code: 0831. Colour map 5, grid C5.*

Aihole was the first Chalukyan capital, but the site was developed over a period of more than 600 years from the sixth century AD and includes important Rashtrakuta and Late Chalukyan temples, some dedicated to Jain divinities. It is regarded as the birthplace of Indian temple architectural styles, and the site of the first built temples, as distinct from those carved out of solid rock. Most of the temples were dedicated to Vishnu, though a number were subsequently converted into Saivite shrines.

Sights ① *The main temples are now enclosed in a park, open sunrise to sunset, foreigners US$2, Indians Rs 5, flash photography prohibited.* There are about 140 temples – half within the fort walls – illustrating a range of developing styles from Hoysala, Dravida, Jain, Buddhist, Nagara and Rekhanagara. There is little else. All the roads entering Aihole pass numerous temple ruins, but the road into the village from Pattadakal and Bagalkot passes the most important group of temples which would be the normal starting point for a visit. Some prefer to wander around the dozens of deserted (free) temples around town instead of joining the crowds in the park!

Durgigudi Temple is named not after the Goddess Durga but because it is close to the *durga* (fort). Dating from the late seventh century, it has an early *gopuram* structure and semi-circular apse which imitates early Buddhist chaitya halls. It has numerous superb sculptures, a series contained in niches around the ambulatory: walking clockwise they represent Siva and Nandi, Narasimha, Vishnu with Garuda, Varaha, Durga and Harihara.

Lad Khan Temple has been dated, according to recent research, from approximately AD 700, not from AD 450 as suggested by the first Archaeological Survey of India reports in 1907. This is indicated by the similarity of some of its sculptures to those of the Jambulinga temple at Badami, which has been dated precisely at AD 699. Originally an assembly hall and *kalyana mandapa* (marriage hall) it was named after Lad Khan, a pious Muslim who stayed in the temple at the end of the 19th century. A stone ladder through the roof leads to a shrine with damaged images of Surya, Vishnu and Siva carved on its walls. It bears a striking resemblance to the megalithic caves which were still being excavated in this part of the Deccan at the beginning of the period. The roof gives an excellent view of the village.

Gaudar Gudi Temple, near the Lad Khan temple, is a small, rectangular Hindu temple, probably dating from the seventh century. It has a rectangular columned *mandapa*, surrounded on three sides by a corridor for circumambulation. Its roof of stone slabs is an excellent example of North Indian architecture. Beyond the Gaudar Gudi Temple is a small temple decorated with a frieze of pots, followed by a deep well. There are others in various states of repair. To see the most important of the remaining temples you leave the main park. Excavations are in progress, and the boundaries of the park may sometimes be fenced. Turning right out of the main park, the Bagalkot road leads to the **Chikki Temple**. Similar in plan to the Gaudar Gudi, this temple has particularly fine carved pillars. The beams which support the platform are also well worth seeing.

Ravan Phadi Cave Temple is reached from the main park entrance on the left, about 300 m from the village. The cave (formerly known as the Brahman) itself is artificial, and the sixth century temple has a variety of carvings of Siva both outside and inside. One is in the *Ardhanarisvara* form (half Siva, half Parvati), another dancing between Parvati and Ganesh. There is a huge lotus carved in the centre of the hall platform. There are two small eighth century temples at the entrance, the one to the northwest dedicated to Vishnu and that to the south, badly weathered, may have been based on an older Dravidian style temple.

The Buddhist Temple is a plain two-storeyed Buddhist temple on a hill beyond the end of the village on the way to the Meguti Temple. It has a serene smiling Buddha with the Bodhi Tree emerging from his head, on the ceiling of the upper floor. Further uphill is the **Jain temple**, a plain structure lacking the decorations on the plinth, columns and no *gopuram* as on some of the Hindu temples. It has a statue of Mahavira in the shrine within. Climb up through the roof for a good view of Aihole.

The **Meguti Temple** (AD 634) is reached from the Buddhist Temple down a path leading to a terrace. A left hand route takes you to the foot of some stairs leading to the top of a hill which overlooks the town. This is the site of what is almost certainly the oldest building in Aihole and one of the oldest dated temples in India. Its 634 date is indicated by an inscription by the court poet to the king Ravikirtti. A Dravidian style temple, it is richly decorated on the outside, and although it has elements which suggest Saivite origins, it has an extremely impressive seated Jain figure, possibly Neminath, in the sanctuary which comprises a hall of 16 pillars.

The Kunti Group is a group of four Hindu temples (seventh to ninth centuries). To find them you have to return down to the village. The oldest is in the southeast. The external columns of its *mandapa* are decorated with *mithuna*, or erotic couples. The temple to the northwest has beautifully carved ceiling panels of Siva and Parvati, Vishnu and Brahma. The other two date from the Rashtrakuta period.

Beyond these temples is the **Hucchappayya Math,** dating from the seventh century, which has sculptures of amorous couples and their servants, while the beams inside are beautifully decorated. There is a *Tourist Rest House* close to the temples should you wish to stay.

★ Pattadakal

On the banks of the Malaprabha River, Pattadakal, a World Heritage Site was the second capital of the Chalukyan kings between the seventh and eighth centuries and the city where the kings were crowned. Ptolemy referred to it as 'Petrigal' in the first century AD. Two of their queens imported sculptors from Kanchipuram.

Sights ⓘ *Sunrise to sunset, foreigners US$2.* Most of the temples cluster at the foot of a hill, built out of the pink-tinged gold sandstone, and display a succession of styles of the southern Dravida temple architecture of the Pallavas (even miniature scaled-down models) as well as the North Indian Nagara style, vividly illustrating the region's position at the crossroads of North and South Indian traditions. With one exception the temples are dedicated to Siva. Most of the site is included in the archaeological park. Megalithic monuments dating from the third-fourth centuries BC have been found in the area.

Immediately inside the entrance are the very small **Jambulinga** and **Kadasiddheshvara Temples** (eighth century). Now partly ruined, the curved towers survive and the shrine of the Jambulinga Temple houses a figure of the dancing Siva next to Parvati. The gateways are guarded by *dvarapalas*.

Just to the east is the eighth century **Galaganatha Temple**, again partly damaged, though its curved tower characteristic of North Indian temples is well preserved, including its *amalaka* on top. A relief of Siva killing the demon Andhaka is on the south wall in one of three original porches.

The **Sangamesvara Temple** dating from the reign of Vijayaditya (696-733) is the earliest temple. Although it was never completed it has all the hallmarks of a purely Dravidian style. Beautifully proportioned, the mouldings on the basement and pilasters divide the wall. The main shrine, into which barely any light is allowed to pass, has a corridor for circumambulation, and a *lingam* inside. Above the sanctuary is a superbly proportioned tower of several storeys.

To the southwest is the late eighth-century North Indian style **Kashi Vishveshvara Temple**, readily distinguishable by the *Nandi* in front of the porch. The interior of the pillared hall is richly sculpted, particularly with scenes of Krishna.

The largest temples, the **Virupaksha** (740-44) with its three-storeyed *vimana* and the **Mallikarjuna** (745), typify the Dravida style, and were built in celebration of the victory of the Chalukyan king Vikramaditya II over the Pallavas at Kanchipuram by his wife, Queen Trailokyamahadevi. The king's death probably accounted for the fact that the Mallikarjuna temple was unfinished, attested by the failure to do more than mark out some of the sculptures. However, the king's victory over the Pallavas enabled him to express his admiration for Pallava architecture by bringing back to Pattadakal one of the chief Pallava architects. The Virupaksha, a Saivite temple, has a sanctuary surrounded by passageways and housing a black polished stone Siva *linga*. A further Saivite symbol is the huge 2.6-m high chlorite stone *Nandi* at the entrance, contrasting with the pinkish sandstone surrounding it. The three-storeyed tower rises strikingly above the shrine, the outside walls of which, particularly those on the south side, are richly carved. Many show different forms of Vishnu and Siva, including some particularly striking panels which show Siva appearing out of a *linga*. Note also the beautifully carved columns inside. They are very delicate, depicting episodes from the *Ramayana*, *Mahabharata* and the *Puranas*, as well as giving an insight into the social life of the Chalukyas.

❖ Note the ingenuity of the sculptor in making an elephant appear as a buffalo when viewed from a different side.

In the ninth century the Rashtrakutas arrived and built a Jain temple with its two stone elephants a short distance from the centre. The carvings on the temples, particularly on the **Papanatha** near the village which has interesting sculpture on the ceiling and pillars, synthesizes northern and southern architectural styles.

There is no suitable **accommodation** though a new restaurant is opening. Stay either in Badami, Aihole (see above) or at Bagalkot.

Mahakuta, which was reached by early pilgrims over rocky hills from Badami 5 km away, is a beautiful complex of Chalukyan temples dating from the late seventh century; worth a detour. The superstructures reflect both northern and southern influence and one has an Orissan *deul*.

The restored **temple complex** of two dozen shrines dedicated to Siva is built around a large spring-fed tank within an enclosure wall. The old gateway to the southeast has fasting figures of Bhairava and Chamunda. On entering the complex, you pass the *Nandi* in front of the older **Mahakutesvara** Temple which has fine scrollwork and figures from the epics carved on the base. Larger Siva figures appear in wall niches, including an *Ardhanarisvara*. The temple is significant in tracing the development of the superstructure which began to externally identify the position of the shrine in Dravidian temples. Here the tower is domelike and octagonal, the tiers supported by tiny 'shrines'. The **Mallikarjuna** Temple on the other side of the tank is similar with fine carvings at the entrance and on the ceiling of the columned *mandapa* inside, depicting Hindu deities and *mithuna* couples. The enclosure has many smaller shrines, some carrying fine wall carvings. Also worth visiting is the **Naganatha** Temple 2 km away.

→ *Phone code: 08357. Colour map 5, grid C5. Population: 25,900. The area is well worth exploring by bicycle.*
Badami occupies a dramatic site squeezed in a gorge between two high red sandstone hills. Once called Vatapi, after a demon, Badami was the Chalukyan capital from AD 543-757. The ancient city has several Hindu and Jain temples and a Buddhist cave and remains peaceful and charming. The transcendent beauty of the Hindu cave temples in their spectacular setting warrant a visit.

The village with its busy bazar and a large lake has white-washed houses clustered together along narrow winding lanes up the hillside. There are also scattered remains of 18 stone inscriptions (sixth-16th century).

History For a short time in the mid-seventh century the Chalukyas lost control of Badami to the Pallavas and were finally defeated by the Rashtrakutas. They were followed by the Western Chalukyas, the Yadavas, the Vijayanagaras, the Bijapur emperors and the Marathas.

Caves and temples The sites are best visited early in the morning. They are very popular with monkeys, which can be aggressive, especially if they see food. End the day by watching the sun set from the eastern end of the tank.

★ The **South Fort** ① *foreigners US$2*, is famous for its cave temples, four of which were cut out of the hillside in the second half of the sixth century. There are 40 steps to **Cave 1**, the oldest. There are several sculpted figures, including Harihara, Siva and Parvati, and Siva as Nataraja with 18 arms seen in 81 dancing poses. **Cave 2**, a little higher than Cave 1, is guarded by *dvarapalas* (door-keepers). Reliefs of Varaha and Vamana decorate the porch. **Cave 3**, higher still, is dedicated to Vishnu. According to a Kannada inscription (unique in Badami) it was excavated in AD 578. It has numerous sculptures including Narasimha (man-lion), Hari-Hara (Siva-Vishnu), a huge seated Vishnu and interesting friezes. Frescoes, executed in the tempera technique (see box, page 1119) are similar to that used in the Ajanta paintings, and the carved ceilings and brackets. **Cave 4**, probably about 100 years later than the three earlier caves, is the only Jain cave. It has a statue of the seated Parsvanatha with two *dvarapalas* at the entrance. The fort itself above the caves is closed to the public.

The **Buddhist Temple** is in the natural cave near the ancient artificial Bhutanatha Lake (Agasthya Lake), where the mossy green water is considered to cure illnesses. The Yellamma Temple has a female deity, while one of the two Saivite temples is to Bhutanatha (God of souls); in this form, Siva appears angry in the dark inner sanctuary.

The seventh-century **Mallegitti Sivalaya Temple**, one of the finest examples of the early southern style, has a small porch, a *mandapa* (hall) and a narrower *vimana* (shrine), which Harle points out is typical of all early Western Chalukya temples. The slim pilasters on the outer walls are reminders of the period when wooden pillars were essential features of the construction. Statues of Vishnu and Siva decorate the outer walls, while animal friezes appear along the plinth and above the eaves. These are marked by a prominent moulding with a series of purely ornamental small solid pavilions.

Jambulinga Temple is an early temple in the centre of the town near the rickshaw stand. Dating from 699, as attested by an inscription, and now almost hidden by houses, the visible brick tower is a late addition from the Vijayanagar period. Its three chapels, dedicated to Brahma, Vishnu and Siva, contain some fine carving, although the deities are missing and according to Harle the ceiling decoration already shows signs of deteriorating style. The carvings here, especially that of the Nagaraja in the outside porch, have helped to date the Lad Khan temple in Aihole accurately (see above). Opposite the Jambulinga temple is the 10th century Virupaksha Temple.

The **North Fort** temples ① *Rs 2, carry water*, mainly seventh century, give an insight into Badami's history. Steep steps, almost 1 m high, take you to 'gun point' at the top of the fort which has remains of large granaries, a treasury and a watchtower. The **Upper Sivalaya Temple**, though damaged, still has some friezes and sculptures depicting Krishna legends. (The North Fort was taken in a day by Col Munro in 1918, when he broke in through the east side).

Dolmens ⓘ *A local English speaking guide Dilawar Badesha at Tipu Nagar charges about Rs 200.* An ancient dolmen site can be reached by an easy hike through interesting countryside; allow 3½ hours.

Museum Archaeological Survey's **Medieval Sculpture Gallery** ⓘ *closed Fri, 1000-1700, free*, north of the tank, has fine specimens from Badami, Aihole and Pattadakal and a model of the natural bridge at Sidilinapadi, 5 km away.

Hospet to Bidar

The dry and undulating plains are broken by rocky outcrops giving superb sites for commanding fortresses such as Gulbarga and Bidar. *▸ For Sleeping, Eating and other listings, see pages 1016-1020.*

Gulbarga → *Phone code: 08472. Colour map 5, grid B5. Population: 427,900.*
Gulbarga was the first capital of the Bahmanis (from 1347-1525). It is also widely known among South Indian Muslims as the home of Saiyid Muhammad Gesu Daraz Chisti (1320-1422) who was instrumental in spreading pious Islamic faith in the Deccan. The annual Urs festival in his memory attracts up to 100,000 people.

Sights The town sites and hotels are quite spread out so it is worth hiring an auto for half a day. The most striking remains in the town are the fort, with its citadel and mosque, the Jami Masjid, and the great tombs in its eastern quarter – massive, fortress-like buildings with their distinctive domes over 30 m high.

The **fort** is just 1 km west of the centre of the present town. Originally built by Ala-ud-din Bahmani, in the 14th century, most of the outer structures and many of the buildings are in ruins although the outer door of the west gate and the *Bala Hissar* (citadel), a massive structure, remain almost intact though the whole is very overgrown. A flight of ruined steps leads up to the entrance in the north wall. Beware of dogs.

★ **Jami Masjid** The whole area of 3,500 sq m is covered by a dome over the *mihrab*, four corner domes and 75 minor domes, making it unique among Indian mosques. It was built by Firoz Shah Bahmani (1397-1432). Similarities with the mosque at Cordoba have contributed to the legend that it was designed by a North African architect from the Moorish court.

The **tombs** of the Bahmani sultans are in two groups. One lies 600 m to the west of the fort, the other on the east of the town. The latter have no remaining exterior decoration though the interiors show some evidence of ornamentation. The Dargah of the Chisti saint, **Hazrat Gesu Nawaz** – also known as Khwaja Bande Nawaz – who came to Gulbarga in 1413 during the reign of Firoz Shah Tughlaq, is open to visitors, see page 1305. The two-storey tomb with a highly decorated painted dome had a mother of pearl canopy added over the grave. Please note that women are not allowed to enter the tombs. The **Dargah library**, which has 10,000 books in Urdu, Persian and Arabic, is open to visitors.

The most striking of all the tombs near **Haft Gumbaz**, the eastern group, is that of **Taj-ud-Din Firuz** (1422). Unlike the other tombs it is highly ornamented, with geometrical patterns developed in the masonry.

★ Bidar→ *Phone code: 08357. Colour map 5, grid C4. Population: 172,300.*

Bidar's impressive fort is still intact and the town sprawls within and outside its crumbling walls, in places retaining some of its old medieval charm. The palaces and tombs provide some of the finest examples of Muslim architecture in the Deccan. The town is pleasantly traffic free and well worth exploring on foot. ▸▸ *For Sleeping, Eating and other listings, see pages 1016-1020.*

Ins and outs

The branch railway line is too slow to be of much use. Travel instead by bus from Hyderabad or Gulbarga, both under four hours away, or Bijapur, eight hours. The bus stand is 1 km west of the centre. There are no exchange facilities available.

Bidar

■ Sleeping
1 Airlines
2 Ashoka
3 Rest House

● Eating
1 Jyoti Udupi

History

The walled fort town, on a red laterite plateau in North Karnataka, once the capital of the **Bahmanis** and the **Barid Shahis**, remained an important centre until it fell to Aurangzeb in 1656. The Bahmani Empire fragmented into four kingdoms, and the ninth Bahmani ruler, **Ahmad Shah I**, shifted his capital from Gulbarga to Bidar in 1424, rebuilding the old Hindu fort to withstand cannon attacks, and enriching the town with beautiful palaces and gardens. With the decline of the Bahmanis, the Barid Shahi Dynasty founded here ruled from 1487 until Bidar was annexed to Bijapur in 1619.

Sights

The intermingling of Hindu and Islamic styles has been ascribed to the use of Hindu craftsmen, skilled in temple carving in stone, particularly hornblende, who would have been employed by the succeeding Muslim rulers. They transferred their skill to Muslim monuments, no longer carving human figures, forbidden by Islam, but using the same technique to decorate with geometric patterns, arabesques and calligraphy, wall friezes, niches and borders on the buildings for their masters. The pillars, often of wood, were intricately carved and then painted and burnished with gold to harmonize with the *encaustic* tiles.

The **Inner Fort** built by Muhammad Shah out of the red laterite and dark trapstone was later embellished by Ali Barid. The steep hill to the north and east provided natural defence. It was protected to the south and west by a triple moat (now filled). A series of gates and a drawbridge over the moat to the south formed the main entrance from the town. The second gate, the **Sharaza Darwaza** (1503) has tigers carved in bas relief on either side (Shia symbols of Ali as protector), tile decorations on the walls and the *Nakkar Khana* (Drum gallery) above. Beyond this is a large fortified area which brings you to the third gate, the huge **Gumbad Darwaza**, probably built by Ahmad Shah Wali in the 1420s, which shows Persian influence. Note the decorated *gumbad* (dome).

You will see the triple moat to the right and after passing through the gateway, to your left are steps leading to the **Rangin Mahal** (Coloured Palace) where Muhammad Shah moved to, after finding the nearby Shah Burj a safe refuge in 1487 when the Abyssinians attacked. This small palace (an indication of the Bahmanis' declining years) was built by him, elaborately decorated with coloured tiles, later enhanced by Ali Barid with mother-of-pearl inlay on polished black granite walls as well as intricate wood carvings. If locked, ask at the Museum for a key.

The old banyan tree and the **Shahi Matbak** (once a palace, but served as the Royal Kitchens) are to the west, with the **Shahi Hammam** (Royal Baths) next to it, which now houses a small **Museum** ① *0800-1700*. The exhibits include Hindu religious sculptures, stone age implements, cannon balls filled with bits of iron.

The **Lal Bagh**, where remains of water channels and a fountain witness to its former glory, and the *zenana*, are opposite the Hammam. The **Sola Khamba** (16 column) or **Zanani Mosque** is to the west (1423). The adjacent **Tarkash Mahal** (possibly refurbished by the Barid Shahis for the harem), to the south of Lal Bagh, is in ruins but still retains some tilework. From behind the Mosque you can get to the **Gagan Mahal** (Heavenly Palace) which once carried fine decorations and is believed to have allowed the ladies to watch animal fights in the moat below from the back of the double hall. Good view from the roof. The **Diwan-i-Am** (Hall of Public Audience) is to the northwest of the Zenana which once held the 'Takht-i-Firoza' (turquoise throne). To the north stands the **Takht Mahal** with royal apartments, audience hall and swimming bath. The steep staircase will take you down to underground chambers.

South of the Royal Apartments is the well which supplied water to the fort palaces through clay pipes. Of the so-called **Hazar** (thousand) **Kothri** ① *cycling is a good way of exploring the site, free,* you can only see a few underground rooms and passages which enabled a quick escape to the moat when necessary. Further south, the **Naubat Khana** probably housed the fort commander and the musicians. The road west from the Royal Apartments leads to the encircling Fort Wall (about 10 km) with bastions carrying vast canyons, the one to the northwest being the most impressive. You can see the ammunition magazine inside the **Mandu Darwaza** to the east before returning to the main Fort entrance.

Old town

As you walk south from the fort you can see the ruins of the **Madrassa of Mahmud Gawan** (1472). It is a fine example of his native Persian architecture and still bears signs of the once brilliant green, white and yellow tiles which covered the whole façade with swirls of floral patterns and bold calligraphy.

The **Chaubara** is a 23-m circular watchtower at the crossroads, south of the town centre (good views from the top). South of this is the **Jami Masjid** (1430) which bears the Barid Shahis' typical chain and pendant motif. The **Kali Masjid** (1694), south of the Talghat Darwaza, is made of black trapstone. It has fine plaster decorations on the vaulted ceiling. There are also a number of **Khanqahs** (monasteries).

The road east from the Dulhan Darwaza, opposite the General Hospital, leads to the eight **Bahmani tombs** at **Ashtur** ① *0800-1700, free, the attendant can use a mirror to reflect sunlight but it is best to carry your own flash light.* These are best seen in the morning when the light is better for viewing the interiors.

The square tombs, with arched arcades all round have bulbous domes. The exteriors have stone carvings and superb coloured tile decoration showing strong Persian influence, while the interiors have coloured paintings with gilding. The tomb of **Ahmad Shah I**, the ninth Bahmani ruler (see above), is impressive with a dome rising to nearly 35 m, and has a particularly fine interior with coloured decorations and calligraphy in the Persian style, highlighted with white borders. To the east and south are minor tombs of his wife and son. The tomb of **Alauddin Shah II** (1458) is possibly the finest. Similar in size to his father's, this has lost its fine painting inside but enough remains of the outer tilework to give an impression of its original magnificence.

On the way back, is the **Chaukhandi of Hazrat Khalil-Ullah** which is approached by a flight of steps. Most of the tilework has disappeared but you can see the fine carvings at the entrance and on the granite pillars.

The **Barid Shahi tombs** each of which once stood in its garden, are on the Nanded Road to the west of the old town. That of **Ali Barid** is the most impressive, with the dome rising to over 25 m, with granite carvings, decorative plasterwork and calligraphy and floral patterns on the coloured tiles, which sadly can no longer be seen on the exterior. Here, abandoning the customary *mihrab* on the west wall, Ali Barid chose to have his tomb left open to the elements. A prayer hall, music rooms, a combined tomb for his concubines and a pool fed by an aqueduct are nearby. There are fine carvings on the incomplete tomb to his son **Ibrahim Barid**, to the west. You can also see two sets of granite *ranakhambas* (lit battleposts) which may have been boundary markers. Other tombs show the typical arched niches employed to lighten the heavy walls which have decorative parapets.

The road north from Ali Barid's tomb descends to **Nanak Jhera**, where a *gurdwara* marks the holy place where Sikhs believe a miracle was performed by Guru Nanak (see page 1346) and the *jhera* (spring) rose.

Raichur → *Phone code: 08532. Colour map 5, grid C5. Population: 205,600.*

The main road from Hospet to Hyderabad passes through the important medieval centre of Raichur, once dominant in the Tungabhadra-Krishna doab but now a dusty peninsula town. An important market town, it is in the middle of a cotton growing area. Cotton takes up more than 20% of the sown area, followed by groundnuts.

The site of the **fort's citadel** at Raichur gives magnificent views over the vast open spaces of the Deccan plateau nearly 100 m below. Built in the mid-14th century Raichur became the first capital of the Bijapur Kingdom when it broke away from the

Bahmani Sultans in 1489. Much of the fort itself is now in ruins, but there are some interesting remains. The north gate is flanked by towers, a carved elephant standing about 40 m away. On the inner walls are some carvings, and a tunnel reputedly built to enable soldiers access to barricade the gate in emergency. Near the west gate is the old palace. The climb to the citadel begins from near the north gate. In the citadel is a shrine with a row of cells with the Jami Masjid in the east. Its eastern gateway has three domes. The top of the citadel is barely 20 sq m.

There are some other interesting buildings in the fort below the hill, including the **Daftar ki Masjid** (Office Mosque), built around 1510 out of masonry removed from Hindu temples. It is one of the earliest mosques in the Deccan to be built in this way, with the bizarre result of producing flat ceilings with pillars carved for Chalukyan temples. The **Ek Minar ki Masjid** ('one-minaret mosque') is in the southeast corner of the courtyard. It has a distinctively *Bahmani* style dome.

Listings: Northern Karnataka and Hampi

● Sleeping

Hospet *p1001, map p1002*
Station Rd has been renamed Mahatma Gandhi Rd (MG Rd).
B-D Shanbhag Towers, College Rd, T25910, F25919, shanbhagtowers@yahoo.com. 64 spacious rooms, 32 a/c with tub, TV, fridge, in brand new hotel, breathtaking Hampi theme, restaurants (one rooftop with great views), bar.
B-F Malligi, 6/143 Jambunatha Rd, T28101, F27038, malligihome@hotmail.com. 140 rooms, 65 a/c, newer **D** are large with bath (4 **B** suites), always inspect first as standard varies enormously, restaurant and bar by pool (economy guests and non-residents pay Rs 25 per hr for pool), health club, exchange, travel (good Hampi tour Rs 80), internet, some adverse comments.
C-E Priyadarshini, V/45 Station Rd, T28838, F24709, www.priyainnhampi.com. 82 fairly good rooms, 25 a/c, rather bare and bit over priced, though friendly service, good restaurants, internet, parking.
D-E Karthik, 252 Sardar Patel Rd, T24938, F20028. 40 good sized, clean rooms, 10 a/c in quiet, modern hotel, garden dining, friendly and good value.
D-E Nagarjuna Residency, Sardar Patel Rd, opposite *Karthik*, T29009. Spotless, modern, excellent value rooms, some a/c, extra bed Rs 30-50, very helpful. Recommended.

E SLV Yatri Nivas, Station Rd, T21525. 15 bright, airy rooms in clean, well-run hotels. Good vegetarian restaurant and bar.
E Sivananda, next to bus stand, T20700. 23 rooms, 4 a/c, simple but clean, astrologer!
F Vishwa, MG Rd, opposite bus station, away from the road, T27172. 42 clean rooms (some 4-bed) with bath, adjacent *Shanthi* restaurant. No frills but good value.

Hampi *p1002, map p1004*
Power cuts are common so a supply of candles is essential. Mosquitos can be a real problem, especially at dusk.

A small selection of over 30 guest houses are listed here. All are fairly similar, converted family houses, usually with common bathroom/toilet, some with roof top restaurant. Few are purpose-built. Most are in the block to the north and northeast of the Virupaksha Temple, and behind the shops on the main street; some are nearer the Bazar bus-stand. All are **E** or **F** category; prices rise 30% during the 'season'.

Hampi Bazar
Archana, T41547. 8 rooms, very clean, quiet, with nets and roof area, attached shop.
Gopi, T41695. 10 rooms with bath, nets, board games.
Rahul, south of the bus stand but reasonably quiet. Basic sleeping under nets, and washing, clean, good simple veg food, good views from rooftop.

● *For an explanation of the sleeping and eating price codes used in this guide, see inside the front cover. Other relevant information is found in Essentials pages 52-57.*

Raju, T41349. Two buildings on either side of river, 2 and 14 rooms. Old with character, and clean, rooftop restaurant.
Shambhu, T41383. 5 rooms with bath and nets, plenty of plants, rooftop restaurants (egg dishes), friendly.
Shanti Guest House, down path to the right of the temple (signed), T41568. 23 rooms with fans around pleasant courtyard with plenty of plants, common shower, roof for overspill, very clean, well run and friendly, cycle hire, good cakes (see below).
Vicky, 200 m north of main road (turn off at tourist office), T41694. 7 rooms (4 with bath), bucket hot water, Indian toilet, good rooftop restaurant, internet Rs 60 per hr.

Kamalapuram
D-E Mayura Bhuvaneswari, 2 km from site, T41574. 32 redecorated rooms (8 a/c, Rs 450), fairly clean, decent food, chilled beer, poor cycle hire.

Bijapur p1006, map p1006
There are few decent hotels and restaurants.
B Madhuvan International, off Station Rd, T55571, F56201. 35 rooms, 10 a/c, very pleasant, good veg garden restaurant and rooftop terrace, beer to rooms only, travel desk, but a bit overpriced.
C-E Kanishka International, Station Rd, T55506. 26 spacious, pleasant rooms, 10 a/c, TV, popular restaurant, car hire. Brand new hotel still establishing itself, clean and friendly.
D-F Godavari, Athni Rd, T53105, F22180. 48 good rooms, friendly staff, good veg and non-veg food. Avoid
D-F Megharaj, MG Rd.
D-F Samrat, Station Rd, T51620. 30 basic rooms, 6 a/c passable, rest battered, good vegetarian garden restaurant but mosquito feast at dinner.
D-F Sanman, opposite Gol Gumbaz, Station Rd, T51866. 24 clean, pleasant rooms with shower, nets, 6 a/c. Very good value. Separate veg restaurant and non-veg with bar. Recommended.
E-F Santosh, T52179. 70 good, clean rooms including some D a/c, quieter at back, convenient, good value.

F Railway Retiring Room and dorm, exceptionally clean, contact Ticket Collector on duty. Recommended.

Bagalkot p1010
E Circuit House, with a/c rooms, 5 km from centre on Bijapur Rd.

Badami p1011
There is no formal money exchange but the hotel *Mukambika* may be persuaded to change small value TCs.
B Badami Court, Station Rd, T20230, F20207, www.hotelbadamicourt.com. 2 km from town (pleasant stroll or frequent buses). 26 clean, modern, though cramped rooms (bath tub), some a/c, good restaurant, pool (small only knee deep; non-residents Rs 80 per hr) gym, garden to relax, friendly, well-managed, rates sometimes negotiable, only accepts Rupees, tour of all nearby sites Rs 800.
C-E Mukambika Deluxe, Station Rd, opposite Bus Stand, T65067, F65106. 6 clean, comfortable rooms with bath, 10 deluxe, some with a/c and TV (Rs 250-950), welcoming, helpful, good value. Recommended, though a little noisy. Adjoining *Kanchan* has a lively bar, good food and cheery service.
E-F Mayura Chalukya (KSTDC), 1 km on Ramdurg Rd, T65046. 10 crumbling rooms with baths, 6 modern cottages, tourist office, well placed, in wooded surrounding, basic restaurant, car hire Rs 650 per day (for Aihole, Pattadakal, Mahakuta).
F Shree Laxmi Vilas. Simple rooms, 3 with balconies with great views back to the temples. Right in the thick of it so interesting if noisy.

Gulbarga p1012
D Pariwar, Humnabad Rd, near station, T21522. Some a/c rooms (Rs 450), some good value E, old but clean, tidy, friendly staff, tasty vegetarian meals (no beer).
D Santosh, University Rd (east of town), T22661. Some a/c rooms, good non veg restaurant (beer). Best in town.
D-E Aditya, Humnabad Rd, T202040. Reasonable rooms, some a/c with bath, good, clean vegetarian restaurant, very good value.
F Railway Retiring Rooms .

● **Phone codes** Hospet: 08394; Hampi: 08394; Bijapur: 08352; Aihole: 0831;
● Badami: 08357; Gulbarga: 08472; Bidar: 08357; Raichur: 08532

Bidar *p1013, map p1013*

E Ashoka, off Udgir Rd, near Deepak Cinema, T26249, F22114. 21 clean, good-sized rooms, hot water, some a/c, restaurant ("bit of a drinking den but good tandoori"), friendly, only decent hotel in town. Recommended. **F Airlines Lodge**, T26883. 18 rooms, some with TV, hot water in morning, clean linen, OK for overnight stay despite first appearances.

Several very basic hotels near Old Bus Station. A roadside Punjabi *dhaba* near the junction of NH9 and the Bidar Rd serves very good meals, clean (including toilet at back). **Jyoti Udupi**, opposite Bus Station, serves good South Indian.

Raichur *p1015*
F Laxmi Lodge at Koppal.
F Railway Retiring Rooms and dorm.

⊘ Eating

Hospet *p1001, map p1002*
The hotels serve chilled beer.
♥♥ Waves, *Malligi's*, by pool. Multicuisine. Good food, bar.
♥ Shanbhag, near the bus station, good South Indian meals.
Iceland, Station Rd, behind the bus station, good South Indian meals.

Hampi *p1002, map p1004*
All restaurants are vegetarian, though eggs are sometimes available.

Hampi Bazar
♥ Boomshankar, on path to Vitthala temple. Well prepared, fresh river fish.
♥ Gopi for good simple, cheap *thalis*.
♥ Mango Tree, river bank, 500 m west of Temple, relaxed and pleasant.
♥ Manju family-run, simple but enticing food (apple *parathas*), take-aways for tiffin boxes (will even lend boxes).
♥ New Shanti does good carrot/apple/banana/chocolate cakes to order.
♥ Om Shiva. Excellent Western and Middle-Eastern dishes. Good hygiene.
♥ Shambhu opposite *Shanti*, for fresh pasta/noodles and espresso plus all the usual; also bus/train tickets for small commission.
♥ Suresh, 30 m from *Shanti*, down a small alley, very friendly family, made to order so takes a while, but worth the wait.

Kamalapuram
♥ Mayura Bhuvaneswari, does cheap adequate meals. Snacks available near the bus stand.

Bijapur *p1006, map p1006*
Eateries include **Kapali**, opposite bus stand, decent South Indian. **Priyadarshini**, for veg snacks; **Shrinidhi**, for quality veg meals.

Badami *p1011*
Sanman, near Bus Stand, has non-vegetarian. **Laxmi Vilas**, near taxi stand, vegetarian meals. *Dhabas* near the Tonga Stand sell snacks.

⊛ Festivals and events

Hampi *p1002, map p1004*
Jan-Feb: Virupaksha Temple Car festival. **Nov 3rd-5th**: Hampi Music festival at Vitthala Temple when hotels get packed.

Bijapur *p1006, map p1006*
Jan: Siddhesvara Temple festival. Music festival accompanied by Craft Mela.

Bagalkot *p1010*
In **Jan** Nrutytsava draws many famous dancers and is accompanied by a Craft Mela. In **Mar-Apr** Temple car festivals at Virupaksha and Mallikarjuna temples.

○ Shopping

Bidar *p1013, map p1013*
Excellent *bidriwork* (see page 1025) here, where it is said to have originated, particularly shops near the Ta'lim of Siddiq Shah. You can see craftsmen at work in the narrow lanes.

⛰ Activities and tours

Hospet *p1001, map p1002*
Tours
From KSTDC, T21008, and *Malligi* hotel, to Hampi, Rs 75 (lunch extra); 0930-1630. English speaking guide but rather rushed.

⊖ Transport

Hospet *p1001, map p1002*
From Hospet to/from **Hampi**, travel via Kamalapuram, especially in the rainy season

when the slower road to Hampi Bazar which winds through villages, is barely passable.

Auto-rickshaw
Local To Hampi, demand Rs 150.
Long distance To Hampi, Rs 50.

Bicycle
Bikes from Hampi Bazar.

Bus
Local Frequent buses to Hampi's two entry points (via Kamalapuram and Museum, Rs 4 and via Hampi Bazar, 30 mins, Rs 3.50), from 0530; last return around 2000.
Long distance Express bus to/from **Bangalore** (road now upgraded), several from 0700, 10 hrs; **Mysore**, 1830, 10½ hrs (Express buses to Belur/Halebid from both). Services to other sites, eg **Badami** (6 hrs), **Bijapur** (6 hrs), **Chitradurga** 0530 (3 hrs). Overnight Karnataka Tourism luxury coaches to various towns. Direct buses to **Panaji** (Goa); the road is being improved – Luxury, 0630 (10½ hrs), State bus, 0830 (reserve a seat in advance); others involve a change in Hubli (4½ hrs). Paulo Travels Luxury Sleeper coach from *Hotel Priyadarshini*, at 1845, Rs 350, daily; West Coast Sleeper, from Hotel Shanbhag, 1830, Rs 350; daily (Oct-Mar only); strangers may be expected to share a bunk. It is better to take a train to Londa (under 5 hrs) and get a bus to Madgaon or Panaji (3 hrs).

Cycle-rickshaw
From Rly station to Bus Stand about Rs 10.

Taxi
KSTDC, T21008, T28537 or from *Malligi Hotel*; about Rs 700 per day (possible to share).

Train
Bangalore, *Hampi Exp, 6591*, 2010 (via Guntakal, 2½ hrs) 10½ hrs. **Guntakal**: *Amaravati Exp, 7226*, 1610, 2½ hrs. For **Belur/Halebid**: *Amaravati Exp, 7225*, 1050 to Hubli; then *Hubli-Arsikere Pass, 884 (S)*, 1440, arrive 2120. To **Badami**: via Gadag, 4 hrs. **Hyderabad** (via Guntakal): *Hampi/Rayalaseema Exp, 6591/7430*, 2010, 14 hrs. **Madgaon**, *7227*, Tue, Fri, depart Hospet 1050, 9 hrs.

Bicycle hire from Hampi Bazar (try stall behind the temple, Rs 30 per day), and Kamalapuram. **Coracles** take passengers across the river from the jetty west of the Virupaksha Temple, Rs 5 (Rs 10 with luggage).

Gadag *p1005*
Train
To **Bijapur**: *Golgumbaz Exp, 7842*, 0715, 4½ hrs. **Guntakal** via **Hospet** (2 hrs): at 0037,1412, 1802 and 2101, 4 hrs; **Hubli**: 8 daily 0322-2030, 1¾ hrs.

Bijapur *p1006, map p1006*
Bus
Local A service runs between the station (2 km east) to west end of town. Horse drawn carriages ply up and down MG Rd; a fine change from autos but bargain hard.
Long distance Buses are frequent between Bijapur and **Bidar**, **Hubli**, **Belgaum** and **Solapur** (2-2½ hrs). Buses to **Badami** 3½ hrs. For **Hospet**, travel via Gadag or Ikal. Reservations can be made on the following daily services to **Aurangabad**: 0600, 1830 (Rs 180), **Hospet**, **Bangalore**:1700, 1800, 1930, 2130 (Rs 193, 12 hrs); Ultra fast at 1900, 2000 (Rs 252), **Belgaum**: 0630 (Rs 71), **Hubli**: 0900, 1400, 1600 (Rs 84), **Hyderabad**: 0600, 1800 (Rs 141); Deluxe at 2130 (Rs 203), **Mumbai (CT)** : 0800, 1600, 1700, 2030 (Rs 215), **Mumbai (Kurla)** : 1900, 2000, 2100 (Rs 210), **Mysore**: 1700 (Rs 230), **Panaji**: 1900 (Rs 126) and **Vasco de Gama**: 0715 (Rs 131). Several private agents also run services to **Bangalore** (Rs 220, 12 hrs), **Mumbai** (Rs 250, 11 hrs) and **Pune** (Rs 200, 7 hrs).

Train
Computerized Reservation Office open 0800-2000, Sun 0800-1400. **Solapur**: 0945, 1635 (2½ hrs). **Gadag**: 5 trains daily for long distance connections. Otherwise, buses are more convenient.

Badami *p1011*
Bicycle
Bike hire: stalls along the main road, Rs 4 per hr; pleasant to visit Banashankari, Mahakuta and Pattadakal.

Bus

Few daily to **Hospet** (6 hrs), very slow and crowded but quite a pleasant journey with lots of stops; **Belgaum** via Bagalkot, 4 hrs; **Bijapur**, 0645-0930 (4 hrs). Several to **Pattadakal** and **Aihole** from 0730. Aihole (2 hrs), from there to Pattadakal (1600). Last return bus from Aihole 1715, via Pattadakal.

Car

Car hire From Badami with driver for Mahakuta, Aihole and Pattadakal, about Rs 650.

Train

The station is 5 km north on the **Bijapur-Gadag** line, with 6 trains daily in each direction (enquire about schedules); frequent buses to town.

Gulbarga *p1012*
Bus

There are bus connections to **Hyderabad** (190 km) and Solapur.

Train

Mumbai (CST): 8 trains daily, 13 hrs. **Bangalore**: *Udayan Exp, 6529,* 1900, 13½ hrs; *Lokmanya Tilak, 1013,* 0905, 13 hrs. **Chennai (MC)**: *Chennai Exp, 6011* (AC/II), 0130, 15 hrs; *Mumbai Chennai Mail, 6009,* 1140, 18 hrs. *Dadar Chennai Exp, 1063,* 0605, 14 hrs. **Hyderabad**: *Mumbai-Hyderabad Exp, 7031* (AC/II), 0020, 5¾ hrs; *Hussainsagar Exp, 7001,* 0740, 5 hrs.

Bidar *p1013, map p1013*
Auto-rickshaw

Easily available, Rs 15 being the going rate for most short hops across town.

Bicycle

Cycle is the best way to get around and see the sights. 'Cycle taxis' can be hired for around Rs 20 per day from several outlets all over town and near the New Bus Station. You may have to ask 2 or 3 before you find a shop that will rent to you, but persevere. Don't waste time with Ganesh Cycle Taxi, near New Bus Station.

Bus

Services from New Bus Station to most regional destinations, but check timings since the last bus is often quite early. Private buses to **Mumbai**: 1700, 5 hrs, Rs 260. **Pune**: 1530, 3½ hrs, Rs 220. Taxi to **Gulbarga** Rs 800.

Train

Bidar is on a branch line from Vikarabad to Parbhani Junction. **Aurangabad**: *Kacheguda-Manmad Exp, 7664,* 2140, 8½ hrs. **Bangalore**: *Hampi Link Exp, 6593,* 1237, 18 hrs. **Secunderabad**: *Manmad-Kacheguda Exp, 7663,* 0352, 5 hrs.

---

❶ Directory

Hospet *p1001, map p1002*
Banks State Bank of India, next to Tourist Office, only changes cash (US $ and UK £). Monica Travel, near Bus Station, changes TCs (3% charge). **Internet** Cybernet, College Rd, next to Shivananda. **Post office** Opposite vegetable market. **Tourist office** KSTDC, Old Fire Station, Taluk Office Circle, near Bus Stand, T28537.

Hampi *p1002, map p1004*
Exchange Several agents on main street. Modi Enterprises, Main road, near Tourist Office, changes TCs and cash. Also **Neha Travels**. **Internet** On main street and some lodges (eg *Shanti, Sree Rama*), Rs 60 per hr; but frequent power cuts.

Bijapur *p1006, map p1006*
Banks State Bank of India in the citadel, Canara Bank, north of market, best for exchange. **Internet** Cyber Park, first floor, Royal Complex, opposite GPO, 0930-2300 fast connections. **Tourist offices** Opposite stadium, T503592, 1030-1330, 1415-1730, Mon-Sat, but next to useless. Better information from the manager of *Mayura Adil Shahi* (see above).

Andhra Pradesh

⁑ Footprint features

Introduction

Away from its lush green coastal deltas much of Andhra
Pradesh is rocky, bare and dry. The thin red soils developed on
the ancient rocks of the peninsula support an often meagre
agricultural subsistence, but Andhra's capital, **Hyderabad**, has
become one of India's dynamic 'electronics cities'. Once the
centre of the largest Muslim ruled princely state in India,
Hyderabad and its nearby fort of **Golconda** are rich in history,
but rural Andhra has its own share of important sites,
including the ancient Buddhist centres of **Nagarjunakonda**
and **Amaravati**, and one of India's most important modern
pilgrimage centres, **Tirumalai**.

★ Don't miss...

❶ There are some interesting sites in Hyderabad but go to **Husain Sagar** and stroll along the bund for a spot of people watching, page 1031.

❷ The **Nehru Zoological Park** is one of the best zoos in the country, page 1033.

❸ Cycle in the early morning to Golconda and the **Qutb Shahi Tombs**, page 1036.

❹ Take the ferry to **Nagajuna Hill**, an island in the middle of an artifical lake. It is merely the tip of what was one of India's richest Buddhist sites, page 1038.

❺ Take the road from Rajahmundry for the **eastern ghats** of Andhra Pradesh. They are strangely reminiscent of Scottish lochs, page 1047.

❻ Join the 10,000 daily pilgrims at **Tirupati** and get a free haircut, page 1054.

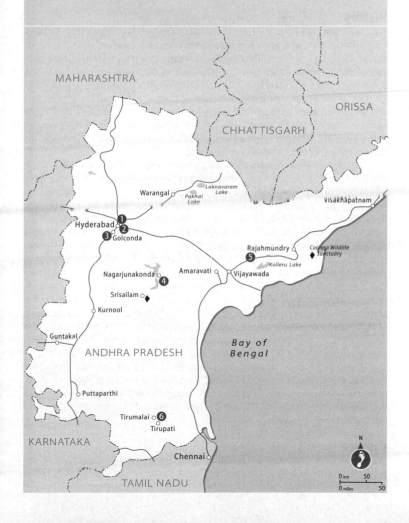

Background → *Population: 75.7 million. Area: 275,000 sq km. www.aptourism.com.*

The land

For much of the year the interior of Andhra looks hot, dry and desolate although the great delta of the Krishna and Godavari rivers retains its lush greenness by virtue of their irrigation water. Water is the state's lifeblood, and the great peninsular rivers have a sanctity which reflects their importance. The **Godavari**, rising less than 200 km north of Mumbai, is the largest of the peninsular rivers. The **Krishna** rises near **Mahabaleshwar** at an altitude of 1,360 m. After the Ganga these two rivers have the largest watersheds in India, and between them they irrigate nearly 6,000,000 ha of farmland.

Climate Andhra Pradesh is hot throughout the year. The interior of the state is in the rain shadow of the Western Ghats and receives less rainfall than much of the coast. All regions have most of their rain between June and October, although the south gets the benefit of the retreating monsoon between October and December. Cyclones sweeping across the Bay of Bengal can wreak havoc in the flat coastal districts in November-December.

History

The first historical evidence of a people called the 'Andhras' came from Emperor Asoka. The first known Andhra power, the **Satavahanas** encouraged various religious groups including Buddhists. Their capital at Amaravati shows evidence of the great skill of early Andhra artists and builders. Around AD 150 there was also a fine university at Nagarjunakonda.

In 1323 Warangal, just to the northeast of the present city of Hyderabad, was captured by the armies of Muhammad bin Tughlaq. Muslim expansion further south was prevented for two centuries by the rise of the **Vijayanagar Empire**, itself crushed at the Battle of Talikota in 1565 by a short-lived federation of Muslim States, and the cultural life it supported had to seek fresh soil.

From then on **Muslim rulers** dominated the politics of central Andhra, Telangana. The Bahmani Kingdoms in the region around modern Hyderabad controlled central Telangana in the 16th century. They were even able to keep the Mughals at bay until Aurangzeb finally forced them into submission at the end of the 17th century. **Hyderabad** was the most important centre of Muslim power in central and South India from the 17th to the 19th centuries. It was founded by the fifth in line of an earlier Muslim Dynasty, **Mohammad Quli Qutb Shah**, in 1591. Through his successors Hyderabad became the capital of a Princely State the size of France, ruled by a succession of Muslim Nizams from 1724 till after India's Independence in 1947.

Through the 18th century **British and French traders** were spreading their influence up the coast. Increasingly they came into conflict and looked for alliances with regional powers. At the end of the 18th century the British reached an agreement with the **Nizam of Hyderabad** whereby he accepted British support in exchange for recognition of British rights to trade and political control of the coastal districts. Thus Hyderabad retained a measure of independence until 1947 while accepting British suzerainty.

There was doubt as to whether the Princely State would accede to India after Partition. The Nizam of Hyderabad would have liked to join fellow Muslims in the newly created Muslim State of Pakistan. However, political disturbances in 1949 gave the Indian Government the excuse to take direct control, and the state was incorporated into the Indian Union.

Culture

Most of Andhra Pradesh's 78 million people are Dravidians. Over 85% of the **population** speak Telugu. However, there are important minorities. Tamil is widely spoken in the extreme south, and on the border of Karnataka there are pockets of

Kanarese speakers. In Hyderabad there are large numbers of Urdu speakers who make up 7% of the state's population.

Hyderabad, the capital of modern Andhra Pradesh, was the seat of government of the Muslim Nizams. Under their rule many Muslims came to work in the court, from North India and abroad. The Nizam's capital was a highly cosmopolitan centre, drawing extensively on Islamic contacts in North India and in west Asia - notably Persia. Its links with the Islamic world and the long tradition of political power that the Nizams had enjoyed encouraged them to hope that they might gain complete Independence from India in 1947. That option was foreclosed by the Indian Government's decision to remove the Nizam by force in 1948 after a half-hearted insurrection.

Andhra **food** stands out as distinct because of its northern influence and larger number of non-vegetarians. The rule of the Muslim Nawabs for centuries is reflected in the rich, spicy local dishes, especially in the area around the capital. Try *haleem* (spiced pounded wheat with mutton), *paya* (soup) or *baghara baigan* (stuffed aubergines). Rice and meat *biryani*, *nahari*, *kulcha,* egg *paratha,* and *kababs* have a lot in common with the northern Mughlai cuisine. Vegetarian biryani replaces meat with cashew nuts and sultanas. The growing of hot chillies has led to its liberal use in the food prepared. Good quality locally-grown grapes (especially *anab-e-shahi*) or *khobani* (puréed apricots) provide a welcome neutralizing effect.

Craft industries

Andhra's **bidriware** uses dark matt gunmetal (a zinc and copper alloy) with silver damascening in beautiful flowing floral and arabesque patterns and illustrates the Persian influence on Indian motifs. The articles vary from large vases and boxes, jewellery and plates to tiny buttons and cuff links. The name is derived from Bidar in Karnataka and dates back to the Bahmani rulers.

Miniature wooden figures, animals, fruit, vegetables and birds are common subjects of *Kondapalli* **toys** which are known for their bright colours. *Nirmal* toys look more natural and are finished with a herbal extract which gives them a golden sheen, *Tirupati* toys are in a red wood while *Ethikoppaka* toys are finished in coloured lacquer. Andhra also produces fine figurines of deities in sandalwood.

Hyderabadi **jewellers** work in gold and precious stones which are often uncut. The craftsmen can often be seen working in the lanes around the Char Minar with shops selling the typical local bangles set with glass to the west. Hyderabadi cultured pearls and silver filigree ware from Karimnagar are another speciality.

The state is famous for **himru shawls** and **fabrics** produced in cotton/silk mixes with rich woven patterns on a special handloom. Silver or gold threads produce even richer 'brocade' cloth. A young boy often sits with the weavers 'calling out' the intricate pattern. The art of weaving special **ikat** fabrics (see page 690) has been revived through the efforts of the All India Handicrafts Board in the villages of Pochampalli, Chirala, Puttapaka and Koyyalagudem among others. The practice of dyeing the warp and weft threads before weaving in such a way as to produce a pattern, additionally used oil in the process when it was woven into pieces of cloth *teli rumal* (literally oil kerchief) to be used as garments. Other towns produce their own special weaves.

Kalamkari paintings (*kalam* refers to the pen used) produced in Kalahasti in the extreme south of Andhra, have a distinctive style using indigo and vegetable dyes extracted from turmeric, pomegranate skin et cetera, on cloth. Fabric is patterned through the medium of dye, then glued. The blues stand out markedly from the otherwise dullish ochre colours. Originally designed to tell stories from mythology (*Mahabharata* and *Ramayana*), they make good wall hangings. *Pallakollu* and *Masulipatam* were particularly famous for printing and painting of floral designs. In addition hand block printed textiles are also produced.

Carpets produced in Warangal and Eluru are known as 'Deccan rugs' with designs that reflect a Persian influence.

Government In 1953 Andhra Pradesh was created on the basis of the Telugu-speaking districts of Madras Presidency. This was not enough for those who were demanding statehood for a united Telugu-speaking region. One political leader, Potti Sreeramulu, starved himself to death in protest at the government's refusal to grant the demand. Finally, in 1956, Andhra Pradesh took its present form. It was the first State to be reorganized when the Indian Government decided to reshape the political map inherited from the British period. In 1956 all Telugu-speaking areas were grouped together in the new State of Andhra Pradesh. This brought together the eastern parts of the old Nizam's territories and the coastal districts which had formerly been in Madras Presidency, whilst Hyderabad became the capital of the new state.

Andhra Pradesh was regarded as a stronghold of the Congress Party until 1983 when a regional party, the **Telugu Desam**, won a crushing victory in the State Assembly elections. The Assembly elections on 5 October 1999 saw a repeat performance, with the highly regarded modernising Chief Minister N Chandrababu Naidu, being swept back to power in the State Assembly with nearly a two thirds majority. Allied with the BJP in the governing coalition in New Delhi, the Telugu Desam has a reputation for pushing ahead with rapid economic modernisation, particularly visible in Hyderabad, but poverty remains endemic in many rural areas. The extremist *Naxalite* movement and the Peoples' War Group (PWG) which have plagued some remote districtsfor over 30 years entered discussions with the government in early 2002.

Economy The last decade has seen a great surge in Hyderabad's focus on IT and computing, but the city already had a significant industrial base. From pharmaceuticals to aerospace electronics, and fertilizers to glass and watches, the city's industrial base has expanded rapidly. However, apart from coal mining in northern Andhra and the extraction of some copper, manganese and mica, the state's economy continues to depend heavily on agriculture which still employs nearly 70% of the population. Rice is by far the most important crop, especially in the fertile coastal districts where good soils also benefit from intensive irrigation. The much drier interior has a quite different range of crops, jowar and millets being dominant. Sugarcane, cotton and tobacco are particularly important cash crops, and forest products also contribute significantly to the state's income.

North Central Andhra

★ Hyderabad-Secunderabad

→ *Phone code: 040 .Colour map 5, grid B6. Population: 5.5 million.*

The twin cities of Hyderabad-Secunderabad are built on the ancient granites and gneisses of the Peninsula, which outcrop in bizarre shapes on hills in this area and which provide building stone for some of the city's most impressive monuments in the dusty and congested Old City to the south of the Musi River. Within the rocks lie some of the region's most valued resources - gem stones. The Golconda Kingdoms which preceded those of Hyderabad produced magnificent diamonds, probably including the Koh-i-Noor. Wealth today comes increasingly from the burgeoning IT sector and there is much evidence of a vibrant economy in the buildings of the commercial sector and the growing attraction of the new landfill areas served by Necklace and Ministers Roads. The Hi-Tec city to the west has attracted Microsoft's first overseas base.▸▸ *For Sleeping, Eating and other listings, see pages 1040-1045.*

Getting there Begumpet (NT Ramaras) airport is just 6 km from Secunderabad station and 15 km from Hyderabad Old City which has most of the sights. It is only a short taxi ride to several luxury hotels and to some cheaper options. Secunderabad station, with trains to major cities, is in the Cantonment area, while the Hyderabad City station at Nampally is close to the Abids district, with the majority of budget accommodation. The large Imbli-Ban Bus terminal for long distance buses is on an island in the Musi River, south of Abids. The Jubilee Bus Terminal is in Secunderabad.

Getting around Autos (or taxis) are the best means of getting about the city north of the Musi and in Secunderabad, but in the congested old quarter you are best off walking, though there are cycle rickshaws. See Transport, page 1043, for further details.

Climate Temperature: May can soar to 40°C and drop to 15°C in Jan. Rainfall: most Jun-Sep (ave 125 mm, minimal for the rest of the year). Best time to visit: Nov-Feb.

History

Hyderabad has a large Muslim minority. Occasionally the political situation can become tense and parts of the city put under curfew. Even though Hyderabad's population was always predominantly composed of Telugu-speaking Hindus, it was ruled by a succession of Muslim Nizams from 1724 when the Nizam-ul-Mulk ('Regulator of the Land') **Asaf Jah**, seized power from the Mughal Governor, founding the dynasty that included some of the richest men in the world. Hyderabad had been founded in 1589 by the fifth Sultan of Golconda of an earlier Muslim Dynasty, Muhammad Quli Qutb Shah, under the original name of Bhagnagar. The founders were famous for their beautiful 'monuments, mosques and mistresses' and also for their diamond markets.

Hyderabad stood on the south bank of the river Musi, in a superb military position. During the Asaf Jahi rule it expanded north. Then in the early 19th century, during the reign of Sikander Jah (1803-30), the cantonment of Secunderabad was developed by the British.

Devastating floods and outbreaks of plague at the beginning of the 19th century were followed by programmes of urban renewal initiated by Nizam Osman Ali Khan. A series of new public buildings date from this period including those from 1914-21, under the British architect **Vincent Esch** who attempted to build in an Indian style. Some of his major buildings are described here.

Sights

The cities Unlike Mughal cities, Hyderabad was planned in a grid pattern with enormous arches and the Char Minar was built in 1591 by the Sultan as the city's prime monument. The streets were lined with stone buildings which had shops below and living quarters above.

If you come out through the western arch of the Char Minar you enter Lad Bazar where shops sell the typical Hyderabadi glass embedded bangles, while to the north you will find jewellers including those with pearls, and cloth merchants.

Close to the Salar Jung Museum, you can see examples of Asaf Jahi architecture. North of the river are the Asafia State Library and Osmania General Hospital and on the south bank the City College and the High Court. Other typical examples are in the Public Gardens behind the Archaeological Museum, where you will find the Ajanta Pavilion, the elaborate Jubilee Hall and the State Assembly Hall.

Old City and Char Minar Facing the river is the **High Court**, on the new roads laid out along the Musi's embankments after the great flood, a splendid Mughal-style building in the old Qutb Shahi gardens, Amin Bagh, near the Afzal Ganj Bridge (New Bridge). Vincent Esch's most striking work, it was built in 1916 of local pink granite, with red sandstone carved panels and columns, a large archway and blue-glazed and gold domes, now painted pink. A further recent change is the enclosure of the verandahs. The detail is Mughal, but as Tillotson argues the structure and internal form are western.

Next door to the High Court is Esch's **City College** (1917-20), originally built as the City High School for boys. Built largely of undressed granite, there are some distinctive Indian decorative features including some marble *jalis*. Esch deliberately incorporated Gothic features, calling his style 'Perpendicular Mogul Saracenic'.

One of the oldest *imambaras* in the country, the **Badshahi** (Royal) **Ashurkhana**, or house of mourning, built in the Qutb Shahi style at the end of the 16th century, has excellent tile mosaics and wooden columns in the outer chamber, both of which were later additions.

South from the bridge is **Charkaman** with its four arches. The eastern Black Arch was for the drums, the western led to the palaces, the northern was the Fish Arch and the southern led to the Char Minar.

★ **Char Minar** This was built between 1591 and 1612 by **Sultan Mohammad Quli Qutb Shah** as a showpiece at the centre of his beautiful city; it has become the city's symbol but is crumbling. With its 56 m tall slender minarets with spiral staircases and huge arches on each side (the whole plastered with lime mortar) it stood at the entrance to the palace complex. Now, standing at the centre of a crossroads, it guards the entry to the main bazar. There is a beautiful mosque on the second floor and a large water tank in the middle. There is a special market on Thursday. Illuminations, 1900-2100. The site is closed to visitors but you can walk under the arches. Best to visit in the morning before the surrounding roads become almost impassable.

★ **Mecca Masjid** Immediately to the southwest, this grand mosque was started in 1614 by the sixth **Sultan Abdulla Qutb Shah** and completed by Aurangzeb when he annexed Golconda in 1692. Built of enormous black granite slabs quarried nearby it

The old city Char Minar

New Bridge

(Afzal Bridge)

Ashurkhana Husaini Alam

Dar Ush Shifa

Musi River

Salar Jang Museum

Railway Reservation

To Vijayawada

High Court

Sayad Ali

Yusuf Bazar

Rajendranagar Rd

Chhatta Bazar St

To Mir Alam Tank & Nehru Zoo

Badshahi Ashurkhana

Munir Ganj

Diwan Deorhi

Purani Haveli Palace

Mahboob Shahi Rd

Sadar Patel Rd

Purani Haveli

PATTHARGATTI

Mir Alam Mandi

Charkaman

Chowk

Jami Masjid

Char Minar

Lad Bazar

Tibbi College

Mecca Masjid

KHILWAT

N

Kishan Prasad Rd

Chaumahalla Palace

0 metres 200
0 yards 200

To Falaknuma Palace (2 km)

has tall pillars, stucco decorations and red bricks on its entrance arches believed to have been made from clay from Mecca mixed with red colouring. The vast mosque can accommodate 10,000 at prayers. The tombs of the Asaf Jahi rulers, the Nizams of Hyderabad, are in a roofed enclosure to the left of the courtyard. The **Jama Masjid** was the second mosque built in the old city at the end of the 16th century.

Lad Bazar area This area has interesting buildings with wood and stone carvings and pink elephant gates. It is at the heart of the Muslim part of the city, so densely packed with people it can be very difficult even to look at the buildings, and some foreign women visitors have found it a bit daunting. You arrive at the **Chowk** which has a mosque and a Victorian Clock Tower. Southeast of the Lad Bazar is the huge complex of the palaces which were built by the different Nizams, including the grand **Chaumahalla Palace** around a quadrangle.

★ **Falaknuma Palace** (1873) Originally a rich nobleman's house, the palace was built in a mixture of classical and Mughal styles. Bought by the Nizam in 1897, it has a superb interior (particularly the state reception room) with marble, chandeliers and paintings. The palace houses oriental and European treasures, including a collection of jade, crystal and precious stones and a superb library. The spectacular building is still being converted into a hotel.

Tomb of Michel Raymond This is off the Vijayawada Road, about 3 km from the Oliphant Bridge. The Frenchman joined the second Nizam's army in 1786 as a common soldier and rose to command 15,000 troops. His popularity with the people earned him the combined Muslim-Hindu name 'Moosa Ram', and even today they remember him by holding a commemorative *Urs* fair at his grey granite tomb which is 7 m high and bears the initials 'JR'.

Mir Alam Tank To the southwest of the old city is this large artificial lake. It was built by French engineers under instructions of the grandfather of Salar Jung III and is a popular picnic spot. It is now part of the **Nehru Zoological Park** which is to its north (see page 1033).

Hyderabad Centre: The New City The **Osmania General Hospital** (1918-21) is the third of Vincent Esch's impressive buildings in Hyderabad. It stands across the river, opposite the High Court. The 200 m long building was one of the largest - and best equipped hospitals in the world when it was opened. Its Indian context is indicated by decorative detail rather than structural plan. To its east, also on the river, is the imposing **Asafia State Central Library** (1929-34) with its priceless collection of Arabic, Persian and Urdu books and manuscripts. The Library was designed by anonymous architects of the PWD. Tillotson states that "Its main front facing the river is dominated by the huge arch of the entrance portal. This is a powerful and also an original motif: round, rather than the usual pointed form, it is rendered Indian by the mouldings on the intrados and by the *chajja* which sweeps over the top".

Public Gardens In Nampally, north of Hyderabad Station, these contain some important buildings including the Archaeological Museum and Art Galleries and the State Legislative Assembly (Vidhan Sabha). The **City Railway Station** (1914) was intended by Esch to be pure Mughal in style but built entirely of the most modern material then available - pre-cast, reinforced concrete. It has a wide range of distinctively Indian features - the *chhattris* of royalty, wide eaves (*chajjas*), and onion domes.

Naubat Pahad (Kala Pahad or Neeladri) These are two hillocks to the north of the Public Gardens. The Qutb Shahis are believed to have had their proclamations read

Hyderabad & Secunderabad

Related maps
A Hyderabad centre,
page 1032
B The old city Char Minar,
page 1028

N
0 metres 500
0 yards 500

■ Sleeping		4 ITC Kakatiya	8 Taj Mahal	12 Youth Hostel
1 Asrani International		5 Karan	9 Taj Residency	13 YMCA
2 Club View		6 Taj Banjara	10 Viceroy	
3 Deccan Continental		7 Taj Krishna	11 Yatri Nivas	

from the hill tops accompanied by the beating of drums. In 1940 pavilions were built and then a hanging garden was laid out on top of one (now occupied by the Birla Planetarium and Science Centre).

Venkatesvara Temple ① *The temple can be reached by a stall-lined path opposite Thomas Cook on Secretariat Rd, summer 0900-1200, 1600-2000, Sun 2030; winter 0700-1200, 1330-2030, photography of inner sanctum prohibited.* The modern, stunning white marble temple with an intricately carved ceiling which overlooks Husain Sagar, was built by the Birlas, the Marwari business family who have been responsible for building important new Hindu temples in several major cities, including the Laxmi Narayan Temple in New Delhi. Completed in 1976, the images of the deities are South Indian, although the building itself drew craftsmen from the north as well, among them some who claimed to have ancestors who built the Taj Mahal.

Vidhan Sabha The massive State Legislative Assembly building, originally the Town Hall, was built by the PWD in 1922. Although Esch had nothing to do with its design, Tillotson records that he greatly admired it for its lightness and coolness, even on the hottest day. He suggests that both the Town Hall and the State Library marked a move away from a Hyderabadi style to a more universal 'Indian' approach to design.

Jubilee Hall (1936) Bhind the Vidhan Sabha, is another remarkable PWD building, with clear simple lines. Tillotson notes the irony in the fact that official contemporary descriptions of these works claim that they represent the natural redevelopment of a Hyderabadi style, when the PWD architects themselves appear to have been aiming for something more genuinely pan-Islamic.

★ **Husain Sagar** ① *Boat trips organised by APTDC leave from Lumbini Park, near the APTDC office on Secretariat Rd. Pedal boats from Public Gardens.* The 16-m deep lake was created in the mid-16th century by building a bund linking Hyderabad and Secunderabad, and was named to mark the gratitude of Ibrahim Quli Qutb Shah to Hussain Shah Wali who helped him recover from his illness. The *bund* is a favourite promenade for the city dwellers. At the far end of the lake is the Nizamia Observatory. The 17.5 m high, 350 tonne granite **statue of the Buddha** was erected in the lake after years of successive disasters and finally inaugurated by the Dalai Lama in 1993. The tank, fed by streams originating from the Musi River, supplies drinking water to Hyderabad. Although it supports a rich

Hyderabad centre

Sleeping			Eating
1 Apsara	5 Saiprakash		1 Asian
2 Brindavan	6 Saptagiri		2 Haridwar
3 Imperial & Kamat	7 Siddharth & South		3 Kamat
Restaurant	Indian Restaurant		4 Liberty
4 Rajmata, Residency &	8 Taj Mahal		5 Softy House
Lakshmi Restaurant	9 YWCA		

birdlife and is used for fish culturing it receives huge amounts of industrial effluent, agricultural waste and town sewage.

Osmania University Built by the Nizam in 1939, this is just outside the city, towards the east. Inaugurated in 1917 in temporary buildings, its sprawling campus with its black granite Arts College combines Moorish and Hindu Kakatiya architectural styles. There is a botanical garden and the **State Archives**.

Malakpet Race Course South of the river, this course is one of the major centres of racing in the country and one of the most modern.

Salar Jung Museum ① *Afzal Ganj, closed Fri and public holidays, 1000-1700, Rs 150 for foreigners, Rs 5 Indians, cameras and bags must be left at counter, tape recorded guides at ticket office, specialist publications and guide books, allow at least 1½ hrs.* Sir Yusuf Ali Salar Jung III was the Wazir (Prime Minister) to the Nizam between 1899-1949, and his collection forms the basis of the modern museum, one of the three national museums in India. Originally housed on the edge of the city in one of the palaces, it was rehoused in a purpose-built if singularly dull and unattractive building just inside the north boundary of the city in 1968. There are informative descriptions of the exhibits in English, Urdu, Hindi and Telugu. The museum is built to a semi-circular plan with the entrance off the reception area. Along the verandah, 19th-century copies of European statuary overlook a small open space. The collection includes Indian textiles, bronzes, sculpture, Indian paintings and fine ivory art pieces, armoury, Far Eastern porcelain and entertaining curiosities.

Other museums Andhra Pradesh State Museum ① *Public Gardens closed public holidays, 1030-1700, nominal entrance fee, photography Rs 10, guide book, Rs 15.* The small museum is near the Lal Bahadur Shastri Stadium, 10 minutes by car from Banjara Hills area. Sections on prehistoric implements, sculptures, paintings, inscriptions, illuminated manuscripts, coins, arms, bidri ware, china, textiles and the crowd-drawing 4,000-year-old Egyptian mummy. Behind the museum, in the Ajanta Pavilion are life-size copies of Ajanta frescoes while the Nizam's collection of rare artefacts are housed in the Jubilee Hall.
Birla Archaeological Museum ① *Malakpet, daily,* has a collection of finds from excavations of historic sites, housed in Asman Ghad Palace, 9 km away. **Birla Planetarium and Science Centre** ① *English shows at 1130, 1600 (1545 Sun) and 1800, Rs 135, Naubat Pahad,* is believed to be 'the most modern planetarium in the country', although rather dubious commentary at times (eg "evidence of microscopic life on Mars billions of years ago shows that humans can colonise the planet in the next century"!). The Science Centre, below, houses an interactive section demonstrating scientific principles (primarily for school groups) and an Art Gallery on the lower ground floor, with many exhibits from Nirmala Birla's personal collection, featuring ivory and porcelain figures (mostly Royal Doulton) plus a section of good temple figures. On the top floor is a small, but well-presented **Dinosaurium** ① *1030-2030 (1530-2030 on last Tue of each month), Rs 10, combined ticket Rs 21,* the centre-piece being a 160 mn year old Sauropod skeleton plus fossils and eggs. **Khazana Museum** On the way to Golconda - stone sculptures, see page 1034.

Parks and zoos ★ Nehru Zoological Park ① *Closed Mon, 0900-1700, Rs 50, camera Rs 10, video Rs 75, bus 7Z from Secunderabad Station and Public Garden Rd.* Occupying 13 ha of a low hilly area with remarkable boulders, the extensive grounds offer a welcome relief from the bustle of the city, and birdwatching here provides a good introduction to Indian avifauna for those new to the country - one of the best zoos in India and well worth a visit. The animals are kept in natural surroundings. Also a lion safari park and a nocturnal house. The Natural History Museum, Ancient Life Museum and Prehistoric Animals Park are here.

Ramoji Film City ① *T08415 46201, F08415-46505 (code 925 from Hyderabad), 0900-1800, Rs 150 weekdays (children under 12, Rs 100), Rs 200 (children, Rs 150) weekends and public holidays, 25 km from Hyderabad on the Vijayawada Road, regular bus services from Hyderabad*, 'World's largest Film City' with a wide variety of sets and landscapes used in film and television.

★ Golconda → *11 km. Open 0900-1630.*

Golconda, one of the most accessible of great medieval fortresses in India, was the capital of the Qutb Shahi kings who ruled over the area from 1507 to 1687. Nizam-ul-Mulk repossessed it in 1724 and restored it to its former glory for a time. Modern day restorations are being carried out by the Archaeological Survey of India.

The fort

① *1000-1630, US$2 foreigners, Rs 5 Indians. Official guides wait at the entrance (Rs 250), unofficial ones greet you with a hand-clap under the Fateh Darwaza, with the 'as you like' monetary arrangement! Allow 2-3 hrs. Both the fort and the tombs are popular sites and can get crowded and very noisy after 1000; if you arrive early it is worth asking to be allowed in. Excellent Sound and Light show, 1 hr, English Nov-Feb 1830; Mar-Oct 1900.Tickets at Golconda 1 hr before start, Rs 25, at Yatri Nivas, 1000-1200; a coach trip from there (minimum number needed) departs at 1615 and returns 2115; Rs 100 includes show ticket.and a couple of other sites. Some buy Sound and Light ticket as soon as the office opens and take a quick tour (45 mins) of the fort before sunset in time for the show. Getting there: see Qutb Shahi Tombs.*

Golconda fort

To Pelta Burj, Banjara Gate,
Katora Hauz & Qutb Shahi Tombs (800m)

To Naya Qila

Magazines

Nagina Bagh

Bala Hissar Gate

Habshi Kamans

Ramdas Jail

Armoury

Mahakali Temple

Badi Baoli

Durbar Hall

Taramati Masjid

Bala Hissar

Baradari

Dad Mahal

To Fateh Darwaza & Hyderabad

Sound & Light Show

Harem

Rani Mahal

Shahi Mahal

Langar Khana

Makki Darwaza Rd

N

To Mecca Gate

0 metres 50
0 yards 50

1 Grand Portico
2 Mortuary Bath
3 Ambar Khana
4 Ibrahim Qutb
  Shahi Masjid
5 Camel Stables

66 99 … the dungeons being used by the Nizam of Hyderabad as a prison for his worst enemies, among whom were several of his sons and two of his wives …

Originally built of mud in the 12th century by the **Hindu Kakatiyas**, the fort was reinforced by masonry by the Bahmanis who occupied it from 1363. The massive fort, built on a granite hill, was surrounded by three walls. One encircled the town, another the hill on which the citadel stood and the last joined huge boulders on the high ridge with parts of masonry wall. The citadel's 5-km double wall had 87 bastions with cannons and eight huge gates with outer and inner doors and guardrooms between. Some of the guns of the Qutb Shahis are still there with fortifications at various levels on the way up. Another of India's supposed underground tunnels is believed by some to run from a corner of the summit, about 8 km to Gosha Mahal. The fort had an ingenious system of laminated clay pipes and huge 'Persian Wheels' to carry water to cool the palace chambers up to the height of 61 m where there were hanging gardens. The famous diamond vault once held the *Koh-i-noor* and *Hope* diamonds. The fort fell to Emperor Aurangzeb after two attempts, an eight month siege and the help of a Qutb General who turned traitor. The English traveller Walter Hamilton described it as being almost completely deserted in 1820: "the dungeons being used by the Nizam of Hyderabad as a prison for his worst enemies, among whom were several of his sons and two of his wives".

The **Fateh Darwaza** or Victory Gate at the entrance, made of teak, with a Hindu deity engraved, is studded with iron spikes as a defence against war elephants. The superb acoustics enabled a drum beat or bugle call or even a clap under the canopy of this gate, to be heard by someone at the very top of the palace; it is put to the test by the visiting crowds today. A couple of glass cases display a map and some excavated finds.

Beyond the gate the **Mortuary Bath** on the right has beautiful arches and a crypt-like ceiling; you see the remains of the three-storeyed **armoury** and the women's palaces on the left. About half way up is a water tank or well and to the north is what was once the most densely populated part of the city. Nearby, the domed store house turned into the **Ramdas Jail** has steps inside that lead up to a platform where there are relief sculptures of deities on the wall, dominated by *Hanuman*. The **Ambar Khana** has a Persian inscription on black basalt stating that it was built between 1626-72. The steps turn around an enormous boulder with a bastion and lead to the top passing the Hindu **Mahakali Temple** on the way. The breezy **Durbar Hall** is on the summit. It is well worth climbing the stairs to the roof here for good views. The path down is clearly signed to take you on a circular route through the **harem** and **Rani Mahal** with its royal baths, back to the main gate. A welcome chilled drink and snack is available at several cafes opposite the gate.

★ Qutb Shahi Tombs

ⓘ *0900-1630 except Fri, Rs 5, camera fee Rs 10, car Rs 10, bicycle Re 1. Allow 2 hrs, or half a day for a leisurely exploration. Inexpensive guidebook available. Bus (Nos 119 or 142M from Nampally or 66G from Charminar) takes 1 hr to the fort. Nos 123 and 142S go direct from Charminar to the Qutb Shahi Tombs, Rs 5. Autos about Rs 150 take 30 mins. Cycling in the early morning is a good option; it is an easy journey.*

One road leaves Golconda Fort to the north through the Banjara Gate. 800 m north-northwest of the fort on a low plateau are the **Qutb Shahi Tombs** which together form an attractive site.

Each tomb of black granite or greenstone with plaster decoration is built on a

66 99 It is appropriate that the man responsible for creating a number of beautiful buildings in Hyderabad should be commemorated by such a remarkable tomb.

square or octagonal base with a large onion dome and arches with fine sculptures, inscriptions and remains of glazed decoration. The larger tombs have their own mosque attached which usually comprises an eastward opening hall with a *mihrab* to the west. The sides have inscriptions in beautiful Naksh script, and remnants of the glazed tiles which used to cover them can still be seen in places. The tombs of the rulers were built under their own supervision but fell into disrepair and the gardens ran wild until the end of the 19th century when *Sir Salar Jang* restored them and replanted the gardens. It is now managed and kept in an excellent state of repair by the Archaeological Survey of India. The gardens are being further improved.

The road from Golconda fort goes north, passing **1** the tomb of **Abdullah Qutb Shah** (1626-72) as it approaches the entrance to the tombs, which is at the east gate of the compound. On the left side of the road just outside the compound is **2** the tomb of **Abul Hasan Tana Qutb Shahi** (ruled 1672-87). He was the last of the kings to be buried here as the final king in the line of the Qutb Shahi Dynasty, Abul Hasan, died in the fort at **Daulatabad** in 1704, see page 1111. To the right of the entrance are **3** the tomb of Princess **Hayat Baksh Begum** (died 1677), the daughter of Ibrahim Qutb Shah, and a smaller mosque, while about 100 m directly ahead is **4** the granite tomb of **Muhammad Qutb Shah** (ruled 1612-26). Tucked away due north of this tomb is **5** that of **Pemamati**, one of the mistresses of Muhammad Qutb Shah, dating from 1663. The path turns south and

Qutb Shahi tombs

N

0 metres 200
0 yards 200

1 Abdullah Qutb Shah	6 Muhammad Quli Qutb Shah
2 Abul Hasan Tana Qutb Shahi	7 Ibrahim Qutb Shah
3 Hayat Baksh Begum	8 Kulsum Begum
4 Muhammad Qutb Shah	9 Jamshid Quli Qutb Shah
5 Pemamati	10 Sultan Quli Qutb Shah

west around the tomb of Muhammad Qutb Shah. About 100 m to the south is a tank which is still open. The *Badshahi Hammam*, the oldest structure in the compound, is the 'bath' where the body of the king was washed before burial. You can still see the channels for the water and the special platforms for washing the body. The Badshahi kings were Shi'a Muslims, and the 12 small baths in the Hammam stand symbolically for the two *imams* revered by the Shi'a community. Next door, a small Archaeological Museum has interesting items in a few glass cases 1000-1630 (closed 1300-1400).

To the south of the Hammam is a series of major tombs. The most striking lies due south, **6** the 54-m high mausoleum of **Muhammad Quli Qutb Shah** (ruled 1581-1612), the poet king founder of Baghnagar (Hyderabad). It is appropriate that the man responsible for creating a number of beautiful buildings in Hyderabad should be commemorated by such a remarkable tomb. The underground excavations here have been turned into a Summer House. You can walk right through the tomb and on to **7**, the tomb of the fourth king of the dynasty, **Ibrahim Qutb Shah** (ruled 1550-80), another 100 m to the south. At the west edge of the compound is the octagonal tomb **8** of **Kulsum Begum** (died 1608), granddaughter of Mohammad Quli Qutb Shah. To its east is **9** the tomb of **Jamshid Quli Qutb Shah** (ruled 1543-50), who was responsible for the murder of his 90 year old father and founder of the dynasty, **Sultan Quli Qutb Shah** (ruled 1518-43), **10**. This has the appearance of a two-storey building though it is in fact a single storey structure with no inscription. There are some other small tombs here.

★ Warangal → *Phone code: 08712. Colour map 6, grid B1. Population: 528,600.*

The capital of the Kakatiya Empire in the 12th and 13th centuries, Warangal's name is derived from the Orugallu (one stone) Hill, a massive boulder with ancient religious significance which stands where the modern town is situated. Warangal is 156 km northeast of Hyderabad.

History

The city, was probably laid out during the reigns of King Ganapatideva (1199-1262) and his daughter Rudrammadevi (until 1294). Warangal was captured by armies from Delhi in 1323, enforcing the payment of tribute. Control of Warangal fluctuated between Hindus and Muslims but between the 14th and 15th centuries it remained in Bahmani hands. Thereafter it repeatedly changed hands, and Michell argues that although the military fortifications were repeatedly strengthened the religious buildings were largely destroyed, including the great Siva temple in the middle of the city. Marco Polo was highly impressed by Warangal's riches, and it is still famous for the remains of its temples and for its three circuits of fortifications though the modern town is not interesting.

Sights

At the centre of the **'fort'** ① *foreigners US$2*, is a circular area about 1.2 km in diameter. Most of it is now farmland with houses along the road. Near the centre are the ruins of the original Siva temple. Remains include the large, beautifully carved stone entrance gateways to the almost square enclosure, aligned along the cardinal directions and beyond are overturned slabs, smashed columns, brackets and ceiling panels.

Nearby Siva temples are still in use, and to the west is the Khush Mahal, a massive royal hall used by the Muslim Shitab Khan at the beginning of the 16th century for state functions. It may well have been built on the site of earlier palaces, near its geometric centre while some structures in the central area may have been granaries.

From the centre, four routes radiate along the cardinal directions, passing through gateways in the three successive rings of fortification. The innermost ring is made of massive granite blocks, and is up to 6 m high with bastions regularly spaced along the wall. The middle wall is of unfaced packed earth, now eroded, while the outermost circuit, up to 5 m high, is also of earth. The four main roads pass through massive gateways in the inner wall, and there are also incomplete gateways in the second ring of fortifications. Some of the original roads that crossed the city have disappeared.

Michell suggests that the plan of Warangal conforms to early Hindu principles of town planning. **'Swastika towns'**, especially suited to royalty, were achieved following the pattern of concentric circles and swastika of the *yantras* and *mandalas*. They were a miniature representation of the universe, the power of god and king recognized symbolically, and in reality, at the centre.

The Chalukya style '1,000-pillar' Siva *Rudresvar* temple on the slopes of the Hanamakonda Hill, 4 km to the north, has beautiful carvings. It is a low, compact temple, built on several stepped platforms with subsidiary shrines to Vishnu and Surya, rock-cut elephants, a large superbly carved *Nandi* in the courtyard and an ancient well where villagers have drawn water for 800 years.

Pakhal, Ethurnagaram and Lakhnavaram Game Sanctuaries

The great artificial lakes that are still in use - from the south, Pakhal, Lakhnavaram, Ramappa and Ghanpur - were created as part of the Kakatiya rulers' water management and irrigation schemes in the 12th and 13th centuries. The lakes are fringed with an emerging marsh vegetation and surrounded by extensive grasslands, tropical deciduous forests and some evergreens. The park was set up in 1952, and although it is well established, some of the significant management problems include grazing by domestic livestock and illegal burning.

This is the richest area for wildlife in the state with tiger, panther, hyena, wild dogs, wild boars, gaur, foxes, spotted deer, jackals, muntjacks, sloth bears and pythons. There is also a large variety of waterbirds and fish, otters and alligators in the lakes. Pakhal Lake, 40 km east of Warangal, is particularly important as an undisturbed site well within the sanctuary, while the Laknavaram Lake is 20 km to the north. They are superb for birdwatching (numerous migratory birds in winter) and occasional crocodile spottings. Tigers and panthers live deep in the forest but are rarely seen. Forest rangers might show you plaster casts of tiger pug marks.

Both the *Forest Rest House* and *Sarovihar* have been reported as destroyed by political activists. Check with Warangal Tourist Office, T32312.

ⓘ *From Hanamakonda or Warangal Bus Station to Narsampet. Regular bus service from Narsampet to Pakhal Lake or take a taxi.*

Palampet

Palampet lies close to the Ramappa Lake. The **Ramappa Temple**, dedicated to Siva as Rudreswara, was built in 1234 and is one of the finest medieval Deccan temples. The black basalt sculpture is excellent (even richer than that at the 1,000-pillar temple) with famous Mandakini figures of female dancers which appear on brackets at the four entrances. The base of the temple has the typical bands of sculpture, the lowest of elephants, the second, a lotus scroll, the third which is the most interesting depicting figures opening a window on the life of the times and finally another floral scroll. There are more fine sculpture inside, some displaying a subtle sense of humour in common with some of the figures outside, and paintings of scenes from the epics on the ceiling. Note that no bottled water is available.

★ Nagarjunakonda

→ *Phone code: 08680. Colour map 6, grid C1. 150 km southeast of Hyderabad.*

One of India's richest Buddhist sites, Nagarjunakonda, now lies almost entirely under the lake created by the Nagarjunasagar Dam, completed in 1960. The remains of a highly cultured Buddhist civilization had remained almost undisturbed for 1,600

Toddy tappers

In many villages of South India palm toddy is a common drink. Known locally as karloo this white, fizzy alcoholic drink is made by collecting sap from the palmyra palm. The tapper climbs the tree and cuts the main fronds of the palm, from which the sap is collected in small earthenware pots. This is poured into a larger pot carried by the toddy tapper on his waist band. If left the juice ferments, but it may also be drunk fresh. It is drunk by holding a folded palm leaf to your mouth in both hands while the juice is poured into it as you drink. Nod vigorously when you have had enough!

years until their discovery by AR Saraswati in March 1926. The reconstructed buildings are on a comparatively small scale, in a peaceful setting on top of the hilltop fort, now an island planted with low trees.

History

Rising from the middle of the artificial lake is the Nagarjuna Hill (*konda* is hill in Telugu) which had been nearly 200 m above the floor of the secluded valley in the northern ranges of the **Nallamalais** ('black hills') which surround the lake on three sides. On the fourth side was the great river **Krishna**, superimposed on the hills as it flows towards the Bay of Bengal.

Early archaeological work showed the remnants of Buddhist monasteries, many limestone sculptures and other remains. The Archaeological Survey carried out a full excavation of the sites for six years before they were covered by the rising waters of the lake. More than 100 distinct sites ranging from the prehistoric early stone age period to the late medieval were discovered. Some of the most important remains have been moved and reconstructed on the hilltop fort. These include nine monuments, rebuilt in their original form, and 14 large replicas of the ruins.

The **Ikshvakus** made Nagarjunakonda the centre of extraordinary artistic activity from the third century AD. In the mid-fourth century AD the Pallavas pushed north from Tamil Nadu and eclipsed the Ikshvaku Kingdom, reducing Nagarjunakonda to a deserted village. However, during the Chalukya period between the seventh and 12th centuries a Saiva centre was built at Yellaswaram, on the other bank of the Krishna. In the 15th and 16th centuries the hill became a fortress in the contest for supremacy between the Vijayanagar, Bahmani and Gajapati kings. After the fall of the Vijayanagar Empire both the hill and the valley below lost all importance.

Sights

The Ikshvaku's capital was a planned city on the right bank of the Krishna - **Vijayapuri** ('city of victory'). The citadel had rampart walls on three sides with the river on the fourth. The buildings inside including houses, barracks, baths and wells were probably destroyed by a great fire. The nine temples show the earliest developments of Brahmanical temple architecture in South India. The Vishnu temple (AD 278) had two beautifully carved pillars which were recovered from its site. Five temples were dedicated to Siva or Karttikeya. The river bank was dotted with **Brahmanical shrines**.

Nagarjunakonda excavations also revealed some of India's finest early **sculptures** and **memorial pillars**. Over 20 pillars were raised in the memory not just of rulers and nobles but also of artisans and religious leaders. The sculptures represent the final phase of artistic development begun at Amaravati in the second century BC.

The **hill fort** (early 14th century) has remnants of the Vijayanagar culture though the present layout of the fort probably dates from as recently as 1565. The main entrance was from the northeast, near where the ferry now lands on the island. In places the walls are still over 6 m high, with regular bastions and six gateways. There are two temples in the east, where the museum now stands.

The **Nagarjunasagar Dam** project, completed in 1966, is one of the largest in India. The 124 m high, 1 km long dam is constructed across the Krishna River out of stone masonry. Two of the irrigation tunnels are said to be among the longest in the world.

Museum

Most of the reconstructed buildings are around the museum on the hill fort. Collection of beads, coins, relic caskets and a variety of ornaments, but most importantly sculptures (including a 3 m-high standing Buddha). Also prehistoric and protohistoric remains and several panels and friezes depicting Buddhist scenes. ① *Closed Fri, 0900-1600, the island is 11 km from Vijayapuri, 2 ferries daily from jetty, 0930 and 1330, other ferries serve APTDC tours organized locally or from Hyderabad.*

Srisailam Wildlife Sanctuary

→ *Colour map 6, grid C1. Altitude: 200-900 m.*
The sanctuary, in an area deeply incised by gorges of the Nallamalai hills, has deciduous and bamboo forest as well as semi-desert scrubland. There are tiger, leopard, Indian pangolins, panther, wild dogs, civet, hyena, jackals, wolves, giant squirrels, crocodiles, lizards, python, vipers, kraits and over 150 species of birds.

Ins and outs

At times it is disturbed due to political activists and can be very difficult to get permission to visit. Check latest position with Forest Officer. Temperature range: 12-42°C. Rainfall: 1,500 mm. Best time to visit: Oct-Mar. Worth visiting AP Dept of Forests (see Hyderabad - Useful Addresses). Cars are not permitted in the Tiger Reserve from 2100-0600.

The largest of the State's wildlife sanctuaries is at Srisailam (201 km from Hyderabad) near Nagarjunasagar. The park, named after the reservoir, is India's largest tiger reserve covering 3,560 sq km in five neighbouring districts. Project Tiger was started here in 1973. Srisailam also attracts visitors to its **fort** and **temple** (originally, circa second century AD) with one of 12 *jyotirlingas* in the country, see page 305. It is a small pilgrimage town in the heart of the vast reserve of hilly dry forest. The ancient **Mahakali Temple** on a hill rising from the Nallamalai forest contains a rare *lingam* which draws large crowds of pilgrims daily and especially at *Sivaratri*, see page 1058. There is a nature trail signposted 1 km short of Srisailam. Otherwise, you can walk the access road and explore from there.

Listings: North Central Andhra

🛏 Sleeping

Hyderabad-Secunderabad
p1026, maps p1030 and p1032
The city suffers frequent electric power cuts. Larger hotels have their own generators, but a/c and lifts in smaller hotels often do not work. Street lighting is also affected: carry a torch.

Hyderabad
AL Taj Banjara, T6669999, F3392218, tbhresv.hyd@tajhotels.com. 121 refurbished rooms, pleasant restaurant overlooking private lake, excellent local cuisine and barbecues, pool, tennis, boating.
AL Taj Krishna, T3392323, F3393079, trn.hyderabad@tajhotels.com. 260 rooms, Presidential suite with private pool, 3 restaurants, large pool and beautiful gardens, immaculately kept, good bookshop.
AL Taj Residency 1 Banjara Hills, T6663939, F3392684, residency.hyderabad@ tajhotels.com. 140 rooms, typical Taj facilities, restaurant (superb local cuisine, faultless

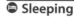

service) attractive 'Gaudi-style' atrium coffee shop, good pool and gardens, quiet.

A-B Amrutha Castle (Best Western), opposite Secretariat, T3243095, F3241850, amruthacastle @pol.net.in. 97 comfortable rooms furnished in individual style, attractive mock medieval public areas, themed restaurant and coffee shop, health club, roof-top pool, helpful staff. Recommended for imagination.

B Residency (Quality Inn), Public Garden Rd, T3204060, F3204020, reservations@ theresidency-hyd.com. 95 a/c rooms on 4 floors, polite service, popular with Indians, good vegetarian restaurant, popular basement pub (see bars below), efficient business hotel.

Abids area

C-D Saiprakash, Nampally Station Rd, T4611726, F4613355. 102 clean, comfortable rooms, some a/c, good *Woodlands* restaurant, efficient business hotel.

D Rajmata, Public Garden Road, opposite Hyderabad Station, T3204111, F3204133. 48 reasonably clean rooms, TV, attached bath, quiet for the area, good *Lakshmi* restaurant (see eating below).

D Taj Mahal, H-1-999 Abids Rd, corner of King Kothi Rd, set back from junction, T4758221, F4760068. 65 good-sized simple rooms, bright, devoid of insects, some a/c, busy restaurant (South Indian vegetarian), room service meals, good value. Recommended.

D-E Brindavan, Nampally Station Road, near the Circle, T3203970. 70 good, clean rooms, reasonable value, good restaurants, popular.

D-E Saptagiri, off Nampally Station Rd, T4603601. 40 clean enough rooms, some big with balcony, some a/c, quiet.

D-E Siddharth, Bank St, T4740222. 90 good rooms, some a/c, quiet location, good South Indian food in coffee shop, Chinese restaurant.

E-F Apsara, Nampally Station Rd, T4602663. 48 small, basic rooms, clean, room service, friendly, good budget choice.

F Imperial, corner of Nampally Station and Public Gardens Rds (5 minutes from Hyderabad station), T3202220. 48 clean rooms, some with bath, avoid roadside rooms, bucket hot water, large Indian hotel, helpful, excellent service.

Secunderabad
(SD Rd is Sarojinidevi Rd).

LL-AL ITC Kakatiya Sheraton (Welcomgroup), Begumpet, 3 km from airport, T3310132, F3311045, grand.kakatiya@welcomgroup.com. 188 rooms in modern luxury hotel, good restaurants, all facilities.

A-B Ramada Manohar, by Airport Exit Rd, T819917, F819801, manohar@hd1.vsnl.net.in. 135 well-designed, sound-proofed rooms, smart, modern business hotel, good value (a meal included) and service.

A-B Viceroy, Tank Bund Rd (taxi Rs 120 from airport), T7538383, F7538797, viceroy@ hd1.vsnl.net.in. 305 a/c rooms, most with fine views of lake, pool, sophisticated restaurant, excellent buffets, good but expensive travel desk, well located, excellent service. Highly recommended.

B Green Park (Quality Inn), Begumpet, Greenlands Arch, 21/2 km airport, T291919, F291900. 148 rooms, typical modern hotel.

C Asrani International, 1-7-179 MG Rd, T842267, F811529. 65 rooms, good restaurants, bar, exchange.

C Baseraa, 9-1, 167/168 SD Rd, T7703200, F7704745. 75 comfortable a/c rooms, restaurants recommended, bar, exchange.

C-D Karan, 1-2-261/1 SD Rd, T840191, F848343. 44 rooms, central a/c, restaurants, coffee shop, exchange, roof-garden.

D Club View, 30 Wellington Rd, behind Secunderabad Club, T7845965. 30 quiet, clean rooms (some a/c), simply appointed, light and airy, pleasant management, meals on room service. Recommended.

D Yatri Nivas (AP Tourism), SP Rd, T7816881, F7729129. 32 rooms, mostly a/c, 3 restaurants, bar, clean, airy, well-kept.

E Taj Mahal, 88 SD Rd, T812105. Adequate, clean rooms, vegetarian restaurant.

F Retiring Rooms, at Rly Station.

F YMCA, SD Rd, T7806049. 15 rooms (mostly singles, but big enough to take an extra bed), shared bath, clean, roomy, friendly, 'treated as family', Rs 75 plus Rs 50 temporary membership.

F Youth Hostel, near Sailing Club, T7540763. 90 beds in dorms (Rs 20, plus Rs 20 temporary membership).

Warangal *p1037*
Hotels with some a/c rooms on Main Rd, Hanamakonda are 8 km from the railway (bus or auto-rickshaw Rs 30).

D-E Ashoka, T78491. 55 clean rooms, good restaurant, bar, friendly service.

E Ratna, Ponchamma Maidan, T23647.
50 rooms some a/c.
E-F Tourist Guest House, Kazipet Rd opposite
Engineering College, 4 km away, T76201. 20
rooms, 6-bed dorm, restaurant. Tourist info.
F hotels near Warangal station are often 'full'
to backpackers.

Palampet *p1038*
This area is mosquito infested, so a
protective net is essential.
F Vanavihar Tourist Rest House,
overlooking the lake. 4 simple, clean rooms,
cook available but bring own provisions.

Nagarjunakonda *p1038*
There are no hotels in Nagarjunakonda, only
at **Nagarjunasagar**. There is no western
style accommodation. Guest houses are
mainly for officials.
E Soundarya Tourist Annexe (APTDC), Hill
Colony. 8 decent rooms, a/c or air-cooled.
F Project House (APTDC), T76240. 25 rooms
on ground floor, 18 rooms upstairs cheaper.
F River View Rest House and cottages.
   Also some on Hill Colony.
F Vijaya Vihar Complex, T76325. 8 a/c rooms,
restaurant, reservations: Assistant Manager.
F Youth Hostel. 12 rooms, contact Executive
Engineer, B & R Hill Colony, T72672,
Resservations, T72635.

Srisailam Wildlife Sanctuary *p1040*
F Rest Houses, contact Project Tiger HQ,
Field Director at Sunnipanta (7 km from
Srisailam), for accommodation, 3 rest houses.
F Saila Vihar (AP Tourism).
F Temple cottages. Cook will prepare meals.

⊘ Eating

Hyderabad-Secunderabad
p1026, maps p1030 and p1032
Hyderabad
▼▼▼ **Taj Banjara**, top hotel. Recommended.
▼▼ **Diwan**, near High Court.
▼▼ **Liberty's**, Nampally Station Rd (Abids).
Continental and Chinese.
▼▼ **Mughal Durbar**, near High Court.
▼▼ **Residency** hotel's *Madhubani* vegetarian.
Lunch buffets popular so à la carte may be
slow, try North Indian *thali*.

▼ **Lakshmi**, by *Rajmata Hotel*, Nampally,
across from railway station. Light meals.
▼ **Palace Heights** (8th floor), Triveni
Complex, Abids.
▼ **Shan Bagh**, Basheerbagh Rd. Good value.
Vegetarian:
Kamat, Nampally Station Rd and 60/1
Saifabad, Secretariat Rd. Simple, quality
food, good value.
Softy House, Chirag Ali Lane. Pizzas, burgers
and good choice of safe ice-cream, a
welcome break from the heat of the day.

Secunderabad
▼▼▼ **Ramada Manohar**, in hotel. International.
Recommended for service, surroundings and
food.
▼▼▼ **Viceroy**, in hotel. International, pleasant
atmosphere, excellent preparations, seafood
treats at *Gaiety*.
▼▼ **Akbar**, 1-7-190 MG Rd. Hyderabadi.
▼▼ **Asrani International**, hotel, good Mughlai.
▼▼ **Baseraa** hotel's Indian vegetarian
restaurant is simple.
▼▼ **Kamat**, Sarojini Devi Rd. Vegetarian.
Simple surroundings, clean, thalis.
▼▼ **Kwality's**, 103 Park Lane. Mixed menu.
▼▼ **Paradise**, 38 Sarojini Devi Rd/MG Rd.
Hyderabadi and others in a brightly lit complex.

⊙ Bars and clubs

Hyderabad-Secunderabad
p1026, maps p1030 and p1032
Larger hotels have pleasant, well-stocked bars.
One Flight Down, below *The Residency*,
opposite Hyderabad Railway Station, Public
Garden Rd, is a modern, British style pub (with
same opening hours, 1100-2300!), snooker
tables and TVs. Dark but popular. 1100-2300.

⊕ Entertainment

Hyderabad-Secunderabad
p1026, maps p1030 and p1032
Sound and Light at Golconda Fort;
spectacular (see details below). Some
cinemas show English language films.
Ravindra Bharati (a/c) regularly stages
dance, theatre and music programmes.
Lalit Kala Thoranam, Public Gardens, hosts
art exhibitions and free film shows daily.

⊛ Festivals and events

Hyderabad-Secunderabad
p1026, maps p1030 and p1032
Jan: Makara Sankranti (13-15) when houses bring out all their collections of dolls. **Mar-Apr**: Ugadi, New Year in Andhra Pradesh - **Chaitra Sudda Padyami. Muharram** and **Ramzan** are celebrated distinctively in Hyderabad.

○ Shopping

Hyderabad-Secunderabad
p1026, maps p1030 and p1032
Most shops open 1000-1900 and some close on Fri. Look for pearls, Bidri ware, crochet work, Kalamkari paintings, himroo and silk saris.

The **bazar** around the Char Minar is a fascinating glimpse into the past. Down the alleys, silver craftsmen work in their tiny rooms.

Antiques
Govind Mukandas, Bank St.
Humayana at *Taj Banjara*.

Books
Akshara, 8-2-273 Pavani Estates, Road No 2, Banjara Hills, T213906. Excellent collection on all aspects of India in English.
Haziq and Mohi, Lal Chowk. Interesting antique bookshop, especially for Arabic and Persian.
Walden, 6-3-871 Greenlands Rd, Begumpet, opposite *Blue Moon Hotel*. Wide choice, open Sun.

Handicrafts
Govt Emporia. **Nirmal Industries**, Raj Bhavan Rd; **Lepakshi** and **Coircraft**, Mayur Complex, Gun Foundry.
Co-optex and several others in Abids.
Khadi, shops in Sultan Bazar and in Municipal Complex, Rashtrapati Rd, Secunderabad.

Others may charge a bit more but may have more attractive items.
Bidri Crafts, Abids.
Kalanjali, Hill Fort Rd, opposite Public Gardens, high quality selection of crafts on 3 floors.
In Secunderabad:
Baba Handicrafts, MG Rd.
Jewelbox, SD Rd.

Jewellery
Especially pearls at **Mangatrai Ramkumar**, *Taj Banjara* and Pathergatti.

Sri Jangadamba Pearls, MG Rd, Secunderabad.
Tibrumal, Basheerbagh.
Totaram Sagarlal, Abids.

▲ Activities and tours

Hyderabad-Secunderabad
p1026, maps p1030 and p1032
Swimming
BV Gurumoorthy Pool, Sardar Patel Rd.
Some hotel pools are open to non-residents.

Tour operators
APTTDC City sightseeing: full day, 0800-1745 from offices at Yatri Nivas and Secretariat Rd, Rs 150; unsatisfactory as it allows only an hour at the Fort and includes unimportant sights.
Golconda: Shilparamam craft village, Hi-Tec city, Golconda (Sound & Light). 1600-2100, Rs 120.
Mercury, Public Gardens Rd, T234441, SD Rd, Secunderabad, T830670.
Nagarjunasagar: daily to Dam, Nagarjunakonda Museum, Right Canal and Ethipothala Falls. 0700-2130, Rs 250.
Ramoji Film City. 0745-1800, Rs 400 including entrance fee. Allows 4-5 hrs at the studios, plus Sanghi Temple and time for shopping!
Sita, 3-5-874 Hyderguda, T233628, F234223, and 1-2-281 Tirumala, SD Rd, Secunderabad, T849155, F849727.
TCI, 680 Somajiguda, Greenlands Rd, T212722.
Thomas Cook, Saifabad, T222689.

Nagarjunakonda *p1038*
AP Tourism's day trip from Hyderabad can be very tiring with 4 hrs on a coach each way, but is convenient and cheap. 0645-2145, Rs 225 including lunch. Nagarjunasagar is the village beside the dam from which boats ferry visitors to the temples and museum on the island (at 0800, 1200, 1500, trip takes 1 hr). If you take the second boat you still have time to visit the sights and return on the next boat. You can leave your luggage for a few hours at this pier provided someone is on duty.

⊝ Transport

Hyderabad-Secunderabad
p1026, maps p1030 and p1032
Air
Transport to town: pre paid taxi Rs 120-150; metered auto-rickshaw, Rs 65 to Banjara Hills, 30 mins. **Indian Airlines**: opposite Ravindra

Bharati, Saifabad, T3299333, Airport, T140. **Bangalore**: 2 daily except Sun; **Kolkata**: some via Bhubaneswar and Nagpur; **Chennai**: 2 or 3 daily; **Delhi**: 2 daily; **Mumbai**: 3 daily; **Visakhapatnam**. Jet Airways, 6-3-1109 Nav Bharat Chambers, Raj Bhavan Rd, T3401222; 201 Gupta Estates, Basheerbagh; airport T7900118. **Bangalore**, **Chennai**, **Delhi**, **Kolkata**, **Mumbai**, **Tirupati**, **Visakhapatnam**, all daily. **Sahara**, opposite Secretariat, Secretariat Rd, T3212767: **Mumbai**.

Auto-rickshaw
(Rs 6 for 2 km), will use meter after mild insistence and cheaper cycle rickshaws.

Bicycle
Bike hire Easily available (ask for "bicycle taxi" shop), Rs 20 per day but may ask for a large deposit; good for visiting Golconda, but the city is only for cyclists who are experienced with heavy, fast-flowing traffic.

Bus
Local City buses are very crowded in rush hrs. Nos 119, 142M: Nampally to Golconda Fort. **Long distance** APSRTC, T4613955. The vast **Imbli-Ban Bus Station**, T4613955, is for long distance buses including **Srisailam** and **Nagarjunasagar Dam**. Private coaches run services to **Aurangabad**, **Bangalore**, **Mumbai**, **Chennai** and **Tirupati**. Reservations: *Royal Lodge*, entrance to Hyderabad Rly Station. Secunderabad has the **Jubilee** Bus Station, T7802203. **Nampally**: buses to **Golconda**. Venus Travel, opposite *Residency Hotel*, runs a bus to **Gulbarga**, 0730, 5 hrs.

Car
Car hire Tourist taxis and luxury cars from AP Tourism, Tank Bund Rd, T3453036, **Ashok Travels**, Lal Bahadur Stadium, T230766, **Travel Express**, Saifabad, T234035. About Rs 550 per 8 hrs or 80 km, Rs 300 per 4 hrs.

Train
Hyderabad (H); Secunderabad (S). South-Central Enquiries: T131. Reservations: T135. Bus No 20 links Hyderabad (Nampally) and Secunderabad stations, Rs 5. From **Hyderabad/Secunderabad** To: **Aurangabad**: *Manmad Exp, 7664* (AC/II), 1800 (S), 12½ hrs. **Bangalore**: *Secunderabad Bangalore Exp, 7085* (AC/II), 1740 (S), 131/2 hrs; *Rajdhani Exp, 2430*, 1910 (Tue, Wed, Thu, Sun) (S), 12 hrs. **Chennai (MC)**: *Charminar Exp, 2760* (AC/II), 1900 (H), 1930 (S), 141/2 hrs; *Hyderabad Chennai Exp, 7054*, 1550, 1625 (S), 141/2 hrs. **Delhi (HN)**: *Rajdhani Exp, 2429*, 0645 (Mon, Tue, Thu, Fri) (S), 221/2 hrs; *Dakshin Exp, 7021*, 2130 (H), 2200 (S), 32 hrs. **Delhi (ND)**: *New Delhi AP Exp, 2723*, 0640 (H), 0700 (S), 26 hrs. All Delhi trains go via **Nagpur** and **Bhopal**. **Guntakal**: (for Hospet and Hampi), *Secunderabad Bangalore Exp, 7085*, 1740, 6 hrs. **Kolkata (Howrah)**: *E Coast Exp, 7046*, 321/2 hrs. **Mumbai (CST)**: *Hyderabad-Mumbai Exp, 7032*, 2040, 17 hrs; *Hussainsagar Exp, 7002*, 1430 (H), 153/4 hrs; *Konark Exp, 1020*, 1050 (S), 171/2 hrs. **Tirupati**: *Krishna Exp, 7406*, 0530 (H), 0600 (S), 16 hrs; *Rayalaseema Exp, 7429* (AC/II), 1730 (H), 151/2 hrs; *Narayanadri Exp, 7424*, 1800 (S), 131/2 hrs.

Warangal *p1037*
Train
Many Express trains stop here. **Nagpur**: Several, 7½-8½ hrs. **Delhi (ND)**: *Tamil Nadu Exp, 2621*, 0724, 24 hrs; *Kerala Exp, 2625*, 1417, 25½ hrs. **Vijayawada**: *Kerala Exp, 2626*, 1140, 3¼ hrs; *GT Exp, 2616*, 1951, 3½ hrs. **Chennai (MC)**: *Tamil Nadu Exp, 2622*, 2101, 10 hrs; *GT Exp, 2616*, 1951, 10½ hrs. **Secunderabad**: *Vijaywada Secunderabad Intercity Exp, 2713*, 0902, 2½ hrs; *Konark Exp, 1020*, 0735, 31/2 hrs; *Golconda Exp, 7201*, 1012, 3½ hrs; *Krishna Exp, 7405*, 1704, 3½ hrs.

Srisailam Wildlife Sanctuary *p1040*
Bus
From Imbli-Ban Bus Station, **Hyderabad**, about 6 hrs.

Train
Marchelna (13 km). Hire jeep beforehand.

Directory

Hyderabad-Secunderabad
p1026, maps p1030 and p1032
Airline offices Air India, Samrat Complex, Secretariat Rd, T237243. **Air France**, Nasir Arcade, Secretariat Rd, T236947. **British Airways**, Chapel Rd, T234927. **Cathay Pacific**, 89 SD Rd, Secunderabad, T840234. **Egypt Air**, Safina International, Public Garden Rd,

T230778. **KLM**, *Gemini Travels*, Chapel Rd, T236042. **Lufthansa**, 86 Shantinagar, T220352. **Saudia**, *Arafath Travels*, Basheerbagh, T238175. **Singapore Airlines** and **Swissair**, Regency Building, Begumpet. **Thai**, Chapel Rd, T236042. **Domestic**: airlines under Transport above.
Banks 1000-1400, Mon-Fri,1000-1200, Sat. In Hyderabad, several banks on Bank St, Mahipatram Rd and Mukaramjahi Market and in Secunderabad on Rashtrapati Rd. **Amex**, Samrat Complex, 5-9-12, Saifabad, T3234591. **Thomas Cook**, Nasir Arcade, 6-1-57, Saifabad, T596521. **Travel Club Forex**, next door, carries Western Union transfers. **Cultural centres and libraries** Alliance Française, near Planetrium, Naubat Pahad, T220296. **British Library**, Secretariat Rd. 1100-1900 Tue-Sat. **Max Müller Bhavan**, Eden Bagh, Ramkote. **Bharatiya Vidya Bhavan**, King Kothi Rd, T237825. **Hospitals** Out-patients usually from 0900-1400. Casualty 24 hrs. **General Hospital** in Nampally, T234344. **Newcity** (Secunderabad), T7805961.
Internet Several in Abids and Charag Ali Lane (Rs 30-40 per hr). Good coverage throughout the twin cities. **Post office** In Hyderabad: **GPO** (with Poste Restante) and **CTO**, Abids. In Secunderabad: Head **PO** in RP Rd and **CTO** on MG Rd. **Tourist offices** Govt of AP, A Block, 3rd floor, Secretariat, T3456717, F3454966; Tank Bund Rd, near Secretariat, T3453036, F3453086. **APTDC**, 3rd floor, FDC Complex, AC Guards, T3399416, F3319886, apttdc@satyam.net.in. 0630-1830; Yatri Nivas, SP Rd, Secunderabad, T7816375. 0630-1930, for tours. Information at Railway Stations and Airport. **India**, Sandozi Building, 26 Himayatnagar, T7630037. **Useful addresses** AP Dept of Forests, Public Garden Rd, near Secretariat (opposite *Reserve Bank*), T4067551. Provides excellent advice, may help with arrangements to visit wildlife reserves - Assistant Conservator of Forests, is very helpful. **Foreigners' Regional Registration Office**: Commissioner of Police, Purani Haveli, Hyderabad, T230191.

Nagarjunakonda *p1038*
Banks and **Post offices** at Hill Colony and Pylon (4 km). State **Tourist office**, Project House, Hill Colony, T76333 (Office). A guide is available through this office; others from the Hyderabad Tourist Office.

Krishna-Godavari Delta

The rice growing delta of the Krishna and Godavari rivers is one of Andhra Pradesh's most prosperous and densely populated regions, and the core region of Andhra culture. The flat coastal plains are fringed with palmyra palms and occasional coconut palms, rice and tobacco. Inland, barely 40% of the land is cultivated. About 120 km to the west of the road south to Chennai run the Vellikonda Ranges, only visible in very clear weather. To the north the ranges of the Eastern Ghats can often be clearly seen.
▸▸ *For Sleeping, Eating and other listings, see pages 1047-1048.*

Vijayawada → *Phone code: 0866. Colour map 6, grid C2. Population: 825,400.*

At the head of the Krishna delta, 70 km from the sea, the city is surrounded by bare granite hills. During the hot dry season these radiate heat, and temperatures of over 45°C are not uncommon in April and May. In winter they can be as low as 20°C. The Krishna delta canal scheme, one of the earliest major irrigation developments of the British period in South India completed in 1855, now irrigates nearly 1,000,000 ha, banishing famine from the delta and converting it into one of the richest granaries of the country. The Prakasam Barrage, over 1,000 m long, carries the road and railways. The name of this city, over 2,000 years old, is derived from the goddess Kanakdurga or Vijaya, the presiding deity. There is a temple to her on a hill along the river.

There are several sites with caves and temples with inscriptions from the first century AD. The **Mogalarajapuram Temple** has an **Ardhanarisvara** statue which is thought to be the earliest in South India. There are two 1,000-year-old **Jain temples** and the **Hazratbal Mosque** which has a relic of the Prophet Mohammed. The **Qutb Shahi** rulers made Vijayawada an important inland port. It has retained its importance as a commercial town, and has capitalized on its position as the link between the interior and the main north-south route between Chennai and Calcutta. A colossal granite Buddha statue (now in Guntur) shows that the site was an important Buddhist religious centre even before the seventh century AD, when it was visited by Hiuen Tsang. **Victoria Jubilee Museum** ① *Bundar Rd, except Fri, 1030-1700, free, camera Rs 5*, collection includes sculpture and paintings.

Excursions

Kondapalli, 20 km northwest, is a famous toy-making centre. The toys are usually made of light wood and laquered in brilliant colours. Craftsmen can be seen working on carvings of human, animal and religious figures.

Amaravati is 30 km west of Vijaywada was the capital of the medieval Reddi kings of Andhra. Some 1,500 years before they wielded power Amaravati was a great Mahayana Buddhist centre (see page 1342). Initially the shrine was dedicated to the Hinayana sect but under Nagarjuna was changed into a Mahayana sanctuary where the Buddha was revered as Amareswara. Its origins go back to the 3rd-2nd centuries BC, though it was enlarged between the first-fourth centuries AD. Very little remains. Excavations were begun by Colonel Colin Mackenzie in 1797. Subsequently most of the magnificent sculpted friezes, medallions and railings were removed, the majority to the museums at Chennai (see Amaravati Gallery, which has finds from excavations from 1797-1905) and Kolkata. The remainder went to the British Museum, London. The **Archaeological Museum** ① *except Fri, 0900-1700 , free, buses via Guntur or by ferry from Krishneveni Hotel*, on site contains panels, mainly broken, railings and sculptures of the Bodhi Tree (some exquisitely carved), *chakras* and caskets containing relics. There are also pottery, coins, bangles and terracotta. Apart from items excavated since 1905, some exhibits relate to other sites in the Krishna and Visakhapatnam districts.

Guntur

From Vijayawada the NH5 southwest crosses the barrage - giving magnificent views over the Krishna at sunset - to Guntur, a major commercial town dealing in rice, cotton and tobacco where the ancient charnockite rocks of the Peninsula meet the alluvium of the coastal plain. In the 18th century it was important as the capital of the region known as the Northern Circars, and was under Muslim rule from 1766 under the Nizam of Hyderabad. The Archaeological Museum exhibits local finds including fourth-century Buddhist stone sculptures and 16th-century bronzes.

Rajahmundry

→ *Phone code: 0883. Colour map 6, grid C3. Population: 313,300. 67 km northeast of Eluru.*

The capital of the Eastern Chalukyas, Rajahmundry was captured by the Muslims from the Vengi kings in 1471, then returned to the Orissan Kingdom in 1512. The Deccan Muslims retook it in 1571 and it was repeatedly the scene of bitter hostilities until being granted to the French in 1753. It is remembered for the poet Nannayya who wrote the first Telugu classic *Andhra Mahabharathamu*. Every 12 years the Pushkaram celebration is held by the river bank. The **Markandaya** and **Kotilingeswara Temples** on the river bank draw pilgrims. Rajahmundry is noted for its coastal districts. There are simple economy hotels in the town.

Rajahmundry is one of two places where you can divert towards the hills of the Eastern Ghats. The Godavari, 80 km northwest of the town, cuts through a gorge and there is a succession of stunningly beautiful lakes, reminiscent of Scottish lochs rather than India, where you can take boat trips.

Listings: Krishna-Godavari Delta

● Sleeping

Vijayawada *p1045*
Bundar Rd is MG Rd.
D Ilapuram, Besant Rd, T571282. 81 large clean rooms, some a/c, **C** suites, restaurants, travel.
D Kandhari International, Bundar Rd, Labbipet, T471311. 73 rooms, some a/c.
D-E Mamata, Eluru Rd (1 km centre), T571251. 59 rooms, most a/c with bath, good a/c restaurants (1 rooftop), bar.
E Krishnaveni (AP Tourism), Gopal Reddy Rd (opposite Old Bus Stand), T426382. Clean rooms, restaurant, tourist office, car hire.
E Santhi, Eluru Rd, T577355. Clean rooms with bath (hot water), good vegetarian restaurant.
There are some **F** hotels near the Bus Stand on Bundar Rd and near the railway station.
F Railway Retiring Rooms, the reasonable restaurant opens at 0600.

Kondapalli *p1046*
F PWD Guest House.

Guntar *p1046*
D Vijayakrishna International, Collectorate Rd, Nagarampalem, T0863-222221, F223541. 42 rooms, some a/c, restaurant.
D-E Annapurna Lodge, opposite the APSRTC bus stand. A/c and non-a/c rooms, quality "unlimited" meals for Rs 22, helpful and obliging.
D-E Sudarsan, Kothapet, Main Rd, T0863-222681. 28 rooms, some a/c, Indian vegetarian restaurant.
F Railway Retiring Rooms.

● Eating

Vijayawada *p1045*
Kandhari, **Krishna** and **Mamata** hotels are recommended. Garden restaurants are very pleasant, especially **Greenlands**, Bhavani Gardens, Labbipet, with 7 huts in lawns.

○ Shopping

Vijayawada *p1045*
Some shops are closed 1300-1600.
Local Kondapalli toys and Machilipatnam Kalamkari paintings are popular. The emporia are in MG Rd, Governorpet and Eluru Rd. **Apco**, Besant Rd, **Handicrafts Shop**, *Krishnaveni Motel*, **Lepakshi**, Gandhi Nagar are recommended.

Books
Ashok, opposite Maris Stella College, T476966. Good collection on India, also English fiction.

▲ Activities and tours

Vijayawada *p1045*
Watersports and boating
KL Rao Vihara Kendram, Bhavani Island on Prakasham Barrage Lake offers rowing, canoeing, water scooters, pedal boats. 0930-1830.

● Transport

Vijayawada *p1045*
Auto rickshaw
Auto rickshaws are available.

Bus
Local Good network in the city but buses do get overcrowded.

For an explanation of the sleeping and eating price codes used in this guide, see inside the front cover. Other relevant information is found in Essentials pages 52-57.

Andhra Pradesh Listings: Krishna-Godavari Delta

Long distance SRTC buses to neighbouring states including **Chennai** (9 hrs). New Bus Stand, Bundar Rd, near Krishna River, has a restaurant and dorm beds. Enquiries T473333. Reservations 24 hrs.

Car
Car hire From AP Tourism.

Cycle rickshaws
Cycle rickshaws are available.

Ferry
Local To **Bhavani Islands**, 0930-1730.
Long distance Services between *Krishnaveni Hotel* and **Amaravati**. Daily 0800. Rs 50 return. Book at hotel or at RTC Bus Station.

Taxi
Very few metered yellow-top taxis.

Tonga
Tongas are available.

Train
Vijayawada is an important junction. Reservations, 0800-1300, 1300-2000; tokens issued 30 mins earlier. **Bhubaneswar**: *Coromandel Exp, 2842* (AC/II), 1600, 11/2 hrs; *Konark Exp, 1019* (AC/II), 1440, 16 hrs. **Kolkata (H)**: *Coromandel Exp, 2842* (AC/II), 1600, 22 hrs. **Chennai (MC)**: *Pinakini Exp, 2711*,), 0600, 7 hrs; *Coromandel Exp, 2841* (AC/II), 1045, 63/4 hrs. **Delhi (ND)**: *GT Exp, 2615*, 2315, 30 hrs; *Kerala Exp, 2625*, 1125, 281/2 hrs. **Hospet**: *Amaravati Exp, 7225*, 2200, 13 hrs. **Secunderabad**: *Satavahana Exp, 2713*, 0610, 51/2 hrs. **Hyderabad**:

Godavari Exp, 7007, 2355, 7 hrs; *Krishna Exp, 7405*, 1330, 81/4 hrs (7 hrs to Secunderabad).

Guntar *p1046*
Bus
APSRTC bus stand is well organized and clean.

Train
Kolkata: *Faluknama Exp, 7201*, 2255, 231/2 hrs. **Chennai**: *Hyderabad Chennai Exp, 7054*, 2200, 8 hrs. **Hospet**: *Amravati Exp, 7225*, 2310, 12 hrs. **Secunderabad**: *Palnad Exp, 2747*, 0525, 5 hrs; *Nagarjuna Exp, 7005*, 3, 61/4 hrs; *Golconda Exp, 7201*, 0530, 8 hrs.

Rajahmundry *p1046*
Train
Kolkata (H): *Coromandel Exp, 2842* (AC/II), 1830, 191/2 hrs. **Vijayawada**: *Coromandel Exp 2841*, 0747, 23/4 hrs; *Chennai Mail, 6003*, 1635, 31/2 hrs; *Ratnachal Exp, 2717*, 1550, 3 hrs. **Visakhapatnam**: *Coromandel Exp 2842*, 1830, 33/4 hrs; *Chennai Howrah Mail, 6004*, 0931, 4 hrs; *Ratnachal Exp, 2718*, 0829, 31/2 hrs.

⊕ Directory

Vijayawada *p1045*
Banks State Bank of India and others on Babu Rajendra Prasad Rd. **Post office** Kaleswara Rao Rd. **Tourist offices** AP, *Hotel Ilapuram Complex*, Gandhi Nagar, T570255. 0600-2000. AP Tourism counter at RTC Bus Stand, Machilipatnam Rd and railway station. **Useful addresses** Foreigners' Regional Registration Office, Superintendent of Police, Bundar Rd.

Northeastern Andhra Pradesh

From Vijayawada the NH5 crosses the lush and fertile delta of the Krishna and Godavari to Rajahmundry and then the narrowing coastal plain with the beautiful hills of the Eastern Ghats rising sharply inland. Check weather forecasts before travelling. The whole pattern of life contrasts sharply with that to the south. Higher rainfall and a longer wet season, alongside the greater fertility of the alluvial soils, contribute to an air of prosperity. Village house styles are quite different, with thatched roofed cottages and white painted walls, distinctive house types and equally distinctive bullock carts. Rice and sugarcane dominate. ⊕ *For Sleeping, Eating and other listings, see pages 1049-1052.*

Although the building of dams on both the Krishna and the Godavari has eliminated the catastrophic flooding common until the mid-19th century, it is still prone to cyclones. In 1864 a cyclone claimed over 34,000 lives. The totally flat delta, lying virtually at sea level, was completely engulfed by a tidal wave in 1883 when the volcano of Mount Krakatoa blew up 5,000 km away. Further catastrophic cyclones in 1977 and 1996 caused massive damage and loss of life. You may notice the increasing number of small concrete buildings on raised platforms along the roadside designed to provide temporary shelter to villagers during cyclones.

The area was brought under Muslim rule by the Golconda kings of the Bahmani Dynasty in 1575 and ceded to the French in 1753. In 1765 the Mughal Emperor granted the whole area to the East India Company, its first major territorial acquisition in India. The region is also the most urbanized part of AP, with a dozen towns with more than 100,000 people. Most are commercial and administrative centres with neither the functions nor the appearance of industrial cities, but they serve as important regional centres for trade, especially in agricultural commodities, and they are the homes of some of the wealthiest and most powerful families in Andhra.

Visakhapatnam → *Phone code: 0891. Colour map 6, grid B4. Population: 969,600.*

Set in a bay with rocky promontories, Visakhapatnam (Vizag) commands a spectacular position between the thickly wooded Eastern Ghats and the sea. It has become one of India's most rapidly growing cities. Already India's fourth largest port it has developed ship building, oil refining, fertilizer, petro-chemical, sugar refinery and jute industries as well as one of India's newest and largest steel mills. This is also the Navy's Eastern Fleet's home base. On the Dolphin's Nose, a cliff rising 174 m from the sea, is a lighthouse whose beam can be seen 64 km out to sea.

Its twin town of **Waltair** to the north used to be thought of as a health resort with fine beaches, though increasing atmospheric pollution is a problem. Ramakrishna Beach, along the 8 km Lawson's Bay and below the 300 m Mount Kailasa, 6 km away, is best. Don't swim at the harbour end of the beach.

Sights

The **Andhra University** founded in 1926 is in the Uplands area of Waltair. The red stone buildings are built like a fortress and are well laid out on a large campus. The country's major **Ship Building Yard** at Gandhigram makes all types of ocean going vessels - passenger liners, cargo vessels as well as naval ships. The **zoo** to the northeast is large and attempts to avoid cages, keeping its animals in enclosures which are close to their natural habitat.

Each of the three hills here is sacred to a different religion. The Hindu Venkateswara Temple on the Venka-teswa Konda was built in 1866 by the European Captain Blackmoor. The Muslims have a mausoleum of the saint Baba Ishaq Madina on the Darga Konda, while the highest Ross Hill has a Roman Catholic Church. A Buddhist relic was discovered at **Dhanipura** nearby.

Simhachalam, 16 km northwest, is noted for its 13th-century Varaha Narasimha Temple, set in the Kailasa Hills, which are also noted for their hot springs.

Listings: Northeastern Andhra Pradesh

◉ Sleeping

Late night arrivals quoted high prices by auto-rickshaws to go to beach. Stay overnight at simple hotel near bus station (walk right from railway station), move next morning.

AL-A Taj Residency, Beach Rd (2 km from centre), T567756, F564370. 95 narrow sea-facing rooms, spacious, light restaurant (pricey but generous), best in town, located at centre of bay, unremarkable public beach across road.

1050 **A Grand Bay Ravi** (Welcomgroup), 15-1-44 Naoroji Rd, Maharanipeta, T566550, F552804. 104 rooms, all business facilities.

B Park, Beach Rd, T554488, F554181. 64 rooms, expensive suites, bookshop, clean pool, well kept gardens, slick management, best for direct beach access (beware of rocks when swimming), popular with German and Czech expatriates.

B-C Dolphin, Daba Gardens, T567027, F567555. 147 rooms, popular restaurants, rooftop has good views, live band, highly recommended (reserve ahead), exchange, pool, family run with excellent service, drawback is distance from beach.

C Green Park, Waltair Main Rd, T56444, F563763. Modern business hotel, rooms vary.

D Apsara, 12-1-17 Waltair Main Rd, T564861. 130 rooms, central a/c, restaurants, bar, exchange, very helpful and friendly staff.

D Daspalla, Surya Bagh, T564825, F562043. 102 rooms, **C** suites, central a/c, 2 good restaurants (continental and thalis, bar, exchange, set back from road, no late-night check-in.

D Punnai Punnami Beach Resort (AP Tourism), Bhimili Beach Rd, Rushikonda beach (15 km away), T790734. New resort up steps from clean beach, rooms with sea views, good food.

D-E Meghalaya, Asilametta Junction (5-min walk from bus, short rickshaw ride from station), T555141, F555824. 65 rooms, some a/c, dull vegetarian restaurant (non-vegetarian on room service), spacious lobby with murals, pleasant roof garden, friendly and helpful, popular with Indian tourists, good value. Recommended.

D-E Ocean View Inn, Kirlampudi (north end of the beach), T554828, F563234. 48 rooms,

Visakhapatnam

Sleeping
1 Apsara
2 Daspalla
3 Dolphin
4 Grand Bay Ravi
5 Green Park
6 Meghalaya
7 Ocean View Inn
8 Palm Beach
9 Park
10 Sarovar
11 Taj Residency

N
Not to scale

some a/c rooms, a/c restaurant, clean and comfortable, location spoilt by high-rise flats, quiet end of town.
D-E Palm Beach, Beach Rd (next to Park), Waltair, T554026. 34 rooms, 30 a/c, restaurant, beer garden, pool, pleasant with shady palm grove but run-down building.
E Lakshmi, next to St Joseph's Hospital, Maryland. 10 rooms a/c, some with bath, clean and welcoming, good Indian restaurant.
E Saga Lodge, off Hospital Rd towards beach. Rooms with balcony, some with bath and sea view, no restaurant but very good room service
E Viraat, Indira Gandhi Stadium Rd, Old Bus Stand, T564821. 42 rooms with bath, some a/c, a/c restaurant and bar, exchange.
E Railway Retiring Rooms decent rooms, men's dorm.

● **Eating**
1 Blue Diamond
2 Rangolli
3 Sarigama

⑦ Eating

Most serve alcohol. Outside hotels there are restaurants on Station Rd.
In Surya Bagh:
Black Dog (near Jagdamba Theatre).
In Dabagardens:
Delight, 7-1-43 Kirlampudi, Beach Rd.
Blue Diamond opposite RTC.

⊛ Festivals and events

Dec: Navy Mela and Navy Day Parade along Beach Rd.

▲ Activities and tours

Swimming
Hotels *Park* and *Palm Beach* are open to non-residents. *Waltair Club* has a pool.

Tours
AP Tourism, RTC Complex. Full day local sightseeing, 0830, Rs 75, Araku Valley, 0700, Rs 80, **Taj Travels**, *Meghalaya Hotel*, T555141 ext 222, F555824.

⊕ Transport

Air
Airport is 16 km from city centre; Taxi (Rs 180) or auto-rickshaw. **Indian Airlines** T565010, Airport, 1558221 and *Air India* agent, *Sagar Travel*, 1000-1300, 1345-1700. Daily except Sun to **Hyderabad**; some to **Bhubaneswar, Kolkata, Chennai Mumbai** Jet Airways, VIP Rd, T/62180, airport T622795, to **Hyderabad**.

Bus
Long distance Aseelmetta Junction Bus Station is well organized. **APSRTC** run services to main towns in the state. Enquiries, T565038, reservations 0600-2000. **Araku Valley**, **Guntur** (0930, 1545, 2045), **Hyderabad** (638 km, 1630), **Kakinda**, **Puri** (0700), **Rajahmundry**, **Srikakulam**, **Vijayawada** (1945, 2015), **Vizianagram** (57 km, 0610-2130).

Ferry
Local Operates from 0800-1700 between the Harbour and Yarada Hills. You can take one to visit the Dolphin Lighthouse.

Long distance Occasional service to **Port Blair** in the Andaman Islands, sometimes at short notice. Enquiries: *M/s AV Banojirow & Co*, PO Box 17, opposite Port Main Gate.

Rickshaw
Auto-rickshaws common (offer Rs 2 over meter-charge to make them use a meter); night fares exorbitant. Only cycle rickshaws in the centre.

Taxi
At the airport, railway station or from hotels: 5 hrs per 50 km, Rs 300; 10 hrs per 100 km, Rs 550 (higher for a/c).

Train
Enquiries, T569421. Reservations T546234. 0900-1700. Advance Reservations, left of building (facing it). Computer reservations close 2100, Sun 1400. Counter system avoids crush at ticket window. City Railway Extension Counter at Turner's Chowltry for Reservations. Taxi from centre, Rs 50. **Chennai**: *Howrah-Chennai Mail, 6003*, 1305, 16 hrs. **Kolkata (H)**: *Coromandel Exp: 2842*, 2235, 15 hrs; *Chennai Howrah Mail, 6004*, 1405, 171/4 hrs; **Secunderabad**: *Godavari Exp, 7007*, 1700, 133/4 hrs; *Palasa Kacheguda Visakha Exp, 7615*, 1635, 151/2 hrs; *East Coast Exp, 7045*, 0525, 14 hrs; *Faluknama Exp 7027*, 0045, Tue, 12 hrs. **Tirupati**: *Tirumala Exp, 7488*, 1430, 16 hrs.

❶ Directory

Banks Several on Surya Bagh. **State Bank of India** is at Old Post Office.
Hospitals Seven Hills, Rockdale Layout; King George, Hospital Rd, Maharani Peta, T564891. **Post office** Head Post Office, Vellum Peta; also at Waltair Railway Station.
Tourist offices AP Tourism, LIC Building, Daba Garden, T713135. 1000-1700, closed Sun and 2nd Sat. Also at Railway Station. Transport Unit, 8 RTC Complex, Dwarka Nagar, T54646. **Useful addresses** Foreigners' Regional Registration Office, SP Police, T562709.

The Tamil Borders

★ Tirupati and Tirumalai

→ *Phone code: 08574 (Tirupati), 08577 (Tirumalai). Colour map 7, grid A5. Population: 245,500.*
The Tirumalai Hills provide a picture-book setting for the famous temple. The main town of Tirupati lies at the bottom of the hill where there are several temples, some centres of pilgrimage in their own right. The seven hills are compared to the seven-headed Serpent God Adisesha who protects the sleeping Vishnu under his hood. The main destination of the 10,000 daily pilgrims is the Sri Venkatesvara Temple in Tirumalai, 18 km away at the top of the ghat road. Tirumalai is remarkably clean and free of beggars. ⇒ *For Sleeping, Eating and other listings, see pages 1056-1057.*

Ins and outs
Getting there Flights from Chennai and Hyderabad arrive at the airport 15 km from Tirupati. The railway station in the town centre has several fast trains from Chennai and other southern towns while the main (central) bus stand is 500 m east of it with express buses from the region. To save time and hassle, buy a through 'Link' ticket to Tirumalai.

Getting around Buses for Tirumalai leave from stands near the station, but there are also share taxis available. Some choose to join pilgrims for a 4-5 hr walk uphill, starting before dawn to avoid the heat though the path is covered most of the way. Luggage is transported free from the toll gate at the start of the 15 km path and may be collected from the reception office at in Tirumalai. See Transport, page 1056, for further details.

Climate Summer, maximum 40°C, minimum 22°C; Winter, maximum 32°C, minimum 15°C. Annual rainfall: 710 mm, mainly Oct-Dec.

Sights

★ **Sri Venkatesvara Temple** ⓘ *There are 2 types of queues for* darshan *or special viewing:* 'Sarvadarsan' *is open to all, while those who pay for* 'Special darshan' *enter by a separate entrance and join a short queue. The actual darshan (from 0600-1100) itself lasts a precious second and a half even though the 'day' at the temple may last 21 hrs.* Suprabhatam *0300-0330 (awakening the deity) costs Rs 100;* Tomala Seva *0330-0415 (flower-offering), Rs 200. Mornings are particularly busy. Mon and Tue are less crowded.* This temple in **Tirumalai** is believed to have been dedicated by the Vaishnava saint Ramanuja and is known as Balaji in the North and Srinivasa Perumalai in the South. Of all India's temples, this draws the largest number of pilgrims. The town of Tirupati, at the base of the hill, was established in approximately AD 1131 under the orders of Ramanuja that the temple functionaries who served in the sacred shrines must live nearby. Although a road runs all the way up the hill to a bus stand at the top, most pilgrims choose to walk up the wooded slope through mango groves and sandalwood forest chanting "Om namo Venkatesaya" or "Govinda, Govinda". Order is maintained by providing 'Q sheds' under which pilgrims assemble.

Every day is festival day with shops remaining open 24 hours. Sri Venkatesvara's image is widely seen across South India, in private homes, cars and taxis and in public places, and is instantly recognizable from its black face and covered eyes, shielded so that the deity's piercing gaze may not blind any who look directly at him. In the temple the deity's body is anointed with camphor, saffron and musk. The holy *prasadam* or consecrated sweet is distributed to well over 50,000 pilgrims at special festivals.

Sri Venkatesvara is a form of Vishnu. Theoretically the inner shrines of the Tirumalai temple are open only to Hindus. However, foreigners are usually welcome. They are sometimes invited to sign a form to show they sympathize with Hindu beliefs. According to the Tourist Information leaflet "All are welcome. The temple welcomes all devotees regardless of formal religions. The only criterion for admission is faith in God and respect for the temple's conventions and rituals".

Tirupati

Sleeping
1 Bhimas
2 Bhimas Deluxe
3 Oorvashi
4 Sri Kumara Lodge
5 TTD Choultries
6 Vasantham Lodge
7 Vishnupriya, Indian Airlines, Laxmi Narayan Bhawan & Dwarka Restaurant

0 metres 100
0 yards 100

⁝ Tirupati haircuts

Architecturally Sri Venkatesvara Temple is unremarkable, but in other respects is extraordinary. It is probably the wealthiest in India, and the devasthanam (or temple trust) now sponsor a huge range of activities, from the Sri Venkatesvara University at Tirupati to hospitals, orphanages and schools. Its wealth comes largely from its pilgrims, on average over 10,000 a day but at major festivals many times that number. All pilgrims make gifts, and the hundi (offering) box in front of the shrine is stuffed full with notes, gold ornaments and other offerings.

Another important source of income is the **haircutting service**. Many pilgrims come to Tirupati to seek a special favour – to seek a suitable wife or husband, to have a child, to recover from illness – and it is regarded as auspicious to grow the hair long and then to offer the hair as a sacrifice. You may see many pilgrims fully shaven at the temple when appearing before the deity. Lines of barbers wait for arriving pilgrims. Once, when coaches unloaded their pilgrims, one barber would line up customers and shave one strip of hair off as many heads as possible in order to maximize the number of customers committed to him before he returned and finished off the job! Now, a free numbered ticket and a razor blade can be collected from the public bath hall which pilgrims take to the barber with the same number to claim a free haircut. The hair is collected, washed and softened before being exported to the American and Japanese markets for wig making.

The Venkatesvara Temple dates from the 10th century, with later additions. The atmosphere is unlike any other temple in India. Turnstiles control the flow of pilgrims into the main temple complex, which is through an intricately carved *gopuram* on the east wall. Much of the *gopuram* is rebuilt. There are three enclosures. The first, where there are portrait sculptures of the Vijayanagar patrons, include Krishnadeva Raya and his queen and a gold covered pillar. The outer colonnades are in the Vijayanagar style; the gateway leading to the inner enclosure may be of Chola origin. The second enclosure has more shrines, a sacred well and the kitchen. The inner enclosure is opened only once every year. The main temple and shrine is on the west side of the inner enclosure.

The sanctuary (ninth-10th centuries), known as 'Ananda Nilayam', has a domed *vimana* entirely covered with gold plate, and gold covered gates. The image in the shrine is a standing Vishnu, richly ornamented with gold and jewels. The 2 m high image stands on a lotus, two of his four arms carry a conch shell and a *chakra* or discus and he wears a diamond crown which is said to be the most precious single ornament in the world. It is flanked by *Sridevi* and *Bhudevi*, Vishnu's consorts. There is a small **museum** with a collection of stone, metal and wooden images (see below).

Govindarajasvami Temple In **Tirupati** itself the Govindarajasvami Temple (16th-17th centuries), is the most widely visited. Built by the Nayakas, the successors to the Vijayanagar Empire, the temple has an impressive outer *gopuram*. Of the three *gopurams* the innermost is also the earliest, dating from the 14th-15th centuries. The main sanctuaries are dedicated to Vishnu and Krishna. The other temple is **Kapilesvarasvami** in a very attractive setting which has a sacred waterfall, Kapila Theertham.

One kilometre away are strange rock formations in a natural arch, resembling a hood of a serpent, a conch and a discus, thought to have been the source of the idol

in the temple. There is a sacred waterfall **Akasa Ganga**, 3 km south of the temple. The
Papa Vinasanam Dam is 5 km north.

Museums At Tirupati, the TTD **Sri Venkatesvara Museum** ⓘ *0800-2000, Re 1*, of temple art at the Sri Govindarajasvamy Temple compound. At Tirumaai, there is an interesting collection of **Indian musical instruments** ⓘ *0800-2000, Re 1*, at the entrance to the temple. **Sri Venkatesvara University Oriental Research Institute** ⓘ *1000-1630, free*, collection includes images of stone, wood and metal, pottery, coins, inscriptions.

Excursions

Chandragiri, 11 km southwest, became the capital of the Vijayanagaras in 1600, after their defeat at the battle of Talikota 35 years earlier. The Palace of Sri Ranga Raya, built in 1639 witnessed the signing by Sri Ranga Raya of the original land grant to the East India Company of Fort St George, but seven years later the fort was captured by Qutb Shahi from Golconda. **The fort** was built on a 180 m high rock where earlier fortifications may date from several hundred years before the Vijayanagar kings took over. You can still see the well preserved fortifications and some palaces and temples. Visit the Rani Mahal and Raja Mahal with its pretty lily pond. Museum, in Raja Mahal, contains Chola and Vijayanagar bronzes. ⓘ *State bus or taxi from Tirupati.*

Sri Kalahasti or Kalahasti ⓘ *state buses run from Tirupati*, 36 km northeast of Tirupati, is very attractively sited on the banks of the Svarnamukhi River at the foot of the extreme southern end of the Vellikonda Ranges, known locally as the Kailasa Hills. The town and temple, built in the 16th and 17th centuries, developed largely as a result of the patronage of the Vijayanagar kings. The **Kalahastisvara Temple** dominates the town with its *gopuram* facing the river. It is built in the Dravida style like the famous temple of Tirumalai. The magnificent detached *gopuram* was built by the Vijayanagar Emperor Krishnadeva Raya. Set within high walls with a single entrance to the south, the temple is particularly revered for the white stone Siva *lingam* in the western shrine, believed to be worshipped by *sri* (spider), *kala* (king cobra) and *hasti* (elephant). The Nayaka style is typified by the columns carved into the shape of rearing animals and the riders. The temple to the Wind God *Vayudeva* is the only one of its kind in India. The bathing ghats of the Swarnamukhi (golden) River and the temple attract a steady flow of pilgrims. In addition to its function as a pilgrim centre, the town is known for its *kalamkaris*, the brightly coloured hand painted textiles used as temple decoration. There are fine examples in the Salar Jung Museum in Hyderabad, see page 1033.

Pulicat Lake, on the coast, 50 km north of Chennai, is the second largest saltwater lagoon in India and one of the most important wetlands for migratory shorebirds on the eastern seaboard of India. The northern area has large concentrations of greater flamingos near the islands of Vendadu and Irukkam. There are also many birds of prey. The shallow brackish waters are rich in crustaceans and **Sriharikotta Island** has patches of residual dry evergreen forest. However, the island today is noted for its rocket launching site. About 20 km north of Suluru is the **Neelapattu Lake**, which was given protected status in 1976 to conserve a large breeding colony of spotbilled pelicans.

Listings: The Tamil Borders

● Sleeping

Tirumalai

Pilgrims are usually housed in well-maintained Temple Trust's *choultries* in Tirumalai which can accommodate about 20,000. They vary from luxury suites and well-furnished cottages to dormitories and unfurnished rooms (some free). Contact PRO, TT Devasthanams, T2753 or Reception Officer 1, T2571.

D **Mayura**, 209 TP Area, Pravasi Soudha, T25925, F25911. 65 rooms, some a/c, Indian restaurant, exchange.

Tirupati

C **Guestline Days**, 14-37 Karakambadi Rd, 3 km from centre, T28366, F27774. 140 rooms, central a/c, restaurants (including non-vegetarian), bar, pool.

C **Quality Inn Bliss**, Renigunta Rd near Overbridge, T25793, F21559. 72 modern clean a/c rooms, restaurants (including non-vegetarian).

D **Bhimas**, 42 Govindaraja Car St, T20766. 59 clean rooms with bath, some a/c, near rly, restaurant (South Indian vegetarian), roof-garden.

D **Bhimas Deluxe**, 38 Govindaraja Car St (near railway), T25521, F25471. 60 rooms, 40 a/c, a/c restaurant (Indian), exchange.

D **Bhimas Paradise**, 33-37 Renigunta Rd, T25747, F25568. 73 clean rooms, some a/c, pool, garden, good restaurant.

D **Mayura**, 209 TP Area, T25925, F25911. 65 rooms, half a/c, veg restaurant, exchange.

D **Sri Oorvasi International**, Renigunta Rd, T20202. 78 rooms, some a/c, 1 km railway, restaurant (vegetarian).

D **Vishnupriya**, opposite APSRTC Central Bus Stand, T25060. 134 rooms, some a/c, restaurants, exchange (Indian Airlines office).

F **Sri Kumara Lodge**, near railway station. Decent rooms.

F **Vasantham Lodge** 141 G Car St, near Railway, T20460. Reasonable rooms with bath.

● Eating

Outside hotels, vegetarian restaurants include **Laxmi Narayan Bhawan** and **Dwarka**, opposite APSRTC Bus Stand, **Konark** Rly Station Rd, **New Triveni**, 139 TP Area and **Woodlands**, TP Area. Tirupathi-Tirumalai Devasthanam Trust (TTD) provides free vegetarian meals at its guest houses. In Tirumalai particularly, the Trust prohibits non-vegetarian food, alcohol and smoking. Near the TTD Canteen and the APSRTC Bus Stand: **Indian Coffee House** and **Tea Board Restaurant**.

● Festivals and events

May/Jun: Govind Brahmotsavam. **Sep-Oct**: Brahmotsavam is the most important, especially grand every 3rd year when it is called **Navarathri Brahmotsavam**. On the 3rd day the Temple Car Festival *Rathotsavam* is particularly popular. In **Oct**: Rayalseema **Food and Dance** follows.

● Shopping

Copper and brass idols, produced at **Perumallapalli** village, 8 km away, and wooden toys are sold locally. Try **Poompuhar** on Gandhi Rd and **Lepakshi** in the TP Area.

▲ Activities and tours

Tours

AP Tourism, Room 15, Srinivasa Choultry, T20602. Local sightseeing tour starts at the APSRTC Central Bus Stand, 1000-1730. Rs 150. Tirupati (not Venkatesvara), Kalahasti, Tiruchanur, Chandragiri and Srinivasamangapuram. From Chennai to Tirumalai, Rs 300.

● Transport

Air

Transport to town: **APSRTC** coach to **Tirupati** (Rs 20) and **Tirumalai** (Rs 30); taxis

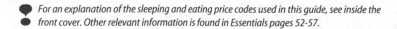
For an explanation of the sleeping and eating price codes used in this guide, see inside the front cover. Other relevant information is found in Essentials pages 52-57.

Rs 150. Indian Airlines, *Hotel Vishnupriya*, opposite Central Bus Stand, T22349. 1000-1730. To **Chennai**: Tue, Thu, Sun and **Hyderabad**: Tue, Thu, Sat. Jet Airways, T56916, airport T71471, to **Hyderabad**.

Bus

Local Service between Tirupati and Tirumalai every 3 mins, 0330-2200. In **Tirupati**: **Sri Venkatesvara** Bus Stand, opposite railway station for passengers with through tickets to Tirumalai; Enquiries: 3rd Choultry, T20132. **Padmavati** Bus Stand in TP Area, T20203; long queues for buses but buying a return ticket from Tirupati (past the railway footbridge) saves time at the ticket queue. The journey up the slow winding hill road - which some find worrying - takes about 45 mins. In **Tirumalai**, arrive at **Kesavanagar** Bus Stand, near Central Reception area, 1/2 km southeast of temple; walk past canteen and shop. Depart from **Rose Garden** Bus Stand, east of the temple.

Long distance Good service through SRTCs from the neighbouring southern states. **Chennai** 4 hrs, **Kanchipuram** 3 hrs, **Vellore** 2½ hrs. Central Bus Stand Enquiries, T22333. 24-hr left luggage.

Rickshaw

Auto-rickshaws: fixed point-to-point fares; **cycle rickshaws**: negotiable.

Taxi

Tourist taxis through AP Tourism from the Bus Stand and Rly Station to Tirumalai, Rs

600 return, for 5½ hrs. Share taxi between Tirupati and Tirumalai, about Rs 65 per person. **Balaji Travels**, 149 TP Area, T24894.

Train

Trains are often delayed. Phone the station in advance if catching a night train as it could be delayed until next morning.
Chennai (C): *Intercity Exp, 6204*, 0645, 3¼ hrs; *Saptagiri Exp, 6058*, 1720, 3¼ hrs.
Mumbai (CST): bus to Renigunta (10 km) for *Chennai- Mumbai Exp, 6012*, 1445, 24 hrs; or direct: *Tirupati-Mumbai CST Bi-Weekly Exp, 6354*, Thu, Sun, 2140, 24 hrs.
Guntakal: *Kacheguda Venkatadri Exp, 7498*, 1750, 6¼ hrs; *Rayalaseema Exp 7430* (AC/II), 1850, 6½ hrs. **Mysore (via Chennai)**: *Saptagiri Exp, 6058*, 1720, 3¼ hrs, wait 2¼ hrs, then *Chennai Mysore Exp, 6222*, 2245, 111/4 hrs (total 16¾ hrs).
Hyderabad: *Narayanadri Exp, 7423*, 1830, 13¾ hrs (for Secunderabad).

❶ Directory

Banks Most are on Gandhi St. State Bank of India, opposite APSRTC. **Tourist offices** AP, Regional, 139 TP Area, near 3rd Choultry, T55386. AP State, Govindraja Car St, T24818. APTDC, Transport Unit, 12 APSRTC Complex, T25602. Karnataka Tourism, Hotel *Mayura Saptagiri* (see above), TTD Information, 1 New Choultry, T22777 and at Railway Station and Airport. **Useful addresses** Foreigners' Regional Registration Office: 499 Reddy Colony, T20503.

The Arid Western Borders

For much of the way the NH7 from Hyderabad to Bangalore crosses the boulder covered plateau of the ancient peninsular granites and gneisses. On either side reddish or light brown soils are cultivated with millets or rice on the patches of irrigated land. ▸▸ *For Sleeping, Eating and other listings, see pages 1059-1060.*

Kurnool → *Colour map 5, grid C6.*

Between 1950-56 Kurnool, 214 km southwest of Hyderabad, was capital of the state of Andhra Desa before Hyderabad was chosen as the capital of the new state of Andhra Pradesh in 1956. Located at the junction of the Hindri and Tungabhadra rivers, it was an administrative centre for the Nawabs of Kurnool. Muslim influence is still evident in the **ruined palace** of the Nawabs on the steep bank of the Tungabhadra.

Srisailam → *Colour map 6, grid C1.*

A longer excursion, 170 km east of Kurnool on the route through Doranala, takes you to this popular site of Saivite pilgrimage on the banks of the Krishna, see page 1040. The wooded Nallamalai Hills are home to the *Chenchu* tribes. The township has been built for workers on a massive dam construction project.

Srisailam's origins are obscure, and the **Mallikarjuna Temple** (14th century) on a hill, containing one of 12 *jyotirlingas*, has often been attacked and damaged. 300 m long (dated to 1456), the outer face is richly decorated with carved figures. These include a portrait of *Krishna Deva Raya*, the Vijayanagar Emperor who visited the site in 1514. The walls and gates have carvings depicting stories from the epics. Non-Hindus are allowed into the inner sanctuary to witness the daily puja ceremony. To avoid the long queue in the middle of the day, it is best to arrive early - first prayers at 0545. *Mahasivaratri Festival* draws large crowds. Srisailam can also be reached straight from Hyderabad (200 km) across the wide open Telangana Plateau.

Gooty → *Phone code: 08553 Colour map 7, grid A4*

Gooty, south of Kurnool, has a dramatic **Vijayanagara Fort** with excellent views on an isolated granite outcrop 300 m high. In the 18th century the fort fell into the hands of a Maratha chief but was captured in 1776 by Haidar Ali after a siege of nine months. Sir Thomas Munro (Governor of Madras), who died nearby in 1827, has his grave in the cemetery on the path leading up to the Fort though his body was moved to Fort St George in Madras.

The town, 4 km from the railway station, is a major crossroads and truck stop. A bypass has taken many of the hundreds of lorries that used to pass through it every day, round its outskirts, leaving it once more as a typically pedestrian-dominated Indian market town.

Guntakal → *Colour map 5, grid C5.*

Guntakal, 95 km west of Gooty, is an important railway junction with little to attract a tourist. It is en route to Bellary to visit Hampi and Hospet (see page 1001). An excellent value

Bellary → *Colour map 5, grid C6*

The first agricultural communities of the peninsula lived around Bellary. The black cotton soils are pierced by islands of granite hills, and the **Neolithic communities** here lived at roughly the same time as the early Indus Valley civilizations. Radiocarbon datings put the earliest of these settlements at about 3,000 BC. **Ash mounds** have been discovered at four places in this area, close to the confluence of the **Krishna** and **Tungabhadra**, and to the south of Bellary. The mounds are where cattle were herded together. Evidence from later sites in Karnataka shows that millets and grain were already widely grown by the first millennium BC. The unusual fort on a single 'pebble' dominates the town (402 steps to the top from the southeast corner of the hill). The 1902 South African POW camp is 150 m north of the Cantonment Railway station, while the British cemetery is east of the rock.

Anantapur

The **Rural Development Trust** ① *FVF Bangalore Highway, T08554-31503, fvfatp@hd2.dot.net.in*, is an NGO working with outcastes in over 1,500 villages. The Director, a former Spanish Jesuit, Vincente Ferrer, started the project over 30 years ago which covers health, education, housing etc. Interested visitors are accommodated (up to 4 days) and will gain a insight into the commendable efforts of the trust.

Puttaparthi

Puttaparthi ① *KSRTC bus from Bangalore takes 4-5 hrs*, just southeast of Dharmavaram, has the principle Sai Baba Ashram, *Prasanthi Nilayam* (open 0400-2100), which attracts his followers from all over India and some from abroad. The present **Sai Baba**, is widely believed to be a reincarnation of the Maharashtrian Sai Baba of Shirdi. He also spends some time at *Whitefields* near Bangalore. The Ashram accommodation is good and open 0800-1900 but it is only open to over 25s and to families. Flights from Chennai and Mumbai were introduced by the former Prime Minister Narasimha Rao, a Sai Baba follower.

Penukonda

The second capital of the Vijaynagara Empire, the city grew in importance between the 14th and 17th century. It is possible to climb Penukonda (literally 'big hill') by a steep path that goes to the top. At the base, east of the hill, are huge walls and gateways of the old fortifications. The **Jain Parsvanatha Temple** has an 11th-century sculpture of Parshvanatha, naked in front of an undulating serpent in late Chalukyan style. There are also two granite Hindu temples from the early Vijayanagar period dedicated to Rama and Siva, the mosque of Sher Ali (circa 1600), the Jama Masjid with a near spherical dome, and the **Gagan Mahal** palace. The last has Islamic style arches, plaster decoration and features that are derived from temple architecture.

Penukonda became the headquarters of the districts ceded to the East India Company by the Nizam of Hyderabad in 1800. There is a well carved 10 m high column in the compound of the sub-collector's office.

Lepakshi

Approaching Lepakshi, 35 km south of Penukonda, from Chilamattur you see a massive sculpture of Siva's bull (*Nandi*), carved out of a granite boulder, 5 m high and 8 m long. This tiny village has a temple of outstanding interest for its murals. The **Virabhadra Temple**, built in 1538 under the Vijayanagar Emperor Achutyadeva Raya, has well-preserved sculptures, but the mural paintings are particularly striking, depicting popular legends from the *Puranas*, see page 1319, and epics. The "Elegant linework and vibrant colours (mostly browns and ochres) and details of costumes and facial types are of outstanding interest" (Michell). On an outcrop of gneiss, the main temple is entered through two *gopurams* with unfinished brick towers. There are pyramidal brick towers over the main shrine. Inside are large sculptures of Nataraja on a column while narrative reliefs on the south walls illustrate Siva legends, including Arjuna's penance. The principal sanctuary has a life-size Virabhadra, decked with skulls and carrying weapons, appropriate to this form of Siva, bent on revenge.

Listings: The Arid Western Borders

⊜ Sleeping

Kurnool *p1057*
D **Raja Vihar Deluxe**, Bellary Rd, T0851-820702. 48 rooms, half a/c, a/c restaurants.
D **Raviprakash**, Railway Station Rd (500 m from railway), T0851- 821116. 46 rooms and bungalows, some a/c with baths, restaurants (Indian), lawns.

Gooty *p1058*
A very basic hotel (with restaurant) is next to the bus stand.

Guntakal *p1058*
F hotel has a South Indian *Restaurant* next door. Local rickshaw drivers will take you there if you have to spend the night.

● *For an explanation of the sleeping and eating price codes used in this guide, see inside the front cover. Other relevant information is found in Essentials pages 52-57.*

Bellary *p1058*
C **Hotel Pola Paradise**, with comfortable a/c
rooms, B suites, restaurant and pool.
D **Ashoka**, which is more modest.

Penukonda *p1059*
F **Sabina Lodge**, near the bus stand has
simple clean rooms.

Lepakshi *p1059*
F **Rest House**, opposite temple. 2 very basic
rooms, and a simple restaurant nearby.
　　Alternatively stay in **Hindupur**, where
there are several hotels by the State Bus
Stand, near some good 'meals' restaurants.

▲▲ Activities and tours

Penukonda *p1059*
Stree Sangsheema Trust, on the main street
north of the centre, organizes tours,
promotes women's co-operative efforts and
sells the guide book, *Penukonda* by Torsten
Otto, 2001, Rs 25.

⊖ Transport

Kurnool *p1057*
Train
Kurnool Town to **Chennai (MC)** via
Tirupati: *Venkatadri/Tirupati- Chennai Exp,*
7497/6054, 2237, 14 hrs. **Guntakal**:
Secunderabad-Bangalore Exp, 7085, 2125,
2 hrs. **Secunderabad**: *Tungabhadra Exp,*
7608, 1510, 4½ hrs; *Bangalore Secunderabad*
Exp, 7086, 0230, 4 hrs.

Gooty *p1058*
Train
Bangalore: *Udyan Exp, 6529,* 0120, 7¼ hrs.
Guntakal: 14 Express/Mail trains daily
including at 0005, 0210, 0700, 0910, 1805,
1950 and 2310, ½ hr. **Chennai (MC)**: *Mumbai*
Chennai Exp, 6011, 0745, 9 hrs; *Mumbai*
Chennai Mail, 6009, 1935, 10 hrs. **Mumbai**
(CST) : *Kanniyakumari Mumbai Exp, 1082,*
0910, 29¾ hrs.

Guntakal *p1058*
Train
Chennai (MC): *Mumbai Chennai Exp, 6011,*
0710, 8½ hrs; *Dadar Chennai Exp, 1063,* 1130,
8½ hrs; *Mumbai Chennai Mail, 6009,* 1835,
11 hrs. **Bangalore**: *Karnataka Exp, 2628,*
0745, 6 hrs; *Hampi Exp/Nanded Bangalore*
Link Exp, 6591, 2300, 7½ hrs.
Kochi/Ernakulam: *Mumbai CST-Trivandrum*
Exp, 6331, Tue, 0540, 20 hrs. **Hospet**: *Hampi*
Exp, 6592, 0510, 3 hrs; *Guntakal Hubli Pass,*
303, 2120, 3¾ hrs; *Amaravati Exp, 7225,* 0815,
2½ hrs; *Haripriya Exp, 7315,* 0245, 2½ hrs.
Secunderabad: *Bangalore Secunderabad*
Exp, 7086, 2345, 6¾ hrs. **Hyderabad**:
Rayalaseema Exp 7430, 0130, 8½ hrs.
Mumbai (CST): *Udyan Exp, 6530,* 0250,
17½ hrs; *Chennai Mumbai Mail, 6010,* 0750,
20½ hrs. **Londa** (for Goa via Hubli): *Haripriya*
Exp, 7315, 0245, 7 hrs; *Amaravati Exp, 7225,*
0815, 5½ hrs.

Bellary *p1058*
Train
To **Gadag**: *Amravathi Exp, 7225,* 0905, 3 hrs. To
Guntakal: *Amravathi Exp, 7226,* 1730, 1¼ hrs.

West India

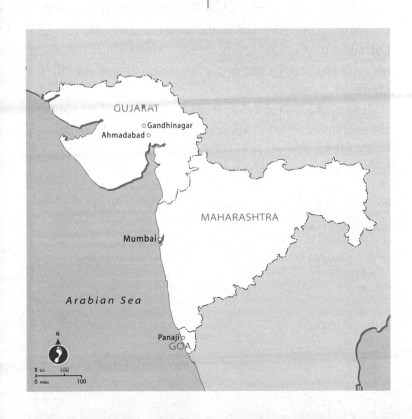

Introduction

West India contains, at the same time, the countries most dynamic city, **Mumbai** (Bombay), and some of its least disturbed rural landscapes. Stretching from the **deserts** bordering Pakistan to the tropical **forested slopes** of the **Western Ghats**, it also includes some of India's most important historical sites.

Maharashtra's Buddhist and Hindu cave paintings and sculptures in **Ajanta** and **Ellora caves** are world famous, but many of its outstanding **forts** are virtually unknown, while the new Konkan railway to Goa and the South is opening up the undiscovered west coast.

Gujarat has both undisturbed beaches and magnificent Jain and Hindu temples, while **Ahmadabad** has some superb examples of Islamic architecture. But the history of Gujarat's people goes back long before the arrival of Islam. The port of **Lothal** on the Gulf of Khambhat served traders from the Mohenjo Daro civilization over 2,000 years before the birth of Christ.

Goa itself is one of India's major tourist attractions, yet although its beaches are drawing increasing numbers of tourists, it too contains many fascinating places completely off the beaten track.

Maharashtra

Introduction

There are some beautiful and fascinating sites in Maharashtra. The earliest of the world famous frescoes and carvings at **Ajanta** and **Ellora Caves** date from the second century BC. Wonderful **ruined forts** built by the Marathas and the Portuguese are scattered along the 500 km of coastline while others are perched precariously on the hilltops of the Western Ghats. From these fastnesses, the 17th-century Marathas, masters in the art of guerrilla warfare, carved out a territory that stretched the width of India. Today Maharashtra boasts not only India's most vibrant city, **Mumbai**, and a diverse and rapidly growing industrial economy, but also a rich agricultural hinterland.

Small beaches offer an escape from the busy city while train buffs can enjoy a ride up the scenic narrow gauge railway to Matheran in the hills. The thriving "modern" city of **Pune** across the Ghats attracts the visitors to the lavish **Osho Commune** which has drawn large numbers of Westerners in search of an alternative spiritual answer.

★ Don't miss...

① Spend a couple of days in **Mumbai**. Try and get a part as a film extra in a Bollywood film, page 1071; take the boat from the Gateway of India to Elephanta Island, page 1093; have a drink in the Taj Mahal Hotel, page 1073, or check out the Mahatma Gandhi or Victoria and Albert museums, page 1078. At the end of the day people watch along Chowpatty Beach, page 1076.

② Marvel at the **Deogiri** fortifications at Daulatabad but try to be there in the late afternoon when the crowds have gone, page 1111.

③ The **Kailasanatha Temple** at Ellora is amongst the most magnificent rock-cut structures in the world, page 1114.

④ The **Ajanta caves** have some fabulous murals retelling the life of the Budhha, page 1116.

⑤ The **Osho Commune** in Pune offers numerous courses in meditation, page 1130.

⑥ The best of the Maratha forts is at **Raigad**. It's extremely atmospheric in the evening and has some great views over the ghats, page 1133.

Background → *Population: 96.8 million. Area: 308,000 sq km.*

The land

The volcanic lavas of the **Deccan Trap**, which poured out over 65 million years ago as the Indian peninsula broke away from the African coast, give rise to the region's very distinctive black soils. East of Nagpur the lava gives way to gently rolling granite hills, 250-350 m above sea level, an extraordinary landscape of huge open spaces and sweeping views. Approaching the ridge of the **Western Ghats**, the vegetation cover is always much lighter than on the Ghats themselves, which often rise as an abrupt and almost impenetrable wall reaching over 1,400 m in places. The undulating **Konkan coastal lowland** is widest near Mumbai, crossed by a series of short streams and rivers. A number of important **rivers** rise in the Western Ghats. Most follow the example of the Godavari and the Krishna, rising within 100 km of the Arabian Sea and then flowing eastwards across the Deccan plateau to the Bay of Bengal.

Climate Most of Maharashtra is hot during the daytime throughout the year, the coast being very humid as well. Daily maximum temperatures are between 28°C in January and 33°C in May, although night-time temperatures fall considerably from November to March. Only the hill stations of the Western Ghats experience much cooler weather, a particular relief in April and May. The southwest monsoon normally breaks on the coast in the second week of June and finishes in September, bringing most of the region's rain in often prolonged and violent storms. The coastal Konkan strip is wet while the interior upland behind is much drier. Mumbai receives over 2,700 mm per year.

History

The name Maharashtra was first used in a seventh century AD inscription, but its origins are unclear. One view is that it is derived from the word *rath* (chariot) whose drivers formed an army (*maharathis*). They are thought to have migrated south and settled in the upland area where they mingled with aboriginal tribes.

The dry western margins of the plateau have sites from the earliest **prehistoric** settlements in India, and Nevasa and Chirki in the Godavari valley, have paleolithic remains. The relatively open lands in the lee of the Ghats were one of the major routes from North to South India but lacked the resources to become the centre of a major political power. In the early period from the eighth to the 14th century there were a number of Hindu kingdoms, followed by the first Muslim Dynasty in 1307. The Muslim use of Persian as a court language left its mark on the development of the Marathi language.

The Marathas divided the country into *Swarajya* (Homeland) and *Mughlai* (territory controlled by foreigners), that was the legitimate object of raids. *Swaraj* ('home rule') re-emerged as one of the watchwords of the Independence struggle in the 20th century. Few Indian leaders have generated such a passionate following as Maharashtra's late 17th-century leader **Sivaji**. The state's modern political life still resonates with the myths of his military abilities, political cunning and Hindu revivalism (see box). Matching the political skills of a Machiavelli to the military ambitions of a Napoleon, within four years of his coronation Sivaji had begun to retake the forts ceded under the treaty with the Mughal Emperor Aurangzeb. By his death in 1680 he had re-established a powerful base around Pune and an expanding Maratha Empire. He died of dysentery at the age of 53. On Aurangzeb's death in 1707, Sivaji's former kingdom became a confederacy under the charge of a hereditary minister called the Peshwa and four main Maratha chiefs – Holkar, Scindia, Gaekwad and Bhonsla. By 1750 their power reached across India to Orissa, which they occupied, and Bengal, which they attacked. Maratha power was only decisively

▮ Sivaji's rise to power

Sivaji was born in 1627 in the then Muslim Sultanate of **Ahmadnagar**. At 19, he gathered an army, took Pratapgarh fort near Pune and soon established a powerful base. He made his reputation by a combination of brilliant campaigns, physical courage and occasional acts of astonishing cruelty towards his opponents.

Sivaji rose rapidly to weld different Hindu groups into a powerful force. Initially attacking their neighbouring Muslim states, his forces expanded their power to confront the Mughal Empire which dominated the north. The Marathas developed the skills of lightning raids and highly mobile military manoeuvres.

Sivaji made his capital at Raigad, and championing the Hindu cause, gained the reputation of being an Indian Robin Hood and regional hero. In 1664 he sacked the Mughal port of Surat. Two years later, the Rajput Jai Singh, sent by Aurangzeb to curb

Sivaji's power, succeeded in defeating him and bringing him back to the Mughal court. At this stage Sivaji obviously thought that he could not take on the Mughals and win, so he agreed to relinquish 23 of the 35 forts he had taken and to accompany Jai Singh to Agra to pay his respects to Aurangzeb.

His reception at the great Mughal's court was muddled. Aurangzeb intended to make him a gift of an elephant but was caught up in his own 50th birthday party celebrations and ignored Sivaji. The Maratha stormed out in protest but was kept under house arrest. By deceiving his guards into thinking that every day he sent a large basket of sweetmeats to Brahmins in the city, he smuggled himself out and returned to Maharashtra, dressed like a Hindu ascetic to avoid recapture. He returned to his own people and was crowned King.

curbed when they were defeated at Panipat by the Afghan Ahmad Shah Abdali. On the death of the young Peshwa, Madhao Rao I, in 1772, the five Maratha powers became increasingly independent of one another. Weakened and divided, they were unable to resist the advance of British power.

Culture

Ethnically, Maharashtra contains a variety of **peoples**. The Bhil, Warli, Gond, Korku and Gowari tribal groups living in the Satpura and Sahyadri ranges in the north are Australoid aboriginals. The Kunbi Marathas found all over the state are believed to be the descendants of immigrants from the north at the beginning of the Christian era. Parsis first arrived in the region in the eighth century from Persia. Just over 80% of the people are Hindus with Islam and Buddhism the most numerous minority religions. The Buddhists are recent converts from among formerly outcaste Hindus.

Marathi is the main regional **language** (spoken by 90% of the population), although both Hindi and English are widely understood, especially in the major cities. Konkani on the west coast and Gondi in the north are important regional languages.

The main regional **dishes** reflect Maharashtra's transition position between the wheat growing regions of the north and the rice growing coastal lands, while millets are grown in the interior. Lightly spiced vegetables and sweet and sour dishes are popular, with a distinctive emphasis on dried and salted fish such as Bombay Duck cooked with lentils. There are also recipes that use sprouting beans. Mumbai has the heaviest concentration of Parsis in the country, so try their cuisine here - *Dhansak*, a special lentil curry with lamb or chicken cooked with five varieties of spice, or *Patrani machli*, fish (often pomfret) stuffed with coconut chutney and coriander, steamed in banana leaves.

Festivals

The majority of Hindu festivals are observed in the state. The highly colourful *Ranga Panchami* and *Holi*, marking the beginning of spring, are very popular. *Janmashtami* (July/August) celebrates the birth of Lord Krishna. Men and boys form human pyramids to break pots of curds that have been hung from high places. On *Ganesh Chaturthi* in Mumbai (August/September) massive figures of the ever popular elephant god Ganesh are immersed in the sea; Pune has special celebrations. *Dasara* is significant because it was the day on which the Marathas usually began their military campaigns. The Muslim festival of *Mohurram* which commemorates the martyrs of Islam, is often observed by Hindus as well.

Modern Maharashtra

The old British administrative region of the Bombay Presidency had never coincided with the area in which Marathi was the dominant language. In 1948 the former princely state of Vadodara and some others were merged into Bombay. The present state did not take shape until 1960, when Gujarati areas in the north and Kannada speaking areas in the south were allocated to Gujarat and Karnataka respectively.

Maharashtra's **legislature** has two houses; the Vidhan Parishad (legislative council) and Vidhan Sabha (legislative assembly). Except for an annual meeting at Nagpur, the old Maratha capital, these meet in Mumbai. The state is represented by 48 members in the Lok Sabha (Lower House) and 19 members in Rajya Sabha (Upper House) of the national parliament in New Delhi. The Hindu -Maratha chauvinist party, the Shiv Sena, under the leadership of the former satirical cartoonist Bal Thackeray, has been a force in Maharastra's politics for over twenty years. However, the Shiv Sena-BJP combination suffered a severe setback in the 1998 Lok Sabha elections when the Congress took 37 of the 48 seats. In the State Assembly elections of October 1999, the Shiv Sena-BJP alliance suffered a further blow when it lost control of the State Assembly to a Congress-led coalition, although it remains in power within Mumbai. The Congress itself had split at the national level, one of Maharashtra's most powerful Congress politicians, Sharad Pawar, leaving to form the National Congress Party, or NCP. However his party remained allied to the Congress state level government under the Chief Ministership of Vilasrao Deshmukh, giving it sufficient support to hold on to power.

Maharashtra has been described as India's **industrial** and **commercial** backbone. The centre of India's stock market, the headquarters of a large number of Indian and multinational companies' operations in India and a major manufacturing state in its own right, Maharashtra has not only India's largest city, Mumbai, but a large number of rapidly industrialising smaller towns. These have been encouraged to develop through Government policies aimed at stimulating decentralised industrial growth. With only 10% of India's population Maharashtra acounts for nearly a quarter of India's total industrial output, with textiles, petro-chemicals, pharmaceuticals, electronics and a wide range of other products. However, agriculture remains important, cash crops like sugar cane accounting for 30% of the country's total sugar production. Alongside sugar, rice, sorghum, millets and gram are all important, while horticultural crops and fruit like mango, banana, oranges and grapes have rapidly grown in importance.

Mumbai → *Phone code: 022. Colour map 5, grid B2 and 3. Population: 16.37 million.*

Mumbai is India's outward looking, commercial face. The countries largest city, sprawling across seven islands joined into an artificial isthmus, its problems are only matched by the enormous drive which makes it unique as the centre of business, fashion and film making in modern India. The 1995 decision of the State government to change Bombay's name to Mumbai – after Mumba Devi, a Koli goddess, a form of Siva's wife Parvati – is now widely accepted, though many people still talk of the city as Bombay. ⟫ *For Sleeping, Eating and other listings, see pages 1079-1092.*

Ins and outs

Getting there Chhatrapati Sivaji International air terminal is 30 km from Nariman Point, the business heart of the city. The domestic terminals at Santa Cruz are 5 km closer. Pre-paid taxis to the city centre are good value and take between 40 mins and 1½ hrs, depending on traffic but there are also cheaper but slower buses. If you arrive late at night without a hotel booking it is best to stay at one of the hotels near the domestic terminal before going into town early in the morning.

Getting around The sights are spread out and you need transport. Taxis are metered and generally good value. There are frequent buses on major routes, and the 2 suburban railway lines are useful out of peak hours on some routes, but get horrendously crowded. Tourism Police Force outposts with trained staff are planned for Gateway of India, Nariman Point, Chowpatty, Juhu Beach and the International Airport which will offer security, distribute maps, guidebooks and tourist literature. Autorickshaws are only allowed in the suburbs. See Transport, page 1089, for further details.

Climate The hottest periods are Mar-May and Oct-Dec. Rainfall is very heavy Jun-Aug (Jun over 980 mm). Best time to visit is Nov-Mar.

History

Hinduism had made its mark on Mumbai long before the Portuguese and then the British transformed it into one of India's great cities. The caves on the island of Elephanta were excavated under the Kalachuris (500-600 AD). Yet, only 350 years ago, the area occupied by this great metropolis comprised seven islands inhabited by Koli fishermen (from whom we have the word 'coolies'). The British acquired these marshy and malarial islands as part of the marriage dowry paid by the Portuguese when Catherine of Braganza married Charles II in 1661. Some suggest that Bombay took its name from the Portuguese *Bom Bahia*, or 'good harbour'. Four years later, the British took possession of the remaining islands and neighbouring mainland area and in 1668 the East India Company leased the whole area from the crown for £10 sterling per year, which was paid for nearly 50 years. The East India Company shifted its headquarters to Mumbai in 1672. Until the early 19th century, Mumbai's fortunes rested on the shipbuilding yards established by progressive Parsis.

Mumbai remained isolated by the sharp face of the Western Ghats and the constantly hostile Marathas. However, it thrived on trade and, in the cosmopolitan city this created, Parsis, Sephardic Jews and the British shared common interests and responded to the same incentives.

Mumbai

To Airports

To Santa Cruz & Vile Parle Stations

Mehboob Studio

DHARAVI

Mahim

Mahim Bay

Matunga Road

Matunga

Dadar

WORLI

Wadala

Sivaji Park

Arabian Sea

Dr Babasaheb Ambedkar Rd

Elphinstone Road

Parel

Sewri

Related map
A Central Mumbai, page 1072

Lower Parel

Curry Rd

Cotton Green

Stadium

Chinchpoli

Reay Road

Dhobi Ghats

Maha Lakshmi

Haji Ali's Tomb

Mahalaxmi Race Course

Victoria Garden

Mahalakshmi Temple

Mumbai Central

Byculla

Catholic Cathedral

Breach Candy

Tata Garden

Dockyard Rd

Kemp's Corner

Pr Ali Khan

Christ Church

Towers of Silence

Grant Road (M Shaukat Ali Rd)

Mani Bhavan

Sandhurst Road

All Saints'

Chor Bazar

S Patel Rd

Masjid

Chowpatty Beach

Charni Road

London Pub

Walkeshwar Temple

Marine Lines

Raj Bhavan

Back Bay

CST

Churchgate

Vir Nariman Rd

Madam Cama Rd

Nariman Point

Gateway of India

Tata Institute of Fundamental Research

World Trade Centre

St John's

Homi Babha Auditorium

Sassoon Dock

Catholic Church

Observatory

N

0 km   1
0 miles   1

Sleeping
1 Anukool D2
2 Heritage C3
3 Kalpana Palace & Café Heaven D2
4 Midtown Pritam D2
5 Parklane B3
6 Red Rose B3
7 YMCA International C2

Eating
1 Biscotti D1
2 Bombay A1 D2
3 Café Olé & Biscotti D1
4 Chinatown, Shalimar & Contemporary Arts D1
5 Chopsticks D2
6 Davaat, Mirch Masala, Moti Mahal & Santraj B2
7 Goa Portuguesa A3
8 Kamat C2
9 NewYorker D1
10 Only Fish A3
11 Rashtriya B3
12 Revival D1
13 Under the Over D1
14 Viva Paschim B2

Maharashtra Mumbai History

The original British community lived within the old fort area. After a devastating fire on 17 February 1803, a new town with wider streets was built. Then, with the abolition of the Company's trade monopoly, the doors to rapid expansion were flung open and Mumbai flourished. Trade with England boomed. Annual exports of raw cotton trebled over the period 1809-16, and with the defeat of the Marathas at Kirkee in November 1817, the economic hinterland of Mumbai was able to expand along revitalized old trade routes onto the Deccan plateau and beyond.

After the opening of the Suez Canal in 1870, Mumbai's greater proximity to European markets gave it an advantage over Kolkata. The port became the commercial centre of the Arabian Sea. The population in 1864 was 816,000, and grew rapidly. With land reclamation the islands were connected, so that Mumbai came to occupy a narrow isthmus.

Modern Mumbai

Mumbai rapidly became the centre of an entrepreneurial as well as a commercial class, drawing from the Parsi as well as the Bania Hindu business community. Mumbai has become the home of India's stock exchange (BSE) and headquarters for many national and international companies and is also a major industrial centre. By the 1880s over 30,000 workers were employed in the cotton and engineering industries. Originally these were concentrated round the ports and railway facilities, but have become more diversified. Other important activities are printing, furniture manufacture, ceramics, food, pharmaceuticals and tobacco. But with the sponsorship of the Tata family Mumbai has also become the primary home of India's nuclear research programme, with its first plutonium extraction plant at Trombay in 1961 and the establishment of the Tata Institute for Fundamental Research the most prestigious science research institute in the country.

Mumbai is still growing fast. One third of the population live in the desperately squalid *chawls* of cramped, makeshift and miserable hovels. There are also many thousands of pavement dwellers. Due to heavy demand for building space, property values are exceedingly high. Mumbai's planners have promoted industrial dispersal since the 1960s and this has had a strong impact. New Mumbai across the Thane Creek has been developed to ease the pressure on the isthmus, but Great Mumbai remains a magnet to people from across India.

Mumbai produces nearly 200 films per year, making **Dollywood** the world's second largest film maker after Hong Kong. The stars live in sumptuous dwellings, many of which are on Malabar Hill, Mumbai's Beverley Hills, and despite the spread of foreign videos their popularity seems undiminished. It is difficult to get permission to visit a studio during filming but you might try **Film City**, Goregaon East, T8401533 or **Mehboob Studios**, Hill Road, Bandra West, T6428045. Alternatively, the staff at the *Salvation Army Hostel* (see Sleeping) may be able to help forcigners get on as 'extras' (blonde and tall preferred!); Rs 500 per day!

Sights

With limited time in the city, for a day tour you might take a boat out to the **Elephanta Caves** from the **Gateway of India** at around 0900, and call in at the *Taj Mahal Hotel* on your return. The excellent **Chhatrapati Sivaji Museum** and the **Jehangir Art Gallery** are only a short walk away. The architecturally interesting **Chhatrapati Sivaji Terminus (CST)** has other Raj buildings around while the bustling **Crawford Market** is just to the north.

Churchgate station can be the start of a half-day tour which takes you down **Marine Drive** past **Chowpatty Beach** and on to the **Gandhi Museum** at Mani Bhavan,

Central Mumbai

Related map
A Gateway of India & Coloba,
page 1074

*Back
Bay*

0 metres   300
0 yards   300

■ **Sleeping**
1 City Palace *C3*
2 Chateau Windsor
   Guest House *C2*
3 Manama *B3*
4 Oberoi Towers
   & Oberoi *D1*
5 Rupam *B3*

● **Eating**
1 Apoorva *C3*
2 Balwas *C2*
3 Berry's & Chopsticks *C1*
4 Copa Cabana *A1*
5 Croissant & British
   Airways *D2*

6 Supreme *E1*
7 West End *B2*

6 Gaylord *D2*
7 George *D3*
8 Kamling &
   Flavours *C1*
9 Mahesh Lunch
   Home *C3*
10 May Rose *B2*
11 Not just Jazz
    by the Bay *C1*
12 Piccolo Café *D3*

13 Rajdhani *B3*
14 Santoor *E1*
15 Sapna *C2*
16 Satkar *C1*
17 Sidewok *D1*
18 Thacker's *C2*
19 West Coast *C3*
20 Woodlands & British
    Council *E1*

the **Hanging Gardens** and the **Jain temple**. Stop on the Mahalaxmi Bridge to see the
extraordinary activity at the **Dhobi Ghats**.

Gateway of India

The Indo-Saracenic-style Gateway of India (1927), designed by George Wittet to
commemorate the visit of George V and Queen Mary in 1911, is modelled in
honey-coloured basalt on 16th-century Gujarati work. The great gateway comprises
an archway with halls on each side capable of seating 600 at important receptions.
The arch was the point from which the last British regiment serving in India signalled
the end of the empire when it left on 28 February 1948. The whole area has a huge
buzz at weekends. Scores of boats depart from here for Elephanta Island, creating a
sea-swell which young boys delight in diving into. Hawkers, beggars and the general
throng of people all add to the atmosphere. A short distance behind the Gateway is
an impressive statue of **Sivaji** (see box).

★ The **Taj Mahal Hotel**, the original red-domed hotel, has been adjoined by a
modern skyscraper (the *Taj Mahal Inter-Continental*). It is worth popping into the *Taj*
for a bite to eat or a drink, or if so inclined go to the disco frequented by well-heeled
young Indians. Unfortunately, drug addicts, drunks and prostitutes frequent the area
behind the hotel.

Colaba

South of the Gateway of India is the crowded southern section of Shahid (literally
'martyr') Bhagat Singh Marg (Colaba Causeway). The Afghan Memorial **Church of St
John the Baptist** (1847-58) is at the northern edge of Colaba itself. Early English in
style, with a 58-m spire, it was built to commemorate the soldiers who died in the First
Afghan War. Fishermen still unload their catch early in the morning at **Sassoon Dock**,
the first wet dock in India; photography prohibited. Beyond the church near the tip of
the Colaba promontory lie the **Observatory** and **Old European cemetery** in the naval
colony (permission needed to enter). Frequent buses ply this route. Sadly, increasing
numbers of beggars target foreign visitors here.

Central Mumbai

The area stretching north from Colaba Causeway to CST (Victoria Terminus) dates
from after 1862, when Sir Bartle Frere became Governor (1862-67). Under his
enthusiastic guidance Mumbai became a great civic centre and an extravaganza of
Victorian Gothic architecture, modified by Indo-Saracenic influences.

Just behind the Chhatrapati Sivaji (Prince of Wales) Museum in South Bhagat
Singh Marg is **St Andrew's Kirk** (1819), a simple neo-classical church. At the south end
of Mahatma Gandhi (MG) Road is the Renaissance style **Institute of Science** (1911)
designed by George Wittet. The Institute, which includes a scientific library, a public hall
and examination halls, was built with gifts from the Parsi and Jewish communities.

★ **Pope Paul (Oval) Maidan** The Oval garden has been restored to a pleasant public
garden. On the east side of the Pope Paul (Oval) Maidan is the Venetian Gothic style
old **Secretariat** (1874), with a façade of arcaded verandahs and porticos faced in
buff-coloured Porbander stone from Gujarat. Decorated with red and blue basalt, the
carvings are in white Hemnagar stone. The University **Convocation Hall** (1874) to its
north was designed by Sir George Gilbert Scott in a 15th-century French decorated
style. Scott also designed the adjacent **University Library** and the **Rajabai Clocktower** (1870s) next door, based on Giotto's campanile in Florence. The sculpted
figures in niches on the exterior walls of the tower were designed to represent the
castes of India. Originally the clock could chime 12 tunes such as Rule Britannia.

The **High Court** (1871-79), in Early English Gothic style, has a 57-m high central
tower flanked by lower octagonal towers topped by the figures of Justice and Mercy.

Gateway of India & Colaba

To Hutatma Chowk

To Horniman Circle

Stock Exchange

Rajabai Tower

Tamil Nadu Handicrafts

Dalal St

Gandhi Rd

Mumbai University

D'Mello Rd

Passports

Rhythm House

Dr V B Gandhi Marg

Rope Walk Lane

Kalkashru Dubash Marg

Shahid Bhagat Singh Marg

City & Civil Courts

Jehangir Art Gallery

Mahatma

National Gallery of Modern Art

Ambedkar Statue

Institute of Science

C Siraji (Prince of Wales Museum)

BNHS

Queen's Rd

Pope Paul (Oval) Maidan

K B Patel Marg

Childrens' Traffic

Madam Cama Rd

Jet Airways

SP Mukharji Chowk (Wellington Circle)

Dockyard

Maharashtra Police HQ

The Cooperage

Cooperage Marg

Regal Cinema

Amex

Cottage Industries

Maharshi Karve Marg

Nathalal Parekh Marg

(Woodhouse Rd)

Convent St

Transport House

Lansdowne Rd

Sivaji Marg

Bus & Elephanta Tours Tickets

Apollo Bunder

Ormiston Rd

Naoroji Marg

Tulloch Rd

ATM

Elephanta Launches

Wesley

OUP Bookshop

Electric House

Mandlik M

Gateway of India

To Elephanta

Shahid Bhagat Singh Marg

(Best Marg)

Cusrow Baug

Barrow Rd

(Colaba Causeway)

Henry Rd

Venture Travels

Walton Rd

Meterweather Rd

Premsingh J Ramchandani Marg (Apollo Bunder)

Arabian Sea

S Barucha Rd

Garden Rd

To Sassoon Dock

Arthur Bunder Rd

Strand Rd

Strand Cinema

N

0 metres 100
0 yards 100

Maharashtra Mumbai Sights

■ Sleeping

1 Apollo
2 Bentley's
3 Diplomat
4 Godwin
5 Lawrence
6 Regent
7 Salvation Army Red Shield Hostel
8 Seashore
9 Suba Palace
10 Strand
11 Taj Mahal
12 Taj Mahal Intercontinental
13 Volga & Kamat Samarambh
14 Whalley's
15 YWCA International Guest House

● Eating

1 Bagdadi
2 Copper Chimney
3 Indigo
4 Kailash Parbat
5 Khyber
6 Leopold
7 Ling's Pavilion
8 Martin's
9 Mondegar
10 Trishna
11 Wayside Inn

The Venetian Gothic **Public Works Office** (1869-72) is to its north. Opposite, and with its main façade to Vir Nariman Road, is the former General Post Office (1869-72). Now called the **Telegraph Office**, it stands next to the original Telegraph Office adding Romanesque to the extraordinary mixture of European architectural styles. The old buildings of the centre are floodlit after 1900.

Horniman Circle From the imposing Horniman Circle, Vir Nariman Road leads to Flora (or Frere) Fountain (1869), now known as **Hutatma Chowk**. Horniman Circle itself was laid out in 1860. On the west edge are the Venetian Gothic **Elphinstone Buildings** (1870) in brown sandstone. The **Cathedral Church of St Thomas** was begun in 1672, opened in 1718, and subject to a number of later additions. Inside are a number of monuments forming a heroic 'Who's Who of India'. The **Custom House** is believed to incorporate a Portuguese barrack block of 1665. Over the entrance is the crest of the East India Company. Parts of the old Portuguese fort's walls can be seen. Many Malabar teak 'East Indiamen' ships were built here.

The **Mint** (1824-29), built on the Fort rubbish dump, has Ionic columns and a water tank in front of it. The **Town Hall** (1820-23) has been widely admired as one of the best neo-classical buildings in India. The original idea of paired columns was abandoned as being too monumental, and half the columns - imported from Britain - were used at Christ Church, Byculla. The Corinthian interior houses the Assembly Rooms and the Bombay Asiatic Society.

★ **CST or 'VT' (Victoria Terminus) Station area** The **Chhatrapati Sivaji Terminus** (formerly Victoria Terminus or **VT**) (1878-87), the most remarkable example of Victorian Gothic architecture in India, was opened during Queen Victoria's Golden Jubilee year. The first train in India had left from this terminus for Thane in April 1853. Known today as 'CST', over half a million commuters use the station every day.

The frontage is symmetrical with a large central dome flanked by two wings. The dome is capped by a 4-m high statue of Progress. The booking hall with its arcades, stained glass and glazed tiles was inspired by London's St Pancras station.

The station was built at a time when fierce debate was taking place among British architects working in India as to the most appropriate style to develop to meet the demands of the late 19th-century boom. One view held that the British should restrict themselves to models derived from the best in western tradition. Others argued that architects should draw on Indian models, trying to bring out the best of Indian tradition and encourage its development. By and large, the former were dominant, but as Tillotson argues, the introduction of Gothic allowed a blending of western traditions with Indian (often Islamic Indian) motifs, which became known as the Indo-Saracenic style. The giant caterpillar-like walkway with perspex awnings looks incongruous against the gothic structure of 'VT'.

Opposite the CST station are the grand Municipal Buildings (1893), built by Stevens. In Mahapalika Marg (Cruickshank Road) are the **Police Courts** (1888), **Cama Albless Hospital** which has interesting Gothic windows with conical iron hoods to provide shade, **St Xavier's College** founded in 1867 and **Elphinstone High School** (1872). On the opposite side of the road is the **Azad Maidan**.

St Xavier's School and Gokuldas Tejpal Hospital (1877), built by Parsi benefactors, are in Lokmanya Tilak Marg (Camac Road). On the southeast and southwest faces are medallions by Rudyard Kipling's father Lockwood Kipling.

★ **Crawford Market** (1865-71), now Jyotiba Phule Market, was designed by Emerson in the 12th-century French Gothic style. Over the entrance is more of Lockwood Kipling's work; the paving stones are from Caithness! The market is divided into sections for fruit, vegetables, fish, mutton and poultry. From Crawford Market you can return to the Gateway of India or take a taxi to either the Victoria and Albert Museum at Byculla, or Malabar Hill.

Maharashtra Mumbai Sights

⁑ The 'Dabbawallahs'

If you go inside Churchgate station at mid-morning or after lunch, you will see the *dabbawallahs*, members of the Bombay Union of Tiffin Box Carriers. Each morning, the 2,500 dabbawallahs call on suburban housewives who pack freshly cooked lunch into small circular stainless steel containers – *dabbas*. Three or four are stacked one on the other and held together by a clip with a handle. Typically the *dabbawallah* will collect 30-40 tiffin boxes, range them out on a long pole and cycle to the nearest station. Here he will hand them over to a fellow *dabbawallah* who will transport them into the city for delivery to the consumer.

Over 100,000 lunches of maybe sabze (vegetable curry), chappattis, dal and pickle make their way daily across town to the breadwinner. The service, which costs a few rupees a day, is a good example of the fine division of labour in India, reliable and efficient, for the dabbawallahs pride themselves on never losing a lunch. He makes sure that the carefully prepared pukka (proper) food has not in any way been defiled.

Between Crawford Market and Mumbai Central Railway Station is **Falkland Road**, the centre of Mumbai's red-light district. Prostitutes stand behind barred windows, giving the area its other name 'The Cages' - many of the girls are sold or abducted from various parts of India and Nepal. Medical reports suggest that AIDS is very widespread.

Marine Drive and Malabar Hill You can do an interesting half-day trip from Churchgate Station, along Marine Drive to the Taraporewala Aquarium, Mani Bhavan (Gandhi Museum), the Babulnath Temple, past the Parsi Towers of Silence to Kamla Nehru Park, the Hanging Gardens and the Jain Temple. If you wish, you can go further towards Malabar Point to get a glimpse of Raj Bhavan and the Walkeshwar Temple, before returning via the Mahalaxmi Temple and Haji Ali's tomb.

Churchgate Station (1894-96) was designed by FW Stevens for the Mumbai, Baroda and Central India Railway. Stevens was a great protagonist of the Indo-Saracenic style. With its domes and façades Churchgate Station is Byzantine in flavour. The statue on the western gable shows a figure holding a locomotive and wheel, symbols of technological progress.

Chowpatty Beach, a long stretch of white sand, looks attractive from a distance, but is polluted. Swimming here is not recommended but there is a lot of interesting beach activity in the evening. Chowpatty was the scene of a number of important 'Quit India' rallies during the Independence Movement. At important festivals like *Ganesh Chaturthi* and *Dasara* (see Festivals), it is thronged with jubilant Hindu devotees. Netaji Subhash Road, better known as Marine Drive, runs round **Back Bay** along Chowpatty from just below the Hanging Gardens on Malabar Hill to Nariman Point. At night, lined with lights, it is a very attractive sight from Malabar Hill, a view which gave rise to the description of it as 'Queen Victoria's Necklace'.

⁑ *Join the crowds at sunset for an entertaining walk: hawkers and sand sculpturers mingle with joggers and Mumbai's high society walking their dogs.*

Mahatma Gandhi Museum is further north towards Nana Chowk, at Mani Bhavan. See Museums below.

The **Towers of Silence** (Parsi 'temple') are in secluded gardens 500 m west of Mani Bhavan. This very private place is not accessible to tourists but it can be glimpsed from the road. Sir Jamshetji Jeejeebhoy gave a large area of land around the towers, thus affording them privacy and allowing the creation of a tranquil garden. Parsis believe that the elements of water, fire and earth must not be polluted by the dead, so they lay

⁝ Washing your dirty linen in public

In Mahalakshmi's municipal *dhobi ghats* you can see a bewildering range of India's contrasts. The *dhobis* (washermen and women) deal with a staggeringly large wash every day. Through the apparent chaos, thousands of pieces of clothing, bedsheets and towels are collected from private houses (marked with a tiny indelible ink symbol, unique to that household), logged in a note book, washed in the small cubicles rented out to several washermen each day, and returned to the owners a week later (except during the rains, when the delivery period may be two weeks or more). Virtually nothing seems to get lost, and equally miraculously most clothes survive the beating they receive on the stones, having spent a night soaking in soapy water which looks positively murky. Surrounded by public squalor, the dhobis deal in cleansing all in public. However, their days may be numbered, for washing machines are spreading fast and there are signs that demand for this most traditional of Indian activities is falling.

The area can be unpleasant and dangerous – beggars pester and gangs have been known to stop lone travellers and demand a large 'ransom'.

their 'vestments of flesh and bone' out on the top of the towers to be picked clean by vultures. The apparent depletion in the number of vultures is a cause for concern.

★ The **Hanging Gardens** (Pherozeshah Mehta Gardens) immediately south of the Towers of Silence, on top of a low hill, are so named since they are located on top of a series of tanks that supply water to Mumbai. The gardens are well kept with lots of topiary animals and there are good views over the city from the children's park across the road. Snake charmers operate from the roadside. Worth a visit.

Nearby is the Church of North India **All Saints' Church** (1882). Across the road from the Hanging Gardens is the **Kamla Nehru Park**, laid out in 1952 and named after the wife of India's first Prime Minister. Very good views over Back Bay.

The **Jain Temple** (1904) was built of marble and dedicated to the first Jain *Tirthankar*. Much of the decoration depicts the lives of the Tirthankars. Visitors can watch various rituals being performed. Jains play a prominent part in Bombay's banking and commerce and are one of the city's wealthiest communities.

Walkeshwar temple One of the oldest buildings in Mumbai, the Walkeshwar Temple ('Lord of Sand') was built about 1000 AD. In legend this was a resting point for Rama on his journey from Ayodhya to Lanka to free Sita from the demon king Ravana. One day Rama's brother Lakshman failed to return from Varanasi at the usual time with a *lingam* which he fetched daily for Rama's worship. Rama then made a *lingam* from the beach sand to worship Siva.

On Bhulabhai Desai Road, Cumballa Hill are the **Mahalakshmi temples**, the oldest in Mumbai and dedicated to three goddesses whose images were found in the sea.

Haji Ali's tomb The tomb and mosque are devoted to a Muslim saint who drowned here. They are reached by a long causeway usable only at low tide. The moneychangers are willing to exchange 1 rupee coins into smaller coins, enabling pilgrims to make several individual gifts to beggars rather than one larger one, thereby reputedly increasing the merit of the gift.

From Haji Ali's Tomb go along Keshavrao Khade Road to SG Maharaj Chowk (Jacob's Circle). From the Mahalakshmi Bridge there is a view of the astonishing Municipal **dhobi ghats**. See box above.

Maharashtra Mumbai Sights

Changed street names

The official address of hotels and restaurants is given in the main text. However, old road names (bold) continue to be widely used and are often much better known. The following list summarizes the most important changes:

Apollo Bunder Road – Sivaji Marg; **Ballard Road** – Shoorji Vallabhas Marg; **Carnac Road** – Lokmanaya Tilak Road;

Churchgate Street – Vir Nariman Road; **Clare Road** – Mirza Ghalib Street; **Club Road** – Maratha Mandir Marg; **Cuffe Parade Road** – Prakash Pethe Marg; **Duncan Road** – Maulana Azad Road; **Elphin Stone Road** – Jagannathrao Bhadkamkar Marg; **Erskine Road** – Brigadier Usman Marg; **Falkland Road** – Patthe Bapurao Marg; **Flora Fountain** – Hutatma Chowk; **Foreshore Road** – Jagannath Bhosle Marg; **Frere Road** – P D'Mello Road; **Gowalia Tank Road** – August Kranti Marg; **Grant Road** – Maulana Shaukat Ali Road; **Gunbow Street** – Rustom Sidhwa Marg; **Harris Road** –

Dr E Moses Road; **Hughes Road** – Sitaram Patkar Marg; **Jacob Circle** – Sant Gadge Maharaj Chowk; **Lamington Road** – Anandrao Nair Marg; **Marine Drive** – Netaji Subhas Chandra Bose Road; **Marine Lines** – Dr Dinshaw Mulla Road; **Nepean Sea Road** – L Jagmohandas Marg; **New Marine Lines Road** – Sir Vithaldas Thackersey Marg; **Ormiston Road** – Best Marg; **Outram Road** – Purshottamdas Thakurdas Marg; **Peddar Road** – Dr Gopalrao Deshmukh Marg; **Proctor Road** – Vadilal A Patel Marg; **Rampart Row** – Kaikashru (K) Dubash Marg; **Sandhurst Road** – Sardar Vallabh Bhai (VB) Patel Road; **Sprott Road** – Shivsagar Ramgulam Marg; **Strand Road** – Sir Premsingh J (PJ) Ramchandani Marg; **Tardeo Road** – Javji Dadaji Marg; **Upper Colaba Road** – Dr Nanabai Moos Marg; **Victoria Terminus (VT)** – Chhatrapati Sivaji Terminus (CST); **Warden Road** – Bhulabhai Desai Road; **Woodhouse Road** – Parekh Marg.

Go down Maulana Azad Road then turn left into Clare Road. On your right is **Christ Church**, Byculla (1835), which incorporated half the pillars originally intended for the Town Hall. Clare Road leads the side of the Victoria Gardens.

Museums

★ **Mahatma Gandhi Museum** (Mani Bhavan) ⓘ *West of Grant Rd, 19 Laburnum Rd, 0930-1800, Rs 3, allow 1 hr.* On map, page 1070. This private house, where Mahatma Gandhi used to stay on visits to Mumbai, is now a memorial museum and research library with 20,000 volumes. There is a diorama depicting important scenes from Gandhi's life – slides without a mount are available, Rs 100. The display of photos and letters on the first floor is more interesting, and includes letters Gandhi wrote to Hitler (1939) asking him not to go to war, Roosevelt and Tolstoy, and there are also letters from Einstein and Tolstoy. Well worth a visit.

★ **Victoria and Albert Museum** (Bhav Daji Laud Museum) ⓘ *North of Byculla Station, Mon, Tue, Thu, Fri, Sat 1030-1700, Sun 0830-1645, closed Wed.* On map, page 1070. Inspired by the V&A in London and financed by public subscription, it was built in 1872 in a Palladian style. The collection covers the history of Mumbai and contains prints, maps and models. In front of the museum is a Clocktower (1865) with four faces (morning, noon, evening and night), and a stone statue of an elephant found by the Portuguese in the harbour. Elephanta Island was named after it. The *Victoria Gardens* are very attractive – marked as Jijamata Udyan on some maps and signs. A list at the entrance shows which trees are in bloom.

★ **Chhatrapati Sivaji (Prince of Wales) Museum** ① *South end of MG Rd, closed Mon, 1015-1730 (Oct-Feb), 1015-1800 (Jul-Sep), 1015-1830 (Mar-Jun), foreigners Rs 350 (includes taped guide), Indians Rs 15, camera fee Rs 15 (no flash or tripods), good guidebooks, cards and reproductions on sale.* This impressive building was designed by George Wittet to commemorate the visit of the Prince of Wales to India in 1905. The dome of glazed tiles has a very Persian and Central Asian flavour. The **archaeological** section has three main groups: Brahminical, Buddhist and Jain; Prehistoric and Foreign. The **art** section includes an excellent collection of Indian miniatures and well displayed *tankhas*. There are also works by Gainsborough, Poussin and Titian as well as Indian silver, jade and tapestries. The **Natural History** section is based on the collection of the Bombay Natural History Society founded in 1833.

Jehangir Art Gallery (in the Chhatrapati Sivaji Museum complex) Holds short term exhibitions of contemporary art (available for sale). Some visitors are disappointed by the small display. The *'Samovar'* café is good for a snack and a drink including chilled beer in a pleasant garden-side setting. There are phones and toilets. Temporary members may use the library and attend lectures. **National Gallery of Modern Art**, Sir Cowasji Jehangir Hall, is opposite the Chhatrapati Sivaji Museum.

Nhava Maritime Museum ① *T7212387 (off); T7212441 (res) for tour.* On Nhava Sheva Island is reached by ferry from Gateway of India. India's oldest maritime museum (1912) traces 4,000 years of maritime history through artefacts, charts, photos, models etc.

⊟ Sleeping

For Paying Guest accommodation contact India Tourist Office, 123 M Karve Rd, T2032932, F2014496. Accommodation in Mumbai is usually very heavily booked. Whenever possible make reservations in advance. If you have not, arrive as early in the day as possible. Most hotels are concentrated in the central area (Marine Drive, Nariman Point, Apollo Bunder and Colaba). See page 1081 for places to stay convenient for the airport. Prices are much higher than elsewhere in India, but there are some moderately priced hotels immediately behind the *Taj Mahal Hotel*. Backpackers usually head for the Colaba area to the south. The alternative is to look around CST and Dadar railway stations. There are several 5-star hotels on Juhu beach and close to the airports.

Gateway of India and Colaba
p1073 and map p1074

Rooms with seaview are more expensive.
L-AL Fariyas, 25 off Arthur Bunder Rd, Colaba,

T2042911, F2834992. 80 upgraded rooms, good restaurants, 'pub', roof garden, pool (open to non-residents), obliging service.
AL Taj Mahal, the original, with great style and character, 294 rooms, and **Taj Mahal Intercontinental**, Apollo Bunder, T2023366, F2872711. 306 rooms, excellent restaurants (no shorts). *Tanjore* (good thalis), Indian dance performance (evenings), open to non-residents (Rs 100, 1 hr). Recommended.
A Strand, 25 PJ Ramchandani Marg, T2882222. Friendly, clean, decent rooms, some with bath and seaview.
B Apollo, 22 Lansdowne Rd, Colaba, behind *Taj*, T2020223, F2871592. 39 rooms, some a/c, not all with sea view, excellent, helpful, friendly.
B Diplomat, 24-26 BK Boman Behram Marg (behind *Taj*), T2021661, F2830000, diplomat@ vsnl.com. 52 a/c rooms, restaurant, quiet, friendly, relaxed atmosphere, good value.
B Gulf Flower, Kamal Mansions, Arthur Bunder Rd, T2833742. Off-putting exterior but modern and clean rooms inside.

● ● *For an explanation of the sleeping and eating price codes used in this guide, see inside the front cover. Other relevant information is found in Essentials pages 52-57.*

B **Regency Inn**, 18 Landsowne Rd behind Regal Cinema, Colaba, T2020292, T2837757. Spacious a/c rooms, fridge, good value.

B **Regent**, 8 Ormiston Rd (Best Marg), T2871854. Well-furnished a/c rooms, no restaurant but good room service.

B **Suba Palace**, Apollo Bunder, T2020636, F2020812, just behind *Taj*. Clean, modern, well run. Recommended.

B-C **Garden**, 42 Garden Rd, T2841476, F2044290. 32 large a/c rooms, restaurant.

B-C **Godwin**, 41 Garden Rd, T2872050, F2871592. 48 large, clean, renovated, a/c rooms (upper floors have better views), good rooftop restaurant (full of wealthy Mumbaiites on Fri and Sat night), very helpful management. Recommended.

B-C **Shelley's**, 30 PJ Ramchandani Marg, Colaba, T2840229, F2840385, shelleyhotel@ vsnl.com. Large comfortable, bright airy a/c rooms, some sea-facing with TV and fridge (more expensive), a 'heritage' building with character, breakfasts only, helpful and friendly owners. Recommended.

C-D **Whalley's**, 41 Mereweather Rd, T2834206. 25 rooms (inspect first), some good a/c with balcony and bath, includes breakfast, accepts TCs, old-fashioned.

C-D **YWCA International Centre**, 2nd Flr, 18 Madam Cama Rd (entrance on side), Fort, T2020122, F2020445. For both sexes, 34 clean, pleasant rooms with bath, breakfast and dinner included, essential to write in advance with Rs 1,300 deposit.

Few budget hotels are left in the area charging under Rs 400 though you may get a dormitory bed for Rs 250.

D **Lawrence**, Rope Walk Lane, behind 'Prince of Wales' Museum, T2843618. 9 rooms, usually full, very good value.

D **Sea Shore**, 4th floor, 1/49 Kamal Mansion, Arthur Bunder Rd, T2874237, F2874238. Has good, clean seafacing rooms (avoid others).

Some **E-F** category hotels are clustered around the *Taj Mahal Hotel*:

Salvation Army Red Shield Hostel, 30 Mereweather Rd, T2841824. Mostly dorm (about Rs 130 including breakfast, Rs 200 including meals), some double rooms (Rs 450, all meals), lockers Rs 30 per item 0800-2200, showers, check out 0900, book in advance or arrive early when others check out, bus ticketing (eg Goa) at Reception desk. Recommended as convenient, friendly, best value but could be cleaner, see 'Film Capital' under 'Modern Mumbai' above.

On Arthur Bunder Rd, Colaba, there are several, often on upper floors, usually shared facilities, cold water only, some windowless rooms; arrive early and inspect room first:

Churchgate, Nariman Point and Marine Drive *p1076, map p1072*

LL-AL **The Oberoi**, Nariman Pt, T2325757, F2041505. 350 large rooms, the newer Oberoi combining modern technology with period furniture, excellent restaurants.

LL-AL **Oberoi Towers**, Nariman Pt, T2324343, F2043282. 650 rooms, superb views from higher floors, good buffets, garden pool, excellent shopping complex.

LL-AL **President**, 90 Cuffe Parade, T2150808, F2151201. 317 rooms, most business facilities, good service but poor value, informal but lacks character.

L-AL **Ambassador**, Churchgate Extn, Vir Nariman Rd, T2041131, F2040004. 127 rooms, all facilities, revolving restaurant and pastry shop, slightly run-down feel.

AL **Nataraj**, 135 Marine Drive, T2044161, F2043864. 83 rooms, some with views over bay, food and live music in restaurant, good but a bit noisy and overpriced.

A-B **West End**, 45 New Marine Lines, T2039121, F2057506, westhotel@vsnl.com. 80 small, pleasant suites but need refurbishing, good restaurant, excellent service, very efficient front desk, well located, good value. Recommended.

B-C **Chateau Windsor Guest House**, 86 Vir Nariman Rd, T2043376, F2851415, info@ chateauwindsor.com. 36 rooms (some a/c) vary, some very small and dark, room service for light snacks and drinks, friendly, clean, good value. Recommended. Cash only.

C **Sea Green**, 145 Marine Drive, T/F2822294. 34 rooms, 22 a/c, pleasant sitting area.

C-D **Astoria**, 4 J Tata Rd, Churchgate, T2852626, F2871765. 75 a/c rooms, restaurant, bar.

C-D **Supreme**, 4 Pandey Rd, near *President*, T2185623. Clean rooms with bath, good service but a little noisy.

CST (VT) and Fort p1075, map p1072

B Grand, 17 Sprott Rd, Ballard Estate, T2618211, F2626581. 73 a/c rooms, exchange, book counter, old-fashioned, built around a central courtyard, helpful service, very relaxing.
B-C City Palace, 121 City Terrace (Nagar Chowk), opposite CST Main Gate, T2615515, F2676897. Tiny though clean, functional rooms (some without window), with bath (Indian WC), some a/c, helpful staff, convenient location. Recommended.
D Popular Place, 104-6 Mint Rd, near GPO, Fort Market, T2695506. Clean rooms with bath (hot water), some a/c, helpful staff good value.
D-E Manama, 221 P D'Mello Rd, T2613412. Reasonable rooms, few with bath and a/c.
D-E Rupam, 239 P D'Mello Rd, T2618298. 37 rooms, some a/c with phone, clean, friendly, comfortable beds.

Dadar, Mumbai Central Station and Grant Road area
map p1070

Dadar can be a good option to stay - plenty of restaurants and good trains to Churchgate and CST.
A-B Midtown Pritam, 20-B Pritam Estates, Senapati Bapat Marg, 2 mins from Dadar station, T4145555, F4143388. 63 rooms, terrace garden.
C Oasis, near CST. Small cell-like, a/c rooms with TV. Friendly, helpful owners.
C Sagar, Nagpada Junction (Bellasin Rd/JB Behram Marg corner), Byculla, T3092727, F3072408. Very clean rooms, good restaurant.
C-D Red Rose, Gokuldas Pasta Rd (behind Chitra Cinema), Dadar East, T4137843. 31 rooms, some a/c, mostly shared but clean baths, flexible checkout, friendly – "welcoming at 0530 with no booking".
D Anukool, 292-8 Maulana Saukat Ali Rd, T30814013, F3078187, hotelanukool@ hotmail.com. 23 rooms, some a/c, friendly, helpful, good value, but inspect room first.
D Heritage, Sant Savta Marg, Byculla, T3714891, F3738844. 84 a/c rooms, restaurant (good Parsi), bar.
D Kalpana Palace, 181 P Bapurao Marg, opposite Daulat Cinema, Grant Rd, T3000846. 30 decent rooms, some a/c.
D Railway Retiring Rooms, Mumbai Central, T3077292. Some a/c with bath.

D-E YMCA International House, 18 YMCA Rd, near Mumbai Central, T3091191. Decent rooms, shared bath, meals included, temp membership Rs 60, deposit Rs 1,300, good value, book 3 months ahead.

Airport, Juhu Beach and Bandra

Juhu Beach (20 km from the centre) used to be quite an attractive and relaxed seaside area but the sea is now polluted. On Sun evenings the beach takes on a fairground atmosphere. Most airport hotels offer free transfer. Tourist Information at the airport will help to book.

Airport
LL-L Leela Palace, near International Terminal, T86363636, F86360606, www.theleela.com. 460 modern rooms, excellent restaurants, pricey but excellent, bar (closed to non-residents after 2300).
L-AL Orchid, 70C Nehru Rd, Vile Parle (east), T6100707, F6105974, 5 mins' walk from domestic terminal. Totally refurbished, attractive rooms, 'eco-friendly' (energy saving, recycling etc), *Boulevard* boasts a '15 min lightening menu' and good midnight buffet.
L Renaissance, near Chinmayanand Ashram, Powai, 9 km from International airport, T6928888, F6928899, www.renaissance hotels.com. 286 stylish rooms, excellent restaurants, pleasant green surroundings, large pool, relaxing.
AL Centaur Airport, Santa Cruz. Poor reports.
A-B Airlink, near Domestic Terminal, Vile Parle (E), T6183695, F6105186. Clean, comfortable.
B-C Airport International, 5/6, Nehru Rd, Vile Parle (east), F6141773, near domestic terminal. 27 rooms, modern business hotel, clean, comfortable.
B-C Atithi, 77A Nehru Rd, Vile Parle (east) 7 mins' walk from domestic terminal, T6116124, F6111998. 47 rooms, functional, clean, set meals included, good value, efficient desk, popular.
B-C Host Inn, opposite Marol Fire Brigade, Andheri-Kurla Rd, Andheri (east), near International airport, T8360105, F8391080. Decent, clean rooms, friendly.
B-C Kumaria Presidency, Andheri-Kurla Rd, facing Leela Palace, Andheri (east), T8352601, F8373850. 32 a/c rooms, 24-hr exchange and room-service, friendly.

B-C Residency, Suren Rd, Andheri (E), T6923000, F6925557, residency@hotmail.com. New hotel 3 km from the airport (request free pick). 72 smallish a/c rooms, good restaurant, on quiet back street, friendly staff. Recommended (often full).
B-C Transit, off Nehru Rd, Vile Parle (east), T6105812, F6105785. 54 rooms, modern, reasonable overnight halt for airport, excellent restaurant (good food and service, draught beer), airport transfer.
D Airport Rest Rooms, old Domestic Terminal, Santa Cruz. For passengers with connecting flights within 24 hrs of arrival, comfortable, clean, but often full.

Bandra

LL Regent, Land's End, Bandra Bandstand, T6551234, F6512471, buscent.regent@lokhandwalahotels.com. Bandra's luxury hotel, very spacious and chic, top facilities.
B Metro Palace, Hill Rd, near Bandra station (W), T6427311, F6431932. Convenient, close to domestic airport and shops, good restaurant.

B Pali Hills, 14 Union Park, Pali Hill, Bandra, T6492995. Quiet location, near market, continental restaurant (see below).

Juhu Beach

Most hotels are under 10 km from the airport.
L-AL Holiday Inn, Balraj Sahani Marg, T6204444, F6204452. 190 rooms, 2 pools, courtesy coach to town, reliable.
AL Sun-n-Sand, 39 Juhu Beach, T6201811, F6202170. 118 rooms, best refurbished, comfortable, though cramped poolside, good restaurant.
A Citizen, 960 Juhu Tara Rd, T6117273, F6227270, citizen@bom2.vsnl.net.in. Despite unexciting appearance, 45 smallish but very well appointed rooms, suites, efficient airport transfer. Recommended.
B Juhu Hotel, Juhu Tara Rd, T6184014. Spacious comfortable cottage-style rooms, sea-facing lawns, good restaurant (try seafood and Mughlai), soundproofed disco.
B Sands, 39/2 Juhu Beach, T6204511, F6205268. 40 rooms, excellent restaurant.

🍴 Eating

Gateway of India and Colaba
p1073 and map p1074

🍴🍴🍴 **Copper Chimney**, 18 K Dubash Marg, T2041661. Indian. Subdued lighting and quietly tasteful, excellent North Indian dishes, must reserve.
🍴🍴🍴 **Excellent Sea**, Ballard Estate, T2668195. Excellent crab, prawn and lobster.
🍴🍴🍴 **Indigo**, 4 Mandlik Rd, behind *Taj Hotel*, T2856316. Excellent Mediterranean in smart new restaurant, good atmosphere, additional seating on rooftop.
🍴🍴🍴 **Khyber**, 145 MG Rd, Kala Ghoda, Fort, T2632174. North Indian. For an enjoyable evening in beautiful surroundings (traditional carved furniture, paintings by Hussain, AE Menon), excellent food, especially lobster and *reshmi* chicken kebabs, try *paya* soup (goats' trotters!), outstanding restaurant, reserve.
🍴🍴🍴 **Ling's Pavilion**, 19/21 KC College Hostel Building, off Colaba Causeway (behind *Taj* and Regal Cinema), T2850023. Stylish décor, good atmosphere and delightful service, colourful menu, seafood specials, generous helpings. Recommended.

🍴🍴🍴 **Trishna**, 7 Rope Walk Lane, behind Kala Ghoda, by Old Synagogue, T2672176. Indian. Good coastline cuisine, seafood, excellent crab. "Swinging, crowded and fun". Recommended.
🍴🍴 **Bagdadi**, Tullock Rd (behind *Taj Hotel*), T2028027. Mughlai. One of the cheapest, first class food, fragrant biryani, delicious chicken, crowded but clean. Recommended.
🍴🍴 **Ming Place**, Apsara Building, Colaba Causeway, T2872820. Chinese. Try 'Shanghai potatoes'.
🍴 **Bade Miyan**, behind Ling's Pavilion. Streetside Kebab corner but very clean. Try *baida roti, shammi* and *boti kebabs*.
🍴 **Kamat Samarambh**, opposite Electric House, SB Singh Marg. Indian vegetarian. Very good *thalis* and snacks, try *chola battura* (*puri* topped with spiced chickpeas).
🍴 **Martin's**, near Strand Cinema. Goan. Simple, authentic Goan food, excellent seafood and pork *sorpotel*.
🍴 **Paradise**, Sindh Chambers, Colaba Causeway. Parsi and others. Spotless, excellent *dhansak*; try *Sali boti* (mutton and 'chips'), closed Mon (not a/c).

Cafés and fast food

Many serve chilled beer; prices have gone up and waiters care too much for large tips from tourist groups.

Churchill, opposite Cusrow Baug, Colaba Causeway, T2844689. Good late breakfasts, continental and steaks served in small a/c café, choice of desserts, ices, shakes, good value.

Food-Inn, 50 m from *Leopold's*. Mainly Indian (some western) snacks. Pleasant (a/c upstairs), reasonably priced, friendly service.

Kailash Parbat, 1st Pasta Lane, Colaba. Excellent snacks and *chaats*.

Leopold's, Colaba, T2830585. Popular and still full of young backpackers for good western food and drink (limited Indian veg), friendly but getting expensive. Similar cafés nearby are far better value.

Mondegar, near Regal Cinema, T2812549. Similar, but a little cheaper.

Wayside Inn, 38 K Dubash Marg, T2844324. Quaint country inn-style good breakfast menu, average continental but perfect for an afternoon beer in heart of the city, breezy, laid back and leisurely, moderately priced.

Churchgate, Nariman Point and Marine Drive *p1076, map p1072*

🍴🍴🍴 **Gaylord**, Vir Nariman Rd,T2821231. Indian. Good food (huge portions) and service, tables inside and out, barbecue, pleasant, good bar, tempting pastry counter.

🍴🍴🍴 **Indian Summer**, 80 Vir Nariman Rd, T2835445. Indian. Excellent food, tasty *kebabs*, interesting modern glass décor, smart dress, reserve.

🍴🍴🍴 **Pearl of the Orient**, *Ambassador Hotel*, T2041131. Excellent Chinese, Japanese and Thai. The *Revolving Restaurant* offers stunning views especially at night (for a less expensive stationary view try the bar on the floor above which does simple meals!).

🍴🍴🍴 **Santoor**, Maker Arcade, Cuffe Parade, near *President Hotel*, T2182262. North Indian. Small place, Mughlai and Kashmiri specialities: creamy chicken *malai* chop, *chana* Peshawari (*puri* with chickpeas), *Kashmiri soda* made with salt and pepper.

🍴🍴🍴 **Sidewok**, next to NCPA theatre, T2818132. Interesting southeast Asian/fusion cuisine. Innovative menu, imaginative cocktails (try non-alcoholic too), surprise entertainment by staff, "longest mosaic mural in Asia", a special, fun dining experience. Reserve.

🍴 **Berry's**, Vir Nariman Rd, near Churchgate Station, T2875691. North Indian. Tandoori specialities, good *kulfi*.

🍴 **Chopsticks**, 90A Vir Nariman Rd, Churchgate, T2832308. Chinese, good, hot and spicy. Offering unusual dishes (taro nest, date pancakes, toffee bananas).

🍴 **Kamling**, 82 Vir Nariman Rd, T2042618. Genuine Cantonese. Simple surroundings, but excellent preparations, try seafood, often busy.

🍴 **May Rose**, Cinema Rd (next to 'Metro'), T2081104. Chinese. Clean a/c, very good food.

🍴 **Sapna**, Vir Nariman Rd. Indian, very traditional Mughlai delicacies, bar, some tables outside, attentive service, good value.

🍴 **Satkar**, Indian Express Building, opposite Churchgate station, T2043259. Indian. Delicious vegetarian, fruit juices and shakes; a/c section more expensive.

🍴 **Balwas**, Maker Bhavan, 3 Sir V Thackersey Marg. Inexpensive, well-prepared food.

🍴 **Piccolo Café**, 11A Sir Homi Mody St. Parsi. 0900-1800, closed Sat afternoon and Sun, profits to charity, homely, clean, good *dhansak*.

🍴 **Purohit's**, Vir Nariman Rd. Indian. Excellent veg *thalis*, also Parsi.

🍴 **Thacker's**, corner Maharshi Karve Rd and 1st Marine St. Indian. Good *thalis*.

🍴 **Woodlands**, Mittal Chambers, Nariman Pt. South Indian. Excellent *idli* and *dosai* and good *thalis*, busy at lunchtime, closed Sun.

Cafés and fast food

Croissants, Vir Nariman Rd, opposite Eros Cinema. Burgers, sandwiches, hot croissants with fillings, ice cream, lively atmosphere.

Fountain, MG Rd. For sizzlers and apple pie in a café atmosphere.

CST (VT) and Fort *p1075, map p1072*

🍴🍴 **Apoorva**, near Horniman Circle, Fort, T2881457. Very good seafood, especially crabs and prawns (more economical downstairs).

🍴🍴 **Bharat**, 317 SB Singh Marg, opposite Fort Market, T2618991. Excellent seafood and crab as well as *naans* and *rotis*: or try fried, stuffed Bombay Duck!

🍴🍴 **George**, 20 Apollo St (near Horniman Circle). Pleasant quiet atmosphere, colonial feel, good service, lunchtime *biriyanis* and *thalis*.

Sadanand, opposite Crawford Market. Excellent *thalis* and veg food, popular with Indian families.

Wall Street, 68 Hamam St, behind Stock Exchange. Coastal cuisine, excellent seafood, try spicy Malabari prawns, squid green garlic, fish patta.

Icy Spicy, off PM Rd, next to *Fort Central Restaurant*. Veg snack bar. Great light meals (from Rs 25).

Ideal Corner, Hornby View, Gunbow St, Fort, CST. Lunchtime Parsi food and snacks in clean café.

Mahesh Lunch Home, Sir PM Rd, Fort. Excellent for Mangalorean, Goan and *tandoori* seafood, a/c, bar, very popular.

West Coast, Rustom Sidhwa Rd, off Sir Perin Nariman Rd. Very good meals. On MG Rd (north end), you can have a good traditional breakfast, often as early as 0600.

Dadar, Mumbai Central Station and Grant Road area
map p1070

Biscotti, Crossroads, Haji Ali, T4955055. Excellent Italian. Wholesome, leisurely dining, try batter-fried calamari, giant prawns in liqueur, flavoured sugar-free soda, zabaglioni, bistro-style complete with fiddler.

Goa Portuguesa, THK Rd, Mahim. Goan. Authentic dishes, taverna-style with guitarist, try *sungto* (prawn) served between *papads*, *kalwa* (oyster), *teesryo* (shell) and clams, lobsters cooked with tomatoes, onions and spices and *bebinca* to end the meal.

Only Fish, *Hotel Rosewood*, J Dadaji Rd, Tulsiwadi, Tardeo, T4940320. Indian regional recipes (including Bengali). Seafood too, small but stylish.

Revival, Chowpatty Sea Face (near footbridge). Classy, good Indian/Continental buffets and desserts.

Bombay A1, 7 Vadilal A Patel Marg (Grant Rd Junc). Parsi. Cheerful, varied menu, try *Patrani machli*.

Chinatown, 99 August Kranti Marg. Szechwan, Cantonese, Mandarin. Varied menu (27 soups), upstairs more comfortable.

Copper Chimney, Dr AB Rd, Worli, T4924488. Indian. Window into kitchen, excellent food from extensive menu, reasonable prices, undiscovered by tourists.

Rajdhani, Mangaldas Rd, opposite Crawford Market. Indian. An a/c oasis, excellent lunch *thali*, very friendly welcome.

Rashtriya, Rd leading to Dadar (East) stairway. South Indian vegetarian. Good food and excellent coffee.

Sindhudurg, RK Vaidya Rd, Dadar. Indian. Try seafood *thali* and fish fry.

Under the Over, 36 Altamount Rd (by flyover). Bistro like, for Mexican, Creole dishes, sizzlers and rich desserts, reasonably priced, no alcohol.

The Village, *Poonam Intercontinental*, near Mahalaxmi racecourse. Gujarati. 'Village' setting, sea views, good authentic food.

Viva Paschim, City View, Dr AB Rd, Worli, T4983636. Quality coastal Maharashtrian. Sunday lunch buffet great value (Rs 225), folk dances at dinner often.

Heaven, corner of Grant Rd/P Bapurao Marg. Very cheap, friendly (eg *aloo matar* Rs 10).

Kamat, Navrose Mansion, Tardeo Rd. Indian. Very inexpensive *thalis* and veg snacks.

Airport, Juhu Beach and Bandra

Bandra, the upcoming area of the moment, has some exciting options.

Gazalee, Kadambari Complex, Hanuman Rd, Vile Parle (E), T8388093. Finest coastal cuisine, try stuffed Bombay Duck, and shellfish.

Independence, at *Metro Palace Hotel*, Bandra, T6427311. Pleasant ambience, wide choice, excellent value buffet lunches (Rs 150).

Just around the Corner, 24th-30th road junction, TPS III, Bandra (W). Bright casual American style diner. Extensive breakfast menu (0800-1100). Pay by the plateful, lots of combination options, excellent salads.

Out of the Blue, at *Pali Hills*. Steak and fondue, great sizzlers, unusual combinations, flavoured ice teas, flambéed desserts, UV lit inside or outside smoke-free.

Trim with Taste, 500 Sant Kutir, Linking Rd, Bandra (lane behind KBN store). Small, spotless, serving unusual health food. Try stuffed idlis, peach and yoghurt smoothies.

China Town, Marol-Maroshi Rd, Andheri (E). Excellent Indian, Chinese, wide choice.

Crunchy Munchy, Agarwal Market, next to Vile Parle (E) station. Open-air café serving veg Indian and Mexican mini-meals. Very clean, good service and portions.

🍴 **Kanchi**, Mittal Industrial Estate, Andheri-Kurla Rd, Marol, Andheri (E). Excellent South Indian vegetarian, unusual daily specials.
🍴 **Lucky**, 9 SV Rd (Hill Rd junction), Bandra (W). Good mughlai especially chicken biriyani and tandooris.
🍴 **Potpourri**, Carlton Court, Turner/Pali Rd junction. Streetside café, great Italian food.

🍸 Bars and clubs

All major hotels and restaurants have bars, others may only serve beer. Many pubs expect couples Fri-Sun. Most pubs charge Rs 175-250 for a 'pitcher' (bottle); cocktails Rs 75-150.

Expensive

Gateway area
Taj Mahal, on top floor of the newer building, has excellent all-round views.
Beyond 1900s, Taj's. Exclusive disco, expensive drinks (Rs 330 entry).

Central Mumbai
Flavors, Ambassador's (Churchgate). Bright 24-hr coffee shop-resto-bar. Chic, interesting cocktails and starters (PSP prawns, Corn and spinach toast), barbecue buffet lunch (Rs 300-800), happy hour (1800-2000), try Graveyard (huge) or Flavothon (a shooter race), big screen, DJ (weekends). Fun at a price.
Not Just Jazz by the Bay, 143 Marine Drive, T2851876. Modern chrome and glass, live music (varied), karaoke, good food menu (grill starters, desserts), generous portions, wide selection of drinks, very lively, a fun place.

Mid-range

Central Mumbai
Café Olé, Ground Floor, Cross Roads, Haji Ali, T4955123. Classic sports bar, chrome and glass, interesting menu (some Indianized), try *Cactus Passion* or *Red Ginger* (non-alcoholic), mini dance floor, DJ at weekends, fun place, affordable drinks.
Copa Cabana, Dariya Vihar, 39/D Girgaum, Chowpatty, T3680274. Small, playing 70s hits and Latino music, packed at weekends so little space for dancing.
Geoffreys, *Hotel Marine Plaza*, Marine Drive, T2851212. Soft music, relaxing for a drink and a bite, no dancing.
Ghetto, B Desai Rd (100 m from Mahalakshmi Temple). Western pop from 60s, 70s, 80s, free entry (couples only), neon graffiti.

Juhu
Paparazzi, opposite Juhu Bus Depot, Juhu Beach Rd, T6602199. Small, cosy disco bar, packed after 2300, drinks and snacks. Closed Mon. **Razzberry Rhinocerus**, *Juhu Hotel*, Juhu Tara Rd, T6184012. Disco, night club. Lots of space for dancing, pool tables, check for live acts.

🎭 Entertainment

Pick up Mumbai This Fortnight, an informative free booklet on everything that is hot in the city. Free from larger bookshops and stores

Art galleries

Usually open 1000-1900: Galleries in *Taj Mahal* and *Centaur* hotels.
Aakar, B Desai Rd, T3671983.
Cymroza, B Desai Rd, T3671983.
JJ School of Art Dr DN Rd.

Piramal, NCPA, Nariman Pt.
Pundole, Hutatma Chowk, T2841837.
    Several near Kemp's Corner including:
Sakshi, 33 Altmount Rd, run by Synergy Art Foundation.

Cinema

Bollywood films are screened in dozens of cinemas.
Eros, opposite Churchgate station. Bollywood films.

☎ *Phone code Mumbai: 022*

Metro, MG Rd, northwest corner of Azad Maidan. Bollywood films.

New Empire, Marzaban Rd, southwest of CST station. English language films.

Regal, Colaba Causeway. English language.

Sterling, Marzaban Rd, southwest of CST station. English language films.

It is best for women to get seats in the Circle.

Theatres

Plays are performed in English, Hindi, Marathi and Gujarati, usually beginning at 1815-1900. Check *Mumbai* or *This Fortnight* for details. See a modern Hindi play at **Privthi Theatre**, T6174118, to sample local culture.

Festivals and events

In addition to the national Hindu and Muslim festivals there are the following:

January

1st weekend. **Banganga Classical Music Festival** at Walkeshwar Temple. Magical atmosphere around temple tank with fine musicians taking part; tickets Rs 50-150 (much in demand).

February

Elephanta Cultural Festival at the caves. Great ambience. Contact MTDC, T2026713, for tickets Rs 150-200 including launch at 1800. **Kala Ghoda Arts Festival** New annual showcase of all forms of fine arts. T2842520; also weekend festival, mid-Dec to mid-Jan includes food and handicrafts at Rampart Row, Fort.

March

Jamshed Navroz, this is New Year's Day for the Parsi followers of the Fasli calendar. The celebrations which include offering prayers at temples, exchanging greetings, alms-giving and feasting at home, date back to Jamshed, the legendary King of Persia.

July-October

Janmashtami, celebrates the birth of Lord Krishna. Boys and young men form human pyramids and break pots of curd hung up high between buildings.

Coconut Day, the angry monsoon seas are propitiated by devotees throwing coconuts into the ocean.

Ganesh Chaturthi Massive figures of Ganesh are worshipped and immersed in the sea on several days following the festival.

Mount Mary's Feast, celebrated at St Mary's Church, Bandra. A fair is also held.

Dasara, during this nationwide festival, in Mumbai there are group dances by Gujarati women in all the auditoria. There are also Ramlila celebrations at Chowpatty Beach.

Diwali (The Festival of Lights) is particularly popular in mercantile Mumbai when the business community celebrate their New Year and open new account books.

December

25 Dec: **Christmas**, Christians across Mumbai celebrate the birth of Christ. A pontifical High Mass is held at midnight in the open air at the Cooperage Grounds.

Shopping

Most shops are open 1000-1900 (closed Sun), the bazars sometimes staying open as late as 2100. Mumbai prices are often higher than in other Indian cities and hotel arcades tend to be very pricey but carry good quality select items. Best buys are textiles, particularly tie-and-dye from Gujarat,

hand-block printed cottons, Aurangabad and 'Patola' silks, gold bordered saris from Surat and Khambat, handicrafts, jewellery and leather goods.

Crossroads & Pyramid, Haji Ali, are modern shopping centres.

'Antiques'

(it is illegal to take anything over 100 years old out of the country).

Natesan in Jehangir Gallery basement and in *Taj Hotel* for fine antiques and copies.

Phillips, Madame Cama Rd opposite Regal Cinema is an Aladdin's cave of bric-a-brac and curios.

Bazars

Chor (Thieves') Bazar, on Maulana Shaukat Ali Rd in central Mumbai. For a different experience, full of finds – from Raj left-overs to precious jewellery. Some claim that the infamous name is unjustified since the original was 'Shor' (noisy) bazaar! On Fri, 'junk' carts sell less expensive 'antiques' and fakes.

Crawford Market, MR Ambedkar Rd (fun for bargain hunting).

Mangaldas Market, MR Ambedkar Rd.

Other shopping streets are South Bhagat Singh Marg, M Karve Rd and Linking Rd, Bandra.

Books

An annual **book fair** takes place at the Cross Maidan near Churchgate each **December**.

Crossword, 22 B Desai Rd (near Mahalakshmi Temple), smart, spacious, good selection.

Danai, 14th Khar Danda Rd is good for books and music.

Dial-a-book, T6495618, for quick delivery.

Nalanda, *Taj Mahal Hotel*, excellent art books, western newspapers/magazines.

Strand Books, off Sir PM Rd near HMV, T2061994, excellent selection, best deals, shipping (reliable), 20% discount on air freight. **Second-hand**: lines of stalls along Churchgate St and near the University.

Carpets

Sadak Ali, behind *Taj* hotel. Good range but bargain.

Clothes

B Desai Rd, Dr DN Rd, Colaba Causeway shops starting near the *Taj Mahal Hotel*. Cheapest at *Fashion St* opposite Mumbai Gymkhana, South Bhagat Singh Marg, but check quality (often export surplus) and bargain vigorously.

For good value and looks:

Benzer, B Desai Rd, Breach Candy (open Sun), good saris and Indian garments.

Cotton World, Mandlik Rd, Colaba.

Fabindia, Navroze Bldg, 66 Pali Hill, nr HDFC Bank, Bandra (W), handloom kurtas etc.

Neeta, 55 Colaba Causeway, opposite Police Station.

Men's

Raymonds, B Desai Rd (also tailoring).

Crafts and textiles

Govt emporia from many states sell good handicrafts and textiles; several at *World Trade Centre,* Cuffe Parade.

Anokhi, 4B August Kranti Marg, opposite Kumbala Hill Hospital. Good gifts.

Bombay Store, Western India House, 1st floor, PM Rd, Fort. Spacious, ethnic lifestyle, gifts (open Sun), value for money.

Contemporary Arts & Crafts, 19 Napeansea Rd. Classy collection (moderate prices).

Cottage Industries Emporium, Apollo Bunder. Represents a nationwide selection, especially Kashmiri embroidery, South Indian handicrafts and Rajasthani textiles. Shop at Colaba Causeway, next to BEST, with additional fabrics, ethnic ware, handicrafts.

Craft Market, K Dubash Marg, Colaba. Street market held on Sun (Nov-Jan).

Good Earth, 104 Kemp's Corner. Smart, trendy, pottery, glass, handmade paper stationery.

Khadi and Village Industries, 286 Dr DN Rd.

Yamini, President House, Wodehouse Rd, Colaba, especially for vibrant textiles.

Leather

Dharavi Market, a kilometre long stretch fronting slum. Export quality but bargain hard.

Music

Groove, West Wing, 1st floor, Eros Cinema, Churchgate. Has café.

Hiro, SP Mehta St. Good Indian classical Cds.

Planet M, opposite CST station. Also has book/poetry readings, gigs.

Rhythm House, north of Jehangir Gallery. Excellent selection of jazz and classical CDs.

Musical instruments

On VB Patel Rd:
RS Mayeka at No 386.
Haribhai Vishwanath at No 419.
Ram Singh at Bharati Sadan.

Photography

Kodak Express,1B East and West Court,
Colaba Causeway (near Churchill café).
Mazda at 231 (Hasselblad, Metz, Nikon)
offers free pick up/delivery, T3004001.
Remedios, opposite Khadi Bhandar,
between CST and Flora Fountain, reliable
repairs. Best buy cameras from DN Rd.

Silks and saris

Many including:
Kala Niketan, MG Rd and Juhu Reclamation.
Sheetal, Tirupati Apartments, B Desai Rd,
saris from all over India; fair prices.
Vama, in Kanchenjunga (next to Kemp's
Corner), tailoring possible.

Tailors

Ensemble, Great Western Bldg, 130-132
South Bhagat Singh Marg, T2872882. Superb
craftsmanship and service for women's
clothes – Indian and 'East meets West'.

▲ Activities and tours

Adventure tourism

Maharashtra Tourism has been active in
encouraging adventure tourism (including
Jungle Safaris and Watersports) by
introducing 'Rent-a-Tent' and hiring out
trekking gear. Prices range from US$35-150
per day/weekend depending upon season
and activity. Some sites provide electricity,
linen, bathrooms and authentic cuisine in
rustic restaurants. It has also set up 27
Holiday Resorts providing cheap
accommodation at hill stations, beaches,
archaeological sites and scenic spots. Details
of packages from tourist offices.

City sightseeing

Approved guides from the India tourist
office, T2036854.
City tour Usually includes visits to The
Gateway of India, the Chhatrapati Sivaji
(Prince of Wales) Museum (closed Monday),
Jain temple, Hanging Gardens, Kamla Nehru
Park and Mani Bhavan (Gandhi Museum).
Suburban tour Includes Juhu Beach,
Kanheri Caves and Lion Safari Park (some
visitors found this 'awful'; closed Mon).
MTDC, Madam Cama Rd, opposite LIC
Building, T2026713.
City tour Daily except Mon, 0900-1300
and 1400-1800, Rs 100.
Suburban tour 0915 (from Dadar
1015)-1815.

Fort walk A heritage walk around CST
and Fort area with the Kala Ghoda
Association, Army & Navy Building,
T2852520; www.artindia.co.in.
Elephanta tours From Gateway of India.
Boat, 0900-1415, Rs 70 return; reserve at
Apollo Bunder, T2026364. If you wish to
sightsee independently with a guide, ask at
the Tourist Office. See page 1093.
Ajanta and Ellora MTDC 4-day tour to
the famous caves at Ajanta and Ellora.

Clubs

Bombay Gymkhana, MG Rd, T2070311. Very
pleasant; reciprocal rights with English clubs
(including Royal Overseas League).
Cricket Club of India, Brabourne Stadium,
Dinshaw Wacha Rd, T2848330, temp
membership (15 days), contact Secretary,
tennis, pool, squash; central with large and
pleasant grounds.
Royal Bombay Yacht Club, Apollo Bunder,
T3094492, temp membership (10 days),
contact Secretary, pleasant garden, rooms
for rent (**B**), "heaven".
Velocity, Film Center Bldg, Tardeo Rd, Haji
Ali, T4912313/022. Spacious, plush interiors
and decor and state-of-the-art sound and
light. Lounge room, Retro Lounge and Main
club. Rs 600 (Rs 400 cover charge and Rs 200
entry) on weekdays and Rs 800 (Rs 600 cover
charge and Rs 200 entry) on weekends.
Closed Mon. Well worth a visit.

Willingdon Club, Haji Ali Rd, T4925802. Very pleasant; reciprocal rights with English clubs (including Royal Overseas League).

Horse racing

Mahalaxmi Race Course, opposite Haji Ali. Season Nov-Mar, Sun and holidays, 1400-1700. Many of India's top races are held at the delightful course (1878), including 'The Derby' in Feb/Mar.

Swimming

Breech Candy Club B Desai Rd, T3612543. For the select set, 2 clean pools including a large one; non-members Rs 250.

Tennis

Maharashtra State Lawn Tennis Association, Cooper, Colaba, T2848102.

Tour companies

Some well established agents:

Cox and Kings, 270-271 Dr DN Rd, T2073066.
Everett, 1 Regent Chambers, Nariman Pt, T2845339.
Mercury, 70VB Gandhi Rd, T2024785.
Sita, 18 Atlanta, Nariman Pt, T2840666, F2044927.
Space Travels, 4th Flr, Sir PM Rd, T2864773, for discounted flights and special student offers, Mon-Fri, 1000-1700, Sat 1030-1500.
TCI, Chandermukhi, Nariman Pt, T2021881.
Thomas Cook, Cooks Building, Dr DN Rd, T2813454.
Venture, Ground Floor, Abubakar Mansion, South Bhagat Singh Marg, T2021304, F2822803, efficient, helpful and friendly.

Yoga

Kaivalyadahama, next to Taraporewala Aquarium, Marine Dr.
The Yoga Institute, Praghat Colony, Santa Cruz (E).
Yoga Training Centre, 51 Jai Hind Club, Juhu Scheme.
Yoga Vidhya Niketan, Sane Guruji Marg, Dadar, T4306258.

⊜ Transport

Air

International Departure Tax, Rs 500 (Rs 250 within South Asia) is often included in the price of your ticket. Look for 'FT' in the tax column.
Chhatrapati Sivaji International airport, T6329090, 8366700. Left Luggage, across the drive from end of Departure terminal, Rs 35-45 per item per day. The Tourist Office counter helps to book rooms in upmarket hotels. There is an Indian Railways reservations and car hire counters inside, and domestic airlines' counters just outside the exit. The **new** domestic terminal (1A), exclusively for *Indian Airlines*, is about 400 m from the **old** terminal (1B), used by others. Enquiries: T140, 143.
Indian Airlines, T6156633, recorded T6114433. A shuttle bus runs between the International and Domestic terminals. ATMs outside terminals. Rupees against cash or TCs can be acquired only inside international terminals.
Transport to and from the airport: Dispatchers at the airport claim that each taxi can take only three passengers. Stand firm as

this law is totally disregarded elsewhere.
Pre-paid taxis into town, from a counter at the exit at the **Chhatrapati Sivaji** International terminal (ignore taxi touts near the baggage hall). Give the exact area or hotel, and the number of pieces of luggage. Hand the receipt to the driver at the end of the journey. There is no need to tip. To Nariman Point or Gateway of India, about Rs 260, 1 hr. During 'rush hour' it can take 2 hrs. Late at night, taxis take about ½ hr - hair-raising! To Juhu Beach Rs 150. From Santa Cruz: metered taxis should charge around the same.
Bus: The red BEST buses connect both terminals with the city.
Touts are very pushy at both terminals but the **hotels** they recommend are often appalling. It is worth making your own telephone call to hotels of your choice from the airport. The rest rooms in the old domestic terminal are clean, comfortable (rooms Rs 500, dorm Rs 200); available for those flying within 24 hrs, but are often full; apply to the Airport Manager.

Domestic Indian Airlines: Nariman Pt, T2023031, flies to all major cities. **Air India:** flies to **Chennai; Delhi; Hyderabad; Kolkata; Thiruvananthapuram.. Jet Airways:** B1 Amarchand Mansions, Madam Cama Rd, T2855788, airport, T6156666, www.jetairways.com, to 23 destinations. **Sahara**, Tulsani Chambers, Nariman Point, T2882718, airport T6134159: **Bangalore, Bhopal, Delhi, Goa, Indore, Jaipur, Kolkata, Lucknow, Patna, Varanasi.**

Bus

Local
Red BEST (Bombay Electrical Supply Co) buses are available in most parts of Greater Mumbai, T4128725. Within the Central Business Dist, buses are marked 'CBD'.

Long distance
Maharashtra RTC operates bus services to all the major centres and Dist HQs in the state as well as to **Ahmadabad, Bangalore, Goa, Mangalore, Indore, Vadodara** and **Hyderabad** in other states. Information on services from MSRTC, Central Bus Stand, Mumbai Central, T3076622. Private buses also travel long distance routes. Some long distance buses also leave from Dadar where there are many travel agents. Information and tickets from Dadar Tourist Centre, just outside Dadar station, T4113398.

Car

Car hire
For 8 hrs or 80 km: Luxury cars, a/c Rs 1,500; Maruti/Ambassador: a/c Rs 1,000, non a/c Rs 800. **Auto Hirers**, 7 Commerce Centre, Tardeo, T4942006; **Blaze**, Colaba, T2020073; **Budget**, T4942644, and **Sai**, Phoenix Mill Compound, Senapati Bapat Marg, Lower Parel, T4942644, F4937524, recommended. **Wheels**, T2822874. Holiday **caravans** with driver, T2024627.

Rickshaw

Not available in central Mumbai (south of Mahim). Metered; about Rs 8 per km, revised tariff card held by the driver (x8, in suburbs) 25% extra at night (2400-0500). Some cunning rickshaw drivers show the revised tariff card for taxis! It's worth buying a card

for a couple of rupees from hawkers at traffic junctions. **Victorias** (horse-drawn carriages), available at Mumbai Central, Chowpatty and Gateway of India. Rates negotiable.

Taxi

Local
Metered yellow-top or blue a/c: easily available. Rs 12 for first km and Rs 12 for each Re 1 on metre. Revised tariff card held by drivers. Taxis called by hotel doormen often arrive with meter registering Rs 12. Always get a prepaid taxi at the airport.

Train

Local
Suburban electric trains are economical. They start from Churchgate for the west suburbs and CST (VT) for the east suburbs but are often desperately crowded (stay near the door or you may miss your stop!); there are 'Ladies' cars. Trains leaving Mumbai Central often have seats at the terminus but soon fill up. **Avoid peak hours** (southbound 0700-1100, northbound 1700-2000), and keep a tight hold on valuables. The difference between 1st and 2nd class is not always obvious although 1st class is 10 times as expensive. Inspectors fine people for travelling in the wrong class or without a ticket.

Long distance
Times for trains are published each Sat in the Indian Express newspaper. To book trains foreign tourists must have either foreign currency or an encashment certificate and passport. Mumbai is the HQ of the Central and Western Railways. **Central Rly**, enquiries, T134/135. Reservations, T2659512, 0800-1230, 1300-1630 (Foreigners' Counter opens 0900; best time to go); **Western Railway**, Churchgate, and Mumbai Central, 0800-1345, 1445-2000. All for 1st Class bookings and Indrail Passes. **Foreign tourists**: Tourist Quota counter on mezzanine floor above tourist office opposite Churchgate Station for Northern Railways. Otherwise, queue downstairs at Reservations. For Southern Railways, at CST, the tourist counter is on the ground floor (towards the left), credit cards upstairs. Railway Tourist Guides at CST and Churchgate (Bus 138 goes between the 2).

The following depart from CST unless specified by these abbreviations: Bandra (B), Central (C), Dadar (D), Lokmanya Tilak (LT): **Ahmadabad** (all from Mumbai Central): *Shatabdi Exp, 2009,* 0625, except Fri, 7 hrs; *Karnavati Exp, 2933,* 1340, except Wed, 7¾ hrs; *Saurashtra Mail, 9005,* 2025, 9 hrs; *Gujarat Mail, 2901,* 2150, 9 hrs. **Allahabad**: *Howrah Mail, 3004,* 2110, 23½ hrs; *Mahanagari Exp, 1093,* 2355, 24¼ hrs. **Agra Cantonment**: *Punjab Mail, 2137,* 1910, 21½ hrs. **Aurangabad** (for Ajanta and Ellora): *Tapovan Exp, 7617,* 0610, 7½ hrs; *Devgiri Exp, 1003,* 2120, 7½ hrs. **Bangalore**: *Udyan Exp, 6529,* 0755, 24¾ hrs; *Coimbatore Exp, 1013,* 2220 (LT), 23¾ hrs. **Bhopal**: *Pushpak Exp, 2133,* 0810, 14 hrs; *Punjab Mail, 2137,* 1910, 14 hrs. **Chennai**: *Dadar Chennai Exp, 1063,* 2020 (D), 23¾ hrs; *Chennai Exp, 6011,* 1400, 26¾ hrs. **Ernakulam** (for Kochi): *Netravati Exp, 6345,* 2300 (LT), 29½ hrs. **Guntakal** (for Hospet/Hampi): *Dadar Chennai Exp, 1063,* 2020 (D), 15 hrs; *Udyan Exp, 6529,* 0755, 16¾ hrs; *Coimbatore Exp, 1013,* 2220 (LT), 16¼ hrs; *Kanniyakumari Exp, 1081,* 1535,

17¾ hrs. **Gwalior**: *Punjab Mail, 2137,* 1910, 19¾ hrs. **Hyderabad**: *Hussainsagar Exp, 7001,* 2155, 15¼ hrs; *Hyderabad Exp, 7031,* 1235, 17½ hrs. **Kolkata** (Howrah): *Gitanjali Exp, 2859,* 0600, 33 hrs; *Howrah Mail, 8001,* 2015, 35½ hrs. **Lucknow**: *Pushpak Exp, 2133,* 0810, 25½ hrs. **Madgaon** (for Goa): The day train is a good option, the night service is heavily booked. Special trains during the winter. *Mandavi Exp, 0103,* 0515, 11 hrs; *Konkan Kanya Exp, 0111,* 2240, 12 hrs. From LT: *Netravati Exp, 6635,* 1640, 13½ hrs. **New Delhi**: *Rajdhani Exp, 2951,* 1655 (C), 17 hrs; *Golden Temple Mail, 2903,* 2130 (C), 21½ hrs; *August Kranti Rajdhani Exp, 2953,* 1740 (C), 17¼ hrs (to Hazrat Nizamuddin). **Pune**: deluxe trains *Shatabdi Exp, 2027,* 0640, 3½ hrs; *Deccan Queen Exp, 2123,* 1710, 3½ hrs, among many. **Thiruvananthapuram**: *Netravati Exp, 6345,* 2300 (LT), 35 hrs. **Ujjain**: *Avantika Exp, 2961,* 1925 (C), 12½ hrs. **Varanasi** *Lokmanya Tilak Varanasi Exp, 2165,* 0520 (LT), Mon, Thu, Sat, 26 hrs; *Muzaffarpur/Darbanga Exp, 5217/5219,* 1125 (LT), 27¼ hrs.

❶ Directory

Airline offices

International

Air India, 1st flr, Nariman Pt (Counters also at *Taj Mahal Hotel (Intercontinental Hotel* and *Santa Cruz*), T2024142, Airport T8366767. **Aeroflot**, Tulsani Chambers, Nariman Pt, T2871942. **Alitalia**, Industrial Assur Bldg, Vir Nariman Rd, Churchgate, T2045023, airport T8379657. **Air Canada**, Amarchand Mansions, Madam Cama Rd, T2027632, Airport T6045653. **Air France**, Maker Chamber VI, Nariman Pt, T2025021, Airport T8328070. **Biman**, 199 J Tata Rd, Churchgate, T2824659. **British Airways**, 202 B Vulcan Ins Bldg, Vir Nariman Rd, T2820888, weekdays, 0800-1300, 1345-1800. Sat, 0900-1300, airport T8329061. **Canadian**, *Taj Intercontinental*, T2029112, Airport T8366205. **Japan**, Raheja Centre, Nariman Pt, T2874940. **Delta**, *Taj Mahal Hotel*, T2885660, Airport T8349890. **Emirates**, Mittal Chamber, Nariman Pt, T2871649. **Gulf Air**, Maker Chambers, 5 Nariman Pt, T2021626. **KLM**, 198 J Tata Rd, T2886973. **Kuwait**, 2A Stadium House, 86 Veer Nariman Rd, Churchgate, T2045351.

Lufthansa, Express Towers, Nariman Pt, T2023430. **PIA**, Mittal Towers, Nariman Pt, T2021455. **Qantas**, 42 Sakhar Bhavan, Nariman Pt, T2020343. **Royal Jordanian**, 199 J Tata Rd, T2823065. **Saudia**, Express Tower, Nariman Pt, T2020199. **Singapore Airlines**, Taj Intercontinental, T2022747. **Sri Lanka**, Raheja Centre, Nariman Pt, T2844148, Airport T8327050. **Thai Airways**, 15 World Trade Centre, Cuffe Parade, T2186502.

Banks

Most are open 1000-1400, Mon-Fri, 1000-1200, Sat. Closed on Sun, holidays, 30 Jun, 31 Dec. Best to change money at the airport, or at Bureau de Change (upstairs) in Air India Building, Nariman Pt or at **Thomas Cook**, 324 Dr DN Rd, T2048556; also at 102B Maker Tower, 10th flr, F Block, Cuffe Parade; TCI, Chander Mukhi, Nariman Pt; A/2 Silver Arch, JB Nagar, Andheri; and at International Airport. **American Express**, Regal Cinema Building, Colaba. ATMs for Visa card holders using their usual PIN at British Bank of the

Middle East, 16 Vir Nariman Rd; **Citibank**, Air India Building, Nariman Pt, 293 Dr DN Rd; **Hongkong Bank**, 52/60 MG Rd, Fort; **Standard Chartered**, 81 Ismaili Building, Dr DN Rd, 264 Annie Besant Rd and elsewhere.

Credit cards

American Express, Lawrence and Mayo Bldg, Dr DN Rd; **Diners Club**, Raheja Chambers, 213 Nariman Pt; **Mastercard**, C Wing, Mittal Tower, Nariman Pt; **Visa**, Standard Chartered Grindlays Bank, 90 MG Rd.

Embassies and consulates

Australia, Maker Tower East, 16th flr, Cuffe Parade, T2181071. **Austria**, Maker Chambers VI, Nariman Pt, T2851066. **France**, Datta Prasad, NG Cross Rd, T4950918. **Germany**, 10th Flr, Hoechst House, Nariman Pt, T2832422. **Indonesia**, 19 Altamount Rd, T3868678. **Israel**, 50 Deshmukh Marg, Kailas, T3862794. **Italy**, Kanchenjunga, 72G Deshmukh Marg, T3804071. **Japan**, 1 ML Dahanukar Marg, T4934310. **Malaysia**, Rahimtoola House, Homji St, T2660056. **Netherlands**, 1 Marine Lines Cross Rd, Churchgate, T2016750. **Philippines**, Sekhar Bhavan, Nariman Pt, T2814103. **Spain**, 6 K Dubash Marg, T2874797. **Sri Lanka**, 34 Homi Modi St, T2045861. **Sweden**, 85 Sayani Rd, Prabhadevi, T4212681. **Thailand**, 43 B Desai Rd, T3631404. **UK**, Maker Chamber IV, Nariman Pt, T2830517. **USA**, Lincoln House, B Desai Rd, T3685483.

Hospitals

The larger hotels usually have a house doctor, the others invariably have a doctor on call. Ask hotel staff for prompt action. The telephone directory lists hospitals and General Practitioners. Admission to private hospitals may not be allowed without a large cash advance (eg Rs 50,000). Guarantees from insurers may not be sufficient. **Prince Aly Khan Hospital**, Nesbit Rd near the harbour, T3754343, has been recommended. **Chemists**: Several open day/night especially opposite Bombay Hospital. **Wordell**, Stadium House, Churchgate; **New Royal Chemist**, New Marine Lines.

Post office

Usually open 1000-1700. Sahar Airport 24 hrs. Post offices all over the city and most 5 star hotels. **GPO**: Nagar Chowk. Mon-Sat, 0900-2000 (**Poste Restante** facilities 0900-1800) and Sun 1000-1730; parcels from 1st flr, rear of building, 1000-1700 (Mon-Sat); cheap 'parcelling' service on pavement outside. **Central telegraph office**: Hutatma Chowk, Churchgate PO, 'A' Rd. Colaba PO, Colaba Bus Station and also at Mandlik Rd, behind *Taj Mahal Hotel*. Foreign PO, Ballard Pier. Counter at Santa Cruz.

Tourist offices

Govt of India, 123 M Karve Rd, opposite Churchgate, T2093229, Mon-Sat 0830-1730 (closed 2nd Sat of month from 1230). Counters open 24 hrs at both airports, and at *Taj Mahal Hotel*, Mon-Sat 0830-1530 (closed 2nd Sat from 1230). Helpful staff who can also issue Liquor Permits (essential for Gujarat); printouts given from computer database of many destinations. **Maharashtra Tourist Development Corporation**, www.mtdcindia.com, ashish37@ indiatimes.com, CDO Hutments, opposite LIC Building, Express Towers, 9th floor, Nariman Pt, T2024482, F2024521; Madam Cama Rd, T2026713; Information and Booking counters at international and domestic terminals. Also at Koh-i-Noor Rd, near *Pritam Hotel*, Dadar T4143200; CST Railway Station, T2622859 and Gateway of India, T2841877. **Goa**, Mumbai Central Station, T3086288; **Gujarat**, Dhanraj Mahal, Apollo Bunder, T2024925; **Madhya Pradesh**, 74 World Centre, Cuffe Parade, Colaba, T2187603, mptourism@bo1.net.in; **Himachal Pradesh**, Himachal Emporium, 36 World Trade Centre, Cuffe Parade, T2181123. **Rajasthan**, 230 Dr DN Rd, T2075603.

Useful addresses

Police Emergency: T100. **Fire**: T101. **Ambulance**: T102. **Foreigners' Regional Registration Office**: Annexe 2, Police Commissioner's Office, Dr DN Rd, near Phule Market. **Passport office**: T4931731.

Excursions from Mumbai

The Hindu caves of Elephanta and the earlier Buddhist caves of Kanheri are within easy reach. You can also cross the bay to Chaul to the south, or head for the clean sandy beaches at Kihim. The old Portuguese fort of Bassein is to the north or go further afield to Mumbai's hill station of Matheran. ▶▶ *For Sleeping, Eating and other listings, see pages 1103-1105.*

Chaul, Kihim and Alibag beaches

① *From the New Ferry Wharf, Gateway, it is a 90-min trip to Rewas. Then, a 6-km bus or auto ride to Kihim; or 30-km bus ride to Chaul. MTDC packages to Kihim include transport.*

A group of Moorish and Portuguese forts lie to the south at the mouth of Mumbai harbour. Chaul was taken in 1522 by the Portuguese. Similar to Bassein with a very attractive fort, it never equalled it in importance. The Marathas took it in 1739 and in 1818 it passed into British hands. Little remains of the settlement apart from ruined churches and broken walls. If you look across the creek you will see the hilltop Muslim fort of Korlai. The clean beach, safe waters and very pleasant surroundings make Kihim very attractive but the summer sun can be killingly hot. The beach is muddy at Alibag and it is possible to walk across to the fort at low tide but it is not worth the US$2 entrance. If you decide to stay, there are a few places on Kihim Beach.

Elephanta Caves

The heavily forested Elephanta Island, often barely visible in the mist from Mumbai only 10 km away, rises out of the bay like a giant whale. The setting is symbolically significant; the sea is the ocean of life, a world of change (Samsara) in which is set an island of spiritual and physical refuge. The 'caves' excavated in the volcanic lava high up the slope of the hill saw Hindu craftsmen over 1,000 years ago, express their view of spiritual truths in massive carvings of extraordinary grace. Sadly a large proportion have been severely damaged, but enough remains to illustrate something of their skill.

Ins and outs

Getting there Maharashtra Tourism launches with good guides leave the Gateway of India every 30 mins from 0900 (last one leaves Elephanta at 1730) except during the monsoon from Jun-Sep. The very pleasant journey takes 1-1½ hrs (Rs 65-85 return).The higher fare is for 'deluxe' boats with an open upper deck. However, the boat boys demand extra payment to sit on top! Reservations,T2026364. Small private boats without guides continue during the monsoon when the seas can be very rough. From the landing place, a 300 m unshaded path along the quayside and then about 110 rough steps lead to the caves at a height of 75 m. The walk along the quay can be avoided when the small train functions (Rs 6 return). The climb can be trying for some, especially if it is hot, though *Doolies* (chairs carried by porters) are available for Rs 300 return, Rs 200 one-way (unnecessary for the reasonably fit). The monkeys can be aggressive. Elephanta is very popular with local day-trippers so avoid the weekend rush. At the start of the climb there are places selling refreshments, as well as lines of stalls with knick-knacks and curios along the way (including models of the Eiffel Tower!). Maharashtra Tourism normally organizes a festival of classical music and dance on the island in the third week of Feb. US$5 for foreigners, Rs 10 Indians. MTDC, T02438-4226, has 2 rooms. Early morning is the best time for light and also for avoiding large groups with guides which arrive from around 1000. The caves tend to be quite dark so carry a powerful torch.

History

The vast majority of India's 1,200 **cave sites** were created as temples and monasteries between the third century BC and the 10th century AD. Jain, Buddhist and Hindu caves often stand side by side. The temple cave on Elephanta island, dedicated to Siva, was probably excavated during the eighth century by the Rashtrakuta Dynasty which ruled the Deccan from 757 to 973 AD, though the caves may have had earlier Buddhist origins. An earlier name for the island was Garhapuri – city of forts – but the Portuguese renamed it after the colossal sculpted elephants when they captured Mumbai from the Sultan of Gujarat in 1535, and stationed a batallion there. They reportedly used the main pillared cave as a shooting gallery causing some of the damage you see. Muslim and British rulers were not blameless either.

The site

The Entrance Originally there were three entrances and 28 pillars at the site. The entrances on the east and west have subsidiary shrines which may have been excavated and used for different ceremonies. The main entrance is now from the north. At dawn, the rising sun casts its rays on the approach to the main shrine (*garbagriha*), housed in a square structure at the west end of the main hall. On your right is a carving of Siva as Nataraj, see page 1330. On the left he appears as Lakulisa in a much damaged carving. Seated on a lotus, the Buddha-like figure is a symbol of the unconscious mind and enlightenment, found also in Orissan temples where Lakulisa played a prominent role in attempting to attract Buddhists back into Hinduism, see page 692. From the steps at the entrance you can see the *yoni-lingam*, the symbol of the creative power of the deity.

The Main Hall The ribbed columns in the main hall, between 5 m and 6 m high and in a cruciform layout, are topped by a capital. At the corner of each pillar is a dwarf signifying the earth spirit (*gana*), and sometimes the figure of Ganesh (Ganapati). To the right, the main **Linga Shrine** has four entrances, each corresponding to a cardinal point guarded by a *dvarpala*. The sanctum is bare, drawing attention to the *yoni-lingam* which the devotee must walk around clockwise.

The wall panels To the north of the main shrine is **Bhairava killing the demon Andhakasura**. This extraordinarily vivid carving shows Siva at his most fearsome, with a necklace of skulls, crushing the power of Andhaka, the Chief of Darkness. It was held that if he was wounded each drop of his blood would create a new demon. So Siva impaled him with his sword and collected his blood with a cup which he then offered to his wife Shakti. In winter this panel is best seen in the early afternoon.

Opposite, on the south side of the main shrine is the damaged panel of **Kalyan Sundari**, in which Siva stands with Parvati on his right, just before their wedding (normally a Hindu wife stands on her husband's left). She looks down shyly, but her body is drawn to him. Behind Parvati is her father Himalaya and to his left Chandramas, the moon god carrying a gift - *soma*, the food of the gods. On Siva's left is Vishnu and below him Brahma.

At the extreme west end of the temple are **Nataraja** (left) and **Yogisvara Siva** (right). The former shows a beautiful figure of Ganesh above and Parvati on his left. All the other gods watch him. Above his right shoulder is the four-headed God of Creation, Brahma. Below Brahma is the elephant-headed Ganesh.

On the south wall, opposite the entrance are three panels. **Gangadhara** is on the west. The holy River Ganga (Bhagirathi) flowed only in heaven but was brought to earth by her father King Bhagiratha (kneeling at Siva's right foot) (see page 228).

Here, Ganga is shown in the centre, flanked by her two tributaries, Yamuna and Saraswati. These three rivers are believed to meet at Allahabad (see page 193).

To the left of these is the centre piece of the whole temple, the remarkable **Mahesvara**, the Lord of the Universe. Here Siva is five-headed, for the usual triple-headed figure has one face looking into the rock and another on top of his head. Nearly 6 m high, he unites all the functions of creation, preservation and destruction. Some see the head on the left (your right) as representing Vishnu, the Creator, while others suggest that it shows a more feminine aspect of Siva. To his right is Rudra or Bhairava, with snakes in his hair, a skull to represent ageing from which only Siva is free, and he has a look of anger. The central face is Siva as his true self, Siva Swarupa, balancing out creation and destruction. In this mode he is passive and serene, radiating peace and wisdom like the Buddha. His right hand is held up in a calming gesture and in his left hand is a lotus bud.

The panel to the left has the **Ardhanarisvara**. This depicts Siva as the embodiment of male and female, representing wholeness and the harmony of opposites. The female half is relaxed and gentle, the mirror in the hand symbolizing the woman reflecting the man. Siva has his 'vehicle', Nandi on the right.

To the east, opposite the *garbha-griha*, was probably the original entrance. On the south is Siva and Parvati **Playing chaupar on Mount Kailash**. Siva is the faceless figure. Parvati has lost and is sulking but her playful husband persuades her to return to the game. They are surrounded by Nandi, Siva's bull, celestial figures and an ascetic with his begging bowl.

On the north is **Ravana Shaking Mount Kailash** on which Siva is seated. Siva is calm and unperturbed by Ravana's show of brute strength and reassures the frightened Parvati. He pins down Ravana with his toe, who fails to move the mountain and begs Siva's forgiveness which is granted.

Sanjay Gandhi National Park, Goregaon

Dense deciduous and semi-evergreen forest provides a beautiful habitat for several varieties of deer, antelope, butterflies and birds. It is also home to hyena and panther, though they are rarely seen, while three lakes have ducks, herons and crocodiles. Nature trails lead from Film City (reached by bus from Goregaon station). A lion safari leaves from the Hotel Sunya near Borivli station.

Kanheri Caves

① *MTDC tours from Mumbai; or by train to Borivli station (from Mumbai Central, 30 mins). From there, by taxi or auto-rickshaw (10 km), or by bus on Sun and public holidays.*

The caves (also known as the **Mahakali Caves**), 42 km north of Mumbai, are on a low hill midway between Borivli and Thane. The hills used to form the central part of Salsette Island, but the surrounding land has long since been extensively built on. Further up the ravine from the caves there are some fine views across the Bassein Fort and out to sea.

The major caves The caves, still shaded by trees, are in the heart of the National Park. The entrance is from the south. There are 109 Buddhist caves, dating from the end of the second to the ninth century AD with flights of steps joining them. The most significant is the **Chaitya cave (3)** circa sixth century. The last Hinayana chaitya hall to be excavated is entered through a forecourt and verandah. The pillared entrance has well carved illustrations of the donors, and the cave itself comprises a 28 m x 13 m colonnaded hall of 34 pillars. At one end these encircle the 5 m-high dagoba. Some of the pillars have carvings of elephants and trees.

Fifty metres up the ravine is **Darbar of the Maharajah cave (10)**. This was a *dharamshala* (resthouse) (22 m x 10 m), which has two stone benches running down the sides and some cells leading off the left and back walls. Above Cave 10 is **Cave 35** which was a *vihara* (monastery) (12 m x 14 m), which has reliefs of a Buddha seated on a lotus and of a disciple spreading his cloak for him to walk on. All the caves have an elaborate drainage and water storage system, fresh rainwater being led into underground storage tanks. Patrons endowed the monasteries so that they could be decorated with carvings.

Above the cave complex is *Ashok Van*, a sacred grove of ancient trees, streams and springs. From there, a three-hour trek leads to "View Point", the highest in Mumbai. There are breathtaking views. Photography is prohibited from the radar station on top of the hill; there are excellent opportunities just below it.

North Konkan → *Colour map 5, grid B3.*

The undulating lowland of the North Konkan coast forms a narrow strip between the Arabian Sea and the often daunting west facing slopes of the Ghats. There are occasional good beaches, scattered mangrove swamps, and rice growing valleys, interspersed with poor laterite covered hills. The beaches to the north, a two-hour journey away, make them a popular getaway from Mumbai, although foreign tourists are virtually unheard of. They are very 'local'. For beaches to the south, see page 1101.
➤➤ *For Sleeping, Eating and other listings, see pages 1103-1105.*

Bassein (Vasai)
ⓘ *Trains go from Mumbai Central to Bassein (Vasai) Road station. From there hire a taxi for 11 km.*

Bassein, at the mouth of the Ulhas River on the mainland, is 60 km north of central Mumbai. Due to silting, the fort on the Bassein Creek is now some distance from the sea. The structure is in ruins, but it is well worth walking round the sea face.

Originally built by Bahadur Shah, Sultan of Gujarat, it was one of a chain of forts against the Portuguese. However, the chain was breached, and the Portuguese remodelled the city along their own lines, renaming it **Vasai**. From 1534 to 1739 it became so prosperous as a centre of shipbuilding and the export of Bassein stone that it was called the Court of the North. As a walled city it contained a cathedral, five convents, 13 churches and the splendid houses and palaces of the aristocracy, or Hidalgos, who with members of the religious orders, alone were allowed to live within the walls. The Marathas took Vasai in February 1739 after a long and desperate siege. Almost the whole Portuguese garrison, 800 strong, was killed in the battle; the Marathas are thought to have lost 5,000 men. In 1780 the British evicted the Marathas, only to return it to them three years later under the Treaty of Salbai.

Approached from the north, the fort in the town contains the ruins of St Joseph's Cathedral (1536), St Anthony's, the Jesuit church and the convents, all belonging to Franciscans, Dominicans, Jesuits or Augustinians. **Nalasopara**, 10 km northwest, is the ancient Konkan capital where Buddhist relics have been found.

Dharavi Island Some 40 km from Mumbai and reached by ferry from the fishing village of Marve, Dharavi Island has three villages, **Manori**, **Gorai** and **Uttan** with a population of 4,000, recently developed for tourism. Portuguese ships docked here some centuries ago but the rural atmosphere remains. It is a laid-place, relaxed place, an escape from the city. It is, however, gaining a reputation for all-night beach parties; you need to book three months ahead for Christmas/New Year holidays. Gorai beach is fairly clean, though crowded at weekends, yet almost empty on weekdays. The **Esselworld Amusement Park** with giant rides for all ages (adults Rs 275) is another attraction. Most of the beach resorts are small, simple and popular with day trippers.

⁝ New Mumbai: a planner's dream?

The challenge of severe overcrowding in Mumbai in the 20 years after Independence led to an increasingly urgent search for ways of reducing the pressure on land and services in the city centre. In 1970 the City and Industrial Development Corporation of Maharashtra (CIDCO) took over responsibility for creating a twin city to Mumbai on the other side of the bay – 'New Mumbai'. In 1979 their plan for a city around a series of 20 different 'nodes' was accepted, each node being planned to have a population of 200,000.

Seven nodes are now completely occupied, including Vashi, the node nearest the Thane Creek Bridge, and the CBD of Belapur to the south. The buildings are modern, the streets widely laid out and the city has begun to feel like a living modern metropolitan centre. **Vashi** has large agricultural wholesale markets (relocating the market from the congested heart of Mumbai itself), a sports complex and large hotels. Belapur CBD is becoming an important commercial centre, while other nodes have specialized functions, such as the Jawaharlal Nehru Port, commissioned in 1989 (India's first fully computerized and automated port) and the Kalamboli Iron and Steel Market. On the sea shore at **Nerul** there is a special housing complex designed for non-resident Indians (NRIs). Yet, while for the rising middle class of India 'Navai Mumbai' may seem like a model for future town living, recent research suggests that it has created a nightmare for the poor and dispossessed, many of whom have lost their homes, land and fishing grounds with no way of sharing the benefits of the new development. Resolving their problems remains one of the planners' biggest challenges.

Rajodi ① *Local train to Virar, ST bus from Virar (W) to Satpala village then auto to Rajodi beach (Rs 20). The uncrowded black sand beach is safe for swimming but is crowded at weekends.*

The Ghats → *Colour map 5, grid B3. Road travel is often disrupted in the rains.*

The Ghats represent an historic divide between the outward looking coastal lowlands with the trading centre of Mumbai at their hub, and the much drier interior, a battle ground of successive Indian dynasties. Today the hilltops are littered with fortified sites, while hill stations offer weekend breaks to Mumbai's élite. The routes through the Western Ghats from Mumbai climb to nearly 1,600 m through the forested slopes, particularly beautiful before the end of the rains in September when wild flowers are everywhere, and rivers and waterfalls are full. The railways through the ghats are spectacular. On the Nashik route alone the line passes through 10 tunnels, over five viaducts and 11 bridges. Between Neral and Lonavla, passing through stunning ravined countryside, the line has gradients of one in 37 to overcome the problems posed by 'the big step' the hills presented. ⊷ *For Sleeping, Eating and other listings, see pages 1103-1105.*

Thane (Thana) Thane, northeast of Mumbai, was the terminus of the first railway in India, built from Mumbai in 1853. As early as 1298, however, Marco Polo had written of Thane as "a great kingdom ... there is much traffic here and many ships and merchants frequent the place". It was an important Portuguese centre until the

⁝ Mumbai to Thane: India's first railway line

The opening of India's first railway line from Mumbai to Thane in 1853 prepared the route through the Ghats to the Deccan Plateau. Mumbai became the hub of regional and international trade. Victoria Terminus (CST now) was the product of a magnificent era of railway building at the end of the 19th century when the British Raj was striding confidently towards the 20th century.

With the disappearance of the East India Company after the Mutiny, the Government of India took over the responsibility for running the railways. On 16 April 1853 the first train made its run from Mumbai along 32 km of line to Thane. Subsequent advances were rapid but often incredible natural obstacles presented great challenges to the railway builders. The 263 km line to Surat encountered 18 rivers and some of the foundations for the bridges had to be driven 45 m in to the ground to cope with the monsoon floodwaters.

Marathas captured it in 1739. The English church in the town dates from 1825 but there is little in the way of tourist attractions.

Akloli Northeast of Thane, 913 km from Mumbai, at the start of the Ghats in Bhiwandi, a road leads up to the hot springs of Akloli, and to **Ganeshpuri**, 6 km from Shirshad, where the Vajreshwari Temple with hot springs is widely visited. There are a few sleeping options.

Matheran → *Phone code: 02148. Colour map 5, grid B3. Population: 5,100. Altitude: 785 m.*

Mumbai's nearest hill station, in an extension of the Sahyadri range, Matheran, meaning 'Mother Forest' or 'Wooded Head', has stunning views, refreshingly cool air and pleasant walks. It maintains its quiet by banning all forms of motor vehicles within the town. It is very much geared towards the Mumbai weekender. A visit is recommended, but stay a night as it is too strenuous to do in a day from Mumbai.

Ins and outs Getting there From Neral, south of Kalyan, the atmospheric narrow gauge train takes 2 hrs to cover 21 km to reach Matheran. The station is in the town centre. A Capitation Tax (Rs 20) is charged on arrival – pay before leaving the station. **Getting around** All motor vehicles must park at Dasturi Naka (near the Holiday Camp), 2 km from town. Porters and ponies charge around Rs 100; 3-man rickshaws Rs 150 after bargaining. See Transport, page 1105, for further details.

Sights Matheran sprawls out along a north-south ridge and from rocky promontories such as The Hart, Panorama Point, Chouk, Duke's Nose and Garbat there are splendid views down the almost sheer hillsides to the valleys below. The best views are from Little Chouk, Louisa and Porcupine, which is also known as Sunset Point. Allow one hour to walk and see the stunning sunsets. From the northernmost vantage points you can see the lights of Mumbai on a clear night. The layout of the town conforms with standard British Hill Station planning with central civic buildings and widely dispersed bungalows. You can sightsee on horseback here.

The most scenic route for this diversion is by the spectacular light railway through the ghats from Neral which may be closed during the monsoon. You will appreciate the problems facing the early railway engineers here, see page 1098. The steam engines are no longer used after working the route for 77 years but you will see one proudly displayed at the station.

→ *Phone code: 02168 (952168). Colour map 5, grid B3. Population: 12,700. Altitude: 1370 m.*

In one of the wettest parts of the Western Ghats during the monsoon, Mahabaleshwar is in a pleasantly wooded setting at the head of the Krishna River. It is the main hill

Matheran

■ Sleeping	4 Hope Hall	8 Royal
1 Alexander	5 Lord's Central	9 Rugby
2 Girivihar	6 MTDC Holiday Camp	10 The Byke
3 Gujarat Bhavan	7 Prasanna & Newsagent	11 Usha Ascot

N

Not to scale

station for Mumbai and Pune. Cool and relaxed with some good walking trails and excellent views from the ghats, it's a good place to have an overnight stop. It is, however, becoming increasingly touristy with crowds of Mumbai holiday makers.

Ins and outs Getting there There are direct buses from Mumbai and Pune. It is approached by road from Surul on the NH4 on the east, or Poladpur on the NH17 to the west. There is a Rs 5 tax to enter the town. **Getting around** The main viewing points are very spread out so it is best to take a MTDC tour or hire a taxi from the ST bus stand. See Transport, page 1105, for further details. **Climate** Best time to visit: Nov-May. The altitude makes the climate very pleasant during the dry season.

Sights 'Discovered' by General Lodwick in 1824, to whom there is still a monument on the Elephant's Head Point, Mahabaleshwar was declared an official British sanatorium in 1828 and was once the summer capital of the Bombay Presidency. These days there are pleasant walks and waterfalls to visit. **Arthur's Seat** (12 km) looks out over a 600 m precipice to the Konkan. The nine-hole Golf Course is built on a cliff side. **Venna Lake** has boating and fishing. From **Mumbai Point** and the hills around the town you can see the sea on a clear day.

There are several typical British hill station buildings: **Christchurch** (1842, enlarged 1867); the cemetery; **Frere Hall** (1864) with its mullioned windows and the Club, founded in 1882; **Government House** (1829) on Mount Malcolm; The **Lodwick Monument** (1874) in honour of the town's founder, and the **Beckwith Monument**.

The old town contains three temples (Krishnabai, Ram and Hanuman) which you can walk to from a turn off Elphinstone Road. **Krishnabai** or Panchganga with a self-formed *linga* resembling a piece of volcanic lava, is said to have five streams, including the Krishna, flowing from it. The 13th-century Yadav King Singhan built a small tank at the Krishna's source which starts its 1,400 km journey across the Deccan to the sea. This part of the 'Deccan Trap' has underground caverns which hold water and give rise to springs.

Panchgani is set among casuarinas and silver oak, in spectacular scenery. At an altitude of 1,334 m, it is surrounded by the five hills from which it takes its name. It has a very compact centre with lovely walks, stunning views and very friendly people, which makes it well worth a visit.

Settled as a hill station before Mahabaleshwar, it is known for its schools and MTDC are happy to arrange for you to visit some of the British and Parsi bungalows. There is a small art gallery on the State Highway, not far from the bus stand. The drive to Mahabaleshwar offers beautiful views; sit on the left of the bus travelling from Panchgani.

Pratapgarh ① *Buses from Mahabaleshwar (22 km), 50 mins.* To the west of Mahabaleshwar, the setting for this Maratha **fort** is spectacular. From the summit (1,080 m) on which it is sited there is a splendid view down the forested hillside. A road leads to the foot of the hill, then 500 steps run up to the top.

The fort comprises a double wall with corner bastions. The gates are studded with iron spikes. Inside, the Bhavani temple in the lower fort has two *dipmal* (lantern towers); their exteriors are covered with regularly placed projections like giant coat hooks. Presumably lanterns were placed on these or hung from them, the towers then acting as beacons. The upper fort has a Siva temple. Its ramparts can be seen nearly all of the way down the very scenic (but slow) road to Poladpur.

Chiplun The NH17 runs south through Khed to Chiplun on the banks of the Vashishti River, fed from the **Koyna Lake**, one of the largest artificial lakes in the Western Ghats. There are spectacular views across the flat valley bottom, criss-crossed by the several courses of the meandering river. After Khed and 10 km before Chiplun, near an attractive small village and temple (difficult to find when travelling north) there is accommodation.

South Konkan Coast → *Colour map 5, B3, C3 and C4.*

The 593 km coast route from Mumbai to Goa, now followed by the Konkan Railway and the NH17, runs through the South Konkan region. It passes a string of small towns which developed at the heads of estuaries. These were transshipment points for cargo brought by sea, then hauled by pack animals over the Ghats. Although lowland, it is far from flat. Many of the densely wooded slopes have been cleared, leaving the laterites bare and unproductive, alternating with patches of intensive rice cultivation and coconut groves. The coastal estuaries support mangrove swamps. Economically a backward region, it is scenically very attractive. ▸▸ *For Sleeping, Eating and other listings, see pages 1103-1105.*

Kashid Beach ⓘ *From Mumbai 4 hrs by car, 21 km south. Also daily 2 'Asiad' coaches from Central Bus Terminal (0545, 1200), Rs 45. Or, Mumbai-Rewas ferry runs hourly in daylight from the Ferry Wharf (Bhaucha Dhakka), 1½ hrs then frequent buses to Kashid, 55 km away, or rickshaws, known locally as 'Vikrams'.* Kashid has an excellent, unspoilt, 3-km silver sand beach near the town of Alibag, which is a popular weekend resort but deserted on weekdays. Unfortunately the sea is polluted and swimming is not advised. A good beach, 2 km away, is suitable for camping and nearby hills are good for walking.

Murud-Janjira Murud is 16 km south of Kashid and is worth a half day excursion. It is a good idea to hire a bike to explore the town. One kilometre north from Murud centre is the temple to the triple-headed **Dattatraya** representing Brahma, Vishnu and Siva. It is worth climbing up 250 steps, not least for the commanding views.

Janjira Fort is reputedly one of the strongest coastal forts in India and was uniquely successful in resisting attempts to capture it. According to legend one such attempt included the digging of a tunnel under the sea. The fort had been built by the Sidis from Abyssinia. Across the bay to the north can be seen Sambhaji's fort, built to combat Janjira, but Janjira was unique in holding out against Maratha attacks. The fort retains a number of remarkable buildings, including mosques, the *topkhana* guarded by canons and a five-storeyed **palace**, which is crumbling. An empty palace of the old nawab, 1 km north of Janjira-Rajpuri, is clearly visitble from the Murud Road. Signs warn tresspassers away, but as the caretaker may allow you to look at the ghost of the once opulent lifestyle of the nawabs, Rs 50 tip expected. Some decaying Muslim tombs stand among baobab trees, 1 km south of Rajpuri jetty. Boats take you from this jetty to the fort for either Rs 10 or Rs 150 on the Tourist boat.

Ratnagiri ⓘ *13 km west off the NH17 at Hathkamba.* Now a rapidly growing unprepossessing port town with a lot of road works, Ratnagiri, 'Jewel hill', was the birthplace of two leaders of the Independence movement, Gangadhar Tilak and GK Gokhale. It was also the internment home for the last king of Burma, King Thibaw, who was held here from 1886 until his death in 1916. His 'palace' is now part of the polytechnic. Sleeping at *Land-mark* as you approach the town.

Ganpatipule Revered and much visited by Hindus for its *swayambhu* ('naturally occurring' or 'self-created') Ganesh, Ganpatipule, north of Ratnagiri, has a beautifully white deserted beach to rival those of Goa which gets busy at weekends. The sea is clean but beware of strong currents. Jaigad Fort, 35 km, makes a pleasant excursion.

Vijayadurg (Viziadurg) A minor road west off the NH17 at Talera leads to the formidable fort guarding the river which was built on an ancient site. The Sultans of Bijapur enlarged it and Sivaji further strengthened it by adding the three outer walls. It has 27 bastions, an inner moat, good water supply and carried 278 guns in 1682. The Maratha pirate Kanhoji Angria made it his base in 1698, plundered European shipping and withstood assaults by the Portuguese and the British.

Malvan A coastal road south from Vijayadurg leads to Malvan. The old town straggles along a crowded little street down to its port. There is an unconventional statue of Sivaji and two well-known temples to Sri Devi Sateri and Rameshwar. It is being developed as a beach resort by MTDC.

Sivaji's coastal fort of **Sindhudurg**, just south of Malvan, now deserted, is on a low-lying island just off the coast. Rowing boats ferry passengers from the tiny port. There are still several shrines – to Maruti, Bhavani, Mahadeo and uniquely to Sivaji.

Vengurla The former trading settlement on an island is now joined to the land. On the NH17, close to the Goa border, the coast here is lined with beautiful white sand beaches. Salt pans provide an important product for export from the region.

Sawantwadi ① *now has an out-of-town station on the Konkan railway*, was the capital of the Bhonsle kings of southern Maharashtra who were constantly trying to extend their territory into Goa. Today it is a large market town, centred on the big tank and palace buildings.

It was once noted for the production of fine hand-painted *gangifa* (playing cards) but this is a dying tradition. The Sawantwadi royal family is actively keeping this ancient art and other local crafts alive, allowing a few artists/craftsmen to work in the once impressive palace darbar hall. They also produce painted lacquered furniture, chessmen, board games and candle sticks.

The brightly coloured *gangifa* were originally produced by pasting layers of cloth together, using tamarind seed gum then coating the 'card' with chalk before polishing it with a stone to provide a smooth white base for decorating the face with natural pigments while the back was stiffened with lacquer. The packs of circular cards come in various sizes and suits. The ten suits of the *Dasavatara* (featuring Vishnu's 10 incarnations), for example, forms a pack of 120 cards while the *Navagraha* (nine planets) has nine suits. The miniature paintings with patterns drawn from mythology, history and nature, often reflect folk traditions. A few towns in Bengal and Orissa continue to produce *gangifa*. Prices range from Rs 800 to 3,000.

Amboli From Sawantwadi, a state road goes up the ghats to the minor hill station of Amboli, at an altitude of 690 m. The road contines on to Belgaum. Set on the flat-topped heights of the Western Ghats overlooking the coastal plain below, Amboli is a quiet and little-visited resort. There are attractive walks and several waterfalls. Bauxite mines, 10 km away, can also be visited.

Redi Beach Just 3 km north of the Goa border and Tiracol, a turn off from NH17, south of Shiroda, leads to Redi Village and beach. An old Maratha Fort, now in ruins but interesting to wander round, dominates the view over a stunning and almost unvisited bay. An idyllic picnic spot, for example for a day trip from Tiracol, but no facilities or shops so carry water and food.

Listings: Excursions from Mumbai

● Sleeping

Manori *p1096*
C-D Manoribel, T2833918. 11 rooms and 8 cottages set under palms, clean, restaurant.
D-E Dominica, 20 rooms, less sedate, catering for young 'revellers', camp fire and jazz evenings by the beach.

Gorai *p1096*
Walk along the beach and check hotels out. Expect to pay around Rs 250 for a double at weekends and less on weekdays. Some resorts insist that you eat their food!
E Di Dimp Shepali, Gorai-Uttan Rd, next to *Shepali Superstore*, T8690125. 2 clean, cosy rooms (1 a/c), home-cooked meals (included), well-kept flower filled garden, small pool, patio, 30-min walk to beach, book ahead.

Uttan *p1096*
Towards Uttan:
D Maxwell Resort, Chavli, Uttan Gorai Rd (7 km by auto from Bhayendar, Rs 50), T8197075 (Mumbai T6285764). Small, clean rooms (some a/c), multicuisine restaurant, only permit room in area, small pool, 3 km from Gorai Beach, 5 km from Esselworld.

Rajodi *p1097*
E-F Sea View Resort, Satpala, T912-587994. Clean, simple rooms, shaded dining (Indian, Chinese), prefers groups at weekends, week-days with meals, Rs 250 (Rs 150 day rate).
F Super Resorts, Rajodi Beach Rd, 100 m from beach, T912-502424. Very simple rooms, meals.

Matheran *p1098, map p1099*
Budget hotels near the station can be very noisy. Prices often include meals and rise considerably during holidays (eg Diwali) but most offer good off-season discounts.
A-B Rugby, Vithalrao Kotwal Rd, T30291. 52 rooms (including large, family rooms), some a/c, gardens, restaurant, professionally run.
A-B Usha Ascot, MG Rd, T30360. 64 rooms, most a/c, a resort hotel.

B The Byke, T30365, F30316. 46 comfortable rooms, 5 a/c, excellent restaurants, good pool.
B-C Lord's Central, MG Marg, T30228. 23 colonial style rooms ('Valley' room best), restaurant (meals included), bar, pool, park, riding, not plush but clean, friendly, with best views in Matheran, perched on the edge of the main ridge. Recommended.
C-D Alexander, Alexander Pt, T30151. 24 rooms, 3 a/c, good restaurant, in unspoilt woodland.
C-D Holiday Camp (MTDC), 30 mins up hill from centre 1 km before Matheran (train stops at camp), T30277, F30566. 39 rooms and cottages for 2 or 4, and dorm, limited catering.
C-D Royal, Kasturba Bhavan, T30247. 61 rooms, 5 a/c, restaurant (Indian veg), bar, health club.
D Gujarat Bhavan, Maulana Azad Rd, T30378. 22 clean rooms (some a/c), restaurant (Indian veg), garden.
E Girivihar, Sivaji Rd, T30231. Peaceful, spacious gardens, some rooms with balconies.
E Hope Hall, MG Marg (opposite Lord's Central), T30253. Good size, clean rooms with bath (bucket hot water), friendly family, pleasant location.
E Prasanna, opposite railway station, T30258. 10 small, clean rooms, restaurant.
Several restaurants have 'Permit' rooms.

Mahabaleshwar *p1099*
Many hotels to choose from; several family-run. The bazar sells local honey which is justly famous, as are jams from fruit grown in area.
A Valley View Resort, Valley View Rd, off James Murray Peth Rd, T60066, F60070. 80 very clean rooms, 40 a/c, real grass to balconies(!), pure veg restaurant (no beer), fabulous views from garden. Recommended.
B-C Brightland, Nakhinda Village (4 km centre), Kates Pt Rd, T60707. 30 rooms, restaurants, bar, pool, gardens.
C Fountain, opposite Koyna Valley, T60227, F60137. 98 rooms, some air-cooled with TV, veg restaurant with a good choice.
C Fredrick, NH71 near Satara Rd junction, T60240. 32 rooms, restaurant, bungalow hotel.
C-D Dinas, Pune Rd. Comfortable rooms, food.

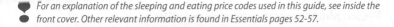
For an explanation of the sleeping and eating price codes used in this guide, see inside the front cover. Other relevant information is found in Essentials pages 52-57.

C-D Dreamland, off MG Rd, behind ST Stand, T60228. 80 rooms, old cottages and newer a/c suites by the pool, restaurant (Indian veg) in large garden.

C-D Holiday Resort (MTDC), T60318, F60300. 100 cottages, rooms and garden suites in large complex, dorm (no beds) Rs 100, restaurant, permit room, pleasant setting and atmosphere, Tourist Office near gate, popular. 2 km from centre (taxi Rs 40).

D Mahabaleshwar Club, off SH71 towards Golf Links. Library attached, quiet, with character, temp membership to stay.

D-E Grand, Woodlawn Rd, away from centre, T60322. Modest rooms with verandah, gardens.

E Sai Niwas, 338 Koli Alley, T60549. Good value, clean rooms.

Panchgani p1100

B-D Five Hills, opposite Dr Ambedkar Nagar, Rajpuri Rd, T40301. 64 doubles and suites, good restaurant, all rooms only Rs 150 on weekdays.

D Summer Palace has clean, modern though characterless rooms.

D-E Amer, 188 Chesson Rd, T40211. Some a/c rooms with bath.

Chiplun p1100

A Riverview Lodge, T2355-52853, F72059. With 37 comfortable rooms, most a/c, very good restaurant, pool to indulge in, helipad, attractive garden setting, peaceful.

There are several very cheap lodges around the town centre.

Kashid Beach p1101

B-C Kashid Beach Resort, T02144-85010. 500 m from beach across main road, has 25 split level rooms, some with good seaviews, bathrooms a bit run-down but rooms clean, restaurant (beer appears as 'snacks' on the bill), in large grounds, bike hire.

Murud-Janjira p1101

B-D Holiday Resort (MTDC/private), T021447-4078. 140 cottages (for 2 or 4) and rooms, basic, restaurant (monotonous menu).

C Golden Swan, Darbar Rd, T021447-4078. Comfortable rooms in cottages near the beach, adequate restaurant.

E Ruchit, Dr Rajendra Prasad Rd, T021447-4219, right on the beach, 2 mins' walk south

of bus station. Lodge with 4 rooms (hot water buckets), garden restaurant, cycle/canoe hire, helpful, friendly owner. Camping allowed.

E Seashore Resort (no sign), 3 rooms, bath, friendly family, lovely garden on beach.

E-F Anan, Darbar Rd, T021447-4297. Simple rooms with bath, hammocks in garden.

Ganpatipule p1101

B-C Abishek, 500 m down dirt track opposite *Landmark*. Typical Indian hotel, restaurant with sea views from patio.

B-C Landmark (on hill side going down to village). Good rooms, excellent Chinese/Indian restaurant, beer.

B-D Resort, T02357-35248, on the beach, among palm trees. 68 clean, comfortable a/c suites to 4-bed rooms (11 and 12 best), poor, grubby restaurant (beer), *Bank of Maharashtra* on site changes TCs, poor service, demands advance payment, but great location, relaxing.

E Tent Resort, T35348. Decent 2 and 4-bed tents with lockers, peaceful location.

Amboli p1102

D JRD International, Vengurla-Belgaon Rd, 1 km from bus stand, T02363-76222, F76224. 30 pleasant, clean rooms, better in 'cottages', reasonable Indian restaurant, bar.

D-E Resort (MTDC/private), T02363-76239, offers a reasonably comfortable base with a choice of 21 rooms including some suites.

❶ Eating

Matheran p1098, map p1099

Kwality Fruit Juice House, MG Rd, south of the train station among many. Excellent honey and *chikki* (a sweet peanut brittle).

Woodlands, Chinoy Rd. Indian.

Mahabaleshwar p1099

Grapevine Restaurant, Masjid Rd. Small eclectic restaurant with Thai, Italian and other non-Indian specials. Try lobster, fresh strawberries washed down with Indian "Chardonnay". Excellent though pricey.

Murud-Janjira p1101

There are some cheap eateries:

Nest, Darbar Rd. Indian including *thalis*.

Vinayak, try Chicken Manchurian Soup.

Ganpatipule p1101

Cheap *thalis* are served in 2 eateries outside the Ganesh Temple in the village shopping street.

▲ Activities and tours

Mahabaleshwar p1099
Tours

MTDC deluxe buses for sightseeing, 1400, Pratapgarh, 0930, 1000, and Panchgani, 1100. Reservations at *Holiday Resort*, T60318, F60300.

⊙ Transport

Uttan p1096

85 km all the way by Western Express Highway, then road west from Bhayendar.

Train

From Churchgate on Suburban West Railway to **Malad**, then auto-rickshaw or bus to **Marve**. Ferry (bikes allowed) across the creek from Marve to Manori, 0515-2215 (15 mins); then bus or auto to 'resort'. Or from Borivli (W), ferry to Gorai, then auto from wharf to beach or Esselworld. For Uttan, local train to Bhayendar then auto from west side to resort.

Matheran p1098, map p1099
Train

It's necessary to book in advance for weekends. From **Neral** 1st Class window seats are Nos 1, 4, 5, 0; some 2nd Class are glazed for better viewing: sit on the right on the way up, for best views. From **Neral**, depart daily at 0840, 1100, 1700 (also 1015, mid Mar-mid-Jun). To connect in the morning: from **Mumbai (CST)**: *Deccan Exp* 1007 at 0640; *Local* 0721; *Koyna Exp* 7307 at 0845; From **Pune** *Sahayadri Exp* at 0730. There are trains from **Karjat Junction** to Neral. From **Matheran**: depart 0545, 1310, 1435, 1620.

Mahabaleshwar p1099
Bus

For the best views, sit on the right of the bus travelling from Pune to Mahabaleshhwar.

Bus station, T60254. Regular services to/from Pune, Rs 30 (4 hrs). MTDC several deluxe buses daily (except monsoons) to Mumbai 1500 (6½ hrs) and from Mumbai (7 hrs), Rs 145. The semi-luxury and luxury buses to Pune stop at Swargate, a Rs 15 auto ride away from the railway station.

Train

Pune is the most convenient railhead.

Panchgani p1100
Bus

Buses run from Mumbai (via Mahad) and Pune ('Luxury' to Swargate stand only).

Train

The nearest railway station is Satara (28 km).

Murud-Janjira p1101

At Kolad (80 km from Panvel) a road leads to the coastal fort of Murud-Janjira.

Bus

From Mumbai, buses cover the 165 km in under 6 hrs but it may be quicker to get a bus to Alibag and pick up a local connection there.

Ferry

Mumbai-Rewas ferry runs hourly in daylight from the Ferry Wharf (Bhaucha Dhakka), 1½ hrs; local buses from there to **Murud**, though there can be a long wait.

Ganpatipule p1101
Bus

Direct State Transport buses run from **Mumbai**, **Pune** and **Ratnagiri**.

Amboli p1102
Bus

From the coastal towns of Ratnagiri (210 km) and Vengurla (50 km).

Train

To Kolhapur or Belgaum, then by local bus.

⊙ Directory

Matheran p1098, map p1099
Useful services Union Bank of India, MG Rd, changes TCs and cash but poor rate; Newsagents in *Hotel Prasanna*, Post Office and Tourist Information Bureau opposite railway station.

Mahabaleshwar p1099
Banks On Dr Sabbana Rd. **Tourist office** At *Holiday Resort*, T60318, F60300, helpful; information near bus stand.

Northwest Maharashtra

Nashik (Nasik) → *Phone code: 0253. Colour map 5, grid A3. Population: 1.08 million.*

Nashik, an unprepossessing mixture of featureless market town, pilgrim centre and sprawling modern industrial estates, nonetheless has an old city area near the ghats with characteristic traditional buildings. It is one of Hinduism's most holy sites, taking its sanctity from its position on the headwaters of the Godavari River. It commands the strategic route from northwestern India to the southern Deccan.
▶▶ *For Sleeping, Eating and other listings, see pages 1107-1108.*

Ins and outs Getting there Trains arrive at Nasik Rd Station, 7 km south of town. City buses run to town (Rs 5), stopping at Shalimar Circle, 3 mins' walk from the Central Bus Stand (CBS) at the town centre; otherwise auto-rickshaws and taxis are around. Buses arrive from Aurangabad at the CBS, close to plenty of budget hotels. Mumbai buses use the Mahamarga Bus Stand, a few kilometres from the centre, where you can get an auto; trains from Mumbai are a faster and better option. **Getting around** Buses to local places of interest use the CBS but few people speak English in case you need to ask the way. See Transport, page 1108, for further details.

Sights Nashik shares the triennial **Kumbh Mela** with Ujjain, Haridwar and Allahabad (see page 195) and every 12 years millions of pilgrims converge on the river Godavari, sometimes referred to as the Ganga of the Deccan, to bathe. The Godavari, which rises 30 km away at Trimbak, is believed to have a common underground source with the Ganga itself. In the last 10 years Nashik has been one of India's fastest growing cities, but the town itself is undoubtedly ancient, and Ghose suggests that it has an unbroken history of over 2,500 years. At Pandu Lena (see below), within a few kilometres of the town centre, palaeolithic settlements have been discovered. Chalcolithic pottery has been found at Gangawadi, 15 km northwest of Nashik. Other finds date from the fifth century BC up to the first century AD and Roman pottery has been found in the third period level. However, none of Nashik's temples are very old. The Vaishnavite **Sundar Narayana Temple** (1756) on the west bank has three black Vishnu images. The **Ramesvara Temple** (18th century) is where Rama is believed to have carried out the funeral rites for his father and to have bathed in the **Rama Kund** nearby. It is a popular place to throw ashes of the dead into the river. The banyan-shaded **Sita Gupha** cave on the east side of town is where Rama's wife hid from Ravana the demon. Nearby is the **Kala** (black) **Rama Temple** (1782) which has a 25-m high *shikhara*.

Around Nashik

Pandu Lena Eight kilometres southwest of Nashik there is a group of 24 rock cut Buddhist monuments on a hillock, the earliest dating from the first century BC. They include over 20 caves. Some have excellent carving, particularly on the exterior doorways. **Cave 3** has 19 monastic cells, a carved Buddha decorates the rear of **Cave 10**, while the exterior of the early **Cave 18**, a chapel (*chaitya*), is finely decorated. Approached by a stepped path, they are cut into the escarpment and overlook the road.

Deolali, 7 km southeast, was the transfer camp for British soldiers going home during the two World Wars. To go 'Doolally Tap' was to go crazy with boredom waiting there. A mental hospital accommodated these casualties.

Trimbak ① *Hourly buses from Nashik take about 45 mins.* The town of Trimbak (30 km west of Nashik) is centred around the beautiful **Gangasagar Tank**. About 690 steps lead up the hill behind Trimbak to the source of the Godavari itself where you get good views. The town is partly surrounded by a fantastic semi-circle of hills, topped by a near vertical scarp. **Trimbakeshwar Temple**, an 18th-century Siva sanctuary with a *jyotirlinga*, is a pilgrimage site. In February/March a large fair is held; the important *Sinhastha Fair* takes place every 12 years. There is a simple hotel here.

Prayag Tirth, on the road to Trimbak, has a beautiful stone-lined tank with two temples. Further on near **Anjaneri**, two 300-m high conical hills are on either side of the road, sweeping round in a broad arc behind the town of Trimbak.

Igatpuri The 'Town of Difficulties' is on the plateau top at the end of the ghat section of railway. **Kalsubai** (1,540 m), the highest mountain in Maharashtra, is visible to the south. About 1 km beyond the town the road passes the end of the beautiful **Beale Lake**.

Jawhar The former capital of a tribal kingdom, Jawhar is noted for its *warli* paintings. Rice paste or poster colours are used to decorate the hut walls. **Jai Vilas**, the palace (ask locally to visit) and **Bhupatgad**, the fort, still show evidence of the tribal kingdom, while there are attractive waterfalls at Dadar Kopra. Ask at *Bank of Baroda* for a small guesthouse.

Listings: Northwest Maharashtra

● Sleeping

Nashik *p1106*
Cheap rooms are hard to come by.
A Residency (Taj), P-17 MIDC Ambad, Mumbai-Agra Rd (14 km from Nasik Rd station, 6 km from city), T384499, F382638, tajnsk@bom2.vsnl.net.in. 64 rooms, large grounds.
A-B Regency (Quality Inn), Pune Rd, Sivaji Nagar, T562444, F562111. 40 rooms, modern, pool, health club.
C Holiday Cottages, Mumbai-Agra Rd, Vilhouli (8 km from centre), T522376, F523009. 40 rooms, 30 a/c, comfortable, restaurant, pool.
C-D Panchavati Elite, Trimbak Rd, near Vinod Auto, T579031, F577869. 26 rooms, some a/c, restaurants (*Kwality, Coffee House*) and a cheaper guesthouse.
C-D Panchavati Yatri, 430 Vakil Wadi, T575771, F571823. 41 rooms, 30 a/c rooms (but cold showers), good restaurants, bar, coffee shop recommended, well run and efficient.
D Green View, 1363 Trimbak Rd, T572231, F579754. 24 rooms, 14 a/c, restaurant, garden, quiet.
E Siddhartha, Nashik Pune Rd, 2 km towards airport, T573288. 32 rooms, some **D** a/c, pleasant garden.
E-F Basera, Shivaji Rd, T575616. 60 clean rooms, hot water.

E-F Pushkraj, near Shalimar City Bus Stop, T74838. 30 rooms, restaurant, helpful.
E-F Rajmahal, opposite the bus stand, T580501, F571096. 28 rooms, friendly, clean.
F Mazda, Old Agra Rd, 5-min walk from CBS, T579720. Basic rooms with bath, café.

● Eating

Nashik *p1106*
Panchavati, hotels, mostly Indian vegetarian, wide choice.
On MG Rd:
Anand, for fast food.
Annapoorna Lunch House for breakfast and South Indian dishes.
Dairy Don for ice creams.
Shilpa Hotel, does excellent Gujarati thalis.
Woodlands, Nashik Pune Rd (opposite *Siddhartha*), recommended for South Indian vegetarian and coffee.

▲ Activities and tours

Nashik *p1106*
Tours
Best to book tours in advance by the evening before at CBS.
Nashik Darshan start from the Central Bus Stand (CBS) 0730-1700, Rs 71 (includes Hindi guide). Visits Pandu Lena, Bhaktidham, Kala Ram Mandir/Sita Gupha, Tapovan, Muktidham

(lunch), Ved Mandir, Somneshwar, Trimbak; good value, well-timed, although the hour's stop at Trimbak allows a visit to the temple but is too short to see the source of the Godavari. Possible to leave the tour at this point and return to Nashik by bus or share taxis (Rs 20) which are available; it is a 30-min walk to the centre.

⊜ Transport

Nashik *p1106*
From Mumbai airport, take taxi to Thane and then a shared taxi (Rs 80) to Nashik (total 4 hrs); also buses from Thane long distance bus stand. For Aurangabad, buses depart 30 mins past the hour, 5 hrs, Rs 85; no share taxis.

Train
Mumbai (CST): *Tapovan Exp, 7618*, 1822, 4½ hrs; *Panchavati Exp, 1402*, 0702, 4¼ hrs; several others scheduled throughout the day. **Bhopal**: *Punjab Mail, 2137*, 2310, 10 hrs; *Kushinagar Exp,1015*, 0227, 12 hrs.

⊙ Directory

Nashik *p1106*
Tourist offices Maharashtra, T/1 Golf Club, Old Agra Rd, T570059. Sightseeing 0730-1500, Rs 80. **Goa**, Kirti Tours, 5 Maru Shopping Centre, Trimbak Rd, opposite Zilla Parishad, T576697. **Useful services** State Bank of India, Vivekananda Rd.

Central Maharashtra

★ Aurangabad → *Phone code: 0240 .Colour map 5, grid A5. Population: 872,700.*

A pleasantly spacious town, Aurangabad is the most common starting point for visiting the superb caves at Ellora and Ajanta. The gates are all that is left of the old city walls. There is a university, medical and engineering colleges and an airport to complement the town's industrial and commercial activities. ▸▸ *For Sleeping, Eating and other listings, see pages 1123-1126.*

Ins and outs
Getting there Chikalthana airport is 10 km east of the town with taxis, Rs 100 (a/c Rs 300) or hotel transport into the town centre. The railway station is on the southern edge of town, within walking distance of most hotels and the central bus stand just under 2 km north on Dr Ambedkar Rd.

Getting around It is easy to navigate. There are plenty of autos to see the sights, most of which are too scattered to see on foot. See Transport, page 1125, for further details.

Climate Temperature highs of 40°C in May down to 14°C in winter. Most rainfall Jun-Sep (ave 160 mm), little during other months. Best time to visit is Nov-Feb.

History
Originally known as **Khadke**, the town was founded in 1610 by Malik Ambar, an Abyssinian slave who became the 'Wazir' (Prime Minister) to the King of Ahmadnagar. It was later changed to Aurangabad in honour of the last great Mughal, Aurangzeb, who built a new citadel. His wife is buried in the Bibi ka Maqbara and he is buried in a simple grave at Rauza. It acted as the centre of operations for his Deccan campaign which occupied him for the second half of his 49-year reign.

Sights
The British **cantonment** area is in the southwest quadrant, along the Kham River and can be seen on the way to Ellora. The old Holy Trinity church is in very poor condition.

To the northwest is the **Begampura** district in which there is the attractive Pan Chakki water mill and the Bibi ka Maqbara, both worth visiting.

Aurangzeb built the 4½-m high, crenellated city walls in 1682 as defence against the Marathas. The **Killa Arrak** (1692), his citadel lay between the Delhi and Mecca Gates. Little remains, though when it was Aurangzeb's capital over 50 Maharajahs and Princes attended the court. With Aurangzeb gone, the city's significance faded. At the centre in a grove of trees lies the **Jama Masjid,** a low building with minarets and a broad band carved with Koranic inscriptions running the length of the façade.

Aurangabad

Sleeping
1 Ajinkya
2 Aurangabad Ashok
3 Devpriya
4 MTDC Holiday Camp
5 Natraj
6 Printravel
7 Shree Maya
8 Taj Residency
9 Tourist Home &
  Tourist Information
10 Vedant
11 Youth Hostel
  & Panchavati

Eating
1 Bhoj
2 Foodwalla's Tandoori
3 Mingling
4 Palace
5 Chanakya

0 metres 800
0 yards 800

Other monuments in the old city are **Kali Masjid** (1600), a six-pillared stone mosque built by Malik Ambar. In the market square is the **Shahganj Masjid** (circa 1720) which has shops on three sides. The **Chauk Masjid** (1665) was built by Shayista Khan, Aurangzeb's uncle, and has five domes. The **Lal Masjid** (1655) is in red-painted basalt. The **City Chowk**, the market in the Old City, is worth visiting.

★ **Bibi ka Maqbara** ① *Sunrise to 2000, US$2 foreigners, Rs 5 Indians, floodlit at night.* Beyond the Mecca Gate lies the mausoleum of Aurangzeb's wife, Rabia Daurani (1678). The classic lines of a garden tomb give it an impressive setting. However, closer is less impressive. Modelled on the Taj Mahal which was completed 25 years earlier, it is about half its size. Far less money was spent – one three-hundredth, by some estimates – and the comparative poverty of the finish is immediately obvious. It uses marble on the bottom 2 m of the mausoleum and four of the jali screens, but plaster elsewhere. The proportions are cramped and the minarets are too heavy in relation to the main mausoleum. Despite its failings it is one of the finest buildings of its period. The brass door carries an inscription which says Ata Ullah was the chief architect and Haibat Rai the maker of the door. On the tomb itself, in place of a marble slab, there is bare earth covered with a decorated cloth, a sign of humility. Light enters through a precisely angled shaft, allowing the early morning sun's rays to light the tomb for three minutes. The second tomb in the corner is said to be that of Rabia Daurani's nurse.

On the same side of the Kham River is the **Pan Chakki** (1696, Water Mill) ① *sunrise to 2000, US$2 foreigners, Rs 5 Indians, refreshments*, which has a white marble shrine to Baba Shah Muzaffar, the devout Aurangzeb's spiritual adviser. The pre-Mughal 17th-century mill for turning large grinding stones was powered by water channelled from a spring some distance away and released through a dam.

★ **Aurangabad Caves** ① *US$2 foreigners, Rs 5 Indians.* Three kilometres north of Aurangabad, the caves are very interesting though not a substitute for Ajanta and Ellora. Overlooking the town they fall into two groups of five each, about 1½ km apart. They date from the Vakataka (fourth and fifth centuries AD) and Kalachuri dynasties (sixth to eighth centuries), though the older Hinayana Cave 4 is believed to be at least first century, if not earlier. Waiting charges for auto-rickshaws can be high – bargain. Or, if it is cool and you are fit, you can walk back to the edge of town and get an auto-rickshaw back.

The **Western Group** are all *viharas* except for the earlier Cave 4 which is a *chaitya*. Cave 1 (incomplete) has finely carved pillars with figures on brackets and ornamentation around doorways and walls. Good views of the country around. Cave 2 has a shrine and columned hallways, a large Buddha and intricately carved panels. The larger Cave 3 has a plain exterior but superb carvings on 12 pillars of the hallway; the sanctuary has panels illustrating *jataka* stories and a fine large Buddha figure on his throne with attendant devotees illustrating contemporary dress and style. Cave 4, the *chaitya* has a rib-vaulted ceiling with a stupa containing relics and a Buddha figure outside. Cave 5 is damaged and retains little of its original carvings.

The **Eastern Group** has more sculptures of women and *Bodhisattvas*. Cave 6 has a large Buddha supporting Ganesh, indicating a later period when Hinduism was gaining in importance over Buddhism. Note the paintings on the ceiling of the balcony. Cave 7 is regarded as the most interesting of both groups. Columned shrines at each end of the verandah house images of *Hariti* (right) and six goddesses, including *Padmini* (left). The central shrine has an ambulatory passage around it and a large preaching Buddha at the back. The wall carvings depict deliverance and numerous female dancers and musicians. The importance of Tara and of Tantric Buddhism is evident here. There is little to see in the unfinished Cave 9; the carvings of pre-Nirvana figures suggest Buddhism was waning. The incomplete Cave 10 illustrates the first stages of cave excavation.

ᛝ Deogiri fortifications

The hillside around Deogiri was made steeper to make scaling the fort extremely difficult. The three concentric walls had strong gates, surrounded by a deep moat and the path climbed through the gates then up the steep slope towards the citadel. Today a new path has been cut to avoid the obstacles that were designed to prevent attackers from gaining entry. There is an L-shaped keep, a long, tortuous tunnel which could be sealed by an iron cover at the top after firing with hot coals, and a chamber which could be filled with noxious fumes. At one point the tunnel divides and meets, to fool attackers to kill each other in the dark. The only genuine access was narrowed so that an invader would have to crawl through the last few metres, making it possible for defenders to kill them on sight. The bodies were disposed of by chutes down into the crocodile infested moat 75 m below. A guide will take you through. Take a torch and allow up to two hours to get the most out of the extraordinary fort and its setting.

Excursions

Ellora, **Daulatabad** and **Rauza** are within easy reach for a full day excursion (see below). **Ajanta's caves** with magnificent paintings and rock-cut cave temples require another day. Conducted tours leave early. **Ghrishneshwara** temple, just outside Ellora, houses one of the 12 *jyotirlinga*, see page 1330.

★ Daulatabad → *Colour map 5, grid A4. 13 km from Aurangabad.*

On a volcanic lava rock towering 250 m above the surrounding countryside is the fort of **Deogiri** which dates from the Yadava period of the 11th-14th centuries although the first fort had probably been built in the ninth century. Before that it had been a Buddhist monastery. It is an extraordinary site, particularly attractive in the late afternoon when the crowds have gone. If you are lucky you may get the resident guide who takes visitors through the dark tunnels with a flaming torch.

The fort ⓘ *0600-1800, US$2 foreigners, Rs 5 Indians, allow 3 hrs, buses from Aurangabad's Central bus stand (platform 8), not all Ellora buses stop at Daulatabad.* From Ala-ud-din Khalji's capture of Deogiri in 1296 until Independence in 1947, by which time it was under the control of the Nizam of Hyderabad, the fort remained in Muslim hands. Muhammad Tughluq - see page 99 - determined to extend his power south, seized Daulatabad, deciding to make it his capital and populate it with the residents from Delhi. Thousands died as a result of his misconceived experiment. The outermost of the three main ring walls and the bastion gates were probably built by the Muslims. For snacks there are numerous dhabas opposite the entrance.

The Persian style **Chand Minar** (1435) stands at the bottom of the fort, towering as a celebration of victory like the Qutb Minar in Delhi. Its original covering of Persian blue tiles must have made it even more striking. Opposite is the **Jama Masjid** (1318), with 106 pillars taken from a Hindu temple, and a large tank. The 31 m high victory tower built by Ala-ud-din Bahmani to celebrate his capture of the fort has at its base 24 chambers and a small mosque. The path passes bastions, studded gates, a drawbridge and the **Chini Mahal** where Abdul Hasan Tana Shah, the last King of Golconda, was imprisoned in 1687 for 13 years. The 6.6-m long Kila Shikan (Fort Breaker) iron cannon is on the bastion nearby. At the end of the tunnel (see box) inside the citadel is a flight of steps leading up to the **Baradari** (Pavilion), said to be the palace of the Yadavi Queen and later Shah Jahan. The **citadel** is reached by climbing 100 further steps and passing through two more gateways. At the top is another cannon with a ram's head on the butt; the Persian inscription around the muzzle reads 'Creator of Storms'. A 'Sound and Light' show is planned.

Rauza or **Khuldabad** ('Heavenly Abode') is 22 km from Aurangabad and was once an important town around which Aurangzeb built a wall with seven gates. He died at the age of 89 on Friday (the day of his choice), 20 February 1707. There is a simple tomb to him and over 20 others of Muslim rulers of the Deccan. Since Aurangzeb wanted a simple grave as a sign of humility, open to the sky, his grave has no canopy. The marble screen around it was erected later by Lord Curzon and the Nizam of Hyderabad. Close to Aurangzeb's tomb are those of various saints, going back to the 14th century. Some are decorated with silver. There are several relics – hairs of the Prophet's beard said to multiply every year, the Prophet's robe, and the supposed remnants of trees miraculously converted to silver by the saint Saiyed Burhan-ud-Din (died 1344).

★ Ellora→ *Phone code: 02437. Colour map 5, grid A4.*

The Hindu, Jain and Buddhist caves carved in the volcanic rocks at Ellora are among the finest in India. Lying near an important ancient trade route between Ujjain in Madhya Pradesh and the west coast, the caves are thought to be the work of priests and pilgrims who used the route. ▸▸ *For Sleeping, Eating and other listings, see pages 1123-1126.*

Ins and outs

Getting there Ellora, 26 km from Aurangabad, takes about 45 mins. Hiring a taxi (Rs 650-1050) gives you flexibility to stop at other sites on the way, auto rickshaws around Rs 350. Alternatively, join a tour group (Rs 150 per person). Car and driver hired through a travel agent will cost around Rs 1,800 return (non a/c). Tour buses usually arrive at the car park, directly in front of the Kailasnatha temple itself. On holidays and in season, it is best to arrive early and see the Kailasnatha first to avoid the very large crowds.

Getting around For visiting Ellora and Ajanta, take lunch (provided by some hotels in Aurangabad) and drinks, wear a sun hat and comfortable shoes and take a strong torch (flash light).

The site

① *Closed Tue, 0900-1730, Kailashnatha entry US$5 foreigners (other caves remain free), Rs 10 Indians. Cameras may be used outside, flash photography and tripods are not allowed inside. Guides available (some European languages and Japanese spoken). 'Light passes' for groups wishing to see darker caves illuminated are available (best to join a group if on your own). Painted caves open at 1000, others at 0900 – light is better in the afternoon. For the elderly and infirm, dhoolies (chairs carried by men) are available.*

Like the caves at Ajanta, Ellora's caves were also abandoned and forgotten. 12 of the 34 caves are Buddhist (created from circa 600-800 AD), 17 Hindu (600-900 AD) and five Jain (800-1100 AD). Most have courtyards in front. They face west and are best seen in the afternoon. To see the caves in chronological order, start at the east end and visit the Buddhist Viharas first. In this way the magnificent Hindu Kailasnatha temple is seen towards the end.

The Buddhist Caves: Nos 1-10 (7th-C) 11-12 (8th-C) These belong to the **Vajrayana** sect of the Mahayana (Greater Vehicle) School. The caves include viharas (monasteries) and chaityas (chapels) where the monks worshipped. It has been suggested that the stone-cut structures were ideally suited to the climate which experienced monsoons, and rapidly became the preferred medium over more flimsy and less durable wood.

Cave 1 A simple *vihara*.

Cave 2 Adjoining is reached by a flight of steps. At the door of the cave are *dwarapala* (guardians) flanked by windows. The interior (14.5 sq m) comprises a hall supported by 12 pillars, some decorated with the pot and foliage motif. In the centre of the back wall is a 3 m high seated Buddha and two standing Buddhas while along each of the side walls are five Buddhas accompanied by Bodhisattvas and *apsaras* (celestial nymphs).

Cave 3 Similar to cave 2, having a square central chamber with a Buddha image, this time seated on a lotus. Around the walls are 12 meditation cells.

Cave 4 Two-storeyed and contains a Buddha sitting under the Bo (pipal) tree.

Cave 5 The **Maharwada**, is the largest of the single storeyed caves in this group (17.6 m by 36 m). Two rows of 10 columns each run the length of the cave, as do two raised platforms which were probably tables, suggesting that this cave was a dining hall. There are very attractive carvings on the first pillar on the left. The Buddha at the back is guarded on the left by *Padmapani*, a symbol of purity. On the right is *Vajrapani* holding a thunderbolt, the symbol of esoteric knowledge and the popular deity of the sect responsible for creating the caves. The Buddha is seated, not cross-legged on the floor as is usual, but on a chair or stool. He demonstrates some of the 32 distinctive marks: three folds in the neck, long ear lobes and the third eye. The *mudra* here signifies the Buddha's first sermon at the Deer Park at Sarnath (see page 190), and is a teaching pose.

The next four caves can be bypassed as they contain nothing new.

Cave 10 Viswakarma, or Carpenter's Cave, is the only *chaitya* (chapel) cave in the group. It was a monastery. This is on the ground floor and above are what are presumed to have been the living quarters of the monks. In front is a large courtyard

Ellora caves

approached by a flight of steps. The galleries around it have square-based pillars at the foot of which was a lion facing outwards. At the back of these galleries are two elaborately carved chapels. The exterior decoration gives the impression that instead of stone, wood was the building material, hence *Viswakarma*. The façade has a trefoil window with *apsara* groups for ornamentation. The main hall is large (26 m by 13 m, 10 m high). The curved fluted 'beams' suggest to some the upturned hull of a ship. The chamber has 28 columns, each with a vase and foliage capital, dividing it up into a nave and aisles. The aisle runs round the decorated stupa (*dagoba*) with a colossal 4.5 m 'Preaching Buddha' carved in front of it. The upper gallery, reached by an internal flight of steps, was supposed to have subsidiary shrines at either end but the left hand one was not finished. Decorating the walls are loving couples, indicating how much Buddhism had changed from its early ascetic days. You can get a view of the friezes above the pillars which show Naga queens, symbolic precursors of the monsoon, and dwarfs as entertainers, dancing and playing musical instruments.

> ❧ *The circular window at the entrance enables sunlight to be cast on it giving the cave a truly ethereal quality.*

Cave 11 (*Do Thal* – two-storeyed) was found to have a third storey in 1876 when the basement was discovered. The lowest level is a verandah with a shrine and two cells at the back of it. The middle level has eight front pillars and five rear cells of which only the central three are completed and decorated. The upper level has a porch opening into a long colonnaded hall with a Buddha shrine at the rear. Images of Durga and Ganesh suggest that the cave was later used by Hindus. Cave 11 and 12 illustrate the use of the upper levels of these caves as a residence for monks and pilgrim hostels.

Cave 12 (*Tin Thal* – three-storeyed) has cells for sleeping (note stone benches) on the lower floors but it is the figures of the Buddha which are of particular interest. The rows of seven Buddhas are symbolic of the belief that he appears on earth every 5,000 years and has already visited it seven times.

The Hindu Caves: (Nos 13-29) These caves lie in the centre of the group and are the most numerous. **Cave 13** is a plain room while **Cave 14** (**Ravana ki khai**, seventh century), is single storeyed and the last of the collection from the early period. River goddesses and guardians stand at the doorway while inside is a broken image of Durga and figurative panels on the walls of the principle deities, Vishnu, Siva, Lakshmi and Parvati. **Cave 15** (*Das Avatara*, mid-eighth century), reached by a flight of steps, has a large courtyard and is two-storeyed.

Kailasanatha Temple (mid-eighth century onwards) This the most magnificent of all the rock-cut structures at Ellora, and is completely open to the elements. It is the only building that was begun from the top. Carved out of 85,000 cubic metres of rock, the design and execution of the full temple plan is an extraordinary triumph of imagination and craftsmanship. Excavating three deep trenches into the rock, carving started from the top of the cliff and worked down to the base. Enormous blocks were left intact from which the porch, the free standing pillars and other shrines were subsequently carved. The main shrine was carved on what became the upper storey, as the lower floor was cut out below. It is attributed to the Rashtrakuta king Dantidurga (725-755 AD) and must have taken years to complete. **Mount Kailasa** (6,700 m), the home of Siva, is a real mountain on the Tibetan plateau beyond the Himalaya. Its distinctive pyramidal shape, its isolation from other mountains, and the appearance to the discerning eye of a swastika etched by snow and ice on its rock face, imbued the mountain with great religious significance to Hindus and Buddhists alike. Kailasa was seen as the centre of the universe, and Siva is Lord of Kailasa, Kailasanatha. To imitate the real snow-covered peaks, the *sikharas* here were once covered with white plaster.

The Entrance The temple is 50 m long and 33 m wide and the tower rises 29 m above the level of the court. At the entrance gate, the threshold between the profane and sacred worlds, the goddesses **Ganga** and **Yamuna** form the door jambs. Just inside are two seated sages: **Vyasa**, the legendary author of the *Mahabharata*, and **Valmiki** to whom the *Ramayana* has been ascribed. In the porch four columns carry the North Indian vase and foliage motif, a symbol of fertility and well-being. On each side of the doorway there are images of **Kubera**, the god of wealth, with other symbols of well-being such as the conch shell and the lotus. Two more figures complete the welcoming party. They are **Ganesh** (left), the elephant headed son of Siva, bringer of good fortune, and **Durga** (right), Siva's wife who fought the demons.

In the antechamber opposite is **Lakshmi**, the goddess of wealth. In the courtyard, to your right and left are free-standing elephants. On the left round the corner is a panel depicting **Kama**, the god of desire, carrying his bow and five arrows, one for each of the senses. On the far wall to your left of the entrance, behind the pillars, is the shrine of the **Three River Goddesses** - Ganga (centre), Yamuna (left) and Sarasvati (right). Symbolically they stand for purity, devotion and wisdom respectively. This is a good place to photograph the central shrine. The two carved monolithic pillars are probably stylized flagstaffs indicating royal patronage - a practice that Asoka popularized in the third century BC.

There are two distinct levels taking the worshipper from the courtyard by two staircases flanking the central hall, to the lower level with its processional path and then rising even higher to the upper level of the *mandapa*.

The Central Assembly Hall Around the central shrine is a colonnaded hall gouged from the rock, which in places overhangs menacingly. Inside this cloister is a series of panels portraying Siva and Vishnu myths. The whole can be viewed as a sort of instructional picture gallery, a purpose it served for worshippers from ancient times who could not read.

The south facing wall has *Ramayana* stories – **Ravana** offering his heads; Siva and Parvati with Nandi the bull and the lingam (creative power); Siva playing the vina; Siva and Parvati playing dice in a spirit of harmony; the marriage of Siva and Parvati; the origin of the lingam, the symbol of Siva and creative (male) energy; Siva dancing and Siva tricking Parvati. The panel on the south of the mandapa of Ravana shaking Mount Kailasa, attempting to carry it off, disturbing Parvati and her attendants, one of whom is seen frightened and fleeing, and Siva restoring order with the movement of his toe.

Along the north facing wall are stories from the *Mahabharata* above and **Krishna** legends below. The panels include **Krishna** stealing buttermilk; Vishnu as **Narasimha**, half man, half lion; Vishnu reclining on **Ananda** the serpent inbetween incarnations; Vishnu the **Preserver** Finally there is **Annapurna**, Goddess of Plenty.

The inner porch contains two panels, Siva as **Lord of Knowledge** and Siva as **Bhairava** killing the Elephant Demon.

The Main Shrine Steps lead to the upper floor which contains a *mandapa* (central hall, 17 m by 16 m) of 16 stout pillars arranged in groups of four, with aisles corresponding to the cardinal points leading to an open central area. At the far end is the *garbhagriha* (shrine) with **Ganga** and **Yamuna** as door guardians. Inside Is the *yoni lingam*, symbol of Siva's creative power. Running around the back is a passageway with five small shrine rooms off it, each with a replica of the main temple. The Nataraja painting on the *mandapa* ceiling. There are remnants of paintings on the porch ceilings (particularly to the west) where you will see *apsaras*, dwarfs and animals.

The temple rises in a pyramid, heavier and more squat looking than later towers in the north. The shape suggests enormous strength. As you leave, the path to the left leads up and around the temple, giving a bird's-eye view of the magnificent complex.

Cave 21 (Ramesvara, late sixth century) has a court with a stone Nandi bull in the middle and side shrines. A *linga* sanctuary leads off the verandah. This cave is celebrated for its fine sculptures of amorous couples and the gods. **Cave 29 (Dhumar Lena**, late sixth century) is very similar to Elephanta (see Mumbai Excursions, page 1093) in concept.

Access is from three sides, there is a spacious hall with a separate small sanctuary with a *lingam* at the end. Wall panels depict Siva legends especially as Destroyer.

Jain Caves (Nos 30-34) These caves are something of an anticlimax after the Hindu ones, but they have an aura of peace and simplicity. **Cave 30 (Chhota Kailasa**, early ninth century) was intended as a smaller scale replica of the Kailasanatha temple but was not completed. The columned shrine has 22 *tirthankaras* with *Mahavira* in the sanctuary.

Cave 32 (Indra Sabha, early ninth century) is the finest of the Jain series and is dedicated to **Mahavir**. A simple gateway leads into an open court in the middle of which stands the shrine. The walls have carvings of elephants, lions and *tirthankaras*. The lower of the two is incomplete but the upper has carvings of Ambika and also Mahavir flanked by guardians of earlier *tirthankaras*. The ceiling is richly carved with a massive lotus at the centre and you can see signs of painted figures among clouds.

★ Ajanta → *Phone code: 02438. Colour map 5, grid A5.*

The caves, older than those at Ellora, date from about 200 BC to 650 AD. They are cut from the volcanic lavas of the Deccan Trap in a steep crescent-shaped hillside in a forested ravine of the Sahyadri hills. After the late seventh century, the jungle took over and they lay unnoticed for centuries. ▶ *For Sleeping, Eating and other listings, see pages 1123-1126.*

Ins and outs

Getting there The bus or taxi drive from Aurangabad (106 km) takes 2½-3 hrs. Good tours are available from Aurangabad for Rs 200 per person (though a hired non a/c car and driver will cost around Rs 3,000). Taxis Rs 800-1000. Shilod (Silod) is a popular halting place and has a number of restaurants. About 10 km from Ajanta, the road descends from the plateau; then there are dramatic views of the Waghora valley, where the caves are located.

Getting around There is a small settlement with a restaurant, curio market and aggressive salesmen at the foot of the approach to the caves, which are carved in a horseshoe shaped cliff face. It is a short uphill walk along a stepped concrete path to the entrance. There are *dhoolis* available for hire if you wish to be carried. You can approach the caves from the river bed in the bottom of the valley, where the bus stops; the View Point, is worth getting to. You have to buy your ticket from the kiosk first, and if there is water in the stream at the bottom you have to wade through, but it is much shadier than the path cut out of the cliff. See Transport, page 1126, for further details.

Ajanta's discovery

In 1819, a party of British army officers from Madras noticed the top of the façade of Cave 10 while tiger hunting. They investigated and discovered some of the caves, describing seeing 'figures with curled wigs'. Others made exploratory trips to the fascinating caves. In 1843, James Fergusson, horrified by the ravages of the elements, requested that the East India Company do something to preserve and protect the deteriorating caves.

In 1844 **Captain Robert Gill**, an artist, was sent to copy the paintings on the cave walls. He spent 27 years living in a small encampment outside, sending each new batch of paintings to Bombay and London. After nearly 20 years his work was almost complete and displayed in the Crystal Palace in London. In December 1866 all but a few of the paintings were destroyed in a fire. Gill soldiered on for another five years before giving up, and died from illness soon afterwards. He is buried in the small European cemetery at **Bhusawal**, 60 km to the north, 27 km from Jalgaon.

66 99 Hiuen-Tsang, recorded in the seventh century (although he did not visit it), a description of the "monastery in a deep defile... large temple with a huge stone image of the Buddha with a tier of seven canopies".

The site

ⓘ *closed Mon, 0900-1730, US$5 foreigners, Rs 10 Indians. Flash photography is forbidden due to the damage caused by direct light to the paintings. Some caves have electric lights for illuminating the paintings while hawkers sell postcards very cheaply and slides for about Rs 100 a set. In the Mahayana caves with paintings there is a restriction on the number of visitors allowed in at any one time. Computer kiosks are planned, designed to show a 'virtual' history of the caves.*

Hiuen-Tsang, recorded in the seventh century (although he did not visit it), a description of the "monastery in a deep defile... large temple with a huge stone image of the Buddha with a tier of seven canopies".

The terrain in which the caves were excavated was a sheer cliff facing a deeply incised river meander. At the height of Ajanta's importance the caves are thought to have housed about 200 monks and numerous craftsmen and labourers. The masterpieces retell the life story of the Buddha and reveal the life and culture of the people of the times, royal court settings, family life, street scenes and superb studies of animals and birds. The *Jatakas* relate the Buddha's previous births – showing the progress of the soul.

Originally the entrance to the caves was along the river bed and most had a flight of stairs leading up to them. The first to be excavated was Cave 10, followed by the

Ajanta caves

⁑ The challenge of preservation

Preservation of the murals poses enormous challenges. Repeated attempts to reproduce and to restore them have faced major problems. After all but five of Robert Gill's paintings were destroyed by fire, the Bombay School of Arts sent out a team to copy the wall paintings under the guidance of the principal John Griffiths in the 1870s. The copies were stored in the Victoria and Albert Museum in London but this also had a fire in 1885, when 87 were destroyed.

In 1918 a team from Kyoto University Oriental Arts Faculty arrived at Ajanta to copy the sculptures. This they did by pressing wet rice paper against the surface to make casts which were then shipped back to Japan. In the early 1920s they were all destroyed by an earthquake.

In 1920 the Ajanta paintings were cleaned by the former Hyderabad Government under whose jurisdiction the caves lay. Two Italian restorers were commissioned, whose first priority was to fix the peeling paintings to the walls of the caves. They first injected casein between the paintings and the plastered wall, then applied shellac as a fixative. The Griffiths team from Bombay had also applied a coat of varnish to bring out the colours of the paintings.

However, these varnishes darkened over the years, rendering the murals less, not more visible. They also cracked, aiding the peeling process and the accumulation of moisture between the wall and the outer membrane. The Archaeological Survey of India is now responsible for all restoration at the site.

first Hinayana caves (in which the Buddha is not depicted in human form), on either side. Later Mahayana caves were discovered, completing the spectrum of Buddhist development in India.

There is a round trip walk, up the side of the valley where all the caves are located then down to the river to cross to the other side. An attractive low level walk through forest brings you back to the roadhead. **Caves 1, 2, 10, 16** and **17** have lights. **11, 19** and **26** are also particularly worth visiting.

Mahayana group **Cave 1** (late fifth century) is one of the finest *viharas* (monasteries), remarkable for the number and quality of its murals. A verandah with cells and porches either side has three entrances leading into a pillared hall. Above the verandah are friezes depicting the sick man, old man, corpse and saint encountered by the Buddha, who is shown above the left porch. The hall has 20 ornamented pillars, a feature of the late period caves. Five small monks' cells lead off three sides, and in the centre of the back wall is a large shrine of the Buddha supported by Indra, the rain god. At the entrance are the river goddesses Yamuna and Ganga and two snake-hooded guardians at the base.

The **murals** are among the finest at Ajanta. In the four corners are panels representing groups of foreigners. The Mahajanaka jataka (where the Buddha took the form of an able and just ruler) covers much of the left hand wall including Renunciation, and the scenes where he is enticed by beautiful dancing girls.

On either side of the entrance to the antechamber of the shrine room are two of the best known murals at Ajanta. On the left is the **Bodhisattva Padmapani** (here holding a blue lotus), in a pose of spiritual detachment, whilst on the right is the **Bodhisattva Avalokitesvara**. Together compassion and knowledge, the basis of Mahayana Buddhism, complement one another. Their size dwarfs the attendants to enhance the godlike stature of the bodhisattva. The Buddha inside the shrine is seated in the teaching position, flanked by the two carved bodhisattvas. Under the

⁞ Tempera techniques in cave painting

To prepare the rock for painting it was chiselled to leave a rough surface. Two layers of mud-plaster containing fibrous material (grain-husk, vegetable fibres and rock grit) was applied, the first coarse, the second fine. Metal mirrors must have been used by the artists, to reflect sunlight into the dark caves. It is thought that the tempera technique was used. On a dry surface, a red cinnabar outline defined the picture, filled in, possibly initially with grey and then numerous colour pigments usually mixed with glue; the completed painting was burnished to give a lustrous finish. The pigments were mainly taken from the land around, the principal ones being red and yellow ochre, white from lime and kaoline, green from glauconite, black from lamp-black and blue from imported lapis lazuli. The shellac used in restoration after 1819 was found to be cracking. Since 1951 this has been removed by the Archaeological Survey of India, with UNESCO's help. PVA is now used.

throne appears the **Wheel of Life**, with deer representing Sarnath where he preached his first sermon, see page 190.

One of the sculptural tricks that a guide will display is that when the statue is lit from the left side (as you face it), the facial expression is solemn, suggesting contemplation. Yet from the other side, there is a smile of joy, while from below it suggests tranquillity and peace. Note the paintings on the ceiling, particularly the elephant scattering the lotus as it rushes out of the pond, and the charging bull. Also look for the 'black princess' and the row of the dancer with musicians. On the way out is a pillar that has four deer sculpted skilfully, sharing the same head.

Cave 2 (sixth century) is also a *vihara* hall, 14.6 sq m with 12 pillars, with five cells on each side of the left and right hand walls and two chapels on each side of the antechamber and shrine room. The verandah in front has a side chapel at each end. The doorway is richly carved. On the left hand wall is the mural depicting **The Birth of The Buddha**. Next to this is **The 'Thousand' Buddhas**, which illustrates the miracle when the Buddha multiplied himself to confuse a heretic. On the right are dancing girls before the king, shown with striking three-dimensional effect.

The cave is remarkable for its painted ceiling, giving the effect of the draped cloth canopy of a tent. The *mandala* (circular diagram of the cosmos) is supported by demon-like figures. The Greek key designs on the border are possibly influenced by Gandharan art, 1st-3rd centuries AD. The ceiling decorations portray a number of figures of Persian appearance apparent from the style of beard and whiskers and their clothing.

The **Yaksha** (nature spirits) Shrine in the left chapel is associated with fertility and wealth. The main shrine is that of Buddha in the teaching position, again flanked by the two bodhisattvas, both holding the royal fly whisk. The **Hariti** Shrine on the right is to the ogress who liked eating children! The panel on your left as you leave the hall is a *jataka* telling the story of the Bodhisattva's life as the Pandit Vidhura.

Caves 3-7 are late fifth century. **Cave 3** has no verandah and **Cave 4** is the largest *vihara* at Ajanta, planned on an ambitious scale and not completed. The hall is 27 sq m and supported on 28 pillars. Along the walls are cells whilst at the rear is a large shrine. **Cave 5** is also unfinished.

Hinayana group A Hinayana group comes next (**Caves 6-10** and **12**, **13** and **15**) dating from the second century BC. **Cave 6** is on two levels with only seven of the 16 octagonal pillars standing. A shrine contains a seated Buddha. **Cave 7** has no hall. The verandah has two porches each supported by heavy octagonal Elephanta-type columns. These lead to four cells. These and the antechamber are profusely carved. The shrine is that of Buddha, his hand raised in blessing. **Cave 8** (first century BC) is a small vihara. **Cave 9** (circa 100 BC), a *chaitya*, is 14 m long, 14 columns run the length of each side and 11 continue round the stupa. The vaulted roof was once wooden ribbed and leads back from a huge arched *chaitya sun* window which throws light on the *stupa* at the rear. Two phases of wall painting have been identified. The earlier ones dating from the construction of the cave can be seen at the far left side and consist of a procession to a stupa as well as a thin band above the left colonnade. Above this are later Buddha figures from the Mahayana period when the figures of the Buddha on either side of the entrance were painted.

Cave 10 (circa 150 BC) is much larger. Like the previous cave the roof was once fitted with wooden ribs which subsequently collapsed. The long hall with an apse housing the *stupa* was one of the first excavated and also the first rediscovered by army officers. An inscription above the façade, now destroyed, dated the excavation to the second century BC through a generous donation by the king. The *dagoba* or *stupa* resembles that of Cave 9 and is a double storey drum. There are also paintings dating from the Hinayana and Mahayana periods. The early ones depict figures in costumes resembling those seen at Sanchi - see page 270. Traces of later paintings survive on the pillars and aisle ceilings and later Buddha figures are often superimposed on earlier works. The main subjects of the Hinayana paintings are *jataka* stories. On the rear wall are the King (in a ceremonial head-dress) and Queen approaching the Sacred Bodhi Tree, one of the earliest Ajanta paintings.

Cave 11 (originally second century BC, with sixth century alterations), has a verandah and roof painted with birds and flowers, a hall supported by four heavy pillars and a stone bench running along the right side. There are five cells and a shrine of a seated Buddha. **Caves 12** (with glauconite rock wall) and **13** (second century BC) are small *viharas*. **Cave 14** (fifth century AD) was planned on a grand scale but not completed and can be missed along with **Cave 15** (fifth century) which is a long hall with a Buddha carved out of the rock.

Later Mahayana period The remaining caves all belong to the Later Mahayana period and date from the fifth century. **Cave 16**, with kneeling elephants at the entrance and the Cobra King, has a 20 m long and 3.5 m deep verandah that carries six plain octagonal pillars. There is a good view of the ravine from here. The magnificent columned hall inside has six cells on each side and a beamed ceiling. The Teaching Buddha is seated on a lion throne. On the left the 'Dying Princess' portrays Nanda's new bride being told that he has been ordained a monk and renounced the world. Her misery is shared by all and everything around her. On the right wall are the remains of a picture of Prince Siddhartha, later the Buddha, using a bow.

Cave 17 (late fifth century) is similar to No. 16 in layout and has the greatest number of murals. On the left of the verandah is a painted Wheel of Life. Over the entrance door is a row of seven Past Buddhas and the eighth, the Maitreya or Future Buddha, above a row of amorous Yaksha couples. Sculpted deities are carved on either side.

Murals show scenes from 17 *jatakas*: the worship of the Buddha, the Buddha preaching; Hansa *jataka*, with paintings of geese; Vessantara *jataka*, where the greedy Brahmin is portrayed, grinning; the miraculous 'Subjugation of the rogue elephant', sent to kill the Buddha; and the ogress who turns into a beautiful maiden by day! There are also panels showing royal processions, warriors, an assembled congregation from which you can get an accurate and detailed picture of the times. **Cave 18** (late fifth century) has little of merit and can be missed.

Cave 19 (late fifth century) is a Mahayana *chaitya* hall and was painted throughout. The façade is considered to be one of the most elegant in terms of execution and elaborate ornamentation, and has the arched *chaitya* window set into it. The interior is in the layout seen before, two rows of richly decorated columns leading up to and around the back of the standing Buddha, which here is in front of the slender stupa. This tall shrine has a triple stone umbrella above it. Note the seated Nagaraja with attendants.

Cave 20 is comparatively small and has imitation beams carved into the ceiling.

Later caves The final few caves belong to the seventh century and are a separate and distinct group at the farthest end of the horseshoe near the waterfall. Only one, **Cave 26**, need be visited. **Cave 21** (early seventh century) has a fallen verandah with flanking chapels. **Cave 24** was intended to be the largest *vihara* but was not completed.

Cave 26 is a large *chaitya hall*. A partly damaged columned façade stretches across the front with the customary side chambers at each end. The 3 m high window is flanked by sculptured Buddha reliefs. Inside, 26 pillars run in an elongated semi circle around the cylindrical *stupa* which is decorated with Buddhas. The walls are decorated with sculpture, including the temptations by Mara's daughters, but the most striking being a 9 m reclining image of the Parinirvana Buddha, about to enter Nirvana, his death mourned by his followers.

The walk back along the promenade connecting the shrines is pleasant enough but the return via the river, waterfall and forest walkway is delightful. Steps lead down from Cave 16 (with the carved elephants). The hilltop opposite the caves offers a fine view of the horseshoe shaped gorge.

Jalgaon Jalgaon, 64 km from Ajanta on the NH6, is the rail junction for the Ajanta Caves. It was once at the centre of a savannah forest region, the habitat of tigers, leopards and other game. Now it has become an important cotton growing area and is quite interesting to walk around.

The Eastern Deccan → *Colour map 5, grid A5, B4 and B5.*

To the east of Aurangabad the road and railway go down the gentle slope of the great basin of the Godavari. Ancient erosion surfaces covered in some of India's richest black lava soils dominate the landscape. Rainfall gradually increases eastwards, and on the lower land the soils are some of the best in the peninsula – rich black soils derived from the lava. Though on the higher land the much poorer red soils surface. Given the relative dryness an extraordinarily high percentage is cultivated. Sorghum (*jowar*) and short stapled cotton dominate. In the west, pearl millet. ▸▸ *For Sleeping, Eating and other listings, see pages 1123-1126.*

Jalna ① *regular buses from Lonar (2 hrs), Aurangabad (2 hrs) and Nanded (5 hrs), Aurangabad trains daily at 0510, 0828, 1259 and 2010, 1-1½ hrs, Mumbai trains* Devgiri Exp, *1004, 2010, 9½ hrs*; Tapovan Exp, *7618, 1259, 10 hrs*, Secunderabad Kacheguda Exp, *7663, 2020, 11¾ hrs*, is the town to which **Abul Fazl**, who wrote the *Ain i Akbari*, was exiled and ultimately murdered by Bir Singh Deo of Orchha, see page 286, at the instigation of Jahangir. The area is dotted with forts. There is a *Dak Bungalow* and a *Rest House* in the town.

Lonar ① *by bus from Jalna (75 km, 2 hrs), Jintur (50 km, 1½ hrs); Ajanta/Fardapur (137 km) via Buldana and Mehkar (total 5 hrs) so best to spend a night,* is famous for its remarkable 2-km wide meteor crater, believed to have formed 50,000 years ago, which has temple ruins at the base. The pool of green water at the bottom, which you can walk down to, has its unique eco-system.

Nanded Guru Gobind Singh, the 10th Sikh guru, was assassinated here in 1708, see page 1345. There is an important *gurudwara* 1,500 m from the station, which is rumoured to be covered in gold in the near future. Today Nanded (Nander), which stands on the river

Godavari, is an important administrative and commercial town. It is also on the main railway line between Hyderabad/Secunderabad and Aurangabad/Nashik.

Paithan One of the oldest cities of the Deccan, Paithan is on the north bank of the Godavari River as it leaves the Nath Sagar reservoir. The **Jayakwadi Project** at Nath Sagar is a large earthen dam and reservoir. The Left Bank scheme is already providing irrigation all the way down the Godavari to Nanded 140 km to the east, and the equivalent Right Bank scheme is in progress.

Paithan is famous for a special kind of silk sari with brocaded gold borders and *pallu* (end-piece). Motifs of geese, parrots, peacocks and stylized leaves, flowers and creepers in dark greens, red and blue are brocaded against the golden background.

Ahmadnagar → *Phone code: 0241. Colour map 5, grid B4. Population: 307,500.*
Ahmadnagar, an historic Muslim town, has several Islamic monuments to visit. The town was founded in 1490 by Ahmad Nizam Shah Bahri, the son of a Brahmin from Vijayanagar who converted to Islam. His dynasty ruled the territory stretching from Aurangabad to Bassein until 1636. Its Islamic history reflects strong Persian influence, both architecturally in the Persian style Husaini Mosque, and theologically in the presence of Shi'a Muslims from Persia in the court.

Sights Alamgir's Dargah is a small enclosure near the cantonment. **Aurangzeb**, who had begun his long Deccan campaign 24 years earlier, died here on 3 March 1707 and the dargah marks his temporary resting place before his body was moved to Aurangabad. To the east is a white marble **Darbar Hall**, well worth visiting for the view from the roof.

The fort (1599) is 1 km to the east of the city, 4 km northeast of the railway station. Circular, it has an 18 m high wall reinforced with 22 bastions. The fort is now occupied by the army, but entry is possible (sign in at gate), to see the 'Leaders' Room' where Nehru and 11 colleagues spent 1942-45, now a small museum. No photography in fort.

Among the numerous **mosques** in the city are the small but attractive Qasim (1500-08), the Husaini, with its Persian style dome, and the Damadi (1567) with its splendid carved stonework. The Malik-i-Maidan cannon now standing on the Lion Bastion at Bijapur (see page 1006), was cast here. The well-preserved **Tomb** of Nizam Shah is in a large garden on the left bank of the Sina River.

Junnar The birthplace of **Sivaji** in 1627, Junnar is another rock-cut cave temple site. The hill fort contains a monument commemorating Sivaji and a temple. On the east side of the hill there are more than 50 **Buddhist caves**. Most are *viharas* (monasteries) and date from the second century BC to the third century AD. They comprise the **Tulja Lena Group**, 2 km west of the town, which includes an unusual circular *chaitya* (chapel, Cave 3) with a dome ceiling. The **Bhuta Lena Group** is on the side of Manmodi Hill, 1,500 m south of the town. The unfinished *chaitya* hall (Cave 40) has a well preserved façade containing reliefs of Laxmi. The **Ganesh Lena Group** is 4 km south of Junnar on the Lenyadri Hill. Cave 7 is a *vihara* with 19 cells leading off the main congregational hall and a colonnaded verandah. The octagonal columns are repeated in the *chaitya* hall next door (Cave 6).

Shivner Fort rises over 300 m above the plain and is approached from the south by a track that passes over the moat, through four gates, then dog-legs up the final stretch to the plateau. Sivaji's birthplace is to the north and not far from it is a ruined mosque. There are four tanks running down the centre. In the third century the site was a Buddhist *vihara* and on the east face there are about 50 rock cells. Maloji Bhonsla, Sivaji's grandfather, was granted the fort in 1599. Sivaji did not remain in it long as it was captured by the Mughals from the early 1630s. Several attempts to win it back failed.

Bhimashankar Completely off the beaten track, the pilgrim site of Bhimashankar can be reached by road from Shivner or from the NH50 at Narayangaon. However, even

Listings: Central Maharashtra

● Sleeping

Aurangabad *p1108, map p1109*
Some hotels offer discounts between Apr
and Sep. Most will provide packed lunch for
trip to the caves. Most are 24-hr check out.
AL-A Residency (Taj), 8N-12 CIDCO (8 km
railway, 9 km airport), T381106, F381053,
trhgm.aug@tajgroup.sprintrpg.ems.vsnl.in.
40 large rooms, quiet swimming, excellent
service, imposing building in lovely gardens,
on outskirts, beautiful gardens, difficult for
the disabled (no lift, some rooms on 1st floor,
reception and restaurant on ground floor).
A Ambassador Ajanta, Airport Rd,
Chikalthana, 4 km centre, T485211, F484367,
amauabad@bom4.vsnl.net.in. 92 rooms,
excellent food (can watch chef preparing
meal), excellent pool in pleasant gardens
(non-residents, Rs 300), squash, tennis, quiet,
good service, generous discount for single
occupancy. Recommended.
A Rama International (Welcomgroup),
Airport Rd, R 3 Chikalthana, 4 km centre,
T485411, F484768, ramaintl@bom4.
vsnl.net.in. 90 rooms, central a/c, restaurant
(mini bar), quiet, large gardens, pool.
A-B President Park, Airport Rd, T486201,
F484823, hpp@bom4.vsnl.net.in. Impressive
newer hotel, large grounds, environment
friendly, 60 a/c rooms focusing around
attractive large pool (non-residents, Rs 150),
excellent vegetarian food, tennis.
B Aurangabad Ashok (ITDC), Dr Rajendra
Prasad Marg, T332491, F331328, aubaashok@
agd2.dot.net.in. 66 a/c rooms, pleasant
restaurant, bar, good shops, small pool,
reliable car hire and travel desk.
B Khemi's Inn, 11 Town Centre, CIDCO (4 km
from town, first left after *Ambassador Ajanta*,
then first right), T484868, khemis@vsnl.com.
10 spotless a/c rooms with hot bath, good
home cooking, quiet, pleasant garden, has
the feel of an English B & B, very hospitable.
C-D Holiday Camp (MTDC), Station Rd,
T331513, F331198. 48 rooms (22 a/c) with bath
and mosquito net, pleasant, busy, but poor
restaurant, bar, Tourist office, checkout 0900.

There are several budget hotels east of the
Central Bus Stand:
D-E Ajinkya, T335601. Ok rooms, some a/c.
D-E Printravel, Dr Ambedkar Rd, T/F352448,
burzin1@vsnl.com. Old-fashioned but large
clean rooms with bath, good *Patang*
restaurant, very well run. Recommended.
E Devpriya, Circular building near Central Bus
Stand Rd, Dr Ambedkar Rd, T339032. 62 ok
rooms in family hotel (hot water in morning),
restaurant, bar, travel desk, good value.
E Shree Maya, Bharuka Complex, behind
Tourist Office, Padampura Rd, T333093,
F331043, shrimaya@bom4.vsnl.net.in.
23 modern, clean, rooms with hot shower,
8 a/c, restaurant, will arrange bus tickets, 24-hr
check out, mixed reports about management.
E-F Railway Retiring Rooms, T331015.
3 rooms (1 a/c), 4 bedded dorm.
F Panchavati, off Station Rd, Padampura,
T328755. 25 clean simple rooms with bath,
good restaurant/bar, friendly, good value.
F Tourist Home, Station Rd, T337212.
26 rooms with bath (Rs 150), friendly, meals.
F Youth Hostel, Station Rd, Padampura,
T334892. 3 rooms, 40 beds in good
segregated dorms (Rs 45), clean, well run,
breakfast/evening meals (gates locked early
so you may need to climb over!), very good
value, recommended, reservations: a week's
notice Aug-Feb with a day's payment.

Ellora *p1112*
C-E Kailas, near the bus stand, T41043,
www.kailas.com. 25 decent rooms in group
of 'cottages', best a/c face the caves, dorm in
annexe, restaurant, very pleasant garden,
good service.
E-F Rock Art Gallery, T44552. 9 very simple,
rooms, 'art' including copies of murals.

Ajanta *p1116*
D Travellers' Lodge (MTDC), T4226. Has
4 clean rooms , chilled beer.

Fardapur
C-F Holiday Resort (MTDC), T/F4230, 5 km
from Ajanta caves. 12 basic rooms with bath

(mosquito net vital, not provided), 16 a/c rooms in gardens are better value, dorm (mattress only, Rs 100), restaurant.
D-E Resort Extension, T4289. 12 rooms and dorm.

Jalgaon *p1121*
D-E Tourist Resort, Nehru Chowk, Station Rd, T225192. 26 clean spacious rooms with bath, 4 a/c, some have TV.
E Plaza, 241 Navi Peth, Station Rd, T227354. 10 air-cooled rooms with bath and TV, very clean, hot water in bucket, very helpful and friendly manager. Highly recommended.
E-F Morako, 346 Navi Path, between railway and Bus Stand, T226621. 50 large rooms, with shared bath, bit shabby but clean enough, restaurant (Indian).

Lonar *p1121*
E-F simple, clean places to stay.

Nanded *p1121*
D-E Ashiana Park, opposite Kala Mandir, off Doctor's Lane, near bus stand, T02462-36412. 21 good rooms, young enthusiastic manager, friendly, good value for a night halt.

Paithan *p1122*
C-D Goradia, off Pimpalwadi Rd, T55257. 80 a/c rooms, Indian restaurant.
D Sai Leela, 9/5 Pimpalwadi Rd, near Temple, T02766-55139, F55270. 72 rooms, some a/c, restaurant, pool.
D-E Pilgrim's Inn (MTDC), near Sai Baba Shrine, T02766-55194, F55198. 50 rooms (10 a/c), Indian restaurant.
E Lakeview Resort, at Jayakwadi, by the dam, has 13 rooms, restaurant, beer.

Ahmadnagar *p1122*
D Sanket, Tilak Path, Station Rd, T/F358701. 30 rooms, some a/c, restaurant.
E-F Swastik, Station Rd, 1 km from station, T357575. 25 rooms.

⊙ Eating

Aurangabad *p1108, map p1109*
⍦⍦⍦ Ambassador, ITDC, in hotel. Good Indian and Western.
⍦⍦⍦ Ashok, ITDC, in hotel.

⍦⍦⍦ President Park. International. Restaurant and coffee shop offer a varied choice of vegetarian dishes.
⍦⍦ Angeethi, next to *Jet Airways*, Jalna Rd, T441988. Excellent Marathi specialities, book ahead.
⍦⍦ Chanakya, Station Rd. North Indian. Fashionable, a/c, well-prepared ("best Malai Kofta"), part outdoors, bar.
⍦⍦ Foodwalla's Tandoori, 500 m from *Holiday Camp*. Indian. A/c, tender chicken preparations, popular, good value, bar.
⍦⍦ Mastercook at *Hotel Mayur*, Jalna Rd, is popular locally.
⍦⍦ Mingling, at *Hotel Rajdoot*, JL Nehru Marg. Chinese.
⍦⍦ Palace, Shahgunj, Indian (Mughlai).
⍦ Bhoj, Ambedkar Marg (above *Manas Hotel*) near Central Bus Stand. Excellent vegetarian food. Friendly (arrive at 1845 to listen to *puja* in the kitchen with chanting and cymbals).
⍦ Guru, Station Rd. Punjabi.
⍦ Youth Hostel, best value *thalis*.

Ellora *p1112*
Numerous restaurants for lunch on the road from Aurangabad.
Hotel Ujwal, 'rice, sambhar and crud'!
Restaurant, MTDC. Unexciting food, chilled beer, garden, souvenirs and postcards.

Ajanta *p1116*
Foodwallas, entrance of *Travellers' Lodge*. Open until 1700, unexciting food, poor service, dirty toilets.

Jalgaon *p1121*
Anjali by the station, great spicy *thalis*.
Bombay, opposite, excellent food, well-stocked bar.
Shreyas, 201 Navi Peth. Inexpensive South Indian vegetarian. Good bakery and ice cream shop on Station Rd.

Nanded *p1121*
Gujarati Bhoj Nalya (sign in Hindi – look for *"High Class Veg Lunch Home"*), near bus stand. Excellent food in unlikely looking *dhaba*.

Ahmadnagar *p1122*
Panchratna, Shivaji Chowk, T359202. Cheap Indian and Continental cuisine.

● *Phone codes   Aurangabad: 0240; Ellora: 02437; Ajanta: 02438; Ahmadnagar: 0241*

● Entertainment

Aurangabad *p1108, map p1109*
Cinema
Goldie Cinema, Station Rd, T328221.
Shows some English language films in a/c
comfort, Rs 20-35, ask hotel reception for
details and programme.

Swimming
Some top hotels open their pools to
non-residents for a fee, eg **Ambassador
Ajanta**, Rs 250 (includes other sporting
facilities), **Aurangabad Ashok**, Rs 125;
President Park, Rs 125; and **Vedant** (Quality
Inn), Station Rd, T350701, Rs 150.

● Festivals and events

Aurangabad *p1108, map p1109*
Feb/Mar: Mahashivratri, large fair at
Ghrishneshwara Temple, near Ellora and
Ellora Yatra.

○ Shopping

Aurangabad *p1108, map p1109*
Shops usually open 1000-2000, closed Sun.
    The city is known for its handwoven Himroo
shawls (brocades occasionally with Ajanta
motifs), and special textile weaves - *Mashru,
Patihani silk* and *Kinkhab* as well as artificial silk.
You can also get good decorative lacquer work,
Bidriware and agate articles. Main shopping
areas are City Chowk, Gulmandi, Nawabpura,
Station Rd, Shahganj, Sarafa, Mondha.
In Shahganj: Cottage Industries.
Station Rd: Silk Loom Fabrics and Govt.
Emporium, opposite *Holiday Resort*.
At Zaffar Gate, Mondha Rd:
Aurangabad Himroo Industry, factory
showroom producing beautiful Ajanta
patterns in silk, the young English speaking
owner is very informative, recommended.

▲ Activities and tours

Aurangabad *p1108, map p1109*
Tour companies
Ashoka Travels, Station Rd, T320816, Mr
Karolkar arranges hotels, cars and excursions,
charges fairly and is dependable.
Classic, TRC Building, Station Rd, T337788,
F338556, classictours@vsnl.com, and at

Ambassador Ajanta. Helpful and efficient; car
hire, ticketing, hotels, Ajanta/Ellora and city
tour, Rs 200/150 per person.
MTDC (and others) operate good
sightseeing to Ajanta, Ellora and the City.
Ajanta tour highly recommended.
Daulatabad and Ellora visits too many places.
From MTDC *Holiday Camp* (pick-up from
major hotels) and then **Central Bus Stand**
(about 45 mins later): Ellora (closed Tue) and
City, 0800-1700, Rs 150; Ajanta (closed Mon)
0800-1700, Rs 200; book at Window 1
(behind book stall) at Bus Stand – check
timing. From **MTDC**. See also Directory.

● Transport

Aurangabad *p1108, map p1109*
Air
The airport is 10 km from city centre.
Transport to town: Taxi, Rs 150 (Rs 300
through travel agents); **Indian Airlines**, near
Rama International, Airport Rd, T485421,
1000-1700, Sun closed. Airport, T482111;
daily flights to **Delhi** and **Mumbai**. Jet
Airways, 4 Vidya Nagar, Jalna Rd, T441770.
0900-1800. Airport T484269. 1830-2130.
Daily flight to **Mumbai**.

Bicycle
Bicycle hire: ('cycle taxi') from shops near Rly
station and Central Bus Stand (CBS), Rs 20
per day.

Bus
Local Services to **Daulatabad**, and **Ellora**
(45 mins) from platform 7; **Ajanta** from
platform 8 (3 hrs), **Jalgaon** (4½ hrs, **Fardapur**
etc) from CBS. Also services to **Bangalore**,
Hubli, Hyderabad, Indore, Nashik and **Pune**.
Long distance MRTC operates a/c luxury
coaches to **Mumbai** (388 km) 10 hrs from
CBS (Central Bus Stand), Dr Ambedkar Rd, Rs
200. To **Pune**, Whilfood Tours (T477844) bus
depart 0730, Rs 100. Others, to **Bidar,
Bijapur, Hyderabad, Indore, Nagpur** and
Nashik (3 hrs), **Solapur** (8-9 hrs).

Car
Car hire: Rs 850 per day (Rs 1050, a/c) from
Aurangabad Transport Syndicate, *Hotel
Rama International,* T486766.

Rickshaw

Auto-rickshaw: Insist on using meter, about Rs 5 per km. Day hire to visit Daulatabad and Ellora Rs 350 from bus station.

Taxi

Rates Rs 350 for 4 hrs, 40 km. Rs 650 for 8 hrs, 80 km.

Train

Beware of touts at the station offering package tours to Ellora and Ajanta. Easier by local bus. **Mumbai**: *Devgiri Exp, 1004*, 2320, 8½ hrs; *Tapovan Exp, 7618*, 1440, 8¼ hrs. **Secunderabad (Hyderabad)**: *Kacheguda Exp 7663*, 1930, 13½ hrs. For **Delhi**: change at **Manmad**. From Aurangabad: 0627, 1010, 1440, 2105, 2-2½ hrs; from Manmad: *Punjab Mail, 2137*, 0020, 20 hrs; *Goa Exp, 2779*, 1010, 20½ hrs (HN); *Karnataka Exp, 2627*, 1550, 20¼ hrs; *Lakshadweep Exp, 2617*, 1900, 21 hrs (HN); *Jhelum Exp, 1077*, 2355, 21½ hrs;

Ajanta *p1116*

Bus

Regular bus service from Fardapur (5 km from Ajanta Caves) to **Ellora** and **Aurangabad** (3 hrs), and **Jalgaon** (1½ hrs). Some buses also go direct from the caves to Aurangabad.

Taxi/rickshaw

Taxis and auto-rickshaws can be hired for the day for visiting the sights.

Train

The caves can also be visited from Jalgaon 59 km, which has the nearest railway station. *Gitanjali Exp* (convenient from Kolkata) does not stop at Jalgaon so best to get off at Bhusawal.

Jalgaon *p1121*

Bus

Local The bus stand is about 1 km from the railway; auto-rickshaws Rs 8-10 for transfer. **Long distance** Direct buses to Ajanta from Bus Stand, 0815, 1030. Private buses from Station Rd for **Aurangabad**, **Indore**, **Hyderabad**, **Nagpur**, **Pune**, most between 2100-2200. Some via **Fardapur** (1½ hrs), go to Ajanta before continuing to Aurangabad (1st dep 0700, 4 hrs, Rs 50); pleasant, interesting journey.

Train

Mumbai (CST): *Punjab Mail* 2138, 2350, 7¾ hrs; *Kushinagar Vidarbha Exp* 1016, 2205, 7¾ hrs. **Delhi** via **Bhopal** and **Agra**: *Punjab Mail*, 2137, 0215, 18 hrs.

Nanded *p1121*

Bus

Connections to many destinations. Several agents by bus stand for private buses.

Train

Aurangabad: Mumbai trains and *Mudkhed Manmad Exp, 7688*, 0510, 5 hrs. **Bangalore**: *Link Exp, 6591A*, 0600, 24½ hrs. **Mumbai (CST)** : *Tapovan Exp, 7618*, 1015, 12½ hrs; *Devgiri Exp, 1004*, 1715, 12½ hrs. **New Delhi**: *Sachkhand Exp, 2715*, 0830 (not Mon, Thu), 29 hrs (onto **Amritsar**, 37¼ hrs).

Ahmadnagar *p1122*

Bus

Regular buses to **Mumbai**, **Pune** and other towns in the state.

Train

Bangalore: *Karnataka Exp, 2628*, 1820, 19½ hrs. **Bhopal**: *Goa Exp, 2779*, 0703, 12 ½ hrs; *Jhelum Exp, 1077*, 2040, 12½ hrs (on to **New Delhi**, 24¾ hrs). **Pune**: *Jhelum Exp* 1078, 1200, 4 hrs; *Goa Exp 2480*, 1300, 4½ hrs (on to **Vasco de Gama (Goa)**, 18¾ hrs).

⊙ Directory

Aurangabad *p1108, map p1109*

Banks State Bank of India, Kranti Chowk, Rajendra Prasad Marg (Adalat Rd), junction of Paithan Darwaza Rd, set back from Rd, deals in foreign currency. **Hospitals** Medical College Hospital, T24411, northwest of town; Govt Hospital, Shahganj. **Post office** GPO: Juna Bazar Chowk. Cantt Post Office. **Tourist offices** Govt of India, Krishna Vilas, Station Rd, T331217. Open 0830-1830 weekdays, 0830-1330 Sat. Airport Counter open at flight times; MTDC, *Holiday Resort*, Station Rd, T331513, F331198. Open 0700-2100. Very helpful with practical information. Also more helpful officer at railway station, 0430-0830, 1100-1600, Tue-Sun 0900-1600.

Southern Maharashtra

Pune → *Phone code: 020. Colour map 5, grid B3. Population: 2.54 million.*

After the small towns and seemingly endless spaces of the Deccan plateau, Pune comes as a vibrant surprise. Touched perhaps by the élan of Mumbai, within commuting distance down the ghat, the town comes to life in the early evening with open-air cafés and pavements crowded with young people out to enjoy themselves in a modern, cosmopolitan atmosphere, a place to see and be seen. It is an important and respected university town and one of the fastest growing IT centres of India, whilst the Osho Commune continues to attract large numbers of westerners seeking spiritual growth, at a price. Descriptions of the city's site range from 'absolutely flat' to 'surrounded by hills', the contrast depending on the direction from which you approach it. ▶▶ *For Sleeping, Eating and other listings, see pages 1135-1141.*

Ins and outs

Getting there The airport, 10 km to the northeast has flights from major cities. There are airport buses, taxis and rickshaws to the city centre. Pune is on the main railway line south from Mumbai and is served by frequent buses. Buses from the north terminate largely at Sivaji Nagar Bus Stand to the northwest of town, and those from the south at Swargate, 3 km to the south. The Railway Bus Stand, just north of the town centre, serving the city and Mumbai, is within walking distance of hotels, restaurants and the MG Rd shops. Another cluster of hotels and popular restaurants are in the Deccan Gymkhana area to the west.

Getting around Pune is very spread out so it is best to hire an auto-rickshaw to get around. The museums and the Osho Commune are a long walk from the hotel areas. See Transport, page 1140, for further details.

Climate The climatic contrast between Pune and the ghats just 70 km away is astonishing. The monsoon winds of Jun-Sep drop most of their rain on the ghats themselves, and rainfall totals fall from over 3,500 mm a year to Pune's 715 mm.

Background

The early home of Sivaji, Pune became the Maratha capital in 1750. After a period under the **Nizam of Hyderabad**'s rule it came under British control in 1817, who then developed it as a summer capital for Mumbai and as a military cantonment. It is now a major growth centre with a booming computer software industry.

For all its connections with the Marathas there are few physical reminders of their power. The Campsite has wide streets with a British colonial feel while old Pune still has narrow streets, old shops and brick and mud houses. The town is renowned for its military cantonment and educational and scientific institutions.

Sights

The city stands on the right bank of the Mutha River before its confluence with the Mula and was divided up into 19 peths (wards). Some were named after the days of their weekly market, others after well-known people.

Near the railway station is the English Gothic style **Sassoon Hospital** (1867). Nearby is the Collectorate and the old Treasury. To the southwest is the **Oleh David Synagogue** (1867), sometimes known locally as the 'Red Mandir', and Sir David Sassoon's Tomb. **St Mary's Church** (1825) to the south was consecrated by Bishop

Heber, who toured the country extensively in the 1830s. St Patrick's Cathedral is beyond the Racecourse. Immediately north are the **Empress Gardens**.

Moving back to the west by the river are **Visram Bagh**, a very attractive Maratha

Sleeping		Eating
1 Blue Diamond	4 Pride	1 Burger King
2 Holiday Inn	5 Saras	2 German Bakery
3 Le Meridien	6 Srimaan	3 Just Baked
	7 Sunderban	

Palace. Now used to house Govt offices and a post office, the entrance and balcony have beautifully carved woodwork. The **Shaniwar Wada** palace (1736) ① *0830-1800, US$2 foreigners, Rs 5 Indians, sound and light show planned*, built by Baji Rao, the

Related maps
A Deccan Gymkhana area, page 1131
B Pune centre, page 1130

4 Sangamitra
5 Zamu's Place

last Peshwa's grandfather, was burnt down in 1827. Only the massive outer walls remain. The main entrance is by the iron-spiked Delhi Gate. Elephants were used for crushing people to death in the nearby street. The gardens were irrigated and contained the **Hazari Karanje** (thousand jet fountain) - in fact there were only 197 jets.

Cross the river by **Sivaji** (Lloyd) **Bridge** into Sivaji Road. Along this are the Pataleshwar Temple and the Military College (1922) – a 9-m high statue of Sivaji (sculpted by VP Karkomar), stands in front. The **Sangam** (Wellesley) **Bridge** (1875) is near the confluence of the rivers. **Garden Reach** (1862-4), 300 m beyond, is the family house of the influential Sassoon family. The main road then passes the **Institute of Tropical Meteorology** and the white domed Observatory.

Raj Bhavan (Government House, 1866) designed by James Trubshawe is in Ganeshkhind. Nearby is the impressive main building of the **University** of Poona in a sprawling campus. Three kilometres north, in Aundha Road, are the **Botanical Gardens**. From here on the way to Holkar's Bridge is **All Saints Church** (1841), which contains the regimental colours of the 23rd Bombay Light Infantry. One kilometre to the southeast is the Roman Catholic **Chapel of St Ignatius**. Cross the river by the Holkar's Bridge to the **Tomb of Vithoji Holkar**, trampled by an elephant in 1802, and the adjacent Mahadeo Temple built in his memory. Sir Henry St Clair Wilkins designed the **Deccan College** (1864).

To the east, on Ahmednagar Road, is the former **Palace of the Aga Khan** (1860) who was attracted to Pune by the horse racing. Mahatma Gandhi was placed under house arrest here and his wife Kasturba died here. The small **Gandhi National Memorial** ① *0900-1745, Rs 2*, museum with personal memorabilia is worth a visit. Kasturba Gandhi's memorial tomb (*samadhi*) is on the estate. South of the Bund Garden (Fitzgerald) Bridge are the riverside **Bund Gardens**, a popular place for an evening stroll.

Pune is home to the **Osho Commune** International (formerly 'Rajneesh Ashram') ① *tours Rs 10 (1-hr part tour, part video "not very interesting"; 1030,1430; booking 0930-1300, 1400-1600), other visitors are screened for HIV (recent certificate or blood test Rs 150-300); day Pass, US$3.25, including meditation, entertainment, discussions, courses cost from US$1,000 per month, full details from www.osho.com*, in Koregaon Park, originally set up by the controversial Bhagwan Rajneesh

Pune centre

Sleeping ■
1 Ashirwad
2 Amir
3 Aurora Towers
4 Dreamland
5 Homeland
6 National
7 Sagar Plaza
8 Woodland

Eating ●
1 Chinese Room & Latif's
2 Coffee House
3 Dorabjee'se
4 George
5 Kamling
6 Kwality
7 Marz-O-Rin
8 Nankin
9 Touché & Manneys Books

66 99 Described by the Wall Street Journal as the "spiritual Disneyland for disaffected First World yuppies", some disenfranchised indigenous followers claim that the commune is remote-controlled from New York!

(Osho). Rajneesh died in 1990. The lushly landscaped 24-acre commune offers numerous programmes with an emphasis on meditation. The commune has gone to great lengths to convert a former rubbish tip in next door Koregaon Park into a beautifully maintained and landscaped garden, the Shunyo Park. Critics point out that "the inmates claim they follow no God, have no temple nor ritual, and are all individuals, yet, they worship the Bhagwan, meet in the same place, at the same time every day to get 'spiritual', dressed in identical robes". The plush 'Club Meditation' with all facilities attracts thousands daily. Described by the Wall Street Journal as the "spiritual Disneyland for disaffected First World yuppies", some disenfranchised indigenous followers claim that the commune is remote-controlled from New York!

Parvati Hill, just south of the Mutha Right Bank Canal, has Hindu temples and commands excellent views over the town and surrounding countryside. Pune also has the **National Defence Academy** which trains cadets for the three defence services. There are parks and gardens dotted around the city.

Deccan Gymkhana area

Museums

Raja Kelkar Museum ① *1378 Shukrawar Peth, closed 26 Jan and 15 Aug, 0830-1800, foreigners Rs 120, Indians Rs 10, good catalogue, worth a visit, has a* private collection focusing on traditional Indian arts including carved temple doors, musical instruments, pottery, miniature paintings, nutcrackers, brass padlocks and lamps. The vast collection can only be displayed in rotation.

Tribal Museum ① *1000-1700, free,* is an excellent, small museum of items relating to Maharashtra's tribal heritage, research encouraged. The 12 sections include domestic life (utensils, ornaments, musical instruments and house patterns), agriculture, weapons and wood carving.

Excursions

Sinhagarh is 24 km southwest of Pune. The 'Lion Fort', situated in the Bhuleshwar range, was a small hill station during the

Map labels:
Fergusson College, Botanical Garden, Ghole Rd, Phule Museum, British Library, Shirole Rd, Paranjpe Path, Prabhat Rd, Bhandarkar Rd, Popular Book House, Deccan Gymkhana, Madhav Chemists, Sai Service, Mutha River, Sambhaji Bridge, Laxmi Rd, Karve Rd, To Chinese Room Oriental, Jangli Maharaj Rd, FC Rd, Gokhale Rd, Bajirao Rd

N

0 metres 200
0 yards 200

■ Sleeping
1 Ajit
2 Ashish Plaza & Ashiyana
3 Ketan
4 Oakwood
5 Shreyas

● Eating
1 Ice Cream Parlour
2 Khyber
3 Roopali
4 Subhadra
5 Vaishali

British period. On the way you pass the **Khadakwasla reservoir** on the Mutha River. The dam was constructed in 1879, the first large dam in the Deccan. The roughly triangular ruined **fort** stands in a beautiful setting on a hill 700 m above the land below. The ascent is steep. To the north and south are cliffs topped with 12-m high basalt walls. There were two entrances, the Pune Gate (northeast) and Kalyan Gate (southwest), both protected by three successive gates. On the west side of the hill the wall was continued across a gorge, creating a dam. Muhammad Tughluq, see page 99, captured the fort in 1328, and in 1486 Malik Ahmad, founder of Ahmadnagar took it. Nearly 200 years later the Marathas captured it in what has become a legendary feat of bravery and skill by the commander scaling the cliffs at night and taking the garrison by surprise. Near the dammed gorge is a monument (1937) to the leader of the campaign, Tanaji Malusara. To the western end is a small, covered, natural spring (known as 'Dev Taki' or 'God's Tank'), which yields cool, fresh sweet water throughout the year. Sinhagarh is a popular day out for people from Pune. Try the locally produced curd served in black clay pots with jeera seeds, salt and sugar.

Lonavla → *Phone code: 02114. Colour map 5, grid B3. Population: 55,700.*

Lonavla's reputation as a hill station for Mumbai is scarcely a preparation for the narrow, densely packed street astride the National Highway. The expressway from Mumbai to Bangalore now shadows the town. Trinket and knick-knack shops and *chikki* stalls piled high with the famous peanut brittle type sweet, is the strung out reality of the town. Yet it has a reasonable range of hotels and pleasant walks and is good as a base for the Karla and Bhaja Caves and also the Rajmachi, Lohagon and Visapur Forts nearby. The railway journey to Kalyan is interesting for rail enthusiasts.

Walks **Ryewood Park** is within a few minutes' reach along Ryewood Road. Further along the same road, 1½ km from the Bazar, the scenic **Monsoon Lake** with a small island and its temple has a kilometre long dam which gives a good bird's eye view. A further 2 km along INS Shivaji Road leads to **Bushy Dam** which attracts crowds who come to soak themselves on monsoon weekends. **Old Khandala Road** which joins the highway near *Fariyas Hotel* was once the main approach to Lonavla. Now it is pleasantly quiet, lined with stately bungalows and is good for an evening stroll. **Tungarli Dam**, a disused water reservoir on a hill, is near *Lion's Den Hotel* and can be reached by taking the left turn from the highway petrol pump near *Jewel Resort*. Clean public toilets are at the start of Ryewood Road (market end). Pleasant circuits around town start at Lonavla Bazar.

Excursions **Ambavane Lake** ⓘ *ST buses to Ambavane village (depart 0915, 1200, 1630, 1815) take 90 mins then walk 1 km beyond 'Sahara', cars, about Rs 500 for half day trip*, is a quiet, small lake ideal for swimming and camping by. It lies at the end of a mud track beyond the Sahara Housing Project; best Nov-Feb but nights can be chilly. The drive there during the monsoon is scenic (but the lake is empty!). You will need to carry all provisions and equipment. **Khandala**, a quiet village overlooking a great ravine from which the Konkan region south of Mumbai can be seen.

★ Karla and Bhaja caves → *Phone code: 02114.*

Karla caves ⓘ *US$2 foreigners, Rs 5 Indians*. This is the largest and best preserved Buddhist *chaitya* (chapel) cave in India, dating from the second to first century BC. Here, as at Bhaja, the stone mason imitated the earlier wooden structures; the main *chaitya* shows evidence of stone supporting a wooden gallery. Unlike Ajanta and Ellora it is off the beaten tourist track for foreigners, though it can be crowded with local tourists at weekends.

The approach is across an excavated court. At the massive entrance stands a stone column topped with four lions (*sinha stambha*). The Hindu temple just outside the entrance may have been built over the remains of a second pillar. The façade contains a large horseshoe shaped window above the three doorways (one for the priest and the other two for pilgrims). In front of the side doors were shallow water-filled troughs through which the pilgrims walked to cleanse their feet. The remarkable sun window diffused the light into the hall, falling gently onto the stupa at the end. Buddha images (circa fifth century) partly decorate the exterior. There are also panels between the doorways depicting six pairs of donors.

The main chamber (38 m by 14 m), entered through a large outer porch, is supported by 37 pillars. It is 8 m from floor to ceiling which is barrel vaulted and ribbed with teak beams. There are 15 octagonal columns along either side, each capital having kneeling elephants carrying an embracing couple carved on it. The stupa is similar to that in Cave No 10 at Ellora but here is topped by a wooden umbrella which is carved with delicate patterns. The other caves to the right of the entrance are of little interest

Bhaja caves There are 18 caves dating from the second century BC. You will need to climb about 170 steps. **Cave No 12** is the best and possibly the first apsidal *chaitya* (a long hall with a semi-circular end) in India. The apse contains a *dagoba*. The vaulted roof of the chapel is supported by 27 columns. The exterior was once covered in a bas-relief, much of this has now been defaced. On either side of the main cave are others which were probably nuns' cells and working quarters. The inner sanctum of the last cave to the south has very fine sculptures, including the 'Dancing Couple'; you will need to tip the caretaker to open the door (surprisingly only the central cell echoes). To the south are 14 *stupas*, five of which are inside the cave.

The ruined **Lohagen Fort** is about 4 km beyond Bhaja and was twice taken and lost by Sivaji. **Visapur Fort**, which stands 600 m from the foot of the hill, is nearby. You can see them from the Bhaja caves.

Bhedsa ⓘ *Drive to Karunjgaon and follow signs for Bhedsa to the base of a hill, from there it is a 20-min walk uphill.* Visit Bhedsa if you have time to spare. There are more early Buddhist rock-cut caves on a hill north of the Pawan Dam but they are much less grand than Karla. The *chaitya* with four columns with animal carvings is similar but may have been built later. The rib vaulted roof is supported by 26 pillars. Seldom visited, the paths to them can be misleading so it is best to ask a local guide to show the way.

★ **Raigad (Raigarh)** ⓘ *Rs 5, foreigners US$ 2; very worthwhile. The Cable Car (Rs 100) avoids the 6-km walk up but power failures can cause delays (diesel generator standby is not dependable). Look for signs for 'Ropeway' leading to a right turn before reaching the end of the paved road and be prepared for a scary ride in a 'cage' for 4-6 passengers. Photos of major Maharashtrian forts are displayed at the base. Getting there: buses go from both Mumbai (via Mahad, 210 km) and Pune (126 km). Pune is the nearest railhead.* (Colour map 5, grid B3). The views from the three-pronged hilltop **fort** are magnificent, especially the stunningly beautiful panorama across the lakes to the north. Difficult to reach, the fort is rarely visited by foreigners though there are plenty of Indian tourists since Sivaji is perhaps the greatest Maratha hero.

These Maratha forts south from Pune are best visited by hiring a car since bus journeys can be slow and tiring. The town was Sivaji's headquarters during the latter part of his reign.

Raigad dates from around the 12th century. Known as 'Rairi' it was the seat of a Maratha chief. Later it passed in turn to the Vijayanagaras, the Nizam of Ahmadnagar, the Bijapuri Adil Shahis until Sivaji regained it in 1648 and made it the home of his much-revered mother, Jiji Bai. In 1674 he chose it for his coronation at the hands of Brahmin priests but died here in 1680. Aurangzeb acquired it in 1690 but it soon reverted back to the Marathas who surrendered it to the British in 1818.

The single path climbs 1,400 steps from its start at **Wadi**. The flat hilltop is about 2,500 m long and 1,500 m across at the widest. A bastioned wall encloses it while two outer curtain walls contour round the hillsides. Heavily fortified in each corner of the irregular triangle, in Sivaji's day the fort was one of the strongest in India. The main gate (Maha Darwaza) is flanked by two large bastions, both 21 m high, one concave, the other convex. Inside the fort, the extensive **Palace** and **Queen's Chamber** are placed between two tanks. In the courtyard is a low platform where the throne stood and after the coronation the title *Chhatrapati* - Lord of the Umbrella was bestowed on Sivaji. In the centre of the town was a market which had more than 40 shops in two parallel rows for the 2,000 people housed in the fort. To the northeast is Sivaji's **Samadhi** (memorial), as well as a *chhattri* for his dog. If you go up in the evening when the heat has died down, it is extremely atmospheric; a *dhoolie* can be hired.

Purandhar Fort (altitude: 1,220 m, 13 km diversion from the NH9) commands a high point on the Western Ghats. It is a double fort, the lower one, **Vajragad** to the east and **Purandhar** itself. Together they command a narrow passage through the hills. Like other hill forts, Purandhar was defended by curtain walls, in this case 42 km in extent, relieved by three gateways and six bastions. The earliest fortifications date from 1350.

Wai stands on the left bank of the Krishna River where the riverside, lined with shady temples, is very attractive, particularly the finely carved *mandapam* in front of the Mahadev temple. Behind the town the hills rise sharply. On top of one is the fort of **Pandavgad**, which according to local tradition was visited by the Pandava brothers of the *Mahabharata*. The town's sanctity is enhanced by its proximity to the source of the Krishna.

Satara lies in a hollow near the confluence of the Krishna and Venna rivers. It is considered a place of great sanctity and there are several temples on the banks at **Mahuli**. The cantonment contains Sir Bartle Frere's **Residency** (1820). A 'New Palace' (1838-44) was built by the engineer responsible for the bridges over the two rivers.

The ruling house of Satara was descended from Sahu, Sivaji's grandson, who was brought up at the Mughal court. Their **mansion**, 200 m from the New Palace, contains a number of Sivaji's weapons. These include the notorious 'tigers' claws (*waghnakh*) with which Sivaji is reputed to have disembowelled Afzal Khan. Other weapons include *Jai Bhavani*, his favourite sword (made in Genoa), and his rhinoceros hide shield. There is an **Historical Museum** (1930) which contains a fine collection of archival material on the Marathas. Satara Road railway station is 6 km from the city and bus stand.

Wasota Fort on the south side of the town can be reached by both road and footpath. Reputedly built by the Raja of Panhala in the 12th century, it's 14-m high walls (which remain only at the gateway) and buttresses contain the remains of the Rajah's Palace, a small temple and a bungalow. It passed to the Mughals under Aurangzeb, for a time, after he besieged the fort in 1699, but returned to the Marathas in 1705 with the help of a Brahmin agent who tricked the Mughals. Sleeping at *Monark*, Pune-Bangalore Rd, Powai Naka, T02162-2789, good restaurant, clean, though traffic noise.

Karad, a thriving industrial and market town on the Pune-Bangalore highway, is a good break point between Kohlapur and Pune.

Kolhapur → *Phone code: 0231. Colour map 5, grid C4. Population: 485,200.*

Set in the wide open plains of the southern Deccan, Kolhapur, founded under the 10th-century Yadavas, was once one of the most important Maratha states. Sivaji's younger son inherited the southern regions of his father's kingdom, but after a history of bitter factional dispute it became an important Princely State under the British. Today it has the unlikely distinction of being at the heart of India's small wine producing region, and is also witnessing a flow of foreign investment, making it one of the major industrial centres of Maharashtra. The area has rich bauxite deposits and the damming of the Koyna, a tributary of the Krishna, is providing electricity for aluminium smelting.

Sights The sacred **Panchganga River** skirts the north of the city, and ghats and temples, including the **Amba Bai** or Mahalaxmi Temple to the mother goddess, stand on its banks. It has 10th-century foundations, a tall pyramidal tower added in the 18th and an impressive carved ceiling to the pillared hall. **Note** Vishnu with the eight *Dikpalas*, see page 694. **Brahmapuri Hill** the Brahmin cremation ground, is in the west.

Much of Kolhapur's architecture can be attributed to the British army engineer Major Charles Mant. His **New Palace** (1881) belongs to the period when all the succession disputes had been resolved and Kolhapur was being governed as a model state. Built out of grey stone around a central courtyard dominated by a clocktower it contains elements from Jain temples and Deeg Palace. In 1871 he had also designed the **cenotaph** on the banks of the Arno River for Maharajah Rajaram, who died in Florence. Among his other buildings in the town are the **Town Hall** (1873), **General Library** (1875), **Albert Edward Hospital** (1878) and **High School** (1879).

Remnants of the pre-British period are found near the town centre. The **Rajwada** (Old Palace), which was badly damaged by fire in 1810, is entered through a traditional drum gallery or music hall (*nakkar khana*). Upstairs in the palace is the Durbar Hall and armoury which contains one of Aurangzeb's swords and other interesting memorabilia. The **Irwin Museum** has a bell taken from the Portuguese at Bassein in 1739. Near Brahmapuri Hill is the **Rani's Garden** where the royal family have memorial *chhattris*.

Excursions **Panhala** (977 m), 19 km northwest of Kolhapur, is where Rajah Bhoj II, whose territory extended to the Mahadeo Hills north of Satara, had his **fort**. However, it is particularly associated with Sivaji, who often stayed here. The Marathas and Mughals occupied it in turn until the British took it in 1844. The fort is triangular with a 7 km wall with three gates around it, in places rising to 9 m. The Tin Darwaza (three gates) leads to a central courtyard or 'killing chamber'; the inner gate leads to the Guard Room. The Wagh Gate (partly ruined) adopts similar principles of defence. Inside are vast granaries, the largest of which covers 950 sq m, has 11 m high walls and enabled Sivaji to withstand a five-month siege. By the ruins is a temple to Maruti, the Wind god. To the north is the two-storey Palace. See below for an overnight stop.

Solapur → Phone code: 0217. Colour map 5, grid B5. Population: 873,000.

In the heart of the cotton growing area Solapur (Sholapur) has been a focus of the cotton trade for over a century. Almost entirely an industrial city it still has an atmospheric area with traditional old buildings along Navee Peth and Rajvadee Chowk.

Excursions From Solapur the main road to Pune follows the Bhima River northwest across the vast open fields and scattered settlements of the plateau. It is a region rich in archaeological sites, as it was a major centre of prehistoric settlement.

Pandharpur, on the south bank of the Bhima River, is regarded by many as the spiritual capital of Maharashtra. It has a shrine to Vithoba, an incarnation of Vishnu, dating from 1228. Although some tourist literature puts its origins as early as 83 AD there is no evidence for this early date. There are 12 bathing ghats on the river bank, and during the main pilgrimage season of July (Kartik Ekadashi Fair), tens of thousands of pilgrims converge on the town. The *Rath Yatra*, or temple car procession, dates back to 1810.

Listings: Southern Maharashtra

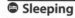 Sleeping

Pune *p1127, maps p1128, p1130 and p1131*
FC Rd is Ferguson Rd;
JM Rd is Jangli Maharaj Rd

AL Blue Diamond (Taj), 11 Koregaon Rd, T6125555, F6127755, www.tajhotels.com. 110 rooms, modern, comfortable, special discounts for business clients with partners.
AL Holiday Inn, 262 Bund Garden, T6137777,

F6134747, hip@holidayinnpune.com. 115 very comfortable rooms, good shops.
AL Le Meridien, RB Mill Rd, T6050505, F6050525, meridien@pn2.vsnl.net.in. 176 rooms in Pune's latest luxury hotel, "feels like being inside a giant wedding cake".
AL Pride, 5 University Rd, Sivajinagar, T55345567, F5533228, www.pridegroup.com. 111 rooms, clean, comfortable, good service, not the best pool but open to non-residents.
B-D Sunderban, 19 Koregaon Park, next to Osho Commune, T6124949, F6123535, tghotels@hotmail.com. 58 rooms (rooms vary, wide range), restaurant planned (veg), exchange, gardens, everything spotless, serenaded by Osho meditations next door.
E Saras, Nehru Stadium, Swargate, T4430499, near bus station. 20 pleasant rooms, 1 a/c, restaurant, good value.

Cheap rooms are hard to find on arrival. Reserve ahead.

Pune Station area
A Sagar Plaza, 1 Bund Garden Rd, T6122622, F6122633, sparkplaza@wmi.co.in. 76 smallish but comfortable rooms, deluxe better, modern concrete and glass tower block, restaurants, exchange, small pool.
A-B Aurora Towers, 9 Moledina Rd, T6131818, F6131826, hotelaurora@usa.net. 68 large rooms with views, good restaurants, friendly service, 24-hr exchange, terraced pool (non-residents Rs 100), good value.
B-C Ashirwad, 16 Connaught Rd, T6128585, F6126121. 44 good rooms, modern, neat, restaurant (good *thali*), exchange, helpful.
B-C Srimaan, 361/5 Bund Garden Rd, T6133535, F6123636, www.littleitalyindia.com. 30 pleasant rooms, clean, Italian restaurant.
B-C Woodland, BJ Rd, T6126161, F6123131, tghotels@hotmail.com. 102 well-kept pleasant rooms, most a/c, restaurant (Indian veg), airport transfer, busy, helpful.
B-D Dreamland, 2/14 Connaught Rd, T6122121, F6122424. 43 rooms, some a/c, good veg *thalis*, well kept.
D Madhav, 6a Tadiwala Rd, T6134219. Simple but friendly.
D-E Homeland, 18 Wilson Garden, T6127158, F6132622, www.hotelhomeland.com. 22 rooms, clean but falling standards.

E National, 14 Sassoon Rd, T6125054. 27 rooms some with bath (quieter in 10 cottages), rooms in old building could be cleaner.

Deccan Gymkhana and Fergusson College area
B Ashish Plaza, 1198 Shivajinagar, FC Rd, T5336541, F5332699, www.hotelashishplaza. com. 35 good rooms, some a/c, impressive reception though not efficient, overpriced.
B Oakwood, Good Luck Square, off FC Rd, T5670011, F5676699, tghotels@hotmail.com. 41 comfortable rooms in plush business hotel, good service, airport transfer, in-room internet.
C Ketan, 917/19A Sivajinagar, FC Rd, T5655081, F5655076. 28 rooms with bath, some spacious a/c, very clean, helpful.
C-D Ashiyana, FC Rd, T5332828, F5332699, www.hotelashishplaza.com. Large, slightly dated, reasonable value.
D Ajit, 766/3 Deccan Gymkhana, T5671212, F5672020. 16 rooms, some a/c (deposit requested), restaurant, small, dark but functional, peaceful location opposite Club.

Sinhagarh *p1131*
B Resort, has 2 pricey rooms.

Lonavla *p1132*
Bombay-Pune Rd is NH4.
L-AL Fariyas Holiday Resort, Tungarli, Frichley Hills, T73852, F72080. 103 luxurious rooms, some newer, solar heated pool, health club.
B Holiday Resort (MTDC/private), Ryewood Park, T73524. 22 rooms and cottages.
B Lakeview Resort, 4 Ryewood, T72141. 22 airy, breezy rooms, very clean, excellent location overlooking lake.
B Rainbow Retreat (*Quality Inn*), on NH4, opposite Valvan Dam (away from town), T72128, F73998. 46 rooms, pricey bar, poolside disco at weekends, pleasant garden, modern.
C Biji's Hill Retreat, New Tungarli Rd, T73025, F72638. 32 spacious rooms (round glass house with round bed!), restaurant, bar, pool.
C Jewel Resort, 80 Tungarli Dam Rd, T70736. 32 rooms, 4 a/c, quiet, clean comfortable, acceptable Indian restaurant, nice garden.
C Rama Krishna, NH4, near Bus Stand, T73600. 45 very clean, comfortable rooms, new well-appointed, suites with tubs.

● *For an explanation of the sleeping and eating price codes used in this guide, see inside the*
● *front cover. Other relevant information is found in Essentials pages 52-57.*

C-D Chandralok, Shivaji Rd, opposite Bus Stand entrance, T/F72921. Large, clean, comfortable airy rooms, some a/c, excellent unlimited thalis (Rs 80-100).

C-D Kadamba Sahyadri, NH4 next to Valvan Dam turning, T73234. Variety of clean rooms, best with a/c, geyser, others spartan, reasonable restaurant.

C-D Lonavla Hotel, NH4, near Bus Stand Lane, T72914. 15 compact, very clean, refurbished rooms with good baths, some a/c, good non-veg restaurant.

D-E Ahuja, Victoria Cottage, off Ryewood Rd, T72123. 18 very clean, comfortable rooms with bath (some 3-4 bedded), optional a/c, dining room, quiet area, modern guest house, very good value.

E DT Shahani Health Home, DT Shahani Rd, behind Bus Stand, T72784. Very clean triples in quiet locality, varied menu in canteen.

E Shamiana, 66 Mumbai Pune Rd, opposite Bajrang Baug, T72356. 7 cottage suites (2-4 beds) set in charming unkempt garden off the highway, nice but noisy, simple but comfortable (no mosquito nets), no food

Khandala

A Duke's Retreat, Mumbai-Pune Rd, 4 km Lonavla Railway (T73817, F73836). 62 rooms, restaurant, bar, lawns, pool, superb views.

Karla caves *p1132*

C-E Holiday Camp (MTDC), off Mumbai Pune Rd (NH4), T82230, F82370. 64 clean rooms in cottages for 2-4 (some comfortable a/c), canteen, bar, vast sylvan surroundings.

E Peshwas Holiday Resort, near Karla Caves. 15 rooms, restaurant.

Karad *p1134*

D Hotel Sangam, 42 rooms, some a/c, restaurant, bar, pool.

D Pankaj, near new Koyna Bridge. 34 modern rooms, reasonable and good restaurant.

Kolhapur *p1134*

B-C Shalini Palace, Rankala, A Ward, T620401, F620407. 41 rooms, some a/c, good value **D** rooms in extension at back, average food but good wine cellar, attractive gardens, built for Maharaja of Kohlapur in 1931 on the lakeside (lots of mosquitors),

real character, old furnishings but comfortable, out of town, very peaceful ("atmospheric but empty"), no exchange, tours arranged, auto-rickshaws at entrance.

C Victor Palace, Rukmini Nagar, Old Pune-Bangalore Rd, T662627, F662632. Modern a/c rooms, good restaurants, full facilities, excellent pool and gym, efficient and helpful, good value, central. Recommended.

D Pearl, New Sahupuri, T650451, F659987. 28 rooms, 20 a/c, restaurant, bar, garden.

D Woodlands, 204E Tarabai Park, T650941. 25 rooms, 8 a/c, restaurant, bar, garden, quiet.

E Opal, Pune-Bangalore Rd, T653622. 9 rooms with TV, restaurant (Maharashtrian).

E-F Maharaja, 514E Station Rd, opposite Bus Station, T650829. 26 rooms, some with bath, veg restaurant.

Panhala

D Mahalaxmi Resort (MTDC/Private), T435048, 7 good rooms and an outdoor restaurant.

D Valley View Grand, has fabulous views from rooms and open air restaurant (very good food), and pretty gardens.

Solapur *p1135*

D Pratham, 560/61 South Sadar Bazar, T729581, F728724. 30 clean, modern, pleasant rooms, half a/c with bath, very good open-air restaurant, friendly and helpful staff.

D Surya Executive, 3/3/2 Murarji Peth, T729880, F620504, hotelsurya1@vsnl.com. Next door to *Surya International*. Good, clean excellent value, air-cooled rooms, restaurant.

D Surya International, 3/2/2 Murarji Peth, 200 m from bus stand, T729501, F729505. 32 rooms, 8 a/c, restaurant, bar, ice cream parlour.

E Srikamal, 77 Rly Lines, T722964. Newish clean rooms, hot shower, good terrace restaurant, run by very helpful, friendly family.

F Railway Retiring Rooms and dorm.

🍴 Eating

Pune *p1127, maps p1128, p1130 and p1131*
Around Pune Station and Osho Commune

🍴🍴 **Blue Diamond**, in hotel. China Town.
🍴🍴 **The Coffee Shop Plush**, in hotel. Good food, relaxing lunch stop, discourages informal dress (men in shorts).

● Phone codes Pune: 020; Lonavla and Karla caves: 02114; Kolhapur: 0231; Solapur: 0217

Sangamitra, North Main Rd, east of Osho. In hotel, Western. Attractive garden, candlelit in evenings, incredible lemon cheesecake, paté, tofu, homemade pasta.

Chinese Room, Gen Thimmaya Rd. Chinese plus bar and ice creams. India's first

Kwality's, Gen Thimmaya Rd (East St). With bar. Good for North Indian, chicken dishes recommended at *Latif's*.

Latif's, Gen Thimmaya Rd (East St). Good for North Indian, chicken dishes recommended at *Latif's*.

Nanking, opposite *Pune Club*, Bund Garden Rd.

The Place, Touché the Sizzler, Clover Centre, 7 Moledina Rd. 1130-1530, 1900-2100. Best sizzlers in town (the sizzler reputedly was invented by the present owner's father!). Also chicken platters, super ice creams (spotless toilets). Recommended.

Shriman, near Osho Commune, North Main Rd. Italian. Recommended for tomato and mozzarella salad, great pizza, pasta, fresh bread, pleasant candlelit atmosphere.

Tamarind Court, 28/2 Koregaon Park, North Main Rd. Western, some Indian. Outdoor, set among huge shady trees.

Zamu's Place, Dhole Patil Rd. Western. Good sizzlers and Parsi dishes.

Kamling, Gen Thimmaya Rd. Chinese.

Shri Krishna Palace, Wilson Gardens, near railway station. Good value South Indian veg.

Fast food

Coffee House, 2 Moledina Rd. Good coffee and South Indian snacks.

George, 2436 Gen Thimmaya Rd. Part a/c, snacks and ice creams.

Jaws, 9 Castelhino Rd. Popular local hangout, pool, chess, in open-air setting. Locals prefer a Jaws burger over the McRival options.

Deccan Gymkhana and Fergusson College area

Chinese Room Oriental, Continental Chambers, Karve Rd. Chinese, bar, ice cream.

Khyber, 1258/2 JM Rd. Indian, some continental, beer bar and ice creams.

Pune Coffee House, 1256/2 Deccan Gymkhana. Large, live music.

Roopali, FC Rd. Good for *thalis*, *dosas*.

Shabree, *Hotel Parichay*, FC Rd. Unlimited Maharashtrian thalis (Rs 60), traditional.

Vaishali, FC Rd. South Indian. Starts early

for breakfast, mainly snacks, their special SPDP (Shev Potato Dahi Puri) is a Pune institution, no one should leave town without trying it, very popular meeting place (queues in evenings for lovely rear garden), spotless. Highly recommended.

Bakeries

ABC Farms, Koregaon Park. Specialist cheese producers, organic veg and rice, restaurant.

German Bakery, North Main Rd. Great coffee, cakes and snacks, suitably in tune with Osho.

Just Baked, Dhole Patil Road. Eat in/take out, baking can be watched through glass screen.

Kayani, East St. Irani bakery specializing in Mawa cakes and Shrewsbury biscuits!

Marz-o-rin, MG Rd. Good sandwiches, cakes, a Pune landmark, "reading and writing not allowed"!

Spicers Health Foods, MG Rd. Brown bread, peanut butter and tofu.

Out of town

All recommended.

Abhiruchi, Singhad Rd, 8 km. Rustic village style restaurant in 40 acres. Unlimited Maharashtrian thali (Rs 100) including 6 types of bread! More a day out than a lunch break.

Garden Court, NDA Rd, 5 km from Gymkhana. Excellent food and ambience overlooking the city.

Sanskruti, Solapur Highway (20 km). Similar to *Abhiruchi*. Palm reading, *mehndi*, *ghazal* singing, dancing, 16 item *thali* (Rs 120).

Lonavla *p1132*

Lonavla Hotel, 1st floor, a/c. Excellent Indian, pleasant ambience (try chicken kebabs), generous helpings, bar (affordable drinks), very clean (about Rs 150 each).

Shivam Garden Restaurant is cheaper but equally good and strictly pure veg.

In the bazar:

Hasty Tasty, for good snacks.

Zeus Bakery MG Rd, near National Chikki. Burger, sandwiches, snacks etc from Rs 25.

⊙ Bars and clubs

Pune *p1127, maps p1128, p1130 and p1131* Check daily 'Pune Times' supplement in The Times of India for listings. Pune has quite an active night life. FC Rd and MG Rd are popular with students in the evenings.

Discos
1000 Oats is more of a family orientated place.
Club Polaris at *Hotel Blue Diamond*.
Crystal Bar, MG Rd.
Cyclone at *Hotel Mayur*.
Kaplia Hotel (opposite *Regency*), has rooftop dancing, once a week (2200-0100).
Nomads, Banjara Hills.
Scream at *Le Meridien*.
TDS (10 Downing Street), Boat Club Rd.

☻ Festivals and events

Pune *p1127, maps p1128, p1130 and p1131*
Aug/Sep: Ganesh Chaturthi 11 day MTDC festival with concerts, food fairs, bullock-cart races, folk shows. **Dec/Jan**: Pune Marathon.

Lonavla *p1132*
Feb/Mar: Sivaratri is celebrated at Mahadev Temple with great ceremony and a fair.

O Shopping

Pune *p1127, maps p1128, p1130 and p1131*
The main shopping centres in Pune are in MG Rd (Camp area), Deccan Gymkhana, Karve Rd, Laxmi Rd (for clothing and textiles) and Hanuman Mandir (for silver jewellery and leather *chappals*).
Nirman Shopping Complex, opposite Shivaji Market, Convent St, is a modern mall.

Books
Crossword, JPN Rd. Very modern, wide range of books and magazines. Recommended.
Manney's, Clover Centre, Moledina Rd, comfortable a/c, well-lit, excellent stock, some bargains.
Modern Book Store, Gen Thimmaya Rd, good selection. Recommended.
Popular Book House, Deccan Gymkhana.

Textiles
Look out for Pune saris (cotton-silk weave).
Kalaniketan, opposite Sancheti Hospital, JM Rd, for premium silkwear.
Kasat, Karve Rd.
    Wholesale sari market at **Raviwarpeth** ("Sunday Lane").

Lonavla *p1132*
Chikki, the candy mix of jaggery and dried fruit and nuts, is the local favourite, with endless variety in the shops in the market along MG Rd. About Rs 40 per kilo; dried fruit chikki, Rs 200 or more.
Cooper's famous for fudges; try coconut or choco walnut.
Maganlal, over 40 types.
National, over 40 types.
Shakti, Shivaji Rd/ Flyover junction. Excellent, unusual concoctions for health seekers; vitamin C rich Indian gooseberry (*awala*), black sesame (*til*), sugar-free cashew and dried fruit is delicious.

▲▲ Activities and tours

Pune *p1127, maps p1128, p1130 and p1131*
Tour operators
Apple Travels, Amir Hotel Building, Connaught Rd, T6128185, F6125421. Agent for *Indian Airlines*, efficient service.
Sita, Akshay Complex, 41 Dhole Patil Rd, T6121707, F6122030.
Sundar, 19 MG Rd, T6131848.
TCI, Dhole Patil Rd, T6122126.
Thomas Cook, Gen Thimmaya Rd.

Karla caves *p1132*
Healing
Atmasantulana, by MTDC Holiday Resort gate, is a holistic treatment centre combining ayurvedic, natural and yogic methods with medications and special dietary preparations produced at the complex; meditation, music therapy and spirituality are also practised. Patients should register a month ahead, about Rs 1000 per day. Visitors 1700-1900.

Lonavla *p1132*
Yoga and vedanta
Kaivalyadhama Yogic Health Care Centre, Valvan Dam approach road, T73039, F71983, www.kdham.com. The 76-year old institute tries to demystify yoga and offers courses (1-yr diploma), cures, research and accommodation.
Vedanta Academy, Malavali Station Rd (T82278, F82327, satva@vsnl.com). A lush haven off the Mumbai Pune Highway offers a free 3-year (or shorter) course for 50 students from around the world. Phone to visit.

⊖ **Transport**

Pune *p1127, maps p1128, p1130 and p1131*
Bangalore (840 km); **Belgaum** (336 km);
Mumbai (184 km); **Delhi** (1,424 km);
Mahabaleshwar (120 km); **Nashik** (184 km).

Air

Transport to town: Ex-Servicemen's coach for
8 km city transfer or airlines bus; taxi Rs 220.
Indian Airlines, T4260932, enquiries T140,
Airport T6689433. To **Bangalore** and **Delhi**,
daily. **Jet Airways**, 243 Century Arcade, B/2
Narangi Bagh Rd, T6137181, Airport,
T6685591. To **Mumbai**, 3 flights per day;
Bangalore and **Delhi**, daily.

Bus

Local City buses: in the city and suburbs
(irregular).
Long distance MSRTC buses connect
Pune with all major towns within the state.
The new Mumbai to Bangalore expressway
connects Pune. Travelling times on these
routes will be cut considerably by those
willing to pay the toll; Enquiry T665516. **Bright
Star**, 13 Connaught Rd, operates luxury
coaches to Ahmadabad, Bangalore, Panaji
(Goa), Mangalore etc. MTDC bus, Rs 125.
Kadamba Transport Corporation (KTC, Goa)
operates the Panaji route at 0630, 1800 and
1900, via Mapusa; buses poor and often dirty;
Booking office open 0900-1200, 1500-1800.
Asiad and *Express* buses run regular services.
City (Railway) Bus Stand, T6126218, for the
city and the South: **Belgaum**; **Chiplun**;
Ganpatipule; **Hubli**; **Kolhapur**;
Mahabaleshwar; **Panaji**; **Ratnagiri**; **Shirdi**;
Solapur. Sivaji Nagar Bus Stand, T5536970,
for the east/northeast: **Ahmadabad**; **Alibag
(Kihim)**; **Amravati**; **Aurangabad**;
Hyderabad; **Indore**; **Jalgaon**; **Nagpur**;
Nashik; **Shirdi**; **Vadodara**. Swargate Bus
Stand, T4441591, for the south and southeast.
An auto from Swargate to Railway Station bus
stand costs Rs 40. **Belgaum**; **Kolhapur**;
Mahabaleshwar; **Mangalore** (starting from
Mumbai); **Ratnagiri**; **Solapur**; **Thane**. Also
private agents run deluxe a/c services direct to
Sahar International Airport, 4 hrs, Rs 450,
0600, 0900, 1200, 1500, 1800, 2100. From the
airport at 0030, 0230, 0430, 0630, 1800.

Car

Car hire: about Rs 800-1250 per day, or from Rs
9,000 per week with driver from **Sai Services**,
Ashoka Pavillion, Dr Ambedkar Rd, T6055603.
Budget cars, T5444118. **Wheels**, *Pride Executive
Hotel*, T3255345; Airport T6683615.

Rickshaw

Auto-rickshaws: best mode for town; driver
carries a rate card, extra charges out-of-town
and between 2400-0500.

Taxi

Local Not metered.
Long distance To/from Mumbai Dadar
station, Rs 750-900.

Train

Rail Bookings: City, Raviwar Peth, and Deccan
Bookings, Karve Rd. Mon-Sat 0900-1200,
1300-1700, computerized. Enquiries T131,
T3126575. **Bangalore via Guntakal**: *Udyan
Exp, 6529*, 1200, 20½ hrs; *Coimbatore Exp,
1013*, 0215, 20 hrs. **Mumbai (CST)**: 17 trains
daily, best are *Deccan Queen, 2124*, 0715,
3½ hrs; *Shatabdi Exp, 2028*, 1735, 3½ hrs;
Indrayani Exp, 1022, 1820, 3¾ hrs; *Pragati Exp,
1026*, 0745, 3¾ hrs; *Sinhagad Exp, 1010*, 0605,
4 hrs; *Deccan Exp, 1008*, 1515, 4½ hrs. **Delhi
(ND)**: *Jhelum Exp, 1077*, 1735, 27¾ hrs;
(Hazrat Nizamuddin) *Goa Exp, 2779*, 0405,
26½ hrs. **Hyderabad**: *Mumbai-Hyderabad
Exp, 7031*, 1650, 13¼ hrs; *Hussainsagar Exp,
7001*, 0150, 11½ hrs. **Secunderabad**: *Konark
Exp, 1019*, 1925, 12¼ hrs. **Jammu Tawi**:
Jhelum Exp, 1077, 1735, 42½ hrs. **Chennai
via Solapur and Guntakal**: *Dadar Chennai
Exp, 1063*, 0010, 20 hrs; *Chennai Exp, 6011*,
1815, 22½ hrs. **Vasco de Gama (Goa)**: *Goa
Exp, 2780*, 1730, 14½ hrs.

Lonavla *p1132*
ST Stand, T72742.

Bus

ST buses to the **Caves**: couple of buses to
Karla in the morning from 0600, last return
about 1900. To **Rajmachi Fort** (north of
Lonavla): buses are unpredictable; **Pune**
(62 km) and **Mumbai** (101 km); special a/c
every 30 mins, last dep 1630, Rs 81. *Lucky
Travels*, Hotel Gulistan, Bombay Pune Rd,
near Flyover, T70332, runs a/c bus to
Mumbai, Rs 170 (non-video preferable).

Rickshaw

Auto-rickshaw: from Lonavla to the Karla and Bhaja Caves including waiting, about Rs 250, more for Bhedsa.

Taxi

Tourist taxis: from near ST Bus Stand, *Ankush Stores*, T74458; *Parekh*, in line with Adarsh Hotel, T73886. Return hire to Ambavane Rs 500; Karla, Bhaja Rs 350 (the caves are some distance from the car park). One way to Mumbai Rs 750-1,000 (under 4 hrs), Pune Rs 500.

Train

Railway Station Enquiry, T72215. Lonavla is on the **Mumbai (CST) - Pune** line with at least 16 trains daily in each direction. To **Mumbai**, 2½-3 hrs; **Pune**, 1-1½ hrs.

Karla caves *p1132*

Tourist taxis charge Rs 350 from Lonavla to visit both caves. From the Karla/Bhaja crossroads on the NH4 at Karla village, turn left (north). The car park is at the bottom of the ridge with a steps up to the caves (20 mins). Buses from Lonavla: a couple from 0600; last return 1900.

Bhaja Caves *p1133*

From Karla village on the NH4, a road to the south goes to Bhaja after crossing the railway at Malavli. Vehicles stop at the car park in new Bhaja 'town', from there follow a path and then climb uphill for about 20 mins to the caves. Heavy rain can close part of the Bhaja Rd to vehicles. Alternatively, take a **train** to Malavli.

Kolhapur *p1134*
Train

To Kolhapur arrive via Miraj. Enquiry, T131. Reservation: T654389. **Mumbai (CST)**: *Mahalaxmi Exp, 1012,* 1905, 11¾ hrs; *Koyna Express 7308,* 0750, 13½ hrs; *Mahalaxmi Sahyadri Exp, 7304,* 2230, 14¼ hrs. **Pune**: *Maharashtra Exp, 7383,* 1405, 8 hrs.

Solapur *p1135*
Bus

Excellent connections to **Mumbai**, **Hyderabad**, **Aurangabad** to the north and **Bijapur** (3 hrs) to the south.

Train

Bangalore: *Udyan Exp, 6529,* 1630, 16 hrs. **Bijapur**, *Golgumbaz Exp, 6541,* 2135, 2½ hrs;

Solapur Bijapur Pass, 245, 1720, 3½ hrs. **Mumbai (Dadar)**: *Chennai Dadar Exp, 1064,* 2115, 9 hrs. **Mumbai (CST)**: *Chennai-Mumbai Mail, 6010,* 1720, 10¾ hrs; *Chennai Mumbai Exp, 6012,* 0425, 10½ hrs; *Siddheswar Exp, 1024,* 2030, 10 hrs. **Hyderabad**: *Mumbai Hyderabad Exp, 7031,* 2200, 8 hrs; *Hussainsagar Exp, 7001,* 0610, 7 hrs. **Chennai**: *Dadar Chennai Exp, 1063,* 0420, 15¾ hrs; *Mumbai Chennai Exp, 6011,* 2340, 17 hrs.

❶ Directory

Pune *p1127, maps p1128, p1130 and p1131*
Banks Amex, 19 MG Rd. Central Bank, MG Rd, accepts Mastercard and Visa. **Thomas Cook**, 13 Thakers House, Gen Thimmaya Rd, T648188 (1000-1700, closed Sun) is best for TCs. **ATMs**: Many across the city, Citibank for Mastercard, ICICI for Visa, HDFC for both. **Internet** Numerous outlets across the city, Rs 20-30 per hr. **Medical services** Jahangir Nursing Home, T6122551. KEM, Rasta Peth, T6125600. Ruby Hall Clinic, T6123391. Sassoon (Govt), JP Narayan Rd, T6128000. **Post office** Head Post Office (city): Laxmi Rd. **Tourist offices** Maharashtra, I Block, Central Bldg, T6126867, F6119434. Information Counter, Pune Railway Station. Lohagaon Airport. Goa, Sam Travels, Karve Rd, T333538. **Useful addresses** Ambulance: T102. Fire: T101. Police: T100. Foreigners' Registration Office, Ground Floor, Main Building, Police Commissioner's Office, Sadhu Waswani Rd, T6128977.

Lonavla *p1132*
Banks Bank of Maharashtra and State Bank of India, Tilak Rd. **Internet** Cybercafé Basement of *Kumar Resort*, Flyover, 1000-2300, Rs 30 for 30 mins. **Medical services** Dahanukar Hospital, T72673; Favourite Medical, Tilak Rd. **Post office** Shivaji Rd. **Tourist office** Maharashtra, near Lonavla Railway Station. **Useful services** Fire: T72286. Police: T72233.

Kolhapur *p1134*
Bank Only State Bank of India, Main Branch, Dasara Chowk Bridge (near railway station), changes cash, TCs from 1130. **Tourist offices** Maharashtra, Kedar Complex, Station Rd, T652935, F650405. Goa, Mohan Travels, 517E Pune-Bangalore Rd, T650911.

Vidharba

Nagpur → *Phone code: 0712. Colour map 6, grid A1. Population: 2 million.*

Nagpur, the former capital of the Central Provinces, is one of the older towns of Central India. Today, although an important commercial centre attracting new businesses and multinationals, most of the industrial units are thankfully located on the outskirts so Nagpur retains a pleasant relaxed feel with friendly inhabitants and signs of fast growing affluence. Sometimes known as the winter capital of Maharashtra, the area is famous for its oranges, giving it the nickname 'The Orange City'. More recently strawberry farms have grown in importance while the surrounding countryside is a major cotton producing area. ⟫ *For Sleeping, Eating and other listings, see pages 1144-1146.*

Ins and outs Getting there The airport is 10 km south of the city centre with taxis for transfer. The main railway station is in the heart of town, within walking distance of several hotels. The New Maharashtra Bus Stand is on Ganesh Peth, about 1,500 km southeast of the railway station,while Madhya Pradesh buses use the stand just south of the station. **Getting around** Nagpur is too big to walk round comfortably, but there are town buses, autos and cycle rickshaws, with tempos on main routes. See Transport, page 1145, for further details.

Sights The city stands on the Nag River and centres on the **Sitabuldi Fort** which is surrounded by cliffs and a moat. At the highest point there is a memorial to those who fell in the Battle of Sitabuldi between the Marathas and the British. The fort, now headquarters of the Territorial Army, is only open to the public on 26 January and 15 August. Among the British buildings scattered around the western half of the city are the red brick Council Hall (1912-13); the Anglican Cathedral of All Saints (1851), and the High Court (1937-42), suggestive of Rashtrapati Bhavan in New Delhi. On the other high hill in the town is the **Raj Bhavan** (Government House).

The **Bhonsla Chhattris** are in the Sukrawari area south of the old city. Around the town there are also a number of 'tanks' (lakes) and parks; **Maharaj Bagh**, west of the Flyover is an attractive park/zoo.

Ramtek ① *Buses from ST Bus Stand, Nagpur, 70 mins, buses run from Ramtek to Khindsey Lake, Ramsagar can be reached by auto-rickshaw.* About 40 km northeast of Nagpur, Ramtek has a **fort** with several Hindu **temples** at its western end, some dating back to the fifth century AD. The fort walls on the well-wooded 'Hill of Rama' were built in 1740 by Raghoji I, the first Bhonsla of Nagpur. The citadel is older and the principal temples are those to Rama and Sita. The fort is approached by a flight of steps from the village of Ambala. The poet Kalidasa wrote his epic *Meghdoot* here. Nearby is Khindsey Lake, 8 km, a popular picnic spot with boating facilities. Ramsagar is another lake closer to town. The 15-day *Ramnavami* fair is held in November.

Wardha → *Phone code: 07152. Colour map 6, grid A1. 62 km southwest.*

After vowing not to return to Sabarmati Ashram in Ahmedabad until India gained its independence, Mahatma Gandhi established his **Sevagram Ashram** (Gandhian Village of Service) here in 1933, 8 km from Wardha. Jamnalal Bajaj, a dedicated follower of Gandhi, provided the land and resources to set up the ashram in which Gandhi remained until 1942 and visited regularly until his death in 1948. It is now a national institution where you can visit the residences *Nivases* and *Kutirs*, see the Mahatma's personal belongings, watch hand-spinning (*khadi* cloth is sold through shops) and attend prayers at the open-air multi-faith Prayer Ground (0430 and 1800). The **Mahatma Gandhi Research Institute of Medical Sciences** and **Kasturba Hospital**

with 325 beds to provide affordable health care for local villagers, is on the bus route.
A path from here leads to the Ashram.

The **Magan Sanghralaya** (Centre of Science for Villages) is an alternative technology museum, on the Nagpur Road at **Duttapur**. Visitors are welcome to see papermaking, pottery, latrine making and other crafts. The **Chetna Organic Farm**, nearby, develops sustainable farming techniques. The **Laxmi Narayan Temple** claims to have been the first in India to have allowed *Harijans* to enter in 1928. The **Viswa Shanti Stupa** (1993), for 'World Peace', with 4 golden statues of Buddha, is a more recent attraction. Prayers are held each evening in the small prayer hall.

At **Paunar**, 10 km north of Wardha, **Vinoba Bhave**, one of Gandhi's keenest disciples, set up his Ashram. He championed the 'land gift' or **Bhoodan Movement**, seeking with remarkable success to persuade large landowners to give away land to the poor. The self-help concept is kept alive by his followers (mostly women) dressed in blue, unlike other ashramites elsewhere in India who conventionally adopt white or saffron. It is possible to hike across from the Sevagram hospital along a village track for about 45 minutes to get there.

Taroba National Park ① *Nearest at Chandrapur (45 km).* Approximately 100 km south of Nagpur, the area around Taroba was once in the possession of the Gond tribals. The compact 120 sq km park has rich deciduous forest – mainly teak with bamboo, gardenia and satinwood. There are several troops of langur monkeys, palm civets, gaur, jackal, wild boar, chital, bison, sambar and a few tigers (although you are more likely to see a leopard in the evening). Waterbirds attracted by the perennial circular lake include cattle egrets, purple moorhens and jacanas. It also has quite a number of marsh crocodiles with a breeding farm for the *pulustris* species.

Minibuses for viewing, which is best in the evening around lake in the dry season. A road runs around the lake, while other roads radiate to the park perimeter. Best season to visit is between November and June. There are no official guides, but a forest guide will accompany you if you hire a searchlight.

Achalpur Until 1853 this important market town was the capital of Berar Kingdom, established in 1484 by Imad Shah. The old cantonment, which had been occupied by a regiment of the Hyderabad infantry, was abandoned in 1903.

To the north, and just before reaching Chikhaldara, is the fort of **Gawilgarh** (Gavilgarh). An important fortress of the 15th-century Shahi Dynasty, it was taken over when the kingdom of Ahmednagar expanded in 1574. Arthur Wellesley, subsequently the Duke of Wellington, who had defeated Tipu Sultan of Mysore at Srirangapatnam just four years previously, captured the fort in 1803 during the second Maratha War. The defences were destroyed after the 'Indian Mutiny' in 1858. Today it is a deserted ruin.

Chikhaldara Known as the only hill station in the Vidharba region and as the northernmost coffee growing region in India, Chikhaldara is high in the Gavilgarh Hills, at an altitude of 1,200 m, a branch of the Satpura mountains. Established as a hill station by the British in 1839, historically the hills marked the southern limits of the core region within which the epics of Hinduism were played out. It remains a tribal region, peopled largely by the Korkus, an Austric tribal group. The settlement is reputed to have taken its name from Kichaka, a prince who was killed by Bhima, one of the Pandava brothers, for having insulted Draupadi. Today, the Satpura Range in which Chikhaldara lies mark the southern boundary of Hindi speech.

The **Melghat Sanctuary** surrounding Chikaldara was one of the earliest to be designated a Project Tiger reserve. Its altitude makes it pleasantly cool during January-June, the best months to visit. The latest count suggests it has 45 tigers, occasionally seen in the dense and dry deciduous teak forest which also supports panther, gaur, chital, sambar and nilgai.

☉ Sleeping

Nagpur *p1142*

C and **D** hotels don't have all usual facilities of the grade but all have restaurants, bars and free transfer for airport

A-B Tuli International, Residency Rd, Sadar, T534784, F534473, www.tuligroup .com. 107 well-appointed rooms and suites, central a/c, executive 'Business' floor, 3 restaurants and bar, excellent pool and health club (residents only), weekend disco. Best in town.

B Pride (was *Jagson's Regency*), Wardha Rd, 500 m from airport, T261102, F260440, www.pridegroup.com. 70 tired rooms, 30 new better, decent restaurant but inefficient reception, unappealing pool next to busy NH7.

B-C Darshan Towers, 60 Central Ave, T726845, F726878, h_darshantowers@ yahoo.com. Well-furnished rooms, central a/c, hot baths (some tubs), double-glazed so quieter than others, good restaurant/bar, friendly and efficient, recommended.

B-C Radhika, Panchsheel Sq, Wardha Rd, T522011, F521179, radhika@ nagpur.dot.net.in. 60 clean rooms, some larger a/c with hot bath, dark corridors, unreliable TV, restaurant, bar.

D Jagsons, 30 Back Central Ave, T728611, F720370. 28 clean carpetted rooms, some a/c, TV, bar/restaurant.

D Skylark (*Tuli* group), 119 Central Ave, T724654, F726193. 48 decent, clean rooms, most a/c, efficient and friendly service, restaurant/bar, good value but suffers from road noise.

D-E Blue Moon, Central Ave, T726061, F727591, micron@bom3.vsnl.net.in. 30 clean rooms, some a/c, TV, room service, quieter rooms at rear.

E Super Deluxe Guest House, Back Central Ave. 32 clean rooms with bath and TV, friendly, away from main road so quieter.

Ramtek *p1142*

D Resort, (MTDC/private), Ramtek, T07114-55620. 17 rooms and a dorm.

E Resort, Khindsey Lake. Smaller with 4 simple rooms and camping.

Wardha *p1142*

E Holiday Resort (MTDC/private), near Bus Stand, T43872. 18 rooms with bath, cheap singles, restaurant. Also some cheap hotels near railway station.

Wardha *p1142*

Sevagram

F Ashram Guest House and **Yatri Niwas**, T2172. Some doubles and dorm, serves cheap veg meals, check-out 0800, friendly, small bookshop of Gandhi's works. Highly recommended (donations welcome), reserve on arrival (or ahead if possible). Alcohol, smoking and non-vegetarian food are prohibited.

Paunar

Yatri Niwas similar to Sevagram but more female oriented.

Taroba National Park *p1143*

E Mayur, Mul Rd. 27 rooms, 1 km railway, restaurant, bar, and three forest rest houses, around the lake. Reserve through the Divisional Forest Officer, Mul Road, Chandrapur. Needs a day's notice.

Chikhaldara *p1143*

B-D Green Vallies Resort (MTDC/private), T07220-20215. 20 suites, wide choice, some a/c.

C-D Convention Complex (MTDC), T07220-202234. 10 4 four-bed rooms, simple though adequate, and dorm with mattresses but no beds (Rs 50), restaurant nearby. Improved accommodation is planned.

 For an explanation of the sleeping and eating price codes used in this guide, see inside the front cover. Other relevant information is found in Essentials pages 52-57.

⦿ Eating

Nagpur *p1142*
Hotel restaurants at **Darshan Towers** and **Tuli International** are recommended. Several others are along Residency Rd and Wardha Rd near the junction with Central Bazar Rd.

Wardha *p1142*
Paunar
Annapurnat, Wardha near station; couple in Saraf Lines.

⊛ Festivals and events

Nagpur *p1142*
Apr/May: Ram Naumi, colourful procession in various parts of the city. **Aug/Sep**: Janmashtami, Krishna's birthday is celebrated with the distinctive tradition of stringing clay pots full of curd high above the streets. Young men try to pull them down by forming human pyramids. **Pola**, the cattle and monsoon harvest festival. **Ganesh Chaturthi**, when idols of Ganesh are immersed in streams and tanks.

⦿ Shopping

Nagpur *p1142*
Main areas are Sitabuldi, Dharampeth, Sadar and Itwari, Mahatma Phule Market. **Gangotri UP Handicrafts**, in Sadar. **Khadi Gramudyog**, in Mahal.

⦿ Transport

Nagpur *p1142*
City **buses**; unmetered **autos**, **cycle-rickshaws**; **taxis** from stand opposite railway station, about Rs 15 per km.

Air
Indian Airlines, Amravati Rd, T523069, airport T260348, flight information T140/141: to **Delhi**, **Mumbai**, **Hyderabad** and **Kolkata**. **Jet Airways**, Shree Mohini Complex, 345 Kingsway, Sitabuldi, T559875, airport T273384: to **Mumbai**.

Bus
Long distance New Maharashtra ST Bus Stand, Ganesh Peth, T726221, to towns in Maharashtra plus **Hyderabad**, **Allahabad** and **Varanasi**. MP Bus Stand, T533695, buses to **Bhopal**, **Indore** and **Raipur**.

Car
Car hire: **Pigale**, Dharampeth, T522291. **Saibaba**, near Pancsheel Cinema, T522416; Rs 600 per 5 hrs.

Train
Nagpur is an important railway junction. Enquiry T131, Reservations T135. **Chennai**: *Tamil Nadu Exp, 2622*, 1410, 16½ hrs; *Grand Trunk Exp, 2616*, 1220, 18 hrs. **New Delhi**: *Andhra Pradesh Exp, 2723*, 1555, 16½ hrs; *Tamil Nadu Exp, 2621*, 1415, 17½ hrs; *Grand Trunk Exp, 2615*, 1015, 18½ hrs. **Kolkata (H)**: *Gitanjali Exp, 2859*, 2015, 18½ hrs; *Mumbai Howrah Mail, 2809*, 1130, 20½ hrs. **Mumbai (CST)**: *Vidarbha Exp, 2106*, 1500, 14¾ hrs; *Howrah Mumbai Mail, 2810*, 1555, 15½ hrs. **Mumbai (Dadar)**: *Sewagram Exp, 1440*, 2020, 16 hrs. **Pune**: *Maharashtra Exp, 7384*, 1100, 19½ hrs. **Secunderabad**: *Andhra Pradesh Exp, 2724*, 1010, 10½ hrs; *Dakshin Exp, 7022*, 1745, 13½ hrs.

Wardha *p1142*
Bus
Several to/from Wardha from **Nagpur**, 77 km, Express 2½ hrs; ask to be dropped off at **Paunar**. Local bus to **Sevagram** (8 km).

Train
Share auto-rickshaws from the station to Sevagram (25 mins). **Ahmedabad**: *Navjivan Exp, 6046*, 0250, 17½ hrs; *Howrah Ahmedabad Exp, 8034*, 2030, 19½ hrs. **Chennai**: *Navjivan Exp, 6045*, 2325, 18 hrs. **Kolkata (H)** via **Nagpur** and **Raipur**: *Mumbai Howrah Mail, 2809*, 0935, 22½ hrs; *Ahmedabad Howrah Exp, 8033*, 0425, 24½ hrs. **Mumbai (CST)**: *Vidarbha Exp, 2106*, 1615, 13½ hrs; *Howrah Mumbai Mail, 2810*, 1715 (1700 from Sevagram), 14½ hrs. **Mumbai (Dadar)**: *Sewagram Exp, 1440*, 2150, 14½ hrs. **Nagpur**: Several fast trains daily; slow passenger trains stop at Sevagram, though the bus is quicker and more convenient. **Pune**: *Maharashtra Exp, 7384*, 1220, 18 hrs.

Bus

State buses from Amaravati, Nagpur, Wardha and Akola. Also, taxis from Amravati (100 km).

Train

Badnera (105 km: Central Railway) on the Mumbai-Kolkata line is a convenient station. Amaravati is on a short spur (10 km) from Badnera.

✪ Directory

Nagpur *p1142*

Banks Kingsway; Sitabuldi and Central Ave. **Hospitals** Private. CIIMS, T236441, Jasleen, T523779, Orange City, T238431. **Internet** Rs 20 per hr. **Post office** GPO, Palm Rd. **Tourist offices** Maharashtra, Sanskruti Bachat Bhavan, opposite *Hardeo Hotel*, near Lakshmie Theatre, Sitabuldi, T533325, F560680. Mainly for booking MTDC accommodation.

Goa

⦂ Footprint features

Introduction

Brilliant lush green fields of irrigated paddy surround villages and hamlets with white painted churches standing out against occasional empty patches of startling red soil. In the background are the **jungle-clad hills**. Piazzas of **churches**, cool **temple tanks**, shady **Goan houses** and elegant **mansions** splashed with the colour of bougainvillea lend the atmosphere of lethargic Portuguese villages.

With some of India's finest **beaches**, Goa has long been popular as a place for relaxation. It also has the Christian pilgrimage centre of **St Francis Xavier's tomb** at Old Goa. Yet inland Goa, predominantly Hindu, has much to offer with interesting **temples** around Ponda and the 12th-13th century site of **Tambdi Surla**.

★ Don't miss...

❶ The flea market at **Anjuna**, although fairly tacky, is a must for most visitors although the market at **Mapusa** is much more local, pages 1179 and 1171.

❷ Take a taxi down to **Old Goa** to see the Portuguese architecture. Scrums form to see St Francis Xavier's Tomb but the other churches are just as rewarding, page 1158.

❸ Walk from **Fort Aguada** to **Baga** and have fish curry and rice at any of the beach shacks along the way, page 1173.

❹ Try to get to tiny **Fort Tiracol** at the northern end of the state and discover rural Goa, page 1173.

❺ Take a day out to visit the **Savoi Spice Plantation** and buy some spices to take home, page 1194.

❻ If you are not visiting the rest of India, try to visit **Tambdi Surla**, the only pre-Portuguese Hindu temple in Goa, page 1194.

❼ **Cabo de Rama Fort**, in the south, evokes a wonderful sense of history and drama, page 1206.

❽ Right at the southern end of the state is **Palolem**. Its palm-fringed golden beach is one of the best in Goa, page 1207.

Goa

Background → *Population: 1.3 million. Area: 3,800 sq km.*

The land

By Indian standards Goa is a tiny state. The coastline on which much of its fame depends is only 97 km long. The north and south of the state are separated by the broad estuaries of the Zuari and Mandovi rivers. Joined at high tide to create an island on which Panaji stands, these short rivers emerge from the high ranges of the Western Ghats less than 50 km from the coast. Alfonso de Albuquerque grasped the advantages of this island site, large enough to give a secure food-producing base but with a defensible moat, at the same time well placed with respect to the important northwestern sector of the Arabian Sea.

Climate Throughout the year Goa is warm, but its position on the coast means that it never suffers unbearable heat. However, from mid-April until the beginning of the monsoon in mid-June, both the temperature and the humidity rise sharply, making the middle of the day steamy hot. The warm clear and dry weather of its tropical winter stretches from October to March, the best time to visit. The six weeks of the main monsoon in June-July often come as torrential storms accompanied by lashing winds, while up in the cooler air of the Ghats the hilltops can be in swirling cloud and mist. It is a good time of year for the waterfalls!

History

Some identify Goa in the *Mahabharata* (the Sanskrit epic) as Gomant, where Vishnu, reincarnated as Parasurama, shot an arrow from the Western Ghats into the Arabian Sea and with the help of the god of the sea reclaimed the beautiful land of Gomant.

Arab geographers knew Goa as Sindabur. Ruled by the Kadamba Dynasty from the second century AD to 1312 and by Muslim invaders from 1312 to 1367, it was then annexed by the Hindu Kingdom of Vijayanagar and later conquered by the Bahmani Dynasty of Bidar in North Karnataka, who founded Old Goa in 1440. When the Portuguese arrived, Yusuf Adil Shah, the Muslim King of Bijapur, was the ruler. At this time Goa was an important starting point for Mecca-bound pilgrims, as well as continuing to be a centre importing Arab horses.

The Portuguese were intent on setting up a string of coastal stations to the Far East in order to control the lucrative spice trade. Goa was the first Portuguese possession in Asia and was taken by **Alfonso de Albuquerque** in March 1510, the city surrendering without a struggle. Three months later Yusuf Adil Shah blockaded it with 60,000 men. In November Albuquerque returned with reinforcements, recaptured the city after a bloody struggle, massacred all the Muslims and appointed a Hindu as Governor. At first they employed Hindus as officials and troops. Mutual hostility towards Muslims encouraged links between Goa and the Hindu Kingdom of Vijayanagar. Religion only became an issue when missionary activity in India increased. Franciscans, Dominicans and Jesuits arrived, carrying with them both religious zeal and intolerance. The Inquisition was introduced in 1540 and all evidence of earlier Hindu temples and worship was eradicated from the territories of the "Old Conquests".

Goa became the capital of the Portuguese Empire in the east and was granted the same civic privileges as Lisbon. It reached its greatest splendour between 1575 and 1600, the age of 'Golden Goa', but when the Dutch began to control trade in the Indian Ocean it declined. The fall of the Vijayanagar Empire in 1565 caused the lucrative trade between Goa and the Hindu state to dry up. Between 1695 and 1775 the population of Old Goa dwindled from 20,000 to 1,600 and by the mid-19th century only a few priests and nuns remained.

where Old Goa is situated, plus the neighbouring areas – Bardez, Ponda, Mormugao and Salcete. The coastal provinces formed the heart of the Portuguese territory and are known as the **Old Conquests**. The **New Conquests** cover the remaining peripheral areas which came into Portuguese possession considerably later, either by conquest or treaty. Initially they provided a refuge for not only the peoples driven from the Old Conquest but also their faith. By the time they were absorbed, the full intolerant force of the Inquisition had passed. Consequently, the New Conquests did not suffer as much cultural and spiritual devastation.

The Portuguese came under increasing pressure in 1948 and 1949 to cede Goa, Daman and Diu to India. The problem festered until 1961 when the Indian Army, supported by a naval blockade, marched in and brought to an end 450 years of Portuguese rule. Originally Goa became a Union Territory together with the old Portuguese enclaves of Daman and Diu, but on 30 May 1987 it became a full state of the Indian Union.

Culture

While in the area of the Old Conquests tens of thousands of people were converted to Christianity, the Zuari River represents a great divide between Christian and predominantly Hindu Goa. Today about 70% of the state's population is Hindu, and there is also a small but significant Muslim minority.

Portuguese used to be much more widely spoken in Goa than was English in most of the rest of India, but local **languages** remained important. The two most significant were Marathi, the language of the politically dominant majority of the neighbouring state to the north, and Konkani, the language commonly spoken on the coastal districts further south. Goa's official language now. English and Hindi are understood in the parts visited by travellers but in rural areas, Konkani predominates.

Cuisine Although Goan food has similarities with that in the rest of India, there are many local specialities. The food in this region is hot, making full use of the small bird's-eye chillies grown locally. However, the main tourist centres offer a good range including western and Chinese dishes. Common ingredients include rice, coconut and cashew nuts, pork, beef (rare in the rest of India) and a wide variety of seafood.

Spicy pork or beef *vindalho*, marinated in garlic, vinegar and chillies is very popular (elsewhere in India 'vindaloo' often refers to a hot, spicy curry). *Chourisso* is Goan sausage made of pork pieces stuffed in tripe, boiled or fried with onions and chillies. It is often eaten stuffed into bread. *Sorpotel*, a highly spiced dish of pickled pig's liver and heart, seasoned with vinegar and tamarind, is perhaps the most famous of Goan **meat dishes**. *Xacutti* is a hot chicken or meat dish prepared with coconut, pepper and star anise. For *Chicken Cafrial,* the meat is marinated in pepper and garlic and braised over a slow fire.

"**Fish curry and rice**", the common Goan meal, has become a catch phrase. Most beach shacks offer a good choice depending on the day's catch and will usually include preparations of kingfish, tuna, mackerel, prawns and often lobster and shark. *Apa de camarao* is a spicy prawn pie and *reichado* is usually a whole fish, cut in half, and served with a hot *masala* sauce. You will find lobsters, baked oysters, boiled clams and stuffed crabs as specialities. *Bangra* is Goa mackerel and *pomfret* a flat fish; fish *balchao* is a preparation of red masala and onions used as a sauce for prawns or kingfish. *Ambot tik* is a hot, sour tamarind and chilli curry made with shark, squid or ray and eaten with rice, while *seet corri* (fish curry) uses the ubiquitous coconut. *Balchao* is prawn, king fish (or meat) in a red chilli and onion sauce. *Kishmur* is ground, dried shrimp mixed with shredded coconut and onion, used as an accompaniment. Spicy pickles and chutneys add to the rich variety of flavours.

Goan **bread** is good and there are pleasant European style **biscuits**. *Undo* is a hard crust round bread, while *kankonn*, hard and crispy and shaped like a bangle is often dunked in tea. *Pole* is like chapatti, often stuffed with vegetables, and Goans prepare their own version of the South Indian *idli*, the *sanaan*. The favourite dessert is *bebinca*, a layered coconut and jaggery delicacy made with egg yolks and nutmeg. Other sweets include *dodol*, a mix of jaggery and coconut with rice flour and nuts, *doce*, which looks like the North Indian *barfi*, *mangada*, a mango jam, and *bolinhas*, small round semolina cakes. There are also delicious **fruits**. Apart from the common coconut and banana and the delicious *alfonso* mangos in season, the extremely rich *jackfruit*, papaya, watermelons and cashew nuts are grown in abundance.

Drinks in Goa remain relatively cheap compared to elsewhere in India. The fermented juice of cashew apples is distilled for the local brew *caju feni* (*fen*, froth) which is strong and potent. Coconut or *palm feni* is made from the sap of the coconut palm. *Feni* is an acquired taste; it is often mixed with soda, salt and lime juice. It can also be taken "on the rocks", as a cocktail or pre-flavoured. 'Port', a very sweet red wine and also dark rum is sold.

Festivals

In addition to the major Hindu, Christian and Muslim festivals, Goa celebrates its own special ones. Check dates with the tourist office.

January 6th *Feast of the Three Kings*, celebrated in Cansaulim (Cuelim), Chandor and Reis Magos. See page 1162.

February/March The *Carnival* is a non-religious festival celebrated all over Goa. On the first day (*Fat Saturday*), 'King Momo' leads a colourful procession of floats with competing 'teams' dressed in flamboyant costumes as they wind through the towns' main streets.

March *Shigmotsav* Similar to *Holi*, at full moon, particularly in Panaji, Mapusa, Vasco da Gama and Margao, is accompanied with plenty of music on drums and cymbals. *Procession of all Saints* in Goa Velha, on the Monday of Holy Week.

April *Feast of Our Lady of Miracles*, Mapusa, on the nearest Sunday, 16 days after Easter.

May 30th *Goa Statehood Day*, when all Government offices and many shops close.

June 13th *Feast of St Anthony*, with songs requesting the gift of rain. *Feast of St John the Baptist (Sao Joao)* (24th). See page 479. *Festival of St Peter* (29th), Fort Aguada, with a pageant on a floating raft.

August *Janmashtami* (birth of Lord *Krishna*) marked with mass bathing in the Mandovi River off Divar Island. *Harvest Festival of Novidade* (different dates from 21st to 27th). The first sheaves of rice are offered to the priests, the Governor and Archbishop, and placed in the Cathedral on the 24th. The festival includes a re-enactment of one of the battles between Albuquerque and the Adil Shah on the lawns of the Lieutenant Governor's Palace.

October *Narkasur* On the eve of Diwali, Goan Hindus remember the victory of Lord Krishna over the demon Narkasur. In Panaji there are processions. *Fama of Menino Jesus* at Colva.

December *Feast of St Francis Xavier* (3rd) at Old Goa. *Liberation Day* (17 December) marking the end of Portuguese colonial rule (public holiday). *Food Festival*, *Christmas* (25 December). Midnight Mass.

Modern Goa

The Goa Legislative Assembly has 40 elected members while the state elects three members to the Lok Sabha. Although the Congress has been the largest single party, **political life** is strongly influenced by the regional issue of the relationship with neighbouring Maharashtra. Regional issues remain important, but there is now also a strong environmental lobby, in which the Catholic Church plays a prominent part.

In common with much of the west coast of India, Goa's rural **economy** depends on rice as the main food crop, cash crops being dominated by coconut, cashewnut and areca nut. Mangos, pineapples and bananas are also important, and forests still give some produce. Seasonal water shortages have prompted the development of irrigation projects, the latest of which was the interstate Tillari Project in Pernem Taluka, completed with the Government of Maharashtra. Iron ore and bauxite have been two of the state's major exports but heavy industrial development has remained relatively limited. Tourism remains one of the state's biggest earners.

★ Panaji (Panjim)

➔ *Phone code: 0832. Colour map 5, grid B7. Population: 58,800. Airport: 29 km.*
Occupying a narrow coastal strip between a low laterite hill – the 'Altinho' – and the mouth of the Mandovi River, Panaji, the capital, still has the feel of quite a small town. There are no great buildings or attractions which would make it a daw for a long stay, but it does retain enough character to warrant a visit. There are very pleasant walks over the Altinho and through the old district of Fontainhas. ➔ *For Sleeping, Eating and other listings, see pages 1165-1171.*

Ins and outs

Getting there From Dabolim airport, across Mormugao Bay, get a prepaid taxi or a bus. Most rail travellers arriving by Konkan Railway from Mumbai and the north, or from coastal Karnataka and Kerala, get to Margao, southeast of the capital; from there taxis and buses go to Panaji (or to your resort). Karmali station (see Old Goa) is nearer, with taxis for transfer. The state Kadamba buses and private coach terminals are in Patto to the east of town. From there it is a 10-min walk across the footbridge over the Ourem Creek to get to guesthouses. The catamaran service from Mumbai remains suspended.

Getting around Auto-rickshaws are the most convenient means for negotiating the city. Motorcycle rickshaws are cheaper but can be more risky. Local buses run along the water front from the city bus stand via the market, towards Miramar.

Climate Best time to visit is Dec-Mar.

Sights

The riverside boulevard (Devanand Bandodkar Marg) runs from the 'new' Patto bridge, past the jetties, to the formerly open fields of the **Campal**. Along it are some of the town's main administrative buildings.

At the east end is the **Idalcao Palace** of the Adil Shahs, once their castle. The Portuguese rebuilt it in 1615 and until 1759 it was the Viceregal Palace. In 1843 it became the Secretariat, and now houses the Passport Office. Next to it is a striking dark statue of the **Abbé Faria** (1756-1819) looming over a prostrate figure of a woman. Abbé José Custodio de Faria, who made a worldwide reputation as an authority on hypnotism, was born near Calangute. At the age of 15 he travelled to Lisbon – a journey that took over nine months – never to return to Goa.

Further west, almost opposite the wharf are the **library** and public rooms of the **Braganza Institute** ① *Mon-Fri 0930-1300, 1400- 1745.* The blue tiled frieze in the entrance, made in 1935, is a 'mythical' representation of the Portuguese colonization of Goa. The tiled panels should be read clockwise from the entrance on the left wall. Each picture is set over a verse from the epic poem by the great Portuguese poet Camoes.

Largo da Igreja, the main square, is south of the Secretariat, dominated by the white-washed **Church of Immaculate Conception** (1541, but subsequently enlarged and rebuilt in 1619), with tall twin towers in the Portuguese Baroque style and modelled on the church at Reis Magos.

On the eastern promontory, beyond the hill, is the **St Thome** quarter with its traditional 18th- and 19th-century houses. Across the square is the old **Mint**. **Fontainhas** lies to the south of San Thome, where you can travel back in time by taking a walk down the narrow lanes between the modest old Portuguese houses. Their colour washed walls, sloping tiled roofs and decorative wrought iron balconies have been preserved and the quarter is ideal for exploring on foot. **San Sebastian Chapel** is small and attractive (built in 1818, rebuilt in 1888), and lies in the heart of Fontainhas. The chapel houses the large wooden crucifix which until 1812 stood in the Palace of the Inquisition in Old Goa. The *Altinho*, meaning hill, to the south of town, offered defensive advantages; it is well worth walking up for the view over the estuary. Most of the buildings on the Altinho today date from the 19th or 20th centuries.

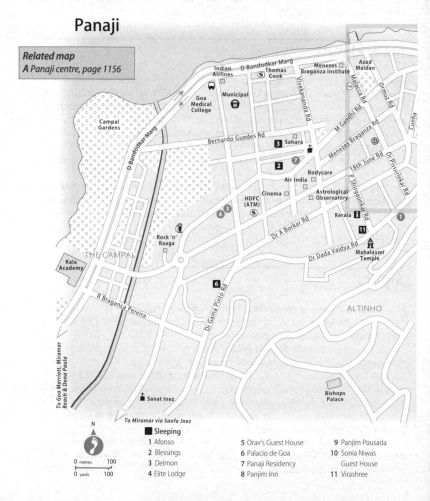

Panaji

Related map
A Panaji centre, page 1156

■ **Sleeping**
1 Afonso
2 Blessings
3 Delmon
4 Elite Lodge
5 Orav's Guest House
6 Palacio de Goa
7 Panaji Residency
8 Panjim Inn
9 Panjim Pousada
10 Sonia Niwas
  Guest House
11 Virashree

The **Goa State Museum** ⓘ *0930-1730, free, Patto, south of Kadamba Bus Stand, a short walk across the Ourem Creek footbridge, take a right across the waste ground, past the State Bank staff training building,* is an impressive building but contains a disappointingly small collection of religious art and antiquities.

Excursions

Mandovi river

The Mandovi and Zuari estuary ⓘ *local fishermen if asked will take you close to the mangroves, pay no more than Rs 100,* is one of the most important mangrove complexes in India, even though today it covers less than 20 hectares. Sea water penetrates a long way inland, especially in the dry season. However, there are approximately 20 species of mangroves, including some rare ones.

Chorao Island and Dr Salim Ali Bird Sanctuary ⓘ *1000-1700, Re 1, best Nov-Feb, ferry from Ribandar to Chorao,* lie opposite Panaji at the confluence of the Mandovi and Mapusa rivers. It is now the focus of a range of conservation measures. The bird

● **Eating**

1 A Pastélaria
2 Avanti
3 Baskin Robbins
4 Coriana
5 Horseshoe
6 Porry & Coolie
7 Shiv Sagar
8 Venite & Vihar

sanctuary occupies 2 sq km of the west tip of the island along the Mandovi River. The mangrove forests form a protective habitat for coastal fauna and in addition to birds it harbours a large colony of flying foxes, crocodiles, turtles and jackals.

Beaches near Panaji

Miramar Panaji's seafront boulevard runs south for 3 km along the Mandovi estuary. Miramar is very 'urban' in character, the water is polluted and the beach is not particularly attractive, so it is not an ideal place for a beach holiday. It is however a pleasant drive offering good views over the sea. Most of the hotels are on, or just off, the D Bandodkar Marg (DB Marg), the road to Dona Paula along the coast.

Dona Paula Dona Paula has a small palm fringed beach with casuarina groves and is very peaceful. It is named after a Viceroy's daughter who reputedly jumped from the

Panaji centre

Sleeping
1 Frank's Inn
2 Keni's
3 La Capitol
4 Mandovi & Riorico Restaurant
5 Manvin's
6 Neptune
7 Nova Goa
8 Rajdhani

Eating
1 Café Moderna
2 Café Tato
3 Delhi Darbar
4 Dominos Pizza
5 Hot Breads
6 Quarterdeck
7 Kamat
8 Mongini's
9 Moti Mahal
10 Rosoyo
11 Satkar
12 Sher-e-Punjab

0 metres 100
0 yards 100

⁝ A drop in the ocean

The watersport industry is still a fledgling enterprise and although agents offer a number of options within easy reach of the major resorts, the easiest to arrange are a choice of boat trips.

Popular trips to view **dolphins** are available from most areas, costing between Rs 200-500. John, of *John's Boat Trips* in Candolim, T277780 (ticket agents at *Bom Sucesso* and *Alma Inn*), is a knowledgeable and friendly host with a good understanding of the dolphins (also provides fishing trips, snorkelling, etc). He charges Rs 500, with guaranteed sighting of usually two species, the bottle-nosed and the hump-backed dolphins. The trip includes the option to have a swim near the Aguada prison, plus lunch at a typical Portuguese house on Coco Beach. Other 'Dolphin Watch' trips are reported to just chase the dolphins and return. Another very good excursion that he offers is a **crocodile spotting** trip, Rs 950 – although there is no guarantee of seeing crocodiles it is still worthwhile. Other agents offer similar trips at varying prices as well as trips to 'Paradise Beach', that is Palolem.

Watersport facilities on the beaches are rare and at present are limited to isolated westerners at various locations with no guarantee that they will be there next year (eg European with the jet ski at Candolim). Splash at Bogmalo seem to be more stable, and parasailing is sometimes available from Candolim and Colva beaches although it is highly erratic. Expect to pay at least Rs 600 for a short parasail. The Taj hotels can arrange these but at a price.

Diving is best after the monsoons from October to April. The local dive sites are relatively shallow (8-15 m) allowing underwater visibility of between two and 20 m. The dive sites on coral or rock beds off several islands are usually between 15 and 30 minutes boat ride away and marine life rich and varied. **PADI** certificated diving is offered by *Barracuda Diving India* at the *Goa Marriot Hotel*, Miramar beach and by *Goa Diving* at *Bogmalo Beach Resort*, where safety standards are high. Diving websites include www.barracudadiving.com and www.travel. Indiamart.com/goa/watersports/. Courses range from Discover Scuba Diving (Rs 3,000) to a two-week Divemaster Course (Rs 25,000).

For those wishing to check for PADI recognised courses in India before arriving, contact PADI International Head Office, Unit 6, Unicorn Park, Whitby Road, Bristol, BS4 4EX. T0117-9711717, F9721821, general@padi.co.uk.

cliffs when refused permission to marry a fisherman, Gaspar Dias. The low laterite cliff forms a headland joined to the mainland by a short causeway.

From the roundabout by the National Oceanography Institute a road runs 600 m up to **Cabo Raj Niwas**, now Raj Bhavan, the State Governor's House. A viewing platform near the entrance gives superb views over the sweep of the coastline across the Mandovi estuary to Fort Aguada.

Vainguinim beach The beach to the east of Dona Paula on which the Cidade de Goa stands is backed by a part of Tiswadi which the Jesuits enjoyed as highly productive agricultural land. There is a small beach but swimming can be unpleasurable when other beach activities take over – especially the noise and fumes from motor boats.

Bambolim Off the NH17 south, 8 km from Panaji, Bambolim's dark-sand beach is secluded, free of hawkers and shaded by palms. Goa University is nearby.

★ Old Goa → *Phone code: 0832. Colour map 5a, grid B2.*

Old Goa (or Velha Goa), on the crest of a low-lying hill on the south bank of the Mandovi, may be regarded as the spiritual heart of Portuguese Goa. Today, it has an air of calm that is revived by a steady flow of tourists and the occasional great pilgrimage to the tomb of St Francis Xavier in the Basilica of Bom Jesus. The major monuments are immediately around the Bus Stop and within easy walking distance. Well worth a visit.

Miramar & Dona Paula

Sleeping		Eating
Miramar & Caranzalem	5 Swimsea Beach Resort	9 Prainha Cottages
1 Bela Goa	6 Youth Hostel	10 Villa Sol
2 Blue Bay		
3 Goa Marriott	**Dona Paula &**	**● Eating**
& Barracuda Diving	**Vaiguinim Beach**	1 Expresso Bar
4 Miramar Beach Resort	7 Cidade de Goa	2 White Horse
& Foodland	8 O Pescador, Dona Paula	
	Beach Resort	

0 metres 200
0 yards 200

Old Goa owes its origin as a Portuguese capital to **Alfonso de Albuquerque,** and some of its early ecclesiastical development to **St Francis Xavier** who was here in the mid-16th century. However, before the Portuguese arrived it was the second capital of the Bijapur Kingdom but all the buildings of that period have disappeared.

Old Goa, enclosed by a fortified wall, had shipyards on the river bank with the administrative and commercial centre nearby. The true centre of the town was filled with magnificent churches. These were built of the local red laterite and basalt with fine white limestone used for decorative detail. The exteriors were coated with lime plaster to protect them from the weather which had to be renewed after each monsoon. When maintenance lapsed, the buildings just crumbled away.

Sights

Holy Hill Approaching Old Goa from the west, you pass 'Holy Hill' with a number of churches. From this site Albuquerque directed the battle against the Adil Shahi forces in 1510. The **Chapel of Our Lady of the Rosary** (1526) belongs to the earliest period of church building. At the time of the conquest of Goa.

Just behind, the **Royal Chapel of St Anthony** (early 17th century) was restored by the Portuguese in 1961. The ruined **Tower of St Augustine** stands nearby. St Augustine's church (begun in 1572), once boasted eight chapels, a convent, and an excellent library. It was abandoned in 1835 due to religious persecution, the vault collapsed in 1842, followed by the façade and main tower in 1931.

Further on is the **Convent of St Monica** (1607-27), the first nunnery in India. The huge three-storey building, built around a sunken central courtyard which contained a formal garden and a church, has, since 1964, been an Institute of Theological Studies. The **Museum of Christian Art** from Rachol has been moved to the attached church ① *Rs 5. 1000-1230, 1500-1830 (check if open through lunch).* More than 150 items have been collected from Goa's churches, convents and Christian homes which reflect a wealth of workmanship in wood, ivory, silver and gold.

Basilica of Bom (the Good) Jesus The laterite façade of Bom Jesus (1594-1605) ① *0900-1830, no photography although this appears to be totally ignored by all,* is the richest in Goa and also the least Goan in character with a single tower at the east end. The Renaissance façade shows transition to Baroque. Apart from the elaborate gilded altars, wooden pulpit and the candy-twist Bernini columns, the interior is very simple. The World Heritage Site contains the treasured remains of **St Francis Xavier,** a pupil of Ignatius Loyola who founded the Order of Jesuits, see page 1347. In 1613 St Francis' body was brought to the adjoining Professed House (see below) from the College of St Paul. It was moved into the church in 1624, and its present chapel in 1655 where it has remained ever since. The tomb lies to the right of the main chancel. St Francis was canonized in 1622. The Order of the Jesuits was suppressed in 1759 but the church was allowed to continue services, and in 1964 it was raised to a minor basilica.

The **Tomb of St Francis Xavier** (1696), the gift of one of the last of the Medicis, Cosimo III, was carved by the Florentine sculptor Giovanni Batista Foggini. It is made of marble and jasper, while the casket containing the remains is silver and has three locks, the keys being held by the Governor, Archbishop and Convent Administrator. Initially the saint's body was exposed for viewing on each anniversary of his death but this ceased in 1707. Since 1859, there has been an **Exposition** every 10 to 12 years; the next is in December 2004 continuing into January. The Saint's Feast Day is on 3rd December.

The body of St Francis has suffered much over the years and has been gradually reduced by the removal of various parts. One devotee is reputed to have bitten off a toe in 1554 and carried it in her mouth to Lisbon. Part of an arm was sent to Rome in

1615 where it is idolized in the 'Gesu', while a part of the right hand was sent to the Christians in Japan in 1619. In 1890 a toe fell away and is displayed in the Sacristy.

The adjoining **Professed House** for Jesuit fathers is a two-storey building with a typically Mediterranean open courtyard garden. After a fire in 1633 destroyed it, it was only partially rebuilt. It now houses a few Jesuits who run a small college.

Se Cathedral Across the square, the Se Cathedral ① *0900-1830*, is dedicated to **St Catherine**. The largest church in Old Goa, it was built by the Dominicans between 1562-1623. Tuscan in style on the exterior and Corinthian inside, the main façade faces east with the characteristic twin towers (one collapsed in 1776, after being struck by lightning). The remaining tower contains five bells including the Golden Bell which is rung at 0530, 1230 and 1830. The vast interior, divided into a barrel-vaulted nave with clerestory and two side aisles, has a granite baptismal font. On each side of the church are four chapels along the aisles. The clerestory windows are on the outside protected by a shield crowned by a balustrade to keep off the sun from the interior. The main altar is superbly gilded and painted, with six further altars in the transept. The marble top table in front of the main altar has been used for the exposition of the relics of St Francis Xavier since 1955 in order to accommodate the vast crowds.

Southwest of the Cathedral are the ruins of the **Palace of the Inquisition**, with dungeons below, where over 16,000 cases were heard between 1561 and 1774. The Inquisition was finally suppressed in 1814.

There are two churches and a museum in the same complex as the Cathedral. The **Church (and Convent) of St Francis of Assisi** is a broad vault of a church with two octagonal towers. The floor is paved with tombstones and on either side of the baroque High Altar are paintings on wood depicting scenes from St Francis' life while the walls above have frescoes with floral designs. A chapel was begun by Franciscan friars in 1517, replaced in 1661 by the present church (restored in 1762-65). The convent now houses the **Archaeological Museum** (see below under Museums). To the west, **St Catherine's Chapel** was built as an act of gratitude on defeating the forces of Bijapur in 1510. The original mud and thatch church was soon replaced by a stone chapel which in 1534 became the Cathedral (renovated in 1952), and remained so until Se Cathedral was built.

Old Goa (Velha Goa)

Sleeping ■	Eating ●
1 Tourist	1 Restaurants
	2 Tea Shop

The Viceroy's Arch To the northeast of the Cathedral on the road towards the river is The Viceroy's Arch, built at the end of the 16th century to commemorate the centenary of Vasco da Gama's discovery of the sea route to India. His grandson Francisco da Gama was Viceoy (1597-1600). On the arrival of each new viceroy this would be decorated. Note the strange figures on the back: a lady with a sword and a book (the Bible?) stands above a 'non-believer' awkwardly resting his head on a bent arm! The arch was rebuilt in 1954.

Church of St Cajetan To the east lies the splendid domed Baroque Convent and Church of St Cajetan (1665), built by Italian friars of the Theatine order, sent to India by Pope Urban III. Shaped like a Greek cross, the church was modelled on St Peter's in Rome. It is rarely visited by groups, and hence more peaceful. There is a well under the dome which the guardian will be pleased to show you. Next door is the beautiful former convent building which is now a pastoral foundation (not open to the public).

The **Gate of the Fortress of the Adil Shahs nearby,** comprises a lintel supported on moulded pillars mounted on a plinth. The now ruined palace was occupied by Adil Shahi sultans of Bijapur, before the arrival of the Portuguese in 1510. It became the Palace of the Viceroys from 1554 to 1695.

Chapel of Our Lady of the Mount On a hill to the east stands this chapel (1510) which was restored in 2001 with help from the Fundação Oriente. It can be approached from the east or the south of the hill. The atmosphere of peace beckons and there are excellent panoramic views across Old Goa. Inside the chapel, the alter gilding has been beautifully restored and there are interesting paintings part of the way up the walls giving the visitor an impression of what the other churches here originally looked like.

Museums
★ **Archaeological Museum** and **Portrait Gallery**, Convent of St Francis of Assisi ① *1000-1700, closed Sun. Rs 5. T286133.* The collection of sculptures covers the period from before the arrival of the Portuguese. Many date from the 12th-13th centuries when Goa came under the rule of the Kadamba Dynasty.

Art Galleries *at Se Cathedral and Basilica of Bom Jesus.* ① *0900-1830 (opens 1030 on Sun), closed Fri and during services. Rs 5.*

Around Panaji

Goa Velha
As Richards says, Goa Velha means "old – being already old when the present-named Old Goa (Velha Goa), was still young and flourishing". Goa Velha, once the centre of international trade along the Zuari, was finally destroyed by the Bahmani Muslims in 1470, although as Gopakapattana or Govapuri it had already suffered from repeated attacks and long term decline due to heavy silting. It is difficult now to spot the exact site. A faded notice board by a cross standing on a pedestal, is the only visible remains. On Monday of Holy Week each year, a colourful *Procession of Saints* starts from St Andrew's Church, just north of the dispersed village.

Pilar
① *Getting there: buses along the NH17, the Panaji-Margao Rd, stop nearby at the bottom of the hillock. From there you can walk uphill through the extension of the seminary. It is best to get a taxi, motorbike or bike to get to Talaulim, 4 km north. Drinks and snacks are available near the church.*

The **Pilar Seminary**, not far from Goa Velha, is on a commanding hilltop site. It was founded by Capuchin monks in 1613, who remained here until 1835. The 17th-century church, dedicated to Our Lady of Pilar still shows faint remains of frescoes on the church walls, and also along the cloisters around the enclosed courtyard of the monastery.

The Carmelites took over and restored the monastery in 1858, but from 1890 it became the headquarters of the Missionary Society of St Francis Xavier. **Father Agnelo de Souza** (1869-1927) who spent 10 years in meditation here before dedicating his life to tireless service, awaits canonization. He is revered and remembered by worshippers at his tomb, especially at services on Thursdays throughout the year.

The museum① *1000-1700,* on the first floor of the seminary, displays some of the finds from the Kadamba period. From the rooftop you can get good views of Mormugao harbour and the Zuari. The more recent extension which houses the present seminary has a small chapel with a fine marble altar and some German stained glass.

Talaulim

Just north of the Pilar Seminary is the ★ **Church of St Anna** (Santana) at Talaulim by the River Siridado, a tributary of the Zuari. Built around 1695, its elaborate Baroque façade is similar in design (though smaller) to the great Church of St Augustine at Old Goa. Once the parish church with a large congregation, it fell into disrepair when Old Goa nearby declined, and had to be refurbished in 1907.

St Anna's feast day (26 July) is celebrated by both Christan and Hindu communities who come to seek blessing from the mother of the Virgin Mary, whose intervention is traditionally sought by childless couples. It is known popularly as the *Toucheam* (or Cucumber) *Feast* because those who come to pray for a baby boy (*menino*) bring with them a *pepino* (cucumber). Unmarried boys and girls also come to pray for partners bringing with them spoons (*colher*) to plead for wives (*mulher*) and *mung* beans (*urid*) in exchange for husbands (*marido*)!

Chandor, Rachol and Loutolim → *Colour map 5a, grid B2.*

There are other excursions which give a variety of insights into the colonial past. These are closer to Margao but can also easily be visited from Panaji or the beaches in central Goa. Buses from Margao will get you to within walking distance of the sights but it is worth considering a taxi.

★ Chandor

① *Getting there: private buses from the Kadamba bus stand in Margao take about 45 mins.*

About 13 km east of Margao, on the site of the 11th-century Kadamba capital of Chandrapur, Chandor is an interesting village. The once navigable tributaries of the Zuari River here allowed trade to flourish with distant Arab ports as early as the seventh century. Even earlier, a fourth century Bhoja king's copperplate inscription dates the existence of an ancient fort which once stood at Chandrapur nearby, taking advantage of the natural defensive moat the two rivers provided.

Today, Chandor is very much a backwater. Succeeding Muslim and Christian rulers destroyed much of Chandor's Hindu past. The **Church of Our Lady of Bethlehem** built in 1645, replaced the principal *Sapta Matrika* (Seven Mothers) temple which was demolished in the previous century. Crowds gather on 6th January each year, for the ★ **Three Kings Festival** at Epiphany, which is similarly celebrated at Reis Magos and Cansaulim (Quelim) in southern Goa. The three villages of Chandor

(Cavorim, Guirdolim and Chandor) come together to put on a grand show. Village 1163
boys dress up as the Three Kings and process through the village on horseback
before arriving at the church.

★ **Menezes Braganza House** ⓘ *Both wings are usually open 0900-1800 everyday
but it is best to confirm by telephone. West Wing: T784201 between 1300-1400 or
early evening after 1830. The front door is usually open; go up the stairs and ring the
bell by the door on the left (you may have to wait a few minutes). A donation of Rs 100
(Rs 50 for students) at the end of the tour will be greatly appreciated. East Wing:
T784227. The East Wing is keener on donations. If you are short of time, a tour of the
West Wing with Aida is recommended.* Chandor also retains several fine Portuguese
mansions. Among them is the enormous Braganza family house which faces one side
of the large Church square, about 400 m from the railway station. Luis de Menezes
Braganza was an influential journalist and politician (1878-1938). The part late-16th
century mansion he inherited (extended in the 18th and 19th), shows the opulent
lifestyle of the old Portuguese families who established great plantation estates.

The West Wing, which is better maintained, is owned by Aida de Menezes
Bragança. The guided tour by this elderly member of the family is fascinating. She has
managed to completely restore the teak ceiling of the 250-year-old library gallery; the
old *mareta* wood floor survives since this native Goan timber can withstand water. In
the Dining Room, the original polished *argamassa* floor has been replaced by new
mosaic though a small section of old tiles have been retained near a window, as an
example. There is much carved and inlaid antique furniture and very fine imported
china and porcelain.

The faded East Wing, occupied by Sr Alvaro de Pereira-Braganza which part
mirrors the West Wing, also has some fine carved furniture, where it requires some
imagination to conjure up the grand occasions it had witnessed in the past. The family
chapel at the back now has a prized relic added to its collection, the decorated nail of St
Francis Xavier which had, until recently, been kept guarded, away from public view.

Loutolim

The small village of Loutolim (Lutolim) has several interesting Goan country houses
around it. Unfortunately after some priceless items were stolen from the chapel of one
of these houses, they are no longer open to the public. The owners, who are often
elderly, do not welcome visitors and would be grateful if tourists did not disturb them
but simply viewed the houses from the road.

The only old house open to the public in Loutolim is **Casa Araujo Alvares** ⓘ *Ask at
Ancestral Goa, see below, for an excellent guided tour, T777034, 1000-1230 and
1500-1800, Rs 100.* The original family home of Maendra Alvares, the founder of
Ancestral Goa (see below), the house has yet to be fully restored yet a well informed
guide can bring the past vividly to life. The house has the feel of a museum with a
collection of typical fixtures and furnishings assimilated from other fine houses,
including Bohemian chandeliers, Chinese porcelain, gilded mirrors, carved wooden
furniture, English prints and Portuguese books. The private chapel contained
precious figures, ivory and plate, while the grand salons and reception rooms for
entertaining had highly polished wooden floors and painted tiles. There is also a
growing collection of interesting domestic and agricultural artefacts.

Miranda House The Mirandas became wealthy as owners of areca plantations and
the garden here still has specimen palms as reminders. Their fine country house built
around 1700 is at the end of a rough track which starts near the church square. The
house has a typical garden courtyard at the back around which runs the family rooms
and bedrooms, protected by shady verandahs. There is also a family chapel with the
kitchen and servants' quarters at the far end.

Ancestral Goa ① *0830-1830 daily. Rs 20. Getting there: from Margao bus to Cortalim (via Fatorda and Racaim) stop at the church square, a few minutes walk from the complex, Rs 6. There is a regular bus to Loutolim from Margao, Rs 5.* The village also has this privately developed open-air site designed to illustrate Goa's traditional past. Well worth a visit. Maendra Alvares, an artist/sculptor has devoted considerable time and energy (and finance) to create a unique centre. Great care and research have gone into constructing authentic replicas of old town and village houses and artisans' huts, with an eye to detail when fitting them out with appropriate tools, utensils and artefacts.

The **fisherman's** shack made out of palm fronds and bamboo with sand and shells on the ground. The **farmer's** house built of mud and laterite blocks, with distinctive small clay tiles on the verandah roof. The **taverna** progresses to being partly white-washed, with larger terracotta "Mangalore tiles" on the roof, a layer of cowdung covers the mud floor. The **landowner's** impressive house shows Portuguese influence in its raised *balcao* (verandah), plastered walls built of laterite and mortar, clay floor tiles, red cement seats, the family altar, and the use of decorative ceramic wall tiles, slatted wood ceilings and oyster-shell windows.

Set on a hill side in very attractive surroundings, visitors are given a guided tour by well-informed guides who lead you through a socio-historical journey. Parts of the trail are shaded but take a hat. An added attraction is a chance to see a range of Goa's spices and fruit trees. At the top of the site is Maendra Alvares' single-handed achievement "Natural Harmony", a sculpture of Sant Mirabai carved out of a horizontal block of laterite (15 m x 5 m). A bakery about 500 m away in a private house sells exceedingly mouth-watering *'Melting moments'* – macaroons made with ground cashew nuts. Ask for directions.

Rachol

Rachol (pronounced *Rashol*) is set in a fertile valley, vivid green during the wet season and into the New Year, but burnt brown in the summer heat. A stone archway crosses the road marking the entrance, the road coming to an abrupt end in a hamlet by the river bank. The seminary is well worth a visit, call in advance.

Rachol Seminary The seminary was established here in 1580 since the site had the protection of the fort (the earlier one at Margao was destroyed by Muslims the previous year). Originally known as the College of All Saints, it was rededicated to **Ignatius Loyola** in 1622. The Rachol complex, principally an ecclesiastical college, also includes a hospital, a primary school, an early printing press which printed the Bible in Konkani and is nearly a self-sufficient community. The seminary was under the Jesuits from 1610 until 1759 when they were expelled, and the 'Oratorians' installed in their place. However, in 1835, when all religious orders lost favour in Portugal they too were removed and the Seminary became the responsibility of the Diocesan Clergy of Goa. For successive generations the seminary has been the most prestigious centre of education in Goa producing some of Goa's secular as well as religious leaders, and now is a forward-looking institution which trains clergy able to meet the challenges of society today. The seminary also contains large galleries and a famous library of rare books on the first floor.

The church ① *daily service at 0700 to which visitors are welcome, at all other times visits only by advance notice, contact Father Ivo de Souza, T776621, icsouza@goatelecom.com,* dating from 1609, was rebuilt in 1622. The impressive interior, beautifully restored and rich with gilding, has nine altars including one to St Constantine containing his relics, and one with the celebrated Menino Jesus statue (which was considered miraculous when it had been installed in Colva, see page 1205). There are many murals in the Seminary and Church.

Listings: Panaji

● Sleeping

Panaji *p1153, maps p1154 and p1156*
Director of Tourism, T226515, has a list of
families who host paying guests.

Dabolim airport

A-B Majestic, just across the Mandovi
bridge, Alto Betim, Porvorim, T410378,
F415715, themajestic@vsnl.net. Rooms with
bath, safes, pool, excellent gym, sauna,
restaurant and coffee shop. Panaji's top
business hotel, free airport transfer.
B Hotel Airport, aimed at business travellers,
28 small but functional a/c rooms, pool.

Panaji centre

B Mandovi, D Bandodkar Marg, T426270,
F225451, mandovi@goatelecom.com
66 large a/c rooms (**A** river-facing), rates
include breakfast, 1st floor *Riorico* restaurant,
popular pastry shop, terrace bar, exchange,
good bookshop, old building with hints of
Art Deco, relaxing but lacks great character.
B Nova Goa, Dr Atmaram Borkar Rd,
T226231, F224958, novagoa@
goatelecom.com. 85 good a/c rooms with
bath, some have fridge and bath tub, best
with pool views, standards have slipped,
rooms and corridors dull and dirty.
B-C Delmon, C de Albuquerque Rd, T226846,
F223527. 50 clean rooms with TV and desk,
some a/c, breakfast included. Modern,
comfortable hotel with popular restaurant.
B-C Panjim Pousada, House 156, Cunha
Gonsalves Rd, T228136, panjimin@
goatelecom.com. 9 rooms (best at rear)
around a permanent gallery in a courtyard,
evocative, attractive renovation, peaceful,
good value. Recommended.
C La Capitol, MG Rd, next to Custom House,
T231050, F223304, lsons@goatelecom.com.
12 renovated rooms (some smallish), TV, neat,
clean, restaurant, friendly and willing staff, but
noisy during the day, check-out 0900.
C Panjim Inn, 31 Janeiro Rd, Fontainhas,
T226523, F228136, panjiminn@
goatelecom.com. 14 rooms (a/c Rs 250

extra), size dictates price so inspect first,
300-year-old character house kept in
traditional style (antique furniture, 4-posters
which make small rooms a bit cramped),
very clean, some rooms on busy (noisy
during day) street corner, long waits for food,
mixed reports on welcome.

Guesthouses have 0800-0930 checkout to
accommodate new arrivals on trains and
buses. A 3rd person in a double room with
or without mattress costs Rs 50-100.
C-D Panaji Residency (GTDC), near
Secretariat, overlooking the river, T227103.
40 good-size rooms with balcony, some a/c
(overpriced at Rs 950), best views from top
floor, good open-air restaurant, often full.
D Manvins, fourth floor, Souza Towers,
T228305, F223231, manvins@
goatelecom.com. 40 good size, clean rooms,
compact baths, TV, great views over city,
relaxing rear terrace. Recommended.
D Palacio de Goa, Gama Pinto Rd, T221785,
F224155. Modern 6-storey building, 55 decent
rooms (phone, TV, good value 4 or 5-bed), a/c
(extra Rs 100), top floor best views, restaurant,
check-out 0800, far from bus stand.
D Rajdhani, Dr Atmaram Borkar Rd,
T225362. 32 smallish clean rooms with bath,
some a/c (Rs 100 extra), in modern Indian
business style hotel, good a/c pure
vegetarian restaurant (closed afternoons).
D-E Blessings, MG Rd, behind Bhatkar
House, T224770, F224155. 18 ordinary
rooms, TV (extra Rs 50), two have huge
terraces instead of balconies, restaurant,
quiet back full of trees.
D-E Virashree, opposite Mahalaxmi Temple,
Dr Dada Vaidya Rd, T226656, tchaitanya@
hotmail.com 12 large, comfortable rooms
with TV but lacking quality finish.
E Afonso, near St Sebastian Chapel, Fontainhas,
T222359. 8 clean rooms with bath, shaded roof
terrace for breakfast, a family-run guesthouse,
obliging and friendly, reserve ahead.
E Orav's Guest House, 31 Janeiro Rd,
T426128. 16 good rooms with shower, some
with pleasant balcony, clean modern block
in old part of town.

*For an explanation of the sleeping and eating price codes used in this guide, see inside the
front cover. Other relevant information is found in Essentials pages 52-57.*

F Frank's Inn, 83 Menezes Braganza Rd, T226716. 10 rooms, shared baths, clean.

Others in Fontainhas (usually rooms belonging to local families), include **Elite Lodge**, T422093 and **Sonia Niwas Guest House**, with 7 rooms with bath.

Miramar p1156, map p1158

AL-A Goa Marriott Resort, on Mandovi River, T437001, F437020. 153 large rooms, good facilities, Barracuda Diving centre, pool (close to public beach), best hotel in Panaji area.
C Blue Bay, on Caranzalem Beach, T228087, F229735. 12 simple modern rooms, some a/c, well kept grounds, friendly owner, quiet and isolated.
D Miramar Beach Resort, close to the beach, T227754. 60 clean rooms, some a/c, better (and cheaper) rooms in newer wing by shaded groves, good restaurant.
D-E Bela Goa, T224575, F224155, 11 simple rooms in an uninspiring building, surprisingly light and airy though no balcony, 2 **C** a/c, restaurant, bar, enthusiastic staff.
F Youth Hostel, away from the beach, T225433. 3 rooms (Rs 60 per person), 5 dorms, maximum 3 nights, YHA members Rs 20, also non-members except in Dec and Jan Rs 40, canteen.
B Swimsea Beach Resort, T227028, F224480, swimsea@satyam.net.in. At the far end of Caranzalem Beach. 28 a/c rooms with small balconies (in need of a makeover), sea facing best, pool, close to black sandy beach.

Dona Paula p1156, map p1158

B Prainha Cottages, T227221, F229959, prainha@goatelecom.com. 42 rooms, 'Madeira cottages' best (a/c, nearer beach and with sea view), spacious, simple but comfortable and quiet (reports of poor sound insulation on upper floor), good views, palm shaded garden, good restaurant, small pool, beautiful secluded beach, helpful staff.
C O Pescador, *Dona Paula Beach Resort*, T227955, F221371, pescador@goa telecom.com. 25 large pleasant rooms in small buildings around a garden (need repainting), rate doubles for a/c and sea-facing balcony, restaurant, good pool, on the beach, quiet, young friendly management.

Vainguinim p1157

LL-AL Cidade de Goa, 26 km from airport, 7 km from Panaji centre, T221133, F223303, hotelcdg@goatelecom.com. 210 rooms (recently refurbished), 4 restaurants, sea-front coffee house, pool, water sports centre, casino, , imaginative development designed by Charles Correa, pleasant and secluded beach but unappealing at low tide.
B Villa Sol, T225852, F220644, villasol@ rediffmail.com 28 rooms with balconies, some overpriced a/c, disco/pub "On The Rocks", restaurant,good size pool, fine sea views but not convenient for beach, grounds now neglected, bit isolated.

Bambolim p1158

B Bambolim Beach Resort is right on the beach, T230927, F230925. There are 120 a/c rooms, some seafacing (Rs 1,925), simple but airy with balcony, open-air beach-side restaurant (breakfast included), bar, palm shaded terrace, pool, taxi necessary (usually available), peaceful, isolated spot. *Sand & Sea Restaurant*, down the beach will cook any kind of fish dish ordered (watch out for price quoted though).

Old Goa p1158, map p1160

E Tourist Hotel (GTDC), near MG (Gandhi) Statue Circle roundabout, T286127. 44 rooms in a poorly maintained building, mosquito prone (bring a net), adequate for an overnight stay for an early visit of the churches avoiding the crowds, friendly restaurant (limited menu). The tea shop near the Palace of the Inquisition Tribunal is a good place for cool drinks.

Rachol p1164

C Naari, nearby, at Maina-Curtorim village. Guesthouse for women among cashew groves, not far from the river, bed and breakfast (US$160 pw double/US$85 single), spacious living space, rooms with bath (hot water), home cooking, garden/terrace, book and pay at least a month ahead, T011-6138316, F6187401, naari@del3.vsnl.net.in.

⊙ Eating

Panaji *p1153, maps p1154 and p1156*
Most restaurants serve some alcohol. Many close between 1500-1900, except for Goan cafés. Several close on Sun evenings.

⍨⍨⍨ Delhi Darbar, MG Rd, T222544. Mainly North Indian, traditional Mughlai, seafood. A/c, excellent carefully prepared dishes, impeccable service, very pleasant, reserve for dinner.

⍨⍨⍨ Goenchin, off Dr Dada Vaidya Rd. Tasty Chinese with spicy seafood (Rs 80-140).

⍨⍨⍨ Rioricoi at the *Mandovi*, D Bandodkar Marg. Good seafood (Tiger prawns Rs 600), Portuguese and Goan dishes, great breakfast.

⍨⍨ Avanti Hotel, Rua de Ourem, T427179, near Old Patto Bridge. Popular local Goan food and chilled beers, a/c, outdoor balcony. Closed Sun. Recommended.

⍨⍨ Horseshoe, Rua de Ourem, T431788. Simple, bright orange decor, lovely high ceilings. Goan and Portuguese dishes, many Rs 60-80. Daily specials, Tiger prawns or Red snapper Rs 300+, Portuguese wines, Rs 600. Reserve weekend evenings. 1200-1430, 1900-1030, closed Sun. Highly recommended.

⍨⍨ Quarterdeck, next to Betim ferry jetty, T432905. Goan, Indian, Chinese. Riverside location is the best in Panaji, very pleasant in the evening occasional live music.

⍨⍨ Venite, 31 Janeiro Rd, T225537. Simple breakfast in peace, good Goan food. Rs 80+ for main dishes, pricier lobsters, beer, arrive early to sit in one of five atmospheric narrow 1st floor balconies, good music, open 0800-2200 (closes in the afternoon and Sun).

⍨ Annapurna, Urmuz Rd. South Indian. Good *thalis* and *dosa* in large, clean eatery upstairs with families relaxing over *chai*.

⍨ Café Tato, off east side of Church Sq. Local institution, busy at lunch time for authentic Goan snacks, a/c upstairs. Closed evenings.

⍨ Corlana, in the lea of New Patto bridge, Goan. Dark purple decor and high backed booths give a slightly seedy feel, but the food is genuine, pleasant owner, excellent fresh fish, chilli fry, sorpotel, roast tongue. Closed Sun.

⍨ Kamat, south end of Municipal Gardens. Very popular dining hall (quiet a/c upstairs), excellent masala dosa (Rs 18) and *thalis* (Rs 28), no alcohol.

⍨ Rosoyo, 18th June Rd. Choice of excellent Gujarati *thalis*, Rs 40-50, generous refills (1130-1530), plus evening special, Rs 80.

⍨ Shiv Sagar, MG Rd. South Indian vegetarian. No *thalis* , tasty Mysore *masala dosa* (Rs 20), clean, popular, a/c upstairs.

⍨ Vihar, R José de Costa. South Indian veg. Well-prepared tasty *thalis* (Rs 50) and good choice of snacks, clean smart a/c upstairs.

Bakeries

A Pastelaria, Dr Dada Vaidya Rd. Good variety of cakes, pastries and breads. *Mandovi Hotel* has a branch too (side entrance).

Hot Breads, MG Rd, behind *State Bank*, near Benetton shop. Bread, mini pizza, croissant and plenty of mouth watering cakes and biscuits, small a/c seating area.

Monginis (popular chain), Dr A Borkar Rd. Assortment of cakes, fresh bread and savoury snacks.

Cafés and fast food

Alternative venues for those tired of *thalis* and Goan seafood. Popular in evenings when the young go out on the town.

Chicky Chocky near Church of the Immaculate Conception. Good fast foods.'Sizzle Point' for speciality sizzlers.

Dominos Pizza, T231166, Church Sq corner. Bright plastic environment, good choice of pizzas (Rs 100-200), delivery service.

Perry & Cookie, MG Rd, west end of town. Takeaway kebab house and roast chicken.

Miramar *p1156, map p1158*
Beach Boogie, Caranzalem Beach, towards Miramar bus stand. Mid-range garden restaurant, varied menu, live music.

Foodland, *Miramar Beach Resort*. Good fastfood available.

Goa Marriott's pastry shop has real continental delights (truffle torte, tiramisu).

Dona Paula *p1156, map p1158*
Goan Delicacy, Hawaii Beach, T224356. (Look for the sign by the rickshaw stand on NIO Circle, follow track to left of Dona Paula road, turn left at the bottom and follow sandy path). Seafood, good local dishes (Rs 60-80 main courses), Tandoori oven, bar, family-run, very friendly. Relaxing evening atmosphere.

White House, near the roundabout, off the road towards the university, has stunning views across Miramar beach and the river.

◑ Bars and clubs

Panaji *p1153, maps p1154 and p1156*
Many bars around Fontainhas are pokey little rooms also serving a few snacks. The *feni* here, delivered in jerry cans, is cheaper than in restaurants.
Café Moderna near Cine National. Popular in evening with young Goan men (women are rarely seen in bars), food not so good, claustrophobic upstairs dining area.

◐ Entertainment

Panaji *p1153, maps p1154 and p1156*
Local papers list all events.
Astronomical Observatory, 7th floor, Junta House, 18th June Rd (entrance in Vivekananda Rd) open 14 Nov-31 May, 1900-2100, in clear weather. Rooftop 6 inch Newtonian reflector telescope and binoculars, plus enthusiastic volunteers. Worth a visit on a moonless night, and for views over Panaji at sunset.
Kala Academy, D Bandodkar Marg, Campal, T223288. The modern and architecturally impressive centre has exhibition galleries, a library and auditoria. Art exhibitions, theatre, and music programmes (from contemporary pop, jazz to Indian classical) are held, mostly during the winter months.

⊛ Festivals and events

Panaji *p1153, maps p1154 and p1156*
In addition to the major festivals in **Feb**, the **Carnival** (3 days preceding Lent in **Feb/Mar**) is somewhat Mediterranean in essence, marked by feasting, colourful processions and floats down streets. **Mar/Apr**, Feat of Jesus of Nazareth, 1st Sun after Easter. **Nov/Dec**, Food & Culture Festival at Miramar Beach (see below). **8 Dec**, Feast of Our Lady of Immaculate Conception. A big fair is held around Church Sq plus an evening (1930) firework display in front of the church during the week before the feast.

○ Shopping

Panaji *p1153, maps p1154 and p1156*
Mapusa and Margao have better Municipal Markets.

Books

Mandovi Hotel bookshop has a good range including American news magazines.
Utopia, Dr A Borkar Rd, near *Dominos Pizza*, Goa tourism booklets and maps, and books on Goan and Indian cuisine, helpful staff, 1000-2000.
Varsha, near Azad Maidan, carries a wide stock in tiny premises, and is especially good for books on Goa, obscure titles are not displayed but ask knowledgeable staff.

Clothes and textiles

For carefully crafted designer wear for women plus accessories, try:
Carey Franklin, Church Sq, next to GOI Tourist Office.
Madame Butterfly opposite Azad Maidan.
Sosa, Rua de Ourem.
Wendell Rodericks, Souza Towers, DR Souza Rd.
  Smart a/c shops near *Delhi Durbar* restaurant have genuine stock of international brands.
  Government Emporia on RS Rd and **Khadi Showroom**, Municipal (Communidade) Building, Church Sq, are good value for clothes, fabric and handicrafts.

Handicrafts

Goa Government handicrafts shops are at the tourist hotels and the Interstate Terminus. There are other emporia on RS Rd.
Kohinoor, 14 Patto Plaza, Shiv Towers. For high class pieces, beautifully displayed.
MusicSinari's, 18 June Rd.
Rock 'n' Raaga, Rizvi Towers, 18 June Rd, T422841. Good CDs (around Rs 575).

Photography

Film, about Rs 100. Developing: fast and high quality (Rs 250 for 36 exp).
Kodak Express, MG Rd. Central Studio, Panaji Residency.
Lisbon Studio, Church Sq.

Provisions

Farm Products, north of Azad Maidan and **Megsons**, 18 June Rd, sell cheese, cooked cold meats, Goan sausages and sweets.
  Many shops sell nuts dried fruit and feni, especially along 18 June Rd.
  Kajuwalla chain has good cashews (around Rs 250 per kilo).

▲ Activities and tours

Panaji *p1153, maps p1154 and p1156*
Soccer
Professional matches are played at the stadium; season Oct-Mar.

Tour operators

Alcon International, D Bandodkar Marg, T/F232267. Quick, efficient and friendly flight bookings.

Goa Tourism tours can be booked at the *Panaji Residency*, MG Rd, T227103; GTDC, Trianora Apartments, Dr Alvares Costa Rd, T226515; Directorate of Tourism, Tourist Home, Patto, T225583; GTDC hotels. The tours which run regularly in season (1 Oct-16 Jun) for min of 8 passengers, leave from *Panaji Residency*. Entrance fees are extra. **North Goa Tour** includes Mapusa, Mayem Lake, beaches Vagator, Anjuna, Calangute, Fort Aguada; **South Goa Tour** includes Old Goa, Shri Mangesh, Ancestral Goa, Loutolim, Margao, Colva, Mormugao, Dona Paula, Miramar; both 0930-1800, Rs 120 (Rs 150, a/c). Similar tours are offered from Margao, Colva, Vasco, Mapusa and Calangute. **Dudhsagar Special** (from Panaji and Calangute) 0900-1800 via Old Goa, Ponda, Tambdi Surla, Rs 500 (a/c Rs 600).

River Cruises by launch are organized on the Mandovi River, sometimes with live bands and sing-along entertainment. Evening cruises are a bit corny but recommended. A bar also operates. *Santa Monivca* (GTDC), Santa Monica Jetty (east of New Patto Bridge): **One hour cruise** 1800-1900, 1915-2015, Rs 100, to Miramar and back.

MGM Travels, MG Rd, T421865, opposite Azad Maidan, reliable and professional, Rs 100 for all rail bookings.

Sita, 101 Rizvi Chambers, 1st floor, C Albuquerque Rd, T220476, F221419, www.sitagoa.com, (0900-1800, Sat 0930-1330).

TCI, "Citicentre", 1st floor, 19 Patto Plaza, T237117, F225152, TCI.goa@gnpun. Travel agents charge Rs 100 -150 to reconfirm international flights. Easy to call the airlines yourself.

Thomas Cook, 8 Alcon Chambers, D Bandodkar Marg, 'ferociously efficient' if slightly expensive.

Walking
There are some beautiful walks through the forested areas of Goa. Contact the **Hiking Assoc of Goa**, 6 Anand Niwas, Swami Vivekenanda Rd.

Watersports
Some large beach resorts, *Cidade de Goa, Vainguinim Beach* and *Fort Aguada Beach Resort*, sailing, water-skiing, windsurfing etc. For diving contact **Barracuda Diving India**, see Miramar.

Yoga
Brahma Kumari, E98 Mala, T226044, 0600-1100, 1600-2000.
Sri Aurobindo Society, Institute Menezes Braganza Building.
Vivekananda Society, 6th floor, Junta House, T224098, 1000-13000, 1500-1800.

Miramar *p1156, map p1158*
Watersports
Barracuda Diving India, at *Goa Marriott Resort*, T437001, 9822-182402 (mob), barracuda@vsnl.com. Highly professional, best diving company in Goa.

Old Goa *p1158, map p1160*
Goa Tourism visit to Old Goa (included in the *South Goa* and *Pilgrim Tours*), spends a short time visiting the sights. It is better to go by bus or share a taxi to give you time to see Old Goa at leisure.

● Transport

Panaji *p1153, maps p1154 and p1156*
Air
The airport is at Dabolim, see page 1200.

Bus
Local Kadamba (KTC) buses and private buses, (often crowded) operate from the Bus Stand in Patto to the east of town, across the Ourem Creek, T222634. Booking 0800-1100, 1400-1630. Tourist Information, 0900-1130, 1330-1700; Sun 0930-1400. The timetable is not strictly kept to as buses often wait until they are full. Frequent service to Calangute 35 mins, Rs 7; **Mapusa** 25 mins, Rs 5. Via Cortalim (Zuari bridge) to **Margao** 1 hr, Rs 8; **Vasco** 1 hr, Rs 8. To **Old Goa** (every 10 mins) 20 mins, Rs 5, continues to **Ponda** 1 hr, Rs 8.

Long distance There are long distance 'Luxury' buses and 'Sleepers' (bunks are shared). **Private operators**: Laxmi Motors, near Customs House, T225745; at Cardozo Building, near KTC Bus Stand: Paulo Tours, *Hotel Fidalgo*, T226291. **State buses** are run by Kadamba TC, Karnataka RTC, Maharashtra RTC. Check times and book in advance at Kadamba Bus Stand. Unlicensed operators use poorly maintained, overcrowded buses; check out beforehand. Buses to **Bangalore**: 1530-1800 (13 hrs), Rs 300; **Belgaum**: 0630-1300 (5 hrs); **Gokarna**; **Hospet (Hampi)**: 0915-1030 (10 hrs), Rs 150 (Rs 350 sleeper); **Hubli** many; **Londa**: 4 hrs, Rs 60; **Mangalore**: 0615-2030 (10 hrs), Rs 180; **Miraj**: 1030 (10 hrs); **Mumbai**: 1530-1700 (15 hrs+), Rs 550 (sleeper), others (some a/c) Rs 300-450; **Pune**: 0615-1900 (12 hrs), Rs 200, Sleeper Rs 400).

Car
Car hire: **Sai Service**, 36/1 Alto Porvorim, just north of the Mandovi Bridge, T417063, or at airport. **Hertz**, T223998; **Joey's**, town centre opposite the *Mandovi Hotel*, T422050, Rs 700 per day (80 km) with driver. **Wheels**, T224304, airport, T512138.

Ferry
Flat-bottomed ferries charge a nominal fee to take passengers (and usually vehicles) when rivers are not bridged. Panaji-Betim (the Nehru bridge over the Mandovi supplements the ferry); Old Goa-Diwar Island; Ribandar-Chorao for Salim Ali Bird Sanctuary; Siolim-Chopdem for Arambol and northern beaches; Keri-Tiracol for Tiracol fort.

Motorcycle
Motorcyle hire: available at all beach resorts, check quality of bike if hiring from a family, rates depend on model, Rs 150-400 per day. For tours, contact **Peter & Friends Classic Adventure** near New Patto Bridge (see also, Mapusa), T254467, F262076, www.classic-bike-india.de.

Rickshaw
Auto-rickshaw: easily available but agree a price beforehand (Rs 20-35), more after dark.

Taxi
Motorcycle-taxi: a bit cheaper. Tourist taxi: (white) can be hired from Goa Tourism,

Trionora Apts, T223396, about Rs 700 per day (80 km). Private taxi: charge similar prices. Share-taxi: run on certain routes; available near the the ferry wharves, main hotels and market places (maximum 5). **Mapusa** from Panaji, around Rs 10 each. **Airport** about 40 mins; Rs 380.

Train
Some Konkan Railways trains stop at **Karmali**, T286398, near Old Goa (20 mins taxi). Rail Bookings, Kadamba Bus Station, 1st floor, T435054, 0930-1300; 1430-1700. The South Central Railway serves the Vasco-Londa/Belgaum line; for details see Transport under Vasco, and under Madgaon (Margao) below.

Miramar and Dona Paula
p1156, map p1158
Bus
From Panaji to Miramar continue to Dona Paula, Rs 8. **NB** In Miramar they turn inland and follow the old road, rejoining the new road just before climbing the hill to Dona Paula.

Old Goa *p1158, map p1160*
From Panaji, frequent **buses** take 15-20 mins (Rs 5). Buses drop you off opposite the Basilica of Bom Jesus; pick up the return bus near the police station. **Auto rickshaws** charge Rs 25, **taxis**, Rs 150 return. Karmali station on the Konkan railway, just east of the centre, has taxis for transfer.

⦿ Directory

Panaji *p1153, maps p1154 and p1156*
Airline offices Air India, 18th June Rd, T431101; **Indian Airlines** and **Alliance Air**, Dempo House, D Bandodkar Marg, T237821; **British Airways**, 2 Exelsior Chambers, opposite Mangaldeep, MG Rd, T224573; **Jet Airways**, Sesa Ghor, 7-9 Patto Plaza, T431472, airport T510354; **Kuwait Airways**, 2 Jesuit House, Dr DR de Souza Rd, Municipal Garden Sq, T224612; **Sahara**, Live-In Appt, Gen Bernard Guedes Rd, airport office, T540043.
Banks Many private agencies change TCs and cash. Sita, transfers money worldwide; **Thomas Cook**, 8 Alcon Chambers, D Bandodkar Marg, T431732, closed Sun. Also for Thomas Cook drafts; money transfers; **Wall Street Finance**, MG Rd, opposite Azad

Maidan; **Amex**, at *Menezes Air Travel*, rua de Ourem, but does not cash TCs. Cash against certain credit cards from: **Central Bank**, Nizari Bhavan; **Andhra Bank**, Dr Atmaram Borkar Rd, opposite EDC House, T223513. **Bank of Baroda**, Azad Maidan. **HDFC**, 18 June Rd, T421922, 24 hr ATM, most convienient way to obtain cash in Panaji. **High commissions** Germany, Hon Consul, c/o Cosme Matias Menezes Group, Rua de Ourem, T223261; **Portugal**, LIC Bldg, Patto, T224233; **UK**, Room 302, 3rd floor, Manguirish Bldg, 18th June Rd, T228571, F232828, bcagoa@goa1.dot.net.

Internet Among many: little.dot.com cyber cafe, 1st floor, Padmavati Towers, 18th June Rd, T427811, 0930-2300. Best in town: **Suraj Business Centre**, T232510, 5 terminals upstairs, excellent fast connection, 0900-2300. **Medical services** Goa Medical College, Av PC Lopez, west end of town, T223026, is very busy; newer College at Bambolim; **CMM Poly Clinic**, Altinho, T225918. **Post office** GPO: Old Tobacco Exchange, St Thome, towards Old Patto Bridge, with Poste Restante on left as you enter. Open Mon-Sat 0930-1730, closed 1300-1400. **Telegraph Office**: Dr Atmaram Borkar Rd. **Tourist offices** Government of India, Municipal Building, Church Sq, T223412. **Goa**, Directorate, Tourist Home, 1st floor, Patto, T225583, F228819, goatour@goa.goa.nic.in for tour but not GTDC accommodation; desk at Panaji Residency; counters at Kadamba Bus Station and Dabolim airport (near Vasco). Goa **Tourism Development Corporation (GTDC)**, Trionora Apartments, Dr Alvares Costa Rd, T226515, F223926, gtdc@goacom.com for GTDC accommodation. **Useful services** Ambulance: T223026, T224601. Fire: T101, T225500. **Police**: T100. **Tourist Police**: T224757. **Foreigners' Regional Registration Office**: Police Headquarters. **Wildlife**: Chief Wildlife Warden, Conservator's Office, Junta House, 3rd floor, 18th June Rd, T224747, and Deputy Conservator of Forests (Wildlife), 4th floor, T229701, for permits and accommodation in the sanctuaries. **World Wildlife Fund**: B-2, Hillside Apartments, Fontainhas (off 31 January St), T226020, advises on trekking with a guide.

North Goa

Bardez and Pernem talukas have a long coastline of wonderful coconut fringed sandy beaches, backed by dunes, and only occasionally interrupted by rocky headland and coves. A string of fishing villages run along the coast. Inland, there are rolling laterite hills covered in open forest. Southern Bardez has saline flood plains which have been managed for centuries through an intricate system of sluice gates. Here salt-tolerant rice varieties co-exist with aquaculture. The Mapusa River was once a transport artery but not anymore; its banks have been reclaimed for building and its waters clogged by urban refuse. ➤ *For Sleeping, Eating and other listings, see pages 1182-1193.*

★ Mapusa → *Phone code: 0832. Colour map 5a, grid A1. Population: 40,100.*

Mapusa (pronounced 'Mahp-sa') is the administrative headquarters of Bardez taluka. It has a busy and colourful Municipal Market, especially interesting on Fridays. The rest of the town is small enough to wander around and observe local activity. Mapusa stands on a long ridge which runs east-west, with fertile agricultural land occupying the flat valley floor right up to the edge of the town. The name may be derived from the extensive swamps which once covered the area; *maha apsa* (great swamps).

Ins and outs
Getting there This is an important junction for interstate and local buses to the northern beaches. Buses arrive at the market square opposite the taxi stand, while the State Kadamba Bus Stand is a bit further south.

Getting around You can walk around the small town and if you should need an auto, Rs 10 should be ample for short hops.

St Jerome's Church, also known as Milagres Church, **Our Lady of Miracles** (1594), was rebuilt in 1674 and in 1839 after it was destroyed by fire. The small church with its scrolled gable and balconied windows in the façade has a belfry at the rear. The main altar is to Our Lady, and those on the two sides to St John and St Jerome. Note also the interesting wooden ceiling. The Church stands near the site of the Shanteri Temple and so is sacred to Hindus as well. See Festival below.

The **Maruti temple** was built on the spot of a firecracker shop in the 1840s which had housed a picture and then the silver image of the Monkey God associated with Rama. Followers of Rama would gather in the shop since the Portuguese destroyed all Hindu temples and none was built for nearly three centuries.

Reis Magos

Reis Magos stands like a watchman facing Panaji across the Mandovi estuary. The small town of some charm is most noted for its 'Royal Fort', built by Don Alfonso de Noronha between 1551 and 1554. In 1703, it was rebuilt; 35 years later it had to face the Maratha onslaught on Bardez and alone with Fort Aguada remained in Portuguese hands.

The Reis Magos **Church** (1555), named after the 'Magi Kings', stands alongside and is one of the early Goan churches which, some believe, was built on the site of a Hindu temple. Dedicated to the three Magi Gaspar, Melchior and Balthazar, the reredos illustrates the story of the Three Kings with a painted wooden panel showing frankincense, myrrh and gold being offered to the baby Jesus. *The Festival of Three Kings* accompanied by a big fair is celebrated here as at Chandor on 6 January each year, see page 1162.

Mapusa

Sleeping
1 Mapusa Residency
2 Satyaheera
3 Sirsat
4 Vilena

Eating
1 Casa Bela
2 Moonlight

★ Northern beaches

Despite the unending stretch of sand that Goa has as its gift, each section has its own distinctive character. The difference reflects in part the nature of the settlements dotted at intervals behind it. Just north of Panaji is the exclusive resort in **Fort Aguada**. Further along is a relatively quiet strip in **Candolim** and then from **Calangute** to **Baga** the coconut palms come closer to the beach with fishing villages nestled among them. This section has close to 200 beach restaurants open during the season. Across the Baga River, **Anjuna** still draws hundreds to the weekly Flea Market, though the beach is too rocky for comfortable swimming. The series of secluded beaches quickly empties towards **Chapora**, and in the far north low rocky headlands create a series of small enclosed bays which are not as easily accessible. Some, like **Arambol** near the northern tip of the state, are being 'discovered' and there is talk of further development.

> ☡ *Oil and litter washed ashore can be a problem, especially on beaches closer to Panaji.*

Ins and outs

There are buses from Mapusa and Panaji to Calangate, Anjuna, Chopora and Arambol but some prefer to hire a motorbike or bike to find their stretch of sand.

Sinquerim beach and Fort Aguada

→ *Phone code: 0832. Colour map 5a, grid B2.*

Sinquerim, 13 km from Panaji, is where the Taj Hotel group set up its *Hermitage Complex* which dominates the headland around the historic Fort Aguada. The Taj complex is at the bottom of the hill where sections of the fortification jut out to the sea. If you want a long beach walk, the firm sand is uninterrupted all the way north to Baga 9 km away.

On the northern tip of the Mandovi estuary with the Nerul River to the east, Fort Aguada, considered essential to keep the Dutch Navy at bay, was completed in 1612, the strongest of the Portuguese coastal forts. A large well and a number of springs provided the fort and ships at harbour with drinking water and gave it its name *'aguada'*, meaning watering place. It saw repeated action against the Marathas. The main fortifications with laterite walls, nearly 5 m high and 1.3 m thick, are still intact; the buildings lower down form the Central Jail.

The motorable road up to the plateau passes the small **Church of St Lawrence** (or Linhares Church, 1630-43). It has an unusual porch with a terrace and balustrades on the towers and parapets.

A 13-m high lighthouse ① *1030-1730, Rs 3,* was added at the top of the fort (84 m above sea level) sometime in the 18th century. It has an oil lamp and there are good views from the top. Next to the fort, there is the 'new' 21-m high concrete lighthouse (1975) ① *1600-1730 (Re 1, no photography)*.

Candolim → *Phone code: 0832. Population: 8,600.*

Candolim has the least developed part of the beach north of Aguada. If you wish to be away from the crowds but within reach of good food, try the beach near *D'Mello's* and *Oceanic* just north. Candolim has no real centre. The beach itself is long and straight, backed by scrub-covered dunes with little shelter. Some beach shacks now fly Union Jacks, Scottish and English flags and play endless Bob Marley. Some hire out sunbeds for around Rs 50.

Calangute → *Phone code: 0832. Colour map 5a, grid A1.*

Calangute, once the remote hippy retreat of the 1960s, is now a busy, rather dirty, commercialized small town with a population 15,800. The centre is crowded and pitifully congested with traffic, especially during the high season as it has become one of the main centres for package tours.

Ins and outs Calangute is 16 km from Panaji and 10 km from Mapusa. Buses from Panaji (35 mins) and Mapusa (20 mins) arrive at the bus stand near the market towards the beach steps. A few continue to Baga to the north, from the crossroads. On market days there are boats from Baga to Anjuna (see under Baga).

Sights There is little of interest in the town but for a fish market and a hexagonal 'Barbeiria' (barbers shop) near the bus stand at the 'T' junction. Immediately north, the narrower **Baga** beach is lined with fishing boats, nets and village huts. A shallow estuary and little headland separate it from **Anjuna**. The main Baga road has several streets off it giving access to the sea. Village houses take in guests but it is a 500-m walk across hot dunes to the beach.

   The beach is okay – no rocks and good swimming but beware of the seaward pulling current. You don't need to go far to see a large number of fishing boats, tackle and fishermen's huts. Hawkers selling sarongs, offering massages or wishing to tell your fortune can be a constant distraction while licensed shacks line the beach, some offering excellent food and a very pleasant evening atmosphere. Behind the busy beach front, coconut trees still give shade to village houses; some offer private rooms to let, while open space is rapidly being covered by new hotels.

Sinquerim Beach & Fort Aguada

N

0 metres 200
0 yards 200

■ **Sleeping**
1 Aguada Hermitage & Fort
   Aguada Beach Resort
2 Aldeia Santa Rita
3 Kamal Retreat
4 Marbella
5 Marfran
6 Palm Shade & Restaurant
7 Per Avel
8 Summerville
9 Taj Holiday Village
10 Village Belle

● **Eating**
1 Banyan Tree
2 Beach House
3 Bon Appetit
4 Octopus Garden
   & Ma's Bakery
5 Palms 'n' Sand
6 Stone House

At weekends the beach near the tourist resort gets particularly crowded with domestic day trippers – some come in the hope of catching a glimpse of scantily clad foreigners.

Baga and Arpora

Sandwiched between Calangute and Anjuna, Baga – really the north end of Calangute beach – has more character. Reached either directly along the beach or by the coconut-shaded road slightly inland, parts of Baga still retain something of its more 'distanced' feel, though even here development has been rapid. It has left behind almost completely the hippy past which brought it to prominence. Arpora, a few kilometres inland is gaining in status by attracting those with ample cash to spare to its exclusive hotel and restaurants.

Sights Although the beach is relatively clean, at high tide the strip is very narrow after accounting for the rows of shacks and fishing boats. It is also far from quiet – with a high concentration of trinket sellers, masseurs and ear cleaners (not hygienic!) who will hassle you for custom at regular intervals. Sun beds are on hire for Rs 50, rising to Rs 100 during the peak season when they are all guaranteed to be occupied.

❂ Many of the beachside restaurants have stalls and there is a good mix of live music played.

To the north, you can wade across the attractive estuary at low tide with care, for a pleasant 45-minute walk round the headland leading to the first of Anjuna's beaches. The ugly concrete bridge across the Baga River adds about 1 km to this walk. Take care when using this bridge at night as there are no lights. The area around Baga River also offers good bird watching. There are thick woods on the hillside on the north side and mangroves along the banks, while the village itself has paddy fields, marshes, water tanks and salt pans.

An Anjuna style "Hippie Market" appears on Saturday evenings from 1700 to midnight when Westerners and local vendors congregate inland towards Arpora, north of the Baga river, to trade shabby "ethnic" goods. Now there is another Saturday market, Ingo's, a few kilometres on the inland road, just off to the right as you drive between Arpora and Anjuna. Both are quite relaxed and have a more of a small festival feel.

Candolim & Sinquerim

0 metres 100
0 yards 100

N

■ Sleeping
1 Alexandra Tourist Centre
2 Casa Sea Shell
3 Costa Nicola
4 D'Mello's Sea View
5 Dona Alcina & Dom Francisco
6 Highland Beach Resort
7 Sea Shell Inn
8 Whispering Palms
9 Xavier

● Eating
1 Club 21
2 Coconut Inn
3 Fisherman's Cove
4 Mermaid
5 Oriental
6 Titus Roma Pisa

Calangute

To Baga

To Arpora & Anjuna

COBRAVADDO

Casa Goa

Our Lady
of Piety

Taxis   WC   Nikki's

Book
Palace   Sports
Field   St John's

UMTAVADDO   Wall St

MGM   SBI   BoB

Buses for Panaji

MADDOVADDO

St Alex

School

Thomas Cook

St Anthony's

GAURAVADDO   Day Tripper Travels

Kerkar Art
Gallery

To Candolim

To Mapusa

N

| 0 metres | 100 |
| 0 yards | 100 |

■ Sleeping
1 Ale-Pas
2 Coco Banana
3 Concha Beach Resort
4 Estrela do Mar
5 Goan Heritage
6 Golden Eye
7 Horizon Resorts
8 Johnny's
9 Martin's Guest Rooms
10 Ondas do Mar

11 Paradise Village
12 Pousada Tauma
13 Santiago Resorts
14 Victorian Heritage
15 Villa Goesa
16 White House

● Eating
1 Delhi Darbar
2 Infanteria
3 Jerry's Place
4 Le Restaurant
5 Master Joel
  Confectioners
6 Pedro's
7 Plantain Leaf
8 Souza Lobo
9 Sportsman

Baga

To Goa Solo Andata, J&A's Italian, Lila Café St Ann's Church (150m), Saturday Market (200m), Sun Village & Anjuna

To Bicycle Hire & Calangute-Anjuna Road

To Calangute

N

| 0 metres | 100 |
| 0 yards | 100 |

Sleeping
1 Alidia Beach Cottages
2 Andrade Guest House
3 Baga Queen
4 Baia do Sol
5 Cavala
6 Lina's Guest House
7 Nani's & Rani's
8 Riverside
9 Ronil Beach Resort
10 Sunshine Beach Resort
11 Venar
12 Villa Fatima

Eating
1 Bernard's Place
2 Blue
3 Britto's
4 Domingo's
5 Fiesta
6 Indian Impact

Anjuna

→ *Phone code: 0832. Colour map 5a, grid A1.*

Anjuna is still one of Goa's most visited beaches. Beach parties continue to attract crowds and the thump of rave/dance music sometime reaches all the way to Vagator. During the day there is a constant traffic of motorbikes and scooters along the roads. Then there is the Wednesday Flea Market. The government proposes to ban all night parties and deal with the unpleasant side effects of related activities.

Ins and outs Getting there: There are frequent buses from Mapusa and a daily bus from Panaji which stop along the main Mapusa Rd. Get down at Starco's crossroads for hotels and guesthouses. Boats ply from Baga and Arambol for the Wednesday Market. **Getting around:** Baga is a 30-min walk away. Motorbikes are easy to hire. See Transport, page 1191, for further details.

Anjuna took over from Calangute as the centre for hippies but they are long gone, leaving their modern equivalent, who often stay on a long term basis. The availability of drugs attracts local police during the high season. They carry out raids on travellers' houses and harass partygoers and sometimes innocent motorcyclists. Note that there are several foreigners serving long sentences.

Anjuna has three centres, De Mello Vaddo, Dando Vaddo and Titayr Vaddo, each with rooms to let and a selection of shops and restaurants. Most places close to the beach are very cheap and have far less character than those tucked away inland away from the busy access roads. The **Wednesday Flea Market** has become very commercialized so can be disappointing (see box page 1179). Some find the Mapusa Market better for local colour.

Vagator and Chapora

→ *Phone code: 0832. Colour map 5a, grid A1. 22 km from Panaji.*

A couple of roads head north from Anjuna into the sprawling village of Vagator, which in turn runs into the small fishing village of Chapora. Vagator has become the centre for most of the Goa Trance party scene. Below the principal view point is '**Disco Valley**' a well-known location during the season. Popular party venues for the last few years have been *Nine Bar*, then on to the *Primrose Café* and *Hilltop Motel*. Vagator has also attracted significant numbers of Italians and Israelis who stay for a time and make a visible presence.

Chapora Fort Chapora Fort commands the hilltop at the north end of the bay, immediately above *Sterling Resorts*. Now in ruins, the fort on the south bank of the Chapora River dominates the estuary. It was originally built by Adil Shah. The Portuguese built it in its present form in 1717 as a secure refuge for the people of Bardez in the face of Maratha attacks, as well as a defence of the river mouth. Despite the fact that none of the original buildings have survived, the fort remains superbly atmospheric. It is quite a climb, so carry some water.

North of the fort along the estuary mouth at Chapora, traditional boat building is carried out on the riverside. North of Chapora, on the Siolim road, **Badem Church** overlooking the estuary is one of the nicest sunset spots.

Anjuna

3 Laguna Anjuna *A2*	2 Basilico Pizza *A1*	10 Pussy Cat *B2*
4 Lolita's *B3*	3 Bean Me Up *A2*	11 Shore Bar *B1*
5 Martha's *B2*	4 Crab Key Foods *B1*	12 Sonic *A1*
6 Red Cab Inn *A1*	5 Gregory's *C3*	13 Sunset *B1*
7 White Negro *B1*	6 Guru Bar *B1*	14 Tin Tin Tibet *B3*
	7 Happy Hours Café *C1*	15 Whole Bean Tofu *B2*
Sleeping	8 Mango Shade *C2*	16 Why Knought *A1*
1 Anjuna Beach Resort *A1*	9 Munche's *A1*	17 Xavier's *C2*
2 Don Joao Resort *A2*	● **Eating & drinking**	
	1 Amigo *A1*	

0 metres 200
0 yards 200

▪ Anjuna flea market

Despite government attempts to regulate it, the Wednesday Flea Market is huge and very popular – some find it colourful and worthwhile for jewellery, souvenirs and ethnic clothes. From its origins as an opportunity for foreign travellers to sell personal possessions in order to get on – or get home – the Flea Market has become an all-India market. Kashmiris and Rajasthanis set up stall alongside stallholders from much closer to home. Everything is geared gaudily and unashamedly at the tourist. Haircuts and henna 'tattoos' are on offer, alongside juggling equipment and chocolate cakes. Prices are extortionate compared to other shops. The best time to visit is the early morning (0800) or just before sunset to avoid the midday crowds who jam the approach roads. In the high season the afternoon can get oppressive and it can be difficult to move around, but at least the beach provides a handy escape valve.

An Englishwoman, Anita Edgar, with the help of a local church, has opened four children's homes and an informal school in Goa since 1997. The El Shaddai trust collects shoes, clothes, spectacles, books etc from charitable departing visitors and welcome volunteers. The Homes in Saligao and Assagao may be visited between 1600-1800. To find out more, contact them at St Anthony Apartments, C Block, Mapusa Clinic Road, Mapusa, T264798, www.elshaddai-trust.org.

Little Vagator Just south of 'Big' Vagator Beach there are two other small beaches which are more popular with younger travellers who fancy a change from Anjuna. Little Vagator is past the *Disco* party spot, while nestling at the bottom of a palm covered cliff is the attractive 'Ozran' (Spaghetti) beach ① *from Starco's restaurant (a well-known meeting place in Anjuna), at the junction of Mapusa and Chapora roads, walk, bike or take a bus to Chapora and get off at the stop at the first paved road to the left (west) where there is a board for the Alcove Restaurant and Disco; the Alcove is perched on the rock just above the beach.* A steep path leads down to the sands where there is a sculpted face of Siva on a rock created by a long-stay visitor in the early 1990s which is partly submerged at high tide – it is a frisbee hang-out.

Siolim ① *The direct route to Arambol and Tiracol passes through Asvem and Mandrem (see below).* The **Church of St Anthony** dominates the square in Siolim (pronounced 'Show-lem') close to the village market. Built in 1606, it replaced an earlier (1568) Franciscan church. The high,flat-ceilinged church has a narrow balustraded gallery and Belgian glass chandeliers. The attractive and typically gabled west end has statues of Jesus and St Anthony. The shady village with its remains of a few fine Portuguese houses retains a leisured feel.

Morjim Morjim lies on the north side of the Chapora River estuary right at its mouth. The beach is still clean and idyllic with minimal development and could be the perfect laid back scene for anyone looking for quiet. However many more people are driving up here on motorbikes from Vagator and Anjuna to escape the hordes of day visitors who descend on their beaches.It has been found to be a **turtle nesting** site. The villagers have been encouraged to protect the southern end of the beach when the eggs are laid from late October. The area is also popular for **bird watching**.

After crossing the estuary by ferry from Siolim to Chopdem, turn left for the beaches. The coast road runs as a narrow village road winding along the edge of the estuary until it reaches the point where the river meets the sea. Just before this, the main road turns north while a small lane continues to a carpark and some beach shacks on the first section of Morjim beach. Further along the main road, a turn on the left, past some guest houses and restaurants, leads down to another section of beach.

The **Shri Morja Devi Temple** in the village is of special interest because of one of its affiliated shrines dedicated to a Jain guru (Jain dynasties ruled over the region from the sixth to the 10th centuries AD).

Asvem The road from Morjim cuts inland over the low wooded hills running parallel to the coast through open farm land and a few isolated settlements. After a few kilometres the road drops down to the coast and runs along the edge of the peaceful palm-fringed Asvem beach.

Mandrem Along the road, the fishing and toddy tapping village occupies a beautifully shaded setting. The beach, usually deserted, has little shade, but a little

Vagator & Chapora

N

0 metres 200
0 yards 200

■ Sleeping		● Eating	
1 Abu John's	6 Leoney Resort	1 Alcove	6 Nine Bar
2 Bethany Inn	7 Noble Nest	2 Bluebird	7 Primrose Café
3 Dolrina	8 Reshma	3 Club Merc	8 Scarlet Bar
4 Garden Villa	9 Royal Resort	4 Mahalaxmi	
5 Hilltop Motel	10 Shertor Villa	5 Mango Tree	
	11 Sterling Vagator		

To Siolim / To Anjuna & Mapusa / To Anjuna

⦂ Safe passage for turtles

Adult turtles come ashore on Morjim beach in Pernem between October and December, to lay their eggs which hatch after 54 days, usually on the night of the full moon. As soon as a nest is discovered, Forest Department staff put a net over the site and mark it with a flag. When the eggs hatch, the officials escort the hatchlings to the sea to allow them a safe run into the unknowns of the ocean. The nesting sites are patrolled day and night to protect them from the worst of humanity.

to the north is a beautiful little 'island' of sand with coconut palms between the sea and the river.

Arambol → *Phone code: 0832. Colour map 5a, grid A1.*

Arambol (Harmal) is a strung out village by the seashore where the main beach is a glorious stretch of curving sand. The once precious quiet of this hidden corner is now broken by the steady flow of buses and motorbikes. The headland is being hacked away to create terraces for yet more guesthouses with spectacular views but for a little while longer this will remain a great place to unwind.

Sights A sign at the crossroads in the village centre near the bus stop points down to the sea. The road passes a school, church and village houses sheltering under coconut palms before reaching cheap trinket stalls and the main southern beach where motorbikes line up in an unruly parking lot. At the north end of the beach, a well-made track runs round the headland past a series of tiny rocky bays to the second relatively quieter beach though there are countless small guest houses on the hillside and restaurants all along the sea margins. Unlike the headlands around Anjuna, the rocks which run into the sea here are basalt, the hexagonal columns tilted almost horizontal but eroded into jagged shapes clearly visible for miles along the coast.

The second beach around the rocky headland holds an attractive fresh water lagoon where the lush forest comes down to the waters edge making it an idyllic spot to pass the day. It can get very busy at weekends though.

Keri Beach, north of Arambol, is a completely unspoilt and rarely visited stretch of sand backed by casuarina trees all the way down to the Arambol highland. It can be reached from the north on foot from the Tiracol ferry terminal, or from the south by walking round the headland from Arambol. At the top end of the beach there are dangerous currents near the mouth of the Tiracol estuary so it is best to avoid swimming there; a five-minute walk south along the beach will get you to safer waters. There are a couple of F guesthouses and simple snacks from kiosks.

★ Tiracol → *Phone code: 0832. Colour map 5a, grid A1.*

Tiracol (Terekhol), the northernmost tip of Goa, an enclave on the Maharashtra border, has a tiny picturesque fort which is now one of the best positioned coastal hotels in India. The views from here are magnificently atmospheric, looking south to Arambol, Chapora and Fort Aguada.

Perched on the north side of the Tiracol River estuary, on a piece of high ground, the fort's battlement walls are clearly visible from the Arambol headland. Originally a Maratha fort, it was protected from attacks from the sea, while the walls on the land side rise from a dry moat. It was captured by the Portuguese in 1776 who built the church here which is worth a look. It has a classic Goan façade with an interesting hinged confessional, and was large enough to have catered for the whole village.

St Anthony's church inside the tiny fort was built in the early 1750s soon after the Portuguese takeover. It has a classic Goan façade and is just large enough to have catered for the small village.

You can explore the fort's battlements and tiny circular turrets which scarcely seem to have been intended for the real business of shooting the enemy. Steps lead down to a terrace on the south side while the north has an open plateau.

Listings: North Goa

● Sleeping

Mapusa *p1171, map p1172*
Most check out at 0900.
C Green Park, Mapusa-Panaji Rd, Bypass Junction (2 km from centre), T250667, F252698. 35 modern, comfortable, rooms, quiet, good pool and restaurants.
D-E Mandarin, near Alankar Cinema, T262579. 21 basic rooms with bath (few a/c), clean rooftop restaurant.
D-E Satyaheera, near Maruti Temple, T262949. 34 reasonable rooms, some a/c, enclosed rooftop restaurant (shared with mosquitoes and the odd mouse!), bar.
E Residency (GTDC), T262794, at the roundabout. 48 adequate rooms for 2-6, some a/c, reasonable restaurant, beer.
E Vilena, opposite the Municipality, T263115. 14 neat, clean rooms, some a/c, good restaurants, bar, very friendly.

Reis Magos *p1172*
C Reis Magos Fort Resort, 44 a/c rooms on 4 floors overlooking the small pool. Shuttle bus to Calangute for the nearest good sand.
Coco Beach on the Nerul River estuary (1.5 km) draws Sun night party goers.

Sinquerim beach and Fort Aguada
p1173, map p1174
Prices vary greatly depending on period (peak 21 Dec-10 Jan, lowest mid Jun-end Sep).
AL Aguada Hermitage, T276201, F276044, fortaguada.goa@tajhotels.com (for all 3). Exclusive and extremely luxurious, 15 fully serviced 1- or 2-room villas (US$600 peak season US$180 in low), private setting away from all the main hotel facilities, terraced tropical gardens, 'Lookout Point' for excellent views.

On the beach
AL-A Fort Aguada Beach Resort, 120 rooms in 2 wings, all with sea views. 3 restaurants, *Caravella* serves excellent sea food and salads, extensive facilities shared by the complex.
AL-A Holiday Village, 300 m away. 144 (most a/c), some well-designed single 'houses', dotted around tropical gardens full of bougainvillea and palms. Restaurant by large pool, plus nearby *Beach House* and the Thai *Banyan Tree* by the entrance. Helpful efficient staff, highly recommended.
B-C Marbella, lane left off road to *Aguada Beach Resort*, T275551, F276509. 6 very clean, well-decorated rooms (priced according to size) in a large in large Portuguese villa, imaginatively designed with antique furniture. Penthouse suite of 3 rooms.
D Marfran, T279274, private house with a few simple rooms, peaceful.
D Palm Shade, Sinquerim, T277429. 5 rooms around a small garden at the back of a popular beach restaurant. Quiet, with direct access to beach.
D Village Belle, near the *Taj Holiday Village*, T/F276153, vbelle@vsnl.com. 8 rooms (some a/c), good, cheap restaurant, among palms, 500 m from the beach, friendly owners, good value for the area.

Candolim *p1173, map p1175*
A Whispering Palms, 300 m from beach (looks a bit like a fortress), T276140, F276142, whispering.palms@gnpun.globalnet.ems. vsnl.net.in. 66 well-equipped rooms, good restaurant, excellent pool (non residents Rs 150), pleasant garden, mainly packages.
A-B Dona Alcina/Dom Francisco, opposite Health Centre, T276936, F276266, alfran@ goatelecom.com. Neighbouring package orientated hotels, most rooms with balcony

● *For an explanation of the sleeping and eating price codes used in this guide, see inside the*
● *front cover. Other relevant information is found in Essentials pages 52-57.*

overlooking pool, more privacy on upper floors, choice of restaurants, cyber café, ayurvedic massages. Indian dance on Sat at *Dom Francisco*, T279034.

B Highland Beach Resort, T276405, F277881. 205 a/c rooms in a rather ugly, sprawling 4-storey complex, 2 restaurants, package choice, Health /Sports club, pool (non residents Rs 100 per hr).

B-C Kamal Retreat, Dando, towards Aguada, T276320, F276282, kmehra@ goatelecom.com. 23 large, quality rooms (half a/c). Spacious site with immaculate grounds, large pool, direct beach access, charming owner.

C Aldeia Santa Rita, towards Aguada, T276868, F276684. 32 rooms with balcony (better upstairs), in colourful 'street' of villas in attractive setting, some a/c, good restaurant, bar, very small pool, friendly management.

C Costa Nicola, near the Health Centre (500 m from beach), T276343, F277343, costanicola@yahoo.com. 7 rooms in old Goan house, full of character, 13 in a functional new block, some with kitchenette, plus 9 rooms in *Sandy Villa* next door. Well-kept grounds, pool, friendly owners.

D Per Avel, 100 m from beach, T277074. 13 simple rooms (a/c Rs 200 extra), courtyard garden for breakfast, among local family houses, friendly.

D Sea Shell Inn, opposite *Canara Bank*, Candolim-Aguada Rd, T276131, seashellyoa@ hotmail.com. 8 spotless, comfortable rooms in new block behind the house, excellent sizzlers and seafood, use of pool at *Casa Sea Shell*.

D Summerville, T277075, F262681, zinia@ goatelecom.com. 15 well-kept rooms, breakfast on rooftop, sunbathing terrace, pool in simple gardens.

D Xavier, round the corner from the *State Bank*. T/F276911, xavieran@goa telecom.com. 16 spacious, well-furnished rooms, fan, balcony, excellent restaurant, close to beach, friendly.

D-E Alexandra Tourist Centre, Morodvaddo, in lane opposite the *Canara Bank*, T/F276250. 12 clean, comfortable rooms, a/c available, better upstairs, restaurant, bar.

E D'Mello's Sea View, turn at Monteiro Rd (towards Calangute), T277395. 7 rooms, good food (tandoori specials), quiet.

Calangute *p1173, map p1176*

LL Pousada Tauma, Porba Vaddo, T277372, www.pousada-tauma.com. 12 unique rooms set in a lush garden around a pool, luxurious setting, discreet management honouring privacy, one of the best hotels in Goa.

A-B Ondas Do Mar, Gauravaddo, T/F277526, alfran@goatelecom.com. Beachfront location, rooms set around pool, some a/c, most with balconies, restaurant.

B Goan Heritage, Gauravaddo, T276253, F276120. 70 large, pleasant rooms but can get stiflingly hot, a/c and fridge (Rs 400 extra), some have sea view, expensive restaurant (others nearby), good pool, beautiful garden, close to beach.

B Paradise Village, South Calangute, near the beach, T276351, F276155. 83 comfortable rooms in 2-storey chalets, pleasant restaurant, large pool, excellent service and management.

B Villa Goesa, Cobravaddo, off Baga Rd, T277535, T/F276182. 57 clean rooms, some a/c, excellent restaurant, lovely gardens, pool, quiet, relaxing, friendly owners, 300m from beach.

B-C Victorian Heritage, Cobravaddo, T276216, 20 compact a/c rooms, TV, small balcony, very clean, pleasant shaded central dining area but stark pool surrounds. Quiet area, but a few mins' walk from beach.

C Concha Beach Resort, Umtavaddo, T/F276056. 13 good sized, clean, comfortable rooms, mosquito nets, best at front with large verandahs, close to beach.

C Estrela do Mar, Calangute-Baga Rd, T276014. 12 clean, well-kept rooms with mosquito nets (rare in these parts), size varies, restaurant, pool, pleasant garden, peaceful location with no buildings nearby, close to beach, good value.

D Ale-Pas, Maddovaddo, T277479, len_ dagama@rediff.com. 10 rooms with bath, fan, small balcony, spartan but clean, pleasant breakfast terrace. Peacefully set among tall palms a short walk from beach.

D Coco Banana, 5/139A Umtavaddo, back from Calangute beach, T/F276478, cocobanana@rediffmail.com. 6 spotless en suite rooms with nets, airy, light and comfortable, helpful Goan/Swiss owners.

D Golden Eye, Gauravaddo, T277308, F276187. 26 clean, comfortable rooms, on the beach, excellent beachside restaurant.

D White House, Gauravaddo (near *Goan Heritage*), T277938, F276308. 8 rooms with seaview, very pleasant.

E Johnny's, Cobravaddo, T277458, johnnys-hotel@rediffmail.com. 12 rooms (1 a/c) with bath, roof top terrace, good restaurant, interesting garden (fruit and spices), yoga, peaceful location, short walk to beach, call for collection from bus stand. Recommended. Also, 2-bed furnished apartments, Rs 8-10,000 per month.

Baga and Arpora *p1175, map p1177*
Most offer big off-season discounts May-Sep; many attract package holidays.

L Nilaya Hermitage, near Arpora, 3 km inland, T276793, F276792, nilaya@goa1. dot.net.in 11 uniquely designed rooms, excellent pool, secluded, peaceful woodland location overlooking Baga headland, health centre, exclusive (US$250).

B Resorte Marinha Dourada, towards Arpora, T276780, F276785, mdourada@ goatelecom.com. 106 a/c rooms, quiet location overlooking small lake 1.5 km from beach (hourly shuttle), restaurant, pool, health centre, close to Sat market but far from beach restaurants.

B Ronil Beach Resort, T276099, F276068, ronil@vsnl.com. 58 a/c rooms, pool, well run with a good local reputation, ideal for all Baga and Calangute nightlife, small grounds.

B Sun Village, Arpora, T279409, F279415, sunvi l@goatelecom.com. 135 spacious suites, TV, bar fridge, balcony, 2 restaurants, 2 pools, pub, health club, good shops. Friendly service, high standards and well maintained. Inland from the beaches, convenient for Anjuna and Baga Sat markets.

C Baia Do Sol, north end, T276084, F731415. 23 very clean rooms, a/c cottages, relaxing, good restaurant, on riverside.

C-D Cavala, Sauntavaddo, Baga-Calangute Rd, away from the beach, T276090, F277340, cavala@goatelecom.com. 22 clean rooms with bath (non a/c Rs 550 with breakfast, double for a/c) best at rear, *Banana Republic*, restaurant, relaxed bar, popular live music evenings, pool across road, friendly.

D Alidia Beach Cottages, behind the church, Sauntavaddo, T276835, F279014, alidia@goaworld.com. 16 good clean rooms with bath, restaurant, secure, friendly owners, beach 2-min walk, excellent value.

D-E Villa Fatima, Calangute-Baga Rd, T277418, Sauntavaddo, fatimavi@ goatelecom .com. 50 rooms set round courtyard, ISD, internet, bike hire, perfect for backpackers, 'fantastic blend of the kitsch and the tropical', helpful management.

E Baga Queen Beach Resort, T276880. 15 good sized, clean rooms with bath close to beach.

F Andrade Guest House, Cobravaddo, behind *Linda Goa*. Really basic rooms with nets, very friendly hostess.

F Venar, Cobravaddo, T276867. 4 basic but clean rooms with shared bath in an old house.

North of Baga Creek, those to the left of the bridge tend to be quieter.

E-F Nani's & Rani's, T277014, T9823088329 (mob). Few simple rooms, some with bath, budget meals in pleasant garden, quiet, relaxed, email, one of the few local budget options with a sea view and a relaxing quiet location. Rooms in houses/cottages are about Rs 300 (discounts for weekly or monthly rental).

Anjuna *p1177, map p1178*
Most budget beachside rooms are occupied by long-stay visitors who pay about Rs 2,000 per month for the most basic.

Prices rise in mid-Nov and Christmas when it may be impossible to find cheap rooms here. Some visitors have been robbed when staying in family houses; it is safer to choose an approved hotel or guesthouse. Good padlocks are sold in a small shop next to the *White Negro Bar* for Rs 150.

AL-A Laguna Anjuna, T274132, F274305, info@lagunaanjuna.com. 22 spacious, attractive apartments in individually designed cottages with 'Swiss interiors' (US$75 for 1-bedroom suite), large pool in lush grounds, but getting run down.

B Grandpa's Inn, Gaunwadi, Mapusa Rd, T273271, F274370, granpas@hotmail.com. 10 comfortable rooms with bath in old Goan house, 2 family blocks, good restaurant, pleasant garden, pool. Experienced friendly management, very comfortable.

C-D Don Joao Resorts, Sorranto, T274325, F273447, luzco@bom2.vsnl.net.in. 48 large rooms with balcony and fridge, some a/c, restaurant, exchange, small pool, friendly, away from beach.

D Anjuna Beach Resort, DeMello Vaddo, opposite Albuquerque Mansion, T274433.

14 rooms with bath, balcony, breakfast, snacks, bike hire, friendly, secure, quiet.
D White Negro, near St Anthony's Church, T273326. 14 rooms with nets, good restaurant and bar, very clean.
D-E Lolita's, by *Oxford Stores*, Monteiro Vaddo, T273289. 5 spacious, clean rooms with fridge and music system (own tapes), some with TV/air cooler, friendly, secure.
D-E Martha's Breakfast Home, Monteiro Vaddo, T273365, mpd8650@hotmail.com. 8 clean, spacious rooms in separate block plus a couple of 2 bedroomed cottages, good brunch, waffles, crêpes. Small garden, quiet (except on Wed), friendly, well run.
D-E Red Cab Inn, De Mello Vaddo, T274427, F273312, redcabinn@rediffmail.com, 5-min walk from Starco X-roads. 4 newly decorated rooms in old house, high ceilings, nice and cool, plus a room on the roof, good for long stay, plus a bright red cottage in the garden. Very clean and neat, own fresh water well, good evening restaurant. 15 mins walk from the beach.

Vagator and Chapora p1177, map p1180
Vagator
The village is quite spread out and most accommodation is hidden away down wooded lanes away from the beaches. Avoid Royal Resort.
B Sterling Vagator (partly time-share), T273276, F274376. Attractive setting at the foot of the Fort, but very run down and overpriced.
B Leoney Resort, T273634, F274343, leoney30@hotmail.com. 13 rooms, 3 cottages, a/c extra Rs 400. Clean, modern, family run, low-key, quiet location, pool, 10 min walk from beach.
B-C Royal Resort, 500 m from beach, T274365. 28 rooms, 10 a/c (overpriced), new management, restaurant, jazz bar, pool.
D Bethany Inn, opposite *Mango Tree*, T273973, bethany@goatelecom.com. 7 clean, comfortable modern rooms with bath (some 4-bedded), central village location.
E Abu John's, 6 small rooms with bath, good restaurant, garden, pleasant, quiet.
E Dolrina, T273382. 13 rooms, most baths shared between 2 rooms, newer **D** rooms best, safe, secure, friendly.
E Hilltop Motel, away from the beach, T273665. 14 small rooms, those with bath reasonable, popular late night venue.

E-F Garden Villa, T273571. 8 clean rooms, some with bath, restaurant.

Chapora
Caters mainly for long-term budget travellers.
F Noble Nest, opposite the Holy Cross Chapel, 274335. 21 rooms, 2 with bath but ample facilities for sharing, basic, but popular, exchange and internet.

Morjim p1179
Brittos Guest House, T784245. Simple rooms, 200 m from sea.
Camp 69, basic bamboo shacks in a large shaded garden, central lounge/dining area in an old house.
Julian's, bar and simple rooms.

Asvem p1180
D-E Palm Grove, towards Morjim. 6 rooms with fan, in a low lying stone building with a verandah, 5 well-built tree-houses close to the beach among casuarinas, plus 2 very basic huts. Shared wash facilities.
E Arabian Sea, Marddiwado, T297432. 2 brick cottages and 3 rickety bamboo huts on stilts (over priced), set back from the beach, shared wash block, beach restaurant.
E Silent Cottages, next door to *Arabian Sea*, have huts on stilts with better views.
F Paradise Cottages, closer to the beach, basic rooms with cold showers.

Mandrem p1180
C Mandrem Beach Resort, Junas Waddo, far end of village, T297115, F297375, prazeres@satyam.net.in. 24 rooms, (fan, lockers), river or sea view, al fresco restaurant, tranquil setting, friendly team. Pool planned, beach to yourself beyond the dunes.
E Dunes Holiday Village, T297219, dunes@rediffmail.com. Simple shacks overlooking the beach, communal wash facilities.
E Fantasy Guest House, T297280. Modern block on the main road (not busy!), but away from the beach.
E Merrylands Paradise, T297446, merrylandsparadise@hotmail.com. Cottages and fragile looking bamboo "tree houses". Right on the lagoon behind the beach.
F Sea Paradise, simple bamboo huts on stilts by the lagoon
F Village rooms, usually signed, rented out to foreigners for up to 6 months through winter.

A Siolim House, Wadi, opposite Wadi Chapel, T0832-272138, F272941, www.siolim house.com. Superb, renovated 300-year old heritage home, seven large, well-furnished suites, some street facing, others around attractive courtyard at rear, no TV or a/c, good Goan food, pool, video library, altogether evocative of a past era.

Arambol *p1181*

Guesthouses higher up on the hill charge more but are poorly maintained and there is a smell of sewage. Touts meet newcomers at the bus stand offering rooms for Rs 80-150 (bargaining expected). Some do not provide bedding. Many lack the security of a hotel compound.

E Ave Maria, inland, down track opposite police post. Well established, one of the best. Simple but recommended.

E Famafa, off the road down to the beach, T292516, famafa_in@yahoo.com. 25 clean rooms, fans, simple restaurant, new purpose built hotel, secure, functional, no views, devoid of character.

E Oasis, far end of beach. 4 rooms, popular restaurant, bar on the cliff face, good evening views. Look out for the hammock shop up the path at the back.

E Oceanic, inland at south end, T292296. Secluded guest house with simple rooms, all hidden behind wall in mature gardens, no drugs, popular. Recommended.

E Welcome, at end of road on sea front, T297733. Clean rooms, bath with hot water, serves the best muesli, taxi hire.

F Blue Fin, north end of beach. 3 rooms, tucked behind a shop, small courtyard, limited views but more privacy than others nearby.

Tiracol *p1181*

B-C Tiracol Fort Heritage, T782240, tiracol@ usa.net. 6 small standard rooms (Rs 800), 4 spacious suites on 1st floor (Rs 1,750), wonderful sea views, one of Goa's most peaceful and romantic places to stay. Restaurant in reclaimed dry moat, birdwatchers' haven, boat trips (dolphins, Redi Beach etc), discounts from 4 May-3 Sep. Part open to visitors (0900-1800).

E Hill Rock, 1 km from the ferry, T268264. 7 rooms in a family hotel, restaurant, good location overlooking fort and Keri beach but neglected.

● Eating

Mapusa *p1171, map p1172*
Little in this area to shout about.

♥♥ **Casa Bela**, near Coscar Corner, specializes in Goan food.

♥♥ **Mahalaxmi**, Anjuna Rd. A/c, South Indian.

♥♥ **Moonlight**, Shalini Building, 1st floor. Good North Indian at lunchtime; rather dark in the evening, used more for drinking than eating.

♥♥ **Vilena**, 2 restaurants (a rooftop and an a/c indoors), serve the best food in town.

Cafes and fast food

Royal-T, Shop 96, near the Shakuntala Fountain, Municipal Market, Goan snacks, sweets and spices.

Other cheap stalls and cafés in the market. From 1630 until late, carts and stalls near the Alankar Cinema, sell popular meat and seafood dishes.

Sinquerim beach and Fort Aguada
p1173, map p1174

♥♥♥ **Banyan Tree** at *Taj Holiday Village* entrance for something special. Excellent Thai food in stylish surroundings, wide verandah, water garden (about Rs 650 each) with an inner sanctum.

♥♥♥ **Beach House** for the "most lavish and complete dinner, served attentively".

Bon Appetit and **Palm Shade** nearby, are also recommended.

Candolim *p1173, map p1175*

♥♥ **After Eight**. Smart decor, professional service, great cuisine.

♥♥ **Casa Manolita**, behind *Dona Alcina*, European bistro, meals served on verandah of restored 19th-century Portuguese villa.

♥♥ **Fisherman's Cove**, opposite *Alexandra Tourist Centre*. Excellent tandooris.

♥♥ **Ma's Bakery** next door to *Octopus Garden*, does great snacks and cakes.

♥♥ **Mermaid**, opposite *Whispering Palms Hotel*, run by a Swedish-Goan couple, superb international and Goan cuisine.

♥♥ **Oceanic**. Spicy, succulent fish grills.

♥♥ **Octopus Garden**, where "cheese *dosas* are an experience".

♥♥ **Oriental**, Costa Nicola, next to Health Centre, original Thai cuisine and selected Western dishes, prepared by Thai master chef, served to soft classical music.

Palms 'n Sand, near the beach. Speciality roast piglet (order the day before).

Stone House, opposite Octopus Garden. Excellent food, wide choice, good service, pleasant music (Blues lapsing into Bob Marley!), boat trips.

Titus Roma Pisa, Candolim Beach Rd. Not just pizzas. Well-prepared food, very friendly staff (good place to ask about fishing trips, flea market etc), *Soccer Bar* for live football, but not rowdy at all, so not just for the younger crowd.

Xavier. Excellent Western meals, Sunday roasts (owner/chef spent 30 years in England), very attentive service (and highly efficient hotel cat!), cocktail bar.

Club 21 on the beach, now crowded in with other shacks, does good breakfasts for about Rs 75, snacks (seafood, pancakes) and drinks.

Coconut Inn, a typical Goan house with indoor and open-air seating (closed May-Sep).

Calangute *p1173, map p1176*

Delhi Darbar, near the beach towards Baga. Excellent North Indian and fish dishes. Upmarket, candle-lit dinner and dancing.

Le Restaurant, one of the regions top restaurants, continental menu, great ambience; closed off-season.

Little Italy, 136/1 Gauravaddo, behind Kelkar Gallery, away from the beach (mock classical front), T275911. Excellent and authentic Italian (Sicilian chef), pastas and pizzas indoors (a/c) or al fresco.

Jerry's Place, near beach, popular lunchtime haunt for package tourists with menu to suit.

Oceanic, Gauravaddo. Well planned setting in neat gardens, varied seafood, pasta, good fun when busy.

Pedro's on the beach behind has authentic, interesting Tibetan dishes to complement a very smartly printed menu.

Souza Lobo on the beach. Excellent fresh seafood, lobsters and sizzlers served on a shaded terrace.

Sportsman, overlooking beach taxi stand, 'full monty' English breakfast, bar and live Premier league football.

Plantain Leaf, main street before beach, (above good jewellers!) near petrol pump. Excellent *thalis* (Rs 40), gigantic *dosas*, plus full range of curries.

Infanteria, near the main crossroads. Recommended for breakfast, baked goodies and snacks all day.

Master Joel Confectioners, 9 Romano Chambers, opposite the petrol pump. Good Goan specialities.

Baga and Arpora *p1175, map p1177*
Some of Goa's best restaurants are here.

Blue, top end of Baga beach, T279473. Delicious Mediterranean cuisine, pitta bread, tacos, all made on site.

Fiesta, Tito's Rd, enviably placed above the beach. Stylish surroundings, unusual Portuguese and Italian dishes, and great desserts. Attract the wealthy crowd before they move on to Tito's.

J&A's Italian, (the original Little Italy), north of Baga river. Excellent, authentic Italian food in a candle-lit garden setting, very romantic, pizza, pasta, pricey by local standards but better value than most.

Nilaya, lunchtime salads by the pool, Rs 230, great view, ideal for a celebration meal.

Brittos, top end of Baga. Upmarket beach shack, curries, seafood, bar, busy in evenings.

Domingo's, Tito's Rd, just off the road next to *Zinho's Guest House*. Well-cooked and tasty, safe (freezes perishables in portions rather than refreezing wholesale), no background music. Friendly, family run

Gou Julu Andata, north bank Baga river, T277802. A newish continental place with Italian cooks.

Indian Impact, CSM Rd. Indian. Curries – "as good as Bradford!", tandoori, friendly.

Lila Café, north bank of Baga river. Slick, German run restaurant, good selection of european dishes, smoked kingfish Rs 110. Homemade cheeses, jams, muesli, croissant etc; slightly small portions. Good coffee, beers. Shaded terrace overlooking the river. Closed evenings. Recommended.

Nisha, Tito's Rd. Watch the chef in action, great choice of fresh seafood, very relaxed.

Anjuna *p1177, map p1178*
A vegetarian's paradise with plenty of western and Tibetan options. Several elderly women set up chai stalls with cakes and king-size rizzlas on sale, making a good profit.

Xavier's, Praias de San Miguel (follow signs from behind small chapel near flea market site; bring a torch at night), T273402. Now a smart restaurant serving excellent fresh seafood, tucked away under palm trees. Good reputation.

¶¶ Basilico Pizza, De Mello Vaddo, opens 1900. Italian outlet set in the grounds of an old house.

¶¶ Bougainvillea, at *Grandpa's Inn*. Excellent food, moist chicken kebabs, salads, bar (wines, imported beer), on the terrace of the old house in a very pretty garden.

¶¶ Gregory's, next to a tennis court. Excellent continental, especially pizzas (try one with prawns); also tennis!

¶¶ La Franza with bar. Good continental. Pleasant, large verandah overlooking attractive tropical garden.

¶ Bean Me Up, Sorranto Vaddo, Soya Station and Salad Bar. Good vegetarian and vegan breakfasts, sandwiches, soups and cakes. All-day veg English, American or continental breakfasts. Open 0830-1700 closed Wed.

¶ Crab Key Foods, Goenkar Vaddo. Seafood and curries, bar, atmospheric split level restaurant above beach.

¶ Munche's, De Mello Vaddo, 24-hr cafe next to Oxford Arcade on Vagator Rd. In peak season, an informal assembly point before heading off to parties, an 'in' place.

¶ Sea Pearl, ideal for breakfast and simple snacks. Good value, pleasant, family run.

¶ Whole Bean Tofu Shop, offers tofu, tempeh and vegetarian snacks.

¶ Why Knought, De Mello Vaddo. Mix of sizzlers and seafood, open air under palms.

Vagator and Chapora *p1177, map p1180*
Hordes of day trippers congregate around the cafés near the beach.

¶¶ Alcove on the cliff above Little Vagator. Smartish, ideal position, excellent food, pleasant ambience in the evening, sometimes live music.

¶¶ Bluebird, T273695, quietly placed, en route to Ozran, does real French food (inventive menu), to be washed down with pricey French wines; one of the best here.

¶¶ Mango Tree, in the village, offers a wide choice of continental favourites.
In **Vagator**:
Several restaurants line the streets to the beach. Some serve good fresh fish including:
Mahalaxmi.
Primrose Café, serves tasty health foods and also hosts "spontaneous" parties.

In **Chapora**:
Scarlet, does good muesli, ice creams and chilled fruity shakes, the place for a morning 'pick-me-up' after a night on the dance floor.

Asvem *p1180*
Café Asvem at the southern end, perched slightly above the beach, does lunches.

Arambol *p1181*
No sign of anything to keep the ingredients cool.

¶ Double Dutch, from the beach turn left off the main beach road before *Ganesh Stores*. Excellent tea, coffee, snacks, imported journals.

¶ Full Moon, secluded shack at south end. Seafood, drinks throughout the day.

¶ Loekie Café, on main beach approach road. Good varied menu and music in the evening.

¶ Pirates Cabin, Indian, succulent *tandoori* grills, popular day time hang out.

¶ Sunset Dream, round headland, above 2nd beach. Fruit juices, seafood. A basic eatery in the village serves delicious authentic Goan fish curry rice for Rs 20. Also doubles up as the village bar.

⊙ Bars and clubs

Candolim *p1173, map p1175*
Rock Your Blues, south end of Candolim near Taj Village. Nightclub, open 2030. Retro music, sensibly priced drinks.

Baga and Arpora *p1175, map p1177*
Many bars here have a "happy hour" from 1700-1930 and show live Premier League football on Sundays. Beach shacks also serve a wide range of drinks and cocktails.
Cavala, Sauntavaddo, genuine bar with friendly atmosphere, attentive staff, great cocktails, and occasional live music evenings.
The Cave Pub, Tito's Rd. European-style pub, good meeting place. Watch out for short measures and sudden price increases.
Sunset, north of Baga river, great place to watch the goings-on of Baga Beach as dusk falls. Prime location but not so busy due to river.
Tito's, is 'the place' for late night drinking and dancing, packed from 2300 to 0300 (Rs 200). Popular with Mumbai yuppies, and also the Indian gay scene.

Anjuna *p1177, map p1178*
Guru, overlooking the beach. A popular bar, picks up late stayers after the flea market.
Shore Bar, Goenkar Vaddo, close to *Guru*, for the Wed après-market hoedown. The good sound system complements the fire jugglers' playground.
Sonic, under the palms on a raised terrace is a great place for a chilled beer at sunset.
Sunset, close to *Shore Bar*. Good raised platform with comfortable sunbeds.

Vagator and Chapora *p1177, map p1180*
Nine Bar, Ozran beach, the place, great sound system, sunset views.
Club Merc, close to Vagator beach, turns into a party venue.

● Entertainment

Calangute *p1173, map p1176*
Kerkar Art Gallery, in a peaceful garden, Gauravaddo, T276017, sells contemporary paintings, sculpture, ceramics and crafts; also holds open-air cultural shows (classical dance) on Tue and Sat from 1830, Rs 150.

Anjuna *p1177, map p1178*
Beach parties Wed and Fri nights tend to be the main evenings, but there is usually something going on each night during Christmas-New Year period – ask around on arrival. Venues are often recognizable by illuminated trees and luminous wall hangings. It is best to walk there and back in a large group. Politicians have tried to impose a ban or a curb on loud music after 2200. A purpose built set, 'Jungle Grove', has been created inland, south of Anjuna.

● Festivals and events

Mapusa *p1171, map p1172*
Feast of our Lady of Miracles, on the Mon of the 3rd week after Easter. The Nossa Senhora de Milagres image is venerated by Christians as well as Hindus who join together to celebrate the feast day of the Saibin. A huge fair and market is held.

Calangute *p1173, map p1176*
Youth Fête (**May**, 2nd week) attracts Goa's leading musicians and dancers.

● Shopping

Mapusa *p1171, map p1172*
Books
Other India Bookstore, 1st floor, St Britto's Apartment, above Mapusa Clinic, T263306, oibs@bom2.vsnl.net.in, different and excellent. It is heavily eco-conscious, has a large catalogue and will post worldwide.

Market
The Municipal Market, 1130-1530, is well planned and operates all week except Sun. It is as colourful and vibrant as the 'Friday Market' which opens earlier and is now firmly on the tourist calendar; 0730 to 0800 is best for photography when the light is good and you can capture the local stalls being set up. Beware of pickpockets.

Calangute *p1173, map p1176*
Books
Book Palace, Beach Rd, near the Bus Stand.
Casa Goa, Baga Rd. Smart upmarket shop, restored Goan antiques plus clothes and gifts, shipping. Be prepared to bargain.

Baga and Arpora *p1175, map p1177*
Books
Jay-Jays, mostly secondhand novels; 50% back if you return the book. Plenty of good quality but over-priced Kashmiri goods in touristy shops.

Anjuna *p1177, map p1178*
Natural Health Food Store, Monteiro Vaddo.
Oxford Stores, for groceries, foreign exchange and photo processing.
Orchard Stores, Monteiro Vaddo. Selection catering for western cravings, at a price. Olive oil, pasta, fresh cheese, frozen meats.
Oxford Arcade, De Mello Vaddo, next to *Munche's*. Good general store close to beach.
Wed Flea Market, attracts hordes of tourists from all over Goa. By mid-morning all approach roads are blocked with taxis, so arrive early.

Vagator and Chapora *p1177, map p1180*
Books
Narayan, bookstall, sells local newspapers.
Rainbow, near Victory House Orphanage, buys, sells and exchanges European language books.

▲▲ Activities and tours

Sinquerim beach and Fort Aguada
p1173, map p1174

Taj Sports Complex, excellent facilities (open to non-residents) at *Taj Holiday Village*, with separate access between *Aguada Beach Resort* and the *Holiday Village*. Rs 450 per day for complex, Rs 350 for pool.
Tennis with markers (Rs 450 per hr); **squash/badminton** (Rs 150 for 30 mins); **mini golf** (Rs 200). **Health centre** offers ayurvedic massage, gym, steam, sauna.
Scuba diving, **sailing/ water skiing/ windsurfing/rod fishing** Rs 450-500 per hr; **parasailing/jet ski** Rs 900-950 per hr.

Candolim *p1173, map p1175*
John's Boats, towards Aguada, T277780, promises 'guaranteed' **dolphin watching**, morning trips start around 0900, Rs 500 (includes meal and hotel pick-up); see page 1157 for details. Also crocodile spotting river trips with lunch.

Occasional **parasailing** is offered independently on Candolim beach, Rs 600-850 for a 5-min flight. **Yoga** teaching and ayurvedic treatment at **Mandala**, off CHOG-M Rd, near Bus Stand, T277104.

Baga and Arpora *p1175, map p1177*
Sailing
Mikes Marine, T279782. Covered boat, dolphin trips, river cruise and bird watching.
Fiesta Yacht, 36 ft, morning and sunset cruises for **dolphin watching**, Rs 400-800. Contact Maneck Contractor at *Fiesta Restaurant*.

Yoga
Rashnu Yoga, Viega Vaddo, Arpora, T276691, maggiehughesyoga@hotmail.com. Equipped to Iyengar specifications, 30-day courses (US$200-250). Rooms for students only, simple, fan cooled, mosquito net, relaxing garden. Recommended.
Natural Health Centre, opposite Tito's Rd, offers alternative therapies including ayurvedic massage and yoga lessons.

Anjuna *p1177, map p1178*
Bungee jumping
Offered by a Mumbai based firm with US trained staff, at Rs 500 per go. Safety is a priority with harnesses, carabinas and air bags

employed. There are pool tables, a bar, an auditorium for slide/film shows and also beach volleyball. Open 1000-1230 and 1730 until late.

Paragliding
Enterprising foreign long-stayers organize this from season to season. Try **Happy Hours Café**, south Anjuna beach, from 1230-1400; Rs 500 (children welcome), or at the hilltop between Anjuna and Baga, (and Arambol).

Windsurfing
Boards are sometimes available for hire at the south end of the beach for about Rs 100 per hr.

Yoga
Purple Valley Yoga Centre, at *Grandpa's Inn*, T273271, www.yogagoa.com. Mainly Ashtanga; offers morning/evening drop-in classes for holidaymakers, "brilliant teachers".

Arambol *p1181*
For **dolphin trips** or **boats** to Anjuna, contact *21 Coconuts Inn*, second restaurant on the left after stepping on to the beach; Rs 150 for Anjuna. Paragliding is arranged from beach shacks.

⊖ Transport

Mapusa *p1171, map p1172*
Bus
Local Several to **Calangute**, some continue on to Baga, some go towards Candolim; check before boarding or change at Calangute. Rs 5. To **Panaji**: non-stop mini buses; buy tickets from booth at market entrance. Check times. For the northern beaches buses to **Calangute** (every 20-30 mins); from there to **Aguada** or **Baga**. Also to **Vagator** and **Chapora** via **Anjuna**. To **Tivim** for Konkan railway and trains to/from Mumbai, Rs 8, (25 mins).
Long distance Private operators lined up opposite the taxi stand offer near identical routes and rates. To **Bangalore**: 1830, 12 hrs, Rs 250 (Luxury), Rs 450 (Sleeper). **Hampi**: 1800, 11 hrs, Rs 450 (sleeper). **Mumbai**: 14 hrs, Rs 250 (Luxury), Rs 450 (Sleeper).

Car
Car hire: **Pink Panther**, T263180.

Rickshaw
Auto-rickshaw: **Calangute**, Rs 50.

Taxi

Motorcycle taxi: to **Anjuna** or **Calangute**, about Rs 40 (bargain). **Taxi**: (shared by up to 5) to **Panaji**, Rs 70; **Calangute/Baga**, Rs 60; **Chapora/Siolim**, Rs 80.

Train

Tivim station on the Konkan railway is convenient if you want to head straight to the **northern beaches** (Calangute, Baga, Anjuna and Vagator), avoiding Panaji and Margao. A bus meets each train and runs to the Kadamba stand in Mapusa. From here you continue on a local bus to the beach, or share a tourist taxi. Enquiries and computerised tickets T298682. To **Ernakulam (Jn)**: *Mangalore Exp 2618*, 1952 (arrive 1345), 18hrs. **Margao**: *Mandovi Exp 0103*, 1650, 1½ hrs; *Konkan Kanya Exp 0111*, 0924, 1½ hrs. **Mumbai (CST)**: *Mandovi Exp 0104*, 1113, 10 hrs; *Konkan Kanya Exp 0112*, 1846, 11 hrs (via Pernem). **Mumbai Kurla (Tilak)** (from Trivandrum): *Netravati Exp, 6346*, 0747, 11 hrs. To **Thiruvananthapuram (Trivandrum)**: *Netravati Exp, 6345*, 2152, 19 hrs (via Margao and Canacona for Palolem beach).

Sinquerim beach and Fort Aguada
p1173, map p1174
Bus

To/from Panaji (via Nerul and some from Candolim) stop near the Taj complex. Aguada Fort is about a 4-km walk uphill though motor cycle taxis sometimes wait at the bus stop.

Candolim *p1173, map p1175*
Bus

To and from **Panaji** stop at the stand at the centre of Candolim; some continue to Calangute to the north, while others go south to the stop near the Taj complex.

Calangute *p1173, map p1176*
Bus

The main bus stand is close to the beach but best to board a bus for Panaji (Rs 8) by the taxi stand near the *State Bank*. For Baga, flag down a bus near St John's chapel.

Scooters and motorbikes

There are plenty of scooters and bikes for hire but bicycles are scarce. Scooters and motorbikes for hire about Rs 250 per day. Kinetic Honda repair shop behind *Samir Electricals*, near the petrol station.

Taxi

To/from Mapusa about Rs 100. **Motorcycle taxis**: a bit cheaper.

Baga and Arpora *p1175, map p1177*
Bicycle

200 m down a small lane past the Hacienda, on the left side. Rs 40 per day, a little extra to keep it overnight.

Boat

From the beach to Anjuna Flea market, Rs 50 (one way), avoid in bad weather.

Bus

Regular to Calangute, some continue to Panjim, others to Mapusa (0700-1830).

Motorbike

Available for hire; ask outside *Brittos* and also *Jay-Jays*.

Taxi

To Mapusa or Anjuna, Rs 100. **Autos**: Cheaper than taxis but few about. **Motorbike taxis**: Not worth risking.

Anjuna *p1177, map p1178*
Motorcycle

Motorcycles are easy to hire; **Peter & Friends Classic Adventure** (Indo-German company) at Casa Tres Amigos, Socol Vado 425, Parra, Assagao, about 5 km east (off the Mapusa Rd), T254467, F262076, www.classic-bike-india.de. Reliable bike hire and tours.

Vagator and Chapora *p1177, map p1180*

Daily **bus** from Panaji, 1½ hrs; frequent from Mapusa to Chapora via Anjuna and Vagator.

Mandrem *p1180*
Bus

Towards Siolem pass along the main road at about 0930 and 1345. Direct services expected to Mapusa and Panaji once the new bridge opens.

Arambol *p1181*
Bicycle

Bike and **taxi hire** from *Welcome Restaurant*.

Bus and ferry

There are regular buses from Mapusa and a frequent service from Chopdem, 12 km along the main road (about 40 mins); the attractive coastal detour via Morjim being slightly longer. From Vagator, walk to Chapora village to find a local ferry across the estuary (Rs 20 each, Rs 40 for a boat), then a 2-hr walk north through Morjim and Mandrem along the coast. Or get a bus to Siolim, cross the river by ferry to Chopdem and then pick up a bus or taxi. The new bridge across the Chopdem estuary opened in 2002.

Tiracol *p1181*
Bus
From **Panaji** direct bus at 1700, arrives 1930, returns to Panaji 0700 next morning. From **Mapusa**, take a bus to Siolim, cross Chapora River by ferry; continue to Keri by bus via Pernem, then cross Tiracol River by ferry (half-hourly, 0600-2130) and walk the remaining 2km! Ferries take cars.

● Directory

Mapusa *p1171, map p1172*
Banks Bank of India, opposite Municipal Gardens, changes TCs; cash Visa and Mastercard. State Bank of India changes cash and TCs, on 1st floor. Pink Panther Agency changes Visa and Mastercard, Mon-Fri, 0900-1700, Sat 0900-1300. **Hospital** Asilo Hospital, T262211. **Internet** Several. LCC, 3rd Floor, Bhavani Apartmentster, 0700-2130. **Pharmacies** Drogaria, near Swiss Chapel, open 24 hrs. **Post office** Sub-Post Office opposite Police Station. **Tourist information** Tourist Shopping Complex, T262390. **Travel agents** Siddhartha, Chandranath Apts, 3 blocks back, Phase II, BS7, opposite the Police Station, T251153, F262076, info@siddharta.de. Arrange special tours, including some for handicapped travellers, and home stays. **Useful numbers** Ambulance: T262372. Fire: T262900. Police: T262231. Tourist Information: T262390.

Candolim *p1173, map p1175*
Medical services Primary Health Centre. **Photography** Many offer same day processing. Foto Finish, next to *Stone House*, stocks slide and black/white films and accessories. **Travel agent** Davidair, Old Post House, Escrivao, Main Rd, T277007,

F276308, davidgoa@goatelecom.com. Licensed to issue air tickets, very efficient, good charter deals to UK; **Traveland**, Laxmi Apartments, T276196, F276124.

Calangute *p1173, map p1176*
Banks State Bank of India changes some TCs but does not accept Visa. Bank of Baroda accepts some credit cards, but get there early. Private dealers offer speedy exchange but a poorer rate. Wall Street, opposite petrol pump, recommended. **Internet** *Nikki's Internet Café*, Calangute Tourist Resort Annexe,T281950. 8 terminals, exchange, pool table, café, 0900-midnight, Rs 40 per hr, back-up power system lasts 8 hrs. One of the best. **Travel agents** Several including **Day Tripper**, Gauravaddo, T276726, daytrip@goatelecom.com. Best deals in the region, Palolem beach Rs 350; Spice plantations Rs 700; Backwaters Rs 1,000, will collect from your hotel. MGM Travels, Umtavaddo, T272273. **Useful services** Police: T278284.

Baga and Arpora *p1175, map p1177*
Banks Exchange, just north of Tito's Rd. **Internet** Everywhere; about Rs 2 per min. Ocean Star Cyber Café, T276492, oceanstar@india.com, has 5 terminals. Recommended. **Travel agents** Fortune Travels, opposite small temple, top end of Baga near bus stand, Sauntavaddo, T276991, fortunet@goatelecom.com. Friendly and very helpful, local dolphin/fishing trips, inland tours etc, cash on credit cards (commission 4%). Lina D'Souza Traveland, Villa Nova, Sauntavaddo, T276196, djtravel@goatelecom.com. Efficient air/rail ticketing.

Anjuna *p1177, map p1178*
Banks Bank of Baroda, Sorranto Vaddo, Mon-Wed, Fri 0930-1330, Sat 0930-1130, accepts most TCs, Visa/Mastercard, 1% commission (min Rs 50); also provide 'Safe Custody Packets'. Thomas Cook agent at Oxford Stores, central, quicker and more efficient. **Medical services** St Michael's Pharmacy, Main Rd, Sorranto, open 24 hrs. **Post office** Poste Restante at post office, open 1000-1600, Mon-Sat; efficient, parcels are also accepted without a fuss. **Travel agents** MGM, T274317; Speedy, near post office, Mazalvaddo, T273208. Very helpful,

comprehensive service, 0900-1830. **Useful services** Police: T273233.

Vagator and Chapora p1177, map p1180
Banks Nearest is in Anjuna. **Health centre** T262211. **Travel agents** Sonya Travels near Holy Cross, Chapora, offers foreign exchange, money transfers, ticketing and internet.

Mandrem p1180
Banks Canara Bank, on the main road accepts TCs.

Arambol p1181
Post office The small village post office is at the 'T' junction, 1½ km from the beach.
Travel agents Delight and Tara, in the village, exchange cash and TCs, get train/bus tickets. **Useful services** Health Centre, T291249. **Police**, T297614.

To the Ghats

This trip gives an attractive picture of the Western Ghats, intensively cultivated rice fields, and some interesting small villages. The forest-rich environment of the foothills nurtures spice plantations and the Bondla Sanctuary. The road east to the Ghat runs through a region of modern and rapid mineral development and industrialization, then to densely forested slopes where ancient Buddhist caves and Hindu temples are tucked away. ▸▸ *For Sleeping, Eating and other listings, see pages 1196-1197.*

Mayem Lake

Mayem is just south of Bicholim and is a very popular local picnic spot. While the pedal boats may not appeal, the setting is very attractive and the *Government Restaurant* on the south side of the lake serves good food, though the buildings are rather run down. E **Lake Resort** provides rooms and dorm facilities ① *from Panaji Bus Stand, buses for Narve pass by the lake, regular service from Bicholim.*

Sanquelim → *Colour map 5a, grid A2.*

Southeast of Bicholim, this is the 'home' of the Rajput **Ranes tribe** who migrated south from Rajasthan in the late 18th century and spent the next century fighting for the Portuguese as mercenaries, then against them for arrears of pay! In 1895 one of their revolts necessitated the despatch of troops from Portugal.

The **Datta Mandir** (1882), north of the bazar, backed by a hillock covered with dense groves of areca palms, has the *trimurthi* (three-headed) image of Dattaraia which is believed to cure insanity. The temple with an interior of white marble, celebrates its annual festival in December. It is one of two temples in Goa where *Devadasis* play no part and are not permitted to enter (the other is the Ananta Temple in Savoi Verem).

Arvalem

About 2 km east of Sanquelim a turn goes south to this small settlement noted now for its waterfalls and small **Buddhist cave temples**. The latter were subsequently converted for Siva worship, the altars which probably originally supported Buddha images now having Siva *lingas* set into them. The caves are believed to date from the third to sixth centuries AD though a Brahmi inscription found was dated to the first century. In a pleasant shaded site with a temple near their foot, the **waterfalls** are formed at the end of a small gorge, and are impressive during the monsoon when the river is in spate. They are concealed from view until the last moment. Steps lead down from the parking place to the foot of the falls, then a track goes along the river and crosses it by a footbridge, leading a short distance to an open cast mine less than 1 km away. Next to the falls is the **Shri Rudreshwar Temple**. Although the present building is comparatively modern the temple itself is ancient, although no one knows exactly when it was founded.

Bondla Wildlife Sanctuary → *Colour map 5a, grid B2.*

The smallest of Goa's three sanctuaries, the Bondla Wildlife Sanctuary① *mid-Sep to mid-Jun; 0900-1730; closed Thu. Rs 5, still camera Rs 25, video camera Rs 100. 2-wheeler Rs 10, car/jeep Rs 50,* is only 80 sq km in area. It is situated in the foothills of the Western Ghats which harbour sambar, wild boar, gaur (Indian bison), monkeys and a few migratory elephants which occasionally wander in from Karnataka during the summer. Sightings can be disappointing.

The park has a well-kept botanical and rose garden, in addition to a zoo and deer park, closed for lunch and on Thursday. The mini-zoo here guarantees sightings of "Goa's wildlife in natural surroundings" although the porcupine and African lion also make an appearance! The number of animals in the zoo has decreased in recent years and those that remain seem to have adequate space compared to other zoos in India. Additions are generally rescued "pets" or animals that have inadvertently fallen down wells! The small and basic Nature Education Centre is closed 1300-1400 and has the facility to show wildlife videos but is rarely used.

Short five-minute elephant rides are offered between 1100-1200 and between 1600-1700 when the mini-zoo is open, and a deer safari (minimum eight people) between 1600-1730, Rs 10.

★ Savoi Spice Plantation → *Colour map 5a, grid B2. For information, T340243.*

Over 200 years old, it was founded by Mr Shetye and is still being run by the family. The plantation is focused around a large irrigation tank with beautiful lilies and kingfishers. Being part wetland and part on a hillside allows cultivation of a wide variety of plants and trees. There are grapefruit, areca nut palms – some 150 years old – and coconuts with pepper vines growing up their trunks, soft and hard skin jackfruit which can become giants weighing over 20 kg, and banana plants which can produce 250 bananas from a single flower, one flower is cut off each plant to be eaten as a vegetable delicacy. On the hillside grow pineapples, 200,000 fruit are cut between June and September, bamboo, basil, cocoa, wood-apple, mangoes, and the surprising nutmeg which you might mistake for lemons! The families employed on the site are housed on the estate and men, women and the older children can be seen working at different seasonal tasks. Retired employees are encouraged to remain active by producing handicrafts for sale to visitors. You can also buy packets of spices. All plants are grown under traditional Goan methods of organic farming. The guided tour ①*Rs 300 for individuals*, along shady paths, takes about an hour and includes soft drinks and lunch and a tot of feni to "give strength" for the return journey to your resort, and the chance to buy packets of spices which make ideal gifts to take home.

Tropical Spice Plantation

Clearly signposted off the NH4A, just south of the Sri Mangesh temple, the Tropical Spice Plantation① *guided tours Rs 300, boats for hire (Rs 100); great for early morning bird watching, information T340329,* is in a picturesque valley in Keri. This is a very pleasant plantation with well-informed guides and friendly staff. They specialise in medicinal uses for the spices, the majority of which seem to be good for the skin.

At the end of the tour an areca nut picker will demonstrate the art of harvesting by shinning up a tall palm with his feet tied together in a circle of rope, and having climbed up one palm, gracefully sways at the crown in order to transfer to the top of a neighbouring tree without having to waste any energy climbing down and up again! The demonstration ends with the equally impressive art of descent, by rapidly sliding down the trunk like a fireman. The tour concludes with a delicious lunch.

★ Tambdi Surla → *Colour map 5a, grid B3.*

From the plantation, it is well worth visiting Tambdi Surla, the small but beautifully preserved temple in Sanguem taluka. The road south from Valpoi goes through

Nanus (2 km) and 2 km further on crosses the upper reaches of the Mandovi River, then following its left bank. After 5 km a right fork leads to Ponda and the left to Molem, nearly 18 km to the southeast. However, after just over 10 km (7.5 km from Molem), an unsignposted road to the left leads to Tambdi Surla, a further 8 km into the dense forest.

Mahadeva Temple Tucked into the forested foothills, the small Mahadeva Temple is the only major remaining example of pre-Portuguese Hindu architecture in Goa. It may well have been saved from destruction by its very remoteness. There is a beautifully preserved miniature example of early Hindu temple architecture from the Kadamba-Yadava period. The place is often deserted, though the compound is well maintained by the Archaeology Department. The entrance to the temple is a short walk from the car park.

The 12th-13th-century black basalt temple stands on a platform with three plain mouldings. The stone used must have been transported some distance as basalt is not available locally. The exterior walls have little decoration save for the breaks provided by the vertical pilasters. However, there are good miniature reliefs and sculptures on the *shikhara* above the *garbagriha*, showing deities including Brahma with Saraswati above, Siva with Uma-Mahesh above, and Vishnu with Kumarashakti above. The low wall near the open-sided entrance hall has finely carved lozenge-with-rosette motifs which still appear crisp.

The *shikharas* of the four niches in the *mandapa* which contain images including *Nagas*, throw light on how the original temple must have looked with its tower over the *garbagriha* complete. A *Naga* with two hoods appears on a separate slab.

Molem

Molem, 12 km south, is the start of hikes and treks in December/January. Popular routes lead to Dudhsagar (17 km), the sanctuary and Atoll Gad, 12 km, Matkonda Hill, 10 km and Tambdi Surla. Contact the Hiking Association, 6 Anand Niwas, Swami Vivekenanda Road, Panaji.

Bhagwan Mahaveer Sanctuary → *Colour map 5a, grid B3.*

The 240 sq km sanctuary contains a herd of gaur (Indian Bison), deer, monkeys and rich birdlife. Occasionally elephants and tigers wander in from neighbouring Karnataka during the summer months, the tigers remaining on higher ground favoured by the few black panthers in the sanctuary but these are rarely spotted. The magnificently attractive **Dudhsagar Falls** are in the southeast corner and the **Devil's Canyon**, an impressive river gorge. The canyon can be visited after getting permission from the Interpretation Centre where you can get directions.

Ins and outs Tickets are available at the Nature Interpretation Centre, 100 m from the police check post, Molem. Entrance to the Molem National Park, within the Sanctuary, 100 m east of the Tourist Complex, is clearly signed but the 14 km of tracks not mapped. Open 0900-1700. Within the Sanctuary, Forest Department jeeps are available; contact the Range Forest Officer, Molem. Motorbikes can manage the rough track but not a scooter.

★ **Dudhsagar Falls** The spectacular falls on the border between Goa and Karnataka, which are the highest in India, measure a total drop of about 600m. The name, 'the sea of milk', is derived from the white foam that the force of the water creates as it drops in stages, forming pools along the way. The falls are best seen just after the monsoon, between October and December, but right up to April there is enough water to make a visit worthwhile.

Colem (Kulem) is a busy small town. Rail passengers have to travel from here by road to the falls as Dudhsagar station has not reopened after gauge conversion (see transport). A viewing area allows you a better appreciation of the falls' grandeur, and to a beautifully fresh pool which is lovely for a swim (take your costume and towel). There are further pools below but you need to be sure-footed. The final section of the journey is a scramble on foot across stream beds with boulders; it is a difficult task for anyone but the most athletic. The really fit and adventurous may wish to make the arduous climb up to the head of the falls with a guide, which is well worth the effort. Allow three hours, plus some time to rest at the top, and make sure of returning before the train you will need to catch. A swim in the pool at the falls is particularly refreshing after a hot and dusty ride. Guides are available but the track is easy to follow even without one.

Listings: The Ghats

●Sleeping

Bondla Wildlife Sanctuary *p1194*
F The Forest Department **Eco-Cottages**. 8 basic rooms with bath (Rs 150), newer ones better. Also 12-bed Dormitories (Rs 30) 1 km inside park entrance (better for seeing wildlife at night). Reserve at Deputy Conservator of Forests, Wildlife Division, 4th Floor, 18th June Rd, Panaji, T229701, although a room or bed is often available to anyone turning up.

Savoi Spice Plantation *p1194*
Savoy Farmhouse, T340243. On a terrace deep in the forest, good for bird watching, an idyllic farmhouse with 2 en suite rooms with verandas built from mud with thick walls.

Tambdi Surla *p1194*
E Shanti Nature Resort, 500 m from the temple, 9 large mud huts with palm-thatched roofs, electricity and running water in forest setting, emphasis on rest, ayurvedic treatment and meditation. Restaurant for all tastes, visits to spice gardens, bird watching, hikes, Dudhsagar etc arranged (2 nights, US$120). Recommended for location and eco-friendly approach. Contact ahead *Passive Active Tourism, Hotel Four Pillars*, Panaji, T422986.

Molem *p1195*
E Forest Resort (GTDC), T0832-600238, has 23 rooms, some a/c, dorm (Rs 50).

●Eating

Bondla Wildlife Sanctuary *p1194*
Cheap eats can be bought at the **Den Bar and Restaurant**, near the entrance, which serves chicken, vegetables or fish with rice and small **cafeteria**, inside the park near the mini-zoo, which has snacks and cold drinks.

● Transport

Bondla Wildlife Sanctuary *p1194*
Bus
From Ponda via Tisk and Usgaon where taxis and motorcycle taxis wait; 5 km beyond, a fork to the right leads to the park. KTC buses may run at weekends from Panaji. During the season the Forest Department minibus is supposed to do 2 daily trips (except Thu) between Bondla and Tisk: from Bondla, 0815, 1745; from Tisk, 1100 (Sun 1030) and 1900. Check at the Tourist Office first.

Motobike
You can hire a motorbike from one of the central beaches for a pleasant ride out. Make sure you have enough petrol. The nearest petrol pump is at Tisk, 15 km away.

Savoi Spice Plantation *p1194*
The plantation north of Ponda is reached via Banastari and is 6 km from Savoi.

Bus
Run from Ponda (towards Volvoi), and also from Banastari; ask for Plantation.

Taxi
Taxis ply from the coastal resorts but travel agents offer competitive rates which include the entrance fee (eg **Day Tripper Tours**, near Kamat Complex, Calangute, T276726, Rs 770). Some include a visit to a local cashew nut processing plant.

Tambdi Surla *p1194*

A **taxi** from Panaji takes about 2½ hrs for the 69 km. From the crossroads at Molem on the NH4A, the road north through dense forest goes to Tambdi Surla; ask local people or follow signs for the *Shanti Nature Resort*. It is also possible to reach the site along minor roads from Valpoi to the north (make sure you have enough petrol before leaving Molem). **Buses** from Ponda (1130-1645) and Panaji (1030-1745) take 2-3 hrs.

Bhagwan Mahaveer Sanctuary *p1197*
From the south, travel via Sanguem. The road from Sanvordem to the NH17 is badly pot-holed and has heavy lorry traffic.

Bus
Buses between Panaji, Ponda or Margao, and Belgaum/Bangalore, stop at Molem.

Jeep
From Colem, jeeps do the rough 45-min ride to Dudhsagar (Rs 300 per head, Rs 1800 return per jeep for 6); then a 5-min walk along a wooded trail to the base of the falls.

Train
Vasco-Colem Passenger from Vasco (0710) or Margao (Madgaon) at 0800 should arrive at Colem around 0930; return around 1640 allowing enough time to visit the falls.

Hindu Heartland

Ponda is Goa's smallest taluka. It is also the richest in Goan Hindu religious architecture. Within 5km of its town centre are some of Goa's most important temples, including the Shri Shantadurga at Queula and the Nagesh Temple near Bandora.
▸▸ *For Sleeping, Eating and other listings, see pages 1198-1199.*

Ponda → *Phone code: 0832 .Colour map 5a, grid B2. Population: 17,700.*

Once a centre of culture, music, drama and poetry, the area around Ponda, with its group of important Hindu temples, was known as Antruz Mahal. Ponda town is now an important transport intersection, where the main road from Margao via Borlim meets the East-West National Highway, NH4A.

The **Safa Mosque** (Shahouri Masjid), the largest of 26 mosques in Goa, was built by Ibrahim 'Ali' Adil Shah in 1560. It has a simple rectangular chamber on a low plinth, with a pointed pitched roof, very much in the local architectural style, but the arches are distinctly Bijapuri. Built of laterite, the lower tier has been quite badly eroded. On the south side is a tank with meherab designs for ritual cleansing.

Priol

★ **Shri Mangesh Temple** is to the northwest of Ponda, on the NH17 leading to Old Goa. The 18th-century temple, set on a wooded hill at Priol just north of Mardol, is sometimes described as the most important Hindu temple in Goa. On 25 February is *Jatra*. During *Mangesh Jatra* the *rath* (temple car) with Shri Mangesh is pulled by crowds of attendants.

The temple complex is architecturally typical of the highly distinctive Goan Hindu temple style. The estate on which the temple depends provides a beautiful setting. Note the attractive tank on the left as you approach which is one of the oldest parts of the site.

The seven-storeyed octagonal *deepmal* in the courtyard is one of the most famous lamp towers in Goa. Around its base are colourful little 'primitif' painted images. Lamps are placed in the niches at festivals. The sacred *tulsi vrindavan* (basil) plant stands nearby. The *mandapa* (assembly hall) has the typical red tiled steeply pitched roof. The highest tower with an octagonal drum topped by a dome is over the sanctum. At the entrance to the shrine itself is a beautifully carved wooden door. The 19th-century Belgian glass chandeliers hang from the ceiling of the main hall, and is usually crowded with pilgrims who make offerings of flowers and coconuts bought at the entrance.

Mardol

The **Mahalsa Narayani Temple** is 2 km from Shri Mangesh. *Mahalsa* is a Goan form of Vishnu's consort Lakshmi or, according to some, his female form *Mohini*. The entrance to the temple complex is through the arch under the *nagarkhana* (drum room). There is a seven-storeyed *deepstambha* and in addition a tall brass Garuda pillar which rests on the back of a turtle, acts as a second lamp tower. The half human-half eagle *Garuda*, Vishnu's vehicle, sits on top. A decorative arched gate at the back leads to the peace and cool of the palm-fringed temple tank. A palanquin procession with the deity marks the *Mardol Jatra*.

Bandora

The **Nagesh Temple** is 4 km west of Ponda. At Farmagudi junction on the NH17, a fork is signposted to Bandora. A narrow winding lane dips down to the tiny hamlet and its temple to Siva as Nagesh (God of Serpents). The temple's origin can be established at 1413 by an inscribed tablet here, though the temple was renewed in the 18th century. The temple tank which is well stocked with carp, is enclosed by a white-outlined laterite block wall and surrounded by shady palms. The five-storey lamp tower near the temple has brightly coloured deities painted in niches just above the base. The main *mandapa* (assembly hall) has interesting painted woodcarvings illustrating stories from the epics *Ramayana* and *Mahabharata* below the ceiling line, as well as the *Ashtadikpalas*, the eight Directional Guardians (Indra, Agni, Yama, Nirritti, Varuna, Vayu, Kubera and Ishana). The principal deity has the usual *Nandi* and in addition there are shrines to Ganesh and Laxmi-Narayan and subsidiary shrines with *lingas*, in the courtyard. The *Nagesh Jatra*, normally in November, is celebrated at full moon to commemorate Siva's victory.

Queula (Kavale)

Just 3 km southwest from Ponda's town centre bus stand is one of the largest and most famous of Goa's temples dedicated to ★ **Shantadurga** (1738), the wife of Siva as the Goddess of Peace. The form of Durga was so named because at the request of Brahma she mediated in a great quarrel between Siva (her husband) and Vishnu, and brought back peace in the Universe. Hence, in the sanctuary she stands between the two other deities. *Jatra* on 15th February.

Steps lead up to the temple complex which has a very large tank cut into the hillside and a spacious courtyard surrounded by the usual pilgrim hostels and administration offices. The temple has a six-storey *deepstambha* (lamp tower) and subsidiary shrines. The part-gilded *rath* (car) is housed in the compound.

Listings: Hindu Heartland

🛏 Sleeping

Ponda *p1197*
C-D Menino, 100 m east of Bus Stand junction, 1st floor, T313146, F315026. 20

rooms, some a/c, pleasant, comfortable, good restaurant serves generous main courses, impressive modern hotel, good value.
E Padmavi, Gaunekar House, 100 m north of bus stand on NH4A, T312144. 20 large clean

🍷 *For an explanation of the sleeping and eating price codes used in this guide, see inside the front cover. Other relevant information is found in Essentials pages 52-57.*

rooms, some with bath with TV.
E President, 1 km east of bus stand, T312287.
11 rooms, basic but clean and reasonable.

Farmagudi (1km north)
C-D Atish, just below the Ganesh Temple on NH4A, T335124, F335249, atishrv@goa telecom.com. 40 comfortable rooms, some a/c, restaurant, large pool in brash open surrounds, gym, modern hotel, many pilgrim groups, friendly staff.
E Farmagudi Resort, attractively located though too close to NH4A, T335122. 39 clean rooms, some a/c, dorm (Rs 80), adequate restaurant (eat at *Atish*).

● Eating

Ponda *p1197*
Amigos, 2 km east of centre on Belgaum road.

Spoon Age, Upper Bazar, T 316191. Garden restaurant, serving Goan meals for local folk, friendly new setup. Occasional live music at weekend.

● Transport

Ponda *p1197*
Bus
To Panaji and Bondla via Tisk, but it is best to have your own transport to see the places nearby.

● Directory

Ponda *p1197*
Internet Fun World.Com, Viradh Building, T316717. **Useful addresses** Community Health Centre, T312115. Deputy Conservator of Forests (North), T312095.

Central Goa

Vasco da Gama → *Phone code: 0832. Colour map 5a, grid B1. Population: 91,300.*

Vasco da Gama (Vasco, in short) is the passenger railway terminus of the Central Goa branch line, and is the industrial heart of modern Goa. It has grown to become Goa's largest town but its only convenience for a visitor is its proximity to the airport.
▶▶ *For Sleeping, Eating and other listings, see pages 1200-1202.*

Ins and outs 3 km away is Dabolim airport. There are taxis or an airport coach. Cheap local buses also pass along the main road. Trains via Londa can now bring visitors from the north (Delhi, Agra) or the south (Hospet, Bangalore). Panaji is 30 km away.

Mormugao (Marmagoa) The natural harbour by the rocky headland jutting into the Arabian Sea, 4 km northwest of Vasco, is one of the busiest ports of India's west coast, mainly handling iron ore exports from the interior of the region.

When chosen as the ideal defensible point to become the capital to succeed Old Goa, a fort was built on the south headland of Mormugao Bay in 1685, and tentative building of a town started. In 1703 the Viceroy actually moved there but subsequently the plan to shift the capital was abandoned. Today, virtually nothing remains of the **fort** and what does is hidden by the industrial development that has taken its place.

Beaches near Vasco Bogmalo, the nearest beach to the airport (4 km, and a 10 minute drive away) is small, palm fringed and attractive, yet it is sparsely visited.

About 2½ km before reaching Bogmalo, the approach road forks. The right fork continues to Bogmalo whilst the left goes to **Hollant Beach**, 2 km away. A small rocky cove, it is fringed with coconut palms.

Santra Beach, further south, can be reached by going through the village behind the *Bogmalo Beach Resort*. Local fishermen are at hand to ferry passengers to two small islands for about Rs 350 per boat, which can be shared by a group.

Goa's airport is south of Panaji, across the Mormugao Bay developed by the Navy, is now shared by domestic and international charter flights from Europe. There are counters at the airport for car hire, foreign exchange (check rate and money carefully) and tourist information, all of which are normally open to meet flights.

Listings: Central Goa

● Sleeping

Vasco de Gama *p1199*
B La Paz Gardens, Swatantra Path, T512121, F513302, lapaz@goatelecom.com. 63 rooms, need redecorating, good a/c restaurants, pleasant bar, health club.
C Bismarck, behind *Auto Service*, T512277, F518524. 22 white-tiled sterile rooms, some a/c, few with bath tubs or balcony, clean linen, TV, small 'slime green' pool and terrace at back with open-air restaurant.
C-D Citadel, near *Tourist Hotel*, Jose Vaz Rd, T512222, F513036, epson@bom2.vsnl.net.in. 42 good size, comfortable rooms, half a/c, restaurant, bar, friendly.
C-D Maharaja, FL Gomes Rd, T514075, F512559, mahahotl@goa1.dot.net.in. 40 smallish rooms, 18 a/c, Gujarati *thalis*, bar.
E Annapurna, D Deshpande Rd, T513735. 33 clean rooms with bath, cool Udipi dining hall.
E Gladstone, FL Gomes Rd, near railway station, T510005. 18 clean functional rooms, some a/c, restaurant, bar.
E Nagina, D Deshpande Rd, T511670. 21 fair sized rooms, some a/c, restaurant serves Goan specialities.

Beaches near Vasco *p1199*
Cheaper family guesthouses in the village are set back from the beach.
AL-A Bogmalo Beach Resort, T556222, F556236. 121 compact rooms with sea view (4th and 5th floors refurbished), choice of restaurants, casino, pool, ayurvedic centre, no direct beach access, cycle hire Rs 50 per hr.
A-B Coconut Creek. 20 rooms (10 a/c) in 2-storey cottages, light and airy, pool, full of character, exemplary hotel, best in the area.
C-D Saritas, T555965, saritasguesthouse@rediffmail.com, short walk from bus stand and beach. 13 rooms with bath, some a/c.

D Joet's Guest House, right on the beach, T555036, joets@goatelecom.com. 2 small airy rooms with shower, good restaurant.

Outside Bogmalo
D Raj Resort by the Sea, Gallin, T555688. 8 airy rooms, restaurant, friendly, clean.

● Eating

Vasco de Gama *p1199*
$$ Goodyland, La Paz. Western fast food joint, pizza, cakes and sweets.
$$ Ginza, Karma Plaza, Rajendra Prasad Ave. Japanese, Chinese and continental, pleasant split level a/c dining area. Good service.
$ Adarsh, Swatantra Path, 100 m south of railway station. Excellent *masala dosa*.
$ Annapurna, D Deshpande Rd. Good *thalis*.
$ La Gosta, D Deshpande Rd. Goan selection plus Chinese, a/c, plenty of veg dishes and fruit juices.
$ Nanking, off Swatantra Path. Good value, authentic Chinese.
$ Temptations, fast food and snacks on the terrace above entrance to *Karma Plaza Hotel*.

Beaches near Vasco *p1199*
The beach cafés **Full Moon** and **Stiff Waves** near *Bogmalo Beach Resort* do excellent seafood.
Joet's, good seafood. "very friendly; sun beds on the beach and hammocks among the palms".

● Entertainment

Beaches near Vasco *p1199*
Naval Aviation Museum, 1 km from beach, on approach road. 1000-1700, closed public holidays, free. A few rusting examples of old planes.

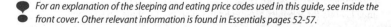
For an explanation of the sleeping and eating price codes used in this guide, see inside the front cover. Other relevant information is found in Essentials pages 52-57.

O Shopping

Beaches near Vasco *p1199*
Ritika Bookshop and Boutique, *Bogmalo Beach Resort's* verandah, a/c, good books and stationery, high quality gifts, good value.

Tailoring
Some beach giftshops offer good-quality, made-to-measure cotton and silk jackets and shirts at reasonable prices.

▲ Activities and tours

Vasco de Gama *p1199*
Gopi Tours, 4 Adarsh Building, Swatantra Path, T514051.
Merces, 6 Vasco Tower, T512268.
Travel Corporation of India, *Bismark Hotel*, T512277.

Beaches near Vasco *p1199*
Watersports
Splash Watersports, T409886, T9822124457 (mob). Run by Derek, a famous Indian champion windsurfer. Operate from a shack on the beach just below *Joets*, providing parasailing, windsurfing, water skiing, trips to nearby island etc; during the high season only. **Bogmalo Beach Resort**, T513291, and **Joet's**, T555036, also offer these; diving is possible through **Goa Diving**, who have a morning office at *Joet's*, and are based at Chapel Bhat, Chicalim, T555117, goadivin@goa telecom.com. PADI certification from Open Water to Assistant Instructor.

● Transport

Vasco de Gama *p1199*
Bus
From City Bus Stand near market, frequent, non-stop service to **Panaji**, and **Margao**, Rs 15, via Airport. Kadamba Bus Stand, northeast of town, with a very helpful information booth, has services to major towns in Goa (not non-stop), and to Bangalore via **Hubli**: 1500, 1645 (15 hrs), Rs 240; **Belgaum**, many, Rs 57; **Hospet**: 1130 (10 hrs) Rs 100; **Hubli** many (6hrs) Rs 65; **Mangalore**: 1700 (10 hrs) Rs 156; **Mumbai**: 1330 (16 hrs) Rs 325. Check timetable in advance.

Taxi
To and from Londa, about Rs 1,500.

Train
Local 3 daily stop at: Dabolim for the airport and Bogmalo; **Cansaulim** for Velsao beach, Seraulim; **Majorda** for Utorda, Majorda, Betalbatim beaches; **Madgaon (Margao)** for Colva, Benaulim and the southern beaches; **Chandorgoa, Sanvordem, Calem, Kulem (Colem), Dudhsagar** for the waterfalls.
Long distance Reservations, T512833. Services via Londa to Belgaum, **Bangalore, Delhi via Agra**, and with **Hospet** (for **Hampi**) among others. To **Londa Junction**: by *Goa Exp 2779*, depart 1400, arrive 1745; by *Vasco Bangalore Exp 7310*, depart 2030, arrive 2353; both 4¼ hrs. To **Delhi (Nizamuddin)** via Agra Cantt: *Goa Exp 2779*, depart 1400, arrive 0635 (after 2 nights), 41¾ hrs. To **Hospet** (for **Hampi**):*Vasco-da-Gama Vijayawada Express 7228,* Wed,Sat, 0640, arrive Hospet 1600. To **Pune** *Goa Exp, 2779*, depart 1400, 14 hrs.

Beaches near Vasco *p1199*
Bus
Erratic service to **Vasco**, passes close to the airport.

Taxi
To Dabolim airport, Rs 140; **Vasco**, 8 km, around Rs 120; half-day hire to visit, say Panaji or Mapusa market, Rs 600.

Dabolim *p1200*
Air
Internal flights Air India, T224081, Mumbai, Thiruvananthapuram. Indian Airlines, T223826, Reservations 1000-1300, 1400-1600, Airport T0834-513863. Flights to **Bangalore, Delhi** (some via **Agra**) and **Mumbai** daily; also **Chennai**; and from **Tiruchirapalli** and to **Pune**. Jet Airways, T431472, Airport T510354, to **Mumbai** and **Bangalore**. Sahara, to **Mumbai** daily, and **Delhi**.
Transport to town Package tour companies and luxury hotels usually arrange courtesy buses for hotel transfer. The pre-paid **taxi** counter immediately outside the arrivals hall has rates clearly displayed (eg Panaji Rs 340 which takes 40 mins; North

Goa beaches from Rs 450; Tiracol Rs 750; south Goa beaches from Rs 240; Palolem Rs 700). State your destination at the counter, pay and get a receipt which will give the registration number of your taxi. Keep hold of this receipt until you reach your destination. There is theoretically no need to tip the driver. The taxi driver may insist that the hotel you have asked for has closed down or is full and will suggest another in order to get a commission from the hotel. Say that you have a reservation at the hotel of your choice (even if you don't!). The public **bus** stop on the far side of the roundabout outside the airport gates has buses to Vasco da Gama, from where there are connections to all major places in Goa. If you want to go straight to the nearest beach, go to the right of the roundabout, cross the road for buses to Bogmalo. *Hotel Airport*, 1 km away, is listed under Panaji Sleeping.

● Directory

Vasco de Gama *p1199*
Internet: Cyberdome, Karma Plaza, T518687, 0930-2200 Mon-Sat, Rs 35 per hr, 0930-1200 Sun, 8 terminals. **Medical services** Salgaocar Medical Research Centre, T512524. **Tourist offices** At *Tourist Hotel*, T512673 with a touch screen help point on Goa (zoom in maps, hotel telephone numbers etc). **Useful services** Ambulance: T512768. Fire: T513840. **Police**: T512304.

Southern Goa

The talukas of Salcete, Quepem and Canacona have a wholly different atmosphere from those of the north. Much of the coastline is lined with village houses scattered beneath coconut palms with rice fields immediately behind. The rising prosperity of Salcete has avoided the packaged pop culture of the northern coast. Here the pace is gentler. While Colva acts as the beach resort for the nearby population of Margao, long stretches of sand are completely deserted. Further south, Canacona has beautiful beaches at Agonda and Palolem. Some of Goa's finest churches and impressive country estates are in the interior of Salcete which was heavily influenced by Portugese culture and virtually anywhere inland is within reach of a day trip of the coast. ➤➤ *For Sleeping, Eating and other listings, see pages 1210-1218.*

★ Margao → *Phone code: 0832. Colour map 5a, grid B2. Population: 78,400.*

Also called Madgaon, this is the largest commercial centre after Panaji and the capital of the state's richest and most fertile taluka, Salcete. A pleasant provincial town, it was given the status of a vila (town) by Royal decree in 1778. The Konkan railway now brings many visitors here as their first port of call, but most head for the beaches, using Margao for an overnight stop.

Ins and outs
Getting there The Konkan Railway connects Margao directly with Mumbai, Mangalore and Kerala. Madgaon station is 1.5 km southeast from the bus stands which are in the Municipal Gardens and the market area where most of the hotels and restaurants are located. Rickshaws charge Rs 15 to transfer while locals walk the 800 m along the rail line! Those arriving by bus from other states and from North Goa use the New Kadamba (State) bus stand 2 km north of town. City buses take you to t he town bus stands for destinations south of Margao. Colva and Benaulim buses leave from the local stand east of the gardens.

Getting around There are plenty of auto-rickshaws and 8-seater van taxis for hire in addition to city buses.

Sights

Tourism has had little impact here. You can still see examples of old Portuguese domestic architecture and some fine churches while also experiencing daily life in a bustling market town going about its business.

The impressive Baroque ★ **Church of the Holy Spirit** with its classic Goan façade dominates the Old Market (*Feast Day* in June) square, the Largo de Igreja. Originally built in 1564, it was sacked by Muslims in 1589 and rebuilt in 1675. A remarkable pulpit on the north wall has carvings of the Apostles. There are statues of St Anthony and of the Blessed Joseph Vaz kept in glass cabinets in the north aisle near the north transept. In the square is a monumental cross with a mango tree beside it.

Many 18th-century houses, though dilapidated, can be seen, especially in and around Abade Faria Road. The **da Silva House** is a fine example of an impressive town house built around 1790 when Inacio da Silva became the Secretary to the Viceroy. It had a long façade with the roof divided into seven separate cropped 'towers' – hence

Margao

Sleeping
1 Goa Woodlands
2 La Flor
3 Margao Residency
4 Nanutel
5 Saaj

Eating
1 Banjara
2 Casa Menino
3 Chinese Pavilion
4 Gaylin
5 Johnny's Cove & Baker's Basket
6 Kamats
7 Longuinhos
8 Tato

its other name, **Seven Shoulders**. Today, however, only three of these 'towers' remain. The house retains an air of grandeur in its lavishly carved dark rosewood furniture, its gilded mirrors and fine chandeliers. The first floor reception rooms which face the street are lit by large wood and oyster shell windows which are protected by wrought iron balconies. The descendants continue to live in a small wing of the diminished house. Intending visitors should contact the local tourist office at the GTDC *Residency* but permission to enter is rarely given.

★ Southern beaches → *Phone code: 0832. Colour map 5a, grid B2 and C2.*

The southern beaches are less distinctive than those of the north. Government regulations have kept nearly all the hotels back from the sea, but the character of the unbroken wide sand nonetheless also varies. The road runs slightly inland, with spurs leading down to the main sections of beach. Some, like **Benaulim** and **Varca** are little more than deserted stretches of dune-backed sand, with isolated fishing hamlets. In contrast **Colva's** coconut palms come down to the beach edge, shading restaurants and a cluster of hotels and shops. At intervals are some luxurious beach resorts. Further south is the newly discovered yet unpoilt beach at **Agonda**, a prelude to the magnificent palm-fringed coast at **Palolem**.

Velsao, Arossim, Utorda, Majorda

These three beaches, broad, flat and open, are among the least heavily used. Around the resort hotels there are small clusters of beach shack restaurants, and occasional fishing villages scattered under the coconut palms.

One of the distinctive features of this section of coast is the strip of land that lies between the main series of villages and the dunes which actually front the sea, used for intensive rice cultivation. The road runs through these villages, set back between 1 and 2 km from the sea. Old mansions of wealthy families still standing in the villages include **Utorda House**. There are also some fine examples dotted about Velsao, in various states of repair. An afternoon spent exploring these quiet back lanes by bicycle provides an insight into village life. The villages from here southwards are noted for the high level of emigration to the Gulf. Some have returned and invested money in many of the new hotels.

Betalbatim

Betalbatim has a pleasant stretch with some coconut palms and a few casuarinas on the low dunes that separate the seaside from the resort development. An afternoon spent on a bicycle seeking out some old Goan villas under the cool of palm trees is a pleasant alternative to lying on the beach. Colva, and a more up beat pace of life, is only a short walk to the south along the beach. At low tide, when the firm sand is exposed, it is possible to cycle for miles along the beach in either direction.

Colva → *Phone code: 0832. Colour map 5a, grid B2.*

Colva is one of the most popular beaches in southern Goa, though not as developed or busy as Calangute in the north. The beach has beautiful sand, coconut palms gently swaying in the breeze and blue waters which can sometimes be rough and grey-green. However, beach sellers and stray dogs can be a nuisance. Colva village is a bit scruffy.

Ins and outs From the airport, taxis charge about Rs 280. Those arriving by train at Margao, 6 km away, can choose between buses, auto-rickshaws and taxis for transfer. Buses pull in at the main crossroads and then proceed down to the beach about a kilometre away before turning around. Auto-rickshaws claim to have a Rs 30 "minimum charge" around Colva itself. See Transport, page 1217, for further details.

Teams of fishermen operate all along the coast, from here down to Benaulim
to the south, with their pitch-boarded boats drawn up on the beach, while motorised
crafts are anchored offshore. They provide added interest and colour and it is worth
waking early to watch them haul in their nets. If you are very early you may even be
invited out on a boat!

The large **Church of Our Lady of the Miracles** (1581) houses an image of Jesus
alleged to have been discovered on the African coast. *Fama of Menino Jesus*
(mid-October) is celebrated with a colourful procession and a fair. Near the church,
specially blessed lengths of string are sold, as well as replicas of limbs which are
offered to the image in thanks for cures effected.

Benaulim → *Phone code: 0832. Population: 10,200.*

This is the more tranquil and pleasant end of Colva beach. However, during the
season, the approach road to the beach can get very busy and some visitors complain
of being plagued by fruit and jewellery vendors. If you want to escape their constant
attention, hire a bike and cycle some distance south along the beach. The 4-km walk
or ride to Colva through idyllic countryside is recommended.

The small **Church of St John the Baptist**, on a hill beyond the village, rebuilt 1596,
is worth a visit. The altar reredos is uniquely decorated and there is a wonderful
Rococo pulpit. See below for *Feast of St John*.

Varca, Fatrade, Cavelossim and Mobor
→ *Phone code: 0832. Colour map 5a, grid B2.*

The beaches south of Benaulim, Varca, Fatrade and Cavelossim, are quieter and
cleaner than Colva. **Varca** and **Fatrade** beaches are a quiet broad section of beach
with no rocks, no mosquitoes or flies, little rubbish and occasional local day trippers.
A bit exposed on windy days and with limited shade they are still good spots with
good swimming. To reach **Cavelossim** beach involves a short walk through scrub

Colva

To Sam's Cottages (250m), Sunshine Restaurant (700m) & Betalbatim
To Betalbatim
Fisherman's Cottages
Sports Field
Paddy Fields
4th Ward
Damodar Bookshop
WC
Taxis
Bike Repairs
School Playing Fields
Weizmann
Meeting Point Travels
BoB
Our Lady of Mercy
Bike Hire
To Margao
To Benaulim

N
0 metres 200
0 yards 200

■ **Sleeping**
1 Colmar
2 Colva Residency
3 Longuinhos Beach Resort
4 Graciano Cottages
5 Star Beach Resort
6 Tourist Nest
7 Vailankanni
8 Vista de Colva
9 White Sands
10 William's Retreat

● **Eating**
1 Johnny Cool's
2 Kentuckee
3 Pasta Palace
4 Pirate's
5 Splash

vegetation and dunes. Further south, **Mobor** lies on the narrow peninsula where the River Sal joins the sea. Access to the beach near the river is somewhat restricted by the sprawling Leela Palace complex. It is well worth walking to the Sal river estuary where a clean spur of sand dividing the river from the sea allows you to enjoy peaceful sun bathing. Be wary of the variable currents though close to the river mouth as the tides turn. The Sal is a busy river and harbour for fishing boats, but it is also very pleasant for boat rides. This relatively quiet backwater has however, been affected by the building boom around Cavelossim.

Betul

Betul, which overlooks the wide estuary, is in an idyllic setting, delightfully shaded by coconut palms, jackfruit, papaya and banana. Betul is an important fishing village which also depends on coir production and labouring. A walk along the 'jetty' past dozens of many-coloured fishing boats will reveal busy fisherfolk loading fish into baskets or their catch of tiny silvery fish glistening in the sun trapped under spread out nets on the bank.

★ Cabo de Rama Fort → *Phone code: 0832. Colour map 5a, grid C2.*

Cape Rama is named after the hero of the Hindu epic the Ramayana, who is said to have lived there with his wife Sita during their period of exile. The Cape was an obvious site for a fort to any power whose interests might be threatened from the sea. Its origins pre-date the arrival of the Portuguese who captured it in 1763 and used it as a prison too.

Benaulim

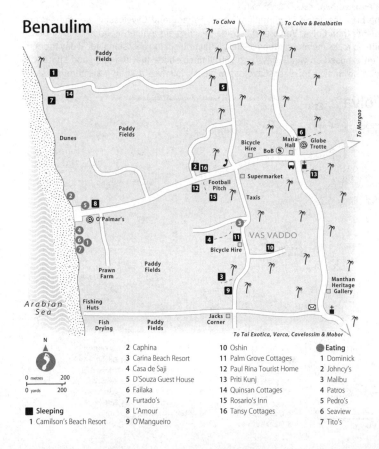

		● Eating
2 Caphina	10 Oshin	1 Dominick
3 Carina Beach Resort	11 Palm Grove Cottages	2 Johncy's
4 Casa de Saji	12 Paul Rina Tourist Home	3 Malibu
5 D'Souza Guest House	13 Priti Kunj	4 Patros
6 Failaka	14 Quinsan Cottages	5 Pedro's
7 Furtado's	15 Rosario's Inn	6 Seaview
8 L'Amour	16 Tansy Cottages	7 Tito's
■ Sleeping	9 O'Mangueiro	
1 Camilson's Beach Resort		

The gatehouse, which has been restored, looks worse for wear than most of the original fortifications. Sadly, it is a grubby mess of broken timbers and walls covered with graffiti. The main entrance seems far from impregnable, considering the scale of the fortifications, but note the strategically positioned hole in the wall, pointing straight at the door, behind which a cannon could be stationed. The outer ramparts are excellently preserved, with several cannons still scattered along their length. There are fine views from several of its major bastions, and you can walk virtually the entire outer length of the fort. From two of the gates it is possible to scramble down to the sea, but great care is needed on the crumbly laterite paths. The most dramatic of the walls is on the landward side, where it rises 10-15 m above the floor of the moat which was dug both to provide laterite blocks from which the fort is constructed, and to create the moat.

The gatehouse is at the lowest point of the whole fort, the ground rising to its highest in the southwest. The view is particularly good to the south in the evening light, across bays stretching down past Palolem to Karnataka easily visible on a clear day.

Varca to Betul

To Benaulim
To Margao
To Varca
Varca Beach
Orlim
To Palolem
Chinchinim
Fatrade Beach
Carmona
Cavelossim
Assolna
Cavelossim Beach
River Sal
To NH17
Betty's Place
Fish Port
Velim
Mobor Beach
Arabian Sea
Betul
Tarrie
To Cabo de Rama
N
0 km 1
0 miles 1

■ Sleeping
1 Club Mahindra
2 Dona Sa Maria
3 Dona Sylvia Resort
4 Gaffino's & Hippo Cool
5 Goa Renaissance Resort
6 José Holiday Home
7 Leela Palace
8 Mobor Beach Resort
9 Octima
10 Resorte de Goa
11 River Sal
12 Sao Domingos
13 Taj Exotica

● Eating
1 Grill Room
2 Jazz Inn
3 Mike's Place
4 River View
5 Shakey's

Agonda

The beautiful beach mid-way between Cabo de Rama and Palolem is totally unspoilt with little development. The bay does not have the picture post card setting of Palolem; casuarinas line the beach rather than palm trees. However the village remains essentially unspoilt with only a couple of small guest houses at the southern end. The swimming is safe, the beach clean and it is a peaceful spot.

★ Palolem

→ *Phone code: 0832. Colour map 5a, grid C2.*

South of Agonda, the beautiful curve of palm-fringed golden sand is one of the best beaches. The search for the remaining unspoilt idyll brought travellers to Palolem a few years ago but it is no longer a deserted bay. There is a line of beach shacks serving food and drink in the season while the range of accommodation increases with demand.

The fairly narrow strip of beach has rather strange rocky outcrops at each end which are locally referred to as 'Pandava's drums' and 'footprints'. An added attraction here is the freshwater stream to the north, as well as the small Canacona Island which can be reached by a short swim or by wading across at low tide.

The main beach is to the north with the bulk of the beach shacks, while the relatively smaller southern section has fishermen's huts and some novel accommodation options. The southern end is also relatively quieter and more relaxed and free from "full moon" parties. The shaded palm tree area is unfortunately becoming increasingly littered. All is worse at weekends when an influx of local trippers bring their picnics, fill the air with loud music and leave behind a pile of garbage and dead whiskey bottles.

Colomb, Patnem and Rajbag beaches

South of Palolem, a walk along the shore over rocky outcrops gives access to the small attractive sandy cove of Colomb Beach with huts of the fishing community nearby. Some take in long-term visitors. *Boom Shankar* overlooks the beach. Red snapper and tuna feature on their menu and is a relaxing place for sunset drinks. *Threemurti Shiva* is a simple small restaurant serving tasty local meals.

At the end of the track there is a collection of huts which marks the start of the fine sweeping Patnem beach where villagers operate a few shacks.

Palolem

Sleeping		
1 Bhakti Kutir	7 Oceanic	2 Boom Shankar
2 Camp Palo	8 Palolem Beach Resort	3 Cool Breeze
3 Ciaran's Camp	9 Premier Cottages	4 Silver Star
4 Cocohuts	10 Waves	5 Sun & Moon
5 Cozy Nook		6 Threemurti Shiva
6 Hi-Tide Beach Huts	● Eating	7 Woody's
	1 Blue Jays	

Further south, by wading across a stream (possible before monsoon), you reach the unspoilt Rajbag Beach backed by dunes and casuarinas which offers excellent swimming. The upmarket *Bharat-Hilton Resort* with 280 rooms, however, opened in 2002 and so the access to the beach from the village side is restricted to a small lane at the south end.

Canacona (Chaudi)

Canacona (pronounced locally Kannkonn) is a crossroads settlement on the NH17 between Panaji and Karwar in Karnataka. The rail link on the Konkan line has brought the idyllic beaches nearby to the attention of developers. For Palolem or Agonda this is the nearest settlement of any significant size with shops and direct transport links. Chaudi, the town's main square, has the bus and auto stands. For a bite to eat there is *Canacona Palace*, 50 m east of the crossroads, serving good Udupi vegetarian food.

Kindlebaga and Galgibaga

Kindlebaga is 2 km from Canacona and has accommodation. South of the Talpona River, which has a ferry crossing, a short strip of land juts out to sea. Galgibaga is a change from the fishing villages across the river as it has well-built houses among lucrative casuarina plantations belonging to the townspeople. Galgibaga beach is visited by Olive Ridley turtles which travel vast distances to return to lay their eggs here each November. The nests are protected by people who in the past, sold the eggs as a delicacy.

Cotigao Wildlife Sanctuary

① *0730-1730 throughout the year (but may not be worthwhile during the monsoon). Rs 5, 2-wheelers Rs 10, cars Rs 50. Still camera Rs 25; Video Rs 100. There is a Nature Interpretation Centre with a small reference library at the entrance. Most visitors come for the day. In theory, overnight stay is possible (with permission) either near the sanctuary office or in a watch tower. Contact the Conservator's Office, Margao, T735361 or at the Sanctuary Interpretation Centre. A kiosk in the hamlet just beyond the entrance sells basic provisions. Getting there: 7 km south of Canacona, a 2-km road along a left turn (east) off the NH17, just after the massive concrete gateway to the Partagali temple, leads to the sanctuary. Buses from Canacona, or hire a motorbike from one of the southern beaches.*

The second largest of Goa's wildlife sanctuaries, Cotigao, 60 km south of Panaji, was established in 1969. One of the most densely forested areas of the state, the 105-sq km sanctuary is in part hilly to the south and east and has the Talpona River flowing through it. There are several small settlements of *Velip* and *Kunbis* who are forest-dwelling groups existing on subsistence farming so it offers a good opportunity to observe traditional rural life.

The sanctuary claims to have a wide range of mammals including panther, sloth, bear and hyena, and several reptiles, but you are really only likely to see wild boar, the odd deer and gaur and many monkeys on a visit, although bird spotting is more rewarding. Birds not easily seen elsewhere in Goa include rufous woodpecker, Malabar crested lark and white-eyed eagle.

You need your own vehicle to reach the tree-top **watch towers** and **water holes** which are signposted, 3 km and 7 km off the main metalled road on a very rough track. There are no guides but the Forest Officer by the Interpretation Centre at the entrance has a map of the park on the wall. The forest paths are easy to follow but make sure you have enough drinking water and petrol. The first tower by a water hole is known as Machan Vhutpal, 400 m off the road. You need to be fit to venture up the steep ladder to the raised platform which offers a great view of the forest canopy. The second tower is more substantial and the best place to spend a night if permission is granted.

Listings: Southern Goa

● Sleeping

Margao *p1202, map p1203*
C Nanutel, Padre Miranda Rd, T733176.
F733175, nanutelmrg@nanuindia.com.
55 smart rooms, comfortable business hotel,
good food, nice pool but unattractive
poolside area, bookshop.
D Margao Residency (GTDC), Luis Miranda
Rd, T715528. 67 acceptable rooms in
6-storey building so some have good view
over the city, a/c better, others are cramped,
simple restaurant (good vegetable *vindaloo*),
tourist information, travel desk.
D-E Goa Woodlands, ML Furtado Rd,
opposite City Bus Stand, T7155218, F738732,
woodland@goatelecom.com. 35 rooms,
18 a/c, clean and spacious with bath,
restaurant, bar, good value.
D-E Saaj, ML Furtado Rd, T711757. 29 rooms,
TV, basic singles, good options for 4-person
rooms, restaurant, bar, near City bus stand,
24 hr check-out.
E La Flor, E Carvalho St, T731402. 35 rooms
with bath, half a/c, restaurant, clean, on a
side street away from the bustle of town.
E-F Railway Retiring Rooms, Margao
Junction. 1st floor. 7 rooms (4 a/c), dorm beds.

Velsao, Arossim, Utorda, Majorda *p1204*
Velsao beach
C Horizon Beach Resort, T0832-754923,
F754977, sales@horizonbeachresort.com.
30 clean, spacious rooms in 2-storey blocks,
(most a/c). Care with interior design, original
paintings and ornaments give it character.
Pool, restaurant, smallish gardens, 5-min
walk to an empty beach.

Arossim
A Heritage Village Club, T0832-754311,
F754324. 100 rooms overlooking a good size
pool, health club, tennis, friendly and helpful.

Utorda
LL Kenilworth Beach Resort (was *Golden
Tulip*), T0832-754180, F754183, www.kenil
worth.allindia.com. 91 a/c rooms,

refurbished but has a slightly shabby feel,
focused on the pool (reputedaly the largest
in Goa), plenty of sports, managed by
enthusiastic New Zealander.

Majorda
AL Majorda Beach Resort, 2 mins' walk
from the beach, T0832-754871, F755382,
majorda@goatelecom.com. 100 rooms, 10
village suites, 10 cottages, 3 restaurants,
pools, designed on a grand scale with a
rather barn-like public area, lush gardens
behind, all very well maintained.
D Shalom Guest House, on corner of road
leading to beach, T0832-881016 (after 1800),
shalome81@satyam.net.in. 1 large family flat
for 4, excellent value.

Betalbatim *p1204*
B Coconut Grove, Ranwaddo (beyond *Alagoa
Guest House*), T880123, F701175, cgrove@
goatelecom.com. 36 clean a/c rooms with
small bath, TV, mini bar, small gardens lead
down to pool and light, airy restaurant (Thai in
evenings, main courses Rs 100). Short walk to
the beach, peaceful setting.
B Nanu Resorts, near the beach and open
fields, T880111, F880120, nanuresort@
nanuindia.com. 72 comfortable and spacious
a/c rooms in 2-storey 'chalet' complex
separated by small patches of green,
imaginatively planned and well managed
with efficient service, good restaurant and
pool, peaceful (time-share blocks are
alongside), very good value May-Sep. Along
Betalbatim Beach road.
E Baptista, Beach Rd. 2 simple rooms, 2
self-catering flats, short walk from beach,
good for long stays.
E Manuelina Tourist House, 1 km from
beach. 5 good clean rooms with bath, TV
lounge, food available, secure, quiet.
E Ray's, T738676. 3 clean rooms, a/c
possible, use of kitchen.

Colva *p1204, map p1205*
B Vista De Colva, 4th Ward, T788144,
F788649, colmar@satyam.net.in. 25 large a/c

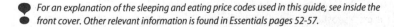
For an explanation of the sleeping and eating price codes used in this guide, see inside the front cover. Other relevant information is found in Essentials pages 52-57.

rooms, breakfast and snacks, small pool (non-residents Rs 50), very comfortable.

B-C Longuinhos Beach Resort, 1 km from 'Colva Circle', T788068, F788070, lbresort@ goatelecom.com. 52 clean rooms with balcony, 6 a/c, (no TV), in plain modern block, restaurant, pool, garden with hammocks, right on the beach, all well maintained but management a bit aloof, used by German charters.

B-C William's Retreat, 500 m from beach, T788153, F788729, wbretreat@satyam.net. 36 clean rooms, some a/c, restaurant, large pool (non-residents Rs 50), tennis, friendly, good value but tired.

C-D Star Beach Resort, just off Colva Beach Rd, T788166, F788020, resortgoa@yahoo.com. 41 large rooms, TV, some a/c, clean pool, childrens pool, best rooms 1st floor poolside with views across paddy fields, bland restaurant setting.

D Colmar, on beach, T788043, atsfernandes @colmarbeachresort.com. 127 rooms, dearer than similar in area but popular, restaurant (see below), travel desk, motorbike hire, bus to Anjuna flea market (Rs 95), exchange.

D Colva Residency (GTDC), T788047. 47 pleasant, clean rooms, 14 a/c, in uninspired complex, good restaurant, bar, garden, friendly, secure, popular with domestic tourists.

E Tourist Nest, 2 km from the sea, T788624, touristnest@indiatimes.com. Old Portuguese house, 12 rooms in new block, fan, secure, some with bath, 2 small self contained cottages, good restaurant. Old part recommended for atmospheric long stay.

E Vailankanni, H No 414/2, 4th Ward, 500 m from beach, T788584, vailancottages@ rediff.com. 10 basic, clean rooms with bath, 5 a/c flats, friendly family run, restaurant.

E White Sands, H No 470, 4th Ward, T788080. 8 clean comfortable rooms with nets, in friendly family run guesthouse, short walk to beach.

F Maria Guest House, 4th Ward, near beach cafés. 7 rooms, some with bath, very friendly, interesting owners, helpful, car-hire, popular with backpackers.

Benaulim *p1205, map p1206*

LL-L Taj Exotica, towards Varca, T705666, F738916, exoticabc@Tajhotels.com. 138 luxurious rooms, all facing 800 m sea frontage, excellent pool, good restaurants, golf course, floodlit tennis, extensive

(maturing) gardens, health club, sumptuously designed.

C-D L'Amour, end of Beach Rd, T737960. 20 rooms in a 2-storey block close to the sea, good terrace restaurant, handy for exchange and booking rail and bus tickets.

C-D Carina Beach Resort, Tambdi-Mati, T770413, F711400. 34 rooms, wing better with solar powered showers, some a/c, light and airy with balcony, restaurant, pool, quiet.

C-E Camilson's Beach Resort, Sernabatim, T771696. 20 simple rooms with bath, better in 2-storey building, restaurant, close to beach.

D Failaka, Adsulim Nagar, near Maria Hall crossing, T770059, hotelfailaka@ hotmail.com. 16 clean comfortable rooms with shower, 4 with TV, quieter at rear, excellent restaurant, friendly family.

D-E Palm Grove Cottages, H No 149, Vasvaddo, T770059, palmgrovecottages@ yahoo.com. 14 clean, spacious rooms, newer block at rear better with shower and balcony, pleasant palm shaded garden, good food, not on beach but bicycle hire from just outside.

All along Benaulim Beach Rd, and in the coconut groves on either side, there are numerous rooms available in private houses and "garden cottages" from Rs 50-150.

E Caphina, set back, midway along Beach Rd, 8 spotless rooms on 2 floors, but no grounds to sit out, friendly and helpful owners good value.

E D'Souza Guest House, T770583. 5 very clean rooms, good food (see below), exchange, garden, friendly family.

E Oshin, Vas Vaddo, T770069. 14 good large rooms with bath on 3 floors, room 11 best, breakfast, evening meals on request, friendly manager, excellent well-kept grounds, bicycle needed to get to beach but peaceful location is well worth it. Recommended.

E Paul Rina Tourist Home, Beach Rd, T770591. 6 large, airy rooms with balcony, good value.

E Rosario's Inn, Beach Rd, T770636. 28 rooms with bath in a peaceful setting with mature trees, simple restaurant, cycle/ motorbike hire, camping possible.

E Tansy, Beach Rd, T770574. 7 very clean, large rooms with bath, some in cottages, good restaurant (super breakfast, seafood sizzlers, Rs 50), friendly, good value.

E-F O Mangueiro, next to *Carina*, 10-min walk to beach, T770408. 5 spartan rooms,

10 newer with bath much better, very clean, peaceful, safe and friendly, very conscientious owner.

F Casa de Saji, 5-min walk from beach, T770228. 5 clean rooms, common bath, better with balcony overlooking fields, very quiet.

F Priti Kunj, south of Maria Hall crossing, 15 m off the main road, behind *Caravan Guest House*. 4 clean, pleasant rooms, 3 with bath, also large 6-bed rooms in family house, meals to order, helpful owners.

Varca and Fatrade *p1205, map p1207*

L Club Mahindra, Varca Village, T744555, F744666, resv.goa@clubmahindra.com. 51 spotless rooms with tubs, 5 suites, spacious public areas, excellent pool, gym etc, direct access to quiet beach, bit isolated. Top class.

AL Goa Renaissance Resort, Fatrade Beach, T745200, F245225, itstimefor@renaissance goa.com. 202 rooms, interesting design, watersports and 9-hole golf, high standards but expensive bland meals and drinks.

B Resorte de Goa, Varca, T745066, F745310, resortedegoa@yahoo.com. 56 rooms and suites in main building and smaller rooms in colourful cottages, tennis, clean deserted beach with some shade, peaceful location but a bit shabby.

D Dona Sa Maria, Tamborim, T745290, F871559, dona_samaria@mailcity.com. 16 good sized clean rooms in modern colonial style villa with private balcony, 1 km from deserted beach, good food, pool, bike hire, internet, friendly family run, quiet.

Cavelossim and Mobor *p1205, map p1207*

A-B Dona Sylvia Resort, T871321, F871320, info@donasylvia.com. 176 comfortable spacious cottages, some a/c, set in lush immaculate grounds with a 'village' feel, mainly packages and buffet meals, tennis. Direct path to the beach, 200 m, new shopping development opposite.

C Mobor Beach Resort, T871167, colinmcf@breathemail.net. 50 well-appointed rooms, fan, balcony, some with view of hills and the sea, restaurant, pool, spacious feel, new, well built, package oriented, aiming for high standards.

C Sao Domingos, quiet lane opposite Dona Sylvia but built-up surrounds, T871461, saodomingos@satyam.net.in. 15 comfortable rooms with fans or a/c and bath, balcony, rooftop breakfast area. Not close to the beach.

D Gaffino's, opposite Dona Sylvia, Mobor, 5 mins' walk from beach, T871441, F730365, bradleygaffino@yahoo.com. 16 clean, simple rooms with bath on 4 floors, 2 a/c, balconies overlook river or sea (far away), bed and breakfast, personal service, package oriented, in the centre of all the action.

D Hippo Cool, next to *Gaffino's*, T871201. 6 clean, very comfortable rooms with fan (a/c on request) and shower, restaurant (a local favourite), 5-min walk from beach.

D Octima, next to Goan Village restaurant, T871462. 3 clean rooms, pleasant 1st floor breakfast balcony, quiet lane only short walk from nightlife but not convenient for beach.

E José Holiday Home, T871127. 10 good clean rooms with attached bath, some a/c, friendly.

Mobor Beach

LL-AL Leela Palace, Mobor, opposite Betul village, T871234, F871352, leela@goatelecom. 137 rooms, luxury villas and pavilions blending Eastern and Western architecture, golf buggies for transport, top facilities, nightclub, casino, watersports, 9-hole golf, spacious lush grounds, very plush.

Betul *p1206*

D River Sal, Kutbona, Zuem Velim, on the river bank, T0832-760276, F760627. 18 simple clean rooms (6 a/c), with perfect river views, bit isolated but very peaceful, offers excellent fresh river fish. Boatmen bring holidaymakers from Mobor to eat here in the evening.

Cabo de Rama Fort *p1206*

Near the fort entrance, very basic rooms, meals (order before visiting the fort to save time waiting later) and drinks: Pinto's Bar, near the entrance to Fort; Millrid Bar, about 1 km back along the road on the dry plateau.

Agonda *p1207*

E Eldfra, T647378. 4 simple rooms with fan and clean baths, bar and simple restaurant, basic roof terrace, no direct seaview.

E Casa Maria, T647237. 4 rooms with clean tiled bath, fan, opening onto a veranda, sea views, but also overlooks the back of Eldfra.

E-F Dersy Beach Resort, T647500. 5 rooms with bath in main block, across road right on beach in palm grove are 12 bamboo huts with spotless shared wash block, limited privacy but idyllic location, restaurant, bar.

F Sun Set Bar, T647381. 7 simple cottages with great views, shared facilities. The restaurant perched high on the rocks has the prime location in Agonda. Recommended. Towards the north end of the beach, close to the school and bus stop, there is a small block of shops, *Fathima stores & restaurant* and *St Annes bookstore*. International calls from a small kiosk near the *Dersy Beach Resort*.

Palolem *p1207, map p1208*
Have a good look before choosing. Only a few budget places have beach views and make a real effort to provide value for money and security. Prices tend to rise on 1 Dec. There may be a shortage of electricity.
D Bhakti Kutir, over the hill at the southern end, T643472, F643469. 21 "cabanas", varying sizes, own bath and compost toilet, sympathetically built with local materials, mosquito nets, excellent wholesome food, away from beach and very quiet, emphasizing peace and meditation (yoga, tai chi classes) and plenty to occupy children. Very relaxing.
D Oceanic, inland on the road to Rajbag beach T643059, F739688, breezefjoy@ hotmail.com. 9 clean but uninspiring rooms (4 in another complex), all different so check, light breakfast, friendly, good restaurant (see below), excellent cocktails.
E Cocohuts, towards the southern end, T643296, F233298. 15 breezy, shaded huts built among palm trees, raised on bamboo stilts, each divided into 2 rooms by thin palm leaf partitions, electricity and fan, separate shared toilets on the ground, on the beach, restaurant.
E Ciaran's Camp, T643477, johnciaran@ hotmail. Com. Based on *Cocohuts* model, 20 good huts on the beach front with restaurant, very popular, Recommended.
E Cozy Nook, at northern end, T643550. Plastered bamboo huts, fans, nets, shared toilets, in a good location sandwiched between the sea and freshwater river, ayurvedic centre, art and crafts, friendly.
E Palolem Beach Resort, T/F643054. 9 rooms with bath, tents and basic cottages with shared facilities, shower blocks, excellent seafood tandoori, ISD phones, reliable travel service and exchange. Clean, shaded site, book ahead.
E Hi-Tide Beach Huts, towards southern end, T643104. 18 huts, best on stilts at the beach front, extra ground level huts with no views have been crammed in at the back.

E Waves, has simple huts right on the beach.
F Camp Palo, behind *La Allegro*, T643173 (ask for Irshad). 13 well-built huts set in a pleasant compound.
F Premier Cottages, next to *Dylan's*, towards southern end. Friendly, reliable 'safe deposit'.
F Rooms in village houses, very basic facilities ('pig' toilets, unconnected to sewers, are raised on a platform where pigs do the necessary 'cleaning out' below).
F Camping, parking for campers and travellers (Rs 15-20 per day) at **Palolem Beach Resort** and south of *Cocohuts*.

Kindlebaga *p1209*
C Molyma, off NH17, west from the crossroads, T643028, F643081. Isolated and somewhat surprising. 43 modern, large rooms, airy restaurant with limited menu, bar, friendly service, good value though rather deserted, set among trees within 15 mins walk to a good beach beyond dunes.

● Eating

Margao *p1202, map p1203*
Banjara, T722088. North Indian. Plush but not flashy, a/c, good service but "food so-so".
Casa Menino, LIC Building, Luis Miranda Rd. Goan. Part a/c, with bar.
Chinese Pavilion, M Menezes Rd (400m west of Municipal Gardens). Chinese. Smart a/c, good choice.
Food Affair. North Indian. Basement café, open all day.
Gaylin, 1 V Valaulikar Rd. Chinese. Tasty hot Szechuan, comfortable a/c.
Longuinhos, near the Municipality. Goan, North Indian. Open all day for meals and snacks, also bar drinks and baked goodies.
Tato, G-5 Apna Bazar, Complex, V Valaulikar Rd. Excellent vegetarian, a/c upstairs.
Utsav, *Nanutel Hotel*. Pleasant, serving a large range of Goan dishes.
Café Margao. Good South Indian snacks. Four **Kamats** including a/c '*Milan*', Station Rd. Indian vegetarian. Clean and good value *thalis* and snacks.

Bakery
Baker's Basket and Johnny's Cove at Rangavi Complex, west of Municipal Gardens, have Goan sweets including *bebincas*.

Betalbatim *p1204*

Martin's Corner, T721391. Coming from the south, look for sign on left after village, 500 m down lane on right, opposite open ground. Accommodates over 200 under cover in front of an old house. Extensive menu, excellent lobster Rs 1500, tiger prawns Rs 500-700, crab Rs 300-500. Recommended.

Alfresco Pub, near *Nanu Resort*. Pleasant for drink and snacks, on edge of coconut plantations overlooking paddy fields.

Roytanzil Garden Pub, set back from the beach at end of Majorda beach road past *Martin's Corner*. Neat grounds, al fresco and small covered area. Seafood and Indian.

Whining Riley's, just outside *Nanu Resorts*, with bar (pool table), garden setting.

Colva *p1204, map p1205*

Most restaurants offer Western food and beer.

Joe Con's, 4th Ward. Excellent fresh fish and Goan dishes, good value.

Kentuckee, good seafood, select from fresh fish brought to table.

Pasta Palace, overlooking the beach at the *Colmar*. Good Italian with bar.

Pirate's, near the beach. Recommended for seafood.

Benaulim *p1205, map p1206*

Service can be tediously slow during the season. Most close in the monsoons.

Taj Exotica's, speciality restaurants are faultless; spread of the Mediterranean, gourmet Goan or authentic Chinese.

Cacy Rose, is just off the main road near the bus station.

Pedro's, by the car park above the beach. Good seafood and tandoori. Imaginative menu, friendly.

Tito's, on the beach, offers English breakfasts, Rs 80.

Close by **Patros** and **Seaview** produce a mix of seafood and curries. Place advance orders to get the best fresh fish.

D'Souza's, good juices, lassis and fast food.

Johncey's, varied menu, good seafood, generous portions, *tandoori* recommended (after 1830) but service can be erratic, pleasant atmosphere though (backgammon, scrabble).

Malibu, nice lush garden setting, for spicy fish/meat kebabs.

Varca, Fatrade, Cavelossim and Mobor *p1205, map p1207*

Menu, prices and atmosphere in hotel restaurants vary so check in advance.

Riverside serves Italian on a open deck overlooking the river Sal.

River View, tranquil, open air location, overlooking the river. Wide choice, international menu, good ambience despite being surrounded by ugly hotel developments.

Grill Room, Fatrade beach road, open 1830-2230. Pleasant steak house with a simple menu. Tiger prawns Rs 400, steaks Rs 150.

La Afra (*Dona Sa Maria*) does excellent steaks and fresh fish, sensibly priced. Boatmen ferry holidaymakers to *River Sal* at Betul.

Beach shacks offer Goan dishes and seafood at reasonable prices. Around *Dona Sylvia*, several come alive in the evening.

Goan Village, lane opposite Dona Sylvia. The best here for all cuisines.

Others recommended for good food, drink and service in a pleasant atmosphere are: **Get Down, Mike's Place**, and **Walk In**.

Jazz Inn, 500 m towards Mobor. For authentic Goan fish *thalis* (Rs 25), try the first house on the left past the church in Cavelossim if heading north.

Outside the *Goa Renaissance Resort*, **Agnelo Bar**, and **Jo Inn**, are open in the evenings and offer a pleasant alternative menu and atmosphere to the hotel.

Palolem *p1207, map p1208*

The southern end offers ample choice.

Bhakti Kutir, tasty western dishes, home-grown organic produce and fresh juices, very pleasant relaxed seating away from the beach and loud sound systems.

Blue Jays, bar, sound system, snacks including fresh avocados and Nilgiri cheese.

Cool Breeze. Unusual mix of Spanish tapas and premier league football on offer.

Oceanic, raised open terrace under palm trees. Excellent seafood and cocktails. Popular in the evening. Closed during the monsoon.

Silver Star, with hammocks in the shade.

Sun & Moon, T643314. Set back from beach, under palms. Friendly, popular, great atmosphere, large helpings of well-cooked Goan food plus internet.

Woody's, set back from the beach on the approach road. Relaxed set up offering range of organic health foods.

● Bars and clubs

Colva *p1204, map p1205*
Several beach hotels have bars.
Johnny Cool's, half way up busy Beach Rd.
Scruffy surroundings but popular for chilled
beer and late night drinks.
Splash, 'the' place for music, dancing and late
drinking, open all night, trendy, very busy on
Sat (full after 2300 on weekdays in season),
good cocktails, poor bar snacks – may not
appeal to all especially unaccompanied girls.
Sunshine, bar and restaurant, north end of the
beach, popular evenings, hammocks overlooking beach, pool table, 60s music, small
dance floor, nice gardens. Relaxed atmosphere.

● Festivals and events

Benaulim *p1205, map p1206*
Feast of St John the Baptist (*Sao Joao*), **24th
Jun**, gives thanks for the arrival of the
monsoon. Young men wearing crowns of
leaves and fruits tour the area singing for
gifts. They jump into wells (which are usually
full) to commemorate the movement of St
John in his mother's womb when she was
visited by Mary, the mother of Jesus!

● Shopping

Margao *p1202, map p1203*
The Old Market was rehoused in the 'New'
(Municipal) Market in town. The covered
market (Mon-Sat, 0800-1300, 1600-2000) is
interesting to wander around. It is not at all
touristy although holidaymakers come on
their shopping trip to avoid paying inflated
prices in the beach resorts. To catch a glimpse
of the early morning arrivals at the Fish Market
head south from the Municipal Building.

Books
Golden Heart, Confident Building, off Abbé
Faria Rd, behind the GPO, (closed 1300-1500).
Small shop at *Nanutel* hotel.

Music
Trevor's, 5 Luis Miranda Rd. Sells Cds.

Photography
Lorenz, opposite the Municipality.
Wonder Colour Lab, Garden View Building.

Textiles
MS Caro, Caro Corner, has an extensive range
including 'suiting', and will advise on tailors.

Tailor
J Vaz, Martires Dias Rd, near Hari Mandir,
T720086. Good quality reliable men's tailor.

Benaulim *p1205, map p1206*
Khazana at *Taj Exotica*, a veritable treasure
chest (gifts, books, crafts, clothes) culled from
across India. High class with prices to match.
Manthan Heritage Gallery, main road.
Quality collection of art items.

Palolem *p1207, map p1208*
The approach roads are now hemmed in by
the usual array of Kashmiri, Tibetan and
Karnataka trinket shops selling clothes,
chillums, music tapes and mineral water.
Everything to set yourself up for a long stay.

▲▲ Activities and tours

Benaulim *p1205, map p1206*
Dolphin watching
The trips are scenic and chances of seeing
dolphin are high, but it gets very hot (take hat,
water and something comfy to sit on). Groups
of dolphins here are usually seen swimming
near the surface and do not oblige with
performing tricks. Boats from **Café Dominick**
(signs on the beach) and several others
charge about Rs 300. **Globe Trotte**, next to
Failaka. New night club (also internet).

Yoga
Taj Exotica, indoors or on the lawn. Also
aromatherapy and reflexology.

**Varca, Fatrade, Cavelossim and
Mobor** *p1205, map p1207*
Dolphin watching
Most hotels arrange river trips and dolphin
viewing, or call T871455. River trips last from
1600-1730, dolphin trips 0800-1000 and sunset
cruises depart at 1700. Expect to pay Rs 250.
Aqua, *Leela Palace*, is a gaming room and
cigar lounge which turns into a late night
disco after 2000.
Betty's Place, in road opposite *Holiday Inn*,
arranges boat trips for fishing, dolphin
viewing, trips up river Sal from 1030-1630
(food included), which is recommended.

Margao *p1202, map p1203*
Choice Tours, V Valaulikar, Grace Church,
T731332.
Paramount Travels, Luis Miranda Rd (opposite
GTDC *Residency*), T731150, also exchange.

Colva *p1204, map p1205*
Meeting Point, opposite, T723338, F732004,
for very efficient, reliable travel service, Mon-
Sat, 0830-1900 (sometimes even later, if busy).

Palolem *p1207, map p1208*
Dolphin watching and fishing trips
Offered by fishermen; mornings between
0830-1230 best. Arrange through *Palolem
Beach Resort*, travel agents or a fisherman;
4 people for about Rs 600 for 1-hr trip,
Rs 1500 for 3 hrs. Take sun-block, shirt, hat
and drinking water. You may be able to see
some dolphins from the headland to the
south of Palolem, just before sunset.

Tour operators
Rainbow Travels, T643912. Efficient flight
and train bookings, exchange, Western
Union money transfer, safe deposit lockers
(Rs 10 per day), good internet connection.

⊝ Transport

Margao *p1202, map p1203*
Bus
Local The local bus stand is by the municipal
gardens. You can usually board buses near the
Kamat Hotel, southeast of the gardens.
Long distance The Kadamba (New) Bus
Stand is 2 km north of town (city buses to the
centre, or motorcycle taxi Rs 8); buses arriving
before 1000 and after 1900, proceed to the
centre. To **Benaulim**; **Cabo da Rama**: 0730 (2
hrs); **Canacona and Palolem**, several; **Colva**:
hourly; **Gokarna**, 1300 daily. **Non-stop KTC
buses** to Panaji: 1 hr. Buy tickets from booth
at stand number 1. **Private buses** (eg Paulo,
Metropole Hotel, T721516), Padre Miranda
Rd: to **Bangalore**: (15 hrs); **Mangalore**: 1800,
2130 (8-10 hrs), Rs 140; **Mumbai (Dadar/
CST)**: 1400, 1700 (16 hrs), Rs 600 (sleeper);
Pune: 1700 (13 hrs), Rs 450 (sleeper).

Car
Car hire: Rs 700-900 per day with driver from
Sai Service, T735772.

Rickshaw
Auto-rickshaw: to **Colva**, Rs 30; beach, Rs 50.

Train
Enquiries, T732255. The new station on the
broad gauge network is 500m south of the
old station which is no longer in use. The
reservation office on the first floor of the new
station is usually quick and efficient, with short
queues. Open 0800-1400, 1415-2000,
Mon-Sat, 0800-1400, Sun. Tickets for Mumbai
and Delhi should be booked well ahead.
Confirm Indrail Pass reservations in Vasco,
Mumbai or Mangalore. *Konkan Kanya Express*
(night train) and *Mandovi Express* (day train)
from **Mumbai** also stop at **Tivim** (for northern
beaches; take the local bus into Mapusa and
from there catch another bus or take a taxi)
and **Karmali** (for Panaji and Dabolim airport)
before terminating at **Margao**. Both are very
slow and take nearly 12 hrs. From **Mumbai
(CST)**: *Mandovi Exp 0103*, 0515 (arr 1815),
11 hrs (2nd class 3-tier Rs 670), doesn't stop at
Pernem; *Konkan Kanya Exp 0111*, 2250 (arr
1045). **Delhi (Nizamuddin)**: *Rajdhani Exp
2431*, 1145, Wed, Fri; *Goa Exp 2779*, 1427, 35
hrs. **Ernakulam (Jn)**: *Mangalore Exp 2618*,
2055, 17 hrs. **Hospet (for Hampi)**:
Vasco-da-Gama Vijayawada Exp, 7228, 0720,
Wed, Sat, 8½ hrs. **Mumbai (CST)**: *Mandovi Exp
0104*, 1030, 11½ hrs (via Karmali, Tivim);
Konkan Kanya Exp 0112, 1800, 12 hrs (via
Karmali, Tivim, Pernem). **Mumbai Kurla
(Tilak)**: *Netravati Exp, 6346*, 0640, 12 hrs (via
Karmali, Tivim). **Thiruvananthapuram
(Trivandrum)**: *Rajdhani Exp 2432*, 1300, Mon,
Wed, 18 hrs. *Netravati Exp, 6345*, 2255, 18 hrs
(via Canacona for Palolem beach).

The broad gauge line between Vasco and
Londa in Karnataka, runs through Margao
and Dudhsagar Falls, connects stations on
the line with **Belgaum**. There are services to
Bangalore *Vasco Bangalore Exp 7310*, 2059,
Mon, Thu. See under Vasco.

Taxi
The **pre-paid taxi stand** is to the right of
the exit (charges are for 1 person with 1 piece
of luggage); to Margao centre Rs 50, Panaji Rs
480 (45 mins), Anjuna Rs 670; Calangute Rs
600; Colva Rs 130, Palolem Rs 480; rates are
clearly displayed outside the office. **Autos** to
Colva Rs 100, to Panaji Rs 320. Avoid tourist
taxis, they can be five times the price.

Velsao, Arossim, Utorda, Majorda
p1204, map p1207

Cansaulim station on the Vasco-Margao line is convenient for Velsao and Arossim beaches and Majorda station for Utorda and Majorda beaches. **Autorickshaws** meet all trains. The Margao-Vasco **bus** service also passes through the centre.

Betalbatim *p1204*
Bus
From **Margao** (12 km); **motorcycle taxis** charge Rs 35.
Taxi
To/from **airport**, 20 mins (Rs 300); **Margao** 15 mins (Rs 200). From **Nanu Resort** Panaji Rs 500, Anjuna Rs 750, or Rs 700 for 8 hrs, 80 km.

Colva *p1204, map p1205*
Bicycle
Mostly through hotels, Rs 20-25 per day.

Bus
To **Anjuna** Wed for the Flea Market, tickets through travel agents, depart 0930, return 1730, Rs 90-100; to **Margao** half-hourly, take 30 mins, Rs 3 (last bus 1915, last return, 2000). Also to **Margao**, **motorcycle taxi**, Rs 20-25 (bargain hard); **auto-rickshaw**, Rs 30-40.

Motorbike
For hire through most hotels (see also Panaji), Rs 200 per day (less for long term rental), more for Enfields, bargain hard.

Benaulim *p1205, map p1206*
Buses from all directions arrive at the hub of all the village activity at Maria Hall crossing which is just over a kilometre from the beach. **Bicycle** and **scooter** hire, Rs 35 and Rs 150 per day. **Taxis** from the beach esplanade near *Pedro's* and at Maria Hall crossing. To/From **Margao**: taxis Rs 100; autos Rs 80; bus Rs 5. **Anjuna** Wed flea market: bus 0930, return 1530, about Rs 95, 2 hrs.

Varca, Fatrade, Cavelossim and Mobor *p1205, map p1207*
Bicycle
Bike hire from **Rocks** outside *Dona Sylvia*, cycles Rs 10 per hr, Rs 150 a day; scooters Rs 300 a day without petrol, Rs 500 with 7 litres of fuel.

Bus
From Margao to Cavelossim, are uncomfortably slow; autos transfer from bus stand to resorts.

Ferry
Crosses river Sal, southeast of Cavelossim and **Assolna**, where you can find petrol, and the lane from the river joins the main road, NH17.

Taxi
From Margao charge around Rs 200, from Dabolim airport to the resorts take under 1 hr.

Betul *p1206*
Bus
From Margao to Betul can be very slow, but there is a fairly regular service stopping in all the settlements along the way (a couple continue as far as Cabo de Rama). Confirm the route when boarding the bus in Margao.

Ferry
From Cavelossim the shortest route to Betul is by taking the ferry across the Sal (signposted, just southeast) to Assolna; turn left off the ferry, then turn right in the village to join the main road towards Betul. From Margao, the NH17 forks right (6 km) towards Assolna at Chinchinim. A further 6 km on, there is a second turning in Cuncolim for Assolna.

Cabo de Rama Fort *p1206*
From Margao, **buses** for the fort leave at 0730 from the southeast corner of the Municipal Gardens (2 hrs); ask the driver for precise timings of the return service. From Palolem, you could hire a motorbike, but take care; there are a lot of blind corners.

Agonda *p1207*
Bus
First direct bus for **Margao** leaves between 0600-0630, last at 1000, takes about 1 hr. Alternatively, arrange a lift to the main road and flag down the next bus (last bus for Margao passes by at around 2000, but it is advisable to complete your journey before dark). Hourly buses between Betul and Palolem call at Agonda (and Cabo de Rama). Easy to visit for the day by taxi, motorbike or bicycle from Palolem beach. **Dunhills Hotel**, Agonda hire out scooters, motorbikes and cars.

Rickshaw
From Palolem/Chaudi Junc, **auto-rickshaws** charge Rs 120-150; turn off the road by the *Niki bar* and restaurant.

Palolem *p1207, map p1208*
Bicycle hire from village for Rs 4 per hr or Rs 35 per day. From Canacona (see below), **taxis** and **auto-rickshaws** charge Rs 40-60.

Bus
Direct buses for Margao leave at around 0615, 0730, 0930, 1415, 1515, 1630 and take 1 hr. Alternatively, take a taxi or rickshaw to the main road and flag down the next private bus.

Train
3 km from Canacona Junction station, which is now on the Konkan line (*Netravati Exp*).

Canacona (Chaudi) *p1209*
Bus
To Palolem and Margao and also to Karnataka.

Train
From Canacona Junction (2 km away from Palolem). The booking office opens 1 hr before trains depart. A few rickshaws and taxis meet trains or wait at *chaurasta* (walk down the approach road and turn left under the railway bridge). Rickshaw to Palolem (Rs 50) or Agonda beach; double for a taxi. To **Ernakulam Junction**, *Netravati Exp 6345*, 2325, 15 hrs, sleeper Rs 280, 3 tier a/c Rs 790, and on to **Thiruvananthapuram** (20 hrs). **Mangalore**, *Matsyagandha Exp 2619*, 0105, 6hrs. **Margao (Madgaon)**, *KAM 2up*, 0630, *KAR 2up*, 1237, 45 mins, Rs 11. **Mumbai (Tilak)**, *Netravati Exp 6346*, 0548, 13 hrs, 2nd class sleeper Rs 300, 3 tier a/c Rs 800; via **Margao (Madgaon)** 45 mins. **Mumbai (Thane)**, *Matsyagandha Exp 2620*, 1910, 12 hrs.

❶ Directory

Margao *p1202 , map p1203*
Banks Bank of Baroda, behind Grace Church; also in Market, Station Rd. Bank of India, exchanges cash, TCs, Visa and Mastercard. State Bank of India, west of the Municipal Gardens. HDFC, 24 hr ATM for Mastercard. Get exchange before visiting beaches to the south where it is more difficult. International money transfer is possible through **Weizmann**, 650 Costa Dias Building, NH 17 (Mon-Sat 1000-1800). There is also a branch in Colva. **Internet** Cyber Link, Shop 9, Rangavi Complex. Cyber Inn, 105 Karnika Chambers, V Valauliker Rd, 0900-2000, Rs 30 per hr. **Medical services** JJ Costa Hospital, Fatorda, T722586. Hospicio, T722164. Holy Spirit Pharmacy, 24 hrs. **Post office** GPO, north of Children's Park. Poste Restante, near the Telegraph Office, down lane west of park, 0830-1030 and 1500-1700 Mon-Sat. **Tourist offices** GTDC Residency, T722513, 0800-1800 (lunch 1300-1400), daily. **Useful addresses** Ambulance: T722722. Fire: T720168. Police: T722175.

Betalbatim *p1204*
Monte Communications, next to *Rays*. Email and international phone calls.

Benaulim *p1205, map p1206*
Bank Bank of Baroda, near Maria Hall, best rates (better than at travel agents and STD booths). **Communications** GK Communications, Beach Rd. 24 hr phone, money exchange and Internet with 4 terminals, book ahead when very busy, Rs 100 per hr. **Medical services** Late night **chemists** near the main crossroads.

Varca, Fatrade, Cavelossim and Mobor *p1205, map p1207*
Banks Bank of Baroda, near the church in Cavelossim, accepts Visa, Mastercard and TCs, helpful staff, open 0930-1330, Mon-Wed, Fri, Sat.

Palolem *p1207, map p1208*
Banks No bank, but exchanges along the beach approach road give cash against credit cards, commission 3-5%. **Post office** Nearest is at Chaudi. Internet widely available, Rs 60 per hr. **Medical facilities** T643339. **Useful services** Police: T643357.

Canacona (Chaudi) *p1209*
Banks State Bank of India, next to Canacona Palace, has no foreign exchange facility. **Post office** 200 m down the highway towards Karnataka. **Medical services** Pai Chemists, 100m east of the crossroads. **Useful services** Petrol: Aryadurga HP station 1km north of the Palolem turning, towards Margao.

Gujarat

‡ Footprint features

Introduction

Gujarat has some fascinating and distinctive architecture, a wide variety of scenery, ranging from vast salt marsh and desert in the northwest, irrigated fields in the southeast, and some good beaches.

The major industrial, commercial and cultural city, **Ahmadabad**, retains excellent examples of Gujarati provincial architecture. The state also has a rich treasury of Jain and Hindu buildings, including the superb temples at **Palitana** and **Modhera**.

Gujarat's ports have been important centres of trade and embarkation points for Muslim pilgrims bound for Mecca, while European colonial nations established factories and trading bases around the coast from the late 15th century onwards.

Gujarat also has some vivid historical associations. Mahatma Gandhi was born at **Porbandar** and had his ashram at **Sabarmati** near Ahmadabad. There is an increasing interest in the unexplored delights to be found in the state which is prompting a number of the old princely mansions to open their doors to guests, as Heritage Hotels.

Kachchh is returning to normal after the devastation of the January 2001 earthquake. Despite the harsh environment, Kachchh people have developed an astonishingly vibrant identity, and tourism is an increasingly important source of earnings.

In addition to abundant birdlife in the state, the Rann of Kachchh has the only surviving wild asses in India and the **Velavadhar** conserves the rare, swift-footed black buck. The last Asiatic lions are found in **Gir National Park**.

Gujarat

★ Don't miss...

1. **Modhera**, quiet and off the beaten track, has the remains of one of the best Hindu temples in Gujarat, page 1232.

2. Stay at **Balaram**, one of the best kept Palace hotels in Gujarat and and take a trip to the **Jessore Bear Sanctuary**, page 1235.

3. Take a ride on the **Vadodara-Dabhoi-Chandod line**, the oldest surviving narrow gauge railway in the world, page 1245.

4. The vast Sunday market in **Ahmadabad** may be the place to pick up some of Gujarat's famous embroidery and other handicrafts, page 1240.

5. **Sasan Gir National Park** is the last refuge of the Asiastic Lion. There are panthers here, too, making it India's best big cat sanctuary, page 1268.

6. The fort museum at **Jamnagar** is a pleasant place to stop and hear the chanting from Bala Hanuman temple wafting across the lake, page 1275.

Background → *Population: 50.6 million. Area: 196,000 sq km.*

The land

Gujarat has nearly 1,600 km of coastline, and no part of the state is more than 160 km from the sea. **Kachchh** (Kutch) on the northwest border of the peninsula, rises to heights of around 300 m, and like the plains of the Indus into which it drops almost imperceptibly, it is almost desert. It has a central ridge of Jurassic sandstones, with underlying basalts breaking through from place to place. To the north is the Great Rann of Kachchh, a 20,700 sq km salt marsh. To the south is the Little Rann. During the monsoon the Rann floods, virtually making Kachchh an island, while during the hot dry summer months it is a dusty plain. **Earthquakes** have had dramatic effects on the landscape. A particularly large quake in 1819 formed a new scarp up to 6 m high and 80 km long, diverting the old channels of the Indus. It has become known as Allah's Bund – *God's embankment*. Another severe earthquake hit Gujarat on the morning of 26 January 2001 and claimed around 20,000 lives. With its epicentre near Bhuj, the tremors which hit 7.7 on the Richter scale virtually flattened the town and several nearby villages. Limbdi, Halvad and Morvi in Saurashtra were also badly damaged.

Saurashtra is to the southeast of the Gulf of Kachchh, and between it and the Gulf of Khambhat (Cambay), is the **Kathiawad** peninsula. Rarely rising to more than 180 m, it is flanked by sandstones in the north. Over most of Kathiawad are great sheets of Deccan lavas, cut across by lava dykes. Around the ancient and holy city of Dwarka in the west and Bhavnagar in the east are limestones and clays, separated by a 50-km belt of alluvium, whose creamy-coloured soft stone is widely used as 'Porbandar stone'.

Northeast Gujarat is a continuation of central Kachchh and is characterized by small plains and low hills. The railway line from Mumbai to Delhi runs through these hills which surround Ahmadabad. The **Western Ghats** extend into southeast Gujarat, the wettest region of the state.

Climate In Ahmadabad the maximum winter temperature is 27°C, although nights are cold and sub-zero cold spells have been recorded. In summer it is extremely hot and maximum temperatures can reach 48°C. Further south the winter temperatures never fall as far, and the summer temperatures are slightly more moderate. In the far south around Daman rainfall is still strongly affected by the southwest monsoon and totals often exceed 1,500 mm, nearly all between June and October. However, because Gujarat is marginal to the main rain-bearing winds the total amounts are highly variable, decreasing rapidly northwards. Ahmadabad normally receives about 900 mm a year while Kachchh, on the borders of the true desert, has recorded under 25 mm.

History

Over the last one million years Gujarat has experienced alternating periods of greater and less rainfall. In these marginal areas some of India's earliest stone age settlements developed, for example at Rojadi near Rajkot and Adamgarh near the border with Madhya Pradesh. Other stone age settlements have been found around the Sabarmati and Mahi rivers in the south and east of the state.

Indus Valley and **Harappan** centres have been discovered at a number of sites, including **Lothal**, **Dhoravira**, **Rangpur**, **Amri**, **Lakhabaval** and **Rozdi**. Lothal, a remarkable Indus Valley site, is 10 km up the Gulf of Khambhat. In 1988 an exciting new Harappan discovery was made at **Kuntasi**, 30 km from Morvi. It has several apparently new features. Like Lothal, Kuntasi was a port, but it had a 'factory' associated with it. Its importance as a trading port is suggested by the discovery of a copper ring with a spiral motif very similar to that found in Crete. The unusual double fortifications seem to date from two periods (circa 2200 BC and 1900-1700 BC).

:: Cyclone hazard

Although cyclones are far more common on India's east coast than in the Arabian Sea hugely damaging storms can strike the Gujarat coast in the warmer months of the year. In 1998 the port of Kandla and the surrounding area was devastated by the high winds, torrential rain and storm surge which accompanied an early summer cyclone. At the end of May 2001 a similar cyclone moved towards the Kachchh and Saurashtra coasts, threatening further damage. In an area which has suffered three years of drought the rains are a mixed blessing, and when the same area has already been devastated by the earthquake, one official pointed out that "even the rains can be a nightmare as most people are living in tents and makeshift quake-damaged houses".

Rock edicts in the Girnar Hills indicate that Asoka extended his domain into Gujarat. The Sakas (Scythians; AD 130-390) controlled it after the fall of the Mauryan Empire. During the fourth and fifth centuries it formed part of the Gupta Empire. Gujarat attained its greatest territorial extent under the Solanki Dynasty, from the ninth century. The Vaghela Dynasty which followed was defeated by the Muslim Ala-ud-din Khalji, the King of Delhi. There then followed a long period of Muslim rule. Ahmad Shah I, the first independent Muslim ruler of Gujarat founded Ahmadabad in 1411.

The Mughal Humayun took Malwa and Gujarat in a brilliant campaign in 1534-35 but soon lost them. His son, Akbar, reclaimed both in a similarly daring and inspired military operation, securing the region for the Mughals for nearly two centuries, a rule terminated by the Marathas in the mid-18th century.

In the scramble for trading bases the Dutch, English, French and Portuguese all established bases along the coast in the 17th century. The British East India Company's first headquarters in India was at Surat. It was later moved to Bombay. As British maritime supremacy became established all but the Portuguese at Daman and Diu withdrew. The state came under the control of the East India Company in 1818 and after the 1857 Mutiny (Rebellion), government authority was assumed by the Crown. The state was then divided into Gujarat province (25,900 sq km), with the rest comprising numerous princely states. Until Independence Kathiawad was one of the most highly fragmented regions of India, having 86 distinct political units. The largest, Junagadh, had an area of less than 9,000 sq km and a population of under 750,000 in 1947.

Art and architecture

Gujarati provincial architecture flowered between 1300 and 1550. The new Muslim rulers made full use of the already highly developed skills of Hindu and Jain builders and craftsmen. The mosques and tombs that resulted reflect the new combination of Muslim political power and Hindu traditions. Thus, although the mosques obey strict Islamic principles they contain important features that are derived directly from Hindu and Jain precedents.

Culture

About 15% of the **population** is tribal, the Bhil, Bhangi, Koli, Dhubla, Naikda and Macchi-Kharwa tribes all being represented. Gujarat is one of the modern strongholds of Jainism. Mahatma Gandhi was strongly influenced by Jain principles, including that of *ahimsa* – see page 1344. He found the deep divisions between high and low caste Hindus deeply repugnant. Renaming the former untouchables as 'Harijans' (God's people), he fought for their rights and dignity. Caste division remains a potent political force in Gujarat today. In the 19th century many Gujaratis went to East Africa and

⁞ The Wild West

A visit to Gujarat can be a rewarding experience but you must be prepared for slow and arduous journeys on public transport and be aware that English is rarely spoken outside the larger cities. A good option is to hire a car with driver or alternatively splash out and let the train take the strain...

The '*Royal Orient*' is Gujarat's answer to the famous 'Palace on Wheels'. It uses the metre-gauge carriages no longer needed in Rajasthan, and runs an eight-night tour from Delhi visiting Chittaurgarh, Udaipur, Junagadh, Somnath, Sasan Gir, Diu, Palitana, Ahmadabad and Jaipur. Contact *The Royal Orient*, A/6 Emporia Building, Baba Kharak Singh Marg, New Delhi, T3364724, F3734015, tcgl.del@rmt. sprintrpg.emvsnl.net.in

Heritage Hotels, in atmospheric old palace and fort conversions offer the unique opportunity to stay in off-the-beaten-track locations but they should be booked in advance. Tour operators such as *North West Safaris*, T079-6302019, F6300962, ssibal@ad1.vsnl.net.in specialize in visiting these unusual properties.

subsequently scattered to England, Canada and New Zealand. At home, Gujaratis are prominent in the business community. The majority of the people speak Gujarati, an Indo-Aryan **language** derived from Sanskrit. Maritime contacts with Persia, Arabia, Portugal and England led to the introduction of many words from these languages.

Whilst Gujarat has a long coastline and an almost endless supply of fish and shellfish, strict Jainism in the past and orthodox Hinduism today have encouraged the widespread adoption of a vegetarian **diet**. Gujaratis base their diet on rice, wholemeal *chapati*, a variety of beans and pulses rich in protein, and coconut and pickles; a thali would include all these, the meal ending with sweetened yoghurt. The dishes themselves are not heavily spiced, though somewhat sweeter than those of neighbouring states. Popular dishes include: *kadhi*, a savoury yoghurt curry with chopped vegetables and a variety of spices; *undhyoo*, a combination of potatoes, sweet potatoes, aubergines (egg plants) and beans cooked in an earthenware pot in the fire; Surat *paunk* made with tender kernels of millet, sugar balls, savoury twists and garlic chutney. Eating freshly prepared vegetable snacks from street vendors is popular. A large variety of *ganthia* or *farsan* (light savoury snacks prepared from chickpea and wheat flour), is a speciality in the state. Desserts are very sweet. Surat specializes in *gharis* made with butter, dried fruits and thickened milk and rich *halwa*. *Srikhand* is saffron-flavoured yoghurt with fruit and nuts.

Modern Gujarat

At Independence in 1947, Gujarat proper was incorporated into Bombay state. In 1956 Saurashtra and Kachchh were added. On 1 May 1960 Bombay state was split into present day Maharashtra and Gujarat states and in 1961 India forcibly annexed Daman and Diu. After Partition the possession of the Rann of Kachchh was disputed by India and Pakistan. In 1965 they fought over it, and following the ceasefire on 1 July, division of the area was referred to an international tribunal. In 1968 the tribunal recommended that 90% should remain with India and 10% pass to Pakistan.

With the sole exception of 1977, Gujarat remained one of the Congress Party's chief strongholds throughout the period after Independence until 1989. It produced a number of national leaders after Mahatma Gandhi, including the first Prime Minister of the Janata Government in 1977, Morarji Desai. However, since the State Assembly elections of March 1995 the BJP has held control. In October 1999 the BJP bucked the national trend by winning 19 of the 26 Lok Sabha seats while the Congress (I) suffered further setbacks. The Lok Sabha results gave the Gujarat Chief Minister a breathing space in the internal strife within the state's BJP, where about 50 of the party's 117 Legislative Members had threatened to stage a revolt. In March 2002 clashes erupted between Hindus and Muslims in Gujarat directly related to the Hindu nationalistcampaign to build a temple to Ram on the site of the Babri mosque at Ayodhya in Uttar Pradesh. Weeks of violence and riots followed and the Indian parliament was deadlocked by the opposition's determination to force Narendra Modi, Gujarat's BJP Chief Minister, out of office for failing to take any effective steps to protect the minority communities.

Gujarat is one of India's leading industrial states. Building on the cotton textile industry established in the 19th century, chemicals and petrochemicals, fertilizers and cement and engineering industries all have a major role. The state also has huge petrochemical complexes, Reliance's new factory at Jamnagar being one of the biggest oil-refining and petrochemical complexes in the world. Agriculture remains important, with cotton, tobacco and groundnut important cash crops and wheat and millets important cereals. Perhaps Gujarat's most striking agricultural development has been its dairy industry. India, now the world's largest milk producer, experienced a revolution in the dairy industry originating in Gujarat's dairy co-operatives' and their milk, butter and cheese now have India-wide markets. It is Gujarat's farmers who are the driving force behind the Indian Government's commitment to complete the Narmada dam projects, now nearing completion after a succession of bitter legal disputes and the high profile opposition of the novelist Arundhati Roy and the social campaigner from Mumbai Medhar Patkar.

Northern Gujarat

Ahmadabad

→ *Phone code: 079 (from Gandhinagar 089). Colour map 2, C3. Population: 3.5 million.*
Ahmadabad, the former state capital (Gandhinagar is the new capital), is a very congested city which spreads out along both banks of the Sabarmati River in a chaotic fashion. The Old City, however, has a maze of narrow winding alleys with carved wooden house fronts and thriving bazars. The Calico Museum and Mahatma Gandhi's Sabarmati Ashram attract visitors though some find the city's noise and pollution unpleasant. ▶▶ *For Sleeping, Eating and other listings, see pages 1236-1243.*

Ins and outs
Getting there The airport is 13 km northeast of town. Regular City buses collect passengers from the airport and arrive at Lal Darwaza, close to many budget hotels. Taxis charge Rs 180-230, and autos about Rs 90-100, to transfer. Train travellers arrive at the Junction Station to the east of the Old City, while long distance buses use the Rajpur Gate Terminus to the south. There are taxis and autos at both to get you to a hotel. See Transport, page 1241, for further details

Getting around Ahmadabad is far too sprawling to be able to cover all the sights on foot so you will need to struggle with local buses or hire an auto-rickshaw or taxi.

Climate Summer, maximum 42°C; winter, minimum 11°C. Most rain received Jun-Sep (average 180 mm). Best time to visit is Nov-Feb.

Ahmadabad retains a highly distinctive feel born out of a long and continuously evolving social history. Recent developments in urban design have contributed important new experiments to its architectural tradition. It was founded in 1411 by **Ahmad Shah I**, then King of Gujarat. He made Asaval, an old Hindu town in the south, his seat of power, then expanded it to make it his capital. Almost constantly at war with the neighbouring Rajputs, fortifications were essential. The **Bhadra** towers and the square bastions of the royal citadel were among the first to be built. The city walls had 12 gates, 139 towers and nearly 6,000 battlements.

Although most of the **Old City** walls have gone, many monuments remain, some of them striking examples of Indian Islamic architecture. The **provincial Gujarati style** flourished from the mid-15th century, and in addition to the religious buildings many of the houses have façades beautifully decorated with wood carving. The Swami Narayan Temple, Kalipur, Rajani Vaishnav Temple and Harkore Haveli, near Manek Chowk as well as *havelis* on Doshiwadani Pol, illustrate traditional carving skills. Sadly, much of the old carving has been dismantled to be sold off to collectors.

The **'new' city**, lying on the west bank, has the site of Mahatma Gandhi's famous Sabarmati Ashram from where he began his historic Salt March in protest against the Salt Law in 1915. Modern Ahmadabad has its own share of showpieces designed by famous architects, among them Le Corbusier, Louis Kahn, Doshi and Correa. The School of Architecture, the National Institute of Design and the Indian Institute of Management (IIM) are national centres of learning.

With a long tradition in craftsmanship under Gujarati Sultans and Mughal Viceroys, Ahmadabad was one of the most brilliant Indian cities. Its jewellers and goldsmiths are renowned, copper and brassworkers produce very fine screens and carpenters produce fine *shisham* wood articles. There are skilled stonemasons, lacquer artists, ivory/bone carvers, hand-block printers and embroiderers producing exquisite pieces with beads and mirrors.

Sights

In the Jami Masjid, Ahmadabad has one of the best examples of the second period of Gujarat's provincial architectural development. In 1411, Ahmad Shah I, the founder of a new dynasty, laid the foundations of the city which was to be his new capital. By 1423 the Jami Masjid, regarded by many as one of the finest mosques in India, was completed. He encouraged others to construct monumental buildings as well. Mahmud I Begarha (ruled 1459-1511) established the third phase of Gujarati provincial architecture, building some of India's most magnificent Islamic monuments.

The central city The citadel of the planned city formed a rectangle facing the river. A broad street was designed to run from Ahmad Shah's fortified palace in the citadel to the centre of the city, lying due east. The ancient citadel built by Ahmad Shah I in 1411, now known as the **Bhadra** (see above), lies between the Nehru and Ellis bridges. In the east face is the **Palace**, now the post office. **Sidi Sayid's Mosque** (circa 1570) formed part of the wall on the northeast corner but now stands isolated in a square. Ten windows of wonderful stone tracery depicting a branching tree are famous here. Note particularly those on the west wall.

Jami Masjid The essential orientation of the Qibla wall to Mecca meant that the main entrance to the mosque itself had to be in its east wall. The mosque was aligned so that the present Mahatma Gandhi Road passed its north entrance. This is still the point at which you enter by a flight of steps. It is pleasantly quiet and peaceful inside. The vegetable and fruit market near the south entrance is worth visiting for the artistic display of stallholders' wares.

❖ Ahmadabad's 'pols'

The old parts of the city are divided into unique, self-contained *pols*, or quarters, fascinating to wander round. Huge wooden doors lead off from narrow lanes into a section of houses with decorative wooden screens and brackets where small communities of people practising a craft or skill once lived. Merchants, weavers, woodworkers, printers and jewellers – each had their *pol*, their houses along winding alleys which met in common courtyards and squares. Today, these old quarters are being developed rapidly, with tower blocks rising up from just inside the old city walls.

The beauty of the sanctuary is emphasized by the spacious courtyard paved in marble, with a tank in the middle. The façade has a screen of arches flanked by a pillared portico. The two 'shaking minarets', once 26 m high, were destroyed by earthquakes in 1819 and 1957. Over 300 graceful pillars are organized in 15 square bays. The whole rises from a single storey through the two-storeyed side aisles to the three-storey central aisle. The central octagonal lantern, rising through both storeys and covered by a dome, was also strikingly original.

Teen Darwaza is immediately to the east of the entrance to Ahmad Shah's mosque – the triumphal archway also known as the Tripolia (Triple gateway). Now crowded by shops, its effect is considerably diminished.

Northeast of the Astodia Gate and a short distance south of the railway station are **Sidi Bashir's Shaking Minarets,** two tall towers connected by a bridge which was once the entrance to the old mosque (now replaced by a modern one). The minarets were believed to 'shake' or vibrate in sympathy as they are cleverly built on a flexible sandstone base to protect against earthquake damage. **Bibi-ki-Masjid** (1454), Gomtipur, southeast of the railway station, also has a shaking minaret. If you climb up the 78 steps to a parapet 25 m high, and hold on to the minaret, your guide may be able to make it gently sway by putting his weight against it!

The north Sayid Usman's mausoleum Across the Gandhi bridge, immediately west of Ashram Road, the *rauza* (circa 1460) is one of the first examples of the Begarha style. Northwest of the Old City near Shahpur Gate, the **Mosque of Hasan Muhammad Chishti** (1565) has some of the finest tracery work in Ahmadabad.

There are several **Jain temples** in the city. The highly decorated, white marble **Hathi Singh Temple** (1848) just north of the Delhi Gate, dedicated to Dharamanath, the 15th Jain *Tirthankar*, is perhaps the most visited. Along the streets of Ahmadabad, it is quite common to see Jain *parabdis* (bird sanctuaries).

The **Rani Rupmati Masjid**, early 16th century, in Mirzapur district, southwest of Delhi Gate and just south of the *Grand Hotel*, incorporates Hindu and Islamic design. Rupmati was the Sultan's Hindu wife. The carvings in the gallery and the *mihrabs* are particularly attractive. To the southeast is the **Pinjrapol**, or Asylum for Animals.

At **Asarva**, about 1 km northeast of Daryapur Gate, are the *baolis*, which often serve a dual purpose of being a cool, secluded source of water during the summer and a place of religious sanctity. The most highly decorated, however, is at **Adalaj Vav**, 19 km away.

The British **Cantonment** lies about 4 km to the northeast of the city, where there is an Anglican Church. On the west bank of the Sabarmati there is the Ahmadabad Textile Mill Owners' Association (**ATMA**) and the **Museum**, both of which were designed by Le Corbusier – see also page 440.

Gujarat Northern Gujarat Ahmadabad

Ahmadabad

Related map
A Ahmadabad centre,
page 1230

To Adalaj Vav & Gandhinagar (NH 8)   To Airport

Sleeping ■
1 Fortune Landmark
2 Inder Residency
3 Karnavati
4 Klassik Gold
5 Moti Mahal
6 Moti Manor
7 Nalanda

8 Panshikura &
  Toran Restaurant
9 Poonam Palace
10 President
11 Radisson

Eating ●
1 Bhagwati Chaats
  & Havmor
2 Black Knight
3 Chills, Thrills & Spills
4 Gopi & Mehta
5 Havmor
6 Khana Khazana

N

0 metres   400
0 yards   400

★ **Sabarmati Ashram** ⓘ *Some 6 km north of the centre. 0830-1900 (1 Apr-30 Sep), otherwise 0830-1830. Last admission: 30 mins before closing, free. Daily Son et Lumière Sun, Wed, Fri (English 2100), closed during monsoons, Rs 5. Donations for upkeep are gratefully received and an ornately printed receipt provided.* Gandhi's Ashram, originally known as Satyagraha and then Harijan Ashram, was founded in 1917. It was the starting point for Gandhi's celebrated, 385-km Salt March to Dandi in March 1930. He vowed not to return to the Ashram till India gained independence. Gandhi and 81 supporters began the march; by the end of it there were 90,000 protesters marching against the unpopular British Salt Tax Laws. Salt manufacture, a government monopoly, was chosen for the protest as it was a commodity every peasant used and could understand. At Dandi beach on 6 April Gandhi went down to the sea and made a small amount of salt, for which he was promptly arrested. In the following months, thousands of Indians followed his example and were arrested by the British. The **Sangrahalaya** includes a library, archives and a picture gallery depicting Gandhi's life in photographs and paintings. A five-minute film on his life is shown several times daily. The peace, quiet and simple style of the Ashram is impressively maintained. Some of the original ashram's work, such as a school for Harijan girls, continues. **Hridaya Kunj**, Gandhi's home for 15 years, containing simple mats, desk, spinning wheel and some personal belongings, overlooks the central prayer corner and the river and remains undisturbed, as does the unfurnished room of his wife Kasturba.

Museums and galleries

★ **Calico Museum**, a part of the Sarabhai Trust, is in an attractive old *haveli* in the botanically interesting Shahi Bagh gardens, 3 km north of Delhi Gate. It is one of the finest museums of its kind in the world. Some exhibits date from the 17th century and include rich displays of

7 Mirch Masala
8 Purohit
9 Rasrajan
10 Sankalp
11 Sheeba
12 Ten & Colours of Spice
13 Tomato
14 Upper Crust

heavy brocades, fine embroideries, saris, carpets, turbans, Maharajahs' costumes and a royal Mughal tent. It illustrates weaving techniques but not weaving equipment. The setting is superb. Secular pieces are housed in traditional old *havelis* which have been reassembled around the chowk.

Religious galleries ① *Daily except Wed and holidays. Free. Tours from 1030-1230 (religious textiles), 1445-1645 (secular textiles); report 15 mins before; they are different and complementary. Guided tour of the garden is by appointment only. Open for research. The guides are friendly and charming - "gorgeous collection, excellent library of textiles, highly recommended". The museum shop sells cards of exhibits, reproductions and books.* Moti Manor Hotel *is the only place nearby, for lunch.* These exhibit outstanding medieval Jain manuscripts, 14th-19th century Jain icons, *pichhwais* and *pattachitras*. The **Secular section** contains Indian textiles that featured in trade, historic pieces of tie-and-dye, embroidery and beadwork from Gujarat, *phulkari* embroideries of Punjab, *patola* silk sarees from Patan, Pashmina shawls from Kashmir, Chamba *rumals* from Himachal, silks from Orissa and South India.

LD Institute of Indology Museum, Gujarat University Campus, contains over 3,300 pieces of medieval sculpture, many of 11th-13th century, an outstanding Jain section and archaeological finds.

Shreyas Museum ① *Open winter, 1030-1730, summer 0830-1300, closed Mon, Diwali, Christmas and during school summer vacation. Rs 35 (foreigners).*, near Shreyas Railway Crossing, has a comprehensive collection of contemporary rural textiles from all parts of Gujarat – excellent beadwork, embroideries, utensils, religious objects and bullock cart accessories. Children's section upstairs exhibits folk art (dance costumes, masks, puppets). The guided tour also takes you around the campus.

Ahmadabad centre

Sleeping		**Eating**
1 Balwas & ZK Restaurant	8 King's Palace	1 Agashiye & Green Home
2 Cadillac	9 Kingsway	2 Chetna
3 Cama	10 Mascot	3 Havmor & Bakery
4 Capri & Volga	11 Nataraj	4 Kalapi
5 Esquire & Metropole	12 Rivera	5 Paramount
6 Goodnight	13 Royal Highness	6 Vadilal
7 Holiday Inn & Mascot	14 Sarita	
	15 Stay Inn	- - - - Heritage trail

0 metres 100
0 yards 100

1800, closed Mon, entry free. Summer timings change so check before visiting., Paldi, an award-winning design by Le Corbusier, with ramps of steps leading up from a fountained pool, houses an excellent collection of old and contemporary art, superbly exhibited. The **NC Mehta Gallery** here, has a vast collection of miniatures from the Rajasthan, Mewar, Mughal, Kangra and other schools. The series of 150 paintings on the Gita Govinda theme and a set from the Gujarat Sultanate period are rare exhibits.

Tribal Research Institute Museum ① *1130-1930, Sat 1130-1430, closed Sun. Gujarat Vidyapith, Ashram Rd.*has re-creations of tribal hamlets of Gujarat, besides weapons, implements, wall art, terracotta figurines and textiles.

The 'caves' of **Amdavad-ni-Gufa** ① *University Campus.*, were an inspirational venture by the architect Doshi and the artist MF Hussain to display their work. Tribal paintings and other works of art are being added.

Contemporary Art Gallery and **Gujarat Kala Mandir**, near Ellis Bridge exhibit contemporary art.

Parks and zoos
Kamala Nehru Zoological Park ① *Daily except Mon, Satellite Rd, off M Dayanand Rd, Kankaria*, was masterminded by the late Reuben David, a 'captive breeding' genius – note the albino porcupine, squirrel and deer here. **Sundervan** is a pleasant nature orientation park, snake demonstrations on their importance to the environment, walk-in aviary, library.

Excursions
Vishala, 5 km away, is a purpose-built collection of traditional Gujarati village huts. Lunch *thalis* and evening meal (2100), accompanied by music. There is traditional dancing after dinner and light is provided in the evening entirely by lanterns. You sit cross-legged at low tables (low stools also provided), eat off green leaves or metal *thalis*, and drink from clay tumblers. Fixed menu, full dinner under Rs 120 and lunch Rs 80. Hospitable, friendly staff. Air-cooled seating for lunch and snacks. The Utensils Museum, renovated and expanded in a courtyard with a pool, has a very well-displayed collection of milking vessels (cattle, camel), Rajasthani pottery, Hindu prayer lamps, jewel boxes and betel nut crackers.① *1700-2300 weekdays, 1000-1300, 1700-2200 Sun. Sarkhej Rd, Vasana. Fix a return price with an auto.*

Indroda Village Deer Park, next to Sarita Udyan by Sabarmati River, has an interesting reptile collection and well marked nature trails through forests where you may spot nilgai, porcupine, jackal, crested honey buzzard, paradise fly-catcher etc. There is a tented campsite.

★ **Adalaj** (1502) is the hamlet where, in a garden setting, one of the finest step wells in India can be found ① *Taxi drivers pretend not to know of it because of poor access road! It is 17 km north of Ahmadabad near Gandhinagar cross-road.*. The Vav (*baoli*) shows a combination of Hindu, Muslim and Buddhist styles. A long flight of steps descends over 30 m to the water. It has four floors, each cooler than the one above. Ornately carved pillars, niches and cross beams create large octagonal landings (now inaccessible) which served as resting places. Remains of the bullock ramp used for drawing water are still visible. Queen Rupabai is believed to have had it built to provide the traveller with a cool and pleasant refuge from the summer heat. Highly recommended. For a bite to eat on Gandhinagar Highway there is *Bageshree* for Gujarati thalis in lovely garden setting; and *Gokul* with a village theme, *havelis* and huts, folk concerts, Gujarati *thalis*. *Kathiawadi*, near crossroads does highly spiced *thalis*.

North of Ahmadabad

The fertile irrigated land immediately north of Ahmadabad becomes increasingly arid northwards towards Rajasthan. When approaching Mehsana there are signs of the growing economy, including natural gas, fertilizers, milk products and rape seed oil processing as well as a few modern places serving drinks and snacks.

Gandhinagar → *Phone code: 02712 (082 from Ahmadabad). Colour map 2, C3.*
Population: 195,900.

When Bombay state was divided along linguistic lines into Maharashtra and Gujarat in 1960, a new capital city was planned for Gujarat named after Mahatma Gandhi. As with Chandigarh, Le Corbusier was instrumental in the design. The 30 residential sectors around the central government complex are similarly impersonal. Construction began in 1965 and the Secretariat was completed in 1970. It is now an established town with over a quarter of a million people. Gandhinagar has become a popular place for day trippers from Ahmadabad with good multiplex theatre complexes and parks. It is situated 23 km north of Ahmadabad.

Akshardham ① *in Sector 20, 0900-1830 (Nov-Feb); 1000-2000 (Mar-Oct), part closed on Mon; 'tickets' for "generous support", Rs 25. Temple Information Counter and shop has maps, guidebooks and post cards.* This temple with a cultural complex and entertainment park, is run by volunteers. The pink sandstone main building, floodlit at dusk, houses a 2 m gold leaf idol and some relics of Sri Swaminarayan, who led a Vedic revivalist movement 200 years ago. The three halls feature a variety of informative sound and light presentations relating to Sri Swaminarayan, the *Vedas* and the Hindu epics. Sahajanabad Vun, the garden for meditation, is impressive and has 'singing fountains' and a restaurant. .

Mehsana (Mahesana)

The town, 80 km north of Ahmadabad, has an impressive Jain temple, built in the 1980s but in the traditional architectural style. Mehsana is used by visitors to Modhera and Patan for an overnight stop. Women travellers have reported being hassled by men near the bus station.

★ Modhera → *Colour map 2, C2.*

Virtually a deserted hamlet 25 km west of Mehsana, Modhera has the remains of one of the finest Hindu temples in Gujarat. Quite off the beaten track, it retains a great deal of its atmosphere and charm.

The temple ① *Rs 200 foreigners; video camera Rs 150. Getting there: for transport see Mehsana above. Visit early in the day.* Gujarat Tourism Toran restaurant *serves drinks and snacks. A* Classical Dance Festival *is held in Jan. See under Festivals.*

The partially ruined **Surya** (Sun) **Temple** (1026), built during the reign of Bhimdev I and consecrated in 1026-27, two centuries before the Sun Temple at Konark, is a product of the great Solanki period (8th-13th centuries). Despite the temple's partial destruction by subsequent earthquakes which may have accounted for the collapse of its tower, it remains an outstanding monument, set against the backdrop of a barren landscape. Superb carvings of goddesses, birds, beasts and blossoms decorate the remaining pillars. Over the last 20 years the complex has undergone major restoration by the Archaeological Survey of India which is continuing as funds permit. Unlike the Temple at Konark, the main temple stands well above the surrounding land, raised by a high brick terrace faced with stone.

The **entrance** A rectangular pool (*kund*, now dry), over 50 m long and 20 m wide, with flights of steps and subsidiary shrines, faces the front of the temple. A remarkable structure, despite the damage caused by weathering it is still possible to gain an impression of the excellence of the carving. On the west side of the tank a steep flight of steps leads up to the main entrance of the east *mandapa* through a beautifully carved *torana*, of which only the pillars now remain. The **sabha mandapa**, a pillared hall, is 15 sq m. Note the cusped arches which became such a striking feature of Mughal buildings 600 years later. The corbelled roof of this entry hall, which has been reconstructed, is a low stepped pyramid. Beautiful columns and magnificent carvings decorate the hall. The western part of the oblong temple contains the raised **inner sanctuary**. The upper storeys have been completely destroyed, though it clearly consisted of a low pyramidal roof in front of the tall *sikhara* (tower) over the sanctuary itself. Surya's image in the sanctuary (now missing) was once illuminated by the first rays of the rising sun at each solar equinox (proof of the mathematical and astronomical knowledge of the designers). Images of Surya and Agni are among the better preserved carvings on the external walls which also contain some erotic scenes. The interior walls were plain other than for niches to house images of Surya.

Patan

Little visited, Patan has over 100 beautifully carved Jain temples and many attractive traditionally carved wooden houses. It remains a centre for fine textiles, particularly silk *patola* saris produced by the characteristic *ikat* technique which involves tie-dyeing the warp threads before weaving to create designs on the finished fabrics. Only three extended families (at Salvivad and Fatipal Gate) can be seen at work on the highly prized double *ikat* weaving where both the warp and the weft threads are tie-dyed before being set on traditional looms – only to be found in Indonesia and Japan outside India. It takes three to six months to weave a sari, hence each sells at least Rs 50,000, samples are Rs 1,000. Patan is 35 km northwest of Mehsana and can be reached either by bus or train. Buses also run from Modhera.

★ The spectacular **Rani ki Vav** (late 11th century) ⓘ *Rs 200 foreigners; video camera Rs 150*, named after a Solanki queen, is one of the largest stepwells in India with superb carvings on seven storeys. Flights of steps lead down to the water level, lined by stringcourses of sculptured voluptuous women, Vishnu avatars and goddesses. The **Sahasralinga Talao** is a cluster of Solanki period (11th-12th century) shrines facing a small lake. Excavations are in progress.

Vadnagar

The town, 40 km northeast of Mehsana, has the finest example of the *torana* arches that characterise North Gujarat. Beautiful sculptures decorate two of the original four 12th-century arched gateways on *kirti stambha* pillars. The Solanki period city gates are beautifully sculpted, the best being near the lake. The impressive 17th-century **Haktesvar temple**, the most important Siva temple in Gujarat, has fine carvings, erotic sculpture and a silver shrine. Tana-Riri, two poetess-singers from Vadnagar, are said to have saved Tansen from the burning effects of the Deepak Raga (Song of Fire) by singing the Maldaar Raga (Song of Rain). Akbar invited the sisters to sing in his court, but rather than refuse to sing for a Muslim emperor (which was against their custom) they immolated themselves. Their shrine can be seen at Vadnagar.

Taranga

Named after Tara Devi, Taranga (55 km northeast of Mehsana by bus, or slow train, 3 hrs) has a wonderful complex of well preserved 12th-century Jain temples surrounded by spectacular hills. The large central sandstone temple to Adinatha is beautifully carved with sensual dancing figures, Hindu deities and Jain *Tirthankaras*. Inside is a bejewelled central statue carved out of a single piece of alabaster. There is a scenic trek from the main Adinath temple, passing some dramatic rock formations, to the hilltop Shilp Temple where one of the Jain saints meditated. Panthers have been sighted near the temple complex. There are four rooms in a 100-year old home set on a hill with village and woodland views where you can stay, Rajput family run, delicious food, 1000 acre farm with Marwari/Kathiawadi horses, riding, horse safaris. Recommended. Cheap Gujarati *thalis* Rs 9 (for Jains), Rs 15 (for non-Jains!).

Ambaji

Close to the Rajasthan border, en route to Mount Abu, Ambaji is known for its marble mines ⓘ *Ahmadabad-Mt Abu buses stop at Ambaji.* You can see marble artisans at work at this temple town (and at Khedbrahma nearby) where *Bhadra Purnima* fair is held, with processions of flag bearing pilgrims followed by musicians and dancers. A picturesque rope-way goes to Gabbar hill, a holy pilgrimage for Hindus (Rs 40).

The five 11th- and 12th-century Jain temples just east of Ambaji at **Kumbhariya** ⓘ *0630-1930; Aarti worship 0900-0930 and 1900, tea canteen, Jain thalis for Rs 12. Getting there: Jeeps (Rs 50) from Ambaji bus stand, Rs 5 for sharing*, are worth visiting for their exquisite marble carvings.

Danta

Enroute from Taranga to Ambaji, the princely state of Danta was known for its cavalry. It is dominated by the medieval Parmara Rajput fort. The jungles and rocky hills harbour panther, nilgai and 4-horned antelopes, and there is extensive birdlife; cycles for hire in the village. At **B** *Bhavani Villa* on a hilltop, tourists are welcomed like family guests. There are four new a/c rooms facing the hills, plus two private guest rooms in colonial period mansion, delicious Rajput meals, friendly hosts, great for nature lovers, game drives, riding (Rs 250 per hour), horse safaris (Rs 5000 per person). Reservations: *North West Safaris*, T079-6302019, F6300962.

Poshina

The small 15th-century Poshina **fort**, 45 km south of Abu Road, stands at the confluence of two holy rivers (Sai and Panhari) with views over the hills. It was the capital of the North Gujarat branch of Vaghela Rajputs. There are ancient Jain and Siva temples nearby as well as tribal villages where you can watch arrowmaking, basketwork, silversmiths and potters. The area is home to Bhils, colourful Garasias and Rabaris who herd camels, cattle and goats. The busy and interesting market centre is well worth stopping at; the last stretch of the approach road is very poor. Ahmadabad-Ambaji buses stop at Kheroj from where it is possible to get shared jeeps to Poshina (12 km). *Chitra Vichitra Fair* is held a fortnight after *Holi* at **Gunbakhari**, 8 km away. It is attended by Bhils, Garasias and Rabaris (some of whom are now abandoning their traditional *dhotis* and turbans). The fair is very colourful with much revelry, dancing and singing, food stalls etc. Matchmaking is often followed by elopements. *Florican Tours*, T5506590, F6426545, can arrange. Try staying in a tent (Gujarat Tourism) during fair. Delicious flavoured *lassi* near the village entrance but ask to prepare with your own mineral water.

Palanpur

ⓘ *There are a few D places to choose from. Getting there: trains between Ahmadabad and Delhi stop at Palanpur. See also under Bhuj. Direct buses go to Mount Abu; Ambaji (also share jeeps, Rs 20); Poshina through attractive countryside and tribal areas, 1200 (1 hr), Rs 7.* The *maqbara* with fine mausolea in this old Nawabi capital stands rather neglected. The palace is now the court; look in to see the fabulous ceiling paintings and sandalwood carvings. The 1915 Kirti Stambha has the 700-year long history of the Nawabs of Palanpur inscribed on it.

Balaram

Balaram has one of the best kept Palace hotels in Gujarat 3 km off the highway and 14 km north of Palanpur. About 20 km from there, the **Jessore Bear Sanctuary** in the Aravallis has sloth bear (occasionally spotted), panther, nilgai, sambhar, four-horned antelope etc, but these are best seen by climbing Jessore hill. Contact Forest Office, T57084.

East of Ahmadabad

Balasinore

A former Nawabi capital, Balasinore, 84 km east of Ahmadabad, is now a crowded town centred around a lake, and has some old Islamic architecture. It has come into international geological limelight after dinosaur fossils were found nearby; eggs and fossils are still being excavated. If you wish to stay

South of Ahmadabad

Vautha

Here the *Vautha Mela*, starting at *Kartik Purnima*, is held at the confluence of Sabarmati and Vatrak rivers, some 46 km south of Ahmadabad. Less colourful than Pushkar fair it is also far less touristy. About 4,000 donkeys, painted in vivid colours, and over 2,000 camels are traded. There is a great atmosphere on the river banks early in the morning, and in addition to the haggling over animals there are craft sales. Gujarat Tourism puts up twin bedded tents with catering.

Nalsarovar Bird Sanctuary

ⓘ *Best season: Nov-Feb. Increased entry fees now control visitor numbers. Try a boat ride for birding (Rs 25 per person per hr) for an experience. Contact Forest Office at Gandhinagar. Getting there: direct buses from Ahmadabad (0700, 1500) take 2 hrs. Last return from park 1800.*

The sanctuary, 65 km southwest of Ahmadabad, is noted for waterbirds including migratory ducks, flamingos and geese. The lake and the Surendranagar Reservoirs were declared a bird sanctuary in 1969. Uniquely in Saurashtra, Nalsarovar is surrounded by reed beds and marshes though the lake often dries out before the rains. Bharwad and Jat herdsmen and their water buffaloes live on the reed islands – you can get hot millet buttered chapatis and chutney with sweet tea or lassi from some shacks. Padhar fisherfolk who live around the lake are good artisans. *Forest Dept Bungalows* have two or three simple rooms, views of lake.

Lothal 'Mound of the dead'

Southeast of Moenjodaro, 720 km as the crow flies, Lothal has some of the most substantial remains of the Harappan culture in India dating from circa 2500-1700 BC. Once a port sandwiched between the Sabarmati River and the Bhogavo River, it is now 10 km inland from the Gulf of Khambhat on a flat, often desolate looking plain. Thorn scrub and parched soils surround the site, and even in February a hot desiccating wind picks up flurries of dust.

Ins and outs Trains and buses from Ahmadabad or Bhavnagar go close to Lothal; see below. It can be a long, hard day, with not much to see at the end of it. Hiring a taxi or motorbike makes it easier. There is no shade and no proper drinks outlet. Carry bottled water. Closed on Fri. See Transport, page 1242, for further details.

The site Lothal's location and function as a port have led most authorities to argue that it was settled by Harappan trading communities who came by sea from the mouths of the Indus. Others suggest that the traders came by an overland route. The site is surrounded by a mud-brick embankment 300 m north-south and 400 m east-west. Unlike the defensive walls at Harappa and Moenjodaro, the wall at Lothal enclosed the workers' area as well as the citadel. The presence of a dry dock and a warehouse further distinguish it from other major Harappan sites.

The dry dock This massive excavated structure runs along the east wall of the city. A 12 m wide gap in the north side is believed to have been the entrance by which boats came into the dock, while a spillway over the south wall allowed excess water to overflow. The city wall at this point may have been a wharf for unloading. Excavations of the warehouse suggest that trade was the basis of Lothal's existence. The building at the southwest corner of the wharf had a high platform made of cubical mud-brick blocks, the gaps between them allowing ventilation. Over 65 Indus Valley seals discovered here show pictures of packing material, bamboo or rope, suggestive of trade; one from Bahrain is evidence of overseas trade.

The city Excavations show a planned city in a grid pattern, with an underground drainage system, wells, brick houses with baths and fireplaces. The raised brick platform to the southeast may have been a kiln where seals and plaques were baked. Objects found include painted pottery, terracotta toys, ivory, shell, semi-precious stone items, bangles and even necklaces made of tiny beads of gold. Rice and millet were clearly in use, and there is some evidence that horses had been domesticated. The cemetery to the northwest had large funerary vessels indicating pit burials.

Wadhwan

Wadhwan, northwest of Limbdi, was a princely state of the Jhalas, a Rajput clan. The fortified old township has plenty of interesting architecture including two old stepwells with attractive carvings, some fine 11th-16th century temples. It is an ideal place to watch and shop for *bandhani*, wood and stone carving, silver and brass work, and textiles.

The opulent 19th-century Raj Mahal (*Bal Vilas*) occupied by the royal family, surrounded by parkland, has a grand Durbar hall with chandeliers, frescoes, carved furniture, crystal and velvet curtains, and a Sheesh Mahal library and billiard room. The vast landscaped gardens have tennis courts, lily ponds and fountains. Maharajah Chaitanya Dev is a keen restorer of classic cars and has a personal vintage car collection.

Listings: Northern Gujarat

⊜ Sleeping

Ahmadabad *p1225, maps p1228 and p1230*
Most are near the centre, about 3 km from railway station. Budget travellers may not find any room with bath for under Rs 150
AL Taj Residency Ummed, Airport Circle, Hansol, T2864444, F2864454. 88 rooms and some expensive suites, tastefully decorated with traditional embroideries and art pieces, usual facilities, good pool, restaurant, hotel sometimes overbooked.
A-B Comfort Inn, Airport Circle, T2862591, F2861627, cisunset@satyam.net.in. 33 rooms,

usual modern facilities, airport pick up.
A-B Cama Park Plaza, Khanpur Rd, T5505281, F5505285, camahotel@vsnl.com. 50 a/c rooms, totally renovated and upgraded on 1st and 2nd floors with long bathrooms, some with riverview, less expensive rooms on 3rd floor, new restaurant, pool, good coffee shop, friendly management.
A-B Fortune Landmark, Ashram Rd, T7552929. One of the best but on busy main road, massive, varied rooms, good restaurants (buffet breakfast to set you up for the day), health club.

A-B Holiday Inn, Khanpur Rd near Nehru Bridge, T5505505, F5505501. 63 rooms, good restaurants (*Waterfall* for buffets), dance floor, good indoor pool.

A-B Inder Residency, Ellis Bridge, T6425050, F6560407. 79 rooms, modern, very comfortable, very good Indian restaurant (avoid western), pool.

B Klassik Gold, CG Rd, T6445508. 33 rooms, excellent restaurant, efficient management, best in category.

B Moti Manor (Best Western), Shahibagh Under Bridge, T2869701, F2866414. 28 good rooms (day rate Rs 1000), excellent restaurant, near Calico Museum, friendly owner.

B Radisson, Gujarat College Cross Rds, T6426967, F6560022. Reopened after renovation. 68 rooms, pool.

B-C Nalanda, Mithakhali 6 Rds, T6426262, F6426090, www.hotelnalanda online.com. 38 clean rooms (standard rooms small; bath tubs and fridge in best), very good restaurant.

C Karnavati (Quality Inn), Shri Cinema Building, Ashram Rd, T6582162. 48 rooms, restaurant.

C Mascot, Khanpur Rd, T5503848, F5503221. Very comfortable, good value.

C President, CG Rd, Swastik Char Rasta, T6421421, F6421414. 58 good rooms, friendly staff, average décor, excellent restaurants.

C Rivera, Khanpur Rd, T5504201, F5502327. 69 clean, comfortable rooms (some overlook river), restaurant, free airport transfer, lawn, quiet.

C-D King's Palace, opposite Camu, T/F5500275. 37 very clean rooms, some a/c, good value, good restaurant, friendly staff.

Khanpur

D grade hotels with some a/c rooms with shower and TV. Those without restaurants provide good room service.

D Stay-Inn, near Gate, T5500724, F5504053. 14 colourful, clean rooms, friendly, eager to please.

Tilak (Relief) Rd

Most **D** hotels in between *Chetna Restaurant* and Sidi Sayid Mosque are similar in standard and facilities; most rooms have phone and bath with hot water, some a/c, though room sizes and prices differ.

D Balwas, 6751 Relief Rd, near Electricity House, T5507135. 21 clean rooms, 6 small at rear (side entrance), some economical non-a/c **E**, good restaurant attached but crowded, noisy area.

D Goodnight, Dr Tankaria Rd, opposite Sidi Sayid, Lal Darwaza, T5506997. 35 clean rooms, good restaurant, good service.

D Kingsway, near GPO, T5501215. 33 large rooms with fan, bath (hot water), modern, small breakfast menu and snacks.

D-E Metropole, Hanuman Lane, opposite Electricity House, T5507988. 19 clean rooms (small singles) some a/c, good room service.

E Volga, near Electricity House, T5509497, F5509636, Volga@icenet.net. Decent rooms, car rentals, internet.

F Cadilac, opposite Electricity House, Lal Darwaza, T5507558. Good value rooms with shared facilities, helpful travel desk.

F Sarita, near Khanpur Gate, T5501569. Clean, large rooms with bath, some a/c, fairly quiet.

West of the river

D Dimple International, Panchkuva, T2141849, F2113276. 30 rooms with modern facilities.

D Panshikura, near Town Hall, Underbridge, Ellis Bridge, T402960. 24 a/c rooms, quieter at rear, excellent restaurant.

D Poonam Palace, off Ashram Rd, near Dipali Cinema. Good value rooms.

E Esquire, opposite Sidi Sayid Mosque. Clean and popular.

E Nataraj, Dada Mavlankar Rd, near Ahmad Shah Mosque. Simple rooms with bath, hostel-like but good value.

E Swagat, near Arya Samaj, Rajpur-Kankaria Rd, T2111314. Rooms on 1st floor, practically windowless and claustrophobic, bit noisy, but very clean, shared shower, good room service from nearby restaurant, bus tickets, unused to foreigners but friendly, eager to please.

Gandhinagar *p1232*

C Haveli, Sector 11, opposite Sachivalaya, T24052, F24057. 84 rooms, restaurants, exchange, car hire, free airport transfer, day rates available, rooms below standard.

F Pathik Ashram, Govt, Sector 11.

F Youth Hostel, Sector 16, T22364. 2 rooms, 42 beds in 6-bed and 8-bed dorms, very good, no reservations.

For an explanation of the sleeping and eating price codes used in this guide, see inside the front cover. Other relevant information is found in Essentials pages 52-57.

Mehsana *p1232*

A-C Water World Resort, 25 mins' drive out of town, T02762-82351, F82352. A/c cottages, modern, Mughal garden with a/c 'royal tents', vegetarian restaurant, wine shop, wave pool and sports complex, artificial lake.

D-E Vijay Guest House, NH8, T02762-20041, near bus stop, on left going north. Good clean rooms with bath, some a/c, quieter at rear, friendly staff but no English spoken.

Others are Indian style:

E Apsara, *Janta Supermarket*, opposite bus station, T02762-20027. Reasonable rooms, some a/c, *thali* meals.

D-E Natraj, 1 km from Bus Stand. 12 rooms ranging from basic dorm to comfortable a/c with bath, very good veg restaurant.

F Railway Retiring Rooms, decent rooms (Rs 40) with bath.

Patan *p1233*

E-F Neerav, near bus and rly station. Rooms with bath (bucket hot water and room service, mornings only), some a/c with TV, clean, Gujarati *thali* and North Indian food, best but noisy area.

F Navjivan, GIDC Char Rasta. Rooms with bath (hot water), veg restaurant (Gujarati *thali* Rs 25-40; north Indian Rs 45-60)

F Toran Tourist Bungalow (Gujarat Tourism), 2 simple rooms, basic cafeteria, convenient for stepwell.

Poshina *p1234*

B Darbargarh (Heritage Hotel), in 17th-century wing of the fort complex. Pleasant with open courtyards and hill views, old world charm, now renovated with antiques, Rajasthani miniatures and rare Tanjore paintings (rather haphazardly), 15 comfortable, air-cooled rooms (some complaints about cleanliness), spicy Indian meals, camel rides, folk entertainment, friendly hosts, owner is very knowledgeable about local tribes, crafts etc, good village safaris, advance reservations.

Balaram *p1235*

B Balaram Palace Resort, Chitrasani, splendid riverside location surrounded by hills. Impeccably restored 1930s palace, 17 a/c

rooms (interiors too modern and characterless for some), choose between 4 colonial rooms with old fireplaces (some windowless) and rooms upstairs with views; *Nawab Suite* has huge arched windows, excellent terrace restaurants, lovely formal Nawabi garden, fountains, period swimming pool fed by natural cascading spring, good gym, bike hire. Recommended. Contact T079-6582191, F6578412, bprhot@ad1.vsnl.net.in.

Balasinore *p1235*

B Balasinore Garden Palace (Heritage Hotel), T02690-62008. 6 refurbished rooms in an early 20th-century building, delicious Mughlai meals, one of few Nawab-family run heritage hotels, pleasant orchard garden, personal attention, tours of 650-million year old dinosaur site and tribal villages.

● Eating

Ahmadabad *p1225, maps p1228 and p1230*
Thalis are around Rs 50 ('Kathiawadi' has more chilly and garlic, while 'Gujarati' is sweetened with sugar and jaggery).

Centre

⑪⑪⑪ Holiday Inn. Very good Indian; also
⑪⑪⑪ 24 Carats for high tea - excellent 'club' and grilled sandwiches.

⑪⑪ Agashiye, opposite Sidi Sayid Mosque, Lal Darwaja. Attractive Gujarati *thali* restaurant on the terrace of a 1920s heritage building. Unique atmosphere, local music, Gujarati *thalis* (Rs 170-200).

⑪⑪ HBM, lounge here is cool (a/c) and attractive and ideal for relaxing, for Rs 70 cover charge, coffee and snacks available, books and TV.

⑪⑪ Green House courtyard coffee shop.

⑪⑪ Bhagyodaya, GPO Rd (opposite *Kingsway*). Good food, varied choice, pleasant outlook.

⑪⑪ Goodnight's *Food Inn* downstairs serves good Indian (unlimited *thali*) but freezing a/c.

⑪⑪ Paramount, MG Rd near Bhadra. Indian. Famous for mutton/chicken biryanis, tikkas, a/c but lacks atmosphere.

⑪ Chetna, Krishna Cinema, Relief Rd (upstairs). Unlimited Gujarati *thalis*.

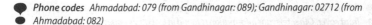

● **Phone codes** *Ahmadabad: 079 (from Gandhinagar: 089); Gandhinagar: 02712 (from Ahmadabad: 082)*

Elsewhere

Colours of Spice, Swastik Crossroads. International (including Thai/Indonesian), pleasant a/c interior, courteous service, about Rs 300 each. Cama Park Plaza does excellent salads, club sandwiches and great value buffets (Rs 200-250).

Fortune Landmark, pleasant rooftop restaurant with city views, open after dark. Great atmosphere, live music, specialises in kebabs, tandoori, grills/roasts (Rs 500 each). Downstairs for good buffets. (Rs 200-275), enormous breakfast (Rs 175).

Black Knight, CG Rd. Good Indian, Chinese, continental, medieval European theme décor.

China Town, Stadium Circle. Good Chinese (including non-vegetarian). Try fish Manchurian or Chicken in hot garlic.

City Gold Multiplex, Ashram Rd. The modern entertainment complexes have several adventurous outlets (Western, oriental) to which the young gravitate.

Fun Republic, Satellite Rd and

Mirch Masala, CG Rd. Very spicy North Indian, Bollywood theme in Juhu beach-shack mock-up with filmland posters and music to match, also tempting and hygienic (usually forbidden!) 'street snacks'.

Rajwadu, Jivraj Park. A rural theme restaurant. Rajasthani/Gujarati dinner, delightful open-air setting, water courses, gardens, folk entertainment, large meals in brass/copper vessels, refills galore, a bit like a Bollywood film set but very pleasant, not quite as authentic as *Vishala* but more comfortable and accessible.

Sheebah, opposite Telephone Exchange, Navrangpura. International, a/c, excellent north Indian (try fish, paneer or chicken *tikkas*), friendly. Continental and Chinese fast food counter (to avoid excess spices, request when ordering). Highly recommended.

Ten, the Restaurant, Swastik Crossroads, CG Rd. Indian and continental, a/c, one of the best in town, ship-breakers yard décor, friendly, occasional live Indian music. Great fish meunière, fried fish, methi chicken, kebab platters, but avoid Chinese. For dessert try the '10-special pudding'. Good cake shop.

Tomato, CG Rd. Western, a/c, 1950s American diner theme, Rock-and-Roll era décor and music, good atmosphere, young crowd; also Mexican/Italian. Coffee shop serves great coffee, nachos, tacos, sandwiches.

Gopi, Ashram Rd. A/c, mildly spiced *thalis* specially for foreigners, good service, family run.

La-Bela, Mirzapur. Mutton/chicken curry and other dishes cooked up by a family. Lady owner treats visitors like part of her family.

Navrang, Vijay Crossroads. Punjabi thalis, a/c.

Sankalp, CG Rd. South Indian, rooftop terrace garden with fountain, good *dosas*.

Shiv Sagar off CG Rd. Thalis (Rs 60), less spicy than elsewhere. Very cheap (under Rs 30) Indian meals and snacks are available at Bhatiar Gali, Law Garden, Raipur Gate and IIM Rd.

Azad Halwai, Revdi Bazar. North Indian sweets, try *Daal-Pakwan*, a Sindhi favourite.

Mehta, Ellis Bridge, *thalis* and snacks.

New Swagath, Babha Complex, near Gujarat Vidyapith. Good South Indian, *Puri-bhaji*.

Tulsi, near Gujarat University. North Indian thalis and à la carte, a/c.

Vallabha, 1 Jeet Complex, opposite 'Shilip', C G Rd. Excellent Gujarati thalis.

Cafés and fast food

Panchwati: **Bhagwati Chaats**, great Indian snacks and sweets, try *paneer tikkas, gulab jamuns* and *jalebis*.

Chills, Thrills, Frills. Veg/cheese burgers, excellent coffee, grilled and toasted sandwiches, ice creams, thick shakes, disappointing pizzas, young crowd (Rs 150 for 2).

Dominos, Stadium Circle. Good pizzas at a few tables outdoors (mainly take-away), also desserts and side dishes.

Periera Takeaways and **Icy Pick**, both near Vijay Crossroads. Cold meats, kebabs, tikkas.

Pizza Hut, Swastik Crossroads. Vegetarian. Young trendy crowd, a/c. Good salad bar and delicious ice creams but disappointing pizzas.

Rasrajan, Vijay Crossroads (a/c). Self service, a/c upstairs. good vegetarian salad bar, Indian and Chinese veg meals.

Upper Crust, Vijay Crossroads, (a/c). Good breads, cakes and desserts, *kathi kabab* rolls, sizzlers, Sun breakfast (Rs 50).

Drinks

Lucky, Lal Darwaza, and stalls near IIM, ID and Times of India Building are known for their masala tea. Ellis Bridge area, for refreshing fresh coconut milk.

Girish, CG Rd, near Jami Masjid and elsewhere, and **Jamalpur**, Revdi Bazar, for fresh fruit juices and good milkshakes.

Ice creams

Ahmadabad is famous for its ice creams. It is India's ice cream capital!
Vadilal, **Baskin Robins**, **Havmor** branches are all over town. Shreyas Crossing is a massive ice cream market.
Patel, Panchwati, and **Rajasthan**, near Shreyas Railway Crossing, do fresh home-made ice cream.

Sweets

Kamal, Revdi Bazar, near the station. For excellent Indian sweets.
Kamdhenu, near VS Hospital. For good Gujarati sweets.
Jai Sitaram, near Paldi Railway Crossing. Delicious *kesar pedas* (saffron-flavoured milk sweets).

Gandhinagar *p1232*

♥ **Relief**, excellent Indian and Continental.
♥ **Premawati**, Akshardham Complex. Veg Gujarati food, Indian snacks, lime tea and delicious ice creams.
♥ **Torana**, Sector-28. Punjabi, South Indian snacks, in a garden.
♥ **Chills, Thrills & Spills**, Sector-21 Shopping Centre. Pizzas, sandwiches, veg *thalis*.
♥ **Regent**, does good Indian. Sector 21 has street-side vendors who offer good snacks. Ask for the 'Bhatiar' couple who make *bajra ka rotla* (millet *chapatis*) and chicken curry, meat samosas and daal in a little shack, not too far from Akshardham.

Mehsana *p1232*

♥ **Kudarat**, near *Vijay* (Hindi sign with a triangular tree symbol), best of the highway cafés. South Indian and Punjabi. Open-air, so you may have a monkey for company.
♥ **Sher-e-Punjab** by a petrol station, east of NH8, does good omelettes.

♦ Bars and clubs

Ahmadabad *p1225, maps p1228 and p1230*
Prohibition is in force. Ask for a 'liquor permit' on arrival in India at the airport tourist counter; getting one in the city is very tortuous. Larger hotels may be authorized to issue 'spot' permits.

⊕ Festivals and events

Ahmadabad *p1225, maps p1228 and p1230*
14-15 Jan: Makar Sankranti marks the end of winter. It is celebrated with kite flying by people of all ages, accompanied by colourful street markets and festivities Kites come in all colours, shapes and sizes, the best varieties reputedly being available in Manek Chowk and Tankshala, Kalupur. The flying continues after sunset, when the kites are lit with candles. See Box. **Sep/Oct**: Navratri, honouring Goddess Amba (*Shakti*), has special significance here and at Vadodara. Nine days of music and traditional '*Garba Ras*' dancing. The custom of women balancing clay pots while they dance is still practised.

⊙ Shopping

Ahmadabad *p1225, maps p1228 and p1230*
Shops usually open from 0900-1900, most close on Sun. Manek Chowk is the main bazar. Other centres are Relief Rd, Ashram Rd, Lal Darwaza and Kapasia Bazar.

Art galleries

Visit Law Gardens after 1600 to browse through stalls of artists and craftsmen.

Books

Art Book Centre, Madalpur, near Inder Residency.
Book Shelf, 16 City Centre, near *10-the Restaurant*, CG Rd, Navrangpura. A/c.
Books Plaza, near Raymond show room, CG Rd. Also CDs.
Crossword, B6 Sri Krishna Centre, Mithakhali 6 Rds, T6425186. A/c, also CDs and café.
Mapin, Darpana Academy, Usmanpura, Ashram Rd. Specialises in Indian arts.
Natraj, Ashram Rd, with branches all over the city. Books and CDs.

Handicrafts

Good bargains at **Satellite Rd**, where Kachchhi and Saurashtrian artisans sell embroideries, block prints and handicrafts – appliqué bedspreads, wall hangings etc, but bargain hard.
To to the huge **Sunday Market**, on the river bank at Ellis Bridge in the morning to pick up 'antiques', handicrafts and second-hand books.

Garvi and Gujari, Ashram Rd. Govt.
Embroidered dresses, block-printed bedspreads, lacquered furniture etc, well displayed,
open 1030-1400, 1500-1900, closed Wed.
Honeycomb at *Cama hotel*.
Kamdhenu Ambawadi, has showrooms of
several State Handicraft Co-ops.
Shringar, near *Honeycomb*, up-market
'antiques'.
Treasure, near Judge's bungalow, Satellite Rd,
is a gallery for art and handicrafts. Brassware
and wood carvings are sold at Manek Chowk.

Photography
Numerous 1-hr processing shops:
Camera Clinic, Vijay Plaza, Kankaria. Good
camera repairs.
Dolphin, Ambawadi, T6465665.
Rangoli, near Gujarat Vidyapith, Ashram Rd.
Sukruti Q Lab, Ashram Rd, T6587335.

Textiles
Gujarat's famous embroideries, *bandhani*
and block prints are sold at Rani-no-Haziro
and Dalgarwad near Manek Chowk in the
walled city. There are '*Khadi Bhandars*' and
Handloom Houses for textiles on Ashram Rd,
between Gandhi Ashram and Natraj Theatre.
Revdi Bazar and Sindhi Market have
semi-wholesale textile shops.
Sewa, east of Ellis Bridge. A commendable
women's co-op producing very fine shadow
embroidery and clothes. CG Rd is the upmarket shopping area for quality garments.

▲ Activities and tours

Ahmadabad *p1225, maps p1228 and p1230*
Ahmadabad Municipal Transport Service,
Lal Darwaza, where you can reserve the
following: Tour 1 0830-1830: Sidi Sayid
mosque, Shaking minarets, Huteehsinh Jain
temples, Gandhi Ashram, Gujarat Vidyapit,
ISKCON temple, Sundarvan, Shreyas
museum, Gandhinagar (also Akshardham)
and Adalaj stepwell; Rs 160 a/c coach. Tour 2
0900-1700, slightly different, Rs 125
(non-a/c). Tours 3, 4 0930-1300, 1330-1730,
split the sights; Rs 75, Rs 85 a/c. Heritage
Walking Tours Mar-Aug 0730 to 1030,
Sep-Feb 0800-1030. Excellent tour with
qualified architects/conservationists; starts at
Swaminarayan temple, Relief Rd, Kalupur, of
havelis, *pols*, artisans' workshops etc, for Rs

50. Check ahead at CRUTA, at the temple
complex, T337058. Highly recommended.
Forican Tours, opposite Electricity House,
Lal Darwaza, T5506590, F6426545, for
bookings for Poshina.
North West Safaris, 91-92 Kamdhenu
Complex, opposite Sahajanand College,
T6302019, F6300962, ssibal@ad1.vsnl.net.in
Knowledgeable, efficient.
Sita, Suflam Building, Mithakhali, Ashram
Rd, T409105.
TCI, near Natraj Theatre, behind Handloom
House, Ashram Rd, T407061.

⊖ Transport

Ahmadabad *p1225, maps p1228 and p1230*
Air
International flights to **Abu Dhabi**, **Bangkok**,
Copenhagen, **Dhaharan**, **Dubai**, **Geneva**
and **Hong Kong**. Indian Airlines, Lal
Darwaza, near Roopalee Cinema, T5503061.
1000-1315, 1415-1715. Airport T140. **Delhi**,
Mumbai, **Calcutta**, **Kolkota** via **Bangalore**,
Hyderabad, **Jaipur**. Jet Airways, Income Tax
Char Rasta, Ashram Rd, T7543304, Airport
T2866240: **Mumbai**, **Delhi**.

Bus
Local City service available from main bus
station, Lal Darwaza, railway station and all
major points in the city.
Long distance Central Bus Station, Geeta
Mandir, T2144764. Reservations 0700-1900.
Advance booking for night services
1500-2300, luxury coach services 1030-1800.
Arrive early to find your bus. ST buses to
Mehsana (Rs 20) on very poor road,
Mumbai (492 km, 11 hrs), **Palitana** 217 km,
Porbandar 394 km, **Rajkot** 216 km, **Sasan
Gir** 217 km, **Surat** 120 km, and **Vadodara**
113 km. **Udaipur** 287 km. Private operators
coaches, from suburban stands, often run at
night. Punjab Travels, K Gandhi Rd, Delhi
Darwaza, and Embassy Market, Ashram Rd,
T6589200. Pawan, Pritamnagar 1st Dhal, Ellis
Bridge. Tanna, Paldi, for Bhavnagar.
Shajanand, Shefali Complex, Paldi, for buses
to Diu; Mt Abu, 7 hrs (via Khed Brahma).

Motorbike
Shaikh Agency, *Swastik Supermarket*,
Ashram Rd.

Rickshaw

Auto-rickshaws: minimum Rs 4 (ask to see rate card). About Rs 2 per km inflated to Rs 5-10 for foreigners. Night charges are quite high.

Taxi

Tourist taxis: for hire from TCGL, T6589683 or **Sai**, 23 Aniket, Navrangpura; Rs 500 (4 hrs), Rs 900 (8 hrs).

Train

Always confirm from which station train departs. Ahmadabad is on a broad gauge line to Mumbai (Platforms 1-4, near the main entrance) and a metre gauge line to Delhi (Platforms 7-12). Platforms 5 and 6 serve both, according to demand, and has 3 rails! Ahmadabad Junction (Kalupur) Station, enquiries T131. Computerized reservations at Junction and Gandhigram stations: 1st Class 0800-1530, 2nd Class 0800-1430, 1500-2000, T135. If you don't have a reservation, last-minute berths can be booked for some trains at a temporary counter on the platform; premium charged. *Dairy Den*, Platform 1, Junction station, fast food, 24 hours, grilled sandwiches, burgers, pizzas, ices.

    Agra Cantt: *Ahmadabad Gorakhpur Exp, 5045*, 0545, Tue, 25 hrs. **Ajmer**: *Ahmadabad Delhi Mail, 9105*, 0955, 10½ hrs (to Jaipur); *Ashram Exp 2915*, 1745, 7 hrs. **Bangalore**: *Ahmadabad Bangalore Exp,* 1800, Sun, 13¾ hrs. **Bhavnagar**: *Bhavnagar Exp 9936*, 0705, 5½ hrs; *Shetrunji Exp, 9910*, 1710, 5½ hrs. **Bhopal**: *Rajkot-Bhopal Jabalpur Exp, 1269/1263*, 1900, 14 hrs. **Chennai**: *Navjivan Exp, 6045*, 0630, 22¾ hrs. **Delhi (OD)**: *Ashram Exp, 2915*, 1745, 16½ hrs. **Jaipur**: *Aravali Exp, 9707*, 0620, 13¾ hrs; *Ashram Exp, 2915*, 1745, 11 hrs. **Kolkata (H)**: *Howrah Exp, 8033*, 0920, 20 hrs. **Jamnagar**: *Jamnagar Exp, 9153*, 1815, not Mon, 6 hrs; *Mumbai Porbandar Saurashtra Exp, 9215*, 2015, 7½ hrs; *Mumbai Okha Saurashtra Mail, 9005*, 0550, 7½ hrs (all stop at **Rajkot**, 2 hrs before Jamnagar). **Jodhpur**: *Ranakpur Exp, 4708*, 0030, 10 hrs (continues to **Bikaner**, 6 hrs). **Junagadh**: *Veraval Girnar Exp, 9946*, 2155, 8½ hrs; *Veraval Somnath Mail, 9924*, 2300, 10 hrs (both continue to **Veraval**, 2 hrs). **Mehsana**: *Aravali Exp, 9707*, 0620, 1¾ hrs; *Delhi Mail, 9105*, 0955, 2 hrs; *Ashram Exp, 2915*, 1745, 1½ hrs. **Mumbai Central**: *Shatabdi Exp, 2010*, 1435, not Fri, 7¼ hrs; *Gujarat Mail, 2902*, 2210, 8¾ hrs. **Porbandar**: *Mumbai Porbandar Saurashtra Exp, 9215*, 2015, 10½ hrs. **Udaipur City**: *DSR Express, 9944*, 2240, 9 hrs. **Vadodara**: *Gandhidham Vadodara Exp, 9104*, 0518, 2 hrs; *Ahmadabad Vadodara Exp, 9130*, 1445, 2½ hrs.

Gandhinagar *p1232*

Train and **buses** to Ahmadabad take 1 hr. ST Bus Station, Sector 11, T22842.

Mehsana *p1232*
Bus

To **Ahmadabad** on a very poor road (2½ hrs) and **Patan**. To **Modhera**: bus from ST Bus Stand (infrequent and uncertain timetable), ¾ hr, Rs 8; or bus from NH8/SH41 junction (Modhera Rd) but often full. Last return from Modhera, 1730 (sometimes delayed by up to 2 hrs).

Rickshaw

Auto-rickshaws Rs 5 from town to *Vijay*.

Train

Rajasthan and Delhi bound trains from Ahmadabad stop at Mehsana.

Lothal *p1235*
Bus

There are a few buses from Ahmadabad; change at Dholka. Luxury and State buses can drop you at **Gundi** railway crossing; from there *chhakras* charge Rs 5 each for the drop to Lothal. Get back on the highway to get a bus back to Ahmadabad or Bhavnagar. Ideally hire a car from Ahmadabad (Rs 800-1000) for the 80 km drive to Lothal; travel 52 km to Bagodra on the NH8A, then turn left on SH1 towards Bhavnagar (73 km), go across the level crossing and immediately turn left. Lothal is signposted as 7 km (appalling section). From Bhavnagar follow the SH1 via Vallabhipur and Barwala. The turn off is 127 km from Bhavnagar.

Train

Some trains from Ahmadabad to Bhavnagar stop at Lothal-Burkhi station; shared motorbike trailers (*chhagras* or *chhakras*) drop you at Lothal or Utelia for a few rupees.

❶ Directory

Ahmadabad *p1225, maps p1228 and p1230*
Airline offices Domestic airlines under
Transport. **Air India**, Premchand House, near
High Court, T425644. **Air France**, T442391.
British Airways, T465621. **Delta**, T448143. **Gulf
Air**, T463812. **Kuwait Airways**, T465848.
Lufthansa, T464122. **Malaysian**, T425840.
Singapore Airlines, T461335. **Swissair**,
T449149. **United**, T401909. **Banks** Bank of
Baroda and Andhra Bank, Ashram Rd, Visa
and TCs. Some on CG Rd and Ashram Rd,
change TCs and currency. **Amex, Wall St
Finance, Foreign Exchange Bureau**, all on CG
Rd; **Thomas Cook**, near the High Court,
involve less paper-work and open till late.
Cultural centres West of Ellis Bridge,
Alliance Française, behind Gujarat College,
T441551. British Library, near Law Garden,
T350686, a/c; clean toilets. **Hospitals** Civil
Hospital, Asarwa, T376351; ESIC General,
Bapunagar, T363734; **Sardar Patel**, Maninagar;

Sarbhai General, Ellis Bridge; Victoria
Jubilee, Panchkuwa Darwaza, T361080.
Internet/email Cyber Café, Shri Krishna
Centre, Mithakhali. Log-In, 92 Kamdhenu
Complex, Polytechnic Rd, Ambawadi,
T6302019, also printouts. **Random Access**,
Ambawadi, 10 terminals. **Post office** GPO:
off Relief Rd. Others at Navrangpura, Ellis
Bridge, Gandhi Ashram, Gandhi Rd, Gujarat
University, IIM, Madhavpura market,
Polytechnic and Ambawadi – all with Speed
Post. **Tourist offices** Gujarat (TCGL), HK
House, opposite Bata, Ashram Rd, T6589172,
F6582183, tcgl.ahm@rmt.sprintrpg.
ems.vsnl.net.in; 1030-1830, closed Sun, 2nd
and 4th Sat each month. Also at airport and
railway station. Goa, Indata, Vaveli Building,
Fantasa Pole, Gandhi Rd. MP, T6589172. UP,
Smrutikunj Soc, opposite Asia Engineering
School. **Useful addresses** Ambulance:
T102. Fire: T101. Police: T100. Foreigners'
Regional Registration Office: Police
Commissioner's Office, Shahi Bagh.

Vadodara and the Old Forts

→ *Colour map 2, C3 and C4.*
*The route south from Ahmadabad crosses the fertile alluvial plains of the Sabarmati
and Mahi rivers before entering the Konkan region. The plains gradually give way
south to broken hills while inland, parallel ridges reach between 500-600 m where
strategically placed atmospheric old forts were sited. Rice dominates agriculture
further south, but ragi (finger millet) and pulses are also common. A pleasant day trip
by car from Vadodara could include the forts of Champaner in the foothills and
Pawagadh on a hilltop, and Dabhoi Fort, 146 km via Bodeli, see page 1245.*
▸▸ *For Sleeping, Eating and other listings, see pages 1250-1254.*

★ Vadodara → *Phone code: 0265. Colour map 2, C3. Population: 1.3 million.*

Formerly Baroda, Vadodara was the capital of one of the most powerful princely
states. It is now a rapidly expanding Industrial town, yet the older part is pleasant and
interesting to wander through. The Gaekwad stood high in the order of precedence
among rulers, being one of only five to receive a 21-gun salute. He was reputedly so
rich that he had a carpet woven of diamonds and pearls, and cannons cast in gold.

Ins and outs

Getting there The airport, with flights from Ahmadabad, Delhi and Mumbai, is 9 km
away with taxis (Rs 250, a/c Rs 350) and auto-rickshaws to town. Better hotels offer
free airport transfer. Railway and the Long Distance bus stations are to the northwest
of town, close to hotels. From the railway station, walk under the bridge; then for 5
mins to find several to the left of the main road and in the streets behind. See
Transport, page 1255, for further details.

Getting around The local bus station is just opposite the railway station. There are taxis and autos to take you to the town centre and the sights.

Climate Temperature: summer maximum 36°C, minimum 22°C; winter maximum 25°C, minimum 8°C. Rainfall: Jul-Aug, 300mm; Nov-May, hardly a spot. Best time to visit Nov-Feb.

Sights
Much of the city's treasures, which can be seen in the palaces and museums reflect the wealth of the Gaekwads, a dynasty established by the powerful 18th-century Maratha General, Damaji. See page 1066.

The **Laxmi Vilas Palace** (1880-90) was built by RH Chisholm. The magnificent palace is somewhat neglected but the interiors are decorated with Venetian mosaic, Italian marble, porcelain, antique furniture, European stained glass, sculptures, a royal armoury etc. ① *Rs 100 (no photography)*. Nearby is the **Naulakhi Well**, a well-preserved *baoli* which has galleried levels.

Just to the south of the Palace is the **Maharajah Fateh Singh Museum** with a prized collection of paintings by the 19th-century Indian artist Raja Ravi Verma (see Museums below). Further south, beyond the railway, the **Pratap Vilas** (circa 1910, known as Lalbagh Palace), with a baroque façade, is now the Railway Staff College; permission from Principal needed to visit the small rail museum. The beautiful **Shiv Mahal Palace**, near the race course, is being renovated.

In the town centre, the **Kirti Mandir** (early 20th century), the Gaekwad *samadhi* (memorial ground) has murals by Nandlal Bose and marble busts. The **Kothi** Building (late 19th century) is to the west and now houses the Secretariat. Across the road is the **Nyaya** (Law) **Mandir** (1896), not a temple but the High Court, in Mughal and Gothic styles. The **Jama Masjid** is next door.

Further along the road away from the lake is the **Mandvi** (1736), a Muslim Pavilion and the **Nazar Bagh Palace** (1721), which has a Shish Mahal (mirror palace), and is rather dilapidated now. The **College of Fine Art** is an institute of national renown.

Vadodara

Sleeping		
1 Apsara, Surya & Tradewings	3 Green	Eating
	4 Rama Inn & Ambassador	1 Alka
2 Express & Sahayog Restaurant	5 Utsav	2 Gokul
	6 Vadodara	3 Havmor
		4 Kalyan

0 metres 500
0 yards 500

⁘ Bullock Train – the oldest narrow gauge!

The Vadodara-Dabhoi-Chandod line is the world's oldest surviving narrow gauge railway. The 19th-century line was commissioned for bullock drawn locomotives in 1863. Later turned to steam, it is now run by a diesel engine. There are some vintage locomotives including steam engines in the Dabhoi station yard dating back to 1902. Take a ride on this line from Vadodara to Chandod via Dabhoi for the experience!

Half-way down Raj Mahal Road are the remarkable buildings of the Khanderao Market. One of the old painted **havelis**, the four-storey Tambekarwada, residence of the Diwan of Vadodara (1849-54), acquired by the Archaeological Survey, is well worth visiting. It is between Raopura Road and Dandia Bazar; rickshaw-wallahs appear not to know it so ask near the GPO and walk two minutes.

Sayaji Bagh is an extensive park, popular for evening strolls. **Kammati Bagh** is also beautiful. There is a fairly interesting zoo and a planetarium.

Museums

Maharajah Sayajirao Museum (Vadodara Museum) and **Art Gallery** ① *in the Victoria Diamond Jubilee Institute, Sayaji Bagh, 1000-1700, Sat 1000-1645.*, designed by RF Chisholm. Archaeology, art, ethnology and ancient Jain sculptures; also Industrial arts, Mughal miniatures and European paintings. **Maharajah Fateh Singh Museum** ① *Nehru Rd, Laxmi Vilas Palace, 1000-1730 (1600-1900 Apr-Jun), closed Mon, Rs 15,* guidebook Rs 35, has a good display of royal state collection of European art (copies of some Murillo, Titian, Raphael, Rubens), Ravi Verma, Chinese and Japanese statuary and porcelain, European porcelain. **Archaeology and Ancient History** ① *MS University, 1400-1700, closed Sun and public holidays*, contains Buddhist antiquities, archaeological finds from North Gujarat, and good pre-history of Gujarat.

Champaner

Champaner, 47 km northeast of Vadodara, stands at 880 m in the Girnar Hills. ① *Shared jeeps and ST buses from Vadodara and Ahmadabad go to Machi where cable cars start for the ascent to the monuments on the hill; Rs 45 return (only hand baggage of 5 kg allowed), 0900-1300, 1400-1700.* The fortress was the old capital of the local Rajputs who lost it in 1484 to Mahmud Beghara, who renamed it Muhammadabad and took 23 years to build his new city. In his campaign in Gujarat, the Mughal Emperor Humayun personally led a small team that scaled the walls of the city using iron spikes and then let the rest of the army in through the main gate. With the collapse of the Empire, Champaner passed to the Marathas.

In the **old city**, the remains of many 15th- and 16th-century mosques and palaces show a blend of Islamic and Jain traditions, a unique style encouraged by Champaner's relative isolation. The **Jami Masjid** (1523), a large, richly ornamented mosque is exemplary of the Gujarati style with interesting features such as oriel windows. Few older structures of the Chauhan Rajputs remain – **Patai Rawal** palace, the domed granary Makai Kota, the 11th-12th-century Lakulisha temple and some old wells.

Pawagadh Fort ① *4 km southwest of Champaner at 880 m, US$2*, dominates the skyline and is visible for miles around. According to myth Pavagadh was believed to have been part of the Himalaya carried off by the monkey god Hanuman. Occupying a large area, it rises in three stages; the ruined fort, the palace and middle fort, and finally the upper fort with Jain and Hindu temples, which are important places of pilgrimage. Parts of the massive walls still stand. The ascent is steep and passes several ruins including the Buria Darwaza (Gate), and the Champavati Mahal, a three-storey summer pavilion. The temple at the summit had its spire replaced by a shrine to the Muslim saint Sadan Shah.

Dabhoi Fort

Dabhoi, 29 km southwest of Vadodara, was fortified by the Solanki Rajputs from 1100 and the fort was built by a King of Patan in the 13th century. Dabhoi is regarded as the birthplace of the Hindu Gujarati architectural style. The fort is a particularly fine example of military architecture with its four gates, a reservoir fed by an aqueduct and farms to provide food at times of siege. The **Vadodara Gate** (northwest) is 9-m high with pilasters on each side and carved with images depicting the reincarnation of Vishnu. The **Nandod Gate** (south) is similarly massive. The **Hira Gate** (east) with carvings, is thought to have the builder buried beneath it. **Mori Gate** (north) lies next to the old palace and on the left of this is the **Ma Kali Temple** (1225), shaped like a cross, with profuse carvings.

Sankheda

Sankheda, 20 km east of Dabhoi off the Indore Road, is famous for its distinctive colourful lacquered wood furniture which is sold in sections to be assembled into chairs and tables. There are also attractive small temples. *Sher-e-Punjab* does good omelettes and spicy North Indian food.

Chandod

South of Dabhoi, this is the meeting place of the Narmada's two tributaries with picturesque bathing ghats and several temples. You can get mechanized country style river boats to visit temples, passing some spectacular ravines and water sculpted rocks.

Chhota Udepur

Around 100 km east of Vadodara, picturesque Chhota Udepur (Chotta Udaipur), centred around a lake, was once the capital of a Chauhan Rajput princely state. The town has palaces and numerous colonial period buildings. It is the capital of a colourful tribal district where Bhils and Ratwas live in secluded hamlets of a handful of mud huts each. The huts are decorated with wall paintings called *pithoras* (tigers and other animals are favourite subjects) and protected from evil spirits by small terracotta devotional figures.

There are colourful weekly tribal *haats* or **markets** in nearby villages which offer an insight into tribal arts, crafts and culture. (The one in town is held by the lake on Saturday.) The government-run tribal **museum** in Diwan Bungalow has interesting examples of *pithoras*, folk costumes, artefacts, aboriginal weapons and handicrafts, but the labelling is in Gujarati and the attendant knows little English. West of Chhota Udepur is the tribal institute at Tejgadh, which is working to document aboriginal languages and culture in the entire country.

The imposing Rajput **Kusum Vilas** palace, set in 40 acre grounds, though Mughal in architectural style, has some impressive European decorative features inside. The large Mughal-style gardens have fountains, ponds, European marble statuary, a colonnaded art deco swimming pool and tennis courts, while the garages have old cars and interesting carriages.

Dasara Fair here is famous. Other fairs held around *Holi* (March/April) in nearby villages like Kawant, with dancing, music, gymnastics and craft stalls, offer a glimpse of tribal life. *Bhagwati* is popular for Gujarati *thalis*.

Khambhat (Cambay) → *Population: 80,400.*

Situated at the mouth of the Mahi River, Khambhat was Ahmadabad's seaport but later declined as it got silted up. Well known to Arab traders, it was governed until

1400 by the kings of Anhilwara (Patan). An English factory was established in the Nawab's Kothi in 1600 in the wake of Dutch and Portuguese ones. The **Jama Masjid** (1325) is built from materials taken from desecrated Hindu and Jain temples. The stone carvers, polishers and enamellers produce attractive jewellery and souvenirs; Dhuvaran hill has agate and jasper mines.

Surat → *Phone code: 0261. Colour map 5, A3. Population: 2.434 million.*

Situated on the banks of the Tapti River, Surat was already an important trading centre by 1600 but went into decline in the 19th century. Today it is again a rapidly growing industrial and commercial city, but despite its historic significance there is little to attract a tourist.

Ins and outs

Getting there The railway, and the confusion of ST and Private bus stations, are all a couple of kilometres east of the busy central Chowk. Sufi Baug with some hotels and restaurants are within easy reach for all arrivals. See Transport, page 1254, for further details.

Getting around The city is very spread out but there are auto-rickshaws a-plenty. From the station area they ask around Rs 10 to the Chowk and Rs 25 to the Athwa gate. **Tourist office**, Athugar St.

Background

The **Parsis**, driven from Persia, first arrived in India in the late eighth century and many moved to Surat in the 12th century. Under the Mughals the Portuguese, British, Dutch and French in turn established trading outposts. The British were the first to establish a 'factory' having arrived in 1608, and Surat remained their headquarters until they moved to Bombay in 1674 but Surat remained the mercantile capital of West India until the 18th century. The tide turned, however, in the next century, when a fire destroyed the city centre to be followed by floods when the river Tapti burst its banks This led many Parsis to move to Mumbai. Surat specializes in jewellery and diamond cutting. It also produces gold and silver thread, *kinkhab* brocades, wood and ivory inlay work. Silk weaving is a cottage industry producing the famous *Tanchoi* and *Gajee* saris. Ask the Tourist Office for details.

Sights

The **museum,** near the castle, has an interesting collection of textiles, furniture, paintings, stamps, coins and ceramics. ① *Wed-Sat 1045-1345, 1445-1745; Tue, Sun 1445-1745; Mon closed. Photography prohibited.* The tombs in the Dutch, English and Armenian **cemeteries**, however, are rather neglected and overgrown though some, like the Aungier and Oxinden mausolea, are imposing. The strong Muslim influence is evident in several 16th- and 17th-century **mosques**. There are two Parsi **Fire Temples** (1823) and the triple-domed Swami Narayan **Temple**. The Chintamani Jain temple, dating from the 15th century, has some fine wood carvings.

Excursions

Navsari, 39 km from Surat, has a historic Parsi fire temple which is one of the most important Zoroastrian pilgrim places in India. You cannot enter the temple but the building and garden are worth seeing from outside. **Dandi**, 13 km from Navsari, where Gandhiji ended his Salt March from Ahmadabad to the south Gujarat coast, and picked up a handful of salt, see page 1229. A monument marks the spot and a photo gallery depicts events in Gandhi's life.

Karadi is nearby where Gandhi was arrested after the Dandi March; his hut is still preserved. There is a small Gandhi Museum. Sleeping at the *Guest House*, very peaceful and friendly; contact '*Om Shanti*', Matwad (English spoken).

Bharuch

At the mouth of the Narmada River, Bharuch (Broach) 72 km south of Vadodara, which flourished in the first century AD, is one of the oldest seaports in Western India. Mentioned as Barugaza by the Romans around 210 AD it was ruled by a Gurhara Prince and much later came under the rule of the Solanki Rajputs.**The Bhrigu Rishi Temple** from which the town got its name 'Bhrigukachba', is on the bank of the river Narmada. It subsequently developed at the lowest crossing of the river, a point of strategic importance. The current walls were built by the Marathas in 1675 and 1686. The **fort** overlooks the Narmada. Within it are the Collector's Office, Civil Courts, the old Dutch factory, a church and the Victoria Clocktower. Below the fort is the **Jama Masjid** (early 14th century), built from a demolished Jain temple in accordance with conventional mosque design. Just over 3 km west of the fort are some early **Dutch tombs**, overlooked by some Parsi Towers of Silence.

Saputara → *Phone code: 02631. Colour map 5, A3. Altitude: 50-1083 m.*

Saputara, a pleasant hill resort created after independence in the Sahayadri hills, is Gujarat's only hill station. Set in a tribal region, there is an attractive lake and forests nearby. It is a relaxing place to enjoy walks, scenic places and folklore but it gets very crowded during weekends and holidays.

Ins and outs

Getting there State buses run from Surat (135 km) and Nashik (Maharashtra, 80 km). Trains on the Mumbai-Ahmadabad line get you as far as Billimora (110 km), with buses to Saputara. See Transport, page 1254, for details.

Getting around The resort is ideal for walking. Best season Nov-May (monsoon Jun-Oct).

Sights

The name Saputara is derived from the snake deity which is worshipped here by the tribal people. The hub of activity at Saputara is the **lake** which has boating facilities and lake view eating places. The plateau is rather barren and not particularly appealing but there are some lovely walks around the hill resort. You could find attractive quartzite rocks, orchids and wild flowers on the trails.

Good **views** are to be had of the valley from Sunset Point, with a 10-minute ropeway service, and from Valley View Point which involves a strenuous 1.5-km climb. There are also some old Maratha hill forts which involve steep climbs – only recommended for serious trekkers. The Hatgadh fort offers superb views and a chance to see rock chats, martens and wolf snakes in cracks on the fort walls. Carry water.

The **Dangs** district comprises more than 300 villages with a population of over 150,000, more than 94% of them belonging to tribal communities. The Bhils, Kunbis, Warlis and Gamits depend on the forest for their livelihood, obtaining timber, honey and lac. They are known for their traditional musical instruments and vigorous dances performed wearing wooden masks. Most villages have a shrine to Wagha-Deva, the tiger God, sculpted on stone. The Dangs Cultural and Ecological **Museum**, with a stone serpent at the entrance, offers an insight into the tribal area and the natural history of the Dangs. There are interesting dioramas, folk costumes, tribal weaponry and musical instruments. The Artists' Village conducts workshops of bamboo crafts, *papier maché* and pottery.

Excursion

The *Dangs Darbar* held at Ahwa, 32 km north, is celebrated with a **tribal fair** around March/April. Tribal chieftains called Bhil Rajas and Kunbi Rajas, who still receive privy purses from the government, are honoured during this festival. For *Nag Panchami* tribal huts are decorated with paintings.

Daman → *Phone code: 02636. Colour map 5, A3. Population: 35,700.*

Daman, on the coast, retains something of the atmosphere of its distinctive Portuguese inheritance which linked it both with Mediterranean Europe and Africa. A few people still use Portuguese in everyday speech.

Ins and outs

Getting there The nearest railway station is at Vapi (13 km southeast) on the Mumbai-Ahmadabad line. From there you can get taxis for transfer (Rs 20 entry fee) or walk about 600m for a bus. Long distance buses run from the major cetnres. All,

Daman town

N

0 metres 200
0 yards 200

Sleeping
1 Diamond
2 Gurukripa
3 Paradise
4 PWD Bungalow
5 Sovereign

Eating
1 Samrat

including those from Vapi, arrive at the main bus stand in Nani Daman. See Transport, page 1255, for further details. Avoid the Indian holiday periods.

Getting around The settlement north of the river, still known as *Nani* (small) Daman, is where most of the accommodation is. To the south, within walking distance across the river, *Moti* (large) Daman has a few colonial remains. Bicycles can be hired in Nani Daman bazar. **Tourist offices** On Main Devka Rd, Dena Bank Building, T255104.

History

The 380 sq km enclave of Daman, along with Diu and Goa, were Portuguese possessions until taken over by the Indian Government in 1961. Its association with Goa ceased when the latter became a 'State' in 1987. It is now a Union Territory with its own Pradesh Council. Daman developed at the mouth of the tidal estuary of the Daman Ganga River as a trading centre from 1531. Much of its early commerce was with the Portuguese territories in East Africa. Later (1817-1837), it was a link in the opium trade chain until this was broken by the British.

Sights

Moti Daman retains something of the Portuguese atmosphere. The landward (east) side has a moat and drawbridge. The shaded main street inside the **fort** wall runs north-south between attractive arched gateways which have Portuguese arms carved on them. One shows a saint carrying a sword but the sculpted giants on the doorways are modelled on the guardian *dwarpalas* at entrances to Hindu temples.

The former **Governor's Palace** and other administrative buildings are along the main road while towards the south end is the old **Cathedral Church of Bom Jesus**, started in 1559 but consecrated in 1603. Large and airy when the main south door is open, the chief feature is its painted and gilt wooden altar reredos and pulpit. Much of the ornamentation, notably the gold crowns of the saints, have been stolen. On the west side of the small square is the old **jail**, still in use. To the south, against the fort wall, is the **Rosario Chapel**, formerly the Church of the Madre Jesus, with a unique feature in Indian churches of carved and gilded wooden panels illustrating stories from the life of Christ. These include the adoration of the Magi, Jesus teaching in the synagogue as a child, and Mary's ascension. The carved ceiling features charming cherubs.

Jampore beach, planted with casuarina groves, 3 km south of Moti Daman, has a sandy beach with safe swimming but is otherwise not particularly appealing. **Nani Daman**, north of the river, is reached by a bridge across Daman Ganga which gives attractive views of Moti Daman's walls and the country fishing boats on either bank. The smaller **fort** here encloses a church, now used as a school, and a cemetery. Some of the old houses retain beautifully carved wooden doors and lintels. The crowded town is thick with bars trading on Gujarat's prohibition of alcohol.

Listings: Vadodara and the Old Forts

 Sleeping

Vadodara *p1243, map p1244*
AL-A Vadodara (Welcomgroup), RC Dutt Rd (west from station), T330033, F330050, vadodara@itchotel.co.in 102 rooms, some cramped, golf arranged.
B-C Express, RC Dutt Rd near *Vadodara*, T337001, F330980. Central a/c, 65 rooms, restaurants (excellent *thalis*), cake/Indian

sweet shop, good travel desk, helpful staff, day tariff, unimpressive exterior but pleasant atmosphere.
C Rama Inn (Best Western), Sayajiganj, T362831. 74 modern rooms, half a/c, near railway, 'wine shop', small gym (sauna extra), small pool.
C-D Kaviraj, RC Dutt Rd, T323401. 30 rooms, some a/c, some with hot water, restaurant, 'Wine shop' issues permits (closes 1830).

C-D Sayaji, Sayajiganj, T363030. 53 a/c rooms, restaurants, pleasant rooftop dining (good *thalis*), business centre.

C-D Surya, Sayajiganj, T361361. 82 rooms (most a/c), restaurant (wide choice, good thalis), friendly.

C-D Surya Palace, opposite Parsi Agiari, Sayajiganj, T363366. 105 a/c rooms, extensive buffet lunch in a/c restaurant, efficient business services.

C-D Yuvraj, near ST stand, T795252. 45 a/c rooms, restaurant, pool, gym, business centre.

D Ambassador, Sayajiganj, near railway station, T362726. Good sized rooms with bath, some a/c, could be cleaner, travel desk.

D-E Utsav, Prof Amnekrao Rd, T435859. 28 a/c rooms, restaurants, exchange, good value, courtesy coach.

E Rajdhani, Dandia Bazar, T421113. 22 rooms, some a/c, restaurant (good *thalis* and Chinese), helpful travel desk. Cheap hotels near the railway.

E Apsara, Sayajiganj near railway station, T362051. All rooms with bath and phone, some a/c, popular.

E-F Green, opposite Circuit House, T336111. 22 rooms, in old building, a bit run-down, but clean and good value for budget travellers, surprisingly free from fly nuisance.

Champaner *p1245*

E Hotel Champaner, T45641, is on a plateau reached by cable car, 32 rooms and dorm, pleasant garden. The Cafeteria with good views, serves snacks.

In **Machi**: like other entrances to pilgrim spots, Machi has a plethora of food stalls and cheap guesthouses.

Chandod *p1246*

D-E Sarita Haveli, 10 mins walk from the river, 19th century, simple rooms, some a/c, dorm beds (Rs 150),library, period furniture, homecooked Indian food in courtyard, bullock cart tours of Juna Mandwa village, walking tours in the ravines, friendly, a bit shabby but good value.

Chhota Udepur *p1246*

B-C Prem Bhuvan. 7 rooms with bath (hot showers) in the renovated *Kusum Vilas*

outhouse, modernized interiors, (5 more are being renovated), pool, sports, set meals, (packages Rs 1500-2000).

C Tribal Huts, set beside a stream. Simple cottages designed along the lines of tribal huts but with aircooler and modern bathrooms, economical restaurant.

E-F Gita, Shradha and **Bhagwati Lodge**, near the bus station, offer spartan rooms (Indian squat toilets, hard beds).

Khambhat *p1246*

E Premalaya, originally the Nawab's bungalow, now a government guesthouse, has a/c rooms, pleasant dining room and galleries with seaviews, good value.

Surat *p1247*

A Holiday Inn, Athwa Lines, Parle Point, T226565, F227294. 140 rooms, good restaurant (breakfast included), modern, attractive location, riverside pool, health club, efficient, courteous staff, the most pleasant stay in town.

B Lord's Park Inn, Ring Rd, T418300, F413921, lordsint@bom6.vsnl.net.in. 102 rooms, a popular new business hotel.

B-C Embassy, Sufi Baug, near station, T443170, F443173. 60 a/c rooms, some with tubs, popular restaurant (North Indian, Gujarati *thalis*), modern, pleasant.

B-D Central Excellency, opposite railway station, T425324, F441271. 46 rooms (mostly a/c) with TV, fridge and other modern facilities.

C Yuvraj, opposite railway station, near Sufi Baug, T413001, F413007. 35 rooms, central a/c, good restaurant, rooftop garden café, modern with business services.

C-D Tex Palazzo, Ring Rd, T623018, F620980. 39 rooms, half a/c, restaurants, on a crowded main road.

D Oasis, near Vaishali Cinema, Varachha Rd, T641124. 25 rooms, some a/c, restaurants, garden, permit room, pool, favoured by diamond merchants!

D Bellevue, Sumul Dairy Rd, near railway station, T437807, F412640. 34 modern rooms with baths, some **C**, business hotel.

D Everyday Inn, near Civil Court, T665154, F664230. 8 a/c doubles with bath (hot water) and TV in a house by the main road.

Gujurat Listings: Vadodara & the Old Forts

● *For an explanation of the sleeping and eating price codes used in this guide, see inside the*
● *front cover. Other relevant information is found in Essentials pages 52-57.*

Opposite the station:
E Sarvajanik, T426434. Clean rooms with bath, hot water.
F Vihar. Has rooftop views of the city, friendly and safe.

Saputara *p1248*

B Patang, T37631, comfortable a/c rooms, the plushest in town.
B-C Vaity, Chimney Ropeway near Sunset Point, T37210, F37213. Superbly situated on a hill with a panoramic views, clean, comfortable rooms, lawn, friendly staff but 'unsophisticated' management, guides for surrounding excursions on weekdays.
B-C Shavshanti Lake Resort, Nageshwar Mahadev Rd, T37292, F37245. 25 rooms with modern facilities.
C-D Anando, T37202. 23 rooms with baths set on different levels facing the lake, vegetarian restaurant, good views.
C-D Toran Hill Resort (Gujarat Tourism), near Bus Stand T/F37226. Cottages and log huts, dorms, restaurant (thalis Rs 25-35). Book at any Tourism office.
D Chitrakut, T37221. Well situated with view of hills, average rooms with bath.
Other cheaper places near the bus stand.
E Shilpi, T37231. 10 rooms, clean and comfortable, attached baths, set back from main road towards the hills, restaurant (meals included). The restaurant *Vaity*, offers the widest choice including non-veg, and good views and outdoor seating.

Daman *p1249, map p1249*

Nani Daman (on crowded Seaface Rd)
C-D Gurukripa, T255046. 25 large a/c rooms with bath, good restaurant (wide choice of Punjabi, Gujarati, some Chinese), roof garden, car hire.
C-D Suruchi Beach Resort, Daman-Vapi Rd, T55134. 53 a/c rooms with a range of modern facilities, rooftop restaurant, with river views, pool, lawn, but not near a beach and no sea views.
D Sovereign, T55023. 24 a/c rooms, clean, secure, friendly, veg restaurant (good Gujarati *thali*), chilled beer, travel desk.
Plenty of cheap places on the seafront.
E Sanman, Tin Batti, T255730. Rooms facing a busy main road, some a/c.

Jampore Beach

D China Town, T254920. 20 rooms (some a/c), few with sea view but short beds, shower and toilets could improve, friendly helpful staff, good restaurant serves Chinese/Indian food (fresh Pomfret and other fish, prawns/shrimps in season), bar does pinacoladas with fresh coconuts, both handy for visitors to beach.

Devka Beach

B-C Cidade de Daman, T250590. 72 breezy, a/c rooms in impressive hotel, pool, popular for conferences.
B-C Silver Sands, T54376 silversa@bom3.vsnl.net.in. 32 rooms, modern facilities, pool, bar, disco, across the road from the beach.
C Dariya Darshan, T54476, F54826. 38 modern a/c rooms, well fitted (TV, fridge), good outdoor restaurant (but piercingly loud Hindi film music heard throughout hotel), bar, pool, gym.
C Miramar, T544971, F54934, miramar@cybervapi.com. 58 rooms (some a/c), some in cottages, sea-facing outdoor restaurant plays loud Indian film music, a/c indoors, discotheque, holiday camp atmosphere.
C Princess Park, T254323, F250800. 27 rooms, some a/c, modern facilities, restaurant, good outlook facing the sea.
C-D Sandy Resort, T254751, F254744. 46 rooms, some a/c (best upstairs), restaurant, disco, pool, the quietest and most pleasant here but across the road from the beach.
E Rahee Guest House (PWD), Marwad Rd, between Nani Daman and Devka Beach, T254614. 15 rooms in neglected old building, some with bath and hot water, cheaper with Indian WCs.

⊘ Eating

Vadodara *p1243, map p1244*
♦♦♦ Vadodara. Extensive menu, polished service, plush and pricey, but try lunch buffet; alcohol against passport or permit.
♦♦ Goodies, Race Course Rd. Parsee couple offer great baked goods.
♦♦ Kansa, Sayajiganj. Gujarati and Rajasthani *thalis*. Traditional décor, turbaned waiters.
♦♦ Kwality, Sayajiganj. Wide choice, including good Italian and Peshwari dishes served indoors or in garden.

Oriental Spice, Tilak Rd, Sayajiganj. Chinese.
Pizza King, Alkapuri. Italian. justly popular.
Surya Palace. Sumptuous buffets.
International spread, range of desserts, Rs 200.
Volga, Alankar Cinema, Sayajiganj. Good
Mughlai kebabs and Chinese.
Gokul, Kothi Char-rasta. Indian. Good
Gujarati *thalis*, small place, large local clientele.
Sahayog, 1st left past *Express Hotel*. Good
South Indian *thali* (Rs 45) and Punjabi..

Fast food
Kalyan, Fatehganj and Sayajiganj. Veg, plus
varied. Choice of the young. Bengali sweets,
savouries to take away, opposite *Express* hotel.

Surat *p1247*
China Gate, Shikar Complex, Ichhcanath Rd.
Tex Palazzo, wide choice, good *thalis* in
revolving restaurant but views not spectacular.
Yuvraj. Rooftop garden café.
Saatvik opposite rly station. Excellent,
unlimited Gujarati *thalis*, Rs 45.

Fast food
Lots of places for pizza, Indian snacks, and ice
cream on Ring Rd and Athwa Lines.

Sweets
Surat is famous for its *Nan-katai* (a bit like
shortbread) and twisty biscuits, best bought
at Parsi bakeries like **Mehr** and **Mazda** in
Bhagat Talao area and **Dotiwala** at Parle Pt.

Daman *p1249, map p1249*
You can get fresh fish lunches/dinners at
most hotels, also fish snacks at the bars.
Duke, Devka Beach. Parsi and *tandoori*
food outdoors (also rooms to let in the old
Parsi bungalow next door, Rs 400).
Damanganga Lake Garden on the
Daman-Vapi Rd. Popular lake facing restaurant,
with gardens all round and fountains. Unusual,
though garish, bar has a Mughal theme with
miniature paintings of royal drinking parties on
the bar stools, tables and chairs. Good
atmosphere and reasonable food.
Kadliya Lake Resort is an island
restaurant created by Daman Tourism, with
lawns, gardens, cascades, fountains and
boating facilities. The food upstairs is not bad
and there is a bar and snacks place
downstairs by the lake, but the service is
slow and suffers an occasional scourge of

flies and mosquitoes from the lake. Entry fee
Rs 10, camera Rs 10, car parking Rs 10.
Jampore Beach Resort, cafeteria, bar,
meals/snacks upstairs with view of sea,
outdoor dining area, hammocks for relaxing.
Samrat, Seaface Rd. Simple and clean, does
excellent *thalis*. You will find cheap Chinese
food at night outside the main gates of Moti
Daman fort.

Entertainment

Vadodara *p1243, map p1244*
MS University's Fine Arts College holds
exhibitions.

Festivals and events

Vadodara *p1243, map p1244*
Navratri is very colourful when local Garba,
Dandia and Raas performances are held, and
pilgrims head for Pawagadh.
Ganesh Chaturthi is celebrated by the large
Maharashtrian population here.

Shopping

Vadodara *p1243, map p1244*
Vadodara is a centre for silver jewellery.
Shopping areas are Raopura, Mandvi, Teen
Darwaza, National Plaza, Leheripura Mandir
Bazar and Alkapuri Arcade.
Khadi Bhandar, Kothi Rd, for handlooms
and local handicrafts.

Activities and tours

Vadodara *p1243, map p1244*
Swimming
Lal Bagh and Sardar Bagh pools, Alkapuri;
also at *Vadodara* and *Surya Palace* hotels.

Tourist offices
Gujarat Tourism, Narmada Bhawan,
C-Block, Indira Ave, T427489, F431297;
1030-1810, closed Sun, instant reservations
for Tourism and other hotels in Gujarat.
Prominent, 7/12 Race Course Circle, T300120,
F342333. Recommended for ticketing.
Sita, Sapna Centre, Alkapuri, T311280, F314334.
Tradewings, Sayajiganj, T327127, changes
money (even on Sat).
Vadodara Tourist, Municipal Corp opposite
railway station, T329656. 0900-1800.

☉ Transport

Vadodara *p1243, map p1244*
Air
Indian Airlines, Fatehgunj, T794747, 1000-1330, 1415-1700; Airport, T443262. **Mumbai, Delhi.** Jet Airways, 11 Panorama Complex, opposite Welcomgroup, Alkapuri, T337051, Airport T443938.

Bus
Local From opposite the railway station. **Long distance** State Transport (SRTCs) to **Ujjain** (403 km), **Mumbai** (425 km), **Pune, Udaipur** and **Mount Abu**, among others. Central Bus Stand, opposite railway station, T327000. Reservations 0700-2200. Advance booking 0900-1300, 1330-1700.

Taxi
Minimum Rs 10 (metered). **Tourist taxi**: from tourist office and travel agents, **Hotel Vadodara**. Non a/c Ambassador, Rs 4 per km, airport drop Rs 150, airport pick-up Rs 200, 80 km per 8 hrs, Rs 700-900. **Wheels**, TCI, T437866.

Train
Vadodara is on the Western Railways' Delhi-Mumbai broad gauge line. Sayajiganj Enquiries, T131. Reservations T135. 0800-2000 (2nd Class) and 0800-1800 (1st Class). **Ahmadabad**: many including *Gujarat Queen Exp, 9109,* 0813, 2¼ hrs; *Gujarat Exp, 9011,* 1303, 2¼ hrs; *Vadodara Ahmadabad Exp, 9129,* 1810, 2½ hrs. **Mumbai Central**: *Golden Temple Mail, 2904,* 2349, 6¼ hrs; *Kutch Exp, 9032,* 0508, 6½ hrs; *Paschim Exp, 2926,* 0852, 6¼ hrs. **New Delhi**: *Paschim Exp, 2925,* 1755, 16¾ hrs; *Rajdhani Exp, 2951,* 2153, 11 hrs. See narrow-gauge railway under Dabhoi. **Porbandar**: Mumbai *Porbandar Saurashtra Exp,* 9215, 1655, 14 hrs.

Surat *p1247*
Train
Ahmadabad: *Shatabdi Exp, 2009,* 0955, not Fri, 3½ hrs; *Gujarat Exp, 9011,* 1045, 4¾ hrs; **Mumbai Central**: *Kranti Rajdhani, 2954,* 0635, 3¾ hrs; *Paschim Exp, 2926,* 1055, 4¼ hrs. **New Delhi**: *Janata Exp, 9023,* 1325, 24 hrs; *Paschim Exp, 2925,* 1542, 19 hrs. **Porbandar**: *Mumbai Porbandar Saurashtra Exp, 9215,* 1408, 16½ hrs. **Rajkot** and **Jamnagar**: *Janata Exp, 9017,* 2132, 10½ hrs (Rajkot), 12½ hrs (Jamnagar).

Saputara *p1248*
From the NH8, the turn off for cars is at Chikhli to the west. Petrol is only available at Waghai (51 km northwest), and at a pump 40 km from Saputara, on the Nashik road. From Mumbai, there are private luxury buses (*Modern Travels*) on alternate days during the season.

Train
From Ahmadabad (400 km) or Mumbai (255 km) to **Billimora** and then local bus or taxi; or a narrow gauge train to **Waghai**.

Daman *p1249, map p1249*
Bus
For the **Bus stand**: turn right out of Vapi station, walk 500 m along main road to a T-junction; the stand is nearby, on the left.

Taxi
Taxis into Daman but shared with 8 others can be a squeeze (Rs 10 each); Rs 80 per taxi. By car, turn off the NH8 at Karmbeli between Bhilad and Vapi.

Train
Not all trains stop at **Vapi** from Mumbai. *Gujarat Exp 9011,* 0545, 3 hrs; *Saurashtra Exp 9215,* 0745, 3½ hrs. From **Ahmadabad**: *Karnavati Exp 2934,* 0500, 5¼ hrs; *Shatabdi Exp,* 2010, 1435 (except Wed) 4¾ hrs.

☉ Directory

Vadodara *p1243, map p1244*
Banks Bank of Baroda, only Sayajiganj branch changes money; also **Trade Wings** on same street, fast and efficient. **Hospital** Sayaji Hospital, Sayajiganj; **Maharani Jamunabai Hospital**, Mandvi. **Post office** GPO: Raopura. **Useful addresses** Forest office: T429748. Foreigners' Regional Registration Office: Collector's Office, Kothi Kacheri.

Surat *p1247*
Banks Exchange at State Bank of India, Chowk Rd. **Internet** Cyber Cafés, at Belgian Sq, Athwa Lines, Ambaji Rd and Bellevue Hotel, near the station.

Daman *p1249, map p1249*
Banks State Bank of India, Kabi Kabarda Rd. **Post office** GPO: near bridge to Moti Daman.

Saurashtra

Around the coastal region of the Saurashtra peninsula are some of India's most remarkable religious sites, from Dwarka in the west to Palitana in the east, while the coastline itself is fringed with some attractive beaches which includes the former Portuguese territory of Diu. The historic town of Junagadh and the wildlife parks also draw visitors. Northern Saurashtra with Rajkot at its centre, is one of the major groundnut growing regions of India. In January 2001, a massive earthquake left Limbdi, Halvad, Dhrangadra and Morvi severely damaged. Visitors should check before visiting these towns. ▸▸ For Sleeping, Eating and other listings, see pages 1262-1265.

Rajkot → *Phone code: 0281. Colour map 2, C2. Population: 966,600.*

Rajkot is a bustling commercial city with a large number of shopping complexes and accompanying heavy road traffic but there are also some fine late 19th-century colonial buildings and institutions since the British Resident for the Western Indian States lived here. It has seen rapid industrialization in the last two decades, based especially in the processing of agricultural products.

Rajkot

■ Sleeping		● Eating
1 Babha Guesthouse	4 Kavery	1 Havmor
2 Galaxy & Step-in	5 Samrat International	2 Rainbow
Fast Food	6 Tulsi & Kanchan	
3 Himalaya	Restaurant	

0 metres 300
0 yards 300

Ins and outs

Getting there The airport, 4 km northwest, has airlines' buses for transfer to town. The ST bus station is just south of the busy Dhebar Chowk at the centre, while more comfortable private long distance coaches arrive at the operators just behind it. Most hotels are central but 2-3 km from the Junction station. See Transport, page 1264, for further details.

Getting around It is possible to walk to the few sights in town quite easily from the centre. There are auto-rickshaws and taxis if you prefer.

Sights

Although there is an early Palaeolithic site at Rajkot, there is very little evidence of the settlement. Rajkot was the capital of the Jadejas, who ruled earlier from a place named Sardhar on the Rajkot-Bhavnagar road, and later set up this new city which became the headquarters of the British representatives in Saurashtra. The British impact can be seen in the impressive **Rajkumar College** in its vast grounds, a famous public school founded in 1870, and the richly endowed **Watson Museum**. The **Memorial Institute** has the crumbling Lang Library in the Jubilee Gardens in the Old Civil Lines. Rajkot was the early home of Mahatma Gandhi. **Gandhi Smriti** (Kaba Gandhino Delo) is in Ghee Kanta Road, between MG Road and Lakahjiraj Road (rickshaw-wallahs know the way). **Rashtriya Shala**, where Mahatma Gandhi went to school, is now trying to promote one of Gandhi's greatest ideals – handloom and handicrafts. Among the textiles being promoted is Patola style *ikat* silk weaving.

Museums

Watson Museum ① *0900-1230, 1430-1800, closed Wed, 2nd and 4th Sat, each month. Rs 2, camera charges Rs 2 per photo, Jubilee Gardens*, has exhibits from Indus Valley civilization, medieval sculpture, pottery and crafts, and colonial memorabilia. **Gandhi Museum** ① *Dharmandra Rd. 0900-1200; 1500-1800. Closed Sun. Descriptions are mainly in Hindi and Gujarati; guides speak no English*, in the Gandhi family home (1880), contains photographs and a few personal effects.

Excursion

Tarnetar (75 km) A betrothal fair centres around the Trineteshwar Mahadev Temple whose pond is considered auspicious as the place where Arjuna is said to have won the hand of princess Draupadi in marriage. Religious rites, bhajans and ritual bathing are a feature of the fair, as are handicraft and food stalls. Bharwad and other herdsmen sport colourful dress and ornaments during the fair to attract a suitable match. They carry *chhattris* with mirrorwork to signify bachelorhood (September). There is a Gujarat Tourism tent village.

Wankaner

On the bend of Machchu River, Wankaner (*wanka* - curve, *ner* - river), another capital of the Jhala Rajputs, was founded in 1605. The old ruler, Amar Sinhji was known for his flamboyant lifestyle but also introduced many wide-ranging reforms (in farmers' co-operatives, education, roads, tramways and internal security). He was also responsible for building the **Ranjitvilas Palace** (1907 extension to the 1880s British Residents' bungalow), visible for miles across the plains. It is built in a strange mix of styles (Venetian façades, a Dutch roof, *jarokha* balconies, a 'Mughal' pavilion, minarets, English clocktower etc) yet all is very well integrated. The garage has an interesting collection of models from the 1930s and 40s and a 1921 Silver Ghost, jeeps, wagons and old buggies. Kathiawadi horses in the stables. A part of the palace is now a **museum** brim full of royal memorabilia of a bygone lifestyle. There is an interesting stepwell with marble balustrade staircases, cool, subterranean chambers and marble statues of Vishnu and a fountain.

Morvi

The tiny princely state, Morvi, dominated access to the peninsula. It developed into a modern state under Thakur Sahib Waghaji (ruled 1879-1948). His aggressive reforms made it one of the most affluent princely states of Saurashtra. A suspension bridge connects the two palaces.

The 1880s **Darbargadh** palace with a riverside façade, inspired by the merchant mansions of Venice, was badly damaged in the 2001 earthquake. It has now undergone repairs. There are rooms if you wish to stay. **B**, facing courtyard, outdoor restaurant, or a good value, cheaper option, **D-E** *Thacker Lodge*, on the main Bhuj Road.

Dhrangadra

The pretty little village town of Dhrangadra is the government Forest Department's headquarters for the Little Rann of Kachchh Wild Ass Sanctuary, T02754-23016. It was also the capital of a very progressive princely state, which had English and vernacular schools in 1855 and free education in the early 1900s. After it has recovered from the 2001 earthquake damage it should be possible to visit the Wild Ass Sanctuary from here. Wildlife guide DP Arts, T50560, is very knowledgeable and friendly. Full day jeep tour of Little Rann – wild asses, salt mining communities, bird sanctuary – is Rs 1,800 for two, including delicious homecooked lunch.

Bhavnagar → *Phone code: 0278. Colour map 5, A2. Population: 511,000.*

Bhavnagar was ruled by progressive rulers since it was founded in 1723. Surrounded by flat and richly cultivated land, it is now a major industrial town and cotton export centre, and is rapidly becoming one of India's most important ship-building ports. However, most of its character is preserved in the bazars of the Old City where you can pick your way through the crowded lanes amongst the old merchants' havelis.

Ins and outs

Getting there The airport is 5 km southeast of town; auto-rickshaws to town insist on Rs 60-70. Hotels are scattered around with no budget option close to the ST bus station and only one within easy reach of the railway. Private bus operators have offices spread around town. See Transport, page 1265, for further details.

Getting around It is best to hire an auto or taxi to see the town.

History

The Gohil Rajputs came to Gujarat from Rajasthan in the 1240s and set up rule along the coast of southeastern Saurashtra. Bhavnagar was one of the most affluent states of Saurashtra. The city was developed by a series of progressive rulers, from the flamboyant Maharajah Takth Sinhji, who commissioned European architects to build grand palaces and public buildings, to the humble Bhav Sinhji, who founded this as a port city and introduced educational and judicial reforms. Krishnakumar Sinhji was one of the first Indian princes to hand over his state unconditionally to the nation.

Sights

The palace-like **Takhtsinghji Hospital** (1879-83) was designed by Sir William Emerson. The 18th-century **Darbargadh** (Old Palace, extended 1894-5), in the town centre, now has the State Bank but is scarcely visible in the incredibly overcrowded and dirty Darbargadh Bazar. The unremarkable marble **Takhteshwar Temple** on a hillock has good views over the city and the distant coastline.

Victoria Park, 2 km from centre, is a former royal hunting preserve. Far removed from the image conveyed by its name of a manicured British city park, it has rolling scrub-forests and marshes rich in birdlife. Nilgai, hyena, jackal, jungle cat and monitor lizard can all be seen. A pleasant stroll from the Nilambagh Palace, it is a great place for walks. **Gaurishankar Lake**, a popular escape from the city with parks and steps along the embankments, is good for winter birdwatching when cranes, pelicans and ducks arrive. Plovers, terns etc nest on the islands.

Museums

The complex includes the **Barton Museum** (1895) ① *0900-1300, 1400-1800, Rs 2, photography prohibited*, in an impressive crescent-shaped building, which has a collection of coins, carvings, geological and archaeological finds, farming implements, arms and armour, some handicrafts, miniature paintings and excellent bead and silk embroidery. The better known **Gandhi Smriti** ① *upstairs, 0830-1230, 1500-1900. Free. All are closed Sun, and 2nd and 4th Sat each month. Ask for a leaflet in English at entrance (small fee). Postcards, booklets and local handicrafts are sold at a shop here,* is dedicated to Mahatma Gandhi (he was at university here; his old college is now an Ayurvedic education centre). Photographs portray his life and the freedom struggle. There are also letters and marksheets showing his scores at university. The top floor is dedicated to arts and crafts of India.

Velavadhar National Park

The compact 36-sq km of flat grassland broken by dry open scrubland with some thorn forest was set up to protect the Indian blackbuck of which it has the largest population – about 1,000 within and another 1,000 which come in from the surrounding area. The Bhavnagar royal family came here for cheetah coursing, falconry and hunting, and also harvested grass for fodder for their cattle and horses. ① *Foreigners US$5, still camera US$5; guide (some have no English), US$10 per trip, jeep US$25 per drive. Pay at Forest*

Bhavnagar

Range Office at park entrance. The park is 10 km off the Bhavnagar-Vadodara Highway. Getting there: few buses from Bhavnagar; better to hire a car. Alternatively hire a Jeep/chhakra (motorbike trailer) from Vallabhipur. A new bridge being built near Bhavnagar port to near the park will make access faster and easier.)

The **blackbuck** is the second largest of the antelopes and the fastest long distance runner of all animals. It can keep going at a steady 90 km per hour. The black and white dominant males sport spiral horns; the juvenile males are brown and white while the hornless females are brownish, with lighter parts. It is one of the most hunted animals in India, and so is an endangered species. Impressive males clash horns to establish territory and court females. Wolves, their prime predator, have been reduced to only two families, but they can still be seen. The park also contains a few sounders of wild boar in addition to 50-60 nilgai, usually seen near waterholes, jungle cat, which can be seen at dawn and dusk, and jackal. It has a rich birdlife with numerous birds of prey including the largest harrier roost in the world - some 1,500-2,000 of these light-bodied hawks gather here at sunset in November-December. During the monsoons the park is the best place in India for the lesser florican. Roger Clark (Hawk & Owl Trust), New Hythe House, Reach, Cambridge, England, brings birding tours, specializing in birds of prey. In addition to the two rivers that border the park, there are three waterholes and three small pools which attract animals at midday.

Sihor

Mid-way between Bhavnagar (27 km) and Palitana, the former Gohil Rajput capital has the 17th-century hilltop Darbargadh palace (now government offices). Though rather dilapidated, you can still see some intricate carved wooden balconies and pillars outside and 19th-century wall paintings inside. The **Brahm Kund**, 11th-12th century, 500 m to the south of the main road, about 2 km west of Sihor centre, is a deeply set stepped tank (now empty). It has around 100 sculpted images of deities in small niches, a few of which are still actively worshipped. There are also pillared galleries with rich carvings of musicians. In the village nearby brass utensils are produced as a cottage industry by rolling scrap from the Alang ship breaking yard and beating it into attractive water pots. Villagers are only too happy to show you around their workshops. The Khodiyar temple on the Bhavnagar-Sihor road has a pretty situation among hills

---

★ Palitana → *Phone code: 02848. Colour map 5, A2. Population: 51,900. Area: 13 sq km.*

Palitana is renowned for the extraordinary Jain temple complex on Shatrunjaya Hill which attracts domestic pilgrims as well as foreign visitors. No one is allowed to remain on the hill at night, but even during the day there is a peaceful serenity as you listen to the temple bells and pilgrims chanting in the City of the Gods.

The town

Palitana was the capital of a small princely state founded by Shahji, a Gohel Rajput who belonged to the same clan as the Maharajah of Bhavnagar. The river bisects the town. The east bank has the hotels, eating places and shopping complexes and the bus and railway stations, while the west bank has the Willingdon Vegetable Market, vegetable vendors and some older Raj and royal buildings. The last ruler died leaving wives and sisters to fight over the royal palace and mansions which are now decaying but show signs of impressive architecture. The better houses are on Taleti Road. The busy little town is also known for diamond cutting and horse breeding. South African diamonds are imported from Belgium for cutting and polishing before being re-exported back to Belgium.

ⓘ *0700-1900. Entry by a free permit at the entrance to the southern ridge. Camera Rs 40. Rules: visitors should wear appropriate, clean clothes; leather articles (even watch straps) and food or drink are not allowed in the temple area at the top of the hill, but can be left, along with shoes, at the entrance. Cloth and plastic footwear, and walking sticks, are available for hire at the bottom of the hill. Take lots of water and a sun hat. Foreign visitors are required to sign a register before entering. Arrive by dawn to join the pilgrims, and allow 2 hrs for the climb, and 4 to 5 hrs for the round trip. You can be carried up by a* dhooli *(string chair – Rs 500 return) but the hassle from aggressive touts in the early stages of the climb can be considerable. Rates rise in summer, peaking during fairs and Mahavir Jayanti to Rs 1000.*

Shatrunjaya Hill is 3 km southwest. According to local tradition, Adinatha, the first Tirthankara, visited the hill several times and the first temple was erected by his son. Thereafter, the temple builders could not stop. Jains believe that Pundarika, the chief disciple of Adinatha, attained nirvana here.

Most of the temples are named after their founders and are mostly 16th century although the earliest may date from the 11th. It would appear that many others were destroyed by the Muslims in the 14th and 15th centuries, but later, when Jains obtained religious toleration they began rebuilding.

All the 863 temples are strung along the two ridges of the hill, with further temples in the hollow between, linking them. There are nine enclosures of fortifications (tuks) which provided defence. There are lovely views over the flat, cultivated black soils of the coastal plain, and on a clear day after the rains it is sometimes possible to see the Gulf of Khambat away to the east, and the Chamardi peak and the granite range of Sihor to the north.

There are two routes up the 600 m climb. The main route starts in the town of Palitana to the east of the hill, while a shorter and steeper route climbs up from the villages of Adpur to the west. Both are excellently made stepped paths. The main pilgrim route starts in Palitana. Over 3,500 steps, you will be told more by the *dhoolie* carriers at the bottom, lead up to the temples. There are two long flat stretches, but since some of the path is unshaded, even in winter it can get very hot.

Temples in this southern group include one of **Ramaji Gandharia** (16th century), and the **Bhulavani** (labyrinth, 18th century) which is a series of crypt-like chambers each surmounted with a dome. The **Hathiapol** (Elephant Gate, 19th century) faces southeast. The **Vimalavasi Tuk** occupies the west end of the south Ridge. In it is the **Adishvara Temple** (16th century) which dominates the site. It has a double-storey *mandapa* inside which is a large image of Rishabhanatha with crystal eyes and a gold crown of jewels. The

Palitana

Sleeping
1 Pathik Ashram
2 Rest House
3 Shravak
4 Shrinath
5 Sumeru & Gujarat Tourism

Temple (1836) occupy the middle ground between the ridges.

The **Khartaravasi Tuk** is the largest and highest temple complex, stretched out along the northern Ridge and includes the **Adinatha Temple** (16th century). There are quadruple *Tirthankara* images inside the sanctuary.

If you wish to take the track down to Adpur turn left out of the complex entrance courtyard where you leave your shoes. Follow the sign to Gheti Pag gate.

Alang

① *Getting there: from Bhavnagar: buses from ST Bus Stand, through the day from 0600 (last return 1800), 1¾ hrs, Rs 10. At Alang, tongas go up and down the beach front past the shipyards for Rs 5. Taxis take 1½ hrs, Rs 400-500 return, and auto-rickshaws Rs 300-400 (expect to bargain).*

The beach has turned into the world's largest scrapyard for dead ships, the industry yielding rich pickings from the sale of salvaged metal (bronze, copper) and the complete range of ship's fittings from doors and portholes to diesel engines and lifeboats.

Alang village, 50 km south of Bhavnagar, has developed this surprising specialization because of the unusual nature of its tides. The twice monthly high tides are exceptional, reputedly the second highest tides in the world, lifting ships so that they can be beached well on shore, out of reach of the sea for the next two weeks. During this period the breakers can move in unhindered. Labourers' 'huts' line the coast road though many workers commute from Bhavnagar.

Even though entry to Alang port may not be available, the last few kilometres to the port are lined with the yards of dealers specialising in every item of ships' furniture. Valuable items are creamed off before the 'breaking' begins, but if you want 3 cm thick porthole glass, a spare fridge-freezer or a life jacket, this is the place to browse. However, customs officers always get first choice of valuables as they have to give permission for vessels to be beached, so don't expect too much. Some visitors have found the journey not worth the trouble since they couldn't enter the fenced off 'Lots'.

Alang is only open to tourists with **special permission** – obtained from the Gujarat Maritime Board at Sector 10A, opposite Air Force Station, Gandhinagar, T02842-35222 or Port Officer, New Port, Bhavnagar 5, T293090. Foreigners are finding it difficult to get permission to enter the beach/port area. Hotels in Bhavnagar may be able to help individuals gain entry but permits for groups are virtually impossible. Photography is not allowed. Strong shoes and modest dress are recommended. Take food and drink.

Mahuva

The fairly picturesque town (pronounced Mow-va), south of Palitana, was known for its historic port. Beautiful handcrafted furniture with lacquerwork and intricate hand-painting, is made here. A new port and ship-breaking yard is under construction at **Pip-a-vav** 25 km to the west.

Gopnath

About 30 km northeast of Mahuva, Gopnath is where the 16th-century mystic poet, Narsinh Mehta is said to have attained enlightenment. Near the lighthouse, the 1940s mansion of late Maharajah Krishna Kumar Singhji of Bhavnagar was the summer home, a part of which is now a hotel. There are pleasant rocky, white-sand beaches – dangerous for swimming but good for walking– and a 700-year-old temple, a kilometre away.

Listings: Saurashtra

◉ Sleeping

Rajkot *p1255, map p1255*
There are nondescript cheap hotels near the station and bus stand.

B-C Kavery, near GEB, Kanak Rd, T239331, F231007, kavery@planetace.com. 33 a/c rooms, modern facilities, good restaurants, exchange.

C Aditya, opposite Rajshri Cinema, T222003, F229901. 40 rooms, most with a/c, some dearer suites, restaurant, travel desk.

C-D Galaxy, Jawahar Rd (above Commercial Centre), T222904. 37 very well furnished, clean rooms, most a/c, pleasant roof-garden, exchange (including TCs, credit cards), well run, courteous and efficient, no restaurant but excellent room service to bring in food, access by lift only. Recommended.

C-D Samrat International, 37 Karanpura, T222269. 32 decent rooms, some a/c, a/c vegetarian restaurant, exchange.

D Tulsi, Kante Shree Vikas Guru Rd, T231731, F231735. 33 rooms, some a/c, excellent but bit pricey *Kanchan* restaurant, exchange, clean, modern hotel.

D-E Babha Guest House, Panchnath Rd, T220861, hotelbabha@rajkot.com. Small, good value rooms, some a/c, excellent veg *thali*.

D-E Himalaya, Lakhajiraj Rd, T231736. Cleanish rooms with bath (bucket hot water), good value, very popular.

D-E Railway Retiring Rooms on 1st floor. 3 clean rooms (1 a/c), 4-bed dorm, reasonable veg restaurant, good value.

Wankaner *p1256*
C-D Royal Oasis, T02828-20000, F20002, guest house of the *Ranjitvilas* in large fruit orchards with original 1930s art deco features, interesting rooms but mosquitoes can be a problem, pool, meals at the palace (slow erratic service, "arrives cold") but worth it if presided over by Maharajah Pratap Singh in his 90s, who is a fund of historic anecdotes.

Bhavnagar *p1257, map p1258*
B Neelambagh Palace, Ahmadabad Rd, T429323, F428072, www.fhraindia.com/ hotel/bhavnagar/nilambag. 1850s palace, 27 upmarket a/c rooms, long bathrooms with tubs (main palace better than cottage annexe), lobby with intricate wood carving, chandeliers, royal portraits, grand banquet hall now restaurant, vast gardens with peacocks, beautiful stepped pool.

B Dil Bahar, Waghawadi Rd, opposite Victoria Park, T568391. 2 km out of town with extensive views. Former 1937 royal hunting lodge retaining art deco features, 4 a/c rooms, dated bathrooms, no TV or phone, period furniture (ask to see the 'Indian' room), home-cooked food (Indian, continental), pool (Apr-Jun), memorabilia, friendly staff, peaceful, advance bookings: *North West Safaris*, T079-6302019, F6300962, ssibal@ad1.vsnl.net.in

B-C Sun 'n' shine, Panwadi, T516131, F516130. Attractive hotel with fountains in the lobby but located on busy main road. 46 comfortable rooms, popular vegetarian restaurant, health club (gym, sauna), travel desk, internet.

C Blue Hill, 500 m from bus, Pill Gardens, T426951, F427313. 40 a/c rooms with bath, **B** suites (traditional Gujarati lacquered furniture, best with jacuzzi), a/c vegetarian restaurant, roof garden, popular with businessmen, comfortable hotel with a view of gardens (storks nest on the nearby trees in winter).

C-D Jubilee, next to *Blue Hill*, T430045, F421744. 33 a/c rooms, 10 newer dearer, *Woodlands* a/c restaurant (good for Indian), exchange, car hire.

E-F Vrindavan, Darbargadh, T519149, F513022. Part of the old Darbargadh complex (18th-19th century) converted to a budget hotel, 100 rooms, some with baths but only a few have western toilets, some **D** a/c, also Rs 50 dorm beds, a/c Gujarati restaurant (*thali* Rs 50), rather noisy surroundings, helpful owner.

F Mini, Station Rd, T424415, F421246. Small hotel with clean rooms (some windowless), some a/c with TV (Rs 25), excellent value, very helpful and friendly manager, bus tickets, ISD phone, internet, good restaurant and cycle hire down the road.

F Shital, Amba Chowk, half-way between railway and bus station, entrance in alley at

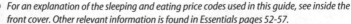

back, T428360. Some rooms with bath (bucket hot water), and men's dorm.

Velavadhar National Park *p1258*
B Kaliyar Bhuvan Forest Lodge, simple but adequate, 5 small rooms, reasonably furnished, but prohibitively priced. Reserve at Forest Office in Bhavnagar.

Sihor *p1259*
There are a few places to eat and for an overnight stop there is:
D-E Vijay Palace, with simple rooms with baths, some a/c.

Palitana *p1259, map p1260*
Difficult to find cheap rooms but dormitory beds are Rs 20-50.
B Vijay Vilas Palace (Heritage Hotel), in Adpur, a cattle herders' village ringed by hills. 3 rooms in 1906 lodge (Italian country house feel), gradually being restored. Delicious homecooked Indian meals (non-residents Rs 250 with advance notice), 7 km from town (rickshaws Rs 50, shared motorbike-rickshaws Rs 4). The shorter but steeper route to the Palitana temple complex starts a few hundred metres away at the temple in Adpur village (follow the milk maids carrying curd!). Book ahead through *North West Safaris*, T079-6302019, F6300962, ssibal@ad1.vsnl.net.in
C-D Sumeru (Gujarat Tourism), Station Rd, near Bus Stand, T2327. 7 rooms, 3 a/c, 5 dorms (Rs 50) with cold water only, limited menu restaurant, Tourist Office, check-out 0900, unfavourable reports.
D-E Shrinath, Natraj Shopping Complex, ST Rd, T2542. 18 tiny rooms, dorm beds, some with western toilets, extremely clean and comfortable, (laundry, international phone nearby).
E Shravak, opposite Central bus station, T2428. 18 rooms with baths (western toilets, hot shower), cheaper with Indian wc, men's dorm but not too clean.
F Patel House, Station Rd, T42441. Run by private farmer's trust, rather basic and impersonal but set around an open courtyard that shuts off some of the traffic noise, double rooms (cold taps, hot water in buckets, Indian toilet), some 4 and 6-bedded.

Numerous **dharamshalas**, some with modern facilities cater mostly for Jain pilgrims.

Gopnath *p1261*
B-C Gopnath Bungalow. Beautiful seaviews, 3 rooms in royal mansion, 4 clean, well-renovated rooms in the "English" bungalow (cheaper) in a rambling complex, great views of sea and cliffs, meals on request, pool, understaffed so expect inconveniences. Contact: Nilambagh Palace, Bhavnagar, T0278-424241.

● Eating

Rajkot *p1255, map p1255*
†† **Havmor**, Jawahar Rd, near *Galaxy Hotel*. Good non-veg food (varied menu, mainly Chinese), a/c.
†† **Lakshmi Lodge** in road opposite *Rainbow*. Good *thalis*.
†† **Royal Orchid**, Kalawad Rd. Variety of vegetarian dishes.
†† **Rainbow** Lakhajiraj Rd. Good South Indian, very busy In the evenings when you may have to queue outside.
†† **Step-In**, Galaxy Centre, Jawahar Rd. Pizzas, Indian fast food and ice creams.

Bhavnagar *p1257, map p1258*
††† **Nilambagh**, Banquet Hall (chandeliers, Belgian mirrors, Burma teak furniture), Wide choice. Good tandoori food. Garden restaurant at night is pleasant, except for loud Hindi film music.
†† **Bageecha**, Waghawadi Rd. Wide choice of vegetarian in attractive garden setting, well appointed.
†† **Greenland**, Krishnanagar, near Barton museum. North Indian and ice creams in a pleasant garden setting.
†† **Live-in**, Waghawadi Rd. Roof garden, Indian/Chinese vegetarian.
†† **Murli**, Panwadi Chowk, T431037. Excellent *thalis*.
†† **Nilgiri**, at *Blue Hill*. Excellent Indian vegetarian (try *palak paneer* and cheese naan), also *idli, dosa* at tea time, a/c.
   Gujarati *thali* places in the main market area include:
† **Evening Point**. Traditional Kathiawadi *thali* in a rustic setting.

● *Phone codes Rajkot: 0281; Bhavnagar: 0278; Palitana: 02848*

Fast food

❤Baker's Basket, Gogha Circle. For cakes and snacks.

❤Black Cat, Gogha Circle. For vegetarian Indian and good cakes.

❤Laxmi, near Pratap Garage, Waghawadi Rd. For homecooked delights, best *'kachoris, gulab jamuns* and *samosas* in Gujarat'.

❤Live-in, Waghawadi Rd. Rooftop café, a young people's hangout.

Das, near Nilambagh, Ramkrishna, near Piramal Chowk, and Khatri, on Waghawadi Rd, have melt-in-the mouth sweets (try *sangam*, a cashew nut candy, or the local *pedas*) and savoury snacks like the famous Bhavnagar *ganthias*.

Palitana *p1259, map p1260*

❤Mansi Park, Bhavnagar Rd. North Indian, Chinese. Pleasant open-air restaurant, tables on the lawn and in kiosks, hill views (main dishes Rs 35-50), also tea time treats (cheese toast, finger chips, *idli, dosa*).

Many eateries in Taleti Rd offer Gujarati *thali* as well as *pau-bhaji* and ice cream. Along Station Rd, *thalis* are Rs 10-15.

Gopnath *p1261*

❤Jai Chamunda, opposite *Gopnath Bungalow*, outdoor eating place though fairly clean, gets rather overcrowded and noisy on Sun. Good Kathiawadi veg thalis with unlimited refills (Rs 45), Rs 10 for local desserts; seafood at night to order (catch of the day lobster Rs 400, shrimps Rs 200 per kg).

⊛ Festivals and events

Palitana *p1259, map p1260*

Teras Fair at Gheti (Adpur-Palitana, 4 km from town) 3 days before *Holi*. Thousands of Jain pilgrims attend, joined by villagers who come for free lunches!

⦾ Shopping

Bhavnagar *p1257, map p1258*

Textiles, locally embroidered cushion covers, shawls, *bandhni* and mock-silver jewellery are good buys. Try Vora Bazar, Radhanpuri Market, Amba Chowk, Darbargadh Lane and Talao fruit-and-veg market. Handlooms and handicrafts are best at Khadi stores in the Barton Museum building.

Palitana *p1259, map p1260*

Local handicrafts include embroidery (saris, dresses, purses, bags, wall hangings etc) and metal engraving. You can watch the craftsmen making harmonium reeds.

Photography: film shops in Main Rd. Nearest processing at Bhavnagar.

▲▲ Activities and tours

Rajkot *p1255, map p1255*
Tourist offices

Department of Information, Jubilee Gardens, T231616. Both open 1030-1400, 1430-1800, closed Sun, 2nd and 4th Sat. Helpful.

Gujarat, Bhavnagar House, Jawahar Rd, behind Bank of Saurashtra (sign in Hindi), T234507. Limited information.

Bhavnagar *p1257, map p1258*

Parag and Tamboli, on Waghawadi Rd, for air tickets.

⦿ Transport

Rajkot *p1255, map p1255*
Air

Indian Airlines, *Angel's Hotel*, Dhebar Chowk, T227916. Jet Airways, 7 Bilkha Plaza, Kasturba Rd, T479623, airport T477014, fly to Mumbai daily.

Bus

ST buses to Junagadh (2 hrs), Veraval (5 hrs), Jamnagar (2 hrs) and Dwarka and Ahna. Eagle Travels run private luxury buses daily to Ahmadabad and Mumbai.

Train

Junction Station Ahmadabad: *Rajkot Ahmadabad Exp, 9154*, 0630, 4¼ hrs; *Saurashtra Exp, 9216*, 0050, 6½ hrs (continues to Vadodara, 3¾ hrs); *Janata Exp, 9018*, 1440, 5¼ hrs (continues to Vadodara, 2½ hrs). Mumbai (Central): *Okha Mumbai Saurashtra Mail, 9006*, 1735, 14½ hrs; *Saurashtra Exp, 9216*, 0050, 18½ hrs. Porbandar: *Saurashtra Exp, 9215*, 0200, 4¾ hrs; *Porbandar Exp, 9264*, 0915, Mon, Thu, 5 hrs. Vadodara: same as Mumbai, 7¼-9 hrs. Veraval: *Rajkot-Veraval Mail 9838*, 1110, 5¼ hrs.

Bhavnagar *p1257, map p1258*
Air
Indian Airlines, T439168, airport T493130,
Jet Airways, Surat House, Waghawadi Rd,
T433371, Airport T517975, flies to **Mumbai**.

Bus
Frequent rickety ST buses to other main
towns;Palitana (1¾ hrs, Rs 10); several to Una
for Diu (6 hrs); Velavadhar (1 hr). Private
operators: **Tanna Travels**, Waghawadi Rd,
T420477, has luxury coaches (reclining seats)
to/from **Ahmadabad**, almost hourly from
0600, 4½ hrs plus short tea break,
recommended; to **Vadodara** 5½ hrs, 3 daily.
Punjab Travels, Kalanala, T424582.

Train
The station in the Old City is about 3 km
north of the ST Bus station in the New Town.
Ahmadabad: a slow journey as the line takes
a circuitous route to skirt the marshes.
Bhavnagar Ahmadabad Exp, 9935, 1530,
5½ hrs; *Shetrunji Exp, 9909*, 0540, 5½ hrs;
Link Exp, 9947, 2300, 7 hrs.

Palitana *p1259, map p1260*
Air
Bhavnagar (51 km northeast) is the
nearest airport.

Bus
ST Bus (0800-1200, 1400-1800) to
Ahmadabad (often with a change at
Dhandhuka), deluxe from Ahmadabad (0700,
0800, 0900); to Bhavnagar (1½ hrs).

Jamnagar, Rajkot, Surat, Una, Vadodara.
Private deluxe coaches to **Surat** and
Mumbai via **Vadodara**; surprisingly, none to
Ahmadabad. Operators: **Paras**, Owen Bridge,
T2370. Opposite ST depot: **Khodiar**, T2586
(to Surat) and **Shah**, T2396.

Taxi
For up to 7, run between **Bhavnagar** (57 km
by State Highway) and Palitana, Rs 15 each.

Train
To **Bhavnagar** about every 3 hrs. From
Ahmadabad, change at Sihor: from Sihor to
Palitana depart 0722, 1525, 1924; to Sihor
0900, 1805, 2030.

❶ Directory

Rajkot *p1255, map p1255*
Post office GPO: MG Rd. **Telegraph office**:
just north of MG Rd opposite Jubilee Gardens.

Bhavnagar *p1257, map p1258*
Banks State Bank of Saurashtra,
Darbargadh, changes currency and TCs.
Useful addresses Forest office, near
Nilambagh Palace, T428644.

Palitana *p1259, map p1260*
Hospital Mansinhji Govt Hospital, Main
Rd; Shatrunjaya Hospital, Taleti Rd. **Post
office** GPO: Main Rd, with Poste Restante;
PO, Bhairavnath Rd. **Tourist office** At
Hotel Toran Sumeru.

Gujurat Western Saurashtra *Gondal*

Western Saurashtra

*The NH8 goes from Rajkot to Junagadh, situated on the edge of the Girnar and Datta
Hills. Millets, sorghum, wheat and cotton dominate the cultivable land between Rajkot
and the coast. To the south are large areas of brackish water and saline earth, but
where the water is sweet, rich crops can be achieved on the alluvial soils. Further west
farming becomes progressively more marginal, and towards Dwarka, clay is
occasionally interspersed with higher limestones.* ▸▸ *For Sleeping, Eating and other listings,
see pages 1277-1283.*

Gondal → *Phone code: 02825. Colour map 5, A1.*

The fascinating old town of Gondal, 38 km south of Rajkot, was the capital of one of
the most progressive, affluent and efficient princely states during the British period.

The exemplary state ruled by Jadeja Rajputs had an excellent road network, free compulsory education for all children including girls, sewage systems and accessible irrigation for farmers. The rulers rejected *purdah*, their palaces have no *zenanas*, and imposed no taxes on their subjects, instead earning revenue from rail connections between the port towns of Porbandar and Veraval with Rajkot and cities inland. The **Naulakha Palace** (1748) with a sculpted façade, pretty *jharoka* windows and carved stone pillars, has an impressive Darbar Hall and a **museum** of paintings, brass and silver. Silver items include caskets, models of buildings and scales used for weighing the Maharajah (he was weighed against silver and gold on his 25th and 50th birthday; the precious metals were then distributed to the poor). A gallery has toys from the 1930s and '40s. The Vintage and Classic **Car Museum** is one of the finest in the country (1910 New Engine, 1920s Delage and Daimler, 1935-55 models, horse-drawn carriages etc). Boating is possible on **Veri Lake** nearby, which attracts large numbers of rosy pelicans, flamingos, demoiselle and common eastern cranes and many others, particularly in January and February. You can visit the Bhuvaneshwari **Ayurvedic Pharmacy** founded in 1910 which still prepares herbal medicines according to ancient principles and runs a hospital which offers massages and treatment. There is also a horse and cattle **stud farm**. The early 20th century **Swaminarayan temple** has painted interiors on the upper floors.

Junagadh → *Phone code: 0285. Colour map 5, A1. Population: 168,700.*

The narrow winding lanes and colourful bazars of this small town, entered by imposing gateways, are evocative of earlier centuries. A large rock with 14 Asokan edicts, dating from 250 BC, stands on the way to the temple-studded Girnar Hill, believed to be a pre-Harappan site. Unfortunately the modern town is marred by ugly new buildings and dirty slums.

Ins and outs

Getting there Trains and long distance buses arrive fairly close to the centre at Chittakhana Chowk with some hotels within easy reach. See Transport, page 1281, for further details.

Getting around The town sites are possible to tackle on foot allowing plenty of time for Uparkot. It is best to get an early start on Girnar Hill with the help of a rickshaw, though.

History

Established by the Mauryans in the fourth century BC, from the second to fourth centuries Junagadh was the capital of Gujarat under the **Kshattrapa** rulers. It is also associated with the **Chudasama Rajputs** who ruled from Junagadh from 875 AD. The fort was expanded in 1472 by Mahmud Beghada, and again in 1683 and 1880. Sher Khan Babi, who took on the title of Nawab Bahadur Khan Babi, declared Junagadh an independent state in the 1700s. At the time of Partition the Nawab exercised his legal right to accede to Pakistan but his subjects were predominantly Hindu and after Indian intervention and an imposed plebiscite their will prevailed. The Nawab was exiled with his hundred dogs.

Sights

The old **Uparkot** citadel① *0700-1900*, on a small plateau is east of the town and was a stronghold in the Mauryan and Gupta Empires. The present walls are said to date from the time of the Chudasama Rajputs (ninth-15th century). The deep moat inside the walls is believe to have once had crocodiles. The Ottoman canons of Suleman Pasha, an ally of the Sultans, were moved here after the Muslim forces were unable to save Diu from Portuguese naval forces. The town was repeatedly under attack so there was a huge granary to withstand a long siege. The **Jama Masjid** was built from the remains of a Hindu palace. The 11th-century **Adi Chadi Vav**, a *baoli* with 172 steps and an impressive spiral staircase, is believed to commemorate two slave girls who were bricked up as sacrifice to ensure the supply of water. The 52-m deep Naghan Kuva is a huge 11th-century well which has steps down to the water level through the rocks, with openings to ventilate the path.

The **Buddhist cave monastery** in this fort complex dates from Asoka's time. Two of the three levels are open to visitors. The drainage system was very advanced as seen in the rainwater reservoir. The ventilation cleverly achieved a balance of light and cool breezes. Other Buddhist caves are hewn into the hillsides near the fort.

In the town, the late 19th-century **Mausolea** of the Junagadh rulers, not far from the railway station, are impressive. The **Maqbara** of Baha-ud-din Bhar with its silver doors and intricate, elaborate decoration, almost has a fairground flamboyance. The **Old Mausolea** at Chittakhana Chowk (opposite *Relief Hotel*, which has views of them from the roof), which were once impressive are now crumbling and overgrown.

Durbar Hall Museum ① *in the Nawab's Palace, circa 1870, Janta Chowk, 0900-1215, 1500-1800, closed Wed, 2nd and 4th Sat of month, Rs 5 plus Rs 2 per photo. Small but recommended; allow 30 mins*, which houses royal memorabilia includes portraits, palanquins, gem-studded carpets, costumes and weapons. Good labelling, particularly in the informative armoury section.

The **Asokan rock edicts** ① *0830-1100, 1400-1800, closed Wed and holidays*, carved in the Brahmi script on a large boulder is at the foot of the Girnar Hill, further east. The

Junagadh

Sleeping ■		
1 Gautum & Madhuwati	4 Relief	2 Poonam
2 National		3 Santoor
3 Railway Retiring Rooms	Eating ●	4 Swati
	1 Geeta & Sharda	

0 metres 300
0 yards 300

Emperor instructed his people to be gentle with women, to be kind to animals, to give alms freely and to plant medicinal herbs. The 13 edicts are summed up in the 14th.

Girnar Hill, rising 900 m above the surrounding plain, 3 km east of town, has been an important religious centre for the Jains from the third century BC. The climb up this worn volcanic cone by 10,000 stone steps takes at least two hours. You start just beyond Damodar Kund in teak forest; at the foot is the Asokan Edict while a group of 16 **Jain temples** surmounts the hill. The climb can be trying in the heat so is best started very early in the morning. You will find tea stalls *en route* and brazen monkeys. *Dhoolis* are available but are expensive. The charge depends on weight; Rs 1,500 for 60 kg!, to the first group of temples, which are the most interesting. There are good views from the top though the air is often hazy.① *Getting there: no 3 or 4 bus from the stand opposite the post office run to Girnar Taleti at the foot of the hill, but are often 'out of order'. Rickshaws, Rs 25 (Rs 40 return), require bargaining. There are plans for a ropeway which will make visiting the summit easier.*

Parks and zoos

Sakkar Bagh Zoo① *0800-1800, closed Mon, Rs 10. Rajkot Rd*, 3½ km north of town centre, is well kept and has a good collection of birds and big cats. Attractive enclosures at the rear are for breeding Asiatic lions. Get permission to visit and photograph from the Superintendent. The garden houses the fine **Junagadh Museum** ① *0900-1215, 1500-1800, closed Wed, 2nd and 4th Sat in the month, Rs 2. Getting there: take bus No 1, 2 or 6.* With local paintings, Nawabi relics, textiles, manuscripts, archaeological finds and natural history.

★ Sasan Gir National Park → *Phone code: 02877. Colour map 5, grid A1.*

The sanctuary covers a total area of 1,412 sq km in the Saurashtra peninsula, of which 258 sq km at the core is the national park. As a result of over-grazing and agricultural colonization, only about 10% of the park is forest. However, much of the natural vegetation in the region was scrub jungle. The area has rocky hills and deep valleys with numerous rivers and streams, and there are extensive clearings covered with savannah-like fodder grasses.

Ins and outs

There are buses from Junagadh, Veraval and Ahmadabad. Sasan railway station (10 mins walk from the Forest Lodge) has convenient trains from Junagadh and Veraval. Temperature: 42-7°C. Rainfall: 1,000 mm. Best time to visit: 15 Oct-15 Jun, best Mar-May, closed during monsoons. Open usually 0700-1200, 1500-1730 from mid-Oct to mid-Feb; 0630-1100, 1600 to sunset from mid-Feb to mid-Jun, depending on sunrise and sunset. Foreigners US$5, still camera US$5; video US$200; guide (some have no English), US$5 per trip; vehicle entry US$10; Jeep US$25 per drive. Permits are only available from Sinh Sadan at Sasan. See Transport, page 1281, for further details. Permits are required.

Wildlife

The **Asiatic Lion** once had a wide range of natural territory running from North to West India through Persia to Arabia. It is now only found in the Gir forest; the last one seen outside India was in 1942, in Iran. Similar to its African cousin, the tawnier Asian is a little smaller and stockier in build with a skin fold on the belly, a thinner mane and a thicker tuft at the end of its tail. The 1913 census accounted for only 18 in the park. The lions' natural habitat was threatened by the gradual conversion of the forest into agricultural land and cattle herders grazing their livestock here. The conservation programme has been remarkably successful. In the mid-90s there were over 300 lions (some suggest, too many for this sanctuary). These, and 294 **panthers**, make Gir

India's best Big Cat sanctuary. There have been attacks on villagers by park lions, these were probably 'provoked' as there are few reported 'maneaters'. Lions are more likely to be seen with the help of a tracker and guide (jeeps and guides available), but some visitors return disappointed. The Interpretation Zone's 'Safari Park' has a few lions. There are six routes in the park, between 22 and 50 km. Jeep (diesel, seats four), from *Sinh Sadan*, bookings between 0700-1100 or 1500-1700 ("a scramble at 0630 as there are not enough jeeps... 8 officials filling forms with one pen between them!").

A **watch tower** camouflaged in the tree canopy at Kamleshwar overlooks an artificial reservoir harbouring wild crocodiles but it is poorly located and overcrowded with bus loads of noisy visitors at weekends. Other towers are at Janwadla and Gola.

For **bird watching**, Adhodiya, Valadara, Ratnaghuna and Pataliyala, are good spots. A walk along Hiran River is also rewarding.

Other sights

The Tulsishyam **hotsprings** in the heart of the forest (Tulsishyam is also a Krishna pilgrimage centre), and Kankai Mata **temple** dedicated to Bhim, the *Mahabharata* hero, and his mother Kunti, add interest.

Gir Interpretation Zone ① *at Devaliya, 12 km west of Sasan. Same rates as for the sanctuary. If you take the mini-bus tour you save US$20 (guide and vehicle fee). Open during Park times except Wed. Getting there: buses run along Sasan-Maliya Rd. Jeeps from Sasan to gate charge Rs 120*, is 16 sq km of Gir habitat fenced in as a 'Safari Park' to show a cross-section of wildlife; the four or five lions here can be easily seen in open scrubland in the area. Photographers will find this a good place to shoot lion behaviour as these lions are less shy than those in the sanctuary. Other Gir wildlife include spotted deer, sambar, nilgai, peafowl. Permits are available at the Reception here.

Crocodile Rearing Centre ① *0800-1200, 1500-1800, free, near entrance to* Sinh Sadan, *and road leading to* Lion Safari Lodge, is full of marsh crocodiles, varying in size from a few centimetres to 1 m for restocking the population in the sanctuary. Eggs are collected in the park and taken to Junagadh for hatching under controlled conditions. All the information is in Gujarati, but it is still worth a look. Unfortunately, keepers prod the crocodiles to make them move.

Veraval

Veraval is a noisy, unbearably smelly and unattractive town which provides a base for visiting the Hindu pilgrimage centre of Somnath at Prabhas Patan. Its importance now is as a fishing port – hence the stench. Sea-going *dhows* and fishing boats are still being built by the sea without the use of any modern instruments, traditional skills being passed down from father to son.

Prabhas Patan (Somnath)

The **Somnath Temple** ① *6km east of Veraval, puja at 0700, 1200 and 1900*, a major Hindu pilgrimage centre, is said to have been built out of gold by Somraj, the Moon God (and subsequently in silver, wood and stone). In keeping with the legend, the stone façade appears golden at sunset. Mahmud of Ghazni plundered it and removed the gates in 1024. Destroyed by successive Muslim invaders, it was rebuilt each time on the same spot. The final reconstruction did not take place until 1950 and is still going on. Unfortunately, it lacks character but it has been built to traditional patterns with a soaring 50 m high tower that rises in clusters. Dedicated to Siva, it has one of the 12 sacred *jyotirlingas* (see page 305).

Nearby is the ruined **Rudreshvara Temple** which dates from the same time as the Somnath Temple and was laid out in a similar fashion. The sculptures on the walls and doorways give an indication of what the original Somnath Temple was like.

Krishna was believed to have been hit by an arrow, shot by the Bhil, Jara, when he was mistaken for a deer at Bhalka Teerth nearby, and was cremated at Triveni Ghat, east of Somnath.

Diu → *Phone code: 02875. Colour map 5, grid A1. Population: 21,600. www.diuindia.com.*

The island of Diu has a fascinating history and a relaxed atmosphere with little traffic. The north side of the island has salt pans and marshes which attract wading birds. The south coast has some limestone cliffs and pleasant, palm-fringed sandy beaches though these cannot compete with Goa and Kerala. The branching Hoka palms, rarely seen on the mainland, were introduced from Africa by the Portuguese. The island is still visited by relatively few foreign travellers though its tavernas attract those deprived of alcohol from neighbouring Gujarat and the bars can get noisy especially at the weekend. It isn't a paradise island but it does offer a welcome break from travelling around the state.

Ins and outs

Getting there Daily flights from Mumbai arrive at the airport 6 km west of the town; auto-rickshaws charge around Rs 50 to transfer. Most visitors arrive by long distance buses either via Una or direct to the island, easiest from Ahmadabad via Bhavnagar. See Transport, page 1282, for further details.

Getting around The small town is best seen on foot to soak in the atmosphere, while the island is ideal for exploring by cycle in the cooler season. State buses use the stand near the Ghogla bridge about a 10-min walk from Bunder Chowk, the main square, with hotels and the market nearby. There are occasional buses from the Local Bus Stand here to the beaches, and to Ghogla and Una.

Background

Like Daman across the gulf, Diu was a Portuguese colony until 1961. In 1987 its administration was separated from Goa (some 1,600 km away), which then became a State – Diu remains a Union Territory. From the 14th to 16th centuries the Sultans of Oman held the reins of maritime power here. The Portuguese failed to take Diu at their first attempt in 1531 but succeeded three years later. Like Daman, it was once a port for the export of opium from Malwa (Madhya Pradesh) but with the decline of Portugal as a naval power it became little more than a backwater.

About 5,000 of the elders here (out of a population of 40,000), still speak fluent Portuguese. There are around 200 Catholic families and the local convent school

Diu Island

To Una, Simbor Beach, Veraval & Somnath   To Una
GUJARAT   Ahmedpur Mandvi
Bucharwada   TAD Village   Bird Sanctuary   Ghogla   Ghogla Beach
Salt Pans   Salt Pans   Fortress of Panikot
Vanakbara   Agricultural   Diu Town
Reserve Forest   Seashell Museum   Kevdi   Malala Mines   Fudam   Sports Complex   Jallandhar Beach
Gomtimata Beach   Nagoa Beach   Gangeshwar   Chakratirtha Beach
Nagoa   Sunset Point
N   Arabian Sea

0 km   2
0 miles   2

■ Sleeping   2 Radhika & Ganga Sagar
1 Kohinoor   3 Resort Hoka

66 99 Unlike Goa, there is little attempt to woo the westerner with touristy 'ethnic' clothes and jewellery although the occasional moonlight beach party is organized.

teaches English, Gujarati, Portuguese and French. The Divechi people remain eligible for Portuguese passports and a few apply daily. Many families have a member working in Lisbon or former Portuguese Africa.

Diu town

The small town is squeezed between the fort on the east and a large city wall to the west. With its attractively ornamented buildings and its narrow streets and squares, it has more of a Portuguese flavour than Daman. While some visitors find it quite dirty and decaying, and are disappointed by the number of liquor shops, others find Diu delightful. Unlike Goa, there is little attempt to woo the westerner with touristy 'ethnic' clothes and jewellery although the occasional moonlight beach party is organized.

St Paul's Church (1601-10) has a fine baroque façade, impressive wood panelling and an attractive courtyard, and the Church of **St Francis of Assisi** (1593), part of which is a hospital (a doctor is available at 0930 for a free consultation). **St Thomas's Church** houses the **museum** with an interesting local collection① *0800-2000*. It has been renovated and now houses a collection including stone sculptures, wood carvings, and shadow clocks (as well as a *café* and pleasant rooms to let). These, and the fort, are floodlit at night.

Diu Fort ① *0700-1800*, (1535-41), considered one of the most important Portuguese forts in Asia, was built after the Mughal Emperor Humayun attacked the Sultan of Gujarat with the help of the Portuguese. Until 1960 it garrisoned 350 Portuguese soldiers. Skirted by the sea on three sides and a rock-cut canal on the fourth, it had two moats, one of which was tidal. The lighthouse stands at one end and parts of the central keep are still used as a jail but has few occupants. Some of the structures (walls, gateways, arches, ramps, bastions), though damaged, still give us an idea of the formidable nature of the defences. It is well worth allowing an hour for a visit.

> **‡** *The night market is a great place to have a drink and to wander around*

Makata Lane or Panchwati, near the Zampa gate, has some impressive old mansions of rich Portuguese and Indian merchants ranging from Venetian-Gothic style bungalows to typical carved wooden or stone *havelis*.

Forte de Mar

Forte de Mar (Fortress of Panikot), built in 1535, was strategically important as an easily defended base for controlling the shipping lanes on the northeast part of the Arabian Sea. It has a lighthouse and a chapel to Our Lady of the Sea. It can be approached from Diu jetty when canoes or motor boats are available although landing is not permitted at present.

The other fort at the eastern end of the island guarded the mint, while two others once guarded the west at Vanakbara and the bay to the south at Nagoa.

Excursions

The creeks to the north of Diu island have been declared a **bird sanctuary**. There are watch towers to spot huge flocks of shore birds including oystercatchers, sanderlings, herons and plovers. Lots of herons and ibises, flamingos, pelicans, ducks etc visit seasonally. Jackals, foxes, jungle cat and porcupine are seen in the evening. Further afield, 80 km along the coast is **Somnath** via Kodinar. An alternative is to go inland to **Sasan Gir** (95 km) to visit the national park.

Beaches

Several beaches on the south side of Diu Island are easy to get to from Diu town by cycle or auto-rickshaw. Beaches between Nagoa and Vanakbara are safe throughout the year except between May and July and are often empty, as is the beach along Ghogla. However, beware of the giant thorns which are hazardous to cycle tyres.

Jallandhar Beach　The beach to the south is pleasant and the nearest to Diu. There have been several reports of groups of teenage boys who not only come to watch and pester tourists but aggressively offer sex.

　　Chakratirtha Beach　Chakratirtha Beach just southwest, has a sunset view point, an open auditorium, and a small beach which is no longer the picture it was. This was a popular promenade for the townspeople until "ruined by the cabins which are, in a way, the beginning of the end of beautiful beaches like Chakratirth".

　　Fudam　Just east of Diu Town, Fudam or Fofrara has the air of a Portuguese village with the crumbling Church of Our Lady of the Remedies. The **Malala Mines** are limestone quarries off the Nagoa road. The **Gangeshwar** temple nearby has an attractive *Nandi* and Siva *linga* washed by the sea at high tide.

Diu Town

Sleeping

1 Alishan	5 Hare Krishna & Ram Vijay	9 Prince
2 Ankur	6 Jayshankar	10 Samrat
3 Apana	7 Nilesh	11 Tourist Cottages
4 Galaxy	8 Pensao Beira Mar	

Nagoa About 7 km from town, facing the Arabian Sea, Nagoa offers the best location for a quiet stay away from Diu town. Its semi-circular palm-fringed beach suitable for swimming is popular with foreigners but also large numbers of Indian tourists who come to watch. There are quieter beaches nearby and the forests are pleasant for walks although the entire stretch from Nagoa is being landscaped for development. A **sea shell museum** ① *Rs 10,* has opened on the road from the airport to Nagoa. It displays a large number of mollusc and crustacean shells, corals, fish and marine life from the world over collected by a retired merchant navy captain.

Ghogla-Ahmedpur Mandvi The fishing village of Ghogla on the mainland is also part of Diu. Its name changes to Ahmedpur Mandvi on crossing to the Gujarat side of the border. The beach is good for swimming and it has splendid views of fishing villages and the fort and churches on Diu island. *Jyoti Watersports* and *Magico Do Mar* offer a variety of watersports here including parasailing, speed boating and waterskiing. Beware of the **rip tide** just a few metres out to sea which has claimed several lives.

Other beaches Bucharwada to the north lacks attractive beaches but has cheap spartan rooms in *Viswas* hotel. **Gomtimata,** a secluded white-sand beach to the west, is where a *Tourist Hostel* is expected to open. **Vanakbara,** the fishing village on the western tip of the island, has the Church of Our Lady of Mercy. Get to the early morning fish market and watch the colourful trawlers unload catches of shark, octopus and every kind of fish imaginable. The drying fish on "washing lines" and waterside activities provide photo opportunities. You can also watch traditional dhow building. There is a ferry service across to Gomtimata. C-D Hotel Maheshwari is on the road to Bucharwada.

Simbor Beach is a pleasant and little known beach. It is 27 km from Diu town, off the Una road, and can be reached in 45 minutes from Diu by hiring a moped or scooter. Carry food and water.

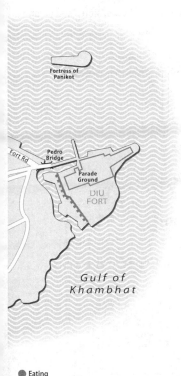

Fortress of Panikot

Fort Rd

Pedro Bridge

Parade Ground

DIU FORT

Gulf of Khambhat

● Eating
1 Deepee Telecom
2 Uma Shakti

Porbandar

→ *Phone code: 0286. Colour map 5, grid A1. Population 133,000. The town is closely associated with Mahatma Gandhi.*

The former capital of the Jethwa Rajput petty princely state, Porbandar was previously named Sudamapuri, after Krishna's devoted friend, and has a temple dedicated to her. The tradition of dhow building which continues on the seashore to the present day reflects its maritime past when it traded with North Africa and Arabia. Today, Porbandar produces gold and silver trinkets, manufactures fine quality silk and cotton and has chemical and cement factories.

Mahatma Gandhi was born in Porbandar in 1869. Next to the family home with its carved balconies is **Kirti Mandir**ⓘ *open from sunrise to sunset, but the guide takes a lunch break from 1300-1400*, a small museum that traces his life and contains memorabilia and a library. **Darbargadh**, a short walk from Kirti Mandir, the old palace of the Maharanas of Porbandar, built in the 1780s, is now deserted and has some intricate carvings and carved balconies. The rooms inside (if you can get in!) have interesting paintings. **Sartanji** (or Rana-no) **Choro** (1785), near the ST stand, is the beautiful pleasure pavilion of Maharajah Sartanji, a great poet, writer and music lover. The pavilion has domes, pillars and carved arches and its four sides represent the four seasons. The Maharana's deserted sprawling **Hazur Palace** is near the seafront. Ask for permission to visit the rooms inside at the office. **Daria Rajmahal**, the splendid turn-of-the-century palace of the Maharana of Porbandar, now a college, has intricate carvings, courtyards, fountains, carved arches and heavily embellished façades. The tower has excellent views of the seashore. **Chaya**, 2 km from Chowpatty sea face, is the old capital of the Jetwas. The Darbargadh Palace with a beautiful carved balcony, is believed to have secret tunnels and passages to temples and places of safety.

The **Bharat Mandir Hall** in Dayananda Vatika garden, is across the Jubilee (Jyubeeli) Bridge. It has a large marble relief map of India on the floor and bas reliefs of heroes from Hindu legends on the pillars. Nearby **Arya Kanya Gurukul** is an experiment in education for girls based on ancient Indian tradition. The dated **Planetarium** has shows in Gujarati only. The architecture incorporates different religious styles illustrating Gandhi's open mind.

Jhavar Creek attracts scores of waterbirds. Flamingos, pelicans, storks and heron

Porbandar

Sleeping			
1 Flamingo	4 Moon Palace	**Eating**	
2 Ilndraprastha	5 New Oceanic	1 Adarsh	
3 Kuber	6 Sheetal	2 Swagath	
	7 Vaibhav		

0 metres 500
0 yards 500

can be seen from the road in the mangrove marshes. Fisheries have appeared around
the creek where the fish put out to dry attract thousands of terns and gulls.

★ Jamnagar → *Phone code: 0288. Colour map 2, grid C1. Population: 447,700.*

Jamnagar, now an expanding town, was a 16th-century pearl fishing centre with one of the biggest pearl fisheries in the world until the beginning of the 20th century. The famous cricketer Ranjitsinghji was its ruler from 1907-33. Although the January 2001 earthquake was strongly felt in the town there was no severe disruption.

Ins and outs
The Bus Stand is about 3 km west of the town centre - if arriving from Rajkot and planning to stay in Bedi Gate area, get off near the Gate (easily spotted) and walk 5 mins or take a rickshaw to the hotel.

Sights
The walled city is famous for its embroidery, silverware and *bandhani* (tie-and-dye) fabrics produced in workshops in the narrow lanes. Pirotan Island in the middle of the Ranmal lake in the Old City, reached by a stone bridge, has the **Lakhota Fort** and **Kotha Bastion** with its arsenal ① *1030-1300, 1500-1730, closed Wed, 2nd and 4th Sun, no photography (unless tipped)*. The fort museum has a collection of sculpture and pottery found in ruined medieval villages nearby. It is also a pleasant, cool and quiet spot just to relax while listening to the strains of '*Shri Ram, Jai Ram, Jai Jai Ram*' wafting across the lake from the **Bala Hanuman Temple**. The temple is worth a visit, especially early evening. The bastion has an old well from which water can be drawn by blowing into a small hole in the floor. The **Solarium** uses solar radiation to cure diseases. The **Jain temples** in the Old City are profusely decorated with glass, gilding and mirrors.

> ♣ Bala Hanuman temple is in the 'Guinness Book of Records' for continuous chanting (13,892 days – over 38 years)

Excursions
Khijadia Lakes, 10 km northeast of Jamnagar, are three freshwater lakes surrounded by salt pans and salt marshes. Entirely flooded in the wet season, the lakes remain fresh throughout the dry season, though they occasionally dry out completely. The lakes, a bird sanctuary, are an important staging post for migratory birds, including swallows, martins and wagtails, and many waterfowl.

Marine National Park, 30 km away, offshore from the southern coast of the Gulf of Kachchh, comprises an archipelago of 42 islands noted for their coral reefs and mangroves. It is possible to see dolphins, finless porpoise and sea turtles and a variety of colourful tropical fish. The area also attracts a host of waterbirds. The best island to visit is 1½ sq km **Pirotan**. ① *Getting there: hire motor boats for 15-45 people from Jamnagar jetty (or from Okha); take a guide. Foreigners US$5, still camera US$5; video US$200; guide US$5. Permit needed from the Director, Marine National Park, Jamnagar.* Pirotan is uninhabited save for lighthouse staff.

★ Dwarka → *Phone code: 02892. Colour map 2, grid C1. Population: 33,600.*

A small coastal town on the tip of the Kathiawad peninsula, Dwarka is one of the most sacred sites for Vaishnavite Hindus. It has the unique distinction of being one of Hinduism's four 'Holy Abodes' as well as one of its seven 'Holy Places'. Heavily geared up to receive pilgrims, the people are easy-going, friendly and welcoming, even to the rarely seen tourist. The beach is good but without any palms for shade.

Archaeological excavations indicate that present day Dwarka is built on the sites of four former cities. Work in 1990 by the marine archaeologist SR Rao discovered triangular anchors weighing 250 kg similar to those used in Cyprus and Syria during the Bronze Age, suggesting that ships of up to 120 tonnes had used the port around the 14th century BC. Marine research in early 2002 revealed evidence of a substantial city off the coast over 100 m below current sea level, reviving the debate about the origins of Dwarka's offshore archaeological sites.

The present town is largely 19th century when the Gaekwad princes developed the town as a popular pilgrimage centre. Celebrated as Krishna's capital after his flight from Mathura, thousands come to observe Krishna's birthday, and also at Holi and Diwali.

Sights

The 12th-century **Rukmini Temple** has beautifully carved *mandapa* columns and a fine sanctuary doorway, but much else is badly weathered.

The mainly 16th-century **Dwarkadisha Temple** ① *0600-1200, 1700-2100*, was supposedly built in one night, and some believe that the inner sanctum is 2,500 years old. The sanctuary walls probably date from the 12th century. The exterior is more interesting. The soaring five-storey tower is supported by 60 columns. Non-Hindus may enter after completing a form to show some level of commitment to Hinduism and to Krishna, but no photography is allowed inside and cameras must be left at the entrance. Some visitors are approached for a 'minimum donation' of Rs 100.

Good humoured lighthouse keepers may treat you to a free private guided tour in exchange for any foreign coin (they all 'collect') ① *1600-1800 or 1 hr before sunset, whichever is earlier, Re 1, no photography*. The views are beautiful - a very peaceful place to rest a while.

Outside Dwarka, the **Nageshwar Mandir** contains one of the 12 *jyotirlingas* in an underground sanctum. Work is in progress. It helps to be fairly agile if you wish to catch a glimpse. **Gopi Talav Teerth** is associated with Krishna (and Arjun) and contains several shrines in the complex.

Excursions

Okha ① *get there from Ahmadabad by Saurashtra Mail 9006, 1120, 10¾ hrs. Local buses to Dwarka, 1 hr. Morning direct bus to Bhuj. From Okha, boats to Beyt Dwarka take 10-15, mins each way*, is a small port at the head of the Gulf of Kachchh, Okha is 32 km north of Dwarka with a few cheap hotels. You can visit the Marine National Park by hiring a motor boat from the jetty (see under Jamnagar). A pilgrimage to Dwarka is

Dwarka

Arabian Sea

To Rukmini Temple & Okha
To Train Station
ST Buses
Okha Rd
Hanuman Talao
To Charak
Sunset Point
Circuit House
Teen Batti Chowk
Bike Hire
Library
Lighthouse
Dwarka Darshan Office
Dwarkadisha Temple
To Jamnagar
Gomati Khadi
N

| metres | 500 |
| yards | 500 |

■ **Sleeping**
1 Radhika
2 Satnam Wadi

● **Eating**
1 Toran

not complete until the island of **Beyt Dwarka** is visited off the coast from Okha. This is where Krishna is believed to have resided while Dwarka was his capital. The 19th-century temple complex contains several shrines and images of Krishna and his 56 consorts. Archaeological excavations have revealed Harappan artefacts dating from the second millennium BC.

Listings: Western Saurashtra

⊜ Sleeping

Gondal *p1265*
The "faultless" Heritage Hotels managed by the ever helpful Mr Kanak Singh ("looks after guests like a father") are worth the experience:
B Riverside Palace (19th century) by river Gondali, T20002, F23332, www.gujarat.net/gondal. With a glassed-in terrace, 11 large, attractive rooms, 4-posters etc.
B Orchard Palace, Palace Rd, near ST bus stand, T24450, overlooking mango and lime groves, 7 rooms in a wing, 2 a/c, with old-fashioned baths, attractive gardens, 35 vintage cars, pool (waiting to be filled), excellent dance performances, mosquito nuisance so burn rings, good food ("bland European dishes; order 'Indian' in advance every time"), good *kebabs* and Gujarati *thalis* but service can be slow (Rs 2,000 includes meals).
B Royal Saloon, standing in garden near Orchard Palace. Beautifully renovated suite in Maharaja's old train, with drawing and dining rooms and sit outs on the platform, meals from the *Orchard Palace*. Sheer nostalgia.
D Bhuvaneswari Rest House, a/c rooms with western baths, Rs 350-700, simple but comfortable, *thali* meals. The Gondal family don't spend time with guests though "the Maharani is delightful company"; request high tea in their private drawing room (French gilt furniture, crystals, Lalique etc). Reservations for all the above: *North West Safaris*, T079-6302019, F6300962, ssibal@ad1.vsnl.net.in.

Junagadh *p1266, map p1267*
Rates double during Diwali (Oct- Nov) when large number of Indians visit Girnar.
C-D Lion Hill View Resort, at the foot of Girnar Hill, is to open.
C-D President, opposite Railway Workshop, T626773. 15 clean rooms, 6 a/c (comfortable

but short beds), all with hot water (winter only) and TV, 'deluxe' front rooms on busy road, noisy, those at rear with view of hills better.
C-D Paramount, Kalwa Chowk, T622119, F650582. 31 rooms (some a/c) with TV and phone, attached baths, car rental, bus ticketing.
D Girnar, Majwadi Darwaja, 2 km north, T621201. 24 decent rooms, some a/c with bath, best with balcony, unattractive building but in good location, poor management.
D-E National, near Kalwa Chowk, T627891. 15 clean, comfortable rooms, 2 a/c dearer, some deluxe with TV, big discount for single, good value though several women visitors have complained of harassment, on noisy road.
E-F Madhuwati, Kalwa Chowk, T620087. 27 spacious rooms, some a/c, attached bath (hot showers in winter only), noisy location above a shopping complex, clean, comfortable, courteous staff.
E-F Relief, Dhal Rd, T620280. 14 rooms (some share bath), hot water, 2 a/c, snacks available, untrained but friendly staff, courteous owner can help with excursions.
F Gautam, Kalwa Chowk, T626432. Located on noisy intersection, small guest house with 12 simple rooms, most with shared bath, bucket hot water, cycle hire.
F Railway Retiring Rooms are clean and well maintained.

Sasan Gir National Park *p1268*
AL-B Gir Lodge (Taj), Sasan, T85521, F85528. 27 comfortable rooms (better upstairs for views from balcony), 9 a/c, pleasant river-facing dining area but average meals at fixed times, slow service though friendly manager and chef, no pool, wildlife library and videos, jeep hire.
B Maneland Jungle Lodge, 2 km before Sasan, T85555, on edge of sanctuary. Well-appointed suites in bungalow (VIP faces

 For an explanation of the sleeping and eating price codes used in this guide, see inside the front cover. Other relevant information is found in Essentials pages 52-57.

jungle), and rooms in cottages resembling royal hunting lodges, restaurant with limited menu delightfully designed, jungle ambience, lions and panthers heard and occasionally spotted nearby, rich birdlife, wildlife videos. Recommended, advance reservations: *North West Safaris*, T079-6302019, F6300962, ssibal@ad1.vsnl.net.in.

B Sinh Sadan Forest Lodge (Govt), T85540, overpriced and run down rooms (foreigners US$30), with Indian toilets, better a/c chalets (US$50), tents with shared bath, 30-bed dorm (US$5), comfortable 2-bed tents, with shared toilet and cold shower - "fell asleep to the sound of a lion roaring nearby!", must order food in advance (mixed reports on quality). Book at least 1 week ahead, Dy CFS Superintendent, Wildlife Div, Sasan Gir, Dist Junagadh T362135.

D Umeng, T85728. Near Sasan bus stop, backdrop of sanctuary but with crowded village on one side (calls from the mosque disturb the peace). 9 decent rooms with mediocre baths, rooftop dining room (order meal well ahead), jeep safaris, knowledgeable owner can help with visits to the sanctuary.

Veraval *p1269*

D Park, Veraval-Junagadh Rd, T02876-22701. Fairly well-appointed rooms, excellent location with spacious grounds, varied menu.

D-E Madhuram, Junagadh Rd, T02876-21938, F43676. Comfortable rooms, some a/c, taxis, travel desk, small cafeteria (limited menu), dorms, run down.

Prabhas Patan *p1269*

D Mayuram, Triveni Rd, T31286. Acceptable rooms, restaurant, good food, clean.

F Shri Somnath Guest House, near Temple, T20212. Has 20 very basic rooms.

Diu *p1270, maps p1270 and p1272*

Most are fairly basic. Some have a few a/c rooms with TV and charge double for the luxury, but offer good discounts when business is slow. High season: *Diwali*, Christmas/New Year and Apr-May.

C Pensáo Beira Mar, Fort Rd, T52342. 6 rooms and suites in pleasant colonial house, sea-facing balcony, rooftop restaurant.

C Prince, near Fish Market, T52265. 11 clean, well kept rooms (some deluxe), dorm (Rs 40), constant hot water, 1st floor rooms can be unbearably hot even at night, friendly staff.

C-D Ankur, Estrada Lacerda, west of town, T52388. 13 basic rooms, 2 a/c (foreigners get good discount since they 'keep rooms cleaner than Indian guests!'), helpful Portuguese owner. Recommended though overpriced.

C-D Apana Guest House, Old Fort Rd, T52112, F52309. 29 clean rooms, 4 a/c, some with bath (best with TV, hot water, seaview and balcony) and dorm, can be noisy (mainly from Hindi films on TV) especially at weekends, roadside terrace with restaurant and bar.

C-D Samrat, Collectorate Rd, T52354. 12 clean rooms, 3 a/c, balconies, good restaurant, helpful manager. Recommended.

C-D Triveni, opposite Sports Complex, T52045. 20 rooms with modern facilities, 4 a/c.

D Galaxy, next to bus station, T53399. Clean rooms in newish 3 storey hotel, some a/c, restaurant, bar.

D-E Hemal Garden, opposite Sports Complex, T52227. 10 simple cottage like rooms, bar, restaurant, family run, pleasant garden, rather basic but pleasant.

F Hare Krishna, opposite Prince, T52213. 9 rooms, basic (hard beds) but clean, some with balcony, friendly staff, popular restaurant, bar can be noisy.

Jallandhar Beach *p1272*

E Jay Shankar Guest House, 1 min from beach, T52424. 15 rooms, some with bath, small dorm (Rs 50).

Fudam *p1272*

B-C Kohinoor, Fofrara, Diu-Nagoa Rd, T52209, F52613, kohinoor_diu @yahoo.com. 28 clean, a/c rooms in ritzy resort (discounts possible), good restaurant serves Portuguese dishes, pool, gym-sauna, modern and pleasant rooms and amenities but no views, pastry shop and disco, gym, pool and water slide complex next door.

F Church Hostel, in the old Fudam church. Simple rooms (Rs 100), use of kitchen, really quiet and pleasant.

Nagoa *p1273*

B Radhika Beach Resort, close to the beach, T52555, F52552. 24 comfortable a/c rooms in modern 2-storey 'villas', excellent a/c restaurant, good pool in well tended garden, prompt service, small provisions store handy for beach. Recommended.

D-E The Resort Hoka, 100 m from the beach among *Hoka* palms and trees, T53036, F52298, resort_hoka@hot mail.com. 10 decent rooms with bath, 3 with shared facilities, clean, pleasant garden restaurant serves excellent fresh fish, bar, laundry, travel, environment conscious and friendly management, discounts for long stays, not luxurious but pleasant and good value.

Ghogla-Ahmedpur Mandvi *p1273*

B-C Magico do Mar, T52116. Charming complex of 14 a/c huts with Saurashtrian décor, around a 1930s mansion of a Junagadh Nawab (best Nos 510-513), cheaper non a/c rooms in unimpressive bungalow needing renovation (with "more wildlife than Sasan Gir... lizards in bed, and beefy cockroaches"), fantastic views, some watersports, charming setting but poor service reported.

B-C Suzlon Beach, T52212. Cluster of attractive bungalows with good sized, well appointed, clean a/c rooms, restaurant, bar, terrace opens onto beach and sea but lacks atmosphere.

D Premalayai, T52270. Simple rooms, serves Indian food.

Porbandar *p1273, map p1274*

C-D Kuber, Bhavsinhji Park, near ST station, T241025, T250164. 19 rooms, most a/c, suites with fridge, good restaurant (residents only), friendly and helpful manager, free airport transfer. Highly recommended.

C-D Indraprastha, near ST Station, T242681, F242682. Large modern hotel, comfortable, some a/c, garden restaurant.

D New Oceanic, 8 Chowpatty, T242917. 17 rooms, some a/c, sea views, modern, good garden restaurant (western, Indian) but rather expensive.

D-E Sheetal, Arya Samaj Rd, opposite GPO, T247596, F241821. Some a/c rooms with shower or tub, limited room service, "a 70s movie motel!".

D-E Host, Blvd Bhavsinhji Park, T241901, F23888. 14 rooms, some a/c, Indian veg meals on the terrace garden, restaurant downstairs.

D-E Flamingo, MG Rd, T247123. Some comfortable rooms (inspect), some larger dearer a/c, a/c restaurant.

D-E Moon Palace, ST Rd, near Bhavsinhji Park, ST Rd, T241172, F243248, moonpalace@ mail.com. Clean, cosy rooms with bath.

Jamnagar *p1275*

B Park Plaza is best in town.

C-D Aram (Heritage Hotel), Pandit Nehru Rd, 3 km northwest from centre, T551701, F554957. Good a/c rooms in 1940s character mansion (bit garish), Raj memorabilia, pleasant veg garden restaurant, friendly, good service.

C-D Express, Motikhavdi, out of town, towards the sea. 120 rooms, pool, gym, modern facilities.

C-D President, Teen Batti, T557491, F558491. 27 clean rooms, some a/c and balcony, relaxing a/c restaurant (wide menu, efficient service), internet.

D-E Aashiana, New Supermarket, Bedi Gate, 3rd floor, T676525. 34 rooms, 14 clean a/c rooms with TV, simple restaurant serving inexpensive Indian veg, good value.

D-E Punit, Pandit Nehru Marg, north of Teen Batti, T670560, F670966. Reasonable, clean rooms, some a/c, better at rear, good value.

Budget hotels are on Old Station Rd and in the New Supermarket area.

Dwarka *p1275, map p1276*

Off-season prices drop dramatically on the appearance of a questioning frown, but most hotels are poorly maintained.

D-E Radhika, opposite ST Bus Stand, T361754. Adequate rooms but poor dining.

E-F Toran (Gujarat Tourism), near Govt Guest House, T361313. 6 clean, well maintained rooms with nets, dorm, courteous service, checkout 0900, "dedicated and friendly manager". Recommended.

F Meera, near railway station, T361335. Friendly, excellent *thalis*.

F Satnam Wadi, near the beach. Rooms with bath and sea view.

⦿ Eating

Junagadh *p1266, map p1267*

⍿ Garden Café, Girnar Rd. Attractive outdoor restaurant with view of hills, among flowering plants and lawns, average food, good atmosphere and service; aquarium and small museum next door (1000-1300, 1500-1800, entry Rs 5), handy for visitors to the hill.

♥ **Geeta** and **Sharda**, both near railway station. Good *thalis*.

♥ **Poonam**, Dhal Rd, Chittakhana Chowk, 1st floor. Unlimited Gujarati *thalis* (Rs 35-60). Excellent food and service.

♥ **Sagar**, Jayshree Talkies Rd. Good Punjabi and Gujarati, vegetarian, Indian breakfast (Rs 50), a/c.

♥ **Santoor**, off MG Rd, near Kalwa Chowk, upstairs. Very good Indian and Chinese veg dishes, a/c, excellent value, 0945-1500, 1700-2300.

♥ **Swati**, Jayshree Talkies Rd. Mainly Punjabi, some South Indian and Chinese, all veg. Good food and lassi, courteous, young enthusiastic staff, clean and comfortable (though smell of spices pervades), a/c, one of town's most popular restaurants.

♥ **Sagar**, offers similar fare. A/c, great breakfasts (poori-aloo, idli, vada, lassi).

Near Kalwa Chowk, try *Dal-Pakwana* (a Sindhi brunch), stuffed parathas, fruit juices. (Kesar mango from April to June). In Azad Chowk, try milk sweets, snacks and curds.

Sasan Gir National Park *p1268*
Order meals at one of the lodges. Nondescript shacks opposite *Sinh Sadan* sell biscuits, toothpaste, ice creams etc and also *chai*; roadside veg *dhabas* serve quite good *thalis*.
Gumalbar, near Sinh Sadan.

Veraval *p1269*
♥ **Ali Baba**, near Park Hotel. Recommended for seafood.

♥ **Sagar**, Riddhi-Siddhi Complex, 1st floor, between Bus Stand and clocktower. A/c, excellent service, veg Punjabi and South Indian.

Diu *p1270, maps p1270 and p1272*
Near the **museum**: some Catholic homes serve traditional 'Portuguese' food to western travellers with an hour's notice (ask directions in the Christian locality near St Paul's Church).

♥♥ **Bom Appetite**, Mrs D'Souza's residence near St Paul's, T53137. To order 'Portuguese' lunches.

♥♥ **Martha's Place**, opposite the museum. Excellent home cooking, good views.

♥♥ **Apana**, Old Fort Rd. Large seafood platters (shark, lobster, kingfish, crab and veg), Rs 300, easily shared by 4-6. Recommended.

♥♥ **Ram Vijay**, near State Bank of Saurashtra. Excellent 'home-made' ice creams, milk shakes and sodas, friendly.

♥♥ **Uma Shakti**, near Samrat. Good food and service (try toasted cheese sandwiches).

Jallandhar Beach *p1272*
Neelkant's Restaurant serves delicious cheap *thalis*, new a/c for continental food, backpackers' meeting place, friendly, family run. Recommended.

Nagoa *p1273*
Radhika Beach Resort. Wide choice of Indian, Chinese, some continental. Well-prepared meals from spotless kitchen, pleasant a/c surroundings and attentive service.
Island Bar, on Nagoa-Diu Rd. Varied, mid-range, cheap menu including Punjabi, Chinese, continental. Food can be excellent or indifferent, service can be slow.

Ghogla-Ahmedpur Mandvi *p1273*
Suzlon Beach. Restaurant, bar, terrace opens onto beach and sea but lacks atmosphere.
Premalayai. Serves Indian food.

Porbandar *p1273, map p1274*
Sudama Chowk near the ST Stand is where locals gather for *samosas, pakodas, bhel, kachori, pau bhaji* etc in the evening.

♥ **Adarsh**, MG Rd. A/c, Indian vegetarian and ice creams.

♥ **Khana Khazana**, MG Rd. Open sunset to past midnight, is recommended for cheese/chutney sandwiches, cheese toasts, burgers and coffee; South Indian snacks (hot *idlis*) on Sun; also takeaway.

♥ **Mehta**, Sudama Chowk. Snacks, ice creams.

♥ **Modern**, near MG Rd. A/c, good non-veg meals, some seafood.

♥ **Raghuvanshi** near Khadi Bhandar. Good Gujarati *thalis*.

♥ **Swagath**, MG Rd. Excellent thalis, pleasant. The bazar sells *khajli* (fried dough snack), *thabdi* and *peda* (milk sweets).

Jamnagar *p1275*
Kalpana, near Teen Batti. Cheap veg dishes, fruit ices from next door.
Rangoli, near Anupam Talkies, near Bedi Gate. A/c, good but more expensive veg Punjabi and South Indian, friendly, open lunch time and evening (except Wed).

Urvee, Supermarket, Town Hall Rd, T671207.
Good Gujarati *thalis* at lunch time.

Dwarka *p1275, map p1276*
Poor choice of rather dhoddy and dirty
eating places.
Dwarkeshwar, is best for tasty, hygienic
thalis but slow service.

◑ Bars and clubs

Diu *p1270, maps p1270 and p1272*
The night market, near post office, very
popular. Kingfisher, Turbo, London Pilsner, Rs
20-30 per bottle; tasty snacks from stalls too.
Most bars close around 2130.
Nilesh stays open until 2300.

❀ Festivals and events

Junagadh *p1266, map p1267*
Feb-Mar: Bhavnath Fair at *Sivaratri* at
Damodar Kund near the Girnar foothills is
very spectacular. Attended by *Naga Bawas*
(naked sages), who often arrive on decorated
elephants to demonstrate strange powers
(including the strength of their penis), and
colourful tribal people who come to worship
and perform *Bhavai* folk theatre. **Nov-Dec**: a
popular 10-day *Fair* is held at the Jain
temples starting at **Kartik Purnima**.

Dwarka *p1275, map p1276*
Aug/Sep: Janmashtami, see page 1086.
Special worship and fair (Aug).

♢ Shopping

Diu *p1270*
The night market is very lively in the
evenings. Govt **Cottage Emporia** near the
jetty sell local crafts of stone, metal and shell;
Jaysukh, Sangaria Lane, has good shell crafts.
Don't be tempted by star tortoise and turtle
shell bangles and souvenirs; they are illegal
under 'Wildlife Protection Act', severe
penalties attached.

▲ Activities and tours

Diu *p1270, maps p1270 and p1272*
Camels: on the dunes at Nagoa Rs 25;
ponies also available.

Cruises
Evening cruises: from Bunder Chowk jetty to
Nagoa Beach, with music, Rs 100 per person;
times from tourist office.

Tour operators
Oceanic, Bunder Chowk, T521800.
Reshma, T52241.

Watersports
At Nagoa and Ahmedpur-Mandvi: 8-seater
speed boat (10-15 mins)/parasailing/wind
surfing, each Rs 500; waterskiing Rs 100 (jet
skiing at Nagoa beach). A new pool/water
slide complex has opened next to *Kohinoor*
on the Diu-Nagoa road.

Dwarka *p1275, map p1276*
Dwarka Darshan a tour of 4 local pilgrimage
sites (Nageshwar Mandir, Gopi Talav Teerth,
Beyt Dwarka, Rukmini Temple) by minibus,
departs 0800, 1400, 5 hrs (can take 7!). Tickets
Rs 30; book a day in advance for morning tour.
Alternatively, visit only Beyt Dwarka for a
worthwhile day spent with pilgrims.

⊖ Transport

Junagadh *p1266, map p1267*
Bycicle
Cycle hire: from shops on Dhal Rd, near
Relief Hotel; Rs 2 per hr, may need to bargain.

Bus
Local Regular bus services to **Ahmadabad**,
Rajkot (2 hrs), **Veraval**, **Porbandar** and
Sasan Gir (2½ hrs).

Train
Ahmadabad: *Somnath Mail 9923*, 1902,
9¼ hrs; *Girnar Exp 9845*, 2120, 9 hrs. Rajkot:
Veraval Rajkot Mail 9837, 1318, 5¼ hrs; *Fast
Pass 341*, 0530, 3¼ hrs; *347*, 1000, 3¾ hrs;
349, 1550, 3¾ hrs. **Veraval**: *Girnar Exp 9846*,
0623, 1¾ hrs. For **Sasan Gir**: take *Fast Pass
352* to Delwada, 0605; a delightful journey.

Sasan Gir National Park *p1268*
Air
Nearest airport is Keshod (86 km).

Bus
Service to/from **Junagadh** (54 km), 2½ hrs,
and **Veraval** (40 km), 2 hrs. Service to **Una**

for Diu is unpredictable, morning dep 1100. Frequent buses from Ahmadabad.

Train
From **Junagadh** to Sasan Gir, *352*, 0650, 3 hrs, continues to **Delwada** near Diu; return to Junagadh, *351*, 1827, so possible to visit for the day. The route is very attractive. **Talala** is the last major station, 15 km before Sasan, so stock up with fruit, biscuits, liquids there. From **Veraval**, take *359* at 1039, or *353* at 1409, both bound for Khijadiya; return to **Veraval**, by *354* at 1138 or *360* at 1535.

Veraval *p1269*
Somnath Travels, Satta Bazar, will obtain tickets for long distance journeys.

Bicycle
Cycle hire: from opposite bus station or railway station, some in poor condition (road between Veraval and Somnath is appalling).

Bus
Long distance To Keshod (1 hr), **Diu**, **Porbandar** (2 hrs), **Bhavnagar** (9 hrs). Deepak Ramchand Taxis, T22591 has non-a/c Ambassador taxis. To **Ahmedpur Mandvi** (via docks) and **Somnath** Rs 550, **Diu** Rs 600, tour of docks and Somnath Rs 250.

Taxi
From Tower Rd and ST bus stands are cheaper than those at the railway station.

Train
Ahmadabad: *Somnath Mail 9923*, 1705, 11¼ hrs; *Girnar Exp 9845*, 1930, 10¾ hrs.

Prabhas Patan *p1269*
From **Veraval**, auto-rickshaw (bargain to Rs 30 return) or frequent bus.

Diu *p1270, maps p1270 and p1272*
Air
Jet Airways, at the airport, Nagoa Rd, T53544, airport T55030, accepts credit card payment; agents: **Oceanic Travels**, Bunder Chowk. **Mumbai**, daily (1050 and 1250 on alternate days), US$80.

Car
Car hire: Rs 900 per day, Rs 300 for Diu sightseeing; Rs 450 includes Nagoa beach.

Bicycle
Cycle hire: about Rs 50 per day. A to Z, near Vegetable Market, Panchwati Rd, T54679; **Shilpa**, Bunder Chowk; **Mayur**, past *Ankur Hotel* (across rough ground, then 20m along alley to left), excellent bikes; **Daud**, Zampa Gate, T418592, well maintained, new bikes; **Krishna Cycles** at Ghogla.

Bus
Local A road bridge connects Diu Town with Ghogla (frequent buses).

ST buses operate from the Jethabai Bus Stand near the bridge to Ghogla. Local Bus Stand: to Nagoa 3 daily; frequent service to Bucharwada-Vanakbara and Una, Rs 4 (minibus Rs 6).

Long distance Most long distance buses operate from the Jethabai Bus Stand just south of the bridge; enquire beforehand. ST services to **Ahmadabad** via Bhavnagar, 0700 (10 hrs); **Jamnagar** via Junagadh, 0600; **Porbandar**, 1300; **Rajkot**, several 0445-1725 (7 hrs); **Vadodara**, 1730; **Veraval**, several 0400-1300 (2½ hrs).

Buses often leave 15-20 mins early. For **Bhavnagar** ask for 'direct bus' (departs 1035), as some go through Mahuva and are packed.

Private agents in the Main Sq offer buses from the private bus stand to **Mumbai** (deluxe) at 1000, and towns in Gujarat which are more reliable than ST buses. To **Ahmadabad**, 1900; from Ahmadabad, a direct bus leaves from Paldi Chowrasta at 2100. **Goa Travels** runs buses to Bhavnagar, Junagadh (5 hrs), Palitana. A daily bus connects with **Mumbai** via Bhavnagar (20 hrs).

Una, 30 mins from Diu (10 km), has more frequent buses to/from **Ahmadabad**, **Bhavnagar**, **Junagadh**, **Rajkot**, **Veraval** etc. **Shiv Shakti**, **Sahajanand** and **Gayatri Travels** run private buses from the main Bus Station to **Ahmadabad**, **Bhavnagar**, **Mumbai**, **Vadodara** etc. From Vanakbara, bus to **Okha**, 0700, 0800.

Motorbike
Motorbike hire in the market area; about Rs 150 a day; **Kismet** has good new scooters Rs 100 per day, Rs 200 deposit, friendly service; repairs off Estrada Lacerda.

Rickshaw
Auto-rickshaw: Rs 30 to Nagoa, Rs 25 to Ghogla.

Train

Delwada, 8 km north is the nearest railhead just south of Una; auto-rickshaws demand Rs 100 from Diu to Una or Delwada. The station is a short walk from the centre of town – follow the locals! Slow train to **Junagadh** (stops at **Sasan Gir**) *351*, 1445. Veraval (90 km): to/from Ahmadabad, *Girnar Exp* and *Somnath Mail* take 12 hrs.

Nagoa *p1273*
Rickshaws from Diu Bus stand, 20 mins, Rs 30, or hire a **bicycle**.

Ghogla-Ahmedpur Mandvi *p1273*
The bus between Una and Ghogla may stop if you request, otherwise take a rickshaw from Ghogla for 3 km, or take a shorter path on foot along the beach. The hotels are 3 km from Diu bridge off the Una Rd (right turn past the gate). Hourly bus from Diu, Rs 3; auto Rs 25.

Porbandar *p1273, map p1274*
Air
Jet Airways, T252774, airport T243343, flies daily to Mumbai.

Bus
ST buses serve most centres of Gujarat. **Bharat** and **Eagle Travels** run regular private luxury buses to **Ahmadabad**, **Jamnagar**, **Junagadh**, **Rajkot** etc.

Train
Mumbai Central: *Saurashtra Exp 9216*, 2000, 23½ hrs. Also to Rajkot and Ahmadabad.

Jamnagar *p1275*
Air
Airport, 10 km west. **Indian Airlines**, T550211; to **Mumbai**.

Bus
STC services to Rajkot (frequent) and Ahmadabad; also Dwarka and Porbandar.

Train
The railway station is 6 km northwest of town. Ahmadabad: *Saurashtra Exp 9216*, 2243, 7¼ hrs; *Saurashtra Mail 9006*, 1445, 7½ hrs. Both to **Mumbai Central**: 20¾ hrs and 17½ hrs via Rajkot: 1¾ hrs and 2¼ hrs.
Vadodara (and Ahmadabad): *Okha-Puri Exp*, 1115.

Dwarka *p1275, map p1276*
Bus
To Jamnagar, Porbandar and Somnath. Private operators run to most major towns in Gujarat.

Train
Ahmadabad and **Vadodara**: *Saurashtra Mail 9006*, 1215, 10 hrs, and **Mumbai Central**: 20 hrs. Also *Okha-Puri Exp*, 0835.

● Directory

Junagadh *p1266, map p1267*
Banks Bank of Baroda, near the town Post Office is very efficient and changes TCs; Bank of Saurashtra, changes currency.

Sasan Gir National Park *p1268*
Useful services The post office in the village has an excellent 'frank' for postcards and letters. Health Centre, Post Office and Bank at Sasan. Market at Talala. Forest Office, T8554.

Diu *p1270, maps p1270 and p1272*
Banks State Bank of Saurashtra, near Fish Market opposite *Nilesh hotel*, accepts TCs but not foreign currency immediately (only encashed after notes are verified by HQ); very slow. Authorised dealers next to *Reshma Travels* and *Alishan Hotel* are more efficient for exchange (sterling and US$ TCs and currency). **Internet** Deepee Telecom and Cyber café, Bunder Chowk. **Medical services** Manesh Medical Store is a pharmacy with a doctor in the building. **Post office** The main Post Office is on Bunder Chowk, the other is at Ghogla. **Tourist offices** At Tourist Complex, Ghogla. Mon-Fri, 0930-1315, 1400-1745. Information Asst, Diu jetty north of Bunder Chowk, T52212.

Porbandar *p1273, map p1274*
Banks Bank of India, Kedareshwar Rd, and State Bank of India, MG Rd (and sometimes Bank of Baroda) change TCs of reputed companies. After frauds and fake notes, they are wary of currency.

Jamnagar *p1275*
Post office Head Post Office at Chandni Chowk. Forestry Office, T552077. **Travel agents**, **exchange** and **internet** are around Teen Batti in the New Town Centre.

★ Kachchh (Kutch)

The scenic Maliya Miyana bridge, across salt marshes often filled with birds, gives a beguilingly attractive impression of the gateway to Kachchh. Yet perhaps this region is climatically the least appealing of Gujarat, and it is certainly the most sparsely populated. It is well and truly off the beaten tourist trail. The various communities such as Rabaris, Ahirs and Meghwals among others, each have a distinct dress and practise a particular craft. ▸▸ *For Sleeping, Eating and other listings, see pages 1290-1292.*

Background

The region, the central peninsula, is surrounded by the seasonally flooded Great and Little Ranns. The Gulf of Kachchh to the south, a large inlet of the Arabian Sea, has a marine national park and sanctuary with 42 islands and a whole range of reefs, mudflats, coastal salt marsh and India's largest area of mangrove swamps.

The **Kachchh Peninsula** is relatively high, covered with sheets of volcanic lava but with often saline soil. Dry and rocky, there is little natural surface water though there are many artificial tanks and reservoirs. Intensive grazing has inhibited the development of the rich vegetation around the tanks characteristic of neighbouring Sindh in Pakistan, and there is only sparse woodland along the often dry river beds. The wetlands are severely over-exploited, but some of the lakes are important seasonal homes for migratory birds including pelicans and cormorants.

The **Rann of Kachchh** in the north runs imperceptibly into the Thar desert. A hard smooth bed of dried mud in the dry season, some vegetation survives, concentrated on little grassy islands called *bets*, which remain above water level when the monsoons flood the mudflats.

With the arrival of the southwest monsoon in June the saltwater of the Gulf of Kachchh invades the Rann and the Rajasthan rivers pour freshwater into it. It then becomes an inland sea and Kachchh virtually becomes an island. From December to February, the Great Rann is the winter home of migratory **flamingos** when they arrive near **Khavda**. There are also sand-grouse, Imperial grouse, pelicans and avocets.

Handicrafts

Local traditional embroidery and weaving is particularly prized. When the monsoons flooded vast areas of Kachchh, farming had to be abandoned and handicrafts flourished which not only gave expression to artistic skills but also provided a means of earning a living. Mirrorwork, Kachchh appliqué and embroidery with beads, *bandhani* (tie-and-dye), embroidery on leather, gold and silver jewellery, gilding and enamelling and colourful wool-felt *namda* rugs are available.

Bhuj → *Phone code: 02832. Colour map 2, grid C1. Population: 120,000.*

The devastating earthquake in January 2001 destroyed much of this old walled town with its tightly packed maze of narrow winding streets. Repairs and restoration are progressing. Most of the heritage buildings suffered extensive damage. It is hoped that some of the structures, as described below, will be restored by experts but many treasures have been lost permanently.

Sights

Among the old buildings in the citadel is the palace of **Rao Lakha** (circa 1752), the fortunate patron of Ramsingh Malam, who after his European adventures became a master clockmaker, architect, glass-blower, tile-maker and much more. A large white

The earthquake

The area around Bhuj was devastated by the severe earthquake which hit Gujarat on the morning of 26th January 2001 and claimed around 20,000 lives. With its epicentre near Bhuj, the tremors which hit 7.7 on the Richter scale virtually flattened the town and several nearby villages and a massive rebuilding programme has begun. Bhuj is trying to attract visitors back to the town and the surrounding villages although the monuments and museums may not have re-opened yet.

mansion with carvings and fretwork, the palace contains a Darbar Hall, State Apartments and the noted **Aina Mahal** (Mirror Palace) which has suffered some damage but is restorable though items such as glass paintings have been destroyed. It has exquisite ivory inlaid doors (circa 1708), china floor tiles and marble walls covered with mirrors and gilt decorations.

The **Fuvara Mahal** (Music Room), next door, is a curiosity. Surrounded by a narrow walkway, the pleasure hall is a shallow tiled pool with a central platform where the Maharao sat in cool comfort to listen to music, watch dancers or recite his poetry. With its entrance shielded from the hot sun, the candlelit interior with embroidered wall hangings provided a welcome refuge. Ingenious pumps,, raised water to the tank above to feed the pool with sprinkling fountains. Some parts, especially the upper floors and roofs, were seriously damaged in January 2001.

Rao Pragmalji's Palace (1865) in red brick is across the courtyard. The elaborate anachronism was designed by the British engineer Colonel Wilkins (though some guides will say by an Italian architect). It contained a vast Darbar Hall, with verandahs, corner towers and *zenanas* all opulently decorated with carving, gilding, Minton tiles and marble. The upper floors suffered serious damage in the earthquake. It is used as Government offices. There are good views of the surrounding countryside from the tall clocktower connected to the palace by covered galleries. The colourful **Swaminarayan Temple** is behind the Palace and near the bazar.

Sarad Bagh Palace, west of Hamirsar, the last residence of the Maharao (died 1991) is set in very lovely gardens. Exhibits include furniture and exotic ornaments.

The **Maharaos' chatedis** (memorial tombs), further south, built of red sandstone were severely damaged in the 1819 earthquake and again in 2001. Some are beyond repair. **Ramkund**, nearby, has a stone lined tank with carvings of Hindu deities.

Museums

The Italianate **Kachchh Museum** (1877), near Mahadev Gate, is the oldest in Gujarat. Exhibits include the largest collection of Kshatrap inscriptions (the earliest, of 89 AD), textiles, weaponry, paintings and an anthropological section. Anyone interested in local traditional folk music and instruments may contact Mr UP Jadia here. Restoration is in progress with the help of Indo-Australian heritage experts.

Bharatiya Sanskriti Darshan ① *Mandvi Rd, near Collector's Office*, is a small, delightful Folk Museum and Reference Library. The collection of 4,500 exhibits includes traditional handicrafts, textiles, weaponry, as well as artefacts of historic or artistic importance, and a recreated village of typical Kachchhi *bhungas* (huts) of different communities. *Kutch – People and their handicrafts* by PJ Jethi (Rs 100), and postcards for sale. For Aina Mahal Museum, see Sights above.

Excursions

Rudrani Dam ① *14 km north, 30-minute drive from Bhuj on the Sumrasar road,* has the colourful Rudramata Temple, originally 17th century, nearby. The goddess Sati's

🎙 Restoration of Bhuj

In 1918 the earthquake destroyed 7,000 houses and killed over 1,000 people. Many more lost their lives in the most recent disaster of 26 January 2001 when much of the town was flattened. Most of the buildings in Bhuj have been destroyed. The people have begun to rebuild their lives but what will emerge will be substantially changed town. Some hotels have now reopened but the museums and monuments will still take time. However, the medieval town atmosphere prevails and Heritage Walks are being organised to bring Bhuj back in the limelight. The surrounding villages and sites – Dholavira and Mandvi – are recovering and are possible to visit. Bhadreswar was badly hit but renovations are progressing at the Jain temples.

'rudra' (frightening) aspect is believed to have fallen on this spot and is hence a place of pilgrimage, see page 1330.

Craft villages nearby are still worth visiting (see below), though some may be disappointed that quality has been sacrificed in order to satisfy increasing demand. You may not see crafts actually being produced and rumours suggest that much is being 'imported' from other areas.

Qasab is an outlet for KMVS (Kutch Mahila Vikas Sangathan), a collective of 1,200 craftswomen from 130 local villages who are practising their traditional skills to produce high quality clothes (Indian and western), home furnishings and some leather goods. The women market the products themselves, bypassing an intermediary, thus achieving a fairer deal for themselves and their producer group (see Shopping page 1291).

Craft villages → *Colour map 2, grid C1. Population: 37,000.*

Handicrafts are a living tradition of Kachchh and the girls of various communities make beautifully embroidered garments for their own trousseaus while women produce attractive fabrics for a second income.

Some visitors to villages near Bhuj are disappointed to find that the previously nomadic tribes are being housed in whitewashed urban housing in expanded older villages which are losing their traditional architecture. Cement and modern materials are replacing mud walls and cow dung. However, the handicrafts of these villages are still of a high standard.

North of Bhuj

ⓘ *Buses from Bhuj go to the main villages from the ST stand, around 0800 (check time), but may involve a 15-min walk. It is better to arrange a taxi or hire a motorbike/scooter.*

The vast grasslands of **Banni** meet the Great Rann in the Khavda region, north of Bhuj. They are home to numerous pastoral nomadic, semi-nomadic and resident people who keep sheep, goats, camels, buffaloes and other livestock. The 40 or so hamlets here are best known for the minute detail of their embroidery. More recently, these villages have started focusing on selling handicrafts as their main source of income and there are signs of modernisation and commercialisation. The traditional thatched huts (*bhungas*) are made from mud plastered with cow dung which are often decorated with hand-painted floral patterns and inlaid with mirrors during festivals. Traditional utensils are still used for cooking, eating and storage in the houses. The area is known for its raptors (eagles, vultures and other birds of prey).

Dhorodo, 80 km north, is the centre for Jat embroidery, using chain stitches inset with small mirrors, leather embroidery as well as silver jewellery.

Sumrasar, 25 km north east, is famous for its Ahir embroidery and Soof embroidery of the Sodhas, done without a plan but by counting the warp and weft of the material. Daya Nathani at Ami Baug is an award-winning artisan, and also an astute businesswoman (taxi-drivers are likely to know her house). *Kala Raksha*, Parkar Vas, Sumrasar Sheikh, near Collector's Office, T77238, is a grassroots organization which maintains a small museum of heirloom textiles. It works with and trains 180 artisans to create contemporary pieces inspired by their own traditions. Now run by Judy Frater, the American author of *Threads of Identity*.

Loria (**Ludia**), 60 km away, has huts with painted and mirror inlaid walls, and is famed for its wood crafts.

Zura, 30 km, produces embroidered footwear and other leather crafts. Copper bells are also made in this village.

Nirona ① *bus from Bhuj, 1½ hrs*, 40 km northwest, has embroidery, lacquered wood crafts, wood carving and is the only home of highly skilful rogan-painting – fabrics painted using iron rods.

Nakhtarana, northwest in the heart of the craft village belt, produces some tie-and- dye work. There is a Chinkara Sanctuary at **Narayan Sarovar**, 75 km away.

Charri Dund Lake, a reservoir near Charri village, offers splendid birdwatching opportunities. Flamingoes, pelicans, cranes, storks, ducks etc gather in large numbers, specially in winter, while nearby grasslands are filled with passerine and ground dwelling birds. The Banni grasslands are known for their huge eagle and vulture congregations. Bombay Natural History Society and other organisations monitor bird migrations in the Banni region, and bird banding camps are set up around Charri lake. The grasslands are home to wolf, hyena, jackal, Indian and desert foxes and lesser wild cats but are imperilled by the government's decision to convert Banni into pastureland.

Dholavira ① *bus from Bhuj via Rapar, 7 hrs,* is the site of excavation of a Harappan town (pre-2500BC) which some estimate to be larger than Moenjodaro, in Pakistan. It was only discovered in 1967 and excavation began in 1990. The drive to Khadir *beyt*, an oasis in the Great Rann, through dazzling salt flats is very scenic. Excavations show the complex to be on three levels (Citadel, Middle and Lower Towns) with pottery, stone cutting, coppersmithing, drainage systems and town planning at an advanced level. The fortifications with walls, bastions and double ramparts reflect danger from invasions or enemies. An inscribed tablet found here bears 10 letters in the Harappan script.

South of Bhuj

① *Buses to Rajkot or Ahmadabad can drop you off at most of the villages.*

There are a number of interesting villages south of Bhuj en route to Gandhidham. All require no permit – Mandvi, Mundra on the coast and Bachau, 84 km east. **Tunda Vandh** is a good place to see typical *bhungas* of Kachchh. Architecture students come to see, study and photograph the traditional architecture adapted to this hostile climate. The interiors have beautiful Rabari cupboards, chests, inlaid mirrors and paintings.

Bhujodi, 10 km southeast, off the main road and a 10-min walk from the bus stand, is the centre for pitloom weaving. The weavers have now been organized into a co-operative. They produce colourful *galichas* (carpets), *durries* (rugs), *dhablos* (blankets), and other items from wool, camel/goat hair, cotton, and even synthetic fibres. Some embroidery and tie-and-dye can be seen here as well. Mr Vanka Kana Rabari, T40005, has reasonably priced local embroidery etc, but not the most select quality. *Shrujan* sells upmarket embroideries and home furnishings.

Padhdhar, 22 km southeast of Bhujodi, produces Ahir embroidery using round mirrors with floral and geometrical patterns.

⦂ A melting pot of tribes

Kachchh is a meeting point of Sindhi, Gujarati, Muslim and Rajasthani cultures; the local language is more Sindhi than Gujarati. The arid grasslands to the north, south and west of Bhuj are home to a number of pastoral tribes – the Bharwad shepherds and goat herds, the Rabari camel and cattle herders, Maldhars who keep buffaloes, Samra and Sindhi Muslim cameleers and others. The communities have the Lohan merchants, Langa musicians of the Indian desert and Kanbi Patel agriculturalists among them. They came from near and far – some, like the Sodha Rajputs, originated from the area neighbouring Rajasthan now in Pakistan, the Jats from Baluchistan, while the Sindhis claim Abyssinian descent.

Dhaneti is a centre for Ahir and Rabari embroidery. Meet Govindbhai, a local entrepreneur, and his friendly family who will show you the embroidered and mirror inlaid fabrics made for their own use. There are some intricate hero stones (*pallias*) by the village lake.

Dhamanka, 50 km east of Bhuj, is famous for its block printed fabrics, table/bed linen, garments etc, using vegetable or chemical dyes. Used blocks can be bought here which make good decorative pieces.

Anjar, 22 km southeast, was an early Jadeja Rajput capital of Kachchh, founded 450 years ago. The Jesal-Toral shrine has a romantic tale of the reform of an outlaw prince through the love of a village girl. Anjar is also known for its metalcrafts, especially betel nut crackers and ornaments, *bandhni* and block printing. The 1818 Bungalow of Captain McMurdoch, the first European to settle in Kachchh, now government offices, has some Kamangari paintings on the ground floor.

Mandvi

Mandvi, 54 km southwest of Bhuj, is a pretty little seaside town, with a reservoir in the centre and a river beyond. During the 18th century the town outclassed Bhuj in importance, the sea-faring people dominating the sea trade, taking cotton, rice, spices etc to the Persian gulf, Arabia and Zanzibar. The skill of building *dhows* and boats using simple tools is being revived along the river – worth watching.

The town is now a centre for handicrafts like *bandhni* tie-and-dyed fabrics, jewellery and shell toys. It is a desert town but important agricultural research for the Kachchh region is being carried out here in the Gujarat Agricultural University and the Vivekenand Research Institute, to improve farming in the often hostile environment.

There is an 18th-century **palace** with an *Aina Mahal* (Mirror Hall) and music rooms which have remains of intricate stone carvings of Dutchmen, tigers and dancing girls and woodcarvings in the courtyard.

The magnificent 1940s **Vijay Vilas palace** ⓘ *Rs 5, camera Rs 20, plus vehicle charge*, with huge domes, combines Indian and European styles. You can see the drawing room with royal memorabilia, and the attractive *jali* windows of the *zenana*. The terrace, reached by a spiral staircase, with excellent sea views, especially at sunset, is ideal for a picnic.

The beaches on the town side are good for swimming and even camel or horse riding. A wind farm next to the beach is working hard to produce an alternative energy source. The *Maharao*'s pleasant private beach with few onlookers is open to visitors ⓘ *Rs 30 (worthwhile for women, to escape hassle from male onlookers)*. Out of town, you can visit a magnificent new Jain temple.

Bhuvad, Kandla and Gandhidham

On the Mundra Road, 19 km southwest of Anjar, Bhuvad has the ruined 13th-century temple of Bhuvaneshwar Mahadev. The *mandapa* (1289-90) is supported by 34 unusual pillars (square base, octagonal middle and circular upper section). A local legend describes how the headless body of the chieftain Bhuvad, who was killed in battle about 1320, fought its way to the village. The District Gazetteer records that a shrine with a red headless figure is dedicated to him, while the nearby tall shrines commemorate warriors killed in the same battle.

Further east along the coast is the port of **Kandla**, built to replace declining Mandvi. After independence, Kandla was further developed by the Government of India, to service the states in northwest India.

Gandhidham, 27 km north of Kandla, was founded by the Maharaos of Kachchh to accommodate refugees from Sindh in Pakistan after Partition in 1947. The enterprising community made a promising start and now the town is a prosperous business centre though the old handloom and embroidery co-operatives for refugees still exist.

The town has developed with the increasing importance of Kandla as a port having lost Karachi sea port to Pakistan. The Institute of Sindhology here is researching on various aspects of Sindhi culture.

★ Little Rann of Kachchh Sanctuary → *Colour map 2 grid C2.*

The 4,950 sq km Wild Ass Sanctuary of the Little Rann of Kachchh (created in 1973) and the 7,850 sq km desert wildlife sanctuary of the great Rann, together would comprise the largest contiguous tract of protected wildlife territory in India were it not divided by a road. The Little Rann is mostly a saline wilderness, broken by beyts – islands during the monsoon – covered with grass, bushes, acacia and thorn scrub. The area is under severe threat from the salt works, which clear the vegetation, release toxic effluents into the wetlands and pollute the air. A fast growing thorn scrub – *Prosopis juliflora* – is destroying most other vegetation.

Ins and outs

Entry The southern part of the sanctuary is accessible. Forest Department fees, US$5 (foreigners), still camera US$5, at Bajana and Dhrangadhra.

Climate Temperature: maximum 42°C, minimum 7°C; Annual rainfall: 1,000 mm. Best season is late-Oct to mid-Mar.

Wildlife

This is the last home of the **Asiatic wild ass** (locally called *khacchar* or *ghorker*), a handsome pale chestnut brown member of the wild horse family with a dark stripe down the back. Wild asses are usually seen as lone stallions, small groups of mares or harems of a male with mares. Large herds of 40-60 are sometimes seen but they are loosely knit. Males fight viciously, biting and kicking, for their females. Nilgai, antelope and chinkara (Indian gazelle) are other mammals seen, but the chinkara numbers have dwindled due to poaching. Blackbucks have become almost extinct in the Little Rann of Kachchh but are seen in villages nearby. Wolf is the primary predator, though not common. You might spot jackal, desert fox, jungle and desert cat on a drive. Birdlife is abundant. Houbara bustard, spotted and common Indian sand grouse, nine species of larks, desert warbler, desert wheatear, Indian and cream coloured courser, grey francolin and five species of quails are spotted at the *beyts*. The salt marshes teem with flamingos, pelicans, storks, ducks, herons and wading birds. Thousands of demoiselle and common eastern cranes spend the winter here.

Excursions

The 13th-century **Jhinjwada fort**, on the edge of Little Rann west of Dasada, has majestic gateways. At the southeast corner of the Rann, **Kalaghoda**, southwest of Dasada on the way to Bajana Lake, is particularly interesting. The principal British salt trading post with an old village-pony express, it retains plenty of colonial architecture including Raj bungalows, a cricket pavilion and a bandstand. **Dasada** is a convenient base for visits to the Little Rann. The interesting village has an old fort with wood carvings, 15th-century tombs, potters, a shepherd's colony and nomadic settlements. The Malik Dynasty who received the 35-mile estate in return for military services to the sultan of Ahmadabad, now live in a 1940s mansion *Fatima Manzil*.

Listings: Kachchh

● Sleeping

Bhuj *p1284*
Several hotels have opened after rebuilding and repairs but check before arriving.
B-D Prince, Station Rd, T20370, F50373. Rooms with bath, restaurant (varied menu), shops (books, clothes, tailoring, Qasab handicrafts), free airport transfer, guided tours of local villages Rs 1,500 per car, crowded area, no credit cards, 'spot' liquor permits.
C-D Lake View Rajendra Park, T53422, F50835. Non-a/c to deluxe a/c comfortable rooms, baths, fridges, garden restaurant, *thalis* indoors, gym, pool (open to non-residents, morning and afternoon), attractive location facing Hamirsar lake (birds in winter).
C-D Anam, end of Station Rd, T21390, F53397. 27 clean rooms, (a/c over-priced; others good value), some 4-bedded, with bath (hot water), TV, phone, comfortable and modern, good a/c veg restaurant (try Kachchhi), inexpensive *thalis*, noisy main road.
D-E Abha International, Siddharth Complex, Station Rd, T54451, F51424. 31 rooms, with bath (hot water), can be noisy, some a/c (non-a/c very good value); veg restaurant.
E-F Gangaram, Darbargadh, T22948, F56474. At intersection near Aina Mahal, extremely noisy. 15 clean, comfortable rooms with TV and baths (tiled floors and walls, showers), new a/c rooms, no restaurant but snacks served.
F Annapurna, Bhid Gate, T20831. Clean rooms, noisy, friendly owners, great Kachchhi cuisine.
F City Guest House, Langa St, near Bazar, T21067. 32 clean, quiet rooms, some with own shower, quiet garden for relaxing, cycle

hire, helpful, well run, very good value, used by foreign backpackers.

Rudrani Dam *p1285*
B Garha Safari Lodge, T079-6579672, F6575201. 14 white-washed *bhungas* (local style huts), tribal furniture, hot water, seven air-cooled, exchange, pool, atmospheric, good views of lake, jeep tours, mixed reports about food, cleanliness and service.

Mandvi *p1288*
D-E Holiday cottages, on the beach, 5 small double bedroom cottages with bath (western toilets), some a/c, and tents (2 cots each, shared toilets), Indian-continental restaurant planned.
F Vinayak, in town, offers simple rooms (Rs 50).

Gandhidham *p1289*
C Desert Palace (Sharma Resort), in Gandhidham-Anjar-Bhuj triangle, T02836-23726, F31891. 35 a/c rooms, resort in local style huts with modern bath, TV, fridge, comfortable, good Punjabi food in outdoor restaurant, pool, gym, boating, ayurvedic treatments, free transfer from airports, good alternative base to Bhuj, reserve ahead.
D Shiv, 360 Ward 12-B (2 km from railway station), T0283-621297, F20985. 39 rooms, some **C** a/c, wide menu restaurant.
D Sayaji, Sector 8, T02836-21297. 40 rooms, central a/c, restaurant and usual facilities.

Little Rann of Kachchh Sanctuary *p1289*
Dasada
B Camp Zainabad, 9 km from Dasada. A cluster of 16 self contained *kooba* huts in a

---

● *For an explanation of the sleeping and eating price codes used in this guide, see inside the front cover. Other relevant information is found in Essentials pages 52-57.*

Eucalyptus grove (beds, hot shower, western toilet) (Rs 2000 each includes meals and safaris), recreating a local village, well located, atmospheric but small cots, hard mattresses and sometimes insipid food, owned and enthusiastically managed by former ruling family of Zainabad, well organised jeep safaris in the Little Rann, also camel/horse/village safaris, boating at nearby lake; contact *Desert Coursers*, Camp Zainabad, via Dasada, Dt Surendranagar.

B Rann Riders, comfortable air-cooled rooms in 15 spacious Kachchhi *bhungas* and Kathiawadi *koobas* (huts) amid plantation and farms, tiled hot showers, comfortable and relaxing, great atmosphere at night, home grown organic vegetables, fresh fish and poultry, delicious home cooking (specially meat dishes), enthusiastic owner good jeeps for tours, contact *North West Safaris* T079-6302019, F6300962, ssibal@ad1.vsnl.net.in.

C Fatima Manzil, English cottage-style outhouse of 1940s mansion damaged by earthquake with renovated and improved rooms and baths. jeep safaris, Sarfraz Malik knows all about Rann wildlife, contact *North West Safaris*, T079- 6302019, F6300962, ssibal@ad1.vsnl.net.in.

E-F Guest Houses, Govt, closer to the Rann, at Bajana and Dhrangadra where a jeep can be hired for visiting the Little Rann.

🍴 Eating

Bhuj *p1284*
¶¶ Green, Shroff Bazar. Punjabi. South Indian vegetarian. Well prepared food, friendly staff.
¶¶ Neelam, Station Rd opposite *Prince*. North Indian (best paneer curries in town), some Chinese and continental. A/c, good variety and quality, friendly staff.
¶¶ Toral at *Prince* has good Gujarati, veg *thalis*; bit more expensive than elsewhere, but in a more comfortable setting.
¶¶ Anando. Excellent for Indian (including Gujarati) snacks. Friendly staff, a/c.
¶¶ Omlette Centre, near Bus Station. Popular for breakfast and snacks, excellent filled omelettes, sandwiches and 'English tea'.
¶¶ Tammu Fast Food, between *Abha* and *Janataghar*, has good hot samosas, South Indian snacks and *batakawadas*.

♨ *Phone code* Bhuj: 02832

¶¶ Noor, behind the bus station. Good, reasonably priced *biryani* and *chicken masala*.
¶¶ Annapurna Guest House, Bhid Gate. Kachchhi. Very cheap, authentic dishes, homely, allow you to sample each dish.

Snacks
Typical local *dhabelis* (spicy burger of peanuts and potatoes, in a roll), and *bhal* (nuts, gram, vegetables in a spicy sauce), can be sampled on Vaniyawad and Station Rd.

Mandvi *p1288*
Rajneesh Osho, near Azad Chowk, best value *thalis* in simple dining area. The bazar has fresh coconuts, biscuits, soft drinks and excellent local corn-on-the-cob. In the evening, hand-carts emerge with popular snacks.

⊛ Festivals and events

Bhuj *p1284*
Feb/Mar: 4-day Rann Utsav (Kachchh Festival) organized by Gujarat Tourism during *Sivaratri* – tribal crafts, folk dances and music, and tours of nearby sights. Fairs in many villages in Feb-Mar (*Nag Panchami*), and around Janmashtami in **Aug-Sep**.

⊙ Shopping

Bhuj *p1284*
Excellent folk embroidery, leather shoes, appliqué, mirrorwork, block-printed fabrics, painted pottery and local weaving are available. The market area stretches from Station Rd to the Darbargadh Palace complex, a maze of alleys specialising in different handicrafts. Most shops are closed from 1200 to 1500.

Crafts and textiles
A number of NGOs have organised craft co-operatives for the benefit of artisans. **Qasab**, 11 Nootan Colony, T22124 and a small shop in *Prince Hotel* (see Excursions above). **Shroff Bazar** has craft shops for hassle-free browsing, and clothes: Uday, T24660, a talented designer (Rs 600 for trousers and top), interesting block-prints, excellent tailoring (made-to-measure in a few hours). In **Danda Bazar**: Al Md Isha for outstanding tie-and-dye; Khatri Daod for block-prints, embroideries.

Kansara bazar, for silver jewellery. Bandhini Ghar, for tie-and-dye. AA Wazir, opposite General Hospital, near High School, selection of old pieces of embroideries; some for sale.

Photography
Pappu, Rashtrabasha Shopping Centre. Pornal, Darbargadh (near palaces), has an outstanding collection of slides of Kachchh.

▲ Activities and tours

Little Rann of Kachchh Sanctuary *p1289*
Naturalist guide Sarfraz Malik (see *Fatima Manzil* in Sleeping) is full of information on history and insights into the area. Tours of Little Rann wildlife sanctuary and nearby areas known for birds and blackbuck (including white mutant bucks) by jeep, charges Rs 500 per person per day, plus jeep hire Rs800 per day.

⊖ Transport

Bhuj *p1284*
Air
Indian Airlines, Station Rd, T50204, airport T22433, and Jet Airways, *Prince Hotel*, T53671, airport T54836, fly to **Mumbai**. Security is tight; pack cameras away in your checked baggage.

Bus
Frequent service to **Ahmadabad**, 411 km. To **Mandvi, Rapar**; **Rajkot**, 5 hrs. Also to **Bhavnagar**; **Jaisalmer**, 8 hrs; **Jamnagar**, 0500, 2040, 2115; **Junagadh, Palitana**,1900; **Porbandar, Veraval** and **Somnath**. Most long distance buses are scheduled to arrive at sunrise or sunset, so times are changed seasonally. 'Luxury buses' with reclining seats, more leg room, comfort stops etc are strongly recommended. Many private operators cluster around the Bus Station, and run infrequent services to major towns in Gujarat.

Train
From Mumbai *Bombay-Gandhidham Kutch Exp 9031*, 1710, 14¾ hrs (from Ahmadabad 0155, 6 hrs); then 2 hrs by bus or train to Bhuj. Trains also to **Kandla Port**. For **Rajasthan**: go to **Palanpur** *JPJ Pass*, 2020, 11½ hrs; trains from there to **Abu Rd, Ajmer, Jaipur** etc or bus; from Abu Rd, bus to **Udaipur**, 5 hrs.

Mandvi *p1288*
Express **bus** from Bhuj, 1 hr; others very slow. From bus station, **auto-rickshaws**, Rs 50 for return trip to Palace after bargaining. Possible to visit Mundra from Mandvi on same day, which also has direct services to Bhuj.

Gandhidham *p1289*
Bus
The station is a 3-min walk – turn right from the railway station. Frequent buses to **Bhuj**, but very crowded.

Train
Gandhidham is the principal railhead of Kachchh. **Mumbai Central**, *Kachchh Exp 9032* (excellent a/c sleeper and chair-car), 2045, 17 hrs via Vadodara. **Kandla Port**, *Fast Pass 177*, 0705; *173*, 0905; *175*, 1500: about 30 mins. **Vadodara**, *Gandhidham Vadodara Exp 9104*, 2305, 7¾ hrs. *Nagercoil-Gandhidham Exp 6336* via Thiruvananthapuram, Kochi etc.

Little Rann of Kachchh Sanctuary *p1289*
Dasada is 33 km northwest of Viramgam station, which has **trains** from Mumbai and Ahmadabad. Hotels arrange transfer at extra cost on prior notice. Dhrangadra has trains from Mumbai. State **buses** from main towns in Gujarat; frequent from Ahmadabad (93 km), 2½ hrs; some continue to Zainabad. From Dasada, Sarfraz Malik arranges transfer; local buses to Zainabad. To Bhuj: short route by narrow road, 267 km; by NH8A, 400 km.

⊕ Directory

Bhuj *p1284*
Banks State Bank of India, Station Rd changes Thomas Cook TCs, 1100-1500 weekdays, till 1300 Sat. Bank of Baroda, almost opposite changes Amex TCs (photocopy of passport needed). **Post office** Head PO: Lal Takri, 0700-1300, 1500-1800 (Mon-Sat). Sub-PO in the chowk at entrance to Aina Mahal. **Tourist offices** Gujarat Tourism, 416 Bahumali Building, T24910. Kachchh Explorer, Aina Mahal, Bhuj. Mr Jethi there is very knowledgeable and enthusiastic, 0900-1200, 1500-1800, closed Sat. **Useful addresses** Fire:T21490. Police: T20892. Forestry Office: T50600.

Background

☃ Footprint features

History

The first village communities in South Asia grew up on the arid western fringes of the Indus Plains 10,000 years ago. Over the following generations successive waves of settlers - sometimes bringing goods for trade, sometimes armies to conquer territory and sometimes nothing more than domesticated animals and families in search of land and peace - moved across the Indus and into India. They left an indelible mark on the landscape and culture of all the countries of modern South Asia.

The first settlers

A site at Mehrgarh, where the Indus Plains meet the dry Baluchistan Hills in modern Pakistan, has revealed evidence of agricultural settlement as early as 8500 BC. By 3500 BC agriculture had spread throughout the Indus Plains and in the thousand years following there were independent settled villages well to the east of the Indus. Between 3000 BC and 2500 BC many new settlements sprang up in the heartland of what became the Indus Valley civilization.

Most cultural, religious and political developments during that period owed more to local development than to external influence, although India had extensive contacts with other regions, notably with Mesopotamia. At its height the Indus Valley civilization covered as great an area as Egypt or Mesopotamia. However, the culture that developed was distinctively South Asian. Speculation continues to surround the nature of the language, which is still untranslated.

India from 2000 BC to the Mauryas

In about 2000 BC Moenjo Daro, widely presumed to be the capital of the Indus Valley Civilization, became deserted and within the next 250 years the entire Indus Valley civilization disintegrated. The causes remain uncertain: the violent arrival of new waves of Aryan immigrants (a theory no one now accepts), increasing desertification of the already semi-arid landscape, a shift in the course of the Indus and internal political decay have each been suggested as instrumental in its downfall. Whatever the causes, some features of Indus Valley culture were carried on by succeeding generations.

Probably from about 1500 BC northern India entered the Vedic period. Aryan settlers moved southeast towards the Ganga valley. Classes of rulers *(rajas)* and priests *(brahmins)* began to emerge. Grouped into tribes, conflict was common. In

BC	Northern South Asia	Peninsular India	External events	BC
900,000			Earliest hominids in West Asia	
500,000	Lower Palaeolithic sites from NW to the Peninsula; Pre-Soan stone industries in NW.	Earliest Palaeolithic sites - Narmada Valley; Karnataka; Tamil Nadu and Andhra.	First occupation of N China. Origin of *homo sapiens* in Africa. *Homo sapiens* in East Asia. First human settlement in Americas (Brazil).	450,000 150,000 100,000 30,000
10,000	Beginning of Mesolithic period.	Continuous occupation of caves and riverside sites.	Earliest known pottery - Kukui, Japan. Ice Age retreats - Hunter gatherers in Europe.	10,500 8,300
8,000	First wheat and barley grown in Indus plains.	Mesolithic.	First domesticated wheat, barley in fertile crescent; first burials in North America.	8,000
7,500	Pottery at Mehrgarh; development of villages.	Increase in range of cereals in Rajasthan.	Agriculture begins in New Guinea.	7,000
6,500	Humped Indian cattle domesticated, farming develops.	Cultivation extends south.	Britain separated from Continental Europe by sea level.	6,500

one battle of this period a confederacy of tribes known as the Bharatas defeated another grouping of 10 tribes. They gave their name to the region to the east of the Indus which is the official name for India today - Bharat.

The centre of population and of culture shifted east from the banks of the Indus to the land between the rivers Yamuna and Ganga, the doab (pronounced *doe-ahb*, literally 'two waters'). This region became the heart of emerging Aryan culture, which, from 1500 BC onwards, laid the literary and religious foundations of what ultimately became Hinduism, spreading to embrace the whole of India.

The Vedas The first fruit of this development was the Rig Veda, the first of four Vedas, composed, collected and passed on orally by Brahmin priests. While some scholars date the oral originsas early as the beginning of the second millennium BC, the date of 1300 BC to about 1000 BC still seems more probable. In the later Vedic period, from about 1000 BC to 600 BC, the Sama, Yajur and Artha Vedas show that the Indo-Aryans developed a clear sense of the Ganga-Yamuna *doab* as 'their' territory.

From the sixth to the third centuries BC the region from the foothills of the Himalaya across the Ganga plains to the edge of the Peninsula was governed under a variety of kingdoms or Mahajanapadhas - 'great states'. Trade gave rise to the birth of towns in the Ganga plains themselves, many of which have remained occupied to the present. Varanasi (Benaras) is perhaps the most famous example, but a trade route was established that ran from Taxila (20 km from modern Islamabad in Pakistan) to Rajgir 1,500 km away in what is now Bihar. It was into these kingdoms of the Himalayan foothills and north plains that both Mahavir, founder of Jainism and the Buddha, were born.

The Mauryas
Within a year of the retreat of Alexander the Great from the Indus in 326 BC, **Chandragupta Maurya** established the first indigenous empire to exercise control over much of the subcontinent. Under his successors, that control was extended to all but the extreme south of peninsular India.

The centre of political power had shifted steadily east into wetter, more densely forested but also more fertile regions. The Mauryans had their base in the region known as Magadh (now Bihar) and their capital at Pataliputra, near modern Patna. Their power was based on massive military force and a highly efficient, centralized administration.

BC	Northern South Asia	Peninsular India	External events	BC
3,500	Potter's wheel in use. Long distance trade.		Sumeria, Mesopotamia: first urban civilization.	3,500
3,000	Incipient urbanization in the Indus plains.	First neolithic settlements in south Deccan (Karnataka). Ash mounds, cattle herding.	First Egyptian state; Egyptian hieroglyphics; walled citadels in Mediterranean Europe.	3,100
2,500	Indus valley civilization cities of Moenjo Daro, Harappa and many others.	Chalcolithic ('copper' age) in Rajasthan; Neolithic continues in south.	Great Pyramid of Khufu China: walled settlements; European Bronze Age begins: hybridization of maize in South America.	2,530 2,500
2,000	Occupation of Moenjo Daro ends.	Chalcolithic in Malwa Plateau, Neolithic ends in south; in Karnataka and Andhra - rock paintings.	Earliest ceramics in Peru. Collapse of Old Kingdom in Egypt. Stonehenge in Britain. Minoan Crete.	2,300 2,150
1,750	Indus Valley civilization ends.	Hill-top sites in south India.	Joseph sold into Egypt - Genesis.	1,750

❖ Indo-Aryans and Dravidians – distinct races?

Recent genetic research suggests that homo sapiens originated in Africa less than 150,000 years ago. Southern and northern Indian types developed distinct genetic characteristics less than 40,000 years ago as they moved out of their central Asian homeland, first into West Asia and then into India, disproving all ideas of racial purity.

Early Mediterranean groups form the main component of the Dravidian speakers of the four South Indian states. Later Mediterranean types also seem to have come from the northwest and down the Indus Valley, but more important were the Indo-Aryans, who migrated from the steppes of Central Asia from around 2000 BC.

Asoka The greatest of the Mauryan emperors, Asoka took power in 272 BC. He inherited a full-blown empire, but extended it further by defeating the Kalingans in modern Orissa, before turning his back on war and preaching the virtues of Buddhist pacifism, see page 698. Asoka's empire stretched from Afghanistan to Assam and from the Himalaya to Mysore.

The state maintained itself by raising revenue from taxation - on everything, from agriculture, to gambling and prostitution. He decreed that 'no waste land should be occupied and not a tree cut down' without permission because all were potential sources of revenue for the state. The *sudras* (lowest of Hindu castes) were used as free labour for clearing forest and cultivating new land.

Asoka (described on the edicts as 'the Beloved of the Gods, of Gracious Countenance') left a series of inscriptions on pillars and rocks across the subcontinent. Over most of India these inscriptions were written in *Prakrit*, using the *Brahmi* script, although in the northwest they were in Greek using the *Kharoshti* script. They were unintelligible for over 2,000 years after the decline of the empire until James Prinsep deciphered the Brahmi script in 1837.

Through the edicts Asoka urged all people to follow the code of **dhamma** or dharma - translated by the Indian historian Romila Thapar as 'morality, piety, virtue and social order'. He established a special force of *dhamma* officers to try to enforce the code, which encouraged toleration, non-violence, respect for priests and those in authority and for human dignity.

However, Romila Thapar suggests that the failure to develop any sense of national consciousness, coupled with the massive demands of a highly paid

BC	Northern South Asia	Peninsular India	External events	BC
1,750 1,500	Successors to Indus Valley. Aryans invade in successive waves. Development of Indo-Aryan language.	Copper Age spreads, Neolithic continues. Gram and millet cultivation. Hill terracing. Cattle, goats and sheep.	Anatolia: Hittite Empire. New Kingdom in Egypt. First metal working in Peru. First inscriptions in China; Linear B script in Greece, 1650.	1,650 1,570 1,500 1,400
1,400	Indo-Aryan spread east and south to Ganga – Yamuna doab.	Horses introduced into south. Cave paintings, burials.	Tutankhamun buried in Valley of Kings.	1,337
1,200	Composition of Rig Veda begins?	Iron age sites at Hallur, Karnataka.	Middle America: first urban civilization in Olmec; collapse of Hittite Empire, 1200.	1,200
1,000	Earliest Painted Grey Ware in Upper Ganga Valley; Brahmanas begin to be written.	Iron Age becomes more widespread across Peninsula.	Australia: large stone-built villages; David King of Israel, Kingdom of Kush in Africa.	

bureaucracy and army, proved beyond the abilities of Asoka's successors to sustain. Within 50 years of Asoka's death in 232 BC the Mauryan Empire had disintegrated and with it the whole structure and spirit of its government.

A period of fragmentation: 185 BC to 300 AD

Beyond the Mauryan Empire other kingdoms had survived in South India. The Satavahanas dominated the central Deccan for over 300 years from about 50 BC. Further south in what is now Tamil Nadu, the early kingdoms of the Cholas and the Pandiyas gave a glimpse of both power and cultural development that was to flower over 1,000 years later. In the centuries following the break up of the Mauryan Empire these kingdoms were in the forefront of developing overseas trade, especially with Greece and Rome. Internal trade also flourished and Indian traders carried goods to China and Southeast Asia.

The classical period - the Gupta Empire: 319-467 AD

Although the political power of Chandra Gupta and his successors never approached that of his unrelated namesake nearly 650 years before him, the Gupta Empire which was established with his coronation in AD 319 produced developments in every field of Indian culture. Their influence has been felt profoundly across South Asia to the present.

Geographically the Guptas originated in the same Magadhan region that had given rise to the Mauryan Empire. Extending their power by strategic marriage alliances, Chandra Gupta's empire of Magadh was extended by his son, Samudra Gupta, who took power in AD 335, across North India. He also marched as far south as Kanchipuram in modern Tamil Nadu, but the heartland of the Gupta Empire remained the plains of the Ganga.

Chandra Gupta II reigned for 39 years from AD 376 and was a great patron of the arts. Political power was much less centralized than under the Mauryans and as Thapar points out, collection of land revenue was deputed to officers who were entitled to keep a share of the revenue, rather than to highly paid bureaucrats. Trade with Southeast Asia, Arabia and China all added to royal wealth.

That wealth was distributed to the arts on a previously unheard of scale. Some went to religious foundations, such as the Buddhist monastery at Ajanta, which produced some of its finest murals during the Gupta period. But Hindu institutions also benefited and some of the most important features of modern Hinduism date from this time. The sacrifices of Vedic worship were given up in favour of personal devotional worship, known as bhakti. Tantrism, both in its Buddhist and Hindu forms, with its emphasis on the female life force and worship of the Mother Goddess, developed. The focus of worship was increasingly towards a personalized and

BC	Northern South Asia	Peninsular India	External events	BC
800	Mahabharata war – Bhagavad Gita; Aryan invaders reach Bengal. Rise of city states in Ganga plains, based on rice cultivation.		First settlement at Rome. Celtic Iron Age begins in north and east of Alps.	850 800
750		Megalithic grave sites.	Greek city states.	750
700	Upanishads begin to be written; concept of transmigration of souls develops; Panini's Sanskrit grammar.		Iliad composed.	700
600	Northern Black Pottery.		First Latin script; first Greek coins.	600
599	Mahavir born – founder of Jainism.		First iron production in China; Zoroastrianism becomes official religion in Persia.	550
563	Gautama Buddha born.			

monotheistic deity, represented in the form of either Siva or Vishnu. The myths of Vishnu's incarnations also arose at this period.

The Brahmins, the priestly caste who were in the key position to mediate change, refocused earlier literature to give shape to the emerging religious philosophy. In their hands the Mahabharata and the Ramayana were transformed from secular epics to religious stories. The excellence of contemporary sculpture both reflected and contributed to an increase in image worship and the growing role of temples as centres of devotion.

Regional kingdoms and cultures

The collapse of Gupta power opened the way for successive smaller kingdoms to assert themselves. After the comparatively brief reign of **Harsha** in the mid-seventh century, which recaptured something both of the territory and the glory of the Guptas, the Gangetic plains were constantly fought over by rival groups, none of whom were able to establish unchallenged authority. Regional kingdoms developed, often around comparatively small natural regions.

The Deccan The Rashtrakutas controlled much of the central Peninsula between 700-950 AD. However, the southern Deccan was dominated by the Chalukyas from the sixth century up to 750 AD and again in the 11th and 12th centuries. To their south the Pandiyas, Cholas and Pallavas controlled the Dravidian lands of what is now Kerala, Tamil Nadu and coastal Andhra Pradesh. The Pallavas, responsible for building the temples at Mamallapuram, just south of modern Madras (Chennai), flourished in the seventh century.

In the eighth century Kerala began to develop its own regional identity with the rise of the **Kulashekharas** in the Periyar Valley. Caste was a dominating feature of the kingdom's social organization, but with the distinctive twist that the **Nayars,** the most aristocratic of castes, developed a matrilineal system of descent.

It was the **Cholas** who came to dominate the south from the eighth century. Overthrowing the Pallavas, they controlled most of Tamil Nadu, south Karnataka and southern Andhra Pradesh from 850 AD to 1278 AD. They often held the Kerala kings under their control. Under their kings **Rajaraja I** (984-1014) and **Rajendra** (1014-44) the Cholas also controlled north Sri Lanka, sent naval expeditions to Southeast Asia and successful military campaigns north to the Ganga plains. They lavished endowments on temples and also extended the gifts of land to Brahmins instituted by the Pallavas and Pandiyas. Many thousands of Brahmin priests were brought

BC	Northern South Asia	Peninsular India	External events	BC
500	Upanishads finished; Taxila and Charsadda become important towns and trade centres.	Aryans colonize Sri Lanka. Irrigation practised in Sri Lanka.	Wet rice cultivation introduced to Japan.	500
326 321	Alexander at Indus. Chandragupta establishes Mauryan Dynasty.	Megalithic cultures.	Crossbow invented in China.	350
300 297	Sarnath and Sanchi stupas. Mauryan power extends to Mysore.	First Ajanta caves in original form.	Mayan writing and ceremonial centres established.	300
272 250 232	Asoka's Empire. Brahmi script. Death of Asoka.	Chola Pandiya, Chera kingdoms: earliest Tamil inscriptions.	Ptolemy. First towns in Southeast Asia. Rome captures Spain.	285 250 206
185	Shunga Dynasty, centred on Ujjain.	Megalithic cultures in hills of south.	Romans destroy Greek states.	146

south to serve in major temples such as those in Chidambaram, and Rajendra wished
to be remembered above all as the king who brought water from the holy Ganga all
the way to his kingdom.

The Rajputs The political instability and rivalry that resulted from the ending of
Gupta power in the north opened the way for new waves of immigrants from the
northwest and for new groups and clans to seize power. Among these were the
Rajputs (meaning '*sons of kings*') who claimed descent from a mythical figure who
rose out of a sacrificial pit near Mount Abu.

From the seventh century AD Rajputs were always a force to be reckoned with in
the northwest, albeit at a comparatively local level. The temples at Khajuraho in
Central India, one of contemporary India's most remarkable sites, were built during
the Rajput dynasty of the Chandelas (916-1203). However, the Rajputs never
succeeded in forging a united front strong enough to establish either effective central
government, control internally or protection from external attack. See page 289.

The spread of Islamic power
The Delhi Sultanate From about 1000 AD the external attacks which inflicted most
damage on Rajput wealth and power came increasingly from the Arabs and Turks.
Mahmud of Ghazni raided the Punjab virtually every year between 1000 and 1026,
attracted both by the agricultural surpluses and the enormous wealth in cash, golden
images and jewellery of North India's temples which drew him back every year. He
sacked the wealthy centres of Mathura (UP) in 1017, Thanesar (Haryana) in 1011,
Somnath (Gujarat) in 1024 and Kannauj (UP). He died in 1030, to the Hindus just
another *mlechchha* ('impure' or sullied one), as had been the Huns and the Śakas
before him, soon to be forgotten. Such raids were never taken seriously as a long term
threat by kings further east and as the Rajputs often feuded among themselves the
northwest plains became an attractive prey.

Muslim political power was heralded by the raids of Mu'izzu'd Din and his defeat
of massive Rajput forces at the Second Battle of Tarain in 1192. Mu'izzu'd Din left his
deputy, Qutb u'd Din Aibak, to hold the territorial gains from his base at Indraprastha.
Mu'izzu'd Din made further successful raids in the 1190s, inflicting crushing defeats
on Hindu opponents from Gwalior to Benaras. The foundations were then laid for the
first extended period of such power, which came under the Delhi sultans.

Qutb u'd Din Aibak took Lahore in 1206, although it was his lieutenant **Iltutmish**
who really established control from Delhi in 1211. Qutb u'd Din Aibak consolidated
Muslim dominion by an even-handed policy of conciliation and patronage. In Delhi he

BC	Northern South Asia	Peninsular India	External events	BC
100	Kharavela King of Kalingans in Orissa. Final composition of Ramayana.	South Indian trade with Indonesia and Rome. Roman pottery and coins in South India.	Indian religions spread to Southeast Asia. Discovery of monsoon winds Introduction of Julian calendar.	100

converted the old Hindu stronghold of Qila Rai Pithora into his Muslim capital and began several magnificent building projects, including the Quwwat-ul-Islam mosque and the Qutb Minar, a victory tower. Iltutmish was a Turkish slave - a *Mamluk* - and the Sultanate continued to look west for its leadership and inspiration. However, the possibility of continuing control from outside India was destroyed by the crushing raids of **Genghis Khan** through Central Asia and from 1222 Iltutmish ruled from Delhi completely independently of outside authority. He annexed Sind in 1228 and all the territory east to Bengal by 1230.

A succession of dynasties followed, drawing on refugees from Genghis Khan's raids and from still further to the west to strengthen the leadership. In 1290 the first dynasty was succeeded by the Khaljis, which in turn gave way to the Tughluqs in 1320. **Mohammad bin Tughluq** (ruled 1324-51) was described by the Moorish traveller Ibn Batuta as 'a man who above all others is fond of making presents and shedding blood'. Despite its periodic brutality, this period marked a turning point in Muslim government in India, as Turkish Mamluks gave way to government by Indian Muslims and their Hindu allies. The Delhi sultans were open to local influences and employed Hindus in their administration. In the mid-14th century their capital, Delhi, was one of the leading cities of the contemporary world but in 1398 their control came to an abrupt end with the arrival of the Mongol Timur.

Timur's limp caused him to be called Timur-i-leng (Timur the Lame, known to the west as Tamburlaine). This self-styled 'Scourge of God' was illiterate, a devout Muslim, an outstanding chess player and a patron of the arts. Five years before his arrival in India he had taken Baghdad and three years before that he had ravaged Russia, devastating land and pillaging villages. India had not been in such danger from Mongols since Genghis Khan had arrived on the same stretch of the Indus 200 years before.

After Timur, it took nearly 50 years for the Delhi Kingdom to become more than a local headquarters. Even then the revival was slow and fitful. The last Tughluqs were succeeded by an undistinguished line of Sayyids, who began as Timur's deputies who were essentially Afghan soldier/administrators. They later called themselves sultans and Lodi kings (1451-1526) and moved their capital to Agra. Nominally they controlled an area from Punjab to Bihar but they were, in fact, in the hands of a group of factious nobles.

The Deccan Kingdoms

The Delhi Sultanate never achieved the dominating power of earlier empires or of its successor, the Mughal Empire. It exercised political control through crushing military raids and the exaction of tribute from defeated kings, but there was no real attempt to

AD	North India	Peninsular India	External events	AD
78	Kushan rulers in Northwest followed by Scythians.	Satavahanas control much of Peninsula up to 300 AD. Thomas brings Christianity to South India. *Tamil Sangram.*	Rome population of 1 mn. Pyramid of the sun at City of Teotihuacan, Mexico.	50
100	Vaishnavism spreads to north and northwest.	Arikamedu – trade with Rome.	Buddhism reaches China. Paper introduced in China; first metal work in Southeast Asia.	68 100
200	Lawbook of Manu Gandharan art. Hinayana/Mahayana Buddhist split.	Mahayana Buddhism spreads. Nagarjunakonda major centre in Andhra Pradesh. First cities on Deccan plateau.	Hadrian's wall in Britain.	125

impose central administration. Power depended on maintaining vital lines of communication and trade routes, keeping fortified strongholds and making regional alliances. In the Peninsula to the south, the Deccan, regional powers contested for survival, power and expansion. The Bahmanis were the forerunners of a succession of Muslim dynasties, who sometimes competed with each other and sometimes collaborated against a joint external enemy.

The Vijayanagar Empire Across West and South India today are the remains of the only major medieval Hindu empire to resist effectively the Muslim advance. The ruins at Hampi demonstrate the power of a Hindu coalition that rose to power in the south Deccan in the first half of the 14th century, only to be defeated by its Muslim neighbours in 1565, see page 1002.

For over 200 years Vijayanagar ('*city of victory*') kings fought to establish supremacy. It was an empire that, in the words of one Indian historian, made it 'the nearest approach to a war state ever made by a Hindu kingdom'. At times its power reached from Orissa in the northeast to Sri Lanka. In 1390 King Harihara II claimed to have planted a victory pillar in Sri Lanka. Much of modern Tamil Nadu and Andhra Pradesh were added to the core region of Karnataka in the area under Vijayanagar control.

The Mughal Empire
In North India it is the impact of the Mughal rule that is most strikingly evident today. The descendants of conquerors, with the blood of both Tamburlaine (Timur) and Genghis Khan in their veins, they came to dominate Indian politics from Babur's victory near Delhi in 1526 to Aurangzeb's death in 1707. Their legacy was not only some of the most magnificent architecture in the world, but a profound impact on the culture, society and future politics of South Asia.

Babur (the tiger) Founder of the Mughal Dynasty, Babur was born in Russian Turkestan on 15 February 1483, the fifth direct descendant on the male side of Timur and 13th on the female side from Genghis Khan. He established the Mughal Empire by leading his cavalry and artillery forces to a stupendous victory over the combined armies of Ibrahim Lodi, last ruler of the Delhi Sultanate and the Hindu Raja of Gwalior, at **Panipat**, 80 km north of Delhi, in 1526. When he died four years later, the Empire was still far from secured, but he had not only laid the foundations of political and military power but had also begun to establish courtly traditions of poetry, literature and art which became the hallmark of subsequent Mughal rulers.

Babur, used to the delights of Persian gardens and the cool of the Afghan hills, was unimpressed by what he saw of India. In his autobiography he wrote: "Hindustan

AD	North India	Peninsular India	External events	AD
300		Rise of Pallavas.	Classic period of Mayan civilization.	300
319	Chandra Gupta founds Gupta Dynasty (Samudra 335, Chandra II 376, Kumara 415).		Constantinople founded.	330
454	Skanda Gupta, the last imperial Gupta, takes power. Dies 467.		End of Roman Empire. Teotihuacan, Mexico, population 200,000.	476 500
540	Gupta rule ends.		Saint Sophia, Constantinople.	532
550		First Chalukya Dynasty, Badami cave temple; last Ajanta paintings.	Buddhism arrives in Japan.	550
578				
600	Period of small Indian states.	Bhakti movement. Chalukyan Dynasty in west and central Deccan. Pallavas in Tamil Nadu.		
629	Hiuen Tsang travels India.		Death of Mohammad.	632
630				

is a country that has few pleasures to recommend it. The people are not handsome. They have no idea of the charms of friendly society, of frankly mixing together, or of familiar intercourse. They have no genius, no comprehension of mind, no politeness of manner, no kindness or fellow-feeling, no ingenuity or mechanical invention in planning or executing their handicraft works, no skill or knowledge in design or architecture; they have no horses, no good flesh, no grapes or musk melons, no good fruits, no ice or cold water, no good food or bread in their bazars, no baths or colleges, no candles, no torches, not a candlestick".

Babur's depressing catalogue was the view of a disenchanted outsider. Within two generations the Mughals had become fully at home in their Indian environment and brought some radical changes. Babur was charismatic. He ruled by keeping the loyalty of his military chiefs, giving them control of large areas of territory.

Humayun However, their strength posed a problem for Humayun, his successor. Almost immediately after Babur's death Humayun was forced to retreat from Delhi through Sind with his pregnant wife. His son Akbar, who was to become the greatest of the Mughal emperors, was born at Umarkot in Sindh, modern Pakistan, during this period of exile, on 23 November 1542.

Akbar Akbar was only 13 when he took the throne in 1556. The next 44 years were one of the most remarkable periods of South Asian history, paralleled by the Elizabethan period in England, where Queen Elizabeth I ruled from 1558 to 1603. Although Akbar inherited the throne, it was he who really created the empire. He also gave it many of its distinguishing features.

Through his marriage to a Hindu princess he ensured that Hindus were given honoured positions in government, as well as respect for their religious beliefs and practices. He sustained a passionate interest in art and literature, matched by a determination to create monuments to his empire's political power and he laid the foundations for an artistic and architectural tradition which developed a totally distinctive Indian style. This emerged from the separate elements of Iranian and Indian traditions by a constant process of blending and originality of which he was the chief patron.

But these achievements were only possible because of his political and military gifts. From 1556 until his 18th birthday in 1560, Akbar was served by a prince regent, Bairam Khan. However, already at the age of 15 he had conquered Ajmer and large areas of Central India. Chittor and Ranthambore fell to him in 1567-68, bringing most of what is now Rajasthan under his control. This opened the door south to Gujarat.

Afghans continued to cause his empire difficulties, including Daud Karrani, who declared independence in East India in 1574. That threat to Mughal power was finally crushed with Karrani's death in 1576. Bengal was far from the last of his conquests.

AD	North India	Peninsular India	External events	AD
			Buddhism reaches Tibet.	645
670	Rajputs become powerful force in northwest.	Mahabalipuram shore temples.		
712	Arabs arrive in Sind.	Nandivarman II in Tamil Nadu. Pandiyas in Madurai.	Muslim invasions of Spain.	711
757		Rashtrakutas dominate central Peninsula.		
775		Kailasanath Temple, Ellora. Rise of Cholas.	Charlemagne crowned. Settlement of New Zealand. Cyrillic script developed.	800 850 863
950	Khajuraho temples started.	Rajendra Chola.		
			Sung Dynasty in China.	979
984		Rajaraja 1st.		

He brought Kabul back under Mughal control in the 1580s and established a presence from Kashmir, Sind and Baluchistan in the north and west, to the Godavari River on the border of modern Andhra Pradesh in the south.

Akbar deliberately widened his power base by incorporating Rajput princes into the administrative structure and giving them extensive rights in the revenue from land. He abolished the hated tax on non-Muslims *(jizya)*-ultimately reinstated by his strictly orthodox great grandson Aurangzeb-ceased levying taxes on Hindus who went on pilgrimage and ended the practice of forcible conversion to Islam.

Artistic treasures abound from Akbar's court - paintings, jewellery, weapons - often bringing together material and skills from across the known world. Akbar's eclecticism had a political purpose, for he was trying to build a focus of loyalty beyond that of caste, social group, region or religion. Like Roman emperors before him, he deliberately cultivated a new religion in which the emperor himself attained divinity, hoping thereby to give the empire a legitimacy which would last. While his religion disappeared with his death, the legitimacy of the Mughals survived another 200 years, long after their real power had almost disappeared.

Jahangir Akbar died of a stomach illness in 1605. He was succeeded by his son, Prince Salim, who inherited the throne as Emperor Jahangir ('*world seizer*'). He added little to the territory of the empire, consolidating the Mughals' hold on the Himalayan foothills and parts of central India but restricting his innovative energies to pushing back frontiers of art rather than of land. He commissioned works of art and literature, many of which directly recorded life in the Mughal court. Hunting scenes were not just romanticized accounts of rural life, but conveyed the real dangers of hunting lions or tigers; implements, furniture, tools and weapons were made with lavish care and often exquisite design.

From early youth Jahangir had shown an artistic temperament, but he also became addicted to alcohol and then to opium. In his autobiography, he wrote: "I had not drunk until I was 18, except in the time of my infancy two or three times my mother and wet nurses gave it by way of infantile remedy, mixed with water and rose water to take away a cough ... years later a gunner said that if I would take a glass of wine it would drive away the feeling of being tired and heavy ... After that I took to drinking wine ... until wine made from grapes ceased to intoxicate me and I took to drinking arrack (local spirits). By degrees my potions rose to 20 cups of doubly distilled spirits, 14 during the daytime and the remainder at night".

Nur Jahan Jahangir's favourite wife, Nur Jahan, brought her own artistic gifts. Born the daughter of an Iranian nobleman, she had been brought to the Mughal court along with her family as a child and moved to Bengal as the wife of Sher Afgan, see page 164. She

AD	North India	Peninsular India	External events	AD
1001	Mahmud of Ghazni raids Indus plains. Rajput dynasties grow.	Chola kings – navies sent to Southeast Asia: Chola bronzes.	Easter Island stone carvings.	1000
1050	Sufism in North India. Rajput dynasties in northwest.		Norman conquest of England.	1066
			First European universities.	1100
1110		Rise of Hoysalas.		
1118	Senas in Bengal.			
			Angkor Wat, Cambodia; paper making spreads from Muslim world.	1150
1192	Rajputs defeated by Mu'izzu'd Din.		Srivijaya Kingdom at its height in Java; Angkor Empire at greatest.	1170

made rapid progress after her first husband's accidental death in 1607, which caused her to move from Bengal to be a lady in waiting for one of Akbar's widows.

At the Mughal court in 1611, she met Jahangir. Mutually enraptured, they were married in May. Jahangir gave her the title Nur Mahal (Light of the Palace), soon increased to Nur Jahan (Light of the World). Aged 34, she was strikingly beautiful and had an astonishing reputation for physical skill and intellectual wit. She was a crack shot with a gun, highly artistic, determined yet philanthropic. Throughout her life Jahangir was captivated by her, so much so that he flouted Muslim convention by minting coins bearing her image.

By 1622 Nur Jahan effectively controlled the empire. She commissioned and supervised the building in Agra of one of the Mughal world's most beautiful buildings, the **I'timad ud-Daula** ('Pillar of government'), as a tomb for her father and mother. Her father, **Ghiyas Beg**, had risen to become one of Jahangir's most trusted advisers and Nur Jahan was determined to ensure that their memory was adequately honoured. She was less successful in her wish to deny the succession after Jahangir's death at the age of 58 to Prince Khurram. Acceding to the throne in 1628, he took the title of Shah Jahan (*Ruler of the World*) and in the following 30 years his reign represented the height of Mughal power.

Shah Jahan The Mughal Empire was under attack in the Deccan and the northwest when Shah Jahan became Emperor. He tried to re-establish and extend Mughal authority in both regions by a combination of military campaigns and skilled diplomacy. Akbar's craftsmen had already carved outstandingly beautiful *jalis* for the tomb of Salim Chishti in Fatehpur Sikri, but Shah Jahan developed the form further. Undoubtedly the finest tribute to these skills is found in the Taj Mahal, the tribute to his beloved wife Mumtaz Mahal, who died giving birth to her fourteenth child in 1631.

Aurangzeb The need to expand the area under Mughal control was felt even more strongly by Aurangzeb ('*The jewel in the throne*'), than by his predecessors, see page 1108. He had shown his intellectual gifts in his grandfather Jahangir's court when held hostage to guarantee Shah Jahan's good behaviour, learning Arabic, Persian, Turkish and Hindi. When he seized power at the age of 40, he needed all his political and military skills to hold on to an unwieldy empire that was in permanent danger of collapse from its own size.

Aurangzeb realized that the resources of the territory he inherited from Shah Jahan were not enough. One response was to push south, while maintaining his hold on the east and north. Initially he maintained his alliances with the Rajputs in the west, which had been a crucial element in Mughal strategy. In 1678 he claimed

AD	North India	Peninsular India	External events	AD
1198	First mosque built in Delhi; Qutb Minar Delhi.		Rise of Hausa city states in West Africa.	1200
1206	Delhi Sultanate established.		Mongols begin conquest of Asia under Genghis Khan.	1206
1206	Turkish 'slave dynasty'.	Pandiyas rise.		
			First Thai kingdom.	1220
1222	Iltutmish Sultan of Delhi.			
1230		Konark, Sun Temple, Orissa		
			Marco Polo reaches China.	1275
1290	Khaljis in Delhi; Jalal ud Din Khalji.			
1320-24	Ghiyas ud Din Tughluq.		Black Death spreads from Asia to Europe.	1348
1324-51	Mohammad bin Tughluq.			

A monument to grief?

The grief that Mumtaz's death caused may have been the chief motivating force behind Shah Jahan's determination to build the Taj Mahal, a monument not just to his love for her, but also to the supremacy of Mughal refinement and power. However, that power had to be paid for and the costs were escalating. Shah Jahan himself had inherited an almost bankrupt state from his father. Expenditure on the army had outstripped the revenue collected by tribute from kings and from the chiefs given the rights and responsibility over territories often larger than European countries. Financial deficits forced Shah Jahan onto the offensive in order to guarantee greater and more reliable revenue.

Major reforms helped to reduce the costs of his standing army. However, maintaining the force necessary to control the huge territories owing allegiance to the emperor continued to stretch his resources to the full. By 1648, when he moved his capital to Delhi, the empire was already in financial difficulties and in 1657 the rumour that Shah Jahan was terminally ill immediately caused a series of battles for the succession between his four sons.

Aurangzeb, the second son and sixth child of Shah Jahan and Mumtaz Mahal – tough, intriguing and sometimes cruel, but also a highly intelligent strategist – emerged the winner, to find that Shah Jahan had recovered. Rather than run the risk of being deposed, Aurangzeb kept his father imprisoned in Agra Fort, where he had been taken ill, from June 1658 until his death in February 1666.

absolute rights over Jodhpur and went to war with the Rajput clans at the same time embarking on a policy of outright Islamisation. However, for the remaining 39 years of his reign he was forced to struggle continuously to sustain his power.

The East India Company and the rise of British power

The British were unique among the foreign rulers of India in coming by sea rather than through the northwest and in coming first for trade rather than for military conquest. The ports that they established - Madras, Bombay and Calcutta - became completely new centres of political, economic and social activity. Before them Indian empires had controlled their territories from the land. The British dictated the emerging shape of the economy by controlling sea-borne trade. From the middle of the 19th century

AD	North India	Peninsular India	External events	AD
1336		Vijayanagar Empire established, Harihara I.		
1347		Ala-ud-Din sets up		
1351-88	Firoz Shah Tughluq.	Bahmani dynasty, independent of Delhi, in Gulbarga.	Ming dynasty in China established.	1368
			Peking the largest city in the world.	1400
1398	Timur sacks Delhi.		Ming sea-going expeditions to Africa.	1405
1412	End of Tughlaq Dynasty.			
1414	Sayyid Dynasty.	Bidar/Bahmani Kingdom in Deccan.		1428
1440	Mystic Kabir born in Benaras.		Aztecs defeat Atzcapatzalco. Incas centralize power.	1438
1451	Afghan Lodi Dynasty established under Bahlul.		Byzantine Empire falls to Ottomans.	1453
1469	Guru Nanak born in Punjab.		Columbus reaches the	1492
1482		Fall of Bahmanis.	Americas; Arabs and Jews expelled from Spain.	

railways transformed the economic and political structure of South Asia and it was those three centres of British political control, along with the late addition of Delhi, which became the foci of economic development and political change.

The East India Company in Madras and Bengal

In its first 90 years of contact with South Asia after the Company set up its first trading post at **Masulipatnam**, on the east coast of India, it had depended almost entirely on trade for its profits. However, in 1701, only 11 years after a British settlement was first established at Calcutta, the Company was given rights to land revenue in Bengal.

The Company was accepted and sometimes welcomed, partly because it offered to bolster the inadequate revenues of the Mughals by exchanging silver bullion for the cloth it bought. However, in the south the Company moved further and faster towards consolidating its political base. Wars between South India's regional factions gave the Company the opportunity to extend their influence by making alliances and offering support to some of these factions in their struggles, which were complicated by the extension to Indian soil of the European contest for power between the French and the British.

Robert Clive The British established effective control over both Bengal and Southeast India in the middle of the 17th century. Robert Clive, in alliance with a collection of disaffected Hindu landowners and Muslim soldiers, defeated the new Nawab of Bengal, the 20-year-old Siraj-ud-Daula, in June 1757. At **Plassey** (Palashi), about 100 km north of Calcutta.

Hastings and Cornwallis The essential features of British control were mapped out in the next quarter of a century through the work of **Warren Hastings**, Governor-General from 1774 until 1785 and **Lord Cornwallis** who succeeded and remained in charge until 1793. Cornwallis was responsible for putting Europeans in charge of all the higher levels of revenue collection and administration and for introducing government by the rule of law, making even government officers subject to the courts.

The decline of Muslim power

The extension of East India Company power in the Mughal periphery of India's south and east took place against a background of the rising power of Sivaji and his Marathas.

Sivaji and the Marathas Sivaji was the son of a Hindu who had served as a small-scale chief in the Muslim-ruled state of Bijapur. The weakness of Bijapur encouraged Sivaji to extend his father's area of control and he led a rebellion. The Bijapur general Afzal Khan, sent to put it down, agreed to meet Sivaji in private to

AD	North India	Peninsular India	External events	AD
1500		Vasco da Gama reaches India.	Inca Empire at its height. Spanish claim Brazil; Safavid Empire founded in Persia.	1498
1506	Sikander Lodi founds Agra.	Vijayanagar dominates South India; Krishnadevraya rules 1509-30.		1500
		Albuquerque seizes Goa; Nizamshahis establish		1510
1526	Babur defeats Ibrahim Lodi to establish Mughal power in Delhi.	independent Ahmadnagar sultanate.	Ottomans capture Syria, Egypt and Arabia.	1516
		Dutch, French, Portuguese and Danish traders.	Spaniards overthrow Aztecs in Mexico.	1519
			Potato introduced to Europe from South America.	1525
1540	Sher Shah forces Humayun into exile.			

reach a settlement. In an act which is still remembered by both Muslims and Marathas, Sivaji embraced him with steel claws attached to his fingers and tore him apart. It was the start of a campaign which took Maratha power as far south as Madurai and to the doors of Delhi and Calcutta.

Although Sivaji himself died in 1680, Aurangzeb never fully came to terms with the rising power of the Marathas, though he did end their ambitions to form an empire of their own. While the Maratha confederacy was able to threaten Delhi within 50 years of Aurangzeb's death, by the early 19th century it had dissolved into five independent states, with whom the British ultimately dealt separately.

Nor was Aurangzeb able to create any wide sense of identity with the Mughals as a legitimate popular power. Instead, under the influence of Sunni Muslim theologians, he retreated into insistence on Islamic purity. He imposed Islamic law, the *sharia*, promoted only Muslims to positions of power and authority, tried to replace Hindu administrators and revenue collectors with Muslims and reimposed the *jizya* tax on all non-Muslims. By the time of his death in 1707 the empire no longer had either the broadness of spirit or the physical means to survive.

Bahadur Shah The decline was postponed briefly by the five year reign of Aurangzeb's son. Sixty-three when he acceded to the throne, Bahadur Shah restored some of its faded fortunes. He made agreements with the Marathas and the Rajputs and defeated the Sikhs in Punjab before taking the last Sikh guru into his service. Nine emperors succeeded Aurangzeb between his death and the exile of the last Mughal ruler in 1858. It was no accident that it was in that year that the British ended the rule of its East India Company and decreed India to be its Indian empire.

Mohammad Shah remained in his capital of Delhi, resigning himself to enjoying what Carey Welch has called "the conventional triad of joys: the wine was excellent, as were the women and for him the song was especially rewarding". The idyll was rudely shattered by the invasion of **Nadir Shah** in 1739, an Iranian marauder who slaughtered thousands in Delhi and carried off priceless Mughal treasures, including the Peacock Throne, see page 103.

The East India Company's push for power

Alliances In the century and a half that followed the death of Aurangzeb, the British East India Company extended its economic and political influence into the heart of India. As the Mughal Empire lost its power India fell into many smaller states. The Company undertook to protect the rulers of several of these states from external attack by stationing British troops in their territory. In exchange for this service the rulers paid subsidies to the Company. The British extended their territory through the 18th century as successive regional powers were annexed and brought under direct Company rule.

AD	North India	Peninsular India	External events	AD
1542		St Francis Xavier reaches		
1555	Humayun re-conquers Delhi.	Goa.		
1556	Akbar Emperor.			
1565		Vijayanagar defeated.	William Shakespeare born.	1564
		First printing press in Goa.		1566
			Dutch East India Co set up.	1602
1603	Guru Granth Sahib compiled.		Tokugawa Shogunate in Japan.	1603
1605	Jahangir Emperor.		First permanent English settlement in America.	1607
1608		East India Co base at Surat.	Telescope invented in Holland.	1609

Progress to direct British control was uneven and often opposed. The Sikhs in Punjab, the Marathas in the west and the Mysore sultans in the south, fiercely contested British advances. **Haidar Ali** and **Tipu Sultan**, who had built a wealthy kingdom in the Mysore region, resisted attempts to incorporate them. Tipu was finally killed in 1799 at the battle of Srirangapatnam, an island fort in the Kaveri River just north of Mysore, where Arthur Wellesley, later the Duke of Wellington, began to make his military reputation.

The Marathas were not defeated until the war of 1816-18. Even then the defeat owed as much to internal faction fighting as to the power of the British-led army. Only the northwest of the subcontinent remained beyond British control until well into the 19th century. Thus in 1799 **Ranjit Singh** was able to set up a Sikh state in Punjab which survived until the late 1830s despite the extension of British control over much of the rest of India.

In 1818 India's economy was in ruins and its political structures destroyed. Irrigation works and road systems had fallen into decay and gangs terrorized the countryside. Thugs and dacoits controlled much of the open countryside in Central India and often robbed and murdered even on the outskirts of towns. The peace and stability of the Mughal period had long since passed. Between 1818 and 1857 there was a succession of local and uncoordinated revolts in different parts of India. Some were bought off, some put down by military force.

A period of reforms

While existing political systems were collapsing, the first half of the 19th century was also a period of radical social change in the territories governed by the East India Company. **Lord William Bentinck** became Governor-General at a time when England was entering a period of major reform. In 1828 he banned the burning of widows on the funeral pyres of their husbands (**sati**) and then moved to suppress **thuggee** (the ritual murder and robbery carried out in the name of the goddess Kali). But his most far reaching change was to introduce education in English.

From the late 1830s massive new engineering projects began to be taken up; first canals, then railways. The innovations stimulated change and change contributed to the growing unease with the British presence. The development of the telegraph, railways and new roads, three universities and the extension of massive new canal irrigation projects in North India seemed to threaten traditional society, a risk increased by the annexation of Indian states to bring them under direct British rule. The most important of these was Oudh.

The Rebellion

Out of the growing discontent and widespread economic difficulties came the Rebellion or 'Mutiny' of 1857. On 10 May 1857 troops in Meerut, 70 km northeast of Delhi, mutinied.

AD	North India	Peninsular India	External events	AD
1628	Shah Jahan Emperor.		Masjid-i-Shah Mosque in Isfahan.	1616
1632-53	Taj Mahal built.			
		Fort St George, Madras, founded by East India Co.		1639
			Manchus found Ch'ing Dynasty.	1644
			Tasman 'discovers' New Zealand.	1645
1658	Aurangzeb Emperor.		Louis XIV of France - the 'Sun King'.	1653-1715

They reached Delhi the next day, where **Bahadur Shah**, the last Mughal Emperor, took sides with the mutineers. Troops in Lucknow joined the rebellion and for three months Lucknow and other cities in the north were under siege. Appalling scenes of butchery and reprisals marked the struggle, only put down by troops from outside.

The Period of Empire

The 1857 rebellion marked the end not only of the Mughal Empire but also of the East India Company, for the British Government in London took overall control in 1858. Yet within 30 years a movement for self-government had begun and there were the first signs of a demand among the new western-educated élite that political rights be awarded to match the sense of Indian national identity.

The Indian National Congress, established in 1885, was the first all-India political institution and was to become the key vehicle of demands for independence. However, the educated Muslim élite of what is now Uttar Pradesh saw a threat to Muslim rights, power and identity in the emergence of democratic institutions which gave Hindus, with their built-in natural majority, significant advantages. Sir Sayyid Ahmad Khan, who had founded a Muslim University at Aligarh in 1877, advised Muslims against joining the Congress, seeing it as a vehicle for Hindu and especially Bengali, nationalism.

The Muslim League The educated Muslim community of North India remained deeply suspicious of the Congress, making up less than 8% of those attending its conferences between 1900-20. Muslims from UP created the All-India Muslim League in 1906. However, the demands of the Muslim League were not always opposed to those of the Congress. In 1916 it concluded the Lucknow Pact with the Congress, in which the Congress won Muslim support for self-government, in exchange for the recognition that there would be separate constituencies for Muslims. The nature of the future Independent India was still far from clear, however. The British conceded the principle of self-government in 1918, but however radical the reforms would have seemed five years earlier, they already fell far short of heightened Indian expectations.

Mahatma Gandhi Into a tense atmosphere Mohandas Karamchand Gandhi returned to India in 1915 after 20 years practising as a lawyer in South Africa. He arrived as the government of India was being given new powers by the British parliament to try political cases without a jury and to give provincial governments the right to imprison politicians without trial. In opposition to this legislation Gandhi proposed to call a *hartal*, when all activity would cease for a day, a form of protest still in widespread use. Such protests took place across India, often accompanied by riots.

On 13 April 1919 a huge gathering took place in the enclosed space of Jallianwala Bagh in Amritsar, see page 454. It had been prohibited by the government and General

AD	North India	Peninsular India	External events	AD
1677		**Shivaji** and Marathas.	Pennsylvania founded.	1681
1690	Calcutta founded.			
1699	Guru Gobind Singh forms Sikh Khalsa.	Regional powers dominate through 18th century.	Chinese occupy Outer Mongolia.	1697
1703	Nawabs of Bengal.	Nawabs of Arcot (1707);	Foundation of St Petersburg,	1703
1707	Death of Aurangzeb; Mughal rulers continue to rule from Delhi until 1858. Nawabs of Avadh.	Maratha Peshwas (1714); Nizams of Hyderabad (1724).	capital of Russian Empire.	
1739	The Persian Nadir Shah captures Delhi and massacres thousands.			
1757	Battle of Plassey; British power extended from East India.	East India Co strengthens trade and political power through 18th century.	US War of Independence.	1775-8

⁑ Mahatma Gandhi

Mohandas Karamchand Ghandi, a westernized, English educated lawyer, had lived outside India from his youth to middle age. He preached the general acceptance of some of the doctrines he had grown to respect in his childhood, which stemmed from deep Indian traditions – notably ahimsa, or non-violence. On his return the Bengali Nobel Laureate poet, Rabindranath Tagore, had dubbed him 'Mahatma' – Great Soul. From 1921 he gave up his Western style of dress and adopted the hand spun dhoti worn by poor Indian villagers.

Yet, he was also fiercely critical of many aspects of traditional Hindu society. He preached against the discrimination of the caste system which still dominated life for the overwhelming majority of Hindus. Often despised by the British in India, his death at the hands of an extreme Hindu chauvinist in January 1948 was a final testimony to the ambiguity of his achievements: successful in contributing so much to achieving India's Independence, yet failing to resolve some of the bitter communal legacies which he gave his life to overcome.

Dyer ordered troops to fire on the people without warning, killing 379 and injuring at least a further 1,200. It marked the turning point in relations with Britain and the rise of Gandhi to the key position of leadership in the struggle for complete independence.

The thrust for Independence Through the 1920s Gandhi developed concepts and political programmes that were to become the hallmark of India's Independence struggle. Ultimately political Independence was to be achieved not by violent rebellion but by *satyagraha* - a "truth force" which implied a willingness to suffer through non-violent resistance to injustice.

In 1930 the Congress declared that 26 January would be Independence day - still celebrated as Republic Day in India today. The Leader of the Muslim League, Mohammad Iqbal, took the opportunity of his address to the League in the same year to suggest the formation of a Muslim state within an Indian Federation. Also in 1930 a Muslim student in Cambridge, **Chaudhuri Rahmat Ali**, coined a name for the new Muslim state **PAKISTAN**. The letters were to stand 'P' for Punjab, 'A' for Afghania, 'K' for Kashmir, 'S' for Sind with the suffix '*stan*', Persian for country. The idea still had little real shape however and waited on developments of the late 1930s and 1940s to bear fruit.

By the end of the Second World War the positions of the Muslim League, now under the leadership of **Mohammad Ali Jinnah** and the Congress led by **Jawaharlal Nehru**, were irreconcilable. While major questions of the definition of separate territories for a Muslim and non-Muslim state remained to be answered, it was clear to General Wavell, the British Viceroy through the last years of the War, that there was no alternative but to accept that independence would have to be given on the basis of separate states.

Independence and Partition

One of the main difficulties for the Muslims was that they made up only a fifth of the total population were scattered throughout India. It was therefore impossible to define a simple territorial division which would provide a state to match Jinnah's claim of a '*two-nation theory*'. On 20 February 1947, the British Labour Government announced its decision to replace Lord Wavell as Viceroy with Lord Mountbatten, who was to oversee the transfer of power to new independent governments. It set a deadline of June 1948 for British withdrawal. The announcement of a firm date made the Indian politicians even less willing to compromise and the resulting division satisfied no one.

⁞ The Indian flag

In 1921, the All Indian Congress considered a red and green flag to represent the two dominant religious groups (Hindu and Muslim); Gandhi suggested white be added to represent the other communities, as well as the charka (spinning wheel) symbolizing the Swadeshi movement, now centred in the party flag.

In 1931, the Indian National Congress adopted the tricolor as the national flag. This was intended to have no communal significance. The deep saffron denoted 'Courage and Sacrifice', the white 'Truth and Peace' and dark green 'Faith and Chivalry'. On the white stripe, the Dharma chakra represented the Buddhist Wheel of Law from Asoka's Lion capital at Sarnath.

Deep saffron

Dark blue

Dark green

When Independence arrived - on 15 August for India and the 14 August for Pakistan, because Indian astrologers deemed the 15th to be the most auspicious moment. Several key Princely States had still not decided firmly to which country they would accede. Kashmir was the most important of these, with results that have lasted to the present day.

Modern India

India, with over one billion people in 2002, is the second most populated country in the world after China. That population size reflects the long history of human occupation and the fact that an astonishingly high proportion of India's land is relatively fertile. Sixty percent of India's surface area is cultivated today, compared with about 10% in China and 20% in the United States.

Although the birth rate has fallen steadily over the last 40 years, initially death rates fell faster and the rate of population increase has continued to be nearly 2% - or 18 million - a year. Today over 280 million people live in towns and cities.

Politics and institutions

When India became Independent on 15 August 1947 it faced three immediate crises. Partition left it with a bitter struggle between Muslims on one side and Hindus and Sikhs on the other which threatened to tear the new country into pieces at birth. An estimated 13 million people migrated between the two new countries of India and Pakistan.

In the years since independence, striking political achievements have been made. With the two year exception of 1975-77, when Mrs Gandhi imposed a state of emergency in which all political activity was banned, India has sustained a democratic system in the face of tremendous pressures. The General Elections of March 1998, which involved an electorate of over 400 million, were the country's 12th. Their results produced a minority government which only survived 15 months, resulting in the 13th general election in September 1999.

The constitution

Establishing itself as a sovereign democratic republic, the Indian parliament accepted Nehru's advocacy of a secular constitution. The President is formally vested with all executive powers exercised under the authority of the Prime Minister.

Parliament has a lower house (the *Lok Sabha*, or 'house of the people') and an upper house (the *Rajya Sabha* - Council of States). The former is made up of directly elected representatives from the 543 parliamentary constituencies (plus two nominated members from the Anglo-Indian community), the latter of a mixture of members elected by an electoral college and of nominated members.

India's federal constitution devolves certain powers to elected state assemblies. Each state has a Governor who acts as its official head. Many states also have two chambers, the upper generally called the Rajya Sabha and the lower (often called the Vidhan Sabha) being of directly elected representatives. In practice many of the state assemblies have had a totally different political complexion from that of the Lok Sabha. Regional parties have played a far more prominent role, though in many states central government has effectively dictated both the leadership and policy of state assemblies.

States and Union Territories Union territories are administered by the President "acting to such an extent as he thinks fit". In practice Union territories have varying

Prime Ministers and Presidents since 1947

Date	Prime Minister	Date	President
1947-64	Jawaharlal Nehru	1948-50	C Rajagopalachari
1964-66	Lal Bahadur Shastri	1950-62	Rajendra Prasad
1966-77	Indira Gandhi	1962-67	S Radhakrishnan
1977-79	Morarji Desai	1967-69	Zakir Hussain
1979-80	Charan Singh	1969-74	V V Giri
1980-84	Indira Gandhi	1974-77	Fakhruddin Ali Ahmed
1984-89	Rajiv Gandhi	1977-82	Neelam Sanjiva Reddy
1989-90	VP Singh	1982-87	Giani Zail Singh
1990-91	S Chandrasekhar	1987-92	R Venkataraman
1991- 96	PV Narasimha Rao	1992-97	Shankar Dayal Sharma
1996 (May)	Atal Behari Vaypayee	1997	K R Narayanan
1996-97 (May)	H D Deve Gowda		
1997-98 (May)	Inder Kumar Gujral		
1998	Atal Bihari Vajpayee		

forms of self-government. Pondicherry has a legislative Assembly and Council of Ministers. The 69th Amendment to the Constitution in 1991 provided for a legislative assembly and council of Ministers for Delhi, elections for which were held in December 1993. The Assemblies of Union Territories have more restricted powers of legislation than full states. Some Union Territories - Dadra and Nagar Haveli, Daman and Diu, all of which separated from Goa in 1987 when Goa achieved full statehood - Andaman and Nicobar Islands and Lakshadweep, have elected bodies known as Pradesh Councils.

Secularism One of the key features of India's constitution is its secular principle. Some see the commitment to a secular constitution as under increasing challenge, especially from the Hindu nationalism of the Bharatiya Janata Party, the BJP.

The judiciary India's Supreme Court has similar but somewhat weaker powers to those of the United States. The judiciary has remained effectively independent of the government except under the Emergency between 1975-77.

The civil service India continued to use the small but highly professional administrative service inherited from the British period. Renamed the Indian Administrative Service (IAS), it continues to exercise remarkable influence across the country. The administration of many aspects of central and regional government is in the hands of this élite body, who act largely by the constitutional rules which bind them as servants of the state. Many Indians accept the continuing efficiency and high calibre of the top ranking officers in the administration while believing that the bureaucratic system as a whole has been overtaken by widespread corruption.

The police India's police service is divided into a series of groups, numbering nearly one million. While the top ranks of the Indian Police Service are comparable to the IAS, lower levels are extremely poorly trained and very low paid. In addition to the domestic police force there are special groups: the Border Security Force, Central Reserve Police and others. They may be armed with modern weapons and are called in for special duties.

The armed forces Unlike its immediate neighbours, India has never had military rule. It has approximately one million men in the army - one of the largest armed forces in the world. Although they have remained out of politics the armed services have been used increasingly frequently to put down civil unrest especially in Kashmir, where there are currently around 400,000 troops.

The Congress Party The Congress won overall majorities in seven of the 10 general elections held before the 1996 election, although in no election did the Congress obtain more than 50% of the popular vote. In 1998 its popular support completely disappeared in some regions and fell below 30% nationally and in the elections of September-October 1999 Sonia Gandhi, Rajiv Gandhi's Italian born widow, failed to achieve the much vaunted revival in the Party's fortunes. Through 2001 into 2002 a sea change began, with the BJP losing power in state assemblies in the north and becoming increasingly unpopular nationally, and the Congress picking up a wide measure of support.

The Non-Congress Parties Political activity outside the Congress can seem bewilderingly complex. There are no genuinely national parties. The only alternative governments to the Congress have been formed by coalitions of regional and ideologically based parties. Parties of the left - Communist and Socialist - have never broken out of their narrow regional bases. The **Communist Party of India** split into two factions in 1964, with the Communist Party of India Marxist **(CPM)** ultimately taking power in West Bengal and Kerala. In the 1960s the **Swatantra Party** (a liberal party) made some ground nationally, opposing the economic centralization and state control supported by the Congress.

At the right of the political spectrum, the **Jan Sangh** was seen as a party of right wing Hindu nationalism with a concentrated but significant base in parts of the north, especially among higher castes and merchant communities. The most organized political force outside the Congress, the Jan Sangh merged with the **Janata Party** for the elections of 1977. After the collapse of that government it re-formed itself as the **Bharatiya Janata Party (BJP)**. In 1990-91 it developed a powerful campaign focusing on reviving Hindu identity against the minorities. The elections of 1991 showed it to be the most powerful single challenger to the Congress in North India. In the decade that followed it became the most powerful single party across northern India and established a series of footholds and alliances in the South. Elsewhere a succession of regional parties dominated politics in several key states, including Tamil Nadu and Andhra Pradesh in the south and West Bengal and Bihar in the east.

Recent developments By mid-2001 the gloss had worn off the popularity of the BJP and it had suffered a series of scandals, but the Prime Minister had kept the core of the government together. In July 2001 Pakistan's military ruler General Pervez Musharraf visited New Delhi and Agra for talks at the Indian Government's invitation, but they ended in a shambles.

The attacks on New York and Washington on 11 September and the US-led "War on Terror" has had major repercussions iin India and Pakistan. While the Taliban's rapid defeat brought a new government to power in Afghanistan, the Kashmir dispute between India and Pakistan deepened. Both India and Pakistan sought political advantage from the war on terror, and when a terrorist attack was launched on the Indian parliament on 13 December 2001 the Indian government pushed massive reinforcements to the Pakistan border from Gujarat and Rajasthan to Kashmir. Demanding the return from Pakistan to India of twenty men wanted on terrorist charges, India also demanded that President Musharraf close down all camps and organisations which India claimed were the source of the attacks in Delhi and Kashmir. Although President Musharraf closed down *Lashkar e Taiba* and *Jaish e Mohammad*, two of the most feared groups operating openly in Pakistan, cross-border firing intensified along the Line of Control in Kashmir and attacks in Kashmir continued. On 16 May 2002 terrorists launched a devastating attack on an army camp in Jammu, killing at least twenty people, and Sonia Gandhi demanded that the Government translate rhetoric into action. The risks of a renewed outbreak of war were higher at the time of writing than at any point since 1971, though enormous pressure is being brought to bear on both India and Pakistan to resolve the disputes by peaceful means. The fact that both countries now have nuclear weapons has raised the stakes dramatically.

India's troubles did not end with its relations with Pakistan. On 27 February 2002 a train returning with militant young Hindus from Ayodhya to Ahmadabad was set on fire and 57 of its occupants killed by a group of Muslim villagers, incensed at what they claimed to have been the rape of a young Muslim girl by youth from the train. While the charge remains unproven the consequences were terrible. Even by mid-May the reprisals had not ceased, as Hindus appeared by many observers to have been given licence to go through Muslim areas of Ahmadabad and some other parts of Gujarat slaughtering any who were found. The BJP Government refused to dismiss their BJP Chief Minister, Narendra Modi, whom the opposition held responsible for allowing the carnage to go unchecked, and while KPS Gill, a senior police office credited with getting on top of violence in the Punjab in the 1990s, was put in charge, the situation remained extremely tense.

Economy

Agriculture

Although agriculture now accounts for less than 30% of India's GDP, it remains the most important single economic activity. More than half of India's people depend directly on agriculture and its success has a crucial effect on the remainder of the economy.

Indian agriculture is enormously varied, reflecting the widely different conditions of climate, soil and relief. Cereal farming dominates most areas. Wheat, grown as a winter crop, is most important in western Uttar Pradesh through Haryana to Punjab. Rice, the most important single foodgrain, is concentrated in the wetter regions of the east and south. The total production of both crops has more than doubled in the last 20 years and 2001-2002 saw production of rice and wheat reach record levels.

Other cereal crops - sorghum and the millets - predominate in central India and unirrigated parts of the north. In addition to its cereals and a range of pulses, India produces important crops of tea, cotton and sugar cane. All have seen significant growth, tea and cotton manufacturers making important contributions to export earnings.

Between independence and the late 1960s most of the increase in India's agricultural output came from extending the cultivated area. In the last 20 years increasingly intensive use of land through greater irrigation and use of fertilizer, pesticides and high yielding varieties of seeds (HYVs) has allowed growth to continue. The area under irrigation has risen to over 35% in 2002, while fertilizer use has increased 25 times since 1961. Indian agriculture is dominated by small holdings. Only 20% of the land is farmed in units of more than 10 ha (compared with 31% 20 years ago), while nearly 60% of farms are less than one hectare.While the "Green Revolution" - the package of practices designed to increase farm output - has had its opponents, it has now transformed the agricultural productivity of many regions of India, allowing a population twice the size of that thirty years ago to be fed without recourse to imports or aid. Much of this has been achieved as the result of seed breeding and agricultural research in India's own agricultural research institutions.

Resources and industry

India has extensive resources of iron ore, coal, bauxite and some other minerals. Reserves of coal at likely rates of use are estimated at well over 100 years (at least 30 billion tonnes, plus 6 billion tonnes of coking coal). Medium and high grade iron ore reserves (five billion tonnes) will last over 200 years at present extraction rates. Although iron ore is found widely across peninsular India, coal is largely restricted to West Bengal, Bihar and Orissa. India's coal output reached over 250 million tonnes in 2002 and iron ore 60 million tonnes, much of which was exported to Japan.

The search for oil intensified after the oil price rises of the 1970s and late 1980s. Development of the Bombay High, off the coast of Gujarat, has contributed to the total output of over 26 million tonnes. Oil, coal and gas provide the energy for just over half of India's 100 million kw electric generation capacity, 20 million kw being hydro and two million mw nuclear.

Power generation By 2002 India's power production had grown to over 470 billion kwh, but demand has risen so fast that many states continue to have power blackouts or 'loadshedding'. Firewood is estimated to provide nearly 30% of the total energy requirement, agricultural waste 9% and cow dung, a universal fuel in some poorer areas, 7%. A recent report highlights the health risk of the continuing dependence on traditional fuels for cooking, suggesting that because of the noxious fumes released in kitchens they are responsible for up to 500,000 deaths a year from cancers and related illnesses.

In the early 1950s India embarked on a programme of planned industrial development. Borrowing planning concepts from the Soviet Union, the government tried to stimulate development through massive investment in the public sector, imposing a system of tight controls on foreign ownership of capital in India and playing a highly interventionist role in all aspects of economic policy. The private sector was allowed to continue to operate in agriculture and in a wide range of 'non-essential' industrial sectors.

Although significant achievements were made in the first two Five Year Plans (1951-56, 1956-61), the Third Five Year Plan failed catastrophically. Agriculture was particularly hard hit by three poor monsoons. After a period of dependence on foreign aid at the end of the 1960s, the economy started moving forward again. The 'Green Revolution' enabled Indian agriculture to increase production faster than demand and through the 1980s it was producing surplus foodgrains, enabling it to build up reserves.

Achievements and problems

India today has a far more diversified industrial base than seemed imaginable at Independence. It produces goods, from aeroplanes and rockets to watches and computers, from industrial and transport machinery to textiles and consumer goods. The influence of India's manufacturing industry reaches every village. The most striking modern development is in the IT sector. According to the London Financial Times since the early 1990s India has become one of the world's leading centres for software development. With an expected seven million Indians on the net in 2002, India is rapidly transforming itself into a computer-based society. Yet despite the economic successes, many in India claim that the weaknesses remain profound. Perhaps half of the population continues to live in absolute poverty and despite surplus grain production many still lack an adequate diet.

Culture

Language

The graffiti written on the walls of any Indian city bear witness to the number of major languages spoken across the country, many with their own distinct scripts. In all the states of North and West India an Indo-Aryan language - the easternmost group of the Indo-European family - is predominant. Sir William Jones, the great 19th-century scholar, discovered the close links between Sanskrit (the basis of nearly all North Indian languages) German and Greek. He showed that they all must have originated in the common heartland of Central Asia, being carried west, south and east by the nomadic tribes who shaped so much of the subsequent history of both Europe and Asia.

Sanskrit As the pastoralists from Central Asia moved into South Asia from 2000 BC onwards, the Indo-Aryan languages they spoke were gradually modified. Sanskrit developed from this process, emerging as the dominant classical language of India by the sixth century BC, when it was classified in the grammar of **Panini**. It remained the language of the educated until about AD 1000, though it had ceased to be in common use several centuries earlier.

Hindi and Urdu The Muslims brought Persian into South Asia as the language of the rulers, where it became the language of the numerically tiny but politically powerful élite. The most striking example of Muslim influence on the earlier Indo-European languages is that of the two most important languages of India and Pakistan, Hindi and Urdu respectively. Most of the other modern North Indian languages were not written until the 16th century or after. Hindi developed into the language of the heartland of Hindu culture, stretching from Punjab to Bihar and from the foothills of the Himalaya to the marchlands of central India.

Bengali At the east end of the Ganga plains Hindi gives way to Bengali (Bangla), the language today of over 50 million people in India, as well as more than 115 million in Bangladesh. Linguistically it is close to both Assamese and Oriya.

Gujarati and Marathi South of the main Hindi and Urdu belt of India and Pakistan is a series of quite different Indo-Aryan languages. Panjabi in both Pakistan and India (on the Indian side of the border written in the Gurumukhi script) and Gujarati and Marathi, all have common features with Urdu or Hindi, but are major languages in their own right.

The Dravidian languages The other major language family of South Asia today, Dravidian, has been in India since before the arrival of the Indo-Aryans. Four of South Asia's major living languages belong to this family group - Tamil, Telugu, Kannada and Malayalam, spoken in Tamil Nadu (and northern Sri Lanka), Andhra Pradesh, Karnataka and Kerala respectively.

Each has its own script. All the Dravidian languages were influenced by the prevalence of Sanskrit as the language of the ruling and educated élite. There have been recent attempts to rid Tamil of its Sanskrit elements and to recapture the supposed purity of a literature that stretches back to the early centuries BC. Kannada and Telugu were clearly established by AD 1000, while Malayalam, which started as a dialect of Tamil, did not develop its fully distinct form until the 13th century. Today the four main Dravidian languages are spoken by over 180 million people.

Scripts

It is impossible to spend even a short time in India or the other countries of South Asia without coming across several of the different scripts that are used. The earliest ancestor of scripts in use today was **Brahmi**, in which Asoka's famous inscriptions were written in the third century BC. Written from left to right, a separate symbol represented each different sound.

Devanagari For about a 1,000 years the major script of northern India has been the Nagari or Devanagari, which means literally the script of the 'city of the gods'. Hindi, Nepali and Marathi join Sanskrit in their use of Devanagari. The Muslim rulers developed a right to left script based on Persian and Arabic.

Dravidian scripts The Dravidian languages were written originally on leaves of the palmyra palm. Cutting the letters on the hard palm leaf made particular demands which had their impact on the forms of the letters adopted. The letters became rounded because they were carved with a stylus. This was held stationary while the leaf was turned. The southern scripts were carried overseas, contributing to the form of the non-Dravidian languages of Thai, Burmese and Cambodian.

Numerals Many of the Indian alphabets have their own notation for numerals. This is not without irony, for what in the western world are called 'Arabic' numerals are in fact of Indian origin. In some parts of South Asia local numerical symbols are still in use, but by and large you will find that the Arabic number symbols familiar in Europe and the West are common.

Literature

Sanskrit was the first all-India language. Its literature has had a fundamental influence on the religious, social and political life of the entire region. Its early literature was memorized and recited. The hymns of the Rig Veda probably did not reach their final form until about the sixth century BC.

The Vedas

The Rig Veda is a collection of 1,028 hymns, not all directly religious. Its main function was to provide orders of worship for priests responsible for the sacrifices which were central to the religion of the Indo-Aryans. Two later texts, the Yajurveda and the Samaveda, served the same purpose. A fourth, the Atharvaveda, is largely a collection of magic spells.

The Brahmanas Central to the Vedic literature was a belief in the importance of sacrifice. At some time after 1000 BC a second category of Vedic literature, the Brahmanas, began to take shape. Story telling developed as a means to interpret the significance of sacrifice. The most famous and the most important of these were the Upanishads, probably written at some time between the seventh and fifth centuries BC.

The Mahabharata The Brahmanas gave their name to the religion emerging between the eighth and sixth centuries BC, Brahmanism, the ancestor of Hinduism. Two of it's texts remain the best known and most widely revered epic compositions in South Asia, the Mahabharata and the Ramayana.

Dating the Mahabharata

Tradition puts the date of the great battle described in the Mahabharata at precisely 3102 BC, the start of the present era, and names the author of the poem as a sage, Vyasa. Evidence suggests however that the battle was fought around 800 BC, at **Kurukshetra**. It was another 400 years before priests began to write the stories down, a process which was not complete until 400 AD. The Mahabharata was probably an attempt by the warrior class, the Kshatriyas, to merge their brand of popular religion with the ideas of Brahmanism. The original version was about 3,000 stanzas long, but it now contains over 100,000 - eight times as long as Homer's Iliad and the Odyssey put together.

Good and evil The battle was seen as a war of the forces of good and evil, the **Pandavas** being interpreted as gods and the **Kauravas** as devils. The arguments were elaborated and expanded until about the fourth century AD by which time, as Shackle says, "Brahmanism had absorbed and set its own mark on the religious ideas of the epic and Hinduism had come into being". A comparatively late addition to the Mahabharata, the Bhagavad-Gita is the most widely read and revered text among Hindus in South Asia today.

The Ramayana

Valmiki is thought of in India as the author of the second great Indian epic, the Ramayana, though no more is known of his identity than is known of Homer's. Like the Mahabharata, it underwent several stages of development before it reached its final version of 48,000 lines.

Sanskrit literature

Sanskrit was always the language of the court and the élite. Other languages replaced it in common speech by the third century BC, but it remained in restricted use for over

⫶ The story of Rama

Under Brahmin influence, Rama was transformed from the human prince of the early versions into the divine figure of the final story. Rama, the 'jewel of the solar kings', became deified as an incarnation of Vishnu. The story tells how Rama was banished from his father's kingdom. In a journey that took him as far as Sri Lanka, accompanied by his wife Sita and helper and friend Hanuman (the monkey-faced God depicted in many Indian temples, shrines and posters), Rama finally fought the king **Ravana**, again changed in late versions into a demon. Rama's rescue of Sita was interpreted as the Aryan triumph over the barbarians. The epic is widely seen as South Asia's first literary poem and is known and recited in all

Ravana, demon king of Lanka

1,000 years after that period. The remarkable Sanskrit grammar of Panini (see page 714) helped to establish grammar as one of the six disciplines essential to understanding the Vedas properly and to conducting Vedic rituals. The other five were phonetics, etymology, meter, ritual practice and astronomy. Sanskrit literature continued to be written in the courts until the Muslims replaced it with Persian, long after it had ceased to be a language of spoken communication. One of India's greatest poets, **Kalidasa**, contributed to the development of Sanskrit as the language of learning and the arts.

Literally 'stories of ancient times', the Puranas are about Brahma, Vishnu and Siva. They were not compiled until the fifth century AD. The stories are often the only source of information about the period immediately following the early Vedas. Each Purana was intended to deal with five themes: "the creation of the world (sarga); its destruction and recreation (pratisarga); the genealogy of gods and patriarchs (vamsa); the reigns and periods of the Manus (manvantaras); and the history of the solar and lunar dynasties".

The Muslim influence

Persian In the first three decades of the 10th century AD Mahmud of Ghazni carried Muslim power into India. For considerable periods until the 18th century, Persian became the language of the courts. Classical Persian was the dominant influence, with Iran as its country of origin and Shiraz its main cultural centre, but India developed its own Persian-based style. Two poets stood out at the end of the 13th century AD, when Muslim rulers had established a sultanate in Delhi, Amir Khusrau, who lived from 1253 to 1325 and the mystic Amir Hasan, who died about AD 1328.

Turki The most notable of the Mughal sponsors of literature, Akbar (1556-1605) was himself illiterate. Babur left one of the most remarkable political autobiographies of any generation, the Babur-nama (History of Babur), written in Turki and translated into Persian. His grandson Akbar commissioned a biography, the Akbar-nama, which reflected his interest in all the world's religions. His son Jahangir left his memoirs, the Tuzuk-i Jahangiri, in Persian. They have been described as intimate and spontaneous and showing an insatiable interest in things, events and people.

The Colonial Period
Persian was already in decline during the reign of the last great Muslim Emperor, **Aurangzeb** and as the British extended their political power so the role of English grew. There is now a very wide Indian literature accessible in English, which has thus become the latest of the languages to be used across the whole of South Asia.

In the 19th century English became a vehicle for developing nationalist ideals. However, notably in the work of **Rabindranath Tagore** , it became a medium for religious and philosophical prose and for a developing poetry. Tagore himself won the Nobel Prize for Literature in 1913 for his translation into English of his own work, Gitanjali. Leading South Asian philosophers and thinkers of the 20th century have written major works in English, including not only MK Gandhi and Jawaharlal Nehru, the two leading figures in India's Independence movement, but S Radhakrishnan, Aurobindo Ghose and Sarojini Naidu, who all added to the depth of Indian literature in English.

Several South Asian regional languages have their own long traditions of both religious and secular literature which are discussed in the relevant sections of this book.

Science

Views of the universe Early Indian views of the universe were based on the square and the cube. The earth was seen as a square, one corner pointing south, rising like a pyramid in a series of square terraces with its peak, the mythical Mount Meru. The sun moved round the top of Mount Meru in a square orbit and the square orbits of the planets were at successive planes above the orbit of the sun. These were seen therefore as forming a second pyramid of planetary movement. Mount Meru was central to all early Indian schools of thought, Hindu, Buddhist and Jain.

However, about 200 BC the Jains transformed the view of the universe based on squares by replacing the idea of square orbits with that of the circle. The earth was shown as a circular disc, with Mount Meru rising from its centre and the Pole Star directly above it.

The science of early India By about 500 BC Indian texts illustrated the calculation of the **calendar**, although the system itself almost certainly goes back to the eighth or ninth century BC. The year was divided into 27 *nakshatras*, or fortnights, years being calculated on a mixture of lunar and solar counting.

Technology The only copy of Kautiliya's treatise on government (which was only discovered in 1909) dates from about 100 BC. It describes the **weapons** technology of catapults, incendiary missiles and the use of elephants, but it is also evident that gunpowder was unknown. Large scale **irrigation** works were developed, though the earliest examples of large tanks may be those of the Sri Lankan King Panduwasa at Anuradhapura, built in 504 BC. During the Gupta period dramatic progress was made in **metallurgy**, evidenced in the extraordinarily pure iron pillar which can be seen in the Qutb Minar in Delhi.

Mathematics Conceptions of the universe and the mathematical and geometrical ideas that accompanied them were comparatively advanced in South Asia by the time of the Mauryan Empire and were put to use in the rules developed for building

temple altars. Indians were using the concept of zero and decimal points in the Gupta
period. Furthermore in AD 499, just after the demise of the Gupta Empire, the astronomer Aryabhatta calculated Pi as 3.1416 and the length of the solar year as 365.358 days. He also postulated that the earth was a sphere rotating on its own axis and revolving around the sun and that the shadow of the earth falling on the moon caused lunar eclipses.

The development of science in India was not restricted to the Gupta court. In South India, Tamil kings developed extensive contact with Roman and Greek thinkers during the first four centuries of the Christian era. Babylonian methods used for astronomy in Greece remained current in Tamil Nadu until very recent times. The basic texts of astronomy (the Surya Siddhanta) were completed by AD 400.

Architecture

Over the 4,000 years since the Indus Valley civilization flourished, art and architecture have developed with a remarkable continuity through successive regional and religious influences and styles. The Buddhist art and architecture of the third century BC left few remains, but the stylistic influence on early Hindu architecture was profound. From the sixth century AD the first Hindu religious buildings to have survived into the modern period were constructed in South and East India.

Hindu temple buildings

The principles of religious building were laid down by priests in the *Sastras*. Every aspect of Hindu, Jain and Buddhist religious building is identified with conceptions of the structure of the universe. This applies as much to the process of building - the timing of which must be undertaken at astrologically propitious times - as to the formal layout of the buildings. The cardinal directions of north, south, east and west are the basic fix on which buildings are planned. George Michell suggests that in addition to the cardinal directions, number is also critical to the design of the religious building. The key to the ultimate scale of the building is derived from the measurements of the sanctuary at its heart.

Indian temples were nearly always built according to philosophical understandings of the universe. This cosmology, of an infinite number of universes, isolated from each other in space, proceeds by imagining various possibilities as to its nature. Its centre is seen as dominated by **Mount Meru** which keeps earth and heaven apart. The concept of *separation* is crucial to Hindu thought and social practice. Continents, rivers and oceans occupy concentric rings around the mountain, while the stars encircle the mountain in another plane. Humans live on the continent of **Jambudvipa**, characterized by the rose apple tree (*jambu*).

Mandalas The Sastras show plans of this continent, organized in concentric rings and entered at the cardinal points. This type of diagram was known as a **mandala**. Such a geometric scheme could be subdivided into almost limitless small compartments, each of which could be designated as having special properties or be devoted to a particular deity. The centre of the mandala would be the seat of the major god. Mandalas provided the ground rules for the building of stupas and temples across India and gave the key to the symbolic meaning attached to every aspect of religious buildings.

Temple design The focal point of the temple, its sanctuary, was the home of the presiding deity, the 'womb-chamber' (*garbhagriha*). A series of doorways, in large temples leading through a succession of buildings, allowed the worshipper to move towards the final encounter with the deity to obtain *darshan* - a sight of the god. Both Buddhist and Hindu worship encourage the worshipper to walk clockwise around the shrine, performing *pradakshina*.

The elevations are symbolic representations of the home of the gods. Mountain peaks such as Kailasa are common names for the most prominent of the towers. In North and East Indian temples the tallest of these towers rises above the *garbagriha* itself, symbolizing the meeting of earth and heaven in the person of the enshrined deity. In later South Indian temples the gateways to the temple come to overpower the central tower. In both, the basic structure is usually richly embellished with sculpture. When first built this would usually have been plastered and painted and often covered in gems. In contrast to the extraordinary profusion of colour and life on the outside, the interior is dark and cramped but here it is believed, lies the true centre of divine power.

Muslim religious architecture

Although the Muslims adapted many Hindu features, they also brought totally new forms. Their most outstanding contribution, dominating the architecture of many North Indian cities, are the mosques and tomb complexes (*dargah*). The use of brickwork was widespread and they brought with them from Persia the principle of constructing the true arch. Muslim architects succeeded in producing a variety of domed structures, often incorporating distinctively Hindu features such as the surmounting finial. By the end of the great period of Muslim building in 1707, the Muslims had added magnificent forts and palaces to their religious structures, a statement of power as well as of aesthetic taste.

European buildings

Nearly two centuries of architectural stagnation and decline followed the demise of Mughal power. The Portuguese built a series of remarkable churches in Goa that owed nothing to local traditions and everything to Baroque developments in Europe. Not until the end of the Victorian period, when British imperial ambitions were at their height, did the British colonial impact on public rather than domestic architecture begin to be felt. Fierce arguments divided British architects as to the merits of indigenous design. The ultimate plan for New Delhi was carried out by men who had little time for Hindu architecture and believed themselves to be on a civilizing mission (see page 85). Others at the end of the 19th century wanted to recapture and enhance a tradition for which they had great respect. They have left a series of buildings, both in formerly British ruled territory and in the Princely States, which illustrate this concern through the development of what became known as the Indo-Saracenic style.

In the immediate aftermath of the colonial period, Independent India set about trying to establish a break from the immediately imperial past, but was uncertain how to achieve it. In the event foreign architects were commissioned for major developments, such as Le Corbusier's design for Chandigarh and Louis Kahn's buildings in Dhaka and Ahmadabad. The latter, a centre for training and experiment, contains a number of new buildings such as those of the Indian architect Charles Correa.

Music and dance

Music Indian music can trace its origins to the metrical hymns and chants of the Vedas, in which the production of sound according to strict rules was understood to be vital to the continuing order of the Universe. Through more than 3,000 years of development and a range of regional schools, India's musical tradition has been handed on almost entirely by ear. The chants of the **Rig Veda** developed into songs in the **Sama Veda** and music found expression in every sphere of life, reflecting the cycle of seasons and the rhythm of work.

Over the centuries the original three notes, which were sung strictly in descending order, were extended to five and then seven and developed to allow freedom to move up and down the scale. The scale increased to 12 with the addition of flats and sharps and finally to 22 with the further subdivision of semitones. Books of musical rules go back at least as far as the third century AD. Classical music was totally intertwined with dance and drama, an interweaving reflected in the term *sangita*.

At some point after the Muslim influence made itself felt in the north, North and South Indian styles diverged, to become Carnatic (Karnatak) music in the south and Hindustani music in the north. However, they still share important common features: *svara* (pitch), *raga* (the melodic structure) and *tala* or *talam* (metre).

Hindustani music probably originated in the Delhi Sultanate during the 13th century, when the most widely known of North Indian musical instruments, the *sitar*, was believed to have been invented. **Amir Khusrau** is also believed to have invented the small drums, the *tabla*. Hindustani music is held to have reached its peak under *Tansen*, a court musician of Akbar. The other important northern instruments are the stringed *sarod*, the reed instrument *shahnai* and the wooden flute. Most Hindustani compositions have devotional texts, though they encompass a great emotional and thematic range. A common classical form of vocal performance is the *dhrupad*, a four-part composition.

The essential structure of a melody is known as a **raga** which usually has five to seven notes and can have as many as nine (or even 12 in mixed ragas). The music is improvised by the performer within certain governing rules and although theoretically thousands of ragas are possible, only around a 100 are commonly performed. Ragas have become associated with particular moods and specific times of the day. Music festivals often include all night sessions to allow performers a wider choice of repertoire.

Carnatic (Karnatak) music Contemporary South Indian music is traced back to Tyagaraja (1759-1847), Svami Shastri (1763-1827) and Dikshitar (1775-1835), three musicians who lived and worked in Thanjavur. They are still referred to as 'the Trinity'. Their music placed more emphasis on extended compositions than Hindustani music. Perhaps the best known South Indian instrument is the stringed *vina*, the flute being commonly used for accompaniment along with the violin (played rather differently to the European original), an oboe-like instrument called the *nagasvaram* and the drums, *tavil*.

Dance The rules for classical dance were laid down in the Natya shastra in the second century BC, which is still one of the bases for modern dance forms. The most common sources for Indian dance are the epics, but there are three essential aspects of the dance itself, Nritta (pure dance), Nrittya (emotional expression) and Natya (drama). The religious influence in dance was exemplified by the tradition of temple dancers, *devadasis*, girls and women who were dedicated to the deity in major temples. In South and East India there were thousands of *devadasis* associated with temple worship, though the practice fell into widespread disrepute and was banned in independent India. Various dance forms (for example Odissi, Manipuri, Bharat Natyam, Kathakali, Mohinyattam) developed in different parts of the country. India is also rich in folk dance traditions which are widely performed during festivals.

The cinema (www.bfi.org.uk/imgineasia) Film goers around the world are taking greater note of Indian cinema, both home-grown and that produced and directed by Indians abroad. Not all fall into the category of a Bollywood '*masala* movie' or 'curry western' churned out by the Mumbai (Bombay) film industry but many offer an insight into what draws millions to watch diverse versions of Indian life on the silver screen. A few titles, both all time favourites as well as new releases are listed here. Some of these are available on video or DVD.

Viewing: *Pather Panchali, Mother India; Titash Ekti Nadir Naam; Sholay; Bombay; Kuch Kuch Hota Hai; Lagaan; Kabhie Khushi Kabhie Cham; Monsoon Wedding; The Guru; The Warrior.*

Religion

It is impossible to write briefly about religion in India without greatly oversimplifying. Over 80% of Indians are Hindu, but there are significant minorities. Muslims number about 125 million and there are over 23 million Christians, 19 million Sikhs, six million Buddhists and a number of other religious groups (see page 99). One of the most persistent features of Indian religious and social life is the caste system. This has undergone substantial changes since Independence, especially in towns and cities, but most people in India are still clearly identified as a member of a particular caste group. The Government has introduced measures to help the backward, or 'scheduled' castes, though in recent years this has produced a major political backlash.

Hinduism

It has always been easier to define Hinduism by what it is not than by what it is. Indeed, the name 'Hindu' was given by foreigners to the peoples of the subcontinent who did not profess the other major faiths, such as Muslims or Christians. While some aspects of modern Hinduism can be traced back more than 4,000 years before that, other features are recent.

Key ideas
According to the great Indian philosopher and former President of India, S Radhakrishnan, religion for the Hindu "is not an idea but a power, not an intellectual proposition but a life conviction. Religion is consciousness of ultimate reality, not a theory about God". There is no Hindu organization, like a church, with the authority to define belief or establish official practice. Not all Hindu groups believe in a single supreme God.In view of these characteristics, many authorities argue that it is misleading to think of Hinduism as a religion at all. Be that as it may, the evidence of the living importance of Hinduism is visible across India. Hindu philosophy and practice has also touched many of those who belong to other religious traditions, particularly in terms of social institutions such as caste, and in post-Independence India religious identity has become an increasingly politicized feature of national life.

Darshan One of Hinduism's recurring themes is 'vision', 'sight' or 'view' - **darshan**. Applied to the different philosophical systems themselves, such as *yoga* or *vedanta*, 'darshan' is also used to describe the sight of the deity that worshippers hope to gain when they visit a temple or shrine hoping for the sight of a 'guru' (teacher). Equally it may apply to the religious insight gained through meditation or prayer.

The four human goals Many Hindus also accept that there are four major human goals; material prosperity (*artha*), the satisfaction of desires (*kama*) and performing the duties laid down according to your position in life (*dharma*). Beyond those is the goal of achieving liberation from the endless cycle of rebirths into which everyone is locked (*moksha*). It is to the search for liberation that the major schools of Indian philosophy have devoted most attention. Together with dharma, it is basic to Hindu thought.

The *Mahabharata* lists 10 embodiments of **dharma**: good name, truth, self-control, cleanness of mind and body, simplicity, endurance, resoluteness of character, giving and sharing, austerities and continence. In *dharmic* thinking these are inseparable from five patterns of behaviour: non-violence, an attitude of equality, peace and tranquillity, lack of aggression and cruelty and absence of envy. Dharma, an essentially secular concept, represents the order inherent in human life.

The four stages of life

Popular Hindu belief holds that an ideal life has four stages: that of the student, the householder, the forest dweller and the wandering dependent or beggar (sannyasi). These stages represent the phases through which an individual learns of life's goals and of the means of achieving them.

One of the most striking sights today is that of the saffron clad *sannyasi* (sadhu) seeking gifts of food and money to support himself in the final stage of his life. There may have been sadhus even before the Aryans arrived. Today, most of these have given up material possessions, carrying only a strip of cloth, a *danda* (staff), a crutch to support the chin during *achal* (meditation), prayer beads, a fan to ward off evil spirits, a water pot, a drinking vessel, which may be a human skull and a begging bowl. You may well see one, almost naked, covered only in ashes, on a city street.

Karma The idea of *karma*, 'the effect of former actions', is central to achieving liberation. As C Rajagopalachari put it: "Every act has its appointed effect, whether the act be thought, word or deed. The cause holds the effect, so to say, in its womb. If we reflect deeply and objectively, the entire world will be found to obey unalterable laws. That is the doctrine of karma".

Rebirth The belief in the transmigration of souls (*samsara*) in a never-ending cycle of rebirth has been Hinduism's most distinctive and important contribution to Indian culture. The earliest reference to the belief is found in one of the *Upanishads*, around the seventh century BC, at about the same time as the doctrine of *karma* made its first appearance.

Ahimsa AL Basham pointed out that belief in transmigration must have encouraged a further distinctive doctrine, that of non-violence or non-injury - *ahimsa*. The belief in rebirth meant that all living things and creatures of the spirit - people, devils, gods, animals, even worms - possessed the same essential soul. One inscription threatens that anyone who interferes with the rights of Brahmins to land given to them by the king will 'suffer rebirth for 80,000 years as a worm in dung'. Belief in the cycle of rebirth was essential to give such a threat any weight!

Schools of philosophy

It is common now to talk of six major schools of Hindu philosophy. *Nyaya*, *Vaisheshika*, *Sankhya*, *Yoga*, *Purvamimansa* and *Vedanta*.

Yoga, can be traced back to at least the third century AD. It seeks a synthesis of the spirit, the soul and the flesh and is concerned with systems of meditation and self denial that lead to the realization of the Divine within oneself and can ultimately release one from the cycle of rebirth.

Vedanta These are literally the final parts of the Vedic literature, the *Upanishads*. The basic texts also include the Brahmasutra of Badrayana, written about the first century AD and the most important of all, the *Bhagavad-Gita*, which is a part of the epic the *Mahabharata*. There are many interpretations of these basic texts. Three are given here.

Advaita Vedanta holds that there is no division between the cosmic force or principle, *Brahman* and the individual Self, *atman* (also referred to as 'soul'). The fact that we appear to see different and separate individuals is simply a result of

⁑ Karma – an eye to the future

According to the doctrine of karma, every person, animal or god has a being or 'self' which has existed without beginning. Every action, except those that are done without any consideration of the results, leaves an indelible mark on that 'self', carried forward into the next life.

The overall character of the imprint on each person's 'self' determines three features of the next life: the nature of his next birth (animal, human or god), the kind of family he will be born into if human and the length of the next life. Finally, it controls the good or bad experiences that the self will experience. However, it does not imply a fatalistic belief that the nature of action in this life is unimportant. Rather, it suggests that the path followed by the individual in the present life is vital to the nature of its next life and ultimately to the chance of gaining release from this world.

ignorance. This is termed *maya* (illusion), but Vedanta philosophy does not suggest that the world in which we live is an illusion. *Jnana* (knowledge) is held as the key to understanding the full and real unity of Self and Brahman. **Shankaracharya**, born at Kalady in modern Kerala, in the seventh century AD, is the best known Advaitin Hindu philosopher. He argued that there was no individual Self or soul separate from the creative force of the universe, or Brahman and that it was impossible to achieve liberation (*moksha*), through meditation and devotional worship, which he saw as signs of remaining on a lower level and of being unprepared for true liberation.

Vishishtadvaita The 11-12th-century philosopher, **Ramanuja**, repudiated such ideas. He transformed the idea of God from an impersonal force to a personal God and viewed both the Self and the World as real but only as part of the whole. In contrast to Shankaracharya's view, Ramanuja saw *bhakti* (devotion) as of central importance to achieving liberation and service to the Lord as the highest goal of life.

Dvaita Vedanta The 14th-century philosopher Madhva believed that Brahman, the Self and the World are completely distinct. Worship of God is a key means of achieving liberation.

Worship

Puja For most Hindus today, worship ('performing puja') is an integral part of their faith. The great majority of Hindu homes will have a shrine to one of the gods of the Hindu pantheon. Individuals and families will often visit shrines or temples and on special occasions will travel long distances to particularly holy places such as Benaras or Puri. Such sites may have temples dedicated to a major deity but may also have numerous other shrines in the vicinity dedicated to other favourite gods.

Acts of devotion are often aimed at the granting of favours and the meeting of urgent needs for this life - good health, finding a suitable wife or husband, the birth of a son, prosperity and good fortune.

Puja involves making an offering to God and *darshan* (having a view of the deity). Hindu worship is generally, though not always, an act performed by individuals. Thus Hindu temples may be little more than a shrine on a river bank or in the middle of the street, tended by a priest and visited at special times when a darshan of the resident God can be obtained. When it has been consecrated, the **image**, if exactly made, becomes the channel for the godhead to work.

Holy places Certain rivers and towns are particularly sacred to Hindus. Thus there are seven holy rivers - the Ganga, Yamuna, Indus and mythical Sarasvati in the north and the Narmada, Godavari and Kaveri in the Peninsula. There are also seven holy places -

Haridwar, Mathura, Ayodhya and Varanasi, again in the north, Ujjain, Dwarka and Kanchipuram to the south. In addition to these seven holy places there are four holy abodes: Badrinath, Puri and Ramesvaram, with Dwarka in modern Gujarat having the unique distinction of being both a holy abode and a holy place.

Rituals and festivals The temple rituals often follow through the cycle of day and night, as well as yearly lifecycles. The priests may wake the deity from sleep, bathe, clothe and feed it. Worshippers will be invited to share in this process by bringing offerings of clothes and food. Gifts of money will usually be made and in some temples there is a charge levied for taking up positions in front of the deity in order to obtain a darshan at the appropriate times.

Every temple has its special festivals. At festival times you can see villagers walking in small groups, brightly dressed and often high spirited, sometimes as far as 80-100 km.

Hindu deities

Today three Gods are widely seen as all-powerful: Brahma, Vishnu and Siva. While Brahma is regarded as the ultimate source of creation, Siva also has a creative role alongside his function as destroyer. Vishnu in contrast is seen as the preserver or protector of the universe. Vishnu and Siva are widely represented have come to be seen as the most powerful and important. Their followers are referred to as Vaishnavite and Shaivites respectively and numerically they form the two largest sects in India.

Brahma Popularly Brahma is interpreted as the Creator in a trinity, alongside Vishnu as Preserver and Siva as Destroyer. In the literal sense the name Brahma is the masculine and personalized form of the neuter word Brahman.

In the early Vedic writing, *Brahman* represented the universal and impersonal principle which governed the Universe. Gradually, as Vedic philosophy moved towards a monotheistic interpretation of the universe and its origins, this impersonal power was increasingly personalized. In the *Upanishads*, Brahman was seen as a universal and elemental creative spirit. Brahma, described in early myths as having been born from a golden egg and then to have created the Earth, assumed the identity of the earlier Vedic deity Prajapati and became identified as the creator.

By the fourth and fifth centuries AD, the height of the classical period of Hinduism, Brahma was seen as one of the trinity of Gods - *Trimurti* - in which Vishnu, Siva and Brahma represented three forms of the unmanifested supreme being. It is from Brahma that Hindu cosmology takes its structure. The basic cycle through which the whole cosmos passes is described as one day in the life of Brahma - the *kalpa*. It equals 4,320 million years, with an equally long night. One year of Brahma's life - a cosmic year - lasts 360 days and nights. The universe is expected to last for 100 years of Brahma's life, who is currently believed to be 51 years old.

By the sixth century AD Brahma worship had effectively ceased (before the great period of temple building), which accounts for the fact that there are remarkably few temples dedicated to Brahma. Nonetheless images of Brahma are found in most temples. Characteristically he is shown with four faces, a fifth having been destroyed by the fire from Siva's third eye. In his four arms he usually holds a copy of the Vedas, a sceptre and a water jug or a bow. He is accompanied by the goose, symbolizing knowledge.

Sarasvati Seen by some Hindus as the 'active power' of Brahma, popularly thought of as his consort, Sarasvati has survived into the modern Hindu world as a far more important figure than Brahma himself. In popular worship Sarasvati represents the goddess of education and learning, worshipped in schools and colleges with gifts of fruit, flowers and incense. She represents 'the word' itself, which began to be deified

⁞ How Sarasvati turned Brahma's head

Masson-Oursel recounts one myth that explains how Brahma came to have five heads. "Brahma first formed woman from his own immaculate substance and she was known as Sarasvati, Savitri, Gayatri or Brahmani. When he saw this lovely girl emerge from his own body Brahma fell in love with her. Sarasvati moved to his right to avoid his gaze, but a head immediately sprang up from the god. And when Sarasvati turned to the left and then behind him, two new heads emerged. She darted towards heaven and a fifth head was formed. Brahma then said to his daughter, 'Let us beget all kinds of living things, men, Suras and Asuras'. Hearing these words Sarasvati returned to earth, Brahma wedded her and they retired to a secret place where they remained together for a hundred (divine) years".

as part of the process of the writing of the Vedas, which ascribed magical power to words. The development of her identity represented the rebirth of the concept of a mother goddess, which had been strong in the Indus Valley Civilization over 1,000 years before and which may have been continued in popular ideas through the worship of female spirits.

In addition to her role as Brahma's wife, Sarasvati is also variously seen as the wife of Vishnu and Manu or as Daksha's daughter, among other interpretations. Normally white coloured, riding on a swan and carrying a book, she is often shown playing a vina. She may have many arms and heads, representing her role as patron of all the sciences and arts.

Vishnu is seen as the God with the human face. From the second century a new and passionate devotional worship of Vishnu's incarnation as Krishna developed in the South. By 1,000 AD Vaishnavism had spread across South India and it became closely associated with the devotional form of Hinduism preached by **Ramanuja**, whose followers spread the worship of Vishnu and his 10 successive incarnations in animal and human form. For Vaishnavites, God took these different forms in order to save the world from impending disaster. AL Basham has summarized the 10 incarnations (see Table).

Rama and Krishna By far the most influential incarnations of Vishnu are those in which he was believed to take recognizable human form, especially as Rama (twice) and Krishna. As the Prince of Ayodhya, history and myth blend, for Rama was probably a chief who lived in the eighth or seventh century BC.

Although Rama is now seen as an earlier incarnation of Vishnu than Krishna, he came to be regarded as divine very late, probably after the Muslim invasions of the 12th century AD. Rama (or Ram - pronounced to rhyme with *calm*) is a powerful figure in contemporary India. His supposed birthplace at Ayodhya became the focus of fierce disputes between Hindus and Muslims in the early 1990's which continue today.

Krishna is worshipped extremely widely as perhaps the most human of the gods. His advice on the battlefield of the *Mahabharata* is one of the major sources of guidance for the rules of daily living for many Hindus today.

Lakshmi Commonly represented as Vishnu's wife, Lakshmi is widely worshipped as the goddess of wealth. Earlier representations of Vishnu's consorts portrayed her as Sridevi, often shown in statues on Vishnu's right, while Bhudevi, also known as Prithvi, who represented the earth, was on his left. Lakshmi is popularly shown in her own right as standing on a lotus flower, although eight forms of Lakshmi are recognized.

Vishnu's ten incarnations

Name	Form	Story
1 *Matsya*	Fish	Vishnu took the form of a fish to rescue Manu (the first man), his family and the Vedas from a flood.
2 *Kurma*	Tortoise	Vishnu became a tortoise to rescue all the treasures lost in the flood, including the divine nectar (Amrita) with which the gods preserved their youth. The gods put Mount Kailasa on the tortoise's back and when he reached the bottom of the ocean they twisted the divine snake round the mountain. They then churned the ocean with the mountain by pulling the snake.
3 *Varaha*	Boar	Vishnu appeared again to raise the earth from the ocean's floor where it had been thrown by a demon, Hiranyaksa. The story probably developed from a non-Aryan cult of a sacred pig.
4 *Narasimha*	Half-man, half lion	Having persuaded Brahma to promise that he could not be killed either by day or night, by god, man or beast, the demon Hiranyakasipu then terrorized everybody. When the gods pleaded for help, Vishnu appeared at sunset, when it was neither day nor night, in the form of a half man and half lion and killed the demon.
5 *Vamana*	A dwarf	Bali, a demon, achieved supernatural power by asceticism. To protect the world Vishnu appeared before him in the form of a dwarf and asked him a favour. Bali granted Vishnu as much land as he could cover in three strides. Vishnu then became a giant, covering the earth in three strides. He left only hell to the demon.
6 *Parasurama*	Rama with the axe	Vishnu was incarnated as the son of a Brahmin, Jamadagni as Parasurama and killed the wicked king for robbing his father. The king's sons then killed Jamadagni and in revenge Parasurama destroyed all male kshatriyas, 21 times in succession.
7 *Rama*	The Prince of Ayodhya	As told in the Ramayana, Vishnu came in the form of Rama to rescue the world from the dark demon, Ravana. His wife Sita is the model of patient faithfulness while Hanuman, is the monkey-faced god and Rama's helper.
8 *Krishna*	Charioteer of Arjuna Many forms	Krishna meets almost every human need, from the mischievous child, the playful boy, the amorous youth to the Divine.
9 The *Buddha*		Probably incorporated into the Hindu pantheon in order to discredit the Buddhists, dominant in some parts of India until the 6th century AD. An early Hindu interpretation suggests that Vishnu took incarnation as Buddha to show compassion for animals and to end sacrifice.
10 *Kalki*	Riding on a horse	Vishnu's arrival will accompany the final destruction of this present age, Kaliyuga, judging the wicked and rewarding the good.

Hanuman The *Ramayana* tells how Hanuman, Rama's faithful servant, went across India and finally into the demon Ravana's forest home of Lanka at the head of his monkey army in search of the abducted Sita. He used his powers to jump the sea channel separating India from Sri Lanka and managed after a series of heroic and magical feats to find and rescue his master's wife. Whatever form he is shown in, he remains almost instantly recognizable.

Siva Professor Wendy Doniger O'Flaherty argues that the key to the myths through which Siva's character is understood, lies in the explicit ambiguity of Siva as the great ascetic and at the same time as the erotic force of the universe.

Siva is interpreted as both creator and destroyer, the power through whom the universe evolves. He lives on Mount Kailasa with his wife **Parvati** (also known as **Uma, Sati, Kali** and **Durga**) and two sons, the elephant-headed Ganesh and the six-headed

Worship of Siva's linga

Worship of Siva's linga – the phallic symbol of fertility, power and creativeness – is universal across India. Its origins lie in the creation myths of the Hindu trinity and in the struggle for supremacy between the different Hindu sects. Saivite myths illustrate the supreme power of Siva and the variety of ways in which Brahma and Vishnu were compelled to acknowledge his supreme power.

One such story tells how Siva, Vishnu and Brahma emerged from the ocean, whereupon Vishnu and Brahma begged him to perform creation. Siva agreed – but then to their consternation disappeared for 1,000 celestial years. They became so worried by the lack of creation that Vishnu told Brahma to create, so he produced everything that could lead to happiness. However, no sooner had Brahma filled the universe with beings than Siva reappeared. Incensed by the usurping of his power by Brahma, Siva decided to destroy everything with a flame from his mouth so that he could create afresh.

As the fire threatened to consume everything Brahma acknowledged Siva's total power and pleaded with him to spare the creation that Brahma had brought forth. "But what shall I do with all my excess power?" "Send it to the sun", replied Brahma, "for as you are the lord of the sun we may all live together in the sun's energy."

Siva agreed, but said to Brahma "What use is this linga if I cannot use it to create?" So he broke off his linga and threw it to the ground. The linga broke through the earth and went right into the sky. Vishnu looked for the end of it below and Brahma for the top, but neither could find the end. Then a voice from the sky said "If the linga of the god with braided hair is worshipped, it will grant all desires that are longed for in the heart." When Brahma and Vishnu heard this, they and all the divinities worshipped the linga with devotion."

Karttikeya, known in South India as Subrahmanya. In sculptural representations Siva is normally accompanied by his 'vehicle', the bull (*Nandi* or *Nandin*).

Siva is also represented in Shaivite temples throughout India by the *linga*, literally meaning 'sign' or 'mark', but referring in this context to the sign of gender or phallus and *yoni*. On the one hand a symbol of energy, fertility and potency, as Siva's symbol it also represents the yogic power of sexual abstinence and penance. The *linga* has become the most important symbol of the cult of Siva. O'Flaherty suggests that the worship of the *linga* of Siva can be traced back to the pre-Vedic societies of the Indus Valley civilization (circa 2000 BC), but that it first appears in Hindu iconography in the second century BC. From that time a wide variety of myths appeared to explain the origin of *linga* worship. The myths surrounding the 12 **jyotirlinga** (*linga* of light) found at centres like Ujjain go back to the second century BC and were developed in order to explain and justify *linga* worship.

Siva's alternative names Although Siva is not seen as having a series of rebirths, like Vishnu, he none the less appears in very many forms representing different aspects of his varied powers. Some of the more common are:

Chandrasekhara The moon (*chandra*) symboilizes the powers of creation and destruction.

Mahadeva The representation of Siva as the god of supreme power, which came relatively late into Hindu thought, shown as the *linga* in combination with the *yoni*, or female genitalia.

Nataraja The Lord of the Cosmic Dance. The story is based on a legend in which Siva and Vishnu went to the forest to overcome 10,000 heretics. In their anger the heretics attacked Siva first by sending a tiger, then a snake and thirdly a fierce black dwarf with a club. Siva killed the tiger, tamed the snake and wore it like a garland and then put his foot on the dwarf and performed a dance of such power that the dwarf and the heretics acknowledged Siva as the Lord.

Rudra Siva's early prototype, who may date back to the Indus Valley Civilization.

Virabhadra Siva created Virabhadra to avenge himself on his wife Sati's father, Daksha, who had insulted Siva by not inviting him to a special sacrifice. Sati attended the ceremony against Siva's wishes and when she heard her father grossly abusing Siva she committed suicide by jumping into the sacrificial fire. This act gave rise to the term *sati* (*suttee*, a word which simply means a good or virtuous woman). Recorded in the *Vedas*, the self immolation of a woman on her husband's funeral pyre probably did not become accepted practice until the early centuries BC. Even then it was mainly restricted to those of the Kshatriya caste.

Nandi Siva's vehicle, the bull, is one of the most widespread of sacred symbols of the ancient world and may represent a link with Rudra, who was sometimes represented as a bull in pre-Hindu India. Strength and virility are key attributes and pilgrims to Siva temples will often touch the Nandi's testicles on their way into the shrine.

Ganesh is one of Hinduism's most popular gods. He is seen as the great clearer of obstacles. Shown at gateways and on door lintels with his elephant head and pot belly, his image is revered across India. Meetings, functions and special family gatherings will often start with prayers to Ganesh and any new venture, from the opening of a building to inaugurating a company, will not be deemed complete without a Ganesh puja.

Shakti, The Mother Goddess Shakti is a female divinity often worshipped in the form of Siva's wife Durga or Kali. As Durga she agreed to do battle with Mahish, an *asura* (demon) who threatened to dethrone the gods. Many sculptures and paintings illustrate the story in which, during the terrifying struggle which ensued, the demon changed into a buffalo, an elephant and a giant with 1,000 arms. Durga, clutching weapons in each of her 10 hands, eventually emerges victorious. As Kali ('black') the mother goddess takes on her most fearsome form and character. Fighting with the chief of the demons, she was forced to use every weapon in her armoury, but every drop of blood that she drew became 1,000 new giants just as strong as he. The only way she could win was by drinking the blood of all her enemies. Having succeeded she was so elated that her dance of triumph threatened the earth. Ignoring the pleas of the gods to stop, she even threw her husband Siva to the ground and trampled over him, until she realized to her shame what she had done. She is always shown with a sword in one hand, the severed head of the giant in another, two corpses for earrings and a necklace of human skulls. She is often shown standing with one foot on the body and the other on the leg of Siva.

The worship of female goddesses developed into the widely practised form of devotional worship called Tantrism. Goddesses such as Kali became the focus of worship which often involved practices that flew in the face of wider Hindu moral and legal codes. Animal and even human sacrifices and ritual sexual intercourse were part of Tantric belief and practice, the evidence for which may still be seen in the art and sculpture of some major temples. Tantric practice affected both Hinduism and Buddhism from the eighth century AD; its influence is shown vividly in the sculptures of Khajuraho and Konark and in the distinctive Hindu and Buddhist practices of the Kathmandu Valley in Nepal.

Skanda The God of War, Skanda (known as Murugan in Tamil Nadu and by other regional names) became known as the son of Siva and Parvati. One legend suggests that he was conceived by the Goddess Ganga from Siva's seed.

Hindu deities

Deity	Association	Relationship
Brahma	Creator	One of Trinity
Sarasvati	Education and culture, "the word"	Wife of Brahma
Siva	Creator/destroyer	One of Trinity
Bhairava	Fierce aspect of Siva	
Parvati (Uma)	Benevolent aspect of female divine power	Consort of Siva, mother of Ganesh
Kali	The energy that destroys evil	Consort of Siva
Durga	In fighting attitude	Consort of Siva
Ganesh/ Ganapati	God of good beginnings, clearer of obstacles	Son of Siva
Skanda (Karttikkeya, Murugan, Subrahmanya)	God of War/bringer of disease	Son of Siva and Ganga
Vishnu	Preserver	One of Trinity
Prithvi/ Bhudevi	Goddess of Earth	Wife of Vishnu
Lakshmi	Goddess of Wealth	Wife of Vishnu
Agni	God of Fire	
Indra	Rain, lightning and thunder	
Ravana	King of the demons	

Ardhanarisvara, the male/female form of Siva

Vishnu, Preserver of the Universe

Krishna, eighth incarnation of Vishnu

Durga, Mother-goddess, destroyer of demons

Attributes	Vehicle
4 heads, 4 arms, upper left holds water pot and rosary or sacrificial spoon, sacred thread across left shoulder	Hamsa (goose/swan)
Two or more arms, vina, lotus, plam leaves, rosary	Hamsa
Linga; Rudra, matted hair, 3 eyes, drum, fire, deer, trident; Nataraja, Lord of the Dance	Bull - Nandi
Trident, sword, noose, naked, snakes, garland of skulls, dishevelled hair, carrying destructive weapons	Dog
2 arms when shown with Siva, 4 when on her own, blue lily in right hand, left hand hangs down	Lion
Trident, noose, human skulls, sword, shield, black colour	Lion
4 arms, conch, disc, bow, arrow, bell, sword, shield	Lion or tiger
Goad, noose, broken tusk, fruits	Rat/ mouse/ shrew
6 heads, 12 arms, spear, arrow, sword, discus, noose cock, bow, shield, conch and plough	Peacock
4 arms, high crown, discus and conch in upper arms, club and sword (or lotus) in lower	Garuda - mythical eagle
Right hand in abhaya gesture, left holds pomegranate, left leg on treasure pot	
Seated/standing on red lotus, 4 hands, lotuses, vessel, fruit	Lotus
Sacred thread, axe, wood, bellows, torch, sacrificial spoon	2-headed ram
Bow, thunderbolt, lances	
10 heads, 20 arms, bow and arrow	

Siva as Nataraj

Ganesh, bringer of prosperity

Parvati, wife of Siva

Kali, the "black" Mother-goddess

Background Religion

Gods of the warrior caste Modern Hinduism has brought into its pantheon over many generations gods who were worshipped by the earlier pre-Hindu Aryan civilizations. The most important is **Indra**, often shown as the god of rain, thunder and lightning. To the early Aryans, Indra destroyed demons in battle, the most important being his victory over Vritra, 'the Obstructor'. By this victory Indra released waters from the clouds, allowing the earth to become fertile. To the early Vedic writers the clouds of the southwest monsoon were seen as hostile, determined to keep their precious treasure of water to themselves and only releasing it when forced to by a greater power. Indra, carrying a bow in one hand, a thunderbolt in another and lances in the others and riding on his vehicle Airavata, the elephant, is thus the Lord of Heaven. His wife is the relatively insignificant **Indrani**.

Mitra and **Varuna** have the power both of gods and demons. Their role is to sustain order, Mitra taking responsibility for friendship and Varuna for oaths and as they have to keep watch for 24 hours a day Mitra has become the god of the day or the sun, Varuna the god of the moon.

Agni, the god of fire, is a god whose origins lie with the priestly caste rather than with the Kshatriyas, or warriors. He was seen in the Vedas as being born from the rubbing together of two pieces of dead wood and as Masson-Oursel writes "the poets marvel at the sight of a being so alive leaping from dry dead wood. His very growth is miraculous". Riding on a ram, wearing a sacred thread, he is often shown with flames leaping from his mouth and he carries an axe, wood, bellows or a fan, a torch and a sacrificial spoon, for he is the god of ritual fire.

Soma The juice of the soma plant, the nectar of the gods guaranteeing eternal life, Soma is also a deity taking many forms. Born from the churning of the ocean of milk in later stories Soma was identified with the moon. The golden haired and golden skinned god **Savitri** is an intermediary with the great power to forgive sin and as king of heaven he gives the gods their immortality. **Surya**, the god of the sun, fittingly of overpowering splendour is often described as being dark red, sitting on a red lotus or riding a chariot pulled by the seven horses of the dawn (representing the days of the week). **Usha**, sometimes referred to as Surya's wife, is the goddess of the dawn, daughter of Heaven and sister of the night. She rides in a chariot drawn by cows or horses.

Devas and Asuras In Hindu popular mythology the world is also populated by innumerable gods and demons, with a somewhat uncertain dividing line between them. Both have great power and moral character and there are frequent conflicts and battles between them.

The **Rakshasas** form another category of semi-divine beings devoted to performing magic. Although they are not themselves evil, they are destined to cause havoc and evil in the real world.

The **Nagas** and **Naginis** The multiple-hooded cobra head often seen in sculptures represents the fabulous snake gods the Nagas, though they may often be shown in other forms, even human. In South India it is particularly common to find statues of divine Nagas being worshipped. They are usually placed on uncultivated ground under trees in the hope and belief, as Masson-Oursel puts it, that "if the snakes have their own domain left to them they are more likely to spare human beings". The Nagas and their wives, the Naginis, are often the agents of death in mythical stories.

Hindu society

Dharma is seen as the most important of the objectives of individual and social life. But what were the obligations imposed by dharma? Hindu law givers, such as those who compiled the code of Manu (AD 100-300), laid down rules of family conduct and social obligations related to the institutions of caste and jati which were beginning to take shape at the same time.

⁝ Auspicious signs

Some of Hinduism's sacred symbols are thought to have originated in the Aryan religion of the Vedic period.

Om The Primordial sound of the universe, 'Om' (or more correctly the three-in-one 'Aum') is the Supreme syllable. It is the opening and sometimes closing, chant for Hindu prayers. Some attribute the three constituents to the Hindu triad of Brahma, Vishnu and Siva. It is believed to be the cosmic sound of Creation which encompasses all states from wakefulness to deep sleep and though it is the essence of all sound, it is outside our hearing.

Svastika Representing the Sun and it's energy, the svastika usually appears on doors or walls of temples, in red, the colour associated with good fortune and luck. The term, derived from the Sanskrit 'svasti', is repeated in Hindu chants. The arms of the symbol point in the cardinal directions which may reflect the ancient practice of lighting fire sticks in the four directions. When the svastika appears to rotate clockwise it symbolizes the positive creative energy of the sun; the anti-clockwise svastika, symbolizing the autumn/winter sun, is considered unlucky.

Six-pointed star The intersecting triangles in the 'Star of David' symbol represents Spirit and Matter held in balance. A central dot signifies a particle of Divinity. The star is incorporated as a decorative element in some Muslim buildings such as Humayun's Tomb in Delhi.

Lotus The 'padma' or 'kamal' flower with it's many petals appears not only in art and architecture but also in association with gods and godesses. Some deities are seen holding one, others are portrayed seated or standing on the flower, or as with Padmanabha it appears from Vishnu's navel. The lotus represents purity, peace and beauty, a symbol also shared by Buddhists and Jains and as in nature stands away and above the impure, murky water from which it emerges. In architecture, the lotus motif occurs frequently.

Om   Svastika   Six-pointed star   Lotus

Caste Although the word caste was given by the Portuguese in the 15th century AD, the main feature of the system emerged at the end of the Vedic period. Two terms - varna and jati - are used in India itself and have come to be used interchangeably and confusingly with the word caste.

Varna, which literally means colour, had a fourfold division. By 600 BC this had become a standard means of classifying the population. The fair-skinned Aryans distinguished themselves from the darker skinned earlier inhabitants. The priestly varna, the Brahmins, were seen as coming from the mouth of Brahma; the Kshatriyas (or Rajputs as they are commonly called in northwest India) were warriors, coming from Brahma's arms; the Vaishyas, a trading community, came from Brahma's thighs and the Sudras, classified as agriculturalists, from his feet. Relegated beyond the pale of civilized Hindu society were the untouchables or outcastes, who were left with the jobs which were regarded as impure, usually associated with dealing with the dead (human or animal) or with excrement.

⁞ From liberal reform to a new fundamentalism

The first major reform movement was launched by the Bengali Brahmin, Ram Mohan Roy (1772-1833). He founded the **Brahmo Samaj**, the Society of God, in 1828, "to teach and to practise the worship of the one God". Services were modelled closely on those of the Unitarian Church, but he never broke with orthodox Hinduism. The Brahmo Samaj became very influential, particularly in Bengal, even though it divided and its numbers remained tiny.

In North India reform was carried out under the leadership of what one writer has called "the Luther of modern Hinduism", Dayananda Saraswati (1824-83). Rejecting idolatry and many of the social evils associated with mid-19th century Hinduism, Dayananda Saraswati established the **Arya Samaj** (the Aryan Society). In the early 19th century the Arya Samaj launched a major attack on the caste system, through recruiting low caste Hindus and investing them with high caste status. At the same time they encouraged a movement for the reconversion of Christians and Muslims (the suddhi movement). By 1931 the Arya Samaj claimed about one million members. With a strongly Hindu nationalist political line, its programme underlay the rise in post-Independence India of the Jana Sangh Party and the present day BJP.

Jati Many Brahmins and Rajputs are conscious of their varna status, but the great majority of Indians do not put themselves into one of the four varna categories, but into a jati group. There are thousands of different jatis across the country. None of the groups regard themselves as equal in status to any other, but all are part of local or regional hierarchies. These are not organized in any institutional sense and traditionally there was no formal record of caste status. While individuals found it impossible to change caste or to move up the social scale, groups would sometimes try to gain recognition as higher caste by adopting practices of the Brahmins such as becoming vegetarians. Many used to be identified with particular activities and occupations used to be hereditary. Caste membership is decided simply by birth. Although you can be evicted from your caste by your fellow members, usually for disobedience to caste rules such as over marriage, you cannot join another caste and technically you become an outcaste.

Right up until Independence in 1947 such punishment was a drastic penalty for disobeying one's dharmic duty. In many areas all avenues into normal life could be blocked, families would disregard outcaste members and it could even be impossible for the outcaste to continue to work within the locality.

The Dalits Gandhi spearheaded his campaign for independence from British colonial rule with a powerful campaign to abolish the disabilities imposed by the caste system. Coining the term *Harijan* (meaning 'person of God'), which he gave to all former outcastes, Gandhi demanded that discrimination on the grounds of caste be outlawed. Lists - or 'schedules' - of backward castes were drawn up during the early part of this century in order to provide positive help to such groups. The term itself has now been widely rejected by many former outcastes as paternalistic and as implying an adherence to Hindu beliefs (Hari being a Hindu deity) which some explicitly reject and today the use of the secular term 'dalits' - the 'oppressed' has been adopted in its place. There are several websites devoted to dalit issues, including www.dalits.org.

Marriage, which is still generally arranged by members of all religious communities, continues to be dictated almost entirely by caste and clan rules. Even in

☷ The sacred thread

The highest three varnas were classified as "twice born" and could wear the sacred thread symbolizing their status. The age at which the initiation ceremony (upanayana) for the upper caste child was carried out, varied according to class – 8 for a Brahmin, 11 for a Kshatriya and 12 for a Vaishya.

The boy, dressed like an ascetic and holding a staff in his hand, would have the sacred thread (yajnopavita) placed over his right shoulder and under his left arm. A cord of three threads, each of nine twisted strands, it was made of cotton for Brahmans, hemp for Kshatriyas or wool for Vaishyas. It was – and is – regarded as a great sin to remove it.

The Brahmin who officiated would whisper a verse from the Rig Veda in the boy's ear, the Gayatri mantra. Addressed to the old solar god Savitr, the holiest of holy passages, the Gayatri can only be spoken by the three higher classes. AL Basham translated it as: "Let us think on the lovely splendour of the god Savitr, that he may inspire our minds".

cities, where traditional means of arranging marriages have often broken down and where many people resort to advertising for marriage partners in the columns of the Sunday newspapers, caste is frequently stated as a requirement. Marriage is generally seen as an alliance between two families. Great efforts are made to match caste, social status and economic position, although the rules which govern eligibility vary from region to region. In some groups marriage between even first cousins is common, while among others marriage between any branch of the same clan is strictly prohibited.

Hindu reform movements

In the 19th-century English education and European literature and modern scientific thought, alongside the religious ideas of Christian missionaries, all became powerful influences on the newly emerging western educated Hindu opinion, That opinion was challenged to re-examine inherited Hindu beliefs and practice.

Some reform movements have had regional importance. Two of these originated, like the **Brahmo Samaj**, in Bengal (see Box). The **Ramakrishna Mission** was named after a temple priest in the Kali temple in Calcutta, Ramakrishna (1834-86), who was a great mystic, preaching the basic doctrine that 'all religions are true'. He believed that the best religion for any individual was that into which he or she was born. One of his followers, **Vivekenanda**, became the founder of the Ramakrishna Mission, which has been an important vehicle of social and religious reform, notably in Bengal (see page 581).

Aurobindo Ghose (1872-1950) links the great reformers from the 19th century with the post-Independence period. Educated in English - and for 14 years in England itself - he developed the idea of India as 'the Mother', a concept linked with the pre-Hindu idea of Shakti, or the Mother Goddess. For him 'nationalism was religion'. After imprisonment in 1908 he retired to Pondicherry, where his ashram became a focus of an Indian and international movement (see page 814).

The Hindu calendar While for its secular life India follows the Gregorian calendar, for Hindus, much of religious and personal life follows the Hindu calendar (see also Festivals). This is based on the lunar cycle of 29 days, but the clever bit comes in the way it is synchronized with the 365 day Gregorian solar calendar of the west by the addition of an 'extra month' (adhik maas), every 21/2-3 years.

Hindus follow two distinct eras. The *Vikrama Samvat* which began in 57 BC (and is followed in Goa), and the *Salivahan Saka* which dates from 78 AD and has been the official Indian calendar since 1957. The *Saka* new year starts on 22 March and has the same length as the Gregorian calendar. In most of South India (except Tamil Nadu) the New Year is celebrated in the first month, *Chaitra* (corresponding to March-April). In North India (and Tamil Nadu) it is celebrated in the second month of *Vaisakh*.

The year itself is divided into two, the first six solar months being when the sun 'moves' north, known as the *Makar Sankranti* (which is marked by special festivals), and the second half when it moves south, the *Karka Sankranti*. The first begins in January and the second in June. The 29 day lunar month with its 'dark' (*Krishna*) and 'bright' (*Shukla*) halves based on the new (*Amavasya*) and full moons (*Purnima*), are named after the 12 constellations, and total a 354 day year. The day itself is divided into eight *praharas* of three hours each and the year into six seasons: *Vasant* (spring), *Grishha* (summer), *Varsha* (rains), *Sharat* (early autumn), *Hemanta* (late autumn), *Shishir* (winter).

Hindu and corresponding Gregorian calendar months:

Chaitra	March-April	*Ashwin*	September-October
Vaishakh	April-May	*Kartik*	October-November
Jyeshtha	May-June	*Margashirsh*	November-December
Aashadh	June-July	*Poush*	December-January
Shravan	July-August	*Magh*	January-February
Bhadra	August-September	*Phalgun*	February-March

Islam

Even after partition in 1947 over 40 million Muslims remained in India and today there are around 120 million. Islamic contact with India was first made around 636 AD and then by the navies of the Arab Mohammad al Qasim in 710-712 AD. These conquerors of Sindh made very few converts, although they did have to develop a legal recognition for the status of non-Muslims in a Muslim-ruled state. From the creation of the Delhi Sultanate in 1206, by Turkish rather than Arab power, Islam became a permanent living religion in India.

The victory of the Turkish ruler of Ghazni over the Rajputs in AD 1192 established a 500 year period of Muslim power in India. By AD 1200 the Turkish sultans had annexed Bihar in the east, in the process wiping out the last traces of Buddhism with the massacre of a Buddhist monastic order, sacked Varanasi and captured Gwalior. Within 30 years Bengal had been added to the Turkish empire and by AD 1311 a new Turkish dynasty, the Khaljis, had extended the power of the Delhi Sultanate to the doors of Madurai.

The early Muslim rulers looked to the Turkish ruling class and to the Arab caliphs for their legitimacy and to the Turkish élite for their cultural authority. From the middle of the 13th century, when the Mongols crushed the Arab caliphate, the Delhi sultans were left on their own to exercise Islamic authority in India. From then onwards the main external influences were from Persia. Small numbers of migrants, mainly the skilled and the educated, continued to flow into the Indian courts. Periodically their numbers were augmented by refugees from Mongol repression in the regions to India's northwest as the Delhi Sultanate provided a refuge for craftsmen and artists from the territories the Mongols had conquered from Lahore westwards.

Muslim populations Muslims only became a majority of the South Asian population in the plains of the Indus and west Punjab and in parts of Bengal. Elsewhere they formed important minorities, notably in the towns of the central heartland such as

⦂ Islamic patronage

The spread of Islam across India was achieved less by forcible conversion than by the patronage offered by the new rulers to Muslim saints and teachers. These were particularly influential in achieving mass conversions among the lower castes of Hindus.

Islam underwent important modifications as it became entrenched in India. From the outset the Muslim invaders had to come to terms with the Hindu majority population. If they had treated them as idolators they would have been forced, under Qur'anic law, to give them the choice of conversion or death. The political impossibility of governing as a tiny minority on those terms encouraged them to give Indian subjects the status of 'protected peoples'.

Lucknow. The concentration at the east and west ends of the Ganga valley reflected the policies pursued by successive Muslim rulers of colonizing forested and previously uncultivated land. In the central plains there was already a densely populated, Hindu region, where little attempt was made to achieve converts.

The Mughals wanted to expand their territory and their economic base. To pursue this they made enormous grants of land to those who had served the empire and particularly in Bengal, new land was brought into cultivation. At the same time, shrines were established to Sufi saints who attracted peasant farmers. The mosques built in East Bengal were the centres of devotional worship where saints were venerated. By the 18th century many Muslims had joined the **Sunni** sect of Islam. The characteristics of Islamic practice in both these regions continues to reflect this background.

In some areas Muslim society shared many of the characteristic features of the Hindu society from which the majority of them came. Many of the Muslim migrants from Iran or Turkey, the élite **Ashraf** communities, continued to identify with the Islamic élites from which they traced their descent. They held high military and civil posts in imperial service. In sharp contrast, many of the non-Ashraf Muslim communities in the towns and cities were organized in social groups very much like the *jatis* of their neighbouring Hindu communities. While the élites followed Islamic practices close to those based on the Qur'an as interpreted by scholars, the poorer, less literate communities followed devotional and pietistic forms of Islam.

Muslim beliefs The beliefs of Islam (which means 'submission to God') could apparently scarcely be more different from those of Hinduism. Islam, often described as having "five pillars" of faith (see box) has a fundamental creed; 'There is no God but God; and Mohammad is the Prophet of God' (*La Illaha illa 'llah Mohammad Rasulu 'llah*). One book, the Qur'an, is the supreme authority on Islamic teaching and faith. Islam preaches the belief in bodily resurrection after death and in the reality of heaven and hell.

The idea of heaven as paradise is pre-Islamic. Alexander the Great is believed to have brought the word into Greek from Persia, where he used it to describe the walled Persian gardens that were found even three centuries before the birth of Christ. For Muslims, Paradise is believed to be filled with sensuous delights and pleasures, while hell is a place of eternal terror and torture, which is the certain fate of all who deny the unity of God.

Islam has no priesthood. The authority of Imams derives from social custom and from their authority to interpret the scriptures, rather than from a defined status within the Islamic community. Islam also prohibits any distinction on the basis of race or colour and most Muslims believe it is wrong to represent the human figure. It is

‼ The five pillars of Islam

In addition to the belief that there is one God and that Mohammed is his prophet, there are four obligatory requirements imposed on Muslims. Daily prayers are prescribed at daybreak, noon, afternoon, sunset and nightfall. Muslims must give alms to the poor. They must observe a strict fast during the month of Ramadan. They must not eat or drink between sunrise and sunset. Lastly, they should attempt the pilgrimage to the Ka'aba in Mecca, known as the Hajj. Those who have done so are entitled to the prefix Hajji before their name.

Islamic rules differ from Hindu practice in several other aspects of daily life. Muslims are strictly forbidden to drink alcohol (though some suggest that this prohibition is restricted to the use of fermented grape juice, that is wine, it is commonly accepted to apply to all alcohol). Eating pork, or any meat from an animal not killed by draining its blood while alive, is also prohibited. Meat prepared in the appropriate way is called Halal. Finally, usury (charging interest on loans) and games of chance are forbidden.

often thought, inaccurately, that this ban stems from the Qur'an itself. In fact it probably has its origins in the belief of Mohammad that images were likely to be turned into idols.

Muslim sects During the first century after Mohammad's death Islam split in to two sects which were divided on political and religious grounds, the Shi'is and Sunni's. The religious basis for the division lay in the interpretation of verses in the Qur'an and of traditional sayings of Mohammad, the Hadis. Both sects venerate the Qur'an but have different *Hadis*. They also have different views as to Mohammad's successor.

The **Sunnis** - always the majority in South Asia - believe that Mohammad did not appoint a successor and that Abu Bak'r, Omar and Othman were the first three caliphs (or vice-regents) after Mohammad's death. Ali, whom the Sunni's count as the fourth caliph, is regarded as the first legitimate caliph by the Shi'is, who consider Abu Bak'r and Omar to be usurpers. While the Sunni's believe in the principle of election of caliphs, Shi'is believe that although Mohammad is the last prophet there is a continuing need for intermediaries between God and man. Such intermediaries are termed Imams and they base both their law and religious practice on the teaching of the Imams.

Akbar, the most eclectic of Mughal emperors, went as far as banning activities like cow slaughter which were offensive to Hindus and celebrated Hindu festivals in court. In contrast, the later Mughal Emperor, Aurangzeb, pursued a far more hostile approach to Hindus and Hinduism, trying to point up the distinctiveness of Islam and denying the validity of Hindu religious beliefs. That attitude generally became stronger in the 20th century, related to the growing sense of the Muslim's minority position within South Asia and the fear of being subjected to Hindu rule.

The Islamic calendar The calendar begins on 16 July 622 AD, the date of the Prophet's migration from Mecca to Medina, the Hijra, hence AH (Anno Hejirae). *Murray's Handbook for travellers in India* gave a wonderfully precise method of calculating the current date in the Christian year from the AH date: "To correlate the Hijra year with the Christian year, express the former in years and decimals of a year, multiply by .970225, add 621.54 and the total will correspond exactly with the Christian year".

The Muslim year is divided into 12 lunar months, totalling 354 or 355 days, hence Islamic festivals usually move 11 days earlier each year according to the solar

Buddhism

India was the home of Buddhism, which had its roots in the early Hinduism, or Brahmanism, of its time. Today it is practised only on the margins of the subcontinent, from Ladakh, Nepal and Bhutan in the north to Sri Lanka in the south, where it is the religion of the majority Sinhalese community. Most are very recent converts, the last adherents of the early schools of Buddhism having been killed or converted by the Muslim invaders of the 13th century. However, India's Buddhist significance is now mainly as the home for the extraordinarily beautiful artistic and architectural remnants of what was for several centuries the region's dominant religion.

India has sites of great significance for Buddhists around the world. Some say that the Buddha himself spoke of the four places his followers should visit. **Lumbini,** the Buddha's birthplace, is in the Nepali foothills, near the present border with India. **Bodh Gaya,** where he attained what Buddhists term his 'supreme enlightenment', is about 80 km south of the modern Indian city of Patna; the deer park at **Sarnath,** where he preached his first sermon and set in motion the Wheel of the Law, is just outside Varanasi; and **Kushinagara,** where he died at the age of 80, is 50 km east of Gorakhpur. There were four other sacred places of pilgrimage - **Rajgir,** where he tamed a wild elephant; **Vaishali,** where a monkey offered him honey; **Sravasti,** associated with his great miracle; and **Sankasya,** where he descended from heaven. The eight significant events associated with the holy places are repeatedly represented in Buddhist art.

In addition there are remarkable monuments, sculptures and works of art, from Gandhara in modern Pakistan to Sanchi and Ajanta in central India, where it is still possible to see the vivid evidence of the flowering of Buddhist culture in South Asia. In Sri Lanka, Bhutan and Nepal the traditions remain alive.

The Buddha's Life Siddharta Gautama, who came to be given the title of the Buddha - the Enlightened One - was born a prince into the warrior caste in about 563 BC. He was married at the age of 16 and his wife had a son. When he reached the age of 29 he left home and wandered as a beggar and ascetic. After about six years he spent some time in Bodh Gaya. Sitting under the Bo tree, meditating, he was tempted by the demon Mara, with all the desires of the world. Resisting these temptations, he received enlightenment. These scenes are common motifs of Buddhist art.

The next landmark was the preaching of his first sermon on 'The Foundation of Righteousness' in the deer park near Benaras. By the time he died the Buddha had established a small band of monks and nuns known as the *Sangha* and had followers across North India. His body was cremated and the ashes, regarded as precious relics, were divided among the peoples to whom he had preached. Some have been discovered as far west as Peshawar, in Pakistan and at Piprawa, close to his birthplace.

After the Buddha's death From the Buddha's death, or *parinirvana*, to the destruction of Nalanda (the last Buddhist stronghold in India) in 1197 AD, Buddhism in India went through three phases. These are often referred to as Hinayana, Mahayana and Vajrayana, though they were not mutually exclusive, being followed simultaneously in different regions.

Hinayana The Hinayana or Lesser Way insists on a monastic way of life as the only path to the personal goal of *nirvana* (see box page 1342) achieved through an austere life. Divided into many schools, the only surviving Hinayana tradition is the **Theravada**

⁝ The Buddha's Four Noble Truths

The Buddha preached Four Noble Truths: that life is painful; that suffering is caused by ignorance and desire; that beyond the suffering of life there is a state which cannot be described but which he termed nirvana; and that nirvana can be reached by following an eightfold path.

The concept of nirvana is often understood in the west in an entirely negative sense – that of 'non-being'. The word has the rough meaning of 'blow out' or 'extinguish', meaning to blow out the fires of greed, lust and desire. In a more positive sense it has been described by one Buddhist scholar as "the state of absolute illumination, supreme bliss, infinite love and compassion, unshakeable serenity and unrestricted spiritual freedom". The essential elements of the eightfold path are the perfection of wisdom, morality and meditation.

Buddhism, which was taken to Sri Lanka by the Emperor Asoka's son Mahinda, where it became the state religion, and spread to southeast Asia as practised in Thailand, Myanmar, Cambodia and Laos today. Suffering, sorrow and dissatisfaction are the nature of ordinary life and can only be eliminated by giving up desire. In turn, desire is a result of the misplaced belief in the reality of individual existence. Theravada Buddhism taught that there is no soul and ultimately no God. *Nirvana* is a state of rest beyond the universe, once found never lost.

Mahayana In contrast to the Hinayana schools, the followers of the Mahayana school (the Great Way) believed in the possibility of salvation for all. They practised a far more devotional form of meditation and new figures came to play a prominent part in their beliefs and their worship - the **Bodhisattvas**, saints who were predestined to reach the state of enlightenment through thousands of rebirths. They aspired to Buddhahood, however, not for their own sake but for the sake of all living things. The Buddha is believed to have passed through numerous existences in preparation for his final mission. Mahayana Buddhism became dominant over most of South Asia and its influence is evidenced in Buddhist art from Gandhara in north Pakistan to Ajanta in Central India and Sigiriya in Sri Lanka.

Vajrayana A new branch of Buddhism, Vajrayana, or the Vehicle of the Thunderbold, appeared which began to lay stress on secret magical rituals and cults of female divinities. This new 'Diamond Way' adopted the practice of magic, yoga and meditation. It became associated with secret ceremonies, chanting of mystical 'mantras' and taking part in orgiastic rituals in the cause of spiritual gain in order to help others. The ideal of Vajrayana Buddhists is to be 'so fully in harmony with the cosmos as to be able to manipulate the cosmic forces within and outside himself'. It had developed in the north of India by the seventh century AD, matching the parallel growth of Hindu Tantrism. The magical

The Buddha in Bhumisparsha-mudra calling the earth to witness

power associated with Vajrayana requires instruction from a teacher or Lama, hence the Tibetan form is sometimes referred to as 'Lamaistic'. See also page 534.

Buddhist beliefs Buddhism is based on the Buddha's own preaching. However, when he died none of those teachings had been written down. He developed his beliefs in reaction to the Brahmanism of his time, rejecting several of the doctrines of Vedic religion which were widely held in his lifetime: the Vedic gods, scriptures and priesthood and all social distinctions based on caste. However, he did accept the belief in the cyclical nature of life and that the nature of an individual's existence is determined by a natural process of reward and punishment for deeds in previous lives - the Hindu doctrine of karma (see page 1325). In the Buddha's view, though, there is no eternal soul. He denied the identification of the Self with the everchanging Mind-Body (here, some see parallels in the Advaita Vedanta philosophy of Self-*Brahman* in Hinduism). In Buddhism, *Anatta* (no-Self), overcame the egoistical Self, given to attachment and selfishness.

Following the Buddha's death a succession of councils was called to try and reach agreement on doctrine. The first three were held within 140 years of the Buddha's death, the fourth being held at Pataliputra (modern Patna) during the reign of the Emperor Asoka (272-232 BC), who had recently been converted to Buddhism. Under his reign Buddhism spread throughout South Asia and opened the routes through Northwest India for Buddhism to travel into China, where it had become a force by the first century AD.

Buddhism's decline The decline of Buddhism in India probably stemmed as much from the growing similarity in the practice of Hinduism and Buddhism as from direct attacks. Mahayana Buddhism, with its reverence for Bodhisattvas and its devotional character, was more and more difficult to distinguish from the revivalist Hinduism characteristic of several parts of North India from the seventh to the 12th centuries AD. The Muslim conquest dealt the final death blow, being accompanied by the large scale slaughter of monks and the destruction of monasteries. Without their institutional support Buddhism faded away.

Jainism

Like Buddhism, Jainism started as a reform movement of the Brahmanic religious beliefs of the sixth century BC. Its founder was a widely revered saint and ascetic, Vardhamma, who became known as **Mahavir** - 'great hero'. Mahavir was born in the same border region of India and Nepal as the Buddha, just 50 km north of modern Patna, probably in 599 BC. Thus he was about 35 years older than the Buddha. His family, also royal, were followers of an ascetic saint, Parsvanatha, who according to Jain tradition had lived 200 years previously.

Mahavir's life story is embellished with legends, but there is no doubt that he left his royal home for a life of the strict ascetic. He is believed to have received enlightenment after 12 years of rigorous hardship, penance and meditation. Afterwards he travelled and preached for 30 years, stopping only in the rainy season. He died aged 72 in 527 BC. His death was commemorated by a special lamp festival in the region of Bihar, which Jains claim is the basis of the now-common Hindu festival of lights, Diwali.

Unlike Buddhism, Jainism never spread beyond India, but it has survived continuously into modern India, claiming four million adherents. In part this may be because Jain beliefs have much in common with puritanical forms of Hinduism and are greatly respected and admired. Some Jain ideas, such as vegetarianism and reverence for all life, are widely recognized by Hindus as highly commendable, even by those who

⁞ The Jain spiritual journey

The two Jain sects differ chiefly on the nature of proper ascetic practices. The Svetambara monks wear white robes and carry a staff, some wooden pots and a woollen mop for sweeping the path in front of them, wool being the softest material available and the least likely to hurt any living thing swept away. The highest level of Digambara monks will go completely naked, although the lower levels will wear a covering over their genitalia. They carry a waterpot made of a gourd and peacock feathers to sweep the ground before they sit.

Jains believe that the spiritual journey of the soul is divided into 14 stages, moving from bondage and ignorance to the final destruction of all karma and the complete fulfilment of the soul. The object throughout is to prevent the addition of new karma to the soul, which comes mainly through passion and attachment to the world. Bearing the pains of the world cheerfully contributes to the destruction of karma.

do not share other Jain beliefs. The value Jains place on non-violence has contributed to their importance in business and commerce, as they regard nearly all occupations except banking and commerce as violent. The 18 m high free-standing statue of Gommateshvara at Sravana Belgola near Mysore (built about 983 AD) is just one outstanding example of the contribution of Jain art to India's heritage.

Jain beliefs Jains (from the word Jina, literally meaning 'descendants of conquerors') believe that there are two fundamental principles, the living (*jiva*) and the non-living (*ajiva*). The essence of Jain belief is that all life is sacred and that every living entity, even the smallest insect, has within it an indestructible and immortal soul. Jains developed the view of ahimsa - often translated as 'non-violence', but better perhaps as 'non-harming'. Ahimsa was the basis for the entire scheme of Jain values and ethics and alternative codes of practice were defined for householders and for ascetics.

The five vows may be taken both by monks and by lay people: not to harm any living beings (Jains must practise strict vegetarianism-and even some vegetables, such as potatoes and onions, are believed to have microscopic souls); to speak the truth; not to steal; to give up sexual relations and practice complete chastity; to give up all possessions-for the *Digambara* sect that includes clothes.

Celibacy is necessary to combat physical desire. Jains also regard the manner of dying as extremely important. Although suicide is deeply opposed, vows of fasting to death voluntarily may be regarded as earning merit in the proper context. Mahavir himself is believed to have died of self-starvation. The essence of all the rules is to avoid intentional injury, which is the worst of all sins. Like Hindus, the Jains believe in *karma*.

Jain sects Jains have two main sects, whose origins can be traced back to the fourth century BC. The more numerous **Svetambaras** - the 'white clad' - concentrated more in eastern and western India, separated from the **Digambaras** - or 'sky-clad'- who often go naked. The Digambaras may well have been forced to move south by drought and famine in the northern region of the Deccan and they are now concentrated in the south of India.

Unlike Buddhists, Jains accept the idea of God, but not as a creator of the universe. They see him in the lives of the 24 **Tirthankaras** (prophets, or literally 'makers of fords' - a reference to their role in building crossing points for the spiritual journey over the river of life), or leaders of Jainism, whose lives are recounted in the Kalpsutra - the third century BC book of ritual for the Svetambaras. Mahavir is regarded as the last of these great spiritual leaders. Much Jain art details stories from these accounts and the Tirthankaras play a similar role for Jains as the Bodhisattvas do for Mahayana Buddhists. The first and most revered of the Tirthankaras, Adinatha, also known as Rishabnath, is widely represented in Jain temples.

Sikhism

Guru Nanak, the founder of the religion was born just west of Lahore and grew up in what is now the Pakistani town of Sultanpur. His followers, the Sikhs, (derived from the Sanskrit word for 'disciples') form perhaps one of India's most recognizable groups. Beards and turbans give them a very distinctive presence and although they represent less than 2% of the population they are both politically and economically significant.

Sikh beliefs The first Guru, accepted the ideas of *samsara* - the cycle of rebirths - and *karma* (see page 1325) from Hinduism. However, Sikhism is unequivocal in its belief in the oneness of God, rejecting idolatry and any worship of objects or images. Guru Nanak believed that God is One, formless, eternal and beyond description.

Guru Nanak also fiercely opposed discrimination on the grounds of caste. He saw God as present everywhere, visible to anyone who cared to look and as essentially full of grace and compassion. Some of Guru Nanak's teachings are close to the ideas of the Benaras mystic **Kabir**, who, in common with the Muslim mystic sufis, believed in mystical union with God. Kabir's belief in the nature of God was matched by his view that man was deliberately blind and unwilling to recognize God's nature. He transformed the Hindu concept of *maya* into the belief that the values commonly held by the world were an illusion.

Guru Nanak preached that salvation depended on accepting the nature of God. If man recognized the true harmony of the divine order (*hookam*) and brought himself into line with that harmony he would be saved. Rejecting the prevailing Hindu belief that such harmony could be achieved by ascetic practices, he emphasized three actions; meditating on and repeating God's name (*naam*), 'giving', or charity (*daan*) and bathing (*isnaan*).

Many of the features now associated with Sikhism can be attributed to **Guru Gobind Singh**, who on 15 April 1699, started the new brotherhood called the *Khalsa* (meaning 'the pure', from the Persian word *khales*), an inner core of the faithful, accepted by baptism (*amrit*). The 'five ks' date from this period: *kesh* (uncut hair), the most important, followed by *kangha* (comb, usually of wood), *kirpan* (dagger or short sword), *kara* (steel bangle) and *kachh* (similar to 'boxer' shorts). The dagger and the shorts reflect military influence.

In addition to the compulsory 'five ks', the new code prohibited smoking, eating *halal* meat and sexual intercourse with Muslim women. These date from the 18th century, when the Sikhs were often in conflict with the Muslims. Other strict prohibitions include: idolatry, caste discrimination, hypocrisy and pilgrimage to Hindu sacred places. The Khalsa also explicitly forbade the seclusion of women, one of the common practices of Islam. It was only under the warrior king Ranjit Singh (1799-1838) that the idea of the Guru's presence in meetings of the Sikh community (the *Panth*) gave way to the now universally held belief in the total authority of the **Guru Granth**, the recorded words of the Guru in the scripture.

Sikh worship The meditative worship Guru Nanak commended is a part of the life of every devout Sikh today, who starts each day with private meditation and a recitation of the verses of Guru Nanak himself, the *Japji*. However, from the time of the third Guru, Sikhs have also worshipped as congregations in Gurudwaras ('gateways to the

Sikhism's Gurus

Guru	Teachings and practice	Developments and events	External powers
1 *Nanak* 1469-1539	The life stories (**janam-sakhis**) of Guru Nanak, written between 50 and 80 years after his death, recorded wide travels, including Bengal and Mecca, studying different faiths.	Devotional and mystic tradition established by Guru Nanak, similar to that of Kabir.	Delhi sultanates
2 *Angad* 1504-1538	Special ceremonies and festivals began to augment individual devotions.		
3 *Amar Das* 1509-1574	Introduction of worship in Gurudwaras.		Portuguese make contact with India.
4 *Ram Das* 1534-1581	Built first lake temple in Amritsar; the first hereditary guru. Widening of congregational worship.	Tolerance for religious experiment.	Akbar
5 *Arjan Dev* 1563-1606	In 1603-4 collected hymns and sayings of the first 3 Gurus, of Sikh mystics and of his father's and his own in a single volume the Adi Granth (the Guru Granth Sahib). Started the Golden Temple at Amritsar.	The Adi Granth comprises nearly 6,000 hymns, 974 attributed to Guru Nanak. Written in Gurumukhi script, developed from Punjabi by the second Guru.	Akbar and Jahangir. Arjan Dev executed by Jahangir at Lahore
6 *Har Gobind* 1595-1645	Jat caste becomes dominant influence. Sikhs began to take up arms, largely to protect themselves against Mughal attacks. Har Gobind decided to withdraw to the Siwalik Hills.	The next 4 Gurus all spent much of their time outside Punjab in the Siwalik Hills, where they developed new martial traditions.	Jahangir and Shah Jahan
7 *Har Rai* 1630-1661			Shah Jahan
8 *Har Krishna* 1656-1664		Died at Delhi.	Aurangzeb
9 *Tegh Bahadur* 1622-1675		Executed by Aurangzeb.	Aurangzeb
10 *Gobind Singh* 1666-1708	Reformed Sikh government introduced the features now universally associated with Sikhism today. Assassinated at Nanded in Maharashtra.	The Khalsa was open to both men and women, who replaced their caste names with the names Singh (lion) and Kaur ('lioness' or 'princess') respectively.	Aurangzeb

Guru'). The Golden Temple in Amritsar, built at the end of the 16th century, is the holiest site of Sikhism.

The present institutions of Sikhism owe their origins to reform movements of the 19th century. Under the Sikh Gurudwaras Act of 1925 all temples were restored to the management of a Central Gurudwara Management Committee, thereby removing them from the administrative control of the Hindus under which many had come. This body has acted as the religion's controlling body ever since. See also, Amritsar.

Christianity

There are about 23 million Christians in India. Christianity ranks third in terms of religious affiliation after Hinduism and Islam and there are Christian congregations in all the major towns of India.

The great majority of the Protestant Christians in India are now members of the Church of South India, formed from the major Protestant denominations in 1947, or the Church of North India, which followed suit in 1970. Together they account for approximately half the total number of Christians. Roman Catholics make up the majority of the rest. Many of the church congregations, both in towns and villages, are active centres of Christian worship.

Origins Some of the churches owe their origin either to the modern missionary movement of the late 18th century onwards, or to the colonial presence of the European powers. However, Christians probably arrived in India during the first century after the birth of Christ. There is evidence that one of Christ's Apostles, **Thomas**, reached India in 52 AD, only 20 years after Christ was crucified. He settled in Malabar and then expanded his missionary work to China. It is widely believed that he was martyred in Tamil Nadu on his return to India in 72 AD and is buried in Mylapore, in the suburbs of modern Chennai. St Thomas' Mount, a small rocky hill just north of Chennai airport, takes its name from him. Today there is still a church of Thomas Christians in Kerala.

The Syrian church Kerala was linked directly with the Middle East, when Syrian Christians embarked on a major missionary movement in the sixth century AD. The Thomas Christians have forms of worship that show very strong influence of the Syrian church and they still retain a Syriac order of service. They remained a close knit community, coming to terms with the prevailing caste system by maintaining strict social rules very similar to those of the surrounding upper caste Hindus. They lived in an area restricted to what is now Kerala, where trade with the Middle East, which some centuries later was to bring Muslims to the same region, remained active.

Roman Catholicism The third major development took place with the arrival of the Portuguese. The Jesuit St Francis Xavier landed in Goa in 1542 and in 1557 Goa was made an Archbishopric (see page 1159). Goa today bears rich testimony to the Portuguese influence on community life and on church building. They set up the first printing press in India in 1566 and began to print books in Tamil and other Dravidian languages by the end of the 16th century.

Northern missions Protestant missions in Bengal from the end of the 18th century had a profound influence on cultural and religious development. On 9 November 1793 the Baptist missionary **William Carey** reached the Hugli River. Although he went to India to preach, he had wide-ranging interests, notably in languages and education and the work of 19th-century missions rapidly widened to cover educational and medical work as well. See page 583.

Converts were made most readily among the backward castes and in the tribal areas. The Christian populations of the tribal hill areas of Nagaland and Assam stem from such late 19th-century and 20th-century movements. But the influence of Christian missions in education and medical work was greater than as a proselytizing force. Education in Christian schools stimulated reformist movements in Hinduism itself and mission hospitals supplemented government-run hospitals, particularly in remote rural areas. Some of these Christian-run hospitals, such as that at Vellore, continue to provide high class medical care.

Christian beliefs Christian theology had its roots in Judaism, with its belief in one God, the eternal Creator of the universe. Judaism saw the Jewish people as the vehicle for God's salvation, the 'chosen people of God' and pointed to a time when God would send his Saviour, or Messiah. Jesus, whom Christians believe was 'the Christ' or Messiah, was born in the village of Bethlehem, some 20 km south of Jerusalem. Very little is known of his early life except that he was brought up in a devout Jewish family. At the age of 29 or 30 he gathered a small group of followers and began to preach in the region between the Dead Sea and the Sea of Galilee. Two years later he was crucified in Jerusalem by the authorities on the charge of blasphemy - that he claimed to be the son of God.

Christians believe that all people live in a state of sin, in the sense that they are separated from God and fail to do his will. They believe that God is personal, 'like a father'. As God's son, Jesus accepted the cost of that separation and sinfulness himself through his death on the cross. Christians believe that Jesus was raised from the dead on the third day after he was crucified and that he appeared to his closest followers. They believe that his spirit continues to live today and that he makes it possible for people to come back to God.

The New Testament of the Bible, which, alongside the Old Testament, is the text to which Christians refer as the ultimate scriptural authority, consists of four 'Gospels' (meaning 'good news') and a series of letters by several early Christians referring to the nature of the Christian life.

Christian worship Although Christians are encouraged to worship individually as well as together, most forms of Christian worship centre on the gathering of the church congregation for praise, prayer and the preaching of God's word, which usually takes verses from the Bible as its starting point. Different denominations place varying emphases on the main elements of worship, but in most church services today the congregation will take part in singing hymns (songs of praise), prayers will be led by the minister, priest or a member of the congregation, readings from the Bible will be given and a sermon preached. For many Christians the most important service is the act of Holy Communion (Protestant) or Mass (Catholic) which celebrates the death and resurrection of Jesus in sharing bread and wine, which are held to represent Christ's body and blood given to save people from their sin.

Zoroastrianism

The first Zoroastrians arrived on the west coast of India in the mid-eighth century AD, forced out from their native Iran by persecution of the invading Islamic Arabs. Until 1477 they lost all contact with Iran and then for nearly 300 years maintained contact with Persian Zoroastrians through a continuous exchange of letters. They became known by their now much more familiar name, the **Parsis** (or Persians).

Although they are a tiny minority (approximately 100,000), even in the cities where they are concentrated, they have been a prominent economic and social influence, especially in West India. Parsis adopted westernized customs and dress and took to the new economic opportunities that came with colonial industrialization. Families in West India such as the Tatas continue to be among India's leading industrialists, just part of a community that in recent generations has spread to Europe and north America.

Origins Zoroastrians trace their beliefs to the prophet Zarathustra, who lived in Northeast Iran around the seventh or sixth century BC. His place and even date of birth are uncertain, but he almost certainly enjoyed the patronage of the father of Darius the Great. The passage of Alexander the Great through Iran severely weakened support for Zoroastrianism, but between the sixth century BC and the seventh century

AD it was the major religion of peoples living from North India to central Turkey. The spread of Islam reduced the number of Zoroastrians dramatically and forced those who did not retreat to the desert to emigrate.

Parsi beliefs The early development of Zoroastrianism marked a movement towards belief in a single God. **Ahura Mazda**, the Good Religion of God, was shown in rejecting evil and in purifying thought, word and action. Fire plays a central and symbolic part in Zoroastrian worship, representing the presence of God. There are eight Atash Bahram - major fire temples - in India; four are in Mumbai, two in Surat and one each in Navsari and Udwada. There are many more minor temples, where the rituals are far less complex - perhaps 40 in Mumbai alone.

Earth, fire and air are all regarded as sacred, while death is the result of evil. Dead matter pollutes all it touches. Where there is a suitable space therefore, dead bodies are simply placed in the open to be consumed by vultures, as at the Towers of Silence in Mumbai. However, burial and cremation are also common.

Land and environment

Geography

India falls into three major geological regions. The north is enclosed by the great arc of the Himalaya. Along their southern flank lie the alluvial plains of the Ganga and to the south again is the Peninsula. The island chains of the Lakshadweep and Minicoy off the west coast of India are coral atolls, formed on submarine ridges under the Arabian Sea.

The origins of India's landscapes
Only 100 million years ago the Indian Peninsula was still attached to the great land mass of what geologists call 'Pangaea' alongside South Africa, Australia and Antarctica. Then as the great plates on which the earth's southern continents stood broke up, the Indian Plate started its dramatic shift northwards, eventually colliding with the Asian plate. As the Indian Plate continues to get pushed under the Tibetan Plateau so the Himalaya continue to rise.

The Himalaya dominate the northern borders of India, stretching 2,500 km from northwest to southeast. They are unparalleled anywhere in the world. Of the 94 mountains in Asia above 7,300 m, all but two are in the Himalaya. Nowhere else in the world are there mountains as high.

The Himalaya proper, stretching from the Pamirs in Pakistan to the easternmost bend of the Brahmaputra in Assam, can be divided into three broad zones. On the

Himalayan profile

southern flank are the Shiwaliks, or Outer Ranges. To their immediate north run the parallel Middle Ranges of Pir Panjal and Dhauladhar and to the north again is the third zone, the Inner Himalaya, which has the highest peaks, many of them in Nepal.

The central core of the Himalayan ranges did not begin to rise until about 35 million years ago. The latest mountain building period, responsible for the Shiwaliks, began less than five million years ago and is still continuing, raising some of the high peaks by as much as 5 mm a year. Such movement comes at a price and the boundary between the plains and the Himalayan ranges is a zone of continuing violent earthquakes and massive erosion.

The Gangetic Plains As the Himalaya began their dramatic uplift, the trough which formed to the south of the newly emerging mountains was steadily filled with the debris washed down from the hills, creating the Indo-Gangetic plains. Today the alluvium reaches depths of over 3,000 m in places (and over 22 km at the mouth of the Ganga in Bangladesh), and contains some of the largest reserves of underground water in the world. These have made possible extensive well irrigation, especially in Northwest India, contributing to the rapid agricultural changes which have taken place.

The Indo-Gangetic plains are still being extended and modified. The southern part of Bengal only emerged from the sea during the last 5,000 years. The Ganga and the Indus have each been estimated to carry over one million tonnes of silt every year - considerably more than the Mississippi. The silts washed down from the Himalaya have made it possible for intensive rice cultivation to be practised continuously for hundreds of years, though they cause problems for modern irrigation development. Dams in the Himalayan region are being rapidly filled by silt, over 33 million tonnes being deposited behind the Bhakra Dam on the Sutlej River alone.

The Peninsula The crystalline rocks of the Peninsula are some of the oldest in the world, the **Charnockites** – named after the founder of Kolkata an enthusiastic amateur geologist, Job Charnock, see page 571 - being over 3,100 million years old. Over 60 million years ago, when India split from Madagascar, a mass of volcanic lava welled up through cracks in the earth's surface and covered some 500,000 sq km of northern Karnataka, Maharashtra, southern Gujarat and Madhya Pradesh.

The fault line which severed India from Africa was marked by a north-south ridge of mountains, known today as the Western Ghats, set back from the sea by a coastal plain which is never more than 80 km wide. In the south, the Nilgiris and Palanis are over 2,500 m high.

From the crest line of the **Western Ghats**, the Peninsula slopes generally eastwards, interrupted on its eastern edge by the much more broken groups of hills sometimes referred to as the **Eastern Ghats**. The east flowing rivers have created flat alluvial deltas which have been the basis of successive peninsular kingdoms.

Climate

India is divided almost exactly by the Tropic of Cancer, stretching from the near-equatorial Kanniyakumari to the Mediterranean latitudes of Kashmir - roughly the same span as from the Amazon to San Francisco, or from Melbourne to Darwin. Not surprisingly, climate varies considerably and high altitudes further modify local climates.

The monsoon The term monsoon refers to the wind reversal which replaces the dry northeasterlies, characteristic of winter and spring, with the very warm and wet southwesterlies of the summer. The arrival of the monsoon is as variable as is the amount of rain which it brings. What makes the Indian monsoon quite exceptional is not its regularity but the depth of moist air which passes over the subcontinent. Over India, the highly unstable moist airflow is over 6,000 m thick compared with only 2,000 m over Japan, giving rise to the bursts of torrential rain which mark out the wet season.

Winter In winter, high pressure builds up over Central Asia. Most of India is protected from the cold northeast monsoon winds that result by the massive bulk of the Himalaya and daytime temperatures rise sharply in the sun. Right across the Ganga plains night temperatures fall to below 5°C in January and February. To the south the winter temperatures increase having a minimum temperature of around 20°C.

Although much of North India often has beautiful weather from November through to March, there are periods when it is cool and overcast. Elsewhere, however, the winter is a dry season through nearly all of India. The low winter night temperatures coupled with increasing pollution in the larger cities such as Delhi and Kolkata, contribute to the growing problem of morning fog in December-January, a major health hazard as well as causing periodic travel chaos.

Summer From April onwards much of India becomes almost unbearably hot. Temperatures of over 50°C are not unknown. It is a time of year to get up to the hills. At the end of May very moist southwesterlies sweep across South India and the Bay of Bengal. They then double back northwestwards, bringing tremendously heavy rain first to the eastern Himalaya then gradually spreading northwestwards.

The wet season The monsoon season, which lasts from between three and five months depending on the region, brings an enveloping dampness which makes it very difficult to keep things dry. Many parts of the west coast get a three-month soaking and the Shillong plateau has received as much as 26 m in one year! If you are travelling in the wetter parts of India during the monsoon you need to be prepared for extended periods of torrential rain and major disruption to travel. However, many parts of India receive a total of under 1,000 mm a year, mainly in the form of heavy isolated showers. Rainfall generally decreases towards the Northwest, Rajasthan and northern Gujarat merging imperceptibly into genuine desert. Tamil Nadu in the southeast has an exceptional rainfall pattern, receiving most of its rain in the period of the retreating monsoon, October-December.

Storms Some regions of India suffer major storms. Cyclones may hit the east coast causing enormous damage and loss of life, the risk being greatest between the end of October and early December. In Northwest India, 'the Loo', between April and June, brings dust storms and very hot winds. In Bengal Nor'westers can cause enormous damage in April-May

Humidity The coastal regions have humidity levels above 70% for most of the year which can be very uncomfortable. However, sea breezes often bring some relief on the coast itself. Moving north and inland, between December-May humidity drops sharply, often falling as low as 20% during the daytime.

Vegetation and wildlife

Vegetation
India's tropical location and its position astride the wet monsoonal winds ensured that 16 different forest types were represented in India. The most widespread was tropical dry deciduous forest. Areas with more than 1,700 mm of rainfall had tropical moist deciduous, semi-evergreen or wet evergreen forest, while much of the remainder had types ranging from tropical dry deciduous woodland to dry alpine

Background Land & environment

scrub, found at high altitudes. However, today forest cover has been reduced to about 13% of the surface area, mainly the result of the great demand for wood as a fuel.

Deciduous forest Two types of deciduous tree remain particularly important, **Sal** (*Shorea robusta*), now found mainly in eastern India and **Teak** (*Tectona grandis*). Most teak today has been planted. Both are resistant to burning, which helped to protect them where man used fire as a means of clearing the forest. See also box below.

Tropical rainforest In wetter areas, particularly along the Western Ghats, you can still find tropical wet evergreen forest, but even these are now extensively managed. Across the drier areas of the peninsula heavy grazing has reduced the forest cover to little more than thorn scrub.

Mountain forests and grassland At between 1,000-2,000 m in the eastern hill ranges of India and in Bhutan, for example, wet hill forest includes evergreen oaks and chestnuts. Further west in the foothills of the Himalaya are belts of subtropical pine at roughly the same altitudes. Deodars (*Cedrus deodarus*) form large stands and moist temperate forest, with pines, cedars, firs and spruce, is dominant, giving many of the valleys a beautifully fresh, alpine feel.

Between 3,000-4,000 m alpine forest predominates. Rhododendron are often mixed with other forest types. Birch, juniper, poplars and pine are widespread.

There are several varieties of coarse grassland along the southern edge of the Terai and alpine grasses are important for grazing above altitudes of 2,000 m. A totally distinctive grassland is the bamboo (*Dendo calamus*) region of the eastern Himalaya.

Trees

Flowering trees Many Indian trees are planted along roadsides to provide shade and they often also produce beautiful flowers. The **Silk Cotton Tree** (*Bombax ceiba*), up to 25 m in height, is one of the most dramatic. The pale greyish bark of this buttressed tree usually bears conical spines. It has wide spreading branches and keeps its leaves for most of the year. The flowers, which appear when the tree is leafless, are cup-shaped, with curling, rather fleshy red petals up to 12 cm long while the fruit produce the fine, silky cotton which gives it its name.

Other common trees with red or orange flowers include the Dhak (also called the 'Flame of the forest' or *Palas*), the Gulmohur, the Indian coral tree and the Tulip tree. The smallish (6 m) deciduous **Dhak** (*Butea monosperma*), has light grey bark and a gnarled, twisted trunk and thick, leathery leaves. The large, bright orange and sweet pea-shaped flowers appear on leafless branches. The 8-9 m high umbrella-shaped **Gulmohur** (*Delonix regia*), a native of Madagascar, is grown as a shade tree in towns. The fiery coloured flowers make a magnificent display after the tree has shed its feathery leaves. The scarlet flowers of the **Indian Coral Tree** (*Erythrina indica*) also appear when its branches with thorny bark are leafless. The tall **Tulip Tree** (*Spathodea campanulata*) (not to be confused with the North American one) has a straight, darkish brown, slender trunk. It is usually evergreen except in the drier parts of India. The scarlet bell-shaped, tulip-like, flowers grow in profusion at the ends of the branches from November to March.

Often seen along roadsides the **Jacaranda** (*Jacaranda mimosaefolia*), has attractive feathery foliage and purple-blue thimble-shaped flowers up to 40 mm long. When not in flower it resembles a Gulmohur, but differs in its general shape. The valuable **Tamarind** (*Tamarindus indica*), with a short straight trunk and a spreading crown, often grows along the roadside. An evergreen with feathery leaves, it bears small clusters of yellow and red flowers. The noticeable fruit pods are long, curved and swollen at intervals. In parts of India, the rights to the fruit are auctioned off annually for up to Rs 4,000 (US$100) per tree.

Of these trees the Silk cotton, the Dhak and the Indian coral are native to India.
Others were introduced mostly during the last century: the Tulip tree from East Africa, the Jacaranda from Brazil and the Tamarind, possibly from Africa.

Fruit trees The familiar apple, plum, apricot and cherry grow in the cool upland areas of India. In the warmer plains tropical fruits flourish. The large, spreading **Mango** (*Mangifera indica*) bears the delicious, distinctively shaped fruit that comes in hundreds of varieties. The evergreen **Jackfruit** (*Artocarpus heterophyllus*) has dark green leathery leaves. The huge fruit (up to 90 cm long and 40 cm thick), growing from a short stem directly off the trunk and branches, has a rough, almost prickly skin and is almost sickly sweet. The **Banana** plant (*Musa*), actually a gigantic herb (up to 5 m high) arising from an underground stem, has very large leaves which grow directly off the trunk. Each large purplish flower produces bunches of up to 100 bananas. The **Papaya** (*Carica papaya*) grows to about 4 m with the large hand-shaped leaves clustered near the top. Only the female tree bears the fruit, which hang down close to the trunk just below the leaves.

Palm trees Coconut Palms (*Cocos nucifera*) are extremely common all round the coast of India. It has tall (15-25 m), slender, unbranched trunks, feathery leaves and large green or golden fruit with soft white flesh filled with milky water, so different from the brown fibre-covered inner nut which makes its way to Europe. The 10-15 m high **Palmyra palms** (*Borassus flabellifer*), indigenous to South and East India, have very distinctive fan-like leaves, as much as 150 cm across. The fruit, which is smaller than a coconut, is round, almost black and very shiny. The **Betel Nut Palm** (*Areca catechu*) resembles the coconut palm, its slender trunk bearing ring marks left by fallen leaf stems. The smooth, round nuts, only about 3 cm across, grow in large hanging bunches. **Wild Date Palms** (*Phoenix sylvestris*), originally came from North Africa. About 20-25 m tall, the trunks are also marked with the ring bases of the leaves which drop off. The distinctive leaflets which stick out from the central vein give the leaf a spiky appearance. Bunches of dates are only borne by the female tree.

All these palm trees are of considerable **commercial importance**. From the fruit alone the coconut palm produces coir from the outer husk, copra from the fleshy kernel from which coconut oil or coconut butter is extracted, in addition to the desiccated coconut and coconut milk. The sap is fermented to a drink called toddy. A similar drink is produced from the sap of the wild date and the palmyra palms which are also important for sugar production. The fruit of the betel nut palm is wrapped in a special leaf and chewed. The trunks and leaves of all the palms are widely used in building and thatching.

Other trees Of all Indian trees the **Banyan** (*Ficus benghalensis*) is probably the best known. It is planted by temples, in villages and along roads. The seeds often germinate in the cracks of old walls, the growing roots splitting the wall apart. If it grows in the bark of another tree, it sends down roots towards the ground. As it grows, more roots appear from the branches, until the original host tree is surrounded by a 'cage' which eventually strangles it. The famous one in Kolkata's Botanical Gardens is more than 400 m in circumference.

Related to the banyan, the **Pipal** or Peepul (*Ficus religiosa*), also cracks open walls and strangles other trees with its roots. With a smooth grey bark, it too is commonly found near temples and shrines. You can distinguish it from the banyan by the absence of aerial roots and its large, heart-shaped leaf with a point tapering into a pronounced 'tail'. It bears abundant 'figs' of a purplish tinge which are about 1 cm across.

The **Ashok** or **Mast** (*Polyalthia longifolia*) is a tall evergreen which can reach 15 m or more in height. One variety, often seen in avenues, is trimmed and tapers towards the top. The leaves are long, slender and shiny and narrow to a long point.

Acacia trees with their feathery leaves are fairly common in the drier parts of India. The best known is the **Babul** (*Acacia arabica*) with a rough, dark bark. The leaves have long silvery white thorns at the base and consist of many leaflets while the flowers grow in golden balls about 1 cm across.

The **Eucalyptus** or **Gum Tree** (*Eucalyptus grandis*), introduced from Australia in the 19th century, is now widespread and is planted near villages to provide both shade and firewood. There are various forms but all may be readily recognized by their height, their characteristic long, thin leaves which have a pleasant fresh smell and the colourful peeling bark.

The wispy **Casuarina** (*Casuarina*) grows in poor sandy soil, especially on the coast and on village waste land. It has the typical leaves of a pine tree and the cones are small and prickly to walk on. It is said to attract lightning during a thunder storm.

Bamboo (*Bambusa*) strictly speaking is a grass which can vary in size from small ornamental clumps to the enormous wild plant whose stems are so strong and thick that they are used for construction and for scaffolding and as pipes in rural irrigation schemes.

Flowering plants

Common in the Himalaya is the beautiful flowering shrub or tree, which can be as tall as 12 m, the **Rhododendron** which is indigenous to this region. In the wild the commonest colour of the flowers is crimson, but other colours, such as pale purple occur too. From March to May the flowers are very noticeable on the hill sides. Another common wild flowering shrub is **Lantana**. This is a fairly small untidy looking bush with rough, toothed oval leaves, which grow in pairs on the square and prickly stem. The flowers grow together in a flattened head, the ones near the middle being usually yellowish, while those at the rim are pink, pale purple or orange. The fruit is a shiny black berry.

Many other flowering plants are cultivated in parks, gardens and roadside verges. The attractive **Frangipani** (*Plumeria acutifolia*) has a rather crooked trunk and stubby branches, which if broken give out a white milky juice which can be irritating to the skin. The big, leathery leaves taper to a point at each end and have noticeable parallel veins. The sweetly scented waxy flowers are white, pale yellow or pink. The **Bougainvillea** grows as a dense bush or climber with small oval leaves and rather long thorns. The brightly coloured part (which can be pinkish-purple, crimson, orange, yellow et cetera) which appears like a flower is not formed of petals, which are quite small and undistinguished, but by large papery bracts.

The unusual shape of the **Hibiscus**. The trumpet shaped flower, as much as 7 or 8 cm across, has a very long 'tongue' growing out from the centre and varies in colour from scarlet to yellow or white. The leaves are somewhat oval or heart-shaped with jagged edges. In municipal flowerbeds the commonest planted flower is probably the **Canna Lily**. It has large leaves which are either green or bronzed and lots of large bright red or yellow flowers. The plant can be more than 1 m high.

On many ponds and tanks the floating plants of the **Lotus** (*Nelumbo nucifera*) and the **Water Hyacinth** (*Eichornia crassipes*) are seen. Lotus flowers which rise on stalks above the water can be white, pink or a deep red and up to 25 cm across. The very large leaves either float on the surface or rise above the water. Many dwarf varieties are cultivated. The rather fleshy leaves and lilac flowers of the water hyacinth float to form a dense carpet, often clogging the waterways.

Crops

Of India's enormous variety, the single most widespread crop is **rice** (commonly *Orysa indica*). This forms the most important staple in South and East India, though other cereals and some root crops are also important elsewhere. The rice plant grows in flooded fields called *paddies* and virtually all planting or harvesting is done by hand. Millets are favoured in drier areas inland, while wheat is the most important crop in the northwest.

There are many different sorts of millet, but the ones most often seen are finger millet, pearl millet (bajra) and sorghum (jowar). **Finger millet**, commonly known as ragi (*Eleusine corocana*), is so-called because the ear has several spikes which radiate out, a bit like the fingers of a hand. Usually less than 1 m high, it is grown extensively in the south. Both **pearl millet** (*Pennisetum typhoideum*, known as *bajra* in the north and *cumbu* in Tamil Nadu) and **sorghum** (*Sorghum vulgare*, known as *jowar* in the north and *cholam* in the south) look superficially similar to the more familiar maize though each can be easily distinguished when the seed heads appear. Pearl millet, mainly grown in the north, has a tall single spike which gives it its other name of bulrush millet. Sorghum bears an open ear at the top of the plant.

Tea (*Camellia sinensis*) is grown on a commercial scale in tea gardens in areas of high rainfall, often in highland regions. Over 90% comes from Assam and West Bengal in the Northeast and Tamil Nadu and Kerala in the South. Left to itself tea grows into a tree 10 m tall. In the tea gardens it is pruned to waist height for the convenience of the tea pluckers and forms flat topped bushes, with shiny bright green oval leaves.

Coffee (*Coffea*) is not as widely grown as tea, but high quality arabica is an important crop in parts of South India. Coffee is also a bush, with fairly long, shiny dark green leaves. The white, sweet smelling flowers, which yield the coffee berry, grow in groups along the stems. The coffee berries start off green and turn red when ripe.

Sugar cane (*Saccharum*) is another commercially important crop. This looks like a large grass which stands up to 3 m tall. The crude brown sugar is sold as jaggery and has a flavour of molasses.

Of the many spices grown in India, the two climbers pepper and vanilla and the grass-like cardamom are the ones most often seen. The **pepper** vine (*Piper Nigrum*) is indigenous to India where it grows in the warm moist regions. As it is a vine it needs support such as a trellis or a tree. It is frequently planted up against the betel nut palm and appears as a leafy vine with almost heart-shaped leaves. The peppercorns cluster along hanging spikes and are red when ripe. Both black and white pepper is produced from the same plant, the difference being in the processing.

Vanilla (*Vanilla planifolium*), which belongs to the orchid family, also grows up trees for support and attaches itself to the bark by small roots. It is native to South America, but grows well in India in areas of high rainfall. It is a rather fleshy looking plant, with white flowers and long slender pods.

Cardamom (*Elettaria cardomomum*) is another spice native to India and is planted usually under shade. It grows well in highland areas such as Sikkim and the Western Ghats. It is a herbaceous plant looking rather like a big clump of grass, with long leafy shoots springing out of the ground as much as 2-3 m in height. The white flowers grow on separate shoots which can be upright, but usually sprawl on the ground. It is from these flowers that the seed bearing capsules grow.

The **cashew nut** tree (*Anacardium occidentale*) was introduced into India, but now grows wild as well as being cultivated. It is a medium sized tree with bright green, shiny, rounded leaves. The nut grows on a fleshy fruit called a cashew apple and hangs down below this. **Cotton** (*Gossypium*) is important in parts of the west and south. The cotton bush is a small knee-high bush and the cotton boll appears after the flower has withered. This splits when ripe to show the white cotton lint inside.

The **castor oil** plant (*Ricinus Communis*) is cultivated as a cash crop and is planted in small holdings among other crops and along roads and paths. It is a handsome plant up to about 2 m in height, with very large leaves which are divided into some 12 'fingers'. The young stems are reddish and shiny. The well known castor oil is extracted from the bean which is a mottled brown in colour.

Wildlife

India has an extremely rich and varied wildlife, though many species only survive in very restricted environments.

Conservation Alarmed by the rapid loss of wildlife habitat the Indian Government established the first conservation measures in 1972, followed by the setting up of national parks and reserves. Some 25,000 sq km were set aside in 1973 for Project Tiger. Tigers have been reported to be increasing steadily in several of the game reserves but threats to their survival continue, notably through poaching. The same is true of other, less well known species. Their natural habitat has been destroyed both by people and by domesticated animals (there are some 250 million cattle and 50 million sheep and goats). There are now nearly 70 national parks and 330 sanctuaries in addition to programmes of afforestation and coastline preservation. Most parks and sanctuaries are open from October-March; those in the northeast are closed from April-September, while many in Madhya Pradesh and Uttar Pradesh close July-September.

The animals

The big cats Of the three Indian big cats the Asiatic lion is virtually confined to a single reserve. The other two, the tiger and leopard, occasionally occur outside. The **tiger** (*Panthera tigris*), which prefers to live in fairly dense cover, is most likely to be glimpsed as it lies in long grass or in dappled shadow. The **asiatic lion** (*Panthera leo*) is now found only in the Gir National Park. Less sleek than the African lion, it has a more shaggy coat and a smaller, often black mane. The **leopard** or **panther** as it is often called in India (*Panthera pardus*), is far more numerous than the tiger, but is even more elusive. The all black form is not uncommon in areas of higher rainfall such as the Western Ghats and Northeast India, though the typical form is seen more often.

Elephant and rhino The **Indian elephant** (*Elephas maximus*) has been domesticated for centuries and today it is still used as a beast of burden. In the wild it inhabits hilly country with forest and bamboo, where it lives in herds which can number as many as 50 or more individuals. They are adaptable animals and can live in all sorts of forest, except those in the dry areas.Wild elephants are mainly confined to reserves, but occasionally move out into cultivation, where they cause great damage. The **great Indian one-horned rhinoceros** (*Rhinoceros unicornis*) has folds of skin which look like rivet covered armour plating. It stands at up to 170 cm at the shoulder.

Deer, antelope, oxen and their relatives Once widespread, these animals are now largely confined to the reserves. The male deer (stags) carry antlers which are branched, each 'spike' on the antler being called a tine. Antelopes and oxen, on the other hand, have horns which are not branched.

    Deer There are several deer species in India, mainly confined to very restricted ranges. Three species are quite common. The largest and one of the most widespread, is the magnificent **sambar** (*Cervus unicolor*) which can be up to 150 cm at the shoulder. It has a noticeably shaggy coat, which varies in colour from brown with a yellowish or grey tinge through to dark, almost black, in the older stags. The sambar is often found on wooded hillsides and lives in groups of up to 10 or so, though solitary individuals are also seen.

    The **barasingha** or **swamp deer** (*Cervus duvauceli*), standing about 130 cm at the shoulder, is also quite common. The females are usually lighter and some are spotted, as are the young. The antlers are much more complex than those of the sambar, having as many as 20 tines, but 12 is more usual. Barasingha prefer swampy habitat, but are also seen in grassy areas, often in large herds.

⦂ Elephants – a future in the wild?

The Indian elephant (Elephas maximas), smaller than the African, is the world's second largest land mammal. Unlike the African elephant, the male rarely reaches a height of over 3 m; it also has smaller ears. Other distinguishing features include the high domed forehead, the rounded shape of the back and the smooth trunk with a single 'finger' at the end. Also the female is often tuskless or bears small ones called tushes and even the male is sometimes tuskless (makhnas). The Indian elephant has five nails on its front feet and four on the back (compared to the African's four and three respectively). There are approximately 6,500 elephants living in the wild in northern West Bengal, Assam and Bhutan. There are a further 2,000 in Central India and 6,000 in the three South Indian states of Kerala, Tamil Nadu and Karnataka.

The loss of habitat has made wild elephants an increasing danger to humans and about 300 people are killed every year by wild elephants, mainly in the northeast. The tribal people have developed skilled techniques for capturing and training wild elephants, which have been domesticated in India for about 5,000 years. They need a lot of feeding – about 18 hours a day. Working elephants are fed on a special diet, by hand straight at the mouth and they eat between 100 and 300 kg per day.

The small **chital** or **spotted deer** (*Axis axis*), only about 90 cm tall, are seen in herds of 20 or so, in grassy areas. The bright rufous coat spotted with white is unmistakable; the stags carry antlers with three tines.

Antelope These animals live in open grasslands, never too far from water. The beautiful **blackbuck** or **Indian antelope** (*Antilope cervicapra*), up to 80 cm at the shoulder, occurs in large herds. The distinctive colouring and the long spiral horns make the stag easy to identify. The coat is chocolate brown above, very sharply demarcated from the white of the underparts. The females do not usually bear horns and like the young, have yellowish brown coats. The larger and heavier **nilgai** or **blue bull** (*Boselaphus tragocamelus*) is about 140 cm at the shoulder and is rather horse-like, with a sloping back. The male has a dark grey coat, while the female is sandy coloured. Both sexes have two white marks on the cheek, white throats and a white ring just above each hoof. The male carries short, forward-curving horns and has a tuft of long black hairs on the front of the neck. They occur in small herds on grassy plains and scrub land.

The very graceful **chinkara** or **Indian gazelle** (*Gazella gazella*) is only 65 cm at the shoulder. The light russet colour of the body has a distinct line along the side where the paler underparts start. Both sexes carry slightly S-shaped horns. Chinkara live in small groups in rather broken hilly countryside.

Oxen The commonest member of the oxen group is the **Asiatic wild buffalo** or water buffalo (*Bubalus bubalis*). About 170 cm at the shoulder, the wild buffalo, which can be aggressive, occurs in herds on grassy plains and swamps near rivers and lakes. The black coat and wide-spreading curved horns, carried by both sexes, are distinctive.

In the high Himalaya, the **yak** (*Bos grunniens*) is domesticated. The wild yak, found on bleak Himalayan hillsides has a shaggy, blackish brown coat and large horns; the domesticated animals are often piebald and the horns much smaller.

The **Indian bison** or **gaur** (*Bos gaurus*) can be up to 200 cm at the shoulder with a heavy muscular ridge across it. Both sexes carry curved horns. The young gaur is a light sandy colour, which darkens with age, the old bulls being nearly black with pale sandy coloured 'socks' and a pale forehead. Basically hill animals, they live in forests and bamboo clumps and emerge from the trees to graze.

Background Land & environment

Others The **bharal** or **blue sheep** (*Pseudois nayaur*) are found on the open slopes around Ladakh. About 90 cm at the shoulder, it has a grey-blue body and horns that curve backwards over the neck.

The rare **asiatic wild ass** (*Equus hemionus*) is confined to the deserts of the Little Rann of Kachchh. The fawn body has a distinctive dark stripe along the back. The dark mane is short and erect. The **wild boar** (*Sus scrofa*) has a mainly black body and a pig-like head; the hairs thicken down the spine to form a sort of mane. A mature male stands 90 cm at the shoulder and, unlike the female, bears tusks. The young are striped. Quite widespread, they often cause great destruction among crops.

One of the most important scavengers of the open countryside, the **striped hyena** (*Hyena hyena*) usually comes out at night. It is about 90 cm at the shoulder with a large head with a noticeable crest of hairs along its sloping back.

The **common giant flying squirrel** are common in the larger forests of India, except in the northeast (*Petaurista petaurista*). The body can be 45 cm long and the tail another 50 cm. They glide from tree to tree using a membrane stretching from front leg to back leg which acts like a parachute.

In towns and villages The **common langur** (*Presbytis entellus*), 75 cm, is a long-tailed monkey with a distinctive black face, hands and feet. Usually a forest dweller, it is found almost throughout India. The **rhesus macaque** (*Macaca mulatta*), 60 cm, is more solid looking with shorter limbs and a shorter tail. It can be distinguished by the orange-red fur on its rump and flanks.

Palm squirrels are very common. The **five-striped** (*Funambulus pennanti*) and the **three-striped palm squirrel** (*Funambulus palmarum*), are both about the same size (30 cm long, about half of which is tail). The five-striped is usually seen in towns.

The two bats most commonly seen in towns differ enormously in size. The larger so-called **flying fox** (*Pteropus giganteus*) has a wing span of 120 cm. These fruit-eating

Major Indian wildlife parks

- ◆ Project Tiger
- ◇ Other National Parks
- ○ Bird Sanctuaries

⁑ Room at the park...

Booking accommodation in national parks can be very frustrating for independent travellers. In many parks it is essential to book in advance. Offices outside may tell you that it is fully-booked, even when outgoing tourists say that the accommodation is empty. This is because cancellation information is not relayed to all offices. The only way in is patient, friendly persistence, asking for just one day inside. This can then be extended once in. Be prepared for a lot of frustration, especially in Ramnagar (Corbett National Park). Where possible go to the park itself and book. You may prefer to try a specialist travel agent in one of the main towns in the region.

bats, found throughout, except in the driest areas, roost in large noisy colonies where they look like folded umbrellas hanging from the trees. In the evening they can be seen leaving the roost with slow measured wing beats. The much smaller **Indian pipistrelle** (*Pipistrellus coromandra*), with a wing span of about 15 cm, is an insect eater. It comes into houses at dusk, roosting under eaves and has a fast, erratic flight.

The **jackal** (*Canis aureus*), a lone scavenger in towns and villages, looks like a cross between a dog and a fox and varies in colour from shades of brown through to black. The bushy tail has a dark tip.

The **common mongoose** (*Herpestes edwardsi*) lives in scrub and open jungle. It kills snakes, but will also take rats, mice and chicken. Tawny coloured with a grey grizzled tinge, it is about 90 cm in length, of which half is pale-tipped tail.

The **sloth bear** (*Melursus ursinus*), about 75 cm at the shoulder, lives in broken forest, but may be seen on a lead accompanying a street entertainer who makes it 'dance' to music as a part of an act. They have a long snout, a pendulous lower lip and a shaggy black coat with a yellowish V-shaped mark on the chest.

If you take a boat trip on the Ganga or the Brahmaputra rivers, look out for the fresh water **gangetic dolphin** (*Platanista gangetica*) as it comes to the surface to breathe.

Birds

Town and village birds Some birds perform a useful function scavenging and clearing refuse. One of the most widespread is the brown **pariah kite** (*Milvus migrans*, 65 cm). The more handsome chestnut and white **brahminy kite** (*Haliastur indus*, 48 cm) is largely confined to the waterside. The common brown **white-backed vulture** (*Gyps bengalensis*, 90 cm) looks ungainly and has a bare and scrawny head and neck. The smaller **scavenger vulture** (*Neophron percnopterus*, 65 cm) is mainly white, but often has dirty looking plumage and the bare head and neck of all vultures. In flight its wedge-shaped tail and black and white colouring are characteristic.

The **house crow** (*Corvus splendens*, 45 cm) on the other hand is a very smart looking bird with a grey body and black tail, wings, face and throat. It occurs in almost every town and village in India. The **jungle crow** (*Corvus macrorhynchos*, 50 cm) originally a bird of the countryside has started to move into populated areas and in the hill stations tends to replace the house crow. Unlike the house crow it is a glossy black all over and has a much deeper, hoarser caw.

The **feral pigeon**, or **blue rock dove** (*Columba livia*, 32 cm), found throughout the world, is generally a slaty grey in colour. It invariably has two dark bars on the wing and a white rump. The **little brown dove** (*Streptopelia senegalensis*, 25 cm) is bluey grey and brown above, with a pink head and underparts and a speckled pattern on the neck. The **collared dove** (*Streptopelia decaocto*, 30 cm) with a distinct half collar on the back of its neck, is common, especially in the drier parts of India.

Background Land & environment

Bulbuls are common in gardens and parks. The **red-vented bulbul** (*Pycnonotus cafer*, 20 cm), a mainly brown bird, can be identified by the slight crest and a bright red patch under the tail. The **house sparrow** (*Passer domesticus*, 15 cm) can be seen in towns throughout the mainland. The ubiquitous **common myna** (*Acridotheres tristis*, 22 cm), feeds on lawns, especially after rain or watering. Look for the white under the tail and the bare yellow skin around the eye, yellow bill and legs and in flight the large white wing patch.

A less common, but more striking bird also seen feeding in open spaces, is the **hoopoe** (*Upupa epops*, 30 cm), easily identified by its sandy plumage with black and white stripes and long thin curved bill. The marvellous fan-shaped crest is sometimes raised. Finally there is a member of the cuckoo family which is heard more often than seen. The **koel** (*Eudynamys scolopacea*, 42 cm), is commonly heard during the hot weather - kuoo-kuoo-kuoo, the double note starts off low and flute-like, rises in pitch and intensity, then suddenly stops, only to start all over again. The male is all black with a greenish bill and a red eye; the female streaked and barred.

Water and waterside birds The *jheels* (marshes or swamps) of India form one of the richest bird habitats in the world. Cormorants abound; the commonest, the **little cormorant** (*Phalacrocorax niger*, 50 cm) is found on most inland waters. An almost entirely black bird with just a little white on the throat, it has a long tail and a hooked bill. The **coot** (*Fulica atra*, 40 cm), another common black bird, seen especially in winter has a noticeable white shield on the forehead.

The magnificent **sarus crane** (*Grus antigone*, 150 cm) is one of India's tallest birds. It is widespread all year round across northern India, almost invariably in pairs. The bare red head and long red legs combined with its height and grey plumage make it easy to identify. The commonest migrant crane is probably the **common crane** (*Grus grus*, 120 cm), present only in winter, often in large flocks. It has mainly grey plumage with a black head and neck. There is a white streak running down the side of the neck and above the eye is a tuft of red feathers.

The **openbill stork** (*Anastomus oscitans*, 80 cm) and the **painted stork** (*Ibis leucocephalus*, 100 cm) are common too and are spotted breeding in large colonies. The former is white with black wing feathers and a curiously shaped bill. The latter, mainly white, has a pinkish tinge on the back and dark marks on the wings and a broken black band on the lower chest. The bare yellow face and yellow down-curved bill are conspicuous.

By almost every swamp, ditch or rice paddy up to about 1,200 m you will see the **paddy bird** (*Ardeola grayii*, 45 cm). An inconspicuous, buff-coloured bird, it is easily overlooked as it stands hunched up by the waterside. As soon as it takes off, its white wings and rump make it very noticeable. The **bronze-winged jacana** (*Metopidius indicus*, 27 cm) has very long toes which enable it to walk on the floating leaves of water-lilies and there is a noticeable white streak over and above the eye. Village ponds often have their resident bird.

The commonest and most widespread of the Indian kingfishers is the jewel-like **common kingfisher** (*Alcedo atthis*, 18 cm). With its brilliant blue upperparts and orange breast it is usually seen perched on a twig or a reed beside the water.

Open grassland, light woodland and cultivated land The **cattle egret** (*Bubulcus ibis*, 50 cm), a small white heron, is usually seen near herds of cattle, frequently perched on the backs of the animals. Equal in height to the sarus crane is the impressive, but ugly **adjutant stork** (*Leptopilos dubius*, 150 cm). This often dishevelled bird is a scavenger and is thus seen near rubbish dumps and carcasses. It has a naked red head and neck, a huge bill and a large fleshy pouch which hangs down the front of the neck.

The **rose-ringed parakeet** (*Psittacula krameri*, 40 cm) is found throughout India up to about 1,500 m while the **pied myna** (*Sturnus contra*, 23 cm) is restricted to northern and central India. The rose-ringed parakeet often forms huge flocks, an impressive sight coming in to roost. The long tail is noticeable both in flight and when the bird is perched. They can be very destructive to crops, but are attractive birds which are frequently kept as pets. The pied myna, with its smart black and white plumage is conspicuous, usually in small flocks in grazing land or cultivation. It feeds on the ground and on village rubbish dumps. The all black **drongo** (*Dicrurus adsimilis*, 30 cm) is almost invariably seen perched on telegraph wires or bare branches. Its distinctively forked tail makes it easy to identify.

Weaver birds are a family of mainly yellow birds, all remarkable for the intricate nests they build. The most widespread is the **baya weaver** (*Ploceus philippinus*, 15cm) which nest in large colonies, often near villages. The male in the breeding season combines a black face and throat with a contrasting yellow top of the head and the yellow breast band. In the non-breeding season both sexes are brownish sparrow-like birds.

Hill birds Land above about 1,500 m supports a distinct range of species, although some birds, such as the ubiquitous **common myna**, are found in the highlands as well as in the lower lying terrain.

The highland equivalent of the red-vented bulbul is the **white-cheeked bulbul** (*Pycnonotus leucogenys*, 20 cm) which is found in gardens and woodland in the Himalaya up to about 2,500 m and as far south as Mumbai. It has white underparts with a yellow patch under the tail. The black head and white cheek patches are distinctive. The crest varies in length and is most prominent in birds found in Kashmir, where it is very common in gardens. The **red-whiskered bulbul** (*Pycnonotus jocosus*, 20 cm) is widespread in the Himalaya and the hills of South India up to about 2,500 m. Its pronounced pointed crest, which is sometimes so long that it flops forward towards the bill, white underparts and red and white 'whiskers' serve to distinguish it. It has a red patch under the tail.

In the summer the delightful **verditer flycatcher** (*Muscicapa thalassina*, 15 cm) is a common breeding bird in the Himalaya up to about 3,000 m. It is tame and confiding, often builds its nest on verandahs and is seen perching on telegraph wires. In winter it is much more widely distributed throughout the country. It is an active little bird which flicks its tail up and down in a characteristic manner. The male is all bright blue green with somewhat darker wings and a black patch in front of the eyes. The female is similar, but duller.

Another species associated with man is the **white wagtail** (*Motacilla alba*, 21 cm), very common in the Himalayan summer up to about 3,000 m. It is always found near water, by streams and lakes, on floating vegetation and among the house boats in Kashmir. Its black and white plumage and constantly wagging tail make it easy to identify.

Yet another species common in Kashmir and in other Himalayan hill stations is the **red-billed blue magpie** (*Urocissa erythrorhyncha*, 65 cm). With a long tail and pale blue plumage, contrasting with its black head, it is usually seen in small flocks as it flies from tree to tree. This is not so much a garden bird, but prefers tea gardens, open woodland and cultivation.

Jungle fowl and pheasants The highlands of India, especially the Himalaya, are the home of the ancestors of domestic hens and also of numerous beautiful pheasants. These are mainly forest dwellers and are not easy to see as they tend to be shy and wary of man.

Last but not least, mention must be made of India's national bird, the magnificent and well-known **Peafowl** (*Pavo cristatus*, male 210 cm, female 100 cm), which is more commonly known as the peacock. Semi-domesticated birds are commonly seen and heard around towns and villages, especially in the northwest of India. In the wild it favours hilly jungles and dense scrub.

India is famous for its reptiles, especially its snakes which feature in many stories and legends. In reality, snakes keep out of the way of people. One of the most common is the **Indian rock python** (*Python molurus*) a 'constrictor' which kills it's prey by suffocation. Usually about 4 m in length, they can be much longer. Their docile nature make them favourites of snake handlers.

The other large snakes favoured by street entertainers are cobras. The various species all have a hood which is spread when the snake draws itself up to strike. They are all highly venomous and the snake charmers prudently de-fang them to render them harmless. The best known is probably the **spectacled cobra** (*Naja naja*), which has a mark like a pair of spectacles on the back of its hood. The largest venomous snake in the world is the **king cobra** (*Ophiophagus hannah*) which is 5 m in length. It is usually brown, but can vary from cream to black and lacks the spectacle marks of the other. In their natural state cobras are generally inhabitants of forest regions.

Equally venomous, but much smaller, the **common krait** (*Bungarus caeruleus*) is just over 1 m in length. The slender, shiny, blue-black snake has thin white bands which can sometimes be almost indiscernible. They are found all over the country except in the northeast where the canniballistic **banded krait** with bold yellowish and black bands have virtually eradicated them.

In houses everywhere you cannot fail to see the **gecko** (*Hemidactylus*). This small harmless, primitive lizard is active after dark. It lives in houses behind pictures and curtain rails and at night emerges to run across the walls and ceilings to hunt the night flying insects which form its main prey. It is not usually more than about 14 cm long, with a curiously transparent, pale yellowish brown body. At the other end of the scale is the **monitor lizard** (*Varanus*), which can grow to 2 m in length. They can vary from a colourful black and yellow, to plain or speckled brown. They live in different habitats from cultivation and scrub to waterside places and desert.

The most widespread crocodile is the freshwater **mugger** or Marsh crocodile (*Crocodilus palustrus*) which grows to 3-4 m in length. The only similar fresh water species is the **gharial** (*Gavialis gangeticus*) which lives in large, fast flowing rivers. Twice the length of the mugger, it is a fish-eating crocodile with a long thin snout and, in the case of the male, an extraordinary bulbous growth on the end of the snout. The enormous, aggressive **estuarine** or **saltwater crocodile** (*Crocodilus porosus*) is now restricted to the brackish waters of the Sundarbans, on the east coast and in the Andaman and Nicobar Islands. It grows to 7 m in length and is much sleeker looking than the rather docile mugger.

Further reading

The literature on India is as huge and varied as the subcontinent itself. India is a good place to buy English language books as foreign books are often much cheaper than the published price. There are also cheap Indian editions and occasionally reprints of out-of-print books. There are excellent bookshops in all the major Indian cities. Below are a few suggestions.

Art and architecture

T Richard Burton *Hindu Art*, British Museum P. Well illustrated; a broad view of art and religion.
Ilay Cooper and Barry Dawson *Traditional Buildings of India*, Thames & Hudson.
George Michell *The Hindu Temple*, Univ of Chicago Press, 1988. An authoritative account of Hindu architectural development.
Henri Sterlin *Hindu India*. Köln, Taschen, 1998. Traces the development from early rock-cut shrines, detailing famous examples; clearly written, well illustrated.

Giles Tillotson *The Rajput Palaces*, Yale, 1987; *Mughal architecture*, London, Viking, 1990; *The tradition of Indian architecture*, Yale 1989. Superbly clear writing on development of Indian architecture under Rajputs, Mughals and the British.

NS Ramaswami *Temples of South India*, Chennai, Maps and Agencies, 1996.

KR Srinivasan's *Temples of South India*, 3rd ed, New Delhi, National Book Trust, 1985, have good background information.

Cities, sites and places

Aurangabad
C Berkson *The caves of Aurangabad*, Mapin, Ahmadabad, 1986.

Delhi
Barton, G, and Malone, L *Old Delhi: 10 easy walks*. Delhi, Rupa, 1988. An interesting companion with which to explore the old city, helpful maps.

Kaul, H, Ed *Historic Delhi: an anthology*. Delhi, OUP, 1985.

Sainty, S *Lost monuments of Delhi*. Delhi, Harper Collins, 1997. A booklet covering Islamic architecture in brief.

Sharma, YD *Delhi and its neighbourhood*. Delhi, ASI, 1972. History, architecture and site details.

Dharamshala
Avedon, *In exile from the land of the snows*.

Dalai Lama *My land and my people* and *Freedom in Exile*.

Nórbu and Turnbull *Tibet: Its history, religion and people*.

Sogyal Rinpoche *The Tibetan Book of Living and Dying*.

Goa
Anthony Hutt *Goa: A Traveller's Historical and Architectural Guide*. An extensive, richly illustrated book.

S Rajagopalan, ASI's *Old Goa*.

Gujarat
Royal Families and Palaces of Gujarat. Scorpion Cavendish,1998. £39 (paperback £29). Beautifully produced.

SH Desai *Junagadh and Girnar*.

KV Soundara Rajan *Junagadh*, an ASI booklet, 1985. Details the edicts and Buddhist caves on Uparkot.

Longhurst's *Hampi Ruins*. Recommended. **Settar**'s *Hampi* (both at *Aspirations Bookshop*, Hampi Bazar).

Kanpur
Manohar Malgaonkar *The Devil's Wind: Nana Saheb's story*, 1988, New Delhi. Largely factual.

George Otto Trevelyan *Cawnpore*, 1992, Delhi.

Andrew Ward *Our bones are scattered*, 1996, New York.

Khajuraho
D Desai's *Religious Imagery of Khajuraho*. Good ASI booklet by Krishna Deva, Rs 5; detailed edition with colour plates, Rs 400. March 2000.

Punja's *A Divine Ecstasy*, Viking (Penguin, India), 1992, carries an original interpretation.

Kullu
Penelope Chetwode *Kulu, to the end of the habitable world*, John Murray, 1972. Chronicles her travels from Narkanda to Ani and over the Jalori Pass to Banjar and Aut in the Tirthan valley. Penelope Chetwode died a peaceful death near Khanag while travelling along this route during the early 1990s.

Ladakh
H Harres *Ladakh*, Innsbruck, 1980.

Andrew Harvey *A Journey in Ladakh*, Cape, London, 1983.

Helena Norberg-Hodge *Ancient Futures: Learning from Ladakh*, Rider, London, 1992.

Paldang *Monasteries of Ladakh*.

J Rizvi *Ladakh, Crossroads of High Asia*, OUP, Delhi, 1983.

Eric Shipton *That Untravelled World*.

M Singh *Himalayan art*, UNESCO, 1971.

DL Snellgrove and T Skorupski *The Cultural Heritage of Ladakh*, Aris & Phillips, Delhi, 1977, 1980.

Lucknow
Rosie Llewellyn-Jones *A fatal friendship: the Nawab, the British and the city of Lucknow*, 1992, OUP, Delhi. A lively guide to the city and its history. Her *A Very Ingenious Man* (1992, Delhi) follows the fortunes of Claude Martin.

PJO Taylor *A Companion to the Indian Mutiny of 1857*, 1996, OUP, Delhi. Includes an annotated bibliography.

Two books about the 'Uprising', particularly at Lucknow, are recommended:

Background Further reading

JG Farrell *The Siege of Krishnapur*, a novel.
Christopher Hibbert *The Great Mutiny: India 1857*, Penguin. A factual history.

Mahabalipuram
Michael Lockwood *Mahabalipuram and the Pandavas* Madras, Christian Literature Society, 1982.
C Sivaramamurti *Mahabalipuram* Fifth edition. New Delhi, Archaeological Survey of India, 1992.

Sanchi
Debala Mitra, *Sanchi*, an Archaeological Survey of India Booklet.

Shekhawati
Ilay Cooper *The painted towns of Shekhawati*, Mapin, Allahabad, 1994, has many colour photos and maps.
P Rakesh and K Lewis *Shekhawati: Rajasthan's painted houses*. Also well illustrated.

Shimla
JG Farrell, *The Hill Station*. This last, unfinished novel describes colonial Shimla of 1871.
Pamela Kanwar's Imperial Simla: the political culture of the Raj, OUP, New Delhi, 1990.
Paul Scott *Staying On*, Booker Prize winning novel set in post Independence Shimla.

Varanasi
Gol *A Pilgrimage to Kashi*, Indica, 1999. Rs 275. An accessible cartoon strip - the city's history and culture as discovered by modern day visitors.
Jonathan P Parry *Death in Banaras*, Cambridge UP, 1994.

Zanskar
Michel Peissel, *Zanskar, the Hidden Kingdom*.
Olivier Folloni *Zanskar, a Himalayan Kingdom*, features superb photos.

Current affairs and politics

Patrick French *Liberty or Death*, Harper Collins, 1997. Well researched and serious yet reads like a novel.
Granta 57 *India: the Golden Jubilee* Superb edition devoted to India's 50th anniversary of Independence, twenty two international writers give brilliant snapshot accounts of India today.

Sunil Khilnani *The idea of India*, Penguin, 1997. Excellent introduction to contemporary India.
Robert B Silver and Barbara Epstein *India: a mosaic*. New York, NYRB, 2000. Distinguished essays on history, politics and literature including Amartya Sen on Tagore, Pankaj Mishra on nuclear India.
Shashi Tharur *India: from midnight to the millennium*. Viking, 1997.
Mark Tully *No full stops in India*, Viking, 1991. An often superbly observed but controversially interpreted view of contemporary India.

History: medieval and modern

John Beames *Memoirs of a Bengal Civilian*. A readable insight into the British Raj in the post-Mutiny period, London, Eland, 1991.
Michael Edwardes *The Myth of the Mahatma*. Presents Gandhi in a whole new light.
Rajmohan Gandhi *The Good Boatman* Viking/Penguin 1995. An excellent biography by one of Gandhi's noted grandson's.
Bamber Gascoigne *The Great Moghuls*, London, Cape, 1987.
John Keay *India: a History*, Harper Collins, 2000. A major new popular history of the subcontinent.
Jawaharlal Nehru *The discovery of India*, New Delhi, ICCR, 1976.
Francis Robinson (ed) *Cambridge Encyclopaedia of India*, Cambridge, 1989. An introduction to many aspects of South Asian society.
Percival Spear & Romila Thapar *A history of India*, 2 vols, Penguin, 1978.
Stanley Wolpert *A new history of India*, OUP, 1990.

History: pre-history and early history

Bridget and Raymond Allchin *Origins of a civilisation*, Viking, Penguin Books, 1997. The most authoritative up-to-date survey of the origins of Indian civilizations.
AL Basham *The Wonder that was India*, London, Sidgwick & Jackson, 1985. Still one of the most comprehensive and readable accounts of the development of India's culture.

Language

Rupert Snell and Simon Weightman *Teach Yourself Hindi*. An excellent, accessible teaching guides with cassette tapes.
H Yule and AC Burnell (eds), *Hobson-Jobson*, 1886. New paperback edition, 1986. A delightful insight into Anglo-Indian words and phrases.

Literature

Upamanyu Chatterjee *English August*. London, Faber, 1988. A wry account of a modern Indian Civil Servant's year spent in a rural posting.
Nirad Chaudhuri Four books give vivid, witty and often sharply critical accounts of India across the 20th century. *The autobiography of an unknown Indian*, Macmillan, London; *Thy Hand, Great Anarch!*, London, Chatto & Windus, 1987.
Firdaus Kanga *Trying to grow*, Bloomsbury, 1989; Mumbai life seen through the experiences of a Parsi family.
Rohinton Mistry *A fine balance*. Faber, 1995. A tale of the struggle to survive in the modern Indian city.
VS Naipaul *A million mutinies now*, Penguin, 1992. Naipaul's 'revisionist' account of India turns away from the despondency of his earlier two India books (*An Area of darkness* and *India: a wounded civilisation*).
RK Narayan has written many gentle and humorous novels and short stories of South India. *The Man-eater of Malgudi* and *Under the Banyan tree and other stories, Grandmother's stories*, among many, London, Penguin, 1985.
AK Ramanuja: *The collected essays*. Ed by V Dhawadker. New Delhi, OUP, 1999. Brilliant essays on Indian culture and literature.
Arundhati Roy *The God of Small Things*. Indian Ink/Harper Collins, 1997. Excellent first novel about family turmoil in a Syrian Christian household in Kerala.
Salman Rushdie *Midnight's children*, London, Picador, 1981. A novel of India since Independence, offering at the same time funny and bitterly sharp critiques of South Asian life in the 1980s. *The Moor's Last Sigh*, Viking, 1996, is of particular interest to those travelling to Kochi and Mumbai.
Paul Scott *The Raj Quartet*, London, Panther, 1973; *Staying on*, Longmans, 1985. Outstandingly perceptive novels of the end of the Raj.
Vikram Seth *A Suitable Boy*, Phoenix House London, 1993. Prize winning novel of modern Indian life.
Simon Weightman (ed) *Travellers Literary Companion: the Indian Sub-continent*. An invaluable introduction to the diversity of Indian writing.

Music and cinema

Raghava R Menon *Penguin Dictionary of Indian Classical Music*, Penguin New Delhi 1995.
Lalit Mohan *Bollywood, Popular Indian Cinema*, Joshi (Dakini).

People

Elisabeth Bumiller *May you be the mother of one hundred sons*, Penguin, 1991. An American woman journalists' account of coming to understand the issues that face India's women today.
Lakshmi Holmstrom *The Inner Courtyard*, a series of short stories by Indian women, translated into English, Rupa, 1992.
Norman Lewis *A goddess in the stones*. An insight into tribal life in Orissa and Bihar.
Sarah Lloyd *An Indian Attachment*, London, Eland, 1992. A very personal and engaging account of time spent in an Indian village.

Religion

Wendy Doniger O'Flaherty *Hindu Myths*, London, Penguin, 1974. A sourcebook translated from the Sanskrit.
JP Jain *Religion and Culture of the Jains*. 3rd ed. New Delhi, Bharatiya Jnanapith, 1981.
IH Qureshi *The Muslim Community of the Indo-Pakistan Sub-Continent 610-1947*, OUP, Karachi, 1977.
Walpola Rahula *What the Buddha Taught*.
H Singh *The heritage of the Sikhs*, 2nd ed. New Delhi, 1983.
R Waterstone *India, the cultural companion*, Duncan Baird, Winchester, 2002. India's spiritual traditions brought up to date, profusely illustrated.
RC Zaehner *Hinduism*, OUP.

William Dalrymple *City of Djinns*, Indus/Harper Collins, 1993, paperback. Superb account of Delhi, based on a year living in the city. *The Age of Kali*, published in edited form in India as *In the court of the fish-eyed Goddess*, is his second anecdotal but insightful account.

Trevor Fishlock *Cobra Road*. London, John Murray, 1991. Impressions of a news journalist.

Alexander Frater *Chasing the monsoon*, London, Viking, 1990. A prize winning account of the human impact of the monsoon's sweep across India.

John Hatt *The tropical traveller: the essential guide to travel in hot countries*, Penguin, 3rd ed 1992. Wide ranging and clearly written common sense, based on extensive experience and research.

John Keay *Into India*. London, John Murray, 1999. Seasoned traveller's introduction to understanding and enjoying India.

Trekking

Bill Aitken *The Nanda Devi Affair*, Penguin India, 1994.

Chris Bonnington *Annapurna South Face*, London, Cassell, 1971; Everest the hard way, London, Hodder & Stoughton, 1979.

P Chabloz N Cremieu *Hiking in Zanskar and Ladakh*, Geneva, Olizane, 1986.

Justine Hardy *The Ochre Border* 1995, Constable, London. An account of crossing the Puri Parvati Pass from Kullu to Spiti.

Edmund Hillary *High Adventure*, New York, Dutton, 1955. Both classic accounts of Himalayan climbs.

Harish Kapadia *Spiti: Adventures in the Trans-Himalaya*, 1996, Indus.

GD Khosla *Himalayan Circuit*. 1989 OUP. An early account of travel into this then virtually unknown region of Kinnaur and Spiti.

Charlie Loram *Leh & Trekking in Ladakh* 1996. Trailblazer, Hindhead, Surrey.

Audrey Salkeld *The History of Great Climbs*, 1995 The Royal Geographical Society. A magnificently illustrated and written account of historic climbs.

William Sax *Mountain Goddess*, OUP, 1991; both about Nanda Devi.

Dhanu Swadi and Deepak Sanan *Exploring Kinnaur and Spiti in the Trans-Himalaya*, 1998, Indus.

More practical publications include:

G Chand and M Puri *Explore Himachal*, New Delhi, International Publishers, 1991. Descriptions of 110 routes and 27 detailed trekking maps.

T Iozawa *Trekking in the Himalayas*, Delhi, Allied Publishers, 1980. *Nest & Wings*, Post Box 4531, New Delhi 110016, T6442245: 'Trekking', 'Holiday & Trekking' and 'Trekking Map' titles (Rs 40-140) cover most trekking destinations in the Indian Himalaya; trekking itineraries are listed in brief but some booklets give additional insight into the history and culture of the area.

Hugh Swift *Trekking in Pakistan and India*, London, Hodder & Stoughton, 1990. Detailed practical guide, based on extensive first hand experience.

Also useful are:

Himalayan Club's *Himalayan Journal* (annual) from PO Box 1905, Mumbai 400001.

Indian Mountaineering Foundation's Indian Mountaineer (six-monthly) from Benito Juarez Rd, New Delhi 110021. *Peaks and passes of the Garhwal Himalaya* published by Alpinists Club, 1990.

Wildlife and vegetation

Salim Ali *Indian hill birds*, OUP.

Salim Ali and S Dillon Ripley *Handbook of the birds of India & Pakistan* (compact ed).

DV Cowen *Flowering Trees and Shrubs in India*.

Martin Ewans *Bharatpur: Bird Paradise*, Lustre Press, Delhi.

R Grimmet and C & T Inskipp *Pocket guide to Birds of the Indian Sub-Continent*. 1999.

Richard Ives *Of tigers and men*, Doubleday, 1995.

Krys Kazmierczak & Raj Singh *A birdwatcher's guide to India*. Prion, 1998, Sandy, Beds, UK. Well researched and carrying lots of practical information for all birders.

SM Nair *Endangered animals of India*, New Delhi, NBT, 1992.

O Polunin & A Stainton *Flowers of the Himalaya*, OUP, 1984.

SH Prater *The Book of Indian Animals*.

S Sippy and S Kapoor *The Ultimate Ranthambhore Guide*, 2001. Informative, practical guide stressing conservation.

Thapar and Rathore *Wild tigers of Ranthambhore* OUP, 2000.

Footnotes

Hindi words and phrases

Pronunciation

a as in ah	i as in bee	nasalized vowels are shown as an un
o as in oh	u as oo in book	

Basics

Hello, good morning, goodbye	namaste
Thank you/no thank you	dhanyavad or shukriya/nahin shukriya
Excuse me, sorry	maf kijiye
Yes/no	ji han/ji nahin
nevermind/that's all right	koi bat nahin

Questions

What is your name?	apka nam kya hai?
My name is...	mera nam... Hai
Pardon?	phir bataiye?
How are you?	kya hal hai?
I am well, thanks, and you?	main thik hun, aur ap?
Not very well	main thik nahin hun
Where is the?	kahan hai?
Who is?	kaun hai?
What is this?	yeh kya hai?

Shopping

How much?	Kitna?
That makes (20) rupees	(bis) rupaye
That is very expensive!	bahut mahanga hai!
Make it a bit cheaper!	thora kam kijiye!

The hotel

What is the room charge?	kiraya kitna hai?
Please show the room	kamra dikhaiye
Is there an airconditioned room?	kya a/c kamra hai?
Is there hot water?	garam pani hai?
... a bathroom/fan/mosquito net	... bathroom/pankha/machhar dani
Is there a large room?	bara kamra hai?
Please clean it	saf karwa dijiye
Are there clean sheets/blanket?	saf chadaren/kambal hain?
Bill please	bill dijiye

Travel

Where's the railway station?	railway station kahan hai?
How much is the ticket to Agra?	Agra ka ticket kitne ka hai?
When does the Agra bus leave?	Agra bus kab jaegi?
How much?	Kitna?
left/right	baien/dahina
go straight on	sidha chaliye
nearby	nazdik

Please wait here	yahan thahariye
Please come at 8	ath bajai ana
quickly	jaldi
stop	rukiye

Restaurants

Please show the menu	menu dikhaiye
No chillis please	mirch nahin dalna
...sugar/milk/ice	...chini/doodh/baraf
A bottle of water please	ek botal pani dijiye
sweet/savoury	mitha/namkin
spoon, fork, knife	chamach, kanta, chhuri

Time and days

right now	abhi	month	mahi
morning	suba	year	sal
afternoon	dopahar	Sunday	raviva
evening	sham	Monday	somvar
night	rat	Tuesday	mangalvar
today	aj	Wednesday	budhvar
tomorrow/yesterday	kal/kal	Thursday	virvar
day	din	Friday	shukravar
week	hafta	Saturday	shanivar

Numbers

1	ek	13	terah
2	do	14	chaudah
3	tin	15	pandrah
4	char	16	solah
5	panch	17	satrah
6	chhai	18	atharah
7	sat	19	unnis
8	ath	20	bis
9	nau	100/200	sau/do sau
10	das	1000/2000	hazar/do hazar
11	gyara	100,000	lakh
12	barah		

Basic vocabulary

Words such as airport, bank, bathroom, bus, doctor, embassy, ferry, hotel, hospital, juice, police, restaurant, station, stamp, taxi, ticket, train are used locally though often pronounced differently eg daktar, haspatal.

and	aur	open	khula
big	bara	police station	thana
café/food stall	dhaba/hotel	road	rasta
chemist	dawai ki dukan	room	kamra
clean	saf	shop	dukan
closed	band	sick (ill)	bimar
cold	thanda	silk	reshmi/silk
day	din	small	chhota
dirty	ganda	that	who

	angrezi	this		yeh	
...ent	bahut achha	town		shahar	
...u/ to eat	khana	water		pani	
...ot (spicy)	jhal, masaledar	what		kya	
hot (temp)	garam	when		kab	
luggage	saman	where		kahan/kidhar	
medicine	dawai	which/who		kaun	
newspaper	akhbar	why		kiun	
of course, sure	zaroor	with		ke sathh	

Food and drink

Eating out is normally cheap and safe but menus can often be dauntingly long and full of unfamiliar names. Here are some Hindi words to help you. Pronunciation is explained on page 1368.

Meat and fish

gosht, mas	meat, usually mutton (sheep)
jhinga	prawns
macchli	fish
murgh	chicken

Vegetables (sabzi)

aloo	potato	khumbhi	mushroom
baingan	aubergine	matar	peas
band gobi	cabbage	piaz	onion
bhindi	okra, ladies' fingers	phool gobi	cauliflower
gajar	carrots	sag	spinach

Styles of cooking

Many items on restaurant menus are named according to methods of preparation, roughly equivalent to terms such as 'Provençal' or 'sauté'.

bhoona in a thick, fairly spicy sauce

chops minced meat, fish or vegetables, covered with mashed potato, crumbed and fried

cutlet minced meat, fish, vegetables formed into flat rounds or ovals, crumbed and fried (eg prawn cutlet, flattened king prawn)

do piaza with onions (added twice during cooking)

dumphuk steam baked

jhal frazi spicy, hot sauce with tomatoes and chillies

jhol thin gravy (Bengali)

Kashmiri cooked with mild spices, ground almonds and yoghurt, often with fruit

kebab skewered (or minced and shaped) meat or fish; a dry spicy dish cooked on a fire

kima minced meat (usually 'mutton')

kofta minced meat or vegetable balls

korma in fairly mild rich sauce using cream /yoghurt

masala marinated in spices (fairly hot)

Madras hot

makhani in butter rich sauce

moli South Indian dishes cooked in coconut milk and green chilli sauce

Mughlai rich North Indian style

Nargisi dish using boiled eggs

navratan curry ('9 jewels') colourful mixed vegetables and fruit in mild sauce
Peshwari rich with dried fruit and nuts (Northwest Indian)
tandoori baked in a tandoor (special clay oven) or one imitating it
tikka marinated meat pieces, baked quite dry
vindaloo hot and sour Goan meat dish using vinegar

Typical dishes

aloo gosht potato and mutton stew
aloo gobi dry potato and cauliflower with cumin
aloo, matar, kumbhi potato, peas, mushrooms in a dryish mildly spicy sauce
bhindi bhaji lady's fingers fried with onions and mild spices
boti kebab marinated pieces of meat, skewered and cooked over a fire
dal makhani lentils cooked with butter
dum aloo potato curry with a spicy yoghurt, tomato and onion sauce
matar panir curd cheese cubes with peas and spices (and often tomatoes)
murgh massallam chicken in creamy marinade of yoghurt, spices and herbs with nuts
nargisi kofta boiled eggs covered in minced lamb, cooked in a thick sauce
rogan josh rich, mutton/beef pieces in creamy, red sauce
sag panir drained curd (panir) sautéd with chopped spinach in mild spices
sarson-ke-sag and **makkai-ki-roti** mustard leaf cooked dry with spices served with maize four roti from Punjab
shabdeg a special Mughlai mutton dish with vegetables
yakhni lamb stew

Rice

bhat/sada chawal plain boiled rice
biriyani partially cooked rice layered over meat and baked with saffron
khichari rice and lentils cooked with turmeric and other spices
pulao/pilau fried rice cooked with spices (cloves, cardamom, cinnamon) with dried fruit, nuts or vegetables. Sometimes cooked with meat, like a biriyani

Roti – breads

chapati (roti) thin, plain, wholemeal unleavened bread cooked on a tawa (griddle), usually made from ata (wheat flour). Makkaikiroti is with maize flour.
nan oven baked (traditionally in a tandoor) white flour leavened bread often large and triangular; sometimes stuffed with almonds and dried fruit
paratha fried bread layered with ghi (sometimes cooked with egg or with potatoes)
poori thin deepfried, puffed rounds of flour

Sweets

These are often made with reduced/thickened milk, drained curd cheese or powdered lentils and nuts. They are sometimes covered with a flimsy sheet of decorative, edible silver leaf.
barfi fudgelike rectangles/diamonds
gulab jamun dark fried spongy balls, soaked in syrup
halwa rich sweet made from cereal, fruit, vegetable, nuts and sugar
khir, payasam, paesh thickened milk rice/vermicelli pudding
kulfi coneshaped Indian ice cream with pistachios/almonds, uneven in texture
jalebi spirals of fried batter soaked in syrup
laddoo lentil based batter 'grains' shaped into rounds
rasgulla (roshgulla) balls of curd in clear syrup
sandesh dry sweet made of curd cheese

KS

, pakora vegetable fritters (onions, potatoes, cauliflower etc) deep-fried in batter

..at sweet and sour fruit and vegetables flavoured with tama rind paste and chillis

nana choor, chioora ('Bombay mix') lentil and flattened rice snacks mixed with nuts and dried fruit

dosai South Indian pancake made with rice and lentil flour; served with a mild potato and onion filling (masala dosai) or without (ravai or plain dosai)

idli steamed South Indian rice cakes, a bland breakfast given flavour by spiced accompaniments

kachori fried pastry rounds stuffed with spiced lentil/ peas/potato filling

samosa cooked vegetable or meat wrapped in pastry triangles and deep fried

utthappam thick South Indian rice and lentil flour pancake cooked with spices/onions/tomatoes

vadai deep fried, small savoury lentil 'doughnut' rings. **Dahi vada** are similar rounds in yoghurt

Glossary

Words in italics are common elements of words, often making up part of a place

A

aarti (arati) Hindu worship with lamps

abacus square or rectangular table resting on top of a pillar

abad peopled

acanthus thick-leaved plant, common decoration on pillars, esp Greek

achalam hill (Tamil)

acharya religious teacher

Adi Granth Guru Granth Sahib, holy book of the Sikhs

Adinatha first of the 24 Tirthankaras, distinguished by his bull mount

agarbathi incense

Agastya legendary sage who brought the Vedas to South India

Agni Vedic fire divinity, intermediary between gods and men; guardian of the Southeast

ahimsa non-harming, non-violence

akhand path unbroken reading of the Guru Granth Sahib

alinda verandah

ambulatory processional path

amla/amalaka circular ribbed pattern (based on a gourd) at the top of a temple tower

amrita ambrosia; drink of immortality

ananda joy

Ananda the Buddha's chief disciple

Ananta a huge snake on whose coils Vishnu rests

anda literally 'egg', spherical part of the stupa

Andhaka demon killed by Siva

anicut irrigation channel (Tamil)

anna (ana) one sixteenth of a rupee (still occasionally referred to)

Annapurna Goddess of abundance; one aspect of Devi

antarala vestibule, chamber in front of shrine or cella

antechamber chamber in front of the sanctuary

apsara celestial nymph

apse semi-circular plan

arabesque ornamental decoration with intertwining lines

aram pleasure garden

architrave horizontal beam across posts or gateways

ardha mandapam chamber in front of main hall of temple

Ardhanarisvara Siva represented as half-male and half-female

Arjuna hero of the Mahabharata, to whom Krishna delivered the Bhagavad Gita

arrack alcoholic spirit fermented from potatoes or grain

aru river (Tamil)

Aruna charioteer of Surya, Sun God; Red

Aryans literally 'noble' (Sanskrit); prehistoric peop/ who settled in Persia and North India

asana a seat or throne (Buddha's) pose

ashram hermitage or retreat

Ashta Matrikas The eight mother goddesses who attended on Siva or Skanda

astanah threshold

atman philosophical concept of universal soul or spirit

atrium court open to the sky in the centre In modern architecture, enclosed in glass

aus summer rice crop (Apr-Aug) Bengal

Avalokiteshwara Lord who looks down; Bodhisattva, the Compassionate

avatara 'descent'; incarnation of a divinity

ayacut irrigation command area (Tamil)

ayah nursemaid, especially for children

B

babu clerk

bada cubical portion of a temple up to the roof or spire

badgir rooftop structure to channel cool breeze into the house (mainly North and West India)

badlands eroded landscape

bagh garden

bahadur title, meaning 'the brave'

baksheesh tip 'bribe'

Balabhadra Balarama, elder brother of Krishna

baluster (balustrade) a small column supporting a handrail

bandh a strike

bandhani tie dyeing (West India)

Bangla (Bangaldar) curved roof, based on thatched roofs in Bengal

bania merchant caste

banian vest

baoli or vav rectangular well surrounded by steps

baradari literally 'twelve pillared', a pavilion with columns

barrel-vault semi-cylindrical shaped roof or ceiling

bas-relief carving of low projection

basement lower part of walls, usually with decorated mouldings

basti Jain temple

batter slope of a wall, especially in a fort

bazar market

bedi (vedi) altar/platform for reading holy texts

begum Muslim princess/woman's courtesy title

beki circular stone below the amla in the finial of a roof

belvedere summer house; small room on a house roof

bhabar coarse alluvium at foot of Himalayas

bhadra flat face of the sikhara (tower)

Bhadrakali Tantric goddess and consort of Bhairav

Song of the Lord; section of the

the king who prayed to Ganga to
to earth
brother

rava Siva, the Fearful

nakti adoration of a deity

bhang Indian hemp

bharal Himalayan blue sheep

Bharata half-brother of Rama

bhavan building or house

bhikku Buddhist monk

Bhima Pandava hero of the Mahabharata, famous for his strength

Bhimsen Deity worshipped for his strength and courage

bhisti a water-carrier

bhogamandapa the refectory hall of a temple

bhumi literally earth; a horizontal moulding of a sikhara

bidi (beedi) Indian cigarette, tobacco wrapped in tendu leaves

bigha measure of land – normally about one-third of an acre

bo-tree (or Bodhi) *Ficus religiosa*, pipal tree associated with the Buddha

Bodhisattva Enlightened One, destined to become Buddha

bodi tuft of hair on back of the shaven head (also *tikki*)

Brahma Universal self-existing power; Creator in the Hindu Triad.

Brahmachari religious student, accepting rigorous discipline (eg chastity)

Brahman (Brahmin) highest Hindu (and Jain) caste of priests

Brahmanism ancient Indian religion, precursor of modern Hinduism

Buddha The Enlightened One; founder of Buddhism

bund an embankment

bundh (literally closed) a strike

burj tower or bastion

burqa (burkha) over-dress worn by Muslim women observing purdah

bustee slum

C

cantonment planned military or civil area in town

capital upper part of a column

caryatid sculptured human female figure used as a support for columns

catamaran log raft, logs (*maram*) tied (*kattu*) together (Tamil)

cave temple rock-cut shrine or monastery

cella small chamber, compartment for the image of a deity

cenotaph commemorative monument, usually an open domed pavilion

chaam Himalayan Buddhist masked dance

chadar sheet worn as clothing

chai tea

chaitya large arched opening in the façade of a hall or Buddhist temple

chajja overhanging cornice or eaves

chakra sacred Buddhist wheel of the law; also Vishnu's discus

chala Bengali curved roof

Chamunda terrifying form of the goddess Durga

Chandra Moon; a planetary deity

chankramana place of the promenade of the Buddha at Bodh Gaya

chapati unleavened Indian bread cooked on a griddle

chaprassi messenger or orderly usually wearing a badge

char sand-bank or island in a river

char bagh formal Mughal garden, divided into quarters

char bangla (char-chala) 'four temples' in Bengal, built like huts

charan foot print

charka spinning wheel

charpai 'four legs' – wooden frame string bed

chatt(r)a ceremonial umbrella on stupa (Buddhist)

chauki recessed space between pillars: entrance

chaukidar (chowkidar) night-watchman; guard

chaultri (choultry) travellers' rest house (Telugu)

chaumukha Jain sanctuary with a quadruple image, approached through four doorways

chauri fly-whisk, symbol for royalty

chauth 25% tax raised for revenue by Marathas

cheri outcaste settlement; slum (Tamil Nadu)

chhang strong mountain beer of fermented barley maize rye or millet or rice

chhatri umbrella shaped dome or pavilion

chhetri (kshatriya) Hindu warrior caste

chikan shadow embroidery on fine cotton (especially in Lucknow)

chikki nut crunch, a speciality of Lonavla

chit sabha hall of wisdom (Tamil)

chitrakar picture maker

chlorite soft greenish stone that hardens on exposure

chogyal heavenly king (Sikkim)

choli blouse

chorten Himalayan Buddhist relic shrine or memorial stupa

chowk (chauk) a block; open place in a city where the market is held

chunam lime plaster or stucco made from burnt seashells

circumambulation clockwise movement around a shrine

clerestory upper section of the walls of a building which allows light in

cloister passage usually around an open square

coir fibre from coconut husk

corbel horizontal block supporting a vertical structure or covering an opening

cornice horizontal band at the top of a wall

crenellated having battlements

crewel work chain stitching

crore 10 million

cupola small dome

curvilinear gently curving shape, generally of a tower

cusp, cusped projecting point between small sections of an arch

D

daal lentils, pulses

dacoit bandit

dada (dadu) grandfather; elder brother

dado part of a pedestal between its base and cornice

dahi yoghurt

dais raised platform

dak bungalow rest house for officials

dak post

dakini sorceress

Dakshineshvara Lord of the South; name of Siva

dan gift

dandi wooden 'seat' carried by bearers

darbar (durbar) a royal gathering

dargah a Muslim tomb complex

darshan (darshana) viewing of a deity or spiritual leader

darwaza gateway, door

Dasara (dassara/dussehra/dassehra) 10 day festival (Sep-Oct)

Dasaratha King of Ayodhya and father of Rama

Dattatraya syncretistic deity; an incarnation of Vishnu, a teacher of Siva, or a cousin of the Buddha

daulat khana treasury

dentil small block used as part of a cornice

deodar Himalayan cedar; from *deva-daru*, the 'wood of the gods'

dervish member of Muslim brotherhood, committed to poverty

deul in Bengal and Orissa, generic name for temple; the sanctuary

deval memorial pavilion built to mark royal funeral pyre

devala temple or shrine (Buddhist or Hindu)

devasthanam temple trust

Devi Goddess; later, the Supreme Goddess

dhaba roadside restaurant (mainly North India) truck drivers' stop

dhansak Parsi dish made with lentils

dharamshala (dharamsala) pilgrims' rest-house

dharma moral and religious duty

dharmachakra wheel of 'moral' law (Buddhist)

dhobi washerman

dhol drums

dhooli (dhooli) swinging chair on a pole, carried by bearers

dhoti loose loincloth worn by Indian men

dhyana meditation

digambara literally 'sky-clad' Jain sect in which the monks go naked

dighi village pond (Bengal)

dikka raised platform around ablution tank

dikpala guardian of one of the cardinal directions mostly appearing in a group of eight

dikshitar person who makes oblations or offerings

dipdan lamp pillar

distributary river that flows away from main channel

divan (diwan) smoking-room; also a chief minister

Diwali festival of lights (Oct-Nov)

diwan-i-am hall of public audience

diwan-i-khas hall of private audience

diwan chief financial minister

do-chala rectangular Bengali style roof

doab interfluve, land between two rivers

dokra tribal name for lost wax metal casting (cire perdu)

dosai (dosa) thin pancake

double dome composed of an inner and outer shell of masonry

Draupadi wife-in-common of the five Pandava brothers in the Mahabharata

drug (*durg*) fort (Tamil, Telugu)

dry masonry stones laid without mortar

duar (dwar) door, gateway

dun valley

dupatta long scarf worn by Punjabi women

Durga principal goddess of the Shakti cult

durrie (dhurrie) thick handloom rug

durwan watchman

dvarpala doorkeeper

dvipa lamp-column, generally of stone or brass-covered wood

E

eave overhang that shelters a porch or verandah

ek the number 1, a symbol of unity

ekka one horse carriage

epigraph carved inscription

eri tank (Tamil)

F

faience coloured tilework, earthenware or porcelain

fakir Muslim religious mendicant

fan-light fan-shaped window over door

fenestration with windows or openings

filigree ornamental work or delicate tracery

finial emblem at the summit of a stupa, tower, dome, or at the end of a parapet

firman edict or grant issued by a sovereign

foliation ornamental design derived from foliage

frieze horizontal band of figures or decorative designs

G

gable end of an angled roof

gadba woollen blanket (Kashmir)

gaddi throne

gadi/gari car, cart, train

gali (galli) lane; an alley

gana child figures in art

Gandharva semi-divine flying figure; celestial musician

Ganesh (Ganapati) elephant-headed son of Siva and Parvati

Ganga goddess personifying the Ganges

ganj market

ganja   Indian hemp

gaon   village

garbhagriha   literally 'womb-chamber'; a temple sanctuary

garh   fort

Garuda   Mythical eagle, half-human Vishnu's vehicle

Gauri   'Fair One'; Parvati

Gaurishankara   Siva with Parvati

ghagra   (ghongra) long flared skirt

ghanta   bell

ghat   hill range, hill road; landing place; steps on the river bank

ghazal   Urdu lyric poetry/love songs, often erotic

ghee   clarified butter for cooking

gherao   industrial action, surrounding home or office of politician or industrial manager

giri   hill

Gita Govinda   Jayadeva's poem of the Krishnalila

godown   warehouse

gola   conical-shaped storehouse

gompa   Tibetan Buddhist monastery

goncha   loose woollen robe, tied at waist with wide coloured band (Ladakh)

Gopala   (Govinda) cowherd; a name of Krishna

Gopis   cowherd girls; milk maids who played with Krishna

gopuram   towered gateway in South Indian temples

Gorakhnath   historically, an 11th-century yogi who founded a Saivite cult; an incarnation of Siva

gosain   monk or devotee (Hindi)

gram   chick pea, pulse

gram   village; gramadan, gift of village

gudi   temple (Karnataka)

gumbaz   (gumbad) dome

gumpha   monastery, cave temple

gur gur   salted butter tea (Ladakh)

gur   palm sugar

guru   teacher; spiritual leader, Sikh religious leader

gurudwara   (literally 'entrance to the house of God'); Sikh religious complex

H

Haj   (Hajj) annual Muslim pilgrimage to Mecca

hakim   judge; a physician (usually Muslim)

halwa   a special sweet meat

hammam   Turkish bath

handi   Punjabi dish cooked in a pot

Hanuman   Monkey devotee of Rama; bringer of success to armies

Hara   (Hara Siddhi) Siva

harem   women's quarters (Muslim), from 'haram', Arabic for 'forbidden by law'

Hari   Vishnu Harihara, Vishnu- Siva as a single divinity

Hariti   goddess of prosperity and patroness of children, consort of Kubera

harmika   the finial of a stupa in the form of a pedestal where the shaft of the honorific umbrella was set

hartal   general strike

Hasan   the murdered eldest son of Ali, commemorated at Muharram

hat   (haat) market

hathi pol   elephant gate

hathi   (hati) elephant

hauz   tank or reservoir

haveli   a merchant's house usually in Rajasthan

havildar   army sergeant

hawa mahal   palace of the winds

Hidimba Devi   Durga worshipped at Manali

hindola   swing

hippogryph   fabulous griffin-like creature with body of a horse

Hiranyakashipu   Demon king killed by Narasimha

hiti   a water channel; a bath or tank with water spouts

Holi   spring festival (Feb-Mar)

hookah   'hubble bubble' or smoking vase

howdah   seat on elephant's back, sometimes canopied

hundi   temple offering

Hussain   the second murdered son of Ali, commemorated at Muharram

huzra   a Muslim tomb chamber

hypostyle   hall with pillars

I

lat   pillar, column

icon   statue or image of worship

Id   principal Muslim festivals

Idgah   open space for the Id prayers

idli   steamed rice cake (Tamil)

ikat   'resist-dyed' woven fabric

imam   Muslim religious leader

imambara   tomb of a Shiite Muslim holy man; focus of Muharram procession

Indra   King of the gods; God of rain; guardian of the East

Ishana   Guardian of the North East

Ishvara   Lord; Siva

iwan   main arch in mosque

J

jadu   magic

jaga mohan   audience hall or ante-chamber of an Orissan temple

Jagadambi   literally Mother of the World; Parvati

Jagannath   literally Lord of the World; particularly, Krishna worshipped at Puri

jagati   railed parapet

jaggery   brown sugar, made from palm sap

jahaz   ship: building in form of ship

jali   literally 'net'; any lattice or perforated pattern

jamb   vertical side slab of doorway

Jambudvipa   Continent of the Rose-Apple Tree; the earth

Jami masjid   (Jama, Jumma) Friday mosque, for congregational worship

Jamuna   Hindu goddess who rides a tortoise; river

Janaka   Father of Sita

jangha   broad band of sculpture on the outside of the temple wall

jarokha   balcony

jataka stories   accounts of the previous lives of the Buddha

jatra   Bengali folk theatre

jauhar   (jauhar) mass suicide by fire of women, particularly in Rajasthan, to avoid capture

jawab   literally 'answer,' a building which duplicates another to provide symmetry

jawan   army recruit, soldier

jaya stambha   victory tower

jheel   (jhil) lake; a marsh; a swamp

jhilmil   projecting canopy over a window or door opening

-ji   (jee) honorific suffix added to names out of reverence and/or politeness; also abbreviated 'yes' (Hindi/Urdu)

jihad   striving in the way of god; holy war by Muslims against non-believers

Jina   literally 'victor'; spiritual conqueror or Tirthankara, after whom Jainism is named

Jogini   mystical goddess

jorbangla   double hut-like temple in Bengal

Jyotirlinga   luminous energy of Siva manifested at 12 holy places, miraculously formed lingams

K

kabalai   (kavalai) well irrigation using bullock power (Tamil Nadu)

kabigan   folk debate in verse

kachcha   man's 'under-shorts' (one of five Sikh symbols)

kacheri   (kutchery) a court; an office for public business

kadal   wooden bridge (Kashmir)

kadhi   savoury yoghurt curry (Gujarat/North India)

kadu   forest (Tamil)

Kailasa   mountain home of Siva

kalamkari   special painted cotton hanging from Andhra

kalasha   pot-like finial of a tower

Kali   literally 'black'; terrifying form of the goddess Durga, wearing a necklace of skulls/heads

Kalki   future incarnation of Vishnu on horseback

kalyanamandapa   marriage hall

kameez   women's shirt

kanga   comb (one of five Sikh symbols)

kankar   limestone pieces, used for road making

kantha   Bengali quilting

kapok   the silk cotton tree

kara   steel bracelet (one of five Sikh symbols)

karma   impurity resulting from past misdeeds

Kartikkeya   (Kartik) Son of Siva, God of war

kashi-work   special kind of glazed tiling, probably derived from Kashan in Persia

kati-roll   Muslim snack of meat rolled in a 'paratha' bread

kattakat   mixed brain, liver and kidney (Gujarat)

keep   tower of a fort, stronghold

kere   tank (Kanarese)

keystone   central wedge-shaped block in a masonry arch

khadi   woven cotton cloth made from home-spun cotton (or silk) yarn

khal   creek; a canal

khana   suffix for room/office/place; also food or meal

khanqah   Muslim (Sufi) hospice

kharif   monsoon season crop

khave khana   tea shop

kheda   enclosure in which wild elephants are caught; elephant depot

khet   field

khola   river or stream in Nepal

khondalite   crudely grained basalt

khukri   traditional curved Gurkha weapon

kirpan   sabre, dagger (one of five Sikh symbols)

kirti-stambha   'pillar of fame,' free standing pillar in front of temple

kohl   antimony, used as eye shadow

konda   hill (Telugu)

kos minars   Mughal 'mile' stones

kot   (kota/kottai/kotte) fort

kothi   house

kotla   citadel

kovil   (koil) temple (Tamil)

Krishna   Eighth incarnation of Vishnu

kritis   South Indian devotional music

Kubera   Chief yaksha; keeper of the treasures of the earth, Guardian of the North

kulam   tank or pond (Tamil)

kumar   a young man

Kumari   Virgin; Durga

kumbha   a vase-like motif, pot

Kumbhayog   auspicious time for bathing to wash away sins

kumhar   (kumar) potter

kund   lake, well or pool

kundan   jewellery setting of uncut gems (Rajasthan)

kuppam   hamlet (Tamil)

kurta   Punjabi shirt

kurti-kanchali   small blouse

kutcha   (cutcha/kacha) raw; crude; unpaved; built with sun-dried bricks

kwabgah   bedroom; literally 'palace of dreams'

L

la   Himalayan mountain pass

lakh   100,000

Lakshmana   younger brother of Rama

Lakshmi   Goddess of wealth and good fortune, consort of Vishnu

Lakulisha   founder of the Pashupata sect, believed to be an incarnation of Siva

lama   Buddhist priest in Tibet

lassi   iced yoghurt drink

lath   monolithic pillar

lathi   bamboo stick with metal bindings, used by police

lena   cave, usually a rock-cut sanctuary

lingam   (linga) Siva as the phallic emblem

Lingaraja   Siva worshipped at Bhubaneswar

lintel   horizontal beam over doorway

liwan   cloisters of a mosque

Lokeshwar   'Lord of the World', Avalokiteshwara to Buddhists and form of Siva to Hindus

lunette   semicircular window opening

lungi wrapped-around loin cloth, normally checked

M

madrassa Islamic theological school or college

mahamandapam large enclosed hall in front of main shrine

maha great

Mahabharata Sanskrit epic about the battle between the Pandavas and Kauravas

Mahabodhi Great Enlightenment of Buddha

Mahadeva literally 'Great Lord'; Siva

mahal palace, grand building

mahalla (mohulla) division of a town; a quarter; a ward

mahant head of a monastery

maharaja great king

maharana Rajput clan head

maharani great queen

maharishi (Maharshi) literally 'great teacher'

Mahavira literally 'Great Hero'; last of the 24 Tirthankaras, founder of Jainism

Mahayana The Greater Vehicle; form of Buddhism practised in East Asia, Tibet and Nepal

Mahesha (Maheshvara) Great Lord; Siva

Mahisha Buffalo demon killed by Durga

mahout elephant driver/keeper

mahseer large freshwater fish found especially in Himalayan rivers

maidan large open grassy area in a town

Maitreya the future Buddha

makara crocodile-shaped mythical creature symbolizing the river Ganga

makhan butter

malai hill (Tamil)

mali gardener

Manasa Snake goddess; Sakti

manastambha free-standing pillar in front of temple

mandala geometric diagram symbolizing the structure of the Universe

mandalam region, tract of country (Tamil)

mandapa columned hall preceding the temple sanctuary

mandi market

mandir temple

mani (mani wall) stones with sacred inscriptions at Buddhist sites

mantra chant for meditation by Hindus and Buddhists

maqbara chamber of a Muslim tomb

Mara Tempter, who sent his daughters (and soldiers) to disturb the Buddha's meditation

marg wide roadway

masjid literally 'place of prostration'; mosque

mata mother

math Hindu or Jain monastery

maulana scholar (Muslim)

maulvi religious teacher (Muslim)

maund measure of weight about 20 kilos

mausoleum large tomb building

maya illusion

medallion circle or part-circle framing a figure or decorative motif

meena enamel work

mela festival or fair, usually Hindu

memsahib married European woman, term used mainly before Independence

Meru mountain supporting the heavens

mihrab niche in the western wall of a mosque

mimbar pulpit in mosque

Minakshi literally 'fish-eyed'; Parvati

minar (minaret) slender tower of a mosque

mitthai Indian sweets

mithuna couple in sexual embrace

mofussil the country as distinct from the town

Mohammad 'the praised'; The Prophet; founder of Islam

moksha salvation, enlightenment; literally 'release'

momos Tibetan stuffed pastas

monolith single block of stone shaped into a pillar

moonstone the semi circular stone step before a shrine (also chandrasila)

mouza (mowza) village; a parcel of land having a separate name in the revenue records

mridangam barrel-shaped drum (musical)

muballigh second prayer leader

mudra symbolic hand gesture

muezzin mosque official who calls the faithful to prayer

Muharram period of mourning in remembrance of Hasan and Hussain, two murdered sons of Ali

mukha mandapa, hall for shrine

mullah religious teacher (Muslim)

mund Toda village

muqarna Muslim stalactite design

mural wall decoration

musalla prayer mat

muta limited duration marriage (Leh)

muthi measure equal to 'a handful'

N

nadi river

nadu region, country (Tamil)

Naga (nagi/nagini) Snake deity; associated with fertility and protection

nagara city, sometimes capital

nakkar khana (naggar or naubat khana) drum house; arched structure or gateway for musicians

nal mandapa porch over a staircase

nallah (nullah) ditch, channel

namaaz Muslim prayers, worship

namaste common Hindu greeting (with joined palms) translated as: 'I salute all divine qualities in you'

namda rug

Nandi a bull, Siva's vehicle and a symbol of fertility

nara durg large fort built on a flat plain

Narayana Vishnu as the creator of life

nata mandapa (nat-mandir; nritya sala) dancing hall in a temple

Nataraja Siva, Lord of the cosmic dance

nath literally 'place' eg Amarnath

natya the art of dance

nautch   display by dancing girls

navagraha   nine planets, represented usually on the lintel or architrave of the front door of a temple

navaranga   central hall of temple

navaratri   literally '9 nights'; name of the Dasara festival

nawab   prince, wealthy Muslim, sometimes used as a title

niche   wall recess containing a sculpted image or emblem, mostly framed by a pair of pilasters

Nihang   literally 'crocodile': followers of Guru Gobind Singh (Sikh)

nirvana   enlightenment; literally 'extinguished'

niwas   small palace

nritya   pure dance

O

obelisk   tapering and usually monolithic stone shaft

oriel   projecting window

P

pada   foot or base

padam   dance which tells a story

padma   lotus flower, Padmasana, lotus seat; posture of meditating figures

paga   projecting pilaster-like surface of an Orissan temple

pagoda   tall structure in several stories

pahar   hill

paisa   (poisa) one hundredth of a rupee

palanquin   covered litter for one, carried on poles

palayam   minor kingdom (Tamil)

pali   language of Buddhist scriptures

palli   village

pan   leaf of the betel vine; sliced areca nut, lime and other ingredients wrapped in leaf for chewing

panchayat   a 'council of five'; a government system of elected councils

pandal   marquee made of bamboo and cloth

pandas   temple priests

pandit   teacher or wise man; a Sanskrit scholar

pankah   (punkha) fan, formerly pulled by a cord

parabdis   special feeding place for birds

parapet   wall extending above the roof

pargana   sub-division of a district usually comprising many villages; a fiscal unit

Parinirvana   the Buddha's state prior to nirvana, shown usually as a reclining figure

parishads   political division of group of villages

Parsi   (Parsee) Zoroastrians who fled from Iran to West India in the eighth century to avoid persecution

parterre   level space in a garden occupied by flowerbeds

Parvati   daughter of the Mountain; Siva's consort

pashmina   fine wool from a mountain goat

Pashupati   literally Lord of the Beasts; Siva

pata   painted hanging scroll

patan   town or city (Sanskrit)

patel   village headman

patina   green film that covers materials exposed to the air

pattachitra   specially painted cloth (especially Orissan)

pau   measure for vegetables and fruit equal to 250 grams

paya   soup

pediment   mouldings, often in a triangular formation above an opening or niche

pendant   hanging, a motif depicted upside down

peon   servant, messenger (from Portuguese *peao*)

perak   black hat, studded with turquoise and lapis lazuli (Ladakh)

peristyle   range of columns surrounding a court or temple

Persian wheel   well irrigation system using bucket lift

pettah   suburbs, outskirts of town (Tamil: *pettai*)

pice   (old form) 1/100th of a rupee

picottah   water lift using horizontal pole pivoted on vertical pole (Tamil Nadu)

pida deul   hall with a pyramidal roof in an Orissan temple

pida   (pitha) basement

pietra dura   inlaid mosaic of hard, semi-precious stones

pilaster   ornamental small column, with capital and bracket

pinjra   lattice work

pinjrapol   animal hospital (Jain)

pipal   Ficus religiosa, the Bodhi tree

pir   Muslim holy man

pitha   base, pedestal

pithasthana   place of pilgrimage

podium   stone bench; low pedestal wall

pokana   bathing tank (Sri Lanka)

pol   fortified gateway

porch   covered entrance to a shrine or hall, generally open and with columns

portico   space enclosed between columns

pradakshina patha   processional passage

prakaram   open courtyard

pralaya   the end of the world

prasadam   consecrated temple food

prayag   confluence considered sacred by Hindus

puja   ritual offerings to the gods; worship (Hindu)

pujari   worshipper; one who performs puja (Hindu)

pukka   literally 'ripe' or 'finished'; reliable; solidly built

punya   merit earned through actions and religious devotion (Buddhist)

Puranas   literally 'the old' Sanskrit sacred poems

purdah   seclusion of Muslim women from public view (literally curtains)

pushkarani   sacred pool or tank

Q

qabr   Muslim grave

qibla   direction for Muslim prayer

qila   fort

Quran   holy Muslim scriptures

qutb   axis or pivot

R

Footnotes Glossary

rabi   winter/spring season crop

Radha   Krishna's favourite consort

raj   rule or government

raja   king, ruler (variations include rao, rawal)

rajbari   palaces of a small kingdom

Rajput   dynasties of western and central India

Rakshakas   Earth spirits

Rama   Seventh incarnation of Vishnu

Ramayana   Sanskrit epic – the story of Rama

Ramazan   (Ramadan) Muslim month of fasting

rana   warrior (Nepal)

rangamandapa   painted hall or theatre

rani   queen

rath   chariot or temple car

Ravana   Demon king of Lanka; kidnapper of Sita

rawal   head priest

rekha   curvilinear portion of a spire or sikhara (rekha deul, sanctuary, curved tower of an Orissan temple)

reredos   screen behind an altar

rickshaw   3-wheeled bicycle-powered (or 2-wheeled hand-powered) vehicle

Rig (Rg) Veda   oldest and most sacred of the Vedas

Rimpoche   blessed incarnation; abbot of a Tibetan Buddhist monastery (gompa)

rishi   'seer'; inspired poet, philosopher

rumal   handkerchief, specially painted in Chamba (Himachal Pradesh)

rupee   unit of currency in India

ryot   (rayat/raiyat) a subject; a cultivator; a farmer

S

sabha   columned hall (sabha mandapa, assembly hall)

sabzi   vegetables, vegetable curry

sadar   (sadr/saddar) chief, main especially Sikh

sadhu   ascetic; religious mendicant, holy man

safa   turban (Rajasthan)

sagar   lake; reservoir

sahib   title of address, like 'sir'

sahn   open courtyard of a mosque

Saiva   (Shaiva) the cult of Siva

sal   a hall

sal   hardwood tree of the lower slopes of Himalayan foothills

salaam   literally 'peace'; greeting (Muslim)

salwar   (shalwar) loose trousers (Punjab)

samadh(i)   literally concentrated thought, meditation; a funerary memorial

sambar   lentil and vegetable soup dish, accompanying main meal (Tamil)

samsara   transmigration of the soul

samudra   large tank or inland sea

sangam   junction of rivers

sangarama   monastery

sangha   ascetic order founded by Buddha

sangrahalaya   rest-house for Jain pilgrims

sankha   (shankha) the conch shell (symbolically held by Vishnu); the shell bangle worn by Bengali women

sanyasi   wandering ascetic; final stage in the ideal life of a man

sarai   caravansarai, halting place

saranghi   small four-stringed viola shaped from a single piece of wood

Saraswati   wife of Brahma and goddess of knowledge

sarkar   the government; the state; a writer; an accountant

sarod   Indian stringed musical instrument

sarvodaya   uplift, improvement of all

sati   (suttee) a virtuous woman; act of self-immolation on a husband's funeral pyre

Sati   wife of Siva who destroyed herself by fire

satyagraha   'truth force'; passive resistance

sayid   title (Muslim)

schist   grey or green finely grained stone

seer   (ser) weight (about 1 kg)

sepoy   (sepai) Indian soldier, private

serow   a wild Himalayan antelope

seth   merchant, businessman

seva   voluntary service

shahtush   very fine wool from the Tibetan antelope

Shakti   Energy; female divinity often associated with Siva

shala   barrel-vaulted roof

shalagrama   stone containing fossils worshipped as a form of Vishnu

shaman   doctor/priest, using magic, exorcist

shamiana   cloth canopy

Shankara   Siva

sharia   corpus of Muslim theological law

shastras   ancient texts defining temple architecture

shastri   religious title (Hindu)

sheesh mahal   palace apartment with mirror work

shehnai   (shahnai) Indian wind instrument like an oboe

sherwani   knee-length coat for men

Shesha   (Sesha) serpent who supports Vishnu

shikar   hunting

shikara   boat (Kashmir)

shisham   a valuable building timber

sikhara   curved temple tower or spire

shloka   (sloka) Sanskrit sacred verse

shola   patch of forest or wood (Tamil)

sileh khana   armoury

sindur   vermilion powder used in temple ritual; married women mark their hair parting with it (East India)

singh   (sinha) lion; Rajput caste name adopted by Sikhs

sinha stambha   lion pillar

sirdar   a guide who leads trekking groups

Sita   Rama's wife, heroine of the Ramayana epic

sitar   classical stringed musical instrument with a gourd for soundbox

Siva   (Shiva) The Destroyer in the Hindu triad of Gods

Sivaratri   literally 'Siva's night'; a festival (Feb-Mar)

Skanda   the Hindu god of war; Kartikkeya

soma   sacred drink mentioned in the Vedas

spandrel   triangular space between the curve of an arch and the square enclosing it

squinch   arch across an interior angle

sri   (shri) honorific title, often used for 'Mr'; repeated as sign of great respect

sridhara pillar with octagonal shaft and square base

stalactite system of vaulting, remotely resembling stalactite formations in a cave

stambha free-standing column or pillar, often for a lamp or figure

steatite finely grained grey mineral

stele upright, inscribed slab used as a gravestone

sthan place (suffix)

stucco plasterwork

stupa hemispheric Buddhist funerary mound

stylobate base on which a colonnade is placed

subahdar (subedar) the governor of a province; viceroy under the Mughals

Subrahmanya Skanda, one of Siva's sons; Kartikkeya in South India

sudra lowest of the Hindu castes

sufi Muslim mystic; sufism, Muslim mystic worship

sultan Muslim prince (sultana, wife of sultan)

Surya Sun; Sun God

svami (swami) holy man; a suffix for temple deities

svastika (swastika) auspicious Hindu/ Buddhist cross-like sign

swadeshi home made goods

swaraj home rule

swatantra freedom

T

tabla a pair of drums

tahr wild goat

tahsildar revenue collector

taikhana underground apartments

takht throne

talao (tal, talar) water tank

taluk administrative subdivision of a district

tamasha spectacle; festive celebration

tandava (dance) of Siva

tank lake dug for irrigation; a masonry- lined temple pool with stepped sides

tapas (tapasya) ascetic meditative self-denial

Tara literally 'star'; a goddess

tarkashi Orissan silver filigree

tatties cane or grass screens used for shade

Teej Hindu festival

tehsil subdivision of a district (North India)

tempera distemper; method of mural painting by means of a 'body,' such as white pigment

tempo three-wheeler vehicle

terai narrow strip of land along Himalayan foothills

teri soil formed from wind blown sand (Tamil Nadu)

terracotta burnt clay used as building material

thakur bari temple sanctuary (Bengal)

thakur high Hindu caste; deity (Bengal)

thali South and West Indian vegetarian meal

thana a police jurisdiction; police station

thangka (thankha) cloth (often silk) painted with a Tibetan Mahayana deity

thug professional robber/murderer (Central India)

tiffin snack, light meal

tika (tilak) vermilion powder, auspicious mark on the forehead; often decorative

tikka tender pieces of meat, marinated and barbecued

tillana abstract dance

tirtha ford, bathing place, holy spot (Sanskrit)

Tirthankara literally 'ford-maker'; title given to 24 religious 'teachers', worshipped by Jains

tonga two-wheeled horse carriage

topi (topee) pith helmet

torana gateway; two posts with an architrave

tottam garden (Tamil)

tribhanga triple-bended pose for standing figures

Trimurti the Hindu Triad, Brahma, Vishnu and Siva

tripolia triple gateway

trisul the trident chief symbol of the god Siva

triveni triple-braided

tsampa ground, roasted barley, eaten dry or mixed with milk, tea or water (Himalayan)

tso lake (Ladakh)

tuk fortified enclosure containing Jain shrines

tulsi sacred basil plant

tykhana underground room for use in hot weather (North India)

tympanum triangular space within cornices

U

Uma Siva's consort in one of her many forms

untouchable 'outcastes', with whom contact of any kind was believed by high caste Hindus to be defiling

Upanishads ancient Sanskrit philosophical texts, part of the Vedas

ur village (Tamil)

usta painted camel leather goods

ustad master

uttarayana northwards

V

vahana 'vehicle' of the deity

vaisya the 'middle-class' caste of merchants and farmers

Valmiki sage, author of the Ramayana epic

Vamana dwarf incarnation of Vishnu

vana grove, forest

Varaha boar incarnation of Vishnu

varam village (Tamil)

varna 'colour'; social division of Hindus into Brahmin, Kshatriya, Vaishya and Sudra

Varuna Guardian of the West, accompanied by Makara (see above)

Vayu Wind god; Guardian of the North-West

Veda (Vedic) oldest known Hindu religious texts

vedi (bedi) altar, also a wall or screen

verandah enlarged porch in front of a hall

vihara Buddhist or Jain monastery with cells around a courtyard

vilas house or pleasure palace

vimana towered sanctuary containing the cell in which the deity is enshrined

vina plucked stringed instrument, relative of sitar

Vishnu a principal Hindu deity; the Preserver (and Creator)

vyala (yali) leogryph, mythical lion-like sculpture

W

-wallah suffix often used with a occupational name, eg rickshaw-wallah

wav (vav) step-well, particularly in Gujarat and western India (baoli)

wazir chief minister of a raja (from Turkish 'vizier')

wazwan ceremonial meal (Kashmir)

Y

yagya (yajna) major ceremonial sacrifice

Yaksha (Yakshi) a demi-god, associated with nature

yali see vyala

Yama God of death, judge of the living

yantra magical diagram used in meditation; instrument

yatra pilgrimage

Yellow Hat Gelugpa Sect of Tibetan Buddhism – monks wear yellow headdress

yeti mythical Himalayan animal often referred to as 'the abominable snowman'

yoga school of philosophy stressing mental and physical disciplines; yogi

yoni a hole symbolising female sexuality; vagina

yura water channel (Ladakh)

Z

zamindar a landlord granted income under the Mughals

zari silver and gold thread used in weaving or embroidery

zarih cenotaph in a Muslim tomb

zenana segregated women's apartments

ziarat holy Muslim tomb

zilla (zillah) district

Main Index

Abbreviations used for state references: **A&N** = Andaman & Nicobar Islands; **AP** = Andhra Pradesh; **Ar** = Arunachal Pradesh; **As** = Assam; **Bi** = Bihar; **Chh** = Chhattisgarh; **Goa** = Goa; **Guj** = Gujarat; **HP** = Himachal Pradesh; **J&K** = Jammu & Kashmir; **Jh** = Jharkhand; **Kar** = Karnataka; **Ke** = Kerala; **Mah** = Maharashtra; **Meg** = Meghalaya; **Miz** = Mizoram; **MP** = Madhya Pradesh; **Man** = Manipur; **Nag** = Nagaland; **Or** = Orissa; **P&H** = Punjab & Haryana; **Raj** = Rajasthan; **Sik** = Sikkim; **TN** = Tamil Nadu; **Tri** = Tripura; **UP** = Uttar Pradesh; **Utt** = Uttaranchal; **WB** = West Bengal.

Map Index

Map symbols

Administration

- ▢ Capital city
- ○ Other city/town
- International border
- Regional border
- Disputed border

Roads and travel

- —— Motorway
- —— Main road
- —— Minor road
- ---- 4WD track
- ······ Footpath
- ⊢▬ Railway with station
- ✈ Airport
- 🚌 Bus station
- Ⓜ Metro station
- ---- Cable car
- ++++ Funicular
- ⚓ Ferry

Water features

- River, canal
- Lake, ocean
- Seasonal marshland
- Beach, sand bank
- Waterfall

Topographical features

- Contours (approx)
- Mountain
- Volcano
- Mountain pass
- Escarpment
- Gorge
- Glacier
- Salt flat
- Rocks

Cities and towns

- Main through route
- Main street
- Minor street
- Pedestrianized street
- Tunnel
- One way street

- ⊪⊪⊪ Steps
- ⇌ Bridge
- Fortified wall
- Park, garden, stadium
- Sleeping
- Eating
- Bars & clubs
- Entertainment
- Building
- Sight
- Cathedral, church
- Chinese temple
- Hindu temple
- Meru
- Mosque
- Stupa
- Synagogue
- Tourist office
- Museum
- Post office
- Police
- Bank
- Internet
- Telephone
- Market
- Hospital
- Parking
- Petrol
- Golf
- A Detail map
- A Related map

Other symbols

- Archaeological site
- National park, wildlife reserve
- Viewing point
- Campsite
- Refuge, lodge
- Castle
- Diving
- Deciduous/coniferous/palm trees
- Hide
- Vineyard
- Distillery
- Shipwreck
- Historic battlefield

Credits

Footprint credits

Text editors: Emma Bryers and Patrick Dawson
Map editor: Sarah Sorensen
Picture editor: Sophie Blacksell

Publisher: Patrick Dawson
Editorial: Alan Murphy, Sophie Blacksell, Claire Boobbyer, Felicity Laughton
Cartography: Robert Lunn, Claire Benison, Kevin Feeney
Series development: Rachel Fielding
Design: Mytton Williams and Rosemary Dawson (brand)
Advertising: Debbie Wylde
Finance and administration: Sharon Hughes, Elizabeth Taylor

Photography credits

Front and back covers: Alamy
Inside colour section:
Alamy, BBC Natural History Picture Library, Eye Ubiquitous, Impact Photo Library, Jamie Marshall, Patrick Dawson, Pictures Colour Library, Robert Harding Picture Library.

Print

Manufactured in Italy by LegoPrint
Pulp from sustainable forests

Footprint feedback

We try as hard as we can to make each Footprint guide as up to date as possible but, of course, things always change. If you want to let us know about your experiences – good, bad or ugly – then don't delay, go to www.footprintbooks.com and send in your comments.

Publishing information

Footprint India
13th edition
© Footprint Handbooks Ltd
June 2004

ISBN 1 904777 00 7
CIP DATA: A catalogue record for this book is available from the British Library

® Footprint Handbooks and the Footprint mark are a registered trademark of Footprint Handbooks Ltd

Published by Footprint

6 Riverside Court
Lower Bristol Road
Bath BA2 3DZ, UK
T +44 (0)1225 469141
F +44 (0)1225 469461
discover@footprintbooks.com
www.footprintbooks.com

Distributed in the USA by

Publishers Group West

Acknowledgements

Thanks go to Emma Bryers and Paul Johnson who struggled manfully to convert the text into Footprint's new design format. We again gratefully acknowledge the generous help we received in preparing the twelth edition.

Sebastian Ballard did a complete overhaul of the Goa section and also sent in feedback and map corrections from Tamil Nadu and Kerala. Cath Croxton and Poonam checked out accommodation options in Delhi. Ian Large covered the new states of Chattisgarh and Jharkhand on his way to revisit Orissa's cities and tribal areas. Catherine Lewis checked through sections of the book for errors and inconsistencies. Tim Makins spent three months visiting the major cities and tourist towns in Tamil Nadu, Karnataka and Kerala. Anil Mulchandani researched parts of Uttaranchal, Himachal, Kerala and Karnataka in addition to updating his home state of Gujarat.

The following local correspondents have been particularly helpful in supplying information for which we record our warmest thanks:

Mr Bardewa, *Singalila Treks*, Gangtok; Pijush Ghosh, *WH Adventures*, Manali; Sanjeev Mehta, *Mohan's Adventure*, Haridwar; Faith Pandian, *Window to the World*, Tiruchirapalli; B Pattnaik and S Acharaya of *Discover Tours*, Bhubaneswar; PR Shetty, *Four Wings International Travels*, Mangalore; Ricky Singh, *Time Travels*, Amritsar; Ran Vijay, *Umaid Bhawan*, Jaipur.

We record our grateful thanks to the HRH Group in Rajasthan, the Taj hotels in Jodhpur, Agra and Delhi, all at Deogarh Mahal, Rajasthan and to Madhya Pradesh Tourism in Orchha, for their kind hospitality.

Thank you also to Dr Charlie Easmon who wrote the health section. His aid and development work has included: Raleigh International (Medical Officer in Botswana), MERLIN (in Rwanda his team set up a refugee camp for 12,000 people), Save the Children (as a consultant in Rwanda), ECHO (The European Community Humanitarian Office review of Red Cross work in Armenia, Georgia and Azerbaijan), board member of International Care and Relief and previously International Health Exchange. In addition to his time as a hospital physician, he has worked as a medical adviser to the Foreign and Commonwealth Office and as a locum consultant at the hospital for tropical diseases travel clinic, as well as being a specialist registrar in Public Health. He now also runs Travel Screening services (www.travelscreening.co.uk) based at 1 Harley Street.

Finally we would like to thank many travellers who have written to us during the year. A special mention for particularly detailed feedback goes to Lynne Anderson, UK; Jeremy Fialko, UK; Jos and Caroline Holtzer, Netherlands; Karine Legeron, France; Steve Scott, UK; Sabine Verheist, Belgium.

Jose Luis Albert, Spain; Kerryn Amery, Australia; Victor Ashe, USA; Neil Ayres, UK; Billy B, email; Prof PJ Bayley, UK; Monica Belalcazar; A. Bianchi, Italy; JF Bodinier, France; Joel Brink, USA; Guy Brusselaers, Belgium; Miquel and Olivia Cabrils, Spain; Lalit Chainwala, email; Massimiliano Cenni, UK; Jonathan Cleaver, email; Chris Cobb, UK; Brian Collins, email; Steve Cooper, email; Bernard Coude, UK; Ranald AM Coyne, UK; Rod Daldry, India; Sheila Darzi, UK; Penny and Biswajit Das, India; Guy Dehn, email; M. Desai, UK; D Desjardins, Canada; Dr Claudia Dimmer, UK; J Dowdeswell, email;

vans, India; Mirella and Gerhard Fabrizi, Austria; Wendy Fehr, Canada; Alan UK; James Flint, UK; Chad Gallagher, email; Günter Gelling, Germany; cesca Gettelman, USA; Marc Gold, USA; Heidi Gordon, email; Bhupendra Singh ur, India; Beaty Grove, New Zealand; Annie Gurton, UK; Veronica Gustavsson, mail; Andrew Harvey, UK.; Marianne van Heerden, South Africa; Lorraine Hellen, UK; Horst Heller, email; Eileen Hewson, UK; Edward Hughes, UK; Sanjay Joshi, email; Helle Juhl, Denmark; Sara Kalvala, email; Alex and Caroline Kristoffersen, UK; Hermann Kurtz, Germany; Jerome Laffon, France; David Langmead., UK; Gillem Lawson, email; Doron Lev, email; Kieran Laurie Lindsay, UK; Shira Luft, email; Jose Luis, Spain; Sally McCarthy, email; Tracy and Niall McCormack, Ireland; Annegret Maier, email; Michael Manser, UK; Susan Marfell, UK; Anthony and Veronica Matthew, UK; Vishwas Mehta, India; Monique and Ari Kovacs Nathan, USA; Helen Nicholson, UK; Paul Nillington, Switzerland; Torsten Otto, India; Ned Pakenham, email; Milan Panchmatia , UK; Bob Pearson, UK; Henry Pfeiffer, India; Henri Picas France; Annedore von Planta, email; Catherine Pollitt email; Paul Prowting, UK.; Maria Giovanna Pugliese, email; Sunil Puri, Canada; Matthias Pusch, USA; GE Quinan, UK; Rajesh Ragoobeer, USA; Vivien Reid, email; Jacques Renaud. France; Hannah Richardson, UK; Blair Robertson, email; Niels Roennest, email; Peter and Sara van Rooijen, Netherlands; Bernard Rottenaicher, Germany; Bruce Rumoge, USA; John Russell, email; Joe and Karen Sabharwal, UK; Simon Sanderson email; Caroline Sapsed, UK; Toby Sargant, UK; Deepthi Sasidharan, India; Ad van Schaik, Netherlands; Johannes Schmidt-Wellenberg. Germany; Willem-Peter Schouten, The Netherlands; Fatema Shamshi, India; Capt Suresh Sharma, India; Penelope Smail, email; Marcos Souza, India; Peter van Spall, Thailand; Aviad Stier, Belgium; Antoine Stoll, Switzerland; Klaus Teufel, email; Nobby Thys, Belgium; Isabel Troy, UK; Robert Trythall, email; Tim Vivian, UK; Jim and Jill Waits, UK; Jane Ward, UK; David Wendland, email; Brian Windsor, India; Elisabeth Zoll, Germany.

Complete title listing

Footprint publishes travel guides to over 150 destinations worldwide. Each guide is packed with practical, concise and colourful information for everybody from first-time travellers to travel aficionados. The list is growing fast and current titles are noted below.
Available from all good bookshops and online

www.footprintbooks.com

(P) denotes pocket guide

Latin America and Caribbean
Argentina
Barbados (P)
Bolivia
Brazil
Caribbean Islands
Central America & Mexico
Chile
Colombia
Costa Rica
Cuba
Cusco & the Inca Trail
Dominican Republic
Ecuador & Galápagos
Guatemala
Havana (P)
Mexico
Nicaragua
Peru
Rio de Janeiro
South American Handbook
Venezuela

North America
Vancouver (P)
New York (P)
Western Canada

Africa
Cape Town (P)
East Africa
Libya
Marrakech & the High Atlas
Marrakech (P)
Morocco
Namibia
South Africa
Tunisia
Uganda

Middle East
Egypt
Israel
Jordan
Syria & Lebanon

Australasia
Australia
East Coast Australia
New Zealand
Sydney (P)
West Coast Australia

Asia
Bali
Bangkok & the Beaches
Cambodia
Goa
Hong Kong (P)
India
Indian Himalaya
Indonesia
Laos
Malaysia
Nepal
Pakistan
Rajasthan & Gujarat
Singapore
South India
Sri Lanka
Sumatra
Thailand
Tibet
Vietnam

Europe
Andalucía
Barcelona
Barcelona (P)
Berlin (P)
Bilbao (P)
Bologna (P)
Britain

Copenhagen (P)
Croatia
Dublin
Dublin (P)
Edinburgh
Edinburgh (P)
England
Glasgow
Glasgow (P)
Ireland
Lisbon (P)
London
London (P)
Madrid (P)
Naples (P)
Northern Spain
Paris (P)
Reykjavík (P)
Scotland
Scotland Highlands & Islands
Seville (P)
Spain
Tallinn (P)
Turin (P)
Turkey
Valencia (P)
Verona (P)

Also available
Traveller's Handbook (WEXAS)
Traveller's Healthbook (WEXAS)
Traveller's Internet Guide (WEXAS)

Footnotes Complete title listing

Check out...

WWW...

100 travel guides, 100s of destinations,
5 continents and 1 Footprint...
www.footprintbooks.com

India

The Government of India state that "the external boundaries of India are neither correct nor authenticated"

Altitude in metres		Highways
3000		Roads
2000		
1500	NH1	Highway number
1000		Railway
500		
200	◆	National Park
100		State border
Ü		International border
Neighbouring Country		

Nubra R

Ladakh Range

Shyok
Tangtse
Lukung
Spangmik

Pangtong Tso

Indus R

Tashigong

RUPSHU

Gardzong

Sarchu
Bara Lacha
Pass

Tso-Moriri

SPITI

Losar
Batal
Kibber
Kaza
Dankar
Lalung
Kunori Gompa
Tabo
Pin Valley
NP
Gulling
Sumdo
Mudh
Sangam
Khabo

HIMACHAL
Puh

Wangtu
Kalpa
Jangi
(Lippa)
Recong Peo
Sarahan
Sangla
Rampur
Bushahr
Chitkul

PRADESH

▲ Kailash

TIBET
(CHINA)

Yamunotri
▲ Gangotri
Barkot
▲ Meru
Kedarnath
Badrinath

Uttarkashi
Hemkund

UTTARANCHAL
Joshimath
Auli

Mussoorie
Tehri

Dehra Dun
Srinagar
Rudraprayag
Karnaprayag
▲ Nanda Devi
▲ Trisul

Rishikesh
Deoprayag
Byasi
Gwaldam

Rajaji
NP
Laksho
Balinath
Kausani

Saharanpur
Haridwar
Ranikhet
Pithoragarh

Roorkee
Kotdwara
Corbett
NP
Almora

Muzaffarnagar
Nathjabad
Ramnagar
Nainital

Khatauli
Nagina
Bhowali
Kathgodam

Bijnor
Kashipur
Haldwani

Meerut
Lalkuan
Tanakpur
Map 3
Mahendranagar

Bilaspur
Kichha
Banbassa

Hapur
Moradabad
Rampur
Pilibhit
Dudwa
NP
Nepalganj
Road

Sambhal
Chandausi
NH24
Puranpur

Bulandshahr
Bareilly
Bisalpur
Mailani
Nanpara

Khurja
Ramganga R

UTTAR
Ganga R

PRADESH
NEPAL

Aligarh
Kasganj
Shahjahanpur
Lakhimpur

Vrindavan
4
5
Sitapur
6

N

0 km 50
0 miles 50

The Government of India state that
"the external boundaries of India
are neither correct nor authenticated"

A

B

C

Chaghana R

Map 4